Proceedings of the Eleventh National Conference on Artificial Intelligence

Proceedings of the Eleventh National Conference on Artificial Intelligence

Sponsored by the
American Association for
Artificial Intelligence

AAAI Press / The MIT Press

Menlo Park • Cambridge • London

Copublished and distributed by The MIT Press, Massachusetts Institute of Technology, Cambridge, Massachusetts and London, England

The trademarked terms that appear throughout this book are used in an editorial nature only, to the benefit of the trademark owner. No infringement of any trademarked term is intended.

ISBN 0-262-51071-5   AAAI-93

Manufactured in the United States of America

Contents

Automated Reasoning / 1

On Computing Minimal Models
Rachel Ben-Eliyahu, University of California, Los Angeles and Rina Dechter, University of California, Irvine / 2

On the Adequateness of the Connection Method
Antje Beringer and Steffen Hölldobler, Intellektik, Informatik, TH Darmstadt / 9

Rough Resolution: A Refinement of Resolution to Remove Large Literals
Heng Chu and David A. Plaisted, University of North Carolina / 15

Experimental Results on the Crossover Point in Satisfiability Problems
James M. Crawford and Larry D. Auton, AT&T Bell Laboratories / 21

Towards an Understanding of Hill-Climbing Procedures for SAT
Ian P. Gent and Toby Walsh, University of Edinburgh / 28

Reasoning with Characteristic Models
Henry A. Kautz, Michael J. Kearns, and Bart Selman, AT&T Bell Laboratories / 34

The Breakout Method for Escaping from Local Minima
Paul Morris, IntelliCorp / 40

An Empirical Study of Greedy Local Search for Satisfiability Testing
Bart Selman and Henry A. Kautz, AT&T Bell Laboratories / 46

Case-Based Reasoning / 53

Projective Visualization: Acting from Experience
Marc Goodman, Brandeis University / 54

Representing and Using Procedural Knowledge to Build Geometry Proofs
Thomas F. McDougal and Kristian J. Hammond, University of Chicago / 60

Case-Based Diagnostic Analysis in a Blackboard Architecture
Edwina L. Rissland, Jody J. Daniels, Zachary B. Rubinstein and David B. Skalak, University of Massachusetts / 66

A Framework and an Analysis of Current Proposals for the Case-Based Organization and Representation of Procedural Knowledge
Roland Zito-Wolf and Richard Alterman, Brandeis University / 73

Complexity in Machine Learning / 79

Cryptographic Limitations on Learning One-Clause Logic Programs
William W. Cohen, AT&T Bell Laboratories / 80

Pac-Learning a Restricted Class of Recursive Logic Programs
William W. Cohen, AT&T Bell Laboratories / 86

Learnability in Inductive Logic Programming: Some Basic Results and Techniques
Michael Frazier and C. David Page, Jr., University of Illinois / 93

Complexity Analysis of Real-Time Reinforcement Learning
Sven Koenig and Reid G. Simmons, Carnegie Mellon University / 99

Constraint-Based Reasoning / 107

Arc-Consistency and Arc-Consistency Again
Christian Bessière, University of Montpellier II and Marie-Odile Cordier, University of Rennes I / 108

On the Consistency of General Constraint-Satisfaction Problems
Philippe Jégou, Université de Provence / 114

Integrating Heuristics for Constraint Satisfaction Problems: A Case Study
Steven Minton, Sterling Software/NASA Ames Research Center / 120

Coping With Disjunctions in Temporal Constraint Satisfaction Problems
Eddie Schwalb and Rina Dechter, University of California, Irvine / 127

Nondeterministic Lisp as a Substrate for Constraint Logic Programming
Jeffrey Mark Siskind, University of Pennsylvania and David Allen McAllester, MIT Artifical Intelligence Laboratory / 133

Slack-Based Heuristics for Constraint Satisfaction Scheduling
Stephen F. Smith and Cheng-Chung Cheng, Carnegie Mellon University / 139

A Constraint Decomposition Method for Spatio-Temporal Configuration Problems
Toshikazu Tanimoto, Digital Equipment Corporation Japan / 145

Extending Deep Structure
Colin P. Williams and Tad Hogg, Xerox Palo Alto Research Center / 152

Diagnostic Reasoning / 159

Multiple Dimensions of Generalization In Model-Based Troubleshooting
Randall Davis and Paul Resnick, Massachusetts Institute of Technology / 160

Hybrid Case-Based Reasoning for the Diagnosis of Complex Devices
M. P. Féret and J. I. Glasgow, Queen's University / 168

An Epistemology for Clinically Significant Trends
Ira J. Haimowitz, MIT Laboratory for Computer Science and Isaac S. Kohane, Harvard Medical School / 176

A Framework for Model-Based Repair
Ying Sun and Daniel S. Weld, University of Washington / 182

Discourse Analysis / 189
A Method for Development of Dialogue Managers for Natural Language Interfaces
Arne Jönsson, Linköping University / 190

Mutual Beliefs of Multiple Conversants: A Computational Model of Collaboration in Air Traffic Control
David G. Norvick and Karen Ward, Oregon Graduate Institute of Science & Technology / 196

An Optimizing Method for Structuring Inferentially Linked Discourse
Ingrid Zukerman and Richard McConachy, Monash University / 202

Distributed Problem Solving / 209
A One-shot Dynamic Coordination Algorithm for Distributed Sensor Networks
Keith Decker and Victor Lesser, University of Massachusetts / 210

Quantitative Modeling of Complex Computational Task Environments
Keith Decker and Victor Lesser, University of Massachusetts / 217

Overeager Reciprocal Rationality and Mixed Strategy Equilibria
Edmund H. Durfee and Jaeho Lee, University of Michigan; Piotr J. Gmytrasiewicz, Hebrew University / 225

Solving the Really Hard Problems with Cooperative Search
Tad Hogg and Colin P. Williams, Xerox Palo Alto Research Center / 231

A Fast First-Cut Protocol for Agent Coordination
Andrew P. Kosoresow, Stanford University / 237

Agents Contracting Tasks in Non-Collaborative Environments
Sarit Kraus, Bar Ilan University / 243

IPUS: An Architecture for Integrated Signal Processing and Signal Interpretation in Complex Environments
Victor Lesser, Izaskun Gallastegi and Frank Klassner, University of Massachusetts; Hamid Nawab, Boston University / 249

An Implementation of the Contract Net Protocol Based on Marginal Cost Calculations
Tuomas Sandholm, University of Massachusetts / 256

Intelligent User Interfaces / 263
Generating Explanations of Device Behavior Using Compositional Modeling and Causal Ordering
Patrice O. Gautier and Thomas R. Gruber, Stanford University / 264

Generating Natural Language Descriptions with Examples: Differences between Introductory and Advanced Texts
Vibhu O. Mittal and Cécile L. Paris, University of Southern California / 271

Building Models to Support Synthesis in Early Stage Product Design
R. Bharat Rao, Siemens Corporate Research, Inc. and Stephen C-Y. Lu, University of Illinois at Urbana-Champaign / 277

A Conversational Model of Multimodal Interaction in Information Systems
Adelheit Stein and Ulrich Thiel, German National Research Center for Computer Science / 283

Large Scale Knowledge Bases / 289
Matching 100,000 Learned Rules
Robert B. Doorenbos, Carnegie Mellon University / 290

Massively Parallel Support for Computationally Effective Recognition Queries
Matthew P. Evett, James A. Hendler, and William A. Andersen, University of Maryland / 297

Case-Method: A Methodology for Building Large-Scale Case-Based Systems
Hiroaki Kitano, Hideo Shimazu and Akihiro Shibata, NEC Corporation / 303

Automated Index Generation for Constructing Large-Scale Conversational Hypermedia Systems
Richard Osgood and Ray Bareiss, Northwestern University / 309

Machine Learning / 315
Probabilistic Prediction of Protein Secondary Structure Using Causal Networks
Arthur L. Delcher, Loyola College; Simon Kasif, Harry R. Goldberg and William H. Hsu, Johns Hopkins University / 316

OC1: A Randomized Induction of Oblique Decision Trees
Sreerama Murthy, Simon Kasif and Steven Salzberg, Johns Hopkins University; Richard Beigel, Yale University / 322

Finding Accurate Frontiers: A Knowledge-Intensive Approach to Relational Learning
Michael Pazzani and Clifford Brunk, University of California, Irvine / 328

Learning Non-Linearly Separable Boolean Functions With Linear Threshold Unit Trees and Madaline-Style Networks
Mehran Sahami, Stanford University / 335

Natural Language Generation / 343
Generating Argumentative Judgment Determiners
Michael Elhadad, Ben Gurion University of the Negev / 344

Bidirectional Chart Generation of Natural Language Texts
Masahiko Haruno and Makoto Nagao, Kyoto University; Yasuharu Den, ATR Interpreting Telecommunication Research Laboratories; and Yuji Matsumoto, Advanced Institute of Science and Technology, Nara / 350

Communicative Acts for Generating Natural Language Arguments
Mark T. Maybury, The MITRE Corporation / 357

Corpus Analysis for Revision-Based Generation of Complex Sentences
Jacques Robin and Kathleen McKeown, Columbia University / 365

Natural Language Sentence Analysis / 373

Machine Translation of Spatial Expressions: Defining the Relation between an Interlingua and a Knowledge Representation System
Bonnie J. Dorr and Clare R. Voss, University of Maryland / 374

Having Your Cake and Eating It Too: Autonomy and Interaction in a Model of Sentence Processing
Kurt P. Eiselt and Kavi Mahesh, Georgia Institute of Technology; Jennifer K. Holbrook, Albion College / 380

Efficient Heuristic Natural Language Parsing
Christian R. Huyck and Steven L. Lytinen, University of Michigan / 386

Towards a Reading Coach that Listens: Automated Detection of Oral Reading Errors
Jack Mostow, Alexander G. Hauptmann, Lin Lawrence Chase and Steven Roth, Carnegie Mellon University / 392

Nonmonotonic Logic / 399

Minimal Belief and Negation as Failure: A Feasible Approach
Antje Beringer and Torsten Schaub, TH Darmstadt / 400

A Context-based Framework for Default Logics
Philippe Besnard, IRISA and Torsten Schaub, TH Darmstadt / 406

Propositional Logic of Context
Sasa Buvac and Ian A. Mason, Stanford University / 412

Generating Explicit Orderings for Non-monotonic Logics
James Cussens, King's College; Anthony Hunter, Imperial College; and Ashwin Srinivasan, Oxford University / 420

Reasoning Precisely with Vague Concepts
Nita Goyal and Yoav Shoham, Stanford University / 426

Restricted Monotonicity
Vladimir Lifschitz, University of Texas at Austin / 432

Subnormal Modal Logics for Knowledge Representation
Grigori Schwarz, Stanford University and Miroslaw Truszczyński, University of Kentucky / 438

Algebraic Sematics for Cumulative Inference Operations
Zbigniew Stachniak, University of Toronto / 444

Novel Methods in Knowledge Acquisition / 451

Question-based Acquisition of Conceptual Indices for Multimedia Design Documentation
Catherine Baudin, RECOM Technologies/NASA Ames Research Center; Smadar Kadar, Sterling Software/Northwestern University/NASA Ames Research Center; Jody Gevins Underwood, Sterling Software Inc./NASA Ames Research Center; and Vinod Baya, Stanford University / 452

Learning Interface Agents
Pattie Maes and Robyn Kozierok, MIT Media Laboratory / 459

Learning from an Approximate Theory and Noisy Examples
Somkiat Tangkitvanich and Masamichi Shimura, Tokyo Institute of Technology / 465

Scientific Model-Building as Search in Matrix Spaces
Raúl E. Valdés-Pérez and Herbert A. Simon, Carnegie Mellon University; Jan M. Żytkow, Wichita State University / 472

Plan Generation / 479

An Average Case Analysis of Planning
Tom Bylander, The Ohio State University / 480

Granularity in Multi-Method Planning
Soowon Lee and Paul S. Rosenbloom, University of Southern California / 486

Threat-Removal Strategies for Partial-Order Planning
Mark A. Peot, Stanford University and David E. Smith, Rockwell International / 492

Postponing Threats in Partial-Order Planning
David E. Smith, Rockwell International and Mark A. Peot, Stanford University / 500

Plan Learning / 507

Permissive Planning: A Machine Learning Approach to Linking Internal and External Worlds
Gerald DeJong, University of Illinois at Urbana-Champaign and Scott Bennett, Systems Research and Applications Corporation / 508

Relative Utility of EBG based Plan Reuse in Partial Ordering vs. Total Ordering Planning
Subbarao Kambhampati and Jengchin Chen, Arizona State University / 514

Learning Plan Transformations from Self-Questions: A Memory-Based Approach
R. Oehlmann, D. Sleeman, and P. Edwards, King's College / 520

On the Masking Effect
Milind Tambe, Carnegie Mellon University and Paul S. Rosenbloom, University of Southern California/Information Sciences Institute / 526

Qualitative Reasoning / 535

Qualitatively Describing Objects Using Spatial Prepositions
Alicia Abella and John R. Kender, Columbia University / 536

Numeric Reasoning with Relative Orders of Magnitude
Philippe Dague, Université Paris Nord / 541

Efficient Reasoning in Qualitative Probabilistic Networks
Marek J. Druzdzel, Carnegie Mellon University and Max Henrion, Rockwell International Science Center / 548

Generating Quasi-symbolic Representation of Three-Dimensional Flow
Toyoaki Nishida, Advanced Institute of Science and Technology, Nara / 554

Real-Time Planning and Simulation / 561
Real-Time Self-Explanatory Simulation
Franz G. Amador, Adam Finkelstein and Daniel S. Weld, University of Washington / 562

A Comparison of Action-Based Hierarchies and Decision Trees for Real-Time Performance
David Ash and Barbara Hayes-Roth, Stanford University / 568

Planning With Deadlines in Stochastic Domains
Thomas Dean, Leslie Pack Kaelbling, Jak Kirman and Ann Nicholson, Brown University / 574

Task Interdependencies in Design-to-time Real-time Scheduling
Alan Garvey, Marty Humphrey, and Victor Lesser, University of Massachusetts / 580

Reasoning about Physical Systems / 587
Sensible Scenes: Visual Understanding of Complex Structures through Causal Analysis
Matthew Brand, Lawrence Birnbaum and Paul Cooper, Northwestern University / 588

Intelligent Model Selection for Hillclimbing Search in Computer-Aided Design
Thomas Ellman, John Keane, and Mark Schwabacher, Rutgers University / 594

Ideal Physical Systems
Brian Falkenhainer, Xerox Corporate Research & Technology / 600

Numerical Behavior Envelopes for Qualitative Models
Herbert Kay and Benjamin Kuipers, University of Texas at Austin / 606

A Qualitative Method to Construct Phase Portraits
Wood W. Lee, Schlumberger Dowell and Benjamin J. Kuipers, University of Texas / 614

Understanding Linkages
Howard E. Shrobe, Massachusetts Institute of Technology / 620

CFRL: A Language for Specifying the Causal Functionality of Engineered Devices
Marcos Vescovi, Yumi Iwasaki and Richard Fikes, Stanford University; B. Chandrasekaran, The Ohio State University / 626

Model Simplification by Asymptotic Order of Magnitude Reasoning
Kenneth Man-kam Yip, Yale University / 634

Representation and Reasoning / 641

Abduction As Belief Revision: A Model of Preferred Explanations
Craig Boutilier and Veronica Becher, University of British Columbia / 642

Revision by Conditional Beliefs
Craig Boutilier, University of British Columbia and Moisés Goldszmidt, Rockwell International / 649

Reasoning about Only Knowing with Many Agents
Joseph Y. Halpern, IBM Almaden Research Center / 655

All They Know About
Gerhard Lakemeyer, University of Bonn / 662

Representation for Actions and Motion / 669

Towards Knowledge-Level Analysis of Motion Planning
Ronen I. Brafman, Jean-Claude Latombe and Yoav Shoham, Stanford University / 670

EL: A Formal, Yet Natural, Comprehensive Knowledge Representation
Chung Hee Hwang and Lenhart K. Schubert, University of Rochester / 676

The Semantics of Event Prevention
Charles L. Ortiz, Jr., University of Pennsylvania / 683

The Frame Problem and Knowledge-Producing Actions
Richard B. Scherl and Hector J. Levesque, University of Toronto / 689

Rule-Based Reasoning / 697

The Paradoxical Success of Fuzzy Logic
Charles Elkan, University of California, San Diego / 698

Exploring the Structure of Rule Based Systems
Clifford Grossner, Alun D. Preece, P. Gokul Chander, T. Radhakrishnan, Ching Y. Suen, Concordia University / 704

Supporting and Optimizing Full Unification in a Forward Chaining Rule System
Howard E. Shrobe, Massachusetts Institute of Technology / 710

Comprehensibility Improvement of Tabular Knowledge Bases
Atsushi Sugiura and Yoshiyuki Koseki, NEC Corporation; Maximilian Riesenhuber, Johann Wolfgang Goethe-University / 716

Search / 723

Time-Saving Tips for Problem Solving with Incomplete Information
Michael R. Genesereth and Illah R. Nourbakhsh, Stanford University / 724

Decomposition of Domains Based on the Micro-Structure of Finite Constraint-Satisfaction Problems
Philippe Jégou, Université de Provence / 731

Innovative Design as Systematic Search
Dorothy Neville and Daniel S. Weld, University of Washington / 737

Generating Effective Admissible Heuristics by Abstraction and Reconstitution
Armand Prieditis, University of California, Davis and Bhaskar Janakiraman, Silicon Graphics Inc. / 743

Iterative Weakening: Optimal and Near-Optimal Policies for the Selection of Search Bias
Foster John Provost, University of Pittsburgh / 749

Pruning Duplicate Nodes in Depth-First Search
Larry A. Taylor and Richard E. Korf, University of California, Los Angeles / 756

Conjunctive Width Heuristics for Maximal Constraint Satisfaction
Richard J. Wallace and Eugene C. Freuder, University of New Hampshire / 762

Depth-First vs. Best-First Search: New Results
Weixiong Zhang and Richard E. Korf, University of California, Los Angeles / 769

Statistically-Based Natural Language Processing / 777
Using an Annotated Language Corpus as a Virtual Stochastic Grammar
Rens Bod, University of Amsterdam / 778

Equations for Part-of-Speech Tagging
Eugene Charniak, Curtis Hendrickson, Neil Jacobson and Mike Perkowitz, Brown University / 784

Estimating Probability Distributions over Hypotheses with Variable Unification
Dekai Wu, Hong Kong University of Science and Technology / 790

Trainable Natural Language Systems / 797
A Case-Based Approach to Knowledge Acquisition for Domain-Specific Sentence Analysis
Claire Cardie, University of Massachusetts / 798

KITSS: A Knowledge-Based Translation System for Test Scenarios
Van E. Kelly and Mark A. Jones, AT&T Bell Laboratories / 804

Automatically Constructing a Dictionary for Information Extraction Tasks
Ellen Riloff, University of Massachusetts / 811

Learning Semantic Grammars with Constructive Inductive Logic Programming
John M. Zelle and Raymond J. Mooney, University of Texas / 817

Vision Processing / 823
Polly: A Vision-Based Artificial Agent
Ian Horswill, MIT AI Laboratory / 824

Range Estimation From Focus Using a Non-frontal Imaging Camera
Arun Krishnan and Narendra Ahuja, University of Illinois / 830

Learning Object Models from Appearance
Hiroshi Murase, NTT Basic Research Labs and Shree K. Nayar, Columbia University / 836

On the Qualitative Structure of Temporally Evolving Visual Motion Fields
Richard P. Wildes, SRI David Sarnoff Research Center / 844

Invited Talks / 851

Tiger in a Cage: The Applications of Knowledge-based Systems (1993)
Edward A. Feigenbaum, Stanford University / 852

Artificial Intelligence as an Experimental Science
Herbert A. Simon, Carnegie Mellon University / 853

Video Abstracts / 855

A Demonstration of the "Circuit Fix-it Shoppe"
D. Richard Hipp and Ronnie W. Smith, Duke University / 856

Instructo-Soar: Learning from Interactive Natural Language Instructions
Scott B. Huffman and John E. Laird, The University of Michigan / 857

Winning the AAAI Robot Competition
David Kortenkamp, Marcus Huber, Charles Cohen, Ulrich Raschke, Clint Bidlack, Clare Bates Congdon, Frank Koss, and Terry Weymouth, The University of Michigan / 858

AIR-SOAR: Intelligent Multi-Level Control
Douglas J. Pearson, Randolph M. Jones, and John E. Laird, The University of Michigan / 860

Selective Perception for Robot Driving
Douglas A. Reece, University of Central Florida and Steven A. Shafer, Carnegie Mellon University / 862

Computer Vision Research at the University of Massachusetts
Edward M. Riseman and Allen R. Hanson, University of Massachusetts; J. Indigo Thomas and Members of the Computer Vision Laboratory, University of Massachusetts / 863

A Fuzzy Controller for Flakey, the Robot
Alessandro Saffiotti, Nicholas Helft, Kurt Konolige, John Lowrance, Karen Myers, Daniela Musto, Enrique Ruspini, and Leonard Wesley, SRI International / 864

Index / 865

Organization of the American Association for Artificial Intelligence

1993 National Conference on Artificial Intelligence (AAAI-93)

Conference Chair
William Swartout, USC/Information Sciences
   Institute

Program Cochairs
Richard Fikes, Stanford University

Wendy Lehnert, University of Massachusetts,
Amherst

Associate Chairs
Paul Cohen, University of Massachusetts, Amherst

Ramesh Patil, USC/Information Sciences Institute

Robot Competition and Exhibition Cochairs
Kurt Konolige, SRI International
Terry Weymouth, University of Michigan

Tutorial Program Chair
Paul Cohen, University of Massachusetts, Amherst

Video Program Cochairs
Walter Hamscher, Price Waterhouse Technology
   Center
Richard Korf, University of California, Los
   Angeles

Workshop Program Chair
Robert Filman, IntelliCorp

Program Committee
Brad Allen, Inference Corporation
Richard Alterman, Brandeis University
Amitava Bagchi, New Jersey Institute of
   Technology
Lawrence Birnbaum, Northwestern University
Craig Boutilier, University of British Columbia
Wray Buntine, NASA Ames Research Center
William Cohen, AT&T Bell Laboratories
Susan E. Conry, Clarkson University
Gary Cottrell, University of California, San Diego
James Crawford, AT&T Bell Laboratories
Mukesh Dalal, Rutgers University

Thomas L. Dean, Brown University
Rina Dechter, University of California, Irvine
Gerald DeJong, University of Illinois
Johan deKleer, Xerox Palo Alto Research Center
Marie desJardins, SRI International
Mark Drummond, NASA Ames Research Center
Michael Dyer, University of California, Los
   Angeles
Charles Elkan, University of California, San
   Diego
Robert S. Engelmore, KSL/Stanford University
Michael Erdmann, Carnegie Mellon University
Brian Falkenhainer, Cornell University
Usama Fayyad, JPL/California Institute of
   Technology
Steven Feiner, Columbia University
Douglas Fisher, Vanderbilt University
Kenneth D. Forbus, Northwestern University
Peter Friedland, NASA Ames Research Center
Les Gasser, University of Southern California
Michael Gelfond, University of Texas
Maria Gini, University of Minnesota
Ken Goldberg, University of Southern California
Diana Gordon, Naval Research Lab
Tom Gruber, KSL/Stanford University
Kristian Hammond, University of Chicago
Steven Hanks, University of Washington
James A. Hendler, University of Maryland
Robert Holte, University of Ottawa
Lawrence Hunter, National Library of Medicine
Leo Joskowicz, IBM T.J. Watson Research Center
Kurt Konolige, SRI International
Benjamin Kuipers, University of Texas, Austin
Vipin Kumar, University of Minnesota
Jean-Claude Latombe, Stanford University
Jay Liebowitz, George Washington University
Victor Lesser, University of Massachusetts,
   Amherst
Mark Maybury, The MITRE Corporation
Eric Mays, IBM T.J. Watson Research Center
Gordon McCalla, University of Saskatchewan
Daniel P. Miranker, University of Texas, Austin
Ray Mooney, University of Texas, Austin
Leora Morgenstern, IBM T.J. Watson Research
   Center

Peter Patel-Schneider, *AT&T Bell Laboratories*
Judea Pearl, *University of California, Los Angeles*
Ed Pednault, *AT&T Bell Laboratories*
Jean Ponce, *University of Illinois*
David Poole, *University of British Columbia*
Bruce Porter, *University of Texas, Austin*
Patti Price, *SRI International*
Lisa Rau, *General Electric Research & Development Center*
Larry Rendell, *University of Illinois*
Jeffrey S. Rosenschein, *Hebrew University*
Alberto Segre, *Cornell University*
Colleen Seifert, *University of Michigan*
Bart Selman, *AT&T Bell Laboratories*
David E. Smith, *Rockwell Palo Alto Science Center*
Steven Smith, *Carnegie Mellon University*
Mark E. Stickel, *SRI International*
Devika Subramanian, *Cornell University*
Ron Sun, *University of Alabama*
Richard S. Sutton, *GTE Labs*
Jeffrey Van Baalen, *University of Wyoming*
Peter van Beek, *University of Alberta*
Pascal Van Hentenryck, *Brown University*
Ralph Weischedel, *BBN Systems & Technology*
Daniel Weld, *University of Washington*
Yorick Wilks, *New Mexico State University*
Beverly Woolf, *University of Massachusetts, Amherst*
Monte Zweben, *NASA Ames Research Center*

Auxiliary Reviewers
Lloyd Greenwald
Jak Kirman, *Brown University*
Shieu-Hong Lin
Ann Nicholson, *Brown University*

AAAI Officials

President
Patrick J. Hayes, University of Illinois

President-Elect
Barbara Grosz, Harvard University

Past President
Daniel G. Bobrow, Xerox Palo Alto Research Center

Secretary-Treasurer
Norman R. Nielsen, SRI International

Councilors (through 1993)
Thomas Dietterich, Oregon State University
Mark Fox, University of Toronto
Barbara Hayes-Roth, Stanford University
Richard Fikes, Stanford University

Councilors (through 1994)
Jaime Carbonell, Carnegie Mellon University
Paul Cohen, University of Massachusetts
Elaine Kant, Schlumberger Laboratory for Computer Science
Candy Sidner, Digital Equipment Corporation

Councilors (through 1995)
Johan deKleer, Xerox Palo Alto Research Center
Benjamin Kuipers, University of Texas, Austin
Paul Rosenbloom, USC/Information Sciences Institute
Beverly Woolf, University of Massachusetts

Standing Committees

Conference Chair
William Swartout, USC/Information Sciences Institute

Finance Chair
Norman R. Nielsen, SRI International

Publications Chair
Mark Fox, University of Toronto

Scholarship Chair
Katia Sycara, Carnegie Mellon University

Symposium Chair
James A. Hendler

Symposium Cochair
Lynn Andrea Stein, MIT AI Laboratory

Workshop Grants Chair
Candace Sidner, Digital Equipment Corporation

Workshop Grants Cochair
Beverly Woolf, University of Massachusetts

AI in Business Subgroup Liaison
Dan O'Leary, University of Southern California

AI and the Law Subgroup Liaison
Edwina Rissland, University of Massachusetts

AI in Medicine Subgroup Liaison
Serdar Uckun, Stanford University

AI in Manufacturing Subgroup Liaison
Karl Kempf, Intel Corporation

AAAI Staff

Executive Director
Carol McKenna Hamilton

Accountant
Julia G. Bowen

Membership & Systems Coordinator
Richard A. Skalsky

Conference Coordinator
Annette Eldredge

Conference & Exhibits Coordinator
Mary Livingston

Administrative
Hasina Aziz, Daphne Black, Sally McLaughlin,
* Arthur Okorie*

AI Magazine

Coeditors
Ramesh Patil, USC/Information Sciences Institute
Elaine Rich, MCC

Editor Emeritus
Robert S. Engelmore, KSL/Stanford University

Associate Editor, Book Reviews
Bruce D'Ambrosio, Oregon State University

Associate Editor, Dissertation Abstracts
Peter Karp, SRI International

Associate Editor, Workshop Reports
Peter Patel-Schneider, AT&T Bell Laboratories

Publishing Director
David Mike Hamilton, The Live Oak Press

Managing Editor
Ellie Engelmore, AAAI

Production Editor
Sunny Ludvik, Ludvik Editorial Services

The AAAI Press

Editor-in-Chief
Kenneth Ford, University of Western Florida

The MIT Press Coliaisons
Robert Prior and Teresa Ehling, The MIT Press

General Manager
David Mike Hamilton, The Live Oak Press

Management Board
William L. Clancey, Institute for Research on
* Learning*
Teresa Ehling, The MIT Press
Kenneth Ford, University of Western Florida
David Mike Hamilton, The Live Oak Press
Robert Prior, The MIT Press
Reid Smith, Schlumberger Laboratory for
* Computer Science*

AAAI Corporate Sponsors

Apple Computers
Digital Equipment Corporation
General Motors Research Laboratory

AAAI Corporate Affiliate

The MITRE Corporation

AAAI–93
Best Written Paper Award

Equations for Part-of-Speech Tagging

Eugene Charniak, Curtis Hendrickson, Neil Jacobson, Mike Perkowitz

Honorable Mentions

Planning With Deadlines in Stochastic Domains

Thomas Dean, Leslie Pack Kaelbling, Jak Kirman, Ann Nicholson

Reasoning with Characteristic Models

Henry A. Kautz, Michael J. Kearns, Bart Selman

The Paradoxical Success of Fuzzy Logic

Charles Elkan

Each year, AAAI's National Conference on Artificial Intelligence honors a handful of papers that exemplify high standards in exposition and pedagogy. Papers are nominated for the Best Written Paper Award by members of the program committee during the NCAI review process. These nominations are then reviewed once again by a smaller subset of the program committee to select a winning paper and honorable mentions. Care is taken during the review process to ensure that our final decisions are based on the opinions of impartial readers who are free from personal biases and conflicts of interest.

Preface

Each year the National Conference on Artificial Intelligence (NCAI) is the primary large scale forum in the United States where the highest quality new research in Artificial Intelligence (AI) is presented and discussed. Quality is maintained by a highly competitive review and selection process in which fewer than one of every four submitted papers is accepted. This volume contains those accepted papers.

For this year's conference, papers were solicited that describe significant contributions to all aspects of AI, including the principles underlying cognition, perception, and action in humans and machines; the design, application, and evaluation of AI algorithms and intelligent systems; and the analysis of tasks and domains in which intelligent systems perform. In recognition of the wide range of methodologies and research activities legitimately associated with AI, the conference program includes papers describing both experimental and theoretical results from all stages of AI research. This year we particularly encouraged submission of papers that present promising new research directions by describing innovative concepts, techniques, perspectives, or observations that are not yet supported by mature results. To be accepted to the conference, such submissions were required to include substantial analysis of the ideas, the technology needed to realize them, and their potential impact.

Because of the essential interdisciplinary nature of AI and the need to maintain effective communication across sub-specialties, authors were encouraged to position and motivate their work in the larger context of the general AI community. While papers concerned with applications of AI were invited, most such papers were presented at the Innovative Applications of AI conference, which was collocated with the NCAI.

Since many papers in the conference involve multiple topics, the task of grouping papers into sessions is generally under constrained and involves significant subjective judgment. For example, one paper might be legitimately presented in a session on case-based reasoning, user interfaces, or natural language processing, while another paper might be presented in a session on search, diagnosis, or planning. So, if you are looking for papers on a particular topic, consider the session titles to be merely suggestive and search broadly throughout the volume. For example, there is only one session this year on case-based

reasoning (CBR), but there are many other CBR papers scattered throughout the proceedings. We did not schedule CBR sessions for those papers where CBR appeared to be used as an enabling technology more than a focal point of the research. Consequently, you will find descriptions of CBR systems (and memory-based systems) in the sessions on Trainable Natural Language Systems, Diagnostic Reasoning, Large Scale Knowledge Bases, Plan Learning, and Novel Methods in Knowledge Acquisition.

When we did find a large number of papers that seemed to be associated with a cohesive community, we grouped those papers into a series of sequentially scheduled sessions so that related papers would not be competing with one another in the parallel sessions. This year we have paper tracks for constraint-based reasoning (2 sessions), distributed problem solving (2 sessions), machine learning (4 sessions), natural language processing (5 sessions), nonmonotonic logic (2 sessions), planning (2 sessions), reasoning about physical systems (2 sessions), and search (2 sessions).

We would like to comment on the review process for papers submitted to the NCAI. The process has evolved in recent years into a unique undertaking that makes extensive use of computing and networking capabilities. For example, this year each of the 75 members of the program committee was sent files containing the title, authors, and abstract of each of the over 500 submitted papers. They were asked to select those papers they were able to review, those they could not review because of conflicts, etc. Those "self selections" were sent back via electronic mail, recorded in a data base, and processed by software that produced a load-balanced draft assignment of two reviewers to each paper for consideration by the program chairs. After papers had been assigned to reviewers, the reviewers used electronic mail to exchange their draft reviews, reach an accept/reject decision, or request an additional reviewer. Finally, a cluster analysis program was used to do the detailed scheduling of the weekend meeting of the program committee so that during that meeting each paper was discussed by its reviewers in a small group of committee members whose interests strongly overlapped with those of the reviewers, as indicated by the self selection data.

Many people have been involved in developing and evolving the paper review process for the NCAI. Special thanks are due to Ramesh Patil for designing and implementing much of the software used in this year's process. That software is a significant contribution to the ongoing life of the AAAI and its ability to produce large scale high quality conferences.

Finally, we would like to thank some of the many people who played a role in creating this program: Paul Cohen and Ramesh Patil, our associate program chairs; Carol Hamilton, Executive Director of the AAAI; Annette Eldredge, the Conference Coordinator; the program committee area chairs who helped recruit the remainder of the program committee and run the program committee meeting; and finally all the members of the program committee, whose time and expertise enabled the selection of this fine representative sampling of current AI research activity.

Richard Fikes and Wendy Lehnert
Program Cochairs

Automated
Reasoning

On Computing Minimal Models*

Rachel Ben-Eliyahu
Cognitive Systems Laboratory
Computer Science Department
University of California
Los Angeles, California 90024
rachel@cs.ucla.edu

Rina Dechter
Information & Computer Science
University of California
Irvine, California 92717
dechter@ics.uci.edu

Abstract

This paper addresses the problem of computing the minimal models of a given CNF propositional theory. We present two groups of algorithms. Algorithms in the first group are efficient when the theory is almost Horn, that is, when there are few non-Horn clauses and/or when the set of all literals that appear positive in any non-Horn clause is small. Algorithms in the other group are efficient when the theory can be represented as an acyclic network of low-arity relations. Our algorithms suggest several characterizations of tractable subsets for the problem of finding minimal models.

1 Introduction

One approach to attacking NP-hard problems is to identify *islands of tractability* in the problem domain and to use their associated algorithms as building blocks for solving hard instances, often approximately. A celebrated example of this approach is the treatment of the propositional satisfiability problem.

In this paper, we would like to initiate a similar effort for the problem of finding one, all, or some of the *minimal models* of a propositional theory. Computing minimal models is an essential task in many reasoning systems in Artificial Intelligence, including propositional circumscription [Lif] and minimal diagnosis [dKMR92], and in answering queries posed on logic programs (under stable model semantics [GL91, BNNS91]) and deductive databases (under the generalized closed-world assumption [Min82]). While the ultimate goal in these systems is not to compute minimal models but rather to produce plausible inferences, efficient algorithms for computing minimal models can substantially speed up inference in these systems.

Special cases of this problem have been studied in the diagnosis literature and, more recently, the logic programming literature. Algorithms used in many diagnosis systems [dKW87, dKMR92] are highly complex in the worst case: To find a minimal diagnosis, they first compute all prime implicates of a theory and then find a minimal cover of the prime implicates. The first task is output exponential, while the second is NP-hard. Therefore, in the diagnosis literature, researchers have often compromised completeness by using a heuristic approach. The work in the logic programming literature (e.g. [BNNS91]) focused on using efficient optimization techniques, such as linear programming, for computing minimal models. A limitation of this approach is that it does not address the issue of worst-case and average-case complexities.

We want to complement these approaches by studying the task of finding all or some of the minimal models in general, independent of any specific domain. We will use the "tractable islands" methodology to provide more refined worst-case guarantees. The two primary "islands" that we use are *Horn theories* and *acyclic theories*. It is known that Horn theories have a unique minimal model that can be found in linear time [DG84]. Our near-Horn algorithms try to associate an input theory with a "close" Horn theory, yielding algorithms whose complexity is a function of this "distance". For acyclic theories, we will show that while finding one or a subset of the minimal models can be done in output-polynomial time, the task of finding all minimal models is more complex. We will set up conditions under which the set of all minimal models can be computed in output-polynomial time and we will present a tree-algorithm that solves this problem in general. Once we have an efficient algorithm for generating minimal models of tree-like theories, we can apply it to any arbitrary theory by first compiling the theory into a tree. The resulting complexity will often be dominated by the complexity of this compilation process and will be less demanding for "near-tree" theories.

---

*This work was partially supported by an IBM graduate fellowship to the first author, by NSF grants IRI-9157636 and IRI-9200918, by Air Force Office of Scientific Research grant AFOSR 900136, and by a grant from Xerox Palo Alto research center.

2 Preliminary definitions

A clause is *positive* if it contains only positive literals and is *negative* if it contains only negative literals. In this paper, a *theory* is a set of clauses. A set of literals *covers* a theory iff it contains at least one literal from each clause in the theory. A set of covers of a theory is *complete* iff it is a superset of all minimal covers of the theory.

A theory is called *positive* if it is composed of positive clauses only. Given a theory Φ and a set of literals S, the operation $\Phi \oslash S$ performs unit propagation on the theory $\Phi \bigcup S$. For each theory Φ, $nf(\Phi)$ denotes $\Phi \oslash \emptyset$. For each model M, $pos(M)$ denotes the set of symbols to which M assigns **true**. We will sometimes refer to a model as a set of literals, where a negative literal $\neg P$ in the model means that the model assigns **false** to P and a positive literal P in the model means that the model assigns **true** to P.

Definition 2.1 (*X*-minimal model) *Let Φ be a theory over a set of symbols $\mathcal{L}$, $X \subseteq \mathcal{L}$, and M a model for Φ. M is an X-minimal model for Φ iff there is no other model M' for Φ such that $pos(M') \bigcap X \subset pos(M) \bigcap X$. If M is an X-minimal model for $X = \mathcal{L}$, it will be called simply a* minimal *model.*

3 General algorithms

Cadoli [Cad92] has shown that the problem of finding an X-minimal model for a theory is $P^{NP[O(\log n)]}$-hard. Roughly, this means that it is at least as hard as problems that can be solved by a deterministic polynomial algorithm that uses $O(\log n)$ calls to an NP oracle. In Figure 1 we show an algorithm for computing X-minimal models that takes $O(n^2)$ steps and uses $O(n)$ calls to an NP oracle (where n is the number of variables in the theory). In Figure 2 we show a variation of this algorithm that uses a procedure for satisfiability that also returns a model in case the theory is satisfiable. The algorithm suggests the following:

Theorem 3.1 *Let C be a class of theories over a language $\mathcal{L}$ having the following properties:*

1. There is an algorithm α such that for any theory $\Phi \in C$, α both decides whether Φ is satisfiable and produces a model for Φ (if there is one) in time $O(t_C)$.

2. C is closed under instantiation, that is, for every $\Phi \in C$ and for every literal L in $\mathcal{L}$, $\Phi \oslash \{L\} \in C$.

Then for any theory $\Phi \in C$, an X-minimal model for Φ can be found in time $O(|X|t_C)$.

Corollary 3.2 *An X-minimal model for a 2-CNF theory Φ can be found in time $O(|X|n)$ where n is the length of the theory.*

However, using a straightforward reduction from VERTEX COVER [Kar72], we can show that if we are interested in finding a minimum cardinality

---

> **Find-X-minimal(Φ, X, M)**
> **Input:** A theory Φ and a subset of the variables in Φ, X. **Output:** **true** if Φ is satisfiable, **false** otherwise. In case Φ is satisfiable, the output variable M is an X-minimal model for Φ.
>
> 1. If $\neg\text{sat}(\Phi)$ return **false**;
> 2. For $i = 1$ to n $M[i] = $ **false**;
> 3. Let $P_1, ..., P_n$ be an ordering on the variables in Φ such that the first $|X|$ variables are all the variables from X.
> 4. For $i := 1$ to n do
>   If $\text{sat}(\Phi \bigcup \{\neg P_i\})$ then $\Phi := \Phi \oslash \{\neg P_i\}$
>   else $\Phi := \Phi \oslash \{P_i\}$, $M[i] = $ **true**;
> 5. return **true**;

Figure 1: Algorithm Find-X-minimal

> **Find-X-minimal2(Φ, X, M)**
> 1. If $\neg\text{model-sat}(\Phi, M)$ return **false**;
> 2. $negX := \{P | P \in X, \neg P \in M\}$; $X := X - negX$;
> $\Phi := \Phi \bigcup \{\neg P | P \in negX\}$;
> 3. While $X \neq \emptyset$ do
>   a. Let $P \in X$;
>   b. If $\neg\text{model-sat}(\Phi \bigcup \{\neg P\}, M')$ then $\Phi := \Phi \oslash \{P\}$
>   else $\Phi := \Phi \oslash \{\neg P\}$, $M := M'$;
>   c. $X := X - \{P\}$;   If $X = \emptyset$ return **true**;

Figure 2: Algorithm Find-X-minimal2

model for a 2-CNF theory (namely, a model that assigns **true** to a minimum number of symbols), the situation is not so bright:

Theorem 3.3 *The following decision problem is NP-complete: Given a positive 2-CNF theory Φ and an integer K, does Φ have a model of cardinality $\leq K$?*

4 Algorithms for almost-Horn theories

In this section, we present algorithms for computing minimal models of a propositional theory which are efficient for almost Horn theories. The basic idea is to instantiate as few variables as possible so that the remaining theory will be a Horn theory and then find a minimal model for the remaining theory in linear time.

4.1 Algorithm for theories with only a few non-Horn clauses

Algorithm MinSAT is efficient when most of the theory is Horn and there are only few non-Horn clauses. Given a theory, MinSAT works as follows: It first tries to solve satisfiability by unit propagation. If the empty clause was not generated and no positive clause is left, the theory is satisfiable, and the unique minimal model assigns **false** to the vari-

```
MinSAT(Φ, M)

Input: A theory Φ. Output: true if Φ is satisfiable,
   false otherwise. In case Φ is satisfiable, the output
   variable M will contain a set of models for Φ that is
   a superset of all the minimal models of Φ.

1.  Φ :=UnitInst(Φ, I, Sat); If not Sat return false;

2.  If Φ contains no positive clauses then begin M :=
    {I ⋃ {¬P | P ∈ Φ}}; return true; end.

3.  M := ∅; Let A be a complete set of covers for the set
    of all the positive clauses in Φ.
    For each S ∈ A do:
              If MinSAT(Φ ⋃ S, M') then
    M := M ⋃ combine(I, M');

4.  If M == ∅ then return false else return true;
```

Figure 3: Algorithm MinSAT

ables in the remaining theory. If a nonempty set of positive clauses is left, we compute a cover for the remaining set of positive clauses, replace them with the cover, and then call MinSAT recursively on the new theory. If the theory is not satisfiable, or if we are interested in *all* minimal models, we have to call MinSAT again with a different cover.

Algorithm MinSAT is shown in Figure 3. The procedure $UnitInst(\Phi, I, Sat)$ gets a theory Φ and returns $nf(\Phi)$. I contains the set of unit clauses used for the instantiations. Sat is false iff the empty clause belongs to the normal form; otherwise Sat is true. The procedure $combine(I, M)$ gets a set of literals I and a set of sets of literals M and returns the set $\{S | S = W \cup I, W \in M\}$.

We can show that MinSAT returns a superset of all the minimal models of the theory. We group all the propositional theories in classes $\Psi_0, \Psi_1, \ldots$ as follows:

- $\Phi \in \Psi_0$ iff $nf(\Phi)$ has no positive clauses or contains the empty clause.

- $\Phi \in \Psi_{k+|C|}$ iff for some A that is a complete set of covers for C and for each S in A, $\Phi \oslash S$ belongs to Ψ_k, where C is the set of positive clauses in $nf(\Phi)$.

Note that if a theory has k non-Horn clauses it belongs to the class Ψ_j for some $j \leq k$ and that all Horn theories belong to Ψ_0. We can show that if $\Phi \in \Psi_k$ then the above algorithm runs in time $O(nm^k)$, where n is the length of the input and m the maximum number of positive literals that appear in any clause. This is also the worst case complexity if we are interested only in deciding satisfiability. Since for every k the class Ψ_k is closed under instantiation, we can use Theorem 3.1 to prove that:

Proposition 4.1 *If a theory Φ belongs to the class Ψ_k for some k, then an X-minimal model for Φ can be found in time $O(|X|nm^k)$.*

Algorithm MinSAT returns a superset of all the minimal models. To identify the set of all minimal

models, we need to compare all the models generated. Therefore, the complexity of finding all minimal models for a theory in the class Ψ_k is $O(nm^{2k})$.

4.2 Algorithms that exploit the positive graph of a theory

In this section we will identify tractable subsets for *satisfiability* and for finding all minimal models by using topological analysis of what we call the *positive graph* of a theory. The positive graph reflects on the interactions of the positive literals in the theory.

Definition 4.2 (positive graph of a theory)
Let Φ be a theory. The positive graph *of Φ is an undirected graph (V, E) defined as follows:*

$\mathbf{V} = \{P | P \text{ is a positive literal in some clause in } \Phi\}$,
$\mathbf{E} = \{(P, Q) | P \text{ and } Q \text{ appear positive in the same clause}\}$.

Note that Φ is a Horn theory iff its positive graph has no edges.

Definition 4.3 (vertex cover) *Let $G = (V, E)$ be a graph. A* vertex cover *of G is a set $V' \subseteq V$ such that for each $e \in E$ there is some $v \in V'$ such that $v \in e$.*

We take "vertex cover of the theory" to mean "vertex cover of the positive graph of the theory".

An algorithm that computes a superset of all minimal models based on a vertex cover of a theory can consider all possible instantiations of the variables in the cover. Each such instantiation yields a Horn theory for which we can find a minimal model (if there is one) in linear time. When we combine the model for the Horn theory with the cover instantiation, a model of the original theory results. We can show that a superset of all minimal models of a theory can be generated in this way. If we are interested only in deciding satisfiability, we can stop once the first model is found. Hence,

Theorem 4.4 *If the positive graph of a theory Φ has a vertex cover of cardinality c, then the satisfiability of Φ can be decided in time $O(n2^c)$, where n is the size of the theory, and an X-minimal model for Φ can be found in time $O(|X|n2^c)$. The set of all minimal models of Φ can be found in time $O(n2^{2c})$.*

In general, the problem of finding a minimum-cardinality vertex cover of a graph is NP-hard. A greedy heuristic procedure for finding a vertex cover could simply remove the node with maximum degree from the graph and continue with the reduced graph until all nodes are disconnected. The set of all nodes removed is a vertex cover.

Algorithm VC-minSAT (Figure 4) integrates the above heuristic into a backtrack algorithm for finding the minimal models. *MaxDegree* takes the positive graph as an input and returns a symbol (node) that has a maximum degree. If there is more

VC-minSAT(Φ, M, G)

Input: A theory Φ and a positive graph of Φ, G.

Output: **true** if Φ is satisfiable, otherwise **false**. If Φ is satisfiable, M contains a superset of all minimal models for Φ.

1. $I := \emptyset$; $\Phi := UnitInst(\Phi, I, Sat)$;

2. If $\neg Sat$ return **false**; $G := Update(\Phi, G)$;

3. If G is disconnected then
    begin $M := I \bigcup \{\neg P | P \in \Phi\}$; return **true**; *end*.

4. $P := MaxDegree(G)$; $Sat :=$ **false**; $M := \emptyset$;

5. If VC-minSAT$(\Phi \bigcup \{P\}, M^+, G)$ then
    $M := combine(I, M^+)$;

6. If VC-minSAT$(\Phi \bigcup \{\neg P\}, M^-, G)$ then
    $M := M \bigcup combine(I, M^-)$;

7. If $M == \emptyset$ return **false** else return **true**

Figure 4: Algorithm VC-minSAT

than one such symbol, it chooses the one that appears in a maximum number of non-Horn clauses in the theory. $Update(\Phi, G)$ returns the positive graph of Φ, by updating G. We can show that algorithm VC-minSAT produces a superset of all the minimal models.

We should mention here that the idea of initializing variables in a theory until the remaining theory is Horn has been suggested, in the context of solving the satisfiability problem, by Gallo and Scutella [GS88] and was recently extended by Dalal and Etherington [DE92]. The advantages of our approach are that we provide an intuitive criteria for how the variables to be instantiated are selected and we classify the performance of the algorithm using a well-understood and largely explored graphical property, vertex cover.

Also note that we could define the *negative graph* of a theory just as we defined the positive graph. We could then write an algorithm that is analogous to VC-minSAT and is efficient for deciding satisfiability of theories for which the negative graph has a small vertex cover. Clearly, algorithm minSAT also has an analogous algorithm that considers negative instead of positive clauses.

5 Computing minimal models on acyclic networks of relations

In this section we provide efficient algorithms for theories that can be represented as acyclic relations of low arity. We next define the notions of *constraint networks* and *relations* and show how they can represent propositional theories and their satisfying models.

Definition 5.1 (relations, networks, schemes) *Given a set of variables* $X = \{X_1, ..., X_n\}$, *each associated with a domain of discrete values*

$D_1, ..., D_n$, *respectively, a relation (or, alternatively, a constraint)* $\rho = \rho(X_1, ..., X_n)$ *is any subset*

$$\rho \subseteq D_1 \times D_2 \times ... \times D_n.$$

The projection of ρ *onto a subset of variables* R, *denoted* $\Pi_R(\rho)$ *or* ρ_R, *is the set of tuples defined on the variables in* R *that can be extended to a tuple in* ρ. *A constraint network* N *over* X *is a set* $\rho_1, ..., \rho_t$ *of such relations. Each relation* ρ_i *is defined on a subset of variables* $S_i \subseteq X$. *We also denote by* $\rho(S_i)$ *the relation specified over* S_i. *The set of subsets* $S = \{S_1, .., S_t\}$ *is called the scheme of* N. *The network* N *represents a unique relation* $rel(N)$ *defined over* X, *which stands for all consistent assignments (or all solutions), namely,*

$$rel(N) = \{x = (x_1, ..., x_n) | \ \forall S_i \in S, \Pi_{S_i}(x) \in \rho_i\}.$$

A partial assignment $T = t$ *is a value assignment to a subset of variables* $T \subseteq X$. *The operator* $\bowtie$ *is the join operator in relational databases. If* $rel(N) = \rho$, *we say that* N *describes or* represents ρ.

Any propositional theory can be viewed as a special kind of constraint network, where the domain of each variable is $\{0, 1\}$ (corresponding to $\{$**false**, **true**$\}$) and where each clause specifies a constraint (in other words, a relation) on its propositional symbols. The *scheme of a theory* is accordingly defined as the scheme of its corresponding constraint network, and the set of all models of the theory corresponds exactly to the set of all solutions of its corresponding constraint network.

Example 5.2 *Consider the theory* $\Phi = \{\neg A \vee \neg B, \neg B \vee \neg C, C \vee D\}$. *This theory can be viewed as a constraint network over the variables* $\{A, B, C, D\}$, *where the corresponding relations are the truth tables of each clause, that is,* $\rho(AB) = \{00, 01, 10\}$, $\rho(BC) = \{00, 01, 10\}$, *and* $\rho(CD) = \{01, 10, 11\}$. *The scheme of the theory* Φ *is* $\{AB, BC, CD\}$. *The set of all solutions to this network (and hence the set of models of* Φ*) is*

$$\rho(ABCD) = \{0001, 0010, 0011, 0101, 1001, 1010, 1011\}.$$

Note that Φ *has two minimal models:* $\{0001, 0010\}$.

The scheme of a theory can be associated with a *constraint graph* where each relation in the scheme is a node in the graph and two nodes are connected iff the corresponding relations have variables in common. The arcs are labeled by the common variables. For example, the constraint graph of the theory Φ of Example 5.2 is as follows:

Theories that correspond to a constraint graph that is a tree are called *acyclic theories*, and their corresponding tree-like constraint graph is called a *join tree*.

We next present two algorithms for computing minimal models for *acyclic* theories. These algorithms will be extended to arbitrary theories via a procedure known as *tree-clustering* [DP89], which compiles any theory into a tree of relations. Consequently, given a general theory, the algorithms presented next work in two steps: A join-tree is computed by tree-clustering, and then a specialized tree-algorithm for computing the minimal models is applied. The complexity of tree-clustering is exponential in the size of the maximal arity of the generated relations, and hence our algorithms are efficient for theories that can be compiled into networks of low-arity relations. We should note, however, that even in the cases where tree-clustering is expensive, it might still be useful since it offers a systematic way of representing the models of the theory in a hierarchical structure capable of supporting information retrieval without backtracking.

5.1 Finding a subset of all minimal models

For the rest of Section 5, we will assume that we are dealing with constraint networks that correspond to propositional theories, and hence the domain of each variable is $\{0,1\}$ and we have the ordering $1 \succ 0$. We will also assume that we are looking for models that are minimal over all the symbols in the language of the theory, namely, X-minimal models where X is the set of all symbols in the theory.

Definition 5.3 *Given a relation ρ defined on a set of variables X, and given two tuples r and t in ρ, we say that $t \succ r$, iff for some X_0 in X, $t_{X_0} \succ r_{X_0}$ and, for all $X_i \in X$, $t_{X_i} \succ r_{X_i}$ or $t_{X_i} = r_{X_i}$. We say that t and r agree on a subset of variables $S \subseteq X$ iff $r_S = t_S$.*

Definition 5.4 (conditional minimal models) *Given a relation ρ over X and a subset of variables $S \subseteq X$, a tuple $t \in \rho$ is conditionally minimal w.r.t. S iff $\not\exists r \in \rho$ such that r agrees with t on S and $t_{X-S} \succ r_{X-S}$. The set of all conditional minimal models (tuples) of ρ w.r.t. $S = s$ is denoted $min(\rho \setminus S = s)$. The set of all conditional minimal models (tuples) of ρ w.r.t. S is denoted $min(\rho \setminus S)$ and is defined as the union over all possible assignments s to S of $min(\rho \setminus S = s)$. $min(\rho \setminus \emptyset)$ is abbreviated to $min(\rho)$.*

Example 5.5 *Consider the relation*

$$\rho(ABCD) = \{0111, 1011, 1010, 0101, 0001\}.$$

In this case, we have $min(\rho) = \{1010, 0001\}$, $min(\rho \setminus \{C, D\}) = \{0111, 1011, 1010, 0001\}$, and $min(\rho \setminus \{A\}) = \{0001, 1010\}$.

One can verify that: (1) any minimal tuple of a projection $\Pi_S(\rho)$ can be extended to a minimal tuple of ρ, but not vice versa; (2) a conditionally minimal tuple is not necessarily a minimal tuple; and (3) a minimal tuple is a conditional minimal tuple w.r.t. to all subsets.

Next we show that, given a join-tree, a subset of all minimal models can be computed in output polynomial time. The idea is as follows: Once we have a rooted join-tree (which is pair-wise consistent[1]), we can take all minimal tuples in the root node and extend them (via the join operation) with the matching conditional minimal tuples in their child nodes. This can be continued until we reach the leaves. It can be shown that all the models computed in this way are minimal and that they are generated in a backtrack-free manner; however, not *all* the minimal models will be generated. In order to enlarge the set of minimal models captured, we can reapply the procedure where each node serves as a root. We can show that if every minimal model has a projection that is minimal in at least one relation of the tree, the algorithm will generate all the minimal models. Formally,

Definition 5.6 (parents of S) *Given a scheme $S = \{S_1, ..., S_t\}$ of a rooted join-tree, we associate each subset S_i with its parent subset $S_{p(i)}$ in the rooted tree. We call an ordering $d = S_1, .., S_t$ a tree-ordering iff a parent node always precedes its child nodes.*

Definition 5.7 *Let T be a rooted join-tree with S_0 at the root. Let ρ_i be the relation associated with S_i and let $d = S_0, S_1, ..., S_t$ be a tree-ordering. We define*

$$\rho^0(T) = min(\rho_0) \bowtie_{i=1..t} (min(\rho_i \setminus S_{p(i)})).$$

Theorem 5.8 *Let T be a rooted join-tree with a tree-ordering $\{S_1, ..., S_t\}$. Then $\rho^0(T)$ is a subset of all the minimal models of T, and $\rho^0(T)$ can be computed in $O(L \sum_{i=1}^{t} |\rho_i|)$ steps where L is the number of minimal models in the output and ρ_i is the input relation associated with S_i.*

Example 5.9 *Consider the join-tree that corresponds to the theory Φ in Example 5.2. Assuming BC is the root, we can use the tree-ordering $d = BC, AB, CD$. Since tuple $(BC = 00)$ is the only minimal model of $\rho(BC)$, it is selected. This tuple can be extended by $A = 0$ and by $D = 1$, resulting in one minimal model of ρ, namely the tuple $(ABCD = 0001)$. If AB plays the role of a root, we will still be computing the same minimal model. However, when CD plays the role of a root, we will*

---

[1] Pair-wise consistency, or arc consistency, is a process that when applied to join-trees will delete from the join-tree all the tuples that do not belong to any solution. Pair-wise consistency can be achieved in polynomial time.

```
min1(Φ)
Input: A theory Φ.
Output: A subset of all the minimal models of Φ.

1. Apply tree-clustering to Φ. If the theory is not satisfi-
   able, stop and exit. Else, generate join-tree T. Apply
   pair-wise consistency to T.

2. For each node R in T do: For each join tree T' rooted
   at R compute ρ⁰(T').

3. Output the union of all models computed.
```

Figure 5: Algorithm min1

compute the tuple (ABCD = 0010), which is also a minimal model of ρ.

From Theorem 5.8, it follows that, given an acyclic network or any general backtrack-free network relative to an ordering d, one minimal model can be computed in time that is linear in the size of the network and the total subset of minimal models $\rho^0(T)$ can be computed in time proportional to the size of the set. We summarize this in algorithm *min1*, given in Figure 5.

Theorem 5.10 (complexity of min1)
The complexity of **min1** *is* $O(n2^k + nL|\rho|)$, *where k is the maximum arity of any relation in the join-tree, n is the number of relations, ρ is the largest relation in the generated tree T, and L is the number of minimal models generated.*

So **min1** is especially efficient when the theory is compiled into a join-tree having relations with low arity. We next present two sufficient conditions for the completeness of algorithm **min1** .

Theorem 5.11 (sufficient condition)
Suppose T is a join-tree having the scheme $S = \{S_1, ..., S_t\}$, and suppose that for every minimal model t of T there is a scheme $S_i \in S$ such that $\Pi_{S_i}(t)$ is in $min(\rho(S_i))$. Then **min1** *, when applied to T, will generate all the minimal models of T.*

Theorem 5.12 (local sufficient condition)
Suppose that for every node S in a join-tree T the set $min(\rho(S) \setminus S')$ is totally ordered, where S' is the set of all variables that are common to S and at least one of its neighbors in the tree. Then **min1** *, when applied to T, will generate all the minimal models.*

5.2   Listing all minimal models

Algorithm *min1* does not necessarily produce all minimal models because, as the following example shows, it is not always the case that all minimal models are minimal within at least one subrelation.

Example 5.13 *Consider the join-tree where the variables are $\{A, B, C, D, E, F, G\}$, the scheme is a tree $\{ABC, BCDEF, EFG\}$, and the corresponding relations are $\rho(ABC) = \{011, 110, 000\}$,*

```
min2(T)
Input: A pair-wise consistent join tree T which corre-
sponds to a theory Φ.
Output: All minimal models of φ.

1. Traverse the tree bottom up and compute Pmin(R)
   for each node R visited using equations (1) and (2).

2. Output Pmin(R⁰), where R⁰ is the root node.
```

Figure 6: Algorithm min2

$\rho(BCDEF) = \{11011, 10100, 00010\}$, *and* $\rho(EFG) = \{110, 000, 101\}$. *The reader can verify that the tuple $\{0110110\}$ is a minimal model for this network, but its projection relative to any of the relations is not minimal.*

We now present a second algorithm, **min2** , that computes all the minimal models but is not as efficient as **min1** in the sense that during processing it may generate models of the theory that are not minimal. Some of those models will be pruned only at the final stage. Nevertheless, we conjecture that the algorithm is optimal for trees.

Basically, algorithm **min2** computes partial minimal models recursively while traversing the join-tree bottom up. When we visit a node R, we prune all the partial models that we already know cannot be extended to a minimal model. The resulting subset of partial models is denoted by $Pmin(R)$. More formally, let T_R denote the network rooted at node R and S_R the set of all variables that R shares with its parent. We define

$$Pmin(R) = min(rel(T_R) \setminus S_R).$$

Since $S_R \subseteq R$,

$$Pmin(R) = min(J_R \setminus S_R) \qquad (1)$$

where J_R is defined to be

$$J_R = min(rel(T_R) \setminus R).$$

Note that for the root node R^0, $Pmin(R^0)$ is the set of all minimal models of the whole tree (conditioning is on the empty set). We can show that J_R can be expressed recursively as a function of $Pmin(U_1), ..., Pmin(U_n)$ where $U_1, ..., U_n$ are R's children:

$$J_R = \rho(R) \bowtie (\bowtie_{i=1}^n Pmin(U_i)). \qquad (2)$$

This allows a bottom-up computation of $Pmin(R)$ starting at the leaf nodes. The algorithm is summarized in Figure 6.

Example 5.14 *Consider again the tree-network of Example 5.9. Algorithm* **min2** *will perform the following computations:*

$$Pmin(AB) = min(\rho(AB) \setminus \{B\}) = \{00, 01\},$$
$$Pmin(CD) = min(\rho(CD) \setminus \{C\}) = \{01, 10\},$$

$$Pmin(BC) = min(\rho(BC) \bowtie$$
$$(Pmin(AB) \bowtie Pmin(CD))) =$$
$$min(\rho(BC) \bowtie (ABCD = \{0001, 0010, 0101, 0110\}))) =$$
$$min(\{0001, 0010, 0101\}) = \{0010, 0001\}.$$

We see that although the theory has 7 models, only 4 intermediate models were generated during the computation.

The reader can also verify that algorithm **min2** produces all the minimal models of Example 5.13. We can show that **min2** computes all and only the minimal models. The complexity of *min2* (without the tree-clustering preprocessing step) can be bounded as follows:

Theorem 5.15 *Let r be the maximum number of tuples in any relation ρ_i in the join-tree, and suppose that for every node R in the join-tree $|J_R| \leq m$. Then the complexity of* **min2** *is $O(nm^2)$, where n is the number of relations.*

Consequently, if the ratio between the number of minimal models, l, and $|J_R|$ is less than some c for every node R in the tree, then the number of models generated will be linear in $c \cdot l$.

6   Conclusion

The task of finding all or some of the minimal models of a theory is at the heart of many knowledge representation systems. This paper focuses on this task and introduces several characterizations of tractable subsets for this problem.

We have presented new algorithms for finding minimal models of a propositional theory. The first group of algorithms is effective for almost-Horn theories. The other group is effective for theories that can be represented as an acyclic network of small-arity relations.

Loveland and colleagues (e.g. [Lov91]) have shown how *SLD* resolution for first-order Horn theories can be modified to be efficient for near-Horn theories. We use different methods and provide worst-case complexities. Cadoli [Cad92] has described a partition of the set of propositional theories into classes for which the problem of finding one minimal model is tractable or NP-hard. His classification is different from ours but, as in Section 5, is also done by considering the set of logical relations that correspond to to the theory. An algorithm that exploits acyclic theories for computing minimum cardinality models is given in [FD92].

The ultimate usefulness of our algorithms must be tested by implementing them in systems that solve real-world problems in diagnosis or logic programming. We believe, however, that in any event the algorithms and the theoretical bounds provided in this paper are of value since the problem of computing minimal models is so fundamental.

Acknowledgments

We thank Yousri El Fattah, Itay Meiri, and Judea Pearl for useful discussions and helpful comments on earlier drafts of this paper. We have benefited from discussions with Adam Grove and Daphne Koller on the topic of computing minimal models. Thanks also to Michelle Bonnice for editing.

References

[BNNS91] C. Bell, A. Nerode, R.T. Ng, and V.S. Subrahmanian. Computation and implementation of non-monotonic deductive databases. Technical Report CS-TR-2801, University of Maryland, 1991.

[Cad92] Marco Cadoli. On the complexity of model finding for nonmonotonic propositional logics. In *Proceedings of the Fourth Italian Conference on Theoretical Computer Science*, October 1992.

[DE92] M. Dalal and D. Etherington. A hierarchy of tractable satisfiability problems. *IPL*, 44:173–180, 1992.

[DG84] W. Dowling and J. Gallier. Linear time algorithms for testing the satisfiability of propositional horn formulae. *journal of Logic Programming*, 3:267–284, 1984.

[dKMR92] J. de Kleer, A.K. Mackworth, and R. Reiter. Characterizing diagnosis and systems. *Artificial Intelligence*, 56:197–222, 1992.

[dKW87] J. de Kleer and B.C. Williams. Diagnosis multiple faults. *Artificial Intelligence*, 32:97–130, 1987.

[DP89] R. Dechter and J. Pearl. Tree clustering for constraint networks. *Artificial Intelligence*, 38:353–366, 1989.

[FD92] Y. El Fattah and R. Dechter. Empirical evaluation of diagnosis as optimization in constraint networks. In *DX-92: Proceedings of the workshop on Principles of Diagnosis*, October 1992.

[GL91] Michael Gelfond and Vladimir Lifschitz. Classical negation in logic programs and disjunctive databases. *New Generation Computing*, 9:365–385, 1991.

[GS88] G. Gallo and M. Scutella. Polynomially solvable satisfiability problems. *IPL*, 29:221–227, 1988.

[Kar72] R. M. Karp. Reducibility among combinatorial problems. In *Complexity of Computer Computations*. Plenum Press, 1972.

[Lif] V. Lifshitz. Computing circumscription. In *IJCAI 1985*.

[Lov91] D. Loveland. Near-horn prolog and beyond. *Journal of Automated Reasoning*, 7:1–26, 1991.

[Min82] J. Minker. On indefinite databases and the closed world assumption. In *Proceedings of the 6th Conference on Automated Deduction*. Springer-Verlag, 1982.

On the Adequateness of the Connection Method

Antje Beringer and **Steffen Hölldobler**
Intellektik, Informatik, TH Darmstadt,
Alexanderstraße 10, D–6100 Darmstadt (Germany)
E-mail: {antje, steffen}@intellektik.informatik.th-darmstadt.de

Abstract

Roughly speaking, adequatness is the property of a theorem proving method to solve simpler problems faster than more difficult ones. Automated inferencing methods are often not adequate as they require thousands of steps to solve problems which humans solve effortlessly, spontaneously, and with remarkable efficiency. L. Shastri and V. Ajjanagadde — who call this gap the artificial intelligence paradox — suggest that their connectionist inference system is a first step toward bridging this gap. In this paper we show that their inference method is equivalent to reasoning by reductions in the well-known connection method. In particular, we extend a reduction technique called evaluation of isolated connections such that this technique — together with other reduction techniques — solves all problems which can be solved by Shastri and Ajjanagadde's system under the same parallel time and space requirements. Consequently, we obtain a semantics for Shastri and Ajjanagadde's logic. But, most importantly, if Shastri and Ajjanagadde's logic really captures the kind of reasoning which humans can perform efficiently, then this paper shows that a massively parallel implementation of the connection method is adequate.

Introduction

Adequateness is one of the assumptions underlying automated deduction. Following W. Bibel [1991], *there is an* adequate *general proof method that can automatically discover any proof done by humans provided the problem (including all required knowledge) is stated in appropriately formalized terms.* Adequateness is, roughly speaking, understood as the property of a theorem proving method that, *for any given knowledge base, the method solves simpler problems faster than more difficult ones.* Furthermore, *simplicity is measured under consideration of all (general) formalisms available to capture the problem* and *intrinsic in this assumption is a belief in the existence of an algorithm that is feasible (from a complexity point of view) for*

the set of problems humans can solve. Later on, Bibel defines general research goals in the field of automated deduction, the first goal being the search for general and adequate proof methods.

This paper is concerned with adequate proof methods. That adequateness is one of the main problems in automated deduction has been realized by many researchers (cf. [Levesque and Brachman, 1985; Levesque, 1989]). L. Shastri and V. Ajjanagadde [1990; 1993] even call the gap between the ability of humans to draw a variety of inferences effortlessly, spontaneously, and with remarkable efficiency on the one hand, and the results about the complexity of reasoning reported by researchers in artificial intelligence on the other hand, the *artificial intelligence paradox.* But they also developed a connectionist computational model — called SAM in the sequel — which can encode a knowledge base consisting of millions of facts and rules, and performs a class of inferences with parallel time bound by the length of the shortest proof and space bound by the size of the knowledge base.[1] Moreover, SAM is consistent with recent neurophysiological findings and makes specific predictions about the nature of reflexive reasoning — ie. spontaneous reasoning as if it were a reflex [Shastri, 1990] — that are psychologically significant. Shastri and Ajjanagadde suggest that their computational model is a step towards resolving the artificial intelligence paradox.

Logically, the knowledge bases considered by Shastri and Ajjanagadde are sets of definite clauses — ie. universally closed clauses of the form $A_1 \wedge \ldots \wedge A_n \Rightarrow A$, where the A, A_i, $1 \leq i \leq n$, are atomic sentences. The knowledge bases are queried by universally closed atomic sentences. Such queries are answered positively if they are logical consequences of the knowledge base, and negatively otherwise. The query as well as the facts and rules are restricted in some particular way, which makes the system both interesting and difficult at the same time. It is difficult to give a semantics

---

[1] SAM shares many features with the connectionist reasoning system ROBIN developed by Lange and Dyer [1989]. They differ mainly in their technique to represent variable bindings.

for the class of problems considered in [Shastri and Ajjanagadde, 1993] and to understand the influence of the various restrictions on the massively parallel computational model. It is interesting as we would like to understand what kind of problems can be handled by a massively parallel computational model in parallel time bound by the length of the shortest proof and in space bound by the size of the knowledge base. In the following section we present the various restrictions in detail and outline the computational model underlying Shastri and Ajjanagadde's approach.

In [Hölldobler, 1993] the suggestion was made that reflexive reasoning is reasoning by reductions and, consequently, that the problems solved by SAM are simpler than the problems investigated by the artificial intelligence community. In this paper we will show that this suggestion holds by comparing SAM with the connection method and its various reduction techniques [Bibel, 1987]. An optimal parallel implementation of these reduction techniques along the lines of CHCL [Hölldobler, 1990a; Hölldobler and Kurfeß, 1992] needs the same space and answers queries at least as fast as SAM. We also demonstrate that there are reflexive reasoning tasks which can be solved in essentially one step by the parallel connection method, whereas SAM needs parallel time bound by the depth of the search space.

We present the connection method and the relevant reduction techniques. To prove our main result we extend the definition of isolated connections [Bibel, 1988] to so-called pointwise isolated connections (PICs). The evaluation of PICs is a general reduction technique applicable to unrestricted first-order formulas. With the help of this technique we can prove our main result relating SAM and the connection method.

Thus, the paper gives a semantics for the class of formulas considered in [Shastri and Ajjanagadde, 1993] and extends the definition of isolated connections such that this reduction technique solves reflexive reasoning tasks in parallel time bound by the length of the shortest proof and space bound by the size of the knowledge base. But, most importantly, if Shastri and Ajjanagadde's logic is the kind of logic needed for representing reasoning tasks which can be solved effortlessly, spontaneously, and with remarkable efficiency by humans, then this paper shows that a parallel implementation of the connection method is adequate. These and related results are discussed in the final section.

Reflexive Reasoning

Shastri and Ajjanagadde [1990; 1993] identified a class of problems computable in space bound by the size of the knowledge base and in parallel time which is at worst sublinear in — and perhaps even independent of — the size of the knowledge base. The was motivated by the observation that humans can perform a limited class of inferences extremely fast although their knowledge base is extremely large.

In this section we introduce the backward reasoning

system SAM. As we are mainly interested in the logic of the system we neither give technical details nor discuss the biological plausibility of the connectionist model underlying SAM or the psychological significance of reflexive reasoning. A detailed discussion of these topics can be found in [Shastri and Ajjanagadde, 1993].

Let $\mathcal{C}$ be a finite set of constants. A knowledge base KB in [Shastri and Ajjanagadde, 1993] is a conjunction of rules and facts. The rules are of the form

$$\forall X_1 \ldots X_m [p_1(\ldots) \wedge \ldots \wedge p_n(\ldots) \Rightarrow \exists Y_1 \ldots Y_k \, p(\ldots)], \quad (1)$$

where p, p_i, $1 \leq i \leq n$, are multi-place predicate symbols, the arguments of the p_i are variables from the set $\{X_1, \ldots, X_m\}$, and the arguments of p are from $\{X_1, \ldots, X_m\} \cup \{Y_1, \ldots, Y_k\} \cup \mathcal{C}$.[2] The facts and queries (or goals) are of the form

$$\exists Z_1 \ldots Z_l \, q(\ldots), \quad (2)$$

where q is a multi-place predicate symbol and the arguments of q are from $\{Z_1, \ldots, Z_l\} \cup \mathcal{C}$. The rules, facts, and goals are restricted as follows.

1. There are no function symbols except constants.
2. Only universally bound variables may occur as arguments in the conditions of a rule.
3. All variables occurring in a fact or goal occur only once and are existentially bound.
4. An existentially quantified variable (occurring in the head of a rule or in a fact) is only unified with variables.
5. A variable which occurs more than once in the conditions of a rule must occur in the conclusion of the rule and must be bound when the conclusion is unified with a goal.
6. A rule is used only a fixed number of times.

From an automated deduction point of view some of these restrictions seem to be rather peculiar. But they are closely related to the mechanism used by Shastri and Ajjanagadde for representing variable bindings. The variable binding problem is one of the major problems in connectionist systems (cf. [Barnden, 1984]). Due to lack of space we cannot discuss connectionist solutions to this problem and the interested reader is referred to [Shastri and Ajjanagadde, 1993]. In this paper we want to concentrate on the semantics of the logic described above. One should observe that restrictions 4-6 cannot be checked statically, but must be checked dynamically. The final restriction is concerned with the problem of how many copies of a rule or fact are needed for a proof of a first-order formula. The dynamic creation of copies is again a major problem in connectionist systems not discussed here. Following [Shastri and Ajjanagadde, 1990], we assume wlog. that each rule may be used at most once. As it is unpredictable how many copies of a rule are needed, SAM is incomplete. A positive answer indicates that the goal G is entailed by the knowledge base KB. A negative answer indicates that either G is not entailed by KB

---

[2]We use uppercase letters for variables and lower case letters for constants, function and predicate symbols.

or it cannot be proven that G is entailed by KB under the given restrictions.

Showing that KB entails G is equivalent to showing that $KB \wedge \neg G$ is unsatisfiable. To determine unsatisfiability we may replace existentially bound variables occurring in $KB \wedge \neg G$ by Skolem terms and obtain a formula $KB' \wedge G'$ which is equivalent to $KB \wedge \neg G$ wrt. unsatisfiability. Let σ be the substitution $\{Y_1 \mapsto f_1(X_1, \ldots, X_m), \ldots, Y_k \mapsto f_k(X_1, \ldots, X_m)\}$ and θ be the substitution $\{Z_1 \mapsto c_1, \ldots, Z_l \mapsto c_l\}$, where the f_i, $1 \leq i \leq k$, are pairwise different Skolem functions and the c_j, $1 \leq j \leq l$, are pairwise different Skolem constants, each of which does not occur in the set C of constants. Then each rule of the form (1) in KB is replaced by the (universally closed) clause $\sigma p(\ldots) \leftarrow p_1(\ldots) \wedge \ldots \wedge p_n(\ldots)$ or, equivalently, by $\sigma p(\ldots) \vee \neg p_1(\ldots) \vee \ldots \vee \neg p_n(\ldots)$ and each fact of the form (2) in KB is replaced by the ground fact $\theta q(\ldots)$. A query of the form (2) corresponds to the (universally closed) goal clause $\neg q(\ldots)$. Altogether, the knowledge base is a set of definite clauses and a query is a goal clause as used in pure PROLOG. Observe that now condition 4 is checked by the unification computation as Skolem constants and functions cannot occur in the goal. Eg. consider the following knowledge base.

$$p(a, Y) \vee \neg q(Y). \qquad p(c, a). \qquad q(b).$$
$$p(b, Z) \vee \neg r(Z). \qquad r(a). \qquad q(c). \qquad (3)$$

If a query like $\neg p(X, a)$ is posed then SAM computes an answer in a three-step process as follows.

1. Constants occurring in the query are recursively propagated to all atoms with the query's predicate symbol; a unification computation is performed. In our example, a is propagated as second argument to $p(a, Y)$, $p(b, Z)$, and $p(c, a)$. The unification computations are succesful and yield the substitutions $\{Y \mapsto a\}$, $\{Z \mapsto a\}$, and ε (the empty substitution), resp. After an application of these substitutions a is propagated from $\neg q(a)$ and $\neg r(a)$ to $q(b)$, $q(c)$, and $r(a)$, resp. The first two unification computations yield failures, whereas the last one is successful. Resulting from this step, each leaf of the search tree is labeled with either *success* or *failure*. Figure 1 shows the example's search tree at this time.

2. The success labels at the leafs are propagated backwards to the root of the search tree. Thereby it is checked whether each condition of a rule is satisfiable, ie. is the root of a successful branch. Otherwise, all branches starting from the conditions of the rule are turned into failure branches.

3. The bindings for the variables occurring in the initial query are now obtained by propagating the variables through the search space along the successful branches. In our example we obtain the bindings $\{X \mapsto c\}$ and $\{X \mapsto b\}$.

Clearly, the first and second step are the most important as they determine the success and failure branches of the search space. The third step only collects the answer substitutions. To define a semantics for SAM

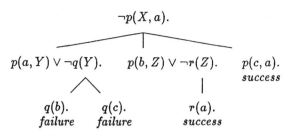

Figure 1: The example's search tree after the first step of SAM. (Substitutions are not applied.)

we will show that the computations performed by SAM are essentially reductions in a standard first-order logic calculus based on the connection method, which we present in the following section.

The Connection Method

The connection method is a formalism to compute the relationships between different statements in a first-order logic language [Bibel, 1987]. Although usually presented as an affirmative method for proving the validity of a formula in first-order logic, we present a dual version for proving the unsatisfiability of a set of Horn clauses, ie. a logic program and a single query. The connection method is based on the observation that a proof of a formula is essentially determined by a so-called spanning set of connections. A *connection* is an unordered pair of literal occurrences with the same predicate symbol but different signs. A literal L is *connected* in a set S of connections iff S contains L as an element of a connection. A set S of connections for a Horn formula of the form $KB \Rightarrow G$ consisting of a knowledge base or logic program KB and a goal G is called *spanning* iff each literal occurring in G is connected in S and, if the head of (a copy of) a clause in KB is connected in S, then each literal occurring in its body is also connected in S. A spanning set is *minimal* iff there is no spanning subset. A spanning set S of connections for $KB \Rightarrow G$ determines a proof iff there is a substitution σ such that σ simultaneously unifies each connection in S. Hence, searching a proof for $P \Rightarrow G$ amounts in generating a spanning set of connections and, then, simultaneously unifying each pair of connected literals.

In Figure 2 the connections for (3) are shown. There are two minimal spanning sets of connections which determine a proof: the sets $\{\langle \neg p(X, a), p(c, a) \rangle\}$ and $\{\langle \neg p(X, a), p(b, Z) \rangle, \langle \neg r(Z), r(a) \rangle\}$ with unifying substitutions $\{X \mapsto a\}$ and $\{X \mapsto b, Z \mapsto a\}$, resp. The other spanning sets $\{\langle \neg p(X, a), p(a, Y) \rangle, \langle \neg q(Y), q(b) \rangle\}$ and $\{\langle \neg p(X, a), p(a, Y) \rangle, \langle \neg q(Y), q(c) \rangle\}$ do not determine proofs as the variable Y cannot be bound to two different constants — viz. a, b and a, c, resp.

The problem whether a goal follows logically from a knowledge base is undecidable as one cannot determine in advance the number of needed copies of program clauses. However, if the number of copies is restricted

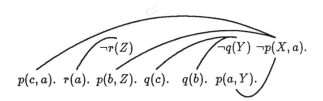

$$\neg r(Z) \qquad \neg q(Y) \ \neg p(X, a).$$

$$p(c, a). \quad r(a). \quad p(b, Z). \quad q(c). \quad q(b). \quad p(a, Y).$$

Figure 2: A simple logic formula with its connections. Each row represents either a fact, a rule, or a goal. Observe that the connection structure corresponds precisely to the search space shown in Figure 1.

as in SAM, then the problem is decidable as now the number of connections — and, hence, the number of spanning sets — is finite. Given a knowledge base and a goal, a procedure like SLD-resolution [Lloyd, 1984] may be used to find a proof if it exists. SLD-resolution is sound and complete, however, it may require exponential time (in the size of the formula) to find a proof. Hence, formulas should first be reduced as far as possible before a rule like SLD-resolution is applied.

The notion of a reduction rule is not uniquely defined. But reduction rules do not change the (un-) satisfiability of a formula while decreasing some complexity measure assigned to formulas. Here we strengthen these conditions by requiring that reduction techniques are applicable in linear parallel time and linear space with respect to the knowledge base. This is in spirit of our ultimate goal to find a class of problems which can be solved extremely fast on a massively parallel machine and has reasonable space requirements. In this paper we are particularly concerned about the following reduction techniques.

- Connections between non-unifiable literals can be removed. Eg. the connections $\langle \neg q(a), q(b) \rangle$ and $\langle \neg q(a), q(c) \rangle$ are non-unifiable.

- Useless clauses may be removed. A clause is *useless* if its conclusion is not connected or its condition contains a subgoal which cannot be solved. Eg. the rule $p(a, a) \vee \neg q(a)$ is useless and, in this case, all connections with this rule can be removed.

- Isolated connections can be evaluated, ie. the connected literals can be unified. A connection $\langle L, L' \rangle$ is *isolated* iff the literals L and L' are either ground or not engaged in any other connection or one of the literals is ground and the other one is not engaged in any other connection. If an isolated connection is unifiable, then the corresponding clauses may be replaced by their resolvent; otherwise, the connection can be removed. In Figure 1, there is the single isolated connection $\langle r(a), \neg r(Z) \rangle$. The literals are unifiable with the substitution $\{Z \mapsto a\}$ and, thus, the rule $p(b, Z) \vee \neg r(Z)$ and the fact $r(a)$ may be replaced by their resolvent $p(b, a)$.

After the reduction of the isolated connection $\langle r(a), \neg r(Z) \rangle$ the formula shown in Figure 2 cannot

be further reduced with the reduction techniques mentioned above. We would have to apply SLD-resolution, which may be exponential. However, as we will show in the sequel, the definition of isolated connections can be extended such that the problem shown in Figure 2 becomes solvable in linear space and linear parallel time with respect to the knowledge base by applying reduction techniques only.

The extension is based on the following observation. If an isolated connection of the form $\langle p(s_1, \ldots, s_n), \neg p(t_1, \ldots, t_n) \rangle$ is to be evaluated, then $p(s_1, \ldots, s_n)$ and $p(t_1, \ldots, t_n)$ are unified. The first step of the unification computation [Robinson, 1965] is to decompose the problem into the unification problems consisting of s_i and t_i, $0 \le i \le n$, and, then, to unify these (sub-)problems simultaneously. The extension consists of anticipating this step and considering *pointwise isolated connections* (PICs) between corresponding arguments of connected literals.

A connection $\langle p(s_1, \ldots, s_n), \neg p(t_1, \ldots, t_n) \rangle$ is called *isolated in its i-th argument* (or *point*) iff either the connected literals are not engaged in any other connection or s_i and t_i are ground or s_i is ground and $\neg p(t_1, \ldots, t_n)$ is not engaged in any other connection or t_i is ground and $p(s_1, \ldots, s_n)$ is not engaged in any other connection. Eg. the connection $\langle p(a, Y), \neg p(X, a) \rangle$ occurring in the example shown in Figure 2 is isolated in its second argument, but not isolated in its first argument. Evaluating the isolated point yields the substitution $\{Y \mapsto a\}$. Applying this substitution yields the connections $\langle q(b), \neg q(a) \rangle$ and $\langle q(c), \neg q(a) \rangle$, both of which are non-unifiable and can be removed. As now the subgoal $\neg q(a)$ is no longer connected, the rule $p(a, a) \vee \neg q(a)$ becomes useless and can be removed as well and we obtain the following reduced formula.

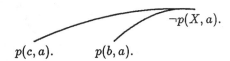

$$\neg p(X, a).$$

$$p(c, a). \qquad p(b, a).$$

Both connections are pointwise isolated and unifiable in their second argument. Both connections define proofs with answer substitutions $\{X \mapsto c\}$ and $\{X \mapsto b\}$. One should observe that this formula corresponds precisely to the successful branches of the search space shown in Figure 1.

The following proposition is an immediate consequence of the definition of PICs.

Proposition 1 *1. A connection is isolated iff it is isolated in each point.*

2. Let F' be obtained from a formula F by evaluating PICs. F is unsatisfiable iff F' is unsatisfiable.

PICs were introduced as an extension of isolated connections [Bibel, 1988]. But they can also be viewed as a special case of the v-rule defined in [Munch, 1988] for the connection graph proof procedure. Whereas the application of the (more complicated) v-rule is expensive to control, the evaluation of PICs is quite efficient.

Reflexive Reasoning is Reasoning by Reductions

The goal of this section is to elucidate the relation between SAM and the connection method. Let KB be a knowledge base, G a goal, F the formula $KB \wedge \neg G$, and F' be obtained by reducing F as far as possible. We assume that KB satisfies the conditions 1-4 defined in the second section. As conditions 5 and 6 must be tested dynamically by a meta-level controller, we assume that they are satisfied.

By definition the search space explored by SAM is defined by the connections of the given formula. As the first and second step of SAM determine the success and failure branches of the search space we have to show that the first and second step of SAM can be simulated by reductions in the connection method. In the first step the constants occurring in the intial goal are propagated through the search space. Recall that following [Shastri and Ajjanagadde, 1990] we have assumed that a rule is used only once. In the connection method this assumption translates into the condition that the conclusion of each rule is connected at most once. Hence, if a constant occurs at the i-th argument of a goal, then the connection between the goal and the conclusion of a rule is isolated in its i-th point. Recall further that facts are always ground as they are skolemized. Thus, if a constant occurs at the i-th argument of a goal, then the connection between the goal and a fact is isolated in its i-th point. Hence, the PICs can be evaluated — ie. unified — as in SAM. One should observe that condition 2 guarantees that after the evaluation of the PICs between the goal and the conclusion of a rule each constant occurring in the conditions of the rule occurs also in the goal. Using these arguments it can be shown by induction on the depth of the search space that SAM's propagation of constants occurring in the initial query corresponds to evaluations of PICs. Thereafter, all non-unifiable connections are eliminated in the connection method. Finally, if a condition of a rule is not the root of a successful branch, then the rule becomes useless and is eliminated. This takes care of the second step of SAM. Altogether we obtain the following result.

Theorem 2 *Let S be the search space after the second step of SAM in an attempt to show the unsatisfiability of F. The connections of F' correspond precisely to the successful branches of S.*

Hence, after reducing F we are left with all the successful branches of the search space. To show that SAM is sound, we have to prove that each minimal spanning set of F' determines a proof, ie. that for each minimal spanning set there is a substitution which simultaneously unifies each connection in the spanning set. By induction on the size of the minimal spanning set it

can be shown that in the unification computation of the connected literals in a minimal spanning set each variable may be bound to at most one constant. By condition 1 no complex data structures can be built up via unification. Conditions 2, 3, and 5 ensure that there are no multiple occurrences of variables in the goal, the facts, the conclusion and the condition of a rule. This implies the following result.

Theorem 3 *Each minimal spanning set of F' determines a proof.*

The soundness of SAM is an immediate consequence of Theorems 2, 3 and Proposition 1. As the knowledge base in [Shastri and Ajjanagadde, 1993] is a logic program, we can define the usual model-theoretic, fixpoint, and operational semantics (based on SLD-resolution) as in [van Emden and Kowalski, 1976] or the S-semantics as in [Falaschi *et al.*, 1989]. Since the connection method is equivalent to SLD-resolution for Horn formulas SAM is sound with respect to these semantics. As already mentioned SAM is incomplete as conditions 5 and 6 cannot be checked in advance. One could easily change the operational and fixpoint semantics such that these conditions are obeyed. Similarly, the model-theoretic semantics can be refined by expressing these conditions as higher-order axioms which have to be satisfied. This, however, is just an exercise in defining semantics.

Discussion

We have extended the reduction technique of evaluating isolated connections. The basic idea of considering PICs is that, whenever a binding for a variable can uniquely be determined, this binding should be applied and propagated. Secondly, we have shown that reflexive reasoning as defined by Shastri and Ajjanagadde [1990; 1993] or [Lange and Dyer, 1989] is reasoning by reduction and, consequently, we have formally established the soundness of reflexive reasoning.

There exists already a connectionist model of the connection method for Horn formulas called CHCL [Hölldobler, 1990a; Hölldobler and Kurfeß, 1992]. In CHCL isolated connections are evaluated, non-unifiable connections and useless clauses are removed in parallel as soon as these reductions become applicable. CHCL can easily be extended to evaluate PICs as CHCL determines the property of being isolated with the help of Proposition 1(1) (although PICs were not introduced in [Hölldobler, 1990a; Hölldobler and Kurfeß, 1992]). Interestingly, CHCL solves some problems even faster than SAM does. For example, if the knowledge base consists of the rules

$$p_1(X_1) \vee \neg p_2(X_1), \ldots, p_{n-1}(X_{n-1}) \vee \neg p_n(X_{n-1})$$

and the fact $p_n(a)$, then the query $p_1(a)$ is solved in essentially one step by CHCL as all connections are isolated and, hence, simultaneously evaluated. SAM needs essentially n steps as the constant a occurring in the goal has to be propagated through the search space. On the other hand, CHCL is less space efficient than SAM. CHCL does not require that formulas obey conditions 1-5 in the second section. Rather, formulas may be arbitrary Horn formulas. Hence, CHCL must solve arbitrary unification problems. This is done by a connectionist unification algorithm [Hölldobler, 1990c], which uses a quadratic number of units with respect to the size of the knowledge base. If the formulas and, consequently, unification was restricted as in SAM, then the design of CHCL could be changed such that it needs the same space and answers queries at least as fast as Shastri and Ajjanagadde's system.

The class of problems considered by Shastri and Ajjanagadde [1990; 1993] does not seem to be the largest class of problems which is computable in space bound by the size of the knowledge base and in parallel time bound by the depth of the search space. The presented reduction techniques are not restricted to Horn formulas, but may be applied to general first-order formulas. The special unification problems solved by Shastri and Ajjanagadde [1990; 1993] are not the largest class of unification problems which can be parallelized in an optimal way. Whereas unification is inherently sequential [Dwork et al., 1984], matching is known to be efficiently parallelizable [Ramesh et al., 1989].

The results of this paper show that SAM computes by reductions. From Shastri and Ajjanagadde's work we learn that automated theorem provers which apply these reduction techniques in parallel are adequate in the sense that they solve simpler problems faster than more difficult ones. [Shastri and Ajjanagadde, 1993] also contains some predictions on the question whether common sense reasoning problems are expressible in Shastri and Ajjanagadde's logic. It remains to be seen whether these predictions hold. In fact, if the predictions hold then the gap between the ability of humans to draw a variety of inferences as if it was a reflex and the results about the complexity of reasoning reported by researchers in artificial intelligence is not a paradox at all. If the problems which can be solved effortlessly, spontaneously, and with remarkable efficiency by humans can be expressed in Shastri and Ajjanagadde's logic, then these problems are just simpler than the problems investigated in the artificial intelligence community.

Acknowledgements

We like to thank S. Brüning for useful comments on earlier drafts of this paper. The first author is supported by the Deutsche Forschungsgemeinschaft (DFG) within project MPS under grant no. HO 1294/3-1

References

J. A. Barnden. On short term information processing in connectionist theories. *Cognition and Brain Theory*, 7:25–59, 1984.

W. Bibel. *Automated Theorem Proving*. Vieweg Verlag, Braunschweig, second edition, 1987.

W. Bibel. Advanced topics in automated deduction. In *Fundamentals of Artificial Intelligence II*, p. 41–59. Springer, LNCS *345*, 1988.

W. Bibel. Perspectives on automated deduction. In *Automated Reasoning: Essays in Honor of Woody Bledsoe*, p. 77–104. Kluwer Academic, Utrecht, 1991.

C. Dwork, P. C. Kannelakis, and J. C. Mitchell. On the sequential nature of unification. *Journal of Logic Programming*, 1:35–50, 1984.

M Falaschi, G. Levi, M. Martelli, and C. Palamidessi. Declarative modelling of the operational behavior of logic languages. *TCS*, 69(3):289–318, 1989.

S. Hölldobler and F. Kurfeß. CHCL – A connectionist inference system. In *Parallelization in Inference Systems*, p. 318 – 342. Springer, LNAI *590*, 1992.

S. Hölldobler. CHCL - A connectionist inference system for Horn logic based on the connection method and using limited resources. TR-90-042, ICSI, Berkeley, 1990.

S. Hölldobler. On high-level inferencing and the variable binding problem in connectionist networks. In *Proc. ÖGAI*, p. 180–185. Springer IFB *252*, 1990.

S. Hölldobler. A structured connectionist unification algorithm. In *Proc. AAAI*, p. 587–593, 1990.

S. Hölldobler. On the artificial intelligence paradox. Journal of Behavioral and Brain Sciences, 1993. (to appear).

T. E. Lange and M. G. Dyer. High-level inferencing in a connectionist network. *Connection Science*, 1:181 – 217, 1989.

H. J. Levesque and R. J. Brachman. A fundamental tradeoff in knowledge representation and reasoning. In *Readings in Knowledge Representation*, p. 41–70. Morgan Kaufmann, 1985.

H. J. Levesque. Logic and the complexity of reasoning. KRR-TR-89-2, Dept. of CS, Univ. of Ontario, Toronto, 1989.

J. W. Lloyd. *Foundations of Logic Programming*. Springer, 1984.

K. H. Munch. A new reduction rule for the connection graph proof procedure. *JAR*, 4:425–444, 1988.

R. Ramesh, R. M. Verma, T. Krishnaprasad, and I. V. Ramakrishnan. Term matching on parallel computers. *Journal of Logic Programming*, 6:213 – 228, 1989.

J. A. Robinson. A machine-oriented logic based on the resolution principle. *JACM*, 12:23–41, 1965.

L. Shastri and V. Ajjanagadde. An optimally efficient limited inference system. In *Proc. AAAI*, p. 563–570, 1990.

L. Shastri and V. Ajjanagadde. From associations to systematic reasoning: A connectionist representation of rules, variables and dynamic bindings using temporal synchrony. *Behavioural and Brain Sciences*, 1993. (to appear).

L. Shastri. Connectionism and the computational effectiveness of reasoning. *Theoretical Linguistics*, 16(1):65–87, 1990.

M. H. van Emden and R. A. Kowalski. The semantics of predicate logic as a programming language. *JACM*, 23(4):733–742, 1976.

Rough Resolution: A Refinement of Resolution to Remove Large Literals*

Heng Chu and **David A. Plaisted**
Department of Computer Science
University of North Carolina
Chapel Hill, NC 27599-3175, USA
{chu|plaisted}@cs.unc.edu

Abstract

Semantic hyper-linking [Plaisted *et al.*, 1992, Chu and Plaisted, 1993, Chu and Plaisted, 1992] has been proposed recently to use semantics with hyper-linking [Lee and Plaisted, 1992], an instance-based theorem proving technique. Ground instances are generated until an unsatisfiable ground set is obtained; semantics is used to greatly reduce the search space. One disadvantage of semantic hyper-linking is that large ground literals, if needed in the proofs, sometimes are hard to generate. In this paper we propose *rough resolution*, a refinement of resolution [Robinson, 1965], to only resolve upon *maximum literals*, that are potentially large in ground instances, and obtain *rough resolvents*. Rough resolvents can be used by semantic hyper-linking to avoid generating large ground literals since maximum literals have been deleted. As an example, we will show how rough resolution helps to prove LIM3 [Bledsoe, 1990], which cannot be proved using semantic hyper-linking only. We will also show other results in which rough resolution helps to find the proofs faster. Though incomplete, rough resolution can be used with other complete methods that prefer small clauses.

Introduction

Semantic hyper-linking has been recently proposed [Plaisted *et al.*, 1992, Chu and Plaisted, 1992, Chu and Plaisted, 1993] to use semantics with hyper-linking [Lee and Plaisted, 1992]. Some hard theorems like IMV [Bledsoe, 1983] and EXQ [Wang, 1965] problems have been proved with user-provided semantics only.

Semantic hyper-linking is a complete, instance-based refutational theorem proving technique. Ground instances of the input clauses are generated and a satisfiability check is applied to the ground instance set. Semantics is used to reduce the search space and keep

---
*This research was partially supported by the National Science Foundation under grant CCR-9108904

relevant ground instances. Size is measured based on the largest literal in the clause and smaller ground instances are generated first. Such an instance generation strategy, however, imposes difficulties generating large ground instances of a literal since there might be many smaller (yet irrelevant) ones that need to be generated first. For example, for some LIM+ problems [Bledsoe, 1990], a correct ground instance of the goal clause

$$(D \leq 0) \vee \sim (|f(xs(D)) - f(a)| + |g(xs(D)) - g(a)| \leq e0)$$

has to be generated by substituting variable D with $min(d1(ha(e0)), d2(ha(e0)))$ to obtain the proof. The ground instance is large and, with normal semantics, semantic hyper-linking generates many irrelevant smaller instances and diverts the search. Similar problems happen when large ground literals need to be generated in axiom clauses.

Rough resolution addresses this problem by resolving upon (and deleting) literals that are potentially large. Thus large ground literals are not needed and proofs are easier to obtain by semantic hyper-linking. However, rough resolution is against the philosophy of hyper-linking, namely, not to combine literals from different clauses. We set restrictions to reduce the number of retained resolvents so duplication of search space is not a serious problem as in ordinary resolution.

In this paper we first describe semantic hyper-linking in brief. Then we discuss in detail the rough resolution technique. An example (LIM3 problem) is given to help illustrate the ideas. Finally we give some more test results and then conclude the paper.

Semantic Hyper-Linking

In this section we briefly describe semantic hyper-linking. For more detailed discussion, please refer to [Chu and Plaisted, 1992, Chu and Plaisted, 1993].

A refutational theorem prover, instead of showing a theorem H logically follows from a set of axiom clauses A, proves A and $\sim H$ is unsatisfiable by deriving contradiction from the input clauses set. Usually we can find *semantics* for the theorem (and the axioms) to be proved. Such semantics can be represented by a *structure* which contains a *domain* of the objects and *interpretations* for constants, functions and predicates. A structure can be viewed as a (possibly infinite) set of all ground literals true in the semantics. A structure I is *decidable* if for a first-order formula F it is decidable whether F is satisfied by I.

According to Herbrand theorem, in the input clauses for a refutational theorem prover, there must be ground instances of some clauses (usually the negation of the theorem) that are false in the semantics; otherwise the input clauses are satisfiable. In general, no matter what semantics is chosen, such false ground instances exist for the input set. This observation is the base of semantic hyper-linking.

The idea of semantic hyper-linking is this: Initially a decidable input structure is given by the user, then the prover systematically *changes* the structure (semantics) by generating ground instances of input clauses that are false in the structure. We have a set U of ground instances, initially empty. Ground instances that are false in the current structure, are generated. User-provided semantics is used to help generate the new ground instances. These ground instances are added to U. Then the structure is changed, if possible, to satisfy U. This procedure is repeated with the new structure until U is unsatisfiable. For details, please see [Plaisted *et al.*, 1992, Chu and Plaisted, 1992, Chu and Plaisted, 1993].

Semantic hyper-linking has been shown to have great potential. Hard theorems like IMV (the intermediate value theorem in analysis) [Bledsoe, 1983, Ballantyne and Bledsoe, 1982] and ExQ (three examples from quantification theory) [Wang, 1965] are proved with the user-provided semantics only. No other human control is needed. However, if large ground literals are needed for the proof, they often are difficult to generate because of the way the ground instances are generated (which is basically an enumeration of the Herbrand base). Many small irrelevant ground literals need to be generated before large ones are generated. This generates a lot of useless smaller ground instances to complicate the proof search and makes many theorems unable to be proved. Rough resolution is designed to address this problem.

Rough Resolution

The basic idea of rough resolution is simple: we only resolve on those literals that are potentially large in ground instances. Those literals resolved upon are deleted in the resolvents and their ground instances need not be generated. If such large ground literals are used in the proof, rough resolution can avoid generating them and help semantic hyper-linking find the proof faster. For example, consider the following clauses (x, y and z are variables):

$C_1 = \{ \sim g(x, y, f(z)), d(z, x) \}$
$C_2 = \{ g(f(x), g(y), z), \sim f(x, y) \}$

If the following two ground instances are needed

in the proof which needs no other instances of $g(f(a), g(h(b)), f(c))$:

$C_1^{'} = \{ \sim g(f(a), g(h(b)), f(c)), d(c, f(a)) \}$
$C_2^{'} = \{ g(f(a), g(h(b)), f(c)), \sim f(a, h(b)) \}$

We can resolve C_1 and C_2 upon the first literals and get

$C = \{ d(z, f(x)), \sim f(x, y) \}$

Then, instead of $C_1^{'}$ and $C_2^{'}$, a smaller ground instance

$C^{'} = \{ d(c, f(a)), \sim f(a, h(b)) \}$

can be used in the proof and avoids the use of larger $g(f(a), g(h(b)), f(c))$ which might be difficult to generate by semantic hyper-linking.

Maximum Literals

Binary resolution on two clauses $C1$ and $C2$ chooses one literal L in $C1$ and one literal M in $C2$ such that $L\theta = \sim M\theta$, where θ is a most general unifier of L and $\sim M$. A *resolvent* $R = (C1 - L)\theta \cup (C2 - M)\theta$ is generated. R is *smooth* if $L\theta\sigma$ is never larger than any literal in $R\sigma$ for any σ; R is *rough* if for some σ, $L\theta\sigma$ is larger than any literal in $R\sigma$. Smooth resolvents are not kept because they only remove small literals (the "smooth" parts of clauses); large literals (the "rough" parts of clauses) remain as a difficulty. Thus we are particularly interested in rough resolvents because they might remove large literals needed for the proof. Rough resolvents can be obtained by resolving upon *maximum literals*.

Definition 1 A literal L in a clause C is an *absolute maximum literal* if, for *all* σ, the size of $L\sigma$ is larger than or equal to that of any literal in $C\sigma$; L is a *likely maximum literal* if for *some* σ, $L\sigma$ is larger than or equal to any literal in $C\sigma$.

A clause can only have one of those two kinds of maximum literals. For example, in clause

$$\{ d(v, k(w, u)), \sim d(v, u), \sim d(v, w) \}$$

where u, v and w are variables, $d(v, k(w, u))$ is the only absolute maximum literal; in clause

$$\{ d(u, q(w, v)), \sim d(f(u, v), w), \sim d(v, w) \}$$

both $d(u, q(w, v))$ and $\sim d(f(u, v), w)$ are absolute maximum literals; clause

$$\{ d(u, v), \sim d(v, u) \}$$

has two absolute maximum literals; in clause

$$\{ d(u, w), \sim d(u, v), \sim d(v, w) \}$$

all three literals are likely maximum literals.

Definition 2 A *rough resolution step* involves simultaneously resolving upon maximum literals $L_1, \ldots, L_n$ of a clause C (called *nuclei*) with some *absolute* maximum literals in other clauses $C_1, \ldots, C_n$ (called *electrons*). A *rough resolvent* is obtained from a rough resolution step.

Nuclei can have absolute or likely maximum literals; electrons can only have absolute maximum literals. Absolute maximum literals in a nucleus are all resolved upon at the same time in one single rough resolution step. This is based on the observation that absolute maximum literals should be eventually all removed since they are always the largest in any instances, and intermediate resolvents might not be saved due to non-negative growths (to be discussed in next section).

Resolving on likely maximum literals in a clause is difficult to handle because it might not delete large literals and, at the same time, could generate too many useless resolvents. For example, the transitivity axiom

$$\sim(x \leq y) \vee \sim(y \leq z) \vee (x \leq z)$$

contains three likely maximum literals and often generates too many clauses during a resolution proof. Their role is obscure in rough resolution. We have used two strategies to do rough resolution on likely maximum literals.

The first is to apply the following heuristics to simultaneously resolve on more than one likely maximum literal: if there are two likely maximum literals in a clause, we resolve upon them one at a time; if there are more than two likely maximum literals, we also resolve upon each possible pair of two of them at the same time. This is based on the observation that usually only few likely maximum literals will become the largest in the ground instances.

Another important strategy is to require that any likely maximum literal resolved upon should still be a likely (or absolute) maximum literal after the proper substitution is applied. Otherwise the resolvent is discarded because it introduces larger literals from those not resolved upon.

For example, consider the clause

$$C = \{ \sim p(x, y), \sim p(y, z), p(x, z) \}$$

where all literals are likely maximum literals. Suppose first two literals are resolved with $p(x, a)$ and $p(a, z)$ respectively with substitution $\theta = \{ y \rightarrow a \}$. Such resolution is not allowed since none of $p(x, a)$ and $p(a, z)$ are maximum literals in $C\theta$, and the literal not resolved upon, $p(x, z)$, becomes an absolute maximum literal in $C\theta$.

Retaining Resolvents

Rough resolution only resolves upon maximum literals. Since usually there are not many absolute maximum literals in a clause, the number of resolvents are greatly reduced. However there are still too many resolvents if no further restriction is applied. In this section we discuss one strategy that we use to retain resolvents more selectively.

From the rough resolvents, we prefer those *smaller* than the parents clauses. Ordering on clauses is needed here and we use ordering of the multisets of all literal sizes in a clause.

Definition 3 $|C|$ is the multiset of sizes of all literals in C. Difference $|C_1| - |C_2|$ is $c1 - c2$ where $c1$ and $c2$ are the largest elements (0 if the multiset is empty) in $|C_1|$ and $|C_2|$ respectively after common elements are deleted.

For example, for clause $C = \{ p(x), p(y), \sim q(x, y) \}$, $|C| = \{ 3, 2, 2 \}$; $\{ 3, 2, 2 \} - \{ 3, 2 \} = \{ 2 \} - \{ \} = 2$ and $\{ 4 \} - \{ 5, 2 \} = -1$.

Definition 4 Suppose in a rough resolution step, resolvent R is obtained from clauses $C_1, \ldots, C_n$. The *growth* of R is $|R| -$ maximum of $(|C_1|, |C_2|, \ldots, |C_n|)$.

Such multiset idea is only used to compute *growth* of a rough resolvent. In other situations the size of a clause is still the largest literal size.

Growth is a useful measurement to retain resolvents from resolving upon likely maximum literals. Intuitively growth indicates the size growth of a rough resolvent relative to the parent clauses before substitution is applied. If growth is negative, the resolvent is smaller than the largest parents clause and "progress" has been made to reduce the number of large literals. On the other hand, if the growth is zero or positive, the resolvent is of the same length or larger than the largest parent clause. There is no progress from this rough resolution step and it is not useful to keep the resolvent.

The algorithm of rough resolution is described in Fig. 1. Resolvents of non-negative growth are retained only when there are no resolvents with negative growth. The procedure repeats until a proof is found. The resolvents are used in semantic hyper-linking in a limited way because many resolvents could be generated. Reasonable time bound is set on the use of rough resolvents in semantic hyper-linking.

The collaboration of rough resolution and semantic hyper-linking is not explicitly shown in Fig. 1. Basically rough resolution executes for some amount of time then stops, and new resolvents are used in later semantic hyper-linking; when executed again, rough resolution picks up from where it left off and continues.

The rough resolvents with negative growth are always kept; among the rough resolvents with non-negative growth, only the smallest (in terms of the largest literal in the resolvent) are saved, if necessary. This allows the resolvents with non-negative growth to be used in a controlled manner.

With restrictions on how rough resolution is applied (by resolving upon maximum literals simultaneously) and how resolvents are retained (based on growth), much less resolvents are retained than those in other similar resolution strategy. And we have found the algorithm practical and useful when used with semantic hyper-linking.

Algorithm *Rough Resolution*
begin
  loop
    for each clause C with absolute maximum literals
      Obtain a new rough resolvent R using C as nucleus
      if R has a negative growth
      then
        save R permanently as a new clause
      else
        save R temporarily
  until there are no new resolvents with growth < 0
  for each clause C having likely maximum literals
  loop
    Obtain a new rough resolvent R using C as nucleus
    if R has negative growth
    then
      save R permanently as a new clause
    else
      save R temporarily
  until no new rough resolvents can be generated
  if in last loop no rough resolvent was generated
    with negative growth
  then
    for each smallest temporarily saved rough
      resolvent R
    save R permanently as a new clause
end

Figure 1: Algorithm: Rough Resolution

An Example

Bledsoe gave LIM+ problems in [Bledsoe, 1990] as challenge problems for automated theorem provers. Because of the large search space they might generate, LIM+ problems are difficult for most theorem provers. However, they are not difficult for Str+ve [Hines, 1992] which has built in inequality inference rules for densed linear ordering.

In this section we will look at the proof of LIM3 using rough resolution. Intermediate results from semantic hyper-linking are omitted.

As mentioned in the introduction, the correct ground instance of the goal clause has to be generated to obtain the proof. However, that ground instance contains a literal so large that semantic hyper-linking cannot generate it early enough in the search for the proof. As a result, the prover got lost even before correct goal instances are generated. Rough resolution helps to delete large literals by resolving upon them; smaller ground literals are generated by semantic hyper-linking. It is interesting to observe that the proof presented here does not need the term $min(d1(ha(e0)), d2(ha(e0)))$ which is essential to human proofs.

We only list clauses used in the proof; literals in boxes are maximum literals and only clauses 14 and 15 (from the same transitivity axiom) have likely maximum literals. Each rough resolution step is denoted by

list of clause numbers, with nuclei in boxes. For example, ([14],3,17) denotes a rough resolution step using clause 14 as nucleus and clauses 3 and 17 as electrons.
Input clauses:

3: $\{\,\boxed{lt(ab(pl(X,Y)),pl(ab(X),ab(Y)))}\,\}$

8: $\{\,\boxed{lt(ab(pl(f(Z),ng(f(a)))),E)},lt(E,o),$
   $\sim\!lt(ab(pl(Z,ng(a))),d1(E))\,\}$

9: $\{\,\boxed{lt(ab(pl(g(Z),ng(g(a)))),E)},lt(E,o),$
   $\sim\!lt(ab(pl(Z,ng(a))),d2(E))\,\}$

10: $\{\,\boxed{lt(ab(pl(xs(D),ng(a))),D)},lt(D,o)\,\}$

13: $\{\,\boxed{lt(X,Y)},\boxed{lt(Y,X)}\,\}$

14: $\{\,\boxed{\sim\!lt(X,Y)},\boxed{\sim\!lt(Y,Z)},lt(X,Z)\,\}$

15: $\{\,\boxed{\sim\!lt(X,Y)},\boxed{lt(X,Z)},\sim\!lt(Y,Z)\,\}$

17: $\{\,\boxed{lt(pl(X,Y),Z)},\sim\!lt(X,ha(Z)),\sim\!lt(Y,ha(Z))\,\}$

18: $\{\boxed{lt(D,o),}$
$\boxed{\sim\!lt(ab(pl(pl(f(xs(D)),ng(f(a))),pl(g(xs(D)),ng(g(a)))),e0)}$

The proof:

21: ([14],3,17)
$\{\,\boxed{lt(ab(pl(X,Y)),Z)},\sim\!lt(ab(X),ha(Z)),$
$\sim\!lt(ab(Y),ha(Z))\,\}$

24: ([18],21)
$\{\,\boxed{\sim\!lt(ab(pl(f(xs(D)),ng(f(a)))),ha(e0))}$
$\boxed{\sim\!lt(ab(pl(g(xs(D)),ng(g(a)))),ha(e0))},lt(D,o)\}$

29: ([24],8,9)
$\{\,\boxed{\sim\!lt(ab(pl(xs(D),ng(a))),d1(ha(e0)))},$
$\boxed{\sim\!lt(ab(pl(xs(D),ng(a))),d2(ha(e0)))},$
$lt(ha(e0),o),lt(D,o)\}$

97: ([15],29,10)
$\{\,\boxed{\sim\!lt(ab(pl(xs(D),ng(a))),d2(ha(e0)))},$
$\sim\!lt(D,d1(ha(e0))),lt(ha(e0),o),lt(D,o)\}$

99: ([15],29,10)
$\{\,\boxed{\sim\!lt(ab(pl(xs(D),ng(a))),d1(ha(e0)))},$
$\sim\!lt(D,d2(ha(e0))),lt(ha(e0),o),lt(D,o)\}$

139: ([10],97)
$\{\,\boxed{\sim\!lt(d2(ha(e0)),d1(ha(e0)))},$
$lt(ha(e0),o),lt(d2(ha(e0)),o)\,\}$

($lt(ha(e0),o)$ and $lt(d2(ha(e0)),o)$ are then unit deleted)

141: ([10],99)
$\{\,\boxed{\sim\!lt(d1(ha(e0)),d2(ha(e0)))},$
$lt(ha(e0),o),lt(d1(ha(e0)),o)\,\}$

($lt(ha(e0),o)$ and $lt(d1(ha(e0)),o)$ are then unit deleted)

([13],139,141)
{ } is obtained and a proof is found.

Unit $\{\sim lt(ha(e0),o)\}$ is generated by model filtering [Chu and Plaisted, 1993] in semantic hyper-linking. Or it can be generated by UR resolution from clause 4 and 7. It is then used with clause 5 to generate $\{\sim lt(d1(ha(e0)),o)\}$; with clause 6 to generate $\{\sim lt(d2(ha(e0)),o)\}$.

4: $\{\sim lt(e0,o)\}$
5: $\{lt(X,o),\sim lt(d1(X),o)\}$
6: $\{lt(X,o),\sim lt(d2(X),o)\}$
7: $\{lt(X,o),\sim lt(ha(X),o)\}$

None of the above three units can be generated by rough resolution. This shows the collaboration of rough resolution with semantic hyper-linking to find the proof.

Results

We have implemented a prover in Prolog. Experiment results show that rough resolution indeed improves the prover and often helps to find proofs faster. Table 1 lists some results (in seconds) that show rough resolution is in general a useful technique used with semantic hyper-linking. AM8 is the attaining maximum (or minimum) value theorem in analysis [Bledsoe, 1983]; LIM1–3 are the first three LIM+ problems proposed by Bledsoe [Bledsoe, 1990]; IMV is the intermediate value theorem in analysis [Bledsoe, 1983]; I1, IP1, P1 and S1 are four problems in implicational propositional calculus [Lukasiewicz, 1948, Pfenning, 1988]; ls37 is the theorem that $\forall x \in$ a ring R, $x * 0 = 0$ where 0 is the additive identity; SAM's lemma is a lemma presented in [Guard et al., 1969]; wos15 proves the closure property of subgroups; wos19 is the theorem that subgroups of index 2 are normal; wos20 is a variant of wos19; wos21 is a variant of ls37; and ExQ problems (including wos31) are three examples from quantification theory [Wang, 1965].

LIM1–3 are considered simpler in [Bledsoe, 1990]. Prover STR+VE, with built in inference rules for densed linear ordering, can easily prove all LIM+ problems. However, few other general-purpose theorem provers can prove LIM1–3 (especially LIM3). METEOR [Astrachan and Loveland, 1991] can prove all three by using special guidance. OTTER [McCune, 1990] and CLIN [Lee and Plaisted, 1992] could not prove any LIM+ problem.

Conclusions

Rough resolution is incomplete but it is useful when used with other complete methods that prefer small clauses. It helps to focus on removing "large" part of the proofs. In particular, we have found that semantic hyper-linking and rough resolution conceptually work well together: semantic hyper-linking solves the "small" and "non-Horn" part of the proof; UR resolution [Chu and Plaisted, 1993] solves the "Horn" part

Problem	with rough resolution	without rough resolution
AM8	2127.3	—*
LIM1	83.0	—
LIM2	63.3	—
LIM3	534.8	—
IMV	374.5	49.8
IPC I1	1.9	344.6
IPC IP1	29.2	1614.1
IPC P1	65.8	—
IPC S1	2.9	805.4
ls37	138.7	65.2
SAM's Lemma	146.5	95.5
wos15	282.7	—
wos19	407.5	1183.2
wos20	5715.7	—
wos21	783.7	93.4
wos31 (ExQ1)	203.5	39.2
ExQ2	84.0	130.1
ExQ3	140.3	112.0

* "—" indicates the run is aborted after either running over 20,000 seconds or using over 30 Megabyte memory

Table 1: Proof results using rough resolution with semantic hyper-linking

of the proof; and rough resolution solves the "large" part of the proof.

Rough resolution is powerful enough to help semantic hyper-linking prove some hard theorems which cannot be obtained otherwise. However we have observed that likely maximum literals are the source of rapid search space expansion in some hard theorems like LIM4 and LIM5. Future research includes further investigation of the role of likely maximum literals and avoid generating unnecessary resolvents from resolving upon likely maximum literals. One possible direction is applying rough resolution idea on paramodulation since equality axioms often contain likely maximum literals. Also, focusing on relevant resolvents should be another important issue to be addressed.

References

Astrachan, O.L. and Loveland, D.W. 1991. METEORs: High performance theorem provers using model elimination. In Boyer, R.S., editor 1991, *Automated Reasoning: Essays in Honor of Woody Bledsoe*. Kluwer Academic Publishers.

Ballantyne, A. M. and Bledsoe, W. W. 1982. On generating and using examples in proof discovery. *Machine Intelligence* 10:3–39.

Bledsoe, W. W. 1983. Using examples to generate instantiations of set variables. In *Proc. of the 8 th IJCAI*, Karlsruhe, FRG. 892–901.

Bledsoe, W. W. 1990. Challenge problems in elementary calculus. *J. Automated Reasoning* 6:341–359.

Chu, Heng and Plaisted, David A. 1992. Semantically guided first order theorem proving using hyper-linking. Manuscript.

Chu, Heng and Plaisted, David A. 1993. Model finding strategies in semantically guided instance-based theorem proving. In Komorowski, Jan and Raś, Zbigniew W., editors 1993, *Proceedings of the 7h International Symposium on Methodologies for Intelligent Systems*. To appear.

Guard, J.; Oglesby, F.; Bennett, J.; and Settle, L. 1969. Semi-automated mathematics. *J. ACM* 16(1):49–62.

Hines, L. M. 1992. The central variable strategy of Str+ve. In Kapur, D., editor 1992, *Proc. of CADE-11*, Saratoga Springs, NY. 35–49.

Lee, Shie-Jue and Plaisted, David. A. 1992. Eliminating duplication with the hyper-linking strategy. *J. Automated Reasoning* 9:25–42.

Lukasiewicz, Jan 1948. The shortest axiom of the implicational calculus of propositions. In *Proceedings of the Royal Irish Academy*. 25–33.

McCune, William W. 1990. *OTTER 2.0 Users Guide*. Argonne National Laboratory, Argonne, Illinois.

Pfenning, Frank 1988. Single axioms in the implicational propositional calculus. In Lusk, E. and Overbeek, R., editors 1988, *Proc. of CADE-9*, Argonne, IL. 710–713.

Plaisted, David. A.; Alexander, Geoffrey D.; Chu, Heng; and Lee, Shie-Jue 1992. Conditional term rewriting and first-order theorem proving. In *Proceedings of the Third International Workshop on Conditional Term-Rewriting Systems*, Pont-à-Mousson, France. Invited Talk.

Robinson, J. 1965. A machine-oriented logic based on the resolution principle. *J. ACM* 12:23–41.

Wang, H. 1965. Formalization and automatic theorem-proving. In *Proc. of IFIP Congress 65*, Washington, D.C. 51–58.

Experimental Results on the Crossover Point in Satisfiability Problems

James M. Crawford
Larry D. Auton
AT&T Bell Laboratories
600 Mountain Ave.
Murray Hill, NJ 07974-0636
jc@research.att.com, lda@research.att.com

Abstract

Determining whether a propositional theory is satisfiable is a prototypical example of an NP-complete problem. Further, a large number of problems that occur in knowledge representation, learning, planning, and other areas of AI are essentially satisfiability problems. This paper reports on a series of experiments to determine the location of the *crossover point* — the point at which half the randomly generated propositional theories with a given number of variables and given number of clauses are satisfiable — and to assess the relationship of the crossover point to the difficulty of determining satisfiability. We have found empirically that, for 3-SAT, the number of clauses at the crossover point is a *linear* function of the number of variables. This result is of theoretical interest since it is not clear why such a linear relationship should exist, but it is also of practical interest since recent experiments [Mitchell et al. 92; Cheeseman et al. 91] indicate that the most computationally difficult problems tend to be found near the crossover point. We have also found that for random 3-SAT problems below the crossover point, the average time complexity of satisfiability problems seems empirically to grow linearly with problem size. At and above the crossover point the complexity seems to grow exponentially, but the rate of growth seems to be greatest near the crossover point.

Introduction

Many classes of problems in knowledge representation, learning, planning, and other areas of AI are known to be NP-complete in their most general form. The best known algorithms for such problems require exponential time (in the size of the problem) in the worst case. Most of these problems can be naturally viewed as *constraint-satisfaction problems*. Under this view, a problem defines a set of constraints that any solution must satisfy. Most known algorithms essentially search the space of possible solutions for one that satisfies the constraints.

Consider a randomly-generated constraint-satisfaction problem. Intuitively, if there are very few constraints, it should be easy to find a solution (since there will generally be many solutions). Similarly, if there are very many constraints, an intelligent algorithm will generally be able to quickly close off most or all of the branches in the search tree. We thus intuitively expect the hardest problems to be those that are neither over- nor under-constrained. Cheeseman et al. have shown empirically that this is indeed the case [91]. Mitchell et al. take this argument further and show empirically that the most difficult problems occur in the region where there are enough constraints so that half of the randomly generated problems have a solution [92]. We refer to this point as the *crossover point*.

The location of the crossover point is of both theoretical and practical importance. It is theoretically interesting since the number of constraints at the crossover point is an intrinsic property of the language used to express the constraints (and in particular is independent of the algorithm used to find solutions). Further, we have found that in the case of 3-SAT the number of constraints required for crossover is a linear function of the number of variables. This leads one to expect there to be some theoretical method for explaining the location of the crossover point (though no satisfactory explanation has yet been proposed).

The crossover point is of practical interest for several reasons. First, since empirically the hardest problems seem to be found near the crossover point, it makes sense to test candidate algorithms on these hard problems. Similarly, if one encounters in practice a problem that is near the crossover point, one can expect it to be difficult and avoid it or plan to devote extra computational resources to it. Furthermore, several algorithms have been proposed [Selman et al. 92; Minton et al. 90] that can often find solutions to constraint-satisfaction problems, but that cannot show a problem unsolvable (they simply give up after some set number of tries). Accurate knowledge about the location of the crossover point provides a method for partially testing such algorithms on larger problems — models should be found for around half of the randomly generated problems at the projected crossover point. Finally, as problem size increases, the transition from satisfiable to unsatisfiable becomes increasingly sharp (see Figures 3-6). This means that if one knows the location of the crossover point, then for random problem (*i.e.*, problems with no regular structure) the number of clauses can be used as a predictor of satisfiability.

In this paper we focus on the prototypical example of an NP-complete problem: 3-SAT — propositional satisfiability of clausal form theories with three variables per clause. We first survey the algorithm used to carry out our experiments (readers primarily interested in the experimental results may skip this section). We then confirm and extend the results of Mitchell et al. [92] by showing that for up to 200 variables the hardest problems do tend to be found near the crossover point. We then show empirically that at the crossover point the number of clauses is a linear function of the number of variables. Finally we show empirically that below the crossover point the complexity of determining satisfiability seems to grow linearly with the number of variables, but above the crossover point the complexity seems to grow exponentially. The exponential growth rate appears to be steepest near the crossover point.

Propositional Satisfiability

The propositional satisfiability problem is the following ([Garey & Johnson 79]):

Instance: A set of clauses[1] C on a finite set U of variables.

Question: Is there a truth assignment[2] for U that satisfies all the clauses in C?

We refer to a set of clauses as a *clausal propositional theory*. 3-SAT is propositional satisfiability for theories in which all clauses have exactly three *terms*.[3]

Tableau Based Satisfiability Checking

Our satisfiability checking program, TABLEAU, began life as an implementation of Smullyan's tableau based inference algorithm [Smullyan, 68]. TABLEAU has since

---

[1] A *clause* is a disjunction of propositional variables or negated propositional variables.

[2] A *truth assignment* is a mapping from U to $\{true, false\}$.

[3] A *term* is a negated or non-negated variable.

evolved significantly and can most easily be presented as a variant of the Davis-Putnam procedure.

The basic Davis-Putnam procedure is the following [Davis et al. 62]:

```
Find_Model(theory)
  unit_propagate(theory);
  if contradiction discovered return(false);
  else if all variables are valued return(true);
  else {
    x = some unvalued variable;
    return(Find_Model(theory AND x) OR
           Find_Model(theory AND NOT x));
  }
```

Unit Propagation

Unit propagation consists of the repeated application of the inference rule:

$$\frac{x \quad \neg x \vee y_1 \ldots \vee y_n}{y_1 \vee \ldots \vee y_n}$$

(similarly for $\neg x$).

Complete unit propagation takes time linear in the size of the theory [Dowling & Gallier 84]. In this section we sketch the data structures and algorithms used for efficient unit propagation in TABLEAU.

We maintain two tables: the *variable table* and the *clause table*. In the variable table, we record the value of each variable (*true*, *false*, or *unknown*) and lists of the clauses in which the variable appears. In the clause table, we keep the text of each clause (*i.e.*, a list of the terms in the clause), and a count of the total number of unvalued variables (*i.e.*, variables whose value is *unknown*) in the clause.

Unit propagation then consists of the following:

1. Whenever a variable's value goes from *unknown* to *true*, decrement the unvalued variable count for all clauses (with non-zero counts) in which the variable appears negated, and set to zero the unvalued variable count for all clauses in which the variable appears positively (this signifies that these clauses are now redundant and can be ignored). Variables going from *unknown* to *false* are treated similarly.

2. Whenever the count for a clause reaches one, walk through the list of variables in the clause and value the one remaining unvalued variable.

The actual implementation has several additional complications for efficiency. Details are given in [Crawford & Auton 93].

Heuristics

On each recursive call to *Find_Model* one must choose a variable to branch on. We have observed that simple variable selection heuristics can make several orders of magnitude difference in the average size of the search tree.

The first observation underlying the heuristics used in TABLEAU is that there is no need to branch on variables which only occur in Horn clauses:[4]

Theorem 1 If a clausal propositional theory consists only of Horn clauses and unit propagation does not result in an explicit contradiction (i.e. x and $\neg x$ for some variable x in the theory) then the theory is satisfiable.

Satisfiability problems are often viewed as constraint-satisfaction problems in which the variables must be given values from $\{true, false\}$, subject to the constraints imposed by the clauses. We take a different approach — we view each non-Horn clause as a "variable" that must take a "value" from among the literals in the clause. The Horn clauses are then viewed as the constraints. It turns out that one can ignore any negated variables in the non-Horn clauses (whenever any one of the non-negated variables is set to *true* the clause becomes redundant and whenever all but one of the non-negated variables are set to *false* the clause becomes Horn). Thus the number of "values" a non-Horn clause can take on is effectively the number of non-negated variables in the clause.

Our first variable-selection heuristic is to concentrate on the non-Horn clauses with a minimal number of non-negated variables. Basically this is just a most-constrained-first heuristic (since the non-Horn clauses with a small number of non-negated variables are viewed as "variables" that can take on a small number of "values"). The first step of TABLEAU's variable-selection algorithm is thus to collect a list, V, of all variables that occur positively in a non-Horn clause with a minimal number of non-negated variables.

The remainder of the variable selection heuristics are used to impose a priority order on the variables in V. Our first preference criterion is to prefer variables that would cause a large number of unit-propagations. We have found that it is not cost-effective to actually compute the number of unit-propagations. Instead we approximate by counting the number of (non-redundant) binary clauses in which the variables appear.[5] This heuristic is similar to one used by Zabih and McAllester [88].

In cases where several variables occur in the same number of binary clauses, we count the number of unvalued *singleton neighbors*.[6] We refer to two terms as *neighbors* if they occur together in some clause.[7] A term is a *singleton* iff it only occurs in one clause in

the theory (this does *not* mean that the clause is of length one — if a theory contains $x \vee y \vee z$ and the term x occurs nowhere else in the theory then x is a singleton). Singleton terms are important because if their clause becomes redundant, their variable will then occur with only one sign and so can be valued:

Theorem 2 If a variable x always occurs negated in a clausal propositional theory Th, then Th is satisfiable iff $Th \wedge \neg x$ is satisfiable.

A similar result holds for variables which only occur positively.

In some cases there is still a tie after the application of both metrics. In these cases we count the total number of occurrences of the variables in the theory.

Heuristic	Nodes	Standard Dev.
Fixed order (no heuristics)	41320	56808
most-constrained-first	14190	17290
binary clauses occurrences	231	145
most singleton neighbors	225	141
most occurrences	195	118

Figure 1: Effects of the search heuristics. The data on each line is for the heuristic listed added to all the previous heuristics.

Figure 1 shows the effects of the search heuristics on 1000 randomly generated 3-SAT problems with 100 variables and 429 clauses.[8] Notice that counting the number of occurrences in binary clauses has quite a dramatic impact on the size of the search space. We have noticed that TABLEAU usually branches down some number of levels (depending on the problem size) and then finds a large number of unit-propagations that lead to a contradiction relatively quickly. This heuristic seems to work by decreasing the depth in the search tree at which this cascade occurs (thus greatly decreasing the number of nodes in the tree).

Figure 2 shows a comparison of TABLEAU with Davis-Putnam on 50-150 variable 3-SAT problems near the crossover point.[9] The experience of the community has been that the complexity of the Davis-Putnam algorithm on 3-SAT problems near the crossover point grows at about $2^{n/5}$ (where n is the number of variables). Our experiments indicate that the complexity of TABLEAU grows at about $2^{n/17}$, thus allowing us to handle problems about three times as large.

---

[4] A clause is *Horn* iff it contains no more than one positive term.

[5] At this point we count appearances in non-Horn *and* Horn clauses since the intent is to approximate the total number of unit-propagations that would be caused by valuing the variables.

[6] This heuristic was worked out jointly with Haym Hirsh.

[7] Recall that a term is a negated or non-negated variable. Thus x and $\neg x$ are different terms but the same variable.

[8] Some of the heuristics are more expensive to compute than others, but we will ignore these differences since they tend to become less significant on larger problems, and since even our most expensive heuristics are empirically only a factor of about three to four times as expensive to compute.

[9] The Davis-Putnam data in this table is courtesy of David Mitchell.

Tableau:

Variables	Clauses	Experiments	Nodes	Time[a]
50	218	1000	26	.02
100	430	1000	204	.47
150	635	1000	1532	3.50

Davis-Putnam:

Variables	Clauses	Experiments	Nodes
50	218	1000	341
100	430	1000	42,407
150	635	164	3,252,280

Figure 2: A Comparison of Davis-Putnam to TABLEAU on 3-SAT problems.

[a]Run times are in seconds and are for the C version of TABLEAU running on a MIPS RC6280, R6000 uni-processor with 128MB ram.

Probabilistic Analysis of Subsumption

The original Davis-Putnam procedure included a test for subsumed clauses (*e.g.*, if the theory includes $x \vee y$ and $x \vee y \vee z$ then the larger clause was deleted). We have found that this test does not seem to be useful near the crossover point.[10]

Consider a clause $x \vee y \vee z$. If we derive $\neg x$, we then unit propagate and conclude $y \vee z$. What is the chance that this new clause subsumes some other clause in the theory ? A simple probabilistic analysis shows that the expected number of subsumed clauses is $3c/2(v-1)$ (where v is the number of variables, and c is the ratio of clauses to variables — empirically this is about 4.24 at the crossover point). The expected number of subsumptions is thus relatively small (.06 for $v = 100$ near the crossover point) and falls as the size of the problem increases.

It seems likely that a similar, but more complex, analysis would show that the expected benefit from enforcing arc and path consistency on 3-SAT problems near the crossover point also decreases with increasing problem size.

Experiment 1: The Relationship Between Crossover and Problem Difficulty

This experiment is intended to give a global view of the behavior of 3-SAT problems as the clause/variable ratio is changed.

Experimental Method

We varied the number of variables from 50 to 200, incrementing by 50. In each case we varied the clause/variable ratio from zero to ten, incrementing the number of clauses by 5 for 50 and 100 variables, by 15 for 150 variables, and by 20 for 200 variables.

[10]We do, of course, do "unit subsumption" — if we generate x, we remove all clauses containing x.

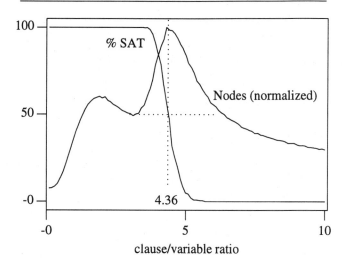

Figure 3: Percent satisfiable and size of the search tree — 50 variables.

At each setting we ran TABLEAU on 1000 randomly generated 3-SAT problems.[11]

Results

The graphs for 50, 100, 150, and 200 variables are shown in Figures 3-6. In each case we show both the average number of nodes in the search tree and the percentage of the theories that were found to be satisfiable.

Discussion

Our data corroborates the results of Mitchell et al. [92] — the most difficult problems tend to occur near the crossover point, and the steepness of both curves increases as the size of the problem is increased. Our data shows a small secondary peak in problem difficulty at about two clauses per variable. This peak does not seem to occur with the Davis-Putnam algorithm and is probably an artifact of the heuristics used to choose branch variables in TABLEAU.

For 3-SAT theories with only three variables, one can analytically derive the expected percent satisfiable for a given clauses/variable ratio. The clauses in a theory with three variables can differ only in the placements of negations (since we require each clause to contain three distinct variables). A theory will thus be unsatisfiable iff it contains each of the eight possible clauses (*i.e.*, every possible combination of negations). If the theory contains n randomly chosen clauses, then the chance that it will be unsatisfiable is equivalent to the chance that picking n times from a bag of eight objects (with replacement) results in getting at least one of each objects. The expected percent satisfiable as a function of the clauses/variables ratio is shown if Fig-

[11]In all our experiments we generated random theories using the method of Mitchell et al. [92] — we made sure that each clause contained three unique variables but did not check whether clauses were repeated in a theory.

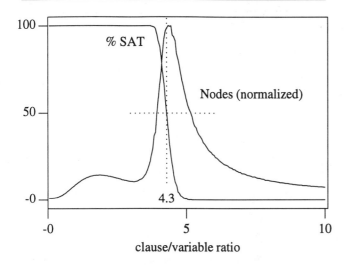

Figure 4: Percent satisfiable and size of the search tree — 100 variables.

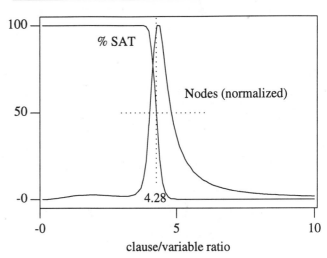

Figure 5: Percent satisfiable and size of the search tree — 150 variables.

ure 7. Notice that the shape of this curve is similar to the experimentally derived curves in Figures 3-6.

Experiment 2: The Location of the Crossover Point

The aim of this experiment is to characterize as precisely as possible the exact location of the crossover point and to determine how it varies with the size of the problem.

Experimental Method

We varied the number of variables from 20 to 260, incrementing by 20. In each case we collected data near where we expected to find the crossover point. We then focused on the data from five clauses below the crossover point to five clauses above the crossover point.[12] For each data point we ran TABLEAU on 10^4 randomly generated 3-SAT problems (10^3 for 220 variables and above).

Results

The results for 20, 100, 180, and 260 variables are shown in Figure 8. Each set of points shows the percentage of theories that are satisfiable as a function of the clause/variable ratio. Notice that the relationship between the percent satisfiable and the clause/variable ratio is basically linear (this is only true, of course, for points very close to the crossover point).

---

[12]To determine whether a point is above or below the crossover point we rounded to one place beyond the decimal point — points at 50.0 were taken to be *at* the crossover point. In most cases we found five points clearly above and five points clearly below the crossover point. The exceptions were: 60 variables — 5 above, 1 at, 4 below, 100 variables — 5 above, 1 at, 4 below, 140 variables — 5 above, 1 at, 4 below, 240 variables — 4 above, 1 at, 5 below, and 260 variables — 4 above, 1 at, and 5 below.

We took the 50 percent point on each of these lines as our experimental value for the crossover point. The resulting points are shown in Figure 9.

Discussion

From the analytical analysis for 3 variables, one can show that the crossover point for 3 variables is at 19.65 clauses. If we add this data to the least-squares fit in Figure 9 we get:

$$clauses = 4.24 vars + 6.21$$

This equation is our best current estimate of the location of the crossover point.

Experiment 3: The Run Time of TABLEAU

The goal of this experiment is to characterize the complexity of TABLEAU below, at, and above the crossover point.

Experimental Method

In these experiments we fixed the ratio of clauses to variables (at 1,2,3 and 10) and varied the number of variables from 100 to 1000 incrementing by 100. At each point we ran 1000 experiments and counted the number of nodes in the search tree.[13] We also used the results from Experiment 2 to calculate the size of the search tree near the crossover point (thus each data point represents an average over 10^5 runs for 20 to 200 variables, and over 10^4 runs for 220 to 260 variables).

Results

The graphs for clause/variable ratios of 1,2, and 3 are shown in Figure 10. The results near the crossover point, and at 10 clauses/variable are shown in Figure 11.

Discussion

---

[13]At 10 clauses/variable we currently only have data up to 600 variables.

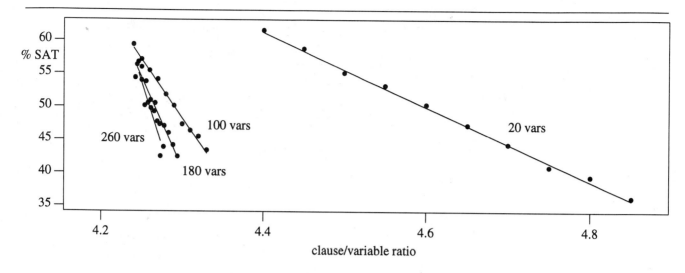

Figure 8: Percent satisfiable as a function of the number of clauses.

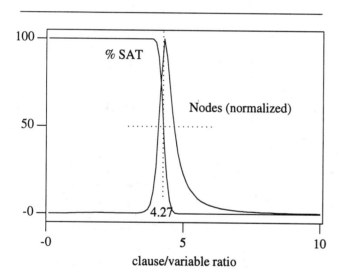

Figure 6: Percent satisfiable and size of the search tree — 200 variables.

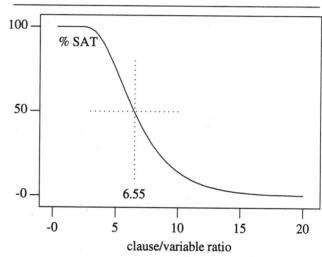

Figure 7: Analytical results for the three variable case.

Below the crossover point, the size of the search tree seems to grow roughly linearly with the number of variables. This is consistent with the results of Broder et al. [93]. However, even in this range there are clearly some problems as hard as those at the crossover point (we observed such problems while trying to gather data beyond 1000 variables). Near the crossover point, the complexity of TABLEAU seems to be exponential in the number of variables. The growth rate from 20 to 260 variables is approximately $2^{n/17}$. Above the crossover point, the complexity appears to grow exponentially (this is consistent with the results of Chvátal and Szemerédi [88]), but the exponent is lower than at the crossover point. The growth rate from 100 to 600 variables at 10 clauses/variable is approximately $2^{n/57}$.

Conclusion

Our experimental results show that the hardest satisfiability problems seem to be those that are *critically constrained* — i.e., those that are neither so under-constrained that they have many solutions nor so over-constrained that the search tree is small. This confirms past results [Cheeseman et al. 91; Mitchell et al. 92]. For randomly-generated problems, these critically-constrained problems seem to be found in a narrow band near the crossover point. Empirically, the number of clauses required for crossover seems to be a *linear* function of the number of variables. Our best current estimate of this function is *clauses* = 4.24*vars* + 6.21. Finally, the complexity of our satisfiability algorithm seems to be on average

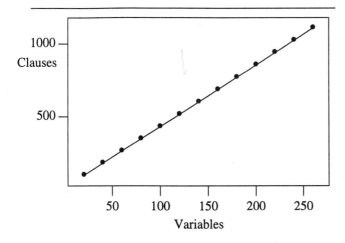

Figure 9: The number of clauses required for crossover.

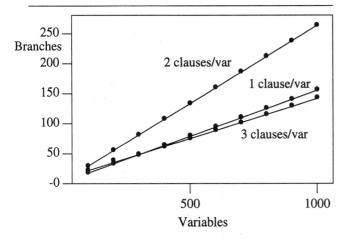

Figure 10: The size of the search tree below the crossover point.

roughly linear on randomly generated problems below the crossover point (though even here there are some problems that are as hard as those at the crossover point). At the crossover point the complexity seems to be about $2^{n/17}$ (where n is the number of variables). Above the crossover point we conjecture that the growth rate will be of form $2^{n/k}$ where k is less than 17 and increases as one gets further from the crossover point. At 10 clauses/variable k seems to be approximately 57.

Acknowledgments

Many people participated in discussions of this material, but we would like to particularly thank Haym Hirsh, Bart Selman, Henry Kautz, David Mitchell, David Etherington, and the participants at the 1993 AAAI Spring Symposium on "AI and NP Hard Problems".

References

Broder, A., Frieze, A., and Upfal, E. (1993). On the Satisfiability and Maximum Satisfiability of Random 3-CNF Formulas. *Fourth Annual ACM-SIAM Symposium on Discrete Algorithms.*

Cheeseman, P., Kanefsky, B., and Taylor, W.M. (1991). Where the really hard problems are. *IJCAI-91*, pp. 163-169.

Chvátal, V. and Szemerédi, E. (1988). Many Hard Examples for Resolution. *JACM* 35:4, pp. 759-768.

Crawford, J.M. and Auton L.D. (1993). Pushing the edge of the satisfiability envelope. In preparation.

Davis, M., Logemann, G., and Loveland, D. (1962). "A machine program for theorem proving", *CACM*, 5, 1962, 394-397.

Dowling, W.F. and Gallier, J.H. (1984). Linear-time algorithms for testing the satisfiability of propositional Horn formulae. *Journal of Logic Programming*, **3**, 267–284.

Garey, M.R. and Johnson D.S. (1979). *Computers and Intractability.* W.H. Freeman and Co., New York.

Minton, S., Johnson, M.D., Philips, A.B. and Laird, P. (1990). Solving large-scale constraint-satisfaction and scheduling problems using a heuristic repair method. *AAAI-90*, pp. 17-24.

Mitchell, D., Selman, B., and Levesque, H. (1992). Hard and easy distributions of SAT problems. *AAAI-92*, pp. 459-465.

Selman, B., Levesque, H., and Mitchell, D. (1992). A new method for solving hard satisfiability problems. *AAAI-92*, pp. 440-446.

Smullyan, R. M. (1968) *First Order Logic.* Springer-Verlag New York Inc.

Zabih, R.D. and McAllester, D.A. (1988). A rearrangement search strategy for determining propositional satisfiability. *AAAI-88*, pp. 155-160.

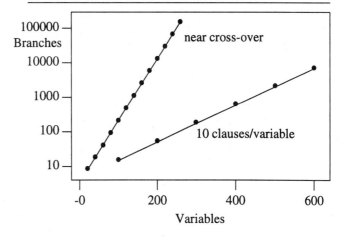

Figure 11: The size of the search tree at and above the crossover point (log scale).

Towards an Understanding of Hill-climbing Procedures for SAT *

Ian P. Gent and **Toby Walsh**
Department of Artificial Intelligence, University of Edinburgh
80 South Bridge, Edinburgh EH1 1HN, United Kingdom
Email:I.P.Gent@edinburgh.ac.uk, T.Walsh@edinburgh.ac.uk

Abstract

Recently several local hill-climbing procedures for propositional satisfiability have been proposed which are able to solve large and difficult problems beyond the reach of conventional algorithms like Davis-Putnam. By the introduction of some new variants of these procedures, we provide strong experimental evidence to support our conjecture that neither greediness nor randomness is important in these procedures. One of the variants introduced seems to offer significant improvements over earlier procedures. In addition, we investigate experimentally how performance depends on their parameters. Our results suggest that runtime scales less than simply exponentially in the problem size.

Introduction

Recently several local hill-climbing procedures for propositional satisfiability have been proposed [Gent and Walsh, 1992; Gu, 1992; Selman *et al.*, 1992]. Propositional satisfiability (or SAT) is the problem of deciding if there is an assignment for the variables in a propositional formula that makes the formula true. SAT was one of the first problems shown to be NP-hard [Cook, 1971]. SAT is of considerable practical interest as many AI tasks can be encoded quite naturally into it (*eg.* planning [Kautz and Selman, 1992], constraint satisfaction, vision interpretation [Reiter and Mackworth, 1989], refutational theorem proving). Much of the interest in these procedures is because they scale well and can solve large and difficult SAT problems beyond the reach of conventional algorithms like Davis-Putnam.

These hill-climbing procedures share three common features. First, they attempt to determine the satisfiability of a formula in conjunctive normal form (a conjunction of clauses, where a clause is a disjunction of literals). Second, they hill-climb on the number of satisfied clauses. Third, their local neighbourhood (which they search for a better truth assignment) is the set of truth assignments with the assignment to *one* variable changed. Typical of such procedures is GSAT [Selman *et al.*, 1992], a greedy random hill-climbing procedure. GSAT starts with a randomly generated truth assignment, and hill-climbs by changing (or "flipping") the variable assignment which gives the largest increase in the number of clauses satisfied. Given the choice between equally good flips, it picks one at random.

In [Gent and Walsh, 1992] we investigated three features of GSAT. Is greediness important? Is randomness important? Is hill-climbing important? One of our aims is to provide stronger and more complete answers to these questions. We will show that neither greediness nor randomness is important. We will also propose some new procedures which show considerably improved performance over GSAT on certain classes of problems. Finally, we will explore how these procedures scale, and how to set their parameters. As there is nothing very special about GSAT or the other procedures we analyse, we expect that our results will translate to any procedure which performs local hill-climbing on the number of satisfied clauses (for example SAT1.1 and SAT6.0 [Gu, 1992]). To perform these experiments, we use a generalisation of GSAT called "GenSAT" [Gent and Walsh, 1992].

procedure GenSAT(Σ)
   for i := 1 **to** Max-tries
      T := *initial*(Σ) ; generate a truth assignment
      for j := 1 **to** Max-flips
         if T satisfies Σ **then return** T
         else Poss-flips := *hill-climb*(Σ, T)
               ; compute best local neighbours
             V := *pick*(Poss-flips) ; pick one to flip
             T := T with V's assignment flipped
   end
  end
return "no satisfying assignment found"

GSAT is an instance of GenSAT in which *initial* generates a random truth assignment, *hill-climb* returns those variables whose truth assignment if flipped gives

*This research was supported by SERC Postdoctoral Fellowships to the authors. We thank Alan Bundy, Bob Constable, Judith Underwood and the members of the Mathematical Reasoning Group for their constructive comments and their estimated 100 trillion CPU cycles.

the greatest increase in the number of clauses satisfied (called the "score" from now on) and *pick* chooses one of these variables at random. An important feature of GSAT's hill-climbing is sideways flips – if there is no flip which increases the score, a variable is flipped which does not change the score. GSAT's performance degrades greatly without sideways flips.

Greediness and Hill-climbing

To study the importance of greediness, we introduced CSAT [Gent and Walsh, 1992], a cautious variant of GenSAT. In CSAT, *hill-climb* returns all variables which increase the score when flipped, or if there are no such variables, all variables which make no change to the score, or if there are none of these, all variables. Since we found no problem sets on which CSAT performed significantly worse than GSAT, we conjectured that greediness is not important [Gent and Walsh, 1992]. To test this conjecture, we introduce three new variants of GenSAT: TSAT, ISAT, and SSAT.

TSAT is timid since *hill-climb* returns those variables which increase the score the least when flipped, or if there are no variables which increase the score, all variables which make no change, or if there are none of these, all variables. ISAT is indifferent to upwards and sideways flips since *hill-climb* returns those variables which do not decrease the score when flipped, or if there are none of these, all variables. SSAT, however, is a sideways moving procedure since *hill-climb* returns those variables which make no change to the score when flipped, or if there are no such variables, all those variables which increase the score, or if there are none of these, all variables.

We test these procedures on two types of problems: satisfiability encodings of the n-queens and random k-SAT. The n-queens problem is to place n-queens on an $n \times n$ chessboard so that no two queens attack each other. Its encoding uses n^2 variables, each true iff a particular square is occupied by a queen. Problems in random k-SAT with N variables and L clauses are generated as follows: a random subset of size k of the N variables is selected for each clause, and each variable is made positive or negative with probability $\frac{1}{2}$. For random 3-SAT the ratio L/N = 4.3 has been identified as giving problems which are particularly hard for Davis-Putnam and many other algorithms [Mitchell *et al.*, 1992; Larrabee and Tsuji, 1992]. This ratio was also used in an earlier study of GSAT [Selman *et al.*, 1992]. Since GenSAT variants typically do not determine unsatisfiability, unsatisfiable formulas were filtered out by the Davis-Putnam procedure.

In every experiment (unless explicitly mentioned otherwise) Max-flips was set to 5 times the number of variables and Max-tries to infinity. In Table 1, the figures for "Tries" are the average number of tries taken until success, while the figures for "Flips" give the average number of flips in successful tries only. The final two columns record the total number of flips (including

Problem	Proc	Tries	Flips	Total	s.d.
Random 50 vars	GSAT	5.87	93.8	1310	2200
	TSAT	5.32	96.4	1180	2090
	ISAT	6.35	127	1460	2560
Random 70 vars	GSAT	10.7	158	3550	6090
	TSAT	10.2	161	3390	5980
	ISAT	11.9	208	4030	7890
Random 100 vars	GSAT	25.7	261	12600	22800
	TSAT	26.1	272	12800	22000
	ISAT	34.6	327	17100	43200
6 queens	GSAT	2.14	65.0	271	267
	TSAT	2.26	74.1	301	296
	ISAT	2.22	78.8	298	310
8 queens	GSAT	1.18	84.5	141	170
	TSAT	1.20	101	165	171
	ISAT	1.21	112	178	173
16 queens	GSAT	1.03	253	288	251
	TSAT	1.04	282	326	295
	ISAT	1.02	339	365	226

Table 1: Comparison of GSAT, TSAT, and ISAT

unsuccessful tries) and their standard deviations. 1000 experiments were performed in each case, all of which were successful. To reduce variance, all experiments used the same randomly generated problems.

The results in table 1 confirm our conjecture that greediness is not important. Like cautious hill-climbing [Gent and Walsh, 1992], timid hill-climbing gives very similar performance to greedy hill-climbing. The differences between GSAT and TSAT are less than variances we have observed on problem sets of this size. ISAT does, however, perform significantly worse than GSAT. ISAT's performance falls off much more quickly as the problem size increases. We conjecture that as the problem size increases, the number of sideways flips offered increases and these are typically poor moves compared to upwards flips. Combined with other heuristics, however, some of these sideways flips can be good flips to make, as we show in a later section where a variant of ISAT gives improved performance over GSAT. As well as SSAT, we tried a variant of ISAT which is indifferent to flips which increase the score, leave it constant or decrease it by 1. Both this variant and SSAT failed to solve any of 25 random 3-SAT 50 variable problems in 999 tries. We therefore conclude that you need to perform some sort of hill-climbing.

Greediness has also been used in several local search procedures for the generation of start positions (*eg.* in a constraint satisfaction procedure [Minton *et al.*, 1990], and in various algorithms for the n-queens problems [Sosič and Gu, 1991]). To investigate whether such initial greediness would be useful for satisfiability, we introduce a new variant of GenSAT called OSAT which is opportunistic in its generation of an initial truth assignment. In OSAT, the score function (number of satisfied clauses) is extended to partial truth assignments by ignoring unassigned variables. OSAT incrementally builds an initial truth assignment by considering the variables in a random order and picking those truth values which maximize the score; the use of a random order helps prevent any variable from dominating. In addition, if the score is identical for the assignment of a variable to true and false, a truth assignment is chosen at random. OSAT is identical to GSAT in all other respects. A comparison of OSAT and GSAT is given in table 2. In this and subsequent tables, percentages give the total flips as a percentage of the comparable figure for GSAT, and standard deviations are omitted for reasons of space.

Problem	Proc	Tries	Flips	Total	%
Rand 50 vars	OSAT	6.82	78.6	1530	120%
Rand 70 vars	OSAT	9.50	139	3110	88%
Rand 100 vars	OSAT	32.6	235	16000	130%
6 queens	OSAT	2.15	62.0	270	100%
8 queens	OSAT	1.18	67.8	126	89%
16 queens	OSAT	1.02	145	165	57%

Table 2: Comparison of GSAT and OSAT

OSAT always takes less flips on average than GSAT on a successful try. OSAT also takes the same or slightly more tries as GSAT. The total number of flips performed by OSAT can therefore be slightly less than GSAT on the same problems. However, if we include the $O(N)$ computation necessary to perform the greedy start, OSAT is nearly always slower than GSAT.

To conclude, our results confirm that greediness is neither important in hill-climbing nor in the generation of the initial start position. Any form of hill-climbing which prefers up or sideways moves over downwards moves (and does not prefer sideways over up moves) appears to work.

Randomness

GSAT uses randomness in generating the initial truth assignment and in picking which variable to flip when offered more than one. To explore the importance of such randomness, we introduced in [Gent and Walsh, 1992] three variants of GenSAT: FSAT, DSAT, and USAT. FSAT uses a fixed initial truth assignment but is otherwise identical to GSAT. DSAT picks between equally good variables to flip in a deterministic but fair way, whilst USAT picks between equally good variables to flip in a deterministic but unfair way[1]. On random k-SAT problems both USAT and FSAT performed poorly. DSAT, however, performed considerably better than GSAT (as well as [Gent and Walsh, 1992] see figures 4 & 5). We therefore concluded that there is nothing essential about the randomness of picking in GSAT (although fairness is important) and that the initial truth assignment must vary from try to try.

---

[1] A procedure is *fair* if it eventually picks any variable that is offered continually. USAT picks the least variable in a fixed ordering. DSAT picks variables in a cyclical order.

To explore whether the initial truth assignment can be varied deterministically, and to determine if randomness can be eliminated simultaneously from all parts of GenSAT, we introduce three new variants: NSAT, VSAT, VDSAT. NSAT generates initial truth assignments in "numerical" order. That is, on the n-th try, the m-th variable in a truth assignment is set to true iff the m-th bit of the binary representation of n is 1. VSAT, by comparison, generates initial truth assignments to maximize the variability between successive assignments. On the first try, all variables are set to false. On the second try, all variables are set to true. On the third try, half the variables are set to true and half to false, and so on. See [Gent and Walsh, 1993] for details. Since this algorithm cycles through all possible truth assignments, VSAT is a complete decision procedure for SAT when Max-tries is set to 2^N. NSAT and VSAT are identical to GSAT in all other respects. VDSAT uses the same start function as VSAT and is identical to DSAT in all other respects. Unlike all previous variants, VDSAT is entirely deterministic.

As table 3 demonstrates, NSAT's performance was very poor on 50 variable problems. Its performance on larger problems was even worse. We conjecture that this poor performance is a consequence of the lack of variability between successive initial truth assignments. VSAT and VDSAT have initial truth assignments which vary much more than initial truth assignments in NSAT. VSAT's performance is very close to GSAT's. VDSAT performs very similarly to DSAT, and better than GSAT, on random problems. VDSAT's performance on the 16 queens problem is poor because VDSAT is entirely deterministic and the first try happens to fail.

Problem	Proc	Tries	Flips	Total	%
Random 50 vars	NSAT	40.1	106	9870	750%
	VSAT	6.18	91.6	1390	110%
	VDSAT	4.32	74.1	904	69%
Random 70 vars	VSAT	10.4	155	3440	97%
	VDSAT	6.90	124	2190	62%
Random 100 vars	VSAT	30.4	270	14900	120%
	VDSAT	14.7	227	7090	56%
6 queens	NSAT	2.07	65.1	258	95%
	VSAT	2.27	76.0	305	110%
	VDSAT	2	50	230	85%
8 queens	NSAT	1.17	74.4	128	91%
	VSAT	1.17	77.5	132	94%
	VDSAT	1	30	30	21%
16 queens	NSAT	1.03	156	190	66%
	VSAT	1.03	160	196	68%
	VDSAT	2	296	1576	550%

Table 3: Comparison of NSAT, VSAT, and VDSAT

To conclude, randomness is neither important in the initial start position nor in picking between equally good variables. However, it is important that successive initial start positions vary on a large number of variables.

Memory

Information gathered during a run of GenSAT can be used to guide future search. For example, [Selman and Kautz, 1993] introduced a variant of GSAT in which a failed try is used to weight the emphasis given to clauses by the score function in future tries. They report that this technique enables GSAT to solve problems that it otherwise cannot solve.

In [Gent and Walsh, 1992] we introduced MSAT, which is like GSAT except that it uses memory to avoid making the same flip twice in a row except when given no other choice. MSAT showed improved performance over GSAT particularly on the n-queens problem, although the improvement declines as problems grow larger. This is, of course, not the only way we can use memory of the earlier search. In this section we introduce HSAT and IHSAT. These variants of GenSAT use historical information to choose deterministically which variable to pick. When offered a choice of variables, HSAT always picks the one that was flipped longest ago (in the current try): if two variables are offered which have never been flipped in this try, an arbitrary (but fixed) ordering is used to choose between them. HSAT is otherwise like GSAT. IHSAT uses the same *pick* as HSAT but is indifferent like ISAT. Results for HSAT and IHSAT are summarised in table 4.

Problem	Proc	Tries	Flips	Total	%
Random	HSAT	3.82	58.7	763	58%
50 vars	IHSAT	3.38	96.0	690	53%
Random	HSAT	4.93	101	1480	42%
70 vars	IHSAT	3.84	165	1160	33%
Random	HSAT	8.11	184	3740	30%
100 vars	IHSAT	6.95	274	3250	26%
6 queens	HSAT	1.11	43.3	62.9	23%
	IHSAT	1.08	55.8	70.6	26%
8 queens	HSAT	1.09	44.1	73.9	52%
	IHSAT	1.08	66.2	90.5	64%
16 queens	HSAT	1.02	156	183	64%
	IHSAT	1.02	220	245	85%

Table 4: Comparison of HSAT and IHSAT

Both HSAT and IHSAT perform considerably better than GSAT. Indeed, both perform better than any previous variant of GenSAT. Many other variants of HSAT also perform very well (*eg.* HSAT with cautious hill-climbing, with timid hill-climbing, with VSAT's start function). Note also that, unlike MSAT, the improvement in performance does not appear to decline as the number of variables increases.

To conclude, memory of the current try can significantly improve the performance of many variants. In particular, picking variables based on the history of the try rather than randomly is one such improvement.

Running GenSAT

We have studied the behaviour of GenSAT as the functions *initial*, *hill-climb*, and *pick* are varied. However, we have not discussed the behaviour of GenSAT as we vary its explicit parameters, Max-tries and Max-flips. The setting of Max-tries is quite simple – it depends only on one's patience. Increasing Max-tries will increase one's chance of success.

The situation for Max-flips is different to that for Max-tries. Although increasing Max-flips increases the probability of success on a given try, it can decrease the probability of success in a given run time. To understand this fully it is helpful to review some features of GenSAT's search identified in [Gent and Walsh, 1992]. GenSAT's hill-climbing is initially dominated by increasing the number of satisfied clauses. GSAT, for example, on random 3-SAT problems is typically able to climb for about 0.25N flips, where N is the number of variables in the problem, increasing the percentage of satisfied clauses from 87.5% ($\frac{7}{8}$ of the clauses are initially satisfied by a random assignment) to about 97%. From now on, there is little climbing; the vast majority of flips are sideways, neither increasing nor decreasing the score. Occasionally a flip can increase the score; on some tries, this happens often enough before Max-flips is reached that all the clauses are satisfied.

In Figure 1, we have plotted the percentage of problems solved against the total numbers of flips used by HSAT for 50 variable random problems, with Max-flips is 150. The dotted lines represent the start of new tries. During the initial climbing phase almost no problems are solved: in fact no problems were solved in less that 10 flips on the first try. Note that 10 is 0.2N, approximately the length of the initial climbing phase. This behaviour is repeated during each try: very few problems are solved during the first 10 flips of a try. After about 10 flips, there is a dramatic change in the gradient of the graph. There is now a significant chance of solving a problem with each flip. Again, this behaviour is repeated on each try. Finally, after about 100 flips of a given try, the gradient declines noticeably. From now on, there is a very small chance of solving a problem during the current try if it has not been solved already.

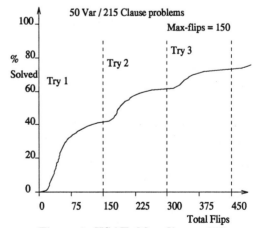

Figure 1: HSAT, Max-flips = 150

Different values of Max-flips offer a trade-off between the unproductive initial phase at the start of a try and the unproductive phase at the end for large Max-flips. To determine the optimal value, we have plotted in Figure 2 the average total number of flips used on 50 variable problems against integer values of Max-flips from 25 to 300 for HSAT, DSAT, and GSAT. For small values of Max-flips, not enough flips remain after the hill-climbing phase to give a high chance of success on each try. Each variant performs much the same. This is to be expected as each is performing the same (greedy) hill-climbing. The optimum value for Max-flips is about 60. Since this minimum is not very sharp, it is not, however, too important to find the exact optimal value. For Max-flips larger than about 100, the later flips of most tries are unsuccessful and hence lead to wasted work. As Max-flips increases, the amount of wasted work increases almost linearly. For everything but small values of Max-flips, HSAT takes fewer flips than DSAT, which in turn takes fewer than GSAT. The type of picking performed thus seems to have a significant effect on the chance of success in a try if more than a few flips are needed.

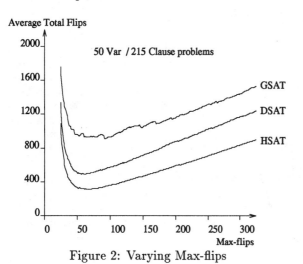

Figure 2: Varying Max-flips

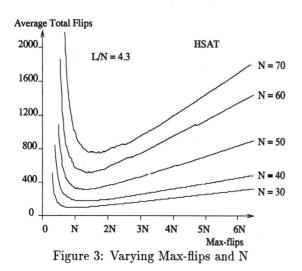

Figure 3: Varying Max-flips and N

Similar results are observed when the problem size is varied. In Figure 3, we have plotted the average total number of flips used by HSAT on random problems against integer values of Max-flips for differing numbers of variables N. The optimal value of Max-flips appears to increase approximately as N^2. Even with 100 variable random problems, the optimal value is only about 2N flips. Figure 3 also supports the claim made in [Selman *et al.*, 1992] and [Gent and Walsh, 1992] that these hill-climbing procedures appear to scale better than conventional procedures like Davis-Putnam.

To investigate more precisely how various GenSAT variants scale, Figure 4 gives the average total number of flips used by GSAT, DSAT and HSAT on random problems against the number of variables N at 10 variable intervals. Although the average total flips increases rapidly with N, the rate of growth seems to be less than a simple exponential. In addition, the improvement in performance offered by HSAT over DSAT, and by DSAT over GSAT increases greatly with N. One cause of variability in these results is that Max-flips is set to 5N and not its optimal value. In Figure 5 we have therefore plotted the *optimal* values of the average total flips against the number of variables at 10 variable intervals using a log scale for clarity. The performances of GSAT, DSAT and HSAT in Figure 5 are consistent with a small (less than linear) exponential dependence on N. Note that the data does not rule out a polynomial dependency on N of about order 3. Further experimentation and a more complete theoretical understanding are needed to choose between these two interpretations. We can, however, observe (as do [Selman *et al.*, 1992]) that these hill-climbing procedures have solved some large and difficult random 3-SAT problems well beyond the reach of conventional procedures. At worst, their behaviour appears to be exponential with a small exponent. Note again that HSAT offers a real performance advantage over GSAT and DSAT, not just a constant factor speed-up.

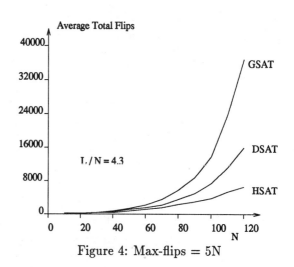

Figure 4: Max-flips = 5N

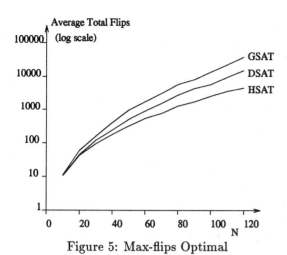

Figure 5: Max-flips Optimal

Related and Future Work

Hill-climbing search has been used in many different domains, both practical (*eg.* scheduling) and artificial (*eg.* 8-puzzle). Only recently, however, has hill-climbing been applied to SAT. Some of the first procedures to hill-climb on the number of satisfied clauses were proposed in [Gu, 1992]. Unfortunately, it is difficult to compare these procedures with GenSAT directly as they use different control structures.

These experiments have been performed with just two types of SAT problems: random k-SAT for $k = 3$ and $L/N = 4.3$, and an encoding of the n-queens. Although we expect that similar results would be obtained with other random and structured problem sets, we intend to confirm this conjecture experimentally. In particular, we would like to try other values of k and L/N, and other non-random problems (*eg.* blocks world planning encoded as SAT [Kautz and Selman, 1992], boolean induction, standard graph colouring problems encoded as SAT). To test problem sets with large numbers of variables, we intend to implement GenSAT on a Connection Machine. This will be an interesting exercise as GenSAT appears to be highly parallelizable.

One aspect of GenSAT that we have not probed in detail is the scoring function. The score function has always been the number of clauses satisfied. Since much of the search consists of sideways flips, this is perhaps a little insensitive. We therefore intend to investigate alternative score functions. Finally, we would like to develop a better theoretical understanding of these experimental results. Unfortunately, as with simulated annealing, we fear that such a theoretical analysis may be rather difficult to construct.

Conclusions

Recently, several local hill-climbing procedures for propositional satisfiability have been proposed [Selman *et al.*, 1992; Gent and Walsh, 1992]. In [Gent and Walsh, 1992], we conjectured that neither greediness nor randomness was essential for the effectiveness of the hill-climbing in these procedures. By the introduction of some new variants, we have confirmed this conjecture. Any (random or fair deterministic) hill-climbing procedure which prefers up or sideways moves over downwards moves (and does not prefer sideways over up moves) appears to work. In addition, we have shown that randomness is not essential for generating the initial start position, and that greediness here is actually counter-productive. We have also proposed a new variant, HSAT, which performs much better than previous procedures on our problem sets. Finally, we have studied in detail how the performance of these procedures depends on their parameters. At worst, our experimental evidence suggests that they scale with a small (less than linear) exponential dependence on the problem size. This supports the conjecture made in [Selman *et al.*, 1992] that such procedures scale well and can be used to solve large and and difficult SAT problems beyond the reach of conventional algorithms.

References

Cook, S.A. 1971. The complexity of theorem proving procedures. In *Proceedings of the 3rd Annual ACM Symposium on the Theory of Computation.* 151–158.

Gent, I. and Walsh, T. 1992. The Enigma of SAT Hill-climbing Procedures. Research Paper 605, Dept. of AI, University of Edinburgh.

Gent, I. and Walsh, T. 1993. Towards an Understanding of Hill-climbing Procedures for SAT. Research Paper, Dept. of AI, University of Edinburgh.

Gu, J. 1992. Efficient local search for very large-scale satisfiability problems. *SIGART Bulletin* 3(1):8–12.

Kautz, H.A. and Selman, B. 1992. Planning as Satisfiability. In *Proceedings of the 10th ECAI.* 359–363.

Larrabee, T. and Tsuji, Y. 1992. Evidence for a Satisfiability Threshold for Random 3CNF Formulas. Technical Report UCSC-CRL-92-42, UC Santa Cruz.

Minton, S.; Johnston, M.; Philips, A.; and Laird, P. 1990. Solving large-scale constraint satisfaction and scheduling problems using a heuristic repair method. In *Proc. 8th National Conference on AI.* 17–24.

Mitchell, D.; Selman, B.; and Levesque, H. 1992. Hard and easy distributions of SAT problems. In *Proc. 10th National Conference on AI.* 459–465.

Reiter, R. and Mackworth, A. 1989. A logical framework for depiction and image interpretation. *Artificial Intelligence* 41(3):123–155.

Selman, B. and Kautz, H. 1993. Domain-independent extensions to GSAT. Technical report, AI Principles Research, AT & T Bell Laboratories, Murray Hill, NJ.

Selman, B.; Levesque, H.; and Mitchell, D. 1992. A New Method for Solving Hard Satisfiability Problems. In *Proc. 10th National Conference on AI.* 440–446.

Sosič, R. and Gu, J. 1991. Fast search algorithms for the N-queens problem. *IEEE Transactions on Systems, Man, and Cybernetics* 21(6):1572–1576.

Reasoning With Characteristic Models

Henry A. Kautz, Michael J. Kearns, and Bart Selman

AI Principles Research Department
AT&T Bell Laboratories
Murray Hill, NJ 07974
{kautz, mkearns, selman}@research.att.com

Abstract

Formal AI systems traditionally represent knowledge using logical formulas. We will show, however, that for certain kinds of information, a model-based representation is more compact and enables faster reasoning than the corresponding formula-based representation. The central idea behind our work is to represent a large set of models by a subset of *characteristic* models. More specifically, we examine model-based representations of Horn theories, and show that there are large Horn theories that can be exactly represented by an exponentially smaller set of characteristic models.

In addition, we will show that deduction based on a set of characteristic models takes only linear time, thus matching the performance using Horn theories. More surprisingly, *abduction* can be performed in polynomial time using a set of characteristic models, whereas abduction using Horn theories is NP-complete.

Introduction

Logical formulas are the traditional means of representing knowledge in formal AI systems [McCarthy and Hayes, 1969]. The information implicit in a set of logical formulas can also be captured by expliciting recording the set of models (truth assignments) that satisfy the formulas. Indeed, standard databases are naturally viewed as representations of a single model. However, when dealing with incomplete information, the set of models is generally much too large to be represented explicitly, because a different model is required for each possible state of affairs. Logical formulas can often provide a compact representation of such incomplete information.

There has, however, been a growing dissatisfaction with the use of logical formulas in actual applications, both because of the difficulty in writing consistent theories, and the tremendous computation problems in reasoning with them. An example of the reaction against the traditional approach is the growing body of research and applications using case-based reasoning (CBR) [Kolodner, 1991]. By identifying the notion of a "case" with that of a "model", we can view the CBR enterprise as an attempt to bypass (or reduce) the use of logical formulas by storing and directly reasoning with a set of models. While the practical results of CBR are promising, there has been no formal explanation of how model-based representations could be superior to formula-based representations.[1]

In this paper, we will prove that for certain kinds of information, a model-based representation is much more compact and enables much faster reasoning than the corresponding formula-based representation. The central idea behind our work is to represent a large set of models by a subset of *characteristic* models, from which all others can be generated efficiently. More specifically, we examine model-based representations of Horn theories, and show that there are large Horn theories that can be exactly represented by exponentially smaller sets of characteristic models.

In addition, we will show that deduction based on a set of characteristic models takes only linear time, thus matching the performance using Horn theories [Dowling and Gallier, 1984]. More surprisingly, *abduction* can be performed in polynomial time using a set of characteristic models, whereas abduction using Horn theories is NP-complete [Selman and Levesque, 1990]. This result is particularly interesting because very few other tractable classes of abduction problems are known [Bylander *et al.*, 1989; Selman, 1990].

Horn Theories and Characteristic Models

We assume a standard propositional language, and use a, b, c, d, p, and q to denote propositional variables. A *literal* is either a propositional variable, called a positive literal, or its negation, called a negative literal. A *clause* is a disjunction of literals, and can be represented by the set of literals it contains. A clause C *subsumes* a clause C' iff all the literals in C appear in C'. A set (conjunction) of clauses is called a *clausal theory*, and is represented by the Greek letter Σ. We use n to denote the length of a theory (*i.e.*, number of literals). A clause is *Horn* if and only if it contains at most one positive literal; a set of such clauses is called a *Horn theory*. (Note that we are not restricting our attention to definite clauses, which contain exactly one positive literal. A Horn clause may be completely negative.)

---

[1] This is, of course, an oversimplified description of CBR; most CBR systems incorporate both a logical background theory and a set of cases.

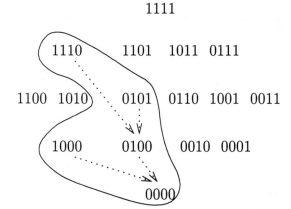

Figure 1: The circled models are M_0', which is the closure of the example set of models M_0.

A *model* is a complete truth assignment for the variables (equivalently, a mapping from the variables to $\{0, 1\}$). We sometimes write a model as a bit vector, *e.g.*, $[010\ldots]$, to indicate that variable a is assigned false, b is assigned true, c is assigned false, etc. A model *satisfies* a theory if the the theory evaluates to "true" in the model. Another way of saying this is that the theory is *consistent* with the model. When we speak of the "models of a theory Σ," we are refering to the set of models that satisfy the theory. This set is denoted by *models*(Σ).

We begin by developing a model-theoretic characterization of Horn theories. The *intersection* of a pair of models is defined as the model that assigns "true" to just those variables that are assigned "true" by both of the pair. The *closure* of a set of models is obtained by repeatedly adding the intersection of the elements of the set to the set until no new models are generated.

Definition: Intersection and Closure
The intersection of models m_1 and m_2 over a set of variables is given by

$$[m_1 \cap m_2](x) \stackrel{def}{=} \begin{cases} 1 & \text{if } m_1(x) = m_2(x) = 1 \\ 0 & \text{otherwise} \end{cases}$$

Where M is a set of models, *closure*(M) is the smallest set containing M that is closed under $\cap$.

To illustrate the various definitions given in this section, we will use an example set M_0 of models throughout. Let $M_0 = \{[1110], [0101], [1000]\}$. The closure of this set is given by $M_0' = M_0 \cup \{[0100], [0000]\}$. See Figure 1.

The notion of closure is particularly relevant in the context of Horn theories:

Theorem 1 [McKinsey 1943][2] *A theory Σ is equivalent to a Horn theory if and only if models(Σ) is closed under intersection.*

---
[2]The proof in McKinsey is for first-order equational theories,

Thus there is a direct correspondence between Horn theories and sets of models that are closed under intersection. For example, consider the closure M_0' of the models in set M_0 defined above. It is not difficult to verify that the models in the closure are exactly the models of the the Horn theory $\Sigma_0 = \{\neg a \vee \neg b \vee c, \neg b \vee \neg c \vee a, \neg a \vee \neg d, b \vee \neg d, b \vee \neg c\}$.

Next, we define the notion of a *characteristic* model. The characteristic models of a closed set M can be thought of as a minimal "basis" for M, that is, a smallest set that can generate all of M by taking intersections. In general, the characteristic models of any finite M can be defined as those elements of M that do not appear in the closure of the rest of M:

Definition: Characteristic Model
Where M is a finite set of models, the set of characteristic models is given by

$$char(M) \stackrel{def}{=} \{m \in M \mid m \notin closure(M - \{m\})\}$$

For example, the characteristic models of M_0' are [1110], [1000], and [0101]. The other two models in of M_0' can be obtained from these characteristic models via intersection.

Note that according to this definition the characteristic elements of any set of models are unique and well-defined. Furthermore, we will prove that characteristic models of a set can generate the complete closure of the set. Now, because the set of models of a Horn theory is closed (Theorem 1), it follows that we can identify a Horn theory with just the characteristic elements among its models. (In fact, henceforth we will simply say "the characteristic models of a Horn theory" to mean the characteristic subset of its models.) In general, this set may be much smaller than the set of all of its models. In summary:

Theorem 2 *Let M be any finite set of models. Then, (1) the closure of the characteristic models of M is equal to the closure of M; and (2) if M is the models of a Horn theory, then the closure of the characteristic models of M is equal to M.*

Proof: That $closure(char(M)) \subseteq closure(M)$ is obvious. To prove equality, for a given M and distinct $m_1, m_0 \in M$, define $m_1 >_M m_0$ iff there exists $m_2, ..., m_n \in M$ such that $m_0 = m_1 \cap m_2 \cap \ldots \cap m_n$, while $m_0 \neq m_2 \cap \ldots \cap m_n$. Define $\geq_M$ as the reflexive and transitive closure of $>_M$. We make the following three claims: (*i*) The directed graph corresponding to $>_M$ is acyclic, because if $m_1 >_M m_0$ then the number of variables set to "true" in m_1 is greater than the number set to "true" in m_0. (*ii*) The elements of M that are maximal under $>_M$ are characteristic. This is so because if $m \in closure(M - \{m\})$, there must be some $m_1, \ldots, m_n \in M$ such that $m = m_1 \cap \ldots \cap m_n$. But then (in particular) $m_1 >_M m$, so m is not maximal under $>_M$. (*iii*) For any $m \in M$, there is a subset M' of elements of M maximal under $>_M$ such that $m = \bigcap M'$. This set is simply defined by $M' = \{m' \mid m' \geq_M m$ and m' is maximal under $>_M\}$. In graphical terms, M' consists of the sources of the graph

---
and in fact led to the original definition of a Horn clause. A simpler, direct proof for the propositional case appears in [Dechter and Pearl, 1992].

obtained by restricting the graph of $>_M$ to nodes that are $\geq_M m$. Therefore, $M \subseteq closure(char(M))$, so $closure(M) = closure(char(M))$. Claim (2) then follows from the previous observations together with Theorem 1. ∎

As an aside, one should note that notion of a characteristic model is not the same as the standard definition of a maximal model. By definition, any $m \in M$ is a maximal model of M iff there is no $m' \in M$ such that the variables assigned to "true" by m' are a superset of those assigned to "true" by m. It is easy to see that all maximal models of a set (or theory) are characteristic, but the reverse does not hold. For example, the model [1000] in M_0 is an example of a non-maximal characteristic model.

Size of Representations

In this section we will examine the most concise way of representing the information inherent in a Horn theory. We have three candidates: a set of Horn clauses; the complete set of models of the theory; and the set of characteristic models of the theory.

We can quickly eliminate the complete set of models from contention. Obviously, it is as least as large as the set of characteristic models, and often much larger. Furthermore, every Horn theory with K models over n variables can be represented using at most Kn^2 Horn clauses [Dechter and Pearl, 1992]. Thus up to a small polynomial factor, the complete set of models is also always at least as large as the clausal representation.

Neither of the other two representations strictly dominates the other. We first show that in some cases the representation using characteristic models can be exponentially smaller than the *best* representation that uses Horn clauses.

Theorem 3 *There exist Horn theories with $O(n^2)$ characteristic models where the size of the size of the smallest clausal representation is $O(2^n)$.*

Proof: Consider the theory $\Sigma = \{\neg x_1 \lor \neg x_2 \lor \ldots \lor \neg x_n \mid x_i \in \{p_i, q_i\}\}$. The size of Σ is $O(2^n)$. Moreover, one can show that there is no shorter clausal form for Σ, by using a proof very similar to the one in [Kautz and Selman, 1992], but the size of its set of characteristic models is polynomial in n. This can be seen as follows. Write a model as a truth assignment to the variables $p_1 q_1 p_2 q_2 \ldots p_n q_n$. From the clauses in Σ, it is clear that in each model there must be some pair p_i and q_i where both letters are be assigned false (otherwise, there is always some clause eliminating the model). Without loss of generality, let us consider the set of models with p_1 and q_1 are both assigned false. Each of the clauses in Σ is now satisfied, so we can set the other letters to any arbitrary truth assignment. The characteristic models of this set are

[00111111 . . . 11]		[00111111 . . . 11]
[00011111 . . . 11]	. . . . . .	[00111111 . . . 01]
[00101111 . . . 11]		[00111111 . . . 10]

The three models in the first column represent all the settings of the second pair of letters. (Note that 00 can be obtained by intersecting the 2nd and the 3rd model.) Each triple handles the possible settings of one of the pairs. From these $3(n-1)$ models, we can generate via intersections all possible truth assignments to the letters in all pairs other than the first pair.

For each pair, we have a similar set of models with that pair set negatively. And, again each set can be generated using $3(n-1)$ models. So, the total number of characteristic models is at most $O(n^2)$. ∎

The following theorem, however, shows that in other cases, the set of characteristic models can be exponentially *larger* than the best equivalent set of Horn clauses.

Theorem 4 *There exist Horn theories of size $O(n)$ with $O(2^{(n/2)})$ characteristic models.*

Proof: Consider the theory Σ given by the clauses $(\neg a \lor \neg b)$, $(\neg c \lor \neg d)$, $(\neg e \lor \neg f)$, etc. The set M of characteristic models of this theory contains all the models where each of the variables in each consecutive pair, such as (a, b), (c, d), (e, f), etc., are assigned opposite truth values (*i.e.*, either [01] or [10]). So, we get the models [010101 . . .], [100101 . . .], [011001 . . .], . . ., [101010 . . .]. There are $2^{(n/2)}$ of such such models, where n is the number of variables. It is easy to see that these are all maximal models of the theory, and as we observed earlier, all such models are characteristic. (One can go on to argue that there are no other characteristic models in this case.) ∎

Thus we see that sometimes the characteristic model set representation offers tremendous space-savings over the clausal representation, and vice-versa. This suggests a strategy if one wishes to compactly represent the information in a closed set of models: interleave the generation of both representations, and stop when the smaller one is completed.

The characteristic models in a closed set can be efficiently found by selecting each model which is not equal to the intersection of any two models in the set. This operation takes $O(K^2 n)$ time, where K is the total number of models and n the number of variables. The clausal theory can be found using the algorithms described in [Dechter and Pearl, 1992] and [Kautz *et al.*, to appear].

Deduction using Characteristic Models

One of the most appealing features of Horn theories is that they allow for fast inference. In the propositional case, queries can be answered in linear-time [Dowling and Gallier, 1984]. However, there is no *apriori* reason why a representation based on characteristic models would also enable fast inference. Nevertheless, in this section, we show that there is indeed a linear-time algorithm for deduction using characteristic models.

We will take a query to be a formula in conjunctive normal form — that is, a conjunction of clauses. It is easy to determine if a query follows from a complete set of models: you simply verify that the query evaluates to "true" on every model. But if the representation is just the set of characteristic models, such a simple approach does not work. For example, let the query α be the formula $a \lor b$, and let the characteristic set of models be $M_0 = \{[1110], [0101], [1000]\}$, as defined earlier. It is easy to see that α evaluates to true in each member of M_0. However, α does not logically follow from the Horn theory with characteristic model set M_0; in other words, α does not hold in every model in the closure of M_0. For example, the query is false in $[0101] \cap [1000] = [0000]$.

There is, however, a more sophisticated way of evaluating queries on the set of characteristic models, that does yield an efficient sound and complete algorithm. Our approach is based on the idea of a "Horn-strengthening", which we introduced in [Selman and Kautz, 1991].

Definition: Horn-strengthening

A Horn clause C_H is a Horn-strengthening of a clause C iff C_H is a Horn clause, C_H subsumes C, and there is no other Horn clause that subsumes C and is subsumed by C_H.

Another way of saying this is that a Horn-strengthening of a clause is generated by striking out positive literals from the clause just until a Horn clause is obtained. For example, consider the clause $C = p \lor q \lor \neg r$. The clauses $p \lor \neg r$ and $q \lor \neg r$ are Horn-strengthenings of C. Any Horn clause has just one Horn-strengthening, namely the clause itself.

Suppose the query is a single clause. Then the following theorem shows how to determine if the query follows from a knowledge base represented by a set of characteristic models.

Theorem 5 *Let Σ be a Horn theory and M its set of characteristic models. Further let C be any clause. Then $\Sigma \models C$ iff there exists some Horn-strengthening C_H of C such that C_H evaluates to "true" in every model in M.*

Proof: Suppose $\Sigma \models C$. By Lemma 1 in [Selman and Kautz, 1991], $\Sigma \models C_H$ for some Horn-strengthening C_H of C. So C evaluates to "true" in every model of Σ, and thus in every member of M. On the other hand, suppose that there exists some Horn-strengthening C_H of C such that C_H evaluates to "true" in every model in M. By Theorem 1, because the elements of M are models of a Horn theory C_H, the elements of the closure of M are all models of C_H. But the closure of M is the models of Σ; thus $\Sigma \models C_H$. Since $C_H \models C$, we have that $\Sigma \models C$. ∎

In the previous example, one can determine that $a \lor b$ does not follow from the theory with characteristic models M_0 because neither the Horn-strengthening a nor the Horn-strengthening b hold in all of $\{[1110], [0101], [1000]\}$.

A clause containing k literals has at most k Horn-strengthenings, so one can determine if it follows from a set of characteristic models in k times the cost of evaluating the clause on each characteristic model. In the more general case the query is a conjunction of clauses. Such a query can be replaced by a sequence of queries, one for each conjunct. We therefore obtain the following theorem:

Theorem 6 *Let a Horn theory Σ be represented by its set of characteristic models M, and let α be a formula in conjunctive normal form. It is possible to determine if $\Sigma \models \alpha$ in time $O(|M| \cdot |\alpha|^2)$, where $|M|$ is the total length of the representation of M.*

Finally, using more sophisticated data structures we can bring the complexity down to truely linear time, $O(|M| + |\alpha|)$ [Kautz *et al.*, 1993].

Abduction using Characteristic Models

Another central reasoning task for intelligent systems is abduction, or inference to the best explanation [Peirce, 1958].

In an abduction problem, one tries to *explain* an observation by selecting a set of assumptions that, together with other background knowledge, logically entail the observation. This kind of reasoning is central to many systems that perform diagnosis or interpretation, such as the ATMS.

The notion of an explanation can be formally defined as follows [Reiter and de Kleer, 1987]:

Definition: [Explanation] Given a set of clauses Σ, called the background theory, a subset A of the propositional letters, called the assumption set, and a query letter q, an explanation E for q is a minimal subset of unit clauses with letters from among A such that

1. $\Sigma \cup E \models q$, and
2. $\Sigma \cup E$ is consistent.

Note that an explanation E is a set of unit clauses, or equivalently, a single conjunction of literals.

For example, let the background theory be $\Sigma = \{a, \neg a \lor \neg b \lor \neg c \lor d\}$ and let the assumption set $A = \{a, b, c\}$. The conjunction $b \land c$ is an explanation for d.

It is obvious that in general abduction is harder than deduction, because the definition involves both a test for entailment and a test for consistency. However, abduction can remain hard even when the background theory is restricted to languages in which both tests can be performed in polynomial time. Selman and Levesque [1989] show that computing such an explanation is NP-complete even when the background theory contains only Horn clauses, despite the fact that the tests take only linear time for such theories. The problem remains hard because all known algorithms have to search through an exponential number of combinations of assumptions to find an explanation that passes both tests.

There are very few restricted clausal forms for which abduction is tractable. One of these is *definite* Horn clauses, which are Horn clauses that contain exactly one positive literal — completely negative clauses are forbidden. However, the expressive power of definite Horn is much more limited than full Horn: In particular, one cannot assert that two assumptions are mutually *incompatible*.

It is therefore interesting to discover that abduction problems can be solved in polynomial time when the background theory is represented by a set of characteristic models. We give the algorithm for this computation in Figure 2.

The abduction algorithm works by searching for a characteristic model in which the query holds. Then it sets E equal to the strongest set of assumptions that are compatible with the model, and tests if this E rules out all models of the background theory in which the query does not hold. This step is performed by the test

$$closure(M) \models (\textstyle\bigwedge E) \supset q$$

and can be performed in polynomial time, using the deduction algorithm described in the previous section. (Note that the formula to be deduced is a single Horn clause.) If the test succeeds, then the assumption set is minimized, by deleting unnecessary assumptions. Otherwise, if no such

```
Explain(M, A, q)
    For each m in M do
        If m ⊨ q then
            E ← all letters in A that
                are assigned "true" by m
            if closure(M) ⊨ (⋀ E) ⊃ q then
                Minimize E by deleting as many
                    elements as possible while
                    maintaining the condition
                    that closure(M) ⊨ (⋀ E) ⊃ q.
                return E
            endif
        endif
    endfor
    return "false"
end.
```

Figure 2: Polynomial time algorithm for abduction. M is a set of characteristic models, representing a Horn theory; A is the assumption set; and q is the letter to be explained. The procedure returns a subset of A, or "false", if no explanation exists.

characteristic model is in the given set, then no explanation for the query exists. Note that the minimization step simply eliminates redundant assumptions, and does not try to find an assumption set of the smallest possible cardinality, so no combinatorial search is necessary.

It is easy to see that if the algorithm does find an explanation it is sound, because the test above verifies that the query follows from the background theory together with the explanation, and the fact that the model m is in M (and thus also in the closure of M) ensures that the background theory and the explanation are mutually consistent. Furthermore, if the algorithm searched through *all* models in the closure of M, rather than just M itself, it would be readily apparent that the algorithm is complete. (The consistency condition requires that the the explanation and the query both hold in at least one model of the background theory.) However, we will argue that it is in fact only necessary to consider the *maximal* models of the background theory; and since, as we observed earlier, the maximal models are a subset of the characteristic models, the algorithm as given is complete.

So suppose m is in *closure*(M), and E is a subset of A such that q and all of E hold in m. Let m' be any maximal model of M (and thus, also a maximal model of *closure*(M)) that subsumes m — at least one such m' must exist. All the variables set to "true" in m are also set to "true" in m'; and furthermore, q and all of E consist of only *positive* literals. Therefore, q and E both hold in m' as well.

Thus the algorithm is sound and complete. In order to bound its running time, we note that the outer loop executes at most $|M|$ times, the inner (minimizing) loop at most $|A|$ times, and each entailment test requires at most $O(|M| \cdot |A|^2)$ steps. Thus the overall running time is bounded by $O(|M|^2 \cdot |A|^3)$. In summary:

Theorem 7 *Let M be the set of characteristic models of a background Horn theory, let A be an assumption set, and q be a query. Then one can find an abductive explanation of q in time $O(|M|^2 \cdot |A|^3)$.*

Again, using better data structures, we can reduce the complexity to be quadratic in the combined length of the query and knowledge base.

The fact that abduction is hard for clausal Horn theories, but easy when the same background theory is represented by a set of characteristic models, does not, of course, indicate that $P = NP$! It only means that it may be difficult to generate the characteristic models of a given Horn theory: there may be exponentially many characteristic models, or even if there are few, they may be hard to find. None the less, it may be worthwhile to invest the effort to "compile" a useful Horn theory into its set of characteristic models, just in case the latter representation does indeed turn out to be of reasonable size. This is an example of "knowledge compilation" [Selman and Kautz, 1991], where one is willing to invest a large amount of off-line effort in order to obtain fast run-time inference. Alternatively, one can circumvent the use of a formula-based representation all together by constructing the characteristic models by hand, or by learning them from empirical data.[3]

Conclusions

In this paper, we have demonstrated that, contrary to prevalent wisdom, knowledge-based systems can efficiently use representations based on sets of models rather than logical formulas. Incomplete information does not necessarily make model-based representations unwieldy, because it possible to store only a subset of characteristic models that are equivalent to the entire model set. We showed that for Horn theories neither the formula nor the model-based representation dominates the other in terms of size, and that sometimes one other can offer an exponential savings over the other.

We also showed that the characteristic model representation of Horn theories has very good computational properties, in that *both* deduction and abduction can be performed in polynomial time. On the other hand, all known and foreseeable algorithms for abduction with Horn clauses are of worst-case exponential complexity.

This paper begins to provide a formal framework for understanding the success and limitations of some of the more empirical work in AI that use model-like representations. Earlier proposals to use models in formal inference, such as Levesque's proposal for "vivid" representations [Levesque, 1986], rely on using a single, database-like model, and thus have difficulty handling incomplete information. As we

---

[3] As mentioned earlier, if all models are given, finding the characteristic models takes only polynomial time. However, the complexity of learning the characteristic models where the algorithm can only sample from the complete set of models is an interesting open problem. Some preliminary results on the compexity of this problem have recently been obtained by D. Sloan and R. Schapire (personal communication).

have seen, our approach is more general, because we represent a *set* of models. We are currently investigating extensions of the notion of a characteristic model to other useful classes of theories.

References

Bylander, Tom; Allemang, Dean; Tanner, Michael C.; and Josephson, John R. 1989. Some results concerning the computational complexity of abduction. In *Proceedings of KR-89*, Toronto, Ontario, Canada. Morgan Kaufmann. 44.

Dechter, Rina and Pearl, Judea 1992. Structure identification in relational data. *Artificial Intelligence* 58(1–3):237–270.

Dowling, William F. and Gallier, Jean H. 1984. Linear time algorithms for testing the satisfiability of propositional Horn formula. *Journal of Logic Programming* 3:267–284.

Kautz, Henry and Selman, Bart 1992. Speeding inference by acquiring new concepts. In *Proceedings of AAAI-92*, San Jose, CA.

Kautz, Henry; Kearns, Michael; and Selman, Bart 1993. Reasoning with characteristic models. Technical report, AT&T Bell Laboratories, Murray Hill, NJ.

Kautz, Henry A.; Kearns, Michael J.; and Selman, Bart ppear. Horn approximations of empirical data. *Artificial Intelligence*.

Kolodner, Janet L. 1991. Improving human decision making through case-based decision aiding. *AI Magazine* 12(2):52–68.

Levesque, Hector 1986. Making believers out of computers. *Artificial Intelligence* 30(1):81.

McCarthy, J. and Hayes, P. J. 1969. Some philosophical problems from the standpoint of artificial intelligence. In Michie, D., editor 1969, *Machine Intelligence 4*. Ellis Horwood, Chichester, England. 463ff.

McKinsey, J. C. C. 1943. The decision problem for some classes of sentences without quantifiers. *Journal of Symbolic Logic* 8(3):61.

Peirce, Charles S. 1958. *Collected Papers of Charles Sanders Peirce*. Harvard University Press, Cambridge, MA.

Reiter, Raymond and Kleer, Johande 1987. Foundations of assumption based truth maintance systems: Preliminary report. In *Proceedings of AAAI-87*. 183.

Selman, Bart and Kautz, Henry 1991. Knowledge compilation using Horn approximations. In *Proceedings of AAAI-91*, Anaheim, CA. 904–909.

Selman, Bart and Levesque, Hector J. 1990. Abductive and default reasoning: a computational core. In *Proceedings of AAAI-90*, Boston, MA.

Selman, Bart 1990. Tractable default reasoning. Ph.D. Thesis, Department of Computer Science, University of Toronto, Toronto, Ontario.

The Breakout Method For Escaping From Local Minima

Paul Morris

IntelliCorp

1975 El Camino Real West

Mountain View, CA 94040

morris@intellicorp.com

Abstract

A number of algorithms have recently been proposed that use *iterative improvement* (a form of hill-climbing) to solve constraint satisfaction problems. These techniques have had dramatic success on certain problems. However, one factor limiting their wider application is the possibility of getting stuck at non-solution local minima. In this paper we describe an iterative improvement algorithm, called *Breakout*, that can escape from local minima. We present empirical evidence that this method is very effective in cases where previous approaches have difficulty. Although Breakout is not theoretically complete, in practice it appears to almost always find solutions for solvable problems. We prove that an idealized (but less efficient) version of the algorithm is complete.

Introduction

Several recent papers have studied iterative improvement methods for solving constraint satisfaction and optimization problems. (See [Minton *et al.* 1990], [Zweben 1990], [Sosic & Gu 1991], [Minton *et al.* 1992], [Selman, Levesque, & Mitchell 1992].) These methods work by first generating an initial, flawed "solution" (i.e., containing constraint violations) to a problem. They then try to eliminate the flaws by making local changes that reduce the total number of constraint violations. Thus, they perform hill-climbing in a space where goodness is measured in terms of how few constraints are violated, in the hope that eventually a point will be reached that provides an acceptable solution to the problem. The papers provide empirical and analytical evidence that such methods can lead to rapid solutions for important classes of problems.

One drawback of such methods, however, is the possibility of becoming stuck at locally optimal points that are not acceptable as solutions. (We will henceforth call these "local minima," viewing the local changes as movements on a *cost surface* where the height reflects the current number of constraint vi-

olations.) While the above approaches incorporate some techniques to mitigate this problem, these are at best only moderately successful. For example, the Minton *et al.* and Selman *et al.* algorithms can escape from plateaus on the cost surface, since they allow random "sideways" local changes. However, they still get caught in other local minima. This causes them to miss solutions in many difficult SAT and K-coloring problems. While the random walk character of the Zweben algorithm would seem to ensure almost certain eventual movement to a solution, this kind of probabilistic guarantee may not be very useful.[1] The Sosic and Gu approach formulates the search space in a way that avoids local minima. However, the method is specific to N-queens, and has no obvious generalization to other problems.

Another remedy for the local minimum problem is to repeatedly restart the iterative improvement process from new random starting points until an acceptable solution is reached, as is done in the Selman *et al.* algorithm. This amounts to randomly searching the local minima for a solution. Figure 1 illustrates why this is computationally impractical in many cases. Iterative improvement methods derive their power from an assumption that the number of constraint violations is a rough indicator of the closeness to a solution. In general, we might expect some noise in the estimate, suggesting a cost surface with a cross-section something like that shown in the upper part of the figure. (The lowest point in the surface represents a solution.) Now consider an algorithm that gets stuck at each of the local minima shown. Notice that repeated restarting will perform no better on the upper surface than it would on the lower surface shown in the figure. That is, it fails to take advantage of the overall *trend* of the surface. Looking only at the lower surface, it is easy to see that the average time to a solution depends on the number of local minima in a region around the solution (and thus indirectly on the "volume" of the

---

[1] As an analogy, if two flasks are connected by a tube, the air molecules will, with probability 1, eventually all pile up in one flask. However, the mean time before this happens is enormous.

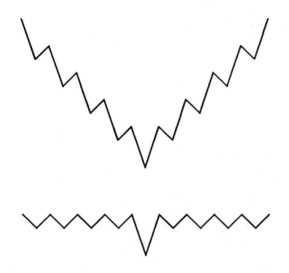

Figure 1: Why escaping is better than restarting.

region). For CSPs, the dimension of the cost surface (i.e., the number of states adjacent to a given state) increases linearly with the size of the problem. This makes the "volume" (and hence, presumably, the expense of a restart search) increase rapidly with the size. Now consider an algorithm that can escape from the local minima shown. This should perform better on the upper surface, since it takes advantage of the general trend towards a solution. For this type of surface, the time required to find a solution should be largely independent of the dimensionality.

It is known that for certain problems, like N-queens, almost all the local minima are narrow plateaus (Morris [1992]). The above analysis suggests that plateau-escaping algorithms (like that of Minton *et al.*) would solve such problems very efficiently. Indeed, this does appear to be the case.

In this paper we present a deterministic algorithm for solving finite constraint satisfaction problems using an iterative improvement method. The algorithm includes a technique called *breakout* for escaping from local minima. In the following sections, we will define the algorithm, and compare its performance to that of other methods. Finally, we will prove a theoretical result that helps explain the success of the algorithm.

The Breakout Algorithm

We now discuss the Breakout algorithm in more detail and consider how it applies to a constraint satisfaction problem (CSP). The essential features of this algorithm were first introduced in Morris [1990], where it was applied to the Zebra problem (see Dechter [1990]).[2]

---

[2]Selman and Kautz [1993] have independently developed a closely related method.

Informally, a CSP consists of a set of variables, each of which is assigned a value from a set called the *domain* of the variable. A *state* is a complete set of assignments for the variables. The solution states must satisfy a set of *constraints*, which mandate relationships between the values of different variables. We refer the reader to Dechter [1990] for the formal definition of a CSP. In this paper we will consider only *finite* CSPs, i.e., where there is a finite set of variables, and the domain of each variable is finite. Constraint satisfaction problems are generally expressed in terms of sets of tuples that are allowed. For our purposes, it is convenient to instead focus attention on the *no-goods*, i.e., the tuples that are prohibited.

The intuition for the breakout algorithm comes from a physical force metaphor. We think of the variables as repelling each other from values that conflict. The variables move (i.e., are reassigned) under the influence of these forces until they reach a position of equilibrium. This corresponds to a state where each variable is at a value that is repelled the least by the current values of the other variables. In physical terms, an equilibrium state is surrounded by a potential barrier that prevents further movement. If this is not a solution, we need some way of breaking through that barrier to reach a state of lower energy.

In an equilibrium state, the variables that are still in conflict are stable because they are repelled from alternative values at least as much as from their current values. Suppose, however, the repulsive force associated with the current nogoods is boosted relative to the other nogoods. As the repulsive force on current values increases, at some point, for some variable, it will exceed that applied against the alternative values. Then the variable will no longer be stable, and the iterative improvement procedure can continue. The boosting process has effectively changed the topography of the cost surface so that the current state is no longer a local minimum. We refer to this as a *breakout* from the equilibrium position.

In iterative improvement, the cost of a state is measured as the number of constraints that it violates, i.e., the number of nogoods that are matched by the state. For the Breakout algorithm, we associate a weight with each nogood, and measure the cost as the sum of the weights of the matched nogoods. The weights have 1 as their initial value. Iterative improvement proceeds as usual until an equilibrium state (i.e., a local minimum) is reached.[3] At that point, the weight of each current nogood is increased (by unit increments) until breakout occurs. Then iterative improvement resumes. Figure 2 summarizes the algorithm.

We note that the algorithm does not specify the initial state. In our experiments we used random start-

---

[3]Plateau points are treated just like any other local minima. Thus, the algorithm relies on breakouts to move it along plateaus.

```
UNTIL current state is solution DO
IF current state is not a local minimum
THEN make any local change that reduces the total
    cost
ELSE increase weights of all current nogoods
END
```

Figure 2: The Breakout Algorithm.

ing points. The results of Minton *et al.* suggest that it may be worthwhile to use a greedy preproccessing algorithm to produce an initial point with few violations. This will generally shorten the time required to reach the first local minimum.

The algorithm also does not specify which local change to make in a non-equilibrium state. In our implementation, we simply use the first one found in a left-to-right search.

Experimental Results

We tested the breakout algorithm on several types of CSP, including Boolean 3-Satisfiability, and Graph K-Coloring. We describe the results here.

Boolean Satisfiability

For Boolean 3-satisfiability, we generated random *solvable* formulas. The results we report here are for 3-SAT problems where the *clause density*[4] has the critical value of 4.3 that has been identified as particularly difficult by Mitchell *et al.* [1992]. We use the same method of generating random problems as theirs except for the following: to ensure the problems are solvable, we select a desired solution[5] in advance and modify the generation process so that at least one literal of every clause matches it. Specifically, we reject (and replace) any clauses that would exclude the desired solution.[6] The variables are then initialized to random values before starting the breakout solution procedure. Note that for Boolean satisfiability problems, the nogoods are just the clauses expressed negatively.

The results are shown in table 1 for a range of problem sizes, averaged over 100 trials in each case. We wish to emphasize that the algorithm never failed to find a solution in any of the trials. Note that the growth of total hill-climbing (HC) steps appears to be a little faster than linear, but less than quadratic. The timing figures shown are the average elapsed time for

---

[4]The number of clauses divided by the number of variables.

[5]By symmetry, it doesn't matter which one.

[6]In an earlier version of this paper, instead of using a rejection method, the negated/unnegated status of one literal was directly chosen to match the solution. That method produced very easy problems.

Vars	Breakouts	HC steps	Time (sec.)
100	60	168	3.2
300	180	795	17.7
500	320	1678	46.9
700	325	2165	68.0
900	475	3215	122.2
1100	575	4508	182.9

Table 1: Breakout on 3-SAT problems with prearranged solution.

Vars	Tries	Total Flips	Time (sec.)
100	3.6	1505	10.4
150	4.2	4093	38.2
200	6.5	11,901	138.7
250	4.3	11,789	166.6
300	6.9	28,782	473.9

Table 2: GSAT on similar problems.

the (combined) creation and solution of 3-SAT problems, running in Lisp on a Sun 4/110.

A recent paper [Williams & Hogg 1993] has noted that using a prespecified solution when generating random problems introduces a subtle bias in favor of problems with a greater number of solutions, and thus is likely to produce easier problems. (On the other hand, it is a convenient way of producing large known-solvable problems, which are otherwise difficult to obtain.) Selman *et al.* [1992] use a different random generation process for testing their GSAT algorithm. First they generate formulas that may or may not be satisfiable. Unsolvable formulas are then filtered out by an exhaustive search (using a variant of the Davis-Putnam algorithm). Thus, the results in table 1 cannot be directly compared to those reported for GSAT. To obtain a better comparison, we reimplemented GSAT and tested it on problems generated in the same way as those used for testing Breakout. The results are shown in table 2 (averaged over 100 trials). The Tries parameter here is the number of restarts (including the final successful one). The Total Flips parameter is the number of local changes needed to reach a solution (summed over all the Tries). This figure is roughly comparable to the number of hill-climbing steps for the Breakout algorithm. In GSAT, each Try phase is limited to *Max-Flips* steps; for these experiments, Max-Flips was set to $n^2/20$, where n is the number of variables.[7]

In terms of the machine-independent parameters,[8] the problems we use are clearly easier for GSAT than those on which it was originally tested. In particular, the Tries figure appears to stay roughly constant

---

[7]An $O(n^2)$ setting was suggested by Bart Selman (personal communication).

[8]The sun 4/110 is slower than the MIPS machine used by Selman *et al.*

Density	3	4	5	6	7
Breakouts	6.4	36	74	23	8.1
HC steps	41	115	248	143	99

Table 3: Breakout for different clause densities

Nodes	30	60	90	120	150	180
Breakout Algorithm:						
Breakouts	12	24	48	46	54	80
HC steps	35	77	159	191	245	363
MCHC:						
% solved	46.5	12.13	1.75	0.5	0.25	0.12

Table 4: Breakout and MCHC on 3-coloring

Nodes	30	60	90	120	150
Breakouts	8	47	189	655	1390
HC steps	49	308	1257	3959	8873

Table 5: Breakout on 4-coloring

as the problem size increases. Nevertheless, the performance of Breakout seems significantly better than that of GSAT, and avoids the inconvenience of having to set the Max-Flips parameter. We remark that testing with a variant of the Davis-Putnam algorithm shows exponential growth for these problems.

We also ran Breakout for different values of the clause density, keeping the number of variables fixed at 100. Instead of a peak centered at 4.3, we found one in the neighbourhood of 5. (Testing at higher resolution indicates a range from 4.8 to 5.2 as the region of greatest difficulty.) The results shown in table 3 are each averaged over 1,000 trials.

In preliminary testing of Breakout on problems generated in the same way as those in Selman *et al.* [1992], average performance appears to degrade to exponential, like that of GSAT, and the peak difficulty occurs at the 4.3 value of the density. Remarkably, the average appears dominated by a small number of very difficult problems. The average over 100 trials has been observed to fluctuate by an order of magnitude, depending on how many of the very difficult problems are encountered. These problems may have cost surfaces that more closely resemble the lower surface in figure 1.

Graph Coloring

For graph K-coloring, we generated random solvable K-coloring problems with n nodes and m arcs in essentially the same way as described in Minton *et al.* [1992] (and attributed there to Adorph and Johnson [1990]). That is, we choose a coloring in advance that divides the K colors as equally as possible between the nodes. Then we generate random arcs, rejecting any that violate the desired coloring, until m arcs have been accepted. The entire process is repeated until a connected graph is obtained.

We used two sets of test data, one with $K = 3$ and $m = 2n$, and the other with $K = 4$ and $m = 4.7n$. The first set are the "sparse" problems for which Minton *et al.* report poor performance of their Min-Conflicts hill-climbing (MCHC) algorithm. The second represents a critical value of the arc density identified by Cheeseman *et al.* [1991] as producing particularly difficult problems.

Table 4 shows the results on the first set of test data. Each figure is averaged over 100 trials. The algorithm never failed to find a solution on any of the trials. We note the number of breakouts seems to increase roughly linearly (with some fluctuation). The number of transitions per breakout also appears to be slowly

growing. This performance can be contrasted with that of MCHC, which shows an apparent exponential decline in the frequency with which solvable sparse 3-coloring problems are solved (within a bound of $9n$ steps), as the number of nodes increases.[9]

Table 5 shows the results on the second set of test data. In this case, each figure is averaged over 100 trials, except for N = 120 and 150, which were averaged over only 99 trials each. This really does seem to be a more difficult task for Breakout. For the omitted trials, the algorithm failed to reach a solution even after 100,000 breakouts, and was terminated. This may be a further instance of the phenomenon of a small number of very difficult problems sprinkled among the majority of easier problems.

A Complete Algorithm

The experimental results show that Breakout has remarkable success on important classes of CSPs. This is partially explained by the discussion regarding figure 1. However, one point has not yet been answered. Since Breakout modifies the cost function, it appears plausible that it could often get trapped in infinite loops; yet the experimental data shows this almost never occurs (at least, for randomly generated problems). In this section, we provide some insight into this by showing that a closely related algorithm is theoretically *complete*; that is, it is guaranteed to eventually find a solution if one exists.

Consider the effect of a breakout on the cost surface: the cost of the current state, and perhaps several neighbouring states (that share nogoods with the current state), is increased. However, all that is really needed to escape the local minimum is that the cost of the *current* state itself increase. We are thus led to consider an idealized version of Breakout where that is the only state whose cost changes. To facilitate this, we assume every state has a stored cost associated with it that can be modified directly. (The initial costs would be the same as before.) This ideal-

---

[9] We thank Andy Philips for providing this data.

UNTIL *current state is solution* DO
IF *current state is not a local minimum*
THEN *make* any *local change that reduces the cost*
ELSE *increase stored cost of current state*
END

Figure 3: The Fill Algorithm.

ized algorithm is summarized in figure 3. We will call this the *Fill* algorithm because it tends to smoothly fill depressions in the cost surface.

It turns out that this idealized version of Breakout is complete, as we prove here.[10] In the following, we say two states are *adjacent* if they differ in the value of a single variable, a state is *visited* when it occurs as the current state during the course of the algorithm, and a state is *lifted* when its stored cost is incremented as a result of the action of the algorithm. Note that lifting only occurs at a local minimum.

Theorem 1 *Given a finite CSP, the Fill algorithm eventually reaches a solution, if one exists.*

Proof: Suppose the algorithm does not find a solution. Then we can divide the state space into states that are lifted infinitely often, and states that are lifted at most a finite number of times. Let $\mathcal{S}$ be the set of states that are lifted infinitely often. A *boundary state* of $\mathcal{S}$ is one that is adjacent to a state not in $\mathcal{S}$. To see that $\mathcal{S}$ must have a boundary state, consider a path that connects any state in $\mathcal{S}$ to a solution. Let s be the last state that belongs to $\mathcal{S}$ on this path. Clearly s is a boundary state of $\mathcal{S}$.

As the algorithm proceeds, there must eventually come a time when all the following conditions hold.

1. The states outside $\mathcal{S}$ will never again be lifted.

2. The cost of each state in $\mathcal{S}$ exceeds the cost of every state not in $\mathcal{S}$.

3. A boundary state of $\mathcal{S}$ is lifted.

Notice that at the moment the last event occurs, the boundary state involved must be a local minimum. But this contradicts the fact that the state is adjacent to a state not in $\mathcal{S}$, which (by the second condition) has a lower cost. Thus, the assumption that a solution is not found must be false. ■

The Breakout algorithm may be regarded as a "sloppy," or approximate version of the Fill algorithm, where some of the increase in cost spills onto neighbouring states. Note that Breakout is much more efficient because of the compact storage of the increased costs.

---

[10]The reader may wonder whether a simpler algorithm that just marked local minima, and never visited them again, would be complete. It turns out this is not the case because of the possibility of "painting oneself into a corner." Note that Fill may revisit states.

The Fill algorithm is itself related to the LRTA* algorithm of Korf [1990], which has also been proved complete. The latter algorithm has been studied in the context of shortest path problems, rather than CSPs. In a path problem, the goal state is usually known ahead of time. Note, however, that this is not essential as long as a suitable heuristic distance function is available. Iterative improvement implicitly treats a CSP as a path problem by seeking a path that transforms an initial state into a solution state, thereby obtaining the solution state as a side product. From this viewpoint, the number of conflicts serves as a heuristic distance function. (However, this heuristic is not *admissible* in the sense of the A* algorithm, because it may occasionally overestimate the distance to a solution.)

Both Fill and LRTA* have the effect of increasing the stored cost of a state when at a local minimum. We note the following technical differences between the two algorithms.

1. LRTA* transitions to the neighbour of *least* cost, whereas the Fill algorithm is satisfied with any lower cost neighbour.

2. LRTA* may modify costs at states that are not local minima, and may decrease costs as well as increasing them.

Item 1 suggests Fill/Breakout is more suited for CSPs, where the number of states adjacent to a given state is generally very large.

One might consider using the Fill algorithm directly to solve CSPs. However, the only obvious advantage of this over Breakout is the theoretical guarantee of completeness. It appears that, in practice, Breakout almost always finds a solution anyway, and has a much lower overhead with regard to storage and retrieval costs. The Fill algorithm requires storage space proportional to $n \times l$, where n is the number of variables, and l is the number of local minima encountered on the way to a solution. By contrast, Breakout only requires storage proportional to the fixed set of no-goods derived from the specification of the problem. Moreover, preliminary experiments suggest that Fill requires many more steps than Breakout to reach a solution. This may be due to a beneficial effect of the cost increase spillovers in Breakout—presumably depressions get filled more rapidly.

It is known that Breakout itself is not complete. As a counterexample, consider a Boolean Satisfiability problem with four variables, x, y, z, w, and the clause

$$x \lor y \lor z \lor w$$

together with the 12 clauses

	$\neg x \lor y$	$\neg x \lor z$	$\neg x \lor w$
$\neg y \lor x$		$\neg y \lor z$	$\neg y \lor w$
$\neg z \lor x$	$\neg z \lor y$		$\neg z \lor w$
$\neg w \lor x$	$\neg w \lor y$	$\neg w \lor z$	

Note that these clauses have a single solution, in which all the variables are *true*.

Suppose the initial state sets all the variables to *false*. It is not hard to see that the Breakout algorithm will produce oscillations here, where each variable in turn moves to *true*, and then back to *false*.

To understand this better, consider the three states S_1, S_2, and S_3, such that x is *true* in S_1, y is *true* in S_2, and both x and y are *true* in S_3. All of the other variables are *false* in each case.

Each time S_1 occurs as an local minimum, the weight of each of its nogoods is incremented. Thus, the total cost of S_1 increases by 3. Since S_1 shares two nogoods with S_3, the cost of the latter increases by 2 at the same time. Similarly, when state S_2 becomes a local minimum, the cost of S_3 increases by 2. This means that S_3 undergoes a combined increase of 4 during each cycle, which exceeds the increase for each of S_1 and S_2. Thus, S_3 is never visited, and this path to a solution is blocked.

Thus, the basic reason for incompleteness is that the cost increase spillovers from several local minima can conspire to block potential paths to a solution. However, this kind of blockage requires nogoods to interact locally in a specific "unlucky" manner. For large random CSPs, the number of possible exits from a region of the state space tends to be very large, and the probability that all the exits get blocked in this way would appear to be vanishingly small. This may explain why we did not observe infinite oscillations in our experiments.

Conclusions

The class of Boolean 3-Satisfiability problems is of importance because of its central position in the family of NP-complete problems. We have seen that the Breakout algorithm performs very successfully on 3-SAT problems with prearranged solutions, including those at the critical clause density. Breakout also performs quite well on K-coloring problems, and appears superior to previous approaches for both of these classes.

We have provided analyses that explain both the efficiency of the algorithm, and its apparent avoidance of infinite cycles in practice. In particular, an idealized version of the algorithm has been proved to be complete.

Several possibilities for future work suggest themselves. The relationship to LRTA* ought to be explored in greater detail, particularly in view of the attractive learning capabilities of LRTA*. One might also consider applying some form of Breakout to other classes of search problems where a cost measure can be distributed over individual "flaws" in a draft solution. More generally, the metaphor of competing forces that inspired Breakout may encourage novel architectures for other computational systems.

Acknowledgements The author is grateful to Rina Dechter, Bob Filman, Dennis Kibler, Rich Korf, Steve Minton and Bart Selman for beneficial discussions, and would also like to thank the anonymous referees for their useful comments.

References

Adorph, H. M., and Johnson, M. D. A discrete stochastic neural network for constraint satisfaction problems. In *Proceedings of IJCNN-90*, San Diego, 1990.

Cheeseman, P.; Kanefsky, B.; and Taylor, W. M. Where the *really* hard problems are. In *Proceedings of IJCAI-91*, Sydney, Australia, 1991.

Dechter, R. Enhancement schemes for constraint processing: backjumping, learning, and cutset decomposition. *Artificial Intelligence*, 41(3), 1990.

Korf, R. E. Real-time heuristic search. *Artificial Intelligence*, 42(2-3), 1990.

Minton, S.; Johnston, M. D.; Philips, A. B.; and Laird, P. Solving large scale constraint satisfaction and scheduling problems using a heuristic repair method. In *Proceedings of AAAI-90*, Boston, 1990.

Minton, S.; Johnston, M. D.; Philips, A. B.; and Laird, P. Minimizing conflicts: a heuristic repair method for constraint satisfaction and scheduling problems. *Artificial Intelligence*, 58(1-3), 1992.

Mitchell, D.; Selman, B.; and Levesque, H. Hard and Easy Distribution of SAT Problems. In *Proceedings of AAAI-92*, San Jose, California, 1992.

Morris, P. Solutions Without Exhaustive Search: An Iterative Descent Method for Solving Binary Constraint Satisfaction Problems. In *Proceedings of AAAI-90 Workshop on Constraint-Directed Reasoning*, Boston, 1990.

Morris, P. On the Density of Solutions in Equilibrium Points for the Queens Problem. In *Proceedings of AAAI-92*, San Jose, California, 1992.

Selman, B.; Levesque, H.; and Mitchell, D. A New Method for Solving Hard Satisfiability Problems. In *Proceedings of AAAI-92*, San Jose, California, 1992.

Selman, B., and Kautz, H. Domain-Independent Extensions to GSAT: Solving Large Structured Satisfiability Problems. In *Proceedings of IJCAI-93*, Chambéry, France, 1993.

Sosic, R., and Gu, J. 3,000,000 Queens in Less Than One Minute. *Sigart Bulletin*, 2(2), 1991.

Williams, C.P., and Hogg, T. Exploiting the Deep Structure of Constraint Problems. Preprint, Xerox PARC, 1993.

Zweben, M. A Framework for Iterative Improvement Search Algorithms Suited for Constraint Satisfaction Problems. In *Proceedings of AAAI-90 Workshop on Constraint-Directed Reasoning*, Boston, 1990.

An Empirical Study of Greedy Local Search for Satisfiability Testing

Bart Selman and Henry A. Kautz

AI Principles Research Department
AT&T Bell Laboratories
Murray Hill, NJ 07974
{selman, kautz}@research.att.com

Abstract

GSAT is a randomized local search procedure for solving propositional satisfiability problems. GSAT can solve hard, randomly generated problems that are an order of magnitude larger than those that can be handled by more traditional approaches, such as the Davis-Putnam procedure. This paper presents the results of numerous experiments we have performed with GSAT, in order to improve our understanding of its capabilities and limitations.

We first characterize the space traversed by GSAT. We will see that for nearly all problem classes we have encountered, the space consists of a steep descent followed by broad flat plateaus. We then compare GSAT with simulated annealing, and show how GSAT can be viewed as an efficient method for executing the low-temperature tail of an annealing schedule. Finally, we report on extensions to the basic GSAT procedure. We discuss two general, domain-independent extensions that dramatically improve GSAT's performance on structured problems: the use of clause weights, and a way to average in near-solutions when initializing the procedure before each try.

Introduction

Selman *et al.* (1992) introduced a randomized greedy local search procedure called GSAT for solving propositional satisfiability problems. Experiments showed that this procedure can be used to solve hard, randomly generated problems that are an order of magnitude larger than those that can be handled by more traditional approaches, such as the Davis-Putnam procedure or resolution. GSAT was also shown to perform well on propositional encodings of the N-queens problem, graph coloring problems, and Boolean induction problems.

This paper presents the results of numerous experiments we have performed with GSAT, in order to improve our understanding of its capabilities and limitations. We will begin with an exploration of the shape of the search space that GSAT typically encounters. We will see that for nearly all problem classes we have examined, the space consists of a steep descent followed by broad plateaus. We then compare GSAT with simulated annealing, and show how GSAT can be viewed as a very efficient method for executing the low-temperature tail of an annealing schedule.

A common criticism of randomized algorithms like GSAT is that they might not do as well on problems that have an intricate underlying structure as they do on randomly generated problems. Based on our understanding of the shape of GSAT's search space, we developed two general, domain-independent extensions that dramatically improve its performance: the use of clause weights, and a way to average in near-solutions when initializing the procedure before each try. We will also describe other local search heuristics which appear promising, but did not improve performance on our test problems.

This paper is unabashidly empirical. Although we will point to relevant results in the theoretical literature, we will not present an abstract analysis of our results. It would obviously be highly desirable to characterize precisely the class of problems for which GSAT succeeds, and to provide precise bounds on its running time. Unfortunately, such results are extremely rare and difficult to obtain in work on incomplete algorithms for NP-hard problems. The situation is similar, for example, in research on simulated annealing, where the formal results show convergence in the limit (*i.e.,* after an arbitrary amount of time), but few address the *rate* of convergence to a solution. In fact, a good, general characterization of the rate of convergence appears to be beyond the current state of the art of theoretical analysis (Bertsimas and Tsitsiklis 1992; Jerrum 1992). Current theory does, however, explain why GSAT performs well on certain limited classes of formulas (*e.g.* 2-SAT and over-constrained formulas), and the range of applicability of such formal results will certainly increase over time (Papadimitriou 1991; Koutsoupias and Papadimitriou 1992). We believe that experimental work should proceed in parallel with theoretical work, because real data can point out the problem-solving techniques that are worthy of formal analysis, and can help distinguish the asymptotic results that carry over to practical cases from those that do not.

The GSAT Procedure

GSAT performs a greedy local search for a satisfying

Procedure GSAT
Input: a set of clauses α, MAX-FLIPS, and MAX-TRIES
Output: a satisfying truth assignment of α, if found
    for $i := 1$ **to** MAX-TRIES
        $T :=$ a randomly generated truth assignment
        for $j := 1$ **to** MAX-FLIPS
            if T satisfies α **then return** T
            $p :=$ a propositional variable such that a change
                in its truth assignment gives the largest
                increase in the total number of clauses
                of α that are satisfied by T
            $T := T$ with the truth assignment of p reversed
        end for
    end for
    return "no satisfying assignment found"

Figure 1: The GSAT procedure.

assignment of a set of propositional clauses.[1] The procedure starts with a randomly generated truth assignment. It then changes ('flips') the assignment of the variable that leads to the largest increase in the total number of satisfied clauses. Such flips are repeated until either a satisfying assignment is found or a pre-set maximum number of flips (MAX-FLIPS) is reached. This process is repeated as needed up to a maximum of MAX-TRIES times. See Figure 1. (For a related approach, see Gu (1992).)

GSAT mimics the standard local search procedures used for finding approximate solutions to optimization problems (Papadimitriou and Steiglitz 1982) in that it only explores potential solutions that are "close" to the one currently being considered. Specifically, we explore the set of assignments that differ from the current one on only one variable. The GSAT procedure requires the setting of two parameters, MAX-FLIPS and MAX-TRIES, which determine, respectively, how many flips the procedure will attempt before giving up and restarting, and how many times this search can be restarted before quitting. As a rough guideline, setting MAX-FLIPS equal to about ten times the number of variables is sufficient. The setting of MAX-TRIES will generally be determined by the total amount of time that one wants to spend looking for an assignment before giving up.

In our experience so far, there is generally a good setting of the parameters that can be used for all instances of an application. Thus, one can fine-tune the procedure by experimenting with various parameter settings. It is important to understand that we are *not* suggesting that the parameters need to be reset for each individual problem — only for a broad class, for example, coloring problems, random formulas, *etc.* Practically all optimization algorithms for intractable problems have parameters that must be set this way,[2] so this is not a particular disadvantage of GSAT. Furthermore, one could devise various schemes to auto-

matically choose a good parameter setting by performing a binary search on different parameter settings on a sequence of problems.

Summary of Previous Results

In Selman *et al.* (1992), we showed that GSAT substantially outperforms backtracking search procedures, such as the Davis-Putnam procedure, on various classes of formulas. For example, we studied GSAT's performance on hard randomly generated formulas. (Note that generating hard random formulas for testing purposes is a challenging problem by itself, see Cheeseman *et al.* (1991); Mitchell *et al.* (1992); William and Hogg (1992); Larrabee and Tsuji (1993); and Crawford and Auton (1993).) The fastest backtrack type procedures, using special heuristics, can handle up to 350 variable hard random formulas in about one hour on a MIPS workstation (Buro and Kleine Büning 1992; Crawford and Auton 1993). Nevertheless, the running time clearly scales exponentially, for example, hard 450 variable formulas are undoable. Our current implementation of GSAT, using the random walk option discussed in Selman and Kautz (1993), solves hard 1500 variable formulas in under an hour. Selman *et al.* also showed that GSAT performs well on propositional encodings of the N-queens problem, hard instances of graph coloring problems (Johnson *et al.* 1991), and Boolean induction problems (Kamath *et al.* 1992).

The Search Space

Crucial to a better understanding of GSAT's behavior is the manner in which GSAT converges on an assignment. In Figure 2, we show how the GSAT's search progresses on a randomly generated 100 variable problem with 430 clauses. Along the horizontal axis we give the number of flips, and along the vertical axis the number of clauses that still remained unsatisfied. (The final flip reduces this number to zero.) It is clear from the figure that most of the time is spent wandering on large plateaus. Only approximately the first 5% of the search is spent in pure greedy descent. We have observed qualitatively similar patterns over and over again. (See also the discussion on "sideway" moves in Selman *et al.* (1992), and Gent and Walsh (1993).)

The bottom panel in Figure 2 shows the search space for a 500 variable, 2150 clause random satisfiable formula. The long tableaus become even more pronounced, and the relative size of the pure greedy descent further diminishes. In general, the harder the formulas, the longer the tableaus.

Another interesting property of the graphs is that we see no upwards moves. An upward move would occur when the best possible flip increases the number of unsatisfied clauses. This appears to be extremely rare, especially for the randomly generated instances.

The search pattern brings out an interesting difference between our use of GSAT and the standard use of local search techniques for obtaining good *approximate* solutions to combinatorial optimization problems (Lin and Kernighan 1973; Papadimitriou and Steiglitz 1982; Papadimitriou *et al.* 1990). In the latter, one generally halts the local search procedure as soon as no more improvement is found. Our

---

[1] A clause is a disjunction of literals. A literal is a propositional variable or its negation. A set of clauses corresponds to a formula in conjunctive normal form (CNF): a conjunction of disjunctions. Thus, GSAT handles CNF–SAT.

[2] For example, see the discussion on integer programming methods in Fourer (1993).

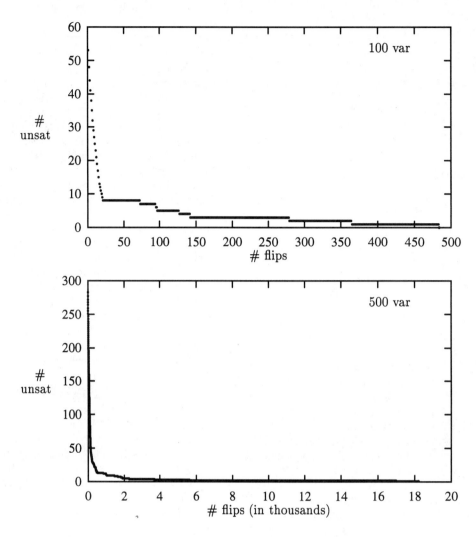

Figure 2: GSAT's search space on a 100 and 500 variables formulas.

figure shows that this is appropriate when looking for a *near-solution*, since most of the gain lies in the early, greedy descent part. On the other hand, when searching for a global minimum (*i.e.*, a satisfying assignment) stopping when flips do not yield an immediate improvement is a poor strategy — *most* of the work occurs in satisfying the last few remaining clauses.

Note that finding an assignment that satisfies all clauses of a logical theory is essential in many reasoning and problem solving situations. For example, in our work on planning as satisfiability, a satisfying assignment correspond to a correct plan (Kautz and Selman 1992). The near-satisfying assignments are of little use; they correspond to plans that contain one of more "magical" moves, where blocks suddenly shift positions.

Simulated Annealing

Simulated annealing is a stochastic local search method. It was introduced by Kirkpatrick *et al.* (1983) to tackle combinatorial optimization problems. Instead of pure greedy local search, the procedure allows a certain amount of "noise" which enables it to make modifications that actually *increase* the cost of the current solution (even when this is not the best possible current modification). In terms of finding satisfying assignments, this means that the procedure sometimes allows flips that actually increase the total number of unsatisfied clauses. The idea is that by allowing random occurrences of such upwards moves, the algorithm can escape local minima. The frequency of such moves is determined by a parameter T, called the temperature. (The higher the temperature, the more often upward moves occur.)

The parameter T is set by the user. Normally, one follows a so-called annealing schedule in which one slowly decreases the temperature until T reaches zero. It can be shown formally that provided one "cools" slowly enough, the system will find a global minimum. Unfortunately, the analysis uses an exponentially long annealing schedule, making it only of theoretical interest (Hajek 1988). Our real interest is in the rate of convergence to a global minimum for more practical annealing schedules. Current formal methods, however, appear too weak to tackle this question.[3]

It is interesting to compare the plot for GSAT (Figure 2) with that for annealing (Figure 3) on the same 100 variable random formula.[4] In the early part of the search, GSAT performs pure greedy descent. The descent is similar to the initial phase of an annealing schedule, although more rapid, because GSAT performs no upward moves. In the next stage, both algorithms must search along a series of long plateaus. GSAT makes mostly sideways moves, but takes advantage of a downward move whenever one arises. Annealing has reached the long, low-temperature "tail" of its schedule, where it is very unlikely to make an upward move, but allows both sideways and downward moves. Because much of the effort expended by annealing in the initial high temperature part of the schedule is wasted, it typically takes longer to reach a solution. Note, for example, that after less than 500 moves GSAT has reached a satisfying assignment, while the annealing algorithm still has 5 unsatisfied clauses. A more rapid cooling schedule would, of course, more closely mimick GSAT.

Thus we can view GSAT as a very efficient method for executing the low-temperature tail of an annealing schedule. Furthermore, our experiments with several annealing schedules on hard, random formulas confirmed that most of the work in finding a true satisfying assignment is in the tail of the schedule. In fact, we were unable to find an annealing schedule that performed better than GSAT, although we cannot rule out the possiblity that such a schedule exists. This is an inherent difficulty in the study of annealing approaches (Johnson et al. 1991).

Extensions

The basic GSAT algorithm is quite elementary, and one might expect that more sophisticated algorithms could yield better performance. We investigated several extensions to GSAT, and found a few that were indeed successful. But it is important to stress that the basic GSAT algorithm is very robust, in the sense that many intuitively appealing modifications do not in fact change its performance. We have found that experimental study can help reveal the assumptions, true or false, implicit in such intuitions, and can lead

to interesting questions for further empirical or theoretical research.

Improving the Initial Assignment

One natural intuition about GSAT is that it would be better to start with an initial assignment that is "close" to a solution, rather than with a totally random truth assignment. Indeed, the theoretical analysis of general greedy local search presented in (Minton et al. 1992) shows that the closer the initial assignment is to a solution, the more likely it is that local search will succeed.

Therefore we tried the following method for creating better initial assignments: First, a variable is assigned a random value. Next, all clauses containing that variable are examined, to see if the values of any unassigned variables are then determined by unit propagation. If so, these variables are assigned, and again unit propagation is performed. (If a clause is unsatisfied by the current partial assignment, it is simply ignored for the time being.) When no more propagations are possible, another unassigned variable is given a random value, and the process repeats.

Experiments revealed that this strategy did *not* significantly reduce the time required to find a solution. In retrospect, this failure can be explained by the shape of the search space, as discussed above. The descent from an initial state in which many clauses are unsatisfied to one which only a few are unsatisfied occupies only a tiny fraction of the overall execution time, and initial unit propagation helps only in this phase of the search.

The problem is that the number of unsatisfied clauses is a fairly crude measure of the distance to a solution, measured in terms of the number of flips required to reach a satisfying assignment. (Minton et al. (1992) make a similar observation regarding coloring problems. See also Gent and Walsh (1993).) This led us to consider another strategy for generating good initial assignments. Since GSAT typically performs many tries before finding a solution, we make use of the information gained from previous tries to create an initial assignment that is already some distance out on a low plateau, and thus actually closer to a solution. We do this by initializing with the *bitwise average* of the best assignment found in the two previous tries.

The bitwise average of two truth assignments is an assignment that agrees with the assignment of those letters on which the two given truth assignments are identical; the remaining letters are randomly assigned truth values. After many tries in which averaging is performed, the initial and final states become nearly identical. We therefore reset the initial assignment to a new random assignment every 10 to 50 tries.[5]

In Selman and Kautz (1993), we give an empirical evaluation of the averaging strategy. We considered propositional encodings of hard graph coloring problems used by Johnson et al. (1991) to evaluate specialized graph coloring

---

[3]Recent work by Pinkas and Dechter (1992) and Jerrum (1992) provides some interesting formal convergence results for a special class of optimization problems.

[4]We use the annealing algorithm given in Johnson et al. (1991). Start with a randomly generate truth assignment; repeatedly pick a random variable, and compute how many more clauses become satisfied when the truth value of that variable is flipped — call this number δ. If $\delta \geq 0$, make the flip. Otherwise, flip the variable with probability $e^{\delta/T}$. We slowly decrease the temperature from 10 down to 0.05.

[5]We thank Geoffrey Hinton and Hector Levesque for suggesting this strategy to us. The strategy has some of the flavor of the approaches found in genetic algorithms (Davis 1987).

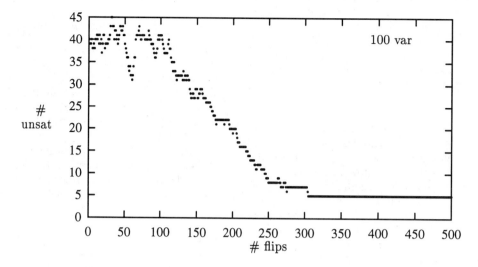

Figure 3: Simulated annealing's search space on a 100 variable formula.

algorithms. Our experiments show that GSAT with the averaging strategy compares favorably with some of the best *specialized* graph coloring algorithms as studied by Johnson. This is quite remarkable because GSAT does not use any special techniques for graph coloring.

Handling Structure with Clause Weights

As we noted in the introduction, the fact that GSAT does well on randomly-generated formulas does not necessarily indicate that it would also perform well on formulas that have some complex underlying structure. In fact, Ginsberg and Jónsson (1992) supplied us with some graph coloring problems that GSAT could not solve, even with many tries each with many flips. Their dependency-directed backtracking method could find solutions to these problems with little effort (Jónsson and Ginsberg 1993). In running GSAT on these problems, we discovered that at the end of almost every try the same set of clauses remained unsatisfied. As it turns out, the problems contained strong *asymmetries*. Such structure can lead GSAT into a state in which a few violated constraints are consistently "out-voted" by many satisfied constraints.

To overcome asymmetries, we added a weight to each clause (constraint).[6] A weight is a positive integer, indicating how often the clause should be counted when determining which variable to flip next. Stated more precisely, having a clause with weight L is equivalent to having the clause occur L times in the formula. Initially, all weights are set to 1. At the end of each try, we increment by 1 the weights of those clauses not satisfied by the current assignment. Thus the weights are dynamically modified *during* problem solving, again making use of the information gained by each try.

---

[6]Morris (1993) has independently proposed a similar approach.

# unsat clauses	# of times reached	
at end of try	basic	weights
0	0	80
1	2	213
2–4	0	0
5–9	90	301
10+	908	406

Table 1: Comparison of GSAT with and without weights on a highly asymmetrical graph coloring problem (see text for explanation).

Using weights, GSAT solves a typical instance of these coloring problems in a second or two. This is comparable with the time used by efficient backtrack-style procedures. Table 1 shows the distribution of the number of unsatisfied clauses after each try for GSAT with and without weights on Ginsberg and Jónsson's 50 node graph (200 variables and 2262 clauses). We used a total of 1000 tries with 1000 flips per try. For example, basic GSAT never found an assignment that had no unsatisfied clauses, but GSAT with weights found one in 80 tries out of 1000. Similarly, basic GSAT found an assignment with one unsatisfied clause only twice, while GSAT with weights found such an assignment 213 times.

The weight strategy turns out to help not only on problems handcrafted to fool GSAT (including the similarly "misleading" formulas discussed in Selman *et al.* (1992)), but also on many *naturally occuring* classes of structured satisfiability problems. A case in point are formulas that encode *planning problems*. As we reported in Kautz and Selman (1992), the basic GSAT algorithm had difficulty in solving formulas that encoded blocks-world planning problems. However, using weights GSAT's solution times are comparable with those of the Davis-Putnam procedure on these formulas. Details appear in Selman and Kautz (1993).

The regularities that appear in certain non-random classes of generated formulas tend to produce local minima that can trap a simple greedy algorithm. The weights, in effect, are used to *fill in* local minima while the search proceeds, and thus *uncover* the regularities. Note that this general strategy may also be useful in avoiding local minima in other optimization methods, and provides an interesting alternative to the use of random noise (as in simulated annealing).

Conclusions

The experiments we ran with GSAT have helped us understand the nature of the search space for propositional satisfiability, and have led us to develop interesting heuristics that augment the power of local search on various classes of satisfiability problems. We saw that search space is characterized by plateaus, which suggests that the crucial problem is to develop methods to quickly traverse broad flat regions. This is in contrast, for example, to much of the work on simulated annealing algorithms, which support the use of slow cooling schedules to deal with search spaces characterized by jagged surfaces with many deep local minima.

We discussed two empirically successful extensions to GSAT, averaging and clause weights, that improve efficiency by re-using some of the information present in previous near-solutions. Each of these strategies, in effect, helps uncover hidden structure in the input formulas, and were motivated by the shape of GSAT's search space. Given the success of these strategies and the fact that they are not very specific to the GSAT algorithm, it appears that they also hold promise for improving other methods for solving hard combinatorial search problems. In our future research we hope to improve our formal understanding of the benefits and applicability of these techniques.

Finally, we should note that we do not claim that GSAT and its descendants will be able to efficiently solve all interesting classes of satisfiability problems. Indeed, no one universal method is likely to prove successful for all instances of an NP-complete problem! Nonetheless, we believe it is worthwhile to develop techniques that extend the *practical* range of problems that can be solved by local search.

References

Bertsimas, D. and Tsitsiklis, J. (1992). Simulated Annealing, in *Probability and Algorithms*, National Academy Press, Washington, D.C., 17–29.

Buro, M. and Kleine Büning, H. (1992). Report on a SAT Competition. Technical Report # 110, Dept. of Mathematics and Informatics, University of Paderborn, Germany, Nov. 1992.

Cheeseman, Peter and Kanefsky, Bob and Taylor, William M. (1991). Where the Really Hard Problems Are. *Proc. IJCAI-91*, 1991, 163–169.

Crawford, J.M. and Auton, L.D. (1993) Experimental Results on the Cross-Over Point in Satisfiability Problems. *Proc. AAAI-93*, to appear.

Davis, E. (1987) *Genetic Algorithms and Simulated Annealing*, in Pitman Series of Research Notes in Artificial Intelligence, London: Pitman; Los Altos, CA: Morgan Kaufmann.

Davis, M. and Putnam, H. (1960). A Computing Procedure for Quantification Theory. *J. Assoc. Comput. Mach.*, 7, 1960, 201–215.

Feynman, R.P., Leighton, R.B. , and Sand, M. (1989). *The Feynman Lectures on Physics, Vol. I*, Addison-Wesley Co, Reading, MA.

Fourer, R. , Gay, D.M., and Kernighan, B.W. (1993). *AMPL: A Modeling Language for Mathematical Programming*, San Francisco, CA: The Scientific Press.

Gent, I.P. and Walsh, T. (1993). Towards an Understanding of Hill-Climbing Procedures for SAT. *Proc. AAAI-93*, to appear.

Ginsberg, M. and Jónsson, A. (1992). Personal communication, April 1992.

Gu, J. (1992). Efficient Local Search for Very Large-Scale Satisfiability Problems. *Sigart Bulletin*, vol. 3, no. 1, 1992, 8–12.

Hajek, B. (1988). Cooling Schedules for Optimal Annealing. *Math. Oper. Res.*, 13, 311–329.

Jerrum, M. (1992) Large Cliques Elude the Metropolis Process. *Random Structures and Algorithms,* vol. 3, no. 4, 347-359.

Johnson, J.L. (1989). A Neural Network Approach to the 3-Satisfiability Problem. *Journal of Parallel and Distributed Computing*, 6, 435–449.

Johnson, D.S., Aragon, C.R., McGeoch, L.A., and Schevon, C. (1991) Optimization by Simulated Annealing: an Experimental Evaluation; Part II, Graph Coloring and Number Partioning. *Operations Research*, 39(3):378–406, 1991.

Jónsson, A.K., and Ginsberg, M.L. (1993) Experimenting with New Systematic and Nonsystematic Search Techniques. *Working Notes of the AAAI Spring Symposia*, 1993.

Kamath, A.P., Karmarkar, N.K., Ramakrishnan, K.G., and Resende, M.G.C. (1992). A Continuous Approach to Inductive Inference. *Mathematical Programming*, 57, 215–238.

Kautz, H.A. and Selman, B. (1992). Planning as Satisfiability. *Proc. ECAI-92*, Vienna, Austria.

Kirkpatrick, S., Gelett, C.D., and Vecchi, M.P. (1983). Optimization by Simulated Annealing. *Science*, 220, 621–630.

Larrabee, T. and Tsuji, Y. (1993) Evidence for a Satisfiability Threshold for Random 3CNF Formulas. *Working Notes AAAI Spring Symposia*, 1993.

Lin, S. and Kernighan, B.W. (1973). An Efficient Heuristic Algorithm for the Traveling-Salesman Problem. *Operations Research,* 21, 498-516.

Koutsoupias, E. and Papadimitriou C.H. (1992) On the Greedy Algorithm for Satisfiability. *Information Processing Letters*, 43, 53-55.

McCarthy, J. and Hayes, P.J. (1969) Some Philosophical Problems From the Standpoint of Artificial Intelligence, in *Machine Intelligence 4*, Chichester, England: Ellis Horwood, 463ff.

Minton, S., Johnston, M.D., Philips, A.B., Johnson, M.D., and Laird, P. (1992) Minimizing Conflicts: a Heuristic Repair Method for Constraint Satisfaction and Scheduling Problems, *Artificial Intelligence*, (58)1–3, 1992, 161–205.

Mitchell, D., Selman, B., and Levesque, H.J. (1992). Hard and Easy Distributions of SAT Problems. *Proc. AAAI-92,* San Jose, CA, 459–465.

Morris, P. (1993). Breakout Method for Escaping from Local Minima. *Proc. AAAI-93*, to appear.

Papadimitriou, C.H. (1991). On Selecting a Satisfying Truth Assignment. *Proc. FOCS-91*, 163–169.

Papadimitriou, C.H., Shaffer, A., and Yannakakis, M. (1990). On the Complexity of Local Search. *Proc. STOC-90*.

Papadimitriou, C.H., Steiglitz, K. (1982). *Combinatorial optimization.* Englewood Cliffs, NJ: Prentice-Hall, Inc., 1982.

Pinkas, G. and Dechter, R. (1992). *Proc. AAAI-92*, 434–439.

Selman, B. and Levesque, H.J., and Mitchell, D.G. (1992). A New Method for Solving Hard Satisfiability Problems. *Proc. AAAI-92*, San Jose, CA, 440–446.

Selman, B. and Kautz, H. (1993). Domain-Independent Extensions to GSAT: Solving Large Structured Satisfiability Problems. *Proc. IJCAI-93*, to appear.

William, C.P. and Hogg, T. (1992) Using Deep Structure to Locate Hard Problems. *Proc. AAAI-92*, 472–477.

Case-Based Reasoning

Projective Visualization: Acting from Experience

Marc Goodman*

Cognitive Systems, Inc.
234 Church Street
New Haven, CT 06510

Computer Science Department
Brandeis University
Waltham, MA 02254

Abstract

This paper describes *Projective Visualization*, which uses previous observation of a process or activity to project the results of an agent's actions into the future. Actions which seem likely to succeed are selected and applied. Actions which seem likely to fail are rejected, and other actions can be generated and evaluated. This paper presents a description of the architecture for Projective Visualization, preliminary results on learning to act from observations of a reactive system, and a comparison of two types of *Case Projection* (how situations are projected into the future).

Introduction

An agent must balance a variety of competing goals. An action which satisfies one goal may cause other goals to become unsatisfiable. For example, while standing on a street corner I may have two competing goals: 1) cross the street, and 2) avoid getting hit by a car. If I step out into the street towards the other side, an oncoming car might hit me. On the other hand, if I stand on the corner, I'm in little risk of getting hit, but I won't be getting to the other side of the street.

One method of selecting an action is to *project* the situation into the future. If I project to a state where both goals are satisfied (I've crossed the street without getting hit), then I know the action is appropriate. On the other hand, if one or more goals are defeated (I get hit by a car, or I fail to cross the street within a certain time period), then I know the action is unlikely to succeed. [Goodman, 1989] uses a simple version of projection where a battlefield commander can evaluate the effectiveness of battle plans by projecting the outcome of the battle. The focus in the battle planning example, as in this paper, is on how observation of previous experience can be used to project and to guide action.

---
*Thanks to David Waltz and Richard Alterman for useful discussion. This work was supported in part by DARPA under contract no. DAAH01-92-C-R376.

Two approaches to representing experience are: 1) to track perceptual observations of an environment (a *concrete* approach), and 2) to extract semantically or causally relevant features from the experience and represent those (an *abstract* approach). For example, Troop movements could be represented either as a series of observations of the positions and orientations of individual soldiers (the concrete approach) or as summary information about the number of soldiers, the type of maneuver (i.e. frontal, enveloping, etc.), and their overall distance to the front (an abstract approach). Previous CBR work has focussed on applying abstract representations of experience to planning [Hammond, 1986; Alterman, 1988; Alterman *et al.*, 1991].

A concrete approach to representation is preferable because of:

- **Knowledge Engineering Difficulty.** An abstract approach requires that an expert interpret each situation to extract the relevant semantic and causal features. A concrete approach stores experience directly from sensor readings or a perceptual system without human intervention. As the number of cases in a system rises, the bottleneck created by an abstract representation becomes severe.

- **Information Loss.** An abstract representation discards features which are deemed irrelevant by a knowledge engineer or domain expert. Unfortunately, what the knowledge engineer or domain expert decide is irrelevant may turn out to be quite relevant. A concrete representation tracks all available information lessening the possibility of information loss.

- **Psychological Evidence.** [Gentner, 1989], suggests that the most common type of reminding is based on surface-level features rather than abstract features. A representation which facilitates surface-level remindings at the expense of additional required work for abstract remindings is, therefore, plausible. A concrete representation satisfies these requirements since surface level features are immediately available for retrieval, but abstract features must be extracted from the representation for ab-

Figure 1: A picture from *The Bilestoad*. Should the agent (light grey) continue fighting or disengage from its opponent?

stract reminding. [Waltz, 1989] points out that since the perception-cognition-action loop typically takes 100ms or less, not much time is available for extracting abstract features from the perceptual world. A concrete representation avoids this problem by dealing directly with perceptual features.

The method of projection presented in this paper uses a concrete representation of a process or activity to create concrete projections into the future. Since these projections have the same structure and content as perceptual observations of the world, we consider this a form of imagery and call the technique *Projective Visualization* by analogy to a form of spatial, visual imagery in humans.

This paper will present results which indicate that Projective Visualization can be used to learn to act through observation. This paper also presents some experiments on evaluating different techniques for *Case Projection*, the underlying engine through which imagery is achieved.

Test Domain

A new version of the video game entitled *The Bilestoad*, which was published by Datamost Software in 1983, serves as the test-bed for the projective visualizer (a picture of a game in progress appears in Figure 1). The game is a simulation of combat between two gladiators armed with battle axes and shields on islands which contain strategic devices. A reactive system was designed and built as an opponent for human players, and serves as a standard of performance for the projective system.

At each frame of the game, approximately 200 pieces of perceptual information about the agent and its environment are collected and processed. This information includes the Cartesian coordinates of each joint in the

bodies of the agents, absolute angles of those joints, state information about the joints and the agent overall, the location of devices in the simulation, motor-control of the agents, etc.

The agent must satisfy conflicting goals to succeed. Consider a scenario where the agent wishes to engage a fleeing opponent. One course of action is to chase the opponent. Another course of action is to navigate to a transportation device, and then chase the opponent. Projection can be used in this situation to determine that approaching the opponent directly will fail to cause engagement, since the opponent is moving away from the agent at the same rate of speed as the agent is approaching. The agent visualizes itself chasing the opponent until the opponent reaches its goal. Navigating to the transportation device will result in engagement, and the agent visualizes itself catching its opponent. Action must be initiated quickly, since the longer the agent spends deciding what to do, the more of a lead the opponent will have.

The agent must also successfully anticipate the actions and objectives of its opponent. Consider a situation where the agent is pursuing its opponent and the opponent begins to alter its bearing. If the agent reacts to this by approaching its opponent directly, the agent may reduce the distance to its opponent but allow the opponent to circle around the agent. On the other hand, if the agent projects the effects of the opponent's bearing change, visualizes the opponent circling around, and maintains a position between the opponent and the goal device, the agent will prevent its opponent's escape. Hence, reacting to the opponent's actions is not enough, the agent must anticipate as well.

Case Projection

In the Battle Planner, abstract representations of historical battles were used to project the outcome of a new battle. The system induced a discrimination tree where features of the historical cases (such as ratio of attacking and defending troops, air superiority, amount of artillery, etc.) which were good predictors of the winner of the battle served as indices for case retrieval. There are several techniques for inducing such a discrimination tree, including ID3 [Quinlan, 1986], CART [Brieman *et al.*, 1984], and Automatic Interaction Detection [Hartigan, 1975]. Though each algorithm has slightly different characteristics with respect to convergence, noise sensitivity, and sensitivity to representation, they all share the characteristic of asymptotically approaching an accuracy limit as the number of examples increases, and they can be automatically reapplied as more experience is gathered without additional knowledge engineering.

Projecting a single result (e.g. the outcome of a battle) from a situation description in one step is inappropriate for the following reasons:

- **Sensitivity to Initial Conditions.** Consider Ben

Franklin's old adage, "For want of a nail, the shoe was lost; For want of the shoe, the horse was lost..." which demonstrates that minor differences between situations can compound as the situation evolves. Capturing this sensitivity to initial conditions in a single discrimination tree requires a fairly exhaustive set of examples. The world, being a complex place, makes having an exhaustive set of examples impractical.

- **Interactions between Features.** In battle planning, having more tanks than your opponent is generally beneficial. However, if you are fighting in marshy, heavily wooded, or urban terrains, your tanks will get bogged down, and having more tanks may actually hurt you. To learn this interaction with a single discrimination tree requires that you see cases with many tanks in urban terrain, few tanks in urban terrain, many tanks in flat terrain, few tanks in flat terrain, etc. Once again, the system requires a fairly exhaustive set of examples.

A Projective Visualizer avoids these problems by creating a projected situation which is temporally (and causally) near to the current situation. Instead of simply jumping to the outcome of the battle from the initial conditions, the system simulates how the situation evolves over time. Each step of projection lessens the causal distance between a situation and its conclusion. In The Bilestoad, the agent might have 2 hits of damage to the shoulder of its arm which holds the axe, while its opponent only has 1 hit of damage. Even if we know the relative locations and orientations of the agent and the opponent it may be hard to say which will win the fight. It's easier to say that since the opponent's axe is in contact with the agent's shoulder, on the next time step the agent's shoulder will have 3 hits of damage. Meanwhile, the opponent continues to have only 1 hit of damage, since the agent's axe is not in contact with its shoulder. Continuing to project, we visualize the agent with 4 hits, 5 hits, 6 hits, 7 hits, until the agent's axe arm is severed at the shoulder. At this point, it's much easier to say that the agent will lose its battle. We have reduced the causal distance between a situation and its conclusion by projecting the situation forward in time.

Projective Visualization uses *Case Projection* as an underlying engine for imagery. Case Projection is the process of creating a projected situation from a current situation. A Case Projector is built from a library of experiences by inducing a separate discrimination tree for each feature of a situation. The decisions in the tree correspond to features of the current situation which are good predictors of the *next* value of the feature we wish to predict. Given k concrete features which represent a situation, we induce k discrimination trees.

Projection consists of traversing these k discrimination trees with a case representing the current situation, making a prediction on the next value of each feature, and storing these predictions into a new case.

This projected case then serves as a basis for further projection. Hence, a current situation can be driven forward arbitrarily far, at a cost of compounding errors from earlier retrieval. This process continues until the system is able to make an evaluation of the projected situation (is the projected result good or bad), or until some pre-defined limit on projection is reached.

Cases include observations of the world as well as "operators." Each case in the system represents a fine-grained approximation of a continuously evolving situation, in the same way as a motion picture is a fine-grained approximation of the recorded experience. In any particular case, agents are in the process of carrying out actions. For example, in a situation representing a quarterback throwing a football, in one case the quarterback might be moving his left leg backwards, moving his right hand forward, and squeezing with the fingers on his right hand. "Operator" refers to this pattern of control signals. There is, therefore, a one-to-one mapping between operators and cases. Note that a linguistic term like "throw" or "dodge" actually corresponds to a sequence of cases and their corresponding operators.

The indices used for Projective Visualization in The Bilestoad and in comparisons of techniques for Case Projection are generated inductively from the case library with an extended version of the Automatic Interaction Detection algorithm [Hartigan, 1975]. Induction is guided and enhanced in a variety of ways, including methods for enriching the case representation and methods for preselecting good discriminators. Each of these enhancements reduces the amount of experience needed to reach a given level of accuracy, but does not change the property that accuracy will asymptotically approach a fixed limit. Therefore, the same ultimate effects as reported in this work can be reproduced using off-the-shelf versions of CART, ID3, AID, or other learning algorithms, even without these enhancements, but a larger base of examples may be needed.

Dynamics of Projective Visualization

Projective Visualization layers on top of Case Projection to provide a framework for controlling action. The basic idea of Projective Visualization is to pick a likely operator to perform and run the situation forward into the future until one of three things happens: 1) the system will run into an obviously bad situation, in which case the operator should be avoided and another operator tried, 2) the system will run into an obviously good situation, in which case the operator should be applied and real action taken in the world, 3) the system projects the case farther and farther into the future, without conclusive evidence one way or another. If the system is unable to reach a conclusion by the time it's projected a prespecified amount of time, it can make a guess as to whether the operator is good or bad by retrieving the closest case and chasing pointers until the case was resolved either positively or negatively.

Case Retrieval can be used to select likely operators. Given all the cases which lead to the successful satisfaction of a goal, we build a discrimination tree where the discriminations in the tree are features of the current situation which are good indicators of the type of operation. Suggesting an operation to apply becomes a matter of traversing this discrimination tree and collecting operations that were applied in the retrieved cases (we refer to this process as *Action Generation*). Different discrimination trees built from cases where different goals were satisfied can be used to suggest different operators. For example, in The Bilestoad, one action generator may consist of all the actions which led directly to using a transportation device, another action generator may consist of actions which led to killing the opponent, a third action generator may consist of actions which prevented the agent from taking damage, etc.

Evaluating whether a situation is good or bad can be treated as a case retrieval task. For example, in battle planning, a projected situation where 90% of your soldiers have been killed might retrieve a different battle where 90% of the soldiers were killed, and the mission failed. Since the mission failed in this retrieved case, we conclude that the mission will fail in the current (projected) situation as well, a bad thing. In a process control domain, where continuous feed roasters are being used to roast coffee beans, evaluation might be based on Neuhaus color readings on the ground beans as well as by moisture content of the beans. If the projected coffee beans retrieved cases where the color and moisture content differed from ideals specified in the roasting recipe, then the evaluation would be negative. In The Bilestoad, retrieving cases where the opponent is dead indicates a positive outcome, and retrieving cases where the agent is dead indicates a negative outcome.

The "branching factor," or number of different paths the system pursues in projection can depend on both the number of different operators which are suggested by a set of retrieved cases and the number of possible projected values for key features of the case. [Goodman, 1989] indicates that by ignoring predictions where only a few examples are retrieved yields a higher overall accuracy. This suggests that a measurement of confidence can be generated from the number and distribution of retrieved cases, and this confidence measure can be used to prune the search tree so that only the most likely paths are explored.

When the system is in a time-critical situation, response-time can be improved by reducing the window of projection (how far the situation is projected into the future) as well as by considering fewer alternative actions (reducing the branching factor). Such a system behaves more and more as a purely situated or reactive system would [Suchman, 1987; Agre and Chapman, 1987; Chapman, 1990]. On the other hand, when more time-resources are available, the system can project the effects of its actions farther and farther, and

consider a greater number of alternatives, causing the system to exhibit more and more planful behavior.

This type of system can learn in several ways. First, through observation of an agent performing a task, it can learn to suggest new candidate actions. It can also refine its ability to suggest actions based on improvements in indexing as more experience is gathered. Next, by carrying along projections and matching them against the world as the situation plays out, it can detect where projection has broken down. Projection can then be improved by storing these experiences into the appropriate projectors and generating new indices to explain these failures. Finally, it can improve its ability to evaluate situations by noting whether its evaluations match outcomes in the real world. Through observation, it can both add new evaluations as well as refine its ability to evaluate by improving evaluation indices.

Evaluation of Projective Visualization

Approximately 28,000 frames of two reactive agents competing in hand-to-hand combat were captured as raw data from The Bilestoad. This represents approximately 1 hour and 18 minutes of continuous play. A case projector was built using this data which predicts whether the agent will cause damage to its opponent in the next frame. Cases representing situations where the agent caused damage to its opponent in the next frame were selected (approximately 3,300 such case existed in the 28,000 frames), and used to build an action generator. The action generator consists of eight sets of indices, one for each control signal for the agent. These control signals include moving the axe clockwise, moving the axe counterclockwise, moving the shield clockwise or counterclockwise, turning the torso clockwise or counterclockwise, and walking forward or backward. Given these controls, there are $3^4 = 81$ significant patterns of control signals which the agent can receive. Cases representing situations where the agent successfully avoided damage (as indicated by a frame where damage was taken followed by a frame where no damage was taken) were selected (amounting to 1,100 cases out of the original 28,000 frames) and used to build an additional action generator. Projection was used to mediate between these two of action generators, such that if the agent could cause damage to its opponent in the next frame it would, otherwise it would use the avoidance action generator.

The mean difference in score between the projective agent and the reactive agent favored the projective agent by 18.01 points, with a standard error of 12.93 for 1000 games. Since the mean difference of 18.01 is within the 95% confidence interval of 25.34, we accept the null hypothesis that there is no significant difference between the reactive and projective agents. We have, therefore, successfully learned to act as well as the reactive agent through observation of the reactive agent, a result which Chapman was unable to achieve in [Chapman, 1990].

Evaluation of Case Projection

If we wish to project a situation k steps into the future (which we refer to as a *Projection Window* of k steps), two contrasting techniques exist for performing this projection. The first technique, called *Projective Simulation*, projects the situation forward 1 step, then projects the projection 1 step, and so on, until the situation has been projected k steps. The second technique, termed *One-Step Projection*, performs one retrieval for each feature of the situation, to predict what the value of that feature will be k steps in the future. For example, if we wish to project a situation 5 steps into the future we can perform 5 steps of projection of 1 time unit each (Projective Simulation), or perform 1 step of projection of 5 time units (One-Step Projection).

One of the exhibits at the Boston Museum of Science is a big enclosed table with a circular hyperbolic slope in it, leading to a hole. Steel balls are released from the edge of the table and go around and around the slope until their orbits decay enough that they fall into the hole. One of the things that makes this exhibit fun to watch is that when the ball is heading toward the hole it accelerates, and if it misses the hole it "sling-shots" around, leading to much visual surprise and merriment. After watching, however, one quickly learns to predict how the steel ball will move around the track, a form of case projection. One-Step Projection and Projective Simulation were compared in the domain of prediction of the position of an object in Newtonian orbit around a gravity source (which is what the exhibit represents). For a full treatment of the physics involved, see [Halliday and Resnick, 1978].

For the following tests, the Gravitational Constant, the mass of the gravity source, the mass of the object in orbit and the initial velocity of the object were chosen to yield a reasonable level of granularity in the orbit. The initial position of the object was varied randomly within a fixed range. For the values chosen, the average number of time steps for an object to complete an orbit around the gravity source was 44.75. A training set of 20 orbits was created by randomly selecting the initial position and deriving subsequent positions from a quantitative model, yielding 895 cases. The set of features on each case was limited to the current position of the object in two-dimensional Cartesian coordinates, the change in position from the previous observation for each coordinate, and the previous change in position for each coordinate. No reference to the position of the gravity source, the masses of the object and source, or the laws of physics, were given to the system for use in projection.

Figure 2 shows the percentage of orbits where One-Step Projection was more accurate than Projective Simulation, for Projection Windows of varying size, given a training set of 20 orbits. When the Projection

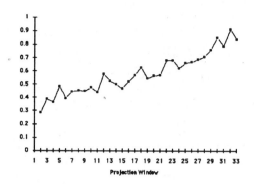

Figure 2: Percentage of Trials where One-Step Projection is More Accurate than Projective Simulation, Size of Training Set=20 Orbits.

Window is equal to 1 time step, Projective Simulation and One-Step Projection are functionally equivalent. For Projection Windows between 2 and 20, 300 initial starting positions were randomly selected and the mean error per orbit was determined and compared. The resulting percentages are accurate to within 4.8%, given a 95% confidence interval based on a one-tailed distribution. For Projection Windows between 21 and 33, 100 initial starting positions were used, yielding a 95% confidence interval of at most 8.3%, based on a one-tailed distribution.

Projective Simulation was more accurate than One-Step Projection for small Projection Windows. Specifically, for Projection Windows between 2 and 11, the null hypothesis that the two methods are equivalent could be rejected for 8 of the 10 points with 95% confidence. On the other hand, One-Step Projection was more accurate than Projective Simulation for large Projection Windows. For Projection Windows between 22 and 33, the null hypothesis could be rejected for all points with 95% confidence.

Figure 3 shows the mean of the mean error per orbit for Projective Simulation and One-Step Projection with training sets of size 5 Orbits and 20 Orbits, as the size of the Projection Window is varied. These data points are based on a random sample of 200 initial positions. The error rate is roughly linear in the size of the Projection Window for small Projection Windows. The slope of these linear components of the errors is slightly smaller for Projective Simulation, hence Projective Simulation is more accurate for small Projection Windows. For larger Projection Windows, the change in error rate for One-Step Projection begins to decrease, and One-Step Projection becomes more accurate than Projective Simulation.

Discussion

The central difference between One-Step Projection and Projective Simulation explains these results. At

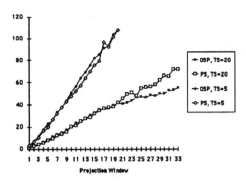

Figure 3: Error VS. Projection Window for Training Sets of Size Five Orbits (TS=5) and Twenty Orbits (TS=20) for One-Step Projection (OSP) and Projective Simulation (PS).

each step in Projective Simulation, the system is free to select new previous situations for subsequent projection, where One-Step Projection is forced to follow one set of previous situations to their conclusion. This benefits Projective Simulation in the short term, since Projective Simulation can account for cascading differences that would render any one previous situation obsolete. In other words, as minor initial differences between the current situation and a retrieved situation begin to compound, Projective Simulation automatically chooses better predictors of future values. One-Step Projection does not have this flexibility, and must follow one set of precedents no matter how much the current situation begins to deviate. Hence, the slope of the error rate for Projective Simulation will be less than the slope of the error rate for One-Step Projection.

On the other hand, One-Step Projection offers a benefit which is lacking in Projective Simulation. One-Step Projection guarantees that the projected situation will be *internally consistent*. Specifically, the space of possible projections is bounded by the case base, and since One-Step Projection relies on a single set of precedents, the projection can never "break out" of these bounds. For domains where there are inherent limitations on values of features, this imposes a maximum error rate for any particular orbit. For example, in the orbit domain, given a range of initial positions and a fixed initial velocity, the minimum and maximum Cartesian coordinates of an object are bounded in a fixed space. As the size of the Projection Window grows, the mean error rate will approach the error resulting from a random selection of points from the fixed space for projection, which is constant for sufficiently large samples. Hence, the error rate for One-Step Projection will asymptotically approach a constant limit. The constant will, of course, depend on the particular domain. The flexibility inherent in Projective Simula-

tion allows it to break out of these bounds, and the error rate retains its linear characteristic.

Conclusions

We have demonstrated that systems can learn to project the effects of their actions through observation of processes and activities. We have demonstrated two techniques for projection, One-Step Projection and Projective Simulation, and have indicated that Projective Simulation is appropriate for projecting effects in the short-term and that One-Step Projection is appropriate for projecting effects in the long-term. Finally, we have demonstrated that a system which controls an agent acting in an environment can benefit from projection, even when projection is not 100% accurate.

References

Philip E. Agre and David Chapman. Pengi: An implementation of a theory of activity. In *Proceedings of the Sixth National Conference on Artificial Intelligence*, pages 268–272, 1987.

Richard Alterman, Roland Zito-Wolf, and Tamitha Carpenter. Interaction, comprehension, and instruction usage. *Journal of the Learning Sciences*, 1(4), 1991.

Richard Alterman. Adaptive planning. *Cognitive Science*, 12:393–421, 1988.

L. Brieman, J. Friedman, R. Olshen, and C. Stone. *Classification and Regression Trees*. Wadsworth, 1984.

David Chapman. *Vision, Instruciton, and Action*. PhD thesis, Massachusetts Institute of Technology, Cambridge, Mass, April 1990.

Dedre Gentner. Finding the Needle: Accessing and Reasoning from Prior Cases. In *Proceedings the Second DARPA Workshop on Case Based Reasoning*, pages 137–143, 1989.

Marc Goodman. CBR In Battle Planning. In *Proceedings the Second DARPA Workshop on Case Based Reasoning*, pages 312–326, 1989.

David Halliday and Robert Resnick. *Physics, Parts 1 and 2*. John Wiley and Sons, 1978.

Kristian J. Hammond. CHEF: A model of case-based planning. In *Proceedings of the Fifth National Conference on Artificial Intelligence*, pages 267–271, 1986.

J. Hartigan. *Clustering Algorithms*. John Wiley and Sons, 1975.

J. Ross Quinlan. Induction of decision trees. *Machine Learning*, 1:81–106, 1986.

Lucy A. Suchman. *Plans and Situated Actions*. Cambridge University Press, Cambridge, 1987.

David Waltz. Is Indexing Used for Retrieval? In *Proceedings the Second DARPA Workshop on Case Based Reasoning*, pages 41–44, 1989.

Representing and using procedural knowledge to build geometry proofs[1]

Thomas F. McDougal and Kristian J. Hammond

Department of Computer Science
University of Chicago
1100 E. 58th St.
Chicago, IL 60637
mcdougal@cs.uchicago.edu, hammond@cs.uchicago.edu

Abstract

What is the nature of expertise? This paper posits an answer to that question in the domain of geometry problem-solving. We present a computer program called POLYA which makes use of explicit planning knowledge to solve geometry proof problems, integrating the processes of parsing the diagram and writing the proof.

Introduction

This paper describes a computer program called POLYA that solves high school geometry proof problems. High school geometry first attracted our interest when the first author was student teaching geometry in a public high school as part of a teacher certification program. We were curious about what kinds of knowledge enabled him and other experienced mathematicians to solve geometry proof problems very quickly, in contrast to his students, who solved the same problems only with great effort. That knowledge had to involve more than the formal rules of geometry (the theorems, axioms, definitions), since, by virtue of their ability to solve the problems at all, the students clearly knew those rules. We conjectured that geometry expertise involves an ability to recognize when those rules *should* be used, in contrast to when the rules *can* be used. Such expertise generally arises from exposure to and experience with a large number of problems. The problem for us then was to define that knowledge concretely and to build a computer model of geometry problem-solving that made use of that knowledge. We call our computer program POLYA.

Although POLYA's task is to write geometry proofs, our desire to model human expertise led us away from some of the traditional concerns of automated theorem-proving. We are not concerned, for instance, with solving hard problems; rather, we are concerned with capturing the knowledge that allows experts to solve easy problems easily.

Our research has led us to address a broad range of important AI issues: visual reasoning and the use of diagrams in problem-solving; representation of planning and problem-solving knowledge; how to store, efficiently retrieve, and apply plans; how to integrate planning and action; how to use the world as a memory aid; how to direct a limited focus of attention to gather information; and what it means to know *how* to solve a problem as distinct from knowing the solution.

This paper describes our representation for geometry problem-solving knowledge and the computer program, POLYA, which uses that knowledge to write proofs.

Recognizing when rules should apply

Central to our model of human geometry theorem-proving expertise is a distinction between when a rule *may* be applied (as determined by its preconditions) and when a rule *should* be applied. A novice with complete understanding of the rules and their preconditions can still have trouble with a relatively easy problem. The novice may get lost in a large number of legitimate but useless inferences, or she may be reluctant to make a single inference without knowing how it will contribute to the final proof. The expert, on the other hand, shows a remarkable ability to make exactly those inferences relevant to the solution without knowing *a priori* what that solution is. [Koedinger & Anderson 1990] documents the tendency of geometry experts to make inferences from the given information without regard to the goal; [Larkin et al. 1980] documents analogous forward reasoning by physics experts.

We hold that most of the expert's decision-making is based on cues in the diagram. This thesis, so broadly stated, is not new; [Koedinger & Anderson 1990] presented a model of geometry problem-solving called DC in which the diagram is parsed into *configuration schema*, each of which defines a restricted subset of applicable rules. Their model contrasts with earlier systems [Gelernter 1959, Nevins 1975, Greeno 1983] which used the diagram primarily as a source of heuristic search control information.

---

[1]This research is supported by the Office of Naval Research under contract N00014-91-J-1185, by the Defense Advanced Research Projects Agency monitored by the Air Force Office of Scientific Research under contract F30602-91-C-0028, and by the University of Chicago School Mathematics Project Fund for Support of Research in Math Education.

We believe that our model addresses two shortcomings in the DC model. First, while the DC model makes a significant contribution in terms of knowledge representation for geometry problem-solving, it still says very little about the problem-solving process. The authors note that once the diagram has been parsed, finding the inference chain is trivial, which suggests that most, if not all, of the problem-solving task involves recognizing the relevant schema. Yet they consciously side-step the question of how people do this, with only a brief argument that perhaps the diagram parsing and schema search processes could be coordinated.

We also disagree with DC's model of schema application. Although DC's configuration schema significantly reduce the rule space, the model still falls back on inference chaining to decide, for each schema, which rule or rules should apply. The problem is that DC's schemas are overly general. Just as human experts are able to commit to specific inferences early in the problem-solving process, more specific schema would make it possible to decide exactly which rule should apply without a second phase of inference chaining.

In contrast, POLYA builds up the proof at the same time that it builds up its understanding of the diagram. It uses schema-like knowledge to parse the diagram on demand, and it recognizes highly specific configurations in the diagram which enable it to make concrete inferences likely to contribute to the final proof. The next sections provide an overview of POLYA's operation and a detailed description of its geometry problem-solving knowledge.

An overview of POLYA

POLYA comprises three basic modules: a memory retriever, a plan interpreter, and a module for simulated vision (figure 1). The memory retriever takes a steady stream of features and uses them to trigger plans in memory. The plan interpreter selects a plan and executes the steps in the plan. The vision module computes features in response to the actions called for by the plan. The next sections discuss these modules in detail.

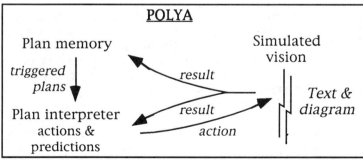

Figure 1: POLYA's three modules. The plan interpreter sends commands to the vision module, which computes a description of some part of the problem and sends that description both to the memory module and back to the plan interpreter.

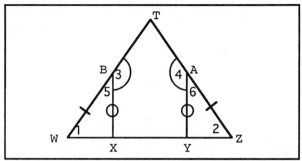

Figure 2: a triangle which appears isosceles. Angles 1 and 2 are the base angles. Angles 3 and 4 are marked congruent, as are two pairs of segments. This represents the initial conditions for one problem POLYA can solve.

The input

As in textbooks, a geometry proof problem for POLYA consists of givens, a goal, and a diagram. The givens and goal are predicates such as (congruent-segments (segment s x) (segment t y)). The diagram is a composite of lines and labelled points. Each line is defined by the coordinates of its endpoints, and labelled points are listed by their coordinate locations, as: (x y <label>), where <label> is a letter (A, B, etc.). The labels are irrelevant to the problem-solving process; they are used only to define the givens and the goal and to generate the proof in human-readable form.

Simulated vision

POLYA accesses the diagram by way of a simulated visual system. The visual system provides over 120 operators by which POLYA can specify which object or objects in the diagram it wishes to inspect; the visual system returns a description of that object including its exact location and a list of aspects.

The operator LOOK-AT-LEFT-BASE-ANGLE, for example, takes as its argument the vertices of a triangle which *appears* isosceles[2] and returns a description of one of its base angles (e.g. angle 1 in figure 2). That description includes the (x, y) location of the vertex, the compass directions of the rays, a symbolic description of the approximate size of the angle (e.g. ACUTE>45), a symbolic description of the pattern of rays at the vertex (SIMPLE-ANGLE), a count of the number of rays interior to the angle (zero), and, if there are no interior rays, a description of the space unto which the angle opens (TRIANGLE). The description also includes whether the angle is marked (e.g. angles 3 and 4 in figure 2 are each marked with SINGLE-ARC congruency marks).

POLYA can itself make annotations such as angle marks on the diagram. There are several benefits from such annotations. Looking at angles 3 and 4, it

---

[2]Based on euclidean distances between the vertices.

Figure 3: POLYA can look at Zs to see if the angles are congruent or the lines parallel.

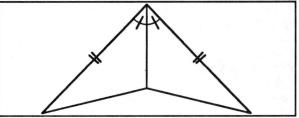

Figure 4: Two triangles share a side, and each triangle has one side marked and one angle marked. This pattern triggers the P-SAS-SHARED-SIDE proof plan, which checks that the marked angle is between the marked side and the shared side.
isosceles.

is apparent from the marks that the angles are congruent to each other. Thus POLYA, like a person, need not remember which angles are congruent, since it can always get that information directly from the diagram. Furthermore, having a mark associated with an individual angle streamlines some inferencing. Looking at angles 3 and 5, POLYA can guess that angle 5 is probably congruent to some other angle (angle 6).

In addition to angles, POLYA can focus on and describe any of the visual objects involved in geometry proofs: points, segments, triangles, quadrilaterals. It can compare pairs of objects—two triangles, for example, or a segment and an angle—to see how they relate to each other spatially. When POLYA looks at a triangle, the visual system computes its shape (RIGHT, ISOSCELES, EQUILATERAL) and counts the number of sides and angles annotated with congruency marks. Thus marks on segments and angles are reflected in the descriptions of all larger objects which contain those segments or angles. So, for example, POLYA can recognize when all sides of a triangle are marked, suggesting the applicability of the side-side-side triangle congruency theorem. This is the other benefit of angle and segment annotations.

POLYA can also look at composite shapes sometimes mentioned in textbooks but never mentioned in proofs. One textbook, for example, explicitly teaches students Z and F patterns involving parallel lines cut by a transversal [Rhoad, Whipple & Milauskas 1988]. POLYA can look at Zs to see if the angles are marked congruent or if the lines are marked parallel (figure 3).

Operators can sometimes fail. FIND-ADJACENT-MARKED-ANGLE, for instance, can fail if no such angle exists. Such operators are nonetheless useful for efficiently locating objects of interest.

Geometry plans

To parse the diagram and write a proof concurrently, POLYA needs to gather information in an organized way while still responding flexibly to what it sees. POLYA has a large memory of geometry plans which structure visual search and instantiate rules; plans are triggered and executed on the basis of configurations in the diagram.

A geometry plan defines a sequence of actions which can be directly executed by the plan interpreter. A typical action looks like this:

```
((COMPARE-TRIANGLES ?tri1 ?tri2)
 :predict (tri-pair (extents shared-side))
 :unbind (?tri1 ?tri2)
 :bind ?tri-pair)
```

The first item is an action for the visual system whose arguments are defined by local plan variables. The prediction partially specifies what the result of that action should look like; if the result fails to match the prediction, the plan aborts. A typical use of predictions is to check preconditions of a rule. Each step may bind the result of the action to a local plan variable and may unbind variables no longer needed.

There are two types of plans: search plans and proof plans. *Search plans* direct the focus of attention to potentially relevant parts of the diagram, gathering information for the memory module. *Proof plans* instantiate formal rules of geometry and add them to the proof. Search and proof plans are structured and handled in the same way, except that POLYA runs proof plans preferentially. (See **plan selection,** below.)

S-ISOSCELES[3] is a typical search plan. It directs attention to the legs and base angles of a triangle which looks isosceles. This reflects knowledge that if the triangle is actually isosceles, the legs and base angles are more likely to provide useful information, and more likely to play a role in the proof, than the apex angle or the base side. P-SAS-SHARED-SIDE[3] is a typical proof plan: if POLYA detects two triangles each of which has one angle marked and one side marked such that the triangles also share a side (figure 4), the plan verifies that the angle between the marked side and the shared side is marked, then adds to the proof a statement that the triangles are congruent.

Search plans gather features which trigger proof plans and other search plans in an interacting cycle of plan selection and execution. To build a proof for an easy-to-moderate geometry problem, POLYA may make use of 12 to 28 plans, causing between 50 to 120 actions to be performed.

POLYA's geometry plans define what it means to know how to solve geometry problems. Once a plan has been triggered, execution is straightforward. This is consistent with our view of geometry problem-solving as being primarily a task of recognizing when a rule or other piece

---

[3]By convention, we use prefixes S- and P- to distinguish search and proof plans.

of knowledge should apply. Next we consider how POLYA recognizes which plans are relevant.

Plan memory and retrieval

We have said that plan execution generates visual results which in turn trigger other plans. In this section we describe specifically how plans are triggered.

POLYA's plan indexing scheme is based on the marker-passing scheme used in DMAP, a case-based natural language understanding system [Martin 1990]. Each plan has a plan index having two parts: an index pattern and index constraints. An *index pattern* consists of a sequence of partially-specified visual results. A typical index pattern looks like this one for the P-SAS-SHARED-SIDE proof plan:

```
( (triangle (angle-mark-count 1)
            (seg-mark-count   1))
  (tri-pair (extents shared-side)) )
```

This pattern detects a triangle with one marked side and one marked angle, and a triangle pair sharing a side. The index constraints specify that the triangle must be part of the triangle pair:

```
( ((?1) = (?2 triangle-1)) )
```

The memory module matches visual results against the index pattern using DMAP's marker-passing scheme. A marker is placed on a node representing the first element of the pattern. When a visual result matches that node, the marker is advanced to the next element in the pattern. When the last element has been matched, the plan is *triggered,* posted to a list as eligible for execution.

We wish to emphasize that a plan index should not be thought of as the antecedent of a rule. Relative to most rules, plan indices are both over- and under-specified: over-specified in the sense that they seek to recognize not only when a rule *may* be applied but when it *should* be applied; under-specified in that they do not always guarantee the applicability of the rule. In the case of the P-SAS-SHARED-SIDE proof plan, for instance, the marked angle must lie between the marked side and the shared side in each triangle, a constraint which is not easily captured by the raw descriptions of the triangle and the triangle pair. It would be possible to design the visual system to capture that information as one aspect of the triangle pair. That would subsume an important part of geometry knowledge in the vision module. We prefer, however, to represent explicitly as much geometry knowledge as possible in the plans.

As stated earlier, an important part of geometry expertise is the ability to make the inferences which are most likely to contribute to the final solution. POLYA makes an assumption which seems to work well for easy to medium problems: If some features in the diagram cause a search plan to focus attention on an object, then the object is likely to be relevant to the proof. For the P-SAS-SHARED-SIDE proof plan to be triggered, some other script must have directed POLYA's attention to the triangles. This does not guarantee that it will be useful to prove the triangles congruent, but it seems to be true most of the time.

Plan selection

When the plan interpreter module finishes a plan, POLYA chooses another from the list of triggered plans. Typically there are several search plans to choose from, and perhaps one proof plan. Proof plans are chosen ahead of search plans, since after all the task is to write a proof; and plans triggered more recently are chosen ahead of plans triggered less recently. This plan-selection algorithm is too simple to work in the long run, and we are experimenting with ways to incorporate knowledge about which plans should run first. In some cases one plan subsumes another; by annotating the larger plan we can ensure that POLYA runs it and not the other.

Issues

One of our objectives with POLYA was to integrate diagram parsing with the process of constructing a proof. In so doing, we have had to address issues associated more with planning, robotics, and vision than with traditional theorem-proving.

Planning and action

POLYA treats planning as memory retrieval, in the spirit of case-based planning [Hammond 1989]. Because feature extraction is a major part of POLYA's task, POLYA cannot solve problems by retrieving and adapting a single case, as a prototypical CBR system does. Instead, POLYA accesses memory constantly, retrieving and using tens of plans over the course of a single problem. POLYA plans and re-plans in response to what it sees.

This responsiveness to visual features is characteristic of situated activity [Chapman & Agre 1986, Agre 1988]. Yet POLYA is not purely reactive; its behavior is better characterized as *reactive planning* [Firby 1989]. It executes each plan to completion so long as its predictions are met. The plans provide necessary structure for apprehending complex relationships in the diagram and for writing a formal mathematical argument. POLYA strikes a balance between top-down memory-based planning and bottom-up reactivity.

Active sensing

In the computer vision community, researchers are acknowledging that it is both intractable and unnecessary to identify everything in an image [e.g. Ballard 1991, Clark & Ferrier 1988, Swain 1991]. Particular tasks require attention to only particular aspects of the image. One may be interested only in the object at the center of the image, or one may be concerned only with detecting rapid motion. Similarly, a robot may have a ring of sonars, but for moving forward across mostly-empty space it makes sense to ignore the sonars pointing aft.

Geometry diagrams are simpler and more constrained than an arbitrary image or a cluttered room, but the idea for POLYA is the same: different parts of the diagram are relevant for different tasks, and some parts of the diagram can be ignored altogether.

Furthermore, we suspect that POLYA's problem of coordinating multiple sensing operations is relevant to vision and robotics as well, and that the solution of using short plans for information-gathering, with top-down predictions, may apply.

Example

Figure 2 above is one example of a problem POLYA can solve. Here we show the diagram with all given information already marked on the diagram; one of the first things POLYA does is annotate the diagram to reflect the given information. The goal in this problem is to prove that the large triangle is isosceles, i.e. that its left and right sides are congruent (have equal lengths).

At startup, POLYA computes a general description of the diagram as a whole, capturing the left/right symmetry of the diagram and the basic shape: a triangle with corner triangles. Two search plans are immediately triggered based on this description: S-ISOSCELES, described above, and S-CORNER-TRIANGLES.

After marking the given information, POLYA executes the S-CORNER-TRIANGLES search plan, which focuses attention on the corner triangles. The descriptions of those triangles triggers S-SIDE+SIDE, which looks at angles 5 & 6 and at sides WX and YZ. The pattern of rays at the vertex of angle 5 triggers S-PIER, which compares angle 5 with its adjacent angle, angle 3. Because angle 3 is marked, plan P-LINEAR-PAIR-PAIR is triggered, which proves that angles 5 and 6 are congruent. Shortly thereafter, POLYA proves the corner triangles congruent using P-SAS-SIMPLE, which instantiates the side-angle-side theorem.

At this point POLYA makes the equivalent of a leap of reasoning. A very specialized plan, P-CORNER-TRIANGLES->ISOSCELES, is triggered by the combination of the shape of the diagram (isosceles with corner triangles) and the assertion that the triangles are congruent.[4] Though POLYA has not yet read the goal statement, this plan represents the knowledge one might have from having seen this problem before: the large triangle is almost certainly isosceles, and, furthermore, that is probably a key conclusion (though not necessarily the goal) in this problem. The plan steps through the argument, adding inferences to the proof: because the corner triangles are congruent, the corner angles are congruent (1 and 2), and therefore the sides of the large triangle are congruent.

Finally, POLYA reads the goal, discovering that the proof is complete.

Discussion

Theorem-proving is usually done from scratch, using a minimalist representation of the problem and the rules. In

---

[4]Inferences are passed to memory in the same way that visual descriptions are, and can be used for indexing.

light of that tradition, what POLYA does in the problem above might seem like cheating.

In the foregoing example, POLYA makes use of two very specialized plans: S-CORNER-TRIANGLES and P-CORNER-TRIANGLES->ISOSCELES. If we remove the P-CORNER-TRIANGLES->ISOSCELES proof plan from memory, POLYA is still able to solve the problem, though it takes longer. (It cannot solve it without S-CORNER-TRIANGLES.) But to remove that plan would be contrary to the main point of this research.

The point is not to build a system which knows very little but can solve problems by working very hard. That has been done many times before. The point is to build a system which knows a lot and which can solve problems easily. The point is to model what an expert knows, including his memory of problems he has solved before. This is what POLYA's plans represent.

Conclusion

At current writing, POLYA has 68 search and proof plans. These plans constitute POLYA's knowledge about how to solve geometry proof problems, covering roughly one-fifth of the simple triangle congruence problems in a textbook and a very few examples involving parallel lines. Expanding POLYA's knowledge to cover quadrilaterals, other parallel line examples, and other aspects of geometry will at least double or treble the number of plans. Rapid growth of plan memory is not a bad thing, provided that we can continue to index the plans efficiently.

While many of POLYA's plans correspond fairly directly to general rules, some of POLYA's plans relate to specific problems in much the same way that a person might remember a specific problem. We believe that it is both necessary and appropriate that geometry expertise comprise knowledge at many levels of generality. When POLYA has a specific plan for a particular problem, fewer plans are needed and fewer actions are performed in solving that problem. Thus it is the case with POLYA, as with an expert, that the more knowledge it has, the more easily it can solve problems.

References

Agre, P.E. 1988. The Dynamic Structure of Everyday Life. Ph.D. diss., Artificial Intelligence Laboratory, MIT.

Ballard, D. H. 1991. Animate vision. *Artificial intelligence* 48.

Chapman, D., and Agre, P.E. 1986. Abstract reasoning as emergent from concrete activity. In *Reasoning about Actions and Plans, Proceedings of the 1986 Workshop, Timberline, Oregon,* Georgeff, M.P., Lansky, A.L., eds. Los Altos, CA.: Morgan-Kaufmann.

Clark, J. J. & Ferrier, N. J. 1988. Modal control of an attentive vision system. In Proceedings of the International Conference on Computer Vision.

Firby, R.J. 1989. Adaptive execution in complex dynamic worlds. Ph.D. diss., Yale University.

Gelernter, H. 1959. Realization of a geometry theorem proving machine. In *The Proceedings of the International Conference on Information Processing,* UNESCO, Reprinted in E.A. Feigenbaum & J. Feldman, (Eds.) (1963), *Computers and thought.* McGraw-Hill.

Greeno, J.G. 1983. Forms of understanding in mathematical problem solving. In Paris, S.G., Olson, G.M., and Stevenson, H.W., 1983. *Learning and Motivation in the Classroom.* Erlbaum.

Hammond, K. 1989. *Case-Based Planning: Viewing Planning as a Memory Task.* Academic Press, San Diego, CA , Vol. 1, Perspectives in Artificial Intelligence.

Koedinger, K.R. and Anderson, J.R. 1990. Abstract planning and perceptual chunks: Elements of expertise in geometry. *Cognitive Science* 14:511-550.

Larkin, J.H., McDermot, J., Simon, D.P., and Simon, H.A. 1980. Models of competence in solving physics problems. *Cognitive Science* 4:317-348.

Martin, C.E. 1990. Direct Memory Access Parsing. Ph.D. diss., Yale University.

Nevins, A.J. 1975. Plane geometry theorem proving using forward chaining. *Artificial Intelligence* 6.

Rhoad, R., Whipple, R., and Milauskas, G. 1988. *Geometry for enjoyment and challenge.* McDougal, Littell.

Swain, M. J. 1991. Low resolution cues for guiding saccadic eye movements. *SPIE advances in intelligent robot systems.*

Case-Based Diagnostic Analysis in a Blackboard Architecture*

Edwina L. Rissland, Jody J. Daniels, Zachary B. Rubinstein, and **David B. Skalak**

Department of Computer Science
University of Massachusetts
Amherst, MA 01003
rissland@cs.umass.edu

Abstract

In this project we study the effect of a user's high-level expository goals upon the details of how case-based reasoning (CBR) is performed, and, *vice versa*, the effect of feedback from CBR on them. Our thesis is that case retrieval should reflect the user's ultimate goals in appealing to cases and that these goals can be affected by the cases actually available in a case base. To examine this thesis, we have designed and built FRANK (Flexible Report and Analysis System), which is a hybrid, blackboard system that integrates case-based, rule-based, and planning components to generate a medical diagnostic report that reflects a user's viewpoint and specifications. FRANK's control module relies on a set of generic hierarchies that provide taxonomies of standard report types and problem-solving strategies in a mixed-paradigm environment. Our second focus in FRANK is on its response to a failure to retrieve an adequate set of supporting cases. We describe FRANK's planning mechanisms that dynamically re-specify the memory probe or the parameters for case retrieval when an inadequate set of cases is retrieved, and give an extended example of how the system responds to retrieval failures.

Introduction

This project places case-based reasoning (CBR) in a workaday context, as one utility for gathering, analyzing, and presenting information in service of a user's high-level task and viewpoint. A user's ultimate task might be to prepare a medical consultation as a specialist to an attending physician, to write a legal memorandum as a lawyer to a client, or to create a policy brief as an advisor to a decision-maker. For each task, what the writer (and his or her audience) plans to do with the information gathered affects the kind of information desired, the way it is found and analyzed, and the style in which it is presented. For instance, to generate a balanced, "pro-con" analysis of a situation, one would present in an even-handed manner the cases, simulations, and/or other analyses that support the various points of view. On the other hand, to create a "pro-position" report that advocates one course of action over all others, one would present information deliberately biased toward that point of view. Furthermore, if, in either situation, the retrieved cases only partially or meagerly support the intended presentation form, the user may have to temper his or her high-level goal by the information actually found, perhaps to the extent of radically revising a presentation stance or even abandoning it. Such revision may be required, for instance, if the cases destined for a balanced report are heavily skewed toward one side of an argument, or compelling cases for an opposing viewpoint subvert a proposed one-sided presentation.

To accommodate a variety of user task orientations, strategies, and viewpoints, we have designed and implemented a blackboard architecture that incorporates case-based and other reasoning mechanisms, a hierarchy of "reports" appropriate to different tasks, and a flexible control mechanism to allow the user's top-level considerations to filter flexibly throughout the system's processing. Our system, which is called FRANK (Flexible Report and Analysis System), is implemented using the Generic Blackboard toolkit (GBB) [Blackboard Technology Group, Inc., 1992] in the application domain of back-injury diagnosis.

Specifically, our goals in pursuing this project focus on two kinds of evaluation and feedback:

1. To investigate the effect of a failure to find useful cases upon the current plan or the user's task orientation; and, *vice versa*, the effects of the context provided by the user's task and viewpoint on case retrieval and analysis.

2. To build a CBR subsystem that can dynamically change its case retrieval mechanisms in order to satisfy a failed query to case memory.

We first give a broad sense of FRANK's overall architecture in the System Description and Implementation section, where we describe its control and planning mechanisms, particularly the two kinds of evaluation and feedback within the system. That section also describes the task hierarchies that are used by the control modules of the system: a reports hierarchy, a problem-solving strategies hierarchy, and a presentation strategies hierarchy. We follow this with an extended example where we present a scenario of FRANK's

---

*This work was supported in part by the National Science Foundation, contract IRI-890841, and the Air Force Office of Sponsored Research under contract 90-0359.

responses to case retrieval failure. A discussion of related research and a summary close the paper.

System Description and Implementation

Overview of FRANK

FRANK is a mixed-paradigm, report planning and generation system with a CBR component that has been implemented in a blackboard architecture. While we have selected the diagnosis of back injuries as the initial domain to illustrate its capabilities, the architecture is not specific to diagnostic tasks. In this domain, the user provides a description of a patient's symptoms and selects from a hierarchy of report types the type of report the system is to generate. The output of the system is a natural language report with appropriate supporting analysis of the problem.

The system's architecture is divided into the three basic components of control, domain reasoning, and report generation (see Figure 1). Control is provided by a planner that selects an appropriate plan from its library and then performs the hierarchical planning needed to instantiate it. Plan selection is based on the report type. Domain reasoning capabilities currently implemented include a CBR module with several processing options (e.g., similarity metrics) and an OPS5 production system, as well as knowledge sources that incorporate procedural reasoning. The domain reasoning capabilities are flexibly invoked by the planner to execute the plan. In particular, different types of case retrieval probes are created as necessary to complete query tasks set up by the plan. Finally, a report generator uses rhetorical knowledge to generate a report for the user. To support the various components, we have developed several hierarchies, which we describe next.

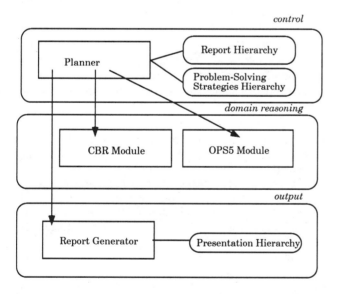

Figure 1: Overview of FRANK Architecture

Hierarchies

To support different expository goals, we have devised three hierarchies. The first hierarchy – the *Report hierarchy* – differentiates among reports based on expository goals. The second – the *Problem-Solving Strategies hierarchy* – represents the different problem-solving strategies inherent in finding, analyzing, and justifying the data that go into a report. A third hierarchy – the *Presentation Strategies hierarchy* – contains the methodologies and policies for presenting the material in its final form. The first two hierarchies support the planner, while the third helps guide report generation.

Report Hierarchy. Our first consideration in classifying reports is their overall goals. This is reflected in the first level in our hierarchy (see Figure 2). Reports are categorized based on whether they are *argumentative* or *summarizing* in nature, although in this paper we discuss the argumentative reports only. Argumentative reports are further subdivided into those that take a *neutral stance* and those that are *pro-position*, that is, endorse particular positions. Further subdivisions within the argumentative reports that take a neutral stance differentiate between reports that provide conclusions and those that do not.

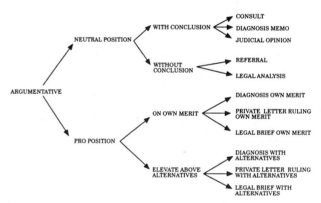

Figure 2: Report Hierarchy (partial)

Within the portion of the hierarchy that supports pro-position argumentative reports, there is a subdivision between reports that justify a position based soley on similar resulting conclusions (the *on own merit* category) and those that justify by additionally examining and discounting possible alternatives (the *elevate above alternatives* category). Examples of reports in these two subcategories are medical reports written from a pro-position viewpoint where there is a predisposition toward a particular conclusion: the *Diagnosis-Own-Merit* and the *Diagnosis-with-Alternatives* reports. A *Diagnosis-Own-Merit* report justifies a diagnosis, in part, by drawing analogies between the current situation and like cases. A *Diagnosis-with-Alternatives* report not only draws analogies to like cases but also discounts or distinguishes alternative diagnoses. Besides these reports from the medical domain, our report hierarchy contains similarly categorized reports for law [Statsky and Wernet, 1984] and policy analysis.

Associated with each report on a leaf node in this hierarchy is a list of groups of strategies. Each group serves as a retrieval pattern for accessing plans to carry out the processing needed to create the report. Currently, the plan that matches the greatest number of strategies is selected first.

Problem-Solving Strategies Hierarchy. Problem-solving strategies encode knowledge about how to perform the analysis necessary to generate a report. These strategies provide guidance on such matters as how to deal with contraindicative data and anomalies, the domain indices (e.g., factors) to use, how extensively to pursue the search for relevant data, what methodologies to use when correlating the data (e.g., pure CBR or CBR with rule-based support), and whether to include or exclude arguments that support alternative conclusions (see Figure 3).

Figure 3: Problem-Solving Strategies Hierarchy (partial)

Presentation Strategies Hierarchy. Presentation strategies guide the system in which aspects of a case to discuss and how to do so. They cover how to handle contraindicative information and anomalies in the output presentation, as well as how to report weaknesses in a position. Presentation strategies also suggest alternative orders for presentation of material within a report. Example presentation strategies are: (1) give the strongest argument first while ignoring alternatives, (2) state alternatives' weaknesses, then expound on the strengths of the desired position, or (3) concede weaknesses if unavoidable and do not bother discussing anomalies.

Control Flow

Top-Level Control. The top-level control flow in FRANK is straightforward. Each processing step in FRANK corresponds to the manipulation by knowledge sources (KSs) of data (units) in its short-term memory, which is implemented as a global blackboard (see Figure 4). The following knowledge sources represent the steps in the top-level control:

1. *Create-Input-KS:* Initially, FRANK is provided with a problem case, the domain, and user preferences for problem-solving and report presentation. The user may also specify the report type and a position to take as part of the preferences. This information is stored on an Input unit.

2. *Process-Input-KS:* This KS analyzes the problem case for quick, credible inferences that are then also stored on the Input unit. In addition, it creates a Report-Envelope

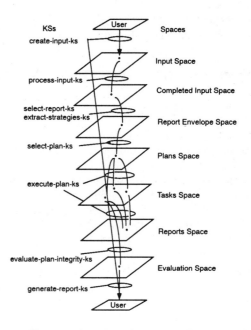

Figure 4: Top-Level Control Flow

unit that contains pointers to the Input unit, the problem case, and the domain, and has additional slots to maintain information about the current state of the problem solving. The Report-Envelope unit represents the context for the current problem-solving session.

3. *Select-Report-KS:* Using information from the Input unit and the Report-Envelope unit, this KS selects a report type and stores it on the Report-Envelope. Currently, the preferred report type must be input by the user.

4. *Extract-Strategies-KS:* Associated with each report type is a list of groups of strategies; these groups act as indices into a library of plans. This KS extracts a group from the list of groups and adds it to a Report-Envelope unit.

5. *Select-Plan-KS:* Using the extracted group of strategies, this KS selects and then stores a specific plan on the Report-Envelope unit. Initially, the plan having the greatest overlap of strategies with the Report-Envelope strategies is selected. (The selection process is described in the Plan Re-Selection section.)

6. *Execute-Plan-KS:* This KS instantiates the selected plan into a set of Goal units. The plan is executed by activating the top-level Goal unit. Leaf Goal units can use a variety of reasoning mechanisms such as model-based reasoning, OPS5, procedural reasoning, or CBR to achieve their respective tasks. The first step in all plans is to create a Report unit that specifies the presentation template to be used and contains slots for the necessary information to complete that template.

7. *Evaluate-Plan-Integrity-KS:* Upon plan completion, the results are evaluated by this KS to determine if the overall cohesiveness of the report is acceptable. Various alternatives, such as switching the plan or report type, are

available should the results be unacceptable.

8. *Generate-Report-KS:* The report is generated by filling out the template with the information stored on the Report unit.

Planning Mechanism

The planning mechanism directs the system's overall efforts to achieve the top-level expository goal. Plans can have dependent, independent, ordered, and unordered goals. Goal parameters may be inherited from supergoals and updated by subgoals. Ultimately, leaf goals invoke tasks through specified KS triggerings. Like plan goals, KSs can be dependent, independent, ordered, or unordered.

The KSs triggered by the leaf goals may use any of a variety of reasoning paradigms suitable for solving the corresponding leaf goal. A goal may be solved by procedural, rule-based, model-based, or case-based reasoning. Procedural and model-based reasonings are Lisp and CLOS modules. The rule-based element is OPS5. The CBR component is the CBR-task mechanism, described below.

Evaluation and Feedback

The analysis and report generation process has several layers. From the highest-level processing abstraction down to the actual executables, there are: reports, plans, goals/subgoals, and tasks/queries (see Figure 5). Currently, a user selects the report type, which indexes an initial plan based on a group of problem-solving strategies. The plan consists of a hierarchy of goals with leaf goals submitting tasks or queries for execution. The tasks/queries are the methodology-specific plan steps such as making inferences using rule-based reasoning (RBR) or finding the best cases using CBR. Replanning may be done at each level to achieve the report's expository goals.

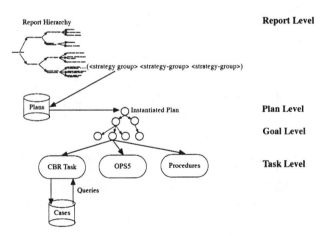

Figure 5: Levels of FRANK

There is a need to provide evaluation and feedback throughout the entire process of gathering, analyzing, and presenting information, rather than waiting until a report is finished to review the final product. Lower-level tasks attempt to rectify any problems they observe in order to lessen the impact on higher-level ones. However, if a process at a lower level has exhausted all its possible remedies, then it returns that feedback to its superior, which can then try a different approach. This type of feedback occurs at all levels of the system. For example, if a report relies on a particular type of information, like good supporting cases to make a pro-position argument, and the necessary information is not found through an (initial) query, then the report (initially) fails at the lowest level. Immediate reparations (e.g., changing particular CBR retrieval parameters) could be made at this level based on evaluation feedback to allow processing to resume without having to abort the whole reporting process.

The mechanism supporting this evaluation-feedback cycle is modeled on operating system vectored interrupts. In our case, the interrupts are unmet expectations detected by goals and the interrupt service routines (ISRs) are the remedies for the various interrupts. Instead of maintaining a single, global table of ISRs, FRANK supports multiple tables, found at the various levels, to permit specialization. When an interrupt occurs, the most local ISR is found by looking first at the table associated with the current goal, then the table of next super goal and so on. If no ISR is found, then a global table is used. While the global table is created at system initialization, the goal ISR tables are specified as part of the goal definition and are created at goal instantiation time.

Report Failures. A report fails only after all the possible plans for it have failed. If the user has not requested a specific report type, FRANK will automatically switch to a potentially more suitable type based on feedback from the failed plans. Otherwise, the user is prompted concerning the deficiencies in the report and he or she can request a new report type.

Plan Re-Selection. There are two general ways to select a new plan when the current plan fails. In the first, a priority-based (or local search of plans) approach, if there are more plans available under the current group of strategies stored on the Report-Envelope unit, the system can use one of these. Failing that, the system checks if there are any other groupings of strategies available under the report type to use as indices in selecting a new plan. Finally, if no other plans are available, then failure occurs, the problem(s) noted, and the system attempts to change the report type.

The second method of selecting a new plan is to use information about the failure to select a better alternative. For example, the *Diagnosis-with-Alternatives* report type requires cases supporting the advocated position to compare favorably to cases supporting alternative diagnoses. If no cases supporting the advocated position can be found, then no plan associated with the *Diagnosis-with-Alternatives* report type will be successful. If this failure occurs, the system switches the report type to *Diagnosis-Own-Merit*, which does not require supporting cases for the advocated position.

Leaf Goals and CBR Methodologies. FRANK supports several CBR methodologies. Currently, two basic methodologies have been implemented: nearest-neighbor and HYPO-style CBR [Ashley, 1990]. Each CBR methodology brings with it different means of retrieving cases, measuring similarity, and selecting best cases. Having multiple types of CBR available allows the system to invoke each type to support the others and to lend credibility to solutions. The flexibility of having different CBR approaches to draw upon also allows the system to apply the best type in a particular context. For example, if no importance rankings can be attached to a set of input-level case features, but a collection of important, derived factors can be identified, a HYPO claim lattice can identify a set of best cases, whereas nearest neighbor retrieval based on input-level features may be less successful if many features are irrelevant. A HYPO claim lattice is a data structure used to rank cases in a partial ordering by similarity to a problem situation according to higher-level domain factors [Ashley, 1990].

FRANK tries to satisfy the current leaf goal's CBR requirement with the most suitable methodology. Should feedback indicate that another methodology may be better suited to the problem, FRANK automatically makes the transition while retaining the feedback about each method. Should no method be able to satisfy the requirement, or only partially satisfy it, then the higher-level goals receive that feedback and decide how to proceed.

CBR-Task Mechanism. The CBR-task mechanism is one of the KSs operating at the lowest level of the planning hierarchy. It controls queries to the case base. Depending on the plan being used to generate a report, a CBR query may be more or less specific or complete. By grouping queries into classes according to what they are asking and what they need as input, this mechanism is able to fill out partial queries. It completes them with viable defaults and then submits them. If a query is unsuccessful, then the CBR-task mechanism alters the values it initially set and resubmits the query, unless prohibited by the user. Again, this level of processing provides feedback concerning the success, partial success, or failure to the next higher process.

Extended Example

The following example demonstrates some of the flexibility of FRANK. In particular, it shows evaluation and reparation at the various levels of the system. The overall motivation for this example is to illustrate how top-level goals influence the type of CBR analysis done and how results during CBR analysis can affect the top-level goals.

Suppose the user wants a pro-position report justifying the diagnosis of spinal stenosis for a problem case. The first step is to select a report type and problem-solving strategies. Given the user input, FRANK selects a pro-position report type called *Diagnosis-with-Alternatives*. Since the user does not specify a problem solving strategy, a default one is used. FRANK selects stronger problem-solving strategies when given a choice. In this case, the default strategy is to make an equitable comparison of an advocated position and the viable alternatives. In particular, the advocated position is considered justified if it is supported by "Best Cases."

There are a variety of definitions for "Best Case" and, as for the problem-solving strategies, FRANK is predisposed to selecting stronger (less inclusive) definitions over weaker (more inclusive) ones. Initially, a Best Case must satisfy three criteria: (1) be a Most On-Point Case (MOPC), (2) support the advocated position, and (3) not share its set of dimensions with other equally on-point cases that support an alternative position (i.e., there can be no equally on-point "competing" cases). In turn, FRANK currently has two definitions for a MOPC: (1) a case that shares the maximal number of overlapping symptoms with the problem situation ("maximal overlap"), or (2) a case in the first tier of a HYPO claim lattice. (These definitions are distinct because cases in the first tier of a claim lattice can share different subsets of dimensions with the problem and these subsets may have different cardinalities.)

FRANK uses the default problem-solving strategy and the above Best Case definition to select a plan associated with the *Diagnosis-with-Alternatives* report type. The selected plan generates goals for finding the Best Cases, collecting the diagnoses associated with them, and then comparing and contrasting these cases.

First Query. The subgoal for finding the Best Cases creates a *Best-Cases* query, specifying the above Best Case definition. Two other case retrieval parameters, (1) whether nearly applicable ("near miss") dimensions are considered during case retrieval and (2) the MOPC definition, are unassigned and are set by the CBR-task mechanism to the defaults of "no near misses" and the maximal overlap definition. The first attempt to satisfy the query results in no Best Cases because all the MOPCs found support diagnoses other than spinal stenosis, thereby violating criterion (3) of the Best Case definition.

Local Modifications. The CBR-task mechanism then alters one of the parameters it set, in this case allowing near misses, and resubmits the query. Again, no Best Cases are found because of competing cases so the CBR-task mechanism changes the MOPC definition from "maximal overlap" to "HYPO Claim Lattice" and resubmits the query. The CBR-task mechanism continues to alter the parameters it has control over and resubmitting the query until either some Best Cases are found or it has exhausted the reasonable combinations it can try. In this example, the query fails to find any Best Cases and returns "no cases" back to the subgoal.

CBR-Task Mechanism Interrupt. When the query returns "no cases" back to the subgoal to find Best Cases, an interrupt is generated to handle the failure. The interrupt is caught by the ISR table related to the subgoal and a remedy to weaken the definition of Best Cases is tried.

New Best Case Definition. The *Best-Cases* query is modified to remove Best Case criterion (3) above, to include as Best Cases those for which equally on-point competing cases may exist. The revised query is submitted and, this time, it returns a set of Best Cases. The subgoal is marked as satisfied and the next goal of the plan is activated.

The next subgoal analyzes each diagnosis used in the set of MOPCs to determine which symptoms of the problem case are and are not covered by the diagnosis. That is, a table is created in which each row contains a viable diagnosis and the columns are the problem case's symptoms. If there is a MOPC for a diagnosis and the MOPC shares the problem case's symptom, then the entry is marked.

Since the current plan compares the strengths of the diagnoses, the symptoms covered by spinal stenosis are compared to the symptoms covered by the alternative diagnoses. The strategy employed here is to conclude that if a symptom is only found in the MOPCs supporting spinal stenosis, then the importance of that symptom is elevated. Unfortunately, in this example, all of the symptoms covered by the spinal stenosis diagnosis are also covered by other diagnoses.

Global Interrupt. Because there are no distinguishing symptoms, at this point an interrupt is generated signifying that the alternatives are too strong. The "too strong alternatives" interrupt is caught by the global ISR table and the corresponding remedy is tried, to try a report type based on the position's own merits. Since the user initially requested a comparison of her position against alternatives, FRANK asks the user if it can make a switch from *Diagnosis-with-Alternatives*. The user agrees and FRANK selects the *Diagnosis-Own-Merit* report type. FRANK now selects and instantiates a plan associated with the *Diagnosis-Own-Merit* report type. Suppose that this time the plan does complete satisfactorily. The resulting data representation of the justification is used by the text generation module to create the actual report and present it to the user.

Related Research

This work extends our previous work on case-based reasoning, mixed-paradigm reasoning, and argumentation, particularly our work on hybrid-reasoning systems that use a blackboard to incorporate a CBR component, including ABISS [Rissland *et al.*, 1991] and STICKBOY [Rubinstein, 1992]. FRANK uses opportunistic control analogous to HEARSAY II [Erman *et al.*, 1980] to better incorporate both top-down and bottom-up aspects of justification than in our previous, rule-based approach to control in CABARET [Rissland and Skalak, 1991]. FRANK also extends our task orientation from mostly argumentative tasks, as in HYPO and CABARET, to more general forms of explanation, justification, and analysis. Other mixed-paradigm systems using blackboard architectures to incorporate cases and heterogeneous domain knowledge representations are the structural redesign program FIRST [Daube and Hayes-Roth, 1988], and the Dutch landlord-tenant law knowledge-based architectures PROLEXS [Walker *et al.*, 1991] and EXPANDER [Walker, 1992].

ANON [Owens, 1989] uses an integrated top-down and bottom-up process to retrieve similar cases. Abstract features are extracted from a current problem and each feature is used to progressively refine the set of similar cases. As the set of similar cases changes, it is used to suggest the abstract features that may be in the current problem and used for further refinement.

TEXPLAN [Maybury, 1991], a planner for explanatory text, provides a taxonomy of generic text types, distinguished by purpose and their particular effect on the reader. This system also applies communicative plan strategies to generate an appropriately formed response corresponding to a selected type of text. TEXPLAN is designed as an addition to existing applications, rather than as an independent domain problem solver.

While FRANK explains failures as part of the evaluation and reparation it performs at various levels, the explanation is not used to determine the appropriateness of a case as in CASEY [Koton, 1988] and GREBE [Branting, 1988], nor is it used to explain anomalies as in TWEAKER [Kass and Leake, 1988] and ACCEPTER [Kass and Leake, 1988]. FRANK's use of explanation in plan failure is similar to CHEF's [Hammond, 1989] in that it uses the explanation of a failure as an index into the possible remedies. However, CHEF's explanation is provided by a domain-dependent casual simulation, whereas FRANK's failure analysis is based on the generic performance of its own reasoning modules, such as the failure of the CBR module to retrieve an adequate collection of supporting cases.

Summary

Our general focus in this paper has been the interaction between a user's high-level expository goal and its supporting subgoal tasks, such as to retrieve relevant cases. Having set ourselves two research goals in the introduction, we have shown first how the FRANK system, a hybrid blackboard architecture, can create diagnostic reports by tailoring case-based reasoning tasks to the user's ultimate goals and viewpoint. In particular, we have given an example of how FRANK uses feedback from tasks such as CBR to re-select a plan. Finally, in pursuit of our second research goal, we have demonstrated how FRANK can re-specify the way case retrieval is performed to satisfy a plan's failed request for case support.

References

Ashley, Kevin D. 1990. *Modelling Legal Argument: Reasoning with Cases and Hypotheticals*. M.I.T. Press, Cambridge, MA.

Blackboard Technology Group, Inc., 1992. *GBB Reference: Version 2.10*. Amherst, MA.

Branting, L. Karl 1988. The Role of Explanation in Reasoning from Legal Precedents. In *Proceedings, Case-Based Reasoning Workshop*, Clearwater Beach, FL. Defense Advanced Research Projects Agency, Information Science and Technology Office. 94–103.

Daube, Francois and Hayes-Roth, Barbara 1988. FIRST: A Case-Based Redesign System in the BB1 Blackboard Architecture. In Rissland, Edwina and King, James A., editors 1988, *Case-Based Reasoning Workshop*, St. Paul, MN. AAAI. 30–35.

Erman, Lee D.; Hayes-Roth, Frederick; Lesser, Victor R.; and Reddy, D. Raj 1980. The Hearsay-II Speech-

Understanding System: Integrating Knowledge to Resolve Uncertainty. *Computing Surveys* 12(2):213–253.

Hammond, Kristian J. 1989. *Case-Based Planning: Viewing Planning as a Memory Task.* Academic Press, Boston, MA.

Kass, Alex M. and Leake, David B. 1988. Case-Based Reasoning Applied to Constructing Explanations. In *Proceedings, Case-Based Reasoning Workshop*, Clearwater Beach, FL. Defense Advanced Research Projects Agency, Information Science and Technology Office. 190–208.

Koton, Phyllis A. 1988. *Using Experience in Learning and Problem Solving.* Ph.D. Dissertation, Department of Electrical Engineering and Computer Science, MIT, Cambridge, MA.

Maybury, Mark Thomas 1991. *Planning Multisentential English Text using Communicative Acts.* Ph.D. Dissertation, University of Cambridge, Cambridge, England.

Owens, Christopher 1989. Integrating Feature Extraction and Memory Search. In *Proceedings: The 11th Annual Conference of The Cognitive Science Society*, Ann Arbor, MI. 163–170.

Rissland, Edwina L. and Skalak, David B. 1991. CABARET: Rule Interpretation in a Hybrid Architecture. *International Journal of Man-Machine Studies* 1(34):839–887.

Rissland, E. L.; Basu, C.; Daniels, J. J.; McCarthy, J.; Rubinstein, Z. B.; and Skalak, D. B. 1991. A Blackboard-Based Architecture for CBR: An Initial Report. In *Proceedings: Case-Based Reasoning Workshop*, Washington, D.C. Morgan Kaufmann, San Mateo, CA. 77–92.

Rubinstein, Zachary B. 1992. STICKBOY: A Blackboard-Based Mixed Paradigm System to Diagnose and Explain Back Injuries. Master's thesis, Department of Computer and Information Science, University of Massachusetts, Amherst, MA.

Statsky, William P. and Wernet, R. John 1984. *Case Analysis and Fundamentals of Legal Writing.* West Publishing, St. Paul, MN, third edition.

Walker, R. F.; Oskamp, A.; Schrickx, J. A.; Opdorp, G. J. Van; and Berg, P. H.van den 1991. PROLEXS: Creating Law and Order in a Heterogeneous Domain. *International Journal of Man-Machines Studies* 35:35–67.

Walker, Rob 1992. *An Expert System Architecture for Heterogeneous Domains: A Case-Study in the Legal Field.* Ph.D. Dissertation, Vrije Universiteit te Amsterdam, Amsterdam, Netherlands.

A Framework and an Analysis of Current Proposals for the Case-Based Organization and Representation of Procedural Knowledge

Roland Zito-Wolf and **Richard Alterman**
Computer Science Department/Center for Complex Systems
Brandeis University, Waltham, MA 02254
rjz@cs.brandeis.edu, alterman@cs.brandeis.edu

Abstract

Case-based reasoning refers to the class of memory-based problem solving methods which emphasize the adaptation of recalled solutions (explanations, diagnoses, plans) over the generation of solutions from first principles. CBR has become a popular methodology, resulting in a proliferation of case organization and representation proposals. The goal of this paper is to sort through some of these proposals. Using the formal models of "procedure" and "case-based reasoning" introduced in Zito-Wolf and Alterman (1992), we compare three current proposals for the organization of procedural case-bases: individual cases, microcases, and multicases. We give a worst-case analysis that shows the advantages of the multicase in terms of case storage and retrieval costs. The model predicts that multicases reduce case storage and retrieval costs as compared to the other two models. We then provide some empirical evidence from an implemented system that suggests that the trends observed in the formal model are also observable in case bases of practical size.

1 Introduction

In recent years, Artificial Intelligence researchers have become increasingly interested in techniques for reasoning directly from examples rather than from the abstract knowledge one might distill from them. *Case-based reasoning* (CBR) refers to the class of memory-based problem-solving methods which emphasize the adaptation of recalled solutions (explanations, diagnoses, plans) over the generation of solutions from first principles (such as a domain theory). People rely heavily on such techniques both in expert domains, such as medical diagnosis, legal reasoning, and in coping with the more mundane problems that arise in everyday life (Kolodner & Simpson, 1989).

The variety of applications of CBR has resulted in a proliferation of case organization and representation proposals. Until now the evaluation of proposals has been informal making comparisons difficult. The goal of this paper is to put some of these issues on a firmer foundation.

Because it is difficult to discuss these issues in any detail independent of specific tasks, this paper will focus on the organization of procedural knowledge for planning tasks. Because procedures are typically executed many times, providing large numbers of related yet distinct cases, and they are complex, with many interrelated components (i.e., steps), procedural domains are a good test domain for examining these issues. It is also an area where perhaps the largest number of different proposals have been made, which we interpret as reflecting the difficulty of the representational problem.

We will present a formal model which will allow for the comparison of case-base organization proposals. We discuss three existing proposals, the third of which, the *multicase*, combines the benefits of the other two. We give a worst-case analysis that shows the advantages of the multicase in terms of case storage and retrieval costs. We also provide some empirical evidence that suggests that the trends observed in the formal model are also observable in case bases of practical size. For an extended analysis that also discusses additional factors (e.g., adaptation costs) see Zito-Wolf (1993).

2 Representing Procedures

Let a *problem* as presented to the system consist of a *situation* (a world state) plus a *goal* to be achieved. The solution to a problem will be a *procedure*, that is, a sequence of steps that achieves the goal in that situation. Assume we are given a set of examples of some procedure. What shall we call a case? In this paper we will use the terms *example* or *episode* for an instance of a problem and a solution procedure. The term *case* will be reserved for the unit of storage and retrieval from memory. Many CBR systems, especially early ones (e.g., CHEF, CYRUS) have equated the two; however, they are logically distinct, and it is useful to distinguish them.

Storage Requirements Although memory is becoming increasingly plentiful, at any given time memory is a finite resource which needs to be traded off against possible uses. Consequently, one significant issue is the amount of memory required to store all the cases. As the quality of solution retrieved by a case-based reasoner is expected to be monotonically increasing with the number of distinct, relevant cases available to it, one wants to accommodate as many cases as possible. On the other hand, the number of potential cases can be very large – it is exponential in the complexity (number of features) of the cases.

Retrieval Cost Retrieval cost is a function of the number of cases examined and the effort required to determine their relevance to the current situation. Both the number of cases to examine and the cost of deciding among them can be large in practical case-bases. When the number of cases becomes large, retrieval normally relies on *indexes*. An index is an auxiliary data structure that provides a direct mapping from each specific feature of interest to cases having that feature. Complete indexing may not be practical for all features, however; for example, the type of data involved may not admit of simple indexes, or the feature of interest may be computed only at execution time. Hence, we will look at both indexed and unindexed retrieval.

3 Modelling Procedure Organizations

In this section we will compare the behavior of three representations for procedural case-bases, based on the formal models of "procedure" and "case-based reasoning" introduced in Zito-Wolf and Alterman (1992). The results of this section are summarized in Table 1.

We assume the procedural knowledge to be captured has the form of a complete binary decision tree T of uniform depth n. Each node $i \in T$ contains a *step* to be performed plus a *decision* selecting the next node to be executed. T therefore contains $|T| = 2^n - 1$ steps and $2^{n-1} - 1$ decisions (those in the leaves are ignored). Each procedure execution *episode* will consist of $n - 1$ decisions selecting n steps along some path in T from the root to a leaf node.

Let the input to the decision at a node i be the set of binary features F_i, so that $F = \bigcup_{i \in T} F_i$ is the set of all features referenced by the procedure. We assume there exists some upper bound $f = \max_{i \in T} |F_i|$ on the number of features tested by any specific decision, and that f is small compared to F.[1] To estimate F we choose $(n-1)f$. This corresponds (for example) to a procedure composed of $n - 1$ distinct decisions occurring in a fixed order.

Storage Case-based reasoning for procedure generation is the example-based selection of a sequence of steps to achieve a given goal. Each occasion for selection is a *problem* P_i, the process of searching through

the case-base to solve a problem is a *retrieval*, and the number of steps determined by each problem is the *problem size* S_P. The solution to each problem will be encoded in memory as some set of *cases* C_P. Each case pairs a problem solution with a conjunction of features for which it applies. Since it has been stipulated that a given decision references at most f features, at most 2^f cases will be required to represent a decision, one for each possible conjunction of the features and their negations. The union of all the C_P is the case-base C. The *case-base size* $S(C)$ will be measured as the number of step instances in the case base C, that is, the product of the number of cases $|C|$ and the problem size. The set of examples from which a given case base is derived will be denoted E.

Retrieval and Indexing Consider a linear search model of case retrieval, in which the *retrieval effort per problem* R_P is proportional to the number of feature tests made. R_P is the product of the number of cases to be searched through and the number of features to be tested per case. If P is the number of problems per episode, then the *total retrieval effort* per episode $R = R_P P$.

Because case-retrieval via linear search involves effort exponential in the procedure size (n), most CBR systems use some form of *indexing* for faster retrieval.[2] We will model an index as a boolean discrimination network which tests just enough features to discriminate all the cases. Assuming that the index is well-constructed, the decision cost per problem R_{XP} is proportional to the depth d of the index, that is, log base 2 of the number of cases entering into a given decision, and the pre-episode cost $R_X = R_{XP} P$ The size of an index (in nodes) is $2^d - 1$, of the same order as the number of cases indexed.

3.1 Individual Cases

The first representation we will consider is the storage of individual cases (CHEF, Hammond 1990; COOKIE, McCartney 1990). In this method the unit of retrieval from memory, the case, is taken to be the same as the unit of knowledge presentation, the episode. Procedure execution over such a case base consists of a single up-front decision among alternative cases (Figure 1a). That is, case retrieval returns a single complete example episode for the target task, which (usually after some tweaking) is interpreted as a procedure for the desired task. Also in this class are MOP-based systems (Kolodner, 1983; Lebowitz, 1983; Turner, 1989).

---

[1] For simplicity, in the remainder of the paper we will write X for $|X|$ where there is no likelihood of confusion.

[2] The term "indexing" is used in the CBR literature in at least three distinct senses: to refer to *performance* methods that accelerate access to subsets of the case base; to refer to *organizing* methods that group cases observed to have similar features, typically in the service of generalization (cf. CYRUS and IPP); and to refer to the process of *encoding knowledge* by adding features to a case-base to define sets of cases with related content. Our analysis focuses on the first of these meanings.

MOPs indexes, though more complex then our model index, serve the same function. The key similarity is that cases are stored and accessed as wholes; for the purpose of this paper the indexing differences can be ignored.

Storage Each episode of (i.e., path through) T is a case, so the problem size $S_P = n$. The entire mapping from features to procedure is performed in one retrieval ($P = 1$) with 2^{n-1} potential outcomes. The number of potential cases can be estimated from the total number of features referenced, yielding $C = 2^{(n-1)f}$, $S(C) = nC$, and $R_P = FC$).

Retrieval Cost Unindexed retrieval cost is determined by the number of feature comparisons made, which is the size of the case base times the number of features per case. Only one retrieval is required, so that $R = R_P P = F2^F$. Using an index, the decision cost is the log base 2 of the number of cases entering into a given decision, or $O(F)$, hence the popularity of indexing. A simple index requires on the order of as many nodes as there are cases indexed, so its storage can be ignored.[3]

Most notable here is the rapid growth in possible cases as either the number of features or procedure steps increases. This is due to the fact that the cases are significantly redundant – each case instantiates a complete path through the tree. To represent procedural knowledge in an individual-case-based system, for, say, one's knowledge of procedures for telephoning, one would have to store a case for every possible event sequence and every situation type that could be encountered in executing one's phone-call procedure, or at least a significant number of them. Note that as the case-base fills up with variant episodes, retrieval also becomes more expensive.

3.2 Microcases

The second class of procedure representations is the *microcase*. In this method, each example presented to the system is converted into *many* cases, typically one for each step of the episode. All the cases so created go into a common case-base. At execution time, procedures are not so much retrieved as incrementally reconstructed, steps being selected sequentially by separate retrievals over the case-base. (Figure 1b). Microcases avoid the redundant storage and difficulty with transfer that we encountered with individual cases. Micro-case-based systems have been applied to planning (Langley and Allen, 1990), parsing (Goodman, 1991), and word pronunciation (NetTalk, Stanfill and Waltz 1986).

---

[3]Note that whereas in a simple index the path to a case is unique (enumerating each case's features in some specific order), methods involving multiple indexing – such MOPs-based systems – will require significantly more storage.

Storage To encode procedure T using microcases we make each selection of a step a separate problem. Then $S_P = 1$, and $C_P = 2^f$ cases per problem. There are $P = n$ problems per episode, but $2^n - 1$ problems to be encoded to represent the entire procedure, giving $C = 2^f(2^n - 1)$.

Retrieval Cost The price of the microcase's additional flexibility and reduced storage is increased retrieval costs: a case retrieval occurs at every procedure step. Each such decision has to select among a large number of options, namely, all possible steps. Unindexed retrieval effort per problem is $R_P = (F+n)2^{n+f}$. Note that n additional features are added to distinguish the 2^{n-1} potential "current positions" within the represented procedure; that is, the structure of the procedure T needs to be encoded implicitly as extra features referenced by the cases. Total retrieval effort R is n times the per-problem figure, or $O(n^2 2^{n+f})$. Indexed decision cost is the log base 2 of the number of cases entering into a given decision, or $O(n+f)$. There is a single index of size $|C|$, or $O(2^{n+f})$.

3.3 The Multicase

We have proposed a third organization, the *multicase* (Zito-Wolf and Alterman 1992). By a multicase we mean a structure which merges many individual episodes but retains a representation of the overall structure of those episodes. Episodes are merged through the introduction of conditionals, so that the details of the individual episodes can be retained (Figure 1c). Each example is represented by some specific path through the procedure graph. Episodic memory is organized around the underlying procedure, which serves to partition the procedure into many individual decisions. This organization efficiently accommodates variation among episodes, and is moreover a convenient vehicle for organizing related knowledge, such as unexpected events or episodes where the plan failed.

The key difference between individual cases and multicases is that individual cases store episodes in memory as separate structures linked by indexes or abstraction hierarchies, whereas multicases index them at a finer-grained level by segmenting them and distributing them across the partonomic (i.e., step) structure of the procedure.

The key difference between the multicase and microcase is that for multicases the decision overhead is reduced by partitioning the pool of cases according to the structure of the procedure, whereas for microcases all the cases go into a single pool, so that each decision must decide among a much larger range of options.

The historical antecedents of all of the case models discussed here are the ideas of scripts (Schank & Abelson, 1977), MOPs, and their elements, scenes and tracks (Schank, 1982). The issue is how to organize an agent's episodic memory using ideas like this in the most effective manner. This is the problem the multicase addresses.

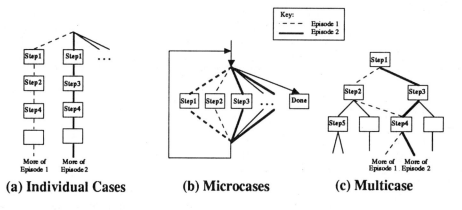

Figure 1: Three Methods of Representing Episodes

Storage The case base is partitioned both by the type of decision (e.g., next-step, role-choice); the structure of the procedure is expressed explicitly in the structure of the multicase. We have $S_P = 1$, $|P| = n-1$ problems per episode, with $|C_P| = 2^f$ and $2^{n-1} - 1$ problems overall, for a total of $|C| = O(2^{n+f-1})$.

Retrieval Cost Because the multicase focuses on only one decision at a time, the number of cases that must be searched through and the number of features needing to be consulted at any given decision point are greatly reduced. For the multicase, only f features need be consulted per decision, so only 2^f cases need be examined; the rest of the cases are only relevant to *other* decisions. Thus $R_P = f \cdot 2^f$ and $R = O(nf \cdot 2^f)$. Indexed decision cost is the log base 2 of the number of cases entering into a given decision, or $O(f)$. For multicases there may be as many 2^{n-1} indexes, one for each decision, the total index size is 2^{n+f-1}.

4 Empirical Demonstration

Our source data derives from a sample of runs of the FLOABN system on problems involving the operation of household and office devices such as telephones, copiers, and vending machines (Alterman, Zito-Wolf, and Carpenter 1990; Alterman, Carpenter, and Zito-Wolf 1990). FLOABN was provided initially with a skeleton multicase for a simple procedure for the usage of each class of device. It was then presented with a sequence of 50 problem situations involving these procedures; for example, phone calls varied in destinations, locations, call types, and phone features. There were on average 25 steps per episode, yielding in excess of 1200 cases. For each episode we collected over 60 items of data about the evolution of memory and procedure performance. Each run of the example sequence required approximately 8 hours on an 8 Mbyte Macintosh IIx under Allegro Common Lisp.

4.1 Comparing Representation Methods

Our methodology for comparing the three case-organization models will be to use our formal model of procedures to define mappings between the multicase model and the individual-case and microcase models. We will gather data from runs of FLOABN to estimate practical values for the relevant parameters of the model: the total number of different features that were observed (F), the average number of features referenced in making a decision (f), the average number of decisions needing to be made per episode, and the number of cases C. We then run this data through the model to derive costs for the three methods.

It would have been preferable in some sense to compare implementations of the three methods directly rather than comparing projections based on a single implementation. Problems emerged from such an attempt. Several operations that were facilitated by the multicase – for example, instruction-processing and plan-modification operations – were hard to do, and in some cases even to define, on other representations. This is because these functions required an evolving plan schema representation, which the multicase provides and the other organizations do not.

4.2 Storage Costs

Figure 2 compares memory requirements for case storage. The greatest storage requirements are for the individual case method. Individual cases save much redundant information with each nominally different case. In contrast, case memory growth for the microcase and multicase methods tail off as as the memory becomes familiar with the range of variation of its procedures. The multicase method uses less storage than the microcase method. This is because the multicase partitions its space of decisions much more finely, and consequently, many more decisions have only one option and hence do not require that any cases be stored for them. Figure 3 compares the number of decisions with > 1 option for each method. The graph for microcases represents something of an upper bound, since

Item	Individual cases		Microcases		Multicases	
	formula	example	formula	ex.	formula	ex.
1. Total cases $|C|$	2^F	256	$O(2^{n+J})$	124	$O(2^{n+J-1})$	75
2. CB size	$n2^F$	1280	$O(2^{n+J})$	124	$O(2^{n+J-1})$	75
3. Effort/problem R_P	$F2^F$	2048	$O(F2^{n+J})$	1612	$f2^J$	8
4. Effort/problem R_{XP}	F	8	$O(n+f)$	7	f	2
5. Effort/episode R	$F2^F$	2048	$O(nF2^{n+J})$	8060	$(n-1)f2^J$	40
6. Effort/episode R_X	F	8	$O(n^2+F)$	35	F	8

Table 1: Storage and Retrieval Cost Summary

microcases strive to have as many options as possible at each decision. Comparison with the graph for multicases shows that in our example situations, anywhere from 50-75% of these decisions are unnecessary. This suggests that microcases overemphasize transfer at the cost of greatly increasing the amount of knowledge required to "learn" the procedure.

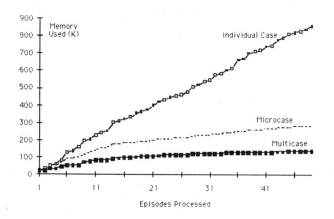

Figure 2: Memory Usage Comparisons

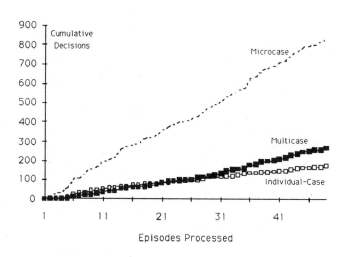

Figure 3: Cumulative Decisions per Episode

4.3 Decision Cost

Now we wish to use our empirical data to compare decision costs. Recall that our model of unindexed decision cost R_P was the product of features tested and cases examined per problem, whereas for indexed retrieval, we took R_{XP} to be the depth of the smallest index needed to discriminate the cases under consideration. The required quantities were determined from the example sequence. Figure 4 shows the number of cases available per decision for the three methods. The number of features referenced per case was measured at the end of the problem sequence to be $f \approx 7$ per case and total $F \approx 16$. Lastly, the number of retrievals per episode was presented in the previous section (Figure 3).

Individual cases introduce a difficulty here. It is unreasonable to assume that only one up-front case retrieval is needed per episode, because it ignores the cost of the runtime decision-making which the other methods are being "charged" for. Thus, since each such unanticipated circumstance incurs at least one additional retrieval, we have added to the count of retrievals per episode in Figure 3 one retrieval per unanticipated decision event or relevant situation feature.

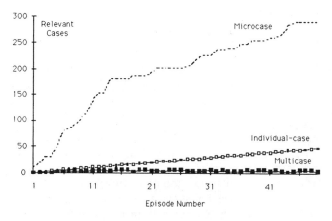

Figure 4: Choices Per Decision

Figure 5 graphs indexed retrieval effort for the three methods. The first result we observe is that microcases have much larger retrieval effort – an order of magnitude larger than multicases even in the fully indexed case. This difference is the product of the two differences shown above: the number of cases requiring a decision, and the number of cases examined per decision. Secondly, we observe that multicases require effort less than (but roughly comparable to) that for individual cases. The individual-case method's advantage of making fewer decisions per episode is more than offset by the extra costs of handling more contingencies and sorting through more cases per decision. For unindexed retrieval (not shown), the multicase has about 1% of the cost of individual cases, while the microcase remains the most costly of the three.

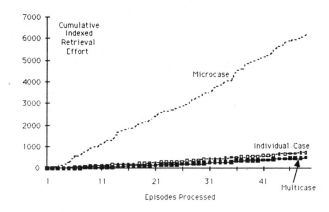

Figure 5: Indexed Retrieval Effort Comparisons

5   Concluding Remarks

The paper has presented a framework for comparing case-based procedure models over issues concerning case representation and organization. The framework is a formal model of procedures and their representation that enables us to characterize analytically several important properties of each method. In this paper we focused on storage cost and retrieval effort.

Three current proposals were analyzed within this framework: microcases, individual cases, and multicase. The formal analysis addressed the large scale behavior of the different models, a kind of worst-case analysis. Results of this analysis can be summarized: the multicase has the least storage requirements and individual cases are worse by an exponential factor. For retrieval cost, multicase and individual cases have comparable costs, with microcases a factor of n worse (where n is the depth of the procedure).

To evaluate the behavior in a more average case, empirical data was collected from a run of FLOABN in which over a thousand cases were collected. The results of this data can be summarized: The empirical data qualitatively confirms the the formal analysis with regard to storage and retrieval costs. We note, however, that the difference in indexed decision cost between individual cases and multicases, though of the expected polarity, was not as significant as the formal model leads us to expect. This is because the number

of cases was not yet large enough for the proliferation of cases to dominate retrieval cost.

Both our formal analysis and our empirical data emphasize that representational choices in CBR systems have significant effects on system performance. We feel that this paper is the first step of a larger project in the exploration and characterization of efficient and useful case-base organizations, and an essential step in the development of truly large-scale CBR systems.

References

[1] Richard Alterman, Tamitha Carpenter, and Roland Zito-Wolf. An architecture for understanding in planning, action, and learning. *SIGART Bulletin*, 2(4):14–19, 1991. Special Issue on *Integrated Cognitive Architectures*.

[2] Richard Alterman, Roland Zito-Wolf, and Tamitha Carpenter. Interaction, comprehension, and instruction usage. *Journal of the Learning Sciences*, 1(4), 1991.

[3] Marc Goodman. A case-based, inductive architecture for natural language processing. In *AAAI Spring Symposium on Machine Learning of Natural Language and Ontology*, 1991.

[4] Kristian J. Hammond. Case-based planning: A framework for planning from experience. *Cognitive Science*, 14:385–443, 1990.

[5] Janet L. Kolodner. Reconstructive memory: A computer model. *Cognitive Science*, 7:281–328, 1983.

[6] Janet L. Kolodner and Robert L. Simpson. The MEDIATOR: Analysis of an early case-based problem solver. *Cognitive Science*, 13:507–549, 1989.

[7] Michael Lebowitz. Generalization from natural language text. *Cognitive Science*, 7:1–40, 1983.

[8] Robert McCartney. Reasoning directly from cases in a case-based planner. In *Proceedings of the Twelfth Annual Conference of the Cognitive Science Society*, pages 101–108, Hillsdale, NJ, 1990. Lawrence Erlbaum Associates.

[9] R. Schank and R. Abelson. *Scripts, Plans, Goals, and Understanding*. Lawrence Erlbaum Associates, Hillsdale, NJ, 1977.

[10] Roger Schank. *Dynamic Memory: A Theory of Reminding and Learning In Computers and People*. Cambridge University Press, Cambridge, 1982.

[11] Craig Stanfill and David Waltz. Toward memory-based reasoning. *Communications of the ACM*, 29(12):1213–1239, 1986.

[12] Roy M. Turner. A schema-based model of adaptive problem solving. Technical Report GIT-ICS-89/42, Georgia Institute of Technology, 1989.

[13] Roland Zito-Wolf. Case-based representations for procedural knowledge. Unpublished doctoral dissertation, 1993.

[14] Roland Zito-Wolf and Richard Alterman. Multicases: A case-based representation for procedural knowledge. In *Proceedings of the Fourteenth Annual Conference of the Cognitive Science Society*, pages 331–336. Lawrence Erlbaum Associates, 1992.

Complexity in
Machine Learning

Cryptographic Limitations on Learning One-Clause Logic Programs

William W. Cohen
AT&T Bell Laboratories
600 Mountain Avenue Murray Hill, NJ 07974
wcohen@research.att.com

Abstract

An active area of research in machine learning is learning logic programs from examples. This paper investigates formally the problem of learning a single Horn clause: we focus on generalizations of the language of constant-depth determinate clauses, which is used by several practical learning systems. We show first that determinate clauses of logarithmic depth are not learnable. Next we show that learning indeterminate clauses with at most k indeterminate variables is equivalent to learning DNF. Finally, we show that recursive constant-depth determinate clauses are not learnable. Our primary technical tool is the method of prediction-preserving reducibilities introduced by Pitt and Warmuth [1990]; as a consequence our results are independent of the representations used by the learning system.

Introduction

Recently, there has been an increasing amount of research in learning restricted logic programs, or *inductive logic programming (ILP)* [Cohen, 1992; Muggleton and Feng, 1992; Quinlan, 1990; Muggleton, 1992a]. One advantage of using logic programs (rather than alternative first-order logic formalisms [Cohen and Hirsh, 1992]) is that its semantics and computational complexity have been well-studied; this offers some hope that learning systems based on it can also be mathematically well-understood.

Some formal results have in fact been obtained; the strongest positive result in the pac-learning model [Valiant, 1984] shows that a single constant-depth determinate clause is pac-learnable, and that a non-recursive logic program containing k such clauses is learnable against any "simple" distribution [Džeroski et al., 1992]. Some very recent work [Kietz, 1993] shows that a single clause is *not* pac-learnable if the constant-depth determinacy condition does not hold; specifically, it is shown that neither the language of indeterminate clauses of fixed depth nor the language of determinate clauses of arbitrary depth is pac-learnable. These negative results are of limited practical importance because they assume that the learner is required

to output a *single* clause that covers all of the examples; however, most practical ILP learning systems do not impose this constraint. Such negative learnability results are sometimes called *representation-dependent*.[1]

This paper presents representation *independent* negative results for three languages of Horn clauses, all obtained by generalizing the language of constant depth determinate clauses. These negative results are obtained by showing that learning is as hard as breaking a (presumably) secure cryptographic system, and thus are not dependent on assumptions about the representation used by the learning system. Specifically, we will show that determinate clauses of log depth are not learnable, and that recursive clauses of constant depth are not learnable. We will also show that indeterminate clauses with k "free" variables are exactly as hard to learn as DNF.

Due to space constraints, detailed proofs will not be given; the interested reader is referred to a longer version of the paper [Cohen, 1993a]. We will focus instead on describing the basic intuitions behind the proofs.

Formal preliminaries

Learning models

Our basic notion of learnability is the usual one introduced by Valiant [1984]. Let X be a set, called the *domain*. Define a *concept* C over X to be a representation of some subset of X, and a *language* $\mathcal{L}$ to be a set of concepts. Associated with X and $\mathcal{L}$ are two *size complexity measures*; we use the notation X_n (respectively $\mathcal{L}_n$) to stand for the set of all elements of X (respectively $\mathcal{L}$) of size complexity no greater than n. An *example of C* is a pair (x, b) where $b = 1$ if $x \in C$ and $b = 0$ otherwise. If D is a probability distribution

---

[1]The prototypical example of a learning problem which is hard in a representation-dependent setting but not in a broader setting is learning k-term DNF. Pac-learning k-term DNF is NP-hard if the hypotheses of the learning system must be k-term DNF; however it is tractable if hypotheses can be expressed in the richer language of k-CNF.

function, a *sample of C from X drawn according to D* is a pair of multisets S^+, S^- drawn from the domain X according to D, S^+ containing only positive examples of C, and S^- containing only negative ones.

Finally, a language $\mathcal{L}$ is *pac-learnable* iff there is an algorithm *LEARN* and a polynomial function $m(\frac{1}{\epsilon}, \frac{1}{\delta}, n_e, n_t)$ so that for every $n_t > 0$, every $n_e > 0$, every $C \in \mathcal{L}_{n_t}$, every $\epsilon : 0 < \epsilon < 1$, every $\delta : 0 < \delta < 1$, and every probability distribution function D, for any sample S^+, S^- of C from X_{n_e} drawn according to D containing at least $m(\frac{1}{\epsilon}, \frac{1}{\delta}, n_e, n_t)$ examples

1. *LEARN*, on inputs S^+, S^-, ϵ, and δ, outputs a hypothesis H such that

$$Prob(D(H - C) + D(C - H) > \epsilon) < \delta$$

2. *LEARN* runs in time polynomial in $\frac{1}{\epsilon}$, $\frac{1}{\delta}$, n_e, n_t, and the number of examples; and

3. The hypothesis H of the learning systems is in $\mathcal{L}$.

The polynomial function $m(\frac{1}{\epsilon}, \frac{1}{\delta}, n_e, n_t)$ is called the *sample complexity* of the learning algorithm *LEARN*.

With condition 3 above, the definition of pac-learnability makes a relatively strong restriction on the hypotheses the learner can generate; this can lead to some counterintuitive results.[2] If a learning algorithm exists that satisfies all the conditions above except condition 3, but does output a hypothesis that can be evaluated in polynomial time, we will say that $\mathcal{L}$ is *(polynomially) predictable*.[3]

These learning models have been well-studied, and are quite appropriate to modeling standard inductive learners. However, the typical ILP system is used in a somewhat more complex setting, as the user will typically provide both a set of examples and a *background theory K*: the task of the learner is then to find a logic program P such that P, together with K, is a good model of the data. To deal with this wrinkle, we will require some additional definitions. If $\mathcal{L}$ is some language of logic programs[4] and K is a logic program, then $\mathcal{L}[K]$ denotes the set of all pairs of the form (P, K) such that $P \in \mathcal{L}$: each such pair represents the set of all atoms e such that $P \wedge K \vdash e$. If $\mathcal{K}$ is a set of background theories, then the *family of languages* $\mathcal{L}[\mathcal{K}]$ represents the set of all languages $\mathcal{L}[K]$ where $K \in \mathcal{K}$. We will consider $\mathcal{L}[\mathcal{K}]$ to be predictable (pac-learnable) only when every $\mathcal{L}[K] \in \mathcal{L}[\mathcal{K}]$ is predictable (pac-learnable.) This requires one slight modification to the definitions of predictability pac-learnability: we must now assume a

size complexity measure for background theories, and allow the sample and time complexities of the learner to also grow (polynomially) with the size complexity of the background theory provided by the user.

Reducibilities among prediction problems

Our main analytic tool in this paper is *prediction-preserving reducibility*, as described by Pitt and Warmuth [1990]. This is essentially a method of showing that one language is no harder to predict than another. If $\mathcal{L}_1$ is a language over domain X_1 and $\mathcal{L}_2$ is a language over domain X_2, then we say that *predicting $\mathcal{L}_1$ reduces to predicting $\mathcal{L}_2$*, written $\mathcal{L}_1 \trianglelefteq \mathcal{L}_2$, if there is a function $f_i : X_1 \rightarrow X_2$, henceforth called the *instance mapping*, and a function $f_c : \mathcal{L}_1 \rightarrow \mathcal{L}_2$, henceforth called the *concept mapping*, so that the following all hold:

1. $x \in C$ if and only if $f_i(x) \in f_c(C)$ — i.e., concept membership is preserved by the mappings;

2. the size complexity of $f_c(C)$ is polynomial in the size complexity of C — i.e. the size of concepts is preserved within a polynomial factor; and

3. $f_i(x)$ can be computed in polynomial time.

Intuitively, $f_c(C_1)$ returns a concept $C_2 \in \mathcal{L}_2$ that will "emulate" C_1 (i.e., make the same decisions about concept membership) on examples that have been "preprocessed" with the function f_i. If predicting $\mathcal{L}_1$ reduces to predicting $\mathcal{L}_2$ and a learning algorithm for $\mathcal{L}_2$ exists, then one possible scheme for learning a concept $C_1 \in \mathcal{L}_1$ would be to preprocess all examples of C_1 with f_i, and then use these preprocessed examples to learn some H that is a good approximation of $C_2 = f_c(C_1)$. H can then be used to predict membership in C_1: given an example x from the original domain X_1, one can simply predict $x \in C_1$ to be true whenever $f_i(x) \in H$. Pitt and Warmuth [1990] give a rigorous argument that this approach leads to a prediction algorithm for $\mathcal{L}_1$, leading to the following theorem.

Theorem 1 (Pitt and Warmuth) *If $\mathcal{L}_1 \trianglelefteq \mathcal{L}_2$ and $\mathcal{L}_2$ is polynomially predictable, then $\mathcal{L}_1$ is polynomially predictable. Conversely, if $\mathcal{L}_1 \trianglelefteq \mathcal{L}_2$ and $\mathcal{L}_1$ is not polynomially predictable, then $\mathcal{L}_2$ is not polynomially predictable.*

Restrictions on Logic Programs

In this paper, logic programs will always be function-free and (unless otherwise indicated) nonrecursive. A background theory K will always be a set of ground unit clauses (aka relations, a set of atomic facts, or a model) with arity bounded by the constant a; the symbol a-$\mathcal{K}$ ($\mathcal{K}$ if a is an arbitrary constant) will denote the set of such background theories. The size complexity of a background theory K is its cardinality, and usually will be denoted by n_b. Examples will be represented by a single atom of arity n_e or less; thus we allow the

---

[2]In particular, it may be that a language is hard to learn even though an accurate hypothesis can be found, if it is hard to encode this hypothesis in the language $\mathcal{L}$.

[3]Such learning algorithms are also sometimes called *approximation algorithms*, as in the general case an approximation to the target concept may be produced.

[4]We assume that the reader is familiar with the basic elements of logic programming; see Lloyd [1987] for the necessary background.

head of a Horn clause to have a large arity, although literals in the body have constant arity.[5]

Muggleton and Feng [1992] have introduced several additional useful restrictions on Horn clauses. If $A \leftarrow B_1 \wedge \ldots \wedge B_r$ is an (ordered) Horn clause, then the *input variables* of the literal B_i are those variables appearing in B_i which also appear in the clause $A \leftarrow B_1 \wedge \ldots \wedge B_{i-1}$; all other variables appearing in B_i are called *output variables*. A literal B_i is *determinate* (with respect to K and X) if for every possible substitution σ that unifies A with some $e \in X$ such that $K \vdash (B_1 \wedge \ldots \wedge B_{i-1})\sigma$ there is at most one substitution θ so that $K \vdash B_i \sigma \theta$. Less formally, a literal is determinate if its output variables have only one possible binding, given K and the binding of the input variables. A clause is determinate if all of its literals are determinate.

Next, define the *depth* of a variable appearing in a clause $A \leftarrow B_1 \wedge \ldots \wedge B_r$ as follows. Variables appearing in the head of a clause have depth zero. Otherwise, let B_i be the first literal containing the variable V, and let d be the maximal depth of the input variables of B_i; then the depth of V is $d+1$. The depth of a clause is the maximal depth of any variable in the clause.

A determinate clause of depth bounded by a constant i over a background theory $K \in j\text{-}\mathcal{K}$ is called *ij-determinate*. The learning program GOLEM, which has been applied to a number of practical problems [Muggleton and Feng, 1992; Muggleton, 1992b], learns *ij*-determinate programs. Closely related restrictions also have been adopted by several other inductive logic programming systems, including FOIL [Quinlan, 1991], LINUS [Lavrač and Džeroski, 1992], and GRENDEL [Cohen, 1993c].

As an example, in the determinate clause

multiply(X,Y,Z) ←
    decrement(Y,W) ∧
    multiply(X,W,V) ∧
    plus(X,V,Z).

W has depth one and V has depth two; thus the clause is 23-determinate.

Learning log-depth determinate clauses

We will first consider generalizing the definition of *ij*-determinacy by relaxing the restriction that clauses have constant depth. The key result of this section is an observation about the expressive power of determinate clauses: *there is a background theory K such that every depth d boolean circuit can be emulated by a*

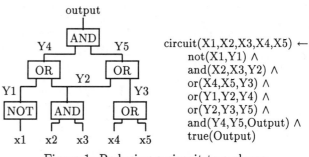

circuit(X1,X2,X3,X4,X5) ←
    not(X1,Y1) ∧
    and(X2,X3,Y2) ∧
    or(X4,X5,Y3) ∧
    or(Y1,Y2,Y4) ∧
    or(Y2,Y3,Y5) ∧
    and(Y4,Y5,Output) ∧
    true(Output)

Figure 1: Reducing a circuit to a clause

depth d determinate clause over K. The background theory K contains these facts:

and(0,0,0)	*and(0,1,0)*	*and(1,0,0)*	*and(1,1,1)*
or(0,0,0)	*or(0,1,1)*	*or(1,0,0)*	*or(1,1,1)*
not(0,1)	*not(1,0)*	*true(1)*	

The emulation is the obvious one, illustrated by example in Figure 1. Notice an example from the circuit domain is a binary vector $b_1 \ldots b_n$ encoding an assignment to the n boolean inputs to the circuit, and hence must be preprocessed to the atom $circuit(b_1, \ldots, b_n)$.

The learnability of circuits has been well-studied. In particular, the language of log-depth circuits (also familiar as the complexity class NC^1) is known to be hard to learn, under cryptographic assumptions [Kearns and Valiant, 1989]. Thus we have the following theorem; here $\mathcal{C}_{ij\text{-}DET}$ denotes the language of logic programs containing a single non-recursive *ij*-determinate clause.

Theorem 2 *There is a small background theory $K \in 3\text{-}\mathcal{K}$ such that $NC^1 \trianglelefteq \mathcal{C}_{(\log n_e)3\text{-}DET}[K]$. Thus, for $j \geq 3$, the family of languages $\mathcal{C}_{(\log n_e)j\text{-}DET}[j\text{-}\mathcal{K}]$ is not polynomially predictable, and hence not pac-learnable, under cryptographic assumptions.*

It has recently been shown that NC^1 is not predictable even against the uniform distribution [Kharitonov, 1992], suggesting that distributional restrictions will not make log-depth determinate clauses predictable.

Learning indeterminate clauses

We will now consider relaxing the definition of *ij*-determinacy by allowing indeterminacy. Let the *free variables* of a Horn clause be those variables that appear in the body of the clause but not in the head; we will consider the learnability of the language $\mathcal{C}_{k\text{-}FREE}$, defined as all nonrecursive clauses with at most k free variables. Clauses in $\mathcal{C}_{k\text{-}FREE}$ are necessarily of depth at most k; also restricting the number of free variables is required to ensure that clauses can be evaluated in polynomial time.

Notice that $\mathcal{C}_{1\text{-}FREE}$ is the *most restricted language possible* that contains indeterminate clauses. We begin with an observation about the expressive power of

---

[5]It should be noted that the parameters n_e, n_b, and n_t (the complexity of the target concept) all measure different aspects of the complexity of a learning problem; as the requirement on the learner is that it is polynomial in all of these parameters, the reader can simply view them as different names for a single complexity parameter $n = \max(n_e, n_b, n_t)$.

Background theory:
for $i = 1, \ldots, k$
    $true_i(b, y)$ for all $b, y : b = 1$ or $y \in 1, \ldots, r$ but $y \neq i$
    $false_i(b, y)$ for all $b, y : b = 0$ or $y \in 1, \ldots, r$ but $y \neq i$

DNF formula: $(v_1 \wedge \overline{v_3} \wedge v_4) \vee (\overline{v_2} \wedge \overline{v_3}) \vee (v_1 \wedge \overline{v_4})$

Equivalent clause:
dnf(X_1,X_2,X_3,X_4) ←
    $true_1(X_1,Y) \wedge false_1(X_3,Y) \wedge true_1(X_4,Y) \wedge$
    $false_2(X_2,Y) \wedge false_2(X_3,Y) \wedge$
    $true_3(X_1,Y) \wedge false_3(X_4,Y).$

Figure 2: Reducing a DNF formula to a clause

---

this language: *for every r, there is a background theory K_r such that every DNF formula with r or fewer terms can be emulated by a clause in $\mathcal{C}_{1\text{-FREE}}[K_r]$.* The emulation is a bit more indirect than the emulation for circuits, but the intuition is simple: it is based on the observation that a clause $p(X) \leftarrow q(X, Y)$ classifies an example $p(a)$ as true exactly when $K \vdash q(a, b_1) \vee \ldots \vee K \vdash q(a, b_r)$, where $b_1, \ldots, b_r$ are the possible bindings of the (indeterminate) variable Y; thus indeterminate variables allow some "disjunctive" concepts to be expressed by a single clause.

Specifically, K_r will contain sufficient atomic facts to define the binary predicates $true_1, false_1, \ldots, true_r, false_r$ which behave as follows:

- $true_i(X, Y)$ succeeds if $X = 1$,
  or if $Y \in \{1, \ldots, i-1, i+1, \ldots, r\}$.

- $false_i(X, Y)$ succeeds if $X = 0$,
  or if $Y \in \{1, \ldots, i-1, i+1, \ldots, r\}$.

The way in which a formula is emulated is illustrated in Figure 2. The free variable in the emulating clause is Y, and the r possible bindings of Y correspond to the r terms of the emulated DNF formula. Assume without loss of generality that the DNF has exactly r terms[6] and let the i-th term of the DNF be $T_i = \bigwedge_{j=1}^{s_i} l_{ij}$; this will be emulated by a conjunction of literals $C_i = \bigwedge_{j=1}^{s_i} Lit_{ij}$ designed so that C_i will succeed exactly when T_i succeeds and Y is bound to i, or when Y is bound to some constant other than i. This can be accomplished by defining

$$Lit_{ij} \equiv \begin{cases} true_i(X_k, Y) & \text{if } l_{ij} = v_k \\ false_i(X_k, Y) & \text{if } l_{ij} = \overline{v_k} \end{cases}$$

Now, assume that X_i is bound to the value of the i-th boolean variable v_i that is used in the DNF formula; then the conjunction $\bigwedge_{i=1}^{r} C_i$ will succeed when Y is bound to 1 and T_1 succeeds, or when Y is bound to 2 and T_2 succeeds, or ... or Y is bound to r and T_r succeeds. Hence, if we assume that each example $b_1 \ldots b_n$ is preprocessed to the atom $dnf(b_1, \ldots, b_n)$, the clause

---

[6]If necessary, null terms $v_1 \overline{v_1}$ can be added to make the DNF r terms long.

$dnf(X_1, \ldots, X_n) \leftarrow \bigwedge_{i=1}^{r} C_i$ (in which Y can be bound to any of the r values) will correctly emulate the original formula.

As a consequence, we have the following theorem:

Theorem 3 *Let DNF_n denote the language of DNF expressions of complexity n or less; for all n there is a polynomial sized background theory K_n such that $DNF_n \trianglelefteq \mathcal{C}_{1\text{-FREE}}[K_n]$. Thus, for all constant k, the family of languages $\mathcal{C}_{k\text{-FREE}}[\mathcal{K}]$ is predictable only if DNF_n is predictable.*

An important question is whether there are languages in $\mathcal{C}_{k\text{-FREE}}$ that are *harder* to learn than DNF. The answer to this questions is no: *for every k and every background theory $K \in a\text{-}\mathcal{K}$, every clause in $\mathcal{C}_{k\text{-FREE}}[K]$ can be emulated by a DNF formula.* Let $Cl = A \leftarrow B_{c_1} \wedge \ldots \wedge B_{c_l}$ be a clause in $\mathcal{C}_{k\text{-FREE}}[K]$. As we assume clauses are nonrecursive, Cl covers an example e iff

$$\exists \sigma : K \vdash (B_{c_1} \wedge \ldots \wedge B_{c_l})\sigma \theta_e \qquad (1)$$

where θ_e is the most general unifier of A and e. However, since the background theory K is of size n_b, and all predicates are of arity a or less, there are at most an_b constants in K, and hence only $(an_b)^k$ possible substitutions $\sigma_1, \ldots, \sigma_{(an_b)^k}$ to the k free variables. Also (as we assume clauses are function-free) if K defines l different predicates, there are at most $l \cdot (n_e + k)^a < n_b \cdot (n_e + k)^a$ possible literals $B_1, \ldots, B_{n_b \cdot (n_e+k)^a}$ that can appear in the body of a $\mathcal{C}_{k\text{-FREE}}$ clause.

So, let us introduce the boolean variables v_{ij} where i ranges from one to $n_b \cdot (n_e + k)^a$ and j ranges from one to $(an_b)^k$. We will preprocess an example e by constructing an assignment η_e to these variables: v_{ij} will be true in η_e if and only if $K \vdash B_i \sigma_j \theta_e$. This means that Equation 1 is true exactly when the DNF formula

$$\bigvee_{j=1}^{(an_b)^a} \bigwedge_{i=1}^{l} v_{c_i j}$$

is true; hence the clause Cl can be emulated by DNF over the v_{ij}'s.

We can thus strengthen Theorem 3 as follows:

Theorem 4 *The family of languages $\mathcal{C}_{k\text{-FREE}}$ is predictable if and only if DNF is predictable.*

This does not actually settle the question of whether indeterminate clauses are predictable, but does show that answering the question will require substantial advances in computational learning theory; the learnability and predictability of DNF has been an open problem in computational learning theory for several years.

Learning recursive clauses

Finally, we will consider learning a single *recursive ij-determinate clause*. A realistic analysis of recursive clauses requires a slight extension of our formalism: rather than representing an example as a single atom of arity n_e, we will (in this section of the paper only) represent an example as a ground *goal atom*, e, plus a set of up to n_e ground *description atoms* $D = \{d_1, \ldots, d_{n_e}\}$ of arity bounded by a. A program P now classifies an example (e, D) as true iff $P \wedge K \wedge D \vdash e$. This also allows structured objects like lists to be used in examples; for example, an example of the predicate *member(X,Ys)* might be represented as the goal atom $e = member(b, list\_ab)$ together with the description

$D = \{$ head(list_ab,a), tail(list_ab,list_b),
head(list_b,b), tail(list_b,nil) $\}$

This formalism follows the actual use of learning systems like FOIL. Finally, in order to talk sensibly about one-clause recursive programs, we will also assume that the non-recursive "base case" of the target program is part of D or K.

Again, the key result of this section is an observation about expressive power: *there is a background theory K_n such that every log-space deterministic (DLOG) Turing machine M can be emulated, on inputs of size n or less, by a single recursive ij-determinate clause.* Since DLOG Turing machines are cryptographically hard to predict, this will lead to a negative predictability result for recursive clauses.

Before describing the emulation, we will begin with some basic facts about DLOG machines. First, we can assume, without loss of generality, that the tape alphabet is $\{0, 1\}$. Then a DLOG machine M accepting only inputs of size n can be encoded by a series of *transitions* of the following form:

if $x_i = b$ and CONFIG$=c_j$ **then** let CONFIG$:=c'_j$

where x_i denotes the value of the i-th square of the input tape, $b \in \{0, 1\}$, and c_j and c'_j are constants from a polynomial-sized alphabet $CON = \{c_1, \ldots, c_{p(n)}\}$ of constant symbols denoting *internal configurations* of M.[7] One can also assume without loss of generality that there is a unique starting configuration c_0, a unique accepting configuration c_{acc}, and a unique "failing" configuration c_{fail}, and that there is exactly one transition of the form given above for every combination of $i : 1 \leq i \leq n$, $b \in \{0, 1\}$, and $c_j \in CON - \{c_{acc}, c_{fail}\}$. On input $X = x_1 \ldots x_n$ the machine M starts with CONFIG$=c_0$, then executes transitions until it reaches CONFIG$=c_{acc}$ or CONFIG$=c_{fail}$, at which point X is accepted or rejected (respectively).

To emulate M, we will preprocess an example $S = b_1 \ldots b_n$ into the goal atom e and the description D defined below:

$$e \equiv tm(new_S, c_0)$$

[7]An internal configuration encodes the contents of M's worktape, along with all other properties of its internal state relevant to the computation. Since M's worktape is of length $\log n$ it can have only n different contents; thus there are only a polynomial number $p(n)$ of internal configurations for M.

$$D \equiv \{bit_i(new_S, b_i)\}_{i=1}^n \cup \{tm(new_S, c_{acc})\}$$

Now we will define the following predicates for the background theory K_n. First, for every possible $b \in \{0, 1\}$ and $j : 1 \leq j \leq p(n)$, the predicate $stat_{b,j}(B, C, Y)$ will be defined so that given bindings for variables B and C, $stat_{b,j}(B, C, Y)$ will fail if $C = c_{fail}$; otherwise it will succeed, binding Y to *active* if $B = b$ and $C = c_j$ and binding Y to *inactive* otherwise. Second, for $j : 1 \leq j \leq p(n)$, the predicate $next_j(Y, C)$ will be true if $Y = active$ and $C = c_j$, or if $Y = inactive$ and $C = c_{acc}$. It is easy to show that these definitions require only polynomially many facts to be in K_n.

$$TRANS_{ibj} \equiv bit_i(S, B_{ibj}) \wedge stat_{b,j}(C, B_{ibj}, Y_{ibj}) \wedge$$
$$next_{j'}(Y_{ibj}, C1_{ibj}) \wedge tm(S, C1_{ibj})$$

Given K_n and D, and assuming that S is bound to new_S and C is bound to some configuration c, this conjunction will fail if $c = c_{fail}$; otherwise, it will succeed trivially if $x_i \neq b$ or $c \neq c_j$[8]; finally, if $x_i = b$ and $c = c_j$, $TRANS_{ibj}$ will succeed only if the atom $tm(new_S, c_{j'})$ is provable.[9] From this it is clear that the one-clause logic program

$$tm(S, C) \leftarrow \bigwedge_{\substack{i \in \{1, \ldots, n\}, \, b \in \{0,1\} \\ j \in \{1, \ldots, p(n)\}}} TRANS_{ibj}$$

will correctly emulate the machine M. Thus, letting $\mathcal{R}_{ij\text{-DET}}$ denote the language of one-clause *ij*-determinate recursive logic programs, and letting $DLOG_n$ represent the class of problems on inputs of size n computable in deterministic space $\log n$, we have the following theorem.

Theorem 5 *For all n there is a background theory K_n such that $DLOG_n \trianglelefteq \mathcal{R}_{33\text{-DET}}[K_n]$. Thus the family of languages $\mathcal{R}_{ij\text{-DET}}[\mathcal{K}]$ is not polynomially predictable, and hence not pac-learnable, under cryptographic assumptions.*

Although this result is negative, it should be noted that (unlike the case in the previous theorems) the preprocessing step used here distorts the distribution of examples: thus this result does not preclude the possibility of distribution-specific learning algorithms for recursive clauses.

Concluding remarks

This paper presented three negative results on learning one-clause logic programs. These negative results are stronger than earlier results [Kietz, 1993] in a number of ways; most importantly, they are not based on restricting the learner to produce hypotheses in some

[8]In this case Y_{ibj} will be bound to *inactive* and $C1_{ibj}$ will be bound to c_{acc}—the recursive call to $tm/2$ succeeds because $tm(new_S, c_{acc}) \in D$.

[9]In this case, Y_{ibj} will be bound to *active* and $C1_{ibj}$ will be bound to $c_{j'}$.

designated language. Instead, they are obtained by showing that learning is as hard as breaking a secure cryptographic system.

In particular, we have shown that several extensions to the language of constant-depth determinate clauses lead to hard learning problems. First, allowing depth to grow as the log of the problem size makes learning a single determinate clause as hard as learning a log-depth circuit, which is hard under cryptographic assumptions; this shows that all learning algorithms for determinate clauses will require time worse than exponential in the depth of the target concept. Second, indeterminate clauses with k "free" variables (a restriction of the language of constant-depth indeterminate clauses) are exactly as hard to learn as DNF; the learnability of DNF is a long-standing open problem in computational learning theory.

Finally, adding recursion to the language of ij-determinate clauses makes them as hard to learn as a log-space Turing machine; again, this learning problem is cryptographically hard. There are however, learnable classes of one-clause linearly recursive clauses; a discussion of this is given in a companion paper [Cohen, 1993b].

Acknowledgements

Thanks to Mike Kearns and Rob Schapire for several helpful discussions, and to Susan Cohen for proofreading the paper.

References

(Cohen and Hirsh, 1992) William W. Cohen and Haym Hirsh. Learnability of description logics. In *Proceedings of the Fourth Annual Workshop on Computational Learning Theory*, Pittsburgh, Pennsylvania, 1992. ACM Press.

(Cohen, 1992) William W. Cohen. Compiling knowledge into an explicit bias. In *Proceedings of the Ninth International Conference on Machine Learning*, Aberdeen, Scotland, 1992. Morgan Kaufmann.

(Cohen, 1993a) William W. Cohen. Learnability of restricted logic programs. In *Proceedings of the Third International Workshop on Inductive Logic Programming*, Bled, Slovenia, 1993.

(Cohen, 1993b) William W. Cohen. A pac-learning algorithm for a restricted class of recursive logic programs. In *Proceedings of the Tenth National Conference on Artificial Intelligence*, Washington, D.C., 1993.

(Cohen, 1993c) William W. Cohen. Rapid prototyping of ILP systems using explicit bias. In preparation, 1993.

(Džeroski *et al.*, 1992) Savso Džeroski, Stephen Muggleton, and Stuart Russell. Pac-learnability of determinate logic programs. In *Proceedings of the 1992 Workshop on Computational Learning Theory*, Pittsburgh, Pennsylvania, 1992.

(Kearns and Valiant, 1989) Micheal Kearns and Les Valiant. Cryptographic limitations on learning Boolean formulae and finite automata. In *21th Annual Symposium on the Theory of Computing*. ACM Press, 1989.

(Kharitonov, 1992) Michael Kharitonov. Cryptographic lower bounds on the learnability of boolean functions on the uniform distribution. In *Proceedings of the Fourth Annual Workshop on Computational Learning Theory*, Pittsburgh, Pennsylvania, 1992. ACM Press.

(Kietz, 1993) Jorg-Uwe Kietz. Some computational lower bounds for the computational complexity of inductive logic programming. In *Proceedings of the 1993 European Conference on Machine Learning*, Vienna, Austria, 1993.

(Lavrač and Džeroski, 1992) Nada Lavrač and Sašo Džeroski. Background knowledge and declarative bias in inductive concept learning. In K. P. Jantke, editor, *Analogical and Inductive Inference: International Workshop AII'92*. Springer Verlag, Daghstuhl Castle, Germany, 1992. Lecture in Artificial Intelligence Series #642.

(Lloyd, 1987) J. W. Lloyd. *Foundations of Logic Programming: Second Edition*. Springer-Verlag, 1987.

(Muggleton and Feng, 1992) Steven Muggleton and Cao Feng. Efficient induction of logic programs. In *Inductive Logic Programming*. Academic Press, 1992.

(Muggleton, 1992a) S. H. Muggleton, editor. *Inductive Logic Programming*. Academic Press, 1992.

(Muggleton, 1992b) Steven Muggleton. Inductive logic programming. In *Inductive Logic Programming*. Academic Press, 1992.

(Pitt and Warmuth, 1990) Leonard Pitt and Manfred Warmuth. Prediction-preserving reducibility. *Journal of Computer and System Sciences*, 41:430–467, 1990.

(Quinlan, 1990) J. Ross Quinlan. Learning logical definitions from relations. *Machine Learning*, 5(3), 1990.

(Quinlan, 1991) J. Ross Quinlan. Determinate literals in inductive logic programming. In *Proceedings of the Eighth International Workshop on Machine Learning*, Ithaca, New York, 1991. Morgan Kaufmann.

(Valiant, 1984) L. G. Valiant. A theory of the learnable. *Communications of the ACM*, 27(11), November 1984.

Pac-Learning a Restricted Class
of Recursive Logic Programs

William W. Cohen

AT&T Bell Laboratories

600 Mountain Avenue Murray Hill, NJ 07974

wcohen@research.att.com

Abstract

A crucial problem in "inductive logic programming" is learning recursive logic programs from examples alone; current systems such as GOLEM and FOIL often achieve success only for carefully selected sets of examples. We describe a program called FORCE2 that uses the new technique of "forced simulation" to learn two-clause "closed" linear recursive ij-determinate programs; although this class of programs is fairly restricted, it does include most of the standard benchmark problems. Experimentally, FORCE2 requires fewer examples than FOIL, and is more accurate when learning from randomly chosen datasets. Formally, FORCE2 is also shown to be a pac-learning algorithm in a variant of Valiant's [1984] model, in which we assume the ability to make two types of queries: one which gives an upper bound on the depth of the proof for an example, and one which determines if an example can be proved in unit depth.

Introduction

An increasingly active area of research in machine learning is *inductive logic programming (ILP)*. ILP systems, like conventional concept learning systems, typically learn classification knowledge from a set of randomly chosen examples; however, ILP systems use *logic programs*—typically some subset of function-free Prolog—to represent this learned knowledge. This representation can be much more expressive than representations (such as decision trees) that are based on propositional logic; for example, Quinlan [1990] has shown that FOIL can learn the transitive closure of a directed acyclic graph, a concept that cannot be expressed in propositional logic.

A crucial problem in ILP is that of learning *recursive* logic programs from examples alone. Early work in ILP describes a number of systems that learn recursive programs, and some of them have convergence proofs [Shapiro, 1982; Banerji, 1988; Muggleton and Buntine, 1988]; however, these systems rely on fairly powerful queries (e.g. membership and subset queries) to achieve these results. More recent systems, such as FOIL [Quinlan, 1990] and GOLEM [Muggleton

and Feng, 1992] have been experimentally successful in learning recursive programs from examples alone. While the results obtained with these systems are impressive, they are limited in two ways.

Non-random samples. In most published experiments in which recursive concepts are learned, the samples used in learning are not randomly selected examples of the target concept; instead, the samples are carefully constructed. For example, in using FOIL to learn the recursive concept *member*, Quinlan gives as examples all membership relations over the list $[a, b, [c]]$ and its substructures; providing examples for all substructures makes it relatively easy for FOIL's information gain metric to estimate the usefulness of a recursive call. It is unclear to what extent recursive programs can be learned from a random, unprepared sample.

Lack of formal justification. Although parts of the GOLEM algorithm have been carefully analyzed, both FOIL and GOLEM make use of a number of heuristics, which makes them quite difficult to analyze. Ideally, one would like rigorous formal justification for an algorithm for learning recursive concepts, as well as experimental results on problems of practical interest.[1]

In this paper, we will describe a new algorithm called FORCE2 for learning a restricted class of recursive logic programs: namely, the class of two-clause "closed" linear recursive ij-determinate programs. This class is fairly restricted, but does include many of the standard benchmark problems, including list reversal, list append, and integer multiply. FORCE2 uses a new technique called *forced simulation* to choose the recursive call in the learned program. Formally, FORCE2 will be shown to be a *pac-learning* algorithm for this class; hence it learns against any distribution of examples in polytime, and does not require a hand-prepared sample. Experimentally, FORCE2 requires fewer examples than FOIL, has much less difficulty with samples that have not been prepared, and

---

[1] Recently, the pac-learnability of the class of programs learned by GOLEM has been studied; however, for recursive programs the analysis assumed membership and subset queries [Džeroski *et al.*, 1992].

is fast enough to be practical.

Although FORCE2 makes no queries *per se*, it does require a certain amount of extra information. In particular, FORCE2 must be given both a characterization of the "depth complexity" of the program to be learned, and also a procedure for determining when an instance is an example of the base case of the recursion. For example, to learn the textbook definition of *append*, one might supply the following

MAXDEPTH(append(Xs,Ys,Zs)) ≡
   length(Xs)+1.
BASECASE(append(Xs,Ys,Zs)) ≡
   if null(Xs) then **true** else **false**

The user need give only an upper bound on the depth complexity, not a precise bound, and need give only sufficient (not necessary and sufficient) conditions for membership in the base case. Later we will discuss, from both a formal and practical viewpoint, the degree to which this extra information is needed; there are circumstances under which both the depth bound and the base-case characterization can be dispensed with. First, however, we will describe the class of logic programs that FORCE2 learns, and present the FORCE2 algorithm and its accompanying analysis.

The class of learnable programs

In a typical ILP system, the user will provide both a set of examples and a *background theory* K: the learning system must then find a logic program P such that $P \wedge K \vdash e^+$ for every positive example e^+, and $P \wedge K \nvdash e^-$ for every negative example e^-. As a concrete example, if the target concept is a function-free version of the usual definition of *append*, the user might provide a background theory K defining the predicate *null(A)* to be true when A is the empty list, and defining the predicate *components(A,B,C)* to be true when A is a list with head B and tail C. The learned program P can then use these predicates: for example, P might be the program

append(Xs,Ys,Ys) ←
   null(Xs).
append(Xs,Ys,Zs) ←
   components(Xs,X,Xs1),
   components(Zs,X,Zs1),
   append(Xs1,Ys,Zs1).

FORCE2, like both GOLEM and FOIL, requires the background theory K to be a set of ground unit clauses (aka relations, a set of atomic facts, or a model.) Like FOIL, our implementation of FORCE2 also assumes that the program to be learned contains no function symbols; however this restriction is not necessary for our formal results.

The actual programs learned by the FORCE2 procedure must satisfy four additional restrictions. First, a learned program must contain *exactly two clauses:* one recursive clause, and one clause representing the base

case for the recursion. Second, the recursive clause must be *linearly recursive:* that is, the body of the clause must contain only a single "recursive literal", where a recursive literal is one with the same principle functor as the head of the clause. Third, the recursive literal must be *closed*: a literal is closed if it has no "output variables".[2] Finally, the program must contain no function symbols, and must be *ij-determinate*. The condition of *ij*-determinacy was first used in the GOLEM system, and variations of it have subsequently been adopted by FOIL [Quinlan, 1991], LINUS [Lavrač and Džeroski, 1992], and GRENDEL [Cohen, 1993b]. It is defined in detail by Muggleton and Feng [1992].[3]

The FORCE2 learning algorithm

The FORCE2 algorithm is summarized in Figure 1. The algorithm has two explicit inputs: a set of positive examples S^+, and a set of negative examples S^-. There are also some additional inputs that (for readability) we have made implicit: the user also provides a function MAXDEPTH(e) that returns an upper bound on the depth complexity of the target program, a function BASECASE(e) that returns "true" whenever e is an example of the base clause, a background theory K (defining only predicates of arity j or less), and a depth bound i. The output of FORCE2 is a two-clause linear and closed recursive *ij*-determinate logic program.

The FORCE2 algorithm takes advantage of an important property of *ij*-determinate clauses: for such clauses, the *relative least general generalization*[4] (rlgg) of a set of examples is of size polynomial in the number of predicates defined in K, is unique, and can be tractably computed. FORCE2 actually uses two rlgg operators: one that finds the least general clause that covers a set of examples, and one that takes an initial clause C_0 and a single example e and returns the least general clause $C_1 \supseteq C_0$ that covers e.

The first step of the algorithm is to use the BASE-CASE function to split the positive examples into two

---

[2]If B_i is a literal of the (ordered) Horn clause $A \leftarrow B_1, \ldots, B_l$, then the *input variables* of the literal B_i are those variables appearing in B_i that also appear in the clause $A \leftarrow B_1, \ldots, B_{i-1}$; all other variables appearing in B_i are called *output variables*.

[3]Briefly, a literal B_i is *determinate* if its output variables have at most one possible binding, given the binding of the input variables. If a variable V appears in the head of a clause, then the depth of V is zero, and otherwise, if B_i is the first literal containing the variable V and d is the maximal depth of the input variables of B_i, the depth of V is $d + 1$. Finally, a clause is *ij-determinate* if its body contains only literals of arity j or less, if all literals in the body are determinate, and if the clause contains only variables of depth less than or equal to i. Muggleton and Feng argue that many common recursive logic programs are *ij*-determinate for small i and j.

[4]The rlgg of a set of examples S (with respect a background theory K) is the least general clause C such that $\forall e \in S, C \wedge K \vdash e$.

```
program FORCE2($S^+, S^-$)                          subroutine force-sim($e, C_{base}, C_{rec}, L_r$)
  $C_{base}$ := rlgg($\{e \in S^+ : BASECASE(e)\}$)     if BASECASE($e$) then
  $C_{rec}$ := rlgg($\{e \in S^+ : \neg BASECASE(e)\}$)    $C_{base}$ := rlgg($C_{base}, e$)
  for each recursive literal $L_r$ over variables($C_{rec}$) do   else
    for each $e^+ \in S^+$ do                            $C_{rec}$ := rlgg($C_{rec}, e$)
      force-sim($e^+, C_{base}, C_{rec}, L_r$)           if any variable in $L_r$ is not in the new $C_{rec}$ or
      $P$ := the logic program containing the             force-sim has recursed more than MAXDEPTH($e_0$)
        clauses $C_{base}$ and $A \leftarrow B_1, \ldots, B_l, L_r$,     times, where $e_0$ is the example $e$ used in the
        where $C_{rec} = A \leftarrow B_1, \ldots, B_l$    top-level call of force-sim
      if an error was signaled in force-sim then       then
          reset $C_{base}$ and $C_{rec}$ to their original values    signal an error and exit
          break from inner "for" loop and try the next $L_r$   else
      endif                                              $A$ := the head of $C_{rec}$
    endfor                                               $B_1, \ldots, B_l$ := the body of $C_{rec}$
    if $P$ consistent with $S^-$ then return $P$         $e'$ := $L_r\theta$, where $\theta$ is such that $A\theta = e$
  endfor                                                   and $K \vdash B_1\theta, \ldots, B_l\theta$
  return "no consistent program"                         force-sim($e', K, C_{base}, C_{rec}, L_r$)
end                                                    endif
                                                     endif
                                                   end
```

Figure 1: The FORCE2 algorithm

---

sets: the examples of the base clause, and the examples of the recursive clause. The rlggs C_{base} and C_{rec} of these two sets of examples are then computed; informally, these rlggs will be used as initial guesses at the base clause and the recursive clause respectively. (More accurately, C_{rec} is a guess at the *non-recursive portion* of the recursive clause being learned.) As an example, we used FORCE2 to learn the *append* program (given as an example on page 2) from a small set of examples; the BASECASE and MAXDEPTH functions were as given on page 2. The rlgg of the three positive examples of the base case was the following:[5]

C_{base}: append(A,B,C) ←
        components(B,D,E),
        null(A),
        B=C.

The rlgg of the non-base case positive examples was the following:

C_{rec}: append(A,B,C) ←
        components(A,D,E),
        components(C,F,G),
        D=F.

Notice that C_{base} is over-specific, since it requires B to be a non-empty list, and also that C_{rec} does *not*

---

[5]As the examples show, our algorithm for constructing lgg's is a bit nonstandard. A distinct variable is placed in every position that could contain an output variable, and equalities are then expressed by explicitly adding equality literals (like $A=C$ and $D=F$ in the examples above.) This encoding for an lgg is not the most compact one; however it is only polynomially larger than necessary, and simplifies the implementation. With the usual encoding the enumeration of recursive literals must be interleaved with the force-sim routine.

---

contain a recursive call. The remaining steps of the algorithm are designed to find an appropriate recursive call.

From the way in which C_{base} and C_{rec} were constructed, one might suspect that adding a recursive literal L_r to C_{rec} would yield the least general program (in our class) that uses that recursive call and is consistent with the positive data; however, this is false. Consider adding the (correct) recursive call $L_r = append(E, B, G)$ to C_{rec}, to yield the program

append(A,B,C) ←
    components(B,D,E),
    null(A),
    B=C.
append(A,B,C) ←
    components(A,D,E),
    components(C,F,G),
    D=F,
    append(E,B,G).

Now consider the non-basecase positive example $e = append([2],[],[2])$. Example e is covered by C_{rec}, but not by the program above; the problem is that the subgoal $e' = append([],[],[])$ is not covered by the base clause.

The subroutine *force-sim* handles this problem. Conceptually, it will simulate the hypothesized logic program on e, except that when the logic program would fail on e or any subgoal of e, the rlgg operator is used to generalize the program so that it will succeed. The effect is to construct the least general program with the recursive call L_r that covers e.

We will illustrate this crucial subroutine by example. Suppose FORCE2 has chosen the (correct) recursive literal $L_r = append(E, B, G)$, using the C_{base}

and C_{rec} given above, and consider forcibly simulating the positive example $append([1,2],[],[1,2])$. The subroutine *force-sim* determines that e is not a BASECASE; thus it will generalize C_{rec} to cover e by replacing C_{rec} with the rlgg of C_{rec} and e; in this case C_{rec} is unchanged. The next step is to continue the simulation by determining what subgoal would be generated by the proposed recursive call; in this case, the recursive call $append(E,B,F)$ would generate the subgoal $e' = append([2],[],[2])$. The subroutine *force-sim* is then called on e', and determines that it is not a BASECASE; again, replacing C_{rec} with its rlgg against e' leaves C_{rec} unchanged. Finally, the routine again computes the recursive subgoal $e'' = append([],[],[])$, and recursively calls *force-sim* on e''. It determines that e'' is a BASECASE, and generalizes C_{base} to cover it, again using the rlgg operator. The final result is that C_{rec} is unchanged, and that C_{base} has been generalized to

append(A,B,C) ← null(A),B=C.

This is the least generalization of the initial program (in the class of closed linear recursive two-clause programs) that covers the example $append([1,2],[],[1,2])$.

For an incorrect choice of L_r, forced simulation may fail: for example, if FORCE2 were testing the incorrect recursive literal $L_r = append(A,A,C)$, then given the example $append([1,2],[],[1,2])$ *force-sim* would loop, repeatedly generating the same subgoal $e' = e'' = e''' \ldots$. This loop would be detected when the depth bound was violated, and an error would be signaled, indicating that no valid generalization of the program covers the example. For incorrect but non-looping recursive literals, forced simulation may lead to an overgeneral hypothesis: for example, given the incorrect recursive literal $L_r = append(B,A,E)$ and the example $append([1,2],[],[1,2])$ *force-sim* would subgoal to $e' = append([],[1,2],[2])$, and generalize C_{base} to the clause $append(A,B,C) ← null(A)$. With sufficient negative examples, this overgenerality would be detected.

The remainder of the algorithm is straightforward. The inner **for** loop of the FORCE2 algorithm uses repeated forced simulations to find a least general hypothesis that covers all the positive examples, given a particular choice for a recursive literal L_r; if this least general hypothesis exists and is consistent with the negative examples, it will be returned as the hypothesis of the learner. The outer **for** loop exhaustively tests all of the possible recursive literals; it is not hard to see that for a fixed maximal arity j there are polynomially many possible L_r's.[6]

---

[6]Since C_{rec} is of polynomial size, it contains polynomially many variables. Let $p(n)$ be the number of variables in C_{rec} and t be the arity of the target predicate; there are at most $p(n)^t \leq p(n)^j$ recursive literals.

Formal results

Formalizing the preceding discussion leads to the following theorem.

Theorem 1 *If the training data is labeled according to some two-clause linear and closed recursive ij-determinate logic program, then FORCE2 will output a least general hypothesis consistent with the training data. Furthermore, assuming that that MAXDEPTH and BASECASE can be computed in polynomial time, for any fixed i and j, FORCE2 runs in time polynomial in the number of predicates defined in K, the number of training examples, and the largest value of MAXDEPTH for any training example.*

It is known that ij-determinate clauses are of size polynomial in the number of background predicates; this implies that the VC-dimension [Blumer *et al.*, 1986] of the class of 2-clause ij-determinate programs over a background theory K is polynomial in the size of K. Thus an immediate consequence of the preceding theorem is the following:

Corollary 1 *For any background theory K, FORCE2 is a pac-learning algorithm [Valiant, 1984] for the concept class of two-clause linear and closed recursive ij-determinate logic programs over K.*

To our knowledge, this is the first result showing the polynomial learnability of any class of recursive programs in a learning model disallowing queries.

It might be argued that the MAXDEPTH and BASECASE functions act as "pseudo-queries", and hence that our learning model is not truly passive. It should be noted, however, that the MAXDEPTH bound is not needed for the formal results, as the constant depth bound of $(j|K|)^j$ is sufficient to detect looping. (In practice, however, learning is much faster with an appropriate depth bound.) The BASECASE function is harder to dispense with, but even here a positive formal result is obtainable. If one assumes that the base clause is part of K, it is reasonable to consider the learnability of the class of *one-clause* linear and closed recursive ij-determinate logic programs over K. It can be shown that this class is pac-learnable, using a slightly modified version of FORCE2 that never changes the base clause.

This pac-learnability result can also be strengthened in a number of technical ways. A variant of the FORCE2 algorithm can be shown to achieve exact identification from equivalence queries; this learning criterion is strictly stronger than pac-learnability [Blum, 1990]. Another extension is suggested by the fact that FORCE2 returns a program that is maximally specific, given a particular choice of recursive call. Instead of returning a single program, one could enumerate all (polynomially many) consistent least programs; this could be used to tractably encode the version space of all consistent programs using the $[S, N]$ representation for version spaces [Hirsh, 1992].

%full	FOIL error	FORCE2 error	FORCE2 (cpu)	%full	FOIL error	FORCE2 error	FORCE2 (cpu)
2	6.10%	2.60%	(20)	40	1.70%	0.00%	(121)
5	5.10%	1.10%	(21)	60	0.84%	0.00%	(167)
10	4.80%	0.73%	(33)	80	0.19%	0.00%	(216)
20	3.00%	0.14%	(63)	100	0.00%	0.00%	(294)

Table 1: FORCE2 *vs.* FOIL on subsets of a good sample of *multiply*

Problem	"natural" samples FOIL	"natural" samples FORCE2	comment	variant distributions FOIL	variant distributions FORCE2	Straw1	Straw2
append	1.7%	0.0%	near miss	27.7%	0.0%	27.3%	40.3%
heapsort	3.7%	0.0%	near miss	7.5%	0.0%	19.7%	0.0%
member	13.4%	0.0%	length< 10	15.1%	0.0%	41.1%	0.0%
reverse1	5.4%	0.0%	near miss	13.9%	0.0%	8.4%	8.0%

Table 2: FORCE2 *vs.* FOIL on random samples

Experimental results

To further evaluate FORCE2, the algorithm was implemented and compared to FOIL4, the most recent implementation of FOIL. The first experiment we performed used the *multiply* problem, which is included with Quinlan's distribution FOIL4.[7] We presented progressively larger random subsets of the full dataset to FOIL and FORCE2 and estimated their error rates using the usual crossvalidation techniques. The results, shown in Table 1, show that FORCE2 generalizes more quickly than FOIL. For this dataset, guessing the most prevalent class gives about a 4.5% error rate; thus FOIL's performance for datasets less than 20% complete is actually quite poor.

CPU times[8] are also given for FORCE2, showing that FORCE2's run time scales linearly with the number of examples. No systematic time comparison with FOIL4 was attempted, as FORCE2 is implemented in Prolog, and FOIL4 in C. However we noted that even though FORCE2 is about 30 times slower than FOIL4 on the full hand-prepared dataset (294 seconds to 9 seconds) their speeds are were comparable on random subsamples of *multiply*: overall, FORCE2 averaged 91.6 seconds a run, and FOIL4 averaged 88.6 seconds a run. Run times for FORCE2 on other benchmarks (reported below) were also comparable: FORCE2 averaged 7 seconds for problems in Table 2 to FOIL4's 10.9 seconds.

Table 2 compares FORCE2 to FOIL on a number of other benchmarks, using training sets of 100 examples; the intent of this experiment was to evaluate performance on randomly-selected samples, and to determine how sensitive performance is to the distri-

bution. First we presented FOIL and FORCE2 with samples generated by what seemed to us the most natural random procedures.[9] These results are shown in the left-hand column. Next, we compared FORCE2 and FOIL on some harder variations of the "natural" distribution;[10] these results are shown in the right-hand column. FOIL's performance degraded noticeably on these distributions, but FORCE2's was unchanged.

There are (at least) two possible explanations for these results. First, FORCE2 has a more restricted bias for FOIL; thus the well-known generality-power tradeoff would predict that FORCE2 would outperform FOIL. Second, FORCE2 uses a more sophisticated method of choosing recursive literals than FOIL. FORCE2 evaluates a recursive literal by using forced simulation of the positive examples, followed by a consistency test against the negative examples. FOIL uses *information gain* (a heuristic metric based on cover-

---

[7]The distributed dataset contains 1056 examples: all positive examples of *mult(X,Y,Z)* where X and Y are both less than seven, and all negative examples *mult(X,Y,Z)* where X, Y, and Z appear as arguments to some positive example. All results are averaged over five trials.

[8]In seconds on a Sparc 1+.

[9]For *member*, a random list was generated by choosing a number L uniformly between one and four, then building a random list of length L over the atoms $a,\ldots,z$; positive examples were constructed by choosing a random element of the list, and negative examples by choosing a random non-element of the list. For *append*, positive examples were generated by choosing two lists at random (here allowing null lists) as the first two arguments, and negative examples by choosing three lists at random. Examples for *reverse1* and *heapsort* were generated a similar way; *reverse1* is a naive reverse program where the background theory defines a predicate that appends a single element to the tail of a list. Equal numbers of positive and negative examples were generated for all problems, and error rates were estimated using 1000 examples generated from the same distribution.

[10]On *member*, we increased the maximum length of a list from five to ten. On the remaining problems, we generated negative examples by taking a random positive example and randomly changing one element of the final argument; these "near miss" examples provide more information, but are harder to distinguish from the positive examples.

age of the positive and negative examples) to choose all literals, including recursive ones. Application of any coverage-based metric to recursive literals is not straightforward: in general one does not know if a recursive call to a predicate P will succeed or fail, because the full definition for P has not been learned. To circumvent this problem, FOIL uses the examples of P as an oracle for the predicate P: a subgoal of P is considered to succeed when there is a positive example that unifies with the subgoal.

A disadvantage of FOIL's method is that for random samples, the dataset can be a rather noisy oracle. In addition to making it harder to choose the right recursive literals, this means that FOIL's assessment of which examples are covered by a clause may be inaccurate, causing FOIL to learn redundant or inaccurate clauses.

To clarify the reasons for the difference in performance, we performed a final study in which we ran two "strawmen" learning algorithms on the harder distributions. *Straw1* outputs FORCE2's initial non-recursive hypothesis without adding any recursive literal; *Straw2* adds a single closed recursive literal chosen using the information gain metric.

Our study indicates that both explanations are partially correct. On the *member* and *heapsort* problems, the good performance of Straw2 indicates that information gain is sufficient to choose the correct recursive literal, and hence the primary reason for FORCE2's superiority is its more restrictive bias.[11] However, for *reverse1* and *append*, even the strongly-biased Straw2 does poorly, indicating that on these problems information gain is not effective at choosing an accurate recursive literal; for these problems, particularly *append*, FOIL's broader bias may actually be helpful.[12]

Concluding remarks

This paper has addressed the problem of learning recursive logic programs from examples alone against an arbitrary distribution. We presented FORCE2, a procedure that learns the restricted class of two-clause linear and closed recursive ij-determinate programs; this class includes many of the standard benchmark problems. Experimentally, FORCE2 requires fewer examples than FOIL, and is less sensitive to the distribution of examples.

More importantly, FORCE2 can be proved to pac-learn any program in this class. This result is surprising, as previous positive results have either considered only nonrecursive concepts (e.g. [Page and Frisch, 1992]) or have assumed the ability to make membership or subset queries (e.g. [Shapiro, 1982; Banerji, 1988; Džeroski *et al.*, 1992]). We make use of two additional sources of information, namely the BASECASE and MAXDEPTH functions; however only one of these (the BASECASE function) is necessary for our formal results. Also, as noted in the discussion following Theorem 1 a positive result can be obtained for a slightly more restricted language from labeled examples alone.

There are a number of possible extensions to the FORCE2 algorithm. Although the BASECASE function is formally necessary for pac-learning,[13] it is probably unnecessary in practice, given a distribution that provides a reasonable number of instances of the base case. Learners like GOLEM and FOIL can learn non-recursive clauses relatively easily; thus one might first learn the base case(s), and then use a slightly modified version of FORCE2 to learn the recursive clause.[14] Such a learner would be more useful, albeit harder to analyze.

It would also be highly desirable to extend the class of learnable programs. FORCE2 can be easily modified to learn 2-clause programs with k closed recursive calls: one simply enumerates all k-tuples of recursive literals $L_{r_1}, \ldots, L_{r_k}$, and modifies *force-sim* to subgoal from an example to the appropriate k subgoals $e'_1, \ldots, e'_k$. This learning algorithm generates a consistent clause, but can take time exponential in the depth bound given in MAXDEPTH and hence is suitable only for problems with a logarithmic depth bound.[15]

Although space does not permit a full explanation, it is also possible to extend FORCE2 to learn non-closed 2-clause recursive programs. (In brief, an initial recursive clause is found by computing an rlgg and guessing a recursive call L_{rec} as before, and then adding to the clause all additional ij-determinate literals that use the output variables of L_{rec} and that succeed for every non-BASECASE positive example. The forced simulation procedure is also replaced with a procedure that actually simulates the execution of the program P on each positive example e, generalizing P as necessary by deleting failing literals.)

On the other hand, several hardness results are known if the ij-determinacy condition is relaxed, or if

---

[11]Examining traces of FOIL4 on these problems also supports this view. For *member*, FOIL4 learned the correct program twice and non-recursive approximations with high error rates three times; due to the "noisy oracle problem" FOIL4 believes the correct program to have an error rate of more than 30%, so has no good reason for preferring it. On the *heapsort* problem FOIL4 typically learns several redundant clauses. Thus, for both problems, a bias toward two-clause recursive programs would be beneficial.

[12]Unlike Straw2, FOIL has the option of learning a non-recursive approximation of the target concept, rather than making a forced choice among recursive literals based on inadequate statistics.

[13]Without it, learning 2-clause ij-determinate programs is as hard as learning 2-term DNF, which is known to be intractable [Kearns *et al.*, 1987].

[14]The modification is to disallow changes to the base clause(s).

[15]This is unsurprising, since the time complexity of the learned program can be exponential in its depth complexity.

less limited recursion is allowed; for example, learning a 2-clause ij-determinate program with a polynomial number of recursive calls is cryptographically hard, even if the base case for the recursion is known [Cohen, 1993a]. In another recent paper [Cohen, 1993c] we also show that learning an ij-determinate program with a polynomial number of linear recursive clauses is cryptographically hard. However, the learnability of ij-determinate programs with a constant number of clauses, each with a constant number of recursive calls, remains open.

Acknowledgements

Thanks to Haym Hirsh for comments on a draft of this paper, and Susan Cohen for help in proofreading.

References

(Banerji, 1988) Ranan Banerji. Learning theories in a subset of polyadic logic. In *Proceedings of the 1988 Workshop on Computational Learning Theory*, Boston, Massachusetts, 1988.

(Blum, 1990) Avrim Blum. Separating PAC and mistake-bound learning models over the boolean domain. In *Proceedings of the Third Annual Workshop on Computational Learning Theory*, Rochester, New York, 1990. Morgan Kaufmann.

(Blumer *et al.*, 1986) Anselm Blumer, Andrezj Ehrenfeucht, David Haussler, and Manfred Warmuth. Classifying learnable concepts with the Vapnik-Chervonenkis dimension. In *18th Annual Symposium on the Theory of Computing*. ACM Press, 1986.

(Cohen, 1993a) William Cohen. Cryptographic limitations on learning one-clause logic programs. In *Proceedings of the Tenth National Conference on Artificial Intelligence*, Washington, D.C., 1993.

(Cohen, 1993b) William Cohen. Rapid prototyping of ILP systems using explicit bias. In preparation, 1993.

(Cohen, 1993c) William W. Cohen. Learnability of restricted logic programs. In *Proceedings of the Workshop on Inductive Logic Programming*, Bled, Slovenia, 1993.

(Džeroski *et al.*, 1992) Savso Džeroski, Stephen Muggleton, and Stuart Russell. Pac-learnability of determinate logic programs. In *Proceedings of the 1992 Workshop on Computational Learning Theory*, Pittsburgh, Pennsylvania, 1992.

(Hirsh, 1992) Haym Hirsh. Polynomial-time learning with version spaces. In *Proceedings of the Tenth National Conference on Artificial Intelligence*, San Jose, California, 1992. MIT Press.

(Kearns *et al.*, 1987) Micheal Kearns, Ming Li, Leonard Pitt, and Les Valiant. On the learnability of boolean formulae. In *19th Annual Symposium on the Theory of Computing*. ACM Press, 1987.

(Lavrač and Džeroski, 1992) Nada Lavrač and Sašo Džeroski. Background knowledge and declarative bias in inductive concept learning. In K. P. Jantke, editor, *Analogical and Inductive Inference: International Workshop AII'92*. Springer Verlag, Daghstuhl Castle, Germany, 1992. Lecture in Artificial Intelligence Series #642.

(Muggleton and Buntine, 1988) Steven Muggleton and Wray Buntine. Machine invention of first order predicates by inverting resolution. In *Proceedings of the Fifth International Conference on Machine Learning*, Ann Arbor, Michigan, 1988. Morgan Kaufmann.

(Muggleton and Feng, 1992) Steven Muggleton and Cao Feng. Efficient induction of logic programs. In *Inductive Logic Programming*. Academic Press, 1992.

(Page and Frisch, 1992) C. D. Page and A. M. Frisch. Generalization and learnability: A study of constrained atoms. In *Inductive Logic Programming*. Academic Press, 1992.

(Quinlan, 1990) J. Ross Quinlan. Learning logical definitions from relations. *Machine Learning*, 5(3), 1990.

(Quinlan, 1991) J. Ross Quinlan. Determinate literals in inductive logic programming. In *Proceedings of the Eighth International Workshop on Machine Learning*, Ithaca, New York, 1991. Morgan Kaufmann.

(Shapiro, 1982) Ehud Shapiro. *Algorithmic Program Debugging*. MIT Press, 1982.

(Valiant, 1984) L. G. Valiant. A theory of the learnable. *Communications of the ACM*, 27(11), November 1984.

Learnability in Inductive Logic Programming: Some Basic Results and Techniques

Michael Frazier* and C. David Page Jr.[†]
Department of Computer Science and Beckman Institute
University of Illinois
Urbana, IL 61801

Abstract

Inductive logic programming is a rapidly growing area of research that centers on the development of inductive learning algorithms for first-order definite clause theories. An obvious framework for inductive logic programming research is the study of the *pac-learnability* of various restricted classes of these theories. Of particular interest are theories that include *recursive* definite clauses. Because little work has been done within this framework, the need for initial results and techniques is great. This paper presents results about the pac-learnability of several classes of simple definite clause theories that are allowed to include a recursive clause. In so doing, the paper uses techniques that may be useful in studying the learnability of more complex classes.

1. Introduction

Inductive logic programming is a rapidly-growing area of research at the intersection of machine learning and logic programming [Muggleton, 1992]. It focuses on the design of algorithms that learn (first-order) definite clause theories from examples. A natural framework for research in inductive logic programming is the investigation of the learnability/predictability of various classes of definite clause theories, particularly in the models of *pac-learnability* [Valiant, 1984] and *learning by equivalence queries* [Angluin, 1988]. Surprisingly little work has been done within this framework, though interest is rising sharply [Džeroski et al., 1992; Cohen and Hirsh, 1992; Ling, 1992; Muggleton, 1992; Page and Frisch, 1992; Arimura et al., 1992].

This paper describes new results on the learnability of several restricted classes of simple (two-clause) definite clause theories that may contain *recursive* clauses; theories with recursive clauses appear to be the most difficult to learn. The positive results are proven for

*mfrazier@cs.uiuc.edu. Supported in part by NSF Grant IRI-9014840, and by NASA Grant NAG 1-613.

[†]dpage@cs.uiuc.edu. Supported in part by NASA Grant NAG 1-613.

learning by equivalence queries, which implies pac-learnability [Angluin, 1988]. In obtaining the results, we introduce techniques that may be useful in studying the learnability of other classes of definite clause theories with recursion.

The results are presented with the following organization. Section 2 describes the learning model. Section 3 shows that the class $\mathcal{H}_1$, whose concepts are built from unary predicates, constants, variables, and unary functions, is learnable. Section 4 shows that the class $\mathcal{H}_*$, an extension of $\mathcal{H}_1$ that allows predicates of arbitrary arity, is not learnable under a reasonable complexity-theoretic assumption.[1] Nevertheless, Section 4 also shows that each subclass $\mathcal{H}_k$ of $\mathcal{H}_*$, in which predicates are restricted to arity k, is learnable *in terms of* a slightly more general class, and is therefore *pac-predictable*. The prediction algorithm is a generalization of the learning algorithm in Section 3. The results of Section 4 leave open the questions of whether (1) $\mathcal{H}_*$ is *pac-predictable* and (2) $\mathcal{H}_k$ is *pac-learnable*. Section 5 relates our results to other work on the learnability of definite clause theories in the pac-learning or equivalence query models [Džeroski et al., 1992; Page and Frisch, 1992].

2. The Model

The examples provided to algorithms that learn concepts expressed in *propositional logic* traditionally have been truth assignments, or models. Such an example is positive if and only if it satisfies the concept. But concepts in first-order logic may (and almost always do) have infinite models. Therefore, algorithms that learn definite clause theories typically take logical formulas, usually ground atomic formulas, as examples instead. Such an example is positive if and only if it is a logical consequence of the concept. The algorithms in this paper use ground atomic formulas (atoms) as examples in this manner. A concept is used to classify ground atoms according to the atoms'

[1]The classes $\mathcal{H}_1$ and $\mathcal{H}_k$ (discussed next) have one other restriction, that variables are *stationary*. This restriction is defined later.

truth value in the concept's least Herbrand model,[2] which is to say, according to whether the atoms logically follow from the concept. For example, the concept $\forall x[p(f(g(x)))] \wedge \forall x[p(f(x)) \to p(f(h(x)))]$, which is in $\mathcal{H}_1$, classifies $p(f(g(c)))$ and $p(f(h(h(h(g(c))))))$ as true or *positive* while it classifies $p(f(c))$ as false or *negative*. If A and B are two concepts that have the same least Herbrand model, we say they are *equivalent*, and we write $A \cong B$.

In a learning problem, a concept C, called the *target*, is chosen from some class of concepts $\mathcal{C}$ and is hidden from the learner. Each concept classifies each possible example element x from a set X, called the *instance space*, as either *positive* or *negative*. We require the existence of an algorithm that, for every $C \in \mathcal{C}$ and every $x \in X$, efficiently (polynomial-time) determines whether C classifies x as positive. (Such an algorithm exists for each concept class introduced in this paper.) The learner infers some concept C' based on information about how the target C classifies the elements of the instance space X. For each of our learning problems, the concept class $\mathcal{C}$ is a class of definite clause theories, and we require that any learning algorithm, $\mathcal{A}$, must for any $C \in \mathcal{C}$ produce a concept $C' \in \mathcal{C}$ such that $C' \cong C$, that is, that C and C' have the same least Herbrand model. (For *predictability* we remove the requirement that C' belong to $\mathcal{C}$, though we still must be able to efficiently determine how C' classifies examples.) The instance space X is the Herbrand universe of C, and the learning algorithm $\mathcal{A}$ is able to obtain information about the way C classifies elements of X only by asking *equivalence queries*, in which $\mathcal{A}$ conjectures some C' and is told by an oracle whether $C' \cong C$. If $C' \not\cong C$, $\mathcal{A}$ is provided a *counterexample* x that C' and C classify differently.

We close this section by observing that the union of several classes can be learned by interleaving the learning algorithms for each class.

Fact 1 *Let $p(n)$ be a polynomial in n, and let $\{C_i : 1 \leq i \leq p(n)\}$ be concept classes with learning algorithms $\{A_i : 1 \leq i \leq p(n)\}$ having time complexities $\{T_{A_i} : 1 \leq i \leq p(n)\}$ respectively. Then the concept class $\bigcup_{i=1}^{p(n)} C_i$ can be learned in time $max_{1 \leq i \leq p(n)}\{p(n)T_{A_i}\}$.*

3. The Class $\mathcal{H}_1$

The concept class $\mathcal{H}_1$ is the class of concepts that can be expressed as a conjunction of at most two simple clauses, where a simple clause is a positive literal (an

atom) composed of unary predicates and unary or 0-ary functions or an implication between two such positive literals.

As an example, the following is a concept in $\mathcal{H}_1$ that we have seen already.

$$\forall x[p(f(g(x)))] \wedge \forall x[p(f(x)) \to p(f(h(x)))]$$

Since our conjuncts are always universally quantified, we henceforth leave the quantification implicit. Thus the above concept is written

$$[p(f(g(x)))] \wedge [p(f(x)) \to p(f(h(x)))]$$

We can divide $\mathcal{H}_1$ into two classes: trivial concepts, which are equivalent ($\cong$) to conjunctions of at most two atoms, and non-trivial, or recursive, concepts. The trivial concepts of $\mathcal{H}_1$ can be learned easily.[3] We next describe an algorithm that learns the non-trivial, or recursive, concepts in $\mathcal{H}_1$. It follows that $\mathcal{H}_1$ is learnable, since we can interleave this algorithm with the one that learns the trivial concepts of $\mathcal{H}_1$.

It can be shown that the recursive concepts in $\mathcal{H}_1$ have the form

$$[p(t_1)] \wedge [p(t_2(x)) \to p(t_3(x))] \qquad (1)$$

where t_1 is a term, and $t_2(x)$ and $t_3(x)$ are terms ending in the same variable, x.[4] The fact that the functions and predicates are unary leads to a very concise description of a recursive concept in $\mathcal{H}_1$. Specifically, we can drop all parentheses in and around terms. Further, since we are discussing recursive concepts, all predicate symbols are the same and can likewise be dropped. Thus any concept having the form of concept (1) may be written $[\alpha e] \wedge [\beta x \to \gamma x]$, or

$$\begin{cases} \alpha e \\ \beta x \to \gamma x \end{cases} \qquad (2)$$

where α, β, and γ are strings of function symbols, x is a variable, and e is either a constant or a variable. Using this notation, determining whether, for example, αe unifies with βx requires only determining whether either α is a prefix of β or β is a prefix of α. For any strings α and β, if α is a prefix of β then we write $\alpha < \beta$.

Since we are speaking now of recursive concepts only, we refer to the two parts of the concept as the *base atom* and the *recursive clause*. The atoms in the least Herbrand model that are not instances of the base

---

[2]The least Herbrand model of a set of definite clauses (every such set has one) is sometimes referred to as *the model* or the *unique minimal model* of the set. The set of definite clauses entails a logical sentence if and only if the sentence is true in this model. It is often useful to think of this model as a set, namely, the set of ground atoms that it makes true.

[3]The basic idea is that the learning algorithm, by using equivalence queries, is able to obtain one example for each of the (at most two) atoms in the concept. Only a few atoms are more general than (that is, have as instances) each example, and the algorithm conjectures all combinations of these atoms, one for each of the (at most two) examples.

[4]The proof of this is omitted for brevity, as are some other proofs; see [Frazier and Page, 1993; Frazier, 1993] for missing proofs.

atom in the concept are generated by applying the recursive clause. A concept is equivalent to a conjunction of two atoms if its recursive clause can be applied at most once. For the recursive clause to apply at all, α must unify with β, and for it to apply more than once, β must unify with γ. Hence a concept is nontrivial only if (1) either $\alpha<\beta$ or $\beta<\alpha$ and (2) either $\beta<\gamma$ or $\gamma<\beta$. In light of Fact 1, to show that the nontrivial concepts can be learned in polynomial time, we need only show that the class of non-trivial concepts can be partitioned into a polynomial number of concept classes, each of which can be learned in polynomial time. Therefore, we carve the class of non-trivial concepts into five different subclasses defined by the prefix relationships among α, β, and γ. The five possible sets of prefix relationships that can yield recursive concepts, based on our earlier discussion, are (1) $\alpha<\beta$ and $\beta<\gamma$, (2) $\alpha<\beta$, $\gamma<\beta$, and $\alpha<\gamma$, (3) $\alpha<\beta$, $\gamma<\beta$, and $\gamma<\alpha$, (4) $\beta<\alpha$ and $\beta<\gamma$, (5) $\beta<\alpha$ and $\gamma<\beta$. (We do not need to divide case (4) into two cases because the relationship between α and γ is insignificant here.) The approach for each subclass is similar—generalize the first positive example in such a way that the oracle is forced to provide a positive example containing whatever pieces of α, β, or γ are missing from the first example. For brevity, we present only the proof of the most difficult case.

$\beta<\alpha$ **and** $\gamma<\beta$. This class consists of concepts having the form

$$\begin{cases} \phi\psi\omega e \\ \phi\psi x \to \phi x \end{cases} \tag{3}$$

Concepts of this form generate smaller and smaller atoms by deleting copies of ψ at the front of ω; if ψ is not a prefix of ω, the concept can delete only one copy of ψ. Any concept of this form has the least Herbrand model described by

$$\phi\psi^k\zeta e \quad \text{for } 1 \leq k \leq n+1, \text{ where } \omega = \psi^n\zeta$$

Lemma 2 *This class can be learned in polynomial time.*

Proof: To learn this class an algorithm needs to obtain an example that contains ϕ, ψ, ω, and ζ. It then must determine n. We give an algorithm that makes at most two equivalence queries to obtain ϕ, ψ, ω, and ζ. It then guesses larger and larger values for n until it guesses the correct value. This value of n is linearly related to the length of the base atom, so overall the algorithm takes polynomial time.

1. Conjecture the false concept to obtain counterexample ρe

2. Dovetail the following algorithms
   - Assuming $\rho = \phi\psi^j\zeta\xi e$ for some $j \geq 1$
   (a) Select ϕ, ψ, ζ, ξ from ρ

(b) Guess the value of n
(c) Halt with output

$$\begin{cases} \phi\psi^{n+1}\zeta e \\ \phi\psi x \to \phi x \end{cases}$$

   - Assuming $\rho = \phi\zeta\xi e$
   (a) Select ϕ, ζ, ξ from ρ
   (b) Conjecture

$$\begin{cases} \phi\zeta e \end{cases}$$

to obtain counterexample $\rho'e'$. Note that ρ' necessarily contains ψ as a substring.
   (c) Select ψ from ρ'
   (d) Guess n
   (e) Halt with output

$$\begin{cases} \phi\psi^{n+1}\zeta e \\ \phi\psi x \to \phi x \end{cases}$$

When the algorithm *selects* substrings from a counterexample, it is in reality dovetailing all possible choices; nevertheless, we observe that there are only $O(|\rho|^5)$ (respectively $O(|\rho'|)$) choices to try. Similarly, when the algorithm guesses the value of n, it is actually making successively larger and larger guesses for n and testing whether it is correct with an equivalence query. It will obtain the correct value for n in time polynomial in the size of the target concept. At that point it outputs the necessarily correct concept and halts. $\square$

It is worth noting that the algorithm above uses only two of the counterexamples it receives, though it typically makes more than two equivalence queries. This is the case with the algorithms for the other subclasses as well. It is also worth noting that when the algorithm above guesses the value of n, it is guessing the number of times the recursive clause is applied to generate the earliest generated atom of which either example is an instance.

By the preceding arguments, we have Theorem 3.

Theorem 3 *The concept class $\mathcal{H}_1$ is learnable.*

4. Increasing Predicate Arity

It is often useful to have predicates of higher arity, but otherwise maintain the form of the concepts in $\mathcal{H}_1$. For example

$$\begin{cases} plus(x, 0, x) \\ plus(x, y, z) \to plus(x, s(y), s(z)) \end{cases}$$

$$\begin{cases} greater(s(x), 0) \\ greater(x, y) \to greater(s(x), s(y)) \end{cases}$$

In this section we remove the requirement that predicates be unary. Specifically, let $\mathcal{H}_*$ be the result of allowing predicates of arbitrary arity but requiring functions to remain unary, with the additional restriction, which we define next, that variables be *stationary*. Notice that because functions are unary, each argument has at most one variable (it may have a constant instead), and that variable must be the last symbol of the argument. A concept meets the *stationary variables* restriction if for any variable x, if x appears in argument i of the consequent of the recursive clause then x also appears in argument i of the antecedent. This class does include the preceding arithmetic concepts built with the successor function and the constant 0, but does not include the concept $[p(a,b,c)] \wedge [p(x,y,z) \to p(z,x,y)]$ because variables "shift positions" in the recursive clause. Unfortunately, we have the following result for the class $\mathcal{H}_*$.

Theorem 4 $\mathcal{H}_*$ *is not learnable, assuming $R \neq NP$.*[5]

The result follows from a proof that the *consistency problem* [Pitt and Valiant, 1988] for $\mathcal{H}_*$ is NP-hard. Our conjecture is that the class is not even predictable (that is, learnable *in terms of* any other class), though this is an open question.

Nevertheless, we now show that if we fix the predicate arity to any integer k, then the resulting concept class $\mathcal{H}_k$ is learnable in terms of a slightly more general class, called $\mathcal{H}_k'$, and is therefore predictable (the question of learnability of $\mathcal{H}_k$ in terms of $\mathcal{H}_k$ itself remains open). Concepts in $\mathcal{H}_k'$ may be any union of a concept in $\mathcal{H}_k$ and two additional atoms built from variables, constants, unary functions, and predicates with arity at most k. An example is classified as positive by such a concept if and only if it is classified as positive by the concept in $\mathcal{H}_k$ or is an instance of one of the additional atoms. The learning algorithm is based on the learning algorithm for $\mathcal{H}_1$, and central to it are the following definition and lemma. In the lemma, and afterward, we use G_0 to denote the base atom and, inductively, G_{i+1} to denote the result of applying the recursive clause to G_i.

Definition 5 *Let*

$$\left\{ \begin{array}{l} p(\alpha_1 e_1, ..., \alpha_k e_k) \\ p(\beta_1 e_1', ..., \beta_k e_k') \to p(\gamma_1 e_1'', ..., \gamma_k e_k'') \end{array} \right.$$

be a concept in $\mathcal{H}_k$. Then we say the *subconcept at argument i*, for $1 \leq i \leq k$, of this concept is

$$\left\{ \begin{array}{l} \alpha_i e_i \\ \beta_i e_i' \to \gamma_i e_i'' \end{array} \right.$$

For example the subconcepts at arguments 1 through 3, respectively, of the concept *plus* are:

$$\left\{ \begin{array}{l} x \\ x \to x \end{array} \right. \qquad \left\{ \begin{array}{l} 0 \\ y \to s(y) \end{array} \right. \qquad \left\{ \begin{array}{l} x \\ z \to s(z) \end{array} \right.$$

Notice that an atom $G_i = plus(t_1, t_2, t_3)$ is the ith atom generated by the concept *plus* if and only if for all $1 \leq k \leq 3$, the ith term generated by subconcept

[5]That is, $\mathcal{H}_*$ is not pac-learnable, and therefore is not learnable in polynomial time by equivalence queries. R is the class of problems that can be solved in random polynomial time.

k of *plus* is t_k. This is the case because the argument positions in the definition of *plus* never disagree on the binding of a variable. Not all concepts in $\mathcal{H}_k$ have this property; concepts that do are said to be *decoupled*.

Lemma 6 (Decoupling Lemma) *Let*

$$\left\{ \begin{array}{l} p(\alpha_1 e_1, ..., \alpha_k e_k) \\ p(\beta_1 e_1', ..., \beta_k e_k') \to p(\gamma_1 e_1'', ..., \gamma_k e_k'') \end{array} \right.$$

be a concept in $\mathcal{H}_k$. For any $1 \leq j \leq k$, if e_j' is a variable x then for any $n \geq 2$: if $G_n = p(t_1, ..., t_k)$ unifies with $p(\beta_1 e_1', ..., \beta_k e_k')$, the binding generated for x by this unification is the same as the binding generated for x by unifying t_j with $\beta_j x$. Equivalently, for any $1 \leq i \neq j \leq k$, if e_i' and e_j' are the same variable, x, then for any $n \geq 2$: unifying t_i with $\beta_i x$ yields the same binding for x as does unifying t_j with $\beta_j x$.

The lemma says, in effect, that every concept in $\mathcal{H}_k$ behaves in a decoupled manner after the generation of G_2. Therefore, by the Decoupling Lemma, any concept C in $\mathcal{H}_k$ that generates $G_0, G_1, ...$ can be rewritten as the union of three concepts (only polynomially larger than C), two of which are the atoms G_0 and G_1. The third concept is some $\tilde{C}$ in $\mathcal{H}_k$ whose base atom $\tilde{G}_0$ is G_2 and whose recursive clause (if any) generates $\tilde{G}_1 = G_3, ..., \tilde{G}_m = G_{m+2}, ...$ meeting the following condition: for all $m \geq 0$ and any variable x in the antecedent of the recursive clause, no two argument positions impose different bindings on x when generating $\tilde{G}_{m+1}$ from $\tilde{G}_m$. In other words, $\tilde{C}$ is decoupled, so the behavior of $\tilde{C}$ can be understood as a simple composition of the independent behaviors of the subconcepts at arguments 1 through k. As an example, the concept *plus* can be rewritten as the union of $G_0 = plus(x, 0, x)$, $G_1 = plus(x, s(0), s(x))$, and $\tilde{C} =$

$$\left\{ \begin{array}{l} plus(x, s(s(0)), s(s(x))) \\ plus(x, y, z) \to plus(x, s(y), s(z)) \end{array} \right.$$

Of course, the definition of *plus* is such that even without this rewriting, the concept is decoupled. Consider instead the concept

$$\left\{ \begin{array}{l} p(z, s(w), z) \\ p(x, x, y) \to p(x, s(s(s(0))), s(y)) \end{array} \right.$$

In generating G_1 from G_0, the first argument binds x to z while the second binds x to $s(w)$, and the third binds y to z. Thus the concept is not decoupled. The result is that x and y are bound to $s(w)$, so G_1 is $p(s(w), s(s(s(0))), s(s(w)))$. Furthermore, in generating G_2 from G_1, the first argument binds x to $s(w)$, while the second binds x to $s(s(s(0)))$, and the third binds y to $s(s(w))$. The result is that x is bound to $s(s(s(0)))$, and y is bound to $s(s(s(s(0))))$. (But from this point on, the first and second arguments always agree on the binding for x.) We would like the concept, instead, to be such that the bindings generated by the arguments are *independent*, that is, the concept is decoupled. The following, equivalent concept in $\mathcal{H}_k{}'$ has this property: $G_0 = p(z, s(w), z)$, $G_1 = p(s(w), s(s(s(0))), s(s(w))$, and $\tilde{C} =$

$$\left\{ \begin{array}{l} p(s(s(s(0))), s(s(s(0))), s(s(s(s(s(0)))))) \\ p(x, x, y) \rightarrow p(x, x, s(y)) \end{array} \right.$$

These observations motivate an algorithm that learns $\mathcal{H}_k$ in terms of $\mathcal{H}_k{}'$ and is therefore a prediction algorithm for $\mathcal{H}_k$.

Theorem 7 *For any constant k, the class $\mathcal{H}_k$ is predictable from equivalence queries alone.*

Proof: (Sketch) Any target concept C is equivalent to some concept in $\mathcal{H}_k{}'$ that consists of G_0, G_1 and $\tilde{C} =$

$$\left\{ \begin{array}{l} p(\alpha_1 e_1, ..., \alpha_k e_k) \\ p(\beta_1 e_1', ..., \beta_k e_k') \rightarrow p(\gamma_1 e_1'', ..., \gamma_k e_k'') \end{array} \right.$$

that is only polynomially larger than C, where $\tilde{C}$ is decoupled. Our algorithm will obtain such an equivalent concept. $\tilde{C}$ generates some sequence of atoms $\tilde{G}_0, \tilde{G}_1, ...$ (this sequence may or may not be finite). Notice that the subconcepts, $S_1, ..., S_k$, of $\tilde{C}$ are, respectively:

$$\left\{ \begin{array}{l} \alpha_1 e_1 \\ \beta_1 e_1' \rightarrow \gamma_1 e_1'' \end{array} \right. \quad \cdots \quad \left\{ \begin{array}{l} \alpha_k e_k \\ \beta_k e_k' \rightarrow \gamma_k e_k'' \end{array} \right.$$

Let $g_{i,j}$ be the jth term generated by subconcept i. Then because $\tilde{C}$ is decoupled, for all $j \geq 0$ we have $\tilde{G}_j = p(g_{1,j}, ..., g_{k,j})$.

At the highest level of description, the prediction algorithm poses equivalence queries in such a way that it obtains, as examples, instances of G_0, G_1, and $\tilde{G}_i$ and $\tilde{G}_j$ for distinct i and j. The algorithm determines G_0, G_1, $\tilde{G}_i$, and $\tilde{G}_j$ from their examples, and it determines $\tilde{C}$ from $\tilde{G}_i$ and $\tilde{G}_j$. To determine $\tilde{C}$ the algorithm uses the learning algorithm for $\mathcal{H}_1$ to learn the subconcepts $S_1, ..., S_k$ of $\tilde{C}$. The only subtlety is that some subconcept S_i may be equivalent to a conjunction of two terms, and the learning algorithm for $\mathcal{H}_1$ might return such a concept. Such a concept cannot serve as a subconcept for a member of $\mathcal{H}_k$. But it is straightforward to verify that the only case in which this can occur is the case in which all $g_{i,j}$, $j \geq 1$, are identical. And the examples the learning algorithm receives do not include $g_{i,0}$ (it receives only examples extracted from G_2, G_3, ...). Therefore, if the concept returned by the learning algorithm is a conjunction of at most two atoms, it is in fact a single atom—$g_{i,1}$ ($= g_{i,j}$, for all $j \geq 1$)—in which case we may use the concept in $\mathcal{H}_1$ whose base atom, recursive clause antecedent, and recursive clause consequent are all $g_{i,1}$. We now fill in the details of the algorithm.

The algorithm begins by conjecturing the empty theory, and it necessarily receives a positive counterexample in response. This counterexample is an instance of some more general atom, A_1, that is either G_0, G_1, or some $\tilde{G}_i$. The algorithm guesses A_1 and guesses whether A_1 is G_0, G_1, or some $\tilde{G}_i$. It then conjectures A_1 in an equivalence query and, if A_1 is not the target, necessarily receives another positive example. (As earlier, by *guess* we mean that the algorithm dovetails the possible choices.) This example is also an instance of G_0, G_1, or some $\tilde{G}_i$, but it is *not* an instance of A_1. Again, the algorithm guesses that atom—call it A_2—and guesses whether it is an instance of G_0, G_1, or some $\tilde{G}_i$. Following the second example, and following each new example thereafter, the algorithm has at least two of of G_0, G_1, $\tilde{G}_i$, and $\tilde{G}_j$ (some $i \neq j$). It conjectures the union of those that it has, with the following exception: if it has both $\tilde{G}_i$, and $\tilde{G}_j$ (any $i \neq j$), it uses a guess of $\tilde{C}$ in place of $\tilde{G}_i$ and $\tilde{G}_j$. Again, in response to such a conjecture, either the algorithm is correct or it receives a positive counterexample. It remains only to show how (1) the atoms G_0, G_1, $\tilde{G}_i$, and $\tilde{G}_j$ are "efficiently guessed", and (2) $\tilde{C}$ is "efficiently guessed" from $\tilde{G}_i$ and $\tilde{G}_j$.

Given *any* example that is an instance of G_0, the number of possibilities for G_0 is small (because no function has arity greater than 1). For example, if A is $plus(s(s(s(0))), s(0), s(s(s(s(0)))))$, then the first argument of G_0 must be $s(s(s(0)))$, $s(s(s(x)))$, $s(s(x))$, $s(x)$, or x. Similarly, the other arguments of G_0 must be generalizations, or prefixes, of the other arguments of A. Finally, there are at most 5 possible choices of variable co-references, or patterns of variable names, for the three arguments (all three arguments end in the same variable, all three end in different variables, etc.). By this reasoning, there are fewer than $O((2|A|)^k)$ generalizations of A to consider, all of which can be tried in parallel. Note that, because k is fixed, the number of possible generalizations is polynomial in the size of the example. G_1, $\tilde{G}_i$, and $\tilde{G}_j$ are efficiently guessed in the same way.

To learn $\tilde{C}$, the algorithm first determines the "high-level structure" of $\tilde{C}$; specifically, it guesses which of $e_1, ..., e_k, e_1', ..., e_k', e_1'', ..., e_k''$ are variables, and which of these are the *same* variable, e.g. that e_1'' and e_2'' are the same variable x. (In other words, it guesses variable co-references; since $\tilde{C}$ is decoupled, these are only important for ensuring proper co-references in generated atoms that contain variables.) There are fewer than k^{3k} possibilities, where k is fixed. The algorithm then is left with the task of precisely determining the subconcepts $S_1, ..., S_k$ of $\tilde{C}$. Because it has two examples of distinct atoms generated by $\tilde{C}$—$\tilde{G}_i$ and $\tilde{G}_j$—it has two examples of each subconcept. For example, where $\tilde{G}_j$ is $p(g_{1,j}, ..., g_{k,j})$, for each $1 \leq i \leq k$ we know $g_{i,j}$ is an example of subconcept S_i. The algorithm uses the learning algorithm for $\mathcal{H}_1$ to learn the subconcepts from these examples, with the following slight modification. While the learning algorithm for $\mathcal{H}_1$ would ordinarily conjecture a concept in $\mathcal{H}_1$, the present learning algorithm must conjecture a concept in $\mathcal{H}_k{}'$. Therefore, the algorithm conjectures every concept in $\mathcal{H}_k{}'$ that results from any combination of conjectures, by the learning algorithm for $\mathcal{H}_1$, for the subconcepts; that is, it tries all combinations of subconcepts. Because k is fixed, the number of such combinations is polynomial in the sizes of the counterexamples seen thus far.

Finally, recall that for concepts having the form of concept 3 the learning algorithm for $\mathcal{H}_1$ must guess the value for n, where n is the number of times the recursive clause was applied to generate the earlier of the two examples it has. Therefore, the present learning algorithm may have to guess n. (The n sought is necessarily the same for all subconcepts. Thus only one n needs to be found.) This is handled by initially guessing $n = 1$ and guessing successively higher values of n until the correct n is reached. This approach succeeds provided that the target truly contains a type 3 subconcept. In the case that the target does not contain a type 3 subconcept, the potentially non-terminating, errant search for a non-existent n halts because we are interleaving the steps from *all* pending guesses of *all* forms—including the correct (not type 3) form—of the subconcept. □

5. Related Work

The concept classes studied in this paper are incomparable to—that is, neither subsume nor are subsumed by—the other classes of definite clause theories whose learnability, in the *pac-learning* and/or *equivalence query* models, has been investigated [Džeroski et al., 1992; Page and Frisch, 1992].[6] Page and Frisch investigated classes of definite clauses that may have predicates and functions of arbitrary arity but explicitly do *not* have recursion [Page and Frisch, 1992]. In that work, a *background* theory was also allowed; allowing such a theory in the present work is an interesting topic for future research. Džeroski, Muggleton, and Russell [Džeroski et al., 1992] investigated the learnability of classes of function-free *determinate* k-clause definite clause theories under simple distributions, also in the presence of a background theory.[7] This class includes recursive concepts; to learn recursive concepts, the algorithm requires two additional kinds of queries (*existential queries* and *membership queries*). Rewriting definite clause theories that contain functions to function-free clauses allows their algorithm to learn in the presence of functions. Nev-

ertheless, the restriction that clauses be *determinate* effectively limits the depth of function nesting; their algorithm takes time exponential in this depth. So, for example, while the algorithm can easily learn the concept *even integer*, or *multiple of 2*, from $\mathcal{H}_1$ — $[even(0)] \wedge [even(x) \rightarrow even(s(s(x)))]$—the time it requires grows exponentially in moving to a concept such as *multiple of 10* or *multiple of 1000*, also in $\mathcal{H}_1$. It is easy to show that the classes $\mathcal{H}_1$, $\mathcal{H}_k$, and $\mathcal{H}_*$, rewritten to be function-free, are not determinate.

References

Angluin, D. (1988). Queries and concept learning. *Machine Learning*, 2:319–342.

Angluin, D., Frazier, M., and Pitt, L. (1992). Learning conjunctions of horn clauses. *Machine Learning*, 9:147–164.

Arimura, H., Ishizaka, H., and Shinohara, T. (1992). Polynomial time inference of a subclass of context-free transformations. In *COLT-92*, pages 136–143, New York. The Association for Computing Machinery.

Cohen, W. W. and Hirsh, H. (1992). Learnability of description logics. In *COLT-92*, pages 116–127, New York. The Association for Computing Machinery.

Džeroski, S., Muggleton, S., and Russell, S. (1992). Pac-learnability of logic programs. In *COLT-92*, pages 128–135, New York. The Association for Computing Machinery.

Frazier, M. (1993). *Forthcoming.* PhD thesis, University of Illinois at Urbana-Champaign.

Frazier, M. and Page, C. D. (1993). Learnability of recursive, non-determinate theories: Some basic results and techniques. Submitted to the Third International Workshop on Inductive Logic Programming (ILP93).

Ling, C. X. (1992). Logic program synthesis from good examples. In Muggleton, S. H., editor, *Inductive Logic Programming*, pages 113–129. Academic Press, London.

Muggleton, S. H. (1992). Inductive logic programming. In Muggleton, S. H., editor, *Inductive Logic Programming*, pages 3–27. Academic Press, London.

Page, C. D. and Frisch, A. M. (1992). Generalization and learnability: A study of constrained atoms. In Muggleton, S. H., editor, *Inductive Logic Programming*, pages 29–61. Academic Press, London.

Pitt, L. and Valiant, L. G. (1988). Computational limitations on learning from examples. *Journal of the ACM*, 35(4):965–984.

Shapiro, E. Y. (1983). *Algorithmic Program Debugging*. MIT Press, Cambridge, MA.

Valiant, L. G. (1984). A theory of the learnable. *Communications of the ACM*, 27(11):1134–1142.

---

[6]Theoretical work on the learnability of definite clauses in other models includes Shapiro's [Shapiro, 1983] work on learning in the limit, Angluin, Frazier, and Pitt's [Angluin et al., 1992] work with propositional definite clause theories, and Ling's [Ling, 1992] investigation of learning from *good examples*.

[7]The restriction to simple distributions is a small one that quite possibly can be removed.

Complexity Analysis of
Real-Time Reinforcement Learning*

Sven Koenig and Reid G. Simmons
School of Computer Science
Carnegie Mellon University
Pittsburgh, PA 15213-3891
skoenig@cs.cmu.edu, reids@cs.cmu.edu

Abstract

This paper analyzes the complexity of on-line reinforcement learning algorithms, namely asynchronous real-time versions of Q-learning and value-iteration, applied to the problem of reaching a goal state in deterministic domains. Previous work had concluded that, in many cases, tabula rasa reinforcement learning was exponential for such problems, or was tractable only if the learning algorithm was augmented. We show that, to the contrary, the algorithms are tractable with only a simple change in the task representation or initialization. We provide tight bounds on the worst-case complexity, and show how the complexity is even smaller if the reinforcement learning algorithms have initial knowledge of the topology of the state space or the domain has certain special properties. We also present a novel *bi-directional Q-learning algorithm* to find optimal paths from all states to a goal state and show that it is no more complex than the other algorithms.

Introduction

Consider the problem for an agent of finding its way to one of a set of goal locations, where actions consist of moving from one intersection (state) to another (see Figure 1). Initially, the agent has no knowledge of the topology of the state space. We consider two different tasks: reaching any goal state and determining shortest paths from every state to a goal state.

Off-line search methods, which first derive a plan that is then executed, cannot be used to solve the path planning tasks, since the topology of the state space is initially unknown to the agent and can only be discovered by exploring: executing actions and observing their effects. Thus, the path planning tasks have to be solved on-line. On-line search methods, also called **real-time search** methods [Korf, 1990], interleave search with action execution. The algorithms we describe here perform minimal computation between action executions, choosing only which action to execute next, and basing

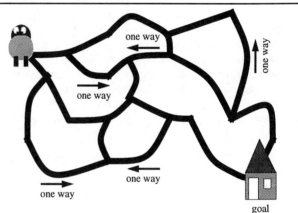

Figure 1: Navigating on a map

this decision only on information local to the current state of the agent (and perhaps its immediate successor states).

In particular, we will investigate a class of algorithms which perform *reinforcement learning*. The application of reinforcement learning to on-line path planning problems has been studied by [Barto *et al.*, 1991], [Benson and Prieditis, 1992], [Pemberton and Korf, 1992], [Moore and Atkeson, 1992], and others. [Whitehead, 1991] showed that reaching a goal state with reinforcement learning methods can require a number of action executions that is exponential in the size of the state space. [Thrun, 1992] has shown that by augmenting reinforcement learning algorithms, the problem can be made tractable. In fact, we will show that, contrary to prior belief, reinforcement learning algorithms are tractable without any need for augmentation, i.e. their run-time is a small polynomial in the size of the state space. All that is necessary is a change in the way the state space (task) is represented.

In this paper, we use the following notation. S denotes a finite set of states, and $G \subseteq S$ is the non-empty set of goal states. $A(s)$ is the finite set of actions that can be executed in $s \in S$. The size of the state space is $n := |S|$, and the total number of actions is $e := \sum_{s \in S} |A(s)|$. All actions are determinis-

*This research was supported in part by NASA under contract NAGW-1175. The views and conclusions contained in this document are those of the authors and should not be interpreted as representing the official policies, either expressed or implied, of NASA or the U.S. government.

tic. $succ(s, a)$ is the uniquely determined successor state when $a \in A(s)$ is executed in state s. The state space is strongly connected, i.e. every state can be reached from every other state. $gd(s)$ denotes the goal distance of s, i.e. the smallest number of action executions required to reach a goal state from s. We assume that the state space is totally observable[1], i.e. the agent can determine its current state with certainty, including whether it is currently in a goal state.

Formally, the results of the paper are as follows. If a good task representation or suitable initialization is chosen, the worst-case complexity of reaching a goal state has a tight bound of $O(n^3)$ action executions for Q-learning and $O(n^2)$ action executions for value-iteration. If the agent has initial knowledge of the topology of the state space or the state space has additional properties, the $O(n^3)$ bound can be decreased further. In addition, we show that reinforcement learning methods for finding *shortest* paths from *every* state to a goal state are no more complex than reinforcement learning methods that simply reach a goal state from a single state. This demonstrates that one does not need to augment reinforcement learning algorithms to make them tractable.

Reinforcement Learning

Reinforcement learning is learning from (positive and negative) rewards. Every action $a \in A(s)$ has an immediate reward $r(s, a) \in \mathcal{R}$, that is obtained when the agent executes the action. If the agent starts in $s \in S$ and executes actions for which it receives immediate reward r_t at step $t \in \mathcal{N}_0$, then the total reward that the agent receives over its lifetime for this particular behavior is

$$U(s) := \sum_{t=0}^{\infty} \gamma^t r_t \qquad (1)$$

where $\gamma \in (0, 1]$ is called the discount factor. If $\gamma < 1$, we say that discounting is used, otherwise no discounting is used.

Reinforcement learning algorithms find a behavior for the agent that maximizes the total reward for every possible start state. We analyze two reinforcement learning algorithms that are widely used, namely Q-learning [Watkins, 1989] and value-iteration [Bellman, 1957]. One can interleave them with action execution to construct asynchronous real-time forms that use actual state transitions rather than systematic or asynchronous sweeps over the state space. In the following, we investigate these on-line versions: 1-step Q-learning and 1-step value-iteration.

---

[1] [Papadimitriou and Tsitsiklis, 1987] state results about the worst-case complexity of every algorithm for cases where the states are partially observable or unobservable.

1. Set $s :=$ the current state.
2. If $s \in G$, then stop.
3. Select an action $a \in A(s)$.
4. Execute action a.
   /* As a consequence, the agent receives reward $r(s, a)$ and is in state $succ(s, a)$. Increment the number of steps taken, i.e. set $t := t + 1$. */
5. Set $Q(s, a) := r(s, a) + \gamma U(succ(s, a))$.
6. Go to 1.

where $U(s) := \max_{a \in A(s)} Q(s, a)$ at every point in time.

Figure 2: The (1-step) Q-learning algorithm

Q-Learning

The 1-step **Q-learning** algorithm[2] [Whitehead, 1991] (Figure 2) stores information about the relative goodness of the actions in the states. This is done by maintaining a value $Q(s, a)$ in state s for every action $a \in A(s)$. $Q(s, a)$ approximates the optimal total reward received if the agent starts in s, executes a, and then behaves optimally.

The action selection step (line 3) implements the exploration rule (which state to go to next). It is allowed to look only at information local to the current state s. This includes the Q-values for all $a \in A(s)$. The actual selection strategy is left open: It could, for example, select an action randomly, select the action that it has executed the least number of times, or select the action with the largest Q-value. Exploration is termed **undirected** [Thrun, 1992] if it uses only the Q-values, otherwise it is termed **directed**.

After the action execution step (line 4) has executed the selected action a, the value update step (line 5) adjusts $Q(s, a)$ (and, if needed, other information local to the former state). The 1-step look-ahead value $r(s, a) + \gamma U(succ(s, a))$ is more accurate than, and therefore replaces, $Q(s, a)$.

Value-Iteration

The 1-step **value-iteration** algorithm is similar to the 1-step Q-learning algorithm. The difference is that the action selection step can access $r(s, a)$ and $U(succ(s, a))$ for every action $a \in A(s)$ in the current state s, whereas Q-learning has to estimate them with the Q-values. The value update step becomes "Set $U(s) := \max_{a \in A(s)} (r(s, a) + \gamma U(succ(s, a)))$".

Whereas Q-learning does not know the effect of an action before it has executed it at least once, value-iteration only needs to enter a state at least once to discover all of its successor states. Since value-iteration is more powerful than Q-learning, we expect it to have a smaller complexity.

---

[2] Since the actions have deterministic outcomes, we state the Q-learning algorithm with the learning rate α set to one.

Task Representation

To represent the task of finding shortest paths as a reinforcement learning problem, we have to specify the reward function r. We let the lifetime of the agent in formula (1) end when it reaches a goal state. Then, the only constraint on r is that it must guarantee that a state with a smaller goal distance has a larger optimal total reward and vice versa. We consider two possible reward functions with this property.

In the **goal-reward representation**, the agent is rewarded for entering a goal state, but not rewarded or penalized otherwise. This representation has been used by [Whitehead, 1991], [Thrun, 1992], [Peng and Williams, 1992], and [Sutton, 1990], among others.

$$r(s, a) = \begin{cases} 1 & \text{if } succ(s, a) \in G \\ 0 & \text{otherwise} \end{cases}$$

The optimal total discounted reward of $s \in S - G := \{s \in S : s \notin G\}$ is $\gamma^{gd(s)-1}$. If no discounting is used, then the optimal total reward is 1 for every $s \in S - G$, independent of its goal distance. Thus, discounting is necessary so that larger optimal total rewards equate with shorter goal distances.

In the **action-penalty representation**, the agent is penalized for every action that it executes, i.e. $r(s, a) = -1$. This representation has a more dense reward structure than the goal-reward representation (i.e. the agent receives non-zero rewards more often) if goals are relatively sparse. It has been used by [Barto *et al.*, 1989], [Barto *et al.*, 1991], and [Koenig, 1991], among others.

The optimal total discounted reward of $s \in S$ is $(1 - \gamma^{gd(s)})/(\gamma - 1)$. Its optimal total undiscounted reward is $-gd(s)$. Note that discounting can be used with the action-penalty representation, but is not necessary.

Complexity of Reaching a Goal State

We can now analyze the complexity of reinforcement learning algorithms for the path planning tasks. We first analyze the complexity of reaching a goal state for the first time.

The worst-case complexity of reaching a goal state with reinforcement learning (and stopping there) provides a lower bound on the complexity of finding *all shortest* paths, since this cannot be done without knowing where the goal states are. By "worst case" we mean an upper bound on the total number of steps for a tabula rasa (initially uninformed) algorithm that holds for all possible topologies of the state space, start and goal states, and tie-breaking rules among actions that have the same Q-values.

Assume that a Q-learning algorithm is **zero-initialized** (all Q-values are zero initially) and operates on the goal-reward representation. Note that the first Q-value that changes is the Q-value of the action that leads the agent to a goal state. For all other actions, no information about the topology of the state space is remembered and all Q-values remain zero. Since the action selection step has no information on which to base

its decision if it performs undirected exploration, the agent has to choose actions according to a uniform distribution and thus performs a random walk. Then, the agent reaches a goal state eventually, but the average number of steps required can be exponential in n, the number of states [Whitehead, 1991].

This observation motivated [Whitehead, 1991] to explore cooperative reinforcement learning algorithms in order to decrease the worst-case complexity. [Thrun, 1992] showed that even non-cooperative algorithms have polynomial worst-case complexity if reinforcement learning is augmented with a directed exploration mechanism ("counter-based Q-learning"). We will show that one does not need to augment Q-learning: it is tractable if one uses either the action-penalty representation or different initial Q-values.

Using a Different Task Representation

Assume we are still using a zero-initialized Q-learning algorithm, but let it now operate on the action-penalty representation. Although the algorithm is still tabula rasa, the Q-values change immediately, starting with the first action execution, since the reward structure is dense. In this way, the agent remembers the effects of previous action executions. We address the case in which no discounting is used, but the theorems can easily be adapted to the discounted case. [Koenig and Simmons, 1992] contains the proofs, additional theoretical and empirical results, and examples.

Definition 1 *Q-values are called **consistent** iff, for all $s \in G$ and $a \in A(s)$, $Q(s, a) = 0$, and, for all $s \in S - G$ and $a \in A(s)$, $-1 + U(succ(s, a)) \leq Q(s, a) \leq 0$.*

Definition 2 *An undiscounted Q-learning algorithm with action-penalty representation is called **admissible**[3] iff its initial Q-values are consistent and its action selection step is "$a := argmax_{a' \in A(s)} Q(s, a')$".*

If a Q-learning algorithm is admissible, then its Q-values remain consistent and are monotonically decreasing. Lemma 1 contains the central invariant for all proofs. It states that the number of steps executed so far is always bounded by an expression that depends only on the initial and current Q-values and, more over, "that the sum of all Q-values decreases (on average) by one for every step taken" (this paraphrase is grossly simplified). A time superscript of t in Lemmas 1 and 2 refers to the values of the variables immediately before executing the action during step t.

Lemma 1 *For all steps $t \in \mathcal{N}_0$ (until termination) of an undiscounted, admissible Q-learning algorithm with*

---

[3] If the value update step is changed to "Set $Q(s, a) := \min(Q(s, a), -1 + \gamma U(succ(s, a)))$", then the initial Q-values need only to satisfy that, for all $s \in G$ and $a \in A(s)$, $Q(s, a) = 0$, and, for all $s \in S - G$ and $a \in A(s)$, $-1 - gd(succ(s, a)) \leq Q(s, a) \leq 0$. Note that $Q(s, a) = -1 - h(succ(s, a))$ has this property, where h is an admissible heuristic for the goal distance.

action-penalty representation,

$$U^t(s^t) + \sum_{s \in S} \sum_{a \in A(s)} Q^0(s,a) - t \geq$$

$$\sum_{s \in S} \sum_{a \in A(s)} Q^t(s,a) + U^0(s^0) - loop^t$$

and

$$loop^t \leq \sum_{s \in S} \sum_{a \in A(s)} (Q^0(s,a) - Q^t(s,a)),$$

where $loop^t := |\{t' \in \{0, \dots, t-1\} : s^{t'} = s^{t'+1}\}|$ *(the number of actions executed before t that do not change the state).*

Lemma 2 *An undiscounted, admissible Q-learning algorithm with action–penalty representation reaches a goal state and terminates after at most*

$$2 \sum_{s \in S-G} \sum_{a \in A(s)} (Q^0(s,a) + gd(succ(s,a)) + 1) - U^0(s^0)$$

steps.

Theorem 1 *An admissible Q-learning algorithm with action-penalty representation reaches a goal state and terminates after at most $O(en)$ steps.*

Lemma 2 utilizes the invariant and the fact that each of the e different Q-values is bounded by an expression that depends only on the goal distances to derive a bound on t. Since the sum of the Q-values decreases with every step, but is bounded from below, the algorithm must terminate. Because the shortest distance between any two different states (in a strongly connected graph) is bounded by $n-1$, the result of Theorem 1 follows directly. Note that Lemma 2 also shows how prior knowledge of the topology of the state space (in form of suitable initial Q-values) makes the Q-learning algorithm better informed and decreases its run-time.

If a state space has *no duplicate actions*, then $e \leq n^2$ and the worst-case complexity becomes $O(n^3)$. This provides an upper bound on the complexity of the Q-learning algorithm. To demonstrate that this bound is tight for a zero-initialized Q-learning algorithm, we show that $O(n^3)$ is also a lower bound: Figure 3 shows a state space where at least $1/6n^3 - 1/6n$ steps may be needed to reach the goal state. To summarize, although Q-learning performs undirected exploration, its worst-case complexity is polynomial in n. Note that Figure 3 also shows that every algorithm that does not know the effect of an action before it has executed it at least once has the same big-O worst-case complexity as zero-initialized Q-learning.

Using Different Initial Q-values

We now analyze Q-learning algorithms that operate on the goal-reward representation, but where all Q-values are initially set to one. A similar initialization has been used before in experiments conducted by [Kaelbling, 1990].

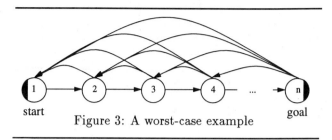

Figure 3: A worst-case example

If the action selection strategy is to execute the action with the largest Q-value, then a discounted, one-initialized Q-learning algorithm with goal-reward representation behaves identically to a zero-initialized Q-learning algorithm with action-penalty representation if all ties are broken in the same way.[4] Thus, the complexity result of the previous section applies and a discounted, one-initialized Q-learning algorithm with goal-reward representation reaches a goal state and terminates after at most $O(en)$ steps.

Gridworlds

We have seen that we can decrease the complexity of Q-learning dramatically by choosing a good task representation or suitable initial Q-values. Many domains studied in the context of reinforcement learning have additional properties that can decrease the worst-case complexity even further. For example, a state space topology has a **linear upper action bound** $b \in \mathcal{N}_0$ iff $e \leq bn$ for all $n \in \mathcal{N}_0$. Then, the worst case complexity becomes $O(bn^2) = O(n^2)$.

Gridworlds, which have often been used in studying reinforcement learning [Barto *et al.*, 1989] [Sutton, 1990] [Peng and Williams, 1992] [Thrun, 1992] have this property. Therefore, exploration in unknown gridworlds actually has very low complexity. Gridworlds often have another special property. A state space is called **1-step invertible** [Whitehead, 1991] iff it has no duplicate actions and, for all $s \in S$ and $a \in A(s)$, there exists an $a' \in A(succ(s,a))$ such that $succ(succ(s,a),a') = s$. (We do not assume that the agent knows that the state space is 1-step invertible.) Even a zero-initialized Q-learning algorithm with goal-reward representation (i.e. a random walk) is tractable for 1-step invertible state spaces, as the following theorem states.

Theorem 2 *A zero-initialized Q-learning algorithm with goal-reward representation reaches a goal state and terminates in at most $O(en)$ steps on average if the state space is 1-step invertible.*

This theorem is an immediate corollary to [Aleliunas *et al.*, 1979]. If the state space has no duplicate actions,

---

[4]This is true only for the task of reaching a goal state. In general, a discounted, "one-initialized" Q-learning algorithm with goal-reward representation behaves identically to a "(minus one)-initialized" Q-learning algorithm with action-penalty representation if in both cases the Q-values of actions in goal states are initialized to zero.

Initially, $Q_f(s,a) = Q_b(s,a) = 0$ and $done(s,a) = false$ for all $s \in S$ and $a \in A(s)$.

1. Set $s :=$ the current state.
2. If $s \in G$, then set $done(s,a) := true$ for all $a \in A(s)$.
3. If $done(s) = true$, then go to 8.
4. /* forward step */
   Set $a := \text{argmax}_{a' \in A(s)} Q_f(s,a')$.
5. Execute action a. (As a consequence, the agent receives reward -1 and is in state $succ(s,a)$.)
6. Set $Q_f(s,a) := -1 + U_f(succ(s,a))$ and $done(s,a) := done(succ(s,a))$.
7. Go to 1.
8. /* backward step */
   Set $a := \text{argmax}_{a' \in A(s)} Q_b(s,a')$.
9. Execute action a. (As a consequence, the agent receives reward -1 and is in state $succ(s,a)$.)
10. Set $Q_b(s,a) := -1 + U_b(succ(s,a))$.
11. If $U_b(s) \leq -n$, then stop.
12. Go to 1.

where, at every point in time,
$U_f(s) := \max_{a \in A(s)} Q_f(s,a)$,
$U_b(s) := \max_{a \in A(s)} Q_b(s,a)$, and
$done(s) := \exists_{a \in A(s)}(Q_f(s,a) = U_f(s) \wedge done(s,a))$.

Figure 4: The bi-directional Q-learning algorithm

then the worst-case complexity becomes $O(n^3)$. This bound is tight. Thus, the average-case complexity of a random walk in 1-step invertible state spaces is polynomial (and no longer exponential) in n. For 1-step invertible state spaces, however, there are tabula rasa on-line algorithms that have a smaller big-O worst-case complexity than Q-learning [Deng and Papadimitriou, 1990].

Determining Optimal Policies

We now consider the problem of finding *shortest* paths from *all* states to a goal state. We present a novel extension of the Q-learning algorithm that determines the goal distance of every state and has the same big-O worst-case complexity as the algorithm for finding a single path to a goal state. This produces an optimal deterministic policy in which the optimal behavior is obtained by always executing the action that decreases the goal distance.

The algorithm, which we term the **bi-directional Q-learning algorithm**, is presented in Figure 4. While the complexity results presented here are for the undiscounted, zero-initialized version with action-penalty representation, we have derived similar results for all of the previously described alternatives.

The bi-directional Q-learning algorithm iterates over two independent Q-learning searches: a forward phase that uses Q_f-values to search a state s with $done(s) = true$ from a state s' with $done(s') = false$, followed by a backward phase that uses Q_b-values to search

a state s with $done(s) = false$ from a state s' with $done(s') = true$. The forward and backward phases are implemented using the Q-learning algorithm from Figure 2.

The variables $done(s)$ have the following semantics: If $done(s) = true$, then $U_f(s) = -gd(s)$ (but not necessarily the other way around). Similarly for the variables $done(s,a)$ for $s \in S - G$: If $done(s,a) = true$, then $Q_f(s,a) = -1 - gd(succ(s,a))$.

If the agent executes a in s and $done(succ(s,a)) = true$, then it can set $done(s,a)$ to $true$. Every forward phase sets at least one additional $done(s,a)$ value to $true$ and then transfers control to the backward phase, which continues until a state s with $done(s) = false$ is reached, so that the next forward phase can start. After at most e forward phases, $done(s) = true$ for all $s \in S$. Then, the backward phase can no longer find a state s with $done(s) = false$ and decreases the U_b-values beyond every limit. When a U_b-value reaches or drops below $-n$, the agent can infer that an optimal policy has been found and may terminate. See [Koenig and Simmons, 1992] for a longer description and a similar algorithm that does not need to know n in advance, always terminates no later than the algorithm stated here, and usually terminates shortly after $done(s) = true$ for all $s \in S$.

Theorem 3 *The bi-directional Q-learning algorithm finds an optimal policy and terminates after at most $O(en)$ steps.*

The proof of Theorem 3 is similar to that of Theorem 1. The theorem states that the bi-directional Q-learning algorithm has exactly the same big-O worst-case complexity as the Q-learning algorithm for finding a path to a goal state. The complexity becomes $O(n^3)$ if the state space has no duplicate actions.[5] That this bound is tight follows from Figure 3, since determining an optimal policy cannot be easier than reaching a goal state for the first time. It is surprising, however, that the big-O worst-case complexities for both tasks are the same.

Empirical Results

Figures 5 and 6 show the run-times of various reinforcement learning algorithms in reset state spaces (i.e. state spaces in which all states have an action that leads back to the start state) and one-dimensional gridworlds of sizes $n \in [2, 50]$, in both cases averaged over 5000 runs.

The x-axes show the complexity of the state space (measured as en) and the y-axes the number of steps needed to complete the tasks. We use zero-initialized algorithms with action-penalty representation, with ties broken randomly. For determining optimal policies, we distinguish two performance measures: the number of steps until an optimal policy is found (i.e. until $U(s) =$

---

[5]The bi-directional Q-learning algorithm can be made more efficient, for example by breaking ties intelligently, but this does not change its big-O worst-case complexity.

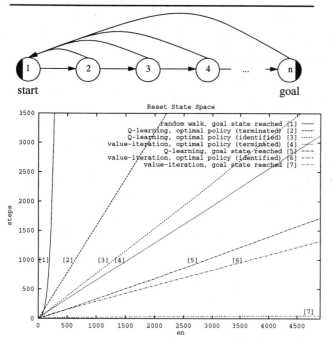

Figure 5: Reset state space

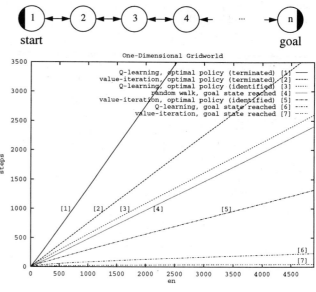

Figure 6: One-dimensional gridworld

$-gd(s)$ for every state s), and the number of steps until the algorithm realizes that and terminates.

These graphs confirm our expectation about the various algorithms. For each algorithm, Q-learning and value-iteration, we expect its run-time (i.e. number of steps needed) for reaching a goal state to be smaller than the run-time for finding an optimal policy which we expect, in turn, to be smaller than the run-time for terminating with an optimal policy. We also expect the run-time of the efficient[6] value-iteration algorithm to be smaller than the run-time of the efficient Q-learning algorithm which we expect to be smaller than the run-time of a random walk, given the same task to be solved. In addition to these relationships, the graphs show that random walks are inefficient in reset state spaces (where they need $3 \times 2^{n-2} - 2$ steps on average to reach a goal state), but perform much better in one-dimensional gridworlds (where they only need $(n-1)^2$ steps on average), since the latter are 1-step invertible. But even for gridworlds, the efficient Q-learning algorithms continue to perform better than random walks, since only the former algorithms immediately remember information about the topology of the state space.

Extensions

The complexities presented here can also be stated in terms of e and the depth of the state space d (instead of n), allowing one to take advantage of the fact that

---

[6] "Efficient" means to use either the action-penalty representation or one-initialized Q-values (U-values).

the depth often grows sublinearly in n. The **depth of a state space** is the maximum over all pairs of different states of the length of the shortest path between them. All of our results can easily be extended to cases where the actions do not have the same reward. The result about 1-step invertible state spaces also holds for the more general case of state spaces that have the following property: for every state, the number of actions entering the state equals the number of actions leaving it.

Reinforcement learning algorithms can be used in state spaces with probabilistic action outcomes. Although the results presented here provide guidance for modeling probabilistic domains, more research is required to transfer the results. [Koenig and Simmons, 1992] contains a discussion of additional challenges encountered in probabilistic domains.

Conclusion

Many real-world domains have the characteristic of the task presented here – the agent must reach one of a number of goal states by taking actions, but the initial topology of the state space is unknown. Prior results which indicated that reinforcement learning algorithms were exponential in n, the size of the state space, seemed to limit their usefulness for such tasks.

This paper has shown, however, that such algorithms are tractable when using either the appropriate task representation or suitable initial Q-values. Both changes produce a dense reward structure, which facilitates learning. In particular, we showed that the task of reaching a goal state for the first time is reduced from exponential to $O(en)$, or $O(n^3)$ if there are no duplicate actions. Furthermore, the complexity is further reduced if the domain has additional properties, such as a linear

Tight bounds on the number of steps required in the worst case for reaching a goal state using a zero-initialized algorithm with action-penalty representation or a one-initialized algorithm with goal-reward representation; the same results apply to determining optimal policies

State Space	Q-Learning	Value-Iteration
general case	$O(en)$	$O(n^2)$
no duplicate actions	$O(n^3)$	$O(n^2)$
linear upper action bound	$O(n^2)$	$O(n^2)$

Figure 7: Complexities of Reinforcement Learning

upper action bound. In 1-step invertible state spaces, even the original, inefficient algorithms have a polynomial average-case complexity.

We have introduced the novel *bi-directional Q-learning algorithm* for finding shortest paths from all states to a goal and have shown, somewhat surprisingly, that its complexity is $O(en)$ as well. This provides an efficient algorithm to learn optimal policies. While not all reinforcement learning tasks can be reformulated as shortest path problems, the theorems still provide guidance: the run-times can be improved by making the reward structure dense, for instance, by subtracting some constant from all immediate rewards.

The results derived for Q-learning can be transferred to value-iteration [Koenig, 1992] [Koenig and Simmons, 1992]. The important results are summarized in Figure 7. Note that a value-iteration algorithm that always executes the action that leads to the state with the largest U-value is equivalent to the LRTA* algorithm [Korf, 1990] with a search horizon of one if the state space is deterministic and action penalty representation is used [Barto *et al.*, 1991].

In summary, reinforcement learning algorithms are useful for enabling agents to explore unknown state spaces and learn information relevant to performing tasks. The results in this paper add to that research by showing that reinforcement learning is tractable, and therefore can scale up to handle real-world problems.

Acknowledgements

Avrim Blum, Long-Ji Lin, Michael Littman, Joseph O'Sullivan, Martha Pollack, Sebastian Thrun, and especially Lonnie Chrisman (who also commented on the proofs) provided helpful comments on the ideas presented in this paper.

References

Aleliunas, R.; Karp, R.M.; Lipton, R.J.; Lovász, L.; and Rackoff, C. 1979. Random walks, universal traversal sequences, and the complexity of maze problems. In *20th Annual Symposium on Foundation of Computer Science*, San Juan, Puerto Rico. 218–223.

Barto, A.G.; Sutton, R.S.; and Watkins, C.J. 1989. Learning and sequential decision making. Technical Report 89–95, Department of Computer Science, University of Massachusetts at Amherst.

Barto, A.G.; Bradtke, S.J.; and Singh, S.P. 1991. Real-time learning and control using asynchronous dynamic programming. Technical Report 91–57, Department of Computer Science, University of Massachusetts at Amherst.

Bellman, R. 1957. *Dynamic Programming.* Princeton University Press, Princeton.

Benson, G.D. and Prieditis, A. 1992. Learning continuous-space navigation heuristics in real-time. In *Proceedings of the Second International Conference on Simulation of Adaptive Behavior: From Animals to Animats.*

Deng, X. and Papadimitriou, C.H. 1990. Exploring an unknown graph. In *Proceedings of the FOCS.*

Kaelbling, L.P. 1990. *Learning in Embedded Systems.* Ph.D. Dissertation, Computer Science Department, Stanford University.

Koenig, S. and Simmons, R.G. 1992. Complexity analysis of real-time reinforcement learning applied to finding shortest paths in deterministic domains. Technical Report CMU–CS–93–106, School of Computer Science, Carnegie Mellon University.

Koenig, S. 1991. Optimal probabilistic and decision-theoretic planning using Markovian decision theory. Master's thesis, Computer Science Department, University of California at Berkeley. (Available as Technical Report UCB/CSD 92/685).

Koenig, S. 1992. The complexity of real-time search. Technical Report CMU–CS–92–145, School of Computer Science, Carnegie Mellon University.

Korf, R.E. 1990. Real-time heuristic search. *Artificial Intelligence* 42(2-3):189–211.

Moore, A.W. and Atkeson, C.G. 1992. Memory-based reinforcement learning: Efficient computation with prioritized sweeping. In *Proceedings of the NIPS.*

Papadimitriou, C.H. and Tsitsiklis, J.N. 1987. The complexity of Markov decision processes. *Mathematics of Operations Research* 12(3):441–450.

Pemberton, J.C. and Korf, R.E. 1992. Incremental path planning on graphs with cycles. In *Proceedings of the First Annual AI Planning Systems Conference.* 179–188.

Peng, J. and Williams, R.J. 1992. Efficient learning and planning within the Dyna framework. In *Proceedings of the Second International Conference on Simulation of Adaptive Behavior: From Animals to Animats.*

Sutton, R.S. 1990. Integrated architectures for learning, planning, and reacting based on approximating dynamic programming. In *Proceedings of the Seventh International Conference on Machine Learning.*

Thrun, S.B. 1992. The role of exploration in learning control with neural networks. In White, David A. and Sofge, Donald A., editors 1992, *Handbook of Intelligent Control: Neural, Fuzzy and Adaptive Approaches.* Van Nostrand Reinhold, Florence, Kentucky.

Watkins, C.J. 1989. *Learning from Delayed Rewards.* Ph.D. Dissertation, King's College, Cambridge University.

Whitehead, S.D. 1991. A complexity analysis of cooperative mechanisms in reinforcement learning. In *Proceedings of the AAAI.* 607–613.

Constraint-Based Reasoning

Arc-Consistency and Arc-Consistency Again

Christian Bessière

LIRMM, University of Montpellier II
161, rue Ada
34392 Montpellier Cedex 5, FRANCE
Email: bessiere@lirmm.fr

Marie-Odile Cordier

IRISA, University of Rennes I
Campus de Beaulieu
35042 Rennes, FRANCE
Email: cordier@irisa.fr

Abstract

Constraint networks are known as a useful way to formulate problems such as design, scene labeling, temporal reasoning, and more recently natural language parsing. The problem of the existence of solutions in a constraint network is NP-complete. Hence, consistency techniques have been widely studied to simplify constraint networks before or during the search of solutions. Arc-consistency is the most used of them. Mohr and Henderson [Moh&Hen86] have proposed AC-4, an algorithm having an optimal worst-case time complexity. But it has two drawbacks: its space complexity and its average time complexity. In problems with many solutions, where the size of the constraints is large, these drawbacks become so important that users often replace AC-4 by AC-3 [Mac&Fre85], a non-optimal algorithm. In this paper, we propose a new algorithm, AC-6, which keeps the optimal worst-case time complexity of AC-4 while working out the drawback of space complexity. More, the average time complexity of AC-6 is optimal for constraint networks where nothing is known about the semantic of the constraints. At the end of the paper, experimental results show how much AC-6 outperforms AC-3 and AC-4.

1. Introduction

There is no need to show the importance of arc-consistency in Constraint Networks. Originating from Waltz [Waltz72], who developed it for vision problems, it has been studied by Mackworth and Freuder [Mackworth77], [Mac&Fre85], by Mohr and Henderson [Moh&Hen86] who have proposed an algorithm having an optimal worst-case time complexity: $O(ed^2)$, where e is the number of constraints (or relations) and d the size of the largest domain. In [Bessière91] its use has been extended to Dynamic constraint networks. Recently, Van Hentenryck, Deville and Teng [Dev&VanH91], [VanH&al92], have proposed a generic algorithm which can be implemented with all known techniques, and have extracted classes of networks on which there exist algorithms running arc-consistency in $O(ed)$. In 1992, Perlin [Perlin92] has

given properties of arc-consistency on factorable relations.

Everybody now looks for arc-consistency complexity in particular classes of constraint networks because AC-4 [Moh&Hen86] has an optimal worst-case complexity and it is supposed that we cannot do better.

But AC-4 drawbacks are its average time complexity which is too much near the worst-case time complexity and more, its space complexity which is $O(ed^2)$. In applications with a large number of values in variables domains and with weak constraints, AC-3 is often used instead of AC-4 because of its space complexity. Such situations appear for example when domains encode discrete intervals and constraints are defined as arithmetic relations ($\geq$, $<$, $\neq$,...). Constraint Logic Programming (CLP) languages [Din&al88] which are big consumers of arc-consistency (arc-consistency has some good properties in CLP) are concerned by these problems.

In problems with many solutions, where the constraints are weak, AC-4 initialization step is very long because it requires to consider the relations in their whole to construct its data structure. In those cases, AC-3 [Mac&Fre85] runs faster than AC-4 in spite of its non-optimal time complexity.

In this paper we propose a new algorithm, AC-6, which while keeping $O(ed^2)$ optimal worst-case time complexity of AC-4, discards the problem of space complexity (AC-6 space complexity is $O(ed)$) and checks just enough data in the constraints to compute the arc-consistent domain. AC-4 looks for all the reasons for a value to be in the arc-consistent domain: it checks, for each value, all the values compatible with it (called its supports) to prove this value is viable. AC-6 only looks for one reason per constraint to prove that a value is viable: it checks, for each value, one support per constraint, looking for another one only when the current support is removed from the domain.

The rest of the paper is organized as follows. Section 2 gives some preliminaries on constraint networks and arc-consistency. Section 3 presents the algorithm AC-6. In section 4, experimental results show how much AC-6 outperforms the algorithms AC-3 and AC-4[1]. A conclusion is given in section 5.

2. Background

A *network of binary constraints (CN)* is defined as a set of n variables $\{i, j,...\}$, a domain $D=\{D_i, D_j,...\}$ where D_i is the set of possible values for variable i, and a set of binary constraints between variables. A *binary constraint* (or relation) R_{ij} between variables i and j is a subset of the Cartesian product $D_i \times D_j$ that specifies the allowed pairs of values for i and j. Following from Montanari [Montanari74], a binary relation R_{ij} between variables i and j is usually represented as a (0,1)-matrix (or a matrix of booleans) with $|D_i|$ rows and $|D_j|$ columns by imposing an ordering on the domains of the variables. Value true at row a, column b, denoted $R_{ij}(a, b)$, means that the pair consisting of the ath element of D_i and the bth element of D_j is permitted; value false means the pair is not permitted. In all the networks of interest here $R_{ij}(a, b)=R_{ji}(b, a)$. In some applications (constraint logic programming, temporal reasoning,...), R_{ij} is defined as an arithmetic relation $(=, \neq, <, \geq,...)$ without giving the matrix of allowed and not allowed pairs of values.

A *graph G* can be associated to a constraint network, where nodes correspond to variables in the CN and an edge links nodes i and j every time there is a relation R_{ij} on variables i and j in the CN. For the purpose of this paper, we consider G as a symetric directed graph with arcs (i, j) and (j, i) in place of the edge $\{i, j\}$.

A *solution* of a constraint network is an instanciation of the variables such that all the constraints are satisfied.

> **Definition.** Having the constraint R_{ij}, value b in D_j is called a *support* for value a in D_i if the pair (a, b) is allowed by R_{ij} (i.e. $R_{ij}(a, b)$ is true).
>
> A value a for a variable i is *viable* if for every variable j such that R_{ij} exists, a has a support in D_j.
>
> The domain D of a CN is *arc-consistent* if for every variable i in the CN, all the values in D_i are viable.

3. Arc-consistency with unique support

3.1. Preamble

As Mohr and Henderson underlined in [Moh&Hen86], arc-consistency is based on the notion of support. As long as a value a for a variable i (denoted (i, a)) has supporting values on each of the other variables j linked to i in the constraint graph, a is considered a viable value for i. But once there exists a variable on which no remaining value satisfies the relation with (i, a), then a must be eliminated from D_i.

The algorithm proposed in [Moh&Hen86] makes this support explicit by assigning a counter $counter[(i, j), a]$ to each arc-value pair involving the arc (i, j) and the value a on the variable i. This counter records the number of supports of (i, a) in D_j. For each value (j, b), a set S_{jb} is constructed, where $S_{jb}=\{(i, a)/(j, b)$ supports $(i, a)\}$. Then, if (j, b) is eliminated from D_j, $counter[(i, j), a]$ must be decremented for each (i, a) in S_{jb}.

This data structure is at the origin of AC-4 optimal worst-case time complexity. But computing the number of supports for each value (i, a) on each constraint R_{ij} and recording all the values (i, a) supported by each value (j, b) implies an expensive space complexity of $O(ed^2)$ (the size of the support sets S_{jb}) and an average time complexity increasing with the number of allowed pairs in the relations since the number of supports is proportional to the number of allowed pairs in the relations.

The purpose of AC-6 is then to avoid the expensive checking of the relations to find all the supports for all the values. AC-6 keeps the same principle as AC-4, but instead of checking all the supports for a value, it only checks one support (the first one) for each value (i, a) on each constraint R_{ij} to prove that (i, a) is currently viable. When (j, b) is found as the smallest support of (i, a) on R_{ij}, (i, a) is added to S_{jb}, the list of values currently having (j, b) as smallest support. If (j, b) is removed from D_j then AC-6 looks for *the next* support in D_j for each value (i, a) in S_{jb}. The only requirement in the use of AC-6 is to have a total ordering in all domains D_j. But this is not a restriction since in any implementation, a total ordering is imposed on the domains. This ordering is independent of any ordering computed in a rearrangement strategy for searching solutions.

3.2. The algorithm

The algorithm proposed here works with the following data structure:

• A table M of booleans keeps track of which values of the initial domain are in the current domain or not ($M(i, a)=$**true** $\Leftrightarrow a \in D_i$). In this table, each initial D_i is considered as the integer range $1..|D_i|$. But it can be a set of values of any type with a total ordering on these values. We use the following

---

[1]AC-5 [VanH&al92] is not discussed here since it is not an improvement but a generic framework in which all previous algorithms can be written.

constant time functions to handle D_i sets that are considered as lists:

- $first(D_i)$ returns the smallest value in D_i.
- $last(D_i)$ returns the largest value in D_i.
- $next(a, D_i)$ returns the value a' in D_i such that every value a'' larger than a and smaller than a' is out of D_i.

• $S_{jb}=\{(i, a)/(j, b)$ is the smallest value in D_j supporting (i, a) on $R_{ij}\}$ while in AC-4 it was containing all the values supported by (j, b).

• Counters for each arc-value pair in AC-4 are not used in AC-6.

• A list $List$ contains values deleted from the domain but for which the propagation of the deletion has not been processed yet.

In AC-4, when a value (j, b) was deleted, it was added to $List$ waiting for the propagation of the consequences of its deletion. These consequences were to decrement $counter[(i, j), a]$ for every (i, a) in S_{jb} and to delete (i, a) when $counter[(i, j), a]$ becomes equal to zero. In AC-6, the use of $List$ is not changed but the consequence of (j, b) deletion is now to find another support for every (i, a) in S_{jb}. Having an ordering on D_j we look after b (the old support) for another value c in D_j supporting (i, a) on R_{ij} (we know there is no such value before b). When such a value c is found, (i, a) is added to S_{jc} since (j, c) is the new smallest support for (i, a) in D_j. If no such value exists, (i, a) is removed and put in $List$.

AC-6 uses the following procedure to find the smallest value in D_j not smaller than b and supporting (i, a) on R_{ij}:

procedure nextsupport(**in** i, j, a : integer; **in out** b : integer; **out** *emptysupport* : boolean);
  begin
    {search of the smallest value as large as b that belongs to D_j; this part is not needed in the call of the procedure done in the initialization step since b already belongs to D_j}
    while not $M(j, b)$ **and** $b < last(D_j)$ **do** $b \leftarrow b + 1$;
    emptysupport $\leftarrow$ **not** $M(j, b)$;

    {search of the smallest support for (i, a) in D_j}
    while not $R_{ij}(a, b)$ **and not** *emptysupport* **do**
      if $b < last(D_j)$ **then** $b \leftarrow next(b, D_j)$
      else *emptysupport* $\leftarrow$ **true**
  end;

The algorithm AC-6 has the same framework as AC-4. In the initialization step, we look for a support for every value (i, a) on each constraint R_{ij} to prove that (i, a) is viable. If there exists a constraint R_{ij} on which (i, a) has no support, it is removed from D_i and put in $List$.

In the propagation step, values (j, b) are taken from $List$ to propagate the consequences of their deletion: finding another support (j, c) for values (i, a)

they were supporting (values (i, a) in S_{jb}). When such a value c in D_j is not found, (i, a) is removed from D_i and put in $List$ at its turn.

{initialization}
for $(i, a) \in D$ **do** $S_{ia} \leftarrow \varnothing$; $M(i, a) \leftarrow$ **true** ;
for $(i, j) \in arcs(G)$ **do**
  for $a \in D_i$ **do**
    begin
    if $D_j = \varnothing$
    then *emptysupport* $\leftarrow$ **true**
    else $b \leftarrow first(D_j)$;
        nextsupport(i, j, a, b, *emptysupport*) ;
    if *emptysupport*
    then $D_i \leftarrow D_i \setminus \{a\}$; $M(i, a) \leftarrow$ **false** ;
        Append($List, (i, a)$)
    else Append($S_{jb}, (i, a)$)
    end

{propagation}
while $List \neq \varnothing$ **do**
  begin
  choose (j, b) from $List$ and remove (j, b) from $List$;
  for $(i, a) \in S_{jb}$ **do**   {before its deletion (j, b) was the
    begin   smallest support in D_j for (i, a) on R_{ij}}
    remove (i, a) from S_{jb} ;
    if $M(i, a)$ **then**
      begin
      $c \leftarrow b$; nextsupport(i, j, a, c, *emptysupport*) ;
      if *emptysupport*
      then $D_i \leftarrow D_i \setminus \{a\}$; $M(i, a) \leftarrow$ **false** ;
         Append($List, (i, a)$)
      else Append($S_{jc}, (i, a)$)
      end
    end
  end

3.3. Correctness of AC-6

Here are the key steps for a complete proof of the correctness of AC-6. In this section we denote *maxAC* the maximal arc-consistent domain which is expected to be computed by an arc-consistency algorithm.

• In AC-6, value (i, a) is removed from D_i only when it has no support in D_j on a constraint R_{ij}. If all previously removed values are out of *maxAC* then (i, a) is out of *maxAC*. *maxAC* was trivially included in D when AC-6 started. Then, by induction, (i, a) is out of *maxAC*. Thus, $maxAC \subseteq D$ is an invariant property of AC-6.

• Every time a value (j, b) is removed, it is put in $List$ until the values it was supporting are checked for new supports. Every time a value (i, a) is found without support on a constraint, it is removed from D. Thus, every value (i, a) in D has at least one support in $D \cup List$ on each constraint R_{ij}. AC-6 terminates with $List$ empty. Hence, after AC-6, every value in D has a support in D on each constraint. Thus, D is arc-consistent.

• $maxAC \subseteq D$ and D arc-consistent at the end of AC-6 imply that D is the maximal arc-consistent domain at the end of AC-6. ❑

3.4. Time and space complexity

In both the initialization step and the propagation step, the inner loop is a call to the procedure *nextsupport* which compute a support for a value on a constraint, starting at the current value. Hence, for each arc-value pair $[(i, j), a]$, each value in D_j will be checked at most once. There are ed arc-value pairs, thus $O(ed^2)$ is the worst-case time complexity for AC-6, as for AC-4.

The matrix M has a size proportional to the number of values in D, $O(nd)$. Arc-value pairs $[(i, j), a]$ have at most one support (j, b) with (i, a) belonging to S_{jb}; hence the total size of the S_{jb} sets is at most equal to the number of arc-value pairs: $O(ed)$. Therefore, the worst-case space complexity of AC-6 is $O(ed)$. The problem of the space complexity of AC-4 is worked out.

Having no information on the semantic of the constraints this algorithm is the best in time we can expect. It stops the processing of a value just when it has the proof it is viable (i.e. the first support). If we know something about the constraint (e.g. functional) we can locally improve the search of the support (e.g. for a functional constraint finding a support for a value is in constant time) but this is not in the topic of this paper.

4. Experimental results

Having produced an algorithm making just enough processing to ensure that each value is viable, we expect it to outperform AC-3 and AC-4 on all the problems.

We have tested the performances of the three algorithms on a large spectrum of problems. For each problem, we have counted the number of atomic operations and tests done by each algorithm.

The first comparison has been done on the zebra problem (see Appendix) which has strong similitudes with real-life problems. With the representation of this problem given in [Dechter88], we obtain the following results:

AC-3: 4008
AC-4: 3824
AC-6: 1998

Afterwards, in fig. 1, we have compared the three algorithms on a problem often used for algorithms comparisons: the *n*-queens (i.e. a *n*x*n* chessboard on which we want to put *n* queens, none of them being attacked by any other). We can encode it in a CN by representing each column by a variable which values are the rows. The graph associated to the CN is complete, each pair $\{i, j\}$ of variables being linked by a constraint that specifies the allowed positions for the two queens in the columns i and j. This CN is very particular since it is extremely symetrical and all the constraints are weak (note that arc-consistency does not discard any value in this CN). So, results obtained here cannot be generalized to other kinds of CNs. However, this CN is interesting to illustrate the behavior of the algorithms on CNs with weak constraints where arc-consistency discards few values. On these CNs, AC-4 fails while AC-3 and AC-4 have an $O(ed)$ average time complexity.

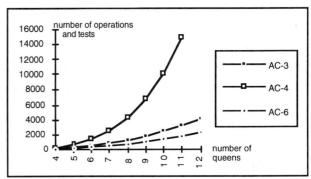

Figure 1. Comparison of AC-3, AC-4 and AC-6 on the *n*-queens problem

Finally, we defined classes of randomly generated constraint networks and we showed in fig. 2, 3 and 4 the behavior of the three algorithms on these different types of constraint networks. Four parameters were taken into account: n the number of variables, d the number of values per variable, pc the probability that a constraint R_{ij} between two variables exists and pu the probability in existing relations R_{ij} that a pair of values $R_{ij}(a, b)$ be allowed. The result given for each class is the average for ten instances of problems in the class, to be more representative of the class.

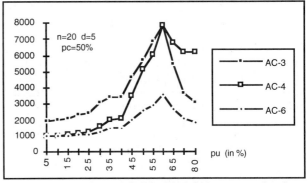

Figure 2. AC-3, AC-4 and AC-6 on randomly generated CNs with 20 variables having 5 possible values and where the probability pc to have a constraint between two variables is 50 per cent

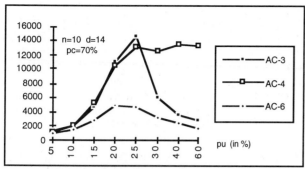

Figure 3. AC-3, AC-4 and AC-6 on randomly generated CNs with 10 variables having 14 possible values and where the probability pc to have a constraint between two variables is 70 %

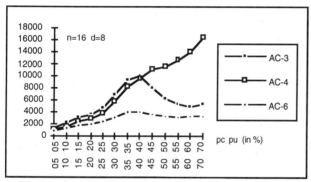

Figure 4. AC-3, AC-4 and AC-6 on randomly generated CNs with 16 variables having 8 possible values

Let summarize roughly those results:

• AC-4 performances decrease when d or pu grow. The larger the domains and the weaker the constraints, the worse AC-4. When we take a look at those figures, AC-4 seems to be not interesting. But, being good when arc-consistency discards many values, randomly generated CNs are not favourable to it. In practical cases, constraints are less homogeneous than in randomly generated CNs and AC-4 is better. Many applications, like SYNTHIA [Jan&al90] to design peptide synthesis plans, prefer AC-4 to AC-3.

• AC-3 is never very bad but it can check several times a pair of values because of its non-optimal time complexity. So, when propagation of deletions is long: in "middle" CNs (i.e. not too much constrained and not under-constrained), AC-3 becomes inefficient. However, CNs treated in practice are often "middle" CNs since under-constrained CNs and too much constrained CNs are easy to solve, a solution or a contradiction being quickly found.

• AC-6 has kept the optimal worst-case time complexity of AC-4 while working out the problem of considering the relations in their whole. Hence, it is very good on CNs with weak constraints contrary to AC-4, and remains efficient on CNs where the constraints are tighten or on "middle" CNs, contrary to AC-3.

5. Conclusion

We have provided an algorithm, AC-6, to achieve arc-consistency in binary constraint networks. It keeps the $O(ed^2)$ optimal worst-case time complexity of AC-4 while working out the two drawbacks of this algorithm: its space complexity ($O(ed^2)$), and its average time complexity on constraint networks with weak constraints. AC-6 has an $O(ed)$ space complexity and its running-time decreases when the weakness of the constraints grows. Experimental results are given, showing that AC-6 outperforms AC-3 and AC-4 (the two other best algorithms to achieve arc-consistency) on all the problems tested.

Acknowledgments

We want to thank Amit Bellicha for his useful comments on the previous draft.

Appendix: The zebra problem

1. There are five houses, each of a different color and inhabited by men of different nationalities, with different pets, drinks, and cigarettes.
2. The Englishman lives in the red house.
3. The Spaniard owns a dog.
4. Coffee is drunk in the green house.
5. The Ukranian drinks tea.
6. The green house is immediatly to the right of the ivory house.
7. The Old-Gold smoker owns snails.
8. Kools are being smoked in the yellow house.
9. Milk is drunk in the middle house.
10. The Norwegian lives in the first house on the left.
11. The Chesterfield smoker lives next to the fox owner.
12. Kools are smoked in the house next the house where the horse is kept.
13. The Lucky-Strike smoker drinks orange juice.
14. The Japanese smokes Parliament.
15. The Norwegian lives next to the blue house.

The query is: Who drinks water? and who owns the Zebra?

This problem can be represented as a binary constraint network involving 25 variables, one for each of the five houses, five nationalities, five pets, five drinks, and five cigarettes. Each of the variables has domain values {1, 2, 3, 4, 5}, each number corresponding to a house position (e.g. assigning the value 2 to the variable *horse* means that the horse owner lives in the second house) [Dechter88].

References

Bessière, C. 1991. *"Arc-Consistency in Dynamic Constraint Satisfaction Problems"*; Proceedings 9th National Conference on Artificial Intelligence, Anaheim CA, 221-226

Dechter, R. 1988. *"Constraint Processing Incorporating Backjumping, Learning, and Cutset-Decomposition"*; Proceedings 4th IEEE Conference on AI for Applications, San Diego CA, 312-319

Deville, Y. and Van Hentenryck, P. 1991. *"An Efficient Arc Consistency Algorithm for a Class of CSP Problems"*; Proceedings 12th International Joint Conference on Artificial Intelligence, Sydney, Australia, 325-330

Dincbas, M., Van Hentenryck, P., Simonis, H., Aggoun, A., Graf, T. and Berthier, F. 1988. *"The constraint logic programming language CHIP"*; Proceedings International Conference on Fifth Generation Computer Systems, Tokyo, Japan

Janssen, P., Jégou, P., Nouguier, B., Vilarem, M.C. and Castro, B. 1990. *"SYNTHIA: Assisted Design of Peptide Synthesis Plans"*; New Journal of Chemistry, 14-12, 969-976

Mackworth, A.K. 1977. *"Consistency in Networks of Relations"*; Artificial Intelligence 8, 99-118

Mackworth, A.K. and Freuder, E.C. 1985. *"The Complexity of Some Polynomial Network Consistency Algorithms for Constraint Satisfaction Problems"*; Artificial Intelligence 25, 65-74

Mohr, R. and Henderson, T.C. 1986. *"Arc and Path Consistency Revisited"*; Artificial Intelligence 28, 225-233

Montanari, U. 1974. *"Networks of Constraints: Fundamental Properties and Applications to Picture Processing"*; Information Science 7, 95-132

Perlin, M. 1992. *"Arc-consistency for factorable relations"*; Artificial Intelligence 53, 329-342

Van Hentenryck, P., Deville, Y. and Teng, C.M. 1992. *"A generic arc-consistency algorithm and its specializations"*; Artificial Intelligence 57, 291-321

Waltz, D.L. 1972. *"Understanding Line Drawings of Scenes with Shadows"*; in: The Psychology of Computer Vision, McGraw Hill, 1975, 19-91 (first published in: Tech.Rep. AI271, MIT MA, 1972)

On the Consistency of General Constraint-Satisfaction Problems

Philippe Jégou

L.I.U.P. - Université de Provence

3,Place Victor Hugo

F13331 Marseille cedex 3, France

jegou@gyptis.univ-mrs.fr

Abstract

The problem of checking for consistency of Constraint-Satisfaction Problems (CSPs) is a fundamental problem in the field of constraint-based reasonning. Moreover, it is a hard problem since satisfiability of CSPs belongs to the class of NP-complete problems. So, in (Freuder 1982), Freuder gave theoretical results concerning consistency of binary CSPs (two variables per constraints). In this paper, we proposed an extension to these results to general CSP (n-ary constraints). On one hand, we define a partial consistency well adjusted to general CSPs called *hyper-k-consistency*. On the other hand, we proposed a measure of the connectivity of hypergraphs called *width of hypergraphs*. Using width of hypergraphs and hyper-k-consistency, we derive a theorem defining a sufficient condition for consistency of general CSPs.

Introduction

Constraint-satisfaction problems (CSPs) involve the assignment of values to variables which are subject to a set of constraints. Examples of CSPs are map coloring, conjunctive queries in a relational databases, line drawings understanding, pattern matching in production rules systems, combinatorial puzzles... In the general case checking for the satisfiability (i.e. consistency) of a CSP is a NP-complete problem. A well known method for solving CSP is the Backtrack procedure. The complexity of this procedure is exponential in the size of the CSP, and consequently, this approach frequently induces "combinatorial explosion". So, many works try to improve the search efficiency. Three important classes of methods has been proposed:

1. Improving Backtrack search: eg. dependency-directed backtracking, Forward Checking (Haralick & Elliot 1980), etc.

2. Improving representation of the problem before search: eg. technics of achieving local consistencies using arc-consistent filtering (Mohr & Henderson 1986).

3. Decomposition methods: these technics are based on an analysis of topological features of a the constraint network related to a given CSP; these methods have generally better complexity upper bound than Backtrack methods.

The two first classes of methods do not improved theoretical complexity of solving CSP, but give on many problems, good practical results. The methods of the third class are based on theoretical results due to Freuder (Freuder 1982) (eg. the cycle-cutset method (Dechter 1990)) or research in the field of relational databases theory (Beeri et al. 1983) (eg. tree-clustering (Dechter & Pearl 1989)). These theoretical results associate a structural property of a given constraint network (eg. an acyclic network) to a semantic property related to a partial consistency (eg. arc-consistency). These two properties permit to derive a theorem concerning global consistency of the CSP and its tractability. Intuitivly, more the network is connected, more the CSP must satisfies a large consistency, and consequently, more the problem is hard to solve. These theoretical results have two practical benefits: on one hand, to define polynomial classes of CSPs, and on the other hand, to elaborate decomposition methods.

In this paper, we propose a theoretical result that is a generalization of the results given in (Freuder 1982) and in relational databases theory (Beeri et al. 1983). Indeed, the theorem given by Freuder concerns binary CSPs (only two variables per constraint), and so this limitation induces practical problems to its application. On the contrary, the property given in the field of relational databases concerns n-ary CSPs (no limitation to the number of variables per constraint), but only CSPs with no cycle. The theorem given in this paper concerns binary and n-ary CSPs, and cyclic constraint networks. It permits to define a sufficient condition to global consistency of general CSPs. This property associates a structural measure of the connectivity of the network, called *width of hypergraph* (in the spirit of Freuder), to a semantic property of CSPs related to partial consistency of n-ary CSPs, that is called *hyper-k-consitency*.

It is known that any non-binary CSP can be treated as a binary CSP if one look at the dual representation or join-graph (this representation has been defined in the field of relational databases: constraints are variables and binary constraints impose equality on common variables). But this approach if of limited interest: it does not allow to realize extension of all theorems and algorithms to non-binary CSPs. For example, the width of an n-ary CSP cannot be defined exactly as the width of its join graph (see example in figure 3). So, original definitions are introduced in this paper.

The second section presents definitions and preliminaries. In the third section, we defined hyper-k-consitency while in next section we introduce the notion of width of hypergraphs. The last section exposes the consistency theorem and give comments about its usability.

Definitions and preliminaries

Finite Constraint-Satisfaction Problems

A *General Constraint-Satisfaction Problem* involves a set X of n variables $X_1, X_2, \ldots X_n$, each defined by its finite domain values $D_1, D_2, \ldots D_n$ (d denotes the maximum cardinality over all the D_i). D is the set of all domains. C is the set of constraints $C_1, C_2, \ldots C_m$. A constraint C_i is defined as a set of variables $(X_{i_1}, X_{i_2}, \ldots X_{i_{j_i}})$. To any constraint C_i, we associate a subset of the cartesian product $D_{i_1} \times \ldots \times D_{i_{j_i}}$ that is denoted R_i (R_i specifies which values of the variables are compatible with each other; R_i is a relation, so it is a set of tuples). R is the set of all R_i. So, we denote a CSP $\mathcal{P} = (X, D, C, R)$. A solution is an assignment of value to all variables satisfying all the constraints.

Given a CSP $\mathcal{P} = (X, D, C, R)$, the hypergraph (X, C) is called the constraint hypergraph (nodes are variables and hyper-edges are defined by constraints). A binary CSP is one in which all the constraints are binary, i.e. only pairs of variables are possible, so (X, C) is a graph called constraint graph. For a given CSP, the problem is either to find all solutions or one solution, or to know if there exists any solution. The decision problem (existence of solution) is known to be NP-complete. We use two relationnal operators. *Projection of relations*: if $X' \subseteq C_i$, the projection of R_i on X' is denoted $R_i[X']$ and *join of relations* denoted $R_i \bowtie R_j$; see formal definitions in (Maier 1983).

Partial consistencies in CSPs

Different levels of consistency have been introduced in the field of CSPs. The methods to achieve these local consistencies are considered as filtering algorithms: they may lead to problem simplifications, without changing the solution set. They have been used as well to improve the representation prior the search, as to avoid backtrack during the search (Haralick & Elliot 1980). Historically, the first partial consistency

proposed was *arc-consistency*. Its generalization was given in (Freuder 1978).

Definition 1 (Freuder 1978). A CSP is *k-consistent* iff for all set of $k - 1$ variables, and all consistent assignments of these variables (that satisfy all the constraints among them), for all k^{th} variable X_k, there exists a value in the domain D_k that satisfies all the constraints among the k variables. A CSP is *strongly k-consistent* iff the CSP is j-consistent for $j = 1, \ldots k$.

Given a CSP and a value k, the complexity of the algorithm achieving k-consistencyis $O(n^k d^k)$ (Cooper 1989). But achieving k-consistency on a binary CSP generally induces new constraints, with arity equal to $k - 1$. Consequently, a binary CSP can be tranformed in an n-ary CSP using this method (eg. achieving 4-consistency).

An other partial-consistency has been defined particularly for n-ary CSPs: the *pairwise-consistency* (Janssen et al. 1989) also called *inter-consistency* (Jégou 1991). This consistency is based on works concerning relational databases (Beeri et al. 1983). Whereas k-consistency is a local consistency between variables, domains and constraints, inter-consistency defines a consistency between constraints and relations. On the contrary of k-consistency, that does not consider structural features of the constraint network, inter-consistency is particularly adjusted to the connections in n-ary CSPs, because connections correspond to intersections between constraints.

Definition 2 (Beeri et al. 1983)(Janssen et al. 1989). We said that $\mathcal{P} = (X, D, C, R)$ is *inter-consistent* iff $\forall C_i, \forall C_j, R_i[C_i \cap C_j] = R_j[C_i \cap C_j]$ and $\forall R_i, R_i \neq \emptyset$.

In (Janssen et al. 1989), a polynomial algorithm achieving this consistency is given. This algorithm is based on an equivalent binary representation given in the next section.

Binary representation for n-ary CSPs

In this representation, the vertices of the constraint graph are n-ary constraints C_i, their domains are the associated relations R_i, and the edges, that are new constraints, are given by intersections between C_i. The compatibility relations are then given by the equality constraints between the connected R_i. This binary representation is called the *constraint intergraph associated to a constraint hypergraph* (Jégou 1991).

Definition 3. A *hypergraph* H is a pair (X, C) where X is a finite set of vertices and C a set of hyper-edges, i.e. subsets of X. When the cardinality of any hyper-edges is two, the hypergraph is a graph (necessary undirected). Given a CSP (X, D, C, R), we consider its associated hypergraph denoted (X, C).

Definition 4 (Bernstein & Goodman 1981). Given a hypergraph $H = (X, C)$, an *intergraph* of H is a graph $G(H) = (C, E)$ such as:

- $E \subseteq \{\{C_i, C_j\} \subset C / i \neq j \text{ and } C_i \cap C_j \neq \emptyset\}$
- $\forall C_i, C_j \in C$, if $C_i \cap C_j \neq \emptyset$, there is a chain $(C_i = C_1, C_2, \ldots C_q = C_j)$ in $G(H)$ such as $\forall k, 1 \leq k < q, C_i \cap C_j \subseteq C_k \cap C_{k+1}$

Intergraphs are also called *line-graphs*, *join-graphs* (Maier 1983) and *dual-graphs* (Dechter & Pearl 1989).

Definition 5 (Jégou 1991). Given a CSP (X, D, C, R), we defined an equivalent (equivalent sets of solutions) binary CSP (C, R, E, Q):

- (C, E) is an intergraph of the hypergraph (X, C).
- $C = \{C_1, \ldots C_m\}$ is a set of variables defined on domains $R = \{R_1, \ldots R_m\}$.
- if $\{C_i, C_j\} \in E$, then we have an equality constraint: $Q_k = \{(r_i, r_j) \in R_i \times R_j / r_i[C_i \cap C_j] = r_j[C_i \cap C_j]\}$

Given a hypergraph, it can exists several associated intergraphs. Some of them can contain redundant edges that can be deleted to obtain an other intergraph. The maximal one is called *representative graph*. In the field of CSPs, we are naturally interested with minimal intergraphs: all edges are necessary, i.e. no edge can be deleted conserving the property of chains in intergraphs. So an algorithms have been proposed to find minimal intergraphs in (Janssen et al. 1989). A study of combinatorial properties of minimal intergraphs is given in (Jégou & Vilarem 1993). In the next example two minimal intergraphs are given:

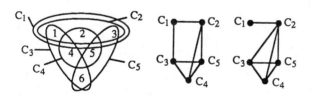

Figure 1. Hypergraph (a) and two minimal intergraphs.

A sufficient condition for CSPs consistency

Freuder has identified sufficient conditions for a binary CSP to satisfy consistency, ie. satisfiability. These conditions associate topology of the constraint graph with partial consistency.

Definition 6 (Freuder 1982). An *ordered constraint graph* is a constraint graph in which nodes are linearly ordered. The *width of a node* is the number of edges that link that node to previous nodes. The *width of an order* is the maximum width of all nodes. The *width of a graph* is the minimum width of all orderings of that graph.

This definition is illustrated in figure 1: the width of the graph (b) is 2 and the width of the graph (c) is 3. On this example, we can remark that the width of an hypergraph cannot be defined as the width of its minimal intergraph, because all minimal intergraphs has not the same width.

Theorem 7 (Freuder 1982). Given a CSP, if the level of strong consistency is greater than the width of the constraint graph, then the CSP is consistent and it is possible to find solutions without backtracking (in polynomial time).

Freuder also gave an algorithm to compute the width of any graph (in $O(n+m)$). So given a CSP, it is sufficient to know the width of the constraint graph, denoted $k - 1$, then to achieve k-consistency. But a problem appears: this approach is possible only for acyclic constraint graphs (width equal to one) and a subclass of graphs the width of which is two (called regular graphs of width two in (Dechter & Pearl 1988)). The cause of that problem: achieving k-consistency generally induces n-ary constraints (arity can be equal to $k-1$), so the corresponding problem is a constraint hypergraph, and the theorem can not be applied. Nevertheless, the result concerning acyclic CSPs is applied in the cycle-cutset method (Dechter 90) and we can consider Freuder's theorem as a vehicle to give a lower bound for complexity of a binary CSP: to the order of d^k if its width is $k - 1$, because complexity of achieving k-consistency is $O(n^k d^k)$ (Cooper 1989).

A result of relational database theory

A similar property has been derived in the field of relational databases. This property is related to acyclic hypergraphs.

Definition 8 (Beeri et al. 1983). A hypergraph is acyclic iff $\exists$ a linear order $(C_1, C_2, \ldots C_m)$ such as $\forall i, 1 < i \leq m. \exists j_i < i / (C_i \bigcap \cup_{k=1}^{i-1} C_k) \subseteq C_{j_i}$, (this property is called *running intersection property*)

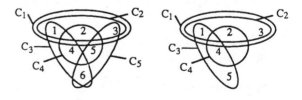

Figure 2. Cyclic (a) and acyclic (b) hypergraphs.

(Beeri et al. 1983) gave a fundamental property of acyclic database schemes that concerns consistency of such databases, namely *global consistency*. This result is presented below using CSPs terminology:

Definition 9. Let $\mathcal{P} = (X, D, C, R)$ be a CSP. We say that $\mathcal{P}$ is *globally consistent* if there is a relation S over the variables X (S is the set of solutions) such as $\forall i, 1 \leq i \leq m, R_i = S[C_i]$. It is equivalent to $\forall i, 1 \leq i \leq m, (\bowtie_{j=1}^{m} R_j)[C_i] = R_i$ since $S = (\bowtie_{j=1}^{m} R_j)$.

Note that global consistency of CSPs implies satisfiability of CSPa. Indeed, a CSP is globally consistent iff every tuple of relations appears at least in one solution. Furthermore, it is clear that global consistency implies inter-consistency but the converse is false. We give the interpretation in the field of CSP to the property given by (Beeri et al. 1983):

Theorem 10 (Beeri et al. 1983). If $\mathcal{P}$ is such as its constraints hypergraph is acyclic, then

$\mathcal{P}$ is inter-consistent $\Leftrightarrow$ $\mathcal{P}$ is globally consistent.

An immediate application of this theorem concerns the consistency checking of CSPs. We know polynomial algorithms to achieve inter-consistency while to check global consistency is a NP-complete problem. So, knowing this theorem, if the database scheme is acyclic, it is possible to check global consistency in a polynomial time achieving inter-consistency. This result is applied in the tree-clustering method (Dechter & Pearl 1989).

Some remarks

Theorems 7 and 10 are significant. First, they can be used to solve CSP; immediatly if the considered CSP is acyclic, or for all CSP, using decomposition methods as the cycle-cutset method, or tree-clustering scheme. Second, because they define polynomial subclasses of CSPs. Nevertheless, there is two significant limitations to these theoretical results. On one hand, theorem 7 is only defined on binary CSPs, and so, it can not be applied, nor on n-ary CSPs, nor on constraints graph with width greater than 2. On the other hand, theorem 11 concerns only acyclic n-ary CSPs. So, a generalization to cyclic n-ary CSPs is necessary to extend this kind of theoretical approach to all CSPs.

A new consistency for n-ary CSPs: Hyper-k-consistency

When Freuder defined k-consistency, the definition is related to assignments: "given a consistent assignment of variables $X_1, X_2, \ldots X_{k-1}$, it is possible to extend this assignment for all k^{th} variable". To generalize k-consistency to n-ary CSPs, we consider the same approach but with constraints and relations: we can consider "assignment" of constraints $C_1, C_2, \ldots C_{k-1}$, and their extension to any k^{th} constraint. Our definition of hyper-k-consistency is given in this spirit:

Definition 11. A CSP $\mathcal{P} = (X, D, C, R)$ is *hyper-k-consistent* iff $\forall R_i, R_i \neq \emptyset$ and $\forall C_1, C_2, \ldots C_{k-1} \in C$,

$$(\bowtie_{i=1}^{k-1} R_i)[(\cup_{i=1}^{k-1} C_i) \cap C_k] \subseteq R_k[(\cup_{i=1}^{k-1} C_i) \cap C_k]$$

$\mathcal{P}$ is *strongly hyper-k-consistent* iff $\forall i, 1 \leq i \leq k$, $\mathcal{P}$ is hyper-i-consistent.

We can note that hyper-2-consistency is equivalent to inter-consistency. So, hyper-k-consistency constitutes really a generalization of inter-consistency to greater levels. Actually, this definition can be considered as a formulation of k-consistency on the constraint intergraph: $(\bowtie_{i=1}^{k-1} r_i) \in (\bowtie_{i=1}^{k-1} R_i)$ signifies that $(r_1, r_2, \ldots r_{k-1})$ is a consistent assignment of constraints $C_1, C_2, \ldots C_{k-1}$, and if there is $r_k \in R_k$ such as:

$$(\bowtie_{i=1}^{k-1} r_i)[(\cup_{i=1}^{k-1} C_i) \cap C_k] = r_k[(\cup_{i=1}^{k-1} C_i) \cap C_k]$$

then $(r_1, r_2, \ldots r_{k-1}, r_k)$ is a consistent assignment of constraints $C_1, C_2, \ldots C_{k-1}, C_k$, i.e. k variables of the constraint intergraph. This particularity induces a method to achieve hyper-k-consistency, that is based on the same approach of achieving k-consistency on binary CSPs. So, we have the same kind of problems: achieving hyper-k-consistency can modified constraint hypergraph. A second problem concerns the complexity of achieving hyper-k-consistency: the complexity is in the order of r^k if r is the maximum size of R_i. These problems are discussed in (Jégou 1991).
Another remark about hyper-k-consistency concerns its links with global consistency; we easily verify that if a CSP $\mathcal{P}$ is hyper-m-consistent, then $\mathcal{P}$ is globally consistent while the converse is generally false.

The definition of hyper-k-consistency in n-ary CSP concerns connections in hypergraphs, i.e. intersections between hyper-edges. So the definition of width of hypergraph is based on the same principles.

Width of Hypergraphs

Connections in hypergraphs concerns intersections between hyper-edges. So, the consistency of a n-ary CSP is intimately connected to the intersections between hyper-edges. The definition of width of hypergraph allows us to define a degree of cyclicity of hypergraphs. Using this width, we shall work out links between structural properties of hypergraphs and the global consistency of n-ary CSPs.

Before to give our definition of the width of an hypergraph, we must explain why this definition is not immediatly related to intergraphs. A first reason has already been given: all minimal intergraphs of a hypergraph have not necessary the same width (see figure 1). An other reason is the next one: if we define the width of an hypergraph as the width of one of its intergraph (not necessary a minimal one), we cannot obtain the same properties than we have with Freuder's theorem that is based on a good order for the assignment of the variables:

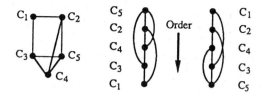

Figure 3. Problem of order on variables.

The hypergraph considered in the figure 4 is the one of the figure 1. We consider two possible orders on this intergraph. The first one is not a possible order for the assignment of the variables. Indeed, when the variable corresponding to C_3 is assigned, the variable 1 of the hypergraph has already been assigned and so, it is possible to assign C_3 with an other value for 1. This is possible because C_2 is given before C_3 in the order and because there is no edge between C_2 and C_3. So, we can obtain two different assignments for the variable 1, and finally, we can obtain a consistent assignment on $C_1, C_2, \ldots C_5$, and consequently an assignment on variables $X_1, X_2, \ldots X_6$ that is not a solution of the problem. The second order of width 3 does not induce such problems.

Definition 12. Given a hypergraph $H = (X, C)$, $\mathcal{O}$ the set of linear orders on C, and a linear order $\tau = (C_1, \ldots C_m) \in \mathcal{O}$:

- the *width of C_i in order τ on H* is the number of maximal intersections with predecessors of C_i in τ; $\mathcal{L}_\tau(C_i)$ denotes the width of C_i in order τ: $\mathcal{L}_\tau(C_i) = |\{C_i \cap C_j / j < i \land \neg \exists k, k < i / C_i \cap C_j \subset \neq C_i \cap C_k\}|$

- the *width of τ* is $\mathcal{L}_H(\tau) = max\{\mathcal{L}_\tau(C_i)/C_i \in C\}$

- the *width of H* is $\mathcal{L}(H) = min\{\mathcal{L}_H(\tau)/\tau \in \mathcal{O}\}$

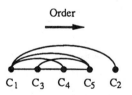

Figure 4. Width of the hypergraph.

In the fugure 4, we see the width of the hypergraph H given in figure 1-a. Here, $\mathcal{L}_H(\tau) = 3$ since $\mathcal{L}_\tau(\{3, 5, 6\}) = 3$; we can verify that $\forall \tau \in \mathcal{O}, \mathcal{L}_H(\tau) = 3$, and consequently that $\mathcal{L}(H) = 3$. A property relies width and cyclicity:

Proposition 13. H is acyclic $\Leftrightarrow \mathcal{L}(H) = 1$
Proof. *H acyclic satisfies the running intersection property*
$\Leftrightarrow \exists order (C_1, C_2, \ldots C_m)$ *such as*
$\forall i, 1 < i \leq m, \exists j_i < i/(C_i \bigcap (\cup_{k=1}^{i-1} C_k)) \subseteq C_j,$

$\Leftrightarrow \exists order (C_1, C_2, \ldots C_m)$ *such as* $\forall i, 1 < i \leq m,$
$|\{C_i \cap C_j/j < i \land \neg \exists k, k < i/C_i \cap C_j \subset \neq C_i \cap C_k\}| \leq 1$
$\Leftrightarrow \exists order (C_1, C_2, \ldots C_m)/\mathcal{L}_H(\tau) \leq 1 \Leftrightarrow \mathcal{L}(H) \leq 1.$
Moreover, it is clear that if H is connected and if C possesses more than one hyper-edge, the inequality $\mathcal{L}(H) \leq 1$ necessary holds.

Given a hypergraph (X, C) and an order on C, it is not hard to find the width of this order. It is just necessary to compute for each C_i the number of maximal intersections with predecessors, and to select the greater. On the contrary, finding an order that give the minimal width of a hypergraph is an optimization problem; this problem seems us to be open concerning its complexity: does it belong to NP-hard problems ? This question is at present an open question. In (Jégou 1991), an heuristic is proposed to find small width, ie. just an approximation of the width of a given hypergraph.

Consistency Theorem

In this section, we derive a sufficient condition to consistency of general CSPs. This condition concerns the width of the hypergraph associated to the CSP, and the hyper-k-consistency that the relations satisfy (i.e. the value k).

Theorem 14. Let $\mathcal{P} = (X, D, C, R)$ be a CSP and $H = (X, C)$. If $\mathcal{P}$ is strongly hyper-k-consistent and if $\mathcal{L}(H) \leq k - 1$, then $\mathcal{P}$ is consistent.
Proof. *We must show that $\mathcal{P}$ is consistent, i.e. $\forall i, 1 \leq i \leq m, \exists r_i \in R_i/(\bowtie_{i=1}^m r_i) \in (\bowtie_{i=1}^m R_i)$. That is $(r_1, r_2, \ldots r_m)$ can be considered as a consistent assignment on $(C_1, C_2, \ldots C_m)$: $\forall i, j, 1 \leq i, j \leq m, r_i[C_i \cap C_j] = r_j[C_i \cap C_j]$.*

We proove this property by induction on p, such as $1 \leq p \leq m$.

If $p = 1$, the property trivially holds.

We consider now a linear order $(C_1, C_2, \ldots C_m)$ associated to the width $\mathcal{L}(H) \leq k - 1$. Suppose that the property holds for $p - 1$ such as $1 < p \leq m$. That is we have $(r_1, r_2, \ldots r_{p-1})/\forall i, 1 \leq i \leq p - 1, r_i \in R_i$ and $\forall i, j, 1 \leq i, j \leq p - 1, r_i[C_i \cap C_j] = r_j[C_i \cap C_j]$.

By definition of the width, C_p possesses at most $k-1$ maximal intersections with predecessors in the order. Let $C_{i_1}, C_{i_2}, \ldots C_{i_q}$ be the corresponding C_i, with necessary $q \leq k - 1$, considering only one C_i for every maximal intersection. $\mathcal{P}$ being strongly hyper-k-consistent, and since $q \leq k - 1$, we have

$$(\bowtie_{j=1}^q R_{i_j})[(\cup_{j=1}^q C_{i_j}) \cap C_p] \subseteq R_p[(\cup_{j=1}^q C_{i_j}) \cap C_p]$$

and for the r_{i_j}'s appearing in $(r_1, r_2, \ldots r_{p-1})$

$$(\bowtie_{j=1}^q r_{i_j})[(\cup_{j=1}^q C_{i_j}) \cap C_p] \in R_p[(\cup_{j=1}^q C_{i_j}) \cap C_p]$$

So, $\exists r_p \in R_p$ such as r_p is consistent with $(r_{i_1}, r_{i_2}, \ldots r_{i_q})$, that is: $\forall j, 1 \leq j \leq q, r_{i_j}[C_{i_j} \cap C_p] = r_p[C_{i_j} \cap C_p]$.

We show now, that r_p is also consistent for all the r_i's, i.e. $r_i[C_i \cap C_p] = r_p[C_i \cap C_p]$.

Consider C_i such as $1 \leq i < p$ and $C_i \cap C_p \neq \emptyset$. By the definition of the width, $\exists j, 1 \leq j \leq q$ such as $C_i \cap C_p \subseteq C_{i_j} \cap C_p$ because the C_{i_j}'s are maximal for the intersection with C_p. Consequently, we have $C_i \cap C_p \subseteq C_i \cap C_{i_j}$.

By hypothesis, we have $r_i[C_i \cap C_{i_j}] = r_{i_j}[C_i \cap C_{i_j}]$, a fortiori, we have $r_i[C_i \cap C_p] = r_{i_j}[C_i \cap C_p]$. We seen that $r_{i_j}[C_{i_j} \cap C_p] = r_p[C_{i_j} \cap C_p]$; this emplies that $r_{i_j}[C_i \cap C_p] = r_p[C_i \cap C_p]$. Consequently, $r_i[C_i \cap C_p] = r_{i_j}[C_i \cap C_p] = r_p[C_i \cap C_p]$. So, $(r_1, r_2, \ldots r_{p-1}, r_p)$ is consistent assignment on $(C_1, C_2, \ldots C_{p-1}, C_p)$.

So the property holds for p, and consequently, $\mathcal{P}$ is consistent.

If we recall the property given about acyclic database schemes (Beeri et al. 1983), it is clear that theorem 10 is a corollary of theorem 14 (because k = 2). A more interesting result is the next corollary:

Corollary 15. Let $\mathcal{P} = (X, D, C, R)$ be a CSP such as (X, C) is a graph (i.e. all hyper-edges have cardinality 2). If $\mathcal{P}$ is strongly hyper-3-consistent, then $\mathcal{P}$ is consistent.
Proof. *It is sufficient to remark that if (X, C) is a graph, its width is at most 2, because all hyper-edges of (X, C) are edges, and an edge has no more than 2 maximal intersections.*

Nevertheless, this surprising corollary is not allways usable, because achieving hyper-k-consistency can modify the hypergraph associated to a n-ary CSP. Freuder's theorem has the same kind of problems: try to obtain its preconditions can modify these preconditions. So, concerning the practical use of the theorem, a problem is given by the verification of hyper-k-consistency in a CSP. On one hand, the theorem gives a sufficient condition to consistency, and not a necessary condition; on the other hand, given a value k, it is possible to obtain hyper-k-consistency using filtering mecanisms (Jégou 1991) in polynomial time in k, in the size of the CSP. But this process can modify the hypergraph with additions of new hyper-edges, and so modify the width. Nevertheless, contrary to Freuder's theorem, the consistency theorem can be tried to apply after modification of the width because it is directly defined on n-ary CSPs.
Consequently, the theorem must be considered in a first time as a theoretical result, with, at this moment, only one practical application: the corollary given in (Beeri et al. 1983), and not as a directly usable result.
The next research must be to exploit the theorem, on one hand to try to find new polynomial classes of C-SP, and on the other hand to propose new methods to solve practically n-ary CSPs.

References

Beeri, C., Fagin, R., Maier, D. and Yannakakis, M. 1983. On the desirability of acyclic database schemes. *Journal of the ACM* 30:479-513.

Dechter, R. 1990. Enhancement Schemes fo Constraint Processing: Backjumping, Learning and Cutset Decomposition. *Artificial Intelligence* 41:273-312.

Dechter, R. and Pearl, J. 1988. Network-based heuristics for constraint satisfaction problems. *Artificial Intelligence* 34:1-38.

Dechter, R. and Pearl, J. 1989. Tree Clustering for Constraint Networks. *Artificial Intelligence* 38:353-366.

Freuder, E.C. 1978. Synthesizing constraint expressions. *Communications of the ACM* 21:958-967.

Freuder, E.C. 1982. A sufficient condition for backtrack-free search. *Journal of the ACM* 29(1):24-32.

Haralick, R.M. and Elliot, G.L. 1980. Increasing tree search efficiency for constraint-satisfaction problems. *Artificial Intelligence* 14:263-313.

Janssen, P., Jégou, P., Nouguier, B. and Vilarem, M.C. 1989. A filtering process for general constraint satisfaction problems: achieving pairwise-consistency using an associated binary representation. In Proceedings of the IEEE Workshop on Tools for Artificial Intelligence, 420-427. Fairfax, USA

Jégou, P. 1991. Contribution à l'étude des probèmes de satisfaction de contraintes... Thèse de Doctorat, Université Montpellier II, France.

Jégou, P. and Vilarem, M.C. 1993. On some partial line graphs of a hypergraph and the associated matroid. *Discrete Mathematics*. To appear.

Maier, D. 1983. The Theory of Relational Databases. Computing Science Press.

Mohr, R. and Henderson, T.C. 1986. Arc and path consistency revisited. *Artificial Intelligence* 28(2):225-233.

Integrating Heuristics for
Constraint Satisfaction Problems: A Case Study

Steven Minton
Sterling Software
NASA Ames Research Center, M.S. 269-2
Moffett Field, CA 94035-1000
minton@ptolemy.arc.nasa.gov

Abstract

This paper describes a set of experiments with a system that synthesizes constraint satisfaction programs. The system, MULTI-TAC, is a CSP "expert" that can specialize a library of generic algorithms and methods for a particular application. MULTI-TAC not only proposes domain-specific versions of its generic heuristics, but also searches for the best combination of these heuristics and integrates them into a complete problem-specific program. We demonstrate MULTI-TAC's capabilities on a combinatorial problem, "Minimum Maximal Matching", and show that MULTI-TAC can synthesize programs for this problem that are on par with hand-coded programs. In synthesizing a program, MULTI-TAC bases its choice of heuristics on the instance distribution, and we show that this capability has a significant impact on the results.

Introduction

AI research on constraint satisfaction has primarily focused on developing new heuristic methods. Invariably, in pursuing new techniques, a tension arises between efficiency and generality. Although efficiency can be gained by designing very specific sorts of heuristics, there is little to be gained scientifically from devising ever more specialized methods. One attractive option is to devise generic algorithms that can be made efficient by incorporating additional information. A good example of this is AC-5 [Van Hentenryk *et al.*, 1992a], a generic arc-consistency method that can be specialized for functional, anti-functional or monotonic constraints to yield a very efficient algorithm.

The idea of specializing generic algorithms for a particular application can be carried much further. In this paper we evaluate a system, MULTI-TAC (Multi-Tactic Analytic Compiler), that can specialize a library of generic algorithms and heuristics to synthesize programs for constraint-satisfaction problems (CSPs). MULTI-TAC not only proposes specialized versions of its generic heuristics, but also searches for a good combination of these heuristics, and integrates them into a complete application-specific search program.

The issues we explore are quite different from those traditionally investigated in the CSP paradigm; our focus is on the specialization and integration of well-known heuristics for a given application rather than the development of new heuristics. For instance, few authors have explicitly considered that many CSP applications require solving repetitive instances of a problem (such as scheduling a factory) and are not "1-shot" problems. However, in our work we take this into account when selecting heuristics, because, as we will show, the relative utility of different heuristics can depend on the population of instances encountered.

We begin this paper with an overview of the MULTI-TAC system. We then present a case study showing the system's performance on a particular problem and illustrating the utility of automatically tailoring a program to an instance distribution.

The Problem

The input to MULTI-TAC consists of a problem specification and an instance generator for that problem. The instance generator serves as a "black box" that generates instances according to some distribution. The system is designed for a scenario where some combinatorial search problem must be solved routinely, such as a staff scheduling application where each week jobs are assigned to a set of workers.

MULTI-TAC outputs a Lisp program that is tailored to the particular problem and the instance distribution. The objective is to produce as efficient a program as possible for the instance population. In practice, our goal is to do as well as competent programmers, as opposed to algorithms experts. Achieving this level of performance on a wide variety of problems could be quite useful; there are many relatively simple applications that are not automated because programming time is expensive.

For our case study we chose an NP-complete problem, "Minimum Maximal Matching" (MMM), described in [Garey and Johnson, 1979]. The problem is simple to specify, but interesting enough to illustrate the system's performance. An instance of MMM consists of a

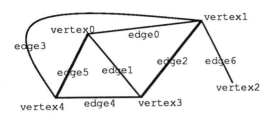

```
(declare-parameter 'K 2)
(declare-type-size 'edge 7)
(declare-type-size 'vertex 5)
(declare-relation-data
  '((endpoint edge0 vertex0)
    (endpoint edge0 vertex1)
    (endpoint edge1 vertex0)
    (endpoint edge1 vertex3)...))
```

Figure 1: An instance of MMM with $K = 2$. A solution $E' = \{$edge2 edge5$\}$ is indicated in boldface. The instance specification is on the right.

```
(iff (satisfies Edgeᵢ Val)
  (and (implies (equal Val 1)
          (forall Vrtx suchthat (endpoint Edgeᵢ Vrtx)
          (forall Edgeⱼ suchthat (endpoint Edgeⱼ Vrtx)
            (or (equal Edgeⱼ Edgeᵢ)
                (assigned Edgeⱼ 0)))))
       (implies (equal Val 0)
          (exists Vrtx suchthat (endpoint Edgeᵢ Vrtx)
          (exists Edgeⱼ suchthat (endpoint Edgeⱼ Vrtx)
            (and (not (equal Edgeⱼ Edgeᵢ))
                 (assigned Edgeⱼ 1)))))
       (exists Solset (set-of Edge suchthat
                       (assigned Edge 1))
       (exists Solsize suchthat (cardinlty Solset Solsize)
          (leq Solsize K)))))
```

Figure 2: Description of MMM Constraints

graph $G = (V, E)$ and an integer $K \leq |E|$. The problem is to determine whether there is a subset $E' \subseteq E$ with $|E'| \leq K$ such that no two edges in E' share a common endpoint and every edge in $E - E'$ shares a common endpoint with some edge in E'.

In order to present a problem to MULTI-TAC, it must be formalized as a CSP. Our CSP specification language is relatively expressive. Variables have an integer range. A *problem specification* defines a set of types (*e.g.*, vertex and edge) and a set of constraints described in a predicate logic. An *instance specification* (see Figure 1) instantiates the types and relations referred to in the problem description.

To formulate MMM as a CSP, we employ a set of boolean variables, one for each edge in the graph. If a variable is assigned the value 1, this indicates the corresponding edge is a member of the subset E'. A value of 0 indicates the corresponding edge is not a member of E'. Figure 2 shows how the constraints are stated in the MULTI-TAC problem specification. The statement specifies the conditions under which a value Val satisfies the constraints on a variable $Edge_i$. We can paraphrase these conditions as follows:

1. If Val equals 1, then for every $edge_j$ such that $edge_j$ shares a common endpoint with $edge_i$, it must be the case that $edge_j$ is assigned the value 0.

2. If Val equals 0, then there must exist an $edge_j$ such

that $edge_i$ and $edge_j$ share a common endpoint, and $edge_j$ is assigned the value 1.

3. The cardinality of the set of edges assigned the value 1 must be less than or equal to K.

The constraint language includes two types of relations, problem-specific *user-defined relations* such as **endpoint**, and built-in *system-defined relations*, including **assigned**, **equal**, **leq**, and **cardinality**. The **assigned** relation has special significance since the system uses it to maintain its state. During the search for a solution, variables are assigned values. Thus, for every variable Var there is at most one value Val such that (**assigned** Var Val) is true at any time. A *solution* consists of an assignment for each variable such that the constraints are satisfied.

MULTI-TAC's specification language enables us to represent a wide variety of combinatorial problems, including many scheduling problems and graph problems. There are, of course, limitations imposed by the specification language. Currently only decision problems are specifiable, since one cannot state "optimization criteria". (We plan to include this in the future.) Furthermore, the system's expertise is limited in many respects by the pre-defined relations. So, for example, geometric concepts such as "planarity" present difficulties.

The MULTI-TAC Architecture

MULTI-TAC rests on the supposition that intelligent problem solving can result from combining a variety of relatively simple heuristics. At the top level, the synthesis process is organized by an "algorithm schema" into which the heuristics are incorporated. Currently only a backtracking schema is implemented (although we also plan to include an iterative repair [Minton *et al.*, 1992] schema), so the remainder of the paper assumes a backtracking search. As in the standard backtracking CSP search[Kumar, 1992] variables are instantiated sequentially. Backtracking occurs when no value satisfies the constraints on a variable.

Associated with an algorithm schema are a variety of generic heuristics. For backtracking, these can be divided roughly into two types: heuristics for variable/value selection and heuristics for representing and propagating information. Let us consider variable and value selection first. Below we list five generic variable/value ordering heuristics used by MULTI-TAC:

- Most-Constrained-Variable-First: This variable ordering heuristic prefers the variable with the fewest possible values left.

- Most-Constraining-Variable-First: A related variable ordering heuristic, this prefers variables that constrain the most other variables.

- Least-Constraining-Value-First: A value-ordering heuristic, this heuristic prefers values that constrain the fewest other variables.

- Dependency-directed backtracking: If a value choice is independent of a failure, backtrack over that choice without trying alternatives.

Specialized versions of these heuristics are generated by refining a meta-level description of the heuristic, as described in [Minton, 1993]. The refinement process incorporates information from the problem description in a manner similar to partial evaluation. Alternative approximations are generated by dropping conditions. For example, one of the specializations of Most-Constraining-Variable-First that MULTI-TAC produces for MMM is: Prefer the edge that has the most adjacent, unassigned edges. An approximation of this is: Prefer the edge that has the most adjacent edges.

MULTI-TAC also employs heuristic mechanisms for maintaining and propagating information during search. These include:

- Constraint propagation: MULTI-TAC selects whether or not to use forward checking. If forward checking is used, then for each unassigned variable the system maintains a list of *possible values* – the values that currently satisfy the constraints on the variable.

- Data structure selection: MULTI-TAC chooses how to represent user-defined relations. For example, it chooses between list and array representations.

- Constraint simplification: The problem constraints are rewritten (as in [Smith, 1991] and [Minton, 1988]) so they can be tested more efficiently.

- Predicate invention: MULTI-TAC can "invent" new relations in order to rewrite the constraints, using test incorporation [Braudaway and Tong, 1989; Dietterich and Bennett, 1986] and finite-differencing [Smith, 1991]. For example, in MMM the system can decide to maintain a relation over edges which share a common endpoint (i.e., the "adjacent" relation).

We are currently working on a variety of additional heuristic mechanisms, such as identifying semi-independent subproblems.

Compiling a target program

The specialization and approximation processes may produce many candidate heuristics that can be incorporated into the algorithm schema. For MMM, MULTI-TAC generates 52 specialized variable- and value-selection heuristics. In order to find the best combination of candidate heuristics, MULTI-TAC's evaluation module searches through a space of *configurations*. A configuration consists of an algorithm schema together with a list of heuristics. Multiple heuristics of the same type are prioritized by their order on the list. For example, if two variable-ordering heuristics are included, then the first heuristic has higher priority; the second heuristic is used only as a tie-breaker when the first heuristic does not determine a unique "most-preferred" candidate. A configuration can be directly compiled into a LISP target program by the MULTI-TAC code generator and then tested on a collection of instances.

As mentioned earlier, MULTI-TAC's objective is to find the most efficient target program for the instance distribution. For the experiments reported here, "most efficient" is defined as the program that solves the most instances given some fixed time bound per instance. If two programs solve the same number of instances, the one that requires the least total time is preferred. Although this is a simplistic criterion, it is sufficient for our purposes.

The evaluation module carries out a parallel hill-climbing search (essentially a beam search) through the space of configurations, using a set of training instances, a per-instance time bound and an integer B, the "beam width". The evaluator first tests each heuristic individually by compiling a program with only the single heuristic; the system records the number of problems solved within the time bound and the total time for the training instances solved. The top B configurations are kept. For each of these configurations, the system then evaluates all configurations produced by appending a second heuristic, and so on, until either the system finds that none of the best B configurations can be improved, or the process is manually interrupted. In our experiments with MMM, the search took anywhere from one hour to several hours, depending on B, the time-limit and the difficulty of the training instances.

One drawback to this scheme is that occasionally two heuristics may interact synergistically, even though they are individually quite poor, and MULTI-TAC's evaluator will never discover such pairs. This is a general problem for hill-climbing utility-evaluation schemes [Minton, 1988; Gratch and DeJong, 1992], which Gratch calls the *composability problem* [Gratch and DeJong, 1991]. To overcome this, we have experimented with a preprocessing stage in which MULTI-TAC evaluates pairs of heuristics in order to find any positive interactions, and then groups these pairs together during the hill-climbing search. Unfortunately, this can be time-consuming if there are several hundred candidate heuristics. We believe that meta-knowledge can be used to control the search, so that only the pairs most likely to interact synergistically are evaluated.

Experimental Results

This section describes a set of experiments illustrating the performance of our current implementation, MULTI-TAC1.0, on the MMM problem and contrasting the synthesized programs to programs written by NASA computer scientists. In our initial experiment, two computer scientists participated, one a MULTI-TAC project member (PM) and the other, a Ph.D. working on an unrelated project (Subject1). We also evaluated a simple, unoptimized CSP engine for comparative purposes.

The subjects were asked to write the fastest programs they could. Over a several-day period Subject1 spent about 5 hours and PM spent 8 hours working on their respective programs. The subjects were given access to a "black box" instance generator. The instance generator randomly constructed solvable instances (with approximately 50 edges) by first generating E' and then adding edges. MULTI-TAC employed the same instance generator, and required approximately 1.5 hours to find its "best" configuration.

Table 1, Experiment1, shows the results on 100 randomly-generated instances of the MMM problem, with a 10-CPU-second time bound per instance. The first column shows the cumulative running time for all 100 instances and the second column shows the number of unsolved problems. The results indicate that PM (the project member) wrote the best program, followed closely by MULTI-TAC and then by Subject1. The unoptimized CSP program was by far the least efficient. These conclusions regarding the relative efficiencies of the four programs can be justified statistically using the methodology proposed by Etzioni and Etzioni [1993]. Specifically, any pairwise comparison of the four programs' completion times using a simple sign test is statistically significant with $p \leq .05$. In fact, we note that for the rest of the experiments summarized in Table 1, a similar comparison between MULTI-TAC's program and any of the other programs is significant with $p \leq .05$, so we will forgo further mention of statistical significance in this section.

We also tried the same experiment on another problem selected from [Garey and Johnson, 1979], K-Closure, with very similar results (see [Minton, 1993]). We were encouraged by our experiments with these two problems, especially since MULTI-TAC performed well in comparison to our subjects. It is easy to write a learning system that can improve its efficiency; it is more difficult to write a learning system that performs well when compared to hand-coded programs. [1] (Published MMM algorithms would provide a further basis for comparison, but we are not aware of any such algo-

---

[1] However, we should note that MMM and K-Closure were not "randomly" chosen from [Garey and Johnson, 1979], but were selected because they could be easily specified in MULTI-TAC's CSP language and because they appeared amenable to a backtracking approach.

Outline of Subject1's algorithm:
Procedure Solve(E', EdgesLeft, K)
if the cardinality of E' is greater than K return failure
  else if EdgesLeft $= \emptyset$ return solution
    else for each edge e in EdgesLeft
      if Solve($E' \cup \{e\}$,
          EdgesLeft $-\{e\} - \{$AdjcntEdges $e\}$,
          K)
          return solution
      finally return failure

Outline of PM's algorithm:
Procedure Solve(E', SortedEdgesLeft, SolSize, K)
if SortedEdgesLeft $= \emptyset$ return solution
  else if SolSize $= K$ return failure
    else for each edge e in SortedEdgesLeft
      SortedEdgesLeft $\leftarrow$ SortedEdgesLeft $-\{e\}$
      if Solve($E' \cup \{e\}$,
          SortedEdgesLeft $-\{$AdjcntEdges $e\}$,
          1 + SolSize,
          K)
          return solution
      finally return failure

Figure 3: Subject1's algorithm and PM's algorithm

rithms.) It is also notable that none of the MULTI-TAC project members was familiar with either MMM or K-closure prior to the experiments. Problems that are "novel" to a system's designers are much more interesting benchmarks than problems for which the system was targeted [Minton, 1988].

One of the interesting aspects of the experiment is that it demonstrates the critical importance of program-optimization expertise. Consider Subject1's algorithm shown in Figure 3 (details omitted). The recursive procedure takes three arguments: the edges in the subset E', the set of remaining edges $E - E'$, and the parameter K. The algorithm adds edges to E' until either the cardinality of E' exceeds K or a solution is found. PM's algorithm, also shown in Figure 3, improves upon Subject1's algorithm in several respects:

- **Pre-sorted Edges:** The most significant improvement involves sorting the edges in a preprocessing phase, so that edges with the most adjacent edges are considered first. Interestingly, Subject1 reported trying this as well, but apparently he did not experiment sufficiently to realize its utility.

- **No redundancy:** Once PM's algorithm considers adding an edge to E', it will not reconsider that edge in subsequent recursive calls. (This is a source of redundancy in Subject1's program. For example, in Subject1's program, if the first edge in EdgesLeft fails it may be reconsidered on each recursive call.)

- **Size of E' incrementally maintained:** PM's program uses the counter $SolSize$ to incrementally track the cardinality of E', rather than recalculating it on each recursive call.

- **Efficiently updating SortedEdgesLeft:** Al-

	Experiment 1		Experiment 2		Experiment 3	
	CPU sec	unsolved	CPU sec	unsolved	CPU sec	unsolved
MULTI-TAC	4.6	0	27.8	1	449	7
Project member (PM)	3.4	0	76.8	2	1976	33
Subject1	166	6	-	-	-	-
Subject2	-	-	8.9	0	-	-
Subject3	-	-	-	-	1035	7
Simple CSP	915	83	991	98	4500	100

Table 1: Experimental results for three distributions

though Figure 3 does not show it, PM used a bit vector to represent SortedEdgesLeft. This vector can be efficiently updated via a bitwise-or operation with a stored adjacency matrix.

- **Early failure:** PM's program backtracks as soon as E' is of size K, which is one level earlier than Subject1's program.

MULTI-TAC's program behaves similarly to the hand-coded programs in many respects. The program iterates through the edges, assigning a value to each edge and backtracking when necessary. In synthesizing the program, MULTI-TAC selected the variable-ordering heuristic: "prefer edges with the most neighbors". This is a specialization of "Most-constrained-Variable-First". The system also selected a value-ordering rule: "try 1 before 0", so that in effect, the program tries to add edges to E'. This rule is a specialization of "Least-Constraining-Value-First", since the value 1 is least-constraining with respect to the second constraint (see Section 2). MULTI-TAC also included many of the most significant features of PM's algorithm:

- **Pre-sorted Edges:** MULTI-TAC's code generator determined that the variable-ordering heuristic is *static, i.e.,* independent of variable assignments. Therefore, the edges are pre-sorted according to the heuristic, so that edges with the most adjacent edges are considered first.

- **No redundancy:** MULTI-TAC's program is free of redundancy simply as a result of the backtracking CSP formalization.

- **Size of E' incrementally maintained:** This was accomplished by finite differencing the third constraint (which specifies that $|E'| \leq K$).

Whereas the other two programs are recursive, MULTI-TAC's program is iterative, which is typically more efficient in LISP. There are additional minor efficiency considerations, but space limitations prevent their discussion.

A followup study was designed with a different volunteer, another NASA computer scientist (Subject2). We intended to make the distribution harder, but unfortunately, we modified the instance generator rather naively – we simply made the instances about twice as large, and only discovered later that the instances

were actually not much harder. Table 1, Experiment2, shows the results, again for 100 instances each with a ten-CPU-second time limit. The program submitted by PM was the same as that in Experiment1, since PM found that his program also ran quickly on this distribution, and he didn't think any futher improvements would be significant. MULTI-TAC also ended up with essentially the same program as in Experiment1. Our second subject rather quickly (3-4 hours) developed a program which performed quite well. The program was similar to PM's program but simpler; the main optimizations were the same, except that no bit array representation was used. Surprisingly, Subject2's program was the fastest on this experiment, and MULTI-TAC's program finished second. PM's program was slower than the others, apparently because it copied the state inefficiently, an important factor with this distribution because of the larger instance size.

Finally, we conducted a third experiment, this time being careful to ensure that the distribution was indeed harder. We found (empirically) that the instances were more difficult when the proportion of edges to nodes was decreased, so we modified the instance generator accordingly. The results for 100 instances, this time with a 45-second time bound per instance, are shown in Table 1, Experiment3.

Our third subject spent about 8 hours total on the task. His best program used heuristic iterative repair [Minton et al., 1992], rather than backtracking. The edges in E' are kept in a queue. Let us say that an edge is *covered* if it is adjacent to any edge in E'. If E' is not a legal solution, then the last edge in the queue is removed. The program selects a new edge that is adjacent to the most uncovered edges (and not adjacent to any edge in E') and puts it at the front of the queue.

PM spent approximately 4 hours modifying his program for this distribution. The modified program uses iteration rather than recursion, and instead of presorting the edges, on each iteration the program selects the edge that has the most adjacent uncovered edges and adds it to E'. Other minor changes were also included.

For this distribution, MULTI-TAC's program is, interestingly, quite different from that of the previous distributions. MULTI-TAC elected to order its values

	Experiment2 Instances		Experiment3 Instances	
	secs	unslvd	secs	unslvd
MULTI-TAC prgrm2	27.8	1	1527	22
MULTI-TAC prgrm3	804	69	449	7

Table 2: Results illustrating distribution sensitivity

so that 0 is tried before 1. Essentially, this means that when the program considers an edge, it first tries assigning it so it is *not* in E'. Thus, we can view this program as incrementally selecting edges to include in the set $E - E'$. For variable ordering, the following three rules are used:

1. Prefer edges that have no adjacent edges along one endpoint. Since this rule is static, the edges can be pre-sorted according to this criterion.
2. Break ties by preferring edges with the most endpoints such that all edges connected via those endpoints are assigned. (I.e, an edge is preferred if all the adjacent edges along one endpoint are assigned, or even better, if all adjacent edges along both endpoints are assigned).
3. If there are still ties, prefer an edge with the fewest adjacent edges.

Each of the above heuristics is an approximation of "Most-Constrained Variable First". Intuitively speaking, these rules appear to prefer edges whose value is completely constrained, or edges that are unlikely to be in E' (which makes sense given the value-ordering rule).

As shown in Table 1, MULTI-TAC's program solved the same number of problems as Subject3's program, and had by far the best run time in this experiment. Interestingly, MULTI-TAC also synthesized a configuration similar to PM's program, which was rejected during the evaluation stage.

One of the interesting aspects of this experiment is that none of our human subjects came up with an algorithm similar to MULTI-TAC's. Indeed, MULTI-TAC's algorithm initially seemed rather mysterious to the author and the other project members. In retrospect the algorithm seems sensible, and we can explain its success as follows. In a depth-first search, if a choice is wrong, then the system will have to backtrack over the entire subtree below that choice before it finds a solution. Thus the most critical choices are the early choices – the choices made at a shallow depth. We believe that MULTI-TAC's algorithm for the third distribution is successful because at the beginning of the search its variable-ordering heuristics can identify edges that are very unlikely to be included in E'. We note that the graphs in the third distribution are more sparse than the graphs in the other two distributions; so, for instance, the first rule listed above is more likely to be relevant with the third distribution.

An underlying assumption of this work is that tai-

loring programs to a distribution is useful. This is supported by Table 2, which shows that MULTI-TAC's program2, which was synthesized for the instances in the second experiment, performs poorly on the instances from the third experiment, and vice-versa. (The hand-coded programs show the same trends, but not as strongly.) This appears to be due to two factors. First, there is a relationship between heuristic power and evaluation cost. The programs tailored to the easy distribution employ heuristics that are relatively inexpensive to apply, but less useful in directing search. For example, pre-sorting the edges according to the number of adjacent edges is less expensive than picking the edge with the most adjacent uncovered edges on each iteration, but the latter has a greater payoff on harder problems.

Second, some heuristics may be qualitatively tailored to a distribution, in that their advice might actually mislead the system on another distribution. There is some evidence of this in our experiments. For example, the third variable-ordering rule used by MULTI-TAC in Experiment3 degrades the program's search on the second distribution! The program actually searches fewer nodes when the rule is left out.

Discussion

MULTI-TAC's program synthesis techniques were motivated by work in automated software design, most notably Smith's KIDS system [Smith, 1991], and related work on knowledge compilation [Mostow, 1991; Tong, 1991] and analytical learning [Minton *et al.*, 1989; Etzioni, 1990]. There are also a variety of proposed frameworks for efficiently solving CSP problems that are related, although less directly, including work on constraint languages [Guesgen, 1991; Lauriere, 1978; Van Hentenryk *et al.*, 1992b], constraint abstraction [Ellman, 1993], and learning [Day, 1991]. Perhaps the closest work in the CSP area is Yoshikowa and Wada's [1992] approach for automatically generating "multi-dimensional CSP" programs. However, this work does not deal with the scope of heuristic optimizations we deal with. In addition, we know of no previous CSP systems that employ learning techniques to synthesize distribution-specific programs.

In the future, we hope to use the system for real applications, and also to characterize the class of problems for which MULTI-TAC is effective. Currently we have evidence that MULTI-TAC performs on par with human programmers on two problems, MMM and K-closure. (MULTI-TAC is also capable of synthesizing the very effective Brelaz algorithm [Turner, 1988] for graph-coloring). However, we do not yet have a good characterization of MULTI-TAC's generality, and indeed it is unclear how to achieve this, short of testing the program on a variety of problems as in [Lauriere, 1978].

This study has demonstrated that automatically specializing heuristics is a viable approach for synthesizing CSP programs. We have also shown that the utility of heuristics can be sensitive to the distribution of instances. Since humans may not have the patience to experiment with different combinations of heuristics, these results suggest that the synthesis of application-specific heuristic programs is a promising direction for AI research.

In our experiments, we also saw that MULTI-TAC can be "creative", in that the system can take combinatorial problems that are unfamiliar to its designers and produce interesting, and in some respects unanticipated, heuristic programs for solving those problems. This is purely a result of the system's ability to specialize and combine a set of simple, generic building blocks. By extending the set of generic mechanisms we hope to produce a very effective and general system. At the same time, we plan to explore the issues of organization and tractability that arise in an integrated architecture.

Acknowledgements

I am indebted to several colleagues for their contributions to MULTI-TAC. Jim Blythe helped devise the specialization theories and search control mechanism, Gene Davis worked on the original CSP engine and language, Andy Philips co-developed the code generator, Ian Underwood developed and refined the utility evaluator, and Shawn Wolfe helped develop the simplifier and the utility evaluator. Furthermore, Ian and Shawn did much of the work running the experiments reported in this paper. Thanks also to my colleagues at NASA who volunteered for our experiments, to Oren Etzioni for his advice, and to Bernadette Kowalski-Minton for her help revising this paper.

References

Braudaway, W. and Tong, C. 1989. Automated synthesis of constrained generators. In *Proceedings of the Eleventh International Joint Conference on Artificial Intelligence.*

Day, D.S. 1991. Learning variable descriptors for applying heuristics across CSP problems. In *Proceedings of the Machine Learning Workshop.*

Dietterich, T.G. and Bennett, J.S. 1986. The test incorporation theory of problem solving. In *Proceedings of the Workshop on Knowledge Compilation.*

Ellman, T. 1993. Abstraction via approximate symmetry. In *Proceedings of the Thirteenth International Joint Conference on Artificial Intelligence.*

Etzioni, O. and Etzioni, R. 1993. Statistical methods for analyzing speedup learning experiments. *Machine Learning.* Forthcoming.

Etzioni, O. 1990. *A Structural Theory of Explanation-Based Learning.* Ph.D. Dissertation, School of Computer Science, Carnegie Mellon University.

Garey, M.R. and Johnson, D.S. 1979. *Computers and Intractability: A Guide to the Theory of NP-Completeness.* W.H. Freeman and Co.

Gratch, J and DeJong, G. 1991. A hybrid approach to guaranteed effective control strategies. In *Proceedings of the Eighth International Machine Learning Workshop.*

Gratch, J and DeJong, G. 1992. An analysis of learning to plan as a search problem. In *Proceedings of the Ninth International Machine Learning Conference.*

Guesgen, H.W. 1991. A universal progamming language. In *Proceedings of the Twelfth International Joint Conference on Artificial Intelligence.*

Kumar, V. 1992. Algorithms for constraint satisfaction problems. *AI Magazine* 13.

Lauriere, J.L. 1978. A language and a program for stating and solving combinatorial problems. *Artificial Intelligence* 10:29–127.

Minton, S.; Carbonell, J.G.; Knoblock, C.A.; Kuokka, D.R.; Etzioni, O.; and Gil, Y. 1989. Explanation-based learning: A problem solving perspective. *Artificial Intelligence* 40:63–118.

Minton, S.; Johnston, M.; Philips, A.B.; and Laird, P. 1992. Minimizing conflicts: A heuristic repair method for constraint satisfaction and scheduling problems. *Artificial Intelligence* 58:161–205.

Minton, S. 1988. *Learning Search Control Knowledge: An Explanation-based Approach.* Kluwer Academic Publishers.

Minton, S. 1993. An analytic learning system for specializing heuristics. In *Proceedings of the Thirteenth International Joint Conference on Artificial Intelligence.*

Mostow, J. 1991. A transformational approach to knowledge compilation. In Lowry, M.R. and McCartney, R.D., editors, *Automating Software Design.* AAAI Press.

Smith, D.R. 1991. KIDS: A knowledge-based software development system. In Lowry, M.R. and McCartney, R.D., editors, *Automating Software Design.* AAAI Press.

Tong, C. 1991. A divide and conquer approach to knowledge compilation. In Lowry, M.R. and McCartney, R.D., editors, *Automating Software Design.* AAAI Press.

Turner, J.S. 1988. Almost all k-colorable graphs are easy to color. *Journal of Algorithms* 9:63–82.

Van Hentenryk, P.; Deville, Y.; and Teng, C-M. 1992a. A generic arc-consistency algorithm and its specializations. *Artificial Intelligence* 57:291–321.

Van Hentenryk, P.; Simonis, H.; and Dincbas, M. 1992b. Constraint satisfaction using constraint logic programming. *Artificial Intelligence* 58:113–159.

Yoshikawa, M. and Wada, S. 1992. Constraint satisfaction with multi-dimensional domain. In *Proceedings of the First International Conference on Planning Systems.*

Coping With Disjunctions
in Temporal Constraint Satisfaction Problems *

Eddie Schwalb, Rina Dechter
Department of Information and Computer Science
University of California at Irvine, CA 92717
eschwalb@ics.uci.edu, dechter@ics.uci.edu

Abstract

Path-consistency algorithms, which are polynomial for discrete problems, are exponential when applied to problems involving quantitative temporal information. The source of complexity stems from specifying relationships between pairs of time points as disjunction of intervals. We propose a polynomial algorithm, called ULT, that approximates path-consistency in *Temporal Constraint Satisfaction Problems* (TCSPs). We compare ULT empirically to *path-consistency* and *directional path-consistency* algorithms. When used as a preprocessing to backtracking, ULT is shown to be 10 times more effective then either DPC or PC-2.

1. Introduction

Problems involving temporal constraints arise in various areas of computer science such as scheduling, circuit and program verification, parallel computation and common sense reasoning. Several formalisms for expressing and reasoning with temporal knowledge have been proposed, most notably Allen's interval algebra (Allen 83), Vilain and Kautz's point algebra (Vilain 86, Vanbeek 92), and Dean & Mcdermott's Time Map Management (TMM) (Dean & McDermott 87).

Recently, a framework called *Temporal Constraint Problem (TCSP)* was proposed (Dechter Meiri & Pearl 91), in which network-based methods (Dechter & Pearl 88, Dechter 92) were extended to include continuous variables. In this framework, variables represent time points and *quantitative* temporal information is represented by a set of unary and binary constraints over the variables. This model was further extended in (Meiri 91) to include *qualitative* information. The advantage of this framework is that it facilitates the following tasks: (1) finding all feasible times a given event can occur, (2) finding all possible relationships between two given events, (3) finding one or more scenarios consistent with the information provided, and (4) representing the data in a *minimal network* form that can pro-

vide answers to a variety of additional queries.

It is well known that all these tasks are NP-hard. The source of complexity stems from specifying relationships between pairs of time points as disjunctions of intervals. Even enforcing path-consistency, which is polynomial in discrete problems, becomes worst-case exponential in the number of intervals in each constraint. On the other hand, simple temporal problems having only one interval per constraint are tractable and can be solved by path-consistency. Consequently, we propose to exploit the efficiency of processing simple temporal problems for approximating path consistency. This leads to a polynomial algorithm, called *ULT*.

We compare ULT empirically with path-consistency (PC-2) and directional path-consistency (DPC). Our results show that while ULT is always a very efficient algorithm, it is most accurate (relative to full path-consistency enforced by PC-2) for problems having a small number of intervals and high connectivity. When used as a preprocessing procedure before backtracking, ULT is 10 times more effective then DPC or PC.

The paper is organized as follows. Section 2 presents the TCSP model. Section 3 presents algorithm ULT; Section 4 presents the empirical evaluation and the conclusion is presented in Section 5.

2. The TCSP Model

A TCSP involves a set of variables, $X_1, \ldots, X_n$, having continuous domains, each representing a time point. Each constraint T is represented by a set of intervals $T \equiv (I_1, \ldots, I_n) = \{[a_1, b_1], \ldots, [a_n, b_n]\}$. For a unary constraint T_i over X_i, the set of intervals restricts the domain such that $(a_1 \leq X_i \leq b_1) \cup \ldots \cup (a_n \leq X_i \leq b_n)$. For a binary constraint T_{ij} over X_i, X_j, the set of intervals restricts the permissible values for the distance $X_j - X_i$; namely it represents the disjunction $(a_1 \leq X_j - X_i \leq b_l) \cup \ldots \cup (a_n \leq X_j - X_i \leq b_n)$. All intervals are pairwise disjoint.

A *binary TCSP* can be represented by a *directed con-*

---
*This work was partially supported by NSF grant IRI-9157636, by Air Force Office of Scientific Research, AFOSR 900136, and by Xerox grant.

straint graph, where nodes represent variables and an edge $i \rightarrow j$ indicates that a constraint T_{ij} is specified. Every edge is labeled by the interval set (Figure 1). A special time point X_0 is introduced to represent the "beginning of the world". Because all times are relative to X_0, thus we may treat each unary constraint T_i as a binary constraint T_{0i} (having the same interval representation). For simplicity, we choose $X_0 = 0$.

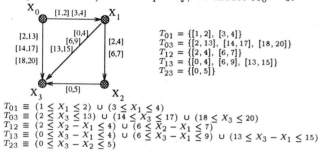

$T_{01} \equiv (1 \leq X_1 \leq 2) \cup (3 \leq X_1 \leq 4)$
$T_{03} \equiv (2 \leq X_3 \leq 13) \cup (14 \leq X_3 \leq 17) \cup (18 \leq X_3 \leq 20)$
$T_{12} \equiv (2 \leq X_2 - X_1 \leq 4) \cup (6 \leq X_2 - X_1 \leq 7)$
$T_{13} \equiv (0 \leq X_3 - X_1 \leq 4) \cup (6 \leq X_3 - X_1 \leq 9) \cup (13 \leq X_3 - X_1 \leq 15)$
$T_{23} \equiv (0 \leq X_3 - X_2 \leq 5)$

Figure 1: A graphical representation of a TCSP where $X_0 = 0$, $X_1 = 1.5$, $X_2 = 4.5$, $X_3 = 8$ is a solution.

A tuple $X = (x_1, \ldots, x_n)$ is called a *solution* if the assignment $X_1 = x_1, \ldots, X_n = x_n$ satisfies all the constraints. The network is *consistent* iff at least one solution exists. A value v is a *feasible value* of X_i if there exists a solution in which $X_i = v$. The *minimal domain* of a variable is the set of all *feasible values* of that variable. The *minimal constraint* is the tightest constraint that describes the same set of solutions. The *minimal network* is such that its domains and constraints are minimal.

Definition 1: Let $T = \{I_1, \ldots, I_l\}$ and $S = \{J_1, \ldots, j_m\}$ be two sets of intervals which can correspond to either unary or binary constraints.

1. The *intersection* of T and S, denoted by $T \oplus S$, admits only values that are allowed by both of them.

2. The *composition* of T and S, denoted by $T \otimes S$, admits only values r for which there exists $t \in T$ and $s \in S$ such that $r = t + s$.

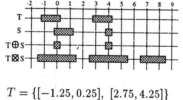

$T = \{[-1.25, 0.25], [2.75, 4.25]\}$
$S = \{[-0.25, 1.25], [3.77, 4.25]\}$
$T \oplus S = \{[-0.25, 0.25], [3.75, 4.25]\}$
$T \otimes S = \{[-1.50, 1.50], [2.50, 5.50], [6.50, 8.50]\}$

Figure 2: A pictorial example of the $\oplus$ and $\otimes$ operations.

The $\otimes$ operation may result in intervals that are not pairwise disjoint. Therefore, additional processing may be required to compute the disjoint interval set.

Definition 2: The *path-induced* constraint on variables X_i, X_j is $R_{ij}^{path} = \oplus_{\forall k}(T_{ik} \otimes T_{kj})$. A con-

straint T_{ij} is *path-consistent* iff $T_{ij} \subseteq R_{ij}^{path}$ and *path-redundant* iff $T_{ij} \supseteq R_{ij}^{path}$. A network is *path-consistent* iff all its constraints are *path-consistent*.

A general TCSP can be converted into an equivalent *path-consistent* network by applying the relaxation operation $T_{ij} \leftarrow T_{ij} \oplus T_{ik} \otimes T_{kj}$, using algorithm PC-2 (Figure 3). Some problems may benefit from a weaker version, called DPC, which can be enforced more efficiently.

Algorithm PC-2
1. $Q \leftarrow \{(i, k, j) | (i < j) and (k \neq i, j)\}$
2. **while** $Q \neq \{\}$ **do**
3.   select and delete a path (i, k, j) from Q
4.   **if** $T_{ij} \neq T_{ik} \otimes T_{kj}$ **then**
5. $T_{ij} \leftarrow T_{ij} \oplus (T_{ik} \otimes T_{kj})$
6.   **if** $T_{ij} = \{\}$ **then** exit (inconsistency)
7. $Q \leftarrow Q \cup RELATED\text{-}PATHS((i, k, j))$
8.   **end-if**
9. **end-while**

Algorithm DPC
1. **for** $k \leftarrow n$ downto 1 by -1 **do**
2.   **for** $\forall i, j < k$ such that $(i, k), (k, j) \in E$ **do**
3.   **if** $T_{ij} \neq T_{ik} \otimes T_{kj}$ **then**
4. $E \leftarrow E \cup (i, j)$
5. $T_{ij} \leftarrow T_{ij} \oplus (T_{ik} \otimes T_{kj})$
6.   **if** $T_{ij} = \{\}$ **then** exit (inconsistency)
7.   **end-if**
8.   **end-for**
9. **end-for**

Figure 3: Algorithms PC-2 and DPC (Dechter Meiri & Pearl 91).

3. Upper-Lower Tightening (ULT)

The relaxation operation $T_{ij} \leftarrow T_{ij} \oplus T_{ik} \otimes T_{kj}$ increases the number of intervals and may result in exponential blow-up. As a result, the complexity of PC-2 and DPC is exponential in the number of intervals, but can be bounded by $O(n^3 R^3)$ and $O(n^3 R^2)$, respectively, where n is the number of variables and R is the range of the constraints. When running PC-2 on random instances, we encountered problems for which path-consistency required 11 minutes on toy-sized problems with 10 variables, range of [0,600], and with 50 input intervals in each constraint. Evidently, PC-2 is computationally expensive (also observed by (Poesio 91)).

A special class of TCSPs that allow efficient processing is the Simple Temporal Problem (STP) (Dechter Meiri & Pearl 91). In this class, a constraint has a single interval. An STP can be associated with a directed edge-weighted graph, G_d, called a *distance graph*, having the same vertices as the constraint graph G; each edge $i \rightarrow j$ is labeled by a weight w_{ij} representing the constraint $X_j - X_i \leq w_{ij}$ (Figure 4). An STP is consistent iff the corresponding d-graph G_d has no negative cycles and the minimal network of the STP

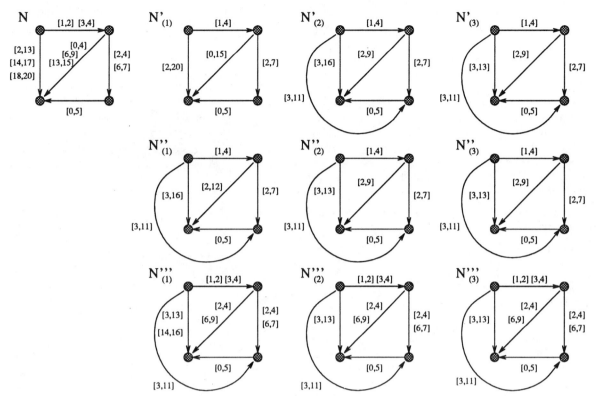

Figure 5: A sample run of ULT. We start with N (Figure 1) and compute $N'_{(1)}$, $N''_{(1)}$, $N'''_{(1)}$. Thereafter, we perform a second iteration in which we compute $N'_{(2)}$, $N''_{(2)}$, $N'''_{(2)}$ and finally, in the third iteration, there is no change. The first iteration removes two intervals, while the second iteration removes one.

corresponds to the *minimal distances* of G_d. For a processing example, see figure 4. Alternatively, the minimal network of an STP can be computed by PC-2 in $O(n^3)$ steps.

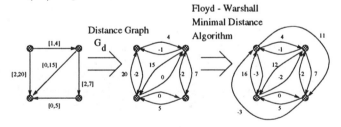

Figure 4: Processing an STP. The minimal network is in Figure 5, network $N''_{(1)}$

Motivated by these results, we propose an efficient algorithm that approximates path-consistency. The idea is to use the extreme points of all intervals associated with a single constraint as one big interval, yielding an STP, and then to perform path-consistency on that STP. This process will not increasing the number of intervals.

Definition 3: Let $T_{ij} = [I_1, \ldots, I_m]$ be the constraint over variables X_i, X_j and let L_{ij}, U_{ij} be the lowest and highest value of T_{ij}, respectively. We define N', N'', N''' as follows (see Figure 5):

Algorithm Upper-Lower Tightening (ULT)

1.   **input:** N
2. $N''' \leftarrow N$
3.   **repeat**
4. $N \leftarrow N'''$
5.   compute N', N'', N'''.
6.   **until** $\forall ij \; (L'''_{ij} = L_{ij})$ and $(U'''_{ij} = U_{ij})$
                or $\exists ij \; (U'''_{ij} < L'''_{ij})$
7.   **if** $\forall ij \; (U'''_{ij} > L'''_{ij})$ **output:** "Inconsistent."
                otherwise   **output:** N'''

Figure 6: The ULT algorithm.

- N' is an STP derived from N by relaxing its constraints to $T'_{ij} = [L_{ij}, \, U_{ij}]$.
- N'' is the minimal network of N'.
- N''' is derived from N'' and N by intersecting $T'''_{ij} = T''_{ij} \oplus T_{ij}$.

Algorithm ULT is presented in Figure 6. We can show that ULT computes a network equivalent to its input network.

Lemma 1: *Let N be the input to ULT and R be its output. The networks N and R are equivalent.*

Regarding the effectiveness of ULT, we can show that

Lemma 2: *Every iteration of ULT (excluding the last) removes at least one interval.*

This can be used to show that

Theorem 1: *Algorithm ULT terminates in $O(n^3ek + e^2k^2)$ steps where n is the number of variables, e is the number of edges, and k is the maximal number of intervals in each constraint.*

In contrast to PC-2, ULT is guaranteed to converge in $O(ek)$ iterations even if the interval boundaries are not rational numbers. For a sample execution see Figure 5.

Algorithm ULT can also be used to identify *path-redundancies*.

Definition 4: A constraint T_{ij} is *redundant-prone* iff, after applying ULT, T_{ij}''' is redundant in N'''.

Lemma 3: T_{ij}''' is path-redundant in N''' if $T_{ij}'' \subseteq T_{ij}$ and $T_{ij}'' = \oplus_{\forall k}(T_{ik}'' \otimes T_{kj}'')$.

Corollary 1: *A single interval constraint T_{ij} is redundant-prone iff $T_{ij}'' = \oplus_{\forall k}(T_{ik}'' \otimes T_{kj}'')$.*

Consequently, after applying ULT to a TCSP, we can test the condition in Corollary 1 and eliminate some redundant constraints.

A brute-force algorithm for solving a TCSP decomposes it into separate STPs by selecting a single interval from each constraint (Dechter Meiri & Pearl 91). Each STP is then solved separately and the solutions are combined. Alternatively, a naive backtracking algorithm will successively assign an interval to a constraint, as long as the resulting STP is consistent.[1] Once inconsistency is detected, the algorithm backtracks. Algorithm ULT can be used as a preprocessing stage to reduce the number of intervals in each constraint and to identify some *path-redundant* constraints. Since every iteration of ULT removes at least one interval, the search space is pruned. More importantly, if ULT causes redundant constraints to be removed, the search space may be pruned exponentially in the number of constraints removed. Note however that the number of constraints in the initial network is e while following the application of ULT, DPC or PC-2, the constraint graph becomes complete thus the number of constraints is $O(n^2)$.

4. Empirical Evaluation

We conducted two sets of experiments. One comparing the efficiency and accuracy of ULT and DPC relative to PC-2, and the other comparing their effectiveness as a preprocessing to backtracking.

Our experiments were conducted on randomly generated sets of instances. Our random problem generator uses five parameters: (1) n, the number of variables, (2) k, the number of intervals in each constraint, (3)

---

[1]We call this process "labeling the TCSP".

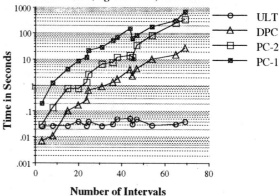

Efficiency of ULT, DPC, PC-2, PC-1 (20 reps) on 10 variables, tightness .95, Pc=0.14

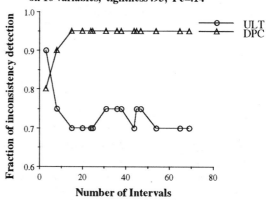

Approximation Quality relative to PC on 10 variables, tightness .95, Pc=.14

Figure 8: The execution time and quality of the approximation obtained by DPC and ULT to PC. Each point represents 20 runs on networks with 10 variables, .95 tightness, connectivity $P_C = .14$ and range $[0, 600]$.

$R = [\text{Inf}, \text{Sup}]$, the range of the constraints, (4) T_I, the tightness of the constraints, namely, the fraction of values allowed relative to the interval $[\text{Inf}, \text{Sup}]$, and (5) P_C, the probability that a constraint T_{ij} exists. Intuitively, problems with dense graphs and loose constraints with many intervals should be more difficult.

To evaluate the quality of the approximation achieved by ULT and DPC relative to PC-2, we counted the number of cases in which ULT and DPC detected inconsistency given that PC-2 detected one. From Figure 8, we conclude that when the number of intervals is small, DPC is faster than ULT but produces weaker approximations. When the number of intervals is large, DPC is much slower but is more accurate. In addition, we observe that when the number of intervals is very large, DPC computes a very good approximation to PC-2, and runs about 10 times faster.

In Figure 9 we report the relative quality of ULT and DPC for a small (3) and for a large (20) number of intervals, as a function of connectivity. As the connectivity increases, the approximation quality of both

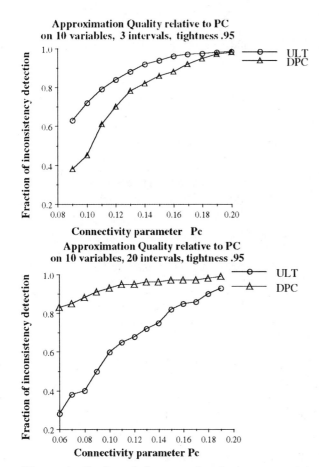

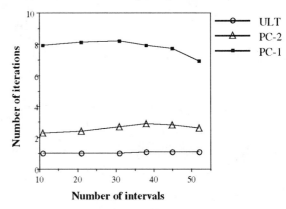

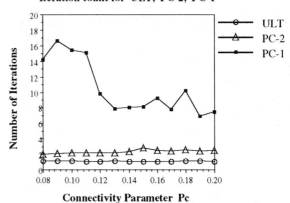

Figure 9: Quality of the approximation vs connectivity on problems with 10 variables, tightness .95 and range [0, 600]. We measured on problems of 3 intervals (top) where each point represents 1000 runs, and on 20 intervals (bottom) where each point represents 100 runs.

Figure 10: The number of iterations ULT, PC-2 and PC-1 performed (excluding the termination iteration) on problems with 10 variables, 20 intervals, $P_C = .14$, and tightness .95. Each point represents 20 runs.

ULT and DPC increases. Note again that ULT is more accurate for a small number of intervals while *DPC* dominates for large number of intervals.

We measured the number of iterations performed by ULT, PC-2, and PC-1[2] (Figure 10). We observe that for our benchmarks, ULT performed 1 iteration (excluding the termination iteration) in most of the cases, while PC-1 and PC-2 performed more (DPC performs only one iteration).

In the second set of experiments we tested the power of *ULT, DPC* and *PC-2* as preprocessing to backtracking. Without preprocessing, the problems could not be solved using the naive backtracking. Our preliminary tests ran on 20 problem instances with 10 variables and 3 intervals and none terminated before 1000000 STP checks. We therefore continued with testing backtracking following preprocessing by ULT, DPC and PC-2.

---

[2] A brute force path-consistency algorithm (Dechter Meiri & Pearl).

Testing the consistency of a labeling requires solving the corresponding STP. An inconsistent STP represents a dead-end. Therefore, we counted the number of inconsistent STPs tested before a single consistent one was found and the overall time required (including preprocessing). The results are presented in Figure 11 on a **logarithmic scale**. We observe that ULT was able to remove intervals effectively and appears to be the most effective as a preprocessing procedure. For additional experiments with path-consistency for qualitative temporal networks see (Ladkin & Reinefeld 92).

Summary and conclusion

In this paper we presented a polynomial approximation algorithm to path-consistency for temporal constraint problems, called ULT. Its complexity is $O(n^3ek+e^2k^2)$, in contrast to path-consistency which is exponential in k, where n is the number of variables, e is the number of constraints and k is the maximal number of intervals per constraint. We also argued that *ULT* can be used to effectively identify some *path-redundancies*.

We evaluated the performance of DPC and ULT em-

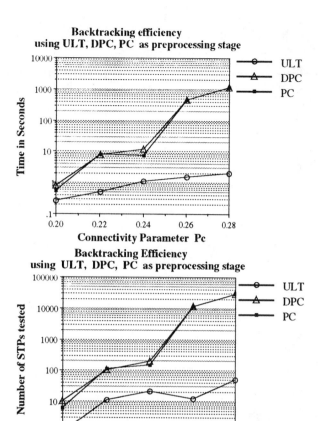

Figure 11: Backtracking performance following preprocessing by ULT, PC-2 and PC-1 respectively, on problems with 10 variables, 3 intervals, and tightness .95. Each point represents 20 runs. The time includes preprocessing.

pirically by comparing their run-time and quality of output relative to PC-2. The results show that while *ULT* is always very efficient, it is most accurate (i.e. it generates output closer to PC-2) for problems having a small number of intervals and high connectivity. Specifically, we saw that: 1. The complexity of both PC-2 and DPC grows exponentially in the number of intervals, while the complexity of ULT remains almost constant. 2. When the number of intervals is small, DPC is faster but produces weaker approximations relative to *ULT*. When the number of intervals is large, DPC is much slower but more accurate. 3. For a large number of intervals, DPC computes a very good approximation to PC-2, and runs about 10 times faster. 4. When used as a preprocessing procedure before backtracking, ULT is shown to be 10 times more effective then either DPC or PC-2.

Finally, our experimental evaluation is by no means complete. We intend to conduct additional experiments with wider range of parameters and larger problems.

References

Allen, J.F. 1983. Maintaining knowledge about temporal intervals. *CACM* 26(11):832-843.

Dechter, R.; Meiri, I.; Pearl, J. 1991. Temporal Constraint Networks. *Artificial Intelligence* 49:61-95.

Dechter, R.; 1992. "Constraint Networks", *Encyclopedia of Artificial Intelligence*, (2nd ed.) (Wiley, New York, 1992) 276-285.

Dechter, R.; Pearl, J. 1988. Network-based heuristics for constraint satisfaction problems. *Artificial Intelligence* 34:1-38.

Dechter, R. 1990. Enhancement schemes for constraint processing: Backjumping, learning and cutset decomposition. *Artificial Intelligence* 41:273-312.

Dechter, R.; Dechter, A. 1987. Removing redundancies in constraint networks. In *Proc. of AAAI-87*, 105-109.

Dean, T.M.; McDermott, D. V. 1987. Temporal data base management. *Artificial Intelligence* 32:1-55.

Freuder, E.C. 1985. A sufficient condition of backtrack free search. *JACM* 32(4):510-521.

Ladkin, P. B.; Reinefeld, A. 1992. Effective solution of qualitative interval constraint problems. *Artificial Intelligence* 57:105-124.

Meiri, I. 1991. Combining qualitative and quantitative constraints in temporal reasoning. In *Proc. of AAAI-91*, 260-267.

Meiri, I.; Dechter, R.; Pearl, J. 1991. Tree decomposition with application to constraint processing. In *Proc. of AAAI-91*, 241-246.

Kautz, H.; Ladkin, P. 1991. Intergating metric and qualitative temporal reasoning", In *Proc. of AAAI-91*, 241-246.

Koubarakis, M. 1992. Dense time and temporal constraints with $\neq$. In *Proc. KR-92*, 24-35.

Poesio, M.; Brachman, R. J. 1991. Metric constraints for maintaining appointments: Dates and repeated activities. In *Proc. AAAI-91*, 253-259.

Van Beek, P. 1992. Reasoning about qualitative temporal information. *Artificial Intelligence* 58:297-326.

Vilain, M.; Kautz, H. 1986. Constraint propagation algorithms for temporal information. In *Proc AAAI-86*, 377-382.

Nondeterministic Lisp as a Substrate for Constraint Logic Programming

Jeffrey Mark Siskind*
University of Pennsylvania IRCS
3401 Walnut Street Room 407C
Philadelphia PA 19104
215/898–0367
internet: Qobi@CIS.UPenn.EDU

David Allen McAllester†
M. I. T. Artificial Intelligence Laboratory
545 Technology Square Room NE43–412
Cambridge MA 02139
617/253–6599
internet: dam@AI.MIT.EDU

Abstract

We have implemented a comprehensive constraint-based programming language as an extension to COMMON LISP. This constraint package provides a unified framework for solving both numeric and non-numeric systems of constraints using a combination of local propagation techniques including binding propagation, Boolean constraint propagation, generalized forward checking, propagation of bounds, and unification. The backtracking facility of the nondeterministic dialect of COMMON LISP used to implement this constraint package acts as a general fallback constraint solving method mitigating the incompleteness of local propagation.

Introduction

Recent years have seen significant interest in constraint logic programming languages. Numerous implementations of such languages have been described in the literature, notably CLP($\Re$) (Jaffar and Lassez 1987) and CHIP (Van Hentenryck 1989). The point of departure leading to these systems is the observation that the unification operation at the core of logic programming can be viewed as a method for solving equational constraints between logic variables which range over the universe of Herbrand terms. A natural extension of such a view is to allow variables to range over other domains and augment the programming language to support the formulation and solution of systems of constraints appropriate to these new domains. The notion of extending a programming language to support constraint-based programming need not be unique to logic programming. In this paper we present the constraint package included with SCREAMER, a nondeterministic dialect of COMMON LISP described by Siskind and McAllester (1993). This package provides functionality analogous to CLP($\Re$) and CHIP in a COMMON LISP framework instead of a PROLOG one.

SCREAMER augments COMMON LISP with the capacity for writing nondeterministic functions and expressions. Nondeterministic functions and expressions can return multiple values upon backtracking initiated by failure. SCREAMER also provides the ability to perform *local* side effects, ones which are undone upon backtracking. Nondeterminism and local side effects form the substrate on top of which the SCREAMER constraint package is constructed.

Variables and Constraints

SCREAMER includes the function `make-variable` which returns a data structure called a *variable*. SCREAMER variables are a generalization of PROLOG logic variables. Initially, new variables are unbound and unconstrained. Variables may be bound to values by the process of solving constraints asserted between sets of variables. Both the assertion of constraints and the ensuing binding of variables is done with local side effects. Thus constraints are removed and variables become unbound again upon backtracking.

SCREAMER provides a variety of primitives for constraining variables. Each constraint primitive is a "constraint version" of a corresponding COMMON LISP primitive. For example, the constraint primitive `+v` is a constraint version of `+`. An expression of the form `(+v x y)` returns a new variable z, which it constrains to be the sum of x and y by adding the constraint $z = (+ \ x \ y)$. By convention, a SCREAMER primitive ending in the letter `v` is a constraint version of a corresponding COMMON LISP primitive. Table 1 lists the constraint primitives provided by SCREAMER. All of these primitives have the property that they accept variables as arguments—in addition to ground

*Supported in part by a Presidential Young Investigator Award to Professor Robert C. Berwick under National Science Foundation Grant DCR–85552543, by a grant from the Siemens Corporation, by the Kapor Family Foundation, by ARO grant DAAL 03–89–C–0031, by DARPA grant N00014–90–J–1863, by NSF grant IRI 90–16592, and by Ben Franklin grant 91S.3078C–1

†Supported in part by the Advanced Research Projects Agency of the Department of Defense under Office of Naval Research contract N00014-91-J-4038.

Type Restrictions:	numberpv realpv integerpv
	booleanpv memberv
Boolean:	andv orv notv
Numeric:	<v <=v >v >=v =v /=v
	+v -v *v /v minv maxv
Expression:	equalv
Functions:	funcallv applyv

Table 1: The constraint primitives provided by SCREAMER.

values—and return a variable as their result. The constraint primitive installs a constraint between the arguments and the returned variable stating that, under any interpretation of the variables involved, the value of the result variable must equal the corresponding COMMON LISP primitive applied to the values of the arguments. As another example, the expression $(<v\ x\ y)$ returns a variable z and adds the constraint $z = (<\ x\ y)$. This constraint is satisfied when z is either t or nil depending on whether x is less than y. For the most part, each constraint primitive obeys the same calling convention as the corresponding COMMON LISP primitive. SCREAMER performs a variety of optimizations to improve run time efficiency. In particular, if the value of a variable returned by a constraint primitive can be determined at the time the function is called then that value is returned directly without creating a new variable.

In SCREAMER, most constraints are of the form $z = (f\ x_1\ \ldots\ x_n)$ where f is the COMMON LISP primitive corresponding to some constraint primitive. Constraints of this form can imply type restrictions on the variables involved. For example, a constraint of the form $z = (<\ x\ y)$ implies that z is "Boolean", i.e., either t or nil. Furthermore, this constraint implies that x and y are numeric. In practice, a variable usually has a well defined type, e.g., it is known to be Boolean, known be real, known to be a cons cell, etc. Knowledge about the type of a variable has significant ramifications for the efficiency of SCREAMER's constraint satisfaction algorithms. SCREAMER has special procedures for inferring the types of variables. Because knowledge of the types of variables is important for efficiency, in contrast to the COMMON LISP primitives and, or, and not which accept any arguments of any type, the SCREAMER constraint primitives andv, orv, and notv require their arguments to be Boolean. This allows the use of Boolean constraint satisfaction techniques for any constraints introduced by these primitives. Similarly, constraint "predicates" return Boolean variables. For example, in contrast to the COMMON LISP primitive member which can return the sub-list of the second argument whose head satisfies the equality check, the result of the memberv primitive is constrained to be Boolean.

SCREAMER includes the primitive assert! which can be used to add constraints other than those added by the constraint primitives. Evaluating the expression (assert! x) constrains x to equal t. This can be used in conjunction with other constraint primitives to install a wide variety of constraints. For example, (assert! $(<v\ x\ y)$) effectively installs the constraint that x must be less than y.[1] Certain constraint primitives in table 1, in conjunction with assert!, can be used to directly constrain the type of a variable. For example, evaluating (assert! (numberpv x)) effectively installs the constraint that x must be a number. Likewise evaluating (assert! (booleanpv x)) installs the constraint that x must be Boolean. This is effectively the same as evaluating (assert! (memberv x '(t nil))).

All constraints in SCREAMER are installed either by assert! or by one of the constraint primitives in table 1. A constraint installed by assert! states that a certain variable must have the value t. A constraint installed by a constraint primitive always has the form $z = (f\ x_1\ \ldots\ x_n)$ where f is either a COMMON LISP primitive or a slight variation on a COMMON LISP primitive. The variations arise for constraint primitives such as orv and memberv where the semantics of the constraint version differs slightly from the semantics of the corresponding COMMON LISP primitive as discussed above.

An attempt to add a constraint fails if SCREAMER determines that the resulting set of constraints would be unsatisfiable. For example, after evaluating (assert! $(<v\ x\ 0)$) a subsequent evaluation of (assert! $(>v\ x\ 0)$) will fail. A call to a constraint primitive can fail when it would generate a constraint inconsistent with known type information. For example, if x is known to be Boolean then an evaluation of $(+v\ x\ y)$ will fail.

Constraint Propagation

In this section we discuss the five kinds of constraint propagation inference processes performed by SCREAMER. First, SCREAMER implements binding propagation, an incomplete inference technique sometimes called value propagation. Second, SCREAMER implements Boolean constraint propagation (BCP). This is an incomplete form of Boolean inference that can be viewed as a form of unit resolution. Third, SCREAMER implements generalized forward checking (GFC). This is a constraint propagation technique for discrete constraints used in the CHIP system. Fourth, SCREAMER implements bounds propagation on numeric variables. Such bounds propagation when combined with the divide-and-conquer technique

---

[1] To mitigate the apparent inefficiency of this conceptually clean language design, the implementation optimizes most calls to assert!, such as the calls (assert! (notv (realpv x))) and (assert! (<=v x y)), to eliminate the creation of the intermediate Boolean variable(s) and the resulting local propagation.

discussed later in this paper—implements a generalization of the interval method of solving systems of nonlinear equations proposed by Hansen (1968). Finally, SCREAMER implements unification. Unification is viewed as a constraint propagation inference technique which can be applied to equational constraints involving variables that range over S-expressions. The constraint propagation techniques are incrementally run to completion whenever a new constraint is installed by `assert!` or one of the constraint primitives. The five forms of constraint propagation are described in more detail below.

Each form of constraint propagation can be viewed as an inference process which locally derives information about variables. All forms of propagation are capable of inferring values for variables. For example, after evaluating (`assert!` (`orv` x y)) and (`assert!` (`notv` x)) BCP will infer that y must have the value `t`. If some constraint propagation inference process has determined a value for some variable x then we say that x is *bound* and the inferred value of x is called the *binding* of x.

Binding Propagation: As noted above, most constraints in SCREAMER are of the form $z = $ (`f` x_1 ... x_n) where f is a COMMON LISP primitive, z is a variable, and each x_i is either a variable or a specific value. For any such constraint SCREAMER implements a certain value propagation process. More specifically, if bindings have been determined for all but one of the variables in the constraint, and a binding for the remaining variable follows from the constraint and the existing bindings, then this additional binding is inferred. This general principle is called *binding propagation*. Binding propagation will always bind the output variable of a constraint primitive whenever the input variables become bound. For example, given the constraint $z = $ (`+` x y), if x is bound to 2 and y is bound to 3, then binding propagation will bind z to 5. Often, however, binding propagation will derive a binding for an input from a binding for the output. For example, given the constraint $z = $ (`+` x y), if z is bound to 5 and x is bound to 2, then binding propagation will bind y to 3.

Boolean Constraint Propagation: BCP is simply arc consistency (cf. Mackworth 1992) relative to the Boolean constraint primitives `andv`, `orv`, and `notv`. BCP, like arc consistency, is semantically incomplete. For example, after evaluating (`assert!` (`orv` z w)) and (`assert!` (`orv` (`notv` z) w)), any variable interpretation satisfying the installed constraints must assign w the value `t`. However, BCP will not make this inference. Semantic incompleteness is necessary in order to ensure that the constraint propagation process terminates quickly. Later in the paper we discuss how we interleave backtracking search with constraint propagation to mitigate the incompleteness of local propagation.

Generalized Forward Checking: GFC applies

to variables for which a finite set of possible values has been established. Such a set is called an *enumerated domain*. Variables with enumerated domains are called *discrete*. For example, after evaluating (`assert!` (`memberv` x '(a b c d))) the variable x is discrete because its value is known to be either `a`, `b`, `c`, or `d`. Boolean variables are a special case of discrete variables where the enumerated domain contains only `t` and `nil`. Similarly, bounded integer variables are considered to be discrete. For each discrete variable SCREAMER maintains a list representing its enumerated domain. The enumerated domain for a given variable can be updated by the GFC inference process. The GFC inference process operates on constraints of the form $z = $ (`funcall` f x_1 ... x_n). These constraints are generated by the constraint primitive `funcallv`. Unlike most constraint primitives, the primitive `funcallv` will signal an error—rather than fail— if its first argument is bound to anything but a deterministic procedure. Now consider the constraint $z = $ (`funcall` f x_1 ... x_n). GFC will only operate on this constraint when f is bound and all but one of the remaining variables in the constraint have been bound. If the unbound variable is the output variable z, then GFC simply derives a binding for z by applying f. If the unbound variable is one of the arguments x_i then GFC tests each element v of the enumerated domain of the discrete variable x_i for consistency relative to this constraint. Elements of the enumerated domain of x_i that are inconsistent with the constraint are removed. For example, suppose that we have evaluated (`assert!` (`memberv` x '(1 5 9))), (`assert!` (`memberv` y '(3 7 12))) and (`assert!` (`funcallv` #'< x y)). In this case the output variable of the `funcallv` constraint is bound to `t`. Now suppose that some constraint propagation inference process infers that y is 3. In this case GFC will run on the `funcallv` constraint and remove 5 and 9 from the enumerated domain of x. Whenever the enumerated domain of a discrete variable is reduced to a single value, GFC binds the variable to that value. An example of GFC running on the N-Queens problem is given later in the paper.

Bounds Propagation: Bounds propagation applies to numeric variables. For each numeric value the system maintains an upper and lower bound on the possible values of that variable. These bounds propagate through constraints generated by numeric constraint primitives such as `+v`, `*v` and `<v`. For example, after evaluating (`assert!` (`=v` z (`+v` x y))), if z is known to be no larger than 5.7, and x is known to be no smaller than 2.2, then bounds propagation will infer that y is no larger than 3.5. Bounds propagation can also derive values for the Boolean output variables of numeric constraint predicates such as `<v` and `=v`. For example, if we have the constraint $z = $ (`<` x y)) and the system has determined that x is at least 2.0 but y is no larger than 1.0, then the system will infer that z

is `nil`.

Bounds propagation will not infer a new bound unless the new bound reduces the known interval of the variable involved by at least a certain minimum percentage. This ensures that the bounds propagation process terminates fairly quickly. For example, SCREAMER avoids the very large number of bounds updates that would result from the constraints `(assert! (>v x 0))`, `(assert! (<v x 1000))` and `(assert! (<v x (-v x 0.001)))`.

Unification: Unification operates on constraints of the form $w = $ (`equal` u v) which are generated by the constraint primitive `equalv`. At any given time there is a system of equations defined by the set of `equalv` constraints whose output variable has been bound to `t`. SCREAMER incrementally maintains a most general unifier σ for this system of equations. For example, evaluating (`assert!` (`equalv` (`cons` x x) (`cons` y w))) will result in a unifier σ that equates x, y, and w, i.e., a unifier σ such that $\sigma[x]$, $\sigma[y]$, and $\sigma[w]$ are all equal. SCREAMER also implements disunification as in PROLOG-II (Colmerauer 1984). Thus, after evaluating (`assert!` (`notv` (`equalv` x y))), any attempt to bind x or y to be equal will fail.

The different forms of constraint propagation can interact with each other. For example, a given variable can be both discrete and numeric. The system removes non-numeric elements from the enumerated domains of discrete numeric variables. Furthermore, if a bound is known for a discrete numeric variable then elements violating that bound are eliminated from its enumerated domain. SCREAMER also derives bounds information from the enumerated domains of discrete numeric variables. Unification also interacts with SCREAMER bindings. For example, if σ is the most general unifier maintained by SCREAMER, and x and y are two variables such that $\sigma[x]$ equals $\sigma[y]$, then any binding for x becomes a binding for y and vice versa. If $\sigma[x]$ equals $\sigma[y]$, and x and y have incompatible bindings, then a failure is generated.

Solving Systems of Constraints

By design, all of the constraint primitives described so far use only fast local propagation techniques. Such techniques are necessarily incomplete; they cannot always solve systems of constraints or determine that they are unsolvable. SCREAMER provides a number of primitives for augmenting local propagation with backtracking search to provide a general mechanism for solving systems of constraints. One such primitive, `linear-force`, can be applied to a variable to cause it to nondeterministically take on one of the values in its domain. `Linear-force` can be applied only to discrete variables or integer variables. Constraining a variable to take on a value using `linear-force` may cause local propagation. Thus a single call to `linear-force` may cause a number of variables to be

bound, or alternatively may fail if the variable cannot consistently take on any value. A second primitive, `divide-and-conquer-force`, can be applied to a variable to nondeterministically reduce the set of possible values it may take on. `Divide-and-conquer-force` can be applied only to discrete variables or real variables with finite upper and lower bounds. When applied to discrete variables, the enumerated domain is split into two subsets and the variable nondeterministically constrained to take on values from either the first or second subset. When applied to bounded real variables, the interval is split in half and the variable nondeterministically constrained to take on values in either of the two subintervals.

The above two functions operate on single variables. More generally, one must find the values of several variables which satisfy the given constraints. SCREAMER provides two primitives to accomplish this. Both are higher-order functions which take a single variable force function as an argument (e.g. `linear-force` or `divide-and-conquer-force`) and produce a function capable of forcing a list of variables using that force function. Each incorporates a different strategy for choosing which variable to force next. The first, `static-ordering`, simply forces the variables in the order given. The single variable force function is repeatedly applied to each variable, until that variable takes on a ground value, before proceeding with the next variable. All variables are bound upon termination. The second, `reorder`, selects the variable with the smallest domain, applies the single variable force function to this variable, and repeats this process until all variables are bound. Since the choice of single variable force function is orthogonal to the choice of variable ordering strategy, SCREAMER thus provides four distinct constraint solving strategies. More can easily be added.

Examples

We will illustrate the power of the SCREAMER constraint language with two small examples. The first, shown in figure 1, solves the N-Queens problem. The function `n-queensv` creates a variable for each row and constrains each row variable to take on an integer between 1 and n indicating the column occupied by a queen in that row. The function (`a-member-ofv` s) is simply syntactic sugar for the following.

```
(let ((v (make-variable)))
(assert! (memberv v s))
v)
```

The SCREAMER primitive (`solution` x f) gathers all of the variables nested inside the structure x, applies the multiple variable forcing function f to this list of variables, and returns a copy of x where the variables have been replaced by their bound values.

In the above example, SCREAMER applies GFC as the technique for solving the underlying constraint sat-

```
(defun attacks? (qi qj distance) (or (= qi qj) (= (abs (- qi qj)) distance)))
(defun n-queensv (n)
 (solution (let ((q (make-array n)))
            (dotimes (i n) (setf (aref q i) (an-integer-betweenv 1 n)))
            (dotimes (i n)
             (dotimes (j n)
              (if (> j i) (assert! (notv (funcallv #'attacks? (aref q i) (aref q j) (- j i)))))))
            (coerce q 'list))
           (reorder #'domain-size #'(lambda (x) (declare (ignore x)) nil) #'< #'linear-force)))
(defun nonlinear ()
 (let ((x (a-real-betweenv -1e40 1e40))
       (y (a-real-betweenv -1e40 1e40))
       (z (a-real-betweenv -1e40 1e40)))
  (assert! (andv (=v (+v (*v 4 x x y) (*v 7 y z z) (*v 6 x x z z)) 1356.14)
                 (=v (+v (*v 3 x y) (*v 2 y y) (*v 5 x y z)) -141.375)
                 (=v (*v (+v x y) (+v y z)) -7.7625)))
  (solution (list x y z)
            (reorder #'range-size #'(lambda (x) (< x 1e-6)) #'> #'divide-and-conquer-force))))
```

Figure 1: Two constraint-based SCREAMER programs, one for solving the N-Queens problem and one for solving a system of nonlinear equations using numeric bounds propagation.

isfaction problem. SCREAMER chooses this technique since all of the variables involved are discrete.

The second example, shown in figure 1, illustrates how bounds propagation can be used to solve systems of nonlinear equations expressed as constraints between numeric variables. The function nonlinear finds a solution to the following system of nonlinear equations.

$$
\begin{aligned}
4x^2y + 7yz^2 + 6x^2z^2 &= 1356.14 \\
3xy + 2y^2 + 5xyz &= -141.375 \\
(x+y)(y+z) &= -7.7625
\end{aligned}
$$

The expression (a-real-betweenv -1e40 1e40) creates a variable constrained to be a real number between the given upper and lower bounds. After the constraints have been asserted between the variables, divide and conquer search—interleaved with bounds propagation—is used to find a solution to the equations. One such solution is $x \approx -7.311$, $y \approx 6.113$, $z \approx 0.367$. Note that unlike the simplex method used in CLP($\Re$)—which is limited to solving linear systems of equations—the combination of divide and conquer search interleaved with bounds propagation allows SCREAMER to solve complex nonlinear systems of equations. These techniques also enable SCREAMER to solve numeric constraint systems with both inequalities and equational constraints. Furthermore, since all of the constraint satisfaction techniques are integrated, SCREAMER can solve disjunctive systems of equations as well as systems which mix together numeric, Boolean, and other forms of constraints.

We wish to point out the intentional similarity in the names of the SCREAMER primitives a-member-of and a-member-ofv.[2] Both describe a choice between a set of possible alternatives. The former enumerates that set nondeterministically by backtracking. The latter instead, creates a variable whose value is constrained to be a member of the given set. The former lends itself to a generate-and-test style of programming.

```
(let (($x_1$ (a-member-of $s_1$))
      ⋮
      ($x_n$ (a-member-of $s_n$)))
 (unless Φ[$x_1 ... x_n$] (fail))
 (list $x_1 ... x_n$))
```

The latter lends itself to constraint-based programming.

```
(let (($x_1$ (a-member-ofv $s_1$))
      ⋮
      ($x_n$ (a-member-ofv $s_n$)))
 (assert! (funcallv
           #'(lambda ($x_1 ... x_n$) Φ[$x_1 ... x_n$])
           $x_1 ... x_n$))
 (solution (list $x_1 ... x_n$)
           (static-ordering #'linear-force)))
```

Though these two program fragments are structurally very similar, and specify the same problem, they entail drastically different search strategies. The latter constitutes a *lifted* variant of the former. A future paper will we discuss the possibilities of performing such lifting transformations automatically. Such

---

[2] We adopt the (unenforced) convention that the names of all nondeterministic generator functions begin with the prefix a- or an- and that functions beginning with the prefix a- or an-, and also ending with v, denote lifted generators, functions which deterministically return a variable ranging over the stated domain instead of nondeterministically returning a value in that domain.

lifting is not limited to the **a-member-of** primitive. SCREAMER includes the following syntactic sugar for (**an-integer-betweenv** l h).

```
(let ((v (make-variable)))
 (assert!
  (andv (integerpv v) (<=v v h) (>=v v l)))
 v)
```

The function **an-integer-betweenv** is a lifted analog to the SCREAMER primitive **an-integer-between**. All SCREAMER generators have lifted analogs.

Related Work

Most of the individual techniques described in this paper are not new. What is novel is their particular combination. Programming languages which allow stating numeric constraints date back to SKETCHPAD (Sutherland 1963). Local propagation for solving systems of constraints was used by Borning (1979) in THINGLAB. Steele (1980) constructs constraint primitives very similar to ours and implements local propagation by procedural attachment. These techniques were expanded on by the MAGRITTE system (Gosling 1983). The above systems differ from SCREAMER in two ways. First, they handled only numeric constraints, lacking the GFC capacity of SCREAMER embodied in **memberv** and **funcallv**, as well as unification and disunification embodied in **equalv**. More importantly, the constraint solving techniques incorporated in all of these systems were incomplete, particularly those based on local propagation. None of these systems could resort to interleaving backtracking search with local propagation—as SCREAMER can—to provide a slow but complete fallback to faster but incomplete local propagation techniques when applied alone.

More recently, numerous systems such as CLP($\Re$) and CHiP have been constructed in the logic programming framework which add some form of constraint satisfaction—sometimes based on local propagation—to the backtracking search mechanism already present in logic programming languages. SCREAMER differs from such systems in a number of ways, some minor and some major. First, SCREAMER uses only fast local propagation techniques as part of its constraint mechanism. The numeric constraint mechanism of CLP($\Re$) instead uses more costly techniques based on the simplex method for linear programming. These techniques are incomplete for nonlinear constraints. CLP($\Re$) and CHiP do not provide mechanisms for dealing with this incompleteness. SCREAMER, on the other hand, can solve nonlinear constraints using **divide-and-conquer-force** combined with local propagation. The second difference lies in using COMMON LISP instead of PROLOG as a substrate for constructing constraint-based programming languages. Given the substrate of nondeterministic COMMON LISP—especially its capacity for local side effects—the SCREAMER constraint package can be written totally in COMMON LISP. This gives

SCREAMER three advantages over CLP($\Re$) and CHiP. First, SCREAMER is portable to any COMMON LISP implementation. Second, SCREAMER can be easily modified and extended, to experiment with alternative constraint types and constraint satisfaction methods. Finally, SCREAMER can coexist and inter-operate with other current or future extensions to COMMON LISP such as CLOS and CLIM.

The current version of SCREAMER, including the full constraint package, is available by anonymous FTP from the file **/com/ftp/pub/screamer.tar.Z** on the host **ftp.ai.mit.edu**. We encourage you to obtain a copy of SCREAMER and give us feedback on your experiences using it.

References

Alan Hamilton Borning. THINGLAB—*A Constraint-Oriented Simulation Laboratory*. PhD thesis, Stanford University, July 1979. Also available as Stanford Computer Science Department report STAN-CS-79-746 and as XEROX Palo Alto Research Center report SSL-79-3.

A. Colmerauer. Equations and inequations on finite and infinite trees. In *2d International Conference on Fifth Generation Computer Systems*, pages 85–99, 1984.

James Gosling. *Algebraic Constraints*. PhD thesis, Carnegie-Mellon University, 1983.

E. R. Hansen. On the solution of linear algebraic equations using interval arithmetic. *Mathematical Computation*, 22:153–165, 1968.

Joxan Jaffar and Jean-Louis Lassez. Constraint logic programming. In *Proceedings of the 14th ACM Symposium on the Principles of Programming Languages*, pages 111–119, 1987.

Alan K. Mackworth. Constraint satisfaction. In Stuart C. Shapiro, editor, *Encyclopedia of Artificial Intelligence*, pages 285–293. John Wiley & Sons, Inc., New York, 1992.

Jeffrey Mark Siskind and David Allen McAllester. SCREAMER: a portable efficient implementation of nondeterministic COMMON LISP. Technical Report IRCS–93–03, University of Pennsylvania Institute for Research in Cognitive Science, 1993.

Ivan E. Southerland. SKETCHPAD: *A Man-Machine Graphical Communication System*. PhD thesis, Massachusetts Institute of Technology, January 1963.

Guy Lewis Steele Jr. *The Definition and Implementation of a Computer Programming Language Based on Constraints*. PhD thesis, Massachusetts Institute of Technology, August 1980. Also avilable as M. I. T. VLSI Memo 80–32 and as M. I. T. Artificial Inteligence Laboratory Technical Report 595.

Pascal Van Hentenryck. *Constraint Satisfaction in Logic Programming*. M. I. T. Press, Cambridge, MA, 1989.

Slack-Based Heuristics For Constraint Satisfaction Scheduling *

Stephen F. Smith
The Robotics Institute
Carnegie Mellon University
Pittsburgh, PA 15213
sfs@isl1.ri.cmu.edu

Cheng-Chung Cheng
The Robotics Institute
Carnegie Mellon University
Pittsburgh, PA 15213
ccen@isl1.ri.cmu.edu

Abstract

In this paper, we define and empirically evaluate new heuristics for solving the job shop scheduling problem with non-relaxable time windows. The hypothesis underlying our approach is that by approaching the problem as one of establishing sequencing constraints between pairs of operations requiring the same resource (as opposed to a problem of assigning start times to each operation) and by exploiting previously developed analysis techniques for limiting search through the space of possible sequencing decisions, simple, localized look-ahead techniques can yield problem solving performance comparable to currently dominating techniques that rely on more sophisticated analysis of resource contention. We define a series of attention focusing heuristics based on simple analysis of the temporal flexibility associated with different sequencing decisions, and a similarly motivated heuristic for determining how to sequence a given operation pair. Performance results are reported on a suite of benchmark problems previously investigated by two advanced approaches, and our simplified look-ahead analysis techniques are shown to provide comparable problem solving leverage at reduced computational cost.

Introduction

In this paper, we propose and evaluate the performance of new look-ahead heuristics for solving the job shop scheduling problem with non-relaxable time windows. The problem originates from the manufacturing domain, and, as classically defined, involves synchronization of the production of N jobs in a facility with M machines. The production of a given job requires the execution of a sequence of operations (its process plan in manufacturing parlance). Each operation has a specified processing time and its execution requires the

exclusive use of a designated machine for the duration of its processing (i.e. machines have unit processing capacity). Each job has an associated ready time and a deadline, and its production must be accomplished within this interval. The problem can be extended in various ways - to include selection among designated resource alternatives for each operation, to associate multiple resource requirements (e.g. machine, operator) with operations, etc. In any case, the objective is to determine a schedule for production that satisfies all temporal and resource capacity constraints.

The job shop scheduling with non-relaxable time windows problem is known to be NP-Complete (Garey & Johnson 1979). Accordingly, the development of effective heuristic procedures for solving this constraint satisfaction problem (CSP) has been the subject of considerable previous research. This work, with few exceptions, has sought to exploit the special structure of the problem, in particular the structure of resource capacity constraints, to enhance consistency enforcement and early search space pruning capabilities, to support more-informed backtracking, and to focus attention in elaborating the search (our principal interest in this paper). Most frequently, the job shop scheduling problem has been formulated as one of finding a consistent assignment of start times for each operation of each job (Johnston 1990), (Keng & Yun 1989), (Minton et al. 1990), (Sadeh 1991), and (Zweben et al. 1990). Here, the development of focus of attention (or variable ordering) heuristics has focused fairly exclusively on use of contention-based metrics. One recent approach which has produced strong comparative experimental results, relies on a dynamic variable ordering heuristic that maintains profiles of resource demand over time, repeatedly identifies the resource and time period of greatest expected contention, and focuses attention on scheduling the operation that contributes most to this "bottleneck" (Sadeh 1991).

A smaller number of efforts have alternatively treated the problem as one of posting sufficient additional sequencing constraints between pairs of operations contending for the same resource so as to ensure feasibility with respect to time and capacity con-

*This research reported in this paper has been sponsored in part by DARPA under contract F30602-90-C-0119, NASA under contract NCC 2-707, and the Robotics Institute.

straints. The solutions generated in this way typically represent a set of feasible schedules (i.e., the sets of operation start times that remain consistent with posted sequencing constraints), as opposed to a single assignment of operation start times. In (Erschler et al. 1976, 1980) the structure of resource capacity constraints is exploited to define dominance conditions for pruning the set of feasible sequencing alternatives at each stage of the search. More recently, (Muscettola 1993) has demonstrated the utility of global resource capacity analysis techniques (similar in spirit to the approach in (Sadeh 1991)) as a focusing mechanism within this alternative search space; in this case sequencing constraints are repeatedly posted between sets of conflicting operations until resource capacity analysis indicates no further possibility of resource contention.

Like (Muscettola 1993), we believe that the inherent flexibility gained by providing sets of feasible solutions offers considerable pragmatic value over typically over-constrained fixed times solutions. The principal claim of this paper, however, is that this second formulation of the problem also provides a more convenient search space in which to operate. When the problem is cast as a search for orderings between pairs of operations vying for the same resource, we argue that it is possible to obtain the look-ahead benefits of global resource capacity analysis through the use of simpler, local analysis of the sequencing possibilities associated with unordered operation pairs. We define a series of variable ordering heuristics based on measures of temporal slack which, when integrated with the search space pruning techniques developed in (Erschler et al. 1976), are shown to yield comparable problem solving performance to contention-based heuristics at a fraction of the computational cost.

The remainder of the paper is organized as follows. In Section 2, we specify the problem as a CSP search for operation pair orderings, and review dominance conditions that enable search space pruning relative to this model. In Sections 3 through 5, we propose a series of variable ordering heuristics and present comparative results on a previously studied suite of 60 test problems. Finally, in Section 6, we outline current work in applying the approach to schedule optimization.

Problem Representation and Search Framework

In more precise terms, a solution to the basic job shop scheduling CSP requires a consistent assignment of values to start time variables st_i for each operation i, under the following constraints:

- **sequencing restrictions** - for every precedence relation $i \rightarrow j$ specified between operations i and j in the process plan of a given job $\mathcal{J}$, $st_i + p_i \leq st_j$, where p_i is the processing time required by operation i of job $\mathcal{J}$.

- **resource capacity constraints** - for any two operations i and j requiring the same resource, $st_i + p_i \leq st_j \lor st_j + p_j \leq st_i$

- **ready times and deadlines** - for each operation i of job $\mathcal{J}$, $r_{\mathcal{J}} \leq st_i$ and $st_i + p_i \leq d_{\mathcal{J}}$, where $r_{\mathcal{J}}$ and $d_{\mathcal{J}}$ are the ready time and deadline respectively associated with job $\mathcal{J}$.

While this problem representation provides a direct basis for problem solving search (and in fact has been taken as the starting point of most previous research), the problem can be alternatively formulated as one of establishing sequencing constraints between pairs of operations contending for the same resource over time. In this case, we define a decision variable $ordering_{i,j}$ for each pair of operations i and j that require the same resource, which can take on either of two values: $i \rightarrow j$ (implying the constraint $st_i + p_i \leq st_j$) and $j \rightarrow i$ (implying $st_j + p_j \leq st_i$). A solution then is a consistent assignment of values to all ordering variables. There are several potential advantages to this formulation. The advantage emphasized in this paper is that the simpler structure of the search space enables more straightforward accounting of resource capacity constraints and the use of simpler, localized analysis of current solution structure as a basis for variable and value ordering.

Our problem solving framework assumes a backtrack search procedure in which the solution is incrementally extended through the repeated selection and binding of an as yet unconstrained $ordering_{i,j}$ variable (referred to as the posting of a new precedence relation). Whenever a new precedence relation is posted, constraint propagation is performed to ensure continued temporal consistency and maintain current bounds on the earliest start time and latest finish time of each operation. [1] If the decision $i \rightarrow j$ is taken, for example, then est_j (the earliest start time of j) and lft_i (the latest finish time of i) are updated by

$$est_j = \max\{est_j, est_i + p_i\}, \text{ and} \qquad (1)$$

$$lft_i = \min\{lft_i, lft_j - p_j\}, \qquad (2)$$

and these new values are then propagated forward or backward respectively through all pre-specified and posted temporal precedence relations. If during this process, $est_k + p_k$ becomes greater than lft_k for any operation k then an inconsistent set of assignments has been detected.

As indicated at the outset, our approach to directing the search integrates a procedure previously developed by Erschler *et al*, referred to as *Constraint-based Analysis (CBA)*, which exploits dominance conditions to prune the space of possible ordering assignments. To summarize their basic idea, assume that est_i and lft_i

---

[1] Since we are assuming in this paper that operation processing times are fixed, we could equivalently reason in terms of earliest and latest start times.

designate the current earliest start time and latest finish time respectively of a given operation i. Then, for any unordered pair of operations, i and j, contending for a particular resource, we can distinguish four different cases:

1. If $lft_i - est_j < p_i + p_j \leq lft_j - est_i$ then i must be scheduled before j in any feasible extension of the current ordering decisions. (case 1)

2. If $lft_j - est_i < p_i + p_j \leq lft_i - est_j$ then j must be scheduled before i in any feasible extension of the current ordering decisions. (case 2)

3. If $p_i + p_j > lft_j - est_i$ and $p_i + p_j > lft_i - est_j$ then there is no feasible schedule. (case 3)

4. If $p_i + p_j \leq lft_j - est_i$ and $p_i + p_j \leq lft_i - est_j$ then either sequencing decision is still possible. (case 4)

These dominance conditions of course provide only necessary conditions for determining a set of feasible schedules, and thus interleaved application of CBA and temporal constraint propagation yields an underspecified search procedure. What is needed to generate solutions are heuristics for resolving the undecided states specified in case 4. In this regard, previous use of CBA has emphasized fuzzy integration of sets of different scheduling rules. In (Bensana & Dubois 1988), a voting procedure based on fuzzy set theory and approximate reasoning was developed and used in conjunction with a set of fuzzy scheduling rules. In (Kerr & Walker 1989), fuzzy arithmetic together with fuzzy scheduling rules was utilized instead. Our goal, alternatively, is to investigate the effectiveness of CBA in conjunction with simple look-ahead analysis of current ordering flexibility. This leads to the search procedure that is graphically depicted in Figure 1, which we will refer to as precedence constraint posting (PCP). In the following sections, we define and evaluate a specific set of variable and value ordering heuristics.

Exploiting Estimates of Sequencing Flexibility

Intuitively, in situations where CBA leaves the search in a state with several unresolved ordering assignments (i.e., for each unordered operation pair, both ordering decisions are still feasible), we would like to focus attention on the ordering decision that is currently most constrained. Since the posting of any sequence constraint is likely to further constrain other ordering decisions that remain to be made, delaying the currently most constrained decision increases the chances of arriving at an infeasible problem solving state.

Implementation of such a variable ordering strategy requires a means of estimating the current flexibility associated with a given unresolved ordering decision. One simple indicator of flexibility is the amount of temporal slack that is retained by a given operation pair if a decision to sequence them is taken. To this end,

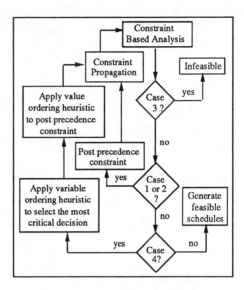

Figure 1: PCP Search Procedure

we define two measures, corresponding to the two possible decisions that might be taken. For a given pair of currently unordered operations (i, j) contending for the same resource, we define the "temporal slack remaining after sequencing i before j" as

$$slack(i \rightarrow j) = lft_j - est_i - (p_i + p_j), \qquad (3)$$

and similarly the "temporal slack remaining after sequencing j before i" as

$$slack(j \rightarrow i) = lft_i - est_j - (p_i + p_j). \qquad (4)$$

Figure 2 provides a graphic illustration of $slack(i \rightarrow j)$ and $slack(j \rightarrow i)$. Note that in either case the remaining slack is shared by both i and j. Thus, the larger the temporal slack, the greater the chance that subsequent ordering decisions involving i and j can be feasibly imposed.

Given these measures of temporal slack, we now have a basis for identifying the most constrained or "most critical" decision and for specifying an initial variable ordering heuristic. We define the ordering decision with the **overall minimum slack**, to be the decision $ordering_{i,j}$ for which

$$\min\{slack(i \rightarrow j), slack(j \rightarrow i)\} =$$
$$\min_{(u,v)}\{\min\{slack(u \rightarrow v), slack(v \rightarrow u)\}\}$$

for all unassigned $ordering_{u,v}$. Using this notion of criticality, we define a variable ordering heuristic that selects this decision at each unresolved state of the search.

With respect to the decision of which sequencing constraint to post (i.e., value assignment), we intuitively prefer the decision that leaves the search with the most degrees of freedom. Thus we post the sequencing constraint that retains the largest amount of temporal slack.

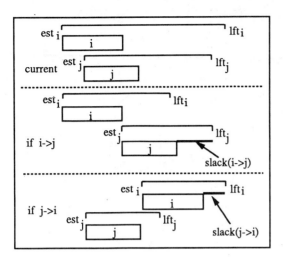

Figure 2: Slack(i → j) and Slack(j → i)

Summarizing then, our initial configuration of variable and value ordering heuristics is defined as follows:

I. Min-Slack variable ordering: Select the sequencing decision with the overall minimum temporal slack. Suppose this decision is $ordering_{i,j}$.

II. Max-Slack value ordering: choose the sequencing constraint $i \rightarrow j$ if $slack(i \rightarrow j) > slack(j \rightarrow i)$; otherwise choose $j \rightarrow i$.

A Computational Study

In this section we evaluate the performance of the above heuristics in conjunction with the PCP search procedure on a suite of job shop scheduling CSPs studied by two recently developed scheduling procedures: ORR/FSS (Sadeh 1991) and CPS (Muscettola 1993). Both ORR/FSS and CPS rely on global estimations of resource contention to dynamically direct their respective search processes. In the former case, profiles of resource demand over time are deterministically constructed according to probabilistic assumptions, and inspected to identify contention "peaks". In the case of CPS, expected resource "conflicts" are identified from demand profiles constructed via stochastic simulation in a relaxed solution space where resource constraints are ignored. ORR/FSS and CPS also differ in the type of decision that is taken at each step of the search. ORR/FSS takes a decision to fix the start time of the operation contributing most to the highest contention peak. CPS identifies the set of operations involved in the most severe resource conflict, and posts a sequencing constraint to reduce the level of contention among these operations. Unlike our approach, which establishes orderings between pairs of operations, CPS posts precedence constraints between sets of operations and attempts to post only as many constraints as are necessary to eliminate the possibility of resource contention (thus retaining additional flexibility in the final solu-

tion). Both ORR/FSS and CPS have reported very strong results on the set of scheduling problems used in this study.

As an additional point of comparison, we also include results obtained with three priority dispatch rules from the field of Operations Research: EDD, COVERT, and ATC (Vepsalainen & Morton 1987). These heuristics are frequently used and have been determined to work very well in job shop scheduling circumstances where expected job tardiness is low (as would likely be the case if a feasible solution exists).

The set of problems used in this study come from the dissertation of Sadeh (Sadeh 1991). The problem set consists of 60 randomly generated scheduling problems. Each problem contains 10 jobs and 5 resources. Each job has 5 operations. In all problems, deadlines were generated randomly within a specified range. A controlling parameter was used to generate problems in three different deadline ranges: wide (w), median (m), and tight (t). A second parameter was used to generate problems with both 1 and 2 "bottleneck" resources. Combining these two parameters, 6 different categories of scheduling problems were defined, and 10 problems were generated for each category. The problem categories were carefully defined to cover a variety of manufacturing scheduling circumstances. While each problem has at least one feasible solution, they range in difficulty from easy to hard.

The results obtained on these problems, along with those previously reported, are given in Table 1 (where problem difficulty increases from top to bottom). The number of problems solved by each approach by problem category are indicated. In the case of ORR/FSS runs, search was terminated on a given problem if a solution was not found after a pre-determined number of search states had been expanded. Two sets of results are reported for this procedure, Sadeh's original dissertation results using simple chronological backtracking and a subsequent study (labeled ORR/FSS+) where the original procedure was augmented with the "intelligent" backtracking techniques described in (Xiong et al. 1992). In the case of CPS, which operates with a stochastic resource analysis, the search was restarted from scratch upon detection of an infeasible state. In the case of our approach, no backtracking mechanism was employed and the search was terminated in failure if an infeasible solution state was reached.

Examining the results, we see that our simple slack-based variable and value ordering heuristics, in conjunction with the search space pruning techniques provided by CBA, perform remarkably well in comparison to both contention-based scheduling procedures, and while not solving all 60 problems, provide evidence in support of our hypothesis that comparable performance can be obtained with localized and less sophisticated look-ahead analysis techniques. From the standpoint of computational performance, average solution times of 128 and 78 seconds were obtained

	PCP	ORR FSS	ORR FSS+	CPS	Edd	Co-vert	Atc
w/1	10	10	10	10	10	7	7
w/2	10	10	10	10	10	8	8
m/1	10	8	10	10	8	5	5
m/2	10	9	10	10	8	8	8
t/1	10	7	10	10	3	6	6
t/2	6	8	10	10	8	8	8
sum	56	52	60	60	47	42	42

Table 1: Results of the experiments

with ORR/FSS+ and CPS respectively in these experiments. Our approach averaged 0.2 seconds for each solved problem.[2]

In the next section we attempt to refine our initial variable and value ordering heuristics to improve problem solving performance. We note in passing that the priority rules perform rather poorly on this set of scheduling problems.

Incorporating Additional Search Bias

While **Min-Slack** performed quite well over the tested problem set, it does not in fact utilize all of the information provided by the temporal slack data. In particular, it relies exclusively on the smaller slack value in determining the criticality of a ordering decision $ordering_{i,j}$, and ignores any information that might be provided by the larger one.

The most common problem created by disregarding this additional value appears in a form of tie-breaking. Consider the following example. Suppose that we have two unsequenced operation pairs, one with associated temporal slack values of $(20, 3)$, and the other with values of $(4, 3)$. **Min-Slack** does not distinguish between the criticality of these two ordering decisions, since the minimum value in both cases is 3. In the event that the overall minimum slack over all candidate decisions is also 3, then **Min-Slack** will choose randomly. But, in this case sequencing the second operation pair is certainly more critical since the flexibility that will be left after the decision is made will be considerably less than the flexibility that will remain if the first unsequenced operation pair is instead chosen and sequenced.

Given this insight, we define a second variable ordering heuristic, which operates exactly as **Min-Slack** except in situations where more than one pending decision $ordering_{i,j}$ is identified as a decision with overall minimum temporal slack. In these situations, ties are broken by selecting the decision with the minimum larger temporal slack value. Applying the PCP procedure with this extended heuristic to the same suite of 60 problems yielded 57 solved problems. Although this

[2] All computation times were obtained on a Decstation 5000. Both ORR/FSS and CPS are Lisp-based systems; our procedure is implemented in C.

improvement is slight, it suggests the potential advantage of incorporating additional information.

A more subtle problem created by the information ignorance inherent in **Min-Slack** is the problem of similarity. Let's again consider an example. Suppose that we are again deciding between two unsequenced operations pairs. This time the temporal slack values associated with the first are $(3, 3)$, and the values associated with the second are $(5, 5)$. Which one is more critical? Without any ambiguity, the first one is more critical than the second one, and this is also the answer provided by **Min-Slack**. But what if we change the values for the first pair to $(20, 3)$. Is the first pair still more critical than the second one? The answer is not obvious. The point is that there exists a tradeoff between relying on minimum slack values and relying on information relating to the degree of similarity of both slack values in determining criticality. The strong performance of **Min-Slack** suggests that minimum slack values should remain the dominant consideration. But we hypothesize that the introduction of bias to increase criticality as the similarity of large and small slack values increases and decrease criticality as the slack values become more dissimilar might provide more effective search guidance.

Let us define a measure of similarity in the range $[0, 1]$ such that for slack value pairs with identical values, the similarity value is 1 and as the distance between large and small slack values increases, the similarity value approaches 0. More precisely, we estimate the similarity between two slack values by the following ratio expression:

$$ S = \frac{min\{slack(i \rightarrow j), slack(j \rightarrow i)\}}{max\{slack(i \rightarrow j), slack(j \rightarrow i)\}} \quad (5) $$

Given the definition of S and the direction of bias desired, we now define a new criticality metric, referred to as biased temporal slack, as follows:

$$ Bslack(i \rightarrow j) = \frac{slack(i \rightarrow j)}{f(S)}, \quad (6) $$

where f is a monotonically increasing function.

With little intuition as to the appropriate level of bias to exert on the criticality calculation, but assuming that the level of bias should not be too great, we use $\sqrt[n]{S}, n \geq 2$, to define a set of alternatives, yielding

$$ Bslack(i \rightarrow j) = \frac{slack(i \rightarrow j)}{\sqrt[n]{S}}. \quad (7) $$

By empirical reasoning, we also define a composite form of the metric with two different parameters, n_1 and n_2, as

$$ Bslack(i \rightarrow j) = \frac{slack(i \rightarrow j)}{\sqrt[n_1]{S}} + \frac{slack(i \rightarrow j)}{\sqrt[n_2]{S}}. \quad (8) $$

Table 2 presents results obtained using **overall minimum Bslack** as a variable ordering criterion for different values of n in Eqn. (7) and n_1 and n_2 in Eqn. (8)

	$n = 2$	$n = 3$	$n = 4$	$n_1 = 2$ $n_2 = 3$	$n_1 = 3$ $n_2 = 4$
w/1	10	10	10	10	10
w/2	10	10	10	10	10
m/1	10	10	10	10	10
m/2	10	10	10	10	10
t/1	10	10	10	10	10
t/2	8	8	8	10	9
total	58	58	58	60	59

Table 2: Performance using Min-Bslack heuristic

on the same suite of 60 problems. From the results, we can see that use of $Bslack(i \rightarrow j)$ as a variable ordering criterion does in fact yield improved performance on this suite of 60 problems. As expected, performance is sensitive to the amount of bias specified. In the case where all 60 problems are solved, average solution time was 0.3 seconds.

Conclusions

In this paper, we have proposed and evaluated new heuristics for solving the job shop scheduling problem with non-relaxable time windows. Our hypothesis has been that by approaching the problem as one of establishing sequencing constraints between pairs of operations requiring the same resource and by exploiting analysis techniques for limiting the search of possible sequencing decisions, simple, localized look-ahead techniques can yield problem solving performance comparable to techniques that rely on more sophisticated analysis of resource contention. We defined a series of attention focusing heuristics based on simple analysis of the temporal flexibility associated with different sequencing decisions, and a similarly motivated heuristic for determining how to sequence a given operation pair. Evaluation of these heuristics on a suite of benchmark problems previously investigated by two contention-based scheduling procedures has shown that our heuristics provide comparable results at very low computational expense.

Our current interest is in adapting the PCP approach to solve more common, optimization-based formulations of scheduling problems. In this context, certain problem constraints (e.g., due dates) are not interpreted as rigid, but instead specify preferred values over which objective criteria are defined (e.g., minimizing tardiness cost). To adapt the PCP procedure to this class of problems, two basic issues must be addressed. First, since CBA depends on the assumption that time and capacity constraints are non-relaxable, its advantage as a search space pruning mechanism is lost. We are exploring use of an alternative mechanism, inspired by standard branch and bound search procedures, which bases pruning on a dynamically refined upper bound solution. The second issue concerns the inappropriateness of temporal slack as a basis

for estimating the criticality of various ordering decisions. This metric, however, can be straightforwardly replaced by the objective function itself (e.g., computing the increase in tardiness cost resulting from alternative ordering decisions for a given pair of operations), giving rise to variants of the variable and value ordering heuristics defined in this paper.

References

Bensana, E., Bel, G., and Dubois, D. 1988. OPAL: A multi-knowledge based system for job-shop scheduling. Int. J. Production Research, 26(5), 795-819.

Erschler, J., Roubellat, F., and Vernhes, J. P. 1976. Finding some essential characteristics of the feasible solutions for a scheduling problem. *Operations Research*, 24, 772-782.

Erschler, J., Roubellat, F., and Vernhes, J. P. 1980. Characterizing the set of feasible sequences for n jobs to be carried out on a single machine. *European Journal of Operational Research*, 4, 189 - 194.

Garey, M. R. and Johnson, D. S. 1979. *Computers and Intractability, a Guide to the Theory of NP-Completeness*, W.H. Freeman Company.

Johnston, M. D. 1990. SPIKE: AI scheduling for NASA's Hubble Space Telescope. In *Proc. 6th IEEE Conference on AI Applications, Santa Barbara, CA*.

Keng, N. and Yun, D. Y. Y. 1989. A planning/scheduling methodology for the constrained resource problem. In *Proc. IJCAI-89*, Detroit, MI.

Kerr, R. M. and Walker, R. N. 1989. A job shop scheduling system based on fuzzy arithmetic. In *Proc. 3rd Int. Conf. on Expert Systems and the Leading Edge in Production and Operations Management*. M.D. Oliff, Ed. 433-450, Hilton Head Island, SC.

Minton, S., Johnston, M. D., Philips, A. B., and Laird, P. 1990. Solving large-scale constraint satisfaction and scheduling problems using a heuristic repair method. In *Proc. AAAI-90*, Boston, MA.

Muscettola, N. 1993. Scheduling by Iterative Partition of Bottleneck Conflicts. In *Proc. 9th IEEE Conference on AI Applications*, Orlando, FL.

Sadeh, N. 1991. Look-ahead Techniques for Micro-Opportunistic Job Shop Scheduling. CMU-CS-91-102, School of Comp. Sci., Carnegie Mellon Univ.

Vepsalainen, A. P. J. and Morton, T. E. 1987. Priority rules for job shops with weighted tardiness costs. *Management Science*, 33(8), August, 1035-1047.

Xiong, Y., Sadeh, N, and Sycara, K. 1992. Intelligent Backtracking Techniques for Job Shop Scheduling. In *Proc. 3rd Int. Conf. on Principles of Knowledge Representation*, Cambridge, MA.

Zweben, M., Deale, M., and Gargan, R. 1990. Anytime Rescheduling. In *Proc. DARPA Workshop on Innovative Approaches to Planning, Scheduling and Control*, Morgan Kaufmann Pub.

A Constraint Decomposition Method
for Spatio-Temporal Configuration Problems

Toshikazu Tanimoto

Digital Equipment Corporation Japan
1432 Sugao, Akigawa, Tokyo, 197 Japan
tanimoto@jrd.dec.com

Abstract

This paper describes a flexible framework and an efficient algorithm for constraint-based spatio-temporal configuration problems. Binary constraints between spatio-temporal objects are first converted to constraint regions, which are then decomposed into hierarchical data structures; based on this constraint decomposition, an improved backtracking algorithm called HBT can compute a solution quite efficiently. In contrast to other approaches, the proposed method is characterized by the efficient handling of arbitrarily-shaped objects, and the flexible integration of quantitative and qualitative constraints; it allows a wide range of objects and constraints to be utilized for specifying a spatio-temporal configuration. The method is intended primarily for configuration problems in user interfaces, but can effectively be applied to similar problems in other areas as well.

Introduction

Spatio-temporal configuration problems based on constraints arise in many important application areas of artificial intelligence, such as planning, robotics and user interfaces. Although most generic problems are known to be NP-complete, a number of practical techniques suitable for special cases have been developed. In addition to frameworks for constraint-based geometric reasoning [13, 14], potentially useful formalisms have been developed for temporal reasoning [1, 4]. As far as configuration problems are concerned, temporal and spatial frameworks share many important features. In fact, a qualitative formalism for temporal reasoning [1] has been extended to spatial qualitative formalisms [9, 19]; a quantitative formalism based on linear binary inequalities [4] has been extended to a multi-dimensional formalism in a similar way [22].

The multi-dimensional extension of temporal formalisms is certainly an attractive approach to spatio-temporal problems. The approach is based on the expectation that a seemingly difficult multi-dimensional problem can be decomposed into a set of 1-dimensional problems, which can be solved much more easily than the original problem. However, direct extensions attempted in [9, 22] have restricted target problems to orthogonal domains; in other words, objects must be rectangular in a certain coordinate system. Obviously, this restriction is not always desirable in practical situations. Thus arises the need for a framework to handle arbitrarily-shaped objects, with little sacrifice in computing resources. Techniques to handle spatial objects have been studied in the area of computational geometry. Spatial objects can be handled efficiently by hierarchical data structures; many powerful techniques have been devised [20]. However, further study will be needed to fit the techniques into the constraint-based framework.

Another attractive feature of the multi-dimensional extension of temporal formalisms is the possibility of integrating qualitative and quantitative constraints. In many practical situations, qualitative expressions are not enough to specify spatio-temporal constraints. This is particularly true when we must solve a configuration problem for user interface objects [8]. On the other hand, it is also true that there are cases where qualitative constraints suffice. It is therefore desirable to handle both qualitative and quantitative constraints in the same framework. There have been attempts to integrate qualitative and quantitative formalisms for temporal reasoning [12, 18]. However, it is not immediately obvious how to extend these frameworks to spatial counterparts.

In this paper, we propose a framework and an algorithm to address these issues; in common with other constraint-based formalisms, the proposed method handles spatio-temporal configurations based on constraints between objects. The method has three stages. Firstly, a binary constraint between two spatio-temporal objects, such as left and after, is converted to a constraint region; this step is called the interpretation of a constraint. Secondly, the constraint region is decomposed into a hierarchical data structure called a constraint region tree; this representation enables the use of metric features of spatio-temporal constraints. Finally, a hierarchical backtracking algorithm called

HBT is applied to region trees; HBT is effective either by itself or in combination with other algorithms, including PC-2.

The proposed method can be characterized by two major advantages; it can efficiently handle arbitrarily-shaped objects, not just rectangular ones; and it integrates quantitative and qualitative constraints through the interpretation of constraints. Although the proposed method is intended primarily for constraint-based spatio-temporal configuration problems in areas such as user interface management, automated animation and multimedia presentation generation, it would be possible to apply the method to a wider range of configuration problems in areas such as scheduling and space planning.

Constraint Regions

In typical spatio-temporal configuration problems, important constraints are binary constraints such as disjoint, left, after and before. If we do not consider the transformation of an object, such as rotation and scaling, this type of constraint can be represented by a region where a displacement between the two objects is restricted. Having mentioned that, we begin by defining several concepts (for generality, we will use real numbers in definitions, rather than integers). Let a be a d-dimensional object, and A be a set of objects; a *configuration* on A is defined as mapping $\omega: A \rightarrow R^d$; for each object a, $\omega(a) \in R^d$ is called its *location*. Given objects a_1 and a_2, *constraint* c between a_1 and a_2 is written as $c(a_1, a_2)$. Let C be a set of constraints, and D be a set of subsets of R^d; an *interpretation* on C is defined as mapping $\varphi: C \rightarrow D$; $\varphi(c) \in D$ is called the *(constraint) region* of constraint c. A *constraint satisfaction problem* defined by A, C and φ is written as $CSP(A, C, \varphi)$. A concept similar to the constraint region was first suggested by [15]; another was discussed by the name of *admissible region* in [23]. In this paper, we use this concept to handle d-dimensional linear binary constraints.

Definition 1 Given a set of objects A, a set of constraints C and interpretation φ, configuration ω is said to *satisfy* constraint $c(a_1, a_2) \in C$, iff $\omega(a_2) - \omega(a_1) \in \varphi(c)$ holds. If configuration ω satisfies all the constraints in C, it is said to be a *solution* of $CSP(A, C, \varphi)$. ∎

In general, a solution of $CSP(A, C, \varphi)$ can take two forms. One is a configuration satisfying the constraints as in Definition 1, and the other is a set of configurations to bound the locations of objects. The latter form is more generic, but in many situations, the former form suffices. The generic form could be obtained by merging all single solutions.

Below we define a set of *canonical constraints* and their interpretations used in our framework, but constraints and/or interpretations are not necessarily limited to those given. We can define a new constraint (either qualitative or quantitative) and/or interpretation with no changes to our framework. One of the advantages of this approach is flexibility in defining constraints specific to the problem being addressed (see Example 2).

The canonical constraints consist of eight topological and two directional constraints. Topological constraints are defined based on the relationships given in [7]: *disjoint, contains, inside, equal, meet, covers, coveredby* and *overlap*. Directional constraints *less* and *greater* are also defined for each dimension; they can be called *left, right, below, above, before* and *after*, depending on context. Figure 1 shows all the canoni-

constraint	interpretation (constraint region)	depiction
$disjoint(a_1, a_2)$	$\{x \in R^d \mid x = \omega(a_2) - \omega(a_1),\ a_1 \cap a_2 = \varnothing\}$	
$contains(a_1, a_2)$	$\{x \in R^d \mid x = \omega(a_2) - \omega(a_1),\ a_1 \subseteq a_2^\circ\}$	
$inside(a_1, a_2)$	$\{x \in R^d \mid x = \omega(a_2) - \omega(a_1),\ a_1^\circ \supseteq a_2\}$	
$equal(a_1, a_2)$	$\{x \in R^d \mid x = \omega(a_2) - \omega(a_1),\ a_1 = a_2\}$	
$meet(a_1, a_2)$	$\{x \in R^d \mid x = \omega(a_2) - \omega(a_1),\ a_1^\circ \cap a_2^\circ = \varnothing,\ \partial a_1 \cap \partial a_2 \neq \varnothing\}$	
$covers(a_1, a_2)$	$\{x \in R^d \mid x = \omega(a_2) - \omega(a_1),\ a_1^\circ \subset a_2^\circ,\ \partial a_1 \cap \partial a_2 \neq \varnothing\}$	
$coveredby(a_1, a_2)$	$\{x \in R^d \mid x = \omega(a_2) - \omega(a_1),\ a_1^\circ \supset a_2^\circ,\ \partial a_1 \cap \partial a_2 \neq \varnothing\}$	
$overlap(a_1, a_2)$	$\{x \in R^d \mid x = \omega(a_2) - \omega(a_1),\ a_1^\circ \cap a_2^\circ \neq \varnothing,\ a_1^- \cap a_2^- \neq \varnothing\}$	
$less_i(a_1, a_2)$	$\{x \in R^d \mid x = \omega(a_2) - \omega(a_1),\ \forall l_i,\ sup_i(l_i \cap a_1^\circ) > sup_i(l_i \cap a_2^\circ)\}$	
$greater_i(a_1, a_2)$	$\{x \in R^d \mid x = \omega(a_2) - \omega(a_1),\ \forall l_i,\ inf_i(l_i \cap a_1^\circ) < inf_i(l_i \cap a_2^\circ)\}$	

Figure 1. Canonical Constraints a_1 a_2

cal constraints (*contains*(a_1,a_2) should be read as "a_2 contains a_1" etc.), their interpretations and exemplary depictions. We assume that all objects are embedded in R^d and are homeomorphic to closed solid spheres. In Figure 1, ∂a, a° and a^- denote the boundary, interior and exterior of object a. For *less*$_i$ and *greater*$_i$ ($i=1,...,d$), l_i indicates a line parallel to i-th coordinate. If $\forall l_i, l_i \cap a_1^\circ = \varnothing \vee l_i \cap a_2^\circ = \varnothing$, the constraint region is defined as $\varnothing$.

It is easy to see that the logical closure (by $\neg$, $\wedge$ and $\vee$) of the canonical constraints for $d=1$ over single intervals contains Allen's 13 relationships [1] (e.g. "a_2 started-by a_1" in Allen's notation can be written as "*covers*(a_1,a_2)$\wedge$*less*(a_2,a_1)" in our notation). As a spatial formalism, the canonical constraints are much more powerful than linear constraints between the surfaces of polyhedra [17], but in some cases, cross-product relationships of Allen's 13 relationships can be more suitable [9]. Note that the cross-product relationships are in fact interpretable and can be added to our framework as well.

Example 1 Suppose the following binary constraints between 2-dimensional objects a_1, a_2, a_3 and a_4 shown in Figure 2 (in this paper, for simplicity, all examples are taken from $d=2$ cases, though they appear spatial rather than spatio-temporal):

c_1: *inside*(a_1,a_2)$\vee$*coveredby*(a_1,a_2)
c_2: *inside*(a_1,a_3)$\vee$*coveredby*(a_1,a_3)
c_3: *inside*(a_1,a_4)$\vee$*coveredby*(a_1,a_4)
c_4: *disjoint*(a_2,a_3)$\wedge$*right*(a_2,a_3)
c_5: *disjoint*(a_3,a_4)$\wedge$*below*(a_3,a_4)
c_6: *disjoint*(a_2,a_4)

A possible solution ω satisfying the above constraints is also shown in Figure 2. In order to find ω, we first have to obtain the constraint regions of the above constraints as follows:

1) determine the reference points of objects (usually their bottom-left corners); $\omega(a)$ is represented by coordinate values of the reference point of a.
2) compute a constraint region for each item in a constraint expression using the interpretations in Figure 1.
3) if the constraint expression contains logical operations, perform corresponding set operations between the regions.

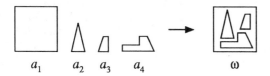

a_1 $\quad$ a_2 $\quad$ a_3 $\quad$ a_4 $\quad\quad$ ω

Figure 2. A Sample Configuration Problem

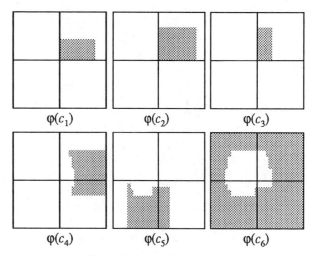

$\varphi(c_1)$ $\quad\quad$ $\varphi(c_2)$ $\quad\quad$ $\varphi(c_3)$

$\varphi(c_4)$ $\quad\quad$ $\varphi(c_5)$ $\quad\quad$ $\varphi(c_6)$

Figure 3. Constraint Regions

The objects are usually pre-processed to employ algorithms such as plane sweeping [20] in Step 2 (in some cases, however, it can be more efficient to compute a constraint region directly from the arithmetic definitions of objects). Figure 3 shows the resulting constraint regions (meshed area) obtained after discretizing the objects. ∎

In our framework, all constraints are eventually represented by their constraint regions, which are simply subsets of R^d. The interpretation of constraints is basically a geometric problem. This framework is much simpler than existing approaches to integrate qualitative and quantitative constraints. The following example is quantitative constraints which can be used in combination with the canonical constraints:

Example 2 Distance constraints could be defined as:

$near(a_1,a_2) \Leftrightarrow disjoint(a_1,a_2) \wedge |\omega(a_2) - \omega(a_1)| < \delta_1$
$far(a_1,a_2) \Leftrightarrow disjoint(a_1,a_2) \wedge |\omega(a_2) - \omega(a_1)| > \delta_2$

where δ_1 and δ_2 are constants. ∎

Note that a unary constraint to specify an absolute location of an object can be represented as a binary quantitative constraint between the object and a special object used as a reference frame.

Constraint Region Trees

Once all constraints are converted to constraint regions, the next step is to construct data structures suitable for constraint satisfaction algorithms. Due to metric features of spatio-temporal problems, we expect that points located close to each other within a constraint region will behave similarly as far as constraint satisfaction is concerned (in other words, as far as the existence of a solution including the point is concerned). We define a partial order relation between problems to make use of this similarity. Given $CSP(A,C,\varphi)$ and $CSP(A,C,\varphi')$, if the inconsistency of

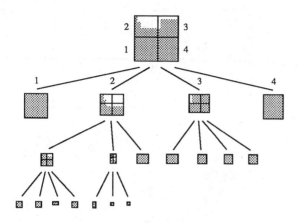

Figure 4. A Constraint Region Tree

$CSP(A,C,\varphi)$ implies the inconsistency of $CSP(A,C,\varphi')$, $CSP(A,C,\varphi)$ is said to *dominate* $CSP(A,C,\varphi')$. Clearly, if $\forall c \in C$, $\varphi(c) \supseteq \varphi'(c)$ holds, $CSP(A,C,\varphi)$ dominates $CSP(A,C,\varphi')$.

If we can construct a hierarchy of problems where any higher level problem dominates its lower level problems, the entire problem will be solved in a hierarchical way. In order to construct such a hierarchy, we employ hierarchical data structures developed in computational geometry. There are many such structures designed for specific purposes [2, 5, 6, 11, 20], but all of them have in common the use of recursive decomposition. We define one of the variations, called a (*constraint*) *region tree*.

Definition 2 Given a constraint region $\varphi(c)$, the *region tree* of $\varphi(c)$ is a tree where each node corresponds to a *d*-rectangle; it is recursively constructed as follows:

1) if the region is a *d*-rectangle, return a node corresponding to the *d*-rectangle.
2) create a node corresponding to the minimum *d*-rectangle including the region.
3) divide each edge of the *d*-rectangle into two intervals.
4) obtain sub-regions by dividing the region with 2^d sub-*d*-rectangles.
5) do 1-5 for all the sub-regions (children nodes).
6) return the node with its children. ∎

If each edge is always divided into two intervals of the same length, the region tree is equivalent to a quadtree ($d=2$) or octree ($d=3$) corresponding to the constraint region [20]. However, in cases where constraint regions are dominantly rectilinear, division at the corner of constituent rectangles can reduce the size of the region tree and can significantly improve computational efficiency. The maximum length of the edges of rectangles corresponding root nodes is written as r, which is called *range* (the multi-dimensional extension of *range* in [4]).

Note that by bounding and dividing each interval using rational numbers, all extreme points of rectangles can be represented by multiples of a unit interval; we assume this condition in the rest of this paper (a unit *d*-rectangle will be called a *pixel*).

Example 3 Figure 4 shows a constraint region tree constructed from $\varphi(c_5)$ in Figure 3; non-leaf nodes are divided in a similar way to quadtrees and all nodes correspond to rectangles. ∎

A hierarchy of problems is constructed as follows: given $CSP(A,C,\varphi)$ and its region trees, by selecting a node from the region tree of $\varphi(c)$ and defining $\varphi'(c)$ as the rectangle corresponding to the node, we obtain $CSP(A,C,\varphi')$ as a *sub-problem* of $CSP(A,C,\varphi)$.

Lemma 1 Given $CSP(A,C,\varphi)$ and its region trees, for two sub-problems $CSP(A,C,\varphi_1)$ and $CSP(A,C,\varphi_2)$, if $\forall c \in C$, the node corresponding to $\varphi_2(c)$ is a descendant of the node corresponding to $\varphi_1(c)$, $CSP(A,C,\varphi_1)$ dominates $CSP(A,C,\varphi_2)$. ∎

Proof By definition, if the node corresponding to $\varphi_2(c)$ is a descendant of the node corresponding to $\varphi_1(c)$, $\varphi_1(c) \supseteq \varphi_2(c)$. Therefore, $CSP(A,C,\varphi_1)$ dominates $CSP(A,C,\varphi_2)$. ∎

A constraint region can be any subset of R^d. However, if all constraint regions are *simple polygons* (polygons with non-intersecting edges and without holes [20]; we assume that the size of their boundaries is $O(r^{d-1})$), a problem becomes much easier to solve. Space and time requirements for the region tree are as follows:

Theorem 1 [20] The region tree of a constraint region has $O(r^{d-1})$ nodes (rectangles) if the region is a simple polygon, and $O(r^d)$ nodes (rectangles) in general. The construction time is $O(dr^{d-1})$ and $O(dr^d)$ respectively. ∎

Hierarchical Backtracking

We can now move on to constraint satisfaction algorithms. Based on the results obtained in the previous section, constraint regions in $CSP(A,C,\varphi)$ are represented by a set of constraint region trees. The primary method adopted here is the framework developed in [4]. Let us briefly review their framework.

A simple temporal constraint satisfaction problem *STP* is defined by a set of variables A and a set of constraint intervals C. *STP* is represented by a *constraint network* where nodes are $a_1,..., a_n \in A$ and each edge $i \rightarrow j$ is labeled with $c_{ij} \in C$. Its constraint network can be transformed into a directed distance graph G by labeling edge $i \rightarrow j$ with $sup(c_{ij})$ and edge $j \rightarrow i$ with $-inf(c_{ij})$. An *STP* is consistent, iff its directed distance graph G has no negative cycles. If $c'_{ij} \subseteq c_{ij}$ for any corresponding intervals $c_{ij} \in C$ and $c'_{ij} \in C'$ of STP and STP', STP' is said to be tighter than STP. A constraint network of the tightest problem of all equivalent (having the same set of solutions) problems to an STP is called its *minimal network*. A solution of an STP can be constructed from its minimal network, which can be computed by Warshall-Floyd's algorithm:

Theorem 2 [4] STP can be solved in $O(n^3)$ time, where $n=|A|$. ∎

Getting back to our own framework, if all the constraint regions of $CSP(A,C,\varphi)$ are d-rectangular, $CSP(A,C,\varphi)$ is said to be *simple*. Simple $CSP(A,C,\varphi)$ is the multi-dimensional counterpart of STP and can be solved by decomposing it into d STPs and solving the STPs separately.

Theorem 3 [22]   Simple $CSP(A,C,\varphi)$ can be solved in $O(dn^3)$ time, where $n=|A|$. ∎

A general problem can be solved by applying a backtracking algorithm to the meta constraint satisfaction problem, where a domain for each variable is a set of leaf nodes (d-rectangles) in the region tree. By using a classical backtracking algorithm (referred as BT) given in [4], we obtain:

Theorem 4   A solution of $CSP(A,C,\varphi)$ is obtained in $O(dn^3 r^{m(d-1)})$ time if all the constraint regions are simple polygons and in $O(dn^3 r^{md})$ time in general, where $n=|A|$ and $m=|C|$. ∎

Proof   According to Theorem 1, $\varphi(c)$ has $O(r^{d-1})$ rectangles if it is a simple polygon. In the worst case, the backtracking algorithm checks all combinations, which are $O(r^{m(d-1)})$. Each step takes $O(dn^3)$ time according to Theorem 3. Thus total time complexity is $O(dn^3 r^{m(d-1)})$. Similarly, total time complexity is $O(dn^3 r^{md})$ in general. ∎

Backtracking algorithms incorporating techniques such as variable ordering, value ordering and network-based heuristics have been used to improve average performance in constraint satisfaction [3, 10]. However, most of them are designed for discrete domain problems and cannot utilize metric features of a problem. As described in the previous section, after constructing region trees from constraint regions, each node in a constraint region tree corresponds to a rectangle; any sub-problem is in fact simple and can be solved in polynomial time (according to Theorem 3). By using this characteristic, average running time can be significantly improved.

Based on the preparation we have made so far, we define a hierarchical backtracking algorithm (abbreviated as HBT). *SOLVE-SIMPLE* computes a solution for each simple sub-problem and returns *true* if the sub-problem is consistent and *false* if inconsistent. Al-

gorithm HBT consists of two functions: *Forward* and *Backward*. It uses a stack to store a search path as a set of pairs (S,T), where S and T are sets of nodes. Given all the region trees, it starts by calling *Forward* with initial stack (S_0,T_0), where $S_0=\{all\ children\ of\ one\ of\ the\ root\ nodes\}$ and $T_0=\{all\ the\ root\ nodes\ except\ for\ the\ parent\ of\ S_0\}$.

Once a sub-problem is known to be inconsistent, HBT does not search sub-problems dominated by the inconsistent sub-problem. The performance of HBT depends on the distribution of possible solutions over constraint regions. The worst case happens when all non-terminal sub-problems are consistent.

Algorithm HBT

Forward
    do
      if S is not empty then select and delete s from S
      else Backward
    until SOLVE-SIMPLE($T \cup \{s\}$)
    $T \leftarrow \{all\ non\text{-}leaf\ nodes\ in\ T \cup \{s\}\}$
    if T is empty then return
    else select and delete t from T
      $S \leftarrow \{all\ children\ of\ t\}$
      pushdown (S,T) and Forward

Backward
    if stack is empty then exit
    else popup (S,T)
    if S is not empty then Forward
    else Backward ∎

HBT is independent of other performance improvement schemes and can be used in combination with them; in the above algorithm description, a value ordering scheme can be applied to select s from S, and a variable ordering scheme can be applied to select t from T. HBT can also be used in combination with other algorithms such as path consistency algorithms, which will be discussed in the next section.

Path Consistency

Computing a path consistent network of the original $CSP(A,C,\varphi)$ is a powerful pre-processing technique for constraint satisfaction problems [15, 16]. Path consistency in our framework is defined as follows:

Definition 3   A path $i(1),..., i(k)$ is consistent iff for any pair of $\omega_{i(1)}$, $\omega_{i(k)}$ such that $\omega_{i(k)} - \omega_{i(1)} \in \varphi_{i(1)i(k)}$ there exists configuration ω such that $\omega(a_{i(1)}) = \omega_{i(1)}$, $\omega(a_{i(k)}) = \omega_{i(k)}$, $\omega_{i(j+1)} - \omega_{i(j)} \in \varphi_{i(j)i(j+1)}$, $j=1,...,k-1$, where φ_{ij} is the constraint region of constraint $c_{ij}=c(a_i,a_j)$. ∎

$CSP(A,C,\varphi)$ is path-consistent iff every path is path consistent. Path consistency algorithms do not guarantee finding a solution; however, they are quite useful for pre-processing. These algorithms require two operations: intersection $\varphi_1 \oplus \varphi_2$ and composition $\varphi_1 \otimes \varphi_2$.

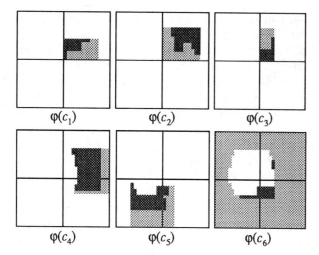

$\varphi(c_1)$ $\varphi(c_2)$ $\varphi(c_3)$

$\varphi(c_4)$ $\varphi(c_5)$ $\varphi(c_6)$

Figure 5. Path Consistent Regions

The two operations in our framework are defined as:

$$\varphi_1 \oplus \varphi_2 = \{x \in \mathbf{R}^d | x \in \varphi_1, x \in \varphi_2\}$$
$$\varphi_1 \otimes \varphi_2 = \{x \in \mathbf{R}^d | x = x_1 + x_2, x_1 \in \varphi_1, x_2 \in \varphi_2\}$$

The distributivity of $\otimes$ over $\oplus$ does not hold except in cases where both φ_1 and φ_2 are rectangles. Moreover, when performed between region trees, $\oplus$ does not preserve the simplicity of regions. With regard to the efficiency of the two operations, we obtain:

Lemma 2 When performed between region trees, $\varphi_1 \oplus \varphi_2$ and $\varphi_1 \otimes \varphi_2$ can be obtained in $O(dr^{2d})$ time. ∎

Proof In general, φ_1 and φ_2 have $O(r^d)$ nodes (or corresponding rectangles). $\varphi_1 \oplus \varphi_2$ and $\varphi_1 \otimes \varphi_2$ require $O(r^{2d})$ operations between two rectangles and create $O(r^{2d})$ rectangles; the resulting region tree can be constructed from the rectangles in $O(dr^{2d})$ time. ∎

Note that if quadtrees (or their d-dimensional equivalents) are used as region trees, $\varphi_1 \oplus \varphi_2$ can be obtained by comparing corresponding nodes in two trees, and the time complexity of $\varphi_1 \oplus \varphi_2$ can be reduced to $O(dr^d)$.

An efficient path-consistency algorithm called PC-2 is described in [15]. Relaxation operation *REVISE((i,k,j))* is defined as $\varphi_{ij} \leftarrow \varphi_{ij} \oplus \varphi_{ik} \otimes \varphi_{kj}$, using intersection and composition defined above. *REVISE* returns *true* if φ_{ij} is modified, otherwise it returns *false*. *RELATED-PATHS* returns the set of 2-length paths relevant to the changed path (see [15] for details). PC-2 is formulated as:

Algorithm PC-2 [15]

    $Q \leftarrow \{(i,k,j) | (i<j) \wedge (k \neq i,j)\}$
    while Q is not empty do
      select and delete a path (i,k,j) from Q, and
      if REVISE((i,k,j)) then
        $Q \leftarrow Q \cup RELATED\text{-}PATHS((i,k,j))$ ∎

With regard to the efficiency of PC-2, we obtain:

Theorem 5 Algorithm PC-2 computes the path consistent network of $CSP(A,C,\varphi)$ in $O(dn^3 r^{3d})$ time. ∎

Proof Algorithm PC-2 needs $O(n^3 r^d)$ steps to terminate, because in the worst case, for each constraint region, which can have $O(r^d)$ pixels, may be decreased by only a pixel in a single *REVISE* operation. According to Lemma 2, each *REVISE* operation consumes $O(dr^{2d})$ time. Total time is therefore $O(dn^3 r^{3d})$. ∎

Theorem 5 is the multi-dimensional counterpart of Theorem 5.7 in [4].

Example 4 PC-2 can be applied to the sample problem as follows:

1) construct region trees as in Figure 4 from the constraint regions in Figure 3, which are used as initial values for PC-2.
2) each time *REVISE* is called, $\oplus$ and $\otimes$ operations are performed between sets of rectangles in the region trees.

At the termination of PC-2, we obtain resulting path consistent constraint regions (constraint regions of a path consistent network) illustrated as in Figure 5 (darkly meshed area). ∎

Discussions

Table 1 summarizes the above results about worst-case time complexity (the left cell of (H)BT is complexity when all constraint regions are simple polygons; the right is complexity in general). However, by storing solutions of non-terminal sub-problems (for HBT) or partial instantiations (for BT), we can reduce the worst-case time complexity of (H)BT to $O(dn^2 r^{m(d-1)})$ and $O(dn^2 r^{md})$ respectively.

Empirical results from 192 small-scale problems ($d=2$, range=16, the number of objects=4, quadtrees are used as region trees) are shown in Table 2. Performance is measured by the number of times *SOLVE-SIMPLE* is called to find a solution (denominated by 1,000 calls) and is averaged over 192 cases (the average number of rectangles corresponding to leaf nodes in a region tree was 33, and PC-2 could reduce it to 19). Although a full-scale experimental analysis should be done in the future, Table 2 well suggests

Table 1. Worst-Case Time Complexity

(H)BT		*REVISE*	PC-2
$O(dn^3 r^{m(d-1)})$	$O(dn^3 r^{md})$	$O(dr^{2d})$	$O(dn^3 r^{3d})$

Table 2. Performance Comparisons

BT	PC-2+BT	HBT	PC-2+HBT
156	5	2	1

that HBT is more efficient than the combination of PC-2 and BT. In combination with PC-2, HBT works even better. Taking into consideration that PC-2 is not inexpensive, HBT without PC-2 would suffice for many practical problems.

Conclusion

In this paper, we have proposed a new method to solve constraint-based spatio-temporal configuration problems; the method centers around the interpretation of constraints and the decomposition of constraint regions into region trees. In contrast to other approaches, our method is more flexible and efficient; the flexibility lies in defining interpretation procedures most suitable for given problems; the efficiency results from employing region trees as the basis for the hierarchical backtracking algorithm HBT. It is suggested that HBT is more efficient than the combination of classical backtracking and path consistency algorithms. However, further research in a couple of different directions will be necessary to refine the proposed framework and algorithm: the capability of handling a wider range of geometric operations such as rotation and scaling; and the empirical evaluation of performance when HBT is used in combination with other techniques including network-based heuristics.

References

[1] Allen, J.F. Maintaining Knowledge about Temporal Intervals. *Commun. ACM*, 26 (1983), 832-843.

[2] Chiang, Y.-J. and Tamassia, R. Dynamic Algorithms in Computational Geometry. *Proc. IEEE*, 80 (1992), 1412-1434.

[3] Dechter, R. and Pearl, J. Network-Based Heuristics for Constraint-Satisfaction Problems. *Artificial Intelligence*, 34 (1988), 1-38.

[4] Dechter, R., Meiri, I. and Pearl, J. Temporal Constraint Networks. *Artificial Intelligence*, 49 (1991), 61-95.

[5] Edelsbrunner, H. A New Approach to Rectangle Intersections Part I. *Intern. J. Computer Math.*, 13 (1983), 209-219.

[6] Edelsbrunner, H. A New Approach to Rectangle Intersections Part II. *Intern. J. Computer Math.*, 13 (1983), 221-229.

[7] Egenhofer, M.J. and Al-Taha, K.K. Reasoning about Gradual Changes of Topological Relationships. In Frank, A.U., Campari, I. and Formentini, U. (eds.) *Theories and Methods of Spatio-Temporal Reasoning in Geographic Space*, Springer-Verlag, Berlin, Germany, 1992.

[8] Freeman-Benson, B.N., Maloney, J. and Borning, A. An Incremental Constraint Solver. *Commun. ACM*, 33 (1990), 54-63.

[9] Guesgen, H.W. and Hertzberg, J. *A Perspective of Constraint-Based Reasoning*. Springer-Verlag, Berlin, Germany, 1992.

[10] Haralick, R.M. and Elliott, G.L. Increasing Tree Search Efficiency for Constraint Satisfaction Problems. *Artificial Intelligence*, 14 (1980), 263-313.

[11] Hunter, G.M. and Steiglitz, K. Operations on Images Using Quad Trees. *IEEE Trans. Pattern Anal. and Machine Intell.*, 1 (1979), 145-153.

[12] Kautz, H.A. and Ladkin, P.B. Integrating Metric and Qualitative Temporal Reasoning. In *Proc. AAAI '91* (Anaheim, CA, 1991), 241-246.

[13] Kin, N., Takai, Y. and Kunii, T.L. PictureEditor II: A Conversational Graphical Editing System Considering the Degree of Constraint. In Kunii, T.L. (ed.) *Visual Computing*. Springer-Verlag, Tokyo, Japan, 1992.

[14] Kramer, G.A. A Geometric Constraint Engine. *Artificial Intelligence*, 58 (1992), 327-360.

[15] Mackworth, A.K. Consistency in Networks of Relations. *Artificial Intelligence*, 8 (1977), 99-118.

[16] Mackworth, A.K. and Freuder, E.C. The Complexity of Some Polynomial Network Consistency Algorithms for Constraint Satisfaction Problems. *Artificial Intelligence*, 25 (1985), 65-74.

[17] Malik, J. and Binford, T.O. Reasoning in Time and Space. In *Proc. IJCAI '83* (Karlsruhe, Germany, 1983), 343-345.

[18] Meiri, I. Combining Qualitative and Quantitative Constraints in Temporal Reasoning. In *Proc. AAAI '91* (Anaheim, CA, 1991), 260-267.

[19] Mukerjee, A. and Joe, G. A Qualitative Model for Space. In *Proc. AAAI '90* (Boston, MA, 1990), 721-727.

[20] Samet, H. *The Design and Analysis of Spatial Data Structures*. Addison-Wesley, Reading, MA, 1990.

[21] Shahookar, K. and Mazumder, P. VLSI Cell Placement Techniques. *ACM Computing Surveys*, 23 (1991), 143-220.

[22] Tanimoto, T. Configuring Multimedia Presentations Using Default Constraints. In *Proc. PRICAI '92* (Seoul, Korea, 1992), 1086-1092.

[23] Tokuyama, T., Asano, T. and Tsukiyama, S. A Dynamic Algorithm for Placing Rectangles without Overlapping. *J. of Information Processing*, 14 (1991), 30-35.

Extending Deep Structure

Colin P. Williams and Tad Hogg

Xerox Palo Alto Research Center
3333 Coyote Hill Road
Palo Alto, CA 94304, U.S.A.
CWilliams@parc.xerox.com, Hogg@parc.xerox.com

Abstract

In a previous paper we defined the "deep structure" of a constraint satisfaction problem to be that set system produced by collecting the nogood ground instances of each constraint and keeping only those that are not supersets of any other. We then showed how to use such deep structure to predict where, in a space of problem instances, an abrupt transition in computational cost is to be expected. This paper explains how to augment this model with enough extra details to make more accurate estimates of the location of these phase transitions. We also show that the phase transition phenomenon exists for a much wider class of search algorithms than had hitherto been thought and explain theoretically why this is the case.

1. Introduction

In a previous paper (Williams & Hogg 1992b) we defined the "deep structure" of a constraint satisfaction problem (CSP) to be that set system produced by collecting the nogood ground instances of each constraint and keeping only those that are not supersets of any other. We use the term "deep" because two problems that are superficially different in the constraint graph representation might in fact induce identical sets of minimized nogoods. Hence their equivalence might only become apparent at this lower level of representation. We then showed how to use such deep structure to predict where, in a space of problem instances, the hardest problems are to be found. Typically, this model led to predictions that were within about 15% of the empirically determined correct values. Whilst this model allowed us to understand the observed abrupt change in difficulty (in fact a phase transition) in general terms in this paper we identify which additional aspects of real problems account for most of the outstanding numerical discrepancy. This is particularly important because as larger problems are considered, the phase transition region becomes increasingly spiked. Hence, an acceptable error for small problems could become unacceptable for larger ones.

To this end we have identified 2 types of error; modelling approximations (such as the assumption that the values assigned to different variables are uncorrelated or that the solutions are not clustered in some special way) and mathematical approximations (such as the assumption that, for a function $f(x)$, $\langle f(x) \rangle \approx f(\langle x \rangle)$, known as a mean-field approximation). In addition we also widen the domain of applicability of our theory to CSPs solved using algorithms such as heuristic repair (Minton et al. 1990), simulated annealing (Johnston et al. 1991, Kirkpatrick 1983) and GSAT (Selman, Levesque & Mitchell 1992), that work with sets of complete assignments at all times.

In the next section we summarize our basic deep structure theory. Following this, we shall show how to make quantitatively accurate predictions of the phase transition points for 3–COL, 4–COL (graph colouring) and 3–SAT. Our results are summarized in Table 1 where the best approximations are highlighted. Finally in Section 4 we present experimental evidence for a phase transition effect in heuristic repair and adapt our deep structure theory to account for these observations.

2. Basic Deep Structure Model

Our interest lies in predicting where, in a space of CSP instances, the harder problems typically occur, more or less regardless of the algorithm used. Because the exact difficulty of solving each instance can vary considerably from case to case it makes more sense to talk about the average difficulty of solving CSPs that are drawn from some pool (or ensemble) of similar problems. This means we need to know something about how the difficulty of solving CSPs changes as small modifications are made to the structure of the constraint problem.

There are many possible types of ensemble that one could choose to study. For example, one might restrict consideration to an ensemble of problems each of whose member instances are guaranteed to have at least one solution. Alternatively, one could study an ensemble in which this requirement is relaxed and each instance may or may not have any solutions. Similarly one could choose whether the domain sizes of each variable should or should not be the same or whether the constraints are all of the same size etc. The possibilities are endless. The best choice of ensemble cannot be determined by mere cogitation but depends on what the CSPs arising in the "real world" happen to be like and that will inevitably vary from field to field. Lacking any compelling reason to choose one ensemble over another, we made the simplest choice of using an ensemble of CSPs whose instances are not guaranteed to be soluble and having variables with a uniform domain size, b.

Given an ensemble of CSPs, then, the deep structure model allows us to predict which members will typically be harder to solve than others. The steps required to do this can be broken down into:

1. CSP → Deep Structure
2. Deep Structure → Estimate of Difficulty

CSP → Deep Structure

The first step consists of mapping a given CSP instance into its corresponding deep structure. We chose to think of CSPs that could be represented as a set of constraints over μ variables, each of which can take on one of b values. Each constraint determines whether a particular combination of assignments of values to the variables are consistent ("good") or inconsistent ("nogood"). Collecting the nogoods of all the constraints and discarding any that are supersets of any other we arrive at a set of "minimized nogoods" which completely characterize the particular CSP. By "deep structure" we mean exactly this set of minimized nogoods.

Unfortunately, reasoning with the explicit sets of minimized nogoods does not promote understanding of generic phenomena or assist theoretical analysis. We therefore attempt to <u>summarize</u> the minimized nogoods with <u>as few parameters as possible</u> and yet still make reasonably accurate quantitative predictions of quantities of interest such as phase transition points and computational costs. As we shall see, such a crude summarization can sometimes throw away important information e.g. regarding the correlation between values assigned to tuples of variables. Nevertheless, it does allow us to identify which parameters have the most important influence on the quantities of interest. Moreover, one is always free to build a more accurate model, as in fact we do in Section 3.

In our basic model, we found that the minimized nogoods could be adequately summarized in terms of their number, m, and average size, k. Thus we crudely characterize a CSP by just 4 numbers, (μ, b, m, k).

Deep Structure → Estimate of Difficulty

Having obtained the crude description of deep structure we need to estimate how hard it would be to solve such a CSP. The actual value of this cost will depend on the particular algorithm used to solve the CSP. In our original model we assumed a search algorithm that works by

Parameter	Meaning
μ	number of variables
b	number of values per variable
m	number of minimized nogoods
k	average size of minimized nogoods

Fig. 1. A coarse description of a CSP.

extending partial solutions (either in a tree or a lattice) until a complete solution is found. However, the important point is not so much the actual value of the cost but in predicting where it will attain a maximum as this corresponds to the point of greatest difficulty. In Section 4 we extend our model to cover the possibility of solving the CSP using an algorithm that works with complete states e.g heuristic repair, simulated annealing or GSAT which requires a different cost measure (still related to the minimized nogoods) to be used.

To obtain a definite prediction, we defined "difficulty" to be the cost to find the first solution or to determine there are no solutions, C_s. Analytically, this is a hard function to derive and in the interests of a more tractable analysis we opted to use a proxy instead that was the cost to find all solutions divided by the number of solutions (if there were any) or else the cost to determine there were no solutions, which we approximated as[1]:

$$\langle C_s \rangle \approx \begin{cases} \langle C \rangle / \langle N_{soln} \rangle & \text{if there are solutions} \\ \langle C \rangle & \text{otherwise} \end{cases} \quad (1)$$

We analyzed what happens to this cost, on average, as the number of minimized nogood ground instances, $m = \beta\mu$, is increased. Note that we merely write m like this to emphasize that the number of minimized nogoods will grow as larger problems are considered (i.e. as μ increases). The upshot of this analysis was the prediction that, as $\mu \to \infty$, the transition occurs where $\langle N_{soln} \rangle = 1$ and so the hardest problems are to be found at a critical value of β given by:

$$\beta_{crit} = -\frac{\ln b}{\ln(1 - b^{-k})}. \quad (2)$$

In other words, if all we are told about a class of CSPs is that there are μ variables (with $\mu \gg 1$), each variable takes one of b values and each minimized nogood is of size k then we expect the hardest examples of this class to be when there are $m_{crit} = \beta_{crit}\mu$ nogoods.

---

[1]N.B. this approximation will fail if the solutions are tightly clustered.

3. More Accurate Predictions

We have tested this formula on two kinds of CSPs: graph colouring and k-SAT and compared its predictions against experimental data obtained by independent authors. Typically this formula gave predictions that were within about 15% of the empirically observed values. The remaining discrepancy can be attributed to one of two basic kinds of error: First, there can be errors in the model (e.g. due to assuming that the values assigned to different variables are uncorrelated). Second there can be errors due to various mathematical approximations (e.g. the mean-field approximation that $\langle C/N_{soln} \rangle \simeq \langle C \rangle / \langle N_{soln} \rangle$). Interestingly, graph colouring is more affected by errors in the model whereas k-SAT is more affected by errors in the mean-field approximation. These two CSPs then will serve as convenient examples of how to augment our basic deep structure model with sufficient extra details to permit a more accurate estimation of the phase transition points.

Graph Colouring

A graph colouring problem consists of a graph containing μ nodes (i.e. variables) that have to be assigned certain colours (i.e. values) such that no two nodes at either end of an edge have the same colour. Thus the edges provide implicit constraints between the values assigned to the pair of nodes they connect. Therefore, if we are only allowed to use b colours, then each edge would contribute exactly b nogoods and every nogood would be of size 2, so $k = 2$. Plugging these values into equation 2 gives the prediction that the hardest to colour graphs occur when $\beta_{crit} = 9.3$ (3–COL) and $\beta_{crit} = 21.5$ (4–COL) in contrast to the experimentally measured values of 8.1 ± 0.3 and 18 ± 1 respectively. This approximation isn't too bad, nevertheless, we will now show how to make it even better by taking more careful account of the structure of the nogoods that arise in graph colouring.

Imprecision due to Model

The key insight is to realize that in our derivation of formula 2 we assume the nogoods are selected independently. Thus each set of m nogoods is equally likely. However, in the context of graph colouring this is not the case because each edge introduces nogoods with a rather special structure. Specifically, each edge between nodes u and v introduces b minimal nogoods of the form $\{u = i, v = i\}$ for i from 1 to b, which changes, for a given number of minimized nogoods, the expected number of solutions, as follows.

Consider a state at the solution level, i.e., an assigned value for each of μ variables, in which the value i is used c_i times, with $\sum_{i=1}^{b} c_i = \mu$. In order for this state to be a solution, none of its subsets must be among the selected nogoods. This requires that the graph not contain an edge between any variables with the same assignment. This excludes a total of $\sum_{i=1}^{b} \binom{c_i}{2}$ edges. With random graphs with e edges, the probability that this given state will be a solution is just

$$p(\{c_i\}) = \frac{\binom{\binom{\mu}{2} - \sum_{i=1}^{b} \binom{c_i}{2}}{e}}{\binom{\binom{\mu}{2}}{e}} \qquad (3)$$

By summing over all states at the solution level, this gives the expected number of solutions:

$$\langle N_{soln} \rangle = \sum_{c_1 \dots c_b} \binom{\mu}{c_1 \dots c_b} p(\{c_i\}) \qquad (4)$$

where the multinomial coefficient counts the number of states with specified numbers of assigned values.

For the asymptotic behaviour, note that the multinomial becomes sharply peaked around states with an equal number of each value, i.e., $c_i = \mu/b$. This also minimizes the number of excluded edges $\sum \binom{c_i}{2}$ giving a maximum in $p(\{c_i\})$ as well. Thus the sum for $\langle N_{soln} \rangle$ will be dominated by these states and Stirling's approximation[2] can be used to give

$$\ln \langle N_{soln} \rangle \sim \mu \left[\ln b + \frac{\beta}{b} \ln \left(1 - \frac{1}{b} \right) \right] \qquad (5)$$

because the number of minimal nogoods is related to the number of edges by $m = \beta\mu = eb$.

With this replacement for $\ln \langle N_{soln} \rangle$ our derivation of the phase transition point proceeds as before by determining the point where the leading term of this asymptotic behaviour is zero, corresponding to $\langle N_{soln} \rangle = 1$, hence:

$$\beta_{crit} = -\frac{b \ln b}{\ln \left(1 - \frac{1}{b} \right)} \qquad (6)$$

which is different from the prediction of our basic model as given in equation 2. This result can also be obtained more directly by assuming conditional independence among the nogoods introduced by each edge (Cheeseman, Kanefsky & Taylor 1992). For the cases of 3 and 4–colouring, equation 6 now allows us to predict $\beta_{crit} = 8.1$ and 19.3, respectively, close to the empirical values given by Cheeseman et al.

---

[2] i.e. $\ln x! \sim x \ln x - x$ as $x \to \infty$.

k-SAT

Empirical studies by Mitchell, Selman & Levesque (Mitchell, Selman & Levesque 1992) on the cost of solving k-SAT problems using the Davis-Putnam procedure (Franco & Paull 1983), allow us to compare the predictions of our basic model against a second type of CSP.

In k-SAT, each of the μ variables appearing in the formula can take on one of two values, *true* or *false*. Thus there are $b = 2$ values for each variable. Each clause appearing in the given formula is a disjunction of (possibly negated) variables. Hence the clause will fail to be true for exactly one assignment of values to the k variables appearing in it. This in turn gives rise to a single nogood, of size k. Distinct clauses will give rise to distinct nogoods, so the number of these nogoods is just the number of distinct clauses in the formula.

Thus, using equation 2, our basic model, with $b = 2$, $k = 3$ predicts the 3–SAT transition to be at $\beta_{crit} = 5.2$ which is above empirically observed value of 4.3. However, as we show below, the outstanding error is largely attributable to the inaccuracy of the mean-field approximation and there is a simple remedy for this.

Imprecision due to Mean-field Approximation

Cheeseman et al. observed that the phase transition for graph colouring occurred at the point when the probability of having at least one solution fell abruptly to zero. In a longer version of this paper (Williams & Hogg 1992a) we explain why this is to be expected. One way of casting this result, which happens to be particularly amenable to mathematical analysis, is to hypothesize that the phase transition in cost should occur when $\left\langle \frac{1}{1+N_{soln}} \right\rangle$ transitions from being near zero to being near 1. In order to estimate this point, we consider the Taylor series approximation (Papoulis 1990, p129):

$$\left\langle \frac{1}{1+N_{soln}} \right\rangle \approx \frac{1}{1+\langle N_{soln} \rangle} + \frac{\text{var}(N_{soln})}{(1+\langle N_{soln} \rangle)^3} \quad (7)$$

In figure 2 we plot measured values of $\left\langle \frac{1}{1+N_{soln}} \right\rangle$ together with its truncated Taylor series approximation versus β for increasing values of μ. This proxy sharpens to a step function as $\mu \to \infty$ apparently at the same point as that reported by Cheeseman et al. Fortunately although the truncated Taylor series approximation overshoots the true value of $\left\langle \frac{1}{1+N_{soln}} \right\rangle$ before finally returning to a value of 1 at high β, it nevertheless is accurate in the vicinity of the phase transition point as required and may therefore be used. Hence, the true transition point can be estimated as the value of β at which the right hand side of equation 7 equals $\frac{1}{2}$. As the true transition point precedes the old one (predicted using equation 2), i.e. $\beta_{crit}^{true} < \beta_{crit}$ and as

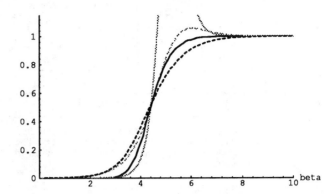

Fig. 2. Behaviour of $\langle 1/(1+N_{soln}) \rangle$ vs β for $b = 2$, $k = 3$ (3–SAT). The dark curves show empirical data for $\mu = 10$ (dashed) and $\mu = 20$ (solid). The light curves show the corresponding two-term Taylor series approximation to $\langle 1/(1+N_{soln}) \rangle$.

there are exponentially many solutions for $\beta < \beta_{crit}$ the first term in the above approximation must be negligible at the true transition for large enough values of μ. In this case we can estimate β_{crit}^{true} as the value of β at which

$$\text{var}(N_{soln}) = \frac{1}{2} \left(1 + \langle N_{soln} \rangle\right)^3. \quad (8)$$

By the same argument as that in (Williams & Hogg 1992b) we can show,

$$\langle N_{soln} \rangle = b^\mu \frac{\left(\binom{\mu}{k} b^k - \binom{\mu}{k} \right)}{\binom{\binom{\mu}{k} b^k}{\beta \mu}} \quad (9)$$

$$\text{var}(N_{soln}) = \langle N_{soln}^2 \rangle - \langle N_{soln} \rangle^2$$

with

$$\langle N_{soln}^2 \rangle = b^\mu \sum_{r=0}^{\mu} \binom{\mu}{r} (b-1)^{\mu-r} \frac{\left(\binom{\binom{\mu}{k} b^k - 2\binom{\mu}{k} + \binom{r}{k}}{\beta \mu} \right)}{\binom{\binom{\mu}{k} b^k}{\beta \mu}} \quad (10)$$

The $\langle N_{soln}^2 \rangle$ term is obtained by counting how many ways there are of picking $m = \beta\mu$ nogoods of size k such that a given pair of nodes at the solution level are both good and have a prescribed overlap r weighted by the number of ways sets can be picked such that they have this overlap. Finally, this is averaged over all possible overlaps. With these formulae the phase transition can be located as the fixed point solution (in β) to equation 7. For $\mu = 10$ or 20 this gives the transition point at $\beta = 4.4$. Asymptotically, one can obtain an explicit formula for the new critical point by applying Stirling's formula to equations 9 and 10, approximating equation 10 as an integral with a single dominant term and factoring a coefficient as a numerical integral. This gives a slightly higher critical point of

Problem	Expt	Basic Theory(2)	Basic + Correlations(6)	Basic + Corrections(7)
3-col	8.1 ± 0.3	9.3	8.1	N/A
4-col	18 ± 1	21.5	19.5	N/A
3-sat	4.3	5.2	N/A	4.5

Table 1. Comparisons of our basic theory and various refinements thereof with empirical data obtained by other authors. The numbers in the column headings refer to the equations used to calculate that columns' entries.

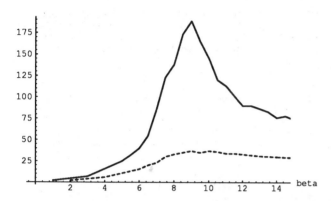

Fig. 3. Median search cost for heuristic repair as a function of β for the case $b = 3$, $k = 2$. The solid curve, for $\mu = 20$, has a maximum at $\beta = 9$. The dashed curve, for $\mu = 10$, has a broad peak in the same region.

$\beta_{crit} = 4.546$ and predicts the new functional form for the critical number of minimized nogoods as $m_{crit} = \beta_{crit}\mu + \text{const} + O\left(\frac{1}{\mu}\right)$ with const = 3.966.

The results for our basic model, the correlation model (for graph colouring) and the correction to mean field model (for k-SAT) are collected together in Table 1 where the best results are highlighted.

4. Heuristic Repair Has Phase Transition Too

The above results show that the addition of a few extra details to the basic deep structure model allows us to make quantitatively accurate estimates of the location of phase transition points. However, the question of the applicability of these results to other search methods, in particular those that operate on complete states, such as heuristic repair, simulated annealing and GSAT remains open. In this section we investigate the behaviour of such methods and show theoretically and empirically that they also exhibit a phase transition in search cost at about the same point as the tree based searches.

In figure 3 we plot the median search cost for solving random CSPs with $b = 3$, $k = 2$ versus our order parameter β (the ratio of the number of minimized nogoods to

the number of variables) using the heuristic repair algorithm. As for other search algorithms we see a characteristic easy-hard-easy pattern with the peak sharpening as larger problem instances are considered.

To understand this recall that heuristic repair, simulated annealing and GSAT all attempt to improve a complete state through a series of incremental changes. These methods differ on the particular changes allowed and how decisions are made amongst them. In general they all guide the search toward promising regions of the search space by emphasizing local changes that decrease a cost function such as the number of remaining conflicting constraints. In our model, the number of conflicting constraints for a given state is equal to the number of nogoods of which it is a superset. A complete state is minimal when every possible change in value assignment would increase or leave unchanged the number of conflicts.

These heuristics provide useful guidance until a state is reached for which none of the local changes considered give any further reduction in cost. To the extent that many of these local *minimal* or *equilibrium* states are not solutions, they provide points where these search methods can get stuck. In such situations, practical implementations often restart the search from a new initial state, or perform a limited number of local changes that leave the cost unchanged in the hope of finding a better state before restarting. Thus the search cost for difficult problems will be dominated by the number of minimal points, $N_{minimal}$, encountered relative to the number of solutions, N_{soln}. Thus our proxy is:

$$\left\langle \frac{N_{minimal}}{N_{soln}} \right\rangle \approx \frac{\langle N_{minimal} \rangle}{\langle N_{soln} \rangle} \qquad (11)$$

with $\langle N_{minimal} \rangle = b^{\mu} p_{minimal}$ where $p_{minimal}$ is the probability that a given state (at the solution level) is minimal. This in turn is just given by the ratio of the number of ways to pick m nogoods such that the given state is minimal to the total number of ways to pick m nogoods. Of course, we should be aware that the mean-field approximation will again introduce some quantitative error.

In figure 4 we plot this cost proxy and the mean-field approximation to it, for $\mu = 10$, $b = 3$, $k = 2$. This predicts that the hardest problems occur around $\beta = 9.5$. Compare this with empirical data, in figure 3. We see that heuristic repair does indeed find certain problems harder than others and the numerical agreement between predicted and observed critical points is quite good, suggesting that $\langle N_{minimal}/N_{soln} \rangle$ is an adequate proxy for the true cost. Thus our deep structure theory applies to sophisticated search methods beyond the tree search algorithms considered previously.

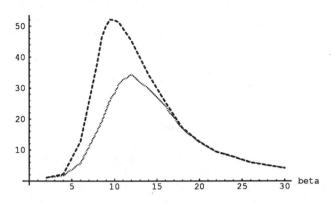

Fig. 4. Ratio of number of minimal points to number of solutions vs. β for the case of $\mu = 10$, $b = 3$, $k = 2$ (dashed curve, with maximum at $\beta = 9.5$) and its mean-field approximation (grey, with maximum at 12).

5. Conclusions

The basic deep structure model (Williams & Hogg 1992) typically led to predictions of phase transition points that were within about 15% of the empirically determined values. However, both empirical observations and theory suggest that the phase transition becomes sharper the larger the problem considered making it important to determine the location of transition points more precisely. To this end, we identified modelling approximations (such as neglecting correlations in the values assigned to different variables) and mathematical approximations (such as the mean field approximation) as the principal factors impeding proper estimation of the phase transition points. We then showed how to incorporate such influences into the model resulting in the predictions reported in Table 1. This shows that the deep structure model is capable of making quantitatively accurate estimates of the location of phase transition points for all the problems we have considered. However, we again reiterate that the more important result is that our model predicts the qualitative existence of the phase transition at all as this shows that fairly simple computational models can shed light on generic computational phenomena. A further advantage of our model is that it is capable of identifying the coarse functional dependencies between problem parameters. This allows actual data to be fitted to credible functional forms from which numerical coefficients can be determined, allowing scaling behaviour to be anticipated.

Our belief that phase transitions are generic is buoyed by the results we report for heuristic repair. This is an entirely different kind of search algorithm than the tree or lattice-like methods considered previously and yet it too exhibits a phase transition at roughly the same place as the tree search methods. We identified the ratio of the number of minimal states to the number of solutions as an adequate cost proxy which can be calculated from the minimized nogoods. Moreover, our experience suggests the exact form for the proxy is not that critical, provided it tracks the actual cost measure faithfully.

6. References

Cheeseman, P.; Kanefsky, B.; and Taylor, W. M. 1991. Where the Really Hard Problems Are. In Proceedings of the Twelfth International Joint Conference on Artificial Intelligence, 331–337, Morgan Kaufmann.

Cheeseman, P.; Kanefsky, B.; and Taylor, W. M. 1992. Computational Complexity and Phase Transitions. In Proc. of the Physics of Computation Workshop, IEEE Computer Society.

Franco and Paull 1983. Probabilistic Analysis of the Davis Putman Procedure for Solving Satisfiability Problems, Discrete Applied Mathematics 5:77–87.

Huberman, B.A. and Hogg, T. 1987. Phase Transitions in Artificial Intelligence Systems, *Artificial Intelligence*, 33:155–171.

Johnson, D., Aragon, C., McGeoch L., Schevon, C., 1991. Optimization by Simulated Aneealing: An experimental evaluation; part ii, graph coloring and number partitioning, *Operations Research*, 39(3):378–406, May-June

Kirkpatrick S., Gelatt C., Vecchi M., 1983. Optimization by Simulated Annealing. Science 220:671–680.

Minton S., Johnston M., Philips A., Laird P. 1990. Solving Large-scale Constraint Satisfaction and Scheduling Problems using a Heuristic Repair Method. In Proc. AAAI-90, pp17–24.

Mitchell D., Selman B., Levesque H., 1992. Hard & Easy Distributions of SAT Problems. In Proceedings of the 10th National Confernce on Artificial Intelligence, AAAI–92, pp459–465, San Jose, CA.

Morris P., 1992. On the Density of Solutions in Equilibrium Points for the N-Queens Problem, In Proceedings of the 10th National Confernce on Artificial Intelligence, AAAI–92, pp428–433, San Jose, CA.

Papoulis A., 1990. Probability & Statistics, p129, Prentice Hall

Selman B., Levesque H., Mitchell D., 1992. A New Method for Solving Hard Satisfiability Problems, In Proceedings of the 10th National Confernce on Artificial Intelligence, AAAI–92, pp440–446, San Jose, CA.

Williams, C. P. and Hogg, T. 1991. Typicality of Phase Transitions in Search, Tech. Rep. SSL-91–04, Xerox Palo Alto Research Center, Palo Alto, California (to appear in *Computational Intelligence* 1993)

Williams, C. P. and Hogg, T. 1992a. Exploiting the Deep Structure of Constraint Problems. Tech. Rep. SSL-92–24, Xerox Palo Alto Research Center, Palo Alto, CA.

Williams, C. P. and Hogg, T. 1992b Using Deep Structure to Locate Hard Problems, in Proc 10th National Conf. on Artificial Intelligence, AAAI–92,pp472–477,San Jose CA.

Diagnostic
Reasoning

Multiple Dimensions of Generalization In Model-Based Troubleshooting

Randall Davis
davis@ai.mit.edu
MIT Artificial Intelligence Lab

Paul Resnick
presnick@eagle.mit.edu
MIT Center for Coordination Science

Abstract

Two observations motivate our work: (a) model-based diagnosis programs are powerful but do not learn from experience, and (b) one of the long-term trends in learning research has been the increasing use of knowledge to guide and inform the process of induction. We have developed a knowledge-guided learning method, based in EBL, that allows a model-based diagnosis program to selectively accumulate and generalize its experience.

Our work is novel in part because it produces several different kinds of generalizations from a single example. Where previous work in learning has for the most part intensively explored one or another specific kind of generalization, our work has focused on accumulating and using multiple different grounds for generalization, i.e., multiple domain theories. As a result our system not only learns from a single example (as in all EBL), it can learn multiple things from a single example.

Simply saying there ought to be multiple grounds for generalization only opens up the possibility of exploring more than one domain theory. We provide some guidance in determining which grounds to explore by demonstrating that in the domain of physical devices, causal models are a rich source of useful domain theories. We also caution that adding more knowledge can sometimes degrade performance. Hence we need to select the grounds for generalization carefully and analyze the resulting rules to ensure that they improve performance. We illustrate one such quantitative analysis in the context of a model-based troubleshooting program, measuring and analyzing the gain resulting from the generalizations produced.

1 Introduction

Two observations motivate our work: (a) model-based diagnosis programs are powerful but do not learn from experience, and (b) one of the long-term trends in learning research has been the increasing use of knowl-edge to guide and inform the process of induction. We have developed a knowledge-guided learning method that allows a model-based reasoner to selectively accumulate and generalize its experience.

In doing so we have continued in the line of work demonstrated by programs that use knowledge to guide the induction process and thereby increase the amount of information extracted from each example. Previous work in this line includes the comprehensibility criterion used in [10] (a constraint on the syntactic form of the concept), the notion of a near-miss [15], and the use of knowledge from the domain to aid in distinguishing plausibly meaningful events from mathematical coincidences in the data [2]. Work on explanation-based learning (EBL) [12,3,9] has similarly emphasized the use of domain specific knowledge as the basis for generalizations, allowing the system to develop a valid generalization from a single example.

While these systems have used increasing amounts of knowledge to guide the induction process, they have also for the most part intensively explored methods for doing one or another specific type of generalization. In addition, EBL generally takes the domain theory as given. Yet as is well known, the type of generalizations EBL can draw is determined by the domain theory, in particular by what the theory parameterizes and what it builds in as primitive. Our work can be seen in these terms as showing the domain theory author how to find and use multiple different theories, thereby extending the range of generalizations that can be drawn.

We report on experiments with an implemented set of programs that produce several distinctly different generalizations from a single example; as a result the system not only learns from a single example, it can learn a lot from that example.

For instance, given a single example of an adder misbehaving to produce $2 + 4 = 7$, the system can produce a number of generalizations, including: the pattern of inputs and outputs consistent with a stuck-at-1 on the low order input bit, the N patterns of inputs/outputs consistent with a stuck-at-1 on any of the N input bits, as well as the pattern of inputs/outputs consistent with a stuck-at-0 on any of the input bits. We show why this last example is both a sensible and useful generalization even though no stuck-at-0 fault can explain the original example.

Simply saying there ought to be multiple grounds for generalization only opens up the possibility of exploring more than one space. We provide some guidance in determining which grounds to explore by demonstrating that in the domain of physical devices, causal models are a rich source of useful grounds for generalization and can help spur the creation of systems that generalize in ways we might not have thought of otherwise.

Finally, not everything we can learn will improve performance; sometimes adding more knowledge will only slow us down. Hence we need to select the grounds for generalization carefully and analyze the resulting rules to ensure that the new knowledge actually improves performance. We illustrate one such quantitative analysis in the context of a model-based troubleshooting program that improves its performance over time as it learns from experience.

2 A View Of Learning From Experience

Learning from experience means seeing a new problem as in some way "the same as" one previously encountered, then using what was learned in solving the old problem to reduce the work needed to solve the new one. What it means to be "the same" is a fundamental issue in much of learning. The simplest definition is of course exact match, i.e., the simplest form of learning by experience is literal memorization. Any more interesting form of learning requires a more interesting definition of "same;" we explore several such definitions in Section 3.

Clearly the more (different) definitions of similarity we have, the more use we can make of a previously solved problem: Each new definition allows the transfer of experience from the old problem to another, different set of new problems.

This issue of the definition of "same" lies at the heart of all inductive learning. It is most obvious in systems like case-based reasoners (e.g., [8]), where a distance metric selects from the library the case that is most nearly the same as the new one. But the identical issue underlies all forms of generalization: every generalization embodies and is a commitment to one or another definition of similarity. For example, generalizing a concept by dropping a single conjunct from its definition is a commitment to defining two instances as "the same" if they share all the remaining conjuncts. Different and more elaborate forms of generalization yield correspondingly different and more elaborate definitions of "same," but the issue is unavoidable: every generalization embodies a definition of "same."

As we explain in more detail below, we have found it useful to view learning from experience in model-based diagnosis as an exercise in finding and using several different definitions of same.

3 Multiple Dimensions of Generalization: Examples

Our approach has been to study the device models used in model-based reasoning, looking for useful ways in which two examples might be viewed as the same, then create generalization machinery that can make that similarity easily detected from available observations.

Consider for instance the familiar circuit, misbehavior, and diagnosis shown in Example 1. What general lessons can we learn from this example? We show that at least five distinct generalizations are possible. We explore each of these in turn, describing them in terms of the dimension of generalization they use (i.e., what definition of "same" they employ), what gets generalized and how, and the rules that result, allowing the program to carry over experience from this single example to multiple different situations it may encounter in the future.

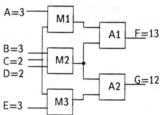

Example 1: Inputs and observed outputs shown; either A1 or M1 is broken.

The contribution here is not machinery, since small variations on traditional EBL suffice for the task at hand. Our focus is instead on finding multiple ways to view the device and thereby provide guidance to the person writing the domain theory (or theories) that EBL will use to produce generalizations.

3.1 The Same Conflict Set

Imagine that we troubleshoot Example 1 using a diagnostic engine in the general style of [5]: we use the behavior rules for each component to propagate values and keep track of which components each propagated value depends on. The prediction that F should be 12 in Example 1, for instance, depends on values propagated through M1, M2 and A1. When two propagations (or an observation and a propagation) offer two different values for the same spot in the circuit, we construct a conflict set, the set of all components that contributed to both predictions.[1] Conflict sets are useful raw material from which single and multiple point of failure hypotheses can be constructed [5]. Our concern in this paper is with single points of failure; the consequences for multiple points of failure are

---

[1]The intuition is that at least one of the components in a conflict set must be malfunctioning. If they were all working properly (i.e., according to their behavior rules), there would have to be two different values at the same point in the circuit, which is of course impossible. Hence at least one is broken.

discussed in [14].

In Example 1 two conflict sets are constructed: (M1 M2 A1) and (M1 M3 A1 A2). Now consider Example 2.

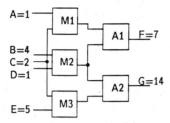

Example 2.

Even though the symptoms are different the pattern of reasoning (i.e., the set of propagations) is the same, and hence so are the resulting conflict sets. There are also numerous other sets of symptoms which produce the same reasoning pattern and conflict sets. Thus if we can determine from Example 1 the general conditions on the values at input/output ports that will produce those conflict sets, we would in future examples be able to check those conditions at the outset, then jump immediately to the result without having to replay that pattern of reasoning (and hence save the work of propagating through the components).

3.1.1 Mechanism and Results

We find those conditions by replacing the specific values at the inputs and outputs with variables, then re-running the propagations, thereby generalizing the pattern of reasoning that led to that answer. Our algorithm is a small variation on standard explanation-based learning (see, e.g., [4]), described in detail in [14] and omitted here for reasons of space. For the first conflict set the result is the generalized rule:[2]

```
R1: (IF (NOT (= ?F (+ (* ?A ?C) (* ?B ?D))))
    (THEN (CONFLICT-SET '(M1 M2 A1)))
```

For the second conflict set we get:

```
R2: (IF (NOT (= (+ (- ?F (* ?A ?C)) (* ?C ?E))
        ?G))
    (THEN (CONFLICT-SET '(M1 M3 A1 A2)))
```

As a result of this process, from Example 1 the system has produced in R1 the condition on the I/O ports for which the pattern of reasoning will lead to the conflict set (M1 M2 A1) (viz., AC + BD ≠ F), and in R2 the condition leading to the conflict set (M1 M3 A1 A2) (viz., F − AC + CE ≠ G). Both of these rules derived from Example 1 are applicable to Example 2, hence the system would now be able to derive the conflict sets for Example 2 in one step each. While these particular rules simply encapsulate in one expression the steps of the derivation, they still provide useful speedup (28%, a figure we document and analyze in Section 4.2).

---

[2]Symbols preceded by question marks are variables.

The same technique was also applied to the more realistic carry-lookahead adder circuit in Example 3, where it produced a 20% speedup.

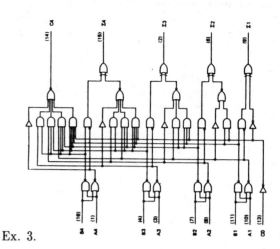

Ex. 3.

3.2 The Same Fault in Same Component

There is another, different sense in which Examples 1 and 2 are the same: they can both be explained by the same fault (a stuck-at-1) in the same component (the low order output of M1). Hence another, different generalization that we can draw from Example 1 is **the set of examples consistent with the hypothesis that the low order bit of M1 is stuck-at-1**.

As before, there are numerous sets of symptoms consistent with this hypothesis, so if we can determine the general conditions and check them at the outset, we may be able to save work. In this case the machinery we use to derive the general rules is symbolic fault envisionment: the system simulates the behavior of the circuit with the fault model in place, but uses variables in place of actual values. The result in this case is:

```
R3:
(IF (AND (= ?F (+ (stuck-at-1 0 (* ?A ?C))
            (* ?B ?D)))
        (= ?G (+ (* ?B ?D) (* ?C ?E))))
    (THEN (fault-hypothesis
        '(stuck-at-1 0 (OUTPUT M1)))))
```

The resulting rule[3] in this case is not particularly deep (it simply encapsulates the fault simulation) but it can still provide useful speedup. In Section 6 we suggest what would be required to enable deriving a rule that used terms like "**the value at F is high-by-1**," which would be both more interesting and more powerful.

The main point here is that Example 1 has been generalized in a new and different way, based on a differ-

---

[3]stuck-at-1 takes two arguments: a number indicating which bit is affected, and the value affected; hence (stuck-at-1 0 (OUTPUT M1)) means the 0th (low order) bit of the output of M1 is stuck at 1.

ent domain theory. Where the previous generalization arose from a domain description phrased in terms of correct behavior (and conflict sets), this generalization comes from a domain theory described in terms of fault modes (and their consistency with observations). The system can now use that generalization to apply the experience of Example 1 to a different set of problems: those with the same fault in the same component (M1).

3.3 The Same Fault in a Component Playing the Same Role

Example 1 can be generalized in yet another way: given the additional information that M1 and M3 play similar roles, we can derive the general conditions consistent with the hypothesis that the low order output bit of M3 (rather than M1) is stuck-at-1. That is, the fault is the same but it is occurring in a different component, a component that happens to be playing the same role.[4]

We use symbolic fault envisionment once again to produce the rule:

```
R4:
(IF (AND (= ?F (+ (* ?A ?C) (* ?B ?D)))
         (= ?G (+ (* ?B ?D)
                  (stuck-at-1 0 (* ?C ?E)))))
(THEN (fault-hypothesis
         '(stuck-at-1 0 (OUTPUT M3)))))
```

A more interesting and realistic example is the application of this to the inputs of an N-bit carry-chain adder (Example 4): given the symptoms $2 + 4 = 7$, the diagnosis of a stuck-at-1 on the low order bit of one of the inputs, and the knowledge that all the input bits play the same role, we can produce rules for a stuck-at-1 on any of the 2N input bits.

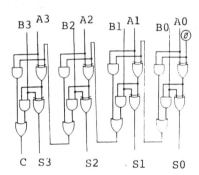

Example 4: A malfunctioning four-bit carry chain adder: $2 + 4 = 7$.

Two comments about this dimension of generalization help make clear the nature of the undertaking

---

[4]The role of a component refers to what it does in the device. The symmetry of the circuit in Example 1, for instance, means that M1 and M3 play the same role, while Example 4 can be viewed as a collection of 4 bit slices, each of which plays the same role, *viz.*, adding its inputs to produce a sum and carry bit.

and the role of domain knowledge. First, the generalizations created are guided and informed by knowledge about this device. In Example 4, the jump was not from a stuck-at-1 on the low order bit input to a stuck-at-1 on every wire in the device. The example was instead generalized to a small subset of the wires that "made sense" in the current context, namely those that were playing analogous roles.

This restriction makes sense because we are relying on the heuristic that role equivalent components are likely to fail in similar ways. Hence if we create generalizations only for the analogous components, we improve the chances that the generalizations will in fact prove useful in the future (i.e., the component will actually break in that fashion).

Second, note that while our current system must be told explicitly which components are playing equivalent roles, the information about structure and function in the device model is just the sort of knowledge needed to derive that. More important, it is by examining such models and asking how to see different examples as the same that we are led to notions like role equivalence as potentially useful dimensions of generalization.

3.4 Same Family of Fault

Example 1 can be generalized in yet another way: given the additional information that stuck-at-1 is a member of a family of faults that also includes stuck-at-0, we can generalize across the fault family.[5] From the single example with a stuck-at-1, we can generalize to the other member of the family, deriving the general conditions under which it is consistent to believe that the output of M1 is stuck-at-0. We use symbolic fault envisionment to produce the rule:

```
R5:
(IF (AND (= ?F (+ (stuck-at-0 0 (* ?A ?C))
                  (* ?B ?D)))
         (= ?G (+ (* ?B ?D) (* ?C ?E)))))
(THEN (fault-hypothesis
         '(stuck-at-0 0 (OUTPUT M3))))
```

This generalization is motivated by the heuristic that if we encounter a device affected by one of the faults in a family, it is likely in the future to be affected by others in the family as well, hence it is worthwhile to create the corresponding generalizations.

3.5 The Same Family of Fault in A Component Playing the Same Role

Example 1 can be generalized in yet one final way, by simply composing the ideas in Sections 3.3 and 3.4. From the original fault in the observed location, we move to a hypothesized fault in the same family in an analogous location. That is, while the experience in

---

[5]The family here is the simple but real hierarchy with stuck-at at the root and stuck-at-1 and stuck-at-0 as child nodes.

Example 1 was a `stuck-at-1` in `M1`, the system next derives the conditions that indicate a `stuck-at-0` in `M3` (using the same fault envisionment machinery):

```
R6:
(IF (AND (= ?F (+ (* ?A ?C) (* ?B ?D)))
         (= ?G (+ (* ?B ?D)
                  (stuck-at-0 0 (* ?C ?E))))))
(THEN (fault-hypothesis
            '(stuck-at-0 0 (OUTPUT M3))))
```

If this approach is applied to the carry-chain adder in Example 4, we have the first step toward the generalization from the single example $2 + 4 = 7$ to the general rule **an adder that is off by a power of two indicates a stuck-at on one of the bits.** We comment in 6.1 on the prospects for this next level of generalization.

4 Comments on the Examples

4.1 Multiple Dimensions of Generalization
Several things stand out about the sequence of examples reviewed. First is the number and diversity of the lessons that have been learned. A number of different kinds of generalizations were derived from the single instance in Example 1, by relying on the notion that problems encountered in the future might be "the same" as Example 1 with respect to: (i) the conflict set generated, (ii) the kind and location of fault, (iii) the role of the faulty component, and (iv) the family the fault belonged to, as well as combinations of those.

Each lesson learned means that the single experience in Example 1 can be seen as applicable to a new and different set of examples in the future. We can view the results in terms of the Venn diagram in Fig. 5: The universe is the set of all possible diagnostic problems (I/O values) for the circuit in Example 1; the sets are the generalizations captured by rules `R1` thru `R6` (and are labeled with the rule name). The specific problem presented by Example 1 is noted by a point marked **+**.

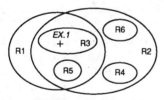

R1: any example in which M1, M2, or A2 is a candidate.
R2: any example in which M1, M3, A1, A2 is a candidate.
R3: any example in which M1 SA-1 is a candidate.
R4: any example in which M3 SA-1 is a candidate.
R5: any example in which M1 SA-0 is a candidate.
R6: any example in which M3 SA-0 is a candidate.
Fig. 5.

Sets `R1` and `R2` are produced by traditional use of EBL on Example 1, while sets `R3`–`R6` are produced because the system has available a variety of different descriptions of (i.e., a variety of domain theories for) the device. `R3`–`R6` are also more specific than `R1` and

`R2`. In the case of sets `R1`–`R3` the process of generalizing from Example 1 can be seen as different ways to expand Example 1 into distinct circles. Note that `R4`–`R6` are appropriately produced by the system even though they don't explain the original example.

We discover multiple ways in which to generalize by examining the models of structure and behavior to determine what kinds of similarities can be exploited, and by developing methods for recognizing those similarities. Hence we are not simply suggesting using multiple generalizations, we are suggesting in addition where they might be found: Causal models have turned out to be a particularly useful source of inspiration, supplying a rich set of different dimensions along which examples can be generalized.

Despite the number of different generalizations, the machinery we have used to create them is both simple and relatively uniform. It is simple in the sense that straightforward application of explanation-based generalization (for `R1` and `R2`) and symbolic simulation (for the rest) sufficed to produce the generalizations; it is relatively uniform in the sense that two mechanisms suffice across a range of different grounds for generalization.

Note also that each of these dimensions of generalization provides significant guidance. The system is aggressive in the number and variety of generalizations it draws, but is still far from doing exhaustive search. For instance, when given a stuck bit in an input wire of a 32 bit adder and generalizing to components playing the same role, it will explore faults in the 63 other input bits, but that is far less than the total number of wires in the device. The subset of wires selected is guided by knowledge from the domain about component role and function.

Finally, our emphasis on domain knowledge as a source of guidance and inspiration appears to be in keeping with the increasing trend toward more informed varieties of inductive learning. The earliest efforts attempted to find statistical regularities in a large collection of examples and hence might be said to be regularity based; later efforts became explanation based. The approach described here, with its reliance on domain-specific information is in the spirit of knowledge guided generalization.

4.2 Useful Dimensions of Generalization
Thus far through the discussion we have implicitly assumed that if we are guided by the domain knowledge, every lesson learned will improve performance. But this need not be true: sometimes it's cheaper to re-derive an answer than even to *check* whether we have relevant experience (i.e., examine the generalizations to see if we have one that matches), much less actually apply that experience.

We suggest that to be useful a dimension of generalization must capture situations that are *recurrent, manifest,* and *exploitable.*[6] By recurrent we mean that the situations the rule applies to must reoccur often enough in the future to make the rule worth checking; if the rule describes a situation the problem solver will never encounter, the rule can't produce any benefit and will only slow us down. By manifest we mean the situations must be relatively inexpensive to recognize; if recognizing costs more than rederiving the answer, the rule can only slow us down. By exploitable we mean that the rule must provide some power in solving the problem, i.e., some discrimination in the diagnosis.

This style of analysis is illustrated in general terms by examining the idea in Section 3.3 of generalizing to the same fault in a component playing an equivalent role. The rules are likely to be useful because the situations they describe should reoccur: role equivalent components are likely to fail in similar ways. The situations they describe are exploitable: if the rule applies we get a specific location for the fault. But the situations are not all that easy to check, primarily because for the N bit carry-chain adder we have 2N separate rules rather than one that captures the appropriate level of generalization (viz., **a result high by a power of two**). We return to this question of level of generalization and level of language in Section 6 below.

A more quantitative analysis is provided by the data in Table I (below). We report tests on 200 cases of the circuit in Example 1 (100 training cases, 100 test cases) and 300 cases of the carry-lookahead adder (150 training, 150 testing).[7] The results demonstrate that a troubleshooter with these generalizations provides a speedup of 28% and 20% on the circuits of Examples 1 and 3.

The speedup shown in Table I arises in small part due to the "encapsulation" effect of rules **R1** and **R2**: i.e., arriving at the conflict sets from the single arithmetic calculation in the rule premise, without the overhead of TMS-style recording of intermediate calculations required when running the standard diagnostic system.

A larger part of the speedup arises from the focus provided by the generalized rules. In Example 1, for instance, two of the generalized rules narrow the possible candidates down to (**A1 M1**) at the outset. The system still has to check each of these, since it can not assume that its set of generalized rules is complete. As this is in fact the minimal set of single fault candidates, no additional conflict sets are derived when checking these candidates, and a large part of the speedup arises from avoiding the deriving (and re-deriving) of conflict sets that occurs in the standard diagnostic system.[8]

Finally, the data also provide a basis for quantitative calibration of the cost/benefit involved in learning. Additional measurement indicated that of the 5.66 seconds taken on average case in Example 3, an average of .70 seconds was devoted to checking the generalized rules. Hence those rules cost .70 sec., but saved $7.07 - (5.66 - .70) = 2.11$ sec. Had the rules been three times as expensive to check, there would have been negligible benefit from having them; any more expense would have meant that learning was disadvantageous, it would on average slow down the system.

Alternatively we can determine that having the generalized rules saved on average $\frac{7.07 - (5.66 - .70)}{3.15} = .67$ sec per generalization rule used, but each rule cost $\frac{.70}{221} = .0032$ sec on average. This produces a cost benefit ratio of .67/.0032 or 211. Hence generalized rules that are on average applicable in fewer than 1 out of 211 examples will slow down the system.

The basic message here is that it is important to be both creative and analytical: we need to be creative in discovering as many dimensions of generalization as possible, but we also then need to be analytical (as above) in checking each dimension to determine whether in fact it is in fact going to provide a net gain in performance.

	Example 1 (100 cases)			Example 3 (150 cases)		
	Sol'n Time (secs)	Rules Created	Rules Applicable	Sol'n Time (secs)	Rules Created	Rules Applicable
Non-learning	.76	(n/a)	(n/a)	7.07	(n/a)	(n/a)
Learning	.55	3.00	2.00	5.66	221	3.15

Table I. In Example 1 there are only 3 conflict sets (and hence 3 generalized rules) possible; the third conflict set is (**M3 M2 A2**). Due to the symmetry of the circuit, two of the rules are always applicable to any single-fault diagnosis.

In the more realistic circuit of Example 3, there are 221 different rules possible; on average 3.15 of them are applicable to any single-fault problem.

---

[6] These three factors have also been independently identified in [11].

[7] Each case was a randomly chosen set of inputs and outputs for the circuit, constrained only by the criterion that the I/O values had to be consistent with a single stuck-at failure somewhere in the device.

[8] Our original implementation used a JTMS, but a second implementation using an ATMS demonstrated the same basic result, due to savings in bookkeeping of environments.

5 Related Work

This work fits in the tradition of the long trend noted earlier: the increasing use of domain knowledge to guide learning. It also shares with other work the notion of using a simulation model to support learning. Work in [13], for instance, uses a simulation model to guide rule revision in the face of diagnostic failure. Work in [1] uses a simulation model as a convenient generator of test cases. There are a number of minor differences: unlike [13], we learn from success rather than failure, and unlike [1] we are in a relatively simple noise-free domain and hence can learn from a single example.

A more important difference, however, is our emphasis on learning multiple things from the model. The point is not simply that a device model can be used to support learning, but that there is a considerable body of knowledge in such models that can be used in multiple ways.

Work in [9] is in some ways similar to ours, exploring learning from experience in model-based diagnosis. That work relied on EBL as the mechanism to produce its generalization but had a single theory of the world and hence produced only a single generalization. By comparison our work, seen in EBL terms, urges using multiple theories, suggests that causal models can be a rich source of those theories, and provides a framework for evaluating the likely utility of each theory.

Work in [11] demonstrated some of the first efforts to quantify the costs and benefits of learning. Our discussion in Section 4.2 offers additional data on that subject.

Finally, some work in EBL has explored the "multiple explanation problem" (e.g., [3]), suggesting ways to find a valid explanation when the theory supports multiple, possibly invalid explanations (because the theories may be incomplete or approximate). This work explores instead the "multiple explanation *opportunity*:" we want to learn as much as possible from the example and use a variety of correct theories to derive multiple useful and valid generalizations.

6 Limitations and Future Work

The current implementation is an early step in the directions outlined here and has some important limitations. The results cited, for instance, come from a set of programs and experiments rather than from a single well-integrated body of code. In addition, as noted earlier, the domain knowledge used to guide the system must be supplied directly: to generalize across components that play the same role, the system must be told explicitly which components match; when generalizing across fault families the system must be told explicitly which faults are in the family.

Most fundamentally, we have supplied the human with a set of guidelines for thinking about the world, rather than a program that automates such thinking. When our system draws multiple generalizations, it is because we have told it what to do. Our work is thus a first step in making such knowledge explicit, because we can specify the general framework that led to the results, but have not yet automated its application.

As with all EBL systems, our program could in principle produce all of its generalizations before encountering any actual example [6,7]. The heuristic of allowing experience to trigger generalization depends on the belief that the past is a good predictor of the future, hence past experience is a useful "seed" from which to generalize. This also highlights the utility of multiple domain theories: It can be difficult to say in what way the past will be a good predictor of the future. Will the same conflict sets occur? Will the same components fail in the same way? The use of multiple domain theories allows us to hedge the bet that lies at the heart of this heuristic, by simply making several such bets about how the past will predict the future.

Another interesting and pervasive limitation becomes evident in examining the language in which the rules are stated. The good news is that, like EBL, our system does not need an externally supplied inductive bias; the language used to construct the generalizations comes from the domain theory. But all we can do is use that language as it stands; some of the rules could be made both more intuitive and easier to check if we could develop the appropriate elaborations of the language.

It would be useful, for example, to be able to rewrite R3 in simpler terms. In this case the crucial non-trivial knowledge is the recognition that stuck-at-1 at the low order input to an adder (in this case A1) will result in a symptom that might be called high-by-1. Once given this, it is relatively simple to rewrite the rule into a form far closer to the normal intuition about this case, viz., "if F is high by 1 and G is correct, then possibly M1 is stuck at 1 in the low order bit." The difficult task is deriving the initial insight about adder behavior, i.e., the connection between behavior described at the level of *bits* (stuck-at) and described at the level of *numbers* (high by 1).

A second example arises in generalizing to the same fault in role equivalent components. As Example 4 illustrated, when creating those generalizations the system can do only one at a time, rather than capturing the entire set of analogous components in a single rule that referred to a result "high by a power of two". This is difficult in general; for Example 4 the difficulty is recognizing the relevant generalization: each bit represents a different power of two. We have speculated elsewhere [14] that a design verification might already have the information needed.

7 Conclusion

All of these are potential directions for useful further development. The primary utility in the notion of multiple dimensions of generalization, however, is not that we can make the process entirely autonomous when it is given only a description of structure and behavior. The primary utility is rather that the notion of multiple kinds of generalizations and the use of such models provides to the researcher a source of inspiration, urging the creation of domain theories that can be generalized in ways we might not have thought of otherwise. The machinery used to produce those generalizations can be improved in many ways; the issue here is one of having suggested a set of directions in which to work.

We displayed the result of those new directions by showing how five distinctly different general lessons can be learned from the single example in Figure 1, provided a framework in which those generalizations can be evaluated for effectiveness, and documented the quantitative speedup provided by one of them.

Acknowledgments

This report describes research done at the Artificial Intelligence Laboratory of the Massachusetts Institute of Technology. Support for the laboratory's artificial intelligence research is provided in part by the Advanced Research Projects Agency of the Department of Defense under Office of Naval Research contract N00014-91-J-4038. Additional support for this research was provided by Digital Equipment Corporation, an NSF Graduate Fellowship, McDonnell Douglas Space Systems, and General Dynamics Corp.

References

[1] Buchanan B, et al., Simulation-assisted inductive learning, *Proc AAAI-86*, pp. 552–557.

[2] Buchanan B, Mitchell T, Model-directed learning of production rules, in *Pattern-Directed Inference Systems*, Waterman, Hayes-Roth (eds.), Academic Press, 1978.

[3] Cohen W, Abductive explanation based learning: a solution to the multiple explanation problem, TR ML-TR-26, Rutgers Univ CSD, 1989.

[4] DeJong G, Mooney R, Explanation-based learning, *Machine Learning*, 1(2), 1986.

[5] deKleer J, Williams B, Diagnosing multiple faults, *AI Jnl*, April 1987, pp. 97–130.

[6] Etzioni O, Why PRODIGY/EBL works, *Proc AAAI-90*, pp. 916–922.

[7] Etzioni O, STATIC – A problem space compiler for prodigy, *Proc AAAI-91*, pp. 533–540.

[8] Kolodner J, et al., A process model of case-based reasoning, *Proc IJCAI-85*, pp. 284–290.

[9] Koseki Y, Experience learning in model-based diagnostic systems, *Proc IJCAI-89*, pp. 1356–1362.

[10] Michalski R, A theory and methodology of inductive learning, in *Machine Learning*, Michalski, Carbonell, Mitchell (eds.), Tioga Press, 1983.

[11] Minton S, Quantitative results concerning the utility of explanation-based learning, *Proc AAAI-88*, pp. 564–569.

[12] Mitchell T, et al, Explanation-based generalization, *Machine Learning*, 1(1), 1986, pp.47–80.

[13] Pazzani, Refining the knowledge base of a diagnostic expert system, *Proc AAAI-86*, pp 1029–1035.

[14] Resnick P, Generalizing on multiple grounds, MIT AI Lab TR-1052 (MS Thesis), May 1988.

[15] Winston P H, Learning structure descriptions from examples, in Winston (ed.), *The Psychology of Computer Vision*, McGraw-Hill, 1975.

Hybrid Case-Based Reasoning for the Diagnosis of Complex Devices

M. P. Féret and J. I. Glasgow

Department of Computing & Information Science,
Queen's University, Kingston,
Ontario, Canada, K7L 3N6
{feret,janice}@qucis.queensu.ca

Abstract

A novel approach to integrating case-based reasoning with model-based diagnosis is presented. The main idea is to use the model of the device and the results of diagnostic tests to index and match cases representing past diagnostic situations with the current one. The initial diagnostic methodology is presented as well as the problems encountered while applying this methodology to two real-world devices. The incorporation of a case-based reasoning system is then motivated and described in detail. Experimental results show the effectiveness of both the indexing schema and the matching algorithm. The paper also discusses how and why these results can be generalized to a multiple fault situation, to other types of device models and to other applications in the field of artificial intelligence.

Introduction

This paper presents an approach to integrating case-based reasoning with a traditional diagnostic method for complex devices. This generic approach to diagnosis is based on a hierarchical decomposition of mechanical devices and uses sensor data, collected in real-time and stored in a database, to guide the search towards hypothetical diagnoses [6, 7, 8, 16]. Some of the difficulties encountered while applying a model-based reasoning (MBR) diagnostic method to two real-world devices are identified. These difficulties arose from imperfections of the device model, due to human errors or misconceptions. These imperfections lead to incorrect models which produced inadequate diagnostic performance. In this paper we further develop ideas initially introduced in [7], providing additional motivations for

our approach, and experimental results that support the claims of the paper.

CBR has traditionally been used as a stand-alone problem-solving method [13, 14], sometimes applied to diagnostic problems (e.g. [20]). Only recently has CBR been used in association with other problem-solving paradigms [15, 10, 19]. Our approach is novel in that it uses CBR only *after* the MBR process has taken place, and in that it uses the model and the results of the MBR process to index the cases.

The hybrid CBR/MBR methodology described in this paper incorporates a critique of the results of the model-based approach in the light of past experience and provides the human operator with a means for exploring alternative hypotheses. The integration of CBR with the structural isolation process allows for a simple and effective indexing schema as well as a computationally inexpensive similarity measure for cases.

This paper initially presents the structural isolation process. It then lists some of the problems arising when trying to apply any MBR diagnostic method to complex devices. The hybrid approach combining CBR and MBR is presented along with some experimental results. The final discussion summarizes the contributions of the research.

Generic Diagnosis

Our approach to generic diagnosis has been fully implemented in the Automated Data Management System (ADMS), which has previously been described and compared to other techniques for diagnosis in [6]. This section describes the structural isolation process and outlines the problems that arose in applying it to two real-world devices, a robotic system called the Fairing Servicing Subsystem, and a Reactor Building Ventilation System [6, 7]. The first device is a robot placed at the rear of a ship to automatically replace damaged fairings on a cable which drags an underwater detec-

*This research was supported through a contract from the Canadian Space Agency (STEAR program), a scholarship and an operating grant from the Natural Sciences and Engineering Research Council (NSERC) of Canada. We also would like to thank Spectrum Engineering Corporation Ltd., Peterborough, Ontario, Canada.

tion system. The fairings prevent the detection system from drifting away from the axis of the ship. The Reactor Building Ventilation System is a modified model of a ventilation system for an existing nuclear power plant.

Structural Isolation Process

Govindaraj and Su suggested that empirical constraints should direct the formation of knowledge representation in a format that reflects how experts solve problems [12]. They also observed that human diagnosis proceeds in a hierarchical manner, starting at higher levels of abstraction to generate hypotheses that guide the diagnosis at lower levels. Hierarchical, structural and conceptual data structures have already been found useful for diagnostic applications (e.g. [11, 12, 25]).

The ADMS methodology for diagnosis of mechanical devices is based on considering the device as a hierarchy of components or groups of components. This hierarchy is expressed using a frame language and constitutes the backbone of the knowledge base built for individual applications of the ADMS to a mechanical device. All recognizable components that can be diagnosed as sources of failure are situated at the bottom of the hierarchy. Each component has associated failure mechanism patterns. These patterns are conjunctions of sensor functions, testing specific conditions on the sensor data stored in a database [16]. Between these top and bottom levels, the device is decomposed into meaningful substructures, associated with test conditions indicating whether these substructures are potentially faulty.

While structural knowledge is usually available from engineering design documents and easily encoded, the knowledge about failure modes and patterns tends to be complex and of various types. In the case of sensor-based diagnosis, the queries to the database and their use in the sensor functions lead to numerous difficulties. These difficulties constitute the major differences between complex devices and electronic circuits, where failures and their consequences are straightforward to characterize.

The models used by the ADMS methodology therefore consist of a structural decomposition of the devices, along with necessary conditions for substructures and basic components being potential diagnoses. They are fault models in which all testing conditions use the real-time sensor data stored in the database through a set of predefined queries.

In the context described above, performing diagnosis involves traversing the hierarchy according to results of necessary conditions applied to the substructures represented in the hierarchy. At a given node in the hierarchy, if there is no evidence that the substructure can be faulty, then the whole substructure can be pruned from the search space of potentially faulty components. If there is such evidence, the substructure is examined further and more local conditions are applied to subnodes of the current node. This process is known as the structural isolation process [17]. It also handles multiple faults by simultaneously investigating multiple paths in the model.

The output of the diagnostic algorithm is a ranked list of potential diagnoses from which the operator can (or not) select the final (supposedly correct) diagnosis. The ranking involves relative levels of confidence in each potential diagnosis as well as criteria related to the history of each component (such as meantime between failures, time to life expectancy, etc.).

Model-Based Diagnosis Weaknesses

Diagnosis from first-principles is believed to be NP-hard in the general case [19, 21, 22]. Many researchers have tried to focus the search for minimal diagnoses in the diagnosis from first-principle approach [2, 3, 4, 5] or to reduce the complexity of similar methods (e.g. [9, 18]).

Analyzing and compiling human diagnostic problem-solving capabilities is difficult. Misunderstandings, incorrect specifications, typos, etc. typically lead to partially incorrect models which are difficult to debug, especially when there is no simulation program available for the device. Moreover, device models are not always the most natural or efficient representation for diagnosing faulty components [23]. These knowledge acquisition and validation problems clearly weaken the reliability of model-based systems such as the ADMS and need to be addressed before the system can be used for critical, real-world applications. Fault models consisting of necessary conditions (for parts to be faulty) are simpler to express and to implement than correct behavior models. However, fault models have a well-known drawback: they only model foreseen, predictable faults. Therefore, diagnostic systems based on fault models are ineffective in the presence of unforeseen faults.

The process of human diagnostic problem-solving is often suboptimal [12, 26]. Resulting shortcomings are likely to be found in any model designed and implemented by humans. In our experience, we have found such mistakes in the experts' explanations and reasoning processes. This leads to models that are either incomplete or inconsistent because they incorporate human limitations.

Recalling past relevant decisions (diagnostic cases) is an effective way of reducing the impact of both the model's and the human's inadequacies. The next section describes the addition of a CBR system to the approach described above. This hybrid approach assists in overcoming the bottlenecks of knowledge acquisition and human reasoning imperfections that limit the capabilities of current model-based approaches to diagnosis.

CBR and Structural Isolation

The philosophy behind CBR is that "raw", unabstracted experiences can be used as a source of knowledge for problem-solving [14, 24]. A CBR system stores past experiences in the form of cases. When a new problem arises, the system retrieves the cases most similar to the current problem, then combines and adapts them to derive and criticize a solution. If the solution is not satisfactory, new cases are retrieved to further adapt it in the light of new constraints, expressed from the non-satisfactory parts of the proposed solution. The process is iterated until the proposed solution is judged acceptable. After a problem is solved, a new case can be created and stored in the casebase. The main issues to address when building CBR systems are to define an effective indexing schema, efficient retrieval and storage mechanisms, a reliable similarity measure for cases and an adaptation mechanism.

CBR is limited by the difficulty of indexing, retrieving and evaluating previous experiences. This is especially true in the case of diagnostic applications, where similar symptoms can have very different or multiple causes. Techniques that work for small problems do not necessarily handle scaled-up versions of the same problem. Model-based approaches are limited by the fact that complete and consistent models of complex devices are difficult to produce.

Researchers have previously combined CBR with other problem solving paradigms. Rajamoney and Lee use CBR to decompose a novel, large problem into smaller known ones that are then solved with a model-based reasoning (MBR) system [19]. They use CBR for a separate task than the one the MBR system is used for. Koton's CASEY system uses CBR to speed up a model-based diagnosis system by storing previous experiences and recalling them when appropriate [15]. In this system, CBR is tried first as an attempt to reason by analogy. The cases are directly derived from the MBR system and are used, once created, in isolation from the MBR system. In these two systems, the paradigms are used independently from one another. Golding and Rosenbloom use CBR to improve the accuracy of a rule-based system [10]. Their cases denote exceptions to rules and are indexed by the rules they confirm and by the rules they contradict. Cases do not store the same information as the rules, but provide a different source of information for decision making. These systems all show that CBR does improve the performance of the whole system by either speeding up the same process without bringing new information or by storing a different type of experiential knowledge that is used to improve the accuracy of the overall system. However, all these systems have to face critical problems in retrieving and matching their cases, problems that are typical of CBR systems.

The ADMS hybrid approach to diagnosis is unique in that it uses the results of the structural isolation process to index cases. There is little overhead in retrieving relevant cases and matching is simplified since it is only applied to similar cases. We are considering CBR as a tool for assisting the operator in the final stage of a diagnostic session. Once the structural isolation has produced a list of potential diagnoses, the operator can call on the CBR component of the system to validate diagnoses or investigate other paths in the search tree.

The remainder of this section describes the content of cases, the retrieval process and the matching algorithm currently being used to evaluate case similarity.

What is a case?

In general, a case stores a fragment of a past experience. In the context of the ADMS, a case stores a past diagnostic scenario, consisting of a description of the fault that occurred (fault type, fault time, detecting sensor), the series of pruning steps used to produce a list of potential diagnoses (i.e. the tests performed during diagnosis and their values), the list of potential diagnoses produced by the structural isolation process and the correct diagnosis selected by the operator. A successful case is a case where the correct diagnosis was produced by the structural isolation process and confirmed by the human operator. A failure case is a case where the diagnosis failed to find the correct diagnosis, and for which the operator chose a component that was not in the list of proposed diagnoses.

Indexing and Storage of Cases

The structural isolation process can be seen as a rough estimate of the location of a component whose failure explains the observed symptoms. The list of potential diagnoses is used as a means of indexing the casebase, leaving the values of the associated sensor functions for

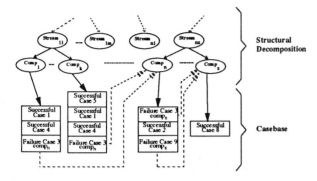

Figure 1: The casebase and the structural decomposition.

the matching step which is a finer judgement of similarity. For either a successful or a failure case, we use each potential diagnosis produced by the structural isolation process as an index for the case. Figure 1 illustrates this indexing schema. Each case is stored at the bottom of the structural decomposition under the basic components it contains as potential diagnoses. The dashed arrows originate from failure cases and point to the components representing the correct diagnoses for those cases.

This indexing schema is satisfying because of the interdependencies that exist among "neighboring" components. Such components often share the same characteristics and are likely to appear in each other's lists of potential diagnoses. They will likely share the same cases, or cases that are very similar to each other, except for failure cases. This ensures a useful grouping of similar cases with "bridges" from one grouping to the next provided by failure cases. This indexing schema, based on the information generated by the structural isolation process, is therefore both simple and effective.

Retrieval and Matching of Cases

Cases are retrieved from the casebase to evaluate and criticize the current list of potential diagnoses. The operator can ask the ADMS to explore its casebase and to criticize or confirm a potential diagnosis or to suggest new diagnoses that were not generated by the structural isolation process. If the current potential diagnosis is supported by a previous successful case, the level of confidence in this potential diagnosis can be raised. If the correct diagnosis for the most similar case disagrees with all the suggested diagnoses, and points towards a failure case that matches sufficiently well with the current situation, the validity of the current diagnosis is lowered. The diagnosis stored in the failure case is extracted from the casebase and presented to

the user as a new potential diagnosis that can, in turn, be evaluated.

Retrieved cases are matched with the current situation, using finer criteria to evaluate similarity. Such criteria include state information from both the past case and the current situation. The measure of similarity yielded by the matching algorithm is a normalized, weighted sum of the number of sensor functions sharing the same value, the number of substructures shared in the path followed during the session represented by the past case and during the current session, the common characteristics of the symptoms, etc. All steps in the matching algorithm involve comparisons of booleans or of reals and are computationally inexpensive.

Because of the indexing method described above, components at the bottom of the hierarchy serve as pointers to cases that represent diagnostic sessions caused by similar or related failures. The matching is effective because the knowledge contained in those cases and on which the matching is based is relevant in both the current and the past cases. The matching algorithm is focused on the part of the system that is the most relevant to the current situation.

Experimental Results

The thesis of this paper and the hypothesis for our experiments is that the analysis of past experiences can aid in the diagnostic process. In particular, CBR can be used to effectively validate or critique a diagnostic decision resulting from an imperfect system model. Testing the effectiveness of the hybrid approach to diagnosis requires an initial casebase of diagnostic cases. Such a casebase could be created with the normal running of the system. For testing purposes, however, a simulator was constructed for the Fairing Servicing Subsystem to automatically generate sensor data and the corresponding sensor function boolean values, representing single faults. This simulator was used to generate initial casebases and to simulate test cases for evaluating the CBR component of the system.

Some simplifying assumptions were made in carrying out the two experiments. First, we assumed that all failure modes for components are equally probable. Although this does not reflect reality, it does present - to some degree - a worst case scenario. Secondly, we assume that the sensor information is accurate, i.e. the sensors are not included among the components that may fail.

The hybrid approach described above is implemented as an interactive process where the human operator explores the casebase indexed by the structural decomposition of the device. To test our approach, we have implemented a non-interactive version of the same program that retrieves all the cases stored under the potential diagnoses produced by the structural isolation. We progressively degrade the model, starting from a model that produces perfect diagnosis performance, and moving towards models that contain errors. This degradation process takes place in the sensor functions, which are randomly selected and failed. A failed sensor function returns an incorrect result, falsely describing the state of the device. The model for the Fairing Servicing Subsystem contains 19 sensor functions, describing 15 failure patterns (conjunctions of sensor functions) for 100 components of 8 different component types, e.g. motors (4 failure patterns), cables (2 failure patterns). The following experiments involved running 77 simulations of faults occurring in two modules of the Fairing Servicing Subsystem containing 36 components and 7 sensors.

Experiment 1

The first experiment's goal is to measure the diagnostic performance degradation in relation to model degradation and to show the effectiveness of the indexing mechanism for CBR. The hypothesis is that the diagnostic performance becomes worse as the model degrades. Another goal of this experiment is to show how many potential diagnoses the CBR system contributes to the final result of the integrated approach.

Method. The simulations are run twice. The first pass does not use a casebase but generates one. The second pass uses the casebase containing 77 cases. A casebase containing the same cases as the ones that are currently being run is a not a good test for measuring the performance of the CBR system. However, the goal of this experiment is not to measure diagnostic performance itself but rather its degradation.

Results. Figure 2.a shows that the degradation is approximately linear in the number of failed sensor functions. Figure 2.b shows the number of potential diagnoses produced in the same experiment. In this experiment, all retrieved cases are considered similar enough to the current situation. Figure 2.b shows the influence of the CBR system in generating new potential diagnosis. The number of potential diagnoses produced by both the hybrid method and the single model-based method are linear in the number of failed sensor functions.

The linearity of the degradation in Figure 2.a is the result of a balanced use of sensor functions in the failure patterns. Failure patterns consist of **3** to **6** sensor functions, possibly negated. Figure 2.b shows the number of retrieved cases, when the casebase contains

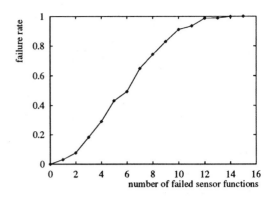

Figure 2.a) Performance Degradation from Model Degradation

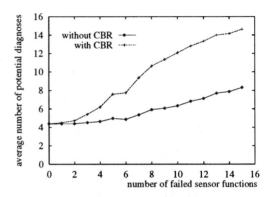

Figure 2.b) Number of Potential Diagnoses

all the cases that were generated by the simulations. This gives an indication of the computational cost of the CBR system. This cost increases linearly when the quality of the model decreases. Although significant, this cost remains within reasonable bounds. This experiment also shows the effectiveness of the retrieval process. Regardless of the quality of the model, the appropriate cases were always retrieved. Intuitively, Figures 2.a and 2.b correspond to the intuition that the worse the device model is, the less accurate it is and the more experience is required to compensate for erroneous knowledge.

Experiment 2

The hypothesis of the second experiment is that the hybrid approach, including a CBR component performs better than a the model-based approach alone, for a small additional computational cost and without over-

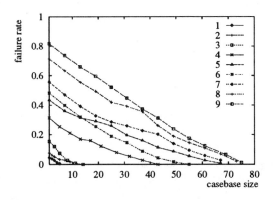

Figure 3.a) Failure Rates

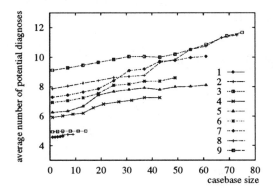

Figure 3.b) Average Number of Potential Diagnoses

whelming the operators with potential diagnoses. It also aims at showing the influence of experience (cases) on the diagnostic performance. Experiment 1 already showed that the number of retrieved matches remains within reasonable bounds.

Method. In this experiment, casebases of different sizes are used for different numbers of failed sensor functions. For each combination of failed sensor functions, and for each casebase size, the 77 simulations are run on 10 different casebases. The matching algorithm described above is used to measure the similarity and the plausibility of the retrieved matches compared to the current diagnostic situation.

Results. The horizontal axes in Figure 3.a and 3.b represent the size of the casebase. Each curve represents a number of failed sensor functions. Figure 3.a shows that the improvement is linear in the size of the casebase. Figure 3.b shows that the average number of potential diagnoses increases only marginally with the size of the casebase. This experiment shows that the

performance of the hybrid diagnostic system increases linearly with the size of the casebase. The matching algorithm is itself generic and does not use any specific knowledge about the Fairing Servicing Subsystem. We therefore believe that it could be applied, with similar results, to the Reactor Building Ventilation System, or to any other complex device. Figure 3.b illustrates its effectiveness in pruning the cases that are irrelevant to the current situation. The number of potential diagnoses is almost constant as the casebase grows larger. Figure 3.a shows the failure rates decreasing linearly with the increasing size of the casebase. Better results could be achieved if the retrieval and the matching algorithms allowed for generalizations over component types. For example, most motors in the Fairing Servicing Subsystem share the same installation configuration and are monitored by similar sensors. Therefore cases related to one motor could be adapted to other motors in the device.

Closing Remarks on the Experiments

There are other possible ways to test this approach. The size of the models could be decreased by removing sensor functions. This simulates a decreasing number of sensors as opposed to a decreasing number of working sensors. This would show how important the model, even a partially incorrect model, is in the indexing. This approach could also be tested for incorrect failure patterns, or for erroneous structural knowledge. Our experience shows that these types of errors are typically easier to detect than errors in sensor functions.

Discussion

This paper presents a hybrid approach to diagnosis. It is based on a structural isolation search for potential diagnoses, enhanced by contributions from an integrated CBR component that assists the human operators in their final decision by using both successful and failure experiences. Such assistance is useful because the structural decomposition and the pruning rules associated with it are not guaranteed to be either consistent or complete and because human operators might not consider all the cues that are available to them.

Compared to an all-model-based approach to diagnosis, a hybrid approach addresses a number of problems. CBR allows the system to improve on the model built by humans. It overrules some mistakes that can be made in the design and implementation of this model. This is accomplished in a computationally inexpensive way, by using the decomposition tree as the basis for indexing previous cases. This original indexing method allows for an accurate and effective retrieval of relevant previous cases and avoids the problems of computational complexity encountered by other hybrid CBR systems in their retrieval and matching tasks (e.g. [15, 19]).

Experimental results show that the performance gain brought by the CBR system is significant. The CBR system improves the failure rate of partially incorrect models without overwhelming the operator with potential diagnoses. These results show that considering CBR as a way to improve an existing search method is a valid approach. This solidifies the results presented in [10]. The power of Golding and Rosenbloom's method as well as ours comes mostly from the indexing schema provided by the other problem-solving algorithm. Cases are indexed by relevant pieces of knowledge, organized in a hierarchical manner. The other problem-solving algorithm (be it rules triggering or a structural isolation process) can be seen as an indexing schema that extensively uses background knowledge. Both systems can therefore be seen as constrained instances of explanation-based indexing [1].

The CBR component does not depend on the device nor on which type of model is used. The structural decomposition of the device is device dependent. Its completion or correction by the CBR component is not. In fact, this hybrid approach can also be incorporated in other model-based approaches to diagnosis, including first-principle approaches based on correct behavior device models. This is a definite advantage, both in the framework of the genericity of the ADMS as a diagnostic system and for the applicability of CBR as a complement to other problem-solving techniques. The Reactor Building Ventilation System's model is an acyclic digraph (instead of a tree for the Fairing Servicing Subsystem). We have found that both the indexing and the matching apply to the Fairing Servicing Subsystem are directly applicable to the Reactor Building Ventilation System's model, which also includes the possibility of failing sensors.

It is clear that this approach is applicable to a whole range of searching and problem-solving methods. An interesting extension to our work would be to apply this hybrid approach to other domains such as natural language parsing and understanding, planning, or game playing, where hierarchies and context information expressed by context functions, equivalent to the sensor functions, are readily available.

Cases could also effectively be used in diagnosing multiple faults. We have not tested this aspect of our approach yet. If a fault is confirmed by a case X, another case Y could also be retrieved that has case X's

final diagnosis as one of its potential, or final diagnoses. The final diagnosis of Y could be examined as a potential diagnosis for the current situation, potentially uncovering a double fault situation. Multiple faults could therefore be diagnosed using the same hybrid approach with no added complexity.

This paper describes how a hybrid model-based/case-based methodology permits the relaxation of the completeness and consistency constraints imposed by the model-based diagnosis approach, and helps overcome shortcomings in human capabilities. We show how CBR can guide the human operator in the last phase of the diagnostic process, using previous experiences indexed by the state of the device. The paper also contributes to the area of CBR, by showing that CBR is well suited to applications where it is combined with an already existing, but imperfect, method or paradigm for problem-solving.

References

[1] R. Barletta and W. Mark. Explanation-based indexing of cases. In *Proceedings of the 6th National Conference on Artificial Intelligence*, pages 541–546, 1988.

[2] L. Console, L. Portinale, and D. Theseider Dupre. Focusing abductive diagnosis. *AI Communications*, 4(2/3):88–97, 1991.

[3] J. de Kleer. Diagnosis with behavioral modes. In *Proceedings of the 11th International Joint Conference on Artificial Intelligence*, pages 1324–1330, Detroit, 1989.

[4] J. de Kleer. Using crude probability estimates to guide diagnosis. *Artificial Intelligence*, 45(3):381–391, 1990.

[5] J. de Kleer. Optimizing focusing model-based diagnosis. In *Proceedings of the 3rd International Workshop on Principles of Diagnosis*, pages 26–29, Rosario, Washington, 1992.

[6] M. P. Féret and J. I. Glasgow. Generic diagnosis for mechanical devices. In *Proceedings of the 6th International Conference on Applications of Artificial Intelligence in Engineering*, pages 753–768, Oxford, UK, July 1991. Computational Mechanics Publications, Elsevier Applied Science.

[7] M. P. Féret and J. I. Glasgow. Case-based reasoning in model-based diagnosis. In *Proceedings of the 7th International Conference on Applications of*

Artificial Intelligence in Engineering, pages 679–692, Waterloo, Canada, July 1992. Computational Mechanics Publications, Elsevier Applied Science.

[8] M. P. Féret, J. I. Glasgow, D. Lawson, and M. A. Jenkins. An architecture for real-time diagnosis systems. In *Proceedings of the Third International Conference on Industrial and Engineering Applications and Expert Systems*, pages 9–15, Charleston, SC, July 1990.

[9] G. Friedrich. Theory diagnoses: A concise characterization of faulty systems. In *Proceedings of the 3rd International Workshop on Principles of Diagnosis*, pages 117–131, Rosario, Washington, 1992.

[10] A. R. Golding and P. S. Rosenbloom. Improving rule-based systems through case-based reasoning. In *Proceedings of the 9th National Conference on Artificial Intelligence*, pages 22–27. AAAI Press, MIT Press, July 1991.

[11] F. Gomez and B. Chandrasekaran. Knowledge organization and distribution for medical diagnosis. *IEEE Transactions on Systems, Mans and Cybernetics*, 11:34–42, 1981.

[12] T. Govindaraj and Y. L. Su. A model of fault diagnosis performance of expert marine engineers. *International Journal on Man Machine Studies*, 29:1–20, 1988.

[13] K. J. Hammond. Chef. In Riesbeck C. and Schank R., editors, *Inside Case-Based Reasoning*. Lawrence Erlbaum Associates, 1989.

[14] J. L. Kolodner. Improving human decision making through case-based decision aiding. *AI Magazine*, 12(2):52–68, 1991.

[15] P. Koton. Reasoning about evidence in causal explanations. In *Proceedings of AAAI-88*, pages 256–261, 1988.

[16] T. P. Martin, J. I. Glasgow, M. P. Féret, and T. G. Kelley. A knowledge-based system for fault diagnosis in real-time engineering applications. In *Proceedings of DEXA'91 - International Conference on Database and Expert System Applications*, pages 287–292, Berlin, Germany, August 1991.

[17] R. Milne. Strategies for diagnosis. *IEEE Transactions on Systems, Man, and Cybernetics*, SMC-17(3):333–339, 1987.

[18] I. Mozetic. Reduction of diagnostic complexity through model abstractions. In *Proceedings of the 1rst International Workshop on Principles of Diagnosis*, pages 102–111, Stanford, CA, July 1990, 1990.

[19] S. A. Rajamoney and H. Y. Lee. Prototype-based reasoning: An integrated approach to solving large novel problems. In *Proceedings of the 9th National Conference on Artificial Intelligence*, pages 34–39, Anaheim, CA, July 1991. AAAI Press, MIT Press.

[20] M. Redmond. Distributed cases for case-based reasoning; facilitating use of multiple cases. In *Proceedings of the National Conference on Artificial Intelligence (AAAI-90)*, Boston, MA, 1990. Morgan Kaufmann.

[21] J.A. Reggia, D.S. Nau, and P.Y. Wang. A formal model of diagnosis inference. *Information Sciences*, 37:227–256, 1985.

[22] R. Rymon. A final determination of the complexity of current formulations of model-based diagnosis (or maybe not final). Technical Report MS-CIS-91-13, LINC LAB 194, Department of Computer and Information Science, School of Engineering and Applied Science, University of Pennsylvania, Philadelphia, PA 19104-6389, 1991.

[23] V. Sembugamoorthy and B. Chandrasekaran. Functional representation of devices and compilation of diagnostic problem-solving systems. Technical Report Tech. Rep., Ohio State University, Colombus, Ohio, 1985.

[24] S. Slade. Case-based reasoning: A research paradigm. *AI Magazine*, 12(1):42–55, 1991.

[25] P. Slovic, B. Fischoff, and S. Lichtenstein. Behavorial decision theory. *Annual Review of Psychology*, 28:1–39, 1977.

[26] W. C. Yoon and J. M. Hammer. Deep-reasoning fault diagnosis: An aid and a model. *IEEE Transactions on Systems, Man, and Cybernetics*, 18(4):659–675, 1988.

An Epistemology for Clinically Significant Trends

Ira J. Haimowitz

MIT Laboratory for Computer Science
545 Technology Square, Room 414
Cambridge, MA 02139
ira@medg.lcs.mit.edu

Isaac S. Kohane

Children's Hospital, Harvard Medical School
300 Longwood Avenue
Boston, MA 02115
gasp@medg.lcs.mit.edu

Abstract

We have written a computer program called $TrenD_x$ for automated trend detection during process monitoring. The program uses a representation called *trend templates* that define disorders as typical patterns of relevant variables. These patterns consist of a partially ordered set of temporal intervals with uncertain endpoints. Attached to each temporal interval are value constraints on real-valued functions of measurable parameters. As $TrenD_x$ receives measured data of the monitored process, the program creates hypotheses of how the process has varied over time.

We introduce the importance of a distinct trend representation in knowledge-based systems. Then we demonstrate how trend templates may represent trends that occur at fixed times or at unknown times, and their utility for domains that are quantitatively both poorly and well understood. Finally we present experimental results of $TrenD_x$ diagnosing pediatric growth disorders from heights, weights, bone ages, and pubertal data of twenty patients seen at Boston Children's Hospital. [1]

Introduction

Our work is part of the growing body of artificial intelligence (AI) research on diagnostic process monitoring. Specifically, we have written a program that automatically detects *trends:* sequences of time-ordered data that together are clinically significant. These trends may be multivariate, and may consist of several distinct phases. Our trend detection program, called $TrenD_x$, can classify the trend and give a chronology of when the data was in each phase.

In another paper [Haimowitz and Kohane 1993] we defined our *trend template* representation of clinically significant trends, and illustrated our trend diagnosis program $TrenD_x$ on a single pediatric growth patient. In this paper we demonstrate how trend templates may represent trends that occur at fixed times or at unknown times. We argue for the utility of trend templates for domains that are

quantitatively poorly or well understood. Then we present experimental results of a clinical trial where $TrenD_x$ diagnosed pediatric growth patterns of twenty patients at Boston Children's Hospital.

Need for Trend Representation

Diagnostic knowledge based systems are programs that can reason abductively from symptoms in a patient to the disorders that cause them. However, the vast majority of these programs treat symptoms as fixed in time. These symptoms may be boolean, as in "chest pain = true" or one of a series of qualitative categories for a measurable parameter, as in "serum sodium = low."

Such a stationary representation of findings is insufficient for monitoring a process (such as a patient) being monitored over any period of time. A human expert monitoring a process has notions of *trends:* how the measured parameters should vary over time under the current hpothesis.When the measurements vary from the expected, that expert may consider an alternative diagnosis. For a computer program to behave similarly, it must represent the expected trend.

Merely checking laboratory values against a reference interval can lead to ignoring a trend where the parameter is markedly decreasing, increasing, or periodically fluctuating within that range. A prime example of this comes from the domain of pediatric growth, where heights and weights are measured at least once a year and plotted on growth charts of standard deviations (SDs) for each measurement by age of United States children [Hamil et. al 1979]. A height that decreases from the mean for some age to -1 SD two years later is still within a range of "normal" yet may strongly indicate either an endocrinological or nutritional disorder.

In domains like pediatric growth where one cannot construct a predictive causal model, experts still demonstrate knowledge of how measured parameters vary under different diagnoses. This is the motivation behind our representation for trends called trend templates and our trend diagnosis program $TrenD_x$ that uses them.

---

1. This work has been supported (in part) by NIH grant R01 LM 04493, NICHHD 5T32 HD07277-9, and by a U.S. Office of Naval Research Graduate Fellowship.

Trend Templates

A *trend template* is an archetypal pattern of data variation in a process disorder. Each trend template has a *temporal component* and a *value component*. The temporal component includes *landmark points* and *intervals*. Landmark points represent significant events in the lifetime of the monitored process. They may be uncertain in time, and so are represented with time ranges *(min max)* expressing the minimal and maximal times between them. Intervals represent periods of the process that are significant for diagnosis or therapy. Intervals consist of begin and end points whose times are declared either as:

* offsets of the form *(min max)* from a landmark point, or
* offsets of the form *(min max)* from another interval's begin or end point.

TrenD$_x$ represents time using the Temporal Utility Package (TUP) of [Kohane 1987]. TUP is a temporal reasoning program with both time points and time intervals; interval structures include a begin point and an end point.

The value component of a trend template is a set of *value constraints* bound to each interval. Each value constraint states that some function of a set of measurable parameters must fall within a certain range. Thus each value constraint is an expression of the form

$$m \le f(D) \le M \qquad \text{(EQ 1)}$$

where f is some real valued function defined on patient data, m is a minimum (possibly $-\infty$), and M is a maximum (possibly $+\infty$). In the diagnostic program TrenD$_x$, the function f is evaluated on the set D of multi-parameter data currently assigned to that interval and the result is compared to the bounds m and M.

Another aspect of trend templates models failure-driven triggering of alternate diagnoses. Trend templates include a function *TRIGGER* that computes a set of alternative trend templates for each value constraint and the direction of failure.

$$TRIGGER: vc \times \{low, high\} \rightarrow \{TT_1, TT_2, ..., TT_k\} \qquad \text{(EQ 2)}$$

This function prunes the diagnosis space by localizing small sets of alternate diagnoses to specific temporal intervals and failures.

Trend Template for Normal Growth

An example trend template (Figure 1) expresses the constraints of male average prepubertal growth. Time constraints, expressed in the years of age of a child, are drawn horizontally, and value constraints on real variables are drawn vertically. There are three landmark points: *Birth* occurs at age zero, *Puberty Onset* occurs between ages ten and fifteen years, and *Growth Stops* occurs between ages seventeen and nineteen years. The temporal

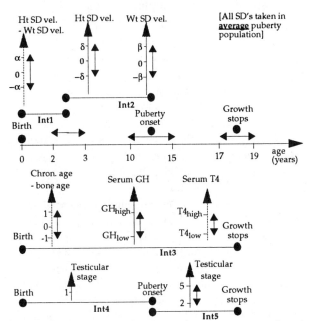

Figure 1 Trend template for male average pre-pubertal growth. Ht is height, Wt is weight, GH is growth hormone, T4 is thyroid hormone, and SD is standard deviation.

uncertainty in these points is depicted with horizontal arrows that span the possible time range.

This trend template contains five intervals. Interval Int1 denotes the time when height and weight standard deviations are established. Int1 begins at *Birth* and ends between ages two and three years. We encode that height and weight standard deviations (SDs) vary in the same way by constraining the difference between the average velocity of height SDs and the average velocity of weight SDs to be within a small number α of zero. Interval Int2 represents the period of the boy staying in his established height and weight channels. Int2 begins at the endpoint of Int1, and Int2 ends at *Puberty Onset*. There are two value constraints: both the average velocities of height SDs and that of weight SDs are close to zero. Because Int1 and Int2 represent consecutive processes of growth, these intervals meet, and we represent the end point of Int1 equal in time to the begin point of Int2. Intervals Int3, Int4 and Int5 constrain other patient parameters: serum growth hormone (GH), serum thyroid hormone (T4), bone age, testicular stage, and other screening tests.

Trigger sets are bound to value constraints of several intervals. For example, if the height SD constraint of Int2 fails low, then the trend template for delayed puberty (termed as "constitutional delay") is suggested. If the constraint fails high, then the trend template for advanced puberty is suggested.

Diagnosis with Trend Templates: TrenD$_x$

The program TrenD$_x$ diagnoses trends by matching process data to trend templates. A TrenD$_x$ hypothesis includes a trend template, an assignment of patient data to the intervals of the template, and a set of temporal assertions that further constrain the endpoints of the template's intervals. TrenD$_x$ initializes a hypothesis for a patient by *anchoring* a landmark point of the trend template as equal to some time in the life of the process. For example, TrenD$_x$ assigns a patient the average normal growth hypothesis by anchoring the *Birth* landmark point of the trend template to the birth date of the patient.

The algorithms for matching a datum *d* to a hypothesis *hyp* are detailed in [Haimowitz and Kohane 1993]. In brief, if *d* meets all value constraints on all intervals that must temporally include that datum, then *hyp* is retained. TrenD$_x$ assigns *d* to all intervals that may contain it. If there are multiple intervals that may include the datum, the program branches to consider distinct data assignments for that same trend template. Because each interval represents a significant process stage, the distinct assignments in fact correspond to alternate hypotheses.

If *d* fails some value constraint on an interval to which it must temporally belong, then *hyp* is removed. The failed value constraint produces a set S of potential new disorders to trigger. The disorders in S are triggered if and only if there exist no other active hypotheses with trend template equal to that of *hyp*. Thus as long as there is some data assignment that is valid for a disorder, TrenD$_x$ does not trigger another disorder.

TrenD$_x$ activates new disorders with a generate and test paradigm. TrenD$_x$ generates the set S of trend templates with the function *TRIGGER*, and tests those templates for matching the patient data. A triggered template becomes an active hypothesis if and only if it matches the patient data.

As TrenD$_x$ monitors a patient, the number of hypotheses increases exponentially in the number N of patient data that may be assigned to multiple intervals of the same trend template. N will be large only if the sampling period of the data is small relative to the uncertainty in the time of interval endpoints. In our experience testing pediatric growth patients with TrenD$_x$ we have always had N ≤ 2. Furthermore hypotheses have been repeatedly pruned when later data fail some value constraint of a hypothesis with a spurious data assignment.

Expressiveness of Trend Templates

Trend templates are capable of representing trends whether or not the onset time is known beforehand. They may also represent trends in areas of either scant or detailed quantitative models.

Intervening Trends

Thus far we have illustrated a trend template for a pattern where one knows the onset time (birth) of the trend beforehand. Statistical curve-fitting models of pediatric growth [Thissen and Bock 1990] are limited in describing only patterns beginning from birth. However, some trends in process monitoring can appear at any unanticipated time, perhaps due to an unexpected event or as the result of a stimulus not modeled. We call these *intervening trends*. In medicine intervening trends often signify a new disorder.

Pediatric growth disorders marked by intervening trends include nutritional disorders such as malnutrition or obesity. Also included are endocrine disorders such as *acquired growth hormone deficiency*. In this disorder serum growth hormone levels unexpectedly decrease, with a consequent decrease in rate of bone elongation and height. On the growth chart, the child loses height standard deviations, even on standards for patients with delayed puberty. The child also appears heavier over time, which can be detected with an by increase in the body mass index (BMI), calculated as weight/(height)^2, expressed in kg/m^2.

We represent an intervening trend such as in acquired growth hormone deficiency with a trend template that includes a landmark point for the uncertain onset time. Anchoring this landmark point to the patient history requires additional reasoning. TrenD$_x$ must shift the landmark point back in time until all subsequent patient data meets the constraints of the intervening trend's template. Note that because intervening trends represent unanticipated faults, the corresponding template is triggered due to the failure of a value constraint of another hypothesis. TrenD$_x$ must anchor the landmark point (onset time) of the intervening trend's template earlier in time than the data failing the value constraint.

Below is the trend template for acquired growth hormone deficiency:

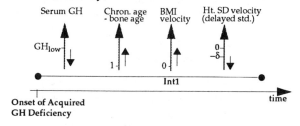

Figure 2   Trend template for acquired growth hormone deficiency. BMI is body mass index.

The landmark point for this trend template denotes the onset time of the growth hormone deficiency. Int1 is an interval beginning at that time and contains four value constraints: serum GH is less than the lower threshold mentioned in Figure 1, bone age is at least one year behind chronological age. Also, height SDs are falling significantly, even compared to the standards for children with delayed puberty, and the velocity of body mass index is greater than zero.

We are just beginning to incorporate trend templates for intervening trends into $TrenD_x$. We plan to have the template for acquired GH deficiency triggered for three failed value constraints for the constitutional delay template: if the height SDs are falling too fast, if the weight SDs are falling too fast, or if the bone age is delayed more than 4 years behind chronological age. In this way $TrenD_x$ diagnoses a growth patient in the sequence: average growth, constitutional delay, growth hormone deficiency. This diagnosis sequence is familiar to expert pediatric endocrinologists.

Trends with Value Ranges Over Time

As noted in (EQ 1), value constraints specify that real-valued functions evaluated on the data within a certain time interval must stay between minimum and maximum bounds. This form was chosen to correspond to those constraints on laboratory values that make up much of the working knowledge of monitoring medical patient data.

For example, in the section on "Diagnostic Procedures in Liver Disease" in *Harrison's Principles of Internal Medicine* [Podolsky and Isselbacher 1991] describe laboratory results of patients with liver disorders. Of primary importance are the hepatic enzymes that aid decomposing and rebuilding of amino acids. One of these is aspartate transferase (AST). The authors note:

> in the patient with massive hepatic necrosis, there may be marked elevations [perhaps over 500 IU] in the early phase (i.e., 24 to 48 hours) , but by the time the patient is tested 3 to 5 days later the levels may be in the range of 200 to 350 IU [page 1309].

The levels of AST are ill-specified in both time and value primarily because the text aims to summarize a pattern for all hepatic necrosis patients.

We represent the above description as a trend template as shown below. Note that this is an intervening trend.

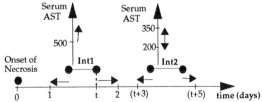

Figure 3 Trend template for serum AST pattern in hepatic necrosis. The time of the endpoint of Int2 is labeled t.

The lone landmark point for this template is the onset time of hepatic necrosis. Interval Int1 represents the period where AST levels are above 500 IU. Int1 begins 1 day or later after the onset of necrosis and ends (at time *t*) 2 days or sooner after the onset of necrosis. Interval Int2 represents the period where AST levels are between 200 and 350 IU. Int2 begins 3 days or later after *t* and Int2 ends 5 days or sooner after *t*.

Trends with Known Quantitative Models

Although value constraints were originally intended to represent constraints in highly uncertain areas like hepatic necrosis above, they may also be used in representing processes whose quantitative processes are better known. A value constraint can specify, for example, acceptable bounds for process data to match a time series model. Consider expressing the constraint that height standard deviations vary minimally from one point to the next as a first order autoregressive (AR(1)) model:

$$H_t = H_{t-1} + \varepsilon_t \qquad \text{(EQ 3)}$$

where H_t is a random-variable for the height SD at time t, and ε_t is a white noise random variable; $\varepsilon_t \sim N(0, \sigma)$. We can equivalently recast the AR(1) model of (EQ 3) as stating that the first difference of height SDs is a white noise variable:

$$H_t - H_{t-1} = \varepsilon_t \sim N(0, \sigma) \qquad \text{(EQ 4)}$$

When using this AR(1) model for trend detection of patient data, one must specify a confidence interval for believing that the actual patent data does conform to this model. For example, if we require a 95% confidence interval to establish a match, the value constraint is:

$$-1.96 \times \sigma \le f(D) = (H_t - H_{t-1}) \le 1.96 \times \sigma \qquad \text{(EQ 5)}$$

This is quite similar to the height SD value constraint on Int2 of Figure 1, with the exception that the value constraint in the figure divides f(D) by the time between the two data, since in general we can not assume that the height data are equally spaced as autoregressive models do.

One can similarly represent as a value constraint that a ceratin parameter P_t must be close to a curve model function g(t) over some time interval by using the value constraint:

$$-\delta \le f(D) = (P_t - g(t)) \le \delta \qquad \text{(EQ 6)}$$

The positive number δ is a noise threshold that may be chosen as in the previous equation. Examples of potentially useful g(t) are polynomials, exponentials, and trigonometric functions.

Clinical Trial with TrenD$_x$

Methods

We conducted a pilot clinical trial of TrenD$_x$ to evaluate its performance and to determine the weakness of the current representation and knowledge engineering. Data sets on 30 patients seen at the Division of Endocrinology at Children's Hospital were retrieved from the Clinician's Workstation (CWS), an on-line charting system [McCallie et. al. 1990]. The data sets included height, weight, sexual staging and bone age measurements. The patients were selected by filtering the problem list associated with each patient record in the CWS. Since this was an exploratory experiment rather than a rigorous test of efficacy, we specifically selected those problems and patient types for which we had engineered trend templates, as well as growth hormone deficiency, to explore how best to implement templates for intervening trends.

The first ten patient data sets were used as training sets. As errors in the performance of TrenD$_x$ on the training set were identified, we modified the trend templates by changing time ranges of the interval end points, by changing bounds of the value constraints, and by adding new intervals with new value constraints.

The remaining twenty data sets were used as test cases. These included patients with growth hormone deficiency, constitutional delay, average tempo of development, and early puberty. The data was read by TrenD$_x$ in chronological order. TrenD$_x$ recorded all the diagnoses and the age of the patient when they were considered or rejected. At the time of this trial, we had not developed trend templates for intervening trends like that for acquired growth hormone deficiency. All constitutional delay trend templates which TrenD$_x$ eventually rejected for any of these reasons:

1. the velocity of the height SD was too low,

2. the velocity of the weight SD was too low, or

3. the bone age was too far behind chronological age

were scored as diagnosing growth hormone deficiency when the constitutional delay trend template was ruled out.

Concurrently, a panel of three expert endocrinologists was given the same data sets and the task of diagnosing each patient. The endocrinologists were given the benefit of seeing the full data set at once rather than a point at a time. They too were required to judge the earliest age at which they could make their diagnosis. Note that this level of growth chart scrutiny is unusual in a busy general pediatric office. Several of the important contextual clues to the diagnosis that are usually gleaned from the patient history or laboratory results (e.g. results of a serum growth hormone test) were not available to either the clinicians or TrenD$_x$. Given the limitations of the data set, even in those cases where the panel consensus was different from the diagnosis stored in the CWS we took the panel consensus as the expert standard for a "correct" diagnosis.

Results

10 of the 20 patients were diagnosed by the panel as having one of these six disorders: normal growth, short stature, constitutional delay, early puberty, precocious puberty, and obesity. Of these TrenD$_x$ diagnosed 9 of 10 correctly. In 8 of the 9 correct diagnoses the clinicians reached the diagnoses at the same time as TrenD$_x$; in one case the clinicians were earlier. In the one case misdiagnosed by TrenD$_x$ the panel diagnosed constitutional delay, and the program diagnosed average prepubertal growth. This occurred because the patient's velocity of height standard deviation never crossed the lower bound of the value constraint on the average prepubertal growth trend template ($-\delta$ in Figure 1). We can correct this error by increasing the value of this lower bound.

The other 10 patients were diagnosed by the panel as having growth hormone deficiency. Of these, TrenD$_x$ diagnosed 5 of 10 correctly. In 3 of the 5 misdiagnosed cases a constraint on proportionality (such as body mass index) could have been used to correctly trigger growth hormone deficiency. For instance, TrenD$_x$ misdiagnosed one case of growth hormone deficiency as having constitutional delay. In this case, the clinicians noted that the weight and height did stay within a broad channel of their standard deviation. However they also noted that the weight standard deviation of the patient was creeping upwards at the same time that her height standard deviation was creeping downwards. As we had not encoded in the constitutional delay template any constraints on the proportionality of height and weight after infancy, TrenD$_x$ did not notice these subtle but significant opposing trends in height and weight. From this we have learned to add a constraint on proportionality to the constitutional delay template and to the acquired growth hormone deficiency template.

The results of this trial were encouraging in that they demonstrated that TrenD$_x$ could diagnose a few trends. However, the number of test cases, and the nature of the cases do not permit us to make any conclusions regarding the performance of TrenD$_x$ in general pediatric practice. We are planning larger trials in one of the primary care clinics at Children's Hospital to rigorously quantify the sensitivity and specificity of TrenD$_x$ as compared to clinicians.

Related Literature

We find that our pattern matching approach to trend detection fills a new niche in the work on monitoring from time-ordered data. Several other projects may have results complementary to ours.

Traditional temporal logics [Allen 1984] have been used to encode the truth of logic propositions over time intervals. TrenD$_x$ extends this research by representing constraints on primary numerical data, as well as representing an entire process as phases.

Much of the work in diagnostic process monitoring has been in combined qualitative and quantitative simulations [Uckun and Dawant 1992]. This approach requires a domain where one can construct a causal model of the monitored process while TrenD$_x$ does not. Also, trend templates may supplement these qualitative simulation programs by indicating which sets of future qualitative states correspond to the same trend hypothesis. This may help to reduce branching of qualitative behaviors and thus improve monitoring efficiency.

Temporal abstraction programs [Shahar 1992] accept time-stamped laboratory data and create temporal intervals over which a parameter has attained a significant qualitative state (low, normal, markedly increasing, etc.). Unguided abstraction suffers in that it has very little context of what parameters are useful to abstract under a given hypothesis. For TrenD$_x$ this context is provided by the trend template of that hypothesis.

Conclusions and Future Work

A trend template represents a multi-variate trend in data from a monitored process (e.g. a medical patient) and incorporates both temporal and value uncertainty. A template may be anchored to specific dates on the calendar or to a specific patient age, or it may be offset from the onset time of an unexpected fault. Each interval of a trend template corresponds to a significant stage of the monitored process. Thus the constraints of a trend template may be more understandable to experts and knowledge engineers than differential equations or statistical curve-fitting models [Thissen and Bock 1990]. Among representations for disorders of monitored processes, the trend template is rare in requiring no pathophysiological model.

Our trend detection program TrenD$_x$ reached plausible diagnoses in most pediatric growth patients from a sample at Boston Children's Hospital. While these are promising results, we plan several epistemological improvements to make the program diagnose even more like an expert. Probabilistic bounds on value constraints would be useful for assigning numerical scores to the match of a datum to a template. Adding standard errors (due to measurement) on data values would make matching more flexible, and would allow more realistic projection of values over time [Dean and Kanazawa 1988].

We also plan improvements to the TrenD$_x$ diagnostic algorithms. The program should be able to ignore markedly aberrant data that do not fit a general trend. It should also be able to distinguish between competing hypotheses by ranking them. For two closely ranked disorders, TrenD$_x$ should request a laboratory test with high information content to distinguish between them, or suggest a waiting period after which the patient's data should differ under the two hypothesized disorders.

References

Allen, J. F. (1984). "Towards a General Theory of Action and Time." *Artificial Intelligence*, **23:**(2) 123-154.

Dean, T. and K. Kanazawa (1988). "Probabilistic Temporal Reasoning." *National Conference on Artificial Intelligence*, 524-528.

Haimowitz, I.J., and I. S. Kohane (1993). "Automated Trend Detection with Multiple Temporal Hypotheses." *International Joint Conference on Artificial Intelligence*, to appear.

Hamil, P. V. V., T. A. Drizd, C. L. Johnson, R. B. Reed, A. F. Roche and W. M. Moore (1979). "Physical Growth: National Center for Health Statistics Percentiles." *The American Journal of Clinical Nutrition*, **32**: 607-629

Kohane, I. S. (1987). *Temporal Reasoning in Medical Expert Systems*. MIT Laboratory for Computer Science technical report TR-389.

McCallie, D. P. Jr., D. M. Margulies, I. S. Kohane, R. Stalhut, and B. Bergeron (1990)."The Children's Hospital Workstation." *Symposium on Computer Applications in Medical Care*, 755-759.

Podolsky, D. K. and K. J. Isselbacher. (1991). "Diagnostic Procedures in Liver Disease." In *Harrison's Principles of Internal Medicine, Twelfth Edition*. McGraw Hill.

Shahar, Y., S. Tu and M. Musen (1992). "Knowledge Acquisition for Temporal Abstraction Mechanisms." *Knowledge Acquisition*, **1:**(4) 217-236.

Thissen, D. and R. D. Bock (1990). "Linear and Nonlinear Curve Fitting." *Statistical Methods in Longitudinal Research, Volume II: Time Series and Categorical Longitudinal Data*. Academic Press, Inc.

Uckun, S. and B.M. Dawant (1993). "Model-Based Reasoning in Intensive Care Monitoring, the YAQ Approach" *Artificial Intelligence in Medicine*, **5:**(1) 31-48.

Acknowledgments

Peter Szolovits, Mario Stefanelli, and Howard Shrobe have supplied valuable comments on this work. Doctors John Crigler, Samir Najjar, and Joseph Majzoub of Boston Children's Hospital Endocrinology Division kindly diagnosed the test cases. Khuram Faizan, Nadya Adjanee, and Phillip Le helped prepare the patient data for testing.

A Framework for Model-Based Repair

Ying Sun & Daniel S. Weld[*]
Department of Computer Science and Engineering, FR-35
University of Washington
Seattle, WA 98195
ysun, weld@cs.washington.edu

Abstract

We describe IRS, a program that combines partial-order planning with GDE-style, model-based diagnosis to achieve an integrated approach to repair. Our system makes three contributions to the field of diagnosis. First, we provide a unified treatment of both information-gathering and state-altering actions via the UWL representation language. Second, we describe a way to use part-replacement operations (in addition to probes) to gather diagnostic information. Finally, we define a cost function for decision making that accounts for both the eventual need to repair broken parts and the dependence of costs on the device state.

Introduction

Although researchers have investigated model-based diagnosis for many years, only recently has attention turned to what should, perhaps, have been the central question all along: repair. When field-replaceable parts contain multiple components, focusing on determining the exact component responsible for faulty behavior can be counterproductive, since the final probes may not distinguish between repair actions. Furthermore, most diagnosis research has assumed that all probes have the same cost, leading to diagnostic strategies guided solely by estimated information gains.

In this paper we argue that both of these problems are best addressed by integrating theories of perception and action. In other words, we claim that repair is best thought of as a marriage of diagnosis and planning. The planner needs to call diagnosis as a subroutine to determine which observations will best improve its incomplete information, and the diagnoser needs to call the planner to estimate the cost of observations that are not directly executable (*e.g.*, probing a location inside a closed cabinet). A rational approach to repair requires accounting for both the cost/benefit tradeoff of actions as well as the synergistic changes in device state that allow one action to facilitate others.

In this paper, we describe an integrated repair system called IRS[1], and discuss three important aspects of its operation.

- Fundamentally, there is no difference between actions that gather information (*i.e.*, probes) and actions that change the device state; they should be treated uniformly. This allows representation of actions that have both state-changing and information-gathering aspects. When estimating the cost of an action that is not directly executable, an agent should add the costs of the primitive actions in a plan that achieves the desired effect.

- The ability to replace parts and repeat observations provides new diagnostic opportunities, similar to those provided by test generation systems. Our integrated theory of action and observation allows a diagnostic agent to combine replacement and observation actions synergistically. A comprehensive utility model selects between strategies.

- When estimating the cost of an operation, it is crucial to consider the eventual cost of repairing broken parts, not just the cost of diagnosis.

The next section of the paper defines an action representation language that distinguishes between observations of and changes to the device state. Then we show how to extend GDE to handle diagnosis of devices with changing state using both traditional observations as well as replacement operations. We decompose our cost function into two parts: the cost of executing the substeps of the current operation, and the expected cost of future diagnosis and repair operations. We show

[*]This research was funded in part by National Science Foundation Grant IRI-8957302, Office of Naval Research Grant 90-J-1904, and a grant from the Xerox corporation. Our implementation is built on pieces of code that were written in part by Johan de Kleer, Denise Draper, Ken Forbus, Steve Hanks, and Scott Penberthy. In addition to those mentioned above, we benefited from conversations with and comments by Oren Etzioni, Walter Hamscher, Nick Kushmerick, Neal Lesh, Mark Shirley, and Mike Williamson.

[1]IRS stands for Integrated Repair System, but its concern with cost evokes images of another basis for the acronym.

how the UCPOP planner [Penberthy and Weld, 1992] can be used to calculate this cost function, and we illustrate our algorithm on two simple refrigerator [Althouse et al., 1992] examples. After discussing the implementation, we close with a discussion of related and future work.

Modeling Action and Change

The first step in creating a unified theory of repair is to select a generalized model of action that distinguishes between causal and information-gathering effects. For example, it is crucial to differentiate between an *observation* that the voltage of a node is zero and an action that *grounds* the node. Even though the agent knows the voltage is zero in both cases, the effects are very different. Traditional diagnosis systems do only the former, while most implemented planners handle only the latter; an integrated repair system needs both. Even though a whole AI research subfield is devoted to representations of action [McCarthy and Hayes, 1969], most existing theories do not meet our needs:

1. Ability to represent incomplete information.
2. Distinguish between observations (which increase information, but don't change the world state) and actions with causal effects.
3. Computationally tractable.

For example, although the STRIPS representation satisfies the last criterion, it assumes complete information and thus renders the notion of observation meaningless. [Moore, 1985] develops a first-order modal logic that codifies actions that supply an agent with information, and [Morgenstern, 1987] presents a more expressive language that allows actions to have knowledge preconditions, but neither researcher considers algorithms for generating plans using their models of action.

Our UWL representation [Etzioni et al., 1992] is perfectly suited to the needs of repair. An extension of STRIPS that handles incomplete information, UWL was originally designed to represent UNIX commands for a Softbot [Etzioni and Segal, 1992]. The novel aspects of the language include annotations to differentiate causal from observational effects and informational from causational goals, T, F, and U truth values, and run-time variables.

For example, one might write the goal or precondition of setting the voltage of V to 220 with (satisfy (value-of V 220)) while the goal of determining the current voltage at that probe point can be written as (findout (value-of V ?x)). Similarly, the effect of an action that grounds a node might be (cause (value-of V 0)) while a step that just observes the value without changing it would be written as (observe (value-of V !y)). In these examples, ?x denotes a plan-time variable whose value may be constrained during subsequent planning decisions [Stefik, 1981], but !y denotes a run-time variable that is

treated as an (unknown) constant by the planner and whose value is only established when the plan is executed. Abstractly, a UWL step schemata contains a step name, a set of preconditions, and a set of postconditions (with associated cost). Preconditions and goals are annotated with satisfy or findout; postconditions are annotated with cause and observe. Initial conditions are represented with a dummy step that has no preconditions and whose postconditions cause all propositions to take on some truth value, U in the case of incomplete information. Complete details and formal semantics are provided in [Etzioni et al., 1992].

To illustrate the use of UWL, we show a simplified version of part of our refrigerator domain theory. When the argument ?x of a measure step is an internal voltage, the probe cost is 5.[2] A measure step also causes the proposition (probed ?x) to be true and sets ?x to !v, a run-time variable whose value will be determined during plan execution.

```
(define-step (measure ?x)
  :when (and (satisfy (internal-voltage ?x))
             (satisfy (not (backplane-on))))
  :effect (and (cause (probed ?x))
               (observe (value-of ?x !v)))
  :cost 5)
```

Diagnosis with Changing State

As discussed in [Sun and Weld, 1992], a variety of architectures are possible for a repair agent. We choose to put a diagnostic reasoner at the top level with the planner as a subroutine. The diagnosis code maintains a model of the most probable modes of the device's components (candidate sets) and uses the planner to suggest useful action sequences. The most utile action is chosen, the device state and candidate sets are updated, and the process is repeated until the stop criterion is satisfied.

In the remainder of this section, we describe how this planner allows estimation of the costs of different operations in a manner that accounts for both the eventual repair need and the state-dependence. We illustrate our algorithm on two troubleshooting episodes with a domestic refrigerator [Althouse et al., 1992] whose schematic is shown in Figure 1.

Calculating Costs

Suppose that the refrigerator is in state S_1: the refrigerator door is closed, the backplane is attached, the refrigerator is located near the wall, and the power is on; the temperature inside the refrigerator is too warm yet the compressor is not running. In this example, it will turn out that the actual fault is the thermostat (which is stuck open), although IRS, of course, does not know this yet. Assuming that the power supply is

---

[2]Measuring the compressor status or other ?x might incur a different cost and have different preconditions.

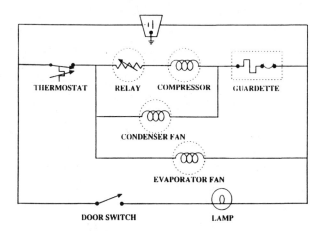

Figure 1: Wiring diagram for a domestic refrigerator

ok and every component has identical prior failure rate (pfr = 0.001), the most probable candidates are:

$$p([\text{thermostat1}]) = p([\text{relay1}]) = \\ p([\text{compressor1}]) = p([\text{guardette1}]) \simeq 0.25$$

To find the best operation O_i, various costs must be computed and compared. IRS employs a cost function using n-step lookahead:

$$C_{\text{total}}(O_i, \mathbf{S}, \mathbf{n}) = \quad C_{\text{exec}}(\mathcal{P}(\mathbf{S}, O_i)) + \qquad (1) \\ \sum_j p(\mathbf{S}_{ij}) EC(\mathbf{S}_{ij}, \mathbf{n} - 1)$$

The total cost of executing operation O_i in state $\mathbf{S}$ as estimated using n-step lookahead is equal to the cost of directly executing a plan that achieves the operation plus the weighted sum of the estimated expected costs of the resulting outcomes. $\mathcal{P}$ denotes the planning function that takes an initial state and goal conjunct (encoding a diagnosis or repair operation) as arguments and returns a plan (linearized sequence of primitive actions). Thus, $C_{\text{exec}}(\mathcal{P}(\mathbf{S}, O_i))$ denotes the cost of executing a plan that achieves an operation O_i (e.g., a probe or a replacement) given device state $\mathbf{S}$. The expected cost of future operations depends on the outcome of the current operation. For each possible state $\mathbf{S}_{ij}$ resulting from executing the plan for O_i, we compute the expected cost with $(\mathbf{n} - 1)$-step lookahead; the cost is then weighted by the probability of each outcome.

The following recursive function computes the expected cost of device state $\mathbf{S}$ with n-step lookahead:

$$EC(\mathbf{S}, \mathbf{n}) = 0 \qquad if\ Reliab(\mathbf{S}) > 1 - \epsilon \quad (2)$$
$$EC(\mathbf{S}, \mathbf{n}) = EC_{\text{repair}}(\mathbf{S}, C) + EC_{\text{diag}}(\mathbf{S}, C) \quad (3)$$
$$= \sum_{c \in C} p(c) C_{\text{exec}}(\mathcal{P}(\mathbf{S}, \Re(c))) + \\ EC_{\text{op}}(C)[-\sum_{c \in C} p(c) log(p(c))] \\ if\ \mathbf{n} = 0$$

$$EC(\mathbf{S}, \mathbf{n}) = \min_{O_i} C_{\text{total}}(O_i, \mathbf{S}, \mathbf{n}) \qquad (4) \\ if\ \mathbf{n} > 0$$

The function $Reliab(\mathbf{S})$ estimates the reliability of the device in state $\mathbf{S}$; repair terminates when the reliability is above the threshold $1 - \epsilon$. In the base case, when the lookahead step $\mathbf{n} = 0$, IRS estimates the remaining costs for candidate discrimination and part repair, and sums them. To estimate the repair cost, IRS iterates through the candidates and asks the planner for a plan that replaces all the parts containing a component in that candidate; the cost of that plan is weighted by the probability of the candidate. In the equation above, C denotes the set of candidates in state $\mathbf{S}$; $\Re(c)$ denotes the conjunctive goal formula that specifies "Replacement" of all the parts with a component in candidate c. The remaining repair cost also includes the cost of placing any removed but working parts back in the device. The remaining cost for partitioning the candidates is estimated using minimum entropy, where $EC_{\text{op}}(C)$ is the estimated average cost of such an operation (which may expand to multiple actions). When $\mathbf{n} > 0$, IRS estimates the cost to be the minimum cost of the possible operations at each step.

For example, to estimate the cost of probing the status of **condenser-fan1**, IRS calls the planner with the goal (**findout (value-of status-of-cond-fan1 !vcf)**) and the initial state of the refrigerator. In this case the planner returns[3] a plan, γ_1, with execution cost $C_{\text{exec}}(\gamma_1) = 4$:

```
(move-refrigerator-away-from-wall)  cost = 2
(measure status-of-condenser-fan1)  cost = 4
```

There are two possible outcomes of probing the status of **condenser-fan1**: with probability 0.5 **!vcf** is **on**, which results in most probable candidates $p([\text{relay1}]) = p([\text{compressor1}]) \simeq 0.5$; and with probability 0.5 **!vcf** is **off**, which results in most probable candidates $p([\text{thermostat1}]) = p([\text{guardette1}]) \simeq 0.5$. If 1-step lookahead is used, IRS arrives at the base case at this point.

When **condenser-fan1** is on, the estimated repair cost is 56:

```
(disconnect-power)                     cost = 1
(remove-backplane)                     cost = 20
(remove-part relay1/compressor1)       cost = 6
(place-part  relay2/compressor2)       cost = 6
(attach-backplane)                     cost = 20
(move-refrigerator-back-to-wall)       cost = 2
(connect-power)                        cost = 1
```

When **condenser-fan1** is **off**, the estimated repair cost is 18 if **thermostat1** turns out to be broken

---

[3]Space limitations preclude a complete description of our UCPOP partial-order planning algorithm, but it has several desirable attributes: sound, complete, and efficient. The details can be found in [Penberthy and Weld, 1992].

$(p \simeq 0.5)$ or 56 if `guardette1` turns out to be broken $(p \simeq 0.5)$, resulting in an average of 37. In both cases, the estimated cost to discriminate among the remaining candidates is $3.0 * [-(2 * 0.5 log 0.5)] = 3.0$, where 3.0 is the estimated average cost of such an operation. Therefore, the estimated total cost of diagnosis and repair starting with a probe to the status of `condenser-fan1` is $4 + (0.5 * 56 + 0.5 * 37) + 3.0 = 53.5$.

All other operations cost more at this point, so IRS chooses to probe the status of `condenser-fan1`.

The plan γ_1 is executed, putting the device into state S_2. `condenser-fan1` is observed to be **off**, causing the set of most probable candidates to be updated to:

$$p([\texttt{thermostat1}]) = p([\texttt{guardette1}]) \simeq 0.4995$$
$$p([\texttt{relay1, cond-fan1}]) \simeq 0.0005$$
$$p([\texttt{compressor1, cond-fan1}]) \simeq 0.0005$$

At this point, the costs of all the possible operations are computed again. In addition to considering the option of probing the status of `thermostat1` or `guardette1`, IRS also considers the possibility of *replacing* one of the components. In this case, replacing `thermostat1` happens to be the cheapest operation, with a plan, γ_2, of cost $C_{\text{exec}}(\gamma_2) = 16$ and estimated total cost $C_{\text{total}} = 52$:

(disconnect-power)	cost = 1
(open-refrigerator-door)	cost = 1
(remove-part thermostat1)	cost = 6
(place-part thermostat2)	cost = 6
(close-refrigerator-door)	cost = 1
(connect-power)	cost = 1

Executing this plan leads the device to state S_3.

Computing the costs of all the possible operations reveals that probing the status of `compressor1` (*i.e.*, checking if it is running) has the lowest total cost, so the corresponding plan, γ_3, is executed:

(measure status-of-compressor1)	cost = 1

The device state is updated to S_4. Observing `compressor1` running exonerates `guardette1` and yields the final candidate:

$$p([\texttt{thermostat1}]) \simeq 0.999$$

Since `thermostat1` has already been replaced, IRS simply moves the refrigerator back to the original location. At this point, the reliability of the device is 0.999, which is above the preset threshold 0.99, so we are done.

Table 1 summarizes the changing reliability of the device, the possible operations, their costs, and the candidates generated from the executed operations. (If a probe is executed, the value measured is shown after an arrow.) Note how IRS handles the state-dependent probe costs and takes into account the eventual repair cost throughout the diagnosis process.

A Different Example

Interestingly, if we adjust the prior failure rates of the components such that the failure rate of the `guardette` is three times higher than that of the other components, IRS would generate a different sequence of operations. After IRS measures `condenser-fan1` to be **off**, the most probable candidates are $p([\texttt{guardette1}]) \simeq 0.75$ and $p([\texttt{thermostat1}]) \simeq 0.25$. At this point, replacing `thermostat1` is the cheapest operation to execute because there is no need to remove the `backplane`, which is an expensive action. However, IRS realizes that other operations have cheaper total costs when taking into account projected diagnosis and repair operations. Due to the higher failure rate of the `guardette`, the `backplane` will probably need to be opened anyway. Thus, IRS correctly chooses to probe the status of `guardette1` before replacing any components as summarized in Table 2.

Representing Time-Varying State

Due to the inadequacy of the notion of minimal diagnoses, we implemented a diagnosis engine based on the *alibis* principle proposed by [Raiman, 1992]. As a complement to minimal conflicts, minimal alibis specify conditions such as a component must be working if n other components are known to be working. IRS works by incrementally generating minimal alibis, minimal conflicts, and the corresponding set of prime diagnoses.

In addition, we were forced to extend the normal component model to handle devices with changing state. Assumptions such as `ok(relay1)` are unchanged because of the non-intermittency assumption. However, IRS's structural primitives require a temporal component. We distinguish between the role a component plays in a device (*i.e.*, the slot it occupies) and the device instance itself. IRS's system description is written in terms of roles (*e.g.*, the `relay-function`, etc.) A separate set of axioms indicates what instances fill what roles at what times, *e.g.*, (`fills-role relay-function relay1` t_0). The assumptions that distinguish possible worlds involve instances, *e.g.*, `ok(relay1)`, and time tokens.

With these extensions, IRS can reason about swapping out a part, collecting evidence with a replacement part, swapping the original back in, collecting more evidence and so on. As a result, IRS can combine evidence collected at multiple times and involving different sets of component instances.

The IRS implementation has been run on the refrigerator example and several others, including a modified 3-inverter example [Sun and Weld, 1992]. It took approximately 2 minutes to run the refrigerator example on a SUN SPARC.

Related Work

Since IRS's behavior is to choose the operation with the maximum expected utility, it *could* be seen as a

most probable candidates	relia-bility	possible operations	exec cost	total cost	operation executed
p([thermostat1]) $\simeq$ .25 p([relay1]) $\simeq$ .25 p([compressor1]) $\simeq$ .25 p([guardette1]) $\simeq$ .25	0	probe cond-fan1-status probe relay1-status probe guardette1-status ...	4 27 27	53.5 67.1 67.1	X $\rightarrow$ off
p([thermostat1]) $\simeq$ .50 p([guardette1]) $\simeq$ .50 ...	0	replace thermostat1 probe guardette1-status replace guardette1 ...	16 25 34	52.0 62.0 70.0	X
p([thermostat1]) $\simeq$ .50 p([guardette1]) $\simeq$ .50 ... pfr(thermostat2)=.001	.495	probe compressor1-status probe cond-fan1-status ...	1 2	37.0 38.0	X $\rightarrow$ on
p([thermostat1]) $\simeq$ .999	.999 DONE	move refrigerator back	2	2.0	X

Table 1: pfr(all components) = 0.001

most probable candidates	relia-bility	possible operations	exec cost	total cost	operation executed
p([guardette1]) $\simeq$ .500 p([relay1]) $\simeq$ .167 p([compressor1]) $\simeq$ .167 p([thermostat1]) $\simeq$ .167	0	probe cond-fan1-status probe guardette1-status ...	4 27	56.3 65.7	X $\rightarrow$ off
p([guardette1]) $\simeq$ .75 p([thermostat1]) $\simeq$ .25 ...	0	probe guardette1-status replace guardette1 replace thermostat1 ...	25 34 16	61.5 63.0 69.0	X $\rightarrow$ open
p([guardette1]) $\simeq$ 1.0	0	replace guardette1	34	36.0	X
p([guardette1]) $\simeq$ 1.0 pfr(guardette2)=.003	.997 DONE	move refrigerator back	2	2.0	X

Table 2: pfr(guardette) = 3 * pfr(other components)

straightforward application of decision theory to the repair problem. From this perspective, our contribution is a program that *automates* both the identification of alternatives being compared and the cost estimation for those alternatives. In the past this problem (called decision *analysis*) has been left as a task that requires human solution [Howard *et al.*, 1976]. See [Breese *et al.*, 1991] for other work on automating the construction of decision models.

The standard cost evaluation in model-based diagnosis is based on the number of probes needed to distinguish a set of hypotheses. Although [Raiman *et al.*, 1991] and [de Kleer *et al.*, 1991] generalize this notion, both approaches assume fixed probe costs that are specified *a priori*, whereas the costs in our evaluation function are state-dependent. Compared with some work on allowing multiple observation sets and diagnosing devices with changing states [Raiman *et al.*, 1991, Hamscher, 1991, Friedrich and Lackinger, 1991, Ng, 1991], our focus is on extending an intelligent agent to plan for state change rather than having a passive agent diagnose devices with dynamic behavior. Several researchers have attempted to represent system purpose explicitly and integrate repair with diagnosis. For example, [Friedrich *et al.*, 1991] formal-izes a repair process with time-dependence, [Poole and Provan, 1991] focuses on the utility and granularity associated with the repair actions, while [McIlraith and Reiter, 1991] discusses how to recognize the relevance of a probe given a goal; but none of these researchers incorporate planning explicitly into their framework. We use planning explicitly to estimate the costs and execute diagnosis and repair operations. We avoid explicit representation of system purpose because repair (replacement) is already intermingled with the diagnosis process. Reconfiguration might be an interesting extension for IRS; we plan to investigate [Crow and Rushby, 1991] more carefully. Planning to minimize breakdown costs is another ability that complements IRS's strengths; it would be straightforward to incorporate [Friedrich *et al.*, 1992]'s time-dependent cost function into our system, but their greedy algorithms are unlikely to extend gracefully to handle the state-dependent probe costs addressed by IRS.

Our research is also similar to work on test generation programs which may also be thought of as a kind of planner that needs to distinguish between controlling and observing the node values in a circuit. Unlike our situation, the goal/subgoal graph for test generation is largely static; this allows predefinition and optimization which are impossible in our case, but see [Shirley, 1986, Shirley, 1988].

Conclusion

We have reported on IRS, our preliminary integration of diagnostic and planning algorithms, and argued that it represents progress towards a general theory of repair. Our contributions are three-fold:

- A unified treatment of information-gathering and state-altering actions with the UWL action representation language.

- A method for using part-replacement operations (as well as simple probes) to gather diagnostic information.

- Decision making based on a cost function that takes into account both the eventual cost of repair and the dependence of cost on device state.

In future work, we hope to investigate heuristics for approximating C_{total}, incorporate the cost of computation into the cost function, and integrate UWL's treatment of incomplete information with UCPOP's ability to handle universal quantification.

References

A. D. Althouse, C. H. Turnquist, and A. F. Bracciano. *Modern Refrigeration and Air Conditioning*. The Goodheart-Willcox Company, Inc., 1992.

J. Breese, R. Goldman, and M. Wellman, editors. *Notes from the Ninth National Conference on Artificial Intelligence (AAAI-91) Workshop on Knowledge-Based Construction of Probabilistic and Decision Models*. AAAI, July 1991.

Judith Crow and John Rushby. Model-Based Reconfiguration: Toward an Integration with Diagnosis. In *Proceedings of AAAI-91*, pages 836–841, July 1991.

J. de Kleer, O. Raiman, and M. Shirley. One Step Lookahead is Pretty Good. In *Proceedings of the 2nd International Workshop on Principles of Diagnosis*, October 1991.

Oren Etzioni and Richard Segal. Softbots as testbeds for machine learning. In *Working Notes of the AAAI Spring Symposium on Knowledge Assimilation*, Menlo Park, CA, 1992. AAAI Press.

Oren Etzioni, Steve Hanks, Daniel Weld, Denise Draper, Neal Lesh, and Mike Williamson. An Approach to Planning with Incomplete Information. In *Proceedings of KR-92*, October 1992.

G. Friedrich and F. Lackinger. Diagnosing Temporal Misbehavior. In *Proceedings of IJCAI-91*, August 1991.

G. Friedrich, G. Gottlob, and W. Nejdl. Formalizing the Repair Process. In *Proceedings of the 2nd International Workshop on Principles of Diagnosis*, October 1991.

G. Friedrich, , and W. Nejdl. Choosing Observations and Actions in Model Based Diagnosis / Repair Systems. In *Proceedings of KR-92*, October 1992.

W.C. Hamscher. Modeling Digital Circuits for Troubleshooting. *Artificial Intelligence*, 51(1–3):223–272, October 1991.

R. Howard, J. Matheson, and K. Miller. *Readings in decision analysis*. Stanford Research Institute, Menlo Park, CA, 1976.

J. McCarthy and P. J. Hayes. Some Philosophical Problems from the Standpoint of Artificial Intelligence. In *Machine Intelligence 4*, pages 463–502. Edinburgh University Press, 1969.

S. McIlraith and R. Reiter. On Experiments for Hypotherical Reasoning. In *Proceedings of the 2nd International Workshop on Principles of Diagnosis*, October 1991.

R.C. Moore. A Formal Theory of Knowledge and Action. In *Formal Theories of the Commonsense World*. Ablex, 1985.

Leora Morgenstern. Knowledge preconditions for actions and plans. In *Proceedings of IJCAI-87*, 1987.

H.T. Ng. Model-based, Multiple Fault Diagnosis of Dynamic, Continuous Physical Devices. *IEEE Expert*, December 1991.

J.S. Penberthy and D. Weld. UCPOP: A Sound, Complete, Partial Order Planner for ADL. In *Proceedings of KR-92*, pages 103–114, October 1992.

D. Poole and G. Provan. Use and Granularity in Consistent-Based Diagnosis. In *Proceedings of the 2nd International Workshop on Principles of Diagnosis*, October 1991.

O. Raiman, J. de Kleer, V. Saraswat, and M. Shirley. Characterizing Non-intermittent Faults. In *Proceedings of AAAI-91*, July 1991.

O. Raiman. *The Alibi Principle*, pages 66–70. Morgan Kaufmann, 1992.

M. Shirley. Generating Tests by Exploiting Designed Behavior. In *Proceedings AAAI-86*, pages 884–890, August 1986.

M. Shirley. Generating Circuit Tests by Exploiting Designed Behavior. AI-TR-1099, MIT AI Lab, December 1988.

M. Stefik. Planning with Constraints (MOLGEN: Part 1). *Artificial Intelligence*, 14(2), 1981.

Y. Sun and D. Weld. Beyond Simple Observation: Planning to Diagnose. In *Proceedings of the 3rd International Workshop on Principles of Diagnosis*, pages 67–75, October 1992.

Discourse
Analysis

A Method for Development of Dialogue Managers for Natural Language Interfaces

Arne Jönsson*

Department of Computer and Information Science

Linköping University

S- 58183 Linköping, Sweden

arj@ida.liu.se

Abstract

This paper describes a method for the development of dialogue managers for natural language interfaces. A dialogue manager is presented designed on the basis of both a theoretical investigation of models for dialogue management and an analysis of empirical material. It is argued that for natural language interfaces many of the human interaction phenomena accounted for in, for instance, plan-based models of dialogue do not occur. Instead, for many applications, dialogue in natural language interfaces can be managed from information on the functional role of an utterance as conveyed in the linguistic structure. This is modelled in a dialogue grammar which controls the interaction. Focus structure is handled using dialogue objects recorded in a dialogue tree which can be accessed through a scoreboard by the various modules for interpretation, generation and background system access.

A sublanguage approach is proposed. For each new application the Dialogue Manager is customized to meet the needs of the application. This requires empirical data which are collected through Wizard of Oz simulations. The corpus is used when updating the different knowledge sources involved in the natural language interface. In this paper the customization of the Dialogue Manager for database information retrieval applications is also described.

Introduction

Research on computational models of discourse can be motivated from two different standpoints. One is to develop general models and theories of discourse for all kinds of agents and situations. The other approach is to account for a computational model of discourse for a specific application, say a natural language interface (Dahlbäck and Jönsson, 1992). It is not obvious that the two approaches should present similar computational theories for discourse. Instead the different motivations should be considered when presenting theories of dialogue management for natural language interfaces. Many models for dialogue in natural language interfaces are not only models for dialogue in

such interfaces but they also account for general discourse. The focus in this work is on dialogue management for natural language interfaces and not general discourse. Thus, the focus is on efficiency and habitability, i.e. a dialogue manager must correctly and efficiently handle those phenomena that actually occur in typed human-computer interaction so that the user does not feel constrained or restricted when using the interface. This also means that a dialogue manager should be as simple as possible and not waste effort on complex computations in order to handle phenomena not relevant for natural language interfaces. For instance, the system does not necessarily have to be psycholinguistically plausible or able to mimic all aspects of human dialogue behaviour such as surprise or irony, if these do not occur in such dialogues.

Grosz and Sidner (1986) presented a general computational theory of discourse, both spoken and written, where they divide the problem of managing discourse into three parts: linguistic structure, attentional state and intentional state.

The need for a component which records the objects, properties and relations that are in the focus of attention, the attentional state, is not much debated, although the details of focusing need careful examination.

However, the role that is given to the intentional state, i.e. the structure of the discourse purposes, and to the linguistic structure, i.e. the structure of the sequences of utterances in the discourse, provide two competing approaches to dialogue management:

- One approach is the plan-based approach. Here the linguistic structure is used to identify the intentional state in terms of the user's goals and intentions. These are then modelled in plans describing the actions which may possibly be carried out in different situations (cf. Cohen and Perrault, 1979; Allen and Perrault, 1980; Litman, 1985; Carberry, 1990; Pollack, 1990).

- The other approach to dialogue management is to use only the information in the linguistic structure to model the dialogue expectations, i.e. utterances are interpreted on the basis of their functional relation to the previous interaction. The idea is that these constraints on what can be uttered allow us to write a grammar to manage the dialogue (cf. Reichman, 1985; Polanyi and Scha, 1984; Bilange, 1991;

---

*This research was financed by the Swedish National Board for Technical Development and the Swedish Council for Research in the Humanities and Social Sciences.

Jönsson, 1991).

For the strong AI goal or the computational linguistics goal to mimic human language capabilities the plan recognition approach might be necessary. But, for the task of managing the dialogue in a natural language interface, the less sophisticated approach of using a dialogue grammar will do just as well, as will be argued below.

The work presented in this paper is restricted to studying written human-computer interaction in natural language, and natural language interfaces for different applications which belong to the domain that Hayes and Reddy (1983) called simple service systems. Simple service systems "require in essence only that the customer or client identify certain entities to the person providing the service; these entities are parameters of the service, and once they are identified the service can be provided" (*ibid.* p. 252).

A method for customization

The method presented in this paper proposes a sublanguage approach (Grishman and Kittredge, 1986) to the development of dialogue managers. A dialogue manager should not account for the interaction behaviour utilized in every application, instead it should be designed to facilitate customization to meet the needs of a certain application.

Kelley (1983) presents a method for developing a natural language interface in six steps. The first two steps are mainly concerned with determining and implementing essential features of the application. In the third step, known as the first Wizard of Oz-step, the subject interacts with what they believe is a natural language interface but which in fact is a human simulating such an interface (cf. Dahlbäck *et al.*, 1993; Fraser and Gilbert, 1991). This provides data that are used to build a first version of the interface (step four). Kelley starts without grammar or lexicon. The rules and lexical entries are those used by the users during the simulation. In step five, Kelley improves his interface by conducting new Wizard of Oz simulations, this time with the interface running. However, when the user/subject enters a query that the system cannot handle, the wizard takes over and produces an appropriate response. The advantage is that the user's interaction is not interrupted and a more realistic dialogue is thus obtained. This interaction is logged and in step six the system is updated to be able to handle the situations where the wizard responded.

The method used by Kelley of running a simulation in parallel with the interface was also used by Good *et al.* (1984). They developed a command language interface to an e-mail system using this iterative design method, UDI (User-Derived Interface). Kelley and Good *et al.* focus on updating the lexical and grammatical knowledge and are not concerned with dialogue behaviour.

The Dialogue Manager presented in this paper is customized to a specific application using a process inspired by the method of User-Derived Interfaces. The starting point is a corpus of dialogues collected in Wizard of Oz-experiments. From this corpus the knowledge structures used by the Dialogue Manager are customized.

The Dialogue Manager

The Dialogue Manager was initially designed from an analysis of a corpus of 21 dialogues, other than the 30 used for customization (see below) collected in Wizard of Oz-experiments using 5 different background systems[1]. It can be viewed as a controller of resources for interpretation, database access and generation. The Dialogue Manager receives input from the interpretation modules, inspects the result and accesses the background system with information conveyed in the user input. Eventually an answer is returned from the background system access module and the Dialogue Manager then calls the generation modules to generate an answer to the user. If clarification is needed from any of the resources it is dealt with by the Dialogue Manager.

The Dialogue Manager uses information from dialogue objects which model the dialogue segments and moves and information associated with them. The dialogue objects represent the constituents of the dialogue and the Dialogue Manager records instances of dialogue objects in a dialogue tree as the interaction proceeds. The dialogue objects are divided into three main classes on the basis of structural complexity. There is one class corresponding to the size of a dialogue, another class corresponding to the size of a discourse segment (cf. Grosz and Sidner, 1986) and a third class corresponding to the size of a single speech act, or dialogue move. Thus, a dialogue is structured in terms of discourse segments, and a discourse segment in terms of moves and embedded segments. Utterances are not analysed as dialogue objects, but as linguistic objects which function as vehicles of one or more moves.[2]

The dialogue object descriptions are domain dependent and can be modified for each new application. The Dialogue Manager is customized by specifying the dialogue objects; which parameters to use and what values they can take. From the perspective of dialogue management the dialogue objects modelling the discourse segment are the most interesting. An initiative-response (IR) structure is assumed (cf. adjacency-pairs, Schegloff and Sacks, 1973) where an initiative opens a segment by introducing a new goal and the response closes the segment (Dahlbäck, 1991). The parameters specified in the dialogue objects reflect the information needed by the various processes accessing information stored in the dialogue tree.

A dialogue object consists of a set of parameters for specifying the initiator, responder, context etc. needed

---

[1] For further details of the Dialogue Manager, see (Ahrenberg *et al.*, 1990); (Jönsson, 1991) and (Jönsson, 1993).

[2] The use of three categories for hierarchically structuring the dialogue is motivated from the analysis of the corpora. However, there is no claim that they are applicable to all types of dialogue, and even less so, to any type of discourse. When a different number of categories are utilized, the Dialogue Manager can then be customized to capture these other categories.

in most applications. Another set of parameters specify content. Two of these, termed Objects and Properties, account for the information structure of a move (query), where Objects identify a set of primary referents, and Properties identify a complex predicate ascribed to this set (cf. Ahrenberg, 1987). These are focal parameters in the sense that they can be in focus over a sequence of IR-units.

Two principles for maintaining the focus structure are utilized. A general heuristic principle is that everything not changed in an utterance is copied from one IR-node in the dialogue tree to the newly created IR-node. Another principle is that the value for Objects will be updated with the value from the module accessing the database, if provided.

The dialogue objects are used to specify the behaviour of the Dialogue Manager and thus the specification of the dialogue objects must include information on what actions to take in certain situations. This is modelled in two non-focal content parameters, Type and Topic.

Type corresponds to the illocutionary type of the move. Hayes and Reddy (1983, p 266) identify two sub-goals in simple service systems: 1) "specify a parameter to the system" and 2) "obtain the specification of a parameter". Initiatives are categorized accordingly as being of two different types 1) update, U, where users provide information to the system and 2) question, Q, where users obtain information from the system. Responses are categorized as answer, A, for database answers from the system or answers to clarification requests. Other Type categories are Greeting, Farewell and Discourse Continuation (DC) (Dahlbäck, 1991) the latter of which is used for utterances from the system whose purpose is to keep the conversation going.

Topic describes which knowledge source to consult. In information retrieval applications three different topics are used: the database for solving a task (T), acquiring information about the database, system-related, (S) or, finally, the ongoing dialogue (D).

The empirical basis for customization

The Dialogue Manager is customized on the basis of a corpus of 30 dialogues collected in Wizard of Oz-experiments using the actual applications. Three different applications were used and each application utilized 10 dialogues for customization. The simulations were carefully designed and carried out using a powerful simulation environment, (Dahlbäck *et al.*, 1993).

In the experiments there were 14 female and 16 male subjects with varying familiarity with computers. Most subjects were computer novices. The average age was 26 (min. 15, max. 55). Most of the subjects were students but there were also others with varying backgrounds, such as cleaning staff and administrative assistants. The subjects did not realize that it was a simulation and they all, in post-experimental interviews, said that they felt very comfortable with the "system".

In the simulations a scenario is presented to the subjects. In one of the simulations, CARS, the scenario presents a situation where the subject, and his/her accompanying person, have just got the message that their old favourite Mercedes had broken down beyond repair and that they would have to consider buying a new car. They had a certain amount of money available and using the computerized CARS system were asked to select three cars, and also to provide a brief motivation for their choice.

The CARS database is implemented in INGRES, and output from the database can be presented directly to the subjects. Thus, answers from the system, after successful requests, are tables with information on properties of used cars. The users/subjects found this type of output very convenient as they could view a particular car in the context of other similar cars. This can be seen as an argument favouring an approach to natural language interfaces where complex reasoning is replaced with fast output of structured information. Possibly more information than asked for is provided, but as long as it can be presented on one screen, it is convenient.

The dialogues in the other domain, TRAVEL, were collected using two scenarios, one where the subjects were asked to gather information on charter trips to the Greek Archipelago and another where they have a certain amount of money available and were asked to use the TRAVEL system to order such a charter trip. In TRAVEL it is also possible to provide graphical information to the subjects, i.e., maps of the various islands.

The use of empirical material

An important question is how to use empirical material on the one hand and common sense and prior knowledge on human-computer interaction and natural language dialogue on the other. Dahlbäck (1991) claims that this partly depends on the purpose of the study, whether it is aimed at theory development or system development. In the latter case, one always has the possibility to design the system to overcome certain problems encountered in the corpus.

In this work empirical material is used for system development from two different perspectives. The first is to develop a dialogue manager for a natural language interface which can be used in various applications. Here the empirical material needs to be analysed with the aim of designing a dialogue manager general enough to cover all the dialogue phenomena that can occur in realistic human-computer dialogues using various background systems. Thus, phenomena which occur in the empirical material must be accounted for and also certain generalizations must be made so that the Dialogue Manager can later be customized to cover phenomena that are not actually present in the corpus but are likely to occur for other applications.

Empirical material is also used for customizing the Dialogue Manager to actual applications. Here generalization is less emphasized, instead many details of how to efficiently deal with the phenomena in the implementation are more interesting.

How can empirical material be used for customization? One can take the conservative standpoint and say that only those phenomena actually occurring in the dialogues are to be handled by the Dialogue Manager, (cf. Kelley, 1983). This has the advantage that a minimal model is developed which is empirically well motivated and which does not waste time on handling phenomena not occurring in the corpus. The drawback is that a very large corpus is needed for coverage of the possible actions taken by a potential user. This was also pointed out by Ogden (1988, p 296), who claims that "The performance of the system will depend on the availability of representative users prior to actual use, and it will depend on the abilities of the installer to collect and integrate the relevant information".

The other extreme standpoint is to only use the linguistic knowledge available. One problem with this approach is that it is plausible that much effort is spent on handling phenomena which will never occur in the dialogue, while at the same time not account for actually occurring phenomena. However, as pointed out by Brown and Yule (1983, p 21) "A dangerously extreme view of 'relevant data' for a discourse analyst would involve denying the admissibility of a constructed sentence as linguistic data".

For the purpose of customization, two kinds of information can be obtained from a corpus:

- First, it can be used as a source of phenomena which the designer of the natural language interface was not aware of from the beginning.

- Second, it can be used to rule out certain interesting phenomena which are complicated but which do not occur in the corpus.

The first point also includes the use of the corpus to make the system behaviour more accurate. This can be illustrated by the use of clarification subdialogues. In the CARS dialogues, when the user initiative is too vague and the system needs a clarification, it first explicitly states the alternatives available and then asks for a clarification. Subjects using the CARS system follow up such a clarification subdialogue as intended. However, in the TRAVEL system there are certain system clarification requests which are less explicit, and which do not state any alternatives. These clarifications do not always result in a follow up answer from the user.

To illustrate the second point, consider the use of singular pronouns. Singular pronouns can be used in various ways to refer to a previously mentioned item. One could argue that if a user utters something like *What is the price of a Toyota Corolla?*, and the answer is a table with two types of cars of different years, then the user may form a conceptualization of Toyota as a generic car and can therefore utter something like *How fast is it?* referring to properties of a Toyota Corolla of any year.

In the work on developing the Dialogue Manager, the use of pronouns in the corpus in various situations motivates the need for designing the Dialogue Manager to capture both uses of singular pronouns. However, when customizing the Dialogue Manager the situation is different. For instance, in the CARS dialogues the users restrict their use of singular pronouns. Thus, the customized Dialogue Manager for the CARS database is not provided with specific means for managing the use of singular pronouns if presented in the context above. If they occur they will result in a clarification subdialogue. However, the "normal" use of singular

pronouns is allowed. There is another motivation for this position. Excluding the generic use of a singular pronoun leads to a simpler Dialogue Manager. On the other hand including the normal use of singular pronouns will not increase the complexity of the Dialogue Manager.

The principle utilized in the customization of the Dialogue Manager is obviously very pragmatic. If the phenomenon is present in the corpus then it should be included. If it is not present, but if it is present in other Wizard of Oz-studies using similar background systems and scenarios and implementation is straightforward, the Dialogue Manager should be customized to deal with it. Otherwise, if it is not present and it would increase the complexity of the Dialogue Manager, then it is not included.

This does not prevent the use of knowledge from other sources (cf. Grishman *et al.*, 1986). In the customization of the Dialogue Manager for the CARS and TRAVEL systems, knowledge on how the database is organised and also how users retrieve information from databases is used in the customization.

Customizing the Dialogue Manager

Customization of the Dialogue Manager involves two major tasks: 1) Defining the focal parameters of the dialogue objects in more detail and customizing the heuristic principles for changing the values of these parameters. 2) Constructing a dialogue grammar for controlling the dialogue.

The focus structure

In the CARS application, task-related questions are about cars which means that the Objects parameter holds various instances of sets of cars and Properties, are various properties of cars. In TRAVEL, on the other hand, users switch their attention between objects of different kinds: hotels, resorts and trips. This requires a slightly modified Objects parameter. It can be either a hotel or a resort. However, in TRAVEL the appropriate resort can be found from a hotel description by following the relation in the domain model from hotel to resort. Finding the hotel from a resort can be accomplished by a backwards search in the dialogue tree. Therefore, one single focused object – a hotel or a resort – will suffice. The value need not be a single object, it can be a set of hotels or resorts.

The general focusing principles need to be slightly modified to apply to the CARS and TRAVEL applications. For the CARS application the heuristic principles apply well to the Objects parameter. An intensionally specified object description provided in a user initiative will be replaced by the extensional specification provided by the module accessing the database, which means that erroneous objects will be removed, as they will not be part of the response from the database manager. For the TRAVEL application the principles for providing information to the Objects parameter are modified to allow hotels to be added if the resort remains the same.

The heuristic principles for the Properties parameter for the CARS application need to be modified. The principle is that if the user does not change Objects to a set of cars which is not a subset of Objects, then the attributes provided in the new user initiative are added to the old set of attributes. This is based on the observation that users often start with a rather large set, in this case a set of cars, and then gradually specify a smaller set by adding restrictions (cf. Kaplan 1983), for instance in CARS using utterances like *remove all small size cars*. For the TRAVEL application the copy principle holds without exception.

The modifications of the general principles are minor and are carried out during the customization.

The results from the customizations showed that the heuristic principles applied well. In CARS 52% of the user initiatives were fully specified, i.e. they did not need any information from the context to be interpreted. 43% could be interpreted from information found in the current segment as copied from the previous segment. Thus, only 5% required a search in the dialogue tree. For the TRAVEL application without ordering, 44% of the user initiatives were fully specified and 50% required local context, while in the ordering dialogues 59% were fully specified and 39% needed local context.

In the TRAVEL system there is one more object; the order form. A holiday trip is not fully defined by specifying a hotel at a resort. It also requires information concerning the actual trip: Travel length, Departure date and Number of persons. This information is needed to answer questions on the price of a holiday trip. The order form also contains all the information necessary when ordering a charter trip. In addition to the information on Resort, Hotel, Departure date, etc. the order form includes information about the name, address and telephone number of the user. Furthermore, information on travel insurance, cancellation insurance, departure airport etc. is found in the order form. The order form is filled with user information during a system controlled phase of the dialogue.

The dialogue structure

The dialogue structure parameters Type and Topic also require customization. In the CARS system the users never update the database with new information, but in the TRAVEL system where ordering is allowed the users update the order form. Here another Type is needed, CONF, which is used to close an ordering session by summarizing the order and implicitly prompt for confirmation. For the ordering phase the Topic parameter O for order is added, which means that the utterance affects the order form.

The dialogue structure can be modelled in a dialogue grammar. The resulting grammar from the customizations of both CARS and TRAVEL is context free, in fact, it is very simple and consists merely of sequences of task-related initiatives followed by database responses, Q_T/A_T[3], sometimes with an embedded clarification sequence, Q_D/A_D. In CARS 60% of the initiatives are of this type. For TRAVEL 83% of the initiatives in the non-ordering dialogues and 70% of the ordering dialogues

---
[3] For brevity, when presenting the dialogue grammar, Topic type will be indicated with a subscript to the Type. The Initiative is the first TypeTopic-pair while the Response is the second separated by a slash (/).

are of this type. Other task related initiatives result in a response providing system information, Q_T/A_S, or a response stating that the intitiative was too vague, Q_T/A_D. There are also a number of explicit calls for system information, Q_S/A_S. The grammar rules discussed here only show two of the parameters of the dialogue objects. In fact, a number of parameters describing speaker, hearer, objects, properties, etc are used. These descriptors provide additional information for deciding which actions to carry out. However, the complexity of the dialogue is constrained by the grammar.

The dialogue grammar is developed by first constructing a minimal dialogue grammar from an analysis of dialogues from the application, or an application of the same type, e.g. information retrieval from a database. This grammar is generalized and extended, using general knowledge on human-computer natural language interaction, with new rules to cover "obvious" additions not found in the initial grammar. In the CARS dialogues it included, for instance, Greetings and Farewells, which did not appear in the analysis of the dialogues. In the TRAVEL system it involved, among other things, allowing for multiple clarification requests and clarification requests not answered by the user. Some extensions not found in any of the dialogues were also added, for instance, a rule for having the system prompt the user with a discourse continuation if (s)he becomes unsure who has the initiative. However, if a phenomenon requires sophisticated and complex mechanisms, it will be necessary to consider what will happen if the grammar is used without that addition. This also includes considering how probable it is that a certain phenomenon may occur.

For each new application, new simulations are needed to determine which phenomena are specific for that application. This is illustrated in the TRAVEL system dialogues where ordering is not allowed. In these dialogues some users try to state an order although it is not possible. This resulted in a new rule, U_O/A_S, informing the users that ordering is not possible.

In the work by Kelley (1983) and Good *et al.* (1984), on lexical and grammatical acquisition, the customization process was saturated after a certain number of dialogues. The results presented here indicate that this is also the case for the dialogue structure. From a rather limited number of dialogues, a context free grammar can be constructed which, with a few generalizations, will cover the interaction patterns occurring in the actual application (Jönsson, 1993).

Summary

This paper has presented a method for the development of dialogue managers for natural language interfaces for various applications. The method uses a general dialogue manager which is customized from a corpus of dialogues, with users interacting with the actual application, collected in Wizard of Oz-experiments. The corpus is used when customizing dialogue objects with parameters and heuristic principles for maintaining focus structure. It is also used when constructing a dialogue grammar which controls the dialogue.

The customization of the Dialogue Manager for two

different applications – database information retrieval and database information retrieval plus ordering – was also presented. Customization was carried out for two different domains: properties of used cars and information on holiday trips. For both domains questions can be described as queries on specifications of domain concepts about objects in the database and simple heuristic principles are sufficient for modelling the focus structure. A context free dialogue grammar can accurately control the dialogue for both applications. The results on customization are very promising for the approach to dialogue management presented in this paper. They show that the use of dialogue objects which can be customized for various applications in combination with a dialogue grammar is a fruitful way to build application-specific dialogue managers.

Acknowledgements

I am indebted to Lars Ahrenberg and Nils Dahlbäck for many valuable discussions. I will also thank Brant Cheikes, Jalal Maleki, Magnus Merkel and Ivan Rankin for commenting on previous versions of the paper. Åke Thurée did most of the implementation of the Dialogue Manager for the CARS system.

References

Ahrenberg, Lars; Jönsson, Arne; and Dahlbäck, Nils 1990. Discourse representation and discourse management for natural language interfaces. In *Proceedings of the Second Nordic Conference on Text Comprehension in Man and machine, Täby.*

Ahrenberg, Lars 1987. *Interrogative Structures of Swedish. Aspects of the Relation between grammar and speech acts.* Ph.D. Dissertation, Uppsala University.

Allen, James F. and Perrault, C. Raymond 1980. Analysing intention in utterances. *Artificial Intelligence* 15:143–178.

Bilange, Eric 1991. A task independent oral dialogue model. In *Proceedings of the Fifth Conference of the European Chapter of the Association for Computational Linguistics, Berlin.*

Brown, Gillian and Yule, George 1983. *Discourse Analysis.* Cambridge University Press.

Carberry, Sandra 1990. *Plan Recognition in Natural Language Dialogue.* MIT Press, Cambridge, MA.

Cohen, Philip. R. and Perrault, C. Raymond 1979. Elements of a plan-based theory of speech acts. *Cognitive Science* 3:177–212.

Dahlbäck, Nils and Jönsson, Arne 1992. An empirically based computationally tractable dialogue model. In *Proceedings of the Fourteenth Annual Meeting of The Cognitive Science Society, Bloomington, Indiana.*

Dahlbäck, Nils; Jönsson, Arne; and Ahrenberg, Lars 1993. Wizard of Oz studies - why and how. In *Proceedings from the 1993 International Workshop on Intelligent User Interfaces, Orlando, Florida.*

Dahlbäck, Nils 1991. *Representations of Discourse, Cognitive and Computational Aspects.* Ph.D. Dissertation, Linköping University.

Fraser, Norman and Gilbert, Nigel S. 1991. Simulating speech systems. *Computer Speech and Language* 5:81–99.

Good, Michael D.; Whiteside, John A.; Wixon, Dennis R.; and Jones, Sandra J. 1984. Building a user-derived interface. *Communications of the ACM* 27(10):1032–1043.

Grishman, Ralph and Kittredge, Richard I. 1986. *Analysing language in restricted domains.* Lawrence Erlbaum.

Grishman, Ralph; Hirshman, Lynette; and Nhan, Ngo Thanh 1986. Discovery procedures for sublanguage selectional patterns: Initial experiments. *Computational Linguistics* 12(3):205–215.

Grosz, Barbara J. and Sidner, Candace L. 1986. Attention, intention and the structure of discourse. *Computational Linguistics* 12(3):175–204.

Hayes, Philip J. and Reddy, D. Raj 1983. Steps toward graceful interaction in spoken and written man-machine communication. *International Journal of Man-Machine Studies* 19:231–284.

Jönsson, Arne 1991. A dialogue manager using initiative-response units and distributed control. In *Proceedings of the Fifth Conference of the European Chapter of the Association for Computational Linguistics, Berlin.*

Jönsson, Arne 1993. *Dialogue Management for Natural Language Interfaces – An Empirical Approach.* Ph.D. Dissertation, Linköping University.

Kaplan, S. Jerrold 1983. Cooperative responses from a portable natural language database query system. In *Computational Aspects of Discourse.* MIT Press. 167–208.

Kelley, John F. 1983. *Natural Language and Computers: Six Empirical Steps for Writing an Easy-to-Use Computer Application.* Ph.D. Dissertation, The Johns Hopkins University.

Litman, Diane J. 1985. *Plan Recognition and Discourse Analysis: An Integrated Approach for Understanding Dialogues.* Ph.D. Dissertation, University of Rochester.

Ogden, William C. 1988. Using natural language interfaces. In Helander, M., editor 1988, *Handbook of Human-Computer Interaction.* Elsevier Science Publishers B. V. (North Holland).

Polanyi, Livia and Scha, Remko 1984. A syntactic approach to discourse semantics. In *Proceedings of the 10th International Conference on Computational Linguistics, Stanford.*

Pollack, Martha E. 1990. Plans as complex mental attitudes. In Cohen, Philip R.; Morgan, Jerry; and Pollack, Martha E., editors 1990, *Intentions in Communication.* MIT Press.

Reichman, Rachel 1985. *Getting Computers to Talk Like You and Me.* MIT Press, Cambridge, MA.

Schegloff, Emanuel A. and Sacks, Harvey 1973. Opening up closings. *Semiotica* 7:289–327.

Mutual Beliefs of Multiple Conversants:
A Computational Model of Collaboration in Air Traffic Control

David G. Novick and Karen Ward

Oregon Graduate Institute of Science & Technology
19600 N.W. von Neumann Drive
Beaverton, OR 97006-1999 USA
novick@cse.ogi.edu, wardk@cse.ogi.edu

Abstract

This work develops a computational model for representing and reasoning about dialogue in terms of the mutuality of belief of the conversants. We simulated cooperative dialogues at the speech act level and compared the simulations with actual dialogues between pilots and air traffic controllers engaged in real tasks. In the simulations, addressees and overhearers formed beliefs and took actions appropriate to their individual roles and contexts. The result is a computational model capable of representing the evolving context of complete real-world multiparty task-oriented conversations in the air traffic control domain.[1]

Introduction

This paper addresses the question of how mutuality is maintained in conversation and specifically how mutuality can be usefully modeled in multiparty computational dialogue systems. The domain we studied and modeled is air traffic control (ATC). The problem we are solving is related to the distributed artificial intelligence research on ATC communications (e.g., Findler & Lo 1988), except that we are explicitly dealing with the mutuality aspects of interaction. While other ATC studies have developed domain models suitable for distributed processing via cooperating agents, we are interested in fundamental knowledge about how such cooperation is achieved through linguistic interaction. Interestingly, we find that the mutuality model by itself explains a great deal of the ATC communications that we observed.

This model and its associated representation of mutuality are not specific to ATC. While ATC served as a domain for the simulation, the mutuality maintenance mechanism presented here does depend on the domain's specifics. Thus, the representation should be useful for other multiparty interaction in, for example, applications of distributed artificial intelligence.

We define and validate a speech act model of ATC dialogue built around the mutuality of beliefs among conversants and overhearers. Complete actual dialogues between air traffic controllers and pilots were explicated in terms of task, belief, and event. The model was tested by computational simulation and was found to be successful in pre-

1. This research was supported by National Science Foundation grant No. IRI-9110797.

dicting and explaining the course of real-world conversation at the speech act level. In particular, we replicated a number of actual conversations using speech-act models of air traffic control and conversational mutuality. The simulations account for and produce the effects of belief formation in computational agents representing both conversants and overhearers.

Motivation

Spoken language understanding systems require dialogue-level language models that are capable of representing and reasoning about the course of real-world task-oriented conversation. Speech act theory (Austin 1962; Searle 1969; Searle 1975; Searle & Vanderveken 1985) suggests that we can motivate dialogue and explain conversational coherence by modeling conversation in terms of the conversants' goals and their plans for reaching those goals. Language as action provides conversants with means for achieving mutual goals (Winograd & Flores, 1986). This approach accords well with findings that the structure of discourse about a particular task closely follows the structure of the task itself (e.g., Oviatt & Cohen 1988; Cohen & Perrault 1979; Grosz & Sidner 1986). In this view, language is just another tool to be used in accomplishing some goal, and utterance planning becomes incorporated into the larger task planning (e.g., Power 1979; Cohen 1984; Litman & Allen 1987).

Clark and his colleagues have proposed a theory of conversation as a collaborative process in which conversants collaborate in building a mutual model of the conversation (Clark & Marshall 1981; Clark & Wilkes-Gibbs 1986; Schober & Clark 1989; Clark & Schaefer 1989). The conversants' beliefs about the mutuality of their knowledge serves to motivate and explain the information that conversants exchange. The collaborative view of conversation offers an explanation for conversational coherence by viewing conversation as an ensemble work in which the conversants cooperatively build a model of shared belief (Suchman 1987; Clark & Schaefer 1989).

Our model is based on a synthesis of these principles, in that conversation is viewed as an attempt to establish and build upon mutual knowledge using speech acts. This synthesis was first proposed by Novick (1988) to explain conversational control acts. More recently, Traum and Hinkelman (1992) have developed a similar model of mutuality maintenance as part of their theory of "conversation acts." In this study, we use these principles to explain and motivate domain-level acts in a real-world task.

This article, then, explores the domain of air traffic control as a speech-act model, produces a computational representation of the beliefs, actions and inferences of the conversants, and validates the model and representation through detailed simulation of observed ATC dialogue. We pay particular attention to the maintenance of mutuality of belief in both conversants and overhearers. The next section of this article discusses the ATC domain and describes the dialogues we analyzed and modeled. We present the computational model, discussing the goals of the agents in the domain and presenting our representation of their beliefs. We next present inference rules for speech acts in the ATC domain, including detailed discussion of their mutuality effects. Based on the representation and inference rules, we then simulate observed dialogue in a multi-agent rule-based environment; we describe the simulation environment and procedure and discuss the results of the simulations.

The Air Traffic Control Domain

Developing and validating a model of mutuality of belief in conversation, particularly for multiple party interaction, requires a domain in which there are naturally occurring cooperative tasks, relative ease of determining initial beliefs, and multiple conversants. For this study, we chose to examine air traffic control dialogue. Because we wanted the model to represent actual dialogue and not just encode the formalisms suggested by the Federal Aviation Administration (FAA 1989), we studied protocols of actual pilot-controller conversation (Ward, Novick, & Sousa 1990) rather than simply encoding the FAA's rules for ATC communication.

In this study we examined four complete ATC dialogues, which ranged in size from 14 to 19 transmissions. Each of the four dialogues represent the entire conversation between an approach controller and the pilot of a commercial flight approaching the airport to land. Controller and pilot are cooperatively performing the task of guiding the aircraft through the controller's airspace to the approach gate, a point from which the pilot can complete the approach and landing without further guidance from the controller. This task is referred to as an Instrument Landing System (ILS) approach procedure. For a detailed description of the ILS approach procedure from the controller's standpoint, see *Air Traffic Control* (FAA 1989). The pilot's view is described in *Airman's Information Manual* (FAA 1991). Rosenbaum (1988) provides a good explanation for the non-pilot.

In ATC dialogue, the conversants often hold strong expectations about what the other knows and what the other will say. Pilot and controller are both trained in ILS approach procedures and each knows at least approximately what the other should do under normal circum-

stances. The system is not infallible, however, and circumstances are not always normal. The purpose of much of their dialogue, then, is to establish and confirm the mutuality of information that each thinks the other probably already knows or expects. Our goal, then, is to build a working model of mutuality that reflects this process, with representations that are usefully able to express differences among beliefs held by a single party, mutually held by some combination of parties, and perceived as held by the same or other combinations. The speech acts of the parties should reflect the natural consequences of their individual needs to achieve mutual understanding: Conversants with goals that require mutuality for their achievement should act appropriately; similarly capable conversants with goals that do not need mutuality should refrain from such actions.

A Computational Model of ATC Dialogue

Our model of mutuality in multiparty dialogue encompasses relations among acts, utterances, and beliefs. Figure 1 summarizes this conceptual model. Conversants are modeled as autonomous agents, each having a separate belief space. An agent's beliefs may include beliefs about another agent's beliefs, depicted as smaller areas within an agent's belief space. Agents communicate in a multi-step process:

- Agent A forms the intention to perform an act directed toward Agent B. This intention is based on A's beliefs about B's beliefs along with other beliefs that A holds.
- A's intended act is expressed as an utterance. This utterance is transmitted to other agents in the system.
- B interprets this utterance as an act based on B's own beliefs and B's beliefs about A's beliefs. Note that if B's beliefs about A are in error or incomplete, B may infer a different act than A intended (misunderstanding).
- Agent B's belief space is updated to reflect the effects that A's act had on B's beliefs.

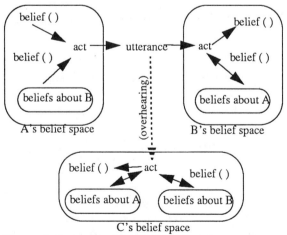

Figure 1. Conceptual Model of Agent Interaction

Agent C represents an overhearer, an agent who hears A's utterance but is not the intended target (shown by a gray line from utterance to agent). Agent C interprets the overheard utterance in light of C's beliefs, including C's beliefs about the beliefs of A and B. Of course, C may arrive at an interpretation of the utterance that differs from that of either A or B; overhearers are at a disadvantage in following a conversation in that they do not actively participate in the collaborative process of reaching mutual belief (Schober & Clark 1989). However, overhearing plays a crucial role in ATC communications. Pilots maintain their situational awareness by monitoring the transmissions of others on the frequency and may respond or refer to dialogue that was not directed to them (Dunham 1991). The representation therefore explicitly supports multiple conversants by accounting for the effect that an utterance has on overhearers, including mutuality of belief judgements involving multiple agents.

Misunderstanding is modeled in terms of inconsistent beliefs; conversants' mental models of the conversation may have diverged without the conversants realizing it. A person may then take an action intended to embody a certain speech act, only to be surprised when the other's response indicates that a completely different speech act was understood. Similarly, disagreements can be modeled in terms of the conversants' beliefs about other conversants' differing beliefs. This model therefore supports both recognized and unrecognized belief inconsistency.

This conceptual model is similar in style to that proposed by Allen and Traum (Allen 1991; Traum 1991; Traum & Hinkelman 1992), in that a distinction is made between privately-held and shared knowledge in understanding a task-oriented conversation. Allen's TRAINS model is built around the negotiation and recognition of plans, however, and explicitly assumes that there are exactly two agents: system and person. The *ViewGen* algorithm (Ballim, Wilks, & Barden 1991) uses multiple environments to permit the system to ascribe and reason about conflicting beliefs among multiple agents. *ViewGen*'s emphasis is on understanding metaphor in text, however, and not on understanding task-oriented conversations. Here, we complement these approaches by providing a systematic representation for mutuality of belief.

Representing Belief

An agent's understanding of the world is represented as a set of beliefs of the form

belief (*proposition, truth-value, belief-groups*).

The *proposition* clause represents the item about which a belief is held. An agent may hold beliefs about the state of the world, about acts that have **occurred**, and about acts that agents **intend**; these last two represent an agent's memory of past actions and expectations of future actions.

The *truth-value* clause represents the truth value that the belief-group assigns to the *proposition* (as understood by the agent in whose belief space the belief appears). This clause may take the values **true, false,** or **unknown.**

Clauses which do not appear in the agent's belief space are considered to have a truth-value of **unknown**. The *truth-value* does not indicate the agent's opinion about the "fact" represented in the *preposition*; rather, it reflects the agent's understanding of the beliefs of the belief group. This indirection allows an agent to ascribe beliefs to other agents.

A *belief-group* is a set of agents who mutually hold the belief. Each belief thus has one or more associated *belief-groups* that express the agent's view of the mutuality status of the proposition. For example, the belief

belief(altitude([sun512],5000),
    true,
    [[approach],[sun512],[approach,sun512]])

means the agent believes that the approach controller, and the pilot of Sundance 512 each believe (individually) that Sundance 512 is at 5000 feet; the agent also believes that controller and pilot have established that they mutually believe the pilot is at 5000 feet.

While we have paid special attention to mutuality, this representation clearly does not solve every problem associated with beliefs about actions in the world. Nevertheless, the representation is adequate for the purposes of demonstrating the effectiveness of our theory of conversational mutuality; its limitations mainly concern "domain" knowledge, particularly with respect to temporal and conditional actions. Thus the belief representation does not accommodate conditions that are in the process of changing from one state to another—that, for example, an aircraft is slowing from 190 knots to 170 knots. It does not capture notions of time; a more general representation would add a time interval argument to indicate when the agent believed the action would or did occur. It also does not capture events that take place without being triggered by the actions of some agent. As we have noted, though, these limitations are acceptable for this representation because our purpose is to model mutuality dialogue and not to model events in general.

Core Speech Acts

In implementing and testing the belief model, we defined a small set of speech acts augmented with a preliminary set of domain acts and states sufficient to represent the dialogues being studied. These acts are: **acknowledge, authorize, contact, direct, report, request.** Acts are modeled at a high level, with preconditions and effects represented only to the degree necessary to understand the communication. The speech act representation is defined more fully in Ward (1992). Note that this is not a complete list of the acts needed to explain all ATC dialogue; it represents only the acts needed to explain typical dialogues seen in the ILS approach task.

Dialogue Rules

ATC dialogue exhibits a strong task orientation that is reflected in the structure of the dialogue. Intentions to perform some act are assumed to be are motivated by task considerations, while the intentions to respond to others' acts are motivated primarily by mutuality considerations. The rules defined for the approach task dialogue are summarized in Table 1. Nine rules in four categories were needed to account for the four dialogues studied.

Mutuality rules establish and update agents' beliefs about the mutuality of knowledge. Included in this category are rules to translate an agent's perception of some act into a belief that the act occurred. These represent a rudimentary first step toward act recognition and interpretation.

Expectation rules capture expectations about an agent's response to another agent's acts. Like planning rules, they build expectations about agents' intended actions. Where planning rules seek to capture the procedures of complex domain tasks, however, expectation rules attempt to embody more basic rules of behavior in this domain: that agents acknowledge acts directed toward them; that agents follow instructions if able to do so; that agents confirm information that is reported to them.

Planning rules attempt to capture the procedural aspects of the domain's communications-oriented tasks, thus representing a rudimentary planning function.

Performative rules translate agents' intentions into acts. This category currently includes only a single, very general rule, **Perform Intentions**; it embodies the principle that agents carry out their intentions if possible. It locates an agent's unfulfilled intention to perform an act, checks that the preconditions for performing that act are satisfied, then does it.

Simulating ATC Dialogue

To validate the mutuality model, we built a working implementation and tested it in saso (Novick 1990), a rule-based shell developed in Prolog as a tool for modeling multi-agent problems involving simultaneous actions and subjective belief. The conversants are represented by computational agents (rules implemented as saso operators) that communicate using the acts defined in the model. Saso uses forward-chaining control to simulate the parallel execution of multiple rule-based agents with separate belief spaces. A user-defined set of extended STRIPS-style operators is used to specify the behavior of agents in terms of preconditions and effects. Agents communicate through acts; when an agent performs an act, clauses representing the action are posted to the memories of all agents in the system. The conflict resolution strategy was defined in terms of the rule types: Mutuality rules are applied in preference to expectation rules, expectation rules in preference to planning rules, and performative rules are triggered only when no other rules apply. This conflict resolution strategy reflects the idea that agents first update beliefs about their knowledge, then form expectations about the future behavior of agents, plan their own actions, and finally act.

For each dialogue, the inputs to the simulation were an initial state for each agent, a list of external non-conversation domain events that each agent would encounter, and a set of rules representing knowledge of mutuality and the domain task. The outputs were speech acts and changes in the agents' beliefs. The simulations were allowed to run to completion.

The simulations were validated by comparing their speech-act outputs on an act-for-act basis with a speech-act coding of the original ATC dialogues. To determine effects of overhearing, the internal belief states of the agents were compared with a manual analysis of mutuality of beliefs in the original dialogues.

Our first concern was to validate the basic model and rule set by simulating a single dialogue. The model's ability to track the belief states of overhearers was then tested by enlarging the simulation to include an agent who lis-

Table 1: Dialogue Rules for the Approach Task

	Rule	**Purpose**	**Effect**
Mutuality Rules	• Act to Belief • Mark Belief Mutual • Mark Act Mutual	• Perceive acts. • Form beliefs about the mutuality of information. • Form beliefs about the mutuality of acts.	• Adds belief that act occurred • Updates mutuality of information • Updates mutuality of belief that act occurred
Expectation Rules	• Expect Acknowledge Act • Expect Follow Instructions • Expect Confirm Report	• Expect agents to acknowledge acts directed toward them. • Expect agents to follow instructions. • Expect agent to confirm information that is reported to them.	• Adds expectation that agent will acknowledge act. • Adds expectation that agent will follow instructions. • Adds expectation that agents will confirm report.
Planning Rules	• Plan Initial Contact • Plan Approach Clearance	• Pilot intends to contact controller. • Controller intends to authorize pilot to fly approach procedure	• Breaks task into a series of subgoals. • Breaks task into a series of subgoals.
Performative Rules	• Perform Intentions	• Agents attempt to carry out their intentions.	• Agent performs act.

tened but did not participate in the conversation. Next, the model was tested against each of the other three dialogues from the protocol. Finally, the model was tested against the four dialogues as they were actually interleaved in the corpus.

Results

The simulations ran to completion and correctly tracked the belief states of conversants and overhearers. With the exceptions noted below, the speech acts produced in the simulation corresponded on an act-for-act basis with the baseline codings. Agents' beliefs about the current state of all ongoing conversations were maintained, with agents responding appropriately to acts directed toward them and to events affecting them. Using the same rules as the active conversants, the overhearing agents "recognized" acts, formed expectations about the next actions of the conversants, and made judgments about the mutuality of knowledge and the evolving conversational state of the conversants.

Some aspects of the original dialogues were not reproduced in the simulations. As a consequence of the decision to avoid detailed event simulation, the model does not currently support directives that are not intended to be carried out immediately, such as an instruction to contact another controller when the aircraft reaches a certain point in its route. Such instructions were simulated as if they were to be carried out immediately. Also, the current rule set does not allow for an agent's inability to perform some action, e.g., a pilot's inability to see another aircraft; this aspect of the test dialogues was not reproduced. The model does not currently represent ranges of conditions, so ranges were instead represented as single values. Because saso simulates perfect understanding by conversants, correction subdialogues were not investigated in these simulations.

The model addresses only one aspect of the approach controller's responsibilities; it should be extended with substantial domain-task information to encompass a significant fraction of ATC dialogue. Also, there is clearly a need for many rules that weren't required for simulating the particular dialogues in this corpus, such as rules for reporting that an agent does not intend to comply with a direction. Another limitation to the generality of this model is the lack of a domain-specific planner. In the present study, this detailed planning function is simulated by introducing agents' intentions through saso's event queue. Although a detailed planner on the level of Wesson's (1977) expert-level simulation of controller functions is probably not required for speech understanding, a certain level of knowledge of expected outcome of domain events is needed to motivate certain aspects of ATC dialogue.

Conclusion

This work is a step toward developing a computational representation multiparty mutuality, which we have shown to be adequate for typical air traffic control dialogues. Complete conversations were computationally simulated at the speech act level, demonstrating that real-world collaborative conversations can be motivated and represented in terms of belief and expectation, task and event. The goal of this study was to develop a computational model of air traffic control dialogue that would:

- Support reasoning about the beliefs and intentions of the conversants.
- Model agents' beliefs about other agents' beliefs.
- Capture sufficient domain and physical context to model the exchanges, particularly the evolving context of the dialogue itself.
- Support multiple (more than two) conversants, including overhearers.
- Permit different agents to hold different, possibly inconsistent, beliefs, and to support reasoning about the mutuality or inconsistency of conversants' beliefs.

We tested the model against these goals by simulation. Using a small set of rules, several actual dialogues were successfully simulated at the speech act level. The belief states of multiple conversational participants and overhearers were modeled through the course of several overlapping dialogues. Agents' beliefs were updated in response to the evolving conversational context as agents negotiated their tasks while maintaining a situational awareness of other agents' activities.

In modeling complete ATC dialogues in terms of the beliefs and goals of the conversants, typical patterns emerged. Conversants separately form similar beliefs based on separate inputs, then attempt to confirm the mutuality of the belief. As utterances are made and acknowledged, speaker and hearer form beliefs about what speech acts are intended by the utterance and form expectations that the act will be acknowledged and confirmed. These expectations form a strong context that permit the conversants to easily recognize the speech acts motivating nonstandard responses that might otherwise be ambiguous.

A key contribution of this model is the representation of mutuality of belief in terms of belief sets. Belief sets capture both an agent's understanding of who believes a given piece of information and the mutuality that the agents holding that belief have established among themselves. This representation allows an agent to hold beliefs about other agents' possibly conflicting beliefs ("I believe A but he believes B.") as well as allowing agents to hold beliefs about the mutuality of their knowledge ("She and I have established that we both believe A; he should also believe A, but we have not yet confirmed that."). The belief set representation is flexible enough to represent and reason about mutuality combinations involving any number of agents, thus supporting the modeling of multi-agent conversations.

In this paper, then, we have proposed a representation for mutuality of belief that supports reasoning and action by multiple agents. We have shown the utility of the belief-groups representation through its use in a simulation of ATC dialogues. As part of the simulation, we developed a set of rules that maintain mutuality in this domain and that re general enough to support straightforward extension to other domains involving cooperative tasks.

Acknowledgments

The authors gratefully acknowledge the assistance of Larry Porter and Caroline Sousa.

References

Allen, J. F. 1991. Discourse Structure in the TRAINS Project. In Proceedings of the Fourth DARPA Workshop on Speech and Natural Language.

Austin, J. L. 1962. *How To Do Things With Words*. London: Oxford University Press.

Ballim, A.; Wilks, Y.; and Barnden, J. 1991. Belief Ascription, Metaphor, and Intensional Identification. *Cognitive Science* 15:133-171.

Clark, H. H., and Marshall, C. R. 1981. Definite Reference and Mutual Knowledge. In I. A. Sag (Ed.), *Elements of discourse understanding*. Cambridge: Cambridge University Press.

Clark, H. H., and Wilkes-Gibbs, D. 1986. Referring as a Collaborative Process. *Cognition* 22:1-39.

Clark, H. H., and Schaefer, E. F. 1989. Contributing to Discourse. *Cognitive Science* 13:259-294.

Cohen, P. R., and Perrault, C. R. 1979. Elements of a Plan-based Theory of Speech Acts. *Cognitive Science* 3(3):177-212.

Cohen, P. R. 1984. The Pragmatics of Referring and the Modality of Communication. *Computational Linguistics* 10(2):97-146.

Dunham, S. 1991. Personal communication.

Federal Aviation Administration 1989. *Air Traffic Control* 7110.65f.

Federal Aviation Administration 1991. *Airman's Information Manual*.

Findler, N., and Lo, R. 1988. An Examination of Distributed Planning in the World of Air Traffic Control. In A. Bond and L. Gasser (eds.), *Readings In Distributed Artificial Intelligence*. San Mateo, Ca: Morgan Kaufman.

Grosz, B. J., and Sidner, C. L. 1986. Attention, Intentions, and the Structure of Discourse. *Computational Linguistics* 12(3):175-204.

Litman, D. J., and Allen, J. F. 1987. A Plan Recognition Model for Subdialogues in Conversations. *Cognitive Science* 11:163-200.

Novick, D. G. 1988. *Control Of Mixed-initiative Discourse Through Meta-locutionary Acts: A Computational Model*, Technical Report No. CIS-TR-88-18, Department of Computer and Information Science, University of Oregon.

Novick, D. G. 1990. Modeling Belief and Action in a Multi-agent System. In B. Zeigler & J. Rozenblit (eds.), *AI Simulation and Planning in High Autonomy Systems*. Los Alamitos, CA: IEEE Computer Society Press.

Oviatt, S. L., and Cohen, P. R. 1988. Discourse Structure and Performance Efficiency in Interactive and Noninteractive Spoken Modalities. Technical Note 454, SRI International.

Power, R. 1979. The Organization Of Purposeful Dialogues, *Linguistics* 17:107-152.

Rosenbaum, S. L. 1988. *A User's View Of The Air Traffic Control (ATC) System*. Internal Memorandum 46321-881130-01.IM, AT&T Bell Laboratories.

Schober, M. F., and Clark, H. H. 1989. Understanding by Addressees and Overhearers. *Cognitive Psychology* 21:211-232.

Searle, J. R. 1969. *Speech Acts: An Essay In The Philosophy Of Language*. Cambridge: Cambridge University Press.

Searle, J. R. 1975. Indirect Speech Acts. In J. L. Morgan (ed.) *Syntax and Semantics, Volume 3: Speech Acts*. New York: Academic Press.

Searle, J. R., and Vanderveken, D. 1985. *Foundations of Illocutionary Logic*. Cambridge: Cambridge University Press.

Suchman, L. A. 1987. *Plans and Situated Actions*. Cambridge: Cambridge University Press.

Traum, D. R. 1991. Towards a Computational Theory of Grounding in Natural Language Conversation, Technical Report No. 401, Computer Science Department, University of Rochester.

Traum, D., and Hinkelman, E. 1992. Conversation Acts in Task-Oriented Spoken Dialogue, Technical Report 425, Department of Computer Science, University of Rochester. (To appear in *Computational Intelligence*, 8(3)).

Ward, K.; Novick, D. G.; and Sousa, C. 1990. Air Traffic Control Communications at Portland International Airport, Technical Report, CS/E 90-025, Department of Computer Science and Engineering, Oregon Graduate Institute.

Ward, K. 1992. A Speech Act Model of Air Traffic Control Dialogue. M.S. thesis, Department of Computer Science and Engineering, Oregon Graduate Institute.

Wesson, R. B. 1977. Problem-solving with Simulation in the World of an Air Traffic Controller. Ph.D diss., University of Texas at Austin.

Winograd, T., and Flores, F. 1986. *Understanding Computers and Cognition*. Norwood, NJ: Ablex.

An Optimizing Method for Structuring Inferentially Linked Discourse[*]

Ingrid Zukerman and Richard McConachy
Department of Computer Science
Monash University
Clayton, Victoria 3168, AUSTRALIA
{ingrid,ricky}@bruce.cs.monash.edu.au

Abstract

In recent times, there has been an increase in the number of Natural Language Generation systems that take into consideration a user's inferences. The statements generated by these systems are typically connected by inferential links, which are opportunistic in nature. In this paper, we describe a discourse structuring mechanism which organizes inferentially linked statements as well as statements connected by certain prescriptive links. Our mechanism first extracts relations and constraints from the output of a discourse planner. It then uses this information to build a directed graph whose nodes are rhetorical devices, and whose links are the relations between these devices. The mechanism then applies a search procedure to optimize the traversal through the graph. This process generates an ordered set of linear discourse sequences, where the elements of each sequence are maximally connected. Our mechanism has been implemented as the discourse organization component of a system called WISHFUL which generates concept explanations.

Introduction

Consideration of the inferences an addressee is likely to make from discourse is an essential part of discourse planning. In recent times, there has been an increase in the number of Natural Language Generation (NLG) systems which address the inferences a user is likely to make from the information presented by these systems, e.g., [Joshi et al. 1984; Zukerman 1990; Cawsey 1991; Horacek 1991; Lascarides & Oberlander 1992; Zukerman & McConachy 1993].

A system that addresses a user's possible inferences poses a new set of problems for the discourse structuring component of the system. Consider, for example, the following discourse:

1 The first step in Bracket Simplification is addition or subtraction.
2 For example, $2(3x + 5x) = 2 \times 8x$.
3 *Indeed*, Bracket Simplification applies to Like Terms.

4 *In addition*, as you know, it applies to Numbers.
5 *However*, it does not always apply to Algebraic Terms.
6 For instance, you cannot add the terms in brackets in $3(2x + 7y)$.

This discourse features inferential relations in lines 2-3, 3-4 and 4-5 (signaled by italicized conjunctions). The sentence in line 3 realizes a generalization from the example in line 2, the sentence in line 4 expands on the information in line 3, and the sentence in line 5 violates an expectation established in line 4.

The two main methods for text organization considered to date are the schema-based approach, e.g., [Weiner 1980; McKeown 1985; Paris 1988], and the goal-based approach, e.g., [Hovy 1988; Moore & Swartout 1989; Cawsey 1990]. Both of these methods are designed to accomplish a single discourse goal. However, inferential relations are opportunistic rather than prescriptive, and therefore cannot be easily cast as contributing to a single communicative goal. Hence, these approaches are ill equipped to cope adequately with inferential links.

In this paper, we present a mechanism which organizes inferentially linked information into maximally connected discourse. This mechanism also copes with prescriptive discourse relations between the intended information and the prerequisite information that is needed to understand the intended information. Our mechanism has been implemented as a component of a system called WISHFUL which generates concept explanations [Zukerman & McConachy 1993].

In the following section, we discuss previous research in discourse structuring. Next, we outline the operation of our discourse planner as background to the description of our discourse structuring mechanism. We then discuss our results and present concluding remarks.

Related Research

The schema based approach was introduced in [Weiner 1980]. It was later formalized in [McKeown 1985] and expanded in [Paris 1988]. This approach consists of compiling rhetorical predicates into a *schema* or template which reflects normal patterns of discourse. Since schemas represent compiled knowledge, they are com-

---

[*]This research was supported in part by grant A49030462 from the Australian Research Council.

putationally efficient. However, they do not cope well with the need to exhibit dynamic and adaptive behaviour. This shortcoming is overcome by the goal-based approach.

The two main techniques which represent the goal-based approach are described in [Hovy 1988; Hovy & McCoy 1989] and in [Moore & Swartout 1989]. Both techniques involve converting discourse relations identified in Rhetorical Structure Theory (RST) [Mann & Thompson 1987] into discourse plan operators, and then applying a hierarchical planner [Sacerdoti 1977] to produce a discourse plan. This plan is a tree whose leaves are propositions and whose non-leaf nodes are relations between propositions. Moore's mechanism takes as input a communicative goal, and uses discourse plan operators both to decide what to say and to organize the discourse. Hovy's structurer, on the other hand, is given a set of propositions to be communicated as well as one or more communicative goals. [Hovy & McCoy 1989] later combined Hovy's discourse structurer with *Discourse Focus Trees* proposed in [McCoy & Cheng 1991] in order to enhance the coherence and flexibility of the generated discourse.

The goal-based approach is particularly suitable for situations where a communicative goal may be achieved by whatever means are available, e.g., convincing a user to do something [Moore & Swartout 1989]. However, when the objective is to convey information about a concept, e.g., teach Distributive Law, this approach may omit information that does not fit in the proposed rhetorical structure. For instance, the system described in [Hovy 1988] tries to include as much information as possible in a generated RST tree, but leaves out information that does not fit. The system described in [Cawsey 1990] includes only certain types of information in the discourse operators, and therefore, other relevant information may never be mentioned.

A different approach was taken in [Mann & Moore 1981], where discourse organization is viewed as a problem solving task whose objective is to satisfy some optimality criterion. They implemented a hill-climbing procedure which iteratively selects the best pairwise combination of an available set of *protosentences*. Due to the use of the hill-climbing function, this approach produces locally optimal discourse. In this research, we also view discourse organization as a problem solving task, but we generate discourse which satisfies globally our optimality criterion.

Finally, [Mooney et al. 1991] and [Cerbah 1992] consider the discourse structuring problem at a different level. [Mooney et al. 1991] generate extended discourse by first applying a bottom-up strategy to partition a large number of information items into groups, and then applying a goal-based technique to structure the discourse in each group. [Cerbah 1992] uses global discourse strategies, such as parallel-explanation and concession, to guide the organization of discourse relations in order to generate discourse that achieves a desired overall effect. An interesting avenue of investigation is the adaptation of the mechanism presented in this paper as a component of these systems.

Operation of the Discourse Planner

Our discourse planner receives as input a *concept* to be conveyed to a hearer, e.g., Bracket Simplification; a list of *aspects* that must be conveyed about this concept, e.g., operation and domain; and an *attitude*, which determines a desired level of expertise. It generates a set of *Rhetorical Devices (RDs)*, where an RD is composed of a rhetorical action, such as Assert or Instantiate, applied to a proposition. To this effect, it performs the following steps.

Step 1: WISHFUL first consults a model of the user's beliefs in order to determine which propositions must be presented to convey the given aspects. This step selects for presentation propositions about which the user has misconceptions, and propositions that are believed by the user but not to the extent demanded by the given attitude. Table 1 contains the propositions selected to convey the operation and domain of Bracket Simplification.

p_1: [Bracket-Simplification step-1 +/−]
p_3: [Bracket-Simplification apply-to Like-Terms]
p_5: [Bracket-Simplification ¬(always) apply-to Algebraic-Terms]

Table 1: *Propositions to be Conveyed*

Step 2: Next, WISHFUL applies inference rules in backward reasoning mode in order to generate alternative RDs that can be used to convey each proposition. It then applies inference rules on these RDs in forward reasoning mode in order to conjecture which other propositions are indirectly affected by these RDs. If propositions that are currently believed by the user are adversely affected by inferences from the proposed RDs, they will be added to the set of propositions to be conveyed, e.g., proposition p_4 in Table 2.

Step 3: In this step, the generation process is applied recursively with a revised attitude and new aspects for each of the concepts mentioned in each of the alternative sets of RDs generated in Step 2. This is necessary, since it is possible that the hearer does not understand the concepts mentioned in a particular set of RDs well enough to understand this set. This process generates subordinate sets of RDs, each of which is an alternative way of conveying a concept that was not sufficiently understood by the hearer.

Rhetorical Action	Proposition
Assert _(A)_	p_3: [Bracket-Simplification apply-to Like-Terms]
Mention _(M)_	p_4: [Bracket-Simplification apply-to Numbers]
Assert+Instantiate $2(3x + 5x)$ _(A+I)_	p_1: [Bracket-Simplification step-1 +/−]
Negate+Instantiate[+] $3(2x + 7y)$ _(N+I[+])_	p_5: [Bracket-Simplification always apply-to Algebraic-Terms]

Table 2: *The Set of RDs Selected by WISHFUL*

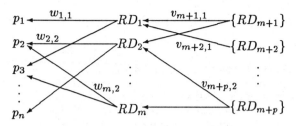

Figure 1: *A 2-layer RD-Graph*

Step 4: For each concept used in each alternative set of RDs, WISHFUL now generates a set of RDs that *evokes* this concept, if the user model indicates that the user and the system do not have a common terminology for it[1]. To ensure that the available discourse options are not constrained unnecessarily, Evocative RDs are generated *before* the organization of the discourse. Further, they are used to generate constraints for the discourse organization process. For instance, consider a situation where the only possible evocation of the concept Like-Terms is "a kind of Algebraic Expression where all the variables are the same." Now, if the organization procedure had been applied before the evocation step, it could have arbitrarily determined that Algebraic-Expressions should be introduced long after Like-Terms. In this case, the resulting discourse would be awkward at best. This situation is avoided by constraining Algebraic-Expressions to appear either before or immediately after Like-Terms. The generation of access referring expressions, on the other hand, must be performed after the organization of the discourse, since decisions regarding pronominalization depend on the structure of the discourse.

Step 5: Owing to the interactions between the inferences from the RDs in each set of RDs generated so far, it is possible that some of the proposed RDs are no longer necessary. In order to remove the redundant RDs, WISHFUL applies an optimization process to each set of RDs. It then selects the set with the least number of RDs among the resulting sets.

The output of the discourse planner is an *RD-Graph*, which is a directed graph that contains the following components: (1) the set of propositions to be conveyed ($p_1, \ldots, p_n$ in Figure 1); (2) the selected set of RDs ($RD_1, \ldots, RD_m, \{RD_{m+1}\}, \ldots, \{RD_{m+p}\}$); (3) the inferential relations between the RDs and the propositions (labelled $w_{i,j}$); and (4) the prescriptive relations between the sets of RDs that generate prerequisite and evocative information and the RDs that are connected to the propositions (labelled $v_{m+k,j}$). The inferential relations are generated in Step 2 above. The weight $w_{i,j}$ contains information about the effect of RD_i on the user's belief in proposition p_j. The prerequisite information is generated in Step 3, and the evocative information in Step 4.

Table 2 contains the set of RDs generated by WISHFUL for the input in Table 1. The rhetorical action

---

[1]Evocation pertains to the first time a concept is mentioned in a piece of discourse, as opposed to *access*, which pertains to subsequent references to this concept [Webber 1983].

Mention indicates that the user is familiar with the proposition in question. **Instantiate**[+] stands for an Instantiation annotated with a short explanation, such as that in line 6 in the sample discourse in the Introduction. The algebraic expressions $2(3x + 5x)$ and $3(2x+7y)$ in the Instantiations are the objects on which the corresponding propositions are instantiated.

Operation of the Discourse Structurer

Our discourse structuring mechanism generates an optimal ordering of the RDs in the RD-Graph generated by the previous steps of WISHFUL. Our optimality criterion is *maximum connectivity*, which stipulates that the generated discourse should include the strongest possible relations between the RDs in the graph.

Our procedure first uses the relations in the RD-Graph to derive constraints and relations that affect the order of the generated RDs. The constraints are strict injunctions regarding the relative ordering of these RDs, while the relations are suggestions regarding the manner in which the RDs should be connected. These constraints and relations are then represented as a *Constraint-Relation Graph*, which is a directed graph whose nodes are RDs and whose links are relations and constraints. Finally, we apply a search procedure which finds the optimal traversal through the graph, i.e., the traversal which uses the strongest links and violates no constraints.

Extracting Constraints and Relations

The constraints extracted by our mechanism are BE-FORE and IMMEDIATELY-AFTER. They are obtained directly from the prescriptive links in the RD-Graph (the links in the right-hand layer of the graph in Figure 1) by applying the following rule:

If $\exists$ a link between $\{RD_{m+k}\}$ and RD_j $(v_{m+k,j} \neq 0)$
Then BEFORE($\{RD_{m+k}\}, RD_j$) or
    IMMEDIATELY$-$AFTER($\{RD_{m+k}\}, RD_j$).

These constraints stipulate that a set of RDs that is used to evoke or explain a concept must be presented in the discourse either at any time before this concept is presented or immediately after it.

The relations extracted by our mechanism are CAUSE, REALIZE, ADD and VIOLATE. The first three relations represent corroborating information, where the causal relation is the strongest, and the additive relation the weakest. The fourth relation represents conflicting information. In order to derive these relations, the system first obtains *support* and *soundness* information from the weights $w_{i,j}$ of the inferential links in the RD-Graph (the links in the left-hand layer of the graph in Figure 1).

Support indicates whether an inference from an RD supports or contradicts a proposition. Inferences that support a proposition are *positive (+)*, while inferences that contradict it are *negative (−)*.

Soundness indicates the level of soundness of an inference from an RD. We distinguish between three types of positive inferences based on the soundness of the inference rules that yield these inferences: *sound (s), acceptable (a)* and *unacceptable (u)*. Negative inferences are not affected by this distinction, since the

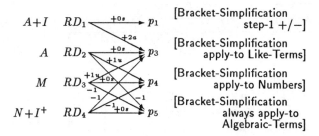

$$
\begin{array}{lll}
A+I & RD_1 \xrightarrow{+0s} p_1 & \text{[Bracket-Simplification} \\
& & \qquad\qquad \text{step-1} +/-] \\
A & RD_2 \xrightarrow{+0s}_{+1u} p_3 & \text{[Bracket-Simplification} \\
& & \qquad \text{apply-to Like-Terms]} \\
M & RD_3 \xrightarrow{+1u} p_4 & \text{[Bracket-Simplification} \\
& & \qquad \text{apply-to Numbers]} \\
N+I^+ & RD_4 \xrightarrow{+0s} p_5 & \text{[Bracket-Simplification} \\
& & \qquad \text{always apply-to} \\
& & \qquad \text{Algebraic-Terms]}
\end{array}
$$

Figure 2: *RD-Graph for the Selected Set of RDs*

manner in which they are addressed is not influenced by their soundness.

Sound inferences are logically sound, e.g., a specialization from a positive statement or a generalization from a negative statement.

Acceptable inferences are sensible, and their results hold often, e.g., a generalization from an instance to a class, a generalization from a positive statement, or a specialization from a negative statement.

Unacceptable inferences hold only occasionally, and hence should not be reinforced, e.g., inferences based on the superficial similarity of two items.

In addition, the discourse structurer requires **directness** information, which conveys the length of the inference chain which infers a proposition from an RD. A directness of level 0 corresponds to a direct inference, level 1 corresponds to inferences drawn from the application of one inference rule such as generalization or specialization, level 2 corresponds to the combination of two inference rules, etc. Directness reflects the intentionality of the discourse, since direct inferences are usually the ones intended by the speaker. Hence, an RD that conveys a proposition by means of a direct inference always has a positive support for this proposition[2]. Directness information is obtained directly from the inference rules used by the system.

Figure 2 depicts support, soundness and directness information for the RD-Graph which corresponds to the set of RDs in Table 2. For instance, the label $+2a$ represents an acceptable inference of positive support and directness 2.

The relations between the RDs are derived from these factors by means of the procedure *Get-Inferential-Relations*. For each proposition, the algorithm builds a set of binary relations of the form $Rel(RD_i, DirRD)$. Each binary relation contains one RD that conveys this proposition directly ($DirRD$), and another that affects it indirectly (RD_i). As stated above, the possible values of Rel considered by our mechanism are: VIOLATE, CAUSE, REALIZE and ADD. The relation VIOLATE is obtained first from the RDs that affect a proposition indirectly with a negative support, i.e., $DirRD$ is at odds with each of these RDs. The remaining RDs, which have a positive support, corroborate $DirRD$. They are divided into those from

----
[2]The Negation of proposition p has a positive support for the intended proposition $\neg p$.

which the proposition is derived by means of a sound inference, those from which the proposition is inferred by an acceptable inference, and those which yield the proposition through an unacceptable inference. These RDs are related to $DirRD$ by means of the relations CAUSE, REALIZE and ADD, respectively. Table 3 contains the binary relations generated by our algorithm for the RD-Graph in Figure 2.

Procedure **Get-Inferential-Relations**(RD-$Graph$)
For each proposition $p \in RD$-$Graph$ do:

1. $DirRD \leftarrow$ the RD from which p is inferred directly.

2. $IndRD \leftarrow$ the RDs from which p is inferred indirectly.

3. If $IndRD \neq \emptyset$ and $DirRD \neq \emptyset$ Then
   $\{$VIOLATE$(RD_i, DirRD)|$ RD_i affects p with
   $\qquad\qquad$ a *negative* inference$\}$
   $\{$CAUSE$(RD_i, DirRD)|$ RD_i affects p with
   $\qquad\qquad$ a *sound* and *positive* inference$\}$
   $\{$REALIZE$(RD_i, DirRD)|$ RD_i affects p with
   $\qquad\qquad$ an *acceptable* and *positive* inference$\}$
   $\{$ADD$(RD_i, DirRD)|$ RD_i affects p with
   $\qquad\qquad$ an *unacceptable* and *positive* inference$\}$

Building the Constraint-Relation Graph

After the ordering constraints and relations have been extracted from the RD-Graph, they are combined in order to generate the Constraint-Relation Graph used in the next step of the discourse organization process. This is done by iteratively adding each constraint and relation to a graph that starts off empty, without disrupting the links built previously. In order to support a numerical optimization process, the links in the Constraint-Relation Graph are assigned weights. Constraints (BEFORE and IMMEDIATELY-AFTER) are assigned a weight of ∞, since constraints must never be violated. Relations are assigned weights according to their support and soundness as follows: CAUSE 4, REALIZE 2, VIOLATE 2 and ADD 1. Figure 3 illustrates the Constraint-Relation Graph built from the relations in Table 3.

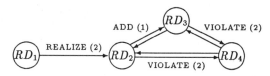

Figure 3: *The Constraint-Relation Graph*

Generating the Optimal Traversal

The procedure for generating the optimal traversal of the Constraint-Relation Graph consists of three stages: (1) *path extraction*, (2) *filtering*, and (3) *optimization*.

The **path extraction** stage generates all the *terminal paths* starting from each node in the Constraint-Relation Graph, where a terminal path is one that continues until a dead-end is reached. For instance, node RD_1 in Figure 3 has two alternative terminal paths: (1) RD_1 – REALIZE – RD_2 – VIOLATE – RD_4 – VIOLATE – RD_3, and (2) RD_1 – REALIZE – RD_2 – ADD – RD_3 – VIOLATE – RD_4.

	p_1	p_3	p_4	p_5
$DirRD$	RD_1	RD_2	RD_3	RD_4
$IndRD\ (-)$	$-$	RD_4	RD_4	$\{RD_2, RD_3\}$
$IndRD\ (+s)$	$-$	$-$	$-$	$-$
$IndRD\ (+a)$	$-$	RD_1	$-$	$-$
$IndRD\ (+u)$	$-$	RD_3	RD_2	$-$
Relation		REALIZE(RD_1,RD_2) ADD(RD_3,RD_2) VIOLATE(RD_4,RD_2)	ADD(RD_2,RD_3) VIOLATE(RD_4,RD_3)	VIOLATE(RD_2,RD_4) VIOLATE(RD_3,RD_4)

Table 3: *Relations Extracted from the RD-Graph*

The **filtering** stage deletes *redundant* and *irregular* paths, where a path is redundant if there exists another path which subsumes it; and a path from node RD_i to node RD_j is irregular if it contains consecutive VIOLATE links, and there exists another path from node RD_i to node RD_j that is composed of positive links only. For example, the path RD_2 – ADD – RD_3 – VIOLATE – RD_4 is redundant, since it is subsumed by path (2) above. The first path above is irregular, since there is a positive link, namely ADD, between RD_2 and RD_3. The deletion of redundant paths cuts down the search, and the deletion of irregular paths prevents the generation of sentences of the form "RD_2, but RD_4. However RD_3" if a sentence of the form "RD_2 and RD_3. However RD_4" is possible.

The **optimization** stage consists of applying algorithm A* [Nilsson 1980], where the goal is to select an ordered set of terminal paths which covers all the nodes in the Constraint-Relation Graph, so that the sum of the weights of the links in these paths is maximal. The operators for expanding a node in the search graph are defined as follows:

Operator O_i traces the terminal path $path_i$ through the Constraint-Relation Graph, and removes from the graph the nodes along the traced route and the links incident upon these nodes. The application of O_i generates discourse that connects the RDs in $path_i$.

After the application of an operator, the problem state consists of (1) the terminal paths removed so far from the Constraint-Relation Graph, and (2) the remaining part(s) of the Constraint-Relation Graph. The remaining parts of the graph must then be processed similarly until the graph is empty.

A* uses the evaluation function $f(n) = g(n) + h(n)$ for each node n in the search graph, and terminates the search at the node with the highest value of f. In order to satisfy the admissibility conditions of A*, g and h are set to the following values:

$$g = \sum_{path \in Paths} \sum_{\{RD_i, RD_j\} \in path} weight(link_{RD_i, RD_j})$$

$$h = \sum_{RD_i \in \{CRG - Paths\}} Weight_{RD_i} - \min_{RD_i \in \{CRG - Paths\}} Weight_{RD_i}$$

where *Paths* are the paths removed so far from the Constraint-Relation Graph CRG; $weight(link_{RD_i, RD_j})$ is the weight of the link which connects RD_i and RD_j; and $Weight_{RD_i}$ is the maximum of the weights of the links incident on RD_i.

The h function estimates the best possible outcome based on the remaining parts of the Constraint-Relation Graph. This outcome corresponds to the discourse that would result if the strongest link incident on each node could be used in the terminal path that covers the remaining graph. The weakest among these links is subtracted from the h function, since $n-1$ links are needed to connect n nodes.

The result of applying this procedure to the Constraint-Relation Graph in Figure 3 is the ordered discourse sequence RD_1 – REALIZE – RD_2 – ADD – RD_3 – VIOLATE – RD_4 which has a total weight of $2 + 1 + 2 = 5$. This sequence yields the following output, which corresponds to the sample text in the Introduction.

Assert+Instantiate$\{2(3x + 5x)\}$
    [Bracket-Simplification step-1 $+/-$]
REALIZE
Assert [Bracket-Simplification apply-to Like-Terms]
ADD
Mention [Bracket-Simplification apply-to Numbers]
VIOLATE
Negate+Instantiate$^+\{3(2x + 7y)\}$
[Bracket-Simplification always apply-to Algebraic-Terms]

Handling Constraints

Our mechanism also handles the constraints BEFORE and IMMEDIATELY-AFTER. Recall that these constraints involve a set of RDs which evokes or explains a singleton RD, e.g., BEFORE$(\{RD_{m+k}\}, RD_j)$. The discourse structurer extracts constraints and relations from the set $\{RD_{m+k}\}$ and builds a Constraint-Relation Graph as explained above. This graph is subordinate to the node RD_j in the main graph, and it is linked to RD_j by a BEFORE/IMMEDIATELY-AFTER hyper-link. The optimization process is applied separately to this graph, resulting in a connected sequence of RDs for the set $\{RD_{m+k}\}$.

This sequence is treated as a single entity when the terminal paths are built for the main graph. When the BEFORE link is followed, this sequence yields an introductory segment that appears at some point before RD_j. Alternatively, when the IMMEDIATELY-AFTER link is followed, it yields a subordinate clause. In this case, if the subordinate graph contains only a few RDs, the main path may continue after the subordinate clause. For example, "Bracket Simplification applies to Like Terms, *which are Algebraic Terms such as* $3(2x + 5x)$. In addition, it applies to Numbers." However, if the subordinate graph is large, the terminal path must stop immediately after it in order to avoid an unwieldy tangential discussion.

Results

As stated above, the mechanism described in this paper is part of a system for the generation of concept explanations. This system is implemented in Sun Common Lisp on a SPARCstation 2. The example discussed throughout this paper takes approximately 4 CPU seconds to reach the stage shown in Table 2, and an additional second to produce the final ordered output sequence of rhetorical devices and relations. Since the discourse organization problem is exponential, the mechanism is slowed down by larger input patterns with many inter-relationships which produce large, highly connected Constraint-Relation Graphs. For example, it takes about twenty seconds to structure one sample input of twenty RDs.

The preliminary testing of our mechanism has been performed in the domains of algebra (14 examples) and zoology (7 examples). Our mechanism was also informally evaluated by showing hand-generated English renditions of its output to staff and tutors in the Department of Computer Science at Monash University. The general opinion of the interviewed staff was that the text was logically constructed. In addition, a comparison of the output of our mechanism with texts in prescribed textbooks showed that this output follows the layout of published instructional material.

Conclusion

We have offered a discourse structuring mechanism that organizes inferentially linked rhetorical devices as well as rhetorical devices linked by prerequisite relations. Our mechanism extracts ordering constraints and inferential relations from the output of a discourse planner, and optimizes the ordering of the generated rhetorical devices based on the principle of maximum connectivity. The output of this mechanism captures sufficient rhetorical features to support continuous discourse.

References

Cawsey, A. 1990. Generating Explanatory Discourse. In Dale, R., Mellish, C., and Zock, M. eds. *Current Research in Natural Language Generation*. Academic Press.

Cawsey, A. 1991. Using Plausible Inference Rules in Description Planning. In Proceedings of the Fifth Conference of the European Chapter of the ACL.

Cerbah, F. 1992. Generating Causal Explanations: From Qualitative Models to Natural Language Texts. In Proceedings of the Tenth European Conference on Artificial Intelligence, 490-494, Vienna, Austria.

Horacek, H. 1991. Exploiting Conversational Implicature for Generating Concise Explanations. In Proceedings of the Meeting of the European Association for Computational Linguistics.

Hovy, E.H. 1988. Planning Coherent Multisentential Text. In Proceedings of the Twenty-Sixth Annual Meeting of the Association for Computational Linguistics, 163-169, Buffalo, New York.

Hovy, E.H.; and McCoy, K.F. 1989. Focusing Your RST: A Step Toward Generating Coherent Multisentential Text. In Proceedings of the Eleventh Annual Meeting of the Cognitive Science Society, 667-674, Ann Arbor, Michigan.

Joshi, A.; Webber, B.L.; and Weischedel, R.M. 1984. Living Up to Expectations: Computing Expert Responses. In Proceedings of the National Conference on Artificial Intelligence, 169-175, Austin, Texas.

Lascarides, A. and Oberlander, J. 1992. Abducing Temporal Discourse. In Dale, R., Hovy, E., Rösner, D., and Stock, O. eds. *Aspects of Automated Language Generation*. Springer-Verlag, Berlin, Heidelberg.

Mann, W.C.; and Moore, J.A. 1981. Computer Generation of Multiparagraph English Text. *American Journal of Computational Linguistics* 7(1): 17-29.

Mann, W.C.; and Thompson, S.A. 1987. Rhetorical Structure Theory: A Theory of Text Organization, Technical Report No. ISI/RS-87-190. Information Sciences Institute, Los Angeles, California.

McKeown, K. 1985. Discourse Strategies for Generating Natural Language Text. *Artificial Intelligence* 27(1): 1-41.

McCoy, K.F.; and Cheng, J. 1991. Focus of Attention: Constraining What Can Be Said Next. In Paris, C.L., Swartout, W.R., and Mann, W.C. eds. *Natural Language Generation in Artificial Intelligence and Computational Linguistics*. Dordrecht, The Netherlands: Kluwer Academic Publishers.

Mooney, D.J.; Carberry, S.; and McCoy, K.F. 1991. Capturing High-level Structure of Naturally Occurring, Extended Explanations Using Bottom-up Strategies. *Computational Intelligence* 7(4): 334-356.

Moore, J.D.; and Swartout, W.R. 1989. A Reactive Approach to Explanation. In Proceedings of the Eleventh International Joint Conference on Artificial Intelligence, 1504-1510, Detroit, Michigan.

Nilsson, N. 1980. *Principles of Artificial Intelligence*. Palo Alto, California: Tioga Publishing Company.

Paris, C.L. 1988. Tailoring Object Descriptions to a User's Level of Expertise. *Computational Linguistics* 14(3): 64-78.

Sacerdoti, E. 1977. *A Structure for Plans and Behaviour*. New York, New York: Elsevier, North-Holland Inc.

Webber, B.L. 1983. So What Can We Talk About Now? In Brady, M., and Berwick, R.C. eds. *Computational Models of Discourse*. MIT Press.

Weiner, J. 1980. Blah, A System Which Explains Its Reasoning. *Artificial Intelligence* 15: 19-48.

Zukerman, I. 1990. A Predictive Approach for the Generation of Rhetorical Devices. *Computational Intelligence* 6(1): 25-40.

Zukerman, I.; and McConachy, R.S. 1993. Generating Concise Discourse that Addresses a User's Inferences. Proceedings of the Thirteenth International Joint Conference on Artificial Intelligence, Chambery, France. Forthcoming.

Distributed
Problem Solving

A One-shot Dynamic Coordination Algorithm for Distributed Sensor Networks *

Keith Decker and Victor Lesser
Department of Computer Science
University of Massachusetts
Amherst, MA 01003
Email: DECKER@CS.UMASS.EDU

Abstract

This paper presents a simple, fast coordination algorithm for the dynamic reorganization of agents in a distributed sensor network. Dynamic reorganization is a technique for adapting to the current local problem-solving situation that can both increase expected system performance and decrease the variance in performance. We compare our dynamic organization algorithm to a static algorithm with lower overhead. 'One-shot' refers to the fact that the algorithm only uses one meta-level communication action.

The other theme of this paper is our methodology for analyzing complex control and coordination issues without resorting to a handful of single-instance examples. Using a general model that we have developed of distributed sensor network environments [Decker and Lesser, 1993a], we present probabilistic performance bounds for our algorithm given any number of agents in any environment that fits our assumptions. This model also allows us to predict exactly in what situations and environments the performance benefits of dynamic reorganization outweigh the overhead.

Introduction

The distributed sensor network (DSN) domain has been a fertile source of examples for the study of cooperative distributed problem solving [Carver and Lesser, 1991; Durfee *et al.*, 1987; Lesser, 1991]. A key result of the early work in DSNs has been the demonstration of the advantages available to groups of agents that communicate about their current problem solving situation. Algorithms for coordinating DSN agents can be divided into two classes on the basis of their communication patterns: *static* algorithms communicate only the results of tasks and no other information about the local state of problem solving; *dynamic* algorithms use meta-level communication about their local problem-solving states to adapt to a situation (examples

---
*This work was supported by ARPA under ONR contract N00014-92-J-1698, ONR contract N00014-92-J-1450, and NSF contract CDA 8922572. The content of the information does not necessarily reflect the position or the policy of the Government and no official endorsement should be inferred.

of this include partial global planning [Durfee and Lesser, 1991] and many negotiation algorithms).

This paper presents a simple one-shot dynamic algorithm for reorganizing agents' areas of responsibility in response to a particular DSN problem-solving episode, and analyzes the agents' resulting behaviors. The class of one-shot dynamic algorithms is interesting because it is the class of coordination algorithms with the lowest communication overhead (only one meta-level communication action) that still allows agents to adapt to a particular situation during problem solving. This low overhead allows dynamic algorithms to be used in environments where the higher costs of multiple meta-level communications and negotiation are not warranted. The particular algorithm presented here, called *one-shot dynamic reorganization*, allows agents to very quickly resolve to a new organization by limiting each agents' area of responsibility to a rectangular shape.

We will analyze the performance of the dynamic algorithm relative to a static one, the effect of some environmental assumptions such as the cost of communication, and the reduction of variance in performance caused by dynamic adaptation (which can be exploited by real-time scheduling algorithms[Decker *et al.*, 1990; Garvey and Lesser, 1993]). The model we will use for our analysis[Decker and Lesser, 1993a] grew out of the set of single instance examples of distributed sensor network (DSN) problems presented in [Durfee *et al.*, 1987]. The authors of that paper compared the performance of several different coordination algorithms on these examples, and concluded that no one algorithm was always the best. This is the classic type of experimental result[Cohen, 1991] that our modeling and analysis method was designed to address—we wish to *explain* this result, and better yet, to *predict* which algorithm will do the best in each situation. We wish to identify the characteristics of the DSN environment, or the organization of the agents, that cause one algorithm to outperform another. Our approach relies on a statistical characterization of an environment rather than single instance examples.

The first section will summarize our model of DSN environments and the results of our previous analysis of static coordination algorithms. The next section will discuss dynamic coordination in general, and then we will present the one-shot dynamic reorganization algorithm and confidence intervals on its performance. Finally, we will present our relative performance, communication cost, and variance reduction results.

A Simple Model of DSN Environments

Our task environment model assumes that several independent *task groups* arrive at multiple physical locations over a period of time called an *episode*. In a distributed sensor network (DSN) episode a single vehicle track corresponds to a task group. The movements of several independent vehicles will be detected over a period of time (the episode) by one or more distinct sensors, where each sensor is associated with an agent. For example, on the left side of Figure 2 we see a single episode with 5 vehicle tracks and the outlines of 9 non-overlapping sensor areas.

The performance of agents in such an environment will be based on how long it takes them to process all the task groups (vehicle tracks), which will include the cost of communicating data, task results, and meta-level communication, if any. The organizational structure of the agents will imply which subsets of which task groups (which portions of which vehicle tracks) are available to which agents and at what cost (an agent can get information from its own sensor more cheaply than by requesting information from another agent's sensor). Usually DSN agents have overlapping sensors, and either agent can potentially work on data that occurs in the overlapping area without any extra communication costs. We make several simplifying assumptions: that the agents are homogeneous (have the same capabilities with respect to receiving data, communicating, and processing tasks), that the agents are cooperative (interested in maximizing the system performance over maximizing their individual performance), that the data for each episode is available simultaneously to all agents as specified by their initial organization, and that there are only structural (precedence) constraints within the subtasks of each task group.[1]

Any single episode can be specified by listing the task groups (vehicle tracks), and what part of each task group was available to which agents, given the organizational structure. Our analysis will be based on the statistical properties of episodes in an environment, not any single instance of an episode. The properties of the episodes in a simple DSN environment are summarized by the tuple $\mathcal{D} = <A, \eta, r, o, \mathcal{T}>$ where A specifies the number of agents, η the expected number of task groups, r and o specify the structural portion of the organization by the physical *range* of each agent's sensor and the physical *overlap* between agent sensors[2], and $\mathcal{T}$ specifies the homogeneous task group structure (an example of the task group structure is shown in Figure 1). A particular episode in this environment can be described by the tuple $\mathcal{D} = <A, r, o, \mathcal{T}_1, \ldots, \mathcal{T}_n>$

---

[1]In general there are usually more complex interrelationships between subtasks that affect scheduling decisions, such as *facilitation* [Decker and Lesser, 1991].

[2]We will also assume the sensors start in a square geometry, i.e, 4 agents in a 2×2 square, 25 agents arranged 5×5.

where n is a random variable drawn from a Poisson distribution with an expected value of η.

In a DSN episode, each vehicle track is modeled as a task group. The structure of each task group is based loosely on the processing done by a particular DSN, the Distributed Vehicle Monitoring Testbed (DVMT)[Lesser and Corkill, 1983]. Our simple model is that each task group $\mathcal{T}_i$ is associated with a track of length l_i and has the following structure: (l_i) vehicle location methods (VLM's) that represent processing raw signal data at a single location resulting in a single vehicle location hypothesis; ($l_i - 1$) vehicle tracking methods (VTM's) that represent short tracks connecting the results of the VLM at time t with the results of the VLM at time $t + 1$; (1) vehicle track completion method (VCM) that represents merging all the VTM's together into a complete vehicle track hypothesis. Non-local precedence relationships exist between each method at one level and the appropriate method at the next level as shown in Figure 1—two VLMs precede each VTM, and all VTM's precede the lone VCM. Besides executing methods, agents may also execute communication actions and information gathering actions (such as getting data from the sensors or communications from other agents). We assume that communication and information gathering are no more time consuming that problem solving computation (in practice they are often much quicker—see the analysis in the final section of this paper). A more complete description of our modeling framework, which can handle much more complexity than this simple model illustrates, can be found in [Decker and Lesser, 1993b], in this volume.

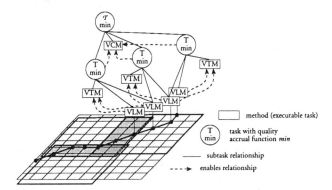

Figure 1: Task structure associated with a single vehicle track.

Later analysis in this paper will be verified by comparing model-based predictions against a DSN simulation, which generates and simulates the execution of arbitrary environments $\mathcal{D}$. In the simulation we assume that each vehicle is sensed at discrete integer locations (as in the DVMT), randomly entering on one edge and leaving on any other edge. Inbetween the vehicle travels along a *track* moving either horizontally, vertically, or diagonally each time unit using a simple DDA line-drawing algorithm (for example, see Figure 2). Given the organization (r, o, and A, and the geometry), we can calculate what locations are seen by the sensors of each agent. This information can then be used along with the locations traveled by each vehicle to determine what part of each task group is initially available to each agent. The analysis summaries in the next section were also verified by simulation; please see [Decker and Lesser, 1993a] for the derivation and verification of these early results; later in this paper we will discuss our verification methodology.

Environmental Analysis Summary

The termination of the system as a whole can be tied to the completion of all tasks at the most heavily loaded agent. Normally, we would use the *average* number of methods to be executed, but since the focus of our analysis is the termination of problem solving, we need to examine the *expected maximum* size $(\hat{S})$ of an initial data set seen by some agent as a random variable. This basic environmental analysis result is taken from the derivation in [Decker and Lesser, 1993a]; it is equivalent to the expected number of VLM methods seen by the maximally loaded agent in an episode. This value also depends on the expected number of task groups $(\hat{N})$ seen by that same agent, another random variable. For example, the observed value of the random variable $(\hat{S})$ in the particular episode shown on the left side of Figure 2 is 22 sensed data points at agent $A4$, and the number of task groups (tracks) seen by that same agent is 4 $(\hat{N} = 4)$. The average number of agents that see a single track (which we represent by the variable a) is 3.8 in the the same episode.

If the system of agents as a whole sees n total task groups, then the discrete probability distributions of $\hat{N}$ and $\hat{S}$ are:

$$\Pr[\hat{N} = N | n] = g_{A,n,\frac{a}{A}}(N) \qquad (1)$$

$$\Pr[\hat{S} = s | \hat{N} = N] = g_{a,N,0.5}(s) \qquad (2)$$

$$\hat{S} = (r\hat{S} + (r/2)(N - \hat{S})) \qquad (3)$$

The function $g_{a,n,p}(s)$ is called the max binomial order statistic, and is defined in terms of the simple binomial probability function $b_{n,p}(s)$ as follows:

$$
\begin{array}{lll}
b_{n,p}(s) & = \binom{n}{s} p^s (1-p)^{n-s} & [\Pr[S = s]] \\
B_{n,p}(s) & = \sum_{x=0}^{s} b_{n,p}(x) & [\Pr[S \le s]] \\
g_{a,n,p}(s) & = B_{n,p}(s)^a - B_{n,p}(s-1)^a & [\Pr[\hat{S} = s]]
\end{array}
$$

The variable a represents the average number of agents that see a single task group, and is estimated as follows:

$$a = A^{(\frac{r^2 + o^2}{2r^2})} \qquad (4)$$

These results, derived and verified in [Decker and Lesser, 1993a], will be used in the following sections within formulae for the predicted performance of coordination algorithms.

Static Coordination Algorithm Analysis summary

In our static algorithm, agents always divide up the overlapping sensor areas evenly between themselves so that they do not do redundant work, and never have to communicate about their areas of responsibility. The total time until termination for an agent receiving the maximum initial data

set (of size $\hat{S}$) is the time to do local work, combine results from other agents, and build the completed results, plus two communication and information gathering actions. Because this agent has the *maximum* amount of initial data, it will not finish any more quickly than any other agent and therefore we can assume it will not have to wait for the results of other agents. The termination time of this agent (and therefore the termination time of the entire statically organized system) can be computed from the task structure shown earlier, and a duration function $d_0(M)$ that returns the duration of method M:

$$
\begin{aligned}
T_{\text{static}} = \\
\hat{S}\mathbf{d}_0(\text{VLM}) + (\hat{S} - \hat{N})\mathbf{d}_0(\text{VTM}) + \\
(a - 1)\hat{N}\mathbf{d}_0(\text{VTM}) + \hat{N}\mathbf{d}_0(\text{VCM}) + \\
2\mathbf{d}_0(I) + 2\mathbf{d}_0(C) \qquad (5)
\end{aligned}
$$

We can use Eq. 5 as a predictor by combining it with the probabilities for the values of $\hat{S}$ and $\hat{N}$ given in Eqns. 3 and 1. Again, we refer the interested reader to [Decker and Lesser, 1993a] for derivations and verification.

Analyzing Dynamic Organizations

In the dynamic organizational case, agents are not limited to the original organization and initial distribution of data. Agents can re-organize by changing the initial static boundaries (changing responsibilities in the overlapping areas), or by shipping raw data to other agents for processing (load balancing). We will assume in this section that the agents do not communicate with each other about the current local state of problem solving directly. A clearer distinction is that in a one-shot dynamic organization each agent makes its initial decision (about changing boundaries or shipping raw data) without access to non-local information. By contrast, in a full meta-level communication algorithm (like Partial Global Planning) the agent has access to both its local information and a summary of the local state of other agents. In this paper the decision to dynamically change the organization is made only once, at the start of an episode after the initial information-gathering action has occurred.

In the case of reorganized overlapping areas, agents may shift the initial static boundaries by sending a (very short) message to overlapping agents, telling the other agents to do more than the default amount of work in the overlapping areas. The effect at the local agent is to change its effective range parameter from its static value of $r' = r - o/2$ to some value r'' where $r - o/2 \ge r'' \ge r - o$, changing the first two terms of Equation 5, and adding a communication action to indicate the shift and an extra information gathering action to receive the results. The following section discusses a particular implementation of this idea that chooses the partition of the overlapping area that best reduces expected differences between agent's loads and averages competing desired partitions from multiple agents.

In the load balancing case, an agent communicates some proportion ρ of its initial sensed data to a second agent, who does the associated work and communicates the results back. Instead of altering the effective range and overlap, this method directly reduces the first two terms of Equation 5 by the proportion ρ. The proportion ρ can be chosen dynamically in a way similar to that of choosing where to partition the overlap between agents (see the next section).

Whether or not a dynamic reorganization is useful is a function of both the agent's local workload and also the load at the other agent. The random variable S again represents the number of initially sensed data points at an agent. Looking first at the local utility, to do local work under the initial static organization with n task groups, any agent will take time:

$$S\mathbf{d}_0(\text{VLM}) + (S - n)\mathbf{d}_0(\text{VTM}) \qquad (6)$$

When the static boundary is shifted before any processing is done, the agent will take time

$$\mathbf{d}_0(C_{\text{short}}) + S''\mathbf{d}_0(\text{VLM}) + (S'' - n)\mathbf{d}_0(\text{VTM}) + \mathbf{d}_0(I) \quad (7)$$

to do the same work, where C_{short} is a very short communication action which is potentially much cheaper than the result communications mentioned previously, and S'' is calculated using the new range r''. When balancing the load directly, local actions will take time

$$\mathbf{d}_0(C_{\text{long}}) + \rho S\mathbf{d}_0(\text{VLM}) + \rho(S - n)\mathbf{d}_0(\text{VTM}) + \mathbf{d}_0(I) \quad (8)$$

where $\mathbf{d}_0(C_{\text{long}})$ is potentially much more expensive than the communication actions mentioned earlier (since it involves sending a large amount of raw data). If the other agent had no work to do, a simple comparison between these three equations would be a sufficient design rule for deciding between static and either dynamic organization.

Of course, we cannot assume that the other agent is not busy; the best we can do *a priori* (without an extra meta-level communication during a particular episode) is to assume the other agent has the *average* amount of work to do. We can derive *a priori* estimates for the average local work at another agent from Equation 6 by replacing S with $\bar{S}$, the probability distribution of the *average* initial sensed data at an agent. This probability distribution is the same as Eq. 3 except that we replace the probability function of the max order statistic $g_{a,N,p}(s)$ in Eq. 2 with the simple binomial probability function $b_{N,p}(s)$ (we'll restate the equations for our implementation in the next section). Therefore without any meta-level communication an agent can estimate how busy its neighbors are, and a system of agents could choose intelligently between static, dynamic overlap reorganization, and dynamic load balancing given these constraints.

One-shot Dynamic Coordination Algorithm for Reorganization

This section describes a particular implementation of the general idea described earlier of dynamically reorganizing the partitions between agents for the DSN simulation. This implementation will keep each agent's area of responsibility rectangular, and relaxes competing constraints from other agents quickly and associatively (the order of message arrival does not affect the eventual outcome). To do this, the message sent by an agent requests the movement of the four *corridors* surrounding an agent. The northern corridor of Agent 1, for example, is the northern agent organizational responsibility boundary shared by every agent in the same

row as Agent 1. As can be seen in Figure 2, a 3x3 organization has four corridors (between rows 1 and 2, 2 and 3, and between columns 1 and 2, 2 and 3).

The coordination algorithm described here works with the static local scheduling algorithm described in [Decker and Lesser, 1993a]. This is consistent with our view of coordination as a *modulating* behavior [Decker and Lesser, 1991]. This simple local scheduler basically runs a loop that finds all local methods that can currently be executed that are also tied to data within the agent's static, non-overlapping sensor area, and then executes one. If no methods can be executed, the current set of results (if new) are broadcast to the other agents, and an information gathering action is executed to receive any new communication from other agents. The only modification to the local scheduler for the dynamic system is that we prevent it from scheduling local method execution actions until our initial communications are completed (the *initial* and *reception* phases, described below).

The coordination algorithm is then as follows. During the *initial* phase the local scheduler schedules the initial information gathering action, and we precede to the second phase, *reception*. In the second phase we use the local information to decide what organizational design to use, and the parameter values for the design we choose. To do this we calculate the duration of our (known) local work under the default static organization (Eq. 6), and then estimate that duration under the alternative organizations (dynamic reorganization or load-balancing). When a parameter needs to be estimated, we do so to minimize the absolute expected difference between the amount of work to be done locally and the amount of work done at the remote agent that is impacted the most by the proposed change.

For example, when dynamically restructuring, if the overlap between agents is more than 2 units, we have a choice of reducing the area an agent is responsible for by more than 1 unit (this is the organizational design parameter ρ in question). To decide on the proper reduction (if any), each agent computes its known local work W using Eq. 6 with the actual (not estimated) S and N computed assuming the agent's area is reduced by ρ. Then the agent finds the value of ρ that minimizes the difference in its known local work $W(r - \rho, S, N)$ and the *average* work $\bar{W}(r + \rho, \bar{S}, \bar{N})$ at the other agent:

$$S(r, s, N) = \left(rs + \frac{r}{2}(N - s)\right)$$

$$W(r, s, N) = S(r, s, N)\mathbf{d}_0(\text{VLM})$$
$$+ (S(r, s, N) - N)\mathbf{d}_0(\text{VTM})$$

$$E[\bar{W}|r] = \sum_{N=0}^{n}\sum_{s=0}^{N} b_{n,\frac{a}{A}}(N)b_{N,0.5}(s)W(r, s, N) \quad (9)$$

If $\rho = 0$, then the agent will not restructure. If $\rho \neq 0$, then the agent sends a message to all affected agents requesting a reduction of amount ρ in each corridor (north, east, south, and west). The agent sets its current area of interest to include only the unique (non-overlapping) portion of its area (if any), and enters the *unique-processing* phase. During this phase the regular local scheduler described earlier controls method execution actions.

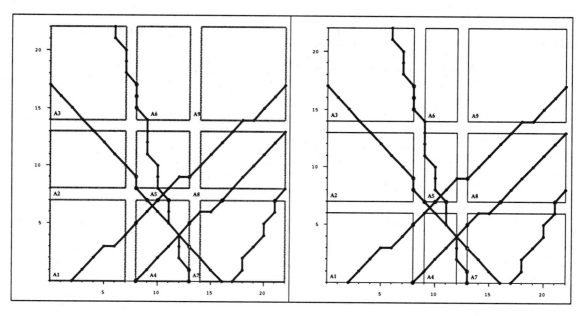

Figure 2: On the left is a 3x3 static organization, on the right is the dynamic reorganization result after agents 3, 4, 5 and 7 attempt to reduce their areas of responsibility by one unit. These are actual screen visualizations (originally in color) from our simulation package.

When no more methods unique to this agent can be executed, the coordination algorithm checks the current time. If enough time has passed for the messages from other agents (if any) to arrive (this depends on the communication delays in the system), the coordination algorithm schedules an information-gathering action to retrieve the messages. Note that every agent may reach this point at a different time; agents with a large amount of unique local work may take some time, agents with no work at all will wait idle for the length of communication delay time in the system.

At this point each agent will relax its borders according to the wishes of the other agents. The relaxation algorithm we have chosen is fairly simple and straightforward, though several similar choices are possible. The algorithm is symmetric with respect to the four corridors surrounding the agent, so we will just discuss the relaxation of the northern corridor. There will be a set of messages about that corridor, some wanting it moved up by some amount and some wanting it moved down by some amount—we will consider these as positive and negative votes of some magnitude. The relaxation algorithm sums the votes, and returns the sum unless it is larger than the maximum vote or smaller than the minimum vote, in which case the max or min is returned, respectively. Competing votes of the same magnitude sum to zero, and cancel each other. The summed value becomes the final direction and amount of movement of that corridor. Figure 2 shows a particular example, where four agents each vote to reduce their areas of responsibility by one unit.

At this point the agent has a new static area that does not overlap with any other agent (since all agents will see the same information and follow the same decision procedure), and it enters the final *normal processing* phase, and the local scheduler schedules all further actions as described earlier (scheduling only tasks in the new, non-overlapping range).

To summarize: the agents first perform information gathering to discover the amount of local sensor data in the episode. They then use this local information to decide how to divide up the overlapping regions they share with other agents, using the assumption that the other agents have the average amount of local work to do. This parameter is then communicated to all the affected agents, and the agent works on data in its unique area (if any)—the part of the agent's sensor range that is never the subject of negotiation because only that agent can sense it. After completing and communicating this unique local work, the agent performs another information gathering action to receive the parameter values from the other agents, and a simple algorithm produces a compromise for the way the overlap will be divided up. The agents now proceed as in the static case until the end of the episode.

Analyzing the Dynamic Restructuring Algorithm

As we did in [Decker and Lesser, 1993a], we can develop an expression for the termination time of any episode where the agents follow this algorithm. To do so, we start with the basic termination time given all of the random variables:

$$T_{\text{dynamic}} = \max[T_{\text{static}}[r = r - \rho], T_{\text{static}}[r = r + \rho, \hat{S} = \bar{s}, \hat{N} = \bar{N})] \tag{10}$$

where ρ is computed as described in the last section using the values of $(r, \hat{S}, \hat{N}, \bar{s}, \bar{N})$. To turn this into a predictive formula, we then use the expressions for the probabilities of the terms $\hat{S}$, $\hat{N}$, $\bar{s}$, and $\bar{N}$ (from Eqns. 3 and 1). For example, we can produce an expression for the expected termination of the algorithm:

$$\sum_{\bar{N}=0}^{n}\sum_{\hat{S}=0}^{\hat{N}}\sum_{\bar{N}=0}^{n}\sum_{\bar{s}=0}^{\bar{N}} g_{A,n,\frac{o}{A}}(\hat{N}) \cdot g_{a,\hat{N},0.5}(s) \cdot$$

$$b_{n,\frac{o}{A}}(\bar{N}) \cdot b_{\bar{N},0.5}(\bar{s}) \cdot T_{\text{dynamic}}[r,\hat{S},\hat{N},\bar{s},\bar{N}] \quad (11)$$

We tested the predictions of Equation 11 versus the mean termination time of our DSN simulation over 10 repetitions in each of 10 randomly chosen environments from the design space $[2 \leq r \leq 10, 0 \leq o \leq r, 1 \leq \sqrt{A} \leq 5, 1 \leq N \leq 10]$. The durations of all tasks were set at 1 time unit, as were the duration of information gathering and communication actions, with the exception of the 4 environments shown in the next section. We used the simulation validation statistic suggested by Kleijnen [Kleijnen, 1987] (where $\hat{y}$ = the predicted output by the analytical model and y = the output of the simulation):

$$z = \frac{y - \hat{y}}{(\text{Var}(y) + \text{Var}(\hat{y}))^{1/2}} \quad (12)$$

where $\text{Var}(\hat{y})$ is the predicted variance.[3] The result z can then be tested for significance against the standard normal tables. In each case, we were unable to reject the null hypothesis that the actual mean termination equals the predicted mean termination at the $\alpha = 0.05$ level, thus validating our formal model.[4]

Increasing task durations

Figure 3 compares the termination of static and dynamic restructuring organizations on identical episodes in four different environments. From left to right, the environments were $[A = 9, r = 9, o = 9, n = 7]$, $[A = 4, r = 9, o = 3, n = 5]$, $[A = 16, r = 8, o = 5, n = 4]$, $[A = 9, r = 10, o = 6, n = 7]$. Ten different episodes were generated for each environment. In order to see the benefits of dynamic restructuring more clearly, we chose task durations for each environment similar to those in the DVMT: $\mathbf{d}_0(\text{VLM}) = 6$, $\mathbf{d}_0(\text{VTM}) = 2$, and $\mathbf{d}_0(\text{VCM}) = 2$.[5] Note that the dynamic organization often does significantly better than the static organization, and rarely does much worse—remember that in many particular episodes that the dynamically organized agents will decide to keep the static organization, although they pay a constant overhead when they keep the static organization (one extra communication action and one extra information gathering action, given that the time for a message to reach all agents is no longer than the communication action time).

Comparative Analyses

The next figure demonstrates the effect of the ratio of computation duration to communication duration. This and

---

[3]The predicted variance of Equation 5 can be easily derived from the statistical identity $\text{Var}(x) = E[x^2] - (E[x])^2$.

[4]For non-statisticians: the null hypothesis is that our prediction is the same as the actual value, we did not wish to reject it, and we did not.

[5]The idea being that the VLM methods correspond to lowest three DVMT KSIs as a group, and the other methods correspond to single DVMT KSIs, and that a KSI has twice the duration of a communication action.

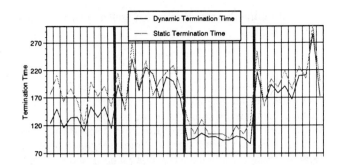

Figure 3: Paired-response comparison of the termination of static and dynamic systems in four different environments (ten episodes in each). Task durations are set to simulate the DVMT (see text).

subsequent figures assume that the dynamic restructuring shrinkage parameter ρ is set to minimize the difference between maximum and average local work as described in the previous section. Figure 4 shows how the expected value and 50% confidence interval on system termination changes as the duration of a method execution action changes from equal to (1x) a communication action to 10 times (10x) that of a communication action. The task structure remains that of the DSN example described in Section . In Figure 4 we see a clear separation emerge between static and dynamic termination. The important point to take from this example is not this particular answer, but that we can do this analysis for *any* environment $\mathcal{D}$.

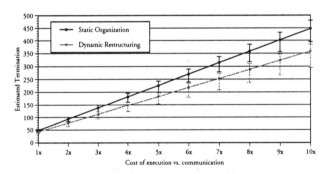

Figure 4: Predicted effect of decreasing communication costs on expected termination under a static organization and dynamic restructuring (expected value and 50% confidence interval, $A = 25, r = 9, o = 9, n = 7$).

Decreasing Performance Variance

The earlier figure assumes that the number of task groups n is known beforehand. The reason for this is to highlight the variance implicit in the organization, and minimize the influence of the external environment. Figure 5 shows how much extra variance is added when only the expected value of n, which is η, is known. We assume that the number of task groups n (in the DSN example, vehicle tracks) that occur during a particular episode has a Poisson distribution with an expected value of η. The discrete probability function for the Poisson distribution, given in any statistics book, is then:

$$p_\eta(y) \;=\; \frac{n^y}{y!}e^{-y} \quad [\text{Pr}\,[n=y]]$$

We can use this probability in conjunction with Eqns. 3, 6, and 9 to calculate the expected value, 50%, and 95% confidence intervals on termination in the static or dynamic organizations. An example of this calculation for one environment is shown in Figure 5. Note in Figure 5 both the large increase in variance when n is random, and the small decrease in variance in the dynamic restructuring organization. Note also that the mean termination time for the dynamic organization is less than that for the static organization.

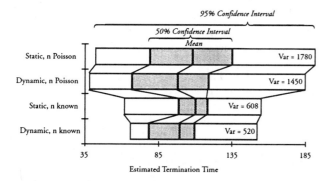

Figure 5: Demonstration of both the large increase in performance variance when the number of task groups n is a random variable, and the small decrease in variance with dynamic restructuring coordination [$A = 9, r = 22, o = 9$]. Where n is known, $n = 5$. Where n is a random variable, the expected value $\eta = 5$.

Conclusions

This paper described a one-shot dynamic coordination algorithm for reorganizing the areas of responsibility for a set of distributed sensor network agents. When performance is measured in terms of the time for a system of agents to terminate, the class of dynamic algorithms can often outperform static algorithms, and reduce the variance in performance (which is a useful characteristic for real-time scheduling [Decker *et al.*, 1990; Garvey and Lesser, 1993]). This paper presented a formula for the expected value (or variance, or confidence interval) of the termination time for a particular one-shot dynamic reorganization algorithm. It showed how this result can be used to predict whether the extra overhead of the dynamic algorithm was worthwhile compared to a static algorithm in a particular environment. Other questions were examined, such as the effect of decreasing communication costs, or increased uncertainty about the task environment.

We hope these results can be used directly by designers of DSNs to choose the number, organization, and control algorithms of agents for their particular environments, and

that they inspire the DAI community to move beyond the development of ideas using single-instance examples.

We are currently analyzing a simple extension of this algorithm that uses two meta-level communication actions to provide agents with non-local information with which to make decisions about how to reorganize. We have observed only a small reduction in mean performance but a greater reduction in variance. Future work we have planned includes the analysis of a multi-stage communication, PGP-style dynamic coordination algorithm, and the use of our expanded model that includes faulty sensors and ghost tracks [Decker and Lesser, 1993b].

References

Carver, N. and Lesser, V.R. 1991. A new framework for sensor interpretation: Planning to resolve sources of uncertainty. In *Proceedings of the Ninth National Conference on Artificial Intelligence*. 724–731.

Cohen, Paul R. 1991. A survey of the eighth national conference on artificial intelligence: Pulling together or pulling apart? *AI Magazine* 12(1):16–41.

Decker, K.S. and Lesser, V.R. 1991. Analyzing a quantitative coordination relationship. Technical Report 91–83, University of Massachusetts. To appear, *Group Decision and Negotiation*, 1993.

Decker, K.S. and Lesser, V.R. 1993a. An approach to analyzing the need for meta-level communication. In *Proc. of the Thirteenth International Joint Conference on Artificial Intelligence*, Chambéry.

Decker, K.S. and Lesser, V.R. 1993b. Quantitative modeling of complex computational task environments. In *Proc. of the Eleventh National Conference on Artificial Intelligence*, Washington.

Decker, K.S.; Lesser, V.R.; and Whitehair, R.C. 1990. Extending a blackboard architecture for approximate processing. *The Journal of Real-Time Systems* 2(1/2):47–79.

Durfee, E.H. and Lesser, V.R. 1991. Partial global planning: A coordination framework for distributed hypothesis formation. *IEEE Trans. on Systems, Man, and Cybernetics* 21(5):1167–1183.

Durfee, E.H.; Lesser, V.R.; and Corkill, D.D. 1987. Coherent cooperation among communicating problem solvers. *IEEE Trans. on Computers* 36(11):1275–1291.

Garvey, A.J. and Lesser, V.R. 1993. Design-to-time real-time scheduling. *IEEE Trans. on Systems, Man, and Cybernetics* 23(6). Special Issue on Scheduling, Planning, and Control.

Kleijnen, J.P.C. 1987. *Statistical Tools for Simulation Practitioners*. Marcel Dekker, New York.

Lesser, V.R. and Corkill, D.D. 1983. The distributed vehicle monitoring testbed. *AI Magazine* 4(3):63–109.

Lesser, V.R. 1991. A retrospective view of FA/C distributed problem solving. *IEEE Trans. on Systems, Man, and Cybernetics* 21(6):1347–1363.

Quantitative Modeling of Complex Computational Task Environments *

Keith Decker and Victor Lesser
Department of Computer Science
University of Massachusetts
Amherst, MA 01003
DECKER@CS.UMASS.EDU

Abstract

Formal approaches to specifying how the mental state of an agent entails that it perform particular actions put the agent at the center of analysis. For some questions and purposes, it is more realistic and convenient for the center of analysis to be the task environment, domain, or society of which agents will be a part. This paper presents such a task environment-oriented modeling framework that can work hand-in-hand with more agent-centered approaches. Our approach features careful attention to the quantitative computational interrelationships between tasks, to what information is available (and when) to update an agent's mental state, and to the general structure of the task environment rather than single-instance examples. A task environment model can be used for both analysis and simulation; it avoids the methodological problems of relying solely on single-instance examples, and provides concrete, meaningful characterizations with which to state general theories. This paper will give an example of a model in the context of cooperative distributed problem solving, but our framework is used for analyzing centralized and parallel control as well.

Introduction

This paper presents a framework, TÆMS (Task Analysis, Environment Modeling, and Simulation), with which to model complex computational task environments that is compatible with both formal agent-centered approaches and experimental approaches. The framework allows us to both analyze and quantitatively simulate the behavior of single or multi-agent systems with respect to interesting characteristics of the computational task environments of which they are part. We believe that it provides the correct level of abstraction for meaningfully evaluating centralized, parallel, and distributed control algorithms for sophisticated knowledge based systems. No previous characterization formally

captures the range of features, processes, and especially interrelationships that occur in computationally intensive task environments.

We use the term *computational task environment* to refer to a problem domain in which the primary resources to be scheduled or planned for are the computational processing resources of an agent or agents, as opposed to physical resources such as materials, machines, or men. Examples of such environments are distributed sensor networks, distributed design problems, complex distributed simulations, and the control processes for almost any distributed or parallel AI application. A job-shop scheduling application *is not* a computational task environment, but the **control**[1] of multiple distributed or large-grain parallel processors that are jointly responsible for solving a job shop scheduling problem *is*. Distributed sensor networks use resources such as sensors, but they are typically not the primary scheduling consideration. Computational task environments are the problem domain for control algorithms like many real-time and parallel local scheduling algorithms [Boddy and Dean, 1989; Garvey and Lesser, 1993; Russell and Zilberstein, 1991] and distributed coordination algorithms [Decker and Lesser, 1991; Durfee *et al.*, 1987].

The *reason* we have created the TÆMS framework is rooted in the desire to produce general theories in AI [Cohen, 1991]. Consider the difficulties facing an experimenter asking under what environmental conditions a particular local scheduler produces acceptable results, or when the overhead associated with a certain coordination algorithm is acceptable given the frequency of particular subtask interrelationships. At the very least, our framework provides a featural characterization and a concrete, meaningful language with which to state correlations, causal explanations, and other forms of theories. The careful specification of the computational task environment also allows the use of very strong analytic or experimental methodologies, including paired-response studies, ablation experiments, and parameter optimization. TÆMS exists as both a language for stating general hypotheses or theories *and* as a system for simulation. The simulator supports the graphical display of generated subjective and objective task structures, agent actions, and statistical data collection in CLOS on the TI

---

*This work was supported by DARPA contract N00014-92-J-1698, Office of Naval Research contract N00014-92-J-1450, and NSF contract CDA 8922572. The content of the information does not necessarily reflect the position or the policy of the Government and no official endorsement should be inferred.

[1]Planning and/or scheduling of computation.

Explorer.

The next section will discuss the general nature of the three modeling framework layers. The following sections discuss the details of the three levels. After describing each layer, we will give an example of a model built with this framework. This example grows out of the set of single instance examples of distributed sensor network (DSN) problems presented in [Durfee et al., 1987] using the Distributed Vehicle Monitoring Testbed (DVMT). The authors of that paper compared the performance of several different coordination algorithms on these examples, and concluded that no one algorithm was always the best. This is the classic type of result that the TÆMS framework was created to address—we wish to explain this result, and better yet, to predict which algorithm will do the best in each situation. The level of detail to which you build your model will depend on the question you wish to answer—we wish to identify the characteristics of the DSN environment, or the organization of the agents, that cause one algorithm to outperform another. In a DSN problem like the DVMT, the movements of several independent vehicles will be detected over a period of time by one or more distinct sensors, where each sensor is associated with an agent. The performance of agents in such an environment is based on how long it takes them to create complete vehicle tracks, including the cost of communication. The organizational structure of the agents will imply the portions of each vehicle track that are sensed by each agent.

General Framework

The principle thing that is being analyzed, explained, predicted, or hypothesized is the performance of a system or some component. While TÆMS does not establish a particular performance criteria, it focuses on providing two kinds of performance information: the temporal location of task executions, and the quality of the execution or its result. Quality is an intentionally vaguely-defined term that must be instantiated for a particular environment and performance criteria. Examples of quality measures include the precision, belief, or completeness of a task result. We will assume that quality is a single numeric term with an absolute scale, although the algebra can be extended to vector terms. In a computationally intensive AI system, several quantities—the quality produced by executing a task, the time taken to perform that task, the time when a task can be started, its deadline, and whether the task is necessary at all—are affected by the execution of other tasks. In real-time problem solving, alternate task execution methods may be available that trade-off time for quality. Agents do not have unlimited access to the environment; what an agent believes and what is really there may be different.

The model of environmental and task characteristics proposed has three levels: objective, subjective, and generative. The objective level describes the essential, 'real' task structure of a particular problem-solving situation or instance over time. It is roughly equivalent to a formal description of a single problem-solving situation such as those presented in [Durfee and Lesser, 1991], without the

information about particular agents. The subjective level describes how agents view and interact with the problem-solving situation over time (e.g., how much does an agent know about what is really going on, and how much does it cost to find out—where the uncertainties are from the agent's point of view). The subjective level is essential for evaluating control algorithms, because while individual behavior and system performance are measured objectively, agents make decisions with only subjective information. Finally, the generative level describes the statistical characteristics required to generate the objective and subjective situations in a domain (how likely are particular task structures, and what variation is present?).

Objective Level

The objective level describes the essential structure of a particular problem-solving situation or instance over time. It focuses on how task interrelationships dynamically affect the quality and duration of each task. The basic model is that task groups appear in the environment at some frequency, and induce tasks T to be executed by the agents under study. Task groups are independent of one another, but tasks within a single task group have interrelationships. Task groups or tasks may have deadlines $D(T)$. The quality of the execution or result of each task influences the quality of the task group result $Q(T)$ in a precise way. These quantities can be used to evaluate the performance of a system.

An individual task that has no subtasks is called a method M and is the smallest schedulable chunk of work (though some scheduling algorithms will allow some methods to be preempted, and some schedulers will schedule at multiple levels of abstraction). There may be more than one method to accomplish a task, and each method will take some amount of time and produce a result of some quality. Quality of an agent's performance on an individual task is a function of the timing and choice of agent actions ('local effects'), and possibly previous task executions ('non-local effects').[2] The basic purpose of the objective model is to formally specify how the execution and timing of tasks affect this measure of quality.

Local Effects: The Subtask Relationship

Task or task group quality ($Q(T)$) is based on the subtask relationship. This quality function is constructed recursively—each task group consists of tasks, each of which consists of subtasks, etc.—until individual executable tasks (methods) are reached. Formally, the subtask relationship is defined as subtask($T, \mathbf{T}, Q$), where $\mathbf{T}$ is the set of all direct subtasks of T and Q is a quality function $Q(T, t) :$ [tasks × times] $\mapsto$ [quality] that returns the quality associated with T at time t. In a valid model, the directed graph induced by this relationship is acyclic (no task has itself for a direct or indirect subtask).

---

[2]When local or non-local effects exist between tasks that are known by more than one agent, we call them coordination relationships[Decker and Lesser, 1991]

The semantics of a particular environment are modeled by the appropriate choice of the quality function Q (e.g., minimum, maximum, summation, or the arithmetic mean). For example, if subtask$(T_1, \mathbf{T}, Q_{\min})$, then $Q(T_1, t) = Q_{\min}(T_1, t) = \min_{T \in \mathbf{T}} Q(T, t)$. In this case the quality that is associated with task T_1 is the minimum quality associated with any of its subtasks. This is sometimes referred to as an AND because the quality of the parent remains at a minimum until every subtask has been completed. Other functions are used for modeling particular environments. Functions like sum and average indicate the possibility that not all tasks in the environment need to be carried out. We have now described how quality is modeled at tasks that have subtasks, but what about methods?

Local Effects: Method Quality

Each method M at a time t will potentially produce (if executed by an agent) some *maximum quality* $\mathbf{q}(M, t)$ in some amount of elapsed time $\mathbf{d}(M, t)$ (we will defer any further definition of the functions $\mathbf{d}$ and $\mathbf{q}$ until we discuss non-local effects). The execution of methods is interruptible, and if multiple methods for a single task are available, the agent may switch between them (typically alternative methods tradeoff time and quality).[3]

Let $\mathsf{P}(M, t)$ be the current amount of progress on the execution of M. If M were not interruptible and $\mathsf{S}(M)$ and $\mathsf{F}(M)$ were the execution start time and finish time, respectively, of M, then:

$$\mathsf{P}(M, t) = \begin{cases} 0 & t \leq \mathsf{S}(M) \\ t - \mathsf{S}(M) & \mathsf{S}(M) < t < \mathsf{F}(M) \\ \mathsf{F}(M) - \mathsf{S}(M) & t \geq \mathsf{F}(M) \end{cases}$$

We typically model the quality produced by a method $Q(M, t)$ using a linear growth function Q_{lin}:

$$Q_{\mathrm{lin}}(M, t) = \begin{cases} \frac{\mathsf{P}(M,t)}{\mathbf{d}(M,t)} \cdot (\mathbf{q}(M, t)) & \mathsf{P}(M, t) < \mathbf{d}(M, t) \\ \mathbf{q}(M, t) & \mathsf{P}(M, t) \geq \mathbf{d}(M, t) \end{cases}$$

Other models (besides linear quality functions) have been proposed and are used, such as concave quality functions (must execute most of a task before quality begins to accumulate), convex quality functions (most quality is achieved early on in a method, and only small increases occur later), and 'mandatory and optional parts' quality functions [Liu *et al.*, 1991]. The desired $Q(M, t)$ can be easily defined for any of these.

As an example of the power of this representation, we consider the two main schools of thought on quality accumulation: the anytime algorithm camp [Boddy and Dean, 1989] and the design-to-time (approximate processing) camp[Decker *et al.*, 1990; Garvey and Lesser, 1993]. We can represent their ideas succinctly; in the anytime algorithm model partial results are always available,[4] as in the definition of $Q_{\mathrm{lin}}(M, t)$ above, while in the design-to-time

---

[3]We model the effect of interruptions, if any, and the reuse of partial results as non-local effects .

[4]In Boddy's paper, the assumption is made that $Q(M, t)$ has monotonically decreasing gain.

model results are not available (quality does not accrue) until the task is complete, as in the definition of $Q_{\mathrm{DTT}}(M, t)$:[5]

$$Q_{\mathrm{DTT}}(M, t) = \begin{cases} 0 & \mathsf{P}(M, t) < \mathbf{d}(M, t) \\ \mathbf{q}(M, t) & \mathsf{P}(M, t) \geq \mathbf{d}(M, t) \end{cases}$$

Non-local Effects

Any task T containing a method that starts executing before the execution of another method M finishes may potentially affect M's execution through a *non-local effect* e. We write this relation nle$(T, M, e, p_1, p_2, \ldots)$, where the p's are parameters specific to a class of effects. There are precisely two possible outcomes of the application of a non-local effect on M under our model: *duration effects* where $\mathbf{d}(M, t)$ (duration) is changed, and *quality effects* where $\mathbf{q}(M, t)$ (maximum quality) is changed. An effect class e is thus a function $e(T, M, t, d, q, p_1, p_2, \ldots)$: [task × method × time × duration × quality × parameter 1 × parameter 2 × . . .] $\mapsto$ [duration × quality].

The amount and direction of an effect is dependent on the relative timing of the method executions, the quality of the effect's antecedent task, and whether information was communicated between the agents executing the methods (in multi-agent models). Some effects are continuous, depending on the current quality of the effect's antecedent $Q(T, t)$. Some effects are triggered by a rising edge of quality past a threshold; for these effects we define the helper function $\Theta(T, \theta)$ that returns the earliest time when the quality surpasses the threshold: $\Theta(T, \theta) = \min(t)$ s.t. $Q(T, t) > \theta$.

Communication. Some effects depend on the availability of information to an agent. We indicate the communication of information at time t about task T_a to an agent A with a delay of δ_t by comm(T_a, A, t, δ_t). There are many models of communication channels that we could take for a communication submodel; since it is not our primary concern we use a simple model with one parameter, the time delay δ_t.[6] For defining effects that depend on the availability of information, we define the helper function $Q_{\mathrm{avail}}(T, t, A)$ that represents the quality of a task T 'available' to agent A at time t. If T was executed at A, $Q_{\mathrm{avail}}(T, t, A) = Q(T, t)$. If T was executed (or is being executed) by another agent, then the 'available' quality is calculated from the last communication about T received at agent A prior to time t.

Computing $\mathbf{d}(M, t)$ *and* $\mathbf{q}(M, t)$. Each method has an initial maximum quality $\mathbf{q}_0(M)$ and duration $\mathbf{d}_0(M)$ so we define $\mathbf{q}(M, 0) = \mathbf{q}_0(M)$ and $\mathbf{d}(M, 0) = \mathbf{d}_0(M)$. If there is only one non-local effect with M as a consequent nle$(T, M, e, p_1, p_2, \ldots)$, then $[\mathbf{d}(M, t), \mathbf{q}(M, t)] \leftarrow$

---

[5]Another difference between design-to-time (DTT) and other approaches will show up in our generative and subjective additions to this model—DTT does not assume that $Q(M, t)$ is fixed and known, but rather that it is an estimator for the actual method response.

[6]Other parameters, such as channel reliability, can be used. The description of an agent's control and coordination algorithms will describe when and where communication actually occurs (see our discussion of communication actions and the concept of agency in the Subjective Level section).

$e(T, M, t, \mathbf{d}(M, t-1), \mathbf{q}(M, t-1), p_1, p_2, \ldots)$. If there is more than one NLE, then the effects are applied one after the other in an order specified in the model (the default is for effects with antecedents closer in the task structure to M to be applied first).

Non-local Effect Examples Non-local effects are the most important part of the TÆMS framework, since they supply most of the characteristics that make one task environment unique and different from another. Typically a model will define different classes of effects, such as *causes, facilitates, cancels, constrains, inhibits,* and *enables*[Decker and Lesser, 1992]. This section contains definitions for three common classes of effects that have been useful in modeling different environments.

Enables. If task T_a enables method M, then the maximum quality $\mathbf{q}(M, t) = 0$ until T_a is completed and the result is available, when the maximum quality will change to the initial maximum quality $\mathbf{q}(M, t) = \mathbf{q}_0(M)$.

$$\text{enables}(T_a, M, t, d, q, \theta) = \begin{cases} [\infty, 0] & t < \Theta(T_a, \theta) \\ [\mathbf{d}_0(M), \mathbf{q}_0(M)] & t \geq \Theta(T_a, \theta) \end{cases} \tag{1}$$

Facilitates. Another relationship, used by the PGP algorithm [Durfee and Lesser, 1991], is the *facilitates* relationship. Intuitively, one task may provide results to another task that *facilitate* the second task by decreasing the duration or increasing the quality of its partial result. Therefore the *facilitates* relationship has two parameters (called *power* parameters) $0 \leq \phi_d \leq 1$ and $0 \leq \phi_q \leq 1$, that indicate the effect on duration and quality respectively. The effect varies not only through the power parameters, but also through the quality of the *facilitating* task available when work on the *facilitated* task starts.

$$\text{facilitates}(T_a, M, t, d, q, \phi_d, \phi_q) = \\ \begin{cases} [d(1 - f(\phi_d, Q_{\text{avail}}(T_a, t), \mathbf{q}(T_a, t))), \\ \quad q(1 + f(\phi_q, Q_{\text{avail}}(T_a, t), \mathbf{q}(T_a, t)))] & t < S(M) \\ [d(1 - f(\phi_d, Q_{\text{avail}}(T_a, S(M)), \mathbf{q}(T_a, t))), \\ \quad q(1 + f(\phi_q, Q_{\text{avail}}(T_a, S(M)), \mathbf{q}(T_a, t)))] & t \geq S(M) \end{cases} \tag{2}$$

where $f(\phi, Q, \mathbf{q}) = \frac{Q}{\mathbf{q}}\phi$. So if T_a is completed with maximal quality, and the result is received before M is started, then the duration $\mathbf{d}(M, t)$ will be decreased by a percentage equal to the duration power ϕ_d of the *facilitates* relationship. The second clause of the definition indicates that communication after the start of processing has no effect. In other work [Decker and Lesser, 1991] we explored the effects on coordination of a *facilitates* relationship with varying duration power ϕ_d, and with $\phi_q = 0$.

Hinders. The *hinders* relationship is the opposite of *facilitates*, because it increases the duration and decreases the maximum quality of the consequent. This can be used as a high-level model of distraction [Durfee *et al.*, 1987].

Objective Modeling Example

Now that we have discussed the basic components of an objective model, let us turn to an example in which we build a model using the TÆMS framework. In our model of DSN problems, the computation to interpret each vehicle track that occurs in the sensed environment is modeled as a task

group. The simplest objective model is that each task group T_i is associated with a track of length l_i and has the following objective structure, based on the DVMT: (l_i) vehicle location methods (VLM) that represent processing raw signal data at a single location resulting in a single vehicle location hypothesis; ($l_i - 1$) vehicle tracking methods (VTM) that represent short tracks connecting the results of the VLM at time t with the results of the VLM at time $t + 1$; (1) vehicle track completion method (VCM) that represents merging all the VTMs together into a complete vehicle track hypothesis. Non-local enablement effects exist—two VLMs *enable* each VTM, and all VTMs *enable* the lone VCM. A picture can be found in the section "A model of DSN environments" in our companion paper [Decker and Lesser, 1993b] (in this volume).

Expanding the Model We will now add some complexity to the model. Let us assume a simple situation: there are two agents, A and B, and that there is one vehicle track of length 3 sensed once by A alone (T^1), once by both A and B (T^2), and once by B alone (T^3). We now proceed to model the standard features that have appeared in our DVMT work for the past several years. We will add the characteristic that each agent has two methods with which to deal with sensed data: a normal VLM and a 'level-hopping' (LH) VLM (the level-hopping VLM produces less quality than the full method but requires less time; see [Decker *et al.*, 1990; Decker *et al.*, 1993] for this and other approximate methods). Furthermore, only the agent that senses the data can execute the associated VLM; but any agent can execute VTMs and VCMs if the appropriate enablement conditions are met.

Figure 1 displays this particular problem-solving episode. To the description above, we have added the fact that agent B has a faulty sensor (the durations of the grayed methods will be longer than normal); we will explore the implications of this after we have discussed the subjective level of the framework in the next section. An assumption made in [Durfee *et al.*, 1987] is that redundant work is not generally useful; this is indicated by using *max* as the combination function for each agent's redundant methods. We could alter this assumption by simply changing this function (to *mean*, for example). Another characteristic that appeared often in the DVMT literature is the sharing of results between methods (at a single agent); we would indicate this by the presence of a sharing relationship (similar to *facilitates*) between each pair of normal and level-hopping VLMs. Sharing of results could be only one-way between methods.

Now we will add two final features that make this model more like the DVMT. First, low quality results tend to make things harder to process at higher levels. For example, the impact of using the level-hopping VLM is not just that its quality is lower, but also that it affects the quality and duration of the VTM it enables (because not enough possible solutions are eliminated). To model this, we will use the *precedence* relationship (a combination of *enables* and *hinders*) instead of just *enables*: not only do the VLM methods enable the VTM, but they can also hinder its execution if the enabling results are of low quality. Secondly, the first VLM

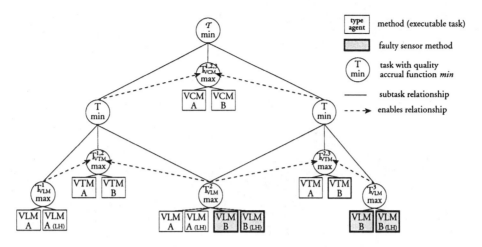

Figure 1: Objective task structure associated with two agents

execution provides information that slightly shortens the executions of other VLMs in the same vehicle track (because the sensors have been properly configured with the correct signal processing algorithm parameters with which to sense that particular vehicle). A similar *facilitation* effect occurs at the tracking level. These effects occur both locally and when results are shared between agents—in fact, this effect is very important in motivating the agent behavior where one agent sends preliminary results to another agent with bad sensor data to help the receiving agent in disambiguating that data [Durfee and Lesser, 1991]. Figure 2 repeats the objective task structure from the previous figure, but omits the methods for clarity. Two new tasks have been added to model facilitation at the vehicle location and vehicle track level.[7] T_{VL} indicates the highest quality initial work that has been done at the vehicle level, and thus uses the quality accrual function *maximum*. T_{VT} indicates the progress on the full track; it uses *summation* as its quality accrual function. The more tracking methods are executed, the easier the remaining ones become. The implications of this model are that in a multi-agent episode, then, the question becomes when to communicate partial results to another agent: the later an agent delays communication, the more the potential impact on the other agent, but the more the other agent must delay. We examined this question somewhat in [Decker and Lesser, 1991].

At the end of the next section, we will return to this example and add to it subjective features: what information is available to agents, when, and at what cost.

Subjective Level

The purpose of a subjective level model of an environment is to describe what portions of the objective model of the situation are available to 'agents'. It answers questions such as "when is a piece of information available," "to whom is it available," and "what is the cost to the agent of that piece

---

[7]Note that these tasks were added to make the model more expressive; they are not associated with new methods.

of information". This is a description of how agents might interact with their environment—what options are available to them.

To build such a description we must introduce the concept of *agency* into the model. Ours is one of the few comprehensive descriptions of computational task environments, but there are many formal and informal descriptions of the concept of agency (see [Gasser, 1991; Hewitt, 1991]). Rather than add our own description, we notice that these formulations define the notion of *computation* at one or more agents, not the environment that the agents are part of. Most formulations contain a notion of *belief* that can be applied to our concept of "what an agent believes about its environment". Our view is that an "agent" is a locus of belief and action (such as computation).

The form of the rest of this section is as follows: how does the environment affect the beliefs of the agents; how do the beliefs of agents affect their actions, and how do the actions affect the environment.

Agent beliefs. We use the symbol Γ_A^t to denote the set of beliefs of agent A at time t. A subjective mapping of an objective problem solving situation $\mathcal{O}$ is a function $\varphi : [A \times \mathcal{O}] \mapsto \Gamma_A$ from an agent and objective assertions to the beliefs of an agent. For example, we could define a mapping φ where each agent has a probability p of believing that the maximum quality of a method is the objective value, and a probability $1 - p$ of believing the maximum quality is twice the objective value. Any objective assertion has some subjective mapping, including **q** (maximum quality of a method), **d** (duration of a method), deadlines, and the relations subtask, nle, and comm.

Control. The beliefs of an agent affect its actions through some control mechanism. Since this is the focus of most of our and others' research on local scheduling, coordination, and other control issues, we will not discuss this further. The agent's control mechanism uses the agent's current set of beliefs Γ_A to update three special subsets of these beliefs (alternatively, *commitments* [Shoham, 1991]) identified as the sets of information gathering, communication,

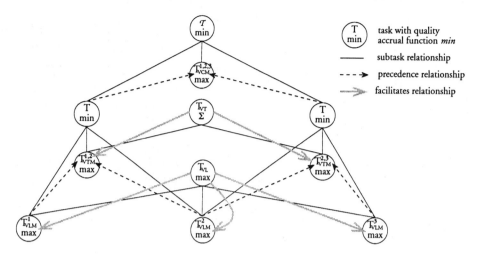

Figure 2: Non-local effects in the objective task structure

and method execution actions to be computed.

Computation. TÆMS can support parallel computation, but for brevity we will just describe single processor computation as a sequence of agent states. Agent A's current state is uniquely specified by Γ_A. We provide a meta-structure for the agent's state-transition function that is divided into the following 4 parts: control, information gathering, communication, and method execution. First the control mechanisms assert (commit to) information-gathering, communication, and method execution actions and then these actions are computed one at a time.

Method Execution. How do the actions of an agent affect the environment? Both the objective environment (i.e. quality of the executing method) and the subjective mapping (i.e., what info is available via φ) can be affected. We use two execution models: simple method execution, and execution with monitoring, suspension, and preemption. These follow from the discussion of Q_{DTT} and Q_{lin} earlier, and are simple state-based models. Basically, for non-interruptible, single processor method executions, the agent enters a method execution state for method M at time $S(M)$ and remains in that state until the time t when $t - S(M) = d(M, t)$. Method execution actions are similar to what Shoham terms 'private actions' like DO [Shoham, 1991].

Communication. How do the actions of an agent affect other agents? Communication actions allow agents to affect each others' beliefs to a limited extent. Many people have worked on formalizing the aspects of communication using ideas such as speech acts. The semantics of communication actions can be freely defined for each environment; most work so far has used speech-act classes of communicative acts, such as Shoham's INFORM and REQUEST. What happens when a communication is 'received'? The reception of information may trigger a non-local effect as we described earlier, and may influence the behavior of an agent as specified by its control algorithm.

Information Gathering. An information gathering action trades-off computational resources (time that could be

spent executing methods) for information about the environment. For example, one useful information gathering action is one that queries the environment about the arrival of new tasks or task groups. Another information gathering action causes any communications that have arrived at an agent to be 'received' (added to the agent's set of beliefs). Both communication and information gathering actions take some period of time to execute, as specified in the model.

Subjective Modeling Example

Let's return to the example we began earlier to demonstrate how adding a subjective level to the model allows us to represent the effects of faulty sensors in the DVMT. We will define the default subjective mapping to simply return the objective value, i.e., agents will believe the true objective quality and duration of methods and their local and non-local effects. We then alter this default for the case of faulty (i.e., noisy) sensors—an agent with a faulty sensor will not initially realize it ($\mathbf{d}_0(\text{faulty-VLM}) = 2\mathbf{d}_0(\text{VLM})$, but $\varphi(A, \mathbf{d}_0(\text{faulty-VLM})) = \mathbf{d}_0(\text{VLM})$).[8] Other subjective level artifacts that are seen in [Durfee *et al.*, 1987] and other DVMT work can also be modeled easily in our framework. For example, 'noise' can be viewed as VLM methods that are subjectively believed to have a non-zero maximum quality ($\varphi(A, \mathbf{q}_0(\text{noise-VLM})) > 0$) but in fact have 0 objective maximum quality, which the agent does not discover until after the method is executed. The strength with which initial data is sensed can be modeled by lowering the subjectively perceived value of the maximum quality $\mathbf{q}$ for weakly sensed data. The infamous 'ghost track' is a subjectively complete task group appearing to an agent as an actual vehicle track, which *subjectively* accrues quality until the hapless agent executes the VCM method, at which point the true (zero) quality becomes known. If the track (subjectively) spans multiple agents' sensor regions,

---

[8]At this point, one should be imagining an agent controller for this environment that notices when a VLM method takes unusually long, and realizes that the sensor is faulty and replans accordingly.

the agent can potentially identify the chimeric track through communication with the other agents, which may have no belief in such a track (but sometimes more than one agent suffers the same delusion).

Generative Level

Space precludes a detailed discussion of the generative level. By using the objective and subjective levels of TÆMS we can model any *individual* situation; adding a *generative* level to the model allows us to go beyond that and determine what the expected performance of an algorithm is over a long period of time and many individual problem solving episodes. Our previous work has created generative models of task interarrival times (exponential distribution), amount of work in a task cluster (Poisson), task durations (exponential), and the likelihood of a particular non-local effect between two tasks [Decker and Lesser, 1993a; Decker and Lesser, 1991; Garvey and Lesser, 1993].

Using the Framework

We have used this model to develop expressions for the expected value of, and confidence intervals on, the time of termination of a set of agents in any arbitrary simple DSN environment that has a static organizational structure and coordination algorithm [Decker and Lesser, 1993a]. We have also done the same for a dynamic, one-shot reorganization algorithm (and have shown when the extra overhead is worthwhile versus the static algorithm) [Decker and Lesser, 1993b] (in this volume). In each case we can predict the effects of adding more agents, changing the relative cost of communication and computation, and changing how the agents are organized. These results were achieved by direct mathematical analysis of the model (a combination of algorithm analysis and derivation of the probability distributions for important parameters) and verified through simulation in TÆMS.

Simulation is also a useful tool for learning parameters to control algorithms, for quickly exploring the behavior space of a new control algorithm, and for conducting controlled, repeatable experiments when direct mathematical analysis is unwarranted or too complex. The simulation system we have built for the direct execution of models in the TÆMS framework supports, for example, the collection of paired response data, where different or ablated coordination or local scheduling algorithms can be compared on identical instances of a wide variety of situations (generated using the generative level of the model). We have used simulation to explore the effect of exploiting the presence of *facilitation* between tasks in a multi-agent real-time environment (no quality is accrued after a task's deadline) [Decker and Lesser, 1991]. The environmental characteristics here included the mean interarrival time for tasks, the likelihood of one task facilitating another, and the strength of the facilitation (ϕ_d).

The TÆMS framework is not limited to experimentation in distributed problem solving. In [Garvey and Lesser, 1993], Garvey and Lesser used the framework to describe the effects of various task environment and agent design features on the performance of their real-time 'design-to-time' algorithm. They show that monitoring does provide a reduction in missed deadlines but that this reduction may be significant only during 'medium' loads. Garvey is now using a more complex model of *enabling* and *hindering* task structures to design an optimal design-to-time algorithm for certain task environments [Garvey et al., 1993] (in this volume).

Related Work and Conclusions

This paper has presented TÆMS, a framework for modeling computationally intensive task environments. TÆMS exists as both a language for stating general hypotheses or theories and as a system for simulation. The important features of TÆMS include its layered description of environments (*objective* reality, *subjective* mapping to agent beliefs, *generative* description of the other levels across single instances); its acceptance of any performance criteria (based on temporal location and *quality* of task executions); and its non-agent-centered point of view that can be used by researchers working in either formal systems of mental-state-induced behavior or experimental methodologies. TÆMS provides environmental and behavioral structures and features with which to state and test theories about the control of agents in complex computational domains, such as how decisions made in scheduling one task will affect the utility and performance characteristics of other tasks.

The basic form of the computational task environment framework—the execution of interrelated computational tasks—is taken from several domain environment simulators [Carver and Lesser, 1991; Cohen et al., 1989; Durfee et al., 1987]. If this were the only impetus, the result might have been a simulator like Tileworld [Pollack and Ringuette, 1990]. However, formal research into multi-agent problem solving has been productive in specifying formal properties, and sometimes algorithms, for the control process by which the mental state of agents (termed variously: beliefs, desires, goals, intentions, etc.) causes the agents to perform particular actions [Cohen and Levesque, 1990; Shoham, 1991; Zlotkin and Rosenschein, 1991]. This research has helped to circumscribe the behaviors or actions that agents can produce based on their knowledge or beliefs. The final influence on TÆMS was the desire to avoid the individualistic agent-centered approaches that characterize most AI (which may be fine) and DAI (which may not be so fine). The concept of agency in TÆMS is based on simple notions of *execution, communication,* and *information gathering.* An agent is a locus of belief (state) and action. By separating the notion of agency from the model of task environments, we do not have to subscribe to particular agent architectures (which one would assume will be adapted to the task environment at hand), and we may ask questions about the inherent social nature of the task environment at hand (allowing that the concept of society may arise before the concept of individual agents).

The TÆMS simulator supports the graphical display of generated subjective and objective task structures, agent actions, and statistical data collection in CLOS on the TI Explorer. It is being used not only for research into the coordination of distributed problem solvers[Decker and Lesser, 1993a; Decker and Lesser, 1991; Decker and Lesser, 1992], but also for research into real-time scheduling of a single agent[Garvey and Lesser, 1993; Garvey et al., 1993], scheduling at an agent with parallel processing resources available, and soon, learning coordination algorithm parameters.

TÆMS does not at this time automatically learn models or automatically verify them. While we have taken initial steps at designing a methodology for verification (see [Decker and Lesser, 1993a]), this is still an open area of research [Cohen, 1991]. Our future work will include building new models of different environments that may include physical resource constraints, such as airport resource scheduling. The existing framework may have to be extended somewhat to handle consumable resources. Other extensions we envision include specifying dynamic objective models that change structure as the result of agent actions. We also wish to expand our analyses beyond the questions of scheduling and coordination to questions about negotiation strategies, emergent agent/society behavior, and organizational self-design.

Acknowledgments

Thanks to Dan Neiman and Alan Garvey for their comments on earlier versions of this paper.

References

Boddy, M. and Dean, T. 1989. Solving time-dependent planning problems. In *Proceedings of the Eleventh International Joint Conference on Artificial Intelligence*.

Carver, N. and Lesser, V. R. 1991. A new framework for sensor interpretation: Planning to resolve sources of uncertainty. In *Proceedings of the Ninth National Conference on Artificial Intelligence*. 724–731.

Cohen, Philip R. and Levesque, H. J. 1990. Intention is choice with commitment. *Artificial Intelligence* 42(3).

Cohen, Paul R.; Greenberg, M.; Hart, D.; and Howe, A. 1989. Trial by fire: Understanding the design requirements for agents in complex environments. *AI Magazine* 10(3):33–48. Also COINS-TR-89-61.

Cohen, Paul R. 1991. A survey of the eighth national conference on artificial intelligence: Pulling together or pulling apart? *AI Magazine* 12(1):16–41.

Decker, K. S. and Lesser, V. R. 1991. Analyzing a quantitative coordination relationship. COINS Technical Report 91–83, University of Massachusetts. To appear in the journal *Group Decision and Negotiation*, 1993.

Decker, K. S. and Lesser, V. R. 1992. Generalizing the partial global planning algorithm. *International Journal of Intelligent and Cooperative Information Systems* 1(2).

Decker, K. S. and Lesser, V. R. 1993a. An approach to analyzing the need for meta-level communication. In *Proceedings of the Thirteenth International Joint Conference on Artificial Intelligence*, Chambéry.

Decker, K. S. and Lesser, V. R. 1993b. A one-shot dynamic coordination algorithm for distributed sensor networks. In *Proceedings of the Eleventh National Conference on Artificial Intelligence*, Washington.

Decker, K. S.; Lesser, V. R.; and Whitehair, R. C. 1990. Extending a blackboard architecture for approximate processing. *The Journal of Real-Time Systems* 2(1/2):47–79.

Decker, K. S.; Garvey, A. J.; Humphrey, M. A.; and Lesser, V. R. 1993. A real-time control architecture for an approximate processing blackboard system. *International Journal of Pattern Recognition and Artificial Intelligence* 7(2).

Durfee, E.H. and Lesser, V.R. 1991. Partial global planning: A coordination framework for distributed hypothesis formation. *IEEE Transactions on Systems, Man, and Cybernetics* 21(5):1167–1183.

Durfee, E. H.; Lesser, V. R.; and Corkill, D. D. 1987. Coherent cooperation among communicating problem solvers. *IEEE Transactions on Computers* 36(11):1275–1291.

Garvey, A. and Lesser, V. R. 1993. Design-to-time real-time scheduling. *IEEE Transactions on Systems, Man, and Cybernetics* 23(6). Special Issue on Scheduling, Planning, and Control.

Garvey, A.; Humphrey, M.; and Lesser, V. R. 1993. Task interdependencies in design-to-time real-time scheduling. In *Proceedings of the Eleventh National Conference on Artificial Intelligence*, Washington.

Gasser, L. 1991. Social conceptions of knowledge and action. *Artificial Intelligence* 47(1):107–138.

Hewitt, C. 1991. Open information systems semantics for distributed artificial intelligence. *Artificial Intelligence* 47(1):79–106.

Liu, J. W. S.; Lin, K. J.; Shih, W. K.; Yu, A. C.; Chung, J. Y.; and Zhao, W. 1991. Algorithms for scheduling imprecise computations. *IEEE Computer* 24(5):58–68.

Pollack, M. E. and Ringuette, M. 1990. Introducing Tileworld: Experimentally evaluating agent architectures. In *Proceedings of the Eighth National Conference on Artificial Intelligence*. 183–189.

Russell, S. J. and Zilberstein, S. 1991. Composing real-time systems. In *Proceedings of the Twelfth International Joint Conference on Artificial Intelligence*, Sydney, Australia. 212–217.

Shoham, Y. 1991. AGENT0: A simple agent language and its interpreter. In *Proceedings of the Ninth National Conference on Artificial Intelligence*, Anaheim. 704–709.

Zlotkin, G. and Rosenschein, J. S. 1991. Incomplete information and deception in multi-agent negotiation. In *Proceedings of the Twelfth International Joint Conference on Artificial Intelligence*, Sydney, Australia. 225–231.

Overeager Reciprocal Rationality and Mixed Strategy Equilibria

Edmund H. Durfee and **Jaeho Lee**
Department of EE and CS
University of Michigan
Ann Arbor, MI 48109
durfee/jaeho@engin.umich.edu

Piotr J. Gmytrasiewicz
Department of Computer Science
Hebrew University
Jerusalem, Israel
piotr@cs.huji.ac.il

Abstract

A rational agent in a multiagent world must decide on its actions based on the decisions it expects others to make, but it might believe that they in turn might be basing decisions on what they believe the initial agent will decide. Such reciprocal rationality leads to a nesting of models that can potentially become intractable. To solve such problems, game theory has developed techniques for discovering rational, equilibrium solutions, and AI has developed computational, recursive methods. These different approaches can involve different solution concepts. For example, the Recursive Modeling Method (RMM) finds different solutions than game-theoretic methods when solving problems that require mixed-strategy equilibrium solutions. In this paper, we show that a crucial difference between the approaches is that RMM employs a solution concept that is overeager. This eagerness can be reduced by introducing into RMM second-order knowledge about what it knows, in the form of a flexible function for mapping relative expected utility of an option into the probability that the agent will pursue that option. This modified solution concept can allow RMM to derive the same mixed equilibrium solutions as game-theory, and thus helps us delineate the types of knowledge that lead to alternative solution concepts.

Introduction

Rational decisionmaking in a multiagent context is a difficult problem when an agent has knowledge that leads it to view other agents as being rational as well. With such *reciprocal rationality*, an agent must decide on its action(s) given what it believes the rational agents around it will do, but inferring that requires it to infer what each of those agents will believe it (and

---

[0]This research was sponsored in part by the NSF under grants IRI-9015423 and IRI-9158473, by DARPA under contract DAAE-07-92-C-R012, and by the Golda Meir Fellowship and the Alfassa Fund administered by the Hebrew University of Jerusalem.

the others) will do, which in turn requires it to assess what each of those agents will believe about what each of the agents will believe the others will do, and so on.

Reciprocal rationality can thus lead to an indefinite (and theoretically infinite) number of levels of recursive modeling. In the Recursive Modeling Method (RMM), for example, we have developed a procedure whereby agents can build this recursive nesting of models and can use the resultant modeling hierarchy to infer rational courses of action for others and for themselves [Gmytrasiewicz *et al.*, 1991]. RMM provides a rigorous foundation for such decisionmaking situations, based on RMM's concept of a solution. However, as we show in this paper, RMM's original formulation leads to decisions that differ from those that would be derived by traditional game-theoretic methods, because those methods employ a different solution concept.

In addition, the original solution concept in RMM could lead to cases where the algorithm that uses the recursive models could arrive at different results depending on the number of recursive levels examined. In our original RMM, we described how such behavior must eventually become cyclic given finite knowledge, and that when such a cycle occurs RMM can probabilistically mix the results to arrive at a single, overall decision. While this is the best that original RMM can do, the question arises as to whether a different solution concept could avoid such cyclic behavior, and could converge more naturally on a single solution. Moreover, the assumption that RMM must run out of knowledge at some finite level might be overly restrictive for some applications, and a solution concept that clearly defines the behavior of RMM in the limit of infinity would be desirable.

In this paper, we suggest these characteristics of original RMM stem from the fact that its solution concept leads to what we call "overeager reciprocal rationality." In a nutshell, our argument is that rationality based on expected payoffs given probabilistic models of what others will do should be tempered by the degree of confidence in those models. We describe one way of introducing this additional knowledge into RMM by using a more flexible function for generating those probabilistic models. Not only can this avoid overeager rationality that leads to oscillations, but that in fact it can make RMM's results converge in the limit of infinite recursion.

More broadly, however, the contributions of this paper extend beyond RMM to examine the nature of game-theoretic rationality as employed in a multiagent reasoning systems [Rosenschein and Breese, 1989; Rosenschein and Genesereth, 1985; Rosenschein *et al.*, 1986; Zlotkin and Rosenschein, 1991]. In particular, the concepts of equilibria and mixed-strategies play a central (although often debated) role in the game-theoretic literature [Shubik, 1982]. In this paper, we show how the recursive algorithm that RMM employs to model reciprocal rationality and the more traditional equilibria solutions can converge, given a particular choice of solution concept.

We begin by defining the game-theoretic notions of equilibria and mixed strategies, showing how rationality is embodied in these models. We then look at original RMM's solution to reciprocal rationality problems and its characteristics. Then we suggest a less eager rationality assumption, embodied in a function for computing probabilities over agents' moves, and describe how introducing it into the original RMM formulation avoids overeager rationality. We conclude by analyzing the performance of our approach and highlighting important open problems.

Game Theoretic Models

Game theoreticians have developed a number of techniques for determining rational combinations of moves for games represented in normal (or strategic) form, where each combination of strategies chosen by the players leads to a particular payoff for each player. The most common solution method involves using (iterated) dominance techniques [Rasmusen, 1989; Shubik, 1982], where players remove from consideration any moves that are clearly inferior (dominated) no matter which of the non-dominated moves others take. By alternating between the players' viewpoints, the number of rational moves can be decreased; in the case where there is a single rational strategy for each player, it can be found. The combination of rational strategies for the players represents an equilibrium solution, since none of the players has an incentive to deviate unilaterally from its own strategy.

In cases where there are multiple equilibrium moves, converging on a single move (a pure strategy) for each player is more complicated. For example, consider the game summarized in Figure 1a, where each combination of moves leads to a matrix entry giving a payoff for P (lower left) and Q (upper right).

In this game, there are two equally good moves for both P and Q. They could each maximize their payoff at 2 by either choosing options *ad* or *bc*. The trouble is, which of these will they choose? One way would be to have P and Q communicate and agree on one of the

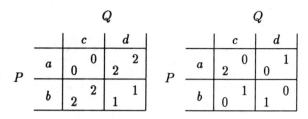

(a) with 2 pure solutions   (b) with no pure solutions

Figure 1: Matrices for Example Games

two possible combinations. Or if they shared common knowledge about how to break such ties, they could employ that knowledge here. But more generally, P and Q cannot be assured of converging for certain on one joint course of action. Game theory says that a mixed strategy equilibrium might thus be a useful solution concept here, where agents adopt probabilistic combinations of the separate pure strategies. One possible derivation for such a mixed strategy, patterned after [Rasmusen, 1989], is the following: Assume that P and Q will adopt mixed strategies $(p_a\ p_b)$ and $(p_c\ p_d)$, respectively.[1] The expected payoff of P (recall that $p_a + p_b = p_c + p_d = 1$) is then:

$$
\begin{aligned}
E[\text{Payoff}_P] &= 2p_a p_d + 2p_b p_c + p_b p_d \\
&= p_a + p_c - 3p_a p_c + 1.
\end{aligned}
$$

Differentiating the above with respect to p_a, and postulating that the result be zero (for the maximization problem), allows us to conclude that in the mixed strategy equilibrium Q must select move c with probability $p_c = 1/3$. That is, it is assumed that a mixed strategy for P is optimal, and P will only adopt a mixed strategy if $p_c = 1/3$ (if higher, P will always choose b, and lower leads to a). By the same arguments, the strategy for player P is $p_a = 1/3$. So, with $p_a = p_c = 1/3$, P and Q would expect payoffs of $4/3$.

Mixed strategies also play a role in games with no equilibrium solutions, such as the game in Figure 1b. In this game, the mixed strategy equilibrium solution has player P choose a with probability $1/2$ and b with probability $1/2$, while player Q chooses c with probability $1/3$ and d with probability $2/3$ [Brandenburger, 1992]. As Brandenburger points out, the concept of mixed strategy, where agents choose probabilistically among possibilities, is somewhat troubling in this kind of game because, for example, if Q believes that P is playing the expected mixed strategy of $(1/2\ 1/2)$, then there is no incentive for Q to play his mixed strategy

---

[1]In the notation in the rest of this paper, a mixture over strategies, represented as $(p_a\ p_b)$, indicates that the option listed first in the matrix has probability p_a and the option listed second has probability p_b.

of (1/3 2/3) over any other mixed (or pure) strategy. Brandenburger cites a history of work involved in viewing mixed strategies not as probabilistic strategy selection by agents playing a game, but instead as probabilistic conjectures that agents have about the pure strategies of others. It is this viewpoint that RMM takes as well.

Recursive Modeling Method

Analyses of normal form games, as described above, can employ various methods, including iterated dominance and adopting assumptions about the agents and solving for optimal mixed strategies. Different analyses might use different solution concepts, and thus (as seen above) different decisions can be rational in the context of different solution concepts. In the Recursive Modeling Method (RMM), our goal has been to develop a general, algorithmic solution to the problem of recursive reciprocal reasoning that generates the recursion explicitly.

In RMM, one agent represents how it thinks another sees the situation by hypothesizing the game matrix (or matrices) that the other agent is seeing. It can also hypothesize the matrices that the other agent might think the first agent sees, and so on, building a hierarchy of models representing, to increasing depths, the view of how the agent thinks that agents think that agents think ... that agents perceive the situation. Beginning at the leaf node(s) of this hierarchy, probabilities over agents' choices from among their options can be propagated upward until, at the top, the agent trying to decide what to do has a more informed model of what others are likely to do. Note that RMM works by assigning an equiprobability distribution among the options at the leaf nodes, corresponding not to a belief that an agent will flip a coin to decide on its strategy, but corresponding rather to the fact that it does not know how the agent will decide on its strategy, leading to the equiprobabilistic distribution that contains no information. RMM then chooses the option(s) with the maximum expected utility at each successive level above.

RMM helps agents converge on informed rational choices in many situations. For example, in situations with single equilibrium solutions, RMM easily converges on solutions computed with iterated dominance. However, in situations without such clear solutions, RMM often must probabilistically mix solutions. Recall the example with two pure equilibrium solutions (Figure 1a). In RMM, the tugging between two solutions leads to oscillating views from level to level. From P's perspective: If he does not consider what Q will prefer to do, then he will choose option *b* since it has the higher average payoff. If he considers Q but does not consider how Q considers P, then he will infer that Q will choose option *d* (highest average) and so P should choose *a*. If he considers Q and how Q considers P but no deeper, then he will infer that Q

will think P will choose *b*, so that Q will choose *c*, so that P should in fact choose *b*. This oscillating of P deciding on *b* and then *a* continues no matter how deep in the hierarchy P searches: If P elaborates the recursion an even number of times, he will prefer *b* (and expect a payoff of 2 since he expects Q to take move *c*), while he will prefer *a* (and again expect a payoff of 2) if he elaborates the recursion an odd number of times.

How do we reconcile this oscillation? Well, what RMM does is to probabilistically mix the derived expectations, and to work from there. So in the example above, when P runs RMM, it will recognize that half the time it expects Q to take action *c*, and half the time it expects Q to take *d*. It ascribes a strategy of (1/2 1/2) to Q, and determines that, if Q is equally likely to take either action, P should take action *b* (for an expected payoff of 1.5) rather than action *a* (which has an expected payoff of 1). Q, when it runs RMM, will go through the same reasoning to decide that it should take action *d*. Thus, each agent will have decided on a single action, and expect a payoff of 1.5; as external observers, however, we can clearly see that their true payoffs will really be 1. Had they instead each derived the mixed strategy of (1/3 2/3), however, we know that they could each expect a payoff of 1.33. Our derivation of this mixed strategy in the previous section assumed additional knowledge that allowed an agent to adopt a mixed strategy based on the understanding that the other agent would be adopting a mixed strategy as well. As we show below, we can incorporate additional knowledge within RMM to change its solution concept such that agents using RMM can derive this mixed strategy.

First, however, let us also revisit the case with no equilibrium solutions (Figure 1b). Here, the results of RMM for successive depths of the recursion will cycle among the four possible joint moves indefinitely. P would believe that Q is equally likely to take action *c* or *d*, and so P would choose action *a* with an expected payoff of 1. Q, on the other hand, would see P as equally likely to take action *a* or *b*, and so Q would be indifferent among its choices, adopting a mixed strategy of (1/2 1/2). This differs from the mixed strategies of (1/2 1/2) for P and (1/3 1/3) for Q derived game theoretically in the previous section.

In summary, RMM's decisions mirror the game-theoretic solutions when the choice is clear, but when several choices are equally rational depending on where one starts in the hierarchy, then RMM treats the possible strategies conjectured for other agents as equally likely. This sometimes leads RMM to adopt strategies that differ from game-theoretic solutions, as we have seen. As we explain next, the reason why RMM makes different conclusions than game theory is because RMM's solution concept does not consider second-order knowledge, and thus RMM's rationality is overeager.

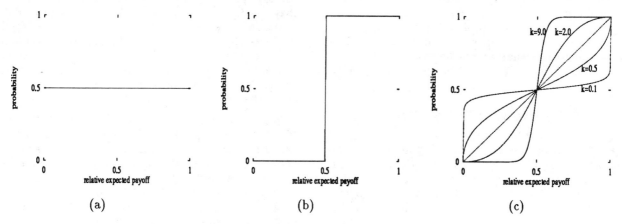

Figure 2: Functions Mapping Relative Payoff to Probability.

Overeager Reciprocal Rationality

We argue here that RMM's solution concept commits too strongly and quickly to the its conjectures—the probabilistic mixtures over options. At the leaves, RMM assigns an equiprobable distribution over the options of the other agent(s). Given this distribution, however, RMM immediately considers desirable only the options that will maximize expected payoffs based on this equiprobable distribution. Because the initial distribution was based on ignorance, it seems premature to place such weight in it, given the opportunity to bring more knowledge to bear at the higher levels of the hierarchy. In other words, RMM applies the utility maximization concept of rationality too eagerly.

Let us look at the probability calculations given relative expected payoffs, graphed for the simple case of two options, shown in Figure 2. At the leaf nodes, we have a flat probability function (Figure 2a), meaning that all options have equal probability because RMM has no knowledge about the relative expected payoffs below the leaf nodes. Above the leaf nodes, we have a step probability function (Figure 2b), which places certainty in the option with the higher expected payoff. Clearly, these are two extremes of a more general mapping function of relative expected payoff to probability.

Consider the more general function to compute probability of option i, given its expected payoff relative to the payoffs of all of the options J (where all payoffs are assumed non-negative):

$$p_i = \text{Payoff}(i)^k / \sum_{j \in J} \text{Payoff}(j)^k \qquad (1)$$

In this function, when k is 0 we get the extreme of a flat probability function, while as k approaches ∞, the function approaches the step function extreme. When k is 1, the function specifies a linear relationship between payoffs and probabilities—that if option a has twice the payoff of option b, for example, then it is

twice as likely to be chosen. The function is graphed for the simple case with two options in Figure 2c.

This function can be incorporated simply into the RMM calculations, provided we can specify a choice for k. The choice of k represents knowledge, and, more importantly, how k changes at different depths of the hierarchy corresponds to second-order knowledge about probabilities at each level. In the original RMM, k was implicitly specified as 0 for computing the probability distribution feeding into the leaves of the hierarchy, and ∞ at all levels above. This abrupt change, however, is what we claim makes the original solution concept in RMM overeager. Instead, k should be 0 at the leaves and become successively larger as one moves up the hierarchy, because k represents knowledge about the certainty RMM should place in conjectures about strategies. Toward the leaves, RMM should only lean slightly toward favoring options that do well given the conjectures at those levels, because those conjectures are based on ignorance. As we work toward the root of the hierarchy, the probabilistic conjectures are based on more and more information (propagated from the levels below), and thus RMM should commit more heavily at these levels. We can think of this approach as a variant of simulated annealing, where early in the process (near the leaves) the algorithm biases the search for rational strategies slightly but still keeps its search options open. As it moves up the hierarchy, the algorithm becomes increasingly committed to better options based on the evidence accumulated from below.

Besides avoiding overeager rationality, this modification also provides a new approach to dealing with the possibility of infinite recursion in RMM. As RMM recurses increasingly deeper, k gets closer and closer to 0, and the influence of deeper levels of knowledge (about what I know about what you know about what I know...) diminishes. In a practical sense, there will be a finite level at which a computing system will lack

```
(defvar *power-reduction-rate* .8)

(defun simple-rmm (matrix1 matrix2 levels &optional (power 1))
  (let* ((column-probs (if (= levels 0)
                           (make-equiprobability-vector (length (first matrix1)))
                           (simple-rmm matrix2 matrix1 (1- levels) (modify-power power levels))))
         (rows-exp-utils (mapcar #'(lambda (row) (compute-expected-utility row column-probs)) matrix1)))
    (mapcar #'(lambda (utility-for-row) (compute-probability utility-for-row rows-exp-utils power)) rows-exp-utils)))

(defun compute-expected-utility (payoffs probs)
  (cond ((null payoffs) 0)
        (t (+ (* (first payoffs) (first probs)) (compute-expected-utility (rest payoffs) (rest probs))))))

(defun compute-probability (payoff all-payoffs power)
  (let ((prob (if power
                  (/ (expt payoff power) (float (let ((current-sum 0))
                                                 (dolist (a-payoff all-payoffs current-sum)
                                                   (setf current-sum (+ current-sum (expt a-payoff power)))))
                                                current-sum)))
                  ; else, nil power means assume original RMM formulation
                  (let ((max-payoff (apply #'max all-payoffs)))
                    (if (= max-payoff payoff) (float (/ 1 (count max-payoff all-payoffs))) 0.0)))))
    (if (<= prob 1.0e-6) 0.0 prob)))

(defun modify-power (power level) ; this version ignores the level....
  (when power (* power *power-reduction-rate*)))
```

Figure 3: Code Fragment For Simple RMM Implementation

sufficient resolution to distinguish deeper levels of the hierarchy, while in a theoretical sense, RMM is well-behaved as it recurses toward infinite levels. Thus, rather than appealing to arguments of finite amounts of knowledge bounding any recursion, we can instead clearly define the behavior of RMM as it moves toward infinite recursive levels.

While it is clear that, in the modified RMM probability calculation, k should approach 0 as more levels are explored, it is less clear what value of k makes sense as we approach the root of the hierarchy. Driving k toward higher values will cause RMM to "lean" increasingly heavily as it goes upward, until it leans hard enough to commit to a specific choice. This is desirable for problems with single equilibrium points, but, when mixed strategies are most rational, having values of k too high will lead to oscillations just like in the unmodified RMM. The remaining questions, therefore, are whether a proper selection of k can lead to appropriate mixed strategies, and if so, how is that selection done.

Mixed Strategies Through RMM

Key functions in a much simplified version of RMM, which does not consider possible horizontal branching representing uncertainty about alternative payoff matrices other agents might subscribe to (see [Gmytrasiewicz et al., 1991]), are shown in Figure 3. Note that this example implementation uses a very simple method to change the value of k at successively lower levels of the hierarchy: it multiplies the value of k at the previous level by a constant (less than 1). This approach allows the algorithm to asymptotically approach 0 toward the leaves assuming sufficient recursive levels and an initial value of k that is not too large.

To see how modifying RMM affects its performance, we begin with the example having two equilibria in Figure 1a. Our game-theoretic analysis determined the optimal mixed strategy would be for P and Q to each select its first option with probability 1/3, and its second option with probability 2/3. Recall, however, that this analysis was based on knowledge that P and Q both assume that the other was adopting a mixed strategy. The modified RMM algorithm outlined in Figure 3 does not assume this knowledge. In Figure 4 we show the probability that P (and Q since the game is symmetric) assigns to its first option derived by modified RMM for runs involving 100 levels of recursion on incrementally larger values of k. The probability of the second option is simply 1 minus that of the first option.

As expected, when k is 0 throughout, the equiprobable mixed strategy is returned. As k increases, however, note that a player will adopt a mixed strategy that approaches the solution computed game-theoretically as (1/3 2/3). Beyond a certain value of k, however, modified RMM diverges from this solution because its solution concept leans so heavily toward particular options even if they are only marginally better, forcing the system into the oscillatory behavior seen in the original RMM formulation.

The other problematic case in which there were no equilibrium solutions (Figure 1b) provides similar results. That is, as k increases, the mixed-strategy solutions derived by RMM approach those derived game-theoretically (P playing (1/2 1/2) and Q (1/3 2/3)), and then begin to diverge and oscillate. The value of k at which convergence ceases differs between this problem and the previous problem, and as yet we have no method to predict ahead of time the value of k that will

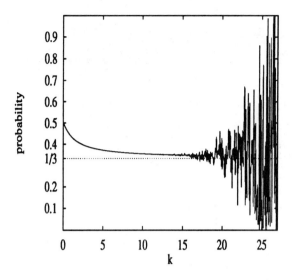

Figure 4: First Option Probability: 2-Equilibria Game.

lead to convergence. Our current formulation thus uses an iterative method: assuming that the new mapping function captures the correct knowledge when modified RMM converges, our formulation increases the value of k until divergence begins.

Conclusions

Our results illustrate how adding additional knowledge about the uncertainty in probabilities over other agents' strategies can lead to a different solution concept, causing reciprocal rationality to be less eager. Under appropriate conditions, this new solution concept can converge on mixed equilibrium solutions that can lead to better actual performance than the solutions derived by the original RMM solution concept. More importantly, the modified solution concept allows us to bring together the equilibrium solution models common in game-theoretic approaches with the recursive modeling approach embodied in RMM. By including the possibility of representing second-order knowledge about the probabilistic conjectures about strategies, we can implement solution concepts ranging from the sometimes overeager rationality of the original RMM, to the less eager solution concepts that approximate those used in game-theoretic methods, all the way to completely indecisive strategies (when $k = 0$).

More generally, our results in this paper serve to underscore how the results of rational decisionmaking are dependent upon the underlying solution concepts and their associated knowledge, even when following the basic concept of maximizing expected utility. Much work along these lines remains to be done, however. With regard to the work presented in this paper, a clear

next step is to examine more precisely the second-order knowledge captured in the new mapping function, using that understanding to analytically derive parameter settings (values of k) that will lead to the optimal converging mixed-strategy equilibria, and possibly embodying that knowledge more explicitly in the RMM algorithm by propagating probabilities about probabilities through the RMM hierarchy. Beyond this, however, is the ongoing challenge of characterizing the different rational solution concepts, so that developers of rational autonomous systems understand the strengths and limitations of the solution concepts that they implement.

References

Brandenburger, Adam 1992. Knowledge and equilibrium in games. *The Journal of Economic Perspectives* 6(4):83–101.

Gmytrasiewicz, Piotr J.; Durfee, Edmund H.; and Wehe, David K. 1991. A decision-theoretic approach to coordinating multiagent interactions. In *Proceedings of the Twelfth International Joint Conference on Artificial Intelligence*.

Rasmusen, Eric 1989. *Games and Information, an Introduction to Game Theory*. Basil Blackwell.

Rosenschein, Jeffrey S. and Breese, John S. 1989. Communication-free interactions among rational agents: A probablistic approach. In Gasser, Les and Huhns, Michael N., editors 1989, *Distributed Artificial Intelligence*, volume 2 of *Research Notes in Artificial Intelligence*. Pitman. 99–118.

Rosenschein, Jeffrey S. and Genesereth, Michael R. 1985. Deals among rational agents. In *Proceedings of the Ninth International Joint Conference on Artificial Intelligence*, Los Angeles, California. 91–99. (Also published in *Readings in Distributed Artificial Intelligence*, Alan H. Bond and Les Gasser, editors, pages 227–234, Morgan Kaufmann, 1988.).

Rosenschein, Jeffrey S.; Ginsberg, Matthew L.; and Genesereth, Michael R. 1986. Cooperation without communication. In *Proceedings of the Fifth National Conference on Artificial Intelligence*, Philadelphia, Pennsylvania. 51–57.

Shubik, Martin 1982. *Game Theory in the Social Sciences: Concepts and Solutions*. MIT Press.

Zlotkin, Gilad and Rosenschein, Jeffrey S. 1991. Cooperation and conflict resolution via negotiation among autonomous agents in non-cooperative domains. *IEEE Transactions on Systems, Man, and Cybernetics* 21(6). (Special Issue on Distributed AI).

Solving the Really Hard Problems with Cooperative Search

Tad Hogg and Colin P. Williams

Xerox Palo Alto Research Center
3333 Coyote Hill Road
Palo Alto, CA 94304, U.S.A.
Hogg@parc.xerox.com, CWilliams@parc.xerox.com

Abstract

We present and experimentally evaluate the hypothesis that *cooperative* parallel search is well suited for hard graph coloring problems near a previously identified transition between under- and overconstrained instances. We find that simple cooperative methods can often solve such problems faster than the same number of independent agents.

Introduction

Many A.I. programs involve search to solve NP hard problems. While intractable in the worst case, of more relevance to many applications is their behavior in typical situations. In fact, for many classes of such problems, most instances can be solved much more readily than might be expected from a worst case analysis. This has led to recent studies to identify characteristics of the relatively hard instances. In particular, observations [Cheeseman et al., 1991, Mitchell et al., 1992] and theory [Williams and Hogg, 1992b, Williams and Hogg, 1992a] indicate that constraint-satisfaction search problems with highest cost (fastest growing exponential scaling) occur near the transition from under- to overconstrained problems. These transitions, becoming increasingly sharp as problems are scaled up, are determined by values of easily measured "order" parameters of the problem, and are analogous to physical phase transitions as in percolation. The transition regions are also characterized by high variance in the solution cost for different problem instances, and for a single instance with respect to different search methods or a single nondeterministic method with e.g., different initial conditions or different tie-breaking choices made when the search heuristic ranks some choices equally. Structurally, these hard problems are characterized by many large partial solutions, which prevent early pruning by many types of heuristics. This phenomenon is also conjectured to appear in other types of search problems.

Can these observations be exploited in practical search algorithms? One immediate application is to use the order parameters to estimate the difficulty of alternate problem formulations as an aid in deciding which approach to take. Another use is based on the observation of high variance in solution cost for problems near the transition region. Specifically, there have been many studies of the benefit of running several methods independently in parallel and stopping when any method first finds a solution [Fishburn, 1984, Helmbold and McDowell, 1989, Pramanick and Kuhl, 1991, Kornfeld, 1981, Imai et al., 1979, Rao and Kumer, 1992, Mehrotra and Gehringer, 1985]. Since the benefit of this approach relies on variation in the individual methods employed, the high variance seen in the transition region suggests it should be particularly applicable for hard problems [Cheeseman et al., 1991, Rao and Kumer, 1992].

Another possibility is to allow such programs to exchange and reuse information found during the search, rather than executing independently. If the search methods are sufficiently diverse but nevertheless occasionally able to utilize information found in other parts of the search space, greater performance improvements are possible. Such "cooperative" methods have been studied in the context of simple constraint satisfaction searches [Clearwater et al., 1991, Clearwater et al., 1992]. In these cases, cooperative methods were observed to give the most benefit precisely for those problems with many large partial solutions that could not be pruned. This was the case even though the information exchanged was often misleading in the sense of not being part of any solution. While this work used fairly simple search methods, it suggests that cooperative search may be useful for much harder problems employing sophisticated search heuristics.

These observations lead us to conjecture that a mixture of diverse search methods that share information will be particularly effective for problems in the transition region. In this paper we test this conjecture experimentally for graph coloring, a particular class of NP-complete problems for which an appropriate order parameter, average connectivity, and the location of the transition region have been empirically determined [Cheeseman et al., 1991]. We also address some practical issues of sharing information, or exchanging "hints", among sophisticated heuristic search methods, which should allow these results to be extended readily to other constraint satisfaction problems.

Hard Graph Coloring Problems

The graph coloring problem consists of a graph, a specified number of colors, and the requirement to find a color for each node in the graph such that no pair of adjacent nodes (i.e., nodes linked by an edge in the graph) have the same color. Graph coloring has received considerable attention and a number of search methods have been developed [Minton et al., 1990, Johnson et al., 1991, Selman et al., 1992]. This is a well-known NP-complete problem whose solution cost grows exponentially in the worst case as the size of the problem (i.e., number of nodes in the graph) increases.

For this problem, the average degree of the graph γ (i.e., the average number of edges coming from a node in the graph) is an order parameter that distinguishes relatively easy from harder problems, on average. In this paper, we focus on the case of 3–coloring (i.e., when 3 different colors are available), for which the transition between under- and overconstrained problems and hence the region of hardest problems occurs near [Cheeseman et al., 1991] $\gamma = 5$. While there are likely to be additional order parameters, such as the variance in the degrees, this one was sufficient to allow us to find a set of graphs that are relatively hard to color with 3 colors.

In our experiments we used two very different search methods. The first was a complete, depth-first backtracking search based on the Brelaz heuristic [Johnson et al., 1991] which assigns the most constrained nodes first (i.e., those with the most distinctly colored neighbors), breaking ties by choosing nodes with the most uncolored neighbors (with any remaining ties broken randomly). For each node, the smallest color consistent with the previous assignments is chosen first, with successive choices made when the search is forced to backtrack. This complete search method is guaranteed to eventually terminate and produce correct results. Moreover, it operates by attempting to extend partial colorings to complete solutions.

Our second method used heuristic repair [Minton et al., 1990] from randomly selected initial configurations. This method, which always operates with complete assignments (i.e., each node is assigned some color), attempts to produce a solution by selecting a node and changing its color to reduce as much as possible, or at least leave unchanged, the number of violated constraints in the problem. If some progress toward actually reducing the number of violations is not made within a prespecified number of steps, the search restarts from a new initial condition. This method is incomplete, i.e., if the problem has no solution it will never terminate. In practice, an upper bound on the total number of tries is made: if no solution is found, the method may incorrectly report there are no solutions.

For hard problems, both methods have a high variance in the number of steps required to find a solution. Moreover, their very different nature suggests a combination of the two methods will give a collection of agents far more diverse than if all agents use the same method. In particular, heuristic repair is often very effective at finding solutions once it starts "near" enough to one.

To generate hard problems we examined many random graphs with connectivity near the transition region. To correspond with the cooperative methods used previously [Clearwater et al., 1991] and simplify the use of hints, we considered only graphs that did in fact have solutions. Specifically, to construct our sample of graphs, we first divided the nodes into three classes (as nearly equal as possible) and allowed only edges that connected nodes in different classes to appear in our graph. This guaranteed that the graphs had a solution. Then trivial cases of underconstrained nodes were avoided by making sure each node had degree at least three. Finally, additional edges required to reach the desired connectivity were then added randomly. Many of the resulting graphs were trivial to search (e.g., for 100 node graphs, the median search cost for the Brelaz heuristic was about 200 steps at the peak). To identify those that were in fact difficult, the resulting graphs were searched repeatedly with both search methods, and only those with high search cost for all these trials were retained. This selection generally produced hard graphs with search costs one to three orders of magnitude higher than typical cases. We should also note that these graphs were hard even when compared to other methods of generating graphs which are known to give harder cases on average. Specifically, the prespecification of a solution state in our method tends to favor graphs with many solutions and hence favors easier graphs than uniform random selection. For 100 node graphs, this latter method gives a peak median search cost of about 350 steps. Even more difficult cases are emphasized by restricting consideration to graphs with no trivial reductions with typical costs of about 1000 steps [Cheeseman et al., 1991].

A Cooperative Search

There are two basic steps in implementing a cooperative search based on individual algorithms. First, the algorithms themselves must be modified to enable them to produce and incorporate information from other agents, i.e., read and write hints. Second, decisions as to exactly what information to use as hints, when to read them, etc. must be made. We should note that the first step may, in itself, change the performance of the initial algorithm or its characteristics (e.g., changing a complete search method into an incomplete one). Since this may change the absolute performance of the individual algorithm, a proper evaluation of the benefit of cooperation should compare the behavior of multiple agents, exchanging hints, to that of a single one running the same, modified, algorithm, but unable to communicate with other agents. In that way, the effect of cooperation, due to obtaining hints from other agents, will be highlighted.

For example, a single agent running the Brelaz algorithm can first be modified so that it may read and write hints (it itself produced) from a private blackboard. This alone leads to slightly improved performance. The effect of cooperation can then be assessed by comparing a society of N agents each running the modified algorithm in isolation with N agents running the same algorithm except that they read and write to a common blackboard. In this way we can subtract out the effects of the changed algorithm and the memory capacity on the performance of the agents, leaving just the effect of cooperation.

While there are many ways to use hints, we made fairly simple choices similar to those used previously [Clearwater et al., 1991], in which hints consisted of partial solutions (thus for graph coloring, these hints are consistent colorings for a subset of the nodes in the graph). A central blackboard, of limited size, was used to record hints produced by the agents. When the blackboard was full, the oldest (i.e., added to the blackboard before any others) of the smallest (i.e., involving colors for the fewest nodes) hints were overwritten with new hints.

Each agent independently writes a hint, based on its current state, at each step with a fixed probability q. When an agent was at an appropriate decision point, described below, it read a hint with probability p. Otherwise, or if there were no available hints, it continued with its original search method. Thus, setting p to zero corresponds to independent search since hints would never be used. We next describe how the two different search methods were modified to produce and incorporate hints.

Using hints with the Brelaz heuristic
At any point in a backtracking search, the current partial state is a consistent coloring of some subset of the graph's nodes. When writing a hint to the blackboard, the Brelaz agents simply wrote their current state.

Each time the agent was about to expand a node in its backtrack search, it would instead, with probability p, attempt to read a compatible hint from the blackboard, i.e., a hint on the blackboard whose assignments were 1) consistent with those of the agent (up to a permutation of the colors[1]) and 2) specified at least one node not already assigned in the agent's current state. Frequently, there was no such compatible hint (especially when the agent was deep in the tree and hence had already made assignments to many of the nodes), in which case the agent continued with its own search.

When a compatible hint was found, its overlap with the agent's current state was used to determine a permutation of the hint's colors that made it consistent with the state. This permutation was applied to the remaining colorings of the hint and then used to extend the agent's current state as far as possible (ordering the new nodes as determined

---

[1]We thus used the fact that, for graph coloring, any permutation of the color assignments for a consistent set of assignments is also consistent.

by the Brelaz heuristic), and retaining necessary backtrack points so that the overall search remained complete. In effect, this hint simply replaced decisions that the Brelaz heuristic would have made regarding the initial colors to try for a number of nodes.

Using hints with heuristic repair
With heuristic repair, the agent's state always has a color assignment for each node, but it will not be fully consistent (until a solution is found). In order to produce a consistent partial assignment for use as a hint, we started with the full state and randomly removed assignments until a hint with no conflicts was obtained.

The heuristic repair agents have a natural point at which to read hints, namely when they are about to start over from a new initial state. At these times, we had each agent read a random hint from the blackboard with probability p, and otherwise randomly generate a new state. This hint, consisting of an assignment to some of the nodes, overwrote the agent's current state.

How Can Cooperation Help?
A simple explanation of the potential benefit of cooperative search is given by observing that the hints provide consistent colorings for large parts of the graph. Agents reading hints in effect then attempt to combine them with their current state. Although not always successful, those cases in which hints do combine well allow the agent to proceed to a solution by searching in a reduced space of possibilities. Even if many of the hints are not successful, this results in a larger variation of performance and hence can still improve the performance of the group when measured by the time for the first agent to finish.

As a more formal, but oversimplified, argument, suppose we view the agents as making a series of choices. Let p_{ij} be the probability that agent i makes choice j correctly (i.e., in the context of its previous choices, this one continues a path to a solution, e.g., by selecting a useful hint). The probability that the series of choices for agent i is correct is then just $p_i = \prod_j p_{ij}$. With sufficient diversity in the hints and agents' choices to prevent the p_{ij} from being too correlated, and viewing them as random variables, this multiplicative process results in a lognormal distribution [Redner, 1990] for agent performance, i.e., a random variable whose logarithm is normally distributed. This distribution has an extended tail compared to, say, a normal distribution or the distribution of the performance of the Brelaz heuristic on many graphs. Hence there is an increased likelihood that at least one agent will have much higher than average performance, leading to an improvement in group performance.

In practice, this simple argument must be modified to account for the possibility of backtracking and the fact that the quality of the hints changes during the search [Clearwater et al., 1992], but nevertheless gives some insight into the reason for the improvement and highlights the importance of maintaining diversity. Because of the high intrinsic variance in performance near the transition point, this in turn suggests why these cooperative methods are likely to be most applicable for the hard problems in the transition region.

Experimental Results

In this section we compare the behavior of independent searches with the cooperative method described above for some hard to color graphs. A simple performance criterion is the number of search steps required for the first agent to find a solution. However, this could be misleading when agents use different search methods whose individual steps have very different computational cost. It also ignores the additional overhead involved in selecting and incorporating hints. Here we present data based on actual execution time of an unoptimized serial implementation of the searches in which individual steps are multiplexed (i.e., each agent in the group takes a single step, with this procedure repeated until one agent finds a solution). The results are qualitatively similar to those based on counting the number of steps [Hogg and Williams, 1993], with the main differences being due to 1) a hint-exchange overhead which made individual cooperative steps about 5% slower than the corresponding independent ones, and 2) heuristic repair steps being about 2.4 times faster than Brelaz ones. This latter fact means that in a parallel implementation of a mixed group, the heuristic repair searches would actually complete relatively more search steps than when run serially. A parallel implementation would also face possible communication bottlenecks at the central blackboard though this is unlikely to be a major problem with the small blackboards considered here due to the relatively low reading rate and the possibility of caching multiple copies of the blackboard which are only slowly updated with new hints. Thus we can expect the cooperative agents to gain nearly the same speedup from parallel execution as the independent agents, i.e., a factor of 10 for our group size. While this must ultimately be addressed by comparing careful parallel implementations, the improvement in the execution time reported below, as well as the reduced number of search steps [Hogg and Williams, 1993], suggest the cooperative methods are likely to be beneficial for parallel solution of large, hard problems.

In Figs. 1 and 2, we compare the performance of groups of 10 cooperative agents with the same number of agents running independently. Note that in both cases, cooperation generally gives better performance than simply taking the best of 10 independent agents. Moreover, cooperation appears to be more beneficial as problem hardness (measured by the performance of a group of independent

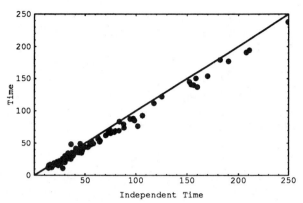

Fig. 1. Performance of groups of 10 cooperating agents vs. that of groups of 10 independent agents, using the Brelaz search method. Each point corresponds to a different graph and is the median, over 10 trials, of the execution time in seconds, on a SparcStation 2, required for the first agent in the group to find a solution. Each second of execution corresponds to about 90 search steps for each of the 10 agents. For comparison, the diagonal line shows the values at which cooperative and independent performance are equal. Cooperation is beneficial for points below this line. In these experiments, the blackboard was limited to hold 100 hints, and we used $p = 0.5$; $q = 0.1$ and graphs with 100 nodes.

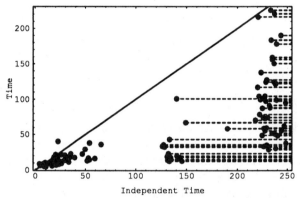

Fig. 2. Cooperation with heuristic repair. Each second of execution corresponds to about 210 search steps for each of the 10 agents. For comparison, the diagonal line shows the values at which cooperative and independent performance are equal. Some of the independent agent searches did not finish within 50000 steps at which point they were terminated. In these cases, the median performance shown in the plot for the independent agents is actually a lower bound: the dashed lines indicate the possible range of independent agent performances. Search parameters are as in Fig. 1.

agents) increases. We obtained a few graphs of significantly greater hardness than those shown in the figures which confirm this trend. We also observed that typically only a few percent of the hints on the blackboard were subsets of *any* solution so it is not obvious *a priori* that using these hints should be helpful at all.

Finally, Fig. 3 shows a combined society of agents. In this case, half the agents use the Brelaz method, half use heuristic repair, and hints are exchanged among all agents. Again, we see the benefit gained from cooperative search. For the graphs we generated, there was little correlation

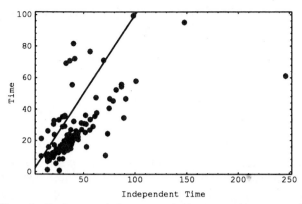

Fig. 3. Performance of groups of 10 cooperating agents, 5 using Brelaz and 5 using heuristic repair vs. the performance of the same groups searching independently. Each second of execution corresponds to about 120 search steps for each of the 10 agents. For comparison, the diagonal line shows the values at which cooperative and independent performance are equal. Search parameters are as in Fig. 1.

between solution cost for the two search methods, so that even when the agents were independent, this mixed society generally performed better than all agents using a single method.

While these results are encouraging, we should note that further work is needed to determine the best ways to exchange hints in societies using multiple methods, as well as the relative amount of resources devoted to different methods. Of particular interest is allowing the mix of agent types to change dynamically based on progress made during the search. More fundamentally for this avenue of research is understanding precisely what aspects of an ensemble of problems (e.g., in this case, determined by the precise method we used to generate the graphs) are important for the benefit of cooperation and the design of effective hints. Possibilities include the variance in individual search performance, the relative hardness of the graph and the proximity to the phase transition point.

Conclusion

In summary, we have tested our conjecture that cooperative methods are particularly well suited to hard graph coloring problems and seen that, even using simple hints, they can improve performance. It is further encouraging that the basic concepts used here, from the existence of regions of hard search problems characterized by order parameters to the use of partial solutions as hints, are applicable to a wide range of search problems.

There are a number of questions that remain to be addressed. An important one is how the observed cooperative improvement scales, both with problem size and, for a fixed size, with changes in the order parameters determining problem difficulty. There is also the question of how much different a parallel implementation is.

Another issue concerns whether these ideas can be applied to problems with no solutions to more quickly de-

termine that fact. This is particularly relevant to the hard problems since they appear to occur at or near the transition from under- to overconstrained problems which have many and no solutions respectively. In cases with no solution, either one must compare complete search methods (e.g., by having at least one agent use a complete search method even when reading hints) or else evaluate both search speed and search accuracy to make a valid comparison. More generally, when applied to optimization problems, one would need to consider quality of solutions obtained as well as time required.

This study also raises a number of more general issues regarding the use of hints. As we have seen, diversity can arise from the intrinsic variation near the transition point and from random differences in the use of hints. Nevertheless, as more agents, using the same basic method, are added diversity does not increase as rapidly [Clearwater et al., 1992]. This suggests more active approaches to maintaining diversity, such as explicitly partitioning the search space or, more interestingly, combining agents using different search methods such as genetic algorithms [Goldberg, 1989] or simulated annealing [Johnson et al., 1991].

From a more practical point of view, a key decision for designing cooperative methods is how hints are generated and used, i.e., the "hint engineering". This involves a number of issues. The first is the nature of the information to exchange. This could consist of any useful information concerning regions of the search space to avoid or likely to contain solutions. The next major question is when during its search should an agent produce a hint. With backtracking, the agent always has a current partial solution which it could make available by placing it on a central blackboard. Generally, agents should tend to write hints that are likely to be useful in other parts of the search space. Possible methods to use include only writing the largest partial solutions an agent finds (i.e., at the point it is forced to backtrack) or only if the hint is at least comparable in size to those already on the blackboard. Complementary questions are when should an agent decide to read a hint from the blackboard, which one should it choose and how should it make use of the information for its subsequent search. Again there are a number of reasonable choices which have different benefits, in avoiding search, and costs for their evaluation, as well as more global consequences for the diversity of the agent population. For instance agents could select hints whenever a sufficiently good hint is available, or whenever the agent is about to make a random choice in its search method (i.e., use the hint to break ties), or whenever the agent is in some sense stuck, e.g., needing to backtrack or at a local optimum. For deciding which available hint to use, methods range from random selection [Clearwater et al., 1991] to picking one that is a good match, in some sense, to the agent's current state. Final issues are the hint memory requirements and what to discard from a full blackboard.

Given this range of choices, is there any guidance for making good use of hints? Theoretical results [Clearwater et al., 1992] emphasize the use of diversity for good cooperative performance. As a note of caution in developing more sophisticated hint strategies, the choices should promote high diversity among the agents [Huberman, 1990, Hogg, 1990] giving many opportunities to try hints in different contexts. This means that choices that appear reasonable when viewed from the perspective of a single agent, could result in lowered performance for the group as a whole, e.g., if all agents are designed to view the same hints as the best to use.

As with other heuristic techniques, the detailed implementation of appropriate choices to maintain diversity of the group of agents while also maintaining reasonable individual performance remains an empirical issue. While we can expect further improvements from more sophisticated use of hints, the fact our relatively simple mechanisms are able to give increased performance suggests that such methods may be quite easily applied.

Acknowledgments

We have benefited from discussions with S. Clearwater.

References

Cheeseman, P., Kanefsky, B., and Taylor, W. M. (1991). Where the really hard problems are. In Mylopoulos, J. and Reiter, R., editors, *Proceedings of IJCAI91*, pages 331–337, San Mateo, CA. Morgan Kaufmann.

Clearwater, S. H., Huberman, B. A., and Hogg, T. (1991). Cooperative solution of constraint satisfaction problems. *Science*, 254:1181–1183.

Clearwater, S. H., Huberman, B. A., and Hogg, T. (1992). Cooperative problem solving. In Huberman, B., editor, *Computation: The Micro and the Macro View*, pages 33–70. World Scientific, Singapore.

Fishburn, J. P. (1984). *Analysis of Speedup in Distributed Algorithms*. UMI Research Press, Ann Arbor, Michigan.

Goldberg, D. E. (1989). *Genetic Algorithms in Search, Optimization and Machine Learning*. Addison-Wesley, NY.

Helmbold, D. P. and McDowell, C. E. (1989). Modeling speedup(n) greater than n. In Ris, F. and Kogge, P. M., editors, *Proc. of 1989 Intl. Conf. on Parallel Processing*, volume 3, pages 219–225, University Park, PA. Penn State Press.

Hogg, T. (1990). The dynamics of complex computational systems. In Zurek, W., editor, *Complexity, Entropy and the Physics of Information*, volume VIII of *Santa Fe Institute Studies in the Sciences of Complexity*, pages 207–222. Addison-Wesley, Reading, MA.

Hogg, T. and Williams, C. P. (1993). Solving the really hard problems with cooperative search. In Hirsh, H. et al., editors, *AAAI Spring Symposium on AI and NP-Hard Problems*, pages 78–84. AAAI.

Huberman, B. A. (1990). The performance of cooperative processes. *Physica D*, 42:38–47.

Imai, M., Yoshida, Y., and Fukumura, T. (1979). A parallel searching scheme for multiprocessor systems and its application to combinatorial problems. In *Proc. of IJCAI-79*, pages 416–418.

Johnson, D. S., Aragon, C. R., McGeoch, L. A., and Schevon, C. (1991). Optimization by simulated annealing: An experimental evaluation; part ii, graph coloring and number partitioning. *Operations Research*, 39(3):378–406.

Kornfeld, W. A. (1981). The use of parallelism to implement a heuristic search. In *Proc. of IJCAI-81*, pages 575–580.

Mehrotra, R. and Gehringer, E. F. (1985). Superlinear speedup through randomized algorithms. In Degroot, D., editor, *Proc. of 1985 Intl. Conf. on Parallel Processing*, pages 291–300, Washington, DC. IEEE.

Minton, S., Johnston, M. D., Philips, A. B., and Laird, P. (1990). Solving large-scale constraint satisfaction and scheduling problems using a heuristic repair method. In *Proceedings of AAAI-90*, pages 17–24, Menlo Park, CA. AAAI Press.

Mitchell, D., Selman, B., and Levesque, H. (1992). Hard and easy distributions of SAT problems. In *Proc. of 10th Natl. Conf. on Artificial Intelligence (AAAI92)*, pages 459–465, Menlo Park. AAAI Press.

Pramanick, I. and Kuhl, J. G. (1991). Study of an inherently parallel heuristic technique. In *Proc. of 1991 Intl. Conf. on Parallel Processing*, volume 3, pages 95–99.

Rao, V. N. and Kumer, V. (1992). On the efficiency of parallel backtracking. *IEEE Trans. on Parallel and Distributed Computing*.

Redner, S. (1990). Random multiplicative processes: An elementary tutorial. *Am. J. Phys.*, 58(3):267–273.

Selman, B., Levesque, H., and Mitchell, D. (1992). A new method for solving hard satisfiability problems. In *Proc. of 10th Natl. Conf. on Artificial Intelligence (AAAI92)*, pages 440–446, Menlo Park, CA. AAAI Press.

Williams, C. P. and Hogg, T. (1992a). Exploiting the deep structure of constraint problems. Technical Report SSL92-24, Xerox PARC, Palo Alto, CA.

Williams, C. P. and Hogg, T. (1992b). Using deep structure to locate hard problems. In *Proc. of 10th Natl. Conf. on Artificial Intelligence (AAAI92)*, pages 472–477, Menlo Park, CA. AAAI Press.

A Fast First-Cut Protocol for Agent Coordination

Andrew P. Kosoresow[*]
Department of Computer Science
Stanford University
Stanford, CA 94305, U.S.A.
kos@theory.stanford.edu

Abstract

This paper presents a fast probabilistic method for coordination based on Markov processes, provided the agents' goals and preferences are sufficiently compatible. By using Markov chains as the agents' inference mechanism, we are able to analyze convergence properties of agent interactions and to determine bounds on the expected times of convergence. Should the agents' goals or preferences not be compatible, they can detect this situation since coordination has not been achieved within a probabilistic time bound and the agents can then resort to a higher-level protocol. The application, used for motivating the discussion, is the scheduling of tasks, though the methodology may be applied to other domains. Using this domain, we develop a model for coordinating the agents and demonstrate its use in two examples.

Introduction

In distributed artificial intelligence (DAI), coordination, cooperation, and negotiation are important in many domains. Agents need to form plans, allocate resources, and schedule actions, considering not only their own preferences, but also those of other agents with whom they have to interact. Making central decisions or deferring to another agent may not be possible or practical, because of design constraints or political considerations. In these situations, agents will need some mechanism for coming to an agreement without reference to an outside authority. There are other advantages to having a distributed negotiator. Communication patterns may become more balanced when a central node or set of nodes do not have to participate in every interaction. Information is localized. Each person's information is only contained by the

local agent and can be more closely controlled. Further, as each person's (or set of persons') schedule is maintained by a separate agent, the system would degrade gracefully if some of the agents were to go off line. Given that there exists at least one satisfactory agreement that satisfies all the agents' constraints, we want to find such an agreement within a reasonable amount of time. If such an agreement does not exist, we would like to find an approximate agreement satisfying as many constraints as possible.

In this paper, we propose a probabilistic method using Markov processes for the coordination of agents, using the domain of scheduling tasks. We make two assumptions about the capabilities of the agents: Agents have a planning system capable of generating sets of possible plans and they have a high-level negotiation system capable of exchanging messages about goals, tasks, and preferences. Each agent has a set of tasks that it has to accomplish. Some of these tasks require the participation of other agents. The agents may have some preference for who does which tasks. While it is possible for the agents to enter into full-scale negotiations immediately, we propose to have the agents first go through a brief phase of trading offers and counteroffers. Should the agents' goals and preferences be sufficiently compatible, the agents will come to an agreement with high probability without the need for full-scale negotiation. Otherwise, the agents would realize this and resort to the higher-level negotiation protocol.[1]

We propose that the agents would simultaneously post their proposed schedules. Based on these postings, the agents would compute their next proposal and repost until they had synchronized on a schedule. In order to calculate each posting, each agent has a Markov process generating its next schedule based

---

[*]This research was supported jointly by the National Aeronautics and Space Administration under grant NCC2-494-S11, the National Science Foundation under grant IRI-9116399, and the Rockwell International Science Center–Palo Alto Facility.

[1]If the high-level protocol takes time T, the low-level protocol takes time t, and the low-level protocol succeeds some fraction p of the time for a set of k tasks, then preprocessing is worthwhile if

$$kT \leq p(kt) + (1-p)(kT)$$

on the current postings of all the agents; this process would involve a lookup operation and possibly a random coin flip. By combining the Markov processes of the individual agents, we obtain a Markov chain for the entire system of agents. We can then analyze the properties of the system by analyzing the Markov chain and determine if the agents will converge to an agreeable schedule and the expected time of convergence.

If the agents have a model of the other agents' tasks and preferences, they can then conjecture a Markov chain corresponding to the entire system of agents. Given this information, the agent can estimate the number of iterations needed to achieve coordination for a given probability. If coordination has not been achieved by this time, the agent then knows that its model of the other agents was incorrect (or that it has been very unlucky) and can then use the higher-level protocol.

In the rest of the paper, we will develop a methodology for using Markov processes and give several illustrative examples of how task scheduling would work using Markov processes. In the next section, we give some basic definitions and lay the groundwork for the use of Markov processes as a method of negotiation. Next, we define convergence properties and expected times. In the following section, we give two examples in a task scheduling domain demonstrating the use of Markov processes. Finally, we discuss related work and summarize our current results.

Basic Architecture

In this paper, we consider a scenario where a group of agents needs to come to an agreement. We assume that the agents communicate by posting messages simultaneously at discrete times called *clock ticks* and that the posted messages are visible to all the agents concerned.[2] At a clock tick, each agent is required to post some message. If it fails to do so for some reason, a default will be specified whose definition depends on the application. First let us consider the process of coming to an agreement from the perspective of an individual agent and then examine the process from the perspective of the entire system of agents.

After each clock tick, an individual agent in the system can examine the current postings of all the agents for that clock tick. Based on this information, the agent needs to generate its proposed schedule by the next clock tick. One method for generating a sched-

ule under this constraint is to use Markov procedures. Informally, a *Markov procedure* is a function that generates an action taking only the agent's current world state as the input.[3] Since many rounds of negotiation may be necessary to come to a satisfactory agreement, Markov procedures are promising candidates for use in such a system; for each iteration, all that is potentially needed is a single lookup or a simple computation.

Each agent is controlled by a *Markov process*, a variant of a Markov procedure. A Markov process is a function that takes the system state and a randomly-generated number and yields an action. In our model, the *system state* is the set of offers made by the agents during the last clock tick. The action is the agent's offer for the next clock tick. Thus, given the set of all offers, $\mathcal{O}$, and a system state, $\mathcal{S}$, we have an evaluation function, $\mathcal{E}_\mathcal{S}$, such that given an $o \in \mathcal{O}$, $\mathcal{E}_\mathcal{S}(o)$ is the probability that the agent should offer o in system state $\mathcal{S}$ and $\sum_{o \in \mathcal{O}} \mathcal{E}_\mathcal{S}(o) = 1$. Let $\mathcal{A}_i^t$ be the state of the ith agent at time t. So, given a random number generator, we can define a Markov process, $\mathcal{M}$ to generate each agent's next offer based on $\mathcal{E}_\mathcal{S}$. Given that there are n agents and ρ is a random number such that $0 \le \rho \le 1$, $\mathcal{A}_i^{t+1} = \mathcal{M}_i(\mathcal{A}_1^t, \mathcal{A}_2^t, \ldots, \mathcal{A}_n^t, \rho)$ for the ith agent. A starting state is specified by each of the agents either by choosing an action randomly or by choosing a preferred action based on some criteria. Practically speaking, the entire Markov process for an agent will probably never be explicitly specified as it could contain an exponential number of states. For example, the number of possible ways to allocate a set of tasks among a group of agents is exponential in the number of tasks. More likely, the system states will be divided into equivalence classes, for which only a single set of actions will be considered. Furthermore, the agents' constraints and preferences may preclude them from even considering many possible ways of allocating the tasks. For an effective system, the number of these classes should be sub-exponential. We shall see an example of how system states collapse into a fewer number of equivalent classes.

In order to learn something of the properties of this system, we can consider all the agents and their Markov processes as a single Markov chain.[4] We call this the *System Markov Chain* or simply the *system chain*. Using the above notation, the system process, $\mathcal{SM}$, can be represented as $\mathcal{S}^{t+1} = \mathcal{SM}(\mathcal{S}^t, P)$ where $\mathcal{S}^t = (\mathcal{A}_1^t, \mathcal{A}_2^t, \ldots, \mathcal{A}_n^t)$ and P is the n-tuple of ρs, as defined above for Markov processes. As it is a Markov chain, certain properties including convergence and the expected times of convergence may be computed in many cases.

---

[2]These assumptions provide a model that is simpler to analyze and may be later extended to cover agent-to-agent messages. They also allow us to postpone considering agents that are Byzantine and otherwise malicious. For example, consider playing a game of Stone, Scissors, Paper. If one player delays slightly, it can win with knowledge of the the opponent's move. Similarly, if the players are communicating through an intermediary, the intermediary can distort the game by passing false information or delaying it.

[3]While ignoring most of the history of an agent may seem to be restrictive, it has been shown to be effective, for example, in cases such as the Tit-for-Tat Algorithm for the Prisoners' Dilemma [Axelrod, 1984].

[4]See [Freedman, 1983] for a more complete discussion of Markov chains and related topics.

Convergence and Expected Times

We now define whether the system chain converges or, in other words, whether the agents come to an agreement. First we need to define absorbing states for a system; a state $\mathcal{S}$ is defined to be an *absorbing state* if and only if given the system is in state $\mathcal{S}$ at time t, it will be in state $\mathcal{S}$ at time $t+1$ with probability 1. If a Markov chain has at least one absorbing state, it is called an *absorbing Markov chain*. If an absorbing Markov chain has a non-zero probability of reaching some absorbing state from every state, let us call it a *converging Markov chain*, since eventually the Markov chain will end up in one of these states. If the system chain is a converging Markov chain and all the absorbing states are possible valid agreements, the agents' Markov processes will lead to one of these agreements. Let us call this chain a *converging system chain*. In this case, a *valid agreement* is one where either all the agents' constraints are satisfied or, if that is not possible, a satisfactory approximate solution is reached. Thus, if we can have the agents generate Markov processes which lead to a converging system chain, we know that they will eventually come to an agreement.

In our case, the convergent states consist of those where all of the agents issue the same offer during one time-step and the subsequent states for all the agents is that same state. We can take advantage of partially convergent states when agents agree on the assignment of subsets of their tasks. If agreeing on these tasks does not preclude reaching an absorbing state, then the agents can reduce their search-spaces, by fixing the agreed-upon task assignments.

We can also try to figure out the expected convergence time. Given a Markov chain $\mathcal{M}$ and a distribution $\mathcal{D}$ of initial system states, the *expected time of convergence*, $\mathcal{T}(\mathcal{M}, \mathcal{D})$ is defined to be:

$$\mathcal{T}(\mathcal{M}, \mathcal{D}) = \sum_{i=0}^{\infty} i P_c(\mathcal{M}, \mathcal{D}, i)$$

where $P_c(\mathcal{M}, \mathcal{D}, t)$ is the probability that the Markov chain $\mathcal{M}$ will reach an absorbing state at time t. This latter quantity can be computed by either solving the recurrence relations derived from the specification of the Markov chain or by framing the Markov chain as a network-flow problem and simulating it. Thus, proving convergence and calculating the time of convergence for the system chain will let us know whether an agreement is guaranteed and, if so, approximately when.

The Scheduling of Multiple Tasks

In this section, we show how to apply Markov processes to scheduling tasks. We will give two examples and an analysis of their expected times of convergence.

Each of the agents in the system has some set of tasks that it has to schedule, possibly the empty set.

1. Exchange task lists with other agents.
2. Using task lists, form a Markov process to generate schedule offers either randomly or weighted according to the agent's preferences or constraints.
3. Form Markov chain using the agent's Markov process and the agent's estimates of the others' Markov processes. Determine estimated time of convergence using the Markov chain.
4. Run Markov process until the time bound, established in Step 3, is reached or a suitable agreement is found.
5. If an agreement is found, return the agreement. Otherwise, resort to higher-level protocol.

Figure 1: Outline of the first-cut coordination protocol.

Assume that there are n agents and they are concerned with a set of m available time slots. For the rest of the paper, we assume that the tasks take unit time and are independent. Each of the tasks requires some number of agents to complete it.

Initially, the agents trade lists of tasks that need to be assigned and the available times for the tasks. By not communicating constraints and preferences in this protocol, agents may avoid having to calculate, communicate, and reason with these types of facts. Each of the agents then generates a Markov process $\mathcal{M}$, as defined above, based on the set of task schedules that it considers valid. Each of the schedules consists of sets of the agents' tasks that should be done during a particular time slot. Thus, the tuple $(\{Aa, Bb\}, \{Bc\}, \{Aa, Bd\})$ indicates that the agent suggests that the agents A and B do tasks a and b in time 1 respectively, B does task c in time 2, and A and B do tasks a and d in time 3 respectively. Since the agent does not know the other agents' constraints, some or all of the schedules generated by one agent may not be valid for other agents. If the agent has some information about the other agents' constraints (or it is willing to make some assumptions in the absence of this information), it can now form a system chain. By calculating the expected time of convergence for the system chain, it now has an estimate on how long the protocol will take and it can use that information to decide when to go to the higher-level protocol. The agents will then trade offers until an agreement is reached or a deadline is passed. This process is outlined in Figure 1.

For this system, there is an exponential number of possible schedules for tasks, and thus both the agents' Markov processes and the system chain could have exponential size if they were represented explicitly. However, often it is possible to store the agents' Markov processes implicitly. Further, we can reduce the number of system chain states by defining equivalence classes over the system states. For example, the set of states where everyone has agreed on a schedule can be dealt with as a single class. In the following example, we show how this fact can be used and give an

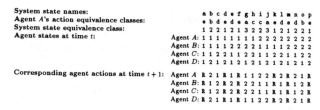

System state names:		a	b	c	d	e	f	g	h	i	j	k	l	m	n	o	p
Agent *A*'s action equivalence classes:		e	b	d	e	d	e	a	a	c	a	e	d	e	d	b	e
System state equivalence class:		1	2	2	1	2	1	3	2	2	3	1	2	1	2	2	1
Agent states at time *t*:	Agent *A*:	1	1	1	1	1	1	1	1	2	2	2	2	2	2	2	2
	Agent *B*:	1	1	1	1	2	2	2	2	1	1	1	1	2	2	2	2
	Agent *C*:	1	1	2	2	1	1	2	2	1	1	2	2	1	1	2	2
	Agent *D*:	1	2	1	2	1	2	1	2	1	2	1	2	1	2	1	2
Corresponding agent actions at time *t* + 1:	Agent *A*:	R	2	1	R	1	R	1	1	2	2	R	2	R	2	1	R
	Agent *B*:	R	1	2	R	2	R	2	2	1	1	R	1	R	1	2	R
	Agent *C*:	R	1	2	R	2	R	2	2	1	1	R	1	R	1	2	R
	Agent *D*:	R	2	1	R	1	R	1	1	2	2	R	2	R	2	1	R

Read system states down vertically.

Figure 2: Markov processes for two teams of two agents coordinating usage of a resource. ('R' in the table above corresponds to a equiprobable random choice between '1' and '2'.)

overview of the procedure. In the second example, we sketch a case where the agents' constraints are partially incompatible.

Example 1: A Constrained Resource

Suppose there are 4 agents: A, B, C, and D. There are two tasks that need to be done: t_1 and t_2. Let A and D be the team that has to do t_1 and let B and C be the team that has to do t_2. Finally, assume that both tasks utilize some resource that can only be used by one set of agents at a time and there are two time slots available: 1 and 2.[5] This example could represent two teams of agents having to use a particular tool in a job-shop or two sets of siblings having to share a television set. Assuming that the agents find the resource equally desirable during both time slots, and that all the agents have equal input into the decision, we need to decide an order in which the agent teams get to use the resource. While workers in a job-shop or family might have other means for coming to a decision, we can abstract the situation and use Markov processes to come to a decision. The agents can specify their choice by a '1' or a '2'. '1' will indicate that the agent offers to do its task first, while a '2' indicates that it offer to go second. Thus, we design the Markov process shown in Figure 2 for each of the agents.

In this Markov process, each of the agents has to react to one of sixteen possible system states. As shown in Figure 2 for Agent A, each of the states falls into one of five equivalence classes for the agents, each of which corresponds to an action: (a) the agents are coordinated; (b) the agents are almost coordinated and to achieve coordination, I need to flip state; (c) the agents are almost coordinated and to achieve coordination, the other person in my pair needs to flip state; (d) the agents are almost coordinated and to achieve coordination, one of the people in the other pair needs

---
[5] A simpler example consists of two agents trying to coordinate on a coin, where both of them decide on heads or tails. This is an example of a consensus problem as in [Aspnes and Waarts, 1992]. The solution for the given example can be easily modified to give a solution to multi-agent consensus.

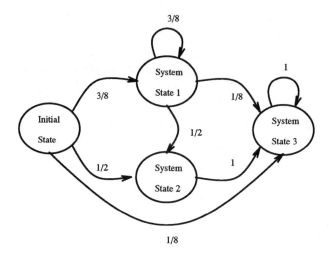

Figure 3: The resulting system chain for Example 1. (State labels correspond to system state equivalence classes from Figure 2 and arc labels are probabilities of transitioning between the two given states.)

to flip state; and (e) the agents are uncoordinated and need to flip randomly. Similarly, the system states fall into three equivalence classes: (1) the agents are uncoordinated, (2) the agents are almost coordinated (and will get coordinated in the next time step), and (3) the agents are coordinated and need to flip randomly. These three equivalence classes are used to form the system chain shown in Figure 3. This Markov chain converges and the expected time to reach a convergent state is $\frac{8}{5}$.[6]

In this example, using Markov processes leads to a satisfactory solution in a relatively short expected time. The solution is fair since both outcomes are equally probable and no agent had more influence than any other agent. While there is no deterministic time bound for the agents coming to an agreement, there is no chance of deadlock which may result from a deterministic protocol. Further, we do not depend on ordering the agents or on an external device for insuring honesty. Of course, there are situations where the agents can sabotage the efficiency or the convergence of such a method. Suppose that Agent D has decided that it prefers the first time slot. It can raise the probability of choosing that slot to greater than $\frac{1}{2}$ or even go to the extreme of choosing it no matter what, thus increasing the expected time of convergence. Further, if Agent A decides that it must have the second time slot, we are left in a situation that has no satisfactory schedule. While such situations appear to lead to inefficiency or inability to come to a satisfactory solution, they may be used to take preferences into account and discover situations where there are irreconcilable conflicts among the agents. An agent can be probabilisti-

---
[6] The details of the expected time calculations is left to the full-length version of this paper.

cally certain that something unexpected is happening when the system has not converged to an agreement within a time bound.

If the agents have a model of each other, then they can construct the system chain for their particular case. Given the chain, the agents can either analytically determine the time of convergence for simple chains or derive it empirically for more complex ones. Similarly, they can use the cutoff for negotiation as an indication that they are not making progress. For example, if they assume the model described above, they would converge to a solution over 90% of the time within seven iterations. Thus, they can use seven as a cutoff to indicate that there might be incompatible preferences such as the ones described above for Agents A and D.

Example 2: Non-compatible Goals

In the second example, we have two agents whose goals are not sufficiently compatible. Even though coordination failures may occur in this system, there is still a significant probability that the agents will coordinate on a plan and thus will not have to resort to a higher level protocol. It further demonstrates how convergence on a partial solution can lead to fast convergence during the remainder of the protocol.

Suppose there are two agents, A and B. Their goal is to move a set of objects to one of three locations: 1, 2, or 3. Agent A would like to have objects a, b, and c at the same location, and Agent B would like to have objects b, c, and d at the same location. There are twelve possible tasks consisting of moving the four objects to the three locations, such as task $a1$ which consists of moving object a to location 1. The agents each have two time steps available during which they can schedule their actions. The initial communications would contain the tasks each agent needs done and the time frame. For example, Agent A would send $((a1, b1, c1, a2, b2, c2, a3, b3, c3), (T1, T2))$ indicating the nine tasks that it is interested in and the two time steps. Note that only the tasks were communicated without any reference to constraints or preferences. The computation and communication of this information is left to the higher-level protocol, should it be necessary.

Since we assume that tasks are of unit time and do not depend on each other, each agent can just enter the new tasks into its list of things to do and expand its Markov process to include them as a possibility. If this operation is not straightforward, as it is in this case, the agents might pop out of this low-level protocol and proceed with a higher-level one at this point.

The agents' offers would consist of the possible ways to do their tasks combined with the possible ways they believe that the other agent's task could be incorporated. For example, Agent A's possible offers, at this point, consists of 216 possibilities: Each of the tasks needs to be assigned an agent, a time, and a location

with the constraint that a, b, and c are assigned the same location. These can be represented by each of the agents implicitly. At each time step, the agents would suggest one of these offers and then compare to see they have made any progress.

At this point, the agents can take advantage of partial coordination. If an assignment of tasks to agents, tasks to time slots, or tasks to locations has been agreed on, the agents then fix those parameters and accordingly reduce the number of offers that they would consider for the next round. Let us first consider the assignment of the objects to locations. There are 81 possible outcomes in this case. With probability $\frac{1}{27}$ the agents will coordinate on a possible assignment of locations; with probability $\frac{2}{27}$, the agents will result in a state from which an acceptable plan cannot be reached; with probability $\frac{8}{27}$, the agents will still be in the initial state; and with $\frac{16}{27}$, the agents will be partially coordinated where the probability is better than $\frac{1}{2}$ that they will eventually agree on an acceptable plan. Thus, the termination of this part of the schedule has an expected time of at most nine steps.

In the other portion of the schedule, where we assign tasks to agents, there is no chance of a partial solution leading to a deadlock state. The agents simply agree on how to put four tasks in four slots. Any partial solutions in this part of the schedule will constrain subsequent actions leading to an agreement.

Thus we see several important features of this methodology. The protocol is able to restrict the space of possible schedules by utilizing partial agreements. Even in an unfavorable situation, it will lead to an acceptable schedule in more than half the cases. Further, we were able to use this coordination protocol even though the two agents were unaware of the constraints of the other agents. By using a quick offer-counteroffer protocol, there would be no need to trade this information and to do the computations associated with incorporating the information into the planner and/or the higher-level coordination protocol's data structures. Even if our protocol was unsuccessful, it may provide us with some useful information for the higher-level protocol.

Summary of Current and Related Work

In this paper, we draw on a variety of sources. Previous work in coordination and cooperation includes the game-theoretic approach taken by Genesereth, Rosenschein, and Ginsberg as in [Ginsberg, 1985], for example. One advantage of our method is that knowledge of explicit payoff matrices is not necessary. Our method is also applicable to the more current work on the Postman Problem[Zlotkin and Rosenschein, 1989]. Our method is more similar contract nets[Davis and Smith, 1983], though our approach is more like haggling than bidding for a contract.

In [Ephrati and Rosenschein, 1991], [Ephrati and Rosenschein, 1992], [Jennings and Mamdani, 1992], and [Wellman, 1992], higher-level protocols are proposed for agent coordination and negotiation. These may be suitable for use with our protocol in part or in their entirety. Other work is related to providing components for a system for coordination and negotiation. For example, [Gmytrasiewicz *et al.*, 1991] provides a framework whereby agents can build up a data structure describing other agents with whom they interact, and [Kraus and Wilkenfeld, 1991] provides a framework for incorporating time as part of a negotiation. Our protocol might also be adapted for use in multi-agent systems such as those described in [Shoham and Tennenholtz, 1992].

Taking these considerations into account, we have decided to use a probabilistic method with Markov processes and chains to try to guarantee that the agents will come to some agreement; the randomness provides us a tool for avoiding potential deadlock among the processes. Further, using Markov processes provides us with methods for determining whether a system of agents will converge to an agreement and, if so, in what expected time. We have demonstrated how Markov processes and Markov chains can be used for coordinating tasks. These techniques may also be useful for other domains involving coordination or negotiation.

We are currently looking at applying Markov processes to the scheduling of elevators, job shops, and other resource allocation problems. We are also working on implementing these procedures to test them empirically. There are also several general problems that need to be examined. In order to make this technique more convenient, we need to look at how to generate Markov chains from a formal specification of a problem and how to recognize equivalence classes. To make the method less restrictive, it would be useful to try to relax the requirement that messages be posted simultaneously. Further, it might be useful to employ direct messages between agents instead of having them post their messages. Finally, we would like to incorporate profit/cost metrics and more complex interdependent tasks with temporal or ordering constraints. As it stands, we see Markov processes as a useful technique for exploring agent coordination and, subsequently, negotiation.

Acknowledgements

I would like to thank Nils Nilsson and Narinder Singh, for their many valuable comments and discussions regarding this paper. In addition, I would like to thank Anil Gangolli, Matt Ginsberg, Michael Genesereth, Andrew Goldberg, Andrew Golding, Ramsey Haddad, Jane Hsu, Joseph Jacobs, George John, Illah Nourbakhch, Oren Patashnik, Greg Plaxton, Devika Subramanian, Vishal Sikka, Eric Torng, Rich Washington, James Wilson, and the members of the Bots, MUGS, and Principia Research Groups at Stanford for many productive conversations.

References

Aspnes, James and Waarts, Orli 1992. Randomized consensus in expected $O(n \log^2 n)$ operations per processor. In *33rd Annual Symposium on Foundations of Computer Science*. IEEE Computer Society Press. 137–146.

Axelrod, Robert 1984. *The Evolution of Cooperation*. Basic Books, Inc., New York.

Davis, Randall and Smith, Reid G. 1983. Negotiation as a metaphor for distributed problem solving. *Artificial Intelligence* 20:63–109.

Ephrati, Eithan and Rosenschein, Jeffrey S. 1991. The clarke tax as a consensus mechanism among automated agents. In *Proceedings of the Ninth National Conference on Artificial Intelligence*. Morgan Kaufmann. 173–178.

Ephrati, Eithan and Rosenschein, Jeffrey S. 1992. Constrained intelligent action: Planning under the influence of a master agent. In *Proceedings of the Tenth National Conference on Artificial Intelligence*. Morgan Kaufmann. 263–268.

Freedman, David 1983. *Markov Chains*. Springer-Verlag.

Ginsberg, Matthew L. 1985. Decision procedures. In Huhns, Michael N., editor 1985, *Distributed Artificial Intelligence*. Morgan Kaufman. chapter 1, 3–28.

Gmytrasiewicz, Piotr J.; Durfee, Edmund H.; and Wehe, David K. 1991. The utility of communication in coordinating intelligent agents. In *Proceedings of the Ninth National Conference on Artificial Intelligence*. Morgan Kaufmann. 166–172.

Jennings, N. R. and Mamdani, E. H. 1992. Using joint responsibility to coordinate collaborative problem solving in dynamic environments. In *Proceedings of the Tenth National Conference on Artificial Intelligence*. Morgan Kaufmann. 269–275.

Kraus, Sarit and Wilkenfeld, Jonathan 1991. The function of time in cooperative negotiations. In *Proceedings of the Ninth National Conference on Artificial Intelligence*. Morgan Kaufmann. 179–184.

Shoham, Yoav and Tennenholtz, Moshe 1992. Emergent conventions in multi-agent systems: initial experimental results and observations. In *Principles of Knowledge Representation and Reasoning: Proceedings of the Third International Conference*. Morgan Kaufmann. 225–231.

Wellman, Michael P. 1992. A general-equilibrium approach to distributed transportation planning. In *Proceedings of the Tenth National Conference on Artificial Intelligence*. Morgan Kaufmann. 282–289.

Zlotkin, Gilad and Rosenschein, Jeffrey S. 1989. Negotiation and task sharing among autonomous agents in cooperative domains. In *Eleventh International Joint Conference on Artificial Intelligence*. Morgan Kaufmann. 912–917.

Agents Contracting Tasks in Non-Collaborative Environments*

Sarit Kraus

Department of Mathematics and Computer Science
Bar Ilan University Ramat Gan, 52900 Israel
sarit@bimacs.cs.biu.ac.il

Abstract

Agents may sub-contract some of their tasks to other agent(s) even when they don't share a common goal. An agent tries to contract some of its tasks that it can't perform by itself, or when the task may be performed more efficiently or better by other agents. A "selfish" agent may convince another "selfish" agent to help it with its task, even if the agents are not assumed to be benevolent, by promises of rewards. We propose techniques that provide efficient ways to reach subcontracting in varied situations: the agents have full information about the environment and each other vs. subcontracting when the agents don't know the exact state of the world. We consider situations of repeated encounters, cases of asymmetric information, situations where the agents lack information about each other, and cases where an agent subcontracts a task to a group of agents. We also consider situations where there is a competition either among contracted agents or contracting agents. In all situations we would like the contracted agent to carry out the task efficiently without the need of close supervision by the contracting agent. The contracts that are reached are simple, Pareto-optimal and stable.

Introduction

Research in Distributed Problem Solvers assumes that it is in the agents' interest to help one another. This help can be in the form of the sharing of tasks, results, or information [Durfee, 1992]. In task sharing, an agent with a task it cannot achieve on its own will attempt to pass the task, in whole or in part, to other agents, usually on a contractual basis [Davis and Smith, 1983]. This approach assumes that agents not otherwise occupied will readily take on the task. Similarly, in information or result sharing, information is shared among agents with no expectation of a return [Lesser, 1991; Conry et al., 1990]. This benevolence is based on the

assumption common to many approaches to coordination: That the goal is for the system to solve the problem as best it can, and therefore the agents have a shared, often implicit, global goal that they are all unselfishly committed to achieving.

It was observed in [Grosz and Kraus, 1993] that agents may sub-contract some of their tasks to other agents also in environments where the agents do not have a common goal and there is no globally consistent knowledge.[1] That is, a selfish agent that tries to carry out its own individual plan in order to fulfill its own tasks may sub-contract some of its tasks to another selfish agent(s). An agent tries to contract some of its tasks that it can't perform by itself, or when the task may be performed more efficiently or better by other agents. The main question is how an agent may convince another agent to do something for it when the agents don't share a global task and the agents are not assumed to be benevolent. Furthermore, we would like the contracted agent to carry out the task efficiently without the need of close supervision by the contracting agent. This will enable the contracting agent to carry out other tasks simultaneously.

There are two main ways to convince another selfish agent to perform a task that is not among its own tasks: threats to interfere with the agent carrying out its own tasks or promises of rewards. In this paper we concentrate on subcontracting by rewards. Rewards may be in two forms. In the first approach one agent may promise to help the other in its tasks in the future in return for current help. As was long ago observed in economics, barter is not an efficient basis for cooperation. In a multi-agent environment, an agent that wants to subcontract a task to another agent may not be able to help it in the future, or one agent that may be able to help in another agent's task may not need help in carrying out its own tasks. In the second approach a monetary system is developed that is used for rewards. The rewards can be used later for other purposes. We will show that a monetary system

---

*This material is based upon work supported by the National Science Foundation under Grant No. IRI-9123460. I would like to thank Jonathan Wilkenfeld for his comments.

[1]Systems of agents acting in environments where there is no global common goal (e.g., [Sycara, 1990; Zlotkin and Rosenschein, 1991; Kraus et al., 1991; Ephrati and Rosenschein, 1991]) are called *Multi-Agent Systems* [Bond and Gasser, 1988; Gasser, 1991].

for the multi-agent environment that allows for side payments and rewards between the agents yields an efficient contracting mechanism. The monetary profits may be given to the owners of the automated agents. The agents will be built to maximize expected utilities that increase with the monetary values, as will be explained below.

The issue of contracts has been investigated in economics and game-theory in the last two decades (e.g., [Arrow, 1985; Ross, 1973; Rasmusen, 1989; Grossman and Hart, 1983; Hirshleifer and Riley, 1992]). They have considered situations in which a person or a company contracts a task to another person or company. In this paper we adjust the models that were developed in economics and game-theory to fit distributed artificial intelligence situations.

We will consider varied situations: In the Section *Contracts Under Certainty* one agent subcontracts a task to another one when the agents have full information about the environment and each other. In the Section *Contracts Under Uncertainty*, we consider contracting when the agents don't know the exact state of the world. The situation in which an agent may subcontract its tasks several times to the same agent is considered in Section *Repeated Encounters*, and situations of asymmetric information or when the agents lack information about each other is dealt with in the Section *Asymmetric and Incomplete Information*. We conclude with the case of an agent subcontracting a task to a group of agents. In all these cases, we consider situations where the contracting agent doesn't supervise the contracted agents' performance and situations where there is a competition among possible contracted agents or possible contracting agents.

Preliminaries

We will refer to the agent that subcontracts one of its tasks to another agent as the *contracting agent* and to the agent that agrees to carry out the task as the *contracted agent*. The *effort* level is the time and work intensity which the contracted agent puts into fulfilling the task. We denote the set of all possible efforts by E. In all cases, the contracted agent chooses how much effort to extend, but its decision may be influenced by the contract offered by the contracting agent. We assume that there is a monetary value $q(e)$ of performing a task which increases with the effort involved. That is, the more time and effort put in by the contracted agent, the better the outcome. The contracting agent will pay the contracted agent a wage w (which can be a function of q). There are several properties we require from our mechanism for subcontracting:

Simplicity: The contract should be simple and there should be an algorithm to compute it.

Pareto-Optimality: There is no other contracted arrangement that is preferred by both sides over the one they have reached.

Stability: We would like the results to be in equilibrium and that the contracts will be reached and executed without delay.

Concerning the simplicity and stability issues, there are two approaches for finding equilibria in the type of situations under consideration here [Rasmusen, 1989]. One is the straight game theory approach: a search for Nash strategies or for perfect equilibrium strategies. The other is the economist's standard approach: set up a maximization problem and solve using calculus. The drawback of the game theory approach is that it is not mechanical. Therefore, in our previous work on negotiation under time constraints, we have identified perfect-equilibrium strategies and proposed to develop a library of meta strategies to be used when appropriate [Kraus and Wilkenfeld, 1991a; Kraus and Wilkenfeld, 1991b]. The maximization approach is much easier to implement. The problem with the maximization approach in our context is that players must solve their optimization problems jointly: the contracted agent's strategy affects the contracting agent's maximization problem and vice versa. In this paper we will use the maximization approach, with some care, by embedding the contracted agent's maximization problem into the contracting agent's problem as a constraint. This maximization problem can be solved automatically by the agent.

The agents' utility functions play an important role in finding an efficient contract. As explained above, we propose to include a monetary system in the multi-agent environment. This system will provide a way for providing rewards. However, it is not always the case that the effort of an agent can be assigned the same monetary values. Each designer of an automated agent needs to provide its agent with a decision mechanism based on some given set of preferences. Numeric representations of these preferences offer distinct advantages in compactness and analytic manipulation [Wellman and Doyle, 1992]. Therefore, we propose that each designer of autonomous agents will develop a numerical utility function that it would like its agent to maximize. In our case the utility function will depend on monetary gain and effort. This is especially important in situations where there is uncertainty in the situation and the agents need to make decisions under risk considerations. Decision theory offers a formalism for capturing risk attitudes. If an agent's utility function is concave, it is risk averse. If the function is convex, it is risk prone, and a linear utility function yields risk neutral behavior [Hirshleifer and Riley, 1992].

We denote the contracted agent's utility function by U which is a decreasing function in effort and an increasing function in wage w. We assume that if the contracted agent won't accept the contract from the contracting agent, its utility, (i.e., its reservation price) which is known to both agents is $\hat{u}$. This outcome can result either from not doing anything or performing some other tasks at the same time. We denote the contracting agent's utility function by V and it is an increasing function with the value of performing the task (q) and decreasing function with the wage w paid to the contracted agent. In our system we assume that the contracting agent rewards the contracted agent *after* the task is carried out. In such situations there should be a technique for enforcing this reward. In case of multiple encounters reputational considerations may yield appropriate behavior. In a single encounter some external intervention may be required to enforce commitments.

Contracts Under Certainty

In this case we assume that all the relevant information about the environment and the situation is known to both agents. In the simplest case the contracting agent can observe and supervise the contracted agent's effort and actions and force it to make the effort level preferred by the contracting agent by paying it only in case it makes the required effort. The amount of effort required from the contracted agent will be the one that maximizes the contracting agent's outcome, taking into account the task fulfillment and the payments it needs to make to the contracted agent.

However, in most situations it is either not possible or too costly for the contracting agent to supervise the contracted agent's actions and observe its level of effort. In some cases, it may be trying to carry out another task at the same time, or it can't reach the site of the action (and that is indeed the reason for subcontracting). If the outcome is a function of the contracted agent's effort and if this function is known to both agents the contracting agent can offer the contracted agent a *forcing contract* [Harris and Raviv, 1978; Rasmusen, 1989]. In this contract, the contracting agent will pay the contracted agent only if it provides the outcome required by the contracting agent. If the contracted agent accepts the contract, he will perform the task with the effort that the contracting agent finds to be most profitable to itself even without supervision. Note that the outcome won't necessarily be with the highest effort on the part of the contracted agent, but rather the effort which provides the contracting agent with the highest outcome. That is, the contracting agent should pick an effort level e^* that will generates the efficient output level q^*. Since we assume that there are several possible agents available for contracting, in equilibrium, the contract must provide the contracted agent with the utility $\hat{u}$.[2] The contracting agent needs to choose a wage function such that $U(e^*, w(q^*)) = \hat{u}$ and $U(e, w(q)) < \hat{u}$ for $e \neq e^*$. We demonstrate this case in the following example.

Example 1: Contracting Under Certainty
The US and Germany have sent several mobile robots independently to Mars to collect minerals and ground

---

[2]We assume that if the contracted agent is indifferent between two actions, it will choose the one preferred by the contracting agent.

samples and to conduct experiments. One of the US robots has to dig some minerals on Mars far from the other US robots. There are several German robots in that area and the US robot would like to subcontract some of its digging. The US robot approaches one of the German robots that can dig in three levels of effort (e): Low, Medium and High denoted by 1,2 and 3 respectively. The US agent can't supervise the German robot's effort since it wants to carry out another task simultaneously. The value of digging is $q(e) = \sqrt{100e}$. The US robot's utility function, if a contract is reached, is $V(q, w) = q - w$ and the German robot's utility function in case it accepts the contract is $U(e, w) = 17 - \frac{10}{w} - 2e$, where w is the payment to the German robot. If the German robot rejects the contract, it will busy itself with maintenance tasks and its utility will be 10. It is easy to calculate that the best effort level from the US robot's point of view is 2, in which there will be an outcome of $\sqrt{200}$. The contract that the US robot offers to the German robot is $3\frac{1}{3}$ if the outcome is $\sqrt{200}$ and 0 otherwise. This contract will be accepted by the German robot and its effort level will be Medium.

There are two additional issues of concern. The first one is how the contracting agent chooses which agent to approach. In the situation of complete information (we consider the incomplete information case in Section *Asymmetric and Incomplete Information*) it should compute the expected utility for itself from each contract with each agent and chooses the one with the maximal expected utility.

Our model is also appropriate in the case in which there are several contracting agents, but only one possible contracted agent. In such a case, there should be information about the utilities of the contracting agents in the event that they don't sign a contract. The contracted agent should compute the level of effort that maximizes its expected utility (similar to the computation of the contracting agent in the reverse case) and make an offer to the contracting agent that will maximize its outcome.

Contracts Under Uncertainty

In most subcontracting situations, there is uncertainty concerning the outcome of an action. If the contracted agent chooses some effort level, there are several possibilities for an outcome. For example, suppose an agent on Mars subcontracts digging for samples of a given mineral and suppose that there is an uncertainty about the depth of the given mineral at the site. If the contracted agent chooses a high effort level but the mineral level is deep underground the outcome may be similar to the case where the contracted agent chooses a low level of effort but the mineral is located near the surface. But, if it chooses a high effort level when the mineral is located near the surface, the outcome may be much better. In such situations the outcome of performing a task doesn't reveal the exact effort level of the contracted agent and choosing a stable and maximal contract is much more difficult.

We will assume that the world may be in one of several states. Neither the contracting agent nor the contracted agent knows the exact state of the world when agreeing on the contract, as well as when the contracted agent chooses the level of effort to take, after agreeing on the contract. The contracted agent may observe the state of the world *after* choosing the effort level (during or after completing the task), but the contracting agent can't observe it. For simplicity, we also assume that there is a set of possible outcomes to the contracted agent carrying out the task $Q = \{q_1, ..., q_n\}$ such that $q_1 < q_2 < ... < q_n$ that depends on the state of the world and the effort level of the contracted agent. Furthermore, we assume that given a level of effort, there is a probability distribution that is attached to the outcomes that is known to both agents.[3] Formally, we assume that there is a probability function $\wp : E \times Q \rightarrow \mathbb{R}$, such that for any $e \in E$, $\sum_1^n \wp(e, q_i) = 1$ and for all $q_i \in Q$, $\wp(e, q_i) > 0$.[4] The contracting agent's problem is to find a contract that will maximize its expected utility, knowing that the contracted agent may reject the contract or if it accepts the contract the effort level is chosen later [Rasmusen, 1989]. The contracting agent's payment to the contracted agent can be based only on the outcome. Let us assume that in the contract that will be offered by the contracting agent, for any q_i $i = 1, ..., n$ the contracting agent will pay the contracted agent w_i. The maximization problem can be constructed as follows (see also [Rasmusen, 1989]).

$$Maximize_{w_1, ... w_n} \sum_1^n \wp(\hat{e}, q_i) V(q_i, w_i) \qquad (1)$$

with the constraints:

$$\hat{e} = argmax_{e \in E} \sum_1^n \wp(e, q_i) U(e, w_i) \qquad (2)$$

$$\sum_1^n \wp(\hat{e}, q_i) U(\hat{e}, w_i) > \hat{u} \qquad (3)$$

Equation (1) states that the contracting agent tries to choose the payment to the contracted agent so as to

---

[3] A practical question is how the agents find the probability distribution. It may be that they have preliminary information about the world, e.g., what is the possibility that a given mineral will be in that area of Mars. In the worst case, they may assume an equal distribution. The model can be easily extended to the case that each agent has different beliefs about the state of the world [Page, 1987].

[4] The formal model in which the outcome is a function of the state of the world and the contracted agent's effort level, and in which the probabilistic function gives the probability of the state of the world which is independent of the contracted agent's effort level is a special case of the model described here [Page, 1987; Ross, 1973; Harris and Raviv, 1978].

maximize its expected utility subject to the constraint that the contracted agent will prefer the contract over rejecting it (3) and that the contracted agent prefers the effort level that the contracting agent prefers, given the contract it is offered (2).

The main question is whether there is an algorithm to solve this maximization problem and whether such a contract exists. This depends primarily on the utility functions of the agents. If the contracting agent and the contracted agent are risk neutral, then solving the maximization problem can be done using any linear programming technique (e.g, simplex, see for example [Pfaffenberger and Walker, 1976].) Furthermore, in most situations, the solution will be very simple: the contracting agent will receive a fixed amount of the outcome and the rest will go to the contracted agent. That is, $w_i = q_i - C$ for $1 \leq i \leq n$, where the constant C is determined by constraint (3) [Shavell, 1979].

Example 2: Risk Neutral Agents Under Uncertainty
Suppose the utility function of the German robot from Example 1 is $U(w, e) = w - e$ and that it can choose between two effort levels Low (e=1) and High (e=2) and its reservation price is $\hat{u} = 1$. There are two possible monetary outcomes to the digging: $q_1 = 8$ and $q_2 = 10$ and the US robot's utility function is as in the previous example, i.e., $V(q, w) = q - w$.

If the German robot chooses the Lower level effort then the outcome will be q_1 with probability $\frac{3}{4}$ and q_2 with probability $\frac{1}{4}$ and if it takes the High level effort the probability of q_1 is $\frac{1}{8}$ and of q_2 it is $\frac{7}{8}$. In such situations, the US robot should reserve to itself a profit of $6\frac{3}{4}$. That is, $w_1 = 1\frac{1}{4}$ and $w_2 = 3\frac{1}{4}$. The German robot will choose the High level effort.

If the agents are not neutral toward risk, the problem is much more difficult. However, if the utility function for the agents are carefully chosen, an algorithm does exist. Suppose the contracted agent is risk averse and the contracting agent is risk neutral (the methods are also applicable when both are risk averse). Grossman and Hart [Grossman and Hart, 1983] presented a three-step procedure to find appropriate contracts. The first step of the procedure is to find for each possible effort level the set of wage contracts that induce the contracted agent to choose that effort level. The second step is to find the contract which supports that effort level at the lowest cost to the contracting agent. The third step is to choose the effort level that maximizes profits, given the necessity to support that effort with a costly wage contract. For space reasons, we won't present the formal details of the algorithm here, and also in the rest of the paper.

Repeated Encounters

Suppose the contracting agent wants to subcontract its tasks several (finite) times. Repetition of the encounters between the contracting and the contracted agents enables the agents to reach efficient contracts if the number of encounters is large enough. The contracting agent could form an accurate estimate of the contracted agent's effort, based on the average outcome, over time. That is, if the contracting agent wants the contracted agent to take a certain effort level $\hat{e}$, in all the encounters, it can compute the expected outcome over time if the contracted agent actually performs the task with that effort level. The contracting agent can keep track of the cumulative sum of the actual outcomes and compare it with the expected outcome. If there is some time T in which the outcome is below a given function of the expected outcome, the contracting agent should impose a big "punishment" on the contracted agent. If the function over the expected outcome is chosen carefully [Radner, 1981], the probability of imposing a "punishment" when the contracted agent is in fact carrying out the desired effort level can be made very low, while the probability of eventually imposing the "punishment" if the agent doesn't do e is one.

Asymmetric and Incomplete Information

In some situations the contracting agent does not know the utility function of the contracted agent. The contracted agent may be one of several types that reflect the contracted agent's ability to carry out the task, its efficiency or the cost of its effort. However, we assume that given the contracted agent's type, its utility function is known to its opponent. For example, suppose Germany builds robots of two types. The specifications of the robots are known to the German robots and to the US robots, however, the US robots don't know the specific type of the German robots that they meet.

As in previous sections the output is a function of the contracted agent's effort level, and the probability function $\wp$ indicates the probability of each outcome, given the effort level and the agent's type. The question remains which contract the contracting agent should offer when it doesn't know the contracted agent's type. A useful technique in such situations is for the contracting agent to search for an optimal mechanism [Demougin, 1989] as follows: the contracting agent offers the contracted agent a menu of contracts that are functions of its type and the outcome. The agents chooses a contract (if at all) and announces it to the contracting agent. Given this contract, the contracted agent chooses an effort level which maximizes its own expected utility. In each of the menu's contracts, the contracted agent's expected utility should be at least as its expected utility if it doesn't sign the contract. We also concentrate only on contracts in which it will always be in the interest of the contracted agent to honestly report its type. It was proven that this requirement is without loss of generality [Myerson, 1982]. It was also shown that in some situations, an efficient contract can be reached without communication [Demougin, 1989], but we omit the dis-

cussion here for space reasons.

If there are several agents whose types are unknown to the contracting agent and it must choose among them, the following mechanism is appropriate: The contracting agent announces a set of contracts based on the agent's type and asks the potential contracted agents to report their types. On the basis of these reports the contracting agent chooses one agent [McAfee and McMillan, 1987].

In other situations, the contracting agent knows the utility function of the contracted agent, but the contracted agent is able to find more information on the environment than the contracting agent. For example, when the German robot reaches the area where it needs to dig, it determines the structure of this area. This information is known only to the German robot and not to the US robot. The mechanism that should be used in this context is the following: The contracting agent offers a payment arrangement which is based on the outcome and the message the contracted agent will send to the contracting agent about the additional information it possesses. If the contracted agent accepts the offer, it will observe the information (by going to the area, or using any of its sensors etc.). Then it will send a message to the contracting agent and will choose its effort level. Eventually, after the task is finished and the outcome is observed, the contracting agent will pay the rewards. Also in this case [Christensen, 1981], the agents can concentrate on the class of contracts that induce the contracted agent to send a truthful message. This is since for any untruthful contracts, a truthful one can be found in which the expected utility of agents is the same. A maximization solvable problem can be constructed here, but we omit it for space reasons.

Subcontracting to a Group

Suppose that the task the contracting agent wants to contract for can be performed by a group of agents. Each of the contracted agents is independent in the sense that it tries to maximize its own utility. The contracting agent offers a contract to each of the possible contracted agents. If one of them rejects the offer, then the contracting agent cannot subcontract the task. Otherwise, the contracted agents simultaneously choose effort levels.

In other situations, the contracting agent can't observe the individual outcome (or such an outcome does not exists) but rather observe only the overall outcome from the effort of all agents [Holmstrom, 1982]. Here, even in the case of certainty, i.e., the state of the world is known, there is a problem in making the contracted agents take the preferred level of action, since there is no way for the contracting agent to find out the effort level of each of the individual agent, given the overall output. For example, suppose two robots agreed to dig minerals, but they both put the minerals in the same truck, so it is not possible to figure out who digs what.

If the contracting agent wants the contracted agents to take the vector of levels effort e^* it can search for a contract such that, if the outcome is $q \geq q(e^*)$ then $w_i(q) = b_i$ and otherwise 0, such that $U(e_i^*, b_i) \geq \hat{u}_i$. That is, if all agents choose the appropriate effort level, each of them gets b_i and if any of them does not, all get nothing.

Conclusions

In this paper we presented techniques that can be used in different cases where sub-contracting of a task by an agent to another agent or a set of agents in non-collaborative environments is beneficial. In all the situations, simple Pareto-optimal contracts can be found by using techniques of maximization with constraints. In the case where the agents have complete information about each other, there is no need for negotiations and a contract is reached without a delay even when the contracting agent doesn't supervise the contracted agent's actions. If there is asymmetric information, or the agents are not sure about their opponents' utility functions, a stage of message exchange is needed to reach a contract.

References

Arrow, K. J. 1985. The economics of agency. In Pratt, J. and Zeckhauser, R., editors 1985, *Principals and Agents: The Structure of Business*. Harvard Business School Press. 37–51.

Bond, A. H. and Gasser, L. 1988. An analysis of problems and research in DAI. In Bond, A. H. and Gasser, L., editors 1988, *Readings in DAI*. Morgan Kaufmann Pub., Inc., Ca. 3–35.

Christensen, J. 1981. Communication in agencies. *Bell Journal of Economics* 12:661—674.

Conry, S.E.; MacIntosh, D. J.; and Meyer, R.A. 1990. DARES: A distributed automated REasoning system. In *Proc. of AAAI90*, MA. 78–85.

Davis, R. and Smith, R.G. 1983. Negotiation as a metaphor for distributed problem solving. *Artificial Intelligence* 20:63–109.

Demougin, D. 1989. A renegotiation-proof mechanism for a principle-agent model with moral hazard and adverse selection. *The Rand Journal of Economics* 20:256–267.

Durfee, E. 1992. What your computer really needs to know, you learned in kindergarten. In *Proc. of AAAI-92*, California. 858–864.

Ephrati, E. and Rosenschein, J. 1991. The clarke tax as a consensus mechanism among automated agents. In *Proc. of AAAI-91*, California. 173–178.

Gasser, L. 1991. Social concepts of knowledge and action: DAI foundations and open systems semantics. *Artificial Intelligence* 47(1–3):107–138.

Grossman, S. and Hart, O. 1983. An anaysis of the principal-agent problem. *Econometrica* 51(1):7–45.

Grosz, B. and Kraus, S. 1993. Collaborative plans for group activities. In *IJCAI93*, French.

Harris, M. and Raviv, A. 1978. Some results on incentive contracts with applications to education and employment, health insurance, and law enforcement. *The American Economic Review* 68(1):20–30.

Hirshleifer, J. and Riley, J. 1992. *The Analytics of Uncertainty and Information*. Cambridge University Press, Cambridge.

Holmstrom, B. 1982. Moral hazard in teams. *Bell Journal of Economics* 13(2):324—340.

Kraus, S. and Wilkenfeld, J. 1991a. The function of time in cooperative negotiations. In *Proc. of AAAI-91*, California. 179–184.

Kraus, S. and Wilkenfeld, J. 1991b. Negotiations over time in a multi agent environment: Preliminary report. In *Proc. of IJCAI-91*, Australia. 56–61.

Kraus, S.; Ephrati, E.; and Lehmann, D. 1991. Negotiation in a non-cooperative environment. *J. of Experimental and Theoretical AI* 3(4):255–282.

Lesser, V.R. 1991. A retrospective view of fa/c distributed problem solving. *IEEE Transactions on Systems, Man, and Cybernetics* 21(6):1347–1362.

McAfee, R. P. and McMillan, J. 1987. Competition for agency contracts. *The Rand Journal of Economics* 18(2):296–307.

Myerson, R. 1982. Optimal coordination mechanisms in generalized principal-agent problem. *Journal of Mathematical Economics* 10:67–81.

Page, F. 1987. The existence of optimal contracts in the principal-agent model. *Journal of Mathematical Economics* 16(2):157–167.

Pfaffenberger, R. and Walker, D. 1976. *Mathematical Programming for Economics and Business*. The IOWA State University Press, Ames, IOWA.

Radner, R. 1981. Monitoring cooperative agreements in a repeated principal-agent relationships. *Econometrica* 49(5):1127–1148.

Rasmusen, E. 1989. *Games and Information*. Basil Blackwell Ltd., Cambridge, Ma.

Ross, S. 1973. The economic theory of agency: The principal's problem. *The American Economic Review* 63(2):134–139.

Shavell, S. 1979. Risk sharing and incentives in the principal and agent relationship. *Bell Journal of Economics* 10:55–79.

Sycara, K. P. 1990. Persuasive argumentation in negotiation. *Theory and Decision* 28:203–242.

Wellman, M. and Doyle, J. 1992. Modular utility representation for decision-theoretic planning. In *Proc. of AI planning Systems*, Maryland. 236—242.

Zlotkin, G. and Rosenschein, J. 1991. Incomplete information and deception in multi-agent negotiation. In *Proc. IJCAI-91*, Australia. 225–231.

IPUS: An Architecture for Integrated Signal Processing and Signal Interpretation in Complex Environments*

Victor Lesser   Hamid Nawab[†]   Izaskun Gallastegi   Frank Klassner

Computer Science Department
University of Massachusetts
Amherst, MA 01003
{lesser izaskun klassner}@cs.umass.edu

[†]ECS Department
Boston University
Boston, MA 02125
hamid@buengc.bu.edu

Abstract

This paper presents the IPUS (*Integrated Processing and Understanding of Signals*) architecture to address the traditional perceptual paradigm's shortcomings in complex environments. It has two premises: (1) the search for correct interpretations of signal processing algorithms' (SPAs) outputs requires concurrent search for SPAs and control parameters appropriate for the environment, and (2) interaction between these search processes must be structured by a formal theory of how inappropriate SPA usage can distort SPA output. We describe IPUS's key components (discrepancy detection, diagnosis, reprocessing, and differential diagnosis) and their instantiation in an acoustic interpretation system. This application, along with another in the radar domain, supports our claim that the IPUS paradigm is feasible and generic.

Introduction

In traditional knowledge-based perceptual systems [8, 17], numeric signal processing is fixed, and interpretation processes are limited to analyzing the single view afforded by this processing. This paradigm assumes that a small set of front-end signal processing algorithms (SPAs) with fixed parameter settings can produce adequate evidence for deriving plausible interpretations under all scenarios. The complex environments that next-generation systems will monitor, however, have variable signal to noise ratios, unpredictable source behaviors, and many sources whose signatures can mask or otherwise distort each other. Under the traditional paradigm, such environments often require combinatorially explosive SPA sets with multiple parameter settings to capture the variety of signals adequately [7] and to handle the variety of processing

*This work was supported by the Rome Air Development Center of the Air Force Systems Command under contract F30602-91-C-0038, and by the Office of Naval Research under contract N00014-92-J-1450. The content does not necessarily reflect the position or the policy of the Government, and no official endorsement should be inferred.

goals the current environment may dictate. To avoid this problem, we argue that knowledge-based perceptual research needs to consider a paradigm incorporating *dynamic SPA reconfiguration*. This term refers not only to reconfiguration for tracking changes in signal behavior, but also to (repeated) reconfiguration for analyzing cached data to reduce uncertainty in signal interpretations.

Research in active vision and robotics has recognized the importance of tracking-oriented reconfiguration [19], and tends to use a control-theoretic approach for making reconfiguration decisions. It is indeed sometimes possible to reduce the reconfiguration of small sets of front-end SPAs to problems in linear control theory. In general, however, the problem of deciding when an SPA (e.g. a shape-from-X algorithm or an acoustic filter) with particular parameter settings is appropriate to a given environment may involve nonlinear control or be unsolvable with current control theory techniques.

Recent systems in other fields [4, 5, 6, 9, 11] have used symbolically-oriented architectures that permit interpretation processes to reconfigure front-end signal processing. However, as the **Related Work** section will show, their architectures have not been general enough. We have developed an architecture to permit more general interaction between signal processing and signal interpretation by explicitly representing the theory underlying front-end SPAs. The *Integrated Processing and Understanding of Signals* (IPUS) architecture has two premises for complex environments. The first is that the search for correct interpretations of numeric SPAs' outputs requires a concurrent search for SPAs and control parameters appropriate for the environment. The second premise is that the interaction between these search processes must be bidirectional and structured by a formal theory of how inappropriate parameter settings or applications of SPAs lead to specific discrepancies in SPA output.

This paper presents (1) the generic architecture, (2) the IPUS components' generic design and interaction, (3) IPUS instantiated in a sound understanding testbed, (4) related work, and (5) conclusions.

The Generic IPUS Architecture

Before describing IPUS we must first discuss SPAs, the basic means for analyzing environmental signals. When applied to a signal, an SPA instance produces correlates, which serve as evidence for hypothesizing features of objects (e.g. sounds or physical objects). An SPA instance is specified by values for a generic SPA's parameters, and these values induce capabilities or limitations with respect to the scenario being monitored. We use "SPA" to refer to SPA instances. Consider the Short-Time Fourier Transform (STFT) [15] in the acoustic domain. An STFT instance has particular values for its parameters, such as analysis window length, frequency-sampling rate, and decimation factor (consecutive analysis windows' separation). Depending on a scenario's spectral features and their time-variant nature, these parameter values increase or decrease the instance's usefulness in monitoring the scenario. Instances with large window lengths provide fine frequency resolution for scenarios containing sounds with time-invariant components, but at the cost of poor time resolution for scenarios containing sounds with time-varying components.

Figure 1a shows the generic IPUS architecture. Two types of signal interpretation hypotheses are stored on the hierarchical blackboard: current signal data's interpretations and expectations about future data's interpretations.

The design of IPUS assumes that signal data is analyzed in blocks. IPUS uses an iterative process to converge to appropriate SPAs and interpretations. The following is a summary (see **Architecture Components** and [12, 14] for more detail). For each data block, the loop starts by processing the signal with an initial SPA configuration. These SPAs are selected not only to identify and track the objects most likely to appear, but also to provide indications of when less likely or unknown objects have appeared. In the next loop step, a *discrepancy detection* process tests for discrepancies between the correlates of each SPA in the current configuration and expectations based on (1) object models, (2) the correlates of other SPAs in the configuration, and (3) application-domain signal characteristics. These comparisons may occur both after SPA output is generated and after interpretations are generated. If discrepancies are detected, a *diagnosis* process then attempts to explain them in terms of a set of distortion hypotheses. This diagnosis uses the formal theory underlying the signal processing. The loop ends with a *signal reprocessing* stage that proposes and executes a search plan to find a new front-end (i.e. a set of SPAs) to eliminate or reduce the hypothesized distortions. After the loop's completion, if there are any similarly-rated competing top-level interpretations, a *differential diagnosis* process selects and executes a reprocessing plan to detect features that will discriminate among the alternatives.

IPUS is intended to integrate the search for interpretations of SPA correlates with the search for SPA parameter values appropriate to the scenario. In complex environments we argue that these searches must interact bidirectionally under the guidance of a domain's formal signal processing theory. The dual search in the framework becomes apparent with the following observations. Each time data is reprocessed, whether for disambiguation or distortion elimination, a new state in the SPA search space is tested for how well it eliminates distortions. The measurement of distortion elimination or disambiguation assumes that the system's current state in the interpretation space matches the scenario being observed. Failure to remove a hypothesized distortion after a bounded search in the SPA space will lead to a new search in the interpretation space. This occurs because the diagnosis and reprocessing results represent attempts at justifying the assumption that the current interpretation is correct. If either diagnosis or reprocessing fails, there is a strong likelihood that the current interpretation is not correct and a new search is required in the interpretation space. Furthermore, the results of failed reprocessing can constrain the new interpretation search by eliminating from consideration objects with features that should have been found during the reprocessing.

We designed IPUS to serve as the basis of perceptual systems that can manage their interpretations' uncertainty levels. Therefore, we had to provide the architecture's control framework with a way to represent factors that affect interpretations' certainties. The control framework also had to support context-sensitive focusing on particular uncertainties in order to control engagement and interruption of the architecture's reprocessing loop.

For these reasons, IPUS uses the RESUN [3] framework to control knowledge source (KS) execution. This framework supports the view of interpretation as a process of gathering evidence to resolve hypotheses' sources of uncertainty (SOUs). It incorporates a language for representing SOUs as structures which trigger the selection of appropriate interpretation strategies. Problem-solving is driven by information in the *problem solving model*, which is a summary of the current interpretations and the SOUs associated with each one's supporting hypotheses. An incremental, reactive planner maintains control using *control plans* and *focusing heuristics*. Control plans are schemas that define the strategies and SPAs available to the system for processing and interpreting data, and for resolving interpretation uncertainties. Focusing heuristics are context-sensitive tests to select SOUs to resolve and processing strategies to pursue.

Architecture Components

This section provides detailed, yet generic, descriptions of the key architectural components. Our focus is on the three roles a domain's formal signal processing theory can play in guiding interpretation and processing in

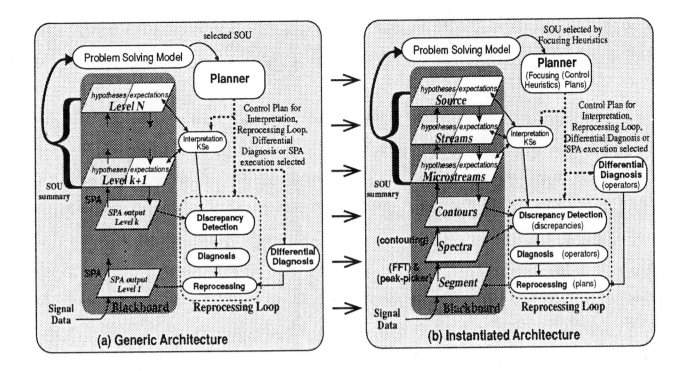

Figure 1: *1a shows the generic IPUS architecture, 1b shows the architecture instantiated for the sound understanding testbed. Solid arrows indicate dataflow relations. Dotted arrows indicate plans that the planner can pursue when trying to reduce SOUs (discrepancies) in the problem solving model that were selected by the focusing heuristics. Knowledge to instantiate the architecture for an application is shown in parentheses in 1b. Reprocessing plans can produce SPA output at any abstraction level, not just the lowest.*

a complex environment: (1) providing methods to determine discrepancies between an SPA's expected correlate set and its computed correlate set, (2) defining distortion processes that explain how discrepancies between expectations and an SPA's computed correlates result when the SPA has inappropriate values for specific parameters, and (3) specifying strategies to reprocess signals so that distortions are removed or ambiguous data is disambiguated.

We relate a signal processing theory to SPAs and their interaction with the environment using *SPA processing models*. An SPA processing model describes how the output of the SPA changes when one of its control parameters is varied while all the others are held fixed.

SPA processing models serve as the basis for defining how the parameter settings of an SPA can introduce distortions into the SPA's computed correlates. These distortions cause SPA output discrepancies. Consider an SPA processing model corresponding to the STFT's WINDOW-LENGTH parameter and how this model can be used to define distortions. Assume that an STFT with an analysis window of length W is applied to a signal sampled at rate R. If the signal came from a scenario containing two or more frequency tracks closer

than R/W, Fourier theory predicts that the tracks will appear as one track in the STFT's correlates.

Discrepancy Detection

Discrepancy detection is crucial to IPUS's iterative approach. Its inclusion in the IPUS loop relies on several observations. An SPA's correlates can be compared with expectations based on object models or on *a priori* environment constraints such as maximum bounds on sounds' rate of temporal change in frequency. Most importantly, a domain's signal processing theory can specify how one SPA's correlates for a context-independent feature can serve as the basis of expectations for another SPA's output correlates. This specification can serve to check an SPA's appropriateness to the environment. It can also serve to decide where to selectively apply another SPA in the signal data stream to obtain correlates for context-dependent features. For example, in the acoustic domain a time-domain energy tracking algorithm can detect impulsive sources whose short-duration frequency components might be smoothed to indetectability in the output of an STFT with a wide analysis window. Thus, the energy algorithm can serve as a standard against which STFT output can be compared.

We categorize discrepancies in focusing heuristics for diagnostic consideration in the following order:

faults A discrepancy detected between an SPA's correlates and correlates from other SPAs applied to the same data. In [2] we discuss several fault discrepancy detection algorithms used in the sound understanding testbed. Faults are considered for diagnosis first since inconsistency among the outputs of two or more SPAs within a front-end almost always indicates a front-end's inappropriate application.

violations A discrepancy detected between an SPA's correlates and environment constraints. Violations are ranked second for diagnosis since they reflect a comparison between only one SPA's output and domain characteristics that may be incompletely specified.

conflicts A discrepancy between an SPA's correlates and the output expected based on previous high-level interpretations. Conflicts are ranked third for diagnosis since they reflect a comparison between SPA output and interpretations which may not be accurate even if they are based on appropriately-processed data.

In IPUS, conflict discrepancy detection is distributed among all KSs that interpret lower-level data as higher-level concepts. Each such KS checks if any data can support a sought-after expectation. If no such data or only partially supportive data is found, the KS records this fact as an SOU in the problem solving model, to be resolved at the discretion of the focusing heuristics. Once a data block's front-end processing is completed, a discrepancy detection KS checks if SPA correlates are consistent with each other, testing for violations and faults defined by the system designer.

An important consideration in discrepancy detection is that expectation hypotheses are sometimes only expressible qualitatively, as in the example, "During the next 400 to 800 msec, a sinusoidal component currently at 1200 Hz will shift to a frequency between 1700 and 2000 Hz." Thus, our testbed discrepancy detection components use a range calculus similar to Allen's [1] to specify discrepancies.

Discrepancy Diagnosis

The discrepancy diagnosis KS is included to take advantage of the fact that a signal domain's SPA processing models can predict the form of an SPA's correlates when the SPA's parameter values are appropriate *or* inappropriate to the current scenario.

The KS models this knowledge in a database of distortion operators. When an operator is applied to a description of undistorted SPA output, it returns the output with the operator's distortion introduced. The KS uses these operators in a means-ends analysis framework [16] to "explain" discrepancies between the expected form of an SPA's correlates and the actual form of the SPA's computed correlates. There are two inputs for this KS: an *initial state* representing the expected correlates' form and a *goal state* representing the computed correlates' form. The formal task of diagnosis is to generate an operator sequence mapping the initial state onto the goal state. Note that there is a difference between discrepancies and distortions. Distortions are used to explain discrepancies. It is also possible for several distortions to explain the same kinds of discrepancies. In the **IPUS Instantiation** section we will see how a "low frequency resolution" distortion explains 'missing' track discrepancies.

The KS's search for a distortion operator sequence is iteratively carried out using progressively more complex abstractions of the initial and goal states, until a level is reached where a sequence can be generated using no more signal information than is available at that level. Thus, the KS mimics expert diagnostic reasoning in that it offers simplest explanations first [18]. Once a sequence is found, the KS enters its *verify* phase, "drops" to the lowest abstraction level, and checks that each operator's pre- and post-conditions are met when all available state information is considered. If verification succeeds, the operator sequence and a diagnosis region indicating the hypotheses involved in the discrepancy are returned. If it fails, the KS attempts to "patch" the sequence by finding operator subsequences that eliminate the unmet conditions and inserting them in the original sequence. If no patch is possible, and no alternative explanations can be generated, the hypotheses hypotheses in the initial state are annotated with an SOU with a very negative rating.

An issue not addressed in earlier work [16] that arose in the development of IPUS is the problem of inapplicable explanations. Sometimes the first explanation offered by the KS will not enable the reprocessing mechanism to eliminate a discrepancy. In these cases, the architecture permits reactivation of the diagnostic KS with the previous explanation supplied as one that must not be returned again. To avoid repeating the search performed for the previous explanation, the KS stores with its explanations the search-tree context it was in when the explanation was produced. The KS's search for a new explanation begins from that point.

Signal Reprocessing

Once distortions have been explained, it falls to the reprocessing KS to search for appropriate SPAs and parameter values that can reduce or remove them. This component incorporates the following phases: *assessment, selection, and execution*. The reprocessing KS input includes a description of the input and output states, the distortion operator sequence hypothesized by the diagnosis KS, and a description of the discrepancies present between the input and output states. The assessment phase uses case-based reasoning constrained by signal processing theory to generate reprocessing plans that have the potential of eliminating the hypothesized distortions present in the current situation. For example, Fourier theory indicates that frequency resolution distortions, if actually present in STFT output, can be eliminated in a reapplication of the SPA with its FFT-SIZE parameter double or quadruple that of the original setting.

In the selection stage, a plan is selected from the retrieved set based on computation costs or other criteria supplied by focusing heuristics. The execution phase consists of incrementally adjusting the SPAs parameters, applying the SPAs to the portion of the signal data that is hypothesized to contain distortions, and testing for discrepancy removal. The execution phase is necessarily incremental because the situation description is at least partially qualitative, and therefore it is generally impossible to predict a priori exact parameter values to be used in the reprocessing.

Execution continues until the distortion causing the discrepancy is removed or plan failure occurs. Plan failure is indicated when either the plan's iterations exceed a fixed threshold or a plan iteration requires a SPA parameter to have a value outside fixed bounds. When failure occurs, the diagnosis KS can be re-invoked to find an alternative explanation for the original distortions. If no alternative explanation can be found, the hypotheses involved in the discrepancy are annotated with SOUs indicating low confidence due to irresolvable discrepancies.

Differential Diagnosis

We include the differential diagnosis KS to produce reprocessing plans that prune the interpretation search space when ambiguous data is encountered. Its input is the ambiguous data's set of alternative interpretations, and it returns the time period in the signal to be reprocessed, the evidence each interpretation requires, and the set of proposed reprocessing plans.

The KS first labels any observed evidence in the interpretation hypotheses' overlapping features as "ambiguous." It then determines the hypotheses' discriminating features (e.g., in the acoustic domain, those frequency tracks of the competing source hypotheses' models which don't overlap any other models' tracks). For each discriminating feature with no observed evidence, the KS posits an explanation for how the evidence could have gone undetected, assuming the source was present. These explanations index into a plan database, and select reprocessing plans to cause the missing evidence to appear. The KS then checks each ambiguous data region for resolution problems based on source models (e.g., a frequency region's peaks could support one source Y component or two source Z components), and selects reprocessing plans to provide finer component resolution in those regions.

The reprocessing plan set returned is the first non-empty set in the sequence: missing-evidence and ambiguous-evidence plan sets' intersection, missing-evidence plan set, ambiguous-evidence plan set. This hierarchy returns the plans most likely to prune many

interpretations from further consideration. The alternative hypotheses' temporal overlap region defines the reprocessing region, and the ambiguous and missing evidence handled by the reprocessing plan set defines the support evidence. A plan from the returned set is then iteratively executed as in the reprocessing KS until either a plan-failure criterion is met or at least one support evidence element is found.

This KS's explanatory reasoning for missing evidence is primitive compared to the discrepancy diagnosis KS's. Only simple, single distortions like loss of low-energy components due to energy thresholding are considered; no multiple-distortion explanations are constructed. This design is justified because the KS's role is to quickly prune large areas of interpretation spaces, *without preference* for any particular interpretation. When a particular interpretation is preferred (rated) over alternatives and a detailed explanation for its missing support is required, IPUS control plans would instead use the discrepancy diagnosis KS, encoding the preferred interpretation in the initial state.

IPUS Instantiation

We have implemented a sound understanding testbed to test the IPUS architecture's realizability and generality (see Figure 1b). In this section we discuss one of the testbed experiment scenarios and how the architecture structured the application of acoustic signal processing knowledge to the scenario's interpretation. The discussion is not intended to illustrate specific control plans' execution or specific SOUs' generation. The testbed version described here is called configuration *C.1*. We are currently developing a second version *C.2* that still relies on the basic IPUS framework but that uses approximate-knowledge KSs to constrain the number of sound models retrieved when large sound libraries are used.

The testbed uses 1500Kb of Common Lisp code and runs on a TI Explorer II+. All SPAs are implemented in software. The testbed SPA database has 3 classes: STFT, energy tracking, and spectral peak-picking. For this experiment the source database contains 5 synthetic and noise-free real-world acoustic source models; the signal is sampled at 10KHz. The scenario and pertinent source models appear in Figure 2. The testbed was initially configured to track a hairdryer sound with two frequency components at 1000 and 1050 Hz. The configuration had a high peak-picking energy threshold to minimize the number of low-energy noise peaks produced by the hairdryer, and STFT parameter settings to provide enough resolution to separate the hairdryer's frequency components. The telephone ring and the door slam represent unexpected source events for which the testbed must temporarily switch SPA configurations if it is to identify them with sufficient certainty.

Because the testbed's SPA settings were originally set for tracking the hairdryer, the testbed must de-

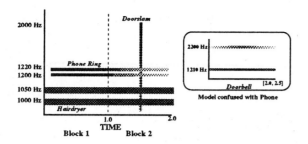

Figure 2: *Scenario and pertinent source definitions. Darker shading indicates higher signal energies.*

tect several discrepancies and perform reprocessing to reasonably analyze the scenario. In block 1's data, the [1200, 1220] Hz region has insufficient resolution to display the phone ring's components due to the frequency-sampling provided by the STFT SPA's FFT-SIZE parameter value. This causes a narrow-band set of peaks with no clear energy trends to appear in the region, thus violating the noise distribution model and raising a discrepancy. The output could support the phone ring, the doorbell, or even both. Had only one candidate interpretation been identified, the testbed would have handled the violation discrepancy via the reprocessing loop. Because more than one interpretation exists, however, the testbed's focusing heuristics select differential diagnosis to resolve the interpretation uncertainty. The diagnosis finds two reasons for the confusion: the peak-picking SPA's high energy threshold designed for the hairdryer would prevent the doorbell's low-energy 2200 Hz component from appearing if it were present and the [1200, 1220] region's low frequency resolution. The uncertainty is resolved in favor of the phone ring interpretation through reprocessing that doubles the FFT-SIZE and decreases the energy threshold. The phone ring's definition and block 1's interpretation generate the expectation for block 2 that it should contain the phone ring's frequencies.

Because the testbed's primary goal is to track the hairdryer, the parameter settings are reset to their original values. In block 2, the testbed detects a fault discrepancy between its time-domain energy-estimator SPA output and its STFT SPA output. The energy-estimator detects the door slam's substantial energy increase followed about 0.1 seconds later by a precipitous decrease. The STFT SPA, however, produces no significant set of peaks to account for the signal energy flux. This is because the SPA's time decimation parameter is too small. The testbed also detects a conflict discrepancy between expectations established from block 1 for the [1200, 1220] frequency region and the STFT SPA's output. The STFT SPA produces a peak set with no energy trends that can support the phone ring's expected continuation because of inadequate frequency sampling in the region. Both discrepancies are resolved by reprocessing based on discrep-

ancy diagnosis explanations. The first discrepancy is resolved through reprocessing with a larger decimation value and smaller STFT windows, while the second is resolved through reprocessing with the finer frequency sampling provided by a 2048 FFT-SIZE.

Related Work

IPUS represents the formalization and extension of concepts explored in our work on a diagnosis system that used formal signal processing theory to debug signal processing systems [16] and in work on meta-level control [10] that used a process of fault-detection, diagnosis, and replanning to choose appropriate parameters for controlling a problem-solving system.

Recent systems have begun to explore interaction between interpretation activity and signal processing. The GUARDIAN system's [9] data management component controls signal sampling rates with respect to real-time constraints. It is designed for monitoring simple signals such as heart rate and does not seem adequate for monitoring signals with complex structures that must be modeled over time. The framework is typical of systems whose input data points already represent useful information and require no formal front-end processing.

Many perceptual frameworks [4, 5, 6] implement the reprocessing concept only as reconfiguration guided by differential diagnosis. Often, they continuously gather data from every available SPA whether required for interpretation improvement or not. Only when ambiguous data is observed are certain SPAs' outputs actually examined to distinguish between competing interpretations. This approach's uncertainty representations attribute deviations between signal behavior and event models solely to chance source variations, never to a signal's interaction with unsuitable SPAs.

In the GOLDIE system [11] interpretation goals guide the choice of image segmentation algorithms, their parameter settings, and their application regions within an image array. The system generates symbolic explanations for an algorithm's (un)suitability to a particular region. In these features the framework approaches the capabilities of IPUS, but notably it does not incorporate diagnosis. If an algorithm's segmentation is unexpectedly poor, the system cannot diagnose the result and use this information to reformulate algorithm search, but simply re-segments with the original search's next rated algorithm.

Conclusion

IPUS provides structured, bidirectional interaction between the search for SPAs appropriate to the environment and the search for interpretations to explain the SPAs' output. The availability of a formal signal processing theory is an important criterion for determining the architecture's applicability to a domain. IPUS allows system developers to organize signal processing knowledge into formal concepts of discrepancy tests, SPA processing models, distortion operators, and reprocessing-SPA application strategies. A major architectural contribution is to unify SPA reconfiguration performed for symbolic-based interpretation processes with that performed for numeric-based processes as a single reprocessing concept.

With respect to scaling, one might argue that the time required by multiple reprocessings under IPUS would be unacceptably high in noisy environments. This view ignores IPUS's advantage over other paradigms in that it *selectively* samples several front-end processings' outputs, avoiding the traditional approach of continuously sampling several front-end processings' results. IPUS also encourages the development of fast, highly specialized, theoretically sound SPAs for reprocessing in appropriate contexts [13]. In this respect the IPUS paradigm decreases the expected processing time for scenarios requiring several processing views for plausible interpretations.

Our acoustic testbed experiments indicate that the basic functionality and interrelationships of the architecture's components are realizable. An indication of the architecture's generality can be seen in its use not only in the acoustic interpretation testbed discussed in this paper but also in a radar interpretation system being developed at Boston University. Our current work in the architecture is concerned with predicting bounds on the amount of reprocessing an environment can induce in IPUS-based systems.

Acknowledgments

We would like to acknowledge Norman Carver for his role in developing IPUS's control framework and evidential reasoning capabilities. Malini Bhandaru and Zarko Cvetanović were important contributors to the testbed's early implementation stages, and Erkan Dorken was an important contributor to the design of testbed SPAs.

References

[1] Allen, J. F.; Hayes, P. J. "A Common-Sense Theory of Time," *Proc. 1985 Int'l Joint Conf. on AI.*

[2] Bitar, N.; Dorken, E.; Paneras, D.; and Nawab, H. "Integration of STFT and Wigner Analysis in a Knowledge-Based Sound Understanding System," *Proc. 1992 IEEE Int'l Conf. on Acoustics, Speech and Signal Processing.*

[3] Carver, N. "A New Framework for Sensor Interpretation: Planning to Resolve Sources of Uncertainty," *Proc. 1991 AAAI.*

[4] Dawant, B.; Jansen, B. "Coupling Numerical and Symbolic Methods for Signal Interpretation," *IEEE Trans. Systems, Man and Cybernetics.* Jan/Feb 1991.

[5] De Mori, R.; Lam, L.; Gilloux, M. "Learning and Plan Refinement in a Knowledge-Based System for Automatic Speech Recognition," *IEEE Trans. Pattern Analysis and Machine Intelligence*, Feb 1987.

[6] Dove, W. *Knowledge-Based Pitch Detection*, PhD Thesis, Computer Science Dept., MIT, 1986.

[7] Dorken, E.; Nawab, H.; Lesser, V. "Extended Model Variety Analysis for Integrated Processing and Understanding of Signals," *Proc. 1992 IEEE Int'l Conf. on Acoustics, Speech and Signal Processing.*

[8] Erman, L.; Hayes-Roth, R.; Lesser, V.; Reddy, D. "The Hearsay II Speech Understanding System: Integrating Knowledge to Resolve Uncertainty," *Computing Surveys*, v. 12, June 1980.

[9] Hayes-Roth, B.; Washington, R.; Hewett, R.; Hewett, M.; Seiver, A. "Intelligent Monitoring and Control," *Proc. 1989 Int'l Joint Conf. on AI.*

[10] Hudlická, E.; Lesser, V. "Meta-Level Control Through Fault Detection and Diagnosis," *Proc. 1984 AAAI.*

[11] Kohl, C.; Hanson, A.; Reisman, E. "A Goal-Directed Intermediate Level Executive for Image Interpretation," *Proc. 1987 Int'l Joint Conf. on AI.*

[12] Lesser, V.; Nawab, H.; et al. "Integrated Signal Processing and Signal Understanding," TR 91-34, Computer Science Dept., University of Massachusetts, Amherst, MA, 1991.

[13] Nawab, H.; Dorken, E. "Efficient STFT Approximation using a Quantization and Difference Method," *Proc. 1993 IEEE Int'l Conf. on Acoustics, Speech and Signal Processing.*

[14] Nawab, H.; Lesser, V. "Integrated Processing and Understanding of Signals," ch 6, *Knowledge-Based Signal Processing*, A. Oppenheim and H. Nawab, eds, Prentice Hall, New Jersey, 1991.

[15] Nawab, H.; Quatieri, T. "Short-Time Fourier Transform," *Advanced Topics in Signal Processing*, Prentice Hall, New Jersey, 1988.

[16] Nawab, H.; Lesser, V.; Milios, E. "Diagnosis Using the Underlying Theory of a Signal Processing System," *IEEE Trans. Systems, Man and Cybernetics*, Special Issue on Diagnostic Reasoning, May/June 1987.

[17] Nii, P.; Feigenbaum, E.; Anton, J.; Rockmore, A.; "Signal-to-Symbol Transformation: HASP/SIAP Case Study," *AI Magazine*, vol 3, Spring 1982.

[18] Peng, Y.; Reggia, J. "Plausibility of Diagnositic Hypotheses: The Nature of Simplicity," *Proc. 1986 AAAI.*

[19] Swain, M.; Stricker, M. eds. *Promising Directions in Active Vision*, NSF Active Vision Workshop, TR CS 91-27, Computer Science Dept, University of Chicago, 1991.

An Implementation of the Contract Net Protocol Based on Marginal Cost Calculations

Tuomas Sandholm

Computer Science Department
University of Massachusetts
Amherst, Massachusetts 01003
sandholm@cs.umass.edu

Abstract

This paper presents a formalization of the bidding and awarding decision process that was left undefined in the original contract net task allocation protocol. This formalization is based on marginal cost calculations based on local agent criteria. In this way, agents having very different local criteria (based on their self-interest) can interact to distribute tasks so that the network as a whole functions more effectively. In this model, both competitive and cooperative agents can interact. In addition, the contract net protocol is extended to allow for clustering of tasks, to deal with the possibility of a large number of announcement and bid messages and to effectively handle situations, in which new bidding and awarding is being done during the period when the results of previous bids are unknown. The protocol is verified by the TRACONET (TRAnsportation COoperation NET) system, where dispatch centers of different companies cooperate automatically in vehicle routing. The implementation is asynchronous and truly distributed, and it provides the agents extensive autonomy. The protocol is discussed in detail and test results with real data are presented.[1]

1   Introduction

The *contract net protocol* (CNP) (Smith 1980; Smith & Davis 1981; Davis & Smith 1988) for decentralized task allocation is one of the important paradigms developed in distributed artificial intelligence (DAI). Its significance lies in that it was the first work to use a negotiation process involving a *mutual selection* by both *managers* and *contractors*. It was initially applied to a simulated distributed acoustic sensor network. In this interpretation

application, the agents were totally cooperative, and selection of a contractor was based on suitability, for example adjacency, processing capability, and current agent load. However, there was no formal model discussed in this work for making task *announcing*, *bidding* and *awarding* decisions. This paper presents such a formal model, where agents locally calculate their marginal costs for performing sets of tasks. The choice of a contractor is based solely on these costs. The pricing mechanism generalizes the CNP to work for both cooperative and competitive agents. Another important issue not covered in previous work on the CNP is the risk attitude of an agent toward being committed to activities it may not be able to honor, or the honoring of which may turn out to be unbeneficial. Additionally, in previous CNP implementations, tasks have been negotiated one at a time. This is not sufficient, if the effort of carrying out a task depends on the carrying out of other tasks. The framework is extended to handle *task interactions* by clustering tasks into sets to be negotiated over as atomic bargaining items. Finally, the practical problem of announcement message congestion is solved.

Our case problem, vehicle routing, is structured in terms of a number of geographically dispersed *dispatch centers* of different companies. Each center is responsible for the deliveries initiated by certain factories and has a certain number of vehicles to take care of the deliveries. The geographical main operation areas of the centers overlap considerably. This provides for the potential for multiple centers to be able to handle a delivery. Every delivery has to be included in the route of some vehicle. The local problem of each agent is a heterogeneous fleet multi-depot routing problem, where the vehicle attributes include cost per kilometer, maximum route duration, maximum route length, maximum load weight and maximum load volume (Sandholm 1992a). The objective is to minimize the transportation costs.

In solving the problem, each dispatch center - represented by one intelligent agent[2] - first solves its local

---

[1]Primary support for this work came from the Technology Development Centre of Finland, during the period which the author was working at the Technical Research Centre of Finland, Laboratory for Information Processing, Lehtisaarentie 2A, SF-00340 Helsinki, Finland. Additional support comes from DARPA contract N00014-92-J-1698. The content of the information does not necessarily reflect the position or the policy of the Government and no official endorsement should be inferred.

[2]Another choice would be that each agent represented one vehicle. This small grain size approach would probably not be as efficient, because such a large number of agents would congest the negotiation network and the method would be too

---

routing problem. After that, an agent can potentially negotiate with other dispatch agents to take on some of their deliveries or to let them take on some of its deliveries for a dynamically constructed charge. In the negotiations the agents exchange sets of deliveries whenever this is profitable, i.e., whenever a contractor is able to carry out the task set with less costs than the manager agent. The negotiations can be viewed as an iterative way of making the routing solution better by going through only feasible solutions.[3] Here 'feasible' means that each center can take care of all of its deliveries. This is how a solution closer to the global optimum is reached although no global optimization run is performed. The use of contract nets as opposed to centralized problem solving is most fruitful in operative decision making in volatile domains such as ours and the factory domain of (Parunak 1987).

The negotiation is real-time since after each contract is made the exchange of deliveries is made immediately. Thus, between individual negotiations some delivery orders may have been dispatched, new orders may have arrived, and the available vehicles may have changed. There is no iteration among the agents until an equilibrium is reached unlike the approach of (Wellman 1992), where the bids include a number of the similar items an agent wants to buy and it is assumed that the purchase of one type of items is independent of the purchase of other types of items. In our system, each item (task set) is different and task sets of different announcements are highly interdependent. In the equilibrium approach of (Kuwabara and Ishida 1992), at each iteration, the seller sets the price based on demand and the buyers state the quantity they want to buy.

Section 2 presents the architecture of our implementation. Section 3 discusses the local control strategy of an agent. In sections 4 to 7, the negotiation phases of announcing, bidding, awarding and award taking are detailed respectively. Section 8 presents test results with real data and section 9 concludes.

2 TRACONET Architecture

The vehicle routing application is implemented in a system called TRACONET (TRAnsportation COoperation NET).[4] The asynchronous automatic negotiations in TRACONET resemble a directed government contracting scheme, where each involved party is allowed to make one bid for each announcement it receives, and the bids of the other parties are not revealed to it. The negotiations are directed in the

sense that an announcement is not sent to all other agents (Parunak 1987), fig. 1. The agents have no fixed hierarchy among themselves. An agent can act both as a manager and a contractor of delivery sets, but it does not have to take both roles, nor is it required to negotiate with all other agents. Further, each agent can reallocate deliveries received from other agents. When announcing, an agent tries to buy some other agent's transportation services at a price, the maximum of which it specifies in the announcement. When bidding, an agent tries to sell its own services at a price, the minimum of which it specifies in the bid. Awarding means actually buying the services of some other center and award taking means actually selling one's services. Unlike the original CNP, in the awarding phase explicit *loser messages* are sent, fig. 1. These messages free the bidder agents from the commitment of their bids, which affects the pricing of new bids and the evaluation of other agents' bids as will be described. Another option would be to consider a bid a loser if it has not received an award within a time limit, but this does not fit our asynchronous approach, because it forces the manager to award within a strict time limit. The time to analyze bids varies depending on the state of the agent and the number of messages received by it. At this point, we do not know how to realistically set an appropriate upper bound for this time. In our approach, we introduce additional message traffic, which hopefully results in more accurate announcing, bidding and awarding, since the agent will know early on, which of its bids it still may have to honor.

Figure 1. Message passing, when agent 1 gives a set of deliveries to agent 2 to be done.

Each agent has two main parts: the *bargaining system* and the *local optimizer*. The bargaining system is divided into four major components: the *announcer*, the *bidder*, the *awarder* and the *award taker*. The bargaining system is not restricted to any specific local optimization algorithm[5], but the local optimizer has to provide five services. These relate to the counting of marginal costs of a set of deliveries (to remove or to add), to optimizing all deliveries of an agent and to removing and adding sets of deliveries to the agent's routing solution. Agents in the same negotiation network can use different local optimization algorithms tuned to the requirements of each center separately. The local optimizer services could also be given manually by a transportation coordinator in dispatch centers that do not use automatic optimization. Interactive routing is discussed in (Waters 1984) and (Powell & Sheffi 1989).

---

opportunistic. When the number of vehicles is small, this approach does work, though. An example is given in (McElroy et al. 1989), where automatically guided vehicles transport items inside a factory.

[3]Centralized versions of iterative routing are discussed in (Waters 1987) and (Wong & Beasley 1984).

[4]The system is implemented in an object-oriented fashion using the C++ language and the X11 Window System on a network of HP 9000 workstations. Each agent is implemented as one HP-UX (UNIX) process. The agents negotiate over the file system and share no memory.

---

[5]A good overview of centralized routing algorithms is given in (Bodin et al. 1983).

3   Local control

In TRACONET, an agent first calls its own local optimizer to make the routing decisions concerning the deliveries and vehicles that belong to the associated dispatch center. Based on these initial solutions, the agents start the negotiations. During the negotiations, the *local control loop* of an agent repeatedly goes through a sequence of invoking the bidder, awarder, award taker and announcer. The bidder, awarder and award taker handle all the messages that have been received by the time of their calls. In contrast, the announcer sends at most one announcement to agents during one local control loop cycle. It is preferable to first handle all received messages before sending a new announcement, so that the agents do not get congested by announcements, and announcements are constructed according to the most up to date view of the agent's local routing decisions. The messages received during the operation of the bidder, awarder or award taker are handled on the next cycle of the local control loop. This prevents the system from getting stuck at any single phase even if large amounts of messages are coming in.

An agent can enter and exit the negotiation network dynamically. When joining the network the agent first deletes all announcements and loser messages that may have accumulated in the incoming message media. Then the agent is ready for the negotiations. However, exiting the negotiation process is not as simple for two reasons. First, some other agent might be awarding a delivery set to the agent and if the agent has exited the negotiations, it will not receive the award. Secondly, some other agent might be making a bid to the agent and if the agent exits the negotiation, the other agent does not receive even a loser message for the bid and will not be freed from the commitment of its bid. The second problem is solved by sending a loser message to the other agents for all unhandled announcements sent to them previously. The first problem is solved by going through a listening phase before logging out of the network. During this phase no announcements and no bids are made. The phase can be ended, when replies (awards or loser messages) have been received for all unhandled bids that have been sent out. If an agent wants to *reoptimize* its local solution, it must first exit the negotiations, reoptimize and then possibly rejoin the negotiations. If the agent did not exit temporarily, the marginal costs calculated before reoptimization would not be valid after it.

4   Announcing

An agent's announcer chooses a set of deliveries from the deliveries of the center and announces them to other centers in order to get bids from them. In the implementation the announcements focus on deliveries ending in the geographical main operation areas of the potential contractors, because these deliveries are most likely to lead to contracts. The announcing methods differ from each other in the number of tasks (deliveries) to be clustered into each announcement, and in whether a delivery set that has already been announced can be reannounced (Sandholm 1992b). Reannouncing leads to better results, but the negotiations are considerably longer. This, however, is not a serious problem, if we assume that actual deliveries are being done during the negotiations and reannouncing is not done immediately. In algorithm 1, a set of deliveries consists of only one (randomly chosen) delivery, and reannouncing is allowed. The $c'_{rem}(T)$ service provided by the local optimizer gives a heuristic approximation of the marginal cost $c_{rem}(T)$ saved if the delivery set T were removed from the routing solution of the agent. The implemented calculation of $c'_{rem}(T)$ will be described in section 6. If the estimate $c'_{rem}(T)$ is too low, the other center's will not bid even though that might be beneficial. On the other hand, if the estimate is too high, the agent will receive also unbeneficial bids. The actual value of $c'_{rem}(T)$ is not as crucial here as it is in the awarding phase, because announcements are not binding. Therefore, even an incorrect calculation of $c'_{rem}(T)$ will not lead to unbeneficial contracting.

Randomly choose one of the deliveries ending in another center's main operation area.

T = {the chosen delivery}.

Maximum price of the announcement $c_{max} = c'_{rem}(T)$.

For all centers except this center itself

If the end stop of the delivery is in the center's main operation area

Then send an announcement to the center.

Algorithm 1. A simple announcer algorithm.

Announcing one delivery at a time is not sufficient in general. This is due to the fact that the deliveries are dependent, i.e., for two disjoint delivery sets T_1 and T_2, for the manager, $c_{rem}(T_1 \cup T_2) \neq c_{rem}(T_1) + c_{rem}(T_2)$. For example, if the removal cost of either of two deliveries alone is small, but the removal cost of both of them together is large, announcing one delivery at a time would probably not lead to a contract, but announcing two at a time probably would. For the tasks to be truly independent, the following would also have to hold for each potential contractor: $c_{add}(T_1 \cup T_2) = c_{add}(T_1) + c_{add}(T_2)$, where $c_{add}(T)$ gives the marginal cost of adding task set T to the agent's routing solution, as will be explained in section 5. The clustering of tasks into (not necessarily disjoint) sets to be bargained over as atomic bargaining items is a complex problem. To solve it, TRACONET's more refined announcer algorithms use domain dependent heuristics. These algorithms and experiments with them in a domain, where all deliveries originate at a common factory have been discussed in (Sandholm 1992b). For example, in one of them, a delivery d_1 was clustered with another delivery d_2, the end stop of which was next to the end stop of d_1 in a route, if $c'_{rem}(\{d_1, d_2\}) > \alpha * c'_{rem}(\{d_1\})$, where α was a constant.

If no more beneficial contracts of any k tasks at a time can be made between any two agents, the solution is called *k-optimal*, which is a necessary, but not a sufficient condition for optimality. Neither does m-optimality guarantee n-optimality, if n ≠ m.

5 Bidding

An agent's bidder reads the announcements sent by other agents. If the maximum price mentioned in the announcement is higher than the price that the deliveries would cost if done by this center, a bid is sent with the latter price. Otherwise, no bid is sent for the specified announcement. Denote an arbitrary bid by b and the set of tasks of that bid by T_b. Let B_{uns} be the set of unsettled bids sent by an agent previously. Define B_{pos} to be the set of possible bids that can be awarded to the agent when b is also awarded to the agent, i.e., $B_{pos} = \{x \mid x \in B_{uns}, T_x \cap T_b = \emptyset\}$. Let T_{cur} be the current set of tasks of the agent. Let function f(T) compute the total cost of the local optimal solution with task set T. Let $c_{add}(T)$ be the marginal cost of adding task set T into the local solution. For any bid b, the cost $c_{add}(T_b)$ is bounded below by

$$c^-_{add}(T_b) = \min_{B \subseteq B_{pos}} [f(T_b \cup T_{cur} \cup \underset{z \in B}{T_z}) - f(T_{cur} \cup \underset{z \in B}{T_z})],$$

and above by

$$c^+_{add}(T_b) = \max_{B \subseteq B_{pos}} [f(T_b \cup T_{cur} \cup \underset{z \in B}{T_z}) - f(T_{cur} \cup \underset{z \in B}{T_z})].$$

Setting the bid price to be $c^-_{add}(T_b)$ is an opportunistic approach, and setting it to be $c^+_{add}(T_b)$ is a safe approach. Assuming that all of the unsettled bids sent by the agent will be awarded to the agent, the bid price can be calculated by

$$c^{all}_{add}(T_b) = f(T_b \cup T_{cur} \cup \underset{z \in B_{pos}}{T_z}) - f(T_{cur} \cup \underset{z \in B_{pos}}{T_z}),$$

and assuming that none of the unsettled bids sent by the agent will be awarded to it, the bid price is as follows:

$$c^{non}_{add}(T_b) = f(T_b \cup T_{cur}) - f(T_{cur}).$$

Clearly, $c^-_{add}(T_b) \leq c^{all}_{add}(T_b) \leq c^+_{add}(T_b)$ and $c^-_{add}(T_b) \leq c^{non}_{add}(T_b) \leq c^+_{add}(T_b)$, but the partial order of $c^{all}_{add}(T_b)$ and $c^{non}_{add}(T_b)$ varies. This is because in this domain, both economies of scale (implying $c^{all}_{add}(T_b) < c^{non}_{add}(T_b)$) and diseconomies of scale (implying $c^{non}_{add}(T_b) < c^{all}_{add}(T_b)$) are present. In (Wellman 1992), only diseconomies of scale are present.

The cost $c^{non}_{add}(T_b)$ is faster to compute than $c^{all}_{add}(T_b)$, and it gives a better approximation of $c_{add}(T_b)$ when bids are seldom awarded to the agent. This is usually the case, if the network has many agents.

In the original CNP, an agent could have multiple bids concerning different contracts pending concurrently in order to speed up the operation of the system (Smith 1980). We have followed this approach for the same reason, although negotiations over only one contract at a time

allow a more precise bid price. If only one bid is allowed to be pending from one agent at a time, $B_{pos} = \emptyset$ and $c^-_{add}(T_b) = c^+_{add}(T_b) = c^{all}_{add}(T_b) = c^{non}_{add}(T_b)$. Fig. 2 compares results of allowing multiple bids and awards simultaneously to those of allowing only one announcement (implying only one award) and one bid at a time.

Calculation of the local utility function takes time. This has not been taken into account in the CNP or in work in game theory. In our domain, calculating the marginal costs (and therefore the announcing, bidding and awarding) takes computational time. Because the calculation of the truly optimizing function f takes exponential time in our domain, we use a heuristic approximation f', for which $f(T) \leq f'(T)$ for any task set T. In our domain, the calculation of $f'(T \cup T_{cur})$ would be very fast if we knew $f(T_{cur})$, because it could be calculated incrementally by just adding the new tasks T to the solution without altering the original solution. The problem is that we do not know the optimal $f(T_{cur})$, but only a heuristic approximation $f'(T_{cur})$ of it. In the tests presented in this paper, the bid price $c'_{add}(T_b)$ was calculated incrementally like this with respect to the current heuristic solution assuming that none of the agent's unsettled bids are awarded to it. This assumption makes the calculation semi-opportunistic. Therefore an agent using this strategy may make unbeneficial contracts now and then. A safe approach would be to use a heuristic upper bound for $c^+_{add}(T_b)$ as the bid price, but its calculation is slower than that of $c'_{add}(T_b)$.

Read in all received announcements and call this set A.
For each announcement a ∈ A
    Call the set of deliveries in a T_a and the maximum price c_{max}.
    If $f'(T_{cur} \cup T_a \cup T_{pos}) < \infty$ (Feasibility check; T_{pos}
        defined w.r.t. a potential bid b with the deliveries of a.)
    Set $c_{bid} = c'_{add}(T_a)$.
    If $c_{bid} < c_{max}$
        Send a bid with the identifier of the announcement, the
        name of this center and cost c_{bid}.

Algorithm 2. The bidding algorithm.

Because of binding bids, a feasibility check in algorithm 2 checks that the agent's transportation solution will be feasible even if all of the previous unsettled possible bids and this bid are awarded to the agent. In domains (unlike ours), where the feasibility check often restricts the bidding, the bidder should choose the most profitable combination among the possible combinations of beneficial bids to send.

Using the previously discussed bidding methods, the negotiation network got congested with announcements, i.e., some of the agents were receiving announcements at a faster pace than they could process. The problem occurred only with announcements, because in our domain the number of them far exceeds the number of other messages. The reason the congested agents could not keep in pace was that the time to handle an announcement increased with the number of previously sent unsettled bids – mainly because of the feasibility check. The more announcements an agent had received, the more bids it was able to make, which slowed it down, and during the bidding process even more announcements kept coming in. The congestion problem was solved by making the bidder consider only announcements newer than a certain time limit. This is sensible also, because bids made on older announcements would probably not get to the managers before the negotiations concerning these announcements would be over.

6   Awarding

An agent's awarder reads the bids of other agents. Before handling the bids concerning a certain announcement, it checks that a fixed time has passed since the sending of the announcement, so that many potential contractors have had time to bid. An award or loser message is sent to every agent to whom an announcement concerning the same contract was sent earlier. The award is sent to the agent with the most inexpensive bid.[6] After an award is sent, the awarder removes the set of deliveries from the agent's current deliveries T_{cur} and from its transportation solution. If no bids for an announcement have been received by the time of the mentioned time limit, the awarding is postponed until the first bid for this announcement is received. If this takes longer than a second time limit, the agent simply forgets that it has made such an announcement and sends loser messages to all agents to whom the announcement was sent previously. Bids received later for this announcement are deleted.

In the awarding phase the manager has a chance to check that awarding is still beneficial to itself, i.e., it does not have to accept any bid. In deciding whether the awarding is beneficial, the manager has to also consider the unsettled bids that it has sent. Awarding to bid b is beneficial iff $c_{rem}(T_b) > c_b$, where c_b is the price mentioned in the bid b, and $c_{rem}(T_b)$ is the cost of removing the tasks T_b from the manager's own local solution. Unlike in the bidding phase, $B_{pos} = B_{uns}$. The cost $c_{rem}(T_b)$ is bounded above by

$$c^+_{rem}(T_b) = \max_{B \subseteq B_{pos}} \ [f(T_{cur} \cup \underset{z \in B}{T_z}) - f((T_{cur} - T_b) \cup \underset{z \in B}{T_z})],$$

and below by

$$c^-_{rem}(T_b) = \min_{B \subseteq B_{pos}} \ [f(T_{cur} \cup \underset{z \in B}{T_z}) - f((T_{cur} - T_b) \cup \underset{z \in B}{T_z})].$$

Assuming that all of the agent's unsettled bids will be awarded to it, $c_{rem}(T_b)$ is calculated by

$$c^{all}_{rem}(T_b) = f(T_{cur} \cup \underset{z \in B_{pos}}{T_z}) - f((T_{cur} - T_b) \cup \underset{z \in B_{pos}}{T_z}),$$

---

[6] If some of the deliveries of the announcement have already been awarded out by an award of some other announcement, all messages sent are loser messages.

and assuming that none of the agent's unsettled bids will be awarded to it, $c_{rem}(T_b)$ is calculated as follows:

$$c^{non}_{rem}(T_b) = \ f(T_{cur}) - f(T_{cur} - T_b).$$

Clearly, $c^-_{rem}(T_b) \leq c^{all}_{rem}(T_b) \leq c^+_{rem}(T_b)$ and $c^-_{rem}(T_b) \leq c^{non}_{rem}(T_b) \leq c^+_{rem}(T_b)$, but the partial order of $c^{all}_{rem}(T_b)$ and $c^{non}_{rem}(T_b)$ varies. If only one bid is allowed to be pending from an agent at a time, then [$c^{all}_{rem}(T_b) = c^-_{rem}(T_b)$ and $c^{non}_{rem}(T_b) = c^+_{rem}(T_b)$] or [$c^{non}_{rem}(T_b) = c^-_{rem}(T_b)$ and $c^{all}_{rem}(T_b) = c^+_{rem}(T_b)$].

Similar to our discussion of f', because calculating the truly optimizing f function takes a long time, we use a heuristic approximation f'', for which $f(T) \leq f''(T)$ for any task set T. In our domain, the calculation of $f''(T_{cur} - T_b)$ would be fast if we knew $f(T_{cur})$, because it could be calculated decrementally by just removing the tasks T_b from the solution without altering the original solution. The problem is that we do not know the optimal $f(T_{cur})$, but only a heuristic approximation $f''(T_{cur})$ of it. In the tests presented in this paper, the benefit check price $c'_{rem}(T_b)$ was calculated decrementally like this with respect to the current heuristic solution assuming that none of the agent's unsettled bids are awarded to it. The assumption makes this calculation semi-opportunistic, and an agent using this strategy may have to take unbeneficial awards later. A safe approach would be to use a heuristic upper bound for $c^+_{rem}(T_b)$ as the benefit check price, but its calculation is slower than that of $c'_{rem}(T_b)$.

In the current implementation, all bids received before the start of the awarding phase are handled in order of receipt before going to any next negotiation phase. If the check for benefit is used, the order of awarding may be important - though this seldom is the case in our domain. The awarding of one task set may disable the beneficial awarding of another. Usually the number of received bids per local control loop cycle is small, so the awarder could try all possible orderings of awarding sets of deliveries and carry out the best ordering.

7   Taking awards

An agent's award taker reads the awards and inserts the deliveries from the awards to the agent's deliveries T_{cur} and its transportation solution. Some contracts may have sneaked in between the bidding for a certain set of deliveries and taking the corresponding award. These contracts have altered the routing solution. If opportunistic pricing is used, taking the award might no longer be profitable for the center. Because bids are binding, the center is committed to take the award anyway. Making bids non-binding would not solve the problem, because the contractor, after receiving an award, would have to inform the manager that it has taken the award or that it will not take it. This would require the manager to keep the delivery set in its routing solution until award taking is confirmed, during which, some changes may have sneaked into its routing solution and the problem rearises.

8   Experimental results

The purpose of the experiments was to validate the distributed problem solving approach in reducing the total transportation costs among autonomous dispatch centers. A detailed presentation of these experiments is given in (Sandholm 1992a). Table 1 provides results of one example experiment. As can be seen, the negotiations led to considerable transportation cost savings in reasonable time even in such a large problem. In the experiment, company A owned the first three centers and company B owned the last two. The centers were located around Finland. The agents had similar local optimization modules and each agent's original local routing solution was acquired heuristically using a parallel insertion algorithm (Sandholm 1992a). Each agent executed on its own HP 9000 s300 workstation. The profit of each contract was divided in half between the agents, i.e., the actual price of a contract was half way between the maximum price mentioned in the announcement and the bid price. A choice closer to a real world competing agent contracting scheme would be to let the contract price equal the bid price. In 30 minutes, each agent goes through its main control loop 100 - 200 times.

Dispatch center	Deliveries	Vehicles	Average delivery length	Cost savings in 15 minutes	Cost savings in 30 minutes
A1	65	10	121 km	5%	6%
A2	200	13	169 km	12%	18%
A3	82	21	44 km	31%	34%
B1	124	18	145 km	11%	23%
B2	300	15	270 km	9%	15%
Total	771	77	187 km	11%	17%

Table 1. Columns 2 - 4 characterize the one week real vehicle and delivery data of the experiments, and the last two columns show results of the negotiations.

Figure 2 presents example runs with two unsafe bidding schemes. Due to the semi-opportunistic pricing explained before, the local costs of the agents do not decrease monotonically in case 1. An agent is forced to take unbeneficial awards now and then. The unbeneficial contracts are somewhat compensated for by other contracting within the time window shown. The cost of an agent in case 1 decreases faster (in the sense of local control loop cycles required) than in case 2. In case 2, the cost decreased monotonically for every agent. To guarantee monotonic decrease of the cost using opportunistic pricing, one bid at a time should be allowed and awarding should be allowed only when no bid is pending from the agent. This would require even more local control loop cycles than case 2, where awarding can happen while a bid is pending.

In case 1, the agents have to consider more messages on each local control loop cycle. Therefore, the previously mentioned time limits were set to be longer in case 1, and in the same actual time, the agents of case 2 go through more main control loop cycles than in case 1.

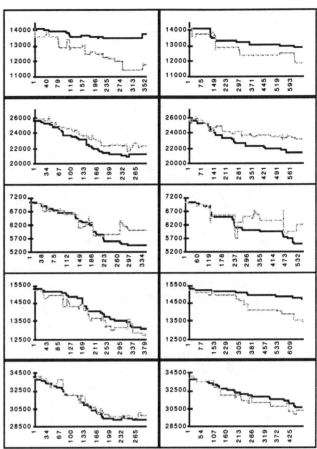

Figure 2. An example run with the results of the five agents one below another. The x-axis show the number of local control loop cycles for each agent. The thin gray line shows the evolution of the total length of the truck routes of an agent in kilometers. The black line shows the evolution of the local cost for each agent, so the black line takes into account the amounts paid by the managers to the contractors for carrying out the transportation tasks. The figures in the left column (case 1) show the normal case, where multiple announcements and bids are allowed simultaneously. The right column (case 2) shows the case, where only one announcement (implying at most one award) and one bid are allowed to be pending from one agent at a time.

9   Conclusions

The role of DAI systems with cooperative and competitive agents is likely to increase in the future. Especially important will be *enterprise cooperation*: allowing autonomous, even competitive, enterprises to cooperate through the on-line, dynamic establishment of contracts among enterprises. The groundwork for computerizing this cooperation is currently being made by building networks of enterprises with electronic data interchange. This paper presents, to our knowledge, the first prototype of an application where different enterprises work together automatically using DAI techniques. Our methodology is presented through a concrete application domain, vehicle routing, but it is applicable to other task allocation problems - assuming that a reasonable local objective function is known for each agent.

TRACONET uses task negotiation. Another solution technique for the same problem is to negotiate over resources. If there are many tasks per resource (eg. many deliveries in one truck route), a higher resolution of cooperation is achieved by exchanging tasks. All possible solutions reached by resource exchange can be reached by task exchange, but not vice versa, so the best possible solution when negotiating tasks is at least as good as the best possible solution when negotiating resources. This does not necessarily imply that after a certain number of iterations, the solution using task negotiation is as good or better than the solution using resource negotiations. Also, if we use a limit on the maximum number of tasks per announcement, it may happen that the best global solution of task negotiations can not be reached at all. If fast computation is crucial, the coarser grain size negotiations - resource negotiations in this case - may be preferred. In domains with many resources per task, the above arguments should be reversed.

We have extended the CNP with a formal model for making announcing, bidding and awarding decisions based on local marginal cost calculations. Additionally, announcing, bidding and awarding are allowed while the results of previous bids are still unknown. Safe and opportunistic pricing policies are discussed: opportunism speeds up the negotiations, but safe policies guarantee monotonic decrease of the local cost. Task interaction is handled by heuristically clustering tasks into announcements negotiated over atomically. The implementation is asynchronous and truly distributed and solves the message congestion problems.

At this stage, the announcing, bidding and awarding decisions do not *anticipate future contracts*. Future research also includes *estimating the marginal costs* when a local solution does not exist, so that the agents could negotiate before they solve the local routing problem, and even if a feasible solution to the local problem does not exist at the moment. In the future we wish to extend the protocol for *contracts involving multiple agents*. In TRACONET, the bidder can only bid for the announced task sets, but allowing *counterproposals* with different content may speed up the negotiations. Currently there is just one focus in the contract space and it is committal. Moving *non-committal foci* in the contract space would enable jumping over local minima, because multiple contracts would be made before the agents have to commit. Finally, other than per centual *profit division* mechanisms, and intelligent *local reoptimization activation* should be implemented.

Acknowledgements

I would like to thank professor Victor Lesser from the University of Massachusetts at Amherst, Computer Science Department, and research professor Seppo Linnainmaa from the Technical Research Centre of Finland, Laboratory for Information Processing, for their support.

References

Bodin, L. et al. 1983. Routing and scheduling of vehicles and crews: The state of the art. *Computers and Operations Research* 10(2):63-211.

Davis, R., and Smith, R.G. 1988. Negotiation as a Metaphor for Distributed Problem Solving. In: Bond, A., and Gasser, L. eds. *Readings in Distributed Artificial Intelligence*, 333-356. San Mateo, Calif.: Morgan Kaufmann.

Kuwabara, K., and Ishida, T. 1992. Symbiotic Approach to Distributed Resource Allocation: Toward Coordinated Balancing. In Proceedings of the European Workshop on Modeling Autonomous Agents and Multi-Agent Worlds '92.

McElroy, J. et al. 1989. Communication and cooperation in a distributed automatic guided vehicle system. In Proceedings of the IEEE Southeastcon '89, 999-1003.

Parunak, H.V.D. 1987. Manufacturing Experience with the Contract Net. In: Huhns, M. ed. *Distributed Artificial Intelligence*, 285-310. Los Altos, Calif.: Morgan Kaufmann.

Powell, W., and Sheffi, Y. 1989. Design and implementation of an interactive optimization system for network design in the motor carrier industry. *Operations Research* 37(1):12-29.

Sandholm, T. 1992a. Automatic Cooperation of Dispatch Centers in Vehicle Routing. M.Sc. Thesis. Research Report No. J-9, Laboratory for Information Processing, Technical Research Centre of Finland.

Sandholm, T. 1992b. Automatic Cooperation of Area-Distributed Dispatch Centers in Vehicle Routing. In Preprints of the International Conference on Artificial Intelligence Applications in Transportation Engineering, 449-467. Institute of Transportation Studies, Univ. of Calif., Irvine.

Smith, R.G. 1980. The Contract Net Protocol: High-Level Communication and Control in a Distributed Problem Solver. *IEEE Trans. on Computers* C-29(12):1104-1113.

Smith, R.G., and Davis, R. 1981. Frameworks for Cooperation in Distributed Problem Solving. *IEEE Trans. on Systems, Man, and Cybernetics* 11(1):61-70.

Waters, C.D. 1984. Interactive vehicle routing. *Journal of the Operational Research Society* 35(9):821-826.

Waters, C.D. 1987. A solution procedure for the vehicle-scheduling problem based on iterative route improvement. *Journal of the Operational Research Society* 38(9):833-839.

Wellman, M. 1992. A General-Equilibrium Approach to Distributed Transportation Planning. Proceedings of the AAAI -92, 282-289.

Wong, K., and Beasley, J. 1984. Vehicle routing using fixed delivery areas. *Omega International Journal of Management Science* 12(6):591-600.

Intelligent
User Interfaces

Generating Explanations of Device Behavior
Using Compositional Modeling and Causal Ordering

Patrice O. Gautier and Thomas R. Gruber

Knowledge Systems Laboratory
Stanford University
701 Welch Road, Building C
Palo Alto, CA 94304
gautier@ksl.stanford.edu

Abstract

Generating explanations of device behavior is a long-standing goal of AI research in reasoning about physical systems. Much of the relevant work has concentrated on new methods for modeling and simulation, such as qualitative physics, or on sophisticated natural language generation, in which the device models are specially crafted for explanatory purposes. We show how two techniques from the modeling research—compositional modeling and causal ordering—can be effectively combined to generate natural language explanations of device behavior from engineering models. The explanations offer three advances over the data displays produced by conventional simulation software: (1) causal interpretations of the data, (2) summaries at appropriate levels of abstraction (physical mechanisms and component operating modes), and (3) query-driven, natural language summaries. Furthermore, combining the compositional modeling and causal ordering techniques allows models that are more scalable and less brittle than models designed solely for explanation. However, these techniques produce models with detail that can be distracting in explanations and would be removed in hand-crafted models (e.g., intermediate variables). We present domain-independent filtering and aggregation techniques that overcome these problems.

1. Introduction

This paper presents a method for generating explanations of device behavior characterized by systems of mathematical constraints over continuous-valued quantities. Such models are widely used in engineering for dynamical systems, such as electromechanical and thermodynamic control systems. Given such a model and initial conditions, conventional simulation software can predict and plot the values of these quantities over time. However, the data can be difficult to interpret because conventional simulators do not explain how the predicted behavior arises from the structure of the modeled system and physical laws.

What we call *explanations* are presentations of information about the modeled system that satisfy three requirements. First, an explanation offers a meaningful *interpretation* of the simulation data, explaining how and why and not just what happened. For engineering tasks such as design and diagnosis, it is useful to provide causal and functional interpretations. In this paper we focus on causal interpretations. Second, an explanation should present information at appropriate levels of abstraction. What is appropriate depends on the system being modeled, the purpose of the model, and the modeling primitives. For our tasks, we need explanations at the level of physical mechanisms and component operating modes, rather than graphs of numeric variables. Third, an explanation is a presentation of information in a format that is comprehensible to the human user. In the context of natural language generation, relevant design issues include choosing an appropriate level of detail, summarizing data, and adapting to information needs of users.

We have developed a system that generates explanations with these properties. It is part of the Device Modeling Environment (DME) [12], which integrates model formulation support, qualitative and numerical simulation, and explanation generation. A separate report introduces the explanation architecture and describes the text generation and human interface techniques [11].

In this paper, we focus on how two techniques from qualitative reasoning research, compositional modeling [6] and causal ordering [13] are applied and combined to produce explanations that satisfy the three criteria outlined above without imposing ad hoc or unscalable modeling formalisms. In Section 3 we present a series of example explanations generated in an interactive session. In Section 3 we describe how compositional modeling is used, and in Section 4 we describe the use of causal ordering. In Section 5 we analyze why it works, explaining how combining the two techniques makes it possible to achieve the three design requirements, and how problems that arise from this design are addressed. The final section compares related work.

2. A Running Example

We will demonstrate the explanation technique using a model of the space shuttle's Reaction Control System (RCS). The RCS is a system of thrusters that are used to steer the vehicle. The system consists of tanks, regulators, valves, thrusters, pipes, and junctions. The RCS system model comprises 160 model fragments that generate 150 equations relating 180 parameters. Figure 1 shows the topological structure of the RCS system. A similar picture

Funding was provided by NASA Grant NCC2-537 and NASA Grant NAG 2-581 (under ARPA Order 6822).

is displayed on the DME user's screen, providing a user interface for monitoring and editing capabilities.

At any time, the user may ask for explanations by clicking the mouse on text or graphics on the screen. Figure 2 shows a sequence of explanations produced in response to user queries. The first presentation, labeled (a), is an explanation of the salient events of the current state. This "what just happened" explanation uses heuristics to filter irrelevant information. Of the 180 variables, only one was mentioned in the explanation of Figure 2a.

All text and graphics presented in DME explanations are mouse-sensitive. By clicking on an icon, word, phrase, or sentence, the user can ask follow-up questions about any part of an explanation. In Figure 2a, the user clicks on the sentence stating that the check valve is now in blocking mode. The system produces a menu of possible queries relevant to this fact, as shown in Figure 2b. The user asks for an explanation by selecting a query from the menu.

The system then generates the explanation shown in Figure 2c, which explains why the selected behavior was observed. In this case, the behavior is determined by a single variable, the pressure differntial of the quad check valve. The user then asks for the influences on that variable by clicking on the sentence describing the value of the variable, and selecting the desired query from the menu shown in Figure 2d.

The resulting explanation, shown in presentation 2e, summarizes the causal influences on the pressure differential variable. The value of this variable is determined by two chains of influences: the upstream pressures from the helium tank through the pressure regulators and the downstream pressures coming from the oxygen tank (see Figure 1). Using heuristics described in Section 4, the system simplifies these chains into two influences. In the ex-

planation, it says that the value of the variable in question, pressure differential, is determined by the input pressure at the oxygen tank and the nominal pressure of the primary pressure regulator. It explains that these were the salient influences because the secondary regulator was in pass-through mode and the primary regulator was in normal mode. It shows the equation that results from this simplification at the bottom of the display.

In Figure 2f, the user follows up by asking for the influences on the input pressure of the oxygen tank. This produces the explanation shown in Figure 2g, which extends the previous explanation. In this case, the system explains that the oxygen pressure is determined by the amount of gas and two exogenous constants "by the ideal gas law for the oxygen tank." Clicking on this phrase would result in an explanation that the oxygen tank is modeled as an ideal gas container, which is why the ideal gas law is governing in this situation.

These are a few of the explanation types that can be generated on demand (others are described in [11]). We now look at the roles of compositional modeling and causal ordering in generating these explanations.

3. Compositional Modeling and Explanation

Engineering models used to describe and predict the behavior of systems like the RCS are typically mathematical models. A set of continuous variables represents the values of physical quantities such as pressures and temperatures. The behavior of the system is defined by a set of equations that constrain these variables. Each model is based on a set of approximations, abstractions, and other assumptions about what is relevant to produce the desired data at a reasonable cost. Model formulation is the task of constructing a model from available primitives to answer some question. In electromechanical domains, these models are often constructed by hand from background knowledge of physics and engineering.

In the compositional modeling approach [6] to model formulation, engineering models are constructed from modular pieces, called *model fragments*. A model fragment is an abstraction of some physical domain, mechanism, structure, or other constituent of a model that contributes constraints to the overall behavior description. Model fragments can represent idealized components, such as resistors, transistors, logical gates, electrical junctions, valves, and pipes, and physical processes such as flows.

Each model fragment has a set of *activation conditions* that specify when an applicable model holds in a given simulation (e.g., the model of a boiling process can only hold when the temperature of the water is above some threshold). Each model fragment contributes a partial description of the behavior that occurs when the conditions hold. The behavior is specified in terms of algebraic and logical constraints on the values of simulation variables.

DME uses a compositional modeling approach for assembling a mathematical model from a library of model fragments. Model formulation and simulation are inter-

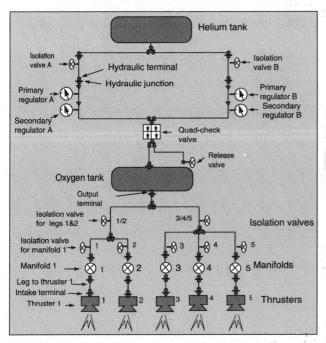

Figure 1: Schematic of the RCS system

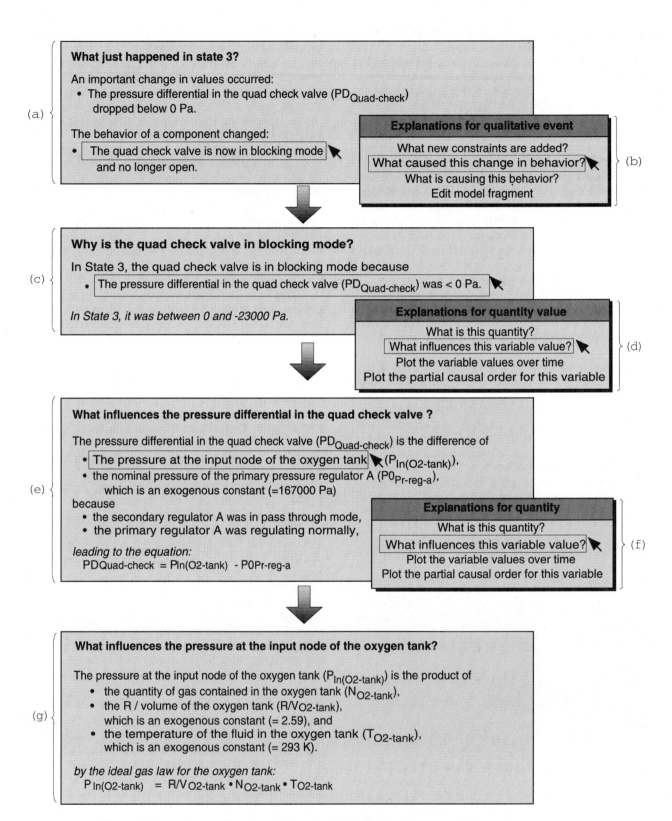

Figure 2: A sequence of explanations produced in response to user queries

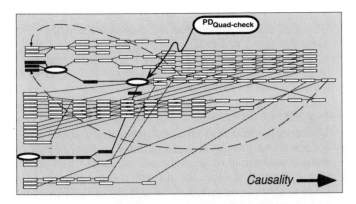

Figure 3: The causal order graph for the RCS in state 3. Nodes are variables. Solid arcs are direct influences, and dashed arcs denote integration relationships.

branching arcs. Influences go roughly from left to right; nodes on the left boundary are either exogenous, constant, or integrated variables. The integrated variables are computed from their derivatives on each numeric integration loop, as depicted by dashed arcs in the figure.

The direct influences on a variable such as $PD_{Quad-check}$ are those connected by single arcs leading into the variable. The subgraph of all influences on a variable is formed by recursively following influence arcs to the left.

To generate the causal explanation of Figure 2e, the system computed the subgraph of influences for the variable to explain, $PD_{Quad-check}$. The subgraph of influences on this variable and the associated equations are shown in Figure 4.

A straightforward application of causal ordering to explanation would be to output the entire subgraph of influences. However, when this subgraph is large the resulting output would not be an effective presentation of information in textual form (violating our third requirement). A second design alternative would be to only output the immediately adjacent nodes in the influence graph. For example, the explanation of Figure 2e would read "$PD_{Quad-check}$ is the difference of the pressure at the output node of the quad check valve ($PD_{In(Quad-check)}$) and the pressure at the input of the quad check valve ($PD_{In(Quad-check)}$) by the definition of pressure differential." Then the user could traverse the next node in influence graph by clicking on one of these two variables and asking for causal influences on it. This approach can distribute a single explanation over several presentations, and requires the user to sort out irrelevant detail.

To overcome this problem, DME applies salience heuristics to select a subset of influences to report in an explanation. The system works back through the subgraph from the influenced variable, collapsing paths called influence chains to a single-step influence. For example, in the influence graph of Figure 4, the chain from $P_{Out(O2-tank)}$ to $PD_{Quad-check}$ and the chain from $P0_{Pr-reg-A}$ to $PD_{Quad-check}$ were collapsed. Instead of describing the graph of 12 potential influences, the explanation says that $PD_{Quad-check}$ is simply the difference between $P_{Out(O2-tank)}$ and $P0_{Pr-reg-A}$.

DME currently uses two salience heuristics to select causal influences, both of which collapse a chain of influences into a virtual, single-step influence.

- *Collapsing equality chains:* Chains in the influence subgraph of the form $v_1=v_2$, $v_2=v_3...=v_n$ are transformed into the equation $v_1 = v_n$, and only these two influences are presented to the user. The path between nodes $P0_{Pr-reg-A}$ and $PD_{Quad-check}$ in Figure 4 was collapsed using this heuristic.

- *Collapsing paths of same dimension:* Chains of variables of the same physical dimension are collapsed into single-step influences. The value of a variable is a physical quantity of some dimension, such as pressure, temperature, or flow. If a sequence of variables all have the same dimension, then they are presumed to be driven as a whole by some influence. For example, the path of fluid flow in the RCS corresponds to sequences of influences of the same dimension (flow).

The influences to report to the user are those connected to the influenced variable by a collapsed sequence or an adjacent node in the influence graph. The resulting influences need not be terminals in the original influence

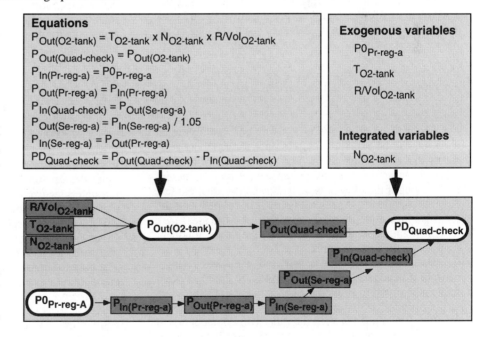

Figure 4: The subgraph of influences on $PD_{Quad-check}$, which are shown in black in Figure 3. The circled variables appear in the explanation of Figure 2e.

leaved. During a simulation, DME monitors the activation conditions of model fragments; at each state, the system combines the equations of active model fragments into a set called the *equation model*. The equation model is then used to drive a conventional numerical simulation. A *qualitative state* is a period during which the equation model remains unchanged. Within a qualitative state, the numeric values of modeled parameters can change. When parameter values cross certain limit points, the activation conditions of some model fragments become true and others become false, leading to qualitative state transitions. DME monitors the numerical simulation for such changes, and updates the equation model for each new state.

The data predicted by simulation are a mathematical consequence of initial values and the constraint equations given in the model. Interpreting the data requires an understanding of the knowledge used in formulating the model, such as the physical mechanisms and component structure underlying the equations. If the engineer looking at the output is not the person who built the model, or if the model is complex and contains hidden assumptions, then it can be difficult for the engineer to make sense of the simulation output. DME's explanation services are intended to address this problem by relating predicted data to the underlying modeling choices.

Compositional modeling plays an essential role for explanation by providing the *derivation* of the equations from model fragments. DME uses the derivation information in several ways.

First, transitions between qualitative states are explained as a change in the set of active model fragments. For example, the summary of salient events (Figure 2a) describes those variables whose values have crossed limit points and lists the model fragments that have become active (quad check valve closed) and inactive (quad check valve open). To explain what caused such a change in behavior, the system shows how the activation conditions of the model fragment were satisfied (Figure 2c). Furthermore, DME uses the analysis of limit points in the activation conditions as a *salience heuristic*, focusing the summary on just those parameters that could lead to qualitative state transitions.

Second, the principles or assumptions underlying an equation can be explained by reference to the model fragments that contributed them. For example, when the user asked the system to describe the influences on the pressure at the input of the oxygen tank, it showed the ideal gas law equation applied to the tank (Figure 2g). It knew that the ideal gas law equation was contributed by the ideal-tank model fragment, which is inherited by the model fragment representing the oxygen tank.

Derivation knowledge is also used when simplifying a causal influence path. As shown in Figure 2e, the system relates the pressure at the quad check valve to the pressure at the primary regulator by explaining that the secondary regulator (which is between the other two components) is in pass-through mode. The model fragment for the pass-through mode specifies that the input and output pressures are equal, and the system removes this equation in the explanation (see Section 4). Knowing the source of this equation—the pass-through operating mode—helps explain why the pressure at the quad check valve is determined by the pressure at the primary regulator.

4. Causal Ordering

The equations in the model used for simulation in DME do not specify any causal orientation; they are purely mathematical constraints on the values of variables. The pressure differential variable, for instance, is related mathematically to almost every other variable in the model. To generate a causal explanation of the influences on this variable, one needs to determine which variables directly influence this variable.

One approach is to build ad hoc models specifically for explanation, in which the causal influences on all variables are fixed in advance. We reject this option because it is brittle and does not scale with the size of the model. Another approach would be to use compositional modeling, but build an assignment of direct influences into the model fragments. This is done in QP theory [8], in which causality is specified explicitly through *direct influences*. Using the QP approach, the model fragments representing processes each contribute causal dependency and orientation information, which can be propagated through functional dependencies (*indirect influences*) to produce a global ordering for the composed model. The only problem with this scheme is that it requires the model fragment writers to anticipate all plausible causal influences in advance.

Instead, we assume that causal influences can be *inferred* at run time. We use an adaptation of the causal ordering procedure developed by Simon and Iwasaki [13] to infer a graph of the influence relation. Given a set of equations constraining a set of model parameters, and the knowledge of which parameters are exogenous (i.e., determined outside the modeled system), the algorithm produces a dependency graph over the remaining parameters. For each variable in an equation model, its causal influences are determined as follows. If it is an exogenous variable and/or a constant, then by definition it is influenced by no other variable. If it is a discrete variable, then it can only be changed by the effect of a discrete mode fragment (e.g., the triggering of a relay), by an operator action (the opening of a valve), or by forward chaining through rules from one of these events. If a variable is integrated from its derivative, then it is influenced by the derivative (e.g., acceleration causes change in velocity). Otherwise, the influences on the variable are the variables that were used to compute it in the numeric simulation. The order of computation is exactly the order given by the causal ordering graph.

Figure 3 shows the causal order graph of the equation model in effect for the explanations of Figure 2. Each node in the graph corresponds to a variable in the model. Each arc represents an influence given by an equation; equations relating more than two variables appear as

graph (i.e., variables that are not influenced). For example, the variable $P_{Out(O2\text{-}tank)}$ is reported as an influence on $PD_{Quad\text{-}check}$, but the former is in turn influenced by three other parameters of the oxygen tank. The user can ask for these influences by invoking a follow-up question, as shown in parts f and g of Figure 2.

In explanations where sequences are collapsed, the system displays the equation that results from symbolically solving the set of relevant equations. For example, the equations shown in Figure 4 are reduced to the equation $PD_{Quad\text{-}check} = P_{Out(O2\text{-}tank)} - P0_{(Pr\text{-}reg\text{-}a)}$.

Presenting a chain of influences as a single-step influence imposes a view of the data that suggests a causal interpretation. The system gives the "reasons" for this causal relationship by listing the model fragments that contributed a collapsed equation and that have activation conditions dependent on time-varying variables. Typically these are operating modes of components. For example, the system justified the single-step jump to the nominal pressure of the primary regulator "because the secondary regulator A was in pass through mode and the primary regulator A was regulating normally" (from Figure 2e).

5. Summary and Analysis

The use of compositional modeling and causal ordering techniques is responsible for several desired properties of the explanation approach we have presented.

First, it is possible to generate causal interpretations (our first design requirement) from models that are designed for engineering analysis and simulation, rather than being crafted specially for explanation. Because causal influences can be inferred from equation models using causal ordering, they need not be built in to the model. Because explanation is integrated with compositional modeling, explanations of the causes of changes in qualitative state (e.g., discrete events like the quad check valve becoming blocked) can be determined by an analysis of the logical preconditions of model fragments that are activated and deactivated. The set of conditions to report need not be anticipated in advance, and it can change as the model fragment library evolves.

Second, the explanations can be presented at useful levels of abstraction (requirement 2), even though they are driven by numerical simulation data. Low-level events such as changes in variable values and mathematical constraints on variables are explained in terms of the model fragments that contributed the constraints; the model fragments represent abstractions such as components, operating modes, and processes. This capability is possible because the derivation of equations from the original model fragments is known to the system.

Third, the explanations can be presented in a suitable format for human consumption (requirement 3). DME's simple text generation procedures are adequate to produce small explanations; the capability to ask interactive follow-up questions gives the user control over the level of detail and lessens the need for advanced text planning and user modeling.

The pedagogical quality of the explanations is a function of the quality of the models. If the model builder divides a system model into modular fragments that make sense in the domain (e.g., components, connections, and operating modes), then the explanation system will be able to describe them. None of the explanation code knows anything about flows, pressures, or even junctions. It knows about the structure of model fragments—activation conditions, behavior constraints, quantity variables—and some algorithms for text generation.

Furthermore, the model builder may add textual annotations incrementally, and the explanations will improve gracefully. For example, if components are not named with text annotations, the system will generate names based on the Lisp atoms used to specify the model fragments. As the textual annotations are added, the system can compose them into more useful labels, such as the subscripted variable notation. This capability is possible because of the modularity and compositionality enabled by the compositional modeling.

The major problem with the use of causal ordering and compositional modeling is the introduction of irrelevant detail. A model built specially for explanation can include only those variables and causal relations that are relevant to the target explanations. A model composed from independent model fragments includes intermediate variables and equations such as those modeling the flows and pressures at junctions. Since the causal ordering algorithm is domain-independent and works bottom-up from equations, rather than top-down from model fragments, these intermediate variables are included in the determination of causal influences on a variable.

The solution taken in DME was the application of salience heuristics, as described in Section 4. Although these are not specific to any domain, they are aimed at eliminating the intermediate variables and equations that occur when modeling circuits using constraint equations. Additional heuristics may be needed in other classes of models. Fortunately, it is possible to degrade smoothly when the heuristics fail. If an influence chain should have been collapsed but was not, the user can easily traverse it with a few clicks of the mouse.

6. Related Work

Existing systems for generating explanations of device behavior typically depend on models built explicitly for the explanation or tutoring task [10,19]. When explanations are generated from more general behavior models, the explanations typically follow from hard-coded labeling of causal influence [21] or component function [14].

Much of the work in explanation has concentrated on the generation of high-quality presentations in natural language based on discourse planning and user modeling [7,17,18,19]. These presentation techniques are independent of the modeling method or technique for determining causal influence, and so could be adapted for the explanation approach presented in this paper.

The task of giving a causal interpretation to device behavior has been addressed from several perspectives [3,13,20]. Alternatives to the causal ordering algorithm have been developed, such as context sensitive causality [16] and a method based on bond graphs [20]. These methods differ in the information they require and the class of models they accept. Given a model like the RCS and the same exogenous labeling, these methods should all produce the same ordering graph. Any of these methods could be used by the explanation technique we have described.

The idea of using such a causal interpretation for generating explanations has been previously proposed. In QUALEX [4], a causal graph is computed from a set of confluences [2], and the graph is used to explain the propagation of perturbations ("if X goes up, Y goes down"). This system is limited by the modeling representation: the confluence equations can only predict the sign of the first derivative and do not scale.

Qualitative models have been used to generate explanations in tutoring and training systems [10,21]. DME's explanation system can also generate explanations on such models (using QSIM [15] for simulation). Qualitative models have known limitations of scale.

Work on the SIMGEN systems [5,9] was the first to achieve the effect of qualitative explanation using numerical simulation models. SIMGEN also uses a compositional modeling approach, and explains simulation data using the derivation of equations from model fragments. The SIMGEN strategy is to build parallel qualitative and quantitative model libraries, analyze the possible qualitative state transitions for a given scenario description, and compile out an efficient numeric simulator. While DME determines model fragment activation and assembles equation models at run time, SIMGEN precomputes and stores the information relating the quantitative model and the qualitative model (which we call the derivation information). For causal explanations, the SIMGEN systems use the causal assignment that is built into the direct and indirect influences of the qualitative model. If the directly influenced variables are exogenous, this produces the same causal ordering as the Iwasaki and Simon algorithm. To answer questions such as "what affects this variable?", SIMGEN currently shows the single-step influences and does not summarize chains of influences.

In principle, the DME explanation method could use the model derivation information from a SIMGEN model library, and SIMGEN could use DME's text composition, causal ordering, user interface, and filtering techniques. Furthermore, QSIM-style qualitative models can be derived from quantitative models as used in DME. We are working with the authors of SIMGEN and QPC [1] (which is similar to DME and uses QSIM) on a common modeling formalism that might make it possible to exchange model libraries and test these conjectures.

Acknowledgments

The DME system is the product of members of the How Things Work project, including Richard Fikes, Yumi Iwasaki, Alon Levy, Chee Meng Low, Fritz Mueller, James Rice, and Pandu Nayak. Brian Falkenhainer and Ken Forbus have been very influential.

Bibliography

[1] J. Crawford, A. Farquhar, & B. Kuipers. QPC: A Compiler from Physical Models into Qualitative Differential Equations. *AAAI-91*, pp. 365-371, 1990.

[2] J. de Kleer & J. S. Brown. A qualitative physics based on confluences. *Artificial Intelligence*, 24:7-83, 1984.

[3] J. de Kleer & J. S. Brown. Theories of Causal Ordering. *Artificial intelligence*, 29(1):33-62, 1986.

[4] S. A. Douglas & Z.-Y. Liu. Generating causal explanation from a cardio-vascular simulation. *IJCAI-89*, pp. 489-494, 1989.

[5] B. Falkenhainer & K. Forbus. Self-explanatory simulations: Scaling up to large models. *AAAI-92*, pp. 685-690, 1992.

[6] B. Falkenhainer & K. D. Forbus. Compositional modeling: Finding the right model for the job. *Artificial Intelligence*, 51:95-143, 1991.

[7] S. K. Feiner & K. R. McKeown. Coordinating text and graphics in explanation generation. *AAAI-90*, pp. 442-449, 1990.

[8] K. D. Forbus. Qualitative Process Theory. *Artificial Intelligence*, 24:85-168, 1984.

[9] K. D. Forbus & B. Falkenhainer. Self-explanatory simulations: An integration of qualitative and quantitative knowledge. *AAAI-90*, pp. 380-387, 1990.

[10] K. D. Forbus & A. Stevens. Using qualitative simulation to generate explanations. *Proceedings of the Third Annual Conference of the Cognitive Science Society*, 1981.

[11] T. R. Gruber & P. O. Gautier. Machine-generated explanations of engineering models: A compositional modeling approach. *IJCAI-93*, 1993.

[12] Y. Iwasaki & C. M. Low. Model Generation and Simulation of Device Behavior with Continuous and Discrete Changes. *Intelligent Systems Engineering*, 1(2)1993.

[13] Y. Iwasaki & H. Simon. Causality in device behavior. *Artificial Intelligence*, 29:3-32, 1986.

[14] A. M. Keuneke & M. C. Tanner. Explanations in knowledge systems: The roles of the task structure and domain functional models. *IEEE Expert*, 6(3):50-56, 1991.

[15] B. Kuipers. Qualitative simulation. *Artificial Intelligence*, 29:289-388, 1986.

[16] M. Lee, P. Compton, & B. Jansen. Modelling with Context-Dependent Causality. In R. Mizoguchi, Ed., *Proceedings of the Second Japan Knowledge Acquisition for Knowledge-Based Systems Workshop*, Kobe, Japan, pp. 357-370, 1992.

[17] J. D. Moore & W. R. Swartout. Pointing: A way toward explanation dialog. *AAAI-90*, pp. 457-464, 1990.

[18] C. Paris. *The Use of Explicit User Models in Text Generation: Tailoring to a User's Level of Expertise*. PhD Thesis, Columbia University, 1987.

[19] D. Suthers, B. Woolf, & M. Cornell. Steps from explanation planning to model construction dialogues. *AAAI-92*, pp. 24-30, 1992.

[20] J. Top & H. Akkermans. Computational and Physical Causality. *IJCAI-91*, pp. 1171-1176, 1991.

[21] B. White & J. Frederiksen. Causal model progressions as a foundation for Intelligent learning. *Artificial Intelligence*, 42(1):99-155, 1990.

Generating Natural Language Descriptions with Examples: Differences between Introductory and Advanced Texts

Vibhu O. Mittal and Cécile L. Paris

USC/Information Sciences Institute
4676 Admiralty Way
Marina del Rey, CA 90292

Department of Computer Science
University of Southern California
Los Angeles, CA 90089

Abstract

Examples form an integral and very important part of many descriptions, especially in contexts such as tutoring and documentation generation. The ability to tailor a description for a particular situation is particularly important when different situations can result in widely varying descriptions. This paper considers the generation of descriptions with examples for two different situations: introductory texts and advanced, reference manual style texts. Previous studies have focused on any the examples or the language component of the explanation in isolation. However, there is a strong interaction between the examples and the accompanying description and it is therefore important to study how both these components are affected by changes in the situation.

In this paper, we characterize examples in the context of their description along three orthogonal axes: the information content, the knowledge type of the example and the text-type in which the explanation is being generated. While variations along either of the three axes can result in different descriptions, this paper addresses variation along the text-type axis. We illustrate our discussion with a description of a `list` from our domain of LISP documentation, and present a trace of the system as it generates these descriptions.

Introduction

Examples are an integral part of many descriptions, especially in contexts such as tutoring and documentation generation. Indeed, the importance of using illustrative examples in communicating effectively has long been recognized, e.g., (Greenwald, 1984; Doheny-Farina, 1988; Norman, 1988). People like examples because examples tend to put abstract, theoretical information into concrete terms they can understand. In fact, one study found that 76% of users looking at system documentation initially ignored the description and went straight to the examples (LeFevre and Dixon, 1986). A system that generates descriptions must

The authors gratefully acknowledge support from NASA-Ames grant NCC 2-520 and DARPA contract DABT63-91-C-0025. Cécile Paris also acknowledges support from NSF grant IRI-9003087.

thus be able to include examples. Furthermore, the ability to tailor a description for a particular situation is particularly important as different situations can result in widely varying descriptions, where both the textual descriptions and the accompanying examples vary. Some researchers have already looked at how a textual description can be affected by different situations (or different users), e.g. (Paris, 1988; Bateman and Paris, 1989). Others have studied how to construct or retrieve appropriate examples, e.g. (Rissland and Soloway, 1980; Ashley and Aleven, 1992; Rissland, 1983; Suthers and Rissland, 1988). However, the issue of tailoring descriptions that include examples for the situation at hand has not been addressed. Yet, it is clear that one cannot plan a description tailored to a user, and then independently and as an afterthought, add some examples to the description: Sweller and his colleagues found that if the examples and the descriptive component were not well integrated, the combination could result in reduced user comprehension (Chandler and Sweller, 1991; Ward and Sweller, 1990). Examples and text must be presented to the user as a coherent whole, and *together*, appropriately tailored to the situation.

Because examples are crucial in documentation (Charney *et al.*, 1988; Feldman and Klausmeier, 1974; Klausmeier and Feldman, 1975; Reder *et al.*, 1986), and documentation is a critical factor in user acceptance of a system, we chose automatic documentation as our domain to investigate the issue of generating descriptions that include examples. This domain has additional advantages: there is a large body of work on documentation writing, a lot of actual material that we can study, including numerous examples of the text types we are concerned with (introductory and advanced). In previous work, we have described the issues that must be addressed for a system to be able to generate descriptions with well integrated examples (Mittal and Paris, 1992). In this paper, we show how two specific situations, introductory texts and advanced texts, result in two different such descriptions.

This paper is structured as follows: Section 2 briefly reviews the issues that arise when generating text with examples. Section 3 presents a categorization of example types that allows us to provide a characterization of the differences between the texts in introductory *vs* references manuals and Section 4 discusses these differences. Section 5 describes our text planning framework, and Section 6 presents a trace of the algorithm.

A list always begins with a left parenthesis. Then come zero or more pieces of data (called the elements of a list) and a right parenthesis. Some examples of lists are:

```
(AARDVARK)
(RED YELLOW GREEN BLUE)
(2 3 5 11 19)
(3 FRENCH FRIES)
```

A list may contain other lists as elements. Given the three lists:

```
(BLUE SKY) (GREEN GRASS) (BROWN EARTH)
```

we can make a list by combining them all with a parentheses.

```
((BLUE SKY) (GREEN GRASS) (BROWN EARTH))
```

Figure 1: A description of list in an introductory text from (Touretzky, 1984), p.35

A list is recursively defined to be either the empty list or a CONS whose CDR component is a list. The CAR components of the CONSes are called the elements of the list. For each element of the list, there is a CONS. The empty list has no elements at all.

A list is annotated by writing the elements of the list in order, separated by blank space (space, tab, or return character) and surrounded by parentheses. For example:

```
(a b c)        ; A list of 3 symbols
(2.0s0 (a 1) #\*) ; A list of 3 things:a
               ; floating point number,
               ; another list, and a
               ; character object
```

Figure 2: A description of list from a reference manual from (Steele Jr., 1984), p.26

---

2 examples. Finally, the examples in Fig. 1 do not contain prompts, while those in Fig. 2 do.

Integrating Examples in Descriptive Texts

Many issues need to be considered when generating descriptions that integrate descriptive text and examples, because both these components co-constrain and affect each other. The inclusion of examples in an explanation can sometimes cause additional text to be generated; at other times, it can cause certain portions of the original explanation to be elided. A generation system must therefore take into account the interaction between the descriptive text and the examples, as well as effects from other factors, such as the presentation order of the examples, the placement of the examples with respect to each other, as well as the descriptive text, etc.

While we have discussed these issues elsewhere (Mittal and Paris, 1992; Mittal, 1993 forthcoming), we review some of them here:

- What should be in the text, in the examples, in both?

- What is a suitable example? How much information should a single example attempt to convey? Should there be more than one example?

- If multiple examples are to be presented, what is the order of presentation?

- If an example is to be given, should the example be presented immediately, or after the whole description is presented? This will determine whether the example(s) appear *within*, *before*, or *after* the descriptive text.

- Should prompts[1] be generated along with the examples?

Answers to these questions will depend on whether the text is an introductory or advanced text. Consider, for example, the descriptions of list given in Fig. 1 taken from (Touretzky, 1984), an introductory manual, and Fig. 2 taken from (Steele Jr., 1984), a reference manual: they contain very different information in both their descriptive portions as well as their examples; while Fig. 1 contains 8 lists (which are used either as examples or as background to the examples), Fig. 2 has only

---

[1] 'Prompts' are attention focusing devices such as arrows, marks, or even additional text associated with examples (Engelmann and Carnine, 1982).

Categorizing Example Types in Context

In order to provide appropriately tailored examples, we must first characterize the type of examples that can appear in descriptions. This will then help the system in choosing appropriate examples to present as part of a description.

While some example categorizations (Michener, 1978; Polya, 1973) have already been proposed, we found these inadequate as they do not take the context of the whole explanation into account. This is because previous attempts at categorizing example types were done in an *analytical* rather than a *generational* context, and, as a result, these categorizations suffered from two drawbacks from the standpoint of a computational generation system: (*i*) they do not explicitly take into account the context in which the example occurred, and (*ii*) they did not differentiate among different dimensions of variation.

An example of how important the context is in determining the category of the example can be seen if we look at the two descriptions of a list, shown in Fig. 3, taken from our LISP domain. The empty list NIL is an anomalous example for the first definition, while it is a positive example for the second one. Thus it is clear that categorization depends upon not only the example, but the surrounding context (which includes the descriptive text accompanying the example) as well.

Based on our analysis of a number of instructional texts, numerous reference manuals and large amounts of system documentation, we formulated a three dimensional system to categorize examples by explicitly taking the context into account. The three dimensions are:[2]

1. the polarity of the example with respect to the description: It can be: (*i*) positive, i.e., the example is an instance of the description, (*ii*) negative, i.e., the example is *not* an instance of the description, or (*iii*) anomalous, i.e., the example either looks positive and is actually negative, or vice-versa.

---

[2] Further details on this classification of examples into a three dimensional space may be found in (Mittal and Paris, 1993).

A left parenthesis followed by zero or more S-expressions followed by a right parenthesis is a list.

From (Shapiro, 1986)

A `list` is recursively defined to be either the empty list or a `CONS` whose `CDR` component is a `list`. The `CAR` components of the `CONS`es are called the elements of the list. For each element of the list, there is a `CONS`. The empty list has no elements at all. The empty list `NIL` therefore can be written ( ), because it is a list with no elements.

From (Steele Jr., 1984)

Figure 3: Two definitions that cause `NIL` to be classified differently as an illustrative example.

---

2. the knowledge type being communicated: for example, a concept, a relation or a process is being described.

3. the genre or text-type to be generated: For now, we only take into consideration two text-types:[3] (*i*) descriptions in introductory texts, and (*ii*) descriptions in reference manuals. These are, in our case, closely related to the user types: introductory texts are intended for beginners and naive users while advanced texts are intended for expert users.[4]

Note that each of these axes can be further sub-divided (for instance, concepts can be further specified as being single-featured or multi-featured concepts, etc.).

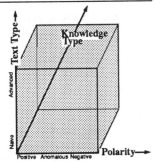

Figure 4: Three dimensions for example categorization.

Such a categorization is essential to narrow the search space for suitable examples during generation. Furthermore, it allows us to make use of the numerous results in educational psychology and cognitive science, on how to best choose and present examples for a particular text- and knowledge-type. For example, results there suggest constraints that can be taken into consideration with respect to the number of examples to present, e.g., (Markle and Tiemann, 1969), their order of presentation, e.g., (Carnine, 1980; Engelmann and Carnine, 1982), whether anomalous examples should be presented, e.g., (Engelmann and Carnine, 1982), etc.

---

[3]We make use of the notion of a text-type here only in a very broad sense to define distinct categories that affect the generation of examples in our framework for the automatic documentation task. However, these text-types can be refined further. Indeed, several detailed text typologies have been proposed by linguists e.g., (Biber, 1989; de Beaugrande, 1980).

[4]We have in fact referred to this axis as 'user type' in other work.

Introductory *vs* Advanced Texts

We now consider how descriptions that contain examples differ, when we move along the text-type axis of our categorization, from introductory to advanced text. We address each of the questions presented in Section 2:

The descriptive component: In the case of the introductory text-type, the descriptive component contains surface or syntactic information; in the case of the reference text-type, the description must include complete information, including the internal structure of the concept.

The actual examples: Examples in both text-types illustrate critical features[5] of the surface or syntactic form of the concept or its realization. In introductory texts, however, examples are simple and tend to illustrate only one feature at a time. (Sometimes it is not possible to isolate one feature, and an example might illustrate two features; in this case, the system will need to generate additional text to mention this fact.) On the other hand, examples in reference texts are multi-featured.

The number of examples: Since introductory texts contain usually single-featured examples, the number of examples depend upon the number of critical features that the concept possesses. In contrast, reference texts contain examples that contain three or four features per example (Clark, 1971), and, therefore, proportionately fewer examples need to be presented.

The polarity of the examples: Introductory texts make use of both positive and negative examples, but not anomalous examples. Advanced texts on the other hand, contain positive and anomalous examples.

The position of the examples: In introductory texts, the examples are presented immediately after the point they illustrate is mentioned. This results in descriptions in which the examples are interspersed in the text. On the other hand, examples in reference texts must be presented only after the description of the concept is complete.

Prompts: The system needs to generate prompts for examples that contain more than one feature. The system must also generate prompts in the case of recursive examples (they use other instances which are also instances of the concept), and anomalous examples if background text has not yet been generated (as is done for introductory texts).

These guidelines are summarized in Fig. 5.

In the following section, we will illustrate how a system can use these guidelines to generate descriptions (text and examples) for both introductory and advanced texts, in our domain of the programming language LISP.

The Generation System

Our system is part of the documentation facility we are building for the Explainable Expert Systems (EES) framework (Swartout *et al.*, 1992). The framework implements the integration of text and examples within a text-generation system. More specifically, we use a text-planning system that constructs text by explicitly reasoning about the communicative

---

[5]Critical features are features that are *necessary* for an example to be considered a positive example of a concept. Changes to a critical feature cause a positive example to become a negative example.

goal to be achieved, as well as how goals relate to each other rhetorically to form a coherent text (Moore and Paris, 1989; Moore, 1989; Moore and Paris, 1992). Given a top level communicative goal (such as (KNOW-ABOUT HEARER (CONCEPT LIST)),[6] the system finds plans capable of achieving this goal. Plans typically post further sub-goals to be satisfied. These are expanded, and planning continues until primitive speech acts are achieved. The result of the planning process is a discourse tree, where the nodes represent goals at various levels of abstraction, with the root being the initial goal, and the leaves representing primitive realization statements, such as (INFORM ...) statements. The discourse tree also includes *coherence relations* (Mann and Thompson, 1987), which indicate how the various portions of text resulting from the discourse tree will be related rhetorically. This tree is then passed to a grammar interface which converts it into a set of inputs suitable for input to a grammar.

Plan operators can be seen as small schemas which describe how to achieve a goal; they are designed by studying natural language texts and transcripts. They include conditions for their applicability, which can refer to the system knowledge base, the user model, or the context (the text plan tree under construction and the dialogue history). In this framework, the generation of examples is accomplished by explicitly posting the goal of providing an example while constructing the text.

A Trace of the system

We now describe a trace of the system as it plans the presentation of descriptions similar to the ones presented in Fig. 1 and 2.

First, assume we want to produce a description of a list for an introductory manual. The system is given a top-level goal: (KNOW-ABOUT HEARER (CONCEPT LIST)). The text planner searches for applicable plan operators in its plan-library, and it picks one based on the applicable constraints such as the text-type (introductory), the knowledge type (concept), etc.[7] The text-type restricts the choice of the features to present to be syntactic ones. The main features of list are retrieved, and two subgoals are posted: one to list the critical features (the left parenthesis, the data elements and the right parenthesis), and another to elaborate upon them.

At this point, the discourse tree has only two nodes apart from the initial node of (KNOW-ABOUT H (CONCEPT LIST)): namely (*i*) (BEL H (MAIN-FEATURES LIST (LT-PAREN DATA-ELMT RT-PAREN))), and (*ii*) (ELABORATION FEATURES),[8] which will result in a goal to describe each of the features in turn.

The planner searches for appropriate operators to satisfy these goals. The plan operator to describe a list of features indicates that the features should be mentioned in a sequence. Three goals are appropriately posted at this point. These

For each issue, the effect of the text-type is:

- Examples:

   introductory: simple, single critical-feature
   advanced: complex, multiple critical-features

- Accompanying Description:

   introductory: surface, syntactic information
   advanced: complete information, including internal structure

- Number of Examples:

   introductory: depends upon number of critical features
   advanced: few (each example contains three to four features)

- Positioning the Examples:

   introductory: immediately after points being illustrated
   advanced: after the description is complete

- Prompts:

   introductory: prompt if example has more than one feature
   advanced: prompts if anomalous and recursive examples

Figure 5: Brief description of differences between examples in introductory and advanced texts.

goals result in the planner generating a plan for the first two sentences of Fig. 1. The other sub-goal (the ELABORATION) also causes three goals to be posted for describing each of the critical features. Since two of these are for elaborating upon the parentheses, they are not expanded because no further information is available. So only the goal of describing the data elements remains. A partial representation of the resulting text plan is shown in Fig. 6.[9]

Data elements can be of three types: numbers, symbols, or lists. The system can either communicate this information by realizing an appropriate sentence, or through examples – since it can generate examples for each of these types, or both. The text type (introductory text) constraints cause the system to pick examples. (If the text-type had been 'reference,' the system would have delayed the presentation of examples, and text would have been generated at that point instead of the examples.) The system posts two goals to illustrate the two dimensions along which the data elements can vary: the number of elements and the type.

Information about a particular feature can be communicated by the system through examples efficiently by using pairs (or groups) of examples as follows:

- if the feature to be communicated happens to be a *critical* feature, the system generates pairs of examples, *one positive and one negative*, which are identical except for the feature being communicated, and

- if the feature to be communicated happens to be a *variable*[10]

---

[6]See the references given above for details on the notation used to represent these goals.

[7]When several plans are available, the system chooses one using *selection heuristics* designed by (Moore, 1989).

[8]ELABORATION is one of the coherence relations defined in (Mann and Thompson, 1987).

[9]All the text plans shown in this paper are simplified versions of the actual plans generated: in particular, the communicative goals are not written in their formal notation, in terms of the hearer's mental states, for readability's sake.

[10]Variable features are features that can *vary* in a positive example. Changes to variable features creates different positive examples.

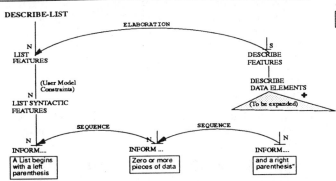

Figure 6: Skeletal plan for listing main features of `list`.

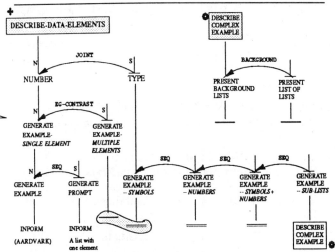

Figure 7: Skeletal plan for generating examples of `lists`.

feature, the system generates pairs of examples that are *both positive* and are widely different in that feature

Thus, to communicate the fact that there can be any number of elements, the system posts two goals to generate two differing positive examples, one with a single element and another with multiple elements. The example generation algorithm ensures that the examples selected for related sub-goals (such as the two above) differ in *only* the dimension being highlighted. However, as the examples contain two critical features (i.e., type is illustrated as well), the system generates prompts to focus the attention on the reader on the number feature ("a list of one element" *vs* "a list of several elements").

The goal to illustrate the *type* dimension is handled in similar fashion, with four sub-goals (one each for the types: symbols, numbers, symbols and numbers, and sub-lists) being posted. The last data type, *sub-lists*, is marked by the algorithm as a *recursive* use of the concept, and is handled specially because the text-type is introductory. In the case of an introductory text, such examples must be introduced with appropriate explanations added to the text. (If the text-type had been 'reference,' the system would have generated a prompt denoting the presence of the sub-list.) The resulting skeletal text-plan generated by the system is shown in Fig. 7.

Consider the second case now, when the text-type is specified as being 'reference.' In this case, the system starts with the same top-level goal as before, but the text-type constraints cause the planner to select both the structural representation of a `list`, as well as the syntactic structure for presentation. The system posts two goals, one to describe the underlying structure, and one to describe the syntactic form of a `list`. The two goals expand into the first two paragraphs in Fig. 2. Note that the examples occur at the end of the description. The two examples generated are much more complex than the previous case, and they contain a number of variable features (the second example shows the variation in element types, as well as the variation in number possible). Since the second example generated contains a list as a data element, the system generates prompts for the examples. For lack of space, the resulting text plan is not presented here.[11]

In both of the above cases, the completed discourse tree is passed to an interface which converts the INFORM goals into the appropriate input for the sentence generator. The interface chooses the appropriate lexical and syntactic constructs to form the individual sentences and connects them appropriately, using the rhetorical information from the discourse tree.

Conclusions

We have presented an analysis of the differences in descriptions that integrate examples for introductory and advanced texts. To be able to do this, we first presented a brief description of our characterization of examples, explicitly taking into account the surrounding context. Variation along any of these axes causes the explanation generated to change accordingly. This variation occurs not just in the descriptive part of the explanation, but also in the examples that accompany it. Since the examples and the descriptive component are tightly integrated and affect each other in many ways, a system designed to generate such descriptions must take into account these interactions and be able to structure the presentation accordingly. We have presented information necessary to generate descriptions for two text-types: introductory and advanced. The algorithm used by the system was illustrated by tracing the generation of two descriptions of the LISP `list`.

The issues we have described are not specific to a particular framework or implementation for generation of either text or examples. In fact, the algorithm described is implemented in our system as constraint specification across different plan operators. We have successfully combined two well-known generators (one for text and one for examples) in our system to produce the explanations described in this paper.

References

Ashley, K. D. and Aleven, V., 1992. Generating Dialectical Examples Automatically. In *Proceedings of AAAI-92*, 654–660. San Jose, CA.

Bateman, J. A. and Paris, C. L., 1989. Phrasing a text in terms the user can understand. In *Proceedings of IJCAI 89*. Detroit, MI.

---

[11] See (Mittal, 1993 forthcoming) for more details.

Biber, D., 1989. A typology of English Texts. *Linguistics* 27:3–43.

Carnine, D.W., 1980. Two Letter Discrimination Sequences: High-Confusion-Alternatives first versus Low-Confusion-Alternatives first. *Journal of Reading Behaviour*, XII(1):41–47, Spring.

Chandler, P. and Sweller, J., 1991. Cognitive Load Theory and the Format of Instruction. *Cognition and Instruction* 8(4):292–332.

Charney, D. H., Reder, L. M., and Wells, G. W., 1988. Studies of Elaboration in Instructional Texts. In Doheny-Farina, S.(Ed.), *Effective Documentation: What we have learned from Research*, 48–72. Cambridge, MA. The MIT Press.

Clark, D. C., 1971. Teaching Concepts in the Classroom: A Set of Prescriptions derived from Experimental Research. *Journal of Educational Psychology Monograph* 62:253–278.

de Beaugrande, R., 1980. *Text, Discourse and Process.* Ablex Publishing Co.

Doheny-Farina, S., 1988. *Effective Documentation : What we have learned from Research.* MIT Press.

Engelmann, S. and Carnine, D., 1982. *Theory of Instruction: Principles and Applications.* New York: Irvington Publishers, Inc.

Feldman, K. V. and Klausmeier, H. J., 1974. The effects of two kinds of definitions on the concept attainment of fourth- and eighth-grade students. *Journal of Educational Research* 67(5):219–223.

Greenwald, J., 1984. How does this #%$! Thing Work? *Time.* (Page 64, Week of June 18, 1984).

Klausmeier, H. J. and Feldman, K. V., 1975. Effects of a Definition and a Varying Number of Examples and Non-Examples on Concept Attainment. *Journal of Educational Psychology* 67(2):174–178.

Klausmeier, H. J., 1976. Instructional Design and the Teaching of Concepts. In Levin, J. R.*et al.*(Eds.), *Cognitive Learning in Children.* New York: Academic Press.

LeFevre, J.-A. and Dixon, P., 1986. Do Written Instructions Need Examples? *Cognition and Instruction* 3(1):1–30.

Mann, W. and Thompson, S., 1987. Rhetorical Structure Theory: a Theory of Text Organization. In Polanyi, L. (Ed.), *The Structure of Discourse.* Norwood, New Jersey: Ablex Publishing Co..

Markle, S.M. and Tiemann, P.W., 1969. *Really Understanding Concepts.* Stipes Press, Urbana, IL.

Michener, E. R., 1978. Understanding Understanding Mathematics. *Cognitive Science Journal* 2(4):361–383.

Mittal, V.O. and Paris, C.L., 1992. Generating Object Descriptions which integrate both Text and Examples. In *Proc.9th Canadian A.I. Conference*, pp.1–8. Morgan Kaufmann Publishers.

Mittal, V. O. and Paris, C. L., 1993. Categorizing Example Types in Context: Applications for the Generation of Tutorial Descriptions. To appear in the *Proceedings of AI-ED 93.* (Edinburgh, Scotland).

Mittal, V.O., 1993 (forthcoming). *Generating descriptions with integrated text and examples.* PhD thesis, University of Southern California, Los Angeles, CA.

Moore, J. D. and Paris, C. L., 1989. Planning text for advisory dialogues. In *Proceedings of ACL 89.* Vancouver, B.C.

Moore, J.D. and Paris, C.L., 1992. Planning text for advisory dialogues: Capturing intentional, rhetorical and attentional information. TR 92-22, Univ. of Pittsburgh, CS Dept., Pittsburgh, PA, 1992.

Moore, J. D., 1989. A Reactive Approach to Explanation in Expert and Advice-Giving Systems. Ph.D. thesis, UCLA, CA.

Norman, D., 1988 *The Psychology of Everyday Things.* New York: Basic Books.

Paris, C. L., 1988. Tailoring Object Descriptions to the User's Level of Expertise. *Computational Linguistics* 14(3):64–78.

Polya, G., 1973. *Induction and Analogy in Mathematics*, volume 1 of *Mathematics and Plausible Reasoning*. Princeton, N.J.: Princeton University Press.

Reder, L. M., Charney, D. H., and Morgan, K. I., 1986. The Role of Elaborations in learning a skill from an Instructional Text. *Memory and Cognition* 14(1):64–78.

Rissland, E. L. and Soloway, E. M., 1980. Overview of an Example Generation System. In *Proc. AAAI 80*, pp. 256–258.

Rissland, E. L., 1980. Example Generation. In *Proceedings of the 3rd Conference of the Candian Society for Computational Studies of Intelligence*, 280–288. Toronto, Ontario.

Rissland, E. L., 1983. Examples in Legal Reasoning: Legal Hypotheticals. In *Proc. IJCAI 83*, pp. 90–93. Karlsruhe, Germany.

Shapiro, S.C., 1986. *LISP: An Interactive Approach.* Rockville, MD.: Computer Science Press.

Steele Jr., G. L., 1984. *Common Lisp: The Language.* Digital Press.

Suthers, D. D. and Rissland, E. L., 1988. Constraint Manipulation for Example Generation. COINS TR 88-71, CIS Dept, Univ. of Massachusetts, Amherst, MA.

Swartout, W. R., Paris, C. L., and Moore, J. D., 1992. Design for Explainable Expert Systems. *IEEE Expert* 6(3):58–64.

Touretzky, D. S., 1984. *LISP: A Gentle Introduction to Symbolic Computation.* New York: Harper & Row Publishers.

Ward, M. and Sweller, J., 1990. Structuring Effective Worked Examples. *Cognition and Instruction* 7(1):1 – 39.

Building Models to Support Synthesis in Early Stage Product Design

R. Bharat Rao
Learning Systems Department
Siemens Corporate Research, Inc.

Stephen C-Y. Lu
Knowledge-based Engg. Systems Res. Lab
University of Illinois at Urbana-Champaign

Abstract

Current computer-aided engineering paradigms for supporting synthesis activities in engineering design require the designer to use analysis simulators iteratively in an optimization loop. While optimization is necessary to achieve a good final design, it has a number of disadvantages during the *early* stages of design. In the *inverse engineering* methodology, machine learning techniques are used to learn a multidirectional model that provides vastly improved synthesis (and analysis) support to the designer. This methodology is demonstrated on the early design of a diesel engine combustion chamber for a truck.

Introduction

A design engineer's primary task is to develop designs that can achieve specified performances. For example, an engine designer may be required to design a "combustion chamber that delivers at least 600hp while minimizing the fuel consumption." The horsepower and fuel consumption are the performance parameters. In a parameterized domain, the designer sets the values of the decision/design parameters (e.g., engine rpm) so as to meet the performance. Under current computer-aided engineering (CAE) paradigms, design support is typically provided by computer simulators. These simulators are computerized *analysis* models that analyze a design and map decisions to performances. However, engineering design is largely a *synthesis* task that requires mapping the performance space, P, to the decision space, D. In the absence of models that provide synthesis support, the designer must use the simulator, F, in an iterative generate and test paradigm, namely, in an optimization loop. The designer begins with an initial design (a point in D), evaluates the design with F, and moves to a new design, based on the difference between the actual and required performances. A common way of moving within D is by response surface fitting, where the designer exercises F repeatedly in the neighborhood of the current design, fits a surface to the performances, and moves based on this surface.

While the above methodology is essential for the final stages of design, it has serious drawbacks during *early* design. First, a poor starting design can result in a large number of optimization steps, which can be very time-consuming. The designer would prefer to rapidly develop a good initial design to use as the starting point in the optimization. Second, the simulator is a point to point simulator. This means that the designer must assign values to every decision variable at the outset of the design. Ideally, the designer would specify or restrict only the variables in which he was interested, leaving the others to be automatically specified as the design progresses. Third, every new performance objective must be set up as a separate design problem. For example, instead of designing an engine that generates 600hp, perhaps there exists an engine that delivers 590hp but with markedly improved fuel consumption, or another that delivers 640hp with slightly less efficient fuel consumption. If the designer had a synthesis model, he could apply and retract conditions on some of the performance variables and quickly determine their effects on the other variables. Similarly he could constrain the decision variables to reflect cost concerns, inventory stocks, or simply as part of a "What-if" analysis. The ability to treat decision and performance variables more or less identically would prove extraordinarily valuable during early design. The synthesis model, once learned, could be used repeatedly for different designs.

The *inverse engineering* methodology [Rao, 1993] provides solutions to all the above problems by building an accurate *multidirectional* model of the problem domain. The designer uses the model directly to prototype a design quickly by successively refining the problem space, $D \cup P$ (as opposed to the traditional CAE paradigm where the designer works only in D). A single invocation of F at the end of the process is sufficient to check the design. The foundation of inverse engineering is KEDS, the Knowledge-based Equation Discovery System [Rao and Lu, 1993]. KEDS ability to learn accurate models in representations that can be converted into constraints (i.e., as piece-wise linear models) makes inverse engineering a viable proposi-

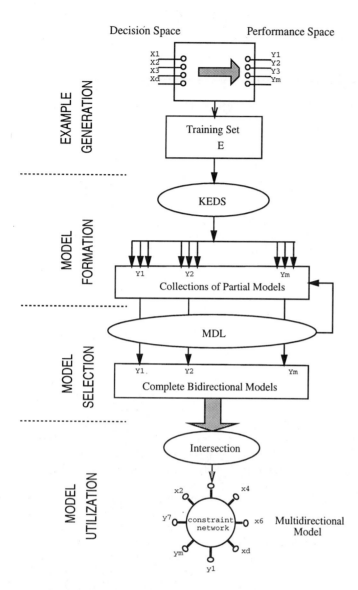

Figure 1: The Inverse Engineering Methodology

Table 1: Decision and Performance variables in DESP

Variable		Min	Max
STBR	Stroke-to-Bore Ratio	0.8	1.2
TIM	Injection Timing (deg)	320.0	335.0
FMIN	Fuel Mass Injected (gm/cyc)	0.1	0.4
CR	Compression Ratio	13.0	17.0
ERPM	Engine Speed (rpm)	1000.	2400.
DVOL	Displacement Volume (l)	0.005	0.015
BSFC	Brake Specific Fuel Consumption		
ENBHP	Engine Brake Horsepower (HP)		

both analysis and synthesis support. The 4 phases of inverse engineering (see Figure 1) are described below.

Example Generation Phase The Diesel Engine Simulation Program, DESP [Assanis and Heywood, 1986], provides the data for KEDS. DESP solves mass and heat balance equations from Thermodynamics and uses finite difference techniques to provide data that is representative of real-world engines. The 6 decision and 2 performance (real-valued) variables for a 6-cylinder, diesel combustion engine are shown in Table 1. The decision variables are randomly varied to generate 145 events. This results in two data sets (one for each performance variable, BSFC and ENBHP in Table 1), such that each event is a two-tuple of a decision vector $X \in D$ and a corresponding performance variable, $y_j \in P$. These data sets are input to KEDS to learn multidirectional models.

Model Formation Phase KEDS is a model-driven empirical discovery system that learns models in forms restricted to $\mathcal{F}$, a user-defined class of parameterized model families (both linear and non-linear $\mathcal{F}$ are permitted). For the purposes of inverse engineering, $\mathcal{F}$ is restricted to the class of linear polynomials, $y = \sum(a_i x_i) + b$. However, it is unlikely that a simple linear representation will be sufficient to accurately model most real-world domains. KEDS can simultaneously be viewed as a conceptual clustering system, which partitions the data based upon the mathematical relationships that it discovers between the variables. Each call to KEDS results in a single *partial model* (R, f), that consists of a region (hyperrectangle), $R \subset D$, associated with an equation, $f \in \mathcal{F}$, that predicts y for all $X \in R$. The KEDS algorithm (described in [Rao and Lu, 1993]) involves recursing through equation discovery (fitting) and partitioning (splitting) and combines aspects of fit-and-split [Langley *et al.*, 1987] and split-and-fit [Friedman, 1991; Quinlan, 1986] modeling systems as KEDS refines both the region and the equation. A sample partial model is shown below.

[321.0< TINJ] [.2482< FMIN <.3941] [13.16< CR <16.8]
[1074< RPM] [.0103< VOL] [.813< STBR] ::>
::> BSFC = 1.3 FMIN -.003 TIM -.008 CR +1.5E-5 RPM -27. VOL +1.5

tion. This rest of this paper describes this methodology, and demonstrates (through an example) how these techniques provides improved support for early design.

The Inverse Engineering Methodology

The essential problem with current CAE paradigms for design is the lack of synthesis support. The barrier between analysis and synthesis activities is especially unbearable in a concurrent engineering framework, where speed and timely execution of tasks is paramount. As directly learning synthesis models is a very hard task [Rao, 1993], the inverse engineering approach is to *learn analysis models in representations that provide synthesis support*. For example, if the analysis model for $y_j \in P$ can be accurately represented as a linear function of some $x_i \in D$ (i.e., $y_j = \sum(a_i x_i) + b$), it can then be converted into a constraint that provides

Model Selection Phase KEDS is invoked repeatedly to generate a collection of overlapping partial models. KEDS-MDL [Rao and Lu, 1992] is a resource-bounded incremental algorithm that uses the minimum description length [Rissanen, 1986] principle to select partial models to build a piece-wise complete model. This is a collection of disjoint partial models that describes the entire decision space.

Model Utilization Phase Each partial model (region-equation pair) is equivalent to a linear constraint that maps a region in D to an interval in y_j. KEDS-MDL learns piece-wise linear models for ENBHP and BSFC. The constraints for ENBHP are intersected with the constraints for BSFC to produce a set of *intersections*. An intersection maps a region in D to a region in P, and also supports reasoning from P to D. No two intersections overlap within the decision space, but the regions in performance space do typically overlap (as several different designs can achieve the same performance). Unlike the traditional CAE paradigm, the designer works in the problem space, $D \cup P$. The designer can *refine* any intersection by refining a variable, i.e., by shrinking the interval associated with that variable. Refining a decision variable leads to *forward* propagation along a constraint and the new intervals for the other variables can be determined in a straightforward fashion. Refining a performance variable requires *inverse* propagation along constraints. One possibility is to solve the intersection to find the new feasible region in D (for example, by using Simplex). Instead, this is done by computing the projection of the feasible region onto the decision variables (i.e., the enclosing hyperrectangle) in a single step computation [Rao, 1993]. Inverse propagations can lead to forward propagations, and vice versa.

The DESP domain has 15-30 intersections, depending upon the model formation parameters used in KEDS. While it would be a great strain, it is remotely possible that a designer would be able to work individually with each intersection. However, other domains can give rise to many more intersections (a process planning application for a turning machine has 1000+ intersections). Instead of working with each individual intersection, the designer refines a single composite region that consists of the union of the intervals for all intersections. A truth maintenance system keeps track of the effects of refinements on each intersection, and the designer only sees the composite interval for each variable. This occasionally leads to *gaps* in the problem space, when two or more disjoint decision regions have similar performance.

A number of CAD/CAM [Finger and Dixon, 1989; Vanderplaats, 1984] and AI [Dixon, 1986] techniques have been developed to support engineering design. A complementary approach to inverse engineering for breaking the analysis-synthesis barrier for early design is to develop representations and theories for multidirectional models [Herman, 1989] that could replace existing analysis simulators. However, this fails to take advantage of past research efforts in developing computer simulators. Another approach is to speed up the iterative optimization process by replacing slow computer simulators with faster models [Yerramareddy and Lu, 1993]. For a detailed review of related machine learning and design research, see [Rao, 1993].

Product Design Demonstration

The inverse engineering interface is shown in Figure 2. There are 6 function windows. The *Control Panel* is used primarily to initialize the domain by loading models created offline by KEDS-MDL , and to simulate the final design. The original intervals of the multidirectional model are displayed in the *Original Model* Window. The *Messages Window* displays detailed domain information. The *Lisp Listener* is for development.

The *Decision Panel* is the window in which the designer does virtually all his work. Clicking on the "Refine" button brings up a pop-up menu of the variable names. Clicking on a variable (e.g., ENBHP) brings up an Emacs window titled "Ranges for parameter: ENBHP" that displays the current ranges for that variable. After refining the values with Emacs commands, hitting the return key causes the refinement to be quickly propagated through all of the intersections creating a new *world*. In Figure 2 the designer has just refined the ENBHP variable in the Decision Panel to demand that the engine deliver at least 600hp. The *Worlds Display Panel* (WDP) shows a *world view* reflecting the state of the world after the ENBHP refinement. The first three columns in the world view show the names of the variables and the current intervals. The last two columns, "Dmin" and "Dmax," in the world view represent the change (i.e., the delta) in the intervals relative to the previous world. Figure 2 shows that after the ENBHP refinement both boundaries of the compression ratio were moved inwards, the lower bound of the engine speed was increased, and there was no influence on the fuel consumption (see Table 1 for acronyms). Successive world views occlude previous views in the WDP. The Messages Window indicates that the designer cannot refine STBRAT to fall completely within the gap,]0.969, 0.988[. Clicking on the "Retract" button in the Decision Panel retracts the last refinement, and uncovers the previous world view. This interface was built on the interfaces for the HIDER [Yerramareddy and Lu, 1993] and IDEEA [Herman, 1989] systems.

Forming an Early Design

The designer's task is to design a combustion chamber for a 6-cylinder diesel engine for a truck. The engine should deliver at least 600hp, though this could be slightly relaxed based on the designer's judgment. In general, good designs have high ENBHP with a low BSFC. There are other cost concerns that may come

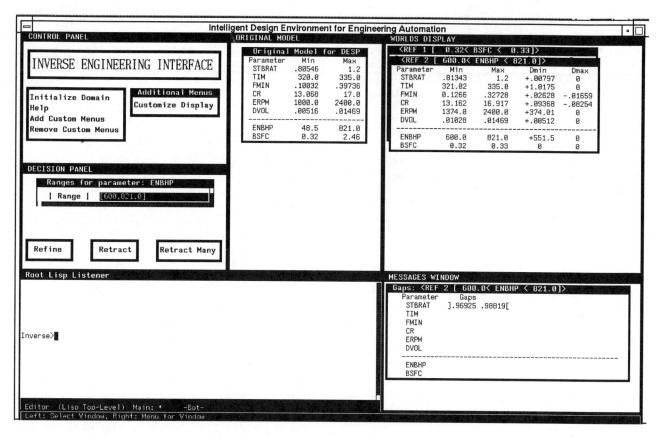

Figure 2: User Interface for Inverse Engineering Environment

into play as the designer applies his background knowledge. In this section we follow a designer step by step, as he uses the inverse engineering interface to come up with a complete early design. Each refinement step is indexed by a number indicating the level of refinement.

- (1) *Refine BSFC to a max of 0.33.* The designer exploits the synthesis support to set fuel consumption to a low value. The screen bitmap of the corresponding world view is shown in Figure 3(a).

- (2) *Refine ENBHP to a min of 600.* Figure 3(b) shows that this refinement influences many other variables (see "Dmax" and "Dmin" fields).

While the designer does not have to begin all designs by restricting P, the importance of being able to directly constrain the performance parameters is tremendous. From this point onwards the designer can make any changes in D, and is assured that the propagation mechanisms will constrain the remaining variables to meet the performance specifications.

- (3) *Refine ERPM to a max of 1400.* Engines that run at lower speeds have higher manufacturing tolerances and thus lower costs associated with them. Unfortunately, restricting the speed to a very low value adversely affects other decision variables as shown in Figure 3(c). In order to deliver 600hp with BSFC< .33, the CR must be a minimum of 16.3.

Higher CR's requires thicker engine cylinder walls, increasing the cost of the engine.

- *Retract Refinement 3.* The system returns to the state shown in Figure 3(b).

- (3) *Refine CR to a value of 15.0.* See Figure 3(d).

While the designer can restrict the CR to a range, the ability to set a variable to an exact value is very useful. Typically, the values of the variables are optimized by exploring the terrain in the problem space. Even though decision variables, such as STBRAT and CR, are continuous-valued, the engine is most easily manufactured if these variables are set to values that can be easily machined. These settings could also cut down on manufacturing costs and time by using existing inventory and machine setups, rather than retooling factories for every new design.

- (4) *Refine DVOL = 0.0145* (cylinder displacement volume is 14.5 liters).

- (5) *Refine STBRAT = 1.0.* The designer notices a gap in the range]0.969, 0.988[. He chooses 1.0 as an easily machined value of STBRAT.

- (6) *Refine TIM = 334.5.* See Figure 3(e).

- (7) *Refine ERPM = 2060.* The designer conservatively picks central values that meet manufacturing requirements for the last two unspecified variables.

<REF 1 [0.32< BSFC < 0.33]>

Parameter	Min	Max	Dmin	Dmax
STBRAT	.80546	1.2	0	0
TIM	320.0	335.0	0	0
FMIN	.10032	.34388	0	-.05348
CR	13.068	17.0	0	0
ERPM	1000.0	2400.0	0	0
DVOL	.00516	.01469	0	0
ENBHP	48.5	821.0	0	0
BSFC	0.32	0.33	0	-2.13

(a) Refining BSFC

<REF 1 [0.32< BSFC < 0.33]>
<REF 2 [600.0< ENBHP < 821.0]>

Parameter	Min	Max	Dmin	Dmax
STBRAT	.81343	1.2	+.00797	0
TIM	321.02	335.0	+1.0175	0
FMIN	0.1266	.32728	+.02628	-.01659
CR	13.162	16.917	+.09368	-.08254
ERPM	1374.0	2400.0	+374.01	0
DVOL	.01028	.01469	+.00512	0
ENBHP	600.0	821.0	+551.5	0
BSFC	0.32	0.33	0	0

(b) Refining ENBHP

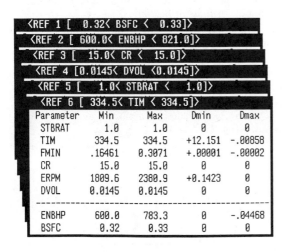

<REF 1 [0.32< BSFC < 0.33]>
<REF 2 [600.0< ENBHP < 821.0]>
<REF 3 [1374.0< ERPM <1400.0]>

Parameter	Min	Max	Dmin	Dmax
STBRAT	.81343	.96925	0	-.23075
TIM	333.98	335.0	+12.959	0
FMIN	.31305	.32728	+.18645	0
CR	16.384	16.694	+3.2224	-.22374
ERPM	1374.0	1400.0	0	-1000.0
DVOL	.01458	.01469	+0.0043	0
ENBHP	600.0	605.27	0	-215.73
BSFC	0.32	0.33	0	0

(c) Refining ERPM

<REF 1 [0.32< BSFC < 0.33]>
<REF 2 [600.0< ENBHP < 821.0]>
<REF 3 [15.0< CR < 15.0]>

Parameter	Min	Max	Dmin	Dmax
STBRAT	.81343	1.2	0	0
TIM	321.02	335.0	0	0
FMIN	.16437	.31547	+.03778	-.01181
CR	15.0	15.0	+1.8382	-1.9175
ERPM	1516.2	2400.0	+142.18	0
DVOL	.01028	.01469	0	0
ENBHP	600.0	797.22	0	-23.785
BSFC	0.32	0.33	0	0

(d) Refining CR

<REF 1 [0.32< BSFC < 0.33]>
<REF 2 [600.0< ENBHP < 821.0]>
<REF 3 [15.0< CR < 15.0]>
<REF 4 [0.0145< DVOL <0.0145]>
<REF 5 [1.0< STBRAT < 1.0]>
<REF 6 [334.5< TIM < 334.5]>

Parameter	Min	Max	Dmin	Dmax
STBRAT	1.0	1.0	0	0
TIM	334.5	334.5	+12.151	-.00858
FMIN	.16461	0.3071	+.00001	-.00002
CR	15.0	15.0	0	0
ERPM	1809.6	2380.9	+0.1423	0
DVOL	0.0145	0.0145	0	0
ENBHP	600.0	783.3	0	-.04468
BSFC	0.32	0.33	0	0

(e) Refining TIM

<REF 1 [0.32< BSFC < 0.33]>
<REF 2 [600.0< ENBHP < 821.0]>
<REF 3 [15.0< CR < 15.0]>
<REF 4 [0.0145< DVOL <0.0145]>
<REF 5 [1.0< STBRAT < 1.0]>
<REF 6 [334.5< TIM < 334.5]>
<REF 7 [2060.0< ERPM <2060.0]>
<REF 8 [0.247< FMIN < 0.247]>

Parameter	Min	Max	Dmin	Dmax
STBRAT	1.0	1.0	0	0
TIM	334.5	334.5	0	0
FMIN	0.247	0.247	+.00235	-.05719
CR	15.0	15.0	0	0
ERPM	2060.0	2060.0	0	0
DVOL	0.0145	0.0145	0	0
ENBHP	603.03	603.03	+3.0258	-73.573
BSFC	.32225	.32225	+.00225	-.00775

(f) Refining FMIN

Figure 3: Engine Design Example: World views from the Inverse Interface

- (8) *Refine FMIN = 0.247*. The initial design (henceforth, D1) is complete. The world-view in Figure 3(f) indicates that according to the model, D1 delivers 603hp at a fuel consumption of 32.3%.

The designer uses the "Simulate Design" option in the Control Panel to run DESP on the design. The performance of D1 is computed to be 612.55 hp at 32.9% fuel consumption, which meets the performance constraints of Refinements 1 and 2 above. Note that any optimization of D1 with DESP will almost certainly result in a superior design in the neighborhood of D1.

Exploring alternate designs

The designer chooses the "Retract Many" option to retract Refinement 1 limiting the BSFC to 0.33. The designer is willing to loosen up slightly on the BSFC requirement if improvements appear elsewhere, for instance in the form of increased horsepower. The designer now sets the minimum ENBHP to 650hp and proceeds in a similar fashion to that described in the previous section. The resulting engine, parameterized by D2=(1.0 334.5 0.247 13.5 2380.0 0.0145), delivers 681hp at 34.2% consumption. The designer had earlier (while designing D1) unsuccessfully tried to lower the engine speed so as to reduce manufacturing costs (see Figure 3(c)). In a further attempt to achieve this, the designer relaxes the ENBHP constraint (Refinement 2 above) while imposing low BSFC and RPM constraints. The resulting design, D3=(1.0 334.5 0.247 17.0 1800.0 0.0145), has 32.09% consumption but delivers only 555hp. Another design, D4=(0.85 334.5 0.247 15.0 2000.0 0.0145), is created when the designer constrains STBRAT=0.85, CR$\leq$15, and BSFC$\leq$0.33. This design delivers 592hp at 33.0% consumption.

Of the 4 designs, D1–4, D3 is discarded because the horsepower delivered by that engine is too low (555hp), and D4 is eliminated because its performance is worse than D1 for both horsepower (590hp versus 603hp) and fuel consumption (33.0% versus 32.9%). The designer can make a choice between D1 and D2 at this point; for example, he can eliminate D2 if he deems that the extra 69hp (=681-612) is not worth the 1.3% drop in fuel efficiency. Alternatively, he could choose to optimize both D1 and D2 using the traditional CAE paradigm and defer the decision. He could then decide to manufacture two lines of trucks or search for more designs with the user interface. Whichever option the designer chooses, his choice is likely to be more informed, than would have been the case had he worked with the traditional CAE paradigm.

Conclusions

This research demonstrates that machine learning techniques can be used to provide vastly improved design support in parameterized domains. The designer is able to refine both decision and performance variables and can reuse the model for new performance specifications. The inverse engineering methodology has also been applied to process design as a *model translator* to convert a point-to-point simulator into a region-to-region model in a process planner for a turning machine. In a few design scenarios the design task is precisely defined and can be automated. This is the approach we are applying to support "worst-case" design of analog MOS circuits. The inverse engineering methodology opens up unexplored paradigms in knowledge processing by harvesting existing analysis-based simulators to ease the knowledge acquisition bottleneck. This methodology shows tremendous promise for solving a wide variety of problems in engineering decision making.

Acknowledgments

This work was begun while R. Bharat Rao was at the University of Illinois at Urbana-Champaign (UIUC) and was partially supported by the Department of Electrical Engineering. We are grateful to Sudhakar Yerramareddy, Allen Herman, and Prof. Dennis Assanis, all from the Department of Mechanical Engineering, UIUC.

References

Assanis, D.N. and Heywood, J.B. 1986. *The Adiabatic Engine: Global Developments*. 95–120.

Dixon, J.R. 1986. Artificial intelligence and design: A mechanical engineers view. In *AAAI-86*. 872–877.

Finger, S. and Dixon, J.R. 1989. A review of research in mechanical engineering design. part i: Descriptive, prescriptive, and computer-based models of design processes. *Research in Engineering Design* 1(1):51–67.

Friedman, J.H. 1991. Multivariate adaptive regression splines. *Annals of Statistics*.

Herman, A. E. 1989. An artificial intelligence based modeling environment for engineering problem solving. Master's thesis, M&IE, University of Illinois, Urbana, IL.

Langley, P.; Simon, H.A.; Bradshaw, G.L.; and Zytkow, J.M. 1987. *Scientific Discovery: Computational Explorations of the Creative Processes*. MIT Press.

Quinlan, J.R. 1986. Induction of decision trees. *Machine Learning* 1(1):81–106.

Rao, R. B. 1993. *Inverse Engineering: A Machine Learning Approach to Support Engineering Synthesis*. Ph.D. Dissertation, ECE, University of Illinois, Urbana.

Rao, R. B. and Lu, S. C-Y. 1992. Learning engineering models with the minimum description length principle. In *AAAI-92*. 717–722.

Rao, R. B. and Lu, S. C-Y. 1993. KEDS: A Knowledge-based Equation Discovery System for learning in engineering domains. *IEEE Expert* (to appear).

Rissanen, J. 1986. Stochastic complexity and modeling. *Annals of Statistics* 14(3):1080–1100.

Vanderplaats, G. N. 1984. *Numerical Optimization Techniques for Engineering Design - With Applications*. McGraw-Hill.

Yerramareddy, S. and Lu, S.C-Y. 1993. Hierarchical and interactive decision refinement methodology for engineering design. *Research in Engineering Design* (to appear).

A Conversational Model of Multimodal Interaction in Information Systems

Adelheit Stein, Ulrich Thiel

German National Research Center for Computer Science
Integrated Publication and Information Systems Institute (GMD-IPSI)
Dolivostrasse 15, 6100 Darmstadt, Germany
Email: {stein, thiel}@darmstadt.gmd.de

Abstract

We propose a comprehensive framework for modeling and specifying multimodal interactions. To this end, we employ an extended notion of 'dialogue acts' which can be realized by linguistic and non-linguistic means. First, a set of constraints is presented that describes the temporal structure and all patterns of exchange during a cooperative information-seeking dialogue. Second, we introduce a strategic level of description which allows the specification of the topical structure according to an information-seeking strategy. The model was used to design and implement the MERIT system, and led to a reduction in the complexity of the user interface while preserving most of the useful, but sometimes confusing, dialogue options of advanced direct manipulation interfaces.

Introduction

Multimodal user interfaces of contemporary information systems use various means of conveying information, e.g. text, graphics, forms, tables, and pictures. If the presented information items become complex, in most systems users are allowed to investigate the items directly. Thus, the distance between the users' intentions and the objects is reduced to a minimum (cf. Hutchins, Hollan & Norman 1986).

However, this exploratory approach to information retrieval has to overcome the problems arising from browsing in a large information space. These difficulties, which are well known in hypertext applications, can be attacked by combining the direct manipulation of objects by the user with cooperative system responses. To date, cooperation has mostly been investigated in the context of natural language interfaces which regard user-machine interaction as a dialogue between two partners. As this notion is often referred to as the *conversation metaphor* (cf. Reichman 1986, 1989), the proposed hybrid interaction style, which integrates graphical and natural language components in a multimedial environment, will be called *multimodal conversation* in the following.

In this paper, we will introduce a comprehensive model of multimodal conversations. The next section outlines the notion of multimodal dialogue acts, whereas in the third section the constraints that govern the structure of a cooperative multimodal dialogue are discussed. In the fourth section, we present an overview of the prototypical information system MERIT, which was designed and implemented as an application of the conversational model. Some of the benefits of this approach are sketched in the concluding part of the paper.

The Notion of Multimodal Dialogue Acts

In the conversational approach, user inputs such as mouse clicks, menu selections, etc. are not interpreted as invocations of methods that are executed independent of the dialogue context. Instead, the direct manipulation of an object is considered to be a *dialogue act* expressing a discourse goal of the user. Therefore, the system can respond in a more flexible way by taking into account the illocutionary and semantic aspects of the user's input. Additionally, this approach to human-computer interaction provides a basis for the integration of different interaction styles, such as natural language and graphics, in a multimodal information system (cf. e.g. Arens & Hovy 1990, Feiner & McKeown 1990, Maybury 1991, Oei et al. 1992).

Based on a representation of the dialogue history, *dialogue acts* of the user, which are performed by directly manipulating the display structure, can be identified. For this reason, the user's manipulations (e.g. mouse clicks) are not only executed as methods sent to the graphical surface objects, but they affect transformations of the underlying internal representation of the ongoing dialogue.

The reactions of the system are instances of generic dialogue acts like 'inform', 'offer', or 'reject', which are modeled as frames. Since we use an object-oriented presentation style, a system's dialogue act is performed by creating or changing *informational objects*. An informational object represents a fragment extracted from the underlying database together with a specification of its graphical and/or textual presentation. In general, the system responds by visualization of new graphical objects on the screen in combination with the generation and presentation of a 'comment' in natural language.

Structure of Multimodal Dialogues

While the notion of dialogue acts captures the essence of single contributions to a multimodal interaction, a conversational model has also to address the problem of combining these actions to coherent sequences. Our approach takes local as well as global patterns of dialogues into account. The local structures are governed by the interrelations of *dialogue roles* and *tactics* of the information seeker and the information provider, and described by a complex network of interrelated generic dialogue acts. The global aspect relates the sequence of dialogue contributions to *information-seeking strategies*.

Thus, a system is able to plan the content of subsequent dialogue steps according to principles of topical coherency.

The Conversational Roles Network

A formal schema of information-seeking dialogues allows dialogues to be modeled at the discourse act level or – in terms of Speech Act Theory – the illocutionary level (cf. Searle & Vanderveken 1985).

In order to capture the temporal structure of the dialogue, we introduce the notion of *dialogue states*. During a dialogue, the dialogue acts performed by the dialogue partners change the dialogue state. Since there may be several possible continuations, our model for possible dialogues resembles a network, whereas each actual dialogue is represented as a sequence of singular acts. The network we developed for our problem domain of information-seeking dialogues is called COR (modeling "<u>C</u>onversational <u>R</u>oles"). For a detailed description of the formalism and the theoretical framework we refer to Sitter & Stein (1992), and Maier & Sitter (1992).

COR can be regarded as a recursive state-transition network like the "Conversation for Action Model" of Winograd and Flores (1986). In addition, our model for information-seeking processes adopts some concepts from Systemic Linguistic approaches to discourse modeling (cf. Fawcett et al. 1988, Halliday 1984) and Rhetorical Structure Theory (Mann & Thompson 1987). Basically, the COR network defines the generic dialogue acts available (e.g. asking, offering, promising, answering, evaluating), their possible interrelations, and the mutual role-changes of speaker and addressee.

Figure 1 shows the basic schema of COR: the circles represent *states* on the top-level of the dialogue, the squares terminal states. Arrows represent transitions between two states, i.e. the *dialogue contributions*. Parameter A refers to the in-

formation seeker, B to the information provider. The order of the parameters indicates the speaker - hearer roles; the first parameter indicates the speaker, the second the addressee.

Note, *first*, that the dialogue contributions (transitions) are themselves transition networks which may contain sub-dialogues of the type of the basic schema. We distinguish between two types of networks of dialogue contributions (cf. fig. 2 and fig. 3) which are described below. *Second*, one should keep in mind that in COR all dialogue contributions – except the inform contribution – can be 'implicit', i.e. they may be omitted (a 'jump') when the implicit intention can be inferred from the current context.

The bold arrows between the states <1> and <5> represent two 'idealized' straightforward courses of a dialogue:

- A utters a request for information, B promises to look it up (possibly skips the promise) and presents the information, A is satisfied and finishes the dialogue.

- B offers to provide some information (anticipating an information need of A), A accepts the offer (or part of it), B provides the information, A finishes the dialogue.

However, such simple courses of actions are very rare in more problematic situations. Participants often depart from such a straight course, and perceive their departure as quite natural. Information-seeking dialogues are also highly structured and normally contain a lot of corrections and clarification sequences. The interactions of the participants build a complex net of mutually related commitments and "role expectations" (cf. e.g. Halliday 1984). Simple question-answer dialogue models (like those applied in most of the classical interfaces to information systems) cannot cover this complexity.

Instead, we need a description of a flexible interaction which allows both dialogue partners to correct, withdraw, or confirm their intentions, and to insert clarifying sub-dialogues. To this end, we invented several transitions for with-

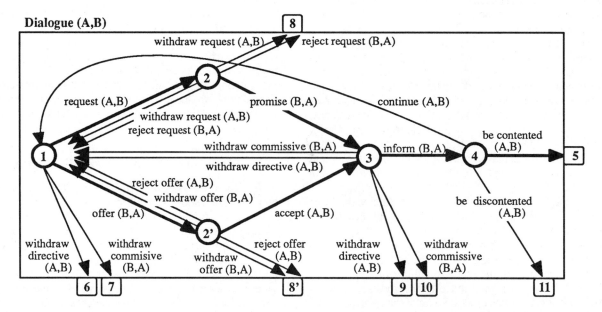

Figure 1: The basic COR 'dialogue' schema

directives: request, accept; *commissives:* offer, promise

drawing or rejecting a contribution. In every dialogue state <from 2 to 4>, A and B may return either to state <1>, thus preparing a new dialogue *cycle*, or they may quit the current dialogue (states <5-11>).

The embedding of clarifying sub-dialogues is described by the two networks below:

Figure 2 displays the schema for the 'inform' contribution, i.e. the transition between <3> and <4> in the basic dialogue network. A more general term is 'assert', indicating an assertion or a statement, but in our context of information-seeking dialogues we use the more specific term.

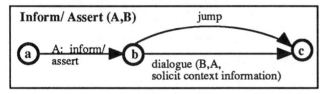

Figure 2: Schema of an 'inform' ('assert') contribution

A starts with an atomic inform (atomic acts are expressed by the notation A: ....). This inform act (its locution) could be quite a long monologue, i.e. a text, or a graphical presentation comprising several propositions. Of course, in that case it would have a semantic sub-structure and consist of several elements, such as sentences. But the illocutionary point would not change, i.e. no new commitments or expectations are expressed or imposed on the addressee. The atomic inform act can either lead directly to state <c> (jump to <c> and at the same time in the dialogue network to <4>). Or B may decide to initiate a sub-dialogue to solicit more context information about A's inform act, e.g. asking a question related to the inform act. This transition between <b> and <c> is a traversal of a basic dialogue network.

The network in figure 3 is more complex. All dialogue contributions, except 'inform', follow this pattern. When A intends, for instance, to make a request, she can follow one of the two possible paths: <a-b-c> or <a-b'-c>. On the first path A formulates the request and either 'jumps' to <c>, or appends an 'assert' (network of fig. 2), supplying voluntarily some context information related to the request. If this con-

text information is not given by A, B might decide to start a sub-dialogue to solicit such context information, e.g. asking for details, or the background of the request. The other path is similar, but with a revised order. After an assert of A supplying some context information about the intended request (or jump), she can either formulate the request now explicitly, but also skip it (jump). The latter would create the situation of an indirect request which is reminiscent of the term "indirect speech act" coined in Speech Act Theory (cf. Searle 1975). A simple example is: A: *"I don't know much about this RACE funding program."* Even if A does not then ask directly *"What is it about?"*, B might infer that A has expressed an indirect request by the first statement.

We distinguish between two main types of components within these dialogue contribution networks (cf. in detail Sitter & Stein 1992). The first expresses the function (illocutionary point) of the whole dialogue contribution. This is normally an atomic dialogue act, e.g. the request or inform act in our example. The second serves for exchanging additional context information which is either supplied voluntarily (assert contributions) or requested in a sub-dialogue.

Using the terminology of Rhetorical Structure Theory – RST (cf. Mann & Thompson 1987) we call a component of the first type a "nucleus" and a component of the second type a "satellite". Both, nucleus and satellite, are related to one another by rhetorical or semantic relations. The set of relations described by RST was developed for the analysis of written texts, i.e. monologues, and has been extended in other approaches in the field of Computational Linguistics (overview in: Maier & Hovy 1993). However, there exist some recent attempts to combine research done in the text-linguistic field with dialogue modeling approaches (cf. Maier & Sitter 1992, Fawcett & Davis 1992). Maier and Sitter, for instance, extended the set of necessary relations, especially "interpersonal relations", for the dialogue situation and combined it with the COR approach. This proved to be very useful in our context of human-computer retrieval dialogues, because their specifications can be directly integrated in our application, the MERIT system.

Modeling Information-Seeking Plans

The COR network covers the illocutionary structure of dialogues, but does not supply means for a specification on the thematic level. Since the thematic level governs the selection of the contents communicated in the dialogue acts, it plays an essential role in dialogue planning. If we want the system to engage in a meaningful cooperative interaction with the user, we have to address this question by supplying a prescriptive addition to the – thus far descriptive – dialogue model. We perceive actual dialogues as instantiations of more abstract entities, each of which represents a class of concrete dialogues. This is similar to approaches to the generation of multimodal utterances using plan operators (e.g. Maybury 1991, Rist & André 1992). However, the abstract representations of dialogue classes are more complex. The classes comprise dialogues that show a similar basic pattern. Usually these patterns are closely related to certain strategies which are pursued by the user during her interaction. In the case of information systems, Belkin, Marchetti, and Cool

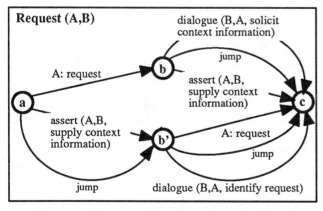

Figure 3: Schema of a 'request' contribution

(1993) suggested a classification of dialogues with respect to information-seeking strategies. Based on this approach, we developed a set of typical dialogue plans or "scripts" (cf. Schank & Abelson 1977) for a given domain and task (cf. Belkin, Cool, Stein & Thiel 1993). A collection of dialogue plans is the basis for selecting an appropriate plan for a given information need. Once a plan has been chosen, it provides suggestions to the user on how to continue in a given dialogue situation, and specifies cooperative system reactions.

On the implementation level, we represent dialogues as sequences of *dialogue steps*. The internal structure of a dialogue step is given by two parameters: the *perspective* of the step, and its *implementation*. The perspective determines the topical spectrum that can be addressed in this step without destroying the thematical coherence of the dialogue in general. Similar notions have been proposed by McCoy (1986) in the area of natural language interfaces and Reichman (1986) who takes a discourse analysis approach to multimodal dialogues. The second component of a step describes the possible and actual ways to implement the corresponding dialogue step. It may be implemented by a single dialogue act. In this case the variety is provided by the different forms the utterance may have. For instance, the presentation of a certain set of data may take the form of a list of the data records, a table, or a graphical presentation. However, the step may also be a certain sequence of dialogue acts which then build a sub-dialogue that may – in accordance with the COR model – replace the single act. Thus, we have a means to prescribe a certain act as appropriate in the given situation, which allows the user to perform it in a way she prefers, e.g. by requesting context or help information.

An approach to problem solving based on past experiences is pursued in the area of case-based reasoning (CBR). In our experimental work, we adapted the ideas of CBR to the requirements of a user-guidance component (for details cf. Tißen 1991, 1993, Stein, Thiel & Tißen 1992) which was developed as part of a prototypical information system.

An Application – the MERIT System

MERIT (Multimedia Extensions of Retrieval Interaction Tools) is a prototypical knowledge-based user interface to a relational database on European research projects and their funding programs (cf. Stein, Thiel & Tißen 1992). The database contains textual and factual information (a subset of the CORDIS databases which are offered online by the ECHO host). These data were extended by interactive maps and scanned-in documents and pictures the user may request as additional context information in certain situations (cf. for example fig. 5 below). The system features form-based query formulation (various form sheets for different 'perspectives' on the data), and the visualization of retrieval results in different situation-dependent graphical presentation forms. One major system component is a case-based dialogue manager (CADI, cf. Tißen 1991) which controls the retrieval dialogue and provides a library of "cases" stored after previous sessions with MERIT. The cases are used to guide the user through the current session, proposing thematic progression basically by suggesting a specific order of query and result steps focusing on a specific perspective in each step.

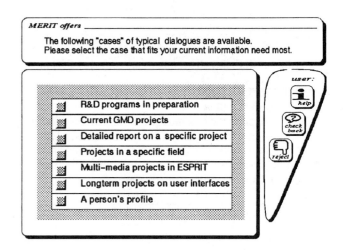

Figure 4: A system's 'offer'

The example in figure 4 shows an offer made at the beginning of a dialogue session. Here the user is asked to choose the case that suits her information need best. The graphical presentation of complex dialogue contributions – like offers, requests, inform acts – is composed of several distinct elements: the label in the upper left corner identifies the contributor and dialogue act type (e.g. "MERIT offers", "user requests", "MERIT presents"). A short text, mostly elliptic, summarizes the content of the dialogue act or gives some meta-information ("Please select ..."). Further, the concrete proposition is displayed below (here in the form of several alternatives among which the user may choose). The right bar is reserved for icons representing possible (local) user actions that refer to the current system's contribution. The user may, for instance, *reject* the offer, *request help*, or pose clarifying questions (*checkback-icon*).

A Coherent Interaction Model of MERIT

Like most advanced graphical interfaces, MERIT offers a wide variety of dialogue control options to the user (cf. icons in fig. 4 and fig. 5). In a given situation, the user may proceed in the current case, start sub-dialogues within the current step, switch to another case, etc. Usually, in conventional interfaces dialogue options are presented to the user as additional components of the interface. However, such additions are disturbing in a direct manipulation interface, since they require context-dependent method evaluation.

In the following, we outline how our conversational model allows us to integrate even complex meta-dialogic options into a coherent interpretation of the multimodal interaction.

Local, i.e. case- or situation-dependent, options are:

help, check back: From the conversational perspective the user engages in a sub-dialogue related to the system's current dialogue contribution (soliciting context information). Thus, the parameter setting of the meta-function is determined in a natural way.

reject offer, withdraw ..., continue: The meaning of these icons is intuitively grasped. They comply with transitions in the basic COR schema (cf. fig. 1). For instance, 'continue' would lead to state <1>, whereupon the user either formu-

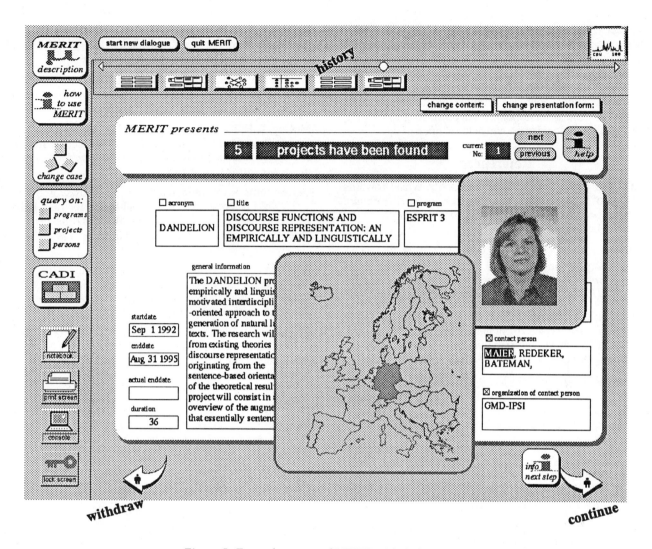

Figure 5: Example screen of MERIT with dialogue control objects

lates a new request (a query), or the system comes up with a new offer and/or information (presentation of data).

change content/ presentation: Here the user can enter a sub-dialogue related to the system's inform act and request a paraphrase and/or solicit context information (cf. fig. 2). The available options in a given dialogue state are, for instance, to ask for more detailed information about the currently presented items, to restrict the presentation to a subset of objects and attributes, or simply to replace a given presentation form by another one (e.g. a table by a graph).

The following actions are interpreted as user requests that initiate inserted meta-dialogues:

info on next step: Before the user decides whether to continue she may click on this icon and start a meta-dialogue about the system's strategy. MERIT generates situation-dependent information (a text), describing the next and subsequent steps proposed in this situation by the current case.

history: By clicking one of the history icons the user starts a short meta-dialogue referring to inform or query states of previous dialogue cycles. The respective information (her

query or the retrieved data) will be displayed. The user can then compare it to the current state and decide whether to return to the current state or to go back in the history.

query on ...: At any time the user has the opportunity to insert a short retrieval dialogue. She can pose a query and inspect the retrieved data, then return to the current path/ case.

change case: The user finishes her current path, returns to the top-level dialogue (state <1>) and initiates a new dialogue cycle to choose a new case.

Conclusions

The outlined comprehensive model of multimodal interaction is based on an extended notion of *dialogue acts* which can be realized by linguistic or non-linguistic means. The structure of multimodal interaction is considered under local as well as global aspects. A comprehensive set of constraints in terms of a recursive transition network describes all (local) patterns of exchange which can occur during interaction. The (global) topical structure of the dialogue is defined according to a selected information seeking strategy. The model was applied to design and implement the MERIT system, and led to a reduction of the complexity of the user interface while preserving most of the useful, but sometimes confusing, dialogue options of advanced direct manipulation interfaces. The conversational approach permits dialogue features to be handled in an *integrative manner*, but not as separated extensions such as undo, history, and help functions.

References

Arens, Y. & Hovy, E. 1990. How to Describe What? Towards a Theory of Modality Utilization. In: *Proc. of the 12th Annual Conference of the Cognitive Science Society*, 487-494. Hillsdale, NJ: Erlbaum.

Belkin, N.J., Cool, C., Stein, A. & Thiel, U. 1993. Scripts for Information Seeking Strategies. Paper presented at: *AAAI Spring Symposium '93 on Case-Based Reasoning and Information Retrieval, Stanford University, CA, March 23-25.*

Belkin, N.J., Marchetti, P.G. & Cool, C. 1993. BRAQUE: Design of an Interface to Support User Interaction in Information Retrieval. *Information Processing & Management. Special Issue on Hypertext* 29(4) (in press).

Fawcett, R.P., van der Mije, A. & van Wissen, C. 1988. Towards a Systemic Flowchart Model for Discourse. In: Fawcett, R.P. & Young, D. (eds.): *New Developments in Systemic Linguistics. Vol. 2*, 116-143. London: Pinter.

Fawcett, R.P. & Davies, B. 1992. Monologue as Turn in Interactive Discourse: Towards an Integration of Exchange Structure and Rhetorical Structure Theory. In: *Proc. of the 6th International Workshop on Natural Language Generation, Trento, Italy*, 151-166. Berlin: Springer.

Feiner, S.K. & McKeown, K.R. 1990. Coordinating Text and Graphics in Explanation Generation. In: *Proc. of the 8th National Conference on Artificial Intelligence, Vol. I*, 442-449. Menlo Park: AAAI Press / MIT Press.

Halliday, M.A.K. 1984. Language as Code and Language as Behaviour: A Systemic-Functional Interpretation of the Nature and Ontogenesis of Dialogue. In: Fawcett, R.P. et al. (eds.): *The Semiotic of Culture and Language. Vol. 1*, 3-35. London: Pinter.

Hutchins, E.L., Hollan, J.D. & Norman, D. 1986. Direct Manipulation Interfaces. In: Norman, D.A. & Draper, S.A. (eds.): *User Centered System Design: New Perspectives on Human-Computer Interaction*, 87-124. Hillsdale, NJ: Erlbaum.

Maier, E. & Hovy, E. 1993. Organising Discourse Structure Relations Using Metafunctions. In: Horacek, H. & Zock, M. (eds.): *New Concepts in Natural Language Processing*, 69-86. London: Pinter.

Maier, E. & Sitter, S. 1992. An Extension of Rhetorical Structure Theory for the Treatment of Retrieval Dialogues. In: *Proc. of the 14th Annual Conference of the Cognitive Science Society, Bloomington, Indiana*, 968-973. Hillsdale, NJ: Erlbaum.

Mann, W.C. & Thompson, S.A. 1987. Rhetorical Structure Theory: A Theory of Text Organization. In: Polanyi, L. (ed.): *Discourse Structure*. Norwood, NJ: Ablex.

Maybury, M. 1991. Planning Multimedia Explanations Using Communicative Acts. In: *Proc. of the 9th National Conference on Artificial Intelligence, Anaheim, CA.*

McCoy, K.F. 1986. The ROMPER System: Responding to Object-Related Misconceptions Using Perspective. In: *Proc. of the 24th Annual Meeting of the Association for Computational Linguistics, New York.*

Oei, S., Smit, R., Schreinemakers, J., Marinos, L. & Sirks, J. 1992. The Presentation Manager, A Method for Task-Driven Concept Presentation. In: Neumann, B. (ed.): *Proc. of the European Conference on Artificial Intelligence*, 774-775. Chichester: John Wiley.

Reichman, R. 1986. Communication Paradigms for a Window System. In: Norman, D.A. & Draper, S.A. (eds.): *User Centered System Design: New Perspectives on Human-Computer Interaction*, 285-313. Hillsdale, NJ: Erlbaum.

Reichman, R. 1989. Integrated Interfaces Based on a Theory of Context and Goal Tracking. In: Taylor, M.M., Neel, F. & Bouwhuis, D.G. (eds.): *The Structure of Multimodal Dialogue*, 209-228. Amsterdam: North-Holland.

Rist, T. & André, E. 1992. From Presentation Tasks to Pictures: Towards a Computational Approach to Graphics Design. In: Neumann, B. (ed.): *Proc. of the European Conference on Artificial Intelligence*, 765-768. Chichester: John Wiley.

Schank, R. & Abelson, R. 1977. *Scripts, Plans, Goals and Understanding*. Hillsdale, NJ: Erlbaum.

Searle, J.R. 1975. Indirect Speech Acts. In: Davidson, D. & Harman, G. (eds.): *The Logic of Grammar*, 59-82. Encino, CA: Dickinson Publishing Co.

Searle, J.R. & Vanderveken, D. 1985. *Foundations of Illocutionary Logic*. Cambridge, GB: Cambridge University Press.

Sitter, S. & Stein, A. 1992. Modeling the Illocutionary Aspects of Information-Seeking Dialogues. *Information Processing & Management* 28(2):165-180.

Stein, A., Thiel, U. & Tißen, A. 1992. Knowledge-Based Control of Visual Dialogues in Information Systems. In: Catarci, T., Costabile, M.F. & Levialdi, S. (eds.): *Proc. of the 1st International Workshop on Advanced Visual Interfaces, Rome, Italy*, 138-155. Singapore: World Scientific Press.

Tißen, A. 1991. A Case-Based Architecture for a Dialogue Manager for Information-Seeking Processes. In: A. Bookstein et al. (eds.): *Proc. of the 14th Annual International Conference on Research and Development in Information Retrieval, Chicago*, 152-161. New York: ACM Press.

Tißen, A. 1993. Knowledge Bases for User Guidance in Information Seeking Dialogues. In: Wayne, D.G. et al. (eds.): *Proc. of the 1993 International Workshop on Intelligent User Interfaces, Orlando, FL*, 149-156. New York: ACM Press.

Winograd, T. & Flores, F. 1986. *Understanding Computers and Cognition*. Norwood, NJ: Ablex.

Large Scale
Knowledge Bases

Matching 100,000 Learned Rules

Robert B. Doorenbos

School of Computer Science
Carnegie Mellon University
Pittsburgh, PA 15213-3891
Robert.Doorenbos@CS.CMU.EDU

Abstract

This paper examines several systems which learn a large number of rules (productions), including one which learns 113,938 rules — the largest number ever learned by an AI system, and the largest number in any production system in existence. It is important to match these rules efficiently, in order to avoid the machine learning *utility problem*. Moreover, examination of such large systems reveals new phenomena and calls into question some common assumptions based on previous observations of smaller systems. We first show that the Rete and Treat match algorithms do not scale well with the number of rules in our systems, in part because the number of rules affected by a change to working memory increases with the total number of rules in these systems. We also show that the sharing of nodes in the beta part of the Rete network becomes more and more important as the number of rules increases. Finally, we describe and evaluate a new optimization for Rete which improves its scalability and allows two of our systems to learn over 100,000 rules without significant performance degradation.[1]

1. Introduction

The goal of this research is to support large learned production systems; i.e., systems that learn a large number of rules. Examination of such systems reveals new phenomena and calls into question some common assumptions based on previous observations of smaller systems. In large systems it is crucial that we match the rules efficiently; otherwise the systems will be very slow. In particular, we don't want the match cost to increase significantly as new rules are learned. Such an increase is one cause of the *utility problem* in machine learning (Minton, 1988) — if the learned rules slow down the matcher, the net effect of learning can be to slow down the whole system, rather than speed it up. For example, learned rules may reduce the number of basic steps a system takes to solve problems (e.g., by pruning the

search space), but the slowdown in the matcher increases the time per step, and this can outweigh the reduction in the number of steps. This has been observed in several machine learning systems (Minton, 1988; Etzioni, 1990; Tambe, Newell, & Rosenbloom, 1990; Cohen, 1990; Gratch & DeJong, 1992).

This paper examines several systems which learn a large number of rules, including one which learns 113,938 rules — the largest number ever learned by an AI system, and the largest number in any production system in existence. Recent work on large production systems has investigated their integration with databases (Sellis, Lin, & Raschid, 1988; Acharya & Tambe, 1992; Miranker et al., 1990). Much of this work is aimed at scaling up production systems to have large working memories, but only a relatively small number of rules. Scalability along the dimension of the number of rules, on the other hand, has been largely neglected. This dimension is of interest for machine learning systems, as noted above; it is also of interest for another class of production systems: those used for cognitive models. In such systems, the productions model human long-term memory. Since the capacity of human long-term memory is vast, production systems used for cognitive models may require a very large number of rules.

(Doorenbos, Tambe, & Newell, 1992) examined various aspects of a single system, Dispatcher-Soar, which learned 10,000 rules; no increase in match cost was observed. The current paper focuses entirely on matching, and studies three other systems in addition to Dispatcher-Soar; the four systems learn 35,000-100,000 rules. We begin by showing that the best currently available match algorithms, Rete (Forgy, 1982) and Treat (Miranker, 1990), do not scale well with the number of rules. Section 2 shows that using the standard Rete algorithm, all these systems suffer a substantial increase in match cost. This was previously overlooked in Dispatcher-Soar due to the smaller number of rules learned and the way match cost was measured.

Previous studies of smaller production systems suggest that Rete and Treat *should* scale well with the number of rules, because only a few rules are affected by changes to working memory, no matter how many rules are in the system. Section 3 shows that this does not hold in any of the four systems studied here. Since the work done by the

---

[1]The research was sponsored by the Avionics Laboratory, Wright Research and Development Center Aeronautical Systems Division (AFSC), U. S. Air Force, Wright-Patterson AFB, OH 45433-6543 under Contract F33615-90-C-1465, ARPA Order No. 7597, and by the National Science Foundation under a graduate fellowship award. The views and conclusions contained in this document are those of the authors and should not be interpreted as representing the official policies, either expressed or implied, of the Defense Advanced Research Projects Agency or the U.S. government.

Treat algorithm is at least linear in the number of affected productions, we conclude that Treat would not scale well with the number of rules in these systems. We suggest reasons for this difference in the number of affected productions, and note its possible implications for parallel production systems.

In Section 4, we examine the sharing of nodes in the beta part of the Rete network and show that it becomes increasingly important as the number of rules increases. This sharing has previously been considered relatively unimportant, and some match algorithms have been designed without incorporating it. Our results here demonstrate that for certain classes of large learning systems, efficient match algorithms must incorporate sharing.

Finally, we show that the scalability of the Rete algorithm can be improved by applying a new optimization, *right unlinking*, which eliminates one source of slowdown in the match as the number of rules increases. Section 5 describes and evaluates this optimization, which can improve the scalability of Rete and reduce the match cost by a factor of ~40. In Section 6, we suggest ways to reduce or eliminate other sources as well.

The results in this paper concern several large learning systems, each implemented using Soar (Laird, Newell, & Rosenbloom, 1987; Rosenbloom et al., 1991). Soar provides a useful vehicle for this research because in addition to providing a mechanism for learning new rules (*chunking*), it incorporates one of the best existing match algorithms (Rete). Soar is an integrated problem-solving and learning system based on formulating every task as search in *problem spaces*. Each step in this search — the selection of problem spaces, states and operators, plus the immediate application of operators to states to generate new states — is a *decision cycle*. The knowledge necessary to execute a decision cycle is obtained from Soar's knowledge base, implemented as a production system. If this knowledge is insufficient to reach a decision, Soar makes use of recursive problem-space search in subgoals to obtain more knowledge. Soar learns by converting this subgoal-based search into *chunks*, productions that immediately produce comparable results under analogous conditions (Laird, Rosenbloom, & Newell, 1986).

Four large learning systems are examined in this paper. The first system, Dispatcher-Soar (Doorenbos, Tambe, & Newell, 1992), is a message dispatcher for a large organization; it makes queries to an external database containing information about the people in the organization. It uses twenty problem spaces, begins with ~1,800 rules, and learns ~114,000 more rules. The second system, Assembler-Soar (Mertz, 1992) is a cognitive model of a person assembling printed circuit boards. It is smaller than Dispatcher-Soar, using six problem spaces, starting with ~300 rules and learning ~35,000 more. Neither of these systems was designed with these experiments in mind. In addition to these two

"natural" systems, two very simple "artificial" systems, Memory1 and Memory2, were built for these experiments. They each use two problem spaces (the minimum necessary for learning in Soar) and are based on the memorization technique described in (Rosenbloom & Aasman, 1990); they differ in the structure of the objects being memorized, with the learned rules in Memory1 more closely resembling some of those learned in Dispatcher-Soar, and those in Memory2 resembling Assembler-Soar. The two systems learned ~102,000 rules and ~60,000 rules, respectively. For each system, a problem-generator was used to create a set of problem instances in the system's domain. The system was then allowed to solve the sequence of problems, learning new rules as it went along.

2. Performance of Standard Rete

Before presenting performance results, we briefly review the Rete algorithm. As illustrated in Figure 1, Rete uses a dataflow network to represent the conditions of the productions. The network has two parts. The alpha part performs the constant tests on working memory elements; its output is stored in *alpha memories* (AM), each of which holds the current set of working memory elements passing all the constant tests of an individual condition. The beta part of the network contains *join nodes*, which perform the tests for consistent variable bindings between conditions, and *beta memories*, which store partial instantiations of productions (sometimes called *tokens*). When working memory changes, the network is updated as follows: the changes are sent through the alpha network and the appropriate alpha memories are updated. These updates are then propagated over to the attached join nodes (*activating* those nodes). If any new partial instantiations are created, they are propagated down the beta part of the network (activating other nodes). Whenever the propagation reaches the bottom of the network, it indicates that a production's conditions are completely matched.

The figure is drawn so as to emphasize the *sharing* of nodes between productions. This is because our focus here is on matching a large number of productions, not just a few, and in this case the sharing becomes important, as we demonstrate in Section 4. When two or more productions have a common prefix, they both use the same network nodes. Due to sharing, the beta part of the network shown in Figure 1 forms a tree. (In general, it would form a forest, but by adding a dummy node to the top of a forest, we obtain a tree.)

The figure also omits the details of the alpha part of the network (except for the alpha memories). In this paper we focus only on the beta part of the network. Previous studies have shown that the beta part accounts for most of the match cost (Gupta, 1987), and this holds for the systems examined here as well.

Figure 2 shows the performance of the basic Rete algorithm on our systems. For each system, it plots the average match cost per decision cycle as a function of the

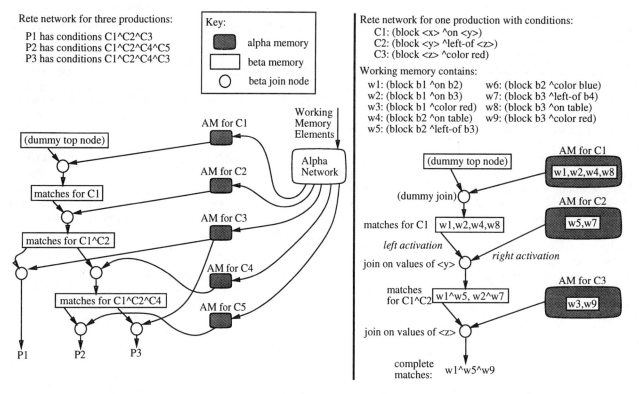

Figure 1: Rete network for several productions (left) and instantiated network for one production (right).

number of rules in the system.[2] It clearly demonstrates that as more and more rules are learned, the match cost increases significantly in all four systems. Thus, the standard Rete algorithm does not scale well with the number of learned rules.

3. Affect Set Size

The data shown in Figure 2 may come as a surprise to readers familiar with research on parallelism in production systems. This research has suggested that the match cost of a production system is limited, *independent* of the number of rules. This stems from several studies of OPS5 (Forgy, 1981) systems in which it was observed that only a few productions (20-30 on the average) were affected by a change to working memory (Oflazer, 1984; Gupta, 1987). A production is *affected* if the new working memory element matches (the constant tests of) one of its conditions. This small *affect set size* was observed in systems ranging from ~100 to ~1000 productions. Thus, the match effort is limited to those few productions, regardless of the number of productions in the whole system.

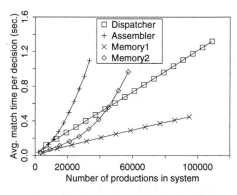

Figure 2: Match time with standard Rete.

This result does not hold for the systems we have studied. Figure 3 shows a lower bound[3] on the number of productions affected per match cycle (recognize-act cycle) for the four systems, plotted as a function of the number of productions. Each point on the figure is the mean taken over 100,000 match cycles. (Recall that the

---

[2]The *decision cycle* is the natural unit of measurement in Soar; each decision cycle is a sequence of a few match cycles (recognize-act cycles). The numbers reported here are based on Soar version 6.0, implemented in C, running on a DECstation 5000/200. The Rete implementation uses hashed alpha and beta memories (Gupta, 1987); the alpha part of the network is implemented using extensive hashing so that it runs in approximately constant time per working memory change.

[3]The graph shows that the lower bound is linearly increasing. An upper bound on the affect set size is the total number of productions, which of course is also linearly increasing. Measuring the *exact* affect set size is computationally expensive, but since both the lower bound and upper bound are linearly increasing, one can assume the actual mean affect set size is linearly increasing also — if it weren't, it would eventually either drop below the (linearly increasing) lower bound, or else rise above the (linearly increasing) upper bound.

number of productions is gradually increasing as the system learns. The exact affect set size varies greatly from one cycle to the next.) In each system, the average affect set size increases fairly linearly with the number of productions. Moreover, each system grows to where the average affect set size is ~10,000 productions — considerably more than the total number of productions any of them started with.

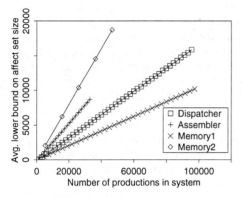

Figure 3: Affect set size.

Why does the affect set size increase in these systems but not in the aforementioned OPS5 systems? (Gupta, 1987) speculates: "The number of rules associated with any specific object-type or any situation is expected to be small (McDermott, 1983). Since most working-memory elements describe aspects of only a single object or situation, then clearly most working-memory elements cannot be of interest to more than a few of the rules." While this reasoning may hold for many OPS5 systems, it does not hold for systems that extensively use problem space search. In such systems, a few working memory elements indicate the active goal, state (or search node), and operator; these working memory elements are likely to be of interest to many rules. In the Soar systems studied here, many rules have the same first few conditions, which test aspects of the current goal, problem space, state, or operator. This same property appears to hold in Prodigy, another search-oriented problem-solving and learning system, for the rules learned by Prodigy/EBL (Minton, 1988). Whenever a working memory element matching one of these first few conditions changes, a large number of rules are affected. More generally, if a system uses a few general working memory elements to indicate the current problem-solving context, then they may be of interest to a large number of rules, so the system may have large affect sets.

(Gupta, 1987) also speculates that the limited affect set size observed in OPS5 programs may be due to particular characteristics of human programmers; but these need not be shared by machine learning programs. For example, people often hierarchically decompose problems into smaller subproblems, then write a few rules to solve each lowest-level subproblem. Consequently, the few working memory elements relevant to a given subproblem affect only those few rules used to solve it. However, if we add a knowledge compilation mechanism to such a program, it may generate rules that act as "macros," solving many subproblems at once. This would tend to increase the number of rules in the system affected by those working memory elements: they would now affect both the original rules and the new macro-rules.

More work needs to be done to better understand the causes of a large affect set size. However, the above arguments suggest that this phenomenon is likely to arise in a large class of systems, not just these particular Soar systems.

Note that a limited affect set size is considered one of the main reasons that parallel implementations of production systems yield only a limited speedup (Gupta, 1987). The results here suggest that parallelism might give greater speedups for these systems. However, if sequential algorithms can be optimized to perform well in spite of the large number of affected productions, then speedup from parallelism will remain limited. So the implications of these results for parallelism are unclear.

4. The Importance of Sharing

Given the increase in the number of productions affected by changes to working memory, how can we avoid a slowdown in the matcher? One partial solution can already be found in the existing Rete algorithm. When two or more productions have the same first few conditions, the same parts of the Rete network are used to match those conditions. By *sharing* network nodes among productions in this way, Rete avoids the duplication of match effort across those productions.

In our systems, sharing becomes increasingly important as more rules are learned. Figure 4 shows the factor by which sharing reduces the number of tokens (partial instantiations) generated by the matcher. The y-axis is obtained by taking the number of tokens that would have been generated if sharing were disabled, and dividing it by the number that actually were generated with sharing. The figure displays this ratio as a function of the number of rules in each of the systems. (As mentioned before, we focus on the beta portion of the match — the figure shows the result of sharing in the beta memories and join nodes only, not the alpha part of the network. CPU time measurements would be preferable to token counts, but it would have taken months to run the systems with sharing disabled.) The figure shows that in the Dispatcher and Memory1 systems, sharing accounts for a tremendous reduction in the number of tokens; at the end of their runs, sharing reduces the number of tokens by two and three orders of magnitude, respectively. In the Assembler and Memory2 systems, sharing is not as effective, reducing the number of tokens by factors of 6 and 8, respectively. (In Figure 4, their points are very close to the horizontal axis.)

Why is sharing so important in Dispatcher and Memory1? As mentioned above, in each of these systems, many of the learned rules have their first few

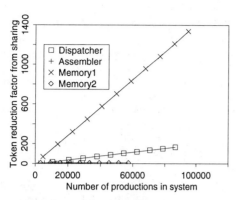

Figure 4: Reduction in tokens due to sharing.

conditions in common. Thus, newly learned rules often share existing parts of the Rete network. In particular, nodes near the top of the network tend to become shared by more and more productions, while nodes near the bottom of the network tend to be unshared (used by only one production) — recall that the beta portion of the network forms a tree. The sharing near the top is crucial in Dispatcher and Memory1 because nodes near the top are activated more often (on average) than nodes near the bottom. Thus, the token counts are dominated by the tokens generated near the top of the network, where sharing increases with the number of rules. In the Assembler and Memory2 systems, however, there is a significant amount of activity in lower parts of the network where nodes are unshared. (The difference is because the lower part of the network forms an effective discrimination tree in one case but not the other.) So sharing is not as effective in Assembler and Memory2. In Section 6, we give ideas for reducing the activity in lower parts of the network. If they prove effective, the activity near the top of the network would again dominate, and sharing would be increasingly important in the Assembler and Memory2 systems as well.

Interestingly, work in production systems has often ignored sharing. Previous measurements on smaller production systems have found sharing of beta nodes to produce only very limited speedup (Gupta, 1987; Miranker, 1990). This is probably due to the limited affect set size in those systems. An important example of the consequences of ignoring sharing can be found in the Treat algorithm. Treat does not incorporate sharing in the beta part of the match, so on each working memory change, it must iterate over all the affected rules. Thus, Treat requires time at least linear in the affect set size. So it would not scale well for the systems examined here — like Rete as shown in Figure 2, it too would slow down at least linearly in the number of rules.

Moreover, work on machine learning systems has also often failed to incorporate sharing into the match process. For example, the match algorithm used by Prodigy (Minton, 1988) treats each rule independently of all the others. As more and more rules are learned, the match cost increases, leading to the utility problem in Prodigy.

Prodigy's approach to this problem is to discard many of the learned rules in order to avoid the match cost. The results above suggest another approach: incorporate sharing (and perhaps other optimizations) into the matcher so as to alleviate the increase in match cost.

5. Right Unlinking

While sharing is effective near the top of the Rete network, it is, of course, uncommon near the bottom, since new productions' conditions match those of existing productions only up to a certain point. (In these systems, it is rare for two productions to have *exactly* the same conditions.) Consequently, as more and more rules are learned, the amount of work done in lower parts of the network increases. This causes an overall slowdown in Rete, as shown in Figure 2. What can be done to alleviate this increase? The match cost (in the beta part of the network) can be divided into three components (see Figure 1): (1) activations of join nodes from their associated alpha memories (henceforth called *right activations*), (2) activations of join nodes from their associated beta memories (henceforth called *left activations*), and (3) activations of beta memory nodes. This section presents an optimization for the Rete algorithm that reduces (1), which turns out to account for almost all of the Rete slowdown in the Dispatcher and Memory1 systems. Some ways to reduce (2) and (3) are discussed in Section 6.

Our optimization is based on the following observation: on a right activation of a join node (due to the addition of a working memory element to its associated alpha memory), if its beta memory is empty then no work need be done. The new working memory element cannot match any items in the beta memory, because there aren't any items there. So if we know in advance that the beta memory is empty, we can skip the right activation of that join node. We refer to right activations of join nodes with empty beta memories as *null right activations*.

We incorporate *right unlinking* into the Rete algorithm as follows: add a counter to every beta memory to indicate how many items it contains; update this counter whenever an item is added to or deleted from the memory. If the counter goes from 1 to 0, *unlink each child join node from its associated alpha memory*. If the counter goes from 0 to 1, *relink each child join node to its associated alpha memory*. On each alpha memory there is a list of associated join nodes; the unlinking is done by splicing entries into and out of this list. So while a join node is unlinked from its alpha memory, it never gets activated by the alpha memory. Note that since the only activations we are skipping are null activations — which would not yield a match anyway — this optimization does not affect the set of complete production matches that will be found.

Figure 5 shows the results of adding right unlinking to Rete. Like Figure 2, it plots the average match time per decision cycle for each of the systems as a function of the number of rules. Note that the scale on the vertical axis is different; all four systems run faster with right unlinking. Figure 6 shows the speedup factors obtained from right unlinking in the systems. (This is the ratio of Figure 2 and Figure 5.)

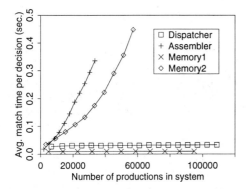

Figure 5: Match cost with right unlinking.

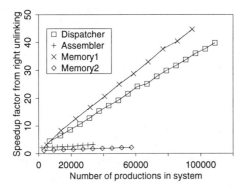

Figure 6: Speedup factors from right unlinking.

Why is this optimization effective? At first glance it seems like a triviality, since it merely avoids null right activations, and a null right activation takes only a handful of CPU cycles. What makes right unlinking so important is that *the number of null right activations per working memory change can grow linearly in the number of rules* — and as the number of rules becomes very large, this can become the dominant factor in the overall match cost in Rete. We first explain why the number of right activations can grow linearly, then explain why almost all of these are null right activations.

Recall from Section 3 that the average affect set size increases with the number of rules. For each affected production, there is some join node that gets right activated. Of course it may be that all the affected productions share this same join node, so that there is only one right activation. But as the beta part of the network forms a tree, sharing is only effective near the top; whenever a new working memory element matches the *later* conditions in many productions, many different join nodes are activated. As an extreme example, consider the case where the last condition is the same in every one of *n* productions. A single alpha memory will

be used for this last condition; but if earlier conditions of the productions differ, the productions cannot share the same join node for the last condition. Thus, the alpha memory will have *n* associated join nodes, and a new match for this last condition will result in *n* right activations. Right unlinking is essentially a way to reduce this potentially large fan-out from alpha memories. Although reordering the conditions would avoid the problem in this particular example, in many cases no such reordering exists.

Now, as more and more rules are learned, the number of join nodes in the lower part of the network increases greatly, since sharing is not very common there. However, at any given time, almost all of them have empty beta memories. This is because usually there is some join node higher up that has no matches — some earlier condition in the rule fails. To see why, consider a rule with conditions $C_1, C_2, \ldots, C_k$, and suppose each C_i has probability p_i of having a match. For the very last join node to have a non-empty beta memory, all the earlier conditions must match; this happens with the relatively low probability $p_1 p_2 \cdots p_{k-1}$. Since most of the lower nodes have empty beta memories at a given time, most right activations of them are in fact null right activations.

In the Dispatcher and Memory1 systems, right unlinking yields a speedup factor of 40-50 when the number of rules is ~100,000. The factor increases with the number of rules. Comparing Figures 2 and 5, we see that right unlinking eliminates almost all of the slowdown in the Dispatcher and Memory1 systems. Thus, the slowdown in the standard Rete for those systems is almost entirely due to increasing null right activations. In the Assembler and Memory2 systems, however, there are additional sources of slowdown in the standard Rete: left and beta memory activations are also increasing. Right unlinking eliminates just one of the sources, so the speedup factors it yields are lower (2-3).

Note that the match cost measurements here are done directly in terms of CPU time. The token or comparison counts commonly used in studies of match algorithms would not reflect the increasing match cost in Rete or Treat, since a null right activation requires no comparisons and generates no new tokens. This prevented (Doorenbos, Tambe, & Newell, 1992) from noticing any increase in match cost in an earlier, shorter run of Dispatcher-Soar. The machine- and implementation-dependent nature of CPU time comparisons is avoided here by running the same implementation (modulo the right unlinking optimization) on the same machine.

6. Conclusions and Future Work

We have shown that the Rete and Treat match algorithms do not scale well with the number of rules in our systems, at least in part because the affect set size increases with the total number of rules. Thus, it is important to reduce the amount of work done by the matcher when the affect set size is large. Both the right unlinking optimization and the sharing of beta nodes can be viewed as members of a family of optimizations that do this. Right unlinking avoids the work for right activations associated with many of the affected rules which cannot match. The sharing of beta nodes allows the matcher to do work once for large groups of affected rules, rather than do work repeatedly for each affected rule.

Another possible optimization in this family is *left unlinking*: whenever a join node's associated alpha memory is empty, the node is unlinked from its associated beta memory. This is just the opposite of right unlinking; while right unlinking reduces the number of right activations by reducing the fan-out from alpha memories, left unlinking would reduce the number of left activations by reducing the fan-out from beta memories. Unfortunately, left and right unlinking cannot simply be combined in the same system: if a node were ever unlinked from both its alpha and beta memories, it would be completely cut off from the rest of the network and would never be activated again, even when it should be.

Another optimization in this family is incorporated in Treat. Treat maintains a *rule-active* flag on each production, indicating whether all of its alpha memories are non-empty. If any alpha memory is empty, the rule cannot match, so Treat does not perform any of the joins for that rule. This essentially reduces the number of left activations and beta memory activations. But since Treat must at least check this flag for each affected rule, the number of right activations remains essentially the same. Right and left activations and beta memory activations together account for the entire beta phase of the match, so this suggests that the slowdown observed in the Assembler and Memory2 systems might be eliminated by some hybrid of Rete (with right unlinking) and Treat, or by adding to Treat an optimization analogous to right unlinking. Of course, much further work is needed to develop and evaluate such match optimizations.

7. Acknowledgements

Thanks to Anurag Acharya, Jill Fain Lehman, Dave McKeown, Paul Rosenbloom, Milind Tambe, and Manuela Veloso for many helpful discussions and comments on drafts of this paper, to the anonymous reviewers for helpful suggestions, and to Joe Mertz for providing the Assembler-Soar system.

8. References

Acharya, A., and Tambe, M. 1992. *Collection-oriented Match: Scaling Up the Data in Production Systems*. Technical Report CMU-CS-92-218, School of Computer Science, Carnegie Mellon University.

Cohen, W. W. 1990. Learning approximate control rules of high utility. *Proceedings of the Sixth International Conference on Machine Learning*, 268-276 .

Doorenbos, R., Tambe, M., and Newell, A. 1992. Learning 10,000 chunks: What's it like out there? *Proceedings of the Tenth National Conference on Artificial Intelligence*, 830-836 .

Etzioni, O. 1990. *A structural theory of search control*. Ph.D. diss., School of Computer Science, Carnegie Mellon University.

Forgy, C. L. 1981. *OPS5 User's Manual*. Technical Report CMU-CS-81-135, Computer Science Department, Carnegie Mellon University.

Forgy, C. L. 1982. Rete: A fast algorithm for the many pattern/many object pattern match problem. *Artificial Intelligence 19*(1), 17-37.

Gratch, J. and DeJong, G. 1992. COMPOSER: A probabilistic solution to the utility problem in speed-up learning. *Proceedings of the Tenth National Conference on Artificial Intelligence*, 235-240 .

Gupta, A. 1987. *Parallelism in Production Systems*. Los Altos, California: Morgan Kaufmann.

Laird, J.E., Newell, A., and Rosenbloom, P.S. 1987. Soar: An architecture for general intelligence. *Artificial Intelligence 33*(1), 1-64.

Laird, J. E., Rosenbloom, P. S. and Newell, A. 1986. Chunking in Soar: The anatomy of a general learning mechanism. *Machine Learning 1*(1), 11-46.

McDermott, J. 1983. Extracting knowledge from expert systems. *Proceedings of the Eighth International Joint Conference on Artificial Intelligence*, 100-107 .

Mertz, J. 1992. Deliberate learning from instruction in Assembler-Soar. Proceedings of the Eleventh Soar Workshop.

Minton, S. 1988. *Learning Effective Search Control Knowledge: An Explanation-Based Approach*. Ph.D. diss., Computer Science Department, Carnegie Mellon University.

Miranker, D. P. 1990. *TREAT: A New and Efficient Match Algorithm for AI Production Systems*. San Mateo, California: Morgan Kaufmann.

Miranker, D. P., Brant, D. A., Lofaso, B., and Gadbois, D. 1990. On the performance of lazy matching in production systems. *Proceedings of the Eigth National Conference on Artificial Intelligence*, 685-692 .

Oflazer, K. 1984. Partitioning in parallel processing of production systems. *Proceedings of the IEEE International Conference on Parallel Processing*, 92-100 .

Rosenbloom, P.S. and Aasman J. 1990. Knowledge level and inductive uses of chunking (EBL). *Proceedings of the National Conference on Artificial Intelligence*, 821-827 .

Rosenbloom, P. S., Laird, J. E., Newell, A., and McCarl, R. 1991. A preliminary analysis of the Soar architecture as a basis for general intelligence. *Artificial Intelligence 47*(1-3), 289-325.

Sellis, T., Lin, C-C., and Raschid, L. 1988. Implementing large production systems in a DBMS environment: Concepts and algorithms. *Proceedings of the ACM-SIGMOD International Conference on the Management of Data*, 404-412 .

Tambe, M., Newell, A., and Rosenbloom, P. S. 1990. The problem of expensive chunks and its solution by restricting expressiveness. *Machine Learning 5*(3), 299-348.

Massively Parallel Support for Computationally Effective Recognition Queries

Matthew P. Evett,[1] James A. Hendler,[2] William A. Andersen[3]

Department of Computer Science
University of Maryland
College Park, MD 20742

Abstract

PARKA, a frame-based knowledge representation system implemented on the Connection Machine, provides a representation language consisting of concept descriptions (frames) and binary relations on those descriptions (slots). The system is designed explicitly to provide extremely fast property inheritance inference capabilities. PARKA performs fast "recognition" queries of the form "find all frames satisfying p property constraints" in $O(d+p)$ time—proportional only to the depth, d, of the knowledge base (KB), and independent of its size. For conjunctive queries of this type, PARKA's performance is measured in tenths of a second, even for KBs with 100,000+ frames, with similar results for timings on the Cyc KB. Because PARKA's run-time performance is independent of KB size, it promises to scale up to arbitrarily larger domains. With such run-time performance, we believe PARKA is a contender for the title of "fastest knowledge representation system in the world".

1. Introduction

Currently, AI is experiencing a period of soul-searching. Critics contend that the promise of the AI techniques of the 80's evaporated because those techniques did not deliver. It wasn't that their formalisms and theory were unacceptable (in fact, they worked fine for relatively small, contrived domains). Real-life domains, however, are orders of magnitude larger, and the run-time performance of these earlier AI techniques is often completely unacceptable for such domains (and even much smaller ones); that is, these techniques, while quite useful, are *computationally ineffective* (Shastri 1986).

The field of knowledge representation (KR) offers many problems for which these classic AI techniques have yielded unacceptably slow performance. One example is *recognition*, the problem of identifying those frames that satisfy a given set of property constraints. For example, "Find all x such that x is yellow, alive, and flies." Existing KR systems efficiently solve the converse problem—retrieving the properties of any given frame—but cannot do the same for recognition. In general, they answer recognition queries by traversing the entire knowledge base (KB), collecting the set of frames satisfying the given constraints. Their run-time for recognition queries is no better than linear in the size of the KB, i.e., $O(n)$.

It has been our goal to design a KR system fast enough to provide computationally effective recognition queries (and

other types of queries) on KBs large enough to support real world commonsense reasoning. Such a system will serve as a foothold for the development of realistic AI applications requiring rapid response time. Our system, PARKA, is a symbolic, frame-based KR system that takes advantage of the Connection Machine's (CM) massive parallelism to deliver high run-time performance. It effects recognition queries in time virtually independent of the size of the KB, and dependent only on the KB's depth, d. (For large KB's, usually $d \approx lg(n)$.)

In the remainder of this paper, we discuss the design and implementation of PARKA, and present a short analysis of the expected and observed run-time performance of those operations used in answering recognition queries. To validate PARKA's inference mechanisms on a KB of realistic size and topology, we test PARKA's performance on the *Cyc* KB and argue that the performance shows that PARKA offers computationally effective recognition queries on realistically large KBs.

2. Description of PARKA

PARKA was designed as a general-purpose KB, for use by other AI systems. We chose a frame-based symbolic representation paradigm for two main reasons: first, frame systems have been used in KR for year and remain a common paradigm in contemporary AI research (Sowa 1991; *J.CMA* 1992, e.g.); second, semantic nets readily lend themselves to the data-level parallelism design so important in efficient parallel implementation.

Most KR systems have two primary goals: expressiveness and formality. The authors of these systems want to express as many semantic concepts as possible with an unambiguous, rigorous formalism. For them, run-time efficiency is of secondary importance. They emphasize classic search and rule-based approaches, consequently suffering run-time that is at best linear, and at worst exponential, in the size of the problem. While these methodologies have a place in AI, their application to large KB's leads to unacceptable run-time performance, and it is expected that realistic KB's will be *very* large, indeed—on the order of 10's or 100's of millions of frames (Lenat & Guha 1990; Stanfill & Waltz 1986, etc.) Such KB's would be orders of magnitude larger than any existing today.

To achieve computational effectiveness on large KBs, we designed PARKA with run-time performance as a primary goal of the system. Thus, we somewhat constrained PARKA's expressiveness—this was unavoidable because many operations, are, in general, *NP* or even undecidable for term-subsumption languages that are sound and complete.

[1]Email: evett@cs.umd.edu

[2]Email: hendler@cs.umd.edu

[3]Email: waander@cs.umd.edu

Recognition, in particular, is *NP*, though it is a special case of classification, which can be undecidable (Nebel 1990). So, although PARKA's semantics are roughly based upon those of NETL (Fahlman 1979) and KL-ONE (Brachman & Schmolze 1985), we avoided semantic constructs lacking a computationally effective implementation. We believe PARKA's run-time performance on even very large KBs more than compensates for its slighlty restricted expressiveness when compared to that of other, serial, KR systems.

2.1 Design specifics

PARKA is a basic frame system: each frame corresponds to a concept represented in the KB and the collection of relations to which it belongs. Relations among concepts are represented as directed graphs whose arcs (or links) are stored as frame pointers in the *slots* of frames. Properties of frames are represented as relations for which the domain is the frames having the property, and the range is the corresponding property values. The KB can be viewed as the network formed by the frames and the links that connect them, similar to a semantic network (Fahlman 1979, e.g.)

Ontological relations among frames are encoded via the IS-A ("is a") relation, which is intimately involved in the calculation of property inheritance inferences (see below) As such, it has special status in PARKA. The subgraph consisting of all IS-A links and frames is referred to as the *IS-A hierarchy* of the net. All PARKA IS-A hierarchies are rooted and acyclic.

A small subset of a frame network is shown in Figure 1. The frames are shown as ovals. The properties of each frame are represented by the arcs emanating from them. Unlabelled arcs are IS-A links.

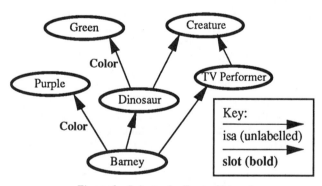

Figure 1: Subset of a Frame Network

2.2 Inheritance Mechanism.

PARKA employs a property inheritance mechanism on its IS-A hierarchy. A frame is said to be *explicitly-valued* for a given property if it is incident on a property link of that type—that is, if the frame contains a slot by that name. Any frame not explicitly-valued for a given property *inherits* the value of its nearest ancestor(s) (using a metric based on Touretzky's *inferential distance ordering* (IDO)) that *is* explicitly-valued for that property. Because PARKA supports multiple inheritance, it is possible to have more than one

such node. In that case, PARKA disambiguates among viable ancestors.

The first version of PARKA (Evett, Spector & Hendler 1993; Evett & Hendler 1992) handled multiple-inheritance—as have other frame-based KR systems (i.e., Brachman & Schmolze 1985, e.g.)—by using inheritance path length to disambiguate multiple inheritance paths. The system chooses the ancestor having the shortest IS-A path from the inheritor. This inheritance paradigm suffers from redundancy, ambiguity, and other problems, and has been soundly criticized in the philosophical community as being epistemologically inadequate. Many of these criticisms are detailed in (Touretzky 1986) and (Brachman 1985).

The current implementation uses a top-down, path-based, credulous inheritance mechanism based on Touretzky's IDO metric to disambiguate multiple inherited values that works like this: assume the frame in question, X, is not explicitly valued for the given property, P. Let B be the set of ancestors $\{B_1, B_2, ...\}$ of X that are explicitly valued for P. X takes B_i's value for P as its own, provided B_i is an element of B such that there is no B_j ($j \neq i$) such that B_j is an IS-A descendant of B_i. If more than one element of B meets this criterion, X is said to be ambiguously valued for property P.

Unfortunately, many retrieval operations involving top-down, path-based inheritance mechanisms, including IDO, have been shown to be NP-hard (Selman & Levesque 1989). To calculate these operations in a timely manner, we adopted a slightly weaker ordering scheme for inheritance disambiguation. Again, let B be the set of ancestors of X that are explicitly valued for property P. X takes B_i's value for P as its own, where B_i is that element of B with the largest *topological number*. The topological number, $topo(Z)$, of a frame Z, is defined inductively: $topo(rootNode)=0$ and for all other frames, Z, $topo(Z) = 1 + \max_{y \in C}(topo(y))$ where C is the set of frames that are parents of Z.

Though PARKA's disambiguation mechanism is not quite as powerful as complete IDO, it enjoys many of the same advantages and is considerably stronger than a simple path-length based scheme. It does not suffer from the problems of *redundancy* noted in (Touretzky 1986) and in only one case does our inheritance scheme differ from IDO: in full IDO, if there are two explicitly valued ancestors, X and Y, but X is also an ancestor of Y, then Y is "more specific" than X, and so its property value is chosen. Our topological disambiguation scheme, however, may arbitrarily disambiguate among the two ancestors, even when neither is an IS-A ancestor of the other. In the vast majority of cases, though, PARKA's mechanism is equivalent to IDO. PARKA's encoding of the Cyc commonsense KB (see Section 3.4) revealed no cases in which PARKA disambiguates an inheritance relation that is ambiguous via IDO. If Cyc turns out to be typical of future KBs, this shortcoming of topologicial disambiguation will have little impact on most inferences.

2.3 Implementation

PARKA's internal representation of a frame consists of a block of processors, one for each of that frame's IS-A parents. These processors are contiguous across the CM's processor address space. One processor of each block is distinguished as a referent for all other frames pointing to the represented frame.

The slots of each frame are encoded in a *slot table*, stored in one of the processors of that frame's block. The table is a list of pairs (<property>, <property-value>), each component being a processor address. Figure 2 illustrates the internal representation on the CM of part of the net shown in Figure 1. The large rectangles represent the distinguished processor of each block of processors corresponding to a particular frame. The smaller rectangles represent the remaining processors of those blocks. The square-bracketed values represent the address of the processor representing the property of that corresponding name.

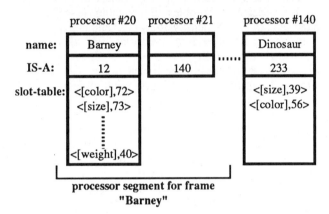

Figure 2: Internal CM representation of a small subset of a frame network

To determine if a frame, Y, is explicitly valued for a given property, P, PARKA determines the (explicit) value of P for every frame in the KB by scanning through every frame's slot table in parallel, seeking an entry corresponding to P. If a matching entry is found in frame Y's slot table, the corresponding value stored there is the address of the processor representing the frame that is the value of property P for frame Y. In general, slot retrieval is proportional to the size of the largest slot table in the KB. Because property values tend to be scattered across inheritance paths, these tables are typically quite small. The largest slot table in our implementation of the Cyc KB had only 43 entries. Even so, PARKA maintains a cache of the most recently accessed properties to accelerate explicit property look-up.

3. Performance

To demonstrate that PARKA provides computationally effective KR, we implemented and timed several retrieval operations on very large KBs which included inheritance queries on very large, pseudo-random KB's and recognition queries on the Cyc KB.

3.1 Inheritance Queries

Almost all KB queries involve some inferencing along the IS-A hierarchy because almost all involve calculating the inherited value of a set of properties for a set of frames. PARKA uses several data structures to make such inheritance inferencing very fast, including using multiple processors to represent frames having multiple parents. PARKA uses an activation wave propagation algorithm to calculate the value for a given property of every frame in the KB in time independent of the size of the network.

First, the IS-A root frame is "activated", forming a nascent *activation wave*. At each iteration, this wave is passed downward along IS-A links. The activation wave propagates synchronously; all nodes in the current "wave front" simultaneously activating the incident nodes that have not yet been activated. Each such iteration is a *propagation step*. Because PARKA is implemented on the CM, each propagation step is accomplished with a single parallel operation. In detail, at propagation step i:

1. Frames with a topological value of i (i.e., those at *topological level* i) that are explicitly valued for the property set their wave value to k, where k's high order bits are i, and k's low order bits are the frame's property value.

2. Every frame (processor) not explicitly valued for the property in question that has parent nodes at topological level i-1 "pulls" down the value of the activation wave from those parents.

3. Non-explicitly valued frames at topological level i choose as their own activation wave value the largest of those pulled down from the parent frames. Because the high order bits of each wave value are the topological level of the origin node, the selected value conforms to the inheritance scheme outlined in section 2.2.

Figure 3: The Basic Inheritance Algorithm

The number of propagation steps required to calculate a property value is equivalent to the depth, d, of the network's IS-A hierarchy. Consequently, PARKA's run-time for queries such as "what things are black?", is $O(d)$, and is independent of the size of the KB. We refer to such queries as "top-down", and they are the bane of most serial KR systems, requiring $O(n)$ time to effect, where n is the size of the KB. Serial systems use *indexing* schemes to mitigate this computational morass, but indexing can be unsatisfactory for a variety of reasons (as we discuss in (Kettler, Hendler & Andersen 1993b)) including that it is typically infeasible to explicitly index all properties.

The comparison between serial and parallel run-times is more striking when realizing that for realistic networks $d \approx lg(n)$. It is commonly believed that such network shallowness will persist and probably be accentuated as net size increases. Our PARKA implementation of the Cyc commonsense KB (see section 3.4), enjoys a similarly shallow IS-A topology.

To compare PARKA against a serial representation system, we created a serial version of PARKA, called SPARKA ("serial-PARKA"). To make the comparison as fair as possible, we implemented SPARKA as a severely stripped-down version of a more complete serial implementation (detailed in (Spector, Evett & Hendler 1990)). It has very little functionality other than for simple property inheritance calculations, but is optimized to effect those calculations as quickly as possible.

We tested our analytical predictions of PARKA's run-time performance of simple property inheritance queries by timing PARKA's response to example queries on topologies of varying size and depth. Then, we timed SPARKA on the same queries and networks. The networks were quite large—up to 128K nodes[4]. Because encoding such large networks by hand was not possible, we developed algorithms for generating pseudo-random networks with certain topological characteristics. These techniques are described in (Evett, Spector & Hendler 1993; Evett & Hendler 1992). Our experience with the Cyc KB (see section 3.4) has affirmed our belief that the topologies used to measure PARKA's performance reflect those of realistic KBs.

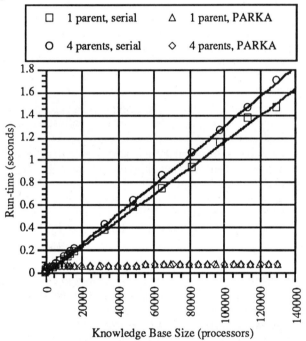

Figure 4: Run-time performance of inheritance queries on 8-level networks of varying sizes.

Figure 4 shows PARKA's run-time for frame networks of depth 8, and of varying size. This timing suite isolates the effect of network size on run-time. These timings support our supposition that PARKA's computation of inheritance queries is independent of network size[5]. Thus,

---

[4]Timings were made on a "quarter" CM-2, consisting of only 16K processors.

[5]Actually, we observed a correlation between PARKA's run-time and the size of the networks. We examined this degradation away from our theoretical performance predictions (the results of this study are detailed in (Evett & Hendler 1993)). The degradation is completely accounted for by the performance of

PARKA's performance should scale up to arbitrarily larger KBs. The serial system's run-time, on the other hand, was linear with respect to network size. The figure contains best-fit curves to highlight this linear relation.

The networks used in the timings were of two topological types: trees (each frame with exactly one parent) and directed graphs (each frame with between one and four parents). We used different topologies to demonstrate that PARKA's run-time is independent of upward IS-A fan-out.

A comparison between the performance figures of SPARKA and PARKA in Figure 4 demonstrates that the latter remains computationally effective even for very large KBs, while the former's performance is unacceptable for large networks. We anticipate that this contrast will become increasingly stark for much larger KBs of applications in real-world domains.

3.2 Recognition Queries

The ability to solve *recognition queries* has driven much of PARKA's design. The problem of recognition is well-known in the field of KR (Wilensky 1986, e.g.) and is the problem of answering KB queries of the form: "find all frames x such that $P_1(x,c_1) \wedge P_2(x,c_2) \wedge ... \wedge P_p(x,c_p)$", where $P_i(x,c_i)$, $\forall i$, is a unary predicate true for all frames, x, that have value c_i for property P_i. E.g.: "What object is most characterized by this list of property values? ...." and "what have trunks, tusks, and are big and gray?" Such queries are extremely time-consuming for serial-based systems, often running in time no better than $O(pn)$, even on systems employing a highly constrained description language.

PARKA's ability to execute inheritance inferences quickly makes it particularly suitable to recognition. Because PARKA determines which objects have a given value for a given property in $O(d)$ time, PARKA determines which objects satisfy a *set* of p property constraints in no more than $O(dp)$ time, where d is the depth of the net.

But PARKA does even better, using a pipelining technique to evaluate recognition queries in time $O(d+p)$. Because each wave propagation step of an inheritance inference occurs "in lockstep"—all frames at the same topological level calculating their property value simultaneously—pipelining can be added to the basic process outlined in Figure 3. At each propagation step i, all frames at topological level j, such that $p \geq j \geq i$, retrieve from their parent(s) the wave activation value having to do with the $(j-i)$-th element of the set of properties being inferred. Thus, the complete propagation requires $d+p-1$ propagation steps.

3.3 Using Cyc for Validation of PARKA

We tested our run-time predictions by timing PARKA's performance for recognition queries on an implementation of the Cyc KB (Lenat & Guha 1990). Our motivation for using Cyc to evaluate PARKA's performance is twofold. First, we want to validate PARKA's inference mechanisms on a KB of large size and realistic topology. Because Cyc

---

the CM's interprocessor communication operations. The run-time of these operations degrades proportionally with router network load.

is the largest and most comprehensive commonsense KB in existence, it is an obvious choice. A second and more exciting motivation is that we envision some future version of Cyc being built on top of a massively parallel substrate, like PARKA, to make its reasoning services fast enough to be used by an intelligent agent operating in the world in real time.

On the lowest level, Cyc consists of a frame system (frames are called "units" in Cyc), representing assertions (in the form of binary relations, or slots) about entities in the world. Above that level is the CycL "constraint language", which allows the specification of inferences to be made about units in the KB. The inference mechanisms provided by CycL range from the very simple, such as the slot inverse mechanism (e.g. father(John,Mary)→ fatherOf(Mary,John)), to theorem proving using general "wffs", and to unsound inference methods such as analogy.

PARKA implements only some of the inference capabilities provided by CycL, particularly those having to do with property inheritance. For our tests we represented only that subset of Cyc that involved IS-A based property inheritance and ontologies. This subset contained a total of 26,214 units, 8591 (33%) of which were collections, and 17,623 (67%) instances. Of the instances, 4031 (15% of the total) were slots (slots are explicitly represented in the Cyc ontology). To accommodate a KB of this size, we used a 16,384 processor CM-2 with a virtual processor ratio of 4:1. The maximum depth of the KB along the IS-A relation was 23, (i.e., shallow relative to KB size, as expected.)

3.4 Performance of Recognition Queries

To test recognition query performance, we timed queries similar to those used by CycL to find units "similar" to a given unit. Units are considered similar if they share the same values for a number of properties exceeding some threshold. First, we selected a Cyc unit (#%Burma-1986) with a relatively large number (22) of local assertions (i.e., explicitly-valued properties), assigning an arbitrary ordering to those properties. We then ran recognition queries in PARKA to identify those frames that matched at least 50% of the first n slots ($1 \leq n \leq 22$) of #%Burma-1986. The recognition queries themselves, then, involved between 1 and 22 conjuncts. The run-time performance of these queries is plotted in Figure 5.

As Figure 5 clearly shows, the time required to perform recognition queries grows only linearly in the number of conjuncts, p, and overall performance, even for a query of 22 conjuncts, is excellent. The run-time matches the $O(d+p)$ performance predicted by analysis. This performance compares very favorably with recognition queries on serial systems, which require $O(pn)$ time for the same queries, where n is the size of the KB. Recognition queries in PARKA are independent of KB size, and should scale up to arbitrarily larger domains. Indeed, in (Kettler et al 1993a) we report sub-second run-time performance of recognition queries in a case-based planning system using KB's of over 100,000 frames. This is a speed-up of more than 10,000 over the highly optimized serial version of PARKA.

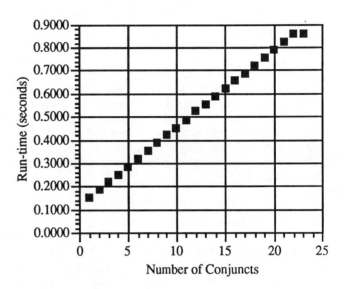

Figure 5: Run-time of recognition queries of various sizes on the PARKA implementation of the Cyc KB

This experiment was designed not ony to demonstrate the $O(d+p)$ complexity of conjunctive recognition queries in PARKA, but also to show that PARKA can supply fast matching for analogy-related functions, a task that traditionally has been difficult for serial systems. For example, the CycL query that most nearly corresponds to those of Figure 5 finds only an arbitrary subset of the matching units. By exhaustively matching the probe against the entire KB simultaneously, PARKA finds *all* appropriate matches.

4. Future & Related Work

PARKA is intended as a basis for large AI systems. The implementation of the Cyc KB in PARKA is the first of a series of uses of PARKA in other large AI systems. Potential uses for PARKA include case-based AI systems, as the basis of a massively parallel knowledge server, and as part of a knowledge-mining system. We plan to examine how PARKA might be more fully integrated into the Cyc representation system, proper.

Also, we implemented a simple version of PARKA on the MIMD CM-5. Preliminary results show that we should be able to represent KBs of over 1M frames on a 1K-processor CM-5 and obtain run-time performance nearly an order of magnitude better than the results in this paper. Because the CM-5 is a MIMD machine (though we use it as a SPMD machine), we can use several inferencing techniques that aren't possible on the SIMD CM-2. In particular, we plan to use an *active messaging* scheme (Von Eicken et al 1992) to increase the flexibility of PARKA's memory association schemes, and to increase the use of pipelining in inferencing.

There are a few other parallel KR systems (Geller 1991; Moldovan, Lee & Lin 1989 to name two) and these are discussed more fully in (Evett 1993).

5. Conclusion

Using KBs with over 100,000 frames, we have shown that PARKA computes property inheritance and recognition queries in time independent of the size of the KB and dependent only on network depth. The run-time of these operations is in the tenths of seconds. This performance compares very favorably to serial representation systems. Because empirical evidence to date supports our analytical claims, we believe that PARKA's performance will scale up to larger KBs, even to the those necessitated by memory based reasoning[6] technology. Thus, we argue that PARKA can supply computationally effective recognition queries for realistic KBs.

Acknowledgments

The author wishes to thank the Systems Research Center at the University of Maryland, for their early support in this research, and for the continuing use of their hardware in the development of PARKA. The authors also wish to thank the University of Maryland Institute for Academic Computing Services (UMIACS) and Thinking Machines Corp. for the use of their Connection Machines. The support staff at both institutions was very helpful during the development of PARKA.

This work has been supported by AFOSR grant 01-5-28180, ONR grant N0014-88-K-0560, and NSF grant 1R1-8907890.

References

Brachman, R.J. I Lied about the Trees. *AI Mag.* **6**, 3 (Fall, 1985).

Brachman, R.J. and Schmolze, J.G. An Overview of the KL-ONE Knowledge Representation System. *Cog. Sci.*, **9**, 2 (April-June 1985).

J. Computers and Mathematics with Applications — special issue on semantic networks, **2 3**(2-5), 1992.

Evett, M.P. PARKA: A System for Massively Parallel Knowledge Representation. Ph.D. diss., Dept. of Computer Science, Univ. Maryland, College Park, 1993. Forthcoming.

Evett, M.P., Spector, L. and Hendler, J.A. Massively Parallel Frame-Based Property Inheritance in PARKA. To appear in *Journal for Parallel and Distributed Computing*.

Evett, M.P. and Hendler, J.A. Degradation of Interprocessor Communication Operations on the Connection Machine. Tech. Rep., Department of Computer Science, Univ. Maryland, College Park, March, 1993.

Evett, M.P. and Hendler, J.A. An Update of PARKA, a Massively Parallel Knowledge Representation System. Tech. Rep., CS-TR-2850, Department of Computer Science, Univ. Maryland, College Park, February, 1992.

Fahlman, S.E. *NETL: A System for Representing and Using Real World Knowledge.* MIT Press, Cambridge, MA, 1979.

Geller, J. Advanced Update Operations in Massively Parallel Knowledge Representation. Tech. Rep. CIS-91-28, Dept. Computer and Information Science, New Jersey Institute of Technology, Newark, NJ, 1991.

Hammond, K. *Case-Based Planning: Viewing Planning as a Memory Task.* Academic Press, 1989.

Kettler, B.P., Hendler, J.A., Andersen, W.A., and Evett, M.P. (1993a) "Massively Parallel Support for a Case-based Planning System". In Proceedings of the Ninth IEEE Conference on AI Applications, IEEE 1993.

Kettler, B.P., Hendler, J.A. and Andersen, W.A. (1993b) Why Explicit Indexing Can't Work. Tech. Rep., Department of Computer Science, Univ. Maryland, College Park, April, 1993.

Kitano, H. and Higuchi, T. Massively Parallel Memory-Based Parsing. *Proceedings of IJCAI-91*, 1991.

Lenat, D.B. and Guha, R.V. *Building Large Knowledge-Based Systems.* Addison Wesley, Reading, Mass., 1990.

Moldovan, D., Lee, W., and Lin, C. SNAP: A Marker-Propagation Architecture for Knowledge Processing. Tech. Rep. CENG 89-10, Dept. Electrical Engineering-Systems, Univ. of Southern California, Los Angeles, CA, 1989.

Nebel, B. Terminological Reasoning Is Inherently Intractable. *AIJ*, **4 3**, 2 (May, 1990).

Selman, B. and Levesque, H. The Tractability of Path-Based Inheritance. *Proceedings of IJCAI-89*, Morgan-Kaufman, San Mateo, CA, 1989.

Shastri, L. Massive Parallelism in Artificial Intelligence. Tech. Rep. MS-CIS-86-77 (LINC LAB 43), Dept. of Computer and Information Science, University of Pennsylvania, Philadelphia, PA, 1986.

Sowa, J. (ed.) *Principles of Semantic Networks.* Morgan-Kaufman, San Mateo, CA, 1991.

Spector, L., Evett, M. and Hendler, J.. Knowledge Representation in PARKA. Tech. Rep. TR-2409, Department of Computer Science, University of Maryland, College Park, MD, Feb. 1990.

Stanfill, C. and Waltz, D. Toward Memory-Based Reasoning. *Communications of the ACM*, Vol. 29, No. 12, December 1986, pp. 1213-1228.

Touretzky, D.S. *The Mathematics of Inheritance Systems.* Morgan Kaufmann, Los Altos, CA, 1986.

Von Eicken, T., Culler, D., Goldstein, S. and Schauser, K. Active Messages: a Mechanism for Integrated Communication and Computation. Tech. Rep. UCB/CSD 92/#675, Computer Science Division, EECS, University of California, Berkeley, CA, 1992.

Wilensky, R. Some Problems and Proposals for Knowledge Representation. Tech. Rep. UCB/CSD 86/294, University of California, Berkeley, May 1986.

---

[6]We use the term "MBR" in a broader sense than in (Stanfill & Waltz 1986) to include such paradigms as case-based reasoning (Hammond 1989; Kettler et al 1993; Kitano & Higuchi 1991.)

Case-Method:
A Methodology for Building Large-Scale Case-Based Systems

Hiroaki Kitano
Case Systems Laboratory
NEC Corporation
2-11-5 Shibaura, Minato
Tokyo 108 Japan
`kitano@ccs.mt.nec.co.jp`

Hideo Shimazu   **Akihiro Shibata**
C&C Information Technology Research Laboratories
NEC Corporation
4-1-1 Miyazaki, Miyamae
Kawasaki 216 Japan
`shimazu,shibata@joke.cl.nec.co.jp`

Abstract

Developing large-scale systems are major efforts which require careful planning and solid methodological foundations. This paper describes CASE-METHOD, the methodology for building large-scale case-based systems. CASE-METHOD defines the procedure which managers, engineers, and domain experts should follow in developing case-based systems, and provides a set of supporting tools. An empirical study shows that the use of CASE-METHOD attains significant workload reduction in system development and maintenance (more than 1/12) as well as qualitative change in corporate activities.

1 Introduction

This paper describes CASE-METHOD, a methodology for building and maintaining case-based reasoning (CBR:[Riesbeck and Schank, 1989]) systems. CASE-METHOD has been inductively defined through a corporate-wide case-based system actually deployed at NEC corporation. It is now being applied to several case-based systems, ranging from division-wide systems to corporate-wide and nation-wide case-based systems.

Despite increasing expectations for using case-based reasoning as a practical approach to building cost-effective problem-solvers and corporate information access systems, no research has been made on how to develop and maintain case-based systems. In the software engineering community, particularly among practitioners, methodology development or selection is regarded as one of the most important development decisions to make.

In general, software development methodologies define how to organize a project, how each development procedures should be carried out, and how to describe interface between development processes. Often, the methodology provides automated tools, which support some of the development processes involved [Downs et. al., 1988, Wasserman et. al., 1983]. A number of methodologies have been formulated by mainframe manufactures and by consulting firms. Some of these are AD/Cycle by IBM, Method/1 by Andersen consulting, SUMMIT by Coopers and Librant, and NAVIGATOR by Ernst and Young.

If CBR systems are to be integrated into mainstream information systems, a solid methodological support is essential. Unfortunately, however, no methodological support has been provided from CBR community ([Acorn and Walden, 1992] is the possible exception, but only a part of the entire process has been defined). Although there are a few methodologies for building expert systems, such as HSTDEK by NASA[Freeman, 1987], KEMRAS by Alvey project, KADS by ESPRIT, and EX/METHOD by NEC, these methodologies are not applicable for CBR system development, because underlying principles are so different between expert systems and CBR.

Thus, the authors had to develop their own methodology, optimized for case-based systems. CASE-METHOD was designed to be consistent with methodologies for non-CBR systems, so that the corporate information systems division would be able to use the methodology without major trouble. Also, CASE-METHOD was inductively defined based on several CBR projects actually carried out. Thus, CASE-METHOD is already a field-tested methodology. While it is not possible to describe all the details for a full set CASE-METHOD due to space limitation, this paper describes basic components of CASE-METHOD — vision, process definition, and tools.

2 Experience Sharing Architecture

Although CASE-METHOD can be applied to various ranges of projects, from task-specific problem-solvers to nation-wide case-based systems, the main target for CASE-METHOD is corporate-wide information systems. It is acknowledged that the mainstream corporate information system has been designed based on the idea of *Strategic Information System (SIS)*[Wiseman, 1988]. However, how SIS should be designed and how the system should be operated has only been vaguely defined. In addition, SIS confined itself within a traditional information processing paradigm of corporate behavior [Simmon, 1976]. Thus, how knowledge can be transferred and reformulated in the organization has not been the issue of the traditional systems. CBR community, on the other hand, viewed CBR mainly as a new problem-solving mechanism, and have not discussed how the CBR idea impacts corporate information systems.

In order to bridge these gaps, the authors propose the *Experience Sharing Architecture (ESA)* concept. ESA facilitates sharing of experiences corporate-wide, thereby promoting organizational knowledge creation, and improves core skills in the corporation. This will be attained through the use of case-based systems integrated with mainstream information systems, such as existing SIS. While the authors agree the importance of SIS and effectiveness of the information processing paradigm of corporate behavior, the authors argue that a new dimension should be added, in order to further enhance the power of corporate information systems.

Since people and organization learn from experiences (see [Badaracco, 1991, Ishikura, 1992, Meen and Keough, 1992, Nonaka, 1991, Nonaka, 1990, Senge, 1990] for discussion on corporate knowledge creation and organizational learning), collecting, sharing, and mining experiences collected in form of *case* is the best approach to improving knowledge level and skills of the organization. In [Kitano, et. al., 1992], effectiveness of case-based systems to support organizational knowledge creation and learning, particularly for Nonaka's theory, has been discussed.

CASE-METHOD provides how to build and maintain the system to support the organizational knowledge creation. In addition, CASE-METHOD defines how organizational knowledge creation can be carried out, in the light of modern information technology. It is a methodology to develop case-based systems, as well as a methodology to implement the knowledge creation cycle.

3 Case-Method Cycle

The methodology employs an iterative approach, which allows the system to evolve as process iterates. Figure 1 shows the system evolution cycle in CASE-METHOD. CASE-METHOD defines the system development process, the case-base development process, the system operation process, the database mining process, the management process, and the knowledge transfer process.

System Development Process This process employs a standard software engineering approach, such as waterfall model or flower model [Humphrey, 1989]. As a development methodology, the goal is to design and develop a CBR system, which can store and retrieve a case-base created in the case-base development process.

Case-Base Development Process The goal of this process is to develop and maintain a large-scale case-base. Details will be described in the next section.

System Operation Process This process defines installation, deployment, and user supports for the CBR system. This follows standard software engineering and RDB management procedures.

Data-Base Mining Process Data-base mining will be carried out using the case-base. Statistical analysis, rule-extraction and other appropriate techniques will be applied. The current model defines how to analyze case-base, using standard statistical procedures, and rule extraction, using decision tree [Quinlan, 1992]. This process is a subject for further research.

Management Process This process defines how the project task force should be formed, what kind of organizational support should be provided to the project,

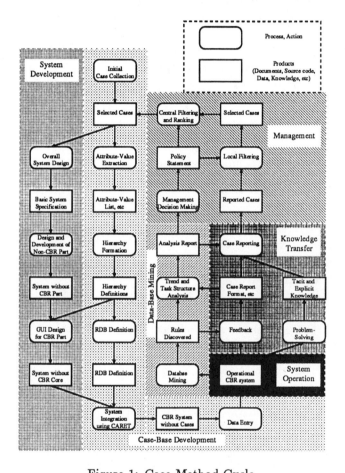

Figure 1: Case-Method Cycle

and what kind of management control should be carried out to obtain a constant flow of high quality cases. The authors have defined a mixed scheme involving bottom-up/top-down control, incentive systems, central/local controls, and case filtering committee. This process should be rearranged for each organization.

Knowledge Transfer Process This process defines methods to transfer knowledge (cases and extracted rules) to related divisions. Network-based system deployment, incentive systems, management control, and newsletter publications have been defined. In addition, how to create a case report format, which is one of the major feed back means, is defined.

These processes form one cycle in the knowledge creation and system evolution. Because of case structure reformulation in the case base development process and rule extraction in the data-base mining process, the quality of knowledge to be stored and transfered improves as the cycle iterates. When the system reached the maturity stage, the system should hold a case-base consisting of appropriately represented and indexed high quality cases and a set of extracted rules specific to the application domain.

4 Major Process Definitions

Case Collection The first phase in the development requires collecting seed cases. The seed cases provide an initial concept regarding the application domain landscape. In case of SQUAD system[Kitano, et. al., 1992], the authors started with 100 seed cases, to define a crude case format and data structure. In case of the nationwide case retrieval system, the authors are working on several hundred cases from the beginning. As a start up phase in the project, cases are generally collected in unstructured and ununiformed style, such as full-text and other domain-specific forms.

From the second cycle, this phase involves (1) collection of cases which are consistent with the pre-defined case report format, and (2) filtering of cases so that only cases with minimum acceptable quality will be sent to the next phase. Cases are reported in structured style, using pre-defined case report form and full-text with specified writing style.

Products of this phase are (1) a set of case report forms, and (2) a set of case reports in full-text.

Attribute-Value Extraction The goal of the attribute-value extraction phase is to extract all possible elements in case representation and indexing. In the initial cycle, this phase consists of three processes; (1) keyword listing, (2) attribute identification, and (3) value grouping.

The process can be semi-automatic, but a certain amount of human monitoring would be necessary, as new keywords and compound nouns need to be identified by human experts. Each attribute and value is examined, to determine whether or not it is independent from other attributes and values. Ideally, a set of attributes is expected to be a linearly independent set. However, in reality, this is not always possible. Thus, some dependency would be allowed. However, an excessive degree of dependency makes case representation and indexing less transparent.

Products of this phase are (1) a list of attributes, (2) a list of possible values for each attribute, (3) a thesaurus of keywords to be the value of each attribute, and (4) a set of normalized units for problem description and evaluation.

Hierarchy Formation The hierarchy formation phase defines relationships among keywords and attributes. For each attribute identified in the previous phase, a set of keywords has already been grouped. In this phase, relationships between keywords will be defined, mostly by using IS-A relation. The process of defining the relationship will be carried out in both bottom-up and top-down manner. Generally, it starts as a bottom-up process involving sub-grouping a set of keywords, and creates a super-class of one or more keywords. Then, the IS-A relation will be defined between the created super-class and keywords. One or more superclass will be grouped and a superclass for them will be defined. Then, the IS-A relation will be defined between them. This iterative process builds up an IS-A hierarchy in a bottom-up manner. This bottom-up process creates a minimally sufficient hierarchy to cover values for a set of existing cases. However, it does not guarantee whether the defined hierarchy can cope with unknown, but possible, cases. Thus, the top-down process will be carried out to incorporate a set of class and values to cover possible unknown cases. In the top-down process, the domain expert checks to determine whether or not all possible subclass are assigned for each class. If possible subclasses are missing, the missing class will be added.

After a set of hierarchies is defined, the relative importance of each attribute and the distance between individual values will be assigned. Ideally, this weight and distance assignment process needs to be carried out, using a sound statistical and empirical basis. However, in many cases, obtaining such statistical data would be unfeasible. In fact, none of the in-house projects is capable of obtaining such statistics. This is mainly due to the nature of domains and constraints on development and deployment schedules. Plus, in some systems, assigning pre-fixed weights works against achieving the system. Particularly when the user's goals for using the system differ greatly, pre-fixed attribute weights undesirably bias the search space in an unintended fashion. Thus, decisions on how to assign weights and how to value distance measures must reflect characteristics of the domain and an actual deployment plan.

A product of this phase is a set of concept hierarchies created for each attribute. The hierarchies are assigned with similarities between values.

Database Definition and Data Entry Then, database definition will be created using the set of hierarchies just defined. There are several methods to map the hierarchy into relational data-base (RDB). Which method is to be used is up to the system designer. However, CARET case-base retrieval shell supports flat record style database definition, as opposed to structured indexing [Hammond, 1986, Kolodner, 1984], due to the maintenance ease [Kitano, et. al., 1992]. Using RDBMS is an important factor in bringing CBR into the mainstream information system environment. At the end of these processes, a defined RDB contains a set of cases. The system should be operational after this phase.

Feedback The goal of the feedback phase is to provide explicit knowledge to case reporters, so that the quality of cases to be reported could be improved. In addition, it is expected that, by providing the explicit knowledge after extensive knowledge engineering, tacit and explicit knowledge regarding each case reporter may be reformulated in a more consistent manner. This is an important phase in the proposed methodology.

One way of providing a feedback is to create a case report format. The case report format should be created from the hierarchy used to index the case. There are three major benefits for distributing the case report format. First, by looking at items in the case report format, case reporters may be able to understand an overall picture of the domain in which they are involved. In the corporate-wide system, the level of expertise the case reporter has may vary significantly, and some reporter are not aware of the correct classification applicable to problems and counter measures. Distribution of the case report format is expected to improve the quality of reported cases. In fact, improvement in the quality has been confirmed in the SQUAD system applied for the software quality control (SWQC:[Mizuno, 1990]) domain. Second, using the case report format reduces data entry cost. Since all attribute-values are covered in the case report format, a simple bulk data entry strategy can be applied to register reported cases. This leads to substantial cost saving, as will be reported later. Third, by allowing free-form description for items, which can not be represented using the predefined attribute-values, new attributes and values can be identified easily and efficiently. These new attributes and values are added to the indexing hierarchies, and the case report format in the next cycle will include new attribute-values.

The products of this phase is a new case report format to be used for reporting cases in the next cycle.

5 Supporting Tools

A set of tools to support the process has been developed. Some of them are: CARET RDB-based CBR Shell [Shimazu, et. al., 1993], Canae/Yuzu GUI Construction Kit, Hierarchy Editor to help develop concept hierarchies using graphical interface, CAPIT Case-Based Natural Language Interface [Shimazu, et. al., 1992] which generate seed SQL specifications to be used by CARET, and Database Mining Tools to accomplish trend and statistical analysis. Figure 2 shows a list of tools for each part of the system development. The key supporting tool is CARET, the RDB-based CBR shell.

CARET is a CBR shell which operates on commercial relational database management systems (RDBMS), such as ORACLE. When the user specifies attributes and values representing the problem, CARET produces a set of SQL (Standard Query Language) specifications, which will be dispatched to RDBMS. Since SQL cannnot be used to achieve similarity-based retrieval, CARET produces several SQL specifications, ranked by similarity measure calculated using indexing hierarchies. For example, let us assume `Computer` is defined to have subclass `Parallel` and `Serial`, `Parallel` has instances `CM-2` and `PARAGON`, and `Serial` has an instances `SparcStation`. If the us-

Part of system	Tools	Process Definition
User Interface	Canae/Yuzu GUI, CAPIT NLI,...	
Case-Base Building	Hierarchy Editor, ...	Case-Method (Case-base building process)
Case-Retrieval	CARET RDB-based CBR Shell	Case-Method (CBR system integration)
Adapation Rule-Based Part	Excore Inference engine, ...	EX/Method, Case-Method
Non-AI Part	CASELAND CASE Tools,...	SEA/I, OMT

Figure 2: Tools and Process Definitions in Case-Method

er specified `CM-2` as a value for one of the attribute such as `Run-Time-Machine`, a SQL specification with highest similarity should contain `Run-Time-Machine = CM-2`. However, other SQLs with slightly lower similarity value may contain `Run-Time-Machine = PARAGON`. Even lower similarity SQL specifications may contain `Run-Time-Machine = SparcStation`. Such a relaxation strategy has been incorporated in CARET so that nearest neighbour similarity retrieval can be carried out using commercial RDBMS. One question which may be raised is whether or not such an approach can attain reasonable response time in large-scale case-based systems. As will be described later in Fig. 3, a practically acceptable response time has been obtained, using real data.

Users may describe the problem by chosing values for each attribute from menus provided by the graphical user interface, or by sending seed SQL specification. The seed SQL specification may be generated by CAPIT natural language user interface[Shimazu, et. al., 1992], so that users may interact with the system in natural language.

6 Empirical Results

Although several on-going projects employ the methodology and tools described in this paper, an empirical result is reported on the effectiveness of the approach using a corporate-wide case-based system applied for software quality control (SWQC). The project was initiated in 1981 as a corporate-wide quality control project, and the case-based system was introduced recently. The authors have accumulated over 25,000 cases as of December 1992, and 3,000 cases are now being reported every year by over 15,000 active participants. The case-based system was called SQUAD and its motivation and the system architecture have been described in [Kitano, et. al., 1992].

System Development The authors have observed a significant reduction in the system development cost. For this kind of system, the expected workload for developing the entire system (but excluding a knowledge-base) is about 10 man-months. However, the system was completed with less than 4 man-months of workload. Since this workload includes successive up-grading of the CARET CBR shell itself, the real workload for the SQUAD itself is estimated to be about 1.5 man-months. Since CARET reached the well-defined state, the authors expect the next system can be built within a 1 man-month workload. There are two major contributing factors for this workload reduction.

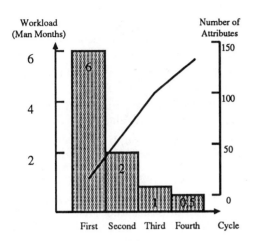

Figure 3: Case-Base Building Workload

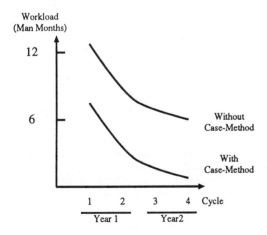

Figure 4: Total Workload

First, use of RDBMS in CARET offered a significant workload saving for building a specific case storage mechanism. All necessary functionalities and performance tuning facilities have been provided by the commercial RDBMS.

Second, Canae/Yuzu, a GUI construction environment, dramatically reduced the workload needed for user interface development. Since SQUAD extensively uses menus and tables for user interface, pre-defined parts for the user interface eliminated requirements for coding these parts of the software. The authors assessment indicates that the user interface development workload was reduced to 1/10.

Case-Base Building and Maintenance Application of the methodology resulted in qualitative and quantitative change in case-base building and maintenance.

On the quantitative side, the authors have observed a reduction in workload for building case-based from cases reported from various divisions. Before the methodology was introduced, the case report format was free-form with about 20 items. One domain expert has been working on the case-base building for her full-time job. Yet, it took almost 6 months to add 1,500 cases reported twice a year. There are two activity cycles in a year. Thus, processing over 3,000 reported cases for each year took a whole year. This is almost 6 man-months workload for 1,500 cases, which represents the cases needed to be processed in one cycle. By introducing the methodology described in this paper, the workload began to decrease. After a fourth cycle, the total workload was reduced to 0.5 man-months for 1,500 cases, 1/12 of initial workload. At this cycle, the number of attributes used reached 130. Figure 3 shows the history of workload reduction. Thus, total system development cost and maintenance cost has been reduced dramatically (Figure 4).

There are qualitative effects as well. As the number of attributes and possible values increases, more case have been covered by a set of values which are already on the case report form. Current coverage is over 95%. Thus, the case-base building process became less expertise-demanding. It was turned into a simple data entry task, which can be automated in the next step. However, there are cases which still need special handing. These are cases which cannot be covered by the values and attributes defined in the case reports. A knowledge engineer on the development team analyzes and registers these cases. At the same time, new values or new attributes are added to the case report form, so that the coverage can be increased in the next cycle.

In addition, quick turnaround for data entry enabled the SWQC division to carry out detailed analysis of the new cases. This also enabled the SWQC division to inspect the quality of cases, using extra-time created as a result of workload reduction.

Run Time Performance The CARET performance on commercial RDBMS has attained a practically acceptable speed. Using Oracle RDBMS on SparcStation2, the average response time for a query to a case-base of up to 1,500 cases (with 130 indexing attributes) is about 2.0 seconds. Figure 5 shows response time for various queries on various case-base sizes. Queries -2 and -3 are normal queries, and query-1 is the worst case performance.

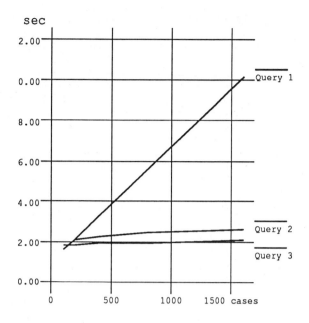

Figure 5: Case-Base Retrieval Time

7 Conclusion

This paper has described CASE-METHOD, a methodology for building large-scale case-based systems. This is the first methodology defined for case-based systems development. The methodology was defined inductively through actual development projects, ranging from task-specific systems to corporate-wide and nation-wide systems. It is the battle-proven methodology.

CASE-METHOD provides a set of process definitions and supporting tools. Empirical study demonstrates that CASE-METHOD effectively reduced system development and maintenance cost, as well as offering qualitative changes in the corporate activities. However, the authors have yet to define an effective means to validate and verify the system behavior due to the same reason pointed out in [Hennessy and Hinkle, 1992]. In order for the proposed methodology to be accepted as a mainstream system development methodology, these issues and consistency with the ISO-9000-3 need to be addressed. However, CASE-METHOD has been sucessfuly deployed, and would be the first step toward a methodology for building large-scale case-based systems.

References

[Acorn and Walden, 1992] Acorn, T. and Walden, S., "SMART: Support Management Automated Reasoning Technology for Compaq Customer Service," *Innovative Applications of Artificial Intelligence 4*, AAAI Press, 1992.

[Badaracco, 1991] Badaracco, J., *The Knowledge Link*, Harvard Business School Press, 1991.

[Downs et. al., 1988] Downs, E., Clare, P., and Coe, I., *Structured Systems Analysis and Design Method*, Prentice Hall International, 1988.

[Freeman, 1987] Freeman, M., "HSTDEK: Developing A Methodology for Construction of Large-scale,

Multi-use Knowledge Bases," *NASA Conference Publication 2492*, NASA/Marshall Space Flight Center, 1987.

[Hammond, 1986] Hammond, C., *Case-Based Planning: An Integrated Theory of Planning, Learning, and Memory*, Ph.D. Thesis, Yale University, 1986.

[Hennessy and Hinkle, 1992] Hennessy, D. and Hinkle, D., "Applying Case-Based Reasoning to Autoclave Loading," *IEEE Expert*, Oct. 1992.

[Humphrey, 1989] Humphrey, W., *Managing the Software Process*, Addison-Wesley, 1989.

[Ishikura, 1992] Ishikura, Y., *Building Core Skills of the Organization*, NTT Publishing, 1992 (in Japanese).

[Kitano, et. al., 1992] Kitano, H., Shibata, A., Shimazu, H., Kajihara, J., and Sato, A., "Building Large-Scale and Corporate-Wide Case-Based Systems," *Proc. of AAAI-92*, San Jose, 1992.

[Kolodner, 1984] Kolodner, J., *Retrieval and Organizational Strategies in Conceptual Memory: A Computer Model*, Lawrence Erlbaum Assoc., 1984.

[Meen and Keough, 1992] Meen, D. and Keough, M., "Creating the learning organization," *The McKinsey Quarterly*, No. 1, 1992.

[Mizuno, 1990] Mizuno, Y., *Total Quality Control for Software*, Nikka-giren, 1990 (in Japanese).

[Nonaka, 1991] Nonaka, I., "The Knowledge Creating Company," *Harvard Business Review*, Nov.-Dec., 1991.

[Nonaka, 1990] Nonaka, I., *A Theory of Organizational Knowledge Creation*, Nikkei, 1990 (in Japanese).

[Quinlan, 1992] Quinlan, R., *C4.5: Programs for Machine Learning*, Morgan-Kaufmann, 1992.

[Riesbeck and Schank, 1989] Riesbeck, C. and Schank, R., *Inside Case-Based Reasoning*, Lawrence Erlbaum Associates, 1989.

[Senge, 1990] Senge, P., *The Fifth Discipline: The Art & Practice of The Learning Organization*, Doubleday, 1990.

[Shimazu, et. al., 1992] Shimazu, H., Arita, S., and Takashima, Y., "Design Tool Combining Keyword Analyzer and Case-Based Parser for Developing Natural Language Database Interfaces," *Proc. of COLING-92*, Nantes, 1992.

[Shimazu, et. al., 1993] Shimazu, H., Kitano, H., and Shibata, A., "Retrieving Cases from Relational Data-Base: Another Stride Towards Corporate-Wide Case-Based Systems," *Proc. of IJCAI-93*, 1993.

[Simmon, 1976] Simmon, H., *Administrative Behavior*, 3rd edition, Free Press, 1976.

[Wasserman et. al., 1983] Wasserman, A., Freeman, P., and Pacella, M., "Characteristics of Software Development Methodologies," (Eds.) Olle, T., Sol, H., and Tully, C., *Information Systems Design Methodologies*, North Holland, 1983.

[Wiseman, 1988] Wiseman, C., *Strategic Information Systems*, Irwin, 1988.

Automated Index Generation for Constructing Large-scale Conversational Hypermedia Systems*

Richard Osgood and **Ray Bareiss**
The Institute for the Learning Sciences
Northwestern University
Evanston, Illinois 60201
osgood@ils.nwu.edu and bareiss@ils.nwu.edu

Abstract

At the Institute for the Learning Sciences we have been developing large scale hypermedia systems, called ASK systems, that are designed to simulate aspects of conversations with experts. They provide access to manually indexed, multimedia databases of story units. We are particularly concerned with finding a practical solution to the problem of finding indices for thes units when the database grows too large for manual techniques. Our solution is to provide automated assistance that proposes relative links between units, eliminating the need for manual unit-to-unit comparison. In this paper we describe eight classes of links, and show a representation and inference procedure to assist in locating instances of each.

Introduction

Interaction with a knowledge-based system typically provides a user with only limited information. For example, a diagnostic system typically returns a classification in response to a sequence of situational features. If an explanation is provided, it is usually a trace of the system's inference process. In contrast, consultation with a human expert typically provides a wealth of information. An expert knows which questions to ask in a problem solving situation, why those questions are important, which questions not to ask, how to interpret and justify the actual results, alternative methods of data collection, *et cetera*. Unfortunately, these aspects of expertise have proven difficult to represent

---
*This research was supported, in part, by the Defense Advanced Research Projects Agency, monitored by the Air Force Office of Scientific Research under contract F49620-88-C-0058 and the Office of Naval Research under contract N00014-90-J-4117, by the Office of Naval Research under contract N00014-89-J-1987, and by the Air Force Office of Scientific Research under contract AFOSR-89-0493. The Institute for the Learning Sciences was established in 1989 with the support of Andersen Consulting, part of The Arthur Andersen Worldwide Organization. The Institute receives additional support from Ameritech and North West Water which are Institute partners, and from IBM.

with current AI formalisms. As a practical alternative, builders of knowledge-based systems have turned to hypermedia to capture such knowledge in a partially represented form [Spiro and Jehng, 1990].

For the last three years, we have been developing a class of large-scale hypermedia systems called ASK systems [Ferguson *et al.*, 1992], that are designed to capture important aspects of a conversation with an expert. An ASK system provides access to a multimedia database containing short video clips of interviews with experts, archival video material, and text passages. Currently, these systems are indexed in two ways. ASK systems can be built by human "indexers" (our term for knowledge engineers) who use a question-based methodology and some supporting tools to create relative links between pieces of the material [Osgood and Bareiss, 1992]. Our experience shows that as the size of the system's database grows beyond about 100 stories, (depending on the degree of interrelatedness) the process of identifying relevant connections between stories becomes prohibitively difficult for indexers. (The term *story* refers to an individual content unit in the database and is not limited to the traditional narrative sense.) We call this phenomenon the *indexer saturation problem*: an indexer cannot remember enough about the contents of the database to make all appropriate connections, and the prospect of exhaustive search for all connections is onerous [Conklin, 1987]).

The second way in which the problem arises is when authors must index their own stories. School Stories is a collaborative hypermedia authoring environment for telling and interconnecting stories about grade K-12 experiences in US public schools. There is no separate indexer role in the system. Authors notice a connection between a story in the system and one they know. This new story is entered into the system and linked directly by its author to the eliciting story at the point it is told. Unfortunately, no easy way exists for an author to find links between a new story and the rest of the database.

We are beginning to provide automated assistance to achieve more complete interconnectivity in all our ASK systems than is possible with our current manual indexing methods. The contents of each story are represented as input to a computerized search process which compares simple representations of the input story to that of other stories in the story base and proposes connections between them to an indexer or author. Although fully automated indexing of stories would be ideal, we do not believe it to be practical, given the current state of the art of knowledge representation. It will require a more complete representation of story content as well as large amounts of commonsense knowledge to infer automatically the same set of the connections typically made by human indexers.

Given our desire to build a practical tool today, we have decided to employ a partial representation of story contents and very limited auxiliary knowledge. The cost of this decision is the requirement to keep a skilled human "in the loop", to determine the relevance of proposed links, and to maintain a story representation that can be easily processed by both machines and humans (see, *e.g.*, semiformal knowledge structures [Lemke and Fischer, 1990]). This decision balances the strengths of humans (*e.g.*, feature extraction and categorization) and computers (*e.g.*, rapid search and record keeping), enabling us to build a useful tool and solve a problem intractable to either machine or human alone.

The remainder of this paper discusses the ASK model of hypermedia, our representation of stories, the specific procedures for inferring links between stories, and our ongoing research.

The ASK Model of Hypermedia

ASK systems are based on a simple theory of the memory organization that might underlie conversation about problem solving.[Schank, 1977; Ferguson *et al.*, 1992]. This general theory argues that coherence in a conversation comes from the connectivity of human memory, *i.e.*, there is alignment between expression and thought (see *e.g.*, [Chafe, 1979]). We hypothesize that after hearing a piece of information in such a conversation, there are only a few general categories of follow-up information that represent a natural continuation of the thread of the conversation rather than a major topic shift. The categories can be thought of the poles of four axes or dimensions. These eight poles represent the most general kinds of questions that a user is likely to have in a conversation about problem solving. The browsing interface of an ASK system reifies this model of conversation by placing each relative link between stories in one of these eight general categories [Ferguson *et al.*, 1992]. Users can find their specific questions in the category that best describes the question.

The four dimensions are *Refocusing, Causality, Comparison,* and *Advice.* The *Refocusing* dimension concerns both adjustments to the specificity of topic under consideration as well as relevant digressions like clarifying of the meanings of terms or describing situ-

ations in which the topic arises. One pole, **Context,** points to the big picture within which a piece of information fits. The other, **Specifics,** points to examples of a general principle, further details of a situation, definitions of terms, or descriptions of parts of the whole, *et cetera.*

The *Causality* dimension arises directly out of the human desire to understand a situation in terms of its antecedents and consequences. We group temporal order and the causal chain because people typically collapse the distinction. The **Causes (or earlier events)** pole points to how a situation developed. The **Results (or later events)** pole points to the outcome of a situation.

The *Comparison* dimension concerns questions of similarity and difference, analogy and alternative, at the same level of abstraction as the reference story. The pole, **Analogies,** points to similar situations from other contexts or from the experiences of other experts. The **Alternatives** pole points to different approaches that might have been taken in a situation or differences of opinion between experts.

Finally, the *Advice* dimension captures the idea of carrying away a lesson, either negative or positive, for use in the problem solver's situation. The **Opportunities** pole points to advice about things a problem solver should capitalize upon in a situation. The **Warnings** pole points to advice about things that can go wrong in a problem solving situation.

The Partial Representation of Stories

Our approach to devising a representation for stories has been to provide a domain-independent representational frame that is instantiated with domain-specific fillers (Figure 1). A primary purpose of the frame is to enforce consistency of feature selection by an indexer. The representation is simple, indexical, and natural for human indexers to employ. It is just detailed enough to support the types of inference needed to recognize relationships between stories. In this and subsequent sections, we will describe a model of naive intentionality expressed in this frame structure and inference procedures specific to the conversational categories. We will offer examples of each from the School Stories application.

Because all of the stories of interest in the School Stories domain (K-12 school experiences) concern human intentional behavior, our representation is based upon the intentional chain [Schank and Abelson, 1975]. This is the simple model implicit in the design of the upper section of the frame shown in Figure 1. First, agents play roles and have beliefs that influence their selection of a course of action. Second, to play out those roles, agents establish goals and plans to achieve them. Finally, actions based on those plans and goals yield both intended and unintended results.

When representing a story, an indexer must instantiate the slots of this domain-independent frame with

AgentRole: *athlete*—the role the agent plays in the story
BeliefType: *strong doesn't mean dumb*—the agent's belief inducing the goal
IntentionLevel: *actually did*—the level of intentionality(goal, plan, or act)
IntentionType: *get good grades*—the goal, plan or action of an agent
OutcomeTypes: *positive emotional*—the results of the IntentionType

SituationType: *conflict with others*—a name linking multiple interacting frames
TimeOfOccurrence: *after reference*—sequencing information for frames
StoryType: *literal example*—story application information

Figure 1: A representational frame for describing one scene of a story

Figure 2: IntentionType Slot Fillers Near *Get Good Grades*

fillers representing the key domain concepts of the story. To achieve representational consistency, fillers are chosen from pre-enumerated taxonomies—one for each slot. Each filler exists in a domain specific hierarchy. The semantics of the hierarchies are intentional for the **IntentionType** slot, for example, *getting good grades* is a way to *graduate* (Figure 2) and categorical for the rest, *e.g.,* for the **AgentRole** slot, *a teacher without leverage* is a kind of *teacher*. Figure 1 also shows examples of fillers drawn from the School Stories domain.

A priori enumeration of all slot fillers is not intended. Rather our idea is to provide an indexer-extensible set for which the initial enumeration serves as an example. Indexers can enter a new term in the hierarchy by determining its similarity to pre-existing fillers. Assessment of the similarity of fillers during representation works because it is conducted by indexers in the target system's task context—the same one in which they would have judged the appropriateness of hand-crafted relative links between stories. In effect, the similarity of concepts is represented in equivalence classes, not computed from features [Porter, 1989], *i.e.,* similar concepts have a common parent in the hierarchy. To infer links, these hierarchies of equivalence classes are processed by inference procedures described in the next section.

The representational frame or *scene* captures the intentionality of a single agent. The upper portion the Figure 1 frame says: *an athlete actually did get good grades* by believing that *being strong doesn't mean being dumb* and this had a *positive emotional* impact on him/her.

In the frame's lower part in Figure 1 we include three additional slots. The **SituationType** slot functions both to group frames together and to describe the kind of agent interaction in those frames enabling

the representation of interactions among multiple agents, sometimes with conflicting goals [Schank and Osgood, 1991]. Indexers employ multiple frames—one or more for each agent, filling just the slots in each that they feel apply as in Figure 3. For example, a situation about how to handle student boredom is captured by selecting *Being Bored* to fill the **SituationType** slots of two frames of the same story, one about a *Student* who *Shows Lack of Interest* and the other about a *Teacher* who *Assigns An Independent Activity*.

The frame representation deliberately overspecifies situations. This makes feasible inferences of the same type at two different levels of abstraction. For example, similarity between stories can be assessed at the level of an entire situation through the fillers of the **SituationType** slot. Similarity can also be assessed between stories at the level of agent activity through fillers of the top section of the frame in Figure 1.

The **TimeOfOccurrence** slot supports sequencing of scenes in stories to establish intrastory causal/temporal relationships. For example, the term *at reference* indicates the relative point in time of the main action of the story, while drawing a lesson from the story happens *after reference,* another time designation.

The **StoryType** slot allows the indexer to advise the inferencing mechanism to identify what the story might be useful for and what the level of abstraction of the story content is. For example, if a story contains useful cautionary advice this slot will contain the value *Warnings*. If a story is a good explicit of example of something, *Literal Example* would fill this slot.

Inference Procedures

We have implemented inference procedures for all of the link types specified by the ASK model of hypermedia. In concept, inference procedures compare one of the representation frames of a reference story with all other frames in the story base. Operationally, inference is implemented as path finding, not exhaustive search and test. Links from slot fillers in the reference story frames are traversed in the concept hierarchy to identify sibling fillers which instantiate slots of other stories. Inference procedures are implemented as deductive retrieval rules which exploit the relationships between slot fillers. Each rule can create one of

AgentRole	Student		AgentRole	Teacher
BeliefType			BeliefType	
IntentionLevel	Actually Did		IntentionLevel	Actually Did
IntentionType	Show Lack of Interest		IntentionType	Assign Independent Activity
OutcomeTypes	Successful		OutcomeTypes	Successful Positive
SituationType	Being Bored		SituationType	Being Bored
TimeOfOccurrence	At Reference		TimeOfOccurrence	At Reference
StoryType	Opportunity		StoryType	Opportunity

Figure 3: Two scenes for the story Entertaining the Troublemaker

more links depending on whether or not the link type is symmetric, e.g., analogies/analogies, or complementary, e.g., context/specifics.

There are many senses of each link type. A particular rule finds only one. Summaries of each rule we have implemented are listed. Each is described as a process which indexes a new story, the reference story, with respect to existing stories in the the database which are potential follow-up stories.

Context, Specifics, and Examples are the implemented **Refocusing** rules. In a reference story scene if the parent concept of the situation or the agent's activity (e.g., in the concept hierarchy for situations, interpersonal struggles is the parent of being bored) occurs in a potential follow-up story scene, the context link is proposed. If on the other hand it is a child concept that is present in the follow-up story scene, then the specifics link is proposed. When a specifics link has been proposed and the follow-up story scene also has the story type of literal example, then an examples link is also proposed.

Earlier Events, Later Events, Causes and Results are the **Causality** rules. When absolute temporal information is available in a reference story scene, and a potential follow-up story scene describes the same situation or similar agent activity and has an earlier absolute time designation, the earlier events link is proposed. The later events link is proposed analogously. When absolute temporal information is not available in a reference story scene, and a potential follow-up story scene has the same agent activity but an earlier position in the intentional chain (e.g., in Figure 2, graduate is earlier in the intentional chain than get good grades), a causes link is proposed. A results link is proposed if the follow-up is later than the reference story scene in the intentional chain. Also, when a reference story scene is missing a belief to explain an agent's activity or situation, causes links are proposed to all follow-up story scenes that can supply one. A results link is proposed if the reference and follow-up story scenes are about similar situations or have similar agent activity and the follow-up story scene can provide the reference scene with missing outcome information.

Analogies and Alternatives are the **Comparison** rules. If a reference and follow-up story scene have agents with similar beliefs, situations, or activities (as determined taxomomically, e.g., in Figure 2, pass ex-

ams is a peer of get good grades), then an analogies link is proposed between them. However, if in otherwise similar story scenes, a dissimilar value is found in exactly one of the slots used above to compute similarity, then an alternatives link is proposed instead.

Warnings and Opportunities are the **Advice** rules. In similar reference and follow-up story scenes, if one has a story type of one of the advice link types and the other does not, then a link of that type is proposed from the former to the latter. The indexer provides these story type values when representing the story.

When we first defined the system, the information needs of these inference procedures determined the definition of the frame as well as the parts of domain concept hierarchy vocabulary that are explicitly mentioned in the rules, e.g., a story type of, literal example, used in the examples link inference. Likewise these rules operate in conjunction with the representations of similarity built into the equivalence classes of the hierarchy. The effectiveness of machine-assisted relative indexing is dependent upon the tuning of this relationship between rules and representation. Experience with tuning the School Stories system indicates that this task is within the capabilities of our indexers.

An Example: Indexing School Stories

Automated inference helps the authors working on School Stories find appropriate links between stories. While our work in this area is ongoing, the examples below illustrate the kinds of links between stories that can be inferred from the simple representation of stories described above.

One story entitled Entertaining the Troublemaker begins:

> One problem for smart kids is to keep from boring them in school. Each year that I was in school, my teachers had to find some way to keep me out of trouble since I was both bored and rambunctious. In the second grade I ran messages for the teacher. In the third I built baseball parks out of oak tag. In the fourth I wrote songs. These events turn out to be most of what I remember from those years. School for me was one long attempt to avoid boredom and trouble.[1]

The author has represented it in two scenes in Figure 3. As part of its search for links, the system runs

[1]This story was written by Roger Schank for Group-Write: School Stories.

AgentRole	Student
BeliefType	
IntentionLevel	Actually Did
IntentionType	Disrupt Class
OutcomeTypes	Successful
SituationType	Being Bored
TimeOfOccurrence	At Reference
StoryType	Literal Example

Figure 4: A Scene from A Different Bag of Tools

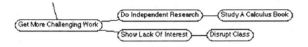

Figure 5: IntentionType Fillers Near *Disrupt Class*

its inference procedure for finding examples links listed above against the frames in Figure 3 and Figure 4. The rule for examples first specializes the fillers for each of the slots of the frame for the reference story (Figure 3). For instance, one causal specialization of the **IntentionType** slot with filler, *Show Lack of Interest* is *Disrupt Class, i.e.,* one way to show lack of interest is to the disrupt class (Figure 5). Because the candidate follow-up story frame in Figure 4 has the **StoryType** slot filler *Literal Example,* the system proposes an examples link to story *A Different Bag of Tools,* the story represented partially by the frame in Figure 4, which reads:

> I had learned to do integrals by various methods shown in a book that my high school physics teacher, Mr. Bader, had given me.
> One day he told me to stay after class. "Feynman," he said, "you talk too much and you make too much noise. I know why. You're bored. So I'm going to give you a book. You go up there in the back, in the corner, and study this book, and when you know everything that's in this book, you can talk again"[2]

AgentRole	Student
BeliefType	
IntentionLevel	Actually Did
IntentionType	Leave Class
OutcomeTypes	Successful
SituationType	Getting What You Want
TimeOfOccurrence	At Reference
StoryType	Literal Example

Figure 6: A Scene from the story A Deal's a Deal

In this simple case, our representation was sufficient to infer a possible *examples* link.[3] The system continues its search and finds additional ways in which to

[2]This story was extracted by Ian Underwood for Group-Write: School Stories from Feynman, R (1985) *Surely you're joking, Mr. Feynman: adventures of a curious character.* New York: W. W. Norton.

[3]In a group story-telling environment authors do not

connect these same two stories. It finds a *similarity* link (one sense of *analogies*) as well through **SituationType**: *Being Bored.* The human indexer can accept one or both of these links for inclusion in School Stories. The system goes on to propose as many other links as the story representations and rules will permit. The author accepts or rejects them as appropriate.

The representation-rule combination excludes some close yet still inappropriate links, as well. The frame for the story *A Deal's a Deal* in Figure 6 does not qualify as an *examples* link for our original story because, while it is has the **StoryType** slot filler *Literal Example,* the **IntentionType** filler *Leave Class* is not a specialization of *Show Lack of Interest* (Figure 5). In the story a *Deal's a Deal* the students were upset because a teacher had broken a promise. It was not that they were bored.

How well the approach excludes near misses depends on the assignment of filler terms to equivalence classes in the concept hierarchies. This assumes that agents do similar things for the same reasons. This kind of similarity limits inadvertent feature matching, because similarities are derived within the context of a specific unambiguous hierarchy locale. In the above example, one construal of *Leave Class* could conceivably be to *Show Lack of Interest,* but that is not the reason in *A Deal's a Deal.* In that story the agents *Leave Class* as a way to *Refuse to Cooperate with a Teacher. Showing Lack of Interest* is a weaker reason and is not represented as similar, *i.e.,* not placed in the same local context of the intentional hierarchy (Figure 5).

These simple examples illustrate how richly connected the stories in our test domain are and how, with a simple representation and processes, these links can be inferred. Given the human commitment to fill out frames for stories and to verify each system-proposed link, such a method significantly reduces the cognitive load human indexers face.

Ongoing Research

This work raises a number of research issues: balancing a fine grained representation against the ability to do simple syntactic feature matching, extending domain concept hierarchies consistently, and testing the effectiveness of the inference rules for machine assisted indexing.

It is difficult to determine just how much detailed domain knowledge should be represented in the content hierarchies to support the kinds of inferencing we have envisioned. There is a trade-off between the coarseness of the representation and its usefulness for infer-

maintain strong causal/temporal threads by telling a sequence of related stories. Therefore the conversational categories have analogical semantics. In the case of an examples link (one sense of **specifics**), one story is an example of the kind of thing discussed in general terms by a story which is probably about another situation written by another author.

ring links by feature matching. At one extreme we could have used fine grained representations that enrich expressiveness but make overall determination of similarity between stories very difficult, because the representations must be processed deeply to compensate for acceptable variation in representation. At the other extreme we could have reified complex relationships into flat propositional features which reduces inferencing to simple feature matching. For example, we rejected the use of complex role relations as a way to represent multiple interacting agents in the **AgentRole** slot, *e.g.*, *student who is infatuated with the teacher but the teacher does not respond favorably*. Use of such unduly extended filler names flattens the representation lessening the ability to infer links, because the internal structure of the filler is not accessible to inference [Domeshek, 1992]. We have tried to find an acceptable balance in our representation between flat and deep representation. Our principle is to provide just the amount of representation needed by the inference rules we have defined.

It is the indexer's job to define the domain concept hierarchies and to use these as fillers in frames for stories. These fillers establish equivalence classes for inferencing. Also where they are placed in the hierarchy represents a prediction about where future indexers will find fillers to describe their stories. Therefore, consistency and economy in the selection of the hierarchy vocabulary is required by both machine and human. We do not yet know how consistent the human extension of domain hierarchies will be. Our experience to date suggests that indexers sometimes overlook or misinterpret the semantics of existing fillers. In many domains, different vocabularies tend to be used in different situations. The result is the creation of synonymous categories. Indexers may also misuse the hierarchy by placing elements of widely divergent levels of abstraction at the same level in the hierarchy. Our current solution is to use the simplest partial concept hierarchy that will support the desired inferences—a corollary of the principle governing representation for rules stated above.

Finally, we have not yet subjected the conversational category-based inference rules for machine assisted linking to a systematic comparison with the link sets derived by human indexers independently. We have however conducted some informal checks on the system's performance in one domain (School Stories). The automated approach found a superset of the links human indexers found in a sample of 16 stories selected at random from the database. We are beginning to apply our technique in a very different domain, *i.e.*, military transportation planning.

These open issues have not prevented us from seeing some significant benefits to indexers already from machine-assisted knowledge acquisition as described herein. Ideally, as our inference procedures are improved and as our confidence grows that the indexes generated converge with those humans would produce, we may be able to grant autonomy to some of them, enabling our ASK hypermedia systems to generate some classes of relative links dynamically. Whether or not that proves possible, we are creating an optimal partnership between human and tool, enabling large-scale relative indexing which neither human nor machine can do alone.

Acknowledgments: The dynamic indexing tool was written by Paul Brown and Paul Rowland.

References

Chafe, W. 1979. The flow of thought and the flow of language. In Givon, T., editor 1979, *Discourse and syntax*. Academic Press, New York. 159–181.

Conklin, E. 1987. Hypertext: An introduction and survey. *IEEE Computer* 2:17–41.

Domeshek, E. 1992. *Do the Right Thing: Component Theory for Indexing Stories as Social Advice*. Ph.D. Dissertation, Yale University, New Haven, CT.

Ferguson, W.; Bareiss, R.; Birnbaum, L.; and Osgood, R. 1992. ASK systems: An approach to the realization of story-based teachers. *The Journal of the Learning Sciences* 2:95–134.

Lemke, A. and Fischer, G. 1990. A cooperative problem solving system for user interface design. In *Proceedings of the Eighth National Conference on Artificial Intelligence*, Menlo Park, CA. AAAI Press/The MIT Press.

Osgood, R. and Bareiss, R. 1992. Index generation in the construction of large-scale conversational hypermedia systems. AAAI-93 Spring Symposium on Case-Based Reasoning and Information Retrieval.

Porter, B. 1989. Similarity assessment: Computation vs. representation. In *Proceedings: Case-Based Reasoning Workshop*, San Mateo, CA. Morgan Kaufman Publishers.

Schank, R. and Abelson, R. 1975. *Scripts, Plans, Goals and Understanding*. Lawrence Erlbaum Associates, Hillsdale, NJ.

Schank, R. and Osgood, R. 1991. A content theory of memory indexing. Technical Report 2, The Institute for the Learning Sciences, Northwestern University, Evanston, IL.

Schank, R. 1977. Rules and topics in conversation. *Cognitive Science* 1:421–441.

Spiro, R. and Jehng, J. 1990. Cognitive flexibility and hypertext: Theory and technology for the non-linear traversal of complex subject matter. In Nix, D. and Spiro, R., editors 1990, *Cognition, Education, and Multimedia: Exploring Ideas in High Technology*. Lawrence Erlbaum Associates, Hillsdale. 163–205.

Machine
Learning

Probabilistic Prediction of Protein Secondary Structure
Using Causal Networks
(Extended Abstract)

Arthur L. Delcher*
Computer Science Dept.
Loyola College
Baltimore, MD 21210

Simon Kasif*
Dept. of Computer Science
Johns Hopkins University
Baltimore, MD 21218

Harry R. Goldberg
Mind-Brain Institute
Johns Hopkins University
Baltimore, MD 21218

William H. Hsu
Dept. of Computer Science
Johns Hopkins University
Baltimore, MD 21218

Abstract

In this paper we present a probabilistic approach to analysis and prediction of protein structure. We argue that this approach provides a flexible and convenient mechanism to perform general scientific data analysis in molecular biology. We apply our approach to an important problem in molecular biology—predicting the secondary structure of proteins—and obtain experimental results comparable to several other methods. The causal networks that we use provide a very convenient medium for the scientist to experiment with different empirical models and obtain possibly important insights about the problem being studied.

Introduction

Scientific analysis of data is an important potential application of Artificial Intelligence (AI) research. We believe that the ultimate data analysis system using AI techniques will have a wide range of tools at its disposal and will adaptively choose various methods. It will be able to generate simulations automatically and verify the model it constructed with the data generated during these simulations. When the model does not fit the observed results the system will try to explain the source of error, conduct additional experiments, and choose a different model by modifying system parameters. If it needs user assistance, it will produce a simple low-dimensional view of the constructed model and the data. This will allow the user to guide the system toward constructing a new model and/or generating the next set of experiments. We believe that flexibility, efficiency and direct representation of causality are key issues in the choice of representation in such a system.

As a first step, in this paper we present a probabilistic approach to analysis and prediction of protein structure. We argue that this approach provides a flexible and convenient mechanism to perform general sci-

entific data analysis in molecular biology. We apply our approach to an important problem in molecular biology: predicting the secondary structure of proteins [Chou and Fasman, 1978; Garnier et al., 1978]. A number of methods have been applied to this problem with various degree of success [Holley and Karplus, 1989; Cost and Salzberg, 1993; Qian and Sejnowski, 1988; Maclin and Shavlik, 1992; Zhang et al., 1993; Muggleton and King, 1991]. In addition to obtaining experimental results comparable to other methods, there are several theoretically and practically important observations that we have made in experimenting with our system.

- It has been claimed in several papers that probabilistic (statistical) approaches have been outperformed by neural network methods and memory-based methods by a wide margin. We show that probabilistic methods are comparable to other methods in prediction quality. In addition, the predictions generated by our methods have precise quantitative semantics which is not shared by other classification methods. Specifically, all the causal and statistical independence assumptions are made explicit in our networks thereby allowing biologists to study causal links in a convenient manner. This generalizes correlation studies that are normally used in statistical analysis of data.

- Our method provides a very flexible tool to experiment with a variety of modelling strategies. This flexibility allows a biologist to perform many practically important statistical queries which can yield important insight into a problem.

- From the theoretical point of view we found that different ways to model the domain produce practically different results. This is an experience that AI researchers encounter repeatedly in many knowledge-representation schemes: different coding of the problem in the architecture results in dramatic differences in performance. This has been observed in production systems, neural networks, constraint networks and other representations. Our experience re-

---
* Supported by NSF DARPA Grant CCR-8908092 and AFOSR Grant AFOSR-89-1151

inforces the thesis that while knowledge representation is a key issue in AI, a knowledge-representation system typically provides merely the programming language in which a problem must be expressed. The coding, analogous to an algorithm in procedural languages, is perhaps of equally great importance. However, the importance of this issue is grossly underestimated and not studied as systematically and rigorously as knowledge representation languages.

- Previous methods for protein folding were based on the window approach. That is, the learning algorithm attempted to predict the structure of the central amino acid in a "window" of k amino acids residues. It is well recognized that in the context of protein folding, very minimal mutations (amino acid substitutions) often cause significant changes in the secondary structure located far from the mutation cite. Our method is aimed at capturing this behavior.

Protein Folding

Proteins have a central role in essentially all biological processes. They control cellular growth and development, they are responsible for cellular defense, they control reaction rates, they are responsible for propagating nerve impulses, and they serve as the conduit for cellular communication. The ability of proteins to perform these tasks, *i.e.*, the *function* of a protein, is directly related to its *structure*. The results of Christian Anfinsen's work in the late 1950's indicated that a protein's unique structure is specified by its aminoacid sequence. This work suggested that a protein's conformation could be specified if its amino acid sequence was known, thus defining the protein folding problem. Unfortunately, nobody has been able to put this theory into practice.

The biomedical importance of solving the protein folding problem cannot be overstressed. Our ability to design genes—the molecular blueprints for specifying a protein's amino acid sequence—has been refined. These genes can be implanted into a cell and this cell can serve as the vector for the production of large quantities of the protein. The protein, once isolated, potentially can be used in any one of a multitude of applications—uses ranging from supplementing the human defense system to serving as a biological switch for controlling abnormal cell growth and development. A critical aspect of this process is the ability to specify the amino acid sequence which defines the required conformation of the protein.

Traditionally, protein structure has been described at three levels. The first level defines the protein's amino acid sequence, the second considers local conformations of this sequence, *i.e.*, the formation of rod-like structures called α-helices, planar structures called β-sheets, and intervening sequences often categorized as coil. The third level of protein structure specifies the global conformation of the protein. Due to limits on

our understanding of solutions to the protein folding problem, most of the emphasis on structure prediction has been at the level of secondary structure prediction.

There are fundamentally two approaches that have been taken to predict the secondary structure of proteins. The first approach is based on theoretical methods and the second is based on data derived empirically. Theoretical methods rely on our understanding of the rules governing amino acid interactions, they are mathematically sophisticated and computationally time-intensive. Conversely, empirically based techniques combine a heuristic with a probabilistic schema in determining structure. Empirical approaches have reached prediction rates approaching 70%—the apparent limit given our current base of knowledge.

The most obvious weakness of empirically based prediction schemes is their reliance on exclusively local influences. Typically, a window that can be occupied by 9-13 amino acids is passed along the protein's amino acid sequence. Based on the context of the central amino acid's sequence neighbors, it is classified as belonging to a particular structure. The window is then shifted and the amino acid which now occupies the central position of the window is classified. This is an iterative process which continues until the end of the protein is reached. In reality, the structure of an amino acid is determined by its local environment. Due to the coiled nature of a protein, this environment may be influenced by amino acids which are far from the central amino acid in sequence but not in space. Thus, a prediction scheme which considers the influence of amino acids which are, in sequence, far removed from the central amino acid of the window may improve our ability to successfully predict a protein's conformation.

Notation

For the purpose of this paper, the set of proteins is assumed to be a set of sequences (strings) over an alphabet of twenty characters (different capital letters) that correspond to different amino acids. With each protein sequence of length n we associate a sequence of secondary structure descriptors of the same length. The structure descriptors take three values: h, e, c that correspond to α-helix, β-sheet and coil. That is, if we have a subsequence of $hh \ldots h$ in positions $i, i+1, \ldots, i+k$ it is assumed that the protein sequence in those positions folded as a helix. The classification problem is typically stated as follows. Given a protein sequence of length n, generate a sequence of structure predictions of length n which describes the secondary structure of the protein sequence. Almost without exception all previous approaches to the problem have used the following approach. The classifier receives a window of length $2K + 1$ (typically $K < 12$) of amino acids. The classifier then predicts the secondary structure of the central amino acid (*i.e.*, the amino acid in position K) in the window.

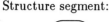

Structure segment:

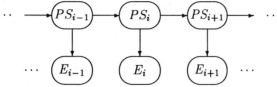

Evidence segment:

Figure 1: Causal tree model.

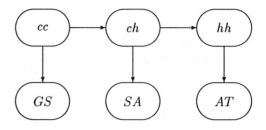

Figure 2: Example of causal tree model using pairs, showing protein segment $GSAT$ with corresponding secondary structure $cchh$

A Probabilistic Framework for Protein Analysis

When making decisions in the presence of uncertainty, it is well-known that Bayes rule provides an optimal decision procedure, assuming we are given all prior and conditional probabilities. There are two major difficulties with using the approach in practice. The problem of reasoning in general Bayes networks is $\mathcal{NP}$-complete, and we often do not have accurate estimates of the probabilities. However, it is known that when the structure of the network has a special form it is possible to perform a complete probabilistic analysis efficiently. In this section we show how to model probabilistic analysis of the structure of protein sequences as belief propagation in causal trees. In the full version of the paper we also describe how we dealt with problems such as undersampling and regularization. The general schema we advocate has the following form. The set of nodes in the networks are either protein-structure nodes (PS-nodes) or evidence nodes (E-nodes). Each PS-node in the network is a discrete random variable X_i that can take values which correspond to descriptors of secondary structure, *i.e.*, segments of h's, e's and c's. With each such node we associate an evidence node that again can assume any of a set of discrete values. Typically, an evidence node would correspond to an occurrence of a particular subsequence of amino acids at a particular location in the protein. With each edge in the network we will associate a matrix of conditional probabilities. The simplest possible example of a network is given in Figure 1.

We assume that all conditional dependencies are represented by a causal tree. This assumption violates some of our knowledge of the real-world problem, but provides an approximation that allows us to perform an efficient computation. For an exact definition of a causal tree see Pearl [Pearl, 1988].

Protein Modeling Using Causal Networks

As mentioned above, the network is comprised of a set of protein-structure nodes and a set of evidence nodes.

Protein-structure nodes are finite strings over the alphabet $\{h, e, c\}$. For example the string $hhhhhh$ is a string of six residues in an α-helical conformation, while $eecc$ is a string of two residues in a β-sheet conformation followed by two residues folded as a coil. Evidence nodes are nodes that contain information about a particular region of the protein. Thus, the main idea is to represent physical and statistical rules in the form of a probabilistic network. We note that the main point of this paper is advocating the framework of causal networks as an experimental tool for molecular biology applications rather than focusing on a particular network. The framework allows us flexibility to test causal theories by orienting edges in the causal network.

For our initial experiments we have chosen the simplest possible models. In this paper we describe two that we feel are particularly important: a classical Hidden Markov Model using the Viterbi algorithm and causal trees using Pearl's belief updating. We shall show that the second approach is better and matches in accuracy other methods that have a less explicitly quantitative semantics.

In our first set of experiments we converged on the following model that seems to match in performance many existing approaches. The network looks like a set of PS-nodes connected as a chain. To each such node we connect a single evidence node. In our experiments the PS-nodes are strings of length two or three over the alphabet $\{h, e, c\}$ and the evidence nodes are strings of the same length over the set of amino acids. The following example clarifies our representation. Assume we have a string of amino acids $GSAT$. We model the string as a network comprised of three evidence nodes GS, SA, AT and three PS-nodes. The network is shown in Figure 2. A correct prediction will assign the values cc, ch, and hh to the PS-nodes as shown in the figure.

Let $X_0, X_1, \ldots, X_n$ be a set of PS-nodes connected as in Figure 1. Generally, speaking the distribution for the variable X_i in the causal network as below can be computed using the following formulae. Let $e_{X_i}^- = e_i, e_{i+1}, \ldots, e_n$ denote the set of evidence nodes to the

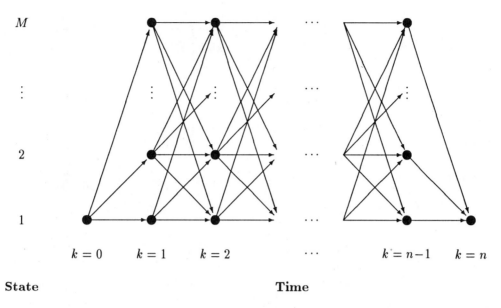

$$k=0 \qquad k=1 \qquad k=2 \qquad \cdots \qquad k=n-1 \qquad k=n$$

State   **Time**

Figure 3: Modelling the Viterbi algorithm as a shortest path problem.

right of X_i, and let $e_{X_i}^+ = e_1, e_2, \ldots, e_{i-1}$ be the set of evidence nodes to the left of X_i. By the assumption of independence explicit in the network we have

$$P(X_i | X_{i-1}, e_{X_i}^+) = P(X_i | X_{i-1})$$

Thus,

$$P(X_i | e_{X_i}^+, e_{X_i}^-) = \alpha P(e_{X_i}^- | X_i) P(X_i | e_{X_i}^+)$$

where α is some normalizing constant. For length consideration we will not describe the algorithm to compute the probabilities. The reader is referred to Pearl for a detailed description [Pearl, 1988]. Pearl gives an efficient procedure to compute the belief distribution of every node in such a tree. Most importantly, this procedure operates by a simple efficient propagation mechanism that operates in linear time.

Protein Modeling Using the Viterbi Algorithm

In this section we describe an alternative model for prediction. This model has been heavily used in speech understanding systems, and indeed was suggested to us by Kai Foo Lee whose system using similar ideas achieves remarkable performance on speaker-independent continuous speech understanding.

We implemented the Viterbi algorithm and compare its performance to the method outlines above. We briefly describe the method here. We follow the discussion by Forney [Forney, 1973].

We assume a Markov process which is characterized by a finite set of state transitions. That is, we assume the process at time k can be described by a random variable X_k that assumes a discrete number of values (states) $1, \ldots, M$. The process is Markov, *i.e.*, the

probability $P(X_{k+1} | X_0, \ldots X_k) = P(X_{k+1} | X_k)$. We denote the process by the sequence $X = X_0, \ldots, X_k$. We are given a set of observations $Z = Z_0, \ldots, Z_k$ such that Z_i depends only on the transition $T_i = (X_{i+1}, X_i)$. Specifically, $P(Z|X) = \prod_{k=0}^{n} (Z_i | X_i)$. The Viterbi algorithm is a solution to the maximum aposteriori estimation of X given Z. In other words we are seeking a sequence of states X for which $P(Z|X)$ is maximized.

An intuitive way to understand the problem is in graph theoretic terms. We build a n-level graph that contains nM nodes (see Figure 3). With each transition we associate an edge. Thus, any sequence of states has a corresponding path in the graph. Given the set of observations Z with any path in the graph we associate a length $L = -\ln P(X, Z)$. We are seeking a shortest path in the graph. However, since

$$
\begin{aligned}
P(X, Z) &= P(X)P(Z|X) \\
&= \prod_{k=0}^{n-1} P(X_{k+1}|X_k) \prod_{k=0}^{n-1} P(Z_k|X_{k+1}, X_k)
\end{aligned}
$$

if we define $\lambda(T_k) = -\ln P(X_{K+1}|X_K) - \ln P(Z_k|T_k)$ we obtain that $-\ln P(Z, X) = \sum_{k=0}^{n-1} \lambda_k$.

Now we can compute the shortest path through this graph by a standard application of shortest path algorithms specialized to directed acyclic graphs. For each time step i we simply maintain M paths which are the shortest path to each of the possible states we could be in at time i. To extend the path to time step $i+1$ we simply compute the lengths of all the paths extended by one time unit and maintain the shortest path to each one of the M possible states at time $i+1$.

Our experimentation with the Viterbi algorithm was completed in Spring 1992. We recently learned that

David Haussler [Haussler *et al.*, 1992] and his group suggested the Viterbi algorithm framework for protein analysis as well. They experimented on a very different problem and also obtain interesting results. We document the performance of Viterbi on our problem even though, as described below, the causal-tree method outperformed Viterbi. The difference between the methods is that the Viterbi algorithm predicts the most likely complete sequence of structure elements, whereas the causal-tree method makes separate predictions about individual *PS*-nodes.

Experiments

The experiments we conducted were performed to allow us to make a direct comparison with previous methods that have been applied to this problem. We followed the methodology described in [Zhang *et al.*, 1993; Maclin and Shavlik, 1992] which did a thorough cross-validated testing of various classifiers for this problem. Since it is known that two proteins that are homologous (similar in chemical structure) tend to fold similarly and therefore generate accuracies of predictions that are often overly optimistic, it is important to document the precise degree of homology between the training set and the testing set. In our experiments the set of proteins was divided into eight subsets. We perform eight experiments in which we train the network on seven subsets and then predict on the remaining subset. The accuracies are averaged over all eight experiments. This methodology is referred to as *k*-way cross validation.

Experimental Results

We report the accuracy of prediction on individual residues and also on predicting runs of helices and sheets. Table 1 shows the prediction accuracy of our methods using the causal network method for each one of the eight trials in our 8-way cross-validation study. In the pairs column we document the performance of the causal network described earlier using *PS*-nodes and *E*-nodes that represent protein segments of length 2. The triples column gives the results for the same network with segments of length 3. The decrease in accuracy for triples is a result of undersampling.

Table 2 shows the performance of our method in predicting the secondary structure at each amino acid position in comparison with other methods. In Table 3 we report the performance of our method on predicting runs of helices and sheets and compare those with other methods that were applied to this problem. To summarize, our method yields performance comparable to other methods on predicting runs of helices and sheets. It seems to have particularly high accuracy in predicting individual helices.

Discussion

In this paper we have proposed causal networks as a general and efficient framework for data analysis in

Trial	Positions	Correct Using:	
		Pairs	Triples
1	2339	1518 (64.9%)	1469 (62.8%)
2	2624	1567 (59.7%)	1518 (57.9%)
3	2488	1479 (59.5%)	1435 (57.7%)
4	2537	1666 (65.7%)	1604 (63.2%)
5	2352	1437 (61.1%)	1392 (59.2%)
6	2450	1510 (61.6%)	1470 (60.0%)
7	2392	1489 (62.3%)	1447 (60.5%)
8	2621	1656 (63.2%)	1601 (61.1%)
All	19803	12322 (62.2%)	11936 (60.3%)

Table 1: Causal tree results for 8-way cross-validation using segments of length 2 and length 3.

Method	Total	Helix	Sheet	Coil
Chou-Fasman	57.3%	31.7%	36.9%	76.1%
ANN	61.8%	43.6%	18.6%	86.3%
w/ state	61.7%	39.2%	24.2%	86.0%
FSKBANN	63.4%	45.9%	35.1%	81.9%
w/o state	62.2%	42.4%	26.3%	84.6%
Viterbi	58.5%	48.3%	47.0%	69.3%
Chain-Pairs	62.2%	55.9%	51.7%	67.4%
Chain-Triples	60.3%	53.0%	45.5%	70.8%

Table 2: Overall prediction accuracies for various prediction methods. Comparative method results from [Maclin and Shavlik, 1992].

molecular biology. We have reported our initial experiments applying this approach to the problem of protein secondary structure prediction. One of the main advantages of the probabilistic approach we described here is our ability to perform detailed experiments where we can experiment with different causal models. We can easily perform local substitutions (mutations) and measure (probabilistically) their effect on the global structure. Window-based methods do not support such experimentation as readily. Our method is efficient both during training and during prediction, which is important in order to be able to perform many experiments with different networks.

Our initial experiments have been done on the simplest possible models where we ignore many known dependencies. For example, it is known that in α-helices hydrogen bonds are formed between every i^{th} and $(i+4)^{\text{th}}$ residue in a chain. This can be incorporated in our model without losing efficiency. We also can improve our method by incorporating additional

Description	Chain-Pair	FSkbann	ANN	Chou-Fasman
Average length of predicted helix run	9.4	8.52	7.79	8.00
Average length of actual helix run	10.3	–	–	–
Percentage of actual helix runs overlapped by predicted helix runs	66%	67%	70%	56%
Percentage of predicted helix runs that overlap actual helix runs	62%	66%	61%	64%
Average length of predicted sheet run	3.8	3.80	2.83	6.02
Average length of actual sheet run	5.0	–	–	–
Percentage of actual sheet runs overlapped by predicted sheet runs	56%	54%	35%	46%
Percentage of predicted sheet runs that overlap actual sheet runs	60%	63%	63%	56%

Table 3: Precision of run (segment) predictions. Comparative method results from [Maclin and Shavlik, 1992].

correlations among particular amino acids as in [Gibrat et al., 1987]. We achieve prediction accuracy similar to many other methods such as neural networks. We are confident that with sufficient fine tuning we can improve our results to equal the best methods. Typically, the current best prediction methods involve complex hybrid methods that compute a weighted vote among several methods using a combiner that learns the weights. E.g., the hybrid method described by [Zhang et al., 1993] combines neural networks, a statistical method and memory-based reasoning in a single system and achieves an overall accuracy of 66.4%.

Bayesian classification is a well-studied area and has been applied frequently to many domains such as pattern recognition, speech understanding and others. Statistical methods also have been used for protein structure prediction. What characterizes our approach is its simplicity and the explicit modeling of causal links. We believe that for scientific data analysis it is particularly important to develop tools that clearly display all the causal independence assumptions. Causal networks provide a very convenient medium for the scientist to experiment with different empirical models and obtain possibly important insights into a problem.

References

Chou, P. and Fasman, G. 1978. Prediction of the secondary structure of proteins from their amino acid sequence. *Advanced Enzymology* 47:45–148.

Cost, S. and Salzberg, S. 1993. A weighted nearest neighbor algorithm for learning with symbolic features. *Machine Learning* 10(1):57–78.

Forney, G. D. 1973. The Viterbi algorithm. *Proceedings of the IEEE* 61(3):268–278.

Garnier, J.; Osguthorpe, D.; ; and Robson, B. 1978. Analysis of the accuracy and implication of simple methods for predicting the secondary structure of globular proteins. *Journal of Molecular Biology* 120:97–120.

Gibrat, J.-F.; Garnier, J.; and Robson, B. 1987. Further developments of protein secondary structure predicition using information theory. *Journal of Molecular Biology* 198:425–443.

Haussler, D.; Krogh, A.; Mian, S.; and Sjolander, K. 1992. Protein modeling using hidden markov models. Technical Report UCSC-CRL-92-23, University of California, Santa Cruz.

Holley, L. and Karplus, M. 1989. Protein secondary structure prediction with a neural network. In *Proceedings of the National Academy of Sciences USA*, volume 86. 152–156.

Maclin, R. and Shavlik, J. 1992. Refinement of approximate domain theories by knowledge-based neural networks. In *Proceedings Tenth National Conference on Artificial Intelligence*. 165–170.

Muggleton, S. and King, R. 1991. Predicting protein secondary structure using inductive logic programming. Technical report, Turing Institute, University of Glasgow, Scotland.

Pearl, J. 1988. *Probabilistic Reasoning in Intelligent Systems*. Morgan Kaufmann.

Qian, N. and Sejnowski, T. 1988. Predicting the secondary structure of globular proteins using neural network models. *Journal of Molecular Biology* 202:865–884.

Zhang, X.; Mesirov, J.; and Waltz, D. 1993. A hybrid system for protein secondary structure prediction. *Molecular Biology (to appear)*.

OC1: Randomized induction of oblique decision trees

Sreerama Murthy[1], Simon Kasif[1], Steven Salzberg[1], Richard Beigel[2]

[1]Dept. of Computer Science, Johns Hopkins University, Baltimore, MD 21218
[2]Dept. of Computer Science, Yale University, New Haven, CT 06520
[1]lastname@cs.jhu.edu, [2]beigel-richard@cs.yale.edu

Abstract

This paper introduces OC1, a new algorithm for generating multivariate decision trees. Multivariate trees classify examples by testing linear combinations of the features at each non-leaf node of the tree. Each test is equivalent to a hyperplane at an oblique orientation to the axes. Because of the computational intractability of finding an optimal orientation for these hyperplanes, heuristic methods must be used to produce good trees. This paper explores a new method that combines deterministic and randomized procedures to search for a good tree. Experiments on several different real-world data sets demonstrate that the method consistently finds much smaller trees than comparable methods using univariate tests. In addition, the accuracy of the trees found with our method matches or exceeds the best results of other machine learning methods.

1   Introduction

Decision trees (DTs) have been used quite extensively in the machine learning literature for a wide range of classification problems. Many variants of DT algorithms have been introduced, and a number of different goodness-of-split criteria have been explored. Most of the research to date on decision tree algorithms has been restricted to either (1) examples with symbolic attribute values [Quinlan, 1986] or (2) univariate tests for numeric attributes [Breiman et al., 1984], [Quinlan, 1992]. Univariate tests compare the value of a single attribute to a constant; i.e., they are equivalent to partitioning a set of examples with an axis-parallel hyperplane. Although Breiman et al [1984] suggested an elegant method for inducing multivariate linear decision trees, there has not been much activity in the development of such trees until very recently [Utgoff and Brodley, 1991], [Heath et al., 1992]. Because these trees use oblique hyperplanes to partition the data, we call them oblique decision trees.

This paper presents a new method for inducing oblique decision trees. As it constructs a tree, this method searches at each node for the best hyperplane to partition the data. Although most of the searching is deterministic hill-climbing, we have introduced randomization to determine the initial placement of a hyperplane and to escape from local minima. By limiting the number of random choices, the algorithm is guaranteed to spend only polynomial time at each node in the tree. In addition, randomization itself has produced several benefits. Our experiments indicate that it successfully avoids local minima in many cases. Randomization also allows the algorithm to produce many different trees for the same data set. This offers the possibility of a new family of classifiers: k-decision-tree algorithms, in which an example is classified by the majority vote of k trees (See [Heath, 1992]).

Two other methods for generating oblique trees, that have been introduced recently, are perceptron trees [Utgoff and Brodley, 1991] and simulated annealing (SADT) [Heath et al., 1992]. The former shows that much smaller trees can be induced when oblique hyperplanes are used. However, theirs is a deterministic algorithm, and Heath [1992] shows that the problem of finding an optimal oblique tree is NP-Complete.[3] This work also introduces a completely randomized technique for finding good hyperplanes. The motivation for randomization is given in [Heath et al., 1992], but the idea can briefly be explained as follows. Consider the hyperplane associated with the root of a decision tree. The optimal (smallest) decision tree may use non-optimal decision plane at the root. Obviously this is true for each node of the tree; this observation suggests a randomized strategy where we try to construct the smallest tree using several candidate hyperplanes at each node. This idea can be facilitated by using a randomized algorithm to find good separating hyperplanes. That is, if a randomized algorithm is executed repeatedly, it will find different hyperlanes each time. [Heath et al., 1992] use an algorithm based on simulated annealing to generate good splits. Our

---

[3]More precisely, Heath [Heath, 1992] proves that the problem of finding an optimal oblique split is NP-Complete, using the number of misclassified examples as the error measure.

method is also randomized, but it includes a substantial directed search component that allows it to run much faster. In our experiments, our method ran much faster than SADT without sacrificing accuracy in the resulting classifier.

The algorithmic content of this paper focusses on the question of how to partition a given sample space into homogeneous regions. A complete description of any DT building method should also include discussion of its choices regarding the pruning strategies and the stop-splitting criteria. However, we do not address these issues here, because our choices for them are quite straightforward and standard in the literature. We stop splitting when the sample space associated with the current node has zero impurity (see Section 2.4). The only pruning done by our method consists of cutting off subtrees at nodes whose impurity measure is less than a certain threshold. For a good review and comparison of pruning strategies, see [Mingers, 1989] and [Quinlan, 1992].

The problem of partitioning the sample space involves the following related issues:

- restrictions on the location and orientation of hyperplanes,

- goodness measures for evaluating a split,

- strategies to search through the space of possible hyperplanes for the best hyperplane, and

- methods for choosing a hyperplane from which the above search begins.

These issues are fundamental to the design of a DT algorithm [Breiman *et al.*, 1984], and many existing DT algorithms can be classified on the basis of how they make these choices. Section 2 elaborates our algorithm with respect to each of these issues. Section 3 presents the results of using our method to classify several real-world data sets, and compares our results to those of some existing methods. Section 4 summarizes the lessons learned from these experiments.

2 The OC1 Algorithm

In this section we discuss details of our oblique decision tree learning method. We call this algorithm OC1, for **O**blique **C**lassifier **1**. OC1 imposes no restrictions on the orientation of the hyperplanes. This is the main difference between OC1 and methods such as ID3 and CART, which use only axis-parallel hyperplanes. However, OC1 cannot distinguish between two hyperplanes that have identical sets of points on both sides. In other words, if the sample space consists of n examples in d dimensions (d attributes), then our algorithm recognizes only $\binom{n}{d}$ distinct hyperplanes.

The initial hyperplane at each node in the decision tree is chosen randomly by OC1. Even if such a randomly placed hyperplane has a very poor location, it is usually improved greatly in the first few perturbations.

2.1 Search Strategies

The strategy of searching through the space of possible hyperplanes is defined by the procedure that perturbs the current hyperplane into a new location. As there are an exponential number, $\binom{n}{d}$, of possible hyperplane locations, any procedure that simply enumerates all of them will be unreasonably costly. The two main alternatives considered in the past have been to use a non-deterministic search procedure, as in SADT [Heath *et al.*, 1992], or to use a heuristic deterministic procedure, as in CART [Breiman *et al.*, 1984]. OC1 combines these two approaches, using heuristic search until it finds a local minimum, and then using a non-deterministic search step to get out of the local minimum.

We will start by explaining how we perturb a hyperplane to split the sample space P at a node of a DT. P contains n examples, each with d attributes. Each example belongs to a particular category. The equation of the current hyperplane H can be written:

$$\sum_{i=1}^{d}(a_i X_i) + a_{d+1} = 0$$

Let $P_j = (x_{j1}, x_{j2}, \ldots, x_{jd})$ be the jth example from the sample space P. If we substitute P_j into the equation for H, we get: $\sum_{i=1}^{d}(a_i x_{ji}) + a_{d+1} = V_j$, where the sign of V_j tells us whether the point P_j is above or below the hyperplane H. If H splits the sample space P perfectly, then all points belonging to the same category in P will have the same sign i.e., $sign(V_j) = sign(V_k)$ iff $category(P_i) = category(P_j)$

OC1 perturbs the coefficients of H one at a time. If we consider the coefficient a_m as a variable, and all other coefficients as constants, V_j can be viewed as a function of a_m. If U_j is defined as

$$U_j = \frac{a_m x_{jm} - V_j}{x_{jm}} \qquad (1)$$

then the point P_j is above H if $a_m > U_j$, and below otherwise. Thus, by fixing the values of the coefficients $a_1 \ldots a_{d+1}$, except a_m, we can obtain n constraints on the value of a_m, using the n points in the set P (assuming no degeneracies).

The problem then is to find a value for a_m that satisfies as many of these constraints as possible. (If all the constraints are satisfied, then we have a perfect split.) This problem is easy to solve; in fact, it is just an axis parallel split in 1-D. The value a_{m_1} obtained by solving this one dimensional problem is a good candidate to be used as the new value of the coefficient a_m. Let H_1 be the hyperplane obtained by changing a_m to a_{m_1} in H. If H has better (lower) impurity than H_1, then H_1 is discarded. If H_1 has lower impurity, H_1 becomes the new location of the hyperplane. If H and H_1 have identical impurities, and different locations, then H_1 is accepted with probability *stag_prob*.

```
Perturb(H,m)
{
  for j = 1 to n
      Compute U_j (Eq. 1)
  Sort U_1 ... U_n in nondecreasing order.
  a_{m_1} = best univariate split of the sorted U_j s.
  H_1 = result of substituting a_{m_1} for a_m in H.
  If (impurity(H) < impurity(H_1))
      { a_m = a_{m_1} ; stagnant = 0 }
  Else if (impurity(H) = impurity(H_1))
      { a_m = a_{m_1} with probability
              stag_prob = e^{-stagnant}
  stagnant = stagnant + 1 }
}
```

Figure 1: Perturbation Algorithm

The parameter $stag\_prob$, denoting "stagnation probability", is the probability that a hyperplane is perturbed to a location that does not change the impurity measure. To prevent the impurity from remaining stagnant for a long time, $stag\_prob$ decreases exponentially with the number of "stagnant" perturbations. It is reset to 1 every time the global impurity measure is improved. Pseudocode for our perturbation procedure is given in Fig. 1.

Now that we have a method for locally improving a coefficient of a hyperplane, we need a method for deciding which of the $d+1$ coefficients to pick for perturbation. We experimented with three different orders of coefficient perturbation, which we labelled Seq, Best, and R-50:

Seq : Repeat until none of the coefficient values is
    modified in the **for** loop:
        For $i = 1$ to $d+1$, Perturb(H, i)
Best: Repeat until coefficient m remains unmodified :
        m = coefficient which when perturbed,
            results in the maximum improvement
            of the impurity measure.
        Perturb(H,m)
R-50: Repeat a fixed number of times :
        (50 in our experiments)
        m = random integer between 1 and $d+1$
        Perturb(H,m)

As will be shown in our experiments (Section 3), the order of perturbation of the coefficients does not affect the classification accuracy as much as other parameters, especially the number of iterations (see Section 2.2.2). But if the number of iterations and the impurity measure are held constant, the order can have a significant effect on the performance of the method. In our experiments, though, none of these orders was uniformly better than any other.

A sequence of perturbations stops when the split

reaches a local minimum (which may also be a global minimum) for the impurity measure. Our method uses randomization to try to jump out of local minima. This randomization technique is described next.

2.2 Local Minima

A big problem in searching for the best hyperplane (and in many other optimization problems, as well) is that of local minima. The search process is said to have reached a local minimum if no perturbation of the current hyperplane, as suggested by the perturbation algorithm, decreases the impurity measure, and the current hyperplane does not globally minimize the impurity measure.

We have implemented two ways of dealing with local minima: perturbing the hyperplane in a random direction, and re-running the perturbation algorithm with additional initial hyperplanes. While the second technique is a variant of the standard technique of multiple local searches, the first technique of perturbing the hyperlane in a random direction is novel in the cont ext of decision tree algorithms. Notably, moving the hyperlane in a random direction rather than modifying one of the coefficients one at a time does not modify the time complexity of the algorithm.

2.2.1 Perturb coefficients in a random direction
When a hyperplane $H = \sum_{i=1}^{d} a_i * x_i + a_{d+1}$ can not be improved by deterministic perturbation, we do the following.

- Let $R = (r_1, r_2, \ldots, r_{d+1})$ be a random vector. Let α be the amount by which we want to perturb H in the direction R. i.e., Let $H_1 = \sum_{i=1}^{d} (a_i + \alpha r_i) x_i + (a_{d+1} + \alpha r_{d+1})$ be the suggested perturbation of H.

- The only variable in the equation of H_1 is α. Therefore each of the n examples in P, depending on its category, imposes a constraint on the value of α (See Section 2.1). Use the perturbation algorithm in Fig. 1 to compute the best value of α.

- If the hyperplane H_1 obtained thus improves the impurity measure, accept the perturbation. Continue with the coefficient perturbation procedure. Else stop and output H as the best possible split of P.

We found in our experiments that a single random perturbation, when used at a local minimum, proves to be very helpful. Classification accuracy improved for every one of our data sets when such perturbations were made.

2.2.2 Choosing multiple initial hyperplanes
Because most of the steps of our perturbation algorithm are deterministic, the initial randomly-chosen hyperplane determines which local minimum will be encountered first. Perturbing a single initial hyperplane deterministically thus is not likely to lead to the best split of a given dataset. In cases where the random perturbation method may have failed to escape

from local minima, we thought it would be useful to start afresh, with a new initial hyperplane.

We use the word *iteration* to denote one run of the perturbation algorithm, at one node of the decision tree, using one random initial hyperplane; i.e., one attempt using either Seq, Best, or R-50 to cycle through and perturb the coefficients of the hyperplane. One iteration also includes perturbing the coefficients randomly once at each local minimum, as described in Section 2.2.1. One of the input parameters to OC1 tells it how many iterations to use. If it uses more than one iteration, then it always saves the best hyperplane found thus far.

In all our experiments, the classification accuracies increased with more than one iteration. Accuracy seemed to increase up to a point and then level off (after about 20–50 iterations, depending on the domain). Our conclusion was that the use of multiple initial hyperplanes substantially improved the quality of the best tree found.

2.3 Comparison to Breiman et al.'s method

Breiman et al [1984, pp. 171–173] suggested a method for inducing multivariate decision trees that used a perturbation algorithm similar to the deterministic hill-climbing method that OC1 uses. They too perturb a coefficient by calculating a quantity similar to U_j (Eq. 1) for each example in the data, and assign the new value of the coefficient to be equal to the best univariate split of the U_js. In spite of this apparent similarity, OC1 is significantly different from the above algorithm for the following reasons.

- Their algorithm does not use any randomization. They choose the best univariate split of the dataset as their only choice of an initial hyperplane. When a local minimum is encountered, their deterministic algorithm halts.

- Their algorithm modifies one coefficient of the hyperplane at a time. One step of our algorithm can modify several coefficients at once.

- Breiman et al. report no upper bound on the time it takes for a hyperplane to reach a (perhaps locally) optimal position. In contrast, our procedure only accepts a limited number of perturbations. The number of changes that reduce the impurity is limited to n, the number of examples. The number of changes that leave impurity the same is limited by the parameter *stag_prob* (Section 2.1). Due to these restrictions, OC1 is guaranteed to spend only polynomial time on each hyperplane in a tree.[4]

In addition, the procedure in [Breiman *et al.*, 1984] is at best an outline: though the idea is elegant, many details were not worked out, and few experiments were performed. Thus, even without the significant changes to the algorithm we have introduced, there was a need for much more experimental work on this algorithm.

2.4 Goodness of a hyperplane

Our algorithm attempts to divide the d-dimensional attribute space into homogeneous regions, i.e., into regions that contain examples from just one category. (The training set P may contain two or more categories.) The goal of each new node in the tree is to split the sample space so as to reduce the "impurity" of the sample space. Our algorithm can use any measure of impurity, and in our experiments, we considered four such measures: information gain [Quinlan, 1986], max minority, sum minority, and sum of impurity (all three defined in [Heath, 1992]). Any of these measures seem to work well for our algorithm, and the classification accuracy did not vary significantly as a function of the goodness measure used. More details of the comparisons are given in Section 3 and Table 2.

2.4.1 Three new impurity measures
The impurity measures max minority, sum minority, and sum of impurity were all very recently introduced in the context of decision trees. We will therefore briefly define them here. For detailed comparisons, see [Heath, 1992]. For a discussion of other impurity measures, see [Fayyad and Irani, 1992] and [Quinlan and Rivest, 1989].

Consider the two half spaces formed by splitting a sample space with a hyperplane H, and call these two spaces L and R (left and right). Assume that there are only two classes of examples, though this definition is easily extended to multiple categories. If all the examples in a space fall into the same category, that space is said to be *homogeneous*. The examples in any space can be divided into two sets, A and B, according to their class labels, and the size of the smaller of those two sets is the *minority*. The *max minority* (MM) measure of H is equal to the larger of the two minorities in L and R. The *sum minority* measure (SM) of H is equal to the sum of the minorities in both L and R.

The *sum of impurity* measure requires us to give the two classes numeric values, 0 and 1. Let $P_1, .., P_L$ be the points (examples) on the left side of H. Let C_{P_i} be the category of the point P_i. We can define the average class *avg* of L as $avg = \frac{\sum_{i=1}^{L} C_{P_i}}{L}$. The *impurity* of L is then defined as $\sum_{i=1}^{L} (C_{P_i} - avg)^2$ The sum of impurity (SI) of H is equal to the sum of the impurity measures

---

[4]The theorethical bound on the amount of time OC1 spends on perturbing a hyperplane is $O(dn^2 \log n)$. To guarantee this bound, we have to reduce *stag_prob* to zero after a fixed number of changes, rather than reducing it exponentially to zero. The latter method leaves an expo- nentially small chance that a large number of perturbations will be permitted. In practice, however, hyperplanes were never perturbed more than a small (< 12) times. The expected running time of OC1 for perturbing a hyperplane appears to be $O(kn \log n)$, where k is a small constant.

Table 1: Comparisons with other methods

Data	Method	Accuracy (%)	Tree Size	Impurity Measure
Star Galaxy (Bright)	OC1	99.2	15.6	SI
	CSADT	99.1	18.4	SI
	ID3	99.1	44.3	SI
	1-NN	98.8	—	—
	BP	99.8	—	—
Star Galaxy (Dim)	OC1	95.8	36.0	SI
	1-NN	95.1	—	—
	BP	92.0	—	—
IRIS	OC1	98.0	3.0	SI
	CSADT	94.7	4.2	SM
	ID3	94.7	10.0	MM
	1-NN	96.0	—	—
	BP	96.7	—	—
Cancer	OC1	97.4	2.4	SI
	CSADT	94.9	4.6	SM
	ID3	90.6	36.1	SI
	1-NN	96.0	—	—

Table 2: Effect of parameters on accuracy and DT size

Iter	Imp. Meas.	Order	Prune Thresh.	Acc. (%)	Tree Depth & Size
1	SI	R-50	10	96.4	3.0,4.9
10	SM	Best	4	97.0	3.3,4.3
10	SM	Seq	10	96.6	2.3,3.3
20	SM	R-50	8	96.8	3.1,4.3
50	MM	Best	6	97.1	1.9,2.8
100	SI	Best	8	96.9	1.9,2.3
1	MM	Seq	0	93.7	6.2,19.6
1	MM	Seq	2	93.8	4.9,14.3
1	MM	Seq	10	92.5	2.9,5.6
1	MM	Best	10	89.2	3.9,6.7
1	MM	R-50	10	92.3	2.8,5.0

on both L and R.

3 Experiments

In this section, we present results of experiments we performed using OC1 on four real-world data sets. These results, along with some existing classification results for the same domains, are summarized in Table 1. All our experiments used 10-fold cross-validation trials. We built decision trees for each data set using various combinations of program parameters (such as the number of iterations, order of coefficient perturbation, impurity measure, impurity threshold at which a node of the tree may be pruned). The results in Table 1 correspond to the trees with the highest classification accuracies.

The results for the CSADT and ID3 methods are taken from Heath [Heath, 1992]. CSADT is an alternative approach to building oblique decision trees that uses simulated annealing to find good hyperplanes. These prior results used identical data sets to the ones used here, although the partitioning into training and test partitions may have been different. In each case, though, we cite the best published result for the algorithm used in the comparison.

Star/galaxy discrimination. Two of our data sets came from a large set of astronomical images collected by Odewahn et al [Odewahn et al., 1992]. In their study, they used these images to train perceptrons and back propagation (BP) networks to differentiate between stars and galaxies. Each image is characterized by 14 real-valued attributes and one identifier, viz., "star" or "galaxy". The objects in the image were divided by Odewahn et al. into "bright" and "dim" data

sets based on the image intensity values, where the "dim" images are inherently more difficult to classify. The bright set contains 3524 objects and the dim set contains 4652 objects.

Heath [Heath, 1992] reports the results of applying the SADT and ID3 algorithms only to the bright images. We ran OC1 on both the bright and dim images, and our results are shown in Table 1. The table compares our results with those of CSADT, ID3, 1-nearest-neighbor (1-NN), and back propagation on bright images, and with 1-NN [Salzberg, 1992] and back propagation on the dim images.

Classifying irises. The iris dataset has been extensively used both in statistics and for machine learning studies [Weiss and Kapouleas, 1989]. The data consists of 150 examples, where each example is described by four numerical attributes. There are 50 examples in each of three different categories. Weiss and Kapouleas [Weiss and Kapouleas, 1989] obtained accuracies of 96.7% and 96.0% on this data with back propagation and 1-NN, respectively.

Breast cancer diagnosis. A method for classifying using pairs of oblique hyperplanes was described in [Mangasarian et al., 1990]. This was applied to classify a set of 470 patients with breast cancer, where each example is characterized by nine numeric attributes plus the label, benign or malignant. The results of CSADT and ID3 are from Heath [Heath, 1992], and those of 1-NN are from Salzberg [Salzberg, 1991].

Table 2 shows how the OC1 algorithm's performance varies as we adjust the parameters described earlier. The table summarizes results from different trials using the cancer data. We ran similar experiments for all our data sets, but due to space constraints this table is shown as a representative. The most important parameter is the number of iterations; we consistently found better trees (smaller and more accurate) using 50 or more iterations. There was no significant correlation between pruning thresholds and accuracies, and the sum minority (SM) impurity measure almost always produced the smallest (though not always the most accurate) trees. We did not find any other significant sources of variation, either in the impurity measure or the order of perturbing coefficients.

4   Conclusions

Our experiments seem to support the following conclusions:

- The use of multiple iterations; i.e., several different initial hyperplanes, substantially improves performance.

- The technique of perturbing the entire hyperplane in the direction of a randomly-chosen vector is a good means for escaping from local minima.

- No impurity measure has an overall better performance than the other measures for OC1. The nature of the data determines which measure performs the best.

- No particular order of coefficient perturbation is superior to all others.

One of our immediate next steps in the development of OC1 will be to use the training set to determine the program parameters (e.g., number of iterations, best impurity measure for a dataset, and order of perturbation).

The experiments contained here provide an important demonstration of the usefulness of oblique decision trees as classifiers. The OC1 algorithm produces remarkably small, accurate trees, and its computational requirements are quite modest. The small size of the trees makes them more useful as descriptions of the domains, and their accuracy provides a strong argument for their use as classifiers. At the very least, oblique decision trees should be used in conjunction with other methods to enhance the tools currently available for many classification problems.

Acknowledgements

Thanks to David Heath for helpful comments. S. Murthy and S. Salzberg were supported in part by the National Science Foundation under Grant IRI-9116843.

References

Breiman, L.; Friedman, J.H.; Olshen, R.A.; and Stone, C.J. 1984. *Classification and Regression Trees.* Wadsworth International Group.

Fayyad, U. and Irani, K. 1992. The attribute specification problem in decision tree generation. In *Proceedings of AAAI-92*, San Jose CA. AAAI Press. 104–110.

Heath, D.; Kasif, S.; and Salzberg, S. 1992. Learning oblique decision trees. Technical report, Johns Hopkins University, Baltimore MD.

Heath, D. 1992. *A Geometric Framework for Machine Learning.* Ph.D. Dissertation, Johns Hopkins University, Baltimore MD.

Mangasarian, O.; Setiono, R.; and Wolberg, W. 1990. Pattern recognition via linear programming: Theory and application to medical diagnosis. In *SIAM Workshop on Optimization.*

Mingers, J. 1989. An emperical comparison of pruning methods for decision tree induction. *Machine Learning* 4(2):227–243.

Odewahn, S.C.; Stockwell, E.B.; Pennington, R.L.; Humphreys, R.M.; and Zumach, W.A. 1992. Automated stargalaxy descrimination with neural networks. *Astronomical Journal* 103(1):318–331.

Quinlan, J.R. and Rivest, R.L. 1989. Inferring decision trees using the minimum description length principle. *Information and Computation* 80:227–248.

Quinlan, J.R. 1986. Induction of decision trees. *Machine Learning* 1(1):81–106.

Quinlan, J.R. 1992. *C4.5 Programs for Machine Learning.* Morgan Kaufmann.

Salzberg, S. 1991. Distance metrics for instance-based learning. In *Methodologies for Intelligent Systems: 6th International Symposium, ISMIS '91.* 399–408.

Salzberg, S. 1992. Combining learning and search to create good classifiers. Technical Report JHU-92/12, Johns Hopkins University, Baltimore MD.

Utgoff, P.E. and Brodley, C.E. 1991. Linear machine decision trees. Technical Report 10, University of Massachusetts, Amherst MA.

Weiss, S. and Kapouleas, I. 1989. An emperical comparison of pattern recognition, neural nets, and machine learning classification methods. In *Proceedings of Eleventh IJCAI*, Detroit MI. Morgan Kaufmann.

Finding Accurate Frontiers:
A Knowledge-Intensive Approach to Relational Learning

Michael Pazzani and Clifford Brunk

Department of Information and Computer Science
University of California
Irvine, CA 92717
pazzani@ics.uci.edu, brunk@ics.uci.edu

Abstract

An approach to analytic learning is described that searches for accurate entailments of a Horn Clause domain theory. A hill-climbing search, guided by an information based evaluation function, is performed by applying a set of operators that derive frontiers from domain theories. The analytic learning system is one component of a multi-strategy relational learning system. We compare the accuracy of concepts learned with this analytic strategy to concepts learned with an analytic strategy that operationalizes the domain theory.

Introduction

There are two general approaches to learning classification rules. Empirical learning programs operate by finding regularities among a group of training examples. Analytic learning systems use a domain theory[1] to explain the classification of examples, and form a general description of the class of examples with the same explanation. In this paper, we discuss an approach to learning classification rules that integrates empirical and analytic learning methods. The goal of this integration is to create concept descriptions that are more accurate classifiers than both the original domain theory (which serves as input to the analytic learning component) and the rules that would arise if only the empirical learning component were used. We describe a new analytic learning method that returns a frontier (i.e., conjunctions and disjunctions of operational[2] and non-operational literals) instead of an operationalization (i.e., a conjunction of operational literals) and we demonstrate there is an accuracy advantage in allowing an analytic learner to dynamically select the level of generality of the learned concept, as a function of the training data.

In previous work (Pazzani, et al., 1991; Pazzani & Kibler, 1992), we have described FOCL, a system that extends Quinlan's (1990) FOIL program in a number of ways, most significantly by adding a compatible explanation-based learning (EBL) component. In this paper we provide a brief review of FOIL and FOCL, then discuss how operationalizing a domain theory can adversely affect the accuracy of a learned concept. We argue that instead of operationalizing a domain theory, an analytic learner should return the most general implication of the domain theory, provided this implication is not less accurate than any more specialized implication. We discuss the computational complexity of an algorithm that enumerates all such descriptions and then describe a greedy algorithm that efficiently addresses the problem. Finally, we present a variety of experiments that indicate replacing the operationalization algorithm of FOCL with the new analytic learning method results in more accurate learned concept descriptions.

FOIL

FOIL learns classification rules by constructing a set of Horn Clauses in terms of known operational predicates. Each clause body consists of a conjunction of literals that cover some positive and no negative examples. FOIL starts to learn a clause body by finding the literal with the maximum information gain, and continues to add literals to the clause body until the clause does not cover any negative examples. After learning each clause, FOIL removes from further consideration the positive examples covered by that clause. The learning process ends when all positive examples have been covered by some clause.

FOCL

FOCL extends FOIL by incorporating a compatible EBL component. This allows FOCL to take advantage of an initial domain theory. When constructing a clause body, there are two ways that FOCL can add literals. First, it can create literals via the same empirical method used by FOIL. Second, it can create literals by operationalizing a target concept, i.e., a non-operational definition of the concept to be learned (Mitchell, et al., 1986). FOCL uses FOIL's information-based evaluation function to determine whether to add a literal learned empirically or a conjunction of literals learned analytically. In general FOCL learns clauses of the form $r \leftarrow O_i \wedge O_d \wedge O_f$ where O_i is an initial conjunction of operational literals learned empirically, O_d is a conjunction of literals found by operationalizing the domain theory, and O_f is a final conjunction of literals learned empirically[3]. Pazzani, et al. (1991) demonstrate

---

1. We use *domain theory* to refer to a set of Horn-Clause rules given to a learner as an approximate definition of a concept and *learned concept* to refer to the result of learning.

2. We use the term *operational* to refer to predicates that are defined *extensionally* (i.e., defined by a collection of facts). However, the results apply to any satirically determined definition of operationality.

3. Note the target concept is operationalized at most once per clause and that either O_i, O_d, or O_f may be empty.

that FOCL can utilize incomplete and incorrect domain theories. We attribute this capability to its uniform use of an evaluation function to decide whether to include literals learned empirically or analytically.

Operationalization in FOCL differs from that of most EBL programs in that it uses a set of positive and negative examples, rather than a single positive example. A non-operational literal is operationalized by producing a specialization of a domain theory that is a conjunction of operational literals. When there are several ways of operationalizing a literal (i.e., there are multiple, disjunctive clauses), the information gain metric is used to determine which clause should be used by computing the number of examples covered by each clause. Figure 1 displays a typical domain theory with an operationalization (f∧g∧h∧k∧l∧p∧q) represented as bold nodes.

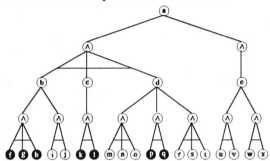

Figure 1. The bold nodes represent one operationalization (f∧g∧h∧k∧l∧p∧q) of the domain theory. In standard EBL, this path would be chosen if it were a proof of a single positive example. In FOCL, this path would be taken if the choice made at a disjunctive node had greater information gain (with respect to a set of positive and negative examples) than alternative choices.

Operationalization

The operationalization process yields a specialization of the target concept. Indeed, several systems designed to deal with overly general theories rely on the operationalization process to specialize domain theories (Flann & Dietterich, 1990; Cohen, 1992). However, fully operationalizing a domain theory can result in several problems:

1. Overspecialization of correct non-operational concepts. For example, if the domain theory in Figure 1 is completely correct, then a correct operational definition will consist of eight clauses. However, if there are few examples, or some combinations of operationalizations are rare, then there may not be a positive example corresponding to all combinations of all operationalizations of non-operational predicates. As a consequence, the learned concept may not include some combinations of operational predicates (e.g., i∧j∧k∧l∧r∧s∧t), although there is no evidence that these specializations are incorrect.

2. Replication of empirical learning. If there is a literal omitted from a clause of a non-operational predicate, then this literal will be omitted from each operationalization involving this predicate. For

example, if the domain theory in Figure 1 erroneously contained the rule b←f∧h instead of b←f∧g∧h, then each operationalization of the target concept using this predicate (i.e., f∧h∧k∧l∧m∧n∧o, f∧h∧k∧l∧p∧q, and f∧h∧k∧l∧r∧s∧t) will contain the same omission. FOCL can recover from this error if its empirical component can find the omitted literal, g. However, to obtain a correct learned concept description, FOCL would have to find the same condition independently three times on three different sets of examples. This replication of empirical learning is analogous to the replicated subtree problem in decision trees (Pagallo & Haussler, 1990). This problem should be most noticeable when there are few training examples. Under this circumstance, it is unlikely that empirical learning on several arbitrary partitions of a data set will be as accurate as learning from the larger data set.

3. Proofs involving incorrect non-operational predicates may be ignored. If the definition of a non-operational predicate (e.g., c in Figure 1) is not true of any positive example, then the analytic learner will not return any operationalization using this predicate. This reduces the usefulness of the domain theory for an analytic learner. For example, if c is not true of any positive example, then FOCL as previously described can find only two operationalizations: u∧v and w∧x. Again, we anticipate that this problem will be most severe when there are few training examples. With many examples, the empirical learner can produce accurate clauses that mitigate this problem.

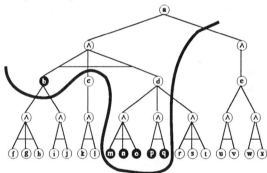

Figure 2. The bold nodes represent one frontier of the domain theory, b∧((m∧n∧o)∨(p∧q)).

Frontiers of a Domain Theory

To address the problems raised in the previous section, we propose an analytic learner that does not necessarily fully operationalize target concepts. Instead, the learner returns a *frontier* of the domain theory. A frontier differs from an operationalization of a domain theory in three ways. The frontier represented by those nodes immediately above the line in Figure 2, b∧((m∧n∧o)∨(p∧q)), illustrates these differences:

1. Non-operational predicates (e.g., b) can appear in the frontier.

2. A disjunction of two or more clauses that define a non-operational predicate (e.g., $(m \wedge n \wedge o) \vee (p \wedge q)$) can appear in the frontier.

3. A frontier does not necessarily include all literals in a conjunction (e.g., neither c, nor any specialization of c, appears in the frontier).

Combined, the first two distinguishing features of a frontier address the first two problems associated with operationalization. Overspecialization of correct non-operational concepts can be avoided if the analytic component returns a more general concept description. Similarly, replication of empirical learning can be avoided if the analytic component returns a frontier more general than an operationalization. For example, if the domain theory in Figure 2 erroneously contained the rule $b \leftarrow f \wedge h$ instead of $b \leftarrow f \wedge g \wedge h$ and frontier $f \wedge h \wedge k \wedge l \wedge d$ was returned, then an empirical learner would only need to be invoked once to specialize this conjunction by adding g. Of course, if one of the clauses defining d were incorrect, it would make sense to specialize d. However, operationalization is not the only means of specialization. For example, if the analytic learner returned $f \wedge h \wedge k \wedge l \wedge ((m \wedge n \wedge o) \vee (p \wedge q))$, then replication of induction problem could also be avoided. This would be desirable if the clause $d \leftarrow r \wedge s \wedge t$ were incorrect.

The third problem with operationalization can be addressed by removing some literals from a conjunction. For example, if no positive examples use $a \leftarrow b \wedge c \wedge d$ because c is not true of any positive example, then the analytic learner might want to consider ignoring c and trying $a \leftarrow b \wedge d$. This would allow potentially useful parts of the domain theory (e.g. b and d) to be used by the analytic learner, even though they may be conjoined with incorrect parts.

The notion of a frontier has been used before in analytic learning. However, the previous work has assumed that the domain theory is correct and has focused on increasing the utility of learned concepts (Hirsh, 1988; Keller, 1988; Segre, 1987) or learning from intractable domain theories (Braverman & Russell, 1988). Here, we do not assume that the domain theory is correct.

We argue that to increase the accuracy of learned concepts, an analytic learner should have the ability to select the generality of a frontier derived from a domain theory. To validate our hypothesis, we will replace the operationalization procedure in FOCL with an analytic learner that returns a frontier. In order to avoid confusion with FOCL, we use the name FOCL-FRONTIER to refer to the system that combines this new analytic learner with an empirical learning component based on FOIL. In general, FOCL-FRONTIER learns clauses of the form $r \leftarrow O_i \wedge F_d \wedge O_f$ where O_i is an initial conjunction of operational literals learned empirically, F_d is a frontier of the domain theory, and O_f is a final conjunction of literals learned empirically. We anticipate that due to its use of a frontier rather than an operationalization, FOCL-FRONTIER will be more accurate than FOCL, particularly when there are few training examples or the domain theory is very accurate.

Enumerating Frontiers of a Domain Theory

Formally, a frontier can be defined as follows. Let b represent a conjunction of literals and p represent a single literal.

1. The target concept is a frontier.
2. A new frontier can be formed from an existing frontier by replacing a literal p with $b_1 \vee ... \vee b_i \vee ... \vee b_n$ provided there are rules $p \leftarrow b_1, ..., p \leftarrow b_i, ..., p \leftarrow b_n$.
3. A new frontier can be formed from an existing frontier by replacing a disjunction $b_1 \vee ... \vee b_{i-1} \vee b_i \vee b_{i+1} \vee ... \vee b_n$ with $b_1 \vee ... \vee b_{i-1} \vee b_{i+1} \vee ... \vee b_n$ for any i. This deletes b_i.
4. A new frontier can be formed from an existing frontier by replacing a conjunction $p_1 \wedge ... \wedge p_{i-1} \wedge p_i \wedge p_{i+1} \wedge ... \wedge p_n$ with $p_1 \wedge ... \wedge p_{i-1} \wedge p_{i+1} \wedge ... \wedge p_n$ for any i. This deletes p_i.

One approach to analytic learning would be to enumerate all possible frontiers. The information gain of each frontier could be computed, and if the frontier with the maximum information gain has greater information gain than any literal found empirically, then this frontier would be added to the clause under construction. Such an approach would be impractical for all but the most trivial, non-recursive domain theories. Since each frontier specifies a unique combination of leaf nodes of an and-or tree (i.e., selecting all leaves of a subtree is equivalent to selecting the root of the subtree and selecting no leaves of a subtree is equivalent to deleting the root of a subtree), there are 2^k frontiers of a domain theory that has k nodes in the and/or tree. For example, if every non-operational predicate has n clauses, each clause is a conjunction of m literals, and inference chains have a depth of d and-nodes, then the number of frontiers is $2^{m^d n^d}$.

Deriving Frontiers from the Target Concept

Due to the intractability of enumerating all possible frontiers, we propose a heuristic approach based upon hill-climbing search. The frontier is initialized to the target concept. A set of transformation operators is applied to the current frontier to create a set of possible frontiers. If none of the possible frontiers has information gain greater than that of the current frontier[4], then the current frontier is returned. Otherwise, the potential frontier with the maximum information gain becomes the current frontier and the process of applying transformation operators is repeated. The following transformation operators are used[5]:

- *Clause specialization*:
  If there is a frontier containing a literal p, and there are exactly n rules of the form $p \leftarrow b_1, ..., p \leftarrow b_i, ..., p \leftarrow b_n$, then n frontiers formed by replacing p with b_i are evaluated.

---

4. The information gain of a frontier is calculated in the same manner than Quinlan (1990) calculates the information gain of a literal: by counting the number of positive and negative examples that meet the conditions represented by the frontier.

5. The numeric restrictions placed upon the applicability of each operator are for efficiency reasons (i.e., to ensure that each unique frontier is evaluated only once).

- *Specialization by removing disjunctions*:
  a. If there is a frontier containing a literal p, and there are n rules of the form $p{\leftarrow}b_1, ..., p{\leftarrow}b_i, ..., p{\leftarrow}b_n$, then n frontiers formed by replacing p with $b_1{\vee}...{\vee}b_{i-1}{\vee}b_{i+1}{\vee}...{\vee}b_n$ are evaluated (provided $n{>}2$).
  b. If there is a frontier containing a disjunction $b_1{\vee}...{\vee}b_{i-1}{\vee}b_i{\vee}b_{i+1}{\vee}...{\vee}b_m$, then m frontiers replacing this disjunction with $b_1{\vee}...{\vee}b_{i-1}{\vee}b_{i+1}{\vee}...{\vee}b_m$ are evaluated (provided $m{>}2$).

- *Generalization by adding disjunctions*:
  If there is a frontier containing a (possibly trivial) disjunction of conjunction of literals $b_1{\vee}...{\vee}b_{i-1}{\vee}b_{i+1}{\vee}...{\vee}b_m$ and there are rules of the form $p{\leftarrow}b_1, ..., p{\leftarrow}b_{i-1}, p{\leftarrow}b_i, p{\leftarrow}b_{i+1}, ..., p{\leftarrow}b_n$ and $m{<}n{-}1$, then $n{-}m$ frontiers replacing the disjunction $b_1{\vee}...{\vee}b_{i-1}{\vee}b_{i+1}{\vee}...{\vee}b_m$ with $b_1{\vee}...{\vee}b_{i-1}{\vee}b_i{\vee}b_{i+1}{\vee}...{\vee}b_m$ are evaluated. This is implemented efficiently by keeping a derivation of each frontier, rather than by searching for frontiers matching this pattern.

- *Generalization by literal deletion*:
  If there is a frontier containing a conjunction of literals $p_1{\wedge}...{\wedge}p_{i-1}{\wedge}p_i{\wedge}p_{i+1}{\wedge}...{\wedge}p_n$, then n frontiers replacing this conjunction with $p_1{\wedge}...{\wedge}p_{i-1}{\wedge}p_{i+1}{\wedge}...{\wedge}p_n$ are evaluated.

There is a close correspondence between the recursive definition of a frontier and these transformation operators. However, there is not a one-to-one correspondence because we have found empirically that in some situations it is advantageous to build a disjunction by adding disjuncts and in other cases it is advantageous to build a disjunction by removing disjuncts. The former tends to occur when few clauses of a predicate are correct while the latter tends to occur when few clauses are incorrect.

Note that the first three frontier operators derive logical entailments from the domain theory while the last does not. Deleting literals from a conjunction is a means of finding an abductive hypothesis. For example, in EITHER (Ourston & Mooney, 1990), a literal can be assumed to be true during the proof process of a single example. One difference between FOCL-FRONTIER and the abduction process of EITHER is that EITHER considers all likely assumptions for each unexplained positive example, and FOCL-FRONTIER uses a greedy approach to deletion based on an evaluation of the effect on a set of examples.

Evaluation

In this section, we report on a series of experiments in which we compare FOCL using empirical learning alone (EMPIRICAL), FOCL using a combination of empirical learning and operationalization, and FOCL-FRONTIER. We evaluate the performance of each algorithm in several domains. The goal of these experiments is to substantiate the claim that analytic learning via frontier transformations results in more accurate learned concept descriptions than analytic learning via operationalization. Throughout this paper, we use an analysis of variance to determine if the difference in accuracy between algorithms is significant.

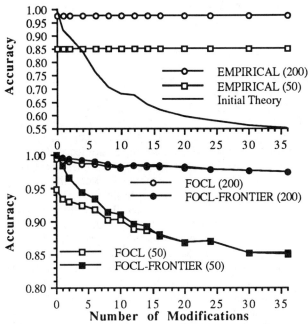

Figure 3. A comparison of FOCL's empirical component (EMPIRICAL), FOCL using both empirical learning and operationalization, and FOCL-FRONTIER in the chess end gain domain. **upper:** The accuracy of EMPIRICAL (given training sets of size 50 and 200) and the average accuracy of the initial theory as a function of the number of changes to the domain theory. **lower:** The accuracy of FOCL and FOCL-FRONTIER on the same data.

Chess End Games

The first problem we investigate is learning rules that determine if a chess board containing a white king, white rook, and black king is in an illegal configuration. This problem has been studied using empirical learning systems by Muggleton, et al. (1989) and Quinlan (1990). Here, we compare the accuracy of FOCL-FRONTIER and FOCL using a methodology identical to that used by Pazzani and Kibler (1992) to compare FOCL and FOIL.

In these experiments the initial theory given to FOCL and FOCL-FRONTIER was created by introducing either 0, 1, 2, 4, 6, 8, 10, 12, 14, 16, 20, 24, 30 or 36 random modifications to a correct domain theory that encodes the relevant rules of chess. Four types of modifications were made: deleting a literal from a clause, deleting a clause, adding a literal to a clause, and adding a clause. Added clauses are constructed with random literals. Each clause contains at least one literal, there is a 0.5 probability that a clause will have at least two literals, a 0.25 probability of containing at least three, and so on.

We ran experiments using 25, 50, 75, 150, and 200 training examples. On each trial the training and test examples were drawn randomly from the set of 8^6 possible board configurations. We ran 32 trials of each algorithm and measured the accuracy of the learned concept description on 1000 examples. For each algorithm the curves for 50 and 200 training examples are presented. Figure 3 (upper) graphs the accuracy of the initial theory and the concept description learned by FOCL's empirical component as functions of the number of modifications to the correct domain theory. Figure 3 (lower) graphs the accuracy of FOCL and FOCL-FRONTIER.

The following conclusions may be drawn from these experiment. First, FOCL-FRONTIER is more accurate than FOCL when there are few training examples. An analysis of variance indicates that the analytic learning algorithm has a significant effect on the accuracy (p<.0001) when there are 25, 50 and 75 training examples. However, where there are 150 or 200 training examples, there is no significant difference in accuracy between the analytic learning algorithms because both analytic learning algorithms (as well as the empirical algorithm) are very accurate on this problem with larger numbers of training examples. Second, the difference in accuracy between FOCL and FOCL-FRONTIER is greatest when the domain theory has few errors. With 25 and 50 examples, there is a significant interaction between the number of modifications to the domain theory and the algorithm (p<.0001 and p<.005, respectively).

During these experiments, we also recorded the amount of work EMPIRICAL, FOCL and FOCL-FRONTIER performed while learning a concept description. Pazzani and Kibler (1990) argue that the number of times information gain is computed is a good metric for describing the size of the search space explored by FOCL. Figure 4 graphs these data as a function of the number of modifications to the domain theory for learning with 50 training examples. FOCL-FRONTIER tests only a small percentage of the 225 frontiers of this domain theory with 25 leaf nodes. The frontier approach requires less work than operationalization until the domain theory is fairly inaccurate. This occurs, in spite of the larger branching factor because the frontier approach generates more general concepts with fewer clauses than those created by operationalization (see Table 1). When the domain theory is very inaccurate, FOCL and FOCL-FRONTIER perform slightly more work than EMPIRICAL because there is a small overhead in determining that the domain theory has no information gain.

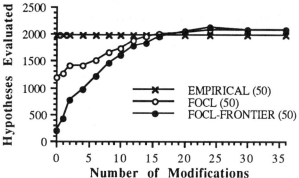

Figure 4: The number of times the information gain metric is computed for each algorithm.

FOCL (92.6% accurate)

```
illegal(WKr,WKf,WRr,WRf,BKr,BKf)←equal(BKf,WRf).
illegal(WKr,WKf,WRr,WRf,BKr,BKf)←equal(BKr,WRr).
illegal(WKr,WKf,WRr,WRf,BKr,BKf)←near(WKr,BKr) ∧
                                  near(WKf,BKf).
illegal(WKr,WKf,WRr,WRf,BKr,BKf)←equal(WKr,BKr) ∧
                                  equal(WKr,BKr) ∧
                                  near(WKf,BKf).
illegal(WKr,WKf,WRr,WRf,BKr,BKf)←equal(WKr,WRr) ∧
                                  equal(WKf,WRf).
```

FOCL-FRONTIER (98.3% accurate)

```
illegal(WKr,WKf,WRr,WRf,BKr,BKf)←k_attack(WKr,WKf,BKr,BKf) ∨
                                  r_attack(WRr,WRf,BKr,BKf).
illegal(WKr,WKf,WRr,WRf,BKr,BKf)←equal(BKf,WRf).
illegal(WKr,WKf,WRr,WRf,BKr,BKf)←same_pos(WKr,WKf,WRr,WRf).
```

Table 1. Typical definitions of illegal. The variables refer to the rank and file of the white king, white rook, and the black king. The domain theory was 91.0% accurate and 50 training examples were used.

Educational Loans

The second problem studied involves determining if a student is required to pay back a loan based on enrollment and employment information. This theory was constructed by an honors student who had experience processing loans. This problem, available from the UC Irvine repository, was previously used by an extension to FOCL that revises domain theories (Pazzani & Brunk, 1991). The domain theory is 76.8% accurate on a set of 1000 examples.

We ran 16 trials of FOCL and FOCL-FRONTIER with this domain theory on randomly selected training sets ranging from 10 to 100 examples and measured the accuracy of the learned concept by testing on 200 distinct test examples. The results indicate that the learning algorithm has a significant effect on the accuracy of the learned concept (p<.0001). Figure 5 plots the mean accuracy of the three algorithms as a function of the number of training examples.

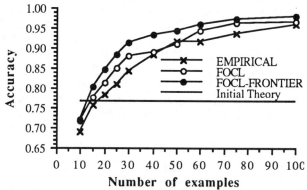

Figure 5. The accuracy of FOCL's empirical component alone, FOCL with operationalization and FOCL-FRONTIER on the student loan data.

Nynex Max

Nynex Max (Rabinowitz, et al., 1991) is an expert system that is used by NYNEX (the parent company of New York Telephone and New England Telephone) at several sites to determine the location of a malfunction for customer-reported telephone troubles. It can be viewed as solving a classification problem where the input is data such as the type of switching equipment, various voltages and resistances and the output is the location to which a repairman should be dispatched (e.g., the problem is in the customer's equipment, the customer's wiring, the cable facilities, or the central office). Nynex Max requires some customization at each site in which it is installed.

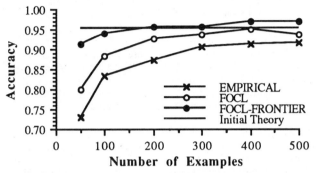

Figure 6. The accuracy of the learning algorithms at customizing the Max knowledge-base.

In this experiment, we compare the effectiveness of FOCL-FRONTIER and FOCL at customizing the Nynex Max knowledge-base. The initial domain theory is taken from one site, and the training data is the desired output of Nynex Max at a different site. Figure 6 shows the accuracy of the learning algorithms (as measured on 200 independent test examples), averaged over 10 runs as a function of the number of training examples. FOCL-FRONTIER is more accurate than FOCL (p<.0001). This occurs because the initial domain theory is fairly large (about 75 rules), very disjunctive, and fairly accurate (about 95.4%). Under these circumstances, FOCL requires many examples to form many operational rules, while FOCL-FRONTIER learns fewer, more general rules. FOCL-FRONTIER is the only algorithm to achieve an accuracy significantly higher than the initial domain theory.

Related Work

Cohen (1990; 1991a) describes the ELGIN systems that makes use of background knowledge in a way similar to FOCL-FRONTIER. In particular, one variant of ELGIN called ANA-EBL, finds concepts in which all but k nodes of a proof tree are operational. The algorithm, which is exponential in k, learns more accurate rules from overly general domain theories than an algorithm that uses only operational predicates. A different variant of ELGIN, called K-TIPS, selects k nodes of a proof tree and returns the most general nodes in the proof tree that are not ancestors of the selected nodes. This enables the system to learn a set of clauses containing at most k literals from the proof tree. Some of the literals may be non-operational and some subtrees may be deleted from the proof tree. In some ways, ELGIN is like the optimal algorithm we described above that enumerates all possible frontiers. A major difference is that ELGIN does not allow disjunction in proofs, and for efficiency reasons is restricted to using small values of k. FOCL-FRONTIER is not restricted in such a fashion, since it relies on hill-climbing search to avoid enumerating all possible hypotheses. In addition, the empirical learning component of FOCL-FRONTIER allows it to learn from overly specific domain theories in addition to overly general domain theories.

In the GRENDEL system, Cohen (1991b) uses a grammar rather than a domain theory to generate hypotheses. Cohen shows that this grammar provides an elegant way to describe the hypothesis space searched by FOCL. It is possible to encode the domain theory in such a grammar. In addition, it is possible to encode the hypothesis space searched by FOIL in the grammar. GRENDEL uses a hill-climbing search method similar to the operationalization process in FOCL to determine which hypothesis to derive from the grammar. Cohen (1991b) shows that augmenting GRENDEL with advice to prefer grammar rules corresponding to the domain theory results in concepts that are as accurate as those of FOCL (with operationalization) on the chess end game problem. The primary difference between GRENDEL and FOCL-FRONTIER is that FOCL-FRONTIER contains operators for deleting literals from and-nodes and for incorporating several disjunctions from or-nodes. However, due to the generality of GRENDEL's grammatical approach, it should be possible to extend GRENDEL by writing a preprocessor that converts a domain theory into a grammar that simulate these operators. Here, we have shown that these operators result in increased accuracy, so it is likely that a grammar based on the operators proposed here would increase GRENDEL's accuracy.

FOCL-FRONTIER is in some ways similar to theory revision systems, like EITHER (Ourston & Mooney, 1990). However, theory revision systems have an additional goal of making minimal revisions to a theory, while FOCL-FRONTIER uses a set of frontiers from the domain theory (and/or empirical learning) to discriminate positive from negative examples. EITHER deals with propositional theories and would not be able to revise any of the relational theories used in the experiments here. A more recent theory revision system, FORTE (Richards & Mooney, 1991), is capable of revising relational theories. It has been tested on one problem on which we have run FOCL, the illegal chess problem from Pazzani & Kibler (1992). Richards (1992) reports that with 100 training examples FOCL is significantly more accurate than FORTE (97.9% and 95.6% respectively). For this problem, FOCL-FRONTIER is 98.5% accurate (averaged over 20 trials). FORTE has a problem with this domain, since it contains two overly-general clauses for the same relation and its revision operators assume that at most one clause is overly general. Although it is not possible to draw a general conclusion form this single example, it does indicate that there are techniques for taking advantage of information contained in a theory that FOCL utilizes that are not incorporated into FORTE.

Future Work

Here, we have described one set of general purpose operators that derive frontiers. We are currently experimenting with more special purpose operators designed to handle commonly occurring problems in knowledge-based systems. For example, one might wish to consider operators that negate a literal in a frontier (since we occasionally omit a not from rules) or that change the order of arguments to a predicate. Initial experiments (Pazzani, 1992) with one such operator in FOCL (replacing one predicate with a related predicate) yielded promising results.

Conclusion

In this paper, we have presented an approach to integrating empirical and analytic learning that differs from previous approaches in that it uses an information theoretic metric on a set of training examples to determine the generality of the concepts derived from the domain theory. Although it is possible that the hill-climbing search algorithm will find a local maximum, experimentally we have demonstrated that in situations where there are few training examples, the domain theory is very accurate, or the domain theory is highly disjunctive this approach learns more accurate concept descriptions than either empirical learning alone or a similar approach that integrates empirical learning and operationalization. From this we conclude that there is an advantage in allowing the analytic learner to select the generality of a frontier derived from a domain theory both in terms of accuracy and in terms of the amount of work required to learn a concept description.

Acknowledgments

This research is supported by an Air Force Office of Scientific Research Grant, F49620-92-J-030, and by the University of California, Irvine through an allocation of computer time. We thank Kamal Ali, William Cohen, Andrea Danyluk, Caroline Ehrlich, Dennis Kibler, Ray Mooney and Jim Wogulis for comments on an earlier draft of this paper.

References

Braverman, M. & Russell, S. (1988). Boundaries of operationality. Proceedings of the Fifth International Conference on Machine Learning (pp. 221–233). Ann Arbor, MI: Morgan Kaufmann.

Cohen, W. (1990). Explanation-based generalization as an abstraction mechanism in concept learning. Technical Report DCS-TR-271 (Ph.D. dissertation). Rutgers University.

Cohen, W. (1991a). The generality of overgenerality. Proceedings of the Eighth International Workshop on Machine Learning (pp. 490–494). Evanston, IL: Morgan Kaufmann.

Cohen, W. (1991b). Grammatically biased learning: Learning Horn Theories using an explicit antecedent description language. AT&T Bell Laboratories Technical Report 11262-910708-16TM (available from the author).

Cohen, W. (1992). Abductive explanation-based learning: A solution to the multiple inconsistent explanation problem. Machine Learning.

Flann, N., & Dietterich, T. (1990). A study of explanation-based methods for inductive learning. Machine Learning, 4, 187–226.

Hirsh, H. (1988). Reasoning about operationality for explanation-based learning. Proceedings of the Fifth International Conference on Machine Learning (pp. 214–220). Ann Arbor, MI: Morgan Kaufmann.

Keller, R. (1988). Operationality and generality in explanation-based learning: Separate dimensions or opposite end-points. AAAI Spring Symposium on Explanation-Based Learning. Stanford University.

Mitchell, T., Keller, R., & Kedar-Cabelli, S. (1986). Explanation-based learning: A unifying view. Machine Learning, 1, 47–80.

Muggleton, S., Bain, M., Hayes-Michie, J., & Michie, D. (1989). An experimental comparison of human and machine learning formalisms. Proceedings of the Sixth International Workshop on Machine Learning (pp. 113–118). Ithaca, NY: Morgan Kaufmann.

Ourston, D., & Mooney, R. (1990). Changing the rules: A comprehensive approach to theory refinement. Proceedings of the Eighth National Conference on Artificial Intelligence (pp. 815–820). Boston, MA: Morgan Kaufmann.

Pagallo, G., & Haussler, D. (1990). Boolean feature discovery in empirical learning. Machine Learning, 5, 71–100.

Pazzani, M., & Brunk, C. (1991). Detecting and correcting errors in rule-based expert systems: an integration of empirical and explanation-based learning. Knowledge Acquisition, 3, 157–173.

Pazzani, M., Brunk, C., & Silverstein, G. (1991). A knowledge-intensive approach to learning relational concepts. Proceedings of the Eighth International Workshop on Machine Learning (pp. 432–436). Evanston, IL: Morgan Kaufmann.

Pazzani, M., & Kibler, D. (1992). The role of prior knowledge in inductive learning. Machine Learning.

Pazzani. M., (1992). When Prior Knowledge Hinders Learning. AAAI workshop on constraining learning with prior knowledge. San Jose.

Quinlan, J.R., (1990). Learning logical definitions from relations. Machine Learning, 5, 239–266.

Rabinowitz, H., Flamholz, J., Wolin, E., & Euchner, J. (1991). Nynex Max: A telephone trouble screening expert system. In R. Smith & C. Scott (Eds.) Innovative applications of artificial intelligence, 3, 213–230.

Richards, B. (1992). An Operator-Based Approach to First-Order Theory Revision. Ph.D. Thesis. University of Texas, Austin.

Richards, B. & Mooney, R. (1991). First-Order Theory Revision. Proceedings of the Eight International Workshop on Machine Learning (pp. 447–451). Evanston, IL: Morgan Kaufmann.

Segre, A. (1987). On the operationality/generality trade-off in explanation-based learning. Proceedings of the Tenth International Joint Conference on Artificial Intelligence (pp. 242–248). Milan, Italy: Morgan Kaufmann.

Learning Non-Linearly Separable Boolean Functions With Linear Threshold Unit Trees and Madaline-Style Networks

Mehran Sahami

Department of Computer Science
Stanford University
Stanford, CA 94305
sahami@cs.Stanford.EDU

Abstract

This paper investigates an algorithm for the construction of decisions trees comprised of linear threshold units and also presents a novel algorithm for the learning of non-linearly separable boolean functions using Madaline-style networks which are isomorphic to decision trees. The construction of such networks is discussed, and their performance in learning is compared with standard Back-Propagation on a sample problem in which many irrelevant attributes are introduced. Littlestone's Winnow algorithm is also explored within this architecture as a means of learning in the presence of many irrelevant attributes. The learning ability of this Madaline-style architecture on non-optimal (larger than necessary) networks is also explored.

Introduction

We initially examine a non-incremental algorithm that learns binary classification tasks by producing decision trees of linear threshold units (LTU trees). This decision tree bears some similarity to the decision trees produced by ID3 (Quinlan 1983) and Perceptron Trees (Utgoff 1988), yet it seems to promise more generality as each node in our tree implements a separate linear discriminant function while only the leaves of a Perceptron Tree have this generality and the remaining nodes in both the Perceptron Tree and the trees produced by ID3 perform a test on only one feature. Recently, Brodley and Utgoff (1992) have also shown that the use of multivariate tests at each node of a decision tree often provides greater generalization when learning concepts in which there are irrelevant attributes.

Furthermore, as presented in (Brent 1990), we show how such an LTU tree can be transformed into a three-layer neural network with two hidden layers and one output layer (the input layer is not counted) and can often be trained much more quickly than the standard Back-Propagation algorithm applied to an entire network (Rumelhart, Hinton, & Williams 1986). After examining this transformation, a new incremental learning algorithm, based on a Madaline-style architecture (Ridgway 1962, Widrow & Winter 1988), is presented in which learning is performed using such three-layer networks. The effectiveness of this algorithm is assessed on a sample non-linearly separable boolean function in order to perform comparisons with the LTU tree algorithm and a similar network trained using standard Back-Propagation.

Being primarily interested in functions in which many irrelevant attributes exist, we also explore the performance of the Winnow algorithm (Littlestone 1988, 1991) (which has proven effective in learning linearly separable functions in the presence of many irrelevant attributes) within the Madaline-style learning architecture. We contrast how it performs in learning our sample non-linearly separable function with the classical fixed increment (Perceptron) updating method (Duda & Hart 1973). We also examine the effectiveness of such learning procedures in "non-optimal" Madaline-style networks, and comment on possible future extensions of this learning architecture.

The LTU Tree Algorithm

The tree building algorithm is non-incremental requiring that the set of all training instances, S, be available from the outset.[1] We begin with the root node of the tree and produce a hyperplane to separate our training set using any means we wish (in our trials, Back-Propagation was applied to one node to produce a single separating hyperplane) into the sets S_0 and S_1, where S_i ($i = 0, 1$) indicates the set of instances classified as i by the separating hyperplane. If there are instances in S_0 which should be classified as 1 (called "incorrect 0's") we then create a left child node and recursively apply the algorithm on the left child using S_0 as the training set. Similarly, if any instances in S_1 should be classified as 0 ("incorrect 1's") we create a right child node and again recursively apply our algorithm on the right child using S_1 as the training set. Thus the algorithm normally terminates when all of the instances in the original training set, S, are correctly classified by our tree.

The classification procedure using the completed tree requires us to simply begin at the root node and determine whether the given instance is classified as a 0 or 1 by the hyperplane stored there. A classification of 0 means we follow the left branch, otherwise we follow the right, and recursively apply this procedure with the hyperplane stored at the appropriate child node. The classification given at a leaf node in the tree is the final output of the classification procedure. Note that the leaves in this decision tree do not

---

[1]Notation and naming conventions in the description of the LTU tree algorithm are from Brent (1990).

classify all instances into one labeling, rather the classification for the instance is the result of applying the linear discriminator stored in the leaf node.

For our experiments, certain (reasonable) limiting assumptions were placed on the building of such LTU trees in order to prevent needlessly complex trees, thereby helping to improve generalization and reduce the algorithm's execution time. These included setting a maximum tree depth of 10 layers and tolerating a certain percentage of error in each individual node. This toleration condition was set after some empirical observations which indicated that given some number of similarly classified instances in a node, n, a certain percentage of erroneous classifications, E, would be acceptable (thus precluding further branching for that particular classification from the node). These values are as follows:

- if $n \leq 25$ then $E = 25\%$
- if $n > 25$ & $n \leq 100$ then $E = 12\%$
- else $E = 6\%$

Initial testing was performed within this LTU tree architecture using a variety of methods for learning the linear discriminant at each node of the tree (Sahami 1993). Wishing to minimize the number of erroneous classifications made at each node in the tree, Back-Propagation appeared to be the most promising of these weight updating procedures. While this heuristic of minimizing errors at each node can occasionally produce larger than optimal trees[2], it generally produces trees of optimal or near-optimal size, and was shown to produce the smallest trees on a number of sample functions when compared with other weight updating procedures. Since we are only allowed to store one hyperplane at each node (and not an entire network, although this might be an interesting angle for further research) we apply the Back-Propagation algorithm to only one unit at a time. To make this unit a linear *threshold* unit, a threshold is set at 0.5 *after* training is completed (this threshold is not used during training). Thus the output of the unit trained with Back-Propagation is given by:

$$O_{LTU_n} = \begin{cases} 1 & O_n \geq 0.5 \\ 0 & \text{otherwise} \end{cases}$$

$$O_n = \frac{1}{1 + e^{-N_k}}, \text{ where } N_k = \vec{w}_k^t \vec{x}_k + \theta_{k-1}$$

where O_n is the actual real valued output of the nth trained unit on any instance and O_{LTU_n} is the output of our "linear threshold unit." θ represents the "bias" weight of the unit.

The updating procedure used in training each node is:

$$\vec{w}_{k+1} = \vec{w}_k + \Delta\vec{w}_k + (momentum)\Delta\vec{w}_{k-1}$$
$$\Delta\vec{w}_k = (lrate * \vec{x}_k * O_k * (1 - O_k) * (d - O_k))$$
$$\text{where } O_k = \frac{1}{1 + e^{-N_k}}, \ N_k = \vec{w}_k^t \vec{x}_k + \theta_{k-1}$$
$$\text{and } \theta_{k+1} = \theta_k + \Delta\theta_k$$
$$\Delta\theta_k = (lrate * O_k * (1 - O_k) * (d - O_k))$$

Where **w** is the weight vector being updated and **x** is a given instance vector. We set *lrate* = 1.0 and *momentum* = 0.5 in our experiments.

There are many possible extensions to this LTU tree-building algorithm including irrelevant attribute elimination (Brodley & Utgoff 1992), producing several hyperplanes at each node using different weight updating procedures and selecting the hyperplane which causes the fewest number of incorrect classifications, using Bayesian analysis to determine instance separations (Langley 1992), post-processing of the tree to reduce its size, etc. These modifications are beyond the scope of this paper however, and generally are only fine tunings to the underlying learning architecture which is not changed by them.

Creating Networks From LTU Trees

The trees which are produced by the LTU tree algorithm can be mechanically transformed into three-layer connectionist networks that implement the same functions. Given an LTU tree, T, with m nodes, we can construct an isomorphic network containing the m nodes of the tree in the first hidden layer (each fully connected to the set of inputs). The second hidden layer consisting of n nodes (*AND* gates), where n is the number of possible distinct paths between the root of T and a leaf node (a node without two children). And the output layer merely being an *OR* gate connected to all n nodes in the previous layer. The connections between the first and second hidden layers are constructed by traversing each possible path from the root to a leaf in the tree T, and at each node recording which branch was followed to get to it. Thus each node in the second hidden layer represents a single distinct path through T by being connected to those nodes in the first layer which correspond to the nodes that were traversed along the given path. Since the nodes in the second hidden layer are merely *AND* gates, the inputs coming from the first hidden layer must first be inverted if a left branch was traversed in T at the node corresponding to a given input from the first hidden layer. Two examples are given below.

As pointed out in (Brent 1990), it is more efficient to do classifications using the tree structure than the corresponding network since the only computations which must be performed are those which lie on a single path from the root of the tree to a leaf. Conveniently, when we later examine how to incrementally train a network which corresponds to an LTU tree, we may then transform the trained network into a decision tree to attain this computational benefit during classification.

---

[2]An optimal tree would contain the minimum number of linear separators (nodes) necessary to successfully classify all instances in the training set, S.

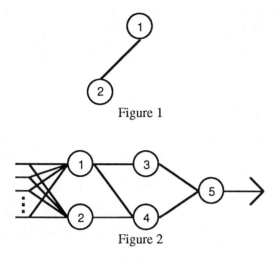

Figure 1

Figure 2

Figure 1 shows a two node tree produced by the LTU tree algorithm, while Figure 2 shows the corresponding network after performing the transformation described above. Nodes 1 and 2 in Figure 1 correspond directly to nodes 1 and 2 in Figure 2. Node 3 simply has the output of node 1 as its input (since there is a path of length 1 in the tree from the root to node 1 which is considered a leaf.) Node 4 is a conjunct of the *inverted* output of node 1 (since we must follow the left branch from node 1 to reach node 2 in the tree) and the output of node 2. Node 5 is simply an *OR* gate.

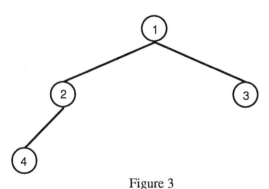

Figure 3

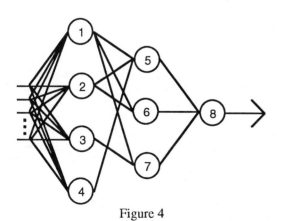

Figure 4

Figure 3 shows a more complex tree produced by the LTU tree algorithm, and Figure 4 represents the corresponding network. Nodes 1, 2, 3, and 4 in Figure 3 correspond directly to the same nodes in Figure 4. In Figure 4, node 5 represents the path 1-2-4 in the tree, with the *inverted* output of node 1, *inverted* output of node 2 and output of node 4 as inputs. Node 6 represents the path 1-2 (as node 2 in the tree is also considered a leaf) with the *inverted* output of node 1 and the output of node 2 as inputs. Node 7 corresponds to the path 1-3 and has the outputs of nodes 1 and 3 as inputs. Again, node 8 is simply a disjunction of the outputs of nodes 5, 6 and 7.

Madaline-Style Learning Algorithm

The updating strategy in this Madaline-style architecture is based upon modifying the weight vectors in the first hidden layer of nodes by appropriately *strengthening* and *weakening* them based on incorrect predictions by the network. We also make use of knowing the structure of the LTU tree, T, which corresponds to the network we are training. When an instance is incorrectly classified as a 0, we know that no nodes in the second hidden layer corresponding to a leaf in T fired. Thus we look for the node corresponding to a leaf node in T which is closest to threshold and strengthen it. We also examine any nodes corresponding to non-leaf nodes in T that we would know exists along the path from the root of T to the given leaf node closest to threshold. If these nodes were over threshold but the given leaf is down their left child in T, then the node in the network corresponding to the particular non-leaf node in T is weakened. Similarly if the node corresponding to a non-leaf node in T was under threshold, but the leaf node is on a path down its right child in T, then the node in the network corresponding to the non-leaf node in T is strengthened. When an instance is misclassified as a 1, we simply find the node in the second hidden layer of the network which misfired (there can only be one) and weaken all nodes which are inputs to it and also correspond to leaf nodes in T. In the case of the network in Figure 2, this translates in to the following updating procedure:

On a misclassified 0, determine if node 1 or node 2 is closer to threshold:
  • If node 1 is closer to threshold, then strengthen node 1, else strengthen node 2.

On a misclassified 1, only node 3 or 4 (but not both) misfired in this case:
  • If the output of node 3 is 1, then weaken node 1, else weaken node 2.

How nodes are strengthened and weakened is based upon what learning method was being used on the Madaline-style networks. Both the classical fixed increment (referred to simply as Madaline below) and Littlestone's Winnow algorithm (referred to as Mada-winnow) were employed in our tests as follows:

Algorithm	Updating Method
Fixed Increment	Strengthen:
(Madaline)	$$\vec{w}_{k+1} = \vec{w}_k + \vec{x}$$
	Weaken:
	$$\vec{w}_{k+1} = \vec{w}_k - \vec{x}$$
Winnow	Strengthen:
(Mada-winnow)	$$\vec{w}_{k+1}^{\,i} = \alpha^{\vec{x}^i}\!\left(\vec{w}_k^{\,i}\right)$$
	Weaken:
	$$\vec{w}_{k+1}^{\,i} = \beta^{\vec{x}^i}\!\left(\vec{w}_k^{\,i}\right)$$

Where $\mathbf{w}$ is the weight vector ($\mathbf{w}^i$ is the ith component of $\mathbf{w}$) at the node being modified and $\mathbf{x}$ is the instance vector which was misclassified. Note that $\alpha = 2.0$ and $\beta = 0.5$ (Winnow also uses a fixed threshold which was set to 4.0 in our initial experiments).

Experimental Results

In testing the LTU tree algorithm and the corresponding network for their abilty to learn, a non-linearly separable 5-bit boolean function was used. This function was defined as:

$$\left(\sum_{i=1}^{5} \vec{x}^{\,i} \le 1\right) \vee \left(\sum_{i=1}^{5} \vec{x}^{\,i} \ge 4\right)$$

This function, effectively being the disjunction of two r-of-k threshold functions, is not linearly separable, but can be optimally learned using *two* hyperplanes to separate the instance space. Thus in testing our various learning methods on this function, we compare the LTU tree algorithm against training networks configured similarly to Figure 2 (as this is the optimal size network to learn the given function). In training the networks, we compare standard Back-Propagation applied to the *entire* network (using preset fixed weights in the second hidden and output layers to simulate the appropriate *AND* and *OR* gates) against our novel Madaline-style learning method (discussed above). Note that our learning procedure is effectively only learning the separating hyperplanes in the first hidden layer of the network (corresponding to learning the nodes of an LTU tree).

On a technical note, the instance vectors presented to both the LTU tree and Back-Propagation applied to an *entire* network include the original boolean vector (comprised of 1's and 0's) with the complements of the original vector to create a "double length" instance vector (as preliminary testing showed that the use of complements helped improve learning performance with these algorithms.) In the Madaline-style tests, the instance vectors presented when using fixed increment updating were composed of 1's and -1's without the addition of complements, whereas when using Winnow the instance vectors were similar to those with the LTU tree (complementary attributes were added).

The number of instances presented for training, as well as the number of dimensions in the input vector were varied. Note that only the first 5 bits of the instance vector are relevant to its proper classification and the added bits are simply random, irrelevant attributes. The dimensions given in the graphs below measure the size of the original instance vector (not including complementary attributes). The graphs below represent 5 test runs on each algorithm in each case. Testing is done on an independent, randomly generated set of instances, numbering the same as the training set. The "% error (average)" refers to the percentage of errors made during testing by each algorithm over the 5 test runs. The "% error (best)" refers to the smallest percentage of errors made during testing over the 5 test runs.

We see that, in the average case (Figure 5), when trained using 1000 instances (which are each seen only once), the Madaline network (using fixed-increment updating) outperforms all other algorithms as the number of irrelevant attributes is increased. The LTU tree (called BP tree here) performs without errors up to 15 dimensions (during which time it was consistently producing optimal trees of 2 nodes) and quickly begins to degenerate in performance as the trees it produces get larger due to poor separating hyperplanes being produced at each node. Not surprisingly, it is at this same point when using Back-Propagation over an entire network also begins to degenerate quickly leading us to realize that the network is getting too small to properly deal with irrelevant attributes. Mada-winnow also performs very erratically, due primarily to seeing too few instance vectors to settle into a good "solution state." The best case analysis (Figure 6) indicates a simple linear increase in the number of errors made by Madaline (caused by a linear increase in the sum of weights from irrelevant attributes) as opposed to an erratic increase indicating that the boolean function was not learned. Similarly, Mada-winnow seems to be capable of learning the function up to 35 dimensions and quickly degenerates indicating that learning is not effectively taking place, as opposed to occasional misclassifications caused by added irrelevant attribute weights. We find the BP network still unable to learn beyond 15 dimensions, while the BP tree is still effective up to 30 dimensions.

When we examine the results of using 3000 training instances (each of which is seen once), the effectiveness of the Madaline-style architecture becomes much more clear. In the average case (Figure 7) we still find the standard BP network degenerating after 15 dimensions. However, we see extremely low error rates in Madaline all the way through, indicating that not only has the target function been learned, but the effect of irrelevant attribute weights has also been minimized. Moreover, we find that Mada-winnow is successful in learning the target function with instances up to 35 dimensions in length before its predictive accuracy begins to fall. Similarly, the BP tree is effective for instances up to 40 dimensions before once

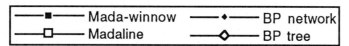

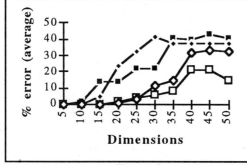

Trained using 1000 randomly generated instances

Figure 5

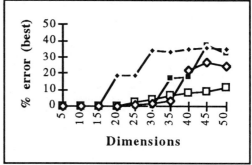

Figure 6

Trained using 3000 randomly generated instances

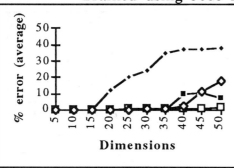

Figure 7

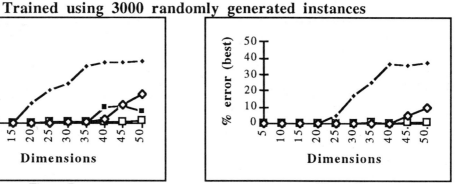

Figure 8

again tree sizes grow too large as the linear separators at each node provide poorer splits. In the best case (Figure 8) we see the most striking results as Madaline still continues a very low error rate, and Mada-winnow has 0% errors over the entire range of dimensions tested! This would indicate that by training a number of such Mada-winnow networks and using cross-validation techniques to determine which has the highest predictive accuracy, we can learn non-linearly separable boolean functions with an extremely high degree of accuracy even in the presence of many irrelevant attributes. This of course does require some knowledge as to what network size would provide the best results, but initially running the LTU tree algorithm on our data set could provide us with good ballpark approximations for this.

Non-Optimal Networks

Having seen the predictive accuracy of the Madaline-style networks in learning when the optimal network size[3] was known, it is important to get an idea for the accuracy of such networks when they are non-optimal. In examining

---

[3]The notion of optimal network size stems from the transformation of an optimal LTU tree.

the effects of using a network that is larger than necessary, the network in Figure 4 was used to learn the same 5-bit non-linearly separable problem. The updating procedure for this network is described below:

On a misclassified 0, determine if node 2, 3 or 4 is closest to threshold:
  • If node 2 is closest to threshold, then strengthen node 2 and if node 1 is over threshold then weaken node 1.
  • If node 3 is closest to threshold, then strengthen node 3 and if node 1 is not over threshold then strengthen node 1.
  • If node 4 is closest to threshold, then strengthen node 4 and if node 1 is over threshold then weaken node 1.

On a misclassified 1, determine if node 5, 6 or 7 misfired:
  • If the output of node 5 is 1, then weaken node 4.
  • If the output of node 6 is 1, then weaken node 2.
  • If the output of node 7 is 1, then weaken node 3.

Now we compare the previous results of Madaline and Mada-winnow using the smaller network, denoted (S), with the larger network, denoted (L). Again looking at the average of 5 test runs on 1000 training instances (Figure 9), we see that the performance of both Madaline and Mada-winnow are worse when learning using a larger network (as

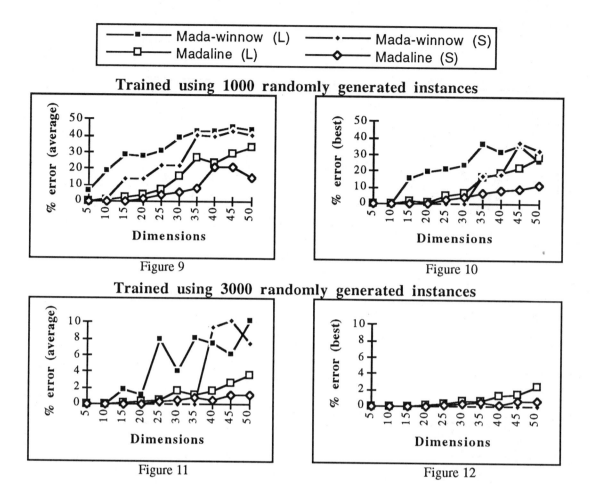

Figure 9

Figure 10

Figure 11

Figure 12

we would expect, since there is greater possibility for confusion among which nodes to update). This is also seen in the best case graph (Figure 10) where we still see the erratic behavior of learning using the Mada-winnow (L) algorithm, which cannot properly learn the target function even with only a few irrelevant dimensions. The Madaline (L) algorithm still holds some promise as it maintains a relatively low error rate until about the 30 dimension mark before it too begins to quickly degenerate in its predictive ability.

Again the most striking differences are seen when examining the graphs of learning runs using 3000 training instances. Noting that the "% error" scale on Figures 11 and 12 is much less than the previous figures (to make the graph more readable), we see that in the average case, while Mada-winnow (L)'s behavior is still erratic (caused by the way the Winnow algorithm greatly modifies weights between each update, leading to instability in the resultant weight vector when training ceases), but the error rate stays below 10%. Moreover, Madaline (L) only shows a small linear decrease in its predictive ability over the entire graph, reflecting again that the target function was effectively learned and misclassifications are arising from the cumulative sum of small irrelevant attribute weights. Finally, Figure 12 shows the most impressive results.

First, Madaline(L) has only a slightly higher error rate that Madaline (S). And more impressively, the Mada-winnow (L) algorithm is able to maintain 0% error over the entire range of irrelevant attributes, reflecting that network size is not entirely crucial for effectively learning within this paradigm. An examination of the weights in the larger network indicated that, in fact, two nodes in the first hidden layer contained the appropriate hyperplanes required to learn the target function and the other two nodes had somewhat random but essentially "unused" weights in terms of instance classification.

It is important to note that the fixed threshold used with the Winnow algorithm was dependent on the number of irrelevant attributes in the instance vectors presented. This reflects a problem inherent in the Winnow algorithm (in which threshold choice can have a large impact upon learning) and is not a shortcoming of the Madaline-style architecture.

Future Work

There is still a great deal of work that needs to be done in examining and extending both the LTU tree and the Madaline-style learning algorithms. In terms of the LTU tree, new methods for finding better separating hyperplanes as well as the incorporation of post-learning pruning techniques would be very helpful in determining proper network size both for Madaline-style and standard neural networks. As for the Madaline-style networks, clearly more work needs to be done in examining larger networks and learning more complex functions. Another interesting problem arises in looking at methods to prune the network *during* training to produce better classifications. Also theoretical measures are needed for the number of training instances to present for adequate learning.

Acknowledgments

The author is grateful to Prof. Nils Nilsson, without whose ideas, guidance, help and support, this work would never have been done. Additional thanks go to Prof. Nilsson for reading and commenting on an earlier draft of this paper. Dr. Pat Langley also provided a sounding board for ideas for extending research dealing with LTU trees.

References

Brent, R. P. 1990. Fast training algorithms for multi-layer neural nets. Numerical Analysis Project Manuscript NA-90-03, Dept. of Computer Science, Stanford Univ.

Brodley, C. E., and Utgoff, P. E. 1992. Multivariate Versus Univariate Decision Trees. COINS Technical Report 92-8, Dept. of Computer Science, Univ. of Mass.

Duda, R. O., and Hart, P. E. 1973. *Pattern Classification and Scene Analysis.* New York: John Wiley & Sons.

Langley, P. 1992. Induction of Recursive Bayesian Classifiers. Forthcoming.

Littlestone, N. 1988. Learning quickly when irrelevant attributes abound: a new linear-threshold algorithm. *Machine Learning* 2:285-318.

Littlestone, N. 1991. Redundant noisy attributes, attribute errors, and linear-threshold learning using Winnow. In Proceedings of the Fourth Annual Workshop of Computational Learning Theory, 147-156. San Mateo, CA: Morgan Kaufmann Publishers, Inc.

Nilsson, N. J. 1965. *Learning machines.* New York: McGraw-Hill.

Quinlan, J. R. 1986. Induction of decision trees. *Machine Learning* 1:81-106.

Ridgway, W. C., 1962. An Adaptive Logic System with Generalizing Properties. Stanford Electronics Laboratories Technical Report 1556-1, prepared under Air Force Contract AF 33(616)-7726, Stanford Univ.

Rumelhart, D. E.; Hinton, G. E.; and Williams, R. J. 1986. Learning internal representations by error propagation. *Parallel Distributed Processing, Vol. 1*, eds. D. E. Rumelhart and J. L. McClelland, 318-62. Cambridge, MA: MIT Press.

Rumelhart, D. E. and McClelland, J. L. eds. 1986. *Parallel Distributed Processing, Vol. 1.* Cambridge, MA: MIT Press.

Sahami, M. 1993. An Experimental Study of Learning Non-Linearly Separable Boolean Functions With Trees of Linear Threshold Units. Forthcoming.

Utgoff, P. E. 1988. Perceptron Trees: A Case Study in Hybrid Concept Representation. In AAAI-88 Proceedings of the Seventh National Conference on Artificial Intelligence, 601-6. San Mateo, CA: Morgan Kaufmann.

Widrow, B., and Winter, R. G. 1988. Neural Nets for Adaptive Filtering and Adaptive Pattern Recognition. *IEEE Computer, March*:25-39.

Winston, P. 1992. *Artificial Intelligence, third edition.* Reading, MA: Addison-Wesley.

Natural Language
Generation

Generating Argumentative Judgment Determiners

Michael Elhadad

Ben Gurion University of the Negev
Dept of Mathematics and Computer Science
Beer Sheva, 84105, Israel
elhadad@bengus.bgu.ac.il *

Abstract

This paper presents a procedure to generate *judgment determiners, e.g., many, few.* Although such determiners carry very little objective information, they are extensively used in everyday language. The paper presents a precise characterization of a class of such determiners using three semantic tests. A conceptual representation for sets is then derived from this characterization which can serve as an input to a generator capable of producing judgment determiners. In a second part, a set of syntactic features controlling the realization of complex determiner sequences is presented. The mapping from the conceptual input to this set of syntactic features is then presented. The presented procedure relies on a description of the speaker's *argumentative intent* to control this mapping and to select appropriate judgment determiners.

Introduction

There are cases when answering *many* is a sign of ignorance:

Teacher: How many neutrons are there in an atom of Uranium?
Child: many...

In other cases, though, uttering a precise number is of no help to the hearer:

Q: how difficult is Topology 101?
A1: It has six assignments.
A2: It requires many assignments.

In A1, the precise number of assignments in the class can be seen as an awful lot or a pretty average workload. In all cases, the precise number does not satisfy the communicative need expressed by the question, and answer A2, with a determiner like *many* is more felicitous. This paper addresses the issue of producing such *judgment determiners* (JDs) in a text generation system, focusing on a class I call *argumentative judgment determiners.*

---

*This paper reports on work pursued while the author was at Columbia University, Dept of Computer Science

This problem has been mostly ignored in previous work in generation for two reasons: first, most of the previous work on determiner generation has focused on the difficult decision definite/indefinite; second, most existing generation systems, except for Dale's EPICURE (Dale 1988), do not focus on the issue of non-singular NPs. Consequently, the generation of JDs, although it fulfills an important pragmatic function, has remained largely unexplored.

The determiner generation procedure presented here is implemented as part of ADVISOR II, a generation system which provides advice to university students preparing their course schedule (Elhadad 1993). In this domain, an analysis of a corpus of 40,000 words containing transcripts of recordings of advising sessions with human academic advisors shows the following distribution of determiners:

Determiner type	# Occurrences
Article (a, the)	1540
Demonstrative (this, that)	950
Cardinal	210
Judgment det	300

In this table, judgment dets include *(many, few, all, no, a lot, a large number of, lots of).* This distribution indicates that, at least in this domain, whenever a quantity must be referred to, JDs are used more often than exact determiners, and highlights the need to cover JDs in a generation system like ADVISOR II.

The paper starts by defining JDs and provides a semantic characterization of JDs. I derive from this characterization a set of requirements on the form of the input representation that must be sent to a generator to allow it to produce JDs. I then discuss the syntax of judgment determiners and explain how the generator maps the input conceptual representation of sets to a set of syntactic features controlling the selection of JDs.

Semantic Characterization of Judgment Determiners

Observing that *242* and *many* do not satisfy the same pragmatic function, one gets the intuition that *many* is a member of a "different" class of determiners - ones that do not express only objective information. This section uses three semantic properties defined in (Barwise & Cooper 1981) and (Keenan & Stavi 1986) in order to precisely identify the class of *judgment determiners* (JDs) and derive constraints on the form of the input required by a generator to produce JDs.

Non Extensionality and Argumentation

The first property of JDs is that they are *non-extensional*, in the sense defined in (Keenan & Stavi 1986, p.257):

> To say that a det *d* is extensional is to say, for example, that whenever the doctors and the lawyers are the same individuals then *d doctors* and *d lawyers* have the same properties, *e.g.*, *d doctors attended the meeting* necessarily has the same truth value as *d lawyers attended the meeting*.

The following example shows that *many* for example, is not extensional:

> Imagine that in the past the annual doctors meeting has been attended by tens of thousands of doctors, and only two or three lawyers. But, during the course of the year, and unbeknownst to everyone, all the doctors get law degrees and all the lawyers get medical degrees (so that doctors and lawyers are now the same) and at this year meeting only 500 doctors/lawyers show up. Reasonably then (a) is true and (b) is false:
> (a) Many lawyers attended the meeting this year.
> (b) Many doctors attended the meeting this year.
> Thus *many (few)* cannot be treated extensionally. (Keenan & Stavi 1986, pp.257-8)

Keenan & Stavi, therefore, propose to consider an expression such as *many Xs* as "simply indeterminate in truth value." In other words, using a non-extensional determiner such as *many Xs* does not say much about the number of *X*s, but instead, expresses *a decision by the speaker* to highlight the number of *X*s as significant. The input to a generator must therefore record this decision if any non-extensional determiner is to be produced.

The work presented here uses the notion of *argumentative intent* to account for this speaker's decision. An argumentative intent is the goal to convince a hearer of a certain conclusion. Following Anscombre & Ducrot (1983), it is hypothesized that simple evaluations, of the form *(X is high/low on scale S)*, and simple argumentative rules, of the form *(the higher X is on P, the higher Y is on Q)* are sufficient to account

for many linguistic phenomena related to argumentation. In previous work, I have discussed the impact of the speaker's argumentative intent on different generation tasks: content selection and organization (Elhadad 1992), connective selection (Elhadad & McKeown 1990), adjective selection (Elhadad 1991). The same general mechanism can be applied to the selection of JDs. In this case, I assume that the generator's input includes argumentative evaluations of the form *(X is high/low on S)* where *X* is a finite set of discrete individuals and *S* is the scale of cardinality. When this is the case, a feature *degree* is set in the description of the set *X*, which records the speaker's argumentative intent regarding the number of elements in the set *X*.

Monotonicity: the orientation feature

Barwise & Cooper define the notion of *monotonicity* using the following linguistic test (Barwise & Cooper 1981, pp.184-191): consider two verb-phrases VP_1 and VP_2, such that the denotation of VP_1 is a subset of the denotation of VP_2, that is, in logical terms, $VP_1(x) \Rightarrow VP_2(x)$. Then by checking whether the following seem logically valid, one can determine if the determiners are monotonic:

> If NP VP_1, then NP VP_2.
> (NP is monotonic increasing.)
> If NP VP_2, then NP VP_1.
> (NP is monotonic decreasing.)

Barwise & Cooper give the following examples, taking VP_1 to be *entered the race early* and VP_2 to be *entered the race* (Barwise & Cooper 1981, p.185):

$$\text{If} \left\{ \begin{array}{ll} some & Republican \\ every & linguist \\ John & \\ most & farmers \\ many & men \end{array} \right\} \text{entered the race early,}$$

$$\left\{ \begin{array}{ll} some & Republican \\ every & linguist \\ John & \\ most & farmers \\ many & men \end{array} \right\} \text{entered the race.}$$

All these implications are valid, while the reverse implications do not hold. Similarly, the following implications indicate that the determiners *no, few* and *neither* are monotonic decreasing:

$$\text{If} \left\{ \begin{array}{ll} no & plumber \\ few & linguists \\ neither & Democrat \end{array} \right\} \text{entered the race,}$$

$$\left\{ \begin{array}{ll} no & plumber \\ few & linguists \\ neither & Democrat \end{array} \right\} \text{entered the race early.}$$

Note that the determiners *exactly two* and *at most three* are not monotonic at all, since there is no implicative relation between *exactly three men entered the race early* and *exactly three men entered the race*.

All argumentative JDs must be monotonic. The feature *orientation* is required in the input specification of a set to indicate the orientation of an argumentative evaluation. Its value can be +, - or none, and it corresponds exactly to the distinction between monotonic increasing, decreasing, and non-monotonic quantifiers. Note that orientation is distinct from degree, because different degrees can be expressed for the same orientation:

AI has a little programming:	orient + degree -
AI has a lot of programming:	orient + degree +
AI has little programming:	orient - degree -
AI has almost no programming:	orient - degree +

The Intersection Condition

Following (Barwise & Cooper 1981, Sect.1.3), NPs *as a whole* are viewed as the expression of *generalized quantifiers*, as opposed to simply determiners like *all* or *some*. Consequently, the input to the determiner generation procedure is a complete set specification. Sets are characterized in intension by a domain and the properties that must be satisfied by all elements. These properties are in general mapped to modifiers of the NP realizing the set using a procedure similar to that discussed in (Elhadad 1993). This section presents the *intersection condition*, defined in (Barwise & Cooper 1981, p.190) and explains why a distinction between two types of modifiers must be enforced to allow for the generation of JDs.

The linguistic test corresponding to the formal definition of the *intersection condition* is the following: let P_1 and P_2 be two properties; then if a determiner D satisfies the intersection condition, the sentences *there are D P_1 P_2 N* and *D P_1 N are P_2* are semantically equivalent. For example:

There are exactly 3 interesting AI topics.
Exactly 3 interesting topics are in AI.
Exactly 3 AI topics are interesting.

These three forms are equivalent, indicating that *exactly n* satisfies the intersection condition. In contrast, consider:

(1) There are many interesting topics which are in AI.
(2) There are many AI topics which are interesting.

These NPs are not equivalent, as shown, for example, by considering the following situation: a person has interest in 100 topics; AI covers 10 topics; the intersection between the interesting topics and the AI topics contains 7 elements. Then (1) is probably not valid (7 topics out of 100 is not many) while (2) is valid (7

out of 10 is many). Note that the "classical" quantifiers, corresponding to the mathematical $\exists$ and $\forall$, both satisfy the intersection condition, but JDs, *e.g., many, few, most*, do not satisfy it.

Consider now the fact that in both (1) and (2) the NPs with the *many* determiner denote the same set of individuals (the 7 topics of the intersection). The validity of the sentences, however, is different when the scope of the *many* changes from one modifier to the other. This indicates again that *many* is not extensional, but also, that the input conceptual description of sets must attribute a different status to the two modifiers if modifier generation is to interact properly with determiner selection and prevent the generation of invalid sentences like (1).

I distinguish between *reference* and *intension* modifiers to account for this difference in status. For example, consider the set defined by:
$S = \{x \in \text{TOPICS} \mid Interest(x, student) \land Area(x, AI)\}$
Different perspectives can be held on this set: when the *interest* property is the intension and the *area* property is the reference, the definition can be written as follows:
$S1 = \{x \in \text{AI-TOPICS} \mid Interest(x, student)\}$
And, under normal circumstances this representation leads to the English realization: *Most AI topics are interesting.*

If in contrast the perspective is switched, and *interest* becomes the reference and *area* the intension, then the definition and realization become:
$S2 = \{x \in \text{INTERESTING-TOPICS} \mid Area(x, AI)\}$
Few of the topics that interest you are in AI.
In this example, the same observation of a set of topics satisfying two properties can lead to the generation of two contradictory argumentative evaluations. This indicates that, because JDs do not satisfy the intersection condition, the structuring of properties in a set specification between *reference* and *intension* must be present in the input to the generator (as in S1 and S2), and that a neutral representation for sets such as S would not be appropriate.

In summary, the following three properties characterize argumentative JDs: (1) they are non-extensional; (2) they are monotonic; (3) they do not satisfy the intersection condition. Consequently, the conceptual description of sets sent as input to a generator must contain the features *degree* and *orientation* and distinguish between *reference* and *intension* modifiers if the generator is to be able to produce JDs.

Input/Output

The overall architecture of the generation part of AD-VISOR II is the following: the input is a conceptual representation encoded in a KL-ONE-like network enriched with pragmatic annotations describing the speaker's intentions and assumptions. This conceptual network is passed to a *lexical chooser* which selects open-class words and performs *phrase planning* to combine them into phrase structures such as NPs and clauses. These structures are finally passed to the *syntactic realization grammar* SURGE for closed-class word selection, agreements and linearization. In this paper, I only describe the *determiner selection* subprocess of the lexical chooser.

The input to the determiner generation procedure, therefore, is a set specification. The output is a set of syntactic features appearing at the NP level and controlling the selection of the determiner sequence in the SURGE grammar.

Conceptual Representation for Generalized Quantifiers

ADVISOR II is implemented in FUF, an extension of the functional unification formalism of Kay (1979) described in (Elhadad 1993, Chap.3 and 4). This section describes the conceptual representation of sets as a FUF functional description input to the generator. The input specification contains objects of four types: individuals, sets, relations and argumentative evaluations. I briefly present here the representation of sets and evaluations.

Sets are described by the following features (all are optional except `cat` and `index`):

```
((cat set)
 (index <unique-id>)
 (kind <prototype>)
 (cardinality <n>)
 (extension <list-of-individuals>)
 (intension <a-relation>)
 (reference <a-set>))
```

`kind` is used for sets of objects of the same type. `extension` is the explicit list of the set elements. The logical definition of a set described by `intension` and `reference` is the following:
$S = \{x \in \text{Reference} \mid \text{Intension}(x)\}$ where `intension` is a relation, and `reference`, recursively, a set and the distinction between `intension` and `reference` is justified above.

Argumentative evaluations encode the speaker's argumentative intent:

```
((cat evaluation)
 (evaluated <path-to-set-or-individual>)
 (scale <a-scale>)
 (orientation <+ or ->))
```

This indicates that the speaker judges the element pointed to by `evaluated` as high (or low) on `scale`.

An input for the following set is shown below with the argumentative evaluation that the set is high on the scale of cardinality:
$S1 = \{x \in \text{AI-TOPICS} \mid \text{Interest}(x, student)\}$ Intuitively, this set contains the 7 topics that are of interest to the user among the 10 topics which are covered in AI.

```
((topics
  ((cat set) (kind ((cat topic)))
   (cardinality 7)
   (reference
    ((cat set) (kind ((cat topic)))
     (cardinality 10)
     (intension
      ((cat class-relation) (name area)
       (1 {^ argument})
       (2 ((cat field) (name AI)))))))
   (intension
    ((cat user-relation) (name interest)
     (1 {^ argument})
     (2 ((cat student)))))))
 (argumentation
  ((cat evaluation) (evaluated {topics})
   (scale ((name cardinality)))
        (orientation +))))
```

Output: Syntax of the Determiner Sequence

The determiner sequence is a subconstituent of NPs. It is also in itself a complex constituent. It has the specificity that it is mainly a *closed system* - *i.e.*, the lexical elements are part of a small set of words which are determined completely by a small set of syntactic features. When implementing the SURGE realization grammar, the issue was to identify a minimal set of features accounting for the variety of determiner sequences observable in English. The syntactic description implemented in SURGE is an augmented version of that presented in (Halliday 1985, pp.159-176), with additions derived from observations in (Quirk et al. 1972, pp.136-165). A set of 24 features controlling the realization of the determiner sequence was thus identified, which is presented in detail in (Elhadad 1993, Sect.5.4). I only present here a brief overview of the grammar for determiners, and focus on the features relevant to the realization of JDs.

The structure of the determiner sequence is shown in Fig.1. Pre-determiners can be one of the following elements: *all, both* or *half*, multipliers (*twice, three times*) or fractions (*one fourth*). Complex co-occurrence restrictions exist between the different predeterminers and different classes of nouns (mass, count nouns denoting a number or an amount) and between prede-

pre-det	(of)	det	deictic2	ord	card
all	*of*	*the*	*famous*	*first*	*ten*
half	*of*	*my*			
twice as					

quant	NP-head
	commandments
many	*properties*
much	*work*

Figure 1: Syntactic structure of the NP

terminers, cardinals and quantifiers. There are also special cases of noun classes that take zero articles, including seasons, institutions, transport means, illnesses (Quirk et al 1972, pp.156-159). The implementation of such co-occurrence restrictions explains the complexity of SURGE's determiner grammar.

To control the selection of the various elements of the determiner sequence, I make use of Halliday's distinction between three functions of the determiner sequence:

1. Deictic: to identify whether a subset of the thing is denoted, and if yes, which subset. The relevant decisions are depicted below, in Fig.2, in the form of a systemic network, where curly braces indicate choice points between alternatives and square brackets indicate simultaneous decisions which must be taken. The top level distinction is between specific and non-specific determination. A specific deictic denotes a known, well identified subset of the thing. A non-specific deictic denotes a subset identified by quantity.

For specific deictics, the subset can be identified by different means: deixis and distance (near or far from the speaker - *this* vs. *that*), possession (*my, John's*) or not at all (*the*).

Non-specific deictics are either total (*all, no, both, each, every, neither*) or partial. Partial deictics come in two sorts: selective (*one, either, any* and *some* as in *some people*) and non-selective (*a, some* as in *some cheese*).

2. Deictic2: to specify the subset of the thing by "referring to its fame, familiarity or its status in the text" (Halliday 1985, p.162). The deictic2 element is an adjective such as *same, usual, given*. Such adjectives are part of the determiner sequence because they systematically occur before the cardinal element of the determiner, in contrast to any other describing adjective, which must occur after the cardinal.

3. Numerative: to specify the quantity or the place of the thing. The numerative specification can be either quantitative (expressing a quantity, *three*) or

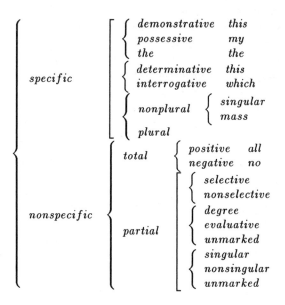

Figure 2: The deictic network

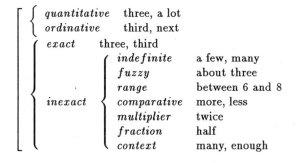

Figure 3: The numerative network

ordinative (expressing a relative position, *third*). In both cases, the expression can be either exact (*one, two..., first, second...*) or inexact (*a lot, the next*). The source of the inexactness can be an approximation device (*about three, roughly third, approximately ten*) or a range expression (*between six and ten*). Alternatively, it can be a context dependent expression like *the next, many, few, more*, and an evaluative expression like *enough, too many, too much*. Figure 3 summarizes the relevant decisions.

The features controlling the selection of JDs are located in the non-specific region of the deictic network and in the inexact region of the numerative network. The subset of SURGE features which trigger the selection of argumentative JDs is `total`, `orientation`, `superlative` and `degree`.

Mapping from Conceptual to Syntactic Features

When mapping from a conceptual description to the features controlling the determiner selection, the first decision is whether the speaker's argumentative intent is to be realized through the use of a JD or with other linguistic devices (such as connotative verbs, scalar adjectives or connectives). This decision can interact with most generation decisions and is discussed at length in (Elhadad 1993).

When argumentation *is* to be expressed in a determiner site, the following mapping rules are applied:

- **Total**: when the set is the object of a positive evaluation, its cardinality is known and equal to that of the reference set, then total is set to +. If the evaluation is negative and the cardinality is known to be 0, total is set to -. In all other cases, total is set to none.

- **Orientation**: when the set is the object of an argumentative evaluation, orientation records whether the evaluation is high or low. Otherwise, it is set to none.

- **Superlative**: set to yes when the reference set is given, its cardinality is known, the cardinality of the set is larger than half that of the reference set, and the set is the object of a positive argumentative evaluation.

The general heuristics behind these rules is to use the pragmatically strongest determiner possible to realize the speaker's argumentative intent. For example, if *all AI topics are interesting* can be produced, it will be preferred to *some AI topics*.

For **Degree**, the determination of a value is more difficult. Degree determines the selection among *a few, some, many, a (large, great, incredible...) number* if orientation is +, and among *few, a (small, tiny, ridiculous...) number* if orientation is -. In ADVISOR II, degree is limited to have values +, - or none. A finer account of the degree of determiners is probably needed, but it creates many problems which, for lack of space, cannot be discussed here.

Conclusion

This paper has presented a method to generate judgment determiners (JDs). It focuses on the use of JDs as one way (among many others) to express the speaker's argumentative intent. The paper provides a semantic characterization of JDs through the use of three tests (non-extensionality, monotonicity and non-satisfaction of the intersection condition) and derives constraints from this characterization on the form of input a generator requires to be capable of producing JDs.

The paper describes the part of a lexical chooser that takes as input a conceptual description of a set with pragmatic annotations such as argumentative evaluations and produces as output a set of syntactic features which control the behavior of the SURGE surface realization component. The component of SURGE responsible for the complex syntax of the English determiner sequence is discussed and a technique to map the conceptual input to the relevant set of features is presented.

Acknowledgments. I am indebted to Kathleen McKeown, Jacques Robin and Rebecca Passonneau for their precious help both during the research and the writing of this paper.

References

J. C. Anscombre and O. Ducrot. *L'argumentation dans la langue.* Pierre Mardaga, Bruxelles, 1983.

J. Barwise and R. Cooper. Generalized quantifiers in english. *Linguistics and Philosophy*, 4:159–219, 1981.

R. Dale. *Generating referring expressions in a domain of objects and processes.* PhD thesis, University of Edinburgh, Scotland, 1988.

M. Elhadad. Types in functional unification grammars. In *Proceedings of the 28th Annual Meeting of the Association for Computational Linguistics*, Detroit, MI, 1990. ACL.

M. Elhadad. Generating adjectives to express the speaker's argumentative intent. In *Proceedings of the 9th Annual Conference on Artificial Intelligence.* AAAI, 1991.

M. Elhadad. Generating argumentative paragraphs. In *Proceedings of COLING'92*, Nantes, France, July 1992.

M. Elhadad. *Using argumentation to control lexical choice: a unification-based implementation.* PhD thesis, Computer Science Department, Columbia University, 1992.

M. Elhadad. Generating complex noun phrases. Technical Report FC-93-05, Dept of Mathematics and Computer Science, Ben Gurion University of the Negev, Israel.

M. Elhadad and K. R. McKeown. Generating connectives. In *Proceedings of COLING'90 (Volume 3)*, pages 97–101, Helsinki, Finland, 1990.

M. Halliday. *An introduction to functional grammar.* Edward Arnold, London, 1985.

M. Kay. Functional grammar. In *Proceedings of the 5th Annual Meeting of the Berkeley Linguistic Society*, 1979.

E. Keenan and Y. Stavi. A semantic characterization of natural language determiners. *Linguistics and Philosophy*, 9:253–326, 1986.

R. Quirk, S. Greenbaum, G. Leech, and J. Svartvik. *A grammar of contemporary English.* Longman, 1972.

Bidirectional Chart Generation of Natural Language Texts

Masahiko Haruno°*   **Yasuharu Den**†   **Yuji Matsumoto**‡   **Makoto Nagao**°

°Department of Electrical Engineering, Kyoto University
†ATR Interpreting Telecommunication Research Laboratories
‡Advanced Institute of Science and Technology, Nara
e-mail: haruno@kuee.kyoto-u.ac.jp

Abstract

This paper presents Bidirectional Chart Generation (BCG) algorithm as an uniform control mechanism for sentence generation and text planning. It is an extension of Semantic Head Driven Generation algorithm [Shieber *et al.*, 1989] in that recomputation of partial structures and backtracking are avoided by using a chart table. These properties enable to handle a large scale grammar including text planning and to implement the algorithm in parallel programming languages.

Other merits of the algorithm are to deal with multiple contexts and to keep every partial structure in the chart. It becomes easier for the generator to find a recovery strategy when user cannot understand the generated text.

Introduction

As opposed to traditional naive top-down or bottom-up mechanism [Wedekind, 1988][van Noord, 1989], the Semantic-Head-Driven (SHD) algorithm[Shieber *et al.*, 1989] combines both top-down and bottom-up derivations effectively. However, a straightforward implementation of the algorithm causes intensive backtracking when the scale of the grammar is large.

Bidirectional Chart Generation (BCG) algorithm avoids the inefficiency of backtracking by using a chart table. Like Chart Parsing algorithm[Kay, 1980], BCG algorithm can be implemented as a no-backtracking program in both parallel and sequential programming languages.

The algorithm is used in our explanation system not only for surface sentence generation but also for RST[Mann and Thompson, 1987] based text planning. As pointed out in [Moore and Paris, 1989], a generation facility must be able to determine what portion of text failed to achieve its purpose when follow-up question (user's feedback) arises. BCG algorithm deals with multiple contexts just like ATMS[de Kleer, 1986] and

---

*Current affiliation is NTT (Nippon Telegraph and Telephone) corporation.

keeps every partial structure in a chart. It is easier for the generator to infer why the explanation fails and to find a recovery strategy.

After reviewing SHD algorithm, we present BCG algorithm comparing with Bottom-up Chart Parsing algorithm. Then, we show an implementation of the algorithm in a parallel logic programming language GHC[Ueda, 1986][1]. Finally, we discuss the application of BCG algorithm to answering user's follow-up questions in a RST based text planning.

Semantic-Head-Driven Algorithm

```
(1) s/Sem --> pp/ga(Sbj),pp/wo(Obj),
        #v(Sbj, Obj)/Sem.
(2) s/Sem -->pp/wo(Obj),pp/ga(Sbj),
        #v(Sbj, Obj)/Sem.
(3) pp/Sem --> np/NP,#p(NP)/Sem.
(4) v(Sbj, Obj)/call(Sbj,Obj) --> [呼ぶ].
(5) np/t --> [太郎].
(6) np/h --> [花子].
(7) p(NP)/ga(NP) --> [が].
(8) p(NP)/wo(NP) --> [を].
```

Figure 1: Sample Grammar

We give a brief outline of SHD algorithm based on the sample Japanese grammar shown in Figure 1. A nonterminal symbol is written in the form of category/semantics. semantic-head (marked by # in the grammar rules) has an important role in the algorithm.

semantic-head When the semantics of a right-hand-side element in a rule is identical to that of the left-hand-side, then the right-hand-side element is called the semantic head of the rule.

Grammar rules are divided into two types: Chain rules that have a semantic-head and non-chain rules[2] that do not. In the sample grammar, (1) through (3) are

---

[1]It is straightforward to transform it into a concurrent program in Prolog.

[2]we consider only lexical rules as non-chain rules for a while.

chain rules and (4) through (8) are non-chain rules. The algorithm proceeds bidirectionally, applying chain rules bottom-up and non-chain rules top-down. Those operations[3] are defined as follows:

Top-down operation A syntactic tree is traversed top-down using non-chain rules. A node that is about to expand is called the *goal*. Select a rule whose left-hand-side semantics is unifiable with that of the goal and make a node (called *pivot*) corresponding to the category of the left-hand-side. Then apply bottom-up operation from the pivot.

Bottom-up operation A syntactic tree is traversed bottom-up using chain rules. Select a rule whose semantic head is unifiable with the pivot, and then make other categories of the right-hand side as new goals. When all these goals are constituted applying operations recursively, the parent node at the left-hand side is introduced. If the parent node is not unifiable with the goal, then apply the bottom-up operation, regarding the parent node as a new pivot.

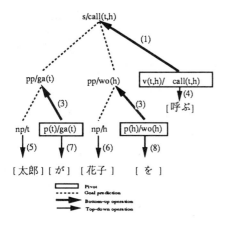

Figure 2: Generation Process

We show a sample generation process starting from semantic representation call(t,h) (Figure 2). First, a pivot v(t,h)/call(t,h) is introduced by applying top-down operation with rule(4). Two bottom-up operations using rules (1) and (2) are applicable to the pivot. Assume that the rule (1) is selected. The new goals pp/ga(t) and pp/wo(h) are introduced from the right-hand side of the rule. Top-down operation introduces new pivots p(t)/ga(t) and p(h)/wo(h) with rules (7) and (8). Going on the same process, a sentence [太郎, が, 花子, を, 呼ぶ] is generated as shown in Figure 2. Another sentence [花子, を, 太郎, が, 呼ぶ] is generated as well applying rule (2) by backtracking. This kind of backtracking causes serious inefficiency when the scale of grammar is large.

As discussed above, SHD algorithm consists of two parts, the top-down operation and the bottom-up oper-

---

[3] Top-down operation is augmented afterwards in order to handle general non-chain rules.

ation. Because the bottom-up operation resembles the basic operation of left-corner parsing algorithm, considering the similarity between left-corner categories and semantic heads, SHD algorithm can be realized in the same way as Bottom-up Chart Parsing algorithm. In the next section, we present BCG algorithm, which avoids the inefficiency caused by backtracking.

BCG Algorithm

Basic Algorithm

Bottom-up Chart Parsing algorithm [Kay, 1980] consists of the following three procedures.

Procedure-1: Let w_i be i-th word. For all rules of the form $b \rightarrow [w_i]$ create new inactive edges between v and w whose term is b provided that v and w are the $(i-1)$-th and i-th vertices.

Procedure-2: Let e_i be an inactive edge of category a incident from vertex v to vertex w. For all rules of the form $b \rightarrow c_1, c_2 \cdots c_n$ in the grammar such that $c_1 = a$, introduce a new edge e_a with the term $[a [?]c_2 \cdots [?]c_n]b$, incident from v to w, provided that there is no such edge in the chart already.

Procedure-3: Let e_a and e_i be adjacent active and inactive edges. e_a is incident from vertex v and e_i is incident to vertex w. Let $[?]\alpha$ be the first open box in e_a. If e_i is of category α, create a new edge between v and w whose term is that of e_a with the first open box replaced by the term of e_i.

Procedure-1 looks up lexical rules at the first stage of the algorithm. Procedure-2 predicts phrase structures by making use of the left-corner category. Procedure-3 fills up a prediction. On the other hand, SHD algorithm discussed in the previous section makes use of semantic head in order to predict new goals and the prediction is filled by recursive top-down operations. BCG algorithm is realized from Bottom-up Chart Parsing algorithm by identifying a semantic-head with a left-corner category. But important differences remain to be considered between generation and parsing as follows:

1. In parsing, all initial inactive edges are introduced at the first place by Procedure-1. This process corresponds to introducing pivots from semantic representation in the case of generation. This means that inactive edges must be built dynamically.

2. If Procedure-2 predicts two distinct goal sequences from one pivot by using two different rules, it happens that the pivot has two distinct adjacents because different goals may introduce different pivots.

The first point demands a dynamic process of introducing pivots. Once a goal is produced, its semantic representation is used to introduce a new pivot. The second point says that adjacent edges in BCG cannot be placed in a linear sequence. We introduce *forward links* to indicate the adjacency relation of edges; that is, when Procedure-1 introduces an inactive edge e_i according to an active edge e_a, it puts a pointer from the tail of e_a to the head of e_i. Two edges are adjacent in generation if there exists a forward link from one to the other. In addition, we must take account of the case where the required pivot has already been introduced before. In such a case, we reuse the previously produced pivot by simply adding a new forward link going to it. Therefore, it occurs that more than one forward link is put to one edge.

BCG algorithm becomes as follows. Procedure-1 realizes the dynamic introduction of pivots. Procedure-2 and Procedure-3 are straightforward augmentations of the bottom-up chart parsing algorithm except for the use of forward links.

Procedure-1: Let e_a be an active edge of category $[a_1 \cdots [?]c_j \cdots [?]c_n]b$ incident from vertex u to v. Let $[?]c_j$ be the first open box in e_a and Sem_j be its semantics. For all rules of the form b/Sem --> $[word]$ such that Sem and Sem_j are unifiable, create new inactive edges between vertex w and vertex w' whose term is b/Sem and put a forward link from vertex v to vertex w. If the same inactive edge ever exists from vertex x to vertex y put a forward link from vertex v to vertex x instead.

Procedure-2: Let e_i be an inactive edge of category a incident from vertex v to vertex w. For all rules of the form b --> $c_1, \ldots, \#c_h, \ldots, c_n$ in the grammar such that Sem_h and Sem are unifiable, introduce a new active edge e_a with the term $[[?]c_1 \cdots a \cdots [?]c_n]b$, incident from v to w, provided that there is no such edge in the chart already. Sem and Sem_h are semantics of a and c_h.

Procedure-3: Let e_a be an active edge with the term $[a_1 \cdots [?]c_j \cdots [?]c_n]b$ incident from vertex u to vertex v and e_i be an inactive edge with the term a incident from vertex w to vertex x. Let $[?]c_j$ be the first open box in e_a. If a forward link exists from vertex v to vertex w such that $c_j = a$, create a new edge between u and x whose term is $[a_1 \cdots a [?]c_{j+1} \cdots [?]c_n]b$.

An example starting from semantic representation call(t,h) is explained in the rest of this section.
The chart constructed in the process is shown in Figure 3 and in Table 1. The first inactive edge v(t,h)/call(t,h) is introduced from rule(4) by Procedure-1 and the process proceeds as shown in Figure 3. The inactive edge4 p(t)/ga(t) is produced from the goal pp/ga(t) of active edge2 and rule(7) by Procedure-1. Then the forward link A is put from the tail of active edge2 to the head of inactive edge4. Inactive edge5 p(h)/wo(h) is produced in the same way from active edge3. After the inactive edge10 pp(t)/ga(t) and 11 pp(h)/wo(h) are generated, which have the same head as inactive edge4 and 5, active edge12 [pp/ga(t) [?]pp/wo(h) v(t,h)/call(t,h)] s/call(t,h) is introduced from

active edge2 and inactive edge10 by Procedure-3. Although inactive edge p(h)/wo(h) is introduced from goal pp/wo(h) of active edge12 and rule(8) by Procedure-1, it is the same as inactive edge5. Then forward link E is put from the tail of active edge12 to the head of inactive edge5 instead of generating a new inactive edge. At the end of the process, inactive edges 14 and 15 are produced, each of which corresponds to a sentence[4]. They are generated with no backtracking.

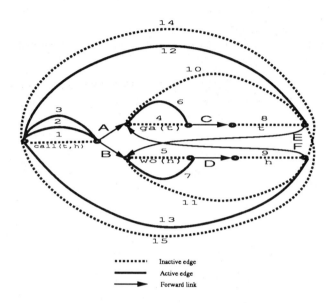

Figure 3: Graph Representation of the Chart

General Non-Chain Rule

We show in this section how general non-chain rules are handled in BCG algorithm, though we have considered only lexical rules as non-chain rules. General non-chain rules are necessary for handling a large scale grammar, particularly for text planning. Consider the following non-chain rule which describes a Japanese relative clause:

```
np/ind(X,[R|Rstr]) -->
        s_rel(X)/R,
        np/ind(X,Rstr).
```

First, we extend the top-down operation defined before:

top-down operation A syntactic tree is traversed top-down using non-chain rules. A node that is about to expand is called the *goal*. Select a non-chain rule whose left-hand-side semantic representation is unifiable with that of the goal and make a node called *pivot* corresponding to the category

---

[4] Note that the order of edges in the chart doesn't mean the surface word order. It is shown explicitly by difference lists as discussed in the next section.

Edge	Term	Procedure	Rule
1	`v(t,h)/call(t,h)`	1	(4)
2	`[[?]pp/ga(t),[?]pp/wo(h),v(t,h)/call(t,h)]s/call(t,h)`	2	(1)
3	`[[?]pp/wo(h),[?]pp/ga(t),v(t,h)/call(t,h)]s/call(t,h)`	2	(2)
4	`p(t)/ga(t)`	1	(7)
5	`p(h)/wo(h)`	1	(8)
6	`[[?]np/t,p(t)/ga(t)]pp/ga(t)`	2	(3)
7	`[[?]np/h,p(h)/wo(h)]pp/wo(h)`	2	(3)
8	`np/t`	1	(5)
9	`np/h`	1	(6)
10	`pp/ga(t)`	3	-
11	`pp/wo(h)`	3	-
12	`[pp/ga(t),[?]pp/wo(h),v(t,h)/call(t,h)]s/call(t,h)`	3	-
13	`[pp/wo(h),[?]pp/ga(t),v(t,h)/call(t,h)]s/call(t,h)`	3	-
14	`s/call(t,h)`	3	-
15	`s/call(t,h)`	3	-

Table 1: Table Representation of the Chart

of the left-hand-side. **In addition, make categories of right-hand side as new goals and apply top-down operation to them recursively.** If the pivot is not unifiable with the goal, then apply bottom-up operation from the pivot.

The bold-face part is supplementary to the original top-down operation. It expands the categories at right-hand side after unifying the goal with left-hand side. Note that this part is almost same as top-down derivation of a syntactic tree. The procedure for the general non-chain rules is formalized in the same way as Top-down Chart Parsing algorithm [Kay, 1980]. The definition of the operation is the following Procedure-1'.

Procedure-1' Let e_a be an active edge with the term $[a_1 \cdots [?]c_j \cdots c_n]d$ incident from vertex u to v. Let $[?]c_j$ be the first open box in e_a and Sem_j be its semantic representation. For every rule of the form $b/Sem \; \texttt{-->} \; c_1, \ldots, c_n$ such that $Sem_j \, and \, Sem$ are unifiable, create a new active edge with the term $[[?]c_1 \cdots [?]c_n]b$ looping at vertex w, and put a forward link from v to w. If the same inactive edge ever exists from y, simply put a forward link from v to y instead.

Implementation

Previous sections show that BCG algorithm is formalized in the similar way to Chart Parsing algorithm. PAX parsing system[Matsumoto, 1986] is an implementation of Bottom-up Chart Parsing algorithm in a parallel logic programming language GHC[5]. We show in this section a GHC implementation of BCG algorithm in the similar way to PAX system. The implemented system consists of the following two parts.

1. The program translated from grammar rules.

---

[5] A GHC clause can be understood just like a Prolog clause if the commit operator '|' is replaced by '!'.

2. The meta-process that introduces inactive edges dynamically. It absorbs the difference between parsing and generation.

Basic Transformation of Grammar Rules

In our implementation, each terminal and non-terminal symbol is realized as a parallel process that communicate with each other for building up larger structures. The communication channel is called a stream. Let us take the following grammar rule.

```
s/Sem -->
      pp/ga(Sbj),
      pp/wo(Obj),
      #v(Sbj,Obj)/Sem.
```

Three non-terminal symbols at right-hand-side are realized as parallel processes and each of them receives a stream from the left and passes an output stream to the right. For transformation, the following modification is done to the grammar rule: Identifiers standing for intermediate positions in a grammar rule are inserted in the rule and the semantic head of the rule is moved to the top of the right-hand-side to be associated with left-corner parsing. Moreover, in order to keep the surface order information, difference lists representing words are added to each symbol. The example rule results in the following form:

```
s(S0-S3)/Sem -->
      v(Sbj, Obj, S2-S3)/Sem,
      id1,
      pp(S0-S1)/ga(Sbj),
      id2,
      pp(S1-S2)/wo(Obj).
```

By translating this rule into following GHC clauses, we can achieve SHD generation in parallel. The behavior of the grammar rule is depicted in Figure 4.
First, `v(Sbj,Obj,S2-S3)` is translated into the program below.

```
v(In,Sbj,Obj,S2-S3,Out) :- true |
      Out = [id1(ga(Sbj),In,Sbj,Obj,S2-S3)].
```

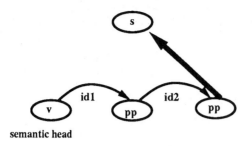

semantic head

Figure 4: Behavior of Processes

When `v(Sbj,Obj,S2-S3)` is produced, tree traverse proceeds to the position of `id1`. It corresponds to the Procedure-2 of BCG algorithm that selects a rule with a semantic head whose semantic representation is unifiable with that of the inactive edge (pivot), and introduces a new active edge (goal). The process `v(In,Sbj,Obj,S2-S3,Out)` generates `id1`, which corresponds to the active edge. In general, processes perform inactive edges and data in streams stands for active edges. The first open box of the new active edge is `pp(S0-S1)`, whose semantics `ga(Sbj)` is passed along with `id1` and used afterwards in the meta-process (Procedure-1 of BCG algorithm).

Secondly, `pp(S0-S1)` is translated as below.

```
pp([id1(_,In,Sbj,Obj,S2-S3)|Tail],S0-S1,Out) :-
    true |
    Out = [id2(wo(Obj),In,Obj,S0-S1,S2-S3)|Out1],
    pp(Tail,S0-S1,Out1).
```

Because `pp(S0-S1)` is to the right of `id1`, tree traverse proceeds to the position of `id2` when `pp(S0-S1)` receives `id1`. This corresponds to the Procedure-3 of BCG algorithm that derives a new active edge from an active edge and an inactive edge. The first open box of the new active edge is `pp(S1-S2)`, the semantics of which is `wo(Obj)` is inserted as the first argument of `id2`. In the same way, `pp(S1-S2)` is translated as below.

```
pp([id2(_,In,Obj,S0-S1,S2-S3)|Tail],S1-S2,Out) :-
    true | s(In, S0-S3,Out1),
    pp(Tail,S1-S2,Out2),merge(Out1,Out2,Out).
```

When `pp(S1-S2)/wo(Obj)` is generated, the parent node `s(S0-S3)/Sem` is generated. The final definition of process `pp` is the collection of all of such clauses each of which corresponds to an occurrence of `pp` in the right-hand-side of grammar rules. The following clauses are necessary to handle exceptional situations:

```
pp([],_,Out) :- true | Out = [].
pp([_|Tail],String,Out):- otherwise |
    pp(Tail,String,Out).
```

Finally, let us take the following non-chain (lexical) rule.

```
v(Sbj, Obj)/call(Sbj,Obj) --> [呼ぶ].
```

This rule is translated into the program below, which generates a process corresponding to `v(Sbj,Obj)` from the semantic representation `call(Sbj,Obj)`.

```
pivot(call(Sbj,Obj),In,Out) :- true |
    v(In,Sbj,Obj,[呼ぶ|S0]-S0,Out).
```

The pivot process is generated dynamically by the meta-process corresponding to the Procedure-1 of BCG algorithm.

Meta-Process

The meta-process monitors the data in all streams and controls the whole generation process. It checks the semantic representation in each identifier (`semantics(Id,Sem)`), and generates or reuses an inactive edges according to the semantic representation, then passes the identifier to the inactive edges. It is attained by calling the pivot process described below. Here, streams perform forward links of BCG algorithm. Forward links are introduced dynamically and a stream is realized by an open list to receive identifiers incrementally. The meta-process maintains the table that consists of pairs like `wait(Sem,Str)`, where Sem is the semantic representation of an ever produced inactive edge and Str is the tail of its input stream. When the meta-process derives Sem_j from an identifier and is about to produce a pivot process, it checks whether Sem_j is already registered in the table. The meta-process generates a new pivot process only if the pair `wait($Sem_j$,Str)` is not registered. The following program realizes the task.

```
meta_proc([],_) :- true | true.
meta_proc([Id|Tail],Table) :-
    semantics(Id,Sem),
    get(wait(Sem,StrTail),Table,Table1) |
    StrTail = [Id|NewStrTail],
    put(wait(Sem,NewStrTail),Table1,NewTable),
    meta_proc(Tail,NewTable).
meta_proc([Id|Tail],Table) :- otherwise |
    semantics(Id,Sem),
    pivot(Sem,[Id|StrTail],Out),
    put(wait(Sem,StrTail),Table,NewTable),
    merge(Out,Tail,Next),
    meta_proc(Next,NewTable).
```

The second clause of `meta_proc` corresponds to the case of reusing the existing process and the third to the case of generating a new process. In the second clause, `get(wait(Sem,StrTail),Table,Table1)` looks up if `wait(Sem,StrTail)` is previously registered in the table. When the table includes the element, `meta_proc` reuses it by instantiating the top of the open list with StrTail. Otherwise `meta_proc` generates a new process by calling `pivot(Sem,[Id|StrTail],Out)` in the third clause, and register the process in the table by `put(wait(Sem,StrTail),Table,NewTable)`.

The pivot process introducing new processes is derived by transforming lexical (non-chain) rules as described in the previous section. The transformation of general non-chain rules are described in the next section.

Transformation of Non-Chain Rules

Let us consider the following rule.

```
np/ind(X,[R|Rstr]) -->
  s_rel(X)/R,
  np/ind(X,Rstr).
```

General non-chain rules are treated by Procedure-1' whose central part is the same as Procedure-1 . The only difference is that Procedure-1' introduces a new active edge, from a semantic representation of a predicted goal. The process is also realized by the pivot process as below:

```
pivot(ind(X,[R|Rstr]),In,Out) :- true |
  Out = [id3(R,In,X,R,Rstr)].
```

The identifier **id3** is inserted just before the leftmost category **s_rel(X)** for top-down traversal of a syntactic tree. The **pivot** process corresponding to the semantic representation **ind(X,[R|Rstr])** generates this identifier. This kind of identifier corresponds to the active edge of Top-down Chart Parsing algorithm. When all categories at right-hand side are constituted, then a new process corresponding to **np** at left-hand side is produced.

Applying BCG Algorithm to RST Based Text Planning

This section examines the applicability of BCG algorithm to text planning. The depth-first search strategy has been used mainly in text planning, in which it is difficult for a generator to select the relevant operator at every choice point. On the other hand, BCG algorithm deals with more than one candidate in parallel until enough information is obtained.

Moreover, in explanation dialogue systems, users often ask follow-up questions when he or she cannot fully understand the explanation. The generator must infer why its explanation has failed to achieve the communicative goal; an error in user model, ambiguity of the meaning and so on. In BCG algorithm, it is easier for a generator to find a recovering strategy because all partial structures are preserved.

Plan Language

Our plan language is based on Rhetorical Structure Theory(RST)[Mann and Thompson, 1987]. Explanation dialogue requests a plan language to express both intentional and rhetorical structures of the text once produced to answer follow-up questions. We adopt the similar representation of RST to Moore's operators [Moore and Paris, 1989], one of which is shown below:

```
EFFECT:(BMB S H ?x)
CONSTRAINTS:nil
NUCLEUS:(INFORM S H ?x)
SATELLITES:(PERSUADE S H ?x)
```

In order to apply BCG algorithm to text planning, such operators are represented in DCG rules, where CONSTRAINTS are inserted as extra conditions. (1) corresponds to the above example.

```
(1) bmb/bmb(Speaker,Hearer,X) -->
      inf/inform(Speaker,Hearer,X),
      psd/persuade(Speaker,Hearer,X).
(2) bmb/bmb(Speaker,Hearer,X) -->
      explain/explain(Speaker,Hearer,X),
      inf/inform(Speaker,Hearer,X).
```

Let the speaker's goal be **bmb(Speaker,Hearer,X)**, there are alternative rules (1) and (2) applicable to this situation. A naive top-down planner recomputes **inf/inform(Speaker,Hearer,X)** due to backtracking. On the other hand, BCG algorithm proceeds in parallel reusing the structures ever constructed. Because most rules are applied top-down in text planning, the behavior of BCG algorithm, in this case, is almost identical to that of Top-down Chart algorithm [Kay, 1980].

Answering Follow-up Questions

BCG algorithm can select the best recovering strategy by comparing multiple contexts when receiving follow-up questions. Suppose user model contains concepts that the user does not actually know, the generator must change the user model and select the proper strategy for explaining the concept. The generator employs partial information in the chart particularly incomplete active edges, which stand for suspended plans. Let us consider the following plan operators and general knowledge.

```
% plan operator
goal/goal(Hearer,do(Hearer,Act)) -->
 recommend/recommend(Speaker,Hearer,Act),
 psd/persuaded(Hearer,goal(Hearer,do(Hearer,Act))).
psd/persuaded(Hearer,goal(Hearer,do(Hearer,Act)))
 --> {step(Act,Goal)},
 motivation/motivation(Act,Goal).
psd/persuaded(Hearer,goal(Hearer,do(Hearer,Act)))
 --> {step(Act,Goal),
 bel(Hearer,benefit(Act,Hearer))},
 inf/inform(benefit(Act,Hearer)).
motivation/motivation(Act,Goal) -->
 {step(Act,Goal)}
 bel/bel(Hearer,step(Act,Goal)).
bel/bel(Hearer,step(Act,Goal)) -->
 {know(Hearer,Goal)},
 inf/inform(Speaker,Hearer,step(Act,Goal)).
bel/bel(Hearer,step(Act,Goal)) -->
 inf/inform(Speaker,Hearer,step(Act,Goal)),
 {\+ know(Hearer,Goal)},
 elaboration/elaboration(Goal).


          % general knowledge
step(insert,optimization).
know(user,optimization).
```

The domain of the dialogue is Prolog programming. The system's goal is **goal(user(do(user,insert)))**, to recommend the user to insert a '!' before a recursive call. **insert** means inserting ! before the recursive call and **optimization** means the tail recursion optimization. The system generates the following texts as the first text (Figure 5).

system: 再帰呼び出しの前にカットを入れて下さい。

末尾最適化に必要です。
```
(Insert a cut symbol before recursive call.
 It is necessary for tail recursive optimi
 zation.)
```

The user cannot understand the explanation and poses the follow-up question.

user: 良く分かりません。
```
(I don't understand very well.)
```

The system accepts the follow-up question and searches the suspended active edges. Now, there are two suspended active edges (1) and (2):

```
(1)[[?]inf/inform(benefit(insert,user))]
     psd/persuaded(user,goal(user,do(user,insert)))
(2)[inf/inform(system,user,step(insert,optimization)),
    [?]elaboration/elaboration(optimization)]
     bel/bel(user,step(insert,optimization))
```

Each of the edges is suspended because of the contradiction to the user model; `bel(user,benefit(insert,user))` and `\+ know(user,insert)`. The generator selects the active edges that require few hypotheses to expand, and gives the relaxation to the user model. In this case, the generator assumes that `\+ know(user,insert)` holds and produces the following additional explanation as shown in Figure 5.

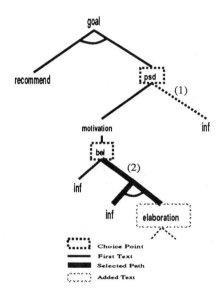

Figure 5: The Explanation Tree

system: 末尾最適化はコンパイラにバックトラックが必要無いことを示し、記憶容量を節約する手法です。
```
(Tail recursive optimization saves memory
 by showing compilers that no backtracking
 is necessary.)
```

The generator can reproduce the explanation by relaxing the user model according to actual state of user's knowledge. This is the similar situation to relaxation based parsing of ill-formed inputs in which chart-based method is powerful[Mellish, 1989] because it maintains all partial structures.

Concluding Remarks

We have presented BCG algorithm as a basic control mechanism of generation system. In contrast to Shieber's SHD algorithm, BCG algorithm deals with multiple contexts at a time. This property resolves two problems: First, the efficiency is remarkably improved in the case of a large scale grammar. Secondly, the comparison between multiple contexts becomes possible. Hence, revision like answering follow-up questions is performed easier by referring to the contexts in the chart. To sum up, we obtain the efficiency and robustness by adopting the BCG algorithm.

We are now studying the patterns of the follow-up questions and investigating the recovery heuristics based on the chart.

References

Johan de Kleer. An assumption-based TMS. *Artificial Intelligence*, 28:127–162, 1986.

Martin Kay. Algorithm schemata and data structure in syntactic processing. Technical Report CLS-80-12, Xerox PARC, 1980.

W. C. Mann and S. A. Thompson. Rhetorical structure theory: Description and construction of text structures. In *Natural Language Generation*, chapter 7, pages 85–96. Martinus Nijhoff Publishers, 1987.

Yuji Matsumoto. A parallel parsing system for natural language analysis. In *Proc. 3rd ICLP*, Lecture Notes in Computer Science 225, pages 396–409. Springer-Verlag, 1986.

Chris Mellish. Some chart-based techniques for parsing ill-formed input. In *Proc. 27th ACL*, pages 102–109, 1989.

Johanna Moore and Cecile Paris. Planning text for advisory dialogues. In *Proc. 27th ACL*, pages 203–211, 1989.

S. M. Shieber, van Noord, R. C. Moore, and F. C. N. Pereira. A semantic-head-driven generation algorithm for unification-based formalisms. In *Proc. 27th ACL*, pages 7–17, 1989.

K Ueda. Guarded Horn Clauses. In E. Wada, editor, *Logic Programming '85*, Lecture Notes in Computer Science 221, pages 168–179. Springer-Verlag, 1986.

van Noord. BUG: A directed bottom-up generator for unification-based formalisms. Working Paper 4, Katholieke Universiteit Leuven Stiching Taaltechnologie Utrecht, the Netherlands, 1989.

J Wedekind. Generation as structure driven derivation. In *Proc. 11th COLING*, pages 732–737, 1988.

Communicative Acts for Generating Natural Language Arguments

Mark T. Maybury

The MITRE Corporation
Artificial Intelligence Center
MS K329, Burlington Road
Bedford, MA 01730
maybury@linus.mitre.org

Abstract

The ability to argue to support a conclusion or to encourage some course of action is fundamental to communication. Guided by examination of naturally occurring arguments, this paper classifies the communicative structure and function of several different kinds of arguments and indicates how these can be formalized as plan-based models of communication. The paper describes the use of these communication plans in the context of a prototype which cooperatively interacts with a user to allocate scarce resources. This plan-based approach to argument helps improve the cohesion and coherence of the resulting communication.

Introduction

Knowledge-based systems are often called upon to support their results or conclusions or to justify courses of action which they recommend. These systems, therefore, are often placed in the position of attempting to influence the beliefs and/or behavior of their users and yet they often do not have sophisticated capabilities for doing so. The first step in arguing for some proposition or some course of action is ensure that it is understood by the addressee. A number of techniques have been developed to automatically generate natural language descriptions or expositions, for example, to describe what is meant by some abstract concept (McKeown 1985) or to explain a complex mechanism in a manner tailored to an individual user (Paris 1987). However, once the addressee understands the point, a system needs to be able to argue for or against that point.

A number of researchers have investigated computational models of representation and reasoning for argument. For example, Birnbaum (1982) represented propositions as nodes in an *argument graph* connected by attack and support relations. He suggested three ways to attack an argument (called *argument tactics*): attack the main proposition, attack the supporting evidence, and attack the claim that the evidence supports the main point.

In contrast, Cohen (1987) investigated the interpretation of deductive arguments and suggested how clue words (e.g., "therefore", "and", "so") could be used to recognize the structure underlying arguments that are presented in "pre-order" (i.e., claim followed by evidence), "post-order" (evidence before claims), and "hybrid-order" format (using both pre-order and post-order). Reichman (1985), on the other hand, characterized natural dialogues using a number

of conversational moves (e.g., support, interrupt, challenge) indicating "clue words" such as "because", "but anyway", and "no but" as evidence.

In contrast, this paper extends previous research in plan-based models of communication generation (Bruce 1975, Cohen 1978, Appelt 1985, Hovy 1988, Moore & Paris, 1989, Maybury 1991ab) by formalizing a suite of communicative acts a system can use to influence user beliefs or actions. The remainder of this paper first outlines several classes of argumentative actions which are differentiated on the basis of their semantics and purpose. Next, several of these actions are formalized as plan operators. The paper then illustrates their use to improve explanations when advising an operator on a course of action during a scheduling task. The paper concludes by identifying limitations and areas for further research.

Arguments as Communicative Acts

There are many conventional patterns of argument, depending upon the goal of the speaker. Aristotle identified several methods of argument including *exemplum* (illustration), *sententia* (maxim), and *enthymeme* (a syllogism with a premise elided because it is assumed to be inferable by the addressee). An Aristotelian example of sentwith is "No man who is sensible ought to have his children taught to be excessively clever." Contemporary rhetoricians (e.g., Brooks & Hubbard 1905, Dixon 1987) similarly enumerate a number of general techniques which can be used to convince or persuade a hearer (e.g., tell advantages, then disadvantages). In addition to discussing general argument forms (e.g., deduction and induction), rhetoricians also indicate presentational strategies such as give the argument which will attract attention first and the most persuasive one last. While these ideas are suggestive, they are not formalized precisely enough to form the basis for a computational theory.

This paper formalizes argument as a series of communicative acts that are intended to perform some communicative goal, such as convincing an addressee to change or modify a belief, or persuading them to perform some action. For example, when attempting to change someone's beliefs, humans provide evidence, give explanations, or disprove counter-arguments to convince an addressee to believe a particular proposition. Arguments may employ descriptive or expository techniques, for

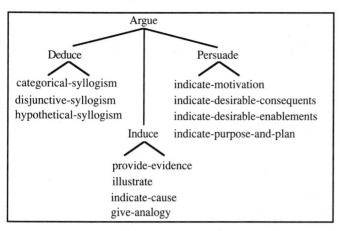

Figure 1. Communicative Acts for Argument

example to define terms (i.e., entities) or to explain propositions.

Just as humans reason about the most efficacious manner in which to achieve their goals, we have formalized and implemented a broad range of communicative acts to achieve communicative goals (Maybury 1991ab). A *communicative act* is a sequence of physical, linguistic or visual acts used to effect the knowledge, beliefs, or desires of an addressee. Linguistic acts include speech acts (Searle 1969) and surface speech acts (Appelt 1985). More abstract *rhetorical acts* coordinate linguistic and other acts. Examples include identifying an entity, describing it, dividing it (into subparts or subtypes), narrating events and situations, and arguing to support a conclusion.

Figure 1 classifies several different kinds of argumentative communicative acts. These actions can be distinguished by their purpose and semantics and are sometimes signalled by surface cues (e.g., "for example", "because"). *Deductive arguments* such as categorical syllogism, disjunctive syllogism and hypothetical syllogism are intended to affect the beliefs of the addressee. The classic example of categorical syllogism is "All men are mortal. Socrates is a man. Therefore, Socrates is mortal." In contrast to arguments which deduce propositions, *inductive arguments* also attempt to convince the hearer of some claim but by providing evidence and examples, or, in the broadest sense of the term, by showing cause and using analogy.

In contrast to these argumentative actions which attempt to affect the beliefs of the addressee, *persuasive argument* has the intention of affecting the goals or plans of the addressee. For example, inducing action in the addressee can be accomplished by indicating (Figure 1):

• the motivation for an act, or its purpose or goal
• the desirable consequents of performing an act
• the undesirable consequents caused by not performing an act
• how the act fits into some more general plan
• how the act enables some important/desirable act or state

Finally, there are many equally effective but perhaps less ethical methods of encouraging action such as threat, coercion, or appeal to authority. In the context of simulating human behavior, several implementations have investigated some of these kinds of persuasive techniques.

For example, characters in Meehan's (1976) TALE-SPIN simulation could persuade one another to perform acts, for example, using threats. Sycara's (1989) PERSUADER program simulated labor negotiations in which three agents (company, union, and mediator) could select from nine persuasive techniques (e.g., appeal to "status quo", appeal to "authority", threat) to effect other agent's plans and goals. While these coercive techniques may be useful in simulations of human behavior, their use by an advisory system is probably not appropriate except in special cases (e.g., persuading someone to take their prescribed medicine). The next section details a plan-based approach to influencing beliefs and encouraging action in human users.

Communicative Plans to Influence Beliefs

We represent communicative actions for argumentation as operators or schemata in a plan library of a hierarchical planner (Sacerdoti 1977). Each plan operator defines the *constraints* and *preconditions* that must hold before a communicative act applies, its intended *effects* (also known as postconditions), and the refinement or *decomposition* of the act into subacts. The decomposition may have optional components. Preconditions and constraints encode conditions regarding the underlying knowledge base (e.g., is there evidence to support a given proposition), the current status of a user model (e.g., does the addressee believe some proposition), and the current status of the discourse (e.g., has a particular piece of evidence already been introduced). Constraints, unlike preconditions, cannot be achieved or planned for if they are false.

For example, the uninstantiated *argue-for-a-proposition* plan operator shown in Figure 2 is one of several methods of performing the communicative action *argue*. Plan operators are encoded in an extension of first order predicate calculus with variables italicized (e.g., *S*, *H*, and *proposition*). As defined in the HEADER of the plan operator, the *argue* action takes three arguments, the speaker (*S*), the hearer (*H*), and a *proposition*. Thus, provided the third argument is indeed a proposition (CONSTRAINTS) and the speaker understands it and wants the hearer to believe it (PRECONDITIONS), the speaker (*S*) will first claim the proposition, optionally explain it to the hearer (*H*) if they don't already understand it (as indicated by the user model, examined by the constraints on the explain act), and finally attempt to convince them of its validity (DECOMPOSITION). The intended effect of this action is that the hearer will believe it (EFFECTS).

NAME	argue-for-a-proposition
HEADER	Argue(*S*, *H*, *proposition*)
CONSTRAINTS	Proposition?(*proposition*)
PRECONDITIONS	KNOW-ABOUT(*S*, *proposition*) ∧
	WANT(*S*, BELIEVE(*H*, *proposition*))
EFFECTS	BELIEVE(*H*, *proposition*)
DECOMPOSITION	Claim(*S*, *H*, *proposition*)
	optional(Explain(*S*, *H*, *proposition*))
	Convince(*S*, *H*, *proposition*)

Figure 2. Uninstantiated Argument Plan Operator

Intensional operators, such as WANT, KNOW, and BELIEVE appear in capitals. KNOW details an agent's specific knowledge of the truth-values of propositions (e.g., KNOW(H, Red(ROBIN-1)) or KNOW(H, ¬Yellow(ROBIN-1))) where truth or falsity is defined by the propositions in the knowledge base. That is, KNOW(H, P) implies P ∧ BELIEVE(H, P). Agents can hold an invalid belief (e.g., BELIEVE(JANE, Yellow(ROBIN-1))). An agent can KNOW-ABOUT an object or event (e.g., KNOW-ABOUT(H, DOG-1) or KNOW-ABOUT(H, MURDER-445)) if they KNOW its characteristics, components, subtypes, or purpose (loosely, if they are "familiar" with it). KNOW-HOW indicates an agent's ability to perform an action.

A number of techniques can be used to explain a proposition. For example, one method is to simply define the predicate and terms of the proposition. For example if the claim is the proposition *Dictator(Hitler)*, then this can be explained by defining dictator and then defining Hitler. As expository techniques are beyond the scope of this paper, see Maybury (1991a) for details.

Even if the hearer understands the proposition, however, they may not believe it is true. To achieve this, the speaker must convince them of it. As indicated above, two types of reasoning can convince a hearer to believe a proposition: deduction and induction. The former moves top-down, from general truisms to specific conclusions whereas the latter builds arguments bottom-up, from specific evidence to a general conclusion. A simple deductive technique is to provide evidence for the proposition. Figure 3 illustrates a slightly more sophisticated deductive technique implemented to support a medical diagnostic application. This first explains how a particular situation could be the case (by detailing the preconditions, motivations, and causes of the proposition) and then informs the hearer of any evidence supporting the proposition (optionally convincing them of this). Evidence is ordered according to importance, a metric based on domain specific knowledge of the relevance and confidence of evidence.

In contrast to deductive techniques, inductive approaches can also be effective methods of convincing an addressee to believe a proposition. These include the use of illustration, comparison/contrast and analogy. For example, you can support a claim that American academics are devalued by comparing American and Japanese education to highlight America's low valuation of the teaching profession. In contrast to this comparison, analogy entails comparing the proposition, P (which we are trying to convince the hearer to believe) with a well-known proposition, Q, which has several properties in common with P. By showing that P and Q share properties α and β, we can claim by analogy that if Q has property χ, then so does P. Maybury (1991c) details similarity algorithms that are used to support this.

Preference Metrics for Argument Choice

Because there may be many methods of achieving a given goal, those operators that satisfy the constraints and essential preconditions are prioritized using *preference metrics*. For example, operators that utilize both text and graphics are preferred over simply textual operators

NAME	convince-by-cause-and-evidence
HEADER	Convince(*S, H, proposition*)
CONSTRAINTS	Proposition?(*proposition*) ∧
	∃*x* | Cause(*x, proposition*) ∧
	∃*x* | Evidence(*proposition, x*)
PRECONDITIONS	∃*x* ∈ *evidence*
	¬ KNOW-ABOUT(*H*,Evidence(*proposition,x*))
EFFECTS	∀*x* ∈ *evidence*
	KNOW-ABOUT(*H*, Evidence(*proposition, x*))
DECOMPOSITION	Explain-How(*S, H, proposition*)
	∀*x* ∈ *evidence*
	Inform(*S, H,* Evidence(*proposition, x*))
	optional(Convince(*S, H, x*))
WHERE	*evidence* =
	order-by-importance(
	∀*x* | Evidence(*proposition, x*) ∧
	BELIEVE(*S,* Evidence(*proposition, x*)))

Figure 3. Uninstantiated Convince Plan Operator

(Maybury 1991b). Also, those operators with fewer subgoals are preferred (where this does not conflict with the previous preference). The preference metric prefers plan operators with fewer subplans (cognitive economy), with fewer new variables (limiting the introduction of new entities in the focus space of the discourse), those that satisfy all preconditions (to avoid backward chaining for efficiency), and those plan operators that are more common or preferred in naturally-occurring explanations (e.g., rhetoricians prefer deductive arguments over inductive ones). While the first three preferences are explicitly inferred, the last preference is implemented by the sequence in which operators appear in the plan library.

Working from this prioritized list of operators, the planner ensures preconditions are satisfied and tries to execute the decomposition of each until one succeeds. This involves processing any special operators (e.g., optionality is allowed in the decomposition) or quantifiers (∀ or ∃) as well as distinguishing between subgoals and primitive acts. For example, if the planner chooses the plan operator in Figure 2 from those that satisfy its constraints, it first ensures its preconditions hold (i.e., the user knows about or "understands" the proposition), which may require backward chaining.

Communicative Plans to Evoke Action

While different forms of argument such as deduction and induction can be belief or action-oriented, the previous sections have defined deductive and inductive forms narrowly as primarily affecting hearer beliefs; this section will similarly define persuasive techniques in the narrow sense as primarily affecting hearer actions. (Of course in the act of convincing someone to believe a proposition using deductive or inductive techniques you can also persuade them to act. Similarly, in the course of persuading someone to act you can change their beliefs.) The following invitation exemplifies arguments that encourage action:

Come to my party tonight. It's at 1904 Park Street. We are serving your favorite munchies and we have plenty of wine and beer. Everybody is going to be there. You'll have a great time.

This text tells the reader what to do, enables them to do it, and indicates why they should do it. This common communicative strategy occurs frequently in ordinary texts intended to get people to do things. It consists of *requesting* them to do the act (if necessary), *enabling* them to do it (if they lack the know-how), and finally *persuading* them that it is a useful activity that will produce some desirable benefit (if they are not inclined to do it). In the above example, the action coming to the party, is enabled by providing the address. The action is motivated by the desirable attributes of the party (i.e., tasty munchies and abundant supply of liquor), the innate human desire to belong, and by the desired consequence of coming to it (i.e., having fun).

This general strategy corresponds to the *request-enable-persuade* plan operator shown in Figure 4. The operator gets the hearer to do some action by requesting, enabling, and then persuading them to do it. *Enable*, the second communicative act in its decomposition, refers to communicative actions which provide the addressee with enough know-how to perform the action (see Maybury 1991a for details). The plan operator in Figure 4 distinguishes among (1) the hearer's knowledge of how to perform the action (i.e., KNOW-HOW, knowledge of the subactions of the action) (2) the hearer's ability to do it (ABLE), and (3) the hearer's desire to do it (WANT). For example, the hearer may want and know how to get to a party, but they are not able to come because they are sick. If the speaker knows this, then they should not use the plan operator below because its constraints fail. The assumption is that a general user modelling/acquisition component will be able to provide this class of information.

NAME	request-enable-persuade
HEADER	Argue(S, H, Do($H, action$))
CONSTRAINTS	Action?($action$) $\land$ ABLE($H, action$)
PRECONDITIONS	WANT(S, Do($H, action$))
EFFECTS	KNOW(H, WANT(S, Do($H, action$))) $\land$
	KNOW-HOW($H, action$) $\land$
	WANT(H, Do($H, action$)) $\land$
	Do($H, action$)
DECOMPOSITION	Request(S, H, Do($H, action$))
	Enable(S, H, Do($H, action$))
	Persuade(S, H, Do($H, action$))

Figure 4. request-enable-persuade Plan Operator

The order and constituents of a communication that gets an individual to act, such as that in Figure 4, can be very different indeed depending upon the conversants involved, their knowledge, beliefs, capabilities, desires, and so on. Thus to successfully get a hearer to do things, a speaker needs to reason about his or her model of the hearer in order to produce an effective text. For example, in an autocratic organization, a request (perhaps in the linguistic form of a command) is sufficient. In other contexts no request need be made because the hearer(s) may share the desired goal, as in the case of the mobilization of the Red Cross for earthquake or other catastrophic assistance. Similarly, if the hearer wants to do some action, is able to do it, and knows how to do it, then the speaker can simply ask them to do it. Because the hearer is able to do it, the speaker need not enable them. And because the hearer wants or desires the outcome of the action, the speaker need not persuade them to do it. Thus we also represent a simple *request* plan operator which argues that the hearer perform an action by simply asking them to do it. A variation on this plan operator could model delegation, whereby the speaker may know the hearer is not willing to do or does know how to perform some task, but the speaker simply asks them because it is expected that they figure out how to do it. As with the autocratic example above, this would require a model of the interpersonal relations of the speaker and hearer (Hovy 1987).

In addition to a request for action, enablement may be necessary if the audience does not know how to perform the task. The following text from the NYS Department of Motor Vehicles *Driver's Manual* (p. 9) informs the reader of the prerequisites for obtaining a license:

To obtain your driver's license you must know the rules of the road and how to drive a car or other vehicle in traffic.

The writer indicates that being knowledgeable of both road regulations and vehicle operation are necessary preconditions for obtaining a license. In some situations, however, the reader may be physically or mentally unable to perform some action, in which case the writer should seek alternative solutions, eventually perhaps consoling the reader if all else fails. On the other hand, if the user is able but not willing to perform the intended action, then a writer must convince them to do it, perhaps by outlining the benefit(s) of the action. Consider this excerpt from the *Driver's Manual*:

The ability to drive a car, truck or motorcycle widens your horizons. It helps you do your job, visit friends and relatives and enjoy your leisure time.

Of course it could be that the hearer already wants to do something but does not know how to do it. In this situation a communicator must explain how to perform the action (see, for example, Moore & Paris (1989) and Maybury (1991a)). However, in some cases the addressee must be persuaded to act and so the next section formalizes several techniques to do so and illustrates their use in an advisory context.

First, however, we briefly compare the *request-enable-persuade* strategy in Figure 4 to Moore & Paris' (1989) "recommend-enable-motivate" strategy. Their plan-based system has three "motivation" strategies: motivating (by telling the purpose and/or means of an action), showing how an action is a step (i.e., subgoal) of some higher-level goal (elaborate-refinement-path), and giving evidence. Some of these techniques are domain specific (e.g., a "motivate-replace-act", where "replace" is specific to the Program Enhancement Advisor domain), and others are architecture/knowledge representation specific (e.g., "elaborate-refinement-path" is a technique based on the Explainable Expert System's architecture (Neches et al. 1985)). In contrast, the strategies presented here are domain and application independent and include persuasion by showing motivation, enablement, cause, and purpose. Furthermore, they distinguish rhetorical acts (e.g., enable, persuade) from illocutionary acts (e.g., request) from surface speech acts (e.g., command, recommend) from the semantic relations underlying these (e.g., enablement, cause). Finally, this paper formalizes communicative acts for both convincing and persuading (i.e., convincing a hearer to believe a proposition versus persuading them to perform an action) and it is the latter which we now detail.

Persuasive Communicative Acts

When an addressee does not want to perform some action, a speaker must often persuade them to act. There are a variety of ways to persuade the hearer including indicating (1) the motivation for the action, (2) how the action can enable some event, (3) how it can cause a desirable outcome, or (4) how the action is a part of some overall purpose or higher level goal.

For example, the plan operator named *persuade-by-desirable-consequents* in Figure 5 gets the hearer to want to do something by telling them all the desirable events or states that the action will cause. An action can either cause a positive result (e.g., approval, commendation, praise) or avoid a negative one (avoid blame, disaster, or loss of self esteem). Advertisement often uses this technique to induce customers to purchase products by appealing to the emotional benefits (actual or anticipated) of possession. An extension of this plan operator could warn the hearer of all the undesirable events or states that would result from their inaction.

NAME	persuade-by-desirable-consequents
HEADER	Persuade(S, H, Do(H, *action*))
CONSTRAINTS	Act(*action*) $\land \exists x$ | Cause(*action*, x)
PRECONDITIONS	$\neg$ WANT(H, Do(H, *action*))
EFFECTS	WANT(H, Do(H, *action*)) $\land$
	$\forall x \in$ *desirable-events-or-states*
	KNOW(H, Cause(*action*, x))
DECOMPOSITION	$\forall x \in$ *desirable-events-or-states*
	Inform(S, H, Cause(*action*, x))
WHERE	*desirable-events-or-states* =
	$\{x$ | Cause(*action*, x) $\land$ WANT(H, x) $\}$

Figure 5. persuade-by-desirable-consequents Plan Operator

Some actions may not cause a desirable state or event but may enable some other desirable action (that the hearer or someone else may want to perform). For example, in the NYS driving example, obtaining a license is a precondition of driving a car, which enables you to visit friends, go shopping, etc. This plan could also be extended to warn the hearer of all the undesirable events or states that would be enabled by their inaction.

NAME	persuade-by-purpose-and-plan
HEADER	Persuade(S, H, Do(H, *action*))
CONSTRAINTS	Act(*action*)
PRECONDITIONS	$\neg$ WANT(H, Do(H, *action*))
EFFECTS	WANT(H, Do(H, *action*)) $\land$
	KNOW(H, Purpose(*action*, *goal*))
DECOMPOSITION	Inform(S, H, Purpose(*action*, *goal*))
	Inform(S, H, Constituent(*plan*, *action*))
WHERE	*goal* = g | Purpose(*action*, g) $\land$ WANT(H, g)
	plan = p | Constituent(p, *action*) $\land$
	WANT(H, Do(p))

Figure 6. persuade-by-purpose-and-plan Plan Operator

One final form of persuasion, *persuade-by-purpose-and-plan*, shown in Figure 6, gets the hearer to perform some action by indicating its purpose or goal(s) and how it is part of some more general plan(s) that the hearer wants to achieve. For example, one subgoal of shopping is writing a check, an action which has the effect or purpose of increasing your liquid assets. These operators give a range of persuasive possibilities. The next section illustrates their application in the context of a cooperative problem solver.

Persuasion in Collaborative Planning

The persuasive plan operators described above (i.e., indicating motivation, enablement, cause, or purpose) were tested using the cooperative Knowledge based Replanning System, KRS (Dawson et al. 1987), a resource allocation and scheduling system. KRS is implemented in a hybrid of rules and hierarchical frames. KRS employs meta-planning (Wilensky 1983) whereby high-level problem solving strategies govern lower-level planning activities. Therefore, it can justify its actions by referring to the higher level strategy it is employing.

Figure 7 illustrates these strategies (e.g., plan an air tasking order, replan an air tasking order, replan an attack mission, and so on) which govern lower-level planning activities (e.g., prescan a package of missions, plan a package of missions, plan an individual mission, and so on). Associated with each meta-plan shown in Figure 7 are several types of information including its name, type, purpose, subgoals, relations among subgoals (e.g., enablement, sequence, etc.), planning history, associated entities (e.g., the name of the mission being replanned), and failure handlers. Therefore when the actions encoded by the plans are executed, the meta-planner knows why particular actions occur when they do. For example, if the user is not persuaded that scanning a plan is a useful activity and they may ask "Why is scanning the plan necessary?" (simulated by posting the action *PERSUADE (#<SYSTEM>, #<USER>, Do(#<SYSTEM>,#<PRESCAN-ATO>)))*. To achieve this action, our explanation planner uses the *persuade-by-purpose-and-plan* operator of Figure 6. This examines the meta-plan structure and produces the response shown in Figure 8 (the surface speech acts, *assert*, which realize the inform acts, are elided). Maybury (1991d) details the linguistic realizer.

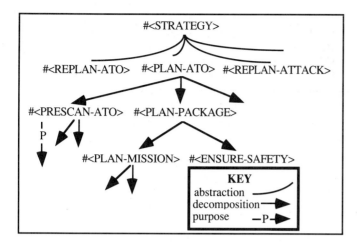

Figure 7. Structure of Plans and Meta-Plans in KRS

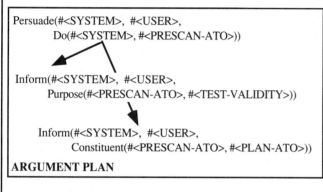

SURFACE FORM:
```
The purpose of prescanning the Air Tasking Order
is to test the validity of the Air Tasking Order.
Prescanning the Air Tasking Order is part of
planning an Air Tasking Order.
```

Figure 8. Argument in support of a Domain Action

Just as showing how an action supports some more general plan or goal can support that action, another way to persuade an addressee to perform (or support) an action is to indicate the cause and/or motivation for the action. Because KRS is a mixed-initiative planner, it cooperates with the user to produce an Air Tasking Order, a package of air missions (e.g., reconnaissance, refueling, escort) that achieve some desired goal (e.g., defend friendly territory). Because of this multi-agent problem solving, the system and user can make choices which result in an ill-formed mission plan. If directed by the user, KRS can replan such an ill-formed mission plan using dependency-directed backtracking (e.g., making changes in the plan by reasoning about temporal and spatial relationships). KRS initially attempts to retract system-supplied choices. As a last resort, KRS suggests to the user that they remove user-supplied choices to recover from the ill-formed plan. In this case the system tries to justify its recommendation on the basis of some underlying rule governing legal plans.

For example, assume the user has interacted with the system to produce the mission shown in Figure 9 (simplified for readability). The frame, OCA1002, is an offensive counter air mission, an instance of (AIO) the class offensive counter air (OCA), with attributes such as a type and number of aircraft, a home airbase, and a target. Each attribute encodes actual and possible values as well as STATUS slot which indicates who supplied the value (e.g., user, planner, meta-planner). Frames also record interactional information, for example in Figure 9 the HISTORY slot records that the user just selected a target and the WINDOW slot indicates where the mission plan is visually displayed. KRS represents domain-dependent relations among slots so that values for some of the slots can be automatically calculated by daemons in reaction to user input (e.g., when the UNIT and ACNUMBER slot of a mission are filled in, the CALL-SIGN slot can be automatically generated).

During planning the system monitors and detects ill-formed mission plans by running rule-based diagnostic tests on the mission plan. For example, in Figure 9 the offensive counter air mission has an incompatible aircraft and target. KRS signals the constraint violation by highlighting the conflicting slots (e.g., AIRCRAFT and TARGET) of the mission frame which is represented visually in a mission window to the user. The built-in explanation component would then simply state the rule-based constraint which detected the error in the mission plan, and then list some of the supporting knowledge (see Figure 10). The first two sentences of the explanation in Figure 10 are produced using simple templates (canned text plus variables for the mission (OCA1002), rule name (TARGET-AIRCRAFT-1), and conflicting slots (TARGET and AIRCRAFT)). The list 1-4 is simply a sequence of information supporting the constraint violation although

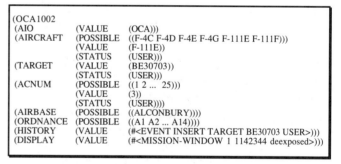

Figure 9. Simplified Mission Plan in FRL

The choice for AIRCRAFT is in question because:

BY TARGET-AIRCRAFT-1: THERE IS A SEVERE CONFLICT BETWEEN TARGET AND AIRCRAFT FOR OCA1002

    1. THE TARGET OF OCA1002 IS BE30703
    2. BE30703 RADIATES
    3. THE AIRCRAFT OF OCA1002 IS F-111E
    4. F-111E IS NOT A F-4G

Figure 10. Current Explanation of Rule Violation

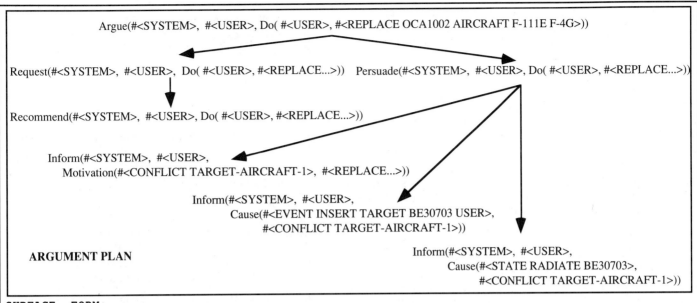

Argue(#<SYSTEM>, #<USER>, Do(#<USER>, #<REPLACE OCA1002 AIRCRAFT F-111E F-4G>))

Request(#<SYSTEM>, #<USER>, Do(#<USER>, #<REPLACE...>))   Persuade(#<SYSTEM>, #<USER>, Do(#<USER>, #<REPLACE...>))

Recommend(#<SYSTEM>, #<USER>, Do(#<USER>, #<REPLACE...>))

Inform(#<SYSTEM>, #<USER>,
   Motivation(#<CONFLICT TARGET-AIRCRAFT-1>, #<REPLACE...>))

Inform(#<SYSTEM>, #<USER>,
   Cause(#<EVENT INSERT TARGET BE30703 USER>,
   #<CONFLICT TARGET-AIRCRAFT-1>))

ARGUMENT PLAN

Inform(#<SYSTEM>, #<USER>,
   Cause(#<STATE RADIATE BE30703>,
   #<CONFLICT TARGET-AIRCRAFT-1>))

SURFACE FORM:

```
You should replace F-111e aircraft with F-4g aircraft in Offensive Counter Air Mission 1002.  A conflict
between the aircraft and the target in Offensive Counter Air Mission 1002 motivates replacing F-111E
aircraft with F-4g aircraft.  You inserted BE30703 in the target slot and BE30703 was radiating which
caused a conflict between the aircraft and the target in Offensive Counter Air Mission 1002.
```

Figure 11. Argument to Encourage User to Act -- Initiated by Rule Violation

there is no indication as to how these relate to each other or to the rule. The fact that BE30703 (Battle Element 30703) is radiating indicates that it is an operational radar. KRS expects domain users (i.e., Air Force mission planners) to know that only anti-radar F-4g ("Wild Weasel") aircraft fly against these targets. Rather than achieving organization from some model of naturally occurring discourse, the presentation in Figure 10 is isomorphic to the underlying inference chain. Because the relationships among entities are implicit, this text lacks cohesion. More important, it is not clear what the system wants the user to do and why they should do it.

In contrast, our text planner was interfaced to KRS by relating rhetorical predicates (e.g., cause, motivation, attribution) to the underlying semantic relations of the domain embodied both in rules justifying constraint violations and in frames representing the mission plan and other domain entities (e.g., aircraft and target frames). Unlike the template and code translation approach used to produce the text in Figure 10, now KRS posts the action *ARGUE(#<SYSTEM>, #<USER>, Do(#<USER>, #<REPLACE OCA1002 AIRCRAFT F-111E F-4G>))* to the text planner. The text planner then instantiates, selects and decomposes plan operators similar to the one in Figure 5 to generate the argument plan and corresponding surface form shown in Figure 11. The output is improved not only by composing the text using communicative acts, but also by linguistic devices, such as the lexical realization "Offensive Counter Air Mission 1002" instead of OCA1002 as well as verb choice, tense and aspect (e.g., "should replace", "inserted"). For example, the recommended

surface speech act is realized using the obligation modal, "should". As above, assertions, the surface speech acts for inform actions, are elided from the argument plan. Finally, note how the surface realizer joins the final two informs into one utterance because they have similar propositional content (i.e., causation of the same conflict).

Conclusion and Future Directions

Argument, perhaps the most important form of communication, enables us to change other's beliefs and influence their actions. This paper characterizes argument as a purposeful communicative activity and formalizes argumentative actions (e.g., deduce, induce, persuade) as plans, indicating their preconditions, constraints, effects, and decomposition into more primitive actions. We illustrate how these plans have been used to improve a communicative interface to a cooperative problem solver.

As the focus of the paper is on the presentation of arguments (i.e., their form), we make no claims regarding their representation, including associated inference or reasoning strategies. Furthermore, no claims are made concerning the representation of intentions and beliefs. Indeed, an important issue that remains to be investigated is how content and context modifies the effect of different communicative plans (e.g., deduction can both change beliefs and move to action depending upon context). This seems analogous to the alteration of the force of illocutionary speech acts by variation in syntactic form or intonation.

Another unresolved issue concerns the multi-functional nature of communicative acts and their interaction. This is more complicated than representing multiple effects of actions, as do our plans. For example, the advertisement below compels the reader to action using a variety of techniques including description, comparison, and persuasion.

> Buy Pontiac. We build excitement. The new Pontiacs have power brakes, power steering, AM/FM stereos, and anti-lock brakes. And if you buy now, you will save $500. An independent study shows that Pontiacs are better than Chevrolet. See your Pontiac dealer today!

In this example, the initial request for action (i.e., purchase) is supported by indicating the desirable attributes of the product, the desirable consequences of the purchase, comparing the action with alternative courses of action/competing products, and finally imploring the hearer to act again. While some of these techniques may be implemented as plan operators in a straightforward manner (e.g., describe desirable attributes), the interaction of various text types remains a complex issue. For example, how is it that some texts can persuade by description, narration or exposition, and entertain by persuasion? What also remains to be investigated is the relationship of linguistic and visual acts to influence beliefs or actions, as in advertisement.

Acknowledgements

I want to thank Karen Sparck Jones and John Levine for detailed discussions on explanation and communication as action.

References

Aristotle. 1926. *The 'Art' of Rhetoric.* trans. J. H. Freese, Cambridge, MA: Loeb Classical Library series.

Appelt, D. 1985. *Planning English Sentences.* England: Cambridge University Press.

Birnbaum, L. 1982. Argument Molecules: A Functional Representation of Argument Structure. In *Proceedings of the Third National Conference on Artificial Intelligence*, 63-65. Pittsburg, PA: AAAI.

Brooks, S. D. and Hubbard, M. 1905. *Composition Rhetoric.* New York: American Book Company.

Bruce, B. C. 1975. Generation as a Social Action. In *Proceedings of Theoretical Issues on Natural Language Processing-1*, 64-67. Urbana-Champaign: ACL.

Cohen, P. R. 1978. On Knowing What to Say: Planning Speech Acts. University of Toronto TR-118.

Cohen, R. 1987. Analyzing the Structure of Argumentative Discourse. *Computational Linguistics* 13(1-2):11-23.

Dawson, B.; Brown, R.; Kalish, C.; & Goldkind, S. 1987. Knowledge-based Replanning System. RADC TR-87-60.

Dixon, P. 1987. *Rhetoric.* London: Methuen.

Hovy, E. 1987. Generating Natural Language Under Pragmatic Constraints. Ph.D. diss., Dept. of Computer Science, Yale University TR-521.

Hovy, E. 1988. Planning Coherent Multisentential Text. In *Proceedings of the 26th Annual Meeting of the ACL*, 163-169. Buffalo, NY: ACL.

Maybury, M. T. 1991a. Generating Multisentential English Text Using Communicative Acts. Ph.D. diss., Computer Laboratory, Cambridge University, England, TR-239. Also available as RADC TR 90-411.

Maybury, M. T. 1991b. Planning Multimedia Explanations Using Communicative Acts. In *Proceedings of the Ninth National Conference on Artificial Intelligence*, 61-66. Anaheim, CA: AAAI.

Maybury, M. T. 1991c. Generating Natural Language Definitions from Classification Hierarchies. In *Advances in Classification Research and Application: Proceedings of the 1st ASIS Classification Research Workshop*, ed. S. Humphrey. ASIS Monographs Series. Medford, NJ: Learned Information.

Maybury, M. T. 1991d. Topical, Temporal, and Spatial Constraints on Linguistic Realization. *Computational Intelligence* 7(4):266-275.

McKeown, K. 1985. *Text Generation.* Cambridge University Press.

Moore, J. D. and C. L. Paris. 1989. Planning Text for Advisory Dialogues. In *Proceedings of Twenty-Seventh Annual Meeting of the ACL*, 203-211, Vancouver.

Neches, R.; Moore, J.; & Swartout, W. November 1985. Enhanced Maintenance and Explanation of Expert Systems Through Explicit Models of Their Development. *IEEE Transactions on Software Engineering* SE-11(11):1337-1351.

Paris, C. 1987. The Use of Explicit User Models in Text Generation: Tailoring to a User's Level of Expertise. Ph.D. diss., Dept. of Computer Science, Columbia University.

Reichman, R. 1985. *Getting Computers to Talk Like You and Me.* Cambridge, MA: MIT Press.

Sacerdoti, E. D. 1977. *A Structure for Plans and Behavior.* New York: Elsevier North-Holland. (Originally SRI TN-109, 1975.)

Searle, J. R. 1969. *Speech Acts.* Cambridge University Press.

Toulmin S.; Rieke, R.; & Janik, A. 1979. *An Introduction to Reasoning.* New York: Macmillan.

Wilensky, R. 1983. *Planning and Understanding.* Reading, MA: Addison-Wesley.

Meehan, J. R. 1977. TALE-SPIN, an Interactive Program that Writes Stories. In *Proceedings of Fifth International Joint Conference on Artificial Intelligence*, 91-98.

Sycara, K. 1989. Argumentation: Planning Other Agents' Plans. In *Proceedings of the Eleventh International Joint Conference on Artificial Intelligence*, 517-523.

Corpus Analysis for Revision-Based Generation of Complex Sentences

Jacques Robin and Kathleen McKeown
Department of Computer Science
Columbia University
New York, NY 10027
{robin,kathy}@cs.columbia.edu

Abstract

The complex sentences of newswire reports contain *floating* content units that appear to be opportunistically placed where the form of the surrounding text allows. We present a corpus analysis that identified precise semantic and syntactic constraints on where and how such information is realized. The result is a set of revision tools that form the rule base for a report generation system, allowing incremental generation of complex sentences.

Introduction

Generating reports that summarize quantitative data raises several challenges for language generation systems. First, sentences in such reports are very complex (*e.g.*, in newswire basketball game summaries the lead sentence ranges from 21 to 46 words in length). Second, while some content units consistently appear in *fixed* locations across reports (*e.g.*, game results are always conveyed in the lead sentence), others *float*, appearing anywhere in a report and at different linguistic ranks within a given sentence. Floating content units appear to be opportunistically placed where the form of the surrounding text allows. For example, in Fig. 1, sentences 2 and 3 result from adding the same streak information (*i.e.*, data about a series of similar outcomes) to sentence 1 using different syntactic categories at distinct structural levels.

Although optional in any given sentence, floating content units cannot be ignored. In our domain, they account for over 40% of lead sentence content, with some content types *only* conveyed as floating structures. One such type is historical information (*e.g.*, maximums, minimums, or trends over periods of time). Its presence in all reports and a majority of lead sentences is not surprising, since the relevance of any game fact is often largely determined by its historical significance. However, report generators to date [Kukich, 1983], [Bourbeau *et al.*, 1990] are not capable of including this type of information due to its floating nature. The issue of optional, floating content is prevalent in

---

1. *Draft sentence:*
   "San Antonio, TX – David Robinson scored 32 points Friday night lifting the San Antonio Spurs to a 127 111 victory over the Denver Nuggets."
2. *Clause coordination with reference adjustment:*
   "San Antonio, TX – David Robinson scored 32 points Friday night LIFTING THE SAN ANTONIO SPURS TO A 127 111 VICTORY OVER DENVER **and handing the Nuggets their seventh straight loss**".
3. *Embedded nominal apposition:*
   "San Antonio, TX – David Robinson scored 32 points Friday night lifting the San Antonio Spurs to a 127 111 victory over THE DENVER NUGGETS, **losers of seven in a row**".

Figure 1: Attaching a **floating content unit** onto different draft sentence SUBCONSTITUENTS

---

many domains and is receiving growing attention (cf. [Rubinoff, 1990], [Elhadad and Robin, 1992], [Elhadad, 1993]).

These observations suggest a generator design where a draft incorporating fixed content units is produced first and then any floating content units that can be accommodated by the surrounding text are added. Experiments by [Pavard, 1985] provide evidence that only such a revision-based model of complex sentence generation can be cognitively plausible[1].

To determine how floating content units can be incorporated in a draft, we analyzed a corpus of basketball reports, pairing sentences that differ semantically by a single floating content unit and identifying the minimal syntactic transformation between them. The result is a set of *revision tools*, specifying precise semantic and syntactic constraints on (1) where a particular type of floating content can be added in a draft and (2) what linguistic constructs can be used for the addition.

The corpus analysis presented here serves as the basis for the development of the report generation sys-

---

[1]cf. [Robin, 1992] for discussion.

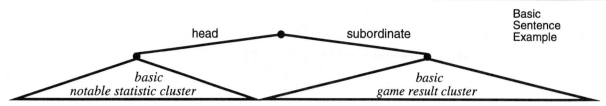

Patrick Ewing scored 41 points Tuesday night   to lead the New York Knicks to a 97–79 win over the Hornets

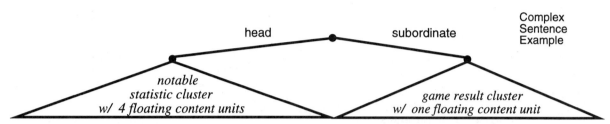

Karl Malone scored 28 points Saturday and John Stockton   leading the Utah Jazz to its fourth straight victory,
added a season–high 27 points and a league–high 23 assists   a 105–95 win over the Los Angeles Clippers

Figure 2: Similarity of basic and complex sentence structures

tem STREAK (Surface Text Revision Expressing Additional Knowledge). The analysis provides not only the knowledge sources for the system and motivations for its novel architecture (discussed in [Robin, 1993]), but also with means for ultimately evaluating its output. While this paper focuses on the analysis, the on-going system implementation based on functional unification is discussed in [Robin, 1992].

After describing our corpus analysis methodology, we present the resulting revision tools and how they can be used to incrementally generate complex sentences. We conclude by previewing our planned use of the corpus for evaluation and testing.

Corpus analysis methodology

We analyzed the lead sentences of over 800 basketball games summaries from the UPI newswire. We focused on the first sentence after observing that all reports followed the *inverted pyramid structure with summary lead* [Fensch, 1988] where the most crucial facts are packed in the lead sentence. The lead sentence is thus a self-contained mini-report. We first noted that all 800 lead sentences contained the game result (*e.g., "Utah beat Miami 105-95"*), its location, date and at least one final game statistic: the most notable statistic of a winning team player. We then semantically restricted our corpus to about 300 lead sentences which contained only these four fixed content units and zero or more floating content units of the most common types, namely:

- Other final game statistics (*e.g., "Stockton finished with 27 points"*).
- Streaks of similar results (*e.g., "Utah recorded its fourth straight win"*).
- Record performances (*e.g., "Stockton scored a season-high 27 points"*).

Complex Sentence Structure We noted that *basic* corpus sentences, containing only the four fixed content units, and *complex* corpus sentences, which in addition contain up to five floating content units, share a common top-level structure. This structure consists of two main constituents, one containing the notable statistic (the *notable statistic cluster*) and the other containing the game result (the *game result cluster*), which are related either paratactically or hypotactically with the notable statistic cluster as head. Hence, the only structural difference is that in the complex sentences additional floating content units are clustered around the notable statistic and/or the game result. For example, the complex sentence at the bottom of Fig. 2 has the same top-level structure as the basic sentence at the top, but four floating content units are clustered around its notable statistic and a fifth one with its game result. Furthermore, we found that when floating elements appear in the lead sentence, their semantics almost always determines in which of the two clusters they appear (*e.g.,* streaks are always in the game result cluster).

These corpus observations show that any complex sentence can indeed be generated in two steps: (1) produce a basic sentence realizing the fixed content units, (2) incrementally revise it to incorporate floating content units. Furthermore, they indicate that floating content units can be attached within a cluster, based on *local* constraints, thus simplifying both generation and our corpus analysis. When we shifted our attention from whole sentence structure to internal cluster structures, we split the whole sentence corpus into two subsets: one containing notable statistic clusters and the other, game result clusters.

Cluster structure To identify syntactic and lexical constraints on the attachment of floating content units within each cluster, we analyzed the syntactic form of each cluster in each corpus lead sentence to derive *realization patterns*. Realization patterns abstract from lexical and syntactic features (e.g., connectives, mood) to represent the different mappings from semantic structure to syntactic structure. Examples of realization patterns are given in Fig. 3. Each column corresponds to a syntactic constituent and each entry provides information about this constituent: (1) semantic content[2], (2) grammatical function, (3) structural status (*i.e.* head, argument, adjunct etc) and (4-5) syntactic category[3]. Below each pattern a corpus example is given.

Realization patterns represent the structure of entire clusters, whether basic or complex. To discover how complex clusters can be derived from basic ones through incremental revision, we carried out a differential analysis of the realization patterns based on the notions of *semantic decrement* and *surface decrement* illustrated in Fig. 4.

A cluster C_d is a semantic decrement of cluster C_i if C_d contains all but one of C_i's content unit types. Each cluster has a set of realization patterns. The surface decrement of a realization pattern of C_i is the realization pattern of C_d that is structurally closest. Figure 3 shows a semantic decrement pairing C_d, a single content unit, with C_i, which contains two content units. Both clusters have two realization patterns associated with them as they each can be realized by two different syntactic structures. These four syntactic structure patterns must be compared to find the surface decrements. Since R_{d1} is entirely included in R_{i1}[4] it is the surface decrement of R_{i1}. To identify the surface decrement of R_{i2}, we need to compare it to R_{d2} and R_{d1} in turn. All the content units common to R_{i2} and R_{d2} are realized by identical syntactic categories in both patterns. In particular, the semantic head (game-result) is mapped onto a noun (*"victory"* in R_{d2}, *"triumph"* in R_{i2}). In contrast, this same semantic head is mapped

onto a verb (*"to defeat"*) in R_{d1}. R_{d2}, rather than R_{d1} is thus the surface decrement of R_{i2}.

We identified 270 surface decrement pairs in the corpus. For each such pair, we then determined the structural transformations necessary to produce the more complex pattern from the simpler *base* pattern. We grouped these transformations into classes that we call *revision tools*.

Revisions for incremental generation

We distinguished two kinds of revision tools. *Simple* revisions consist of a single transformation which preserves the base pattern and adds in a new constituent. *Complex* revisions are in contrast non-monotonic; an *introductory* transformation breaks up the integrity of the base pattern in adding in new content. Subsequent *restructuring* transformations are then necessary to restore grammaticality. Simple revisions can be viewed as elaborations while complex revisions require true revision.

Simple revisions We identified four main types of simple revisions: Adjoin[5], Append, Conjoin and Absorb. Each is characterized by the type of base structure to which it applies and the type of revised structure it produces. For example, Adjoin applies only to hypotactic base patterns. It adds an adjunct A_c under the base pattern head B_h as shown in Fig. 5.

Adjoin is a versatile tool that can be used to insert additional constituents of various syntactic categories at various syntactic ranks. The surface decrement pair $< R_{d1}, R_{i1} >$ in Fig. 3 is an example of **clause rank PP adjoin**. In Fig. 6, the revision of sentence 5 into sentence 6 is an example of **nominal rank pre-modifier adjoin**: *"franchise record"* is adjoined to the nominal *"sixth straight home defeat"*.

In the same figure, the revision of sentence 2 into sentence 3 is an example of another versatile tool, Conjoin: an additional clause, *"Jay Humphries added 24"*, is coordinated with the draft clause *"Karl Malone tied a season high with 39 points"*. In general, Conjoin groups a new constituent A_c with a base constituent B_{c1} in a new paratactic[6] complex. The new complex is then inserted where B_{c1} alone was previously located (cf. Fig. 5). Note how in Fig. 1 paraphrases are obtained by applying Conjoin at different levels in the base sentence structure.

Instead of creating a new complex, Absorb relates the new constituent to the base constituent B_{c1} by demoting B_{c1} under the new constituent's head A_h which is inserted in the sentence structure in place of B_{c1} as

---

[2] An empty box corresponds to a syntactic constituent required by English grammar but not in itself conveying any semantic element of the domain representation.

[3] The particular functions and categories are based on: [Quirk *et al.*, 1985], [Halliday, 1985] and [Fawcett, 1987].

[4] Remember that we compare *patterns*, not sentences.

[5] Our Adjoin differs from the adjoin of Tree-Adjoining Grammars (TAGs). Although, TAGs could implement three of our revision tools, Adjoin, Conjoin and Append, it could *not* directly implement non-monotonic revisions.

[6] Either coordinated or appositive.

C_i: <game-result(winner,loser,score),**streak(winner,aspect,type,length)**>.
C_d: <game-result(winner,loser,score)>.

$R_{i1}(C_i)$:

winner	game-result	loser	score			length	streak+aspect	type
agent	process	affected	score	result				
arg	head	arg	adjunct	adjunct				
proper	verb	proper	number	PP				
				prep	[det	ordinal	adj	noun]
Chicago	beat	Phoenix	99-91	**for**	**its**	**third**	**straight**	**win**

$R_{d1}(C_d)$ surface decrement of $R_{i1}(C_i)$:

winner	game-result	loser	score
agent	process	affected	score
arg	head	arg	adjunct
proper	verb	proper	number
Seattle	defeated	Sacramento	121-93

$R_{i2}(C_i)$:

winner	aspect		type	streak	length			score	game-result	loser
agent	process	affected/located			location	means				
arg	head	arg			adjunct	adjunct				
proper	verb	NP			PP	PP				
		det	participle	noun		prep	[det	number	noun	PP]
Utah	**extended**	**its**	**winning**	**streak**	**to six games**	**with**	**a**	**118-94**	**triumph**	**over Denver**

$R_{d2}(C_d)$ surface decrement of $R_{i2}(C_i)$:

winner			score	game-result	loser
agent	process	range			
arg	head	arg			
proper	support-verb	NP			
		det	number	noun	PP
Chicago	**claimed**	**a**	**128-94**	**victory**	**over New Jersey**

Figure 3: Realization pattern examples

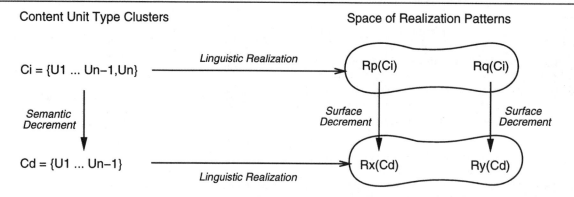

Figure 4: Differential analysis of realization patterns

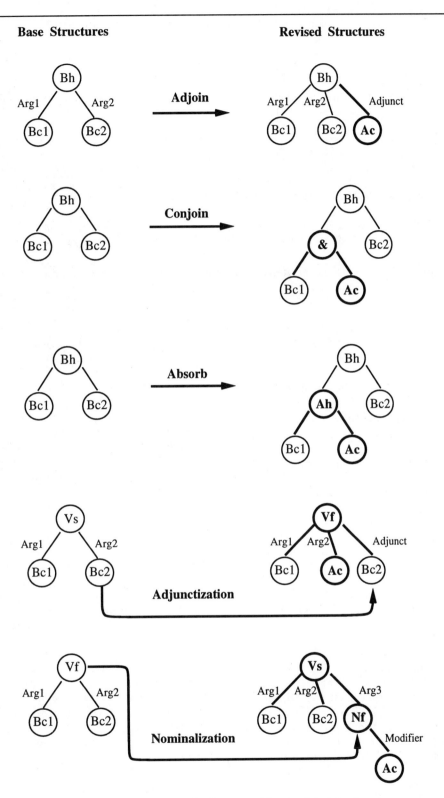

Figure 5: Structural schemas of five revision tools

1. **Initial draft (basic sentence pattern):**
   "Hartford, CT – Karl Malone <u>scored</u> 39 points Friday night as the Utah Jazz defeated the Boston Celtics 118 94."

2. **adjunctization:**
   "Hartford, CT – Karl Malone **tied a season high with** *39 points* Friday night as the Utah Jazz defeated the Boston Celtics 118 94."

3. **conjoin:**
   "Hartford, CT – Karl Malone tied a season high with 39 points **and Jay Humphries added 24** Friday night as the Utah Jazz defeated the Boston Celtics 118 94."

4. **absorb:**
   "Hartford, CT – Karl Malone tied a season high with 39 points and Jay Humphries **came off the bench** *to add 24* Friday night as the Utah Jazz defeated the Boston Celtics 118 94."

5. **nominalization:**
   "Hartford, CT – Karl Malone tied a season high with 39 points and Jay Humphries came off the bench to add 24 Friday night as the Utah Jazz **handed** the Boston Celtics **their sixth straight home** *defeat* 118 94."

6. **adjoin:**
   "Hartford, CT – Karl Malone tied a season high with 39 points and Jay Humphries came off the bench to add 24 Friday night as the Utah Jazz handed the Boston Celtics their **franchise record** sixth straight home defeat 118 94."

Figure 6: Incremental generation of a complex sentence using various revision tools

shown in Fig. 5. For example, in the revision of sentence 3 into sentence 4 Fig. 6, the base VP *"added 24"* gets subordinated under the new VP *"came off the bench"* taking its place in the sentence structure. See [Robin, 1992] for a presentation of **Append**.

Complex revisions We identified six main types of complex revisions: **Recast**, **Argument Demotion**, **Nominalization**, **Adjunctization**, **Constituent promotion** and **Coordination Promotion**. Each is characterized by different changes to the base which displace constituents, alter the argument structure or change the lexical head. Complex revisions tend to be more specialized tools than simple revisions. For example, **Adjunctization** applies only to clausal base patterns headed by a support verb V_s. A support verb [Gross, 1984] does not carry meaning by itself, but primarily serves to support one of its meaning bearing arguments. **Adjunctization** introduces new content by replacing the support verb by a full verb V_f with a new argument A_c. Deprived of its verbal support, the original support verb argument B_{c2} migrates into adjunct position, as shown in Fig. 5.

The surface decrement pair $< R_{d2}, R_{i2} >$ of Fig. 3 is an example of **Adjunctization**: the RANGE argument of R_{d2} migrates to become a MEANS adjunct in R_{i2}, when the head verb is replaced. The revision of sentence 1 into sentence 2 in Fig. 6 is a specific **Adjunctization** example: *"to score"* is replaced by *"to tie"*, forcing the NP *"39 points"* (initially argument of *"to score"*) to migrate as a PP adjunct *"with 39 points"*.

In the same figure, the revision of sentence 4 into sentence 5 is an example of another complex revision tool, **Nominalization**. As opposed to **Adjunctization**, **Nominalization** replaces a full verb V_f by a synony-

mous <support-verb,noun> collocation $< V_s, N_f >$ where N_f is a nominalization of V_f. A new constituent A_c can then be attached to N_f as a pre-modifier as shown in Fig. 5. For example, in revising sentence 4 into sentence 5 (Fig. 6), the full-verb pattern *"X defeated Y"* is first replaced by the collocation pattern *"X handed Y a defeat"*. Once nominalized, *defeat* can then be pre-modified by the constituents *"their"*, *"sixth straight"* and *"home"* providing historical background. See [Robin, 1992] for presentation of the four remaining types of complex revisions.

Side transformations Restructuring transformations are not the only type of transformations following the introduction of new content in a revision. Both simple and complex revisions are also sometimes accompanied by *side* transformations. Orthogonal to restructuring transformations which affect grammaticality, side transformations make the revised pattern more concise, less ambiguous, or better in use of collocations.

We identified six types of side transformations in the corpus: **Reference Adjustment**, **Ellipsis**, **Argument Control**, **Ordering Adjustment**, **Scope Marking** and **Lexical Adjustment**. The revision of sentence 1 into sentence 2 in Fig. 1 is an example of simple revision with **Reference Adjustment**. Following the introduction of a second reference to the losing team *"the Nuggets ..."*, the initial reference is abridged to simply *"Denver"* to avoid the repetitive form *"a 127 111 victory over the Denver Nuggets, handing the Denver Nuggets their seventh straight loss"*. See [Robin, 1992] for a presentation of the other types of side transformations.

Revision tool usage Table 1 quantifies the usage of each tool in the corpus. The total usage is broken

		side transformations		scope ranks		streak	extrema	game stat
adjoin	88	reference adjust	15	clause	16	8	1	7
		ordering adjust	2	nominal	72	23	46	3
append	10	ellipsis	1	clause	8	-	-	8
				nominal	2	-	-	2
conjoin	127	reference adjust	3	clause	91	5	-	86
		scope marking	12	NP coordination	28	-	-	28
		lexical adjust	3	NP apposition	8	8	-	—
		ellipsis	86			-	-	—
absorb	11	argument control	10	clause	10	3	-	7
				nominal	1	-	1	—
recast	4	none		clause	3	2	1	—
				nominal	1	1	-	—
argument demotion	7	none		clause	7	7	-	—
nominalization	1	none		clause	1	1	-	—
adjunctization	20	reference adjust	6	clause	20	8	8	4
constituent promotion	1	none		clause	1	1	-	—
coordination promotion	1	none		clause	1	-	1	—
	270		138		270	67	58	145

Table 1: Revision tool usage in the corpus

down by linguistic rank and by class of floating content units (*e.g.*, Adjoin was used 88 times in the corpus, 23 times to attach a streak at the nominal rank in the base sentence). Occurrences of side transformations are also given.

Figure 6 illustrates how revision tools can be used to incrementally generate very complex sentences. Starting from the draft sentence 1 which realizes only four fixed content units, five revision tools are applied in sequence, each one adding a new floating content unit. Structural transformations undergone by the draft at each increment are highlighted: deleted constituents are underlined, added constituents boldfaced and displaced constituents italicized. Note how displaced constituents sometimes need to change grammatical form (*e.g.*, the finite VP "*added 24*" of (3) becomes infinitive "*to add 24*" in (4) after being demoted).

Conclusion and future work

The detailed corpus analysis reported here resulted in a list of revision tools to incrementally incorporate additional content into draft sentences. These tools constitute a new type of linguistic resource which improves on the realization patterns traditionally used in generation systems (*e.g.*, [Kukich, 1983], [Jacobs, 1985], [Hovy, 1988]) due to three distinctive properties:

- They are compositional (concerned with atomic content additions local to sentence subconstituents).
- They incorporate a wide range of *contextual* constraints (semantic, lexical, syntactic, stylistic).
- They are abstract (capturing common structural relations over sets of sentence pairs).

These properties allow revision tools to opportunistically express floating content units under surface form constraints and to model a sublanguage's structural complexity *and* diversity with maximal economy and flexibility. Our analysis methodology based on surface decrement pairs can be used with any textual corpus.

Revision tools also bring together incremental generation and revision in a novel way, extending both lines of research. The complex revisions and side transformations we identified show that accomodating new content cannot always be done without modifying the draft content realization. They therefore extend previous work on incremental generation [Joshi, 1987] [De Smedt, 1990] that was restricted to elaborations preserving the linguistic form of the draft content. As content-*adding* revisions, the tools we identify also extend previous work on revision [Meteer, 1991] [Inui *et al.*, 1992] that was restricted to content-*preserving* revisions for text editing.

In addition to completing the implementation of the tools we identified as revision rules for the STREAK generator, our plans for future work includes the evaluation of these tools. The corpus described in this paper was used for acquisition. For testing, we will use two other corpora. To evaluate completeness, we will look at another season of basketball reports and compute the proportion of sentences in this test corpus whose realization pattern can be produced by applying the tools acquired in the initial corpus. Conversely, to evaluate domain-independence, we will compute, among the tools acquired in the initial corpus, the proportion of those resulting in realization patterns also used in a test corpus of stock market reports. The example below suggests that the same floating constructions are used across different quantitative domains:

- " Los Angeles – John Paxson hit 12 of 16 shots Friday night to score a season high 26 points **helping the Chicago Bulls snap a two game losing streak** with a 105 97 victory over the Los Angeles Clippers."

- "New York – Stocks closed higher in heavy trading Thursday, as a late round of computer-guided buy programs tied to triple-witching hour **helped the market snap a five session losing streak.**"

Although the analysis reported here was carried out manually for the most part, we hope to automate most of the evaluation phase using the software tool CREP [Duford, 1993]. CREP retrieves corpus sentences matching an input realization pattern encoded as a regular expression of words and part-of-speech tags.

Acknowledgments

Many thanks to Tony Weida and Judith Klavans for their comments on an early draft of this paper. This research was partially supported by a joint grant from the Office of Naval Research and the Defense Advanced Research Projects Agency under contract N00014-89-J-1782, by National Science Foundation Grants IRT-84-51438 and GER-90-2406, and by New York State Center for Advanced Technology Contract NYSSTF-CAT(92)-053 and NYSSTF-CAT(91)-053.

References

Bourbeau, L.; Carcagno, D.; Goldberg, E.; Kittredge, R.; and Polguere, A. 1990. Bilingual generation of weather forecasts in an operations environment. In *Proceedings of the 13th International Conference on Computational Linguistics.* COLING.

De Smedt, K.J.M.J. 1990. Ipf: an incremental parallel formulator. In Dale, R.; Mellish, C.S.; and Zock, M., editors 1990, *Current Research in Natural Language Generation.* Academic Press.

Duford, D. 1993. Crep: a regular expression-matching textual corpus tool. Technical Report CUCS-005-93, Columbia University.

Elhadad, M. and Robin, J. 1992. Controlling content realization with functional unification grammars. In Dale, R.; Hovy, H.; Roesner, D.; and Stock, O., editors 1992, *Aspects of Automated Natural Language Generation.* Springler Verlag. 89–104.

Elhadad, M. 1993. *Using argumentation to control lexical choice: a unification-based implementation.* Ph.D. Dissertation, Computer Science Department, Columbia University.

Fawcett, R.P. 1987. The semantics of clause and verb for relational processes in english. In Halliday, M.A.K. and Fawcett, R.P., editors 1987, *New developments in systemic linguistics.* Frances Pinter, London and New York.

Fensch, T. 1988. *The sports writing handbook.* Lawrence Erlbaum Associates, Hillsdale, NJ.

Gross, M. 1984. Lexicon-grammar and the syntactic analysis of french. In *Proceedings of the 10th International Conference on Computational Linguistics.* COLING. 275–282.

Halliday, M.A.K. 1985. *An introduction to functional grammar.* Edward Arnold, London.

Hovy, E. 1988. *Generating natural language under pragmatic constraints.* L. Erlbaum Associates, Hillsdale, N.J.

Inui, K.; Tokunaga, T.; and Tanaka, H. 1992. Text revision: a model and its implementation. In Dale, R.; Hovy, E.; Roesner, D.; and Stock, O., editors 1992, *Aspects of Automated Natural Language Generation.* Springler-Verlag. 215–230.

Jacobs, P. 1985. PHRED: a generator for natural language interfaces. *Computational Linguistics* 11(4):219–242.

Joshi, A.K. 1987. The relevance of tree-adjoining grammar to generation. In Kempen, Gerard, editor 1987, *Natural Language Generation: New Results in Artificial Intellligence, Psychology and Linguistics.* Martinus Ninjhoff Publishers.

Kukich, K. 1983. The design of a knowledge-based report generation. In *Proceedings of the 21st Conference of the ACL.* ACL.

Meteer, M. 1991. The implications of revisions for natural language generation. In Paris, C.; Swartout, W.; and Mann, W.C., editors 1991, *Natutal Language Generation in Artificial Intelligence and Computational Linguistics.* Kluwer Academic Publishers.

Pavard, B. 1985. La conception de systemes de traitement de texte. *Intellectica* 1(1):37–67.

Quirk, R.; Greenbaum, S.; Leech, G.; and Svartvik, J. 1985. *A comprehensive grammar of the English language.* Longman.

Robin, J. 1992. Generating newswire report leads with historical information: a draft and revision approach. Technical Report CUCS-042-92, Computer Science Department, Columbia Universtity, New York, NY. PhD. Thesis Proposal.

Robin, J. 1993. A revision-based generation architecture for reporting facts in their historical context. In Horacek, H. and Zock, M., editors 1993, *New Concepts in Natural Language Generation: Planning, Realization and Systems.* Frances Pinter, London and New York.

Rubinoff, R. 1990. Natural language generation as an intelligent activity. PhD. Thesis Proposal, Computer Science Department, University of Pennsylvania.

Natural Language
Sentence Analysis

Machine Translation of Spatial Expressions: Defining the Relation between an Interlingua and a Knowledge Representation System*

Bonnie J. Dorr   and   Clare R. Voss
Department of Computer Science
A.V. Williams Building
University of Maryland
College Park, MD   20742
{bonnie,voss}@cs.umd.edu

Abstract: In this paper we present one aspect of our research on machine translation (MT): defining the relation between the *interlingua* (IL) and a knowledge representation (KR) within an MT system. Our interest lies in the translation of natural language (NL) sentences where the "message" contains a spatial relation — in particular, where the sentence conveys information about the location or path of physical entities in the real, physical world. We explore several arguments for clarifying the source of constraints on the particular IL structures needed to translate these sentences. This paper develops one approach to defining these constraints and building an MT system where the IL structures designed to satisfy these constraints may be tested. In this way, we have begun to address one of the basic issues in MT research, providing independent justification for the IL itself.

Keywords: Natural Language Processing, Knowledge Representation, Machine Translation, Lexical Knowledge, Spatial Knowledge

1   Introduction

In this paper we present one aspect of our research on machine translation (MT): defining the relation between the *interlingua* (IL) and a knowledge representation (KR) system within an MT system called LEX-ITRAN. Our interest lies in the translation of natural language (NL) sentences where the "message" contains a spatial relation — in particular, where the sentence conveys information about the location or path of physical entities in the real, physical world.

We will be looking at sentences such as:

(1)   Die Kirche liegt im Süden der Stadt

which may have either of the following interpretations:

(2)   (i)   The church lies in the south of the city

      (ii) The church lies to the south of the city

Here the location of a **church** is ambiguous with respect to the **city**: the church may lie in the southern part of the city, within the city limits, or it may lie south of the city. The need to translate such sentences accurately presents a clear case of where general as well as specific real world knowledge should assist in eliminating inappropriate translations.

For example, had the sentence above been about a **mountain** lying *im Süden* of the **city**, the MT system should be able to use the *default* knowledge in a KR system that mountains typically are physical entities distinct and external to cities, to produce only the second, "outside the city" translation of the sentence.[1] The MT system should also be able, when the information is available, to take advantage of specific facts to override the default reasoning. For example, if the KR system contains a fact, or is able to infer from other facts, that the particular mountain named in the sentence is in a city, the MT system should only produce the first (*i.e.,* "inside the city") translation of the sentence.[2]

What is intriguing about this translation is that the ambiguity concerns such a conceptually clear distinction (*i.e.,* lying inside of, *vs.* outside of, a geographical region), yet this conceptual distinction is not "lexicalized", *i.e.,* it is not readily noticeable in the words of the sentence. This observation has led us to ask how the encoding of spatial relations — such as being lexicalized or not — should result in different formal representations for these relations in the components of an MT system, and what the interdependencies of these encodings should be.

In producing the correct translation of a sentence, an MT system may need to have access to information about a spatial relation that is only logically implicit, *i.e.,* not lexicalized — as was the case with the mountain/city sentence above. We will argue in this paper that, for a particular sentence, its logically implicit relations should be kept distinct from its lexicalized relations. In the sections to follow, we will explain how this position is reflected in our system design by maintaining the main components — the syntax, the interlingua, and the KR system — as separate modules.

In this context we address the question of what the relation between the interlingua (IL) and KR means. In general terms, our discussion will focus on the specific ways a KR system can assist the MT system in filtering out incorrect translations. In particular, of all the IL

---

*This research has been partially supported by the National Science Foundation under grant IRI-9120788, by the DARPA Basic Research Program under grant N00014-92-J-1929, by the Army Research Office under contract DAAL03-91-C-0034 through Batelle Corporation, and by the Army Research Institute under contract MDA-903-92-R-0035 through Microelectronics and Design, Inc.

[1] We are assuming a non-interactive MT system here, not a system that has recourse to asking a person on-line during the translation process which of the possible meanings was intended or is most likely.

[2] One of our reviewers noted, for example, that towns like Edinburgh have mountains in them.

structures built during the analysis phase, where each IL structure represents a distinct interpretation of the input sentence, we ask how the KR system eliminates those interpretations that are incorrect or highly unlikely before the generation phase begins.

The issues we will be examining are:

- What primitives in the domain of spatial relations must be in both the IL and KR components?

- What structures are passed between the IL and KR?

- What relations will the KR need to infer, *i.e.*, that are not in the IL?

The system design of LEXITRAN reflects two research issues. First, we wish to capture the insights of Dorr (1993) and those of Nirenburg *et al.* (1992) in the same model because they are complementary: Dorr has streamlined the syntax-IL mapping and Nirenburg *et al.* (1992) has demonstrated the advantages of including a taxonomic, or ontological, knowledge base (KB) in a MT system. No MT system currently exists that combines these two approaches or is able to make the claims of both Dorr and Nirenburg *et al.*[3]

Second, MT theory has not yet defined the issues surrounding how IL and KR formalisms should be related, either in terms of primitives, structures, or overall MT system computational issues, such as efficiency. In the development of grammatical theory, for example, the "points of contact" between the syntax and the real world knowledge[4] have been addressed in natural language processing (NLP) systems (*e.g.* Winograd (1973), and others in Grosz, Sparck-Jones, and Webber (1987)). However, with respect to a theory of the IL, these issues are more complex because no consensus exists yet on the criteria for evaluating ILs.

It is this second concern for defining the relation between the IL and the KR components of a MT system that we focus on in this paper.

2 Background

This section first describes our system, focusing on certain issues relevant to defining an interlingua, and then introduces the formalism we are using as an interlingua for our system.

2.1 From UNITRAN to LEXITRAN

In translating from the input, *i.e.*, a source language (SL) sentence, to the output, *i.e.*, one or more target language (TL) sentences, an IL-based MT system proceeds through two phases:[5]

- An *analysis phase*: the SL sentence is translated into the IL formalism.

- A *generation phase*: the IL structures are translated into TL sentences.

MT system vary widely with respect to the processing components that are used in these two phases and the manner in which these components exchange intermediate representations during the translation. A syntactic processor is required both for analysis of the SL sentence and synthesis of the final TL sentence. Also in both phases, an IL processor is needed to compose the IL representation (during the interpretation of the SL input) and to decompose the IL representation (during the production of the TL output).

In our current system, LEXITRAN, we have adopted the syntactic and IL processors from UNITRAN (see Dorr (1987, 1990, 1993)). However, our system differs from the UNITRAN design in two ways. First, in terms of the translation steps, LEXITRAN has an intermediary "filter" phase between the analysis of the SL sentence and the generation of the TL sentences. Second, in terms of system components, LEXITRAN has a component containing a KR system, which is separate from the syntactic and IL processors.

The filter phase makes use of a KR component and an MT system IL-KR interface program. During this phase, each structure that is output by the semantic analysis/composition phase is passed separately via the interface program to the KR component.[6] This component in turn filters out, or discards, those structures containing spatial relations that are incompatible with the system's facts; the resulting representations comprise the interlingua. The entire translation process is illustrated in Dorr and Voss (1993).

We should note that an MT system that includes a filter phase, by taking the extra step of having the KR system check its interpretations of a SL sentence (the IL set produced during the analysis phase), tackles two significant problems efficiently: (1) the MT system may be scaled up in terms of the number of natural languages it handles, without requiring changes to the KR system which is isolated from the syntax; and (2) the MT system

---

[3] For an introduction to the various approaches used in MT systems, see Hutchins and Somers (1992), chapter 4. Reference is made to other IL-based MT systems in section 2.2 below.

[4] For example, the notion of selectional restrictions — such as the requirement that the verb *sleep* have an animate subject to explain the anomaly of *The ideas are sleeping* — hinges on one's definition of terms that are taxonomic (or ontological) and syntactic — "animate" and "subject" in the case of *sleep*.

[5] Another type of MT system is the transfer-based model. For examples of this approach, see Abeillé, Schabes, and Joshi (1990), Alonso (1990), Arnold and Sadler (1990), Boitet (1987), Colmerauer *et al.* (1971), Kaplan *et al.* (1989), Mc-

Cord (1989), van Noord *et al.* (1990), Thurmair (1990), among others. Simplifying somewhat, the following pyramid diagram is often used to illustrate a range of levels at which transfer is possible in an MT system, suggesting that as more of the source text is analyzed, the transfer becomes simpler.

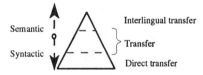

See Hutchins and Somers (1992), chapter 6, for a critical discussion of different MT models.

[6] For the KR component we are using PARKA (Spector, Hendler, and Evett (1990) and Spector *et al.* (1992)), a frame-based KR system which was designed to provide a principled approach to multiple inheritance and the representation of part-whole relations. (Also, see Woods and Schmolze (1992) for an overview of the KL-ONE family of KR systems that PARKA belongs to.) Since at this time our KR needs are quite narrow, we have opted to use this adequate and readily available resource.

may be scaled up in terms of the number of words in a language,[7] without requiring changes to the syntactic component, similarly because that component is isolated from the KR.

2.2 Defining an Interlingua

As mentioned in section 1, the field of MT research lacks a consensus on what evaluation criteria should be applied to IL formalisms. Other IL-based MT systems have drawn on a variety of semantic formalisms as the basis for their IL. For example, the project Rosetta (Appelo and Landsbergen (1986)) uses an IL based on M-grammar, a representation derived from Montague grammar (Dowty, Wall, and Peters (1981)). Barnett *et al.* (1991) at MCC have taken Discourse Representation Theory (DRT) (Heim (1982), Kamp (1984)) as their starting point for an IL. In both these cases, the original representations were developed as a theoretical formalism and then were adapted for an MT system.

This raises the question of how the IL in an MT system relates to a theory of semantics. The semantic or IL structures of MT systems must meet two different types of criteria. First, IL structures must map somehow to KR structures and we must justify what differentiates the representations in the IL and KR components since neither is constrained by perceptual data. Defining a IL-KR mapping is a precondition to building an MT system that can take advantage of the KR capabilities to filter out incorrect translations. Second, the IL structures in an MT system must map to and from syntactic structures of all the languages in the system — not just one language.

Our approach in LEXITRAN has been to assume that the "languages" of the IL and KR systems share many of the same predicates, but are not identical. Instead, the IL predicates are a proper subset of those in the KR system because we wish to allow, in principle, for KR concepts that are not needed for language-to-language translations. This avoids the problem of trying to represent a "full" meaning for each word in a sentence being translated.

Another advantage to making this distinction is that we wish to have the predicates of the IL system be driven by the demands of the syntax-to-IL mapping, rather than by the KR system. This design consideration protects our system from becoming unnecessarily brittle as the KR system grows or changes with the domain of translation. It also reflects our bias toward maintaining the advantages of assumptions made by Dorr (1993) over those of Nirenburg *et al.* (1992) when the two have different consequences for LEXITRAN.

2.3 Lexical Conceptual Structures

LEXITRAN bases its IL formalism on the theory of semantic structures developed by Jackendoff (1983, 1990). The representation he developed, referred to as *lexical conceptual structure* (LCS) and later *conceptual structure* (CS), is defined at the word level. That is, for each word, there exists one or more CSs that defines its meaning as a structure. For the meaning of a sentence, simplifying somewhat, the CSs for the words in

that sentence are composed into one CS. The resulting CS then represents the meaning of the sentence.

When a word has multiple meanings, it has, for each of those meanings, a separate CS associated with it in the lexicon. This occurs, for example, in the case of the English word *under* which is 'overloaded' and can convey several distinct interpretations. For these same interpretations German uses its word *unter* and then relies on the grammatical mechanism of case markings and an additional word to make further distinctions. Consider the translation of the English sentence *The mouse ran under the table* to its three German equivalents:

(3)   (i)   Die Maus ist unter dem Tisch gelaufen
        'The mouse ran (about in the area) under the table'

    (ii)   Die Maus ist unter den Tisch gelaufen
        'The mouse ran (to a place somewhere) under the table'

    (iii)   Die Maus ist unter dem Tisch durch gelaufen
        'The mouse ran (past a place somewhere) under the table'

The English preposition *under* together with the verb *run* conveys ambiguously three possible spatial relations, *i.e.* three different paths that the mouse may take. In German, two of these paths are distinguished from the third by explicit case markings: the accusative and the dative cases show up on the determiner *den* and *dem* of the noun *Tisch*, and distinguish between the path having an endpoint (as when the mouse stops under the table) and the path being open-ended (as when the mouse continues to move either past or about under the table).

The mechanism of a verbal prefix is then also available in German for conveying additional information about the path.[8] Here the prefix *durch* is needed to convey that the path is not only under the table, but that it also continues 'past' or beyond being under the table.

Note that these two ways of explicitly distinguishing the path types — namely, the presence of the word *durch* and the different case marking options in the German translations — give us evidence that we do indeed need to have enough information in our CSs for the English word *under* to differentiate among these path types. Without the path details being stored in the CSs, the information needed to generate the German translations correctly would not appear in the IL and hence would be lost in the analysis phase.

Now consider a change of **window** to **door** in the sentence: *The mouse ran under the door.* This change does not affect the IL composition process in the translation. We would expect however that a KR system would be able to filter out 2 of the 3 interpretations — namely, those corresponding to running to a place under the door and those for running about in a place under the door. These should follow from the assumption that a typical door is upright on its hinges and so has inadequate space for a mouse to run 'to a place under' or 'about in an area under' and yet still be understood as having run *under the door*.

3 Analysis

The aim of the last section was to provide a brief introduction to LEXITRAN and the issues of defining an

---

[7]We assume here that the syntactic categories of those words have already been included in the syntax component.

[8]The grammatical status of these prefixes is subject to debate within linguistic theory (van Riemsdijk (1990)).

interlingua as a level of representation that is distinct from the syntax and the KR components of the system. Now we will examine more carefully the domain of the sentences being translated and the evidence for the representations in the different components.

3.1 Spatial Domain and Spatial Predicates

We have been using the phrase "spatial relation" to refer to the relative positions of objects in 3-dimensional physical space. Thus, when referring to the "spatial relation" of a cup being on a table, we are locating one object, a cup, in terms of the top surface of another object, a table. This phrase is meant to capture a conceptual level of representing such relations. We could describe spatial relations in a mathematical notation, such as with Cartesian coordinates. However the symmetry of mathematical formalizations for spatial relations does not extend to the natural language expressions of spatial relations (Talmy (1978)).

In contrast to "spatial relation" we use term "spatial expression" to mean the linguistic surface structures that express spatial relations.[9] Not all natural languages have or use the same set of linguistic forms to convey the location or path of motion of objects in physical space. For example, the spatial relation expressed in a preposition in English may appear as a verbal prefix in a Russian translation, or as a postfix on the head noun of an NP in a language such as Korean. Or the equivalent of the English preposition may not actually appear as a distinct surface element in a French translation, but instead be incorporated into the meaning of a verb.

In order to identify more narrowly the parts of a spatial expression that we will be discussing, we will use the term *spatial predicate*. A *predicate* is a structure (composed of a predicate-relation and arguments) that exists at the IL or semantic level of representation: it is a theoretical construct.

Modifying the categories of Talmy (1985) and adapting work on PLACEs and PATHs by Jackendoff (1983, 1990) to our MT framework, we identify the following components within spatial predicates:

T1: The type of spatial predicate being conveyed, one of two high-level characterizations we will be examining: a PLACE or a PATH. *Example: he stood on the boat* contains a PLACE, whereas *the cargo was loaded onto the boat* contains a PATH.

T2: The "target" object or event, the item being located. *Example: the boy* in the phrase *the boy is on the boat.*

T3: One or more "reference" objects, items whose locations are known. *Example: the boat* in the phrase *the boy is on the boat.*

T4: The spatial operator, one of a few high-level characterizations, including a LOCATION or a DIRECTION. *Example: a direction such as south, left, down, or away; a location in a physical relation such as against or a geometric configuration such as around*

T5: A "perspective" location or frame of reference. *Example:* German *hin/her* distinction; English *here/there* distinction; also the distinction between *come* and *go* as in *he came into the room* and *he went into the room.*

In a simple sentence such as *the cup is on the table*, the spatial predicate T1, corresponds to a PLACE, meaning that location on the table where the cup is. T2, the target or object being located, and T3, the reference object, correspond to the phrases *the cup* and *the table*, respectively. The spatial operator T4, corresponds to the word *on*. This sentence conveys a spatial relation that is independent of the viewer's perspective and so T5 has no value.

The mapping from T1–T5 to the parts of a sentence is not always one-to-one however. Here are a few examples where the mapping is not so obvious:

Spatial Component	(a) He lifted the box	(b) He went ashore	(c) He fell down
T1	PATH	PATH	PATH
T2	box	he	he
T3	—	shore	ground
T4	up	to	down
T5	—	(the sea)	—

In (a), T4 corresponds to a lexically implicit value (the word *up* does not appear in the sentence). Similarly, in (b) and (c) there are other non-explicit values for the components, T3, T4, and T5.

Currently our IL structures contain spatial predicates corresponding to relations for the T1, T3, and T4 components; we have not yet implemented the T5 relation and have chosen to treat the T2 part of the predicate as an "external argument" (*i.e.*, it is outside the IL spatial predicate constituent structure).[10]

We should note here that the components in our predicates will need to be refined as we develop a richer model of spatial expressions. For example, some languages make fine-grained distinctions with respect to distances in their frames of reference (our T5). We have not dealt with the structure of measurement and quantity, so we have not formalized phrases like *under many tables*. And, in order to extend our work to an intersentential, or discourse level of analysis, our predicates may need additional components for tracking spatial focus (Maybury (1991)).

Dorr and Voss (1993) present a discussion of the changes made to the CSs that were adapted from Jackendoff's framework for LEXITRAN. One critical argument made there concerns the need for within-language synonymy tests, as well as cross-linguistic evaluations, in an iterative approach to developing the lexical-semantics for PATH and PLACE predicates. The results of such tests provide the first step in establishing evidence for the particular structures being hypothesized as IL predicates. The set of structures developed in this way can then be tested across languages. Furthermore, as noted in Dorr and Voss (1993), since there is a finite set of "lexicalization classes" that enumerate where spatial predicates may appear in the spatial expressions of a language, research can proceed by testing structures that fall into each of the relevant lexicalization classes.

3.2 Evidence for Encodings

In order to talk about the encoding of spatial relations in the various parts of the MT system and examine the

---

[9] Many other similar, less inclusive terms exist in the literature. (See Dorr and Voss (1993).)

[10] This is analogous to the syntactic treatment of a sentence subject which is generally considered to be external to the verb phrase.

role of the KR system in filtering out incorrect interpretations during the translation process, we need to clarify which encodings appear in which part of the MT system.

The following terms are used to classify the encoding of spatial relations on the basis of the "evidence" we have for them:

- *lexically explicit:* a spatial relation encoded explicitly in a word.

- *lexically implicit:* a spatial relation encoded implicitly, or internal to the structure representing the meaning of a word.

- *logically inferable:* a spatial relation logically inferred from lexically explicit or implicit relations, but not itself part of the structure representing the meaning of a word.

In the first two cases, the relation appears in the lexical entry for the relevant word; in the third case, the relation does not appear in the lexical entry.

An example of the first case is the direction SOUTH as an abstract concept, which is lexically explicit in the word *south*.[11] An example of the second case is the direction UP as a lexically implicit component of the word *lift*. The implicit presence of this constituent is apparent in tests for synonymy: *he lifted the baby, he lifted the baby up,* and *he lifted up the baby.* Finally, as an example of this last category, the direction FROM is logically inferable in the sentence *John arrived home,* where the lexically implicit relation PATH contains the explicit PLACE from *home,* and where we can infer logically that in a PATH ending at home, there was also a DIRECTION from which the arriver, *John,* came.

The definition of these categories is tied to the way we have modularized LEXITRAN into components. In the chart below, the X's mark which types of encoding of a spatial relation may appear in which of the components in our MT system.

Spatial Relation	Component of LEXITRAN		
	Syntax	IL	KR
lexically explicit	X	X	X
lexically implicit		X	X
logically inferable[12]			X

Following up on the examples above, the relation SOUTH in *south* will be represented at all levels in LEXITRAN, whereas UP in *lift* will only be represented at the IL and KR levels, and FROM in *John arrived home* will only be represented at the KR level (as the result of inferencing).

We can readily see that the Syntax-IL mapping requires tracking which components in the spatial predicates (at the IL level) appear in the surface SL and TL sentences and where in the sentence syntax they will be positioned. The IL-KR mapping involves no such transformation of structures. Instead, the IL structures are passed to the KR component for the checking of its spatial predicates; thus, the term *spatial predicate* extends to these structures once transferred into the KR component as well. However, one must not confuse the spatial

relations that were inferred in the KR system from those brought in by the IL representation.

To clarify this last point, consider the following English sentences:

(4) (i) He took the book to Tanya's table

(ii) He took the book from Florence's floor

If the sentences are translated into German, the *take-to* component of the first sentence translates to *bringen* whereas the *take-from* component in the second sentence translates to *nehmen.* In both sentences there is an implicit PATH relation where a book moves from one location to another. The FROM direction is logically inferable in the first sentence but lexically explicit in the second sentence. The situation is reversed with a TO direction: the TO is lexically explicit in the first sentence, but only logically inferable in the second sentence. If our IL representation of the first sentence were to include the FROM relation — and similarly if our IL representation of the second sentence were to include the TO relation — then at the point in translation where the system must generate a German sentence, we would have lost the information from the lexicalization and could no longer use it to select between the two German verbs.

This last example and the chart above help illustrate the double set of justifications that are required in a theory of the interlingua. In one direction the syntax-IL mapping provides one set of constraints on the IL, and in the other direction, the IL-KR mapping provides another set. Currently no theory of the interlingua defines these constraints and addresses the criteria to be used in evaluating them.

4   Results and Discussion

If we consider the status of the sentence *Daniel drove to the south of Colorado,* we quickly determine that the phrase *the south of Colorado* is ambiguous. One interpretation of this sentence is that Daniel drove to southern Colorado. That is, the phrase *the south of Colorado* refers to the region inside of Colorado that is considered its south. The IL structure for this part-to-whole relation, where the "part" is the meaning of the entire phrase and the "whole" is Colorado, is viewed as a "place-place" relation by the KR component which checks for a part-whole interpretation when it encounters two "place" predicates in an IL structure.

Now consider the following examples:

(5) (i) Maria drove to the south of Florida

(ii) The skipper navigated to the south of Gibraltar.

In the first case, *the south of Florida* refers to a part-whole spatial relation, with an "inside of" Florida interpretation. In the second case, *the south of Gibraltar* does not mean a part-whole relation — it refers to a region "outside of" Gibraltar. This distinction is captured in the translation into Spanish:

(6) (i) Maria manejó hacia el sur de la Florida

(ii) El capitán navejó al sur de Gibraltar

In other words, what appears as a conceptual distinction must be detected in the MT system in order to appropriately select the proper translation into Spanish.

Syntactically the English sentences are identical. At the IL level they are ambiguous. The IL processor will

---

[11]The words in capital letters refer to the spatial relation, the abstract term.

[12]The logically inferrable relations can be broken out into the "logically explicit" facts explicitly encoded in the KB of the KR system and the "logically implicit" facts that are derived from other facts and inference rules in the system.

create the "inside of" as well as the "outside of" IL interpretation for both of these sentences since it has no knowledge of which interpretation makes sense for which sentence. In other words, it does not check the T1–T4 values in predicates against real world knowledge. Rather it is the KR processor that performs this checking in the filter phase of the translation: it must allow for the part-whole IL structure for the first sentence and discard that structure for the second.

The KR processor makes use of the information in the IL structure that, in this case, was contributed by the verbs. Sentences (5)(i) and (6)(i) contain the equivalent of "go by land-vehicle" in its IL structure, whereas sentence (5)(ii) and (6)(ii) contain the equivalent of "go by water-vehicle" in its structure.[13] The KR, using inference rules that disallow a "go by X-vehicle" event composed with a path not on X (X would be "land" or "water" here), would rule out the two anomalous cases that concern us: (1) the IL interpretation of "driving to the south of Florida" as going by car to the outside of Florida, and (2) the IL interpretation of "navigating to the south of Gibraltar" as going by boat to the inside of Gibraltar. This result — enabling the KR to filter out anomalous IL interpretations by virtue of IL structures where it can readily identify the arguments within spatial predicates — also extends to other internal-external distinctions among spatial entities.

Our approach has been to assume that, in general, the syntactic properties of phrases reflect the underlying predicate-argument structural meaning of the words that head those phrases. Since we can "see" and test properties of phrasal structure, but not those of semantic structure, we must take advantage of what information we can glean from phrasal structures. The idea here is to use the differences in word meaning that correlate with syntactic distribution patterns to refine the hypotheses we have for the meaning structure — rather than developing lexical semantic structures solely based on our intuitions.[14]

We have described our approach to translating spatial expressions in an IL-based MT system and presented several arguments for the next steps in developing a theory of the *interlingua*. Such a theory must specify what can count as a constraint on the IL structures and thus provide independent justification for the particular structures being used. Our approach combines promising syntactic and semantic aspects of existing translation systems; we see this as the most appropriate framework for addressing some of the tough issues in MT, including the development of criteria for evaluating IL representations.

References

Abeillé, A., Schabes, Y., and Joshi, A. K. 1990. Using Lexicalized Tags for Machine Translation. In Proceedings of Thirteenth International Conference on Computational Linguistics, 1–6. Helsinki, Finland.

Appelo, L. and Landsbergen, J. 1986. The Machine Translation Project Rosetta. First International Conference on State of the Art in Machine Translation. Saarbruecken, Germany.

Barnett, J., Mani, I., Rich, E., Aone, C., Knight, K., and Martinez, J. C. 1991. Capturing Language-specific Semantic Distinctions in Interlingua-Based MT. In Proceedings of the Machine Translation Summit, 25–32. Washington, DC.

Dorr, Bonnie J. 1987. UNITRAN: An Interlingual Approach to Machine Translation. In Proceedings of the Sixth Conference of the American Association of Artificial Intelligence, 534–539. Seattle, Washington.

Dorr, Bonnie J. 1990. Solving Thematic Divergences in Machine Translation. In Proceedings of the 28th Annual Conference of the Association for Computational Linguistics, 127–134. University of Pittsburgh, Pittsburgh, PA.

Dorr, Bonnie J. 1993. *Machine Translation: A View from the Lexicon*. Cambridge, MA: MIT Press.

Dorr, Bonnie J. and Voss, Clare. 1993. Constraints on the Space of MT Divergences, Working Notes for the AAAI 1993 Spring Symposium, Building Lexicons for Machine Translation, Technical Report SS-93-02, Stanford University, CA.

Dowty, D. R., Wall, R. E. and Peters, S. 1981. *Introduction to Montague Semantics*. Dordrecht, Holland: Reidel.

Fillmore, C. 1968. The Case for Case. In *Universals in Linguistic Theory*, Bach, E. and R. Harms, eds. New York, NY: Holt, Rinehart, and Winston, 1-88.

Grosz, B., Sparck-Jones, K., and Webber, B. eds. 1987. *Readings in Natural Language Processing*. Los Altos, CA: Morgan Kaufmann.

Heim, I. 1982. The Semantics of Definite and Indefinite Noun Phrases. Ph.D. diss., Dept. of Linguistics, University of Massachusetts, Amherst, MA.

Hutchins, J. W. and Somers, H. L. 1992. *An Introduction to Machine Translation*. London, England: Academic Press.

Jackendoff, Ray S. 1983. *Semantics and Cognition*. Cambridge, MA: MIT Press.

Jackendoff, Ray S. 1990. *Semantic Structures*. Cambridge, MA: MIT Press.

Kamp, H. 1984. A Theory of Truth and Semantic Representation. In *Formal Methods in the Study of Language*. Dordrecht, Holland: Foris Publications.

Maybury, M. T. 1991. Topical, Temporal, and Spatial Constraints on Linguistic Realization. *Computational Intelligence* 7(4): 266–275.

Nirenburg, S., Carbonell, J., Tomita, M., and Goodman, K. 1992. *Machine Translation: A Knowledge-Based Approach*. San Mateo, CA: Morgan Kaufmann.

Riemsdijk, H. van 1990. Functional Prepositions. In *Unity in Diversity*, Pinkster, H. and Genee, I., eds. Dordrecht, Holland: Foris Publications, 229-241.

Schank, R. 1973. Identification of Conceptualizations Underlying Natural Language. In *Computer Models of Thought and Language*, R. Schank and K. Colby, eds. San Francisco, CA: W. H. Freeman, 187-247.

Spector, L., Hendler, J. and Evett, M. 1990. Knowledge Representation in PARKA, UMIACS TR 90-23, CS TR 2410, Dept. of Computer Science, University of Maryland, College Park, MD.

Spector, L., Anderson, W., Hendler, J., Kettler, B., Schwartzman, E., Woods, C. and Evett, M. 1992. Knowledge Representation in PARKA - Part 2: Experiments, Analysis, and Enhancements, CS-TR-2837, UMIACS-TR-92-16, Dept. of Computer Science, University of Maryland, College Park, MD.

Talmy, L. 1978. Figure and Ground in Complex Sentences. *Universals of Human Language*, Vol. 4: Syntax J. H. Greenberg, C. Ferguson, and E. Moravcsik, eds. Palo Alto, CA: Stanford University Press, 625–49.

Talmy, L. 1985. Lexicalization Patterns: Semantic Structure in Lexical Forms. *Grammatical Categories and the Lexicon* Timothy Shopen, ed. Cambridge, England: University Press, 57–149.

Winograd, T. 1973. A Procedural Model of Language Understanding. In *Computer Models of Thought and Language*, R. Schank and K. Colby, eds. San Francisco, CA: W. H. Freeman.

Woods, W.A. and Schmolze, J. A. 1992. The KL-ONE Family. *Computers and Mathematics with Applications*, 23(2-5): 133-177.

---

[13] See Dorr (1993) for a more complete discussion of verbs' CS structures.

[14] Two related issues should be addressed here. First, there is the notion that current lexical semantics basically draws on the well-known linguistic work on case (*e.g.* Fillmore (1968)) and so seems uninteresting. The second issue, is that the current computational work done in lexical semantics basically does not go beyond the insights achieved in the 70s work in AI (*e.g.* Schank (1973)), and so again seems uninteresting. However, we argue that this earlier work does not place any constraints on (1) what can be represented as a predicate, (2) the number of arguments, (3) the obligatory or optional nature of those arguments, or (4) the definitions of what constitutes a valid argument, each theory must provide independent justification for its hypothesized structures. It is at the lower level of how the ideas about case are integrated with the rest of modern linguistic theory that the current research challenges exist.

Having Your Cake and Eating It Too: Autonomy and Interaction in a Model of Sentence Processing

Kurt P. Eiselt*
College of Computing
Georgia Institute of Technology
Atlanta, Georgia 30332-0280
eiselt@cc.gatech.edu

Kavi Mahesh*
College of Computing
Georgia Institute of Technology
Atlanta, Georgia 30332-0280
mahesh@cc.gatech.edu

Jennifer K. Holbrook
Department of Psychology
Albion College
Albion, Michigan 49224
jen@cedar.cic.net

Abstract

Is the human language understander a collection of modular processes operating with relative autonomy, or is it a single integrated process? This ongoing debate has polarized the language processing community, with two fundamentally different types of model posited, and with each camp concluding that the other is wrong. One camp puts forth a model with separate processors and distinct knowledge sources to explain one body of data, and the other proposes a model with a single processor and a homogeneous, monolithic knowledge source to explain the other body of data. In this paper we argue that a hybrid approach which combines a unified processor with separate knowledge sources provides an explanation of both bodies of data, and we demonstrate the feasibility of this approach with the computational model called COMPERE. We believe that this approach brings the language processing community significantly closer to offering human-like language processing systems.

The Big Questions

Years of research by linguists, psychologists, and artificial intelligence specialists have provided significant insight into the workings of the human language processor. Still, fundamental questions remain unanswered. In particular, the debate over modular processing versus integrated processing rages on, and experimental data and computational models exist to support both positions. Furthermore, if the integrated processing position is correct, just what exactly is integrated? And if the modular position is the right one, what are the different modules? Do they interact, and if so, to what extent and when? Or are those modules entirely autonomous?

Wrestling with these questions induces considerable frustration in researchers. This frustration stems not only from the research community's apparent inability to answer them satisfactorily, but also from the overwhelming importance of the answers themselves—these answers, once uncovered, undoubtedly will impact thinking in all areas of artificial in-

telligence and cognitive science research, including visual processing, reasoning, and problem solving, to name just a few. In this paper, we intend to provide the reader with answers to some of these questions—answers based on nearly ten years of our own interdisciplinary research in sentence processing, and built upon the work of many others who went before us. In brief, we propose a model of language understanding (or, more specifically, sentence processing) in which all linguistic processing is performed by a single unified process, but the different types of linguistic knowledge necessary for processing are separate and distinct. This model accounts for conflicting experimental data, some of which suggests an autonomous, modular approach to language processing, and some of which indicates an integrated approach. Because it is a closer fit to the experimental data than any model which has gone before, this model consequently points the way to more human-like performance from language processing systems.

Background

Our new model of sentence processing has its roots in work begun nearly ten years ago. That research effort started as an attempt to explain how the human language understander selected the most context-appropriate meaning of an ambiguous word, and then was able to correct both the choice of word meaning and the surrounding sentence interpretation, without reprocessing the input, when later processing showed that the initial choice of word meaning was erroneous.

The resulting computational model, ATLAST (Eiselt, 1987; Eiselt, 1989), resolved word sense ambiguities by activating multiple word meanings in parallel, selecting the meaning which matched the previous context, and deactivating but retaining the unchosen meanings for as long as resources were available for retaining them. If later context proved the initial decision to be incorrect, the retained meanings could be reactivated without reaccessing the lexicon or reprocessing the text. ATLAST proved to have great psychological validity for lexical processing—its use of multiple access was well grounded in the psychological literature (e.g., Seidenberg, Tanenhaus, Leiman, & Bienkowski, 1982), and, more importantly, it made psychological predictions about the retention of unselected meanings that were

---
*During the course of this work, these authors were supported in part by a research grant from Northern Telecom.

experimentally validated (Eiselt & Holbrook, 1991; Holbrook, 1989). ATLAST provided an architecture of sentence processing which was also used to explain recovery from erroneous decisions in making pragmatic inferences as well as explaining individual differences in pragmatic inferences (Eiselt, 1989; cf. Granger, Eiselt, & Holbrook, 1983).

Error recovery in semantic processing had occasionally aroused the attention of researchers in conceptually-based natural language understanding, but the questions that arose were usually dismissed as unimportant or something which could be resolved as an afterthought (Birnbaum & Selfridge, 1981; Lebowitz, 1980; Lytinen, 1984). These researchers were content to assume that the first inference decision made was the correct one. Meanwhile, other researchers investigating syntactically-based approaches had long since concluded that the means by which erroneous syntactic decisions were accommodated had a dramatic impact on the architecture of the syntactic processor being proposed. For example, the backtracking models embodied the theory that only a single syntactic interpretation need be maintained at any given time, so long as the processor could keep track of its decisions, undo them when an erroneous decision was discovered, and then reinterpret the input (e.g., Woods, 1973). The lookahead parsers tried to sidestep the problems inherent in backtracking by postponing any decision until enough input had been processed to guarantee a correct decision, thereby avoiding erroneous decisions to some extent (e.g., Marcus, 1980). Another approach to avoiding erroneous decisions was offered by parallel parsers which maintained all plausible syntactic interpretations at the same time (Kurtzman, 1985). ATLAST, however, was a model of semantic processing and did not address the issue of recovery from erroneous syntactic decisions, nor did it substantially address the issue of syntactic processing at all.

Recently, Stowe (1991) presented experimental evidence showing that in dealing with syntactic ambiguity, the sentence processor accesses all possible syntactic structures simultaneously and, if the structure preferred for syntactic reasons conflicts with the structure favored by the current semantic bias, the competing structures are maintained and the decision is delayed. Furthermore, the work suggests an interaction of the various knowledge types, as in some cases semantic information influences structure assignment or triggers reactivation of unselected structures. This model of limited delayed decision in syntactic ambiguity resolution had much in common with the ATLAST model of semantic ambiguity resolution. Both models proposed an early commitment where possible. Both models had the capability to pursue multiple interpretations in parallel when ambiguity made it necessary. Both models explained error recovery as an operation of switching to another interpretation maintained in parallel by the sentence processor. Finally, both models made decisions by integrating the preferences from syntax and semantics.

One explanation for this high degree of similarity between the syntactic and semantic error recovery mechanisms is that there are two separate processors, one for syntax and one for semantics, each with its corresponding source of linguistic knowledge, and each doing exactly the same thing. A more economical explanation, however, is that there is only one process which deals with syntactic and semantic information in the same manner. We have chosen to explore the latter explanation, as others have done, but we have also chosen to maintain the separate knowledge sources for reasons which will be explained below. (See also Holbrook, Eiselt, & Mahesh, 1992.)

Overview of COMPERE

Our new model of sentence processing, called COMPERE (Cognitive Model of Parsing and Error Recovery), consists of a single unified process operating on independent sources of syntactic and semantic knowledge. This is made possible by a uniform representation of both types of knowledge. The unified process applies the same operations to the different types of knowledge, and has a single control structure which performs the operations on syntactic and semantic knowledge in tandem. This permits a rich interaction between the two sources of knowledge, both through transfer of control and through a shared representation of the interpretations of the input text being built by the unified process.

An advantage of representing the different kinds of knowledge in the same form is that the boundaries between the different types of knowledge can be ill-defined. Often it is difficult to classify a piece of knowledge as belonging to a particular class such as syntactic or semantic. With a uniform representation, such knowledge lies in between and can be treated as belonging to either class.

Syntactic and semantic knowledge are represented in separate networks in which each node is a structured representation of all the information pertaining to a syntactic or semantic category or concept. A link, represented as a slot-filler pair in the node, specifies a parent category or concept of which the node can be a part, together with the conditions under which it can be bound to the parent, and the expectations that are certain to be fulfilled should the node be bound to the parent. In addition, nodes in either network are linked to corresponding nodes in the other network so that the unified process can build on-line interpretations of the input sentence in which each syntactic unit has a corresponding representation of its thematic role and its meaning. In addition, there is a lexicon as well as certain other minor heuristic and control knowledge that is part of the process. (COMPERE's architecture and knowledge representation are displayed graphically in Figures 1 and 2.)

The unified process is a bottom-up, early-commitment parsing mechanism integrated with top-down guidance through expectations. The operators and the control structure that constitute the unified process are described briefly in the algorithm shown in Figure 3.

The COMPERE prototype has been implemented in Common LISP on a Symbolics LISP Machine. At this time, its unified process can perform on-line interpretations of its input, and can recover from erroneous syntactic decisions when necessary. COMPERE is able to process relatively complex syntactic structures, including relative clauses, and

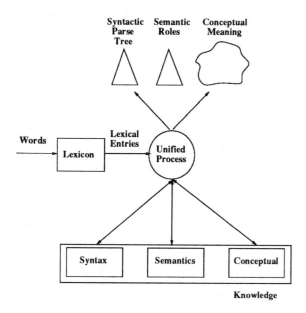

Figure 1: Architecture of COMPERE.

1. Access lexical entries of next word.
2. Create instance nodes for syntactic category, meaning, and (primitive) thematic role.
3. Compute feasible bindings to parents for syntactic instance node and role instance node. (This operation checks any conditions to be satisfied to make the binding feasible; it also takes existing expectations into account.)
4. Rank syntactic and semantic feasible bindings by their respective preference criteria.
Combine feasible bindings and select the most preferred binding.
5. Make the binding by creating parent node instances and appropriate links, and generating any expectations. Create links between corresponding instances in syntax and their thematic roles and meanings.
6. Retain alternative bindings for possible error recovery.
7. If there is no feasible binding for a node, explore previously retained alternatives to recover from errors.
8. Continue to bind the parent nodes to nodes further up as far as possible (such as until the S node in syntax or the Event node in semantics).

Figure 3: Unified Process: Algorithm.

can resolve the associated structural ambiguities.

Autonomy and interaction effects from one process

COMPERE is able to exhibit seemingly modular processing behavior that matches the results of experiments showing the autonomy of different levels of language processing (e.g., Forster, 1979; Frazier, 1987). It is also able to display seemingly integrated behavior that matches the results of experiments showing semantic influences on syntactic structure assignment (e.g., Crain & Steedman, 1985; Tyler & Marslen-Wilson, 1977). For example, consider the processing of the following sentence:

(1) *The bugs moved into the new lounge were found quickly.*

This sentence has a lexical semantic ambiguity at the subject noun *bugs* that could mean either insects or electronic microphones. In addition, it is also syntactically ambiguous locally at the verb *moved* since there is no distinction between its past-tense form and its past-participle form. In the simple past reading of *moved*, it would be the main verb with the corresponding interpretation that "the bugs moved themselves into the new lounge." On the other hand, if *moved* is read as a verb in its past-participle form, it would be the verb in a reduced relative clause corresponding to the meaning "the bugs which were moved by somebody else into the new lounge...." Parse trees for the two structural interpretations and the corresponding thematic-role assign-

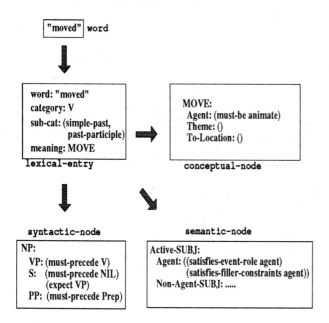

Figure 2: Knowledge Representation in COMPERE.[1]

---

[1]The arrows in Figure 2 simply indicate which types of knowledge point to which other types; they do not mean that the specific nodes shown point to the other nodes.

ments are shown in Figures 4 and 5.[2]

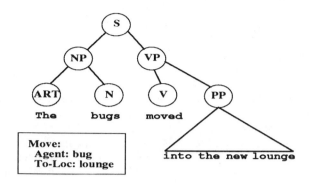

Figure 4: Garden Path: Main-Clause Interpretation.

Null Context: When sentence (1) is presented to COMPERE in a null semantic context, one where there is no bias for either meaning of the noun *bugs*, COMPERE reads ahead without resolving the lexical ambiguity at the word *bugs*. When it encounters the structural ambiguity at the verb *moved*, COMPERE does not have the necessary information to decide which of the two structures in Figures 4 and 5 is the appropriate one to pursue.

However, COMPERE has a syntactic preference for the main-verb interpretation over the relative clause one. Though this preference can be explained by the minimal attachment principle (Frazier, 1987), COMPERE offers a more general explanation. Extrapolating from Stowe's model, we have endowed COMPERE with the pervasive goal of completing an incomplete item at any level of processing. In syntactic processing, it has a goal to complete the syntactic structure of a unit such as a phrase, clause, or a sentence. COMPERE prefers the alternative which helps complete the current structure (called the Syntactic Default) over one that adds an optional constituent leaving the incompleteness intact. For instance, in (1), a VP is required to complete the sentence after seeing *The bugs*. Since the main-clause interpretation helps complete this requirement and the relative-clause interpretation does not, the main-clause structure gets selected. In other words, COMPERE would rather use the verb to begin the VP that is required to complete the sentence structure than treat it as the verb in a reduced relative clause which would leave the expectation of the VP unsatisfied. This behavior is the same as the one explained by the "first analysis" models of Frazier and colleagues (Frazier, 1987) using a minimal-attachment preference. COMPERE can produce this behavior by applying structural preferences independently since it maintains separate representations of syntactic and semantic knowledge.

As a consequence of choosing the main-clause interpretation, the lexical ambiguity is also resolved. The electronic

bug meaning is now ruled out since there is a selectional restriction on the verb *moved* that is not satisfied by electronic bugs (namely, they cannot move by themselves).[3]

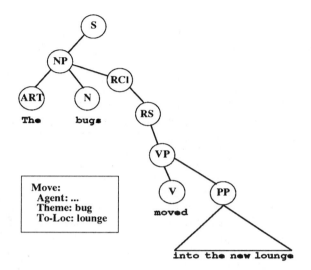

Figure 5: Garden-Path: Reduced Relative Clause.

Thus, until seeing the word *were*, the verb *moved* is treated as the main verb since it satisfies the expectation of a VP that is required to complete the sentence. However, at this point, the structure is incompatible with the remaining input. COMPERE recognizes the error and now tries the alternative of attaching the VP as a reduced relative clause so that there is still a place for a main verb. This results in a garden-path effect upon reading this sentence. That is, the sentence processor is led up a garden path and has to backtrack when later information shows that it was the wrong path to take. This behavior is not influenced by semantic or conceptual preferences and can be perceived as a modular behavior. COMPERE's error recovery method was first developed in the ATLAST model (Eiselt, 1987). It was also experimentally validated (Eiselt & Holbrook, 1991).

As a consequence of switching to the new syntactic interpretation, COMPERE makes corresponding changes to thematic role assignments and also "unresolves" the lexical ambiguity. There is no longer any reason to eliminate the electronic bug meaning since either kind of bugs can be moved by others.

Semantically Biasing Context: Now consider sentence (1) in a semantically biasing context such as the one in (2).[4]

---

[3]COMPERE's program does not resolve lexical semantic ambiguities at this time. We are currently rectifying this by incorporating lexical ambiguity resolution strategies from our earlier model ATLAST (Eiselt, 1989) in COMPERE.

[4]At present, COMPERE is not capable of using context effects in its ambiguity resolution process. However, its architecture supports the inclusion of such effects and we are working on providing context information to the unified process.

---

[2]For simplicity, these figures show the parse trees and the thematic roles separate from each other. In COMPERE's actual output, the parse trees and thematic roles are interlinked.

(2) *The Americans built a new wing to the embassy. The Russian spies quickly transferred the microphones to the new wing. The bugs moved into the new lounge were found quickly.*

The semantic context in (2) resolves the lexical ambiguity by choosing the electronic bug meaning. This decision helps COMPERE resolve the structural ambiguity at the verb *moved*. Using its conceptual knowledge, represented as a selectional restriction, that only animate agents can move by themselves, COMPERE decides that *moved* cannot be a main verb and goes directly to the reduced relative clause interpretation (Fig. 5), thereby avoiding the garden path. This shows how the same unified process that previously exhibited modular processing behavior can also produce interactive processing behavior when semantic information is available. Syntax and semantics interact in COMPERE to help resolve ambiguities in each other.

COMPERE can also use independent syntactic preferences in other types of sentences such as those with prepositional attachment ambiguities. The COMPERE prototype thus demonstrates that the range of behaviors that the interactive models account for (Crain & Steedman, 1985; Tyler & Marslen-Wilson, 1977), and the behaviors that the "first analysis" models account for (Frazier, 1987), can be explained by a unified model with a single processor operating on multiple independent sources of knowledge.

Comparative evaluation

There is certainly nothing unique about a unified process model of language understanding—the integrated processing hypothesis has been visited and revisited many times, for good reason, and with significant results (e.g., Jurafsky, 1992; Lebowitz, 1980; Riesbeck & Martin, 1986). Yet each of these models labors under the assumption that the integration of processing necessarily goes hand in hand with the integration of the knowledge sources. While this design decision may make construction of the corresponding computational model easier, it also makes the model incapable of easily explaining the autonomy effects demonstrated by Forster (1979), Frazier (1987), and others. As shown above, COMPERE's unified processing mechanism combined with its separate sources of linguistic knowledge offers an explanation for observed autonomy effects as well as the interaction effects reported by Marslen-Wilson and Tyler (Tyler & Marslen-Wilson, 1977). Furthermore, the integrated models noted above cannot capture syntactic generalizations.

Another form of the modularity debate concerns the effect of context on syntactic decisions—does context affect structure assignment, or are context effects absent until later in language processing (Taraban & McClelland, 1985)? Though we do not have a model of context effects in COMPERE, we believe that contextual information can be incorporated as an additional source of preferences in COMPERE's architecture.

An added benefit of COMPERE's sentence processing architecture is that it offers an explanation for the effects of linguistic aphasias. In reviewing the aphasia literature, Caramazza and Berndt (1978) concluded that the evidence pointed strongly to the functional independence of syntactic and semantic processing. COMPERE suggests an alternate explanation—the different aphasic behaviors are not due to damage to the individual processors, but are instead due to damage to the individual knowledge sources or, perhaps, to the communications pathways between the knowledge sources and the unified processor.

We believe that COMPERE's architecture accounts for the wide variety of seemingly conflicting data on linguistic behavior better than any previously proposed model of sentence processing. Yet COMPERE is not the first sentence processing model to be configured as a single process interacting with independent knowledge sources. The localist or punctate connectionist models of Pollack (1987; Waltz and Pollack, 1985) and Cottrell (1985; Cottrell and Small, 1983) resemble COMPERE at a gross architectural level, but these models did not offer the range of explanation of different behaviors that COMPERE does; for example, these models do not recover from errors, nor can they deal with complex syntactic structures such as relative clauses.

Despite all its theoretical advantages over other models, the prototype implementation of COMPERE is not yet fully developed and suffers from some weaknesses. Its role knowledge is fairly limited, and its conceptual knowledge is even more so. Also, the implementation currently diverges slightly from theory. The divergence appears in the process itself: the theoretical model has a single unified process, while the prototype computational model consists of two nearly-identical processes—one for syntax and one for semantics. These two processes share identical control structures, but they are duplicated because we have not yet completed the task of representing the different types of information in a uniform format. Some readers may take this as an indication that we are doomed to failure, but the connectionist models mentioned earlier serve as existence proofs that finding a uniform format for representing different types of linguistic knowledge is by no means an impossible task.

Conclusion

Is the human language understander a collection of modular processes operating with relative autonomy, or is it a single integrated process? This ongoing debate has polarized the language processing community, with two fundamentally different types of model posited, and with each camp concluding that the other is wrong. One camp puts forth a model with separate processors and distinct knowledge sources to explain one body of data, and the other proposes a model with a single processor and a homogeneous, monolithic knowledge source to explain the other body of data. In this paper we have argued that a hybrid approach which combines a unified processor with separate knowledge sources provides an explanation of both bodies of data, and we have demonstrated the feasibility of this approach with the computational model called COMPERE. We believe that this approach brings the language processing community significantly closer to offering human-like language processing systems.

Acknowledgement: We would like to thank Justin Peterson for his comments on this work and his help in finding good examples.

References

Birnbaum, L., and Selfridge, M. 1981. Conceptual analysis of natural language. In Schank, R. C., and Riesbeck, C. K. eds. Inside computer understanding: Five programs plus miniatures, 318-353. Hillsdale, NJ: Lawrence Erlbaum.

Caramazza, A., and Berndt, R. S. 1978. Semantic and syntactic processes in aphasia: A review of the literature. *Psychological Bulletin* 85:898-918.

Cottrell, G. W. 1985. A connectionist approach to word sense disambiguation, Technical Report, 154, Computer Science Department, University of Rochester.

Cottrell, G. W., and Small, S. L. 1983. A connectionist scheme for modelling word sense disambiguation. *Cognition and Brain Theory* 6:89-120.

Crain, S., and Steedman, M. 1985. On not being led up the garden path: The use of context by the psychological syntax processor. In Dowty, D. R., Kartunnen, L., and Zwicky, A. M. eds. Natural language parsing: Psychological, computational, and theoretical perspectives, 320-358. Cambridge, England: Cambridge University Press.

Eiselt, K. P. 1987. Recovering from erroneous inferences. In Proc. AAAI-87 Sixth National Conference on Artificial Intelligence, 540-544. San Mateo, CA: Morgan Kaufmann.

Eiselt, K. P. 1989. Inference processing and error recovery in sentence understanding, Technical Report, 89-24, Ph.D. diss., Dept. of Computer Science, University of California, Irvine.

Eiselt, K. P., and Holbrook, J. K. 1991. Toward a unified theory of lexical error recovery. In Proc. of the Thirteenth Annual Conference of the Cognitive Science Society, 239-244. Hillsdale, NJ: Lawrence Erlbaum.

Forster, K. I. 1979. Levels of processing and the structure of the language processor. In Cooper, W. E., and Walker, E. C. T. eds. Sentence processing: Psycholinguistic studies presented to Merrill Garrett, 27-85. Hillsdale, NJ: Lawrence Erlbaum.

Frazier, L. 1987. Theories of sentence processing. In Garfield, J. L. ed. Modularity in knowledge representation and natural-language understanding. Cambridge, MA: MIT Press.

Granger, R. H., Eiselt, K. P., and Holbrook, J. K. 1983. STRATEGIST: A program that models strategy-driven and content-driven inference behavior. In Proc. of the National Conference on Artificial Intelligence, 139-147. San Mateo, CA: Morgan Kaufmann.

Holbrook, J. K. 1989. Studies of inference retention in lexical ambiguity resolution. Ph.D. diss., School of Social Sciences, University of California, Irvine.

Holbrook, J. K., Eiselt, K. P., and Mahesh, K. 1992. A unified process model of syntactic and semantic error recovery in sentence understanding. In Proc. of the Fourteenth Annual Conference of the Cognitive Science Society, 195-200. Hillsdale, NJ: Lawrence Erlbaum.

Jurafsky, D. 1992. An on-line computational model of human sentence interpretation. In Proc. of the Tenth National Conference on Artificial Intelligence, 302-308. San Mateo, CA: Morgan Kaufmann.

Kurtzman, H. S. 1985. Studies in syntactic ambiguity resolution. Ph.D. diss., Dept. of Psychology, Massachusetts Institute of Technology.

Lebowitz, M. 1980. Generalization and memory in an integrated understanding system, Research Report, 186, Dept. of Computer Science, Yale University.

Lytinen, S. L. 1984. The organization of knowledge in a multi-lingual, integrated parser, Research Report, YALEU/CSD/RR 340, Dept. of Computer Science, Yale University.

Marcus, M. P. 1980. *A theory of syntactic recognition for natural language.* Cambridge, MA: MIT Press.

Pollack, J. B. 1987. On connectionist models of natural language processing, Technical Report, MCCS-87-100, Computing Research Laboratory, New Mexico State University.

Riesbeck, C. K., and Martin, C. E. 1986. Towards completely integrated parsing and inferencing. In Proc. of the Eighth Annual Conference of the Cognitive Science Society, 381-387. Hillsdale, NJ: Lawrence Erlbaum.

Seidenberg, M. S., Tanenhaus, M. K., Leiman, J. M., and Bienkowski, M. 1982. Automatic access of the meanings of ambiguous words in context: Some limitations of knowledge-based processing. *Cognitive Psychology* 14:489-537.

Stowe, L. A. 1991. Ambiguity resolution: Behavioral evidence for a delay. In Proc. of the Thirteenth Annual Conference of the Cognitive Science Society, 257-262. Hillsdale, NJ: Lawrence Erlbaum.

Taraban, R., and McClelland, J. L. 1988. Constituent attachment and thematic role assignment in sentence processing: Influences of content-based expectations. *Journal of Memory and Language* 27:597-632.

Tyler, L. K., and Marslen-Wilson, W. D. 1977. The on-line effects of semantic context on syntactic processing. *Journal of Verbal Learning and Verbal Behavior* 16:683-692.

Waltz, D. L., and Pollack, J. B. 1985. Massively parallel parsing: A strongly interactive model of natural language interpretation. *Cognitive Science* 9:51-74.

Woods, W. A. 1973. An experimental parsing system for transition network grammars. In Rustin, R. ed. Natural language processing. New York: Algorithmics Press.

Efficient Heuristic Natural Language Parsing

Christian R. Huyck   Steven L. Lytinen
Artificial Intelligence Laboratory
The University of Michigan
1101 Beal Ave.
Ann Arbor, MI 48109
(313)936-3667
e-mail: chris@engin.umich.edu

Abstract

Most artificial natural language processing (NLP) systems make use of some simple algorithm for parsing. These algorithms overlook the inextricable link between parsing natural language and understanding it.

Humans parse language in a linear fashion. Our goal is to develop an NLP system that parses in a linear and psychologically valid fashion. When this goal is achieved, our NLP system will be efficient, and it will generate the correct interpretation in ambiguous situations.

In this paper, we describe two NLP systems, whose parsing is driven by several heuristics. The first is a bottom-up system which is based on the work of (Ford, Bresnan & Kaplan 1982). The second system is a more expansive attempt, incorporating the initial heuristics and several more. This system runs on a much larger domain and incorporates several new syntactic forms. It has its weaknesses, but it shows good progress toward the goal of linearity.

Keywords: Natural Language Processing, Parsing, Heuristic Reasoning

Introduction

Natural language is inherently ambiguous. Even unambiguous sentences often contain local ambiguities, which cannot be resolved without taking into account the overall context. However, despite the prevalance of ambiguity, humans are able to process natural language in linear time in the average case. How can we develop a natural language processing (NLP) system that is as efficient as humans?

One common area of NLP research is in grammar formalisms. Unfortunately, there seems to be a tradeoff between the expressiveness of formalisms and the efficiency of the parsing algorithms that they yield. While there is disagreement as to the expressiveness required to describe the syntax of English and other natural languages, most computational linguists seem to agree that grammar formalisms which are expressive enough to capture the full syntax of natural languages are too powerful to yield efficient parsing algorithms. Even context-free grammars, one of the simpler formalisms widely used, can only be parsed in $O(n^3)$ time. Other, more powerful formalisms, yield even more inefficient parsing algorithms.

A common approach to improving parsing efficiency is to devise an algorithm which cannot parse all possible sentences, but which efficiently parses those sentences which it can parse. Let us call this the *restricted parser* approach to efficiency. The hope is that the parsable sentences correspond to those constructions which people use most commonly, and are able to successfully understand; while sentences that cannot be parsed, although perhaps technically in the language, correspond to pathological examples (for people) such as garden paths. For example, Marcus achieved determinism in his PARSIFAL system (Marcus 1980) by limiting the parser's lookahead to at most three constituents, and argued that many English garden paths require a larger lookahead window. Similarly, Blank's register vector grammar parser (Blank 1989) used a finite (and small) number of registers to store previous parser states, thereby restricting the parser's backtracking capabilities.

While it is beyond the scope of this paper to argue in detail against the restricted parser approach, we feel it suffers from two difficulties. First, it is not clear that the sentences that these parsers can successfully process really do correspond to those sentences which are commonly used by people. In particular, psycholinguistic evidence indicates that some sentences predicted to be garden paths by theories of limited lookahead or limited backtracking are in fact easily understood by people (e.g., Crain & Steedman 1985). Second, these systems do not gracefully degrade: either a sentence is parsable in linear time, or it cannot be parsed at all.[1] NLP systems should be capable of parsing unusual syntactic constructions, even if they cannot be parsed as efficiently as more commonly used constructions.

As an alternative to the restricted grammar approach, we offer an approach based on the use of parsing *heuristics*, which are used to select which grammar rules to apply at each step in the parse. The heuristics utilize a combination of syntactic and semantic information to determine which rule to apply next. While these heuristics do not improve our parser's worst-case complexity, we have found that they do improve the system's average-case performance. Empirical testing has indicated that the system parses sentences in linear time on average. In addition to achieving improved average-case complexity, our system also degrades gracefully. Those sentences which mislead the heuristics are still successfully parsed, though not in linear time. Another major benefit is that when our heuristics succeed, the correct interpretation is generated; i.e., the one that a human would generate.

Our heuristic approach has been implemented as part of the LINK system (Lytinen 1992), which is one of several unification-based grammar systems (Shieber 1986). This system uses a bottom-up parser with a unification-based grammar and a chart mechanism. The particular heuristics we have encoded have been inspired by the work of Ford, Bresnan, and Kaplan (1982), although we are using an extension of the set of heuristics proposed by them.

In the rest of this paper, we first review some prior work on parsing natural language. Then we describe an initial system which we implemented, that uses heuristics to parse a small subset of English in linear time. Next, we describe initial attempts at heuristic parsing in a 'real' domain. Finally, we conclude with a discussion of some problems we have encountered and future directions.

Prior Work

The knowledge of grammars and the ability to parse input using these grammars has advanced rapidly since the advent of the computer. Work in parsing formal

---

[1] Marcus (1980) discusses possible techniques for parsing garden path sentences, but these were not implemented in PARSIFAL.

languages advanced rapidly in the 1960s, and this advancement aided the development of programming languages and compilers for these languages. These formal methods have been applied to natural languages, but they have met with less success.

In this section we first discuss some algorithmic approaches to parsing, including some results from formal language theory. After this, we discuss some other work that has been done in heuristic approaches to natural language parsing.

Algorithmic Approaches

Early work on formal languages was done by (Chomsky 1956), where he introduced context free grammars. Backus adapted context-free grammars into BNF notation, which was used for formally describing Algol 60 (Naur 1963). Efficient algorithms were designed to parse regular languages in linear time, significant subsets of context-free languages in linear time, and all context-free languages in cubic time.

However, natural language is not easily understood in formal language terms. The position of natural languages on the scale of complexity of formal languages is under debate, though most current systems assume that natural language is at least context-free. This assumption is implied by the use of context-free grammar rules. Others, e.g. (Blank 1989), feel that natural language is a regular language. Blank's argument is that humans are finite; therefore, our language can be defined by a finite automata. We are indeed finite, but our language may be more easily described by context free rules.

There has also been work in fast algorithms for parsing natural language. Tomita (1987) has developed a parser which on average case behaves in n-logn time, though it is an n-squared worst case algorithm. This work is based on Earley's (Earley 1970) fast algorithm work. Its weakness is threefold: first, it functions on a restricted context-free grammar. Second, while more efficient than many parsers, it is not linear. Third and most important, it is not psychologically valid. It generates all grammatically valid parses, and humans do not do this. Similarly, it has no means of choosing the correct interpretation (the interpretation humans produce) from all of the grammatical interpretations.

Heuristic Approaches

Early studies of heuristics focused on a small number of heuristics which specified parsing decisions. Kimball (1973) was a pioneer in this field and introduced the principles of right association, early closure, and others. These heuristics are quite useful, but nothing is said about how they are related to each other.

Another approach was to build a heuristic parser to account for linear parsing. Marcus (1980) built PARSIFAL, Ford, Bresnan and Kaplan (1982) built a system which exploited their lexical preference heuristic, and Frazier and Fodor (1978) built the sausage machine.

The main drawback of all of these systems is that they functioned only in small domains. It is not clear that they would scale up to a larger domain.

Blank (1989) designed a system with linearity in mind. His system used a regular grammar with registers to account for embedded constructs. This approach has certain limitations since some constructs can be indefinitely embedded. Furthermore, the number of rewrite rules needed for any significant subset of English would be enormous. Blank's heuristics are embedded into his parsing mechanism, so he really has nothing to say about heuristics. His work does, however, provide an excellent statement on linearity. Blank's results are impressive, but again his system only works on a small subset of English.

A System for a Small Domain

Our first attempt at an efficient heuristic parser was based on the work of (Ford, Bresnan & Kaplan 1982). The heuristics they implemented included the final arguments, syntactic preference, and lexical preference heuristics. The final arguments heuristic has been mentioned by others including Kimball (1973). It states that the attachment of the final argument of a verb phrase should have low priority; this delayed attachment allows the final argument to have extra modifiers attached to it. The syntactic preference heuristic states that a word which is in multiple lexical categories should be expanded to the strongest category first. For instance, the word *that* can be a pronoun or a complementizer; the pronoun is the stronger category so its interpretation as a pronoun should be preferred.

The most important heuristic is the lexical preference heuristic; it states that lexical items will have a preference for certain semantic items. For instance, in the sentence *The woman positioned the dress on the rack,* the lexical item *positioned* will prefer a location phrase. For this reason, *on the rack* should be attached to the verb phrase *positioned*, instead of being attached to the noun phrase *the dress*. It is important to note that this heuristic utilizes both syntactic and semantic information.

We implemented Ford *et al.'s* heuristics in the LINK system, enhanced with several others of our own. One of our heuristics, the *phrase creation* heuristic, is a special case of Kimball's (1973) right attachment rule. The heuristic prefers to attach incoming lexical items to the most recent open constituent, provided that constituent is an 'elementary' one (e.g., noun phrase, prepositional phrase, ...) rather than a more complex constituent (e.g., subordinate clause). Thus, in *The air force pilots*, although *force* and *pilots* could be interpreted as verbs, this heuristic prefers to interpret them as nouns, since then the string can be parsed as a single noun phrase. Note that this heuristic applies only to simple phrases and would not apply to a phrase like *the house on the hill* which contains two simple phrases. This heuristic is not perfect, because it

is strictly syntactic. For example, in the sentence *The document will reiterate, will* is initially read as part of the noun phrase *The document will.* While this is valid a more robust method would read *will* as a modal verb. Eventually the correct interpretation is made, but in this example heuristic parsing breaks down.

Another of our heuristics, the *left to right* heuristic, causes the parser to build constituents further left in the sentence before those further right. These heuristics were simply implemented as a Lisp subroutine. The routine was passed a list of the possible rules that could be applied at each point in the parse, and returned the rule which should apply.

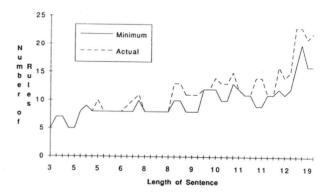

Figure 1: Near-Optimal Heuristic Parses

Figure 1 shows the performance of this simple system on a set of sentences from (Ford, Bresnan & Kaplan 1982). The horizontal axis of Figure 1 shows the length of the sentence, and the vertical axis shows the number of rules applied in parsing the sentence. The dotted line signifies the number of rules that the system applies, and the solid line signifies the minimum number of rules that can be applied to get the correct parse. In general, the minimum number of rules increases linearly with the length of the sentence.

For more than half of the sentences, our system generates the correct parse in the minimum number of rule applications. The system does no worse than 1.5 times the minimum number of sentences needed. All of these unnecessary rule applications are due to the nature of the phrase creation heuristic.

The success of this system is not surprising. Bresnan implemented these heuristics on a top-down system and came up with the appropriate results. It simply shows that these heuristics can be implemented in a bottom-up parser, using a unification-based grammar.

A System for an Open Domain

After completing this simple implementation, we started scaling up our system to a more complex set of sentences. We chose the corpus from the Fourth Message Understanding Competition (MUC-4) (DARPA

1992), a collection of 1600 articles from newspapers and other sources that describe terrorist events which occurred in Latin America during 1989-1991. Here is a typical sentence from this corpus for which our heuristics successfully guide the parse:

> Farabundo Marti National Liberation Front detachments have conducted the largest military operation in the entire history of the Salvadoran conflict in the country's capital.

To see if our simple heursitic parsing system would scale up, we randomly chose a set of 100 sentences from the MUC-4 corpus. Using our simple rule selection heuristics in this test resulted in a miserable failure. Unlike Ford *et al.*'s examples, the MUC-4 sentences tend to be much longer, and contain a much wider variety of syntactic phenomena not encountered in the earlier examples. In fact, not one sentence was completely parsed by the above heuristics; instead the parser had to fall back into general search to arrive at a complete interpretation. It was readily apparent that the few heuristics that we had used would be insufficient to handle all of these new sentences.

Expanding the System

The new system consisted of many parsing heuristics. All heuristics from the earlier system were ported to this system. This included the left to right mechanism, the simple phrase creation heuristic, the minimal attachment heuristic, the syntactic preference heuristic, and the lexical preference heuristic.

We also augmented the system with several new heuristics. The least complex heuristic was the *particle grabbing* heuristic, which is a method to handle compound verbs. For instance, in sentences containing the phrasal verb *blow up*, often the particle *up* is separated from the verb *blow*. Thus, in the sentence *The terrorists will blow the car up*, there is an ambiguity when *up* is encountered as to whether this word should be interpreted as a particle (attached to *blow*) or a preposition (in which case a noun phrase should follow). In this situation, the particle grabbing heuristic prefers to interpret *up* as a particle.

We also added several heuristics for determining when verbs should be interpreted as part of a subordinate clause, as opposed to the main verb of the sentence. For example, if a noun phrase was followed by a comma and a verb, the verb was interpreted as beginning a passive relative clause. For example, in *two soldiers, shot...*, the passive interpretation of *shot* would be preferred. On the other hand, without an explicit marker such as a comma or a relativizer ('who' or 'that'), the active interpretation of the verb was preferred. Similar heuristics were added for other types of clauses, such as infinitive clauses.

In summary the heuristics that were implemented in the extended system were:

- Psychological Parsing Mechanism Heuristics

  1. Left-to-Right Parsing
  2. Delay Attaching a Phrase Until it is Complete

- Syntactic Combination Heuristics

  1. Simple Phrase Creation
  2. Particle Grabbing
  3. Conjunctions of Noun Phrases

- Semantic Syntactic Phrase Combination Heuristics

  1. Create a Pre-Subject
  2. Create a Relative Clause
  3. Create a Sentential Compliment
  4. Create an Infinitival Compliment
  5. Combine a Verb-Phrase with the Subject

- Search Control Heuristics

  1. Combine Large Phrases
  2. Apply a Rule Which Will Complete The Parse

Another heuristic that we added was a search control heuristic. It was only used after standard heuristic parsing broke down. It did not function in a left to right manner, but combined large adjacent phrases. In this context, large phrases are anything that is a simple phrase or larger. This counterbalanced the effects of syntactic constructs that were not explicitly accounted for by the parsing heuristics. This type of heuristic can be very useful in a natural language system, but it should only be used as a last resort; since it is not psychologically valid, it may give the wrong answer among ambiguous interpretations.

Test Results

Figure 2 shows the results of our test on the MUC-4 corpus using our enhanced heuristics. The horizontal axis shows the length of the sentence, and the vertical axis shows the number of rules applied in parsing the sentence. The solid line shows the minimum number of rules needed to generate the correct parse. Our system's performance is broken down into two parts. First, the dotted line represents the number of rules applied when the heuristics succeed in generating a correct parse. On other sentences, the heuristics fail to generate a complete parse, and the system falls back into undirected bottom-up chart parsing. These sentences are represented by the bold dotted line. In these cases, there is still an improvement over parsing without heuristics, because some structure has been built by the heuristics before the system reverts to its undirected processing. The result of a completely undirected parsing (i.e., parsing without our heuristics) is shown by the dashed and dotted line. Note that there is a ceiling on the chart, and this is represented by the top line labeled 500. As sentences get longer, depth-first search can lead to thousands of rules being generated.

The heuristics perform quite well, particularly when they succeed in generating a complete parse. The system with heuristics performs better than without them on all of the sentences. More importantly, when the heuristics succeed, statistical analysis shows that the number of rules applied increases linearly with sentence length. On the 35 successfully parsed sentences, using a weighted R^2 analysis, the best fit polynomial was $4.16 + 2.15x$ (x = sentence length); $R^2 = 0.929$. The ratio is 2.15 the length of the sentence. As in the first system, most of these extra rules are due to the nature of the simple phrase creation heuristic.

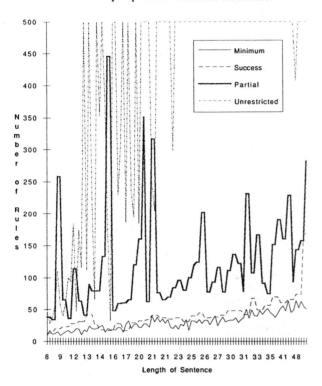

Figure 2: Heuristic Parsing Results from an Open Domain

Even when the heuristics fail, the number of rules applied is significantly less than without heuristics. The reason for this is that the heuristics have built up some partial structure. When this is the correct partial structure, search from this point is much shorter than general search. The heuristics have, in effect, reduced the size of the search space.

Analysis of Test Results

Although our test data shows several successes, it also shows a number of failures. These failures are an improvement upon prior systems, but they do not achieve the desired linear parsing time. There are two reasons for the failures. First, our heuristics still fail at several points, indicating that they are incomplete. Second, many constructs are not accounted for by the heuristics.

Virtually all of the heuristics occasionally fail. For instance, the relative clause heuristic may not complete a relative clause. In the sentence fragment *the two people who were killed in the attack*, the heuristics

guide the parser to find an interpretation in which the relative clause is finished after *killed* and *in the attack* becomes the location of the people. Similarly, the simple phrase creation heuristic occasionally fails; it sometimes incorrectly combines two adjacent noun phrases into one phrase. For instance, in the fragment *alleged terrorists today killed*, *alleged terrorists* is grouped with *today*. This eventually leads to a missing subject. In our current system, this type of failure is particularly harmful, because the phrase combination heuristics depend on the correct simple phrases; all phrase combinations are tried before the original phrases are broken into smaller phrases.

The reason for the failures of these heuristics is their lack of semantic knowledge. Except for the lexical preference heuristic and the filling of verb frames, all of the heuristics we used are purely syntactic. To make them more effective, they must use more semantics. In section 3 We explained how the phrase creation heuristic fails because of its strictly syntactic basis. A given rule is preferred because it is syntactically and semantically the strongest rule. In this preliminary study my heuristics were mostly syntactic.

The largest problem is that several constructs are not handled by the heuristic parser. For instance, only the simplest types of conjunction are handled. This leads to a deterioration in performance when other constructs are encountered. When a conjunctive verb phrase is encountered, the system has no choice but to fall into general search. The solution for this problem is simply encoding more heuristics.

Finally, it must be noted that this test was run on what is still a relatively small domain. The lexicon and the set of grammatical rules is insufficient for a larger sample of sentences, because lexical, syntactic, and semantic ambiguity would all increase. As the system is made more general, its performance will degrade. Occasionally we can fall back on cheap heuristics and general search, but, in the long run, we will need a much broader range of heuristics to be successful.

Conclusion

We have provided evidence that parsing guided by heuristics can be performed on natural language in linear time in the average case. While we found many of the heuristics suggested in the psychological literature to be useful, these heuristics by themselves were inadequate for the range of constructions found in our limited domain. Our work indicates that a complete system would require a great number of heuristics. These include very broad heuristics, such as the left to right heuristic; heuristics which apply to several constructs, such as the lexical preference heuristics; and narrow heuristics, such as particle grabbing. The left to right heuristic is so intimately related to the serial nature of human natural language processing that it could actually be built into the parsing algorithm. On the other hand, the particle grabbing heuristic is so dependent on a given lexical item that a special heuristic may be needed for each case. Although our current set of heuristics is still not adequate to handle all English constructions, those that it does handle are parsed in linear time by our system. We expect that additional heuristics will extend this result to a wider variety of constructions.

Heuristic parsing mechanisms have proven successful in small domains, but in larger domains, many more heuristics will be required. The problem then becomes one of software engineering. How do we encode all of these parsing heuristics, and how do we handle the potential interactions among them?

The need for a useful method of encoding parsing heuristics becomes even more apparent in real domains. In addition to the large variety of syntactic and semantic phenomenon that are encountered in such domains, there is a greater likelihood of encountering ungrammatical texts. From the system's point of view, a sentence may be ungrammatical for two reasons. First, the input may simply be improper English. Second, the grammar that was provided may be insufficient. In either case, there will be a mismatch between the grammar rules and the structure of the input, and in either case, the system will have to use some kind of search techniques to find a reasonable match between grammar and input. Another problem is encountering unknown words. An intelligent parser can aid or solve all of these problems.

A final note must be made on the encoding of preferences in the form of heuristics. If a sentence is not parsed by an NLP system the way humans parse it, it is not parsed correctly. In an ambiguous grammar, it may be that several grammatically valid interpretations can be generated, but if people only generate one, then the NLP system must only generate one. Since the reason for interpreting sentences is to interpret them the way that humans do, our systems must parse like humans. Thus, any biases in interpretation by people must be reflected in search heuristics used in an NLP system.

References

Blank, Glenn D. 1989. A Finite and Real-Time Processor for Natural Language. In *Comm. ACM* 32:10 pp. 1174-1189.

Chomsky, Noam. 1956. Three models for the description of language. In *IRE Trans. on Information Theory* pp. 113-124.

Crain, S. and Steedman, M. 1985. On not being led up the garden path: the use of context by the psychological syntax processor. In Dowty, D., Karttunen, L., and Zwicky, A. (eds.), *Natural Language Parsing: Psychological, Computational, and Theoretical Perspectives.* New York: Cambridge University Press, pp. 320-358.

Defense Advanced Research Projects Agency. 1992. *Proceedings of the Fourth Message Understanding Conference (MUC-4)*, McLean VA, June 1991. San Mateo, CA: Morgan Kaufmann Publishers.

Earley, J. 1970. An efficient context-free parsing algorithm. *Comm. ACM* 13:2 pp. 94-102.

Ford, Marilyn, Joan Bresnan, and Ronald Kaplan. 1982. A competence-based theory of syntactic closure. In *The mental representation of grammatical relations,* ed. by Joan Bresnan. Cambridge, MA: MIT Press.

Frazier, Lyn. and Janet Dean Fodor. 1978. The sausage machine: A new two-stage parsing model. *Cognition,* 6:291-295

Kimball, John P. 1973. Seven principles of surface structure parsing. In natural language. *Cognition,* 2(1):15-47

Lytinen, S. 1992. A unification-based, integrated natural language processing system. *Computers and Mathematics with Applications, 23*(6-9), pp. 403-418.

Marcus, Mitchell P. 1980. *A theory of syntactic recognition for natural language.* Cambridge, MA: MIT Press.

Naur, P. ed. 1963. Revised report on the algorithmic language Algol 60. *Comm. ACM* 6:1 pp. 1-17

Shieber, Stuart M. 1986. *An Introduction to Unification-Based Approaches to Grammar* Stanford, CA: Center for the Study of Language and Information.

Tomita, M. 1987. *Efficient Parsing for Natural Language* Norwell, MA: Kluwer Academic Publishers.

Towards a Reading Coach that Listens:
Automated Detection of Oral Reading Errors

Jack Mostow, Alexander G. Hauptmann, Lin Lawrance Chase, and Steven Roth

Project LISTEN, CMT-UCC 215, Carnegie Mellon University
5000 Forbes Avenue, Pittsburgh, PA 15213-3891
mostow@cs.cmu.edu

Abstract[1]

What skill is more important to teach than reading? Unfortunately, millions of Americans cannot read. Although a large body of educational software exists to help teach reading, its inability to hear the student limits what it can do.

This paper reports a significant step toward using automatic speech recognition to help children learn to read: an implemented system that displays a text, follows as a student reads it aloud, and automatically identifies which words he or she missed. We describe how the system works, and evaluate its performance on a corpus of second graders' oral reading that we have recorded and transcribed.

1. Introduction

Deficiency in reading comprehension has become a critical national problem; workplace illiteracy costs over $225 billion dollars a year (Herrick, 1990) in corporate retraining, industrial accidents, and reduced competitiveness. Although intelligent tutoring systems might help, their inability to see or hear students limits their effectiveness in diagnosing and remediating deficits in comprehension.

In an attempt to address this fundamental limitation, we are building on recent advances in automated speech processing, reading research, and high-speed computing. We have dubbed this effort Project LISTEN (for "Language Instruction that Speech Technology ENables"). This paper reports our initial results.

To place these results in context, imagine how automated speech recognition may eventually be used in an interactive system for assisting oral reading. The system displays text on the screen and listens while the student (a child, illiterate adult, or foreign speaker) reads it aloud. When the student gets stuck or makes a serious mistake, the system intervenes with the sort of assistance a parent or teacher might provide, such as saying the word, giving a hint, or explaining unfamiliar vocabulary. Afterwards, it reviews the passages where the student had difficulty, giving an opportunity to reread them, and providing appropriate feedback.

This paper reports on a scaled-down version of such a system. Along the way it points out some current limitations and directions for future improvement.

2. What Evelyn does (and doesn't)

Our implemented prototype, named Evelyn, displays a page of text on a screen, and listens while someone reads it. While the user is reading, Evelyn dynamically displays what it thinks is the reader's current position in the text, by highlighting the next word to read. This position does not necessarily progress linearly through the text, since the reader may repeat, misread, sound out, insert, or skip words. Due to the nature of the speech recognition process, the display lags behind the reader; it is intended to show us what the system is doing, rather than to be of pedagogical benefit.

When the reader finishes, Evelyn identifies substitutions, deletions, and insertions relative to the original text. Evelyn treats these phenomena as follows:

- **Substitutions:** Evelyn provides contrastive feedback. To focus the reader's attention, it visually highlights the misread passage of the text on the screen. It plays back what the reader said, and then speaks the same passage correctly using synthesized or pre-digitized speech.

- **Deletions:** Evelyn provides corrective feedback. It highlights and speaks the text it thinks the reader skipped. For this case there is nothing to play back.

- **Insertions:** Evelyn deliberately ignores them. Insertions are usually hesitations, sounding out, self-corrections, repetitions, or interjections, rather than genuine misreadings of the text.

Notice that Evelyn uses "missed words" -- words in the text that were not read correctly at least once -- as its criterion for what to give feedback on. This criterion is based on the pedagogical assumption that whether the reader eventually succeeded in reading the word matters more than whether he or she got it right on the first try. Although word misses are a reasonable first-order approximation, finer-grained criteria will be needed to

[1]This research was supported in part by the National Science Foundation under Grant Number MDR-9154059; in part by the Defense Advanced Research Projects Agency, DoD, through DARPA Order 5167, monitored by the Air Force Avionics Laboratory under contract N00039-85-C-0163; in part by a grant from the Microelectronics and Computer Technology Corporation (MCC); in part by the Rutgers Center for Computer Aids to Industrial Productivity, an Advanced Technology Center of the New Jersey Commission on Science and Technology, at Rutgers University; and in part by a Howard Hughes Doctoral Fellowship to the third author from the Hughes Research Laboratory, where she is a Member of Technical Staff. The views and conclusions contained in this document are those of the authors and should not be interpreted as representing the official policies, either expressed or implied, of the sponsors or of the United States Government.

trigger an expanded range of pedagogically useful interventions.

We make no claims for the pedagogical efficacy of Evelyn's feedback. Rather, its purpose is to show us what the speech analysis is doing, and to test the feasibility of features that might later support various interventions. To identify more effective forms of feedback to implement, we are currently performing "Wizard of Oz" studies in which a human experimenter controls the display by hand to simulate possible system behavior -- including interrupting the reader to provide assistance in the context where it is needed.

3. Relation to previous work

There have been some uses of automated speech recognition in language learning. For example, the Indiana Speech Training Aid (Watson et al, 1989) helps hearing-impaired people improve their speech, by comparing their pronunciation of problem words to that of fluent speakers. (Newton, 1990) describes a commercial product that uses automated speech recognition for a similar purpose in foreign language training. However, these systems are based on isolated word recognition technology, which requires as input a single word or phrase chosen from a fixed vocabulary. The techniques used in isolated word recognition do not handle the continuous speech that occurs in reading connected text.

Some more recent work has used continuous speech recognition. (Bernstein et al, 1990) automatically estimated the intelligibility of foreign speakers based on how well their readings of a few sentences matched models trained on native speakers. A system developed at MIT uses a connected speech recognizer to follow the reading of a known text, providing verbal feedback via DECtalk (McCandless, 1992, Phillips et al, 1992). However, systematic evaluation of its accuracy has been limited by the lack of a corpus of disfluent reading. Instead, fluent utterances were used to simulate disfluent reading by pretending that one word in each utterance should have been some other word selected randomly from the lexicon -- a methodology that admittedly fails to capture important characteristics of disfluent reading (McCandless, 1992, p. 12).

There has been more use of speech in the system-to-student direction, thanks to the availability of synthesized or digitized speech. In particular, previous research has documented the benefits of making speech feedback on demand available to children with reading difficulties (Wise et al, 1989, Roth & Beck, 1987, McConkie & Zola, 1987, Reitsma, 1988), and this capability is now available in some commercial educational software (e.g., (Discis, 1991)). Pronouncing a word on demand supports students' reading comprehension -- both directly, by relaxing the bottleneck caused by their deficits in word recognition, and indirectly, by freeing them to devote more of their attentional resources to comprehension processes. Although such assistance can therefore be very useful, its utility is limited by the students' ability and willingness to ask for help when they need it; struggling readers often misread words without realizing it (McConkie, 1990).

Alternatives to the approach reported here include using an eyetracker or a user-controlled pointing device to track the reader's position in the text. These alternatives might indeed facilitate text tracking, but at best they could only indicate what the reader was trying to read -- not whether the outcome was successful.

Our project differs from previous efforts by drawing on the best available technology, in the form of Bellcore's ORATOR[TM] speech synthesizer[2] (Spiegel, 1992) and CMU's Sphinx-II speech recognizer (Huang et al, 1993). ORATOR produces high-quality speech, and is especially good at pronouncing names. Sphinx-II represents the current state of the art in speaker-independent connected speech recognizers, insofar as it was ranked at the top in DARPA's November 1992 evaluations of such systems. However, analysis of oral reading differs from speech recognition in an important way. In speech recognition, the problem is to reconstruct from the speech signal what sequence of words the speaker said. In contrast, the problem addressed in this paper is to figure out, given the text, where the speaker departed from it.

4. How Evelyn works

In this section we explain how the Evelyn system works. Since Evelyn is built on top of the Sphinx-II speech recognizer, we start with a minimal description of Sphinx-II to distinguish what it already provides from what Evelyn contributes. (For a more detailed description of Sphinx-II, please see (Huang et al, 1993).) Then we explain how we use the Sphinx-II recognizer within the Evelyn system -- that is, how we generate Sphinx-II's knowledge sources from a given text, and how we process Sphinx-II's output.

4.1. Speech recognition with the Sphinx-II system

Sphinx-II's input consists of digitized speech in the form of 16,000 16-bit samples per second from a microphone via an analog-to-digital converter. Sphinx-II's output consists of a segmentation of the input signal into a string of words, noises, and silences.

Sphinx-II uses three primary knowledge sources: a database of phonetic Hidden Markov Models, a dictionary of pronunciations, and a language model of word pair transition probabilities. The Hidden Markov Models use weighted transitions between a series of states to specify the acoustic probability of a given phone or noise. The pronunciation dictionary represents the pronunciation of each word as a sequence of phonemes. The language model specifies the linguistic probability that the second word in each pair will follow the first.

Sphinx-II operates as follows. The digitized speech is compressed to produce four 16-bit numbers every 10 msecs. This stream of values is matched against the Hidden Markov Models to compute the acoustic probability of each phone at each point in the speech signal. Hypothesized phones are concatenated into words

---

[2]ORATOR is a registered trademark of Bellcore.

using the pronunciation dictionary, and hypothesized words are concatenated into word strings using the language model. Beam search is used to pursue the most likely hypotheses, while unlikely paths are pruned. At the end of the utterance, Sphinx-II outputs the highest-rated word string as its best guess.

4.2. How Evelyn applies Sphinx-II to oral reading

In order to use Sphinx-II, we must supply the phonetic, lexical, and linguistic knowledge it requires to recognize oral reading of a given text.

Evelyn's phonetic knowledge currently consists of Sphinx-II's standard 7000 Hidden Markov Models trained from 7200 utterances produced by 84 adult speakers (42 male and 42 female). Sphinx-II uses separate models for male and female speakers. The results reported here used the female models, which we assume work better for children's higher-pitched speech.

Evelyn's lexical knowledge is created by a combination of lookup and computation. First the given ASCII text is segmented into individual words, and the words are sequentially numbered in order to distinguish multiple occurrences of the same word. The phonetic pronunciation of each word is then looked up in a pronunciation lexicon of about 32,000 words. However, some words may not be found in this lexicon, such as idiosyncratic words or proper names. Pronunciations for these missing words are generated by the ORATOR speech synthesizer. Finally, the pronunciation lexicon is augmented with individual phonemes to allow recognition of non-word phonetic events that occur when readers sound out difficult words.

Evelyn's linguistic knowledge consists of a probabilistic word pair transition grammar. This grammar is generated automatically from the numbered word sequence. It consists of pairs of (numbered) words and the likelihood of a transition from one word to the next. There are currently three kinds of transitions in our language model. The highest-probability transition is from one word to the next one in the text, which models correct reading. Second, a transition to an arbitrary other word in the text models a repetition or skip. Third, a transition to a phoneme models a non-word acoustic event.

The constraint provided by this grammar is critical to the accuracy of the speech recognition. If the grammar weights transitions to correct words too strongly, then word misses will not be detected when they occur. However, if it weights them too weakly, recognition accuracy for correct words will be low. To represent a particular tradeoff, Evelyn uses a linear combination of the three kinds of transitions.

As Figure 4-1 shows, the recognized string is Sphinx-II's best guess as to what the reader actually said into the microphone, given the phonetic, lexical, and linguistic knowledge provided. Evelyn compares this string against the original text, and segments the input utterance into correctly spoken words from the text, substitutions, deletions, and insertions. Based on this analysis, Evelyn provides the feedback described earlier in Section 2.

4.3. Text following

Although Evelyn provides corrective feedback only after the reader finishes the page, in the future we would like to interrupt with help when appropriate. Evelyn does provide one prerequisite capability for making such interruptions, namely text following. At present this capability is used merely to provide a visible dynamic indication of where Evelyn thinks the reader is. However, experience with this capability has exposed some challenging technical issues.

In order to track the reader's position in the text, Evelyn obtains partial recognition results from Sphinx-II four times a second in the form of the currently highest rated word string. However, these partial results are subject to change. For example, suppose the word "alter" was spoken. The first partial hypothesis may be the determiner "a". After more speech has been processed, the word "all" might be a candidate. It is not until the whole spoken word has been processed that Sphinx-II will return the correct hypothesis. Moreover, if the subsequent word is "candle", the hypothesis may be revised to reflect the high probability of the phrase "altar candle". In contrast, the phrase "alter ego" would require no modification of the earlier hypothesis of "alter".

The point of this discussion is that one cannot merely look at the last word in the current partial recognition result for a reliable estimate. Our initial text following algorithm, which did just that, caused the cursor that indicates the current location in the text to skip around wildly as it tried to follow the reader. The problem is that in order to select reliably among competing hypotheses, the recognizer needs to know the context that follows. This **"hindsight dependency"** suggests that for some time to come, a real-time speech recognizer will have to lag behind the speaker by a word or two to reduce inaccuracy -- *no matter how fast the machine it runs on.* Thus pedagogical interruptions triggered by recognition will face a tradeoff between interrupting promptly and waiting for more reliable recognition results.

To attack this problem, we developed a more sophisticated heuristic text-following algorithm. It exploits the expectation that the reader will step through the text in a sequential fashion, and yet allows for reading errors without considering short-lived spurious candidates. The revised algorithm has a certain amount of inertia. As it digests partial results, it refrains from moving the cursor until at least n (currently $n=2$) consecutive words in the text have been recognized. This heuristic gives us reasonable confidence that a portion of the text has been read correctly and that recognition is stable. If Sphinx-II recognizes a word other than the expected next one, this method prevents the cursor from immediately jumping to a new location in the text, since it is likely to represent either a misreading by the reader or a misrecognition by the recognizer. However, when the reader really does skip to another place in the text, the method allows the cursor to catch up, after a short delay during which consecutive words from the new location in the text are recognized.

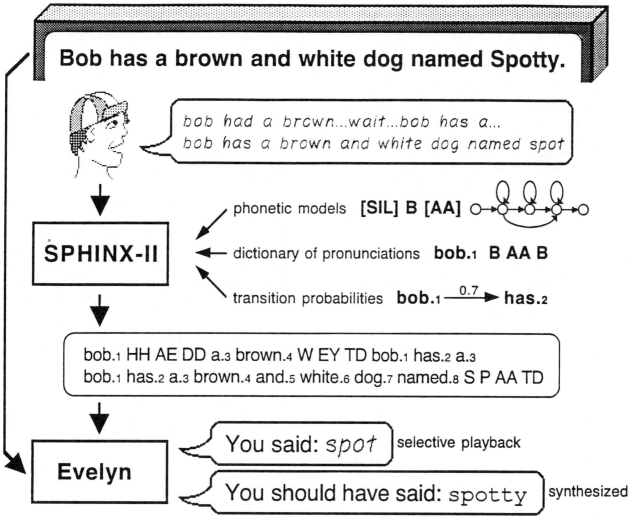

Bob has a brown and white dog named Spotty.

*bob had a brown...wait...bob has a...
bob has a brown and white dog named spot*

phonetic models **[SIL] B [AA]**

SPHINX-II ← dictionary of pronunciations **bob.₁ B AA B**

transition probabilities **bob.₁ $\xrightarrow{0.7}$ has.₂**

bob.₁ HH AE DD a.₃ brown.₄ W EY TD bob.₁ has.₂ a.₃
bob.₁ has.₂ a.₃ brown.₄ and.₅ white.₆ dog.₇ named.₈ S P AA TD

Evelyn

You said: *spot* selective playback

You should have said: spotty synthesized

In this example, the reader self-corrected "had" to "has", but misread "Spotty" as "spot".
Sphinx-II's actual recognition was much less accurate than the ideal result shown.

Figure 4-1: Example of how Evelyn should detect a word miss

5. How well Evelyn works

Since Evelyn is only a precursor of an educational system, a true pedagogical evaluation of it would be premature. However, we did measure its performance in a way that would help guide our work. In particular, we needed a suitable evaluation scheme to help us develop, assess, and improve the language models described in Section 4.2 by allowing us to test alternative language models against the same data. We now describe the data we collected for this purpose, the methodology we used to measure performance, and the results we obtained.

5.1. Corpus of oral reading

To evaluate Evelyn's performance, we collected and transcribed a corpus of oral reading, which we are continuing to expand. This paper is based on readings by second graders at two schools in Pennsylvania. Of the 27 speakers, 17 are from Turner School, a public school in

Wilkinsburg with a predominantly minority student body. The other 10 are from the Winchester Thurston School, a private school in Pittsburgh.

We made the recordings at the schools, using special-purpose software running on a NeXT workstation to display the texts and digitally record the speech. We used a Sennheiser close-talking headset microphone to reduce the amount of non-task information in our acoustic signal, but did not by any means eliminate it. Our corpus contains many sounds, both speech and non-speech, that are not examples of a reader decoding a text. (Teachers and children are talking in the hallway, doors are slamming, and readers are shuffling and bumping the microphone with their chins.)

We selected the reading materials from the Spache graded reading tests (Spache, 1981), since their levels of difficulty are well calibrated and their accompanying comprehension probes have been carefully validated. To accommodate a large display font, we split each text into two or three one-page passages, advancing to each "page" when the child finished the previous one, and administering a comprehension probe when the child completed the text. To obtain examples of reading errors, we chose texts for each subject somewhat above his or her independent reading level, which we estimated by administering Spache's word list test. We wanted text challenging enough to cause errors, but easy enough to produce complete readings.

The evaluation corpus used for this paper consists of 99 spoken passages, totalling 4624 text words. The passages average about 47 words in length and 45 seconds in duration. The pace -- about one text word per second -- reflects the slow reading speed typical of early readers. The number of actual spoken words is higher, due to repetitions and insertions.

We carefully transcribed each spoken passage to capture such phenomena as hesitations, "sounding out" behaviors, restarts, mispronunciations, substitutions, deletions, insertions, and background noises. The transcripts contain correctly spoken words, phonetic transcriptions of non-words, and noise symbols such as [breath].

5.2. Accuracy of recognition and missed-word detection

Using the original texts, transcripts, and recognizer outputs over the corpus, we measured both "raw" recognition accuracy and missed-word detection accuracy.

To compute recognition accuracy, we compared the string of symbols output by the recognizer against the string of symbols obtained from the transcript. We used a standard dynamic programming algorithm to align symbols from these two strings and count substitutions, deletions, and insertions. These "raw" scores appear mediocre: 4.2% substitutions, 23.9% deletions, and 0.5% insertions. Thus 28.1% of the transcribed symbols are misrecognized, and the total error rate, including insertions, is 28.6%.

However, since Evelyn's purpose is to detect missed words, a more useful criterion in this domain is the accuracy of this detection. (Recall that a word that is misread or "sounded out", but eventually produced correctly, is not considered a missed word.) To measure the *accuracy of missed-word detection*, we counted the words in the text that Evelyn misclassified, either as correct, or as missed.

Measuring the accuracy of missed-word detection requires a three-way comparison between the original text (what the reader was supposed to say), a transcript of the utterance (what the reader actually said), and the recognizer's output (what the recognizer thinks the reader said). First, the actual word misses in the corpus are identified by comparing the transcripts against the original text, using the alignment routine described earlier. Then the hypothesized misses are identified by comparing the recognizer output against the original text, using the same alignment routine. Finally we check the hypothesized misses against the actual ones.

Table 5-1: Accuracy of Missed-Word Detection

Reader Disfluency	Evelyn Coverage	Evelyn Precision
2.5%	63.6%	60.9%

Disfluency = (missed words) / (words in text)

Coverage = (misses detected) / (words missed)

Precision = (misses detected) / (missed-word reports)

Table 5-1 summarizes Evelyn's ability to detect word misses in our current corpus: how frequently word misses occurred, what fraction of them Evelyn reported, and what fraction of such reports were true. We computed these three numbers separately for each reading, and then averaged them across the readings, so as to avoid counting the longer, more difficult texts more heavily than the shorter, easier ones. (This methodology also served to discount some "outlier" runs in which our language model caused the recognizer to get lost without recovering.) The first number measures reading disfluency as the percentage of words actually missed by the reader, which varied from zero to 20%, but averaged only 2.5%. That is, the average reader missed only about one word in 40. The second number shows that Evelyn detected these misses almost two thirds of the time -- probably enough to be pedagogically useful. The third number reflects a moderate rate of false alarms. For each properly reported miss, Evelyn often classified a correctly read word as a miss, but a majority of such reports were true.

It is instructive to compare these numbers against a "strawman" algorithm that classifies 2.5% of the words in the text as missed, but chooses them randomly. That is, how well can we do if all we know is the average reader's disfluency? Since the strawman chooses these words independently of whether they are actual misses, its expected coverage and precision will also each be 2.5%. How well does Evelyn do by comparison? Its coverage and precision are each about twenty-five times better. Thus the additional information contributed by speech recognition, although imperfect, is nevertheless significant.

These results represent the best of the few language models we have tested so far on the corpus. Further improvements in accuracy may require devising better language models of oral reading and training new phonetic models on a large number of young readers.

Besides accuracy, we are concerned with speed, since timely intervention will require keeping up with the reader. For our language model and corpus, the recognizer already runs consistently in between real time and two times real time on a 100+ MIPS DEC Alpha workstation. A modest increase in processing power due to faster hardware should therefore produce the speed required for real time response.

6. Conclusion

The principal contribution of this work is an **implemented system for a new task** -- automatically following the reading of a known text so as to detect an important class of oral reading errors (namely, missed words). Its **model of oral reading** constitutes an initial solution to the problem of constraining a speech recognizer's search when the text is known but the reading is disfluent. We identified **hindsight dependency** as causing an intrinsic tradeoff between accuracy and immediacy for recognition-driven interrupts, and developed a **heuristic text-following algorithm** based on this tradeoff.

To establish an initial baseline for performance at this new task, we **evaluated the performance** of Evelyn and its underlying model. We defined **performance evaluation criteria** that are more appropriate for the task of detecting word misses than is the traditional definition of accuracy in speech recognition. To evaluate our algorithms, we recorded and transcribed a **corpus of oral reading** by second graders of varying fluency. This corpus is a contribution in itself, since the speech recognition community has not previously had access to a corpus of disfluent oral reading. It is essential to our continued efforts to improve on the baseline defined by Evelyn.

The social significance of our work, if it succeeds, will be its impact on illiteracy: even a one percent reduction in illiteracy would save the nation over two billion dollars each year. But in the long run, the broader scientific significance of this work may be its role in helping to open a powerful new channel between student and computer based on two-way speech communication.

Acknowledgements

We thank Marcel Just, Leslie Thyberg, and Margaret McKeown for their expertise on reading; Matthew Kane, Cindy Neelan, Bob Weide, Adam Swift, Nanci Miller, and Lee Ann Galasso for their various essential contributions; the entire CMU Speech Group for their advice on speech in general and Sphinx in particular; Murray Spiegel and Bellcore for use of their ORATOR speech synthesis system; CTB Macmillan/McGraw-Hill for permission to use copyrighted reading materials from George Spache's *Diagnostic Reading Scales*; the pupils we recorded at Irving School in Highland Park, NJ, Winchester Thurston School in Pittsburgh, PA, and Turner School in Wilkinsburg, PA, and the educators who facilitated it; and the many friends who provided advice, encouragement, and assistance to get Project LISTEN started.

References

J. Bernstein, M. Cohen, H. Murveit, D. Rtischev, and M. Weintraub. (1990). Automatic evaluation and training in English pronunciation. *International Conference on Speech and Language Processing (ICSLP-90)*. Kobe, Japan.

Discis Knowledge Research Inc. *DISCIS Books*. 45 Sheppard Ave. E, Suite 802, Toronto, Canada M2N 5W9. Commercial implementation of Computer Aided Reading for the MacIntosh computer.

E. Herrick. (1990). *Literacy Questions and Answers.* Pamphlet. P. O. 81826, Lincoln, NE 68501: Contact Center, Inc.

X. D. Huang, F. Alleva, H. W. Hon, M. Y. Hwang, K. F. Lee, and R. Rosenfeld. (1993). The SPHINX-II speech recognition system: An overview. *Computer Speech and Language*, (in press).

M. McCandless. (May 1992). *Word Rejection for a Literacy Tutor*. S.B. Thesis. Cambridge, MA: MIT Department of Electrical and Computer Engineering.

G. W. McConkie. (November 1990). Electronic Vocabulary Assistance Facilitates Reading Comprehension: Computer Aided Reading. Unpublished manuscript.

G. W. McConkie and D. Zola. (1987). Two examples of computer-based research on reading: Eye movement tracking and computer aided reading. In D. Reinking (Eds.), *Computers and Reading: Issues for Theory and Practice*. New York: Teachers College Press.

F. Newton. (1990). Foreign language training. *Speakeasy*, Vol. *1*(2). Internal publication distributed to customers by Scott Instruments, 1111 Willow Springs Drive, Denton, TX 76205.

M. Phillips, M. McCandless, and V. Zue. (September 1992). *Literacy Tutor: An Interactive Reading Aid* (Tech. Rep.). Spoken Language Systems Group, 545 Technology Square, NE43-601, Cambridge, MA 02139: MIT Laboratory for Computer Science.

P. Reitsma. (1988). Reading practice for beginners: Effects of guided reading, reading-while-listening, and independent reading with computer-based speech feedback. *Reading Research Quarterly*, *23*(2), 219-235.

S. F. Roth and I. L. Beck. (Spring 1987). Theoretical and Instructional Implications of the Assessment of Two Microcomputer Programs. *Reading Research Quarterly*, *22*(2), 197-218.

G. D. Spache. (1981). *Diagnostic Reading Scales*. Del Monte Research Park, Monterey, CA 93940: CTB Macmillan/McGraw-Hill.

M. F. Spiegel. (January 1992). *The Orator System User's Manual - Release 10*. Morristown, NJ: Bell Communications Research Labs,

C. S. Watson, D. Reed, D. Kewley-Port, and D. Maki. (1989). The Indiana Speech Training Aid (ISTRA) I: Comparisons between human and computer-based evaluation of speech quality. *Journal of Speech and Hearing Research*, *32*, 245-251.

B. Wise, R. Olson, M. Anstett, L. Andrews, M. Terjak, V. Schneider, J. Kostuch, and L. Kriho. (1989). Implementing a long-term computerized remedial reading program with synthetic speech feedback: Hardware, software, and real-world issues. *Behavior Research Methods, Instruments, & Computers*, *21*, 173-180.

Nonmonotonic
Logic

Minimal belief and negation as failure: A feasible approach

Antje Beringer and **Torsten Schaub**

FG Intellektik, TH Darmstadt, Alexanderstraße 10,

D-6100 Darmstadt, Germany

{antje,torsten}@intellektik.informatik.th-darmstadt.de

Abstract

Lifschitz introduced a logic of minimal belief and negation as failure, called MBNF, in order to provide a theory of epistemic queries to nonmonotonic databases. We present a feasible subsystem of MBNF which can be translated into a logic built on first order logic and negation as failure, called FONF. We give a semantics for FONF along with an extended connection calculus. In particular, we demonstrate that the obtained system is still more expressive than other approaches.

Introduction

Lifschitz [1991; 1992][1] introduced a logic of minimal belief and negation as failure, MBNF, in order to provide a theory of epistemic queries to nonmonotonic databases. This approach deals with self-knowledge and ignorance as well as default information.

From one perspective, MBNF relies on concepts developed by Levesque [1984] and Reiter [1990] for database query evaluation. In these approaches, databases are treated as first order theories, whereas queries may also contain an epistemic modal operator. In addition to query-answering *from* a database, this modal operator allows for dealing with queries *about* the database. From another perspective, Lifschitz' approach relies on the system GK developed by Lin and Shoham [1990], which uses two epistemic operators accounting for the notion of "minimal belief" and "negation as failure". Thus, MBNF can be seen as an extension of GK, which identifies their epistemic operator for minimal belief with the ones used by Levesque and Reiter.

MBNF is very expressive. Apart from asking what a database knows, it permits expressing default knowledge and axiomatizing the closed world assumption [Reiter, 1977] and integrity constraints [Kowalski, 1978]. Furthermore, Lifschitz [1992] established close relationships to logic programming, default logic [Reiter, 1980] and circumscription [McCarthy, 1980].

However, Lifschitz' approach is purely semantical and mainly intended to provide a unifying framework

---

[1]In what follows, we rely on the more recent approach.

for several nonmonotonic formalisms. Consequently, there is no proof theory yet. We address this gap by identifying a subsystem of MBNF and translating it into a feasible system by relying on the fact that in many cases negation as failure is expressive enough to account for the different modalities in MBNF. The resulting system is called FONF (first order logic with negation as failure). We demonstrate that it provides a versatile approach to epistemic query answering for nonmonotonic databases, which are first order theories enriched by beliefs and default statements. Furthermore, we give a clear semantics of FONF along with an extended connection calculus for FONF. Also, we show that FONF is still more expressive than PROLOG and a competing approach [Reiter, 1990].

Minimal belief and negation as failure

MBNF deals with an extended first order language including two independent modal operators B and not. B is of epistemic nature and represents the notion of "minimal belief", whereas not captures the notion of "negation as failure". A theory T, or *database*, is a set of sentences. α, β denote sentences; F, G denote formulas. A *positive* formula (or theory) does not contain not. An *objective* one contains neither B nor not.

For instance, given an ornithological database, we can formalize the default that "we believe that birds fly, unless there is evidence to the contrary", as

$$\forall x (\mathsf{B}\mathit{bird}(x) \land \mathsf{not}\neg\mathit{fly}(x) \rightarrow \mathsf{B}\mathit{fly}(x)).$$

Now, the idea is to interpret our beliefs by a set of "possible worlds", ie. $\mathsf{B}\mathit{bird}(\mathit{Tweety})$ is true iff Tweety is a bird in all possible worlds and $\mathsf{not}\neg\mathit{fly}(\mathit{Tweety})$ is true iff Tweety flies in some possible world.

Formally, the truth of a formula is defined wrt a triple $(w, W_\mathsf{B}, W_\mathsf{not})$, where w is a first order interpretation, or simply *world*, representing "the real world", W_B is a set of "possible worlds" defining the meaning of beliefs formalized with B, and W_not serves for the same purpose in case of not. w, W_B and W_not share the same universe, but W_B and W_not do not necessarily include w. Intuitively, this means that beliefs need not be consistent with reality. Thus, Tweety may be believed to fly without actually flying.

Then, the truth of a formula F in MBNF is defined for the language of MBNF extended by names for all elements of the common universe.[2]

1. For atomic F, $(w, W_\mathsf{B}, W_\mathsf{not}) \models_\mathsf{MBNF} F$ iff $w \models F$.

2. $(w, W_\mathsf{B}, W_\mathsf{not}) \models_\mathsf{MBNF} \neg F$ iff $(w, W_\mathsf{B}, W_\mathsf{not}) \not\models_\mathsf{MBNF} F$.

3. $(w, W_\mathsf{B}, W_\mathsf{not}) \models_\mathsf{MBNF} F \wedge G$ iff
$(w, W_\mathsf{B}, W_\mathsf{not}) \models_\mathsf{MBNF} F$ and $(w, W_\mathsf{B}, W_\mathsf{not}) \models_\mathsf{MBNF} G$.

4. $(w, W_\mathsf{B}, W_\mathsf{not}) \models_\mathsf{MBNF} \exists X F(X)$ iff
for some name ξ, $(w, W_\mathsf{B}, W_\mathsf{not}) \models_\mathsf{MBNF} F(\xi)$.

5. $(w, W_\mathsf{B}, W_\mathsf{not}) \models_\mathsf{MBNF} \mathsf{B} F$ iff
$\forall w' \in W_\mathsf{B} : (w', W_\mathsf{B}, W_\mathsf{not}) \models_\mathsf{MBNF} F$.

6. $(w, W_\mathsf{B}, W_\mathsf{not}) \models_\mathsf{MBNF} \mathsf{not} F$ iff
$\exists w' \in W_\mathsf{not} : (w', W_\mathsf{B}, W_\mathsf{not}) \not\models_\mathsf{MBNF} F$.

The definition of a model in MBNF is restricted to the case where $W_\mathsf{B} = W_\mathsf{not}$. Therefore, Lifschitz introduces structures (w, W), where w is a world and W a set of worlds corresponding to W_B and W_not. In particular, he is only interested in $<$-maximal structures, where $(w, W) < (w', W')$ iff $W \subset W'$, since they express *"the idea of 'minimal belief': The larger the set of 'possible worlds' is, the fewer propositions are believed"* [Lifschitz, 1992]. Formally, a model in MBNF is defined by means of a fixed-point operator $\Gamma(T, W)$, which, given a theory T and a set of worlds W, denotes the set of all $<$-maximal structures (w, W') such that T is true in (w, W', W). Then, a structure (w, W) is an MBNF-*model* of T iff $(w, W) \in \Gamma(T, W)$.

In MBNF, theoremhood is only defined for positive formulas: A positive formula F is entailed by T, $T \models_\mathsf{MBNF} F$, iff F is true in all models of T. Thus, query answering is also restricted to positive queries.[3] Notice that models of T need not be models of F. For instance, $\mathsf{B}p$ is true in all models of $\mathsf{B}(p \wedge q)$ and, hence, $\mathsf{B}(p \wedge q) \models_\mathsf{MBNF} \mathsf{B}p$. However, no MBNF-model of $\mathsf{B}(p \wedge q)$ is an MBNF-model of $\mathsf{B}p$, since none of them is $<$-maximal in satisfying $\mathsf{B}p$. So, we have to distinguish carefully between formulas in a given theory and formulas being posed as queries to that theory.

FONF: A feasible approach to MBNF

We develop a feasible approach to MBNF by identifying a large subclass of MBNF, which allows for equivalent formalizations in first order logic plus negation as failure. This is the case whenever a theory T is complete for believed sentences, ie. whenever we have either $T \models_\mathsf{MBNF} \mathsf{B}\alpha$ or $T \models_\mathsf{MBNF} \neg \mathsf{B}\alpha$ for each α. In this case, first order logic with negation as failure is strong enough to capture also the notion of "minimal belief".

We thus identify a feasible subclass of MBNF for which we provide a translation into FONF, a first order logic with an additional negation as failure operator not. This translation preserves the above notion

of completeness in the sense, that an MBNF-theory is complete for believed sentences iff the corresponding FONF-theory is.

As mentioned above, we have to distinguish between queries and sentences in a database. Accordingly, we define the following feasible subset of MBNF for queries and databases separately:

- A *feasible query* is an MBNF-formula q satisfying:

  1. q is positive.
  2. Each scope of an $\exists$ or $\neg$ in q is either purely subjective or purely objective.
  3. If the scope of a $\neg$ in q is subjective, then it must not contain free variables.

- A *feasible database* (FDB) is an MBNF-theory containing only *rules* of the form

  $$F_1 \wedge \ldots \wedge F_m \wedge \mathsf{not}\, F_{m+1} \wedge \ldots \wedge \mathsf{not}\, F_n \rightarrow F_{n+1}$$

  where for $n, m \geq 0$ each F_i $(i = 1, \ldots, n+1)$ is

  - either a disjunction-free MBNF-formula where the scope of $\neg$ is minimal and objective,[4]
  - or of the form $\mathsf{B}(G_1 \vee \ldots \vee G_k)$ where the G_i $(i = 1, \ldots, k)$ are objective formulas.

  F_{n+1} may also be an unrestricted objective formula.

These restrictions are not as strong as it seems at first sight: Even default rules, integrity constraints, and closed world axioms can be formalized within FDBs.

In [Lifschitz, 1992] an MBNF-formula F is translated into a first order formula F° to relate MBNF- and first order entailment: A second sort of so-called "world variables" is added to the first order language; appending one of them to each function and predicate symbol (as an additional argument), and introducing a unary predicate B whose argument is such a world variable. A world variables denotes the world in which a certain predicate or function symbol is interpreted and B accounts for the "accessibility" of a world from the actual world. However, the translation $^\circ$ is insufficient for creating a deduction method for MBNF. First, it deals only with positive formulas and, therefore, discards a substantial half of MBNF: The modal operator not. Second, only first order entailment carries over to MBNF but not vice versa. That is, roughly speaking, even for positive T and α, $T^\circ \models \alpha^\circ$ implies $T \models_\mathsf{MBNF} \alpha$ but not vice versa. In this sense, the translation $^\circ$ is sound but incomplete.

Our approach addresses this shortcoming by translating feasible queries and databases into FONF. This has the following advantages: First, we deal with a much larger subset of MBNF. In particular, we can draw nonmonotonic conclusions by expressing B and not by a first order predicate *bel* and a negation as failure operator not. Second, our translation is truth-preserving. That is, for feasible queries and databases, FONF-entailment carries over to MBNF *and* vice versa.

---

[2] $\models$ without any subscript denotes first order entailment.

[3] As regards MBNF-queries, we rely on this restriction throughout the paper.

[4] Observe that one cannot distribute $\neg$ over B.

In this sense, the translation is sound and complete for feasible queries and databases. In the sequel, we give this translation and prove that it is truth-preserving.

Now, FONF-*formulas* are all formulas that can be built using the connectives and construction rules of first order logic and the unary operator not. The only constraint on FONF-formulas is that variables must not occur free in the scope of not.

The translation $\star$ of feasible MBNF-queries and -databases into FONF-formulas is developed in analogy to [Lifschitz, 1992]. We use the predicate *bel* to translate the MBNF-operator B. Then, a feasible MBNF-formula F, ie. either a feasible query or a formula belonging to a FDB, is translated into the FONF-formula $F^\star$ in the following way.

- If F is objective, then

1. $F^\star$ is obtained by appending the world variable V to each function and predicate symbol in F.

- else (ie. if F is non-objective)

2. $(\neg F)^\star = $ not $F^\star$.
3. $(F \circ G)^\star = F^\star \circ G^\star$ for $\circ = \wedge, \vee$ or $\rightarrow$.
4. $(\mathcal{Q}\, F)^\star = \mathcal{Q}\, F^\star$ for $\mathcal{Q} = \exists$ or $\forall$.
5. $(\mathsf{B}F)^\star = \forall V\, (bel(V) \rightarrow F^\star)$.
6. $($not $F)^\star = $ not$(\mathsf{B}F)^\star$.

Observe that feasible queries must not contain not, so that then Condition 6 does not apply. The translation $\star$ depends on the notion of feasible formulas which obey syntactical restrictions. Thus, we have to account for all connectives. As an example, translating $\neg\alpha \vee \neg\mathsf{B}\beta$ (α, β objective) into FONF yields $\neg\alpha^\star \vee$ not$(\forall V\, (bel(V) \rightarrow \beta^\star)$, which shows that the combination $\neg\mathsf{B}$ is translated using negation as failure, namely not, whereas pure negation $\neg$ is kept.

In order to show that this translation is truth-preserving, we look at the semantics of FONF and define satisfiability wrt a set of worlds W:

$$W \models_{\text{FONF}} \alpha \quad \text{iff} \quad \forall w \in W : (w, W) \models_{\text{FONF}} \alpha,$$

where the truth value of a FONF-formula wrt a structure (w, W) is defined in the following way:

- If F is objective, then

1. $(w, W) \models_{\text{FONF}} F$ iff $w \models F$.

- else (ie. if F is non-objective)

2. $(w, W) \models_{\text{FONF}} \neg F$ iff $(w, W) \not\models_{\text{FONF}} F$.
3. $(w, W) \models_{\text{FONF}} F \wedge G$ iff
$\qquad (w, W) \models_{\text{FONF}} F$ and $(w, W) \models_{\text{FONF}} G$.
4. $(w, W) \models_{\text{FONF}}$ not$F$ iff $\exists w' \in W : (w', W) \not\models_{\text{FONF}} F$.

FONF can be seen as an extension of extended logic programs [Gelfond and Lifschitz, 1990]. Accordingly, FONF-models extend the semantics of extended logic programs to the first order case: For a FONF-theory T, and a set of worlds W, we develop a set of objective formulas T^W from T by

1. deleting all rules, where not α occurs in the body while $W \models_{\text{FONF}} \alpha$ holds.

2. deleting all remaining subformulas of the form not α.

Then, W is a FONF-*model* for T if it consists of all first order models of T^W. A sentence α is entailed by a FONF-theory T, $T \models_{\text{FONF}} \alpha$, iff α is true in all FONF-models of T. Then, we obtain the equivalence between query-answering in MBNF and FONF for $FDBs$.

Theorem 1 *For feasible* MBNF-*databases* T *and feasible* MBNF-*queries* α: $T \models_{\text{MBNF}} \alpha$ *iff* $T^\star \models_{\text{FONF}} \alpha^\star$.

As a corollary, we get that the translation $\star$ preserves completeness for believed sentences in the above sense. The translation proposed in [Lifschitz, 1992] satisfies only one half of the above result since it only provides completeness for "monotonically answerable queries". Moreover, Lifschitz deals with a more restricted fragment of MBNF, which excludes, for example, the use of negation as failure for database sentences.

A connection calculus for FONF

We develop a calculus for FONF based on the connection method [Bibel, 1987], an affirmative method for proving the validity of a formula in disjunctive normal form (DNF). These formulas are displayed two-dimensionally in the form of *matrices*. A matrix is a set of sets of literals. Each element of a matrix represents a *clause* of a formula's DNF. In order to show that a sentence α is entailed by a sentence T, we have to check whether $\neg T \vee \alpha$ is valid. In the connection method this is accomplished by path checking: A *path* through a matrix is a set of literals, one from each clause. A *connection* is an unordered pair of literals with the same predicate symbol, but different signs. A connection is *complementary* if both literals are identical except for their sign. Now, a formula, like $\neg T \vee \alpha$, is valid iff each path through its matrix contains a complementary connection under a global substitution.

First, we extend the definition of matrices and literals. An *NM-Literal* is an expression not M, where M is an *NM*-matrix. An *NM-matrix* is a matrix containing normal and *NM*-literals. Although these structures seem to be rather complex, we only deal with normal form matrices, since *NM*-literals are treated in a special way during the deduction process.

The definition of classical normal form matrices relies on the DNF of formulas. Here, we deal with formulas in *disjunctive* FONF-*normal form* (FONF-DNF) by treating subformulas like not α as atoms while transforming formulas into DNF. Then these α's are transformed recursively into FONF-DNF and so forth. An *NM*-matrix M_F represents a quantifier-free FONF-formula F in FONF-DNF as follows.

1. If F is a literal then $M_F = \{\{F\}\}$.
2. If $F = $ not G then $M_F = \{\{$not $M_G\}\}$.
3. If $F = F_1 \wedge \ldots \wedge F_n$ then $M_F = \{\bigcup_{i=1}^{n} M_{F_i}\}$.

4. If $F = F_1 \vee \ldots \vee F_n$ then $M_F = \bigcup_{i=1}^{n} M_{F_i}$.

For instance, $p(X) \vee (q(a) \wedge \text{not } (r(Y) \wedge q(Y) \vee p(a)))$ has the following matrix representation:

$$\begin{bmatrix} p(X) & & q(a) \\ & \text{not} & \begin{bmatrix} r(Y) & p(a) \\ q(Y) & \end{bmatrix} \end{bmatrix}$$

In order to define a nonmonotonic notion of complementarity, we introduce so-called *adjunct matrices*. They are used for resolving the complex structures in *NM*-matrices during the deduction process. Given an *NM*-matrix $M = \{C_1, \ldots, C_n\}$ where $C_n = \{L_1, \ldots, L_m, \text{not } N\}$ the adjunct matrix M_N is defined as $M_N = (M \setminus C_n) \cup N$, or two-dimensionally:

$$\text{M} \qquad\qquad \text{M}_N$$

$$\begin{bmatrix} \vdots & & \vdots & & L_1 \\ C_1 & \cdots & C_{n-1} & & \vdots \\ \vdots & & \vdots & \text{not} & [\text{N}] \end{bmatrix} \qquad \begin{bmatrix} \vdots & & \vdots & \\ C_1 & \cdots & C_{n-1} & \text{N} \\ \vdots & & \vdots & \end{bmatrix}$$

An *NM*-matrix is *NM-complementary* if each path through the matrix is *NM*-complementary. A path p is *NM*-complementary if

- p contains a connection $\{K, L\}$ which is complementary under unification or

- p contains an *NM*-literal not N with N being an *NM*-matrix. If the adjunct matrix M_N is not *NM*-complementary, then p is *NM*-complementary.

The deduction algorithm relies on the standard connection method, except that if a path contains an *NM*-literal then the same deduction algorithm is started recursively with the corresponding adjunct matrix. Let M be an *NM*-matrix and let $\mathcal{P}^M$ be the set of all paths through M. Then the *NM*-complementarity of M is checked by checking all paths in $\mathcal{P}^M$ for *NM*-complementarity. This is accomplished by means of the procedure nmc in the following informal way for a set of paths $\mathcal{P}'$ and a matrix M'.

nmc$(\mathcal{P}', M')$

- If $\mathcal{P}' = \emptyset$, then nmc$(\mathcal{P}', M')$="yes"

- else choose $p \in \mathcal{P}'$.

  - If p is classically complementary with connection $\{K\sigma, L\sigma\}$ and unifier σ, then nmc$(\mathcal{P}', M') = $ nmc$((\mathcal{P}' - \{p \mid \{K, L\} \in p\})\sigma, M')$

  - else
    * if there exists an *NM*-literal not $N \in p$ such that nmc$(\mathcal{P}^{M_N}, M_N)$="no",
      then nmc$(\mathcal{P}', M')$=nmc$(\mathcal{P}' - \{p \mid \text{not } N \in p\}, M')$
    * else nmc$(\mathcal{P}', M')$="no"

Initially, nmc is called with $\mathcal{P}^M$ and M, namely nmc$(\mathcal{P}^M, M)$. Then, we obtain the following result.

Proposition 1 *If the algorithm terminates with "yes", then the NM-matrix is NM-complementary.*

So far, we have only considered quantifier-free FONF-formulas in FONF-DNF. But how can an arbitrary FONF-formula F be treated within this method? First of all, F must be transformed into FONF-*Skolem normal form*, analogously to [Bibel, 1987]. We denote the result of FONF-skolemization of a formula F by $\mathcal{S}(F)$.

Now, FONF-formulas can be represented as matrices. If we have a FONF-database, we require that rules containing free variables in the scope of not (which is actually not allowed in FONF) are replaced by the set of their ground instances before skolemization.

However, the above algorithm has its limitations due to its simplicity. First, in MBNF and FONF, it is necessary to distinguish between sentences occurring in the database and those serving as queries. Representing a database together with a query as an *NM*-matrix removes this distinction. Second, the above algorithm cannot deal with FONF-theories possessing multiple FONF-models. This requires a separate algorithmic treatment of alternative FONF-models.

We address this shortcoming by slightly restricting the definition of feasible queries and databases instead of providing a much more complicated algorithm. Thus, we introduce *determinate* queries and databases.[5] Determinate queries are feasible MBNF-queries in DNF which are either objective or consist only of one non-objective disjunct. Determinate databases are *FDBs* which do not contain circular sets of rules, like $\{\text{not } p \rightarrow Bq, \text{ not } q \rightarrow Bp\}$, because only such circular sets cause multiple models in FONF. This restriction is not as serious as it might seem at first sight: First, non-objective disjunctive queries can be posed by querying the single disjuncts separately. Second, we doubt that we loose much expressiveness by forbidding circular rules. So, if we consider this kind of databases and queries, we can use the nonmonotonic connection method for query-answering:

Proposition 2 *For determinate FONF-theories T and FONF-sentences α: $T \models_{\text{FONF}} \alpha$ iff the NM-matrix of $\mathcal{S}(\neg T \vee \alpha)$ is NM-complementary.*

Together with Theorem 1, we obtain the following.

Theorem 2 *For determinate MBNF-databases T and determinate MBNF-queries α: $T \models_{\text{MBNF}} \alpha$ iff the NM-matrix of $\mathcal{S}(\neg T^\star \vee \alpha^\star)$ is NM-complementary.*

Hence, we obtain a deduction method for a quite large subset of MBNF: Given a determinate MBNF-database T and -query α, we check whether $T \models_{\text{MBNF}} \alpha$ holds by

1. translating T into $T^\star$ and α into $\alpha^\star$,

2. replacing free variables with all constants occurring in the database,

3. skolemizing $\neg T^\star \vee \alpha^\star$ yielding $\mathcal{S}(\neg T^\star \vee \alpha^\star)$,

4. testing the resulting matrix for *NM*-complementarity.

---

[5]This expression will also be used for the corresponding FONF-queries and -databases.

Finally, let us consider an example illustrating our approach. Consider the following MBNF-database T:

$$B(teaches(anne, bio) \lor teaches(sue, bio))$$
$$not\ teaches(X, bio) \to \neg\ teaches(X, bio)$$

which we write in short notation as

$$B(t(a, b) \lor t(s, b)) \land (not\ t(X, b) \to \neg t(X, b)).$$

Recall that the second conjunct is considered as an abbreviation for the set of its ground instances. Consider the following query:

Is it true that Anne doesn't teach biology?

This query, say α, is formalized in MBNF as $\neg t(a, b)$. Notice that T and α constitute determinate MBNF-expressions. Now, we have to verify whether $T \models_{\text{MBNF}} \alpha$ holds. According to the closed world axiom given by $not\ t(X, b) \to \neg t(X, b)$, saying that a person does not teach biology unless proven otherwise, we expect a positive answer.

Following the four steps above, we first translate T and α into FONF and obtain the FONF-theory $T^\star$

$$\forall V\ bel(V) \to t(a, b, V) \lor t(s, b, V)$$
$$not\ [\forall V\ bel(V) \to t(X, b, V)] \to \neg t(X, b, V)$$

along with the query $\alpha^\star = \neg t(a, b, V)$. Then, the theory is negated yielding $\neg T^\star$. After replacing X by the constants a, s and b[6] in $\neg T^\star$, we obtain $S(\neg T^\star \lor \alpha^\star)$ by FONF-skolemization which is (with Skolem constants w_i $(i = 1, 2, 3)$)

$$bel(V) \land \neg t(a, b, V) \land \neg t(s, b, V)$$
$$not\ [\neg bel(w_2) \lor t(a, b, w_2)] \land t(a, b, w_1)$$
$$not\ [\neg bel(w_3) \lor t(s, b, w_3)] \land t(s, b, w_1)$$
$$\neg t(a, b, w_1).$$

This FONF-formula has the following matrix representation (if we ignore the drawn line)

$$\begin{bmatrix} bel(V) & not\ N_1 & not\ N_2 & \neg t(a, b, w_1) \\ \neg t(a, b, V) & t(a, b, w_1) & t(s, b, w_1) & \\ \neg t(s, b, V) & & & \end{bmatrix}$$

with the submatrices $N_1 = [\neg bel(w_2)\quad t(a, b, w_2)]$ and $N_2 = [\neg bel(w_3)\quad t(s, b, w_3)]$.

It remains to be checked whether this matrix is *NM*-complementary in order to prove $T \models_{\text{MBNF}} \alpha$. The first connection starting from the query $\neg t(a, b, w_1)$ is shown by the drawn line. It remains to be tested, if all paths through the *NM*-literal $not\ N_1$ are *NM*-complementary. So, the adjunct matrix has to be built yielding the following matrix (with N_2 as above), which must not be *NM*-complementary for a successful proof.

$$\begin{bmatrix} bel(V) & \neg bel(w_2) & t(a, b, w_2) & not\ N_2 & \neg t(a, b, w_1) \\ \neg t(a, b, V) & & & t(s, b, w_1) & \\ \neg t(s, b, V) & & & & \end{bmatrix}$$

[6]For simplicity, we omit the last case in this example, as it obviously does not contribute to the proof.

During the proof for the above adjunct matrix a copy of the first clause has to be generated. We get the substitution $\sigma = \{V_1\backslash w_1, V_2\backslash w_2\}$, where V_1 occurs in the first copy and V_2 in the second one. The resulting matrix contains the (non-complementary) path

$$\{\neg t(a, b, w_1),\quad \neg t(s, b, w_2),\quad \neg bel(w_2),$$
$$t(a, b, w_2),\quad t(s, b, w_1),\quad \neg t(a, b, w_1)\}.$$

The first two literals stem from the two copies of the first clause of the adjunct matrix. The four others belong to the remaining clauses of the adjunct matrix.

Since this path through the adjunct matrix is not complementary, the *NM*-literal $not\ N_1$ in the original matrix is *NM*-complementary. Therefore, all paths through the original matrix are *NM*-complementary. Accordingly, we have proven that $T \models_{\text{MBNF}} \alpha$ holds and thus that Anne doesn't teach biology.

In order to illustrate the difference between queries to and about the database in presence of the closed world assumption (CWA), consider the query, say β,

Is it known that Anne doesn't teach biology?

Now, we expect a negative answer, since the used formalization of the CWA only affects objective formulas. It avoids merging propositions about the world (like objective formulas in the database) and propositions about the database, which causes inconsistencies when using the "conventional" CWA [Reiter, 1977] in the presence of incomplete knowledge.

β is formalized in MBNF as $B\neg t(a, b)$ yielding the skolemized FONF-formula $\neg bel(w_4) \lor \neg t(a, b, w_4)$. Treating β and the above formula T according to the four aforementioned steps results in the following matrix with submatrices N_1 and N_2 as defined above:

$$\begin{bmatrix} bel(V) & not\ N_1 & not\ N_2 & \neg bel(w_4) & \neg t(a, b, w_4) \\ \neg t(a, b, V) & t(a, b, w_1) & t(s, b, w_1) & & \\ \neg t(s, b, V) & & & & \end{bmatrix}$$

Looking at the three paths without *NM*-literals, it can be easily seen that at least one of them will never be complementary (regardless of how V is instantiated). Consequently, the matrix is not *NM*-complementary, which tells us that β is not an MBNF-consequence of T. That is, even though we were able to derive that Anne does not teach biology, we cannot derive that it is *known* that Anne does not teach biology. This is because the used closed world axioms merely affect what is derivable and not what is known. However, observe that the opposite query, namely $\neg B\neg t(a, b)$ is answered positively. Certainly, we could obtain different answers by using different closed world axioms.

The above algorithm has been implemented using a PROLOG implementation of the connection method. The program takes *NM*-matrices and checks whether they are *NM*-complementary. It consists only of five PROLOG-clauses. Interestingly, the first four clauses constitute a full first order theorem prover, and merely the fifth clause deals with negation as failure. This extremely easy way of implementation is a benefit of the restriction to determinate queries and -databases.

Conclusion

MBNF [Lifschitz, 1992] is very expressive and thus very intractable. Therefore, we have presented a feasible approach to minimal belief and negation as failure by relying on the fact that in many cases negation as failure is expressive enough to capture additionally the (nonmonotonic) notion of minimal belief. We have identified a substantial subsystem of MBNF: Feasible databases along with feasible queries. This subsystem allows for a truth-preserving translation into FONF, a first order logic with negation as failure. However, feasibility has its costs. For instance, FONF does not allow for "quantifying-in" not. Also, we have given a semantics of FONF by extending the semantics of extended logic programs [Gelfond and Lifschitz, 1990].

We have developed an extended connection calculus for FONF, which has been implemented in PROLOG. To our knowledge, this constitutes the first connection calculus integrating negation as failure. We wanted to keep our calculus along with its algorithm as simple as possible, so that it can be easily adopted by existing implementations of the connection method, like SETHEO [Letz et al., 1992]. The preservation of simplicity has resulted in the restriction to determinate theories, which possess only single FONF-models. This restriction is comparable with the one found in extended logic programming, where one restricts oneself to well-behaved programs with only one model.

As a result, we can compute determinate queries to determinate databases in MBNF. This subset of MBNF is still expressive enough for many purposes: Apart from asking what a database knows, determinate queries and databases allow for expressing default rules, axiomatizing the closed world assumption and integrity constraints. Also, it seems that the restriction to determinate queries and databases can be dropped in the presence of a more sophisticated algorithm treating multiple FONF-models separately.

Moreover, our approach is still more expressive than others: First, FONF is more expressive than PROLOG: Since it is build on top of a first order logic, it allows for integrating disjunctions and existential quantification. Second, Reiter [1990] has proposed another approach, in which databases are treated as first order theories, whereas queries may include an epistemic modal operator. As shown in [Lifschitz, 1992], this is equivalent to testing whether $BT \models_{MBNF} BF$ holds for objective theories T and positive formulas F of MBNF. Obviously, Reiter's approach is also subsumed by determinate queries and databases, so that we can use our approach to implement his system as well.

Although we cannot account for MBNF in its entirety, our approach still deals with a very expressive and, hence, substantial subset of MBNF. Moreover, from the perspective of conventional theorem proving, our translation has shown how the epistemic facet of negation as failure can be integrated into automated theorem provers. To this end, it is obviously possible to implement FONF by means of other deduction methods, like resolution. In particular, it remains future work to compare resolution-based approaches to negation as failure to the approach presented here.

Acknowledgements

We thank S. Brüning, M. Lindner, A. Rothschild, S. Schaub, and M. Thielscher for useful comments on earlier drafts of this paper. This work was supported by *DFG, MPS (HO 1294/3-1)* and by *BMfT, TASSO (ITW 8900 C2)*.

References

Bibel, W. 1987. *Automated Theorem Proving*, Vieweg, 2nd edition.

Gelfond, M. and Lifschitz, V. 1990. Logic programs with classical negation. In Proc. *International Conference on Logic Programming*. 579–597.

Kowalski, R. 1978. Logic for data description. In Gallaire, H. and Minker, J., eds., In Proc. *Logic and Databases*, Plenum. 77–103.

Letz, R.; Bayerl, S.; Schumann, J.; and Bibel, W. 1992. SETHEO: A high-performance theorem prover. *Journal on Automated Reasoning*.

Levesque, H. 1984. Foundations of a functional approach to knowledge representation. *Artificial Intelligence* 23:155–212.

Lifschitz, V. 1991. Nonmonotonic databases and epistemic queries. In Myopoulos, J. and Reiter, R., eds., In Proc. *International Joint Conference on Artificial Intelligence*, Morgan Kaufmann 381–386.

Lifschitz, V. 1992. Minimal belief and negation as failure. Submitted.

Lin, F. and Shoham, Y. 1990. Epistemic semantics for fixed–points nonmonotonic logics. In Parikh, Rohit, ed., In Proc. *Theoretical Aspects of Reasoning about Knowledge*. 111–120.

McCarthy, J. 1980. Circumscription — a form of nonmonotonic reasoning. *Artificial Intelligence* 13(1–2):27–39.

Reiter, R. 1977. On closed world data bases. In Gallaire, H. and Nicolas, J.-M., eds., In Proc. *Logic and Databases*, Plenum. 119–140.

Reiter, R. 1980. A logic for default reasoning. *Artificial Intelligence* 13(1–2):81–132.

Reiter, R. 1990. On asking what a database knows. In Lloyd, J. W., ed., *Computational Logic*, Springer. 96–113.

A context-based framework for default logics

Philippe Besnard
IRISA, Campus de Beaulieu
F-35042 Rennes Cédex, France
besnard@irisa.fr

Torsten Schaub
TH Darmstadt, Alexanderstraße 10
D-6100 Darmstadt, Germany
torsten@intellektik.informatik.th-darmstadt.de

Abstract

We present a new context-based approach to default logic, called contextual default logic. The approach extends the notion of a default rule and supplies each extension with a context. Contextual default logic allows for embedding all existing variants of default logic along with more traditional approaches like the closed world assumption. A key advantage of contextual default logic is that it provides a syntactical instrument for comparing existing default logics in a unified setting. In particular, it reveals that existing default logics mainly differ in the way they deal with an explicit or implicit underlying context.

Introduction

Default logic has become the prime candidate for formalizing consistency-based default reasoning since its introduction in [Reiter,1980]. Since then, several variants of default logic have been proposed, eg. [Lukaszewicz,1988; Brewka,1991; Delgrande *et al.*,1992]. Each such variant rectified purportedly counterintuitive features of the original approach. However, the evolution of default logic is diverging. Although it has resulted in diverse variants sharing many interesting properties, it has altered the notion of a default rule. In particular, most of the aforementioned variants deal with a different notion of consistency. For instance, Reiter's default logic employs some sort of local consistency, whereas others employ some sort of global consistency.

Up to now, we are then compelled to choose among one of the respective variants whenever we want to represent default knowledge. At first sight, this seems to be a good solution, since we may select one of the variants depending on its properties. However, our choice fixes the notion of a default rule. More freedom would be desirable: We should not be forced to commit ourselves to just a single variant of default logic, because all facets of default logic are worth considering. Instead, an integrated approach is proposed below, which is based on a very general notion of a default rule.

Thus, the primary purpose of this work is to integrate the different variants of default logic in a more general but uniform system, which combines the expressiveness of the various default logics. The basic idea is twofold. First, we supply each default extension (ie. a set of default conclusions) with an underlying context. Second, we extend the notion of a default rule in order to allow for a variety of different application conditions which arise naturally from the distinction between the initial set of facts, the default extension at hand, and its context.

Notions of consistency in default logics

Classical default logic was defined by Reiter in [1980] as a formal account of reasoning in the absence of complete information. It is based on first-order logic, whose sentences are hereafter simply referred to as formulas (instead of closed formulas). In default logics, default knowledge is incorporated by means of so-called *default rules*. A default rule is any expression of the form $\frac{\alpha\,:\,\beta}{\gamma}$, where α, β and γ are formulas. α is called the *prerequisite*, β the *justification*, and γ the *consequent* of the default rule. Accordingly, a *default theory* (D, W) consists of a set of formulas W and a set of default rules D. Informally, an *extension* of the initial set of facts W is defined as the set of all formulas derivable from W by applying classical inference rules and all applicable default rules. Usually, a default rule $\frac{\alpha\,:\,\beta}{\gamma}$ is applicable, if its prerequisite α is derivable and its justification β is *consistent* in a certain way.

In all "conventional" default logics, the prerequisite α of a default rule $\frac{\alpha\,:\,\beta}{\gamma}$ is checked wrt an extension E by requiring $\alpha \in E$. However, all of the aforementioned variants differ in the way they account for the consistency of the justification β. For instance, in classical default logic [Reiter,1980] the consistency of the justification β is checked wrt the extension E by $\neg\beta \notin E$, whereas in constrained default logic [Delgrande *et al.*,1992] the same is done wrt a set of constraints C, containing the extension E, by checking $\neg\beta \notin C$.

In default logics, there are thus two extreme notions of consistency: Individual and joint consistency. The former one is employed in classical default logic, whereas the latter can be found in cumulative and constrained default logic. Individual consistency requires that no justification of an applying default rule is contradictory with a given extension, whereas joint consistency stipulates that all justifications of all applying default rules are jointly consistent with the extension at hand. As an example, consider the default theory

$$\left(\left\{ \frac{:B}{C}, \frac{:\neg B}{D} \right\}, \emptyset \right). \tag{1}$$

In classical default logic, this default theory has one extension $Th(\{C, D\})$. Both default rules apply, although they have contradictory justifications. This is because each justification is separately consistent with $Th(\{C, D\})$. In this case, the extension is somehow embedded in a "context" which gathers two incompatible "subcontexts": One containing the extension and the justification of the first default rule, $Th(\{C, D, B\})$, and another one containing the justification of the second default rule, $Th(\{C, D, \neg B\})$.

This is different from the approach taken in constrained default logic. There, we obtain two constrained extensions. We obtain one extension $Th(\{C\})$ which is supplied with a set of constraints $Th(\{C, B\})$ consisting of the justification B and the consequent C of the first default rule. We also obtain another extension $Th(\{D\})$ whose constraints $Th(\{D, \neg B\})$ contain the justification $\neg B$ and the consequent D of the second default rule. Each set of constraints contains the extension and additionally all justifications of all applying default rules. Thus, each extension is embedded in a "context" given by the set of constraints.

In order to combine the variants of default logic, we have to compromise the notions of individual and joint consistency. In particular, we have to deal with joint consistency requirements in the presence of inconsistent individual consistency requirements. Therefore, we allow for "contexts" containing contradictory formulas, like B and $\neg B$ as in the previous example in classical default logic, without containing all possible formulas. Thus, we admit contexts which are not deductively closed. In the previous example, the extension $Th(\{C, D\})$ will then have the context $Th(\{C, D, B\}) \cup Th(\{C, D, \neg B\})$, which is composed of two incompatible subcontexts. A useful notion is then that of *pointwise closure* $Th_S(T)$.

Definition 1 *Let T and S be sets of formulas. The pointwise closure of T under S is defined as $Th_S(T) = \bigcup_{\phi \in T} Th(S \cup \{\phi\})$.*

If S is a singleton set $\{\varphi\}$, we simply write $Th_\varphi(T)$ instead of $Th_{\{\varphi\}}(T)$. Given two sets of formulas T and S, we say that T is *pointwisely closed under S* iff $T = Th_S(T)$. We simply say that T is pointwisely closed whenever $T = Th_\top(T)$ for any tautology $\top$.

Observe that the aforementioned context can now be represented as the pointwise closure of $\{B, \neg B\}$ under $\{C, D\}$, namely $Th_{\{C,D\}}(\{B, \neg B\})$.

Contextual default logic

We introduce a new approach to default logic by extending the notions of default rules and extensions. The resulting system is called *contextual default logic*. We consider three sets of formulas: A set of facts W, an extension E, and a certain *context* C such that $W \subseteq E \subseteq C$. The set of formulas C is somehow established from the facts, the default conclusions (ie. the consequences of the applied default rules), as well as all underlying consistency assumptions (ie. the justifications of all applied default rules). That is, our approach trivially captures the above application conditions for "conventional" default rules, eg. $\alpha \in E$ and $\neg\beta \notin E$ in the case of classical default logic.

This approach allows for even more ways of forming application conditions of default rules. Consider a formula φ and three consistent, deductively closed sets of formulas W, E, and C such that $W \subseteq E \subseteq C$. Six more or less strong application conditions are obtained which can be ordered from left to right by decreasing strength; whereby $>$ is read as "implies":
$$\varphi \in W > \varphi \in E > \varphi \in C > \neg\varphi \notin C > \neg\varphi \notin E > \neg\varphi \notin W$$
We can think of W as a deductively closed set of facts, E as a default extension of W, and C as the above mentioned context for E. Then, the first condition $\varphi \in W$ stands for first-order derivability from the facts W. The second condition $\varphi \in E$ stands for derivability from W using first-order logic and certain default rules. This is used in conventional default logics as the test for the prerequisite of a default rule. The third condition, $\varphi \in C$, is the strangest one. It expresses "membership in a context of reasoning". The last three conditions are consistency conditions. The fourth condition $\neg\varphi \notin C$ corresponds to the consistency condition used in constrained default logic, the fifth one $\neg\varphi \notin E$ is used in classical default logic. Finally, the last condition $\neg\varphi \notin W$ is the one used for the closed world assumption [Reiter,1977], where it is restricted to ground negative literals.

This variety of application conditions motivates an extended notion of a default rule.

Definition 2 *A contextual default rule δ is an expression of the form*
$$\frac{\alpha_W \mid \alpha_E \mid \alpha_C : \beta_C \mid \beta_E \mid \beta_W}{\gamma}$$
where α_W, α_E, α_C, β_C, β_E, β_W, and γ are formulas. α_W, α_E, α_C are called the W-, E-, and C-prerequisites, also noted $Prereq_W(\delta)$, $Prereq_E(\delta)$, $Prereq_C(\delta)$, β_C, β_E, β_W are called the C-, E-, and W-justifications, also noted $Justif_C(\delta)$, $Justif_E(\delta)$, $Justif_W(\delta)$, and γ is called the consequent, also noted $Conseq(\delta)$. [1]

The six antecedents of a contextual default rule are to be treated along the above intuitions. Accordingly, a contextual default theory is a pair (D, W), where D is a set of contextual default rules and W is a deductively

---

[1] These projections extend to sets of default rules in the obvious way (eg. $Justif_E(\Delta) = \bigcup_{\delta \in \Delta} \{Justif_E(\delta)\}$).

closed[2] set of formulas.

Now, a *contextual extension* is to be a pair (E, C), where E is a deductively closed set of formulas and C is a pointwisely closed set of formulas, as follows.

Definition 3 *Let* (D, W) *be a contextual default theory. For any pair of sets of formulas* (T, S) *let* $\nabla(T, S)$ *be the pair of smallest sets of formulas* (T', S') *such that* $W \subseteq T' \subseteq S'$ *and the following condition holds:*

For any $\frac{\alpha_W \mid \alpha_E \mid \alpha_C \,:\, \beta_C \mid \beta_E \mid \beta_W}{\gamma} \in D$, *if*

   1. $\alpha_W \in W$ *2.* $\alpha_E \in T'$ *3.* $\alpha_C \in S'$

   4. $\neg\beta_C \notin S$ *5.* $\neg\beta_E \notin T$ *6.* $\neg\beta_W \notin W$

then   *7.* $Th_\gamma(T') \subseteq T'$

        8. $Th_{\beta_E}(T') \subseteq S'$

        9. $Th_{\beta_C}(S') \subseteq S'$

A pair of sets of formulas (E, C) *is a contextual extension of* (D, W) *iff* $\nabla(E, C) = (E, C)$.

Notice that the operator ∇ is in fact parameterized by (D, W). Furthermore, observe that Conditions *1-6* basically correspond to those given above.

Intuitively, we start from (W, W) (ie. we take the facts W as our initial version of E and C) and try to apply a contextual default rule by checking conditions *1-6* and, if we are successful, we enforce *7-9*, ie. we add γ to our current version of E and we add $\phi \wedge \beta_E$ and $\varphi \wedge \beta_C$ to our current version of C, for each ϕ in the final E and for each φ in the final C.

Consider the contextual default theory

$$\left(\left\{ \frac{A \mid\mid : \mid B \mid}{C}, \frac{\mid C \mid : E \mid \neg B}{D} \right\}, Th(A) \right)$$

along with its only contextual extension (E, C), where

$E \;=\; Th(\{A, C, D\})$

$C \;=\; Th(\{A, C, D, E, B\}) \cup Th(\{A, C, D, E, \neg B\})$.

E represents the extension and C provides its context. This contextual extension is generated from the facts by applying first the first contextual default rule and then the second one.

Now, $\frac{A \mid\mid : \mid B \mid}{C}$ applies if its prerequisite A is monotonically derivable (ie. if A is derivable without contextual default rules according to Condition 1 in Definition 3) and if its E-justification B is consistent with the extension E (according to Condition 5). In other words, B has to be individually consistent. This being the case, we derive C. That is, C is nonmonotonically derivable by means of the first contextual default rule (cf. Condition 2). Thus, C establishes the prerequisite of the second contextual default rule, $\frac{\mid C \mid : E \mid \neg B}{D}$. In order to derive D, we have to verify the consistency of the two justifications E and $\neg$B, ie. E has to be jointly consistent (ie. according to Condition 4, it has to be consistent with the context C), whereas $\neg$B has to be individually consistent (ie. according to Condition 5, it has to be consistent with the extension E). Since this is fulfilled, we obtain the above contextual extension satisfying our consistency requirements.

---

[2]This is no real restriction, but it simplifies matters.

Observe that the context C is composed of two incompatible subcontexts, $Th(\{A, C, D, E, B\})$ and $Th(\{A, C, D, E, \neg B\})$. All such subcontexts contain a common "kernel" given by the extension and all jointly consistent C-justifications, here $Th(\{A, C, D\})$ and E. The E-justifications, B and $\neg$B, create different subcontexts. Why is the joint consistency of E not affected by these two incompatible formulas? This is because in our approach joint consistency only requires the consistency of a justification with each subcontext in turn, whereas individual consistency requires the consistency of a justification with at least one such subcontext.

Embedding default logics

We show that classical [Reiter,1980], justified [Łukaszewicz,1988] and constrained default logic [Delgrande *et al.*,1992] are embedded in contextual default logic. Since cumulative default logic [Brewka,1991] is closely connected to constrained default logic, neglecting representational issues, we obtain that variant too.

As mentioned in the introductory section, *classical default logic* employs a sort of local consistency (which we also called individual consistency), as can be seen from the following definition of *classical extensions*.

Definition 4 *Let* (D, W) *be a default theory. For any set of formulas* T *let* $\Gamma(T)$ *be the smallest set of formulas* T' *such that*

  1. $W \subseteq T'$,   *2.* $Th(T') = T'$,

  3. For any $\frac{\alpha \,:\, \beta}{\gamma} \in D$, *if* $\alpha \in T'$ *and* $\neg\beta \notin T$ *then* $\gamma \in T'$.

A set of formulas E *is a classical extension of* (D, W) *iff* $\Gamma(E) = E$.

In order to have a comprehensive example throughout the text, we extend default theory (1) by introducing an additional default rule:

$$\left(\left\{ \frac{: \neg B}{C}, \frac{: \neg B}{D}, \frac{: \neg C \wedge \neg D}{E} \right\}, \emptyset \right) \qquad (2)$$

This default theory still has one classical extension $Th(\{C, D\})$. As shown above, the first two default rules apply, although they have contradictory justifications, and then block the third default rule.

In order to relate classical with contextual default logic, let us identify default theories in classical default logic with contextual default theories as follows.

Definition 5 *Let* (D, W) *be a default theory. Define*

$$\Phi_{DL}(D, W) = \left(\left\{ \frac{\mid \alpha \mid : \mid \beta \mid}{\gamma} \;\middle|\; \frac{\alpha \,:\, \beta}{\gamma} \in D \right\}, Th(W) \right).$$

Then, classical default logic corresponds to this fragment of contextual default logic.

Theorem 1 *Let* (D, W) *be a default theory and let* E *be a set of formulas. Then,* E *is a classical extension of* (D, W) *iff* (E, C) *is a contextual extension of* $\Phi_{DL}(D, W)$ *for some* C.

Given a classical extension E, the context C is the pointwise closure of the justifications of the generating[3] default rules under E.

---

[3]Informally, the generating default rules are those which apply in view of E.

Consider the contextual counterpart of default theory (2):

$$\left(\left\{\frac{||:|B|}{C}, \frac{||:|\neg B|}{D}, \frac{||:|\neg C \wedge \neg D|}{E}\right\}, Th(\emptyset)\right)$$

We obtain one contextual extension $(Th(\{C, D\}), Th(\{C, D, B\}) \cup Th(\{C, D, \neg B\}))$ whose extension corresponds to the classical extension of default theory (2). The common kernel of the two subcontexts of the context is given by the extension. In addition, the first subcontext, $Th(\{C, D, B\})$, contains the E-justification of the first contextual default rule, whereas the second one, $Th(\{C, D, \neg B\})$, contains additionally the E-justification of the second contextual default rule. As in classical default logic, the third contextual default rule is blocked by the other ones.

Further evidence for the generality of our approach is that it also captures *justified default logic* [Lukaszewicz,1988]. In this approach, the justifications of the applying default rules are attached to extensions in order to strengthen the applicability condition of default rules. A *justified extension* is defined as follows.

Definition 6 *Let (D, W) be a default theory. For any pair of sets of formulas (T, S) let $\Psi(T, S)$ be the pair of smallest sets of formulas T', S' such that*

1. $W \subseteq T'$, 2. $Th(T') = T'$,
3. *For any $\frac{\alpha : \beta}{\gamma} \in D$, if $\alpha \in T'$ and $\forall \eta \in S \cup \{\beta\}$. $T \cup \{\gamma\} \cup \{\eta\} \nvdash \bot$ then $\gamma \in T'$ and $\beta \in S'$.*

A pair of sets of formulas (E, J) is a justified extension of (D, W) iff $\Psi(E, J) = (E, J)$.

Let us return to default theory (2). This default theory has two justified extensions: $(Th(\{C, D\}), \{B, \neg B\})$ and $(Th(\{E\}), \{\neg C \wedge \neg D\})$. The first one corresponds to the extension obtained in classical default logic. However, it is supplied with a set of justifications, $\{B, \neg B\}$ (which, incidentally, is inconsistent). The second extension stems from applying the third default rule whose justification blocks the two other default rules by contradicting their consequents.

Now, let us identify default theories in justified default logic with contextual default theories:

Definition 7 *Let (D, W) be a default theory. Define*
$$\Phi_{JDL}(D, W) = \left(\left\{\frac{|\alpha|:\gamma|\beta \wedge \gamma|}{\gamma} \mid \frac{\alpha:\beta}{\gamma} \in D\right\}, Th(W)\right).$$

This leads to the following correspondence.

Theorem 2 *Let (D, W) be a default theory and let E be a set of formulas. Then, (E, J) is a justified extension of (D, W) for some J iff (E, C) is a contextual extension of $\Phi_{JDL}(D, W)$ for some C.*

J consists of the justifications of the generating[4] default rules for E, whereas C is given by the pointwise closure of the same set of justifications under E.

It is interesting to observe how the relatively complicated consistency check in justified default logic is accomplished in contextual default logic. For a justified extension (E, J) and a default rule $\frac{\alpha:\beta}{\gamma}$ the condition is

---

[4]In the sense of justified default logic.

$\forall \eta \in J \cup \{\beta\}$. $E \cup \{\gamma\} \cup \{\eta\} \nvdash \bot$. In fact, it is two-fold: It consists of a joint and an individual consistency check, ie. $\forall \eta \in J$. $E \cup \{\gamma\} \cup \{\eta\} \nvdash \bot$ and $E \cup \{\gamma\} \cup \{\beta\} \nvdash \bot$. Transposed to the case of a contextual extension (E, C) the two subconditions are $\neg\gamma \notin C$ and $\neg(\beta \wedge \gamma) \notin E$. The first check cares about the joint consistency of the consequent γ, whereas the second one checks whether the conjunction of the justification and consequent of the default rule is individually consistent.

Now, let us see what happens to default theory (2) if we apply translation Φ_{JDL}:

$$\left(\left\{\frac{||:C|B \wedge C|}{C}, \frac{||:D|\neg B \wedge D|}{D}, \frac{||:E|\neg C \wedge \neg D \wedge E|}{E}\right\}, Th(\emptyset)\right)$$

As in justified default logic, we get two contextual extensions: $(Th(\{C, D\}), Th(\{C, D, B\}) \cup Th(\{C, D, \neg B\})\})$ and $(Th(\{E\}), Th(\{E, \neg C, \neg D\}))$, whose extensions correspond to the extensions obtained in justified default logic. Observe that the respective subcontexts differ exactly in the justifications attached to the extensions in justified default logic.

Finally, we turn to *constrained default logic* [Delgrande *et al.*,1992], which employs a sort of joint consistency. In constrained default logic, an extension comes with a set of constraints. A *constrained extension* is defined as follows.

Definition 8 *Let (D, W) be a default theory. For any set of formulas S let $\Upsilon(S)$ be the pair of smallest sets of formulas (T', S') such that*

1. $W \subseteq T' \subseteq S'$, 2. $T' = Th(T')$ and $S' = Th(S')$,
3. *For any $\frac{\alpha:\beta}{\gamma} \in D$, if $\alpha \in T'$ and $S \cup \{\beta\} \cup \{\gamma\} \nvdash \bot$ then $\gamma \in T'$ and $\beta, \gamma \in S'$.*

A pair of sets of formulas (E, C) is a constrained extension of (D, W) iff $\Upsilon(C) = (E, C)$.

As we have seen above, constrained default logic detects inconsistencies among the justifications of default rules. Thus, we obtain three constrained extensions, $(Th(\{C\}), Th(\{C, B\}))$, $(Th(\{D\}), Th(\{D, \neg B\}))$, $(Th(\{E\}), Th(\{E, \neg C, \neg D\}))$, of default theory (2). They are formed as described above.

A default theory in constrained default logic is identified with a contextual default theory as follows.

Definition 9 *Let (D, W) be a default theory. Define*
$$\Phi_{CDL}(D, W) = \left(\left\{\frac{|\alpha|:\beta \wedge \gamma||}{\gamma} \mid \frac{\alpha:\beta}{\gamma} \in D\right\}, Th(W)\right).$$

This yields the following correspondence.

Theorem 3 *Let (D, W) be a default theory and let E and C be sets of formulas. Then, (E, C) is a constrained extension of (D, W) iff (E, C) is a contextual extension of $\Phi_{CDL}(D, W)$.*

Notice that C is always deductively closed whenever (E, C) is an extension in either sense.

Consider the contextual counterpart of default theory (2) from the perspective of constrained default logic:

$$\left(\left\{\frac{||:B \wedge C||}{C}, \frac{||:\neg B \wedge D||}{D}, \frac{||:\neg C \wedge \neg D \wedge E||}{E}\right\}, Th(\emptyset)\right)$$

As a result, we obtain three contextual extensions: $(Th(\{C\}), Th(\{C, B\}))$, $(Th(\{D\}), Th(\{D, \neg B\}))$,

and $(Th(\{E\}), Th(\{E, \neg C, \neg D\}))$. These are identical to the respective constrained extensions.

Contextual default logic: Expressiveness

This section is devoted to the novel application conditions of contextual default rules and how their interplay may influence the contents of extensions.

Let us first consider the difference between W- and E-prerequisites. In general, W-prerequisites should be preferred over E-prerequisites whenever a prerequisite has to be verified, ie. whenever it should not be derivable by default inferences. This cannot be modelled in conventional default logics, since they do not distinguish between monotonic and nonmonotonic conclusions.

As an example, consider the assertion "usually, we can transplant an organ provided that the person is proven to be dead". Of course, the antecedent of this rule should be more than merely concluded by default. For instance, a person whose body is fully covered with a medical blanket is usually dead, but it takes more evidence for doctors to remove organs. Now, the above rule can be formalized by means of the contextual default rule $\frac{D \,\|\,:\, O \,\|}{O}$, saying that an organ, O, can be transplanted, if this is consistent with the current context, and provided that the death, D, of the person has been verified. Importantly, adding the contextual default rule $\frac{\,|\,C\,|\,:\,|\,D\,|}{D}$ (saying that a person whose body is covered, C, with a blanket is usually dead, D) does not allow $\frac{D \,\|\,:\, O \,\|}{O}$ to apply, even in the case where $W = Th(\{C\})$.

C-prerequisites are a means for weakening antecedents of default rules. This is because a C-prerequisite allows us not only to refer to default conclusions but also to their underlying consistency assumptions: A C-prerequisite is satisfied iff it belongs to some subcontext. Accordingly, certain contextual default rules can only be applied if a certain context has been established. For instance, a contextual default rule $\frac{\,\|\,:\,|\,A\,|}{B}$ may establish, without actually asserting, a consistency assumption A on which other contextual default rules, like $\frac{\,\|\,A\,:\,|\,D\,|}{D}$, rely.

Let us now turn to the difference between C- and E-justifications of contextual default rules. Notably, it can serve for imposing priorities between two implicit assumptions. This cannot be modelled easily in conventional default logics. For instance, in default theory (1) a precedence among the two implicit assumptions can be modelled in contextual default logic in a very straightforward way by weakening the implicit assumption B compared to its negation:

$$\left(\left\{ \frac{\,\|\,:\,|\,B\,|}{C}, \frac{\,\|\,:\, \neg B \,\|}{D} \right\}, Th(\emptyset) \right)$$

This yields one contextual extension, $(Th(\{C\}), Th(\{B, C\}))$.

The use of W-justifications is closely related to CWA, the closed world assumption [Reiter,1977]. CWA has

been introduced in order to complete a given set of facts W. In CWA, a ground negative literal is derivable iff the original atom is not derivable from W. Considering a database about taxpayers, for instance, an individual is not a dead person unless stated otherwise. Given no other knowledge about an individual, we derive that he is not dead. This can be modelled by means of the contextual default rule $\frac{\,\|\,:\,\|\, \neg D}{\neg D}$.

Contextual default logic: The formal theory

In the sequel, we give alternative characterizations of contextual extensions and describe their structure in more detail. First, we define the set of generating contextual default rules.

Definition 10 *Let (D, W) be a contextual default theory and T and S sets of formulas. The set of generating contextual default rules for (T, S) wrt (D, W) is defined as*

$$GD_{(D,W)}^{(T,S)} = \left\{ \frac{\alpha_W \,|\, \alpha_E \,|\, \alpha_C \,:\, \beta_C \,|\, \beta_E \,|\, \beta_W}{\gamma} \in D \;\middle|\; \begin{array}{l} \alpha_W \in W, \quad \alpha_E \in T, \quad \alpha_C \in S, \\ \neg\beta_C \notin S, \quad \neg\beta_E \notin T, \quad \neg\beta_W \notin W \end{array} \right\}$$

Now, we can make precise the claim made before Definition 3: In a contextual extension (E, C), the set E is deductively closed and the set C is pointwisely closed.

Theorem 4 *Let (E, C) be a contextual extension of (D, W) and $\Delta = GD_{(D,W)}^{(E,C)}$. Then,*
$$Th(W \cup Conseq(\Delta)) = Th(E) = E$$
$$Th_{E \cup Justif_C(\Delta)}(Justif_E(\Delta)) = Th_{\top}(C) = C.$$

The first inclusion shows that extensions of contextual default theories are formed in the same way as in conventional default logics. That is, they consist of the initial facts along with the consequents of all applying contextual default rules. The second inclusion describes the respective contexts. A context is the pointwise closure of the E-justifications of the applying contextual default rules (corresponding to the individual consistency requirements) under the extension and the C-justifications of the applying contextual default rules (corresponding to the joint consistency requirements). It follows that whenever (E, C) is a contextual extension, C contains the deductive closure of E and all formulas involved in joint consistency requirements. In symbols, $Th\left(E \cup Justif_C\left(GD_{(D,W)}^{(E,C)} \right) \right) \subseteq C$. Since this set is shared by all subcontexts of a context, we call it the *kernel* of a context.

Theorem 5 *Let (D, W) be a contextual default theory and let E and C be sets of formulas. Define $E_0 = W$ and $C_0 = W$ and for $i \geq 0$*
$$\Delta_i = \left\{ \frac{\alpha_W \,|\, \alpha_E \,|\, \alpha_C \,:\, \beta_C \,|\, \beta_E \,|\, \beta_W}{\gamma} \in D \;\middle|\; \begin{array}{l} \alpha_W \in W, \quad \alpha_E \in E_i, \quad \alpha_C \in C_i, \\ \neg\beta_C \notin C, \quad \neg\beta_E \notin E, \quad \neg\beta_W \notin W \end{array} \right\}$$
$$E_{i+1} = Th(W \cup Conseq(\Delta_i))$$
$$C_{i+1} = Th_{E_i \cup Justif_C(\Delta_i)}(Justif_E(\Delta_i))$$

Then, (E, C) is a contextual extension of (D, W) iff $(E, C) = (\bigcup_{i=0}^{\infty} E_i, \bigcup_{i=0}^{\infty} C_i)$.

The extension E is built by successively introducing the consequents of all applying contextual default rules. Also, the deductive closure is computed at each stage. For each partial context C_{i+1}, the previous partial extension E_i is unioned with the C-justifications of all applying contextual default rules. This set is unioned in turn with each E-justification of all applying contextual default rules. Again, the deductive closure is computed when appropriate. In this way, each partial context C_{i+1} is built upon the kernel of the previous partial context, $Th(E_i \cup Justif_C(\Delta_i))$.

A possible worlds semantics

In analogy to [Besnard and Schaub,1993], we employ Kripke structures for characterizing contextual extensions. A Kripke structure has a distinguished world, the "actual" world, and a set of worlds accessible from it.

The idea is roughly as follows. In a class of Kripke structures, the actual worlds characterize an extension, whereas the accessible worlds characterize its context consisting of a number of subcontexts. In concrete terms, given a contextual extension (E, C) and a Kripke structure m, we require that the actual world ω_0 of m be a model of the extension, E, and demand that each world in m accessible from ω_0 be a model of some subcontext of C. Thus, each world of m accessible from the actual world ω_0 is to be a model of the kernel of C.

First, we define the class of K-models[5] associated with W as $\mathfrak{M}_W = \{m \mid m \models \gamma \wedge \Box\gamma, \gamma \in W\}$. We will semantically characterize contextual extensions by maximal elements of a strict partial order on classes of K-models. Given a contextual default rule δ, its application conditions and the result of applying it are captured by an order $>_\delta$ as follows.

Definition 11 Let $\delta = \frac{\alpha_W \mid \alpha_E \mid \alpha_C : \beta_C \mid \beta_E \mid \beta_W}{\gamma}$. Let $\mathfrak{M}$ and $\mathfrak{M}'$ be distinct classes of K-models. Define $\mathfrak{M} >_\delta \mathfrak{M}'$ iff

$$\mathfrak{M} = \{m \in \mathfrak{M}' \mid m \models \gamma \wedge \Box\gamma \wedge \Box\beta_C \wedge \Diamond\beta_E\}$$

and

1. $\mathfrak{M}_W \models \alpha_W$ 2. $\mathfrak{M}' \models \alpha_E$ 3. $\mathfrak{M}' \models \Diamond\alpha_C$
4. $\mathfrak{M}' \not\models \Diamond\neg\beta_C$ 5. $\mathfrak{M}' \not\models \Box\neg\beta_E$ 6. $\mathfrak{M}_W \not\models \neg\beta_W$

Given a set of contextual default rules D, the strict partial order $>_D$ is defined as the transitive closure of the union of all orders $>_\delta$ such that $\delta \in D$.

Then, we obtain soundness and completeness:[6]

Theorem 6 Let (D, W) be a contextual default theory. Let $\mathfrak{M}$ be a class of K-models, E a deductively closed set of formulas, C a pointwisely closed set of formulas, and $C_K = Th\left(E \cup Justif_C\left(GD_{(D,W)}^{(E,C)}\right)\right)$ and $C_J = Justif_E\left(GD_{(D,W)}^{(E,C)}\right)$ such that

$$\mathfrak{M} = \{m \mid m \models E \wedge \Box C_K \wedge \Diamond C_J\}.$$

(E, C) is a consistent contextual extension of (D, W) iff $\mathfrak{M}$ is a $>_D$-maximal non-empty class above $\mathfrak{M}_W$. Observe that the requirements on a maximal class of K-models correspond to the aforementioned intuitions. Clearly, E is the extension, C the context, C_K the kernel and C_J consists of E-justifications distinguishing the subcontexts from each other.

Conclusion

Contextual default logic provides a unified framework for default logics by extending the notion of a default rule and supplying each extension with a context. Such contexts are formed by pointwisely closing certain consistency assumptions under a given extension.

We isolated six different application conditions for default rules. We showed that only three of them are employed in conventional default logics, even though two of the three remaining ones correspond to well-known notions, namely first-order derivability and the closed world assumption. The remaining condition expresses "membership in a context" and needs further elaboration.

Among various advantages, contextual default logic explicates the context-dependency of default logics and reveals that existing default logics differ mainly in the way they deal with an explicit or implicit underlying context. As a result, we saw that justified default logic compromises individual and joint consistency, whereas other variants strictly employ either of them.

Acknowledgements

We would like to thank Bob Mercer for valuable discussions. This work was supported by *CEC, DRUMS II (6156)* and by *BMfT, TASSO (ITW 8900 C2)*.

References

Besnard, P. and Schaub, T. 1993. Possible worlds semantics for default logics. *Fundamenta Informaticae.* Forthcoming.

Brewka, G. 1991. Cumulative default logic: In defense of nonmonotonic inference rules. *Artificial Intelligence* 50(2):183–205.

Delgrande, J.; Jackson, K.; and Schaub, T. 1992. Alternative approaches to default logic. *Artificial Intelligence.* Submitted for publication.

Łukaszewicz, W. 1988. Considerations on default logic – an alternative approach. *Computational Intelligence* 4:1–16.

Reiter, R. 1977. On closed world data bases. In Gallaire, H. and Nicolas, J.-M., eds., *Logic and Databases.* Plenum. 119–140.

Reiter, R. 1980. A logic for default reasoning. *Artificial Intelligence* 13(1–2):81–132.

---

[5] K-models stand for models of the modal logic K.

[6] Given a set of formulas T let $\Box T$ stand for $\wedge_{\alpha \in T} \Box\alpha$ and $\Diamond T$ stand for $\wedge_{\alpha \in T} \Diamond\alpha$.

Propositional Logic of Context

Saša Buvač   &   Ian A. Mason

Computer Science Department
Stanford University
Stanford
California 94305-2140
{buvac, iam}@sail.stanford.edu

Abstract

In this paper we investigate the simple logical properties of *contexts*. We describe both the syntax and semantics of a general propositional language of context, and give a Hilbert style proof system for this language. A propositional logic of context extends classical propositional logic in two ways. Firstly, a new modality, $\text{ist}(\kappa, \phi)$, is introduced. It is used to express that the sentence, ϕ, holds in the context κ. Secondly, each context has its own vocabulary, i.e. a set of propositional atoms which are *defined* or *meaningful* in that context. The main results of this paper are the soundness and completeness of this Hilbert style proof system. We also provide soundness and completeness results (i.e. correspondence theory) for various extensions of the general system.

Introduction

In this paper we investigate the simple logical properties of *contexts*. Contexts were first introduced into AI by John McCarthy in his Turing Award Lecture, [McCarthy, 1987], as an approach which might lead to the solution of the problem of *generality* in AI. This problem is simply that existing AI systems *lack* generality.

Since then, contexts have found a large number of uses in various areas of AI. R. V. Guha's doctoral dissertation [Guha, 1991] under McCarthy's supervision was the first in-depth study of context. Guha's context research was primarily motivated by the Cyc system [Guha and Lenat, 1990] (a large common-sense knowledge-base currently being developed at MCC). Without using contexts it would have been virtually impossible to create and successfully use a knowledge base of the size of Cyc.

Large knowledge bases are not the only place where contexts have found practical use. The knowledge sharing community has accepted the need for explicating context when transferring information from one agent to another. Currently, proposals for introducing contexts into the Knowledge Interchange Format or KIF [Genesereth and Fikes, 1992] are being considered.

Furthermore, it seems that the context formalism can provide semantics for the process of translating facts into KIF and from KIF, one of the key tasks that the knowledge sharing effort is facing.

The meaning of an utterance depends on the context in which it is uttered. Computational linguists have developed various ways of describing this context. For example, Barbara Grosz in her Ph.D. thesis, [Grosz, 1977], implicitly captures the context of a discourse by *focusing* on the objects and actions which are most relevant to the discourse. This representation is similar to an ATMS context [de Kleer, 1986], which is simply a list of propositions that are *assumed* by the reasoning system.

However till now no formal logical explication of contexts has been given. The aim of this paper is to rectify this deficiency. We describe both the syntax and semantics of a general propositional language of context, and give a Hilbert style proof system for this language. The main results of this paper are the soundness and completeness of this Hilbert style proof system. We also provide soundness and completeness results (i.e. correspondence theory) for various extensions of the general system.

Notation

We use standard mathematical notation. If X and Y are sets, then $X \rightarrow_p Y$ is the set of partial functions from X to Y. $\mathbf{P}(X)$ is the set of subsets of X. X^* is the set of all finite sequences, and we let $\bar{x} = [x_1, \ldots, x_n]$ range over X^*. ϵ is the empty sequence. We use the infix operator $*$ for appending sequences. We make no distinction between an element and the singleton sequence containing that element. Thus we write $\bar{x} * x_1$ instead of $\bar{x} * [x_1]$. As is usual in logic we treat X^* as a tree (that grows downward). $\bar{x}_1 < \bar{x}_0 \leq \epsilon$ iff $\bar{x}_1$ properly extends $\bar{x}_0$ (i.e. $(\exists \bar{y} \in X^* - \{\epsilon\})(\bar{x}_1 = \bar{x}_0 * \bar{y})$). We say $Y \subseteq X^*$ is a subtree rooted at $\bar{y}$ to mean

1. $\bar{y} \in Y$ and $(\forall \bar{z} \in Y)(\bar{z} \leq \bar{y})$

2. $(\forall \bar{z} \in Y)(\forall \bar{w} \in X^*)(\bar{z} \leq \bar{w} \leq \bar{y} \rightarrow \bar{w} \in Y)$

The General System

A propositional logic of context extends classical propositional logic in two ways. Firstly, a new modality, $ist(\kappa, \phi)$, is introduced. It is used to express that the sentence, ϕ, holds in the context κ. Secondly, each context has its own vocabulary, i.e. a set of propositional atoms which are *defined* or *meaningful* in that context. The vocabulary of one context may or may not overlap with another context.

Syntax

We begin with two distinct countably infinite sets, $\mathbb{K}$ the set of all contexts, and $\mathbb{P}$ the set of propositional atoms. The set, $\mathbb{W}$, of well-formed formulas (wffs) is built up from the propositional atoms, $\mathbb{P}$, using the usual propositional connectives (negation and implication) together with the ist modality.

Definition ($\mathbb{W}$):

$$\mathbb{W} = \mathbb{P} \cup (\neg \mathbb{W}) \cup (\mathbb{W} \to \mathbb{W}) \cup ist(\mathbb{K}, \mathbb{W})$$

The operations $\wedge$, $\vee$ and $\leftrightarrow$ are defined as abbreviations in the usual way. The term *literal* is used to refer to a propositional atom or the negation of a propositional atom. We use $\pm\phi$ to represent either the formula ϕ, or its negation $\neg\phi$. We also use the following abbreviations:

$$ist(\overline{\kappa}, \phi) \quad := ist(\kappa_1, ist(\kappa_2, \ldots, ist(\kappa_n, \phi)))$$
$$ist^{\pm}(\overline{\kappa}, \phi) \quad := \pm ist(\kappa_1, \pm ist(\kappa_2, \cdots \pm ist(\kappa_n, \phi) \cdots))$$

when $\overline{\kappa}$ is the context sequence $[\kappa_1, \kappa_2, \ldots, \kappa_n]$. In the definition of $ist^{\pm}$ all the ist's need not be of the same parity. PROP is the set of all well formed formulas which do not contain ist's. If ψ is a formula containing distinct atoms $p_1, \ldots, p_n$, then we write $\psi(\phi_1, \ldots, \phi_n)$ for the formula which results from ψ by simultaneously replacing all the occurrences of p_i in ψ by ϕ_i. We say that $\psi(\phi_1, \ldots, \phi_n)$ is an *instance* of ψ.

Semantics

We begin with a system which makes as few semantic restrictions as possible. Other systems are obtained by placing restrictions on the models. The semantics of the general system has the following three features:

Firstly, the nature of a particular context may itself be context dependent. For example, in the context of the 1950's, the context of car racing is different than than the context of car racing viewed from today's context. This leads naturally to considering sequences of contexts rather than a solitary context. We refer to this feature of the system as *non-flatness*. It reflects on the intuition that what holds in a context can depend on how this context has been reached, i.e. from which perspective it is being viewed. For example, non-flatness will be desirable if we represent the beliefs of an agent as the sentences which hold in a context. A system of flat contexts can easily be obtained by placing certain

restrictions on what kinds of structures are allowed as models, as well as enriching the axiom system.

Secondly, a context is modelled by a set of truth assignments, that describe the possible states of affairs of that context. Therefore the ist modality is interpreted as validity: $ist(\kappa, \rho)$ is true iff the propositional atom ρ is true in all the truth assignments associated with context κ. Treatment of ist as validity corresponds to Guha's proposal for context semantics, which was motivated by the Cyc knowledge base. A system which models a context by a single truth assignment, thus interprets ist as truth, can be obtained by placing simple restrictions on the definition of a model, and enriching the set of axioms.

Thirdly, since different contexts can have different vocabularies, some propositions can be meaningless in some contexts, and therefore the truth assignments describing the state of affairs in that context need to be partial.

Definition ($\mathfrak{M}$): In this system a model, $\mathfrak{M}$, will be a function which maps a context sequence $\overline{\kappa} \in \mathbb{K}^*$ to a set of partial truth assignments,

$$\mathfrak{M} \in \mathbb{K}^* \to_p \mathbf{P}(\mathbb{P} \to_p 2),$$

with the added conditions that

1. $(\forall \overline{\kappa})(\forall \nu_1, \nu_2 \in \mathfrak{M}(\overline{\kappa}))(\text{Dom}(\nu_1) = \text{Dom}(\nu_2))$

2. $\text{Dom}(\mathfrak{M})$ is a subtree of $\mathbb{K}^*$ rooted at some context sequence $\overline{\kappa}_0$.

We write $\overline{\kappa}^{\mathfrak{M}}$ to denote the set of partial truth assignments $\mathfrak{M}(\overline{\kappa})$. Note that $\overline{\kappa}^{\mathfrak{M}}$ can be empty. The collection of all such models will be denoted by $\mathbb{M}$.

We could have assumed the existence of a *fixed outermost context* which would result in $\text{Dom}(\mathfrak{M})$ being a tree rooted at empty sequence ϵ (i.e. the fixed outermost context). This would result in slightly simpler notation and proofs. However, although more complicated, our definition is based on the intuition that there is no *outermost* context.

Vocabularies The truth assignments in our model are partial. The atoms which are given a truth value in a context are defined by a relation $\text{Vocab} \subseteq \mathbb{K}^* \times \mathbb{P}$.

Definition (*Vocab* of $\mathfrak{M}$): We define a function $Vocab : \mathbb{M} \to \mathbf{P}(\mathbb{K}^* \times \mathbb{P})$ which given a model returns the vocabulary of the model:

$$Vocab(\mathfrak{M}) := \{ <\overline{\kappa}, \rho> \mid \overline{\kappa} \in \text{Dom}(\mathfrak{M}) \text{ and } \rho \in \text{Dom}(\mathfrak{M}(\overline{\kappa})) \}$$

We say that a model $\mathfrak{M}$ is *classical on vocabulary* Vocab iff $\text{Vocab} \subseteq Vocab(\mathfrak{M})$.

The notion of vocabulary can also be applied to sentences. Intuitively, the vocabulary of a sentence relates a context sequence to the atoms which occur in the scope of that context sequence. In the definition we also need to take into account that sentences are not given in isolation but in a context.

Definition (Vocab of ϕ in $\overline{\kappa}$): We define a function Vocab : $\mathbb{K}^* \times \mathbb{W} \to \mathbb{P}(\mathbb{K}^* \times \mathbb{P})$ which given formula in a context, returns the vocabulary of the formula. Vocab$(\overline{\kappa}, \phi)$ is defined inductively by:

$\{<\overline{\kappa}, \phi>\}$	$\phi \in \mathbb{P}$
Vocab$(\overline{\kappa}, \phi_0)$	$\phi = \neg\phi_0$
Vocab$(\overline{\kappa} * \kappa, \phi_0)$	$\phi = \text{ist}(\kappa, \phi_0)$
Vocab$(\overline{\kappa}, \phi_0) \cup$ Vocab$(\overline{\kappa}, \phi_1)$	$\phi = \phi_0 \to \phi_1$

It is extended to sets of formulas in the obvious way.

Note that it is only in the propositional case that we can carry out this *static* analysis of the vocabulary of a sentence. It will not be possible in the quantified versions. Also note that our definition of vocabulary of a sentence is somewhat different from Guha's notion of definedness. Guha proposes to treat $\text{ist}(\kappa, \phi)$ as false if ϕ is not in the vocabulary of the context κ.

Satisfaction We can think of partial truth assignments as total truth assignments in a three-valued logic. Our satisfaction relation then corresponds to Bochvar's three valued logic [Bochvar, 1972], since an implication is meaningless if either the antecedent or the consequent are meaningless. We chose Bochvar's three valued logic because we intend meaningfulness to be interpreted as syntactic meaningfulness, rather than semantic meaningfulness along the lines of Kleene's three valued logic [Kleene, 1952].

Definition ($\models$):
If $\nu \in \overline{\kappa}^{\mathfrak{M}}$ and Vocab$(\overline{\kappa}, \varphi) \subseteq Vocab(\mathfrak{M})$, then

$\mathfrak{M}, \nu \models_{\overline{\kappa}} \rho$ iff $\nu(\rho) = 1$, $\rho \in \mathbb{P}$

$\mathfrak{M}, \nu \models_{\overline{\kappa}} \neg\phi$ iff not $\mathfrak{M}, \nu \models_{\overline{\kappa}} \phi$

$\mathfrak{M}, \nu \models_{\overline{\kappa}} \phi \to \psi$ iff $\mathfrak{M}, \nu \models_{\overline{\kappa}} \phi$ implies $\mathfrak{M}, \nu \models_{\overline{\kappa}} \psi$

$\mathfrak{M}, \nu \models_{\overline{\kappa}} \text{ist}(\kappa_1, \phi)$ iff $\forall\nu_1 \in (\overline{\kappa}*\kappa_1)^{\mathfrak{M}}$ $\mathfrak{M}, \nu_1 \models_{\overline{\kappa}*\kappa_1} \phi$

In the last point note that $\overline{\kappa} * \kappa_1 \in \text{Dom}(\mathfrak{M})$ since the Dom$(\mathfrak{M})$ is a rooted subtree, and Vocab$(\overline{\kappa}, \phi) \subseteq Vocab(\mathfrak{M})$.

We write $\mathfrak{M} \models_{\overline{\kappa}} \phi$ iff $\forall\nu \in \overline{\kappa}^{\mathfrak{M}}$ $\mathfrak{M}, \nu \models_{\overline{\kappa}} \phi$.

Formal System

We now present the formal system. To do this we fix a particular vocabulary, Vocab $\subset \mathbb{K}^* \times \mathbb{P}$, and define a provability relation, $\vdash_{\overline{\kappa}}^{\text{Vocab}}$. Since Vocab will remain fixed throughout we omit explicitly mentioning it and write $\vdash_{\overline{\kappa}} \phi$ instead. Similarly, to avoid constantly stating lengthy side conditions we make the following convention.

Definedness Convention: *In the sequel, whenever we write $\vdash_{\overline{\kappa}} \phi$ we will be assuming implicitly that* Vocab$(\overline{\kappa}, \phi) \subseteq$ Vocab.

Axioms and inference rules are given in table 1. Note that the rules of inference preserve the (**definedness convention**).

Assuming that our system was limited to only one context, the rule (**CS**) would be identical to the rule of necessitation in normal systems of modal logic, and axiom schema (**K**) would be identical to the the standard axiom schema K. Thus in the single context case, ignoring axiom schemas ($\triangle_+$) and ($\triangle_-$), our formal system is identical to what is usually called the *normal system* of modal logic, characterized by (**PL**), (**MP**), (**K**), and the rule of necessitation. The axiom schemas ($\triangle_+$) and ($\triangle_-$) are needed in order to accommodate the validity aspect of the ist modality. It turns that they derivable in the system which treats ist as truth and does not allow inconsistent contexts.

Provability A formula ϕ *is provable in context $\overline{\kappa}$ with vocabulary* Vocab (formally $\vdash_{\overline{\kappa}} \phi$) iff $\vdash_{\overline{\kappa}} \phi$ is an instance of an axiom schema or follows from provable formulas by one of the inference rules; formally, iff there is a sequence $[\vdash_{\overline{\kappa}_1} \phi_1, \ldots, \vdash_{\overline{\kappa}_n} \phi_n]$ such that $\overline{\kappa}_n = \overline{\kappa}$, and $\phi_n = \phi$ and for each $i \leq n$ either $\vdash_{\overline{\kappa}_i} \phi_i$ is an axiom, or is derivable from the earlier elements of the sequence via one of the inference rules. In the case of assumptions, formula ϕ is provable from assumptions T in context $\overline{\kappa}_0$ with vocabulary Vocab (formally T$\vdash_{\overline{\kappa}_0}^{\text{Vocab}}$, or again taking into account that Vocab is fixed T $\vdash_{\overline{\kappa}_0} \phi$) iff there are formulas $\phi_1, \ldots, \phi_n \in$ T, such that $\vdash_{\overline{\kappa}_0} (\phi_1 \wedge \cdots \wedge \phi_n) \to \phi$. Note that due to the definedness convention if T $\vdash_{\overline{\kappa}_0} \phi$ then Vocab(T) $\subseteq$ Vocab.

Consequences

Some simple theorems and derivable rules of the system are:

(C) $\vdash_{\overline{\kappa}} \text{ist}(\kappa_1, \phi) \wedge \text{ist}(\kappa_1, \psi) \to \text{ist}(\kappa_1, \phi \wedge \psi)$

(Or) $\vdash_{\overline{\kappa}} \text{ist}(\kappa_1, \phi) \vee \text{ist}(\kappa_1, \psi) \to \text{ist}(\kappa_1, \phi \vee \psi)$

(M) $\vdash_{\overline{\kappa}} \text{ist}(\kappa_1, \phi \wedge \psi) \to \text{ist}(\kappa_1, \phi) \wedge \text{ist}(\kappa_1, \psi)$

(K*) $\vdash_{\overline{\kappa}} \text{ist}(\overline{c}, \phi \to \psi) \to \text{ist}(\overline{c}, \phi) \to \text{ist}(\overline{c}, \psi)$

(REP)
$$\frac{\vdash_{\overline{\kappa}} \phi_1 \leftrightarrow \phi_1' \cdots \vdash_{\overline{\kappa}} \phi_n \leftrightarrow \phi_n'}{\vdash_{\overline{\kappa}} \psi(\phi_1, \ldots, \phi_n) \leftrightarrow \psi(\phi_1', \ldots, \phi_n')}$$

provided $\psi(p_1, \ldots p_n) \in \text{PROP}$.

A slightly deeper result is that any formula is provably equivalent to one in a certain syntactic form. This equivalence plays an important role in the completeness proof.

Definition (CNF): A formula ϕ is in conjunctive normal form (CNF) iff it is of the form $E_1 \wedge E_2 \wedge \cdots \wedge E_k$, and each E_i is of the form $\alpha_{i1} \vee \alpha_{i2} \vee \cdots \vee \alpha_{ir_i}$, where each α_{ij} is either a literal, or $\text{ist}^{\pm}(\overline{c}, \beta)$ for some disjunction of literals β. Note that i and k can be 1.

Lemma (CNF): For any formula ϕ, context sequence $\overline{\kappa}$, there exists a formula ϕ^* which is in CNF, such that $\vdash_{\overline{\kappa}} \phi \leftrightarrow \phi^*$.

(PL)	$\vdash_{\overline{\kappa}} \phi$ provided ϕ is an instance of a tautology.

(K) $\vdash_{\overline{\kappa}} \text{ist}(\kappa_1, \phi \to \psi) \to \text{ist}(\kappa_1, \phi) \to \text{ist}(\kappa_1, \psi)$

$(\triangle_+)$ $\vdash_{\overline{\kappa}} \text{ist}(\kappa_1, \text{ist}(\kappa_2, \phi) \lor \psi) \to \text{ist}(\kappa_1, \text{ist}(\kappa_2, \phi)) \lor \text{ist}(\kappa_1, \psi)$

$(\triangle_-)$ $\vdash_{\overline{\kappa}} \text{ist}(\kappa_1, \neg\text{ist}(\kappa_2, \phi) \lor \psi) \to \text{ist}(\kappa_1, \neg\text{ist}(\kappa_2, \phi)) \lor \text{ist}(\kappa_1, \psi)$

(MP) $\dfrac{\vdash_{\overline{\kappa}} \phi \quad \vdash_{\overline{\kappa}} \phi \to \psi}{\vdash_{\overline{\kappa}} \psi}$ (CS) $\dfrac{\vdash_{\overline{\kappa} * \kappa_1} \phi}{\vdash_{\overline{\kappa}} \text{ist}(\kappa_1, \phi)}$

Table 1: Axioms and Inference Rules

Theorem (soundness): If $\vdash_{\overline{\kappa}} \phi$, then for all models $\mathfrak{M}$ classical on Vocab $\mathfrak{M} \models_{\overline{\kappa}} \phi$. If $T \vdash_{\overline{\kappa}} \phi$, then for all models $\mathfrak{M}$ classical Vocab if for all $\psi \in T$ $\mathfrak{M} \models_{\overline{\kappa}} \psi$, then $\mathfrak{M} \models_{\overline{\kappa}} \phi$.

Completeness

We begin by introducing some concepts needed to state the completeness theorem.

Definition (satisfiability): A set of formulas T is *satisfiable in context $\overline{\kappa}$ with vocabulary* Vocab iff there exists a model $\mathfrak{M}$ classical on Vocab, such that for all $\phi \in T$, $\mathfrak{M} \models_{\overline{\kappa}} \phi$.

Definition (consistency): A formula ϕ is *consistent in $\overline{\kappa}$ with* Vocab, where $\text{Vocab}(\overline{\kappa}, \phi) \subseteq$ Vocab iff not $\vdash_{\overline{\kappa}} \neg\phi$. A finite set T is consistent in $\overline{\kappa}$ with Vocab iff $\bigwedge T$ is consistent in $\overline{\kappa}$ with Vocab. An infinite set T is consistent in $\overline{\kappa}$ with Vocab iff every finite subset of T is consistent in $\overline{\kappa}$ with Vocab. A set T is inconsistent in $\overline{\kappa}$ with Vocab iff the set T is not consistent in $\overline{\kappa}$ with Vocab.

A set T is maximally consistent in $\overline{\kappa}$ with Vocab iff T is consistent in $\overline{\kappa}$ with Vocab and for all $\phi \notin T$ such that $\text{Vocab}(\overline{\kappa}, \phi) \subseteq$ Vocab, $T \cup \{\phi\}$ is inconsistent in $\overline{\kappa}$ with Vocab.

As is usual, an important part of the completeness proof is the Lindenbaum lemma allowing any consistent set of wffs to be extended to a maximally consistent set.

Lemma (Lindenbaum): If T is consistent in $\overline{\kappa}$ with Vocab, then T can be extended to a maximally consistent set T_0 in $\overline{\kappa}$ with Vocab.

Now we proceed to state and prove the completeness of the system.

Theorem (completeness): For any set of formulas T, T is consistent in $\overline{\kappa}_0$ with Vocab iff T is satisfiable in $\overline{\kappa}_0$ with Vocab.

Proof (completeness): Assume T is consistent in $\overline{\kappa}_0$ with Vocab. By the (**Lindenbaum lemma**) we can extend T to a maximally consistent set T_0. From T_0 we will construct the model $\mathfrak{M}_0$. For each $\overline{\kappa} = \overline{\kappa}_0 * \overline{c} \in \mathbb{K}^*$ define

$$T_{\overline{\kappa}+} := \{\phi \,|\, T_0 \vdash_{\overline{\kappa}_0} \text{ist}(\overline{c}, \phi), \phi \in \text{PROP}\}.$$

Lemma ($T_{\overline{\kappa}+}$): $T_{\overline{\kappa}+}$ is closed under logical consequence: for all ϕ where $\text{Vocab}(\overline{\kappa}, \phi) \subseteq$ Vocab, if ϕ tautologically follows from $T_{\overline{\kappa}+}$ then $\phi \in T_{\overline{\kappa}+}$.

Note that $T_{\overline{\kappa}+}$ need not be either maximally consistent or even consistent. Now, using only the sets $T_{\overline{\kappa}+}$ of formulas from PROP, we will define a model $\mathfrak{M}_0$ for the set of formulas T_0. We define the domain of $\mathfrak{M}_0$

$$\text{Dom}(\mathfrak{M}_0) := \{\overline{\kappa} \,|\, \overline{\kappa} \leq \overline{\kappa}_0, \exists \overline{\kappa}' \in \text{Dom}(\text{Vocab}), \overline{\kappa}' \leq \overline{\kappa}\}$$

and for all $\overline{\kappa} \in \text{Dom}(\mathfrak{M}_0)$

$$\mathfrak{M}_0(\overline{\kappa}) := \{\nu \,|\, \text{Dom}(\nu) = \text{Vocab}(\overline{\kappa}), \forall \phi \in T_{\overline{\kappa}+}, \overline{\nu}(\phi) = 1\}.$$

In the above, $\overline{\nu}$ is the unique homomorphic extension of ν with respect to the propositional connectives. To see that $\mathfrak{M}_0$ as defined is a model, we first note that it clearly meets condition 1, since all the truth assignments associated with a context must have the same domain. Condition 2 is met since $\text{Dom}(\mathfrak{M}_0)$ as defined is a subtree rooted at $\overline{\kappa}_0$. Note that if $T_{\overline{\kappa}+}$ is empty (which corresponds to the case where $\text{Vocab}(\overline{\kappa}) = \emptyset$), then $\mathfrak{M}_0(\overline{\kappa})$ is a singleton set, whose only member is the *empty truth assignment*. Finally, to establish completeness we need only prove the truth lemma. The proof of the truth lemma is based on the CNF construction and is the novel aspect of this completeness proof.

Lemma (truth):
For any ϕ such that $\text{Vocab}(\overline{\kappa}_0, \phi) \subseteq$ Vocab,

$$\phi \in T_0 \quad \text{iff} \quad \mathfrak{M}_0 \models_{\overline{\kappa}_0} \phi.$$

Clearly, if $\phi \in T$ then also $\phi \in T_0$ and therefore by truth lemma we get $\mathfrak{M}_0 \models_{\overline{\kappa}_0} \phi$. $\square$**completeness**

Before we give the proof of the truth lemma, we need to state a property of the model $\mathfrak{M}_0$ which is needed in the `ist` case of the truth lemma.

Lemma ($\mathfrak{M}_0$): Let $\mathfrak{M}_0$ be a model as defined from T_0 in the completeness proof. Then for all $\phi \in \text{PROP}$ where $\text{Vocab}(\overline{\kappa_0} * \overline{c}, \phi) \subseteq \text{Vocab}$,

$$T_0 \vdash_{\overline{\kappa_0}} \texttt{ist}(\overline{c}, \phi) \text{ iff for all } \nu \in \mathfrak{M}_0(\overline{\kappa_0} * \overline{c}) \quad \nu(\phi) = 1.$$

A frequently used instance of the $\mathfrak{M}_0$ lemma is that $T_0 \vdash_{\overline{\kappa_0}} \texttt{ist}(\overline{c}, \phi \wedge \neg\phi)$ iff $\mathfrak{M}_0(\overline{\kappa_0} * \overline{c}) = \emptyset$, for all ϕ satisfying the (**definedness condition**).

Proof (truth lemma): Instead of proving $\phi \in T_0$ iff $\mathfrak{M}_0 \models_{\overline{\kappa_0}} \phi$ we will prove the statement

(TL) $\quad \psi$ is in CNF implies $(\psi \in T_0$ iff $\mathfrak{M}_0 \models_{\overline{\kappa_0}} \psi)$.

To see that the former follows from the latter, assume $\phi \in T_0$. By the (**CNF lemma**), there exists formula ϕ^* in CNF such that $\vdash_{\overline{\kappa_0}} \phi \leftrightarrow \phi^*$. Using maximal consistency of T_0, it follows that $\phi^* \in T_0$. Therefore by (**TL**) it must be the case that $\mathfrak{M}_0 \models_{\overline{\kappa_0}} \phi^*$. Our logic is sound: $\mathfrak{M}_0 \models_{\overline{\kappa_0}} \phi^*$ iff $\mathfrak{M}_0 \models_{\overline{\kappa_0}} \phi$, and thus we conclude that $\mathfrak{M}_0 \models_{\overline{\kappa_0}} \phi$. We can simply reverse the steps of the argument to prove the other direction of the biconditional.

We prove the (**TL**) by induction on the structure of the formula ψ. In the base case ψ is an atom, and thus in CNF. From the definition of $\mathfrak{M}_0(\overline{\kappa_0})$ it follows that $\rho \in T_0 \Leftrightarrow \mathfrak{M}_0 \models_{\overline{\kappa_0}} \rho$. In proving the inductive step we first examine $\psi = \chi \vee \mu$. The inductive hypothesis is that the lemma is true for formulas χ and μ. Assume $\chi \vee \mu$ is in CNF. Then both χ and μ must also be in CNF. Since T_0 is maximally consistent $\chi \vee \mu \in T_0$ iff either $\chi \in T_0$ or $\mu \in T_0$. By the inductive hypothesis this will be true iff either $\mathfrak{M}_0 \models_{\overline{\kappa_0}} \chi$ or $\mathfrak{M}_0 \models_{\overline{\kappa_0}} \mu$, and by the definition of satisfaction iff $\mathfrak{M}_0 \models_{\overline{\kappa_0}} \chi \vee \mu$. The inductive step for conjunction and negation is similar. We make use of the fact that if $\chi \wedge \mu$ is in CNF, then so are both χ and μ; and if $\neg\chi$ is in CNF, then so is χ. The interesting case is when ψ is an `ist`. Assume that ψ is in CNF. Then ψ must be of the form

$$\psi = \texttt{ist}^{\pm}(\overline{c}, \chi),$$

where χ is a disjunction of literals. The context sequence $\overline{c}$ will sometimes be written as $\kappa_1 * \cdots * \kappa_n$. We will examine two cases, depending on whether or not any of the sets of sentences $T_{(\overline{\kappa_0} * \overline{c}')+}$ where $\overline{c} \leq \overline{c}'$, are inconsistent. The sets $T_{(\overline{\kappa_0} * \overline{c}')+}$, where $\overline{c} \leq \overline{c}'$, are all consistent iff the formula

$(D_{\overline{c}}) \quad \texttt{ist}(\overline{c}, \neg\phi) \rightarrow \neg\texttt{ist}(\overline{c}, \phi)$

is in T_0, for any wff ϕ which satisfies the definedness condition. The proof of this is identical to the soundness and completeness proofs of a context system with

axiom schema (**D**) w.r.t. the set of consistent models, dealt with shortly. Formula $(D_{\overline{c}})$ is equivalent to

$$\neg\texttt{ist}(\overline{c}, \phi \wedge \neg\phi) \in T_0,$$

for all ϕ satisfying the definedness condition; the proof carries over from normal systems of modal logic. Now we state a useful consequence of $(D_{\overline{c}})$'s.

Lemma ($D_{\overline{c}}$):
Let $\overline{c}$ be $\kappa_1 * \cdots * \kappa_n$. If $D_{(\kappa_1 * \cdots * \kappa_{n-1})} \in T_0$, then

$$\texttt{ist}^{\pm}(\overline{c}, \phi) \in T_0 \quad \text{iff} \quad \pm\,\texttt{ist}(\overline{c}, \phi) \in T_0$$

for any formula ϕ which satisfies the definedness convention. The sign on the right hand side is positive iff there is an even number of negations in the $\texttt{ist}^{\pm}$ on the left hand side.

Now we examine the two cases need to prove the inductive step for `ist` of the truth lemma.

Case $D_{(\kappa_1 * \cdots * \kappa_{n-1})} \in T_0$: In this case we assume $D_{(\kappa_1 * \cdots * \kappa_{n-1})} \in T_0$ and that $\psi \in T_0$. Then by the $D_{\overline{c}}$ lemma:

$$\texttt{ist}^{\pm}(\overline{c}, \chi) \in T_0 \quad \text{iff} \quad \pm\,\texttt{ist}(\overline{c}, \chi) \in T_0$$

We only include the positive case.

$$\texttt{ist}(\overline{c}, \chi) \in T_0 \quad \text{iff} \quad T_0 \vdash_{\overline{\kappa_0}} \texttt{ist}(\overline{c}, \chi)$$

Now by ($\mathfrak{M}_0$ **lemma**) and the definedness condition $\text{Vocab}(\overline{\kappa_0} * \overline{c}) \subseteq \text{Vocab}$ we have

$$T_0 \vdash_{\overline{\kappa_0}} \texttt{ist}(\overline{c}, \chi) \quad \text{iff} \quad (\forall \nu \in \mathfrak{M}_0(\overline{\kappa}))(\overline{\nu}(\chi) = 1)$$

By the definition of satisfaction:

$$(\forall \nu \in \mathfrak{M}_0(\overline{\kappa}))(\overline{\nu}(\chi) = 1) \quad \text{iff} \quad \mathfrak{M}_0 \models_{\overline{\kappa_0}} \texttt{ist}(\overline{c}, \chi)$$

Now since $D_{(\kappa_1 * \cdots * \kappa_{n-1})} \in T_0$, and by ($\mathfrak{M}_0$ **lemma**) we obtain:

$$\mathfrak{M}_0 \models_{\overline{\kappa_0}} \texttt{ist}(\overline{c}, \chi) \quad \text{iff} \quad \mathfrak{M}_0 \models_{\overline{\kappa_0}} \texttt{ist}^{\pm}(\overline{c}, \chi)$$

Case $D_{(\kappa_1 * \cdots * \kappa_{n-1})} \notin T_0$: Let j be the index of the first inconsistent context; formally $D_{(\kappa_1 * \cdots * \kappa_j)} \notin T_0$ and $D_{(\kappa_1 * \cdots * \kappa_{j-1})} \in T_0$. Then for all ϕ satisfying the definedness condition we have $\neg\texttt{ist}(\kappa_1 * \cdots * \kappa_j, \phi \wedge \neg\phi) \notin T_0$. Now by maximal consistency of T_0, (K*) and (**MP**)

$$\texttt{ist}(\kappa_1 * \cdots * \kappa_j, \phi \wedge \neg\phi) \in T_0 \text{ iff } \texttt{ist}(\kappa_1 * \cdots * \kappa_j, \psi) \in T_0$$

Thus, $T_{(\overline{\kappa_0} * \kappa_1 * \cdots * \kappa_j)+}$ is inconsistent, $\mathfrak{M}_0(\overline{\kappa_0} * \kappa_1 * \cdots * \kappa_j) = \emptyset$, and consequently

$$\texttt{ist}(\kappa_1 * \cdots * \kappa_j, \phi) \in T_0 \quad \text{iff} \quad \mathfrak{M}_0 \models_{\overline{\kappa_0}} \texttt{ist}(\kappa_1 * \cdots * \kappa_j, \phi)$$

for all ϕ such that $\text{Vocab}(\overline{\kappa_0} * \kappa_1 * \cdots * \kappa_j, \phi) \subseteq \text{Vocab}$. Then by reasoning similar to the previous case we get:

$$\texttt{ist}^{\pm}(\overline{c}, \chi) \in T_0 \quad \text{iff} \quad \mathfrak{M}_0 \models_{\overline{\kappa_0}} \texttt{ist}^{\pm}(\overline{c}, \chi).$$

Note that in the entire proof of the inductive step for `ist`, we did not need the inductive hypothesis, making use only of the special form of χ which is guaranteed because ψ is in CNF. $\square$**truth–lemma**

Correspondence Results

In this section we provide soundness and completeness results for several extensions of the general system. correspond to certain intuitive principles concerning the nature of contexts. In each extension the syntax and semantics is the same as in the general case, and the (**definedness convention**) still holds. Only the class of models and axioms are modified.

Consistency

Sometimes it is desirable to ensure that all contexts are consistent.

In this system we examine the class, $\mathfrak{Consistent}$, of *consistent models*. A model $\mathfrak{M} \in \mathfrak{Consistent}$ iff for any context sequence $\overline{\kappa} \in \mathrm{Dom}(\mathfrak{M})$,

$$\mathfrak{M}(\overline{\kappa}) \neq \emptyset.$$

The following axiom schema is sound with respect to the class of consistent models $\mathfrak{Consistent}$:

(D) $\vdash_{\overline{\kappa}} \mathtt{ist}(\kappa, \neg\phi) \to \neg\mathtt{ist}(\kappa, \phi)$

Axiom schema (D) is also commonly used in modal logic, and is sound and complete for the set of serial Kripke frames, in which for each world there is another world from which it is accessible from. Note that axiom (D) is equivalent to

$$\vdash_{\overline{\kappa}} \mathtt{ist}(\kappa, \phi \wedge \neg\phi).$$

Theorem (completeness):   The general context system with (D) axiom schema is complete with respect to the set of models $\mathfrak{Consistent}$.

Flatness

For some applications all contexts will be identical regardless of where they are examined from. This type of situation will often arise when we use a number of independent databases. For example, if I am booked on flight 921 in the context of the Northwest airlines database, then regardless of which travel agent I choose, in the context of that travel agent, it is true that in the context of Northwest airlines I am booked on flight 921.

In this system we examine a class, $\mathfrak{Flat}$, of what we call *flat models*. A model $\mathfrak{M}$ is flat, formally $\mathfrak{M} \in \mathfrak{Flat}$ iff $\mathrm{Dom}(\mathfrak{M}) = \mathbb{K}^*$ and for any context sequences $\overline{\kappa}_1$ and $\overline{\kappa}_2$, and any context κ,

$$\mathfrak{M}(\overline{\kappa}_1 * \kappa) = \mathfrak{M}(\overline{\kappa}_2 * \kappa).$$

When dealing with flat models it might be more intuitive to think of individual contexts rather then context sequences. Then $\mathfrak{M} \in \mathfrak{Flat}$ can be viewed as a function which maps contexts to finite sets of partial truth assignments, in other words

$$\mathfrak{M} \in \mathbb{K} \cup \{\epsilon\} \mapsto \mathbf{P}(\mathbb{P} \to_{\mathrm{p}} 2).$$

with the side condition of general models that still applies:

$$(\forall \overline{\kappa} \in \mathbb{K} \cup \{\epsilon\})(\forall \nu_1, \nu_2 \in \mathfrak{M}(\overline{\kappa}))(\mathrm{Dom}(\nu_1) = \mathrm{Dom}(\nu_2))$$

The following flatness axiom schemas are sound with respect to the class of flat models $\mathfrak{Flat}$:

(Fl$_+$) $\vdash_{\overline{\kappa}} \mathtt{ist}(\kappa_2, \mathtt{ist}(\kappa_1, \phi)) \leftrightarrow \mathtt{ist}(\kappa_1, \phi)$

(Fl$_-$) $\vdash_{\overline{\kappa}} \mathtt{ist}(\kappa_2, \neg\mathtt{ist}(\kappa_1, \phi)) \to \neg\mathtt{ist}(\kappa_1, \phi)$

providing the vocabulary also satisfies the flatness condition: for any context sequences $\overline{\kappa}_1$ and $\overline{\kappa}_2$, and any context κ,

$$\mathrm{Vocab}(\overline{\kappa}_1 * \kappa) = \mathrm{Vocab}(\overline{\kappa}_2 * \kappa).$$

The backward direction of the flatness axiom schemas (**Fl$_+$**) corresponds of the modal logic axiom schema S4 (provided that κ_1 is the same as κ_2). Similarly, the converse of (**Fl$_-$**) corresponds to the modal logic axiom schema S5. Note that the converse of (**Fl$_-$**) is a theorem in the system.

It is interesting to observe that in every system with (**Fl$_+$**) and (**Fl$_-$**), (**D**) is also derivable. In semantic terms, this means that any flat model is also a consistent model; a reasonable property for if a context was inconsistent, then in that context it would be true that all other contexts are also inconsistent. Due to flatness, this would really make all the other contexts inconsistent.

Theorem (completeness):   The general context system with (Fl$_+$) and (Fl$_-$) axiom schemas is complete with respect to the set of flat models $\mathfrak{Flat}$.

Truth

It might be more intuitive to define the $\mathtt{ist}$ modality to correspond to truth rather than validity; incidently this is also where the $\mathtt{ist}$ predicate got its name: is true. Truth based interpretation of the basic context modality also corresponds to the original suggestions by McCarthy [McCarthy, 1993]. In this case a context is associated with a single truth assignment rather than a set of truth assignments.

We examine the class, $\mathfrak{Truth}$, of *truth models*. A model $\mathfrak{M}$ is a truth model, formally $\mathfrak{M} \in \mathfrak{Truth}$ iff for any context sequence $\overline{\kappa} \in \mathrm{Dom}(\mathfrak{M})$,

$$|\mathfrak{M}(\overline{\kappa})| \leq 1.$$

The following axiom schema is sound with respect to the class of truth models $\mathfrak{Truth}$:

(Tr) $\vdash_{\overline{\kappa}} \mathtt{ist}(\kappa, \phi) \vee \mathtt{ist}(\kappa, \neg\phi)$

Note that (**Tr**) is the converse of (**D**).

Theorem (completeness):   The general context system with (Tr) axiom schema is complete with respect to the set of truth models $\mathfrak{Truth}$.

Previously we said that $(\triangle_+)$ and $(\triangle_-)$ are derivable in a system which contains (**D**) and (**Tr**). In fact, a stronger formula is true of this system:

$$\vdash_{\overline{\kappa}} \mathtt{ist}(\kappa, \phi \vee \psi) \leftrightarrow (\mathtt{ist}(\kappa, \phi) \vee \mathtt{ist}(\kappa, \psi)).$$

Meaninglessness as Falsity

In this section we examine a slightly more elaborate modification of the general system. This modification closely models the semantics described, but not investigated, in [Guha, 1991]. The general idea here is that if ϕ is not in the vocabulary of κ, then $\mathtt{ist}(\kappa, \phi)$ is taken to be false instead of meaningless or undefined. To cater faithfully to this interpretation, two changes must be made to the semantics of the general system. Firstly, the $\mathtt{ist}$ clause in the definition of $\mathrm{Vocab} : \mathbb{K}^* \times \mathbb{W} \rightarrow \mathbf{P}(\mathbb{K}^* \times \mathbb{P})$ must be altered to reflect the fact that $\mathtt{ist}(\kappa, \phi)$ will always be in the vocabulary of any context. Secondly, the $\mathtt{ist}$ clause in the definition of satisfaction must also be modified. The appropriate new clause in the definition of Vocab is:

$$\mathrm{Vocab}(\overline{\kappa}, \phi) = \emptyset \text{ if } \phi \text{ is } \mathtt{ist}(\kappa, \phi_0)$$

While the new clause in the definition of satisfaction is:

$$\mathfrak{M}, \nu \models_{\overline{\kappa}} \mathtt{ist}(\kappa_1, \phi) \text{ iff } \mathrm{Vocab}(\phi, \overline{\kappa} * \kappa_1) \subseteq Vocab(\mathfrak{M})$$
$$\text{and for all } \nu_1 \in (\overline{\kappa} * \kappa_1)^{\mathfrak{M}} \quad \mathfrak{M}, \nu_1 \models_{\overline{\kappa} * \kappa_1} \phi$$

The other clauses in both definitions remain the same, modulo the fact that all occurrences of Vocab in the definition of satisfaction now refer to the new definition. We maintain the (**definedness convention**) in stating the proof system for this version, but again we point out that all occurrences of Vocab now refers to the new definition. The proof system for this version consists of the axioms and rules of the general system, together with the new axiom:

$$(\mathbf{MF}) \quad \vdash_{\overline{\kappa}} \neg \mathtt{ist}(\kappa_1, \phi) \qquad \text{if } \mathrm{Vocab}(\overline{\kappa} * \kappa_1, \phi) \nsubseteq \mathrm{Vocab}$$

The completeness proof for this system is structurally similar to the one described in this paper. The only new points are those that arise out of the liberal definition of Vocab.

Related Work

Our work is largely based on McCarthy's ideas on context. McCarthy's research [McCarthy, 1987; McCarthy, 1993] in formalizing common sense has led him to believe that in order to achieve human-like generality in reasoning, we need to develop a formal theory of context. The key idea in McCarthy's proposal was to to treat contexts as formal objects, which enables one to state that a proposition is true in a context: $\mathtt{ist}(\kappa, \phi)$ where ϕ is a proposition and κ is a context. This permits axiomatizations in a limited context to be expanded so as to *transcend* their original limitations.

There has been other research done in this area, most notable is the work of Lifschitz, Shoham, and Guha. We briefly treat each in turn.

Two contexts can differ in, at least, three ways: they may have different vocabularies; or they may have the same vocabulary but describe different states of affairs, or (in the first order case) they may have the same vocabulary (i.e. language) but treat it differently (i.e the arities may not be the same). The first two differences were studied in [Buvač, 1992], and led to two different views on the use of context. Lifschitz's early note on formalizing context [Lifschitz, 1986] concentrates on the third difference. Shoham, in his work on contexts, concentrates on the second difference [Shoham, 1991]. Every proposition is meaningful in every context, but the same proposition can have different truth values in different contexts. Shoham approached the task of formalizing context from the perspective of modal and non-classical of logics. He defines a propositional language with an analogue to the $\mathtt{ist}$ modality, and a relation $\kappa_1 \bullet \supset \kappa_2$, expressing that context κ_1 is as general as context κ_2. Drawing on the intuitive analogy between a context κ and the proposition *current-context*(κ), Shoham identifies the set of contexts with the set of propositions. This enables him to define truth in a context $\mathtt{ist}(\kappa, p)$, in terms of the the the conditional *current-context*$(\kappa) \rightarrow p$, where $\rightarrow$ is interpreted as as some form of intuitionistic or relevance implication. His paper gives a list of 14 benchmark sentences which characterize this implication.

Guha's dissertation contains a number of examples of context use. These demonstrate how reasoning with contexts should behave, and which properties a formalization of context should exhibit. The Cyc knowledge base [Guha and Lenat, 1990], which is the main motivation for Guha's context research, is made up of many theories, called *micro-theories*, describing different aspects of the world. Guha has tailored the design of micro-theories after contexts.

There is also a clear parallel between the logic of context and the modal logics of knowledge and belief [Halpern and Moses, 1992]. The modality $\mathtt{ist}(\kappa, \phi)$ may be interpreted as expressing that the agent κ knows or believes the sentence ϕ. In the case where there is only one context, our formal system collapses to a normal system of modal logic (with two additional axiom schemas $(\triangle_+)$ and $(\triangle_-)$). This is analogous to the way logics of knowledge and belief collapse to a normal system of modal logic in case of a single agent. However, the logics of knowledge and belief differ from our logic of contexts in a number of ways: Firstly, logics of knowledge and belief do not deal with variable vocabularies and the corresponding partiality. Furthermore, logics of knowledge and belief are usually ascribed possible world semantics. Consequently, an agent's belief is modeled by relations between worlds. Modeling truth or validity in a context by a relation between worlds would not be intuitive because we want contexts to be reified as first class objects in the semantics. This will allow us (in the predicate case) to state relations between contexts, define operations on contexts, and specify how sentences from one context can be *lifted* into another context.

Conclusions and Future Work

Our goal is to extend the system to a full quantification logic. One advantage of quantificational system is that it enables us to express relations between context, operations on contexts, and state *lifting rules* which describe how a fact from one context can be used in another context. However, in the presence of context variables it might not be possible to define the vocabulary of a sentence without knowing which object a variable is bound to. Therefore the first step in this direction is to to examine propositional systems with dynamic definitions of meaningfulness.

We also plan to define non-Hilbert style formal systems for context. Probably the most relevant is a natural deduction system, which would be in line with McCarthy's original proposal of treating contextual reasoning as a strong version of natural deduction. In such a system, entering a context would correspond to making an assumption in natural deduction, while exiting a context corresponds to discharging an assumption.

Finally, it would be interesting to show some formal properties of our logic. These include defining a decision procedure, in the style of [Mints, 1992].

Acknowledgements

The authors would like to thank Tom Costello, R. V. Guha, Furio Honsell, John McCarthy, Grigorii Mints and Carolyn Talcott for their valuable comments. This research is supported in part by the Advanced Research Projects Agency, ARPA Order 8607, monitored by NASA Ames Research Center under grant NAG 2-581, by NASA Ames Research Center under grant NCC 2-537, NSF grant CCR-8915663 and Darpa contract NAG2-703.

References

Bochvar, D. A. 1972. Two papers on partial predicate calculus. Technical Report STAN-CS-280-72, Department of Computer Science, Stanford University. Translation of Bochvar's papers originally published in 1938 and 1943.

Buvač, Saša 1992. Context in AI. Unpublished manuscript.

de Kleer, Johan 1986. An assumption-based truth maintenance system. *Artificial Intelligence* 28:127–162.

Genesereth, Michael R. and Fikes, Richard E. 1992. Knowledge interchange format, version 3.0, reference manual. Technical Report Logic Group Report Logic-92-1, Stanford University.

Grosz, Barbara J. 1977. A representation and use of focus in a system for understanding dialogs. In *Proceedings of the Fifth International Joint Conference on Artificial Intelligence*. Morgan Kaufmann Publishers Inc.

Guha, Ramanathan V. and Lenat, Douglas B. 1990. Cyc: A midterm report. *AI Magazine* 11(3):32–59.

Guha, Ramanathan V. 1991. *Contexts: A Formalization and Some Applications*. Ph.D. Dissertation, Stanford University. Also published as technical report STAN-CS-91-1399-Thesis.

Halpern, Joseph Y. and Moses, Yoram 1992. A guide to completeness and complexity for modal logics of knowledge and belief. *Artificial Intelligence* 54:319–379.

Kleene, Steven C. 1952. *Introduction to Metamathematics*. North-Holland Publishing Company.

Lifschitz, Vladimir 1986. On formalizing contexts. Unpublished manuscript.

McCarthy, John 1987. Generality in artificial intelligence. *Comm. of ACM* 30(12):1030–1035. Reprinted in [McCarthy, 1990].

McCarthy, John 1990. *Formalizing Common Sense: Papers by John McCarthy*. Ablex Publishing Corporation, 355 Chesnut Street, Norwood, NJ 07648.

McCarthy, John 1993. Notes on formalizing context. In *Proceedings of the Thirteenth International Joint Conference on Artificial Intelligence*. To appear.

Mints, Grigorii E. 1992. Lewis' systems and system T (1965-1973). In *Selected Papers in Proof Theory*. Bibliopolis and North-Holland.

Shoham, Yoav 1991. Varieties of context. In Lifschitz, Vladimir, editor 1991, *Artificial Intelligence and Mathematical Theory of Computation: Papers in Honor of John McCarthy*. Academic Press.

Generating Explicit Orderings for Non-monotonic Logics

James Cussens
Centre for Logic and Probability in IT
King's College
Strand
London, WC2R 2LS, UK
j.cussens@elm.cc.kcl.ac.uk

Anthony Hunter
Department of Computing
Imperial College
180, Queen's Gate
London, SW7 2BZ, UK
abh@doc.ic.ac.uk

Ashwin Srinivasan
Programming Research Group
Oxford University Computing Laboratory
11, Keble Road
Oxford, OX1 3QD, UK
ashwin.srinivasan@prg.ox.ac.uk

Abstract

For non-monotonic reasoning, explicit orderings over formulae offer an important solution to problems such as 'multiple extensions'. However, a criticism of such a solution is that it is not clear, in general, from where the orderings should be obtained. Here we show how orderings can be derived from statistical information about the domain which the formulae cover. For this we provide an overview of prioritized logics—a general class of logics that incorporate explicit orderings over formulae. This class of logics has been shown elsewhere to capture a wide variety of proof-theoretic approaches to non-monotonic reasoning, and in particular, to highlight the role of preferences—both implicit and explicit—in such proof theory. We take one particular prioritized logic, called SF logic, and describe an experimental approach for comparing this logic with an important example of a logic that does not use explicit orderings of preference—namely Horn clause logic with negation-as-failure. Finally, we present the results of this comparison, showing how SF logic is more skeptical and more accurate than negation-as-failure.

Keywords: non-monotonic reasoning, statistical inference, prioritized logics, machine learning.

Introduction

Within the class of non-monotonic logics and associated systems such as inheritance hierarchies, there is a dichotomy between those formalisms that incorporate explicit notions of preference over formulae, and those that do not. Even though using explicit orderings offers an effective mechanism for obviating certain kinds of 'multiple extension' problems, their use remains controversial. A major criticism is that it is unclear where the orderings come from. We address this criticism by arguing that the orderings should be derived from statistical information generated from the domain over which they operate. If we delineate the kind of information about the domain that we require, then there are generic mappings from this information into the set of orderings over data.

The structure of the paper is as follows. First, we provide an overview of prioritized logics—a general class of logics that incorporate explicit preferences over formulae. Second, we take one particular prioritized logic, SF logic, and describe an experimental approach to comparing this logic with an important example of a logic that does not use explicit orderings of preference—namely Horn clause logic with negation-as-failure. Third, we take SF logic and show how we can generate explicit orderings over the data using statistical inference, and finally, we present the results of the comparison, showing how SF logic is more skeptical and more accurate than negation-as-failure.

Overview of prioritized logics

In order to provide a general framework for logics with explicit orderings, we use the family of prioritized logics [Hunter, 1992; Hunter, 1993]. Within this family, each member is such that:

- Each formula of the logic is labelled.
- The rules of inference for the logic are augmented with rules of manipulation for the labels.
- The labels correspond to a partially-ordered structure.

A prioritized logic is thus an instance of a labelled deductive system [Gabbay, 1991a; Gabbay, 1991b; Gabbay and de Queiroz, 1993].

A prioritized logic can be used for non-monotonic reasoning by defining a consequence relation that allows the inference of the formula with a label that is 'most preferred' according to some preference criterion. Furthermore, we can present a wide variety of existing non-monotonic logics in this framework. In particular, we can explore the notion of implicit or explicit preference prevalent in a diverse class of non-monotonic logics. For example, by adopting appropriate one-to-one rewrites of formulae into prioritized logic formulae, we can show how the propositional form of a number of key non-monotonic logics including negation-as-failure with general logic programs, ordered logic, LDR, and a skeptical version of inheritance hierarchies, can be viewed as using preferences in an essentially equivalent fashion [Hunter, 1993].

For this paper, we use a member of the prioritized logics family called SF logic and defined as follows. The language is composed of labelled formulae of the following form, where $\alpha_0, \ldots, \alpha_n, \beta$ are unground literals, i is a unique label, and $n \geq 0$.

$$i : \alpha_0 \wedge \ldots \wedge \alpha_n \to \beta$$

We call these formulae SF *rules*. We also allow uniquely labelled ground positive and negative literals which we call SF *facts*. A database Δ is a tuple $(\Gamma, \Omega, \succeq, \sigma)$, where Γ is a set of SF rules and facts, Ω is $[0,1] \times [0,1]$, $\succeq$ is some partial-ordering relation over Ω, and σ is a map from labels into Ω. This means each label corresponds to a pair of reals, and in this sense the ordering is two-dimensional. We use $[0,1] \times [0,1]$ only as a convenient representation for two-dimensional partial orderings. For the SF facts, σ maps to $(1,1)$.

There is more than one intuitive way of combining these two dimensions of values to generate a single poset $(\Omega, \succeq)$. We define the $\succeq$ relation in terms of $\geq$, the usual ordering relation for the real numbers. Consider the following definitions for the $\succeq$ relation.

Definition 1 $(i,p) \succ (j,q)$ *iff* $(i > j)$ *or* $(i = j$ *and* $p > q)$

Definition 2 $(i,p) \succ (j,q)$ *iff* $(i > j$ *and* $p > q)$

Definition 1 imposes a total ordering on Ω, where the ordering on the first label takes precedence, and the second label is only used as a 'tie-breaker'. Definition 2 defines a non-total subset of the first relation, where both dimensions play an equally important rôle.

The $\succ$ relation can be used to resolve conflicts in the arguments that emanate from Γ and is used as

such in the consequence relation for a prioritized logic. The SF consequence relation $\vdash$ allows an inference α if α is *proposed* and *undefeated* or if α is a fact. It is *proposed* if and only if there is an argument for α, such that all conditions for α are satisfied by recursion. It is *undefeated* if and only if there is no more preferred arguments for the complement of α. For all databases Δ, atomic labels i, unground literals α, groundings μ, and ground literals δ, the $\vdash$ relation is defined as follows, where, if δ is a positive literal then $\hat{\delta} = \neg\delta$ and $\widehat{\neg\delta} = \delta$:

Definition 3

$\Delta \vdash \delta$ *if* $i : \delta \in \Delta$ *and* $\sigma(i) = (1,1)$

$\Delta \vdash \delta$ *if* $\exists i [proposed(\Delta, i, \delta)$ *and* $undefeated(\Delta, i, \delta)]$

$proposed(\Delta, i, \delta)$ *iff*
   $\exists \beta_0, \ldots, \beta_n, \mu \ [i : \beta_0 \wedge \ldots \wedge \beta_n \to \alpha \in \Delta$
      and $\mu(\alpha) = \delta$
      and $\Delta \vdash \mu(\beta_0), \ldots, \Delta \vdash \mu(\beta_n)]$

$undefeated(\Delta, i, \delta)$ *iff*
   $\forall j [proposed(\Delta, j, \hat{\delta}) \Rightarrow \sigma(i) \succ \sigma(j)]$

Suppose $\Gamma = \{r : \alpha(a), \ p : \alpha(x) \to \beta(x), \ q : \alpha(x) \to \neg\beta(x)\}$, where $\sigma(p) = (0.6, 0.7)$, $\sigma(q) = (0.5, 0.8)$ and $\sigma(r) = (1,1)$. Using Definition 1, $\sigma(p) \succ \sigma(q)$, so $\Delta \vdash \beta(a)$ and $\Delta \vdash \alpha(a)$ hold. Using Definition 2, however, we have that $\sigma(p) \not\succ \sigma(q)$ and $\sigma(q) \not\succ \sigma(p)$ so $\Delta \not\vdash \beta(a)$ and $\Delta \not\vdash \neg\beta(a)$, but still $\Delta \vdash \alpha(a)$. This illustrates how Definition 2 captures a more skeptical logic.

Generating Rules

To show the value of generating explicit orderings, we now want to compare SF logic with existing non-monotonic logics. However, instead of undertaking this comparison purely on theoretical grounds, we do an empirical comparison with Horn clause logic augmented with negation-as-failure (Prolog). To support this, we use a machine learning algorithm, Golem [Muggleton and Feng, 1990], to generate definite clauses. Golem is an inductive logic programming approach to learning [Muggleton, 1991; Muggleton, 1992]. Using Golem means that significantly large numbers of examples can be used to generate these clauses. This facilitates the empirical study, and supports the statistical inference used for generating the explicit ordering. The definite clauses are used directly by Prolog, and used via a rewrite by SF logic.

We assume a set of ground literals D which express relevant facts about the domain in question and we also assume a target predicate symbol β. Since Prolog does not allow classical negation, we adopt the following non-logical convention: for a predicate symbol β, we represent negative examples using the predicate symbol not_β. Golem learns definite clauses where the head of the clause has the target predicate symbol β. This is done by using a training set Tr of N randomly chosen literals from D, where each of these literals has either β or not_β as predicate symbol. To learn these clauses Golem uses background knowledge, which is another subset of D, where none of the literals has β or not_β as a predicate symbol. The literals in the antecedents of the learnt clauses use the predicate symbols from the background knowledge.

For example, given background knowledge $\{\alpha(c_1), \alpha(c_2), \alpha(c_4), \alpha(c_7), \delta(c_1)\}$ and training examples $\{\beta(c_1), \beta(c_2), \text{not\_}\beta(c_3)\}$, Golem would learn the clause $\alpha(x) \rightarrow \beta(x)$, which has *training accuracy* 100%. In practice we use significantly larger sets of background knowledge and training examples. Also, we allow Golem to induce clauses with training accuracy below 100%, since learning completely accurate rules is unrealistic in many domains.

The induced clauses are tested using testing examples—ground literals with predicate symbol either β or not_β, which are randomly selected from $D \setminus Tr$. In the normal execution of Golem these testing examples are treated as queries to the induced set of definite clauses and are evaluated using $\vdash_p$, the Prolog consequence relation.

We define a function f to evaluate each test example. f takes Δ, the union of the learnt rules and the background knowledge, and the test example $\beta(\bar{c})$ or not_$\beta(\bar{c})$, where $\bar{c}$ is a tuple of ground terms and returns an evaluation of Δ's prediction concerning the test example. (Recall that none of the ground literals in the background knowledge have β as a predicate symbol.)

Definition 4

$$
\begin{aligned}
f(\Delta, \beta(\bar{c})) &= correct & \text{if } \Delta \vdash_p \beta(\bar{c}) \\
f(\Delta, \beta(\bar{c})) &= incorrect & \text{if } \Delta \nvdash_p \beta(\bar{c}) \\
f(\Delta, \text{not\_}\beta(\bar{c})) &= correct & \text{if } \Delta \nvdash_p \beta(\bar{c}) \\
f(\Delta, \text{not\_}\beta(\bar{c})) &= incorrect & \text{if } \Delta \vdash_p \beta(\bar{c})
\end{aligned}
$$

To continue the above example, suppose that $\{\beta(c_4), \text{not\_}\beta(c_5), \beta(c_6), \text{not\_}\beta(c_7)\}$ were the test examples, then we would have $f(\Delta, \beta(c_4)) = f(\Delta, \text{not\_}\beta(c_5)) = correct$ and $f(\Delta, \beta(c_6)) = f(\Delta, \text{not\_}\beta(c_7)) = incorrect$. The clause $\alpha(x) \rightarrow \beta(x)$ would then have the extremely poor *test accuracy* of 50%.

We generate SF rules in two stages. First, we run Golem with target predicate β, then we rerun it with target predicate not_β. To get the SF rules, we take the union of the two sets of clauses, rewrite the not_β symbol to the negated symbol $\neg\beta$, uniquely label each clause, and provide a map σ from the labels into Ω. This map is determined by information contained in the training data, and methods for defining it are described in the next section.

Let Δ denote the union of the SF rules with the background data. The examples from the test set are then used to query Δ. Suppose $\gamma(\bar{c})$ were such an example, where either $\gamma = \beta$ or $\gamma = \neg\beta$, then one of the following obtains (1) $\Delta \vdash \gamma(\bar{c})$; (2) $\Delta \vdash \widehat{\gamma(\bar{c})}$; or (3) ($\Delta \nvdash \gamma(\bar{c})$ and $\Delta \nvdash \widehat{\gamma(\bar{c})}$). We define the function g to evaluate each example (note that for SF logic we have extra category 'undecided').

Definition 5

$$
\begin{aligned}
g(\Delta, \gamma(\bar{c})) &= correct & \text{if } \Delta \vdash \gamma(\bar{c}) \\
g(\Delta, \gamma(\bar{c})) &= incorrect & \text{if } \Delta \vdash \widehat{\gamma(\bar{c})} \\
g(\Delta, \gamma(\bar{c})) &= undecided & \text{if } \Delta \nvdash \gamma(\bar{c}), \Delta \nvdash \widehat{\gamma(\bar{c})}
\end{aligned}
$$

Generating preference orderings

We now describe how to elicit a preference ordering over formulae by using facts about the domain, specifically facts from that subset of them which constitutes the training set of examples. To construct a preference ordering over the induced formulae, we find a pair of values which measure how well *confirmed* each SF rule $i : \alpha \rightarrow \beta$ is by the training data. We then map the unique label associated with each SF rule to this pair of values in Ω via the mapping σ.

For the first value, we calculate an estimate, denoted $\tilde{p}$, of the probability $P(\beta|\alpha) = p$. p is the probability that a (randomly chosen) example, given that it satisfies α, also satisfies β. Equivalently, it is the proportion of those examples that satisfy α which also satisfy β. p is an obvious choice as a measure of preference, it is the probability that the rule $\alpha \rightarrow \beta$ correctly classifies examples which it covers, i.e. examples which satisfy its antecedent α. Unfortunately, the value p can not be determined without examining all individuals in the domain that satisfy α and determining what proportion of them also satisfy β. This is infeasible for any domain large enough to be of interest. We show below how various estimates $\tilde{p}$ are constructed.

Clearly, we want $\tilde{p}$ close to p, i.e. we want to minimise $l = |\tilde{p} - p|$. The value l would be an ideal measure of the precision of the estimate $\tilde{p}$, but it will be unknown, since p is unknown. Instead, we either use *relative cover* (see below) or $P(l < t)$ for some fixed t, as a measure of the reliability of $\tilde{p}$. This gives us our second value.

For details of the various estimates used, see [Cussens, 1993]. We give only a brief sketch here, since the important point is that we can use straightforward and established statistical techniques to derive labels.

Relative Frequency We simply set $\tilde{p} = r/n$, where n is the number of training examples satisfying α and r the number satisfying $\alpha \wedge \beta$. The reliability of relative frequency as an estimate was measured by *relative cover* (n/N), which is simply the proportion of training examples which satisfy α and hence 'fire' the rule $\alpha \rightarrow \beta$. We use relative cover, since, for example, an estimate of $p = 1$ is more reliable with $r = 100, n = 100$ than with $r = 2, n = 2$ (recall the example in the previous section, which had $r/n = 1$ but test accuracy of only 50%).

Bayesian In Bayesian estimation of probabilities, a prior probability distribution over possible values of p is used. This is then updated to give a posterior distribution, the mean of which is used as a point estimate $\tilde{p}$ of p. Let λ be the mean of the prior distribution, we then have

$$\tilde{p} = \left(\frac{n}{n + \hat{K}}\right)\frac{r}{n} + \left(\frac{\hat{K}}{n + \hat{K}}\right)\lambda$$

The balance between r/n and λ is governed by the value $\hat{K}$, $\hat{K} = 0$ renders $\tilde{p} = r/n$. Various values for $\hat{K}$ have been employed in the statistical and machine learning literature [Bishop *et al.*, 1975; Cestnik, 1990; Cestnik and Bratko, 1991; Džeroski *et al.*, 1992]. Below we have used the value $\hat{K} = \sqrt{n}$; for the properties of this particular estimate see [Bishop *et al.*, 1975]. The value λ can be seen as a 'guess' at p prior to looking at domain information. We used an estimate of the value $P(\beta)$ for λ, an approach common in the machine learning literature. $P(l < t)$ was calculated by integrating between $\tilde{p} - t$ and $\tilde{p} + t$ on the posterior distribution. The actual value of t is not crucial. It affects the magnitude of $P(l < t)$, but rarely affects the preference ordering. In our experiments t was set to 0.025.

Pseudo-Bayes Like Bayesian, but

$$\hat{K} = \frac{r(n - r)}{(n\lambda - r)^2}$$

Such an approach is *pseudo*-Bayesian because $\hat{K}$, which is usually seen as a prior parameter is a function of r/n—which is a parameter of the training data.

Generating preference orderings in this way provides an alternative to orderings based on specificity (for example [Poole, 1985; Nute, 1988]). In the context of prioritized logics, some of the issues of specificity and accuracy have been considered in [Cussens and Hunter, 1991; Cussens and Hunter, 1993], but there is a clear need to further clarify this relationship by building on more general results relating non-monotonic reasoning and probabilistic inference [Pearl, 1990; Bacchus, 1990; Bacchus *et al.*, 1992].

A preliminary empirical comparison

In our preliminary comparison, we considered two domains. The first was for rules that predict whether a protein residue is part of an alpha-helix. These rules were defined in terms of relative position in a protein and various biochemical parameters. We call this domain the protein domain. The second was for rules that predict the relative activity of drugs. These rules were defined in terms of the structure of the drug and they provided a partial ordering over the degrees of activity of the drugs. We call this domain the drugs domain.

For the protein domain, from a training set of 1778 examples together with background knowledge consisting of 6940 ground literals, Golem generated 100 clauses

for the predicate symbol *alpha_helix* and 99 clauses for the predicate symbol *not_alpha_helix* and hence 199 SF clauses for *alpha_helix* and $\neg alpha\_helix$. For the drugs domain, from a training set of 1762 examples together with background knowledge consisting of 2106 ground literals, Golem generated 23 clauses for the binary predicate *greater_activity* and 24 for the predicate symbol *not_greater_activity*, giving 47 SF rules for *greater_activity* and $\neg greater\_activity$.

For the protein domain, Table 1 was formed using a test set of 401 *not_alpha_helix* examples and 322 *alpha_helix* examples. For the drugs domain, Table 2 was formed according to a test set of 513 *greater_activity* examples and 513 *not_greater_activity* examples.

Accuracy The key observation from these tables is that if we define accuracy by the ratio correct/(correct + incorrect), as we do in the 'Accuracy' column, then the performance of Prolog is inferior to that of SF logic. Furthermore, the difference in accuracy between the two variants of SF is negligible.

The marked improvement in accuracy of SF logic over Prolog is contingent on the assumption that we can ignore the examples classified as undecided. In other words, in this interpretation, the increased skepticism of the SF logic is not regarded negatively. However, this is only one way of interpreting the undecided category. If accuracy is defined as the percentage of correct examples, as in the 'Correct' column, then SF is markedly less accurate.

Comparing Definitions 1 and 2 When comparing the variants of SF logic, we find, after rounding, that the same results are obtained using Definition 1 for the three different estimation techniques—this is because they all return similar values. Also, since Definition 1 gives a total ordering on the labels, only those examples that are not covered by any rule are undecided. Using the more skeptical Definition 2, we find that accuracy was close or equal to Definition 1 in all cases.

Skepticism and the Protein Domain In the proteins domain, skepticism, as measured by the percentage of undecided examples, increases significantly as we move from Definition 1 to Definition 2. This increase was greatest using relative frequency, since there, the first value of its label, $\tilde{p} = r/n$, which estimates the accuracy of a rule, can be high even if n and consequently n/N is low. Using Definition 2 with relative frequency, a rule is preferred over another if and only if both the first value of its label ($\tilde{p} = r/n$) *and* the second (n/N) are greater than the respective parts of the label of the competing rule. So many rules with high r/n values but low n values will be preferred over competing rules using Definition 1, but not when using Definition 2.

In contrast, for $\hat{K} = \sqrt{n}$ and pseudo-Bayes, values for $\tilde{p}$ substantially higher than the prior mean λ are only possible if n is reasonably high. If n is high then,

	Correct	Incorrect	Undecided	Accuracy
Prolog with *alpha_helix* clauses	58	42	0	58
Prolog with *not_alpha_helix* clauses	59	41	0	59
Definition 1 using relative frequency	53	31	16	63
Definition 2 using relative frequency	45	25	30	64
Definition 1 using $\hat{K} = \sqrt{n}$	53	31	16	63
Definition 2 using $\hat{K} = \sqrt{n}$	48	27	25	64
Definition 1 using pseudo-Bayes	53	31	16	63
Definition 2 using pseudo-Bayes	50	29	21	63

Table 1: The Protein Domain (all values are percentages)

	Correct	Incorrect	Undecided	Accuracy
Prolog with *greater* clauses	79	21	0	79
Prolog with *not_greater* clauses	80	20	0	80
Definition 1 using relative frequency	70	5	25	93
Definition 2 using relative frequency	70	5	25	93
Definition 1 using $\hat{K} = \sqrt{n}$	70	5	25	93
Definition 2 using $\hat{K} = \sqrt{n}$	70	5	25	93
Definition 1 using pseudo-Bayes	70	5	25	93
Definition 2 using pseudo-Bayes	70	5	25	93

Table 2: The Drugs Domain (all values are percentages)

usually, so will be the second part of the label, $P(l < t)$. So in these cases, the second part of the label is usually high when the first part is, which explains the smaller increase in skepticism as we move from Definition 1 to Definition 2.

Skepticism and the Drugs Domain In the drugs domain, we have, after rounding, the same results for both variants of SF logic and all estimates. This is because conflicts between arguments in Γ occurred only for relatively few test examples.

Summary of Empirical Comparison If we allow increased skepticism, the results given here indicate how a richer formalism such as prioritized logics can be used for increased accuracy in reasoning. Furthermore, this shows how a clearer understanding of generating explicit orderings in terms of statistical inference can support this improved capability.

Discussion

It has been widely acknowledged that non-monotonic logics are of critical importance for artificial intelligence, yet there is some dissatisfaction with the rate and nature of progress in the development of non-monotonic logics that address the needs of artificial intelligence.

Many developments in non-monotonic logics have been based on a set of reasoning problems concerning, for example, inheritance, multiple extensions, and cumulativity. Existing non-monotonic logics can be used

to capture these problems in an intuitive fashion by appropriate encoding. Yet for the user of these kinds of formalism, it is not clear which is the most appropriate.

We believe that developing non-monotonic logics for artificial intelligence is, in part, an engineering problem and that the space of possible logics that could constitute a solution is enormous. It is therefore necessary to augment theoretical analyses of non-monotonic logics with sound empirical analyses. This should then focus the endeavour on improving the performance of reasoning with uncertain information, and as a matter of course should raise further important and interesting theoretical questions.

Acknowledgements

This work has been funded by UK SERC grants GR/G 29861 GR/G 29878 and GR/G 29854. The authors are grateful for helpful feedback from Dov Gabbay, Donald Gillies and Stephen Muggleton, and also from two anonymous referees.

References

Bacchus, Fahiem; Grove, Adam; Halpern, Joseph Y.; and Koller, Daphne 1992. From statistics to belief. In *Tenth National Conference on Artificial Intelligence (AAAI-92)*. 602–608.

Bacchus, Fahiem 1990. *Representing and Reasoning with Probabilistic Knowledge: A Logical Approach to Probabilities*. MIT Press, Cambridge, MA.

Bishop, Yvonne M. M.; Fienberg, Stephen E.; and Holland, Paul W. 1975. *Discrete Multivariate Analysis: Theory and Practice*. MIT Press, Cambridge, Mass.

Cestnik, Bojan and Bratko, Ivan 1991. On estimating probabilities in tree pruning. In Kodratoff, Yves, editor 1991, *Machine Learning—EWSL-91*. Lecture Notes in Artificial Intelligence 482, Springer-Verlag. 138–150.

Cestnik, Bojan 1990. Estimating probabilities: A crucial task in machine learning. In Aiello, L., editor 1990, *ECAI-90*. Pitman. 147–149.

Cussens, James and Hunter, Anthony 1991. Using defeasible logic for a window on a probabilistic database: some preliminary notes. In Kruse, R. and Seigel, P., editors 1991, *Symbolic and Quantitative Approaches for Uncertainty*. Lecture Notes in Computer Science 548, Springer-Verlag. 146–152.

Cussens, James and Hunter, Anthony 1993. Using maximum entropy in a defeasible logic with probabilistic semantics. In *Information Processing and the Management of Uncertainty in Knowledge-Based Systems (IPMU '92)*. Lecture Notes in Computer Science, Springer-Verlag. Forthcoming.

Cussens, James 1993. Bayes and pseudo-Bayes estimates of conditional probability and their reliability. In *European Conference on Machine Learning (ECML-93)*. Springer-Verlag.

Džeroski, Sašo; Cestnik, Bojan; and Petrovski, Igor 1992. The use of Bayesian probability estimates in rule induction. Turing Institute Research Memorandum TIRM-92-051, The Turing Institute, Glasgow.

Gabbay, Dov and de Queiroz, Ruy 1993. Extending the Curry-Howard interpretation to linear, relevance and other resource logics. *Journal of Symbolic Logic*. Forthcoming.

Gabbay, Dov 1991a. Abduction in labelled deductive systems: A conceptual abstract. In Kruse, R. and Seigel, P., editors 1991a, *Symbolic and Quantitative Approaches for Uncertainty*. Lecture Notes in Computer Science 548, Springer-Verlag. 3–11.

Gabbay, Dov 1991b. Labelled deductive systems. Technical report, Centrum für Informations und Sprachverarbeitung, Universität München.

Hunter, Anthony 1992. A conceptualization of preferences in non-monotonic proof theory. In Pearce, D. and Wagner, G., editors 1992, *Logics in AI*. Lecture Notes in Computer Science 633, Springer-Verlag. 174–188.

Hunter, Anthony 1993. Using priorities in non-monotonic proof theory. Technical report, Imperial College, London. Submitted to the *Journal of Logic, Language, and Information*.

Muggleton, Stephen and Feng, Cao 1990. Efficient induction of logic programs. In *Proc. of the First Conference on Algorithmic Learning Theory*, Tokyo. 473–491.

Muggleton, Stephen 1991. Inductive logic programming. *New Generation Computing* 8:295–318.

Muggleton, Stephen, editor 1992. *Inductive Logic Programming*. Academic Press.

Nute, Donald 1988. Defeasible reasoning and decision support systems. *Decision Support Systems* 4(1):97–110.

Pearl, Judea 1990. Probabilistic semantics for nonmonotonic reasoning: A survey. In Shafer, Glen and Pearl, Judea, editors 1990, *Readings in Uncertain Reasoning*. Morgan Kaufmann, San Mateo, CA, USA.

Poole, David L. 1985. On the comparison of theories: Preferring the most specific explanation. In *Ninth International Joint Conference on Artificial Intelligence (IJCAI-85)*. 144–147.

Reasoning Precisely with Vague Concepts*

Nita Goyal and Yoav Shoham

Robotics Laboratory, Computer Science Department
Stanford University
Stanford, CA 94305
{nita,shoham}@cs.stanford.edu

Abstract

Many knowledge-based systems need to represent vague concepts. Although the practical approach of representing vague concepts as precise intervals over numbers is well-accepted in AI, there is no systematic method to delimit the boundaries of intervals, only *ad hoc* methods. We present a framework to reason precisely with vague concepts based on the observation that the vague concepts and their interval-boundaries are constrained by the underlying domain knowledge. The framework is comprised of a constraint language to represent logical constraints on vague concepts, as well as numerical constraints on the interval-boundaries; a query language to request information about the interval boundaries; and a computational mechanism to answer the queries. A key step in answering queries is preprocessing the constraints by extracting the numerical constraints from the logical constraints and combining them with the given numerical constraints.

1 Introduction

The input to an AI system embedded in a real-world environment is often numerical whereas the reasoning is done with abstract symbols. Many abstract symbols embody vague concepts over continuous numerical ranges. To quote Davis, "In some respects, the concepts of commonsense knowledge are *vague*,... Many categories of common sense have no well-marked boundary lines; there are clear examples and clear nonexamples, but in between lies an uncertain region that we cannot categorize, even in principle." [Davis 1990]. For example, there is no minimum precise body temperature that a doctor considers high and there is no maximum number of hairs that a person might have and still be considered bald.

The representation of such vagueness poses a problem. "From a theoretical point of view, this vagueness is extremely difficult to deal with, and no re-

ally satisfactory solutions have been proposed." [Davis 1990]. Some of the approaches that try to address this theoretical difficulty are fuzzy logic [Zadeh 1983] and vague predicates [Parikh 1983]. However, it is commonly accepted in AI that, though inadequate theoretically, in practice it is often adequate to assume that a vague concept *is* precise and that there is indeed a well-defined boundary. In fact, most system builders who encounter the vagueness problem [Hayes-Roth *et al.* 1989; Shahar, Tu & Musen 1992] adopt a similar approach of representing a vague concept as an interval over the range of numbers. This practical approach is illustrated by an example from [Davis 1990]: "Suppose that "bald" did refer to some specific number of hairs on the head, only we do not know which number. We know that a man with twenty thousand hairs on his head is not bald, and that a man with three hairs on his head is bald, but somewhere in between we are doubtful." This precise representation of the vague concept bald is still useful for reasoning.

Despite the pervasiveness of the vagueness problem, and the pervasiveness of the practical approach of representing vague concepts as intervals, there has been no effort in AI to provide a systematic account of this practical approach. We propose a framework for representing and reasoning with vague concepts as intervals that has the advantages of (1) improving our understanding of the issues involved in the practical approach, and (2) replacing the *ad hoc* approach used by system designers to delimit the interval-boundaries.

The framework is based on the observation that vague concepts and their interval-boundaries (also referred to as *thresholds*) are constrained by the underlying domain knowledge that must be used to reason about the thresholds. We motivate the components of the framework by extending Davis' baldness example.

Example 1: "Anyone with 3 or fewer hairs is bald and anyone with 20000 or more hairs is not bald"
"All old people are bald" (note that "old" itself is a vague concept that we will assume has a well-defined boundary)
"Anyone who is 50 years or younger is not old whereas anyone over 80 is old"

---
*This research has been supported by grant AFOSR-89-0326.

"All presidents of companies are old"
"Tom's age is 70 years, he has 500 hairs and is the president of a company"
"Jim's age is 75 years and he has 800 hairs"
"Sam's age is 45 and he has 650 hairs"

Is Tom bald? Logical reasoning tells us that since Tom is president of a company, he is old and therefore bald. Note that here we used only the logical relations between the concepts *president*, old and bald, where old and bald are vague concepts but *president* is not.

Is Jim bald? We can reason that since Tom is old, the oldness threshold[1] can be at most 70. Since Jim's age is 75 which is over the oldness threshold, he must be old and therefore bald. Note that here we needed numerical reasoning with Tom and Jim's ages and oldness threshold, as well as logical reasoning that since Jim is old he must be bald.

We can ask if the baldness threshold is necessarily more than 800? Since Jim is bald and has 800 hairs, the baldness threshold must be at least 800. Therefore, the answer to the query is *yes* and hence anyone with less than 800 hairs is bald. Here we needed numerical reasoning about Jim's hairs and the baldness threshold.

Is Sam bald? Since anyone with less than 800 hairs is bald, and Sam has only 650 hairs, he must be bald. Here we needed numerical reasoning with number of hairs on Sam's head and the baldness threshold. ∎

As illustrated by this example, we need to *represent* both logical relations between symbolic concepts and numerical relations on thresholds. Also, logical as well as numerical *reasoning* is required to answer the interesting queries. Hence, the proposed framework facilitates this representation and supports queries about the thresholds.

Framework: The framework is comprised of three main parts – a constraint language to express domain knowledge, a query language to query the domain knowledge and a computational mechanism to answer the queries.

The first part of the framework is a *constraint language* that captures the domain knowledge. The language enables the expression of logical constraints on the vague concepts as well as numerical constraints on the thresholds of these concepts. Explicit representation of the thresholds is important to represent the numerical constraints and as we shall see, to ask queries.

The second part of the framework is a *query language* that extracts relevant information about the thresholds implied by the domain knowledge. In particular, the queries enable us to delimit the thresholds based on the information provided in the domain knowledge[2].

---

[1]By oldness threshold we mean that age such that everyone of higher age is old whereas everyone of lower age is not old. The baldness threshold is defined analogously.

[2]Note that it is not necessary to assign specific values to the thresholds to answer any queries, although this as-

This is exactly what a system designer needs to define intervals for a vague concept that are consistent with the domain knowledge. For example, the answer to the query "what is the minimum permissible value for the baldness threshold?" provides the designer with useful information to define the interval for bald.

The third part of the framework is a *computational mechanism* to answer the queries in the query language using the domain knowledge expressed in the constraint language.

In Sections 2 and 3, we introduce particular constraint and query languages. In Section 4, we describe a computational mechanism to answer queries for these languages. It includes a sound and complete algorithm, a discussion of the complexity, and experimental results illustrating the applicability of the framework. Our experiments were carried out in the domain of medical diagnosis where numerical measurements of parameters such as blood pressure and heart rate are abstracted to vague concepts such as high and low blood pressure and used for the diagnosis of the patient's condition. In this paper, for the sake of clarity and understanding, we stick to the more everyday example of bald people.

2   Constraint Language

To express the domain knowledge, the constraint language must have an explicit representation of thresholds, a language to express numerical constraints and a language to express the logical constraints. We present such a language here, chosen for its familiarity as well as to strike a tradeoff between expressivity and efficiency of answering queries.

The vague predicates in the logical language are distinguished from the other predicates. We refer to the vague predicates, which must all be unary, as *interval-predicates* and to all other predicates as *noninterval-predicates*. The set of *interval-predicates* is denoted by $\mathcal{IP}$, and the set of *noninterval-predicates* by $\mathcal{NIP}$. With every $P \in \mathcal{IP}$ we associate two *threshold terms* P^- and P^+, called the *lower* and *upper thresholds* of P, respectively. The set of all threshold terms is denoted by $\mathcal{T}$ ($\mathcal{T} = \{P^-, P^+ \mid P \in \mathcal{IP}\}$). The interval-predicates will be interpreted in a special way to reflect our intuition about the vague predicates: P will be interpreted as the interval $[P^-, P^+]$ over $\Re$, the set of real numbers. We will refer to this interpretation as the *predicate-as-interval assumption*.

1. **Numerical Constraints:** The language of numerical constraints is that of linear arithmetic inequalities where the threshold terms in $\mathcal{T}$ are the variables of the inequalities. A numerical constraint must be reducible to the form $(a_1 x_1 + \ldots + a_n x_n) \ rel \ b$, where $a_1, \ldots, a_n, b \in \Re$, $x_1, \ldots, x_n \in \mathcal{T}$, and $rel \in \{\leq, \geq, <, >, =\}$. We denote the set of numerical constraints by NC.

---

signment is made much easier in our framework.

2. **Logical Constraints:** These are definite Horn clauses without function symbols (also called Datalog sentences in the deductive database literature [Ullman 1988]). The predicates of these logical constraints are interval-predicates $\mathcal{IP}$ as well as noninterval-predicates $\mathcal{NIP}$. We denote the set of logical constraints by LC.

The constraints in Example 1 are represented in the language as follows. We extend the example to include another constraint that all rich VPs become presidents of companies.

Example 2:

$$\mathcal{IP} = \{\text{bald, old, rich}\}$$

$$\mathcal{NIP} = \{age,\ hairs,\ pres,\ money,\ was\_VP\}$$

$NC = \{\text{bald}^- = 0,\ 3 \leq \text{bald}^+ \leq 20000,\ \text{old}^+ = \infty,$
$\quad\quad 50 \leq \text{old}^- \leq 80,\ 0.1 \leq \text{rich}^- \leq 1,\ \text{rich}^+ = \infty\ \}$
$\quad\quad \cup\ \{\text{P}^- \leq \text{P}^+\ |\ \text{P} \in \mathcal{IP}\}$

The unit for bald is number of hairs, for old is age in years, and for rich is money in millions of dollars.

$LC = \{pres(x) \leftarrow was\_VP(x) \wedge money(x, y) \wedge \text{rich}(y)$
$\quad\quad \text{bald}(z) \leftarrow \text{old}(y) \wedge age(x, y) \wedge hairs(x, z)$
$\quad\quad \text{old}(y) \leftarrow pres(x) \wedge age(x, y)$
$\quad\quad age(\text{Tom}, 70),\ hairs(\text{Tom}, 500),\ was\_VP(\text{Tom}),$
$\quad\quad money(\text{Tom}, 6),\ age(\text{Jim}, 75),\ hairs(\text{Jim}, 800)$
$\quad\quad age(\text{Sam}, 45),\ hairs(\text{Sam}, 650)\}$ ∎

There are other languages that combine quantitative and qualitative constraints. For instance, Williams' qualitative algebra [Williams 1988] expresses operations on reals and signs of reals, but is not concerned with logical constraints. Similarly, [Meiri 1991] and [Kautz & Ladkin 1991] present frameworks for expressing and processing both quantitative and qualitative temporal constraints. Their language limits the constraints, whether numerical or logical, to be binary whereas our language does not. On the other hand, their language can express disjunctive relations between intervals which our language does not.

Most closely related to our language are languages for *constraint logic programming* (CLP) in the style of Lassez *et al.* [Jaffar & Lassez 1987]. CLP considers general Horn theories, as opposed to our limited Datalog theories. However, CLP does not allow numerical constraints in the head of a clause. In our language the interval-predicates can occur in the head which, if represented in CLP, would correspond to numerical constraints occurring in the head.

3 Query Language

The purpose of the query language is to enable a user to extract information about the thresholds that is implied by the domain constraints. It is a useful tool for a system designer to find the threshold values allowed by the constraints. The kind of queries supported are informally described below. Here $\text{P}_1^{th}, \ldots, \text{P}_n^{th} \in \mathcal{T}$, $\text{a}_1, \ldots, \text{a}_n \in \Re$, $rel_1, \ldots, rel_n \in \{\leq, \geq, <, >, =\}$, and $i \in \{1, \ldots, n\}$.

1. Is it *necessarily* the case that $(\text{P}_1^{th}\ rel_1\ \text{a}_1) \wedge \ldots \wedge (\text{P}_n^{th}\ rel_n\ \text{a}_n)$?

2. Is it *possibly* the case that $(\text{P}_1^{th}\ rel_1\ \text{a}_1) \wedge \ldots \wedge (\text{P}_n^{th}\ rel_n\ \text{a}_n)$?

3. What is the *minimum* value that P_i^{th} can take?

4. What is the *maximum* value that P_i^{th} can take?

Many queries may be derived using the above primitives. For example, the query "P(a) ?" can be cast as "Is it necessarily the case that $(\text{P}^- \leq \text{a}) \wedge (\text{P}^+ \geq \text{a})$?". If the answer is *yes* then P(a) is *true*, otherwise it is unknown. If the answer to "Is it possibly the case that $(\text{P}^- \leq \text{a}) \wedge (\text{P}^+ \geq \text{a})$?" is *no* then P(a) is *false*, otherwise it is unknown.

In addition, it is possible to request a specific assignment of values to the thresholds that satisfies the constraints. For Example 2, assigning the value 2000 to the baldness threshold is consistent with the given constraints. We will indicate briefly in Section 4.3 how this assignment is made. This procedure is particularly useful for a system designer who assigns specific numbers to the thresholds in the design stage of the system.

4 Computational Mechanism for Answering Queries

The final component of our framework is the computational mechanism responsible for answering queries on constraints. A key step in answering queries is preprocessing the constraints by extracting the numerical constraints from the logical constraints and combining them with the given numerical constraints. The preprocessing is a two-step procedure: first, using the predicate-as-interval assumption, the procedure extracts the numerical information on the interval-predicates from the logical constraints LC. This derived information is in the form of disjunctions of numerical constraints. Next, the procedure combines these disjunctive constraints with the given numerical constraints NC. We describe the procedure to extract numerical information from LC in Section 4.1. In Section 4.2 we prove that the procedure is sound and complete and also discuss the complexity issues. In Section 4.3 we describe how to combine the numerical information from LC with NC.

4.1 Extracting Numerical Information from Logical Constraints

The algorithm *Symb_to_Numeric* described in this section takes as input the logical constraints LC and the sets of interval and noninterval-predicates $\mathcal{IP}$ and $\mathcal{NIP}$, and returns a set of numerical constraints *quant_LC*. This process of conversion from logical to numerical constraints preserves the information about the thresholds of interval-predicates but discards the information on the noninterval-predicates. A formal discussion is deferred to Section 4.2.

Function $Symb\_to\_Numeric(LC, \mathcal{IP}, \mathcal{NIP}) : quant\_LC$
  $S \leftarrow \emptyset;$
  for every clause $c \in LC$ such that $head(c) \in \mathcal{IP}$ **do**
    $S_c \leftarrow Expand(c, LC, \mathcal{IP}, \mathcal{NIP});$
    $S \leftarrow S \cup S_c;$ /* S has no $\mathcal{NIP}$ predicates */
  endfor
  $quant\_LC \leftarrow \emptyset;$
  for every clause $c \in S$ **do**
    $quant\_LC \leftarrow quant\_LC \cup Convert\_LC\_to\_NC(c);$
  return$(quant\_LC)$
endfunction

Figure 1: Numerical Information from Logical Constraints

The algorithm $Symb\_to\_Numeric$ is described in Figure 1. Starting with all those clauses in LC that have interval-predicates at the *head*, we *expand* their bodies using other clauses in LC until all noninterval-predicates are eliminated from the body. *Expand* is very similar to SLD resolution [Lloyd 1987] but with two differences: (1) only noninterval-predicates are expanded (2) all possible expansions are computed. Thus, each clause in set S of Figure 1 has only interval-predicates. Using the predicate-as-interval assumption, we convert the resultant clauses to numerical constraints as described by function $Convert\_LC\_to\_NC$ in Figure 2. This function works by fragmenting each clause into subclauses such that each subclause has at most one variable and no two subclauses have the same variable[3]. For example, the clause $P(a) \leftarrow Q(x) \wedge R(x) \wedge S(b)$ is a disjunction of three subclauses: "$P(a)$", "$\leftarrow Q(x) \wedge R(x)$" and "$\leftarrow S(b)$". In general, each subclause thus obtained will be one of the six basic types described in Figure 2. Each type of subclause is converted to numerical constraint by using the predicate-as-interval assumption, and by interpreting the connectives $\neg, \vee, \wedge$ as complement, union and intersection of intervals, respectively.

An application of the algorithm on Example 2 is illuminating:

Example 3: The first step in the procedure is to locate clauses with interval-predicates at the head in LC and expand them until all noninterval-predicates are eliminated. Here there are two such clauses with old and bald at the head. On expansion, we obtain set S:

bald(500) $\leftarrow$ old(70)	old(70) $\leftarrow$ rich(6)
bald(800) $\leftarrow$ old(75)	bald(650) $\leftarrow$ old(45)

On applying the function $Convert\_LC\_to\_NC$, each of these clauses fragments into subclauses of the first two types: "$P(a)$" and "$\leftarrow P(a)$". On conversion we obtain the set $quant\_LC$[4]:

$quant\_LC =$
$\{(\text{bald}^- \leq 500 \leq \text{bald}^+) \vee (70 < \text{old}^-) \vee (\text{old}^+ < 70)$

---

[3]Note that this is always possible because all interval-predicates are unary.

[4]Note that each of the 4 clauses obtained here will actually split into 2 clauses.

Function $Convert\_LC\_to\_NC(lc) : nc$
  $nc \leftarrow \emptyset;$
  $lc\_subclauses \leftarrow Make\_Subclauses(lc);$ /* Every
    subclause of lc with a constant or the same variable */
  for every subclause $subcl \in lc\_subclauses$ **do**
    Case $subcl$ **of**:   /* a is a constant */
      "P(a)": $subcl' \leftarrow (\text{P}^- \leq \text{a} \leq \text{P}^+)$
      "$\leftarrow$ P(a)": $subcl' \leftarrow (\text{a} < \text{P}^-) \vee (\text{a} > \text{P}^+)$
      "P(x)": $subcl' \leftarrow (\text{P}^- = -\infty) \wedge (\text{P}^+ = +\infty)$
      "$\leftarrow$ P(x)": $subcl' \leftarrow \text{P}^- > \text{P}^+$
      "$\leftarrow \text{P}_1(x), \ldots, \text{P}_n(x)$":
        $subcl' \leftarrow \vee_{i=1}^n \vee_{j=1}^n (\text{P}_i^- > \text{P}_j^+)$
      "$\text{P}(x) \leftarrow \text{Q}_1(x), \ldots, \text{Q}_n(x)$":
        $subcl' \leftarrow (\vee_{i=1}^n \text{P}^- \leq \text{Q}_i^-) \wedge (\vee_{i=1}^n \text{P}^+ \geq \text{Q}_i^+)$;
    $nc \leftarrow nc \vee subcl'$
  endfor
  return(nc)
endfunction

Figure 2: Conversion from Logical to Linear Arithmetic Constraint

$(\text{old}^- \leq 70 \leq \text{old}^+) \vee (6 < \text{rich}^-) \vee (\text{rich}^+ < 6)$
$(\text{bald}^- \leq 800 \leq \text{bald}^+) \vee (75 < \text{old}^-) \vee (\text{old}^+ < 75)$
$(\text{bald}^- \leq 650 \leq \text{bald}^+) \vee (45 < \text{old}^-) \vee (\text{old}^+ < 45)\}$ ∎

4.2 Formal results on conservation of numerical information

We establish formally that no numerical information is lost in the conversion performed by algorithm $Symb\_to\_Numeric$. We begin by defining the models of LC that are faithful to the predicate-as-interval assumption; we call these the *standard models*. Specifically, in all standard models $M = (D, \mu)$ over a domain D, the interpretation function μ will have to map interval-predicates to intervals over the reals. In the following, $\Re$ denotes the set of real numbers.

Definition 1: Given a set of logical constraints LC, the set of interval-predicates $\mathcal{IP}$, and the set of threshold terms $\mathcal{T}$, a *standard model* of LC w.r.t. $\mathcal{IP}$ is a model $M = (D, \mu)$ such that $M \models LC$, and for every $\text{P} \in \mathcal{IP}$ there exist $\text{P}^-, \text{P}^+ \in \mathcal{T}$ and it is the case that $\mu(\text{P}^-), \mu(\text{P}^+) \in \Re$ and $\mu(\text{P}) = \{x \mid \mu(\text{P}^-) \leq x \leq \mu(\text{P}^+),\ x \in \Re\}$. ∎

Definition 2: Given LC, $\mathcal{IP}$ and $\mathcal{T}$ as above, a *numerical submodel* of LC w.r.t. $\mathcal{IP}$ is a model $M = (\Re, \mu)$ such that there is some standard model $M' = (D, \mu')$ of LC w.r.t. $\mathcal{IP}$, and μ is the restriction of μ' to terms in $\mathcal{T}$. ∎

The following theorem establishes that the algorithm $symb\_to\_numeric$ is sound and complete w.r.t. the numerical information (complete proof in [Goyal 1993]).

Theorem 4: (Soundness and Completeness) *The class of numerical submodels of LC w.r.t. $\mathcal{IP}$ is identical to the class of models of $quant\_LC$.*

Proof: *(Sketch for Completeness)* An arbitrary model M of $quant\_LC$ is extended to a standard model M' of

LC such that its numerical submodel is exactly M. M' is constructed by first building a dependency graph of predicates in LC and then by defining the interpretation of the predicates in $\mathcal{NIP}$ in the topological order of the graph. The intuition is that when a clause in LC is used to build the interpretation of the predicate in the head from the predicates in the body, the body predicates would have been already interpreted because of the order of interpretation. The equivalence of the numerical submodel of M' and the model M is proved through mathematical induction on the topological order of predicates. ∎

In the worst case, the space and time complexity of computing $quant\_LC$ is exponential in the size of LC. This is not surprising, since in the worst case, $quant\_LC$ is of exponential size. However, we have identified syntactic restrictions on the constraint language for which we can avoid such exponential blowup. In practice, the performance of the algorithm has been found to be quite acceptable for the following reasons. First, we observe that the algorithm is exponential only in the size of the non-ground constraints. Typically, the number of non-ground constraints is small compared to the number of ground literals. Second, this algorithm is invoked only once for all the queries on a given set of constraints; hence, the cost is amortized over all the queries. Thus, the overall performance of the system is not severely affected despite the apparent intractability. A more detailed discussion of the complexity issues may be found in [Goyal 1993].

4.3 Combining with Numerical Constraints

The constraints in the set $quant\_LC$, obtained by converting the logical constraints to numerical constraints, are disjunctive. These constraints must be combined with the set of given numerical constraints NC to answer the queries. In principle, we can convert the set $quant\_LC$ to disjunctive normal form (DNF) and add the constraints NC to each disjunct. The disjunction thus obtained is referred to as $output\_C$. However, in practice, we leave $quant\_LC$ in its conjunctive normal form to save space, and generate the disjuncts of $output\_C$ one by one through backtracking. Furthermore, to make the process more efficient, we first reduce the size of the set $quant\_LC$ using the constraints NC. We elaborate on these below and also discuss how existing methods are applicable to answer queries on a single disjunct of $output\_C$.

Pruning $quant\_LC$: We have developed a procedure that uses the constraints in NC to reduce the size of the set $quant\_LC$ significantly. This procedure, called $reduce$, uses the upper and lower bounds of all thresholds implied by the constraints in NC to prune $quant\_LC$ in two ways. First, if a disjunct of a constraint in $quant\_LC$ is already satisfied by the bounds, then that constraint can be deleted from $quant\_LC$. In

Example 3, the lower and upper bounds for old^- are 50 and 80 respectively, hence ($old^- > 45$) is already satisfied. Second, if a disjunct is inconsistent with the bounds, then that disjunct can be deleted. For instance, ($old^- > 82$) is inconsistent with the bounds for old^-.

The experimental results confirm that the procedure $reduce$ reduces the size of $quant\_LC$ significantly. In Example 3, $quant\_LC$ has 8 constraints with 3 disjuncts each that should give rise to 3^8 disjuncts (in DNF) in the worst case. Applying procedure $reduce$ eliminates all but 1 disjunct, that is:

$$output\_C = NC \cup \{(old^- \leq 70), (bald^+ \geq 800)\}$$

When the procedure was applied to the medical diagnosis domain, in the first application $quant\_LC$ had 12 constraints with 3 disjuncts each, giving rise to 3^{12} disjuncts in the worst case. Procedure $reduce$ eliminated all but 2 disjuncts. In a second medical application, $quant\_LC$ had 416 constraints with 2 or 3 disjuncts per constraint that would have given rise to at least 2^{416} disjuncts. Procedure $reduce$ eliminated all but 2592 disjuncts.

Generating disjuncts of $output\_C$: Once the set $quant\_LC$ has been pruned, queries are answered by generating the remaining disjuncts of $output\_C$ one at a time through backtracking. We avoid generating redundant disjuncts in $output\_C$ by recognizing the presence of common disjuncts in the constraints of $quant\_LC$. For instance, in the second medical application, only 184 disjuncts had to be generated out of the 2592 that were possible.

In practice, most queries do not require backtracking even over all possible distinct disjuncts that are generated. For instance, a query whether a constraint is *possibly* true or not, has to find any one disjunct over which the constraint is satisfied. Furthermore, even for queries where all disjuncts have to be checked, an approximate answer can be obtained by computing only on a few disjuncts. For instance, a query to find the minimum value of a threshold can return the minimum over only a few disjuncts. This approximate answer is still useful since it supplies a lower bound on the threshold, even though not the tightest lower bound. Thus, this procedure gives a useful approximate answer any time that an answer is required, and the approximation gets closer to the optimal as the allowed time increases. The experimental results on answering queries are available in [Goyal 1993].

We can even assign a specific value to the thresholds using heuristic criteria. For Example 3, the baldness threshold ($bald^+$) could be 10400 which is halfway between its bounds of 800 and 20000, and satisfies all the given constraints. When a large amount of ground data is available, clustering techniques are utilized to assign a specific value.

Answering for each disjunct: We have discussed previously how the set $quant\_LC$ is pruned *a priori* to eliminate redundant disjuncts and how the disjuncts of *output_C* are generated. Each disjunct thus generated is a set of linear arithmetic constraints. We now discuss how any query is answered on a single disjunct. The queries for maximum and minimum values of thresholds (queries 3 and 4 in Section 3) require the computation of lower and upper bounds of thresholds. Queries for checking a constraint for consistency (queries 1 and 2 in Section 3) require a consistency check on a set of constraints. Thus, any existing method for computing bounds and checking consistency of linear arithmetic constraints can be used. If NC has only simple order relations or bounded differences, we can use an efficient $\mathcal{O}(n^3)$ procedure (where n is the number of variables) from [Davis 1987] or [Meiri 1991]. Sacks' *bounder* [Sacks 1990] is applicable but more useful for nonlinear constraints. For more general linear constraints, we have to use a linear programming method that is still tractable $\mathcal{O}(n^{3.5}L)$ (L is size of input) [Karmarkar 1984]. Lassez's work on canonical form of generalized linear constraints [Huynh *et al.* 1990] has potential applications, though the advantage of a canonical form would be offset by the cost of maintaining the canonical form because we backtrack on disjunctive constraints.

5 Conclusions

We have provided a systematic account of the practical approach of representing vague concepts as precise intervals over numbers. Based on the observation that the vague concepts and their interval-boundaries are constrained by the underlying domain knowledge, we motivated and proposed a framework to reason precisely with vague concepts. The framework is comprised of a constraint language to represent the domain knowledge; a query language to request information about the interval boundaries; and a computational mechanism to answer the queries.

We described the constraint and query languages and a computational mechanism to answer queries. A key step in answering queries is preprocessing the constraints by extracting the numerical constraints from the logical constraints and combining them with the given numerical constraints. We proved this algorithm to be sound and complete and also discussed the complexity issues. Some experimental results of applying this framework to a medical domain were discussed.

The main contribution of our work is in providing a systematic framework to understand the common though *ad hoc* approach of representing vague predicates as intervals. This work is particularly applicable to a knowledge base during its development stage where the vague concepts over numbers need to be defined precisely.

Acknowledgements We would like to thank Surajit Chaudhuri, Ashish Gupta, Alon Levy, Pandu Nayak, Moshe Tennenholtz, Becky Thomas and the anonymous reviewers.

References

Davis, E. 1987. Constraint Propagation with Interval Labels. *Artificial Intelligence* 32(3):281–331.

Davis, E. 1990. *Representations of Commonsense Knowledge*. Morgan Kaufmann Publishers, 19–20.

Goyal, N. 1993. A Framework for Reasoning Precisely with Vague Concepts. Ph.D. diss. (in preparation), Dept. of Computer Science, Stanford University.

Hayes-Roth, B.; Washington, R.; Hewett, R.; Hewett, M.; and Seiver, A. 1989. Intelligent Monitoring and Control. In *Proc. of Eleventh International Joint Conference on Artificial Intelligence*, 43–249.

Huynh, T.; Joskowicz, L.; Lassez, C.; and Lassez, J-L. 1990. Reasoning about Linear Constraints using Parametric Queries. In *Proc. of Tenth FST TCS*, Bangalore, India.

Jaffar, J.; and Lassez, J-L. 1987. Constraint Logic Programming. In *Proc. of 14th ACM Symposium on Principles of Programming languages*, 111–119.

Karmarkar, N. 1984. A New Polynomial-Time Algorithm for Linear Programming. *Combinatorica* 4:373–395.

Kautz, H.A.; and Ladkin, P.B. 1991. Integrating Metric and Qualitative Temporal Reasoning. In *Proc. of Ninth National Conference on Artificial Intelligence*, 241–246.

Lloyd, J.W. 1987. *Foundations of Logic Programming, 2nd. ed.*. Springer-Verlag.

Meiri, I. 1991. Combining Qualitative and Quantitative Constraints in Temporal Reasoning. In *Proc. of Ninth National Conference on Artificial Intelligence*, 260–267.

Parikh, R. 1983. The problem of Vague Predicates. In Cohen and Wartofsky (eds.), *Language, Logic, and Method*. Reidel Publishers, 241–261.

Sacks, E. 1990. Hierarchical Reasoning about Inequalities. In *Readings in Qualitative Reasoning about Physical Systems*, eds. D.S. Weld and J. de Kleer. Morgan Kaufmann Publishers, 344–350.

Shahar, Y.; Tu, S.W.; and Musen, M.A. 1992. Knowledge Acquisition for Temporal-Abstraction Mechanisms. *Knowledge Acquisition* 4:217–236.

Ullman, J.D. 1988. *Principles of Database and Knowledge-Base Systems, Vol. 1*. Computer Science Press.

Williams, B.C. 1988. MINIMA: A Symbolic Approach to Qualitative Algebraic Reasoning. In *Proc. of Seventh National Conference on Artificial Intelligence*, 264–269.

Zadeh, L.A. 1983. Commonsense and Fuzzy Logic. In *The Knowledge Frontier: Essays in the Representation of Knowledge*, eds. N. Cercone and G. McCalla. New York: Springer-Verlag, 103–136.

Restricted Monotonicity

Vladimir Lifschitz*

Department of Computer Sciences
and Department of Philosophy
University of Texas at Austin
Austin, TX 78712

Abstract

A knowledge representation problem can be sometimes viewed as an element of a family of problems, with parameters corresponding to possible assumptions about the domain under consideration. When additional assumptions are made, the class of domains that are being described becomes smaller, so that the class of conclusions that are true in all the domains becomes larger. As a result, a satisfactory solution to a parametric knowledge representation problem on the basis of some nonmonotonic formalism can be expected to have a certain formal property, that we call *restricted monotonicity*. We argue that it is important to recognize parametric knowledge representation problems and to verify restricted monotonicity for their proposed solutions.

Introduction

This paper is about the methodology of representing knowledge in nonmonotonic formalisms. A knowledge representation problem can be sometimes viewed as an element of a family of problems, with parameters corresponding to possible assumptions about the domain under consideration. When additional assumptions are made, the class of domains that are being described becomes smaller, so that the class of conclusions that are true in all the domains becomes larger. As a result, a satisfactory solution to a parametric knowledge representation problem on the basis of some nonmonotonic formalism can be expected to have a certain formal property, that we call *restricted monotonicity*.

The idea of restricted monotonicity is first illustrated here by examples. Then the precise definition of this property is given, and methods for proving it are discussed. Finally, we apply the concept of restricted monotonicity to the analysis of some of the recent work on representing action and change in nonmonotonic formalisms.

---

*This work was partially supported by National Science Foundation under grant IRI-9101078.

Examples

Here is a simple knowledge representation problem involving a default:

Formalize the assertions:

Birds normally fly.
Penguins are birds.
Penguins do not fly.

We will compare two solutions, one based on default logic [Reiter, 1980], the other on circumscription [McCarthy, 1986].

The first formalization is the default theory whose postulates are the axioms

$$\forall x (Penguin(x) \supset Bird(x)) \qquad (1)$$

and

$$\forall x (Penguin(x) \supset \neg Flies(x)), \qquad (2)$$

and the default

$$Bird(x) : Flies(x) \ / \ Flies(x). \qquad (3)$$

The second is the circumscriptive theory with the axioms (1), (2) and

$$\forall x (Bird(x) \wedge \neg Ab(x) \supset Flies(x)), \qquad (4)$$

in which Ab is circumscribed and $Flies$ varied.

There is an important difference between the two formalizations that becomes obvious when we apply the default *birds normally fly* to specific objects. Although the postulates of the two theories do not use any object constants, let us assume that their languages include an object constant, say, *Joe*. Since Joe is not postulated to be a bird, the formula $Flies(Joe)$ is undecidable both in the default logic formalization T_1 and in the circumscriptive formalization T_2. We are interested in the theories obtained from T_1 and T_2 by adding some of the possible assumptions

$$\begin{array}{c} Bird(Joe), \neg Bird(Joe), \\ Penguin(Joe), \neg Penguin(Joe) \end{array} \qquad (5)$$

to their axiom sets.

For some subsets p of (5), adding p to the axiom set of T_1 will have the same effect on the status of the formula $Flies(Joe)$ as adding p to T_2. If, for instance, p is $\{Bird(Joe), \neg Penguin(Joe)\}$, then $Flies(Joe)$ is provable both in $T_1 \cup p$ and $T_2 \cup p$. If, on the other hand, p is $\{Penguin(Joe)\}$, then this formula is refutable in both theories.

The situation will be different, however, if we take p to be $\{Bird(Joe)\}$. Now Joe is known to be a bird, but it is not known whether he is a penguin. The default logic formalization sanctions the conclusion that Joe flies: $T_1 \cup \{Bird(Joe)\}$ entails $Flies(Joe)$. In the corresponding circumscriptive formalization, $T_2 \cup \{Bird(Joe)\}$, the formula $Flies(Joe)$ remains undecidable.

The theories T_1 and T_2 can be viewed as somewhat different interpretations of the given set of assumptions about the ability of birds to fly. Whether or not T_1 is considered too strong—or T_2 too weak—depends on which of the two identically worded, but slightly different knowledge representation problems we had in mind in the first place.

The circumscriptive solution T_2 can be viewed as reasonable, and the default logic solution T_1 as excessively strong, if the absence of both $Penguin(Joe)$ and $\neg Penguin(Joe)$ among the axioms is supposed to indicate our willingness to take into consideration both the domains in which Joe is a penguin and the domains in which he isn't, and to sanction only the conclusions that are true in domains of both kinds. We will express this knowledge representation convention by saying that these two literals function in this example as "parameters." A parameter is an additional postulate whose presence in the axiom set is supposed to make the set of domains under consideration smaller, and thus to increase the set of conclusions sanctioned by the formalization.

The knowledge representation problem stated at the beginning of this section would be described more precisely if we specified that the ground literals containing $Bird$ or $Penguin$ should be treated as parameters. This statement implies that a formalization T will be considered adequate only if it has the following property: *For any subsets p, q of (5) such that $p \subset q$, each consequence of $T \cup p$ is a consequence of $T \cup q$.* In particular, if T is adequate, then all theorems of $T \cup \{Bird(Joe)\}$ will be among the theorems of $T \cup \{Bird(Joe), Penguin(Joe)\}$, so that $Flies(Joe)$ will not be one of them.

This property is an example of what we call "restricted monotonicity." It is satisfied for the circumscriptive formalization T_2, but not for the default theory T_1. We will see that, in general, there is no correlation between restricted monotonicity and the choice of a nonmonotonic formalism; what matters is which postulates are included in the formalization and, in case of circumscription, what circumscription policy is ap-

plied. For instance, we will give a default logic formalization of the same example that satisfies the restricted monotonicity condition.

There is nothing wrong, of course, with a different interpretation of the flying birds problem: If the axioms do not tell us whether Joe is a penguin, we may treat the domains in which this is the case as "secondary," and be prepared to jump to the conclusion that we are not in such a domain, at least when we decide whether Joe can fly. But it is important to be clear about how the problem is interpreted before discussing the adequacy of a particular solution.

We argue in this paper that many knowledge representation problems can be described as parametric, and that, when we deal with such a problem, it is important to recognize this fact and to verify restricted monotonicity for its proposed solutions.

A class of examples that is discussed here in some detail is given by *initial conditions* in temporal projection problems. In various versions of the "Yale shooting" story [Hanks and McDermott, 1987], the initial situation is described by including some of the formulas

$$Holds(Loaded, S0), \neg Holds(Loaded, S0), \\ Holds(Alive, S0), \neg Holds(Alive, S0) \qquad (6)$$

in the axiom set. We can think of these formulas as parameters. Every consistent subset of (6) represents an instance of a "parametric problem"; the larger the subset is, the more conclusions about the values of fluents in future situations can be justified. This is again an example of restricted monotonicity.

Definition

We would like to give a definition of restricted monotonicity applicable to many nonmonotonic formalisms. In order to make it general, we will first introduce the notion of a "declarative formalism."

A *declarative formalism* is defined by a set S of symbolic expressions called *sentences*, a set P of symbolic expressions called *postulates*, and a map Cn from sets of postulates to sets of sentences. A set of postulates is a *theory*. A sentence A is a *consequence* of a theory T if $A \in Cn(T)$. The formalism is *monotonic* if Cn is a monotone operator, that is, if $Cn(T) \subset Cn(T')$ whenever $T \subset T'$.

Here are some examples. Any first-order or higher-order language of classical logic can be viewed as a declarative formalism. Its postulates are identical to its sentences—they are arbitrary closed formulas of the language; $Cn(T)$ is the set of sentences that are true in all models of T. The use of circumscription amounts to defining $Cn(T)$ to be the set of sentences that are true in the models of T which are minimal relative to some circumscription policy. In case of default theories, a sentence is a closed formula, and a postulate is either a closed formula or a default. (Note that here P differs from S.) For a default theory T, $Cn(T)$ is the intersection of the extensions of T.

When a declarative formalism $\langle S, P, Cn \rangle$ is used to solve a parametric knowledge representation problem, a subset S_0 of its sentences is designated as the set of *assertions*, and a subset P_0 of its postulates is designated as the set of *parameters*. The idea of a parameter was discussed above: A parameter is an additional postulate whose presence in a theory is supposed to make the class of domains under consideration smaller. An assertion is a sentence that can be interpreted as true or false in a domain described by the theory. The need to distinguish between assertions and arbitrary sentences arises when the language contains auxiliary symbols, such as Ab, that have no "observable" meaning in the domains under consideration. We may wish to specify, for instance, that a sentence is an assertion if it does not contain Ab. Some formalizations do not use auxiliary symbols; in such cases, we view every sentence as an assertion.

Let $\langle S, P, Cn \rangle$ be a declarative formalism. Let a subset S_0 of S be designated as the set of assertions, and a subset P_0 of P as the set of parameters. We say that a theory T satisfies the *restricted monotonicity condition* if, for any sets $p, q \subset P_0$,

$$p \subset q \Rightarrow Cn(T \cup p) \cap S_0 \subset Cn(T \cup q) \cap S_0. \quad (7)$$

In words: *If more parameters are added to T as additional postulates, no assertions will be retracted.*

Note that (7) is trivially true if Cn is a monotone operator. Consequently, restricted monotonicity becomes an issue only when a nonmonotonic formalism is used.

Condition (7) is weaker than the monotonicity of Cn in two ways. First, it applies only to theories of the form $T \cup p$ for the subsets p of P_0, rather than to arbitrary theories. Second, it refers not to the set of all consequences of a theory, but only to the assertions that belong to it.

Methods for Proving Restricted Monotonicity

The mathematical apparatus required for proving restricted monotonicity will vary depending on the declarative formalism on which the solution is based. In this section we discuss some of the methods that can be used for verifying the restricted monotonicity condition in circumscriptive theories and in extended logic programs.

Circumscriptive Theories

For simplicity, we restrict attention to finite circumscriptive theories without prioritization. Let S be the set of all sentences of some first-order language, R a list of distinct predicate constants of that language, and Z a list of distinct function and/or predicate constants disjoint from R. By $Cn_{R;Z}$ we denote the consequence operator corresponding to the circumscription which circumscribes R and varies Z. This means that, for any finite subset T of S, $Cn_{R;Z}(T)$ is the set of sentences entailed by CIRC$[\bigwedge_{A \in T} A; R; Z]$.

Proposition 1. *Let T be a finite theory in the formalism $\langle S, S, Cn_{R;Z} \rangle$. If the set of parameters is finite, and the parameters do not contain symbols from R or Z, then T satisfies the restricted monotonicity condition.*

Proof. For any set p of parameters, $Cn_{R;Z}(T \cup p)$ is the set of sentences entailed by

$$\text{CIRC}[\bigwedge_{A \in T} A \wedge \bigwedge_{A \in p} A; R; Z].$$

Since $\bigwedge_{A \in p} A$ does not contain symbols from R or Z, this formula is equivalent to

$$\text{CIRC}[\bigwedge_{A \in T} A; R; Z] \wedge \bigwedge_{A \in p} A.$$

If $p \subset q$, then this conjunction is entailed by the corresponding condition for q:

$$\text{CIRC}[\bigwedge_{A \in T} A; R; Z] \wedge \bigwedge_{A \in q} A.$$

It follows that $p \subset q$ implies

$$Cn_{R;Z}(T \cup p) \subset Cn_{R;Z}(T \cup q),$$

and consequently

$$Cn_{R;Z}(T \cup p) \cap S_0 \subset Cn_{R;Z}(T \cup q) \cap S_0.$$

In case of the circumscriptive theory T_2 defined above, R is Ab, Z is $Flies$, P_0 is (5), and S_0 is the set of sentences not containing Ab. By Proposition 1, the restricted monotonicity of T_2 follows from the fact that the parameters (5) contain neither Ab nor $Flies$.

Note that the statement of Proposition 1 imposes a restriction on the set of parameters, but not on the set of assertions. It follows, in particular, that T_2 would have satisfied the restricted monotonicity condition even if all sentences were considered assertions. We will see below that, for some other solutions to the same knowledge representation problem, the fact that Ab is not allowed in assertions is crucial for the verification of restricted monotonicity.

Consider, on the other hand, the theory T_2', which differs from T_2 in that the predicates $Bird$ and $Penguin$ are allowed to vary, along with $Flies$. This theory is stronger than T_2, and it allows us to justify, among others, the conclusion that there are no penguins in the world: $\forall x \neg Penguin(x)$. This result may be viewed as undesirable. Peculiarities of this kind in circumscriptive theories are well known ([McCarthy, 1986], Section 5). In fact, T_2' has a more fundamental defect: It does not satisfy the restricted monotonicity condition. Indeed, $\neg Penguin(Joe)$ is a consequence of T_2' which is lost when $Penguin(Joe)$ is added to its axiom set. Proposition 1 does not apply here, because the predicates $Bird$ and $Penguin$, varied in T_2', occur in the parameters.

Extended Logic Programs

According to [Gelfond and Lifschitz, 1991], an *extended logic program* is a set of rules of the form

$$L_0 \leftarrow L_1, \ldots, L_m, not\ L_{m+1}, \ldots, not\ L_n, \qquad (8)$$

where each L_i is a literal, that is, an atom possibly preceded by $\neg$. ("General" logic programs are, syntactically, the special case when classical negation $\neg$ is not used.) The rule (8) has the same meaning as the default

$$L_1 \wedge \ldots \wedge L_m : \overline{L_{m+1}}, \ldots, \overline{L_n} / L_0, \qquad (9)$$

where $\overline{L}$ stands for the literal complementary to L, so that the language of extended programs can be viewed as a subsystem of default logic. A ground literal L is a *consequence* of an extended program Π if it belongs to all extensions of Π. Extended logic programs can be viewed as theories in a declarative formalism, if ground literals are taken to be sentences, and rules of the form (8) are considered postulates.

The knowledge representation problem described at the beginning of the paper can be solved in the language of extended programs as follows:

$$\begin{aligned} &Flies(x) \leftarrow Bird(x), not\ Ab(x), \\ &Bird(x) \leftarrow Penguin(x), \\ &\neg Flies(x) \leftarrow Penguin(x), \\ &Ab(x) \leftarrow not\ \neg Penguin(x). \end{aligned} \qquad (10)$$

Note the last rule, which plays an important part in this program. Without it, adding the fact $Penguin(Joe)$ to the program would have made it inconsistent. Note also the use of the combination $not\ \neg$ in that rule. The simpler rule

$$Ab(x) \leftarrow Penguin(x) \qquad (11)$$

would have canceled the applicability of the first rule of the program to x only when x is known to be a penguin; with $not\ \neg$ inserted in front of $Penguin(x)$, this is accomplished for every x that is not known to satisfy $\neg Penguin(x)$. (Compare this with the discussion of the cancelation rule for *Noninertial* in Section 4 of [Gelfond and Lifschitz, 1992].) In particular, even with the fact $Bird(Joe)$ added to (10), the formula $Flies(Joe)$ remains undecidable. We see that (10) is similar in this respect to the circumscriptive formalization T_2, rather than to the default theory T_1.

Written as defaults, the rules (10) are:

$$\begin{aligned} &Bird(x) : \neg Ab(x) / Flies(x), \\ &Penguin(x) / Bird(x), \\ &Penguin(x) / \neg Flies(x), \\ &: Penguin(x) / Ab(x). \end{aligned} \qquad (12)$$

The first of these defaults is reminiscent of the approach to the use of default logic advocated by Morris [1988].

The theorem about restricted monotonicity in extended logic programs stated below is based on the notion of a "signing." This notion was originally defined for general logic programs [Kunen, 1989], and then extended by Turner [1993] to programs that may contain classical negation.

The *absolute value* of a literal L (symbolically, $|L|$) is L if L is positive, and $\overline{L}$ otherwise. A *signing* for an extended logic program Π without variables is a set X of ground atoms such that

(i) for any rule (8) from Π, either

$$|L_0|, \ldots, |L_m| \in X, |L_{m+1}|, \ldots, |L_n| \notin X$$

or

$$|L_0|, \ldots, |L_m| \notin X, |L_{m+1}|, \ldots, |L_n| \in X;$$

(ii) for any atom $A \in X$, $\neg A$ does not appear in Π.

It is easy to see, for example, that the set of ground instances of $Ab(x)$ is a signing for the set of ground instances of the rules (10).

The following lemma is a special case of Theorem 1 from [Turner, 1993].

Lemma. *Let Π_1 be an extended program without variables, and let X be a signing for Π_1. Let Π_2 be a program obtained from Π_1 by dropping some of its rules (8) such that $|L_0| \notin X$. If a ground literal L is a consequence of Π_2 and $|L| \notin X$, then L is a consequence of Π_1 also.*

Proposition 2. *Let Π be an extended logic program, and let X be a signing for the set of ground instances of the rules of Π. If all parameters and assertions are ground literals whose absolute values do not belong to X, then Π satisfies the restricted monotonicity condition.*

Proof. Since a program has the same consequences as the set of all ground instances of its rules, we can assume, without loss of generality, that the rules of Π do not contain variables. Let p and q be sets of parameters such that $p \subset q$. By applying the lemma to $\Pi \cup q$ as Π_1 and $\Pi \cup p$ as Π_2, we conclude that, for any ground literal L such that $|L| \notin X$, if $L \in Cn(\Pi \cup p)$ then $L \in Cn(\Pi \cup q)$. It follows that

$$Cn(\Pi \cup p) \cap S_0 \subset Cn(\Pi \cup q) \cap S_0.$$

Proposition 2 implies, for instance, that (10) satisfies the restricted monotonicity condition.

Restricted Monotonicity in Theories of Action

As observed above, temporal projection problems can be thought of as parametric, with initial conditions as parameters. It is interesting to look from this perspective at the existing approaches to describing actions in nonmonotonic formalisms and to see how successful they are in achieving restricted monotonicity. (For the methods based on stating frame axioms explicitly and then applying classical logic, the problem does not arise, because any theory based on a monotonic logic satisfies the restricted monotonicity condition.)

Minimizing Change

The first attempt to solve the frame problem using circumscription ([McCarthy, 1986], Section 9) was shown by Hanks and McDermott [1987] to lead in some cases to "overweak disjunctions." The analysis of McCarthy's method from the point of view of restricted monotonicity shows that it has also another flaw.

The following key observation was made by Fangzhen Lin in connection with the temporal minimization method (personal communication, October 31, 1992). Let A be an action whose effect is to make a propositional fluent F false if it is currently true. The initial value of F is not given. Minimizing change will lead to the conclusion that F was initially false, because in this case nothing has to change as A is executed.

This undesirable conclusion presents a difficulty that is perhaps even more fundamental than the one uncovered by Hanks and McDermott. Minimizing change may lead not only to conclusions that are too weak; sometimes, its results are much too strong. Since the only action considered in this example is performed in the initial situation, it does not matter whether the minimization criterion is simple or temporal, as in [Kautz, 1986], [Lifschitz, 1986] and [Shoham, 1986].

We will describe Lin's example formally and show that it can be viewed as a violation of restricted monotonicity. Instead of the situation calculus language, we will use the simpler syntax of a *theory of a single action* ([Lifschitz, 1990], Section 2). Theories of this kind include situation variables and fluent variables, but they do not have variables for actions. The function *Result* is replaced by two situation constants: S^i for the initial situation, in which a certain fixed action is executed, and S^r for the result of the action. If the only fluent constant in the language is F, then the possible initial conditions are

$$Holds(F, S^i), \quad \neg Holds(F, S^i). \tag{13}$$

The assumption that the action in question makes F false if executed when F is true is expressed by the formula

$$Holds(F, S^i) \supset \neg Holds(F, S^r). \tag{14}$$

Minimizing change, in this simplified language, is expressed by postulating the "commonsense law of inertia" in the form

$$\neg Ab(f) \supset Holds(f, S^r) \equiv Holds(f, S^i), \tag{15}$$

and circumscribing Ab.

Let T be the circumscriptive theory with axioms (14) and (15), in which Ab is circumscribed and *Holds* varied. Take the formulas (13) to be parameters, and all closed formulas not containing Ab to be assertions. Lin's observation shows that T does not satisfy the restricted monotonicity condition. Indeed, $\neg Holds(F, S^i)$ is a consequence of T, but not a consequence of $T \cup \{Holds(F, S^i)\}$.

Mathematically, the lack of restricted monotonicity in this example is not surprising: The predicate *Holds*, varied in T, occurs in parameters, so that Proposition 1 does not apply.

Other Approaches to the Frame Problem

Two other ways to apply circumscription to the frame problem are proposed in [Lifschitz, 1987] and [Baker, 1991]. Unlike McCarthy's original proposal and the temporal minimization approach, these methods have reasonable restricted monotonicity properties, although this fact does not follow from Proposition 1. A restricted monotonicity theorem for Baker-style formalizations can be proved using Theorem 3 from [Kartha, 1993].

The logic programming method of [Gelfond and Lifschitz, 1992] and [Baral and Gelfond, 1993] builds on the ideas of [Morris, 1988], [Eshghi and Kowalski, 1989], [Evans, 1989] and [Apt and Bezem, 1990]. A restricted monotonicity theorem for this method can be derived from Proposition 2.

Sandewall [1989] proposed to apply a nonmonotonic formalism to a set of axioms that does not include initial conditions ("observations") and to get first "the set of all possible developments in the world *regardless of* any observations," and then " to take that whole set and 'filter' it with the given observations." A mechanism of this kind may achieve restricted monotonicity by removing the initial conditions from the scope of the nonmonotonic consequence operator. Some of the ideas of [Lin and Shoham, 1991] seem to be in the same group.

High-Level Languages for Describing Actions

The "high-level" language $\mathcal{A}$ [Gelfond and Lifschitz, 1992], designed specifically for describing action and change, has propositions of two kinds. "Value propositions" specify the values of fluents in particluar situations. "Effect propositions" are general statements about the effects of actions. A "domain description" is a set of propositions. The semantics of domain descriptions is defined in terms of "models." A model of a domain description D consists of two components: One specifies the "initial state" of the system, and the other is a "transition function," describing how states are affected by performing actions. The effect propositions from D determine what can be used as the transition function in a model of D. The value propositions limit possible choices of the initial state. Details of the syntax and semantics of $\mathcal{A}$ can be found in [Gelfond and Lifschitz, 1992].

A value proposition is a *consequence* of a domain description D if it is true in all models of D. This definition allows us to treat the language $\mathcal{A}$ as a declarative formalism, with value propositions as sentences, and both value propositions and effect propositions as postulates.

This formalism is nonmonotonic. Indeed, adding an effect proposition to a domain description D, generally, changes the set of models of D in a nonmonotonic way, so that the set of consequences of D changes nonmonotonically also. However, adding value propositions to D merely imposes additional constraints on the choice of the initial state in a model, so that it can only make the set of models smaller, and the set of consequences larger. If we agree to identify both parameters and assertions with value propositions, then this fact can be expressed as follows:

Proposition 3. *Every domain description in $\mathcal{A}$ satisfies the restricted monotonicity condition.*

Since initial conditions in a temporal projection problem are represented in $\mathcal{A}$ by value propositions, we conclude that the problem of restricted monotonicity for temporal projection is resolved in $\mathcal{A}$ in a satisfactory way.

The extensions of $\mathcal{A}$ introduced in [Baral and Gelfond, 1993] and [Lifschitz, 1993] have similar restricted monotonicity properties.

Acknowledgements

I have benefitted from discussing the ideas presented here with Robert Causey, Michael Gelfond, G.N. Kartha, Fangzhen Lin, Norman McCain, Luis Pereira, Hudson Turner and Thomas Woo. My special thanks go to Fangzhen Lin for permission to include his unpublished counterexample.

References

Apt, Krzysztof and Bezem, Marc 1990. Acyclic programs. In Warren, David and Szeredi, Peter, editors 1990, *Logic Programming: Proc. of the Seventh Int'l Conf.* 617–633.

Baker, Andrew 1991. Nonmonotonic reasoning in the framework of situation calculus. *Artificial Intelligence* 49:5–23.

Baral, Chitta and Gelfond, Michael 1993. Representing concurrent actions in extended logic programming. In *Proc. of IJCAI-93*. To appear.

Eshghi, Kave and Kowalski, Robert 1989. Abduction compared with negation as failure. In Levi, Giorgio and Martelli, Maurizio, editors 1989, *Logic Programming: Proc. of the Sixth Int'l Conf.* 234–255.

Evans, Chris 1989. Negation-as-failure as an approach to the Hanks and McDermott problem. In *Proc. of the Second Int'l Symp. on Artificial Intelligence.*

Gelfond, Michael and Lifschitz, Vladimir 1991. Classical negation in logic programs and disjunctive databases. *New Generation Computing* 9:365–385.

Gelfond, Michael and Lifschitz, Vladimir 1992. Representing actions in extended logic programming. In Apt, Krzysztof, editor 1992, *Proc. Joint Int'l Conf. and Symp. on Logic Programming.* 559–573.

Hanks, Steve and McDermott, Drew 1987. Nonmonotonic logic and temporal projection. *Artificial Intelligence* 33(3):379–412.

Kartha, G. N. 1993. Soundness and completeness theorems for three formalizations of action. In *Proc. of IJCAI-93*. To appear.

Kautz, Henry 1986. The logic of persistence. In *Proc. of AAAI-86*. 401–405.

Kunen, Kenneth 1989. Signed data dependencies in logic programs. *Journal of Logic Programming* 7(3):231–245.

Lifschitz, Vladimir 1986. Pointwise circumscription: Preliminary report. In *Proc. AAAI-86*. 406–410.

Lifschitz, Vladimir 1987. Formal theories of action (preliminary report). In *Proc. of IJCAI-87*. 966–972.

Lifschitz, Vladimir 1990. Frames in the space of situations. *Artificial Intelligence* 46:365–376.

Lifschitz, Vladimir 1993. A language for describing actions. In *Working Papers of the Second Symposium on Logical Formalizations of Commonsense Reasoning.*

Lin, Fangzhen and Shoham, Yoav 1991. Provably correct theories of action (preliminary report). In *Proc. AAAI-91*. 349–354.

McCarthy, John 1986. Applications of circumscription to formalizing common sense knowledge. *Artificial Intelligence* 26(3):89–116. Reproduced in [McCarthy, 1990].

McCarthy, John 1990. *Formalizing common sense: papers by John McCarthy.* Ablex, Norwood, NJ.

Morris, Paul 1988. The anomalous extension problem in default reasoning. *Artificial Intelligence* 35(3):383–399.

Reiter, Raymond 1980. A logic for default reasoning. *Artificial Intelligence* 13(1,2):81–132.

Sandewall, Erik 1989. Combining logic and differential equations for describing real-world systems. In Brachman, Ronald; Levesque, Hector; and Reiter, Raymond, editors 1989, *Proc. of the First Int'l Conf. on Principles of Knowledge Representation and Reasoning.* 412–420.

Shoham, Yoav 1986. Chronological ignorance: Time, nonmonotonicity, necessity and causal theories. In *Proc. of AAAI-86*. 389–393.

Turner, Hudson 1993. A monotonicity theorem for extended logic programs. In *Proc. of the Tenth Int'l Conference on Logic Programming*. To appear.

Subnormal modal logics for knowledge representation

Grigori Schwarz
Robotics Laboratory
Computer Science Department
Stanford University
Stanford CA 94305-4110

Mirosław Truszczyński
Department of Computer Science
University of Kentucky
Lexington, KY, 40506

Abstract

Several widely accepted modal nonmonotonic logics for reasoning about knowledge and beliefs of rational agents with introspection powers are based on strong modal logics such as KD45, S4.4, S4F and S5. In this paper we argue that weak modal logics, without even the axiom K and, therefore, below the range of normal modal logics, also give rise to useful nonmonotonic systems. We study two such logics: the logic N, containing propositional calculus and necessitation but no axiom schemata for manipulating the modality, and the logic NT — the extension of N by the schema T. For the nonmonotonic logics N and NT we develop minimal model semantics. We use it to show that the nonmonotonic logics N and NT are at least as expressive as autoepistemic logic, reflexive autoepistemic logic and default logic. In fact, each can be regarded as a common *generalization* of these classic nonmonotonic systems. We also show that the nonmonotonic logics N and NT have the property of being conservative with respect to adding new definitions, and prove that computationally they are equivalent to autoepistemic and default logics.

Introduction

Several nonmonotonic logics have been proposed as formalisms for common-sense reasoning [Reiter, 1980; McCarthy, 1980; McDermott and Doyle, 1980]. Some of the most interesting and powerful logics (default logic and autoepistemic logics among them) can be obtained from the approach originated by McDermott and Doyle [1980] and further refined by McDermott [1982]. The idea is to introduce a modality L which is read as "is known", "is believed", or 'is provable", and to define a set T of consequences of a given theory in such a way that if a sentence ψ does not belong to T, then the sentence $\neg L\psi$ is in T.

Formally, let I be a set of sentences representing the initial knowledge of an agent, and let $\mathcal{S}$ be a monotonic logic. A set T is called an $\mathcal{S}$-*expansion* of I, if

$$T = \{\varphi : I \cup \{\neg L\psi : \psi \notin T\} \vdash_{\mathcal{S}} \varphi\}, \qquad (1)$$

where $\vdash_{\mathcal{S}}$ denotes derivability in $\mathcal{S}$.

In [McDermott and Doyle, 1980] expansions were defined and investigated with the classical propositional logic in place of $\mathcal{S}$. In this case the notion of expansion has counterintuitive properties. Expansions of I are meant to serve as candidates for a knowledge or belief set based in I. However, a consistent expansion (in the sense of [McDermott and Doyle, 1980]) may contain both ψ and $\neg L\psi$, contrary to the intended interpretation of L. Already in [McDermott and Doyle, 1980], where expansions were first introduced, this undesirable phenomenon was observed. As a way out of the problem, McDermott [1982] suggested to replace in (1) the propositional derivability by the derivability $\vdash_{\mathcal{S}}$ in a modal logic $\mathcal{S}$. If $\mathcal{S}$ contains the inference rule of necessitation, then the counterintuitive properties, like the one indicated above, disappear.

A crucial question is what modal logic $\mathcal{S}$ should be used. McDermott [1982] considered three well-known logics: T, S4 and S5. He noted that, intuitively, all the axioms of S5 seem to be acceptable. On the other hand, he proved that nonmonotonic S5 collapses to the monotonic logic S5 and, hence, cannot be used as a formal description of defeasible reasoning. Logics S4 and T yield "true" nonmonotonic systems adequate for handling some examples of common-sense reasoning [Shvarts, 1990]. But it is hard to justify why we should give up some of the axioms of S5 while retaining the others if all of them seem to be intuitively justified.

It was proved in [McDermott, 1982] that if a logic $\mathcal{S}$ contains the necessitation rule, then each $\mathcal{S}$-expansion contains all theorems of S5. Hence, the presence or absence of some of the axioms of S5 has no effect on the fundamental property of expansions that they are closed under provability in S5. This result may be regarded as an evidence that the search for modal logics which may yield useful nonmonotonic systems should focus on two classes of modal logics: those close to S5, satisfying many of the axioms of S5, and those which satisfy none or few of them.

So far, logics close to S5 have received substantially more attention most notably the modal logics KD45, S4.4, S4F. It has been shown [Shvarts, 1990; Schwarz, 1991a; Truszczyński, 1991b] that if we disregard inconsistent expansions, the nonmonotonic modal logic KD45 is equivalent to the celebrated autoepistemic logic by Moore, logic S4.4 is equivalent to the autoepistemic logic of knowledge introduced in [Schwarz, 1991a], and Reiter's default logic can be naturally embedded in the nonmonotonic logic logic S4F, which, in turn, has a natural interpretation as a logic of minimal (or grounded) knowledge [Schwarz and Truszczyński, 1992].

The logics KD45, S4.4 and S4F share several common features. They are close to S5 and admit natural epistemic interpretation as logics of belief (KD45), true belief (S4.4), knowledge (S4F). Finally, each is maximal with respect to some property of nonmonotonic logics. The logics KD45 and S4.4 are maximal with respect to the property of producing exactly one expansion for modal-free theories [Schwarz, 1991a]. The logic S4F is a maximal logic for which theories without positive modalities (like the theory $\{Lp \supset p\}$ considered by Konolige [1988]) have a unique expansion [Schwarz and Truszczyński, 1992].

Logics close to S5 are normal, that is, they contain the necessitation rule and the modal axiom scheme $L(\varphi \supset \psi) \supset (L\varphi \supset L\psi)$. Normal modal logics possess an elegant and natural semantics, namely, the possible world semantics introduced by Kripke [1963]. Kripke semantics makes it easy to investigate normal modal logics, and was fruitfully exploited in investigations of nonmonotonic logics based on normal modal logics [McDermott, 1982; Moore, 1984; Levesque, 1990; Shvarts, 1990; Marek et al., 1991].

In this paper we will focus our attention on the other end of the spectrum of modal logics. We will consider nonmonotonic logics that correspond to weak modal logics that satisfy none or only few axioms of S5. Namely, we will consider logics *not satisfying the axiom K*. Such logics are not normal. We will refer to them as *subnormal*. Some non-normal logics have been investigated by philosophers [Kripke, 1965; Segerberg, 1971]. (In fact, the first three modal logics introduced, S1, S2 and S3, were not normal; see [Feys, 1965] for a historical survey). Because these logics were aimed at eliminating the so-called "paradoxes of material implication", they do not contain the necessitation rule, but contain the axiom K or some of its weaker versions. Hence, they are different from the subnormal modal logics considered in this paper.

There are at least two reasons why it is important to consider nonmonotonic logics based on weak modal logics. First, according to one of the results of [McDermott, 1982], if $\mathcal{T}$ and $\mathcal{S}$ are two modal logics such that $\mathcal{T} \subseteq \mathcal{S} \subseteq S5$, then each $\mathcal{T}$-expansion is an $\mathcal{S}$-expansion but the converse does not hold in general. In other words, when we replace a logic $\mathcal{S}$ by a weaker

one, say $\mathcal{T}$, then often some of the expansions disappear. Hence, using weak modal logics in the schema (1) offers a possible solution to the problem of ungrounded expansions (see Konolige [1988]). Secondly, the assumption that a reasoner has a power of reasoning in a strong modal logic such as KD45, S4.4 or S4F may not be a realistic one. Therefore, it is important to study what types of reasoning can be modeled if weak modal logics are used instead. It turns out that in the nonmonotonic case we do not loose anything by restricting an agent's reasoning capabilities. Namely, and it is perhaps the most surprising result of our work, we show that nonmonotonic modal logics KD45 and S4.4 (that is, essentially, autoepistemic logic and autoepistemic logic of knowledge) can be embedded into nonmonotonic modal logics corresponding to some very weak modal logics containing necessitation. A similar result is also known to hold for default logic [Truszczyński, 1991b].

In this paper we study two modal logics. Both logics are assumed to be closed under the uniform substitution rule and contain propositional calculus and the rule of necessitation. These requirements specify the first of them, the logic N of *pure necessitation*. It was first introduced and investigated in [Fitting et al., 1992] but its nonmonotonic counterpart had been studied earlier in [Marek and Truszczyński, 1990]. The second logic is obtained from N by adding the axiom schema T: $Lp \supset p$. It will be referred to as the logic NT.

The logic N is clearly distinguished among all modal logics contained in S5 and containing the necessitation rule. It is the *weakest* one. It is also the weakest logic without counterintuitive expansions containing ψ and $\neg L\psi$. It is interesting to note that N-expansions were introduced already in the pioneer work of Moore [1985] under the name "modal fixed points". He also noticed that all N-expansions are stable expansions, but not vice versa, and suggests the interpretation of "nonmonotonic N" as a logic of "justified belief". In [Marek and Truszczyński, 1990] nonmonotonic N was studied in detail under the name *strong autoepistemic logic*.

The reasons we are interested in the logic NT are the following. First, while KD45 is quite commonly accepted as a logic of belief, there is no consensus as for the "right" modal logic of knowledge. For example, in the monograph [Lenzen, 1978] among all the modal axioms of S5 only the axiom T is essentially unquestionable (you cannot *know* a false proposition, you can only *believe* that it is true). Hence, NT may be regarded as a part of any reasonable logic of knowledge.

Another reason is more formal in nature. Often modal formulas describing examples of common-sense reasoning have no nested modalities, and no negative occurrences of L. For example, "p is true by default" is usually expressed as $\neg L \neg p \supset p$. For such theories many nonmonotonic logics coincide. For example, it is proved in [Marek and Truszczyński, 1990] that for theories without negative occurrences of L, $\mathcal{S}$-expansions coincide for all modal logics $\mathcal{S}$ between N and KD45. Similarly, $\mathcal{S}$-expansions coincide for all modal logics $\mathcal{S}$ between NT and S4.4. Recall that KD45 and S4.4 are maximal logics which do not produce "ungrounded" expansions for objective theories. Thus, it seems that T is, probably, the only axiom which makes a difference. Hence, it is important to study the nonmonotonic modal logic corresponding to the weakest modal logic containing the schema T.

The problem with logics like N or NT is, that *they are not closed under the equivalence substitution rule.* For example, $\vdash_N p \equiv \neg\neg p$, but $\nvdash_N Lp \equiv L\neg\neg p$. This means, that algebraic semantics for such logics are impossible (if we want $\equiv$ to be interpreted as equality in the algebra of truth values). On the other hand, a Kripke-style semantics for N has been found in [Fitting *et al.*, 1992]. The key idea used in this paper was to treat N as a logic with infinitely many modalities, so L in $L\varphi$ and L in $L\psi$ represent two different modalities, if φ and ψ are syntactically different.

For a long time nonmonotonic modal logics, even if an underlying modal logic was normal, lacked an intuitively clear semantics. Recently, such a semantics has been found [Schwarz, 1992]. In this paper we combine ideas from [Fitting *et al.*, 1992] and [Schwarz, 1992] and obtain a possible world semantics for the nonmonotonic logics N and NT. We apply these semantics to prove that the nonmonotonic modal logics KD45 and S4.4 can be embedded into the nonmonotonic logics N and NT. What is more, the embeddings are very simple. For example, to embed the nonmonotonic logic KD45 (that is, the autoepistemic logic) into the nonmonotonic logic N, it is enough to replace each occurrence of L with $\neg L\neg L$. Consequently, the nonmonotonic logic N is at least as expressive as nonmonotonic KD45: the modality $\neg L\neg L$ can be viewed as the "modality of nonmonotonic KD45". In the same time, no faithful embedding of nonmonotonic N (or NT) into nonmonotonic KD45 is known so far. We regard our "embedding" results as the most important results of our paper. They show that subnormal modal logics such as N and NT can easily be used (in the nonmonotonic setting) to simulate other nonmonotonic formalisms and, thus, are viable and powerful knowledge representation tools.

Perhaps even more importantly, the expressive power of nonmonotonic logics N and NT comes at no additional cost in terms of computational complexity, In this paper we study computational properties of the logics N and NT and their nonmonotonic counterparts. It turns out that the logics N and NT behave similarly to logics close to S5 (such as S5 itself, KD45, S4.4 and S4.3.2). Namely, in the monotonic case, it is NP-complete to decide if a theory is consistent in N (or NT) and it is Σ_2^P-complete to decide existence of an N(NT)-expansion. Since the complexity of reasoning

with autoepistemic and default logics is also located on the second level of the polynomial hierarchy [Gottlob, 1992], nonmonotonic logics N and NT are computationally equivalent to these two classic nonmonotonic systems. It is worth noting that logics "in the middle" of the spectrum, that is, those containing K but still "far away" from S5, such as K, or T, are much more complex (satisfiability is PSPACE-complete). Hence, our complexity results provide yet another justification for focusing on logics that are either very weak (subnormal) or very strong (close to S5).

Some properties which are quite easy to prove for monotonic modal logics are not at all obvious for nonmonotonic modal logics. For example, adding explicit definitions of the form $q \equiv \varphi$ does not affect the q-free fragment of the set of logical consequences of a theory. Some nonmonotonic logics, for example logic of moderately grounded expansions, do not have this property [Schwarz, 1991b]. It is rather unfortunate since it means that simply introducing a new notation can change the fragment of agent's knowledge that does not involve this new notation at all. In this paper we prove that for every (even subnormal) modal logic $\mathcal{S}$, introducing an explicit definition of the form $q \equiv \varphi$ does not affect the q-free fragments of $\mathcal{S}$-expansions.

Kripke semantics for the logics N and NT

In this section we recall the semantics introduced in [Fitting *et al.*, 1992] and [Truszczyński, 1992] for the logics N and NT.

By a *multi-relational Kripke model* (or, simply, *m-r Kripke model*) we mean a triple

$$\langle M, \{R_\varphi\}_{\varphi \in \mathcal{L}_L}, V \rangle,$$

where M is a nonempty set, commonly referred to as the set of (possible) *worlds* of a model, R_φ, where $\varphi \in \mathcal{L}_L$, is a binary relation on M, and V is a function on M, called a *valuation function*, assigning to each world $\alpha \in M$ a subset $V(\alpha)$ of propositional variables of the language. Hence, the only difference between multi-relational Kripke models and standard Kripke models is that the former have infinitely many accessibility relations while the latter have just one.

The notion of *truth* of a formula φ in a world α of a multi-relational Kripke model $\mathcal{M} = \langle M, \{R_\varphi\}_{\varphi \in \mathcal{L}_L}, V \rangle$, denoted $(\mathcal{M}, \alpha) \models \varphi$, is defined recursively on the length of a formula. The only case where the definition differs from the usual one is the case of modal operator L. If φ is of the form $L\psi$, we define $(\mathcal{M}, \alpha) \models \varphi$ if and only if for every $\beta \in M$ such that $\alpha R_\psi \beta$ we have $(\mathcal{M}, \beta) \models \psi$.

A formula φ is *valid* in a multi-relational Kripke model $\mathcal{M}$ if $(\mathcal{M}, \alpha) \models \varphi$ for every $\alpha \in M$.

Theorem 1 ([Fitting *et al.*, 1992]) *Let* $I \subseteq \mathcal{L}_L$ *and let* $\varphi \in \mathcal{L}_L$. *Then* $I \vdash_N \varphi$ *if and only if* φ *is valid in every multi-relational Kripke model in which* I *is valid.*

A multi-relational Kripke model is *reflexive* if each of its accessibility relations is reflexive.

Theorem 2 ([Truszczyński, 1992]) *Let $I \subseteq \mathcal{L}_L$ and let $\varphi \in \mathcal{L}_L$. Then $I \vdash_{NT} \varphi$ if and only if φ is valid in every reflexive multi-relational Kripke model in which I is valid.*

Minimal model semantics for the nonmonotonic logics N and NT

We will follow the approach of [Schwarz, 1992], where minimal model semantics was proposed for the non-monotonic logic $\mathcal{S}$ for a wide class of *normal* modal logics. Speaking more precisely, we will consider universal S5-models as special m-r Kripke models (with the same, universal, accessibility relation for every formula) and we will adapt the notion of minimality introduced in [Schwarz, 1992] to the class of all m-r models and the class of all *reflexive* m-r models.

Let $\mathcal{M}' = \langle M', \{R'_\varphi\}_{\varphi \in \mathcal{L}_L}, V' \rangle$ and $\mathcal{M}'' = \langle M'', M'' \times M'', V'' \rangle$ be an m-r Kripke model and Kripke S5-model, respectively. Assume also that M' and M'' are disjoint. By the *concatenation* of $\mathcal{M}'$ and $\mathcal{M}''$, denoted $\mathcal{M}' \circ \mathcal{M}''$, we mean an m-r Kripke model

$$\langle M' \cup M'', \{R_\varphi\}_{\varphi \in \mathcal{L}_L}, V' \cup V'' \rangle,$$

where $R_\varphi = R'_\varphi \cup ((M' \cup M'') \times M'')$.

A Kripke S5-model $\mathcal{M}$ is N-*minimal* (NT-*minimal)* model of I, if $\mathcal{M} \models I$ and there does not exist an m-r Kripke model (reflexive m-r Kripke model) $\mathcal{M}'$ such that

1. $\mathcal{M}' \circ \mathcal{M} \models I$,
2. for some $\beta \in M'$, V'_β differs from V''_α for all $\alpha \in M''$.

Speaking informally, an S5-model $\mathcal{M}''$ is N-minimal, if it is not a common final cluster for all the accessibility relations of any $\mathcal{N}$-model with at least one world different from all the worlds of M''.

This notion of minimality may seem a bit exotic at first. In particular, it is different from the notion of a minimal universal S5-model as discussed by Halpern and Moses [1985] who consider minimality in the class of universal S5-models with respect to the inclusion relation on the sets of worlds of models. On the other hand, a careful examination of our notion of minimality shows that it is very closely related to the notion of minimality used by Moore [1984] and Levesque [1990] in their characterizations of stable expansions in the autoepistemic logic. We refer the reader to [Schwarz, 1992; Schwarz and Truszczyński, 1992] for a more detailed discussion of the minimal knowledge paradigm and comparisons between existing approaches. Similar intuitions behind the notions of minimality studied here will be provided in the full paper.

Theorem 3 *For every theory $I \subseteq \mathcal{L}_L$ and for every consistent theory $T \subseteq \mathcal{L}_L$, T is an N-expansion for I if and only if T is the set of all formulas valid in some N-minimal model for I.*

Theorem 4 *For every theory $I \subseteq \mathcal{L}_L$ and for every consistent theory $T \subseteq \mathcal{L}_L$, T is an NT-expansion for I if and only if T is the set of all formulas valid in some NT-minimal model for I.*

These two results show that the semantic notion of N- (NT-) minimal models is in the exact correspondence with the syntactic notion of an N- (NT-) expansion as specified by the equation (1).

Expressive power of nonmonotonic logics N and NT

In the monotonic setting the logics N and NT are very weak. In fact, the logic N is the weakest modal nonmonotonic logic containing necessitation. Despite of that, nonmonotonic logics N and NT are powerful nonmonotonic formalisms. It is known that default logic can be embedded into the nonmonotonic logics N and NT so that there is a *one-to-one* correspondence between extensions of default theories and N- and NT-expansions of the corresponding modal theories [Truszczyński, 1991b; Truszczyński, 1991a]. The main goal of this section is to show that also the autoepistemic logic can be embedded into the nonmonotonic modal logics N and NT.

The autoepistemic logic represents the modality L as the belief modality. The interpretation that logics N and NT give to the operator L is more that of knowledge than belief. Having a formula $L\varphi$ in the set of consequences of a theory I (in either of these logics) means that we are able to provide a very rigorous proof of $L\varphi$ from our initial assumptions I. In the case of logic N, in such a proof we only use propositional calculus and necessitation. Hence, in particular, if I is modal-free, the only way to have a formula $L\varphi$ in the set of consequences of I is to have φ among the propositional consequences of I. In the case of the logic NT the situation is similar. The only difference is that we are also allowed to make use of the axiom schema T ($Lp \supset p$) which seems to be an uncontroversial property of knowledge modality.

For a formula φ, by φ^N we denote the result of simultaneously replacing each occurrence of L in φ by $\neg L \neg L$. For a theory I, we define $I^N = \{\varphi^N : \varphi \in I\}$.

The following theorem shows that under the mapping $I \mapsto I^N$, stable expansions for I are precisely N(NT)-expansions for I^N.

Theorem 5 *Let $T \subseteq \mathcal{L}_L$ be consistent. Let $I \subseteq \mathcal{L}_L$. Then T is an autoepistemic expansion for a theory I if and only if T is an N-expansion for I^N, and if and only if T is an NT-expansion for I^N.*

A similar correspondence between autoepistemic logic and reflexive autoepistemic logic (the nonmonotonic logic S4.4) under the same translation has been discovered earlier in [Schwarz, 1991a]

Reflexive autoepistemic logic of [Schwarz, 1991a] is faithfully embedded into Moore's logic by means of the translation which rewrites each $L\varphi$ as $\varphi \wedge L\varphi$. Combaining these two translations, we obtain easily the translation of reflexive autoepistemic logic into non-monotonic N, too.

Algorithmic aspects of reasoning with nonmonotonic logics N and NT

Reasoning in modal logics is often very complex. For example, it is PSPACE-complete to decide whether for a given theory I and a formula φ, $I \vdash_{S4} \varphi$ (where $\vdash_{S4}$ denotes the provability operator in the logic S4). For stronger logics such as KD45, S4.4, S4F and S5 the problem of deciding whether a formula φ is a consequence of a theory I becomes easier namely, NP-complete (assuming PSPACE does not collapse to the first level of the polynomial hierarchy). In this section, we will study the complexity of reasoning in the logics N and NT.

Theorem 6 *Problems of deciding for a given finite set I of formulas, if I is consistent with logic N, or with logic NT, are NP-complete (in the length of I). Problems of deciding, for given finite set I and formula φ, if $I \vdash_{\mathcal{S}} \varphi$, is co-NP-complete, for $\mathcal{S}$ being N or NT.*

Our complexity results have direct implications of on the complexity of reasoning in nonmonotonic logics N and NT. The results for the case of the logic N have been obtained by Gottlob [1992]. Therefore, we derive here only the results for the nonmonotonic logic NT. As the main tool in our argument we will use a syntactic characterization of NT-expansions which follows from general results given in [Shvarts, 1990; Marek *et al.*, 1991]. Adapting this characterization to the case of logic NT, we obtain complexity results for the following algorithmic problems associated with the nonmonotonic logic NT:

EXISTENCE Given a finite theory $A \subseteq \mathcal{L}_K$, decide if A has an NT-expansion;

IN-SOME Given a finite theory $A \subseteq \mathcal{L}_K$ and a formula $\varphi \in \mathcal{L}_K$, decide if φ is in some NT-expansion of A;

NOT-IN-ALL Given a finite theory $A \subseteq \mathcal{L}_K$ and a formula $\varphi \in \mathcal{L}_K$, decide if there is an NT-expansion for A not containing φ;

IN-ALL Given a finite theory $A \subseteq \mathcal{L}_K$ and a formula $\varphi \in \mathcal{L}_K$, decide if φ is in all NT-expansions of A.

Theorem 7 *Problems* EXISTENCE, IN-SOME *and* NOT-IN-ALL *are* Σ_2^P-*com-plete. Problem* IN-ALL *is* Π_2^P-*complete.*

For the case of the logic N the same complexity results have been obtained by Gottlob [1992]. Since reasoning in default and autoepistemic logics is also Σ_2^P- or Π_2^P-complete (depending on the type of question) [Gottlob, 1992], it follows that computationally our nonmonotonic logics are equivalent to these two "classic" nonmonotonic formalisms.

Explicit definitions

All standard logics are conservative with respect to adding explicit definitions. Speaking informally, naming a formula by a *new* propositional symbol does not change the set of theorems in the original language. Since logics are supposed to model general principles of reasoning and be applicable in a wide spectrum of domains, the property that the set of conclusions is (essentially) invariant under new names seems to be natural and desirable to have.

It is known (see [Schwarz and Truszczyński, 1992]) that those nonmonotonic logics in the McDermott and Doyle's family which are based on normal modal logics are conservative with respect to adding new names. That is, after a new name is introduced, each expansion of the resulting theory is a conservative extension of an expansion of the original theory. In this paper we will show, using different means than in [Schwarz and Truszczyński, 1992] (the proof given there does not carry over to the case of subnormal modal logics) that every modal nonmonotonic logic in the family of McDermott and Doyle, in particular the nonmonotonic logics N and NT, share this desirable property.

For a theory $I \subseteq \mathcal{L}_L$, we define

$$I^{q,\eta} = I \cup \{q \equiv \eta\}.$$

Let p be a propositional variable and let ψ and φ be formulas. we write $\psi(p/\varphi)$ to denote the result of substituting φ for p uniformly in ψ. Clearly, if p does not occur in ψ then $\psi(p/\varphi) = \psi$. Let q be an atom not in $\mathcal{L}_L$ and let η be a formula from $\mathcal{L}_L$. For a theory $T \subseteq \mathcal{L}_L$ define

$$T^{q,\eta} = \{\psi \in \mathcal{L}_L^q : \psi(q/\eta) \in T\},$$

where $\mathcal{L}_L^q$ denotes the extension of the language $\mathcal{L}_L$ by q.

The following theorem states that nonmonotonic N and NT admit explicit definitions.

Theorem 8 *Let $\mathcal{S}$ be a modal logic. Let $I \subseteq \mathcal{L}_L$. A theory S is an $\mathcal{S}$-expansion for $I^{q,\eta}$ if and only if $S = T^{q,\eta}$ for some $\mathcal{S}$-expansion T of I. Moreover, S is a conservative extension of T, that is, T is exactly the q-free part of S.*

Conclusions

In this paper we have studied the nonmonotonic logics that can be obtained by the method of McDermott and Doyle from two very weak modal monotonic logics: the logic N of pure necessitation and its extensions, the logic NT. We argued that despite the fact that these logics lack several of the axiom schemata that characterize properties of knowledge and belief, the resulting nonmonotonic systems are at least as suitable for representing these notions as are autoepistemic, reflexive autoepistemic and default logics.

We developed a minimal model semantics for the nonmonotonic logics N and NT. We proved that autoepistemic logics can be embedded into either of these two logics (the same result for the default logics has been already known earlier). We showed that both our nonmonotonic logics have a desirable property of being conservative with respect to adding new names. We also showed that reasoning with monotonic logics N and NT is computationally equivalent to reasoning in propositional logic, and established the complexity of reasoning with nonmonotonic logics N and NT. Our results show that the complexity of reasoning with nonmonotonic logics N and NT is located on the second level of the polynomial hierarchy and, thus, is the same as the complexity of reasoning with autoepistemic, reflexive autoepistemic and default logics.

Finally, nonmonotonic logics N and NT are conservative with respect to adding explicit definitions. All these results indicate that nonmonotonic logics N and NT are viable and powerful nonmonotonic formalisms.

Acknowledgements

The second author was partially supported by National Science Foundation under grant IRI-9012902.

References

Feys, R. 1965. *Modal Logics*. Louvain E. Nauwelaerts, Paris.

Fitting, M. C.; Marek, W.; and Truszczynski, M. 1992. Logic of necessitation. *Journal of Logic and Computation* 2:349–373.

Gottlob, G. 1992. Complexity results for nonmonotonic logics. *Journal of Logic and Computation* 2:397–425.

Halpern, J.Y. and Moses, Y. 1985. Towards a theory of knowledge and ignorance: preliminary report. In Apt, K., editor 1985, *Logics and Models of Concurrent Systems*. Springer-Verlag. 459 – 476.

Konolige, K. 1988. On the relation between default and autoepistemic logic. *Artificial Intelligence* 35:343–382.

Kripke, S. 1963. Semantic analysis of modal logic I: Normal modal propositional calculi. *Zeitschrift für mathematische Logic und Grundlagen der Mathematik* 67 – 96.

Kripke, S. 1965. Semantic analysis of modal logic II: Non-normal modal propositional calculi. In Addison, J.W.; Henkin, L.; and Tarski, A., editors 1965, *The Theory of Models*, volume 9. North-Holland, Amsterdam. 206 – 220.

Lenzen, W. 1978. *Recent Work in Epistemic Logic*, volume 30 of *Acta Philosophica Fennica*. North-Holland, Amsterdam.

Levesque, H. J. 1990. All I know: a study in autoepistemic logic. *Artificial Intelligence* 42:263–309.

Marek, W. and Truszczynski, M. 1990. Modal logic for default reasoning. *Annals of Mathematics and Artificial Intelligence* 1:275 – 302.

Marek, W.; Shvarts, G.F.; and Truszczyński, M. 1991. Modal nonmonotonic logics: ranges, characterization, computation. In *Second International Conference on Principles of Knowledge Representation and Reasoning, KR '91*, San Mateo, CA. Morgan Kaufmann. 395–404. An extended version of this article will appear in the Journal of the ACM.

McCarthy, J. 1980. Circumscription — a form of nonmonotonic reasoning. *Artificial Intelligence* 13:27–39.

McDermott, D. and Doyle, J. 1980. Nonmonotonic logic I. *Artificial Intelligence* 13:41–72.

McDermott, D. 1982. Nonmonotonic logic II: Nonmonotonic modal theories. *Journal of the ACM* 29:33–57.

Moore, R.C. 1984. Possible-world semantics for autoepistemic logic. In Reiter, R., editor 1984, *Proceedings of the workshop on non-monotonic reasoning*. 344–354. (Reprinted in: M.Ginsberg, editor, *Readings on nonmonotonic reasoning*. pages 137 – 142, 1990, Morgan Kaufmann.).

Moore, R.C. 1985. Semantical considerations on nonmonotonic logic. *Artificial Intelligence* 25:75–94.

Reiter, R. 1980. A logic for default reasoning. *Artificial Intelligence* 13:81–132.

Schwarz, G.F. and Truszczyński, M. 1992. Modal logic **S4F** and the minimal knowledge paradigm. In *Proceedings of TARK 1992*, San Mateo, CA. Morgan Kaufmann.

Schwarz, G. 1991a. Autoepistemic logic of knowledge. In Nerode, A.; Marek, W.; and Subrahmanian, V.S., editors 1991a, *Logic Programming and Non-monotonic Reasoning*. MIT Press. 260–274.

Schwarz, G.F. 1991b. Bounding introspection in nonmonotonic logics. In *Third International Conference on Principles of Knowledge Representation and Reasoning, KR '92*, Cambridge, MA.

Schwarz, G.F. 1992. Minimal model semantics for nonmonotonic modal logics. In *Proceedings of LICS-92*.

Segerberg, K. 1971. *An essay in classical modal logic*. Uppsala University, Filosofiska Studier, 13.

Shvarts, G.F. 1990. Autoepistemic modal logics. In Parikh, R., editor 1990, *Proceedings of TARK 1990*, San Mateo, CA. Morgan Kaufmann. 97–109.

Truszczyński, M. 1991a. Embedding default logic into modal nonmonotoninc logics. In Nerode, A.; Marek, W.; and Subrahmanian, V.S., editors 1991a, *Logic Programming and Non-monotonic Reasoning*. MIT Press. 151–165.

Truszczyński, M. 1991b. Modal interpretations of default logic. In *Proceedings of IJCAI-91*, San Mateo, CA. Morgan Kaufmann. 393–398.

Truszczyński, M. 1992. A generalization of Kripke semantics to the case of logics without axiom K. A manuscript.

Algebraic Semantics for Cumulative Inference Operations

Zbigniew Stachniak [*]

Department of Computer Science
University of Toronto
Toronto, Ontario, M5S 1A4 Canada
zbigniew@cs.yorku.ca

Abstract

In this paper we propose preferential matrix semantics for nonmonotonic inference systems and show how this algebraic framework can be used in methodological studies of cumulative inference operations.

Introduction

The notion of a cumulative inference operation arose as a result of formal studies of properties of nonmonotonic inference systems, more specifically, as a result of the search for desired and natural formal properties of such inference systems. In this paper we propose an algebraic semantics for cumulative inference systems and show how this new semantic framework can be used for the methodological studies of nonmonotonic reasoning. The point of departure for our presentation are the studies of nonmonotonic inference systems undertaken in (Brown & Shoham 1988, Gabbay 1985, Kraus, Lehmann, & Magidor 1990, Makinson 1988). All these works share a common preferential model-theoretic view on semantics. In (Makinson 1988) and (Makinson 1989) this unified semantic framework assumes the form of the theory of preferential model structures. If $\mathcal{L}$ is the language of an inference system, then a preferential model structure for $\mathcal{L}$ is a triple $M = <\mathcal{U}, \models, \prec>$, where $\mathcal{U}$ is a nonempty set the elements of which are called models, $\prec$ is a binary relation on $\mathcal{U}$, called the preference relation of M, and $\models$ is a binary relation between models in $\mathcal{U}$ and formulas of $\mathcal{L}$ called the satisfaction relation of M. No properties of $\mathcal{U}$, of the satisfaction relation $\models$, nor of the preference relation $\prec$ are assumed. Makinson shows that cumulative inference systems are exactly those defined by the class of (stoppered) preferential model structures.

---

[*]On leave from the Department of Computer Science, York University, Canada. Research Supported by the Natural Sciences and Engineering Research Council of Canada.

The study of general properties of cumulative inference systems can be based on a less general and more structured notion of a model structure. The key feature of our semantic proposal is the truth-functional interpretation of logical connectives, the idea well-developed in the context of logical calculi which can also be exploited in the studies of nonmonotonic reasoning. We define a preferential model, or as it is called in this paper, a *preferential matrix*, as an algebra of truth-values augmented with a family $\mathcal{D}$ of sets of designated truth-values. We model a desired degree of nonmonotonicity by selecting an appropriate preference relation on $\mathcal{D}$. Preferential matrices have the same semantic scope as Makinson's preferential model structures. Evident similarities between 'classical' logical matrices and preferential matrices provide an access to reach algebraic techniques available for methodological studies of deductive proof systems. In this context, the present paper examines a list of properties of nonmonotonic inference systems, starting with characterization of *cumulativity* and *loop-cumulativity* in terms of preferential matrices. We introduce a handy notion of the *monotone base* of an inference system and study the *distributivity* property in terms of this notion. Finally, we look at the *consistency preservation* property in the context of finding automated theorem proving methods for cumulative inference systems. We give a criterion for such systems to have a refutationally equivalent automated proof system based on the resolution rule.

In this paper we study inference systems on propositional level only. It is assumed that the reader is familiar with (Gabbay 1985, Kraus, Lehmann, & Magidor 1990, Makinson 1988). The familiarity with (Brown & Shoham 1988, Makinson 1989) and the basic facts on logical matrices, as presented in (Wójcicki 1988), is an asset.

Preferential Matrices

We begin this section with a brief description of the class

of cumulative inference systems. To avoid a lengthy exposition of facts available elsewhere, this description is just a list of definitions with rather scarce commentaries. The reader may refer to (Gabbay 1985, Kraus, Lehmann, & Magidor 1990, Makinson 1988, Makinson 1989, Wójcicki 1988) where all these definitions are fully motivated and discussed.

A *propositional language* $\mathcal{L}$ is defined in the usual way in terms of a finite set $\{f_0, ...f_k\}$ of logical connectives and a countable infinite set of propositional variables. By L we denote the set of all well-formed formulas of $\mathcal{L}$. From algebraic point of view, $\mathcal{L}$ is an algebra $< L, f_0, ..., f_k >$ of formulas while logical substitutions are simply endomorphisms of $\mathcal{L}$. [1]

Following (Makinson 1988), we say that an operation $C : 2^L \rightarrow 2^L$ is a *cumulative inference operation* if it satisfies the following two conditions: for all $X, Y \subseteq L$,

(c1) $X \subseteq C(X)$,   (*inclusion*)

(c2) $X \subseteq Y \subseteq C(X)$ implies $C(Y) = C(X)$

                               (*cumulativity*).

These (or equivalent) conditions were discussed in depth in (Gabbay 1985, Kraus, Lehmann, & Magidor 1990, Makinson 1988, Makinson 1989). Let us note, that (c1) and (c2) imply:

(c3) $C(C(X)) = C(X)$ (*indempotence*).

If $\alpha \in L$ and $X \subseteq L$, then we read '$\alpha \in C(X)$' as 'X entails α'. An inference operation C is a *consequence operation* if, in addition to (c1) and (c3), it satisfies the following condition: for every $X, Y \subseteq L$,

(c4) $X \subseteq Y$ implies $C(X) \subseteq C(Y)$ (*monotonicity*).

Every system $< \mathcal{L}, C >$, where C is a cumulative inference operation on $\mathcal{L}$ is called an *inference system*. If C is a consequence operation, then $< \mathcal{L}, C >$ is called a *logic*. If C_0, C_1 are two inference operations on $\mathcal{L}$, then we shall write $C_0 \leq C_1$ if for every $X \subseteq L, C_0(X) \subseteq C_1(X)$.

We begin our voyage towards the notion of a preferential matrix by analyzing the classical notion of a logical matrix (cf. Wójcicki 1988). Let $\mathcal{L} =< L, f_0, ..., f_k >$ be an arbitrary language fixed for the rest of this paper. A *logical matrix* is a pair $M =< \mathcal{A}, \mathcal{D} >$, where $\mathcal{A} =< A, F_0, ..., F_k >$ is an algebra of truth-values, with the set A of truth-values and with the operations $F_0, ..., F_k$ serving as interpretations of the connectives $f_0, ..., f_k$, respectively. [2] The role of $\mathcal{A}$ is to provide the interpretation of logical connectives and to define the space of truth-values – the possible meanings of formulas of $\mathcal{L}$. $\mathcal{D}$ is a family of sets of truth-values (i.e.

subsets of A). We consider every $d \in \mathcal{D}$ a *set of designated truth-values*. Interpretations of formulas of $\mathcal{L}$ are defined in terms of *valuations* of $\mathcal{L}$ into M, which are simply homomorphisms of $\mathcal{L}$ into the algebra $\mathcal{A}$ of truth-values. Every logical matrix M defines the consequence operation Cn_M in the following way: for every $X \cup \{\alpha\} \subseteq L$,

(M) $\alpha \in Cn_M(X)$ *iff* for every valuation h and every $d \in \mathcal{D}, h(X) \subseteq d$ implies $h(\alpha) \in d$.

The matrix consequence operation Cn_M is always *structural*, i.e. it satisfies the following property: for every $X \subseteq L$ and every substitution e,

(c5) $e(Cn_M(X)) \subseteq Cn_M(e(X))$.

Structurality allows us to regard an entailment $\alpha \in C(X)$ as the schema representing all entailments of the form $e(\alpha) \in C(e(X))$, where e is any substitution. Moreover, the set of tautologies of a structural inference operation is closed under arbitrary substitutions. In fact, the majority of propositional logics considered in the literature, in addition to being monotonic, are structural. Nonmonotonic formalisms depart not only from the monotonicity, but frequently from the structurality as well. One way of extending matrix semantics to cover all consequence operations (not just structural) is described in (Piochi 1983) and (Stachniak 1988). The key idea is to base the semantic entailment on a set of 'admissible valuations', i.e., to consider *generalized matrices* of the form $< \mathcal{A}, \mathcal{D}, \mathcal{H} >$, where $\mathcal{A}$ and $\mathcal{D}$ are as before, and $\mathcal{H}$ is a subset of the set of all valuations of $\mathcal{L}$ into $\mathcal{A}$. In this semantic framework, every consequence operation can be defined by a generalized matrix. Let us note that in (Kraus, Lehmann, & Magidor 1990) a similar idea (of restricting the set of possible interpretations) is used to go beyond structural nonmonotonic inference systems. Our main problem with semantic modeling of cumulative inference systems, however, is not structurality but monotonicity. To get over this problem, we employ the idea of a *preference relation* so successfully used in preferential model-theoretic semantics discussed in (Brown & Shoham 1988, Kraus, Lehmann, & Magidor 1990, Makinson 1988, Makinson 1989). We call a system

$$M =< \mathcal{A}, \mathcal{D}, \mathcal{H}, \sqsubset >,$$

a *preferential matrix* of $\mathcal{L}$ if $\mathcal{A}, \mathcal{D}$, and $\mathcal{H}$ are as described earlier, and $\sqsubset$ is a binary relation on $\mathcal{D}$. We call $\sqsubset$ the *preference relation* of M and for every pair $d_0, d_1 \in \mathcal{D}$ we read '$d_0 \sqsubset d_1$' as 'd_0 is preferred over d_1'.

EXAMPLE 2.0: Let $\mathcal{L}$ be a language with one binary connective $\lor$, one unary connective f, and two logical

---

[1] In fact, $\mathcal{L}$ is an absolutely free algebra generated by propositional variables of $\mathcal{L}$.

[2] We assume that $\mathcal{L}$ and $\mathcal{A}$, as algebras, are of the same similarity type.

constants **3** and **4**. The preferential matrix M we define in this example is rather artificial; however, it is designed to provide simple illustrations of some of the properties of inference operations discussed in this paper. The truth-values of M are $0, 1, 2, 3$. The constants **3** and **4** are interpreted as the truth-values 3 and 4, respectively, while $\vee$ and f are interpreted as the operations V and F defined in the following tables:

V	0	1	2	3
0	0	3	2	1
1	0	3	1	3
2	0	3	2	2
3	1	3	2	1

p	$F(p)$
0	3
1	2
2	1
3	0

The family $\mathcal{D}$ of designated truth-values has three sets: $\{0, 2, 3\}, \{0, 1, 3\}$, and $\{1, 2, 3\}$. The preference relation of M is defined by: $\{0, 1, 3\} \sqsubset \{0, 2, 3\}$ and $\{1, 2, 3\} \sqsubset \{0, 2, 3\}$. Finally, the set $\mathcal{H}$ consists of all valuations of $\mathcal{L}$ into $\mathcal{A}$. □

Let $M = \langle \mathcal{A}, \mathcal{D}, \mathcal{H}, \sqsubset \rangle$ be a preferential matrix. For every set $X \subseteq L$, every set d of designated truth-values of M, and every valuation $h \in \mathcal{H}$, we shall write $Sat_M(h, X, d)$ iff $h(X) \subseteq d$ and for every $d' \sqsubset d, h(X) \not\subseteq d'$. Intuitively, '$Sat_M(h, X, d)$' means that d is a most preferred set of designated truth-values containing $h(X)$. With M we associate the inference operation C_M on $\mathcal{L}$ by rewriting the definition (M) in the following way: for every $X \cup \{\alpha\} \subseteq L$,

$\alpha \in C_M(X)$ *iff* for every $h \in \mathcal{H}$ and every $d \in \mathcal{D}$, $Sat_M(h, X, d)$ implies $h(\alpha) \in d$.

One of the conceptual distinctions between preferential model structures of Makinson and preferential matrices is the fact that in our approach the preference relation does not 'work' on models but on sets of designated truth-values – components of models. In the definition of the predicate $Sat_M(h, X, d)$, we search $\mathcal{D}$ for a minimal d (with respect to the preference relation) while keeping h and the algebra $\mathcal{A}$ of truth-values fixed. However, every preferential matrix $\langle \mathcal{A}, \mathcal{D}, \mathcal{H}, \sqsubset \rangle$ can be 'decomposed' into a preferential model structure $\mathcal{M} = \langle \mathcal{U}, \models, \prec \rangle$, where $\mathcal{U} = \{\langle \mathcal{A}, h, d \rangle : h \in \mathcal{H}, d \in \mathcal{D}\}$, and $\langle \mathcal{A}, h_0, d_0 \rangle \prec \langle \mathcal{A}, h_1, d_1 \rangle$ if and only if $h_0 = h_1$ and $d_0 \sqsubset d_1$. The satisfaction relation $\models$ is defined by the equivalence:

$$\langle \mathcal{A}, h, d \rangle \models \alpha \quad iff \quad h(\alpha) \in d.$$

Hence, preferential matrices can be considered special cases of preferential model structures. As we shall see shortly, for methodological studies of cumulative inference systems, preferential matrices are just what we need.

We call a preferential matrix $M = \langle \mathcal{A}, \mathcal{D}, \mathcal{H}, \sqsubset \rangle$ *stoppered* iff for every set A of truth-values of M, the set $\mathcal{D}_A = \{d \in \mathcal{D} : A \subseteq d\}$ is empty or has the smallest element, i.e., there exists $d_A \in \mathcal{D}_A$ such that for every $d \in \mathcal{D}_A, d \neq d_A$ implies $d_A \sqsubset d$; moreover, for no $d \in \mathcal{D}_A, d \sqsubset d_A$ is true. The notion of a stoppered matrix is a counterpart of a stoppered preferential model structure (cf. Makinson 1988, Makinson 1989): a model structure $\langle \mathcal{U}, \models, \prec \rangle$ is said to be *stoppered* iff for every set A of propositions and every $m \in \mathcal{U}$, if $m \models A$, then there is a minimal $n \in \mathcal{U}$ (minimal with respect to $\prec$) such that $n \models A$ and either $n = m$ or $n \prec m$. As it was pointed out by Makinson, this notion is

> partially metamathematical, as it refers to sets A of propositions and the satisfaction relation $\models$ as well as to the non-linguistic components $\mathcal{U}$ and $\prec$ of the model structure. There does not appear to be any exactly equivalent purely mathematical condition. (Makinson 1989)

In contrast to this situation, the notion of a stoppered preferential matrix is defined in purely set-theoretic terms. Let us also note, that if a preferential matrix M is stoppered, then so is the preferential model structure $\mathcal{M}$ defined as in the previous paragraph.

THEOREM 2.1: If $M = \langle \mathcal{A}, \mathcal{D}, \mathcal{H}, \sqsubset \rangle$ is a preferential stoppered matrix, then C_M is cumulative inference operation. Moreover, if $\mathcal{H}$ is closed under the composition with all substitutions of $\mathcal{L}$, then C_M is structural.

THEOREM 2.2: For every cumulative inference operation C there is a preferential stoppered matrix $M = \langle \mathcal{A}, \mathcal{D}, \mathcal{H}, \sqsubset \rangle$ such that $C = C_M$. Moreover, if C is structural then $\mathcal{H}$ can be assumed to consists of all valuations.

Theorems 2.1 and 2.2 give us a representation theorem for cumulative inference systems in terms of preferential matrices. One of the matrices that satisfy Theorem 2.2 is $M_\mathcal{L} = \langle \mathcal{L}, \{C(X) : X \subseteq L\}, \{id\}, \sqsubset \rangle$, where id is the identity function on $\mathcal{L}$, and $C(X) \sqsubset C(Y)$ iff $C(X) \neq C(Y)$ and for some $X' \subseteq C(Y), C(X) = C(X')$. Its construction resembles that of the so-called Lindenbaum matrix for a logical system (cf. Wójcicki 1988). Henceforth, we shall call it the *Lindenbaum matrix* for C. A model structure similar to $M_\mathcal{L}$ is used in (Makinson 1988) to characterize the class of cumulative inference operations in terms of preferential model structures.

There are obvious connections between preferential matrices and logical matrices (for every preferential matrix $\langle \mathcal{A}, \mathcal{D}, \mathcal{H}, \sqsubset \rangle, \langle \mathcal{A}, \mathcal{D} \rangle$ is a logical matrix). Hence, one may expect to transfer some of the algebraic tools and techniques developed for logical matrices to study cumulative inference systems. In this and the following sections we will try to do just that.

Let us consider the so-called *loop principle* (cf. Kraus, Lehmann, & Magidor 1990, Makinson 1988, Makinson 1989):

(loop) $X_0 \subseteq C(X_1), X_1 \subseteq C(X_2), ..., X_{n-1} \subseteq C(X_n),$
$X_n \subseteq C(X_0)$ implies $C(X_0) = C(X_n).$

In (Kraus, Lehmann, & Magidor 1990) and (Makinson 1989) this principle has been found the counterpart of transitivity of preference relation in stoppered preferential models. In preferential matrix semantics, loop can be related to the following property of preference relations. We say that a preferential matrix $< \mathcal{A}, \mathcal{D}, \mathcal{H}, \sqsubset >$ is *loop-free* if and only if there is no sequence $d_0 \sqsubset d_1 \sqsubset ... \sqsubset d_n \sqsubset d_0$ of sets in $\mathcal{D}$. Following (Kraus, Lehmann, & Magidor 1990), we call every inference operation satisfying (loop) *loop-cumulative*. Our last theorem of this section characterizes the loop principle in the class of cumulative systems.

THEOREM 2.3. *Representation Theorem for Loop-Cumulative Inference Operations.* An inference operation C is loop-cumulative if and only if it is defined by a stoppered loop-free matrix.

Monotone Bases of Inference Operations

Nonmonotonic inference systems are build 'on top' or 'on the basis of' some monotonic logical systems; they depart from their deductive counterparts by giving up monotonicity for some other principles of inference. The system $\mathcal{C}$ presented in (Kraus, Lehmann, & Magidor 1990) is based on the classical logic $< \mathcal{L}_2, C_2 >$ and so are all the inference systems $< \mathcal{L}_2, C >$ such that $C_2 \leq C$. Frequently, nonmonotonic inference systems are based on non-classical logics: on Kleene's three-valued logic (cf. Doherty 1991), on modal logics (cf. McDermott 1982, Moore 1985), on constructive logic (cf. Pearce 1992), etc. This suggests the following definition:

> the *monotone base* of a cumulative inference operation C is the largest structural consequence operation C_B such that $C_B \leq C$ (the largest with respect to $\leq$).

To the best of our knowledge, no formal discussion of the monotone base of inference systems is present in the literature, although many important properties of nonmonotonic inference systems were implicitly defined in terms of this notion. Two of such properties, distributivity and consistency preservation, will be studied soon.

The fact that all structural consequence operations on $\mathcal{L}$ form a lattice under the ordering $\leq$ (cf. Wójcicki 1988) implies the following theorem:

THEOREM 3.0: Every inference operation has the unique monotone base.

In (Makinson 1989), a cumulative inference operation C is called *supraclassical* if $C_2 \leq C$, where C_2 denotes the consequence operation of the classical logic. If C is nontrivial, then the above condition is equivalent to the statement that C_2 is the monotone base of C, i.e. that $C_B = C_2$. Namely, C_2 is a maximal structural consequence operation, i.e. for every structural consequence operation $C^* \geq C_2$, $C^* = C_2$ or C^* is trivial, i.e., $C^*(X) = L$, for all $X \subseteq L$. Since C is nontrivial, by Theorem 3.0, we must have $C_B = C_2$.

Before we state our next theorem, let us introduce the following notation. If $M =< \mathcal{A}, \mathcal{D}, \mathcal{H}, \sqsubset >$ is a preferential matrix, then C_M denotes the inference operation defined by M and Cn_M denotes the consequence operation defined by the logical matrix $< \mathcal{A}, \mathcal{D} >$.

THEOREM 3.1: For every preferential matrix M, $Cn_M \leq C_M$.

Unfortunately, Cn_M is not always the monotone base of C_M. As the next example shows, we can easily find two preferential matrices M_0 and M_1 such that $C_{M_0} = C_{M_1}$ but $Cn_{M_0} \neq Cn_{M_1}$.

EXAMPLE 3.2: Let M_0 be as in Example 1.0 and let M_1 be obtained from M_0 by the addition of $\{3\}$ to the family of designated truth-values and by making this set the maximal with respect to the preference relation. The inference operations C_{M_0} and C_{M_1} are identical while $4 \in Cn_{M_0}(\{3\}) - Cn_{M_1}(\{3\})$. The reason while $C_{M_0} = C_{M_1}$ is that the addition of the set $\{3\}$ is 'useless', i.e., it does not modify the inference engine of M_0. However, this addition modifies the 'monotone base' of M_0 represented by Cn_{M_0}. $\square$

THEOREM 3.3: Let C be a cumulative inference operation and let M be the Lindenbaum matrix for C. Then $C_B = Cn_M$.

By Theorem 3.3, the monotone base of a cumulative inference operation C is defined by the 'logical part' of the Lindenbaum matrix for C. If C is introduced by an arbitrary matrix M, then frequently $C_B = Cn_M$, provided that M has no 'useless' sets of designated truth-values. The details are as follows. Let $M =< \mathcal{A}, \mathcal{D}, \mathcal{H}, \sqsubset >$ be a preferential matrix. We call a set $d \in \mathcal{D}$ *useless* if for some $d^* \in \mathcal{D}, d^* \sqsubset d$ and $d \subseteq d^*$. The next theorem shows that all the useless sets can be safely eliminated.

THEOREM 3.4: Let M be a preferential matrix and let N be the matrix obtained from M by removing all useless sets. Then $C_M = C_N$.

THEOREM 3.5: Let C be a cumulative inference operation defined by a matrix $M = <\mathcal{A}, \mathcal{D}, \mathcal{H}, \sqsubset>$ without useless sets. If $\mathcal{H}$ contains a valuation of $\mathcal{L}$ onto $\mathcal{A}$, then $C_B = Cn_M$.

Theorems 3.4 and 3.5, when applied to a preferential matrix M with the full set of valuations, say that the monotone base of C_M is defined by M with all the useless sets removed.

As we have settled the problem of semantic definition of monotone bases, let us turn to the problem of an interplay between cumulative inference operations and their monotone bases. In (Makinson 1988, Makinson 1989) it is shown that every supraclassical inference system C defined by a *classical* preferential model structure (i.e. the satisfaction relation preserves the intended meanings of classical logical connectives) satisfies the following principle of distributivity: for every $X, Y \subseteq L$,

(d) $C_2(X) = X$ and $C_2(Y) = Y$ implies $C(X) \cap C(Y) \subseteq C(X \cap Y)$.

Makinson's proof exploits the following property of classical models: a disjunction α is satisfied in a model M iff one of the disjuncts of α is satisfied in M. The preferential matrix counterpart of this property, called well-connectivity, is defined as follows. Let $M = <\mathcal{A}, \mathcal{D}, \mathcal{H}, \sqsubset>$ be a preferential matrix for $\mathcal{L}$ and let us suppose that $\vee$ is one of the binary connectives of $\mathcal{L}$. We say that M is *well-connected* (with respect to $\vee$) iff for every pair a, b of truth-values of M and every $d \in \mathcal{D}$:

$a \vee b \in d$ iff $a \in d$ or $b \in d$.

Well-connectivity is, in fact, a property of the logical matrix $< \mathcal{A}, \mathcal{D} >$, since its definition is independent of the preference relation of M. Moreover, if M is well-connected, then Cn_M is disjunctive with respect to $\vee$, i.e., for every $X \cup \{\alpha, \beta\} \subseteq L$, $Cn(X \cup \{\alpha \vee \beta\}) = C(X \cup \{\alpha\}) \cap C(X \cup \{\beta\})$. We say that a cumulative inference operation C is *distributive* if it satisfies (d) with C_2 replaced by C_B. Our next theorem extends Makinson's result to a larger class of cumulative operations.

THEOREM 3.6: Every cumulative inference operation defined by a well-connected preferential matrix is distributive.

Another result, first formulated and proved for supraclassical cumulative inference systems, which, when expressed in terms of monotone bases, holds for a larger class of such systems is presented in the following theorem.

THEOREM 3.7: Every distributive cumulative inference operation is loop-cumulative.

Consistency Preservation

An inference operation C satisfies the *consistency preservation property* if for every $X \subseteq L$,
$$C(X) = L \quad iff \quad C_B(X) = L.$$

In other words, this property, when satisfied, sets the limit on how much a given inference operation C and its monotone base C_B may differ. In the context of supraclassical inference systems this property was investigated in (Makinson 1989), where the reader is referred to for examples of inference systems with this property. Let us note that:

THEOREM 4.0: Every cumulative structural inference operation satisfies the consistency preservation property.

The satisfaction of the consistency preservation principle enables the application of rich refutational automated theorem proving techniques available for logical systems, such as non-clausal resolution or signed tableau (cf. Hähnle 1991, Stachniak 1991, Stachniak 1992), to cumulative inference systems. In fact, following (Stachniak 1991), we can characterize the class of cumulative inference systems for which a refutationally equivalent resolution proof system can be found. Informally, a logic $\mathcal{P}$ is said to be a *resolution logic* if there exists a resolution-based proof system Rs refutationally equivalent to $\mathcal{P}$, i.e. for every finite set X of formulas, X is inconsistent in $\mathcal{P}$ if and only if X can be refuted in Rs (cf. Stachniak 1991, Stachniak 1992). This definition can be extended to cumulative inference systems in the following way: a cumulative inference system $< \mathcal{L}, C >$ with the consistency preservation property is said to be a *resolution inference system* if and only if the logic $< \mathcal{L}, C_B >$ is a resolution logic. In the light of this definition, the characterization of the class of resolution logics given in (Stachniak 1991) can be extended to resolution inference systems as follows:

THEOREM 4.1: Let C be a cumulative inference operation with the consistency preservation property. Then the following conditions are equivalent:

(i) $< \mathcal{L}, C >$ is a resolution inference system;

(ii) there exists a finite logical matrix M such that C and Cn_M have the same inconsistent sets;

(iii) for some integer $k \geq 0$, $L^{(k)}/\Theta$ is finite and for every finite set $X \subseteq L$,

$$C(X) = L \quad iff \quad C(e(X)) = L, \text{ for every substitution } e$$
$$\text{that maps } L \text{ into } L^{(k)}.$$

In this theorem, $L^{(k)}$ denotes the set of all formulas of L which are built up by means of the connectives of $\mathcal{L}$ and the propositional variables $p_0, ..., p_k$. Θ denotes the congruence relation of $\mathcal{L}$ defined in the following way: for every $\alpha, \beta \in L$,

$$\alpha \Theta \beta \; iff \text{ for every } X \subseteq L \text{ and every } \gamma(p) \in L,$$
$$C(X \cup \{\gamma(p/\alpha)\}) = L \leftrightarrow C(X \cup \{\gamma(p/\beta)\}) = L.$$

If C is a structural cumulative inference operation whose monotone base is defined by a finite logical matrix N, then, by Theorems 4.0 and 4.1, $< \mathcal{L}, C >$ is a resolution inference system. Moreover, a resolution based automated proof system for $< \mathcal{L}, C >$ can be effectively constructed from N following, for example, the algorithm described in (Stachniak 1991).

Let us close this section with the following general remark. The application of refutational theorem proving techniques to a particular cumulative inference system $< \mathcal{L}, C >$ hinges upon the availability of an effective procedure that reduces the problem of validation of an inference to the problem of inconsistency checking. What is required is an algorithm which for every finite set X of formulas and every formula α constructs a finite set X_α such that the following *reduction principle* holds:

$$\alpha \in C(X) \quad iff \quad C(X_\alpha) = L.$$

For example, in the case of the classical propositional logic we can just put $X_\alpha = X \cup \{\neg\alpha\}$. The reduction principle, however, is not universally available to all cumulative inference systems, as it is not available to all logics.

Acknowledgment

I am grateful to David Makinson for comments on the first draft of this paper.

References

A. BROWN, A. L., AND SHOHAM, Y. 1988. New Results on Semantical Nonmonotonic Reasoning. In Proceedings of the Second International Workshop on Non-Monotonic Reasoning, 19-26. Lecture Notes in Computer Science 346.

DOHERTY, P. 1991. NML3 – A Nonmonotonic Formalism with Explicit Defaults. Ph.D. diss., Dept. of Computer Science, Thesis, Univ. of Linköping.

GABBAY, D. M. 1985. Theoretical Foundations for Non-Monotonic Reasoning in Expert Systems. In *Logics and Models of Concurrent Systems* (K. Apt ed.). Springer-Verlag.

HÄHNLE, R. 1991. Uniform Notation of Tableaux Rules for Multiple-Valued Logics. In Proceedings of the Twenty-First International Symposium on Multiple-Valued Logics, 238-245. IEEE Press.

KRAUS, S.; LEHMANN, D.; MAGIDOR, M. 1990. Nonmonotonic Reasoning, Preferential Models and Cumulative Logics. *Artificial Intelligence* 44: 167-207.

MAKINSON, D. 1988. General Theory of Cumulative Inference. In Proceedings of the Second International Workshop on Non-Monotonic Reasoning, 1-18. Lecture Notes in Computer Science 346.

MAKINSON, D. 1989. General Patterns in Nonmonotonic Reasoning. In *Handbook of Logic in Artificial Intelligence and Logic Programming. Vol 2. Nonmonotonic and Uncertain Reasoning* (Gabbay, D. M., Hogger, C.J., and Robinson J.A. eds.) Forthcoming.

MCDERMOTT, D. 1982. Nonmonotonic Logic II: Nonmonotonic Modal Theories. *Journal of the Association for Computing Machinery* 29: 33-57.

MOORE, R. C. 1985. Semantic Considerations on Nonmonotonic Logic. *Artificial Intelligence* 25: 75-94.

PEARCE, D. 1992. Default Logic and Constructive Logic. In Proceedings of the Tenth European Conference on Artificial Intelligence, 309-313. John Wiley.

PIOCHI, B. 1983. Logical Matrices and Non-Structural Consequence Operations. *Studia Logica* 42: 33-42.

STACHNIAK, Z. 1991. Extending Resolution to Resolution Logics. *Journal of Experimental and Theoretical Artificial Intelligence* 3: 17-32.

STACHNIAK, Z. 1992. Resolution Approximation of First-Order Logics. *Information and Computation* 96: 225-244.

STACHNIAK, Z. 1988. Two Theorems on Many-Valued Logics. *Journal of Philosophical Logic* 17: 171-179.

WÓJCICKI, R. 1988. *Theory of Logical Calculi: Basic Theory of Consequence Operations.* Kluwer.

Novel Methods in
Knowledge Acquisition

Question-based Acquisition of Conceptual Indices for Multimedia Design Documentation

Catherine Baudin* Smadar Kedar** Jody Gevins Underwood***
Artificial Intelligence Research Branch
NASA Ames Research Center, Mail Stop 269-2
Moffett Field, CA 94035
baudin@ptolemy.arc.nasa.gov, kedar@ptolemy.arc.nasa.gov,
gevins@ptolemy.arc.nasa.gov

Vinod Baya
Center For Design Research
Bldg. 530, Duena street
Stanford University
baya@sunrise.stanford.edu

Abstract

Information retrieval systems that use conceptual indexing to describe the information content perform better than syntactic indexing methods based on words from a text. However, since conceptual indices represent the semantics of a piece of information, it is difficult to extract them automatically from a document, and it is tedious to build them manually. We implemented an information retrieval system that acquires conceptual indices of text, graphics and videotaped documents. Our approach is to use an underlying model of the domain covered by the documents to constrain the user's queries. This facilitates question-based acquisition of conceptual indices: converting user queries into indices which accurately model the content of the documents, and can be reused. We discuss Dedal, a system that facilitates the indexing and retrieval of design documents in the mechanical engineering domain. A user formulates a query to the system, and if there is no corresponding index, Dedal uses the underlying domain model and a set of retrieval heuristics to approximate the retrieval, and ask for confirmation from the user. If the user finds the retrieved information relevant, Dedal acquires a new index based on the query. We demonstrate the relevance and coverage of the acquired indices through experimentation.

1. Motivation

Information retrieval systems based on conceptual indexing can access the underlying meaning of text, graphics or videotaped documents. Conceptual indices focus on the important concepts of a domain (the semantics) rather than on the multiple ways these concepts are represented in a document (the syntax). This facilitates information retrieval [Salton et al. 89][Hayes et al. 89] because: (1) the number of concepts in a document is smaller than the number of

their possible syntactic representations, thus facilitating vocabulary selection when formulating queries to a system, and (2) since conceptual indices represent the *content* of a piece of information they can be used by a reasoning component to facilitate the match between a query and the information in the documents [Baudin et al. 92b]. The following example, extracted from a technical design report, illustrates the difference between conceptual and syntactic indexing.

"The inner hub holds the steel friction disks and causes them to rotate when the road input is transmitted through the connecting link to the rotating inner shaft...

This paragraph can be indexed by words from the text such as *inner hub, friction disk, inner shaft, connecting links.* However, the content of this text refers to concepts like the *function of the inner-hub,* or the *relation between the road input* and *the way the device works.* Accessing these concepts enables an information retrieval system to accurately answer questions about the function of each part of the device, their operation and the way they interact. Conceptual indexing combined with knowledge of the relations among the objects in a domain can be used by a reasoning component to draw *inferences* about how to locate a piece of information. In this example, the content of the above paragraph can be summarized by one concept: "operation of disk stack" to convey the fact that it describes how the disk stack device works. A reasoning component can then infer that the paragraph might describe the function of each part of the disk stack and the way they interact. In this case, the component *hub* is a subpart of the *disk stack* mechanism and its function is referenced in the paragraph.

However, since conceptual indices represent the underlying meaning of a piece of information, the language used to build these indices is usually different from the language in the documents. In particular, conceptual indices can be complex entities taht involve several objects and relations. This abstraction level mismatch between the indexing language and the language used to convey the information makes it difficult to automatically extract

---

(*) employee of RECOM Technologies.
(**) Research performed while employed by Sterling Software Inc. and while a visiting scientists at the Institute for the Learning Sciences, Northwestern University.
(***) employee of Sterling Software Inc.

conceptual indices, for instance by interpreting sentences in a text [Mauldin 91] [Tong et al. 89]. On the other hand, the creation of conceptual indices by human indexers is a labor intensive task that is difficult to perform exhaustively. This is particularly true for a large volume of documentation where concepts are closely interrelated, as is the case for technical documents that describe the operation, diagnosis or design of complex artifacts.

2. Question-based Acquisition of Conceptual Indices

Our approach is to use a *conceptual query language* plus feedback from the user on the relevance of the documents retrieved in response to a query, to incrementally acquire new conceptual indices for that document. The user formulates a query to the system. If no document description exactly matches the query, the system approximates the retrieval and prompts the user for feedback on the relevance of the references retrieved. If a reference is confirmed, the query is turned into a new index. This extends *relevance feedback* techniques [Salton et al. 68][Salton et al. 88] to the acquisition of *conceptual indices*.

This approach uses a *question-based indexing* paradigm [Osgood et al. 91][Schank 91][Mabogunje 90] where the query language and the indexing language have the same structure and use the same vocabulary. The assumption is that the questions asked by users indicate the objects and relationships that are relevant to describe the content of the documents at a conceptual level appropriate for a class of users. However, in order to use the queries to acquire new indices the following conditions must be met by the query language:

1. Reusability: The query language must be general enough to create indices that will match a class of queries.

2. Relevance: The query language must be able to describe the information that the user is interested in. Articulating queries to acquire information in order to achieve a goal is in general a difficult task [Croft et al. 90][Graesser et al. 85]. In our approach, the query formulation is *constrained* by a model of the domain covered by the documents and a model of the type of information designers are interested in (see section 3).

3. Context independence: The query language must be able to generate indices that can be reused in different situations - that is, for different users and different tasks.

In the next two sections we describe Dedal, a system that acquires conceptual indices to facilitate the reuse of multimedia design documents in the mechanical engineering domain. In section 5 we discuss three experiments conducted at Stanford's Center for Design Research and at NASA Ames where conceptual indices were created by Dedal while mechanical engineers used the system to access information about a shock absorber design.

3. Background

We developed Dedal, an information retrieval system that uses conceptual indexing to represent the content of multimedia text, graphics and videotaped design information. Dedal is currently applied to documents of mechanical engineering design. It is an interface to records such as meeting summaries, pages of a designer's notebook, technical reports, CAD drawings and videotaped conversations between designers.

3.1 Conceptual Language to Query and Index Design Information

Based on studies of the information seeking behavior of designers conducted at Stanford's Center for Design Research and NASA Ames [Baya et al. 92], we identified a language to describe and query design information [Baudin et al. 92a]. This language combines concepts from a model of the artifact being designed with a task vocabulary representing the classes of design topics usually covered by design documents. For instance, "function," "operation," or "alternative" are topics of the task vocabulary.

A conceptual index can be seen as a structured entity made of two parts: the *body* of the index which represents the content of a piece of information and the *reference* part that point to a region in a document. In Dedal the body of an index has the following form: <topic **T** subject **S** level of detail **L** medium **M**> where S is a list of subjects from a domain model and T, L and M are member of the task vocabulary. The reference part of an index contains a pointer to the *record* and *segment* corresponding to the starting location of the information in a document (e.g. document name and page number or video counter). A segment of information is described by several conceptual indices, each of which partially describing its content.

For instance: "The inner hub holds the steel friction disks and causes them to rotate" is part of a paragraph in page 20 of the record: report-333. It can be described by two indexing patterns:

```
<topic function subject inner-hub level-
    of-detail configuration medium text in-
    record report-333 segment 20>
<topic relation subject inner-hub and
    steel-friction-disks level-of-detail
    configuration medium text in-record
    report-333 segment 20>.
```

The queries have the same structure as the body of an index and use the same vocabulary. A question such as: "How does the inner hub interact with the friction disks?" can be formulated in Dedal's language as:

```
<get-information-about topic relation
    regarding subject inner-hub and steel-
    friction-disks with preferred medium
    equation>.
```

3.2 The domain model

In the mechanical engineering design domain, the model includes a representation of the artifact structure, some aspects of its function, the main decision points and alternatives considered. It also includes concepts that are part of the problem but external to the device representation. The main relations in the model are *isa*, *part-of*, *attribute-of*, and *depends-on* (see Figure 1). The *isa* and *part-of/ attribute-of* hierarchies are used by Dedal to compare a query with a given index. For instance in Figure 1, given that *metal-disk* is part of the *disk-stack* the pattern: "function of metal-disk" will be considered more specific than the pattern "function of disk-stack". In the same way, the subject: "resistive-force of disk-stack" is more specific than the subject "disk-stack".

3.3 Retrieval strategy

The retrieval module takes a query from the user as input, matches the question to the set of conceptual indices and returns an ordered list of references related to the question. The retrieval proceeds in two steps: (1) <u>exact match:</u> find the indices that exactly match the query and return the associated list of references. If the exact match fails: (2) <u>approximate match:</u> activate the *proximity retrieval heuristics*.

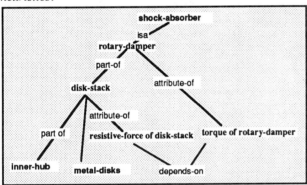

Figure 1: Objects and relations in the domain model

Dedal currently uses fourteen proximity retrieval heuristics to find related answers to a question. For instance, segments described by concepts like *"decision* for lever material" and *"alternative* for lever material" are likely to be located in nearby regions of the documentation. The heuristics are described in detail in [Baudin et al. 92b].

Each retrieval step returns a list of references ordered according to a set of priority criteria. The user selects a reference and if the document is on line, goes to the corresponding segment of information (using the hypertext facility that supports the text and graphics documents). A user dissatisfied with the references retrieved can request more information and force Dedal to resume its search and retrieve other references.

4. Index Acquisition in Dedal

Dedal acquires a new index in two phases: (1) an index creation phase, and (2) an index refinement phase.

4.1. Index Creation

Figure 2 illustrates with an example how Dedal acquires a new index. Given a user query and feedback from the user on the relevance of the documents retrieved. The index creation phase goes through the following steps:

1. <u>Query formulation:</u> The user's question in English is "what is the function of the hub?". After the user selects the subject *inner-hub* from the domain model and the topic *function* from the task vocabulary, the corresponding query in Dedal is: < topic: function of subject: inner-hub>(In the following paragraphs we will use a shortened syntax for queries where the words topic and subjects are omitted and where domain concepts are indicated in bold).

2. <u>Query-Index mapping:</u> Dedal tries to find an index that exactly matches the query. In this case, it does not find an exact match and applies a proximity heuristic to guess where the required information may be located. The heuristic states that any information describing how a mechanism works might also describe the function of its parts. In this case, given that *inner-hub* is a subpart of the *disk-stack* mechanism, Dedal matches the query "function of **inner-hub**" with two indices I1 and I2 pointing to two information regions describing the "operation of **disk-stack**".

3. <u>Relevance Feedback:</u> The user looks at the two references retrieved, finds that the reference pointed to by the index I2 (page 12 in the record report-333) describes the function of the inner hub while the document associated with index I1 does not. The user rates the reference I2 as relevant.

4. <u>Index Acquisition:</u> The query: "function of inner-hub" is more specific (see section 3) than the index "operation of disk-stack". In this case Dedal creates a new index I3. The system now knows that page 12 of report-333 explicitly describes the function of the inner-hub.

Each time a reference is retrieved by the approximate match and is relevant, Dedal attaches the reference of the selected index to the query, turning the query into a new index (as shown in step 4 in figure 2). In addition, the procedure records the type of inference that relates each subject of the new question to the subject of the matching index. There are four types of inferences: *identity, specialization, generalization* and *extension*. These inferences determine the type of the subjects associated with the new index created.

The type of a new subject is *identity* if this subject is identical to a subject of the matching index. The type of the new subject is a *specialization* if it is related to a subject of the matching index by a <u>subpart</u> or <u>isa</u> relationship, or if its value <u>depends-on</u> the value of the matching subject. The type of subject is a *generalization* if the matching subject is related to the new subject by a subpart or isa relation, or if its value depends-on the value of the new subject. The type of the new subject is an *extension* if it has no relations with any of the matching subjects. Finally if an index is defined manually by a user, the type of its subjects is: *human-indexer*.

For instance, if the query : "relation between **solenoid** and **lever**" matches the index: <topic: operation, subject: solenoid, reference: (meeting-10/2/91, 12)>, the new index will be: <topic: relation, subject1: solenoid and subject2: lever, reference(meeting-10/2/91, 12)>, where type(subject1) = identity and type(subject2)= extension.

When a query is matched to a new index created by Dedal, the type of each subject is taken into account in the determination of the ordering coefficient. The greatest confidence is attached to subjects in the following order: human-indexer, identity, specialization, generalization and extension. This means that there is high confidence in a new index created by a human while little confidence if the index is overgeneralized or provides an unrelated reference.

4.2 Index Refinement

Two factors may impact the ability of an acquired index to accurately describe the associated information:

(1) *incompleteness of the domain model:* If the model is missing the particular subject the user is interested in and the user selects a related subject, the approximate match might still retrieve a relevant document. In this case the user query does not exactly describe the information required by the user and the resulting index will be inaccurate;

(2) *multiple subject problem:* when a query involves several subjects from the model, the user might feel satisfied with a document that refers to a *subset* of these subjects. For instance, if the query is of the form "relation between **outer-cage, solenoid** and **lever**" the user might feel satisfied with a reference which only describes the relation between outer-cage and solenoid, the third argument: lever will then incorrectly describes the content of the referenced document.

The index refinement phase keeps track of the relevance of each subject in the newly acquired indices. Each time a query Q matches an acquired index I, and a subject Sq of Q is related to the subject Si of the index I (where related means either is the identity, a specialization, a generalization or an extension), the following procedure is activated: if the corresponding reference is relevant, the success rate of Si is incremented. If the reference retrieved is irrelevant, the failure rate of Si is incremented. The idea is that after some time, the indices that are suspect (whose failure rate is above a certain threshold) will be presented to a human indexer who will decide what indices should be maintained or deleted and what subjects should be dropped from the index.

For example, if the question is "what component interacts with the lever?", the corresponding query : < relation (between) **lever** and $X> (where $X is a variable) matches the body of the index I: < relation (between) **solenoid, lever, shaft** >. If the match is rated by the user as relevant, the coefficient of success of the subject lever in index I will be reinforced. If the user indicates that the reference retrieved is not relevant, the coefficient of failure of subject lever in I will be reinforced. Eventually if the index I fails to match any query about lever, the subject lever will be dropped.

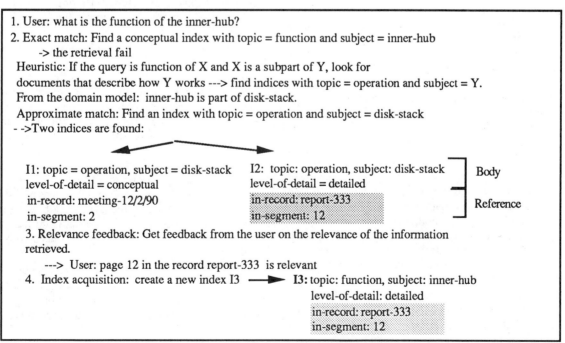

1. User: what is the function of the inner-hub?
2. Exact match: Find a conceptual index with topic = function and subject = inner-hub
    -> the retrieval fail
Heuristic: If the query is function of X and X is a subpart of Y, look for
documents that describe how Y works ---> find indices with topic = operation and subject = Y.
From the domain model: inner-hub is part of disk-stack.
Approximate match: Find an index with topic = operation and subject = disk-stack
- ->Two indices are found:

I1: topic = operation, subject = disk-stack   I2: topic: operation, subject: disk-stack   Body
level-of-detail = conceptual   level-of-detail = detailed
in-record: meeting-12/2/90   in-record: report-333
in-segment: 2   in-segment: 12   Reference

3. Relevance feedback: Get feedback from the user on the relevance of the information retrieved.
    ---> User: page 12 in the record report-333 is relevant
4. Index acquisition: create a new index I3 ⟶ **I3:** topic: function, subject: inner-hub
    level-of-detail: detailed
    in-record: report-333
    in-segment: 12

Figure 2: Creating a new index

```
index: EXP1-Q17                              index: EXP1-Q59
 in-record: DAMPER-DRD-WINTER-1990,           in-record: DAMPER-DRD-SPRING-1990,
 in-segment: 23                               in-segment: 12
 Topic: LOCATION of Subject: ARM             Topic: RELATION of Subjects:
 created by rule: PART-OF                                 (SUSPENSION-SYSTEM, DAMPER)
 from question: Q15                           created by rule: OR-RULE
 from index G205:                             from question: Q58
    Topic: DESCRIPTION                        from index G329:
        of Subject: ROTARY-DAMPER                Topic: RELATION of Subject:
                                                         (SUSPENSION-SYSTEM, CAR)
```

          (a)   (b)

Figure 3: Two indices generated by Dedal

5. Experiments and Preliminary Results

In this section we report on experiments and preliminary results to evaluate the effectiveness of Dedal's index acquisition. Index Acquisition is considered *effective* by three criteria: *reusability*, *relevance* and *context independence* of the indices in future retrieval (see section 2 for a description of these criteria).

We conducted experiments where we observed mechanical engineers using Dedal to ask questions in the context of a modification of a shock absorber designed at Stanford's Center for Design Research for Ford Motor Corporation [Baudin et al. 92a]. The engineers rated the references retrieved by Dedal as relevant or irrelevant. In these experiments we considered three contextual factors: the *user*, the *problem* being solved, and the specific *goal* that motivates each query.

Experiment 1: In the first experiment a mechanical designer unfamiliar with the shock absorber design queried the system during redesign. In this experiment we measured the *relevance* and the *reusability* of the indices acquired within the same problem solving process. As the new indices were created, they were reused to answer slightly different questions. Out of 71 indices created, 13 were reused and out of those 70% were found relevant by the user. The main causes of irrelevance were the incompleteness of the model and the multiple subjects problem, where indices that involve relations among multiple subjects need more training to be refined (see Section 4.2).

Experiment 2: An expert designer used the system for a similar redesign task. In this study we observed how the indices created during experiment1 were reused in experiment2. This gave us an idea of the *reusability* and *relevance* of these indices, with a user of different design experience, and during the course of another problem solving process. In this experiment many questions were about the relation among multiple subject and we focused on the reusability and relevance of indices that have more than one subject. Each time a multiple subject index is reused, the success or failure coefficients of its subjects are updated by the system. We found that:

(1) The number of irrelevant new indices retrieved outweighed the number of new indices that were relevant, thus degrading the performance of the system. In this experiment 30 indices created during experiment1 were reused and out of these, 40% were relevant. As expected, this degradation was due to the multiple subject problem, mainly to the introduction of incorrect subject extensions.

(2) In the new indices, each incorrect subject was showing positive failure rates and no success rates. The new indices created were shown to another designer that confirmed the trend that the system recorded. This suggests that the accuracy of the indices created is improving and will lead to a better performance in future retrieval.

Figure 3b shows an index generated during the first experiment, in this index the subject "damper" is an incorrect extension of the original index "relation (between) suspension-system, car". The rating (not shown on the figure) of the subject "damper" showed a positive failure rating and no success rating after we conducted the second experiment.

Experiment 3: We presented the 71 indices created (see Figure 3) during experiment 1 along with the associated information regions to a designer familiar with the shock absorber documentation. The designer rated each of these indices as relevant or irrelevant depending on his appreciation of the ability of the index to describe (part of)the associated information. In this experiment, the designer reviewed the *relevance* and *context independence* of the indices created. The three contextual factors (user, problem and goals) in our experiment were removed: the designer was different from the users who conducted the experiments, he rated the indices independently of any problem solving task, and he had no access to the English version of the questions that motivated the queries. The designer rated 86% of the acquired indices as relevant. Here again the irrelevant indices acquired were due to the incompleteness of the domain model and the introduction of incorrect subject extensions in indices with more than one argument.

The three criteria, reusability, relevance and context independence, of the acquired indices don't give us a direct measure of the impact of these indices on the global retrieval performance in terms of the precision and recall of the retrieval[1]. However, when the newly acquired indices are reusable and relevant across contexts, the references associated with them can be retrieved through an exact match instead of an approximate match. Our assumption is that this provides better performance since the precision of the exact match retrieval is higher than the precision of the approximate retrieval [Baudin et al. 92b] and since the exact match will now retrieve more references. The intuition is that the user will see more relevant references sooner while more irrelevant inferences will be pruned form the first set of documents proposed to the user. For instance in the example discussed in Section 4.1, the system retrieved two references in response to the query "function of **inner-hub**", only one of this reference being relevant the precision of this retrieval was 50%. After Dedal acquired the new index I3 and the next time the same question is asked, only the relevant reference will be retrieved through an exact match in the first set of answers proposed to the user.

6 Future work

Performance evaluation: Our preliminary experimental results are mostly qualitative. They are useful in indicating the main features of the effectiveness of the index acquisition in terms of the reusability, relevance and context independence of the acquired indices. In order to have a more precise notion of the effectiveness of the method we plan to quantitatively evaluate the impact of these indices on the global performance of the system in terms of the gain in the precision and recall of Dedal. However, The quantitative evaluation of the method on a meaningful sample of queries is a difficult task because: (1) the questions submitted to the system during the experiments must be motivated by specific goals (such as the redesign of the shock absorber in our first experiment); and (2) the questions asked during these experiments must overlap so as to involve the new indices created.

Index refinement: Our refinement algorithm is preliminary and can be expanded in two directions. One direction is to add to the refinement procedure the capability to automatically analyze which subjects cause the success or failure of an index so that, after multiple queries, Dedal can automatically decide how to modify an index based on the rating of its subjects. Another direction is to increase the interaction between the system and the user in order to elicit more knowledge about the causes of failure when a new index led to the retrieval of an irrelevant reference. This would be similar to the dialogue triggered by retrieval failure in Protos [Porter et al. 90].

---

[1] These are two criteria used to measure the performance of information retrieval systems,. Precision is the number of relevant references retrieved over the total number of references retrieved in response to a query. Recall is the number of relevant references retrieved in response to a query over the total number of existing relevant references.

Interactive modification of the domain model: The query language is designed to describe as much as possible the information required by the user. However, any language that uses concepts from a model is inherently incomplete. A missing domain subject forces the user to fall back on a related subject and is a source of inaccuracy in the use of queries for indexing purposes. One way of alleviating this problem is to allow the user to define new domain subjects when he cannot find a suitable concept in the model. We implemented a question formulation component that interacts with the user to understand how a new subject relates to the domain model and we plan to test this functionality with a user.

Definition of the domain model: Our conceptual query language is (1) task dependent: It is adapted to the type of questions that designers are interested in when they access design documents, and (2) is constrained by a domain model and requires this model to be built for each new design project. With respect to this method, an advantage of technical domains that relate to the operation, diagnostic or design of engineered artifacts, is that the scope of the domain model is usually well defined. For instance, in the engineering design domain a large part of technical documentation can be indexed using terms from a structural model (*part-of* hierarchy of components) of the designed artifact. The domain model becomes a design glossary whose terms are linked by different types of relations. Although model building might be considered a burden when compared to domain independent information retrieval systems, it is interesting to note that this type of "super glossary" is actually useful to the members of a design project as it explicitly defines what is meant by the vocabulary used by each member of the team.

7. Related work

Information retrieval systems have used relevance feedback techniques for two purposes: (1) to help refine user queries, and (2) to help refine indices associated with textual documents. Approaches such as [Salton 68][Croft et al. 90][Tou et al. 82] are domain independent methods that operate at the syntactic level in that they use a combination of words from a text to index and query the information. By comparison we constrained the query language and we use the queries to index the documents at a *conceptual level* appropriate to represent the content of the information in a given domain.

The CID project [Boy 89] starts with words from the text to index pages of textual documents. Index acquisition is performed by attaching contextual information such as the user profile to restrict the applicability of the indices. In our approach, the queries partially describe the content of the target information at the "appropriate" conceptual level and can directly be turned into an index. In this respect contextual factors such as the domain relations or the type of user are already embedded in the model underlying the query language and therefore become part of the acquired indices.

RUBRIC (Tong 89) uses *evidential reasoning* and *natural language processing* techniques to infer the content of a text. For instance, an evidential rule can define which words and relations among words suggest a given concept. It is not clear, at this point, how much background knowledge would be needed to automatically extract the document descriptions from our text-based documents.

8. Summary

We applied the use of relevance feedback to the acquisition of conceptual indices. We turn user queries into indices that partially describes the content of text, graphics and videotaped information at a conceptual level appropriate for a given class of users in a given domain. Using queries to describe pieces of information is made possible by: (1) constraining the query language: this requires studying the information needs of users in a given domain to identify generic types of questions this class of users is interested in, and (2) using a model of the domain to be able to match the queries with more general or related conceptual indices.

Although the principle of our approach is domain independent, its implementation requires to build a domain model. Our approach is particularly well adapted to the indexing of technical documents that describe the operation, diagnosis or design of complex artifacts where the domain model can be clearly circumscribed.

Acknowledgments: Thanks to Ade Mabogunje, Guy Boy and Nathalie Mathé for discussions on indexing and relevance feedback. We are grateful to Fred Lakin from the Performing Graphics Company for his support of the Electronic Design Notebook system that interacts with Dedal. Thanks to Michel Baudin for his help on early drafts of this paper.

References

Baudin, C., Gevins, J, Baya, V, Mabogunje, A. 1992a "Dedal: Using Domain Concepts to Index Engineering Design Information", Proceedings of the Meeting of the Cognitive Science Society, Bloomington, Indiana.

Baudin, C., Gevins, J., Baya, V., "Using Device Models to Facilitate the Retrieval of Multimedia Design Information", in proceedings of IJCAI 93 Chambéry, 1992b.

Baya, V, Gevins, J, Baudin, C, Mabogunje, A, Leifer, L., Toye, G.,"An Experimental Study of Design Information Reuse", in proceedings of the 4th International Conference on Design Theory and Methodology, 1992.

Boy, G., "The block representation in knowledge acquisition for computer integrated documentation", in: Proceedings Knowledge Acquisition for Knowledge-based systems, AAAI Workshop, Banff, Canada - 1989.

Croft, W.B, Das, R., "Experiments with Query Acquisition and Use in Document Retrieval Systems". in Proceedings of SIGIR 1990.

Graesser, A.; Black, J., 1985. The Psychology of Questions. Lawrence Elrlbaum associates.

Hayes, P., Pepper, J. "Towards An Integrated Maintenance Advisor" in Hypertext '89 Proceedings.

Mabogunje, A. "A conceptual framework for the development of a question based design methodology", Center for Design Research Technical Report (19900209), February 1990.

Mauldin, M. L., "Retrieval Performance in Ferret, A Conceptual Information Retrieval System". in Proceedings of SIGIR 1990.

Osgood, R., Bareiss, R. "Question-based indexing", Technical report 1991, The Institute for the Learning Sciences, Northwestern University.

Porter, B, Bareiss R., Holte C. "Concept learning and heuristic classification in weak-theory domains" in the AI Journal 45 1990 p 229-263.

Salton, G. Automatic Information Organization and Retrieval". Mc Graw-Hill, New York; 1968

Salton, G., Buckley, C. "Improving Retrieval Performance by Relevance Feedback", Technical Report, Cornell University, 1988

Schank, R., Ferguson, W., Birnbaum, L., Barger, J., Greising, M., "ASK TOM: An Experimental Interface for Video Case Libraries" ILS technical report, March 1991.

Tong, M. R., Appelbaum, A., and Askman V. "A Knowledge Representation for Conceptual Information Retrieval", International Journal of Intelligent Systems. vol. 4, 259-283, 1989

Tou, F.M. et al. "RABBIT: An intelligent database assistant". Proceedings AAAI-82, 314-318, 1982.

Learning Interface Agents

Pattie Maes

MIT Media Laboratory
20 Ames Street Rm. 401a
Cambridge, MA 02139
pattie@media.mit.edu

Robyn Kozierok

MIT Media Laboratory
20 Ames Street Rm. 401c
Cambridge, MA 02139
robyn@media.mit.edu

Abstract

Interface agents are computer programs that employ Artificial Intelligence techniques in order to provide assistance to a user dealing with a particular computer application. The paper discusses an interface agent which has been modelled closely after the metaphor of a *personal assistant*. The agent learns how to assist the user by (i) observing the user's actions and imitating them, (ii) receiving user feedback when it takes wrong actions and (iii) being trained by the user on the basis of hypothetical examples. The paper discusses how this learning agent was implemented using *memory-based learning* and *reinforcement learning* techniques. It presents actual results from two prototype agents built using these techniques: one for a meeting scheduling application and one for electronic mail. It argues that the machine learning approach to building interface agents is a feasible one which has several advantages over other approaches: it provides a customized and adaptive solution which is less costly and ensures better user acceptability. The paper also argues what the advantages are of the particular learning techniques used.

Introduction

Computers are becoming the vehicle for an increasing range of everyday activities. Acquisition of news and information, mail and even social interactions become more and more computer-based. At the same time an increasing number of (untrained) users are interacting with computers. Unfortunately, these developments are not going hand in hand with a change in the way people interact with computers. The currently dominant interaction metaphor of *direct manipulation* [Schneiderman 1983] requires the user to initiate all tasks and interactions and monitor all events. If the ever growing group of non-trained users has to make effective use of the power and diversity the computer provides, current interfaces will prove to be insufficient. The work presented in this paper employs Artificial Intelligence techniques, in particular semi-intelligent semi-autonomous agents, to implement a complementary style of interaction, which has been referred to as *indirect management* [Kay 1990]. Instead of unidirectional interaction via commands and/or direct manipulation, the user is engaged in a cooperative process in which human and computer agent(s) both initiate communication, monitor events and perform tasks. The metaphor used is that of a *personal assistant* who is *collaborating with the user* in the same work environment.

The idea of employing agents in the interface to delegate certain computer-based tasks was introduced by people such as Nicholas Negroponte [Negroponte 1970] and Alan Kay [Kay 1984]. More recently, several computer manufacturers have adopted this idea to illustrate their vision of the interface of the future (cf. videos produced in 1990-1991 by Apple, Hewlett Packard, Digital and the Japanese FRIEND21 project). Even though a lot of work has gone into the modeling and construction of agents, currently available techniques are still far from being able to produce the high-level, human-like interactions depicted in these videos. Two approaches for building interface agents can be distinguished. Neither one of them provides a satisfactory solution to the problem of how the agent acquires the vast amounts of knowledge about the user and the application which it needs to successfully fulfill its task.

The first approach consists in making the end-user program the interface agent. Malone and Lai's *Oval* (formerly *Object-Lens*) system [Lai, Malone, & Yu 1988], for example, has "semi-autonomous agents" which consist of a collection of user-programmed rules for processing information related to a particular task. For example, the Oval user can create an electronic mail sorting agent by creating a number of rules that process incoming mail messages and sort them into different folders. Once created, these rules perform tasks for the user without having to be explicitly invoked by the user. The problem with this approach to building agents is that it requires too much insight, understanding and effort from the end-user. The user has to (1) recognize the opportunity for employing an agent, (2) take the initiative to create an agent, (3) endow the agent with explicit knowledge (specifying this knowledge in an abstract language) and (4) maintain the agent's rules over time (as work habits change, etc.).

The second approach, also called the "knowledge-based approach", consists in endowing an interface agent with a lot of domain-specific background knowledge about its application and about the user (called a domain model and user model respectively). This approach is adopted by the majority of people working on intelligent user interfaces [Sullivan & Tyler 1991]. At run-time, the interface agent uses its knowledge to recognize the user's plans and find opportunities for contributing to them. For example, UCEgo [Chin 1991] is an interface agent designed to help a user solve problems in using the UNIX operating system. The UCEgo agent has a large knowledge base about how to use UNIX, incorporates goals and meta-goals and does planning, for example to volunteer information or correct the user's misconceptions. One problem with this approach to building interface agents is that it requires a huge amount of work from the knowledge engineer: a large amount of application-specific and domain-specific knowledge has to be entered and little of this knowledge or the agent's control architecture can be used when building agents for other applications. A second problem is that the knowledge of the agent is fixed once and for all: it is possibly incorrect, incomplete, not useful, and can be neither adapted nor customized (e.g. to individual user differences or to the changing habits of one user). Finally, it can be questioned whether it is possible to provide all the knowledge an agent needs to always be able to "make sense" of the user's actions (people do not always behave rationally, unexpected events might happen, the organization might change, etc.).

A Machine Learning Approach

In our work we explore an alternative approach to building interface agents which heavily relies on Machine Learning. The scientific hypothesis that is tested is that under certain conditions, an interface agent can "program itself", i.e. it can acquire the knowledge it needs to assists its user. The agent is given a minimum of background knowledge and it learns appropriate "behavior" from the user. The particular conditions that have to be fulfilled are (1) the use of the application has to involve a lot of repetitive behavior, and (2) this repetitive behavior is very different for different users. If the latter condition is not met, i.e. the repetitive behavior demonstrated by different users is the same, a knowledge-based approach might prove to yield better results than a learning approach. If the former condition is not met, a learning agent will not be able to learn anything (because there are no regularities in the user's actions to learn about).

Our machine learning approach is inspired by the metaphor of a personal assistant. Initially a personal assistant is not very "customized" and may not even be very useful. Some amount of time will go by before the assistant becomes familiar with the habits, preferences and particular work methods of the person and organization at hand. However, with every experience, the assistant learns, and gradually more tasks that were initially performed by the person directly, can be taken care of by the assistant.The goal of our research is to demonstrate that a learning interface agent can in a similar way become gradually more "helpful" to its user. In addition, we attempt to prove that the learning approach has several advantages. First, it requires less work from the end-user and application developer. Second, the agent is more adaptive over time and the agent automatically becomes customized to individual user preferences and habits. The results described in a later section support all of the above hypotheses and predictions.

A particular additional advantage of the learning approach to building interface agents is that the user and agent can gradually build up a *trust relationship*. Most likely it is not a good idea to give a user an interface agent that is from the start very sophisticated, qualified and autonomous. Schneiderman has convincingly argued that such an agent would leave the user with a feeling of loss of control and understanding [Myers 1991]. On the other hand, if the agent gradually develops its abilities – as is the case in our approach – the user is also given time to gradually build up a model of how the agent makes decisions. A particular advantage of the machine learning technique we use, namely *memory-based learning* [Stanfill & Waltz 1986], is that it allows the agent to give "explanations" for its reasoning and behavior in a language that the user is familiar with, namely in terms of past examples which are similar to the current situation. ("I thought you might want to take this action because this situation is similar to this other situation we have experienced before, in which you also took this action.")

We have developed a generic architecture for building "learning interface agents". The following section discusses the design and implementation of this architecture. For more technical detail, the reader should consult [Kozierok & Maes 1993]. We also built concrete examples of interface agents using this generic architecture. These include (i) a "mail clerk", which learns how a specific user prefers to have electronic messages handled and (ii) a "calendar manager" which learns to manage the calendar of a user and schedule meetings according to his or her preferences. Figure 1 shows some screen snaps from the calendar agent implementation. The last section discusses the status of these prototypes and discusses the results obtained so far.

Learning Techniques

The interface agent uses several sources for learning (1) learning by observing the user, (2) learning from user feedback and (3) learning by being trained. Each of these methods for learning is described in more detail below. More detail on the learning algorithms used can be found in [Kozierok & Maes 1993].

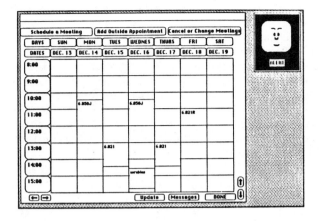
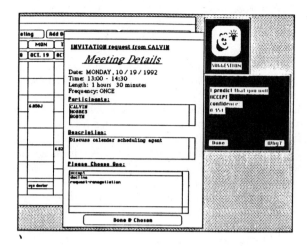

Figure 1: The alert agent observes and memorizes all of the user's interactions with the calendar application (left picture). When it thinks it knows what action the user is going to take in response to a meeting invitation, it may offer a suggestion (right picture), or even automate the action if its confidence is high enough (not shown).

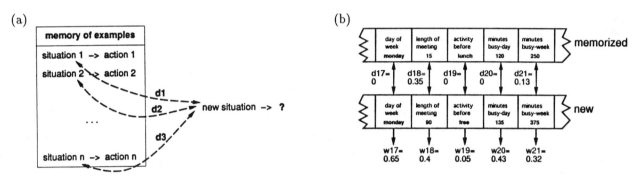

Figure 2:
(a) The agent suggests an action to perform based on the similarity of the current situation with previous (memorized) situations. d_i is the distance between the ith memorized situation and the new situation.
(b) The distance between two situations is computed as a weighted sum over the features. The weight of a feature and the distance between the two values for it depend upon the correlation statistics computed by the agent. The figure shows some possible feature weights and distances from the calendar manager agent.

Learning by Observing the User

The interface agent learns by continuously "looking over the shoulder" of the user as the user is performing actions. The interface agent can monitor the activities of the user, keep track of all of his/her actions over long periods of time (weeks or months), find recurrent patterns and offer to automate these. For example, if an electronic mail agent notices that a user almost always stores messages sent to the mailing-list "intelligent-interfaces" in the folder `pattie:email:int-int.txt`, then it can offer to automate this action next time a message sent to that mailing-list has been read.

The main learning technique used in our implementation is a variant on nearest-neighbor techniques known as *memory-based learning* [Stanfill & Waltz 1986] (see illustration in Figure 2(a)). As the user per-

forms actions, the agent memorizes all of the situation-action pairs generated. For example, if the the user saves a particular electronic mail message after having read it, the mail clerk agent adds a description of this situation and the action taken by the user to its memory of examples. Situations are described in terms of a set of features, which are currently handcoded. For example, the mail clerk keeps track of the sender and receiver of a message, the Cc: list, the keywords in the Subject: line, whether the message has been read or not, whether it has been replied to, and so on. When a new situation occurs, the agent compares it against the memorized situation-action pairs. The most similar of these memorized situations contribute to the decision of which action to take or suggest in the current situation.

The distance between a new situation and a memorized situation is computed as a weighted sum of the distances between the values for each feature as detailed in [Stanfill & Waltz 1986] (see Figure 2(b)). The distance between feature-values is based on a metric computed by observing how often in the example-base the two values in that feature correspond to the same action. The weight given to a particular feature depends upon the value for that feature in the new situation, and is computed by observing how well that value has historically correlated with the action taken. For example, if the `Sender:` field of a message has shown to correlate to the action of saving the message in a particular folder, then this feature (i.e. whether or not it is the same in the old and new situation) is given a large weight and thus has a high impact on the distance between the new and the memorized situation. At regular times, the agent analyzes its memory of examples and computes the statistical correlations of features and values to actions, which is used to determine these feature-distances and -weights.

Once all the distances have been computed, the agent predicts an action by computing a score for each action which occurs in the closest N (e.g. 5) memorized situations and selecting the one with the highest score. The score is computed as

$$\sum_{s \in S} \frac{1}{d_s}$$

where S is the set of memorized situations predicting that action, and d_s is the distance between the current situation and the memorized situation s.

Along with each prediction it makes, the agent computes a confidence level for its prediction, as follows:

$$\left(1 - \frac{\frac{d_{predicted}}{n_{predicted}}}{\frac{d_{other}}{n_{other}}} \right) \times \frac{n_{total}}{N}$$

where:

- N is, as before, the number of situations considered in making a prediction,
- $d_{predicted}$ is the distance to the closest situation with the same action as the predicted one,
- d_{other} is the distance to the closest situation with a different action from the predicted one,
- $n_{predicted}$ is the number of the closest N situations with distances less than a given maximum with the same action as the predicted one,
- n_{other} is the minimum of 1 or the number of the closest N situations with distances within the same maximum with different actions than the predicted one, and
- $n_{total} = n_{predicted} + n_{other}$, i.e. the total number of the closest N situations with distances below the maximum.

If the result is < 0, the confidence is truncated to be 0. This occurs when $d_{predicted}/n_{predicted} < d_{other}/n_{other}$ which is usually the result of several different actions occurring in the top N situations. If

every situation in the memory has the same action attached to it, d_{other} has no value. In this case the first term of the confidence formula is assigned a value of 1 (but it is still multiplied by the second term, which in this case is very likely to lower the confidence value as this will usually only happen when the agent has had very little experience). This computation takes into account the relative distances of the best situations predicting the selected action and another action, the proportion of the top N situations which predict the selected action, and the fraction of the top N situations which were closer to the current situation than the given maximum.

If the confidence level is above a threshold $T1$ (called the "tell-me" threshold), then the agent offers its suggestion to the user. The user can either accept this suggestion or decide to take a different action. If the confidence level is above a threshold $T2 > T1$ (called the "do-it" threshold), then it automates the action without asking for prior approval. The agent keeps track of all the automated actions and can provide a report to the user about its autonomous activities whenever the user desires this. The two thresholds are set by the user and are action-specific, thus the user may, for example, set higher "do-it" thresholds for actions which are harder to reverse. (A similar strategy is suggested for computer-chosen thresholds in [Lerner 1992].) The agent adds the new situation-action pair to its memory of examples, after the user has approved of the action.

Occasionally the agent "forgets" old examples so as to keep the size of the example memory manageable and so as to adapt to the changing habits of the user. At the moment, the agent deletes the oldest example whenever the number of examples reaches some maximum number. We intend to investigate more sophisticated "forgetting" methods later.

One of the advantages of this learning algorithm is that the agent needs very little background knowledge. Another advantage is that no information gets lost: the agent never attempts to abstract the regularities it detects into rules (which avoids problems related to the ordering of examples in incremental learning). Yet another advantage of keeping individual examples around is that they provide good explanations: the agent can explain to the user why it decided to suggest or automate a particular action based on the similarity with other concrete situations in which the user took that action – it can remind the user of these prior situations and point out the ways in which it finds them to be similar to the current situation. Examples provide a familiar language for the agent and user to communicate in. There is no need for a more abstract language and the extra cognitive burden that would accompany it.

One could argue that this algorithm has disadvantages in terms of computation time and storage requirements. We believe that the latter is not an issue because computer memory becomes cheaper and more available every day. The former is also less of a problem in practice. Computing the statistical correlations in the examples is an expensive operation ($O(n^2)$), but it can be performed off-line, for example at night or during lunch breaks. This does not mean that the agent does not learn from the examples it has observed earlier the same day: new examples are added to memory right away and can be used in subsequent predictions. What does not get updated on an example basis are the weights used in computing distances between examples. The prediction of an action is a less computation intensive operation ($O(n)$). This computation time can be controlled by restricting the number of examples memorized or by structuring and indexing the memory in more sophisticated ways. Furthermore, in a lot of the applications studied real-time response is not needed (for example, the agent does not have to decide instantly whether the user will accept a meeting invitation). In the experiments performed so far, all of the reaction times have been more than satisfactory. More details and results from this algorithm are described in a later section and in [Kozierok & Maes 1993].

Learning from User Feedback

A second source for learning is direct and indirect user feedback. Indirect feedback happens when the user neglects the suggestion of the agent and takes a different action instead. This can be as subtle as the user not reading the incoming electronic mail messages in the order which the agent had listed them in. The user can give explicit negative feedback when inspecting the report of actions automated by the agent ("don't do this action again"). One of the ways in which the agent learns from negative feedback is by adding the right action for this situation as a new example in its database.

Our agent architecture also supports another way in which the agent can learn from user feedback. The architecture includes a database of priority ratings which are relevant to all situations. For example, the calendar manager keeps a database of ratings expressing how important the user thinks other users of the system are, and how relevant the user feels certain keywords which appear in meeting descriptions are. These ratings are used to help compute the features which describe a situation. For example, there is an "initiator importance" feature in the calendar manager, which is computed by looking up who initiated the meeting, and then finding the importance rating for that person. When the agent makes an incorrect suggestion, it solicits feedback from the user as to whether it can attribute any of the blame to inaccuracy in these priority ratings, and if so in which ones. It can then adjust these ratings to reflect this new information, increasing or decreasing them as the difference in the "positiveness" of the suggested versus actual action dictates. The details of

how this is done are described in [Kozierok & Maes 1993].

Learning by Being Trained

The agent can learn from examples given by the user intentionally. The user can teach/train the agent by giving it hypothetical examples of events and situations and showing the agent what to do in those cases. The interface agent records the actions, tracks relationships among objects and changes its example base to incorporate the example that it is shown. For example, the user can teach the mail clerk agent to save all messages sent by a particular person in a particular folder by creating a hypothetical example of an email message (which has all aspects unspecified except for the sender field) and dragging this message to the folder in question. Notice that in certain cases it is necessary to give more than one hypothetical example (e.g. if the user wants to train the system to save messages from different senders in the same folder).

This functionality is implemented by adding the example in memory, including "wildcards" for the features which were not specified in the hypothetical situation. The new situation-action pair will match all situations in which an email message has been received from a user with the same name. One of the unresolved questions is how such hypothetical examples should be treated differently both when selecting an action and when compiling statistics. [Kozierok 1993] explores this issue, and describes how both *default* and *hard-and-fast rules* can be implemented within the memory-based learning framework. This paper also discusses how rules may be used to compress the database, when either all or most of the situations the rule would represent have occurred.

Results

The generic architecture for a learning interface agent is implemented in CLOS (Common Lisp Object System) on a Macintosh. We have evaluated the design and implementation of this architecture by constructing agents for several application programs. We currently have a prototype of a mail clerk as well as a calendar manager agent. The application software (the meeting scheduling system and electronic mail system) was implemented from scratch, so as to make it easier to provide "hooks" for incorporating agents. Both applications have a graphical direct manipulation interface (also implemented in Macintosh CLOS). The agent itself is hardly visible in the interface: a caricature face in the corner of the screen provides feedback to the user as to what the current state of the interface agent is. Figure 3 lists some of these caricatures. They help the user to quickly (in the blink of an eye) find out "what the agent is up to".

We have performed testing of both agents with simulated users. We are currently testing the calendar agent on real users in our own office environment, and

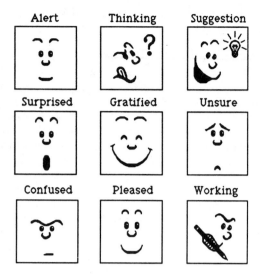

Figure 3: Simple caricatures convey the state of the agent to the user. The agent can be (a) alert (tracking the user's actions, (b) thinking (computing a suggestion), (c) offering a suggestion (when above tell-me threshold) (a suggestion box appears under the caricature), (d) surprised the suggestion is not accepted, (e) gratified the suggestion is accepted, (f) unsure about what to do in the current situation (below tell-me threshold) (suggestion box only shown upon demand), (g) confused about what the user does, (h) pleased that the suggestion it was not sure about turned out to be the right one and (i) working or performing an automated task (above do-it threshold).

will begin real-user testing of the email agent shortly as well. These users will be observed and interviewed over a period of time. The results obtained so far with both prototypes are encouraging. The email agent learns how to sort messages into the different mailboxes created by the user; when to mark messages as "to be followed up upon" or "to be replied to", etc. Current results on the meeting scheduling agent are described in detail in [Kozierok & Maes 1993]. A collection of seven such agents has been tested for several months worth of meeting problems (invitations to meetings, scheduling problems, rescheduling problems, etc). All seven agents learned over time to make mostly correct predictions, with high confidence in most of the correct predictions, and low confidence in almost all of the incorrect ones. Figure 4 shows the results for a representative agent. Again, the results obtained demonstrate that the learning interface agent approach is a very promising one. From this graph one can see that the correct predictions tend to increase in confidence level, while the incorrect ones tend to decrease. (We expect to see similar results in our real-user tests, but the inconsistencies and idiosyncrasies of real users will probably cause the agents to take longer to converge on such positive results. However, the memory-based

learning algorithm employed is designed to allow for inconsistencies, so we have confidence that the agents will indeed be able to perform competently within a reasonable timeframe.) Providing the user with access to this type of performance information allows him to easily set the thresholds at reasonable levels, as shown in the figure.

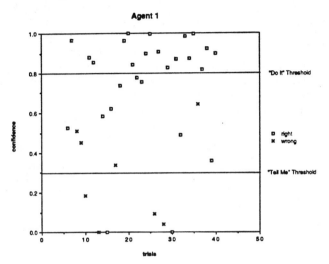

Figure 4: Results of a representative agent from the meeting scheduling application. The graph shows the right and wrong predictions made by the agent as plotted over time (X-axis). The Y-axis represents the confidence level the agent had in each of predictions. The picture also shows possible settings for the "tell-me" (T1) and "do it" (T2) thresholds.

Related Work

The work presented in this paper is related to a similar project under way at CMU. Dent et. al. [Dent et al. 1992] describe a personal learning apprentice which assists a user in managing a meeting calendar. Their experiments have concentrated on the prediction of meeting parameters such as location, duration and day-of-week. Their apprentice uses two competing learning methods: a decision tree learning method and a backpropagation neural network. One difference between their project and ours is that memory-based learning potentially makes better predictions because there is no "loss" of information: when suggesting an action, the detailed information about individual examples is used, rather than general rules that have been abstracted beforehand. On the other hand, the memory-based technique requires more computation time to make a particular suggestion. An advantage of our approach is that our scheduling agent has an estimate of the quality or accuracy of its suggestion. This estimate can be used to decide whether the prediction is good enough to be offered as a suggestion to the user or even to automate the task at hand.

The learning agents presented in this paper are also related to the work on so-called *demonstrational interfaces*. The work which is probably closest is Cypher's "eager personal assistant" for Hypercard [Cypher 1991]. This agent observes the user's actions, notices repetitive behavior and offers to automate and complete the repetitive sequence of actions. Myers [Myers 1988] and Lieberman [Lieberman 1993] built demonstrational systems for graphical applications. One difference between the research of all of the above authors and the work described in this paper is that the learning described here happens on a longer time scale (e.g. weekly or monthly habits). On the other hand a system like Eager forgets a procedure after it has executed it. A difference with the systems of Lieberman and Myers is that in our architecture, the user does not have to tell the agent when it has to pay attention and learn something.

Conclusion

We have modelled an interface agent after the metaphor of a personal assistant. The agent gradually learns how to better assist the user by (1) observing and imitating the user, (2) receiving feedback from the user and (3) being told what to do by the user. The agent becomes more helpful, as it accumulates knowledge about how the user deals with certain situations. We argued that such a gradual approach is beneficial as it allows the user to incrementally build up a model of the agent's behavior. We have presented a generic architecture for constructing such learning interface agents. This architecture relies on memory-based learning and reinforcement learning techniques. It has been used to build interface agents for two real applications. Encouraging results from tests of these prototypes have been presented.

Acknowledgments

Cecile Pham, Nick Cassimatis, Robert Ramstadt, Tod Drake and Simrod Furman have implemented parts of the meeting scheduling agent and the electronic mail agent. The authors have benefited from discussions with Henry Lieberman, Abbe Don and Mitch Resnick. This work is sponsored by the National Science Foundation (NSF) under grant number IRI-92056688. It has also been partially funded by Apple Computer. The second author is an NSF fellow.

References

Chin D. 1991. Intelligent Interfaces as Agents. In: J. Sullivan and S. Tyler eds. *Intelligent User Interfaces*, 177-206. New York, New York: ACM Press.

Crowston, K., and Malone, T. 1988. Intelligent Software Agents. *BYTE* 13(13):267-271.

Cypher, A. 1991. EAGER: Programming Repetitive Tasks by Example. In: CHI'91 Conference Proceedings, 33-39. New York, New York: ACM Press.

Don, A. (moderator and editor). 1992. Panel: Anthropomorphism: From Eliza to Terminator 2. In: CHI'92 Conference Proceedings, 67-72. New York, New York: ACM Press.

Kay, A. 1984. Computer Software. *Scientific American.* 251(3):53-59.

Kay, A. 1990. User Interface: A Personal View. In: B. Laurel ed. *The Art of Human-Computer Interface Design,* 191-208. Reading, Mass.: Addison-Wesley.

Kozierok, R., and Maes, P. 1993. A Learning Interface Agent for Scheduling Meetings. In: Proceedings of the 1993 International Workshop on Intelligent User Interfaces, 81-88. New York, New York: ACM Press.

Kozierok, R. 1993. Incorporating Rules into a Memory-Based Example Base, Media Lab Memo. Dept. of Media Arts and Sciences, MIT. Forthcoming.

Lai, K., Malone, T., and Yu, K. 1988. Object Lens: A "Spreadsheet" for Cooperative Work. *ACM Transactions on Office Information Systems* 5(4):297-326.

Laurel, B. 1990. Interface Agents: Metaphors with Character. In: B. Laurel ed. *The Art of Human-Computer Interface Design,* 355-366. Reading, Mass.: Addison-Wesley.

Lerner, B.S. 1992. Automated customization of structure editors. *International Journal of Man-Machine Studies* 37(4):529-563.

Lieberman, H. 1993. Mondrian: a Teachable Graphical Editor. In: A. Cypher ed. *Watch what I do: Programming by Demonstration.* Cambridge, Mass.: MIT Press. Forthcoming.

Dent, L., Boticario, J., McDermott, J., Mitchell, T., and Zabowski D. 1992. A Personal Learning Apprentice. In: Proceedings, Tenth National Conference on Artificial Intelligence, 96-103. Menlo Park, Calif.: AAAI Press.

Myers, B. 1988. *Creating User Interfaces by Demonstration.* San Diego, Calif.: Academic Press.

Myers, B. (moderator and editor). 1991. Panel: Demonstrational Interfaces: Coming Soon? In: CHI'91 Conference Proceedings, 393-396. New York, New York: ACM Press.

Negroponte, N. 1970. *The Architecture Machine; Towards a more Human Environment.* Cambridge, Mass.: MIT press.

Schneiderman, B. 1983. Direct Manipulation: A Step Beyond Programming Languages. *IEEE Computer* 16(8):57-69.

Stanfill, C., and Waltz, D. 1986. Toward Memory-Based Reasoning. *Communications of the ACM* 29(12):1213-1228.

Sullivan, J.W., and Tyler, S.W. eds. 1991. *Intelligent User Interfaces.* New York, New York: ACM Press.

Learning from an Approximate Theory and Noisy Examples

Somkiat Tangkitvanich and Masamichi Shimura
Department of Computer Science, Tokyo Institute of Technology
2-12-1 Oh-Okayama, Meguro, Tokyo 152, JAPAN
sia@cs.titech.ac.jp

Abstract

This paper presents an approach to a new learning problem, the problem of learning from an approximate theory and a set of noisy examples. This problem requires a new learning approach since it cannot be satisfactorily solved by either indictive, or analytic learning algorithms or their existing combinations. Our approach can be viewed as an extension of the minimum description length (MDL) principle, and is unique in that it is based on the encoding of the refinement required to transform the given theory into a better theory rather than on the encoding of the resultant theory as in traditional MDL. Experimental results show that, based on our approach, the theory learned from an approximate theory and a set of noisy examples is more accurate than either the approximate theory itself or a theory learned from the examples alone. This suggests that our approach can combine useful information from both the theory and the training set even though both of them are only partially correct.

Introduction

Previous machine learning approaches learn either empirically from noise-free [Mitchell, 1978] or noisy examples [Quinlan, 1983], or analytically from a correct theory and noise-free examples [Mitchell et al., 1986; DeJong and Mooney, 1986], or empirically and analytically from an approximate theory and noise-free examples [Richards, 1992; Pazzani et al., 1991; Cohen, 1990; Wogulis, 1991; Ginsberg, 1990; Cain, 1991; Bergadano and Giordana, 1988].

This paper discusses the problem of learning from an approximate theory and a set of noisy examples, a new learning problem which cannot be satisfactorily solved by the previous approaches. In this problem, it is harmful to place full confidence in either the given theory or the training set. Thus, an analytic approach will not learn successfully since it places full confidence in the theory which is only approximately correct. An inductive approach does not satisfactorily solve the problem since it cannot take advantage of the theory for biasing the learning. The approaches that combine analytic with inductive techniques, and modify the given theory to fit the examples, will not learn correctly since they place full confidence in the noisy training set. Consequently, we require a new learning approach that can balance the confidence in the theory against that in the examples.

Our approach, presented in this paper, can take advantage of the given theory for biasing the learning and can tolerate noise in the training examples. In our approach, the given theory is refined as little as necessary while its ability to explain the examples is increased as much as possible. The amount of the refinement and the ability of the theory to explain the examples are judged by the encoding lengths required to describe the refinement and the examples with the help of the theory, respectively. By keeping a balance between the amount of refinement and the ability to explain the examples, our approach places full confidence in neither the given theory nor the examples.

Although our approach can be applied to the learning of a theory represented in any language, we demonstrate its application to the learning of a relational theory. The prototype system, which we call LATEX (Learning from an Approximate Theory and noisy EXample), has been tested in the chess endgame domain in both knowledge-free and knowledge-intensive environments. The results show that a theory learned by LATEX from an approximate theory and a set of noisy examples is remarkably more accurate than the approximate theory itself, a theory learned by LATEX from the examples alone, or a theory learned by the FOIL learning system [Quinlan, 1990]. This suggests that our system can combine useful information from the theory and the training set even though both of them are only partially correct.

Description of the Problem

Our learning problem can be defined as follows:

- Given:
  - a prior knowledge in form of an approximate theory,

- a set of noisy positive and negative examples.

- Find:
  - a theory which is similar to the given theory but is expected to be more accurate in classifying the unseen examples.

The fundamental assumption of learning from an initial theory is that although the theory is flawed, it is still relatively "close" or "approximates" to the target theory [Mooney, To appear]. Intuitively, an approximate theory is supposed to facilitate the learning rather than hinder it. Such a theory can be obtained from a human expert, a prior learning [Muggleton *et al.*, 1992], a textbook [Cohen, 1990] or other sources. It has been pointed out that the accuracy of a theory is not a good criterion to quantify its approximateness [Mooney, To appear; Pazzani and Kibler, 1992]. Unfortunately, there has been no satisfactory criterion yet. In the next section, we show that the notion of an approximate theory can be precisely defined based on the encoding length of the refinement.

Our Approach

We present a new learning approach based on encoding a refinement and examples. The approach can be viewed as an extension of the minimum description length (MDL) principle [Wallace and Boulton, 1968; Rissanen, 1978], a general principle applicable to any inductive learning task involving sufficient examples. According to the principle, the simplest theory that can explain the examples well is the best one. Simplicity of a theory is judged by its length under an encoding scheme chosen subjectively by the experimenter. The ability of a theory to explain the given examples is judged by the length of the examples encoded with the help of the theory, with shorter length indicating more ability to explain. From the MDL perspective, learning occurs only when the sum of these encoding lengths is less than the explicit encoding length of the examples, that is when there is a compression.

General as it is, the MDL principle in its original form cannot take advantage of a prior knowledge in the form of an initial theory. This is a weakness since the information in the theory may be essential for an accurate learning when sufficient examples are not available. Our approach extends the MDL principle so that it can take advantage of an initial theory.

Extending MDL to Learn from an Approximate Theory

In our approach, the theory that is most similar to the given theory and can explain the examples well is the best theory. Similarity between a theory T' and the given theory T is judged by the length under some encoding scheme to describe the *refinement* required to transform T into T'. The ability of a theory to explain the examples is judged by the length

of the examples encoded with the help of the theory, with shorter length indicating more ability to explain. Qualitatively, the best theory is the theory with the minimum description length calculated from the sum of

1) the description length of the refinement, and

2) the description length of the examples encoded with the help of the refined theory.

The refined theory in 2) can be obtained from the initial theory and the description of the refinement. When the bias for a similar theory is appropriate, as in the case of learning from an approximate theory, a learning algorithm based on our approach will achieve a higher accuracy than an algorithm that cannot learn from a theory. It should be noted that when there is no initial theory, the bias reduces to one that prefers the simplest theory that can explain the examples, and our approach degenerates to the MDL approach.

The emphasis on encoding refinement is a unique feature of our approach. It has the following advantages for our learning problem.

1. It can balance the confidence in the theory against that in the training set. Consequently, our approach can take advantage of the information in both the theory and the training set while being able to avoid the pitfalls of placing full confidence in either of them. From a Bayesian perspective, our approach can be interpreted as assigning a prior probability to each theory in the hypothesis space, favoring the ones which are similar to the given theory, updating the probability by using the training examples, and selecting the theory that has a maximum posterior probability. However, in comparison with a Bayesian approach, an approach based on the MDL principle provides the user with the conceptually simpler problem of computing code lengths, rather than estimating probabilities [Quinlan and Rivest, 1989].

2. It provides a precise way to define an approximate theory. Intuitively, an approximate theory is a theory that facilitates the learning rather than hinder it. Since learning is related to producing a compression in the encoding length, an approximate theory can be judged based on the help it provides in shortening the description length of the target theory. Given an approximate theory, the encoding of the target theory as a sequence of refinements of that theory should be shorter than a direct encoding of the target theory. This leads to the following definition.

Definition 1 Approximate Theory
A theory T_0 is an approximate theory of T_* under an encoding scheme E iff $l_E(T_0, T_*) < l_E(\phi, T_*)$, where $l_E(T_i, T_j)$ is the length required to encode the transformation from T_i into T_j, and ϕ is an empty theory.

How can such a theory facilitate learning? Within the PAC learnability framework [Valiant, 1984], the following theorem shows that it reduces the sample complexity of any algorithm that accepts an initial theory T_0 and i) never examines a hypothesis h_1 before another hypothesis h_2 if $l_E(T_0, h_2) < l_E(T_0, h_1)$, and ii) outputs a hypothesis consistent with the training examples. Such an algorithm reflects important elements of a number of existing algorithms (e.g., [Ginsberg, 1990; Cain, 1991]) that modify the initial theory to fit the examples.

Theorem 1 *Let L be any algorithm that satisfies i) and ii). For a finite hypothesis space, L with an approximate theory T_0 has less sample complexity than L with an empty theory ϕ.*

The above theorem is applicable when the examples are noise-free. The proof of the theorem and an analogous theorem for learning from noisy examples is given in [Tangkitvanich and Shimura, 1993].

Learning a Relational Theory

In learning a relational theory, the examples and the theory are represented in form of tuples and a set of function-free first-order Horn clauses, respectively.

Encoding Training Examples

From the MDL perspective, learning occurs when there is a compression in the encoding length of the examples. In learning a relational theory, although both the positive and negative examples are given, it is a common practice to learn a theory that characterizes only the positive examples [Quinlan, 1990; Muggleton and Feng, 1990]. In encoding terms, this suggests that it is appropriate to compress only the encoding length of the positive examples.[1] One way to produce a compression is to encode the examples with the help of an approximate theory.

From Shannon's information theory, the optimal code length for an object e that has a probability p_e is $-\log_2 p_e$ bits. Without the help of an initial theory, the optimal code length required to indicate that an example is positive is thus $-\log_2 p_0$ bits, where p_0 is the probability that an example left in the training set is a positive example. In contrast, with the help of Cl, a clause in an approximate theory that covers the example, the optimal code length becomes $-\log_2 p_{cl}$ bits, where p_{cl} is the probability that an example covered by Cl is a positive example. Consequently, there is a compression produced by Cl in encoding a positive example if $p_{cl} > p_0$, that is when the positive examples are more concentrated in the clause than in the training set. The total compression obtained in encoding n positive examples covered by Cl is

$$Compress(Cl) = n \times (\log_2 p_0 - \log_2 p_{cl}). \quad (1)$$

---

[1]On the contrary, if a theory that characterizes both types of examples (e.g., a relational decision tree [Watanabe and Rendell, 1991]) is to be learned, it would be appropriate to compress the encoding length of both types.

The compression produced by a theory is the sum of the compressions produced by all the clauses in the theory. By using a more accurate theory to encode the examples, we can obtain further compressions. Such a theory can be obtained by means of refinement. However, the compression is not obtained without any cost since we have to encode the refinement as well.

Encoding Refinements

We assume that the head of each clause in the theory is identical. This limits the ability to learn an intermediate concept but simplifies the encoding of a refinement. With this assumption, it is possible to encode any refinement by using only two basic transformations: a literal addition and a literal deletion. Other forms of transformation can be encoded by using these. For example, literal replacement can be encoded by using a combination of a literal addition and a literal deletion. Clause addition can be encoded by using a combination of literal additions. The head of a new clause need not be encoded since it is identical to that of an existing clause. Clause deletion can be encoded in a similar way by using a combination of literal deletions. Thus, the overall refinement can be encoded by the following self-delimiting code:

$\|n_1\|$ $refine_{1,1}\|$ $refine_{1,2}\|...\|refine_{1,n_1}\|$
$\|n_2\|$ $refine_{2,1}\|$ $refine_{2,2}\|...\|refine_{2,n_2}\|$
$\vdots \qquad \vdots \qquad \vdots$
$\|n_k\|$ $refine_{k,1}\|$ $refine_{k,2}\|...\|refine_{k,n_k}\|$

In the above encoding scheme, n_i is the encoding of an integer indicating the number of refinements applied to clause i (with $n_i = 0$ indicating no refinement), $refine_{i,j}$ is the encoding of the j-th refinement to clause i. $refine_{i,j}$ is composed of a one-bit flag indicating whether the refinement is a literal addition or a literal deletion, and the encoding of the content of the refinement. For a literal addition, the encoding of the content contains the information required to indicate whether the literal to be added is negated or not, and from which relation and variables the literal is constructed. For a literal deletion, the encoding of the content contains the information required to indicate which literal in the clause is to be deleted. Note that the encoding scheme is natural for our learning problem in that it requires a shorter encoding length for a refinement that has a littler effect on the theory. For example, adding a literal requires a shorter length than adding a clause.

We now quantify the relationship between the refinement and its effect on the compression in the encoding length. Let Cl_i be a clause in the initial theory, $Length(refine_{i,j})$ be the length required for $refine_{i,j}$, and Cl_i' be the refined clause obtained from Cl_i and $refine_{i,j}$. The compression produced by the refinement can be estimated by

$$Compression(refine_{i,j}) = Compress(Cl'_i) -$$
$$Compress(Cl_i) - Length(refine_{i,j}). \quad (2)$$

The Learning Algorithm

The algorithm of LATEX is very simple. In each iteration, the theory is refined by using all the possible applications of the following refinement operators: a clause-addition operator, a clause-deletion operator, a literal-addition operator and a literal-deletion operator. The literal-addition operator adds to an existing clause a literal in the background knowledge. The literal must contain at least one existing variable and must satisfy constraints to avoid problematic recursion. The clause-addition operator adds to the theory a new clause containing one literal. Among all the possible refinements, LATEX selects one that produces maximal positive compression. The system terminates when no refinement can produce a positive compressions. The refined theory is then passed to a simple post-processing routine which removes clauses that cover more negative than positive examples.

Admittedly, the current greedy search strategy and the simple refinement operators prevent LATEX from learning some theories, e.g., those contain literals that do not discriminate positive from negative examples. We are now incorporating a more complex search strategy and better operators to overcome this limitation.

Experimental Evaluations

LATEX has been experimented on the king-rook-king board classification domain described in [Quinlan, 1990; Richards, 1992]. In this domain, there are two types of variable, representing row and column. For each type, there are three relations given as the background knowledge: $eq(X,Y)$ indicating that X is the same as Y, $adj(X,Y)$ indicating that X is adjacent to Y and $lessthan(X,Y)$ indicating that X is less than Y.

In our experiments, the training sets are randomly generated and noise are randomly introduced into them. To introduce noise, we adopt the classification noise model used in [Angluin and Laird, 1988]. In this model, a noise rate of η implies that the class of each example is replaced by the opposite class with probability η. The test set is composed of 10,000 examples selected independently to the training set.

The experiments are made on 5 initial theories which are the operationalized version of those used by FORTE [Richards, 1992]. The theories are generated by corrupting the correct theory with six operators: clause-addition, clause-deletion, literal-addition, literal-deletion, literal-replacement and variable-replacement operators. Each corrupted theory is an approximate theory according to our definition and is averagely 45.79% correct. The average number of clauses in an operationalized theory is 14.2, and the average number of literals in a clause is 2.8.

Figure 1 compares the learning curves of LATEX with an initial theory (LATEX-Th), LATEX without an initial theory (LATEX-NoTh), and FOIL [Quinlan, 1990], for $\eta = 10\%$. The curves demonstrate many interesting points. First, throughout the learning session, the theory learned by LATEX from an initial theory and the examples is significantly more accurate than that learned by LATEX from the examples alone. Further, although the training examples are considerably noisy, the theory learned from the initial theory and the examples is much more accurate than the initial theory itself. This means that LATEX can extract useful information from the noisy examples to improve the accuracy of the theory.

In other words, the experiments show that by combining the information in the theory and the examples, LATEX achieves a higher accuracy than it could with either one alone. Both are beneficial to the system. This suggests a dual view of our approach: as a means of refining an initial theory using examples, or as a means of improving the learning from examples using an initial theory.

It is also interesting to compare the learning curve of LATEX with that of FOIL. Without an initial theory, LATEX degenerates to an ordinary inductive learning system based on the MDL principle. Throughout the training sessions, the theory learned by LATEX is significantly more accurate than that learned by FOIL. However, another experiment which is not reported here shows that there are no significant differences in the accuracies achieved by the two systems when there is no noise in the training set. Hence, the differences can be attributed to the differences in the noise-handling mechanisms of the two systems. Investigation reveals that, when the examples are noisy, the theories learned by FOIL contain more literals and require longer encoding lengths than those learned by LATEX. In other words, the theories learned by FOIL are much more complex.

Related Work

In this section, we discuss three related approaches for learning a relational theory from noisy examples. Other approaches (e.g., [Towell et al., 1990; Drastal et al., 1989; Ginsberg, 1990]) will be discussed in the full paper.

- FOIL

  Unlike LATEX, FOIL [Quinlan, 1990] is a relational learning system that cannot take advantage of an initial theory. However, it is informative to compare the two systems from an inductive learning perspective. FOIL uses an information-based heuristic called Gain to select a literal and uses another information-based heuristic as its stopping criterion to handle noise. In contrast, LATEX uses a single compression-based criterion for both tasks. When used to select a literal, our criterion and Gain are

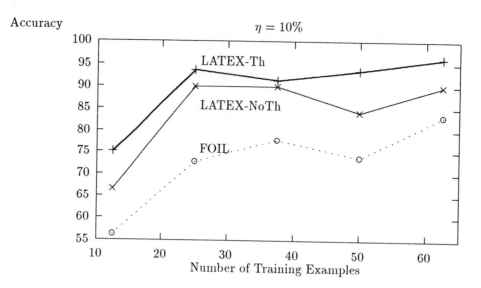

Figure 1: Learning curves of LATEX and FOIL

similar in that they suggest selecting a literal that discriminates positive from negative examples. However, when used to handle noise, our criterion and FOIL's stopping criterion have different effects. The experiments reveal that a theory learned by FOIL is much more complex than that learned by LATEX. This is because FOIL's stopping criterion allows the building of long clauses to cover a small number of examples. Former study [Dzeroski and Lavrac, 1991] also arrived at the same conclusion.

- FOCL

  FOCL extends FOIL to learn from an initial theory in an interesting way. However, the original algorithm of FOCL [Pazzani and Kibler, 1992] is unsuitable for learning from noisy examples since it refines the given theory to be consistent with them. Two extensions of FOCL are designed to deal with noise: one with FOIL's stopping criterion, the other with a pruning technique [Brunk and Pazzani, 1991].

  Currently, we are not aware of any experimental results of testing any FOCL algorithms in learning from an initial theory and noisy examples. However, it should be noted that while FOCL with the pruning technique requires another training set for pruning, and both extensions of FOCL use separate mechanisms for selecting literals and handling noise, LATEX requires a single training set and uses a single mechanism for both tasks.

- Muggleton et. al.'s Learning System

  Recently, Muggleton et. al. [Muggleton et al., 1992] proposed an approach to learn a theory represented as a logic program from noisy examples. The system based on their approach receives as an input an

overly general theory learned by the GOLEM system [Muggleton and Feng, 1990]. It then specializes the theory by using a technique called closed-world specialization [Bain and Muggleton, 1990]. If there are several possible specializations, the one that yields maximal compression is selected. Since the system attempts to minimize the encoding length, it can be viewed as incorporating the MDL principle.

From the point of view of learning from an initial theory, there is an important difference between the theory acceptable by their system and that acceptable by LATEX. While their system assumes an overly general theory produced by a prior learning of GOLEM, LATEX requires no such assumptions. LATEX can accept a theory that is overly general, overly specific, or both. The theory can be obtained from an expert, a textbook, a prior learning and other sources.

Conclusion

We presented an approach for learning from an approximate theory and noisy examples. The approach is based on minimizing the encoding lengths of the refinement and the examples, and can be viewed as an extension of the MDL principle that can take advantage of an initial theory. We also demonstrated the applicability of our approach in learning a relational theory, and showed that the system based on our approach can tolerate noise in both the knowledge-free and knowledge-intensive environment. In the knowledge-free environment, our system compares favorably with FOIL. In the knowledge-intensive environment, it combines useful information from both the theory and the training set and achieves a higher accuracy than it could with either one alone. Consequently, our approach can be viewed either as a means to improve the accuracy of an initial theory using training examples, or as a means to improve the learning from examples using an initial theory.

Directions for future work include experimenting with other models of noise in the examples and comparing an approximate theory according to our formalization with a theory obtained from a knowledge source in a real-world domain.

Acknowledgments

We would like to thank Hussein Almuallim for his insightful comments. We are also indebted to Boonserm Kijsirikul for his excellent help in implementing LA-TEX, Tsuyoshi Murata and Craig Hicks for their help in preparing the paper.

References

Angluin, D. and Laird, P. 1988. Learning from noisy examples. *Machine Learning* 2:343–370.

Bain, M. and Muggleton, S. 1990. Non-monotonic learning. In *Machine Intelligence12*. Oxford University Press.

Bergadano, F. and Giordana, A. 1988. A knowledge intensive approach to concept induction. In *Proc. the Fifth International Conference on Machine Learning*. Morgan Kaufmann. 305–317.

Brunk, C. and Pazzani, M. 1991. An investigation of noise-tolerant relational concept learning algorithms. In *Proc. the Eighth International Workshop on Machine Learning*. Morgan Kaufman. 389–393.

Cain, T. 1991. The DUCTOR: A theory revision system for propositional domains. In *Proc. the Eighth International Workshop on Machine Learning*. Morgan Kaufman. 485–489.

Cohen, W. 1990. Learning from textbook knowledge: A case study. In *Proc. the Eighth National Conference on Artificial Intelligence*. AAAI Press/MIT Press. 743–748.

DeJong, G. and Mooney, R. 1986. Explanation-based learning: An alternative view. *Machine Learning* 1(2):145 – 176.

Drastal, G.; Czako, G.; and Raatz, S. 1989. Induction in an abstract space: A form of constructive induction. In *IJCAI 89*. Morgan Kaufman. 708–712.

Dzeroski, S. and Lavrac, N. 1991. Learning relations from noisy examples: an empirical comparison of LINUS and FOIL. In *Proc. the Eighth International Workshop on Machine Learning*. Morgan Kaufman. 399–402.

Ginsberg, A. 1990. Theory reduction, theory revision, and retranslation. In *AAAI 90*. Morgan Kaufman. 777–782.

Mitchell, T.M.; Keller, R.M.; and Kedar-Cabelli, S.T. 1986. Explanation-based learning: A unifying view. *Machine Learning* 1(1):47 – 80.

Mitchell, T. M. 1978. Version spaces: An approach to concept learning. Technical Report HPP-79-2, Stanford University, Palo Alto, CA.

Mooney, R. To appear. A preliminary PAC analysis of theory revision. In Petsche, T.; Judd, S.; and Hanson, S., editors, *Computational Learning Theory and Natural Learning Systems*, volume 3. MIT Press.

Muggleton, S. and Feng, C. 1990. Efficient induction of logic programs. In *Proc. the First Conference on Algorithmic Learning Theory*. OHMSHA. 368–381.

Muggleton, S.; Srinivasan, A.; and Bain, M. 1992. Compression, significance and accuracy. In *Proc. the Ninth International Conference on Machine Learning*. Morgan Kaufmann. 339–347.

Pazzani, M. and Kibler, D. 1992. The utility of knowledge in inductive learning. *Machine Learning* 9:57–94.

Pazzani, M.; Brunk, C.; and Silverstein, G. 1991. A knowledge-intensive approach to learning relational concepts. In *Proc. the Eighth International Workshop on Machine Learning*. Morgan Kaufman. 432–436.

Quinlan, J.R. and Rivest, R.L. 1989. Inferring decision trees using the minimum description length principle. *Information and Computation* 80:227–248.

Quinlan, J. R. 1983. Learning from noisy data. In *Proc. the 1983 International Machine Learning Workshop*. 58 – 64.

Quinlan, J.R. 1990. Learning logical definitions from relations. *Machine Learning* 5:239–266.

Richards, B. 1992. *An Operator-based Approach to First-order Theory Revision*. Ph.D. Dissertation, The University of Texas at Austin. AI92-181.

Rissanen, J. 1978. Modeling by shortest data description. *Automatica* 14:465–471.

Tangkitvanich, S. and Shimura, M. 1993. Theory refinement based on the minimum description length principle. Technical Report 93TR-001, Department of Computer Science, Tokyo Institute of Technology.

Towell, G. G.; Shavlik, J. W.; and Noordewier, M. O. 1990. Refinement of approximate domain theories by knowledge-based neural networks. In *AAAI 90*. AAAI Press / The MIT Press. 861–866.

Valiant, L. 1984. A theory of the learnable. *CACM*. 27:1134–1142.

Wallace, C. and Boulton, D. 1968. An information measure for classification. *Computer J.* 11:185–194.

Watanabe, L. and Rendell, L. 1991. Learning structural decision trees from examples. In *IJCAI 91*. Morgan Kaufman. 77–776.

Wogulis, J. 1991. Revising relational theory. In *Proc. the Eighth International Workshop on Machine Learning*. Morgan Kaufman. 462–466.

Scientific Model-Building as Search in Matrix Spaces

Raúl E. Valdés-Pérez
School of Comp. Sci. &
Center for Light Microscope
Imaging and Biotechnology
Carnegie Mellon Univ.

Jan M. Żytkow
Dept. of Comp. Sci.
Wichita State Univ.

Herbert A. Simon
Dept. of Psychology
Carnegie Mellon Univ.

Abstract

Many reported discovery systems build discrete models of hidden structure, properties, or processes in the diverse fields of biology, chemistry, and physics. We show that the search spaces underlying many well-known systems are remarkably similar when re-interpreted as search in matrix spaces. A small number of matrix types are used to represent the input data and output models. Most of the constraints can be represented as matrix constraints; most notably, conservation laws and their analogues can be represented as matrix equations. Typically, one or more matrix dimensions grow as these systems consider more complex models after simpler models fail, and we introduce a notation to express this. The novel framework of matrix-space search serves to unify previous systems and suggests how at least two of them can be integrated. Our analysis constitutes an advance toward a generalized account of model-building in science.

Introduction

The discovery of models of atomic and molecular structure, of chemical processes, and of genetic transmission are celebrated events in the history of science. Far from being isolated historical instances, discovery of hidden structure in the form of discrete models is a universal and current task across the natural sciences.

Several discovery systems reported in the AI literature discover models of discrete, hidden structure. These systems include DALTON [Langley *et al.*, 1987], GELL-MANN [Fischer and Zytkow, 1990], MECHEM [Valdes, 1992; 1993 (in press)], MENDEL [Fischer and Zytkow, 1992], BR-3/PAULI [Kocabas, 1991; Valdes, accepted], STAHL [Zytkow and Simon, 1986] and its descendents STAHLp [Rose and Langley, 1986] and REVOLVER [Rose, 1989]. Of these, DALTON, MECHEM, and STAHL perform in chemistry, GELL-MANN and BR-3/PAULI in physics, and MENDEL in biology.

Despite the diversity of scientific domains that these systems treat, there lurk striking similarities in the representation of models, problem-solving methods, and domain knowledge used in model construction. Some of these similarities were pointed out elsewhere [Fischer and Zytkow, 1992]. These similarities may eventually allow us to develop a unified discovery system able to search for many types of discrete models. As a prerequisite, we should study existing systems that have already demonstrated a degree of competence on historical or current science. An important theoretical task of comparative analysis, which is relatively scarce in the AI literature, is to identify a unitary core among these systems. Without this, progress is limited to the accumulation of special-purpose programs.

The purpose of this paper is to identify a common representation of discrete models and a systematic analysis of the search spaces and domain constraints using the language of matrices. Our analysis introduces a small set of matrix types that represent the input data, the output models, and the spaces to be searched by the discovery system. Models are proposed by assigning numeric values to entries in a matrix, most assignments being ruled out by the domain constraints. The matrix representation enables the use of powerful methods of matrix algebra and combinatorial algorithms to improve the search for discrete models.

We also introduce a new notation to express how discovery systems carry out the search for models by postulating new entities, processes, and properties. This notation is used later to show how two specific systems that were developed separately can be integrated.

Systems

In this section we will re-interpret six discovery systems and show that they have a surprising degree of similarity. Three types of matrices used in these systems will be highlighted: a reaction matrix $\mathcal{R}$, a structure matrix $\mathcal{S}$, and a property matrix $\mathcal{P}$, defining them in the context of each system. We use the language of matrices and matrix algebra to describe the constraints in these systems. We also show how each system systematically changes the sizes of some few matrices in the course of performing its task.

The emphasis in this paper is on the spaces searched

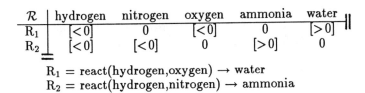

$\mathcal{R}$	hydrogen	nitrogen	oxygen	ammonia	water
R_1	[<0]	0	[<0]	0	[>0]
R_2	[<0]	[<0]	0	[>0]	0

R_1 = react(hydrogen,oxygen) $\rightarrow$ water
R_2 = react(hydrogen,nitrogen) $\rightarrow$ ammonia

Figure 1: Reaction Matrix in DALTON

$\mathcal{S}$	N	O	H
hydrogen	0	0	[>0]
nitrogen	[>0]	0	0
oxygen	0	[>0]	0
ammonia	[>0]	0	[>0]
water	0	[>0]	[>0]

Figure 2: Structure Matrix in DALTON

by the systems, and not on the detailed ways each system carries out its search, which varies across systems and sometimes even within systems, since several of the programs possess more than one internal search space. One view of problem-solving in science is that it typically proceeds over several spaces which can be quite heterogeneous. Initially proposed by Lea and Simon [Lea and Simon, 1974], this idea has been expanded and applied in the discovery system FAHRENHEIT [Zytkow, 1987], while Klahr and Dunbar [Klahr and Dunbar, 1988] have investigated it as a psychological model.

Some comments on notation follow. Matrices will be represented as tables with two intersecting perpendicular line segments, one to mark the rows, the other the columns. Additional marks are used to show whether a matrix dimension grows, shrinks, or is static: an outgoing (ingoing) arrow means that the dimension grows (shrinks), and a cap means that it is static during problem solving. We will see that most of the systems progressively enlarge their matrix models when smaller models prove inadequate.

DALTON

DALTON's task is to find structural models of chemical reactions and substances in terms of atoms [Langley *et al.*, 1987]. For example, given the following data:

1. two volumes of hydrogen and one volume of oxygen react to form two volumes of water;

2. three volumes of hydrogen and one volume of nitrogen react to form two volumes of ammonia;

3. hydrogen, oxygen, and nitrogen are elementary substances;

4. water consists of hydrogen and oxygen, and ammonia consists of hydrogen and nitrogen;

DALTON uses its bias for simplicity, conservation laws, and the Gay-Lussac law to report correctly that (1) two hydrogen molecules react with one of oxygen to form two water molecules, while three hydrogen molecules combine with one nitrogen molecule to form two ammonia molecules, and that (2) hydrogen, oxygen and nitrogen are diatomic, water is H_2O and ammonia is NH_3.

In making these inferences, DALTON can be interpreted as filling in two matrices. The first matrix describes inputs and outputs for each reaction; the example discussed in [Langley *et al.*, 1987] has the initial

form shown in Figure 1. The bracketed constraints represent conventional matrix depictions of reactions [Aris and Mah, 1963]: the reactants have negative entries, and the products have positive entries. All nonparticipating substances have zero entries. In this paper, we will always denote such a reaction matrix by $\mathcal{R}_{r \times s}$, where r is the number of reactions, and s is the number of chemical substances.

A second, structure matrix in DALTON (Figure 2) represents the structure of the chemical substances in terms of atomic elements. Initially, some of the entries are zero to indicate that certain substances do not contain certain atoms. The remaining entries in the matrix are constrained to positive integers. We denote this structure matrix as $\mathcal{S}_{s \times e}$, where s as before is the number of substances, and e is the number of chemical elements involved.

The sizes of the $\mathcal{R}$ and $\mathcal{S}$ matrices are fixed, as indicated in the figures by a "double cap" notation that prevents the matrix from changing size. DALTON does not conjecture new reactions, substances, nor chemical elements, so it never enlarges the two matrices which it receives as input.

DALTON's task is to fill in the reaction matrix and the structure matrix completely with integer entries, subject to the constraints stated above, a criterion of simplicity of entries, and a conservation law on atoms, which is expressed in matrix algebra as follows:

$$\mathcal{R}_{r \times s} \times \mathcal{S}_{s \times e} = 0_{r \times e} \qquad (1)$$

This equation implies that each of r reactions must conserve the atoms of all e elements: the product $\mathcal{R} \times \mathcal{S}$ gives the zero matrix 0 of dimensions $r \times e$. Conservation means that the net production of atoms of each element is zero for each reaction. Simplicity has a role in choosing the magnitudes of the entries (integers of smaller magnitude are simpler). Equation 1 is the standard way to express linear conservation conditions in sciences such as chemistry.

In our example, DALTON outputs the two matrices in Figure 3 (the output matrix $\mathcal{R}$ is shown transposed to fit on the page). The matrix $\mathcal{R}$ quantifies the qualitative reaction matrix input to DALTON, e.g., three hydrogen molecules enter into the ammonia reaction. The output matrix $\mathcal{S}$ specifies the elementary constituents of each substance. For example, a value of 2 for the matrix entry (*hydrogen*, H) in $\mathcal{S}$ means that hydrogen molecules include two atoms of hydrogen. Since all other entries in the hydrogen row are

$\mathcal{R}^T$	water reaction	ammonia reaction
hydrogen	-2	-3
nitrogen	0	-1
oxygen	-1	0
ammonia	0	2
water	2	0

$\mathcal{S}$	N	O	H
hydrogen	0	0	2
nitrogen	2	0	0
oxygen	0	2	0
ammonia	1	0	3
water	0	1	2

Figure 3: Output of DALTON

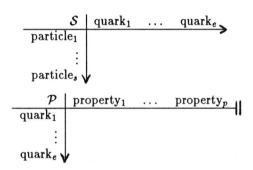

Figure 4: Matrix Structure of GELL-MANN

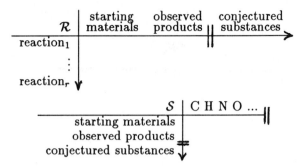

Figure 5: Matrix Structure of MECHEM

zero, the hydrogen molecule is diatomic, i.e., has structure H_2.

GELL-MANN

GELL-MANN's task is to propose quark models that account for the known property values of the particles in elementary-particle families [Fischer and Zytkow, 1990]. The models constructed by GELL-MANN are filled-in pairs of matrices shown in Figure 4. The structural $\mathcal{S}$ matrix is analogous to the $\mathcal{S}$ matrix in DALTON: s particles (or "substances") will contain e quarks (or "elements"). The second matrix in GELL-MANN is a property matrix $\mathcal{P}$ which assigns values of p properties to e quarks. The domain constraints on the $\mathcal{S}$ matrix are:

- The matrix entries are non-negative integers.

- The sum of entries over each row equals k, which is the number of quarks contained in each particle.

- The number of k-combinations of the set of e quarks (with infinite repetition number), which by a theorem in elementary combinatorics [Brualdi, 1981] equals $C(e-1+k,k)$, satisfies $s \le C(e-1+k,k) \le 3s$, where s is the number of input particles.

Contrary to DALTON, GELL-MANN enlarges the number of columns in the first matrix (and perforce the number of rows in the second) if it cannot find an acceptable model for the current number of quarks. Adding another column corresponds to postulating one more quark. During its search for an acceptable model, GELL-MANN also increments the value of k, the number of quarks per particle. Each k leads to $C(e-1+k,k)$ possible quark combinations, each represented by one row in the expanded $\mathcal{S}$ matrix. The number of input particles is constant, and equals s.

The quark models proposed by GELL-MANN must also be consistent with the observed property values of the particles. For example, since a proton has a charge of 1, the sum of charges for quarks which constitute the proton must be also 1. This constraint is called an "additivity law" in [Fischer and Zytkow, 1990], and is analogous to laws of conservation. Whereas conservation in DALTON (and generally) is expressed by a constraint of the form $\mathcal{R} \times \mathcal{S} = 0$, additivity in GELL-MANN is expressed as $\mathcal{S}_{s \times e} \times \mathcal{P}_{e \times p} = \mathcal{P}'_{s \times p}$. The matrix $\mathcal{P}'$ contains property values of particles, which are constants given as input to the system. Matrices $\mathcal{P}$ and $\mathcal{P}'$ both contain property values: the first for hidden objects postulated in the model, the second for observable objects given in the input.

Those rows in GELL-MANN's $\mathcal{S}$ matrix corresponding to particles input to the program are tested using the additivity law. However, GELL-MANN also predicts unseen particles by taking advantage of those quark combinations (numbering $C(e-1+k,k)-s$) that were not used to model the known particles. In these cases, the properties of these new particles are predicted by simply pre-multiplying the matrix $\mathcal{P}$ by these $C(e-1+k,k)-s$ rows.

MECHEM

MECHEM's task is to discover the simplest pathway able to explain all the experimental evidence about an aggregate chemical reaction [Valdes, 1992; 1993 (in press)]. MECHEM searches the space of two matrices shown in Figure 5. Some constraints on the $\mathcal{R}$ matrix are:

1. matrix entries admit only integer values,

2. For each row, the sum of the negative integers is -1 or -2. The sum of the positive integers is 1 or 2

[*Each reaction has at most two reactants and two products*].

3. Each column contains at least one nonzero entry [*All substances must occur somewhere in the reaction*].

4. For each column corresponding to observed or conjectured products, the top-most nonzero entry is positive [*Each product must be formed before it can be consumed*].

The fourth constraint is used to define a canonical order on reactions in the service of search efficiency [Valdes, 1991]; it is not derived from chemical theory.

New rows and columns can be added in the $\mathcal{R}$ matrix as the program fails with simpler hypotheses, so we see that MECHEM has two dimensions of expansion that guide its search in this matrix space. MECHEM prefers adding new reactions (by incrementing r) over incrementing the number of conjectured substances, so usually the matrix is growing vertically. Three systems considered in this paper (MECHEM, MENDEL, and GELL-MANN) enlarge matrices along two dimensions.

In the $\mathcal{S}$ matrix, the molecular formulas for the starting materials and observed products are known; the program determines the formulas, or matrix entries, for the conjectured substances. This task is common to all systems which fill in entries in the $\mathcal{S}$ matrix. As in DALTON, the conservation conditions can be expressed as the equation $\mathcal{R}_{r \times s} \times \mathcal{S}_{s \times e} = 0_{r \times e}$, in which $\mathcal{S}$ is a structure matrix that contains the molecular formula (involving e chemical elements) of each substance, and $0_{r \times e}$ is the zero matrix.

In addition to conservation of the elements, MECHEM incorporates other chemical constraints that arise from properties of substances, such as free energy or oxidation number. These constraints can be interpreted as an equation $\mathcal{R}_{r \times s} \times \mathcal{P}_{s \times p} = \mathcal{Z}_{r \times p}$, in which the constraint on the entries of the p columns of $\mathcal{Z}$ vary according to the property. For example, in certain oxidation reactions, the oxidation number should never decrease across a reaction, so all the entries under the oxidation-number column of $\mathcal{Z}$ would be non-negative.

The above are not the only search spaces in MECHEM. For example, to perform its task at a modern level of competence, molecular structures must be inferred for the conjectured substances, not only formulas. The space of molecular structures can also be represented as a matrix, similar to the search space in DENDRAL [Lindsay *et al.*, 1980].

MENDEL

MENDEL's task is to devise genetic explanations for observed inheritance patterns (or "reactions") among phenotypes [Fischer and Zytkow, 1992]. Each phenotype is explained by one or more genotypes. MENDEL searches the pair of matrices $\mathcal{R}$ and $\mathcal{S}$ in Figure 6, in analogy to the matrix $\mathcal{R}$ in DALTON, MECHEM,

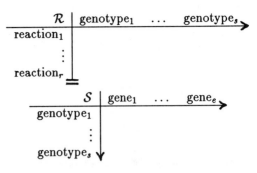

Figure 6: Matrix Structure of MENDEL

and STAHL, and in analogy to $\mathcal{S}$ in DALTON, GELL-MANN, and MECHEM. The domain constraints on $\mathcal{S}$ are identical to GELL-MANN's:

- The matrix entries admit only non-negative integers.

- The sum of entries over each row equals k, which is the number of genes making up a genotype.

- The number $s \stackrel{def}{=} C(e-1+k, k)$ of possible genotypes having k genes (analogous to the constraint in GELL-MANN) satisfies the constraint $f \leq C(e-1+k, k) \leq 3f$, where f is the fixed number of input phenotypes.

MENDEL enlarges the number of columns in $\mathcal{S}$ if it cannot find explanations of genetic reactions within a specific number of genes. Adding one more column to the matrix corresponds to postulating one more gene. MENDEL, like GELL-MANN, carries out a subordinate search by varying the values of the parameter k, which together with the number e of genes leads to postulating $C(e-1+k, k)$ genotypes; these determine the number of rows in the $\mathcal{S}$ matrix and columns in the $\mathcal{R}$ matrix. MENDEL's search for gene combinations into genotypes is similar to GELL-MANN and DALTON, although several genotypes may be needed to explain one phenotype and several genotype reactions may be needed to explain one phenotype reaction.

The relative number of reactions between genotypes which look identical at the phenotype level is acceptable when it is approximately equal to the observed inheritance statistics that govern mating between phenotypes. Rather than using a predefined conservation principle, MENDEL searches for the right conservation/combination principle for genetic reactions, and finds out that one gene per parent is preserved in each offspring.

Since the same genotype can occur on both sides of a genetic reaction, and the occurrences should not cancel out, the entries in the $\mathcal{R}$ matrix need to be pairs (n_r, n_p), where n_r is the number of reactants and n_p is the number of products of a particular genotype.

BR-3/PAULI

PAULI's goal [Valdes, accepted], like its predecessor BR-3 [Kocabas, 1991], is to postulate a small number of

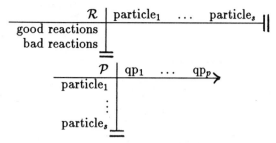

Figure 7: Matrix Structure of BR-3/PAULI

$\mathcal{R}$	lime	quick lime	fixed air	magnesia alba	calcined magnesia
R_1	−	+	+	0	0
R_2	+	−	0	−	+

$$R_1 = \{lime\} \rightarrow \{quick\ lime,\ fixed\ air\}$$
$$R_2 = \{quick\ lime,\ magnesia\ alba\} \rightarrow \{lime,\ calcined\ magnesia\}$$

Figure 8: Reaction Matrix of STAHL

$\mathcal{S}$	quick lime	fixed air	calcined magnesia
lime	+	+	0
quick lime	+	0	0
fixed air	0	+	0
magnesia alba	0	+	+
calcined magnesia	0	0	+

Figure 9: Structure Matrix of STAHL

quantum properties, together with values for the properties for each known elementary particle. New properties must explain how certain reactions in physics do not occur and how others occur. The ("good") reactions that occur must conserve each of the postulated properties, while every ("bad") disallowed reaction must disconserve at least one of the properties.

PAULI's matrix search space is shown in Figure 7. A filled-in $\mathcal{R}$ matrix is input to the program. PAULI fills in the $\mathcal{P}$ matrix, and enlarges its number of columns, i.e., the number of quantum properties that it postulates, when simpler models fail.

The only constraint that applies directly to the $\mathcal{P}$ matrix is that the quantum properties of particle/antiparticle pairs should be of equal magnitude and opposite sign. Further constraints on solutions involve both conservation and disconservation. Letting g and b denote the "good" and "bad" reactions respectively, the following matrix equation must be satisfied:

$$\begin{bmatrix} \mathcal{R}_{g \times s} \\ \mathcal{R}_{b \times s} \end{bmatrix} \times P_{s \times p} = \begin{bmatrix} 0_{g \times p} \\ \mathcal{Z}_{b \times p} \end{bmatrix}$$

The first matrix is input to the program, the sub-matrix $0_{g \times p}$ has only zero entries, and the sub-matrix $\mathcal{Z}_{b \times p}$ enforces the disconservation: each row of $\mathcal{Z}$ must contain a nonzero entry. Like GELL-MANN, BR-3 and PAULI could predict many unseen good and bad reactions by combining particles in various ways and testing whether conservation of all properties holds.

STAHL

Unlike other systems, the STAHL program of [Zytkow and Simon, 1986] discovers qualitative models rather than quantitative ones. Consequently, to describe STAHL's search problem we use qualitative matrix entries rather than numbers.

We use an example from page 128 of [Zytkow and Simon, 1986] for illustration. The input to the program consists of qualitative input/output facts about chemical reactions shown in Figure 8. A negative entry '−' corresponds to a reactant, a positive entry '+' corresponds to a reaction product, while any non-participating substance receives a zero entry. To represent reaction schemes in which the same substance occurs both as a reactant and a product, pairs of signs can be used, e.g., (-, +).

STAHL's task is to discover the elements and the make-up of substances in terms of these elements, i.e., an $\mathcal{S}$ matrix. In the above example, from the first reaction STAHL notices that lime consists of quick lime and fixed air, and then combining the first and the second, that magnesia alba consists of calcined magnesia and fixed air. In effect the $\mathcal{S}$ matrix in Figure 9 is created. If two rows in the $\mathcal{S}$ matrix have the same entries, STAHL concludes that two substances having different names are in fact identical. In such a case, one row in $\mathcal{S}$ (and the column in $\mathcal{R}$) can be deleted to give a simpler model; STAHL is the only system in this paper that can be viewed to shrink matrices. The columns of S can be viewed either as growing and shrinking, or as only shrinking from a maximal possible set of elementary substances. The number of rows in $\mathcal{R}$ grows, since STAHL makes "new" reactions from arithmetic combinations of known ones.

STAHL's $\mathcal{R}$ and $\mathcal{S}$ matrices satisfy a qualitative conservation principle: each element which occurs in a reaction should appear both in its reactants and in its products. This can be expressed identically to DALTON and MECHEM as $\mathcal{R}_{r \times s} \times \mathcal{S}_{s \times e} = 0_{r \times e}$, where matrix multiplication uses qualitative arithmetic following expected rules, for instance $pos \times neg = neg$, $pos + pos = pos$, $pos \times 0 = 0$. The qualitative arithmetic is not associative (e.g., $pos + pos + neg$ could equal pos or 0), but the order of production-rule firing determines how expressions are simplified.

Contradictions can arise when the product $\mathcal{R} \times \mathcal{S}$ has nonzero entries. Such nonzero entries indicate reactions which according to current knowledge (and STAHL's qualitative arithmetic) are unbalanced.

Discussion

The six systems examined in this paper propose discrete underlying models of empirical phenomena across a variety of tasks and sciences. All of the systems find models of either the structure or properties of substances; this is the main task of DALTON, GELL-MANN, MENDEL, BR-3/PAULI, and STAHL. In addition, DALTON, MECHEM, and MENDEL find models of processes (reactions) in terms of hidden objects. DALTON takes a set of qualitative reactions and specifies them quantitatively, while MECHEM finds a simplest set of reactions (a pathway) from scratch.

All of the systems fill in the entries of one or more matrices. All except DALTON enlarge one or more matrix dimensions, and all including DALTON use constraints expressible as matrix equations of the form $AB = C$ or weaker forms of conservation.[1] The concept of simplicity has a strong presence, as reflected especially by growth in the matrices, which corresponds to entertaining more complex models.

Three matrix types are observed to recur. The most frequent is the reaction matrix $\mathcal{R}$, which appears in all of the systems except GELL-MANN. Either the structure matrix $\mathcal{S}$ or the property matrix $\mathcal{P}$ appears in all of the systems; all except DALTON and STAHL postulate either new objects or new properties.

Other discovery systems

DENDRAL [Lindsay et al., 1980] and TETRAD-II [Spirtes et al., 1990] discover models of molecular and causal structure, respectively. These models are in the form of graphs, which as is well known can always be represented as adjacency matrices. However, these two systems use different matrix types and different constraints than the ones discussed here, so we have not included them in the analysis of this paper.

AM [Lenat, 1982], GRAFFITI [Fajtlowicz, 1988], and BACON [Langley et al., 1987] are other notable discovery systems that do not seem to fit the present framework. AM and GRAFFITI find plausible mathematical conjectures in elementary number theory and graph theory. BACON finds descriptive, empirical laws in data. These programs make inductive generalizations and introduce new theoretical terms, but do not build discrete models of hidden structure.

What is gained?

It is always possible to view one thing as another thing. A better understanding of a subject is often claimed as a virtue of a new viewpoint. However, since "understanding" is a slippery notion, it is more convincing if the new viewpoint enables new practical accomplishments or unifies seemingly unrelated phenomena. This section discusses what is gained by the matrix representation of discrete models and the matrix-search viewpoint, and culminates by suggesting ways to integrate separately-developed discovery systems.

There are several gains from the interpretation and notation introduced by this paper. First, they provide

---

[1]The order of matrix multiplication in $AB = C$ has no special significance, since the theorem $(AB)^T = B^T A^T$ allows re-writing the former as $B^T A^T = C^T$.

a unifying framework that demonstrates a broad similarity of input/output representation, constraint representation, and elements of search. These similarities raise the question of whether a more general scheme could incorporate these systems as special cases.

A second benefit from the matrix viewpoint is that several constraints can be expressed and satisfied using explicit algebraic techniques, such as Gaussian elimination or linear programming. MECHEM and PAULI do use matrix manipulation to satisfy some constraints. MECHEM converts pathways to matrices in order to solve for the unknown substances by imposing the conservation law of reaction balance. MECHEM also uses matrix algebra to test whether a pathway can explain observed concentrations data. Finally, MECHEM and PAULI both use the simplex algorithm of linear programming to implement some constraints, and the simplex algorithm uses the matrix representation explicitly in the form of tableaus.

A third benefit is that matrix-based heuristics can guide us to find and address other scientific problems that resemble the current ones. One should look for problems that:

- Progressively enlarge classes of objects, structural elements, processes, or properties. Mention of simplicity or Occam's Razor in this connection is a favorable sign.

- Involve integral numbers of combinations of things.

- Involve linear constraints, e.g., conservation or additivity laws.

Examples of possible matches are Feynman diagrams in particle physics (in which the simplest diagrams are called "leading-edge" diagrams), models of ions, and models of atomic nuclei. Finally, the next section uses the matrix-search viewpoint to demonstrate how an integration of GELL-MANN with BR-3/PAULI could be carried out.

Integrating systems

The concept of search in matrix spaces can be applied to show how the task of GELL-MANN can be integrated smoothly with the task of BR-3/PAULI. GELL-MANN's search fills out the two matrices $\frac{\mathcal{S} \mid \text{quarks}}{\text{particles} \mid}$ and $\frac{\mathcal{P} \mid \text{properties}}{\text{quarks} \mid}$ subject to the constraint

$$\mathcal{S}_{s \times e} \times \mathcal{P}_{e \times p} = \mathcal{P}'_{s \times p}.$$

Given a reaction matrix $\frac{\mathcal{R} \mid \text{particles}}{\text{reactions} \mid}$, BR-3/PAULI's search fills out a property matrix $\frac{\mathcal{P}'' \mid \text{properties}}{\text{particles} \mid}$ subject to the constraint

$$\begin{bmatrix} \mathcal{R}_{g \times s} \\ \mathcal{R}_{b \times s} \end{bmatrix} \times \mathcal{P}''_{s \times p} = \begin{bmatrix} 0_{g \times p} \\ \mathcal{Z}_{b \times p} \end{bmatrix}.$$

A combined system that carries out the tasks of GELL-MANN and BR-3/PAULI simultaneously would fill out the $\mathcal{R}$, $\mathcal{S}$, and $\mathcal{P}$ matrices and would need to satisfy at least the constraint

$$\left[\begin{array}{c} \mathcal{R}_{g \times s} \\ \mathcal{R}_{b \times s} \end{array} \right] \times \mathcal{S}_{s \times e} \times \mathcal{P}_{e \times p} = \left[\begin{array}{c} 0_{g \times p} \\ \mathcal{Z}_{b \times p} \end{array} \right].$$

In the integrated system, *four* distinct matrix dimensions can be enlarged: the two from GELL-MANN, one from BR-3/PAULI, but also a fourth for the reaction dimension, since many new unseen "good" and "bad" reactions can be postulated just as GELL-MANN could postulate unseen particles and their property values. The combined system could accept exactly the $\mathcal{R}$ input to BR-3/PAULI as before, and carry out a substantial theoretical effort by postulating quarks, properties, values, and unseen reactions all within a single system.

Conclusion

We have shown that the search carried out by a number of well-known systems that induce discrete models of hidden structure can be represented by sets of matrices on which constraints are placed. The typical dimensions of the matrices involve reactions (processes), substances (types of objects), and properties of substances. For example, DALTON finds structural models of chemical reactions and substances which can be described by a reaction matrix $\mathcal{R}_{r \times s}$ and a structure matrix $\mathcal{S}_{s \times e}$. $\mathcal{R}_{r \times s}$ describes reactions by the number of molecules of each substance in input and output, and $\mathcal{S}_{s \times e}$ describes the composition of each substance in terms of numbers of atoms of elements. Conservation of atoms is expressed by $\mathcal{R} \times \mathcal{S} = 0$.

The common matrix representation eases comparing these systems, reveals their underlying commonalities and sometimes shows how two systems (e.g., BR-3/PAULI and GELL-MANN) can be integrated into a single one. It also suggests how search algorithms designed for one system could be applied to others.

Hypothesizing new reactions, substances, or properties is accomplished by enlarging a matrix along one or more dimensions. The sizes of the matrices provide an (inverse) measure of a model's simplicity, so that generating small matrices first, then successively enlarging them as required, assures that simpler hypotheses are considered first, and that only as many hidden entities are introduced as are required to account for the data.

Representing model-building as search over a small matrix set does much to reduce the apparent diversity among the various systems, and shows that a few principles are fundamental to the organization and functioning of most of them. Hence, the representation is a significant advance toward a general theory of discrete model-building in scientific discovery.

Acknowledgments. RVP was supported partly by a W.M. Keck Foundation grant for advanced training in computational biology to the University of Pittsburgh, Carnegie Mellon, and the Pittsburgh Supercomputing Center. JMZ contributed to this paper while on sabbatical at Carnegie Mellon.

References

Aris, R. and Mah, R.H.S. 1963. Independence of chemical reactions. *Ind. Eng. Chem. Fundam.* 2:90–94.

Brualdi, Richard A. 1981. *Introductory Combinatorics.* North Holland, New York, NY. (Theorem on page 37).

Fajtlowicz, Siemion 1988. On conjectures of Graffiti. *Discrete Mathematics* 72:113–118.

Fischer, P. and Zytkow, Jan M. 1990. Discovering quarks and hidden structure. *Proc. of 5th International Symposium on Methodologies for Intelligent Systems.*

Fischer, P. and Zytkow, Jan M. 1992. Incremental generation and exploration of hidden structure. *Proc. of the ICML-92 Workshop on Machine Discovery.*

Klahr, D. and Dunbar, K. 1988. Dual space search during scientific reasoning. *Cognitive Science* 12:1–48.

Kocabas, Sakir 1991. Conflict resolution as discovery in particle physics. *Machine Learning* 6(3):277–309.

Langley, P.; Simon, H.A.; Bradshaw, G.L.; and Zytkow, J.M. 1987. *Scientific Discovery: Computational Explorations of the Creative Processes.* MIT Press.

Lea, Glenn and Simon, Herbert A. 1974. Problem solving and rule induction: A unified view. In Gregg, Lee W., editor 1974, *Knowledge and Cognition.*

Lenat, Douglas B. 1982. AM: Discovery in mathematics as heuristic search. In Davis, R. and Lenat, D.B., editors 1982, *Knowledge-based systems in artificial intelligence.*

Lindsay, R.K.; Buchanan, B.G.; Feigenbaum, E.A.; and Lederberg, J. 1980. *Applications of Artificial Intelligence for Organic Chemistry: The Dendral Project.*

Rose, D. and Langley, P. 1986. Chemical discovery as belief revision. *Machine Learning* 1(4):423–451.

Rose, Donald 1989. Using domain knowledge to aid scientific theory revision. In *Proc. of the 6th International Workshop on Machine Learning.*

Spirtes, P.; Glymour, C.; and Scheines, R. 1990. Causality from probability. In Tiles, J.E. et al., editors 1990, *Evolving Knowledge in Natural Science and Artificial Intelligence.* Pitman.

Valdes-Perez, Raul E. Conjecturing hidden entities via simplicity and conservation laws: machine discovery in chemistry. *Artificial Intelligence.* In press.

Valdes-Perez, Raul E. Discovery of conserved properties in particle physics: A comparison of two models. *Machine Learning.* Accepted for publication.

Valdes-Perez, Raul E. 1991. A canonical representation of multistep reactions. *Journal of Chemical Information and Computer Sciences* 31(4):554–556.

Valdes-Perez, Raul E. 1992. Theory-driven discovery of reaction pathways in the MECHEM system. In *Proc. of 10th National Conference on Artificial Intelligence.* 63–69.

Zytkow, J.M. and Simon, Herbert A. 1986. A theory of historical discovery: the construction of componential models. *Machine Learning* 1(1):107–139.

Zytkow, J.M. 1987. Combining many searches in the FAHRENHEIT discovery system. In *Proc. of the 4th International Workshop on Machine Learning.* 281–287.

Plan
Generation

An Average Case Analysis of Planning

Tom Bylander
Laboratory for Artificial Intelligence Research
Department of Computer and Information Science
The Ohio State University
Columbus, Ohio 43210
byland@cis.ohio-state.edu

Abstract

I present an average case analysis of propositional STRIPS planning. The analysis assumes that each possible precondition (likewise postcondition) is equally likely to appear within an operator. Under this assumption, I derive bounds for when it is highly likely that a planning instance can be efficiently solved, either by finding a plan or proving that no plan exists. Roughly, if planning instances have n conditions (ground atoms), g goals, and $O(n \sqrt[g]{\delta})$ operators, then a simple, efficient algorithm can prove that no plan exists for at least $1 - \delta$ of the instances. If instances have $\Omega(n(\ln g)(\ln g/\delta))$ operators, then a simple, efficient algorithm can find a plan for at least $1 - \delta$ of the instances. A similar result holds for plan modification, i.e., solving a planning instance that is close to another planning instance with a known plan. Thus it would appear that propositional STRIPS planning, a PSPACE-complete problem, is hard only for narrow parameter ranges, which complements previous average-case analyses for NP-complete problems. Future work is needed to narrow the gap between the bounds and to consider more realistic distributional assumptions and more sophisticated algorithms.

Introduction

Lately, there has been a series of worst-case complexity results for planning, showing that the general problem is hard and that several restrictions are needed to guarantee polynomial time (Bäckström and Klein, 1991; Bylander, 1991; Bylander, 1993; Chapman, 1987; Erol et al., 1992a; Erol et al., 1992b). A criticism of such worst-case analyses is that they do not apply to the average case (Cohen, 1991; Minsky, 1991).

Recent work in AI has shown that this criticism has some merit. Several experimental results have shown that specific NP-complete problems are hard only for narrow ranges (Cheeseman et al., 1991; Minton et al., 1992; Mitchell et al., 1992) and even the problems within these ranges can be efficiently solved (Selman et

al., 1992). Theoretical results also support this conclusion (Minton et al., 1992; Williams and Hogg, 1992). However, it must be noted that all this work makes a strong assumption about the distribution of instances, namely that the probability that a given constraint appears in a problem instance is independent of what other constraints appear in the instance.

This paper presents an average-case analysis of propositional STRIPS planning, a PSPACE-complete problem (Bylander, 1991). Like the work on NP-complete problems, I make a strong distributional assumption, namely that each possible precondition (likewise postcondition) is equally likely to appear within an operator, and that the probability of a given operator is independent of other operators. Under this assumption, I derive bounds for when it is highly likely that a planning instance can be efficiently solved, either by finding a plan or proving that no plan exists.

Given that planning instances have n conditions (ground atoms) and g goals, and that operators have r preconditions on average and s postconditions on average, I derive the following results. If the number of operators is at most $((2n - s)/s) \sqrt[g]{\delta}$, then a simple, efficient algorithm can prove that no plan exists for at least $1 - \delta$ of the instances. If the number of operators is at least $e^r e^{sg/n}(2n/s)(2 + \ln g)(\ln g/\delta)$, then a simple, efficient algorithm can find a plan for at least $1 - \delta$ of the instances. If r and s are small, e.g., the number of pre- and postconditions remains fixed as n increases, then these bounds are roughly $O(n \sqrt[g]{\delta})$ and $\Omega(n(\ln g)(\ln g/\delta))$, respectively.

A similar result holds for plan modification. If the initial state or goals are different by one condition from that of another planning instance with a known plan, and if there are at least $e^{r+s}(2n/s)(\ln 1/\delta)$ operators, then it is likely $(1 - \delta)$ that adding a single operator converts the old plan into a solution for the new instance.

Thus it would appear that propositional STRIPS planning is hard only for narrow parameter ranges, which complements previous average-case analyses for NP-complete problems. Future work is needed to narrow the gap between the bounds and to consider more realistic distributional assumptions and more sophisticated algorithms.

The rest of the paper is organized as follows. First, definitions and key inequalities are presented. Then, the average-case results are derived.

Preliminaries

This section defines propositional STRIPS planning, describes the distribution of instances to be analyzed, and presents key inequalities.

Propositional STRIPS Planning

An instance of *propositional STRIPS planning* is specified by a tuple $\langle \mathcal{P}, \mathcal{O}, \mathcal{I}, \mathcal{G} \rangle$, where:

$\mathcal{P}$ is a finite set of ground atomic formula, called the *conditions*;

$\mathcal{O}$ is a finite set of *operators*; the preconditions and postconditions of each operator are satisfiable sets of positive and negative conditions;

$\mathcal{I} \subseteq \mathcal{P}$ is the *initial state*; and

$\mathcal{G}$, the *goals*, is a satisfiable set of positive and negative conditions.

Each subset $S \subseteq \mathcal{P}$ is a *state*; $p \in \mathcal{P}$ is true in state S if $p \in S$, otherwise p is false in state S. If the preconditions of an operator are satisfied by state S, then the operator can be applied, and the resulting state is determined by deleting the negative postconditions from S and adding the positive postconditions (cf. (Fikes and Nilsson, 1971)). A solution plan is a sequence of operators that transforms the initial state into a goal state, i.e., a state that satisfies the goals.

Distributional Assumptions

Let n be the number of conditions. Let o be the number of operators. Let r and s respectively be the expected number of pre- and postconditions within an operator. Let g be the number of goals.

For given n, o, r, s, and g, I assume that *random planning instances* are generated as follows:

For each condition $p \in \mathcal{P}$, p is a precondition of an operator with probability r/n. If p is a precondition, it is equally likely to be positive or negative. For postconditions, s/n is the relevant probability.

For each condition $p \in \mathcal{P}$, $p \in \mathcal{I}$ (the initial state) with probability .5.

For the goals, g conditions are selected at random and are set so that no goal is satisfied in the initial state. This latter restriction is made for ease of exposition.

It must be admitted that these assumptions do not approximate planning domains very well. For example, there are only b *clear* conditions for a blocks-world instance of b blocks compared to $O(b^2)$ *on* conditions. However, every blocks-world operator refers to one or more *clear* conditions, i.e., a given *clear* condition appears more often within the set of ground operators than a given *on* condition. Also, there are correlations between the conditions, e.g., $clear(A)$ is more likely to appear with $on(A, B)$ than with $on(C, D)$. Similar violations can be found for any of the standard toy domains.

Ultimately, the usefulness of these assumptions will depend on how well the threshold bounds of the analysis classify easiness and hardness of real planning domains. Until then, I shall note that the assumptions are essentially similar to previous work on NP-complete problems as cited in the introduction, but for a different task (planning) in a harder complexity class (PSPACE-complete). Also, the assumptions permit a clean derivation of interesting bounds, which suggest that hard planning instances are localized to a narrow range of the number of operators (the o parameter). Finally, the gap between the assumptions and reality will hopefully spur further work to close the gap.

Algorithm Characteristics

Each algorithm in this paper is incomplete but sound, i.e., each algorithm returns correct answers when it returns yes or no, but might answer "don't know." Specifically, "success" is returned if the algorithm finds a solution plan, "failure" is returned if the algorithm determines that no plan exists, and "don't know" is returned otherwise.

The performance of a given algorithm is characterized by an accuracy parameter δ, $0 < \delta < 1$. Each result below shows that if the number of operators o is greater than (or less than) a formula on n, r, s, g, and δ, then the accuracy of the algorithm on the corresponding distribution (see Distributional Assumptions section) will be at least $1 - \delta$.

Inequalities

I freely use the following inequalities. For nonnegative x and y:

$$e^{-x/(1-x)} \leq 1 - x \quad \text{for } 0 \leq x < 1$$
$$1 - x \leq e^{-x}$$
$$x/(1+x) \leq 1 - e^{-x}$$
$$1 - e^{-x} \leq x$$
$$xy/(1+xy) \leq 1 - (1-x)^y \quad \text{for } 0 \leq x < 1$$
$$1 - (1-x)^y \leq xy/(1-x) \quad \text{for } 0 \leq x < 1$$

The first two inequalities are easily derivable from (Cormen *et al.*, 1990). The last four inequalities are derivable from the first two.

When Plan Nonexistence is Efficient

If there are few operators, it becomes unlikely that the postconditions of the operators cover all the goals, i.e., that some goal is not a postcondition of any operator. This leads to the following simple algorithm:

POSTS-COVER-GOALS
    for each goal
        if the goal is not a postcondition of any
            operator
        then return failure
    return don't know

The following theorem characterizes when POSTS-COVER-GOALS works.

Theorem 1 *For random planning instances, if $o \leq ((2n - s)/s) \sqrt[g]{\delta}$, then POSTS-COVER-GOALS will determine that no plan exists for at least $1 - \delta$ of the instances.*

Proof: The probability that there exists a goal that is not a postcondition of any operator can be developed as follows. Consider a particular goal to be achieved:

$s/2n$ probability that an operator achieves the goal[1]

$1 - s/2n$ probability that an operator doesn't achieve the goal

$(1 - s/2n)^o$ probability that no operator achieves the goal

$1 - (1 - s/2n)^o$ probability that some operator achieves the goal

$(1 - (1 - s/2n)^o)^g$ probability that *every* goal is achieved by some operator

It can be shown that:

$$(1 - (1 - s/2n)^o)^g \leq (so/(2n - s))^g$$

which is less than δ if:

$$o \leq ((2n - s)/s) \sqrt[g]{\delta}$$

Thus, if the above inequality is satisfied, then the probability that some goal is not a postcondition of any operator is at least $1 - \delta$. □

For fixed δ and increasing n and g, the above bound approaches $(2n - s)/s$. If s is also fixed, the bound is $O(n)$.

Naturally, more complex properties that are efficient to evaluate and imply plan non-existence could be used, e.g., the above algorithm does not look at preconditions. Any algorithm that also tests whether there are postconditions that cover the goals will have performance as good and possibly better than POSTS-COVER-GOALS.

When Finding Plans is Efficient

With a sufficient number of operators, then it becomes likely that some operator will make progress towards the goal. In this section, I consider three algorithms. One is a simple forward search from the initial state to a goal state, at each state searching for an operator

---

[1] For arithmetic expressions within this paper, multiplication has highest precedence, followed by division, logarithm, subtraction, and addition. E.g., $1 - s/2n$ is equivalent to $1 - (s/(2n))$.

that decreases the number of goals to be achieved. The second is a backward search from the goals to a smaller set of goals to the initial state. The third is a very simple algorithm for when the initial state and goals differ by just one condition.

Forward Search

Consider the following algorithm:

FORWARD-SEARCH(S,O)
    if $\mathcal{G}$ is satisfied by S, **then return** success
    repeat
        if O is empty **then return** don't know
        randomly remove an operator from O
    until applying an operator satisfies more goals
    let S' be the result of applying the operator to S
    return FORWARD-SEARCH(S',O)

If FORWARD-SEARCH($\mathcal{I}$,$\mathcal{O}$) is called, then each operator in $\mathcal{O}$ is considered one at a time. If applying an operator increases the number of satisfied goals, the current state S is updated. FORWARD-SEARCH succeeds if it reaches a goal state and is noncommittal if it runs out of operators.

FORWARD-SEARCH only considers each operator at most once. I do not propose that this "feature" should be incorporated into practical planning algorithms, but it does simplify the analysis. Specifically, there is no need to consider the probability that an operator has some property given that it is known that the operator has some other property. Despite this handicap, FORWARD-SEARCH is surprisingly robust under certain conditions. First, I demonstrate a lemma for the number of operators that need to be considered to increase the number of satisfied goals.

Lemma 2 *Consider random planning instances except that d of the g goals are not satisfied. If at least*

$$e^r e^{s(g-d)/n}(1 + 2n/sd)(\ln 1/\delta)$$

operators are considered, then, for at least $1 - \delta$ of the instances, one of those operators will increase the number of satisfied goals.

Proof: The expression for the probability can be developed as follows:

$(1 - r/2n)^n$ probability that a state satisfies the preconditions of an operator, i.e., each of n conditions is not a precondition with probability $1 - r/n$; alternatively, a condition is a matching precondition with probability $r/2n$

$(1 - s/2n)^{g-d}$ probability that the postconditions of an operator are consistent with the $g - d$ goals already achieved

$(1 - s/2n)^d$ probability that the postconditions do not achieve any of the d remaining goals, i.e., for each goal, it is not a postcondition with probability $1 - s/n$; alternatively, it is a precondition of the wrong type with probability $s/2n$

$(1 - (1 - s/2n)^d)$ probability that the postconditions achieve at least one of the d remaining goals

Thus, the probability p that a particular operator can be applied, will not clobber any satisfied goals, and will achieve at least one more goal is:

$$p = (1 - r/2n)^n (1 - s/2n)^{g-d} (1 - (1 - s/2n)^d)$$

$1 - p$ is the probability that the operator is unsatisfactory, and $(1 - p)^o$ is the probability that o operators are unsatisfactory.

If $(1 - p)^o \le \delta$, then there will be some satisfactory operator with probability at least $1 - \delta$. This inequality is satisfied if $o \ge (1/p)(\ln 1/\delta)$ because in such a case:

$$(1 - p)^o \le e^{-po} \le e^{-\ln 1/\delta} = \delta$$

All that remains then is to determine an upper bound on $1/p$, i.e., a lower bound on p. For each term of p:

$$(1 - r/2n)^n \ge e^{-rn/(2n-r)} \ge e^{-r}$$
$$(1 - s/2n)^{g-d} \ge e^{-s(g-d)/(2n-s)} \ge e^{-s(g-d)/n}$$
$$(1 - (1 - s/2n)^d) \ge sd/(2n + sd)$$

Inverting these terms leads to the bound of the lemma.
$\square$

To describe FORWARD-SEARCH, the expression in the lemma must be summed for each d from 1 to g, which leads to the following theorem:

Theorem 3 *For random planning instances, if*

$$o \ge e^r e^{sg/n} (2n/s)(3/2 + \ln g)(\ln g/\delta)$$

then FORWARD-SEARCH *will find a plan for at least* $1 - \delta$ *of the instances after considering the above number of operators.*

Proof: For g goals, the number of satisfied goals will be increased at most g times. If each increase occurs with probability at least $1 - \delta/g$, then g increases (the most possible) will occur with probability at least $1 - \delta$.

Thus, Lemma 2 can be applied using δ/g instead of δ. Summing over the g goals leads to:

$$\sum_{d=1}^{g} e^r e^{s(g-d)/n}(1 + 2n/sd)(\ln g/\delta)$$
$$= e^r e^{sg/n}(\ln g/\delta)$$
$$\left(\left(\sum_{d=1}^{g} e^{-sd/n} \right) + \left(\sum_{d=1}^{g} e^{-sd/n}(2n/sd) \right) \right)$$
$$\le e^r e^{sg/n}(\ln g/\delta)$$
$$\left(\left(\sum_{d=1}^{g} e^{-sd/n} \right) + \left((2n/s) \sum_{d=1}^{g} 1/d \right) \right)$$

For the two sums:

$$\sum_{d=1}^{g} e^{-sd/n} \le \int_0^g e^{-sx/n} dx \le n/s$$
$$\sum_{d=1}^{g} 1/d \le 1 + \int_1^g (1/x) dx = 1 + \ln g$$

which leads to:

$$\left(\sum_{d=1}^{g} e^{-sd/n} \right) + \left((2n/s) \sum_{d=1}^{g} 1/d \right)$$
$$\le n/s + (2n/s)(1 + \ln g)$$
$$= (2n/s)(3/2 + \ln g)$$

Combining all terms results in the bound of the theorem.
$\square$

The bound is exponential in the expected numbers of pre- and postconditions. Naturally, as operators have more preconditions, it becomes exponentially less likely that they can be applied. Similarly, as operators have more postconditions, it becomes exponentially less likely that the postconditions are consistent with the goals already achieved. Note though that if $g \le n/s$, then $e^{sg/n} \le e$, so the expected number of postconditions s is not as important a factor if the number of goals are small.

Backward Search

Consider the following algorithm for searching backward from a set of a goals:

```
BACKWARD-SEARCH(G,O)
    if G = ∅ then return success
    while O ≠ ∅
        randomly remove an operator from O
        let R and S be its pre- and postconditions
        if G is consistent with S, and
            |(G − S) + R| < |G|
        then return
            BACKWARD-SEARCH((G − S) + R, O)
    return don't know
```

Like FORWARD-SEARCH, BACKWARD-SEARCH makes a single pass through the operators, but in this case, BACKWARD-SEARCH starts with the goals and looks for an operator whose preconditions results in a smaller number of goals. In fact, if BACKWARD-SEARCH succeeds, then it will have discovered a sequence of operators that achieves a goal state from any initial state, although note that the first operator in this sequence (the last operator selected by BACKWARD-SEARCH) must not have any preconditions; otherwise $|(G - S) + R|$ would be non-zero. Having such an operator is probably unrealistic; nevertheless, the results below suggest that reducing a set of goals into a much smaller set of goals is often possible, which, of course, can then be followed by forward search.

I first introduce a lemma for the number of operators needed to find one operator that reduces the number of goals. Space limitations prevent displaying the complete proof.

Lemma 4 *For random planning instances with $r \leq n/2$ and $s \leq n/2$, if at least the following number of operators are considered:*

$$e^{2r}e^{sg/n}((3n+sg)/sg)(\ln 1/\delta)$$

then, for $1 - \delta$ of the instances, some operator will reduce the number of goals.

Proof Sketch: The following expression gives the probability p that, for a random operator, the preconditions are a subset of the goals, the postconditions are consistent with the goals, and there is one goal equal to a postcondition, but not in the preconditions.

$$p = (1 - r/n)^{n-g}((1-r/2n)^g(1-s/2n)^g - (1-r/2n-s/n+(3rs/4n^2))^g)$$

Bounding this expression leads to the bound of the lemma. □

Similar to Theorem 3, this expression needs to be summed for g goals down to 1 goal. This is done to prove the next theorem (proof omitted).

Theorem 5 *For random planning instances with $r \leq n/2$ and $s \leq n/2$, if*

$$o \geq e^{2r}(3n/s)(4e^{sg/n} + 3(\ln g) + 3)(\ln g/\delta)$$

then BACKWARD-SEARCH *will find a plan for at least $1 - \delta$ of the instances after considering the above number of operators.*

Comparing the two bounds for FORWARD-SEARCH and BACKWARD-SEARCH, the bound for BACKWARD-SEARCH is worse in that it has a larger constant and has a e^{2r} term as opposed to a e^r term for the FORWARD-SEARCH bound. Because BACKWARD-SEARCH does not use the initial state, some increase would be expected. However, the BACKWARD-SEARCH bound is better in that one component is additive, i.e., $O(e^{sg/n} + \ln g)$; whereas the corresponding subexpression for the FORWARD-SEARCH bound is $O(e^{sg/n} \ln g)$. The reason is that $e^{sg/n}$ (see Lemma 4) is maximum when g is at its maximum, while the maximum value for $(3n + sg)/sg$ is when g is at its minimum.

Of course, it should be mentioned that rather crude inequalities are used in both cases to derive simplified expressions. A careful comparison of the probabilities derived within the Lemmas would perhaps be a more direct route for comparing the algorithms, but I have not done this yet.

Plan Modification

So far I have considered the problem of generating a plan from scratch. In many cases, however, the current planning instance is close to a previously solved instance, e.g., (Hammond, 1990; Kambhampati and Hendler, 1992).

Consider a simplified version of plan modification, specifically, when the initial state or set of goals of the current planning instance differs by one condition from a previously solved instance. In this case, the new instance can be solved by showing how the new initial state can reach the old initial state, or how the old goal state can reach a new goal state. Within the framework of random planning instances then, I shall analyze the problem of reaching one state from another when the two states differ by one condition, i.e., there are n goals, and all but one goal is true of the initial state.

The worst-case complexity of this problem, like the problem of planning from scratch, is PSPACE-complete (Nebel and Koehler, 1993). However, the following theorem shows that it is usually easy to solve this problem if there are sufficient operators.

Theorem 6 *For random planning instances in which there are n goals, where $n - 1$ goals are true of the initial state, if:*

$$o \geq e^r e^s (2n/s)(\ln 1/\delta)$$

then, for at least $1 - \delta$ of the instances, some operator solves the instance in one step.

Proof: First, I develop the probability p that a random operator solves a random instance. The probability that the preconditions are consistent with the initial state is $(1 - \frac{r}{2n})^n$. The probability that the postconditions are consistent with the $n - 1$ goals already achieved is $(1 - s/(2n))^{n-1}$. In addition, the probability that the goal to be achieved is a postcondition is $s/(2n)$.[2] Thus:

$$p = (1 - r/2n)^n (1 - s/2n)^{n-1} s/2n$$

Lower bounds for p are:

$$p \geq e^{-rn/(2n-r)}e^{-sn/(2n-s)}s/2n \geq e^{-r}e^{-s}s/2n$$

The probability that none of o operators solves the instance is $(1 - p)^o$. If o satisfies the inequality stated in the theorem, then:

$$(1-p)^o \leq e^{-po} \leq e^{-\ln 1/\delta} = \delta$$

which proves the theorem. □

Thus, for fixed r, s, and δ, a linear number of operators suffice to solve planning instances that differ by one condition from previously solved instances. So, for at least the distribution of planning instances considered here, plan modification is easier than planning from scratch by roughly $O(\ln^2 g)$.

---

[2]This does not scale up to the case of attaining g goals by a single operator. The probability that the postconditions of a random operator contain the g goals is $(s/2n)^g$, i.e., exponentially small in the number of goals.

Remarks

I have shown that determining plan existence for propositional STRIPS planning is usually easy if the number of operators satisfy certain bounds, and if each possible precondition and postcondition is equally likely to appear within an operator, independently of other pre- and postconditions and other operators. Assuming that the expected numbers of pre- and postconditions are fixed, then it is usually easy to show that instances with n conditions and $O(n)$ operators are unsolvable, and it is usually easy to find plans for instances with n conditions, g goals, and $\Omega(n \ln^2 g)$ operators. In addition, plan modification instances are usually easy to solve if there are $\Omega(n)$ operators. The constants for the latter two results are exponential in the expected numbers of pre- and postconditions.

This work complements and extends previous average-case analyses for NP-complete problems. It complements previous work because it suggests that random planning instances are hard only for a narrow range of a particular parameter, in this case, the number of operators. It extends previous work because the worst-case complexity of propositional STRIPS planning is PSPACE-complete, thus, suggesting that PSPACE-complete problems exhibit similar threshold phenomena.

This work also provides theoretical support for reactive behavior. A main tenet of reactive behavior is that sound and complete planning, besides being too inefficient, is often unnecessary, i.e., states can be mapped to appropriate operators without much lookahead. The analysis of the FORWARD-SEARCH algorithm, which only does a limited one-step lookahead, shows that this tenet is true for a large subset of the planning problem.

Further work is needed to narrow the gap between the bounds derived by this paper and to analyze more realistic distributions. In particular, the assumption that pre- and postconditions are independently selected is clearly wrong. Nevertheless, it would be interesting to empirically test how well the bounds of this paper classify the hardness of planning problems.

References

Allen, J.; Hendler, J.; and Tate, A., editors 1990. *Readings in Planning*. Morgan Kaufmann, San Mateo, California.

Bäckström, C. and Klein, I. 1991. Parallel non-binary planning in polynomial time. In *Proc. Twelfth Int. Joint Conf. on Artificial Intelligence*, Sydney. 268–273.

Bylander, T. 1991. Complexity results for planning. In *Proc. Twelfth Int. Joint Conf. on Artificial Intelligence*, Sydney. 274–279.

Bylander, T. 1993. The computational complexity of propositional STRIPS planning. *Artificial Intelligence*. To appear.

Chapman, D. 1987. Planning for conjunctive goals. *Artificial Intelligence* 32(3):333–377. Also appears in (Allen *et al.*, 1990).

Cheeseman, P.; Kanefsky, B.; and Taylor, W. M. 1991. Where the really hard problems are. In *Proc. Twelfth Int. Joint Conf. on Artificial Intelligence*, Sydney. 331–337.

Cohen, P. R. 1991. A survey of the eighth national conference on artificial intelligence: Pulling together or pulling apart? *AI Magazine* 12(1):17–41.

Cormen, T. H.; Leiserson, C. E.; and Rivest, R. L. 1990. *Introduction to Algorithms*. MIT Press, Cambridge, Massachusetts.

Erol, K.; Nau, D. S.; and Subrahmanian, V. S. 1992a. On the complexity of domain-independent planning. In *Proc. Tenth National Conf. on Artificial Intelligence*, San Jose, California. 381–386.

Erol, K.; Nau, D. S.; and Subrahmanian, V. S. 1992b. When is planning decidable? In *Proc. First Int. Conf. on AI Planning Systems*, College Park, Maryland. 222–227.

Fikes, R. E. and Nilsson, N. J. 1971. STRIPS: A new approach to the application of theorem proving to problem solving. *Artificial Intelligence* 2(3/4):189–208. Also appears in (Allen *et al.*, 1990).

Hammond, K. J. 1990. Explaining and repairing plans that fail. *Artificial Intelligence* 45(1-2):173–228.

Kambhampati, S. and Hendler, J. A. 1992. A validation-structure-based theory of plan modification and reuse. *Artificial Intelligence* 55(2-3):193–258.

Minsky, M. 1991. Logical versus analogical or symbolic versus connectionist or neat versus scruffy. *AI Magazine* 12(2):34–51.

Minton, S.; Johnston, M. D.; Philips, A. B.; and Laird, P. 1992. Minimizing conflicts: A heuristic repair method for constraint satisfaction and scheduling problems. *Artificial Intelligence* 58:161–205.

Mitchell, D.; Selman, B.; and Levesque, H. 1992. Hard and easy distributions of sat problems. In *Proc. Tenth National Conf. on Artificial Intelligence*, San Jose, California. 459–465.

Nebel, B. and Koehler, J. 1993. Plan modification versus plan generation: A complexity-theoretic perspective. In *Proc. Thirteenth Joint Int. Conf. on Artificial Intelligence*, Chambery, France. To appear.

Selman, B.; Levesque, H.; and Mitchell, D. 1992. A new method for solving hard satisfiability problems. In *Proc. Tenth National Conf. on Artificial Intelligence*, San Jose, California. 440–446.

Williams, C. P. and Hogg, T. 1992. Using deep structure to locate hard problems. In *Proc. Tenth National Conf. on Artificial Intelligence*, San Jose, California. 472–477.

Granularity in Multi-Method Planning[*]

Soowon Lee and Paul S. Rosenbloom
Information Sciences Institute and Computer Science Department
University of Southern California
4676 Admiralty Way
Marina del Rey, CA 90292
{swlee,rosenbloom}@isi.edu

Abstract

Multi-method planning is an approach to using a set of different planning methods to simultaneously achieve planner completeness, planning time efficiency, and plan length reduction. Although it has been shown that coordinating a set of methods in a coarse-grained, problem-by-problem manner has the potential for approaching this ideal, such an approach can waste a significant amount of time in trying methods that ultimately prove inadequate. This paper investigates an approach to reducing this wasted effort by refining the granularity at which methods are switched. The experimental results show that the fine-grained approach can improve the planning time significantly compared with coarse-grained and single-method approaches.

Introduction

The ability to find a low execution-cost plan efficiently over a wide domain of applicability is the core of domain-independent planning systems. The key issue here is how to construct a single planning method, or how to coordinate a set of different planning methods, that has sufficient scope and efficiency. Our approach to this issue begins with the observation that no single method will satisfy both sufficiency and efficiency, with the implication therefore that a coordinated set of planning methods will be needed.

We have constructed a system that can utilize six different planning methods, based on the notion of *bias* in planning. A planning bias is any constraint over the space of plans considered that determines which portion of the entire plan space can be the output of the planning.[1] The six planning methods used vary along two independent bias dimensions: goal-protection and

goal-flexibility. The goal-protection dimension determines whether or not a protection bias is used, that eliminates plans in which an operator undoes an initial goal conjunct that is either true a priori or established by an earlier operator in the sequence. The goal-flexibility dimension determines the degree of flexibility the planner has in using new subgoals. Two biases, directness and linearity, are used along this dimension. Directness eliminates plans in which operators are used to achieve preconditions of other operators, rather than just top-level goal conjuncts. Linearity eliminates plans in which operators for different goal conjuncts are interleaved. The 3×2 methods arise from the cross-product of these two dimensions: (directness, linearity, or nonlinearity) $\times$ (protection, or no-protection).[2]

These single-method planners are implemented in the context of the Soar architecture (Laird, Newell, & Rosenbloom, 1987). Plans in Soar are represented as sets of control rules that jointly specify which operators should be executed at each point in time (Rosenbloom, Lee, & Unruh, 1990). Planning time for these methods is measured in terms of *decisions*, the basic behavioral cycle in Soar. This measure is not quite identical to the more traditional measure of number of planning operators executed, but should still correlate with it relatively closely.

The six implemented methods have previously been compared empirically in terms of planner completeness, planning time, and plan length over a test set of 100 randomly generated 3- and 4-conjunct problems in the blocks-world domain. The predominant result obtained so far from the experiments with these methods is that planning time and plan length are both inversely correlated with the applicability of the plan-

---

[*]This work was sponsored by the Defense Advanced Research Projects Agency (DOD) and the Office of Naval Research under contract number N00014-89-K-0155.

[1]The specification here assumes that the plan space contains only totally-ordered sequences of operators, but it

does not rule out a search strategy that incrementally specifies an element of the plan space by refining a partially-ordered plan structure.

[2]The term "nonlinearity" in this context implies that it is allowable to interleave operators in service of different goal conjuncts. It does not necessarily mean that either partial-order or least-commitment planning are being used.

ning method; that is, the more restricted the method, the less time it takes to solve the problems that it can solve, and the shorter are the plans generated. The most restricted method (the method with directness and protection) could solve 68 of them, in an average of 16.3 decisions each, producing plans containing an average of 1.8 operators (Lee & Rosenbloom, 1992). The least restricted method (nonlinear planning without goal protection) could solve all 100 problems; however, planning time and plan length averaged over the same 68 problems solvable by the most restricted method were considerably worse — an average of 39.0 decisions to produce plans containing on average 3.3 operators.

This trade-off between completeness and efficiency implies that the planning system would be best served if it could always opt for the most restricted method adequate for its current situation. In a first step towards this ideal, we have begun exploring multi-method planners that start by trying highly restricted methods, and then successively relax the restrictions until a method is found that is sufficient for the problem. The intuition behind this is based on iterative deepening (Korf, 1985) — if the proportion of problems solvable at a particular level of restriction is large enough, and the ratio of costs for successive levels is large enough, there should be a net gain. Over the set of 100 blocks-world problems, this has yielded broadly applicable multi-method planners (actually, complete for the blocks-world) that on average generate shorter plans than are produced by corresponding (complete) single-method planners, with marginally lower planning times (from 39.9 to 52.5 decisions for single-method planners versus from 33.4 to 42.2 decisions for multi-method planners).

However these results do not necessarily mean that, for all situations, there exists a multi-method planner which outperforms the most efficient single-method planner. In fact, the performance of these planners depends on the biases used in the multi-method planners and the problem set used in the experiments. For example, if the problems are so complex that most of the problems are solvable only by the least restricted method, the performance loss by trying inappropriate earlier methods in multi-method planners might be relatively considerable. On the other hand, if the problems are so trivial that it takes only a few decisions for the least restricted method to solve the problems, the slight performance gain by using more restricted methods in multi-method planners might be overridden by the complexity of the meta-level processing required to coordinate the sequence of primitive planners.

These results suggest that multi-method planning is a promising approach, but that further work is necessary to establish whether robust gains are possible over a wide range of domains. The work reported here is one step in this direction, in which we investigate reducing the wasted effort in multi-method planners by refining the granularity at which the individual planning methods can be switched. This approach has been implemented, and initial experiments in two domains show significant gains in planning time with respect to both single-method and the earlier, coarser-grained, multi-method planners.

Fine-grained Multi-method Planners

The approach to multi-method planning described so far starts with a restricted method and switches to a less restricted method whenever the current method fails. This switch is always made on a problem-by-problem basis. However, this is not the only granularity at which methods could be switched. The family of multi-method planning systems can be viewed on a granularity spectrum. While in coarse-grained multi-method planners, methods are switched for a whole problem when no solution can be found for the problem within the current method, in fine-grained multi-method planners, methods can be switched at any point during a problem at which a new set of subgoals is formulated, and the switch only occurs for that set of subgoals (and not for the entire problem). At this finer level of granularity it is conceivable that the planner could use a highly-restricted and efficient method over much of a problem, but fall back on a nonlinear method without protection for those critical subregions where there are tricky interactions.

With this flexibility of method switching, fine-grained multi-method planning can potentially outperform both coarse-grained multi-method planning and single-method planning. Compared with coarse-grained multi-method planning, it can save the effort of backtracking when the current method can not find a solution or the current partial plan violates the biases used in the current method. Moreover, it can save the extra effort of using a less restricted method on later parts of the problem, just because one early part requires it. As compared with single-method planning, a fine-grained multi-method planner can utilize biases which would cause incompleteness in a single-method planner — such as directness or protection in the blocks-world domain — while still remaining complete. The result is that a fine-grained multi-method planner can potentially be more efficient than a single-method planner that has the same coverage of solvable problems.

One way to construct an efficient multi-method planner is to order the single method planners according to increasing coverage and decreasing efficiency, an approach called *monotonic multi-method planning*. In this paper, we focus on a special type of monotonic multi-method planner, called a *strongly monotonic multi-method planner*, which is based on the de-

Planner	Decisions			Plan length		
	A_1	A_2	A_5	A_1	A_2	A_5
M_1 (directness, protection)	12.50	-	-	1.56	-	-
M_2 (linearity, protection)	13.00	18.90	-	1.56	2.32	-
M_3 (protection)	13.21	26.91	-	1.62	2.49	-
M_4 (directness)	14.48	-	-	1.71	-	-
M_5 (linearity)	14.81	24.47	24.84	2.10	3.22	3.34
M_6	16.23	40.85	40.96	2.02	3.17	3.37

Table 1: The performance of the six single-method planners for the three problem sets defined by the scopes of the planners.

liberate selection and relaxation of effective biases. In the next section, we provide a formal definition of a monotonic multi-method planner, and define a criterion for selecting effective biases from experiments with single-method planners.

Selecting Effective Biases

Let $M_{k_i}(k_i \in \{1, ..., 6\})$ be a single-method planner, as defined in Section 1. A fine-grained multi-method planner that consists of a sequence of n different single-method planners is denoted as $M_{k_1 \to k_2 \to ... \to k_n}$, and the corresponding coarse-grained multi-method planner is denoted as $M_{k_1} \to M_{k_2} \to ... \to M_{k_n}$. Let A be a sample set of problems, and let $A_{k_i} \subseteq A$ be the subset of A which are solvable in principle by M_{k_i}. The functions $s(M_{k_i}, A_s)$ and $l(M_{k_i}, A_s)$ represent respectively the average cost that M_{k_i} requires to succeed and the average length of plans generated by M_{k_i}, for the problems in $A_s \subseteq A_{k_i}$. Let M_{k_0} be a null planner which cannot solve any problems; that is, $A_{k_0} = \phi$.

A multi-method planner which consists of M_{k_1}, M_{k_2}, ..., M_{k_n} is called *monotonic* if the following three conditions hold for each pair of $M_{k_{i-1}}$ and M_{k_i}, for $2 \le i \le n$: (1) $A_{k_{i-1}} \subseteq A_{k_i}$, (2) $s(M_{k_{i-1}}, A_{k_{j-1}}) \le s(M_{k_i}, A_{k_{j-1}})$, for $j \le i$, and (3) $l(M_{k_{i-1}}, A_{k_{j-1}}) \le l(M_{k_i}, A_{k_{j-1}})$, for $j \le i$.[3] The straightforward way to build monotonic multi-method planners is to run each of the individual methods on a set of training problems, and then from the resulting data to generate all method sequences for which monotonicity holds. The approach we have taken here is to generate only a subset of this full set; in particular, we have focused only on multi-method planners in which later methods embody subsets of the biases incorporated into earlier methods, and in which the biases themselves are all *positive*.

Let B_{k_i} be the set of biases used in M_{k_i}. A bias b is called positive in a problem set A and a method set $\{M_{k_i}\}$, if for each pair of M_{k_x} and M_{k_y} in $\{M_{k_i}\}$ such that $B_{k_x} = B_{k_y} + \{b\}$, $s(M_{k_x}, A_{k_j}) \le s(M_{k_y}, A_{k_j})$ and $l(M_{k_x}, A_{k_j}) \le l(M_{k_y}, A_{k_j})$, for every $j \le x$. A multi-method planner which consists of M_{k_1}, M_{k_2}, ..., M_{k_n} is called *strongly monotonic* if $B_{k_{i-1}} \supset B_{k_i}$, for $2 \le i \le n$, and $B_{k_{i-1}} - B_{k_i}$ consists of positive biases only, for $2 \le i \le n$. From this definition, if a multi-method planner is strongly monotonic, it is monotonic, while the reverse is not necessarily true.

To generate a strongly monotonic multi-method planner, it is necessary to determine which biases are positive in the domain. Table 1 illustrates the average number of decisions, $s(M_{k_i}, A_{k_j})$, and average plan lengths, $l(M_{k_i}, A_{k_j})$ for the six single-method planners and the problem sets defined by the scope of these planners over a training set of 30 randomly generated 3- and 4-conjunct problems in the blocks-world domain. In this domain, A_4 is the same as A_1 because if a problem is not solvable with protection, it also is not solvable with directness. A_5 is the same as A_6 because both M_5 and M_6 are complete in this domain, though M_5 may not be able to generate an optimal solution. A_2 and A_3 are different sets in principle, because problems such as Sussman's anomaly cannot be solved by a linear planner with protection (M_2) but can be by a nonlinear planner with protection (M_3). However, among the 30 problems, these "anomaly" problems did not occur, yielding $A_2 = A_3$ for this set of problems. The results imply that directness and protection are positive in this domain, while linearity is not, since $l(M_5, A_1) > l(M_6, A_1)$ and $l(M_5, A_2) > l(M_6, A_2)$. If we use linearity as an independent bias — so that one set of multi-method planners is generated using it and one set without it — and vary directness and protection within the individual multi-method planners, we get a set of 10 strongly monotonic multi-method planners (four three-method planners and six two-method planners).

---

[3]This is a slight redefinition of monotonicity from (Lee & Rosenbloom, 1992) with a minor correction.

Planner	Decisions				Plan length			
	A_1	A_2	A_3	A_5	A_1	A_2	A_3	A_5
M_5	22.21	29.41	29.48	29.22	3.00	3.78	3.83	3.82
M_6	33.40	47.12	48.06	47.93	2.90	3.88	4.07	4.14
Average				38.58				3.98
$M_1 \rightarrow M_2 \rightarrow M_5$	13.26	24.69	25.07	26.13	1.82	2.48	2.54	2.58
$M_1 \rightarrow M_3 \rightarrow M_6$	13.26	26.34	26.55	28.91	1.82	2.52	2.54	2.59
$M_1 \rightarrow M_4 \rightarrow M_5$	13.26	26.16	26.41	26.79	1.82	2.85	2.92	2.94
$M_1 \rightarrow M_4 \rightarrow M_6$	13.26	36.78	37.40	37.30	1.82	2.91	2.99	3.02
$M_1 \rightarrow M_5$	13.26	25.68	25.86	26.04	1.82	2.96	3.02	3.03
$M_1 \rightarrow M_6$	13.26	31.54	31.85	31.77	1.82	2.89	2.94	2.97
$M_2 \rightarrow M_5$	19.54	27.89	28.18	29.34	1.85	2.43	2.49	2.58
$M_3 \rightarrow M_6$	21.22	28.46	28.41	30.67	2.00	2.52	2.52	2.57
$M_4 \rightarrow M_5$	16.85	27.81	27.95	28.38	1.82	2.83	2.88	2.93
$M_4 \rightarrow M_6$	16.85	33.33	33.59	34.47	1.82	2.83	2.85	2.95
Average				29.98				2.82
$M_{1 \rightarrow 2 \rightarrow 5}$	8.63	12.87	13.00	13.01	1.82	2.80	2.84	2.90
$M_{1 \rightarrow 3 \rightarrow 6}$	8.63	13.38	13.43	13.56	1.82	2.53	2.53	2.59
$M_{1 \rightarrow 4 \rightarrow 5}$	8.63	13.19	13.29	13.25	1.82	3.25	3.32	3.34
$M_{1 \rightarrow 4 \rightarrow 6}$	8.63	13.48	13.73	13.63	1.82	2.87	2.96	2.97
$M_{1 \rightarrow 5}$	8.63	12.21	12.36	12.51	1.82	2.63	2.73	2.81
$M_{1 \rightarrow 6}$	8.63	13.22	13.27	13.23	1.82	2.68	2.69	2.73
$M_{2 \rightarrow 5}$	19.19	23.75	23.76	23.80	2.56	3.07	3.11	3.16
$M_{3 \rightarrow 6}$	16.62	23.45	23.56	24.22	2.03	2.56	2.57	2.71
$M_{4 \rightarrow 5}$	13.57	17.24	17.30	17.38	2.44	3.71	3.77	3.77
$M_{4 \rightarrow 6}$	14.10	19.28	19.58	19.83	2.41	3.33	3.43	3.46
Average				16.44				3.04

Table 2: Single-method and coarse-grained multi-method vs. fine-grained multi-method planning in the blocks-world domain.

Experimental Results

Table 2 compares the strongly monotonic fine-grained multi-method planners with the corresponding coarse-grained multi-method planners and (complete) single-method planners over a test set of 100 randomly generated 3- and 4-conjunct blocks-world problems (this test set is disjoint from the 30-problem training set used in developing the multi-method planners). Z-tests on this data reveal that fine-grained multi-method planners take significantly less planning time than both single-method planners ($z=5.35$, $p<.01$) and coarse-grained multi-method planners ($z=6.72$, $p<.01$). This likely stems from fine-grain multi-method planners preferring to search within the more efficient spaces defined by the biases — thus tending to outperform single-method planners — but being able to recover from bias failure without throwing away everything already done for a problem (thus tending to outperform coarse-grained multi-method planners).

Fine-grained multi-method planners also generate significantly shorter plans than single-method planners ($z=3.42$, $p<.01$). They generate slightly longer plans than coarse-grained multi-method planners; however, no significance is found at a 5% level ($z=1.77$). These results likely arise because, whenever possible, both types of multi-method planners use the more restrictive methods that yield shorter plan lengths, while there may be little difference between the methods that ultimately succeed for the two types of multi-method planners.

Table 3 illustrates the performance of these three types of planners over a test set of 100 randomly generated 5-conjunct problems in the machine shop scheduling domain (Minton, 1988). In this domain, no precondition subgoals are required because there is no operator which achieves any of the unmet preconditions. Thus both directness and linearity are irrelevant. However, there are strong interactions among the operators, so protection violations are still relevant. In consequence, the entire table of six planners reduces to only two distinct planners for this domain: with or without protection.

Planner	Decisions		Plan length	
	A_1	A_4	A_1	A_4
M_4, M_5, M_6	31.47	33.97	4.13	4.47
$M_1 \rightarrow M_4,\ M_2 \rightarrow M_5,\ M_3 \rightarrow M_6$	26.17	35.91	2.43	3.58
$M_{1 \rightarrow 4},\ M_{2 \rightarrow 5},\ M_{3 \rightarrow 6}$	18.71	19.07	2.87	3.29

Table 3: Single-method and coarse-grained multi-method vs. fine-grained multi-method planning in the scheduling domain.

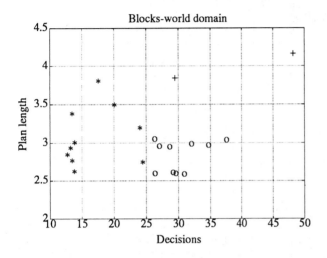

Figure 1: Performance of single-method planners (+), coarse-grained multi-method planners (o), and fine-grained multi-method planners (*) in the blocks-world domain.

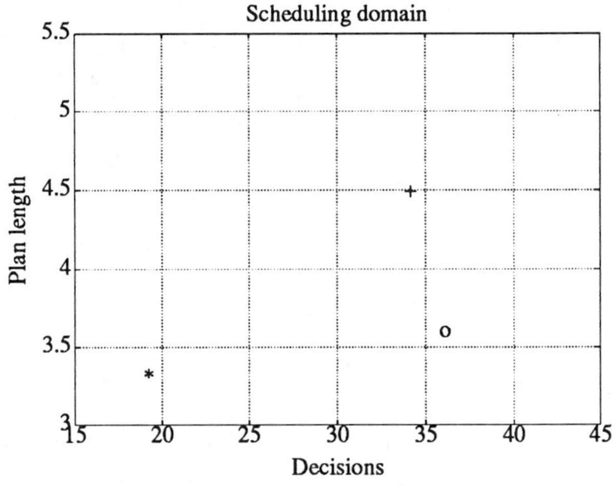

Figure 2: Performance of single-method planners (+), coarse-grained multi-method planners (o), and fine-grained multi-method planners (*) in the scheduling domain.

As with the blocks-world domain, the z-tests in the scheduling domain indicate that fine-grained planners dominate both single-method planners ($z=10.91$, $p<.01$) and coarse-grained planners ($z=8.95$, $p<.01$) in terms of planning time. Fine-grained planners also generate significantly shorter plans than do the single-method planners ($z=6.49$, $p<.01$). They generate slightly shorter plans than coarse-grained multi-method planners; however, no significance is found at a 5% level ($z=1.28$).

Figures 1 and 2 plot the average number of decisions versus the average plan lengths for the data in Tables 2 and 3. These figures graphically illustrate how the coarse-grained approach primarily reduces plan length in comparison to the single-method approach, and how the fine-grained approach primarily improves efficiency in comparison to the coarse-grained approach.

Related Work

The basic approach of bias relaxation in multi-method planning is similar to the shift of bias for inductive con-

cept learning (Russell & Grosof, 1987; Utgoff, 1986). In the planning literature, this approach is closely related to an *ordering modification* which is a control strategy to prefer exploring some plans before others (Gratch & DeJong, 1990). Bhatnagar & Mostow (1990) described a relaxation mechanism for over-general censors in FAILSAFE-2. However, there are a number of differences, such as the type of constraints used, the granularity at which censors are relaxed, and the way censors are relaxed. SteppingStone (Ruby & Kibler, 1991) tries constrained search first, and moves on to unconstrained search, if the constrained search reaches an impasse (within the boundary of ordered subgoals) and the knowledge stored in memory cannot resolve the impasse.

This approach is also related to the traditional partial-order planning, where heuristics are used to guide the search over the space of partially ordered plans without violating planner completeness (McAllester & Rosenblitt, 1991; Barrett & Weld, 1993; Chapman, 1987). For example, using directness in fine-grained multi-method planners is similar to preferring the nodes which reduce the size of the set of open conditions when a new step is added. Relaxing bias in fine-grained multi-method planners only when it is necessary is similar to the least-commitment approach which adds ordering constraints only if a threat to a causal link is detected.

Conclusion

In this paper, we have provided a way to select a set of positive biases for multi-method planning and investigated the effect of refining the granularity at which individual planning methods could be switched. The experimental results obtained so far in the blocks-world and machine-shop-scheduling domains imply that (1) fine-grained multi-method planners can be significantly more efficient than single-method planners in terms of planning time and plan length, and (2) fine-grained multi-method planners can be significantly more efficient than coarse-grained multi-method planners in terms of planning time.

The bias selection approach used here is based on preprocessing a set of training examples in order to develop fixed sequences of biases (and methods). A more dynamic, run-time approach would be to learn, while doing, which biases (and methods) to use for which classes of problems. If such learned information can transfer to the later problems, much of the effort wasted in trying inappropriate methods, as well as the effort for preprocessing, may be reduced (as demonstrated in (Rosenbloom, Lee, & Unruh, 1993)).

Another way to enhance the multi-method planning framework would be to extend the set of biases available to include ones that limit the size of the goal hierarchy (to reduce the search space), limit the length of plans generated (to shorten execution time), and lead to learning more effective rules (to increase transfer) (Etzioni, 1990). Investigations of these topics are in progress.

References

Barrett, A., & Weld, D. S. (1993). Partial-order planning: Evaluating possible efficiency gains. *Artificial Intelligence*. To appear.

Bhatnagar, N., & Mostow, J. (1990). Adaptive search by explanation-based learning of heuristic censors. *Proceedings of the Eighth National Conference on Artificial Intelligence* (pp. 895-901). Boston, MA: AAAI Press.

Chapman, D. (1987). Planning for conjunctive goals. *Artificial Intelligence, 32*, 333-377.

Etzioni, O. (1990). Why Prodigy/EBL works. *Proceedings of the Eighth National Conference on Artificial Intelligence* (pp. 916-922). Boston, MA: AAAI Press.

Gratch, J. M., & DeJong, G. F. (1990). A framework for evaluating search control strategies. *Proceedings of the Workshop on Innovative Approaches to Planning, Scheduling, and Control* (pp. 337-347). San Diego, CA: Morgan Kaufmann.

Korf, R. E. (1985). Depth-first iterative-deepening: An optimal admissible tree search. *Artificial Intelligence, 27*, 97-109.

Laird, J. E., Newell, A., & Rosenbloom, P. S. (1987). Soar: An architecture for general intelligence. *Artificial Intelligence, 33*, 1-64.

Lee, S., & Rosenbloom, P. S. (1992). Creating and coordinating multiple planning methods. *Proceedings of the Second Pacific Rim International Conference on Artificial Intelligence* (pp. 89-95).

McAllester, D., & Rosenblitt, D. (1991) Systematic Nonlinear Planning. *Proceedings of the Ninth National Conference on Artificial Intelligence* (pp. 634-639). Anaheim, CA: AAAI Press.

Minton, S. (1988). Learning effective search control knowledge: An explanation-based approach. (Ph.D. Thesis). Department of Computer Science, Carnegie-Mellon University.

Rosenbloom, P. S., Lee, S., & Unruh, A. (1990). Responding to impasses in memory-driven behavior: A framework for planning. *Proceedings of the Workshop on Innovative Approaches to Planning, Scheduling, and Control* (pp. 181-191). San Diego, CA: Morgan Kaufmann.

Rosenbloom, P. S., Lee, S., & Unruh, A. (1993). Bias in planning and explanation-based learning. S. Chipman & A. L. Meyrowitz (Eds.) *Foundations of Knowledge Acquisition: Cognitive Models of Complex Learning.* (pp. 269-307). Hingham, MA: Kluwer Academic Publishers. (Also available in S. Minton (Ed.) *Machine Learning Methods for Planning and Scheduling.* San Mateo, CA: Morgan Kaufmann. In Press.)

Ruby, D., & Kibler, D. (1991). SteppingStone: An empirical and analytical evaluation. *Proceedings of the Ninth National Conference on Artificial Intelligence* (pp. 527-532). Anaheim, CA: AAAI Press.

Russell, S. J., & Grosof, B. N. (1987). A declarative approach to bias in concept learning. *Proceedings of the Sixth National Conference on Artificial Intelligence* (pp. 505-510). Seattle, WA: Morgan Kaufmann.

Utgoff, P. E. (1986). Shift of bias for inductive concept learning. In R. S. Michalski, J. G. Carbonell, & T. M. Mitchell (Eds.) *Machine Learning: An Artificial Intelligence Approach, Vol. II.* Los Altos, CA: Morgan Kaufmann.

Threat-Removal Strategies for Partial-Order Planning

Mark A. Peot

Department of Engineering-Economic Systems
Stanford University
Stanford, California 94305
peot@rpal.rockwell.com

David E. Smith

Rockwell International
444 High St.
Palo Alto, California 94301
de2smith@rpal.rockwell.com

Abstract

McAllester and Rosenblitts' (1991) systematic nonlinear planner (SNLP) removes threats as they are discovered. In other planners such as SIPE (Wilkins, 1988), and NOAH (Sacerdoti, 1977), threat resolution is partially or completely delayed. In this paper, we demonstrate that planner efficiency may be vastly improved by the use of alternatives to these threat removal strategies. We discuss five threat removal strategies and prove that two of these strategies dominate the other three--resulting in a provably smaller search space. Furthermore, the systematicity of the planning algorithm is preserved for each of the threat removal strategies. Finally, we confirm our results experimentally using a large number of planning examples including examples from the literature.

1 Introduction

McAllester and Rosenblitt (1991) present a simple elegant algorithm for systematic nonlinear planning (SNLP). Much recent planning work (Barrett & Weld, 1993; Collins & Pryor, 1992; Harvey, 1993; Kambhampati, 1993a; Penberthy & Weld, 1992; Peot & Smith, 1992) has been based upon this algorithm (or the Barrett & Weld (1993) implementation of it).

In the SNLP algorithm, when threats arise between steps and causal links in a partial plan, those threats are resolved before attempting to satisfy any remaining open conditions in the partial plan. From a practical standpoint, we know that this is not always the most efficient course. When there are only a few loosely coupled threats in a problem, it is generally more efficient to delay resolving those threats until the end of the planning process.[1] However, if there are many tightly-coupled threats (causing most partial plans to fail), those threats should be resolved early in the planning process to avoid extensive backtracking. These two options, resolve threats immediately, and resolve threats at the end, represent two

extreme positions. There are several other options, such as waiting to resolve a threat until it is no longer separable, or waiting until there is only one way of resolving the threat. Given a reasonable mix of problems, what is the best strategy or strategies?

In this paper, we introduce four alternative threat removal strategies and show that some are strictly better than others. In particular, we show that delaying separable threats generates a smaller search space of possible plans than the SNLP algorithm.

In Section 2 we give preliminary definitions and a version of the SNLP algorithm. In Section 3 we introduce four different threat removal strategies and investigate the theoretical relationships between them. In Section 4 we give empirical results that confirm the analysis of Section 3. In Section 5, we discuss work related to the work in this paper.

2 Preliminaries

Following (Kambhampati, 1992), (Barrett & Weld, 1993), (Collins & Pryor, 1992) and (McAllester & Rosenblitt, 1991), we define causal links, threats and plans as follows:

Definition 1: An open condition, g, is a precondition of an operator in the plan that has no corresponding causal link.

Definition 2: A causal link, L: $s_e \xrightarrow{g} s_c$, protects effect g of the establishing plan step, s_e, so that it can be used to satisfy a precondition of the consuming plan step, s_c.

Definition 3: An ordering constraint O: $s_1 > s_2$ restricts step s_1 to occur after step s_2.

Definition 4: A plan is a tuple $\langle S, L, O, G, B \rangle$ where S denotes the set of steps in the plan, L denotes the set of causal links, O denotes the set of ordering constraints, G denotes the outstanding open conditions, and B denotes the set of equality and inequality constraints on variables contained in the plan.

---

[1] Hacker (Sussman, 1973), Noah (Sacerdoti, 1977), and (to a certain extent) Sipe (Wilkins, 1988), delay the resolution of threats until the end of the planning process. Yang (1993) has also explored this strategy.

Definition 5: A threat T: $s_t \overset{b}{\otimes} (s_e \overset{g}{\to} s_c)$ represents a potential conflict between an effect of a step in the plan, s_t, and a causal link $s_e \overset{g}{\to} s_c$. s_t threatens causal link $s_e \overset{g}{\to} s_c$, if s_t can occur between s_e and s_c and an effect, e, of s_t possibly unifies with either g or $\neg g$ when the additional binding constraints b are added to the plan bindings. Unification of two literals, e and g, under bindings b is denoted by $e \overset{b}{\equiv} g$. If $e \overset{b}{\equiv} g$, we refer to T as a *positive threat*. If $e \overset{b}{\equiv} \neg g$, we refer to T as a *negative threat*.

To make our analysis easier, we will work with the following modified version of the SNLP algorithm given below. The primary difference between this algorithm and the algorithms given in (Barrett, Soderland & Weld, 1991; Collins & Pryor, 1992; and Kambhampati 1993a) is that threat resolution takes place immediately after Add-Link and Add-Step. As a result, the set of partial plans being considered never contains any plans with unresolved threats.

Plan (initial-conditions, goal):

1. **Initialization:** Let Finish be a plan step having preconditions equal to the goal conditions and let Start be a plan step having effects equal to the initial conditions. Let Q be the set consisting of the single partial plan $\langle \{\text{Start}, \text{Finish}\}, \varnothing, \{\text{Start} < \text{Finish}\}, G, \varnothing \rangle$, where G is the set of open conditions corresponding to the goals.

2. **Expansion:** While Q is not empty, select a partial plan $p = \langle S, L, O, G, B \rangle$ and remove it from Q.

   A. **Termination:** If the open conditions G are empty, return a topological sort of S instantiated with the bindings B.

   B. **Establish Open Condition:** Select some $g \in G$ and do the following:

   i. **Add Link:** For each $s \in S$ with an effect e such that $e \overset{b}{\equiv} g$ and s is possibly prior to s_c call
   $$\text{Resolve-Threats}\left(S, L + \left(s \overset{g}{\to} s_c\right), O + (s < s_c), \atop G - g + G_s, B + b\right)$$

   ii. **Add Step:** For each $a \in A$ with an effect e such that $e \overset{b}{\equiv} c$ call
   $$\text{Resolve-Threats}\left(S + s, L + \left(s \overset{g}{\to} s_c\right), O + (s < s_c), \atop G - g + G_s, B + b\right)$$
   where A denotes the set of all action descriptions, s denotes the new plan step constructed by copying a with a fresh set of variables and G_s is the preconditions of S.

Resolve-Threats (S, L, O, G, B):

1. Let T be the set of threats between steps in S and causal links in L.

2. If T is empty add $\langle S, L, O, G, B \rangle$ to Q.

3. If T is not empty select some threat
   $$s_t \overset{b}{\otimes} \left(s_e \overset{g}{\to} s_c\right) \in T \text{ and do the following:}$$

   A. **Demotion:** If $s_t < s_e$ is consistent with O Resolve-Threats $(S, L, O + s_t < s_e, G, B + b)$.[2]

   B. **Promotion:** If $s_c < s_t$ is consistent with O Resolve-Threats $(S, L, O + s_c < s_t, G, B + b)$.

   C. **Separation:** For each $(x_i = y_i) \in b$:
   $$\text{Resolve-Threats} \Big(S, L, O, G \atop B + \{x_k = y_k\}_{k=1}^{i-1} + (x_i \neq y_i) \Big)$$
   where $\{x_k = y_k\}_{k=1}^{i-1}$ denotes the set of the first $i-1$ equality constraints in b.[3]

3 Threat Delay Strategies

In the SNLP algorithm, when threats arise in a partial plan, they are immediately resolved before attempting to satisfy any remaining open conditions. There are three ways that a threat can be resolved: separation, promotion, and

---

[2] The criterion for separation, promotion, and demotion, used in (Barrett & Weld, 1993) and (Collins & Pryor, 1992) are not mutually exclusive. In order to preserve systematicity, one must either restrict separation so that the threatening step occurs between the producer and consumer steps, or restrict the variable bindings for promotion and demotion so that separation is not possible. For our purposes, the latter restriction is simpler.

[3] The addition of equality constraints during separation is required to maintain systematicity [3].

demotion. Separation forces the variable bindings in the clobbering step to be different than those in the threatened causal link. Promotion forces the clobbering step to come before the producing step in the causal link, and demotion forces the clobbering step to come after the consumer of the causal link. If all three of these are possible, there will be at least a three way branch in the search space of partial plans. In fact, it can be worse than this, because there may be many alternative ways of doing separation, and all of them must be considered.

In practice, however, threat removal is often deferred in order to improve planning performance. Harvey (1993) has shown that any threat removal order may be used in the SNLP algorithm without compromising the algorithm's systematicity. In this section, we describe four alternative threat deferral strategies and the effect of these strategies on the size of the planner search space.

3.1 Separable Delay

Many of the threats that occur during planning are ephemeral. As planning continues, variables in both the clobbering step and the causal link may get bound, causing the threat to go away. This causes the promotion and demotion branches for that partial plan to go away, and causes all but one of the separation branches for the plan to go away. Thus, it would seem to make heuristic sense to postpone resolving a threat until the threat becomes definite; that is, until the bindings of the clobbering step and the causal link are such that the threat is guaranteed to occur. Thus we could modify the SNLP algorithm in the following way:

Resolve-Threats (S, L, O, G, B):

1. Let $T = \{s \overset{\varnothing}{\otimes} l\}$ be the set of unseparable threats between steps $s \in S$ and causal links $l \in L$. These threats are those that are guaranteed to occur regardless of the addition of additional binding constraints.

2. If T is empty add $\langle S, L, O, G, B \rangle$ to Q

3. If T is not empty select some threat, $s_t \overset{\varnothing}{\otimes} \left(s_e \overset{g}{\to} s_c \right) \in T$, and do the following:

   A. **Demotion**: If $s_t < s_e$ is consistent with O
      Resolve-Threats$(S, L, O + s_t < s_e, G, B)$

   B. **Promotion**: If $s_c < s_t$ is consistent with O
      Resolve-Threats$(S, L, O + s_c < s_t, G, B)$

We refer to this threat resolution strategy as DSep. Note that DSep is a complete, systematic planning algorithm that does not require the use of separation.

Theorem 1: The space of partial plans generated by DSep is no larger than (and often smaller than) the space of partial plans generated by SNLP. (We are assuming that the two algorithms use the same strategy to decide which open conditions to work on.)

Sketch of Proof: The essence of the proof is to show that each partial plan generated by DSep has a unique corresponding partial plan generated by SNLP. Let $p = \langle S, L, O, G, B \rangle$ be a partial plan generated by DSep and let $Z = z_1, ..., z_n$ be the sequence of planner operations (add-link, add-step, demote, and promote) used by DSep to construct p. For each threat t introduced by an operation z_t in Z, there are three possibilities:

1. t became unseparable and was resolved using a later Promote or Demote operation z_r.

2. t is still separable and hence is unresolved in p

3. t was separable, but eventually disappeared because of binding or ordering constraints introduced by a later operation z_r.

For each threat t, we perform the corresponding modification to the sequence Z indicated below:

1. move z_r to immediately after z_t.

2. add a Separate operation for t immediately after z_t

3. add the appropriate Promote, Demote, or Separate operation immediately after z_t that mimics the way in which the threat is eventually resolved.

In this new sequence Z', all threats are resolved immediately after they are introduced. As a result, Z' is now the sequence of planning operations that would have been generated by SNLP. The plan $p' = \langle S, L, O', G, B' \rangle$ generated by this sequence differs from the original plan only in that 1) B' is augmented with separation constraints for each unresolved threat in p, and 2) O and O' may differ in redundant ordering constraints, but $Closure(O) = Closure(O')$. As a result, the mapping from DSep plans to SNLP plans is one to one, and the theorem follows. ▫

Although the space of partial plans generated by DSep is smaller than that generated by SNLP, we cannot guarantee that DSep will always be faster than SNLP. There are two reasons for this:

1. There is overhead associated with delaying threats because the planner must continue to check separability.

2. When a threat becomes unseparable, DSep must check to see if demotion or promotion are possible. Because the space of partial plans may have grown considerably since the threat was introduced, there might be more of these checks than if resolution had taken place at the time the threat was introduced. (Of course, the reverse can also happen.)

3.2 Delay Unforced Threats

A natural extension of the DSep idea would be to delay resolving a threat until there is only one (or no) threat resolution option remaining. (This is the ultimate least-commitment strategy with regard to threats.) Thus, if demotion were the only possibility for resolving a threat, the appropriate ordering constraint would be added. Alternatively, if separation were the only option, and there was only one way of separating the variables, the appropriate not-equals constraint would be added to the plan. We refer to this threat resolution strategy as DUnf. The threat resolution procedure for DUnf is shown below:

Resolve-Threats (S, L, O, G, B):

1. Let $T = s_t \overset{b}{\otimes} \left(s_e \overset{g}{\to} s_c \right)$ be the set of threats between steps in S and causal links in L such that either:

   A. $s_t < s_e$ is consistent with O, $s_t \leq s_c$, and $b = \varnothing$

   B. $s_c < s_t$ is consistent with O, $s_t \geq s_e$, and $b = \varnothing$.

   C. $s_e \leq s_t \leq s_c$ and b contains exactly one constraint.

2. If T is empty add $\langle S, L, O, G, B \rangle$ to Q

3. If T is not empty select some threat $s_t \overset{b}{\otimes} \left(s_e \overset{g}{\to} s_c \right) \in T$ and do the following:

   A. **Demotion**: If $s_t < s_e$ is consistent with O
   Resolve-Threats $(S, L, O + s_t < s_e, G, B + b)$

   B. **Promotion**: If $s_c < s_t$ is consistent with O
   Resolve-Threats $(S, L, O + s_c < s_t, G, B + b)$.

   C. **Separation**: For the single binding constraint, $(x = y)$,
   Resolve-Threats $(S, L, O, G, B + (x \neq y))$.

It might seem that this strategy would always expand fewer partial plans than DSep. Unfortunately this is not the case

for at least two reasons. First of all, it is possible to construct examples where both promotion and demotion are possible for each individual threat, but the entire set of threats is unsatisfiable (a direct conclusion from the fact that the problem of determining whether a set of threats might be resolved by the addition of ordering constraints is NP-Complete (Kautz, 1993)). For such a case, the DUnf planner would choose not to work on the threats and therefore wouldn't recognize that the plan was impossible. In contrast, SNLP and DSep would commit to either promotion or demotion for each threat, and would therefore discover that the plan was impossible earlier than would the DUnf strategy. In addition, when the DUnf strategy postpones the addition of ordering constraints to a plan, it allows plan branches to be developed that contain Add-links that might have been illegal if those ordering constraints were added earlier in the planning process.

On the other hand, it is also easy to construct domains where DSep is clearly inferior to DUnf. Therefore we can conclude:

Theorem 2: Neither DUnf nor DSep are guaranteed to generate a smaller search space than the other for all planning problems.

Another possible drawback to DUnf is that checking to see if there is only one option for resolving a threat may be costly, whereas the separability criterion used in DSep is relatively easy to check.

3.3 Delay Resolvable Threats

An alternative to DUnf would be to ignore a threat until it becomes impossible to resolve, and then simply discard the partial plan. We refer to this alternative as DRes:

Resolve-Threats (S, L, O, G, B):

1. Let T be the set of threats between steps in S and causal links in L.

2. For all $s_t \overset{b}{\otimes} \left(s_e \overset{g}{\to} s_c \right) \in T$ if either b is nonempty, $s_t < s_e$ is consistent with O, or $s_c < s_t$ is consistent with O, then add $\langle S, L, O, G, B \rangle$ to Q

To see the difference between DUnf and DRes, consider a partial plan with a threat that can only be resolved by demotion. Using DUnf, we would generate a new partial plan with the appropriate ordering constraint. This ordering constraint could, in turn, prevent any number of possible add-link operations, and could reduce the possible ways of resolving other threats. If DRes were used, this additional ordering constraint would not be present. As a result, DUnf will consider fewer partial plans than DRes.

It is relatively easy to show that:

Theorem 3: The space of partial plans generated by DRes is at least as large as the space generated by DUnf.

Since the cost of checking to see if a threat is unresolvable is just as expensive as checking to see if a threat has only one resolution, there should be no advantage to DRes over DUnf.

3.4 Delay Threats to the End

The final extreme approach is to delay resolving threats until all open conditions have been satisfied. We refer to this algorithm as DEnd. Threat resolution strategies similar to DEnd are used in (Sussman, 1973; Sacerdoti, 1977; Wilkins, 1988; and Yang 1993).

The primary advantage to this approach is that there is no cost associated with checking or even generating threats until the plan is otherwise complete. In problems where there are few threats, or the threats are easy to resolve by ordering constraints, this approach is a win. However, if most partial plans fail because of unresolvable threats, this technique will generate many partial plans that are effectively dead.

It is relatively easy to show that:

Theorem 4: The space of partial plans generated by DRes is no larger than (and is sometimes smaller than) the space generated by DEnd.

The search space relationships between the five threat removal strategies is summarized in Figure 1.

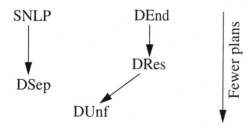

Figure 1: Search space relationships for five threat removal strategies.

4 Empirical Results

We tested the five threat resolution strategies on several problems in each of several different domains; a discrete time version of Minton's machine shop scheduling domain (1988), a route planning domain, Russell's tire changing domain, and Barrett & Weld's (1993) artificial domains D^mS^1 and D^1S^1 (also called the ART-MD and ART-1D domains), and ART-1D-RD and ART-MD-RD, Kambhampati's (1993a) variations on these domains.

Ordinarily, the performance of a planner depends heavily on first, the order in which the partial plans are selected, and second, the order in which open conditions are selected. In order to try to filter out these effects, we tested each domain using several different strategies.

We used the A* search algorithm in our testing. The 'g' function is the length of the partial plan, and 'h' is the number of open conditions. We did not include the number of threats in 'h' because this number varies across different threat resolution strategies. The search algorithm is engineered so that it always searches partial plans with equivalent causal structures (generated by the same chain of add-link and add-step operations) in the same order regardless of the threat resolution strategy selected. These tests demonstrate the relative search space theorems by showing that an inefficient threat resolution strategy (for example, SNLP) generates at least one (and often more than one) partial plan for each equivalent partial plan generated by one of the more efficient threat resolution strategies (for example, DSep).

For selecting open conditions, we used a LIFO strategy, a FIFO strategy, and a more sophisticated least-commitment strategy. The LIFO and FIFO strategies refer to the order that open conditions are attacked: oldest or youngest first. The least-commitment strategy selects the open condition to expand that would result in the fewest immediate children. For example, assume that two open conditions A and B are under consideration. Open condition A can be satisfied by adding either of two different operators to the plan. Condition B, on the other hand, can only be satisfied by linking to a unique initial condition. In this situation, the least-commitment strategy would favor working on B first. Note that the least-commitment strategy violates the assumption of Theorem 1; the action of the least-commitment strategy can depend on previous threat resolution actions.

The planner used for these demonstrations differs from the algorithm described in this paper in that it can ignore positive threats.[4] For most of our testing, we turned off detection of positive threats in order to reduce the amount of time spent in planning.

In the following plots, we have made no attempt to distinguish between individual planning problems. Instead, we have plotted the relative size of the search space of each problem in the sample domain. Each line corresponds to a single problem/conjunct-ordering-strategy pair. The relative size plotted in these figures is the quotient of the number of nodes explored by the planner when using a particular threat resolution strategy and the number of nodes explored when using a reference strategy. For example, in Figure 2, all of the search spaces sizes are normalized relative to the size of the most efficient threat resolution strategy for this domain, DSep. The shapes of these plots demonstrate the superiority of the DSep and DUnf threat resolution strategies over all of the other threat resolution strategies. The pseudoconvex shape of each of these curves illustrates the dominance relationships illustrated in Figure 1.

Figures 2 through 4 illustrate the relative search space size of several problems drawn from the tire changing, machine shop and route planning domains, respectively. Figures 5 and 6 illustrate the relative search space sizes for a variety of problems drawn from the ART-MD-RD and ART-1D-RD domains. The choice of threat delay strategy has no effect on the D^mS^1 and D^1S^1 domains (that is, the relative search space sizes are identical).

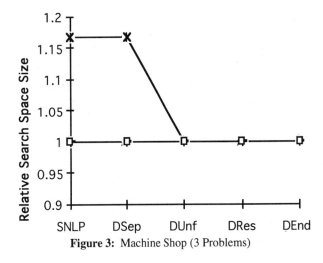

Figure 2: Russell's Tire Changing Domain (3 Problems)

Figure 3: Machine Shop (3 Problems)

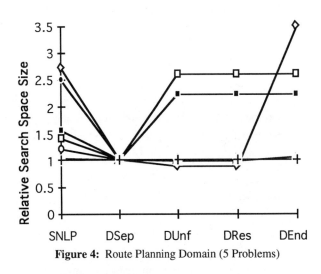

Figure 4: Route Planning Domain (5 Problems)

---

[4] and is, therefore, nonsystematic.

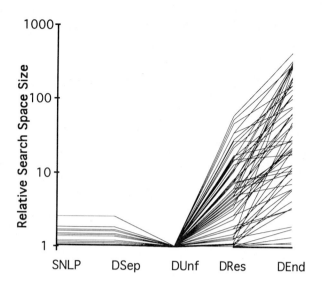

Figure 5: ART-MD-RD Planning Domain (29 Problems)

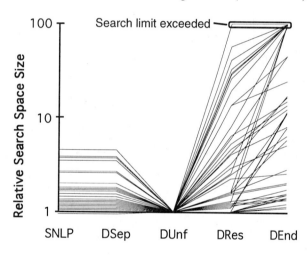

Figure 6: ART-1D-RD Domain (29 Problems)

Note that the artificial domains are propositional. Thus DSep has exactly the same effect as the default SNLP strategy because threats are never separable.

In Figure 7, we plot the CPU time required for planning using three of the threat resolution strategies on an assortment of ART-MD-RD problems. On small problems, the additional computation required for the more complicated threat resolution strategies dominates. For larger problems, however, we expect that these factors will

become unimportant and that we will realize a savings that is roughly exponential in the number of threats.

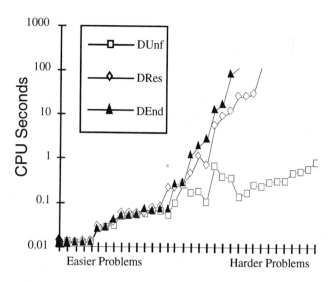

Figure 7: CPU time required for ART-1D-RD Problems

5 Related Work

Recently, Kambhampati (1993a) performed tests with several different planning algorithms, including SNLP, and argues that systematicity reduces the redundancy of the search space at the expense of increased commitment by the planner. He shows data indicating that for some classes of problems SNLP performs more poorly than planners that are nonsystematic.

Although we find these results interesting (and find Kambhampati's multi-contributor planners intriguing) we are left wondering to what extent his results would be affected by a more judicious selection of threat resolution strategies.

In his tests, Kambhampati also considers a variant of SNLP where positive threats are ignored (NONLIN). It is possible to construct examples where ignoring a positive threat in SNLP results in an arbitrarily large increase in search. Conversely, we believe that the consideration of positive threats does not cost a great deal. In particular, if t is the potential number of positive threats in a partial plan, we conjecture that considering positive threats in the delayed separability algorithm will never result in more than a factor of 3^t increase in the size of the search space of partial plans.

Kambhampati (1993b) also observes that the DSep threat resolution strategy is identical to SNLP if the definition for threats is modified. In particular, we would only recognize a threat when the post condition of a potentially threatening operator unifies with a protected precondition regardless of any bindings that might be added to the plan. Thus, with the appropriate threat definition, separation is not required for a complete, systematic variation of SNLP.

In addition, Kambhampati claims that these threat resolution strategies can be applied to planners that use multi-contributor causal structures (Kambhampati, 1992).

Yang (1993) has investigated the use of constraint satisfaction methods for resolving sets of threats. In our experience, the time at which the planner resolves threats has far more impact on performance than the method used for resolving sets of threats.

In (Smith & Peot, 1993), we have been investigating a more involved method of deciding when to work on threats. In particular, we show that for certain kinds of threats it is possible to prove that the threats can always be resolved at the end, and can therefore be postponed until planning is otherwise complete. The work reported in this paper is complementary since it suggests strategies for resolving threats that cannot be provably postponed.

Acknowledgments

This work was supported by DARPA contract F30602-91-C-0031 and a NSF Graduate Fellowship. Thanks to Will Harvey, Rao Kambhampati, and Dan Weld for their contributions to this paper.

References

Barrett, A., and Weld, D., Partial Order Planning: Evaluating Possible Efficiency Gains, to appear in *Artificial Intelligence*, 1993.

Collins, G., and Pryor, L., *Representation and performance in a partial order planner*, technical report 35, The Institute for the Learning Sciences, Northwestern University, 1992.

Harvey, W., Deferring Conflict-Resolution Retains Systematicity, Submitted to AAAI, 1993.

Kambhampati, S., Characterizing Multi-Contributor Causal Structures for Planning, Proceedings of the First International Conference on Artificial Intelligence Planning Systems, College Park, Maryland, 1992.

Kambhampati, S., On the utility of systematicity: understanding trade-offs between redundancy and commitment in partial-ordering planning, submitted to IJCAI, 1993a.

Kambhampati, S., A comparative analysis of search space size, systematicity and performance of partial-order planners. CSE Technical Report, Arizona State University, 1993b.

Kautz, Henry. Personal communication, April 6, 1992.

McAllester, D., and Rosenblitt, D., Systematic nonlinear planning, In *Proceedings of the Ninth National Conference on Artificial Intelligence*, pages 634–639, Anaheim, CA, 1991.

Minton, S., *Learning Effective Search Control Knowledge: An Explanation-Based Approach.* Ph.D. Thesis, Computer Science Department, Carnegie Mellon University, 1988.

Penberthy, J., S., Weld, D., UCPOP: A sound, complete, partial order planner for ADL, In *Proceedings of the Third International Conference on Knowledge Representation and Reasoning*, Cambridge, MA, 1992.

Peot, M., and Smith, D., Conditional nonlinear planning, In *Proc. First International Conference on AI Planning Systems*, College Park, Maryland, 1992.

Sacerdoti, E., *A Structure for Plans and Behavior*, Elsevier, North Holland, New York, 1977.

Smith, D. and Peot, M., Postponing conflicts in nonlinear planning, AAAI Spring Symposium on Foundations of Planning, Stanford, CA, 1993, to appear.

Sussman, G., *A Computational Model of Skill Acquisition*, Report AI-TR-297, MIT AI Laboratory., 1973.

Wilkins, D., *Practical Planning: Extending the Classical AI Planning Paradigm*, Morgan Kauffman, San Mateo, 1988.

Yang, Q., A Theory of Conflict Resolution in Planning, *Artificial Intelligence*, 58 (1992) pg. 361-392.

Postponing Threats in Partial-Order Planning

David E. Smith

Rockwell International
444 High St.
Palo Alto, California 94301
de2smith@rpal.rockwell.com

Mark A. Peot

Department of Engineering Economic Systems
Stanford University
Stanford, California 94305
peot@rpal.rockwell.com

Abstract

An important aspect of partial-order planning is the resolution of threats between actions and causal links in a plan. We present a technique for automatically deciding which threats should be resolved during planning, and which should be delayed until planning is otherwise complete. In particular we show that many potential threats can be provably delayed until the end; that is, if the planner can find a plan for the goal while ignoring these threats, there is a guarantee that the partial ordering in the resulting plan can be extended to eliminate the threats.

Our technique involves: 1) construction of an *operator graph* that captures the interaction between operators relevant to a given goal, 2) decomposition of this graph into groups of related threats, and 3) postponement of threats with certain properties.

1 Introduction

In (McAllester & Rosenblitt 1991), the authors present a simple elegant algorithm for systematic partial-order planning (SNLP). Much recent planning work (Barrett & Weld 1993, Collins & Prior 1992, Kambhampati 1992, Penberthy & Weld 1992, Peot & Smith 1992) has been based upon this algorithm.

In the SNLP algorithm, when threats arise between steps and causal links in a partial plan, those threats are resolved before attempting to satisfy any remaining open conditions in the partial plan. In (Peot & Smith 1993) we investigate several other strategies for resolving threats. Although some of these strategies work much better than the SNLP strategy, they are all fixed, dumb strategies. In practice, we know that some threats that occur during planning are easy to resolve, while others are difficult to resolve. What we would like is a smarter threat-selection strategy that can recognize and delay resolution of the easy threats in order to concentrate effort on the difficult ones.

In this paper, we present techniques for automatically deciding whether threats should be resolved during partial-order planning, or delayed until planning is otherwise complete. In particular, we show that certain threats can be provably delayed until the end; that is, if the planner can find a plan for the goal while ignoring these threats, there is

a guarantee that the partial ordering in the resulting plan can be extended to eliminate the threats.

In Section 2, we construct *operator graph*s that capture the interaction between operators relevant to a goal and set of initial conditions. In Section 3, we develop theorems and decomposition rules that use the operator graph to decide when threats can be postponed. In Section 4 we discuss our experience with these techniques and related work.

For purposes of this paper, we adopt a simple STRIPS model of action, and assume the SNLP model of planning. Many of the results and ideas can be applied to other causal-link planners such as (Kambhampati 1993, Tate 1977). Full proofs of the theorems appear in (Smith & Peot 1993).

2 Operator graphs

Following (McAllester & Rosenblitt 1991), we define special Start and Finish operators for a problem:

Definition 1: The Start operator for a problem is defined as the operator having no preconditions, and having all of the initial conditions as effects. The Finish operator for a problem is defined as the operator having no effects, and having all of the goal clauses as preconditions.

Given these operators we construct an operator graph for a problem recursively, according to the following rules:

Definition 2: An *operator graph* for a problem is a directed bipartite graph consisting of *precondition nodes* and *operator nodes* such that:

1. There is an operator node for the Finish operator.

2. If an operator node is in the graph, there is a precondition node in the graph for each precondition of the operator and a directed edge from the precondition node to the operator node.

3. If a precondition node is in the graph, there is an operator node in the graph for every operator with an effect that unifies with the precondition and there is a directed edge from the operator node to the precondition node.

To illustrate, consider the simple set of operators below (relations, operator names, and constants are capitalized, variables are lower case):

Shape(x)
  Prec's: Object(x), ¬ Fastened(x, z)
  Effects: Shaped(x), ¬ Drilled(x)
Drill(x)
  Prec's: Object(x), ¬ Fastened(x, z)
  Effects: Drilled(x)
Bolt(x, y)
  Prec's: Drilled(x), Drilled(y)
  Effects: Fastened(x, y)
Glue(x, y)
  Prec's: Object(x), ¬ Fastened(x, z),
            Object(y), ¬ Fastened(y, z)
  Effects: Fastened(x, y)

Suppose that the goal is

Shaped(x) ∧ Shaped(y) ∧ Fastened(x, y),

and the initial conditions are:

Object(A) ¬Fastened(A, z)
Object(B) ¬Fastened(B, z)

...   ...

The operator graph for this problem is shown in Figure 1. Note that each operator appears at most once in the

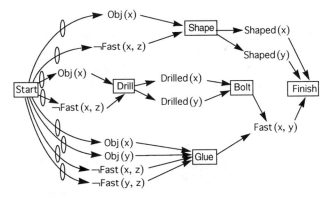

Figure 1: Operator graph for simple machine shop problem. Fastened and Object have been abbreviated for clarity. Circled arcs represent a bundle of arcs.

graph; but a clause such as Object(x) may appear more than once, if it appears more than once as a precondition. Note that the graph can also contain cycles. If the Bolt operator had an effect Drilled(z) there would be directed edges from Bolt(x, y) to both Drilled(x) and Drilled(y), forming loops with the directed edges from Drilled(x) and Drilled(y) to Bolt(x,y). In this paper we will only consider acyclic operator graphs. The basic results and techniques also apply to cyclic graphs, but the definitions

and theorems are more complicated. The full theory is given in (Smith & Peot 1993).

The operator graph tells us what operators are relevant to the goal, and also tells us something about the topology of partial plans that will be generated for the problem. In this example, it tells us that if the Bolt operation appears in the plan, at least one Drill operation will precede it in the plan. The operator graph has an implicit *and/or* structure to it. Predecessors of an operator node are *ands*, since all preconditions of the operator must be achieved. Predecessors of a precondition node are *ors*, since they correspond to different possible operators that could be used to achieve the precondition.

2.1 Use Count

In the example above, the Glue and Bolt operators are used for only one purpose, while the Drill and Shape operators are used for more than one purpose. This information is important for our analysis of operator threats. We therefore introduce the following notion:

Definition 3: The *use count* of a node in the graph is defined as the number of directed paths from the node to Finish.

The use count of an operator is an upper bound on the number of times the operator could appear in a partial plan. It can be infinite for graphs with cycles.

2.2 Threats

So far, operator graphs only tell us which subgoals and operators may be useful for a problem.

Definition 4: Let O be an operator node, and P be a precondition node in an operator graph. If some effect of O unifies with the negation of P we say that O threatens P and denote this by O ⊗ P.

The threats for our example are shown in Figure 2.

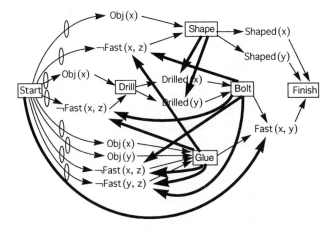

Figure 2: Operator graph with threats (heavy lines).

2.3 Eliminating Threats

Not all threats in the operator graph are important. Some of them will never actually occur during planning. In particular, consider the threat from Start to Fastened(x, y). The initial conditions operator always precedes all other operators in a plan. As a result, there is no possibility that Start can ever clobber an effect produced by another operator. Therefore we can eliminate these threats from the graph.

Theorem 1: Threats emanating from Start can be eliminated.

A related class of threats are those between operators and preconditions that are successors of each other. Consider the threat from Glue(x, y) to its precondition ¬Fastened(x, z). This says that gluing clobbers its precondition. This is not a problem since the clobbering follows the consumption of the precondition. As a result, this threat can be eliminated. Similar arguments can be made for the threat from Bolt(x, y) to the ¬Fastened(x, z) precondition of Drill(x).

Note that our arguments rely on the fact that Glue and Bolt will only appear once in the final plan. If Glue(x, y) appeared more than once, there is a distinct possibility that one gluing operation might clobber the precondition of another gluing operation. As a result, we can only eliminate such threats when the use count of the operator is 1.

Theorem 2: Threats from an operator to any predecessor or successor in the graph can be eliminated if the threatening operator has use count 1.

A third source of superfluous threats are *disjunctive* branches in the operator graph. In our example, there are two different ways of achieving the subgoal Fastened(x, y): bolting and gluing. Only one of these two alternatives will appear in any given plan. As a result, we can ignore threats that go from one branch to the other. This means that the edges from Bolt(x, y) to the ¬Fastened preconditions of Glue(x, y), and from Glue(x, y) to the ¬Fastened(x, z) precondition of Drill(x) can be eliminated.

As with Theorem 2, we need to consider use count. Suppose that there was a second subgoal of the form Fastened(x, y). The planner might choose Bolt(x, y) for one of these subgoals, and Glue(x, y) for the other. In this case, a threat between Bolt(x, y) and the ¬Fastened(x, y) precondition of Glue(x, y) could occur.

Theorem 3: If a threat is between two disjunctive branches in the operator graph, and the threatening operator has use count 1, the threat can be eliminated.

To decide if a threat is between two disjunctive branches we need to look at the nearest common ancestor of the threatening operator and precondition. For the threat between Bolt(x, y) and the ¬Fastened(x, y) precondition of Glue(x, y), the nearest common ancestor is Fastened(x, y). Since this is a precondition node, the threat is between disjunctive branches.

After applying Theorems 1, 2, and 3, there are only four remaining threats, as shown in Figure 3. These are the only possible threats that can actually arise during planning.

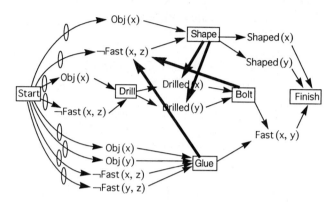

Figure 3: Threats remaining after the elimination theorems have been applied.

3 Postponing Threats

In Figure 3, consider the threats Shape(x) ⊗ Drilled(x) and Shape(x) ⊗ Drilled(y). These threats tell us that allowing Shape operations to occur between Drill and Bolt operations may cause problems. However, in considering the graph, we can see that there is an easy solution. If we add the ordering constraint that Shape operations must occur before Drill operations, both threats are eliminated.

We could have the planner automatically add these constraints every time Shape or Drill operations were added to a partial plan. Although this strategy would work, it is more restrictive than necessary. In our example, if two different objects, A and B are used for x and y, there would be two different Shape operations, and two different Drill operations in the final plan. To get rid of the threats it would only be necessary that Shape(A) precede Drill(A) and Shape(B) precede Drill(B). The other potential threats go away by virtue of the different variable bindings for x and y.

To avoid this over-commitment, it is better to *postpone* the threats between Shape(x) and Drilled(x). No matter what plan is generated, we can always eliminate this threat *later* by imposing the necessary ordering constraints between Shape and Drill operations.

The argument made above relies on two things:

1. There are ordering constraints that will resolve the threats,

2. The other potential threats do not interfere with these ordering constraints.

The first part of this argument is straightforward; in our case, demoting Shape before Drill did the trick, since it prevents Shape from occurring between Drill and Bolt. The second part of the argument is tougher. It requires showing that none of the possible resolutions of the remaining threats will prevent the ordering of Shape operations before Drill operations. To show this, we need to consider all possible ways that the planner might choose to resolve the remaining set of threats.

First consider the threat Bolt(x, y) ⊗ ¬Fastened(x, y). Since Bolt cannot come before Start, demotion is not possible for this threat. However, promotion is possible, since Shape < Bolt is consistent with the operator graph. We therefore need to consider the possibility that this constraint might be added to the operator graph. (Separation is not possible in this case. Even if it were, separation adds no ordering constraints to the graph, and therefore does not concern us.)

Next consider the threat Glue(x, y) ⊗ ¬Fastened(x, y). As before, demotion is not possible since Glue cannot come before Start. However, promotion is possible, since Shape < Glue is consistent with both the operator graph, and with the constraint Shape < Bolt.

Since the addition of Shape < Glue and Shape < Bolt do not interfere with Shape < Drill, condition (2) is also satisfied.

The general form of this argument is summarized in the following theorem:

Theorem 4: Let T be the set of threats in an operator graph, and let P be a subset of those threats. The threats in P can be postponed if there is a set of ordering constraints that resolves the threats in P for every possible resolution of the remaining threats in T − P.

Proof Sketch: Suppose that SNLP ignores all threats corresponding to the threats P in the operator graph. Consider a final plan F produced by SNLP. Let R be the set of threats that were resolved in the construction of F. The threats in R are instances of the threats T-P in the operator graph. Thus there is some resolution of threats in T-P that corresponds to the resolution of R in the plan. By our hypothesis, there is some set of ordering constraints in the operator graph that resolves the threats in P, for each possible resolution of T-P. These ordering constraints will therefore resolve any instances of P ignored during the construction of F. As a result, there is an extension of the partial ordering of F that will resolve all of the postponed threats. Since F was an arbitrary plan, the theorem follows.

Corollary 5: Let T be the set of threats in an operator graph. The (entire) set of threats T can be postponed if there is a set of ordering constraints that resolves the threats in T.

In the machine shop example, we could use Corollary 5 to postpone the entire set of threats at once, since the three ordering constraints Shape < Drill, Shape < Glue, and Shape < Bolt resolve all four of the threats. In general, however, this corollary cannot be applied as frequently as Theorem 4. The reason is that this corollary requires the resolution of all threats by ordering constraints. There may be some threats that can only be resolved by separation during planning or that cannot be resolved. In these cases Corollary 5 cannot be applied, but Theorem 4 may still allow us to postpone some subset of the threats. As an example, consider the operator graph shown in Figure 4.

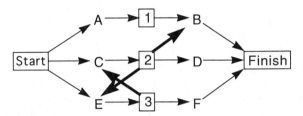

Figure 4: Operator graph where only two of the three threats can be postponed.

In this example, the two threats 2 ⊗ E and 3 ⊗ C can only be resolved by separation. However, the threat 2 ⊗ B can always be resolved by imposing the ordering constraint 2 < 1 (demotion). Since demotion is consistent with the only possible resolution of the remaining threats, the threat 2 ⊗ B can be postponed according to Theorem 4.

3.1 Over-constraining

The primary difficulty with applying Theorem 4 and Corollary 5 is that they both take time that is exponential in the number of threats being considered. In fact it can be shown that:

Theorem 6: Given a partial ordering and a set of threats, it is NP-complete to determine whether there exists an extension to the partial ordering that will resolve the threats.

The proof of this theorem (Kautz 1992) involves a reduction of 3-SAT clauses to a partial ordering and set of threats. The complete proof can be found in (Smith & Peot 1993).

Although the general problem of postponing threats is computationally hard, there are some special cases that are more tractable. The first technique that we consider involves over-constraining the operator graph. In particular, we simultaneously impose both promotion and demotion ordering constraints on the operator graph for all threats in the graph but one. We then check to see if there is an ordering constraint on the remaining threat (demotion or promotion) that is still possible in the over-constrained graph. If so, we know that the ordering constraint will work for all possible resolutions of the remaining threats, and we can therefore postpone the threat. More precisely:

Theorem 7: Let t be the threat $O_t \otimes \left(O_p \overset{g}{\to} O_c \right)$. For each remaining threat $r_t \otimes \left(r_p \overset{g}{\to} r_c \right)$ in the operator graph augment the operator graph with the edges $r_t \to r_p$ and $r_c \to r_t$. The threat t can be postponed if either:

1. $O_t < O_p$ is consistent with the operator graph, and $O_p \notin \text{Predecessors}(O_t)$ in the augmented operator graph.

2. $O_c < O_t$ is consistent with the operator graph, and $O_c \notin \text{Successors}(O_t)$ in the augmented operator graph.

Proof Sketch: Let A be the set of augmentation edges added to the graph. Every consistent way of resolving the set of remaining threats corresponds to some subset of these constraints. Suppose that case 1 holds for the above theorem. Since $O_p \notin \text{Predecessors}(O_t)$ in the augmented graph, we know that it will also hold for every subset of the augmentation edges. As a result, we know that this condition holds for every possible way of resolving the remaining threats in the graph. Furthermore, in a consistent graph, $O_p \notin \text{Predecessors}(O_t)$ implies that t can be resolved by demotion. As a result, Theorem 4 says that t can be postponed. The argument for case 2 is analogous.

To see how this theorem applies, consider the threat $\text{Glue}(x,y) \otimes \neg\text{Fastened}(x,z)$ in Figure 3. To see if this threat can be postponed, we need to augment the operator graph with all ordering constraints that resolve the remaining three threats. For the threat $\text{Bolt}(x,y) \otimes \neg\text{Fastened}(x,z)$ we need to add the edge $\text{Shape}(x) \to \text{Bolt}(x,y)$ to the graph, since it is the only way of resolving the threat. For the other two threats, $\text{Shape}(x) \otimes \text{Drilled}(x)$ and $\text{Shape}(x) \otimes \text{Drilled}(y)$, we need to add the two edges $\text{Shape}(x) \to \text{Drill}(x)$ and $\text{Bolt}(x,y) \to \text{Shape}(x)$. The resulting graph is shown in Figure 5.

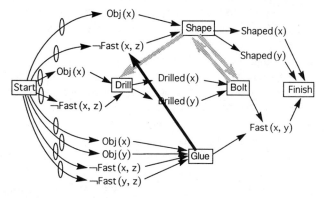

Figure 5: Machine shop example with over-constrained threats. Partial-ordering constraints are shown as grey arrows.

Now consider the two possibilities for resolving $\text{Glue}(x,y) \otimes \neg\text{Fastened}(x,z)$. Glue cannot be ordered before Start in the operator graph, so case 1 is out. Glue can be ordered after Shape, however, so we need to consider case 2. In the augmented graph, the only successor of Glue is Finish. Since Shape is not in this set, the second condition is satisfied. Therefore we can postpone the threat $\text{Glue}(x,y) \otimes \neg\text{Fastened}(x,z)$.

Theorem 7 can also be used to show that each of the remaining threats in the machine shop problem can be postponed. More generally, Theorem 7 can be applied in a serial fashion: after one threat is postponed, it does not need to be considered in the analysis of subsequent threats.

3.2 Threat Blocks

Although Theorem 7 is considerably weaker than Theorem 4, it can be applied in time that is linear in the size of the operator graph. As a result, it can often be used to quickly eliminate many of the easiest threats from consideration. Unfortunately, there are some sets of threats where the full power of Theorem 4 is still needed. Consider the graph shown in Figure 6. The four threats shown in the top half of

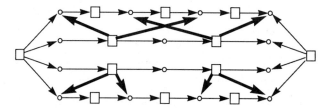

Figure 6: Threat graph with difficult threats.

the graph can be resolved and postponed using Theorem 4 but not Theorem 7. The set of threats in the bottom half of the graph cannot be resolved using only ordering constraints, and therefore cannot be postponed. In a case like this, the top and bottom halves of the graph are independent, and we should be able to examine the threats in the two halves separately.

To do this we first need some definitions. We define a block as a subset of an operator graph having a common beginning and ending. More precisely:

Definition 5: Let Begin and End be two operators such that Begin is a predecessor of End in the operator graph. A *block* is a subset of the operator graph (ignoring threats), such that, for each node N in the block:

1. Begin occurs on all paths from Start to N.

2. End occurs on all paths from N to Finish.

3. Every node and edge on a path from Begin to N is in the block.

4. Every node and edge on a path from N to End is in the block.

In the graph above, each of the four branches constitutes a block. Any two or three of these branches also constitute a block.

Definition 6: A *threat block* is a block where all threats that touch any node in the block are contained completely within the block. A threat block is *minimal* if no subset of the block is a threat block.

According to this definition, there are two minimal threat blocks in the above graph, one containing the top two and one containing the bottom two branches.

Theorems 4 and 7 can now be extended to threat blocks. We restate Theorem 4 for threat blocks.

Theorem 8: Let T be the set of threats in a minimal threat block and let P be a subset of those threats. The threats in P can be postponed if there is a set of ordering constraints that resolves the threats in P for every possible resolution of the remaining threats in T − P.

Proof Sketch: Consider the set of threats not in the threat block. If we consider every possible way of resolving these outside threats it is easy to see that the resulting ordering constraints can have no impact on any ordering decisions within the block. Thus, if the conditions of Theorem 8 hold, we can expand the set T to include the threats outside the block and Theorem 4 will apply.

Using this theorem, we could examine and postpone the threats in the top half of the graph of Figure 6.

It is relatively easy to find minimal threat blocks. We start with one threat, and find the common descendents and ancestors of both ends of the threat. If other threats are encountered in the process, we include the endpoints of these new threats in our search for a common ancestor and descendent. With pre-numbering of the graph, this process can be done in time linear in the size of the graph.

4 Discussion

4.1 Implementation

In our current implementation, we first attempt to eliminate as many individual threats as possible using Theorem 7. After this, we construct minimal threat blocks for the remaining threats. We then use Corollary 5 on each individual threat block. We have not yet implemented the more powerful Theorems 4 or 8, but expect to apply them only after other more tractable alternatives have failed.

Our preliminary testing indicates several things:

1. The number of threats that can be postponed varies widely across problems and domains. As we would expect, many more threats can be post-

poned in domains with loosely-coupled operators. The techniques do little to help highly recursive sets of operators.

2. The time taken to build an operator graph and analyze threats is computationally insignificant in comparison to the time required to do planning. For non-trivial planning problems, this time is less than 10% of planning time, and is often much smaller than that.

Our experience suggests that the speed of these procedures is not a concern and that even the use of Theorem 8 on threat blocks will probably not cause serious computational problems. We speculate that if the threats in a block are so numerous and tangled that the speed of these techniques is a problem, the planner is in deep trouble anyway.

4.2 Related Work

Both (Etzioni 1993) and (Knoblock 1990, 1991) have proposed goal ordering mechanisms to reduce the number of threats that arise during planning. In particular, Etzioni and Knoblock construct and analyze graphs similar to the operator graphs developed here. Etzioni derives goal-ordering rules from this graph, while Knoblock constructs predicate hierarchies to guide a hierarchical planner. Unfortunately, both of these systems were developed for a total-order planner. In a total-order planner the order in which goals are processed affects the ordering of actions in the plan. This, in turn, determines the presence or absence of threats in the plan.

In contrast, for partial-order planning, the order in which goals are processed does not determine the ordering of actions within the plan. As a consequence, goal ordering does not affect the presence or absence of threats in the plan, and cannot be used to help reduce threats. Although goal ordering can be used to reduce search in partial-order planning (Smith 1988, Smith & Peot 1992), it cannot be used to reduce the number of threats. A more detailed critique of Knoblock's technique can be found in (Smith & Peot 1992).

4.3 Extensions

Originally, we thought it was possible to use local analysis techniques to postpone many threats. However, all of our conjectures in this area have proven false. The one area that we think still holds promise is division into threat blocks. We think that there may be criteria that will allow threats to be broken up into smaller blocks.

Another approach that we think holds promise is variable analysis in the operator graph (Etzioni 1993). By a careful analysis of variable bindings in the operator graph, it is often possible to eliminate many phantom threats from the graph. This, in turn, makes it more likely that other threats can be postponed.

There are other possibilities for analysis of the operator graph, including analysis of potential loops. Here, the recognition and elimination of unnecessary loops among the operators can allow the postponement of additional threats. Some of these possibilities are discussed in (Smith & Peot 1993).

4.4 Final Remarks

The techniques developed in this paper have a direct impact on the efficiency of the planning process. Whenever possible, they separate the tasks of selecting actions from the task of ordering or scheduling those actions. This is a natural extension of the least-commitment strategy inherent to partial-order planning.

But perhaps as important as threat postponement is the ability to recognize threats that are difficult to resolve. If a block of threats cannot be postponed, the planner should pay attention to those threats early. This information could be used to help the planner avoid partial plans with difficult threat blocks. It could also be used to help determine the order in which to work on open conditions. In particular, if the planner is faced with a difficult threat block it should probably generate and resolve that portion of the plan early. In our experience, both the choice of partial plan and the choice of open condition can dramatically influence the performance of a planner. For this reason, information about difficult threat blocks could make a significant difference.

Acknowledgments

The idea of analyzing threats in the operator graph was motivated by the work of Craig Knoblock (Knoblock 1990, 1991). Thanks to Mark Drummond, Steve Minton, Craig Knoblock, and Oren Etzioni for comments and discussion. Thanks to Henry Kautz and David McAllester for help with the NP-completeness result. This work is supported by DARPA contract F30602-91-C-0031.

References

Barrett, A. and Weld, D. 1993. Partial-Order Planning: Evaluating Possible Efficiency Gains, Technical Report 92-05-01, Dept. of Computer Science, University of Washington.

Collins, G., and Pryor, L. 1992. Representation and Performance in a Partial Order Planner, Technical Report 35, The Institute for the Learning Sciences, Northwestern University.

Etzioni, O. 1993. Acquiring Search-Control Knowledge via Static Analysis, *Artificial Intelligence*, to appear.

Harvey, W. 1993. Deferring Threat Resolution Retains Systematicity, Technical Note, Department of Computer Science, Stanford University.

Kambhampati, S. 1992. Characterizing Multi-Contributor Causal Structures for Planning, *In Proceedings of the First International Conference on AI Planning Systems*, College Park, Maryland, 116-125.

Kambhampati, S. 1993. On the Utility of Systematicity: Understanding Tradeoffs between Redundancy and Commitment in Partial-Ordering Planning, *In Proceedings of the Thirteenth International Conference on AI*, Chambéry, France.

Kautz, H. 1992, personal communication.

Knoblock, C. 1990, Learning abstraction hierarchies for problem solving. *In Proceedings of the Eight National Conference on AI*, Boston, MA, 923–928.

Knoblock, C. 1991. Automatically Generating Abstractions for Problem Solving, Technical Report CMU-CS-91-120, Dept. of Computer Science, Carnegie Mellon University.

McAllester, D., and Rosenblitt, D. 1991. Systematic non-linear planning, *In Proceedings of the Ninth National Conference on AI*, Anaheim, CA, 634–639.

Penberthy, J. S., and Weld, D. 1992. UCPOP: A Sound, Complete, Partial Order Planner for ADL, *In Proceedings of the Third International Conference on Knowledge Representation and Reasoning*, Cambridge, MA.

Peot, M., and Smith, D. 1992. Conditional Nonlinear Planning, *In Proceedings of the First International Conference on AI Planning Systems*, College Park, MD, 189-197.

Peot, M., and Smith, D. 1993. Threat-removal Strategies for Partial-Order Planning, *In Proceedings of the Eleventh National Conference on AI*, Washington, D.C.

Smith, D. 1988. A Decision Theoretic Approach to the Control of Planning Search., Technical Report 87-11, Stanford Logic Group, Department of Computer Science, Stanford University.

Smith, D., and Peot, M. 1992. A Critical Look at Knoblock's Hierarchy Mechanism, *In Proceedings of the First International Conference on AI Planning Systems*, College Park, Maryland, 307-308.

Smith, D., and Peot, M. 1993. Threat Analysis in Partial-Order Planning. Forthcoming.

Tate, A. 1977. Generating Project Networks, *In Proceedings of the Fifth International Joint Conference on AI*, Boston, MA, 888-893.

Yang, Q., A Theory of Conflict Resolution in Planning, *Artificial Intelligence*, 58:361–392, 1992.

Plan
Learning

PERMISSIVE PLANNING: A MACHINE LEARNING APPROACH TO LINKING INTERNAL AND EXTERNAL WORLDS

Gerald DeJong dejong@cs.uiuc.edu
Computer Science / Beckman Institute
University of Illinois at Urbana/Champaign
405 N. Mathews, Urbana IL 61801

Scott Bennett bennett@sra.com
Systems Research and Applications Corporation

2000 15th St. North
Arlington VA 22201

Abstract

Because complex real–world domains defy perfect formalization, real–world planners must be able to cope with incorrect domain knowledge. This paper offers a theoretical framework for *permissive planning*, a machine learning method for improving the real–world behavior of planners. Permissive planning aims to acquire techniques that tolerate the inevitable mismatch between the planner's internal beliefs and the external world. Unlike the reactive approach to this mismatch, permissive planning embraces projection. The method is both problem–independent and domain–independent. Unlike classical planning, permissive planning does not exclude real–world performance from the formal definition of planning.

Introduction

An important facet of AI planning is *projection*, the process by which a system anticipates attributes of a future world state from knowledge of an initial state and the intervening actions. A planner's projection ability is often flawed. A classical planner can prove goal achievement only to be thwarted by reality. The reactive approach, which has received much attention, avoids these problems by reducing reliance on projection or disallowing it altogether. For all its stimulating effect on the field, however, reactivity is only one path around projection problems. It is important to continue searching for and researching alternatives. In this paper we advance one such alternative termed *permissive planning*. In some ways it is the dual of the reactive approach, relying heavily on a goal projection ability enhanced by machine learning. From a broader perspective, permissive planning embodies an approach to inference which integrates empirical observations into a traditional *a priori* domain axiomatization.

The research reported in this paper was carried out at the University of Illinois and was supported by the Office of Naval Research under grant N0001491–J–1563. The authors also wish to thank Renee Baillargeon, Pat Hayes, Jon Gratch and the anonymous reviewers for helpful comments.

Permissive Planning

The real world is captured within an inference system by some description in a formal language such as the predicate calculus. The system's internal description may only approximate the external real world, giving rise to discrepancies between inferred and observed world behavior. In classical planning, the difficulties with projection can be traced to such a discrepancy, in this case, a discrepancy between an action's *internal* definition (the one represented and reasoned about) and its *external* definition (the mapping enforced by the real world). To concentrate on the discrepancies of action definitions, we will assume in this paper that no difficulty is introduced by the system's sensing or state representation abilities. Then, for simplicity in our figures, we can employ a single universe of states to denote both internal and external sets of states. Figure 1 illustrates a difference between a plan's proj-

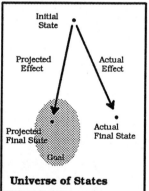

Figure 1: An Action Sequence's
Projected and Actual Mappings

ected and actual mappings from an initial state. The dot labeled *initial state* represents both a particular configuration of the world (which we call the external state) and the system's formal description of it (the internal state). According to the system's internal model, the plan's action sequence transforms the initial state into a goal state. In the real world, however, the actual final state falls well outside the goal region.

One might employ machine learning to improve the system's operator definitions. The result would be a more faithful representation of their real–world effects. This would yield a more accurate projection ability as illustrated in Figure 2. Un-

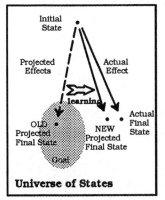
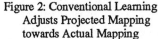

Figure 2: Conventional Learning Adjusts Projected Mapping towards Actual Mapping

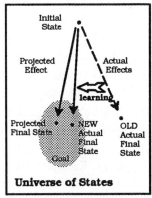

Figure 3: Permissive Planning Adjusts Actual Mapping towards Projected Mapping

fortunately, a trend toward increasingly correct operator definitions is necessarily also a trend towards more complex operator definitions. Increased complexity results in more work for the planner which must rule out concomitantly more negative interactions. Indeed, operator complexity can grow unboundedly as dictated by the qualification problem [McCarthy80]. With sufficient experience, this use of machine learning could paralyze any planner.

There is an alternative machine learning approach. When an apparently sound plan fails to achieve its goal in the real world, it may be possible to find a small alteration of the plan which tends not to influence the *projected* final state but moves the *actual* final state closer to the projected one. Instead of altering the system's representations to better fit the observed world (Figure 2), this approach alters the actions selected so the real–world effects better match the projected effects. This is illustrated in Figure 3. If such a plan can be found, the planner itself might be altered so that when presented with similar future problems, the planner will tend to produce a solution similar to the improved plan rather than repeating the mistakes of the the original plan. Our approach is to alter systematically the planner in response to execution failures so the planner prefers not to employ its domain knowledge in ways that seem to lead to failure. We call the approach "permissive" because it allows the planner to construct plans that work in the real world in spite of flaws in its domain knowledge.

Permissive Planning Principle: Blame the plan and adjust the planner in response to execution failures even though the implementor–supplied domain theory is known to be at fault.

Planner Bias and Permissive Planning Adjustment

In response to the need for breakfast a planner may be able to formulate several acceptable action sequences. One results in pancakes, another in cold raisin bran cereal, still another in hot oatmeal, etc. Of course, most planners will not produce all possible plans. Planning activity typically ceases when the first acceptable solution is found. After constructing an acceptable plan for a hot oatmeal breakfast, the system should not waste effort in working out the details for cooking pancakes.

We call the set of all possible plans that a particular classical planner could produce in principle for a problem, the *competence set* of the planner for that planning problem. We call the particular element of this set which is in fact constructed in response to the problem the *performance* of the planner for that planning problem. We use the term *planner bias* to refer to the preference, no matter how it is realized, for the particular performance plan from the planner's competence set. By systematically altering a planner's bias in response to observed plan execution failures, the same planning competence can yield quite different planning performance, resulting in improved real–world behavior. The permissive adjustment of a planner's bias so as to improve the real–world success of its performance behavior can be seen as applying the permissive planning principle above: the planner is blamed and its bias adjusted even though the offending projection failures are due to inaccurate operator definitions.

In this view of planning, actions may have different *internal* and *external* effects. We will say that an action sequence *ISolves* a planning problem the goal holds in the projection of the initial state through the sequence. The sequence *ESolves* the problem if the goal is achieved in the real world by executing sequence **s** from the initial state.

In the planning literature, it is not uncommon to view a plan as a collection of constraints [Chapman87, Wilkins88]. We subscribe to this notion but carry it a bit further. For us, a *plan* for a planning problem is any set of constraints which *individuates* an action sequence such that the action sequence ISolves the planning problem. The accepted nonlinear view (e.g., [Chapman87, Sacerdoti75, Wilkins88]), is similar but does not require the individuation of an action sequence. A typical non–linear planner imposes constraints only until *all* action sequences consistent with the constraints are guaranteed to reach a goal state (i.e., each ISolves the planning problem). Stopping here allows a notion of minimal planning commitment. Remaining ambiguities are left for plan execution when they are resolved in the most propitious manner available in the execution environment. Our definition of a plan is more restrictive. We allow no ambiguities for later resolution. This requirement follows from our desire to adjust the planner's bias. We wish to incorporate the entire decision procedure resulting in an action sequence within the planner proper. Only then can the permissive adjustment procedure have access to the full bias reflected in the executable actions.

We use the informal term *partial plan* to refer to a set of constraints which is intended to solve a particular planning problem but does not yet individuate an action sequence.

A planner (including its bias) is *adequate* if 1) whenever a plan is produced that ISolves a problem it also ESolves the problem, and 2) whenever the planner fails to find a plan its competence set contains no plan whose action sequence ESolves the problem.

Finally, a *planning computation* is a finite sequence of decisions, $D_i, \{i=1,...n\}$. Each decision selects a constraint, c_i, to be added to the partial plan from a (possibly infinite) set of alternatives $\{a_{i,1}, a_{i,2}, a_{i,3}...\}$ entertained by the planner for that decision, so that $c_i \in \{a_{i,1}, a_{i,2}, a_{i,3}...\}$. The partial plan (which is initially the empty set of constraints) is augmented with the new decision's constraint, resulting in a (possibly) more restrictive constraint set. A planning computation is successful if, at its termination, there is exactly one distinct action sequence consistent with the set of constraints and that action sequence ISolves the planning problem.

Planning, in this framework, is repeatedly entertaining alternative constraint sets and for each, selecting one constraint to be imposed on the partial plan. This is not to say that every planner must *explicitly* represent the alternative constraint sets. But every planner's behavior can be construed in this way. From this perspective, a planner's competence is determined by the sets of alternatives that the planner can entertain. A (possibly empty) subset of alternatives from each constraint set supports successful plan completion. The planner's competence is precisely the set of all possible successful plans given the entertained alternatives. A planner's performance, on the other hand, is determined by its particular choice at each point from among the subset of alternatives which support a successful computation continuation.

The Permissive Planning Algorithm

A planning bias is any strategy for designating a particular element from among sets of valid continuation alternatives. Permissive adjustment of a planner is an empirically–driven search through the space of possible biases. Searching for an alternative bias is evoked whenever inadequate real–world planning behavior is observed.

In practice, the bias space is extremely large and the permissive planning search must be strongly guided by domain knowledge. If such domain knowledge is unavailable, the algorithm continues to have its formal properties. However, we believe that the practical ease with which suitable domain knowledge can be formulated will largely govern when the permissive planning approach will be useful. The permissive planning algorithm:
1. Initialize Candidate_Bias_Set to the space of all biases.
2. Using domain knowledge select an element from the Candidate_Bias_Set, call it Current_Bias.
3. Solve planning problems using Current_Bias. If an executed plan fails to achieve its goal go to 4.
4. Delete all biases from Candidate_Bias_Set that are provably inadequate using domain knowledge (including at least Current_Bias).
5. If Candidate_Bias_Set is not empty, Go To 2.
6. FAIL, no adequate bias exists.

As will become clear in the example, domain knowledge, in the form of qualitative information relating operators' effects to their arguments, can substantially increase the efficiency of permissive planning by guiding the selection of a promising bias in step 2 and increasing the number of untried but guaranteed inadequate biases rejected in step 4.

It can be easily proven when the algorithm terminates an adequate planner has been produced. Further, it can be proven that the algorithm will terminate so long as the bias space possesses some modest properties. On advice from an anonymous reviewer these proofs have been deleted in favor of more substantial discussions of other issues.

An Example of Permissive Planning

Suppose we have a two–dimensional gantry–type robot arm whose task is to move past an obstacle to position itself above a target (see Figure 4). The operators are **LEFT**, **RIGHT**,

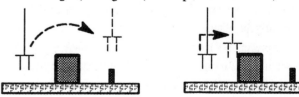

Figure 4: Goal to Move Past an Obstacle

Figure 5: Collision Observed During Execution

OPEN, **CLOSE**, **UP**, and **DOWN**, which each take an amount as an argument. The obstacle is 2.5 units high, the tip of the hand is 1.2 units above the table, and the front face of the target is

4.201 units from the left finger. The planner's native bias results in a plan individuating the action sequence: **UP(1.4) RIGHT(4.2)**. Figure 6 shows the alternatives entertained. Shaded alternatives indicate the competence selections given the constraints already adopted. The performance selection for each decision is outlined in a solid white box.

The first decision selects **UP**. The second decision selects a value for the parameter to **UP**. Any value greater than 1.3 up to the ceiling is possible according to the system's internal world. The value 1.4 is selected. Finally, **RIGHT** is selected with an argument of 4.2.

During execution a collision is detected. Permissive processing is invoked which explains the most likely collision in qualitative terms. The problem deemed most likely is the one requiring the least distortion of the internal projection. In this case, the most likely collision is with the obstacle block; the height of the gripper fingers is judged too low for the height of the obstacle as shown in Figure 5. The planning decisions are examined in turn for alternative competence set elements which can qualitatively reduce the diagnosed error. In this case it amounts to looking for alternatives that, according to the operators' qualitative descriptions, increase the distance between the finger tip and the top of the obstacle. Decision 2 is a candidate for adjustment. Higher values for decision 2 do not influence the projected goal achievement in the internal world but appear qualitatively to improve avoidance of the observed collision. The resulting plan is generalized in standard EBL fashion [DeJong86] resulting in a new schema which might be called **REACH–OVER–OBSTACLE**. It embodies specialized bias knowledge that, in the context of this schema, the highest possible value consistent with the internal world model should be selected as the parameter for the **UP** action. The new performance choice is illustrated in Figure 6 by a dashed white box.

From now on, the robot will retreat to the ceiling when reaching over an obstacle. If other failures are encountered, permissive planning would once again be invoked resulting in additional or alternative refinements. If no further refinement can be constructed, the schema forces a hard planning failure; none of the elements of the systems performance set is empirically adequate. Although the internal model supports solutions, this class of planning problems cannot be reliably solved in the external world. Any adequate planner must fail to offer a plan for such a class of planning problems.

Bias Space

What constitutes a bias space and how does one go about selecting a particular bias? These are important practical questions. If there is no convenient way to construct a searchable bias space, then permissive planning is of little consequence. The required *theoretical* properties are modest and do not significantly restrict what can and cannot serve as a bias space.

In fact it is quite easy to construct an effectively searchable bias space. We employ a method for the example above and for the **GRASPER** system based on problem–solving schemata (generalized macro–operators). Each schema represents a parameterized solution to a class of planning problems (like **REACH–OVER–OBSTACLE**). When the planner is given a new planning problem, the schema library is examined first. If no schema is relevant, a standard searching planner is applied to the problem. If a schema is found, the schema specifies how the problem is to be dealt with, and the native searching planner is not invoked. Thus, the schema library acts as a variable sieve, intercepting some planning problems while letting the native planner deal with the rest.

One practical difficulty with this method of bias adjustment is the utility problem [Minton88]. However, this is a separate issue from planner adequacy. Furthermore, recent research [Gratch92, Greiner92] has shown effective methods for attacking the utility problem that are consistent with this view of permissive planning.

Empirical Evidence

We have implemented a permissive planner, called **GRASPER**, and tested its planning on two domains using a real–world robot manipulator. Here we summarize the results of two experiments. Readers are referred to [Bennett93] for details of the system and the experimental domains.

Experiment 1. The task is to grasp and lift designated objects from the table with the gripper even though the gripper's actual movements are only imprecisely captured by the sys-

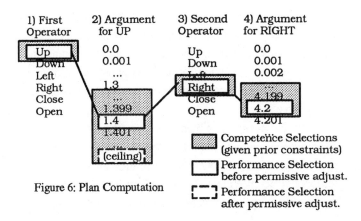

Figure 6: Plan Computation

tem's operator knowledge. Objects are known only by their silhouette as sensed by an over–head television camera. This experiment consists of an experimental and a control condition. Twelve plastic pieces of a children's puzzle were each assigned a random position and orientation within the robot's working envelope. Pieces were successively positioned as assigned on the table. For each, the robot performed a single grasp attempt. In the experimental condition permissive planning was employed; in the control condition permissive planning was turned off. The results are summarized in Figure 7A. In the control condition only two of the twelve attempted grasps succeeded. In the experimental condition ten of the twelve attempts succeeded. Failures due to three dimensional motion of the target, which cannot be correctly sensed by the robot, were excluded. One bias adjustment was sufficient to preclude recurrences of each of the two observed types of grasping failure. The two bias adjustments can be interpreted as 1) preferring to open the gripper as wide as possible prior to approaching the target, and 2) selecting opposing sides for grasp points that are maximally parallel. Other permissive adjustments that have been exhibited by the system in this domain include closing the gripper more tightly than is deemed necessary and selecting grasp points as close as possible to the target's center of geometry.

Experiment 2. Details of this task domain are borrowed from Christiansen [Christiansen90]. It is a laboratory approximation to orienting parts for manufacturing: a tray is tilted to orient a rectangular object free to slide between the tray's sides.. Christiansen employed the domain to investigate stochastic planning to which we compare permissive planning. The tray is divided into nine identical regions. The task is to achieve a desired orientation (either vertical or horizontal) of the rectangular object in a specified region.

We compared 1–step permissive plans to 1– and 3–step optimal stochastic plans. The optimal stochastic plans were generated using the technique described in [Christiansen90]. In the experiment, a sequence of 52 block orientation problems was repeatedly given to the permissive planner 20 times (1040 planning problems in all). Figure 8 shows the improvement

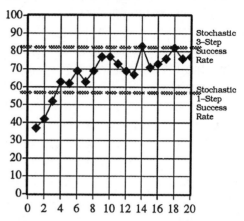

Figure 8: Average Success Rates over 20 Repetitions for 1–Step Permissive vs. 1– and 3–Step Stochastic Plans

in average success rate in the course of the 20 repetitions. Each data point is the average success over the 52 problems. Success rate increased from about 40% to approximately 80%. The final 1–step permissive performance approaches the 3–step stochastic performance, but requires fewer training examples.

Related Work and Conclusions

In this paper we have described our efforts toward formalizing permissive planning. Prior descriptions [Bennett91] have discussed our motivations and how these motivations have guided the implementation of experimental systems. We feel that we now understand the reasons behind the success of our implementations sufficiently to offer a beginning formal account of why our experimental systems work.

Our notion of bias was inspired by the use of the same term in machine learning [Utgoff86]. However, the bias referred to in permissive planning is quite separate from the bias of its underlying machine learning system. Likewise, our competence/performance distinction for planners is borrowed from a similar but fundamentally different notion in linguistics [Chomsky65].

In the current research literature the methods most similar to permissive planning trace their roots to dynamic programming [Bellman57] variously called reinforcement learning, temporal difference methods, and Q learning [92]. Like permissive planning the motivation is to improve real–world goal

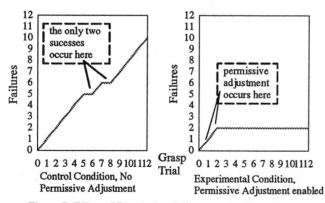

Figure 7: Effect of Permissive Adjustment on Grasp Success

achievement. Some approaches utilize prior operator knowledge. However, like dynamic programming, the goal specification is folded into the acquired knowledge; the improved system is not applicable to other goals without redoing the machine learning. Furthermore, like stochastic planning, (but unlike permissive planning) a coarse discretization of continuous and fine–grained domain attributes is required.

One interesting consequence of permissive planning concerns minimal commitment planning. Permissive planning rejects this apparently attractive and generally accepted planner design goal. The desire to make the fewest necessary planning commitments is motivated by theoretical elegance, planning efficiency, and discrepancies with the real world. However, it denies access to a significant portion of the planning bias.

The primary significance of this work, we believe, lies in combining the internal constraints of a planner's *a priori* domain axiomatization (i.e., its definition of operators) with the external constraints obtained from examining real–world outcomes of action sequences. The machine learning formalism for combining these internal and external world models is problem–independent and domain–independent, although some amount of domain training is introduced. The approach offers real–world robustness previously associated only with reactive interleaving of sensing and action decisions.

The examples described here are modest. For each failure that initiates permissive planning, one could, after the fact, re–craft the operator definitions. But this misses the point. After all of the axiom tuning a human implementor can endure, inaccuracies will still exist in a planner's world knowledge. As long as there are multiple ways of solving a problem, permissive planning can be employed to preferentially generate plans that work in the external world.

References

[Bellman57] R. Bellman, *Dynamic Programming*, Princeton University Press, Princeton, 1957.

[Bennett91] S. Bennett and G. F. DeJong, "Comparing Stochastic Planning to the Acquisition of Increasingly Permissive Plans for Complex Uncertain Domains," *Proceedings of the Eighth International Workshop on Machine Learning*, June, 1991, pp. 586–590.

[Bennett93] S. W. Bennett, "Permissive Planning: A Machine Learning Approach to Planning in Complex Real–World Domains," Ph.D. Thesis, Electrical and Computer Engineering Department, University of Illinois, Urbana, IL, January, 1993.

[Chapman87] D. Chapman, "Planning for Conjunctive Goals," *Artificial Intelligence 32*, 3 (1987), pp. 333–378.

[Chomsky65] N. Chomsky, in *Aspects of the Theory of Syntax*, MIT Press, Cambridge, 1965.

[Christiansen90] A. D. Christiansen and K. Y. Goldberg, "Robotic Manipulation Planning with Stochastic Actions," *Proceedings of the Workshop on Innovative Approaches to Planning, Scheduling and Control*, San Diego, CA, November 1990, pp. 3–8.

[DeJong86] G. F. DeJong and R. J. Mooney, "Explanation–Based Learning: An Alternative View," *Machine Learning 1*, 2 (1986), pp. 145–176.

[Gratch92] J. Gratch and G. DeJong, "COMPOSER: A Probabilistic Solution to the Utility Problem in Speed–up Learning," *Tenth National Conference on Artificial Intelligence*, San Jose, CA, 1992.

[Greiner92] R. Greiner and I. Jurisica, "A Statistical Approach to Solving the EBL Utility Problem," *Proceedings of the National Conference on Artificial Intelligence*, San Jose, CA, July 1992, pp. 241–248.

[McCarthy80] J. McCarthy, "Circumscription – A Form of Non–Monotonic Reasoning," *Artificial Intelligence 13*, 1 (1980), pp. 27–39.

[Minton88] S. Minton, in *Learning Search Control Knowledge: An Explanation–Based Approach*, Kluwer Academic Publishers, Norwell, MA, 1988.

[Sacerdoti75] E. D. Sacerdoti, "The Nonlinear Nature of Plans," *Proceedings of the Fourth International Joint Conference on Artificial Intelligence*, Tiblisi, Georgia, U.S.S.R., 1975, pp. 206–214.

[Sutton92] *Machine Learning (Special Issue on Reinforcement Learning) 8*, 3/4, R. Sutton (ed.), 1992

[Utgoff86] P. E. Utgoff, "Shift of Bias for Inductive Concept Learning," in *Machine Learning: An Artificial Intelligence Approach, Vol. II*, R. S. Michalski, J. G. Carbonell and T. M. Mitchell (ed.), MORGAN, 1986, pp. 107–148.

[Wilkins88] D. E. Wilkins, *Practical Planning: Extending the Classical Artificial Intelligence Planning Paradigm*, Morgan Kaufman, San Mateo, CA, 1988.

Relative Utility of EBG based Plan Reuse in Partial Ordering vs. Total Ordering Planning

Subbarao Kambhampati* and **Jengchin Chen**
Department of Computer Science and Engineering
Arizona State University, Tempe, AZ 85287-5406
Email: rao@asuvax.asu.edu

Abstract

This paper provides a systematic analysis of the relative utility of basing EBG based plan reuse techniques in partial ordering vs. total ordering planning frameworks. We separate the potential advantages into those related to storage compaction, and those related to the ability to exploit stored plans. We observe that the storage compactions provided by partially ordered partially instantiated plans can, to a large extent, be exploited regardless of the underlying planner. We argue that it is in the ability to exploit stored plans during planning that partial ordering planners have some distinct advantages. In particular, to be able to flexibly reuse and extend the retrieved plans, a planner needs the ability to arbitrarily and efficiently "splice in" new steps and sub-plans into the retrieved plan. This is where partial ordering planners, with their least-commitment strategy, and flexible plan representations, score significantly over state-based planners as well as planners that search in the space of totally ordered plans. We will clarify and support this hypothesis through an empirical study of three planners and two reuse strategies.

1. Introduction

Most work in learning to improve planning performance through EBG (explanation based generalization) based plan reuse has concentrated almost exclusively on state-based planners (i.e., planners which search in the space of world states, and produce totally ordered plans;[3, 14, 11, 20].) In contrast, the common wisdom in the planning community (vindicated to a large extent by the recent formal and empirical evaluations [1, 12, 15]), has held that search in the space of plans, especially in the space of partially ordered plans provides a more flexible and efficient means of plan generation. It is natural to enquire, therefore, whether partial order (PO) planning retains its advantages in the context of EBG based plan reuse.

In our previous work [8], we have shown that the explanation-based generalization techniques can indeed be extended in a systematic fashion to partially ordered partially instantiated plans, to give rise to a spectrum of generalization strategies. In this paper, we will address the issue of comparative advantages of doing EBG based plan reuse in a partial order planning framework. We will do this by separating two related but distinct considerations: the advantages of *storing* plans as partially ordered and partially instantiated generalizations and the advantages of *using* the stored generalizations in the context of a PO planning framework.

Storing plans in a partially ordered and partially instantiated form allows for compactness of storage, as well as more flexible editing operations at retrieval time. We will point out, however, that these advantages can be exploited whether the underlying planner is a PO planner or a total ordering planner. We will argue that it is in the ability to *use* the generalized plans during planning, that partial ordering planners have some distinct advantages over total ordering planners. In particular, to be able to flexibly reuse and extend the retrieved plans (when they are only partially relevant in the new problem situation), the planner needs to be able to arbitrarily and efficiently "splice in" new steps and sub-plans into the retrieved macro (and *vice versa*). Partial ordering planners, with their least-commitment strategy, and flexible plan representations, are more efficient than state-based planners as well as planners that search

in the space of totally ordered plans, in doing this splicing. We argue that in many plan reuse situations, this capability significantly enhances their ability exploit stored plans to improve planning performance. We will support our arguments through focused experimentation with three different planners and two different reuse strategies.

The rest of the paper is organized as follows: the next section provides a brief characterization of different planners in terms of how they refine plans during search. Section 3. uses this background to characterize the advantages of partial order planners in exploiting stored plan generalizations to improve performance. Section 4.1. describes an empirical study to evaluate the hypotheses regarding the comparative advantages of PO planning. Section 4.2. presents and analyzes the results of the study. Section 5. argues in favor of basing plan reuse and other speedup learning research in partial order planning, and clears some misconceptions regarding PO planning which seem to have inhibited this in the past. Section 6. concludes with a summary of contributions. All through this paper, we shall refer to stored plan generalizations as *macros*, regardless of whether they get reused as macro-operators, or serve as a basis for library-based (case-based) plan reuse. We also use the terms "efficiency" and "performance" interchangeably to refer to the speed with which a planner solves a problem.

2. A Characterization of Planners in terms of allowable plan refinements

Whatever the exact nature of the planner, the ultimate aim of planning is to find a *ground operator sequence*, which is a *solution* to the given problem (i.e., when executed in a given initial state will take the agent to a desired goal state). From a first principles perspective, the objective of planning is to navigate this space, armed with the problem specification, and find the operator sequences that are solutions for the given problem. Suppose the domain contains three ground actions $a1$, $a2$ and $a3$. The regular expression $\{a1|a2|a3\}^*$ describes the potential solution space for this domain. If we are interested in *refinement planners* (i.e., planners which add but do not retract operators and constraints from a partial plan during planning) which most planners are, then the planner's navigation through the space of potential solutions can be enumerated as a directed acyclic graph (DAG), as illustrated in Figure 1.

When a refinement planner reaches an operator sequence that is not a solution, it will try to refine the sequence further (by adding more operators) in the hopes of making it a solution. Different types of planners allow different types of transitions in the DAG. For example, planners such as STRIPS and PRODIGY that do *forward search in the space of world states*, will only add operators to the end of the partial solution during refinement, and thus only transition via the solid lines in Figure 1.[1] Most planners used in learning research to-date fall in this category. On the other hand, planners

---

*This research is supported by National Science Foundation under grant IRI-9210997.

[1]Notice that the so called *linearity assumption*, which specifies whether the planner manages its list of outstanding goals as a stack or an arbitrary list, has no effect on this. In particular, both PRODIGY, which makes linearity assumption, and its extension NOLIMIT[19] doesn't (and thus allows interleaving of subgoals), are both capable only of refining a partial plan by adding operators to the end of the current plan.

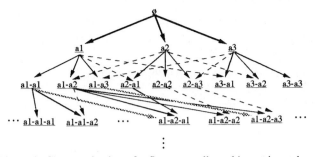

Figure 1: Characterization of refinements allowed by various planning strategies (see text)

ART-IND ($D^0 S^1$): (A_i $prec$: I_i $\underline{add}$: G_i)
ART-MD ($D^m S^1$): (A_i $prec$: I_i $\underline{add}$: G_i $\underline{del}$: $\{I_j\|j < i\}$)
ART-MD-NS ($D^m S^2$): (A_i^1 $prec$: I_i $\underline{add}$: P_i $\underline{del}$: $\{I_j\|j < i\}$) (A_i^2 $prec$: P_i $\underline{add}$: G_i $\underline{del}$: $\{I_j\|\forall j\} \cup \{P_j\|j < i\}$)

Figure 2: The specification of Weld et. al.'s Synthetic Domains

which do backward search in the space of world states, will only add new operators to the beginning of the partial solution during refinement, and thus allow the transitions shown in dashed lines. Finally, planners which *search in the space of plans*, allow new operators to be added *anywhere* in the partial solution, *including in the middle of the existing plan*, and thus allow all of the refinements shown in the figure.

All the planners we discussed above can be called total ordering planners in that the partial plans they maintain during their search is always a totally ordered sequence of operators. However, planners searching in the space of plans have the option to either search in the space of totally ordered plans, or in the space of partially ordered (PO) plans. Many current-day planners such as NOAH, NONLIN, SIPE belong to the latter class, called partial order or PO planners[2] are generally more efficient as they avoid premature commitment to inter-operator orderings, there by improving efficiency over corresponding planners that search in the space of totally ordered plans [1, 15].

3. Advantages of Partial Order planning in plan reuse

3.1. Storage Compaction

A PO plan provides a compact representation for the possibly exponential number of its underlying linearizations by specifying just the steps, the partial ordering between steps and the codesignation and non-codesignation constrains between the variables. This flexible plan representation allows for a spectrum of order, precondition and structure generalizations. Our previous work [8] provides a systematic basis for generating these generalizations. Storing plans in PO form also allows for more sophisticated *editing* operations at retrieval time, when the macro is only partly applicable. Specifically, any irrelevant steps and constraints of the plan can be edited out by retracting the corresponding planning decisions. The retraction itself can be facilitated by justifying individual planning decisions in terms of the plan causal structures. Once such a justification framework is in place, the retraction of irrelevant constraints can be accomplished with the help of a polynomial time greedy algorithm (c.f. [5, 8]).

However, all the advantages of storage compaction and plan editing will hold whether the underlying planner generates a totally ordered or partially ordered (PO) plans. For example, generalization techniques described in our previous work on EBG for PO plans [8] can be used whether the plan was initially produced by a partial ordering or a total ordering planner. Similarly, even in reuse frameworks based on total ordering planners (e.g. [20, 18]), order generalization has been used as a way to separate independent parts of the plan and store them separately, thereby containing the proliferation of macros by reducing the redundancy among them. In other words, although storage considerations motivate the use of PO

plan representation during plan reuse, they do not necessarily argue for the use of PO planning.

3.2. Ability to exploit stored plans during plan reuse

In this section, we argue that the real utility of using partial order planning when doing EBG based plan reuse is that it provides a flexible and efficient ability to interleave the stored plans with new operators, thereby significantly increasing the planner's ability to exploit stored plans. To understand this, we need to look at the various possible ways in which a stored plan can be extended during planning.

When a macro is retrieved to be reused in a new problem situation, it will only be a partial match for the problem under consideration: (*i*) The macro may contain extraneous goals/constraints that are not relevant to the problem at hand. (*ii*) There may be some outstanding goals of the problem that the retrieved macro does not match. The first situation can be handled largely through the editing operations described earlier. In the second case, the planner may have to do some further planning work even after the macro is incorporated into the current plan. The way a planner extends the macro during planning critically affects its ability to reuse stored plans in new situations. This, in turn, depends upon whether the planner searches in the space of world-states or plans (Section 2.).

Suppose a planner is solving a problem involving a set G of goals, and retrieves a macro M which promises to achieve a subset G' of these goals. Let $g \in (G - G')$ be an outstanding goal of the problem. We will say that M is **sequenceable** with respect to the outstanding goal g if and only if there exists a subplan P for achieving g such that $M.P$ or $P.M$ (where "." is the sequencing operator) will be a correct plan for achieving the set of goals $G \cup \{g\}$. M is said to be **interleavable**[3] with respect to g, if and only if there exists a sub-plan P for achieving g such that P can be merged with M without retracting any steps, ordering constraints or binding constraints in M or P. In particular, if M corresponds to a plan $\langle T_M, O_M, B_M \rangle$ (where T_M is the set of steps, O_M is the partial ordering on the steps and B_M is the binding constraints on the variables), and P corresponds to a plan $\langle T_P, O_P, B_P \rangle$, then there exists a plan P' : $\langle T_M \cup T_P, O_M \cup O_P \cup O', B_M \cup B_P \cup B' \rangle$ which achieves the set of goals $G \cup \{g\}$.[4]

Clearly, interleavability is more general than sequenceability. There are many situations when the macros are not sequenceable but only interleavable with respect to the outstanding goals of the planner. Consider the simple artificial domains, ART-IND, ART-MD and ART-MD-NS (originally described in [1]) shown in Figure 2. These domains differ in terms of the serializability [10] of the goals in the domain. ART-IND contains only independent goals (notice that none of the actions have delete lists). The goals in ART-MD are interacting but *serializable* while those in ART-MD-NS are *non-serializable*.[5] In particular, in the latter domain, macros will be

---

[2]Partial order planners have also been called nonlinear planners. We prefer the former term since the latter gives the misleading impression that partial order planning is related to linearity assumption. In fact, as we mentioned earlier linearity assumption is concerned with order in which different goals are attacked, and can be used in *any planner*. Linearity assumption causes incompleteness in planners that search in the space of world states (such as STRIPS and PRODIGY), but does not affect completeness in any way in planners that search in the space of plans.

[3]Note that interleavability here refers to the ability to interleave plan steps. This is distinct from the ability to interleave subgoals. In particular state-based planners that don't use linearity assumption can interleave subgoals, but cannot interleave plan steps

[4]Interleavability of macros, as defined here differs from *modifiability* (c.f. [5, 6]) in that the latter also allows retraction of steps and/or constraints from the macro, once it is introduced into the plan. While modifiability is not the focus of the current work, in our previous work [5], we have shown that PO planners do provide a flexible framework for plan modification. More recently, we have been investigating the utility tradeoffs involved in incorporating a flexible modification capability in plan reuse [4].

[5]From the domain descriptions, it can be seen that a conjunctive goal

	SNLP			TOCL			TOPI	
	scratch	+SEBG	+IEBG	scratch	+SEBG	+IEBG	scratch	+SEBG
ART-MD								
% Solved	100%	100%	100%	100%	100%	100%	100%	100%
Cum. time	80	306	136	92	177	2250	1843	3281
% Macro usage	-	20%	100%	-	20%	100%	-	6%
ART-MD-NS								
% Solved	40%	40%	100%	30%	26%	60%	40%	40%
cum. time	19228	21030	4942	22892	23853	14243	20975	23342
% Macro usage	-	0%	100%	-	0%	100%	-	0%

Table 1: Performance statistics in ART-MD and ART-MD-NS domains.

interleavable, but not sequenceable with respect to any outstanding goals of the planner. To illustrate, consider the macro for solving a problem with conjunctive goal $G_1 \wedge G_2$ in ART-MD-NS, which will be: $A_1^1 \to A_2^1 \to A_1^2 \to A_2^2$. Now, if we add G_3 to the goal list, the plan for solving the new conjunctive goal $G_1 \wedge G_2 \wedge G_3$ will be $A_1^1 \to A_2^1 \to \underline{A_3^1} \to A_1^2 \to A_2^2 \to \underline{A_3^2}$ (where the underlined actions are the new actions added to the plan to achieve G_3). Clearly, the only way a macro can be reused in this domain is by interleaving it with new operators (unless of course it is an exact match for the problem).

Even when the goals are serializable, as is the case in ART-MD, the distribution of stored macros may be such that the retrieved macro is not sequenceable with respect to the outstanding goals. For example, suppose the planner is trying to solve a problem with goals $G_1 \wedge G_2 \wedge G_3$ from ART-MD domain, and retrieves a macro which solves the goals $G_1 \wedge G_3$: $A_1 \to A_3$. Clearly, the outstanding goal, G_2 is not sequenceable with respect to this macro, since the only way of achieving $G_1 \wedge G_2 \wedge G_3$ will be by the plan $A_1 \to \underline{A_2} \to A_3$, which involves interleaving a new step into the retrieved macro.

The foregoing shows that any planner that is capable of using macros only when they are sequenceable with respect to the outstanding goals is less capable of exploiting its stored plans than a planner that can use macros also in situations where they are only interleavable. From our discussion in Section 2., it should be clear that planners that search in the space of world states, such as STRIPS, PRODIGY, and NOLIMIT [19], which refine plans only by adding steps to the beginning (or end, in the case of backward search in the space of states) of the plan, can reuse macros only when they are sequenceable with respect to the outstanding goals. In contrast, planners that search in the space of plans can refine partial plans by introducing steps anywhere in the middle of the plan, and thus can reuse macros even when they are only interleavable with respect to the outstanding goals. Of these latter, partial order planners, which eliminate premature commitment to step ordering through a more flexible plan representation, can be more efficient than total order planners. Based on this, we hypothesize that partial order planners not only will be able to reuse both sequenceable and interleavable macrops, but will also be able to do it more efficiently. This, we believe is the most important advantage of partial ordering planning during reuse.

4. Empirical Evaluation

The discussion in the previous section leads to two plausible hypotheses regarding the utility of PO planning in plan reuse frameworks. (*i*) PO planners are more efficient in exploiting interleavable macros than planners that search in the space of totally ordered plans, as well as state-based planners and (*ii*) This capability significantly enhances their ability to exploit stored macros to improve performance in many situations, especially in domains containing non-serializable sub-goals. We have tested these hypotheses by comparing the performance of three planners -- a partial ordering planner, a total ordering planner, both of which search in the space of plans; and a state-based planner -- in conjunction with two different reuse strategies.[6] In the following two subsections, we describe our experimental setup and discuss the results of the empirical study.

4.1. Experimental Setup

Performance Systems: Our performance systems consisted of three simple planners implemented by Barrett and Weld [1]: SNLP, TOCL and TOPI. SNLP is a causal-link based partial ordering planner, which can arbitrarily interleave subplans. TOCL is a causal link based total ordering planner, which like SNLP can insert a new step anywhere in the plan, but unlike SNLP, searches in the space of totally ordered plans[7]. SNLP, by virtue of its least commitment strategy, is more flexible in its ability to interleave operators than is TOCL. The third planner, TOPI carries out a backward-chaining world-state search. TOPI only adds steps to the beginning of the plan. Thus, unlike SNLP and TOCL, but like planners doing search in the space of plan states, such as STRIPS and PRODIGY, TOPI is unable to interleave new steps into the existing plan. All three planners are *sound* and *complete*. The three planners share many key routines (such as unification, operator selection, and search routines), making it possible to do a fair empirical comparison between them.

Reuse modes: To compare the ability of each planner to exploit the stored plan generalizations in solving new problems, the planners were run in three different modes in the testing phase: **Scratch mode**, **SEBG (or sequenceable EBG) mode** and **IEBG (or interleavable EBG) mode**. In the **scratch** mode, the planner starts with a null plan and refines it by adding steps, orderings and bindings until it becomes a complete plan. In the **SEBG** mode, the planner first retrieves a stored plan generalization that best matches the new problem (see below for the details of the retrieval strategy). The retrieved plan is treated as an opaque macro operator, and is added to the list of operator templates available to the planner. The planner is then called to solve the new problem, with this augmented set of operators. The **IEBG** mode is similar to the SEBG mode, except that it allows new steps and constraints to be introduced between the constituents of the instantiated macro and the rest of the plan, as the planning progresses. To facilitate this, whenever the planner selects a macro to establish a precondition, it consider the macro as a transparent plan fragment, and adds it to the existing partial plan. This operation involves updating the steps, orderings and causal links of the current partial plan with those of the macro. In the case of SNLP, the exact ordering of the steps of the macro with respect to the current plan can be left partially specified (e.g., by specifying the predecessor of the first step of the macro, and the successor of the last step of the macro), while in the case of TOCL, partial plans need to be generated for *each* possible totally ordered interleaving of the steps of the macro with respect to the steps of the current partial

---

$G_i \wedge G_j$ (where $i < j$) can be achieved in ART-IND domain by achieving the two goals in any order, giving rise to two plans $A_i \to A_j$ and $A_j \to A_i$. Only the first of these two plans will be a correct plan in ART-MD domain, since the delete literals in the actions demand that G_i be achieved before G_j. Finally, in ART-MD-NS domain, the subplans for G_i and G_j have to be interleaved to give the plan $A_i^1 \to A_j^1 \to A_i^2 \to A_j^2$.

[6]Code and test data for replicating our experiments can be acquired by sending mail to *rao@asuvax.asu.edu*

[7]Each partially ordered plan produced by SNLP corresponds to a set of totally ordered plans. TOCL generates these totally ordered plans whenever SNLP generates the corresponding partially ordered plans.

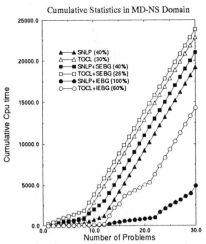

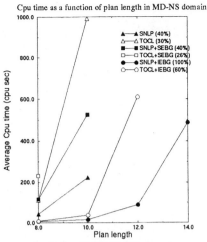

Figure 3: Performance across the three reuse modes in the ART-MD-NS domain

plan. SNLP is thus more efficient and least committed than TOCL in interleaving macros.

It is easy to see that the SEBG strategy can reuse a macro if and only if it is sequenceable with the other outstanding goals of the plan, while the more general IEBG strategy can also reuse a macro whenever it is interleavable with other outstanding goals of the plan. From the description of the three planners above, it should also be clear that only SNLP and TOCL can support IEBG mode. TOPI, like other state-based planners such as STRIPS, PRODIGY and NOLIMIT, cannot support IEBG mode.

Our SEBG and IEBG strategies differ from usual macro operator based reuse strategies in that rather than use the entire plan library as macro-operators, they first retrieve the best matching plan from the library and use that as the macro-operator. The primary motivation for this difference is to avoid the high cost of going through the entire plan library during each operator selection cycle. (This cost increase is due to both the cost of operator matching and instantiation, and the increased branching factor). Instead of a single best match plan, the strategies can be very easily extended to start with two or more best matching plans, which between them cover complementary goal sets of the new problem. This would thus allow for transfer from multiple-plans. Here again, the ability to interleave plans will be crucial to exploit multiple macros.

Storage and Retrieval Strategies: To control for the factors of storage compaction, and flexible plan editing, no specialized storage or editing strategies are employed in either of the planners. The retrieval itself is done by a simple (if unsophisticated) strategy involving matching of the goals of the new problem with those of the macros, and selecting the one matching the maximum number of goals. Although, there is much scope for improvement in these phases (for example, retrieval could have been done with a more sophisticated causal-structure based similarity metric, such as the one described in [6]), our choices do ensure a fair comparison between the various planners in terms of their ability to exploit stored plans.

Evaluation strategy: As noted earlier, sequenceability and inter-leavability of the stored macros with respect to the goals of the encountered problems can be varied by varying the ratio of independent vs. serializable vs. non-serializable goals in the problems. The artificial domains described in Figure 2, and Section 3.2. make ideal testbeds for varying the latter parameter, and were thus used as the test domains in our study. Our experimental strategy involved training all three planners on a set of 50 randomly generated problems from each of these domains. The training problems all have between 0 and 3 goals. During the training phase, each planner generalizes the learned plans using EBG techniques and stores them. In the testing phase, a set of 30 randomly generated problems, that have between 4 and 7 goals (thus are larger than those used in the

training phase) are used to test the extent to which the planners are able to exploit the stored plans in the three different modes. A limit of 1000 cpu sec. per problem is enforced on all the planners, and any problem not solved in this time is considered unsolved (This limit includes both the time taken for retrieval and the time taken for planning). To eliminate any bias introduced by the time bound (c.f. [16]), we used the maximally conservative statistical tests for censored data, described by Etzioni and Etzioni in [2], to assess the significance of all speedups. All experiments were performed in interpreted Lucid Commonlisp running on a Sun Sparc-II.

4.2. Experimental Results

Table 1 shows the cumulative statistics for solving the 30 test problems from each domain for all three planners and all three reuse modes. For each domain, the first row shows the percentage of domain test problems that were correctly solved by each strategy within the 1000 cpu. sec. time bound. The second row shows the cumulative cpu. time. for running through all the test problems (as mentioned, if a problem is not solved in 1000 cpu. seconds, we consider it unsolved and add 1000 cpu. sec. to the cumulative time). The third row shows the percentage of the solved problems whose solutions incorporated retrieved library macros.

In the ART-MD domain, which has subgoals that are easily serializable, none of the planners show much improvement through reuse (although SNLP does perform significantly faster than TOCL in the interleaving EBG mode). All three planners are able to solve all the test problems from scratch within the 1000 cpu sec. time limit. The addition of SEBG and IEBG strategies does not change the solvability horizon. More importantly, the cumulative time taken is slightly worse in both SEBG and IEBG strategies as compared to from scratch planning. This is understandable given that the problems in this domain are easy to solve to begin with, and any improvements provided by reuse strategy are offset by the retrieval costs.

The situation in ART-MD-NS domain is quite different. We see that none of the planners are able to solve more than 40% of the problems in the from-scratch mode. Of the two reuse modes, SEBG remains at the same level of correctness as from-scratch. This is not surprising, since as discussed in Section 3.2., in ART-MD-NS domain, the stored plans are not sequenceable with respect to any remaining outstanding goals of the planner. Thus, unless the macro is an exact match (i.e., solves the full problem), it cannot be reused by an SEBG strategy.

The IEBG strategy on the other hand, dramatically improves the correctness rates of TOCL and SNLP from 40% to 60% and 100% respectively, while TOPI, which cannot support IEBG, stays unaffected. Moreover, as hypothesized, SNLP's improvement is

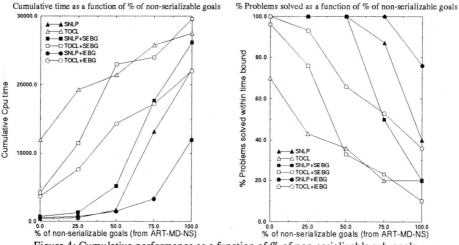

Figure 4: Cumulative performance as a function of % of non-serializable sub-goals

more significant than that of TOCL.[8] The plots in Figure 3 compare the performance of TOCL and SNLP for all three reuse strategies in this domain. The left one plots the cumulative planning time as a function of the problem number (with the problems sorted in the increasing order of difficulty). The right plot shows the average cpu time taken by each planner as a function of the plan length. We see that in IEBG mode SNLP significantly outperforms TOCL in the ability to exploit stored plans both in terms of cumulative time, and in terms of solvability horizon.

Experiments in Mixed Domains: The test domains ART-MD and ART-MD-NS above were somewhat extreme in the sense that the former only has serializable goals while the latter only has non-serializable goals. More typically, we would expect to see a mixture of independent, serializable and non-serializable goals in a problem distribution. To understand how the effectiveness of the various reuse strategies vary for such mixed problem distributions, we experimented with a mixed domain obtained by combining the actions of ART-IND (the domain with independent subgoals) and ART-MD-NS (the domain with non-serializable subgoals) domains (shown in Figure 2). Five different training and testing suites, each containing a different (pre-specified) percentage of non-serializable goals in the problem distribution, were generated. We experimented with problem sets containing 0, 25, 50, 75 and 100% non-serializable goals (where 0% corresponding to the problem set having goals drawn solely from ART-IND, and 100% corresponding to the problem set with goals drawn solely from ART-MD-NS). For each mixture, 50 training problems and 30 testing problems were generated randomly, as discussed before. Given the inability of TOPI to support IEBG, we concentrated on comparisons between SNLP and TOCL.

The plots in Figure 4 summarize the performance in each problem set as a function of the percentage of the non-serializable goals in the problem set. The plot on the left compares the cumulative time taken by each strategy for solving all the problems in the test suite of each of the 5 problem sets The plot on the right shows the percentage problems successfully solved within the time bound by each strategy for each problem set. Once again, we note that SNLP using IEBG shows the best performance in terms of both the cumulative time and the percentage problems solved. IEBG strategy is also the best strategy for TOCL, but turns out to be considerably less effective than the IEBG strategy for SNLP. More interestingly, we see that the

performance of IEBG strategy compared to the base-level planner improves as the percentage of non-serializable goals in the problem set increases for both SNLP and TOCL. By the same token, we also note that the relative performance of SEBG strategy worsens with increased percentage of non-serializable goals for both SNLP and TOCL.

Summary: The results in our empirical studies are consistent with our hypothesis regarding the superiority of PO planners in exploiting stored macros. First, we showed that TOPI fails to improve its performance when faced with interleavable macros, while SNLP and TOCL can both exploit them. Next we showed that SNLP is more efficient in exploiting stored macros than TOCL. In particular, the strategy of using SNLP planner with IEBG reuse strategy significantly outperforms all the other strategies including TOCL+IEBG, in most cases. The higher cost of TOCL+IEBG strategy can itself be explained by the fact that TOCL generates partial plans corresponding to each possible interleaving of the macro with the new steps, while SNLP can maintain partially ordered plan and interleave the steps as necessary.

5. Related Work

Starting with STRIPS, stored plans have traditionally been reused as opaque macro operators that cannot be interleaved during planning. We believe that this was largely due to the limitations imposed by the underlying state-based planners. It is of course possible to get the effect of reuse of interleavable macros within state-based planning indirectly through the use of single operator macros (aka *preference search control rules* [14]). However, it is not clear what are the advantages of starting with a simplistic planner and get interleavability indirectly, when more sophisticated planners, such as PO planners, allow interleavability naturally. More generally, we believe that eager compilation strategies such as search control rules are complementary to rather than competing with more lazy learning strategies such as plan reuse. In some cases, the planner is better served by the lazy strategy of retrieving and modifying a large plan, rather than the eager strategy of compiling each incoming plan into search control rules. In the former, the ability to interleave is essential, and planners like STRIPS would be at a natural disadvantage. Interestingly enough, this was one of the original reasons for the shift from state based planning of STRIPS to plan-space based partial-order planning of NOAH, within the planning community. As McDermott [13, p. 413] remarks, if you want the ability improve performance by piecing large canned plans together, postponing decisions about how these plans will interact, then partial order planning is in some sense the inevitable choice.

In [19, 20], Veloso et. al. advocate basing learning techniques within state-based (total ordering) planning without linearity assumption, rather than within partial order planning. They justify this

---

[8]Using the statistical tests for censored data advocated by Etzioni in [2], we find that the hypothesis that SNLP+IEBG is faster than SNLP as well as the hypothesis that SNLP+IEBG is faster than TOCL+IEBG are both supported with very high significance levels by our experimental data. The *p-value* is bounded above by 0.000 for both the signed test, and the more conservative censored signed-rank test. The hypothesis that TOCL+IEBG is faster than TOCL is however supported with a much lower significance level (with a *p-value* of .13 for sign test and .89 for the censored signed-rank test).

by arguing that the former have all the advantages of PO planners, and also scale up better to more expressive action representations because checking necessary truth of a proposition becomes NP-hard for partially ordered plans containing such actions. To begin with, as we discussed in Section 2., the inability to interleave macros is due to the limited refinement strategies allowed by a state-based planner, and has little to do with whether or not the planner makes linearity assumption. Secondly, the argument regarding the relative difficulty of scaling up the partial ordering planners to more expressive action representations is based on the (mistaken) premise that a PO planner has to interpret the full (necessary and sufficient) modal truth criterion for PO plans during each search iteration. Recent work [7, 12, 15] amply demonstrates that sound and complete partial ordering planners do not necessarily have to interpret the full-blown modal truth criterion at each iteration (since they only need completeness in the space of ground operator sequences rather than in the space of PO plans), and thus can retain their relative advantages over total ordering planners even with more expressive action representations. This, coupled with our experiments showing the superiority of PO planners in exploiting stored plans, make PO planning an attractive framework for doing plan reuse.

The concentration on state-based planning has also been true of much of the speedup learning work within planning, including search control rules and precondition abstraction. In [14, p. 83] Minton et. al. seem to justify this by the observation: *"[..] the more clever the underlying problem solver is, the more difficult the job will be for the learning component"*. Preferring a state-based planning strategy only to make learning easier seems to be somewhat unsatisfactory, especially given that there exist more sophisticated planning strategies that avoid many of the inefficiencies of the state-based planners More over, we believe that the shift to more sophisticated planning strategies is not just an *implementation issue*; it may also lead to qualitatively different priorities in techniques as well as target concepts worth learning. As an example, one source of the inefficiency of STRIPS and other state-based planners stems from the fact that they confound the execution order (i.e., the order in which the goals are achieved during execution) with the planning order (i.e., the order in which the goals are attacked during planning). As we shift to planners that search in the space of plans, such as PO planners, planning order is cleanly separated from execution order; and many of the inefficiencies of state-based planners are naturally avoided. Thus, learning strategies and target concepts that are designed with state-based planners in mind may be of limited utility when we shift to more flexible planners. As an example, *"goal order preference rules"* of the type *"work on $on(y, z)$ before $on(x, y)$"*, learned by EBL strategies in blocks world, are not that useful for partial order planners, which avoid premature step orderings to begin with. Similarly, in [17] Smith and Peot argue that may of the static abstractions generated with state-based planners in mind (e.g. [9]), impose unnecessary and sometimes detrimental ordering constraints, when used in conjunction with the more flexible and efficient partial order planning strategies. All of this, in our view, argues in favor of situating research on learning to improve planning performance within the context of more flexible and efficient planning paradigms such as partial order planning.

6. Concluding Remarks

In this paper, we have addressed the issue of relative utility of basing EBG based plan reuse strategies in partial ordering vs. total ordering planning. We observed that while storage compactions resulting from the use of PO plans can be exploited irrespective of whether the underlying planner is a PO planner or a total ordering planner, the PO planners do have distinct advantages when it comes to the issue of effectively *reusing* the stored plans. In particular, we showed that PO planners are significantly more efficient in exploiting interleavable macros than state-based planners as well as planners that search in the space of totally ordered planners. We also showed that this capability substantially enhances the ability to exploit stored macros to improve performance in many situations, where the domain goals and problem distributions are such that a

significant percentage of stored macros are only *interleavable* with respect to the outstanding goals of the planner. Although this can happen both in domains with serializable subgoals and domains with non-serializable subgoals, our experiments show that the effect is particularly strong in the latter.

When taken in the context of recent work on comparative advantages of PO planners in plan generation [1, 12, 15], our study strongly argues for situating EBG based plan reuse strategies within the context of PO planning framework. We believe that such a move would also benefit other learning strategies such as search control rules and abstractions [4], and are currently working towards verifying these intuitions.

Acknowledgements: We wish to thank Tony Barrett and Dan Weld for distributing the code for SNLP, TOCL and TOPI planners. We also thank Oren Etzioni, Laurie Ihrig, Smadar Kedar, Suresh Katukam, Prasad Tadepalli and (anonymous) reviewers of AAAI-93 and ML-93 for helpful comments on a previous draft.

References

[1] A. Barrett and D. Weld. Partial order planning: Evaluating possible efficiency gains. Technical Report 92-05-01, Department of Computer Science and Engineering, University of Washington, June 1992.

[2] O. Etzioni and R. Etzioni. Statistical methods for analyzing speedup learning experiments. *Machine Learning*. (To Appear).

[3] R. Fikes, P. Hart, and N. Nilsson. Learning and executing generalized robot plans. *Artificial Intelligence*, 3(4):251–288, 1972.

[4] S. Kambhampati. Utility tradeoffs in incremental plan modification and reuse. In *Proc. AAAI Spring Symp. on Computational Considerations in Supporting Incremental Modification and Reuse*, 1992

[5] S. Kambhampati and J.A. Hendler. A validation structure based theory of plan modification and reuse. *Artificial Intelligence*, 55(2-3), June 1992.

[6] S. Kambhampati. Exploiting causal structure to control retrieval and refitting during plan reuse. *Computational Intelligence* (To appear).

[7] S. Kambhampati and D.S. Nau. On the Nature and Role of Modal Truth Criteria in Planning. University of Maryland Inst. for Systems Res. Tech. Rep. ISR-TR-93-30, 1993.

[8] S. Kambhampati and S. Kedar. A unified framework for explanation-based generalization of partially ordered and partially instantiated plans. Technical Report (ASU-CS-TR 92-008), Arizona State University, 1992. (A preliminary version appears in Proc. 9th AAAI, 1991).

[9] Craig Knoblock. Learning abstraction hierarchies for problem solving. In *Proc. 8th AAAI*, pages 923–928, 1990.

[10] R. Korf. Planning as Search: A quantitative approach. *Artificial Intelligence*, 33(1), 1987.

[11] J. Allen and P. Langley and S. Matwin. Knowledge and Regularity in Planning. In *Proc. AAAI Symp. on Computational Consideration in Supporting Incremental Modification and Reuse*, 1992.

[12] D. McAllester and D. Rosenblitt. Systematic nonlinear planning. In *Proc. 9th AAAI*, 1991.

[13] D. McDermott. Regression Planning. *Intl. Jour. Intell. Systems*, 6:357-416, 1991.

[14] S. Minton, J.G. Carbonell, C.A. Knoblock, D.R. Kuokka, O. Etzioni and Y. Gil. Explanation-based Learning: A problem solving perspective. *Artificial Intelligence*, vol 40, 1989.

[15] S. Minton, M. Drummond, J. Bresina, and A. Philips. Total order vs. partial order planning: Factors influencing performance. In *Proc. KR-92*

[16] A. Segre, C. Elkan, and A. Russell. A critical look at experimental evaluation of EBL. *Machine Learning*, 6(2), 1991.

[17] D.E. Smith and M.A. Peot. A critical look at Knoblock's hierarchy mechanism. In *Proc. 1st Intl. Conf. on AI Planning Systems*, 1992.

[18] P. Tadepalli and R. Isukapalli. Learning plan knowledge from simulators. In *Proc. workshop on Knowledge compilation and speedup learning*.

[19] M. M. Veloso, M. A. Perez, and J. G. Carbonell. Nonlinear planning with parallel resource allocation. In *Proc. DARPA Planning workshop* pages 207–212, November 1990.

[20] M.M. Veloso. *Learning by Analogical Reasoning in General Problem Solving*. PhD thesis, Carnegie-Mellon University, 1992.

Learning Plan Transformations from Self-Questions: A Memory-Based Approach

R. Oehlmann   D. Sleeman   P. Edwards
University of Aberdeen, King's College Department of Computing Science
Aberdeen AB9 2UE, Scotland, UK
{oehlmann, sleeman, pedwards}@csd.abdn.ac.uk

Abstract

Recent work in planning has focussed on the re-use of previous plans. In order to re-use a plan in a novel situation the plan has to be transformed into an applicable plan. We describe an approach to plan transformation which utilises reasoning experience as well as planning experience. Some of the additional information is generated by a series of self generated questions and answers, as well as appropriate experiments. Furthermore, we show how transformation strategies can be learned.

Planning, Execution, and Transformation

Over the past few years a new view of planning has emerged. This view is based on the re-use of pre-stored plans rather than on building new plans from first principles.

Debugging of Interaction Problems uses pattern based retrieval of pre-stored programs and subroutines. Programs containing bugs are repaired by *patching* faulty steps, (Sussman 1974).

Adaptive Planning employs abstraction and specialisation of plans as transformation strategies, (Alterman 1988).

Case-Based Planning is an extension of Sussman's ideas of retrieval and repair and the application of these ideas to planning. Hammond's CHEF system modifies a retrieved plan to satisfy those goals which are not already achieved, executes the plan, repairs it when it fails, and stores the planning problems related to the failure in the plan. This approach is characterised as memory-based, because the organisation of the memory of previous plans is changed during the process (Hammond 1989).

These approaches stress the necessity to modify previous plans in order to obtain plans which can be used in a new situation. In particular, the memory-based approach to plan transformation attempts to integrate the phases of building a plan and learning from planning failures.

In addition to the standard features of plan modification, execution, and repair, a planning system should be able to transform plans based on knowledge about actions, with the objective being to improve the system's reasoning about actions as well as plan execution. Furthermore, it should be able to learn the transformation strategy as a higher level plan in order to apply similar methods of modification and repair to the strategy as to other plans. Oehlmann, Sleeman, & Edwards (1992) argue that learning a more appropriate plan can be supported by the generation of appropriate questions and answers which we refer to as self-questions and answers; this is done using case-based planning. If an answer can not be generated, a reasoning component plans and executes an experiment in an attempt to acquire the missing knowledge.

In particular, we address the following planning issues:

- reasoning about plans before plan execution,

- reasoning about all known plans,

- generating self-questions to build a plan transformation,

- learning transformation strategies.

We have implemented our approach to plan transformation in an exploratory discovery system, IULIAN[1] (Oehlmann, Sleeman, & Edwards 1992) and have tested the system in various domains.

In the remainder of this paper, we present a top level view of the IULIAN system followed by an example demonstrating the interaction between case-based question and experimentation planning. We then describe our approach to plan transformation. Finally, we evaluate the approach and indicate various options for future work.

---

[1]IULIAN is the acronym for Interogative Understanding and Learning In AberdeeN.

Reasoning about Actions from Self-Questions

IULIAN uses the planning of self-questions, answers and experiments to model reasoning about plans and actions. The main stages of IULIAN's top level algorithm are given in Figure 1.

---

1. **Question Stage.** Input a description of a new experimental setting (problem), execute a pre-stored question plan about the expected experimental result.
2. **Answer Stage.** Try to generate an Answer for the Question.
3. **Experimentation Stage.** If the answer can not be generated, conduct an experiment to obtain the answer.
   a) Generate a hypothesis about the experimental result.
   b) Retrieve and execute an appropriate pre-stored experimental plan (interacting with a simulator).
   c) Compare the experimental result with the hypothesis and determine the expectation failure.
   d) Store experimental setting and experimental result as a new case.
4. **Question and Answer Loop.** If an expectation failure is found, generate a *why* question about the expectation failure. If the *why* question can be answered, store the answer as a new explanation, otherwise generate a sequence of questions, answers, and experiments in order to answer the *why* question and to obtain an explanation. If during the generation of this sequence a case is retrieved which is not sufficiently similar to the input problem, transform the plan associated with the retrieved case into a new plan and generate a new case by executing that plan.
5. **Model Revision Stage.** Use the final explanation to modify the causal model.

Figure 1: IULIAN's Top Level Algorithm

The main task of the system is the discovery of new explanations to revise an initial theory. The basic data structures of the IULIAN system are cases, causal models, and plans (see Figure 2). A case comprises two components, an experimental setting (e.g. a description of an electric circuit with battery, lamp, and switch) and the result of an experiment such as the statement that *the lamp is on when the battery is switched on.*

Cases are represented by objects and relations between objects. Causal models have a similar representation. However, they are stored in a separate library and their objects are viewed as abstract concepts, eg., the concept "lamp" rather than an actual lamp used in a given experiment (Oehlmann 1992). In addition, causal models use particular relations between concepts to represent causal links. A causal model is linked to the cases used to generate that model. Experimental

plans describe the steps which have to be executed in order to produce an experimental setting and result, i.e. a case. Each case has a link to the experimental plan which generated it. In addition, each plan contains a set of descriptors (indexes), such as goals and planning failures, to enable plan retrieval. Plans are retrieved by matching their index values with the characteristic values of a given situation. The effects of plan execution are simulated by a rule-based simulator. The same basic plan structure is employed for question and answer plans, although the index vocabulary differs. Executing these plans allows the system to connect small parts of questions and answers in order to generate complete questions and answers. Question strategies are higher level plans[2] which organise the execution of single question and answer plans, when it is important to generate questions in a particular sequence.

An Example

Before we describe the details of the transformation process, we will discuss the core of an example focusing on the question and answer loop (stage 4 of the top level algorithm). The entire example and the questions used during the reasoning process are described in (Oehlmann, Sleeman, & Edwards 1992).

We assume that the IULIAN system receives as input the description of a electric circuit with lamp and closed switch in parallel (target domain). Associated with the description of the circuit (target case) is an experimental (target) plan to build the circuit by connecting the various components and to observe the status of the lamp. The lamp is reported as being off, as a result of this experiment. This result is inconsistent with the systems expectation based on a previous case of a serial circuit in which the lamp was on. The situation characterised by this expectation failure (partially) matches the index of a question plan for generating a *why* question which would identify an explanation of the expectation failure (Stage 4 of the top level algorithm). IULIAN is able to retrieve the question plan but not an appropriate answer plan, because the explanation has not been stored. This new situation determines an index for retrieving the question strategy CROSS-DOMAIN-REMINDING which supports analogical case retrieval between domains. Executing the first step of the question strategy initialises the retrieval and execution of a question plan to generate an additional top level question. The answer plan to this question can be executed and the generated answer comprises a (source) case in the domain of water pipes (source domain). The interplay between the execution of question and answer plans has actually lead to a case-retrieval (reminding) across domain boundaries.

---

[2]Note that all planning components in the IULIAN system are case-based planners, see (Oehlmann, Sleeman, & Edwards 1993).

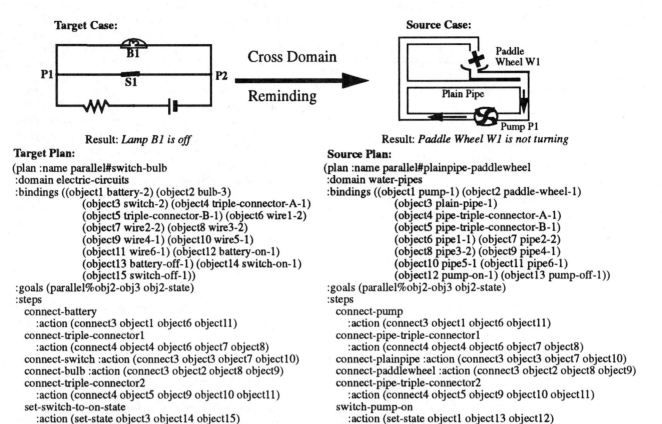

Target Case:

B1

P1   S1   P2

Result: *Lamp B1 is off*

Target Plan:
```
(plan :name parallel#switch-bulb
 :domain electric-circuits
 :bindings ((object1 battery-2) (object2 bulb-3)
            (object3 switch-2) (object4 triple-connector-A-1)
            (object5 triple-connector-B-1) (object6 wire1-2)
            (object7 wire2-2) (object8 wire3-2)
            (object9 wire4-1) (object10 wire5-1)
            (object11 wire6-1) (object12 battery-on-1)
            (object13 battery-off-1) (object14 switch-on-1)
            (object15 switch-off-1))
 :goals (parallel%obj2-obj3 obj2-state)
 :steps
   connect-battery
      :action (connect3 object1 object6 object11)
   connect-triple-connector1
      :action (connect4 object4 object6 object7 object8)
   connect-switch :action (connect3 object3 object7 object10)
   connect-bulb :action (connect3 object2 object8 object9)
   connect-triple-connector2
      :action (connect4 object5 object9 object10 object11)
   set-switch-to-on-state
      :action (set-state object3 object14 object15)
   switch-battery-on
      :action (set-state object1 object13 object12)
   check-bulb-state :action (check-state object2))
```

EXPERIMENTATION PLAN and CASE
Parallel Circuit with Switch and Bulb

Cross Domain Reminding →

Source Case:

Paddle Wheel W1

Plain Pipe

Pump P1

Result: *Paddle Wheel W1 is not turning*

Source Plan:
```
(plan :name parallel#plainpipe-paddlewheel
 :domain water-pipes
 :bindings ((object1 pump-1) (object2 paddle-wheel-1)
            (object3 plain-pipe-1)
            (object4 pipe-triple-connector-A-1)
            (object5 pipe-triple-connector-B-1)
            (object6 pipe1-1) (object7 pipe2-2)
            (object8 pipe3-2) (object9 pipe4-1)
            (object10 pipe5-1) (object11 pipe6-1)
            (object12 pump-on-1) (object13 pump-off-1))
 :goals (parallel%obj2-obj3 obj2-state)
 :steps
   connect-pump
      :action (connect3 object1 object6 object11)
   connect-pipe-triple-connector1
      :action (connect4 object4 object6 object7 object8)
   connect-plainpipe :action (connect3 object3 object7 object10)
   connect-paddlewheel :action (connect3 object2 object8 object9)
   connect-pipe-triple-connector2
      :action (connect4 object5 object9 object10 object11)
   switch-pump-on
      :action (set-state object1 object13 object12)
   check-paddlewheel-state :action (check-state object2))
```

EXPERIMENTATION PLAN and CASE:
Parallel Water Pipes with Plain Pipe and Paddle Wheel

Figure 2

In the source case a plain pipe and a paddle wheel are in parallel. Additionally the observation that the paddle wheel does not turn is stored in the source case, which is associated with both a causal model and the source plan. A summary of the causal model is given below:

In order for the paddle wheel to turn, water must flow over it. There is a plain pipe in parallel with the paddle wheel. The smaller the resistance in a given pipe, the greater is the water flow in this pipe. If one of two parallel pipes has a very low resistance and the other one has a very high resistance, most of the water flows through the pipe with low resistance. Since the paddle wheel offers resistance to the flow and the plain pipe does not, all of the water flow goes through the plain pipe. Since there is no water flow over the paddle wheel, the paddle wheel does not move.

The source model can not be applied to the original electric circuit, because the switch and the plain pipe are not sufficiently similar.[3] Therefore, the source plan

is transformed into a new source plan able to generate a new source case which is sufficiently similar to the target case. The transformation process is described in the following section.

During plan transformation, IULIAN replaces the step which refers to the insertion of a plain pipe by a step which refers to the insertion of a valve. The valve is more similar to the switch in the target domain, because both components are used to pursue the goal "select:flow-interruption/flow-support". In addition, the system inserts a step which opens the valve.[4]

Once the transformation process is finished, two additional reasoning stages are needed. First, the reasoner has to collect evidence that the causal model associated with the source case is valid for the transformed source case. Second, the reasoner has to modify the causal model to make it applicable to the target case, and it then has to ensure that the modified causal model is valid for this case.

(Oehlmann, Sleeman, & Edwards 1992).

[4] The inserted steps are marked in Figure 3 in italics.

[3] For a discussion of how similarity is measured see

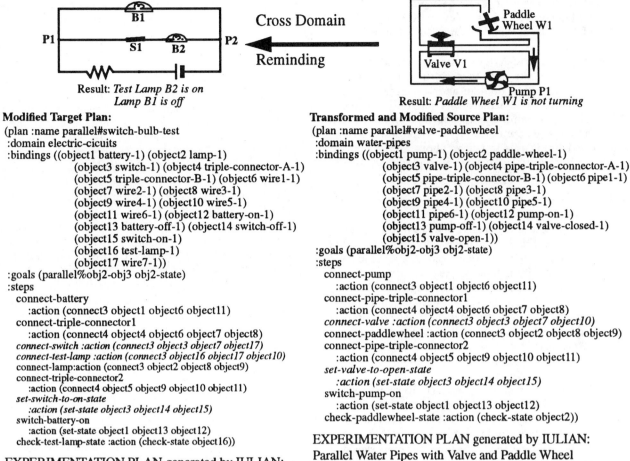

Case:

B1

P1   S1   B2   P2

Result: *Test Lamp B2 is on*
Lamp B1 is off

Cross Domain
Reminding

Case:

Paddle
Wheel W1

Valve V1

Pump P1

Result: *Paddle Wheel W1 is not turning*

Modified Target Plan:
```
(plan :name parallel#switch-bulb-test
 :domain electric-cicuits
 :bindings ((object1 battery-1) (object2 lamp-1)
            (object3 switch-1) (object4 triple-connector-A-1)
            (object5 triple-connector-B-1) (object6 wire1-1)
            (object7 wire2-1) (object8 wire3-1)
            (object9 wire4-1) (object10 wire5-1)
            (object11 wire6-1) (object12 battery-on-1)
            (object13 battery-off-1) (object14 switch-off-1)
            (object15 switch-on-1)
            (object16 test-lamp-1)
            (object17 wire7-1))
 :goals (parallel%obj2-obj3 obj2-state)
 :steps
   connect-battery
     :action (connect3 object1 object6 object11)
   connect-triple-connector1
     :action (connect4 object4 object6 object7 object8)
   connect-switch :action (connect3 object3 object7 object17)
   connect-test-lamp :action (connect3 object16 object17 object10)
   connect-lamp:action (connect3 object2 object8 object9)
   connect-triple-connector2
     :action (connect4 object5 object9 object10 object11)
   set-switch-to-on-state
     :action (set-state object3 object14 object15)
   switch-battery-on
     :action (set-state object1 object13 object12)
   check-test-lamp-state :action (check-state object16))
```

EXPERIMENTATION PLAN generated by IULIAN:
Parallel Electric Circuit with Switch, Lamp and Test Lamp

Transformed and Modified Source Plan:
```
(plan :name parallel#valve-paddlewheel
 :domain water-pipes
 :bindings ((object1 pump-1) (object2 paddle-wheel-1)
            (object3 valve-1) (object4 pipe-triple-connector-A-1)
            (object5 pipe-triple-connector-B-1) (object6 pipe1-1)
            (object7 pipe2-1) (object8 pipe3-1)
            (object9 pipe4-1) (object10 pipe5-1)
            (object11 pipe6-1) (object12 pump-on-1)
            (object13 pump-off-1) (object14 valve-closed-1)
            (object15 valve-open-1))
 :goals (parallel%obj2-obj3 obj2-state)
 :steps
   connect-pump
     :action (connect3 object1 object6 object11)
   connect-pipe-triple-connector1
     :action (connect4 object4 object6 object7 object8)
   connect-valve :action (connect3 object3 object7 object10)
   connect-paddlewheel :action (connect3 object2 object8 object9)
   connect-pipe-triple-connector2
     :action (connect4 object5 object9 object10 object11)
   set-valve-to-open-state
     :action (set-state object3 object14 object15)
   switch-pump-on
     :action (set-state object1 object13 object12)
   check-paddlewheel-state :action (check-state object2))
```

EXPERIMENTATION PLAN generated by IULIAN:
Parallel Water Pipes with Valve and Paddle Wheel

Figure 3

The first stage can be achieved by modifying the transformed plan (Hammond 1989). This stage has the following effect: in executing the modified plan the water pipe circuit is built by connecting the various components and a small test paddle wheel is placed after the valve. The test paddle wheel allows the planner to test whether the water runs through the valve.

In the second stage, the table of similar objects (see the following section) enables the system to replace all objects from the water pipe domain which appear in the causal model with similar objects from the electric circuit domain. The validity of the modified causal model can be tested by modifying the target plan in the same way as the transformed source plan. A step is added to the plan, allowing the planner to insert a test lamp after the switch in the electric circuit in order to test whether the current flows through the path with the switch. The result of plan execution shows that the current flows through the switch rather than through the main lamp and confirms the new causal model.

Plan Transformation from Self-Questions

In this section, we describe our approach to plan transformation by extending the example in the previous section. We will focus in particular on the interaction between self-questions and transformation steps.

The system has to accept that the plan is appropriate for mapping the relevant parts of the knowledge from the water pipe domain to the domain of electrical circuits. Therefore it retrieves a question plan to generate an evaluation question.[5]

Question 1.2:   *Is the retrieved experimental plan (source) appropriate?*

Answer 1.2:   *No, there are steps in the target plan without equivalents in the source plan.*

_____

[5]We assume that the appropriate question and answer plans are available rather than a higher level question strategy representing the transformation process. This strategy will be learned during the process of self-questioning and answering.

The answer reveals that the plan is not completely appropriate; however, it is the best plan IULIAN can obtain. Therefore, the strategy CROSS-DOMAIN-REMINDING is suspended and the plan is transformed into a more appropriate one.[6] It is important to note that the strategy goals are not abandoned, the planner still has the goal to perform a mapping between the water pipe domain and the electric circuit domain. IULIAN will achieve this goal only if it has a plan available to build the appropriate links between source and target domains. It is therefore desirable that the system is able to reason about all the plans it knows (Pollack 1992). The stages of plan transformation are summarised in Figure 4.

---

1. **Match objects** and relations in target and source plan with respect to the abstract descriptor values *goal, task, and belief*. If a match succeeds store the matching object pairs in the object-transformation-table. If one of the matches does not succeed perform the following stages.

2. Instantiate steps in target and source plan using the information from the **object-transformation-table** and **match the steps** in target and source plan according to identical *goals* (omitted in Figures 2 and 3) and *actions*. Build the **step-transformation-table** of matching steps.

3. Identify the non matching steps in the target plan and **search the plan library for matching steps** in plans from the source domain. Store these pairs in the **retrieved-step-table**.

4. **Build a new source plan** by inspecting every step in the target plan. If the step-transformation-table contains a matching source step, copy this step into the new plan. If the retrieved-step-table contains a matching retrieved step, copy this step into the new plan.

5. Collect the abstract indices used to retrieve the appropriate questions and answers during the plan transformation process and **build a new question strategy**.

Figure 4: The Transformation Steps

In order to reason about plans in different domains, a similarity measure has to be established, i.e. the planner has to know which steps in the plan are similar and which steps are different. In a second stage, the planner uses the table of matching objects and the two binding lists to build a table of equivalent steps.

The system is able to generate Answer 1.2, because there are steps which do not appear in the table of equivalent steps. In order to identify these differences, IULIAN retrieves a question plan whose execution re-

---

[6] If the transformation fails, the problem is presented to the user who can add additional knowledge and re-start the process.

sults in Question 1.2.1.

Question 1.2.1: *Which steps in the target plan have no equivalent in the source plan and which steps in the source plan have no equivalent in the target plan?*

Answer 1.2.1: *The step CONNECT-SWITCH in the target plan has no equivalent in the source plan and the step CONNECT-PLAINPIPE in the source plan has no equivalent in the target plan.*

After establishing the exact differences between both plans, the system has a choice between modifying the source plan or the target plan. In our example, IULIAN searches in the water pipe domain for the equivalent to the step CONNECT-SWITCH and uses this equivalence to modify the source plan. The system retrieves and executes a question plan focusing on the step CONNECT-SWITCH.

Question 1.2.2: *What is the equivalent for the step CONNECT-SWITCH in the WATER-PIPE domain?*

Answer 1.2.2: *The step CONNECT-VALVE in the plan SERIAL#VALVE-PADDLEWHEEL.*

The generation of the answer involves the search for an equivalent step in the remaining experimentation plans. The system is looking for a step which supports the same goals it pursued in the circuit domain using the step CONNECT-SWITCH. However, the new step has to be found in the domain of water pipes, because the plan to be transformed describes an experiment in this domain. In addition, the new step and the step CONNECT-SWITCH should perform actions with the same name. IULIAN might have identified additional steps in the source plan without equivalents in the target plan. If this happened, the system would then attempt to find appropriate steps in the plan SERIAL#VALVE-PADDLEWHEEL. If this limited search is not successful, it would start a new general search through the entire plan library. However, it would use similar goal, domain and action constraints as described above. After retrieving the step CONNECT-VALVE, the system has the necessary information to build a new plan. The following question focuses on the plan transformation goal and attempts to combine all the single pieces of information obtained.

Question 1.2.3: *How can I make the source plan more similar to the target plan?*

Answer 1.2.3: *I can make the source plan more similar to the target plan by removing the step CONNECT-PLAINPIPE and replacing it with the step CONNECT-VALVE.*

The new experimental plan PARALLEL#VALVE-PADDLEWHEEL is then generated (see Figure 3). We take the memory-based view that organisation of memory should reflect its function (Hammond 1989) and so memory supporting learning should reflect this process by changing its organisation. The learning task described here involves the transformation of plans. Therefore, the overall transformation process should be reflected by changing the indices of plans. IULIAN improves plan indexing by storing information about equivalent objects or equivalent steps and information about the problem the system had with the source plan. After successful generation of the new plan, the question and answer goals used to retrieve the appropriate questions and answers are packaged to form a strategy which can be executed when a similar problem arises. In this way, the planner learns a new plan, and additionally a new and more efficient way to cope with the problem of an inappropriate plan in the context of cross domain reminding.

With the newly generated plan, IULIAN continues the execution of the suspended question strategy CROSS-DOMAIN-REMINDING which finally leads to the explanation given in the example.

Discussion

Evaluation

The three main goals of our transformation approach are: improving the execution of question strategies, improving plan execution, and learning new transformation strategies. In this section, we discuss the achievements and limitations of our approach in the light of these goals and compare the approach with previous systems discussed in Section 1.

- Execution of the question strategy is improved, because the transformation process generates new plans. These plans enable the system to execute the strategy. In previous approaches, (Alterman 1988; Hammond 1989; Hanks & Weld 1992), plans are transformed to facilitate plan execution. Similarly, approaches to cross domain analogy rely on existing knowledge structures rather than on knowledge newly generated by experimentation (Vosniadou & Ortony 1989). IULIAN additionally views plans as knowledge about actions which facilitates the reasoning process.

- Plan execution is improved in that the transformed plan addresses additional planning situations. In contrast to previous systems, the close integration of reasoning and planning enables IULIAN to transform plans based on its knowledge about the reasoning process, rather than only using its experience with plan execution.

- A new transformation strategy is learned by storing the components of the transformation process in a question strategy. Learning plan transformations in this way is a novel contribution. In previous approaches, e.g. the CHEF system (Hammond 1989), plan transformation is implemented as a set of fixed, pre-stored rules.

- The current scope of our plan transformation approach is limited to the cross domain reminding strategy. However, we expect that new strategies can be easily incorporated because the structure of our transformation approach is highly modular and

each component can be replaced with a new component.

Future Work

Our system evaluation indicates that the current transformation mechanism is restricted to reasoning in the context of cross domain reminding. Although the reasoner is able to apply the approach to a large variety of different situations, we intend to extend our concept of plan transformation to additional reasoning strategies. An important advantage of our approach is the application of case-based planning to the transformation process itself. We will continue to address this question by investigating the modifications needed to adapt a transformation strategy learned in the context of a given reasoning strategy to a second reasoning strategy.

Acknowledgements

We are grateful to Jeff Berger, University of Chicago, for his helpful comments on a previous version of this paper. This research is partially founded by a University of Aberdeen studentship.

References

Alterman, R. 1988. Adaptive Planning. *Cognitive Science* 12:393-421.

Hammond, K. 1989. *Case-Based Planning: Viewing Planning as a Memory Task.* New York: Academic Press.

Hanks, S., and Weld, D. 1992. Systematic Adaptation for Case-Based Planning. In Proceedings of the First International Conference on Artificial Intelligence Planning Systems, 96–105.

Oehlmann, R. 1992. Learning Causal Models by Self-Questioning and Experimentation. In Workshop Notes of the AAAI-92 Workshop on Communicating Scientific and Technical Knowledge, 73–80.

Oehlmann, R., Sleeman, D., and Edwards, P. (1992). Self-Questioning and Experimentation in an Exploratory Discovery System. In Proceedings of the ML-92 Workshop on Machine Discovery, 41–50.

Oehlmann, R., Sleeman, D., and Edwards, P. (1993). Case-Based Planning in an Exploratory Discovery System. In Working Notes of the IEE/BCS Symposium on Case-Based Reasoning, 1/1-1/3.

Pollack, M. 1992. The Uses of Plans. *Artificial Intelligence* 57:43-68.

Sussman, G. 1974. The Virtuous Nature of Bugs. In Proceedings of the First Conference of the Society for the Study of AI and the Simulation of Behaviour.

Vosniadou, S. and Ortony, A. (1989). Similarity and Analogical Reasoning. Cambridge, UK: Cambridge University Press.

On the Masking Effect

Milind Tambe
School of Computer Science
Carnegie Mellon University
5000 Forbes Avenue
Pittsburgh, Pa 15213

e-mail: tambe@cs.cmu.edu

Paul S. Rosenbloom
Information Sciences Institute
& Computer Science Department
University of Southern California
4676 Admiralty Way
Marina del Rey, CA 90292
e-mail: rosenbloom@isi.edu

Abstract

Machine learning approaches to knowledge compilation seek to improve the performance of problem-solvers by storing solutions to previously solved problems in an efficient, generalized form. The problem-solver retrieves these learned solutions in appropriate later situations to obtain results more efficiently. However, by relying on its learned knowledge to provide a solution, the problem-solver may miss an alternative solution of higher quality — one that could have been generated using the original (non-learned) problem-solving knowledge. This phenomenon is referred to as the *masking effect* of learning.

In this paper, we examine a sequence of possible solutions for the masking effect. Each solution refines and builds on the previous one. The final solution is based on cascaded filters. When learned knowledge is retrieved, these filters alert the system about the inappropriateness of this knowledge so that the system can then derive a better alternative solution. We analyze conditions under which this solution will perform better than the others, and present experimental data supportive of the analysis. This investigation is based on a simulated robot domain called Groundworld.[1]

1. Introduction

Knowledge-compilation techniques in the field of machine learning seek to improve the performance of problem-solvers/planners by utilizing their past experiences. Some examples of these knowledge-compilation techniques are explanation-based generalization (EBG/EBL) (DeJong and Mooney, 1986, Mitchell, Keller, and Kedar-Cabelli, 1986), chunking (Laird, Rosenbloom, and Newell, 1986a), production composition (Anderson, 1983, Lewis, 1978), macro-operator learning (Fikes, Hart, and Nilsson, 1972, Shell and Carbonell, 1989), and analogical and case-based reasoning (Carbonell, 1986, Hammond, 1986). These techniques store experiences from previously solved problems in an efficient, generalized form. The problem-solver then retrieves these learned experiences in appropriate later situations so as to obtain results more efficiently, and thus improve its performance.

However, by relying on its learned knowledge to provide a solution, the problem-solver may miss an alternative solution of higher quality — one that could have been generated using the original (non-learned) problem-solving knowledge. For instance, in a planning domain, the problem-solver may miss the derivation of a higher-quality plan, if a lower-quality plan has been learned earlier. The following example from the Groundworld domain (Stobie et al., 1992) illustrates this phenomenon. Groundworld is a two-dimensional, multi-agent simulation domain in which both space and time are represented as continuous quantities. The principal features in this world are walls, which block both movement and vision. Currently, our task in Groundworld involves two agents: an evasion agent and a pursuit agent. The evasion agent's task is to reach its destination from its starting point, without getting caught by the pursuit agent, and to do so as quickly as possible. The pursuit agent's task is to catch the evasion agent. Both agents have a limited range of vision. When the two agents are in visual range, the pursuit agent starts chasing, while the evasion agent attempts to escape by hiding behind some wall, from where it replans to reach its destination.

Figure 1-1-a shows part of an example scenario from Groundworld. The thick straight lines indicate walls. Here, the two agents are within visual range. To avoid capture, the evasion agent uses a map to create a plan (shown by dashed lines) to hide behind a wall. The plan is stored in learned rules, to be retrieved and reused in similar later situations. The situation in Figure 1-1-b is similar and the learned rules directly provide a plan to the hiding spot. However, by relying on these learned rules, the evasion agent misses a closer hiding spot (denoted by **X**). If the evasion agent had confronted the problem in Figure 1-1-b without its previously learned rules, it would have planned a path to the closer hiding spot. However, due to its learned rules, the evasion agent follows a low quality plan. While the lower-quality plan allows it to hide successfully, there is a significant delay in its hiding, which in turn delays it in reaching its real destination.

This effect, of using a low quality learned solution, has been observed for some time in humans, where it is referred to as *Einstellung* (Luchins, 1942). Modeling Einstellung in computer simulations is an important aspect of capturing human skill acquisition (Lewis, 1978). More recently, Clarke and Holte (Clark and Holte, 1992) report this effect in the context of a Prolog/EBG system, where they call it the *masking effect*, because the learned

---

[1]This research was supported under subcontract to Carnegie Mellon University and the University of Southern California from the University of Michigan as part of contract N00014-92-K-2015 from the Defense Advanced Research Projects Agency (DARPA) and the Naval Research Laboratory (NRL). The *Groundworld* simulator used in this paper was developed by Charles Dolan of Hughes AI center. The simulated robots in Groundworld were developed in collaboration with Iain Stobie of the University of Southern California.

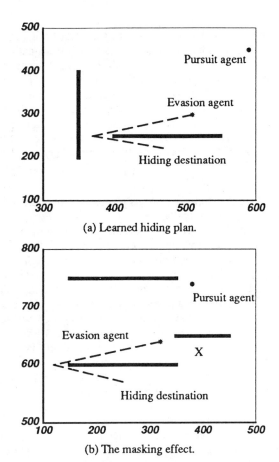

(a) Learned hiding plan.

(b) The masking effect.

Figure 1-1: The masking problem when hiding: approx 15% of the Groundworld scenario is shown.

knowledge masks the original problem-solving knowledge. However, in contrast to the psychological work, Clarke and Holte's goal is not to produce this effect, but to eliminate it.

The hypothesis underlying the work described here is part way between these two perspectives; in particular, the assumption is that masking (Einstellung) is in its essence unavoidable, but that there are effective strategies that an intelligent system can use to minimize its negative consequences. Note that a low-quality solution produced due to masking is not always problematical. For instance, in real-time situations, a low-quality solution may be acceptable, as long as it is produced in bounded time (Korf, 1990). However, in other situations, a good quality solution has a much higher priority and hence avoiding the masking effect assumes importance.

We start by motivating the overall hypothesis by examining the relationship of masking to overgenerality, looking at some of the existing approaches for dealing with this overgenerality and discussing the problems these approaches have. We then propose a sequence of three new approaches to coping with masking, based on the concepts of approximations, filters, and cascades of filters. This is all then wrapped up with some analysis and backup experiments comparing these approaches.

2. Masking and Overgenerality

The masking effect arises because, while generating a new learned rule (i.e., at *generation time*), the system may fail to capture all of the knowledge that was relevant in deriving a high-quality solution. This may occur, for example, because the requisite knowledge is only implicit in the problem solving, or because it is intractable to capture the knowledge. Either way, the learned rule may be missing some knowledge about the exact situations where its application will lead to a high quality solution. Thus, when the learned rule is retrieved (i.e., at *retrieval time*), it may apply even though it leads to a low quality solution.

This is clearly an instance of *overgenerality* (Laird, Rosenbloom, and Newell, 1986b); however, this overgenerality is with respect to producing a high quality solution, not with respect to producing a correct solution. That is, these learned rules do not lead to a failure in task performance. For instance, in Figure 1-1-b, the learned rules that lead to masking do not result in a failure in hiding, even though a closer hiding place is missed.

The two classical types of solutions to overgenerality are: (1) avoid it by learning correct rules, or (2) recover from it by detecting the performance failures they engender and then learning patches for those situations. Clarke and Holte's approach is of the first type. In their Prolog-based system, knowledge about solution quality is implicit in the ordering of the Prolog rules. Their EBG implementation fails to capture this knowledge while learning new rules, and leads to the masking effect. The key feature of their solution is, at generation time, to order the learned and non-learned rules according to solution quality. This ordering is guaranteed to remain valid at retrieval time, so the highest quality solution can be retrieved simply by selecting the topmost applicable rule from the ordering.

In general, solutions of type 1 — which we shall henceforth refer to as *generation-time exact* or GT-exact solutions — require capturing all of the relevant knowledge into the learned rules at generation time. However, in complex domains, it can be extraordinarily difficult to do this; that is, tractability problems result. Consider a second example from the Groundworld domain (Figure 2-1). In Figure 2-1-a, the evasion agent attempts to reach its destination, using a map to plan a path through a set of regions (Mitchell, 1988). The path (shown by a dashed line) is chosen so as to be the shortest one that avoids traveling close to the ends of walls — these are potential ambush points that may not allow the evasion agent sufficient maneuvering space to reach a hiding place before it is caught. In this particular instance, the evasion agent has no information about the pursuit agent's position, and hence cannot take that into account while planning the path; however, the pursuit agent is far enough away that it cannot intercept the evasion agent anyway.

The rule learned from the path-planning process in

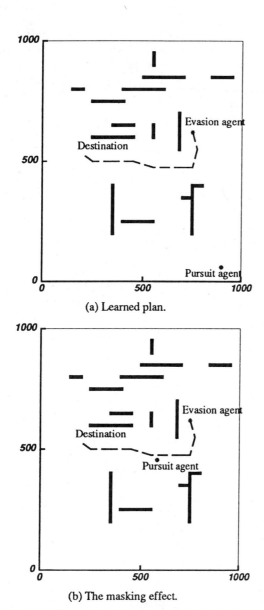

(a) Learned plan.

(b) The masking effect.

Figure 2-1: Masking when trying to reach destination.

Figure 2-1-a captures a plan — a generalized sequence of regions through which the agent must traverse — that transfers to the situation in Figure 2-1-b. In this situation, the plan leads to interception by the pursuit agent. Such interceptions occur in this world, and *are by themselves a non-issue* — interceptions do not lead to failure (capture) as long as there is enough maneuvering space for successful hiding. However, in this case masking occurs because the evasion agent has knowledge about the location of the pursuit agent — from an earlier encounter with it — so it should have been possible to avoid this interception, and the resultant time lost from hiding and replanning. Without the learned rule, the evasion agent would have formed a different plan in Figure 2-1-b, one that would have avoided the area around the pursuit agent, allowing it to reach its destination quickly.

To apply the GT-exact solution to this problem, the

correct learned rule would need to capture exactly the circumstances under which the path is of low quality; that is, those circumstances in which the pursuit agent is in a known location from which it can intercept the evasion agent's path. For example, the overgeneral rule could be augmented with explicit disabling conditions of the form: *(know pursuit agent in region-X), (know pursuit agent in region-Y)* and so on. These disabling conditions avert the retrieval of the learned path if the pursuit agent is known to be in any of the regions from which it could intercept the path traversed.

While this approach seems plausible here, there are two problems which tend to make it intractable. First, locating all possible disabling conditions, i.e., positions of the pursuit agent for which the plan is of low-quality, involves a large amount of processing effort. This is a long path, and there are a variety of positions of the pursuit agent which threaten the path. Second, a large number of disabling conditions can severely increase the match cost of the learned rule, causing an actual slowdown with learning (Tambe, et al., 1990). The problems become even more severe in intractable domains. For example, in the chess end-game domain, it is effectively impossible to correctly condition a learned plan at generation time so as to ensure its exact retrieval (Tadepalli, 1989). As a result, at retrieval time, the learned plan may apply, but it does not always lead to a successful solution. And further in incomplete domains the relevant knowledge may not even be available at generation time. Together these problems limit the feasibility of the GT-exact approach to relatively simple domains.

The second general class of existing solutions to overgenerality are the refinement (or recovery) strategies (Gil, 1992, Huffman, Pearson and Laird, 1991, Chien, 1989, Tadepalli, 1989). However, these solutions all depend on explicit detection of failures at planning or execution time (e.g., failure in forming or executing a plan) to indicate the incorrectness of a rule, and thus to trigger the refinement process (Huffman, Pearson and Laird, 1991). While this works for overgeneral solutions that produce incorrect behavior, with the masking effect the learned solutions are only of low quality, and *do not lead to explicit failure*. Without an explicit failure, the refinement process simply cannot be invoked. (Furthermore, failure-driven learning may not always be the right strategy, e.g., in Groundworld, failure is extremely expensive — it leads to capture by the pursuit agent!) Thus, this class of solutions does not look feasible for masking problems.

3. New Approaches to Masking

The previous section ruled out refinement strategies and raised tractability issues with respect to GT-exact. This section introduces a sequence of three new approaches: (1) GT-approximate takes the obvious step of avoiding the intractability of GT-exact by approximating the disabling conditions; (2) RT-approximate improves on

GT-approximate's real-time characteristics by using the approximations as retrieval-time filters; and (3) RT-cascade refines RT-approximate by reducing the amount of replanning.

3.1. Approximating Disabling Conditions

GT-approximate overcomes the intractability issues faced by GT-exact by using overgeneral approximations (simplifying assumptions) about the exact situations for which the learned rules lead to low quality solutions. In the path-planning example, this involves replacing the set of exact disabling conditions by a single, more general, approximate condition — *(know pursuit agent's position)* — thus disabling the learned rule if any knowledge about the pursuit agent's position is available. Inclusion of only a single disabling condition also alleviates the problem of high match cost.

For this solution to be effective in general, the system must be able to derive good approximations. Fortunately, there is already considerable amount of work on this topic that could provide such approximations, e.g., (Elkan, 1990, Ellman, 1988, Feldman and Rich, 1986). However, there are still two other problems with GT-approximate. First, due to the overgeneral approximations, it may overspecialize a learned rule, disabling it from applying even in situations where it leads to a high quality solution. For instance, suppose the rule learned in 2-1-a is to be reused in 2-1-a, and *(know pursuit agent's position)* is true. In this situation, GT-approximate will disable the learned rule, even though the pursuit agent is far away, and the learned rule is thus appropriate. Second, GT-approximate does not facilitate the speed-quality tradeoff that is essential for real-time performance (Boddy and Dean, 1989). In particular, the disabling conditions used here simply disable learned rules in situations where they lead to low quality solutions, forcing the system to derive a new solution from scratch. However, in some real-time situations, a low quality response is perfectly acceptable (Korf, 1990), e.g., in the hiding situation, the evasion agent may find a low-quality plan acceptable if the pursuit agent is close and there is no time to generate a better plan.

3.2. Approximations as Retrieval-Time Filters

RT-approximate alleviates the real-time performance problem faced by GT-approximate by converting the (approximate) disabling conditions into (approximate) retrieval-time filters.[2] These filters quickly check if a learned solution is of low quality after its retrieval. For instance, *(know pursuit agent's position)* can be used as an approximate filter for the path-planning example. If this filter is true at retrieval time, then the retrieved plan is marked as being one of possibly low quality. In a time-critical situation, such as the hiding situation, the system

can simply ignore this mark and use its learned solution.

Where do these filters come from? One "top-down" possibility is that they arise from explicit generation-time assumptions, much as in GT-approximate. For example, if it is known that the planning proceeded under the assumption that no knowledge is available about the location of the pursuit agent, then this assumption could be captured as a filter and associated with the learned rule. Though existence of such location knowledge at retrieval time does not necessarily mean that the plan will be of low-quality, the filter does at least ensure that the plan will not suffer from the masking effect because of this location information.

A second "data-driven" possibility is to use "significant" external events as the basis for filters. Essentially, the system notices some external object/event which may suggest to it that a retrieved solution is inappropriate. For instance, in the hiding example, if the system notices a closer, larger wall in front, then this may suggest to it that its retrieved hiding plan is inappropriate. This strategy is related to the *reference features* proposed in (Pryor and Collins, 1992), which are tags that the system associates with potentially problematical elements in its environment. Later activation of a reference feature alerts the system to a potential negative (positive) interaction of that element with its current plan.

The biggest problem with RT-approximate is that it suffers from the same overspecialization problem that dogs GT-approximate; that is, the filters are overgeneral, and can eliminate plans even when they would yield high-quality solutions.

3.3. Cascading Filters

RT-cascade overcomes the overspecialization problem of RT-approximate by cascading a more exact filter after the approximate filter. It first applies the approximate filter to the retrieved solution. If this indicates that the solution may be of low quality, then the exact filter is applied to verify the solution. If the exact filter also indicates that the retrieved solution is inappropriate, then the system replans from scratch. (Sometimes, a better alternative may be to modify and re-use the existing plan (Kambhampati, 1990).) If the exact filter indicates that the solution is appropriate, then the original solution is used, thus overcoming the overspecialization introduced by the approximate filter.

As an example, consider what happens when RT-cascade is applied to the two Groundworld scenarios introduced earlier. In the path-planning scenario, the approximate filter is *(know pursuit agent's position)* and the exact filter is a simulation of the plan that verifies whether the pursuit agent's position will lead to an interception. In the hiding scenario, the approximate filter is *(wall in front of evasion agent)*. Here, the exact filter verifies that the wall actually is a hiding place (e.g., it will not be so if the pursuit agent is located between the wall and the evasion agent), and that the wall is close. In both the scenario in Figure 2-1-b and the one in Figure 1-1-b

---

[2]Filtering strategies have also been used in other agent architectures. For example, in IRMA (Bratman, et al., 1988), filters decide if an external event/opportunity is compatible or incompatible with the plan the system has committed to.

the approximate filters detect possibly low quality plans. The exact filters are then run, and since they concur, replanning occurs, yielding the plans in Figure 3-1. In both of these cases RT-cascade yields the same qualitative behavior as would RT-approximate; however, in other circumstances RT-cascade would have stayed with the original plan while RT-approximate replanned. In either event, this experience can be learned so as not to repeat the exact verification (and replanning) on a similar future problem.

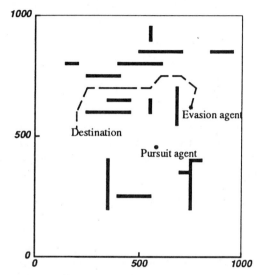

(a) Overcoming the masking effect in path-planning.

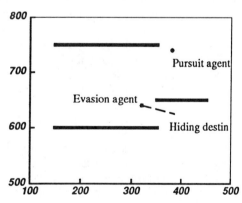

(b) Overcoming the masking effect in hiding.

Figure 3-1: Overcoming the masking effect.

The exact verification in RT-cascade may appear similar to GT-exact; but there is a big difference in their computational costs. In the exact verification process, the system reasons only about the single situation that exists at retrieval time. In contrast, GT-exact reasons about all possible potentially problematical situations that may arise at retrieval time. For instance, in the path-planning example, GT-exact requires reasoning about *all* possible positions of the pursuit agent that can lead to an interception, as opposed to a single position of the pursuit agent. This difference in reasoning costs at generation time and retrieval time have also been observed (and

exploited) in some other systems (Huffman, Pearson and Laird, 1991). Note that this high cost of GT-exact also rules out a GT-cascade solution, which would combine the exact and approximate disabling conditions at generation time.

We have focused on applying the cascaded filters after the retrieval of a learned solution, but before its execution/application. However, the cascaded filters could be employed during or after execution as well. For instance, in the path-planning example, the cascaded filters could be invoked only if the pursuit agent actually intercepts the path. Here, this interception itself acts as a bottom-up approximate filter. The exact filter then verifies if the path is a low quality one (e.g., this path could be the best the system could plan if it had no prior knowledge about the pursuit agent, or this was the only path possible, etc.) This experience can be learned, and retrieved in future instances. However, one key problem with this strategy is that it disallows any preventive action on the problem at hand.

The key remaining question about RT-cascade is how well it performs in comparison to RT-approximate; that is, whether the extra cost of performing the exact verifications in RT-cascade is offset by the replanning effort that would otherwise be necessary in RT-approximate. This is a sufficiently complicated question to be the topic of the next section.

4. RT-approximate vs RT-cascade

Two factors determine whether RT-cascade outperforms RT-approximate. The first is the amount of overspecialization/inaccuracy in the approximate filter. Without such inaccuracy, the exact filter is simply unnecessary. The second factor relates to the cost of (re)derivation. Since the exact filter is intended to avoid the (re)derivation of a solution, it must cost less than the rederivation to generate savings. Winslett (Winslett, 1987) shows that while, in the worst case, derivation and verification processes are of the same complexity, in general, verification may be cheaper.

Let us consider two systems. The first, S-approximate, uses the RT-approximate approach; and a second, S-cascade, uses the RT-cascade approach. Now, consider a problem-instance where the approximate filter is inaccurate, i.e., it indicates that a solution is of low quality, but it is actually not of low quality. Since S-approximate depends on only the approximate filter, it will derive a new solution from scratch, and it will incur the cost of C_{derive}. On the contrary, with S-cascade, the exact filter will be used to verify the quality of the solution. This verification will succeed, indicating that the solution is actually not of low quality. Therefore, S-cascade will not derive a new solution, and will only incur the cost of C_{vsucc} for successful verification. Assuming C_{vsucc} is less than C_{derive} (as discussed above), this situation favors S-cascade. It will obtain a speedup over S-approximate of: C_{derive}/C_{vsucc}.

Thus, a cascaded filter can lead to performance improvements. However, now consider a second problem instance, where the approximate filter is accurate, i.e., it indicates that a solution is of low quality, and it is actually of low quality. S-approximate will again derive a new solution from scratch, with cost of C_{derive}. S-cascade will again use an exact filter to verify the quality of the solution. However, now since the solution is of low quality, the verification will fail, at the cost of C_{vfail}. S-cascade will then derive a new solution, at the cost of C_{derive}, so that the toal cost for S-cascade will be: $C_{derive}+C_{vfail}$. This situation favors S-approximate. It will obtain a speedup over S-cascade of: $(C_{derive}+C_{vfail})/C_{derive}$.

Thus, if the approximate filter functions inaccurately for a problem instance, S-cascade outperforms S-approximate; otherwise, S-approximate performs better. In general, there will be a mix of these two types of instances. Let N_{acc} be the number of instances where the approximate filter performs accurately, and N_{inacc} be the number of instances where it performs inaccurately. Simple algebra reveals that if S-cascade is to outperform S-approximate, then the accuracy of the approximate filter $[N_{acc}/(N_{acc}+N_{inacc})]$ must be bounded above by: $(C_{derive} - C_{vsucc})/(C_{vfail} + (C_{derive} - C_{vsucc}))$. If the approximate filter is any more accurate, S-approximate will outperform S-cascade. (It may be possible to improve this bound further for S-cascade by applying the exact filter selectively; that is, skipping it when C_{derive} is estimated to be cheaper than C_{vsucc}.)

We do not yet know of any general procedures for predicting a priori how accurate an approximate filter will be, nor how low this accuracy must be for RT-cascade to outperform RT-approximate. So, we have instead investigated this question experimentally in the Groundworld domain. Our methodology has been to implement RT-cascade as part of an evasion agent that is constructed in Soar (Rosenbloom, et al., 1991) — an integrated problem-solving and learning architecture, which uses *chunking* (a variant of EBL) to acquire rules that generalize its experience in solving problems — and then to use this implementation to gather data that lets us approximate the parameters of the upper-bound equation, at least for this domain.

Table 4-1 presents the experimental results. Since the values for C_{derive}, C_{vfail}, and C_{vsucc} vary for different start and destination points, five different sets of values were obtained. The first, second and third columns give C_{derive}, C_{vsucc} and C_{vfail} respectively (measured in number of simulation cycles). The fourth column gives the speedup — C_{derive}/C_{vsucc} — obtained by the system due to the cascaded filter, when the approximate filter is inaccurate. The fifth column gives the slowdown — $(C_{derive}+C_{vfail})/C_{derive}$ — observed by the system due to the cascaded filter, when the approximate filter is accurate. The last column in the table is the computed

bound on the accuracy of the approximate filter.

Pr. No	C_{derive}	C_{vsucc}	C_{vfail}	speed cascade	slowdn cascade	Upper bound
1	340	30	11	11.3	1.03	0.96
2	276	38	11	7.3	1.04	0.95
3	234	35	6	6.7	1.02	0.97
4	176	26	8	6.7	1.04	0.95
5	83	16	--	5.2	--	--

Table 4-1: Experimental results for the path-planning example.

The first row in the table shows the data for the start and destination points as shown in Figure 2-1-a. Here, the value of 30 for C_{vsucc} represents a case where the pursuit agent is located far to the north-east of the evasion agent, so that it will not intercept the planned path. The value of 11 for C_{vfail} was obtained for the case where the pursuit agent is located as shown in Figure 2-1-b. The other four rows represent four other problems, with decreasing path lengths.

The table shows that in cases where the approximate filter is inaccurate, the system derives good speedups due to the cascaded filter. In cases where the approximate filter is accurate, the system encounters very small slowdowns due to the cascaded filter. The last column in the table shows that even if the accuracy of the approximate filter is as high as 95-97%, the cascaded filter will continue to provide the system with some performance benefits. The approximate filter that we have used — *(know pursuit agent's position)* — is not as accurate as this. For the five problems above, its actual accuracy varied from about 44% for the first problem to 28% for the last problem. We could employ an alternative filter, but its accuracy would need to be more than 95-97% before the cascaded filters become unuseful for this problem.

The last row in Table 4-1 shows a low C_{derive}, for source and destination points that are close. Here, the speedup due to the cascaded filters has decreased. However, the other entries in this last row are blank. This is because with such close source and destination points, verification failure is instant: the pursuit agent is in visual range and starts chasing. In such cases, the evasion agent abandons its path planning, and instead tries to hide.

For the hiding example, C_{derive} is 14, while C_{vsucc} and C_{vfail} are both 3. These values show little variance with different hiding destinations. This provides a bound of 73% on the accuracy of the approximate filter. If the approximate filter is any more accurate than this, the cascaded filter is not beneficial. We estimate the accuracy of our approximate filter — *(wall in front of evasion agent)* — to be approximately 25%.

5. Summary and Discussion

This paper focused on the masking problem in knowledge compilation systems. The problem arises when a system relies on its learned knowledge to provide a solution, and in this process misses a better alternative solution. In this paper, we examined a sequence of possible solutions for the masking effect. Each solution refined and built on the previous one. The final solution is based on cascaded filters. When learned knowledge is retrieved, these filters alert the system about the inappropriateness of this knowledge so that the system can then derive a better solution. We analyzed conditions under which this solution performs better than the others, and presented experimental data supportive of the analysis.

Much more needs to be understood with respect to masking. Concerns related to masking appear in different systems, including some non-learning systems. One example of this is the *the qualification problem* (Ginsberg and Smith, 1987, Lifschitz, 1987, McCarthy, 1980), which is concerned with the issue that the successful performance of an action may depend on a large number of qualifications. The *disabling conditions* for learned rules (from Section 2) are essentially a form of such qualifications. However, the solutions proposed for the qualification problem have a different emphasis — they focus on higher-level logical properties of the solutions. For instance, one well-known solution is to group together all of the qualifications for an action under a single disabling *abnormal* condition (McCarthy, 1980, Lifschitz, 1987). This condition is assumed false by default, unless it can be derived via some independent disabling rules. However, issues of focusing or limiting the reasoning involved in these disabling rules are not addressed. In contrast, our use of filters to focus the reasoning at retrieval time and the use of two filters (not just one), provide two examples of our concern with more pragmatic issues.

Masking also needs to be better situated in the overall space of learning issues. We have already seen how it is a subclass of overgeneralization that leads to a decrease in solution quality rather than outright solution failure. However, it also appears to be part of a more general family of issues that includes, among others, the utility problem in EBL.

The utility problem concerns the degradation in the speed of problem-solving with learning (Minton, 1988, Tambe, et al., 1990). Clarke and Holte (Clark and Holte, 1992) note that this is distinct from masking, which concerns degradation in solution quality with learning. However, the utility problem can be viewed from a broader perspective, as proposed in (Holder, 1992). In particular, the traditional view of the utility problem is that it involves symbol-level learning (e.g., acquisition of search-control rules), and creates a symbol-level utility problem (degradation in speed of problem-solving) (Minton, 1988). Holder (Holder, 1992) examines the problem of overfitting in inductive learning, and views that as part of a general utility problem. This overfitting problem could actually be viewed as involving knowledge-level (inductive) learning, and creating a knowledge-level utility problem (degradation of the accuracy of learned concepts). Given this perspective, we can create a 2x2 table, with the horizontal axis indicating the type of utility problem, and the vertical axis indicating the type of learning (Figure 5-1).

| | | Type of utility problem | |
		Symbol-level	Knowledge-level
Type of learning	Symbol level	Slowdown in EBL	Masking effect
	Knowledge level	Average growth effect	Overfitting in inductive learning

Figure 5-1: A broader perspective on the utility problem.

The masking effect may now be viewed as involving symbol-level learning (knowledge compilation), but creating a knowledge-level utility problem (degradation in solution quality). Finally, the average growth effect that is observed in some systems (Tambe, 1991) provides an example of knowledge-level learning causing a symbol-level utility problem. Here, a large number of new rules acquired via knowledge-level learning can cause a symbol-level utility problem. We hope that by exploring such related issues, we can obtain a broader understanding of the masking effect.

References

Anderson, J. R. 1983. *The Architecture of Cognition.* Cambridge, Massachusetts: Harvard University Press.

Boddy, M., and Dean, T. 1989. Solving Time-Dependent Planning Problems. Proceedings of the International Joint Conference on Artificial Intelligence. pp. 979-984.

Bratman, M. E., Israel, D. J., and Pollack, M. E. 1988. Plans and resource-bounded practical reasoning. *Computational Intelligence*, Vol. 4(4).

Carbonell, J. G. (1986). Derivational analogy: a theory of reconstructive problem-solving and expertise acquisition. In Mitchell, T.M., Carbonell, J.G., and Michalski, R.S. (Eds.), *Machine Learning: A Guide to Current Research.* Los Altos, California: Kluwer Academic Press.

Chien, S. 1989. Using and refining simplifications: explnation-based learning in intractable domains. Proceedings of the International Joint Conference on Artificial Intelligence. pp. 590-595.

Clark, P., and Holte., R. 1992. Lazy partial evaluation: an integration of explanation-based generalization and partial evaluation. Proceedings of the International conference on Machine Learning. pp. 82-91.

DeJong, G. F. and Mooney, R. 1986. Explanation-based learning: An alternative view. *Machine Learning*, *1*(2), 145-176.

Elkan, C. 1990. Incremental, approximate planning. Proceedings of the National Conference on Artificial Intelligence (AAAI). pp. 145-150.

Ellman, T. 1988. Approximate theory formation: An explanation-based approach. Proceedings of the National Conference on Artificial Intelligence. pp. 570-574.

Feldman, Y., and Rich, C. 1986. Reasoning with simplifying assumptions: a methodology and example. Proceedings of the National Conference on Artificial Intelligence (AAAI). pp. 2-7.

Fikes, R., Hart, P., and Nilsson, N. 1972. Learning and executing generalized robot plans. *Artificial Intelligence*, *3*(1), 251-288.

Gil, Y. 1992. *Acquiring Domain Knowledge for Planning by Experimentation*. Ph.D. diss., School of Computer Science, Carnegie Mellon University.

Ginsberg, M., and Smith, D. E. 1987. Reasoning about Action II: The qualification problem. Proceedings of the 1987 workshop on the frame problem in AI. pp. 259-287.

Hammond, K. 1986. Learning to anticipate and avoid planning problems through the explanation of failures. Proceedings of the Fifth National Conference on Artificial Intelligence (AAAI). pp. 556-560.

Holder, L. 1992. The General Utility problem in EBL. Proceedings of the National Conference on Artificial Intelligence. pp. 249-254.

Huffman, S.B., Pearson, D.J. and Laird, J.E. November 1991. *Correcting Imperfect Domain Theories: A Knowledge-Level Analysis* (Tech. Rep. CSE-TR-114-91) Department of Electrical Engineering and Computer Science, University of Michigan.

Kambhampati, S. 1990. A theory of plan modification. Proceedings of the National Conference on Artificial Intelligence (AAAI). pp. 176-182.

Korf, R. 1990. Real-time heuristic search. *Artificial Intelligence*, Vol. *42*(2-3).

Laird, J. E., Rosenbloom, P.S. and Newell, A. 1986. Chunking in Soar: The anatomy of a general learning mechanism. *Machine Learning*, *1*(1), 11-46.

Laird, J.E., Rosenbloom, P.S., and Newell, A. 1986. Overgeneralization during knowledge compilation in Soar. Proceedings of the Workshop on Knowledge Compilation. pp. 46-57.

Lewis, C. H. 1978. *Production system models of practice effects*. Ph.D. diss., University of Michigan.

Lifschitz, V. 1987. Formal theories of action. Proceedings of the 1987 workshop on the frame problem in AI. pp. 35-57.

Luchins, A. S. 1942. Mechanization in problem solving. *Psychological monographs*, Vol. *54*(6).

McCarthy, J. 1980. Circumsription -- a form of non-monontonic reasoning. *Artificial Intelligence*, *13*, 27-39.

Minton, S. 1988. Quantitative results concerning the utility of explanation-based learning. Proceedings of the National Conference on Artificial Intelligence. pp. 564-569.

Mitchell, J. S. B. 1988. An algorithmic approach to some problems in terrain navigation. *Artificial Intelligence*, *37*, 171-201.

Mitchell, T. M., Keller, R. M., and Kedar-Cabelli, S. T. 1986. Explanation-based generalization: A unifying view. *Machine Learning*, *1*(1), 47-80.

Pryor, L. and Collins, G. 1992. Reference features as guides to reasoning about opportunities. Proceedings of the Conference of the Cognitive Science Society. pp. 230-235.

Rosenbloom, P. S., Laird, J. E., Newell, A., and McCarl, R. 1991. A preliminary analysis of the Soar architecture as a basis for general intelligence. *Artificial Intelligence*, *47*(1-3), 289-325.

Shell, P. and Carbonell, J. 1989. Towards a general framework for composing disjunctive and iternative macro-operators. Proceedings of the Eleventh International Joint Conference on Artificial Intelligence. pp. 596-602.

Stobie, I., Tambe, M., and Rosenbloom, P. 1992. Flexible integration of path-planning capabilities. Proceedings of the SPIE conference on Mobile Robots. pp. (in press).

Tadepalli, P. 1989. Lazy explanation-based learning: A solution to the intractable theory problem. Proceedings of the International Joint Conference on Artificial Intelligence. pp. 694-700.

Tambe, M. 1991. *Eliminating combinatorics from production match*. Ph.D. diss., School of Computer Science, Carnegie Mellon University.

Tambe, M., Newell, A., and Rosenbloom, P. S. 1990. The problem of expensive chunks and its solution by restricting expressiveness. *Machine Learning*, *5*(3), 299-348.

Winslett, M. 1987. Validating generalized plans in the presence of incomplete information. Proceedings of the National Conference on Artificial Intelligence. pp. 261-266.

Qualitative
Reasoning

Qualitatively Describing Objects Using Spatial Prepositions

Alicia Abella   John R. Kender

Department of Computer Science
Columbia University
New York, NY 10027

Abstract

The objective in this paper is to present a framework for a system that describes objects in a qualitative fashion. A subset of spatial prepositions is chosen and an appropriate quantification is applied to each of them that capture their inherent qualitative properties. The quantifications use such object attributes as area, centers, and elongation properties. The familiar zeroth, first, and second order moments are used to characterize these attributes. This paper will detail how and why the particular quantifications were chosen. Since spatial prepositions are by their nature rather vague and dependent on context a technique for *fuzzifying* the definition of the spatial preposition is explained. Finally an example task is chosen to illustrate the appropriateness of the quantification techniques.

Introduction

The work presented in this paper is motivated by an interest in how spatial prepositions may be used to describe space and more interestingly, the spatial relationship among the objects that occupy that space. This work is not concerned with the natural language aspect of spatial prepositions. Given a particular environment and a particular task, where the task and environment may change, we wish for a framework that describes the elements in the environment. It is this framework that is of concern in this paper.

It is known that language meaning is very much dependent on context. An example of a context dependent use of the spatial preposition *next* as taken from [Landau and Jackendoff, accepted for publication] is *the bicycle next to the house.* We would normally not say *the house next to the bicycle.* This is the case because the house is larger in size and as such it serves as an anchor for those objects around it. The house in this example serves as a reference object, or in an environmental context, as a landmark. In the system presented in this paper either description is acceptable since the only concern is in the spatial arrangement of the objects irrespective of the size or the purpose of either of the two objects.

The treatment of objects in our chosen environment is a binary one. There is not a reference object, or landmark, because we wish to avoid choosing a reference object that would require the use of physical attributes such as color, size, or shape and focus solely on two objects' spatial relationship. If we think about the use of a preposition like *near* we realize that the requirement of a particular shape is not needed for its proper use. Landau and Jackendoff [Landau and Jackendoff, accepted for publication] have categorized spatial prepositions into those that describe volumes, surfaces, points, lines, and axial structure. They have pointed out that an object can be regarded as a "lump" or "blob" as far as most of the commonly used spatial prepositions are concerned. For example the preposition *in* or *inside* can regard an object as a blob as long as the blob has the capacity to surround. Likewise, *near* and *at* only require that the blob have some spatial extent. *Along* requires that an object be fairly linear and horizontal with respect to another.

The work presented in [Herskovits, 1986] covers the topic of spatial prepositions fairly extensively from a natural language perspective. The author only suggests the possibility of constructing a computational model for expressing spatial prepositions. The intent here is to demonstrate that a computational model can be constructed and that it indeed captures the vital properties sufficient for a succinct use of the chosen prepositions. We can encode the spatial prepositions fairly concisely because we are treating objects as "blobs" and because most of the properties characterized by these prepositions can be encoded using geometric properties such as alignment and distance. Other related works can be found in [Lindkvist, 1976; Talmy, 1983].

The following sections will provide the details of the encoding we have chosen and demonstrate them though the use of an example.

Notations and Definitions

The prepositions for which we have encoded are *near, far, inside, above, below, aligned, next*. We have defined a preposition as a predicate that maps k objects to true (T) or false (F); true if the k objects meet the requirements imposed by the preposition and false otherwise.

$$p : O^k \longrightarrow \{T, F\}$$

where p is a preposition and O^k is a k-tuple of objects. In this paper we will consider $k = 2$. Nevertheless, prepositions that involve three objects like *between* can also be represented, using a similar formalism.

Now that we have defined a preposition we need to define an object. Formally, each object is represented by a six element vector that depend on an object's area A, center (x_c, y_c), and inertia tensor $\begin{bmatrix} I_{xx} & I_{xy} \\ I_{xy} & I_{yy} \end{bmatrix}$

It is important to scale the elements in this vector so that they have consistent units, in this case units of length, because we will use this vector in the fuzzification procedure described in section 4. Therefore, the kth object is represented by a vector

$$\mu^k = (\sqrt{A^k}, x_c^k, y_c^k, \sqrt[4]{I_{xx}^k}, \sqrt[4]{I_{xy}^k}, \sqrt[4]{I_{yy}^k})$$

The pair of objects μ is represented by a 12-component vector

$$\mu = (\mu^1, \mu^2) \in \mathcal{R}^{12}$$

It is this scaled vector that we will be using in our future calculations.

The parameterization of objects presented above leads to the concept of a bounding box. A bounding box encloses the object using certain criteria. There are various ways in which to compute a bounding box for an object, one of which may be to find the maximum and minimum x and y values belonging to the object. The one we've chosen is defined through the values of ξ_x and ξ_y, that offer a measure of how much an object stretches in the x and y direction. See the Appendix for the derivation.

Two objects define a point in 12D space. A preposition p can be thought of as a set of points $U_p \in \mathcal{R}^{12}$ such that $U_p = \{\mu | p(\mu)\}$. The volume in this 12D space may be able to reveal some of the inherent properties associated with prepositions. In other words, examination of the space occupied by the various sets U_p may tell us something about the spatial prepositions. Vacancies in this 12D space may reveal why we do not have a word to describe certain spatial relationships among objects. The intersection and distances of volumes occupied by various spatial prepositions may reveal a correlation between various prepositions.

We say that objects O^1 and O^2 are in preposition p if $(\mu^1, \mu^2) \in U_p$. This "ideal" set is made up of pairs of object vectors that satisfy the constraints imposed by the preposition p. As we well know, prepositions are inherently vague in their descriptions, and their interpretation may vary from person to person. Because of this, it is important to add some *fuzzifying* agent to our ideal set. The fuzzifying technique is as defined through fuzzy set theory [Klir and Folger, 1988]. The theory of fuzzy sets is used to represent uncertainty, information, and complexity. The theory of classical sets[1] represents certainty. A classical set divides objects in the world into two categories: those that certainly belong to a set and those that certainly do not belong to a set. A fuzzy set, on the other hand, divides the world much more loosely, by introducing vagueness into the categorization process. This means that members of a set belong to that set to a greater or lesser degree than other members of the set. Mathematically, members of the set are assigned a membership grade value that indicates to what degree they belong to the set. This membership grade is usually a real number in the closed interval between 0 and 1. Therefore a member that has a membership grade closer to 1 belongs to the set to a greater degree than a member with a lower membership grade. Because of its properties fuzzy set theory can find application in fields that study how we assimilate information, recognize patterns [Abella, 1992], and simplify complex tasks. In our notation the fuzzified ideal set is defined through a membership function

$$f_{U_p}(\mu) \in [0, 1]$$

We also define a threshold value that depends on how much vagueness we allow before we decide that two objects are no longer describable with the given preposition:

$$f_{U_p}(\mu) \geq \theta_p$$

Computational Model of Spatial Prepositions

The quantification of prepositions entails representing objects through certain physical properties that can then serve as a basis for expressing prepositions. The physical properties we've chosen include object area, centers of mass, and elongation properties. These properties are calculated through the use of the zeroth, first, and second order moments. The basis for this choice of attributes is simplicity and familiarity. What ensues is a brief description of the various prepositions we've chosen to illustrate. Each preposition is defined through a set of inequalities. This results in sets U_p having nonzero measure (i.e. full dimensionality) in $\mathcal{R}^{12}$ which is necessary for the fuzzification procedure described in section 4.

NEAR
We've defined *near* so that objects' bounding boxes

---

[1] Referred to as "crisp" sets in fuzzy set theory.

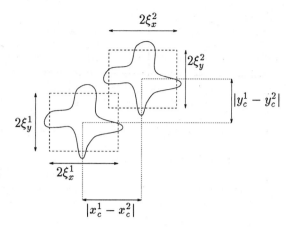

Figure 1: Two objects that are *near* each other

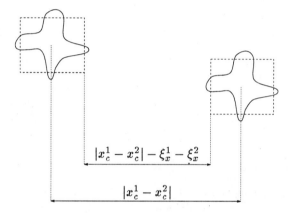

Figure 2: Two objects that are *far* from each other

have a non-empty intersection (see figure 1). Mathematically this is :

$$\xi_x^1 + \xi_x^2 > |x_c^1 - x_c^2| \text{ and } \xi_y^1 + \xi_y^2 > |y_c^1 - y_c^2|$$

FAR

Far is not the complement of *near* as one may initially suspect. We may be faced with a case where an object is neither *near* or *far* from another object, but rather it is *somewhat near* or *somewhat far*. This notion of *somewhat* will be explained more fully when we introduce the concept of *fuzzifying* our "ideal" set. For now it suffices to say that *far* is defined so that the distance between two bounding boxes in either the x extent or the y extent is larger than the maximum length of the two objects in that same x or y extent (see figure 2). Mathematically,

$$|x_c^1 - x_c^2| - (\xi_x^1 + \xi_x^2) > 2\max(\xi_x^1, \xi_x^2) \text{ or}$$
$$|y_c^1 - y_c^2| - (\xi_y^1 + \xi_y^2) > 2\max(\xi_y^1, \xi_y^2)$$

INSIDE

Inside requires that the bounding box of one object

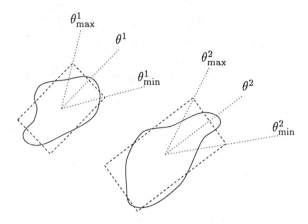

Figure 3: Definition of relevant angles for *aligned*

be completely embedded within the bounding box of another. Formally,

$$\xi_x^1 - \xi_x^2 > |x_c^1 - x_c^2| \text{ and } \xi_y^1 - \xi_y^2 > |y_c^1 - y_c^2|$$

ABOVE, BELOW

Above requires that the projections of bounding boxes on the x axis intersect and that the projections of bounding boxes on the y axis do not intersect. The mathematical relationship is

$$\xi_x^1 + \xi_x^2 > |x_c^1 - x_c^2| \text{ and } \xi_y^1 + \xi_y^2 < y_c^1 - y_c^2$$

Note that *above* is non-commutative. We define *below* similarly. As with *near* and *far*, *above* and *below* are mutually exclusive prepositions. However, not-*above* does not strictly imply *below*.

ALIGNED

The alignment[2] property is angular in nature, therefore its quantification involves inequalities between angles, rather than lengths as the previous prepositions had. For this purpose we define a different type of bounding box that is centered at the object's center of mass and oriented along the object's principal inertia axes with dimensions proportional to the object's maximum and minimum moments of inertia. θ, θ_{min} and θ_{max} are as shown in figure 3. With this in mind, the preposition *aligned* is defined as:

$$\max(\theta_{\min}^1, \theta_{\min}^2) < \theta^i < \min(\theta_{\max}^1, \theta_{\max}^2), \quad i = 1, 2$$

NEXT

We've defined *next* as a combination of the prepositions *near* and *aligned*. Therefore the definition for *next* is:

$$U_{next} = U_{near} \cap U_{aligned}$$

The preposition *next* is an example of a spatial preposition that is a combination of more elementary

---

[2]Although not a preposition from a language perspective we've adopted it as a spatial preposition.

prepositions. This hints at the possibility of a natural hierarchy of spatial prepositions. It also shows evidence of the possible partitioning of the 12D space mentioned previously.

The Fuzzification of Spatial Prepositions

This section describes why and how we fuzzify spatial prepositions. We need to fuzzify spatial prepositions because they are vague by their very nature; they depend on context and depend on an individual's perception of them with respect to an environment. For these reasons we need to allow for some leeway when deciding if two objects are related through a given preposition.

There is a lot of freedom in how we can fuzzify spatial prepositions, or equivalently, the "ideal" set, U_p. The idea we have adopted is to define the membership function $f_{U_p}(\mu)$ where $\mu \in \mathcal{R}^{12}$ as a function of a distance d between μ and U_p.

$$d = \min_{\mu' \in U_p} |\mu - \mu'|$$

Note that $d(\mu, U_p) = 0$ for $\mu \in U_p$. The distance d tells us by how much the defining preposition inequalities are *not* satisfied. Thus,

$$f_{U_p}(\mu) = 1 \text{ for } \mu \in U_p$$

$$f_{U_p}(\mu) \to 0 \text{ as } d(\mu, U_p) \to \infty$$

U_p is a multi-dimensional set defined by complex inequalities, for which computing d may be very burdensome. For this reason we resort to a Monte-Carlo simulation with a set of random points around μ that have given statistical properties. The experiments we've conducted use normally distributed random points with mean μ and covariance matrix diag $(\sigma^2, ..., \sigma^2)$. The exact form for f_{U_p} used is

$$f_{U_p} = \begin{cases} 1, & \mu \in U_p \\ \min(1, 2\frac{N'}{N}), & \mu \notin U_p \end{cases}$$

where N is the total number of random points in the Monte-Carlo simulation and N' is the number of points $\mu' \in U_p$. Note that the formulation of f_{U_p} ensures that f_{U_p} for μ very close to the boundary of U_p will have a value close to 1.

The following section will detail some experiments that use this fuzzification technique and put into effect the inequalities that define the given spatial prepositions.

Qualitative Description Experiments

We will use the image shown in figure 4 to illustrate several uses of the prepositions. Each object has been numbered to ease their reference. The image is read as a grey-scale pixel image. It is then thresholded to produce a binary image and objects are located using a sequential labelling algorithm [Horn, 1989]. Once the objects in the scene have been found, the attributes

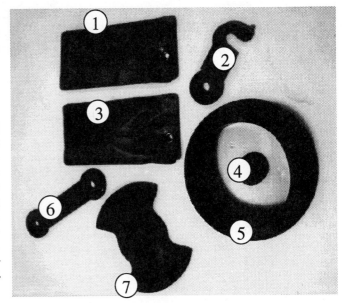

Figure 4: The experimental image

necessary for construction of the 12-dimensional vector are computed (e.g. the area of an object is the sum of all the pixels belonging to the object). Currently the system accepts a spatial preposition and displays all those objects that satisfy the preposition inequalities. The system also accepts as input two objects along with a preposition and it outputs how well those two objects meet the given preposition (the value of f_{U_p} for given σ). All intuitively obvious relations between objects are discovered by the system, e.g. objects 1 and 3 are *next* to each other, etc.

An interesting case, and one that demonstrates the effects of fuzzification is the case of supplying object 2 and object 6 along with the preposition *aligned*. With no fuzzification the system finds that 2 and 6 are not aligned. However, if we allow a certain amount of fuzzification with say $\sigma = 0.03$ the value of $f_{U_{aligned}}$ is 0.8. This value indicates that they may be sufficiently aligned to be regarded as such (which we actually see in the image!), depending on how much leeway we wish to allow. The dependency of $f_{U_{aligned}}$ on σ is shown in figure 5. From this graph we see that the value of the membership function significantly deteriorates for large values of σ. This simply means that the amount of induced uncertainty is so large that the objects cease to possess their original features (such as orientation in this case). This also indicates what the maximal acceptable value for σ should be. In this case, that is $\sigma < 0.1$.

Another interesting case is that of supplying object 2 and object 6 along with the preposition *near* or *far*. Neither satisfies the inequalities precisely. However, if we again, allow for fuzzification, we get a most interesting result, as shown in figure 6. We observe that

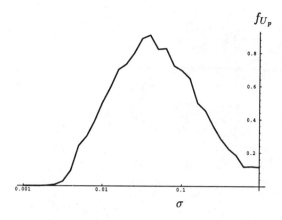

Figure 5: The dependency of $f_{U_{aligned}}(2,6)$ as a function of σ

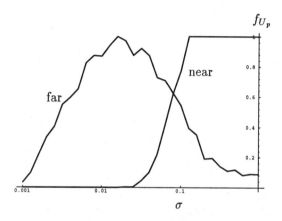

Figure 6: The dependency of $f_{U_{near}}(2,6)$ and $f_{U_{far}}(2,6)$ as a function of σ

although we can not say for certain that object 2 and object 6 are either *near* or *far*, we can say that they are *somewhat near* or *somewhat far*. How we decide which of the two to use can be seen in figure 6. If we examine the slopes of the two curves we see that for small values of σ the slope for *far* is steeper than that for *near*. Therefore it would seem more appropriate to say that 2 is *somewhat far* from 6 as opposed to 2 is *somewhat near* to 6.

Conclusion

The intent of this paper was to establish a computational model for characterizing spatial prepositions for use in describing objects. A quantification was established and demonstrated through the use of an example. A framework to deal with the inherent vagueness of prepositions was also introduced with the use of a fuzzification technique.

An extension of this work would be one in which a user could conduct a dialogue with the system, capable of understanding as well as generating scene de-

scriptions. In other words, we may wish to describe a particular object with as few descriptions as possible through the feedback from the system. The goal would be to home in on the object we are truly referring to through repeatedly supplying additional prepositions to those objects that were singled out after previous inquires. An experiment using this technique may reveal that people naturally describe spatial arrangements in a series of descriptions, rather than once and for all. It may also demonstrate inadequacies in the vocabulary or complexity of a scene. We may also discover that certain environments require that we adopt prepositions that do not exist in the English language for describing a particular sort of spatial arrangement.

References

Abella, A. 1992. Extracting geometric shapes from a set of points. In *Image Understanding Workshop*.

Herskovits, A. 1986. *Language and spatial cognition: An interdisciplinary study of the prepositions in English*. Cambridge University Press.

Horn, Berthold K.P. 1989. *Robot Vision*. The MIT Press.

Klir, G. J. and Folger, T. A. 1988. *Fuzzy Sets, Uncertainty, and Information*. Prentice Hall.

Landau, B. and Jackendoff, R. ation. "What" and "Where" in spatial language and spatial cognition. *BBS*.

Lindkvist, K. 1976. *Comprehensive study of conceptions of locality in which English prepositions occur*. Almqvist & Wiksell International.

Talmy, L. 1983. How language structures space. In *Spatial orientation: Theory, research, and application*. Plenum Press.

Definition of ξ_x and ξ_y

We have used the following two equations to define how much an object stretches in the x and y directions.

$$\xi_x = 2\max\{\sqrt{\frac{I_{max}}{A}}|\cos\theta|, \sqrt{\frac{I_{min}}{A}}|\sin\theta|, \}$$

$$\xi_y = 2\max\{\sqrt{\frac{I_{max}}{A}}|\sin\theta|, \sqrt{\frac{I_{min}}{A}}|\cos\theta|, \}$$

The following is the derivation of the above formulas. The maximal moment of inertia is given by the formula

$$I_{max} = \int\int_A u^2 du dv = k\xi_u^2 A$$

where u and v are axes of maximal and minimal moment of inertia respectively, A is an object's area and ξ_u is an elongation parameter that conveys information regarding how much an object "stretches" along the axis u. Constant k is chosen so that in the case of a circle with radius r we have $\xi_u = r$. Simple calculation gives $k = 2$, and formulas for ξ_x and ξ_y are obtained by projecting ξ_u and ξ_v onto axes x and y.

Numeric Reasoning with Relative Orders of Magnitude

Philippe Dague

L.I.P.N. Université Paris Nord
Avenue Jean-Baptiste Clément
93430 Villetaneuse - France
e-mail: dague@lipn.univ-paris13.fr

Abstract

In [Dague, 1993], a formal system ROM(K) involving four relations has been defined to reason with relative orders of magnitude. In this paper, problems of introducing quantitative information and of ensuring validity of the results in $\mathbb{R}$ are tackled.

Correspondent overlapping relations are defined in $\mathbb{R}$ and all rules of ROM(K) are transposed to $\mathbb{R}$. Unlike other proposed systems, the obtained system ROM($\mathbb{R}$) ensures a sound calculus in $\mathbb{R}$, while keeping the ability to provide commonsense explanations of the results.

If needed, these results can be refined by using additional and complementary techniques: k-bound-consistency, which generalizes interval propagation; symbolic computation, which considerably improves the results by delaying numeric evaluation; symbolic algebra calculus of the roots of partial derivatives, which allows the exact extrema to be obtained; transformation of rational functions, when possible, so that each variable occurs only once, which allows interval propagation to give the exact results.

ROM($\mathbb{R}$), possibly supplemented by these various techniques, constitutes a rich, powerful and flexible tool for performing mixed qualitative and numeric reasoning, essential for engineering tasks.

Introduction

The first attempt to formalize relative order of magnitude reasoning, with binary relations invariant by homothety, appeared with the formal system FOG [Raiman, 1986] (see also [Raiman, 1991] for a more general set-based framework), based on 3 basic relations and described by 32 inference rules, which has been used successfully in the DEDALE system of analog circuit diagnosis [Dague et al., 1987]. Nevertheless, FOG has several limitations which prevent it from being really used in engineering. A first difficulty arises when wanting to express a gradual change from one order of magnitude to another: only a steep change is possible, due to the non overlapping of the orders of magnitude. This can be solved, as described in [Dague, 1993], by introducing a fourth relation "to be distant from" which allows overlapping relations to be defined and used. This has given a formal system ROM(K) with 15 axioms, consistency of

which was proved by finding models in non standard analysis.

But two crucial problems remain: the difficulty to incorporate quantitative information when available (in DEDALE this lack of a numeric-symbolic interface meant writing Ohm's law in an ad hoc form) and the difficulty to control the inference process, in order to obtain valid results in the real world. These problems were pointed out in [Mavrovouniotis and Stephanopoulos, 1987] but the proposed system O(M) does not really solve them. In particular, use of heuristic interpretation semantics just ensures the validity of the inference in $\mathbb{R}$ for one step (application of one rule) but not for several steps (when chaining rules). This paper focuses on solving these two problems by concentrating on how to transpose the formal system ROM(K) to $\mathbb{R}$ with a guarantee of soundness and how to use additional numeric and symbolic algebra techniques to refine the results if needed, in order to build a powerful tool for both qualitative/symbolic and quantitative/numeric calculus for engineering purposes.

The present paper is organized as follows. Section 2 shows through an example how ROM(K), as FOG or O(M), may lead to results that are not valid in $\mathbb{R}$. In section 3 a translation in $\mathbb{R}$ of axioms and properties of ROM(K) is given, which ensures soundness of inference in $\mathbb{R}$. In section 4 the example is revisited with this new formulation; this time correct results are obtained. Nevertheless they may be far from the optimal ones and too inaccurate for certain purposes. In section 5 numeric and symbolic algebra techniques are proposed to refine these results: applications of consistency techniques for numeric CSPs; use of computer algebra to push symbolic computation as far as possible and delay numeric evaluation, which considerably improves the results; symbolic calculus of derivatives and of their roots by using computer algebra alone in order to compute extrema and obtain optimal results; formal transformation of rational functions by changing variables, which allows the exact results to be obtained, in particular cases, by a simple numeric evaluation and opens up future ways of research.

Example: a Heat Exchanger

Let us remember that the formal system ROM(K) (see [Dague, 1993] for a complete description) involves four binary relations $\approx$, $\sim$, $\ll$ and $\nsim$, intuitive meanings of which are "close to", "comparable to", "negligible w.r.t." and "distant from" respectively. The 15 axioms are as follows:

(A1) $A \approx A$
(A2) $A \approx B \mapsto B \approx A$
(A3) $A \approx B, B \approx C \mapsto A \approx C$
(A4) $A \approx B \mapsto B \sim A$
(A5) $A \sim B, B \sim C \mapsto A \sim C$
(A6) $A \approx B \mapsto A \sim B$
(A7) $A \approx B \mapsto C.A \approx C.B$
(A8) $A \sim B \mapsto C.A \sim C.B$
(A9) $A \sim 1 \mapsto [A] = +$
(A10) $A \ll B \longleftrightarrow B \approx (B+A)$
(A11) $A \ll B, B \sim C \mapsto A \ll C$
(A12) $A \approx B, [C] = [A] \mapsto (A+C) \approx (B+C)$
(A13) $A \sim B, [C] = [A] \mapsto (A+C) \sim (B+C)$
(A14) $A \sim (A+A)$
(A15) $A \not\approx B \longleftrightarrow (A-B) \sim A$ or $(B-A) \sim B$

45 properties of ROM(K) have been deduced from these axioms and 7 basic overlapping relations between two positive quantities $A < B$ have been defined:
$A \approx B, \neg(A \not\approx B), \neg(A \approx B) \wedge A \sim B, A \not\approx B \wedge A \sim B, A \not\approx B \wedge \neg(A \ll B), \neg(A \sim B), A \ll B$.
Taking into account signs and identity, these relations give 15 primitive overlapping relations. Adding the 47 compound relations obtained by disjunction of successive primitive relations gives a total of 62 legitimate relations.

Let us try to apply ROM(K) to a simple example of a counter-current heat exchanger as described in [Mavrovouniotis and Stephanopoulos, 1988]. Let FH and KH be the molar-flowrate and the molar-heat of the hot stream, FC and KC the molar-flowrate and the molar-heat of the cold stream. Four temperature differences are defined: DTH is the temperature drop of the hot stream, DTC is the temperature rise of the cold stream, DT1 is the driving force at the left end of the device, and DT2 is the driving force at the right end of the device. The two following equations hold:

(e1) $DTH - DT1 - DTC + DT2 = 0$,
(e2) $DTH \times KH \times FH = DTC \times KC \times FC$.

The first one is a consequence of the definition of the temperature differences, and the second one is the energy balance of the device. Let us take the following assumptions expressed as order of magnitude relations:

(i) $DT2 \sim DT1$, (ii) $DT1 \ll DTH$, (iii) $KH \approx KC$.

The problem is now to deduce from the 2 equations and these 3 order of magnitude relations the 5 missing order of magnitude relations between quantities having the same dimension (4 for temperature differences and 1 for molar-flowrates). Let us take the axioms (Ai) above and the properties (Pi), viewed as production rules of a symbolic deduction system ROM, as stated in [Dague, 1993].

Consider first the relation between DT2 and DTH. Thanks to (P4) $A \ll B, C \sim A \mapsto C \ll B$, ROM infers from (i) and (ii) that (1) $DT2 \ll DTH$.

Consider the relation between DTH and DTC. (P5) $A \ll B \mapsto -A \ll B$ and (P6) $A \ll C, B \ll C$

$\mapsto (A+B) \ll C$ applied to (ii) and (1) imply $-DT1 + DT2 \ll DTH$. From this it can be deduced, using (A10), that $DTH \approx DTH - DT1 + DT2$, i.e. using (e1) that (2) $DTH \approx DTC$.

Consider the relation between DT1 and DTC. From (ii) and (2) it can be deduced, using (A6) and (A11), that (3) $DT1 \ll DTC$.

Consider the relation between DT2 and DTC. It results from (i) and (3), by using (P4), that (4) $DT2 \ll DTC$.

Another deduction path can be found to obtain the same result. In fact, from (A10) $A \approx B \mapsto (B-A) \ll A$ and $A \approx C \mapsto (C-A) \ll A$, using (P5) and (P6), (P) $A \approx B, A \approx C \mapsto (C-B) \ll A$ can be derived. As, from (3) and (A10), it results that $DTC \approx DTC + DT1$, it can be deduced from this and (2), using (P), that $-DTH + DT1 + DTC \ll DTC$, i.e. using (e1) that (4) $DT2 \ll DTC$.

Consider finally the relation between FH and FC. (A7), applied to (iii) and (2), gives $DTH \times KH \approx DTH \times KC$ and $DTH \times KC \approx DTC \times KC$. Applying (A3) then gives $DTH \times KH \approx DTC \times KC$. Applying (A7) again and using (e2) gives (5) $FH \approx FC$.

The five results (1 to 5) have thus been obtained by ROM (identical to those produced by O(M) because $\not\approx$ is not used here):
(1) $DT2 \ll DTH$ (2) $DTH \approx DTC$ (3) $DT1 \ll DTC$ (4) $DT2 \ll DTC$ (5) $FH \approx FC$.

We have now to evaluate them in the real world. For this, it is necessary to fix a numeric scale for the order of magnitude relations. Choose for example $\ll$ represented by at most 10%, $\approx$ by at most (for the relative difference) 10 % and $\sim$ by at most (for the relative difference) 80%. Assumptions thus mean that:
(i') $0.2 \leq DT2/DT1 \leq 5$, (ii') $DT1/DTH \leq 0.1$,
(iii') $0.9 \leq KH/KC \leq 1.112$.
It is not very difficult in this example to compute the correct results by hand. It is found (see also subsections 5.3 and 5.4) that:
(1') $DT2/DTH \leq 0.5$ (2') $0.714 \leq DTH/DTC \leq 1.087$ (3') $DT1/DTC \leq 0.109$ (4') $DT2/DTC \leq 0.358$ (5') $0.828 \leq FH/FC \leq 1.556$.

This shows that only the formal result $DT1 \ll DTC$ is satisfied in practice. For the 4 others, although the inference paths remain short in this example, there is already a non trivial shift, which makes them unacceptable. This is the case for the two $\approx$ relations: DTH may in fact differ from DTC by nearly 30%, and FH may differ from FC by 35%. And the same happens for the two $\ll$ relations: DT2 can reach 35% of DTC and, worse, 50% of DTH. This is not really surprising because we know that there is no model of ROM(K) in $\mathbb{R}$. Here, it is essentially the rule (P4) that causes discrepancy between qualitative and numeric results. Rules such as (P4), or (A11) from which it comes, and also (A3) are obviously being infringed. What this does demonstrate is the insufficiency of ROM for general engineering tasks and the need for a sound relative order of magnitude calculus in $\mathbb{R}$.

Transposing the Formal System to $\mathbb{R}$: ROM($\mathbb{R}$)

In fact, all the theoretical framework developed in [Dague, 1993] is a source of inspiration for this task. Since the rules of ROM capture pertinent qualitative information and may help guide intuition, they will serve as guidelines for inferences in $\mathbb{R}$ ([Dubois and Prade, 1989] addresses the same type of objectives by using fuzzy relations). Let us introduce the natural relations in $\mathbb{R}$, parameterized by a positive real k, "close to the order k":

$A \overset{k}{\sim} B \;\longleftrightarrow\; |A-B| \leq k \times \text{Max}(|A|,|B|)$,
i.e. for $k < 1$, (I) $\;1-k \leq A/B \leq 1/1-k\;$ or $A = B = 0$, "distant at the order k":

$A \overset{k}{\not\sim} B \;\longleftrightarrow\; |A-B| \geq k \times \text{Max}(|A|,|B|)$,
i.e. for $k < 1$, (II) $A/B \leq 1-k$ or $A/B \geq 1/1-k$ or $B = 0$, and "negligible at the order k":

$A \overset{k}{\ll} B \;\longleftrightarrow\; |A| \leq k \times |B|$,
i.e. (III) $-k \leq A/B \leq k$ or $A = B = 0$.

The first one will be used to model both $\approx$ and $\sim$, the second one to model $\not\approx$, and the third one to model $\ll$, by associating a particular order to each relation. When trying to transpose the axioms (Ai) by using these new relations, three cases occur.

Axioms of reflexivity (A1), symmetry (A2,A4), invariance by homothety (A7,A8), and invariance by adding a quantity of the same sign (A12,A13, assuming (A9)) are obviously satisfied by $\overset{k}{\sim}$ for any positive k.

A second group of axioms imposes constraints between the respective orders attached to each of the 4 relations. Coupling of $\sim$ with signs (A9) is true for any order k attached to $\sim$ that verifies $k < 1$. The fact that $\sim$ is coarser than $\approx$ (A6) forces the order for $\approx$ to be not greater than the order for $\sim$. Axiom (A14) is true for $\overset{k}{\sim}$ if $k \geq 1/2$. The left to right implication of (A10) has the exact equivalent: $A \overset{k}{\ll} B \mapsto B \overset{k}{\sim} (B+A)$ for $k < 1$. We can thus take the same order k_1 for $\ll$ and $\approx$. In the same way, the definition of $\not\approx$ in terms of $\sim$ (A15) has its equivalent: $A \overset{k}{\not\approx} B \longleftrightarrow (A-B) \overset{1-k}{\sim} A$ or $(B-A) \overset{1-k}{\sim} B$ provided $k \leq 1/2$, i.e. $1-k \geq 1/2$. If we call k_2 the order for $\not\approx$, we can thus take $1-k_2$ as the order for $\sim$. All the above thus leads to the following correspondences:

$A \approx B \;\longleftrightarrow\; A \overset{k_1}{\sim} B \qquad A \sim B \;\longleftrightarrow\; A \overset{1-k_2}{\underset{k_2}{\sim}} B$

$A \ll B \;\longleftrightarrow\; A \overset{k_1}{\ll} B \qquad A \not\approx B \;\longleftrightarrow\; A \overset{k_2}{\not\sim} B$

with $0 < k_1 \leq k_2 \leq 1/2 \leq 1-k_2 < 1$. Note that, as the formal system ROM(K) depends on two relations, its analog in $\mathbb{R}$ has two degrees of freedom represented by the orders k_1 and k_2.

Remaining axioms are those which are not true in $\mathbb{R}$. For these, the loss of precision on the orders is computed exactly in conclusion. The right to left implication of (A10) gives:

$B \overset{k}{\sim} (B+A) \;\mapsto\; A \overset{k/1-k}{\ll} B$ ($k/(1-k) < 1$ when $k < 1/2$).
Transitivity axioms (A3) and (A5) each give:
$A \overset{k}{\sim} B, \; B \overset{k'}{\sim} C \;\mapsto\; A \overset{k+k'-kk'}{\sim} C$ ($k+k'-kk' < 1$ when $k < 1$ and $k' < 1$).

Finally the coupling between $\approx$ (through $\ll$) and $\sim$ (A11) gives:
$A \overset{k}{\ll} B, \; B \overset{1-k'}{\sim} C \;\mapsto\; A \overset{k/k'}{\ll} C$ ($k/k' < 1$ when $k < k'$).

Like the axioms (Ai), all properties (Pi) deduced in [Dague, 1993] are demonstrated in the same way by computing the best orders in conclusion, when they are not directly satisfied, and constitute all the inference rules of ROM($\mathbb{R}$). For reasons of lack of space, here are the most significant or useful of the 45 properties for our purpose.

(P4), as (A11), gives $A \overset{k}{\ll} B, \; A \overset{1-k'}{\sim} C \;\mapsto\; C \overset{k/k'}{\ll} B$.
(P6) gives $A \ll C, \; B \ll C \;\mapsto\; (A+B) \ll C$ (which can be improved if $[A] = -[B]$ by taking $\max(k,k')$ as order in conclusion) and (P) gives $A \overset{k}{\sim} B, \; A \overset{k'}{\sim} C \;\mapsto\; C-B \overset{k''}{\ll} A$ with $k'' = (k+k'-kk')/(1-\max(k,k'))$ (which can be improved if $[C-B] = [A]$ by taking $k'' = (k+k'-kk')/(1-k')$).
Transitivity of $\ll$ (P11) obviously improves the degree $A \overset{k}{\ll} B, \; B \overset{k'}{\ll} C \;\mapsto\; A \overset{k \times k'}{\ll} C$.

The incompatibility of $\ll$ and $\sim$ (P14) $A \overset{1-k_2}{\sim} B, \; A \overset{k_1}{\underset{k_2}{\ll}} B \;\mapsto\; A = B = 0$ and of $\approx$ and $\not\approx$ (P34) $A \overset{k_1}{\sim} B, \; A \overset{k_2}{\not\sim} B \;\mapsto\; A = B = 0$ are ensured provided $k_1 < k_2$. These two properties will be used to check the consistency of the set of relations describing, for example, an actual behavior of a physical system, or on the contrary to detect inconsistencies coming, from example, from discrepancies between modeled and actual behaviors of a system for tasks such as diagnosis.

Relations between $\approx$ and $\not\approx$ (P37, P38) give $A \overset{k_2}{\not\sim} B$, $C \overset{k_1}{\sim} A \;\mapsto\; C \overset{(k_2-k_1)/(1-k_1)}{\not\sim} B$ and $A \overset{k_2}{\sim} B, \; C \overset{k_1}{\not\sim} A \;\mapsto\; (C-A) \overset{k_1/k_2}{\sim} (C-B)$.
Finally, the completeness of the description is obtained: $A \overset{1-k_2}{\sim} B$ or $A \overset{k_2}{\not\sim} B$ provided that $k_2 \leq 1/2$.

Moreover, it can be proved that adding the assumption $A \overset{1-k_2}{\sim} B$ or $B \overset{1-k_2}{\sim} A$ or $A \overset{k_1}{\ll} B$ or $B \overset{k_1}{\ll} A$ would be equivalent to adding $A \overset{k_1}{\sim} B$ or $A \overset{k_1}{\not\sim} B$ and also equivalent to $k_2 \leq k_1$. This would imply $k_1 = k_2 = e$ as in FOG or in the strict interpretation of O(M) [Mavrovouniotis and Stephanopoulos, 1987], i.e. only one degree of freedom instead or two. In the same way that formal models of ROM(K) could not be reduced to FOG or O(M), the same is obtained for ROM($\mathbb{R}$) by choosing $k_1 < k_2$, i.e. $0 < k_1 < k_2 \leq 1/2$. Note that, in relation to non standard models of ROM(K), one degree of freedom corresponds to what is chosen as the analog in $\mathbb{R}$ of the infinitesimals, and the other to the choice of the analog of the parameter ε [Dague, 1993] of the model, where ε corresponds to k_1/k_2.

The above gives the exact counterpart in $\mathbb{R}_+$ of the 15 primitive relations of [Dague, 1993] (in fact inference rules analog to the previous ones can be defined for these relations, often with some better orders in conclusion by taking into account the signs of the quantities, e.g. (P6) and (P) above), for describing the order of magnitude of A/B w.r.t. 1. These relations correspond to real intervals which overlap (in contrast with the strict interpretation of O(M)) and are built from the landmarks k_1, k_2, $1-k_2$, $1-k_1$, 1, $1/(1-k_1)$, $1/(1-k_2)$, $1/k_2$, $1/k_1$ of $\mathbb{R}_+$ (see Fig. 1). Note that, as in the formal model, intervals (k_1, k_2), $(1-k_2, 1-k_1)$ and their inverse are not acceptable relations. The heuristic interpretation of O(M) [Mavrovouniotis and Stephanopoulos, 1987], which only allows the correct inference to be made for one rule, corresponds to the particular case where $k_1 = k_2/(1+k_2)$. But here k_1 and k_2 are chosen independently, according to the expertise domain.

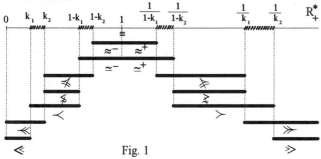

Fig. 1

The orders appearing in each rule of ROM($\mathbb{R}$) have to be considered as variables, with order in conclusion symbolically expressed in terms of orders in premises. Inference by such a rule is made simply by matching relations patterns in premises with existing relations, i.e. by instantiating the orders to real numbers, and computing the orders in conclusion to deduce a new relation. A sound calculus in $\mathbb{R}$ is thus ensured whatever the path of rules used, i.e. any conclusion that can be deduced by application of rules of ROM($\mathbb{R}$) from given correct premises is correct when interpreted in $\mathbb{R}$. This may be entirely hidden from the user, with both data and results being translated via k_1 and k_2 in symbolic order of magnitude relations as in FOG, but this time correctly. But the user may also incorporate numeric information as required by using k orders directly or even introducing numeric values for quantities. In this last case, binary relations between two given numeric quantities are automatically inferred from the equivalent formulation of these relations in terms of intervals (I,II,III).

Control of the inference in order to avoid combinatory explosion remains a problem for large applications. A pragmatic solution is to call on the expert who will possibly prevent a rule from being applied if he considers in the light of its underlying qualitative meaning that the conclusions are not relevant.

The Example Revisited

Let us take the example of the heat exchanger again and follow the same reasoning paths, but this time using the inference rules of ROM($\mathbb{R}$). Take, as in the numeric application, $k_1 = 0.1$ and $k_2 = 0.2$. As (1) is inferred by using (P4) we obtain:
(1a) DT2 $\overset{k3}{\lessapprox}$ DTH with $k3 = k_1/k_2 = 0.5$.
DT2 and $-$DT1 having opposite signs, application of (P6) gives $-$DT1 $+$ DT2 $\overset{k4}{\lessapprox}$ DTH

with $k4 = \max(k_1, k3) = 0.5$. Using left to right implication of (A10) and (e1), we get:
(2a) DTH $\overset{k4}{\approx}$ DTC with $k4 = \max(k_1, k3) = 0.5$.
From (ii) and (2a), it can be deduced, using (A11), that:
(3a) DT1 $\overset{k5}{\lessapprox}$ DTC with $k5 = k_1/(1-k4) = 0.2$.
The first deduction path leading to (4) has as an equivalent, using (P4), DT2 $\overset{k6}{\lessapprox}$ DTC with $k6 = k5/k_2 = 1$, which cannot be used because the order of $\lessapprox$ is assumed to be < 1. We may, however, use the other deduction path. As, from (3a) and (A10), we have DTC $\overset{k5}{\approx}$ DTC $+$ DT1, it can be deduced from this and (2a), using (P) and (e1), that:
(4a) DT2 $\overset{k7}{\lessapprox}$ DTC
with $k7 = (k4 + k5 - k4k5)/(1-k5) = 0.75$.
Note that two different paths leading to the same formal result in ROM may lead here to different results in ROM($\mathbb{R}$). This poses the as yet unsolved problem of defining heuristics in order to obtain the best result, by pruning the paths that lead to less precise ones (the length of the deduction path not necessarily being a good criterion).
From DTH$\times$KH $\overset{k1}{\approx}$ DTH$\times$KC and DTH$\times$KC $\overset{k4}{\approx}$ DTC$\times$KC, (A3) gives DTH$\times$KH $\overset{}{\approx}$ DTC$\times$KC, from which, using (A7) and (e2), we obtain:
(5a) FH $\overset{k8}{\approx}$ FC with $k8 = k_1 + k4 - k_1k4 = 0.55$.
Results (1a to 5a) have thus been obtained by applying rules of ROM($\mathbb{R}$). In terms of intervals, these relations are expressed as:
DT2/DTH ≤ 0.5 $0.5 \leq$ DTH/DTC ≤ 2
DT1/DTC ≤ 0.2 DT2/DTC ≤ 0.75
$0.45 \leq$ FH/FC ≤ 2.223.
They can automatically be translated in terms of formal order of magnitude compound relations w.r.t. scales k_1 and k_2 (with obviously a loss of precision in general), giving:
DT2 $\ll..\prec$ DTH   DTH $\lessapprox ..\succapprox$ DTC   DT1 $\ll$ DTC   DT2 $\ll..\prec$ DTC   FH $\lessapprox ..\succapprox$ FC.
In contrast with results of FOG or O(M) (1 to 5), this time the results are correct. We thus have a sound calculus in $\mathbb{R}$, with all the advantages of the qualitative meaning transmitted by rules of ROM. In particular, each of the above results has its explanation in commonsense reasoning terms given by the rules applied to obtain it. Using symbolic computation, the formal k orders of the results can even be expressed in terms of k_1 and k_2. This can be used for other purposes such as design, so as to tune the values of k_1 and k_2 and thus make sure desired orders of magnitude relations are satisfied.
Nevertheless it can be noticed, by comparing them with exact results (1′ to 5′), that these relations are not in general optimal. In fact, in qualitative terms, the exact results would give:
DT2 $\ll..\prec$ DTH   DTH $\lessapprox ..\approx^+$ DTC   DT1 $\ll$ DTC   DT2 $\ll..\prec$ DTC   FH $\simeq^-..\succapprox$ FC,
improving 3 of the 5 above results. The improvement is even more obvious when comparing ranges given by numeric orders k3 to k8 with exact results. Only DT2/DTH is correctly estimated (i.e. (1a) and (1′) are the same). In fact, this is not surprising. Although each rule of ROM($\mathbb{R}$) has been computed with the

best estimate for order in conclusion, so that each rule taken separately cannot be improved, this does not guarantee optimality through an inference path using several rules that share common variables. In some way, what we have is local optimality, not global optimality. If we estimate that the obtained results, although sound, are not accurate enough for our purpose, we have to supplement ROM($\mathbb{R}$) with other techniques.

Using Numeric or Symbolic Algebra Techniques

Once sound results of ROM($\mathbb{R}$), with the obvious qualitative meaning of the inference paths, have been obtained, several supplementary techniques can be used in order to refine them if needed. These techniques come from two different approaches: numeric ones which transpose well-known consistency techniques for CSPs to numeric CSPs, and symbolic ones which use computer algebra. These approaches are not exclusive and can be usefully combined.

Applying Consistency Techniques for Numeric CSPs

A first way of refining the results is to start from definitions (I,II,III) of the fundamental relations of ROM($\mathbb{R}$) in terms of intervals, a technique that can easily be extended to all 15 primitive relations. Numeric values are also naturally represented by intervals to take into account precision of observation. Interval computation thus offers itself. Moreover, we are not limited to intervals representing the 15 primitive relations or the compound ones, i.e. to the scale of ROM($\mathbb{R}$); we can in fact express any order of magnitude binary relation between two quantities by an interval encompassing the quotient of the quantities. In particular, intervals do not need the specific symmetry properties of those of ROM($\mathbb{R}$) such as in (I,II,III). Since using intervals is thus more accurate when expressing data, it should also be so for the results. But, unfortunately, interval propagation is rarely powerful enough: in the heat exchanger example nothing is obtained by this method.

The idea is to generalize interval propagation in the same way that, in CSPs, k-consistency with $k > 2$ extends arc consistency. This has been done in [Lhomme, 1993], who shows that the consistency techniques that have been developed for CSPs can be adapted to numeric CSPs involving, in particular, continuous domains. The way is to handle domains only by their bounds and to define an analog of k-consistency restricted to the bounds of the domains, called k-B-consistency. In particular 2-B-consistency, or arc B-consistency, which formalizes interval propagation, is extended by the notion of k-B-consistency. The related algorithms with their complexity are given for k = 2 and 3. They have been implemented in Interlog [Dassault Electronique, 1991], above Prolog language. In this section, these techniques are evaluated w.r.t. the heat exchanger example.

Starting from equations (e1) and (e2) and assumptions (i',ii',iii'), bounds for the 5 remaining quotients are looked for. In this case, as already seen, arc B-consistency gives no result. But 3-B-consistency gives the following results for the first 4 quotients (nothing is obtained for FH/FC) with parameters characterizing the authorized relative imprecision at the bounds w1 = 0.02 and w2 = 0.0001 (in about 75s on an IBM 3090):

(1″) DT2/DTH ≤ 0.508
(2″) $0.665 \leq$ DTH/DTC ≤ 1.120
(3″) DT1/DTC ≤ 0.112
(4″) DT2/DTC ≤ 0.559.

It can be noticed that estimates (2″,3″,4″) are better than corresponding results of ROM($\mathbb{R}$) (2a,3a,4a) and, for the first two, not far from optimal ones (2′,3′). 4-B-consistency has also been tried, although execution time increases considerably. For example, $0.710 \leq$ DTH/DTC ≤ 1.090 and DT2/DTC ≤ 0.362, which well approximate (2′) and (4′), are obtained in a few minutes with w1 = 0.01 and w2 = 0.05.

Although interval propagation alone is in general insufficient, k-B-consistency techniques with $k \geq 3$ may thus provide very good results, but some difficulties remain (here, nothing can be done with equation (e2), unless considering at least 5-consistency with efficiency problems).

Using Symbolic Algebra first

The above results reach the limits of purely numeric approaches. If we want to progress towards optimal results, we have to use computer algebra in order to push symbolic computation as far as possible and delay numeric evaluation In a great number of real examples, the total number of equations expressing the behavior of the system and of order of magnitude assumptions equals the number of order of magnitude relations asked for, and the desired dimensionless quotients can be solved in terms of the known quotients, using these equations. These solutions are very often expressed as rational functions and this symbolic computation can be achieved by computer algebra.

For example, from equations (e1) and (e2), known relations
DT2 = Q1×DT1, DT1 = Q2×DTH, KH = Q3×KC,
and searched relations
DT2 = X×DTH, DTH = Y×DTC, DT1 = W×DTC,
DT2 = Z×DTC, FH = U×FC,
MAPLE V [Char, 1988] immediately deduces the formulas (F):
X = Q1×Q2,   Y = 1/(1−Q2+Q1×Q2),
W = Q2/(1−Q2+Q1×Q2),
Z = Q1×Q2/(1−Q2+Q1×Q2),
U = (1−Q2+Q1×Q2)/Q3,
with $1/5 \leq Q1 \leq 5$, $0 \leq Q2 \leq 1/10$, $9/10 \leq Q3 \leq 10/9$.

Numeric CSP techniques can now be applied directly to these symbolic equations. This time, results are obtained just with arc B-consistency, even for U:

(1s) $X \leq 0.5$ (2s) $0.666 \leq Y \leq 1.112$ (3s) $W \leq 0.112$ (4s) $Z \leq 0.556$ (5s) $0.810 \leq U \leq 1.667$.

It can thus be seen that, when starting from solved symbolic expressions, the most simple numeric technique, i.e. analog to interval propagation, gives results which are close to the exact ones (1' to 5') and, in all cases, much better than those given by $ROM(\mathbb{R})$ (1a to 5a). Obviously, using 3-B-consistency improves the results still further, in particular for Z, as follows (with $w1 = 0.001$ in 10s):

(1s') $X \leq 0.5$ (2s') $0.713 \leq Y \leq 1.088$ (3s') $W \leq 0.110$ (4s') $Z \leq 0.358$ (5s') $0.827 \leq U \leq 1.556$,

which are practically optimal.

Using Symbolic Algebra Alone for Computing Optimal Results

Symbolically expressing searched quotients in terms of known ones (Qi) leads to expressions which are continuously differentiable in Qi and most often algebraic (rational functions such as in (F)). The problem to be solved can thus generally be expressed as that of finding the absolute extrema of these expressions on n-dimensional closed convex parallelepipeds defined by the ranges of the known intervals $mi \leq Qi \leq Mi$ for $1 \leq i \leq n$. It is well-known that these extrema occur at points where partial derivatives are null. Thus this is a way to compute them exactly from roots of derivatives by using computer algebra.

More precisely, a necessary (not sufficient because it can correspond in particular to a local extremum) condition for an absolute extremum in a neighborhood is the nullity of all the partial derivatives at the given point. A difficulty arises because extrema may be obtained on a face of dimension < n rather than in the interior of the parallelepiped. Thus derivatives on all faces have to be considered. But, thanks to computer algebra, it is sufficient to symbolically compute partial derivatives once and for all and then, in order to obtain derivatives on any face, to fix the Qi, which determine the face, to their numeric values. Roots of all derivatives (in our case roots of a system of polynomials) are computed, firstly in the interior and then on the different faces in decreasing order of dimension, and the corresponding numeric values of expressions at these points are evaluated up to the vertices. These values are finally compared and only the highest and lowest are kept, which correspond to the absolute extrema.

Let us now apply this method, implemented in MAPLE V, to the heat exchanger example. Expressions X, Y, W and Z depend on the 2 variables Q1 and Q2 and are thus considered w.r.t. the rectangle $1/5 \leq Q1 \leq 5$, $0 \leq Q2 \leq 1/10$; U, which depends on the 3 variables Q1, Q2 and Q3 is considered w.r.t. the parallelepiped based on the previous rectangle with $9/10 \leq Q3 \leq 10/9$. Results are computed immediately and summarized below.

For X, Y, W and Z, it is found that only their derivatives w.r.t. Q1 are null on the edge $Q2 = 0$. Corresponding constant values $X = 0$, $Y = 1$, $W = 0$ and $Z = 0$ are shown, after inspection of vertices, to be the minima for X, W and Z, but not an absolute extremum for Y. Looking now at the vertices, it is found that the maximum of X is obtained at the vertex $Q1 = 5$, $Q2 = 1/10$ and is equal to $1/2$; the minimum of Y is reached at $Q1 = 5$, $Q2 = 1/10$ and is equal to $5/7$, and its maximum is reached at $Q1 = 1/5$, $Q2 = 1/10$ and is equal to $25/23$; the maximum of W is obtained at $Q1 = 1/5$, $Q2 = 1/10$ and is equal to $5/46$ and the maximum of Z is obtained at $Q1 = 5$, $Q2 = 1/10$ and is equal to $5/14$.

The derivative of U w.r.t. Q1 is null both on the edge $Q2 = 0$, $Q3 = 9/10$ corresponding to the constant value $U = 10/9$ and on the edge $Q2 = 0$, $Q3 = 10/9$ corresponding to the constant value $U = 9/10$. But it is finally found that the minimum occurs at the vertex $Q1 = 1/5$, $Q2 = 1/10$, $Q3 = 10/9$ and is equal to $207/250$, and that the maximum occurs at the vertex $Q1 = 5$, $Q2 = 1/10$, $Q3 = 9/10$ and is equal to $14/9$.

Finally computer algebra, which works with rational numbers, gives the exact solutions (S) to our problem:

$0 \leq X \leq 1/2$, $5/7 \leq Y \leq 25/23$, $0 \leq W \leq 5/46$, $0 \leq Z \leq 5/14$, $207/250 \leq U \leq 14/9$.

Floating point approximation with 3 significant digits gives (1' to 5').

The method of roots of derivatives, processed by computer algebra, is thus a very powerful technique to automatically obtain the exact ranges. But, in addition to the complete loss of the qualitative aspect of the inference and the necessity, as in the above subsection, for the system of equations to be algebraically solvable, there are two other drawbacks to this approach. The first one is that roots of a polynomial system cannot in general be obtained exactly. This is solved in practice in a large number of cases by using the most recent modules of computer algebra which are able to deal with algebraic numbers (represented as a couple of a floating point interval and a polynomial, coefficients of which are algebraic numbers, such that the considered number is the only root of the polynomial belonging to the interval). The second one is the exponential complexity of the method: in an n-dimensional space we have 3^n systems of polynomials to look for, from the interior to the vertices. The method becomes intractable very rapidly unless the number of variables (assumed order of magnitude relations) remains very small.

Syntactically Transforming Rational Functions: a Line of Research

There are cases where, after having judiciously syntactically transformed rational functions which are solutions of the set of equations, the simple interval propagation technique gives the exact optima, as illustrated in the example.

Let us consider symbolic formulas (F). The exact result (1s) can be obtained simply by interval propagation for X because variables Q1 and Q2 have only one occurrence in X. It is not the case for the other 4 formulas, which is why, in this case, interval propagation does not give exact results (2s to 5s). However, a simple trick may be found by hand to satisfy this condition. In fact the expression $1-Q2+Q1\times Q2$ in Y, W and U may be rewritten as $1+Q2\times(Q1-1)$, which boils down to changing a variable: $Q1-1$ instead of Q1. A simple interval propagation gives $23/25 \leq 1+Q2\times(Q1-1) \leq 7/5$, from which exact solutions (S) for Y, W and U are immediately obtained. It is not the case for Z because Q1 appears also in the numerator. But Z can be rewritten as $Z=1/(1+(1/Q1)(1/(Q2-1)))$ where each new variable $1/Q1$ and $1/(Q2-1)$ appears only once. The exact result (S) $0 \leq Z \leq 5/14$ follows immediately. This interval propagation may be achieved exactly by manipulating rational numbers, or with a given approximation by manipulating floating point numbers, as is done by Interlog with 10 exact significant digits.

It can be concluded that, when expressions can be rewritten by changing variables, such that each new variable occurs only once, simple interval propagation gives exact solutions. This transformation is obviously not always possible. A line of research would be to characterize the cases where such a transformation of rational functions (or at least a partial one which minimizes the number of occurences of each variable) is possible and to find algorithms to do this.

Conclusion

It has been shown in this paper that the formal system ROM(K) [Dague, 1993] can be transposed in $\mathbb{R}$ in order to incorporate quantitative information easily, and to ensure validity of inferences in $\mathbb{R}$. Rules of ROM($\mathbb{R}$) thus guarantee a sound calculus in $\mathbb{R}$ (which was not the case with FOG, O(M) or ROM(K)), while keeping their qualitative meaning, thus guiding research and providing commonsense explanations for results.

If the loss of precision through inference paths is such that some of these results are judged to be too imprecise for a specific purpose, several complementary techniques can be used to refine them. k-consistency algorithms for numeric CSPs, which generalize for $k > 2$ interval propagation, generally improve the results but may require a large k, in which case they are very time consuming. A better approach is first to use computer algebra to express dimensionless quotients for which approximation is searched in terms of quotients for which given bounds are assumed, and then to apply k-consistency techniques to the symbolic expressions obtained. It has also been shown that computer algebra alone may be used to obtain exact results, by computing roots of partial derivatives in order to obtain the extrema of the expressions on n-dimensional parallelepipeds although this method, which is exponential in n, is tractable only for a small number of

variables (i.e. known quotients). Finally, future work would consist in formally modifying rational functions in order to have a minimal number of occurrences of each variable, thus making interval computation more precise; in particular, when it is possible to have only one occurrence for each variable, simple interval computation gives the exact results.

All this assortment of tools, with ROM($\mathbb{R}$) as the basis, is now available to perform powerful and flexible qualitative and numeric reasoning for engineering tasks, and will be tested soon on real applications in chemical processes.

Acknowledgments

This research was done partly at the Paris IBM Scientific Center, to whom I extend my thanks, and partly at the University Paris 6, where I had very fruitful discussions with Daniel Lazard on computer algebra. I would also like to thank Olivier Lhomme for experiments with Interlog and Emmanuel Goldberger for applying this work to chemical processes. Finally, my thanks go to Rosalind Greenstein for the English version of this paper and to Gilles Dague for the figure.

References

B.W. Char, *MAPLE Reference Manual*, Watcom, Waterloo, Ontario, 1988.

P. Dague, "Symbolic reasoning with relative orders of magnitude," *Proceedings of the Thirteenth IJCAI*, Chambéry, August 1993.

P. Dague, P. Devès, and O. Raiman, "Troubleshooting: when Modeling is the Trouble," *Proceedings of AAAI Conference*, Seattle, July 1987.

Dassault Electronique, INTERLOG 1.0, User's Guide, 1991.

D. Dubois and H. Prade, "Order of magnitude reasoning with fuzzy relations," *Proceedings of the IFAC/IMACS/IFORS International Symposium on Advanced Information Processing in Automatic Control*, Nancy, 1989.

O. Lhomme, "Consistency techniques for numeric CSPs," *Proceedings of the Thirteenth IJCAI*, Chambéry, August 1993.

M.L. Mavrovouniotis and G. Stephanopoulos, "Reasoning with orders of magnitude and approximate relations," *Proceedings of AAAI Conference*, Seattle, July 1987.

M.L. Mavrovouniotis and G. Stephanopoulos, "Formal order of magnitude reasoning in process engineering," *Comput. chem. Engng. 12*, 1988.

O. Raiman, "Order of magnitude reasoning," *Proceedings of AAAI Conference*, Philadelphia, August 1986.

O. Raiman, "Order of magnitude reasoning," *Artificial Intelligence 51*, 1991.

Efficient Reasoning in Qualitative Probabilistic Networks*

Marek J. Druzdzel

Carnegie Mellon University
Department of Engineering
and Public Policy

Pittsburgh, PA 15213

marek+@cmu.edu

Max Henrion

Rockwell International Science Center
Palo Alto Laboratory

444 High Street, Suite 400
Palo Alto, CA 94301

henrion@camis.stanford.edu

Abstract

Qualitative Probabilistic Networks (QPNs) are an abstraction of Bayesian belief networks replacing numerical relations by qualitative influences and synergies [Wellman, 1990b]. To reason in a QPN is to find the effect of new evidence on each node in terms of the sign of the change in belief (increase or decrease). We introduce a polynomial time algorithm for reasoning in QPNs, based on local sign propagation. It extends our previous scheme from singly connected to general multiply connected networks. Unlike existing graph-reduction algorithms, it preserves the network structure and determines the effect of evidence on all nodes in the network. This aids meta-level reasoning about the model and automatic generation of intuitive explanations of probabilistic reasoning.

Introduction

A formal representation should not use more specificity than needed to support the reasoning required of it. The appropriate degree of specificity or numerical precision will vary depending on what kind of knowledge is available and what questions users want it to address. Qualitative Probabilistic Networks (QPNs) can replace or supplement quantitative Bayesian belief networks where numerical probabilities are either not available or not necessary for the questions of interest. QPNs have been found valuable for such tasks as planning under uncertainty [Wellman, 1990b] and for explanation of probabilistic reasoning [Henrion and Druzdzel, 1991]. Like other qualitative schemes, QPNs are weaker than their quantitative counterparts, but they can provide more robust results with much less effort.

QPNs are in essence a qualitative abstraction of Bayesian belief networks and influence diagrams. A QPN requires specification of the graphical belief network, expressing probabilistic dependence and independence relations. In addition, it requires specifica-

tion of the signs of influences and synergies among variables. A proposition A has a positive influence on a proposition B, if observing A to be true makes B more probable. Variable A is positively *synergistic* with variable B with respect to a third variable C, if the joint effect of A and B on the probability of C is greater than the sum of their individual effects. QPNs generalize straightforwardly to multivalued and continuous variables. An expert may express his or her uncertain knowledge of a domain directly in the form of a QPN. This requires significantly less effort than a full numerical specification of a belief network. Alternatively, if we already possess a numerical belief network, then it is straightforward to identify the qualitative relations inherent in it.

In previous work [Henrion and Druzdzel, 1991] we introduced an approach called *qualitative belief propagation*, analogous to message-passing algorithms for quantitative belief networks (e.g., [Kim and Pearl, 1983]), which traces the effect of an observation e on successive variables through a belief network to the target t. Every node on the path from e to t is given a label that characterizes the sign of impact. This was further developed, with particular emphasis on intercausal reasoning in [Wellman and Henrion, 1991]. This approach differs from the graph reduction-based approach [Wellman, 1990b] in that it preserves the original structure of the network. The graph-reduction scheme performs inference by successively reducing the network to obtain the qualitative relation directly between e and t. There are usually several node reduction and arc reversal sequences possible at any step of the algorithm. As some of these sequences may lead to ambiguous signs, the algorithm needs to determine which sequences are optimal with respect to maximum specificity of the result. The computational complexity of this task is unknown [Wellman, 1990c]. The reason why different sequences of operators lead to different specificity of the results, is that, although the operation of arc reversal preserves the numerical properties of the network [Shachter, 1986], it leads to loss of the explicit qualitative graphical information about conditional independencies.

---

*This research was supported in part by the Rockwell International Science Center.

Earlier work on qualitative belief propagation applied only to a restricted class of singly connected belief networks (polytrees). The main contribution of this paper is to extend qualitative belief propagation to arbitrary networks and to present a complete belief propagation algorithm for QPNs.

All random variables that we deal with in this paper are multiple-valued, discrete variables, such as those represented by nodes of a Bayesian belief network. We make this assumption for convenience in mathematical derivations and proofs. Lower case letters (e.g., x) will stand for random variables, indexed lower-case letters (e.g., x_i) will denote their outcomes. In case of binary random variables, the two outcomes will be denoted by upper case (e.g., the two outcomes of a variable c will be denoted by C and $\overline{C}$). Outcomes of random variables are ordered from the highest to the lowest value. And so, for a random variable a, $\forall i < j \; [a_i \geq a_j]$. For binary variables $C > \overline{C}$, or **true**>**false**.

Qualitative Probabilistic Networks

Formally, a QPN is a pair $G = (V, Q)$, where V is a set of variables or nodes in the graph and Q is a set of qualitative relations among the variables [Wellman, 1990b]. There are two types of qualitative relations in Q: *qualitative influences* and *additive synergies*. We reproduce their definitions from [Wellman and Henrion, 1991]. The qualitative influences define the sign of direct influence between two variables and correspond to an arc in a belief network.

Definition 1 (qualitative influence) *We say that a positively influences c, written $S^+(a,c)$, iff for all values $a_1 > a_2$, c_0, and x, which is the set of all of c's predecessors other than a,*

$$\Pr(c \geq c_0 | a_1 x) \geq \Pr(c \geq c_0 | a_2 x).$$

This definition expresses the fact that increasing the value of a, makes higher values of c more probable. *Negative qualitative influence*, S^-, and *zero qualitative influence*, S^0, are defined analogously by substituting $\geq$ by $\leq$ and $=$ respectively.

Definition 2 (additive synergy) *Variables a and b exhibit* positive additive synergy *with respect to variable c, written $Y^+(\{a,b\},c)$, if for all $a_1 > a_2$, $b_1 > b_2$, c_0, and x, which is the set of all of c's predecessors other than a and b,*

$$\Pr(c \geq c_0 | a_1 b_1 x) + \Pr(c \geq c_0 | a_2 b_2 x)$$
$$\geq \Pr(c \geq c_0 | a_1 b_2 x) + \Pr(c \geq c_0 | a_2 b_1 x).$$

The additive synergy is used with respect to two causes and a common effect. It captures the property that the joint influence of the two causes is greater than sum of individual effects. *Negative additive synergy*, Y^-, and *zero additive synergy*, Y^0, are defined analogously by substituting $\geq$ by $\leq$ and $=$ respectively.

If a qualitative property is not $'+$, $'-$, or $'0$, it is by default $'?$ ($S^?$ and $Y^?$ respectively). As all the definitions are not-strict, both $'+$ and $'-$ are consistent with $'0$; for the same reason $'?$ is consistent with $'0$, $'+$, and $'-$. Any qualitative property that can be described by a $'0$ can be also described by $'+$, $'-$, or $'?$. Obviously, when specifying a network and doing any kind of reasoning, one prefers stronger conclusions to weaker ones and this is captured by the canonical order of signs: $'0$ is preferred to $'+$ and $'-$, and all three are preferred to $'?$ [Wellman, 1990b].

Qualitative properties can be elicited directly from a domain expert along with the graphical network using their common-sense interpretation or, alternatively, extracted from the numerical specification of a quantitative belief network using the definitions given above. It is worth noting that most popular probabilistic interactions exhibit unambiguous qualitative properties. It can be easily proven, for example, that bi-valued noisy-OR gates have always positive influences (S^+) and negative additive synergies (Y^-). Linear (Gaussian) models yield well defined qualitative influences (i.e., non-$'?$) and zero additive synergies (Y^0).

Figure 1 shows an example of a QPN. This network is a small fragment of a larger belief network proposed for modeling an Orbital Maneuvering System (OMS) propulsion engine of the Space Shuttle [Horvitz *et al.*, 1992]. The OMS engine's fragment captured by the

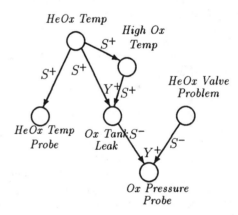

Figure 1: An example of a qualitative probabilistic network.

network consists of two liquid gas tanks: an oxidizer tank and a helium tank. Helium is used to pressurize the oxidizer, necessary for expelling the oxidizer into the combustion subsystem. A potential temperature problem in the neighborhood of the two tanks (*HeOx Temp*) can be discovered by a probe (*HeOx Temp Probe*) built into the valves between the tanks. An increased temperature in the neighborhood of the two tanks can increase the temperature in the oxidizer tank (*High Ox Temp*) and this in turn can cause a leak in the oxidizer tank (*Ox Tank Leak*). A leak may lead to a decreased pressure in the tank. A problem with the valve between the two tanks (*HeOx Valve Problem*) can also be a cause of a decreased pressure in the oxidizer tank. The pressure in the oxidizer tank is measured by a pressure gauge (*Ox Pressure Probe*). Of all the variables in this network, only the values of the two probes (*HeOx Temp Probe* and *Ox Pressure Probe*) are directly observable. The others must be inferred.

Links in a QPN are labeled by signs of the qualitative influences S^δ, each pair of links coming into a node is described by the signs of the synergy between them. Note that all these relations are uncertain. An increased *HeOx Temp* will usually lead to an increased reading from the *HeOx Temp Probe*, but not always — the probe may fail. But the fact that increased *HeOx Temp* makes an increased *HeOx Temp Probe* more probable is denoted by a positive influence S^+.

Qualitative Intercausal Reasoning

In earlier work [Henrion and Druzdzel, 1991] we proposed a third qualitative property, called *product synergy*, which was further studied by Wellman and Henrion [1993]. Product synergy captures the sign of conditional dependence between immediate predecessors of a node that has been observed or has evidential support. The most common pattern of reasoning captured by product synergy is known as *explaining away*. For example, suppose my observed sneezing could be caused by an incipient cold or by a cat allergy. Subsequently observing a cat would explain away the sneezing, and so reduce my fear that I was getting a cold. This is a consequence of the negative product synergy between cold and allergy on sneezing.

A key desired feature of any qualitative property between two variables in a network is that this is invariant to the probability distribution of other neighboring nodes. This invariance allows for drawing conclusions that are valid regardless of the numerical values of probability distributions of the neighboring variables. Previous work on intercausal reasoning concentrated on situations where all irrelevant ancestors of the common effect were assumed to be instantiated. To be able to perform intercausal reasoning in arbitrary belief networks, we extended the definition of product synergy to accommodate this case. We reproduce here only the most important results. The complete derivations and proofs are reported in [Druzdzel and Henrion, 1993].

Definition 3 (half positive semi-definiteness) *A square $n \times n$ matrix* $\mathbf{M}$ *is called half positive semi-definite (half negative semi-definite) if for any non-negative vector* $\mathbf{x}$ *consisting of n elements* $\mathbf{x}^T \mathbf{M} \mathbf{x} \geq 0$ *($\mathbf{x}^T \mathbf{M} \mathbf{x} \leq 0$).*

The following theorem states the sufficient condition for a matrix to be half positive semi-definite. Necessity of this condition in general remains a conjecture, although we have shown that it is necessary for 2×2 and 3×3 matrices.

Theorem 1 (half positive semi-definiteness) *A sufficient condition for half positive semi-definiteness of a matrix is that it is a sum of a positive semi-definite and a non-negative matrix.*

Definition 4 (product synergy) *Let a, b, and x be predecessors of c in a QPN. Let n_x denote the number of possible values of x. Variables a and b exhibit* negative product synergy *with respect to a particular value c_0 of c, regardless of the distribution of x, written* $X^-(\{a, b\}, c_0)$, *if for all $a_1 > a_2$ and for all $b_1 > b_2$, a square $n_x \times n_x$ matrix* $\mathbf{D}$ *with elements*

$$D_{ij} = Pr(c_0|a_1 b_1 x_i)Pr(c_0|a_2 b_2 x_j)$$
$$- Pr(c_0|a_2 b_1 x_i)Pr(c_0|a_1 b_2 x_j).$$

is half negative semi-definite. If $\mathbf{D}$ *is half positive semi-definite, a and b exhibit* positive product synergy *written as* $X^+(\{a, b\}, c_0)$. *If* $\mathbf{D}$ *is a zero matrix, a and b exhibit* zero product synergy *written as* $X^0(\{a, b\}, c_0)$.

Note that product synergy is defined with respect to each outcome of the common effect c. There are, therefore, as many product synergies as there are outcomes in c. For a binary variable c, there are two product synergies, one for C and one for $\overline{C}$.

Although the definition of product synergy may seem rather unintuitive, it simply captures formally the sign of conditional dependence between pairs of direct ancestors of a node, given that the node has been observed. This sign can be easily elicited directly from the expert. It is worth noting that most popular probabilistic interactions, the bi-valued noisy-OR gates exhibit negative product synergy (X^-) for the common effect observed to be present and zero product synergy (X^0) for the common effect observed to be absent, for all pairs of their direct ancestors.

Intercausal reasoning is an important component of the qualitative belief propagation allowing for sign propagation in cases where some of the network variables are instantiated. The following theorem describes the sign of intercausal reasoning for direct evidential support for the common effect node (see Figure 2). We prove an analogue theorem for indirect evidential support in [Druzdzel and Henrion, 1993].

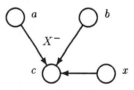

Figure 2: Intercausal reasoning between a and b with c observed.

Theorem 2 (intercausal reasoning) *Let a, b, and x be direct predecessors of c such that a and b are conditionally independent (see Figure 2). A sufficient and* *necessary condition for $S^-(a,b)$ on observation of c_0 is negative product synergy, $X^-(\{a,b\},c_0)$.*

Qualitative Belief Propagation

In singly connected networks, evidence flows from the observed variables outwards to all remaining nodes of the network, and never in the opposite direction. In the presence of multiple connections, this paradigm becomes problematic, as the evidence coming into a node can arrive from multiple directions. For any link that is part of a clique of nodes, it becomes impossible to determine in which direction the evidence flows. Numerical belief propagation through multiply connected graphs, encounters the problem of a possibly infinite sequence of local belief propagation and an unstable equilibrium that does not necessarily correspond to the new probabilistic state of the network [Pearl, 1988, pages 195–223]. Algorithms adapting the belief propagation paradigm to multiply connected belief networks treat loops in the underlying graph separately and essentially reduce the graph to a singly connected one.

It turns out that the qualitative properties of the QPNs allow for an interesting view of qualitative belief propagation. The qualitative influences and synergies are defined in such a way that they are independent of any other nodes interacting with the nodes that they describe. This allows the propagation of belief from a node e to a node n to disregard all such nodes and effectively decompose the flow of evidence from e to n into distinct trails from e to n. On each of these trails, belief flows in only one direction, from e to n, and never in the opposite direction, exactly as it does in singly connected networks.

The belief propagation approach requires that qualitative changes be propagated in both directions. Product synergy is symmetric with respect to the predecessor nodes, so $X^\delta(\{a,b\},c_0)$ implies $X^\delta(\{b,a\},c_0)$. The following theorem shows that a qualitative influence between any two nodes in a network is also symmetric.

Theorem 3 (symmetry) $S^\delta(a,b)$ *implies* $S^\delta(b,a)$.

The theorem follows from the monotone likelihood property [Milgrom, 1981]. It shows merely that the sign of influence is symmetric. The magnitude of the influence of a variable a on a variable b can be arbitrarily different from the magnitude of the influence of b on a.

Of the definitions below, trail, head-to-head node, and active trail are based on [Geiger *et al.*, 1990].

Definition 5 (trail in undirected graph) *A trail in an undirected graph is an alternating sequence of nodes and links of the graph such that every link joins the nodes immediately preceding it and following it.*

Definition 6 (trail) *A trail in a directed acyclic graph is an alternating sequence of links and nodes of the graph that form a trail in the underlying undirected graph.*

Definition 7 (head-to-head node) *A node c is called a* head-to-head *node with respect to a trail t if there are two consecutive edges $a \rightarrow c$ and $c \leftarrow b$ on t.*

Definition 8 (minimal trail) *A trail connecting a and b in which no node appears more than once is called a* minimal trail *between a and b.*

Definition 9 (active trail) *A trail t connecting nodes a and b is said to be active given a set of nodes L if (1) every head-to-head node with respect to t either is in L or has a descendant in L and (2) every other node on t is outside L.*

Definition 10 (evidential trail) *A minimal active trail between an evidence node e and a node n is called an* evidential trail *from e to n.*

Definition 11 (intercausal link) *Let a and b be direct ancestors of a head-to-head node t. An* intercausal link *exists between a and b, if t is in or has a descendant in the set of evidence nodes. The sign of the intercausal link is the sign of the intercausal influence between a and b determined by the product synergy.*

Qualitative signs combine by means of sign multiplication and sign addition operators, defined in Table 1.

$\otimes$	+	−	0	?	$\oplus$	+	−	0	?
+	+	−	0	?	+	+	?	+	?
−	−	+	0	?	−	?	−	−	?
0	0	0	0	0	0	+	−	0	?
?	?	?	0	?	?	?	?	?	?

Table 1: Sign multiplication ($\otimes$) and sign addition ($\oplus$) operators [Wellman, 1990b]

Definition 12 (sign of a trail) *The sign of a trail t is the sign product of signs of all direct and intercausal links on t.*

Theorem 4 (evidential trails) *The qualitative influence of a node e on a node n is equal to the sign sum of the signs of all evidential trails from e to n.*

Proof: (outline) We demonstrate for each of the three qualitative properties that they are insensitive to the probability distribution of neighboring nodes. The presence of another, parallel trail through which evidence might flow changes only the probability distribution of the neighboring nodes, and this does not impact the qualitative properties of other nodes and paths.

This implies that none of the straightforward propagation rules for the singly connected networks will be invalidated by the presence of multiple trails. Qualitative change in belief in a node n given a single evidence node e can be viewed as a sum of changes through individual evidential trails from e to n. It will be well determined only if the signs of these paths are consistent (i.e., the sign sum is not '?'). □

The algorithm for qualitative belief propagation (Figure 3) is based on local message passing. The goal is to determine a sign for each node denoting the direction of change in belief for that node given new evidence for an observed node. Initially each node is set to $'0$, except the observed node which is set to the specified sign. A message is sent to each neighbor. The sign of each message becomes the sign product of its previous sign and the sign of the link it traverses. Each message keeps a list of the nodes it has visited and its origin, so it can avoid visiting any node more than once. Each message travels on one evidential trail. Each node, on receiving a message, updates its own sign with the sign sum of itself and the sign of the message. Then it passes a copy of the message to all unvisited neighbors that need to update their signs.

network to reach stability is less than twice the number of nodes. Each message carries a list of visited nodes, which contains at most the total number of nodes in the graph. Hence, the algorithm is quadratic in the size of the network. Unfortunately, this propagation algorithm does not generalize straightforwardly to quantitative belief networks.

The sign propagation will reach each node in the network that is not d-separated from the evidence node e. It is possible to change the focus of the algorithm to determining the sign of some target node n and all nodes that are located on active trails from e to n. This requires a small amount of preprocessing, consisting of removal of irrelevant barren and ancestor nodes. The methods to do that are summarized in [Druzdzel, 1993].

Given: A qualitative probabilistic network,
      an evidence node e.
Output: Sign of the influence of e
      on each node in the network
Data structures:
{ In each of the nodes }
  sign ch;   { sign of change }
  sign evs;   { sign of evidential support }
Main Program:
    for each node n in the network **do** $ch := '0$;
    Propagate-Sign($\emptyset, e, e, '+$);
Recursive procedure for sign propagation:
 { $trail$ visited nodes,
     $from$ sender of the message,
     to recipient of the message,
     $sign$ sign of influence from $from$ to to }
    Propagate-Sign($trail, from, to, sign$)
    begin
      if $to \uparrow ch = sign \oplus to \uparrow ch$ **then** exit;
        { exit if already made the update }
      $to \uparrow ch := sign \oplus to \uparrow ch$;
        { update the sign of to }
      $trail := trail \cup to$;
        { add to to the set of visited nodes }
      for each n in the Markov blanket of to **do**
      begin
        $s :=$ sign of the link; { direct or intercausal }
        $sn := n \uparrow ch$; { current sign of n }
        if the link to n is active
          and $n \notin trail$
          and $sn \neq to \uparrow ch \otimes s$ **then**
            Propagate-Sign($trail, to, n, to \uparrow ch \otimes s$);
      end
    end

Figure 3: The algorithm for qualitative sign propagation.

The character of the sign addition operator implies that each node can change its sign at most twice — first from $'0$ to $'+$, $'-$, or $'?$ and then, if at all, only to $'?$, which can never change to any other sign. Hence each node receives a request for updating its sign at most twice, and the total number of messages for the

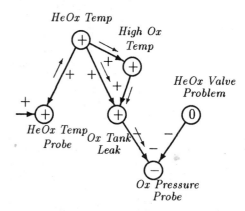

Figure 4: Algorithm for qualitative belief propagation: An example.

Figure 4 shows an example of how the algorithm works in practice. Suppose that we want to know the effect of observing a high reading of the *HeOx Temp Probe* on other variables in the model. We set the signs of each of the nodes to $'0$ and start by sending a positive sign to *HeOx Temp Probe*, which is our evidence node. *HeOx Temp Probe* determines that its parent, node *HeOx Temp*, needs updating, as the sign product of $'+$ and the sign of the link $'+$ is $'+$ and is different from the current value of the node $'0$. After receiving this message, *HeOx Temp* sends messages to its direct descendants *High Ox Temp* and *Ox Tank Leak*, who also need updating. As the sign of *Ox Tank Leak* is already $'+$, *High Ox Temp* does not send any further messages. Seeing that *Ox Pressure Probe* needs updating, *Ox Tank Leak* will send it a message. The sign of this message is $'-$, because the sign of the qualitative influence between *Ox Tank Leak* and *Ox Pressure Probe* is $'-$. *Ox Pressure Probe* will not send any further messages and the algorithm will terminate leaving *HeOx Valve Problem* unaffected. The final sign in each nodes expresses how the probability of this node is impacted by observing a high reading of *HeOx Temp Probe*.

Conclusions and Applications

This paper has described an extension of belief propagation in qualitative probabilistic networks to multiply connected networks. Qualitative belief propagation can be performed in polynomial time. The type of reasoning addressed by QPNs and by the algorithm that we propose, namely determining the sign of evidential impact, is one of the few queries that can be answered in polynomial time in general networks, even when all nodes are of some restricted type, for example noisy-OR or continuous linear (Gaussian). Belief propagation is more powerful than graph reduction approach for two reasons: (1) it uses product synergy, which is a new qualitative property of probabilistic interactions, and (2) it offers a reasoning scheme, whose operators do not lead to loss of qualitative information and whose final results do not depend on the order of their application. Although examples of problems that can be resolved by belief propagation and not by graph reduction can be easily found, it is unfair to compare the strength of the two methods, as belief propagation uses an additional qualitative property, namely product synergy.

Wellman [1990a] describes several possible applications of QPNs, such as support for heuristic planning and identification of dominant decisions in a decision problem. The belief propagation approach proposed in this paper supports these applications, and has the additional advantage over the graph-reduction approach in that it preserves the underlying graph and determines the sign of the node of interest along with the signs of all intermediate nodes. This supports directly two new applications of QPNs. Firstly, it allows a computer program, in case of sign-ambiguity, to reflect about the model at a meta level and find the reason for ambiguity, for example, which paths are in conflict. Hence, it can suggest ways in which the least additional specificity could resolve the ambiguity. This may turn out to be a desirable property, as many multiply-connected networks that we used for testing the algorithm led in some queries, especially those involving intercausal reasoning, to ambiguous results. One reason for that is that the most common value of product synergy appears to be negative, which in loops often leads to conflicts with usually positive signs of links. A second application involves using the resulting signs for generation of intuitive qualitative explanations of how the observed evidence is relevant to the node of interest. The individual signs, along with the signs of influences, can be translated into natural language sentences describing paths of change from the evidence to the variable in question. A method for generation of verbal explanations of reasoning based on belief propagation is outlined in [Druzdzel, 1993].

Acknowledgments

We are most grateful to Michael Wellman and two anonymous reviewers for insightful comments.

References

Druzdzel, M.J., and Henrion, M. 1993. Intercausal reasoning with uninstantiated ancestor nodes. Forthcoming.

Druzdzel, M.J. 1993. *Probabilistic Reasoning in Decision Support Systems: From Computation to Common Sense*. Ph.D. diss., Department of Engineering and Public Policy, Carnegie Mellon University.

Geiger, D.; Verma, T.S.; and Pearl, J. 1990. *d*-Separation: From theorems to algorithms. In Henrion, M.; Shachter, R.D.; Kanal, L.N.; and Lemmer, J.F., eds. 1990, *Uncertainty in Artificial Intelligence 5*. 139–148. North Holland: Elsevier.

Henrion, M., and Druzdzel, M.J. 1991. Qualitative propagation and scenario-based approaches to explanation of probabilistic reasoning. In Bonissone, P.P.; Henrion, M.; Kanal, L.N.; and Lemmer, J.F., eds. 1991, *Uncertainty in Artificial Intelligence 6*. 17–32. North Holland: Elsevier.

Horvitz, E.J.; Ruokangas, C.; Srinivas, S.; and Barry, M. 1992. A decision-theoretic approach to the display of information for time-critical decisions: The Vista project. In *Proceedings of SOAR-92*, NASA/Johnson Space Center, Houston, Texas.

Kim, J.H., and Pearl, J. 1983. A computational model for causal and diagnostic reasoning in inference systems. In *Proceedings of the 8th International Joint Conference on Artificial Intelligence, IJCAI-83*, Los Angeles, Calif. 190–193.

Milgrom, Paul R. 1981. Good news and bad news: Representation theorems and applications. *Bell Journal of Economics* 12(2):380–391.

Pearl, J. 1988. *Probabilistic Reasoning in Intelligent Systems: Networks of Plausible Inference*. San Mateo, Calif.: Morgan Kaufmann

Shachter, R.D. 1986. Evaluating influence diagrams. *Operations Research* 34(6):871–882.

Wellman, M.P. and Henrion, M. 1991. Qualitative intercausal relations, or explaining "explaining away". In *KR-91, Principles of Knowledge Representation and Reasoning: Proceedings of the Second International Conference*, Cambridge, MA. 535–546.

Wellman, M.P., and Henrion, M. 1993. Explaining "explaining away". *IEEE Trans. PAMI* 15(3):287–291.

Wellman, M.P. 1990a. *Formulation of Tradeoffs in Planning Under Uncertainty*. London: Pitman.

Wellman, M.P. 1990b. Fundamental concepts of qualitative probabilistic networks. *Artificial Intelligence* 44(3):257–303.

Wellman, M.P. 1990c. Graphical inference in qualitative probabilistic networks. *Networks* 20(5):687–701.

Generating Quasi-symbolic Representation of Three-Dimensional Flow

Toyoaki Nishida
Graduate School of Information Science
Advanced Institute of Science and Technology, Nara
8916-5, Takayama-cho, Ikoma-shi, Nara 630-01, Japan
nishida@is.aist-nara.ac.jp

Abstract

Understanding flow in the three-dimensional phase space is challenging both to human experts and current computer science technology. To break through the barrier, we are building a program called PSX3 that can autonomously explore the flow in a three-dimensional phase space, by integrating AI and numerical techniques. In this paper, I point out that quasi-symbolic representation called *flow mappings* is effective as a means of capturing qualitative aspects of three-dimensional flow and present a method of generating flow mappings for a system of ordinary differential equations with three unknown functions. The method is based on a finding that geometric cues for generating a set of flow patterns can be classified into five categories. I demonstrate how knowledge about interaction of geometric cues is utilized for intelligently controlling numerical computation.

Flow in Three-Dimensional Phase Space

In this paper, we consider qualitative behavior of systems of ODEs of the form:

$$\frac{\mathrm{d}\mathbf{x}}{\mathrm{d}t} = f(\mathbf{x}), \qquad (1)$$

where $\mathbf{x} \in \mathrm{R}^3$ and $f : \mathrm{R}^3 \to \mathrm{R}^3$. For a while, I focus on systems of piecewise linear ODEs in which f is represented as a collection of linear functions and constants.[1] Although they are but a subclass of ODEs, systems of piecewise linear ODEs equally exhibit complex behaviors under certain conditions. For example, consider a system of piecewise linear ODEs:

$$\begin{cases} \frac{\mathrm{d}x}{\mathrm{d}t} = -6.3x + 6.3y - 9g(x) \\ \frac{\mathrm{d}y}{\mathrm{d}t} = 0.7x - 0.7y + z \\ \frac{\mathrm{d}z}{\mathrm{d}t} = -7y \end{cases} \qquad (2)$$

where,

$$\begin{aligned} g(x) \quad = \quad & -0.5x + 0.3 \ (x < -1) \\ & -0.8x \ (-1 \le x \le 1) \\ & -0.5x - 0.3 \ (1 < x). \end{aligned}$$

System of ODEs (2) results from simplifying the circuit equations of Matsumoto-Chua's circuit (third order, reciprocal, with only one nonlinear, 3-segments piecewise linear resistor v_R; see Figure 1a). In spite of its simplicity in form, (2) exhibits a fairly complex behavior. The phase portrait contains a chaotic attractor[2] with a "double scroll" structure, that is, two sheet-like thin rings curled up together into spiral forms as shown in Figure 1e (Matsumoto *et al.*, 1985). Orbits approach the attractor as time goes and manifest chaotic behaviors as they irregularly transit between the two "rings."

Chaotic attractors may exist only in three or higher dimensional phase space. This fact makes analysis of high dimensional flows significantly harder than two-dimensional flows. Analysis of the double-scroll attractor was reported in a full journal paper (Matsumoto *et al.*, 1985) in applied mathematics.

Flow Mappings as Representation of Flow

We would like to represent flow using finite-length, quasi-symbolic notations. The key idea I present in this paper is to partition orbits into intervals (*orbit intervals*) and aggregate them into "coherent" bundles (hereafter, *bundles of orbit intervals*) so that the flow can be represented as a sum of finitely many bundles of orbit intervals. I define the *coherency* of orbit intervals with respect to a finite set of *sensing planes* arbitrarily inserted into the phase space: a bundle of orbit intervals Φ is *coherent*, if all orbit intervals in Φ come from the same *generalized source* (or *g-source*) and go to the same *generalized sink* (or *g-sink*) without being cut by any sensing plane, where g-source and g-sink are either (a) a fixed point or a repellor/attractor

---

[1] Later, I will discuss how the method presented can be extended to cases in which only general restrictions (continuity) are posed on f.

[2] Roughly, an attractor is a dense collection of orbits that nearby orbits approach as $t \to \infty$. The reader is referred to (Guckenheimer and Holmes, 1983) for complete definition and discussion.

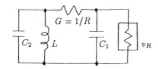

(a) the circuit

(b) characteristic of v_R

$$i_R = g(v_R) = m_0 v_R + \frac{1}{2}(m_1 - m_0)|v_R + B_p|$$
$$+ \frac{1}{2}(m_0 - m_1)|v_R - B_p|$$

(c) the circuit equation

$$\begin{cases} C_1 \frac{dv_{C_1}}{dt} = G(v_{C_2} - v_{C_1}) - g(v_{C_1}) \\ C_2 \frac{dv_{C_2}}{dt} = G(v_{C_1} - v_{C_2}) + i_L \\ L \frac{di_L}{dt} = -v_{C_2} \end{cases}$$

(d) constants and transformation

$C_1 = 1/9, C_2 = 1, L = 1/7, G = 0.7,$
$m_0 = -0.5, m_1 = -0.8, B_p = 1,$
$v_{C_1} = x, v_{C_2} = y, i_L = z$

(e) trace of an orbit near (0, 0, 0)

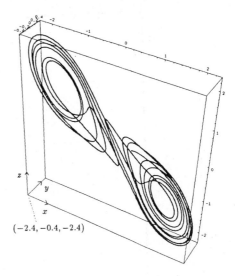

$(-2.4, -0.4, -2.4)$

Figure 1: Matsumoto-Chua's circuit (Matsumoto *et al.*, 1985) and a trace of an orbit near a double scroll attractor

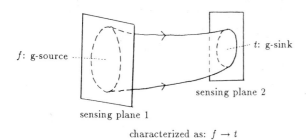

f: g-source

t: g-sink

sensing plane 1

sensing plane 2

characterized as: $f \to t$

Figure 2: A bundle of orbit intervals and its representation by a flow mapping

with more complex structure, or (b) a singly connected region of a sensing plane.

A flow mapping represents a bundle of orbit intervals as a mapping from the g-source to the g-sink. Thus, it is mostly symbolic. However, it is not completely symbolic as we represent the shape of g-sources and g-sinks approximately. Figure 2 schematically illustrates a bundle of orbit intervals and its representation by a flow mapping, where the g-sinks and g-sources are connected regions of a sensing plane. We are interested in minimal partition of flow into coherent bundles of orbit intervals that would lead to minimal description length.

Figure 3 shows minimal partition of the flow of Matsumoto-Chua equation (2) in a three-dimensional region $R : 1 \leq x \leq 3, -2 \leq y \leq 2, -3 \leq z \leq 3, 0.566(x-1.5) - 0.775y + 0.281(z+1.05) \geq 0$ into bundles of orbit intervals. Plane $0.566(x-1.5) - 0.775y + 0.281(z+1.05) = 0$ is a two-dimensional eigenspace and line $p_{26}p_{29}$ is a one-dimensional eigenspace of a fixed

point p_{26}. Orbits in region $0.566(x - 1.5) - 0.775y + 0.281(z + 1.05) > 0$ approach the two-dimensional eigenspace with turning around the eigenspace $p_{26}p_{29}$. As they approach the two-dimensional eigenspace, the spiral becomes bigger and diverges. The flow in R can be partitioned into fifteen bundles of orbit intervals. For example, orbit intervals entering R through region $v_1 v_5 p_{41} p_{40} p_{10}$ can be partitioned into five bundles of orbit intervals:

$\Phi_1 : v_1 p_2 p_3 p_4 p_5 \to v_1 p_1 p_8 p_6 p_5$
$\oplus \quad \Phi_2 : p_2 v_5 p_{43} p_{39} p_{38} p_{30} p_{28} p_4 p_3$
$\qquad \to p_1 p_{51} p_{35} p_{36} p_{34} p_{23} p_{22} p_9 p_8$
$\oplus \quad \Phi_3 : p_5 p_4 p_{28} p_{32} p_{31} p_{10} \to p_{11} p_{15} p_{38} p_{30} p_{31} p_{10}$
$\oplus \quad \Phi_4 : p_{29} p_{30} p_{31} p_{32} p_{28} p_{30} \to p_{25} p_{23} p_{24} p_{23} p_{34} p_{33}$
$\oplus \quad \Phi_5 : p_{39} p_{43} p_{41} p_{40} \to p_{44} p_{43} p_{41} p_{42}.$

Generating Flow Mappings for Three-Dimensional Flow

In order to design an algorithm of generating flow mappings for a given flow, I have studied the relationships between geometric patterns that flow makes on the surface of sensing planes and the topological structure of underlying orbit intervals, and found that they can be classified into five categories called *geometric cue interaction patterns*. My algorithm makes use of geometric cue interaction patterns as local constraints both to focus numerical analysis and interpret the result.

Geometric Cues

Let us consider characterizing flow in a convex region called a *cell* which is bounded by sensing planes by a set of flow mappings. In order to do that we study

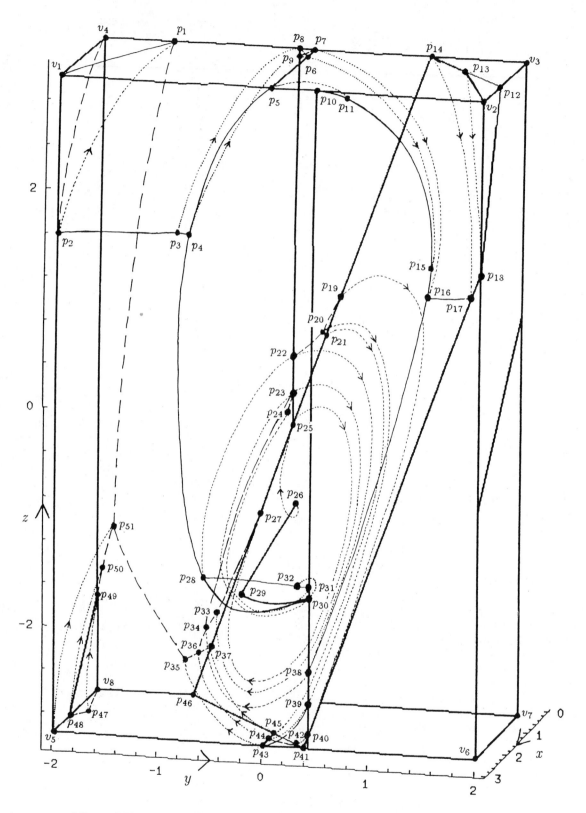

Figure 3: Anatomy of flow of Matsumoto-Chua equation (2) in Region $R : 1 \leq x \leq 3, -2 \leq y \leq 2, -3 \leq z \leq 3, 0.566(x - 1.5) - 0.775y + 0.281(z + 1.05) \geq 0$

geometry that orbits make on the surface of a sensing plane.

I classify the surface in terms of the orientation of orbit there. A contingent section S of the surface is called an *entrance section* if S is on a single sensing plane and orbits enter the cell at all points of S except some places where the orbits are tangent to the surface. An *exit section* is defined similarly. An entrance or exit section (*e.g.*, exit section $v_1 p_5 p_7 v_4$) may be further divided into smaller sections (*e.g.*, sections $v_1 p_1 v_4$, $v_1 p_5 p_6 p_8 p_1$, and $p_6 p_7 p_8$) by one or more *section boundary* (*e.g.*, $v_1 p_1$ and $p_6 p_8$), which may be either (a) an intersection of sensing planes, (b) an image or an inverse image of a section boundary, or (c) an intersection of a two-dimensional eigenspace and the cell surface. Section boundaries play an important role as primary geometric cues on the surface.

Tangent sections separate entrance and exit sections. Tangent sections are further classified into two categories: a *concave section* (*e.g.*, $p_5 p_7$) at which orbits come from the inside the cell, touch the surface, and go back to the cell, and a *convex section* (*e.g.*, $v_1 p_5$ and $p_{10} p_{31}$) at which orbits come from the outside the cell, touch the surface, and leave the cell.

An intersection of an eigenspace and the surface[3] is called a *pole* or a *ground* depending on whether the eigenspace is one-dimensional or two-dimensional, respectively. In Figure 3, point p_{29} is a pole and line segments $p_{41} p_{40}$, $p_{40} p_{18}$, $p_{18} p_{12}$, *etc* are grounds.

A *thorn* is a one-dimensional geometric object which thrusts outward from section boundary into an entrance/exit section. In Figure 3, there are two thorns: $p_{23} p_{24}$ and $p_{30} p_{29}$. Thorns result from peculiarity of eigenspace.

Interaction of geometric cues may result in a *junction* of various types. For example, section boundaries $p_2 p_4$ and $p_5 p_4 p_{28}$ in Figure 3 meet at p_4, making a *T-junction*, while $v_1 p_1 p_{51}$ and $v_4 p_1 p_8$ make an *X-junction* at p_1.

Some geometric cues such as fixed point p_{26} or convex section $p_{10} p_{31}$ are *trivial* in the sense that they can be easily recognized by local computation without tracking orbits, while others such as a T-junction at p_4 are *nontrivial* because they cannot be found without predicting their existence and validation by focused numerical analysis.

Geometric Cue Interaction Patterns

I have classified interactions of geometric cues into five categories, as shown in Figure 4. Each pattern is characterized by a *landmark orbit* such as $X_1 X_2$ in an *X-X* interaction or $T_1 X$ in a *T-X* interaction that connect geometric cues.

A *X-X* ("double X") interaction is an interaction

between boundary sections. In Figure 3, example of a X-X interaction is with the landmark orbit $p_2 p_1$.

A *T-X* and a *T-T* ("double T") interaction co-occurs with a concave section, which "pushes in" or "pops out" bundle of orbit intervals. In Figure 3, example of a T-X interactions is with landmark orbit $p_{28} p_{22} p_{38}$.

A *Pole-T* interaction results from peculiarity of orbits in an eigenspace of a saddle node. The closer the start (or end) point of an orbit approaches the ground, the closer the end (or start) point of an orbit approaches the pole. Special care is needed for searching for a *Pole-T* interaction when the derivative of the flow at the fixed point has complex eigenvalues, for a boundary edge may turn around the pole infinitely many times.

A *Thorn-T* interaction accompanies peculiarity, too. A T-junction consisting of a section boundary, a convex section, and a concave section is mapped to/from the top of a thorn. Points on the section boundary of the T-junction are mapped to/from the concave section, points on which are in turn mapped to/from the body of the thorn.

Analysis Procedure

Roughly, a procedure for generating flow mappings for a given cell consists of four stages: (stage 1) recognition of trivial geometric cues, (stage 2) recognition of nontrivial geometric cues, (stage 3) partitioning of the cell surface into coherent regions, and (stage 4) generation of flow mappings.

Instead of describing the procedure in detail,[4] I will illustrate how it works for the top-left portion of the cell shown in Figure 3. As a result of the initial analysis, the surface is classified with respect to the orientation of flow and trivial geometric cues are recognized as shown in Figure 5a.

Then, orbits are numerically tracked from sampling points on each trivial geometric cue. When the images or/and inverse images are obtained, they are examined to see whether they suggest the existence of a nontrivial geometric cue. For the case in hand, as p_is move downward from vertex v_1, their images $\phi(p_i)$s jump from the top plane to the rear plane, suggesting the existence of an X junction (Figure 5b). Similarly, as q_js go to the right, their inverse images $\phi^{-1}(q_j)$ jump from the left plane to the front plane, suggesting the existence of another X junction (Figure 5c).

Explanation is sought that may correlate the two X junctions, by consulting a library of geometric cue interaction patterns. As a result, a X-X interaction is chosen as the most plausible interpretation. The approximate location of the landmark orbit is computed by focused numerical computation (Figure 5d).

The algorithm is implemented as PSX3 (Nishida, 1993), except procedures for *Pole-T* and *Thorn-T* interactions. We have tested the current version of PSX3

---

[3] For simplicity, I assume that no surface of a cell is an *eigenspace*, which is a special subspace consisting of orbits tending to/from a saddle node.

[4] Interested reader is referred to (Nishida, 1993) for more detail.

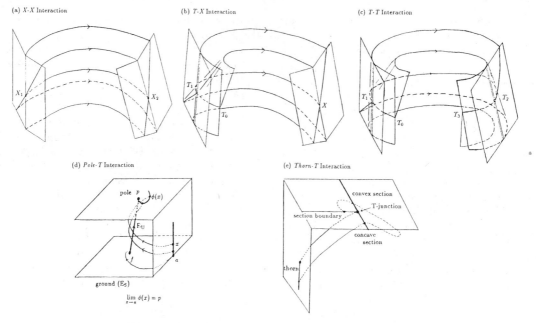

(a) *X-X* Interaction   (b) *T-X* Interaction   (c) *T-T* Interaction

(d) *Pole-T* Interaction   (e) *Thorn-T* Interaction

Figure 4: Geometric Cue Interaction Patterns

against a few systems of piecewise linear ODEs whose flow does not contain *Pole-T* or *Thorn-T* interactions.

Generalization to Nonlinear ODEs

So far, I have carefully limited our attention to systems of piecewise linear ODEs, for which the flow in each cell is linear. However, it is not hard to extend the method to nonlinear ODEs, if we are to handle only non-degenerate (*i.e.*, *hyperbolic*) flows.[5] What to be added is twofold: (a) a routine which will divide the phase space into cells that contain at most one fixed point, and (b) a general nonlinear (non-differential) simultaneous equation solver. Neither of these are very different from those that have been implemented for analyzing two-dimensional flow (Nishida and Doshita, 1991).[6]

Another thing we might have to take into account is the fact that certain assumptions such as planarity of an eigenspace do not hold any more. Fortunately, local characteristic of a nonlinear flow is equivalent to a linear flow, as linear approximation by Jacobian preserves local characteristics of nonlinear flow as far as the flow is hyperbolic. Thus, the local techniques work. Globally, we have not made any assumption that takes advantage of the linearity of local flow, so it also works.

---

[5] Degenerate flows are rare, even though generative property (Hirsch and Smale, 1974) (a proposition that the probability of observing a degenerate flow is *zero*) does not hold for three-dimensional flow.

[6] It should be noted that a nonlinear simultaneous equation solver may not always produce a complete answer. Dealing with incompleteness of numerical computation is open for future research. Some early results are reported in (Nishida *et al.*, 1991).

Implementation of these codes is, however, left for future.

Related Work

This work can be thought of as development of a basic technology for intelligent scientific computation (Abelson *et al.*, 1989; Kant *et al.*, 1992), whose purpose is to automate scientific and engineering problem solving. In this paper, I have concentrated on deriving quasi-symbolic, qualitative representation of ODEs by intelligently controlling numerical analysis. Previous work in this direction involves: POINCARE (Sacks, 1991), PSX2NL (Nishida and Doshita, 1991), Kalagnanam's system (Kalagnanam, 1991), and MAPS (Zhao, 1991). KAM (Yip, 1991) is one of the frontier work, though it is for discrete systems (difference equations). Unfortunately, these systems are severely limited to two-dimensional flows, except MAPS.

Zhao claims MAPS (Zhao, 1991) can analyze *n*-dimensional flows too. MAPS uses polyhedral approximation of collection of orbits as intermediate internal representation. As polyhedral approximation represents rather the shape of flow than the topology, it is not suitable for reasoning about qualitative aspects in which the topology of the flow is a main issue. The more precise polyhedral approximation becomes, the more irrelevant information is contained, making it harder to derive topological information. In contrast, flow mappings only refer to g-sinks and g-sources of bundles of orbit intervals, neglecting the shape of orbit intervals in between. As a result, (a) topological information is directly accessible, and (b) unnecessary computation and memory are suppressed significantly.

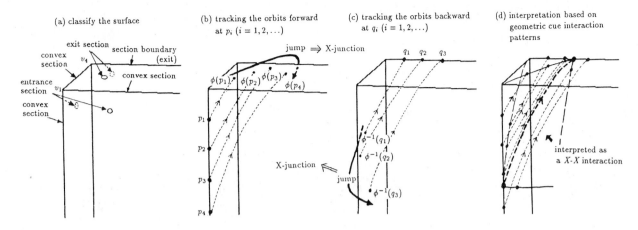

Figure 5: A process of generating flow mappings for (2)

Limitations of the Approach

The method reported in this paper has two major limitations. First, it is not straightforward to extend it to general n-dimensional flow, even though the underlying concepts are general, for I have chosen to improve efficiency by taking advantages of three-dimensional flow. Second, the current approach may be too rigid with respect to the topology of flow. Sometimes, we may have to pay a big cost for complete information, especially when the topology of the flow is inherently complex (*e.g.*, fractal basin boundary (Moon, 1987)).[7] Making the boundary fuzzy might be useful.

Conclusion

Automating qualitative analysis by intelligently controlled numerical analysis involves reasoning about complex geometry and topology under incomplete information. In this paper, I have pointed out that complex geometric patterns of solution curves of systems of ODEs can be decomposed into a combination of simple geometric patterns called geometric cue interaction patterns, and shown how they can be utilized in qualitative analysis of three-dimensional flow.

References

Abelson, Harold; Eisenberg, Michael; Halfant, Matthew; Katzenelson, Jacob; Sacks, Elisha; Sussman, Gerald J.; Wisdom, Jack; and Yip, Kenneth 1989. Intelligence in scientific computing. *Communications of the ACM* 32:546–562.

Guckenheimer, John and Holmes, Philip 1983. *Nonlinear Oscillations, Dynamical Systems, and Bifurcations of Vector Fields*. Springer-Verlag.

Hirsch, Morris W. and Smale, Stephen 1974. *Differential Equations, Dynamical Systems, and Linear Algebra*. Academic Press.

Kalagnanam, Jayant 1991. Integration of symbolic and numeric methods for qualitative reasoning. Technical Report CMU-EPP-1991-01-01, Engineering and Public Policy, CMU.

Kant, Elaine; Keller, Richard; and Steinberg, Stanly, editors 1992. *Working Notes Intelligent Scientific Computation*. American Association for Artificial Intelligence. AAAI Fall Symposium Series.

Matsumoto, Takashi; Chua, Leon O.; and Komuro, Motomasa 1985. The double scroll. *IEEE Transactions on Ciruits and Systems* CAS-32(8):798–818.

Moon, Francis C. 1987. *Chaotic Vibrations — An Introduction for Applied Scientists and Engineers*. John Wiley & Sons.

Nishida, Toyoaki and Doshita, Shuji 1991. A geometric approach to total envisioning. In *Proceedings IJCAI-91*. 1150–1155.

Nishida, Toyoaki; Mizutani, Kenji; Kubota, Atsushi; and Doshita, Shuji 1991. Automated phase portrait analysis by integrating qualitative and quantitative analysis. In *Proceedings AAAI-91*. 811–816.

Nishida, Toyoaki 1993. Automating qualitative analysis of three-dimensional flow. (unpublished research note, in preparation).

Sacks, Elisha P. 1991. Automatic analysis of one-parameter planar ordinary differential equations by intelligent numeric simulation. *Artificial Intelligence* 48:27–56.

Yip, Kenneth Man-kam 1991. Understanding complex dynamics by visual and symbolic reasoning. *Artificial Intelligence* 51(1-3):179–222.

Zhao, Feng 1991. Extracting and representing qualitative behaviors of complex systems in phase spaces. In *Proceedings IJCAI-91*. 1144–1149.

---

[7]Note that this does not mean the current approach is not suitable for analyzing chaos. Remember that the example I have used in this paper is Matsumoto-Chua's double-scroll attractor which is known as a chaotic attractor.

Real-Time Planning
and Simulation

Real-Time Self-Explanatory Simulation

Franz G. Amador and **Adam Finkelstein** and **Daniel S. Weld**[*]

Department of Computer Science and Engineering, FR-35
University of Washington
Seattle, Washington 98195
franz, adam, weld@cs.washington.edu

Abstract

We present Pika, an implemented self-explanatory simulator that is more than 5000 times faster than SimGen Mk2 [Forbus and Falkenhainer, 1992], the previous state of the art. Like SimGen, Pika automatically prepares and runs a numeric simulation of a physical device specified as a particular instantiation of a general domain theory, and it is capable of explaining its reasoning and the simulated behavior. Unlike SimGen, Pika's modeling language allows arbitrary algebraic and differential equations with no prespecified causal direction; Pika infers the appropriate causality and solves the equations as necessary to prepare for numeric integration.

Introduction

Science and engineering have used numeric simulation productively for years. Simulation programs, however, have been laboriously hand-crafted, intricate, and difficult to understand and change. There has been much recent work on automating their construction (*e.g.* [Yang, 1992, Rosenberg and Karnopp, 1983, Abelson and Sussman, 1987, Palmer and Cremer, 1992]). To this, the Qualitative Physics community has contributed the idea of a *self-explanatory simulator* [Forbus and Falkenhainer, 1990, Forbus and Falkenhainer, 1992]. When using such a system, a person need only specify the basic entities, quantities, and equations governing the system to be simulated. From these, the program automatically prepares and runs a numeric simulation. It also keeps a record of its reasoning so it can explain the simulated behavior.

Such a simulator has three primary advantages [Forbus and Falkenhainer, 1990].

- **Improved automation**: Because the user specifies the simulated system declaratively using equations, creating and modifying simulations is much easier.

- **Improved self-monitoring**: The simulator can analyze the equations to produce checks that detect problems with the simulation, such as numerical instability.

- **Better explanations**: Because the simulator records the deductions needed to prepare the simulation, it can generate custom English-language or graphical explanations for the simulated behavior. Such explanations assist debugging the simulated equations, and they can form the core of an automated tutor that allows the user to explore and learn about the behavior of a simulated system.

The first and third of these properties are of particular interest to the Electronic Encyclopedia/Exploratorium (E³) project at the University of Washington. We are constructing a program via which the user may interact with simulated versions of various engineered artifacts to learn how they work [Amador *et al.*, 1993]. The user can perturb the environment of the device to see how it reacts and even modify the device itself as it is "operating," all the while receiving English or graphical explanations for its behavior. Thus a central part of the E³ program is effectively a combined CAD system and self-explanatory simulator.

Unfortunately, existing self-explanatory simulators, namely the SimGen Mk1 and SimGen Mk2 programs [Forbus and Falkenhainer, 1990, Forbus and Falkenhainer, 1992], do not meet our needs.

- **Too slow**: Both compile the equation model of an artifact into a custom program that simulates it. While SimGen Mk2 is much faster than SimGen Mk1, this compilation process still takes much too long to allow prompt response to user manipulations of the artifact model. For example, SimGen Mk2 requires 4 hours to compile a simulator for a model of 9 containers and 12 pipes [Forbus and Falkenhainer, 1992].

- **Restrictive modeling language**: As with their

[*]Many thanks to the members of the E³ project, especially Mike Salisbury and Dorothy Neville. Pandu Nayak kindly provided Common Lisp causal ordering code. Elisha Sacks and Eric Boesch kindly provided the Runge-Kutta numeric integration code. This research was funded in part by National Science Foundation Grant IRI-8957302, Office of Naval Research Grant 90-J-1904, and the Xerox corporation.

predecessor Qualitative Process Theory [Forbus, 1984], the SimGen programs require equations to be written as uni-directional *influences*. Thus the flow of causality and information through the model must be chosen by the modeler and remains fixed. We claim it is easier and more natural to describe a model using ordinary non-directional equations. (See "Equations" below.)

In this paper we present Pika[1], an implemented self-explanatory simulator which overcomes these limitations. Its first, unoptimized implementation prepares the above SimGen Mk2 example simulation in under 3 seconds—more than 5000 times faster. Furthermore, the modeling language is based upon ordinary differential and algebraic equations, which Pika automatically manipulates as necessary to simulate the model.

The modeling language

As with the SimGen programs, our modeling language (known as the Quantified Modeling Language (QML)) derives from the Qualitative Process Theory [Forbus, 1984]. The user defines a model in two parts. The physics that apply to the device are defined in a *domain theory*, which is general and can be reused when modeling different devices. This theory is instantiated according to a *scenario description*, which specifies a particular device for simulation. For example, a domain theory might describe the various types of electrical components while a corresponding scenario description would specify a particular circuit.

QML has two distinguishing features: a simplified modeling language and non-directional equations.

Model Fragments

Qualitative Process Theory's *entity*, *process*, and *view* definitions are replaced by *model fragments* (MFs), of which there are two kinds. *Unquantified* MFs (similar to QP Theory's entities) are instantiated explicitly in the scenario description. *Quantified* MFs (similar to QP Theory's processes and views) are instantiated automatically by the system when their preconditions are met, and their instances are likewise destroyed when those preconditions no longer hold. Here, for example, is a simplistic characterization of boiling.

```
(define-MF boiling (?fluid)
  (preconditions
   (instance-of Liquid ?fluid)
   (>= (temperature ?fluid)
       (boiling-temperature ?fluid)))
  (effects
   (dyn-infl (mass ?fluid)
             (- (/ (heat-absorption-rate ?fluid)
                   (latent-heat ?fluid)))))))
```

The `dyn-infl` (dynamic influence) is a non-directional version of a QP-theory "direct influence"

[1]A pika (pronounced pee-kuh) is a small mammal that lives in alpine rockpiles.

written using terminology first advocated by Woods [Woods, 1991]. Pika sums all dynamic influences upon a quantity to form an equation that constrains its derivative. Thus if `boiling` is the only active MF, the derivative of mass is constrained to be equal to the ratio of absorption rate and latent heat of vaporization. However, if an MF encoding fluid flow into the container were active then that influence would be added to the sum constraining the derivative. Algebraic influences (`alg-infl`) are similar—they specify an implicit summation constraining the influenced quantity itself.

Equations

Pika treats all QML equations as non-directional constraints. This follows standard scientific practice better than do QP Theory's one-directional influences. Scientists express almost all physical laws as constraint equations. Ohm's Law ($V = IR$), for example, makes no commitment as to which variables are dependent and which are independent. In different contexts, such an equation can determine the value of any of its variables. If a resistor MF containing an Ohm's-Law equation appears in a model in which it is connected to a constant-voltage source, Pika will use the equation to find the current through the resistor. If the resistor is instead connected to a constant-current source, the equation determines the voltage drop across it.

Non-directional equation constraints make model writing much easier. The modeler can write the ideal gas law ($PV = nRT$) in its familiar form, without having to decide how it will be used in future simulations. Even QML's "influences" specify non-directional equations. The dynamic influence in the boiling MF above provides the modularity of QP Theory's direct influences without making any commitment to causal direction. Such modular specification of non-directional summation equations provides the modeler with considerable expressive power. For example, to encode Kirchhoff's current rule for electrical nodes, the modeler need simply include the equation (= (net-current ?self) 0) in a **Node** MF, together with (alg-infl (net-current ?node) (current ?terminal)) in an MF that will be instantiated for each connected node and terminal. From this, Pika will create an equation for each node that constrains the sum of the currents of its connected terminals to be zero. Note that the "influenced" quantity remains constant; causality flows among the "influencing" terminal currents as appropriate. This use of influences is impossible in QP Theory.

The simulation algorithm

Unlike the SimGen programs (known collectively hereafter as "SimGen"), Pika does not compile the artifact model before simulating it. However, it does compile the domain theory once after it is written or changed. Pika's domain theory compiler translates each model fragment into a set of functions that speed simulation: a model fragment's preconditions are compiled into functions that query the knowledge base to find bindings for the MF's arguments, that test whether the quantitative part of the preconditions is satisfied, and that generate numeric integration bounding conditions that halt integration when those quantitative preconditions cease to be satisfied (or become satisfied, given that the non-quantitative preconditions are met). The model fragment's effects are compiled into functions that assert those effects when the MF is activated and that retract them when it is deactivated.

This compilation requires little time (less than the LISP compiler requires to compile the resulting code). Furthermore, one need not suffer even this small cost except when the domain theory changes, which happens quite infrequently compared with changes to the model being simulated.

Since Pika is still being integrated with the E^3 user interface [Salisbury and Borning, 1993], its current implementation runs in a "batch" manner. Pika takes as input the compiled domain theory, the scenario description, and a period of time for which to simulate. It simulates for the requested time, recording its reasoning and the device's behavior, and then stops to answer the user's questions.

Pika's simulation algorithm is as follows:

Instantiate unquantified MFs from scenario description
Repeat until time bound reached
    Instantiate and deinstantiate quantified MFs based
      upon world state
    Causally order the equations
    Solve the equations for the quantities they determine
    Create integration bounds from MF preconditions
    Numerically integrate until a bound is violated

Pika's algorithm differs from SimGen's in three important ways: MF activation, numeric integration, and equation manipulation.

Model fragment activation

Both SimGen programs use an assumption-based truth maintenance system (ATMS) [de Kleer, 1986] to perform substantial analysis during model compilation. SimGen Mk1 generates a total envisionment of the model's qualitative state space, which is computationally infeasible for large models. SimGen Mk2 reduces this cost by finding only the "local states" in which each MF is active. This analysis allows them to reduce the run-time checking needed to determine changes in the set of active MFs. If the simulation is in a qualitative state from which there is only one possible transition, then the simulator need check only the limit hypothesis corresponding to that transition, and it can switch directly to the set of active MFs determined during compilation to be active in the next qualitative state. This speeds simulation, but it exacts an enormous cost during compilation.

Since Pika does no such compile-time analysis, it must test all quantified MF preconditions at runtime to determine the active set. For each MF it queries the knowledge base for all argument bindings that meet the non-quantitative preconditions (e.g. the `instance-of` test in the boiling example). In the worst case, this is exponential in the number of MF arguments, but their number is under the modeler's control and is always small.[2] Pika then tests the quantitative preconditions of these candidate MF activations, which requires time linear in the size of the quantitative expressions.

Numeric integration

SimGen uses custom-generated *evolver procedures* (which use Euler's method) to do numeric integration and *state transition procedures* to detect transitions in qualitative state. Because Pika does not compile the model, it must instead use a general-purpose numeric integrator. Its current implementation uses a fourth-order Runge-Kutta integrator with adaptive step-size control [Press *et al.*, 1986], which, at a given accuracy, is much faster than Euler's method.[3]

In addition to the simulation equations, initial quantity values, and integration limit, the integrator also takes as input a set of *integration bounds*. Each bound is an expression and an interval; if the expression's value ever leaves the interval, the integrator halts (at the time step immediately before the bound is violated). Pika supplies bounds representing the quantitative preconditions of all currently active model fragments (known as *deactivation bounds*) and other bounds representing the quantitative preconditions of all MFs that are inactive only because of their quantitative preconditions (*activation bounds*).

Equation manipulation

All the equations in a SimGen model are written either as direct influences or as qualitative proportionalities (indirect influences). SimGen converts these into numeric integration equations by 1) summing the direct influences upon each quantity's derivative, 2) sorting the indirect influences into a graph (causal ordering) such that all quantities are determined, and 3) converting the influence subgraph that determines each quantity into an algebraic equation via a table (known as the math library). Since this table contains a different equation for each possible combination of influences upon each quantity, any given qualitative proportionality can "mean" different things in different contexts.

This arrangement implies a "two-tiered" process of quantitative model construction: the domain theory is instantiated based upon MF preconditions to produce

---

[2]Note that SimGen must also confront this exponential when instantiating MFs into the ATMS.

[3]It is important to emphasize that Pika's performance advantage over SimGen is not due to the underlying integration technology—the important speed-up is in simulation preparation.

a qualitative model, and then the math library is instantiated based upon the qualitative model influences to produce the quantitative model. This structure may make writing some kinds of models easier, but it requires the modeler to write every equation twice: once qualitatively for the domain theory, and once quantitatively for the math library. It also sacrifices possible modularity. Influences allow the modeler to specify qualitative equations in pieces that are automatically assembled by SimGen; however, the modeler must fully specify all possible quantitative model equations.

With Pika, the modeler specifies the domain theory using equations which Pika automatically combines and symbolically manipulates as needed to form the quantitative model. QML thus effectively collapses SimGen's two-tiered structure into one, allowing modular specification of quantitative model equations.

Pika must convert the model's non-directional equations into the following directional form expected by the Runge-Kutta integrator:

$$\frac{dX_1}{dt} = f_1(X_1, \ldots, X_n, t) \quad Y_1 = g_1(X_1, \ldots, X_n, t)$$
$$\vdots \qquad\qquad\qquad \vdots$$
$$\frac{dX_n}{dt} = f_n(X_1, \ldots, X_n, t) \quad Y_m = g_m(X_1, \ldots, X_n, t)$$

The X's are the state variable used by the integrator to advance time; the Y's are all other variables calculated from the state variables. Pika classifies any quantity that has a derivative (generally due to a dyn-infl) as a state variable. It rearranges the equations into the above form by first using a causal ordering routine [Iwasaki and Simon, 1986, Serrano and Gossard, 1987] to find an order in which the equations can be evaluated so as to determine values for all quantities; this ordering may include sets of simultaneous equations. Pika then uses Mathematica's [Wolfram, 1988] Reduce function to solve each equation for the quantity it determines (unless it is already in "solved" form, *i.e.* (= *determined-quantity expression*)). Mathematica also solves any simultaneity for the quantities it determines. However, since causal ordering abstracts equations to sets of quantities, it can falsely group non-independent equations as simultaneities. Here we rely upon the fact that Reduce, if it cannot find a solution, will reformulate the equations, discarding non-independent ones, so that another attempt at causal ordering will not make the same mistake. This process repeats until the causal ordering contains no simultaneities.

The modeler may denote some quantities as constants. Non-constant quantities retain their previous values if they are not determinable from the state variables. Implementing these semantics requires that the equation-directionalizing process make several passes. First, all constants are marked as exogenous, and causal ordering and equation solving discover which quantities are determinable from them. Next, those state variables that remain undetermined (usually all of them) are marked as exogenous, and the algorithm

Q: Summarize the simulated behavior.
A: At time 0, heat started flowing from STOVE to CAN-OF-WATER.
   At time 55.96147, the temperature of CAN-OF-WATER reached 100.0, and it started boiling.
   At time 55.969383, a gas appeared in CAN-OF-WATER.
   At time 95.961464, the liquid in CAN-OF-WATER boiled away, and it stopped boiling.
   At time 165.31618, the pressure of CAN-OF-WATER exceeded 150.0, and the container exploded.

Q: What is the value of (TEMPERATURE CAN-OF-WATER) at time 40?
A: (TEMPERATURE CAN-OF-WATER) is 82.10323 at time 40.

Q: How is (TEMPERATURE CAN-OF-WATER) changing?
A: (TEMPERATURE CAN-OF-WATER) is increasing at time 40.

Q: What happens next?
A: At time 55.96147, the temperature of CAN-OF-WATER reached 100.0, and it started boiling.

Figure 1: Example of explanation generation. Queries are translations from a specialized query language; answers are actual program output.

runs again. Lastly, all remaining undetermined quantities are given their previous values and treated as constants under the current set of equations. A feature of this algorithm is that the modeler can force a state variable to be constant during one operating region while allowing it to vary during another.

Explanations

By keeping a record of its equation manipulations, the history of model fragment activations and deactivations, and the data returned by numeric integration, Pika can answer the class of questions answerable by SimGen Mk2. This includes summarizing so-far-simulated behavior in qualitative terms, reporting the equation that determines the value of any quantity at any simulated time, and reporting the value of a quantity at any simulated time. It objects if the quantity does not exist at the requested time. Because it does no global envisioning, Pika (like SimGen Mk2) cannot answer some questions answerable by SimGen Mk1, such as summarizing currently unsimulated future behavior and describing alternative behaviors. See figure 1 for an example.

Implementation status

PIKA is fully implemented. It is written in Allegro Common Lisp and uses the LOOM knowledge representation system (version 1.4.1) [Brill, 1991], the Mathematica symbolic math system (version 2.0) [Wolfram,

Test	Prep[4]	Total[5]	RK %[6]	Mma %[7]
SimGen Mk2:[8] 9 cont & 12 pipe	2.7s	3.1s	6	0
36 cont & 60 pipe[9]	34s	38s	6	0
2-rung RC ladder[10]	4.9s	5.1s	1.5	70
5-rung RC ladder	38s	38s	0.0006	87
Exploding can[11]	0.5s	1.8s	5	40

Figure 2: Timing data (Sun SPARCstation IPX).

1988], and a Runge-Kutta numeric integration package that is written in C [Press *et al.*, 1986]. See figure 2 for timing data.

The "prep" column is what we are comparing to SimGen's model-compilation time; it gives the time needed to prepare each model for simulation. This table demonstrates PIKA's speed and scalability for models that do not produce large sets of simultaneous equations. However, the 2-rung and 5-rung "RC ladder" electrical circuit tests require solving sets of 21 and 51 simultaneous equations, respectively, and suffer accordingly.

Second prototype

One way to reduce the impact of equation manipulation is to avoid redoing it when unnecessary. Pika regenerates the simulation equations "from scratch" every time the set of active MFs changes. We have reimplemented Pika (as Pika2) using SkyBlue [Sannella, 1992], a hierarchical constraint manager. SkyBlue effectively maintains a causal-ordering graph which can be updated incrementally as MFs activate and deactivate. Only those equations whose causal direction changes (or which form new simultaneities) must Pika2 resolve. Also, Pika2 caches solutions of individual equations, though not of simultaneities.

SkyBlue offers other advantages over "traditional" causal ordering methods. Each constraint (a set of variables) has a specified strength. SkyBlue builds the causal-ordering graph from the highest-strength, consistent set of constraints, leaving some lower-strength constraints unused if necessary. Pika2 uses this strength hierarchy to implement the semantics of con-

stants, state variables, and value persistence without having to repeatedly run a causal-ordering procedure. For example, every quantity has an associated low-strength equation that sets it equal to its most recent simulated value. SkyBlue includes the constraint representing this equation in the causal ordering only if the quantity is not otherwise determined.

SkyBlue also allows one-way constraints, which Pika2 uses to represent the fact that the derivative of a state variable is numerically integrated to determine the state variable's next value, but not vice versa. This allows a more accurate definition of a state variable than Pika uses: a state variable is a quantity having a derivative that can be causally determined if the quantity is assumed to be a state variable (and hence exogenous to each time step). This definition better reflects the cyclic nature of numeric integration, and SkyBlue will use a one-way constraint between derivative and possible state variable only when the definition is satisfied.

Pika2's initial simulation-preparation times are about the same as Pika's, but unfortunately it is not yet stable enough for timings demonstrating the value of incremental constraint management.

Related work

An important inspiration for much work in self-explanatory simulation was the STEAMER project [Holland *et al.*, 1984], which produced an impressive interactive simulator/tutor for a naval propulsion system, though all the simulations and explanations were hand-crafted in advance.

Many people have worked on easing the construction of fast, accurate numeric simulations. The iS-MILE and MISIM systems [Yang and Yang, 1989, Yang, 1992], for example, provide tools for constructing a variety of electrical and optical circuit simulations. The modeler must define new components using a subset of FORTRAN, however, and the systems do no equation manipulation. The ENPORT program [Rosenberg and Karnopp, 1983] generates numeric simulations from the more declarative bond-graph system representation, and the *Dynamicist's Workbench* project [Abelson and Sussman, 1987] generates simulations from equation models. None of these systems, however, allow changes in the equations during simulation.

Besides SimGen, the system closest in spirit to our own is SimLab [Palmer and Cremer, 1992], which allows a model-fragment-like specification of equation-based models that it symbolically manipulates to produce numeric simulations. SimLab does not, however, allow changes in the equations during simulation, nor does it generate explanations.

We note that the "How Things Work" project at Stanford [Fikes *et al.*, 1992] is addressing issues similar to those those tackled by Pika; however, the Stanford work is too preliminary to discuss extensively.

---

[4] Elapsed time spent before the first numeric integration.

[5] Total simulation elapsed time. The container/pipe and RC ladder tests were simulated until "quiescence", *i.e.* until all quantities had completed 99% of their possible change.

[6] Percent of total time spent doing numeric integration.

[7] Percent of total time spent solving equations.

[8] Our implementation of the example described in [Forbus and Falkenhainer, 1992].

[9] The SimGen Mk2 example container grid quadrupled.

[10] Each "rung" of an "RC ladder" is a capacitor with some initial voltage in series with a resistor. All rungs are connected in parallel.

[11] See figure 1.

Future work

Pika is fast, but it isn't quite fast enough to drive a truly interactive simulation for the E³ project. We estimate that we need another factor of ten for practical use and are working on several ways to speed it up.

Pika currently uses LOOM [Brill, 1991] for its knowledge base, but it uses almost none of LOOM's inferencing power. Switching to LOOM's CLOS subset, or abandoning LOOM altogether, should significantly speed Pika.

Using Mathematica to solve equations dramatically slows Pika; solving a set of a dozen linear simultaneous equations can take several seconds. Pika prepares the SimGen Mk2 example in under 3 seconds partly because that model requires no equation solving. Using a dedicated linear-equation solver instead (when possible) should help.

Conclusions

We have presented Pika, a self-explanatory simulator 5000 times faster than SimGen Mk2, the previous state of the art. Pika also provides a more natural and more expressive modeling language based upon non-directional algebraic and differential equation constraints. Pika and the SimGen programs represent points along a continuum: SimGen Mk1 does an enormous amount of model analysis prior to simulation, SimGen Mk2 does less, and Pika does almost none. Pika must therefore pay a greater cost when changing the model during simulation. The highly interactive nature of simulation in the E³ project demands such an architecture. However, the performance results suggest that Pika's strategy may work well for other applications.

References

H. Abelson and G.J. Sussman. The Dynamicist's Workbench: I Automatic Preparation of Numerical Experiments. AI Memo 955, MIT AI Lab, May 1987.

Franz G. Amador, Deborah Berman, Alan Borning, Tony DeRose, Adam Finkelstein, Dorothy Neville, David Notkin, David Salesin, Mike Salisbury, Joe Sherman, Ying Sun, Daniel S. Weld, and Georges Winkenbach. Electronic "How Things Work" Articles: Two Early Prototypes. *IEEE Transactions on Knowledge and Data Engineering*, To Appear 1993.

D. Brill. *LOOM Reference Manual*. USC-ISI, 4353 Park Terrace Drive, Westlake Village, CA 91361, version 1.4 edition, August 1991.

J. de Kleer. An Assumption-based Truth Maintenance System. *Artificial Intelligence*, 28, 1986.

R. Fikes, T. Gruber, and I. Iwasaki. The Stanford How Things Work Project. In *Working Notes of the AAAI Fall Symposium on Design from Physical Principles*, pages 88–91, October 1992.

K. Forbus and B. Falkenhainer. Self-Explanatory Simulations: An integration of qualitative and quantitative knowledge. In *Proceedings of AAAI-90*, pages 380–387, 1990.

K. Forbus and B. Falkenhainer. Self-Explanatory Simulations: Scaling Up to Large Models. In *Proceedings of AAAI-92*, page To Appear, 1992.

K. Forbus. Qualitative Process Theory. *Artificial Intelligence*, 24, December 1984. Reprinted in [Weld and de Kleer, 1989].

J. Holland, E. Hutchins, and L. Weitzman. STEAMER: An interactive inspectable simulation-based training system. *AI Magazine*, Summer 1984.

Y. Iwasaki and H. Simon. Causality In Device Behavior. *Artificial Intelligence*, 29(1):3–32, July 1986. Reprinted in [Weld and de Kleer, 1989].

R.S. Palmer and J.F. Cremer. SimLab: Automatically Creating Physical Systems Simulators. In *ASME DSC-Vol. 41*, November 1992.

W. Press, B. Flannery, S. Teukolsky, and W. Vetterling, editors. *Numerical Recipes*. Cambridge University Press, Cambridge, England, 1986.

R.C. Rosenberg and D.C. Karnopp. *Introduction to Physical System Dynamics*. McGraw Hill, New York, 1983.

M. Salisbury and A. Borning. A User Interface for the Electronic Encyclopedia Exploratorium. In *Proceedings of the 1993 International Workshop on Intelligent User Interfaces*, Orlando, FL, January 1993.

M. Sannella. The SkyBlue Constraint Solver. Technical Report 92-07-02, Department of Computer Science and Engineering, University of Washington, December 1992.

D. Serrano and D.C. Gossard. Constraint Management in Conceptual Design. In *Knowledge Based Expert Systems in Engineering: Planning and Design*, pages 211–224. Computational Mechanics Publications, 1987.

D. Weld and J. de Kleer, editors. *Readings in Qualitative Reasoning about Physical Systems*. Morgan Kaufmann, San Mateo, CA, August 1989.

S. Wolfram. *Mathematica: A System for Doing Methematics by Computer*. Addison-Wesley, Redwood City, CA, 1988.

E. Woods. The Hybrid Phenomena Theory. In *Proceedings of the 5th intenational workshop on qualitative reasoning*, pages 71–76, May 1991.

A.T. Yang and S.M. Yang. iSMILE: A Novel Circuit Simulation Program with Emphasis on New Device Model Development. In *Proceedings of ACM/IEEE 1989 Design Automation Conference*, pages 630–633, 1989.

A.T. Yang. *MISIM User's Manual*. Department of Electrical Engineering, University of Washington, 1992.

A Comparison of Action-Based Hierarchies and Decision Trees for Real-Time Performance*

David Ash   Barbara Hayes-Roth

KSL / Stanford University
701 Welch Rd. Bldg. C
Palo Alto, CA 94304-1709
ash@sumex-aim.stanford.edu

Abstract

Decision trees have provided a classical mechanism for progressively narrowing down a search from a large group of possibilities to a single alternative. The structuring of a decision tree is based on a heuristic that maximizes the value of the information gained at each level in the hierarchy. Decision trees are effective when an agent needs to reach the goal of complete diagnosis as quickly as possible and cannot accept a partial solution. We present an alternative to the decision tree heuristic which is useful when partial solutions do have value and when limited resources may require an agent to accept a partial solution. Our heuristic maximizes the improvement in the value of the partial solution gained at each level in the hierarchy; we term the resulting structure an *action-based hierarchy*. We present the results of a set of experiments designed to compare these two heuristics for hierarchy structuring. Finally, we describe some preliminary work we have done in applying these ideas to a medical domain--surgical intensive care unit (SICU) patient monitoring.

0 Introduction

Traditionally, decision trees have provided a mechanism for progressively narrowing down a search of a wide range of possibilities to a single alternative efficiently. However, in this context efficient has generally meant that the agent needs to reach its goal after consuming the minimal amount of resources. Suppose, however, that its goal is to diagnose one of a number of faults, and that the agent does not have the resources to reach its goal before it needs to act to remedy the situation. If the domain is such that partial information about the correct alternative is much better than nothing, then we will define the effectiveness of our solution not merely by how efficiently the agent reaches its goal but also by the relative worth of the partial answers it finds along the way. In this paper, we present an alternative to the traditional decision tree, *the action-based hierarchy*, which takes into account the value of partial information and performs better when this is factored in.

Our ideas build on several themes in the literature. The basic structure of the action-based hierarchy we will describe is quite similar to that of decision trees as used by Quinlan [QU83]. Other researchers ([FA92], [CH91]) have addressed the question of how to structure a decision tree, as we do, but without specifically concerning themselves with the value of the partial answers reached along the way. We follow the reactive planning approach taken in [AG87], [NI89], [RO89], and [SC87]. The algorithm which is utilized with an action-based hierarchy at run-time may be viewed as a type of *anytime algorithm* [DE88]. Our ideas are also connected to the work on bounded rationality ([DE88], [HO87], [RU91]); we guarantee response without consuming more than a certain maximal amount of expendable resources.

1 Action-Based Hierarchies

Action-based hierarchies are used to discriminate among a set of alternatives or *faults*. Each leaf node in the hierarchy corresponds to a single fault; higher nodes in the hierarchy correspond to classes of faults. The class of faults associated with a node is always the union of the classes of faults associated with its children, and the top node has associated with it the

* This research was supported by DARPA through NASA grant NAG2-581 (ARPA order 8607) and the DSSA project (DARPA contract DAAA21-92-C-0028). We acknowledge the many useful discussions we have had with our Guardian colleagues Adam Seiver, David Gaba, Juli Barr, Serdar Uckun, Rich Washington, Paul-Andre Tourtier, Vlad Dabija, Jane Chien and Alex Macalalad. Thanks to Ed Feigenbaum for sponsoring the work at the Knowledge Systems Laboratory.

set of all faults. In order to help the agent achieve its goal, there are *tests* available that it can perform. Each outcome of a test will identify the correct fault as being in one of a number of not necessarily disjoint subsets of the set of all faults. Each test has an associated *cost* which is a heuristic estimate of the difficulty of performing the test. For instance, in a real-time domain, the cost of a test might be the time consumed by the test.

There are also *actions* which can be performed; the agent tries to identify the correct fault because it needs to find an action to remedy that fault. Therefore, for every (action, fault) pair there is a *value* representing a heuristic estimate of the value of performing a particular action if a particular fault is present. This value ranges from -1 (undesirable action) through 0 (neutral) to +1 (ideal solution).

The main idea behind an action-based hierarchy is that associated with each node in the hierarchy there is a corresponding action which has the highest expected value given that the agent knows the fault falls within the set associated with this node, but has not yet discriminated among the node's children. This action can then be performed if the agent is required to act (e.g. it reaches a deadline) but has not yet completed its diagnosis. The action might be suboptimal (depending upon which fault actually turns out to be present), but is likely to be much better than doing nothing.

Figure 1 shows a sample action-based hierarchy. There is a set of four faults F1, F2, F3, and F4, and the top of the diagram shows a hierarchy with a test used to distinguish among the children of each node. The faults associated with each node, as well as the action with the best expected value, are shown in the boxes at each level in the hierarchy. The box at lower right shows how performing each test enables us to distinguish among faults; the box at lower left gives values for each (action, fault) pair.

2 Hierarchy Structuring

Given a set of faults, and the associated tests, costs of tests, actions, and values of actions, there are many hierarchies that could be constructed, although not all such hierarchies would be equally useful. Indeed, a hierarchy could be constructed by starting with the root node, and recursively selecting tests which help discriminate among the faults associated with the current node, and adding children to the current

node with one child corresponding to each possible outcome of the test. More formally, the following algorithm could be run to structure a hierarchy for use by the agent in real time:

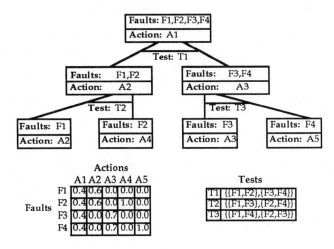

Figure 1: Sample Action-Based Hierarchy

❶ Start at the top of the yet-to-be-built hierarchy, associating the set of all faults with this top node.

❷ Pick a leaf node in the hierarchy in DFS order, or stop if there are no more leaf nodes to expand. Associate with this leaf node the action which has the highest expected value for the set of faults associated with this node.

❸ If the leaf node cannot be expanded further, go back to step 2 and pick another leaf node.

❹ Find all tests relevant to the set of faults associated with the current node.

❺ If no tests were found in step 4, go back to step 2 and pick another leaf node.

❻ Determine which test found in step 4 is best according to some heuristic.

❼ Expand the current node with one child corresponding to each possible outcome of the test found in step 6, and the associated fault sets suitably adjusted.

❽ Go back to step 2 and pick one of the children of the current node.

Note that this algorithm will never get stuck in a local maximum at any node as long as there are relevant tests for expanding a node. Once we have constructed a hierarchy in this manner, it is very simple to use it--the agent simply performs the following algorithm in real time:

❶ Label the root node of the hierarchy as the *current best hypothesis*.

❷ Perform the test associated with the current best hypothesis. If an action is required before this test can be completed, perform the action associated with the current best hypothesis.

❸ When the test results come back, refine the current best hypothesis to the one of its children pointed to by the result of the test.

2.1 Different Heuristics for Hierarchy Structuring

The variable we are most interested in in the current paper is the particular heuristic used in step 6 of the hierarchy structuring algorithm. The traditional decision tree approach is to take the *prior probability* $P(f)$ of each fault f, the set of faults F associated with the current node (a subset of all the faults), and the set of outcomes T of the test (each outcome is a subset of F), and then to compute the following function:

$$\sum_{t \in T} P(t)I(t) \text{ where}$$

$$P(t) = \sum_{f \in t} P_w(f) \ , \ I(t) = \sum_{f \in t} \frac{P_w(f)}{P(t)} \log \left(\frac{P_w(f)}{P(t)} \right)$$

$$\text{and } P_w(f) = \frac{P(f)}{\#\{t \in T : f \in t\}}$$

The effective result of this approach is that the agent maximizes the expected information content of the result of the test. This guarantees that the agent will reach its goal of diagnosing a single fault in the minimum possible time, but does nothing to guarantee that it will find actions of high value along the way. We take a different approach. In addition to the functions defined above, we use a cost function $C(t)$, and a value function $V(f,a)$ giving the value of action a for fault f. The function we wish to maximize is:

$$\frac{V(T) - V(F)}{C(T)} \text{ where } V(F_0) = \max_{a \in A} V(a, F_0)$$

and F_0 is a any set of faults. Also

$$V(T) = \frac{\sum\limits_{t \in T} V(t)P(t)}{\sum\limits_{t \in T} P(t)} \text{ and}$$

$$V(a, F_0) = \frac{W(a, F_0)}{P(F_0)} \qquad W(a, F_0) = \sum_{f \in F_0} V(f, a) P_w(f)$$

(Note that an assumption is being made here that if one fault appears in more than one of the outcomes of a test, then if the fault is present, each of those outcomes is equally likely. This assumption will be made throughout the paper.) The intuition above is that the agent performs the test which will yield the highest expected increase in the value of the best action available to date.

2.2 Evaluating Hierarchy Performance

In order to effectively compare the performance gained through the use of different hierarchies, we need to have a method of evaluating that performance. We assume that the cost of a test (the resources consumed by the test) is equal to the real time consumed by the test, but our ideas apply just as well to other types of cost which can be measured by a real number. Because of the assumed real time flavor, we will refer to the maximum time the agent is allowed to consume before acting as the *deadline*.

On any given occasion where the hierarchy is used and a fault is present, the agent will start at the top of the hierarchy and refine the current best hypothesis until it reaches a leaf node or its deadline. At any given point in time, therefore, there will be a current best hypothesis, an associated action, and a value of that action for the fault. It is this value which forms the basis for our evaluation. The value of the action associated with the current best hypothesis becomes a step function of time representing the performance of the hierarchy in one particular instance.

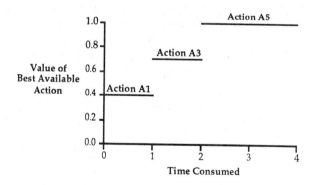

Figure 2: Hierarchy Performance on Fault F4

For example, Figure 2 shows the performance of the hierarchy illustrated in Figure 1 on the fault F4, assuming that all tests have constant time (or cost) of 1. We can now define the average hierarchy performance as follows:

$$E(f,t) = \sum_{p_f} P(p_f)E(f,p_f,t)$$

where the summation is over all paths p_f from the root node to a leaf node corresponding to fault f, and $E(f,p_f,t)$ denotes the performance of the hierarchy over time assuming that the path p_f is taken to the leaf node. The function $P(p_f)$ denotes the probability that path p_f is taken given that fault f is present.

Having defined the performance of the hierarchy for a particular fault, we can define the overall performance of the hierarchy as the weighted average of the performances for each fault:

$$E(t) = \sum_{f \in F} P(f)E(f,t)$$

$E(t)$ gives the performance of the hierarchy at various possible deadlines t.

3 Formal Properties of Action-Based Hierarchies

It is possible to prove that under certain well-defined assumptions, the performance of action-based hierarchies is optimal. Specifically, we need to make the following assumptions:

❶ The values of tests are additive. The value of a test is given by the function $V(T)$ defined in section 2. Two tests T_1 and T_2 may be combined into a single test T by combining their results: $T = \{t_1 \cap t_2 : t_1 \in T_1 \wedge t_2 \in T_2\}$. Additivity means that the value of the combination is the sum of the values of each test: $V(T) = V(T_1) + V(T_2)$. In a similar manner, additivity must also apply to combinations of more that two tests.

❷ The value of any test or combination of tests is constant for all faults. That is, if this constant is 0.7 for a given combination of tests, then for *any* set of faults corresponding to particular outcomes of these test, the best action available will have value 0.7 for all the faults in the set.

❸ The deadline occurs immediately following a successful refinement of the current best hypothesis.

❹ The structuring of the hierarchy conforms with the algorithm given at the start of section 2.

❺ For any set of faults, there is always an action available which has positive expected value so that doing something is better than doing nothing.

The proof is based on the fact that the action-based hierarchy structuring algorithm is a greedy algorithm, and when test values are additive the agent does best by simply performing the apparently best test first without considering lookahead.

4 Formal Experiments

The assumptions outlined in the last section clearly do not hold in general. Therefore, we designed experiments to test the following two hypotheses:

❶ Using the action-based hierarchy will provide substantially better performance than the decision tree when evaluated as described in section 2.
❷ Using the decision tree will provide substantially better performance when only speed in reaching a leaf node matters.

The experimental method was to randomly assign prior probabilities, test outcomes, and values of actions for faults. The prior probabilities were assigned by dividing the interval [0,1] into uniformly distributed partitions. Each test was randomly assigned to divide the fault set into two equal parts (the number of faults was always even). No fault appeared as part of both outcomes of a particular test. The values of actions for faults were also randomly distributed in the interval [0,1].

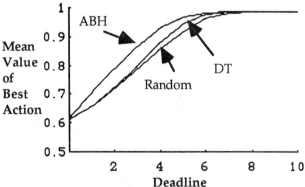

Figure 3: Hierarchy Performance with Different Deadlines and Heuristics

Figure 3 shows the difference in performance, over time, of action-based hierarchies, decision trees, and the randomly structured hierarchies. This shows that action-based hierarchies always do at least as well as the other approaches, no matter what the value of the deadline (the amount of resources available for diagnosis), but that this advantage varies over time from nil at time zero, to a maximum for deadline values of around 3 or 4, back to nil for large deadline values. This corresponds, roughly speaking, to the fact that all hierarchies perform equally well at their root and their leaf nodes, but that at the intermediate nodes there is an advantage for certain hierarchies over others.

The reader may wonder why there are not certain time points at which decision trees would have an advantage over action-based hierarchies. The answer appears to be that for individual performance profiles DT might have an advantage at certain time points, but this charateristic is lost when we compute the average.

Now, suppose we are not interested in intermediate nodes but only in getting to a leaf node as quickly as possible. In Figure 4, we show a graph of the probability that a leaf node has been diagnosed by particular deadline values. Looking at this figure it is apparent that over a relatively small range of the deadline (between about 4 and 7) using a decision tree offers a very significant advantage over the other approaches. However, for other values of the deadline, it makes very little difference.

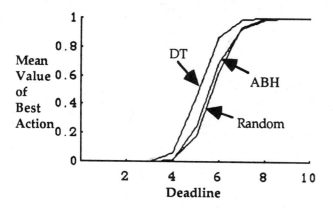

Figure 4: Hierarchy Performance using All-or-Nothing Evaluation

5 Implementation in a Medical Domain (ReAct)

We have used the idea of an action-based hierarchy to structure the knowledge base for a system, called ReAct, designed to provide fast response time in a

surgical intensive care unit (SICU). ReAct is described in detail in [AS93] and is part of the Guardian SICU patient monitoring system [HA92]. Because it uses an action-based hierarchy, ReAct is able to meet deadlines. This is in contrast with other medical AI systems ([BR87], [CL89], [FA80], and [HO89]) which perform diagnosis efficiently but without specifically addressing deadline issues. Knowledge regarding faults, tests, costs of tests, probabilities of faults, etc., has been provided by a medical expert; the hierarchy structuring algorithm has been used to produce an action-based hierarchy. A small part of the hierarchy is shown in Figure 5. In applying these ideas to a real-world domain, we are interested in determining whether the same results as reported earlier in this paper apply. In this domain, the theoretical assumptions made in section 3 will definitely not apply; nor will the variables necessarily fit the random distributions used to run the experiments described in section 4.

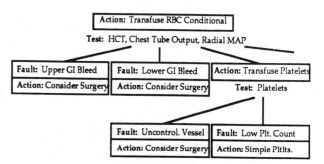

Figure 5: Portion of Medical Action-Based Hierarchy

Figure 6 shows the results of an experiment run using the medical problem similar to the ones described in section 4. In this experiment we assumed that all tests took constant time to come back (30 minutes). As can be seen, for small values of the deadline, action-based hierarchies enjoyed a modest advantage over decision trees. For larger values of the deadline (not shown here) there was no discernable difference. We anticipate that if we took test times into account, the advantage of ABH over DT would be much more noticeable, even for larger values of the deadline.

6 Future Work

In addition to the domain experiments described in section 5, we intend to explore a number of different avenues in our ongoing research. The first question is whether there are other, still better heuristics which could be used to structure the hierarchy. We have tried combining the two heuristics, and we expect that a more sophisticated combining function than we have used could lead to behavior which is better than either algorithm in certain circumstances. Another question is whether better performance could be obtained by altering the basic structure of the solution. At present, only one test is performed at each node in the hierarchy. In the domain described in section 5, this approach would be the exception rather than the rule: generally physicians will order a whole battery of tests to help them distinguish among the children of the current node. Thus, our hierarchies should be able to perform similarly if we hope to achieve performance comparable to that obtained by physicians.

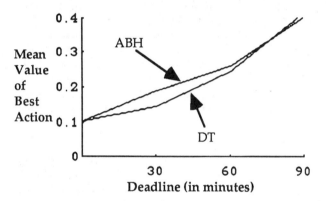

Figure 6: Hierarchy Performance in Medical Problem

Our measures for cost and value (numbers between 0 and 1) are quite crude and may not be sufficient in many domains. Therefore, we intend to explore the process of hierarchy structuring in domains where we have more sophisticated notions of cost and value.

References

[AG87] Agre, P., Chapman, D. Pengi: an implementation of a theory of activity. *Proceedings of the Sixth International Conference on Artificial Intelligence*, 268-272, 1987.

[AS93] Ash, D., et.al. Guaranteeing real-time response with limited resources. *Artificial Intelligence in Medicine*, 5(1):49-66, 1993.

[BR87] Bratko, I., Mozetic, I., Lavrac, N. Automatic synthesis and compression of cardiological knowledge. *Machine Intelligence 11*, pp 435-454, 1987.

[CH91] Chrisman, L., Simmons, R. Sensible planning: focusing perceptual attention. *Ninth National Conference on Artificial Intelligence*, 756-761, 1991.

[CL89] Clarke, J., et.al. TraumAID: a decision aid for managing trauma at various levels of resources. *Proceedings of the Thirteenth Annual Symposium on Computer Applications in Medical Care*, Washington, DC, November, 1989.

[DE88] Dean, T., Boddy, M. An analysis of time-dependent planning. *Seventh National Conference on Artificial Intelligence*, 49-54, 1988.

[FA80] Fagan, L. VM: representing time-dependent relations in a medical setting. PhD Thesis, Computer Science Department, Stanford University, June, 1980.

[FA92] Fayyad, U., Irani, K. The attribute selection problem in decision tree generation. *Tenth National Conference on Artificial Intelligence*, 104-110, 1992.

[HA92] Hayes-Roth, B., et.al. Guardian: a prototype intelligent agent for intensive-care monitoring. *Artificial Intelligence in Medicine*, 4:165-185, 1992.

[HO87] Horvitz, E. Reasoning about beliefs and actions under computational resource constraints. *Proceedings of the 1987 AAAI Workshop on Uncertainty in Artificial Intelligence*, 1987.

[HO89] Horvitz, E., et.al. Heuristic abstraction in the decision-theoretic Pathfinder system. *Proceedings of the Thirteenth Annual Symposium on Computer Applications in Medical Care*, Washington, DC, November, 1989.

[NI89] Nilsson, N.J. Action Networks. *Proceedings from the Rochester Planning Workshop: From Formal Systems to Practical Systems*, J. Tenenberg et al., ed., University of Rochester, 1989.

[QU83] Quinlan, J.R. Inductive inference as a tool for the construction of high-performance programs. In R.S. Michalski, T.M. Mitchell, and J. Carbonell, *Machine Learning*, Palo Alto, Calif.: Tioga, 1983.

[RO89] Rosenschein, S.J. Synthesizing information-tracking automata from environment descriptions. *Proceedings of Conference on Principles of Knowledge Representation and Reasoning*, Morgan Kaufmann, San Mateo, CA, 1989.

[RU91] Russell, S., Wefald, E. Principles of metareasoning. *Artificial Intelligence*, 49:361-395, 1991.

[SC87] Schoppers, M. Universal plans for reactive robots in unpredictable environments. *Tenth International Joint Conference on Artificial Intelligence*, 1987.

Planning With Deadlines in Stochastic Domains

Thomas Dean, Leslie Pack Kaelbling, Jak Kirman, Ann Nicholson
Department of Computer Science
Brown University, Providence, RI 02912
tld@cs.brown.edu

Abstract

We provide a method, based on the theory of Markov decision problems, for efficient planning in stochastic domains. Goals are encoded as reward functions, expressing the desirability of each world state; the planner must find a policy (mapping from states to actions) that maximizes future rewards. Standard goals of achievement, as well as goals of maintenance and prioritized combinations of goals, can be specified in this way. An optimal policy can be found using existing methods, but these methods are at best polynomial in the number of states in the domain, where the number of states is exponential in the number of propositions (or state variables). By using information about the starting state, the reward function, and the transition probabilities of the domain, we can restrict the planner's attention to a set of world states that are likely to be encountered in satisfying the goal. Furthermore, the planner can generate more or less complete plans depending on the time it has available. We describe experiments involving a mobile robotics application and consider the problem of scheduling different phases of the planning algorithm given time constraints.

Introduction

In a completely deterministic world, it is possible for a planner simply to generate a sequence of actions, knowing that if they are executed in the proper order, the goal will necessarily result. In nondeterministic worlds, planners must address the question of what to do when things do not go as expected.

The method of triangle tables [Fikes *et al.*, 1972] made plans that could be executed robustly in any circumstance along the nominal trajectory of world states, allowing for certain classes of failures and serendipitous events. It is often the case, however, that an execution error will move the world to a situation that has not been previously considered by the planner.

Many systems (SIPE, for example [Wilkins, 1988]) can monitor for plan "failures" and initiate replanning. Replanning is often too slow to be useful in time-critical domains, however. Schoppers, in his universal plans [Schoppers, 1987], gives a method for generating a reaction for every possible situation that could transpire during plan execution; these plans are robust and fast to execute, but can be very large and expensive to generate. There is an inherent contradiction in all of these approaches. The world is assumed to be deterministic for the purpose of planning, but its nondeterminism is accounted for by performing execution monitoring or by generating reactions for world states not on the nominal planned trajectory.

In this paper, we address the problem of planning in nondeterministic domains by taking nondeterminism into account from the very start. There is already a well-explored body of theory and algorithms addressing the question of finding optimal policies (universal plans) for nondeterministic domains. Unfortunately, these methods are impractical in large state spaces. However, if we know the start state, and have a model of the nature of the world's nondeterminism, we can restrict the planner's attention to a set of world states that are likely to be encountered on the way to the goal. Furthermore, the planner can generate more or less complete plans depending on the time it has available. In this way, we provide efficient methods, based on existing techniques of finding optimal strategies, for planning under time constraints in non-deterministic domains. Our approach addresses uncertainty resulting from control error, but not sensor error; we assume certainty in observations.

We assume that the environment can be modeled as a stochastic automaton: a set of states, a set of actions, and a matrix of transition probabilities. In the simplest cases, achieving a goal corresponds to performing a sequence of actions that results in a state satisfying some proposition. Since we cannot guarantee the length of a sequence needed to achieve a given goal in a stochastic domain, we are interested in building planning systems that minimize the expected number of actions needed to reach a given goal.

In our approach, constructing a plan to achieve a goal corresponds to finding a *policy* (a mapping from states to actions) that maximizes expected performance. Performance is based on the expected accumulated reward over sequences of state transitions determined by the underlying stochastic automaton. The rewards are determined by a *reward function* (a mapping from states to the real numbers) specially formulated for a given goal. A good policy in our framework corresponds to a universal plan for achieving goals quickly on average.

In the following, we refer to the automaton modeling the environment as the *system* automaton. Instead of generating the optimal policy for the whole system automaton, we formulate a simpler or *restricted* stochastic automaton and then search for an optimal policy in this restricted automaton. The state space for the restricted automaton, called the *envelope*, is a subset of the states of the system automaton, augmented with a special state OUT that represents being in any state outside of the envelope.

The algorithm developed in this paper consists of two basic subroutines. *Envelope extension* adds states to the restricted automaton, making it approximate the system automaton more closely. *Policy generation* computes an optimal policy for the restricted automaton; a complete policy for the system automaton is constructed by augmenting the policy for the restricted automaton with a set of default actions or *reflexes* to be executed for states outside the envelope.

The algorithm is implemented as an *anytime* algorithm [Dean and Boddy, 1988], one that can be interrupted at any point during execution to return an answer whose value at least in certain classes of stochastic processes improves in expectation as a function of the computation time. We gather statistics on how envelope extension and policy generation improve performance and use these statistics to compile expectations for allocating computing resources in time-critical situations.

In this paper, we focus primarily on the details of the algorithm and the results of a series of computational experiments that provide some indication of its merit. Subsequent papers will expand on the representation for goals and deal with more complicated models of interaction that require more sophisticated methods for allocating computational resources.

Planning Algorithm

Definitions We model the entire environment as a stochastic automaton. Let $\mathcal{S}$ be the finite set of world states; we assume that they can be reliably identified by the agent. Let $\mathcal{A}$ be the finite set of actions; every action can be taken in every state. The transition model of the environment is a function mapping elements of $\mathcal{S} \times \mathcal{A}$ into discrete probability distributions over $\mathcal{S}$. We write $\text{PR}(s_1, a, s_2)$ for the probability that the world will make a transition from state s_1 to state s_2 when action a is taken.

A *policy* π is a mapping from $\mathcal{S}$ to $\mathcal{A}$, specifying an action to be taken in each situation. An environment combined with a policy for choosing actions in that environment yields a Markov chain [Kemeny and Snell, 1960].

A *reward function* is a mapping from $\mathcal{S}$ to $\Re$, specifying the instantaneous reward that the agent derives from being in each state. Given a policy π and a reward function R, the *value* of state $s \in \mathcal{S}$, $V_\pi(s)$, is the sum of the expected values of the rewards to be received at each future time step, discounted by how far into the future they occur. That is, $V_\pi(s) = \sum_{t=0}^{\infty} \gamma^t E(R_t)$, where R_t is the reward received on the tth step of executing policy π after starting in state s. The *discounting factor*, γ, is between 0 and 1 and controls the influence of rewards in the distant future. Due to properties of the exponential, the definition of V can be rewritten as

$$V_\pi(s) = R(s) + \gamma \sum_{s' \in \mathcal{S}} \text{PR}(s, \pi(s), s') V_\pi(s') \ . \quad (1)$$

We say that policy π *dominates* (is better than) π' if, for all $s \in \mathcal{S}$, $V_\pi(s) \geq V_{\pi'}(s)$, and for at least one $s \in \mathcal{S}$, $V_\pi(s) > V_{\pi'}(s)$. A policy is optimal if it is not dominated by any other policy.

One of the most common goals is to achieve a certain condition p *as soon as possible*. If we define the reward function as $R(s) = 0$ if p holds in state s and $R(s) = -1$ otherwise, and represent all goal states as being absorbing, then the optimal policy will result in the agent reaching a state satisfying p as soon as possible. *Absorbing* means that all actions result in the same state with probability 1; $\forall a \in \mathcal{A}$, $\text{PR}(s, a, s) = 1$. Making the goal states absorbing ensures that we go to the "nearest" state in which p holds, independent of the states that will follow. The language of reward functions is quite rich, allowing us to specify much more complex goals, including the maintenance of properties of the world and prioritized combinations of primitive goals.

A *partial policy* is a mapping from a subset of $\mathcal{S}$ into actions; the domain of a partial policy π is called its *envelope*, $\mathcal{E}_\pi$. The *fringe* of a partial policy, F_π, is the set of states that are not in the envelope of the policy, but that may be reached in one step of policy execution from some state in the envelope. That is, $F_\pi = \{s \in \mathcal{S} \mid \exists s' \in \mathcal{E}_\pi \ s.t. \ \text{PR}(s', \pi(s'), s) > 0\}$.

To construct a restricted automaton, we take an envelope $\mathcal{E}$ of states and add the distinguished state OUT. For any states s and s' in $\mathcal{E}$ and action a in $\mathcal{A}$, the transition probabilities remain the same. Further, for every $s \in \mathcal{E}$ and $a \in \mathcal{A}$, we define the probability of going out of the envelope as

$$\text{PR}(s, a, \text{OUT}) = 1 - \sum_{s' \in \mathcal{E}} \text{PR}(s, a, s') \ .$$

The OUT state is absorbing.

The cost of falling out of the envelope is a parameter that depends on the domain. If it is possible to re-invoke the planner when the agent falls out of the envelope, then one approach is to assign $V(\text{OUT})$ to be the estimated value of the state into which the agent fell minus some function of the time to construct a new partial policy. Under the reward function described earlier, the value of a state is negative, and its magnitude is the expected number of steps to the goal; if time spent planning is to be penalized, it can simply be added to the magnitude of the value of the OUT state with a suitable weighting function.

Overall Structure We assume, initially, that there are two separate phases of operation: planning and execution. The planner constructs a policy that is followed by the agent until a new goal must be pursued or until the agent falls out of the current envelope. More sophisticated models of interaction between planning and execution are possible, including one in which the planner runs concurrently with the execution, sending down new or expanded strategies as they are developed. Questions of how to schedule deliberation are discussed in the following section (see also [Dean *et al.*, 1993]). Execution of an explicit policy is trivial, so we describe only the algorithm for generating policies.

The high level planning algorithm, given a description of the environment and start state s_0 is as follows:

1. Generate an initial envelope $\mathcal{E}$
2. While ($\mathcal{E} \neq \mathcal{S}$) and (not deadline) do
   2.1 Extend the envelope $\mathcal{E}$
   2.2 Generate an optimal policy π for restricted automaton with state set $\mathcal{E} \cup \{\text{OUT}\}$
3. Return π

The algorithm first finds a small subset of world states and calculates an optimal policy over those states. Then it gradually adds new states in order to make the policy robust by decreasing the chance of falling out of the envelope. After new states are added, the optimal policy over the new envelope is calculated. Note the interdependence of these steps: the choice of which states to add during envelope extension may depend on the current policy, and the policy generated as a result of optimization may be quite different depending on which states were added to the envelope. The algorithm terminates when a deadline has been reached or when the envelope has been expanded to include the entire state space. In the following sections, we consider each subcomponent of this algorithm in more detail.

Generating an initial envelope This high-level algorithm works no matter how the initial envelope is chosen, but if it is done with some intelligence, the early policies are much more useful. In our examples, we consider the goal of being in a state satisfying p

as soon as possible. For such simple goals of achievement, a good initial envelope is one containing a chain of states from the initial state, s_0, to some state satisfying p such that, for each state, there is some action with a non-zero probability of moving to the next state in the chain.

In the implemented system, we generate an initial envelope by doing a depth-first search from s_0 considering the most probable outcome for each action in decreasing order of probability. This yields a set of states that can be traversed with fairly high probability to a goal state. More sophisticated techniques could be used to generate a good initial envelope; our strategy is to spend as little time as possible doing this, so that a plausible policy is available as soon as possible.

Generating an optimal policy Howard's *policy iteration* algorithm is guaranteed to generate the optimal policy for the restricted automaton. The algorithm works as follows: [1]

1. Let π' be any policy on $\mathcal{E}$
2. While $\pi \neq \pi'$ do loop
   2.1 $\pi := \pi'$
   2.2 For all $s \in \mathcal{E}$, calculate $V_\pi(s)$ by solving the set of $|\mathcal{E}|$ linear equations in $|\mathcal{E}|$ unknowns given by equation 1
   2.3 For all $s \in \mathcal{E}$, if there is some action $a \in \mathcal{A}$ s.t. $[R(s) + \gamma \sum_{s' \in \mathcal{E} \cup \{\text{OUT}\}} \text{PR}(s, s', a) V_\pi(s')] > V_\pi(s)$, then $\pi'(s) := a$; otherwise $\pi'(s) := \pi(s)$
3. Return π

The algorithm iterates, generating at every step a policy that strictly dominates the previous policy, and terminates when a policy can no longer be improved, yielding an optimal policy. In every iteration, the values of the states under the current policy are computed. This is done by solving a system of equations; although this is potentially an $O(|\mathcal{E}|^{2.8})$ operation, most realistic environments cannot transition from every state to every other, so the transition matrix is sparse, allowing much more efficient solution of the equations. The algorithm then improves the policy by looking for states s in which doing some action a other than $\pi(s)$ for one step, then continuing with π, would result in higher expected reward than simply executing π. When such a state is found, the policy is changed so that it always chooses action a in that state.

This algorithm requires a number of iterations at most polynomial in the number of states; in practice for for an instance of our domain with 6000 world states, it has never taken more than 16 iterations. When we use this as a subroutine in our planning algorithm, we generate a random policy for the first step, and then for

---

[1]Since $V(\text{OUT})$ is fixed, and the OUT state is absorbing, it does not need to be explicitly included in the policy calculations.

all subsequent steps we use the old policy as the starting point for policy iteration. Because, in general, the policy does not change radically when the envelope is extended, it requires very few iterations (typically 2 or 3) of the policy iteration algorithm to generate the optimal policy for the extended envelope. Occasionally, when a very dire consequence or an exceptional new path is discovered, the whole policy must be changed.

Extending the envelope There are a number of possible strategies for extending the envelope; the most appropriate depends on the domain. The aim of the envelope extension is to judiciously broaden the subset of the world states, by including states that are outside the envelope of the current policy but that may be reached upon executing the policy. One simple strategy is to add the entire fringe of the current policy, F_π; this would result in adding states uniformly around the current envelope. It will often be the case, however, that some of the states in the fringe are very unlikely given the current policy.

A more reasonable strategy, similar to one advocated by Drummond and Bresina [Drummond and Bresina, 1990], is to look for the N most likely fringe states. We do this by simulating the restricted automaton and accumulating the probabilities of falling out into each fringe state. We then have a choice of strategies. We can add each of the N most likely fringe states. Alternatively, for goals of achievement, we can take each element of this subset of the fringe states and find a chain of states that leads back to some state in the envelope. In the experiments described in the following sections, fringe states are added rather than whole paths back to the envelope.

Example In our approach, unlike that of Drummond and Bresina, extending the current policy is coupled tightly and naturally to *changing* the policy as required to keep it optimal with respect to the restricted view of the world. The following example illustrates how such changes are made using the algorithm as described.

The example domain is mobile-robot path planning. The floor plan is divided into a grid of 166 locations, $\mathcal{L}$, with four directional states associated with each location, $\mathcal{D} = \{N, S, E, W\}$, corresponding to the direction the robot is facing, resulting in a total of 664 world states. The actions available to the robot are {STAY, GO, TURN-RIGHT, TURN-LEFT, TURN-ABOUT}. The transition probabilities for the outcome of each action may be obtained empirically. In our experimental simulation the STAY action is guaranteed to succeed. The probability of success for GO and turning actions in most locations were 0.8, with the remainder of the probability mass divided between undesired results such as overshooting, over-rotating, slipping sideways, etc. The world also contains *sinks*, locations that are difficult or impossible to leave. On average each state has 15.6 successors.

Figure 1 shows a subset of our domain, the locations surrounding a stairwell, which is a *complete sink*, *i.e.*, there are no non-zero transitions out of it; also, it is only accessible from one direction, north. In this figure there are four small squares associated with each location, one for each possible heading; thus each small square corresponds to a state, the direction of the arrow shows the policy for the robot in that location and with that heading. Figure 1 (a) shows the optimal policy for a small early envelope; Figures 1(b) and (c) show two subsequent envelopes where the policy changes to direct the robot to circumvent the stairwell, reflecting aversion to the risk involved in taking the shortest path.

Deliberation Scheduling

Given the two-stage algorithm for generating policies provided in the previous section, we would like the agent to allocate processor time to the two stages when faced with a time critical situation. Determining such allocations is called *deliberation scheduling* [Dean and Boddy, 1988]. In this paper, we consider situations in which the agent is given a deadline and an initial state and has until the deadline to produce a policy after which no further adjustments to the policy are allowed. The interval of time from the current time until the deadline is called the *deliberation interval*. We address more complicated situations in [Dean *et al.*, 1993].

Deliberation scheduling relies on compiling statistics to produce expectations regarding performance improvements that are used to guide scheduling. In general, we cannot guarantee that our algorithm will produce a sequence of policies, $\hat{\pi}_0, \hat{\pi}_1, \hat{\pi}_2, \ldots$, that increase in value, *e.g.*, $V_{\hat{\pi}_0}(s_0) < V_{\hat{\pi}_1}(s_0) < V_{\hat{\pi}_2}(s_0) \cdots$, where the $\hat{\pi}_i$ are complete policies constructed by adding reflexes to the partial policies generated by our algorithm. The best we can hope for is that the algorithm produces a sequence of policies whose values increase in expectation, *e.g.*, $E[V_{\hat{\pi}_0}(s_0)] < E[V_{\hat{\pi}_1}(s_0)] < E[V_{\hat{\pi}_2}(s_0)] \cdots$, where here the initial state s_0 is considered a random variable. In allocating processor time, we are concerned with the expected improvement, $E[V_{\hat{\pi}_{i+1}}(s_0) - V_{\hat{\pi}_i}(s_0)]$, relative to a given allocation of processor time.

If envelope extension did not make use of the current policy, we could just partition the deliberation interval into two subintervals, the first spent in envelope extension and the second in policy generation. However, since the two stages are mutually dependent, we have to consider performing multiple rounds where each round involves some amount of envelope extension followed by some amount of policy generation.

Let t_{EE_i} (t_{PG_i}) be the time allocated to envelope extension (policy generation) in the ith round of the algorithm and $\mathcal{E}_i$ be the envelope following the ith round envelope extension. To obtain an optimal deliberation schedule, we would have to consider the expected value

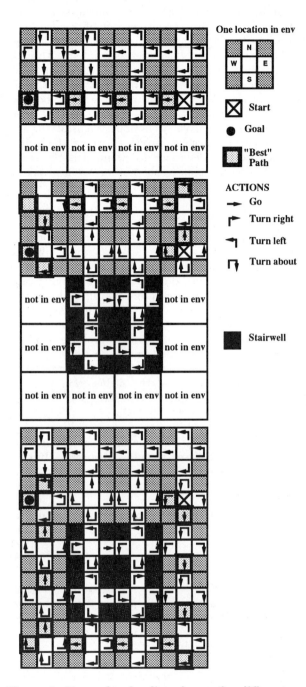

One location in env

	N	
W		E
	S	

⊠ Start

● Goal

▨ "Best" Path

ACTIONS

→ Go

⌐ Turn right

⌐ Turn left

⌐ Turn about

■ Stairwell

Figure 1: Example of policy change for different envelopes near a complete sink. The direction of the arrow indicates the current policy for that state. (a) Sink not in the envelope: the policy chooses the straightforward shortest path. (b) Sink included: the policy skirts north around it. (c) All states surrounding the stairwell included: the barriers on the south, east and west sides allow the policy take a longer but safer path. For this run $\gamma = 0.999999$ and $V(\text{OUT}) = -4000$.

of the final policy given $k = 1, 2, \ldots$ rounds and all possible allocations to t_{EE_i} and t_{PG_i} for $1 \leq i \leq k$. We suspect that finding the optimal deliberation schedule is NP-hard. To expedite deliberation scheduling, we use a greedy algorithm based on the following statistics.

1. The expected improvement starting with an envelope of size m and adding n states: $E[V_{\hat{\pi}_{i+1}}(s_0) - V_{\hat{\pi}_i}(s_0) | m = |\mathcal{E}_i|, m + n = |\mathcal{E}_{i+1}|]$.

2. The expected time required to extend by n states an envelope of size m and compute the optimal policy for the resulting restricted automaton: $E[t_{EE_i + PG_i} | m = |\mathcal{E}_i|, m + n = |\mathcal{E}_{i+1}|]$.

After each round of envelope extension followed by policy generation we have an envelope of some size m; we find that n maximizing the ratio of (1) and (2), add n states, and perform another round, time permitting. If the deadline occurs during envelope extension, then the algorithm returns the policy from the last round. If the deadline occurs during policy generation, then the algorithm returns the policy from the last iteration of policy iteration.

Results

In this section, we present results from the iterative refinement algorithm using the table lookup deliberation scheduling strategy and statistics described in the previous sections. We generated 1.6 million data points to compute the required statistics for the same robot-path-planning domain. The start and goal states were chosen randomly for executions of the planning algorithm using a greedy deliberation strategy, where N, the number of fringe states added for each phase of envelope extension, was determined from the deliberation scheduling statistics.

We compared the performance of (1) our planning algorithm using the greedy deliberation strategy to (2) policy iteration optimizing the policy for the whole domain. Our results show that the planning algorithm using the greedy deliberation strategy supplies a good policy early, and typically converges to a policy that is close to optimal before the whole domain policy iteration method does. Figure 2 shows average results from 620 runs, where a single run involves a particular start state and goal state. The graph shows the average improvement of the start state under the policy available at time t, $V_{\hat{\pi}}(s_0)$, as a function of time. In order to compare results from different start/goal runs, we show the average ratio of the value of the current policy to the value of the optimal policy for the whole domain, plotted against the ratio of actual time to the time, T_{opt}, that the policy iteration takes to reach that optimal value.

The greedy deliberation strategy performs significantly better than the standard optimization method. We also considered very simple strategies such as adding a small fixed N each iteration, and adding the

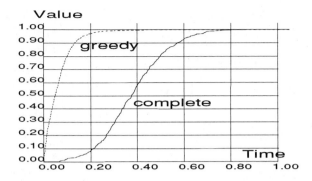

Figure 2: Comparison of planning algorithm using greedy deliberation strategy (dashed line) with the policy iteration optimization method (solid line).

whole fringe each iteration, which performed fairly well for this domain, but not as well as the greedy policy. Further experimentation is required to draw definitive conclusions about the comparative performance of these deliberation strategies for particular domains.

Related Work and Conclusions

Our primary interest is in applying the sequential decision making techniques of Bellman [Bellman, 1957] and Howard [Howard, 1960] in time-critical applications. Our initial motivation for the methods discussed here came from the 'anytime synthetic projection' work of Drummond and Bresina. [Drummond and Bresina, 1990]. We improve on the Drummond and Bresina work by providing (i) coherent semantics for goals in stochastic domains, (ii) theoretically sound probabilistic foundations, (iii) and decision-theoretic methods for controlling inference.

The approach described in this paper represents a particular instance of time-dependent planning [Dean and Boddy, 1988] and borrows from, among others, Horvitz' [Horvitz, 1988] approach to flexible computation. Boddy [Boddy, 1991] describes solutions to related problems involving dynamic programming. Hansson and Mayer's BPS (Bayesian Problem Solver) [Hansson and Mayer, 1989] supports general state-space search with decision-theoretic control of inference; it may be that BPS could be used as the basis for envelope extension thus providing more fine-grained decision-theoretic control. Christiansen and Goldberg [Christiansen and Goldberg, 1990] also address the problem of planning in stochastic domains.

The approach is applicable to stochastic domains with certain characteristics; typically there are multiple paths to the goal and the domain is relatively benign. If there is only one path to the goal all the work will be done by the procedure finding the initial envelope, and extending the envelope only improves the policy if the new states can be recovered from. Our future research plans involve extending the approach in several directions: allowing more complex goals; per-

forming more complicated deliberation scheduling such as integrating online deliberation in parallel with the execution of policies; relaxing the assumption of observation certainty to handle sensor error.

Acknowledgements. Thomas Dean's work was supported in part by a National Science Foundation Presidential Young Investigator Award IRI-8957601, by the Advanced Research Projects Agency of the Department of Defense monitored by the Air Force under Contract No. F30602-91-C-0041, and by the National Science foundation in conjunction with the Advanced Research Projects Agency of the Department of Defense under Contract No. IRI-8905436. Leslie Kaelbling's work was supported in part by a National Science Foundation National Young Investigator Award IRI-9257592 and in part by ONR Contract N00014-91-4052, ARPA Order 8225.

References

Bellman, R. 1957. *Dynamic Programming.* Princeton University Press.

Boddy, M. 1991. Anytime problem solving using dynamic programming. In *Proceedings AAAI-91.* AAAI. 738–743.

Christiansen, A., and Goldberg, K. 1990. Robotic manipulation planning with stochastic actions. In *DARPA Workshop on Innovative Approaches to Planning, Scheduling and Control.* San Diego,California.

Dean, T., and Boddy, M. 1988. An analysis of time-dependent planning. In *Proceedings AAAI-88.* AAAI. 49–54.

Dean, T.; Kaelbling, L.; Kirman, J.; and Nicholson, A. 1993. Deliberation scheduling for time-critical sequential decision making. Submitted to *Ninth Conference on Uncertainty in Artificial Intelligence.*

Drummond, M., and Bresina, J. 1990. Anytime synthetic projection: Maximizing the probability of goal satisfaction. In *Proceedings AAAI-90.* AAAI. 138–144.

Fikes, R. E.; Hart, P. E.; and Nilsson, N. J. 1972. Learning and executing generalized robot plans. *Artificial Intelligence* 3:251–288.

Hansson, O., and Mayer, A. 1989. Heuristic search as evidential reasoning. In *Proceedings of the Fifth Workshop on Uncertainty in AI.* 152–161.

Horvitz, E. J. 1988. Reasoning under varying and uncertain resource constraints. In *Proceedings AAAI-88.* AAAI. 111–116.

Howard, R. A. 1960. *Dynamic Programming and Markov Processes.* MIT Press, Cambridge, Massachusetts.

Kemeny, J. G. and Snell, J. L. 1960. *Finite Markov Chains.* D. Van Nostrand, New York.

Schoppers, M. J. 1987. Universal plans for reactive robots in unpredictable environments. In *Proceedings IJCAI 10.* IJCAII. 1039–1046.

Wilkins, D. E. 1988. *Practical Planning: Extending the Classical AI Planning Paradigm.* Morgan-Kaufmann, Los Altos, California.

Task Interdependencies in Design-to-time Real-time Scheduling *

Alan Garvey and Marty Humphrey and Victor Lesser
Computer Science Department
University of Massachusetts
Amherst, MA 01003
EMAIL: garvey@cs.umass.edu

Abstract

Design-to-time is an approach to real-time scheduling in situations where multiple methods exist for many tasks that the system needs to solve. Often these methods will have relationships with one other, such as the execution of one method enabling the execution of another, or the use of a rough approximation by one method affecting the performance of a method that uses its result. Most previous work in the scheduling of real-time AI tasks has ignored these relationships. This paper presents an optimal design-to-time scheduler for particular kinds of relationships that occur in an actual AI application, and examines the performance of that scheduler in a simulation environment that models the tasks of that application.

Introduction

One of the major difficulties in the real-time scheduling of AI tasks is their lack of predictable durations. This difficulty occurs in non-AI systems, but it is especially prominent in AI problem-solving because of the inherent nondeterminism of most AI problem-solving techniques due to their extensive use of search. For this reason, most AI systems use some form of approximation to reduce the nondeterminism and make system performance more predictable.

At least two broadly different kinds of approximation algorithms have been examined. They are:

- *Iterative refinement*—where an imprecise answer is generated quickly and refined through some number of iterations. There are several variations including *milestone methods* where a procedure explicitly generates intermediate results as often as is deemed useful, and *sieve functions* where intermediate results are refined by running them through a series of functions (known as sieves) that improve the results [Liu *et al.*, 1991].

- *Multiple methods*—where a number of different algorithms are available for a task, each of which is capable

of generating a solution. These algorithms emphasize different characteristics of the problem, which might be applicable in different situations. These algorithms also make tradeoffs of solution quality versus time.

The scheduling problem for approximate algorithms is to decide how to allocate processing time among approximations for different tasks so as to optimize the total performance of the system. Several approaches to this scheduling problem have been described in the literature [Dean and Boddy, 1988; Liu *et al.*, 1991; Russell and Zilberstein, 1991]. Nearly all of these approaches assume that tasks are either totally independent or have only hard precedence constraints between them. However, often AI applications do not consist of independent tasks, but rather of a series of interrelated subproblems whose consistent solution is required for an acceptable answer. The importance of taking these relationships into account in scheduling decisions has been observed in our work in sensor interpretation [Garvey and Lesser, 1993; Lesser and Corkill, 1983]. One important reason why other work has not focused on relationships is undoubtedly the difficulty of scheduling related tasks efficiently. While we don't offer a proof of it here due to space limitations, it is evident that the scheduling problems we are investigating fall into the class of NP-Hard problems, as others have shown for similar problems not involving task interrelationships [Graham *et al.*, 1979; Liu *et al.*, 1991]. As we will discuss below, we have developed a scheduling algorithm for a specific class of approximation algorithms and task structures that in the worst case has exponential performance, but, in practice, is able to schedule tasks effectively.

Our new scheduling algorithm that exploits task interrelationships is appropriate for what we have called the *design-to-time* approach to real-time problem-solving [Decker *et al.*, 1990; Garvey and Lesser, 1993]. Design-to-time (a generalization of what we have previously called approximate processing [Lesser *et al.*, 1988]) is an approach to solving problems in domains where multiple methods are available for many tasks and satisficing solutions are acceptable. These methods make tradeoffs in solution quality versus execution time, and may only be applicable in particular environmental situations.

---
*This work was partly supported by NSF contract CDA 8922572, ARPA under ONR contract N00014-92-J-1698 and ONR contract N00014-92-J-1450. The content of the information does not necessarily reflect the position or the policy of the Government and no official endorsement should be inferred.

The methodology is known as design-to-time because it advocates the use of all available time to generate the best solutions possible. It is a problem-solving method of the type described by D'Ambrosio [D'Ambrosio, 1989] as those which "given a time bound, dynamically construct and execute a problem solving procedure which will (probably) produce a reasonable answer within (approximately) the time available."

Design-to-time can only be successful if the duration and quality associated with methods is fairly predictable. The predictability issue was investigated in detail in a previous paper [Garvey and Lesser, 1993] with the result that the predictability necessary for execution times is based on a complex set of factors that include how busy the agent is and how difficult it is for the agent to determine when a method is not performing as expected. An agent can tolerate uncertainty in its predictions if

- monitoring can be done quickly and accurately, so that when a task will not meet its deadline enough time remains to execute a faster method, or

- intermediate results can be shared among methods, so that when it is necessary to switch to a faster method the intermediate results generated by the previous method can be used, or

- there exists a fall back method that quickly generates an minimally acceptable solution.

The next section presents a model of task structures that supports satisficing real-time tasks. The following section describes a particular class of task structure, then presents an algorithm for scheduling that class and gives an example of that algorithm scheduling a set of task groups. That is followed by a section that examines the performance of that algorithm in a simulation environment. Finally, we summarize our results and discuss future directions.

Task Structures

This section defines a model of task structures that has the complexity necessary to describe the unpredictability of tasks and the interactions among tasks[1]. In this model a problem consists of a set of independent task groups. Each task group contains a structured set of dependent tasks. Task groups T occur in the environment at some frequency, and induce tasks T to be executed by the agent under study. Each task group has a deadline $D(T)$.

In this model the value of performing a task is known as the *quality* of the task. The term quality summarizes several possible properties of actions or results in a real system: certainty, precision, and completeness of a result, for example [Decker *et al.*, 1990]. Task group quality ($Q(T)$) is based on the *subtask* relationship. In the experiments described in this paper tasks accumulate quality using *minimum* or *maximum* functions, i.e., a task's quality at time t is either the minimum or maximum of the qualities of each of its subtasks at time t. This quality function is constructed recursively;

---

[1]A more detailed mathematical description of this model can be found in [Decker *et al.*, 1992].

each task group consists of tasks, each of which consists of subtasks, etc., until individual executable tasks (known as *executable methods*) are reached. Executable methods have a base level quality and duration, which in this work are generated randomly for the experimental evaluation, but are correlated with one another (i.e., higher quality methods tend to take longer than lower quality methods).

Besides task/subtask relationships, tasks can have other relationships to tasks in their task group. Many such relationships are possible including:

- *enables* constraints — Task A must be executed before Task B. This is usually a hard constraint.

- *facilitates* relationships [Decker and Lesser, 1991] — If Task A is executed before Task B, then Task B will have increased quality and/or decreased duration. This could result, for example, from Task A performing part of the work that would have been done by Task B.

- *hinders* relationships — If Task A is executed before Task B, then Task B will have decreased quality and/or increased duration. This could result, for example, from Task A using an approximation that reduces the precision with which Task B can be performed.

These relationships can affect the base level quality and duration of affected methods. In this work we have examined task structures that have acyclic enables and hinders constraints.

For each task in a task structure there may be multiple sets of subtasks that can be combined to solve the task, although a particular scheduling algorithm may not enumerate all such combinations. Each of these sets is known as a *method* for solving the task. At least some of these methods may involve approximations and thus be satisficing.

The scheduling problem for sets of task groups is to find an ordered set of executable methods that

- generate non-zero quality for each task group, T,

- maximize the total quality, $Q(T)$, of all task groups added together (possibly weighted by the *importance* of the task group, although that is not examined in this paper),

- do not execute any executable methods after the deadline of their task group, $D(T)$.

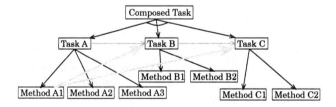

Figure 1: An example task group. The dark lines indicate subtask relationships. The thin gray lines represent enables constraints. The thick gray lines represent hindering constraints. The standard notation for minimum as *and* and maximum as *or* are used.

Figure 1 is an example of a simple task group. In this task group *Composed Task* is solved by solving each of

Task A, *Task B* and *Task C* in order. (In order because of the enables constraints.) Each of these tasks has multiple solution methods available for solving it, where increasing method number means longer, more complete method. The thick gray lines represent hindering constraints from *Method A1* to each of *Task B* and *Task C*. This means that if *Method A1* (presumably a fast, imprecise method) is used to solve *Task A* then *Tasks B* and *C* will take longer to complete and/or produce lower quality results.

A Design-to-time Scheduler

This section describes an algorithm for scheduling the execution of executable methods in environments where:

- The task/subtask relationship forms a tree with a single root for each task group. This means that each task and method has exactly one supertask.

- Tasks generate quality using one of *minimum* (AND) or *maximum* (OR).

- Enables relationships may exist among the subtasks of tasks that accumulate quality using minimum. The enables relationships are mutually consistent (i.e., there are no cycles). This corresponds to the situation where there is a body of work that must be completed to satisfy a task and this work must be done in a particular order.

- Hinders relationships may exist in situations where enables may exist and an enabling subtask has a maximum quality accumulation function. In this situation there may be a hinders relationship from the lowest quality method for solving the subtask to the tasks that the subtask enables. This corresponds to the situation where using a crude approximation for a task can have negative effects on the behavior of tasks that use the result of the approximated task.

These environmental characteristics closely model characteristics seen in a sensor interpretation application. In particular, the enables relationships appear as requirements that low level data be processed before high level interpretations of that data are made, and the hinders relationships appear in the situation where fast, imprecise approximations of low level data processing can both increase the duration and decrease the precision of high level results [Garvey and Lesser, 1993; Lesser and Corkill, 1983].

The Algorithm

Briefly, this algorithm recursively finds all methods for executing each task in the task structure, pruning those methods that are superseded by other methods that generate greater or equal quality in equal or less time. In calculating the expected quality of a method it takes enables and hinders constraints into account. When it has found all unpruned methods for every task group, it orders the task groups by deadline and finds the combination of methods for the task groups that generates the highest total quality while meeting all deadlines. It then schedules the execution of each individual executable method using a simple algorithm that ensures that no enables constraints are violated and avoids

hinders constraints if possible. If no schedule can be found that generates quality for all task groups, the scheduler returns a schedule that generates some quality for as many task groups as possible.

This algorithm works its way up from the leaves of the tree. In all examples in this paper, those leaves are executable methods, however, there is no reason why they could not be higher level tasks (with an estimated duration and quality) whose detailed execution is scheduled at a later time.

The optimality of this algorithm follows from the fact that it is effectively generating all possible alternatives, then choosing the ones that generate the maximum quality possible without missing any deadlines. As the alternatives for each task are generated, ones that could never be chosen because other alternatives exist that are *always* better are pruned. This pruning is effective only because we can make this determination locally, because of the constraints on where relationships can occur.

In the worst case this algorithm takes time exponential in the number of tasks, but, in practice, pruning and a clustering effect (to be described) usually make it much more efficient. The pruning reduces the number of alternatives that need to be considered for each task. In fact, pruning can reduce the number of alternatives for a task to no more than the number of distinct quality values possible. In the case where quality is a real number, this is not particularly helpful. However, if quality values are symbols from a small set of possible values or are somehow otherwise limited, this can significantly reduce the number of alternatives considered. As illustrated by the example in the next section, our experiments achieved a clustering effect by using small integer values for quality and combining them using minimum and maximum, resulting in a small set of possible quality values.

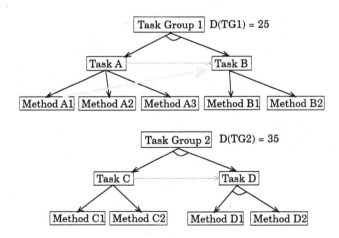

Figure 2: An example problem consisting of two task groups. The dark lines indicate subtask relationships. The thin gray lines represent enables constraints. The thick gray line represents a hinders constraint.

Method	Duration	Quality
Method A1	5	5
Method A2	7	7
Method A3	10	9
Method B1	9	8
Method B2	12	12
Method C1	4	4
Method C2	7	6
Method D1	6	5
Method D2	5	5

Table 1: Duration and quality for the executable methods in the example problem.

An Example

To describe the details of the algorithm more specifically we now show how it would schedule the two task groups shown in Figure 2 with associated durations and qualities shown in Table 1. Task group 1 (TG1) has both a hinders and an enables relationship, while TG2 has only an enables relationship. TG1 and TG2 have deadlines of 25 and 35 respectively. The hinders relationship has the effect of reducing quality by 50% and increasing duration by 25%.

First the algorithm recursively finds all alternatives for each element of the task structure. Each executable method has exactly one alternative, the method itself. Task's A, B, and C each accumulate quality using maximum, so they only need to execute one of their subtasks, giving them 3, 2, and 2 alternatives respectively[2]. Task D accumulates quality using minimum, so it has only one alternative, that which executes both of its subtasks. No pruning is possible in any of these situations. Finally, the algorithm finds the alternatives for each task group by combining alternatives from the associated subtasks. The possible alternatives for TG1 shown in Table 2.

In this case alternatives 1,2 and 4 can be pruned (as indicated by the lines through them) because other alternatives exist that can generate equal or higher quality in equal or shorter time. Note that the effects of the hinders relationship from Method A1 to Task B are shown in the reduced qualities and increased durations of Methods B1 and B2 in alternatives 1 and 2. Similarly the possible alternatives for TG2 (neither of which can be pruned) are shown in Table 3.

Finally, the alternatives for the entire set of task groups are shown in Table 4.

Alternatives 4, 5, and 6 can be pruned because TG2 does not meet its deadline of time 35. Alternative 3 can be pruned because it is redundant with Alternative 2. The scheduler chooses Alternative 2, which generates the maximum possible quality while meeting all deadlines. It then finds an ordering for the chosen alternative that meets all enables

---

[2]There is no need to consider alternatives that involve executing more than one of these subtasks, because no possible gain could result. However, in cases where such gain could result, for example when quality is accumulated in an additive fashion, all possible subgroupings must be considered.

constraints, for example it could choose the schedule: A2, B1, C2, D1, D2.

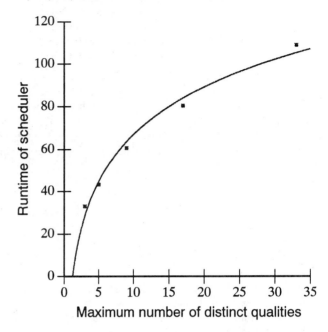

Figure 3: Maximum number of possible quality values versus the average runtime of the scheduler.

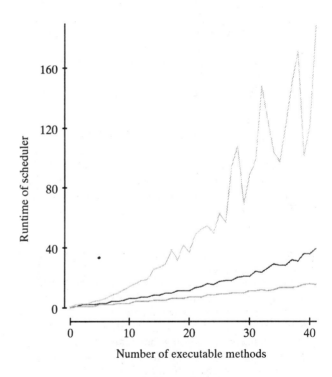

Figure 4: Number of executable methods versus the average runtime of the scheduler. The middle line is the median runtime. The upper and lower line are the 95th and 5th quartiles respectively.

ID	Set of methods	Expected quality	Expected duration
1	{Method A1, Method B1}	$\min(5, 0.5*8) = 4$	$5 + 1.25 * 9 = 16.25$
2	{Method A1, Method B2}	$\min(5, 0.5*12) = 6$	$5 + 1.25 * 12 = 20$
3	{Method A2, Method B1}	$\min(7, 8) = 7$	$7 + 9 = 16$
4	{Method A2, Method B2}	$\min(7, 12) = 7$	$7 + 12 = 19$
5	{Method A3, Method B1}	$\min(9, 8) = 8$	$10 + 9 = 19$
6	{Method A3, Method B2}	$\min(9, 12) = 9$	$10 + 12 = 22$

Table 2: Alternatives for Task Group 1.

ID	Set of methods	Expected quality	Expected duration
1	{C1, D1, D2}	$\min(4, 5, 5) = 4$	$4 + 6 + 5 = 15$
2	{C2, D1, D2}	$\min(6, 5, 5) = 5$	$7 + 6 + 5 = 18$

Table 3: Alternatives for Task Group 2.

Experimental Results

In order to be practically useful, a design-to-time scheduling algorithm needs to be subject to the same kind of controls that it expects from domain level tasks. In particular it needs to be able to tradeoff the quality of its schedules as a function of the time devoted to scheduling.

This section describes two measures of the performance of our scheduling algorithm as a function of the task structures it is scheduling. The first experiment measures the effect of the number of distinct possible quality values on the performance of the scheduler. The second experiment measures the effect of the size of the task structure (as reflected in the number of executable methods) on the performance of the scheduler.

Our experiments were conducted on randomly generated sets of task groups with enables and hinders relationships of the form described above. In the first experiment the number of task groups varied from 1 to 4 (to vary the size of the problems significantly); in the second experiment there was always 1 task group (to isolate the effect of the number of methods on scheduler performance). We controlled the size of the trees generated by having a maximum branching factor and a maximum depth—in these experiments the maximums were set to 5. We also controlled the likelihood that enables and hinders relationships would appear in situations where they were possible—these values were 50% and 100% respectively.

Figure 3 shows the effect of the maximum number of distinct quality values on the performance of the scheduler. This experiment was conducted by generating a task structure, then randomly assigning quality values to the executable methods by choosing them uniformly from the set of possible quality values. As this graph shows the runtime of the scheduler appears to increase in a logarithmic fashion as the number of possible quality values increases.

Figure 4 shows the effect of the number of methods in the task structure on the performance of the scheduler. This experiment was conducted by generating random task structures, scheduling them using the design-to-time scheduling

algorithm, recording a number of statistics including both the runtime of the scheduler and the number of executable methods in the task structure. We then collected together all of the data from each of several thousand runs and found the average runtime for each distinct number of executable methods. This suggests that the performance of the scheduler is polynomial in the number of executable methods, and that performance becomes significantly less predictable as the number of methods increases.

The results of these experiments suggest that a design-to-time scheduler could control its own performance by dynamically modifying the task structures it is scheduling. The result relating to the number of possible quality values suggests that a scheduler could reduce its runtime by reducing the number of distinct quality values in the task structure it is scheduling. It could do this by bucketizing the quality values into a smaller set of buckets and treating all quality values in the same bucket as identical. This approximation will have the effect of reducing the precision of the final schedule, because the scheduler will not consider fine-grained distinctions among methods. However, because it does not throw away any methods, the scheduler will always find a schedule in those situations where it would have found a schedule originally; it just might not be as good a schedule.

The result concerning the number of methods suggests that if a scheduler could reduce the number of methods it had to consider it could reduce its runtime. It could do this by reducing the number of methods considered for tasks that generate quality in a maximum fashion. It is probably best to not remove the fastest method or the highest quality method, but methods in between can be ignored. This approximation will have the effect of reducing the completeness of the schedule. Not all possible schedules will have been considered, so the best schedule may not be found. However, if the scheduler does not throw away the fastest methods, it will always be able to find a schedule in those situations where it could find one originally.

Another approximation that we have thought of, but not

ID	Set of methods	Expected quality	Expected finish times
1	{A2, B1, C1, D1, D2}	$7 + 4 = 11$	$16, 16 + 15 = 31$
2	{A2, B1, C2, D1, D2}	$7 + 5 = 12$	$16, 16 + 18 = 34$
3	{A3, B1, C1, D1, D2}	$8 + 4 = 12$	$19, 19 + 15 = 34$
4	{A3, B1, C2, D1, D2}	$8 + 5 = 13$	$19, 19 + 18 = 37$
5	{A3, B2, C1, D1, D2}	$9 + 4 = 13$	$22, 22 + 15 = 37$
6	{A3, B2, C2, D1, D2}	$9 + 5 = 14$	$22, 22 + 18 = 40$

Table 4: Alternatives for set of task groups.

yet investigated carefully, is to schedule without considering hinders relationships. Preliminary investigation suggests that this has the positive effect of reducing the runtime of the scheduler, but the negative effect of having the scheduler occasionally produce schedules that do not meet deadlines (because the scheduler mis-estimates the duration of executable methods). One approach to this problem is to monitor the execution of methods. For a more detailed discussion of monitoring see [Garvey and Lesser, 1993].

We intend to investigate these issues and build schedulers that take their own performance into account when scheduling. This should result in schedulers for design-to-time tasks that are themselves design-to-time in character.

Conclusions and Future Work

Previously we have examined the scheduling of tasks with multiple methods, but few task interdependencies, in both the Distributed Vehicle Monitoring Testbed (DVMT) and in a simulation environment [Garvey and Lesser, 1993]. Currently we are working on developing a more sophisticated scheduler that efficiently schedules more complex task structures that include additional types of relationships between tasks such as *facilitates*, another relationship that occurs in the DVMT environment. We are also looking at scheduling for distributed agents that are cooperating to solve complex, real-time problems. Finally, we intend to study this scheduler in a sound understanding application [Lesser *et al.*, 1993].

More generally, we would like to investigate the issues raised in the Experimental Results section by moving in the direction of building design-to-time schedulers that can control their own performance. These schedulers should be able to trade off the quality of the schedules they produce with the time it takes to produce them. This will have the effect of creating schedulers for design-to-time tasks that have a design-to-time character.

References

D'Ambrosio, Bruce 1989. Resource bounded-agents in an uncertain world. In *Proceedings of the Workshop on Real-Time Artificial Intelligence Problems*, IJCAI-89, Detroit.

Dean, T. and Boddy, M. 1988. An analysis of time-dependent planning. In *Proceedings of the Seventh National Conference on Artificial Intelligence*, St. Paul, Minnesota. 49–54.

Decker, Keith S. and Lesser, Victor R. 1991. Analyzing a quantitative coordination relationship. COINS Technical Report 91–83, University of Massachusetts. To appear in the journal *Group Decision and Negotiation*, 1993.

Decker, Keith S.; Lesser, Victor R.; and Whitehair, Robert C. 1990. Extending a blackboard architecture for approximate processing. *The Journal of Real-Time Systems* 2(1/2):47–79.

Decker, Keith S.; Garvey, Alan J.; Lesser, Victor R.; and Humphrey, Marty A. 1992. An approach to modeling environment and task characteristics for coordination. In Petrie, Charles J. Jr., editor 1992, *Enterprise Integration Modeling: Proceedings of the First International Conference*. MIT Press.

Garvey, Alan and Lesser, Victor 1993. Design-to-time real-time scheduling. *IEEE Transactions on Systems, Man and Cybernetics* 23(6). To appear.

Graham, R.L.; Lawler, E. L.; Lenstra, J. K.; and Kan, A. H. G. Rinnooy 1979. Optimization and approximation in deterministic sequencing and scheduling: A survey. In Hammer, P. L.; Johnson, E. L.; and Korte, B. H., editors 1979, *Discrete Optimization II*. North-Holland Publishing Company.

Lesser, Victor R. and Corkill, Daniel D. 1983. The distributed vehicle monitoring testbed. *AI Magazine* 4(3):63–109.

Lesser, Victor R.; Pavlin, Jasmina; and Durfee, Edmund 1988. Approximate processing in real-time problem solving. *AI Magazine* 9(1):49–61.

Lesser, Victor; Nawab, Hamid; Gallastegi, Izaskun; and Klassner, Frank 1993. IPUS: An architecture for integrated signal processing and signal interpretation in complex environments. In *Proceedings of the Eleventh National Conference on Artificial Intelligence*.

Liu, J. W. S.; Lin, K. J.; Shih, W. K.; Yu, A. C.; Chung, J. Y.; and Zhao, W. 1991. Algorithms for scheduling imprecise computations. *IEEE Computer* 24(5):58–68.

Russell, Stuart J. and Zilberstein, Shlomo 1991. Composing real-time systems. In *Proceedings of the Twelfth International Joint Conference on Artificial Intelligence*, Sydney, Australia. 212–217.

Reasoning about Physical Systems

Sensible Scenes:
Visual Understanding of Complex Structures
through Causal Analysis*

Matthew Brand, Lawrence Birnbaum, and Paul Cooper

Northwestern University
The Institute for the Learning Sciences
1890 Maple Avenue, Evanston IL 60201
brand@ils.nwu.edu

Abstract

An important result of visual understanding is an explanation of a scene's causal structure: How action—usually motion—is originated, constrained, and prevented, and how this determines what will happen in the immediate future. To be useful for a purposeful agent, these explanations must also capture the scene in terms of the *functional* properties of its objects—their purposes, uses, and affordances for manipulation. Design knowledge describes how the world is organized to suit these functions, and causal knowledge describes how these arrangements work. We have been exploring the hypothesis that vision is an explanatory process in which causal and functional reasoning plays an intimate role in mediating the activity of low-level visual processes. In particular, we have explored two of the consequences of this view for the construction of purposeful vision systems: Causal and design knowledge can be used to 1) drive focus of attention, and 2) choose between ambiguous image interpretations. Both principles are at work in SPROCKET, a system which visually explores simple machines, integrating diverse visual clues into an explanation of a machine's design and function.

Visual understanding

A fundamental purpose of vision is to relate a scene to the viewer's beliefs about how the world ought to be—to "make sense" of the scene. Understanding is the preparation we make for acting, hence our beliefs are fundamentally causal in nature; they describe the world's capacity for action and change. "Making sense" of a scene means assessing its potential for action, whether instigated by the agent, or set in motion by forces already present in the world.

*This work was supported in part by the National Science Foundation, under grant number IRI9110482. The Institute for the Learning Sciences was established in 1989 with the support of Andersen Consulting, part of The Arthur Andersen Worldwide Organization. The Institute receives additional support from Ameritech, North West Water Plc, Institute Partners, and from IBM.

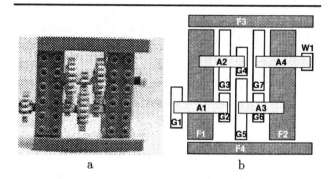

a   b

Figure 1: A scene explored by SPROCKET, and a schematic representation of its explanation.

In the physical world of everyday experience, action is usually motion. One way scenes make sense is that they organize potential motions in a way that addresses some function. At the very least, scene elements must preserve their integrity: Plants, mountains, buildings, and furniture are all structured to address the forces of gravity. Often, scenes are structured for motion: Mechanical devices are structured to contain, direct, and transform motion. Ritual spaces, control panels, and computer interfaces are structured to organize users' gestures into meaningful messages. In every case, the way we visually make sense of these scenes is by explaining their configuration relative to a theory of how the world works. Because we are purposeful, we organize that causality into theories of how scenes are *designed*—how structures are organized to address functions.

We are investigating the role that knowledge of causality and design play in the perception of scenes. In particular, we are building systems for explanation-mediated vision—vision systems whose output is not feature lists, shape descriptions, or model classifications, but high-level explanations of why the scene makes sense: How it addresses its function, how it might causally unfold in the future, how it could be manipulated, or how it might have come to be.

In previous papers, we have shown that the explanation of static scenes in terms of their stability and structural integrity is an important aspect of understanding. In particular, causal analysis of this sort can be used to address such issues as image segmentation [Cooper *et al.* 1993] and focus of visual attention [Birnbaum *et al.* 1993]. Previous systems have worked in the domains of children's blocks and tinkertoys. In this paper, we extend the scope of the approach to encompass more complex mechanical structures. This paper describes a system currently under development—SPROCKET—which explores and explains the design of simple machines. Our previous systems—BUSTER, which explains the stability of stacked blocks towers, BANDU, a variant which plays a rudimentary game of blocks, and FIDO, which resolves occlusions in tinkertoy structures by causal analysis—are discussed briefly at the end of the paper.

These vision systems have several interesting properties. First, they are vertically integrated, i.e. they encompass both low-level and high-level visual processing. Second, the output of these systems is in the form of meaningful explanations about the internal dynamics of the scene. These explanations could potentially be used to make predictions, to plan to enter and manipulate the scene, or to reason about how the scene came to be. Third, these systems employ causal theories which, although relatively small, are sufficiently powerful to generate explanations of highly complex structures. Fourth, they share an explicit model of what is interesting in a scene: They use functional and causal anomalies in ongoing explanations to generate visual queries, thus providing control of focus of attention in low-level visual processing. Fifth, causal and functional explanation forms a framework for the integration of evidence from disparate low-level visual processes. We suggest that these properties are natural consequences of building perception systems around explanation tasks.

Explanation-mediated vision

The goal of explanation-mediated vision is to assign each part in the scene a function, such that all spatial relations between parts in the scene are consistent with all causal relations between functions in the explanation [Brand *et al.* 1992; Birnbaum *et al.* 1993]. In previous papers, we have shown how this constraint can guide the visual perception and interpretation of complex static structures—structures where the possible motions of each part must be arrested. The same basic insight applies to structures in which possible motions are merely constrained. Thus a logical extension for explanation-mediated vision is the visual perception and interpretation of complex dynamical structures.

Visual cognition of machines

The visual understanding of simple machines is an approachable task because (1) causal relations are mediated by proximal spatial relations, and (2) the domain supports a very rich causal/functional semantics. This extends from simple principles of struc-

tural integrity to sophisticated knowledge about the design and layout of drivetrains. Design principles for kinematic machines are abundant generators of scene expectations (see [Brand 1992; Brand & Birnbaum 1992]). For example, a function of a gear is to transmit and alter rotational motion. To find a gear in the image is to find evidence of a design strategy which requires other torque-mediating parts in certain adjacencies and orientations, specifically an axle and one or more toothed objects (e.g., gears or racks).

Understanding machines is a matter of apprehending their design and function. Designs are strategies for decomposing functions into arrangements of parts; thus the overall strategy of SPROCKET is to reconstruct the designer's intent by applying the principles and practicum of machine design to hypotheses about the configuration of parts. As they are discovered, each part is assigned a function, such that (1) causal relationships are consistent with spatial relationships, and (2) the functions of individual parts combine to give the machine a sensible overall purpose.

Gearbox design

To bridge the gap between structure and function, we have developed a surprisingly small qualitative design theory for gearboxes (18 rules, not including spatial reasoning and stability rules). It begins with axioms describing the overall functional mission of a machine, and progresses through design rules to describe the way in which gears, axles, rods, hubs, and frames may be assembled to make workable subassemblies. The rules ground out in the predicates of rigid-body physics and spatial relations: adjacent parts restrict each other's translational motion; varieties of containment limit rotational degrees of freedom; etc. The design theory, adequate for most conventional spur-gear gearboxes, incorporates the following knowledge:

1. Knowledge about explanations:

   (a) An explanation describes a structure of gears, rods, frame blocks, and a ground plane.
   (b) A structure is explained if all parts are shown to be constrained from falling out and are functionally labelled.
   (c) A scene is considered explained if all structures in it are explained and all generated regions of interest have been explored.

2. Knowledge about function:

   (a) A moving part must transduce motion between two or more other parts.
   (b) A singly-connected moving part may serve as input or output.
   (c) A machine has one input and one output.
   (d) A fixed part serves to prevent other parts from disengaging (either by force of gravity or by action of the machine).

3. Knowledge about gears:

(a) In order to mesh, two gears must be coplanar and touching at their circumferences.

(b) Meshed gears are connected, and restrict their rotation to opposite directions and speeds inversely proportioned to their radii.

(c) A gear may transduce motion from a fixed axle (rod) to a meshing gear.

(d) A gear may transduce motion between two meshing gears.

4. Knowledge about axles and hubs:

(a) If a rod intersects an object but does not pass through, then the object (implicitly) contains a hub, which penetrates it. The rod penetrates the hub, restricting the rotational axis of the object. The object and the rod restrict each other's axial translation.

(b) If an object penetrates another object, it eliminates freedom of non-axial rotation, and freedom of translation perpendicular to its axis.

(c) If a rod goes through an object, then it passes through an implicit hub.

(d) If a non-round rod penetrates a non-round hub and the inscribed circle of the hub isn't larger than the circumscribed circle of the rod, then the hub and the object share the same axis and rate of rotation.

(e) If a hub penetrates a rod and either is round or the circumscribed circle exceeds the inscribed circle, then the rod restricts the hub to its principal axis of rotation.

5. Knowledge about frames and stability:

(a) Frames are stable by virtue of attachment to the table or to other frame pieces.

(b) Objects are stable if all of their motions downward are arrested.

Perception and pathologies

Beyond the design theory, much of the domain knowledge necessary to properly interpret mechanical devices resides in the practicum of the mechanical design: common part configurations, design pathologies, and knowledge of typical shapes and textures. This knowledge forms the basis for strategies for scene inspection, hypothesis formation, anomaly detection, and hypothesis revision.

Design pathologies are particularly important in our approach, since evidence gathering and hypothesis revision are driven by anomalies in the explanation [Schank 1986; Ram 1989; Kass 1989]. Anomalies are manifest as gaps or inconsistencies in the explanation. In machine explanations they take the form of inexplicable gears, assemblies that appear to have no function, or assemblies that appear to defeat their own function. These anomalies reflect underlying design pathologies in the system's current model of the machine, if not in the machine itself. We are currently developing a catalogue of gearbox design pathologies.

Each pathology is indexed to a set of repair hypotheses. A repair hypothesis describes previous assumptions that may be suspect, and proposes scene inspections that may obtain conclusive evidence. The example below illustrates at length a repair hypothesis which compensates for a known weakness of one of our visual specialists: Gear inspections will sometimes construe two meshed gears as a single large gear. This generally leads to design pathologies which make the perceived structure dysfunctional or physically impossible.

Visual specialists

Figure 2a shows the output of a visual specialist built to look for groupings of short parallel contrast lines. This "tooth specialist" is used to look for mechanically textured surfaces, which are usually gears. The specialist uses a simple syntactic measure for gear candidates: groups of four or more short parallel contrast edges in the image. Like most specialists, it is meant to be deployed in limited regions of interest in the image to answer spatially specific queries such as, "Is there a gear oriented vertically and centered on this axle?" These queries may include initial guesses as to position, orientation, and scale hints. If a specialist succeeds, it will return more precise information on the location of a part, along with a confidence measure. Other specialists scan regions of interest for shaped areas of consistent color, for example rectangles, parallelograms, and ellipses (see [Brand 1993] for details).

Example

For the purposes of this exposition, the "tooth specialist" has been applied to the entire image (figure 2a). The specialist correctly identified 4 gears, made two spurious reports (that there is a horizontal gear and that there is a small vertical gear in the lower right corner), fused the two middle gears into one large one, and made a partially correct report of small gear in the lower right. To simplify this example, we will ignore reports to the right of the middle and concentrate on the diagnosis and correction of the fused gears.

Figure 2b illustrates the state of the explanation after a first-pass application of the design rules to the candidate gears found by the "tooth specialist." This preliminary model assumes that:

1. An axle **A1** has been surmised to support and connect gear **G1** and gear **G2** from frame piece **F1**.

2. Gear **G1** must be fixed to axle **A1** and apparently lacks a meshing gear.

3. Gear **G2** meshes with gear **G3** and must be fixed to axle **A1** (otherwise it rotates freely on **A1** and a gear must be found below it).

4. An axle **A2** has been surmised to support gear **G3** from frame piece **F1**.

5. An axle **A*** has been surmised to support the large gear **G***. The axle must either connect to frame piece

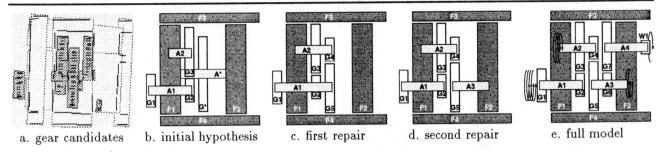

| a. gear candidates | b. initial hypothesis | c. first repair | d. second repair | e. full model |

Figure 2: Three successively more sensible interpretations of the gear specialist's reports.

F1, in which case it runs in front of or behind gears G1 and G2, or to frame piece F2, or to both.

6. Gear G* must be meshed with a two gears above and below, or one gear above or below plus a fixed axle A* which must then connect to some other part of the drivetrain, or gear G* may also be for interface.

7. Frame pieces F1, F2, F3, and F4 are all attached.

These hypotheses are established by explaining how each part satisfies as mechanical function, using the above-described rules about function and configuration. The most productive constraint is that every moving part must have a source and a sink for its motion. Gears, for example, must transduce rotational motion, either between two meshing gears, between one meshing gear and a fixed axle, or between the outside world and a meshing gear or fixed axle (as an interface).[1] Given this constraint, two anomalies stand out immediately: gears G1 and G* are not adequately connected to be useful.

Visual inspection determines that G1 is indeed unmeshed, and spatial reasoning determines that it lies outside of the frame. As a matter of practicum, this suffices to support the hypothesis that G1 is indeed for interfacing, and the anomaly is resolved.

To resolve the anomaly in hypothesis number 6, the system must find at least one meshing gear above or below G*. However, there is no room between G* and frame piece F4 for such a gear, and there is no room for an axle to support a gear above G*. Thus G* is reclassified as an inexplicable gear anomaly.[2]

Since we know that fusion is one of the typical errors made by the gear-finding specialist, we have written a repair method for this anomaly which attempts to split fused gears. The method looks for nearby axles to support the gears resulting from the split, and if present, uses these axles as guides for the division. In this case, G* is split into gear G4, which is put on axle A2, and gear G5, which is put on axle A1. Conjectured axle A* is discarded at the same time. This state of affairs is illustrated in figure 2c. The new gears mesh

with each other, and in order to transmit motion, both are assumed to have fixed axles. This is necessary because there is still no room to place additional meshing gears. It also makes all four gears G2–5 appear functionally viable; each gear will transmit motion to and from another part.

Unfortunately, there is an anomaly in this configuration: gears G2–5 are now in a locked cycle, and will not turn. This is detected when propagation of constraints reveals that each gear is required to spin at two different speeds simultaneously. The three elements of the new hypothesis—that 1) G* is split into G4 and G5, 2) G4 is fixed on axle A2, 3) G5 is fixed on axle A1—must be re-examined. Retracting (1) returns to the original anomaly, so this option is deferred. Retracting (2) deprives G4 of its axle and leaves gear G2 dangling without a sink for its motion. Retracting (3) merely leaves G5 without an axle. This is the cheapest alternative, since, as a matter of practicum, it requires only a single alteration and axle-additions are generally low-overhead alterations. The required axle (A3) can be surmised coming from frame piece F2. This leaves gears G2–4 properly explained, unlocks the drivetrain, and eliminates all design pathologies except for a yet undiscovered sink for G5, which will lead to the discovery of the rest of the mechanism. The repair produces a model illustrated in figure 2d.

Final analysis

Through this process of exploration, hypothesis, anomaly, evidence procurement, and reformulation, SPROCKET develops a functionally and causally consistent explanation of how the individual elements of the mechanism work together to conduct and modify motion. Our goal is to have SPROCKET analyze the resultant model of the drivetrain to provide a functional assessment of the entire device, e.g.: The machine is for the conversion of high-speed low-torque rotation into high-torque low-speed reversed rotation (figure 2e), or vice-versa.

Precursor systems: Seeing stability

The most ubiquitous aspect of our causal world, at least physically, is the force of gravity. Nearly everything in visual experience is structured to suit the twin constraints of stability and integrity. To understand a static scene such as a bridge or building, one explains

---

[1] Currently SPROCKET is ignorant of chains, racks, ratchets, and other more sophisticated uses of gears.

[2] Ostensibly, meshing gears could be *behind* G*. This is beyond SPROCKET's abilities, as it is limited to machines where the drivetrain is laid out in a small number of visually accessible planes.

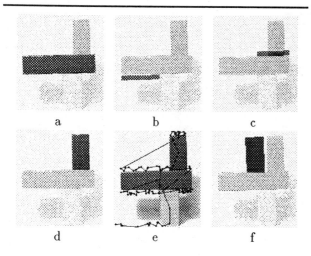

Figure 3: Snapshots of BUSTER's analysis of a three-block cantilever. Regions of interest are highlighted; the rest is faded. See the text for explanation.

how it meets these constraints. We have built a number of vertically integrated end-to-end systems that do this sort of explanation, perusing objects that stand up, asking (and answering) the question, "Why doesn't this fall down?"

Understanding blocks structures

BUSTER [Birnbaum *et al.* 1993] does exactly this sort of visual explanation for structures made out of children's blocks. BUSTER can explain a wide variety of blocks structures, noting the role of each part in the stability of the whole, and identifying functionally significant substructures such as architraves, cantilevers, and balances.

In static stability scenes, the internal function of each part is to arrest the possible motions of its neighbors. BUSTER's treatment of cantilevers provides a simple illustration of this constraint. In figure 3a BUSTER has just discovered the large middle block, and noticed a stability anomaly: It should roll to the left and fall off of its supporting block. To resolve this anomaly, BUSTER hypothesizes an additional support under the left end of the block, but finds nothing in that area (3b). A counterweight is then hypothesized above the block and to the right of the roll point (3c), and a search in that area succeeds, resulting the discovery of a new block (3d). BUSTER thus assesses the structure as a cantilever. Figure 3e shows the attentional trace for the entire scene analysis.

Playing with blocks

One of the immediate uses of causal explanations is in reasoning about actions to take within the scene. Depending on the goals of the vision system, an explanation might also answer such questions as, "How did this scene come to be?" or "Is there a safe path to navigate through the scene?" With a child's goals, the robot may also want to know, "Where can I add

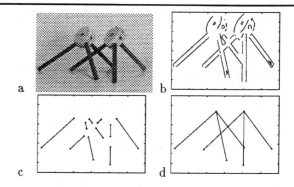

Figure 4: Stages in the explanation of the tinkertoy scene (a). (b) Boundary contours are extracted from stereo pairs. (c) Potential rod segments are extracted from the contours. (d) Rodlets are merged and extended to conform to knowledge about stable structures.

blocks to make the tower more precarious?" "What is the best way to knock it down?" Given that children play blocks partly to learn about structural integrity in the world, these are probably fruitful explanation tasks. BANDU, an augmented version of BUSTER, answers the latter two questions in order to play a rudimentary competitive block-stacking game. The aim is to pile a high and precarious tower, making it difficult or impossible for the opponent to add a block without destabilizing the whole structure. Figure 3f shows an addition that BANDU proposes for the cantilever structure.

Interpreting Tinkertoy assemblies

FIDO [Cooper *et al.* 1993] is a vertically integrated end-to-end vision system that uses knowledge of static stability to segment occluded scenes of three-dimensional link-and-junction objects. Link-and-junction domains are a nice composable abstraction for any complex rigid object. Occlusions tend to be both common and serious in link-and-junction scenes; FIDO uses naive physical knowledge about three-dimensional stability to resolve such problems. Visually, FIDO works with scenes of Tinkertoys assemblies, though its algorithms are generally applicable to a wide variety of shapes.

FIDO's input from early processing is a piecemeal description of the visible scene parts. The footprint of each object is determined to be the convex hull of places where the object touches the ground. If the object's center of mass is in the footprint, it is stable. If a part's object is not stable in this sense, FIDO invokes a series of rules whereby parts try to connect to each other. In this way, invisible connections are hypothesized, parts are extended through unseen regions to touch the ground plane, and entire parts may be completely hallucinated, in order to generate stable subassemblies. FIDO can successfully process relatively complex scenes like that shown in 4a; images b-c show the data this image yielded and the stable structure that was inferred by causal analysis.

Related work

Causal and functional knowledge are enjoying a renaissance in computer vision. Researchers such as [Pentland 1986] and [Terzopoulis & Metaxas 1990] have pointed out that the normal causal processes in the world have consequences for the way objects are shaped. On the functional side, [Stark & Bowyer 1993] have used structural concomitants of function—containment for cups, stability for chairs—to verify category decisions for CAD representations of objects. [Rimey 1992] has developed a system which visually explores table settings, using models of typical arrangements to identify, say, a formal dinner. Although these systems do not have an explicit and generative notion of function—e.g. what cups are for and why they should be cylindrical, or why formal settings have two forks—they do serve as impressive demonstrations of the value of high-level knowledge in visual paradigms.

There is an extensive literature on qualitative causal reasoning about kinematics. [Forbus *et al.* 1987; Faltings 1992] have produced kinematic analyses of ratchets, escapements, and even an entire clock using qualitative reasoning methods. [Joskowicz & Sacks 1991] have developed an algorithm for the kinematic analysis of machines that breaks the devices down into subassemblies, analyzes their configuration spaces, and combines the results into a description of the mechanism's overall kinematic behavior. These approaches feature quantitative shape analysis and rigid-body modelling algorithms that are quite a bit more extensive and more general than we use. Rather than concentrate on the universality of our kinematic models, we have chosen to focus on their compability with perceptual and teleological representations. SPROCKET is limited to machines built of rectangular and cylindrical shapes, with smooth and toothed surfaces, and conjoined by means of attachment, containment, friction, and compression—e.g., Lego machines.

Conclusion

SPROCKET and its sister programs are vertically integrated vision systems that achieve consistent explanations of complex scenes through the application of causal and functional semantics. Using modest generative theories of design and naive physics, these systems purposefully explore scenes of complex structures, gathering evidence to explain the stability, integrity, and functional coherence of what they see. Anomalies in the ongoing explanation drive hypothesis formation, visual exploration, and hypothesis reformulation. Considered as vision systems, they demonstrate the surprising leverage that high-level semantics provide in the control of visual attention, and in the interpretation of noisy and occasionally erroneous information from low-level visual processes. Considered as evidential reasoning systems, they highlight the importance of building content theories that describe not just the possibilities of a domain, but the domain's most likely configurations, the way in which the domain is manifest in perception, and the characteristic errors and confusions of the perceptual system itself.

Acknowledgments

Thanks to Ken Forbus, Dan Halabe, and Pete Prokopowicz for many helpful and insightful comments.

References

[Birnbaum *et al.* 1993] Lawrence Birnbaum, Matthew Brand, & Paul Cooper. Looking for trouble: Using causal semantics to direct focus of attention. To appear in *Proceedings of the Seventh International Conference on Computer Vision*, 1993. Berlin.

[Brand & Birnbaum 1992] Matthew Brand & Lawrence Birnbaum. Perception as a matter of design. In *Working Notes of the AAAI Spring Symposium on Control of Selective Perception*, pages 12–16, 1992.

[Brand *et al.* 1992] Matthew Brand, Lawrence Birnbaum, & Paul Cooper. Seeing is believing: why vision needs semantics. In *Proceedings of the Fourteenth Meeting of the Cognitive Science Society*, pages 720–725, 1992.

[Brand 1992] Matthew Brand. An eye for design: Why, where, & how to look for causal structure in visual scenes. In *Proceedings of the SPIE Workshop on Intelligent Vision*, 1992. Cambridge, MA.

[Brand 1993] Matthew Brand. A short note on region growing by pseudophysical simulation. To appear in *Proceedings of Computer Vision and Pattern Recognition*, 1993. New York.

[Cooper *et al.* 1993] Paul Cooper, Lawrence Birnbaum, & Daniel Halabe. Causal reasoning about scenes with occlusion. 1993. To appear.

[Faltings 1992] Boi Faltings. A symbolic approach to qualitative kinematics. *Artificial Intelligence*, 56(2-3):139–170, 1992.

[Forbus *et al.* 1987] Ken Forbus, Paul Nielsen, & Boi Faltings. Qualitative kinematics: a framework. In *Proceedings of IJCAI-87*, 1987.

[Joskowicz & Sacks 1991] L. Joskowicz & E.P. Sacks. Computational kinematics. *Artificial Intelligence*, 51(1-3):381–416, 1991.

[Kass 1989] Alex Kass. Adaptation-based explanation. In *Proceedings of IJCAI-89*, pages 141–147, 1989.

[Pentland 1986] A.P. Pentland. Perceptual organization and the representation of natural form. *Artificial Intelligence*, 28(3):293–332, 1986.

[Ram 1989] Ashwin Ram. *Question-driven understanding.* PhD thesis, Department of Computer Science, Yale University, 1989.

[Rimey 1992] Ray Rimey. Where to look next using a bayes net: The tea-1 system and future directions. In *Working Notes of the AAAI Spring Symposium on Control of Selective Perception*, 1992. Stanford, CA.

[Schank 1986] Roger Schank. *Explanation Patterns.* L. Erlbaum Associates, NJ, 1986.

[Stark & Bowyer 1993] L. Stark & K. Bowyer. Function-based generic recognition for multiple object categories. To appear in *CVGIP: Image Understanding*, 1993.

[Terzopoulis & Metaxas 1990] Demetri Terzopoulis & Dimitri Metaxas. Dynamic 3d models with local and global deformations: Deformable superquadrics. In *Proceedings of the Fourth International Conference on Computer Vision*, pages 606–615, 1990.

Intelligent Model Selection for Hillclimbing Search in Computer-Aided Design

Thomas Ellman   John Keane   Mark Schwabacher

Department of Computer Science, Hill Center for Mathematical Sciences

Rutgers University, New Brunswick, NJ 08903

{ellman,keane,schwabac}@cs.rutgers.edu

Abstract

Models of physical systems can differ according to computational cost, accuracy and precision, among other things. Depending on the problem solving task at hand, different models will be appropriate. Several investigators have recently developed methods of automatically selecting among multiple models of physical systems. Our research is novel in that we are developing model selection techniques specifically suited to computer-aided design. Our approach is based on the idea that artifact performance models for computer-aided design should be chosen *in light of the design decisions they are required to support.* We have developed a technique called "Gradient Magnitude Model Selection" (GMMS), which embodies this principle. GMMS operates in the context of a hillclimbing search process. It selects the simplest model that meets the needs of the hillclimbing algorithm in which it operates. We are using the domain of sailing yacht design as a testbed for this research. We have implemented GMMS and used it in hillclimbing search to decide between a computationally expensive potential-flow program and an algebraic approximation to analyze the performance of sailing yachts. Experimental tests show that GMMS makes the design process faster than it would be if the most expensive model were used for all design evaluations. GMMS achieves this performance improvement with little or no sacrifice in the quality of the resulting design.

1. Introduction

Models of a given physical system can differ along several dimensions, including the cost of using the model, the accuracy and precision of the results, the scope of applicability of the model and the data required to execute the model, among others. More than one model is often needed because different tasks require different tradeoffs among these dimensions. A variety of criteria and techniques have been proposed for selecting among various alternative models of physical systems. For example, some techniques select appropriate models by analyzing the structure of the query the model is intended to answer [Falkenhainer and Forbus, 1991], [Ling and Steinberg, 1992], [Weld and Addanki, 1991]. Another approach selects an appropriate model by reasoning about the simplifying assumptions underlying the available models [Addanki *et al.*, 1991]. Yet another approach reasons about the accuracy of the results the model must produce [Weld, 1991], [Falkenhainer, 1992].

We are are developing model selection techniques specifically suited to computer-aided design. Our approach is based on the idea that artifact performance models for computer-aided design should be chosen *in light of the design decisions they are required to support.* We have developed a technique called "Gradient Magnitude Model Selection" (GMMS), which embodies this principle. GMMS operates in the context of a hillclimbing search process. It selects the computationally cheapest model that meets the needs of the hillclimbing algorithm in which it operates.

Intelligent model selection is crucial for the overall performance of computer-aided design systems. The selected models must be accurate enough to ensure that the final artifact design is optimal with respect to some performance criterion, or else satisfactory with respect to specific performance objectives. The selected models must also be as computationally inexpensive as possible. Cheaper models enable a design system to spend less time on evaluation and more time on search. Broader search typically leads in turn to superior designs. These facts will remain true, even with the widespread use of supercomputers. The combinatorics of most realistic design problems are such that exhaustive search will probably never be feasible. There will always be an advantage in using the cheapest model that supports the necessary design decisions.

Model selection is a task that arises often in the day to day work of human design engineers. A human engineer's expertise consists, in part, of the ability to intelligently choose among various exact or approximate models of a physical system. In particular, as an engineer accumulates experience over his career, he learns which models are best suited to each modeling task he typically encounters in his work. This knowledge is one of the things that makes him an expert. Therefore, to the extent that GMMS successfully solves the model selection task, it automates a component of the computer-aided design process that is currently handled by human experts. GMMS may also be seen as a technique for attacking a standard AI problem: using knowledge to guide search. In particular, GMMS uses knowledge in the form of exact and approximate models, to guide hillclimbing design optimization. Related knowledge-based techniques for controlling numerical design optimization are described in [Cerbone and Dietterich, 1991] and [Tcheng *et al.*, 1991]

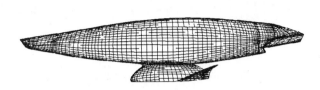

Figure 1: The Stars and Stripes '87 Hull

2. Yacht Design: A Testbed Domain

The GMMS technique has been developed and tested in the domain of 12-meter racing yachts, the class of yachts that race in the America's Cup competition. An example of a 12-meter yacht, the Stars and Stripes '87, is shown in Figure 1. This yacht won the America's cup back from Australia in 1987 [Letcher *et al.*, 1987]. Racing yachts can be designed to meet a variety of objectives. Possible yacht design goals include: *Course Time Goals*, *Rating Goals* and *Cost Goals*. In our research we have chosen to focus on a course time goal, i.e., minimizing the time it takes for a yacht to traverse a given race course under given wind conditions. Our system evaluates *CourseTime* using a "Velocity Prediction Program", called "VPP". The organization of *VPP* is described in Figure 2. *VPP* takes as input a set of B-Spline surfaces representing the geometry of the yacht hull. Each surface is itself represented as a matrix of "control points" that define its shape. *VPP* begins by using the "hull processing models" to determine physically meaningful quantities impacting on the performance of the yacht, e.g., wave resistance (R_w), friction resistance (R_f), effective draft (T_{eff}), vertical center of gravity (Vcg) and vertical center of pressure (Zcp), among others. These quantities are then used in the "velocity prediction model" to set up non-linear equations describing the balance of forces and torques on the yacht. The velocity prediction model uses an iterative method to solve these equations and thereby determine the "velocity polar", i.e., a table giving the velocity of the yacht under various wind speeds and directions of heading. Finally, the "race model" uses the velocity polar to determine the total time to traverse the given course, assuming the given wind speed.

3. Hillclimbing for Design Optimization

Hillclimbing search is useful for attacking design optimization when the number of parameters is so large that exhaustive search methods are not practical. Our system uses steepest-descent as our basic hillclimbing method [Press *et al.*, 1986]. The steepest-descent algorithm operates by repeatedly computing the gradient of the evaluation function. (In the yacht domain, this requires computing the partial derivatives of *CourseTime* with respect to each operator parameter.) The algorithm then takes a step in the direction of the gradient, and evaluates the resulting point. If the new point is better than the old one, the new point becomes the current

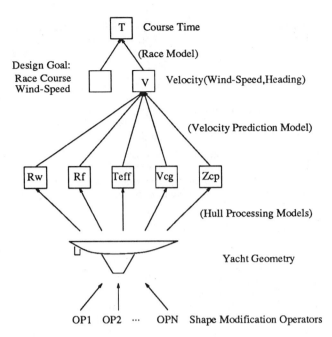

Figure 2: Velocity Prediction Program

one, and the algorithm iterates. The algorithm terminates if the gradient is zero, or if a step in the direction of the gradient fails to improve the design.

A number of enhancements to the hillclimbing algorithm have been adopted to deal with practical difficulties arising in the yacht design domain. The program we use to compute *CourseTime* (VPP) is a commercial software product. Nevertheless, it suffers from a number of deficiencies that make hillclimbing difficult. For example, it may return a spurious root of the balance of force equations that it solves. It may also exhibit discontinuities, due to numerical round-off error, or due to discretization of the (theoretically) continuous yacht hull surface. These deficiencies can produce "noise" in the evaluation function surface over which the hillclimbing algorithm is moving. The algorithm can easily get stuck at a point that appears to be a local optimum, but is nevertheless not locally optimal in terms of the true physics of the yacht design space. To overcome these difficulties, we have endowed the hillclimbing algorithm with some special features. To begin with, we arrange for the algorithm to use a range of different step sizes. The algorithm does not terminate until all of the step sizes fail to improve the design. The algorithm can therefore jump over hills of width less than the maximum step size. In addition, we provide the algorithm with an estimate of the magnitude of the noise in the evaluation function. The algorithm attempts to climb over any hills with height equal to the noise magnitude or lower. The resulting algorithm is more robust than the original algorithm.

4. Modeling Choices in Yacht Design

A number of modeling choices arise in the context of sailing yacht design. These choices are outlined in Figure 3.

- Algebraic Approximations v. Computational Fluid-Dynamics: The effective draft T_{eff} of a yacht can be estimated using an algebraic approximation or by using a potential flow code called "$PMARC$".

- Reuse of Prior Results v. Recomputation of Results: Some physical quantities may not change significantly when a design is modified. For a given physical quantity, its value may be retrieved from a prior candidate design, or its value may be recomputed from scratch.

- Linear Approximations v. Non-Linear Models: Velocity polars can be computed as linear functions of resistances and geometric quantities or by directly solving non-linear force and torque balancing equations.

Figure 3: Modeling Choices in Yacht Design

Probably the most important is the choice of models for estimating the effective draft (T_{eff}) of a yacht. Effective draft is a measure of the amount of drag produced by the keel as a result of the lift it generates. An accurate estimate of this quantity is quite important for analyzing the performance of a sailing yacht. Unfortunately, the most accurate way to estimate effective draft is to run a highly expensive potential flow code called $PMARC$. (This code takes approximately one hour when running on a Sun Microsystems Sparcstation 2 Workstation.) Effective draft can also be estimated using an algebraic approximation with the general form outlined below:

$$T_{eff} = K\sqrt{D^2 - 2A_{ms}/\pi}$$

$$D = Maximum \quad Keel \quad Draft$$

$$A_{ms} = Midship \quad Hull \quad Cross \quad Section \quad Area$$

This algebraic model is based on an approximation that treats a sailing yacht hull as an infinitely long cylinder and treats the keel of the yacht as an infinitely thin fin protruding from the cylinder. The constant K is chosen to fit the algebraic model to data obtained from wave tank tests, or from sample runs using the $PMARC$ potential flow code. Although the algebraic approximation is comparatively easy to use, its results are not as accurate as those produced by the $PMARC$ potential flow code.

Another important modeling choice involves the decision of when to reuse the results of a prior computation. The importance of this type of decision is illustrated by Figure 4. Suppose one is systematically exploring combinations of canoe-bodies and keels of a sailing yacht. In order to evaluate the performance of a yacht, one must evaluate the yacht's wave resistance R_w as well as its effective draft T_{eff}. Wave resistance depends mainly on the canoe-body of the yacht and is not significantly influenced by the keel. When only the keel is modified, wave resistance will not significantly change. Instead of recomputing wave resistance for the new yacht, the system can reuse the prior value. On the other hand, effective draft depends mainly on the keel of the yacht and is not significantly influenced by the canoe-body. When only the canoe-body is modified, effective draft will not significantly change. Instead of recomputing effective draft for the new yacht, the system can reuse

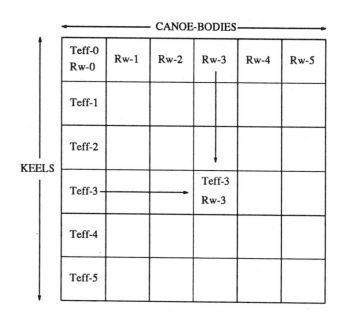

Figure 4: Reuse of Prior Results

the prior value. In fact, the entire matrix of yachts can be evaluated by computing wave resistance for a single row, and computing effective draft for a single column. By intelligently deciding when to reuse prior evaluation results, one can significantly lower the computational costs of design.

5. Gradient Magnitude Model Selection

Gradient Magnitude Model Selection (GMMS) is a technique used in the Design Associate for selecting evaluation models in the context of a hillclimbing search procedure. The key idea behind this technique is illustrated by Figure 5. Suppose the system is running a hillclimbing algorithm to minimize $CourseTime$ as estimated by some approximate model. The values of $CourseTime$ returned by this approximate model are indicated by the curved line. Suppose further that the system is considering the hillclimbing step illustrated in the figure. If the error bars shown with solid lines reflect the uncertainty of the approximate model, the system can be sure that the proposed step will diminish the value of $CourseTime$. On the other hand, using the error bars shown with dotted lines, the system would be uncertain as to whether the true value of $CourseTime$ would improve after taking the proposed hillclimbing step. In the first case, the system could safely use the approximate model to decide whether to take the proposed hillclimbing step, while in the second case, the approximate model would not be safe to use for that decision. Thus GMMS evaluates the suitability of an approximate model by comparing error estimates to the magnitude of the change in the optimization criterion as measured by the approximate model.

GMMS actually operates in a manner that is slightly more general than outlined above. In particular, GMMS is implemented in the form of a function: $ModelSelect(p_1, p_2, K, M_1, ..., M_n)$. The parameters p_1

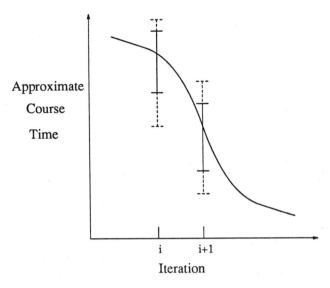

Figure 5: Gradient Magnitude Model Selection

1. Let A be a sparse point set in the design space $(u_1, \ldots, u_n)$.
   (a) Run $PMARC$ to find $T_{eff}(u)$ for each point in set A.
   (b) Fit coefficients in $Alg(A)$ to minimize average error over set A.

2. Let B be a dense point set in the design space $(u_1, \ldots, u_n)$.
   (a) Run $PMARC$ to find $T_{eff}(u)$ for each point in set B.
   (b) Fit coefficients of $Alg(B)$ to minimize average error over set B.

3. Estimate the error of $Alg(A)$ using the $PMARC$ as the "gold standard":
   - $Absolute\text{-}Error(Alg(A))$ = Average error in T_{eff} over all points in $B - A$.
   - $Difference\text{-}Error(Alg(A))$ = Average error in $|T_{eff}(u) - T_{eff}(u')|$ as function of $\Delta u_1, \ldots, \Delta u_n$, over all pairs (u, u') of points in $B - A$.

Figure 6: Error Estimation Technique

and p_2 represent artifacts under consideration during the design process (e.g., two different sailing yachts). The parameters $M_1, \ldots, M_n$ are an ordered list of the available models for evaluating artifact performance, where M_1 is the cheapest, and M_n is the most expensive. The *ModelSelect* routine returns the cheapest model that is sufficient for evaluating the following inequality:

$$M(p_1) - M(p_2) \geq K$$

Thus the selected model is sufficient for determining whether the performance of p_1 and p_2 differ by at least K. In order to evaluate forward progress in steepest-descent hillclimbing, as illustrated in Figure 5, the constant K is chosen to be zero. Our robustness-improving enhancements to steepest-descent hillclimbing occasionally require comparing artifacts using a non-zero tolerance level. In such cases, the *ModelSelect* routine takes a parameter K not equal to zero. GMMS can, in principle, be applied to any search algorithm that needs only to access the physical models in order to evaluate inequalities of the form shown above. Likewise, GMMS can in principle be applied to any of the modeling choices outlined in Figure 3.

6. Model Fitting and Error Estimation

We have experimented with GMMS using the choice of models for effective draft, T_{eff}, as a test case. Thus GMMS chooses between the algebraic approximate model and the $PMARC$ potential flow model described above. The accuracy of the algebraic approximation (relative to the $PMARC$ model) can be optimized by adjusting the value of the coefficient K. Our system fits the algebraic model and obtains an error estimate using the procedure outlined in Figure 6. The procedure takes as input two sets, A and B, of sample points in the space of candidate yacht designs. The set A is a small, sparsely distributed point set, while set B is a larger, more densely distributed point set. The system

constructs two versions of the algebraic model, by choosing values for the fitting coefficient K. $Alg(A)$ is fitted against the "true" values from the sparse point set A. $Alg(B)$ is fitted against the "true" values from the dense point set B. In each case the "true" values are determined using the $PMARC$ as the "gold standard". Since $Alg(B)$ is fitted against the denser point set, this model is actually used during hillclimbing search; however, its error is estimated using $Alg(A)$, which was fitted against the sparser point set. In particular, the error in $Alg(B)$ is estimated by comparing $Alg(A)$ to $PMARC$ for all points in the set $B - A$. Two different error estimates result from this procedure: *Absolute-Error* is based on the assumption that errors in the algebraic model at nearby points in the design space are independent of each other. *Difference-Error* takes into account the possibility that errors for nearby points may be correlated.

GMMS operates in a slightly different manner depending on which type of error estimate is available. Consider first how *Absolute-Error* estimates are used. Given two candidate yacht designs D_i and D_{i+1}, the system first evaluates the effective draft T_{eff} of each candidate using the algebraic approximation. The estimate of *Absolute-Error* is then used to find upper and lower bounds on the T_{eff} of each candidate. Each pair of bounds is then propagated through the rest of the velocity prediction program (Figure 2) to obtain an upper and lower bound on the *CourseTime* of each candidate. If the *CourseTime* intervals do not overlap, then the system knows that the step from D_i to D_{i+1} can be taken using the algebraic model. If the intervals do overlap, then the system must use $PMARC$ to obtain a better estimate of effective draft T_{eff} for each candidate.

When *Difference-Error* estimates are available, GMMS operates differently. After computing the effective draft of each candidate, the system considers two scenarios: (1) All of the *Difference-Error* occurs in the T_{eff} of D_i, and none occurs in the T_{eff} of D_{i+1}; (2) All of the *Difference-Error* occurs in the T_{eff} of D_{i+1}, and none occurs in the T_{eff} of D_i. In each case the system propagates the *Difference-Error* through the rest of the velocity prediction program, to obtain bounds on the *CourseTime* of each candidate. The algebraic model is considered acceptable only if the *CourseTime* intervals are disjoint under *both* scenarios. Similar methods can be used to apply Gradient Magnitude Model Selection to the other modeling choices shown in Figure 3.

Since GMMS is a heuristic method, it is not necessary that the error estimate be exact for each point in the design space. Overestimating the error will result in too little use of the approximate model, raising the cost of evaluation. Underestimating the error will result in overuse of the approximate model, leading the optimization along (possibly) less direct paths to the solution. Nevertheless, hillclimbing with GMMS should lead to a nearly optimal solution even when the approximate model is over-used. Recall that hillclimbing only terminates at local minimum points of the search space. Before stopping, the hillclimber usually encounters a region that is sufficiently flat to require use of the exact model in order to distinguish the performance of candidate designs. GMMS thus forces the hillclimber to switch to the expensive, but exact model in order to verify the presence of a local optimum.

The performance of GMMS can be enhanced by dynamically re-fitting the approximate model during the optimization process. This method proceeds from the observation that the optimal value of the fitting coefficient K in the T_{eff} formula will generally depend on the region of the design space in which the formula is applied. Suppose the algebraic model is periodically re-calibrated during the search process, by adjusting this coefficient. The resulting approximate model will be more accurate in evaluation of designs near the latest recalibration point. It can therefore be used more often and provide greater savings over $PMARC$ than is possible with a fixed approximation.

We have implemented a "recalibrating" version of GMMS, "Recal-GMMS", to test out this strategy. Recal-GMMS operates as follows: Whenever $ModelSelect$ indicates that the current algebraic model cannot be used, the system runs $PMARC$ on the current design. The computed value of T_{eff} is then used to recalibrate the coefficient of the algebraic model. Two different algebraic models are fit to the current region of the design space. In one model, the fitting coefficient K is treated as a constant. In the other model, K is expressed as a linear function of the parameters of the design space. This linear function is fit using $d + 1$ $PMARC$ evaluations for a d dimensional design parameter space. The required $PMARC$ evaluations are obtained by selecting the $d + 1$ most recent $PMARC$ evaluations that yield a non-degenerate fitting problem. (Degeneracy is detected using a standard numerical singular value decomposition code.) In case no such non-degenerate set can be found, the system generates additional design parameter points that yield a non-degenerate set, and then evaluates them in order to carry out the fitting process. Of the two recalibrated algebraic models, the linear model is actually used to compute effective draft T_{eff}. The error of this linear model is estimated to be the absolute value of the difference between the linear model and the constant model.

7. Experimental Results

We have tested our approach to model selection in a series of experiments comparing various model selection strategies. In particular, we investigated the five model selection strategies listed in Figure 7. The five strategies were each run on four separate design optimization problems. The problems differed in both the initial yacht prototypes, and in the yacht design goals. Two shape modification operators were used for the optimizations, i.e., Scale-Keel, which changes the depth of the keel, and Invert-Keel, which alters the ratio between the lengths of the top and bottom edges of the keel. The results of these runs are summarized by the table in Figure 8. For each model selection strategy, the table gives a measure of the quality of the final design, and a measure of the computational cost needed to find the final design, each averaged over all four test problems. The quality of a design D is measured as the difference between the *CourseTime* of D and the *CourseTime* of the "optimal" design, i.e. the best design found by any of the five strategies. The computational cost of finding a design is measured by counting the number of $PMARC$ evaluations needed to carry out the design optimization, since $PMARC$ is by far the most expensive part of the design process.

- **Alg-Only:** Only the algebraic model is used for evaluation of effective draft.

- **PMARC-Only:** Only the $PMARC$ potential flow code is used for evaluation of effective draft.

- **GMMS:** Gradient magnitude model selection is used to select between the algebraic and $PMARC$ models for effective draft. Errors are estimated using the *Difference-Error* formula. Errors are propagated through VPP using the difference error propagation method.

- **Recal-GMMS:** GMMS, with the addition that the algebraic model is recalibrated according to $PMARC$ data collected during the optimization. Errors are estimated by comparing locally fit constant and linear models. Errors are propagated through VPP using the absolute error propagation method.

- **CTO (Cheap-to-Optimal):** Only the algebraic model is used until an initial optimum is reached. Then only the $PMARC$ model is used until a final optimum is reached.

Figure 7: Model Selection Strategies

The results in Figure 8 illustrate a tradeoff between computational cost and the quality of the optimization. In terms of computational expense, measured by the number of $PMARC$ evaluations, the strategies can be ranked in the order shown, with "Alg-Only" being the cheapest and "PMARC-Only" being the most expensive. "Alg-Only" comes out being the cheapest because it never invokes the $PMARC$ potential flow code. "PMARC-Only" is the most expensive because it always invokes the $PMARC$ potential flow code. Notice that each of the three non-trivial model selection strategies ("Recal-GMMS", "GMMS" and "CTO") is cheaper than the "PMARC-Only" strategy. Each avoids some of the *PMARC* runs that occur under the "PMARC-Only" strategy. In fact, the computationally cheapest of the three, "Recal-GMMS", incurs only about 59% of the computational expense of the "PMARC-Only" strategy. Notice that the "Alg-Only" strategy yields yacht designs of lower quality than those produced using the other strategies. Lower quality designs are obtained because the algebraic model causes the hillclimber to terminate at a point that is not a local optimum in terms of the more accurate "*PMARC*" model. In contrast to this, all of the other four strategies achieve the same quality levels. Higher quality designs are obtained because these strategies cause the hillclimber to terminate at points that really are locally optimal in terms of the *PMARC* model.

Strategy	Compute Cost (*PMARC* Evals)	Design Quality (Lag in Seconds)
Alg-Only	0.00	-351
Recal-GMMS	152.00	0
CTO	207.75	0
GMMS	250.00	0
PMARC-Only	257.50	0

Figure 8: Comparison of Model Selection Strategies

The "Alg-Only" and "Recal-GMMS" strategies are Pareto optimal. Neither of these two strategies is dominated in quality and computation cost by any of the other three strategies. In contrast, none of the other three strategies ("PMARC", "GMMS" and "CTO") is Pareto optimal. Each is dominated by the "Recal-GMMS" strategy, since the "Recal-GMMS" strategy achieves the same quality as each at a lower computational cost. In order to choose between "Alg-Only" and "Recal-GMMS" one must supply some criterion for balancing the quality of a design against the amount of computation cost expended during the design process. In the yacht design domain, the choice is fairly easy. America's Cup yacht races are often won and lost by a few seconds. Considerations of quality therefore tend to outweigh considerations of computation cost. In this application domain, our results indicate that "Recal-GMMS" is the best model selection strategy.

8. Ongoing Research

Ongoing research is aimed at applying our GMMS techniques to other model selection choices that arise during hillclimbing search in the yacht design domain, as described in Figure 3. We are especially interested in using GMMS to decide when to reuse prior evaluation results, and when to use linear approximation models. These two types of approximation are very general and can be applied to a wide variety of design problems. If GMMS can be shown useful for these decisions, it will be established as a widely applicable model selection technique. We also plan to test our GMMS techniques in domains other than yacht design.

Longer term research is aimed at investigating model selection problems that arise in parts of the design process other than hillclimbing search. Models of physical systems can be used to support computer-aided design in a variety of ways other than direct evaluation of candidate designs. For example, physical models can be used in sensitivity analyses that enable engineers to decide which design parameters to include in the search space. Each design task that depends on a physical model will lead to a distinct model selection problem. We are therefore attempting to classify the modeling tasks that arise in computer-aided design and to develop model selection methods for each of them.

9. Acknowledgments

This research was supported by the Defense Advanced Research Projects Agency (DARPA) and the National Aeronautics and Space Administration (NASA). (DARPA-funded NASA grant NAG 2-645.) It has benefited from discussions with Saul Amarel, Martin Fritts, Andrew Gelsey, Haym Hirsh, John Letcher, Chun Liew, Ringo Ling, Gerry Richter, Nils Salvesen, Louis Steinberg, Chris Tong, Tim Weinrich, and Ke-Thia Yao.

References

S. Addanki, R. Cremonini, and J. Scot. Graphs of models. *Artificial Intelligence*, 50, 1991.

G. Cerbone and T. Dietterich. Knowledge compilation to speed up numerical optimization. In *Proceedings of the Eighth International Workshop on Machine Learning*, Evanston, IL, 1991.

B. Falkenhainer and K. Forbus. Compositional modeling: Finding the right model for the job. *Artificial Intelligence*, 50, 1991.

B. Falkenhainer. A look at idealization. Working Notes of the AAAI Workshop on Approximation and Abstraction of Computational Theories, San Jose, CA, 1992.

J. Letcher, J. Marshall, J. Oliver, and N. Salvesen. Stars and stripes. *Scientific American*, 257(2), August 1987.

R. Ling and L. Steinberg. Model generation from physical principles: A progress report. Technical Report CAP-TR-9, Department of Computer Science, Rutgers University, 1992.

W. Press, B. Flannery, S. Teukolsky, and W. Vetterling. *Numerical Recipes*. Cambridge University Press, New York, NY, 1986.

D. Tcheng, B. Lambert, S. Lu, and L. Rendell. Aims: An adaptive interactive modeling system for supporting engineering decision making. In *Proceedings of the Eighth International Workshop on Machine Learning*, Evanston, IL, 1991.

D. Weld and S. Addanki. Query-directed approximation. Technical Report 90-12-02, Department of Computer Science and Engineering, University of Washington, Seattle, WA, 1991.

D. Weld. Reasoning about model accuracy. Technical Report 91-05-02, Department of Computer Science and Engineering, University of Washington, Seattle, WA, 1991.

Ideal physical systems

Brian Falkenhainer
Xerox Corporate Research & Technology
Modeling & Simulation Environment Technologies
801-27C, 1350 Jefferson Road, Henrietta, NY 14623

Abstract

Accuracy plays a central role in developing models of continuous physical systems, both in the context of developing a new model to fit observation or approximating an existing model to make analysis faster. The need for simple, yet sufficiently accurate, models pervades engineering analysis, design, and diagnosis tasks. This paper focuses on two issues related to this topic. First, it examines the process by which idealized models are derived. Second, it examines the problem of determining when an idealized model will be sufficiently accurate for a given task in a way that is simple and doesn't overwhelm the benefits of having a simple model. It describes IDEAL, a system which generates idealized versions of a given model and specifies each idealized model's *credibility domain*. This allows valid future use of the model without resorting to more expensive measures such as search or empirical confirmation. The technique is illustrated on an implemented example.

Introduction

Idealizations enable construction of comprehensible and tractable models of physical phenomena by ignoring insignificant influences on behavior. Idealized models pervade engineering textbooks. Examples include frictionless motion, rigid bodies, as well as entire disciplines like the mechanics of materials. Because idealizations introduce approximation errors, they are not credible representations of behavior in all circumstances. In better textbooks, their use is typically restricted by a vague set of conditions and tacit experience. Consider the following from the standard reference for stress/strain equations [18, page 93], which is more precise than most texts:

7.1 Straight Beams (Common Case) Elastically Stressed

The formulas of this article are based on the following assumptions: (1) The beam is of homogeneous material that has the same modulus of elasticity in tension and compression. (2) The beam is straight or nearly so; if it is slightly curved, the curvature is in the plane of bending and the radius of curvature is at least 10 times the depth. (3) The cross section is uniform. (4) The beam has at least one longitudinal plane of symmetry. (5) All loads and reactions are perpendicular to the axis of the beam and lie in the same plane, which is a longitudinal plane of symmetry. (6) The beam is long in proportion to its depth, the span/depth ratio being 8 or more for metal beams of compact section, 15 or more for beams with relatively thin webs, and 24 or more for rectangular timber beams. (7) The beam is not disproportionately wide. (8) The maximum stress does not exceed the proportional limit.

...The limitations stated here with respect to straightness and proportions of the beam correspond to a maximum error in calculated results of about 5%.

Our goal in this research is to provide answers to the following questions:

1. *How are these conditions derived?* What is the process by which a model is converted to a simpler, idealized version? What are the principles behind the form and content of the standard textbook rules of thumb?

2. *What do these conditions mean?* For what "nearly straight", "disproportionately wide" beams will error begin to exceed 5%? How can the conditions be relaxed if only 20% accuracy is needed? What if 1% accuracy is needed?

3. *What is the best method by which an automated modeling system should determine when an approximate model is credible?* The answer to this may not necessarily be the same as the answer to question 1.

This paper examines these issues for algebraic and ordinary differential equation models of up to second order. It describes IDEAL, a system which generates idealized versions of a given model and provides measurable information about the model's error. The key enabler is recognizing the centrality of context in the idealization process - the idealizations that are generated and the limits that are placed on their use reflect the (intended) user's typical cases. We begin by describing how idealized models are derived. Section examines how approximation error should be managed in an automated modeling setting, while Section describes the principles behind the kinds of conditions stated above and a technique, called *credibility domain synthesis*, for generating them. It closes with a discussion of how the same functionality might be achieved for more complex systems. In particular, our ultimate goal is to be able to reproduce the above passage, which requires the analysis of 3-dimensional, 4th-order partial differential equations.

Idealizations

A *model* $\mathcal{M}$ contains a set of (algebraic and ordinary differential) equations E describing the behavior of some physical system in terms of variables $V = \{t, y_2, \ldots, y_{k-1}, p_k, \ldots, p_n\}$, where y_i represents a dependent variable, and p_i represents a constant, model parameter (i.e., p_i is a function of elements external to the model).[1] At most one varying independent variable t is allowed (which typically denotes time). Each model also has an associated set of logical preconditions, as described in [6]. We make the simplification that all analyses occur in a single operating region (i.e., the status of the preconditions does not change and thus can be ignored for the purposes of this paper).

A *behavior* is a vector $\mathbf{v} = [v_1, \ldots, v_n]$ of assignments to V as a function of t over the interval $t \in [0, t_f]$. A set of *boundary conditions* B specify values for t_f, the model parameters, and $y_i(0)$ for all y_i such that B and $\mathcal{M}$ uniquely specify a behavior $\mathbf{v} = \text{BEHAVIOR}(\mathcal{M}, B)$.

An idealized model $\mathcal{M}^*$ arises from the detection of order of magnitude relationships, such as those described in [10; 7], which enable the elimination of negligible terms. This can produce significant simplifications by reducing simultaneities and nonlinearities, and enabling closed-form, analytic solutions. In this paper, we consider the use of the two most common idealization assumptions:

DOMINANCE-REDUCTION: $A + B \approx A$ *given* $|A| \gg |B|$

ISO-REDUCTION: $\frac{dy}{dx} = 0$ *given* $\frac{\frac{dy}{dx}}{y} \approx 0$

Dominance-reduction ignores negligible influences on a quantity and is the basis for idealizations like frictionless motion. When applied to derivative pairs, it offers one approach to time-scale approximation:

TIME-SCALE-REDUCTION: $\frac{dy_2}{dx} = 0$ *given* $|\frac{dy_1}{dx}| \gg |\frac{dy_2}{dx}|$

Iso-reduction assumes constancy and is the basis for idealizations like quasi-statics, homogeneous materials, and orthogonal geometries. It is often the key enabler to obtaining analytic solutions.

In general, order of magnitude reasoning requires a carefully designed set of inference rules (e.g., approximate equality is not transitive [10]). For the class of ODEs currently being studied, algebraic operations across a set of equations are unnecessary and these issues do not arise. Thus, IDEAL currently uses only the

two idealization rules without the associated machinery to propagate their consequences.[2]

Given that $\mathcal{M}^*$ is an idealization of $\mathcal{M}$, the error function $\mathbf{e}$ of $\mathcal{M}^*$'s approximate behavior $\mathbf{v}^*$ is measured with respect to $\mathcal{M}$'s predicted behavior $\mathbf{v}$ and couched in an appropriate scalar *norm* $\mathbf{e} = \| \mathbf{v}^* - \mathbf{v} \|$, the standard measure of goodness of an approximation [3]. The results are independent of the particular norm. In the examples we will use the maximum (L_∞) norm for the relative error

$$e_i(v_i) = \max_{t \in [0, t_f]} | \frac{v_i^*(t) - v_i(t)}{v_i(t)} |$$

where $\mathbf{e} = [e_1, \ldots, e_n]$ and e_i is the error norm for variable v_i. At times (section), the instantaneous error value as a function of t will be used in place of the absolute value norm.

A model is *credible* with respect to error tolerance $\tau = [\tau_a, \ldots, \tau_b]$ if $e_i(v_i) \leq \tau_i$ for every variable v_i for which a tolerance has been specified. Not all variables need have an associated tolerance; the error of these variables is unmonitored and unconstrained. The *credibility domain* of an idealized model is the range of model parameters and t for which the simplified model is a credible representation of the original model [2].

Idealization process

A model may be idealized in at least two settings. In the on-demand setting, idealizations are made during the course of using a model to analyze a specific system. In the compilation setting, a model is idealized into a set of simpler models *a priori* by assuming the different potential relationships that enable use of the idealization rules. Because much of the on-demand setting is a special case of the compilation setting, we will focus solely on the latter. The key then is to pre-identify the set of enabling relationships that might arise. One straw-man approach would be to systematically explore all algebraic combinations and assume hypothetical situations in which the idealizations' conditions would hold. For example, for every pattern $A + B$, we could make one reduction based on $A \gg B$ and another based on $A \ll B$ (when consistent with the given equations). To make *useful* idealizations, we must have information about what relationships are possible or likely in practice. This is critical both in guiding the idealization process and in characterizing each idealized model's credibility domain (as discussed in section).

The more specific the information about what is likely, the more the idealized models may be tuned for one's specific future needs. Information about the population of analytic tasks is represented as a set of distributions over parameter values across problems and their variability within each problem (see Table 1).

---

[1] This is also known as an *exogenous* variable in the economics and AI literature. Throughout, we will try to use standard engineering terminology and indicate synonyms.

[2] The current implementation is in Mathematica, which is a hindrance to implementing the kinds of order of magnitude systems described in [10; 7].

Table 1: Some distributions characterizing an analyst's typical problem set.

Distribution of parameter values	
Simple Ranges	$p \in [0.1..1.5]$
Independent	uniform, normal, truncated
Joint (e.g., A may never be small when B is large)	
Distribution of function types	
Constant	$\frac{dy}{dx} = 0$
Nearly Constant	$\frac{dy}{dx} \approx 0$
Dependent	$y = y(x), \; \left|\frac{dy}{dx}\right| > 0$

Distributions on parameter values indicate which inequalities are likely or possible. They provide information about the population of tasks as a whole. Parameters specified by simple ranges are treated as having uniform distributions over their range. Distributions on function types provide information about the per-task behavior of parameters. For example, material densities may have wide variance across different analyses, but are normally constant throughout the material during any single analysis. These distributions are currently given as input; in the context of a CAD environment, they could easily be obtained by saving information about each analytic session.

IDEAL is guided by two factors - the form of the original equations and the problems to which they are typically applied. Given a model and associated distributions, it proceeds as follows:[3]

1. Syntactically identify candidates for reduction. Based on the two reduction rules, a candidate is either a sum or a derivative.

2. For sums, cluster the addenda into all possible dominant/negligible equivalence classes based on the given distributions. Each parameter's possible range is truncated at three standard deviations (otherwise it could be infinite and lead to spurious order of magnitude relationships).

3. For each possible reduction rule application, derive an idealized model under the assumption of the rule's applicability condition.

4. Repeat for consistent combinations of idealization assumptions (c.f., assumption combination in an ATMS [4]).

Example (sliding motion) Figure 1 illustrates the problem of determining the velocity and position of a block as it slides down an incline. The given model considers the influences of gravity, sliding friction, and air resistance. Due to the nonlinear response to air resistance, the model has no analytic solution.[4] The

---

[3]This is a more complete version of the algorithm described in [13]. For example, the earlier algorithm did not consider the ISO-REDUCTION rule.

[4]Well, at least not one that Mathematica can find.

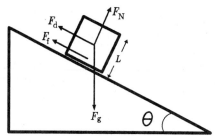

$\mathcal{M}_{gfd}$: $\quad \frac{dv}{dt} = a_g + a_f + a_d$
$\qquad\qquad \frac{dx}{dt} = v$

Gravity: $\qquad\qquad a_g = g \sin \theta$
Sliding Friction: $\; a_f = -\mu_k g \cos \theta \mathrm{sgn}(v)$
Air Resistance: $\; a_d = -C_d \rho_{air} L^2 v^2 \mathrm{sgn}(v)/2M$

Distributions		
parameter	*type*	*pdf*
t	truncated normal	$\frac{1}{e^{\frac{t^2}{20}} 4.52}$
	$(t \in [0..\infty])$	
θ	uniform	$[30°..60°]$
μ_k	truncated, skewed	$\mu_k - \mu_k^3 + 2.54$
	$(\mu_k \in [0.2..0.55])$	
$\frac{dv}{dt}$	dependent	
$\frac{dx}{dt}$	dependent	

Figure 1: A block slides down an inclined plane. Need we model sliding friction, air drag, or both? In the table, pdf = *probability density function*

methods apply to higher-dimensions, but to enable 3-dimensional visualization and simplify the presentation, the initial velocity, $v_0 = 0$, and the air resistance coefficient $(C_d \rho_{air} L^2)$ will be treated as constants.

IDEAL begins by identifying patterns for which the idealization rules may apply. In this case, there is the single sum

$$a_g + a_f + a_d$$

The assumption of $|A| \gg |B|$ is limited by requiring that at least $|A/B| \geq 10$ must be possible. Using this constraint and the given distributions, only one partial ordering is possible: $|a_g + a_f| \gg |a_d|$. This enables, via dominance-reduction, the derivation of a simple linear approximation $\mathcal{M}_{gf}$:

$$\frac{dv}{dt} = A_{gf} = a_g + a_f, \qquad \frac{dx}{dt} = v$$

from which we can derive

$$v(t) = A_{gf}\,t, \quad x(t) = \frac{A_{gf}}{2}t^2 + x_0 \qquad (\mathcal{M}_{gf})$$
$$\text{assuming } A_{gf} \gg a_d$$

Had the distributions covered wider ranges for angle and time, and allowed air resistance to vary, a space of possible models, each with its own assumptions and credibility domain, would be derived. For example, high viscosity, long duration, and low friction would make the friction term insignificant with respect to the drag term, resulting in another idealized model:

$$\frac{dv}{dt} = g\sin\theta - C_d\rho_{air}L^2v^2\mathrm{sgn}(v)/2M \qquad (\mathcal{M}_{gd})$$
$$\text{assuming } A_{gd} \gg a_f$$

Error management for automated modeling

The idealized model $\mathcal{M}_{gf}$ derived in the example offers a considerable computational savings over its more detailed counterpart. Unfortunately, it is also quite non-operational as stated. What does $A_{gf} \gg a_d$ mean? When should one expect 5%, 10%, or 50% error from the model? What we would like is a mechanism for bounding the model's error that is (1) easy to compute at problem solving time – it should require much less time than the time savings gained by making the idealization, and (2) reliable – failure, and subsequent search for a more accurate model, should be the exception rather than the rule.

One appealing approach lay in the kinds of thresholds illustrated in the introduction, but augmented with some clarifying quantitative information. However, it is not as simple as deriving e as a function of A_{gf}/a_d or sampling different values for A_{gf}/a_d and computing the corresponding error. For a specified error threshold of 5%, the meaning of $A_{gf} \gg a_d$ is strongly influenced by the model parameters and the independent variable's interval. Figure 2 illustrates the error in position as a function of $A_{gf} = a_g + a_f$ and time t. The problem is further compounded in the context of differential equations. Not only does a_d change with time, the influence of error accumulation as time progresses can dominate that of the simple $A_{gf} \gg a_d$ relationship. Second, much of the requisite information cannot be obtained analytically (e.g., $\mathrm{e}(A_{gf},t)$). For each value of A_{gf} and t_f, we must numerically integrate out to t_f. Thus, any mechanism for *a priori* bounding the model's error presupposes a solution to a difficult, N-dimensional error analysis problem.

The key lies in the following observation: only an approximate view of the error's behavior is needed – unlike the original approximation, this "meta-approximation" need not be very accurate. For example, a 5% error estimate that is potentially off by 20% means that the error may actually be only as much as 6%. This enables the use of the following simple procedure:

1. Sample the error's behavior over the specified distributions to obtain a set of datapoints.

2. Derive an approximate equation for each e_i as a function of the independent variable and model parameters by fitting a polynomial to the N-dimensional surface of datapoints.

If the error is moderately smooth, this will provide a very reliable estimate of the model's error.[5] For $\mathcal{M}_{gf}$'s

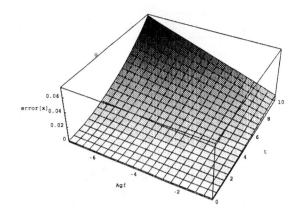

Figure 2: Percentage error in position x over the ranges for $A_{gf} = a_g + a_f$ and time t produced by $\mathcal{M}_{gf}$.

error in position x (shown in Figure 2), the resulting approximating polynomial is

$$\begin{aligned}
e_x = {}& 3.52524\ 10^{-6} + 2.20497\ 10^{-6}\ A_{gf} - 3.18142\ 10^{-6}\ A_{gf}^2 \\
& -4.02174\ 10^{-7}\ A_{gf}^3 - 0.0000179397\ t \\
& -0.0000191978\ A_{gf}\ t - 1.20102\ 10^{-6}\ A_{gf}^2\ t \\
& +3.68432\ 10^{-6}\ t^2 - 0.0000940654\ A_{gf}\ t^2 \\
& +2.83115\ 10^{-8}\ A_{gf}^2\ t^2 - 1.1435\ 10^{-7}\ t^3
\end{aligned}$$

At this point, the specified requirements (easy to compute and reliable) have both been satisfied, without generating explicit thresholds! Although not as comprehensible, from an automated modeling perspective this approximate error equation is preferable because it provides two additional highly desirable features: (3) a continuous estimate of error that is better able to respond to differing accuracy requirements than a simple binary threshold, and (4) coverage of the entire problem distribution space by avoiding the rectangular discretization imposed by thresholds on individual dimensions.

Credibility domain synthesis

The question still remains – where do conditions like "the beam is not disproportionately wide" come from and what do they mean? They are clearly useful in providing intuitive, qualitative indications of a model's credibility domain. Further, for more complex systems, increased dimensionality may render the derivation of an explicit error function infeasible. The basic goal is to identify bounds in the independent variable and model parameters that specify a region within the model's credibility domain for a given error tolerance. This is the *credibility domain synthesis* problem:

find t_f and p_i^-, p_i^+ for every $p_i \in P$ such that
$$0 \le t \le t_f \ \wedge\ [\forall(p_i \in P), p_i^- \le p_i \le p_i^+] \ \rightarrow\ \mathrm{e} < \tau$$

---

[5] As one reviewer correctly noted, global polynomial approximations are sensitive to poles in the function being modeled. For the general case, a more reliable method is needed, such as local interpolation or regression on a more phenomena-specific basis function. There is nothing in the IDEAL algorithm which limits use of these methods.

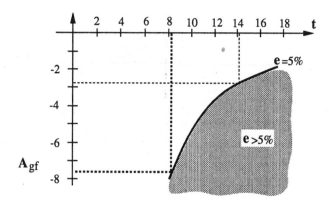

Figure 3: The error function imposes conservation laws on the shape of the credibility domain.

Unfortunately, these dimensions are interdependent. Increasing the allowable interval for p_i decreases the corresponding interval for p_j. Figure 3 illustrates for $\mathcal{M}_{gf}$ subject to a 5% error threshold. A credibility domain that maximizes the latitude for t also minimizes the latitude for A_{gf}. What criteria should be used to determine the shape of the hyperrectangle? Intuitively, the shape should be the one that maximizes the idealized model's expected future utility. We currently define future utility as its prior probability. Other influences on utility, when available, can be easily added to this definition. These include the cost of obtaining a value for p_i and the likely measurement error of p_i. Given distributions on parameter values and derivatives, the credibility domain synthesis problem can be precisely formulated as the following optimization problem:

minimize
$$F(t_f, p_k^-, p_k^+, \ldots, p_n^-, p_n^+) =$$
$$1 - P(0 \le t \le t_f, \ p_k^- \le p_k \le p_k^+, \ldots, p_n^- \le p_n \le p_n^+)$$
subject to $e \le \tau$

For the case of $\mathcal{M}_{gf}$ and the distributions given in Figure 1, the optimal credibility domain is

$$t < 8.35 \ \wedge \ \mu_k > 0.2 \ \wedge \ \theta < 60°$$

which has a prior probability of 0.975.

This formulation has several beautiful properties:

1. The credibility domain is circumscribed by clear and easily computed conditions.

2. It maximizes the idealized model's future utility according to the user's typical needs.

3. It offers a precise explanation of the principles underlying the standard textbook rules of thumb.

In particular, it explains some very interesting aspects of the passage quoted in the introduction. For example, a careful examination of the theory of elasticity [14], from which the passage's corresponding formulas were derived, shows that several influences on

the error are omitted. Why? How is that (likely to be) sound? Consider the conditions synthesized for $\mathcal{M}_{gf}$. The limits for μ and θ cover their entire distribution; they are irrelevant with respect to the anticipated analytic tasks and may be omitted.[6] Only the independent variable's threshold imposes a real limit with respect to its distribution in practice.

Like the textbook conditions, credibility domain synthesis makes one assumption about the error's behavior - it must not exceed τ inside the bounding region. This is guaranteed if it is unimodal and concave between thresholds, or, if convex, strictly decreasing from the threshold. $\mathcal{M}_{gf}$ satisfies the former condition. However, the current implementation lacks the ability to construct such proofs, beyond simply checking the derived datapoints.

Related Work

Our stance, starting with [13], has been that the traditional AI paradigm of search is both unnecessary and inappropriate for automated modeling because experienced engineers rarely search, typically selecting the appropriate model first. The key research question is then to identify the tacit knowledge such an engineer possesses. [5] explores the use of experiential knowledge at the level of individual cases. By observing over the course of time a model's credibility in different parts of its parameter space, *credibility extrapolation* can predict the model's credibility as it is applied to new problems. This paper adopts a generalization stance - computationally analyze the error's behavior *a priori* and then summarize it with an easy to compute mechanism for evaluating model credibility.

This is in contrast to much of the work on automated management of approximations. In the graph of models approach [1], the task is to find the model whose predictions are sufficiently close to a given observation. Search begins with the simplest model, moves to a new model when prediction fails to match observation, and is guided by rules stating each approximation's qualitative effect on the model's predicted behavior. Weld's domain-independent formulation [15] uses the same basic architecture. Weld's derivation and use of *bounding abstractions* [16] has the potential to reduce this search significantly and shows great promise. Like our work, it attempts to determine when an approximation produces sound inferences. One exception to the search paradigm is Nayak [9], who performs a post-analysis validation for a system of algebraic equations using a mix of the accurate and approximate models. While promising, it's soundness proof currently rests on overly-optimistic assumptions about the error's propagation through the system.

---

[6]This occurred because μ and θ were bound by fixed intervals, while t had the ∞ tail of a normal distribution, which offers little probabilistic gain beyond 2-3 standard deviations.

Credibility domain synthesis most closely resembles methods for tolerance synthesis (e.g., [8]), which also typically use an optimization formulation. There, the objective function maximizes the allowable design tolerances subject to the design performance constraints.

Intriguing questions

Credibility domain synthesis suggests a model of the principles behind the form and content of the standard textbook rules of thumb. Their abstract, qualitative conditions, while seemingly vague, provide useful, general guidelines by identifying the important landmarks. Their exact values may then be ascertained with respect to the individual's personal typical problem solving context. This "typical" set of problems can be characterized by distributions on a model's parameters which in turn can be used to automatically provide simplified models that are specialized to particular needs.

The least satisfying element is the rather brute-force way in which the error function is obtained. While it only takes a few seconds on the described examples, they are relatively simple examples (several permutations of the sliding block example described here and the more complex fluid flow / heat exchanger example described in [5]). The approach will likely be intractable for higher-dimensional systems over wider distributions, particularly the 3-dimensional PDE beam deflection problem. How else might the requisite information be acquired? What is needed to reduce sampling is a more qualitative picture of the error's behavior. This suggests a number of possible future directions. One approach would be to analyze the phase space of the system to identify critical points and obtain a qualitative picture of its asymptotic behavior, which can in turn suggest where to measure [11; 12; 17]. Alternatively, one could use qualitative envisioning techniques to map out the error's behavior. The uncertainty with that approach lies in the possibility of excessive ambiguity. For some systems, traditional functional approximation techniques might be used to represent the error's behavior.

Acknowledgments

Discussions with Colin Williams, both on the techniques and on programming Mathematica, were very valuable.

References

[1] Addanki, S, Cremonini, R, and Penberthy, J. S. Graphs of models. *Artificial Intelligence*, 51(1-3):145–177, October 1991.

[2] Brayton, R. K and Spruce, R. *Sensitivity and Optimization*. Elsevier, Amsterdam, 1980.

[3] Dahlquist, G, Bjorck, A, and Anderson, N. *Numerical Methods*. Prentice-Hall, Inc, New Jersey, 1974.

[4] de Kleer, J. An assumption-based TMS. *Artificial Intelligence*, 28(2), March 1986.

[5] Falkenhainer, B. Modeling without amnesia: Making experience-sanctioned approximations. In *The Sixth International Workshop on Qualitative Reasoning*, Edinburgh, August 1992.

[6] Falkenhainer, B and Forbus, K. D. Compositional modeling: Finding the right model for the job. *Artificial Intelligence*, 51(1-3):95–143, October 1991.

[7] Mavrovouniotis, M and Stephanopoulos, G. Reasoning with orders of magnitude and approximate relations. In *Proceedings of the Sixth National Conference on Artificial Intelligence*, pages 626–630, Seattle, WA, July 1987. Morgan Kaufmann.

[8] Michael, W and Siddall, J. N. The optimization problem with optimal tolerance assignment and full acceptance. *Journal of Mechanical Design*, 103:842–848, October 1981.

[9] Nayak, P. P. Validating approximate equilibrium models. In *Proceedings of the AAAI-91 Workshop on Model-Based Reasoning*, Anaheim, CA, July 1991. AAAI Press.

[10] Raiman, O. Order of magnitude reasoning. *Artificial Intelligence*, 51(1-3):11–38, October 1991.

[11] Sacks, E. Automatic qualitative analysis of dynamic systems using piecewise linear approximations. *Artificial Intelligence*, 41(3):313–364, 1989/90.

[12] Sacks, E. Automatic analysis of one-parameter planar ordinary differential equations by intelligent numerical simulation. *Artificial Intelligence*, 48(1):27–56, February 1991.

[13] Shirley, M and Falkenhainer, B. Explicit reasoning about accuracy for approximating physical systems. In *Working Notes of the Automatic Generation of Approximations and Abstractions Workshop*, July 1990.

[14] Timoshenko, S. *Theory of Elasticity*. McGraw-Hill, New York, 1934.

[15] Weld, D. Approximation reformulations. In *Proceedings of the Eighth National Conference on Artificial Intelligence*, Boston, MA, July 1990. AAAI Press.

[16] Weld, D. S. Reasoning about model accuracy. *Artificial Intelligence*, 56(2-3):255–300, August 1992.

[17] Yip, K. M.-K. Understanding complex dynamics by visual and symbolic reasoning. *Artificial Intelligence*, 51(1-3):179–221, October 1991.

[18] Young, W. C. *Roark's Formulas for Stress & Strain, Sixth Edition*. McGraw-Hill, New York, NY, 1989.

Numerical Behavior Envelopes for Qualitative Models*

Herbert Kay and Benjamin Kuipers
Department of Computer Sciences
University of Texas at Austin
Austin, Texas 78712
bert@cs.utexas.edu and kuipers@cs.utexas.edu

Abstract

Semiquantitative models combine both qualitative and quantitative knowledge within a single semiquantitative qualitative differential equation (SQDE) representation. With current simulation methods, the quantitative knowledge is not exploited as fully as possible. This paper describes *dynamic envelopes* – a method to exploit quantitative knowledge more fully by deriving and numerically simulating an *extremal system* whose solution is guaranteed to bound all solutions of the SQDE. It is shown that such systems can be determined automatically given the SQDE and an initial condition. As model precision increases, the dynamic envelope bounds become more precise than those derived by other semiquantitative inference methods. We demonstrate the utility of our method by showing how it improves the dynamic monitoring and diagnosis of a vacuum pumpdown system.

Introduction

Many models of real systems are incompletely specified either because a precise model of the system does not exist or because the parameters of the model span some range of values. Qualitative simulation methods [de Kleer and Brown, 1984; Forbus, 1984; Kuipers, 1984; Kuipers, 1986] permit such systems to be simulated in the face of this incompleteness by transforming the system into a related system in a more abstract space of qualitative values where model imprecision can be dealt with by the rules of qualitative mathematics. Semiquantitative models [Kuipers and Berleant, 1988; Berleant and Kuipers, 1992] reduce model imprecision by adding numerical knowledge to the purely qualitative representation. Predic-

---

*This work has taken place in the Qualitative Reasoning Group at the Artificial Intelligence Laboratory, The University of Texas at Austin. Research of the Qualitative Reasoning Group is supported in part by NSF grants IRI-8905494, IRI-8904454, and IRI-9017047, by NASA contract NCC 2-760, and by the Jet Propulsion Laboratory.

tions from semiquantitative models are more precise (i.e., more tightly bounded), while still retaining the accuracy (i.e., all possible behaviors are found) provided by purely qualitative methods.

This paper presents a new inference method called *dynamic envelopes* that more fully exploits the semiquantitative representation than existing methods. It works by numerically simulating a set of (typically nonlinear) differential equations whose solutions are guaranteed to bound all behaviors of the semiquantitative QDE. This approach captures the benefits of both qualitative and quantitative reasoning as all possible behaviors of the system are simulated [Kuipers, 1986], and tighter numerical bounds are deduced yielding more precise predictions for each behavior. These benefits are especially important in monitoring tasks where early detection of deviations is vital.

We represent semiquantitative models as QSIM QDEs [Kuipers, 1986] augmented with envelopes for all monotonic functions and numeric ranges for all model variables. We call this representation an SQDE (for semiquantitative QDE). Our technique generates a bounding ordinary differential equation (ODE) system derived from the SQDE that is numerically simulated to yield bounds on all model variables. Note that since the ODE system is in general a non-linear vector function defined over a multidimensional state space, it has no closed-form solution and so the integration must be performed numerically. The resulting bounds on the SQDE as a function of t are called the *dynamic envelopes* for the system.

The strength of this method is apparent when compared to other semiquantitative approaches such as FuSim [Shen and Leitch, 1991] and Q2 [Kuipers and Berleant, 1988]. These simulators also use SQDE models, but produce overly conservative bounds because they use a simulation time-step determined by qualitative distinctions. To better understand this, consider simulating the second order model of the two-tank cascade in Figure 1a using Q2, an extension to QSIM [Kuipers, 1986]. Assume that the partially known monotonic function $f \in M^+$ is bounded by the functions (*static envelopes*) shown in Figure 1b. Q2 pro-

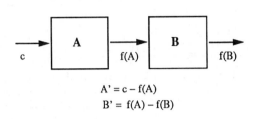

$A' = c - f(A)$

$B' = f(A) - f(B)$

(a) System definition (c is constant).

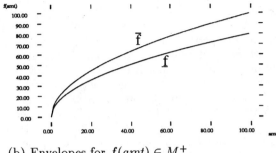

(b) Envelopes for $f(amt) \in M^+$.

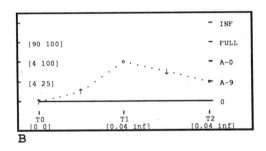

(c) Q2 behavior for $B(t)$ with initial condition A=FULL, B=0.

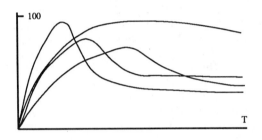

(d) Possible curves corresponding to (c).

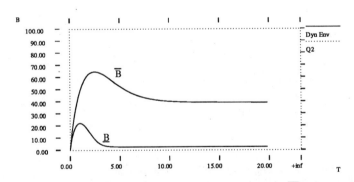

(e) Dynamic envelopes defining the lower bound $\underline{B}(t)$ and the upper bound $\overline{B}(t)$ on $B(t)$. The rectangular Q2 range prediction is superimposed. Note that the dynamic envelopes are much tighter than the Q2 bound.

Figure 1: A second order cascaded tank system and its behaviors.

duces predictions by first constructing a qualitative description of the behavior. This behavior consists of a series of time-points where one or more model variables change qualitative value, and the intervening time-intervals over which the behavior is qualitatively unchanging. It then applies a range propagation algorithm at each time-point which assigns interval values to each model variable at the time-point. These intervals represent the possible range of values that the variable could have at that time-point. Figure 1c shows the Q2 plot of the amount in tank B with the given static functional envelopes and an initial state with tank A full and tank B empty. Note that there are only three time-points in the behavior description and, due to model imprecision, the possible range for each time-point (other than T0) is infinite. There is therefore little than can be said about the possible trajectories described by the prediction. For example, *any* of the behaviors shown in Figure 1d are consistent with the prediction.

The problem is that the precision of a numerical simulation is directly related to the number and density of the time-points in the simulation and a simulator whose time-step is based solely on the qualitative distinctions cannot adequately control these quantities. The dynamic envelope method avoids this problem by using a standard numerical method (such as Runge Kutta) which chooses time-points based on local simulation error estimates. This method results in a much smaller time-step, and hence a more precise simulation. The remaining imprecision – the difference between the dynamic envelopes in Figure 1(e) – more closely reflects the incomplete knowledge in the model itself.

Dynamic Envelopes

To numerically simulate the bounds of an SQDE, bounding equations for each state variable must be generated. Our method attempts to find a set of *extremal equations* for a system. An extremal equation is a bound on the derivative of a state variable (as opposed to a bound on the *value* of the state variable). It may be either *minimal* or *maximal*.

Let $A : \mathbf{x}' = \mathbf{f}(\mathbf{x})$ be an ODE system with state vector $\mathbf{x}$. For each $x_i \in \mathbf{x}$, let $x_i' = f_i(\mathbf{x}_i)$ be the equation for the derivative of x_i where $\mathbf{x}_i \subset \mathbf{x}$ is the set of state variables that f_i depends upon. For each x_i, let $\underline{x}_i$ and $\overline{x}_i$ denote the lower and upper bounds on x_i. We will use the term y_i to refer to either $\underline{x}_i$ or $\overline{x}_i$. We say that $y_i' = g_i(\mathbf{x}_i)$ is a minimal equation for x_i if $y_i = x_i$ implies $y_i' < x_i'$ and maximal if $y_i = x_i$ implies $y_i' > x_i'$. The function g_i is called an *extremal expression* for f_i.

A set of equations is an *extremal system* for the system A if it consists of a minimal and a maximal equation for each $x_i \in \mathbf{x}$.

We can generate a set of extremal equations for any SQDE that is written as a system of equations of the form $x_i' = f(\mathbf{x}_i)$ where f is an expression composed of

e	$L(e)$	$U(e)$
c	$\underline{c}$	$\overline{c}$
x_j	$L(x_j)$	$U(x_j)$
x_i	$\beta(x_i)$	$\beta(x_i)$†
$A + B$	$L(A) + L(B)$	$U(A) + U(B)$
$A \times B$	$L(A) \times L(B)$	$U(A) \times U(B)$‡
$A - B$	$L(A) - U(B)$	$U(A) - L(B)$
$A \div B$	$L(A) \div U(B)$	$U(A) \div L(B)$
$-A$	$-U(A)$	$-L(A)$
$M^+(A)$	$\underline{M}^+(L(A))$	$\overline{M}^+(U(A))$
$M^-(A)$	$\underline{M}^-(U(A))$	$\overline{M}^-(L(A))$

Table 1: Translation table for extremal expressions of the equation $x_i' = f_i(\mathbf{x}_i)$. Let $\beta(f_i)$ be the desired bound on x_i' ($\beta = L$ or $\beta = U$). The table is applied recursively to the subexpressions of f_i. The symbol x_j is any state variable other that x_i, c is a constant, M^+ and M^- are monotonic functions, $\underline{c}$ and $\overline{c}$ return the lower or upper range values of c, $\underline{M}^*$ and $\overline{M}^*$ return the lower or upper functional envelope of the monotonic function. For state variables, $L(x)$ returns the variable $\underline{x}$ and $U(x)$ returns the variable $\overline{x}$.

addition, subtraction, multiplication, division, unary minus, and arbitrary monotonic functions. The algorithm uses the functions $L(e)$ and $U(e)$ which take an expression and return the corresponding minimal or maximal expression as defined in Table 1.

The extremal equations are generated by computing for each x_i the expressions $L(f_i)$ and $U(f_i)$ using Table 1. This yields a set of $2n$ equations which represent an ODE of order $2n$ which is the extremal system for the SQDE.

Let the relation $\mathbf{R_i}$ be $\leq$ when $y_i \equiv \underline{x}_i$ and $\geq$ when $y_i \equiv \overline{x}_i$. In [Kay, 1991], the following theorem is proved:

Let $A : \mathbf{x}' = \mathbf{f}(\mathbf{x})$ be an ODE system. Let $\alpha : \mathbf{y}' = \mathbf{g}(\mathbf{y})$ be an extremal system for A. Assume that for all i y_i $\mathbf{R_i}$ x_i at $t = 0$. Then for all t, $y_i(t)$ $\mathbf{R_i}$ $x_i(t)$.

This states that if the state of the extremal system starts on the "correct side" of the SQDE, then it will remain on that side and hence bound the solution for all time.

Once the extremal system has been found, it can be simulated by a standard numerical simulation technique such as Runge-Kutta. The complete simulation method is thus :

---

†The bound on x_i is the same as that for f_i regardless of whether an $L(x_i)$ or $U(x_i)$ is desired.

‡The expressions for multiplication and division are for the case where A and B are positive. For other cases, the expressions in the table for $L(e)$ and $U(e)$ are computed differently, using information about the signs of A and B.

1. For each initial state of the SQDE, generate its extremal system.

2. Using a numerical simulator, simulate the extremal system for all initial states.

A simple example

To demonstrate the method, we apply it to the second-order model in Figure 1a. The qualitative equations of the system are

$$A' = c - f(A)$$
$$B' = f(A) - f(B)$$

where $c \in (0, \infty)$ and $f \in M^+$. The semiquantitative model also includes numerical bounds on c such that $\underline{c} \leq c \leq \overline{c}$ and static envelope functions $\underline{f}$ and $\overline{f}$ such that $\underline{f} < f < \overline{f}$. The corresponding extremal system is:

$$\underline{A}' = \underline{c} - \overline{f}(\underline{A})$$
$$\underline{B}' = \underline{f}(\underline{A}) - \overline{f}(\underline{B})$$
$$\overline{A}' = \overline{c} - \underline{f}(\overline{A})$$
$$\overline{B}' = \overline{f}(\overline{A}) - \underline{f}(\overline{B})$$

Note that in this case, the extremal system partitions into two separate systems, one for $\underline{A}$ and $\underline{B}$, the other for $\overline{A}$ and $\overline{B}$. This is *not* the case in general. Figure 1e shows the behavior produced by the dynamic envelope method that corresponds to the Q2-produced behavior shown in Figure 1c. Note that the numerical bounds are much tighter than those of Q2.

Using dynamic envelopes to infer behavior characteristics

The dynamic envelope method bases its prediction on the ability to bound the first derivatives of the system. As a result, the extremal systems are not generally members of the class of ODEs represented by the SQDE. Therefore, the dynamic envelopes do not necessarily have the same shape as the behaviors of the SQDE. This means that only "0th order" bounds are predicted. The width of the bounds will increase with increasing imprecision in the SQDE. The prediction may also become weak because the extremal system may be numerically unstable, which results in the envelopes diverging from each other with time. In such a case, the dynamic envelope bounds can eventually be worse than those from Q2.

To combat this effect, we combine the Q2 and dynamic envelope simulation methods and thus gain the benefits of both. Q2 describes behaviors as a series of time-points with intervening time intervals. It places ranges on the location of each time-point and the values of the model variables at the time-point. The time-intervals are defined simply by their adjacent time-points. We gain predictive precision by intersecting dynamic envelopes with Q2 in two ways:

- By intersecting over time-intervals, we improve the precision over the interval. The Q2 time-interval prediction is simply that each model variable is somewhere between the values that it has at the adjacent qualitative time-points. Because it uses a smaller time-step, dynamic envelopes can be more precise over such intervals (as seen in Figure 1).

- By intersecting at time-points, we potentially reduce the ranges of the model variables at the time-points. This not only improves the precision of the prediction, but may also open up gaps into which semi-quantitative time-point interpolation methods such as Q3 [Berleant and Kuipers, 1992] can insert time-points.

Note that since both the dynamic envelope method and Q2 bound all real behaviors of the model, if an intersection is empty, the behavior is refuted. Hence, dynamic envelopes can be used as a behavior filter.

The Vacuum Chamber

In this section we model a complex system, the vacuum chamber, and use the dynamic envelope simulation method to improve the response time of a monitoring system based on the MIMIC system [Dvorak and Kuipers, 1989; Dvorak, 1992].

The production of high vacuum is of great importance to semiconductor fabrication as many of the steps (such as sputtering and molecular beam epitaxy) cannot be performed if there are foreign particles in the process chamber.

Unfortunately, creating such ultra-high vacua can be expensive and time-consuming. To reach ultimate pressures of 10^{-9} Torr can take several hours[3] and something as innocuous as a fingerprint left on the chamber during servicing can cause a huge performance loss.

Because of this risk, it is important to service vacuum equipment only when there is a problem. This suggests a need for a monitoring system that can detect when the system goes out of tolerance. The normal approach to monitoring is to run the pumpdown process until the chamber reaches a steady-state pressure and then to compare this pressure to the expected value. Unfortunately, it can take several hours to reach a steady-state pressure. If the monitoring method could detect failures before the chamber reaches a steady-state pressure, the time and expense of unnecessarily running the pumpdown procedure could be avoided.

A model-based method that can track the state of the system while it is changing is one way to solve this problem. In order to construct such a system, a model of the pumpdown process must be constructed. The difficulty in modeling this process numerically is that

---

[3] Atmospheric pressure is 760 Torr.

there is no practical theory for the sorption [4] of gases. Therefore, any useful model must deal with uncertainties in the underlying modeling assumptions. Qualitative modeling permits reasoning with these types of uncertainties.

The pumpdown process is intuitively very simple. A chamber at atmospheric pressure initially contains some amount of gas. A pump, which can displace a certain amount of gas per unit time and pressure, removes gas from the chamber, hence lowering the pressure. For a simple vacuum pump, this process will continue until the pump reaches its cutoff pressure at which point the minimum pressure within the pump is the same as the pressure within the chamber.

For pumps that operate in the high vacuum range (between 10^{-3} and 10^{-5} Torr), there are additional effects to consider. The most significant of these is that of "outgassing" – a process where gas initially present in the walls of the chamber desorbs and thereby increases the chamber pressure.

Our model takes into account both the effects of the pump and outgassing. The system is described by the following equations :

$$
\begin{aligned}
A' &= -fl(A, B) - ptp(A) + leak(A) \quad (1) \\
B' &= fl(A, B) \quad (2) \\
fl(A, B) &= area \cdot ads(A, B) - des(B) \quad (3) \\
ads(A, B) &= mi(pr(A)) \cdot sf(B) \quad (4) \\
ptp(A) &= pr(A) \cdot speed(pr(A)) \quad (5) \\
leak(A) &= C_{leak} \cdot (p_{atm} - pr(A)) \cdot c_l \quad (6)
\end{aligned}
$$

where A is the amount of gas in the chamber and B is the amount of gas adsorbed in the chamber walls (all other terms are defined in Table 2 in the Appendix).

For a working vacuum chamber, the leak rate is zero and hence $C_{leak} = 0$. For model-based diagnosis, however, fault models of the system must also be created. By setting C_{leak} to a positive value, the above system models a chamber with a leak. The behavior of both the working and leaking models is for A to decrease until it reaches a steady state. With $C_{leak} > 0$ the steady state value of A will be higher than when $C_{leak} = 0$.

Simulation results

The two systems were augmented with envelopes for the functions $speed(p)$, $des(B)$, $mi(A)$, and $sf(B)$ and then simulated with both Q2 and the dynamic envelope method using the values described in Table 3. The resulting envelopes are shown in Figure 2 together with the corresponding Q2 range predictions. First, notice that Q2 predicts identical ranges for the normal and faulty model whereas the dynamic envelope method

---

[4] *Desorption* is the process by which gases trapped on a substance are released. The reverse process is called *adsorption*. Adsorption is different from absorption in that the gases do not dissolve into the substance; they simply "stick" to its surface.

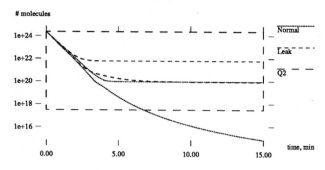

Figure 2: The predicted behaviors of the vacuum chamber A variable as a function of time for both a normal and a leaking model are shown using dynamic envelopes (the dotted and short-dashed envelopes, respectively). The behaviors of the two hypotheses are clearly distinguished after $t = 4$ minutes. For comparison, the Q2 predictions for both hypotheses are also displayed, although since Q2 is unable to disambiguate the behaviors quantitatively, the Q2 results are represented by the same prediction (long-dashed box).

predicts no overlap between the two models after $t = 4$ minutes. Second, notice that the dynamic envelope prediction for the lower envelope of the normal system is less precise than Q2 prediction. This situation is not a problem since the diagnostic algorithm uses the intersection of the Q2 and dynamic envelope predictions.

Our diagnostic program is based on a simplified version of the MIMIC system [Dvorak and Kuipers, 1989]. We provided our own predefined fault models and used dynamic envelopes rather than Q2 to predict variable ranges. We then ran our system against a stream of pressure measurements (taken every minute) that simulated a gasket leak in our vacuum system. Our diagnostic system was able to detect the leak after four measurements, whereas the diagnostic system using only Q2 required nine measurements to detect the fault[5]. Further improvements are possible by recomputing the envelopes of both models after every new measurement is taken. Note that leak model envelopes are predicted based on an assumed leak size range. Because of this, when MIMIC refutes the leak model, it is really partitioning the space of possible leak sizes into three regions (those within the range, those bigger, and those smaller) with the first two regions refuted. This provides a method for converging on the precise leak size through successive partitions based on refining the leak size hypothesis.

---

[5] Q2 detected the fault because of a difference in the qualitative behavior of the two models that is detectable after the chamber pressure becomes constant.

Related Work

There has been considerable interest in the combination of qualitative and quantitative reasoning. This work includes the development of combined qualitative/quantitative representations (see [Williams, 1988; Kuipers and Berleant, 1988; Cheng and Stephanopoulos, 1988; Karp and Friedland, 1989; Simmons, 1986]) and the use of numerical and qualitative knowledge for process monitoring [Dvorak and Kuipers, 1989] and process planning [Fusillo and Powers, 1988; Lakshmanan and Stephanopoulos, 1988; LeClair and Abrams, 1988]. The methods and software described in [Kuipers and Berleant, 1988] and [Dvorak and Kuipers, 1989] (Q2 and MIMIC) are integral parts of this research. Recently Berleant and Kuipers have extended Q2 to provide a single representation for both qualitative and quantitative simulation [Berleant and Kuipers, 1992; Berleant, 1989]. In their method, called Q3, the range of a qualitative parameter is narrowed through an adaptive discretization technique that subdivides qualitative intervals. Q3 and the dynamic envelope method take different approaches to improving the precision of semiquantitative inference. Our experience suggests that the two methods may have complimentary strengths, so we are exploring methods for coordinating their application.

The problem of predicting behavioral bounds on uncertain systems is also addressed in control theory and ecological system simulation. Sensitivity analysis [Deif, 1986] is used to investigate the effect of small-scale perturbations to a model. Tolerance banding [Ashworth, 1982], [Lunze, 1989] is used to predict the effect of larger-scale model uncertainties. Both methods are normally restricted to linear models and hence permit uncertainty in parameter values or initial conditions only. The dynamic envelope method is not restricted by linearity assumptions and so it can also handle models with uncertain (and possibly nonlinear) functional relations. Bounding techniques that do not rely on linearity assumptions have been developed for VLSI simulation [Zukowski, 1986], however they rely on domain-specific assumptions about MOS VLSI circuits.

Interval analysis [Moore, 1979] also provides methods for simulating SQDEs by recasting standard numerical ODE solvers to work with interval arithmetic [Markov and Angelov, 1986]. In contrast, the dynamic envelope method recasts the SQDE into an ODE of higher order and uses a standard numerical ODE solver directly. An advantage of this approach is that model imprecision is separated from the error introduced by the simulator. Another benefit is that we can directly take advantage of advances in the field of numerical analysis by switching to more powerful simulators as they are developed.

This research also relates to the measurement interpretation theories ATMI [Forbus, 1986] and DATMI [DeCoste, 1990]. Both of these methods abstract a measurement stream into qualitative values and then select possible behaviors by comparing measurement segments to states in the total envisionment graph. By hypothesizing measurement errors, DATMI also manages to interpret noisy sensor data. By contrast, the dynamic envelope method augments the qualitative behavior with numerical envelopes that are guaranteed to bound any solution of the system and then compares the measurement data directly. This approach has the advantage that distinctions between models can be detected over intervals where their qualitative behaviors are identical. Furthermore, by recomputing the envelopes as new measurements are received, the bounding solutions can be further tightened. Measurement faults can also be modeled by assuming that the measurement data itself represents a range rather than a precise point.

The work on SIMGEN [Forbus and Falkenhainer, 1990] is also related to the work described in this paper. It, too, generates a standard numerical simulation by extracting the relevant information from a qualitative model. It differs in that it generates an exact numerical model based on a library of predefined functions rather than generating a bounded model expressing the inexactness of the qualitative model. Since it sacrifices accuracy for precision, it is not particularly suited to tasks such as process monitoring in which an exact numerical model cannot be found.

Conclusions

The dynamic envelope method combines qualitative and quantitative simulation so that both representations can be used in problem solving. QSIM produces all behaviors associated with a particular model, and dynamic envelopes provide detailed numerical ranges for each behavior. Because the generation of extremal systems is guided by the qualitative behaviors, the expense of needless numerical simulation is eliminated. Because the envelope systems are automatically generated from the SQDEs used by Q2, the method can be used with any existing Q2 model.

The precision of the dynamic envelope predictions depends on the precision of the SQDE. As model precision increases, dynamic envelope predictions become more precise than Q2 predictions. Even when the model is very imprecise, combining dynamic envelopes with other QSIM prediction techniques leads to improved precision.

In monitoring tasks, the dynamic envelope method improves the predictive power of SQDEs both in accuracy (meaning that fault hypotheses can be more easily eliminated) and failure detection time (meaning that there is more time to recover from failures). In cases where measurement acquisition is expensive, the increased accuracy of the predictions may allow fewer measurements to be made and errors to be detected sooner.

The ultimate goal of our research is to construct a

self-calibrating monitoring and diagnosis system that can learn models directly from observations of a physical system. Part of this task involves developing a semiquantitative simulation method that produces precise predictions without excessive computation. The dynamic envelope method helps address this need by providing a new form of inference especially suited for high precision semiquantitative models.

Acknowledgments

The authors would like to thank Adam Farquhar for his comments on an earlier version of this paper.

Vacuum system terms and SQDE quantitative knowledge

Term	Definition (units)
A	amount of chamber gas (molec)
B	amount of gas in chamber walls (molec)
$area$	surface area of chamber (cm^2)
$pr(A)$	pressure exerted by A molecules [assuming fixed chamber volume v] (Torr)
$ptp(A)$	pump throughput (Torr-liters/min)
$speed(p)$	pump speed (liters/min)
$ads(A, B)$	rate : chamber gas $\rightarrow$ walls (molec/cm^2-min)
$des(B)$	rate : chamber gas $\leftarrow$ walls (molec/cm^2-min)
$fl(A, B)$	net flow of gas out of walls (molec/min)
$mi(A)$	# molecules incident on walls (molec/cm^2-min)
$sf(B)$	sticking factor : fraction of $mi(A)$ that "stick" to walls
$leak(A)$	rate : room air $\rightarrow$ chamber (molec/min)
C_{leak}	leak conductance (liters/min)
P_{atm}	atmospheric pressure (760 Torr)
c_l	constant : Torr-liters $\rightarrow$ molecs

Table 2: Definition of terms used in equations 1 through 6.

Term	Value or envelope description
A	$[2.34 \times 10^{24}, 2.34 \times 10^{24}]$ molec
B	$[1.36 \times 10^{21}, 1.50 \times 10^{21}]$ molec
$area$	$[13100, 14500]$ cm^2
C_{leak}	$[0.01, 0.001]$ liters/min
v	90 liters
$speed(p)$	M^+ piecewise linear with narrowing envelope
$des(B)$	M^+ linear with both envelopes equal
$mi(p)$	M^+ linear with both envelopes equal
$sf(B)$	M^- exponential envelope narrowing from $[2, 0.5]$ to $[0, 0]$ at $B \approx 0.3$

Table 3: Initial ranges and functional envelopes for the vacuum chamber model. These values are based on data from Duval [Duval, 1988].

References

Ashworth, M. J. 1982. *Feedback Design of Systems With Significant Uncertainty*. John Wiley and Sons, New York.

Berleant, Daniel and Kuipers, Benjamin 1992. Combined qualitative and numerical simulation with q3. In Faltings, Boi and Struss, Peter, editors 1992, *Recent Advances in Qualitative Physics*. MIT Press.

Berleant, Daniel 1989. A unification of numerical and qualitative model simulation. In *Proceedings of the Model-based Reasoning Workshop*.

Cheung, Jarvis Tat-Yin and Stephanopoulos, George 1990. Representation of process trends – part I. a formal representation framework. *Computers and Chemical Engineering* 14(4/5):495–510.

de Kleer, Johan and Brown, John Seely 1984. A qualitative physics based on confluences. *Artificial Intelligence* 24:7–83.

DeCoste, Dennis 1990. Dynamic across-time measurement interpretation. In *Proceedings of the Eighth National Conference on Artificial Intelligence (AAAI-90)*. 373–379.

Deif, Assam 1986. *Sensitivity Analysis in Linear Systems*. Springer-Verlag, Berlin.

Duval, Pierre 1988. *High Vacuum Production in the Microelectronics Industry*. Elsevier Science Publishers, Amsterdam.

Dvorak, Daniel Louis and Kuipers, Benjamin 1989. Model-based monitoring of dynamic systems. In *Proceedings of the Eleventh International Joint Conference on Artificial Intelligence*. 1238–1243.

Dvorak, Daniel Louis 1992. Monitoring and diagnosis of continuous dynamic systems using semiquantitative simulation. Technical Report AI92–170, Artificial Intelligence Laboratory, University of Texas at Austin, Austin, Texas 78712.

Forbus, Kenneth D. and Falkenhainer, Brian 1990. Self-explanatory simulations: An integration of qualitative and quantitative knowledge. In *Proceedings of the Eighth National Conference on Artificial Intelligence (AAAI-90)*. 380–387.

Forbus, Kenneth 1984. Qualitative process theory. *Artificial Intelligence* 24:85–168.

Forbus, Kenneth D. 1986. Interpretating meaurements of physical systems. In *Proceedings of the Fifth National Conference on Artificial Intelligence (AAAI-86)*. 113–117.

Fusillo, R. H. and Powers, G. J. 1988. Operating procedure synthesis using local models and distributed goals. *Computer and Chemical Engineering* 12(9/10):1023–1034.

Karp, Peter D. and Friedland, Peter 1989. Coordinating the use of qualitative and quantitative knowledge in declarative device modeling. In Widman, Lawrance E.; Loparo, Kenneth A.; and Nielson, Norman R., editors 1989, *Artificial Intelligence, Simulation and Modeling*. John Wiley and Sons. chapter 7.

Kay, Herbert 1991. Monitoring and diagnosis of multi-tank flows using qualitative reasoning. Master's thesis, The University of Texas at Austin.

Kuipers, Benjamin and Berleant, Daniel 1988. Using incomplete quantitative knowledge in qualitative reasoning. In *Proceedings of the Seventh National Conference on Artificial Intelligence*. 324–329.

Kuipers, Benjamin 1984. Commonsense reasoning about causality : Deriving behavior from structure. *Artificial Intelligence* 24:169–204.

Kuipers, Benjamin 1986. Qualitative simulation. *Artificial Intelligence* 29:289–338.

Lakshmanan, R. and Stephanopoulos, G. 1988. Synthesis of operating procedures for complete chemical plants – i. hierarchical, structured modelling for nonlinear planning. *Computer and Chemical Engineering* 12(9/10):985–1002.

LeClair, Steven R. and Abrams, Frances L. 1988. Qualitative process automation. In *Proceedings of the 27th National Conference on Decision and Control*. 558–563.

Lunze, Jan 1989. *Robust Multivariable Feedback Control*. Prentice Hall.

Markov, S. and Angelov, R. 1986. An interval method for systems of ode. In *Lecture Notes in Computer Science #212 – Interval Mathematics 1985*. Springer-Verlag, Berlin. 103–108.

Moore, Ramon E. 1979. *Methods and Applications of Interval Analysis*. SIAM, Philadelphia.

Shen, Qiang and Leitch, Roy 1991. Synchronized qualitative simulation in diagnosis. In *Working Papers from the Fifth International Workshop on Qualitative Reasoning about Physical Systems*. 171–185.

Simmons, Reid 1986. "commonsense" arithmetic reasoning. In *Proceedings of the Fifth National Conference on Artificial Intelligence (AAAI-86)*. 118–124.

Williams, Brian C. 1988. Minima : A symbolic approach to qualitative algebraic reasoning. In *Proceedings of the Sixth National Conference on Artificial Intelligence*. 264–269.

Zukowski, Charles A. 1986. *The Bounding Approach to VLSI Circuit Simulation*. Kluwer Academic Publishers, Boston.

A Qualitative Method to Construct Phase Portraits[*]

Wood W. Lee
Schlumberger Dowell
P. O. Box 2710
Tulsa, OK 74101
lee@dsn.sinet.slb.com

Benjamin J. Kuipers
Department of Computer Sciences
University of Texas
Austin, TX 78712
kuipers@cs.utexas.edu

Abstract

We have developed and implemented in the QPORTRAIT program a qualitative simulation based method to construct phase portraits for a significant class of systems of two coupled first order autonomous differential equations, even in the presence of incomplete, qualitative knowledge.

Differential equation models are important for reasoning about physical systems. The field of nonlinear dynamics has introduced the powerful phase portrait representation for the global analysis of nonlinear differential equations.

QPORTRAIT uses qualitative simulation to generate the set of all possible qualitative behaviors of a system. Constraints on two-dimensional phase portraits from nonlinear dynamics make it possible to identify and classify trajectories and their asymptotic limits, and constrain possible combinations. By exhaustively forming all combinations of features, and filtering out inconsistent combinations, QPORTRAIT is guaranteed to generate all possible qualitative phase portraits. We have applied QPORTRAIT to obtain tractable results for a number of nontrivial dynamical systems.

Guaranteed coverage of all possible behaviors of incompletely known systems complements the more detailed, but approximation-based results of recently-developed methods for intelligently-guided numeric simulation [Nishida et al; Sacks; Yip; Zhao]. Combining the strengths of both approaches would better facilitate automated understanding of dynamical systems.

Intoduction

This report[1] describes a qualitative simulation based method, implemented in the QPORTRAIT program, to construct phase portraits for a significant class of systems of two first order autonomous differential equations. It is a step towards a useful tool for automated reasoning about dynamical systems (i.e. differential equations), and shows that a dynamical systems perspective can give a tractable overview of a qualitative simulation problem.

Differential equations are important for reasoning about physical systems. While nonlinear systems often require complex idiosyncractic treatments, phase potraits have evolved as a powerful tool for global analysis of them. A state of a system is represented by a point in the phase space; change of the system state over time is represented by a trajectory; and a phase portrait is the collection of all possible trajectories of the system.

Phase portraits are typically constructed for exactly specified system instances by intelligently choosing samples of trajectories for numeric simulation and interpreting the results. This has led to recent development of numeric methods based reasoning in the phase space [Nishida et al; Sacks; Yip; Zhao]. These approaches are able to give good approxiamte results.

Based on qualitative simulation [Kuipers 86], and using knowledge of dynamical systems, QPORTRAIT is able to predict all possible phase portraits of incompletely known systems (in the form of qualitative differential equations, QDEs). Starting with a total envisionment [Forbus 84] of a system, QPORTRAIT progressively identifies, classifies, and combines features of the phase portrait, abstracting away uninteresting distinctions, and filtering out inconsistent combinations of features. Exhaustive search and elimination of only provable inconsistencies enable guaranteed coverage of behaviors. This, and the ability to handle incomplete information about systems complement numeric methods based approaches.

QPORTRAIT is currently applicable to systems of two

[0]This work has taken place in the Qualitative Reasoning Group at the Artificial Intelligence Laboratory, The University of Texas at Austin. Research of the Qualitative Reasoning Group is supported in part by NSF grants IRI-8905494, IRI-8904454, and IRI-9017047, by NASA contract NCC 2-760, and by the Jet Propulsion Laboratory.

[1]This report summarizes the work of [Lee 93].

first order autonomous differential equations with non-degenerate fixed points. Various recently developed techniques have been incorporated to deal with qualitative simulation's potential for intractability. As a result, QPORTRAIT is able to produce tractable results for systems with fixed points at landmark values for the phase variables. We have applied QPORTRAIT to obtain tractable results for QDE versions of several well-known nonlinear systems, including a Lienard equation, a van der Pol equation, an undamped pendulum, and a predator-prey system

In the rest of this report, we will first describe the underlying concepts of our work. Then we will describe the steps of our method, followed by an illustration of the steps using a Lienard equation example. Next we will present an argument that our method provides guarantee of coverage, discuss dependencies and limitations, and describe related work. We then end this report with our conclusion.

Underlying Concepts

Phase Portraits

In the phase portrait representation, a state of a system is represented by a point in the system's *phase space*, defined by a set of phase variables of the system. (A set of *phase variables* of a system is a minimal set of variables that fully describes the state of the system.) Change of the system state over time is represented by a *trajectory* in the phase space. A *phase portrait* is the collection of all possible trajectories of the system. The key characteristics of a phase portrait are the *asymptotic limits* of trajectories (i.e. where trajectories may emerge or terminate), and certain bounding trajectories that divide the phase space into stability regions.

For autonomous two-dimensional systems,

$$\begin{cases} x' = f(x, y) \\ y' = g(x, y), \end{cases}$$

asymptotic limits of trajectories can only be one of: fixed points (where the system is stationary), closed orbits (where the system oscillates steadily forever), unions of fixed points and the trajectories connecting them, and points at infinity. Fixed points are either *sinks* (where trajectories only terminate), *sources* (where trajectories only emerge), *saddles* (where trajectories may either emerge or terminate), or *centers* (where trajectories neither emerge or terminate). Bounding trajectories other than closed orbits are associated with saddles, and are called *separatrices*.

In restricting our attention to system with nondegenerate fixed points (which are noncontiguous), local characteristics of fixed points are essentially linear. This means, in particular, that unions of fixed points and the trajectories connecting them can only be unions of saddles and separatrices connecting them.

Furthermore, the essentially linear characteristics of saddle points means that exactly one separatrix enters a saddle in either of two opposite directions, and exactly one separatrix exits a saddle in either of two opposite directions.

Reasoning in Qualitative Phase Space[2]

To reason about phase portraits in qualitative phase space, we integrate the *total envisionment* and *behavior generation* approaches in qualitative simulation. A total envisionment [Forbus 84], using a coarse state space representation[3], produces a transition graph of the n-dimensional state space for the QDE of the system in question. This includes all possible qualitative states a system can take on, and possible transitions between them, capturing all possible trajectories, and their asymptotic limits. Behavior generation [Kuipers 86] refines trajectory paths for two purposes: to check for each trajectory that not all behavior refinements of it are provably inconsistent, and to depict detailed trends of cyclic paths. These ideas are further discussed in the next section.

A QDE description of a system may apply to instances of a system that give rise to phase portraits with different local characteristics. For example, a nonlinear oscillator may be overdamped, giving rise to non-spiraling (nodal) trajectories into a sink; partially underdamped, with trajectories spiraling an arbitrary finite number of times around a sink; or totally underdamped, spiraling infinitely many times as it converges to the sink. These trajectories are mutually intersecting, and belong to different phase portraits, but the distinctions are local to the cyclic paths around a particular sink.

In order to arrive at a tractable global view of the set of qualitative phase portraits, we abstract such a local configuration into a *spiral-nodal bundle* of trajectories around a given sink or source [Lee93], representing the bundle with one of the constituents. Other examples of abstracting away detailed distinctions are discussed subsequently.

Steps of QPORTRAIT

The major steps of QPORTRAIT are:

1. envision, through total envisionment, to capture all possible trajectories and their asymptotic limits,

2. identify the asymptotic limits (possible origins and destinations) from the envisionment graph,

3. gather trajectories by exhaustively tracing paths between possible origins and destinations,

---

[2]Notable earlier work in this area has been done by [Chiu 88], [Lee & Kuipers 88] and [Struss 88].

[3]The value a variable can take on is from a predetermined set of *landmark values* for the variable, or the set of intervals between these landmarks.

4. compose mutually non-intersecting trajectories into phase portraits.

With a few exceptions identified explicitly below, all steps in this analysis have been automated. These techniques are described in more detail in [Lee93].

Capturing all Trajectories

A QDE is first constructed for the system in question. While this process is manually performed, there are often straightforward transformations between functional relationships and QDE constraints. Next, total envisionment captures all possible trajectories and their asymptotic limits. Fixed points are then identified and checked for nondegeneracy[4]. This involves symbolic algebraic manipulation, and is performed manually (though a simple version can be relatively easily implemented). Potentially degenerate fixed points suggest possible bifurcation, and the system needs to be decomposed along these points.

Before proceeding to identify asymptotic limits, the envisionment graph is projected onto the phase plane, and states not giving rise to distinctions in the phase plane are removed. These techniques are described in [Fouché 92] and [Lee93].

Identifying Asymptotic Limits

The complete set of possible asymptotic limits (origins and destinations) of trajectories for autonomous two-dimensional systems with nondegenerate fixed points can be identified from the total envisionment graph.

1. Fixed points are quiescent states in the envisionment graph. Sinks have only predecessors; sources have only successors; saddles have both; and centers have neither.

2. Closed orbits are closed paths in the graph. (Closed paths may also represent inward or outward spirals. These possibilities are distinguished in the next step, gathering trajectories.)

3. Separatrices are paths connecting to saddle points. The union of saddle points and separatrices connecting them (homoclinic and heteroclinic orbits) can also be asymptotic limits of trajectories.

4. Points at infinity that are asymptotic limits have either ∞ or $-\infty$ as their $qmag$, and either have no predecessors, or have no successors.

Gathering Trajectories

Trajectories are gathered by exhaustively tracing possible paths between origins and destinations, abstracting away unimportant distinctions. Loops representing

---

[4]This is done by checking to see that the eigenvalues of the Jacobian matrix of the system at the fixed points have nonzero real parts.

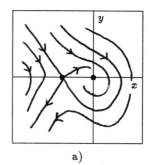 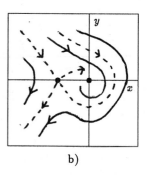

a)   b)

Figure 1: Phase portraits of the Lienard equation: a) from [Brauer & Nohel 69] and [Sacks 90], and b) from QPORTRAIT.

chatter [Kuipers & Chiu 87], and topologically equivalent paths (i.e. sets of mutually homotopic trajectories), are abstracted away and replaced by their simplest representative path.

When one of the resulting trajectories contains a cyclic path in the envisionment graph, its qualitative description is refined through behavior generation in order to determine possible trends of the cycle (spiral inward, spiral outward, and/or periodic). Envisionment-guided simulation [Clancy & Kuipers 92], the energy filter [Fouché & Kuipers 92], and cycle trend extraction [Lee93], are used for this task. Once cycle trends have been established, incomplete cyclic trajectory fragments can be combined in all consistent ways with connecting fragments to form complete trajectories.

Next, trajectories around sinks and sources are analyzed, and spiral-nodal bundles are identified and abstracted. Each trajectory is checked to see that not all behavior refinements are provably inconsistent.

Composing Portraits

Trajectories gathered are first classified as either separatrices, which connect to saddle points (and are bounding trajectories that divide the phase space into stability regions), and flows, which do not. At each saddle, QPORTRAIT composes all possible separatrix sets, each consisting of non-intersecting separatrices with exactly one entering the saddle in each of two opposite directions, and exactly one exiting in each of two opposite directions. The method for enforcing non-intersection of qualitative trajectories is described in [Lee & Kuipers 88].

All possible non-intersecting combinations of separatrix sets between saddle points are then formed, and all possible non-intersecting flows are composed into each combination to form all possible qualitative phase portraits.

A Lienard Equation Example

A particular instance of the Lienard equation takes the form ([Brauer & Nohel 69] pp. 217):

$$x'' + x' + x^2 + x = 0,$$

or equivalently:

$$\begin{cases} x' = y \\ y' = -(x^2 + x) - y. \end{cases}$$

It has an interesting phase portrait, discussed in detail in [Brauer & Nohel 69] pp. 217–220, and used in [Sacks 90] as a main example. Its phase portrait (from [Brauer & Nohel 69] pp. 220) is as shown in Figure 1a. The portarit produced in [Sacks 90] has the same essential qualitative features.

A QDE generalization of this equation has the $x^2 + x$ term replaced by a U^+ function[5]:

$$\begin{cases} x' = y \\ y' = -f(x) - y, \quad f \in U^+_{(a,b),(c,0),(0,0)}; a, b < 0; c < a. \end{cases}$$

QPORTRAIT is able to produce for this QDE the phase portrait in Figure 1b. This portrait has the same essential features as the one in Figure 1a, though ours is applicable to the QDE. We describe briefly below results of intermediate steps for arriving at this portrait.

Applying total envisionment, projecting the envisionment graph onto the phase plane, and removing states not giving rise to interesting distinctions give the envisionment graph in Figure 2a. The potential asymptotic limits are the fixed points at S-26 which is a saddle, the fixed point at S-27 which is a sink, the closed paths around S-27, the paths connecting S-26 to itself (which are separatrices connecting a saddle to itself), and the points at infinity, S-47 and S-57. They are automatically identified from the graph. Both fixed points are nondegenerate.

Trajectory gathering then proceeds progressively. Initially, paths emerging from points at infinity and fixed points are traced. This results in the paths shown in Figure 2b. Note that topologically equivalent paths are abstracted together. The cycle associated with trajectories 7 and 13 is then refined to extract its possible trends. It is found to be inward spiraling, and is consistent with trajectories 7 and 13. Further processing of trajectories 7 and 13 produce trajectories that spiral into the sink in various manners.

Subsequently, when analyzing trajectories for spiral-nodal bundles, spiraling trajectories associated with 7, together with 5 and 6, are bundled. Also bundled are spiraling trajectories associated with 13, together with 11 and 12.

---

[5]A $U^+_{(a,b)}$ function is a QSIM [Kuipers 86] modeling primitive. Intuitively speaking, it is a 'U' shaped function consisting of a monotonically decreasing left segment and a monotonically increasing right segment, with (a,b) the bottom point.

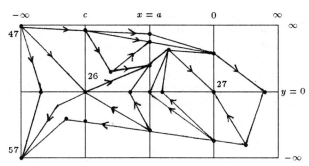

a) Envisionment graph of the Lienard equation in the phase plane.

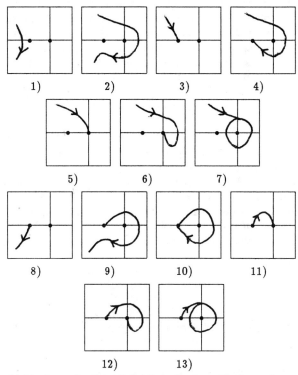

b) Trajectories from initial gathering. Trajectories 7 and 13 are cyclic and incomplete. Trajectory 10 is a homoclinic orbit.

Figure 2: Intermediate results from applying QPORTRAIT to a QDE generalization of a Lienard equation.

Trajectory 10 is a separatrix connecting a saddle to itself (a homoclinic orbit). It is a potential asymptotic limit, and is further processed for trajectories emerging from or terminating on it. Subsequent checking for consistent behavior refinements of trajectories, however, finds trajectory 10 to be inconsistent (violating energy constraints). Trajectory 10 and its associated trajectories are therefore eliminated. Trajectory 9 is also found to violate energy constraints and eliminated.

Trajectories resulting from gathering are 1 through 4, 8, and the two bundles. Of these, 3, 4, 8 and the bundle associated with 13 are separatrices. Composing separatrix set, then phase portrait, give the result in Figure 1b.

Discussions

While some phase portraits produced by QPORTRAIT may be spurious, and some may contain spurious trajectories, the set of portraits that remain consistent after spurious trajectories are removed is guaranteed to capture all real portraits of systems consistent with the given QDE. We have applied QPORTRAIT to obtain tractable results for a set of nontrivial examples to offer reasonable coverage of possible asymptotic limits of systems in our domain. Included are a Lienard equation, a van der Pol equation, an undamped pendulum, and a predator-prey system.

Guarantee of Coverage

Guaranteed coverage follows from the guarantees of the individual steps. First, qualitative simulation is guaranteed to predict all qualitatively distinct solutions. Second, possible asymptotic limits of trajectories are exhaustively identified for systems in our domain. Third, possible flows between asymptotic limits are exhaustively traced, eliminating only provably inconsistent flows. Fourth, in abstracting away uninteresting qualitative distinctions, asymptotic limits and flows are preserved. Fifth, all possible phase portrait compositions are exhaustively explored, eliminating only provably inconsistent compositions. Thus, given a QDE, QPORTRAIT is guaranteed to produce all qualitatively distinct phase portraits of it.

Dependencies and Limitations[6]

While QPORTRAIT is dependent on its supporting techniques, the dependency is in terms of tractability[7]. In other words, improvement in performance of the supporting techniques gives more tractable results, and

---

[6]Aspects concerning construction of QDE, determination of nondegeneracy of fixed points, and system bifurcation have been discussed when describing steps of QPORTRAIT, and will not be repeated here.

[7]The problem with tractability can be due to an intractable number of spurious predictions, or an intractable number of overly detailed distinctions, or both. Refer to [Lee 93] for further discussion.

converse otherwise. Guarantee of coverage, however, is preserved regardless of the performance of the supporting techniques, though the guarantee becomes increasingly less useful as results become increasingly less tractable.

Although QPORTRAIT is able to produce tractable results for the examples we've attempted, it would not be difficult to come up with examples where intractability would result. No general characterization relating system property to the potential for intractability has been developed. Nevertheless, knowledge of system fixed points helps produce tracable results, such as when fixed points are at landmark values for the phase variables.

QPORTRAIT's applicability is limited to autonomous two-dimensional systems with nondegenerate fixed points. Extending QPORTRAIT to apply to systems with degenerate fixed points would require incorporating knowledge of asymptotic limits of such systems. While nonautonomous systems can be transformed into equivalent autonomous systems, systems of higher dimensions will result. Extending QPORTRAIT to higher dimensional systems will be difficult, largely because the qualitative non-intersection constraint [Lee & Kuipers 88] may not apply generally. Furthermore, trajectory flows and their asymptotic limits have more complicated structures in higher-dimensional systems, and are hard to characterize exhaustively.

Related Work

Various numeric methods based approaches to reason in the phase space have recently emerged. These include the work of Nishida et al, Sacks, Yip, and Zhao. They work with exactly specified system instances to produce approximate solutions, and are able to produce qualitative conclusions from underlying numerical results. Although each approach iterates in an attempt to capture all essential qualitative features, none guarantees coverage.

An early attempt to use qualitative simulation to construct phase portraits is the work of [Chiu 88]. Chiu was able to use the few available qualitative simulation techniques to perform complete analysis of various systems. Using his work as our foundation, we are able to take advantage of more recently developed techniques to perform more sophisticated reasoning, and incorporate sufficient knowledge of dynamical systems to handle a significant class of systems.

Conclusion

We have developed a qualitative simulation based method to construct phase portraits of autonomous two-dimensional differential equations with nondegenerate fixed points. It has been implemented in the QPORTRAIT program. It has the attractive property that it is guaranteed to capture the essential qualitative features of all real phase portraits of systems consistent with an incomplete state of knowledge (a QDE). This complements the ability of numeric methods based approaches to produce good approximate results for particular system instances.

While the potential for intractable results remain, we have demonstrated that QPORTRAIT is able to produce tractable results for nontrivial systems. In particular, results will be tractable when fixed points of the system are at landmark values for the phase variables.

Extending our approach to higher-dimensional systems will be hard, and will be a very significant contribution. It will need to proceed in smaller steps (covering a smaller class of systems at a time) due to the more complicated phase space structures of higher-dimensional systems. Integration with numeric methods to combine the power of both approaches appears to be a particularly attractive line of future work.

Despite a concern (notably in [Sacks & Doyle 92a] and [Sacks & Doyle 92b]) that qualitative simulation methods may not be useful for scientific and engineering reasoning, our work represents a significant steps towards automated reasoning about differential equations, which are important for scientists and engineers. Furthermore, our work is a demonstration that a dynamical systems (phase space) perspective can give a tractable overview of a qualitative simulation problem.

References

[**Brauer & Nohel 69**] Brauer, F. and Nohel, J. A., *The Qualitative Theory of Ordinary Differential Equations*, W. A. Benjamin, New York, 1969.

[**Chiu 88**] Chiu, C., Higher Order Derivative Constraints and a QSIM-Based Total Simulation Scheme, technical report AITR88-65, Department of Computer Sciences, University of Texas, Austin, TX, 1988.

[**Clancy & Kuipers 92**] Clancy, D. J. and Kuipers, B. J., Aggregating Behaviors and Tractable Simulation, in: *AAAI Design from Physical Principles Fall Symposium Working Notes*, pp 38–43, Cambridge, MA, 1992.

[**Forbus 84**] Forbus, K. D., Qualitative Process Theory, in: *Artificial Intelligence* **24**, pp 85–168, 1984.

[**Fouché 92**] Fouché, P., *Towards a Unified Framework for Qualitative Simulation*, PhD Dissertation, Université de Technologie de Compiègne, France, 1992.

[**Fouché & Kuipers 92**] Fouché, P. and Kuipers, B. J., Reasoning about Energy in Qualitative Simulation, in: *IEEE Transactions on Systems, Man and Cybernetics* **22**, pp 47–63, 1992.

[**Guckenheimer & Holmes 83**] Guckenheimer, J. and Holmes, P., *Nonlinear Oscillations, Dynamical Systems, and Bifurcations of Vector Fields*, Springer-Verlag, New York, 1983.

[**Hirsch & Smale 74**] Hirsch, M. W. and Smale, S., *Differential Equations, Dynamical Systems, and Linear Algebra*, Academic Press, New York, 1974.

[**Kuipers 86**] Kuipers, B. J., Qualitative Simulation, in: *Artificial Intelligence* **29**, pp 289–338, 1986.

[**Kuipers & Chiu 87**] Taming Intractable Branching in Qualitative Simulation, in: *Proceedings IJCAI-87*, pp 1079–1085, Milan, Italy, 1987.

[**Lee 93**] Lee, W. W. *A Qualitative Based Method to Construct Phase Portraits*, PhD Dissertation, Department of Computer Sciences, University of Texas, Austin, TX, 1993.

[**Lee & Kuipers 88**] Lee, W. W. and Kuipers, B. J., Non-Intersection of Trajectories in Qualitative Phase Space: A Global Constraint for Qualitative Simulation, in: *Proceedings AAAI-88*, pp 286–290, Saint Paul, MN, 1988.

[**Nishida & Doshita 91**] Nishida, T. and Doshita, S., A Geometric Approach to Total Envisioning, in: *Proceedings IJCAI-91*, pp 1150–1155, Sydney, Australia, 1991.

[**Nishida et al 91**] Nishida, T., Mizutani, K., Kubota, A. and Doshita, S., Automated Phase Portrait Analysis by Integrating Qualitative and Quantitative Analysis, in: *Proceedings AAAI-91*, pp 811–816, Los Angeles, CA, 1991.

[**Sacks 90**] Sacks, E. P., Automatic Qualitative Analysis of Dynamic Systems using Piecewise Linear Approximations, in: *Artificial Intelligence* **41**, pp 313–364, 1990.

[**Sacks 91**] Sacks, E. P., Automatic Analysis of One-Parameter Planar Ordinary Differential Equations by Intelligent Numerical Simulation, in: *Artificial Intelligence* **48**, pp 27–56, 1991.

[**Sacks & Doyle 92a**] Sacks, E. P. and Doyle, J., Prolegomena to Any Future Qualitative Physics, in: *Computational Intelligence* **8**, pp 187–209, 1992.

[**Sacks & Doyle 92b**] Sacks, E. P. and Doyle, J., Epilegomenon, in: *Computational Intelligence* **8**, pp 326–335, 1992.

[**Struss 88**] Struss, P., Global Filters for Qualitative Behaviors, in: *Proceedings AAAI-88*, pp 275–279, Saint Paul, MN, 1988.

[**Yip 88**] Yip, K., Generating Global Behaviors using Deep Knowledge of Local Dynamics, in: *Proceedings AAAI-88*, pp 280–285, Saint Paul, MN, 1988.

[**Yip 91**] Yip, K., *KAM: A System for Intelligently Guiding Numerical Experimentation by Computer*, MIT Press, Cambridge, MA, 1991.

[**Zhao 91**] Zhao, F., Extracting and Representing Qualitative Behaviors of Complex Systems in Phase Spaces, in: *Proceedings IJCAI-91*, pp 1144–1149, Sydney, Australia, 1991.

Understanding Linkages*

Howard E. Shrobe

Massachusetts Institute of Technology
NE43-839
Cambridge, MA 02139
hes@zermatt.lcs.mit.edu

Abstract

Mechanical linkages are used to transmit and transform motion. In this paper we investigate what it means for a program to "understand" a linkage. Our system extracts its understanding by analyzing the results of a numerical simulation of the mechanism, finding interesting qualitative features, looking for symbolic relationships between these features and conjecturing a causal relationship between them. Our system is capable of understanding a variety of mechanisms, producing explanations very much like those in standard texts.

1 Motivation

Mechanical linkages are used to transmit and transform motion. They are a subset of the class of "fixed topology mechanisms", those consisting of rigid bodies in constant contact with motion being transmitted through joints, gears and cams. In this paper we investigate how a system can "understand" a linkage, i.e. how it can

- Decompose the mechanism into understandable sub-mechanisms.

- Explain how the behavior of the whole arises from that of the parts.

- Assign a purpose to each of the components.

- Enable redesign by highlighting what interactions lead to the desired behavior.

Although the techniques in this paper apply to the broader class of fixed topology mechanisms, the running example in this paper will consist of a linkage with a single degree of freedom.

---

*This paper describes research done at the Artificial Intelligence Laboratory of the Massachusetts Institute of Technology. Support for the author's artificial intelligence research is provided by the Advanced Research Projects Agency of the Department of Defense under Office of Naval Research contract N00014-91-J-4038.

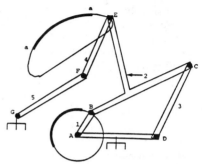

The lengths of the links comply with the conditions: BC = 2 AB, DC = 5.2AC, EC = 3.6AB, EF = 3.6AB, GF = 11.4AB, AD = 6AB, GD = 8.4AB and AG = 11AB. Link 4 is connected by turning pairs E and F to link 2 of *four-bar linkage ABCD* and to link 5 which oscillates about fixed axis G.

When point B of crank 1 travels along the part of the circle indicated by a heavy continuous line, point E of connecting rod 2 *describes a path of which portion a-a approximates a circular arc* of radius FE with its center at point F. During this period link 5 almost ceases to oscillate, i.e. *it practically has a dwell.*

Figure 1: A Dwell Mechanism and Its Explanation

Figure 1 shows a six-bar linkage[1] functioning as a dwell mechanism[2] with its explanation reproduced from [1][3]. (We have highlighted parts of this explanation). This paper presents a system which can "understand" this linkage, producing an explanation like that of the figure.

Several observations about the explanation of figure 1 are worth emphasizing:

- The explanation is compositional. The behavior of the whole is derived by first decomposing the mechanism into modules and by then composing the behaviors of the modules into an aggregate behavior: the device consists of "four-bar linkage ABCD" driving the pair of links 4 and 5.[4] However, the decomposition stops before reaching the primitive elements (joints and links).

---

[1] For those not familiar with linkages, we note that the set of links 1,2, and 3 together with the fixed frame, is a "four-bar linkage" (with joints A,B,C and D) and that the pair of links 4 and 5 (with joints F and G) is a "dyad". Link 2 is the "coupler" of the four-bar linkage; since point E is on the coupler, the curve it traces is called a "coupler curve". Four bar linkages are extremely flexible driving mechanisms; they can create a large number of coupler curves exhibiting a broad variety of shapes. The shape of the curve is a function of the (relative) sizes of the links and the position on the coupler link used to trace the curve.

[2] A dwell mechanism is one in which some part moves (in this case oscillates) most of the time, but for some period of time stands still (i.e. dwells).

[3] In this picture, the links are draw as bars, except that link 2 has a long finger projecting from it to point E making it look like an inverted T. Circles are used to indicate the joints between the links. The "ground" symbols are used to indicate that link AB is rigidly connected to the fixed frame and that joint G connects link 5 to the fixed frame.

[4] Such a pair of links is called a dyad.

The explanation does not attempt to provide a mechanistic explanation of how the shape of the coupler curve of the four bar linkage ABCD is related to the sizes of its links.

- A crucial component of the explanation is a characterization of the qualitative shape of curves traced by "interesting points" in the mechanism: "point E (of link 2) ... traces a path of which portion a-a approximates a *circular arc* of radius FE with its center at point F".

- Although the explanation does not emphasize local causal propagations of the type made popular in [2; 4; 11; 12], it does have a causal flavor at a relatively high level of abstraction: "the shape of the coupler curve causes link 5 to have a dwell".

The system described in this paper is capable of producing such an explanation. Our approach is as follows:

1. We numerically simulate the mechanism at a single time step.

2. The simulator is driven by geometric constraints. While satisfying these constraints, the simulator records its inferences as a "mechanism graph" showing how motion propagates from link to link through the joints of the mechanism.

3. The mechanism graph is "parsed" into a more structured form which decomposes the system into driving and driven modules. To the extent possible the parsed graph consists of standard building blocks (e.g. four-bar linkages, dyads). The system knows which parameters of the standard building blocks are significant and these are identified as *important parameters*. Also the coupling points between the driving and driven modules are identified as *important parameters*.

   A complete simulation of the linkage is run, stepping the mechanism through its full range of positions (in our example this amounts to spinning link 1 through a full 360 degrees and for each step determining the positions and orientations of all the remaining components). During this simulation, the values of all *important parameters* (including the trajectories of the points connecting driving and driven modules) are recorded.

4. The shapes of the captured curves are analyzed and qualitative features extracted.

5. Qualitative relationships between these features are derived and accounted for by geometric reasoning.

Section 2 describes the simulator and how it supports the rest of this process. Section 3 then examines the process of mechanism extraction and section 4 describes curve characterization. Section 5 show how these facilities work together to construct an explanation of the mechanism. Section 6 discusses to what degree the interpretation produced is an adequate "understanding" of the mechanism. Finally, in section 7 we compare our work with other work on understanding mechanisms.

2   The Simulator

Our simulator is based on Kramer's TLA [10]. However, since our work (at least for now) only involves planar mech-

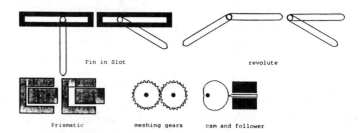

Figure 2: The Joints Modeled in the System

anisms we have simplified TLA to a 2-D simulator. Also we have extended the geometric solution techniques to handle gears and cams as well as pure linkages.

2.1   Basic Object Types

The simulator is at its core a geometric constraint engine. This engine reasons about the following physical objects:

- **Links**: These are rigid bodies connected by joints. All links are assumed to be aligned in parallel planes. Each link has its own local coordinate system. Each link also has a transformation matrix mapping its coordinate system into the global coordinate system. (We will often refer to the global coordinate system as the "fixed frame").

- **Joints**: A joint is a fixed connection between two links which couples their motion. We handle the following joint types (see figure 2):

   1. **Revolute**: The two links are connected at a single point; they rotate relative to each other about this point. A hinge is familiar example. All the joints in our example are revolute joints; these are sometimes called "turning pairs".

   2. **Pin in Slot**: A round "finger" from the first link slides in a guide path in the second link. The first link can translate along the direction of the slot; it can rotate relative to the second link as well. The guide track of a folding door is an example.

   3. **Prismatic**: The first link slides along the second link, but is not free to rotate relative to it. A piston in its cylinder is a familiar example.

   4. **Gears**: The two links are spur gears coupled by the meshing of their teeth. This includes planetary as well as fixed gears.

   5. **Cams**: One link is an irregularly shaped rotational device; the other is constrained to maintain contact with the perimeter of the rotating cam.

Links and joints are modeled by reducing their behavior to the following computational constructs:

- **Markers**: Each marker is associated with a specific link (although each link may have several markers). A marker has two components specified in the local coordinate system of its link: a point and an orientation. A marker can be thought of as a line extending from the point in the direction specified by the orientation. The simulator may restrict a marker to occupy a specific position or to have a specific orientation in the global coordinate system. If this has occured we say that the marker has *invariant* position or orientation.

- **Constraints**: Constraints are the mechanism used to build a computational model of Joints. Each joint is modeled as a bundle of constraints. A constraint is imposed between two links by relating two markers, one from each link. Our simulator has the following constraint types:

  1. **Coincident**: The two markers are forced to be at the same location in the global coordinate system. A revolute joint is modeled as a single coincident constraint.

  2. **Inline**: The location of the first marker is on the line described by the second marker. A Pin-In-Slot joint is modeled by a single Inline constraint.

  3. **Cooriented**: The two markers' orientations are forced to be the same in the global coordinate system. A prismatic joint is modeled as a combination of a Cooriented and an Inline constraint.

  4. **Rotational Multiplication**: Used to model gears. The angular deflection of the first marker from its initial position is a constant (the gear ratio) times the deflection of the second marker from its initial position.

  5. **Perimeter Contact**: Used to model cams. The marker on the follower is constrained to be in contact with the perimeter of the Cam link.

- **Anchors**: An anchor is a distinguished type of marker attached to the global coordinate system rather than to a link. Constraints between anchors and markers on links are used to orient or set the position of a link in the global coordinate system. Input variables are supplied to the system as the position or orientation of an anchor; typically, the anchor controls the position or orientation of a link via a constraint to one of the link's markers.

2.2 The Constraint Engine

As in Kramer's TLA, the constraint engine solves the geometric constraints using local geometric techniques. These techniques take the form of "constraint" and "locus intersection" methods (described below). As the constraint engine runs, it monitors the degrees of freedom remaining to each link; it also records for each marker whether its global position and orientation are *invariant*. As the links' degrees of freedom are reduced and the markers' orientations and positions become invariant, the geometric methods are triggered. Each method moves or rotates a link to satisfy a constraint, further reducing the degrees of freedom available to the link; each method may also cause the global position or orientation of some marker to become invariant. This will trigger other methods. The process terminates when all degrees of freedom are removed.

The **constraint methods** are triggered when the location or orientation of a marker becomes invariant. Its triggering pattern contains the invariant marker, a constraint coupling the invariant marker to some marker on a link, the type of the constraint, and the degrees of translational and rotational freedom remaining to the link. When a constraint method is triggered, it translates or rotates (or

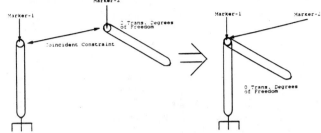

If   There is a coincident constraint between M-1 and M-2
      M-1 has invariant global position
      M-2 is on link L-2
      L-2 has 2 degrees of translational freedom
Then Measure the vector from M-2 to M-1
      Translate L-2 by this vector
      Reduce the translational degrees of freedom of L-2 to 0
      Constrain M-2 to have invariant global position

Figure 3: A Constraint Method for The Coincident Constraint

both) the link to satisfy the constraint. In doing so it reduces the degrees of freedom available to the link; it also causes the global orientation or position of the marker on the link to become invariant. When a link is reduced to 0 degrees of rotational freedom, the orientation of every marker on it becomes *invariant* in the global coordinate system; when a link is reduced to 0 degrees of both rotational and translational freedom, the position of every marker on the link becomes *invariant* in the global coordinate system. Figure 3 shows a constraint method for the coincident constraint used to model a revolute joint.

Locus intersection methods are used after the constraint methods. When a link's degrees of freedom have been sufficiently reduced, the markers on the link are constrained to move in simple curves. For example, if a link has 0 degrees of translational freedom and 1 degree of rotational freedom, then every marker on the link (except the one about which the link rotates) is constrained to move in a circle. If two markers coupled by a constraint are both restricted to move in simple curves, then there are only a small number of locations that the markers can consistently occupy. For example, if two markers coupled by a coincident constraint are both restricted to move in circles, then the markers must be located at one of the two intersection points of the circles. In simulating the linkage of figure 1, driving link 1 is rotated into its desired position, fixing the position of B; this means that link 2 is allowed only to rotate about B. Similarly, the position of D is fixed, so link 3 may only rotate about D. C must, therefore, be at an intersection point of the circular paths allowed to the ends of links 2 and 3.[5][6]

2.3 Animating a Linkage

The motion of a linkage can be simulated by repeatedly incrementing the position or orientation of the driving link and allowing the constraint engine to determine the correct

---

[5] Notice that locus intersection methods lead to ambiguous results, since two circles may intersect at more than one point; the simulator must chose between the geometrically allowable results using physical principles such as continuity of motion.

[6] When there are no further constraint method or locus intersection methods to be employed but the constraints have not been solved, then an iterative numerical solution technique is employed. To save space and maintain continuity of presentation we omit the details; the examples in this paper never require iterative techniques.

locations and orientations for the other links. A simple animation can be produced by showing successive snapshots.

The simulator can attach "probes" to any marker in the mechanism; these record the position and/or orientation of the marker at each time step of the simulation. Thus, a probe captures the complete trajectory of a marker (e.g. the trajectory of point E in figure 1) or the history of values of some property of a marker (e.g. the global orientation of Marker G which is the same as the angular deflection of Link 5). This information is used later in analyzing the mechanism, see section 4.

2.4 Building the Mechanism Graph

The simulator can record its deductions using a truth maintenance facility. The simulator maintains in each link a special data structure called a *link-state-entry*. This contains the number of degrees of rotational and translational freedom available to the link at that point in the process of satisfying the geometric constraints.

When a constraint method entry updates the state of a link, it creates a new link-state-entry for the link. It also creates a *justification*. The antecedents of the justification are the current link-state-entries of the links coupled by the constraint; the consequent of the justification is the new link-state-entry for the affected link. The justification also records the constraint which caused the update. The link-state-entries may be thought of as the nodes of a truth maintenance graph and the justifications as directed arcs from the old link-state-entries to the new one. Locus intersection methods also create new link-state-entries and special justifications connecting them. The resulting graph records the steps of the process of satisfying the geometric constraints by moving (or rotating) then links while reducing their degrees of freedom.

This structure is similar to the "mechanism graph" of [2].

3 Mechanism Extraction

The first step in understanding the linkage mechanism shown in figure 1 is *mechanism extraction*, in which the assembly is decomposed into sub-assemblies and the relationship between driving and driven components is established. The input to this process is the mechanism graph produced by the simulator.

Mechanisms are identified as patterns of constraint solution within the mechanism graph; the patterns are identified by parsing rules like those shown in figure 4. The parsing rules build up a hierarchy of sub-modules. For the linkage of figure 1, the first rule characterizes link 1 as a crank; the third rule characterizes links 2 & 3 as a dyad. The second rule then notices that crank 1 drives the dyad formed by links 2 & 3. The last rule characterizes links 1,2 & 3, together with the fixed frame, as a four-bar linkage. Next, links 4 & 5 are characterized as another dyad which is driven by marker E on the coupler of the four bar linkage.

The rules shown in figure 4 cover most uses of four bar linkages. Pantographs, scotch-yokes, planetary-gear sets, slider-cranks, etc. are identified by similar sets of rules.

The structure produced by the parsing rules is used to identify points of interest in the mechanism. Part of what

```
If    Marker M-1 is on Link-1
      A-1 is an anchor and C-1 is a coincident constraint between M-1 and A-1
      The position of M-1 is determined by satisfying C-1
      A-2 is an anchor providing an input parameter
      C-2 is a cooriented constraint coupling A-2 and M-1
      The orientation of M-1 is determined by satisfying C-2
Then  Link-1 is acting as a crank

If    Marker M-1 is on Link-1
      There is a constraint C between M-1 and M-2
      M-2 is on Link-2
      The position of M-2 is determined by satisfying C
Then  Link-2 is driven by Link-1

If    M-0 and M-1 are on Link-1
      M-2 and M-3 are on Link-2
      The positions of M1 and M2 are determined by a circle-circle locus method
      A-2 is an anchor coupled by a coincident constraint C-2 to M-3
      The position of M-3 is determined by satisfying C-2
      M-4 is a marker coupled to M-0 by a coincident constraint C-1
      The position of M-0 is determined by satisfying C-1
Then  Links 1 and 2 form a Dyad Dyad-1
      Link-1 is the coupler of Dyad-1
      Link-2 is the rocker of Dyad-1

If    Dyad-1 is a Dyad
      C-1 is the coupler of Dyad-1
      R-1 is the rocker of Dyad-1
      Crank-1 is acting as a crank
      C-1 is driven by Crank-1
Then  C1, R-1 and Crank-1 form a four-bar linkage Four-bar-1
      Crank-1 is the crank of the four-bar
      C-1 of Dyad-1 is the coupler of Four-bar-1
      R-1 of Dyad-1 is the rocker of Four-bar-1
```

Figure 4: Rules for Parsing a Mechanism Graph

the system knows about each type of module is what points in the module are likely to play "interesting" roles in the larger mechanism. In particular, the system knows that the trajectory of coupler points of four-bar linkages are usually interesting, particularly if the coupler point drives another identifiable mechanism. Also the system knows that the deflection angle of the rocker arm of a driven dyad is interesting.

4 Characterizing Curve Shape

At this point, mechanism extraction has parsed the linkage into 2 sub-assemblies (a four-bar linkage and a dyad) and established a driver-driven relationship between them (the dyad is driven by a coupler point on the four-bar). However, the overall behavior of the mechanism depends on a specific feature of the shape of the curve traced by point E (it is a circular arc).

The next step of the analysis is to capture the relevant curves and to characterize their shapes. This is done by running a complete simulation of the linkage (i.e. by stepping the driving link through its complete range of motion); during this simulation, probes are attached to those points identified as interesting by the mechanism extraction: the coupler curve traced by point E and the angle of the rocker arm 3.

The following analyses are then performed:

- For each graph, the extrema of values are located (by finding the zero crossings of the first derivatives).

- For each trajectory traced, the system calculates the "Theta-S" representation which maps distance along the trajectory to the orientation at that point on the trajectory (in this representation a circular arc on the original curve appears as a straight line and a straight line in the original curve appears as a horizontal line).

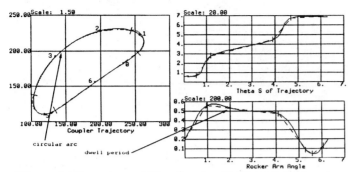

Figure 5: Curvature of The Coupler Curve and Angle of The Rocker Arm

- For each graph (other than traces of the trajectory of a point, but including the Theta-S curve for such a trajectory) a segmentation into linear approximations is performed using the "Split-Merge" technique.

  For each trajectory traced, the segmentation of the Theta-S representation is mapped back into a segmentation of the original curve. This segmentation approximates the original curve with linear and circular segments.

- For each trajectory traced, the system calculates the radius and centers of curvature at each point.

- For each trajectory traced, the system calculates the points of self intersection.

- For each graph, segments of constant value are located.

- Fourier transforms of graphs are calculated if there is reason to suspect that periodic motion is present.

Figure 5 shows the coupler curve of the dwell mechanism of Figure 1. The segmentation of the curve is indicated by "hatch marks"; the approximation of the curve by straight lines and circular arc segments is shown by dashed lines. Dots along the curve with numbers attached indicate the value, in radians, of the driving parameter (the angle of the crank, link 1). Also shown is the Theta-S representation of this curve with its segmentation. The horizontal axis is the distance along the curve normalized to 2Υ, the vertical axis is the orientation (in radians) at that position on the curve. Finally, the figure shows the angle (in radians) of the rocker arm of the dyad (link 5) plotted against the driving parameter same analyses, as is also shown in the figure.

Note that the coupler curve is well approximated by a circular arc (between about 1.1 and 4.0 radians of the driving parameter). Also note that the rocker arm's orientation is very nearly constant between about 1.0 and 4.1 radians of the driving parameter (the vertical scale of the graph is much larger than the horizontal scale, which obscures this fact).

5 Constructing an Understanding of a Mechanism

At this point, we have extracted from the simulation of the device a decomposition into driving and driven components. The decomposition has guided the choice of tra-

jectories and displacement histories to collect. The analysis of these curves leads to a set of qualitative features characterizing the shapes of the curves. In the case of the dwell mechanism of figure 1, the system notes that:

- The angle of the rocker arm has a period of constant value.
- The coupler curve has a segment of constant curvature (i.e. a circular segment).

The final step in constructing an understanding of the mechanism is to notice relationships between these features as well as relationships between the curve features and metric properties of the links of the mechanism. It must then attempt to explain these relationships through geometric reasoning.

In particular, the system notes that:

- The radius of curvature of the circular segment traced by point E, the coupler point of the four bar linkage is nearly equal to the length of link 4, the coupler arm of the dyad.
- The distance from the fixed end of link 5, the rocker of the dyad to the center of curvature of the circular arc traced by point E is nearly equal to the length of link 5, the rocker of the dyad.
- There is a substantial overlap between the period during which the coupler of the four bar traces the circular arc and the period during which the rocker arm's angle holds steady.

Having found these overlaps, the system conjectures that the dyad has a dwell period which is *caused* by the coupler arm moving through a circular arc whose curvature is the same as the length of the driven arm of the dyad and whose center of curvature is at the location occupied by the dyad's joint when the circular arc is entered.

Notice that this conjecture does not itself refer to any specific metric information from the simulation. If we can support the conjecture with reasoning which also does not depend on metric information specific to this linkage, then we will have deduced a universal principle applicable to a broader class of devices.

The final step is to use geometric reasoning to support the conjecture. The geometric knowledge needed to support the conjecture is very basic:

- Two circles intersect in at most two points.
- The center of a circle (the center of curvature of a circular arc) is the unique point equidistant (by the radius) from more than two points on the circle.

The reasoning supporting the conjecture is quite simple (and we omit it for brevity). It completes the interpretation of the mechanism and uses no metric information from the simulation but only qualitative shape features of the curves and symbolic relationships between joint positions. Any other mechanism satisfying these symbolic relationships will have the same behavior. **General information has been extracted from the simulation of a specific device.**

6 Adequacy of the Interpretation

An understanding of a mechanism should:

- Decompose the mechanism into understandable sub-mechanisms.

- Explain how the behavior of the whole arises from that of the parts.

- Assign a purpose to each of the components.

- Enable redesign by highlighting what interactions lead to the desired behavior.

Our explanation of the dwell mechanism meets all these criteria. It decomposes the linkage into two well known sub-linkages and explains how the shape of the coupler curve causes the dyad to dwell. The two sub-linkages have well understood purposes.

We also claim that this explanation of the mechanism enables redesign. Although our system is not a redesign system, we claim that a redesign system could use the kind of information we generate. In particular, it is clear that the four bar linkage could be replaced by any other mechanism which generates a curve with a similar circular arc segment.

We have run our system on several mechanisms from [1] and several other source books of mechanisms. We handle multiple dwells mechanisms, frequency multipliers, quick returns and a variety of stand-alone uses of four bar linkages. The modules understood by the system include planetary gears, scotch-yokes, pantographs, dyads, cams, four-bar linkages, dyads, slider-cranks, etc.

7 Comparison to Other Approaches

There have been other projects on understanding kinematic mechanisms, (e.g. [5; 3; 8; 6]). These have been concerned mainly with determining when state transitions occur, typically when contact between bodies is established and broken. Although this is an important and difficult issue in the general case, it does not occur in the domain of linkages (or more generally fixed topology mechanisms).

Our central concern is deriving qualitative features of the shapes of curves generated by driving mechanisms; and this is quite different from those generated by these systems.

With the exception of [6; 8], most of these systems are based on qualitative simulation.

One system [9] attempts to apply qualitative simulation to linkages. Kim's system conducts a form of envisioning of the behavior of a four-bar linkage. However, the system as described does not predict the shape of coupler curves, nor does it deal with more complex systems which use four bar linkages as driving mechanisms.

The shape of a coupler curve is governed by highly non-linear equations (it is a 6th degree curve). [7] points out the difficulty of relating link sizes to coupler curve shapes and catalogues several thousand coupler curves as a service to designers. Because the equations are highly non-linear, it is unlikely that qualitative simulation can derive the shape properties of coupler curves.

8 Summary

We have shown a system that can "understand" linkages (and other fixed topology devices) producing an explana-

tion very similar to that given in textbooks on mechanical design.

Our system begins with numerical simulation, extracting from this a mechanism graph. The graph is then parsed into familiar modules bearing a driver-driven relationship to one another. This identifies interesting points in the mechanism whose trajectories are extracted and qualitatively characterized. Symbolic relationships between curve features are then noticed and used to generate conjectures about the functioning of the mechanism. Finally, geometric reasoning is used to support the conjecture, establishing the qualitative conditions which must obtain for the observed behavior to result.

This process has been shown to extract general design principles from specific mechanisms.

References

[1] I.I. Artobolevsky. *Mechanisms in Modern Engineering Design*. MIR Publishers, Moscow, 1975.

[2] Johan deKleer. Causal and teleological resoning in circuit recognition. Technical Report TR-529, Massachussetts Institute of Technology, AI Lab., Cambridge, Mass., September 1979.

[3] Boi Faltings. A theory of qualitative kinematics in mechanisms. Technical Report UILU-ENG-86-1729, University of Illinois at Urbana-Champaign, Urbana, Illinois, May 1986.

[4] Kenneth D. Forbus. Qualitative process theory. Technical Report TR-789, Massachussetts Institute of Technology, AI Lab., Cambridge, Mass., July 1981.

[5] Kenneth D. Forbus, Paul Nielsen, and Boi Faltings. Qualitative kinematics: A framework. Technical Report UILU-ENG-87-1739, University of Illinois at Urbana-Champaign, Urbana, Illinois, June 1987.

[6] Andrew Gelsey. The use of intelligently controlled simulation to predict a machine's long-term behavior. In *Proceedings of the National Conference on Artificial Intelligence*, pages 880–887. AAAI, 1991.

[7] J.A. Hrones and G.L. Nelson. *Analysis of The Four-bar Linkage*. MIT Press and John Wiley & Sons, New York, 1951.

[8] L. Joskowicz and E.P. Sacks. Computational kinematics. Technical Report CS-TR-300-90, Princeton University, Princeton, N.J., April 1990.

[9] Hyun-Kyung Kim. Qualitative kinematics of linkages. Technical Report UILU-ENG-90-1742, University of Illinois at Urbana-Champaign, Urbana, Illinois, May 1990.

[10] Glenn A. Kramer. Solving geometric constraint systems. In *Proceedings of the National Conference on Artificial Intelligence*, pages 708–714. AAAI, 1990.

[11] Benjamin J. Kuipers. Qualitative simulation. *Artificial Intelligence*, 29:289–338, 1986.

[12] Brian Williams. Qualitative analysis of mos circuits. *Artificial Intelligence*, 24:281–346, 1984.

CFRL: A Language for Specifying the Causal Functionality of Engineered Devices

Marcos Vescovi   Yumi Iwasaki   Richard Fikes
Knowledge Systems Laboratory
Stanford University
701 Welch Road, Bldg C
Palo Alto, CA 94304
vescovi,iwasaki,fikes@ksl.stanford.edu

B. Chandrasekaran
Laboratory for AI Research
The Ohio State University
217 B, Bolz Hall, 2036 Neil Avenue
Columbus, OH 43210-1277
chandra@cis.ohio-state.edu

Abstract*

Understanding the design of an engineered device requires both knowledge of the general physical principles that determine the behavior of the device and knowledge of what the device is intended to do (i.e., its functional specification). However, the majority of work in model-based reasoning about device behavior has focused on modeling a device in terms of general physical principles or intended functionality, but not both. In order to use both functional and behavioral knowledge in understanding a device design, it is crucial that the functional knowledge is represented in such a way that it has a clear interpretation in terms of actual behavior. We propose a new formalism for representing device functions with well-defined semantics in terms of actual behavior. We call the language CFRL (Causal Functional Representation Language). CFRL allows the specification of conditions that a behavior must satisfy, such as occurrence of a temporal sequence of expected events and causal relations among the events and the behavior of device components. We have used CFRL as the basis for a functional verification program which determines whether a behavior achieves an intended function.

Introduction

Understanding the design of an engineered device requires both knowledge of the general physical principles that determine the behavior of the device and knowledge of what the device is intended to do (i.e., its functional specification). However, the majority of work in model-based reasoning about device behavior has focused on modeling a device in terms of general physical principles *or* intended functionality, but not both. For example, most of the work in qualitative physics has been concerned with predicting the behavior of a device given its physical structure and knowledge of general physical principles. In that work, great importance has been placed on preventing

a pre-conceived notion of an intended function of the device from influencing the system's reasoning methods and representation of physical principles in order to guarantee a high level of "objective truth" in the predicted behavior. In contrast, in their work based on the FR (Functional Representation) language (Sembugamoorthy & Chandrasekaran 1986) (Keuneke 1986), Chandrasekaran and his colleagues have focused mostly on modeling a device in terms of what the device is intended to do and how those intentions are to be accomplished through causal interactions among components of the device.

Both types of knowledge, functional and behavioral, seem to be indispensable in fully understanding a device design. On the one hand, knowledge of intended function alone does not enable one to reason about what a device might do when it is placed in an unexpected condition or to infer the behavior of an unfamiliar device from its structure. On the other hand, knowledge of device structure and general physical principles may allow one to predict how the device will behave under a given condition, but without knowledge of the intended functions, it is impossible to determine if the predicted behavior is a desirable one, or what aspect of the behavior is significant.

In order to use both functional and behavioral knowledge in understanding a device design, it is crucial that the functional knowledge is represented in such a way that it has a clear interpretation in terms of actual behavior. Suppose, for example, that the function of a charge current controller is to prevent damage to a battery by cutting off the charge current when the battery is fully charged. To be able to determine whether this function is actually accomplished by an observed behavior of the device, the representation of the function must specify conditions that can be evaluated against the behavior. Such conditions might include occurrence of a temporal sequence of expected events and causal relations among the events and the components. Without a clear semantics given to a representation of functions in terms of actual behavior, it would be impossible to evaluate a design based on its predicted behavior and intended functions.

While it is important for a functional specification to have a clear interpretation in terms of actual behavior, it is also desirable for the language for specifying functions to be independent of any particular system used for simulation. Though there are a number of alternative

---

* The research by the first three authors is supported in part by the Advanced Research Projects Agency, ARPA Order 8607, monitored by NASA Ames Research Center under grant NAG 2-581, and by NASA Ames Research Center under grant NCC 2-537. Chandrasekaran's research is supported by the Advanced Research Projects Agency by means of AFOSR contract F-49620-89-C-0110 and AFOSR grant 89-0250.

methods for predicting behavior, such as numerical simulation with discrete time steps or qualitative simulation, a functional specification at some abstract level should be intuitively understandable without specifying a particular simulation mechanism. If a functional specification language was dependent on a specific simulation language or mechanism, a separate functional specification language would be needed for each different simulation language, which is clearly undesirable. What is needed is a functional specification language that has sufficient expressive power to support descriptions of the desired functions of a variety of devices. At the same time, the language should be clear enough so that for each simulation mechanism used, it can be given an unambiguous interpretation in terms of a simulated behavior.

An essential element in the description of a function is causality. In order to say that a device has achieved a function, which may be expressed as a condition on the state of the world, one must show not only that the condition is satisfied but also that the device has participated in the causal process that has brought about the condition. For example, when an engineer designs a thermostat to keep room temperature constant, the design embodies her idea about how the device is to work. In fact, the essential part of her knowledge of its function is the expected causal chain of events in which it will take part in achieving the goal. Thus, a representation formalism of functions must provide a means of expressing knowledge about such causal processes.

We have developed a new representational formalism for representing device functions called CFRL (Causal Functional Representation Language) that allows functions to be expressed in terms of expected causal chains of events. We have also provided the language with a well-defined semantics in terms of the type of behavior representation widely used in model-based, qualitative simulation. Finally, we have used CFRL as the basis for a functional verification program which determines whether a behavior achieves an intended function.

This paper is organized as follows: We first describe the representation of behavior over time in terms of which the semantics of CFRL will be defined and our assumptions about the modeling and simulation schemes that produce such a behavior description. We then present the CFRL language and define its semantics in terms of behavior. We close with a discussion and summary.

Behavior Representation

Before describing CFRL, we briefly describe the behavior representation in terms of which the semantics of CFRL will be defined. A physical situation is modeled as a collection of *model fragments*, each of which represents a physical object or a conceptually distinct physical phenomenon, such as a particular aspect of component behavior or a physical process. A model fragment representing a phenomenon specifies a set of conditions under which the phenomenon occurs and a set of consequences of the phenomenon. The conditions specify a set of instances of object classes that must exist and a set of relations that must hold among those objects and their attributes for the phenomenon to occur. The consequences specify the functional relations the phenomenon will cause to hold among the objects and their attributes.

Model fragments can represent phenomena as occurring continuously while the fragment's conditions hold or as events that occur instantaneously when the conditions become true. The consequences of a model fragment that represents an event are facts to be asserted resulting from the event, whereas the consequences of a model fragment that represents a continuous process are sentences (e.g., ordinary differential equations) which are true while the phenomena is occurring.

When there exists at time t a set of objects represented by model fragments m_i to m_j that satisfy the conditions of a model fragment m_0, we say that an instance of m_0 is active at that time. We will call m_i through m_j the *participants* of the m_0 instance.

Representation of physical knowledge in terms of model fragments is a generalization of the representation of physical processes and individuals in Qualitative Process Theory (Forbus 1984). There are several systems, including the Device Modeling Environment (DME) (Iwasaki & Low 1991) the Qualitative Process Engine (QPE) (Forbus 1989), and the Qualitative Process Compiler (QPC) (Crawford, Farquhar & Kuipers), that use similar representations for physical knowledge to predict the behavior of physical devices over time. Though the ways these systems actually perform prediction differ, the basic idea behind all of them is the following: For a given situation, the system identifies active model fragment instances by evaluating their conditions. The active instances give rise to equations representing the functional relations that must hold among variables as a consequence of the phenomena taking place. The equations are then used to determine the next state into which the device must move.

We assume that a behavior is a linear sequence of states. The output of a qualitative simulation system such as QPE, DME, and QPC is usually a tree or a graph of states. Each path through the graph represents a possible behavior over time. We will refer to such a path, i.e., a linear sequence of states, as a *trajectory*.

A state represents a situation in which the physical system being modeled is in at a particular time. "A particular time" here can be a time point or interval. We will not assume any specific model of time in this paper. The only assumptions about time that we make are: (1) the times associated with different states do not overlap; (2) when a state s_j immediately follows s_i in a behavior, there is no other "time" that falls between the times (periods) associated with s_i and s_j; and (3) every state has a unique successor (predecessor) unless it is the final (initial) state, in which case it has none.

In our modeling scheme, each state has a set of variable values and predicates that hold in the state. In addition, each state has a set of active model fragment instances representing the phenomena that are occurring in the state.

An Electrical Power System

This section presents the device that we will use throughout the rest of this paper as an example. The device is the electrical power system (EPS) aboard an Earth orbiting satellite (Lockheed 1984). A simplified schematic diagram of the EPS is shown in Figure 1. The main purpose of the EPS is to supply a constant source of electricity to the satellite's other subsystems. The solar array generates electricity when the satellite is in the sun, supplying power to the load and recharging the battery. The battery is a constant voltage source when it is charged between 6 and 30 ampere-hours. When the charge level is below 6 ampere-hours, the voltage output decreases as the battery discharges. When the charge level is above 30 ampere-hours, the voltage output increases as it is charged.

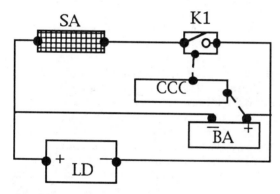

SA: Solar array
LD: Electrical load on board
BA: Rechargeable battery
CCC: Charge current controller
K1: Relay

Figure 1: An Electrical Power System.

Since the battery can be damaged when it is charged beyond its capacity, the charge current controller opens the relay when the voltage exceeds a threshold to prevent the battery from being over-charged. The controller senses the voltage via a sensor connected to the positive terminal of the battery. When the voltage is greater than 33.8 volts, the controller turns on the relay K1. When the relay is energized, it opens and breaks the electrical connection to prevent further charging of the battery, thereby switching the current source for the load from the solar array to the battery. When the relay is open or when an eclipse period begins, the battery's charge-level starts to decrease. When the battery becomes under-charged, the voltage decreases. When it reaches 31.0 volts, the CCC turns relay K1 off to close it.

CFRL

We now describe the syntax and semantics of CFRL. Figures 2 shows an example of the representation of a function of the EPS.

D_F: *?eps*: Electrical-power-system
C_F: Object-set: *?sun*: Sun   *?l*: electrical-load
       Conditions: T

G_F:
  (ALWAYS
    (AND
      (-> (AND (Shining-p ?sun)
             (Closed-p (Relay-component ?eps)))
         CPD1)
      (-> (OR (NOT (Shining-p ?sun))
             (Open-p (Relay-component ?eps)))
         CPD2)
      (-> (AND (> (Electromotive-force
                  (Battery-component ?eps))
                33.8)
             (Closed-p (Relay-component ?eps)))
         CPD3)
      (-> (AND (< (Electromotive-force
                  (Battery-component ?eps))
                31.0)
             (Open-p (Relay-component ?eps)))
         CPD4)))

Figure 2-a: Function F_1 of EPS

We consider a function to be an agent's belief about how an *object* is to be used in some *context* to achieve some *effect*. Thus, our representation of a function specifies the object, the context, and the effect. However, it does not specify an agent, which is implicitly assumed to be whoever is using the representation. Formally, a function is defined as follows:

Definition 1: Function

A function F is a triplet $\{D_F, C_F, G_F\}$, where:

D_F denotes the device of which F is a function.

C_F denotes the context in which the device is to function.

G_F denotes the functional goal to be achieved.

The device specification, D_F, specifies the class of the device and the symbol by which the device will be referred to in the rest of the definition of F. The example in Figure 2-a states that the function is of an Electrical-power-system which will be referred to as *?eps* in the rest of the definition.

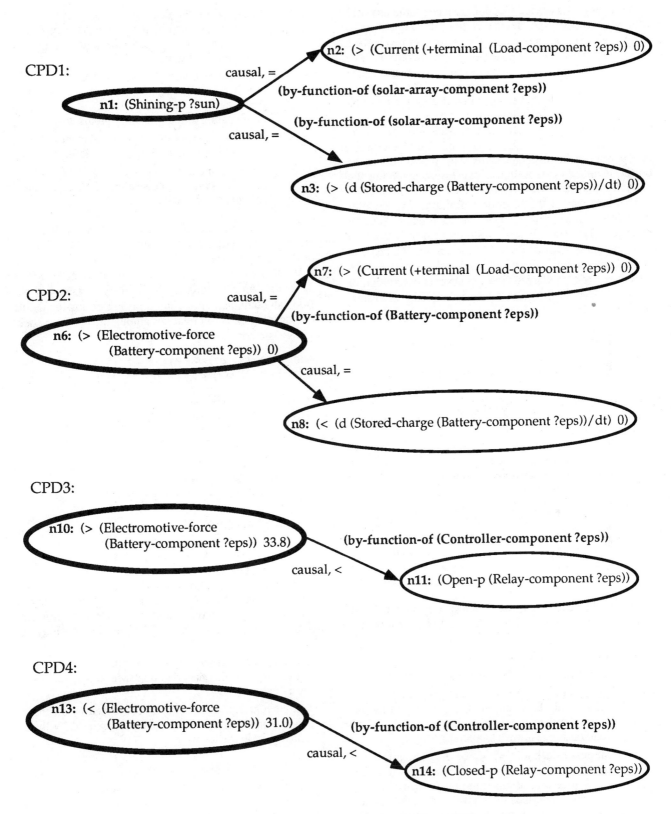

Figure 2-b: CPD's of Function F_1 of EPS.

The notion of a device function assumes some physical context in which the device is placed, and C_F is a specification of such a context. C_F consists of two parts, a set of objects and a set of conditions on those objects. For example, Figure 2-a states that there must exist an instance of Sun and an instance of electrical load. The conditions must hold throughout a behavior in order for the function to be verified in the behavior.

Formally, the *Object-set* of a C_F is a list of pairs *{var, type}*, where *var* is a symbol to be used in the description of *F* to refer to the object, and *type* is the type (class) of the object. *Conditions* is a logical expression involving the variables defined in the *Object-set* and D_F.

The third part of the function definition, G_F, specifies the behavior to be achieved by the device used in a specific manner. G_F of a function is represented as a Boolean combination of *Causal Process Descriptions* (CPDs) and conditions involving the variables defined in D_F and the *Object-set* of C_F. Each CPD is an abstract description of expected behavior in terms of a causal sequence of events. In the following, we formally define a CPD.

Causal Process Descriptions (CPD's)

Figure 2-b shows examples of CPD's which are part of the functional specification of the EPS. A CPD is a directed graph, in which each node describes a state and each arc describes a temporal and (optionally) a causal relation between states.

A node specifies a condition on a state. The condition is a logical sentence about the state of the world at some time using the variables defined in the D_F and C_F portions of the function. For example, the node n_1 in Figure 2-b states the condition that the sun be shining. One or more nodes in each CPD are distinguished as the initial node(s). In the figures, the initial nodes are indicated with a thick oval. A condition specified by a node can contain AND and OR as logical connectives. When the meaning is clear, we will use the name of a node to refer to the condition represented by the node.

The arcs in a CPD are directed and specify temporal and causal relations among nodes. An arc has the following attributes:

source: The node at the tail of the arc.

destination: The node at the head of the arc.

causal-flag: An indicator of whether the relationship between the states described by the source and destination nodes is causal. (The relationship is always temporal.)

temporal-relation: =, <, or ≤, indicating the temporal relation between the states described by the source and destination nodes. = means that the states described by the two nodes are to be the same state, < means the state described by the source node must strictly precede the state

described by the destination node, and ≤ means the state described by the source node must either be the same as or precede the state described by the destination state.

causal-justification: If an arc is "causal", one can attach a justification for the causal relation. A justification takes the form of a Boolean combination of the following predicates:

(**by-function-of** <model-fragment>),
(**with-participation-of** <model-fragment>).

The meaning of these predicates will be explained after we give a precise definition of a *causal relation* among nodes.

In order to refer to attributes of arcs, we will use the attribute name (e.g., source, destination, etc.) as a function of the arc as in "*source(a_1)*".

We will write $n_i \Rightarrow_c n_j$ when there is a causal arc from n_i to n_j. As a condition specified by a node can be a Boolean combination of conditions, the following defines the meaning of causal relations among them, where e_1, e_2, and e_3 are conditions:

a) $(\text{AND } e_1 \ e_2) \Rightarrow_c e_3 \quad \equiv$
$(\text{AND } (e_1 \Rightarrow_c e_3) (e_2 \Rightarrow_c e_3))$

b) $e_1 \Rightarrow_c (\text{AND } e_2 \ e_3) \quad \equiv$
$(\text{AND } (e_1 \Rightarrow_c e_2)(e_1 \Rightarrow_c e_3))$

c) $(\text{OR } e_1 \ e_2) \Rightarrow_c e_3 \quad \equiv$
$(\text{OR } (e_1 \Rightarrow_c e3) (e_2 \Rightarrow_c e_3))$

d) $e_1 \Rightarrow_c (\text{OR } e_2 \ e_3) \quad \equiv$
$(\text{OR } (e_1 \Rightarrow_c e_2) (e_1 \Rightarrow_c e_3))$

Semantics of a CPD

A CPD can be considered to be an abstract specification of a behavior. Unlike a trajectory, it does not specify every state or everything known about each state. It only specifies some of the facts that should be true during the course of the behavior and partial temporal/causal orderings among those facts. The intuitive meaning of a CPD is that:

• For each node in the CPD, there must be a state in the trajectory in which the condition specified by the node is satisfied, and

• For each pair of nodes directly connected by an arc, the causal and temporal relationships specified by the arc must exist in the trajectory.

In order for us to evaluate these conditions against a behavior, we must define their meanings in terms of the languages used to describe a (simulated or actual) behavior. In this paper, we will do so in terms of the behavior representation formalism described earlier.

However, note that CFRL itself is independent of the particular behavior representation language used, and that one would need to provide different definitions in order to evaluate functional specifications in CFRL against behaviors generated by a different scheme.

We first present the definition of a *causal dependency* relation between sentences in a trajectory and the *causality constraints* that can be associated with a CPD arc. We then define the requirements for a trajectory to match a CPD and for a trajectory to match a function goal. Finally, we use those definitions to define the requirements for a trajectory to achieve a function.

A few words about notation: We will attach *[s]* to a sentence to denote the sentence holds in state *s*. Therefore, *p[s]* means that *p* holds in state *s*. We will also associate a state with models and variables to denote sentences as follows:

m[s] : An instance of model fragment *m* is active in *s* .

v[s] : The value of variable *v* in *s*. (i.e., an axiom of the form *(= (value v s) c)* for some constant *c*.)

We will use the relations <, >, =, and ≤ to express temporal ordering among states in a trajectory. For example, for states s_1 and s_2 in a trajectory, "$s_1 < s_2$" means that s_1 strictly precedes s_2 in time. Note that ordering is total for states in a trajectory because a trajectory is a linear sequence of states, while the ordering is partial for states in a CPD.

Intuitively, we say p_2 is *causally dependent* on p_1 in trajectory *Tr*, written $p_1 \Rightarrow p_2$, when it can be shown that p_1 being true in *Tr* eventually leads to p_2 being true in *Tr*.

Definition 2: Causal Dependency

The causal dependency relation, $\Rightarrow$, is a binary relation between sentences in a trajectory with the following properties:

1. For all atomic sentences *p*, states *s*, model fragments *m*, and variables *v*:

   a) If $p[s_0], p[s_1], \ldots p[s]$ (i.e., if *p* is part of the initial conditions and is never changed), then $\emptyset \Rightarrow p[s]$. (And we say that *p[s]* is exogenous.)

   b) If model fragment *m* represents an event and asserts *p*, and if there exists a state s_j such that $s_j < s$, ~$p[s_j]$, $m[s_j]$, and $p[s_k]$ for all $k > j$ (i.e., *p* became true at some point before *s* due to *m*), then $m[s_j] \Rightarrow p[s]$.

   c) If model fragment *m* represents a continuous process and has *p* as a consequence, and if there exists a state s_j such that $s_j < s$, ~$p[s_j]$, $m[s_j]$, and $p[s_k]$ for all $k > j$ (i.e., *p* became true at some point before *s* due to *m*), then $m[s_j] \Rightarrow p[s]$.

   d) If model fragment *m* has *p* as a condition, then $p[s] \Rightarrow m[s]$.

   e) If *v* occurs in *p* as a term and *p* is not *v[s]*, then $v[s] \Rightarrow p[s]$.

   f) If *v* is an exogenous variable, $\emptyset \Rightarrow v[s]$.

   g) For all variables *v'* such that *v' -> v* is in the causal ordering[1] in *s* :

      (i) v'[s] $\Rightarrow$ v[s] ;

      (ii) If *p[s]* is the equation through which *v* depends on *v'*, then $p[s] \Rightarrow v[s]$.

   h) For all variables *v'* such that *v* and *v'* are in a feedback loop in the causal ordering in *s*:

      (i) v'[s] $\Rightarrow$ v[s] and v[s] $\Rightarrow$ v'[s] ;

      (ii) For each equation *p* such that *p* is part of the feedback loop and *v* appears in *p*, $p[s] \Rightarrow v[s]$.

   i) If s_1 is the state immediately following *s*, and *dv* is the time-derivative of *v* in *s*, then $dv[s] \Rightarrow v[s_1]$,

2. $\Rightarrow$ is transitive.

When $p_i \Rightarrow p_j$, we will say that p_j is *causally dependent* on p_i or that p_i *causes* p_j. Given statements $p[s_i]$ and $p[s_j]$ such that $p[s_i] \Rightarrow p[s_j]$, we call the causal sequence of statements starting from $p[s_i]$ and leading to $p[s_j]$ the *causal path* from $p[s_i]$ to $p[s_j]$.

Having defined the meaning of a causal relation among statements, we can now explain the meaning of the predicates used to justify causal arcs in a CPD.

Definition 3: Causality constraints

Given an arc *a* from node n_i to n_j in a CPD and a model fragment *m*, causality constraints of the following form can be associated with *a* :

a) *(by-function-of m)* -- meaning that the causal path from n_i to n_j includes a consequence of an instance of *m*;

b) *(with-participation-of m)* -- meaning that the causal path from n_i to n_j includes a consequence of an instance of a model fragment in which an instance of *m* participates.

These predicates do not imply specific commitments as to *how* the components participate in the causal process. They give the designer the capability of using whatever component has the desired function, independent of its particular mechanism.

We can now present the definitions on which verification of a trajectory with respect to a CPD is based.

Definition 4: Matching of a state and a node

A state *s* in a trajectory and a node *n* in a CPD are said to *match* if the condition specified in *n* is true in *s*.

Having defined the meaning of a causal relation among statements in a trajectory, we can now define the meaning

---

[1] Causal ordering is a technique for determining causal dependency relations among variables in a set of equations (Iwasaki & Simon 1986).

of the causal and temporal relations between linked nodes of a CPD.

Definition 5: Satisfying the constraints of an arc

If a is an arc from node n_i to n_j in a CPD, then the causal and temporal constraints of a are satisfied at states s_i and s_j if both of the following conditions are satisfied:

a) $s_i <$ (= or $\leq$) s_j when $n_i <$ (= or $\leq$) n_j, respectively.

b) If arc a is causal and if n_i and/or n_j are Boolean combinations of conditions, then the causal relation between n_i and n_j can be rewritten as a Boolean combination of causal relations of the form $e_i \Rightarrow_c e_j$, where e_i and e_j are atomic conditions. $e_i[s_i] \Rightarrow_c e_j[s_j]$ is satisfied if for every variable[2] v_i used in e_i and every variable v_j used in e_j, $v_i[s_i] \Rightarrow v_j[s_j]$ and the causal path from $v_i[s_i]$ to $v_j[s_j]$ satisfies the causal justification on a.

Definition 6: Matching of a CPD and a trajectory

Let T be a trajectory consisting of a linear sequence of m states, s_1 through s_m. Let CPD_1 be a CPD consisting of a set of nodes, N_1, and a set of arcs, A_1. CPD_1 and T are said to match iff all the following conditions are satisfied:

a) The initial nodes of CPD_1 match the initial state s_1 in T.

b) For each remaining node n in N_1, there exists a state in T that matches n such that for every arc a in A_1 from nodes n_i to n_j, the temporal and causal constraints specified by a are satisfied by the states matched to n_i and n_j.

Representation of the Functional Goal (G_F)

The functional goal of a function (denoted by G_F) is represented as an expression consisting of CPDs, conditions, quantifiers, and Boolean connectives. Nested expressions using connectives are allowed, but a quantifier cannot appear in the scope of another quantifier. Each CPD must appear in the scope of one and only one quantifier. There are two quantifiers, ALWAYS and SOMETIMES. Connectives are AND, OR, IMPLIES, and NOT. Syntactically, the connectives are used in the same way as ordinary logical connectives. The following are example G_F expressions:

> (ALWAYS (AND cpd_1 cpd_2 (OR cpd_3 cpd_4)))
> (OR (ALWAYS cpd_1)
>   (SOMETIMES (AND cpd_2 cpd_3)))
> (ALWAYS (NOT cpd_1))

---

[2] The variables used in CFRL can be different from the variables in terms of which the trajectory states are defined, since CFRL descriptions represent a device-level perspective, while states in the trajectory represent a component or physical process-level perspective. Correspondences between CPD variables and trajectory variables are made when the function is matched against a specific trajectory.

Quantifiers align the initial nodes of the CPDs in their scope as well as specify whether the described behavior must hold in every subsequence of the trajectory or only in some of them. The connectives and quantifiers are to be interpreted as specified in the following definition of matching a G_F and a trajectory.

Definition 7: Matching of a G_F and a trajectory

Let T be a trajectory consisting of a linear sequence of m states, s_1 through s_m; T_i denote subsequences of T from s_i through s_m; and <cpd-exp> denote a Boolean combination of CPD's and conditions. Then:

a) *(ALWAYS <cpd-exp>)* matches T iff <cpd-exp> matches T_i for each T_i ($i = 1$ to m).

b) *(SOMETIMES <cpd-exp>)* matches T iff <cpd-exp> matches T_i for some T_i ($i = 1$ to m).

c) *(AND <cpd-exp$_0$> <cpd-exp$_1$> ...)* matches T iff every conjunct matches T.

d) *(OR <cpd-exp$_0$> <cpd-exp$_1$> ...)* matches T iff at least one of the disjuncts matches T.

e) *(NOT <cpd-exp>)* matches T iff <cpd-exp> does not match T.

f) *(IMPLIES <cpd-exp$_0$> <cpd-exp$_1$>)* matches T iff <cpd-exp$_0$> does not match T or <cpd-exp$_1$> does match T.

g) Condition c matches T iff c is true in the initial state of T.

Finally, we complete the definition of the meaning of a function, as follows:

Definition 8: A trajectory achieving a function

A trajectory T achieves a function F when the condition specified in C_F holds throughout T and G_F matches T.

Discussion and Summary

In this paper, we have presented CFRL, a language for specifying an expected function of a device and defined its semantics in terms of the type of behavior representation widely used in model-based qualitative simulation. The language allows one to explicitly state the physical context in which the function is to be achieved and to describe the function as an expected causal sequence of events. Since the concept of causal interactions among components is essential to the understanding of a function, the language allows explicit representation of causal interactions and constraints on such interactions.

CFRL is based on the work on Functional Representation (Sembugamoorthy & Chandrasekaran 1986), and it is a further extension of the work presented in (Iwasaki & Chandrasekaran 1992). We have extended the expressive power of the function specification languages described in those papers and have provided a formal foundation for the semantics of the resulting language.

Franke (Franke 1991) also proposed matching design intent with simulated behavior. Unlike other work on functional representation, he focuses on representing the purpose of a design *modification* and not that of a device itself. He developed a representation scheme, called TED, in which he expresses the purpose for making a modification in a structure. TED's representation of a function can be a sequence (not necessarily a linear) of partial descriptions, which is matched against states in a sequence of qualitative states generated by QSIM. To prove that a function is achieved by a modification, he compares the behavior of the original structure and that of the modified structure.

Bradshaw and Young (Bradshaw & Young 1991) also represent the intended function in a manner similar to Functional Representation. They built a system called DORIS, which uses the knowledge generated by qualitative simulation for evaluating device behavior as well as for diagnosis and explanation.

The most important characteristic that distinguishes our work from those by Franke and by Bradshaw and Young is the central role causal knowledge plays in CFRL. We conjecture that causal relations are an essential part of functional knowledge, and that representation of functional knowledge must allow explicit description of the causal processes involved. Furthermore, verification of a function must ascertain that the expected causal chain of events take place, since the satisfaction of the functional goal alone does not necessarily indicate that the device is functioning as intended.

Because the semantics of CFRL is defined in terms of matching between a behavior and a functional specification, the language is immediately useful for the purpose of behavior verification. We have designed and implemented an algorithm that verifies a behavior produced by the DME system with respect to a function specified in CFRL as defined in this paper. Initial testing of the algorithm has included verifying the functional specifications of the EPS as given above. Care must be taken in designing such an algorithm to assure that exponential search is not required to find a match between a trajectory and a CPD. We are currently in the process of analyzing the computational complexity of the problem and our algorithm.

We expect formal functional specifications to have many uses throughout the life cycle of a device (Iwasaki et al. 1993). For example, in the early stages of the design process, designers often do "top down" design by incrementally introducing assumptions about device structure and causality relationships. Such design evolution could be expressed as incremental refinements of a CFRL functional specification. DME could assist a designer in this functional refinement process by assuring that each successive specification is indeed a refinement of its predecessor so that any device that satisfies the refinement also satisfies the predecessor.

References

Bradshaw J.A.; and Young R.M. 1991. Evaluating Design Using Knowledge of Purpose and Knowledge of Structure. *IEEE Expert* April.

Crawford J.; Farquhar A.; and Kuipers B. 1990. QPC : A Compiler from Physical Models to Qualitative Differential Equations. In *Proceedings of the Eight National Conference on Artificial Intelligence*.

Forbus K.D. 1984. Qualitative Process Theory. *Artificial Intelligence* 24.

Forbus, K. D. 1989. The Qualitative Process Engine. In *Readings in Qualitative Reasoning about Physical Systems*. Weld, D. S., and de Kleer, J. Eds. Morgan Kaufmann.

Franke D.W. 1991. Deriving and Using Descriptions of Purpose. *IEEE Expert* April.

Iwasaki Y.; and Simon H.A. 1986. Causality in device behavior. *Artificial Intelligence* 29:3-32.

Iwasaki Y.; and Low C.M. 1991. Model Generation and Simulation of Device Behavior with Continuous and Discrete Change. Technical Report, KSL, Dept. of Computer Science, Stanford University.

Iwasaki Y.; and Chandrasekaran B. 1992. Design Verification through Function and Behavior-Oriented Representations : Bridging the gap between Function and Behavior. In *Proceedings of the Second International Conference on Artificial Intelligence in Design*, Pittsburgh.

Iwasaki Y.; Fikes R.; Vescovi M.; and Chandrasekaran B. 1993. How Things are Intended to Work : Capturing Functional Knowledge in Device Design. In *Proceedings of the Thirteenth International Joint Conference on Artificial Intelligence*.

Keuneke A. 1989. Machine Understanding of Devices; Causal Explanation of Diagnostic Conclusions. Ph.D. thesis, Laboratory for AI Research, Dept. of Computer & Information Science, The Ohio State University.

Lockheed Missiles and Space Company. 1984. SMM Systems Procedure for Electrical Power Subsystem. doc #D889545A, SE-23, Vol. 3.

Sembugamoorthy V.; and Chandrasekaran B. 1986. Functional Representation of Devices and Compilation of Diagnostic Problem-Solving Systems. In Kolodner J.L. and Riesbeck C.K. (editors), *Experience, Memory and Reasoning*, Lawrence Erlbaum Associates, Hillsdale, NJ.

Model Simplification
by Asymptotic Order of Magnitude Reasoning

Kenneth Man-kam Yip*
Department of Computer Science
Yale University
P.O. Box 2158, Yale Station
New Haven, CT 06520.
yip-ken@cs.yale.edu

Abstract

One of the hardest problems in reasoning about a physical system is finding an approximate model that is mathematically tractable and yet captures the essence of the problem. Approximate models in science are often constructed by informal reasoning based on consideration of limiting cases, knowledge of relative importance of terms in the model, and understanding of gross features of the solution. We show how an implemented program can combine such knowledge with a heuristic simplification procedure and an inequality reasoner to simplify difficult fluid equations.

Introduction

Many important scientific and technological problems – from life in moving fluids, to drag on ship hulls, to heat transfer in reentering spacecrafts, to motion of air masses, and to evolution of galaxies – arise in connection with fluid equations. In general, these equations form a system of coupled nonlinear partial differential equations, which presents enormous analytical and numerical difficulties.

We are interested in making computers to help scientists and engineers analyze difficult fluid problems. By this we do not mean the development of new computer technology for more machine cycles and memory nor clever numerical methods nor better turbulence models nor techniques for automatic grid generation or body definition. Advances in all these areas will no doubt enhance the applicability of direct numerical approaches to fluid problems. A thorough understanding of the physics involved, however, requires much more than numerical solutions. The present computers generate too much low-level output and that makes the process of discovering interesting flow phenomena and tracking important structures tedious and error-prone.

Our goal is to build a new generation of smart, expert machines that know how to *represent* – not just present – the important features of the solutions so

that they can talk about them, reason about them, and use them to guide further experiments or build simplified mathematical models. Our programs are not big number-crunchers; nor are they symbolic calculators like Macsyma. Rather we view them as models of what some scientists do when they are investigating physical phenomena. We want our computer programs to simulate how scientists analyze these phenomena; they should be able to formulate approximate models, to perform qualitative and heuristic analyses, to provide a high-level executive summary of these analyses, and to give meaningful information that helps a scientist in understanding the phenomena.

One of the most important skills in developing understanding of a physical phenomenon is the ability to construct approximate models that are mathematically tractable but yet retain the essentials of the phenomenon. The scientist must exercise judgment in choices of what idealizations or approximations to make. Making such judgement often requires an understanding of the gross features of the solution, knowledge of the relative importance of terms in the model, and consideration of limiting cases. The purpose of this paper is to demonstrate how this kind of knowledge can be embodied in a computer program to tackle the difficult problem of model approximation in fluid dynamics.

Related works in AI include research in model selection and model generation. Addanki's *graph of models* guides the selection of an appropriate model from a set of handcrafted models [Addanki *et al.*, 1991]. Weld's *model sensitivity analysis* provides an alternative but more general approach to model selection [Weld, 1992]. Falkenhainer and Forbus automate model generation by composing suitable model fragments [Falkenhainer and Forbus, 1991].

Another relevant line of work concerns order of magnitude reasoning. Raiman introduces *order of magnitude scales* to extend the power of qualitative algebra [Raiman, 1991]. Weld explores related ideas in a technique called *exaggeration* in the context of comparative analysis [Weld, 1990]. Mavrovouniotis and Stephanopoulos combines numerical and symbolic or-

---
*Supported in part by NSF Grant CCR-9109567.

der of magnitude relations in analyzing chemical processes [Mavrovouniotis and Stephanopoulos, 1988].

Our project differs from these works in two major aspects. First, whereas all the previous works deal with either qualitative models or models specified by algebraic or ordinary differential equations, we analyze systems of nonlinear partial differential equations (PDEs). Second, we base our programs on a theory of asymptotic order of magnitude of *functions*, which we believe is closer to what applied mathematicians or fluid dynamicists use. [1]

The Task

We are interested in the task of model simplification, a part of a larger process of modeling-analysis-validation the purpose of which is to establish our confidence in the applicability of an approximate model in describing certain physical phenomenon. Model simplification takes three inputs: (1) a detailed model, (2) a description of the parameters, dependent variables, and independent variables of the model, and (3) essential physical effects to be included. Its output is one or more simplified models with constraints on parameters to represent the applicability of the models.

Detailed fluid models are usually available from standard textbooks and so are the physical meanings of parameters and variables. The description of variables is problem-dependent; it often includes their boundary values and estimated maximum order of magnitude. Knowledge of which physical effects are essential can come from experimental observations concerning the phenomenon. For instance, a model that neglects viscosity will predict zero drag on a solid body in steady flow; results diverge from physical reality.

In general, the simplified model is valid only under a range of parameter values. For instance, the approximation may require the Reynolds number to be large and conditions like this are represented by symbolic constraints among the parameters.

As our model problem, we use Prandtl's boundary layer approximation for high Reynolds number flows, which is probably the single most important approximation made in the history of fluid mechanics. For ease of exposition, we consider the case of two-dimensional, steady, incompressible flow over a flat plate (Fig. 1). The same technique will work for three-dimensional, unsteady flow over arbitrary bodies.

The detailed model is the 2D steady incompressible Navier-Stokes equations (Fig. 2). Equations (1) and (2) are the momentum equations, while (3) is the equation of continuity (or conservation of mass). The model is a system of three coupled PDEs containing three unknowns u, v, and p. The objective is to simplify the model in the limit $Re \to \infty$.

---

[1] The asymptotic theory is also commonly used in the analysis of algorithms.

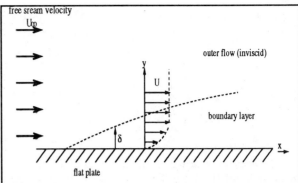

Figure 1: Boundary layer over a flat plate. The velocity gradient near the surface is large because of the no-slip condition. As one moves away from the surface, along the y-direction, the local velocity increases steadily as it approaches the free stream velocity.

$$u\frac{\partial u}{\partial x} + v\frac{\partial u}{\partial y} = -\frac{\partial p}{\partial x} + \frac{1}{Re}\left(\frac{\partial^2 u}{\partial x^2} + \frac{\partial^2 u}{\partial y^2}\right) \quad (1)$$

$$u\frac{\partial v}{\partial x} + v\frac{\partial v}{\partial y} = -\frac{\partial p}{\partial y} + \frac{1}{Re}\left(\frac{\partial^2 v}{\partial x^2} + \frac{\partial^2 v}{\partial y^2}\right) \quad (2)$$

$$\frac{\partial u}{\partial x} + \frac{\partial v}{\partial y} = 0 \quad (3)$$

Figure 2: Two-Dimensional steady, incompressible Navier Stokes Equations: u and v are the horizontal and normal components of the velocity, p is the pressure, and Re is the Reynolds number.

Prandtl's idea is that at high Reynolds numbers viscosity remains important near the body surface even if it could be disregarded everywhere else. As long as the "no-slip" condition holds, i.e., that fluids do not slip with respect to solids, there will be a thin layer around the body where rapid changes of velocity produce notable effects, despite the small coefficient $\frac{1}{Re}$. The layer in question is called *boundary layer*.

To get a feel of the type of reasoning involved in the derivation of the boundary layer approximation, we will quote a passage, slightly edited for our purpose, from a standard fluid dynamics textbook [Yih, 1977]:

To start with we assume that δ^*, the width of the boundary layer, is small compared with L, the length of the flat plate if Re is large. That means $\delta = \frac{\delta^*}{L} \ll 1$, and the range of the boundary layer y is δ. Since u and x are all of order of unity, equation (3) states that v is of order δ. Now the convective terms in equation (1) are all of $O(1)$. A glance at the viscous terms in equation (1) reveals that $\frac{\partial^2 u}{\partial x^2} \ll \frac{\partial^2 u}{\partial y^2}$ so that the first can be neglected and the viscous terms can be replaced by $\frac{1}{Re}\frac{\partial^2 u}{\partial y^2}$. Since in the boundary layer the viscous terms are of the same order of magnitude as the inertial terms, $\frac{1}{Re}\frac{\partial^2 u}{\partial y^2} = O(1)$; this shows that:

$$Re = O(\frac{1}{\delta^2}) \quad (4)$$

To see how p varies, we turn to equation (2). Again the term $\frac{\partial^2 v}{\partial x^2}$ can be neglected since it is added to a much larger term

$\frac{\partial^2 v}{\partial y^2}$. Then all the terms involving v are of $O(\delta)$. Hence the pressure variation with respect to y in the boundary layer is of $O(\delta^2)$, and can be neglected. Thus we take the pressure outside the boundary layer to be the pressure inside. But outside the boundary layer, the pressure distribution $p(x)$ is a function of x only. So we can replace the partial derivative of the pressure term by the total derivative. Thus the flow in the boundary layer is governed by:

$$u\frac{\partial u}{\partial x} + v\frac{\partial u}{\partial y} = -\frac{dp}{dx} + \frac{1}{Re}\frac{\partial^2 u}{\partial y^2} \qquad (5)$$

to which must be added the equation of continuity (3).

Much can be learned from this explanation. First, we notice that the simplified model consists of only two equations (5) and (3), and two unknowns u and v; the momentum equation (2) is discarded. The pressure p becomes a known boundary term to be given by the solution to the outer flow, the farfield approximation, where viscosity can be totally ignored. Second, the explanation refers to physical meanings of the terms in the equations; we have *inertia terms, convective terms, viscous terms,* and *pressure terms.* Third, the reasoning makes heavy use of order of magnitude estimate to justify the elimination of small terms. Fourth, given a few basic order of magnitude estimates (such as those of δ, u, and x), estimates for more complicated quantities involving partial derivatives are automatically inferred. In particular, it derives the important conclusion that the dependency of the pressure on y, i.e., the variation across the thin boundary layer, can be neglected at this level of approximation. Finally, by balancing the inertia terms and the viscous terms, it obtains a quantitative condition on the range of parameter values Re, equation (4), for which the approximation is valid.

Characteristics of the Problem Domain
Some Terminology

Fluids obey Newton's laws of motion. The momentum equations (1) and (2) are just examples of Newton's 2nd Law ($F = ma$). In fluid mechanics, it is customary to have the acceleration or the inertia terms written on the left hand side of the equation, while the remaining force terms on the right. See Fig. 3.

Figure 3: Meaning of terms in the 2D steady incompressible Navier-Stokes Equations.

Since the motion of a fluid particle can change with both time and space, the inertia consists of two parts:

the **local acceleration** (i.e., rate of change of velocity with respect to time), and the **convective acceleration** (i.e., product of velocity and the velocity gradient).

A **steady flow** is one in which the local acceleration is zero. The applied forces on the fluid can be divided into two types: (1) **surface forces**, caused by molecular attractions, include pressure and friction forces due to viscosity, and (2) **body forces** resulting from external force fields like gravity or magnetic field. It is often convenient to define the pressure term to include gravity (i.e., $p + \rho gy$, where ρ is density of fluid, g gravitational constant, and y is the vertical coordinate). When the divergence of the fluid velocity is zero (equation (3)), the flow is called **incompressible**, which just means that the mass of fluid inside a given volume is always conserved.

The momentum equations express a balance of opposing forces on the fluid: the inertia forces keep the fluid moving steadily against the effects of pressure gradient and viscous forces. **Reynolds number** is simply the ratio between the inertia and the viscous forces; it is an indication of the relative importance of viscosity – actually the unimportance since high Reynolds numbers are associated with slightly viscous flow.

Ontology

Description of fluid motion involves a variety of quantities: (1) the fundamental quantities: time, space, and mass, (2) the usual dynamical quantities from particle mechanics such as velocity, acceleration, force, pressure, and momentum, (3) quantities that are less familiar but can be easily derived from the more basic ones: velocity gradient and pressure gradient, convective acceleration, viscous shearing forces, and turbulent stress, (4) dimensionless parameters such as Reynolds number, and (5) scale parameters, such as δ, which determine the length, time, or velocity scale of interest.

Asymptotic Order of Magnitude of Functions

Flows often vary widely in character depending on the relative magnitude of certain parameters or variables. For instance, the flow near a jet may be highly irregular, but at a large distance the mean velocity profile may become quite regular; this is the so-called farfield approximation. Another example is the Reynolds number. Small Reynolds number are often associated with laminar (smooth) flow, whereas large Reynolds numbers flow are quite erratic. So it should not be surprising that most useful approximations in fluid mechanics (and in many other branches of physics) are dependent on a limit process, the approximation becoming increasingly accurate as a parameter tends to some critical value. In our model problem, for example, we would be interested in how the boundary layer velocities u and v behave as Re becomes large.

More generally, we will consider the **asymptotic behavior** of a function $f(\epsilon)$ as ϵ approaches some critical value ϵ_0. Without loss of generality, we can assume $\epsilon_0 = 0$, since translation $(\epsilon - \epsilon_0)$ and inversion $(\frac{1}{\epsilon})$ can be used to handle any non-zero finite and infinite limiting values.

There are several ways to describe the asymptotic behavior of a function with varying degrees of precision. For instance, we could describe the limiting value $f(\epsilon)$ as $\epsilon \to 0$ qualitatively, i.e., whether it is bounded, vanishing, or infinite. Or, we could describe the limiting value *quantitatively* by giving a numerical value for the bound. But it is most useful to describe the *shape of the function qualitatively* as a limit is approached. The description uses the order symbols O ("big oh"), o ("little oh"), and $\sim$ ("asymptotically equal") to express the relative magnitudes of two functions.

Definition 1 $f(\epsilon) = O(g(\epsilon)), \epsilon \to 0$ if $\lim_{\epsilon \to 0} \frac{f(\epsilon)}{g(\epsilon)} = K$ where K is a finite number.

Definition 2 $f(\epsilon) = o(g(\epsilon)), \epsilon \to 0$ if $\lim_{\epsilon \to 0} \frac{f(\epsilon)}{g(\epsilon)} = 0$

Definition 3 $f(\epsilon) \sim g(\epsilon), \epsilon \to 0$ if $\lim_{\epsilon \to 0} \frac{f(\epsilon)}{g(\epsilon)} = 1$

Typically, we will use a convenient set of simple functions inside an order symbol; they are called the **gauge functions** because they are used to describe the shape of an arbitrary function in the neighborhood of a critical point. Common gauge functions include the powers and inverse powers of ϵ. For example, $\sin(\epsilon) = O(\epsilon)$ as $\epsilon \to 0$. For more complicated problems, logarithms and exponentials of powers of ϵ may also be used.

The asymptotic order of magnitude must be distinguished from the numerical order of magnitude. If $f = 10^6 g$, then f and g differ by 6 numerical orders of magnitude, but they are still of the same asymptotic order. However, in a physical problem the variables are normally scaled in such as way that the proportionality constant K will be close to 1.

Below we list some useful rules of operation on order symbols:

1. $O(fg) = O(f)O(g)$
2. $O(f + g) = \max(O(f), O(g))$
3. $O(f) + o(f) = O(f)$
4. $o(fg) = O(f)o(g) = o(f)o(g)$
5. If $f = O(g)$, then $\int_0^\epsilon f(t)dt = O(\int_0^\epsilon \mid g(t) \mid dt)$ as $\epsilon \to 0$.

Order relations cannot in general be differentiated. That is, if $f = O(g)$, then it is not generally true that $f' = O(g')$. However, using the definition of the total differential of a function $f(x, y)$, $df = \underbrace{\frac{\partial f}{\partial x}dx}_{df\text{-}x} + \underbrace{\frac{\partial f}{\partial y}dy}_{df\text{-}y}$ where df-x and df-y are the partial differentials, we can derive some useful rules involving partial derivatives:

1. $O(\frac{\partial f}{\partial x})O(dx) = O(df\text{-}x)$
2. $O(\frac{\partial f}{\partial y})O(dy) = O(df\text{-}y)$

3. $O(df) = \max(O(df\text{-}x), O(df\text{-}y))$

Theory of Simplification

The basic idea in simplification is to identify small terms in an equation, drop these terms, solve the simplified equation, and check for consistency. But this does not always work. Consider the following simple polynomial:

$$3\epsilon^2 x^3 + x^2 - \epsilon x - 4 = 0$$

in the limit $\epsilon \to 0$. We might naively drop the cubic and the linear terms because their coefficients are small. But if we do that, we only get two roots $x = \pm 2$, losing the third root. Thus, the process of simplification leads to a loss of important information.

What went wrong? The problem is that terms that appear small are not really small. The missing root depends inversely on ϵ in such a way that the cubic term is not negligible even its coefficient becomes small. To fix this problem, we introduce three concepts: an **undetermined gauge**, a **significant gauge**, and a **maximal set**. To begin, we will assume $x = O(\epsilon^n)$ where n is still undetermined – hence the name undetermined gauge. The order of each term is then:

$$\underbrace{3\epsilon^2 x^3}_{O(\epsilon^{3n+2})} + \underbrace{x^2}_{O(\epsilon^{2n})} - \underbrace{\epsilon x}_{O(\epsilon^{n+1})} - \underbrace{4}_{O(1)} = 0$$

To determine the relative importance of terms, we use the heuristic that we only retain the smallest number of terms that will balance the equation. Since we must allow the situation where two or more terms may have the same asymptotic order, we group terms into equivalence classes by the relation $\sim$. A maximal set is any such class that is not smaller than any other classes. As an example, the cubic polynomial above has four maximal sets each containing one term. The heuristic can then be stated as follows:

Heuristic of minimal complication (or Method of Dominant Balance):
If the equation has two or more maximal sets, balance two of them; these two maximal sets are called dominant. Assume the remaining sets are negligible. Self-consistent choices of dominant maximal sets correspond to significant simplified equations.

Applying this heuristic to the polynomial, we get six cases to consider. For instance, one possibility is that the first two terms are dominant, i.e., $\epsilon^2 x^3 \sim x^2 \gg \epsilon x, 4$. Equating the two undetermined gauges, we get $3n + 2 = 2n$ and this implies $n = -2$. The remaining terms are $O(\epsilon^{-1})$ and $O(1)$, which is consistent with the assumption that the first two terms are dominant. So this possibility is included. On the other hand, if we assume $\epsilon^2 x^3 \sim \epsilon x \gg x^2, 4$, we get $n = -\frac{1}{2}$. But then $x^2 = O(\epsilon^{-1}) \gg O(\epsilon^{\frac{1}{2}})$, violating the assumption that it should be much smaller than the first term. This possibility must be excluded. A similar analysis shows that only one more possibility, when the second and fourth terms are dominant, i.e., $n = 0$, is self-consistent. So the heuristic concludes that we should consider *two* simplified polynomials:

$$3\epsilon^2 x^3 + x^2 = 0 \Rightarrow x \sim \frac{1}{3\epsilon^2}$$

and

$$x^2 - 4 = 0 \Rightarrow x \sim \pm 2$$

The values of ϵ^n for which we get self-consistent dominant maximal sets are called **significant gauges**. The balancing of the dominant maximal sets produces simplified equations that correspond to qualitatively significant asymptotic behaviors.

Implementation: The Details

Our method has two main parts: (1) a preprocessor, which given the input specification of a model, creates internal representations of quantities, equations, and a constraint network connecting the quantities, and (2) a model-simplifier, which finds all the self-consistent approximate models by the heuristic of minimal complication. The model-simplifier relies on three procedures – a constraint propagator, a graph searcher, and an inequality bounder – to determine the order of magnitude of quantities and their relationships. We describe each of these five pieces in turn.

The Preprocessor

The problem specification is defined by the macro `defmodel`, which takes a name, a list of quantity descriptions, the momentum and continuity equations in infix form, relations defining external pressure and free stream velocities, and a list of estimated orders of magnitude.

```
(defmodel prandtl-boundary-layer-with-pressure-gradient
  (with-independent-variables
    ((x :lower-bound 0 :upper-bound 1
        :physical-features '(space streamwise))
     (y :lower-bound 0 :physical-features '(space transverse)))
    ...
    ;;similar descriptions for U, V, P, Re, etc.;;
    ...
  (with-essential-terms
    (viscous inertia)
    (with-equations
      ((streamwise-momentum-equation
        (U * (d U / d x) + V * (d U / d y)
        = - (d P / d x) + (d2 U / d2 x) / Re + (d2 U / d2 y) / Re))
       (transverse-momentum-equation
        (U * (d V / d x) + V * (d V / d y)
        = - (d P / d y) + (d2 V / d2 x) / Re + (d2 V / d2 y) / Re))
       (continuity
        ((d U / d x) + (d V / d y) = 0)))
    (with-relations
      (constant U 1)
      (constant x 1)
      (constant y 'delta)
      (constant P0 1)))))))
```

Quantities

Quantities are represented by CLOS objects. They are divided into four types: (1) independent variables (space and time), (2) dependent variables (e.g.,

pressure, velocity), (3) controllable parameters (e.g., Reynolds number), and (4) scale parameters (e.g., length scale δ). Each quantity has slots for its upper bound, lower bound, boundary values, physical features, and relations which other quantities. A dependent variable contains additional information about its dependency on the independent variables. For example, the dependent variable U depends on both x and y.

The input specifies nine quantities – $x, y, U, V, U\text{-inf}, P0, P, Re$, and *delta*. But a total of 60 quantities will be created. The reason is that for each dependent variable, quantities corresponding to its total differential, partial differentials, and derivatives are also automatically generated. For instance, the dependent variable U generates 5 additional quantities: dU, $dU\text{-}x$, $dU\text{-}y$, $\frac{\partial U}{\partial x}$, and $\frac{\partial U}{\partial y}$. Quantities are also generated for each term in the equations and relations. An example would be the dependent variable $d2Udx2/RE$ corresponding to the viscous term $\frac{1}{Re}\left(\frac{\partial^2 u}{\partial x^2}\right)$.

Input quantities have associated physical features such as space, velocity, and pressure. These features are used to determine the physical meaning of derived quantities by simple rewrite rules. For instance, a velocity quantity differentiated by a space quantity gives a velocity-gradient quantity. The physical meaning of a term in the equation is determined in a similar fashion. For example, a term that is the product of a velocity quantity and a velocity gradient represents the convective inertia term.

A Constraint Language

Equations involving quantities are represented as constraints so that when all but one quantities are known the value of the remaining one can be computed in terms of the others. Our constraint language has 6 primitives:

1. The equality constraint, `(== q1 q2)`, asserts that $O(q1) = O(q2)$. Example: the continuity equation (3) is represented by `(== dudx dvdy)`.
2. The multiplier constraint, `(multiplier q1 q2 q3)`, specifies that the quantities q1, q2 and q3 must be related by the equation $O(q1) \times O(q2) = O(q3)$. Example: `(multiplier u dudx ududx)`.
3. The maximum constraint, `(maximum q1 q2 q3)`, specifies that $O(q3) = \max(O(q1), O(q2))$. Example: `(maximum du-x du-y du)`.
4. The variation constraint, `(variation f x df-x)`, captures the inference that when the partial differential of a function $f(x, y)$ with respect to x is much less than the value of f at its outer boundary, then f is asymptotically equal to its boundary value. Symbolically, $df\text{-}x = o(f_0) \Rightarrow O(f) = O(f_0)$, where f_0 is the value of f at its outer boundary in the x-direction.
5. The total-variation constraint, `(total-variation f df)`, specifies: $O(df) = O(\text{upperbound}(f) - \text{lowerbound}(f))$.
6. The constant constraint, `(constant q v)`, just says that $O(q) = v$.

The constraint language allows simple inferences about quantities to be made. For instance, using the continuity equation (3) and the known order of magnitudes for the quantities U, x, and y, the value for V is automatically deduced.

Qualitative Order Relations

An important type of inference is the determination of the ordering relationship between two quantities. For instance, in order to drop a term A, the system has to show that A is much smaller than another quantity B in the equation. For models involving a few scale parameters, such as our model problem, the relationship can be determined by relatively simple algebraic manipulations. But for quantities involving three or more scale parameters, the algebra can be quite complicated.

A simpler inference technique is to represent the order relationships explicitly in a directed graph whose nodes are quantities and edges are labeled order relations, and to use a breadth-first search to find paths between quantities. The idea is similar to Simmons' graph search in a quantity lattice [Simmons, 1986], but we generalize it to include symbolic factors in the order relations. Let's look at an example (Fig. 4a). We have 4 quantities: A, B, C, and D. Assume δ is a small parameter. The following relations are also known: (1) $O(A) = O(B)$, (2) $O(B) = \delta O(D)$, and (3) $O(A) = \delta O(C)$. To show that $O(C) = O(D)$, we find the shortest path between them, collecting the symbolic factor of each edge of the path. The symbolic factors are divided into two groups: the $\ll$-factors, and the $\gg$-factors depending on whether the edge is labeled $\ll$ or $\gg$. In the example, the $\ll$-factors consists of one factor δ, while the $\gg$-factors consists of one factor $\frac{1}{\delta}$.

The inference procedure can also handle partial information. For instance, in the graph shown in Fig. 4b, it will correctly conclude that $E \gg H$ even it is not told what the symbolic factor of edge $F \gg G$ is.

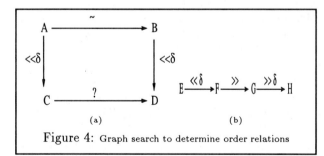

$$\text{(a)} \qquad \text{(b)}$$

Figure 4: Graph search to determine order relations

Inequality Bounder

The constraint propagator and the graph searcher are fast but they cannot determine more subtle ordering relationships. For instance, given $\delta^2 = O(\frac{1}{Re})$ and $\delta \ll 1$, they can't deduce that $\frac{1}{Re} \times \frac{1}{\delta} \ll 1$. This problem in its general form is equivalent to the satisfiability of a set of inequality constraints. To solve this problem, we use a version of the **sup-inf** bounding algorithm first proposed by [Bledsoe, 1975] and extended by [Brooks, 1981] and [Sacks, 1987] to deal with nonlinear inequalities. Our algorithm is simpler because there is no need to deal with nonmonotonic functions such as the trigonometric functions.

Simplification Algorithm

The purpose of the simplification algorithm is to search for all self-consistent simplified models corresponding to a detailed input model. A simplified model is **self-consistent** if the terms neglected are consistent with the dominant balance assumptions, and it contains the essential terms specified by the input. The algorithm determines the maximal sets for each momentum equation, balances all possible pairs of maximal sets, and eliminates the inconsistent ones. It terminates when each momentum equation has only one maximal set.

The principal steps of simplification are:

1. If the model has no unsimplified momentum equation, then return the model.
2. Otherwise, pick the first unsimplified momentum equation and consider all possible pairwise dominant balances.
3. Propagate the effects of the dominant balance and record any assumptions made on parameters due to the balance.
4. If the resulting model is self-consistent, call simplification recursively on it. Otherwise, return nil.

The algorithm will terminate because during each call of simplification, the number of maximal sets is reduced by at least one. So each recursive call will return either a simplified model or nil if the partially simplified model is not self-consistent.

Performance Trace

The following script shows how the program produces the boundary layer approximation for our model problem. The problem generates 60 quantities and 65 constraints; it takes about 60 secs real time on a Sparc 330.

The program builds `model-1` according to the input description. Each momentum equation has three maximal sets. The program simplifies the transverse momentum equation by balancing its maximal sets; there are three possible balances. The first choice – balancing viscous stress and pressure gradient – is not consistent.

```
> (search-simplifications *model*)

Making <MODEL-2: PRANDTL-BOUNDARY-LAYER> from
<MODEL-1: PRANDTL-BOUNDARY-LAYER>...
Balancing two terms:
 D2VDY2/RE (VISCOUS STRESS TRANSVERSE)
 DPDY (PRESSURE-GRADIENT)
in TRANSVERSE-MOMENTUM-EQUATION
with 1 parameter assumption:
```

```
(<< RE (^ DELTA -2))
```
The model is not self-consistent because the simplified equations do not contain the essential INERTIA term.

The second choice – balancing viscous stress and inertia – generates a consistent model `model-3`. Since `model-3` is not completely simplified, the program goes on to simplify its streamwise equation, which now has two maximal sets. So there is only one balancing choice; the result is a consistent model `model-4`. The program also finds the correct condition on the Reynolds number.

```
Making <MODEL-4: PRANDTL-BOUNDARY-LAYER> from
<MODEL-3: PRANDTL-BOUNDARY-LAYER>...
Balancing two terms:
D2UDY2/RE (VISCOUS STRESS TRANSVERSE)
DPDX (PRESSURE-GRADIENT)
in STREAMWISE-MOMENTUM-EQUATION
with 1 parameter assumption:
(= RE (^ DELTA -2))`
<MODEL-4: PRANDTL-BOUNDARY-LAYER> is self-consistent.
```

The final choice of balance for the transverse equation is inconsistent. Let's check that `model-4` has the correct boundary layer equations (equations (5) and (3)):

```
> (model-simplified-equations model-4)

((U * (D U / D X)) + (V * (D U / D Y)) =
    - (D P / D X) + ((D2 U / D2 Y) / RE))
((D U / D X) + (D V / D Y) = 0)
```

Evaluation

The program has been tested on several problems including ODEs and PDEs representing flows in turbulent wake and turbulent jet. The turbulent wake problem, for instance, has 89 quantities and 112 constraints; it takes the program about 90 secs real time to find two simplified models.

When does the simplification heuristic fail?

There are equations for which balancing two maximal sets does not give any self-consistent approximations. For instance, the ODE $\frac{dy}{dx} - \frac{y}{x} = \frac{\cos x}{x^2}$ requires a 3-term balance because all the pairwise balances are inconsistent. Our algorithm incorporates a systematic search starting from 2-term balance until a self-consistent model is found.

How good are the approximate models?

There is no simple answer to this question. It is known that solutions to a self-consistent approximate model derived by dominant balances can be grossly inaccurate. A simple example is an ill-conditioned set of linear algebraic equations, in which a small change in the coefficients can lead to a large change in the solution vector. The situation for PDEs is much worse because, except in rare cases, it is not known whether the approximate model has a solution at all or whether the solution if exists will be unique. The strongest claim one can made seems to be this: An approximate model

that is *not* self-consistent is certainly a poor approximation. In practice, an approximate model is validated by subjecting its predictions to experimental and numerical checks. In fact, there still exists no theorem which speaks to the validity and accuracy of Prandtl's boundary layer approximation, but ninety years of experimental results leave little doubt of its validity and its value.

Conclusion

We have demonstrated how a heuristic simplification procedure can be combined with knowledge of asymptotic order of functions, relative importance of terms, and gross physical features of the solution to capture certain aspects of the informal reasoning that applied mathematicians and fluid dynamicists use in finding approximate models – informal because the approximation is done without firm error estimates. The key to the simplification method is to examine limiting cases where the model becomes singular (i.e., when the naively simplified model has a different qualitative behavior from the original model). This idea of simplification by studying the most singular behaviors is very general: it comprises the core of many powerful approximation and analysis techniques that have proven to be extremely useful in reasoning about behaviors of complicated physical systems.

References

Addanki, S; Cremonini, R; and Penberthy, J.S. 1991. Graphs of models. *Artificial Intelligence* 51.

Bledsoe, W.W. 1975. A new method for proving certain presburger formulas. In *Proceedings IJCAI-75*.

Brooks, R.A. 1981. Symbolic reasoning among 3d models and 2d images. *Artificial Intelligence* 17.

Falkenhainer, B. and Forbus, K.D. 1991. Compositional modelinng: finding the right model for the job. *Artificial Intelligence* 51.

Mavrovouniotis, M.L. and Stephanopoulos, G. 1988. Formal order-of-magnitude reasoning in process engineering. *Computer Chemical Engineering* 12.

Raiman, Olivier 1991. Order of magnitude reasoning. *Artificial Intelligence* 51(1).

Sacks, Elisha P. 1987. Hierarchical reasoning about inequalities. In *American Association for Artificial Intelligence*.

Simmons, Reid 1986. Commonsense arithmetic reasoning. In *Proceedings AAAI-86*.

Weld, D.S. 1990. Exaggeration. *Artificial Intelligence* 43.

Weld, D.S. 1992. Reasoning about model accuracy. *Artificial Intelligence* 56.

Yih, Chia-shun 1977. *Fluid Mechanics*. West River Press.

Representation
and Reasoning

Abduction As Belief Revision:
A Model of Preferred Explanations

Craig Boutilier and Verónica Becher
Department of Computer Science
University of British Columbia
Vancouver, British Columbia
CANADA, V6T 1Z2
email: cebly,becher@cs.ubc.ca

Abstract

We propose a natural model of abduction based on the revision of the epistemic state of an agent. We require that explanations be sufficient to induce belief in an observation in a manner that adequately accounts for factual and hypothetical observations. Our model will generate explanations that *nonmonotonically predict* an observation, thus generalizing most current accounts, which require some deductive relationship between explanation and observation. It also provides a natural preference ordering on explanations, defined in terms of normality or plausibility. We reconstruct the Theorist system in our framework, and show how it can be extended to accommodate our predictive explanations and semantic preferences on explanations.

1 Introduction

A number of different approaches to abduction have been proposed in the AI literature that model the concept of abduction as some sort of deductive relation between an explanation and the explanandum, the "observation" it purports to explain (e.g., Hempel's (1966) *deductive-nomological* explanations). Theories of this type are, unfortunately, bound to the unrelenting nature of deductive inference. There are two directions in which such theories must be generalized. First, we should not require that an explanation deductively entail its observation (even relative to some background theory). There are very few explanations that do not admit exceptions. Second, while there may be many competing explanations for a particular observation, certain of these may be relatively implausible. Thus we require some notion of preference to chose among these potential explanations.

Both of these problems can be addressed using, for example, probabilistic information (Hempel 1966; de Kleer and Williams 1987; Poole 1991; Pearl 1988): we might simply require that an explanation render the observation sufficiently probably and that most likely explanations be preferred. Explanations might thus *nonmonotonic* in the sense that α may explain β, but $\alpha \wedge \gamma$ may not (e.g., $P(\beta|\alpha)$ may be sufficiently high while $P(\beta|\alpha \wedge \gamma)$ may not). There have been proposals to address these issues in a more qualitative manner using

"logic-based" frameworks also. Peirce (see Rescher (1978)) discusses the "plausibility" of explanations, as do Quine and Ullian (1970). Consistency-based diagnosis (Reiter 1987; de Kleer, Mackworth and Reiter 1990) uses abnormality assumptions to capture the context dependence of explanations; and preferred explanations are those that minimize abnormalities. Poole's (1989) assumption-based framework captures some of these ideas by explicitly introducing a set of default assumptions to account for the nonmonotonicity of explanations.

We propose a semantic framework for abduction that captures the spirit of probabilistic proposals, but in a qualitative fashion, and in such a way that existing logic-based proposals can be represented as well. Our account will take as central subjunctive conditionals of the form $A \Rightarrow B$, which can be interpreted as asserting that, if an agent were to believe A it would also believe B. This is the cornerstone of our notion of explanation: if believing A is sufficient to induce belief in B, then A *explains* B. This determines a strong, *predictive* sense of explanation. Semantically, such conditionals are interpreted relative to an ordering of plausibility or normality over worlds. Our conditional logic, described in earlier work as a representation of belief revision and default reasoning (Boutilier 1991; 1992b; 1992c), has the desired nonmonotonicity and induces a natural preference ordering on sentences (hence explanations). In the next section we describe our conditional logics and the necessary logical preliminaries. In Section 3, we discuss the concept of explanation, its epistemic nature, and its definition in our framework. We also introduce the notion of *preferred explanations*, showing how the same conditional information used to represent the defeasibility of explanations induces a natural preference ordering. To demonstrate the expressive power of our model, in Section 4 we show how Poole's Theorist framework (and Brewka's (1989) extension) can be captured in our logics. This reconstruction explains semantically the non-predictive and *paraconsistent* nature of explanations in Theorist. It also illustrates the correct manner in which to augment Theorist with a notion of predictive explanation and how one should capture semantic preferences on explanations. These two abilities have until now been unexplored in this canonical abductive framework. We conclude by describing directions for future research, and how consistency-based diagnosis also fits in our system.

2 Conditionals and Belief Revision

The problem of revising a knowledge base or belief set when new information is learned has been well-studied in AI. One of the most influential theories of belief revision is the *AGM theory* (Alchourrón, Gärdenfors and Makinson 1985; Gärdenfors 1988). If we take an agent to have a (deductively closed) belief set K, adding new information A to K is problematic if $K \vdash \neg A$. Intuitively, certain beliefs in K must be retracted before A can be accepted. The AGM theory provides a set of constraints on acceptable belief revision functions $*$. Roughly, using K_A^* to denote the belief set resulting when K is revised by A, the theory maintains that the least "entrenched" beliefs in K should be given up and then A added to this *contracted* belief set.

Semantically, this process can be captured by considering a *plausibility ordering* over possible worlds. As described in (Boutilier 1992b; Boutilier 1992a), we can use a family of logics to capture the AGM theory of revision. The modal logic CO is based on a propositional language (over variables **P**) augmented with two modal operators $\Box$ and $\overleftarrow{\Box}$. L_{CPL} denotes the propositional sublanguage of this bimodal language L_B. The sentence $\Box \alpha$ is read as usual as "α is true at all *equally or more plausible* worlds." In contrast, $\overleftarrow{\Box} \alpha$ is read "α is true at all *less plausible* worlds."

A CO-model is a triple $M = \langle W, \leq, \varphi \rangle$, where W is a set of worlds with valuation function φ and $\leq$ is a plausibility ordering over W. If $w \leq v$ the w is at least as plausible as v. We insist that $\leq$ be transitive and connected (that is, either $w \leq v$ or $v \leq w$ for all w, v). CO-structures consist of a totally-ordered set of *clusters* of worlds, where a cluster is simply a maximal set of worlds $C \subseteq W$ such that $w \leq v$ for each $w, v \in C$ (that is, no extension of C enjoys this property). This is evident in Figure 1(b), where each large circle represents a cluster of equally plausible worlds. Satisfaction of a modal formula at w is given by:

1. $M \models_w \Box \alpha$ iff for each v such that $v \leq w$, $M \models_v \alpha$.

2. $M \models_w \overleftarrow{\Box} \alpha$ iff for each v such that not $v \leq w$, $M \models_v \alpha$.

We define several new connectives as follows: $\Diamond \alpha \equiv_{df} \neg \Box \neg \alpha$; $\overleftarrow{\Diamond} \alpha \equiv_{df} \neg \overleftarrow{\Box} \neg \alpha$; $\overset{\leftrightarrow}{\Box} \alpha \equiv_{df} \Box \alpha \wedge \overleftarrow{\Box} \alpha$; and $\overset{\leftrightarrow}{\Diamond} \alpha \equiv_{df} \neg \overset{\leftrightarrow}{\Box} \neg \alpha$. It is easy to verify that these connectives have the following truth conditions: $\Diamond \alpha$ ($\overleftarrow{\Diamond} \alpha$) is true at a world if α holds at some more plausible (less plausible) world; $\overset{\leftrightarrow}{\Box} \alpha$ ($\overset{\leftrightarrow}{\Diamond} \alpha$) holds iff α holds at all (some) worlds, whether more or less plausible.

The modal logic CT4O is a weaker version of CO, where we weaken the condition of connectedness to be simple reflexivity. This logic is based on models whose structure is that of a partially-ordered set of clusters (see Figure 1(a)). Both logics can be extended by requiring that the set of worlds in a model include every propositional valuation over

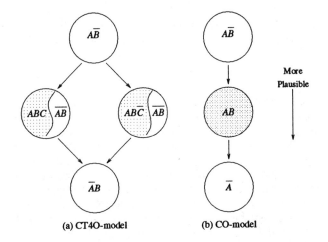

(a) CT4O-model   (b) CO-model

Figure 1: CT4O and CO models

P (so that every logically possible state of affairs is possible). The corresponding logics are denoted CO* and CT4O*. Axiomatizations for all logics may be found in (Boutilier 1992b; Boutilier 1992a). For a given model, we define the following notions. We let $\|\alpha\|$ denote the set of worlds satisfying formula α (and also use this notion for sets of formulae K). We use $min(\alpha)$ to denote the set of *most plausible* α-worlds:[1]

$$min(\alpha) = \{w : w \models \alpha, \text{ and } v < w \text{ implies } v \not\models \alpha\}$$

The revision of a belief set K can be represented using CT4O or CO-models that reflect the degree of plausibility accorded to worlds by an agent in such a belief state. To capture revision of K, we insist that any such K-*revision model* be such that $\|K\| = min(\top)$; that is, $\|K\|$ forms the (unique) minimal cluster in the model. This reflects the intuition that all and only K-worlds are most plausible (Boutilier 1992b). The CT4O-model in Figure 1(a) is a K-revision model for $K = Cn(\neg A, B)$, while the CO-model in Figure 1(b) is suitable for $K = Cn(\neg A)$.

To revise K by A, we construct the revised set K_A^* by considering the set $min(A)$ of most plausible A-worlds in M. In particular, we require that $\|K_A^*\| = min(A)$; thus $B \in K_A^*$ iff B is true at each of the most plausible A-worlds. We can define a conditional connective $\Rightarrow$ such that $A \Rightarrow B$ is true in just such a case:

$$(A \Rightarrow B) \equiv_{df} \overset{\leftrightarrow}{\Box}(A \supset \Diamond(A \wedge \Box(A \supset B)))$$

Both models in Figure 1 satisfy $A \Rightarrow B$, since B holds at each world in the shaded regions, $min(A)$, of the models. Using the *Ramsey test* for acceptance of conditionals (Stalnaker 1968), we equate $B \in K_A^*$ with $M \models A \Rightarrow B$. Indeed, for both models we have that $K_A^* = Cn(A, B)$. If the model in question is a CO*-model then this characterization of revision is equivalent to the AGM model (Boutilier

---

[1] We assume, for simplicity, that such a (limiting) set exists for each $\alpha \in L_{CPL}$, though the following technical developments do not require this (Boutilier 1992b).

1992b). Simply using CT4O*, the model satisfies all AGM postulates (Gärdenfors 1988) but the eighth. Properties of this conditional logic are described in Boutilier (1990; 1991).

We briefly describe the *contraction* of K by $\neg A$ in this semantic framework. To retract belief in $\neg A$, we adopt the belief state determined by the set of worlds $\|K\| \cup min(A)$. The belief set $K^-_{\neg A}$ does not contain $\neg A$, and this operation captures the AGM model of contraction. In Figure 1(a) $K^-_{\neg A} = Cn(B)$, while in Figure 1(b) $K^-_{\neg A} = Cn(A \supset B)$.

A key distinction between CT4O and CO-models is illustrated in Figure 1: in a CO-model, all worlds in $min(A)$ must be equally plausible, while in CT4O this need not be the case. Indeed, the CT4O-model shown has two maximally plausible sets of A-worlds (the shaded regions), yet these are incomparable. We denote the set of such incomparable subsets of $min(A)$ by $Pl(A)$, so that $min(A) = \cup Pl(A)$.[2] Taking each such subset to be a plausible revised state of affairs rather than their union, we can define a weaker notion of revision using the following connective. It reflects the intuition that at *some* element of $Pl(A)$, C holds:

$$(A \to C) \equiv_{df} \overset{\hookrightarrow}{\Box}(\neg A) \vee \overset{\hookrightarrow}{\Diamond}(A \wedge \Box(A \supset C))$$

The model in Figure 1(a) shows the distinction: it satisfies neither $A \Rightarrow C$ nor $A \Rightarrow \neg C$, but both $A \to C$ and $A \to \neg C$. There is a set of comparable most plausible A-worlds that satisfies C and one that satisfies $\neg C$. Notice that this connective is *paraconsistent* in the sense that both C and $\neg C$ may be "derivable" from A, but $C \wedge \neg C$ is not. However, $\to$ and $\Rightarrow$ are equivalent in CO, since $min(A)$ must lie within a single cluster.

Finally, we define the *plausibility* of a proposition. A is at least as plausible as B just when, for every B-world w, there is some A-world that is at least as plausible as w. This is expressed in $\mathbf{L}_B$ as $\overset{\hookrightarrow}{\Box}(B \supset \Diamond A)$. If A is (strictly) more plausible than B, then as we move away from $\|K\|$, we will find an A-world before a B-world; thus, A is qualitatively "more likely" than B. In each model in Figure 1, $A \wedge B$ is more plausible than $A \wedge \neg B$.

3 Epistemic Explanations

Often explanations are postulated relative to some background theory, which together with the explanation entails the observation. Our notion of explanation will be somewhat different than the usual ones. We define an explanation relative to the epistemic state of some agent (or program). An agent's beliefs *and* judgements of plausibility will be crucial in its evaluation of what counts as a valid explanation (see Gärdenfors (1988)). We assume a deductively closed belief set K along with some set of conditionals that represent the revision policies of the agent. These conditionals may represent statements of normality or simply subjunctives (below).

There are two types of sentences that we may wish to explain: beliefs and non-beliefs. If β is a belief held by the agent, it requires a *factual* explanation, some other belief α

that might have caused the agent to accept β. This type of explanation is clearly crucial in most reasoning applications. An intelligent program will provide conclusions of various types to a user; but a user should expect a program to be able to *explain* how it reached such a "belief," to justify its reasoning. The explanation should clearly be given in terms of *other* (perhaps more fundamental) beliefs held by the program. This applies to advice-systems, intelligent databases, tutorial systems, or a robot that must explain its actions.

A second type of explanation is *hypothetical*. Even if β is not believed, we may want a hypothetical explanation for it, some new belief the agent *could* adopt that would be sufficient to ensure belief in β. This counterfactual reading turns out to be quite important in AI, for instance, in diagnosis tasks (see below), planning, and so on (Ginsberg 1986). For example, if A explains B in this sense, it may be that ensuring A will bring about B. If α is to count as an explanation of β in this case, we must insist that α is also not believed. If it were, it would hardly make sense as a predictive explanation, for the agent has already adopted belief in α without committing to β. This leads us to the following condition on epistemic explanations: if α is an explanation for β then α and β must have the same epistemic status for the agent. In other words, $\alpha \in K$ iff $\beta \in K$ and $\neg\alpha \in K$ iff $\neg\beta \in K$.[3]

Since our explanations are to be predictive, there has to be some sense in which α is sufficient to cause acceptance of β. On our interpretation of conditionals (using the Ramsey test), this is the case just when the agent believes the conditional $\alpha \Rightarrow \beta$. So for α to count as an explanation of β (in this predictive sense, at least) this conditional relation must hold.[4] In other words, if the explanation were believed, so too would the observation.

Unfortunately, this conditional is vacuously satisfied when β is believed, once we adopt the requirement that α be believed too. Any $\alpha \in K$ is such that $\alpha \Rightarrow \beta$; but surely arbitrary beliefs cannot count as explanations. To determine an explanation for some $\beta \in K$, we want to (hypothetically) suspend belief in β and, *relative to this new belief state*, eval-

---

[2] $Pl(A) = \{min(A) \cap \mathcal{C} : \mathcal{C} \text{ is a cluster}\}$.

[3] This is at odds with one prevailing view of explanation, which takes only non-beliefs to be valid explanations: to offer a *current* belief α as an explanation is uninformative; abduction should be an "inference process" allowing the derivation of *new* beliefs. We take a somewhat different view, assuming that observations are not (usually) accepted into a belief set until some explanation is found and accepted. In the context of its other beliefs, β is unexpected. An explanation relieves this dissonance when it is accepted (Gärdenfors 1988). After this process both explanation and observation are believed. Thus, the abductive *process* should be understood in terms of *hypothetical* explanations: when it is realized what *could* have caused belief in an (unexpected) observation, both observation and explanation are incorporated. *Factual* explanations are retrospective in the sense that they (should) describe "historically" what explanation was *actually* adopted for a certain belief.

In (Becher and Boutilier 1993) we explore a weakening of this condition on epistemic status. Preferences on explanations (see below) then play a large role in ruling out any explanation whose epistemic status differs from that of the observation.

[4] See the below for a discussion of non-predictive explanations.

uate the conditional $\alpha \Rightarrow \beta$. This hypothetical belief state should simply be the *contraction* of K by β. The contracted belief set K_β^- is constructed as described in the last section. We can think of it as the set of beliefs held by the agent before it came to accept β.[5] In general, the conditionals an agent accepts relative to the contracted set need not bear a strong relation to those in the original set. Fortunately, we are only interested in those conditionals $\alpha \Rightarrow \beta$ where $\alpha \in K$. The AGM contraction operation ensures that $\neg\alpha \notin K_\beta^-$. This means that we can determine the truth of $\alpha \Rightarrow \beta$ relative to K_β^- by examining conditionals in the original belief set. We simply need to check if $\neg\beta \Rightarrow \neg\alpha$ relative to K. This is our final criterion for explanation. If the observation had been absent, so too would the explanation.

We assume, for now, the existence of a model M that captures an agent's objective belief set K and its revision policies (e.g., M completely determines K_A^*, K_A^- and accepted conditionals $A \Rightarrow B$). When we mention a belief set K, we have in mind also the appropriate model M. All conditionals are evaluated with respect to K unless otherwise indicated. We can summarize the considerations above:

Definition A *predictive explanation* of $\beta \in \mathbf{L}_{CPL}$ relative to belief set K is any $\alpha \in \mathbf{L}_{CPL}$ such that: (1) $\alpha \in K$ iff $\beta \in K$ and $\neg\alpha \in K$ iff $\neg\beta \in K$; (2) $\alpha \Rightarrow \beta$; and (3) $\neg\beta \Rightarrow \neg\alpha$.

As a consequence of this definition, we can have the following property of factual explanations:

Proposition 1 *If $\alpha, \beta \in K$ then α explains β iff $\alpha \Rightarrow \beta$ is accepted in K_β^-.*

Thus factual explanations satisfy our desideratum regarding contraction by β. Furthermore, for both factual and hypothetical explanations, only one of conditions (2) or (3) needs to be tested, the other being superfluous:

Proposition 2 *(i) If $\alpha, \beta \in K$ then α explains β iff $\neg\beta \Rightarrow \neg\alpha$; (ii) If $\alpha, \beta \notin K$ then α explains β iff $\alpha \Rightarrow \beta$.*

Figure 2 illustrates both factual and hypothetical explanations. In the first model, wet grass (W) is explained by rain (R), since $R \Rightarrow W$ holds in that model. Similarly, sprinkler S explains W, as does $S \land R$. Thus, there may be competing explanations; we discuss preferences on these below. Intuitively, α explains β just when β is true at the most plausible situations in which α holds. Thus, explanations are *defeasible*: W is explained by R; but, R together with C (the lawn is covered) does not explain wet grass, for $R \land C \Rightarrow \neg W$. Notice that R *alone* explains W, since the "exceptional" condition C is normally false when R (or otherwise), thus need not be stated. This defeasibility is a feature of explanations that has been given little attention in many logic-based approaches to abduction.

The second model illustrates factual explanations for W. Since W is believed, explanations must also be believed. R and $\neg S$ are candidates, but only R satisfies the condition on factual explanations: if we give up belief in W, adding R is

[5]We do not require that this must *actually* be the case.

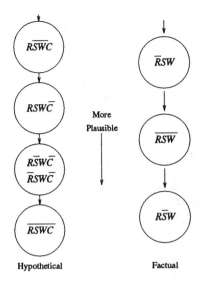

Figure 2: Explanations for "Wet Grass"

sufficient to get it back. In other words, $\neg W \Rightarrow \neg R$. This does not hold for $\neg S$ because $\neg W \Rightarrow S$ is false. Notice that if we relax the condition on epistemic status, we might accept S as a hypothetical explanation for factual belief R. This is explored in (Becher and Boutilier 1993).

Semantic Preferences: Predictive explanations are very general, for any α that induces belief in β satisfies our conditions. Of course, some such explanations should be ruled out on grounds of implausibility (e.g., a tanker truck exploding in front of my house explains wet grass). In probabilistic approaches to abduction, one might prefer most probable explanations. In consistency-based diagnosis, explanations with the fewest abnormalities are preferred on the grounds that (say) multiple component failures are unlikely. Preferences can be easily accommodated within our framework. We assume that the β to be explained is not (yet) believed and rank possible explanations for β.[6] An adopted explanation is not one that simply makes an observation less surprising, but one that is itself as unsurprising as possible. We use the plausibility ranking described in the last section.

Definition If α and α' both explain β then α is *at least as preferred as α'* (written $\alpha \leq_P \alpha'$) iff $M \models \overset{\leftrightarrow}{\Box}(\alpha' \supset \Diamond\alpha)$. The *preferred explanations* of β are those α such that not $\alpha' <_P \alpha$ for all explanations α'.

Preferred explanations are those that are most plausible, that require the "least" change in belief set K in order to be accepted. Examining the hypothetical model in Figure 2, we see that while R, S and $R \land S$ each explain W, R and S are preferred to $R \land S$ (I may not know whether my sprinkler was

[6]We adopt the view that an agent, when accepting β, also accepts its most plausible explanation(s). There is no need, then, to rank factual explanations according to plausibility – all explanations in K are equally plausible. In fact, the only explanations in K can be those that are preferred in K_β^-.

on or it rained, but it's unlikely that my sprinkler was on in the rain). If we want to represent the fact, say, that the failure of fewer components is more plausible than more failures, we simply rank worlds accordingly. Preferred explanations of β are those that predict β and presume as few faults as possible.[7] We can characterize preferred explanations by appealing to their "believability" given β:

Proposition 3 α *is a preferred explanation for* β *iff* $M \models \neg(\beta \to \neg\alpha)$.

In the next section, we discuss the role of $\to$ further.

This approach to preferred explanations is very general, and is completely determined by the conditionals (or defaults) held by an agent.[8] We needn't restrict the ordering to, say, counting component failures. It can be used to represent any notion of typicality, normality or plausibility required. For instance, we might use this model of abduction in scene interpretation to "explain" the occurrence of various image objects by the presence of actual scene objects (Reiter and Mackworth 1989). Preferred explanations are those that match the data best. However, we can also introduce an extra level of preference to capture preferred interpretations, those scenes that are *most likely* in a given domain among those with the best fit.

We should point out that we do not require a complete semantic model M to determine explanations. For a given incomplete theory, one can simply use the derivable conditionals to determine derivable explanations and preferences. This paper simply concentrates on the semantics of this process. All conditions on explanations can be tested as object-level queries on an incomplete KB. However, should one have in mind a complete ordering of plausibility (as in the next section), these can usually be represented as a compact object-level theory as well (Boutilier 1991).

Other issues arise with this semantic notion of explanation. Consider the wet grass example, and the following conditionals: $R \Rightarrow W$, $S \Rightarrow W$ and $S \wedge R \Rightarrow W$ (note that the third does not follow from the others). We may be in a situation where rain is preferred to sprinkler as an explanation for wet grass (it is more likely). But we might be in a situation where R and S are equally plausible explanations.[9] We might then have $W \Rightarrow (S \equiv \neg R)$. That is, S and R are the *only* plausible "causes" for W (and are mutually exclusive). Notice that $S \equiv \neg R$ is a preferred explanation for W, as is $S \vee R$. We say α is a *covering explanation* for β iff α is a preferred explanation such that $\beta \Rightarrow \alpha$. Such an α represents all preferred explanations for β.[10]

Pragmatics: We note that β is always an explanation for itself. Indeed, semantically β is as good as any other explanation, for if one is convinced of this *trivial* explanation, one is surely convinced of the proposition to be explained. There are many circumstances in which such an explanation is reasonable (for instance, explaining the value of a root node in a causal network); otherwise we would require infinite regress or circular explanations.

The undesirability of such trivial explanations, in certain circumstances, is not due to a lack of predictive power or plausibility, but rather its *uninformative* nature. We think it might be useful to rule out trivial explanations as a matter of the *pragmatics* of explanation rather than semantics, much like Gricean maxims (but see also Levesque (1989)). But, we note, that in many cases, trivial (or overly specific) explanations may be desirable. We discuss this and other pragmatic issues (e.g., irrelevance) in the full paper (Becher and Boutilier 1993). We note that in typical approaches to diagnosis this problem does not arise. Diagnoses are usually selected from a pre-determined set of conjectures or component failures. This can be seen as simply another form of pragmatic filtering, and can be applied to our model of abduction (see below).

4 Reconstructing Theorist

Poole's (1989) Theorist system is an assumption-based model of explanation and prediction where observations are explained (or predicted) by adopting certain hypotheses that, together with known facts, entail these observations. We illustrate the naturalness and generality of our abductive framework by recasting Theorist in our model. It shows why Theorist explanations are paraconsistent and non-predictive, how they can be made predictive, and how a natural account of preferred explanation can be introduced to Theorist (and Brewka's (1989) extension of it). Our presentation of Theorist will be somewhat more general than that found in (Poole 1989), but unchanged in essential detail.

We assume the existence of a set $\mathcal{D}$ of *defaults*, a set of propositional formulae taken to be "expectations," or facts that normally hold (Boutilier 1992c). We assume $\mathcal{D}$ is consistent.[11] Given a fixed set of defaults, we are interested in what follows from a given (known) finite set of facts $\mathcal{F}$; we use F to denote its conjunction. A *scenario* for $\mathcal{F}$ is any subset D of $\mathcal{D}$ such that $\mathcal{F} \cup D$ is consistent. An *extension* of $\mathcal{F}$ is any maximal scenario. An *explanation* of β given $\mathcal{F}$ is any α such that $\{\alpha\} \cup \mathcal{F} \cup D \models \beta$ for some scenario D of $\{\alpha\} \cup \mathcal{F}$.[12] Finally, β is *predicted* given $\mathcal{F}$ iff $\mathcal{F} \cup D \models \beta$ for each extension D of $\mathcal{F}$.

In the definition of prediction in Theorist, we find an implicit notion of plausibility: we expect some maximal subset of defaults, consistent with $\mathcal{F}$, to hold. Worlds that violate

---

[7]In consistency-based systems, explanations usually do not *predict* an observation without adequate fault models (more on this in the concluding section).

[8]Direct statements of belief, relative plausibility, integrity constraints, etc. in $\mathbf{L}_B$ may also be in an agent's KB.

[9]We can ensure that $R \wedge S$ is less likely, e.g., by asserting $S \Rightarrow \neg R$ and $R \Rightarrow \neg S$.

[10]Space limitations preclude a full discussion (see (Becher and Boutilier 1993)), but we might think of a covering explanation as the disjunction of all likely causes of β in a causal network (Pearl

---

1988). We are currently investigating *causal explanations* in our conditional framework and how a theory might be used to derive causal influences (Lewis 1973; Goldszmidt and Pearl 1992).

[11]Nothing crucial depends on this however.

[12]Theorist explanations are usually drawn from a given set of conjectures, but this is not crucial.

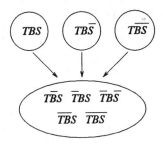

Figure 3: A Theorist Model

more defaults are thus less plausible than those that violate fewer. We define a CT4O*-model that reflects this.

Definition For a fixed set of defaults $\mathcal{D}$, and a possible world (valuation) w, the *violation set* for w is defined as $V(w) = \{d \in \mathcal{D} : w \models \neg d\}$. The *Theorist model* for $\mathcal{D}$ is $M_{\mathcal{D}} = \langle W, \leq, \varphi \rangle$ where W and φ are as usual, and $\leq$ is an ordering of plausibility such that $v \leq w$ iff $V(v) \subseteq V(w)$.

Thus, $M_{\mathcal{D}}$ ranks worlds according to the sets of defaults they violate. We note that $M_{\mathcal{D}}$ is a CT4O*-model, and if $\mathcal{D}$ is consistent, $M_{\mathcal{D}}$ has a unique minimal cluster consisting of those worlds that satisfy each default. It should be clear that worlds w, v are equally plausible iff $V(w) = V(v)$, so that each cluster in $M_{\mathcal{D}}$ is the set of worlds that violate a particular subset $D \subseteq \mathcal{D}$. The α-worlds minimal in $M_{\mathcal{D}}$ are just those that satisfy some maximal subset of defaults consistent with α.

Theorem 4 β *is predicted given* $\mathcal{F}$ *iff* $M_{\mathcal{D}} \models F \Rightarrow \beta$.

Thus, predictions based on $\mathcal{F}$ correspond to the belief set obtained when $\mathcal{D}$ is revised to incorporate $\mathcal{F}$. This is the view of default prediction discussed in (Boutilier 1992c).

We now turn our attention to explanations. Theorist explanations are quite weak, for α explains β whenever there exists *any* set of defaults that, together with α, entails β. This means that α might explain both β and $\neg\beta$. Such explanations are in a sense paraconsistent, for α cannot usually be used to explain the conjunction $\beta \wedge \neg\beta$. Furthermore, such explanations are not predictive: if α explains contradictory sentences, how can it be thought to predict either? Consider a set of defaults in Theorist

$$\mathcal{D} = \{T \supset S, T \wedge B \supset \neg S\}$$

which assert that my car will start (S) when I turn the key (T), unless my battery is dead (B). The Theorist model $M_{\mathcal{D}}$ is shown in Figure 3. Suppose our set of facts $\mathcal{F}$ has a single element B. When asked to explain S, Theorist will offer T. When asked to explain $\neg S$, Theorist will again offer T. If I want my car to start I should turn the key, and if I do not want my car to start I should turn the key. There is certainly something unsatisfying about such a notion of explanation. Such explanations do, however, correspond precisely to *weak explanations* in CT4O using $\rightarrow$.

Theorem 5 α *is a Theorist explanation of* β *given* $\mathcal{F}$ *iff* $M_{\mathcal{D}} \models \alpha \wedge F \rightarrow \beta$.

This illustrates the conditional and defeasible semantic underpinnings of Theorist's weak (paraconsistent) explanations in the conditional framework.

In our model, the notion of predictive explanation seems much more natural. In the Theorist model above, there is a possibility that $T \wedge B$ gives S and a possibility that $T \wedge B$ gives $\neg S$. Therefore, T (given B) *explains* neither possibility. One cannot use the explanation to ensure belief in the "observation" S. We can use our notion of predictive explanation to extend Theorist with this capability. Clearly, predictive explanations in the Theorist model $M_{\mathcal{D}}$ give us:

Definition α is a *predictive explanation* for β given $\mathcal{F}$ iff β is predicted (in the Theorist sense) given $\mathcal{F} \cup \{\alpha\}$.

Theorem 6 α *is a predictive explanation for* β *given* $\mathcal{F}$ *iff* $M_{\mathcal{D}} \models \alpha \wedge F \Rightarrow \beta$ *(i.e., iff* $\mathcal{F} \cup D \cup \{\alpha\} \models \beta$ *for each extension D).*

Taking those α-worlds that satisfy as many defaults as possible to be the most plausible or typical α-worlds, it is clear that revising by α should result in acceptance of those situations, and thus α should (predictively) explain β iff β holds in each such situation. Such explanations are often more useful than weak explanations for they suggest *sufficient* conditions α that *will* (defeasibly) lead to a desired belief β. Weak explanations of the type originally defined in Theorist, in contrast, merely suggest conditions that *might* lead to β.

Naturally, given the implicit notion of plausibility determined by $\mathcal{D}$, we can characterize *preferred* explanations in Theorist. These turn out to be exactly those explanations that force the violation of as few defaults as possible.

Definition Let α, α' be predictive explanations for β given $\mathcal{F}$. α is *at least as preferred as* α' (written $\alpha \leq_{\mathcal{F}} \alpha'$) iff each extension of $\mathcal{F} \cup \{\alpha'\}$ is contained in some extension of $\mathcal{F} \cup \{\alpha\}$.

Theorem 7 $\alpha \leq_{\mathcal{F}} \alpha'$ *iff* $M_{\mathcal{D}} \models \overset{\leftrightarrow}{\Box}((\alpha' \wedge F) \supset \Diamond(\alpha \wedge F))$.

So the notion of preference defined for our concept of epistemic explanations induces a preference in Theorist for predictive explanations that are consistent with the greatest subsets of defaults; that is, those explanations that are most plausible or most normal (see Konolige (1992) who proposes a similar notion).

This embedding into CT4O provides a compelling semantic account of Theorist in terms of plausibility and belief revision. But it also shows directions in which Theorist can be naturally extended, in particular, with predictive explanations and with preferences on semantic explanations, notions that have largely been ignored in assumption-based explanation.

In (Becher and Boutilier 1993) we show how these ideas apply to Brewka's (1989) prioritized extension of Theorist by ordering worlds in such a way that the prioritization relation among defaults is accounted for. If we have a prioritized default theory $D = D_1 \cup \cdots D_n$, we still cluster worlds according to the defaults they violate; but should w violate fewer high priority defaults than v, even if it violates more low priority defaults, w is considered more plausible than v.

This too results in a CT4O*-model; and prediction, (weak and predictive) explanation, and preference on explanations are all definable in the same fashion as with Theorist. We also show that priorities on defaults, as proposed by Brewka, simply prune away certain weak explanations and make others preferred (possibly adding predictive explanations). For instance, the counterintuitive explanation T above, for S given B, is pruned away if we require that the default $T \supset S$ be given lower priority than the default $T \wedge B \supset \neg S$. A model for such a prioritized theory simply makes the world TBS less plausible than $TB\overline{S}$. We note, however, that such priorities need not be provided explicitly if the Theorist model is abandoned and defaults are expressed directly as conditionals. This preference is derivable in CT4O from the conditionals $T \Rightarrow S$ and $T \wedge B \Rightarrow \neg S$ automatically.

5 Concluding Remarks

We have proposed a notion of epistemic explanation based on belief revision, and preferences over these explanations using the concept of plausibility. We have shown how Theorist can be captured in this framework. In (Becher and Boutilier 1993), we show how this model can be axiomatized. We can also capture consistency-based diagnosis in our framework, though it does not usually require that explanations be predictive in the sense we describe. Instead, consistency-based diagnosis is characterized in terms of "might" counterfactuals, or *excuses* that make an observation plausible, rather than likely (Becher and Boutilier 1993). Of course, fault models describing how failures are manifested in system behavior make explanations more predictive, in our strong sense. However, the key feature of this approach is not its ability to represent existing models of diagnosis, but its ability to infer explanations, whether factual or hypothetical, from existing conditional (or default) knowledge. We are also investigating the role of causal explanations in abduction, and how one might distinguish causal from non-causal explanations using only conditional information.

Acknowledgements: Thanks to David Poole for helpful comments. This research was supported by NSERC Research Grant OGP0121843.

References

Alchourrón, C., Gärdenfors, P., and Makinson, D. 1985. On the logic of theory change: Partial meet contraction and revision functions. *Journal of Symbolic Logic*, 50:510–530.

Becher, V. and Boutilier, C. 1993. Epistemic explanations. Technical report, University of British Columbia, Vancouver. forthcoming.

Boutilier, C. 1991. Inaccessible worlds and irrelevance: Preliminary report. In *Proceedings of the Twelfth International Joint Conference on Artificial Intelligence*, pages 413–418, Sydney.

Boutilier, C. 1992a. Conditional logics for default reasoning and belief revision. Technical Report KRR-TR-92-1, University of Toronto, Toronto. Ph.D. thesis.

Boutilier, C. 1992b. A logic for revision and subjunctive queries. In *Proceedings of the Tenth National Conference on Artificial Intelligence*, pages 609–615, San Jose.

Boutilier, C. 1992c. Normative, subjunctive and autoepistemic defaults: Adopting the Ramsey test. In *Proceedings of the Third International Conference on Principles of Knowledge Representation and Reasoning*, pages 685–696, Cambridge.

Brewka, G. 1989. Preferred subtheories: An extended logical framework for default reasoning. In *Proceedings of the Eleventh International Joint Conference on Artificial Intelligence*, pages 1043–1048, Detroit.

de Kleer, J., Mackworth, A. K., and Reiter, R. 1990. Characterizing diagnoses. In *Proceedings of the Eighth National Conference on Artificial Intelligence*, pages 324–330, Boston.

de Kleer, J. and Williams, B. C. 1987. Diagnosing multiple faults. *Artificial Intelligence*, 32:97–130.

Gärdenfors, P. 1988. *Knowledge in Flux: Modeling the Dynamics of Epistemic States*. MIT Press, Cambridge.

Ginsberg, M. L. 1986. Counterfactuals. *Artificial Intelligence*, 30(1):35–79.

Goldszmidt, M. and Pearl, J. 1992. Rank-based systems: A simple approach to belief revision, belief update, and reasoning about evidence and actions. In *Proceedings of the Third International Conference on Principles of Knowledge Representation and Reasoning*, pages 661–672, Cambridge.

Hempel, C. G. 1966. *Philosophy of Natural Science*. Prentice-Hall, Englewood Cliffs, NJ.

Konolige, K. 1992. Using default and causal reasoning in diagnosis. In *Proceedings of the Third International Conference on Principles of Knowledge Representation and Reasoning*, pages 509–520, Cambridge.

Levesque, H. J. 1989. A knowledge level account of abduction. In *Proceedings of the Eleventh International Joint Conference on Artificial Intelligence*, pages 1061–1067, Detroit.

Lewis, D. 1973. Causation. *Journal of Philosophy*, 70:556–567.

Pearl, J. 1988. *Probabilistic Reasoning in Intelligent Systems: Networks of Plausible Inference*. Morgan Kaufmann, San Mateo.

Poole, D. 1989. Explanation and prediction: An architecture for default and abductive reasoning. *Computational Intelligence*, 5:97–110.

Poole, D. 1991. Representing diagnostic knowledge for probabilistic horn abduction. In *Proceedings of the Twelfth International Joint Conference on Artificial Intelligence*, pages 1129–1135, Sydney.

Quine, W. and Ullian, J. 1970. *The Web of Belief*. Random House, New York.

Reiter, R. 1987. A theory of diagnosis from first principles. *Artificial Intelligence*, 32:57–95.

Reiter, R. and Mackworth, A. K. 1989. A logical framework for depiction and image interpretation. *Artificial Intelligence*, 41:125–155.

Rescher, N. 1978. *Peirce's Philosophy of Science: Critical Studies in his Theory of Induction and Scientific Method*. University of Notre Dame Press, Notre Dame.

Stalnaker, R. C. 1968. A theory of conditionals. In Harper, W., Stalnaker, R., and Pearce, G., editors, *Ifs*, pages 41–55. D. Reidel, Dordrecht. 1981.

Revision By Conditional Beliefs

Craig Boutilier
Univ. of British Columbia
Dept. of Computer Science
Vancouver, BC V6T 1Z2
CANADA
cebly@cs.ubc.ca

Moisés Goldszmidt
Rockwell International
444 High Street
Palo Alto, CA 94301
U.S.A.
moises@rpal.rockwell.com

Abstract

Both the dynamics of belief change and the process of reasoning by default can be based on the *conditional belief set* of an agent, represented as a set of "if-then" rules. In this paper we address the open problem of formalizing the dynamics of revising this conditional belief set by *new* if-then rules, be they interpreted as new default rules or new revision policies. We start by providing a purely semantic characterization, based on the semantics of conditional rules, which induces logical constraints on any such revision process. We then introduce logical (syntax-independent) and syntax-dependent techniques, and provide a precise characterization of the set of conditionals that hold after the revision. In addition to formalizing the dynamics of revising a default knowledge base, this work also provides some of the necessary formal tools for establishing the truth of nested conditionals, and attacking the problem of learning new defaults.

Introduction

Consider a child using a single default "typically birds fly", to predict the behavior of birds. Upon learning of the class of penguins and their exceptional nature she considers *revising* her current information about birds to include the information that penguins are birds yet "typically penguins do not fly". This process is different from that usually modeled in approaches to nonmonotonic reasoning and belief revision, where upon discovering that Tweety is a (nonflying) penguin she simply retracts her previous belief that Tweety does fly. Instead, the example above addresses the issue of revising the set of *conditional beliefs*, namely, the default rules that guide the revision of our *factual* beliefs. In this paper we are concerned with the dynamics of such conditional beliefs. Our objective is to characterize how the conditional information in a knowledge base evolves due to the incorporation of the new conditionals, which rules should be given up in case of inconsistency, and what principles guide this process.[1]

One well-known theory addressing the dynamics of factual beliefs is that proposed by Alchourron, Gärdenfors and Makinson (1985; 1988). The *AGM theory* takes epistemic states to be deductively closed sets of (believed) sentences and characterizes how a rational agent should change its set K of beliefs. This is achieved with postulates constraining revision functions $*$, where K_A^* represents the belief set that results when K is revised by A. Unfortunately, the AGM theory does not provide a calculus with which one can realize the revision process or even specify the content of an epistemic state (Boutilier 1992a; Doyle 1991; Nebel 1991). Recent work (Boutilier 1992a; Goldszmidt 1992) shows that AGM revision can be captured by assuming that an agent has a knowledge base (*KB*) containing *subjunctive conditionals* of the form $A \rightarrow B$ (where A and B are objective formulae). These conditionals define the agent's belief set and guide the revision process via the *Ramsey test* (Stalnaker 1968): $A \rightarrow B$ is accepted iff revision by A results in a belief in B. Such conditionals may be given a probabilistic interpretation (Goldszmidt 1992): each $A \rightarrow B$ is associated with a conditional probability statement arbitrarily close to one. They may also be interpreted a statements in a suitable modal logic (Boutilier 1992a). The corresponding logics (and indeed semantics) are identical (Boutilier 1992a), and furthermore there is a strong relation between these conditionals and conditional default rules (Boutilier 1992c; Goldszmidt and Pearl 1992a).

The AGM theory has two crucial limitations. First, the conditionals (or revision policies) associated with K, that determine the form of K_A^*, provide no guidance for determining the conditionals accepted in K_A^* itself. The theory only determines the new *factual* beliefs held after revision. Even if conditionals are contained in K, the AGM theory cannot suggest which conditionals should be retained or retracted in the construction of K_A^*. *Subsequent* revisions of K_A^* can thus be almost arbitrary. Second, the theory provides no mechanism for revising a belief set with new *conditionals*. Thus, the revision policies of an agent cannot, in general, be changed.[2] This paper provides a solution to this second problem, and extends our recent work on a solution to the first problem (Boutilier 1993; Goldszmidt and Pearl 1992b).

---

[1] We will not address the important question of why and when an agent decides to revise its conditional beliefs or defaults.

[2] Surprisingly, these two issues have remained largely unexplored, due largely to the Gärdenfors (1988) triviality result, which points to difficulties with the interpretation of conditional belief sets. But these can be easily circumvented (Boutilier 1992c).

In this paper we focus on a particular model of *conditional revision* that extends propositional natural revision introduced by Boutilier (1993). The *natural revision* model addresses the problem of determining new conditional beliefs after revision by factual beliefs, and extends the notion of minimal change (characteristic of the AGM theory) to the conditional component of a *KB*. Thus, when a factual revision is applied to *KB*, the revised *KB'* contains as much of the *conditional information* from *KB* as possible. The extension to conditional revision presented here preserves these properties and possesses the crucial property that the beliefs resulting from any sequence of (conditional or factual) updates can be determined using only properties of the original ranking, and tests involving simple (unnested) conditionals.[3]

A model for revising *KB* with new conditional belief (e.g., a rule $C \rightarrow D$) is crucial for a number of reasons. The problem of truth conditions for nested conditionals is subsumed by this more general problem. The semantics of conditionals with arbitrary nesting requires an account of revision by *new conditional information*. To test the truth of $(A \rightarrow B) \rightarrow C$, we must first revise *KB* by $A \rightarrow B$ and then test the status of C (Goldszmidt and Pearl 1992b). Also, it is clear that our beliefs do not merely change when we learn new factual information. We need a model that accounts for updating our belief set with new conditional probabilities and new subjunctive conditionals to guide the subsequent revision of beliefs. Given the strong equivalence between conditionals of the type described here and conditional default rules (Boutilier 1992c; Goldszmidt and Pearl 1992a), a model of conditional revision provides an account of updating a *KB* with new default rules. Any specification of how an agent is to learn new defaults must describe how an agent is to incorporate a new rule into its corpus of existing knowledge. Hence, the process we study in this paper is crucial for providing a semantic core for learning new default information.

We first review the basic concepts underlying belief revision. We then describe the basics of conditional belief revision by presenting a set of operations on ranked-models, and an important representation theorem. Finally, we explore a syntax-independent and a syntax-dependent approach to the conditional revision of a *KB*.

Propositional Natural Revision

In this section we briefly review a semantic account of belief revision (we refer the reader to (Gärdenfors 1988; Goldszmidt and Pearl 1992b; Boutilier 1992b) for details). We assume the existence of a deductively closed belief set K

over a classical propositional language $\mathbf{L}_{CPL}$. Revising this belief set with a new proposition A is problematic when $K \models \neg A$, for simply adding the belief A will cause inconsistency. To accommodate A, certain beliefs must be given up before A is added. The AGM theory of revision provides a set of constraints on *revision functions* $*$ that map belief sets K into revised belief sets K_A^*. Any theory of revision also provides a theory of conditionals if we adopt the *Ramsey test*. This test states that one should accept the conditional "If A then B" just when $B \in K_A^*$.

A key representation result for this theory shows that changes can be modeled by assuming an agent has an ordering of *epistemic entrenchment* over beliefs: revision always retains more entrenched propositions in preference to less entrenched ones. Grove (1988) shows that entrenchment can be modeled semantically by an ordering of worlds. This is pursued by Boutilier (1992b) who presents a modal logic and semantics for revision. A *revision model* $M = \langle W, \leq, \varphi \rangle$ consists of a set of worlds W (assigned valuations by φ) and an *plausibility* ordering $\leq$ over W. If $v \leq w$ then v is at least as plausible as w. We insist that $\leq$ be transitive and connected (so $w \leq v$ or $v \leq w$ for all v, w). We denote by $\|A\|$ the set of worlds in M satisfying A (those w such that $M \models_w A$). We define the set of most plausible A-worlds to be those worlds in A minimal in $\leq$; so $min(M, A)$ is just

$$\{w \in W : M \models_w A, \text{ and } M \models_v A \text{ implies } w \leq v\}$$

We assume that all models are *smooth* in the sense that $min(M, A) \neq \emptyset$ for all (satisfiable) $A \in \mathbf{L}_{CPL}$.[4] The *objective belief set* K of a model M is the set of $\alpha \in \mathbf{L}_{CPL}$ such that $min(M, \top) \subseteq \|\alpha\|$ (those α true at each *most* plausible world). Such α are believed by the agent. These objective or *factual* beliefs capture the agent's judgements of true facts in the world. They should be contrasted with the conditional beliefs of an agent, described below.

To capture the revision of a belief set K, we define a K-revision model to be any revision model such that $min(M, \top) = \|K\|$. That is, all and only those worlds satisfying the belief set are most plausible. When we revise K by A, we must end up with a new belief set that includes A. Given our ordering, we simply require that the new belief set correspond to the set of most plausible A-worlds. We can define the truth conditions for a conditional connective as

$$M \models_w A \rightarrow B \quad \text{iff} \quad min(M, A) \subseteq \|B\| \qquad (1)$$

Such *conditional beliefs* characterize the revision policies, hypothetical beliefs or defaults of an agent. Equating $A \rightarrow B$ with $B \in K_A^*$, this definition of revision characterizes the same space of revision functions as the AGM theory (Boutilier 1992b).

The AGM theory and the semantics above show how one might determine a new objective belief set K_A^* from a given K-revision model; but it provides no hint as to what new *conditionals* should be held. To do so requires that a new revision

---

[3] A second method of revision is the model of *J-conditioning* (Goldszmidt and Pearl 1992b): when *KB* is updated with a new fact A, the revised *KB'* is determined by Bayesian conditionalization, giving rise to a qualitative abstraction of probability theory (Adams 1975; Goldszmidt 1992). This mechanism preserves the (qualitative) conditional probabilities in *KB* as much as possible and thus guarantees that the relative strength of the conditionals also remains constant. The extension of J-conditionalization to the conditional revision case is explored in the full version of the paper (Boutilier and Goldszmidt 1993).

[4] Hence, there exist *most* plausible A-worlds. This is not required, but the assumption does not affect the equivalence below.

model, suitable for K_A^*, be specified. *Natural revision*, proposed by Boutilier (1993), does just this. Given a K-revision model M, natural revision specifies a new model M_A^* suitable for the revision of K_A^* (i.e., a K_A^*-revision model). Roughly, this model can be constructed by "shifting" the set $min(M, A)$ to the bottom of the ordering, leaving all other worlds in the same relative relation. This extends the notion of minimal change to the relative plausibility of worlds. To believe A, certainly K_A^*-worlds must become most plausible, but nothing else need change (Boutilier 1993). Hence, natural revision constructs a new ranking to reflect new objective beliefs. With such a ranking one can then determine the behavior of subsequent objective revisions. But no existing model of revision accounts for revision of a ranking to include new conditionals. In the next section we extend natural revision so that new conditional information can be incorporated explicitly in a model.

Conditional Belief Revision: Revising a Model

Given a revision model M, we want to define a new model $M_{A \to B}^*$ that satisfies $A \to B$ but changes the plausibility ordering in M as little as possible. We do this in two stages: first, we define the *contraction* of M so that the "negation" $A \to \neg B$ is not satisfied; then we define the *expansion* of this new model to accommodate the conditional $A \to B$. Let $M = \langle W, \leq, \varphi \rangle$.

Definition 1 The *natural contraction operator* $-$ maps M into $M_{A \to B}^-$, for any simple conditional $A \to B$, where $M_{A \to B}^- = \langle W, \leq', \varphi \rangle$, and:

1. if $v, w \notin min(M, A \wedge \neg B)$ then $v \leq' w$ iff $v \leq w$
2. if $w \in min(M, A \wedge \neg B)$ then: (a) $w \leq' v$ iff $u \leq v$ for some $u \in min(M, A)$; and (b) $v \leq' w$ iff $v \leq u$ for some $u \in min(M, A)$

Figure 1 illustrates this process in the principle case, showing how the model $M_{A \to B}^-$ is constructed when $M \models A \to B$. Clearly, to "forget" $A \to B$ we must construct a model where certain minimal A-worlds do not satisfy B. If M satisfies $A \to B$, we must ensure that certain $A \wedge \neg B$-worlds become at least as plausible as the minimal A-worlds, thus ensuring that $A \to B$ is no longer satisfied. Natural contraction does this by making the most plausible $A \wedge \neg B$-worlds just as plausible as the most plausible A-worlds. Simply put, the minimal $A \wedge \neg B$-worlds (the light-shaded region) are shifted to the cluster containing the minimal A-worlds (the dark-shaded region). We have the following properties:[5]

Proposition 1 *Let M be a revision model.*
(1) $M_{A \to B}^- \not\models A \to B$;
(2) If $M \not\models A \to B$ then $M_{A \to B}^- = M$; and
(3) If $M \not\models A \to \neg B$ then $M_{A \to B}^- \models A \not\to B \wedge A \not\to \neg B$.

Theorem 2 *Let M_A^- denote the natural propositional contraction of M by (objective belief) A (as defined in (Boutilier 1993)). Then $M_A^- = M_{\top \to A}^-$.*

---
[5]We let $\alpha \not\to \beta$ stand for $\neg(\alpha \to \beta)$.

Thus, propositional contraction is a special case of conditional contraction.

We define the *expansion* of M by $A \to B$ to be the model $M_{A \to B}^+$ constructed by making the minimal changes to M required to accept $A \to B$. While we do not require that $M \not\models A \to \neg B$ in the following definition, we will only use this definition of expansion for such models.

Definition 2 The *natural expansion operator* $+$ maps M into $M_{A \to B}^+$, for any simple conditional $A \to B$, where $M_{A \to B}^+ = \langle W, \leq', \varphi \rangle$, and:

1. if $v \notin min(M, A \wedge \neg B)$ then $w \leq' v$ iff $w \leq v$
2. if $v \in min(M, A \wedge \neg B)$ then:
   (a) if $w \in min(M, A \wedge \neg B)$ then $w \leq' v$; and
   (b) if $w \notin min(M, A \wedge \neg B)$ then $w \leq' v$ iff $w \leq v$ and there is no $u \in min(M, A \wedge B)$ such that $u \leq w$

Figure 1 illustrates this process in the principle case, showing how the model $M_{A \to B}^+$ is constructed when $M \not\models A \to B$. Clearly, to believe $A \to B$ we must construct a model where all minimal A-worlds satisfy B. If M fails to satisfy $A \to B$, we must ensure that the minimal $A \wedge \neg B$-worlds become less plausible than the minimal A-worlds, thus ensuring that $A \to B$ is satisfied. Natural expansion does this by making the most plausible $A \wedge \neg B$-worlds (the dark-shaded region) less plausible than the most plausible A-worlds (the light-shaded region). This leaves us with $A \to B$, but preserves the relative plausibility ranking of all other worlds. In particular, while the set of minimal $A \wedge \neg B$-worlds becomes less plausible than those worlds with which it shared equal plausibility in M, its relationship to more or less plausible worlds is unchanged. Once again, the idea is that the conditional belief set induced by A should contain only B-worlds, but that all other conditionals should remain unchanged to the greatest extent possible.

Proposition 3 *Let M be a revision model such that $M \not\models A \to \neg B$. (1) $M_{A \to B}^+ \models A \to B$; and (2) If $M \models A \to B$ then $M_{A \to B}^+ = M$.*

We can now define revision by a conditional $A \to B$. Briefly, to accept such a conditional we first "forget" $A \to \neg B$ and then "add" $A \to B$.

Definition 3 The *natural revision operator* $*$ maps M into $M_{A \to B}^*$, for any simple conditional $A \to B$, where $M_{A \to B}^* = (M_{A \to \neg B}^-)_{A \to B}^+$.

This definition of revision reflects the Levi identity (Levi 1980). Figure 1 illustrates this process in the principle case, showing how the model $M_{A \to B}^*$ is constructed when $M \models A \to \neg B$. Natural revision behaves as expected:

Proposition 4 *Let M be a revision model. (1) $M_{A \to B}^* \models A \to B$; and (2) If $M \models A \to B$ then $M_{A \to B}^* = M$.*

Theorem 5 *Let M_A^* denote the natural propositional revision of M by (objective belief) A (as defined in (Boutilier 1993)). Then $M_A^* = M_{\top \to A}^*$.*

Thus, we can view propositional revision as a special case of conditional revision. We will henceforth take M_A^* as an abbreviation for $M_{\top \to A}^*$.

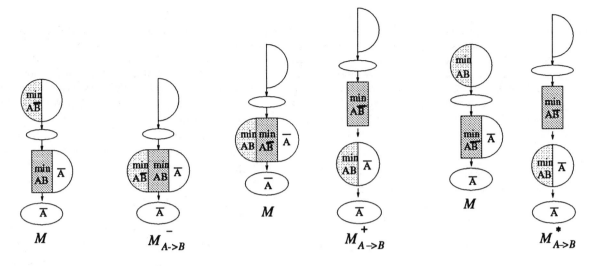

Figure 1: Contraction, Expansion and Revision of a Model

These results show that natural conditional revision can reasonably be called a revision operator. To show that this revision operator is indeed "natural," we must determine its precise effect on belief in previously accepted conditionals. In particular, we would like a precise characterization the simple conditionals $\alpha \to \beta$ satisfied by the revised model $M^*_{A \to B}$. The following result (Thm. 6) shows that the truth of such conditionals in $M^*_{A \to B}$ is completely determined by the set of simple conditionals satisfied by M. Thus, the truth of an arbitrarily nested conditional under natural revision can be determined by the truth of simple conditionals in our original model. We note that revision models are *complete* in that they satisfy every simple conditional or its negation. We do not require that a conditional *KB* be complete in this sense. We describe how this semantic model can be applied to an incomplete *KB* in the next section.

We now show which conditionals are satisfied by a model $M_{A \to B}$. In (Boutilier and Goldszmidt 1993) we also describe similar characterizations of models $M^-_{A \to B}$ and $M^+_{A \to B}$. We begin by noting that if $M \not\models A \to \neg B$, then $M^*_{A \to B} = M^+_{A \to B}$. In particular, if $M \models A \to B$, then $M^*_{A \to B} = M$ and no conditional beliefs are changed. We assume then that $M \models A \to \neg B$, the principle case of revision. We also introduce the notion of *plausibility*: a sentence P is at least as plausible as Q (relative to M) iff the minimal P-worlds are at least as plausible (in the ordering $\leq$) as the minimal Q-worlds. This will be the case exactly when $M \models (P \vee Q) \not\to \neg P$. We write $P <_P Q$ if formula P is more plausible that Q, and $P =_P Q$ if P and Q are equally plausible.[6] To determine whether $\alpha \to \beta$ holds in $M^*_{A \to B}$, we simply need to know how the relative position of worlds in $\|\alpha\|$ is affected by the revision. The relative plausibility of A and α in M is crucial in determining this. If α is more

plausible than A, then shifting $A \wedge B$-worlds down cannot affect the most plausible α-worlds. If α is less plausible, the most plausible α-worlds *might* change, but only if there are α-worlds among the most plausible $A \wedge B$-worlds. Finally, there are several different types of changes that can occur if α and A are equally plausible.

Theorem 6 *Let $M \models A \to \neg B$ and let $\leq_P$ be the plausibility ordering determined by M. Let $\alpha, \beta \in \mathbf{L}_{CPL}$.*

1. *If $\alpha <_P A$ then $M^*_{A \to B} \models \alpha \to \beta$ iff $M \models \alpha \to \beta$.*
2. *If $\alpha >_P A$ then*
   (a) If $M \models A \wedge B \to \neg\alpha$ then
      $M^*_{A \to B} \models \alpha \to \beta$ iff $M \models \alpha \to \beta$.
   (b) If $M \models A \wedge B \not\to \neg\alpha$ then
      $M^*_{A \to B} \models \alpha \to \beta$ iff $M \models A \wedge B \wedge \alpha \to \beta$.
3. *If $\alpha =_P A$ then*
   (a) If $M \models A \wedge B \not\to \neg\alpha$ and $M \models \alpha \to A$ then
      $M^*_{A \to B} \models \alpha \to \beta$ iff $M \models A \wedge B \wedge \alpha \to \beta$.
   (b) If $M \models A \wedge B \not\to \neg\alpha$ and $M \models \alpha \not\to A$ then
      $M^*_{A \to B} \models \alpha \to \beta$ iff
      $M \models A \wedge B \wedge \alpha \to \beta$ and $M \models \alpha \wedge \neg A \to \beta$.
   (c) If $M \models A \wedge B \to \neg\alpha$ and $M \models A \wedge \neg B \to \neg\alpha$ then
      $M^*_{A \to B} \models \alpha \to \beta$ iff $M \models \alpha \to \beta$.
   (d) If $M \models A \wedge B \to \neg\alpha$, $M \models A \wedge \neg B \not\to \neg\alpha$ and $M \models \alpha \to A$ then $M^*_{A \to B} \models \alpha \to \beta$ iff $M \models \alpha \to \beta$.
   (e) If $M \models A \wedge B \to \neg\alpha$, $M \models A \wedge \neg B \not\to \neg\alpha$ and $M \models \alpha \not\to A$ then $M^*_{A \to B} \models \alpha \to \beta$ iff $M \models \alpha \wedge \neg A \to \beta$.

While this characterization results appears complex, it is rather intuitive, for it captures the interactions caused by the relative plausibility of A and other propositions α. As an example, suppose we believe that a power surge will normally cause a breaker to trip ($S \to B$) and this will prevent equipment damage ($S \to \neg D$); but if the breaker doesn't trip there will be damage ($S \wedge \neg B \to D$). Our characterization shows that, should we learn the breaker is faulty ($S \to \neg B$), we should also change our mind about potential

[6]Plausibility is also induced by the κ-ranking of formulae (Goldszmidt and Pearl 1992b): $P \leq_P Q$ iff $\kappa(P) \leq \kappa(Q)$.

damage, and thus accept $S \rightarrow D$. However, information such as $\top \rightarrow \neg S$ will continue to be held (the likelihood of a power surge does not change). Hence, our factual beliefs (e.g., $\neg S$) do not change, merely our conditional belief about the breaker: what will happen *if* S.

Theorem 6 also shows that the conditionals that hold in the revised model $M^*_{A \rightarrow B}$ can be completely characterized in terms of the conditionals in M. This allows us to use the mechanisms and algorithms of Goldszmidt and Pearl (1992b) for computing the new model (Boutilier and Goldszmidt 1993). This also demonstrates that an arbitrary nested conditional sentence (under natural revision) is logically equivalent to a sentence without nesting (involving disjunctions of conditionals). Thus, purely propositional reasoning mechanisms (Pearl 1990) can be used to determine the truth of nested conditionals in a conditional KB. Indeed, in many circumstances, a complete semantic model can be represented compactly and reasoned about tractably (Goldszmidt and Pearl 1992b). We explore this in the full paper.

When we revise by $A \rightarrow B$ we are indicating a willingness to accept B should we come to accept A. Thus, we might expect that revising by $A \rightarrow B$ should somehow reflect propositional revision by B were we to restrict our attention to A-worlds. This is indeed the case. Let $M \backslash \alpha$ denote the model obtained by eliminating all α-worlds from M.

Theorem 7 $(M^*_{A \rightarrow B}) \backslash \neg A = (M \backslash \neg A)^*_B$

This shows that accepting $A \rightarrow B$ is equivalent to accepting B "given" A. Thus, natural revision by conditionals is in fact a conditional form of the propositional natural revision of Boutilier (1993). The only reason the characterization theorem for conditional revision is more complex is the fact that we can "coalesce" partial clusters of worlds, something that can't be done in the propositional case. We also note that $(M^*_{A \rightarrow B}) \backslash A = M \backslash A$; that is, the relative plausibility of $\neg A$-worlds is unaffected by this revision.

Revising a Conditional Knowledge Base

If a conditional KB contains a complete set of simple conditionals (i.e., defines a unique revision model) we can use the definitions above to compute the revised KB. Often we may use techniques to complete a KB as well (Pearl 1990). In practice, however, KB will usually be an incomplete set of premises or constraints. We propose the following method of *logical revision*. Since KB is not complete, it is satisfied by each of a set $\|KB\|$ of revision models, each of these a "possible" ranking for the agent. When a new conditional $A \rightarrow B$ is learned, revision proceeds in the following way. If there are elements of $\|KB\|$ that satisfy $A \rightarrow B$, these become the new possible rankings for the agent.[7] In this case we have $KB^*_{A \rightarrow B} \equiv KB \cup \{A \rightarrow B\}$. If this is not the case, each possibility in $\|KB\|$ must be rejected. To do this, we revise each ranking in $\|KB\|$ and consider the result of this revision to be the set of new possibilities. $KB^*_{A \rightarrow B}$ is then

$$\{C \rightarrow D : M^*_{A \rightarrow B} \models C \rightarrow D \text{ for all } M \in \|KB\|\}$$

---

[7]This is is equivalent to asking if $KB \cup \{A \rightarrow B\}$ is consistent (see Def. 4 and Thm. 8).

The breaker example above exemplifies this approach. Clearly, we do not want to resort to generating all models of KB. Fortunately, our representation theorem allows us to use any logical calculus for simple conditionals alone to determine the set of all such consequences. A simple conditional $\alpha \rightarrow \beta$ will be in the logical revision of KB iff the appropriate set of simple conditionals (from Theorem 6) is derivable from KB (e.g., one may use the calculus of (Boutilier 1992b; Goldszmidt and Pearl 1991)).

The main problem with an approach based on logical revision is that it is extremely cautious. A direct consequence of this cautious behavior is that the syntactic structure of KB is lost: it plays no role in the revision process.[8] For instance, the revisions of either of $\{A \rightarrow B, A \rightarrow C\}$ or $\{A \rightarrow B \wedge C\}$ by $A \rightarrow \neg B$ are identical. Yet, in some cases, conditional revision of the first set should yield a KB equivalent to $\{A \rightarrow \neg B, A \rightarrow C\}$ simply because $A \rightarrow \neg B$ conflicts only with $A \rightarrow B$. Yet logical revision forces into consideration models in which $A \rightarrow C$ is given up as well. This is not unreasonable, in general,[9] but the syntactic structure may also be used in revision.

The strategy we propose isolates the portion of KB inconsistent with the new rule $A \rightarrow B$, which will be denoted by KB_I, and then applies logical revision to KB_I alone. Letting $KB_J = KB - KB_I$, the revised set $KB^*_{A \rightarrow B}$ is the union of KB_J and the logically revised KB_I (with $A \rightarrow B$). We first introduce the notion of consistency:

Definition 4 A set KB is *consistent* iff there exists at least one model M such that, for each $A \rightarrow B \in KB$, $min(M, A) \subseteq \|B\|$ and $min(M, A) \neq \emptyset$.

A conditional $A \rightarrow B$ is *tolerated* by the set $\{C_i \rightarrow D_i\}$, $1 \leq i \leq n$ iff the propositional formula $A \wedge B \bigwedge_{i=1}^{i=n} \{C_i \supset D_i\}$ is satisfiable. The notion of toleration constitutes the basis for isolating the inconsistent set of KB. A set containing a rule tolerated by that set will be called a *confirmable* set. The following theorem presents necessary and sufficient conditions for consistency (Goldszmidt and Pearl 1991):

Theorem 8 KB *is consistent iff every nonempty subset* $KB' \subseteq KB$ *is confirmable.*

Given KB, a subset KB_m is *minimally unconfirmable* iff KB_m is unconfirmable, but every nonempty subset $KB'_m \subseteq KB_m$ is confirmable.[10] Finally, a set KB_I is a *minimal complete inconsistent set* (MCI) with respect to KB iff it is the union of all minimally unconfirmable subsets for KB. Thus, KB_I contains only the conditionals in KB that are responsible for the inconsistencies in KB. In a syntax-directed revision of KB we are primarily interested in uncovering the conditionals in the original KB that are still valid after the revision process. The S operator below serves this purpose (note that S is built

---

[8]E.g., Nebel (1991) has advocated syntax-dependent revision.

[9]Indeed, this is exactly analogous to the generality of the AGM theory. Given $K = Cn\{A, B\}$, it is not known whether $B \in K^*_{\neg A}$ or not. Logically, the possibility of a connection between A and B exists, and should be denied or stated (or assumed) explicitly.

[10]If KB is consistent, then KB_m is the empty set.

on top of a logical revision process). Given a set KB, and a simple conditional $A \rightarrow B$, let $S(KB, A \rightarrow B)$ denote the set of conditionals $C \rightarrow D$ such that: (1) $C \rightarrow D \in KB$ and (2) $KB^L_{A \rightarrow B} \models C \rightarrow D$, where $KB^L_{A \rightarrow B}$ denotes the logical revision of KB by $A \rightarrow B$. We define the syntactic revision of KB by $A \rightarrow B$ as follows:

Definition 5 Let KB be consistent, and let $A \rightarrow B$ be a simple conditional. Let KB'_I denote the MCI of $KB \cup \{A \rightarrow B\}$, $KB_I = KB'_I - \{A \rightarrow B\}$, and $KB_J = KB - KB_I$. The syntactic revision of KB by $A \rightarrow B$, written $KB^*_{A \rightarrow B}$, will be $KB^*_{A \rightarrow B} = S(KB_I, A \rightarrow B) \cup KB_J \cup \{A \rightarrow B\}$.

Note that in the case where $A \rightarrow B$ is consistent with respect to KB, $KB^*_{A \rightarrow B}$ will be simply the union of the original KB and the new conditional $A \rightarrow B$. Also, the syntactic revision of $\{A \rightarrow B, A \rightarrow C\}$ by $A \rightarrow \neg B$ will be the set $\{A \rightarrow \neg B, A \rightarrow C\}$ since $KB_I = \{A \rightarrow B\}$. In the breaker example above, the revision of $\{S \rightarrow B, S \wedge \neg B \rightarrow D, S \rightarrow \neg D\}$ by $S \rightarrow \neg B$ will yield $\{S \rightarrow \neg B, S \wedge \neg B \rightarrow D\}$ which entails the conditional $S \rightarrow D$ (as in the case of logical revision). Given that the revision of KB^* is based on Theorem 6 and notions of propositional satisfiability (i.e., toleration), the resulting set of conditionals can be computed effectively. The major problem in terms of complexity is the uncovering of the MCI set KB_I which seems to require an exponential number of satisfiability tests.

Concluding Remarks

We have provided a semantics for revising a conditional KB with new conditional beliefs in a manner that extends both the AGM theory and the propositional natural revision model. Our results include a characterization theorem, providing computationally effective means of deciding whether a given conditional holds in the revised model. We have also provided a syntactic characterization for the revision of a KB. We remark that, as in the case of proposals for objective belief revision (including the AGM theory), we make no claims or assumptions about the complex process by which an agent decides to incorporate a new conditional belief (or default rule) into its corpus of knowledge. We merely provide the formal means to do so.

Conditional belief revision defines a semantics for arbitrary nested conditionals as proposed in (Goldszmidt and Pearl 1992b), extending the semantics for right-nested conditionals studied in (Boutilier 1993). By describing the process by which an agent can assimilate new information in the form of conditionals, conditional belief revision is proposed as a basis for the learning of new default rules.

We note that the same techniques can be used to model revision by conditionals in a way that respects the probabilistic intuitions of J-conditioning. Analogues of each of the main results for natural revision are shown in the full paper (Boutilier and Goldszmidt 1993). We also explore other mechanisms for revising a KB and the relationship of our models to probabilistic conditionalization and imaging. We discuss further constraints on the revision process to reflect a causal interpretation of the conditional sentences.

Acknowledgements: Thanks to Judea Pearl for helpful comments. This research was supported by NSERC Grant OGP0121843 and by Rockwell International Science Center.

References

Adams, E. W. 1975. *The Logic of Conditionals*. D.Reidel, Dordrecht.

Alchourrón, C., Gärdenfors, P., and Makinson, D. 1985. On the logic of theory change: Partial meet contraction and revision functions. *Journal of Symbolic Logic*, 50:510–530.

Boutilier, C. 1992a. Conditional logics for default reasoning and belief revision. Technical Report KRR-TR-92-1, University of Toronto, Toronto. Ph.D. thesis.

Boutilier, C. 1992b. A logic for revision and subjunctive queries. In *Proc. of AAAI-92*, pages 609–615, San Jose.

Boutilier, C. 1992c. Normative, subjunctive and autoepistemic defaults: Adopting the Ramsey test. In *Proc. of KR-92*, pages 685–696, Cambridge.

Boutilier, C. 1993. Revision sequences and nested conditionals. In *Proc. of IJCAI-93*, Chambery. (to appear).

Boutilier, C. and Goldszmidt, M. 1993. Revising by conditionals. Technical report, University of British Columbia, Vancouver. (Forthcoming).

Doyle, J. 1991. Rational belief revision: Preliminary report. In *Proc. of KR-91*, pages 163–174, Cambridge.

Gärdenfors, P. 1988. *Knowledge in Flux: Modeling the Dynamics of Epistemic States*. MIT Press, Cambridge.

Goldszmidt, M. 1992. Qualitative probabilities: A normative framework for commonsense reasoning. Technical Report R-190, University of California, Los Angeles. Ph.D. thesis.

Goldszmidt, M. and Pearl, J. 1991. On the consistency of defeasible databases. *Artificial Intelligence*, 52:121–149.

Goldszmidt, M. and Pearl, J. 1992a. Rank-based systems: A simple approach to belief revision, belief update, and reasoning about evidence and actions. In *Proc. of KR-92*, pages 661–672, Cambridge.

Goldszmidt, M. and Pearl, J. 1992b. Reasoning with qualitative probabilities can be tractable. In *Proceedings of the Eighth Conference on Uncertainty in AI*, pages 112–120, Stanford.

Grove, A. 1988. Two modellings for theory change. *Journal of Philosophical Logic*, 17:157–170.

Levi, I. 1980. *The Enterprise of Knowledge*. MIT Press, Cambridge.

Nebel, B. 1991. Belief revision and default reasoning: Syntax-based approaches. In *Proc. of KR-91*, pages 417–428, Cambridge.

Pearl, J. 1990. System Z: A natural ordering of defaults with tractable applications to default reasoning. In Vardi, M., editor, *Proceedings of Theoretical Aspects of Reasoning about Knowledge*, pages 121–135. Morgan Kaufmann, San Mateo.

Stalnaker, R. C. 1968. A theory of conditionals. In Harper, W., Stalnaker, R., and Pearce, G., editors, *Ifs*, pages 41–55. D. Reidel, Dordrecht. 1981.

Reasoning about only knowing with many agents*

Joseph Y. Halpern

IBM Almaden Research Center
650 Harry Road
San Jose, CA 95120–6099
halpern@almaden.ibm.com
408-927-1787

Abstract

We extend two notions of "only knowing", that of Halpern and Moses [1984], and that of Levesque [1990], to many agents. The main lesson of this paper is that these approaches do have reasonable extensions to the multi-agent case. Our results also shed light on the single-agent case. For example, it was always viewed as significant that the HM notion of only knowing was based on S5, while Levesque's was based on K45. In fact, our results show that the HM notion is better understood in the context of K45. Indeed, in the single-agent case, the HM notion remains unchanged if we use K45 (or KD45) instead of S5. However, in the multi-agent case, there are significant differences between K45 and S5. Moreover, all the results proved by Halpern and Moses for the single-agent case extend naturally to the multi-agent case for K45, but not for S5.

1 Introduction

There has been over twelve years of intensive work on various types of nonmonotonic reasoning. Just as with the work on knowledge in philosophy in the 1950's and 1960's, the focus has been on the case of a single agent reasoning about his/her environment. However, in most applications, this environment includes other agents. Surprisingly little of this work has focused on the multi-agent case. To the extent that we can simply represent the other agents' beliefs as propositions (so that "Alice believes that Tweety flies" is a proposition just like "Tweety flies"), then there is no need to treat the other agents in a special way. However, this is no longer the case if we want to reason about the other agents' reasoning. In fact, we need to reason about other agents' reasoning when doing multi-agent planning; moreover, much of this reasoning will be nonmonotonic (see [Morgenstern 1990] for examples).

In this paper, we show how to extend to the multi-agent case two related approaches to nonmonotonic reasoning, both based on the notion of "only knowing": that of Halpern and Moses [1984] (hereafter called the HM notion) and that of Levesque [1990]. The main lesson of the paper is that, despite some subtleties, both approaches do have reasonable extensions to the multi-agent case. Our results also shed light on the single-agent case. For example, it was always viewed as significant that the HM notion of only knowing was based on S5, while Levesque's was based on K45.[1] In fact, our results show that the HM notion is better understood in the context of K45. Indeed, in the single-agent case, the HM notion remains unchanged if we use K45 (or KD45) instead of S5. However, in the multi-agent case, there are significant differences between K45 and S5. Moreover, as we show here, all the results proved by Halpern and Moses for the single-agent case extend naturally to the multi-agent case for K45, but not for S5.

2 The HM notion of "all I know"

The intuition behind the HM notion is straightforward: In each world of a (Kripke) structure, an agent considers a number of other worlds possible. In the case of a single agent whose knowledge satisfies S5 (or K45 or KD45), we can identify a world with a truth assignment, and a structure with a set of truth assignments. Truth in these logics is with respect to *situations* (W, w), consisting of a structure W, representing the set of truth assignments (worlds) that the agent considers possible, and a truth assignment w, intuitively representing the "real world".[2] The more worlds an agent considers possible, the less he knows. Thus, (W, w) is the situation where α is all that is known if (1) $(W, w) \models L\alpha$ (so that the agent knows α) and (2) if $(W', w') \models L\alpha$, then

*The work of the author is sponsored in part by the Air Force Office of Scientific Research (AFSC), under Contract F49620-91-C-0080. The United States Government is authorized to reproduce and distribute reprints for governmental purposes.

---

[1] Due to lack of space, we are forced to assume that the reader is familiar with standard notions of modal logic. Details can be found in [Hughes and Cresswell 1968; Halpern and Moses 1992].

[2] For KD45, we require that W be nonempty; for S5, we require in addition that $w \in W$.

$W' \subseteq W$. If there is no situation (W, w) satisfying (1) and (2), then α is said to be *dishonest*; intuitively, it cannot then be the case that "all the agent knows" is α. A typical dishonest formula is $Lp \vee Lq$. To see that this formula is dishonest, let W_p consist of all truth assignments satisfying p, let W_q consist of all truth assignments satisfying q, and let w satisfy $p \wedge q$. Then $(W_p, w) \models Lp \vee Lq$, and $(W_q, w) \models Lp \vee Lq$. Thus, if $Lp \vee Lq$ were honest, there would have to be a situation (W, w') such that $(W, w') \models Lp \vee Lq$ and $W \supseteq W_p \cup W_q$. It is easy to see that no such situation exists. Notice that in the case of one agent, the notions of honesty and "all I know" coincide for K45, KD45, and S5.

We want to extend this intuition to the multi-agent case and—in order to put these ideas into better perspective—to other modal logics. We consider six logics, three that do not have negative introspection, K_n, T_n, and $S4_n$, and three that do, $K45_n$, $KD45_n$, and $S5_n$.[3] Below, when we speak of a modal logic $\mathcal{S}$, we are referring to one of these six logics; we refer to $K45_n$, $KD45_n$ and $S5_n$ as *introspective logics*, and K_n, T_n, and $S4_n$ as *non-introspective logics* (despite the fact that positive introspection holds in $S4_n$). As we shall see, "all I know" behaves quite differently in the two cases.

There are philosophical problems involved in dealing with a notion of "all I know" for the non-introspective logics. What does it mean for an agent to say "all I know is α" if he cannot do negative introspection, and so does not know what he doesn't know? Fortunately, there is another interpretation of this approach that makes sense for arbitrary modal logics. Suppose that a says to b, "All i knows is α" (where i is different from a and b). If b knows in addition that i's reasoning satisfies the axioms of modal logic $\mathcal{S}$, then it seems reasonable for b to say that i's knowledge is described by the "minimal" model satisfying the axioms of $\mathcal{S}$ consistent with $L_i \alpha$, and for b to view a as dishonest if there is no such minimal model.

Of course, the problem lies in defining what it means for a model to be "minimal". Once we consider multi-agent logics, or even nonintrospective single-agent logics, we can no longer identify a possible world with a truth assignment. It is not just the truth assignment at a world that matters; we also need to consider what other worlds are accessible from that world. This makes it more difficult to define a reasonable notion of minimality. To deal with this problem, we define a canonical collection of objects that an agent can consider possible. These will act like the possible worlds in the single-agent case. The kind of objects we consider depends on whether we consider the introspective or the non-

introspective logics, for reasons that will become clearer below. We start with the non-introspective case.

Fix a set Φ of primitive propositions, and agents $1, \ldots, n$. We define a *(rooted) k-tree (over Φ)* by induction on k: A 0-tree consists of a single node, labeled by a truth assignment to the primitive propositions in Φ. A $(k + 1)$-tree consists of a root node labeled by a truth assignment, and for each agent i, a (possibly empty) set of directed edges labeled by i leading to roots of distinct k-trees.[4] We say a node w' is the *i-successor* of a node w in a tree if there is an edge labeled i leading from w to w'. The *depth* of a node in a tree is the distance of the node from the root. We say that the $k + 1$-tree T_{k+1} is an *extension* of the k-tree T_k if T_{k+1} is the result of adding some successors to the depth-k leaves in T_k. Finally, an ω-tree T_ω is a sequence $\langle T_0, T_1, \ldots \rangle$, where T_k is a k-tree, and T_{k+1} is an extension of T_k, for $k = 0, 1, 2, \ldots$. (We remark that ω-trees are closely related to the knowledge structures of [Fagin, Halpern, and Vardi 1991; Fagin and Vardi 1986], although we do not pursue this connection here.)

We now show that with each situation we can associate a unique ω-tree. We start by going in the other direction. We can associate with each k-tree T $(k \neq \omega)$ a Kripke structure $M(T)$ defined as follows: the nodes of T are the possible worlds in $M(T)$, the $\mathcal{K}_i$ accessibility relation of $M(T)$ consists of all pairs (w, w') such that w' is an i-successor of w in T, and the truth of a primitive proposition at a world w in $M(T)$ is determined by the truth assignment labeling w.

We define the *depth* of a formula by induction on structure. Intuitively, the depth measures the depth of nesting of the K_i operators. Thus, we have $depth(p) = 0$ for a primitive proposition p; $depth(\neg \varphi) = depth(\varphi)$; $depth(\varphi \wedge \psi) = \max(depth(\varphi), depth(\psi))$; $depth(K_i \varphi) = 1 + depth(\varphi)$. If M and M' are (arbitrary) structures, w is a world in M, and w' a world in M', we say that (M, w) and (M', w') are *equivalent up to depth k*, and write $(M, w) \equiv_k (M', w')$ if, for all formulas φ with $depth(\varphi) \leq k$, we have $(M, w) \models \varphi$ iff $(M', w') \models \varphi$. For convenience, if w_0 is the root of T, we take $M(T) \models \varphi$ to be an abbreviation for $(M(T), w_0) \models \varphi$, and write $(M, w) \equiv_k M(T)$ rather than $(M, w) \equiv_k (M(T), w_0)$.

Proposition 2.1: *Fix a situation (M, w). For all k, there is a unique k-tree $T_{M,w,k}$ such that such that $(M, w) \equiv_k M(T_{M,w,k})$. Moreover, $T_{M,w,k+1}$ is an extension of $T_{M,w,k}$.*

Let $T_{M,w}$ be the ω-tree $\langle T_{M,w,0}, T_{M,w,1}, T_{M,w,2}, \ldots \rangle$. By Proposition 2.1, $T_{M,w}$ can be viewed as providing a canonical way of representing the situation (M, w) in terms of trees. We use $(\omega\text{-})$trees as a tool for defining what agent i considers possible in (M, w). Thus, we define i's possibilities at (M, w), denoted $Poss_i(M, w)$, to be $\{T_{M,w'} : (w, w') \in \mathcal{K}_i\}$.

---

[3] The subscript n in all these logics is meant to emphasize the fact that we are considering the n-agent version of the logic. We omit it when considering the single-agent case. Details and axiomatizations can be found in [Halpern and Moses 1992].

[4] Since we are allowing a node to have no successors, any k-tree is also a $(k + 1)$-tree.

Intuitively, for α to be i-honest, there should be a situation (M, w) for which i has the maximum number of possibilities. Formally, if S is a non-introspective logic, we say that α is S-i-honest if there is an S-situation (M, w), called an S-i-maximum situation for α, such that $(M, w) \models L_i\alpha$, and for all S-situations (M', w'), if $(M', w') \models L_i\varphi$, then $Poss_i(M', w') \subseteq Poss_i(M, w)$. If α is S-i-honest, we say that agent i knows β if all he knows is α, and write $\alpha \mathrel{\vdash\mkern-7mu\sim}^i_S \beta$, if $(M, w) \models L_i\beta$ for some S-i-maximum situation for α.[5]

How reasonable are our notions of honesty and $\mathrel{\vdash\mkern-7mu\sim}^i_S$? The following results give us some justification for these definitions. The first gives us a natural characterization of honesty.

Theorem 2.2: *If S is a non-introspective logic, then the formula α is S-i-honest iff $L_i\alpha$ is S-consistent, and for all formulas $\varphi_1, \ldots, \varphi_k$, if $\models_S L_i\alpha \Rightarrow (L_i\varphi_1 \vee \ldots \vee L_i\varphi_k)$, then $\models_S L_i\alpha \Rightarrow L_i\varphi_j$, for some $j \in \{1, \ldots, k\}$.*

Thus, a typical dishonest formula in the case of T_n or $S4_n$ is $L_i p \vee L_i q$, where p and q are primitive propositions. If α is $L_i p \vee L_i q$, then $L_i\alpha \Rightarrow (L_i p \vee L_i q)$ is valid in T_n and $S4_n$, although neither $L_i\alpha \Rightarrow L_i p$ nor $L_i\alpha \Rightarrow L_i q$ is valid. However, the validity of $L_i\alpha \Rightarrow (L_i p \vee L_i q)$ depends on the fact that $L_i\alpha \Rightarrow \alpha$. This is not an axiom of K_n. In fact, it can be shown that $L_i p \vee L_i q$ is K_n-i-honest. Thus, what is almost the archetypical "dishonest" formula is honest in the context of K_n. As the following result shows, this is not an accident.

Theorem 2.3: *All formulas are K_n-i-honest.*

A set S of formulas is an S-i-stable set if there is some S-situation (M, w) such that $S = \{\varphi : (M, w) \models K_i\varphi\}$. We say the situation (M, w) corresponds to the stable set S. This definition is a generalization of the one given by Moore [1985] (which in turn is based on Stalnaker's definition [1980]); Moore's notion of stable set corresponds to a $K45$-stable set in the single-agent case. (See [Halpern 1993] for some discussion as to why this notion of stable set is appropriate.) Since a stable set describes what can be known in a given situation, we would expect a formula to be honest if it is in a minimum stable set. This is indeed true.

Theorem 2.4: *If S is a non-introspective logic, then α is S-i-honest iff there is an S-i-stable set S^α containing α which is a subset of every S-i-stable set containing α. Moreover, if α is stable, then $\alpha \mathrel{\vdash\mkern-7mu\sim}^i_S \beta$ iff $\beta \in S^\alpha$.*

This characterization of honesty is closely related to one given in [Halpern and Moses 1984]; we discuss this in more detail below.

Our next result gives another characterizion of what agent i knows if "all agent i knows is α", for an honest formula α. Basically, it shows that all agent i knows are the logical consequences of his knowledge of α. Thus, "all agent i knows" is a monotonic notion for the non-introspective logics.

Theorem 2.5: *If S is a non-introspective logic and α is S-i-honest, then $\alpha \mathrel{\vdash\mkern-7mu\sim}^i_S \beta$ iff $\models_S L_i\alpha \Rightarrow L_i\beta$.*

This completes our discussion of the non-introspective logics. We must take a slightly different approach in dealing with the introspective logics. To see the difficulties if we attempt to apply our earlier approach without change to the introspective case, consider the single-agent case. Suppose Φ consists of two primitive propositions, say p and q, and suppose that all the agent knows is p. Surely p should be honest. Indeed, according to the framework of Halpern and Moses [1984], there is a maximum situation where p is true where the structure consists of two truth assignments: one where both p and q are true, and the other where p is true and q is false. Call this structure M. There is, of course, another structure where the agent knows p. This is the structure where the only truth assignment makes both p and q true. Call this structure M'. Let w be the world where both p and q are true. We can easily construct $T_{M,w}$ and $T_{M',w}$; the trouble is that $Poss_1(M, w)$ and $Poss_1(M', w)$ are incomparable. What makes them incomparable is introspective knowledge: In (M, w), the agent does not know q; so, because of introspection, he knows that he does not know q. On the other hand, in (M', w), the agent does not know this. These facts are reflected in the trees. We need to factor out the introspection somehow. In the single-agent case considered, this was done by considering only truth assignments, not trees. We need an analogue for the multi-agent case.

We define an i-objective k-tree to be a k-tree whose root has no i-successors. We define a i-objective ω-tree to be an ω-tree all of whose components are i-objective. Given a k-tree T, let T^i be the result of removing all the i-successors of the root of T (and all the nodes below it). Given an ω-tree $T = \langle T_0, T_1, \ldots \rangle$, let $T^i = \langle T_0^i, T_1^i, \ldots \rangle$. The way we factor out introspection is by considering i-objective trees. Intuitively, this is because the i-objective tree corresonding to a situation (M, w) eliminates all the worlds that i considers possible in that situation. Notice that in the case of one agent, the i-objective trees are precisely the possible worlds.

We define $IntPoss_i(M, w) = \{T^i : T \in Poss_i(M, w)\}$. ($IntPoss$ stands for *introspective possibilities*.) The following result assures us that we have not lost anything in the introspective logics by considering $IntPoss_i$ instead of $Poss_i$.

Lemma 2.6: *If M is an S-structure, and S is an introspective logic, then $Poss_i(M, w)$ is uniquely determined* *by* $\text{IntPoss}_i(M, w)$.

In the case of the introspective logics, we now repeat all our earlier definitions using *IntPoss* instead of *Poss*. Thus, for example, we say that that α is $\mathcal{S}$-i-honest if there is an $\mathcal{S}$-situation (M, w) such that $(M, w) \models L_i\alpha$, and for all $\mathcal{S}$-situations (M', w'), if $(M', w') \models L_i\varphi$, then $\text{IntPoss}_i(M', w') \subseteq \text{IntPoss}_i(M, w)$. We make the analogous change in the definition of $\vdash_{\mathcal{S}}^i$. Since i-objective trees are truth assignments in the single-agent case, it is easy to see that these definitions generalize those for the single-agent case given in [Halpern and Moses 1984].

We now want to characterize honesty and "all agent i knows" for the introspective logics. There are some significant differences from the non-introspective case. For example, as expected, the primitive proposition p is $\mathcal{S}$-1-honest even if $\mathcal{S}$ is introspective. However, due to negative introspection, $\neg L_1q \Rightarrow L_1\neg L_1q$ is $\mathcal{S}$-valid, so we have $\models_{\mathcal{S}} L_1p \Rightarrow (L_1q \vee L_1\neg L_1q)$. Moreover, we have neither $\models_{\mathcal{S}} L_1p \Rightarrow L_1q$ nor $\models_{\mathcal{S}} L_1p \Rightarrow L_1\neg L_1q$. Thus, the analogue to Theorem 2.2 does not hold.

We say a formula is *i-objective* if it is a Boolean combination of primitive propositions and formulas of the form $L_j\varphi$, $j \neq i$, where φ is arbitrary. Thus, $q \wedge L_2L_1p$ is 1-objective, but L_1p and $q \wedge L_1p$ are not. Notice that if there is only one agent, say agent 1, then the 1-objective formulas are just the propositional formulas. As the following result shows, the analogue of Theorem 2.2 holds for KD45_n and K45_n, provided we stick to i-objective formulas.

Theorem 2.7: *For $S \in \{\text{KD45}_n, \text{K45}_n\}$, the formula α is $\mathcal{S}$-i-honest iff for all i-objective formulas $\varphi_1, \ldots, \varphi_k$, if $\models_{\mathcal{S}} L_i\alpha \Rightarrow (L_i\varphi_1 \vee \ldots \vee L_i\varphi_k)$ then $\models_{\mathcal{S}} L_i\alpha \Rightarrow L_i\varphi_j$, for some $j \in \{1, \ldots, k\}$.*

This result does not hold for S5_n; for example, $\models_{\text{S5}_n} L_1p \Rightarrow (L_1q \vee L_1L_2\neg L_2L_1q)$ (this follows from the fact that $\models_{\text{S5}_n} \neg L_1q \Rightarrow L_1L_2\neg L_2L_1q$). However, it is easy to see that $\not\models_{\text{S5}_n} L_1p \Rightarrow L_1q$ and $\not\models_{\text{S5}_n} L_1p \Rightarrow L_1L_2\neg L_2L_1q$. Since p is S5_n-1-honest, Theorem 2.7 fails for S5_n.

Theorem 2.7 is a direct extension of a result in [Halpern and Moses 1984] for the single-agent case. Two other characterizations of honesty and "all I know" are given by Halpern and Moses, that can be viewed as analogues to Theorems 2.4 and 2.5. As we now show, they also extend to K45_n and KD45_n, but not S5_n.

One of these characterizations is in terms of stable sets. The direct analogue of Theorem 2.4 does not hold for the introspective logics. In fact, as was already shown in [Halpern and Moses 1984] for the single-agent case, any two consistent stable sets are incomparable with respect to set inclusion. Again, the problem is due to introspection. For suppose we have two consistent $\mathcal{S}$-i-stable sets S and S' such that $S \subset S'$, and $\varphi \in S' - S$. By definition, there must be situations (M, w) and (M', w'), corresponding to S and S' respec-

tively, for which we have $(M, w) \models L_i\varphi$ and $(M', w') \not\models L_i\varphi$. By introspection, we have $(M, w) \models L_iL_i\varphi$ and $(M', w') \models L_i\neg L_i\varphi$. This means that $L_i\varphi \in S$ and $\neg L_i\varphi \in S'$. Since $S \subset S'$, we must also have $L_i\varphi \in S$, which contradicts the assumption that S' is consistent.

We can get an analogue of Theorem 2.4 if we consider i-objective formulas. Define the i-kernel of an $\mathcal{S}$-i-stable set S, denoted $\ker_i(S)$, to consist of all the i-objective formulas in S.

Theorem 2.8: *For $S \in \{\text{KD45}_n, \text{K45}_n\}$, a formula α is $\mathcal{S}$-i-honest iff there is an $\mathcal{S}$-i-stable set S_α^i containing α such that for all i-stable sets S containing α, we have $\ker_i(S_\alpha^i) \subseteq \ker_i(S)$. Moreover, α is $\mathcal{S}$-i-honest, then $\alpha \vdash_{\mathcal{S}}^i \beta$ iff $\beta \in S_\alpha^i$.*

As we show in the full paper, Theorem 2.8 does not hold for S5_n. This is not an artifact of our definition of honesty for S5_n, since in fact we can show that for *no* formula α is there an S5_n-i-stable set containing α whose i-kernel is a minimum.

Finally, let us consider the analogue to Theorem 2.5. In contrast to the non-introspective case, inference from "all agent i knows" is nonmonotonic for the introspective logics. For example, we have $p \vdash_{\mathcal{S}} \neg L_1q$, even though $\not\models_{\mathcal{S}} L_1p \Rightarrow L_1\neg L_1q$. This seems reasonable: if all agent 1 knows is p, then agent 1 does not know q and (by introspection) knows that he does not know this. As shown in [Halpern and Moses 1984], there is an elegant algorithmic characterization of "all agent i knows" in the single-agent case. We extend it to the multi-agent case here. We recursively define a set $D_{\mathcal{S}}^i(\alpha)$ that intuitively consists of all the formulas agent i knows, given that agent i knows only α (and reasons using modal logic $\mathcal{S}$):

$$\varphi \in D_{\mathcal{S}}^i(\alpha) \text{ iff } \models_{\mathcal{S}} (L_i\alpha \wedge \varphi^{\alpha, i}) \Rightarrow L_i\varphi,$$

where $\varphi^{\alpha, i}$ is the conjunction of $L_i\psi$ for all subformulas $L_i\psi$ of φ for which $\psi \in D_{\mathcal{S}}^i(\alpha)$, and $\neg L_i\psi$ for all subformulas $L_i\psi$ for which $\psi \notin D_{\mathcal{S}}^i(\alpha)$ (where φ is considered a subformula of itself). Thus, the algorithm says that the agent knows φ if it follows from knowing α, together with the formulas that were decided by recursive applications of the algorithm. Then we have:

Theorem 2.9: *For $S \in \{\text{KD45}_n, \text{K45}_n\}$, the formula α is i-honest iff $D_{\mathcal{S}}^i(\alpha)$ is (propositionally) consistent. If α is $\mathcal{S}$-i-honest, then $\alpha \vdash_{\mathcal{S}}^i \beta$ iff $\beta \in D_{\mathcal{S}}^i(\alpha)$.*

While the analogue to Theorem 2.9 does not hold for S5_n, the algorithm is correct for honest formulas.

Theorem 2.10: *If α is S5_n-i-honest, then $\alpha \vdash_{\text{S5}_n}^i \beta$ iff $\beta \in D_{\text{S5}_n}^i(\alpha)$.*

We now characterize the complexity of computing honesty and "all i knows".

Theorem 2.11: *For $S \in \{\text{T}_n, \text{S4}_n : n \geq 1\} \cup \{\text{KD45}_n, \text{K45}_n, \text{S5}_n : n \geq 2\}$, the problem of computing whether α is $\mathcal{S}$-i-honest is PSPACE-complete.*

Of course, the problem of computing whether α is K_n-i-honest is trivial: the answer is always "Yes".

Theorem 2.12: *For $S \in \{K_n, T_n, S4_n : n \geq 1\} \cup \{KD45_n, K45_n, S5_n : n \geq 2\}$, if α is S-i-honest, then the problem of deciding if $\alpha \models_S^i \beta$ is PSPACE-complete.*

We close this section by briefly comparing our approach to others in the literature. Fagin, Halpern, and Vardi [1991] define a notion of *i-no-information extension* that can also be viewed as characterizing a notion of "all agent i knows" in the context of $S5_n$. However, it is defined only for a limited set of formulas. It can be shown that these formulas are always $S5_n$-i-honest in our sense, and, if α is one of these formulas, we have $\alpha \models_{S5_n}^i \beta$ iff β is true in the i-no-information extension of α. The fact that these two independently motivated definitions coincide (at least, in the cases where the i-no-information extension is defined) provides further evidence for the reasonableness of our definitions.

Vardi [1985] defines a notion of "all agent i knows" for $S4_n$, using the knowledge-structures approach of [Fagin, Halpern, and Vardi 1991], and proves Theorem 2.5 for $S4_n$ in the context of his definition. It is not hard to show that our definition of honesty coincides with his for $S4_n$. However, the knowledge structures approach does not seem to extend easily to the introspective logics. Moreover, using our approach leads to much better complexity results. For example, all that Vardi was able to show was that honesty was (nonelementary-time) decidable.

Parikh [1991] defines a notion of "all that is known" for $S5_n$ much in the spirit of the definitions given here. Among other things, he also starts with k-trees (he calls them *normal models*), although he does not use i-objective trees. However, rather than focusing on all that some fixed agent i knows as we have done, Parikh treats all agents on an equal footing. This leads to some technical differences between the approaches. He was also able to obtain only nonelementary-time algorithms for deciding whether a formula was honest in his sense.

3 Levesque's notion of "only knowing"

Despite the similarity in philosophy and terminology, Levesque's notion of "only knowing" differs in some significant ways from the HM notion (see [Halpern 1993] for a discussion of this issue). Nevertheless, some of the ideas of the previous section can be applied to extending it to many agents.

Levesque considers a K45 notion of belief, and introduces a modal operator O, where $O\alpha$ is read "only believes α". The O operator is best understood in terms of another operator introduced by Levesque denoted N. While $L\alpha$ says "α is true at all the worlds that the agent considers possible", $N\alpha$ is viewed as saying "α is true at all the worlds that the agent does *not* consider possible". Then $O\alpha$ is defined as an abbreviation for $L\alpha \wedge N\neg\alpha$. Thus, $O\alpha$ holds if α is true at all the worlds that the agent considers possible, and only these worlds. We can read $L\alpha$ as saying "the agent knows at least α", while $N\neg\alpha$ says "the agent knows at most α" (for if he knew more, than he would not consider possible all the worlds where α is true).

In the case of a single agent, since worlds are associated with truth assignments, it is easy to make precise what it means that the agent does not consider a world possible: it is impossible if it is not one of the truth assignments the agents considers possible. Thus, Levesque defines:

$$(W, w) \models N\alpha \text{ if } (W, w') \models \alpha \text{ for all } w' \notin W.$$

Two important features of this definition are worth mentioning here. First, the set of all worlds is absolute, and does not depend on the situation: it is the set of all truth assignments. Thus, the set of impossible worlds given that W is the set of worlds that the agent considers possible is just the complement of W (relative to the set of all truth assignments). Second, when evaluating the truth of α at an "impossible world" w', we do not change W, the set of worlds that the agent considers possible. (We remark that it is this second point that results in the main differences between this notion of "all I know" and the HM notion; see [Halpern 1993].)

Of course, the problem in extending Levesque's notion to many agents lies in coming up with an analogue to "the worlds that the agent does not consider possible". This is where our earlier ideas come into play.

Before we go into details on the multi-agent case, we mention one important property of this notion of "only knowing". Moore [1985] defines a *stable expansion of* α to be a (K45-)stable set S such that S is the closure under propositional reasoning of $\{\alpha\} \cup \{L\alpha : L\alpha \in S\} \cup \{\neg L\alpha : \neg L\alpha \in S\}$. Notice that for any stable set S, there is a unique set W_S of truth assignments such that $\varphi \in S$ iff $(W_S, w) \models L\varphi$ for all $w \in W_S$. Levesque shows that S is a stable expansion of α iff $(W_S, w) \models O\alpha$ for all $w \in W_S$.

We now turn to extending Levesque's definitions to the multi-agent case. We first extend the language of knowledge by adding modal operators N_i and O_i for each agent $i = 1, \ldots, n$. Following Lakemeyer, we call the full language $\mathcal{ONL}_n$. We say that a formula in $\mathcal{ONL}_n$ is basic if it does not involve the modal operators O_i or N_i. Finally, we take the language $\mathcal{ONL}_n^-$ to be the sublanguage of $\mathcal{ONL}_n$ where no O_j or N_j occurs in the scope of an O_i, N_i, or L_i, for $i \neq j$. In analogy to Levesque, we define $O_i\alpha$ as the conjunction $L_i\alpha \wedge N_i\neg\alpha$. The problem is to define $N_i\alpha$. As in the single-agent case, we want $N_i\alpha$ to mean that α is true at all the worlds that i does not consider possible. So what are the worlds that i does not consider possible?

Perhaps the most straightforward way of making sense of this, used by Lakemeyer [1993], is to define N_i in terms of the complement of the $\mathcal{K}_i$ relation. We briefly outline this approach here. Given a structure $M = (W, \mathcal{K}_1, \ldots, \mathcal{K}_n, \pi)$, let $\mathcal{K}_i(w) = \{w' : (w, w') \in \mathcal{K}_i\}$. $\mathcal{K}_i(w)$ is the set of worlds that agent i considers possible at w. We write $w \approx_i w'$ if $\mathcal{K}_i(w) = \mathcal{K}_i(w')$. Thus, if $w \approx_i w'$, then agent i's possibilities are the same at w and w'. Finally, Lakemeyer defines:

$(M, w) \models_{Lak} N_i \alpha$ if $(M, w') \models \alpha$ for all w' such that $(w, w') \notin \mathcal{K}_i$ and $w \approx_i w'$.

By restricting attention to worlds w' such that $w \approx_i w'$, Lakemeyer is preserving the second property of Levesque's definition, namely, that when evaluating the truth of a formula at an impossible world, we keep the set of agent i's possibilities unchanged. However, this definition does not capture the first property of Levesque's definition, that the set of impossible worlds is absolute. Here it is relative to the structure. To get around this problem, Lakemeyer focuses on a certain *canonical model*, which intuitively has "all" the possibilities.[6] It is only in this model that the N_i (and thus the O_i) operators seem to have the desired behavior. (We discuss to what extent they really do have the desired behavior in this canonical model below.)

We want to define N_i and O_i in a reasonable way in all models. We proceed as follows:

$(M, w) \models N_i \alpha$ if $(M', w') \models \alpha$ for all (M', w') such that $T^i_{M', w'} \notin IntPoss_i(M, w)$ and $IntPoss_i(M, w) = IntPoss_i(M', w')$.

The analogues to Lakemeyer's definitions should be obvious: we replace $(w, w') \notin \mathcal{K}_i$ by $T^i_{M', w'} \notin IntPoss_i(M, w)$ and $w \approx_i w'$ by $IntPoss_i(M, w) = IntPoss_i(M', w')$.

What evidence do we have that this definition is reasonable? One piece of evidence is that we can extend to the multi-agent case Levesque's result regarding the relationship between only knowing and stable expansions. To do this, we first need to define the notion of stable expansion in the context of many agents. We say that S is a $K45_n$-i-*stable expansion of* α if S is a $K45_n$-i-stable set and S is the closure under $K45_n$ of $\{\alpha\} \cup \{L_i \alpha : L_i \alpha \in S\} \cup \{\neg L_i \alpha : \neg L_i \alpha \in T\}$.[7]

Next, we need to associate a situation with each $K45_n$-i-stable set, as we were able to do in the single-agent case. Given a set S of basic formulas, we say that the $K45_n$-situation (M, w) i-*models* S if, for all basic formulas φ, we have $(M, w) \models L_i \varphi$ iff $\varphi \in S$. In analogy to the single-agent case, the situation that we

would like to associate with a stable set S is one that i-models S. There is, however, a complication. In the single-agent case, a stable set determines the set of possible truth assignments. That is, given a stable set S, there is a unique set W_S such that (for any w) we have $(W_S, w) \models L\varphi$ iff $\varphi \in S$. The analogue does not hold in the multi-agent case. That is, given a stable set S, there is not a unique set $\mathcal{W}$ of i-objective ω-trees such that if (M, w) i-models S, then $IntPoss_i(M, w) = \mathcal{W}$. As we show in the full paper, two structures can agree on all basic formulas, and still differ with regard to formulas of the form $N_i \alpha$ or $O_i \alpha$ under $\models$.[8] A similar phenomenon was encountered by Levesque [1990] when considering only knowing in the first-order case. We solve our problem essentially the same way he solved his. We say that (M, w) is a *maximum i-model of the stable set S* if (M, w) is an i-model of S and for every i-model (M', w') of S, we have $IntPoss_i(M', w') \subseteq IntPoss_i(M, w)$.

Lemma 3.1: *Every $K45_n$-i-stable set has a maximum i-model.*

Theorem 3.2: *Suppose S is a $K45_n$-i-stable set and (M, w) is a maximum i-model of S. Then S is an i-stable expansion of α iff $(M, w) \models O_i \alpha$.*

We remark that an analogous result is proved by Lakemeyer [1993], except that he restricts attention to situations in the canonical model.

More evidence as to the reasonableness of our definitions is given by considering the properties of the operators N_i and O_i. As usual, we say that φ is valid, and write $\models \varphi$, if $(M, w) \models \varphi$ for all situations (M, w). We write $\models_{Lak} \varphi$ if φ is valid under Lakemeyer's semantics *in the canonical model*; we remark that $\models_{Lak}$ is the notion of validity considered by Lakemeyer, since he is only interested in the canonical model.

Theorem 3.3: *For all formulas φ, if $\models \varphi$ then $\models_{Lak} \varphi$. If $\varphi \in \mathcal{ONL}_n^-$, we have $\models \varphi$ iff $\models_{Lak} \varphi$.*

This theorem says that Lakemeyer's notion of validity is stronger than ours, although the two notions agree with respect to formulas in the sublanguage $\mathcal{ONL}_n^-$. In fact, Lakemeyer's notion of validity is strictly stronger than ours. Lakemeyer shows that $\models_{Lak} \neg O_i \neg O_j p$; under his semantics, it is impossible for i to only know that it is not the case that j only knows p. This seems counterintuitive. Why should this be an unattainable state of knowledge? Why can't j just tell i that it is not the case that he (j) only knows p?

We would argue that the validity of this formula is an artifact of Lakemeyer's focus on the canonical model. Roughly speaking, we would argue that the canonical model is not "canonical" enough. Although it includes all the possibilities in terms of basic formulas, it does

---

[6] This canonical model is built using standard modal logic techniques (cf. [Halpern and Moses 1992; Hughes and Cresswell 1968]); the worlds in this canonical model consist of all maximally $K45_n$-consistent subsets of formulas.

[7] In Moore's definition of stable expansion, we could have used closure under K45 instead of closure under deductive reasoning. The two definitions are equivalent in the single-agent case, but modal reasoning is necessary in the multi-agent case so that agent i can capture j's introspective reasoning.

[8] This can be viewed as indicating that basic formulas are not expressive enough to describe ω-trees. If we had had allowed infinite disjunctions and conjunctions into the language, then a stable set would determine the set of trees.

not include all the possibilities in terms of the extended language. The formula $O_i \neg O_j p$ is easily seen to be satisfiable under our semantics.

Lakemeyer provides a collection of axioms that he proves are sound with respect to $\models_{Lak}$, and complete for formulas in $\mathcal{ONL}_n^-$. He conjectures that they are not complete with respect to the full language. It is not hard to show that all of Lakemeyer's axioms are sound with respect to our semantics as well. It follows from Theorem 3.3 and Lakemeyer's completeness result that these axioms are complete with respect to $\mathcal{ONL}_n^-$ for our semantics too. It also follows from these observations that, as Lakemeyer conjectured, his proof system is not complete. This follows since everything provable in his system must be valid under our semantics, and $\neg O_i \neg O_j p$ is not valid under our semantics (although it is valid under his).

4 Discussion

We have shown how to extend two notions of only knowing to many agents. The key tool in both of these extensions was an appropriate canonical representation of the possibilities of the agents. Although we gave arguments showing that the way we chose to represent an agent's possibilities was reasonable, it would be nice to have a more compelling theory of "appropriateness". For example, why is it appropriate to use arbitrary trees for the non-introspective logics, and i-objective trees for the introspective logics? Would a different representation be appropriate if we had changed the underlying language? Perhaps a deeper study of the connections between ω-trees and the knowledge structures of [Fagin and Vardi 1986; Fagin, Halpern, and Vardi 1991] may help clarify some of these issues.

Another open problem is that of finding a complete axiomatization for $\mathcal{ONL}_n$. We observed that Lakemeyer's axioms were not complete with respect to his semantics. In fact, it seems that these axioms are essentially complete for $\mathcal{ONL}_n$ under our semantics.[9] We hope to report on these results in the future.

Acknowledgements: I would like to thank Ron Fagin, Gerhard Lakemeyer, Grisha Schwarz, and Moshe Vardi for their helpful comments on an earlier draft of this paper.

---

[9]The reason we say "essentially complete" here is that one of the axioms has the form

$N_i\alpha \Rightarrow \neg L_i\alpha$ for all basic i-objective α falsifiable in K45$_n$.

We need to extend this axiom to formulas that are not basic. But the axiom system K45$_n$ does not apply to non-basic formulas. We deal with this problem by extending the language so that we can talk about satisfiability within the language. The axiom then becomes

$$\neg Con(\alpha) \Rightarrow (N_i\alpha \Rightarrow \neg L_i\alpha),$$

where $Con(\alpha)$ holds if α is satisfiable.

References

Fagin, R., J. Y. Halpern, and M. Y. Vardi (1991). A model-theoretic analysis of knowledge. *Journal of the ACM 91*(2), 382–428. A preliminary version appeared in *Proc. 25th IEEE Symposium on Foundations of Computer Science*, 1984.

Fagin, R. and M. Y. Vardi (1986). Knowledge and implicit knowledge in a distributed environment: preliminary report. In J. Y. Halpern (Ed.), *Theoretical Aspects of Reasoning about Knowledge: Proc. 1986 Conference*, San Mateo, CA, pp. 187–206. Morgan Kaufmann.

Halpern, J. Y. (1993). A critical reexamination of default logic, autoepistemic logic, and only knowing. In *Proceedings, 3rd Kurt Gödel Colloquium*. Springer-Verlag.

Halpern, J. Y. and Y. Moses (1984). Towards a theory of knowledge and ignorance. In *Proc. AAAI Workshop on Non-monotonic Logic*, pp. 125–143. Reprinted in *Logics and Models of Concurrent Systems*, (ed., K. Apt), Springer-Verlag, Berlin/New York, pp. 459–476, 1985.

Halpern, J. Y. and Y. Moses (1992). A guide to completeness and complexity for modal logics of knowledge and belief. *Artificial Intelligence 54*, 319–379.

Hughes, G. E. and M. J. Cresswell (1968). *An Introduction to Modal Logic*. London: Methuen.

Lakemeyer, G. (1993). All they know: a study in multi-agent autoepestemic reasoning. In *Proc. Thirteenth International Joint Conference on Artificial Intelligence (IJCAI '93)*. Unpublished manuscript.

Levesque, H. J. (1990). All I know: A study in autoepistemic logic. *Artificial Intelligence 42*(3), 263–309.

Moore, R. C. (1985). Semantical considerations on nonmonotonic logic. *Artificial Intelligence 25*, 75–94.

Morgenstern, L. (1990). A theory of multiple agent nonmonotonic reasoning. In *Proc. National Conference on Artificial Intelligence (AAAI '90)*, pp. 538–544.

Parikh, R. (1991). Monotonic and nonmonotonic logics of knowledge. *Fundamenta Informaticae 15*(3,4), 255–274.

Stalnaker, R. (1980). A note on nonmonotonic modal logic. Technical report, Dept. of Philosophy, Cornell University. A slightly revised version will appear in *Artificial Intelligence*.

Vardi, M. Y. (1985). A model-theoretic analysis of monotonic knowledge. In *Proc. Ninth International Joint Conference on Artificial Intelligence (IJCAI '85)*, pp. 509–512.

All They Know About

Gerhard Lakemeyer
Institute of Computer Science III
University of Bonn
Römerstr. 164
5300 Bonn 1, Germany
gerhard@cs.uni-bonn.de

Abstract

We address the issue of agents reasoning about other agents' nonmonotonic reasoning ability in the framework of a multi-agent autoepistemic logic (AEL). In single-agent AEL, nonmonotonic inferences are drawn based on *all* the agent knows. In a multi-agent context such as Jill reasoning about Jack's nonmonotonic inferences, this assumption must be abandoned since it cannot be assumed that Jill knows everything Jack knows. Given a specific subject matter like Tweety the bird, it is more realistic and sufficient if Jill only assumes to know all Jack knows about Tweety in order to arrive at Jack's nonmonotonic inferences about Tweety. This paper provides a formalization of *all an agent knows about a certain subject matter* based on possible-world semantics in a multi-agent AEL. Besides discussing various properties of the new notion, we use it to characterize formulas that are about a subject matter in a very strong sense. While our main focus is on subject matters that consist of atomic propositions, we also address the case where agents are the subject matter.

Introduction

Most of the research on nonmonotonic reasoning has concentrated on the single-agent case. However, there is little doubt that agents who have been invested with a nonmonotonic reasoning mechanism should be able to reason about other agents and their ability to reason nonmonotonically as well. For example, if we assume the common default that birds normally fly and if Jill tells Jack that she has just bought a bird, then Jill should be able to infer that Jack thinks that her bird flies. Other examples from areas like planning and temporal projection can be found in [Mor90].

One of the main formalisms of nonmonotonic reasoning is *autoepistemic logic* (AEL) (e.g. [Moo85]). The basic idea is that the beliefs of agents are closed under *perfect introspection*, that is, they know[1] what

---

[1] We use the terms knowledge and belief interchangeably

they know and do not know. Nonmonotonic reasoning comes about in this framework in that agents can draw inferences on the basis of their own ignorance. For example, Jack's flying-bird default can be phrased as the belief that birds fly unless known otherwise. If Jill tells Jack that she has a bird called Tweety, Jack will conclude that Tweety flies since he does not know of any reason why Tweety should not be able to fly.

Note that in standard AEL agents determine their beliefs and especially their non-beliefs with respect to *everything* they believe. Thus, if we think of Jack's beliefs being represented by a knowledge base (KB), then Jack's belief that Tweety flies follows in AEL because the KB is *all* he believes or, as we also say, because Jack *only-believes* the formulas in the KB. (See [Lev90] for a formalization of AEL with an explicit notion of only-knowing.) If we want to extend autoepistemic logic to the multi-agent case, the strong assumption of having access to everything that is known is not warranted when applied to knowledge about other agents' knowledge. In other words, while an agent may have access to everything she herself knows, it is certainly not the case that she knows everything agents other than herself know. How then should Jill, for example, conclude that Jack autoepistemically infers that Tweety flies without pretending that she knows everything Jack knows? Intuitively, it seems sufficient for Jill to assume that she knows everything Jack knows *about Tweety*, which is quite plausible since Jack heard about Tweety through Jill. Thus if Jill believes that all Jack knows about Tweety is that he is a bird and, hence, that the flying-bird default applies to Tweety, then Jill is justified to conclude that Jack believes that Tweety flies.

In this paper, we present an account of multi-agent AEL which explicitly models the notion of *only-knowing about a subject matter*, which we also call *only-knowing-about*, for short. The work is based on possible-world semantics and takes ideas from a single-agent version of only-knowing-about [Lak92] and combines them with a multi-agent version of only-

---

in this paper for stylistic reasons. However, the formalism presented allows agents to have false beliefs.

knowing [Lak93].

None of the existing approaches to multi-agent AEL [Mor90, MG92, Hal93, Lak93][2] addresses the issue of only-knowing-about and are thus forced, one way or the other, to unrealistic assumptions when it comes to reasoning about the autoepistemic conclusions of other agents. Morgenstern and Guerreiro [Mor90, MG92], for example, run into the problem of what they call *arrogance*, where an agent i ascribes a non-belief to an agent j only on the basis of i herself not knowing whether j has this belief. Their solution is to heuristically limit the use of such arrogant behavior depending on specific applications. In [Lak93, Hal93], the only way to model the Tweety example is to assume that Jill knows *all* Jack knows.

The multi-agent AEL OL_n of [Lak93] is the starting point of this paper. OL_n's syntax and semantics are presented in the next section. We then extend OL_n by incorporating an explicit notion of only-knowing-about. Besides discussing various properties of the new notion, we use it to characterize formulas that are about a subject matter in a very strong sense. While our main focus is on subject matters that consist of atomic propositions, we also address the case where agents are the subject matter. We conclude with a summary of the results and future work.

The Logic OL_n

After introducing the syntax of the logic, we define the semantics in two stages. First we describe that part of the semantics that does not deal with only-knowing. In fact, this is just an ordinary possible-world semantics for n agents with perfect introspection. Then we introduce the necessary extensions that give us the semantics of only-knowing. The properties of only-knowing are discussed briefly. A detailed account is given in [Lak93].

Syntax

Definition 1 *The Language*
The primitives of the language consist of a countably infinite set of atomic propositions (or atoms), the connectives $\vee$, $\neg$, and the modal operators $\mathbf{L}_i$ and $\mathbf{O}_i$ for $1 \leq i \leq n$. (Agents are referred to as $1, 2, \ldots, n$.) Formulas are formed in the usual way from these primitives.[3] $\mathbf{L}_i\alpha$ should be read as "the agent i believes α" and $\mathbf{O}_i\alpha$ as "α is all agent i believes." A formula α is called **basic** *iff there are no occurrences of $\mathbf{O}_i$ ($1 \leq i \leq n$) in α.*

---

[2] Some notes on multi-agent AEL appear also in [HM84]. There has also been work in applying nonmonotonic theories to special multi-agent settings such as speech act theory, e.g. [Per87, AK88]. Yet these approaches do not aim to provide general purpose multi-agent nonmonotonic formalisms.

[3] We will freely use other connectives like $\wedge$, $\supset$ and $\equiv$, which should be understood as syntactic abbreviations of the usual kind.

Definition 2 *A modal operator occurs at* **depth** n *of a formula α iff it occurs within the scope of exactly n modal operators.*

For example, given $\alpha = p \wedge \mathbf{L}_1\mathbf{L}_2(\mathbf{L}_3q \vee \neg\mathbf{O}_2r)$, $\mathbf{L}_1$ occurs at depth 0, $\mathbf{L}_2$ at depth 1, and $\mathbf{L}_3$ and $\mathbf{O}_2$ occur both at depth 2.

Definition 3 *A formula α is called* **i-objective** *(for $i = 1, \ldots n$) iff every modal operator at depth 0 is of the form $\mathbf{O}_j$ or $\mathbf{L}_j$ with $i \neq j$.*

In other words, i-objective formulas talk about the external world from agent i's point of view, which includes beliefs of other agents but not his own.
For example, $(p \vee \mathbf{L}_2q) \wedge \neg\mathbf{O}_3\mathbf{L}_1p$ is 1-objective, but $(p \vee \mathbf{L}_2q) \wedge \neg\mathbf{L}_1\mathbf{O}_3p$ is not.

The Semantics of Basic Formulas

Basic formulas are given a standard possible-world semantics [Kri63, Hin62, Hin71], which the reader is assumed to be familiar with.[4] Roughly, a *possible-world model* consists of *worlds*, which determine the truth of atomic propositions, and binary *accessibility* relations between worlds. An agent's beliefs at a given world w are determined by what is true in all those worlds that are accessible to the agent from w. Since we are concerned with agents whose beliefs are consistent and closed under *perfect introspection*, we restrict the accessibility relations in the usual way. The resulting logic is called $KD45_n$.[5]

Definition 4 *A $KD45_n$-Model*
$M = \langle W, \pi, R_1, \ldots, R_n \rangle$ *is called a $KD45_n$-**model** (or simply* **model***) iff*

1. W *is a set (of worlds).*
2. π *is a mapping from the set of atoms into 2^W.*
3. $R_i \subseteq W \times W$ *for $1 \leq i \leq n$.*
4. R_i *is serial, transitive, and Euclidean[6] for $1 \leq i \leq n$.*

Given a model $M = \langle W, \pi, R_1, \ldots, R_n \rangle$ and a world $w \in W$, the meaning of basic formulas is defined as follows: Let p be an atom and α and β arbitrary basic formulas.

$$
\begin{aligned}
w &\models p &\iff& \quad w \in \pi(p) \\
w &\models \neg\alpha &\iff& \quad w \not\models \alpha \\
w &\models \alpha \vee \beta &\iff& \quad w \models \alpha \text{ or } w \models \beta \\
w &\models \mathbf{L}_i\alpha &\iff& \quad \text{for all } w', \text{ if } wR_iw' \text{ then } w' \models \alpha
\end{aligned}
$$

The Canonical Model

It is well known that, as far as basic formulas are concerned, it suffices to consider just one, the so-called *canonical model* [HC84, HM92]. This canonical model will be used later on to define the semantics of only-knowing.

---

[4] See [HC84, HM92] for an introduction.

[5] We use the subscript n to indicate that we are concerned with the n-agent case.

[6] R_i is Euclidean iff $\forall w, w', w''$, if wR_iw' and wR_iw'', then $w'R_iw''$.

Definition 5 *Maximally Consistent Sets*
Given any proof theory of $KD45_n$ and the usual notion of theoremhood and consistency, a set of basic formulas Γ is called **maximally consistent** *iff Γ is consistent and for every basic α, either α or $\neg\alpha$ is contained in Γ.*

The canonical $KD45_n$-model M_c has as worlds precisely all the maximally consistent sets and a world w' is R_i-accessible from w just in case all of i's beliefs at w are included in w'.

Definition 6 *The Canonical $KD45_n$-Model M_c*
The canonical model is a Kripke structure $M_c = \langle W_c, \pi, R_1, \ldots, R_n \rangle$ such that

1. $W_c = \{w \mid w$ is a maximally consistent set$\}$.

2. For all atoms p and $w \in W_c$, $w \in \pi(p)$ iff $p \in w$.

3. wR_iw' iff for all formulas $\mathbf{L}_i\alpha$, if $\mathbf{L}_i\alpha \in w$ then $\alpha \in w'$.

The following (well known) theorem tells us that nothing is lost from a logical point of view if we confine our attention to the canonical model.

Theorem 1 *M_c is a $KD45_n$-model and for every set of basic formulas Γ, Γ is satisfiable[7] iff it is satisfiable in M_c.*

The Semantics of Only-Knowing

Given this classical possible-world framework, what does it mean for an agent i to only-know, say, an atom p at some world w in a model M? Certainly, i should believe p, that is, all worlds that are i-accessible from w should make p true. Furthermore, i should believe as little else as possible apart from p. For example, i should neither believe q nor believe that j believes p etc. Minimizing knowledge using possible worlds simply means *maximizing* the number of accessible worlds. Thus, in our example, there should be an accessible world where q is false and another one where j does not believe p and so on. It should be clear that in order for w to satisfy only-knowing α this way, the model M must have a huge supply of worlds that are accessible from w. While not essential for the definition of only-knowing, it turns out to be very convenient to simply restrict our attention to models that are guaranteed to contain a sufficient supply of worlds. In fact, we will consider just one, namely the *canonical model* of $KD45_n$. Let us call the set of all formulas that are true at some world w in some model of $KD45_n$ a *world state*. The canonical model has the nice property that it contains precisely one world for every possible world state, since world states are just maximally consistent sets.

With that agent i is said to only-know a formula α at some world w (in the canonical model) just in case

α is believed and any world w' which satisfies α and from which the same worlds are i-accessible as from w is itself i-accessible from w.

Definition 7 *Given a model $M = \langle W, \pi, R_1, \ldots, R_n \rangle$ and worlds w and w' in W, we say that w and w' are* **i-equivalent** *($w \approx_i w'$) iff for all worlds $w^* \in W$, wR_iw^* iff $w'R_iw^*$.*

Given an arbitrary formula α, a world w in a model M, let

$$w \models \mathbf{O}_i\alpha \iff \text{ for all } w' \text{ s.t. } w \approx_i w', wR_iw' \text{ iff } w' \models \alpha.$$

A formula α is a logical consequence of a set of formulas Γ ($\Gamma \models \alpha$) iff for all worlds w in the canonical model M_c, if $w \models \gamma$ for all $\gamma \in \Gamma$, then $w \models \alpha$. As usual, we say that α is valid ($\models \alpha$) iff $\{\} \models \alpha$. A formula α is satisfiable iff $\neg\alpha$ is not valid.

Some Properties of the Logic   Here we can only sketch some of the properties of OL_n. The logic is discussed in more detail in [Lak93].[8] See also Halpern's logic of only-knowing [Hal93], which is closely related to OL_n.

Given Theorem 1, it is clear that the properties of basic formulas (no $\mathbf{O}_i$'s) are precisely those of $KD45_n$. Concerning only-knowing we restrict ourselves to the connection between only-knowing and a natural multi-agent version of the *stable expansions* of autoepistemic logic [Moo85].

Definition 8 *i-Epistemic State*
A set of basic formulas Γ is called an i-epistemic state iff there is a world w in M_c such that for all basic γ, $w \models \mathbf{L}_i\gamma$ iff $\gamma \in \Gamma$.

Given a set of basic formulas Γ, let $\overline{\Gamma} = \{$basic $\gamma \mid \gamma \notin \Gamma\}$, $\mathbf{L}_i\Gamma = \{\mathbf{L}_i\gamma \mid \gamma \in \Gamma\}$, and $\neg\mathbf{L}_i\overline{\Gamma} = \{\neg\mathbf{L}_i\gamma \mid \gamma \in \overline{\Gamma}\}$.

Definition 9 *i-Stable Expansion*
Let A be a set of basic formulas and let $\models_{KD45}$ denote logical consequence in $KD45_n$. Γ is called an i-stable expansion of A iff
$\Gamma = \{$*basic* $\gamma \mid A \cup \mathbf{L}_i\Gamma \cup \neg\mathbf{L}_i\overline{\Gamma} \models_{KD45} \gamma\}$.

Note that the use of $\models_{KD45}$ instead of logical consequence in propositional logic is essentially the only difference between Moore's original definition and this one. The following theorem establishes that the i-stable expansions of a formula α correspond precisely to the different i-epistemic states of agent i who only-knows α.

Theorem 2 *Only-Knowing and i-Stable Expansions*
Let α be a basic formula, $w \in W_c$, and let $\Gamma = \{$basic $\alpha \mid w \models \mathbf{L}_i\alpha\}$. Then $w \models \mathbf{O}_i\alpha$ iff Γ is an i-stable expansion of $\{\alpha\}$.

(See also [Hal93] for an analogous result.)

---

[7]A set of basic formulas Γ is *satisfiable* iff there is a model $M = \langle W, \pi, R_1, \ldots, R_n \rangle$ and $w \in W$ such that $w \models \gamma$ for all $\gamma \in \Gamma$.

[8]As a minor difference, [Lak93] uses $K45_n$ instead of $KD45_n$ as the base logic, that is, beliefs are not required to be consistent.

E-Clauses We end our discussion of OL_n by extending the notion of a clause of propositional logic to the modal case (e-clauses) and show that i-epistemic states are uniquely determined by the i-objective e-clauses they contain. This will be useful in developing the semantics of only-knowing-about in the next section.

Definition 10 *E-Clauses*
An e-clause *is a disjunct of the form*

$$(\bigvee_{i=1}^{u} l_i \vee \bigvee_{i=u+1}^{v} \mathbf{L}_{j_i} c_i \vee \bigvee_{i=v+1}^{w} \neg \mathbf{L}_{j_i} d_i),$$

where the l_i are literals and the c_i and d_i are themselves e-clauses.

Definition 11 *Extended Conjunctive Normal Form*
A basic formula α is in extended conjunctive normal form (ECNF) iff $\alpha = \bigwedge \alpha_i$ and every α_i is an e-clause.

Lemma 1 *For every basic α there is an α^* in ECNF such that $\models \alpha \equiv \alpha^*$.*

Every i-epistemic state is uniquely determined by the i-objective e-clauses it contains.

Theorem 3 *Let Γ and Γ' be two i-epistemic states. If Γ and Γ' agree on all their i-objective clauses, then $\Gamma = \Gamma'$.*

The Logic OL_n^a

We now extend OL_n to a logic that allows us to express things like "x is all agent i knows about subject y." A subject matter is defined as any finite subset π of atoms.[9] For every agent i and subject matter π, let $\mathbf{O}_i\langle \pi \rangle$ be a new modal operator. $\mathbf{O}_i\langle \pi \rangle \alpha$ should be read as "α is all agent i knows about π." If we refer to a subject matter extensionally, we sometimes leave out the curly brackets. For example, we write $\mathbf{O}_i\langle p, q \rangle \alpha$ instead of $\mathbf{O}_i\langle \{p, q\} \rangle \alpha$. Formulas in this extended language are formed in the usual way except for the following restriction: $\mathbf{O}_i\langle \pi \rangle$ may only be applied to **basic** formulas, that is, for any given $\mathbf{O}_i\langle \pi \rangle \alpha$, the only modal operators allowed in α are $\mathbf{L}_1, \ldots, \mathbf{L}_n$. Given a formula α and a subject matter π, we say that α **mentions** π iff at least one of the atoms of π occur in α.

To define the semantics of $\mathbf{O}_i\langle \pi \rangle \alpha$, we follow an approach similar to [Lak92], where only-believing-about is reduced to only-believing after "forgetting" everything that is irrelevant to π. Given a world w and a subject matter π, forgetting irrelevant beliefs is achieved by mapping w into a world $w|_{\pi,i}$ that is just like w except that only those beliefs of i are preserved that are *relevant* to π. Assuming we have such a $w|_{\pi,i}$, then i only-believes α about π at w just in case i believes it at w and i only-believes α at $w|_{\pi,i}$.

-----
[9] The results of the paper do not hinge on π being finite. What matters is that we have a way to refer to each subject matter in our language. If π is finite, this can always be done.

The crucial part of the semantics then is the construction of $w|_{\pi,i}$. It is obtained in two steps. First we collect all the beliefs of i about π in a set $\Gamma_{\pi,i}^w$. Theorem 3 allows us to restrict ourselves to i-objective e-clauses only. What does it mean for i to believe an e-clause c that is relevant to π? A reasonable answer seems to be the following: any formula that is believed by i and that implies c must mention the subject matter. For example, if $\pi = \{p\}$ and all i believes at w is $(p \vee q) \wedge r$, then the clauses selected to be relevant beliefs about π are $(p \vee q)$ and weaker ones like $(p \vee q \vee s)$. However, neither $(p \vee r)$ nor any clause not mentioning p are selected. $(p \vee r)$ is disqualified because it is contingent on r, which is also believed, thus not conveying any information about p.

Given $\Gamma_{\pi,i}^w$ it is then easy to define $w|_{\pi,i}$ in such a way that it believes only the formulas contained in $\Gamma_{\pi,i}^w$.

Definition 12 *Given a world w in the canonical model M_c, let*

$$\Gamma_{\pi,i}^w = \{c \mid c \text{ is an i-objective e-clause, } w \models \mathbf{L}_i c \text{ and}$$
$$\text{for all i-objective basic } \alpha, \text{ if } w \models \mathbf{L}_i \alpha$$
$$\text{and } \models \alpha \supset c \text{ then } \alpha \text{ mentions } \pi \}.$$

Lemma 2 *Given a world w of M_c and a subject matter π, let*
$$\Lambda_1 = \{\mathbf{L}_i \gamma \mid \gamma \text{ is i-objective and } \mathbf{L}_i \Gamma_{\pi,i}^w \models \mathbf{L}_i \gamma\} \cup$$
$$\{\neg \mathbf{L}_i \gamma \mid \gamma \text{ is i-objective and } \mathbf{L}_i \Gamma_{\pi,i}^w \not\models \mathbf{L}_i \gamma\}$$
$$\Lambda_2 = \{l \mid l \text{ is a literal in } w\} \cup \bigcup_{j \neq i} \{\mathbf{L}_j \gamma \mid \mathbf{L}_j \gamma \in w\} \cup$$
$$\bigcup_{j \neq i} \{\neg \mathbf{L}_j \gamma \mid \neg \mathbf{L}_j \gamma \in w\}.$$
Then $\Lambda_1 \cup \Lambda_2$ is consistent.

Definition 13 *Given w, π, and Λ_1 and Λ_2 of the previous lemma, let $w|_{\pi,i}$ be a world (= maximally consistent set) that contains Λ_1 and Λ_2.*

Note that by containing Λ_2, $w|_{\pi,i}$ is exactly like w except for the beliefs of agent i. Furthermore, Λ_1 makes sure that agent i at $w|_{\pi,i}$ believes no more than what follows from $\Gamma_{\pi,i}^w$, that is, the agent believes only what is relevant to the subject matter π.

Lemma 3 *$w|_{\pi,i}$ is unique.*

With this machinery we are finally ready to formally define the semantics of $\mathbf{O}_i\langle \pi \rangle \alpha$ for any basic formulas α and subject matter π:

$$w \models \mathbf{O}_i\langle \pi \rangle \alpha \iff w|_{\pi,i} \models \mathbf{O}_i \alpha \text{ and } w \models \mathbf{L}_i \alpha.$$

Satisfiability, logical consequence, and validity in OL_n^a are defined as for OL_n.

Some Properties of Only-Knowing-About

So far we do not have a complete axiomatization of only-knowing-about. The following properties, which are natural generalizations of the single-agent case [Lak92], suggest that our definitions are reasonable.

Definition 14 *Given a formula α, let $\pi_\alpha = \{p \mid p \text{ is an atom that occurs in } \alpha\}$.*

1) $\models O_i\langle\pi\rangle\alpha \supset L_i\alpha$.

Follows immediately from the definition.

2) $\models\neg O_i\langle\pi\rangle\alpha$ if $\not\models\alpha$ and $\pi \cap \pi_\alpha = \{\}$.

In other words, an agent cannot only-know something about π that is totally irrelevant to π.

3) $\models O_i\langle\pi\rangle\alpha \equiv O_i\langle\pi\rangle\beta$ if $\models \alpha \equiv \beta$.

In other words, the syntactic form of what is only-known about π does not matter.

4) $\models O_i\langle p\rangle(p \vee q) \supset (\neg L_i p \wedge \neg L_i q \wedge \neg L_i \neg p \wedge \neg L_i \neg q)$.

Here, assuming any of the beliefs of the right-hand-side implies that i must know more about p than just $p \vee q$.

5) $\models O_i\alpha \supset O_i\langle\pi_\alpha\rangle\alpha$.

This says that, if all you know is α and if the subject matter spans everything you know (see Definition 14), then surely α is all you know about this subject matter.

The following theorem characterizes cases where reasoning from only-knowing-about is the same as reasoning from only-knowing. This is interesting for at least two reasons. For one, only-knowing has a much simpler definition than only-knowing-about. For another, the theorem tells us that even though one usually does not know all another agent knows, there are cases where one may pretend to know all the other agent knows without drawing false conclusions. This will be very useful in the following section, where we show that Jill is indeed able to infer that Jack believes that Tweety flies.

Theorem 4 *Let α and β be basic formulas such that $\pi_\beta \subseteq \pi_\alpha$. Then $\models O_i\langle\pi_\alpha\rangle\alpha \supset L_i\beta$ iff $\models O_i\alpha \supset L_i\beta$.*

Jack, Jill, and Tweety Revisited

We now demonstrate that our formalism is able to model our initial Tweety example correctly. Let us assume that all Jack believes about Tweety is the flying-bird default for Tweety (α) and the fact that Tweety is a bird (β).

$\alpha = [\text{Bird}(Tweety) \wedge \neg L_{jack}\neg\text{Fly}(Tweety)] \supset \text{Fly}(T.)$
$\beta = \text{Bird}(Tweety)$

The subject matter Tweety can be characterized as the set of relevant predicates that mention Tweety, i.e. $\pi = \{\text{Bird}(Tweety), \text{Fly}(Tweety)\}$. We then obtain

$$\models O_{jack}\langle\pi\rangle(\alpha \wedge \beta) \supset L_{jack}\text{Fly}(Tweety) \qquad (1)$$

Proof : To prove this fact, note that $\pi_{\alpha\wedge\beta} = \pi$. Thus Theorem 4 applies and it suffices to show that $\models O_{jack}(\alpha \wedge \beta) \supset L_{jack}\text{Fly}(Tweety)$. It suffices to show that $\models O_{jack}(\alpha \wedge \beta) \equiv O_{jack}(\text{Bird}(Tweety) \wedge \text{Fly}(Tweety))$, since $\models O_{jack}(\text{Bird}(Tweety) \wedge \text{Fly}(Tweety)) \supset L_{jack}\text{Fly}(Tweety)$ follows immediately from the semantics of O_{jack}.

Let $w\models O_{jack}(\text{Bird}(Tweety) \wedge \text{Fly}(Tweety))$, that is, for all w' such that $w \approx_{jack} w'$, $wR_{jack}w'$ iff $w'\models (\text{Bird}(Tweety) \wedge \text{Fly}(Tweety))$. For all w' s.t. $w \approx_{jack} w'$ we obtain that $w'\models(\text{Bird}(Tweety) \wedge \text{Fly}(Tweety))$ iff $w'\models\alpha \wedge \beta$ since $w'\models\neg L_{jack}\neg\text{Fly}(Tweety)$. Thus $w\models O_{jack}(\alpha \wedge \beta)$.

Conversely, let $w\models O_{jack}(\alpha \wedge \beta)$, that is, for all w' such that $w \approx_{jack} w'$, $wR_{jack}w'$ iff $w'\models (\alpha \wedge \beta)$. Let w' be any world such that $w \approx_{jack} w'$. Let $w'\models\text{Bird}(Tweety) \wedge \text{Fly}(Tweety)$. Then $w\models\alpha \wedge \beta$ and, hence $wR_{jack}w'$. Conversely, let $wR_{jack}w'$. Obviously, $w'\models\text{Bird}(Tweety)$. Assume $w'\not\models\text{Fly}(Tweety)$. Then $w'\models L_{jack}\neg\text{Fly}(Tweety)$ by assumption. Then there is a world w'' such that $w \approx_{jack} w''$ and $w''\models L_{jack}\neg\text{Fly}(Tweety) \wedge \text{Bird}(Tweety) \wedge \text{Fly}(Tweety)$. Hence $w''\models(\alpha \wedge \beta)$ and, therefore, $wR_{jack}w''$, contradicting the assumption that $w'\models L_{jack}\neg\text{Fly}(Tweety)$. Thus $w\models O_{jack}(\text{Bird}(Tweety) \wedge \text{Fly}(Tweety))$. ∎

Given (1) and $\models L_i(\alpha \supset \beta) \supset (L_i\alpha \supset L_i\beta)$ for all α, β and i, we immediately obtain the desired result

$$\models L_{jill}O_{jack}\langle\pi\rangle(\alpha \wedge \beta) \supset L_{jill}L_{jack}\text{Fly}(Tweety),$$

that is, if Jill knows what Jack knows about Tweety, then she also knows what default inferences Jack makes about Tweety.

Strictly π-Relevant Formulas

It seems very hard to define what it means for a formula to be about a subject matter on purely syntactic grounds. For example, while $(p \supset q)$ is intuitively about p, $(p \supset q) \wedge (\neg p \supset q)$ (which is equivalent to q) is not. Also note that, while $(q \vee r)$ by itself is clearly not about p, $(q \vee r)$ becomes nontrivial information about p as part of the formula $(q \vee r) \wedge (p \equiv q)$. Our notion of only-knowing-about captures these subtleties of aboutness and yields a useful definition of formulas that are about a subject matter in a very strong sense.

Definition 15 *Let α be a basic formula such that $\not\models\alpha$ and let π be a subject matter. α is called **strictly π-relevant** iff $O_i\langle\pi\rangle\alpha$ is satisfiable for some i.*

Intuitively, every piece of information conveyed by a strictly π-relevant formula tells us something nontrivial about π.

p, $\neg L_i p \vee (q \wedge r)$, and $(q \vee r) \wedge (p \equiv q)$ are all strictly p-relevant, $(p \supset q) \wedge (\neg p \supset q)$, $p \wedge (p \supset q)$, and $(p \vee \neg p)$, on the other hand, are not. At first glance, one may want to include $(p \vee \neg p)$ among the p-relevant formulas. After all, $O_i\langle p\rangle(p \vee \neg p)$ is satisfiable. However, the mention of p in $p \vee \neg p$ seems merely accidental since $\models(p \vee \neg p) \equiv \alpha$ for every valid α. Thus we feel justified in assuming that $p \vee \neg p$ does not convey any relevant information about p.[10] The following lemma identifies a simple case where formulas are strictly about a subject matter.

Lemma 4 *Let α be a basic i-objective formula such that $\not\models\alpha$ and $\not\models\neg\alpha$. Then α is strictly π_α-relevant.*

Finally, the following theorem allows us to characterize strictly π-relevant basic formulas without appealing to belief or only-believing-about.

---

[10]In this light, $O_i\langle p\rangle(p \vee \neg p)$ is best understood as saying that *nothing* is known about p.

Theorem 5 *Let α be a basic i-objective formula such that $\not\models\alpha$ and let π be a subject matter. Let*

$$\Gamma = \{c \mid c \text{ is a basic i-objective e-clause such that}$$
$$\models\alpha \supset c \text{ and for all basic i-objective } \beta,$$
$$\text{if } \models\alpha \supset \beta \text{ and } \beta \supset c \text{ then } \beta \text{ mentions } \pi\}$$

Then α is strictly π-relevant iff there are $c_1, \ldots, c_k \in \Gamma$ such that $\models \bigwedge_{i=1}^{k} c_i \supset \alpha$.

What Does Jill Know about Jack?

So far, we have assumed that the subject matter is a set of atomic propositions, just as in [Lak92]. In a multi-agent context, there is at least one other possible subject matter, namely other agents. In other words, we may want to ask the question what Jill believes about Jack's beliefs. For example, if all Jill believes is $p \vee (\neg\mathbf{L}_{jack}q \wedge r)$, then all Jill believes about Jack seems to be $p \vee \neg\mathbf{L}_{jack}q$. It turns out to be quite easy to formalize these ideas, requiring only minor changes to the definitions we already have.

For simplicity, we only consider the subject matter of one agent. Thus for all agents i and j with $i \neq j$, let $\mathbf{O}_i\langle j\rangle$ be a new modal operator. As before, we require that $\mathbf{O}_i\langle j\rangle$ only be applied to basic formulas.

Definition 16 *Given a world w in the canonical model M_c, let*

$$\Gamma_{j,i}^{w} = \{c \mid c \text{ is an i-objective e-clause, } w\models\mathbf{L}_i c \text{ and}$$
$$\text{for all i-objective basic } \alpha, \text{ if } w\models\mathbf{L}_i\alpha$$
$$\text{and } \models\alpha \supset c \text{ then } \alpha \text{ mentions } \mathbf{L}_j\}.$$

Given a world w, let $w|_{j,i}$ be defined just as $w|_{\pi,i}$ was defined with $\Gamma_{j,i}^{w}$ now taking the role of $\Gamma_{\pi,i}^{w}$. The semantics of only-knowing about another agent is then simply:

$$w\models\mathbf{O}_i\langle j\rangle\alpha \iff w|_{j,i}\models\mathbf{O}_i\alpha \text{ and } w\models\mathbf{L}_i\alpha.$$

For example, given i's knowledge base $KB = p\wedge(\neg\mathbf{L}_j q\vee q) \wedge \mathbf{L}_k\mathbf{L}_j p$, where i, j, and k denote three different agents, we obtain

$$\models\mathbf{O}_i KB \supset \mathbf{O}_i\langle j\rangle[(\neg\mathbf{L}_j q \vee q) \wedge \mathbf{L}_k\mathbf{L}_j p].$$

Finally, if we were interested only in what i herself knows about j's beliefs, that is, if we want to exclude $\mathbf{L}_k\mathbf{L}_j p$ in the last example, we can do so by modifying the definition of $\Gamma_{j,i}^{w}$ in that we require that α mentions $\mathbf{L}_j$ at *depth 0*.

Conclusion

While an agent i in general does not know all another agent j knows, i may well know all j knows about a specific subject matter π, which suffices for i to infer j's nonmonotonic inferences regarding π. In this paper we formalized such a notion of only-knowing-about for two kinds of subject matters and discussed some of its properties. In addition, we were able to use our new notion of only-knowing-about to specify what it means for a formula to be strictly about a given subject matter.

As for future work, it would be desirable to obtain a complete axiomatization of only-knowing-about, simply because proof theories provide very concise characterizations. The first-order case, of course, needs to be addressed as well. We believe that our work, apart from the specific context of multi-agent autoepistemic reasoning, sheds some light on the concept of *aboutness*. However, much more remains to be done before this intriguing and difficult issue is fully understood.

References

[AK88] Appelt, D. and Konolige, K., A Practical Nonmonotonic Theory of Reasoning about Speech Acts, in *Proc. of the 26th Conf. of the ACL*, 1988.

[Hal93] Halpern, J. Y., Reasoning about only knowing with many agents, these proceedings.

[HM84] Halpern, J. Y. and Moses, Y. O., Towards a Theory of Knowledge and Ignorance: Preliminary Report, in Proceedings of The Non-Monotonic Workshop, New Paltz, NY, 1984, pp. 125–143.

[HM92] Halpern, J. Y. and Moses, Y. O., A Guide to Completeness and Complexity for Modal Logics of Knowledge and Belief, *Artificial Intelligence* **54**, 1992, pp. 319–379.

[HC84] Hughes, G. E. and Cresswell, M. J., *A Companion to Modal Logic*, Methuen & Co., London, 1984.

[Hin62] Hintikka, J., *Knowledge and Belief: An Introduction to the Logic of the Two Notions*, Cornell University Press, 1962.

[Hin71] Hintikka, J., Semantics for Propositional Attitudes, in L. Linsky (ed.), *Reference and Modality*, Oxford University Press, Oxford, 1971.

[Kri63] Kripke, S. A., Semantical Considerations on Modal Logic, *Acta Philosophica Fennica* **16**, 1963, pp. 83–94.

[Lak92] All You Ever Wanted to Know about Tweety, in *Proc. of the 3rd International Conference on Principles of Knowledge Representation and Reasoning*, Morgan Kaufmann, 1992, pp. 639–648.

[Lak93] All They Know: A Study in Multi-Agent Nonmonotonic Reasoning, in *Proc. of the 13th International Joint Conference on Artificial Intelligence (IJCAI-93)*, Morgan Kaufmann, 1993.

[Lev90] Levesque, H. J., All I Know: A Study in Autoepistemic Logic, *Artificial Intelligence*, North Holland, **42**, 1990, pp. 263–309.

[Moo85] Moore, R., Semantical Considerations on Nonmonotonic Logic, *Artificial Intelligence* **25**, 1985, pp. 75–94.

[Mor90] Morgenstern, L., A Theory of Multiple Agent Nonmonotonic Reasoning, in *Proc. of AAAI-90*, 1990, pp. 538–544.

[MG92] Morgenstern, L. and Guerreiro, R., Epistemic Logics for Multiple Agent Nonmonotonic Reasoning I, *Symposium on Formal Reasoning about Beliefs, Intentions, and Actions*, Austin, TX, 1992.

[Per87] Perrault, R., An Application of Default Logic to Speech Act Theory, in *Proc. of the Symposium on Intentions and Plans in Communication and Discourse*, Monterey, 1987.

Representation for
Actions and Motion

Towards Knowledge-Level Analysis
of Motion Planning [*]

Ronen I. Brafman   **Jean-Claude Latombe**   **Yoav Shoham**

Robotics Laboratory

Stanford University

Stanford, CA 94305

e-mail: {brafman,latombe,shoham}@cs.stanford.edu

Abstract

Inspired by the success of the distributed computing community in applying logics of knowledge and time to reasoning about distributed protocols, we aim for a similarly powerful and high-level abstraction when reasoning about control problems involving uncertainty. Here we concentrate on robot motion planning, with uncertainty in both control and sensing. This problem has already been well studied within the robotics community. Our contributions include the following:

- We define a new, natural problem in this domain: obtaining a sound and complete termination condition, given initial and goal locations.
- We consider a specific class of (simple) motion plans in R^n from the literature, and provide necessary and sufficient conditions for the existence of sound and complete termination conditions for plans in that class.
- We define a high-level language, a logic of time and knowledge, to reason about motion plans in the presence of uncertainty, and use them to provide general conditions for the existence of sound and complete termination conditions for a broader class of motion plans.

Introduction

Much research carried on in computer science in general, and AI in particular, concerns the development of powerful abstractions, and their application to problems of interest. In the context of this article, of particular note is the application of logics of knowledge in distributed computing (e.g., [Halpern and Moses, 1990]). The essential insight behind that line of research was that a formal notion of "knowing," developed initially in philosophy [Hintikka, 1962] and later

imported to AI [Moore, 1985], can be coherently and usefully applied to reasoning about (and later also designing) distributed protocols. The reasons for the success of this approach include:

Intuitiveness: The high-level language supported statements of the sort "processor A doesn't know that processor B is faulty," which are precisely the type employed informally by people reasoning about the domain.

Groundedness: The formal notion of knowledge was anything but vague; it was defined precisely in terms of the underlying protocol.

Abstraction and Generality: In principle, the notion of knowledge was dispensable. However, the analysis in terms of knowledge homed in on the essential notion, the knowledge available to the various processors at different points in time, and allowed one to abstract away from the details of how the particular physical protocol implemented that knowledge. This knowledge-level abstraction made it possible to analyze (and later also design) protocols even before their physical implementation was specified; in fact, the same knowledge-level protocol could be implemented differently, without affecting the high-level analysis.

While logics of knowledge have been widely used in AI (e.g., to model human-computer interaction, distributed planning, and nonmonotonic logics), they have so far not been applied in a similar fashion, as a knowledge level corresponding to some specific concrete system. Two exceptions do come to mind – Levesque's knowledge-level analysis of databases [Levesque, 1984], and Rosenschein and Kaelbling's Situated Automata [Rosenschein, 1985, Kaelbling and Rosenschein, 1990]. We claim, however, that there is a much wider arena in which the lessons from distributed computing can be applied, namely planning and control in the presence of uncertainty. In this article we take one step towards exploring this arena, concentrating on robot motion planning.

Robot motion planning with uncertainty is a well researched area [Canny, 1989, Erdmann, 1986, Latombe, 1991, Latombe *et al.*, 1991]. The uncertainty in that domain can arise from several sources, including par-

---

*The work of the first and third author is supported by DARPA grant USC 598240 (DARPA DABT63-91-C0025) and AFOSR grant #F49620-92-J-0547. The work of the second author is supported by DARPA grant N00014-92-J-1809.

tial information about the location of various objects, sloppy control, and noisy sensing. We argue that this domain exhibits all the 'right' properties: (1) One naturally analyzes the situation by saying that "the robot knows that it is at the goal, since it knows that the current reading could only have been obtained if it were either at the goal or beyond the wall, and it knows its motion plan could not possibly have taken it behind the wall"; (2) the notion of knowledge can be grounded precisely in the motion plan of the robot, as well as some additional parameters such as the slop in control and the noise in sensing.

It would have been convenient to start with a given class of motion planning problems, and delve directly into their knowledge-level analysis. However, we were surprised to find that, although much related research has been conducted in robotics, the simple question *we* would like to pursue has not been addressed. A typical question asked in robotics is "Given that the robot must end up in a particular region, and given bounds on the slop in control and noise in sensing, what is the biggest initial area from which the robot can start, and still be guaranteed to arrive at the goal and recognize that it is at the goal?" This initial area is called the *pre-image* of the goal. In a multi-step motion plan, this question is repeated in a backward-chaining fashion, leading to the method of *pre-image backchaining* [Lozano-Pérez *et al.*, 1984]. In contrast, we consider fixed initial and goal regions and a class of simple motion commands 'Go in direction D, until the termination condition, T, is satisfied'. D can be seen as responsible for reaching the goal, while T is responsible for recognizing it. The seemingly more basic question we ask is: "Given a fixed D, and given bounds on the slop in control and sensing of the robot, does there exist a *good* definition of T?" Of course, one could interpret *good* in many ways. We will interpret it by appealing to standard computer-scientific notions; we will be interested in termination conditions that are *sound* and *complete*, that is, ones that guarantee that if the robot stops, it only stops at the goal, and that it does eventually stop.

Before introducing a high-level language, we will give more feel for the problem by considering it in the context of a particular class of motion plans in R^n; we will present some results on necessary and sufficient conditions for the existence of sound and complete termination conditions in that class. We will then consider general motion planning, define a (fairly standard) logic of knowledge and time for reasoning about them, and then, for a broad class of motion planning problems in R^n, provide a knowledge-level characterization of the conditions in which sound and complete termination conditions exist. Our proofs, contained in a longer version of this paper ([Brafman *et al.*, 1993]), are constructive, that is, when such termination conditions exist, the proofs yield ways of computing them.

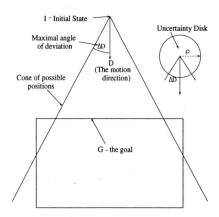

Figure 1: An example domain

We conclude the introduction with a simple path-planning problem in R^1, taken from [Latombe, 1991]. We will use it later to illustrate the various definitions and results, along with more realistic examples, to the extent that space allows.

Example 1 *Assume that our robot is a point moving forward along the positive reals, starting at 0; it moves continuously at finite velocity, until the termination condition is satisfied, at which point it stops. The goal is the interval $[2, 4]$. There is a position sensing uncertainty of 1, so that if the robot is at location l, its sensor may indicate any value between $l - 1$ and $l + 1$.*

In the following let r denote the current position reading of the robot. Clearly '$r > 1$' is a complete termination condition, but not a sound one. Similarly, '$r = 3$' is a sound termination condition, but not a complete one (readings need not be continuous: we may have a sequence of readings that are accurate until we reach 2.5, at which point they might become consistently off by +1, i.e., start from 3.5 and grow). Somewhat surprisingly, there exists a termination condition that is both sound and complete, e.g., '$r \in [3, 5]$'.

Termination Conditions in Motion Planning

We introduce a motion planning domain, with particular types of sensing and control uncertainty, in which we investigate the existence of sound and complete termination conditions.

The problem

Our robot starts its motion from a designated set of locations (possibly a singleton), I, within the workspace $\mathcal{W} \subset R^n$. It proceeds along its commanded direction, D, attempting to reach and stop at the goal, G, a compact subset of $\mathcal{W}$ (see Figure 1). However, *control uncertainty* may cause the tangent of the path to deviate by up to ΔD from this direction. This constrains

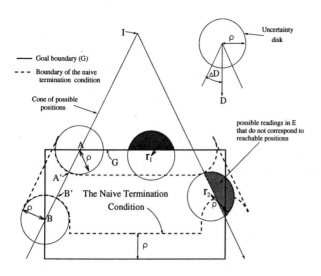

Figure 2: A naive termination condition

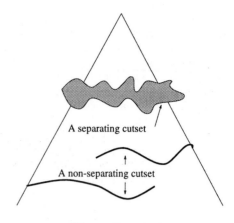

Figure 3: cutsets

the robot to remain within a cone of possible positions defined by the initial state, by D and by ΔD. At each position, q, the robot's sensors supply a position reading, r; but while the robot's motion is continuous, the position readings may not be continuous. The reading, r, must be within a disk of radius ρ, $\Delta R(q)$, centered at q. Consequently, given a position reading, r, the actual position, q, is also within a disk of radius ρ, $\Delta Q(r)$, centered in r, defining the *sensing uncertainty*. If a subset of this disk is outside the cone of possible positions, it can be eliminated as candidates for the actual position. We use the term **motion planning instance** to refer to the domain specified by $\Delta D, \rho, I$, and G. The **termination condition**, T, is a (total) boolean function on the set of possible readings. The first time it evaluates to *true* the robot stops.

An annotated trajectory describes a possible execution of a motion command.

Definition 1 *Given a motion planning instance and a motion command $M=(D,T)$, $\tau=(Q,V)$ is a* **consistent annotated trajectory**, *where Q is a continuous function from $[0,\infty)$ to $\mathcal{W}$ (describing the path), and V is a (not necessarily continuous) function from $[0,\infty)$ to $\mathcal{R}$ (describing the readings), if the the following properties are satisfied:*

- *$Q(0) \in I$;*
- *$\forall s \in [0,\infty): |V(s) - Q(s)| \leq \rho$;*
- *$\forall s \in [0,\infty): |dQ(s) - D| \leq \Delta D$, where $dQ(s)$ is the direction of the tangent to Q at s;*
- *$\forall s \in [0,\infty)$: if $T(V(s))$ is true, then $\forall s' > s$ $Q(s')=Q(s)$.*

Definition 2 *Given a motion planning instance and a motion direction, a termination condition T is* **sound** *if for every consistent trajectory $\tau=(Q,V)$: for $\hat{s} \equiv \inf\{s \in [0,\infty): T(V(s))$ is true$\}$ it is the case that*

$Q(\hat{s}) \in G$. *It is* **complete** *if every consistent trajectory $\tau=(Q,V)$ satisfies $\exists s \in [0,\infty)$ such that $T(V(s))$ is true.*

That is, if the termination condition is complete the robot eventually stops, and if it is sound, if the robot stops, it stops in the goal. A precise formulation of the problem we wish to investigate, is:

```
Given a motion planning instance and a
motion direction D, does there exist a
sound and complete termination condition?
```

The naive termination condition

Let the **forward projection** of I, $\mathcal{F}(I)$, be the set of positions that can be reached from I by a path consistent with D and ΔD. The termination condition '$\Delta Q(r) \cap \mathcal{F}(I) \subset G$' can only be true at positions within the goal or at positions that cannot be reached from I. Hence it is sound. We call it the **naive termination condition**. The naive termination condition in Example 1 is '$r=3$'.

Example 2 *In Figure 2 we see an example of a naive termination condition, bounded by the dashed line. The positions from which the reading r_1 can be obtained are contained in the disk $\Delta Q(r_1)$. Some of them, those in the shaded area, are not in the goal. Thus, a reading of r_1 may be obtained from outside the goal, and r_1 is not within the naive termination condition. r_2 is in the naive termination condition, although part of the positions from which we can obtain a reading of r_2 are outside the goal. These positions are outside $\mathcal{F}(I)$, and cannot be reached by any consistent motion.*

The naive termination condition is not complete. In Example 2, because the distance between the points A' and B' is less than 2ρ, a consistent annotated trajectory, in which the termination condition never evaluates to *true* exists.

Conditions for existence of a sound and complete termination condition

We now derive a number of conditions for the existence of a sound and complete termination condition in *domains containing no obstacles, in which the initial states are in a single connected component.*

Definition 3 *A* **motion cutset** *(w.r.t. a motion direction) is a set of positions, at least one of which must be traversed by every consistent trajectory, assuming the termination condition $T \equiv false$.*

A **separating cutset** *is a motion cutset* **cs** *such that $\mathcal{F}(I) \backslash$**cs** consists of two disjoint connected components, one of which includes the set of possible initial states.*

Figure 3 offers an example of separating and non-separating cutsets.

Theorem 1 *A sufficient condition for the existence of a sound and complete termination condition is that the naive termination condition contains a separating cutset.*

We have a constructive proof of this theorem, which due to length limitations we must omit. The construction relies on the fact that we can disregard positions consistent with our reading if we know that reaching them requires that we pass through earlier positions that satisfy the termination condition. We use the given cutset, cs, to derive a second cutset within the goal, cs', (one that is ρ "farther") and construct a termination condition that guarantees that we never pass cs', thus allowing us to ignore positions that are "beyond" this cutset. Figure 4 illustrates a sound and complete termination condition based on this construction for an example similar to, but more extreme than that of Figure 2 (i.e., A' and B' of Figure 2 are equal).

Example 1 (continued) *The naive termination condition 'r = 3' is a separating cutset (as is any other point). Using the construction provided by the proof of Theorem 1, a sound and complete termination condition is 'r $\in$ [3,5]'. Although a reading in the range of [3,5] can be obtained outside the goal, the first time the termination condition is satisfied will always be within the goal.*

Theorem 2 *A necessary condition for the existence of a sound and complete termination condition is that the naive termination condition be a motion cutset.*

Since for convex goals if the naive termination condition is a motion cutset then it is a separating cutset we obtain:

Consequence 1 *If the goal is convex a necessary and sufficient condition for the existence of a sound termination condition is that the naive termination condition is a motion cutset.*

Using more complex definitions we can prove stronger versions of Theorem 1 (i.e., allow obstacles and relax restrictions on initial states) and Theorem 2 (i.e., relax restriction on initial states).

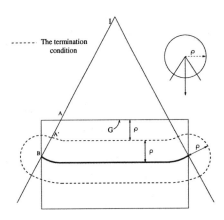

Figure 4: sound & complete termination condition

Knowledge-Level Formalization

We would like to generalize the results of the previous section, by extending our analysis to more general domains, not restricting ourselves to such a limited class of sensors. The notion of knowledge will serve as a powerful abstraction, enabling us to do so.

The motion protocol

We can view our endeavor as the investigation of a class of two-player protocols. Our players are the robot, which follows the motion command, and the environment, which decides nondeterministically, how the robot actually moves and what it senses, within given margins [Taylor *et al.*, 1988]. Let us make this more precise.

Definition 4 *A* **(global) state** *is a pair (e, r), where $e \in \mathcal{E}$ and $r \in \mathcal{R}$. $\mathcal{E}$ is the set of possible (local) states of the environment and $\mathcal{R}$ is the set of possible (local) states of the robot. The set of global states is denoted by $\mathcal{S}$. If a is an agent (i.e., the robot or the environment), the set of local states of a is denoted by $S_{|a}$.*

In the domain of the previous section the local state of the robot consisted of its current sensor reading, while the local state of the environment consisted of the robot's *actual* position.

Definition 5 *A* **run** *R, is a function from $[0, \infty)$ to $\mathcal{S}$. A* **system** *is a set of runs. A run R is* **consistent** *with a system S if $R \in S$.*

A run extends the static description of the world, provided by the state, over time. A system corresponds to some subset of the set of possible runs, those runs that describe behaviors that correspond to the ones we would like to model. The states that are part of a consistent run are called **possible states** (or worlds), and represent states of the world that may hold at some time. To reason about one-step motion plans we look at a parameterized class of systems that includes runs that obey the following restrictions:

$\mathcal{P}(I, D, \Delta D, \Delta R)$

The initial state is in I.
The restriction of the run to the local state of the robot describes a continuous trajectory.
The direction of the tangent to the trajectory at each point q, dq, satisfies $dq \in \Delta D(q)$.
The reading r in q satisfies $r \in \Delta R(q)$.

Note that there are no restrictions on the shape or size of $\Delta R(q)$, the set of readings possible at q. The possible initial states are not constrained, either, nor is $\Delta D(q)$ (thus we are not restricted to cone-like domains).

As an example, in the previous section we looked at a case where $\Delta R(q)$ is a disk of radius ρ centered in q, and $\Delta D(q) = \{D' : |D - D'| \leq \Delta\}$ for a constant Δ.

Knowledge-level analysis of the motion protocol

We introduce a language for reasoning about the motion protocol. This language contains temporal and epistemic modal operators and has intuitive semantics. We use it to formulate and prove new, more general, results.

The language We assume that we have a propositional language $\mathcal{L}$. Given an instance of the above motion protocol, let $\mathcal{S}$ be the set of possible states. Let $\mathcal{I}$ be an *interpretation function*, which is a boolean function on $\mathcal{S}$ and the primitive propositions in $\mathcal{L}$. $\mathcal{I}$ tells us whether a certain primitive proposition is true in a certain possible state. We define the notion of satisfiability of a propositional formula in a state s, under interpretation $\mathcal{I}$ of $\mathcal{S}$.

- $\mathcal{I}, \mathcal{S}, s \models p$ for a primitive proposition p if $\mathcal{I}(s,p) = true$;
- $\mathcal{I}, \mathcal{S}, s \models \neg\alpha \Leftrightarrow \mathcal{I}, \mathcal{S}, s \not\models \alpha$;
- $\mathcal{I}, \mathcal{S}, s \models \alpha \wedge \beta \Leftrightarrow \mathcal{I}, \mathcal{S}, s \models \alpha$ and $\mathcal{I}, \mathcal{S}, s \models \beta$.

We assume that the interpretation function $\mathcal{I}$, is fixed and 'natural', e.g., the proposition g, denoting a goal state, will be satisfied *exactly* by those states in which the position is part of the goal. We will use $\mathcal{S} \models \alpha$ when α is satisfied by all states in $\mathcal{S}$, and $\models \alpha$ when $\mathcal{S}' \models \alpha$ for any $\mathcal{S}'$.

Motion is closely connected with time, thus we add temporal operators:[1]

- $\mathcal{S}, s \models \exists_\square \alpha$ if there exists a run R such that $\exists t \in [0, \infty)$ such that $R(t) = s$ and $\forall t' \geq t\ R(t') \models \alpha$. I.e., all possible states following s (s inclusive) of a certain run containing s, satisfy α.
- $\mathcal{S}, s \models \exists_\diamond \alpha$ if for some run R such that $\exists t \in [0, \infty)\ R(t) = s$, $\exists t' \geq t$ s.t. $R(t') \models \alpha$. I.e., some possible state following s (or s itself) in some run containing s, satisfies α.

These modal operators define two other operators:

$$\forall_\square \alpha \equiv \neg\exists_\diamond \neg\alpha \qquad \forall_\diamond \alpha \equiv \neg\exists_\square \neg\alpha$$

In the above operators the present state is considered a part of the future. We have similar operators for the past. The 8 operator for all tenses are:

Future	Past
$\forall_\diamond, \forall_\square, \exists_\diamond, \exists_\square$	$\forall_{\diamondsuit}, \forall_{\boxdot}, \exists_{\diamondsuit}, \exists_{\boxdot}$

To deal with uncertainty we define the notion of knowledge.

Definition 6 *Let $\mathcal{S}$ be a given set of states, and let $s, s' \in \mathcal{S}$.*
$s \sim_r s' \Leftrightarrow$ the state of the robot is identical in s and s'.

Note that $\sim_r$ is an equivalence relation.

Definition 7 *Let $\alpha \in \mathcal{L}$. The robot **knows** α at $s \in \mathcal{S}$, written $\mathcal{S}, s \models K_r \alpha$ if for any state s', such that $s \sim_r s'$, $\mathcal{S}, s' \models \alpha$.*

From now on we shall assume that our language, $\mathcal{L}$, is closed under the temporal and epistemic operators. All definitions remain unchanged. Although detailed logical investigation is not the thrust of this paper, we note in passing that K is an $S5$ operator. Note that given $\mathcal{S}$, the satisfiability in s of a formula of the form $K_r \alpha$ depends only on the local state of the robot, and can be interpreted as a predicate on its local state. $K_r \alpha$ thus uniquely defines a termination condition (although not necessarily an easily computable one).

The following is our main theorem:

Theorem 3 *Assume that $\mathcal{S} \models (\neg g \wedge \forall_{\diamondsuit} g) \rightarrow \exists_\square \neg g$, where g is the proposition satisfied precisely by the goal states. A sound and complete termination condition exists iff $K_r \forall_{\diamondsuit} g$ defines a sound and complete termination condition.*[2]

<u>Discussion</u>: There are a number of important things to note.
Constructive canonical form: The theorem gives a constructive definition of a sound and complete termination condition, if one exists, so we need only check this condition to verify the existence of a sound and complete termination condition.
Optimality: For any run, this termination condition evaluates to *true* no later than any other sound and complete termination condition.
Generality: The use of knowledge to characterize the termination condition means that it applies to sensing uncertainty of *any* type, i.e., while previously $\Delta R(q)$ was a disk, it can now take on any shape. In fact, we

---

[1] Temporal logic with these operators were investigated by Emerson and Halpern ([Emerson and Halpern, 1985]), among others.

[2] We will assume that $K_r \forall_{\diamondsuit} g$ is a closed set. This is a very weak assumption which we discuss in the longer version of this paper [Brafman *et al.*, 1993].

are *not* constrained to position sensing, and the theorem applies to force sensing, as well as robots with sensing memory. The initial state may be part of a large region or just a point and our domain may contain obstacles. The control uncertainty is not limited to the cone-like behavior of the previous section.

The following lemma shows that Theorem 3 covers a large natural family of domains,

Lemma 1 *For any convex subspace of R^n, if the goal region is convex, $\mathcal{S} \models (\neg g \wedge \forall_{\diamond} g) \rightarrow \exists_{\Box} \neg g$.*

Example 1 (continued) *If you recall our robot moved along the positive reals, its goal was to be in $[2,4]$ and its reading uncertainty was $\rho = 1$. The condition $\forall_{\diamond} g$ is satisfied by positions $q \in [2,\infty)$, thus $K_r \forall_{\diamond} g$ is satisfied by readings $r \in [3,\infty)$, corresponding to a sound and complete termination condition.*

Using the above theorem we have been able to prove the following result about the domain of the previous section.

Theorem 4 *In an empty subspace of R^n with $\Delta R(q)$ a disc of radius $\rho \in R$ and a compact goal, in which the condition $\mathcal{S} \models (\neg g \wedge \forall_{\diamond} g) \rightarrow \exists_{\Box} \neg g$ of Theorem 3 holds for a robot with sensing history; a sound and complete termination condition based on a complete reading history exists, iff there is one dependent only on the cur-rent position reading.*

Conclusion and future work

Knowledge is a powerful tool for reasoning about domains in which uncertainty exists. The temporal-epistemic language we used provides a natural and powerful tool in the domain of motion planning with uncertainty, and enabled us to express and prove results more general than when using geometric specifications. One important task for future research will be to look for interesting temporal/epistemic properties of different sensors and domains (relating the knowledge level and the geometric level), and exploit these properties to prove more specific results. We also hope to be able to lift the restrictions of Theorem 3, and find a general characterization of sound and complete termination conditions.

The present paper has studied one particular problem. However, knowledge can be applied to many natural problems in motion planning, especially ones that deal with multiple agents, where purely geometrical reasoning would become even more complicated. In fact, most interesting aspects of knowledge come out when there are a number of agents. For example, one can look at the problem of *mobile coordinated attack*, in which two robots need to halt at their respective goals at synchronized times. Here, a more complicated notion of *common knowledge* is involved (see [Fagin *et al.*, 1993] for definitions and examples). Various geometric settings of this problem can be explored and it seems that in these complex environments knowledge will be

an essential tool. In fact, motion planning offers all the problems encountered in distributed systems and more, but in a much richer setting.

Acknowledgement We wish to thank Ronny Kohavi and Moshe Tennenholtz for important discussions about this work.

References

Brafman, R. I.; Latombe, J. C.; and Shoham, Y. 1993. Towards knowledge-level analysis of motion planning. Technical report, Stanford University. in preparation.

Canny, J. F. 1989. On computability of fine motion plans. In *Proc. of the 1989 IEEE Int. Conf. on Robotics and Automation*. 177–182.

Emerson, E. A. and Halpern, J. Y. 1985. Decision procedures and expressivenessin the temporal logic of branching time. *J. of Comp. and Sys. Sci.* 30(1):1–24.

Erdmann, M. 1986. Using backprojection for fine motion planning with uncertainty. *Int. J. of Robotics Research* 5(1):19–45.

Fagin, R.; Halpern, J. Y.; Moses, Y.; and Vardi, M. Y. 1993. *Reasoning about Knowledge*. MIT Press. to appear.

Halpern, J. Y. and Moses, Y. 1990. Knowledge and common knowledge in a distributed environment. *J. ACM* 37(3):549–587.

Hintikka, J. 1962. *Knowledge and Belief*. Cornell University Press, Ithaca, NY.

Kaelbling, L. P. and Rosenschein, S. J. 1990. Action and planning in embedded agents. *Robotics and Autonomous Systems* 6:35–48.

Latombe, J. C.; Lazanas, A.; and Shekhar, S. 1991. Robot motion planning with uncertainty in control and sensing. *Artificial Intelligence* 52:1–47.

Latombe, J. C. 1991. *Robot Motion Planning*. Kluwer Academinc Publishers, Boston.

Levesque, H. 1984. Foundations of a functional approach to knowledge representation. *Artificial Intelligence* 23(2):155–212.

Lozano-Pérez, T.; Mason, M. T.; and Taylor, R. H. 1984. Automatic synthesis of fine-motion strategies for robots. *Int. J. of Robotics Research* 3(1):3–24.

Moore, R. C. 1985. A formal theory of knowledge and action. In Hobbs, J. R. and Moore, R. C., editors 1985, *Formal Theories of the Common Sense World*, Norwood, N.J. Ablex Publishing Corporation.

Rosenschein, S. J. 1985. Formal theories of knowledge in ai and robotics. *New Generation Comp.* 3:345–357.

Taylor, R. H.; Mason, M. T.; and Goldberg, K. Y. 1988. Sensor-based manipulation planning as a game with nature. In Bolles, R. and Roth, B., editors 1988, *Robotics Research 4*. MIT Press. 421–429.

EL : A Formal, Yet Natural, Comprehensive Knowledge Representation*

Chung Hee Hwang & Lenhart K. Schubert
Department of Computer Science, University of Rochester
Rochester, New York 14627-0226
{hwang,schubert}@cs.rochester.edu

Abstract

We present *Episodic Logic* (EL), a highly expressive knowledge representation well-adapted to general commonsense reasoning as well as the interpretive and inferential needs of natural language processing. One of the distinctive features of EL is its extremely permissive ontology, which admits situations (episodes, events, states of affairs, etc.), propositions, possible facts, and kinds and collections, and which allows representation of generic sentences. EL is natural language-like in appearance and supports intuitively understandable inferences. At the same time it is both formally analyzable and mechanizable as an efficient inference engine.

Introduction

One of the requirements on knowledge representation is that it should support efficient inference (cf., [Brachman & Levesque, 1985]). Our basic methodological assumption is that this demand on the representation is best met by using a highly expressive logic closely related to natural language itself. The possibility of handling situations, actions, facts, beliefs, attitudes, causes, effects, and general world knowledge simply and directly depends on the expressiveness of the representation. These remarks apply as much to semantic representation of English sentences, as to knowledge representation. In fact, the simplest assumption is that the two are one and the same. On that premise, we have been developing *Episodic Logic* (EL), a highly expressive knowledge and semantic representation well-adapted to commonsense reasoning as well as the interpretive and inferential needs of natural language processing.

EL is a first order, intensional logic that incorporates from situation semantics the idea that sentences describe situations [Barwise & Perry, 1983; Barwise, 1989]. A distinctive feature of the logic, responsible for its name, is the inclusion of *episodic* (situational) variables. (Episodes, as the term is construed in EL, subsume events, states of affairs, circumstances, eventualities, etc.) The adjective "episodic" is intended to emphasize the fact that reasoning about the world and the agents in it often involves inference of the temporal

and causal connections among *transient* types (as opposed to *eternal* types) of situations, i.e., occurrences or state changes.

EL is related to natural language through a Montague-style coupling between syntactic form and logical form, allowing the relationship between surface form and logical form to be specified in a modular, transparent way. EL representations derived from English text are natural and close to English surface form. Episodic variables implicit in English sentences and temporal relations between those episodes are automatically introduced into the logical form in the process of deindexing. Very general inference rules, *rule instantiation* and *goal chaining*, have been developed that allow for deductive and probabilistic inferences.

We first describe the ontology of EL, which provides the necessary ingredients for interpreting an expressive representation, and then show how some of the more unusual kinds of objects are represented using these ingredients. After that we briefly discuss how inferences are made in EL.

EL and its Liberal Ontology

A distinctive feature of EL is its very permissive ontology, which supports the interpretation of a wide range of constructs that are expressible in English. EL can represent conjoined predicates by means of λ-abstraction (e.g., *crack longer than 3 inches*); restricted quantifiers (e.g., *most aircrafts manufactured by Boeing*); predicate modifiers (e.g., *severe* damage); perception (e.g., "Mary *heard* the bomb explode"); attitudes and possible facts (e.g., "Mary *believes that* gasoline is heavier than water"); actions (e.g., "John thought *Mary's dropping the glass* was intentional"); opaque contexts (e.g., "John *wants to design a new engine*"); kinds (e.g., "the two kinds of precious metal, *gold* and *platinum*"), etc. We now describe the ontological basis of this wide expressive range of EL.

Model structures for EL are based on an ontology of *possible individuals* $\mathcal{D}$. Like Hobbs [1985], we believe it is better to expand one's ontology to allow more kinds of entities than complicating the logical form. *Possible* individuals include not only real or actual individuals but also imaginary or nonexistent ones (e.g., "*Tomorrow's lecture* has been cancelled" [Hirst, 1991]). As shown in Figure 1, $\mathcal{D}$ includes many unusual types of individuals

*This research was supported in part by NSF Research Grant IRI-9013160, ONR/DARPA Research Contracts No. N00014-82-K-0193 and No. N00014-92-J-1512, NSERC Operating Grant A8818, and the Boeing Co. in Seattle under Purchase Contract W288104.

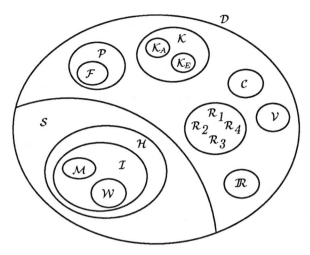

Figure 1: Ontology of Basic Individuals

besides "ordinary" ones. First, unlike situation semantics, EL allows *possible situations* $\mathcal{S}$. These are much like "partial possible worlds," in that predicate symbols are assigned partial extensions (and antiextensions) relative to them. Among the possible situations are informationally maximal *exhaustive situations* $\mathcal{H}$, and among the exhaustive situations are the spatially maximal *possible times* $\mathcal{I}$, which in turn include the spatiotemporally maximal *possible worlds* $\mathcal{W}$ and the spatially maximal, temporally minimal *moments of time* $\mathcal{M}$. The treatment of times and worlds as certain kinds of situations is unusual but quite plausible. Sentences like "Last week was eventful" suggests that times such as *last week* indeed have episodic content. Note that times in the episodic sense are distinguished from *clock times* (in the metric sense). Also, note that *actions* or *activities* are not included in $\mathcal{S}$, since actions are regarded in EL as events paired with their agents. (More on this later.) In general, a situation can be part of many worlds, but an "exhaustive" situation belongs to a unique world.[1] A transitive, reflexive relation *Actual* $\subset \mathcal{D} \times \mathcal{S}$ determines what individuals are actual with respect to a given situation. As well, there is a relation *Nonactual* $\subset \mathcal{D} \times \mathcal{S}$, disjoint from *Actual*, determining the possible but nonactual individuals involved in a situation.

Disjointly from $\mathcal{S}$, we have not only ordinary individuals of our experience, but also propositions $\mathcal{P}$ (including possible facts $\mathcal{F}$ which we identify with consistent propositions), kinds of individuals $\mathcal{K}$ (including kinds of actions $\mathcal{K}_A$, and kinds of episodes $\mathcal{K}_E$), the real numbers $\mathbb{R}$ (augmented with $-\infty$ and $+\infty$), and n-D regions $\mathcal{R}_n$, containing subsets of $\mathbb{R}^n$ ($1 \leq n \leq 4$). Elements

of $\mathcal{R}_4$ are space-time trajectories that may not be connected, and whose temporal projection in general is a multi-interval.[2] This allows for repetitive or quantified events in EL.

Finally, there are collections $\mathcal{C}$ and n-vectors (i.e., tuples) $\mathcal{V}$, $n = 2, 3, \ldots$, of all of these. Space limitations prevent further elaboration, but readers are referred to [Hwang, 1992; Hwang & Schubert, To appear] for a more detailed discussion of the EL ontology and semantics.

Some Essential Resources of EL

We now outline some of the essential resources of EL, emphasizing nonstandard ones intended to deal with events, actions, attitudes, facts, kinds, and probabilistic conditionals.

Events and Actions

We discuss events (situations) and actions first. While doing so, we will also indicate the flavor of EL syntax. We then discuss kinds of events and actions, and describe how properties of events and actions are represented. Consider the following sentences and their logical forms.

(1)a. Mary dropped the glass
   b. (past (The x: [x glass] [Mary drop x]))
   c. ($\exists$e1: [e1 before u1] [[Mary drop Glass1] ** e1])

(2)a. John thought *it* was intentional.
   b. (past [John think (**That** (past [*It* intentional]))])
   c. ($\exists$e2: [e2 before u2]
        [[John think (**That** ($\exists$e3: [e3 at-or-before e2]
                [[[Mary | e1] intentional] ** e3]))]
      ** e2])

Initially, sentence (1a) is translated into an unscoped logical form **ULF**,

   [Mary ⟨past drop⟩ ⟨The glass⟩],

where ⟨ ⟩ indicates unscoped expressions and [ ] indicates infix expressions. (Infix notation is used for readability, with the last argument wrapped around to the position preceding the predicate.) After scoping of the **past** operator and the **The**-determiner, we get **LF** (1b), which is then deindexed to episodic logical form **ELF** (1c). As seen in (1c), we use restricted quantifiers of form (Qα:$\Phi\Psi$), where Q is a quantifier such as $\forall, \exists, \textbf{The}, \textbf{Most}, \textbf{Few}, \ldots$; α is a variable; and restriction Φ and matrix Ψ are formulas. ($\forall\alpha$:$\Phi\Psi$) and ($\exists\alpha$:$\Phi\Psi$) are equivalent to ($\forall\alpha$)[$\Phi \rightarrow \Psi$] and ($\exists\alpha$)[$\Phi \wedge \Psi$], respectively. In (1c), '**' is an episodic, modal operator that connects a formula with the episode/situation it describes. Intuitively, for Φ a formula and η an episodic term, [Φ ** η] means "Φ characterizes (or,

---

[1]Note that if two worlds assign the same truth values to the same unlocated (i.e., eternal) statements, they must be one and the same world. Since exhaustive situations are informationally maximal, any true (or false) unlocated statement in a particular world must be true (or false) in every exhaustive situation that is part of that world. Thus, an exhaustive situation cannot belong to more than one world.

[2]Note that situations occupy such spatiotemporal trajectories, rather than occupying space and time separately. This point is supported by sentences like "It did not snow on the trip from Madison to Chicago" [Cooper, 1985]. As Cooper points out, this sentence "could be true even if it had snowed during the trip on the road between Madison and Chicago and yet had not been snowing at any time at the place where the car was at the time."

completely describes) η."[3] Also notice in (1c) that the past operator is deindexed to the predication [e1 before u1], where u1 denotes the utterance event of sentence (1a). Such temporal deindexing is done by a set of recursive deindexing rules [Hwang & Schubert, 1992; Schubert & Hwang, 1990].

A "characterizing" description of an episode is maximal, or complete, in the sense that it provides *all* the facts that are supported by the episode, except possibly for certain ones entailed by those given. In other words, the episodes so characterized are *minimal* with respect to the characterizing description, in the part-of ordering among situations, i.e., no proper *part* of such an episode supports the same description. We also have a more fundamental episodic operator '*', where [$\Phi * \eta$] means "Φ is true in (or, partially describes) η." '*' is essentially an object-language embedding of the semantic notion of *truth in an episode or situation*. Note that [$\Phi ** \eta$] implies [$\Phi * \eta$]. Thus, for instance, [[Mary drop Glass1] ** e1] implies that e1 is a part (in an informational sense) of some episode e2, coextensive with e1, such that [[Glass1 fall] * e2], [[Mary hold Glass1] * (begin-of e2)], [($\neg$[Mary hold Glass1]) * (end-of e2)], etc. The notion of a complete description (characterization) of a situation using '**' is crucial for representing causal relationships among situations. For instance, if (1a) is followed by "It woke up John," "it" refers to an event *completely* described by (1a), i.e., a *minimal*—spatiotemporally as well as informationally—event supporting (1a), not simply some event *partially* described by (1a). (For more detailed argument, see [Hwang & Schubert, In print].) In (2b), That is a proposition-forming (nominalization) operator to be discussed later. In (2a, b), "it" refers to Mary's *action* of dropping the glass, and is resolved in (2c) to [Mary | e1], "the action whose performance by Mary constitutes event e1."[4] '|' is a pairing function (similar to Lisp "cons") applicable to individuals and tuples.

Thus, actions are represented as agent-event pairs in EL. This representation is motivated by the observation that actions are distinguished from events or episodes in that they have well-defined *agents*. That is why it makes sense to talk about "intentional actions," but not "intentional events." It also seems that the criteria for individuating actions are different from those for individuating episodes. For example, it seems that (3) and (4) below may describe the same episode or event (an

exchange of a boat for a sum of money), but different actions (a buying versus a selling).

(3) John bought the boat from Mary.
(4) Mary sold the boat to John.

Note, in particular, that the buying in (3) may have been performed *reluctantly* and the selling in (4) *eagerly*, but it would be very odd to say that the *events* described in (3) or (4) were reluctant, or eager, or occurred reluctantly or eagerly. Events simply do not have such properties. If we assume they did, we might end up saying, contradictorily, that an event was both reluctant and eager.[5]

Several event- or situation-based formalisms have been proposed within the AI community also. The first was the situation calculus [McCarthy & Hayes, 1969], which introduces explicit situation-denoting terms and treats some formulas and functions (namely, *situational fluents*) as having situation-dependent values. However, situations are viewed as instantaneous "snapshots" of the universe. (They correspond to $\mathcal{M}$ in our ontology.) As such they cannot serve as models of the events and situations of ordinary experience, which can be temporally extended while having limited spatial extent and factual content, can cause each other, etc. Kowalski and Sergot [1986] developed the event calculus in an effort to avoid the frame problem that exists in the situation calculus. Events in the event calculus are local (rather than global), and initiate or terminate "time periods" (probably best understood as circumstances or states of affairs, since they can be concurrent yet distinct). The main limitation is that (as in a Davidsonian approach) events are associated only with simple subject-verb-object(s) tuples, and not with arbitrarily complex descriptions.

Kinds of Events and Actions. As separate categories from situations and events, there are also *kinds* of events and actions. Below are some sample sentences with their logical forms (with certain simplifications). Ka in (5b) and (6b) is a property forming (nominalization) operator that maps monadic predicate intensions to (reified) types of actions and attributes. Ke in (7b) and (7b) is a sentence nominalization operator, which forms (reified) types of *events* from sentence intensions.

(5) a. *Skiing is strenuous*
    b. [[(Ka ski) strenuous] ** E1]
(6) a. Mary wants *to paint the wall*
    b. [[Mary want (Ka (paint Wall3))] ** E2]
(7) a. *For John to be late* is rare
    b. [[(Ke [John late]) rare] ** E3]
(8) a. Bill suggested to John that *he call Mary*
    b. [[Bill suggest-to John (Ke [John call Mary])] ** E4]

---

[3] Our episodic variables are different from Davidsonian [1967] event variables in that they can be "attached" to any formula, whereas Davidsonian ones can be "attached" only to atomic ones. Note that Davidson's method cannot handle sentences with quantifiers or negation. Event variables that are closely related to ours are those of Reichenbach [1947] who, like situation semanticists, viewed a sentence as describing a situation.

[4] Notice the existential variable e1 occurring outside its quantifier scope. This is allowed in EL thanks to the "parameter mechanism," which allows the binding of variables to be carried beyond their quantifier scopes. See [Hwang & Schubert, In print].

[5] Our view appears to resonate with Jacobs' [1987]. Although our conception of actions as agent-event pairs is somewhat different from Jacobs' who regards actions as VIEWs of events, both are based on the intuition that events and actions are different, though closely related.

"Skiing" and "to paint the wall" are *kinds of actions*, while "for John to be late" and "John call Mary" are *kinds of events*.

Properties of Events and Actions.
Typically, properties of actions and attributes (manner, purpose, degree, quality, etc.) are introduced through predicate operators; and those of episodes (duration, frequency, spatiotemporal location, etc.) through sentential operators. Consider the following examples.

(9) a. John fixed the engine with Bill yesterday
    b. (past (The x: [x engine]
        ((adv-e (during Yesterday))
        [John ((adv-a (with-accomp Bill)) (fix x))]))))
    c. (∃e1:[e1 before u1]
        [[$^\vee$(during (yesterday-rel-to u1)) ∧
        $^\vee$λe[[John | e] with-accomp Bill] ∧
        [John fix Engine2]]
        ** e1])

(10) a. Mary bought a brush *to paint the wall*
    b. (past (The x: [x wall]
        [Mary ((adv-a (for-purpose (Ka (paint x))))
            λz(∃y: [y brush] [z buy y]))]))
    c. (∃e2:[e2 before u2]
        [[$^\vee$λe[[Mary | e] for-purpose
                (Ka (paint Wall3))] ∧
        (∃y: [y brush] [Mary buy y])]
        ** e2])

"Yesterday" in (9a) implicitly modifies the *episode* described by "John fix the engine" (its temporal location). "With Bill" in (9a) and "to paint the wall" in (10a), on the other hand, implicitly modify *actions* performed by John and Mary respectively (by specifying their "accompaniment" and "purpose"). As illustrated in the indexical (b)-formulas above, implicit episode modifiers appear as sentential operators of form (adv-e π), where π is a predicate over episodes; implicit action modifiers appear as predicate modifiers of form (adv-a π), where π is a predicate over actions/attributes. Simple deindexing rules for adverbials (which we omit here; see [Hwang & Schubert, 1993a]) convert the (b)-formulas into the nonindexical ELFs shown in (c). Note in (c)-formulas that our treatment of adverbials views them as providing conjunctive information about the described episode (or action), as in Dowty's system [1982]. '$^\vee$' is an extension operator that applies its predicate operand to the "current" episode. For example, $^\vee$(during 1993) or $^\vee$λe[[John | e] with-accomp Bill] is true in situation s iff s occurs during 1993 or the action [John | s] is accompanied by Bill. Notice that the adv-a rule introduces the agent-event pair [x | e] into the formula. The following are some relevant meaning postulates.

For π, π' 1-place predicates, η a term, and Φ a formula:
□ [$^\vee\pi$ ∧ $^\vee\pi'$] ↔ $^\vee$λe[[e π] ∧ [e π']]
□ [[$^\vee\pi$ ∧ Φ] ** η] ↔ [[[η π] ∧ Φ] ** η]

Applying the above meaning postulates to (9c) and (10c), we obtain the following (assuming e1, e2 are skolemized to E1, E2).

(9′) d. [E1 during (yesterday-rel-to u1)]
    e. [[John | E1] with-accomp Bill]
    f. [John fix Engine2] * E1]
    g. (∃e3: [e3 coexten-subep-of E1]
        [[John fix Engine2] ** e3])
(10′) d. [[Mary | E2] for-purpose (Ka (paint Wall3))]
    e. [(∃y: [y brush] [Mary buy y]) * E2]
    f. (∃e4: [e4 coexten-subep-of E2]
        [(∃y: [y brush] [Mary buy y]) ** e4])

[e coexten-subep-of e'] means that e and e' occupy the same spatiotemporal location and that e is an (informational) part of e'.

Intensions, Attitudes and Possible Facts
We now briefly discuss attitude and intensional verbs.

(11) a. John will *design* the engine
    b. (pres (futr [John (design
                λx[x = ⟨The engine⟩])]))
    b′. (pres (futr [John (design
                λx(The y:[y engine][x = y]))]))
(12) a. Mary *told* John *that the engine gave up*
    b. (past (The x: [x engine]
        [Mary tell John (That (past [x give-up]))])))
    c. (∃e1: [e1 before u1]
        [[Mary tell John (That (∃e2: [e2 before e1]
                [[Engine3 give-up] ** e2]))]
        ** e1])

As shown in (11), intensional verbs are treated as predicate modifiers in EL. For objects of intensional verbs, there is generally no presupposition of actual existence — at least not in the "opaque" (*de dicto*) reading. That is, "the engine" in (11), for instance, does not necessarily exist in the world wherein the sentence is evaluated. That is why it is scoped under the intensional verb in (11b′). (We omit the deindexed formula for (11a), but see [Hwang, 1992].) The "transparent" (*de re*) reading can be obtained by choosing wide scope for the unscoped term ⟨The engine⟩, i.e., just inside the tense operator, but outside the intensional verb.

Objects of attitudes are taken to be (reified) propositions in EL. Propositions are formed by a nominalization operator That as shown in (12bc). Recall that we take propositions as subsuming possible facts. Possible facts are just consistent propositions — there are self-contradictory propositions (and these may, for instance, be objects of beliefs, etc.), but there are no self-contradictory possible facts. We should remark here that often events and facts are equated, e.g., by Reichenbach [1947]. As Vendler [1967] has pointed out, this is untenable. Most importantly, events take place over a certain time interval, and may cause and be caused by other events. In contrast, facts do not happen or take place. They are abstractions (like propositions) and as such provide explanations, rather than causes. However, they are so closely related to events (e.g., it may be a fact *that an event occurred* or *will occur*) that people often talk of facts as if they were causes. We regard such talk as metonymic, referring to the "events behind the facts."

Kinds and Probabilistic Conditionals

We have seen operators `Ka` and `Ke`, forming kinds of actions and events. We now consider a more general kind-forming operator, `K`, that maps predicates to individuals. It seems that many generic sentences are best translated into formulas involving kinds. Other kinds of generic sentences are more easily represented as probabilistic (generic) conditionals, and we will discuss these after "kind" expressions. First, consider the following sentences.

(13) a. Gold is expensive, but John buys *it* regularly
   b. [(gpres [(K gold) expensive]) $\wedge$
      (pres ((adv-f regular) [John buy It]))]
   c. [($\exists$e1: [[e1 extended-ep] $\wedge$ [u1 during e1]]
      [[(K gold) expensive] ** e1]) $\wedge$
      ($\exists$e2: [e2 at-about u1]
      [[[e2 regular] $\wedge$ (mult [John buy (K gold)])]
      ** e2])]

(14) a. Wasps are pesky and they spoiled our picnic
   b. [(gpres [(K (plur wasp)) (plur pesky)]) $\wedge$
      (past [They spoil Picnic1])]

Following Carlson [1982] and Chierchia [1982], we translate mass or abstract nominals like *gold, corrosion, welfare*, etc., and bare plurals like *wasps* into *kinds*. In (13a,b) above, 'it' refers to 'gold' in the first clause and is resolved as (K gold) in (13c). In (13b), adv-f (standing for *f*requency adverbial) is an operator that maps predicates over sequences (i.e., composite episodes) to sentence modifiers, and its deindexing rule introduces the `mult` operator shown in (13c). For Φ a formula and η a composite episode, [(mult Φ) ** η] reads "every component episode of η is of type Φ." In (14b), `plur` is an operator that maps predicates applicable to (non-collective) individuals to predicates applicable to collections. That is, (plur P) is true of a collection just in case P is true of each member. (`plur` is similar to Link's [1983] "star" operator.) We omit the deindexed formula for (14a) for space reasons.

Now in (13a), what John buys is apparently quantities of gold, not the "kind" gold. We obtain such "instance" or "realization" interpretations using the following meaning postulates.

For kinds κ and telic, object-level predicates Π:
   $\Box$ [[τ Π κ] $\leftrightarrow$ ($\exists x$: [x instance-of κ] [τ Π x])]
For all monadic predicates π :
   $\Box$ ($\forall x$ [[x instance-of (K π)] $\leftrightarrow$ [x π]])

Then, we have the following equivalences.

   [John buy (K gold)] $\leftrightarrow$ ($\exists x$: [x gold] [John buy x]).

Our uniform treatment of mass terms and bare plurals as kinds in **EL** deals straightforwardly with seemingly problematic sentences like (13a) and (14a), in which kinds and instances appear to co-refer.

Generalizations involving indefinite count singulars (e.g., "*A bicycle* has two wheels") or bare numeral plurals (e.g., "*Two men* can lift a piano") are translated into probabilistic conditionals (i.e., extensionally interpretable generic conditionals), rather than kind-level predications. Such conditionals turn out to be very useful in representing naive physics and causal laws (of the kinds discussed in [Hayes, 1985; Hobbs *et al.*, 1987]) and unreliable knowledge in general, like the following.

(15) a. If one drops an open container containing some liquid, then the container may cease to contain any liquid.
   b. ($\exists x$: [x person]
      ($\exists e_1$:[($\exists y$:[[y container] $\wedge$ [y open]]
         ($\exists z$: [z liquid] [y contain z])) ** e_1]
         ($\exists e_2$: [(begin-of e_2) during e_1]
         [[x drop y] ** e_2])))
      $\longrightarrow_{.3, x, y, e_1, e_2}$
      ($\exists e_3$:[[e_2 cause-of e_3] $\wedge$ [e_3 right-after e_2]]
         [($\neg$ ($\exists v$: [v liquid] [y contain v])) ** e_3])

Here, '.3' attached to the conditional is a lower bound on the *statistical probability*, and $x, y, e1, e2$ are controlled variables.[6] This rule says, roughly, that in at least 30% of the situations in which the antecedent is true, the consequent will also be true.[7] It appears that for many conditional generalizations, a representation in terms of a probabilistic conditional with control over all existentials in the antecedent that occur anaphorically in the consequent leads to intuitively reasonable uncertain inferences. We provide a "first cut" formal semantics in [Hwang, 1992; Hwang & Schubert, To appear].

Inference Rules

The main inference rules in **EL** are *Rule Instantiation* (`RI`) and *Goal Chaining* (`GC`). They are generalizations of "forward chaining" and "backward chaining," in AI terminology.

`RI` allows arbitrarily many minor premises to be matched against arbitrarily deeply embedded subformulas of a "rule" (an arbitrary formula, though typically a conditional with quantified or controlled variables). As such, it is similar to "nested resolution" [Traugott, 1986], but avoids skolemization. Instead of stating the rule formally (which we have done elsewhere [1993b] & [In print]), we illustrate its use with a simple example.

---

[6] As mentioned earlier, the parameter mechanism in **EL** lets the existential variable bindings be carried beyond their quantifier scope. Different choices of controlled variables lead to different readings. (This addresses the "proportion problem"; cf., [Schubert & Pelletier, 1989].)

[7] If the consequent of the rule said "the container will contain less liquid than before," then the conditional would have a much higher lower bound, say, '.95'.

Suppose we have the following rule (with all episodic variables suppressed for simplicity),

$$(\forall x: [x\ person]$$
$$[[[x\ healthy] \land [[x\ rich] \lor (\exists y:[x\ has\text{-}job\ y])]]$$
$$\to [x\ contented]]),$$

For anyone, if he is healthy and is rich or has a job, he is contented

and assume we are given the following facts:

[Joe man] and [Joe has-job Lawyer].

Then RI would trigger on the second fact, matching [Joe has-job Lawyer] to $[x\ has\text{-}job\ y]$, and thus binding x to *Joe* and y to *Lawyer*. This also particularizes $[x\ person]$ in the rule to [Joe person], and this would immediately be verified by the "type specialist," with use of [Joe man] and the implicit subsumption relation between *person* and *man*. Substituting truth for both of the matched subformulas and simplifying, RI would then infer

[Joe healthy] $\to$ [Joe contented],

i.e., Joe is contented provided that he is healthy. Note that the matching process can substitute for either universal variables (provided that the universal quantifier lies in a *positive* environment) or existential variables (provided that the existential quantifier lies in a *negative* environment).[8]

More generally variables controlled by probabilistic conditionals and quantified variables in "facts" may also be bound in the matching process. For instance, suppose that the rule above were slightly reformulated to say "If a person is healthy and either is rich or has a job, then he is *probably* (with lower bound .6 on the probability) contented" (it should not be hard to see how to write this down formally); and suppose [Joe has-job Lawyer] had been replaced by $(\exists z\ [Joe\ has\text{-}job\ z])$, and the additional fact [Joe healthy] given. Then RI would still have applied, and would have yielded conclusion

[Joe contented]$^{.6}$,

i.e., with an epistemic probability of at least 60%, Joe is contented.

While RI is typically used for "spontaneous" (input-driven) inference chaining when new facts are asserted, *goal chaining* (GC) is used for deliberate, goal-directed inference, for instance when answering questions. GC is the exact dual of RI. For example, suppose again that we have the rule and facts given above, and we wish to answer the question, "Is Joe contented?". Then GC would reduce this goal to the subgoal "Is Joe healthy?" in one step. (It would do this either from the original rule and facts, or, if the above result of RI had been asserted into the knowledge base, from the latter.)

In actual use, RI and GC are slightly more subtle than the above examples suggest. First, there are two ver-

sions of each rule, whose (sound) use depends on the configuration of quantifiers for matched variables. Second, goal-directed reasoning is supplemented with natural deduction rules, such as that to prove a conditional, we can assume the antecedent and prove the consequent. And finally, there is some limited use of goal-chaining in input-driven inference, so as to verify parts of rules, and some limited use of input-driven inference in goal-directed reasoning, so as to elaborate consequences of assumptions that have been made.

Concluding Remarks

EL is a very expressive knowledge representation; its ontology allows for possible situations (events, states, states of affairs, etc.), actions, attitudes and propositions, kinds, and unreliable general knowledge, among other things. As such, EL goes beyond the current state of the art as represented by such works as [Alshawi & van Eijck, 1989; Brachman *et al.*, 1991; Hobbs *et al.*, 1987; Shapiro, 1991; Sowa, 1991]. All features of EL are strongly motivated by corresponding expressive devices found in natural languages—i.e., generalized quantifiers, modifiers, nominalization, etc. As a result, knowledge can be cast in a very natural, understandable form and intuitively obvious inferences can be modelled in a direct, straightforward way.

One of the most important remaining problem is the principled handling of probabilities. The state of the art in probabilistic inference (e.g., [Pearl, 1988; Bacchus, 1990]) is not such as to provide concrete technical tools for a logic as general as EL. Our current techniques consist mainly of probabilistic inference chaining, which is demonstrably sound under certain conditions. As well, the implementation applies a "noncircularity principle" which prevents the same knowledge from being used twice to "boost" the probability of a particular conclusion. Apart from this, independence assumptions are used where there are no known dependencies, and lower probabilities are manipulated in accord with the laws of probability. However, we lack a general theory for *combining evidence* for (or against) a given conclusion. Another remaining problem is inference control. Right now EPILOG terminates forward inference chains when either the probability or the "interestingness" of the inferred formulas becomes too low. We are convinced that "interestingness" is a crucial notion here, and that it must allow for context (salience) and for the inherent interestingness of both objects and predicates, and the interaction between these (e.g., an object should become more interesting if it is found to have interesting properties). We have experimented with such measures, but have not achieved uniformly satisfactory inference behavior.

The kinds of EL formulas we have shown are in principle derivable from surface structure by simple, Montague-like semantic rules paired with phrase structure rules. While developing a grammar and semantic rules that would cover most of English would be a very large undertaking, we have developed GPSG-like gram-

---

[8] Positive and negative environments correspond respectively to embedding by an even and odd number of negations, implicational antecedents, and universal quantifier restriction clauses. Only subformulas embedded by extensional operators $\neg, \land, \lor, \to, \forall, \exists$, and generic conditionals may be matched by RI.

mars to cover story fragments and (more ambitiously) sizable dialogs from the TRAINS domain [Allen & Schubert, 1991]. For some such fragments, as well as rules for mapping indexical LFs into nonindexical ELFs, see [Hwang, 1992; Hwang & Schubert, To appear]. The EPILOG implementation [Schaeffer *et al.*, 1991] of EL has been applied to small excerpts from the *Little Red Riding Hood* story, making complex inferences about causation [Schubert & Hwang, 1989]; and it reasons with telex reports for aircraft mechanical problems in a message processing application for the Boeing Commercial Airplane Reliability and Maintainability Project [Namioka *et al.*, In print; Hwang & Schubert, 1993b].

References

[Allen, J. F. & Schubert, L. K. 1991] The TRAINS Project. TR 382, U. of Rochester, Rochester, NY.

[Alshawi, H. & van Eijck, J. 1989] Logical forms in the Core Language Engine. In *Proc. 27th Annual Meeting of the ACL*, Vancouver, Canada. 25–32.

[Bacchus, F. 1990] *Representing and Reasoning with Probabilistic Knowlege: A Logical Approach to Probabilities.* MIT Press, Cambridge, MA.

[Barwise, J. 1989] *The Situation in Logic.* CSLI, CA.

[Barwise, J. & Perry, J. 1983] *Situations and Attitudes.* MIT Press, Cambridge, MA.

[Brachman, R. J. & Levesque, H. J. 1985] Introduction. In *Readings in Knowledge Representation.* Morgan Kaufmann, San Mateo, CA.

[Brachman, R. J., McGuinness, D. L., Patel-Schneider, P. F., Resnick, L. A., & Borgida, A. 1991] Living with Classic: When and how to use a KL-ONE like language. In *Sowa, J. F., editor. 1991*, 401–456.

[Carlson, G. N. 1982] Generic terms and generic sentences. *J. of Philosophical Logic* 11:145–181.

[Chierchia, G. 1982.] On plural and mass nominals. *Proc. West Coast Conf. on Formal Semantics* 1:243-255.

[Cooper, R. 1985] Aspectual classes in situation semantics. CSLI-84-14C, CSLI, CA.

[Davidson, D. 1967] The logical form of action sentences. In Rescher, N., ed. *The Logic of Decision and Action.* U. of Pittsburgh Press.

[Dowty, D. 1982] Tense, time adverbs and compositional semantic theory. *Linguistics & Philosophy* 5:23–55.

[Hayes, P. J. 1985] Naive physics I: Ontology for liquids. In Hobbs, J. R. & Moore, R. C., eds. *Formal Theories of the Commonsense World.* Ablex, Norwood, NJ. 71–108.

[Hirst, G. 1991] Existence assumptions in knowledge representation. *Artificial Intelligence* 49:199–242.

[Hobbs, J. R. 1985] Ontological promiscuity. In *Proc. 23rd Annual Meeting of the ACL.* Chicago, IL. 61–69.

[Hobbs, J. R., Croft, W., Davies, T., Edwards, D., & Laws, K. 1987] Commonsense metaphysics and lexical semantics. *Computational Linguistics* 13:241–250.

[Hwang, C. H. 1992] *A Logical Approach to Narrative Understanding.* Ph.D. Dissertation, U. of Alberta, Canada.

[Hwang, C. H. & Schubert, L. K. 1992] Tense trees as the "fine structure" of discourse. In *Proc. 30th Annual Meeting of the ACL.* Newark, DE. 232–240.

[Hwang, C. H. & Schubert, L. K. 1993a] Interpreting temporal adverbials. In *Proc. Human Language Technology, ARPA Workshop*, Princeton, NJ.

[Hwang, C. H. & Schubert, L. K. 1993b] Meeting the interlocking needs of LF-computation, deindexing, and inference: An organic approach to general NLU. In *Proc. 13th IJCAI*, Chambéry, France.

[Hwang, C. H. & Schubert, L. K. In print] Episodic Logic: A situational logic for natural language processing. In *Situation Theory & its Applications, V. 3*, CSLI, CA.

[Hwang, C. H. & Schubert, L. K. To appear] *Episodic Logic: A comprehensive semantic representation and knowledge representation for language understanding.*

[Jacobs, P. S. 1987.] Knowledge-intensive natural language generation. *Artificial Intelligence* 33:325–378.

[Kowalski, R. & Sergot, M. 1986] A logic-based calculus of events. *New Generation Computing* 4:67–95.

[Link, G. 1983] The logical analysis of plurals and mass terms: A lattice-theoretical approach. In Bäuerle, Schwarze, & von Stechow, eds. *Meaning, Use, and Interpretation of Language.* Walter de Gruyter, Berlin, Germany. 302–323.

[McCarthy, J. & Hayes, P. J. 1969] Some philosophical problems from the standpoint of artificial intelligence. In Meltzeret, et al. eds. *Machine Intelligence, V. 4.* 463–502.

[Namioka, A., Hwang, C. H., & Schaeffer, S. In print] Using the inference tool EPILOG for a message processing application. *Int. J. of Expert Systems.*

[Pearl, J. 1988] *Probabilistic Reasoning in Intelligent Systems.* Morgan Kaufman, San Mateo, CA.

[Reichenbach, H. 1947] *Elements of Symbolic Logic.* Macmillan, New York, NY.

[Schaeffer, S., Hwang, C. H., de Haan, J., & Schubert, L. K. 1991] *The User's Guide to EPILOG.* Edmonton, Canada.

[Schubert, L. K. To appear] Formal foundations of Episodic Logic.

[Schubert, L. K. & Hwang, C. H. 1989] An Episodic knowledge representation for narrative texts. In *Proc. KR '89*, Toronto, Canada. 444–458.

[Schubert, L. K. & Hwang, C. H. 1990] Picking reference events from tense trees: A formal, implementable theory of English tense-aspect semantics. In *Proc. Speech & Natural Language, DARPA Workshop*, Hidden Valley, PA. 34–41.

[Schubert, L. K. & Pelletier, F. J. 1989] Generically speaking, or, using discourse representation theory to interpret generics. In Chierchia, Partee, & Turner, eds. *Property Theory, Type Theory, and Semantics, V.2.* Kluwer, Boston, MA. 193–268.

[Shapiro, S. C. 1991] Cables, paths, and "subconscious" reasoning in propositional semantic networks. In *Sowa, J. F., editor. 1991.* 137–156.

[Sowa, J. F., editor. 1991] *Principles of Semantic Networks: Explorations in the Representation of Knowledge.* Morgan Kaufmann, San Mateo, CA.

[Sowa, J. F. 1991] Toward the expressive power of natural language. In *Sowa, J. F., editor. 1991.* 157–189.

[Traugott, J. 1986] Nested resolution. In *Proc. 8th Int. Conf. on Automated Deduction (CADE-8).* 394–402.

[Vendler, Z. 1967] Causal relations. *J. of Philosophy.* 64:704–713.

The Semantics of Event Prevention

Charles L. Ortiz, Jr. *
Department of Computer and Information Science
University of Pennsylvania
Philadelphia, PA 19104
clortiz@linc.cis.upenn.edu

Abstract

In planning tasks an agent may often find himself
in a situation demanding that he choose an action
that would prevent some unwanted event from occurring. Similarly, in tasks involving the generation of descriptions or explanations of sequences
of events, it is often useful to draw as many informative connections as possible between events
in the sequence; often, this means explaining why
certain events are not possible. In this paper, I
consider the semantics of event prevention and argue that a naive semantics which equates prevention with the elimination of all future possibility
of the event in question is often difficult, if not
impossible, to implement. I argue for a more useful semantics which falls out of some reasonable
assumptions regarding restrictions on the set of
potential actions available to an agent: (1) those
actions about which the agent has formed intentions, (2) those actions consistent with the agent's
attitudes (including its other intentions), and (3)
the set of actions evoked by the type of situation
in which the agent is embedded.

Introduction

Any reasonable theory of action must consider the semantics of preventing events. This is important in
planning: an agent may find himself in a situation demanding that he choose an action that would prevent
some unwanted event from occurring. This is also important to tasks involving the generation of descriptions or explanations of sequences of events: it is often
useful in such descriptions to draw as many informative
connections as possible between events in the sequence.

A naive definition of event prevention motivated by
examples such as (1a) might base the notion on the
creation of circumstances in which the event to be prevented could not occur. Such a definition would count
too few events as legitimately "preventing," excluding

reasonable cases such as (1b) in which intuition suggests that the agent who was prevented was somehow
predisposed to not attempt the desired action in the
new, resulting situation.

(1a) I prevented him from drinking this water by
drinking it myself.

(1b) I prevented him from drinking this water by taking it away.

By examining the use of the verb *prevents* as it occurs
in normal language I will argue that its commonsense
usage is much more restrictive in terms of the set of
possible futures relative to which it is interpreted. I
claim that this more restrictive and more useful notion
is a consequence of reasonable contextual restrictions
that agents place on the set of potential actions available to them: (1) those actions about which the agent
has formed intentions, (2) those actions consistent with
the agent's attitudes (including its other intentions),
and (3) the set of actions evoked by the type of situation in which the agent is embedded (for example,
in a traffic situation, the set of actions defined by the
vehicle code). I will show that many of these properties need not be taken as axiomatic but rather can be
seen as deriving from a set of assumptions regarding
the rational constitution of agents.

Background

One characteristic of the notion of some event, e, preventing another event, e', is that it makes implicit reference to an event that never occurs (e'). This suggests that the semantics must consider future possibility, only a portion of which might be realized. A
first attempt at a definition might therefore base it on
the conditional "if e does not occur, e' will." Unfortunately, there is an obvious problem with this sort of
definition. Consider the statement,

(2) The vaccine prevented him from getting smallpox.

Unintended would be a suggestion that smallpox would
have inevitably eventuated had the person not received
the vaccine. A more acceptable definition in terms of a
model of branching time was suggested by McDermott

*This research was supported by the following grants:
ARO no. DAAL 03-89-C-0031 Prime and DARPA no.
N00014-90-J1863.

[McDermott, 1982]: e prevents e' just in case before e, e' was possible, while after e, e' became impossible. In this paper, I will refer to this definition of prevention as *necessary prevention*, for reasons that will become clear shortly. Sentence (2) is an example of necessary prevention. The problem with the definition of necessary prevention, as I have already noted by way of example (1b), is that it handles too few cases. In fact, in the same paper McDermott quotes James Allen as objecting to its limited usefulness: a literal application of the definition by an agent in the course of planning would make it difficult for that agent to be able to prevent anything, there being so many things in the world outside an agent's control. In the next section I consider the constraining influence that the prevailing context, in the form of the beliefs, desires, and intentions (BDIs) of the agent being prevented, might have on the set of actions that should realistically be considered "possible."

In order to express some of these contextual restrictions, I will draw on a logic of BDI developed by Cohen and Levesque (C&L) [Cohen and Levesque, 1990] to which I will make a few additions. Their logic models belief with a weak S5 modal logic where possible worlds are linear sequences of event types; complex action descriptions are possible by way of statements in dynamic logic. An agent i's belief in some proposition ϕ is expressed by the statement: $Bel(i, \phi)$. An agent's goals (consistent desires) are similarly captured by statements of the form $Goal(i, \phi)$. The semantics of both *Bel* and *Goal* are in terms of two sets of possible worlds: one captures the agent's goals and is a subset of the second set which captures the agent's beliefs. An agent's intentions are then composite objects modeled as *persistent goals* which an agent will maintain until the action intended is achieved or until the agent believes the action is no longer possible. Their temporal model is one based on discrete linear time, indexed by the integers, with modal temporal operators: $\diamond \phi$ means ϕ is eventually true in the current world (which includes the current moment), $\square \phi$ is defined as $\neg \diamond \neg \phi$, and $later(\phi)$ is defined as $\neg \phi \wedge \diamond \phi$. Their action representation is based on dynamic logic in which primitive actions are closed under nondeterministic choice ($\alpha \mid \beta$), sequencing ($\alpha ; \beta$), tests (α?), and iteration ($\alpha *$). Conditional actions are defined by way of the usual if-then-else statement: [if a then α else β] defined as $[a? ; \alpha \mid \neg a? ; \beta]$. Finally, the modal operators $happens(\alpha)$ and $done(\beta)$ refer to the actions α and β as, respectively, happening next or as having just happened in the current world-time point (with an optional extra argument standing for the agent of the action). The reader is referred to [Cohen and Levesque, 1990] for details on the logic.

Since we will need to refer to future *possibility* I will introduce the following branching modal operators to C&L's logic: $\diamond_B \phi$ means that among all of the possible worlds with pasts identical to the real one, there is

some possible future in which ϕ holds. $\square_B$ is defined again as $\neg \diamond_B \neg \phi$. Formally, this can be done as follows. Let the set of worlds *compatible* with world w at time t (written $comp(w, t)$) (where, in C&L, T is the set of possible worlds and each world is a function from times to event types) be: $comp(w, t) = \{w' \in T \mid w'(t') = w(t)$ for all $t' \leq t$ and $M, w, t' \models p$ iff $M, w', t' \models p$ for each primitive proposition$\}$. This collapses all of the worlds with pasts identical to the current world: as such it introduces a forward branching structure. The operators are then defined as follows. $M, w, t \models \diamond_B \phi$ iff for some $w' \in comp(w, t)$ there is a $t^* \geq t$ such that $M, w', t^* \models \phi$. $\square_B$ is then defined in the usual way: $\square_B =_{def} \neg \diamond_B \neg \phi$. I will also make use of an operator, $\not\rightarrow$, which I will define as follows:

$$e \not\rightarrow e' =_{def} happens(e) \supset \neg later(happens(e'))$$

which can be glossed as stating that e is not followed by e'.

In this paper, I will adopt a common convention in which an event can have more than one type or description associated with it [Davidson, 1989; Goldman, 1970; Pollack, 1986]. Alternative descriptions of a particular instance of an event are often conditioned either on the prevailing circumstances at the time of occurrence or on the previous event history. To use a typical example, flipping a switch can also be described as turning on a light just as long as the switch and light are connected and functioning in the appropriate manner and just as long as the light was not already on. C&L allow predications over events in order to support this convention. This requires, however, second order statements in order to quantify over those predications. Instead, in this paper I add a predicate $type(e_1, e_2)$ to their language which is true at a particular world-time point if e_2 is an alternative type for e_1. That is, one might have

$$M, w, t \models happens(e)$$
$$\wedge type(e, flip\_switch) \wedge type(e, turn\_on)$$

The act of preventing some event will then be treated as an act whose type is, among others, a prevention of that event. In general, when referring to a prevention I will be referring to a particular event token (an event type occurring at a specific world-time point) as preventing some event type. Given this, the definition of necessary prevention can be expressed symbolically as:

$$type(e, prevents(e')) \equiv$$
$$happens(e) \wedge \square_B[e \not\rightarrow e'] \wedge \diamond_B happens(e')$$

An alternative, common definition ([Jackendoff, 1991]) equates prevention with causation of a particular sort. Assuming, for the moment, that one has an adequate treatment of negative events, the definition is the following:

$$e_1 \text{ PREVENTS } e_2 \text{ .iff. } e_1 \text{CAUSES (NOT } e_2)$$

As Shoham observes [Shoham, 1988], however, the two behave quite differently counterfactually: e_1 PREVENTS e_2 entails that if e_1 hadn't occurred, e_2 *could* have occurred, but need not have[1]. Whereas e_1 CAUSES (NOT e_2) entails that if e_1 had not occurred e_2 would have. Another approach has been suggested by Shoham, who defines prevention according to the form that the causal rules actually take. Briefly, Shoham's suggestion is to count the "exceptional conditions" in causal rules (usually represented with "abnormality" predicates) as preventing conditions. One problem with this suggestion is that it does not address contextual effects, involving, for example, the agent's mental state in delimiting the space of possibilities that agent is willing to consider.

Finally, note that though many of the examples I will discuss refer to past preventions (for example, (1a), (1b), (2)), the issue of the evaluation of the associated counterfactual — for example, in the case of necessary prevention, "if e had not occurred then e' would have been possible" — is an issue which is, I believe, orthogonal to the matters with which this paper is concerned: namely, the conditions which must hold at some world-time pair (w, t) such that one is justified in claiming that some event, e, occurring at (w, t), will prevent the occurrence of some later e', *irrespective* of how one should counterfactually reconstruct the state, (w, t), from a later state.

Agent-Centered Notions of Event Prevention

In order to derive a more manageable definition of event prevention — one that does not suffer from Allen's objection — I will examine the role of context in the interpretation of natural language statements involving the verb *prevents*. Consider first what appears to be a simple instance of necessary prevention as I have defined it:

(3) I prevented him from drinking this glass of water by drinking it myself.

Previously, I said that before some event was prevented it need only have been possible. However, in (3) in which an *action* is prevented, this does not seem quite right. If the individual in question does not intend to drink the water, say, because he is not even in the room and thereby unaware of the glass of water, then, even if (3) satisfies the conditions of necessary prevention, it hardly seems to represent a justified claim. Consider another example: suppose someone is standing next to a window and I claim that by standing between that person and the window I thereby prevent the person from being shot. This seems justified only if I was aware of someone trying to shoot that person in the first place. Sometimes these beliefs might only be defaults: for example, if the president is visiting a hostile

---

[1] Actually, this is not quite correct if e_2 is an *action*. I will discuss this further in the next section.

country one can claim to prevent an attempt on his life — say, by keeping him indoors — if one is justified in assuming that an attempt might be made in that sort of situation.

Continuing with (3), suggesting that the agent must intend the *specific* action in question and therefore be *committed* to its execution, is not completely right either: consider the situation in which two glasses are in front of the agent and (3) is uttered. For the claim in (3) to hold it seems only necessary that the agent intend to drink (generic) water (call this act-type α), either glass believed by the agent to be an acceptable choice (call one of these e'). The agent may have committed to drinking the referenced glass of water or remained uncommitted; but the agent should not have committed to another choice. That the agent must be aware of these choices is necessary otherwise we could claim an event as prevented even though the agent never believed that event to be a possibility. From this it seems that the following amendment to the definition of necessary prevention of some e_2 by e_1 is needed:

(PR1)
(i) The agent, A, who is the patient of the prevention, intends some act α (ii) there is some act, e', which A believes is of type α, and (iii) e' is of type e_2, (iv) the agent has at most committed to e'.

In (PR1), the qualification in (ii) that it need not be a fact that A can do α by doing e', but rather that A need only believe that the relation holds together with (iii), is crucial for handling cases of the prevention of the unintended side-effects of an agent's intended actions. In the following variation of (3), if the glass actually contains alcohol, but agent A doesn't know it, one is justified in stating that one can prevent the agent from getting drunk (e_2) by drinking the glass oneself, even if the agent does not intend to become drunk but only intends to drink water (α), since, as far as A knows, drinking from that glass (e') will satisfy that intention. In this example I am making the following assumption regarding the agent's rationality: intentions are always as specific as possible. Therefore, if one intends to drink something cold one doesn't also intend to drink some particular water out of some particular glass. So the more general intention is superseded by the more specific one as soon as it is formed. The need for the referenced qualification in (ii) is a consequence of an observation made by [Bratman, 1987] that an agent, in general, does not intend all of the side effects of his actions. It is also meant to capture some sense of agent A's awareness of available possibilities; lack of awareness being modeled by lack of belief that some event is of some specific type.

I will express (PR1) in Cohen and Levesque's logic in the following way. First define a notion of potential action relative to some arbitrary agent i:

$$poss(e_2, i) \equiv$$
$$\exists \alpha \exists e' \exists x . intentional(e') \land intends(i, \alpha)$$
$$\land \neg Bel(i, \neg happens(i, x; e'; type(e', \alpha)?))$$
$$\land \Diamond_B happens(i, x; e'; type(e', e_2)?)$$

these are the actions (e_2) we believe might eventuate by virtue of the fact that they depend on a prior intention on the part of some agent. Note that rather than introduce another accessibility relation for these potential actions, I have chosen to express the restriction with the available modal operators from C&L's logic, much as Moore did in defining ability derivatively, by way of knowledge axioms[Moore, 1985]. The requirement that the e' in the definition of *poss* be "intentional" seems necessary because not all actions are of the sort requiring a prior intention; only those in which the prior intention has "causal force." Consider, the following.

(4) The carpet prevented him from slipping.

This certainly does not suggest that the agent must have had the prior intention to slip. Other cases include the more problematic variety of "intention-in-action" ([Davidson, 1989; Anscombe, 1963]).

Returning to the definition of *poss*, the last three conjuncts capture conditions (i),(ii), and (iii) of (PR1). In order to handle condition (iv) we need some sort of closed-world assumption with respect to intentions. The third conjunct states that there is some possible future in which the agent believes doing e_1 will result in the performance of α. A statement of $Bel(i, happens(x; e'; type(e', \alpha)?))$ would have instead said that agent i was certain that the referenced sequence occurred next. The last conjunct states that the agent might be wrong or might not be aware of other descriptions for that event (e'). We can then define the following notion of *agent-centered prevention*:

$$type(e_1, prevents(e_2, i)) \equiv$$
$$\land happens(e_1)$$
$$\land poss(e_2, i) \land \Box_B(e_1 \not\rightarrow e_2)$$

This says that e_1 prevents e_2 from the point of view of the set of potential actions of agent i, where e_2 is an action the agent might perform as a side-effect of some other action. I refer to this definition as *agent-centered* since its semantics must explicitly appeal to an agent's attitudes. Note that (PR1) immediately suggests a useful *planning strategy*: if we desire to prevent some α and we know that α is not intended, then no action on our part is necessary since, as far as we know, the action we desire to be prevented will never eventuate. A further simple strategy, falls out of the fact that e' is considered a possibility simply by virtue of the fact that it is an option that agent i considers possible. This

suggests that one can also prevent an agent from performing some action by forcing the agent to only *believe* that the conditions for prevention obtain, even if they actually don't; that is if $Bel(i, type(e, prevents(e', i)))$. Of course, agent i can hold the belief that e will prevent e' without having any reason to believe that e will actually occur.

Some statements which refer to an event prevention are inherently statements about the "abilities" of an agent. For example, consider:

(5) Going to the meeting prevented her from attending the seminar.

in which there was no intention to attend the seminar. Contrast this example with:

(6) The phone call prevented her from attending the entire meeting.

in which a prior intention to attend the entire meeting *is* required. Example (5) is a statement that reflects the inherent abilities of the agent while (6) makes a statement about the necessary future. This is clear if one considers the associated counterfactuals. In the case of (5), we can say that "If she hadn't gone to the meeting she *could* have attended the seminar (whether or not she had intended to or not)," whereas in (6), we can say that "If she hadn't received the phone call she *would* have attended the entire meeting.

In certain situations, an agent may not have fixed on any particular intention but might only be deliberating over the various alternatives that could achieve some desired goal. For example, consider an agent embedded in a traffic situation with a goal to arrive at a particular address. Prior to forming any intentions regarding actions to achieve its goal, the agent may consider many possible actions available in that traffic micro-world. In cases such as these, where it is difficult to be certain about which actions might play a role in an agent's plan, we must either weaken the definition of $poss(e, i)$ to actions *desired* — but not necessarily intended — by an agent or consider means for necessary prevention under the restricted causal structure of that particular microworld. Consider the second alternative by way of the following example:

(7) The red light prevents him from turning left.

Suppose that in this example the agent's intentions are not at issue. Here it appears that the current context, prescribed by the content of the vehicle code, constrains the set of actions the agent is disposed to consider, even if the agent is aware of possibilities outside that set. Alternatively, one could explain this example by suggesting that the agent has a constant background maintenance goal or intention to "not break the law" and that this goal is serving to constrain the actions about which it will deliberate. Although, seemingly formally equivalent, it appears that the first alternative is to be preferred on practical grounds: under the second alternative the agent would have to continually deliberate regarding the consistency of a considered action with the maintenance goal in question, and would be forced, at the same time, to consider its entire stock of beliefs and potential actions. Further, in the case of the constant background intention, an agent would normally almost always be "intentionally not breaking the law." This seems somehow to corrupt the use of the concept of prior intention, in the sense that intentions are "formed" for the purposes of guiding future actions until they have been realized.

I propose to handle this case by modifying the temporal portion of the logic so that a model now includes not only the set T of possible worlds but also a set $\{C_1, C_2, ..., C_n\}$, where each set $C_1(w,t)$ is a nonempty subset of T; the case of $n = 1$ reduces to the earlier version of the logic with $comp(w,t)$. Each C_i can be viewed as a sort of context; the entire set of contexts forming a lattice structure closed under meet and join operations, $\sqcap$ and $\sqcup$, corresponding to intersection and union of possible worlds in the model; with a partial order $\preceq$ defined on the set ($C_i \sqcap C_j \preceq C_j$) Each C_i will be consistent with some set of causal rules which constraint the structure of possible worlds in the set. The definition for satisfaction would then be modified as follows:

$$M, w, t \models^{C_i \sqcap C_j} \Diamond_B \phi \text{ iff}$$

$$M, w, t \models^{C_i} \Diamond_B \phi \text{ and } M, w, t \models^{C_j} \Diamond_B \phi$$

where, as before, $M, w, t \models^{C_i} Diamond_B \phi$ iff $M, w', t' \models \phi$ for some $t' \geq t$ and some $w' \in C_i(w,t)$. One could then have a particular set of causal rules in each context which defined the necessary or possible actions sanctioned by that context. For example, consider the following simple set, relative to some model, world, and time:

$$\models^{c_1} obstacle(dir) \supset$$
$$\Box_B \neg(happens(e) \land type(e, turn(dir)))$$

$$\models^{c_2} green(light) \supset \Diamond_B(happens(e) \land type(e, proceed))$$

$$\models^{c_2} red(light) \supset$$
$$\neg \Diamond_B(happens(e) \land type(e, proceed))$$
$$\land \neg \Diamond_B(happens(e) \land type(e, turn(left)))$$

That is, in C_1 if there is an obstacle in some direction, dir, one may not turn into that direction; while in C_2 if there is a green light one can proceed and if there is a red light one may not turn left or proceed forward.

Given these axioms, we then might have:

$$\models^{c_1 \sqcap c_2} happens(e) \land type(e, red(light)) \supset$$
$$type(e, prevents(turn(left)))$$

In other words, in the everyday context of a typical driver, a red light will prevent a driver from turning left while, in a less specific context we might have,

$$\models^{c_1} happens(e) \land type(e, red(light)) \supset$$
$$\neg type(e, prevents(turn(left)))$$

as desired (where $c_1 \sqcap c_2 \preceq c_1$). I explore such a restriction on actions in more detail in [Ortiz, 1993].

Consider now the following, slightly different example which demonstrates an even more restrictive notion of prevention. In the situation following this utterance,

(8) I prevented him from drinking this water by telling him it was poisoned.

the action of drinking the water is still certainly possible though, unlike the case in (3), no longer desirable. So, while in (3) the agent had the intention to drink the water, my statement of (8) causes the agent to drop its intention thereby rendering the action "impossible." In this case, the intention must have been relativized to some belief, as suggested in [Cohen and Levesque, 1990]; such a belief representing a justification or reason for forming and maintaining the intention. The justification might be of the form "the x substance is water and there is nothing abnormal about it."

The balance of an agent's goals and intentions will also serve to filter the options he is disposed to consider [Bratman, 1987]. For example, consider the situation illustrated in Figure 1, abstracted from the video game discussed in [Chapman, 1992]. In this example, there is a character called the Amazon (A) who wishes to get to an object called a Scroll (S). Scrolls are only activated for a limited period of time. The Amazon has two possible routes by which to get to the scroll: either via door d or via door d'. Several demons (D) are blocking door d; although the Amazon is perfectly capable of destroying them she still chooses door d' because it takes time to destroy a demon and in so doing the Amazon would not be able to get to the scroll in time. In this sort of situation, one would be perfectly justified in asserting:

(9) The demons prevented the Amazon from exiting through door d.

even though the action claimed to be prevented is certainly still "possible." Note that crucial to a correct treatment of this example is the previous observation in (PR1) that the Amazon could not have already formed the intention to take some other option (door d'). In that case, we would not be justified in claiming the prevention. This property falls directly out of a theorem from [Cohen and Levesque, 1990] on intentions providing a screen of admissibility:

$$intends(x, b) \land \Box bel(x, a \not\leadsto b) \supset \neg intends(x, a; b)$$

That is, if an agent intends b, but the agent believes that a prevents b then the agent will never form the intention to do $a; b$. Therefore, if the intention is never formed, it cannot be considered a potential action. This example suggests that one can prevent an action either by preventing the physical act behind it or creating circumstances in which the physical act either creates additional unintended effects or does not realize its intended ones. In some cases, the prevailing context

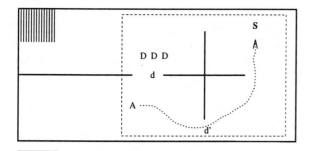

Figure 1: Taking an agent's plans and goals into account. The Amazon wants to get to the readied scroll before it changes state. It is "prevented" from exiting through door d by virtue of its existing commitments.

might render impossible the successful prevention of the physical act itself. For example, if a pitcher wishes to prevent a player from hitting a home run, unavailable to him is the act of tying the hitter's hands behind his back (for the same reason I argued explained (7)); unhappily, he must resort to more traditional means such as by catching the corner of the plate with a fastball.

Conclusions

I began with the observation (originally due to Allen) that cases of necessary prevention are often almost impossible to enforce. In particular, the definition of necessary prevention seemed not to be at the heart of the interpretation of the natural language event descriptions I discussed. This led to my suggestion for a more restrictive, agent-centered version of the definition that took into account an agent's mental state as well as the constraining effect of the current situation on the set of actions an agent was disposed to consider. I argued that an agent's intentions figure prominently in determining the contents of that set of potential actions. I then demonstrated that many cases of prevention fall out of a theory of the rational constitution of agents: agents will generally not consider actions that conflict with current commitments captured in their intentions. I went on to suggest an extension to Cohen and Levesque's BDI logic in which alternative causal microworlds, represented as alternative sets of possible worlds, capture useful and common restrictions that agents make to the set of actions about which they will deliberate. Finally, these observations suggested a number of planning strategies: for example, one can prevent an agent from performing an action by forcing the agent to drop its intention, by causing the agent to believe that the action is no longer possible, by creating circumstances in which the action would either interfere with the realization of other intentions or would introduce unintended effects, or finally by restricting consideration to the smaller micro-world in which we

believe the agent is currently focusing upon. Such strategies never represent sure bets, nevertheless, they do represent good bets and certainly more tractable strategies for getting by in the world.

Acknowledgments

I would like to thank Mark Steedman, Barbara DiEugenio, Jeff Siskind , and Mike White for helpful comments on an earlier draft of this paper.

References

Anscombe, G.E.M. 1963. *Intention.* Cornell University Press.

Bratman, Michael 1987. *Intentions, Plans, and Practical Reason.* Harvard University Press.

Chapman, David 1992. *Vision, Plans, and Instruction.* MIT Press.

Cohen, Philip and Levesque, Hector 1990. Intention is choice with commitment. *Artificial Intelligence* 42:213–261.

Davidson, Donald 1989. *Actions and Events.* Clarendon Press.

Goldman, Alvin 1970. *A Theory of Human Action.* Princeton University Press.

Jackendoff, Ray 1991. *Semantic Structures.* MIT Press.

McDermott, Drew 1982. A temporal logic for reasoning about processes and plans. *Cognitive Science* 6:101–155.

Moore, Robert C. 1985. A formal theory of knowledge and action. In *Formal Theories of the Commonsense World.* Ablex Publishing Corporation.

Ortiz, Charles L. 1993. Event description in causal explanation, forthcoming.

Pollack, Martha 1986. *Infering Domain Plans in Question-Answering.* Ph.D. Dissertation, University of Pennsylvania.

Shoham, Yoav 1988. *Reasoning About Change: Time and Causation from the Standpoint of Artificial Intelligence.* MIT Press.

The Frame Problem and Knowledge-Producing Actions

Richard B. Scherl* and Hector J. Levesque†
Department of Computer Science
University of Toronto
Toronto, Ontario
Canada M5S 3A6
email: scherl@cs.toronto.edu hector@cs.toronto.edu

Abstract

This paper proposes a solution to the frame problem for knowledge-producing actions. An example of a knowledge-producing action is a sense operation performed by a robot to determine whether or not there is an object of a particular shape within its grasp. The work is an extension of Reiter's solution to the frame problem for ordinary actions and Moore's work on knowledge and action. The properties of our specification are that knowledge-producing actions do not affect fluents other than the knowledge fluent, and actions that are not knowledge-producing only affect the knowledge fluent as appropriate. In addition, *memory* emerges as a side-effect: if something is known in a certain situation, it remains known at successor situations, unless something relevant has changed. Also, it will be shown that a form of *regression* examined by Reiter for reducing reasoning about future situations to reasoning about the initial situation now also applies to knowledge-producing actions.

Introduction

The situation calculus provides a formalism for reasoning about actions and their effects on the world. Axioms are used to specify the prerequisites of actions as well as their effects, that is, the fluents that they change. In general, it is also necessary to provide frame axioms to specify which fluents remain unchanged by the actions. In the worst case this might require an axiom for every combination of action and fluent. Recently, Reiter [1991] (generalizing the work of Haas [1987], Schubert [1990] and Pednault [1989]) has given a set of conditions under which the explicit specification of frame axioms can be avoided. In this paper, we extend his solution to the frame problem to cover

knowledge-producing actions, that is, actions whose effects are to change a state of knowledge.

A standard example of a knowledge-producing action is that of reading a number on a piece of paper. Consider the problem of dialing the combination of a safe [McCarthy and Hayes, 1969; Moore, 1980; Moore, 1985]. If an agent is at the same place as the safe, and knows the combination of the safe, then he can open the safe by performing the action of dialing that combination. If an agent is at the same place as both the safe and a piece of paper and he knows that the combination of the safe is written on the paper, he can open the safe by first reading the piece of paper, and then dialing that combination. The effect of the read action, then, is to change the knowledge state of the agent, typically to satisfy the prerequisite of a later action. Another example of a knowledge-producing action is performing an experiment to determine whether or not a solution is an acid [Moore, 1985]. Still other examples are a sensing operation performed by a robot to determine the shapes of objects within its grasp [Lespérance and Levesque, 1990; Lespérance, 1991] and the execution of UNIX commands such as ls [Etzioni *et al.*, 1992].

To incorporate knowledge-producing actions like these into the situation calculus, it is necessary to treat knowledge as a fluent that can be affected by actions. This is precisely the approach taken by Moore [1980]. What is new here is that the knowledge fluent and knowledge-producing actions are handled in a way that avoids the frame problem: we will be able to prove as a consequence of our specification that knowledge-producing actions do not affect fluents other than the knowledge fluent, and that actions that are not knowledge-producing only affect the knowledge fluent as appropriate. In addition, we will show that *memory* emerges as a side-effect: if something is known in a certain situation, it remains known at successor situations, unless something relevant has changed. We will also show that a form of *regression* examined by Reiter for reducing reasoning about future situations to reasoning about the initial situation now also applies to knowledge-producing actions. This

---
*National Sciences and Engineering Research Council of Canada International Postdoctoral Fellow

†Fellow of the Canadian Institute for Advanced Research

has the desirable effect of allowing us to reduce reasoning about knowledge and action to reasoning about knowledge in the initial situation, where techniques such as those discussed in [Frisch and Scherl, 1991; Scherl, 1992] can be used. Finally, we show that if certain useful properties of knowledge (such as positive introspection) are specified to hold in the initial state, they will continue to hold automatically at all successor situations.

In the next section, we briefly review the situation calculus and Reiter's solution to the frame problem. In the following section, we introduce an epistemic fluent into the situation calculus as an accessibility relation over situations, as done by Moore[1980; 1985]. Our solution to the frame problem for knowledge producing actions, based on this epistemic fluent, is developed and illustrated over the next four sections. In the next to the last section, we consider regression for the situation calculus with knowledge-producing actions. Finally, future work is discussed in the last section.

The Situation Calculus and the Frame Problem

The situation calculus (following the presentation in [Reiter, 1991]) is a first-order language for representing dynamically changing worlds in which all of the changes are the result of named *actions* performed by some agent. Terms are used to represent states of the world–i.e. *situations*. If α is an action and s a situation, the result of performing α in s is represented by $do(\alpha, s)$. The constant S_0 is used to denote the initial situation[1]. Relations whose truth values vary from situation to situation, called *fluents*, are denoted by a predicate symbol taking a situation term as the last argument. For example, $Broken(x, s)$ means that object x is broken in situation s.

It is assumed that the axiomatizer has provided for each action $a(\vec{x})$, an *action precondition axiom* of the form given in 1, where $\pi_{a(\vec{x})}(s)$ is the formula for $a(\vec{x})$'s action preconditions.

Action Precondition Axiom

$$Poss(a(\vec{x}), s) \equiv \pi_a(\vec{x}, s) \qquad (1)$$

An action precondition axiom for the action *drop* is given below.

$$Poss(drop(x), s) \equiv Holding(x, s) \qquad (2)$$

Furthermore, the axiomatizer has provided for each fluent F, two *general effect axioms* of the form given

[1]By convention, single lower case letters (i.e. roman), possibly with subscripts or superscripts, are used to represent variables, strings of letters beginning with a capital letter are used for predicate symbols, strings of lower case letters are used for function symbols, and possibly subscripted strings of letters beginning with a capital letter are used for constants. When quantifiers are not indicated, the variables are implicitly universally quantified.

in 3 and 4.

General Positive Effect Axiom for Fluent F

$$Poss(a, s) \wedge \gamma_F^+(a, s) \rightarrow F(do(a, s)) \qquad (3)$$

General Negative Effect Axiom for Fluent F

$$Poss(a, s) \wedge \gamma_F^-(a, s) \rightarrow \neg F(do(a, s)) \qquad (4)$$

Here $\gamma_F^+(a, s)$ is a formula describing under what conditions doing the action a in situation s leads the fluent F to become true in the successor situation $do(a, s)$ and similarly $\gamma_F^-(a, s)$ is a formula describing the conditions under which performing action a in situation s results in the fluent F becoming false in situation $do(a, s)$.

For example, 5 is a positive effect axiom for the fluent *Broken*.

$$Poss(a, s) \wedge [(a = drop(y) \wedge Fragile(y)) \\ \vee ((\exists b) a = explode(b) \wedge Nexto(b, y, s))] \\ \rightarrow Broken(y, do(a, s)) \qquad (5)$$

Sentence 6 is a negative effect axiom for *broken*.

$$Poss(a, s) \wedge a = repair(y) \\ \rightarrow \neg Broken(y, do(a, s)) \qquad (6)$$

It is also necessary to add the *frame axioms* that specify when fluents remain unchanged. The frame problem arises because the number of these frame axioms in the general case is $2 \times \mathcal{A} \times \mathcal{F}$, where $\mathcal{A}$ is the number of actions and $\mathcal{F}$ is the number of fluents.

The solution to the frame problem [Reiter, 1991; Pednault, 1989; Schubert, 1990] rests on a *completeness assumption*. This assumption is that axioms 3 and 4 characterize all the conditions under which action a can lead to R becoming true (respectively, false) in the successor situation. Therefore, if action a is possible and R's truth value changes from *false* to *true* as a result of doing a, then $\gamma_R^+(a, s)$ must be *true* and similarly for a change from *true* to *false*. Additionally, *unique name axioms* are added for actions and situations.

Reiter[1991] shows how to derive a set of *successor state axioms* of the form given in 7 from the axioms (positive effect, negative effect and unique name) and the completeness assumption.

Successor State Axiom

$$Poss(a, s) \rightarrow [F(do(a, s)) \equiv \\ \gamma_F^+(a, s) \vee (F(s) \wedge \neg \gamma_F^-(a, s))] \qquad (7)$$

Similar successor state axioms may be written for functional fluents. A successor state axiom is needed for each fluent F, and an action precondition axiom is needed for each action a. The unique name axioms need not be explicitly represented as their effects can be compiled. Therefore only $\mathcal{F} + \mathcal{A}$ axioms are needed.

From 5 and 6 the following successor state axiom for *Broken* is obtained.

$$Poss(a, s) \rightarrow [Broken(y, do(a, s)) \equiv \\ a = drop(y) \wedge Fragile(y) \vee (\exists b) a = explode(b) \\ \wedge Nexto(b, y, s) \vee Broken(y, s) \wedge a \neq repair(y)] \qquad (8)$$

Now note for example that if $\neg Broken(Obj_1, S_0)$, then it also follows (given the unique name axioms) that $\neg Broken(Obj_1, do(drop(Obj_2), S_0))$.

This discussion has assumed that there are no ramifications, i.e., indirect effects of actions. This can be ensured by prohibiting state constraints, i.e., sentences that specify an interaction between fluents. An example of such a sentence is $\forall s P(s) \leftrightarrow Q(s)$. The assumption that there are no state constraints in the axiomatization of the domain will be made throughout this paper. In [Lin and Reiter, 1993], the approach discussed in this section is extended to work with state constraints by compiling the effects of the state constraints into the successor state axioms.

An Epistemic Fluent

The approach we take to formalizing knowledge is to adapt the standard possible-world model of knowledge to the situation calculus, as first done by Moore[1980]. Informally, we think of there being a binary accessibility relation over situations, where a situation s' is understood as being accessible from a situation s if as far as the agent knows in situation s, he might be in situation s'. So something is known in s if it is true in every s' accessible from s, and conversely something is not known if it is false in some accessible situation.

To treat knowledge as a fluent, we introduce a binary relation $K(s', s)$, read as "s' is accessible from s" and treat it the same way we would any other fluent. In other words, from the point of view of the situation calculus, the last argument to K is the official situation argument (expressing what is known in situation s), and the first argument is just an auxiliary like the y in $Broken(y, s)$.[2]

We can now introduce the notation $\mathbf{Knows}(P, s)$ (read as P is known in situation s) as an abbreviation for a formula that uses K. For example

$$\mathbf{Knows}(Broken(y), s) \stackrel{\text{def}}{=} \forall s' \ K(s', s) \rightarrow Broken(y, s').$$

Note that this notation supplies the appropriate situation argument to the fluent on expansion (and other conventions are certainly possible).

This notation can be generalized inductively to arbitrary formulas so that, for example

$$\exists x \mathbf{Knows}(\exists y[Nexto(x, y) \wedge \neg Broken(y)], s) \stackrel{\text{def}}{=}$$
$$\exists x \forall s' \ K(s', s) \rightarrow \exists y[Nexto(x, y, s') \wedge \neg Broken(y, s')].$$

We will however restrict our attention to knowledge about atomic formulas in both this and the next section.

Turning now to knowledge-producing actions, there are two sorts of actions to consider: actions whose effect is to make known the truth value of some formula, and actions to make known the value of some term.

---

[2] Note that using this convention means that the arguments to K are reversed from their normal modal logic use.

In the first case, we might imagine a $Sense_P$ action for a fluent P, such that after doing a $Sense_P$, the truth value of P is known. We introduce the notation $\mathbf{Kwhether}(P, s)$ as an abbreviation for a formula indicating that the truth value of a fluent P is known.

$$\mathbf{Kwhether}(P, s) \stackrel{\text{def}}{=} \mathbf{Knows}(P, s) \vee \mathbf{Knows}(\neg P, s),$$

It will follow from our specification in the next section that $\mathbf{Kwhether}(P, do(Sense_P, s))$. In the second case, we might imagine an action $Read_t$ for a term t, such that after doing a $Read_t$, the denotation of t is known. For this case, we introduce the notation $\mathbf{Kref}(t, s)$ defined as follows:

$$\mathbf{Kref}(t, s) \stackrel{\text{def}}{=} \exists x \mathbf{Knows}(t = x, s)$$
$$\text{where } x \text{ does not appear in } t.$$

It will follow from the specification developed in the next section that $\mathbf{Kref}(t, do(Read_t, s))$. For simplicity, we assume that each type of knowledge-producing action is associated with a characteristic fluent or term in this way.

Solving the Frame Problem

The approach being developed here rests on the specification of a successor state axiom for the K relation. For all situations $do(a, s)$, the K relation will be completely determined by the K relation at s and the action a.

For non-knowledge-producing actions (e.g. $drop(x)$), the specification (based on Moore [1980; 1985]) is as follows:

$$Poss(drop(x), s) \rightarrow K(s'', do(drop(x), s)) \equiv \atop \exists s'(K(s', s) \wedge (s'' = do(drop(x), s'))) \quad (9)$$

The idea here is that as far as the agent at world s knows, he could be in any of the worlds s' such that $K(s', s)$. At $do(drop(x), s)$ as far as the agent knows, he can be in any of the worlds $do(drop(x), s')$ for any s' such that $K(s', s)$. So the only change in knowledge that occurs in moving from s to $do(drop(x), s)$ is the knowledge that the action $drop$ has been performed.

Now consider the simple case of a knowledge-producing action $Sense_P$ that determines whether or not the fluent P is true (following Moore [1980; 1985]).

$$Poss(Sense_P, s) \rightarrow K(s'', do(Sense_P, s)) \equiv \atop [\exists s'(K(s', s) \wedge (s'' = do(Sense_P, s'))) \atop \wedge (P(s) \equiv P(s'))] \quad (10)$$

Again, as far as the agent at world s knows, he could be in any of the worlds s' such that $K(s', s)$. At $do(Sense_P, s)$ as far as the agent knows, he can be in any of the worlds $do(Sense_P, s')$ for all s' such that $K(s', s)$ and $P(s) \equiv P(s')$. The idea here is that in moving from s to $do(Sense_P, s)$, the agent not only knows that the action $Sense_P$ has been performed (as above), but also the truth value of the predicate P. Observe that the successor state axiom for P guarantees that P is true at

$do(Sense_P, s)$ iff P is true at s, and similarly for s' and $do(Sense_P, s')$. Therefore, P has the same truth value in all worlds s'' such that $K(s'', do(Sense_P, s))$, and so $\textbf{Kwhether}(P, do(Sense_P, s))$ is true.

In the case of a $Read_t$ action that makes the denotation of the term t known, $P(s) \leftrightarrow P(s')$ is replaced by $t(s) = t(s')$. Therefore, t has the same denotation in all worlds s'' such that $K(s'', do(Read_t, s))$, and so $\textbf{Kref}(t, do(Read_t, s))$ is true.

In general, there may be many knowledge-producing actions. Each knowledge-producing action A_i will have associated with it a formula $\varphi_i(s, s')$. In the case of a $Sense$ type of action, the formula is of the form $F_i(s) \equiv F_i(s')$, where F_i is a fluent. In the case of a $Read$ type of action, the formula is of the form $(t_i(s) = t_i(s'))$, where t_i is a situation-dependent term. Assume that there are n knowledge-producing actions $A_1, \ldots, A_n$ and therefore n associated formulas $\varphi_1, \ldots, \varphi_n$. The form of the successor state axiom for K is then as follows:

Successor State Axiom for K

$$
\begin{aligned}
Poss(a, s) \to K(s'', do(a, s)) &\equiv \\
[\exists s' \, (K(s', s) \wedge (s'' = do(a, s'))) &\wedge \\
(((a \neq A_1) \wedge \ldots \wedge (a \neq A_n)) & \\
\vee ((a = A_1) \wedge \varphi_1) & \\
\vdots & \\
\vee ((a = A_n) \wedge \varphi_n)))]
\end{aligned}
\quad (11)
$$

The relation K at a particular situation $do(a, s)$ is completely determined by the relation at s and the action a.

Example

Consider the example of opening a safe whose combination is written on a piece of paper (adapted from Moore[1980], but without the frame axioms). The successor state axiom for the fluent $Open$ (i.e. be open) is:

$$
\begin{aligned}
Poss(a, s) \to [Open(y, do(a, s)) &\equiv \\
(\exists x \, a = dial(x, y) \wedge x = comb(y, s)) & \\
\vee (Open \, (y, s) \wedge a \neq lock(y))]
\end{aligned}
\quad (12)
$$

The preconditions for dial (actually dialing and pulling the handle) are:

$$
\begin{aligned}
Poss(dial(x, y), s) &\equiv Safe(y, s) \wedge \\
At(y, s) \wedge (\forall s' K(s', s) &\to x = comb(y, s'))
\end{aligned}
\quad (13)
$$

The idea here is that the object being dialed needs to be a safe, the agent needs to be at the safe, and the agent needs to know the combination of the safe. The axiomatization of the initial state includes $Safe(Sf_1, S_0)$, $At(Sf_1, S_0))$, $At(Ppr, S_0)$, and $info(Ppr, S_0) = comb(Sf_1, S_0)$. Note that $\neg \exists x Poss(dial(x, Sf_1), S_0)$. It is assumed that there are successor state axioms for $Safe$, At and the functional fluents $info$ and $comb$.

There is a knowledge-producing action $read(x)$, with the following action precondition axiom:

$$
Poss(read(x), s) \equiv At(x, s) \quad (14)
$$

The successor state axiom for K is as follows:

$$
\begin{aligned}
Poss(a, s) \to K(s'', do(a, s)) &\equiv \\
\exists s' (K(s', s) \wedge (s'' = do(a, s'))) &\wedge \\
((a \neq read(x)) \vee (\exists x \, (a = read(x)) & \\
\wedge (info(x, s) = info(x, s'))))
\end{aligned}
\quad (15)
$$

Note that the axiomatization entails:

$$
\begin{aligned}
Kref(info(Ppr), do(read(Ppr), S0)) &\wedge \\
info(Ppr, do(read(Ppr), S0)) &= \\
comb(Sf_1, do(read(Ppr), S0))
\end{aligned}
\quad (16)
$$

Since the successor state axioms ensure that a $read$ action does not change At, $Safe$, $Comb$ and $Info$, it is the case that $\exists x Poss(dial(x, Sf_1), do(read(Ppr), S_0))$ and therefore the axiomatization entails that $\exists x Open(Sf_1, do(dial(x, Sf_1), do(read(Ppr), S_0)))$.

Correctness of the Solution

The following theorem shows that knowledge-producing actions do not change the state of the world. The only fluent whose truth value is altered by a knowledge-producing action is K.

Theorem 1 (Knowledge-Producing Effects)
For all fluents P (other than K) and all knowledge producing actions a, if $P(s)$ then $P(do(a, s))$.

Proof: Immediate from having successor state axioms for each fluent. $\square$

It is also necessary to show that actions only affect knowledge in the appropriate way. The truth of the following theorem ensures that there are no unwanted increases in knowledge.

Theorem 2 (Default Persistence of Ignorance)
If $\neg \textbf{Knows}(P, s)$ then $\neg \textbf{Knows}(P, do(a, s))$ unless $Poss(a, s)$ and either a is an A_i and P is the corresponding φ_i in the successor state axiom for K, or P is a fluent whose successor state axiom specifies that it is changed by action a.

Proof: For $\neg \textbf{Knows}(P, s)$ to be true, it must be the case that $\forall s' K(s', s) \to P(s')$ is false. There must be some s' such that $P(s')$ is false. By sentence 11, for all situations s'' such that $K(s'', do(a, s))$, it is the case that $s'' = do(a, s')$ for some s' such that $K(s', s)$. Since $P(s')$ is false for some s', $P(do(a, s'))$ will (by the successor state axiom for P) also be false, unless either (1) the successor state axiom for P specifies that the effect of a is to make P true, $Poss(a, s)$ is true, and the conditions for this change are satisfied in s, or (2) a is a knowledge-producing action A_i, the corresponding φ_i in the successor state axiom for K is $P(s) \leftrightarrow P(s')$, $P(s)$ is true, and $Poss(a, s)$. If neither is the case by the successor state axiom for K, there will be an s'' such that $K(s'', do(a, s))$ where $P(s'')$ is false and therefore $\neg \textbf{Knows}(P, do(a, s))$ will be true. $\square$

Finally, it is a property of this specification that agents never forget.

Theorem 3 (Memory) *For all fluents P and situations s, if* **Knows**(P, s) *then* **Knows**$(P, do(a, s))$ *unless the effect of a is to make P false.*

The proof is similar to that of the previous theorem.

Consider again the successor state axiom for *broken* given in sentence 8. If **Knows**$(\neg Broken(Obj_1), S_0)$ is true, then **Knows**$(\neg Broken(Obj_1), do(drop(Obj_2), S_0))$ must also be true. Also, note that if **Knows**$(Fragile(Obj_2), S_0)$ and **Knows**$(Poss(drop(Obj_2)), S_0)$ are true, then **Knows**$(Broken(Obj_2), do(drop(Obj_2), S_0))$ must also be true.

Knowledge of Formulas

Up to this point, all results have been stated in terms of fluents. But both the argument to **Kwhether** and **Knows** can be an arbitrary formula.

In the discussion of *sense* type actions, nothing hinged on the argument to **Kwhether** being a fluent, rather than a formula. Thus the effect of a *sense* action performed by a robot [Lespérance and Levesque, 1990; Lespérance, 1991] may be specified as follows:

$$\textbf{Kwhether}(\exists x\,(Object(x) \wedge \neg Holding(x) \wedge Ofshape(x, Shape_1))) \tag{17}$$

Now the formula φ_i associated with each knowledge-producing action is of the form $\alpha_i(s) \equiv \alpha_i(s')$, where α_i is a formula.

Also, the arguments to the **Knows** operator may be arbitrary formulas. Now, we may also want nested **Knows** operators. The situation argument of the operator is then understood contextually. If it is not the outermost operator, the situation argument is understood to be the first argument of the immediately dominating K atom. For example, 18 is understood as an abbreviation for 19.

$$\textbf{Knows}(\textbf{Knows}(P)) \tag{18}$$

$$\forall s_1\, K(s_1, S_0) \rightarrow (\forall s_2\, K(s_2, s_1) \rightarrow P(s_2)) \tag{19}$$

By a simple induction on the size of formulas, Theorems 1, 2, and 3 expressed in terms of fluents, can be generalized to formulas as well. So, the solution to the frame problem for knowledge-producing actions is correct for knowledge understood as the knowledge of arbitrary sentences.

The only remaining issue concerns requiring that the **Knows** operator conform to the properties of a particular modal logic. For example, if the logic chosen is $S4$, then we want positive introspection (sentence 20) to be a property of the logic.

$$\textbf{Knows}(\phi) \rightarrow \textbf{Knows}(\textbf{Knows}(\phi)) \tag{20}$$

Restrictions need to be placed on the K relation so that it correctly models the accessibility relation of a particular modal logic. The problem is to do this in a way that does not interfere with the successor state axioms for K, which must completely specify the K

relation for non-initial situations. The solution is to axiomatize the restrictions for the initial situation and then verify that the restrictions are then obeyed at all situations.

The sort *Init* is used to restrict variables to range only over S_0 and those situations accessible from S_0. It is necessary to stipulate that:

$$Init(s_1) \rightarrow (K(s, s_1) \rightarrow Init(s))$$
$$\neg Init(s_1) \rightarrow (K(s, s_1) \rightarrow \neg Init(s))$$
$$Init(S_0) \qquad \neg Init(do(a, s))$$

The various restrictions are listed below.[3] The reflexive restriction is always added as we want a modal logic of knowledge. Some subset of the other restrictions are then added.

Reflexive $\forall s_1{:}Init\ K(s_1, s_1)$

Euclidian $\forall s_1{:}Init, s_2{:}Inits_3{:}Init$
$\qquad K(s_2, s_1) \wedge K(s_3, s_1) \rightarrow K(s_3, s_2)$

Symmetric $\forall s_1{:}Init, s_2{:}Init\ K(s_2, s_1) \rightarrow K(s_1, s_2)$

Transitive $\forall s_1{:}Init, s_2{:}Init, s_3{:}Init$
$\qquad K(s_2, s_1) \wedge K(s_3, s_2) \rightarrow K(s_3, s_1)$

To model the logic $S4$, for example, one would need to include the axioms for both reflexivity and transitivity.

The next step is to prove that if the K relation over the initial situations satisfies a particular restriction R, that restriction R will also hold over the other situations as well.

Theorem 4 *If the K relation on the set of initial situations is restricted to conform to some subset of the properties of reflexive, symmetric, transitive and euclidian, then the K relation at every level will satisfy the same set of properties.*

The proof involves showing for each restriction that if the restriction holds for s, then it holds for $do(a, s)$.

The significance of this theorem is that if the K relation at the initial situation is defined as satisfying certain conditions, then the K relation at all situations reachable from the initial situation also satisfies those properties. So, if we decide to use, for example, the logic $S4$ to model knowledge, we can go ahead and stipulate that the K relation at the initial situation is reflexive and transitive. Then we are guaranteed that the relation at all reachable situations will also satisfy those properties and our model of knowledge will remain $S4$, without danger of conflicting with the successor state axiom.

Reasoning

Reiter [Reiter, 1991] develops a form of *regression* to reduce reasoning about future situations to reasoning about the initial situation. In this section, a regression operator is developed for knowledge-producing actions and applied to the problem of determining whether

---

[3]$\forall s{:}Init\ \varphi$ is an abbreviation for $\forall s Init(s) \rightarrow \varphi$

or not a particular plan satisfies a particular property. So given a plan, expressed as a ground situation term (i.e. a term built on S_0 with the function do and ground action terms[4]) s_{gr}, the question is whether the axiomatization of the domain $\mathcal{F}$ entails $G(s_{gr})$ where G is an arbitrary sentence. Under these circumstances, the successor state axioms (including 11) are only used to regress the formula $G(s_{gr})$. The result of the regression is a formula in ordinary modal logic—i.e. a formula where the only situation term is S_0. Then an ordinary modal theorem proving method (e.g. that developed in [Frisch and Scherl, 1991; Scherl, 1992]) may be used to determine whether or not the regressed formula holds. In what follows, it is assumed that the formulas do not use the fluent K except as abbreviated by **Knows**.

The regression operator $\mathcal{R}$ is defined relative to a set of successor state axioms Θ. The first four parts of the definition of the regression operator $\mathcal{R}_\Theta$ concern ordinary (i.e. not knowledge-producing) actions [Reiter, 1991; Pednault, 1989].

i When A is a non-fluent atom, including equality atoms, and atoms with the predicate symbol $Poss$, or when A is a fluent atom whose situation argument is a situation variable, or the situation constant S_0, $\mathcal{R}_\Theta[A] = A$.

ii When F is a fluent (other than K) whose successor state axiom in Θ is

$$Poss(a, s) \rightarrow [F(x_1, \ldots, x_n, do(a, s)) \equiv \Phi_F] \quad (21)$$

then

$$\mathcal{R}_\Theta[F(t_1, \ldots, t_n, do(\alpha, \gamma))] = \Phi_F|_{t_1, \ldots, t_n, \alpha, \sigma}^{x_1, \ldots, x_n, a, s} \quad (22)$$

iii Whenever W is a formula, $\mathcal{R}_\Theta[\neg W] = \neg \mathcal{R}_\Theta[W]$, $\mathcal{R}_\Theta[(\forall v)W] = (\forall v)\mathcal{R}_\Theta[W]$, $\mathcal{R}_\Theta[(\exists v)W_1] = (\exists v)\mathcal{R}_\Theta[W_1]$.

iv Whenever W_1 and W_2 are formulas, $\mathcal{R}_\Theta[W_1 \wedge W_2] = \mathcal{R}_\Theta[W_1] \wedge \mathcal{R}_\Theta[W_1]$, $\mathcal{R}_\Theta[W_1 \vee W_2] = \mathcal{R}_\Theta[W_1] \vee \mathcal{R}_\Theta[W_1]$, $\mathcal{R}_\Theta[W_1 \rightarrow W_2] = \mathcal{R}_\Theta[W_1] \rightarrow \mathcal{R}_\Theta[W_1]$.

Additional steps are needed to extend the regression operator to knowledge-producing actions. For simplicity, it is assumed that there are only knowledge-producing operators of type sense—$Sense_1 \ldots Sense_n$. Two definitions are needed for the specification to follow. When ϕ is an arbitrary sentence and s a situation term, then apply(ϕ, s) is the sentence that results from adding an extra argument to every fluent of ϕ and inserting s into that argument position. The reverse operation apply$^{-1}(\phi)$ is the result of removing the last argument position from all the fluents in ϕ.

v Whenever a is not a knowledge-producing action, $\mathcal{R}_\Theta[\mathbf{Knows}(W, do(a, s))] = \mathbf{Knows}(\text{apply}^{-1}(\mathcal{R}_\Theta(\text{apply}(W, do(a, s)))), s)$.

---

[4]It is also assumed that this plan is known to be executable [Reiter, 1991], i.e., each step is possible.

vi $\mathcal{R}_\Theta[\mathbf{Knows}(W, do(Sense_i, s))] = ((\varphi_i(s) \rightarrow \mathbf{Knows}(\varphi_i \rightarrow W, s)) \wedge (\neg\varphi_i(s) \rightarrow \mathbf{Knows}(\neg\varphi_i \rightarrow W, s))$

In the following theorem, $\mathcal{F}$ is the axiomatization of the domain including $\mathcal{F}_{ss}$, the successor state axioms.

Theorem 5 *For any ground situation term s_{gr}*

$$\mathcal{F} \models G(s_{gr}) \quad \leftrightarrow \quad \mathcal{F} - \mathcal{F}_{ss} \models \mathcal{R}_\Theta^* G(s_{gr})$$

The proof is based on an induction over all ground action terms [Reiter, 1993]. Each regression step preserves logical equivalence given an axiomatization of the form developed here (i.e. successor state axioms). The process must terminate as every step removes the outer do from the situation terms and the number of do function symbols making up any such term is finite. Since each step preserves equivalence, the whole process results in an equivalent formula.

The result means that to test if some sentence G is true after executing a plan, it is only necessary to first regress $G(s_{gr})$, where s_{gr} is the plan expressed as a situation term, using the successor state axioms. This is accomplished by repeatedly passing the regression operator through the formula until the only situation term is S_0. Then the successor state axioms (including 11) are no longer needed. At that point an ordinary modal logic theorem proving method can be utilized to perform the test to determine whether or not $\mathcal{F} - \mathcal{F}_{ss} \models \mathcal{R}_\Theta^* G(s_{gr})$.

Consider the following example adapted from [Moore, 1985] (but without the frame axioms). The task is to show that after an agent performs a litmus paper test on an acidic solution, the agent will know that the solution is acidic. The litmus paper turns red if and only if the solution is acidic. The axiomatization includes $Acid(S_0)$. The actions are $Test_1$ and $Sense_R$. As the action preconditions are all $True$, the predicate $Poss$ is ignored in the presentation here. The successor state axiom for Red is given below:

$$Red(do(a, s)) \equiv (Acid(s) \wedge a = Test_1) \vee (Red(s) \wedge a \neq Test_1) \quad (23)$$

The instance of the successor state axiom (11) for the K relation is:

$$\forall a, s, s'', \; K(s'', do(a, s)) \equiv \\ \exists s'(K(s', s) \wedge (s'' = do(a, s'))) \wedge \\ ((a \neq Sense_R) \vee ((a = Sense_R) \\ \wedge (Red(s) \equiv Red(s')))) \quad (24)$$

The formula to be initially regressed is

$$\mathbf{Knows}(Acid, do(Sense_R, do(Test_1, S_0))) \quad (25)$$

Step **vi** of the definition of $\mathcal{R}$ is used with 25 to yield 26.

$$(Red(do(Test_1, S_0)) \rightarrow \\ \mathbf{Knows}(Red \rightarrow Acid, do(Test_1, S_0))) \wedge \\ (\neg Red(do(Test_1, S_0)) \rightarrow \\ \mathbf{Knows}(\neg Red \rightarrow Acid, do(Test_1, S_0))) \quad (26)$$

This is then regressed to sentence 27 by steps **iii**, **iv**, and **v** of the regression definition along with 23.

$$(Acid(S_0) \rightarrow \mathbf{Knows}(Acid \rightarrow Acid, S_0)) \wedge$$
$$(\neg Acid(S_0) \rightarrow \mathbf{Knows}(\neg Acid \rightarrow Acid, S_0))$$
$$(27)$$

Sentence 27 is clearly entailed by $Acid(S_0)$ and so 25 is entailed by the original theory. Note that 27 can be rewritten as a sentence in an ordinary modal logic because the only situation term is S_0.

Conclusion

This paper provides a solution to the frame problem for knowledge-producing actions. As long as the conditions needed for Reiter's solution for ordinary actions can be met, the work presented here provides a solution for knowledge-producing actions as well.

In terms of future work, we are extending the work discussed here so that the knowledge prerequisites and effects of actions can be *indexical* rather than objective knowledge. Following [Lespérance and Levesque, 1990; Lespérance, 1991], this will be done by making situations a composite of agents, times and worlds.

Also, the consideration of logics of *belief* is a topic for future research. The results presented in this paper are limited to logics of knowledge—logics with a possible world semantics in which the accessibility relation is reflexive. Note that in the case of a knowledge-producing action a that causes P to be known at $do(a, s)$, there must be a situation s' such that $K(s', s)$, and $P(s')$. But in the case of a belief-producing action, there is no guarantee that such a situation s' exist. This is why the results do not directly extend to modal logics without a reflexive accessibility relation.

Acknowledgments

We thank Ray Reiter and Fangzhen Lin for useful discussions on the situation calculus and the frame problem. Additionally, we would like to thank both Ray Reiter and Sheila McIlraith for comments on an earlier version of this paper. This research was funded in part by the National Sciences and Engineering Research Council of Canada, and the Institute for Robotics and Intelligent Systems.

References

Etzioni, Oren; Hanks, Steve; Weld, Daniel; Draper, Denise; Lesh, Neal; and Williamson, Mike 1992. An approach to planning with incomplete information. In Nebel, Bernhard; Rich, Charles; and Swartout, William, editors 1992, *Principles of Knowledge Representation and Reasoning: Proceedings of the Third International Conference*, Cambridge, Massachusetts. 115–125.

Frisch, Alan and Scherl, Richard 1991. A general framework for modal deduction. In Allen, J.A.; Fikes, R.; and Sandewall, E., editors 1991, *Principles of Knowledge Representation and Reasoning: Proceedings of the Second International Conference*, San Mateo,CA : Morgan Kaufmann.

Haas, A. R. 1987. The case for domain-specific frame axioms. In Brown, F. M., editor 1987, *The Frame Problem in Artificial Intelligence. Proceedings of the 1987 Workshop*. Morgan Kaufmann Publishers, Inc., San Mateo, California. 343–348.

Lespérance, Yves and Levesque, Hector J. 1990. Indexical knowledge in robot plans. In *Proceedings Eighth National Conference On Artificial Intelligence*. 1030–1037.

Lespérance, Yves 1991. *A Formal Theory of Indexical Knowledge and Action*. Ph.D. Dissertation, University of Toronto.

Lin, Fangzhen and Reiter, Ray 1993. State constraints revisited. Presented at the Second Symposium on Logical Formalizations of Commonsense Reasoning.

McCarthy, J. and Hayes, P. 1969. Some philosophical problems from the standpoint of artificial intelligence. In Meltzer, B. and Michie, D., editors 1969, *Machine Intelligence 4*. Edinburgh University Press, Edinburgh, UK. 463–502.

Moore, R.C. 1980. Reasoning about knowledge and action. Technical Note 191, SRI International.

Moore, R.C. 1985. A formal theory of knowledge and action. In Hobbs, J.R. and Moore, R.C., editors 1985, *Formal Theories of the Commonsense World*. Ablex, Norwood, NJ.

Pednault, E.P.D. 1989. ADL: exploring the middle ground between STRIPS and the situation calculus. In Brachman, R.J.; Levesque, H.; and Reiter, R., editors 1989, *Proceedings of the First International Conference on Principles of Knowledge Representation and Reasoning*. Morgan Kaufmann Publishers, Inc., San Mateo, California. 324–332.

Reiter, Raymond 1991. The frame problem in the situation calculus: A simple solution (sometimes) and a completeness result for goal regression. In Lifschitz, Vladimir, editor 1991, *Artificial Intelligence and Mathematical Theory of Computation: Papers in Honor of John McCarthy*. Academic Press, San Diego, CA. 359–380.

Reiter, R. 1993. Proving properties of states in the situation calculus. *Artificial Intelligence*. to appear.

Scherl, Richard 1992. *A Constraint Logic Approach To Automated Modal Deduction*. Ph.D. Dissertation, University of Illinois.

Schubert, L.K. 1990. Monotonic solution of the frame problem in the situation calculus: an efficient method for worlds with fully specified actions. In Kyberg, H. E.; Loui, R.P.; and Carlson, G.N., editors 1990, *Knowledge Representation and Defeasible Reasoning*. Kluwer Academic Press, Boston, Mass. 23–67.

Rule-Based
Reasoning

The Paradoxical Success of Fuzzy Logic*

Charles Elkan

Department of Computer Science and Engineering
University of California, San Diego
La Jolla, California 92093-0114

Abstract

This paper investigates the question of which aspects of fuzzy logic are essential to its practical usefulness. We show that as a formal system, a standard version of fuzzy logic collapses mathematically to two-valued logic, while empirically, fuzzy logic is not adequate for reasoning about uncertain evidence in expert systems. Nevertheless, applications of fuzzy logic in heuristic control have been highly successful. We argue that the inconsistencies of fuzzy logic have not been harmful in practice because current fuzzy controllers are far simpler than other knowledge-based systems. In the future, the technical limitations of fuzzy logic can be expected to become important in practice, and work on fuzzy controllers will also encounter several problems of scale already known for other knowledge-based systems.

1 Introduction

Fuzzy logic methods have been applied successfully in many real-world systems, but the coherence of the foundations of fuzzy logic remains under attack. Taken together, these two facts constitute a paradox, which this paper attempts to resolve. More concretely, the aim of this paper is to identify which aspects of fuzzy logic render it so useful in practice and which aspects are inessential. Our conclusions are based on a new mathematical result, on a survey of the literature on the use of fuzzy logic in heuristic control, and on our own practical experience developing two large-scale expert systems.

This paper is organized as follows. First, Section 2 proves and discusses the theorem mentioned above, which is that only two truth values are possible inside a standard system of fuzzy logic. In an attempt to understand how fuzzy logic can be useful despite this paradox, Sections 3 and 4 examine the main practical uses of fuzzy logic, in expert systems and heuristic control. Our tentative conclusion is that successful applications of fuzzy logic are successful because of factors other than

---

*This work was supported in part by the National Science Foundation under Award No. IRI-9110813.

the use of fuzzy logic. Finally, Section 5 shows how current work on fuzzy control is encountering dilemmas that are already well-known from work in other areas of artificial intelligence, and Section 6 provides some overall conclusions.

2 A paradox in fuzzy logic

As is natural in a research area as active as fuzzy logic, theoreticians have investigated many different formal systems, and applications have also used a variety of systems. Nevertheless, the basic intuitions are relatively constant. At its simplest, fuzzy logic is a generalization of standard propositional logic from two truth values *false* and *true* to degrees of truth between 0 and 1.

Formally, let A denote an assertion. In fuzzy logic, A is assigned a numerical value $t(A)$, called the degree of truth of A, such that $0 \leq t(A) \leq 1$. For a sentence composed from simple assertions and logical connectives "and" ($\wedge$), "or" ($\vee$), and "not" ($\neg A$ or $\overline{A}$), degree of truth is defined as follows:

Definition 1:

$$t(A \wedge B) = \min\{t(A), t(B)\}$$
$$t(A \vee B) = \max\{t(A), t(B)\}$$
$$t(\neg A) = 1 - t(A)$$
$$t(A) = t(B) \text{ if } A \text{ and } B \text{ are}$$
$$\text{logically equivalent.} \quad \blacksquare$$

In the last case of this definition, let "logically equivalent" mean equivalent according to the rules of classical two-valued propositional calculus. The use of alternative definitions of logical equivalence is discussed at the end of this section.

Fuzzy logic is intended to allow an indefinite variety of numerical truth values. The result proved here is that only two different truth values are in fact possible in the formal system of Definition 1.

Theorem 1: For any two assertions A and B, either $t(B) = t(A)$ or $t(B) = 1 - t(A)$.
Proof: Let A and B be arbitrary assertions. Consider the two sentences $\overline{A} \wedge \overline{B}$ and $B \vee (\overline{A} \wedge \overline{B})$. These are logically equivalent, so

$$t(\overline{A \wedge \overline{B}}) = t(B \vee (\overline{A} \wedge \overline{B})).$$

Now

$$t(\overline{A \wedge \overline{B}}) = 1 - \min\{t(A), 1 - t(B)\}$$
$$= 1 + \max\{-t(A), -1 + t(B)\}$$
$$= \max\{1 - t(A), t(B)\}$$

and

$$t(B \vee (\overline{A} \wedge \overline{B})) = \max\{t(B), \min\{1 - t(A), 1 - t(B)\}\}.$$

The numerical expressions above are different if

$$t(B) < 1 - t(B) < 1 - t(A),$$

that is if $t(B) < 1 - t(B)$ and $t(A) < t(B)$, which happens if $t(A) < t(B) < 0.5$. So it cannot be true that $t(A) < t(B) < 0.5$.

Now note that the sentences $\overline{A \wedge \overline{B}}$ and $B \vee (\overline{A} \wedge \overline{B})$ are both re-expressions of the material implication $A \to B$. One by one, consider the seven other material implication sentences involving A and B

$$\overline{A} \to B$$
$$A \to \overline{B}$$
$$\overline{A} \to \overline{B}$$
$$B \to A$$
$$\overline{B} \to A$$
$$B \to \overline{A}$$
$$\overline{B} \to \overline{A}.$$

By the same reasoning as before, none of the following can be true:

$$1 - t(A) < t(B) < 0.5$$
$$t(A) < 1 - t(B) < 0.5$$
$$1 - t(A) < 1 - t(B) < 0.5$$
$$t(B) < t(A) < 0.5$$
$$1 - t(B) < t(A) < 0.5$$
$$t(B) < 1 - t(A) < 0.5$$
$$1 - t(B) < 1 - t(A) < 0.5.$$

Now let $x = \min\{t(A), 1 - t(A)\}$ and let $y = \min\{t(B), 1 - t(B)\}$. Clearly $x \leq 0.5$ and $y \leq 0.5$ so if $x \neq y$, then one of the eight inequalities derived must be satisfied. Thus $t(B) = t(A)$ or $t(B) = 1 - t(A)$. ∎

It is important to be clear as to what exactly is proved above, and what is not proved. The first point to note is that nothing in the statement or proof of the theorem depends on any particular definition of the meaning of the implication connective, either in two-valued logic or in fuzzy logic. Theorem 1 could be stated and proved without introducing the symbol $\to$, since $A \to B$ is used just as a syntactic abbreviation for $B \vee (\overline{A} \wedge \overline{B})$.

The second point to note is that the theorem also applies to any more general formal system that includes the four postulates listed in Definition 1. Any extension of fuzzy logic to accommodate first-order sentences, for example, collapses to two truth values if it admits the propositional fuzzy logic of Definition 1 as a special case. The theorem also applies to fuzzy set theory, because Definition 1 can be understood as axiomatizing degree of membership for fuzzy set intersections, unions, and complements.

On the other hand, the theorem does not necessarily apply to any version of fuzzy logic that modifies or rejects any of the four postulates of Definition 1. It is however possible to carry through the proof of the theorem in many variant systems of fuzzy logic. In particular, the theorem remains true when negation is modelled by any operator in the Sugeno class [Sugeno, 1977], and when disjunction or conjunction are modelled by operators in the Yager classes [Yager, 1980].[1]

Of course, the last postulate of Definition 1 is the most controversial one, and the postulate that one naturally first wants to modify in order to preserve a continuum of degrees of truth. Unfortunately, it is not clear which subset of classical tautologies and equivalences should be, or can be, required to hold in a system of fuzzy logic. What all formal fuzzy logics have in common is that they reject at least one classical tautology, namely the law of excluded middle (the assertion $\overline{A} \vee A$). Intuitionistic logic [van Dalen, 1983] also rejects this law, but rejects in addition De Morgan's laws, which are entailed by the first three postulates of Definition 1. One could hope that fuzzy logic is therefore a formal system whose tautologies are a subset of the classical tautologies, and a superset of the intuitionistic tautologies. However, Theorem 1 can still be proved even if logical equivalence is restricted to mean intuitionistic equivalence.[2] It is an open question how to choose a notion of logical equivalence that simultaneously (i) remains philosophically justifiable, (ii) allows useful inferences in practice, and (iii) removes the opportunity to prove results similar to Theorem 1.

3 Fuzzy logic in expert systems

Any logical system or calculus for reasoning such as fuzzy logic must be motivated by its applicability to phenomena that we want to reason about. The operations of the calculus must model the behaviour of the ideas in certain classes. One way to defend a calculus is to show that it succeeds in interesting applications, which has certainly been done for fuzzy logic. However, if we are to have confidence that the successful application of the calculus is reproducible, we must be persuaded that the calculus correctly models the interaction of all phenomena in a well-characterized general class.

The basic motivation for fuzzy logic is clear: many ideas resemble traditional assertions, but they are not

---

[1] The postulates of standard fuzzy logic have been used quite widely, but it happens that even the same author sometimes adopts them and sometimes does not. For example (following [Gaines, 1983]) Bart Kosko explicitly uses all four postulates to resolve Russell's paradox of the barber who shaves all men except those who shave themselves [Kosko, 1990], but in later work he uses addition and multiplication instead of maximum and minimum [public lecture at UCSD, 1991].

[2] The Gödel translations [van Dalen, 1983; p. 172] of classically equivalent sentences are intuitionistically equivalent. For any sentence, the first three postulates of Definition 1 make its degree of truth and the degree of truth of its Gödel translation equal. Thus the proof given for Theorem 1 can be carried over directly.

naturally either true or false. Rather, uncertainty of some sort is attached to them. Fuzzy logic is an attempt to capture valid patterns of reasoning about uncertainty. The notion is now well accepted that there exist many different types of uncertainty, vagueness, and ignorance [Smets, 1991]. However, there is still debate as to what types of uncertainty are captured by fuzzy logic.[3] Many papers have discussed at a high level of mathematical abstraction the question of whether fuzzy logic provides suitable laws of thought for reasoning about probabilistic uncertainty. Our conclusion from practical experience in the construction of expert systems is that fuzzy logic is not uniformly suitable for reasoning about uncertain evidence. A simple example shows what the difficulty is.

Suppose the universe of discourse is a collection of melons, and there are two predicates *red* and *watermelon*, where *red* and *green* refer to the colour of the flesh of a melon. For some not very well-known melon x, suppose that $t(red(x)) = 0.5$ and $t(watermelon(x)) = 0.8$, meaning that the evidence that x is red inside has strength 0.5 and the evidence that x is a watermelon has strength 0.8. According to the rules of fuzzy logic, $t(red(x) \wedge watermelon(x)) = 0.5$. This is not reasonable, because watermelons are normally red inside. Redness and being a watermelon are mutually reinforcing facts, so intuitively, x is a red watermelon with certainty greater than 0.5.

The deep issue here is that the degree of uncertainty of a conjunction is not in general determined uniquely by the degree of uncertainty of the assertions entering into the conjunction. There does not exist a function f such that the rule $t(A \wedge B) = f(t(A), t(B))$ is always valid, when t represents the degree of certainty of fragments of evidence. The certainty of $A \wedge B$ depends on the content of the assertions A and B as well as on their numerical certainty. This fact is recognized implicitly in probabilistic reasoning, since probability theory does not assign unique probability values to conjunctions. What probability theory says is that

$$1 - \Big(1 - Pr(A) + 1 - Pr(B)\Big) \leq Pr(A \cap B)$$
$$\leq \min\{Pr(A), Pr(B)\}.$$

The actual probability value depends on further aspects of the situation that have not been stated. For example, if the two assertions A and B are independent, then the probability of their conjunction is $Pr(A) \cdot Pr(B)$.

Although probability theory is more flexible than fuzzy logic, the red watermelon example shows that it is not a universally adequate system of laws of thought for reasoning about all types of uncertainty either. If $t(red(x)) = 0.5$ and $t(watermelon(x)) = 0.8$, then it is natural to want $t(red(x) \wedge watermelon(x)) > 0.5$, which probability theory cannot permit.

---

[3] Misunderstanding on these issues has reached the nontechnical press: see articles based on [Kosko, 1990] in *Business Week* (New York, May 21, 1990), the *Financial Times* (London, June 5, 1990), the *Economist* (London, June 9, 1990), *Popular Science* (New York, June 1990), and elsewhere.

The difficulties identified here with fuzzy logic and probability theory as formalisms for reasoning about uncertainty do occur in practice. We have recently designed, implemented, and deployed at IBM two large-scale expert systems [Hekmatpour and Elkan, 1993; Hekmatpour and Elkan, 1992]. One system, CHATKB, solves problems encountered by engineers while using VLSI design tools. The other system, WESDA, diagnoses faults in machines that polish semiconductor wafers. The knowledge possessed by each system consists of a library of cases and a deep domain theory which is represented as a decision tree where each node corresponds to a fact about the state of the tool being diagnosed. Relevant cases are attached to each leaf of the decision tree. Roughly, the children of each node represent evidence in favour of the parent node, or potential causes of the parent node. CHATKB or WESDA retrieves an old case to solve a new problem by choosing a path through its decision tree. A path from the root to a leaf is chosen by combining *a priori* child node likelihoods with evidence acquired through questioning the user. We have found that this process of combining evidence is a type of reasoning about uncertainty that cannot be modelled adequately by the axioms of fuzzy logic, or by those of probability theory.

Methods for reasoning about uncertain evidence are an active research area in artificial intelligence, and the conclusions reached in this section are not new. Our practical experience does, however, independently confirm previous arguments about the inadequacy of systems for reasoning about uncertainty that propagate numerical factors according only to which connectives appear in assertions [Pearl, 1988].

4 Fuzzy logic in heuristic control

Heuristic control is the area of application in which fuzzy logic has been the most successful. There is a wide consensus that the techniques of traditional mathematical control theory are often inadequate. The reasons for this include the reliance of traditional methods on linear models of systems to be controlled, their propensity to produce "bang-bang" control regimes, and their focus on worst-case convergence and stability rather than typical-case efficiency. Heuristic control techniques give up mathematical simplicity and performance guarantees in exchange for increased realism and better performance in practice. A heuristic controller using fuzzy logic is shown to have less overshoot and quicker settling in [Burkhardt and Bonissone, 1992] for example.

The first demonstrations that fuzzy logic could be used in building heuristic controllers were published in the 1970s [Zadeh, 1973; Mamdani and Assilian, 1975]. Work using fuzzy logic in heuristic control continued through the 1980s, and recently there has been an explosion of industrial interest in this area; for surveys see [Yamakawa and Hirota, 1989] and [Lee, 1990]. One reason why fuzzy controllers have attracted so much interest recently is that they can be implemented by embedded specialized microprocessors [Yamakawa, 1989].

Despite the intense industrial interest (and, in Japan, consumer interest) in fuzzy logic, the technology continues to meet resistance. For example, at the 1991 International Joint Conference on Artificial Intelligence (IJCAI'91, Sydney, Australia) Takeo Kanade gave an invited talk on computer vision in which he described at length Matsushita's camcorder image stabilizing system [Uomori *et al.*, 1990], without mentioning that it uses fuzzy logic.

Almost all currently deployed heuristic controllers using fuzzy logic are similar in five important aspects. A good description of a prototypical example of this standard architecture appears in [Sugeno *et al.*, 1989].

- First, the knowledge base of a typical fuzzy controller consists of under 100 rules; often under 20 rules are used. Fuzzy controllers are orders of magnitude smaller than systems built using traditional artificial intelligence formalisms: the knowledge base of CHATKB, for example, occupies many megabytes.

- Second, the knowledge entering into fuzzy controllers is structurally shallow, both statically and dynamically. It is not the case that some rules produce conclusions which are then used as premises in other rules. Statically, rules are organized in a flat list, and dynamically, there is no run-time chaining of inferences.

- Third, the knowledge recorded in a fuzzy controller typically reflects immediate correlations between the inputs and outputs of the system to be controlled, as opposed to a deep, causal model of the system. The premises of rules refer to sensor observations and rule conclusions refer to actuator settings.[4]

- The fourth important feature that deployed fuzzy controllers share is that the numerical parameters of their rules and of their qualitative input and output modules are tuned in a learning process. Many different learning algorithms have been used for this purpose, and neural network learning mechanisms have been especially successful [Keller and Tahani, 1992; Yager, 1992]. What the algorithms used for tuning fuzzy controllers themselves have in common is that they are gradient-descent "hillclimbing" algorithms that learn by local optimization [Burkhardt and Bonissone, 1992].

- Last but not least, by definition fuzzy controllers use the operators of fuzzy logic. Typically "minimum" and "maximum" are used, as are explicit possibility distributions (usually trapezoidal), and some fuzzy implication operator.

---

[4] Rule premises refer to qualitative ("linguistic" in the terminology of fuzzy logic) sensor observations and rule conclusions refer to qualitative actuator settings, whereas outputs and inputs of sensors and actuators are typically real-valued. This means that two controller components usually exist which map between numerical values and qualitative values. In fuzzy logic terminology, these components are said to defuzzify outputs and implement membership functions respectively. Their behaviour is not itself describable using fuzzy logic, and typically they are implemented procedurally.

The question which naturally arises is which of the features of fuzzy controllers identified above are essential to their success. It appears that the first four shared properties are vital to practical success, because they make the celebrated credit assignment problem solvable, while the use of fuzzy logic is not essential.

In a nutshell, the credit assignment problem is to discover how to modify part of a complex system in order to improve it, given only an evaluation of its overall performance. In general, solving the credit assignment problem is impossible: the task is tantamount to generating many bits of information (a change to the internals of a complex system) from just a few bits of information (the input/output performance of the system). However, the first four shared features of fuzzy controllers make the credit assignment problem solvable for them.

First, since it consists of only a small number of rules, the knowledge base of a fuzzy controller is a small system to modify. Second, the short paths between the inputs and outputs of a fuzzy controller mean that the effect of any change in the controller is localized, so it is easier to discover a change that has a desired effect without having other undesired consequences. Third, the iterative way in which fuzzy controllers are refined allows a large number of observations of input/output performance to be used for system improvement. Fourth, the continuous nature of the many parameters of a fuzzy controller allows small quantities of performance information to be used to make small system changes.

Thus, what makes fuzzy controllers useful in practice is the combination of a rule-based formalism with numerical factors qualifying rules and the premises entering into rules. The principal advantage of rule-based formalisms is that knowledge can be acquired from experts or from experience incrementally: individual rules and premises can be refined independently, or at least more independently than items of knowledge in other formalisms. Numerical factors have two main advantages. They allow a heuristic control system to interface smoothly with the continuous outside world, and they allow it to be tuned gradually: small changes in numerical factor values cause small changes in behaviour.

None of these features contributing to the success of systems based on fuzzy logic is unique to fuzzy logic. It seems that most current applications of fuzzy logic could use other numerical rule-based formalisms instead, if a learning algorithm was used to tune numerical values for those formalisms, as is customary when using fuzzy logic.

Several knowledge representation formalisms that are rule-based and numerical have been proposed besides fuzzy logic. For example, well-developed systems are presented in [Sandewall, 1989] and [Collins and Michalski, 1989; Dontas and Zemankova, 1990]. To the extent that numerical qualification factors can be tuned in these formalisms, we expect that they would be equally useful for constructing heuristic controllers. Indeed, at least one has already been so used [Sammut and Michie, 1991].

5 Recapitulating mainstream AI

Several research groups are attempting to scale up systems based on fuzzy logic, and to lift the architectural limitations of current fuzzy controllers. For example, a methodology for designing block-structured controllers with guaranteed stability properties is studied in [Tanaka and Sugeno, 1992], and methodological problems in constructing models of complex systems based on deep knowledge are considered in [Pedrycz, 1991]. Controllers with intermediate variables, thus with chaining of inferences, are investigated in [von Altrock *et al.*, 1992].

However, the designers of larger systems based on fuzzy logic are encountering all the problems of scale already identified in traditional knowledge-based systems. It appears that the history of research in fuzzy logic is recapitulating the history of research in other areas of artificial intelligence. This section discusses the knowledge engineering dilemmas faced by developers of fuzzy controllers, and then points to dealing with state information as another issue arising in research on fuzzy controllers that has also arisen previously.

The rules in the knowledge bases of current fuzzy controllers are obtained directly by interviewing experts. Indeed, the original motivation for using fuzzy logic in building heuristic controllers was that fuzzy logic is designed to capture human statements involving vague quantifiers such as "considerable." More recently, a consensus has developed that research must focus on obtaining "procedures for fuzzy controller design based on fuzzy models of the process" [Driankov and Eklund, 1991]. Mainstream work on knowledge engineering, however, has already transcended the dichotomy between rule-based and model-based reasoning.

Expert systems whose knowledge consists of *if-then* rules have at least two disadvantages. First, maintenance of a rule base becomes complex and time-consuming as the size of a system increases [Newquist, 1988]. Second, rule-based systems tend to be brittle: if an item of knowledge is missing from a rule, the system may fail to find a solution, or worse, may draw an incorrect conclusion [Abbott, 1988]. The main disadvantage of model-based approaches, on the other hand, is that it is very difficult to construct sufficiently detailed and accurate models of complex systems. Moreover, models constructed tend to be highly application-specific and not generalizable [Bourne *et al.*, 1991].

Many recent expert systems, therefore, including CHATKB and WESDA, are neither rule-based nor model-based in the standard way. For these systems, the aim of the knowledge engineering process is not simply to acquire knowledge from human experts, whether this knowledge is correlational as in present fuzzy controllers, or deep as in model-based expert systems. Rather, the aim is to develop a theory of the situated performance of the experts. Concretely, under this view of knowledge engineering, knowledge bases are constructed to model the beliefs and practices of experts and not any "objective" truth about underlying physical processes. An important benefit of this approach is that the organization of an expert's beliefs provides an implicit organization of knowledge about the external process with which the knowledge-based system is intended to interact.

The more sophisticated view of knowledge engineering just outlined is clearly relevant to research on con-

structing fuzzy controllers more intricate than current ones. For a second example of relevant previous artificial intelligence work, consider controllers that can carry state information from one moment to the next. These are mentioned as a topic for future research in [von Altrock *et al.*, 1992]. Symbolic AI formalisms for representing systems whose behaviour depends on their history have been available since the 1960s [McCarthy and Hayes, 1969]. Neural networks with similar properties (called recurrent networks) have been available for several years [Elman, 1990], and have already been used in control applications [Karim and Rivera, 1992]. It remains to be seen whether research from a fuzzy logic perspective will provide new solutions to the fundamental issues of artificial intelligence.

6 Conclusions

Applications of fuzzy logic in heuristic control have been highly successful, despite the collapse of fuzzy logic as a formal system to two-valued logic, and despite the inadequacy of fuzzy logic for reasoning about uncertainty in expert systems. The inconsistencies of fuzzy logic have not been harmful in practice because current fuzzy controllers are far simpler than other knowledge-based systems. First, long chains of inference are not performed in controllers based on fuzzy logic, so there is no opportunity for inconsistency between paths of reasoning that should be equivalent to manifest itself. Second, the knowledge recorded in a fuzzy controller is not a consistent causal model of the process being controlled, but rather an assemblage of visible correlations between sensor observations and actuator settings. Since this knowledge is not itself consistent and probabilistic, the probabilistic inadequacy of fuzzy logic is not an issue. Moreover, the ability to refine the parameters of a fuzzy controller iteratively can compensate for the arbitrariness of the fuzzy logic operators as applied inside a limited domain.

The common assumption that heuristic controllers based on fuzzy logic are successful because they use fuzzy logic appears to be an instance of the *post hoc, ergo propter hoc* fallacy. The fact that using fuzzy logic is correlated with success does not entail that using fuzzy logic causes success. In the future, the technical limitations of fuzzy logic identified in this paper can be expected to become important in practice. Other general dilemmas of artificial intelligence work can also be expected to become critical—in particular, the issue of designing learning mechanisms that can solve the credit assignment problem when the simplifying features of present controllers are absent.

Acknowledgements. The author is grateful to several colleagues for useful comments on earlier versions of this paper, and to John Lamping for asking if Theorem 1 holds when equivalence is understood intuitionistically.

References

[Abbott, 1988] K. Abbott. Robust operative diagnosis as problem solving in a hypothesis space. In *Proceedings of the National Conference on Artificial Intelligence*, pages 369–374, 1988.

[Bourne et al., 1991] J. R. Bourne et al. Organizing and understanding beliefs in advice-giving diagnostic systems. *IEEE Transactions on Knowledge and Data Engineering*, 3(3):269–280, September 1991.

[Burkhardt and Bonissone, 1992] David G. Burkhardt and Piero P. Bonissone. Automated fuzzy knowledge base generation and tuning. In *Proceedings of the IEEE International Conference on Fuzzy Systems*, pages 179–188, San Diego, California, March 1992.

[Collins and Michalski, 1989] A. Collins and R. Michalski. The logic of plausible reasoning: A core theory. *Cognitive Science*, 13(1):1–49, 1989.

[Dontas and Zemankova, 1990] K. Dontas and M. Zemankova. APPLAUSE: an implementation of the Collins-Michalski theory of plausible reasoning. *Information Sciences*, 52(2):111–139, 1990.

[Driankov and Eklund, 1991] Dimiter Driankov and Peter Eklund. Workshop goals. In *IJCAI'91 Workshop on Fuzzy Control Preprints*, Sydney, Australia, August 1991.

[Elman, 1990] Jeffrey L. Elman. Finding structure in time. *Cognitive Science*, 14(2):179–211, 1990.

[Gaines, 1983] Brian R. Gaines. Precise past, fuzzy future. *International Journal of Man-Machine Studies*, 19:117–134, 1983.

[Hekmatpour and Elkan, 1992] Amir Hekmatpour and Charles Elkan. A multimedia expert system for wafer polisher maintenance. Technical Report CS92-257, Department of Computer Science and Engineering, University of California, San Diego, 1992.

[Hekmatpour and Elkan, 1993] Amir Hekmatpour and Charles Elkan. Categorization-based diagnostic problem solving in the VLSI design domain. In *Proceedings of the IEEE International Conference on Artificial Intelligence for Applications*, pages 121–127, March 1993.

[Karim and Rivera, 1992] M. N. Karim and S. L. Rivera. Comparison of feed-forward and recurrent neural networks for bioprocess state estimation. *Computers and Chemical Engineering*, 16:S369–S377, 1992.

[Keller and Tahani, 1992] J. M. Keller and H. Tahani. Back-propagation neural networks for fuzzy logic. *Information Sciences*, 62(3):205–221, 1992.

[Kosko, 1990] Bart Kosko. Fuzziness vs. probability. *International Journal of General Systems*, 17(2–3):211–240, 1990.

[Lee, 1990] C. C. Lee. Fuzzy logic in control systems–parts 1 and 2. *IEEE Transactions on Systems, Man, and Cybernetics*, 20(2):404–435, March 1990.

[Mamdani and Assilian, 1975] E. H. Mamdani and S. Assilian. An experiment in linguistic synthesis with a fuzzy logic controller. *International Journal of Man-Machine Studies*, 7:1–13, 1975.

[McCarthy and Hayes, 1969] John McCarthy and Patrick J. Hayes. Some philosophical problems from the standpoint of artificial intelligence. In *Machine Intelligence*, volume 4, pages 463–502. Edinburgh University Press, 1969.

[Newquist, 1988] H. P. Newquist. Struggling to maintain. *AI Expert*, 3(8):69–71, 1988.

[Pearl, 1988] Judea Pearl. *Probabilistic Reasoning in Intelligent Systems*. Morgan Kaufmann Publishers, Inc., 1988.

[Pedrycz, 1991] Witold Pedrycz. Fuzzy modelling: fundamentals, construction and evaluation. *Fuzzy Sets and Systems*, 41(1):1–15, 1991.

[Sammut and Michie, 1991] Claude Sammut and Donald Michie. Controlling a "black box" simulation of a space craft. *AI Magazine*, 12(1):56–63, 1991.

[Sandewall, 1989] Erik Sandewall. Combining logic and differential equations for describing real-world systems. In *Proceedings of the First International Conference on Principles of Knowledge Representation and Reasoning (KR'89)*, pages 412–420, 1989.

[Smets, 1991] Philippe Smets. Varieties of ignorance and the need for well-founded theories. *Information Sciences*, 57–58:135–144, 1991.

[Sugeno et al., 1989] Michio Sugeno et al. Fuzzy algorithmic control of a model car by oral instructions. *Fuzzy Sets and Systems*, 32(2):135–156, 1989.

[Sugeno, 1977] Michio Sugeno. Fuzzy measures and fuzzy integrals—a survey. In Madan M. Gupta, George N. Saridis, and Brian R. Gaines, editors, *Fuzzy Automata and Decision Processes*, pages 89–102. North-Holland, 1977.

[Tanaka and Sugeno, 1992] K. Tanaka and M. Sugeno. Stability analysis and design of fuzzy control systems. *Fuzzy Sets and Systems*, 45(2):135–156, 1992.

[Uomori et al., 1990] Kenya Uomori, Autshi Morimura, Hirohumi Ishii, Takashi Sakaguchi, and Yoshinori Kitamura. Automatic image stabilizing system by full-digital signal processing. *IEEE Transactions on Consumer Electronics*, 36(3):510–519, August 1990.

[van Dalen, 1983] Dirk van Dalen. *Logic and Structure*. Springer Verlag, second edition, 1983.

[von Altrock et al., 1992] C. von Altrock, B. Krause, and Hans J. Zimmermann. Advanced fuzzy logic control of a model car in extreme situations. *Fuzzy Sets and Systems*, 48(1):41–52, 1992.

[Yager, 1980] Ronald R. Yager. On a general class of fuzzy connectives. *Fuzzy Sets and Systems*, 4:235–242, 1980.

[Yager, 1992] Ronald R. Yager. Implementing fuzzy logic controllers using a neural network framework. *Fuzzy Sets and Systems*, 48(1):53–64, 1992.

[Yamakawa and Hirota, 1989] Special issue on applications of fuzzy logic control to industry. *Fuzzy Sets and Systems*, 32(2), 1989. Takeshi Yamakawa and K. Hirota (editors).

[Yamakawa, 1989] Takeshi Yamakawa. Stabilization of an inverted pendulum by a high-speed fuzzy logic controller hardware system. *Fuzzy Sets and Systems*, 32(2):161–180, 1989.

[Zadeh, 1973] Lotfi A. Zadeh. Outline of a new approach to the analysis of complex systems and decision processes. *IEEE Transactions on Systems, Man, and Cybernetics*, 3:28–44, 1973.

Exploring the Structure of Rule Based Systems*

Clifford Grossner, Alun D. Preece, P. Gokul Chander,
T. Radhakrishnan and **Ching Y. Suen**
Computer Science Department, Concordia University
1455 De Maisonneuve Blvd. Ouest
Montréal, Québec, Canada H3G 1M8
cliff@cs.concordia.ca

Abstract

In order to measure and analyze the performance of rule-based expert systems, it is necessary to explicate the internal structure of their rule bases. Although a number of attempts have been made in the literature to formalize the structure of a rule base using the notion of a rule base execution path, none of these are entirely adequate. This paper reports a new formal definition for the notion of a rule base execution path, which adequately supports both validation and performance analysis of rule-based expert systems. This definition for the execution paths in a rule base has been embodied in a rule base analysis tool called Path Hunter. Path Hunter is used to analyse a rule base consisting of 442 CLIPS rules. In this analysis, the problem of combinatorial explosion, which arises during path enumeration, is controlled due to the manner in which paths are defined. The analysis raises several issues which should be taken into account in the engineering of rule-based systems.

Introduction and Motivation

Expert systems characteristically achieve a high level of performance in solving ill structured problems [Simon, 1973], using a body of knowledge specific to the problem domain. This knowledge is represented explicitly in the *knowledge base* (KB) of the system, which is kept separate from the mechanism which applies the knowledge to solve problems (the *inference engine*). The intuitive appeal of rules for solving ill structured problems results from rules often being easy for non-programmers to read and write. However, the behaviour of large rule-based systems is almost always hard to predict because, although individual rules can be easy to understand on their own, interactions that can occur between rules are not obvious. As a consequence of this, it is hard to measure and analyze the performance of rule-based expert systems. Tools are required to assist developers in understanding the dependencies that exist between individual rules, and

indicate how sets of rules will operate together to complete tasks in the problem-solving process. This paper describes a formal method for detecting the potential interactions between the rules in a rule base [Grossner *et al.*, 1992a], and the development of a tool embodying this method, called Path Hunter [Gokulchander *et al.*, 1992]. Path Hunter is used to analyse the rule base of the Blackbox Expert, an experimental DAI testbed [Grossner *et al.*, 1991]. The Blackbox Expert is a rule-based expert system designed to solve a puzzle called Blackbox.

Our desire to explicate the structure of rule bases is motivated by work in two related fields of artificial intelligence: expert systems, and distributed artificial intelligence (DAI). We use the term *structure* to refer to the dependencies between the rules and potential interactions that can occur between the rules in the rule base. Mapping the structure of a rule-based expert system has become important for structural validation of expert systems [Rushby and Crow, 1990] as well as performance analysis of cooperative distributed problem solving systems (CDPS) [Durfee *et al.*, 1989]. In *structural validation*, the structure of the rule base of an expert system is used as a guide for the generation of test cases and as an indicator of the "completeness" of the validation process [Rushby and Crow, 1990]. Performance analysis of CDPS systems requires a description of the structure of the rule bases of the expert systems in the CDPS to predict the operations that they will be able to perform given the 'information' (data items) available to them as a part of the CDPS system [Grossner *et al.*, 1992b].

We seek to capture the structure of a rule base in terms of chains of inter-dependent rules called *paths*. If the notion of path in a rule base is to be useful for validation and performance analysis of expert systems, it must possess the following criteria:

- The notion of path must be well-defined and unambiguous, so that it can serve as an adequate specification for an automatic path-enumeration program. Only sequences of rules that depend upon each other for their firing are to be considered part of the same path.

---

*This work was funded in part by Bell Canada Inc.

- When the rules forming a path fire, their combined actions carry out an intended function of the system designer, and can be seen as having significantly advanced the state of the problem being solved.

- The computational effort involved in finding the rules that comprise a path should not be too large to enable efficient automatic enumeration of paths. The number of paths that will be enumerated for a rule base using this definition of path must be computable; that is, we want to prohibit a combinatorial explosion in finding paths.

While researchers in DAI have speculated about the effects of data distribution on the performance of a CDPS system [Lesser and Corkill, 1981; Fox, 1981], there have not been any attempts made at modeling the rule base of an expert system for the purposes of understanding the magnitude of the change in the performance of an expert system given a change in the data distribution of the CDPS. Durfee et al. have observed several of the effects of data distribution on specific test cases of the Distributed Vehicle Monitoring Problem [Durfee *et al.*, 1987]. Other efforts at modeling CDPS systems have been for the purpose of understanding agent behavior and their potential interactions [Shoham, 1991].

The expert system validation literature reports a number of approaches for defining the execution paths in a rule base. The EVA system [Chang *et al.*, 1990] defines a dependency graph (DG) that is used to generate test cases for validating an expert system. The definition of the rule-dependency relation used to construct the DG is unsatisfactory because it allows EVA to consider rules to depend upon each other when in fact they do not; thus, many paths are enumerated which do not reflect 'paths' that will occur when a rule base is executed. Rushby and Crow [Rushby and Crow, 1990] propose a refinement of the EVA DG method, where the rule-dependency relation is improved, but under certain conditions it is still unsatisfactory for the same reason. A stricter method for determining rule dependencies is proposed by Kiper [Kiper, 1992], which models the state of the rule-based system as it would appear when the rules are fired. While this method permits only true rule dependencies to be captured, the rule base states are very costly to compute. Therefore, none of the previous approaches satisfy our criteria.

The Paths of a Rule Base

Conventionally, an expert system $\mathcal{E}$ is built to solve ill structured problems, which we denote by P^I. For our purposes, a rule-based expert system $\mathcal{E}$ is considered to be a triple $\langle E, RB, WM \rangle$ where: E is an inference engine, RB is the rule base used by the inference engine, and WM is the working memory where facts (representing current data) are stored. The facts that are stored in the working memory consists of a predicate name and a list of arguments. Predicates indicate the relationships that exist among the elements of the list in a fact. Let R be the set of all predicates used by $\mathcal{E}$ in solving P^I. We use the notation f_i to represent a fact that may be present in the working memory WM, where: $f_i = \langle \alpha_i, l_i \rangle$ such that l_i is a list of data elements, and $\alpha_i \in R$ identifies the relationship between the elements of l_i. Finally, the *state* of $\mathcal{E}$ is denoted by the set of facts S present in WM at a given time.

The rule base RB of an expert system $\mathcal{E}$ is the set of rules r_i for solving P^I. When a rule fires, it changes the state of the expert system by adding or removing facts from the WM. We consider a rule r_i to be composed of an LHS and an RHS where: the LHS indicates the fact templates such that at least one instance of each template must be present in WM for the rule to fire, denoted by $\mathcal{I}^{r_i}$; the RHS indicates the set of facts that may be asserted by r_i, denoted by $\mathcal{A}^{r_i}$.

The Blackbox expert has been developed using the CLIPS expert system tool [Giarratano and Riley, 1989], and has been designed to solve the Blackbox puzzle. The Blackbox puzzle consists of an opaque square grid (box) with a number of balls hidden in the grid squares. The puzzle solver can fire beams into the box. These beams interact with the balls, allowing the puzzle solver to determine the contents of the box based on the entry and exit points of the beams. The puzzle solver must determine if each location of the grid square is empty or contains a ball, and in addition if the conclusion drawn for the location is certain. As an intermediate step, the puzzle solver can determine that there is evidence indicating that a square is both empty and contains a ball, signalling a conflict. Conflicts may be resolved as additional evidence is obtained. For example, additional evidence may indicate that the ball is certain. Thus, the grid location would be considered to certainly contain a ball, and the evidence suggesting that the location is empty would be disproven. The objective of the Blackbox puzzle-solver is to determine the contents of as many of the grid squares as possible, while minimizing the number of beams fired.

An example rule (`Ball-Certain`) from the CLIPS rule base for the Blackbox Puzzle is shown in Figure 1. Table 1 lists the predicates and user defined functions used by `Ball-Certain` and the other rules from the Blackbox Expert's rule base that will be used for example purposes. The user defined functions represent an indirect access to WM; thus, each function will have a predicate associated with it as shown in Table 1. `Ball-Certain` is activated when ample evidence is gathered to support making certain a ball located in the Blackbox grid. This rule will be activated by the presence of the fact using the predicate BALL_CERTAIN as well as a fact using the predicate CERTAIN_BALLS. Once the rule is activated, it will check to see if the grid location is already certain, in which case no action is needed. Otherwise, the location is made certain; and if a conflict exists, a fact using the predicate RMC_B is

```
; Update the grid to indicate that a ball in a particular location is to be considered
: a certain ball.
(defrule Ball-Certain
    ?var1 <- (BALL_CERTAIN ?sn ?rule-ID ?row ?col)    ;A ball is to be made certain
    ?var2 <- (CERTAIN_BALLS ?cb)                       ;Get number of certain balls located
  =>
    (retract ?var1)
    (if (not (iscertain ?row ?col)) then               ;Is the ball already marked as certain?
      (retract ?var2)
      (assert (CERTAIN_BALLS =(+ ?cb 1)))              ;Increment # of certain balls
      (setcertain ?row ?col)                           ;Update the grid making the ball certain
      (if (eq (status ?row ?col) CONFLICT) then        ;Is There a Conflict?
        (assert (RMC_B ?sn ?rule-ID ?row ?col))        ;Indicate the conflict is to be resolved
))) ; end rule Ball-Certain
```

Figure 1: Sample CLIPS Rule

USER FN	Interpretation	Assoc. Predicate
iscertain	check certainty of a square	GMAP_CERT
setcertain	set a square certain	GMAP_CERT_B
status	check contents of a square	GMAP

PREDICATE	Interpretation
BALL	Ball located
BALL-CERTAIN	A ball is to be made certain
BLANK-GRID	Place an empty in a grid square
CERTAIN-BALLS	Count of certain balls located
CONFLICT_B	Conflict has occurred placing a ball
DISPROVE_E	Evidence for an empty square is disproven
GMAP	Access to the contents of a grid square
GMAP_B	Ball location on the grid
GMAP_C	Conflict location on the grid
GMAP_CERT	Certainty of grid location
GMAP_CERT_B	Ball made certain
GRIDSIZE	Dimension of the grid
P-BALL	Place a ball on the grid
RMC_B	Remove a conflict by placing a ball
SHOT-RECORD	exit and entry point for a beam

Table 1: Predicates and User Defined Function for Blackbox

asserted indicating it can be resolved.

Ball-Certain does not follow the form of rules as we have defined them. Therefore, Path Hunter will abstract Ball-Certain and split it into two rules: Ball-Certain%1, and Ball-Certain%2. The rule Ball-Certain%1 will update the grid to indicate that a ball in a particular location is to be considered a certain ball, a conflict is discovered, and the conflict is to be resolved. $\mathcal{I}^{\text{Ball-Certain\%1}} = \{$GMAP, GMAP_CERT, CERTAIN_BALLS, BALL_CERTAIN$\}$, and $\mathcal{A}^{\text{Ball-Certain\%1}} = \{$GMAP_CERT_B, RMC_B, CERTAIN_BALLS$\}$. The rule Ball-Certain%2 will update the grid to indicate that a ball in a particular location is to be considered a certain ball. $\mathcal{I}^{\text{Ball-Certain\%2}} = \{$GMAP, GMAP_CERT, CERTAIN_BALLS, BALL_CERTAIN$\}$, and $\mathcal{A}^{\text{Ball-Certain\%2}} = \{$GMAP_CERT_B, CERTAIN_BALLS$\}$. The original rule contained a conditional on its RHS

representing two different potential actions: the case that the ball made certain was successfully placed, and the case where there was a conflict when the ball was placed. Thus, Path Hunter created two abstract rules each embodying one of the potential actions taken by the RHS of Ball-Certain. The predicate associated with the user defined function used in the condition that was on the RHS of Ball-Certain has been placed on the LHS of the abstract rules.

In order to reduce the computation and memory requirements needed to solve ill structured problems they are typically decomposed into subproblems [Grossner, 1990], and we denote a subproblem by SP_t. Two of the subproblems for Blackbox are Beam Selection and Beam Trace. Each subproblem SP_t of P^I will have its own set of rules within RB. We refer to the collection of rules $\{ r_i \mid r_i$ used to solve $SP_t \}$ as task T_t. Each subproblem SP_t of P^I will have distinct states that represent acceptable solutions for the subproblem. States which represent an acceptable solution for SP_t are characterized by the presence of facts in WM that use specific predicates called end predicates. We denote the set of end predicates for SP_t by Z_t.

Definition 1 (Logical Completion) *A logical completion for SP_t is a conjunction of selected predicates from Z_t denoting a state which is a meaningful solution to a subproblem.*

We use the notation $SP_t \rightsquigarrow U$ to denote a set of rules U that assert facts using all the predicates of a logical completion for SP_t. A logical completion for Beam Trace would be GMAP_B $\wedge$ BALL.

We now turn our attention to the types of 'dependency' that can exist between two rules. As the original problem P_I is already decomposed into subproblems, we will only consider dependencies between rules in the same task. Intuitively, we say that one rule is dependent upon another if the action taken by one rule facilitates the other rule to become fireable. The simplest form of dependency exists when one rule asserts a fact that is required by the LHS of another rule. At this point, we will consider only this simple form of dependency.

Definition 2 (Depends Upon)
The relation depends upon between two rules r_i and r_j is denoted by $r_i \prec r_j$, and it indicates that the RHS of r_i asserts a fact $\langle \alpha_i, l_i \rangle$ that matches a template in the LHS of r_j, with the constraint that $\alpha_i \notin Z_t$. Formally:
$$r_i \prec r_j \equiv ((\mathcal{A}^{r_i} \cap \mathcal{I}^{r_j}) \neq \emptyset) \wedge (\forall \alpha)((\alpha \in \mathcal{A}^{r_i} \cap \mathcal{I}^{r_j}) \Rightarrow \alpha \notin Z_s)$$

The condition $(\forall \alpha)((\alpha \in \mathcal{A}^{r_i} \cap \mathcal{I}^{r_j}) \Rightarrow \alpha \notin Z_s)$ placed on the *depends upon* relation restricts this relationship to rules that are in the same task.

A set of sample rules from the Blackbox Expert's rule base are shown in Table 2. These rules are part of the `Beam Trace` task. Two examples of the *depends upon* relation exist between `RA-12-Right%1`, `Right-12-Left%1`, and `RA-12-Prep%1`. More precisely, `RA-12-Right%1` $\prec$ `RA-12-Prep%1` and `RA-12-Left%1` $\prec$ `RA-12-Prep%1`.

When considering the dependencies that exist among the rules in a task, we become concerned with grouping the rules according to the dependency relationship. Thus for any rule in a task we desire the ability to identify those rules which it *depends upon*.

Definition 3 (Reachability)
A rule r_j is reachable from a set of rules V, if V contains all the rules that r_j depends upon. We use the notation $V \rightarrow r_j$ to indicate that r_j is reachable from the rules in V. Formally, $V \rightarrow r_j$ iff $(\forall r_i \in T_t)(r_i \prec r_j \Rightarrow r_i \in V)$.

For `RA-12-Prep%1` in Table 2, $V = \{$`RA-12-Right%1`, `Right-12-Left%1`$\}$.

We now consider the set of rules that *enable* a rule to fire. Informally, we say that a set of rules W *enables* a rule r_j when' the rules in W assert facts causing r_j to fire. This set of rules W must satisfy a number of conditions for it to be an *enabling-set* for a rule r_j:

- Given r_j, then $W \subseteq V$; that is, r_j must *depend upon* every rule in W.

- Every rule in W must assert at least one fact that uses a predicate specified by the LHS of r_j where a fact using that predicate is not asserted by any other rule in W. Formally, we say W is *minimal* if $(\forall r_i)(\forall r_k)((r_i \neq r_k) \Rightarrow (\mathcal{A}^{r_i} \not\subseteq \mathcal{A}^{r_k}))$, where $r_i, r_k \in W$.

- For each predicate specified by a template on the LHS of r_j, if that predicate is used in a fact asserted by at least one rule, then some rule that asserts a fact using the predicate must be a member of W. Formally, we say that W is *maximal* if $(\forall \alpha_u)(\alpha_u \in \mathcal{I}^{r_j})((\exists r_k)(r_k \in V \wedge \alpha_u \in \mathcal{A}^{r_k}) \Rightarrow (\exists r_i)(r_i \in W \wedge \alpha_u \in \mathcal{A}^{r_i}))$.

Definition 4 (Enablement)
A set of rules W enables a rule r_j iff W is a minimal set of rules that assert facts matching the maximum number of templates in the LHS of r_j; we write $W \hookrightarrow r_j$ to denote that W is an enabling-set for r_j. Formally, given $r_j \in T_t$ and $V \rightarrow r_j$, $W \hookrightarrow r_j$ iff: $W \subseteq V$, and W is both minimal and maximal.

For `RA-12-Prep%1` in Table 2 there are two enabling-sets: $W_1 = \{$`RA-12-Right%1`$\}$, and $W_2 = \{$`RA-12-Left%1`$\}$. For `Remove-Conflict%1` the enabling-set is $\{$`Place-Ball%1`, `Ball-Certain%1`$\}$.

A path in a rule base of an expert system must identify a sequence of rule firings that can occur when the expert system is solving a subproblem; thus, each path is composed of a sequence of rules that *depend upon* each other. The set of rules comprising a path must be defined such that each rule in the path is *enabled* by a subset of the set of rules comprising that path. It is desirable that each path represent a 'meaningful' thread of execution for the subproblem; thus, the rules in each path must assert facts using all the predicates of a logical completion for the subproblem.

Definition 5 (Path)
P_k^t, *a path k in task T_t is a partially-ordered set of rules $\langle \Phi, \pi \rangle$ where:*

$\Phi = \{r_1, r_2 \ldots r_n\}$ *with $r_i \in T_t$,*
$(\exists U \subseteq \Phi, SP_t \rightsquigarrow U)$,
$(\forall r_i \in \Phi)(\exists W \hookrightarrow r_i, W \subset \Phi)$, *and*
$(\forall r_i \in \Phi) (\exists r_j \in \Phi)$ *such that* $[(\forall a_k)(a_k \in \mathcal{A}^{r_i} \Rightarrow (a_k \in \mathcal{I}^{r_j} \vee (a_k \in Z_t)))]$.

π: *a partial order indicating which rules in path P_k^t depend upon others.*
$(\forall r_i)((r_i \pi r_j) \Rightarrow r_i \prec r_j)$.

The condition $(\forall r_i \in \Phi) (\exists r_j \in \Phi)$ such that $[(\forall a_k)(a_k \in \mathcal{A}^{r_i} \Rightarrow (a_k \in \mathcal{I}^{r_j} \vee (a_k \in Z_t)))]$ which we have placed on the structure of a path ensures that every fact that is asserted by a rule in a path either uses an end predicate, or it must match the template of the LHS of another rule in the path.

The path formed by the rules in Table 2 as found by Path Hunter is shown in Figure 2. This path represents the combined actions of six rules. These rules recognize a particular configuration on the Blackbox grid, indicate that a ball should be placed on the grid, indicate that the ball is certain, indicate that a location is to be marked as empty, resolves a conflict that occurs when the ball is placed, and disproves that the location should be empty. The logical completion that is asserted by this path is `DISPROVE_E` $\wedge$ `GMAP_C` $\wedge$ `GMAP_B` $\wedge$ `BALL` $\wedge$ `CERTAIN-BALLS` $\wedge$ `GMAP_CERT_B`.

Experiences with Path Hunter

Path Hunter has been used to analyse the structure of the Blackbox Expert's rule base. This rule base contains 442 CLIPS rules which formed 512 abstract rules. The abstract rules formed 72 equivalence classes (explained below) as well as 170 rules not in any equivalence class, from which Path Hunter found 516 paths. The paths produced by Path Hunter have been verified by the rule base designer as being accurate and

r_i	$\mathcal{I}^{r_i}$	$\mathcal{A}^{r_i}$	Comment
RA-12-Right%1	{GMAP, GRIDSIZE, SHOT-RECORD, BALL}	{RA-12}	Indicate the occurrence of a specific configuration on the Blackbox grid.
RA-12-Left%1	{GMAP, GRIDSIZE, SHOT-RECORD, BALL}	{RA-12}	Indicate the occurrence of a specific configuration on the Blackbox grid.
RA-12-Prep%1	{RA-12}	{P-BALL, BLANK-GRID, BALL_CERTAIN}	Place a ball, mark a location as empty, and indicate that the Ball is a certain ball.
Place-Ball%1	{GMAP, GMAP_CERT, P-BALL}	{CONFLICT_B, GMAP_C}	Update the grid to indicate that placing a ball has created a conflict.
Place-Empty%2	{GMAP, GMAP_CERT, BLANK-GRID}	{DISPROVE_E}	Update the grid to indicate that evidence for an empty grid square, is disproven.
Remove-Conflict%1	{CONFLICT_B, RMC_B}	{GMAP_B, BALL}	A certain ball is placed in a square with a conflict, and the conflict is resolved by placing a ball.

Table 2: Example Rule Set

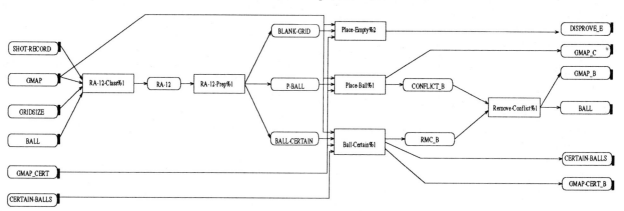

Figure 2: An Example Path

meaningful; that is, they capture the original intent with which the rules in the path were specified and the rules that are depicted in the paths combine together as intended. A typical path contains 5–6 rules, 2–3 branches, and has a length of 4 rules.

The problem of combinatorial explosion will arise when the cardinality of U for many of the rules in a task is large. When the cardinality of U is large, there will be a large number of potential combinations for the rules in a task to form a valid path. Of course, Path Hunter must check all of these combinations. One method that was used to control combinatorial explosion was to form *equivalence classes* of rules. When the rules in a rule base are abstracted, some rules will have the same LHS and RHS. Rules that have the same LHS and RHS are said to form an equivalence class. Rules RA-12-Right%1 and RA-12-Left%1, shown in Table 2, form an equivalence class called RA-12-Class%1. The path shown in Figure 2 contains this equivalence class. Thus, the path shown in Figure 2 represents *two* paths that can be observed when the Blackbox Expert's rule base is executed: one path starting with RA-12-Right%1, and one path starting with RA-12-Left%1. Therefore, equivalence classes reduce the number of paths that must be produced by Path Hunter, with no loss of generality.

Controlling combinatorial explosion can require modifications to the logical completions. When a logical completion is too general, many different paths will be formed that assert this logical completion. Thus, a combinatorial explosion may result. In this case, the rule base designer can control the combinatorial explosion by creating several, more specific, logical completions. This new set of logical completions will lead Path Hunter to create a set of paths for each new logical completion, where the total number of paths for all the new logical completions is less than the paths that were to be created for the original logical completion. In effect, the paths to be created using the original logical completion are broken down into smaller paths where there are fewer potential combinations of rules for creating these smaller paths, resulting in a fewer number of total paths produced. Nevertheless, these smaller paths are still meaningful.

The process of applying Path Hunter to the Blackbox Expert's rule base also served to identify various anomalies: the improper use of predicates, undesired interactions between rules, and rules which were not considered to be part of any path due to programming inconsistencies. In some cases, it was determined that the same predicate had been used within the rule base to reflect slightly different semantics. Thus, it was determined that while the rule base designer had intended to represent two distinct situations, an undetected ambiguity had occurred. These ambiguities also led to undesired potential interactions between the rules in the rule base. One of the rules in the Blackbox Expert's rule base did not appear in any path because it was dependent upon rules in the `Beam Trace` task, but asserted a fact that used an end predicate from the `Beam Selection` task. This situation indicated a poor design for the rule in question. The use of Path Hunter to analyse the Blackbox Expert's rule base also provided a method to validate the design of the rule base by indicating these inconsistencies and ambiguities.

Our experience with Path Hunter points to the need for a well defined approach for the engineering of rule based systems. As the problem to be solved by a rule based system is analysed and a preliminary design for the rule base is created, various issues must be tackled. The modules that will comprise the rule base should be specified as the subproblems that comprise the original problem are understood. The predicates to be used in the construction of the rule base will play a central role in defining the structure of the rule base. It is very important that the semantics attached to each predicate be clear and unambiguous. In addition, predicates must be chosen to ensure that the states which indicate that an acceptable solution to a subproblem are unambiguous. Otherwise, the logical completions will be ambiguous and paths that do not reflect the intent of the rule base designer will be present in the rule base.

Conclusion

The rule base execution paths defined in this paper meet the requirements for the validation and performance analysis of rule based expert systems. Paths are well-defined because our rule-dependency relations *depends upon* and *enablement* are unambiguous and accurately capture potential rule firing sequences. Paths are meaningful because each path is associated with a logical completion indicating a significant state in the problem-solving process. Paths are computable because the system designer, using logical completions and equivalence classes, can control the complexity of path enumeration.

Path Hunter has been used to analyse the structure of the Blackbox Expert's rule base (512 abstract rules). The use of logical completions and equivalence classes proved effective for controlling combinatorial explosion. Our experience with Path Hunter points to the need for a well-defined approach for the engineering of rule-based systems, where the subproblems (or modules) required to solve the problem, the appropriate solutions for the subproblems, and the predicates to be used in constructing the rule base are clearly specified as early as possible during its development.

References

Chang, C. L.; Combs, J. B.; and Stachowitz, R. A. 1990. A report on the Expert Systems Validation Associate (EVA). *Expert Systems with Applications (US)* 1(3):217–230.

Durfee, Edmund H.; Lesser, Victor; and Corkill, Daniel D. 1987. Coherent cooperation among communicating problem solvers. *IEEE Transactions on Computers* C-36(11):1275–1291.

Durfee, Edmund H.; Lesser, Victor R.; and Corkill, Daniel D. 1989. Trends in cooperative distributed problem solving. *Transactions on Knowledge and Data Engineering* 1(1):63–83.

Fox, Mark S. 1981. An organizational view of distributed systems. *IEEE Transactions on Systems, Man, and Cybernetics* SMC-11(1):70–80.

Giarratano, J. and Riley, G. 1989. *Expert Systems: Principles & Programming.* PWS-KENT.

Gokulchander, P.; Preece, A.; and Grossner, C. 1992. Path hunter: A tool for finding the paths in a rule based expert system. DAI Technical Report DAI-0592-0012, Concordia University, Montreal Quebec.

Grossner, C.; Lyons, J.; and Radhakrishnan, T. 1991. Validation of an expert system intended for research in distributed artificial intelligence. In *2nd CLIPS Conference, Johnson Space Center.*

Grossner, C.; Gokulchander, P.; and Preece, A. 1992a. On the structure of rule based expert systems. DAI Technical Report DAI-0592-0013, Concordia University, Montreal Quebec.

Grossner, C.; Lyons, J.; and Radhakrishnan, T. 1992b. Towards a tool for design of cooperating expert systems. In *4th International Conference on Tools for Artificial Intelligence.*

Grossner, C. 1990. Ill structured problems. DAI Technical Report DAI-0690-0004, Concordia University, Montreal Quebec.

Kiper, James D. 1992. Structural testing of rule-based expert systems. *ACM Transactions on Software Engineering and Methodology* 1(2):168–187.

Lesser, Victor R. and Corkill, Daniel D. 1981. Functionally accurate, cooperative distributed systems. *IEEE Transactions on Systems, Man and Cybernetics* SMC-11(1):81–96.

Rushby, John and Crow, Judith 1990. Evaluation of an expert system for fault detection, isolation, and recovery in the manned maneuvering unit. NASA Contractor Report CR-187466, SRI International, Menlo Park CA. 93 pages.

Shoham, Yoav 1991. Agent0: A simple agent language and its interpreter. In *Proc. International Conference on Artificial Intelligence (AAAI 91).* 704–709.

Simon, Herbert A. 1973. The structure of ill-structured problems. *Artificial Intelligence* 4:181–201.

Supporting and Optimizing Full Unification in a Forward Chaining Rule System

Howard E. Shrobe

Massachusetts Institute of Technology

NE43-839

Cambridge, MA 02139

hes@zermatt.lcs.mit.edu

Abstract

The Rete and Treat algorithms are considered the most efficient implementation techniques for Forward Chaining rule systems. These algorithms support a language of limited expressive power. Assertions are not allowed to contain variables, making universal quantification impossible to express except as a rule. In this paper we show how to support full unification in these algorithms. We also show that: Supporting full unification is costly; Full unification is not used frequently; A combination of compile time and run time checks can determine when full unification is not needed. We present data to show that the cost of supporting full unification can be reduced in proportion to the degree that it isn't employed and that for many practical systems this cost is negligible.

1 Introduction

Relatively efficient mechanisms have been developed for the implementation of forward chaining rules [1; 4]. However, these mechanisms have mainly been used in the implementation of the OPS family of production system languages. Languages in this family have limited expressive power: they are pure forward chaining languages in which assertions are restricted to ground terms.[1]

In this paper we explore the use of these mechanisms in more expressive languages in the tradition of [7; 2; 3; 6]. Such languages work by *pattern directed procedure invocation*. They center around a database of assertions accessed by forward and backward chaining rules as well as by normal procedural code using a *Tell* and *Ask* interface. The bodies of rules in such languages may be full procedures. Such languages naturally fall into the full unification case: Assertions containing variables take on the force of universally quantified statements and these may match the patterns of either forward or backward chaining rules.

However, the designers of the OPS family of languages did not choose the limitation to the semi-unification case naively. Full unification significantly complicates the Rete mechanisms and leads to two forms of inefficiency:

- The resulting code executes more slowly.

- The resulting code is significantly larger.

---

[1]In the remainder of the paper, we will refer to a language which only allows ground terms in assertions as a "semi-unification" language. If assertions may contain variables we will refer to the language as a "full-unification" language.

Moreover, in many domains the semi-unification case closely approximates the needed expressive power; full unification is rarely required.

In this paper, we show that one can have both the expressive power of full unification and the efficiency of the techniques developed for the more limited semi-unification case. The mechanisms described here have been implemented and extensively used in the Joshua system[5].

The outline for the remainder of the paper is as follows: In section 2 we begin by reviewing the conventional Rete network, describing it as a mechanism for incrementally computing unifications between a set of patterns and a set of assertions (an unconventional viewpoint). We then show in section 2.1 that conventional Rete networks are an optimization of our viewpoint for the semi-unification case. In section 3, we describe our extensions to support full unification; section 4 presents data to show the degree of inefficiency introduced by our extensions. The next two sections present techniques for addressing the inefficiencies. Section 5 presents a set of run time optimizations that dynamically identify when semi unification alone is adequate; we show that this reduces the first form of inefficiency to negligible levels. Section 6 shows how the rule compiler can statically segregate out portions of the rule system which can be compiled under the semi unification assumption; we show that this reduces the second form of inefficiency to acceptable levels.

2 Rete Networks

We assume that the reader is familiar with Rete networks and related techniques (see, for example, [1]). In describing Rete networks, our terminology will be somewhat nonstandard; we will refer to *unification* rather than matching in an attempt to show how our extensions fit within the pattern of the original algorithm.

Rete networks incrementally maintain the partial triggering states of rules as new assertions are added and deleted. A rule is fully triggered when its set of patterns unify with a set of statements asserted in the database. Partial triggering states contain two kinds of information: 1) The unifications between individual patterns and individual assertions and 2) Extended unifications between subsets of a rule's patterns and sets of assertions. Figure 1 shows a pair of rules and the corresponding Rete network.

The network contains two sections: Match and Join. Each of these incrementally updates its internal state each time a new token is added to (or deleted from) its input nodes.

The match section is a discrimination network whose

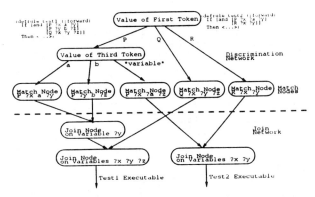

Figure 1: A Typical Rete Network

terminal nodes (the match nodes) compute unifications between rule patterns and assertions in the database. State is stored only at the match nodes (these are the alpha memories of [1]). Patterns from different rules which are *variants* (i.e. identical up to variable renaming) share match nodes; two patterns which share leading terms share a path through the network up to the point of divergence. The tests made by the nodes above the match nodes filter out assertions which cannot possibly unify with the pattern of the match nodes below them.

The Join network begins at the Match nodes. State is stored at all join nodes (these are the beta memories in the terminology of [1]). Each node of the join section merges the partial unifications represented by its two parent nodes, checking that the shared variables are unifiable. Each terminal node of the join network corresponds to a complete set of rule patterns. If two rules share leading patterns, they share join nodes up to the point of divergence.

The rete network compiler emits code for each node in the network to perform the above functions.[2] The code for match and join nodes perform the indicated unifications; they also package up the results into *state tokens* stored at the node.[3]

2.1 Optimizations for the Semi Unification Case

In classic Rete networks all assertions contain only ground terms and therefore no variable in a rule's pattern may ever be bound to another variable. Under these conditions the Rete network can be viewed as computing relational selects (at the match nodes) and relational joins (at the join nodes) (as pointed out in [4]).

Operationally matching reduces to: 1) checking that constants in the assertion are equal to corresponding constants in the pattern and 2) checking that terms of an

---

assertion which match different occurrences of the same variable are equal.

When assertions contain only ground terms the discrimination nodes perform part of the unification by testing for equality between constants in the pattern and constants in the assertion. Therefore, the code at a match node may omit these tests.

Similarly, the tests at the join nodes can be reduced to checking that variables shared between the parents of the join are bound to equal values. Hashing (or other forms of indexing) may be used to speed up the join computation. Each parent of a join node maintains a hash-table of tokens; the key for this table is a list of the values of the shared variables.

In the semi-unification case, a hash probe will find the precise set of unifiable tokens; therefore, no other code is needed at the join nodes.

Finally, in the semi-unification case, the state tokens need not contain a variable binding environment; each variable can be identified with a particular term from one of the matching assertions.

These optimizations are not fully available in the full-unification case.

3 Extending the Rete Network to Support Full Unification

We have described the Rete algorithm in a very general context, that of computing and extending unifications. The semi-unification case allows a variety of optimizations to be made by replacing unification with equality tests. To extend the traditional Rete algorithm to support the full-unification case we must undo these optimizations, replacing equality checks by unifications.

The following questions must be addressed:

1. How are logic variables represented?

2. What code is compiled to conduct the unification matching?

3. How are state-tokens represented and computed?

4. How do auxiliary indices (e.g. hash-tables at join nodes) handle logic variables?

Having made these choices we will then need to see what impact they have on the components of the Rete network.

3.1 Data Structures and Basic Operations

3.1.1 Representation of Logic Variables

We adopt a representation for logic variables based on the Prolog oriented techniques of the Warren Abstract Machine [8].

Logic variables are represented as pointers to their values; an unbound logic variable points to itself. An unbound logic variable is unified with a value by making it to point to the value; this value might be another unbound logic-variable which might later be bound to a value, leading to a chain of logic-variable pointers as shown in figure 3.

To find the value of a logic variable one must follow the chain of pointers until encountering either a value which is not a logic variable or a logic variable which points to

```
(lambda (assertion)
 (with-unification
  (with-unbound-logic-variables (?x)
   (unify 'P (dereference (pop assertion)))
   (unify ?x (dereference (pop assertion)))
   (unify 'a (dereference (pop assertion)))
   (unify (dereference ?x) (dereference (pop assertion)))
   (unify 'b (dereference (pop assertion)))
   ... code to be executed upon success ...)))
```

Figure 2: Full Unification Code Corresponding to [P ?x a ?x b]

itself. This operation is referred to as *dereferencing*. A logic variable must be dereferenced before its use.

When a logic variable is bound, an entry consisting of the logic variable is made on a stack called the *trail*. Before a pattern matching operation is begun, the level of the trail is saved. To return to the binding state which obtained at the beginning of the operation (e.g. when the unification fails) each logic variable above the marked point on the trail is reset to point to itself and the trail level is reset to the marked point. This operation is usually called *unwinding the trail*, or *untrailing*.

3.1.2 Implementation of Unification

The match compiler is responsible for emitting the unification code corresponding to a pattern. When given an assertion to match, the code must *fail* if the pattern and the assertion are not unifiable; otherwise it must *succeed* and bind the logic-variables of the pattern to the values implied by the unification.

Figure 2 shows the code emitted for the pattern [P ?x a ?x b].

In this code, *With-unification* establishes a unification context (i.e. it notes the level of the trail on entry and unwinds the trail to that level upon exit. Also it establishes a catch tag which is thrown to in the event of *failure*. *With-unbound-logic-variables* creates a set of new logic-variables (typically these are stack allocated). Notice that each term of the assertion must be dereferenced before the call to *Unify* since the term might be a logic variable.

Unify is called with atomic elements (including logic variables) as the first argument; when the pattern contains compound terms, the match compiler must recurse into the substructure of these terms. For simplicity of presentation we omit the details, see [8]. The behavior of Unify is as follows:

- If neither argument is a logic-variable, then UNIFY succeeds if the arguments are EQUAL and otherwise fails.

- If exactly one argument is a logic-variable, UNIFY succeeds, the logic-variable is bound to the other argument and a trail entry is made.[4]

- If both arguments are logic-variables then one is bound to the other a trail entry is made and UNIFY succeeds. (If both logic-variables are stored on the stack, then the one pushed more recently must point to the one more deeply nested).

---

[4]The unification is only allowed if the variable does not occur within the structure of the other arguments. Prolog implementations typically skip this "free-for" check for efficiency as do we in our implementation.

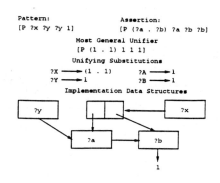

Figure 3: A Unification and its Implementation Level View

Failing is accomplished by throwing the value NIL to a catch-tag for *FAIL*. This is normally established by *with-unification*; this causes the trail to be unwound.[5]

3.1.3 Saving the Binding State in Tokens

The code emitted by the Rete network compiler for a match node tests whether the triggering assertion can be unified with the rule pattern; if so it produces a state-token containing the bindings of the pattern's logic variables.

Consider the unification shown in figure 3. The variable ?x of the rule's pattern is unified with the list (?a . ?b) of the assertion; this list contains variables which are bound to ground terms (e.g. 1). The value of ?x is valid, therefore, only as long as ?a and ?b continue to be bound to 1. However, ?a and ?b are contained in a database assertion whose intent is to state a universal quantification. Therefore, the binding of ?a and ?b must be untrailed and the values of their current bindings must be preserved elsewhere.[6] Notice that this is quite a bit more expensive than the semi-unification case where the assertion can serve as an adequate representation of the binding state as explained in 2.1.

To preserve the volatile binding state over a longer duration, state-tokens maintain an *environment* of logic-variable values with a slot for each variable in the pattern. Each slot is filled with the *unified-value* of its corresponding logic-variable. The unified value of a logic-variable is computed as follows:

- The logic-variable is dereferenced.

- If the variable is unbound, its unified value is a new logic-variable. All occurrence of a particular unbound logic-variable have the same new logic-variable as their unified-value.[7]

---

[5]In the implementations of Joshua on Symbolics equipment, Dereference is a microcoded instruction. In implementations on more conventional machines it would be implemented either as subroutines or an inline code fragment; either approach is both slower and consumes more instructions. Our measurements are made on Symbolics equipment, yielding more favorable results for the full-unification case than would result on more conventional machines.

[6]I.e. our implementation uses a shallow binding scheme for logic variables but needs to preserve their values beyond the dynamic extent.

[7]Unbound logic-variables are replaced by new variables to

- If the variable is bound and the bound value is atomic, then the unified-value is the bound-value.

- If the bound value is a compound data-structure, then the sub-structure is traversed replacing each term by its unified value.

In the example of figure 3 the logic-variable ?x is bound to the pair (?a . ?b). But ?a is bound to ?b which is in turn bound to 1; so the unified value of ?x is (1 . 1), a value which persists even after unwinding the trail.

3.2 Extending the Algorithm

3.2.1 The Discrimination Network

We begin with the discrimination nodes of the Match network. Each discrimination node dispatches on the value of a term in the assertion, see figure1. For large branching factors, a hash table is an appropriate implementation. If the term being dispatched on is a constant then it serves as the hash-key. The value retrieved is the next discrimination node to visit. If there is a branch for the key *variable* (indicating a rule pattern with a variable at this position), this must also be followed.

Notice that the term being discriminated on may itself be a logic-variable. In this case all outgoing branches must be followed, since a variable can match anything.[8]

3.2.2 The Match Nodes

The discrimination network search discards most match nodes that don't unify with the assertion; however, some non-unifiable match nodes may still be reached. For example:

```
Rule Pattern:    (P a  ?c  b ?c)
Assertion:       (P ?x  c ?x  c)
```

The discrimination network treats each occurrence of ?x in the assertion as independent, allowing this assertion to reach the match node although it isn't unifiable with the pattern. Notice that the inconsistency between the assertion and the pattern occurs at constant terms in the pattern. As mentioned in section 2.1, this can never happen in the semi unification case and the match code need only check the positions corresponding to variables.

In contrast, the full unification match code must perform the entire unification as explained in section 3.1.2 (i.e. tests must be generated for both constant and variable positions). It must also save the results in a binding vector by copying out the unified values, as explained in section3.1.3. The match compiler, therefore, emits code containing two sections: The first conducts the unifications, the second creates the binding vector and fill it with the unified values of the logic variables.

3.2.3 The Join Nodes

Join nodes are extended in a similar manner. The rule compiler generates a map for each join node specifying

---

[8]We do not attempt to carry along the variable bindings while traversing the discrimination network.

prevent sharing of logic-variables held in state tokens with those in assertions (or other state-tokens). Were this not done, the unifications performed at join nodes would unintentionally bind the variables in the assertions. Resolution systems rename variables in the resolvent for the same reason.

```
(P ?x ?y ?z) environment ?x → 1 ?y → 2 ?z → 3
(Q ?y ?z ?w) environment ?y → 1 ?z → 2 ?w → 3

(lambda (token-1 token-2)
 (with-unification
  ;; unify ?y from 1 with ?y from 2
  (unify (token-slot token-1 2) (token-slot token-2 1))
  ;; unify ?z from 1 with ?z from 2
  (unify (token-slot token-1 3) (token-slot token-2 2))
  (let ((new-token (make-new-token :n-variables 3)))
   ;; copy ?x
   (setf (token-slot new-token 1) (copy-unified-value (token-slot token-1 1)))
   ;; copy ?y
   (setf (token-slot new-token 2) (copy-unified-value (token-slot token-1 2)))
   ;; copy ?z
   (setf (token-slot new-token 3) (copy-unified-value (token-slot token-1 3)))
   ;; copy ?w
   (setf (token-slot new-token 4) (copy-unified-value (token-slot token-2 3)))
   new-token)))
```

Figure 4: Join Code for The Full Unification Case

which variables from the two parent nodes are to be unified. The compiler emits code to perform these unifications and to copy the unified values of all the variables into a new state-token. Figure 4 shows a join to be performed and the corresponding code generated by the rule compiler.

Many Rete network implementations use hashing (or other indexing) to speed up the join computation, as explained in section 2.1. In the full unification case, any of the shared variables in either token might be an unbound logic-variable. Unlike ground terms, two distinct logic variables might match; a list of the values of the shared variables is, therefore, not an adequate retrieval key. A simple extension which solves this problem is as follows:

- When storing a new token in a node:
  - If any of the shared variables are unbound, then hash the token under a special key: *unbound-variable*.
  - Otherwise use the list of the shared variable values as the key.

- When looking for stored tokens to join with a new token:
  - If any of the new token's shared variables are unbound then look at every token stored in the other parent node.
  - Otherwise form a key which is the list of shared variables and attempt to join with every stored token hashed in the other parent node under this key. Also attempt to join with every token hashed under the key *unbound-variable*.

3.2.4 Compiling Rule Bodies

Forward rule bodies may contain normal procedural code which references the logic variables of the patterns. In the full unification case, variables referenced in the body of a rule may be left unbound by the matching process; they therefore must be treated as logic variables and be dereferenced before being used.

The values of the logic-variables are stored in the environment of the triggering state token. The rule compiler, therefore, first emits a prologue which fetches the variable values from the environment into local variables. The rest of the rule body code is transformed so that every reference to a logic-variable is wrapped within a call to *dereference*.

example	Time in Rete Network		Total Run Time	
	Semi	Full	Semi	Full
Natural Deduction	14,114	84,725	167,816	360,740
Troubleshooting	79,353	346,726	645,634	943,602
Cryptarithmetic	851,288	2,872,276	3,489,086	7,309,309
Planning	209,308	739,605	891,742	1,413,495

Table 1: Run Times of Full and Semi Unification Code

4 Full Unification Support is Costly

These extensions lead to semantically correct behavior in the full unification case. However, as can also be seen, each extension removes a constraint of the semi-unification case which was used in optimizing the original algorithm.

Table 1 shows the relative performance of the matching and merging portions of a a number of demonstration systems. Table 2 shows the relative sizes of the generated code for a variety of systems.

The following are among the causes of this difference:

- Equality tests in the match and join code are replaced by unification.

- The discrimination network in the match network acts only as a partial filter in the full unification case (due to the possibility of logic-variables in the assertions, see section 3.2.1). The match code generator cannot assume that every constant has already been checked and must generate checks for the constants as well as the variables.

- Hashing alone is a sufficient join test in the semi-unification case. In the full-unification case this is not true. A rather bulky merge procedure must be still be generated and called, see section 3.2.3.

- The code generated for rule bodies must replace variable references by calls to *dereference*. This incurs both increased code size and slower performance.

- In the semi-unification case, state tokens need not contain environments. In the full unification case environments must be built and values copied between them.

- Calls to *copy-unified-value* must be used to copy logic-variable values to new state tokens. If variables are bound to compound data-structures this incurs the cost of traversing and incrementally rebuilding those sub-structures containing logic-variables.

- In the semi-unification case, match procedures typically check only the terms corresponding to variables in the pattern; constants in the pattern are ignored since the discrimination nodes check them. This means that two match nodes which have the same pattern of variable occurrences but distinct constants may nevertheless share match procedures. This is not the case for the full unification case, only variant patterns may share match procedures.

5 Dynamic Optimizations

The programming style of typical knowledge based systems infrequently employs the full unification case. Unfortunately, the expressiveness of the full unification case leads to code with much worse run-time performance.

This section addresses one approach to this problem: optimizations performed at run-time.

We have extended the rete network compiler to generate two sets of procedures for each of the match and join nodes. The first of these is the less efficient but more general code capable of handling the full unification case; the second procedure handles only the semi-unification case, but is considerably more efficient. The rete network interpreter is responsible for dispatching to the semi-unification procedure if allowable, otherwise it must call the full unification procedure.

To make this decision, our system checks each newly created assertion for the presence of logic-variables and stores the result in the data-structure representing the assertion. (The check must be made in any event, since all logic-variables in a database assertion must be copied so as to be unique to that assertion). At a match node, the rete interpreter uses this information to determine which procedure to call.

When a new state-token is created, a we check whether any element of the environment is an unbound logic variable; the token is marked with the result of this check. At a join node the semi-unification code is called if both input tokens are marked as logic-variable free. Notice that only the full unification procedures need to check for the presence of unbound logic-variables in the output token since in the semi unification case the output will necessarily contain only ground terms.

The crucial question for a dynamic optimization is whether the cost of detecting the opportunity swamps out the resulting benefit. In this case, the detection cost is that incurred in checking assertions for non-ground terms and (if we're running a full-unification procedure) the cost of a similar check on any newly generated token. Metering indicates that this consumes about 1.5% of total run time.

To test the efficacy of dynamic optimization, we ran a rule-based natural deduction system on three versions of the same problem. The first version uses only ground terms, the second has a mix of ground terms and terms with variables and the third version is completely quantified. In the first case, all matches and joins used the semi-unification code and ran the problem 6.9 times faster than would the full-unification code. In the second case, 86% of the matches and 59% of the joins used the semi-unification code with a resulting speedup of 2.4. In the last case, of course, all matches and joins used the full-unification code. These results show that the system is highly effective in dynamically identifying when the semi unification code can be utilized.

6 Static Optimizations

The dynamic optimizations incur the additional cost of generating two procedures at each node. A traditional production system would generate only the semi unification code; but our system also generates code to support the rarer case of full unification. As table 2 indicates this code is considerably larger. Furthermore, we generate only a single version of the code for rule bodies which is required to be the slower and bulkier code capable of handling full unification.

In this section, we discuss how we use information avail-

example	Rule	Semi Unification					Full Unification				
		Matchers / Size	Mergers / Size	Proc-edures	Rule Body	Matchers / Size	Mergers / Size	Proc-edures	Rule Body		
Circuits	10	2 37	2 44	0	212	7 364	2 260	0	214		
Cryptarithmetic	59	7 188	34 979	307	2251	14 703	34 6816	628	2269		
Midsummer	7	3 56	3 68	46	124	6 264	3 372	73	124		
Discrete Event	7	4 81	4 94	20	237	7 361	4 544	36	237		
Ht Atms	7	4 82	3 66	64	153	8 412	3 390	120	153		
Ht Ltms	15	5 120	6 146	80	391	15 754	6 849	169	397		
NatDed	7	6 266	4 109	0	425	8 508	4 672	0	425		
All Rules	123	36 950	50 1380	587	4009	74 3797	50 9186	1102	4035		

Table 2: Compiled Code Size of Full and Semi Unification Code

able at compile time to help the rule compiler determine which nodes of the network (as well as which rule bodies) will never encounter the full-unification case. This lets us generate only the more efficient semi unification code at any node or rule body so classified.

In the Joshua system, all operations of the system (including the operations of the rule compiler) are driven by the *class* of the assertion (or pattern) being processed. The classes are identified with the predicate of the assertion and are, in fact, CLOS classes; see [5] for details. The data structures used to represent rule patterns and data-base assertions are instances of these CLOS classes.

One such predicate class (which can be "mixed in" to any other assertion class) is *no-variables-in-data-mixin*. If one tries to enter an assertion of this type into the database, an error is signalled. Rule patterns which are instances of this class can therefore reliably assume that any triggering assertion will contain only ground terms. This information is used at rule compilation time to determine that a match node will be "semi unification only". A join node whose parent nodes are both "semi unification only" will also be "semi unification only". If a terminal node of the rete network is "semi unification only" then all rule bodies connected to that node are also "semi unification only".[9]

Table 2 shows the relative sizes of the full-unification and semi-unification code for 7 systems. In aggregate the full unification matchers are 4 times larger than the semi-unification matchers; the full unification mergers are 6.7 times larger. With static optimizations applied, our system generates no full unification code for most of the systems (this is optimum, these systems never use the full unification capability). The system is forced to generate both versions of the code for the one subsystem which does take advantage of the full unification. In aggregate, this save 86% of the matching code and 92% of the merging code.

7 Discussion

We have shown that the expressiveness of full unification can be supported with very limited cost in efficiency. This result depends on the statistics of assertion usage: most assertions contain only ground terms. This allows us to generate optimized procedures for the semi unification case. If the triggering assertions all contain only ground terms then the more efficient semi unification case is called; this is very frequently the case. The system's performance gracefully degrades as universally quantified assertions are entered in the database.

Also we have shown that when extra information is conveyed to the system at compile time, we can avoid generating the bulkier code for the general case. Furthermore, we have indicated that in many practical cases, this *a priori* information is obtainable.

References

[1] C. Forgy. Rete: A fast algorithm for the many pattern/many object pattern match problem. *Artificial Intelligence*, 19:17–38, 1982.

[2] C.E. Hewitt. Description and theoretical analysis (using schemata) of planner: A language for proving theorems and manipulating models in a robot. Technical Report AI-TR-258, MIT Artificial Intelligence Laboratory, 1972.

[3] G.J. McDermott, D.V.and Sussman. The conniver reference manual. Technical Report Memo 259, MIT Artificial Intelligence Laboratory, 1972.

[4] Daniel P. Miranker. *TREAT: A New and Efficient Match Algorithm for AI Production Systems*. Morgan Kaufmann, San Mateo, California, 1990.

[5] S. Rowley, H. Shrobe, R. Cassels, and W. Hamscher. Joshua: Uniform access to heterogeneous knowledge structures (or why joshing is better than conniving or planning). In *National Conference on Artificial Intelligence*, pages 48–52. AAAI, 1987.

[6] G.J. Sussman and D.V. McDermott. Why conniving is better than planning. Technical Report AI Memo 255A, MIT Artificial Intelligence Laboratory, Cambridge Mass., 1972.

[7] G.J. Sussman, T. Winograd, and E. Charniak. The micro-planner reference manual. Technical Report AI Memo 203, MIT Artificial Intelligence Laboratory, Cambridge, MA, 1970.

[8] D.H.D Warren. An abstract prolog instruction set. Technical Report SRI Technical Note 309, SRI International, October 1983.

[9]Our system also supports user supplied procedural condition elements. If such a node's parent is semi-unification only and it introduces no new logic variables, then the node itself is semi-unification only.

Comprehensibility Improvement of Tabular Knowledge Bases

Atsushi Sugiura†   **Maximilian Riesenhuber‡**   **Yoshiyuki Koseki†**

†C&C Systems Res. Lab. NEC Corp.
4-1-1 Miyazaki Miyamae-ku
Kawasaki 216 JAPAN
sugiura@btl.cl.nec.co.jp

‡Inst. of Theoretical Physics
Johann Wolfgang Goethe-Univ.
Robert-Mayer-Strasse 8-10
Frankfurt am Main 60054 Fed. Rep. of GERMANY

Abstract

This paper discusses the important issue of knowledge base comprehensibility and describes a technique for comprehensibility improvement. Comprehensibility is often measured by simplicity of concept description. Even in the simplest form, however, there will be a number of different DNF (Disjunctive Normal Form) descriptions possible to represent the same concept, and each of these will have a different degree of comprehensibility. In other words, simplification does not necessarily guarantee improved comprehensibility. In this paper, the authors introduce three new comprehensibility criteria, *similarity*, *continuity*, and *conformity*, for use with tabular knowledge bases. In addition, they propose an algorithm to convert a decision table with poor comprehensibility to one with high comprehensibility, while preserving logical equivalency. In experiments, the algorithm generated either the same or similar tables to those generated by humans.

Introduction

Two major requirements for knowledge base are that it contain only correct knowledge and that it be comprehensible. Several techniques have been reported regarding the verification of correctness, including the completeness and consistency checking [Cragun 1987, Nguyen et al. 1985]. However, little work has been reported concerning the maintenance or improvement of comprehensibility.

Comprehensibility is critical, because it strongly affects efficiency of construction and maintenance of knowledge bases. However, the actual work of modifying knowledge descriptions so as to improve the comprehensibility can prove to be a serious burden for the knowledge engineers who must manage knowledge bases. Purpose of this research is to automate such tasks.

In past work [Michalski, Carbonell, & Michell 1983, Coulon & Kayser 1978], the one and only method to improve the comprehensibility of a knowledge base was to simplify the concept descriptions in it. Even in the simplest form, however, there will be a number of different DNF descriptions possible to represent the same concept, and each of these will have a different degree of comprehensibility. In other words, simplification does not necessarily guarantee improved comprehensibility.

Let us compare the following two logic functions of attribute-value:

[*Sex Male*] ∨ [*Sex Female*] ∧ [*Pregnant? No*]
→ *Can_Drink_Alcohol*

[*Pregnant? No*] ∨ [*Pregnant? Yes*] ∧ [*Sex Male*]
→ *Can_Drink_Alcohol*

While these are logically equivalent and have the same simplicity, their *concept function forms*, that is formalized by the combination of attribute values, conjunctions (∧) and disjunctions (∨), are different. The second description is incomprehensible, because it describes a case that never happens: [*Pregnant? Yes*] ∧ [*Sex Male*].

In this paper, the authors propose three additional comprehensibility criteria for use in concept function forms on decision tables: similarity among concept functions, continuity in attributes which have ordinal values, and conformity between concept functions and real cases. The first criterion is developed on the basis of an analysis of decision table characteristics. The others are developed on the basis of consideration of meaning embodied in expressions of knowledge.

In addition, the authors describe an algorithm to convert a decision table with poor comprehensibility to one with high comprehensibility, while preserving logical equivalency. This conversion is accomplished by using MINI-like logic minimization techniques [Hong, Cain, & Ostapko 1974], and it involves as well the use of a number of different heuristics.

Decision Table

With regard to knowledge acquisition, completeness checking, and concept comparison, decision tables offer advantages over other methods of knowledge representation (e.g. production rules and decision trees, etc.)

Table 1: Comprehensible expression for bond selection.

	Material			Usage		Bonding-area	
	Paper	Lea-ther	Plas-tic	Nor-mal	Indus-trial	Large	Small
Bond-A	O	×	×	O	O	O	O
Bond-B	O	×	×	O	O	O	O
Bond-B	×	O	×	O	×	O	O
Bond-B	×	O	×	×	O	O	×
Bond-C	×	×	O	O	×	O	O

Table 2: Incomprehensible expression for bond selection.

	Material			Usage		Bonding-area	
	Paper	Lea-ther	Plas-tic	Nor-mal	Indus-trial	Large	Small
Bond-A	O	×	×	O	O	O	O
Bond-B	O	×	×	×	O	×	O
Bond-B	O	O	×	O	O	O	×
Bond-B	O	O	×	O	×	×	O
Bond-C	×	×	O	O	×	O	O

[Cragun 1987, Koseki, Nakakuki, & Tanaka 1991].

A decision table represents a set of concept functions, expressed in DNF. This construct enables the handling of disjunctive concepts which have multiple-value attributes. Each concept function consists of a number of disjuncts, called *cubes*. Each cube consists of a set of values for an attribute. The union of the vertices in logic space, covered by concept function, is called a *cover* for the concept.

An example knowledge base is shown in Table 1. Here, each row forms a cube, and a set of cubes for the same concept name forms a a concept function. For example, the concept function for *Bond-B* consists of three cubes, and each cube consists of three attributes. In a cube, the values specified by the circle (O) in an attribute are ORed, and all attributes are ANDed to form the cube. Don't-Care attributes are designated as an attribute with all Os. A min-term is a cube which has only one O in every attribute.

The decision table facilitates the comparison of different concepts, due to the following reason. Concept comparison means comparing the values of all the attributes which define concepts. In this context, the decision tables, in which description of the same attribute is represented in the same columns and concepts are represented by all attributes, can facilitate concept comparison. In other knowledge representations, for example in the production rules, the same attribute name appears in various positions of each rule, and concepts are represented only by attributes that are necessary to define concepts. This disturbs easy comparison of attribute values.

This advantage is critical for the knowledge base constructions, because, in the classification problems, it is essential to compare and to classify the concepts which have the same cover.

Comprehensibility Criteria

This section presents four criteria for knowledge base comprehensibility. One is simplicity of concept description, which is the conventional criterion. The other three are concerned with concept function forms. Three new criteria are a reflection of the great influence of the concept function forms on its comprehensibility.

The second criteria employs general rules to facilitate the comparison of different concepts, whereas the last two require some background knowledge, which is characteristics of attributes and their values.

Table Size

Preference criteria for human comprehensibility are commonly based on the knowledge description length (for example, [Michalski, Carbonell, & Michell 1983, Coulon & Kayser 1978]). Some inductive learning algorithms [Michalski, Carbonell, & Michell 1983, Quinlan 1986] reduce the knowledge base size to obtain simple knowledge expressions.

As the conventional criteria, the authors define table size as one of the comprehensibility factors. Since the number of attributes to define concepts is fixed in the decision tables, table size can be measured by the number of cubes.

Similarity among Concept Functions

When comparing different concepts, it is desirable to be able to easily ascertain common and different features in each concept. This requires high similarity among concept functions.

Table 1 and Table 2 are example knowledge bases for a bond selection problem. They have the same cover and the same table size, but their concept function forms (cube shapes) are different. In this example, Table 1 is better than Table 2, for the following reasons.

First, compare Bond-B with Bond-A. In the first cube (Bond-A) and the second cube (Bond-B) in Table 1, their forms are exactly the same. Using Table 1, the intersection of the two concepts in logic space can be determined by looking at just two cubes, whereas, using Table 2, this would require considering four cubes.

Next, compare Bond-B with Bond-C. In the third cube (Bond-B) and the fifth cube (Bond-C) in Table 1, descriptions of attributes *Usage* and *Bonding-area* are the same; only those of attribute *Material* are different. This makes it easy to see that these two concepts are discriminated by attribute *Material*. On the other hand, in Table 2, descriptions of most of the attributes are different, making the common and different features unclear.

Overall, comprehensibility of Table 1 arises from the high similarity among the concept function forms: the

Table 3: Comprehensible expression for Scholarship Approval.

	School-record		Student earn?		Parent-income (ten thousand dollars)			
	Good	Poor	Yes	No	-6	6-7	7-8	8-
Approved	O	×	×	O	O	O	O	O
Approved	O	×	O	×	O	O	O	×
Approved	×	O	×	O	O	O	×	×
Approved	×	O	O	×	O	×	×	×
Not_approved	O	×	O	×	×	×	×	O
Not_approved	×	O	×	O	×	×	O	O
Not_approved	×	O	O	×	×	O	O	O

Table 4: Incomprehensible expression for Scholarship Approval.

	School-record		Student earn?		Parent-income (ten thousand dollars)			
	Good	Poor	Yes	No	-6	6-7	7-8	8-
Approved	O	×	×	O	O	×	×	O
Approved	O	O	O	×	O	×	×	×
Approved	×	O	×	O	O	O	×	×
Approved	O	×	O	O	×	O	O	×
Not_approved	O	×	O	×	×	×	×	O
Not_approved	×	O	O	O	×	×	O	O
Not_approved	×	O	O	×	×	O	×	×

first and the second cubes and the third and the fifth cubes.

Continuity in Attributes which have Ordinal Values

In many knowledge bases, attributes with ordinal values are expressed by a range of values (for example, material which is harder than aluminum should be shaped by grinder-A). Therefore, high continuity of Os in such attributes leads to high comprehensibility.

Two example knowledge bases for a scholarship approval are shown in Table 3 and Table 4, which have the same cover and the same table size. Values of the attribute *Parent-income* are ordinal values.

These examples implicitly embody the meaning that students whose parent income is low are granted scholarship, which can be seen clearly in Table 3. By contrast, the first cube in Table 4 shows that some students are granted scholarships, if the parent income is less than $60,000 or more than $80,000. This gives the initial impression that anyone with an income of $60,000-80,000 can not be approved. By examining other cubes this can be seen to be false, but this is time-consuming; Table 3 is preferable to Table 4.

Conformity between Concept Functions and Real Cases

In some knowledge bases, there is a dependency relationship between the attributes, which the authors can divide into *precondition* and *constrained* attributes. Whether the constrained attribute relates to concept definition or not depends on the values of the precondition attribute. In such a situation, the positions of the Don't-Cares are critical, because cases that never happen in the real world may be described in knowledge bases.

Other knowledge bases relating to an earned credit at a university are shown in Table 5 and Table 6; they have the same cover and the same table size. These examples implicitly embody the meaning that only students who failed the first exam are eligible to take the makeup exam. There exists an attribute dependency relationship consisting of the precondition at-

tribute *Exam* and the constrained attribute *Makeup-exam*: taking the makeup exam depends on the result of the exam.

In this example, Table 5 is more comprehensible than Table 6, because of the conformity between concept functions and the real cases. In the first cube in Table 6, a case that never happens is described: an examination result is not less than 60 points and the makeup examination result is less than 80 points. Table 5, however, represents only the real cases.

In general, the precondition attributes should not be Don't-Cares, if the constrained attributes are not Don't-Cares.

Table 5: Comprehensible expression for Credit Earning.

	Exam		Makeup-exam	
	≥60	<60	≥80	<80
Pass	O	×	O	O
Pass	×	O	O	×
Fail	×	O	×	O

Table 6: Incomprehensible expression for Credit Earning.

	Exam		Makeup-exam	
	≥60	<60	≥80	<80
Pass	O	×	×	O
Pass	O	O	O	×
Fail	×	O	×	O

Algorithm

Figure 1 shows an algorithm to improve the comprehensibility of a decision table. It converts a table with poor comprehensibility to one with high comprehensibility, while preserving logical equivalency.

Table conversion is accomplished by the techniques used in logic minimization algorithm MINI: disjoint sharp operation, Expansion, and Reduction [Hong, Cain, & Ostapko 1974]. In these operations, attributes are required to be ordered, and this order affects concept function forms in a resultant table. The proposed algorithm first determines the attribute order σ, where σ is a list of attributes that specifies the

Notation

a_i: attribute $(1 \leq i \leq n)$
C_j: list of the cubes for jth concept $(1 \leq j \leq m)$
p: precondition attribute on attribute dependence relationship
q: constrained attribute on attribute dependence relationship
S: set of attributes which have ordinal values

```
 1   begin
                /* Determination of attribute order */
 2       Calculate n_i (1 ≤ i ≤ n) by (U ⊕ (U ⊕ C_j)) with attribute order (a_i, a_1, a_2 ···, a_{n-1})
 3       List1 ← list of a_i ∈ S sorted in increasing order of n_i
 4       List2 ← list of a_i ∉ S sorted in increasing order of n_i
 5       σ ← connect List2 after List1
 6       for all (p, q) do
 7           if q is placed after p on σ
 8           then  σ ← list which q is moved to previous position of p
 9           endif
10       endfor
                /* Modification of concept functions */
11       for C_j(1 ≤ j ≤ m) do
12           C_j ← (U ⊕ (U ⊕ C_j)) with σ
13       endfor
14       Expand and Reduce the cubes with σ
15   end
```

Figure 1: Algorithm for improving comprehensibility.

order, by some heuristics (in Lines 2-10, Fig. 1), and next modifies the concept function forms by MINI's techniques (in Lines 11-14, Fig. 1).

The main difference between MINI and the proposed algorithm is heuristics to determine the attribute order in each algorithm. While the heuristics in MINI algorithm are mainly for reducing the number of cubes, those in the proposed algorithm are for improving comprehensibility.

For the explanation of heuristics here, consider a decision table constructed solely by min-terms like Table 7. The heuristics for attribute order σ is due to the three out of four comprehensibility criteria:

1. **Table size.**

A small-size table can be obtained by merging as many min-terms as possible. The algorithm pre-scans the table and examines the merging ability of each attribute, measured by n_i, where the number of cubes after merging min-terms for all concepts only on attribute a_i. For example, $n_{Bonding-area} = 7$, as shown in Table 8. Also, $n_{Material} = 10$, $n_{Usage} = 8$. Attributes are ordered in increasing order of n_i (in Lines 2-4, Fig. 1). The algorithm merges the cubes, one attribute at a time, in this order. In other words, first the cubes are merged on attribute with high merging ability and last on attribute with low ability. Table 1 is generated by merging the cubes in Table 7 with the $\sigma = (Bonding\text{-}area,\ Usage,\ Material)$.

2. **Continuity in attributes which have ordinal values.**

Attributes with ordinal values are placed at the beginning of σ (in Line 5, Fig. 1). Cubes are first merged on those attributes, generating the maximum number of $\bigcirc$s in those attributes. As a result, high continuity of $\bigcirc$s in those attributes can be achieved.

3. **Conformity between concept functions and real cases.**

Attribute order is changed so that the constrained attribute is placed before the precondition attribute (in Lines 6-10, Fig. 1). This change prevents Don't-Cares being generated in the precondition attribute, because cubes are merged on the constrained attribute before considering the precondition attribute. In the example of knowledge bases for credit earning, Table 5 and Table 6 are generated by $\sigma = (Makeup\text{-}exam,\ Exam)$ and $\sigma = (Exam,\ Makeup\text{-}exam)$, respectively.

After determining the attribute order σ, concept function forms are modified. In the modification, to achieve high Similarity among concept functions, other heuristics are applied.

4. **Similarity among concept functions.**

High similarity can be achieved, when cubes for many concepts are merged on the same attributes. The algorithm merges the cubes in the same order of attributes for all concepts.

If, in the early stage of merging, cubes are merged on the attributes, in which the cubes only for the specific concepts can be merged, then similarity becomes low. In Table 7, if first merged on *Material*, cubes mainly for concept Bond-B can be merged. Attribute order $\sigma = (Material,\ Usage,\ Bonding\text{-}$

Area) leads to Table 2, whose similarity is low. However, it is expected that such merging would be prevented, because the cubes are first merged on the attributes which many cubes can be merged (See 1.).

If all cubes in the given table were converted to min-terms for the pre-scan and the modification, the algorithm would take exponential time. To reduce this to a modest amount of computational time, it uses disjoint sharp operation $F \oplus G$, where F and G are lists of cubes (details are shown in [Hong, Cain, & Ostapko 1974]).

In the modification, the following feature of the $\oplus$ operation is utilized: $U \oplus G$ with σ generates more Os in the attribute placed in the earlier position of σ, where U is universe. This operation can generate almost the same concept function forms, as merging min-terms in the attribute order σ. However, since the order of the cubes in C_j affects the number of cubes generated by $U \oplus C_j$, the generated table may be redundant. To reduce the table size, cubes are Expanded and Reduced, using the σ order (in Line 14, Fig. 1).

Table 7: Table constructed only by min-terms.

	Material			Usage		Bonding-area	
	Paper	Leather	Plastic	Normal	Industrial	Large	Small
Bond-A	O	×	×	O	×	O	×
Bond-A	O	×	×	O	×	×	O
Bond-A	O	×	×	×	O	O	×
Bond-A	O	×	×	×	O	×	O
Bond-B	O	×	×	O	×	O	×
Bond-B	O	×	×	O	×	×	O
Bond-B	O	×	×	×	O	O	×
Bond-B	O	×	×	×	O	×	O
Bond-B	×	O	×	O	×	O	×
Bond-B	×	O	×	O	×	×	O
Bond-B	×	O	×	×	O	O	×
Bond-C	×	×	O	O	×	O	×
Bond-C	×	×	O	O	×	×	O

Table 8: Table after merging min-terms on attribute *Bonding-area*.

	Material			Usage		Bonding-area	
	Paper	Leather	Plastic	Normal	Industrial	Large	Small
Bond-A	O	×	×	O	×	O	O
Bond-A	O	×	×	×	O	O	O
Bond-B	O	×	×	O	×	O	O
Bond-B	O	×	×	×	O	O	O
Bond-B	×	O	×	O	×	O	O
Bond-B	×	O	×	×	O	O	×
Bond-C	×	×	O	O	×	O	O

Experimental Results

To evaluate concept function forms generated by the proposed algorithm, the authors experimented on 11 real knowledge bases. In addition, they evaluated table size and computational time, using 1 real knowledge base and 24 artificial ones, which are quite large.

Concept Function forms

The proposed algorithm is based on MINI. However, MINI's goal is logic minimization, not knowledge base modification, and the knowledge bases minimized by MINI are incomprehensible.

To confirm the comprehensibility of the generated table, the authors experimented on 11 real knowledge bases, which have 3-7 attributes, 5-20 cubes, 2-6 concepts, and 6-20 columns. Four examples contain attributes with ordinal values and attribute dependency relationships.

Comprehensibility is evaluated by comparing the concept function forms modified by a human with those modified by the algorithm. In seven examples, concept functions produced by the algorithm exactly corresponded to those produced by a human. In the other four examples, results were different, but they were comprehensible to humans.

This difference is mainly due to the limitation in the algorithm: it can only generate cubes which are mutually disjoint. Moreover, the difference might partly be attributed to the heuristics for determining the attribute order. If the calculated n_i values were equal in some attributes, the algorithm would determine the order arbitrarily; it is not guaranteed that expected concept functions are obtained. This situation was observed in two knowledge bases.

Table Size

Experimental results on 24 artificial knowledge bases showed that the algorithm performs logic minimization well. These knowledge bases have 1 concept, 10 cubes, 30 attributes, and 120 columns.

In 21 knowledge bases, size of the generated tables were exactly the same as that by MINI. However, in the other three knowledge bases, MINI was able to generate one or two cubes less than the proposed algorithm. This arises from another limitation in the algorithm: Don't-Cares are collected in the specific attributes, placed in the early position of σ.

The algorithm was also evaluated on a real knowledge base for a grinder selection problem, which has 158 concepts, 1023 cubes, 16 attributes, and 222 columns. In this experiment, the proposed algorithm generated the same number of cubes as MINI.

Computational Time

Pre-scan and modification of a table are based on the disjoint sharp operation. However, it is difficult to estimate the exact cost for the disjoint sharp operation. This is because the cost depends on the concept cover, the attributes order, and the cube order in the right-side cube list of the ⊕.

To confirm the feasibility of the algorithm, the authors experimented on 24 artificial knowledge bases, described in the previous subsection, with a 33 MIPS work-station. The tables were generated in 210 seconds on an average , which is about 50 % of MINI.

The authors also experimented on a real knowledge base for the grinder selection problem. The resultant table can be obtained in 90 seconds (80 seconds by MINI). This time is not too long and actually much shorter than the time required for modification by a knowledge engineer.

Related Work

Inductive learning algorithms, like ID3 [Quinlan 1986], can also improve the comprehensibility of concept functions. However, the produced concept functions are often incomprehensible, because of the lack of background knowledge and the comprehensibility criteria; they only use the description length criteria implicitly. From another viewpoint, most induction algorithms generate decision trees, not decision tables. Generated decision trees may have a minimum number of nodes and leaves. However, this does not mean a minimum number of cubes.

EG2 [Núñez 1991] uses background knowledge, which is IS-A hierarchy of values, to simplify the decision tree and to obtain a more comprehensible knowledge expression. However, EG2 requires much background knowledge for such simplification. In the proposed algorithm, the only background knowledge required concerns the attribute dependency relationships and the orderings of ordinal attribute values.

The orderings of the ordinal attribute values is used in INDUCE [Michalski, Carbonell, & Michell 1983] to generalize concepts. The proposed algorithm does not generalize the concepts, but produces the logically-equivalent concept functions to those described by knowledge engineers.

Conclusion

This paper presented new comprehensibility criteria regarding concept function forms, and an algorithm for automatically producing comprehensible forms of concept functions. This algorithm is implemented on an expert-system shell DT, which handles classification problems on the decision table [Koseki, Nakakuki, & Tanaka 1991]; its usefulness has been demonstrated in several real problems. Since the concept functions on decision table format can be easily converted to the one on production rule format, this algorithm can be applied to the knowledge bases constructed by production rules.

The new criteria are general ones, which can be applied to many knowledge bases. However, comprehensibility criteria differ according to people and domains, and generated tables may not correspond exactly to the tables expected by knowledge engineers. This disagreement, however, can be overcome by a knowledge editor on DT.

Acknowledgement

The authors express their appreciation to Takeshi Yoshimura of NEC Corporation for giving them the opportunity to pursue this research.

References

[Cragun 1987] Cragun,B.J. 1987. A decision-table-based processor for checking completeness and consistency in rule-based expert systems. *International Journals of Man-Machine Studies* 26(5):3-19.

[Hong, Cain, & Ostapko 1974] Hong,S.J.; Cain,R.G.; and Ostapko,D.L. 1974. MINI:A Heuristic Approach for Logic Minimization. *IBM Journal of Research and Development* :443-458.

[Coulon & Kayser 1978] Coulon,D.; and Kayser,D. 1978. Learning criterion and inductive behavior. *Pattern Recognition* 10(1):19-25.

[Koseki, Nakakuki, & Tanaka 1991] Koseki,Y.; Nakakuki,Y.; and Tanaka,M. 1991. DT:A Classification Problem Solver with Tabular-Knowledge acquisition. *Proceedings of Third International Conference on Tools for Artificial Intelligence* 156-163.

[Michalski, Carbonell, & Michell 1983] Michalski,R.S.; Carbonell,J.G.; and Michell,T.M. 1983. A Theory and Methodology of Inductive Leaning, *Machine Learning: An Artificial Intellegence Approach* Chapter 4, Tioga Press, Palo Alto, 83-134.

[Nguyen et al. 1985] Nguyen,T.A.; Perkins,W.A.; Laffey,T.J.; and Pecora,D. 1985 Checking an Expert Systems Knowledge Base for Consistency and Completeness. *Proceedings of the Ninth International Joint Conference on Artificial Intelligence* 375-378.

[Núñez 1991] Núñez,M. 1991. The Use of Background Knowledge in Decision Tree Induction, *Machine Learning* 6(3):231-250.

[Quinlan 1986] Quinlan,J.R. 1986. Induction of Decision Trees. *Machine Learning* 1(1):81-106.

Search

Time-Saving Tips for Problem Solving with Incomplete Information

Michael R. Genesereth
Computer Science Department
Stanford University
Stanford CA 94305

Illah R. Nourbakhsh
Computer Science Department
Stanford University
Stanford CA 94305

Abstract

Problem solving with incomplete information is usually very costly, since multiple alternatives must be taken into account in the planning process. In this paper, we present some pruning rules that lead to substantial cost savings. The rules are all based on the simple idea that, if goal achievement is the sole criterion for performance, a planner need not consider one "branch" in its search space when there is another "branch" characterized by equal or greater information. The idea is worked out for the cases of sequential planning, conditional planning, and interleaved planning and execution. The rules are of special value in this last case, as they provide a way for the problem solver to terminate its search without planning all the way to the goal and yet be assured that no important alternatives are overlooked.

Introduction

In much of the early literature on robot problem solving, the problem solver is assumed to have complete information about the initial state of the world. In some cases, the information is provided to the robot by its programmer; in other cases, the information is obtained through a period of exploration and observation.

In fact, complete information is rarely available. In some cases, the models used by our robots are quantitatively inaccurate (leading to errors in position, velocity, etc.). In some cases, the incompleteness of information is more qualitative (e.g. the robot does not know the room in which an essential tool is located). In this paper, we concentrate on problem solving with incomplete information of the latter sort.

There are, of course, multiple ways to deal with qualitatively incomplete information. To illustrate some of the alternatives, consider a robot in a machine shop. The robot's goal is to fabricate a part by boring a hole in a piece of stock, and it decides to do this by using a drill press. The complication is that there might or might not be some debris on the drill press table.

In some cases, it may be possible to formulate a *sequential* plan that solves the problem. One possibility is a sequential plan that covers many states by using powerful operators with the same effects in those states. In our example, the robot might intend to use a workpiece fixture that fits into position whether or not there is debris on the table. Another possibility is a sequential plan that coerces many states into a single known state. For example, the robot could insert into its plan the action of sweeping the table. Whether or not there is debris, this action will result in a state in which there is no debris.

A second possibility is for the planner to insert a *conditional* into the plan, so that the robot will examine the table before acting, in one case (debris present) clearing the table, in the other case (table clear) proceeding without delay.

A more interesting possibility is for the planner to *interleave planning and execution*, deferring some planning effort until more information is available. For example, the robot plans how to get its materials to the drill press but then suspends further planning until after those steps are executed and further information about the state of the table is available.

The difficulty with all of these approaches is that, in the absence of any good pruning rules, the planning cost is extremely high. In the case of deferred planning, the absence of good termination rules means that the problem solver must plan all the way to the goal, thus eliminating the principal value of the approach.

In this paper, we present some powerful pruning rules for planning in the face of incomplete information. The rules are all based on the simple idea that, if goal achievement is the sole criterion for performance, a planner need not consider one "branch" in its search space when there is another "branch" characterized by equal or greater information.

Fikes introduced interleaved planning and execution in the limited instance of plan modification during execution [Fikes 1972]. Rosenschein's work on dynamic

[1] Funding was provided by the Office of Naval Research under contract number N00014-90-J-1533.

logic formalized conditional planning but paid little attention to computational aspects [Rosenschein 1981]. More recent works do provide domain dependent guidance, but have not uncovered methods that generalize across domains [Hsu 1990], [Olawsky 1990], [Etzioni 1992].

In the next section, we give our definition for problem solving. In section 3, we present a traditional approach to problem solving with complete information. In sections 4-6, we present pruning rules for the three approaches to problem solving mentioned above. Section 7 offers some experimental results on the use of our rules. The final section summarizes the main results of the paper and describes some limitations of this work.

Problem Solving

Our definition of problem solving assumes a division of the world into two interacting parts – an agent and its environment. The outputs of the agent (its actions) are the inputs to the environment, and the outputs of the environment are the inputs to the agent (its percepts).

Formally, we specify the behavior of our agent as a tuple $\langle P, B, A, int, ext, b_1 \rangle$, where P is a set of input objects (the agent's *percepts*), B is a set of internal states, A is a set of output objects (the agent's *actions*), int is a function from $P \times B$ into B (the agent's state transition function), ext is a function from $P \times B$ into A (the agent's action function), and b_1 is a member of B (the agent's initial internal state).

We characterize the behavior of an agent's environment as a tuple $\langle A, E, P, see, do, e_1 \rangle$, where A is a finite set of actions, E is a set of world states, P is a finite set of distinct percepts, see is a function that maps each world state into its corresponding percept, do is a function that maps an action and a state into the state that results from the application of the given action in the given state, and e_1 is an initial state of the world.

Note the strong similarity between our characterization of an agent's behavior and that of its environment. There is only one asymmetry – the see function is a function only of the environment's state, whereas the ext function of an agent is a function of both the percept and the internal state. (For automata theorists, our agent is a Mealy machine, whereas our environment is a Moore machine.) This asymmetry is of no real significance and can, with a little care, be eliminated; it just simplifies the analysis.

The behavior of an agent in its environment is cyclical. At the outset, the agent has a particular state b_1, and the environment is in a particular state e_1. The environment presents the agent with a percept p_1 (based on see), and the agent uses this percept and its internal state to select an action a_1 to perform (based on the ext function). The agent then updates its internal state to b_2 (in accordance with int), and the environment changes to a new state e_2 (in accordance with do). The cycle then repeats.

In what follows, we define a *goal* to be a set of states of an environment. We say that an agent *achieves* a goal G if and only if there is some time step n on which the environment enters a state in the goal set:

$$\exists n \; e_n \in G$$

In problem solving with complete information, the agent has the advantage of complete information about the environment and its goal. In problem solving with incomplete information, some of this information is missing or incomplete. The pruning rules presented here are fully general and apply equally well in cases of uncertainty about initial state, percepts, and actions. However, for the sake of presentational simplicity, we restrict our attention to uncertainty about the robot's initial state. In our version, the robot's job is to achieve a goal G, when started in an environment $\langle A, E, P, see, do, e \rangle$, where e is any member of a set of states $I \subseteq E$.

Problem Solving with Complete Information

The traditional approach to problem solving with complete information is sequential planning and execution. An agent, given a description of an initial state and a set of goal states, first produces a plan of operation, then executes that plan.

In *single state sequential planning*, information about the behavior of the agent's environment is represented in the form of a *state graph*, i.e. a labelled, directed graph in which nodes denote states of the agent's environment, node labels denote percepts, and arc labels denote actions. There is an arc (s_1, s_2) in the graph if and only if the action denoted by the label on the arc transforms the state denoted by s_1 into the state denoted by s_2. By convention, all labelled arcs that begin and end at the same state are omitted.

To find a plan, the robot searches the environment's state graph for a path connecting its single initial state to a goal state. If such a path exists, it forms a sequential plan from the labels on the arcs along the path.

Obviously, there are many ways to conduct this search — forward, backward, bidirectional, depth-first, breadth-first, iterative deepening, etc. If the search is done in breadth-first fashion or with iterative deepening, the shortest path will be found first.

As an illustration of this method, consider an application area known as the *Square World*. The geography of this world consists of a set of 4 cells laid out on a 2-by-2 square. The cells are labelled a,b,c,d in a clockwise fashion, starting at the upper left cell. There is a robot in one of the cells and some gold in another.

One state of the Square World is shown on the left in Figure 1. The robot is in cell a and the gold is in cell c. The picture on the right illustrates another state. In this case, the robot is in cell b and the gold is in cell d.

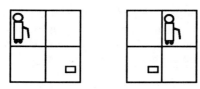

Figure 1: Square World

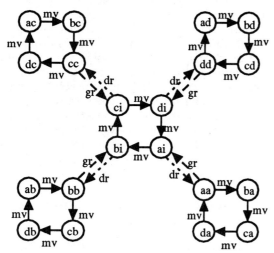

Figure 2: State Graph of Square World

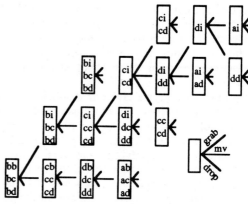

Figure 3: State-set Graph of Square World

If we concentrate on the location of the robot and the gold only, then there are 20 possible states. The robot can be in any one of 4 cells, and the gold can be in any one of 4 cells or in the grasp of the robot (5 possibilities in all).

Given *our* point of view, we can distinguish every one of these states from every other state. By contrast, consider an agent with a single sensor that determines whether the gold is in the grip of the robot, in the same cell, or elsewhere. This sensory limitation induces a partition of the Square World's 20 states into 3 subsets. The first subset contains the 4 states in which the robot grasps the gold. The second subset consists of the 4 states in which the gold and the robot are in the same cell. The third subset consists of the 12 states in which the gold and the robot are located in different cells.

The Square World has four possible actions. The agent has a single movement action *move*, which moves the robot around the square in a clockwise direction one cell at a time. In addition, the agent can grasp the gold if the gold is occupying the same cell, and it can drop the gold if it is holding the gold, leading to 2 more actions *grab* and *drop*. Finally, it can do nothing, i.e. execute the *noop* action.

Our robot's objective in the Square World problem is to get itself and the gold to the upper left cell. In this case, the goal G is a singleton set consisting of just this one state.

Figure 2 presents the state graph for the Square World. The labels inside the nodes denote the states. The first letter of each label denotes the location of

the robot. The second letter denotes the location of the gold using the same notation as for the robot, with the addition of i indicating that the gold is in the grip of the robot. The structure of the graph clarifies the robot's three percepts. The four inner states indicate that the robot is holding the gold. The next four states indicate that the gold is in the same cell as the robot (aa,bb,cc,dd). The outermost twelve states indicate that the robot and the gold are in different locations.

Looking at the graph in Figure 2, we see that there are multiple paths connecting the Square World state ac to state aa. Consequently, there are multiple plans for achieving aa from ac. It is a simple matter for *sssp* to find these paths. If the search is done in breadth-first fashion, the result will be the shortest path — the sequence *move, move, grab, move, move, drop*.

Sequential Planning with Incomplete Information

In problem solving with incomplete information, our robot knows that its initial state is a member of a set I of possible states. How can this robot reach the goal, given a state graph of the world and this set I? One approach is to derive a single sequential plan that is guaranteed to reach the goal no matter which state in I is the actual initial state. The robot can execute such a plan with confidence.

A *multiple state sequential planner* finds a sequential plan if a sequential solution exists using a *state-set graph* instead of the *state graph* that *sssp* uses. In the state-set graph, a node is a set of states. An action arc connects node n_1 to node n_2 if n_2 contains exactly the states obtained by performing the corresponding action in the states of n_1.

Figure 3 illustrates a partial state-set graph for the Square World. In this case, the robot knows at the outset that it is in the upper right cell. However, it does not know the whereabouts of the gold, other than that it is not in its grasp or in its cell. Therefore, the initial state set I consists of exactly three states: *bb*, *bc*, and *bd*.

Note that actions can change the state-set size, both increasing node size and *coercing* the world to decrease node size. The *mssp* architecture begins with node I and expands the state-set graph breadth-first until it encounters a node that is a subset of the goal node. *Msspa* expands nodes using $Results(N)$, which returns all nodes that result from the application of each $a \in A$ to node N. The following is a simple version of such an algorithm. For a more thorough treatment of problem solving search algorithms, see [Genesereth 1992].

MSSPA Algorithm

1. $graph = I$, $frontier = (I)$
2. $S = Pop(frontier)$
3. If $S \subseteq G$ go to 6.
4. $frontier = Append(frontier, Results(S))$
5. Go to 2.
6. Execute the actions of the path from I to S in $graph$.

One nice property of this approach is that it is guaranteed – the robot will achieve its goal if there is a guaranteed sequential plan. Furthermore, it will find the plan of minimal length.

However, the cost of simple *mssp* is very high. Given $i = |I|$, $g = |G|$, $a = |A|$, and search depth k, the cost $cost_{mssp}$ of finding a plan is proportional to iga^k.

Fortunately, many of the paths in the state-set graph can be ignored; these are *useless* partial plans. Any path reaching a node that is identical to some earlier node in that path is accomplishing nothing. Furthermore, any path that leads to a state from which there is no escape is simply trapping the robot. Finally, if we compare two paths and can show that one path is always as good as the other path, we needn't bother with the inferior path. We formally define *useless* in terms of any partial plan that begins at any node in the graph. Therefore, note the distinction between the *root* node, the current node being expanded, and node I, the node at which our solution plan must begin:

A partial plan q is *useless* with respect to *root* (the current node) and *result-node(q)* (the resultant node of executing plan q from *root*) if (1) there is a node n on the path from I to *root* (inclusive) such that n is a subset of *result-node(q)*, (2) there is a state s in *result-node(q)* that has no outgoing arcs in the state graph, or (3) there is a plan r such that q is not a sub-plan of r and *result-node(r)* is a proper subset of *result-node(q)*.

Pruning Rule 1: Sequential Planning

Prune any branch of the state-set graph that leads only to useless plans.

Theorem: *Pruning Rule 1 preserves completeness.*

Furthermore, we can guarantee the minimal solution by modifying condition (3) to (3e): there is some plan r such that $length(r) \le length(q)$ and *result-node(r)* is a proper subset of *result-node(q)*.

Note that once the planner finds a *useless* partial plan, it can prune all extensions of that plan since any solution from the result-node of a useless plan must work either from an earlier node (1) or from some other plan's result-node (3).

This rule can lead to significant cost savings. Recall that $cost_{mssp}$ was iga^k. If the pruning rule decreases the branching factor from a to a/b and searches to depth d for case 3, the cost of *mssp* including the cost of *Pruning Rule 1* is proportional to $(ki^2 + ai + a^d i^2 + ig)a^k/b^k$. We would have savings when:

$$\frac{new\ cost}{old\ cost} = \frac{ki + a + a^d i + g}{gb^k} < 1$$

As a result of the k term in the denominator, $cost_{mssp+heuristics}$ will grow significantly more slowly than $cost_{mssp}$ as the solution length increases.

Conditional Planning

Sequential planning has a serious flaw: some problems require perceptual input for success. In these cases, a sequential planner would fail to find a solution although the system can reach the goal if it consults its sensory input. We need a planner that will find such solutions.

A *multiple state conditional planner* finds the minimal conditional solution using a *conditional state-set graph*. This graph alternates *perceptory* and *effectory* nodes. An effectory node has action arcs emanating from it and percept arcs leading to it. A perceptory node has percept arcs emanating from it and action arcs leading to it. Action arcs connect nodes exactly as in state-set graphs. Percept arcs are labelled with percept names and lead to nodes representing the subset of the originating states that is consistent with the corresponding percept. Figure 4 illustrates part of a conditional state-set graph.

Mscp begins with just the state set I and expands the conditional state-set graph in a breadth-first (or iterative deepening) manner until it finds a solution. The planner uses both *Results* and *Sees*, which expands a perceptory node into a set of nodes, to accomplish the construction. Searching this graph is much less trivial and often more costly than the state-set graph search that *mssp* conducts. This is basically an and-or graph search problem.

Mscp returns a *conditional plan*. This plan specifies a sequence of actions for every possible sequence of inputs. It is effectively a series of nested case statements that branch based upon perceptual inputs. *Mscpa* then executes the conditional plan by checking the robot's percepts against case statements and executing the corresponding sub-plans. Below is a greatly simplified version of the *mscp* algorithm.

MSCPA Algorithm

1. $graph = I$ (a perceptory node)
2. Expand every unexpanded perceptory node n

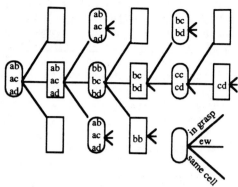

Figure 4: Conditional State-set Graph

using $Sees(n)$.

3. If there is a sub-graph of *graph* that specifies all action arcs and reaches a subset of G for every possible series of percept arcs, then go to 6.

4. Expand every unexpanded effectory node m using $Results(m)$.

5. Go to 2.

6. Execute that sub-graph as a conditional plan.

Mscpa will reach the goal with a minimal action sequence provided that there is a conditional solution.

Unfortunately, greater power has a price. At its worst, $cost_{mscp}$ is even greater than $cost_{mssp}$ because the space contains perceptual branches: $igp^k a^k$. To extend *Pruning Rule 1* to *mscp*, remember that a sequential plan has a single "result node" while a conditional plan has many possible "result nodes." We define the *result-nodes(q)* to be the set of possible resultant nodes (depending upon perceptory inputs) of conditional plan q. Pruning Rule parts (1) and (2) require trivial changes to take this into account. But part (3) now intends to compare two plans, which amounts to comparing two sets of result-nodes.

We define *domination* such that if plan r dominates plan q, then if there is a solution from *result-nodes(q)*, there must be a solution from *result-nodes(r)*. Each node in *result-nodes(r)* is dominating if it is a proper subset of some node in *result-nodes(q)*. But "result-nodes" that maintain goal-reachability and do not introduce infinite loops are also acceptable. Therefore, we also state that n is dominating if it has reached the goal or even if it is a proper subset of *root*. Below, we define *domination* and revisit *useless* in terms of conditional plans:

Formally, conditional plan r *dominates* a conditional plan q if and only if

(A) $\forall(n_q \in \text{result-nodes}(q))$
$\exists(n_r \in \text{result-nodes}(r))\ n_r \subset n_q, and$

(B) $\forall(n_r \in \text{result-nodes}(r)) either$
  1. $\exists(n_q \in \text{result-nodes}(q))n_r \subset n_q, or$
  2. $n_r \subseteq G, or$
  3. $n_r \subset root.$

A partial conditional plan q is *useless* with respect to *root* and *result-nodes(q)* if:

(1) There is a node n on the path from I to *root* (inclusive) and there is a node n_q in *result-nodes(q)* such that n is a subset of n_q, or

(2) There is a node n_q in *result-nodes(q)* such that there is a state in n_q with no outgoing action arcs in the state graph, or

(3) There is a partial conditional plan r such that r dominates q.

Pruning Rule 2: Conditional Planning

Prune any branch of the conditional state-set graph that leads only to useless plans.

Theorem: *Pruning Rule 2 preserves completeness.*

Once again, we can reimpose the minimality guarantee by modifying condition (3): (3e) There is a plan r such that $length(r) \leq length(q)$ and r dominates q without use of case $B3$.

Cost analysis of *mscp* with *Pruning Rule 2* yields results identical to $cost_{mssp}$ with the exception that all a^k terms become $a^k p^k$. The pruning rule again provides search space savings as solution length increases.

Interleaved Planning and Execution

Conditional planning is an excellent choice when the planner can extract a solution in reasonable time. But this is not an easy condition to meet. As the branching factor and solution length increase mildly, conditional planning becomes prohibitively expensive in short order. These are cases in which conditional planning wastes much planning energy by examining simply too much of the search space.

What if the system could cut its search short and execute effective partial conditional plans? The system could track its perceptual inputs during execution and pinpoint its resultant fringe node at the end of execution. The planner could continue planning from this particular fringe node instead of planning for every possible fringe node. This two-phase cycle would continue until the system found itself at the goal.

DPA Algorithm

1. $states = I$.
2. if $states \subseteq G$ exit (success!!!)
3. Invoke terminating *mscp* from *states* and return the resultant conditional plan.
4. Execute the conditional plan, updating *states* during execution.
5. Go to 2.

Dpa will reach the goal provided that there is a conditional solution and the search termination rules preserve completeness.

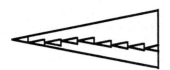

Figure 5: Search Space Savings of DPA

Assume for the moment that our search termination rules return sub-plans of the minimal conditional plan from I to G. We can quantify the dramatic search space savings of delayed planning in this case. Recall that the cost of conditional planning is $igp^k a^k$. The cost of delayed planning is the sum of the costs of each conditional planning episode. If there are j such episodes, then the total cost of delayed planning is $jigp^{k/j}a^{k/j}$. Figure 5 demonstrates the savings, representing *mscpa* with a large triangle and *dpa* by successive small triangles. Note that if the system could terminate search at every step, the search cost would simplify to a linear one: $kigpa$.

Let us return to the search termination problem: how can the planner tell that a particular plan is worth executing although it does not take the system to the goal? The intuition is clear in situations where all our actions are clearly inferior to one action: we might as well execute that one action before planning further. For example, suppose Sally the robot is trying to deliver a package. She is facing the staircase and has two available actions: move forward and turn right 90 degrees. The pruning rules would realize that flying down the stairs is *useless* (deadly) and the planner should immediately return the *turn right* action. We can generalize this rule from single actions to partial plans.

Termination Rule 1 (Forced Plan) *If there exists a plan r such that for all plans q either q is useless or r is a sub-plan of q, then return r as a forced plan.*

Theorem: *Termination Rule 1 preserves completeness and provides a minimal solution.*

The *forced plan* rule has trivial cost when its conditional planner is using *Pruning Rule 2*. Unfortunately, the forced plan criterion can be difficult to satisfy. This rule requires that every non-useless solution from *root* share at least a common first action. This fails when there are two disparate solutions to the same problem. Still, complete conditional planning to the goal may be prohibitively expensive.

We need a termination rule with weaker criteria. The *viable plan* rule will select a plan based upon its own merit, never comparing two plans. The foremost feature of any viable plan is reversibility. We want to insure that the plan does not destroy the ability of the system to reach the goal. This justifies the requirement that each fringe node of a viable plan be a subset of *root*.

A viable plan must also guarantee some sort of progress toward the goal. We guarantee such progress by requiring every fringe node to be a proper subset of *root*. Each viable plan will decrease uncertainty by decreasing the *root* state set size. This can occur at most $|I| - 1$ times.

Termination Rule 2 (Viable Plan) *If there exists a plan r such that for all nodes n_r in result-nodes(r): n_r is a proper subset of root, then return r as a viable plan.*

Theorem: *Termination Rule 2 preserves completeness.*

The fact that the *viable plan* rule does not preserve minimality introduces a new issue: how much of the viable plan should the system execute before returning to planning? Reasonable choices range from the first action to the entire plan. Experimental and qualitative analysis indicates that this variable allows a very mild tradeoff between planning time and execution time.

Average-case cost analysis of *dpa* using the *Viable Plan Rule* yields hopeful results. Recall that pure conditional planning would cost $igp^k a^k$. Suppose a *dpa* system executes n partial plans of depth j, resulting in node I_n with size h. From I_n, there are no search termination opportunities and the planner must plan straight to the goal. Assume that there is some c such that $i = ch$. The cost per node of the *Viable Plan Rule* is i^2.

For case 1, assume $g > h$. The cost from I to I_n is $n(i^2 + ig)p^j a^j$. The worst-case cost from I_n to the goal is $(h^2 + hg)p^k a^k$ when I_n is no closer to the goal than I. This can occur precisely when $g > h$ and *coercion* is not necessary. When we divide the cost of *dpa* by the cost of *mscp* we are left with savings when:

$$\frac{n(i+g)p^j a^j}{gp^k a^k} + \frac{h}{i} + \frac{h^2}{ig} < 1$$

For case 2, assume $g \leq h$. Then a number of *coercive* actions occur along the way from I to G. If we assume that these *coercives* are distributed evenly, then there are $(h - g)/2$ coercives from I_n to the goal and $k - (i - h)/2$ total steps from I_n to the goal. The total cost changes to $n(i^2 + ig)p^j a^j + (h^2 + hg)p^{k-(i-h)/2}a^{k-(i-h)/2}$. The third term, h^2/ig, changes to $h/(gp^{(i-h)/2}a^{(i-h)/2})$, which is now less than one since we assumed that $g \leq h$.

Experimental Results

We implemented these planners in four domains using property space representations, in which sets of properties correspond to sets of states satisfying those properties. For DPA, we implemented both termination criteria and executed the first step of viable plans. MJH World is a realistic indoor navigation problem. Wumpus World is a traditional hero, gold, and monster game. The Bay Area Transit Problem [Hsu 1990] models an attempt to travel from Berkeley to Stanford despite traffic jams. The Tool Box Problem [Olawsky 1990] describes two tool boxes that our robot must bolt. The following depicts p, a, i, and g:

	p	a	i	g
MJH1	2	4	4	4
MJH2	2	4	6	6
MJH3	2	4	6	6
WUM1	4	6	24	4
WUM2	4	6	44	4
BAT	16	4	8172	8172
TBOX	3	14	4	4

Below are running times (in seconds) and plan lengths, including average length in brackets, for all architectures with and without pruning rules. The DPA statistics were derived by running DPA on every initial state and averaging the running times. The dash (-) signifies no solution and the asterisk (*) indicates no solution after 24 hours running time.

	SPA	SPA_h	CPA	CPA_h	DPA
MJH1	34.6	4.1	82.8	21.4	1.6
MJH2	-	-	74.6	24.6	1.5
MJH3	-	-	*	623.6	2.4
WUM1	-	-	877.7	104.5	1.3
WUM2	-	-	*	15111	1.7
BAT	-	-	*	*	3.6
TBOX	-	-	*	*	73.1

	Len_{dpa}	Len_{ideal}
MJH1	9-11[10]	7
MJH2	8-12[10]	6-10[8]
MJH3	8-16[11]	6-12[10]
WUM1	7-15[9.2]	7-11[8.5]
WUM2	7-20[10.8]	7-15[9.8]
BAT	5-12[6.5]	5-12
TBOX	10-13[11.7]	10-13

BAT introduces a huge initial state set and a high branching factor. DPA time results for BAT are based upon a random sampling of thirty actual initial states. TBOX is the hardest problem because the action branching factor is so high that even sequential programming with complete information is impossible without pruning. The TBOX running times are based upon running DPA on every I possible in the Tool Box World. Our DPA planner never issued an *unbolt* command in any TBOX solution. Olawsky regards the use of *unbolt* as a failure and, using that definition, our termination rules produced zero failures in TBOX. A surprising result concerning both of these large domains is that the execution lengths were extremely similar to the ideal execution lengths.

Conclusion

This paper presents some powerful pruning rules for problem solving with incomplete information. These rules are all domain-independent and lead to substantial savings in planning cost, both in theoretical analysis and on practical problems. The rules are of special importance in the case of interleaved planning and execution in that they allow the planner to terminate search without planning to the goal.

Although our analysis concentrates exclusively on uncertainty about initial states, the rules are equally relevant to uncertainty about percepts and actions.

Our analysis also assumes that state sets are represented explicitly, but the pruning rules apply equally well to planners based on explict enumerations of property sets (e.g. Strips) and logic-based methods (e.g. Green's method).

One substantial limitation of this work is our emphasis on state goals. We have not considered the value of these methods or rules on problems involving conditional goals or process goals. We have also not considered the interactions of our rules with methods for coping with numerical uncertainty. Further work is needed in both areas.

Acknowledgements

David Smith introduced the machine shop robot example. Sarah Morse provided a helpful early critique of this paper. Tomas Uribe provided useful late-night suggestions.

References

Etzioni, O., Hanks, S., and Weld, D. 1992. An Approach to Planning with Incomplete Information. In Proceedings of the Third International Conference on Knowledge Representation and Reasoning.

Fikes, R. E., Hart, P.E., and Nilsson, N. J. 1972. Learning and Executing Generalized Robot Plans. *Artificial Intelligence* 3(4): 251–288.

Genesereth, M. R. 1992. *Discrete Systems*. Course notes for *CS 222*. Stanford, CA: Stanford University.

Hsu, J. 1990. Partial Planning with Incomplete Information. In Proceedings of AAAI Spring Symposium on Planning in Uncertain, Unpredictable, or Changing Environments. Menlo Park, Calif.: AAAI Press.

Olawsky, D., and Gini, M. 1990. Deferred Planning and Sensor Use. In Proceedings of the DARPA Workshop on Innovative Approaches to Planning, Scheduling, and Control. Los Altos, Calif.: Morgan Kaufmann.

Rosenschein, S.J. 1991. Plan Synthesis: A Logical Perspective. In Proceedings of the Seventh International Conference on Artificial Intelligence. Vancouver, British Columbia, Canada.

Decomposition of domains based on the micro-structure of Finite Constraint-Satisfaction Problems

Philippe Jégou [*]

L.I.U.P. - Université de Provence
3, place Victor Hugo
F13331 Marseille cedex 3, France
jegou@gyptis.univ-mrs.fr

Abstract

In this paper, we present a method for improving search efficiency in the area of Constraint-Satisfaction-Problems in finite domains. This method is based on the analysis of the "micro-structure" of a CSP. We call micro-structure of a CSP, the graph defined by the compatible relations between variable-value pairs: vertices are these pairs, and edges are defined by pairs of compatible vertices. Given the micro-structure of a CSP, we can realize a pre-processing to simplify the problem with a decomposition of the domains of variables. So, we propose a new approach to problem decomposition in the field of CSPs, well adjusted in cases such as classical decomposition methods are without interest (i.e. when the constraint graph is complete). The method is described in the paper and a complexity analysis is presented, given theoretical justifications of the approach. Furthermore, two polynomial classes of CSPs are induced by this approach, the recognition of them being linear in the size of the instance of CSP considered.

Introduction

Constraint-satisfaction problems (CSPs) involve the assignment of values to variables which are subject to a set of constraints. Examples of CSPs are map coloring, conjunctive queries in a relational databases, line drawings understanding, pattern matching in production rules systems, combinatorial puzzles...

In the general case, finding a solution or testing if a CSP admits a solution is a NP-complete problem. A well known method for solving CSP is the Backtrack procedure. If n is the number of variables, d the size of the domains of variables, and m the number of constraints, the complexity of this procedure is $O(m.d^n)$. A better bound is given using decomposition methods as tree-clustering (Dechter & Pearl 1989) or cycle-cutset method (Dechter 1990). The complexity is then of the order of d^K, K being a parameter function of the structure of the CSP (the constraint graph). If the constraint network is a complete graph, then $K = n$. The decomposition methods are based on the structure of the CSP, i.e. the structure of the constraint graph.

In this paper, we present a decomposition method based on the "micro-structure" of the CSP. We call micro-structure of a CSP, the graph defined by the compatible relations between variable-value pairs: vertices are these pairs, and edges are defined by pairs of compatible vertices (compatible values). Given the graph associated to the micro-structure of a CSP, the problem of finding a solution to the CSP is equivalent to the problem of finding a n-clique (a set of vertices that induces a complete subgraph with these n vertices) in the micro-structure. Considering this property, we use triangulation of graphs (Kjærulff 1990) and clustering of values driven by maximal cliques in the micro-structure to decompose the micro-structure associated to the CSP $\mathcal{P}$ to solve. This approach is motivated by the good algorithmic properties of triangulated graph, particularly to find maximal cliques. Every maximal clique induces a domains decomposition, and so, generates a collection of problems $\mathcal{P}_1, \mathcal{P}_2, \ldots \mathcal{P}_p$, equivalent to the initial problem $\mathcal{P}$. Each problem $\mathcal{P}_i$, corresponds to a sub-problem of $\mathcal{P}$ with a size of domains equal to δ_i, with the inequality $\delta_i \leq d$. So the complexity of solving $\mathcal{P}$, is now the sum of the complexities $O(m.\delta_i^n)$, for $i = 1, 2, \ldots p$. The complexity of the decomposition is linear in the size of the problem $\mathcal{P}$, and the number of new sub-problems is at most linear in the size of $\mathcal{P}$. The quality of the decomposition is related to the value of each δ_i: more the value δ_i is small, more the decomposition is good. For example, if $\delta_i = 1$ or 2, the complexity of the problem $\mathcal{P}_i$ is now polynomial.

The second section introduces some preliminaries about CSPs while the third section defines formally the micro-structure. The method of domains decomposition is presented in the next section. This is followed by a theoretical analysis of the method, concerning a complexity analysis, and showing some polynomial classes of problems associated to the method.

---

[*] This work is supported by the BAHIA project of the PRC-GDR IA of CNRS.

Preliminaries

A finite CSP (Constraint Satisfaction Problem) is defined as a set X of n variables $X_1, X_2,... X_n$, a set D of finite domains $D_1, D_2,... D_n$, and a set C of m constraints $C_1, C_2,...C_m$. A constraint C_i is defined on a set of variables $(X_{i_1},...X_{i_{j_i}})$ by a subset of the cartesian product $D_{i_1} \times ... D_{i_{j_i}}$; we note this subset R_i (R_i specifies which values of the variables are compatible with each other). R is the set of all R_i, for $i=1...m$. So, we denote a CSP $\mathcal{P} = (X,D,C,R)$. A solution is an assignment of value to all variables which satisfies all the constraints. For a CSP $\mathcal{P}$, the hypergraph (X,C) is called the constraint hypergraph. A binary CSP is one in which all the constraints are binary, i.e. they involve only pairs of variables, so (X,C) is then a graph (called constraint graph) associated to (X,D,C,R). This paper deals only with binary CSPs. To simplify notations for binary CSPs, a constraint between variables X_i and X_j is denoted C_{ij}, and the associated relation R_{ij}. For a given CSP, the problem is either to find all solutions or one solution, or to know if there exists any solution; the last problem is known to be NP-complete.

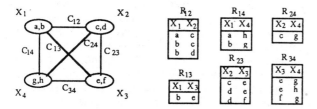

Figure 1. Binary CSP with complete constraint graph.

CSPs are normally solved by different versions of backtrack search. In this case, if d is the size of domains (maximum number of values in domains D_i), the theoretical time complexity of search is then $O(m.d^n)$. Consequently, many works try to improve the search efficiency. They mainly deal with binary CSPs. In (Freuder 1982), Freuder, considering the problem of finding one solution, gives a preprocessing procedure for selecting a good variable ordering prior to running the search. One of his main results is a sufficient condition for backtrack-free search. This condition concerns on one hand a structural property of the constraint graph, and on the other hand a local consistencies. After (Freuder 1982), Dechter and Pearl (Dechter and Pearl 1988) give two classes of polynomially solvable CSPs. For example, they define a property: *if a binary CSP is arc-consistent, and if its constraint graph is acyclic, then the CSP admits a solution and there is a backtrack-free search order.* This property holds for n-ary CSPs with hypergraphs (Janssen et al 1989).

Some methods use decomposition techniques based on structural properties of the CSP. These methods exploit the fact that the tractability of CSPs is intimately connected to the topological structure of their underlying constraint graphs. Moreover, these methods give an upper bound to the complexity of the problem, therefore, an upper bound to the search. The above property gives the goal of the transformation: given a CSP, the result must be an other CSP, equivalent to the first one, whose the structure is a tree. Two methods are based on this principle: the cycle-cutset method (Dechter 1990) and tree-clustering scheme (Dechter & Pearl 1989).

The cycle-cutset method (CCM) is based on the notion of cycle-cutset. The cycle-cutset of a graph, is a set of vertices such as the deletion of these vertices induces an acyclic graph. CCM is based on the fact that variables assignments changes the effective connectivity of the constraint graph. So, as soon as all the variables of the cycle-cutset are assigned, all the cycles of the constraint graph are cut. Therefore, the resulting problem is tree-structured and Freuder's theorem (Freuder 1982) can be applied to solve it. A property summarizes the method: *if all the variables belonging to the cycle-cutset are instanciated, and if the resulting CSP is arc-consistent, then the problem admits solutions and a backtrack-free order.* So, searching a solution, we can consider that the size of cycle-cutset corresponds to the height of the backtracking. More precisely, if K is the size of the cycle-cutset, the complexity of CCM is $O(m.d^{K+2})$.

Tree-clustering (TC) consists in forming clusters of variables such as the interactions between the clusters is tree structured. The hyper-edges of the induced constraint hypergraph are defined by the clusters of variables. The new CSP is equivalent to the first one, but the associated constraint hypergraph is acyclic. So, the property concerning acyclic n-ary CSPs holds for this CSP. If E is the size of the maximal cluster, the complexity of TC is then $O(n.E.d^E)$.

If the constraint network is a complete graph, we have the equality $E = K+2 = n$. So, the complexity of decomposition methods is the same than for classical backtracking, of the order of d^n. Consequently, complete constraint graphs (n-cliques) can be considered as hard instances of CSP for decomposition methods. The decomposition method described in this paper proposes a solution to handle these hard CSPs, but can also be used on incomplete constraints graph. It is based on a decomposition of the micro-structure of a CSP.

Microstructure of CSPs

We call *micro-structure* of a CSP, the graph defined by the compatible relations between variable-value pairs: vertices are these pairs, and edges are defined by pairs of compatible vertices.

Definition 1. Given a binary CSP $\mathcal{P} = (X,D,C,R)$ such as (X,C) is a complete graph, $\mu(\mathcal{P})$ is called *micro-structure* of $\mathcal{P}$ and it is a n-partite graph defined by
- $X_D = \{ (X_i,a) / X_i \in X \text{ and } a \in D_i \}$
- $C_R = \{ \{(X_i,a),(X_j,b)\} / (X_i,X_j) = C_{ij} \in C \text{ and } (a,b) \in R_{ij}\}$
- $\mu(\mathcal{P}) = (X_D,C_R)$

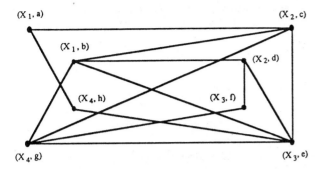

Figure 2. Micro-structure of the CSP given in figure 1.

Necessary, $\mu(\mathcal{P})$ is a n-partite graph because it can not exist edges between vertices of a same domain. In the example in figure 2, we have sets $\{(X_1,a),(X_1,b)\}$, $\{(X_2,c),(X_2,d)\}$, $\{(X_3,e),(X_3,f)\}$ and $\{(X_4,g),(X_4,h)\}$ with no one edge between vertices associated to the same variable, i.e. a set $\{(X_i,\alpha), (X_i,\beta),\dots\}$.

If (X,C) is not a complete graph, i.e. there are two variables X_i and X_j such as the constraint C_{ij} does not exist between variables X_i and X_j, $\mu(\mathcal{P})$ can be completed adding the universal relation between these variables. The universal relation is the relation $R_{ij} = D_i \times D_j$ (all pairs of values are compatible). In this paper we always consider CSPs with complete constraint graph.

Given a CSP $\mathcal{P} = (X,D,C,R)$ and its micro-structure $\mu(\mathcal{P})$, we can derive a basic property.

Property 2. Given a CSP $\mathcal{P} = (X,D,C,R)$ and its micro-structure $\mu(\mathcal{P})$ we have:

$$(a_1,a_2,\dots a_n) \text{ is a solution of } \mathcal{P}$$
$$\Leftrightarrow$$
$$\{(X_1,a_1),(X_2,a_2),\dots (X_n,a_n)\} \text{ is a n-clique of } \mu(\mathcal{P})$$

Proof: $(a_1,a_2,\dots a_n)$ *is a solution of* $\mathcal{P}$
$\Leftrightarrow \forall i, j, 1 \leq i < j \leq n, (a_i,a_j) \in R_{ij}$
$\Leftrightarrow \forall i, j, 1 \leq i \leq j \leq n, \{(X_i,a_i),(X_j,a_j)\} \in C_R$
$\Leftrightarrow \{(X_1,a_1),\dots (X_n,a_n)\}$ *is a n-clique of* $\mu(\mathcal{P})$ □

We remark that a solution of $\mathcal{P}$ corresponds to a covering of n vertices in the constraint graph (X,C): there is exactly one vertex (X_i,a) for each domain D_i, for $i = 1, 2,\dots n$. So, solving a CSP can be considered as the problem of finding a n-clique in its microstructure. The method we present for the decomposition of domains is based on the topological analysis of the microstructure, related to the existence of n-cliques.

Solving CSPs by domains decomposition

We seen that solving a CSP (finding one solution) can be considered as the problem of finding a n-clique in its microstructure. This problem is known to be NP-hard (Karp 1972), but there are classes of graphs such as polynomial (linear) algorithms have been defined. The

method we present is based on one of these classes: *triangulated graphs*. So, some definitions and properties must be recalled.

Definition 3. A graph is *triangulated* iff every cycle of length at least four has a chord, i.e. an edge joining two non-consecutive vertices along the cycle.

Property 4. (Fulkerson & Gross 1965) A triangulated graph on n vertices has at most n maximal cliques (a clique is maximal iff it is not included in an other clique).

Property 5. (Gavril 1972) The problem of finding all maximal cliques in a triangulated graph (X,C) is in $O(n+m)$ if $n = |X|$ and $m = |C|$.

Given the micro-structure of any CSP, it is not possible to immediately use these properties because any micro-structure is not necessary a triangulated graph (eg. the micro-structure in the figure 2).

Nevertheless, it is possible to use these results: given any graph $G = (X,C)$, it is possible to add new edges in C to obtain C', such as the graph $\Gamma(G) = (X,C')$ is a triangulated graph. This addition of edges is called triangulation, and can be realized in a linear time in the size of the graph (Kjærulff 1990).

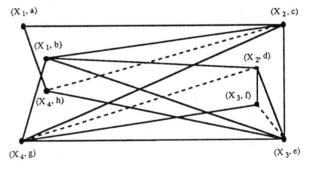

Figure 3. Triangulation of the micro-structure of figure 2. Added edges are given by the dotted lines.

After a triangulation, it is possible to apply the property 5. We show how this approach can be used here.

Suppose we have a CSP $\mathcal{P} = (X,D,C,R)$ and its micro-structure $\mu(\mathcal{P}) = (X_D,C_R)$. Consider a triangulated graph defined by a triangulation of (X_D,C_R). There are three classes of edges in $\Gamma(X_D,C_R)$:
- edges $\{(X_i,a),(X_j,b)\}$ already in $\mu(\mathcal{P})$, i.e. (a,b) is in R_{ij}
- edges $\{(X_i,a),(X_j,b)\} / i \neq j$: adding this edge corresponds to add the tuple (a,b) in R_{ij}
- edges $\{(X_i,a),(X_i,b)\}$: adding this edge has no semantic

Since $\Gamma(X_D,C_R)$. is a triangulated graph, we know that there are no more than n.d maximal cliques in this graph (by property 4), and that it is possible to find them with a linear algorithm (by property 5). Furthermore, we know that if there exist solutions, anyone is in a maximal clique of this triangulated graph, and consequently, the search of solutions of $\mathcal{P}$ will be limited to the search of solutions on separated problems, each one associated to a maximal clique.

Consider Y, a maximal clique in the triangulated graph $\Gamma(X_D, C_R)$; two possibilities must be considered:

• Y is not a covering of all domains: there is at least one variable X_i of X that does not appear in the vertices (X_i, a) of Y. Consequently, the clique Y does not contain a n-clique that is a covering of all domains, and so there is no solution in Y.

• Y is a covering of all domains. Given Y, we can induce a new CSP, by the projection of vertices in Y on each domains. So, we obtain a collection of domains $D_{Y,i}$ such as $D_{Y,i} \subseteq D_i$, each new domain $D_{Y,i}$ being induced by the vertices (X_i, a) in Y. The constraints of the new CSP associated to Y are the old constraints, restricted to the values in new domains. Searching a solution can be realized on this new CSP. Nevertheless, the fact that Y is a covering of all domains does not guarantee that there is a solution, because the triangulation adds some new edges that connect vertices corresponding to incompatible values.

Theoretical foundations of the method are given below.

Definition 6. Given a binary CSP $\mathcal{P} = (X,D,C,R)$, its micro-structure $\mu(\mathcal{P})=(X_D, C_R)$, and Y a subset of X_D. The CSP induced by Y on $\mathcal{P}$, denoted $\mathcal{P}(Y)$ is defined by:
• $D_Y = \{D_{Y,1}, \ldots D_{Y,n}\}$ such as $D_{Y,i} = \{a \in D_i \ / (X_i, a) \in Y\}$
• $R_{Y,ij} = \{ (a,b) \in R_{ij} \ / \ (X_i, a), (X_j, b) \in Y \}$
• $\mathcal{P}(Y) = (X, D_Y, C, R_Y)$

The theorem below define the principle driving the domain decomposition:

Theorem 7. Given a binary CSP $\mathcal{P} = (X,D,C,R)$, its micro-structure $\mu(\mathcal{P})$ and $\mathcal{Y} = \{Y_1, \ldots Y_k\}$, the set of the maximal cliques of $\Gamma(\mu(\mathcal{P}))$, we have:

$$Solutions(\mathcal{P}) = \bigcup_{1 \leq i \leq k} Solutions(\mathcal{P}(Y_i))$$

Proof:
• *With property 2, we know that any solution of the problem $\mathcal{P}$ is associated to a n-clique. So, this n-clique is necessary included in one set Y_i because in a graph, each clique belongs necessary to a maximal clique of the considered graph. Consequently, the considered solution of $\mathcal{P}$ is necessary a solution of $\mathcal{P}(Y_i)$.*
• *Every solution of a problem $\mathcal{P}(Y_i)$ is a clique in $\mu(\mathcal{P})$ because all the edges of this clique are edges induced by*

compatible values in $\mathcal{P}$. Consequently, every solution of $\mathcal{P}(Y_i)$ is a solution of $\mathcal{P}$. □

We remark that a solution of $\mathcal{P}(Y_i)$ can appear as a solution of an other $\mathcal{P}(Y_i)$. In the figure 4, we present the applying of theorem 7 to the example.

Maximal cliques

$$Y_1 = \{(X_1,a),(X_2,c),(X_4,h)\}$$
$$Y_2 = \{(X_1,b),(X_2,c),(X_3,e),(X_4,g)\}$$
$$Y_3 = \{(X_1,b),(X_2,d),(X_3,e),(X_3,f)\}$$
$$Y_4 = \{(X_2,c),(X_3,e),(X_4,h)\}$$
$$Y_5 = \{(X_1,b),(X_3,e),(X_3,f),(X_4,g)\}$$

Decomposed domains

$$D_{Y_1,1} = \{a\}, D_{Y_1,2} = \{c\}, D_{Y_1,3} = \varnothing, D_{Y_1,4} = \{h\}$$
$$D_{Y_2,1} = \{b\}, D_{Y_2,2} = \{c\}, D_{Y_2,3} = \{e\}, D_{Y_2,4} = \{g\}$$
$$D_{Y_3,1} = \{b\}, D_{Y_3,2} = \{d\}, D_{Y_3,3} = \{e,f\}, D_{Y_3,4} = \varnothing$$
$$D_{Y_4,1} = \varnothing, D_{Y_4,2} = \{c\}, D_{Y_4,3} = \{e\}, D_{Y_4,4} = \{h\}$$
$$D_{Y_5,1} = \{b\}, D_{Y_5,2} = \varnothing, D_{Y_5,3} = \{e,f\}, D_{Y_5,4} = \{g\}$$

Figure 4. Applying theorem 7 to the CSP of figure 1. The cliques Y_1, Y_3, Y_4 and Y_5 do not cover all the domains; so the induced sub-problem are not consistent. On the other hand, the cliques Y_2 induces a consistent sub-problem.

Algorithm:

1 - generation of $\mu(\mathcal{P})$

2 - triangulation of $\mu(\mathcal{P})$; we obtain $\Gamma(\mu(\mathcal{P}))$

3 - research of all maximal cliques in $\Gamma(\mu(\mathcal{P}))$; the result of this step is $\mathcal{Y} = \{Y_1, \ldots Y_k\}$

4 - for all Y_i in Y do
    if Y_i is a covering of all the domains in D
    then solve $\mathcal{P}(Y_i)$ else $\mathcal{P}(Y_i)$ has no solution

The first step is realized first with an enumeration of the values of all the domains to obtain the vertices of $\mu(\mathcal{P})$, and secondly, with an enumeration of all the compatible tuples of relations to obtain the edges of $\mu(\mathcal{P})$. If the problem $\mathcal{P}$ has not a complete constraint graph, it is possible to transform it with the addition of the universal constraint between non-connected variables. The second step can be realized using triangulation algorithms - see (Kjærulff 1990). The maximal cliques can be obtained by the algorithm of Gavril (Gavril 1972)(Golumbic 1980).

The last step is first realized with the generation of the problem $\mathcal{P}(Y_i)$: it is sufficient to define new domains based on the vertices in Y_i. Finally, solving $\mathcal{P}(Y_i)$ is possible with a any classical method such as standard backtracking for example.

Theoretical analysis

Complexity analysis

We first give some notations. Given $\mathcal{P} = (X,D,C,R)$ and its micro-structure $\mu(\mathcal{P}) = (X_D, C_R)$.
- n is the number of variables
- d is the maximal number of values in domains, i.e. $\forall i, \ 1 \leq i \leq n, \ |D_i| \leq d$
- N the number of vertices in $\mu(\mathcal{P})$; $N = \displaystyle\sum_{1 \leq i \leq n} |D_i| \leq n.d$
- m is the number of constraints
- M is the number of edges in $\mu(\mathcal{P})$: $M = \displaystyle\sum_{1 \leq i < j \leq n} |R_{ij}|$

and $M \leq N.(N-1)/2 < n^2.d^2$
- p is the number of maximal cliques in $\Gamma(\mu(\mathcal{P}))$

The cost of step 1 of the algorithm is $O(N+M)$. Nevertheless, if (X,C) is not a complete graph, we have $O(n^2.d^2)$. Triangulation step (step 2) is linear is the size of the resultant graph: $O(N+M')$, if M' is the new set of edges after triangulation. Necessary, $M \leq M' < n^2.d^2$. The cost of finding all maximal cliques in $\Gamma(\mu(\mathcal{P}))$ is also linear: $O(N+M')$. By property 4, we know that the number of maximal cliques p satisfies the inequality $p \leq N$.

For the last step, we first evaluate the cost of solving one problem $\mathcal{P}(Y_j)$; it can be bounded by:

$$O\left(m.\left(\prod_{1 \leq i \leq n} |D_{Y_j,i}|\right)\right)$$

So, the cost of the last step, i.e. the cost of solving all sub-problems $\mathcal{P}(Y_j)$, for $j = 1, 2, \dots p$, is:

$$O\left(m.\left(\sum_{1 \leq j \leq p}\left(\prod_{1 \leq i \leq n} |D_{Y_j,i}|\right)\right)\right)$$

The comparison of this cost with respect to the cost of standard backtracking on the initial problem is necessary. The cost of backtracking on $\mathcal{P}$ is

$$O\left(m.\left(\prod_{1 \leq i \leq n} |D_i|\right)\right)$$

If we consider $d = |D_i|$ and $\delta = |D_{Y_j,i}|$, for $i = 1, 2, \dots n$ and $j = 1, 2, \dots p$, the comparison between standard backtracking and domains decomposition is now

$$m.d^n \quad \text{VS} \quad m.p.\delta^n$$

or

$$d^n \quad \text{VS} \quad p.\delta^n$$

We know that p is bounded by $n.d$ (cf. property 4). So we give comparison of exponential terms, d^n and δ^n. Suppose that the decomposition induces a simplification of domains, such as we have for example $d = 2.\delta$. The comparison is now

$$d^n \quad \text{VS} \quad \frac{n.d}{2^n}.d^n$$

because $p.\delta^n = p.(d/2)^n = p.(1/2)^n.d^n \leq [n.d.(1/2)^n].d^n$.

Consequently, the decomposition can be very interesting on the instances of problems such as these kind of hypothesis on d and δ hold, i.e. for the problems such as we have $[n.d.(1/2)^n] \ll 1$.

Two trivial polynomial classes

CSPs with triangulated micro-structures. A first polynomial class induced by the domains decomposition is naturally the class of CSPs such as their micro-structure is already triangulated:

Property 8. Let $\mathcal{P}$ be a CSP, and its micro-structure $\mu(\mathcal{P})$. If $\mu(\mathcal{P})$ is a triangulated graph, then the number of solutions of $\mathcal{P}$ is linear in the size of $\mathcal{P}$ and there is a linear algorithm to find all solutions.

Proof. Applying the algorithm, the first step is linear in the size of $\mathcal{P}$. The second step does not add new edges in the micro-structure $\mu(\mathcal{P})$ because $\mu(\mathcal{P})$ is already triangulated graph. The number of maximal cliques is linear in the size of $\mu(\mathcal{P})$, and in the size of $\mathcal{P}$. Finding all these maximal cliques $Y_1, Y_2, \dots Y_p$, is linear in the size of $\mathcal{P}$. Finally, all the induced sub-problems $\mathcal{P}(Y_j)$ have at most one value in all the domains $D_{Y_j,i}$, for $j = 1, 2, \dots p$ and $i = 1, 2, \dots n$. Consequently, a search for any solution will be linear in the number of variables, that is exactly in $O(m)$. □

The interest of this polynomial class is principally that checking for the adherence to it will be linear in the size of any checked instance.

CSPs such as the triangulation of their micro-structures induces domains of size 1 or 2. We now consider the class of CSPs $\mathcal{P}$ such as the triangulation of their micro-structure $\mu(\mathcal{P})$ connects at most two values belonging to the same domain in every obtained maximal cliques.

Property 9. Let $\mathcal{P}$ be a CSP, and its micro-structure $\mu(\mathcal{P})$. If in $\Gamma(\mu(\mathcal{P}))$ there is at most one new edge $\{(X_i,a),(X_i,b)\}$ per domain D_i in every new maximal cliques then, there is a polynomial algorithm to solve $\mathcal{P}$ (searching for one solution).

Proof. After applying the algorithm for triangulation of the micro-structure $\mu(\mathcal{P})$, the size of domains in all the induced sub-problems $\mathcal{P}(Y_j)$ is at most two. Consequently, all induced sub-problems can be solved applying the result given in (Dechter 1992). One corollary of this theorem deals for binary CSPs with bivalent domains, and provides a polynomial method to solve this class of CSPs. □

For the same reasons than for the first polynomial class, the interest of this class is also that checking for the adherence will be linear in the size of any checked instance. Moreover, one can observe that the first class is a subclass of the second: already triangulated graphs are graphs such as their triangulation do not add any edge, and consequently, the size of domains induces by maximal cliques is so necessary equal to 1.

Conclusion

We proposed a new method to reduce domains in constraint satisfaction problems. This method is based on the analysis of the micro-structure of CSP, i.e. the structure of the relations between compatibles values of the domains. Given the micro-structure of a CSP, we present a scheme to decompose domains of variables, forming a set of sub-problems such as they have necessary less values than domains in the initial problem. This decomposition is driven by combinatorial properties of triangulated graphs. The complexity analysis of the method shown the theoretical advantages of the approach. Indeed, given a CSP $\mathcal{P}$, if d is the size of domains of the n variables, and if this problem is defined on m constraints, the complexity of any search like standard backtracking, is $O(m.d^n)$. We shown that the method induces the complexity $O(m.p.\delta^n)$ with p being the number of induced sub-problems — p is necessary linear in the size of the problem $\mathcal{P}$ — and δ is the size of new domains, always satisfying $\delta \leq d$. Furthermore, two polynomial classes of CSPs has been defined, the recognition of their elements being linear in the size of instances. Nevertheless, an experimental analysis must now be realized to see practical interest of the approach.

The decomposition method is at present only defined on binary CSPs. Nevertheless, an extension to n-ary CSPs is possible. A way to realize this extension consists in using primal constraint graph. Suppose we have a n-ary CSP with a constraint C_l between three variables; that is $C_l = \{X_i, X_j, X_k\}$. To generate the microstructure, we consider three binary constraints: C_{ij}, C_{ik} and C_{jk}. The associated relations are $R_{ij} = R_l[(X_i, X_j)]$, $R_{ik} = R_l[(X_i, X_k)]$ and $R_{jk} = R_l[(X_j, X_k)]$. This primal representation is not equivalent to the initial n-ary CSP because the new problem is less constrained. But it is sufficient to realize domains decomposition, since the constraints finally considered to solve the initial CSP will be the initial n-ary constraints, with possibly, smallest domains.

Acknowledgements

I would like to thank Philippe Janssen for the helpful pastaga discussion we had on the method discribed in this paper.

References

Dechter R., Enhancement Schemes for Constraint-satisfaction problems: Backjumping, Learning and Cutset Decomposition, *Artificial Intelligence*, 41 (1990) 273-312.

Dechter R. & Pearl J., Network-based heuristics for constraint-satisfaction problems, *Artificial Intelligence*, 34 (1988) 1-38.

Dechter R. & Pearl J., Tree Clustering for Constraint Networks, *Artificial Intelligence*, 38 (1989) 353-366.

Freuder E.C., A sufficient condition for backtrack-free search, *JACM*, 29-1 (1982) 24-32.

Fulkerson D.R. & Gross O., Incidence matrices and interval graphs, *Pacific J. Math.*, 15 (1965) 835-855.

Gavril F., Algorithms for minimum coloring, maximum clique, minimum covering by cliques, and maximum independent set of a chordal graph, *SIAM J. Comput*, 1-2 (1972) 180-187.

Golumbic, Algorithmic Graph Theory and Perfect Graphs, *Academic Press, New-York* (1980).

Janssen P., Jégou P., Nouguier B. & Vilarem M.C., A filtering process for general constraint satisfaction problems: achieving pairwise-consistency using an associated binary representation, *Proc. IEEE Workshop on Tools for Artificial Intelligence*, Fairfax, USA (1989) 420-427.

Karp E.C., Reducibility among combinatorial problems, in Complexity of Computer Computation, Miller & Thatcher Eds., Plenum Press, New-York, (1972), 85-103.

Kjærulff U., Triangulation of Graphs - Algorithms Giving Small Total State Space, *Judex R.R. Aalborg*, Denmark (1990)

Innovative Design as Systematic Search

Dorothy Neville & Daniel S. Weld*
Department of Computer Science and Engineering
University of Washington
Seattle, WA 98195
neville, weld @cs.washington.edu

Abstract

We present a new algorithm, SIE, for designing lumped parameter models from first principles. Like the IBIS system of Williams [1989, 1990], SIE uses a qualitative representation of parameter interactions to guide its search and speed the test for working designs. But SIE's *interaction set* representation is considerably simpler than IBIS's space of potential and existing interactions. Furthermore, SIE is both complete and systematic — it explores the space of possible designs in an nonredundant manner.

Introduction

A long standing concern of Artificial Intelligence has been the automation of synthesis tasks such as planning [Allen *et al.*, 1990] and design. Of the many approaches to design (e.g., library design, parameterized design, etc.) innovative (or first principles) design has seemed to present the greatest combinatorial challenge. In this paper, we extend the work of Williams [1989, 1990] on the IBIS innovative design system. Like IBIS we assume the lumped parameter model of components and connections that is common in system dynamics [Shearer *et al.*, 1971].

We take the problem of innovative design to be the following:

- **Input:**

  1. A set of possible components (described in terms of terminals, variables, and equations relating the variables).
  2. Constraints on the number and type of legal connections between terminals.
  3. A description of an existing, incomplete device (specified as a component-connection graph).

4. A set of equations that denote the desired behavior of the complete design.

- **Output:** A component connection graph which subsumes the existing device and whose equations are consistent and imply the desired behavior.

In this paper, we present the Systematic Interaction Explorer (SIE), an algorithm which performs this task of design from first principles. While our algorithm is based on IBIS it has a number of advantages over that algorithm:

- SIE is complete.

- SIE is systematic — it explores the space without repetition. [McAllester and Rosenblitt, 1991].

- SIE shares IBIS's interaction-focused search, yet

- SIE is small, simple, and easy to understand.

In particular, this paper presents a way to perform interaction-based invention without the complexity of IBIS's *space of existing interactions, space of potential interactions*, and the complex links and mappings between spaces. As explained fully below, our interaction set representation is considerably simpler than IBIS's space of potential and existing interactions, allowing us to greatly simplify the whole design algorithm. In addition, our approach results in complete and systematic exploration of the space of possible designs; we believe these properties yield greatly increased search efficiency. Although we remain unsure of the scaling potential for both IBIS and SIE, preliminary empirical results suggest that interaction-based focusing can reduce the search space by up to 95%.

In the next section, we summarize recent work on design from first principles, concentrating on William's IBIS algorithm. Then we describe the SIE algorithm and demonstrate it on the simple punchbowl example. Following that we discuss implementation status and give preliminary empirical results. We conclude with a discussion of limitations and plans for future work.

---

*Thanks to Franz Amador and Tony Barrett for helpful discussions. We gratefully acknowledge Oren Etzioni's emergency faxxing service. This research was funded in part by National Science Foundation Grant IRI-8957302, Office of Naval Research Grant 90-J-1904, and a grant from the Xerox corporation.

Previous Work

While there is a vast literature on design compilation, library approaches, case-based design and other approaches with restricted aims, there has been little work on design from first principles — presumably due to the combinatorics involved. Roylance [1980] backward chains from the specification equations using abstractions of primitive components, but assumes the purpose of each device and so loses completeness. Ulrich's [1988] schematic synthesis algorithm uses heuristic modifications to generate bond graphs from a specification consisting of the parameters to be related, an abstract characterization of the derivative or integral relation between the parameters, and a specification of the lumped parameter model of the input and output.

Rather than searching though the space of possible components, Williams' [1989] IBIS system searches through abstractions of this space. Specifically, IBIS constructs two graphs: the space of existing interactions and the space of potential interactions. The former is a graph whose nodes denote the value of parameters of the existing components (e.g., the pressure at the bottom of the particular vat V_1); hyperedges in the graph signify a set of parameters that are related by an equation in a component description or by a connection law such as the generalized Kirchoff's Current Law. The space of potential interactions is similar except nodes represent classes of parameters (e.g., one class might represent parameters denoting flow through pipes) and hyperedges represent relations that could be added. The two graphs are linked with edges that connect existing parameters with their respective classes. The most elegant aspect of this data structure is the way that the finite space of potential interactions represents an unbounded number of possible additions to the existing structure, yet we argue below that this very feature is also a weakness. Williams uses the interaction topology representation to aid search in three ways:

- Search control — search for interactions that are more likely to relate the parameters of the desired behavior first.

- Hierarchical testing — only consider a device worth testing when there is a path connecting all the parameters of the desired behavior.

- Verification — use information about the path connecting the parameters as a guide for verifying the desired behavior.

The key assumption made by IBIS is that a finite representation (the space of potential interactions) of the unbounded set of addable components leads to efficient search, since "Path tracing in a small graph is fast" [Williams, 1990, p. 354]. However, this ignores the effect of the resulting redundancy in search. The use of the interaction abstraction

space causes IBIS to lose the property of systematic search[1] in two ways:

- There is no coordination between the debugging process of refining an inconsistent candidate and the process of generating and testing a new hyperpath from the original interaction spaces. This is crucial since "Several refinements are normally required for complex structures" [Williams, 1990, p. 355].

- No systematic way is presented for adding multiple components of a single type in service of a single objective. This can only be accomplished by repeated cycles of search and refinement [Williams, 1990, p. 354].

Since SIE searches through the concrete space of possible design topologies rather than through the abstract space of interactions, there is no need for IBIS's debugging-style refinements. This leads to a search we argue is both complete and systematic. Yet like IBIS, SIE uses the interactions of the various parameters both for search control and as a cheap method of partial design verification; thus SIE gets the same computational focus from its simple interaction set representation as does IBIS from its space of existing and potential interactions.

The SIE Design Algorithm

Our technique includes two factors that simplify the design task: interaction set representation to guide search and test potential designs, and a systematic search algorithm. We discuss the details of these below, demonstrating the technique on Williams' punchbowl example.

Defining a Device

Let $\mathcal{D} = \prec \mathcal{C}, \mathcal{N}, \mathcal{I} \succ$ be a device, where $\mathcal{C}$ is a set of *components*, $\mathcal{N}$ is a set of *nodes* (where each node is a pair[2] of component terminals signifying connections between them), and $\mathcal{I}$ is the set of *interaction sets* (explained below). The device can be *partial* if not all terminals are connected or *complete* if all terminals are connected to a node and the connection graph is connected.

For the punchbowl problem, the initial device consists of an unconnected bowl and vat: $\mathcal{C} = \{vat, bowl\}$ and $\mathcal{N} = \{\}$. The key to our algorithm is $\mathcal{I}$, a set of parameter sets; two parameters share an interaction set if and only if a change in the value of one can affect the other, i.e. if there is an interaction path (series of equations) between them. Thus the sets in $\mathcal{I}$ partition the device parameters into equivalence classes that interact causally through one or more equations. Interaction sets maintain information on which parameters can influence each

---

[1]Completeness may be sacrificed also, but this is unclear.

[2]The restriction to two terminals per node is relaxed in the discussion on implementation.

other without the overhead of representing the details on how they interact. Given the primitive device equations of a container:

$$V_c(t) = H_c(t) \times area_c$$
$$Pd_c(t) = fluid\_density_c \times g \times H_c(t)$$
$$\frac{d}{dt}(V_c(t)) = Q_{top(c)}(t) + Q_{bot(c)}(t)$$
$$\frac{d}{dt}(V_c(t)) = \frac{d}{dt}(H_c(t)) \times area_c$$
$$[area_c] = [+]$$
$$[fluid\_density_c] = [+]$$
$$[g] = [+]$$

SIE determines that the variables describing a container form two interaction sets. The derivatives of the fluid height and volume are related to the flow, while the fluid height is related to the pressure difference between the top and bottom of the container. The interaction sets corresponding to each unconnected component are easily generated from the primitive equations defining each component type.

Since the punchbowl initially consists of two containers, the interaction set initially consists of four parameter sets, two each for the vat and bowl.

$$\mathcal{I} = \begin{Bmatrix} \frac{d}{dt}(H_v), \frac{d}{dt}(V_v), Q_{top(v)}, Q_{bot(v)} \\ \{Pd(vat), H_v\} \\ \frac{d}{dt}(H_b), \frac{d}{dt}(V_b), Q_{top(b)}, Q_{bot(b)} \\ \{Pd(bowl), H_b\} \end{Bmatrix}$$

We use a union-find algorithm to maintain consistency of the interaction sets when joining components. When a node connects two terminals, the effort parameters (e.g. voltage or pressure) associated with the terminals get equated and the flow parameters (e.g. current) get closed with Kirchoff's Current Law (KCL). As far as the interaction sets are concerned, the only significant change has been a possible causal connection between these parameters so their respective interaction sets are unioned together.

Specifying & Testing Behavior

The desired behavior can also be considered as a set of parameters that interact in the completed device. Thus, interaction sets form a quick test of a new device's utility: do all the desirable interactions (i.e. all the parameters in the desired behavior equations) actually interact (i.e. are they all in the same interaction set)?[3]

---

[3]There is a potential problem with this technique. Suppose that the desired equations are $A + B = C + D$ then this could be solved by two parallel interactions $A = C$ and $B = D$ without all parameters joining a single interaction set. We can compensate for this of course with a weaker test on the interaction sets, but the focusing power is reduced. More research is necessary to formally prove necessary and sufficient interaction conditions for design validity. The IBIS algorithm has a corresponding problem — the number of hyperpaths that pairwise connect a set of parameters is vastly greater than the number of connected paths.

Algorithm: SIE$(\prec\mathcal{C}, \mathcal{N}, \mathcal{I}\succ, O, S, Max)$

1. **Termination:** If $|\mathcal{C}| \geq Max$ then signal failure and backtrack. Else, If O is empty and $Test(\prec\mathcal{C}, \mathcal{N}, \mathcal{I}\succ, S) = true$ then signal success and return design. Else, signal failure and backtrack.

2. **Select Open Terminal:** Let t be an open terminal in O.

3. **Select Connecting Terminal:** *Either* connect t to another terminal t' in O *or* instantiate new component c with terminal set O_{new} and choose t' from O_{new}. *BACKTRACK POINT: Each existing compatible open terminal and each possible new component and compatible terminal must be considered for completeness.*

4. **Update Device:** If both terminals were chosen from the existing O, let $\mathcal{C}' = \mathcal{C}$. Else, let $\mathcal{C}' = \mathcal{C} \cup \{c\}$. In either case, let $\mathcal{N}' = \mathcal{N} \cup \{(t, t')\}$.

5. **Update Interaction Sets:** If two terminals from existing components were connected, the interaction sets corresponding to the relevant parameters of the terminals are replaced with their union. If a new component was added, all of its interaction sets are added to $\mathcal{I}$, then the relevant ones are joined to reflect the connection.

6. **Update Open Terminal Set:** If both terminals were chosen from O, let $O' = O - \{t, t'\}$. Else, let $O' = O \cup O_{new} - \{t, t'\}$.

7. **Recursive call:** SIE$(\prec\mathcal{C}', \mathcal{N}', \mathcal{I}'\succ, O', S, Max)$

Figure 1: The SIE Algorithm

The desired behavior for the punchbowl is "[change] the height difference in the direction opposite to the difference" [Williams, 1989, p. 59] which can be written as the following $SR1$ equation (in which square brackets denote the sign-of function):

$$\left[\frac{d}{dt}(H_v - H_b)\right] = [H_b - H_v]$$

This equation relates the four parameters H_v, H_b, $\frac{d}{dt}(H_v)$, and $\frac{d}{dt}(H_b)$. The first test of a potential design is to check the interaction sets of the device, ruling it out if the four parameters are not all in the same set. The quick test can definitively rule out some devices, but this is only a necessary condition. It is insufficient for complete verification. If a device passes the interaction set test, the detailed equations are generated and evaluated with respect to the desired behavior.

Generating Designs

The search algorithm takes a partial design $\prec\mathcal{C}, \mathcal{N}, \mathcal{I}\succ$, a list of open terminals O, and the desired behavior specification S. It systematically generates new devices by considering an open terminal and considering all the things to which it can attach: all the compatible[4] open terminals from the

---

[4]Representing and reasoning about compatibility is

existing components, all compatible terminals from the set of possible components and the possibility of not attaching the terminal to anything. For regularity, we consider this case as connecting the terminal to a special virtual terminal called an *endcap*, with exactly one terminal compatible with all terminal types. Figure 1 shows a non-deterministic, tail-recursive version of the algorithm. In practice, depth-first iterative deepening search can be used to implement nondeterminism.

SIE can generate Williams' solution for the punchbowl problem with four recursive calls, given the initial structure and desired behavior described previously and the open terminal set $O = \{top(vat), bot(vat), top(bowl), bot(bowl)\}$. First, SIE decides to connect terminal $bot(vat)$ to a new instance of a pipe. A pipe is defined as having a pressure difference between the ends to be proportional to the flow through the pipe. Therefore the interaction set for a pipe is one set containing the variables pressure difference an the flow at each end.

The resulting device is:

$$
\begin{aligned}
\mathcal{C} &= \{vat, bowl, pipe\} \\
\mathcal{N} &= \{(bot(vat), e_1(pipe))\} \\
\mathcal{I} &= \{\frac{d}{dt}(H_v), \frac{d}{dt}(V_v), Q_{top(v)}, Q_{bot(v)}, Pd_v, \\
&\quad H_v, Pd_p, Q_{e_1(p)}, Q_{e_2(p)}\} \\
&\quad \{\frac{d}{dt}(H_b), \frac{d}{dt}(V_b), Q_{top(b)}, Q_{bot(b)}\} \\
&\quad \{Pd_b, H_b\}
\end{aligned}
$$

The open terminal list is $O = \{top(vat), top(bowl), bot(bowl), e_2(pipe)\}$ and the second call to SIE chooses two open terminals from this set to connect, $bot(bowl)$ and $e_2(pipe)$, giving:

$$
\begin{aligned}
\mathcal{C} &= \{vat, bowl, pipe\} \\
\mathcal{N} &= \{(bot(vat), e_1(pipe)), (bot(bowl), \\
&\quad e_2(pipe))\} \\
\mathcal{I} &= \{H_v, V_v, Q_{top(v)}, Q_{bot(v)}, Pd_v, Pd_p, \\
&\quad Q_{e_1(p)}, Q_{e_2(p)}, H_b, V_b, Q_{top(b)}, Q_{bot(b)}, Pd_b\}
\end{aligned}
$$

The open terminal list is now $\{top(vat), top(bowl)\}$. The last two calls to SIE connect these in turn to a virtual endcap. With the open terminal list empty, the device is "complete" and ready to test. The interaction set test returns true for this device — all four parameters in the desired behavior are in the same interaction set. Further mathematical testing determines that indeed this device has the desired behavior.

Implementation Status & Potential

The basic SIE algorithm has been completely implemented in Common Lisp on a Sun SPARC-IPX. However, since we do not have access to an imple-

mentation of MINIMA, the final mathematical verification of potential solutions is done by hand.[5] We have tested SIE on several design problems in a domain which consists of a dozen fluid, mechanical and electrical components, including a turbine (with fluid and mechanical-rotation terminals) and a generator (with mechanical-rotation and electrical terminals). Our preliminary results are shown in figure 2.

The problems in figure 2 are summarized as follows:

- **Punchbowl.** This is the classical punchbowl example from [Williams, 1990] including the restriction that containers may not be connected directly together, and the partial device requirements that do not allow connections to be made to the tops of the existing containers.

- **Dynamo 1.** The initial device consists of an unconnected vat and a light bulb; the desired behavior relates the flow of liquid through the bottom of the vat with the light output of the bulb. SIE's solution connects the bottom of the vat to a turbine to a generator to the light bulb. The two correct solutions have the bulb's electrical terminals reversed with respect to the polarity of the generator.

- **Dynamo 2.** The same example as the dynamo, but allowing up to 5 components in the device, to illllustrate to combinatorics involved with increasing search depth. The solutions include the two previous ones and many five component solutions that have an "extra" component, such as another light bulb in series with the original one.

- **Dynamo 3.** This dynamo example has the desired behavior that the flow of fluid though the vat influences the light output of *two* lighbulbs. The correct variations have the bulbs in series with the generator.

- **Dynamo 4.** Similar to the above example with two lightbulbs, the implemention is augmented to allow for three terminals to connect to a node. Thus there are two topologically distinct solutions: the bulbs can be in series or in parallel with the generator.

Our experiments suggest that interaction sets provide the greatest performance advantage when used to evaluate devices cross technologies, with hydraulic and electrical components, for example. We predict that devices whose components are contained within one technology, will not benefit as much since all parameters will quickly collapse to the same interaction set. We plan to investigate this hypothesis with further tests.

---

an interesting topic in itself. Although we use a simple type system that restricts terminal connections, one could imagine a more sophisticated system such as Williams' IOTA [Williams, 1989].

---

[5]In the future, we intend to connect SIE to a design verification system built on top of Mathematica [Wolfram, 1988] and our PIKA simulator. [Amador *et al.*, 1993]

	Devices	Satisfy $\mathcal{I}$	Solutions	Max	CPU
Punchbowl	18	3	1	3	0.167
Dynamo 1	150	4	2	4	1.550
Dynamo 2	1640	124	42	5	23.850
Dynamo 3	891	16	8	5	13.617
Dynamo 4	2786	72	14	5	39.600

Figure 2: The number of possible devices created, those that pass the interaction set test, those that pass complete mathematical verification, maximum number of components (search depth), and SPARCstation CPU time in seconds.

More Elaborate Physical Models

To evaluate this line of research, we need a clear understanding of the coverage of physical devices SIE can handle. So far we have limited ourselves to relatively simple devices with simple behavioral specifications and with one operating region. Space precludes a discussion of our algorithmic extensions to multiple behavioral regions, but see [Neville and Weld, 1992].

For simplicity, we started with the requirement that at most two terminals could connect at a node. We have extended this to allow for an arbitrary number of common connections. This increases the types of devices SIE can handle, but induces a correspondingly high combinatorical cost. Note that allowing for three-terminal nodes in the dynamo example triples the amount of time needed and the number of designs tested, while it adds only one interesting solution, the six configurations with the bulbs attached in parallel to the generator. Heuristics and search control are expected to reduce the cost. We are currently investigating the addition of search control.

Another important extension would be to incorporate geometry. While the lumped parameter model is useful and expressive for many physical processes, it fails to capture the geometric reasoning needed to design mechanical devices such as linkages and transmissions. Our design algorithm, however, is well suited for generating devices consisting of kinematic pairs or possibly unity machines [Subramanian *et al.*, 1992]. Capturing and testing geometric contraints and behavior would not be a straightforward application for interaction sets though; for analysis we would hope to draw on the ideas of Subramanian [1992] and Neville & Joskowicz [1992].

Combinatorics and SIE Scaling Potential

The most crucial question to ask of any first principles design algorithm is combinatorial: how does the approach scale? Suppose that there are C types of components, each with two terminals, and there are no restrictions on terminal connectivity except a limit of two terminals per node. Then there are $\mathcal{O}(C^n)$ connected device topologies with n symmetric parts. If more than two terminals can be connected at a node, the number of designs increases — with no limit on the number of terminals per node, then there are about $m^n C^n$ possible topologies (where m denotes the number of nodes). Considering an electric component set of identical batteries, resistors, capacitors and inductors, this suggests that there are about 17 million device topologies with 6 components and 4 nodes. While this is clearly a large number, and would take 78 hours to search with our current implementation, it is reassuring to note that existing chess machines can search this many board positions in under 10 seconds.

Note that this analysis ignores the effect of interaction representations on search. There are two ways that interaction sets increase the speed of SIE. Since the presence of all goal parameters in the same interaction set is a necessary (yet insufficient) condition for design success, interaction sets provide fast, preliminary verification technique. Of course, by itself this results in no search space reduction. The other way that interaction sets can be used is as a heuristic to guide the selection and connection of components in steps 2 and 3 of SIE (figure 1). Various heuristics are possible (maximize size of resulting interaction sets, etc.) and they correspond to search strategies in IBIS's interaction spaces.[6] The question remains: how effective are *heuristics* based on interaction sets? We believe that this question can only be answered empirically. Our hope is that the benefit will equal or surpass the speedup we have achieved in design verification.

---

[6] To see this, note that the combinatorial analysis of the previous section applies to IBIS as it does to SIE. For a moment assume that IBIS used a completely instantiated (infinitely large) interaction graph instead of its finite space of potential interactions. Since each component is described by one or more equations, the number of hyperedges is no less than the number of possible components. This implies that the fundamental idea of an interaction space results in no savings over search in component space — the only possible advantage comes from the use of a finite description. Yet (as we argued in section), this requires multiple refinements and the loss of systematicity. Hence we believe that IBIS searches a space that is strictly larger than SIE's space of components.

Conclusion

In this paper we have described SIE, a new algorithm for innovative design of lumped parameter models from first principles. Our approach is based on Williams IBIS system and represents an incremental advance in the search aspects of that system. We have argued that (unlike IBIS) SIE is complete and systematic. Both algorithms are sound if the subsidiary verification algorithm is sound.

We have implemented SIE and demonstrated that it runs fast enough to use it as a testbed for further research in automated design. We have demonstrated that hierarchical testing using interaction sets can eliminate up to 95 percent of the candidate devices from further expensive testing; thus it is beneficial for some types of design problems.

Our suspicion is that both IBIS's interaction spaces and SIE's interaction sets are only a partial solution to the combinatoric problems of design from first principles. We plan to continue with this research, using SIE as a testbed for search control heuristics in order to gain a better grasp of their power and the corresponding scalability of these innovative design algorithms. We suspect that in truly large design problems a first principles approach must be coupled to a library of past experience. One way to perform this is with a case-based approach that uses a modified first principles design algorithm to adapt past solutions to new problems. In [Hanks and Weld, 1992] we show how this can be done for the synthesis of partial order plans, retaining soundness, completeness and systematicity. Since we expect that it would be easy to perform the same modification on SIE, the construction of an extensive design library and a good indexing system might result in a practical design system.

References

J. Allen, J. Hendler, and A. Tate, editors. *Readings in Planning*. Morgan Kaufmann, San Mateo, CA, August 1990.

F. Amador, A. Finklestein, and D. Weld. Real-Time Self-Explanatory Simulation. *AAAI-93*, Submitted to 1993.

Steven Hanks and Daniel Weld. Systematic adaptation for case-based planning. In *Proceedings of the First International Conference on AI Planning Systems*, June 1992.

D. McAllester and D. Rosenblitt. Systematic Non-linear Planning. In *Proceedings of AAAI-91*, pages 634–639, July 1991.

D. Neville and L. Joskowicz. A Representation Language for Conceptual Mechanism Design. In *Proceedings of the 6th International Workshop on Qualitative Reasoning*, August 1992.

D. Neville and D. Weld. Innovative Design as Systematic Search. In *Working Notes of the AAAI Fall Symposium on Design from Physical Principles*, October 1992.

G. Roylance. A Simple Model of Circuit Design. AI-TR-703, MIT AI Lab, May 1980.

J. Shearer, A. Murphy, and Richardson H. *Introduction to System Dynamics*. Addison-Wesley Publishing Company, Reading, MA, 1971.

D. Subramanian, C. Wang, S. Stoller, and A. Kapur. Conceptual Synthesis of Mechanisms from Qualitative Specifications of Behavior. In S. Kim, editor, *Creativity: Methods, Models, Tools*. 1992.

K. Ulrich. Computation and Pre-Parametric Design. AI-TR-1043, MIT AI Lab, September 1988.

B. Williams. Invention from First Principles via Topologies of Interaction. Phd thesis, MIT Artifical Intelligence Lab, June 1989.

B. Williams. Interaction-Based Invention: Designing Novel Devices from First Principles. In *Proceedings of AAAI-90*, pages 349–356, July 1990.

S. Wolfram. *Mathematica: A System for Doing Methematics by Computer*. Addison-Wesley, Redwood City, CA, 1988.

Generating Effective Admissible Heuristics by Abstraction and Reconstitution[1]

Armand Prieditis
Department of Computer Science
University of California
Davis, CA 95616
prieditis@cs.ucdavis.edu

Bhaskar Janakiraman
Silicon Graphics Inc.
Mountain View, CA 94039
bhaskar@mti.sgi.com

Abstract

Admissible heuristics are worth discovering because they have desirable properties in various search algorithms. Unfortunately, effective ones—ones that are accurate and efficiently computable—are difficult for humans to discover. One source of admissible heuristics is from abstractions of a problem: the length of a shortest path solution to an abstracted problem is an admissible heuristic for the original problem because the abstraction has certain details removed. However, often too many details have to be abstracted to yield an efficiently computable heuristic, resulting in inaccurate heuristics. This paper describes a method to *reconstitute* the abstracted details back into the solution to the abstracted problem, thereby boosting accuracy while maintaining admissibility. Our empirical results of applying this paradigm to project scheduling suggest that reconstitution can make a good admissible heuristic even better.

1 Introduction

Admissible (lower-bound) heuristics are worth discovering because they have desirable properties in various search algorithm. For example, they guarantee shortest path solutions in the A^* [24] and IDA^* [19] algorithms and less expensively produced, but boundedly longer solutions in the *dynamic weighting* [26] and A^*_ϵ [25] algorithms. Moreover, multiples of them can reduce an exponential average time complexity to a polynomial one with A^* [4]. Unfortunately, effective (accurate and efficiently computable) admissible heuristics are difficult for people to discover.

Several researchers have shown that admissible heuristics can be generated from abstractions (transformations that drop certain details) of a problem [12, 10, 25, 16, 23, 27, 28, 29]. As Figure 1 shows, the length of a shortest path solution in the abstracted problem is the admissible heuristic. For such heuristics to be effective, the abstracted problem that generates them should be efficiently solvable and yet close to the original problem [32, 23, 13, 29]. This technique typically yields efficiently computable, but inaccurate heuristics because efficiently solvable abstracted problems often ignore precisely those details that are central to solving the original problem.

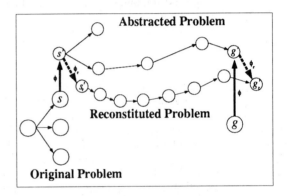

Figure 1 The Length of a Shortest Path Solution to the Abstracted Problem = Admissible Heuristic for the Original Problem; Reconstitution Increases that Length, Thereby Boosting Accuracy of the Heuristic

This paper describes a method called *reconstitution* that adds back such ignored details to the abstracted problem's solution, thereby boosting accuracy heuristic while maintaining admissibility. As Figure 1 shows, the length of a shortest path solution in the abstracted problem is increased with reconstitution to yield a more accurate admissible heuristic. The ultimate goal of this research is to develop an automatic reconstitution system to shift some of the burden of discovery from humans to machines.

2 Project Scheduling

As a vehicle for exploring reconstitution, we investigated *project scheduling* problems because they are of practical importance and are difficult to solve without effective heuristics. A project scheduling problem consists of a finite set of jobs, each with fixed integer duration, requiring one or more resources such as personnel or equipment, and each subject to a set of precedence relations, which specify allowable job orderings, and a set of mutual exclusion constraints, which specify jobs that cannot overlap. No job can be interrupted once started. The objective is to minimize

---
[1] This work is supported by the National Science Foundation grant number IRI-9109796.

project duration. Since this objective arises in nearly every large construction project—from software to hardware to buildings—efficient algorithms that obtain that objective are desirable.

Integer linear programming methods have been used to solve project scheduling problems for years [1, 3, 21, 11]. However, these methods are computationally expensive, unreliable, and applicable only to problems of small size. The underlying reason for the computational expense and limited problem size is that such project scheduling problems are NP-hard [9]. As a result, scheduling problems are typically solved by branch-and-bound algorithms with lower-bound duration estimates (admissible heuristics) to improve efficiency [31, 7, 2].

The only published attempt at discovering admissible heuristics a scheduling domain yielded poor heuristics when abstraction alone was applied [22, 28]. Moreover, the particular scheduling problem (uniprocessor scheduling) to which it was applied did not allow concurrency, which is the *essence* of scheduling.

3 Key Definitions

As shown in Figure 2, a scheduling problem can be represented as graph with jobs as vertices, precedences as single-arrowed edges, and mutual exclusions as double-arrowed edges. For example, the figure shows that job I must be completed before job J can start and that jobs J and K cannot overlap. The single number above each job represents the job's duration. For example, job J takes 10 units of time to complete. The letter to the left of each job represents the resource that the job requires; one job's use of a resource cannot overlap with another job's use of that same resource. For example, jobs I and E, which both require resource s, cannot overlap with each other.

A *precedence graph* is a directed acyclic graph consisting only of the precedence relations and no resource constraints. An *early schedule graph* is derived from the precedence graph, where each job is scheduled as early as possible. The numbers within the square brackets near each job in the figure represent the *earliest start time* and the *earliest completion time* of each job. The *critical path* is the longest path in the early schedule graph; it shows the earliest time by which all jobs can be completed.

No job on the critical path can be delayed, although other jobs on the same early schedule can be delayed as long as they do not increase the critical path length. For example, if job J, which is on the critical path, starts later than 33 units of time, the entire project will be delayed. These jobs may have to be delayed in order to satisfy mutual exclusion constraints. The total completion time of an early schedule is therefore equal to the critical path length, which in our case is 43. An *optimal schedule* is an early schedule which takes the least total time among all possible schedules.

Given only precedence constraints, finding an early schedule reduces to a topological sort of the precedence graph, which can be done in linear time of the number of precedence constraints [15]. Finding the critical path in an early schedule takes linear time of the number of jobs. Therefore, if all other constraints such as mutual exclusion constraints and resource constraints can be recast as precedence constraints, the problem is easily solvable. For example, the mutual exclusion constraint between jobs J and K can be recast in two ways: either J is completed before K or vice versa. Similarly, for resource constraints each pair of jobs sharing the same resource can be recast as a mutual exclusion constraint between the two jobs. Each mutual exclusion constraint can then be recast as one of two precedence constraints as previously described. Henceforth, we assume that all resource constraints have been recast as mutual exclusion constraints.

4 Branch and Bound Project Scheduling

The idea of recasting mutual exclusion and resource constraints as precedence constraints suggests the following simple combinatorial algorithm. Explore all recastings, one at a time, that do not create a cycle and find early schedules for all of these recastings; the early schedule with the minimum critical path length is the optimal one. Unfortunately, this brute-force algorithm is combinatorially explosive: n mutual exclusion constraints results in 2^n possible recastings, which is clearly too large a space to explore exhaustively for large n. One way to reduce this combinatorial explosion is to use a branch-and-bound algorithm with lower-bound estimates to prune certain recastings earlier. If the current duration + the lower-bound estimate exceeds a user-supplied upper-bound, then that schedule can be pruned.

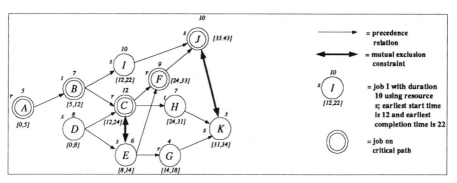

Figure 2 A Project Scheduling Problem

1. Calculate the critical path (CP).
2. Traverse the CP backwards—from late to early jobs. Assume jobs encountered are $j_k, j_i, \ldots$
3. As each job j_k on CP is encountered, look for unsatisfied mutual exclusion constraints between j_k, and some job j_r, where j_r is not on CP. Notice that traversing the graph backwards as in step 2 is more efficient than forwards because we have to reschedule only one job.
4. If in the given schedule, execution of j_k overlaps with j_r, then push j_r to a later time so that there is no overlap.
5. Push other jobs later in time if necessary. This is done by listing all jobs j_p such that j_r must come before j_p according to the precedence relation, and rescheduling j_p so that j_r completes before j_p. Repeat this step until all the precedence relations are satisfied.
6. If the length of CP in the new schedule is greater than the original CP, then terminate the algorithm and return the new bound as original CP length + amount of overlap between j_k and j_r.
7. Else, repeat till a mutual exclusion constraint is found which increases CP length.
8. If no such constraint is found, return the CP length as the new bound.

Figure 3 An Algorithm to Compute the RCP Heuristic

The critical path estimate of an early schedule, which is efficiently computable, is clearly a lower-bound since any early schedule that satisfies *part* of the constraints is a lower bound on the completion time for any optimal schedule satisfying *all* constraints. Moreover, any additional constraint will not result in a decrease in the critical path length. Notice that the critical path (CP) heuristic results from an abstraction of the original problem: all mutual exclusion and resource constraints are ignored.

Although the CP heuristic is admissible and easily computable and has proved to be valuable in evaluating overall project performance and identifying bottlenecks, it can be far from the actual project duration. In the worst case, it can underestimate the actual project duration by a factor of n, where n is the total number of jobs to be scheduled. This case arises when the only possible schedule is a serial schedule. For example, if a scheduling problem has no precedence constraints and has mutual exclusion constraints between every pair of jobs, then the only possible schedule will be a serial one. For this case, the CP heuristic will return length of the longest job, which underestimates the optimal duration by a factor of n. Also, since the critical path estimate ignores the resource constraints, certain sequencing decisions may be required in the actual schedule that increase the project duration well beyond the critical path estimate.

5 Reconstitution-based Heuristics in Project Scheduling

What we would like is an admissible heuristic that is as easily computable as the critical path estimate, but that takes into account the resource and mutual exclusion constraints, which the critical path estimate ignores. We would like to reconstitute these ignored constraints back into the critical path somehow. The RCP (Reconstituted Critical Path) heuristic described below does exactly that.

The basic idea behind the RCP heuristic is to extend the critical path by analyzing all unsatisfied mutual exclusion constraints between jobs in critical path and jobs not in critical path. When possible, all jobs with such unsatisfied constraints are rescheduled at a later time while still

preserving critical path length. If that is not possible, then the critical path length is increased by a time overlap underestimate between the jobs of each type. For example, consider the project scheduling problem in Figure 2, which has a critical path of J, F, C, B, A. First, we examine job J and check for any mutual exclusion constraints involving it. The only such constraint is the one with job K. Next, we check if J overlaps with K, which in fact it does. The object now is to try to delay job K beyond the completion time of job J, which is at 43 time units. Delaying job K will necessarily increase the length of the critical path by 1 time unit. If the rest of the jobs were ignored, the RCP heuristic would return 44, which is the length of critical path (43) plus the overlap of the earliest start time of job J and the earliest completion time of K ($34 - 33 = 1$). The general algorithm is shown in Figure 3 and a pictorial definition of overlap is shown in Figure 4.

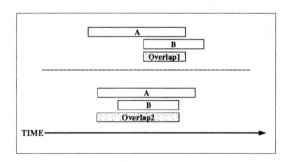

Figure 4 Overlap is the Minimum of Both
Overlaps; Jobs A and B are Mutually Exclusive

To see that the RCP heuristic is admissible, consider a job j_l on the critical path which has a mutual exclusion constraint with job j_m. In the final schedule, either j_l will be scheduled before j_m or vice versa. Note that neither of the two jobs can be scheduled any earlier since the schedule is already an early schedule. If job j_m cannot be scheduled after j_l without increasing the critical path length in the current schedule by pushing jobs ahead which depend on j_m, then neither can it be scheduled after j_l in the final schedule. The reason is that precedence constraints are always added and never removed at each iteration of the search algorithm and adding more precedence constraints cannot invert an existing scheduling order. If j_l is scheduled after j_m, then the critical path length will be increased by *at least* the minimum of the overlap between the earliest start time of j_l and the earliest completion time of j_m or the earliest start time of j_m and the earliest completion time of j_l. The reason is because job j_l is on the critical path: starting it later affects the entire project duration.

Although the RCP heuristic takes slightly longer to compute than the CP heuristic, it prunes more of the space than the CP heuristic. As we will see in the next section, the extra time taken in computing the heuristic is more than compensated by the time saved from pruning the search space. If the current critical path length is optimal, then computation of the RCP heuristic takes longer than that of the CP heuristic, since the algorithm has to examine all jobs on the critical path. The worst case complexity of computing the RCP heuristic is $O(n^2)$ for n jobs, since at most $O(n)$ jobs will be on the critical path and $O(n)$ work will be required to process a mutual exclusion constraint involving a job on the critical path. An analysis of the *average* computational complexity is, however, difficult since the heuristic depends on specific mutual exclusion constraints. The degree of complexity can be controlled by reconstituting fewer mutual exclusion constraints if desired.

The complexity of the RCP heuristic can be further reduced by computing it incrementally. That is, the RCP on a successor state (one with a new precedence constraint added) can be computed more efficiently by reusing a portion of the RCP on the original state. Since new precedence constraints are added and never removed at each iteration of the search algorithm, the critical path up to the point in the graph where the new precedence constraint is added remains the same and the critical path need only be recomputed from that point on.

6 Empirical Results

To get some idea of the effectiveness of the RCP and CP heuristics, we implemented the IDA* algorithm [19], which is a standard branch-and-bound algorithm in which to evaluate admissible heuristics, in Quintus Prolog on a Sun Sparstation 1+ and ran it on a set of random solvable (i.e. no cycles) problem instances with various numbers of jobs, mutual exclusion constraints, and precedence constraints. The algorithm works as follows. All partial schedules whose duration exceeds a certain threshold are pruned. Initially, the threshold is set to the value of the admissible heuristic on the initial state. If no solution is found within that threshold, then the algorithm repeats. On the next iteration, the threshold is set to the minimum of duration plus heuristic estimate over all the previously generated partial schedules whose duration exceeds the threshold. One important property of IDA* is that it guarantees minimal duration solutions with admissible heuristics [19].

A state consists of three items:

1. A precedence graph which includes original precedence constraints and a set of precedence constraints

originating from mutual exclusion constraints which have so far been recast as one of two precedence constraints.

2. An early schedule satisfying the precedence constraints.

3. A set of unsatisfied mutual exclusion constraints.

The goal state is characterized by an empty mutual exclusion constraint set. A state transition is a recasting of a mutual exclusion constraint into one of two precedence constraints followed by the generation of a new early schedule. Search proceeds from an initial schedule satisfying only the original precedence constraints.

We ran two sets of experiments, each with a fixed the number of jobs and precedence constraints and a variable number of mutual exclusion constraints since problem complexity grows as the number of mutual exclusion constraints increases: one with 30 jobs with 112 precedence constraints and the other with 40 jobs with 128 precedence constraints. For the first set, we varied the number of mutual exclusion constraints between 0 and 25; for the second, between 10 and 40. We chose these problems because they were the largest ones we could generate that still could be solved in a reasonable amount of time on our machine.

Table 1 summarizes the results of running IDA* on these two problem sets. For each problem set, the table lists the number of mutual exclusion constraints, the number of states expanded, the CPU time, and the amount of run-time memory used. As the table shows, for problems with few mutual exclusion constraints, the number of states expanded in both cases remain the same and CP consistently takes less time than RCP, since RCP does more work each time. However, for all problems where RCP resulted in a saving in terms of states expanded, RCP always takes less CPU time. RCP also uses slightly more run-time memory in all examples, but always within a factor of 4 when compared to CP. The breakdown between 15 and 20 mutual exclusions in the first data set and 20 and 30 in the second data sets may be sudden because a particular "hard problem" region threshold is cross in those ranges. We have yet to understand what aspect of a scheduling problem determines actual running time, but we suspect that there is some threshold of the average number of mutual exclusions per job that separates the hard from the easy problems. In summary, RCP works better than CP in all cases where the critical path length is not optimal, which is typically the case in real-world (non-artificial) problems, where it is highly probably that constraints other than precedence constraints play a major role in dictating the total project duration. Therefore, RCP will result in better performance in most real-world cases.

We are currently running more extensive experiments. One major problem in this domain is that there is a lack of good benchmark hard problems and that "easy" problems might skew randomly generated data sets unless the easy ones are filtered out. We hope to produce a set of such good benchmark problems.

7 General Reconstitution

This paper has described one instance of reconstitution: use an efficient algorithm to generate a optimal (shortest duration) solution to an abstract problem and then calculate how adding back certain constraints increases the duration of this solution. We have identified one other type of reconstitution, this one involving abstracted problems that are decomposable into independent subproblems. This type of reconstitution involves calculating how the sum of shortest path lengths for each of the independent subproblems increases when abstracted dependencies are added back. For example, the Manhattan distance heuristic for sliding block puzzles is derivable by ignoring (abstracting) the location of the blank—a shortest path solution to the abstracted problem is the Manhattan Distance. Since the rectilinear tile distance to each tile's final destination can be independently computed, the abstracted problem that generates Manhattan Distance can be decomposed into a set of independently solvable subproblems, one for each tile. If the blank is added back to each subproblem then dependencies such as linear conflicts (i.e. two tiles that must pass through each other to their goal destination) can be efficiently detected and the solution path length can be boosted by two for such conflicts. We are currently implementing a general purpose reconstitution algorithm for decomposable abstracted problems.

8 Related Work

The idea that abstraction-derived heuristics can sometimes be made more effective by taking into account certain details ignored by the abstracted problem was first expressed by Hansson, Mayer, and Yung [14]. In particular, they hand-derived a new effective admissible sliding block puzzle heuristic (the LC heuristic) by taking into account those linear tile conflicts (same row or column) ignored by the Manhattan Distance heuristic. We have extended this idea to a problem involving time (project scheduling) rather than solution path length.

Instead of using an abstract solution as a heuristic measure, others (such as[17]) use it as a skeleton for producing a solution; the remaining details are then filled in by re-finement. One drawback of this method is that the abstract solution often cannot be refined—backtracking between the original and abstract level must continue until a refinable solution is found. As a result researchers have tried to find specific types of abstractions that can always be refined, or refined with little backtracking [18]. However, guaranteed refinable abstractions are difficult to find.

In general, heuristics are efficient approximations of lookahead searches [20]. A heuristic approximates the search by either ignoring certain paths or adding additional paths to reduce search complexity. If a full-width lookahead search is used a heuristic for solving the original problem in an algorithm such as A^*, then the complexity of A^* will be worse than that of A^* without any heuristics. What the heuristic does is trade off efficiency for accuracy in approximating this full-width search, thus making it worthwhile for algorithms such as A^* to use the heuristic.

9 Conclusions and Future Work

This paper has described an instance of a general three step problem-solving paradigm: abstract, solve, reconstitute. Certain details of the original problem are removed by abstraction. Next, the abstracted problem is efficiently solved. Finally, the abstracted details are reconstituted back into this solution. This reconstituted solution is then used as a guide for solving the original problem. Our results of applying this paradigm to project scheduling, where reconstitution was used to generate a novel effective admissible heuristic (RCP), suggest that reconstitution can make good admissible heuristics even better.

This paradigm as applied to project scheduling has several shortcomings. First, complex project scheduling problems often involve resource constraints with fixed limits for each job, typically specifying the *number* of fixed resource units that cannot be exceeded, rather than the absolute resource constraints as in our model; it is not clear to us how to recast such resource constraints as mutual exclusion constraints. However, Davis and Heidorn [5] show a branch-and-bound solution to the problem. They describe

Jobs	Precedences	Mutual Exclusions	CP Heuristic			RCP Heuristic		
			States Expanded	*CPU Seconds*	*Bytes*	*States Expanded*	*CPU Seconds*	*Bytes*
30	112	0	0	.25	30820	0	.25	30808
		10	14	5.43	41024	14	8.52	58108
		15	19	5.98	43212	19	9.18	70256
		20	6237	1644.17	45796	49	30.58	109584
		25	6242	1651.53	47188	54	30.67	116068
40	128	10	12	5.15	52928	12	5.63	72228
		20	24	9.73	56988	24	18.52	101936
		30	1084	718.20	71024	431	494.33	194220
		40	1096	727.83	65104	521	521.80	224112

Table 1 Comparative Performance Analysis of the CP and RCP Heuristics with IDA*

a preprocessor algorithm that expands a job with duration k into a sequence of k unit duration jobs each successively linked with a "must immediately precede" precedence relation. After this expansion, a standard branch-and-bound project scheduling algorithm can be run. Unfortunately, such expansion can result in enormous project networks in projects with long duration jobs.

A second shortcoming is that not all scheduling constraints can be recast as precedence constraints. For example, a constraint that a particular job must start only after a certain time cannot be recast as a precedence constraint. Effective admissible heuristics that reflect such general constraints would be an important contribution to scheduling.

How does the amount reconstitution quantitatively relate to the accuracy of the resulting heuristics? How much reconstitution is enough? This paper shows one data point at which reconstitution pays off. Since reconstitution is the inverse of abstraction, results that quantitatively link abstractness to the accuracy of the resulting heuristics should be applicable[6, 30].

Finally, although this paper has described a method for generating better admissible heuristics from existing ones, the process of discovering heuristics such as the RCP heuristic is far from automatic. We are currently extending this method to job-shop scheduling problems of the sort described in [8]. In a job-shop problem, n jobs are to be scheduled on m machines with varying durations per job per machine. We hope to develop a set of general principles that practitioners in the scheduling field can follow to derive effective heuristics and eventually to automate the discovery process.

References

[1] M. L. Balinski. Integer programming: Methods, uses, computation. *Management Science*, November 1965.

[2] C. E. Bell and K. Park. Solving resource-constrained project scheduling problems by A* search. *Naval Research Logistics*, 37:61–84, 1990.

[3] J. D. Brand, W. L. Meyer, and L. R. Schaffer. The resource scheduling problem in construction. Technical Report 5, Dept. of Ciivil Engineering, University of Illinois, Urbana, 1964.

[4] S. Chenoweth and H. Davis. High-performance A* search with rapidly growing heuristics. In *Proceedings IJCAI-12*, Sydney, Australia, August 1991. International Joint Conferences on Artificial Intelligence.

[5] E. W. Davis and G. E. Heidorn. An algorithm for optimal project scheduling under multiple resource constraints. *Management Science*, 17(12), August 1971.

[6] R. Davis and A. Prieditis. The expected length of a shortest path. *Information Processing Letters*, (To appear), 1993.

[7] M. Dincbas, H. Simonis, and P. V. Hentenryck. Solving large combinatorial problems in logic programming. *Journal of Logic Programming*, 8(1 and 2):75–93, 1990.

[8] M. S. Fox. *Constraint-Directed Search: A Case Study of Job-Shop Scheduling*. Pitman, 1984.

[9] M. Garey and D. Johnson. *Computers and Intractability*. W. H. Freeman, San Francisco, 1979.

[10] J. Gaschnig. A problem-similarity approach to devising heuristics. In *Proceedings IJCAI-6*, pages 301–307, Tokyo, Japan, 1979. International Joint Conferences on Artificial Intelligence.

[11] D. Graham and H. Nuttle. A comparison of heuristics for a school bus scheduling problem. *Transportation*, 20(2):175–182, 1986.

[12] G. Guida and M. Somalvico. A method for computing heuristics in problem solving. *Information Sciences*, 19:251–259, 1979.

[13] O. Hansson, A. Mayer, and M. Valtorta. A new result on the complexity of heuristic estimates for the A* algorithm. *Artificial Intelligence*, 55(1), 1992.

[14] O. Hansson, A. Mayer, and M. Yung. Criticizing solutions to relaxed models yields powerful admissible heuristics, 1992. To appear in Information Sciences.

[15] E. Horowitz and S. Sahni. *Fundalmentals of Data Structures*. Computer Science Press, Inc, Rockville, Maryland, 1978.

[16] D. Kibler. Natural generation of heuristics by transforming the problem representation. Technical Report TR-85-20, Computer Science Department, UC-Irvine, 1985.

[17] C. Knoblock. Learning abstraction hierarchies for problem solving. In *Proceedings AAAI-90*, Boston, MA, 1990. American Association for Artificial Intelligence.

[18] C. Knoblock. Search reduction in hierarchical problem-solving. In *Proceedings AAAI-91*, Anaheim, CA, 1991. American Association for Artificial Intelligence.

[19] R. Korf. Depth-first iterative-deepening: An optimal admissible tree search. *Artificial Intelligence*, 27(2):97–109, 1985.

[20] R. Korf. Real-time heuristic search: New results. In *Proceedings AAAI-88*, St. Paul, MN, 1988. American Association for Artificial Intelligence.

[21] C. L. Moodie and D. E. Mandeville. Project resource balancing by assembly line balancing techniques. *Journal of Industrial Engineering*, July 1966.

[22] J. Mostow, T. Ellman, and A. Prieditis. A unified transformational model for discovering heuristics by idealizing intractable problems. In *AAAI90 Workshop on Automatic Generation of Approximations and Abstractions*, pages 290–301, July 1990.

[23] J. Mostow and A. Prieditis. Discovering admissible heuristics by abstracting and optimizing. In *Proceedings IJCAI-11*, Detroit, MI, August 1989. International Joint Conferences on Artificial Intelligence.

[24] N. J. Nilsson. *Principles of Artificial Intelligence*. Morgan Kaufmann, Palo Alto, CA, 1980.

[25] J. Pearl. *Heuristics: Intelligent Search Strategies for Computer Problem-Solving*. Addison-Wesley, Reading, MA, 1984.

[26] I. Pohl. The avoidance of (relative) catastrophe, heuristic competence, genuine dynamic weighting and computational issues in heuristic problem solving. In *Proceedings IJCAI-3*, pages 20–23, Stanford, CA, August 1973. International Joint Conferences on Artificial Intelligence.

[27] A. Prieditis. *Discovering Effective Admissible Heuristics by Abstraction and Speedup: A Transformational Approach*. PhD thesis, Rutgers University, 1990.

[28] A. Prieditis. Machine discovery of effective admissible heuristics. In *Proceedings IJCAI-12*, Sydney, Australia, August 1991. International Joint Conferences on Artificial Intelligence.

[29] A. Prieditis. Machine discovery of effective admissible heuristics. *Machine Learning*, 1993. To appear.

[30] A. Prieditis and R. Davis. Quantitatively relating accuracy to abstractness of abstraction-derived heuristics. *Artificial Intelligence*, (Submitted), 1993.

[31] F. J. Radermacher. Scheduling of project networks. *Journal of Operations Research*, 4(1):227–252, 1985.

[32] M. Valtorta. A result on the computational complexity of heuristic estimates for the A* algorithm. *Information Sciences*, 34:47–59, 1984.

Iterative Weakening: Optimal and Near-Optimal Policies for the Selection of Search Bias

Foster John Provost
Department of Computer Science
University of Pittsburgh
foster@cs.pitt.edu

Abstract

Decisions made in setting up and running search programs bias the searches that they perform. Search *bias* refers to the definition of a search space and the definition of the program that navigates the space. This paper addresses the problem of using knowledge regarding the complexity of various syntactic search biases to form a policy for selecting bias. In particular, this paper shows that a simple policy, *iterative weakening*, is optimal or nearly optimal in cases where the biases can be ordered by computational complexity and certain relationships hold between the complexity of the various biases. The results are obtained by viewing bias selection as a (higher-level) search problem. Iterative weakening evaluates the states in order of increasing complexity. An offshoot of this work is the formation of a near-optimal policy for selecting both breadth *and* depth bounds for depth-first search with very large (possibly unbounded) breadth and depth.

Introduction

For the purposes of this paper, search *bias* refers to the definition of a search space and the definition of the program that navigates the space (*cf.*, *inductive bias* in machine learning [Mitchell, 1980], [Utgoff, 1984], [Rendell, 1986], [Provost, 1992]). Bias choices are purely syntactic if they are not based on domain knowledge, otherwise they are semantic. In this work, except where I refer to the incorporation of *knowledge* into the search program (*e.g.*, the addition of heuristics), *bias* refers to syntactic bias choices. The choice of a depth-first search is a coarse-grained choice; the choice of a maximum depth of *d* is a finer-grained choice. *Search policy* refers to the strategy for making bias choices based on underlying assumptions and knowledge (*cf.*, *inductive policy* [Provost & Buchanan, 1992a]). This paper addresses the problem of selecting from among a set of bias choices, based solely on complexity knowledge. I show that in certain cases, optimal or near-optimal policies can be formed.

The problem is attacked by viewing bias selection as a (higher-level) state-space search problem, where the states are the various biases and the goal is to find a bias which is satisfactory with respect to the underlying search goal (*e.g.*, a search depth sufficient for finding the lower-level goal). For the purposes of the current exposition, let us assume that no knowledge is transferred across biases, *i.e.*, the search with one bias has no effect on the search with another bias. So, the higher-level problem is a search problem where the cost of evaluating the various states is not uniform, and we know (at least asymptotically) the complexity of the evaluation of each state. I will refer to the worst-case time complexity of searching with a given bias as the *complexity* of that bias. Using worst-case time complexity side-steps the problem that some problems may be inherently "easier" than others with a given bias, and allows biases to be ordered independently of the distribution of problems that the search program will encounter.

If we view the strength of a bias to be analogous to the complexity of that bias, we can define the policy *iterative weakening* to be: *evaluate the biases in order of increasing complexity*. (The term *iterative weakening* is borrowed from the *iterative deepening* of [Korf, 1985] and *iterative broadening* of [Ginsberg and Harvey, 1990], which are special cases of the general technique). In cases where the states (biases) can be grouped into equivalence classes based on complexity, where there is an exponential increase in complexity between classes, and where the rate of growth of the cardinality of the classes is not too great (relatively), iterative weakening can be shown to be a near-optimal policy with respect to the complexity of only evaluating the minimum complexity goal state (optimal in simple cases).

Consider an example from machine learning as search, where being able to select from among different search biases is particularly important. The complexity of a non-redundant search of a space of conjunctive concept descriptions with maximum length k is polynomial in the number of features and is exponential in k. Given a fixed set of features, iterative weakening would dictate searching with $k = 1$, $k = 2$, ..., until a satisfactory concept description is found.

However, the size of an ideal feature set might not be manageable. In many chemistry domains the properties and structure of chemicals provide a very large set of features for learning; for example, in the Meta-DENDRAL domain the task is to learn cleavage rules for chemical mass spectrometry [Buchanan & Mitchell, 1978]. In such domains with effectively infinite sets of features, knowledge may be used to order the features by potential relevance. However, it may not be known *a priori* how many of the most relevant features will be necessary for satisfactory learning.

Many existing learning programs represent concept descriptions as sets of rules, each rule being a conjunction of features (*e.g.*, [Quinlan, 1987], [Clark & Niblett, 1989], [Clearwater & Provost, 1990]). The space of conjunctive rules can be organized as a search tree rooted at the rule with no features in the antecedent, where each child is a specialization of its parent created by adding a single conjunct. A restriction on the depth of the search tree restricts the maximum complexity of the description language (the number of conjuncts in a rule's antecedent). A restriction on the breadth of the search restricts the list of features considered. A depth-first search of this space would not only face the classic problem of determining a satisfactory search depth (see Section 3), but also the problem of (simultaneously) determining a satisfactory search breadth. In Section 5 I develop a near-optimal policy for selecting both the depth and the breadth of a depth-first search.

Optimal Policies

The heuristic behind iterative weakening policies is by no means new. As mentioned above, and discussed further below, iterative deepening and iterative broadening are special cases of the general technique. Simon and Kadane [Simon and Kadane, 1975] show that in cases where knowledge is available regarding the cost of a search and the probability of the search being successful, that an "optimal" strategy is to perform the searches in order of increasing probability/cost ratio. In the case where the probability distribution is uniform (or is assumed to be because no probability information is available), this reduces to a cheapest-first strategy. Slagle [Slagle, 1964] also discusses what he calls *ratio-procedures*, where tasks are carried out in order of the ratio of benefit to cost, and shows that these "often serve as the basis of a minimum cost procedure" (p.258).

However, the problem addressed in this paper is a different one from that addressed by Simon and Kadane and Slagle. Their work showed that the cheapest-first strategy was a minimum cost strategy with respect to the other possible orderings of the biases. In this paper, the term *optimal* will be used to denote a policy where the asymptotic complexity is no worse than that of a policy that knows *a priori* the minimum cost bias that is sufficient for finding the (lower-level) goal. To illustrate, given n search procedures, p_1, p_2, ... , p_n, previous work addressed finding an ordering of the p_i's such that finding the goal will be no more expensive than any other ordering of the p_i's. In contrast, I address the problem of ordering the p_i's such that finding the goal will be as inexpensive (or almost as inexpensive) as only using p_{i_m}, the minimum-cost search procedure.

This paper shows that in some cases the cheapest-first strategy is almost as good (asymptotically) as a strategy that *knows* the right bias *a priori*. The implications are that in these cases, it is a better investment to apply knowledge to reduce the complexity of the underlying task (*e.g.*, by introducing heuristics based on the semantics of the domain) than to use it to aid in the selection of (syntactic) search bias (discussed more below).

A Single Dimensional Space

Let us assume the states of our (higher-level) search space can be indexed by their projection onto a single dimension, and that the projection gives us integer values. In a machine learning context this could be the case where the different biases are different types of hypothesis-space search, different degrees of complexity of the description language (*e.g.*, number of terms in the antecedent of a rule), different search depths, etc. From now on, let us refer to the states (biases) by their indices, *i.e.*, i denotes the state that gives value i when projected onto the dimension in question. Without loss of generality, let us assume that $i_1 \leq i_2$ implies that the complexity of evaluating i_1 is less than or equal to the complexity of evaluating i_2. Let $c(i)$ denote the complexity of evaluating i.

Iterative weakening is a rather simple policy in these cases. It specifies that the states should be evaluated in order of increasing i. It may seem that iterative weakening is a very wasteful policy, because a lot of work might be duplicated in evaluating all the states. However, if $c(i)$ is exponential in i, then the arguments of [Korf, 1985] apply. Korf shows that *iterative deepening*, iterative weakening along the search-depth dimension, is an optimal policy with respect to time, space, and cost of solution path. In short, since the cost of evaluating i increases exponentially, the complexity of iterative deepening differs from that of searching with the correct depth by only a constant factor. Thus "knowing" the right bias buys us nothing in the limit. This paper concentrates solely on time complexity.

Theorem: (after [Korf, 1985]) *Iterative weakening is an asymptotically optimal policy, with respect to time complexity, for searching a single-dimensional space where the cost of evaluating state i is $O(b^i)$.*

Iterative Broadening is a similar technique introduced in [Ginsberg and Harvey, 1990], where the dimension in question is the breadth of the search. In this case, the complexity increases only polynomially in i, however the technique is shown to still be useful in many cases (a characterization of when iterative broadening will lead to a computational speedup is given).

Theorem: (after [Ginsberg and Harvey, 1990]) *Iterative weakening is an asymptotically near-optimal policy, with respect to time complexity, for searching a single-dimensional space where the cost of evaluating state i is $O(i^d)$. (It is within a dth-root factor of optimal–see [Provost, 1993].)*

A similar technique is used in [Linial, *et al.*, 1988] for learning with an infinite VC dimension. If a concept class $\mathcal{C}$ can be decomposed into a sequence of subclasses $\mathcal{C} = \mathcal{C}_1 \cup \mathcal{C}_2 \cup \ldots$ such that each $\mathcal{C}_i$ has VC dimension at most i, then iterative weakening along the VC dimension is shown to be a good strategy (given certain conditions).

Thus, previous work helps us to characterize the usefulness of iterative weakening along a single dimension. However, in specifying a policy for bias selection there may be more than one dimension along which the bias can be selected. The rest of this paper considers multi-dimensional spaces.

Multi-Dimensional Spaces

Consider the general problem of a search where the states have different costs of evaluation (in terms of complexity). We want to find a good policy for searching the space. Let each state be indexed according to its projection onto multiple dimensions, and let us refer to the state by its vector of indices $\vec{i}$ (assume, for the moment, that there is a one-to-one correspondence between states and indices). Let $c(\vec{i})$ be the complexity of evaluating state $\vec{i}$. Iterative weakening specifies that the states (biases) should be evaluated by increasing complexity. Let us consider some particular state complexity functions. (For clarity I will limit the remaining discussion to two dimensions, but mention results for n dimensions. A more detailed treatment can be found in [Provost, 1993]).

Dual Searches

Consider a particular $c(\vec{i})$: $c(i,j) = b^i + b^j$. This is the complexity function for the situation where two (depth-first) searches must be performed, and both subgoals must be discovered before the searcher is sure that either is actually correct.

How well will iterative weakening do on this problem? The following theorem shows that it is nearly optimal–within a log factor. For the rest of the paper, let $\vec{i_g} = (i_g, j_g)$ denote the minimum-complexity goal state, and let $b > 1$.

Proposition: *Given a search problem where the complexity of evaluating state (i,j) is $b^i + b^j$, any asymptotically optimal policy for searching the space must have worst-case time complexity $O(b^m)$, where $m = max(i_g, j_g)$ (the complexity of evaluating the minimum-complexity goal state).*

Theorem: *Given a search problem where the complexity of evaluating state (i,j) is $b^i + b^j$, iterative weakening gives a time complexity of $O(mb^m)$, where $m = max(i_g, j_g)$.*

Proof: In the worst case, iterative weakening evaluates all states $\vec{i}$ such that $c(\vec{i}) \leq c(\vec{i_g})$, where $\vec{i_g} = (i_g, j_g)$ is the (minimum-complexity) goal state. Thus the overall complexity of the policy is:

$$\sum_{\{\vec{i} \mid c(\vec{i}) \leq c(\vec{i_g})\}} c(\vec{i}) = \sum_{\{(i,j) \mid b^i + b^j \leq b^{i_g} + b^{j_g}\}} b^i + b^j.$$

The terms that make up the sum can be grouped into equivalence classes based on complexity. Let a term b^k be in class $\mathcal{C}_k$. Then the overall complexity becomes:

$$\sum_{k=1}^{m} |\mathcal{C}_k| b^k,$$

where $|\mathcal{C}_k|$ denotes the cardinality of the set of equivalent terms. The question remains as to the number of such terms (complexity of b^k). The answer is the number of vectors (i, j) whose maximum element is k, plus the number of vectors (i, j) whose minimum element is k. The number of such vectors is $2m$, so the overall complexity is: $\sum_{k=1}^{m} 2mb^k$, which is: $O(mb^m)$.♠

Corollary: *Given a search problem where the complexity of evaluating state (i, j) is $b^i + b^j$, iterative weakening is within a log factor of optimal.*

Proof: The optimal complexity for this problem is $O(N) = O(b^m)$; iterative weakening has complexity $O(mb^m) = O(N \log N)$. ♠

For n dimensions, the proximity to being optimal is dependent on n. In general, for such searches iterative weakening is $O(m^{n-1}b^m) = O(N(\log N)^{n-1})$. (See [Provost, 1993].)

If we have more knowledge about the problem than just the complexity of evaluating the various states, we can sometimes come up with a better policy. In this case, the policy that immediately springs to mind is to let $i = j$ and search to depth $i = 1, 2, \dots$ in each (lower-level) space. This is, in fact, an optimal policy; the amount of search performed is

$$\sum_{k=1}^{m} 2b^k = O(b^m).$$

We have, in effect, collapsed the problem onto a single dimension. The particular extra knowledge we use in specifying this optimal policy is that a solution found in state $\vec{i_1}$ will also be found in $\vec{i_2}$ if $\vec{i_1}$ is componentwise less than or equal to $\vec{i_2}$. (As is the case for a pair of depth-first searches.)

A Search within a Search

Let us consider a search problem where the complexity of evaluating state (i, j) is b^{i+j}. This complexity function is encountered when evaluating the state involves a search within a search. For example, consider a learning problem where there is a search for an appropriate model, with a search of the space of hypotheses for each model (*e.g.*, to evaluate the model). Iterative weakening is once again competitive with the optimal policy.

Proposition: *Given a search problem where the complexity of evaluating state (i, j) is b^{i+j},*

any asymptotically optimal policy for searching the space must have worst-case time complexity $O(b^m)$, where $m = i_g + j_g$ (the complexity of evaluating the minimum-complexity goal state).

Theorem: *Given a search problem where the complexity of evaluating state (i, j) is b^{i+j}, iterative weakening gives a time complexity of $O(mb^m)$, where $m = i_g + j_g$.*

Proof: Similar to previous proof. Note that in this case, the cardinality of the set of equivalent terms is equal to the number of vectors (i, j) whose components sum to k, which is $k-1$ (given positive components). Thus the overall complexity of the policy is: $\sum_{k=1}^{m}(k-1)b^k$, which is: $O(mb^m)$.♠

Corollary: *Given a search problem where the complexity of evaluating state (i, j) is b^{i+j}, iterative weakening is within a log factor of optimal.*

Proof: The optimal complexity for this problem is $O(N) = O(b^m)$; iterative weakening has complexity $O(mb^m) = O(N \log N)$. ♠

For n dimensions, the proximity to being optimal is dependent on n. In general, for such searches iterative weakening has complexity $O(m^{n-1}b^m) = O(N(\log N)^{n-1})$. (See [Provost, 1993].)

In this case, the policy of collapsing the space and iteratively weakening along the dimension $i = j$ does not produce an optimal policy. If we let $m = i_g + j_g$, in the worst case, as $m \to \infty$, the $i = j$ policy approaches b^m times worse than optimal.

Important: Relative Growth

As we have seen from the preceding examples, in general, the important quantity is the growth of the complexity function relative to the growth of the number of states exhibiting a given complexity. In the cases where there is but one state for each complexity (*e.g.*, iterative deepening, iterative broadening) we have seen that the faster the rate of growth of the complexity function, the closer to optimal. In multidimensional cases, as the dimensionality increases the policy becomes further from optimal because the number of states of a given complexity increases more rapidly.

Let us now consider a multidimensional problem with a (relatively) faster growing complexity function, namely $c(\vec{i}) = b^{ij}$. This is another function where the strategy of choosing $i = j$ and searching $i = 1, 2, \dots$ is not optimal, even if we have the extra knowledge outlined above. If we let $m = i_g j_g$, in the worst case, as $m \to \infty$ the ratio of the overall complexity of the $i = j$ policy to the optimal approaches $b^{m^2 - m}$ (very much worse than optimal).

However iterative weakening does very well—even better than in the previous case. The following theorem shows that in this case, it is within a root-log factor of being an optimal policy.

Proposition: *Given a search problem where the complexity of evaluating state (i, j) is b^{ij}, any asymptotically optimal policy for searching the space must have worst-case time complexity $O(b^m)$, where $m = i_g j_g$ (the complexity of evaluating the minimum complexity goal state).*

Theorem: *Given a search problem where the complexity of evaluating state (i, j) is b^{ij}, iterative weakening gives a time complexity of $O(\sqrt{m} b^m)$, where $m = i_g j_g$.*

Proof: Similar to previous proofs. Note that in this case, the cardinality of the set of equivalent terms is equal to the number of factors of k, which is bounded by $\sqrt{k}$. Thus the overall complexity of the policy is: $\leq \sum_{k=1}^{m} \sqrt{k} b^k$, which is: $O(\sqrt{m} b^m)$.♠

Corollary: *Given a search problem where the complexity of evaluating state (i, j) is b^{ij}, iterative weakening is within a root-log factor of optimal.*

Proof: The optimal complexity for this problem is $O(N) = O(b^m)$; iterative weakening has complexity $O(\sqrt{m} b^m) = O(N \sqrt{\log N})$. ♠

For n dimensions, the proximity to being optimal is again dependent on n. In general, for such searches iterative weakening can be shown to have complexity $O(m^{\log n} b^m) = O(N (\log N)^{\log n})$. (See [Provost, 1993].) The above results suggest that this bound may not be tight.

The general problem can be illustrated with the following schema: Complexity(IW) =

$$\sum_{\{\vec{i} | c(\vec{i}) \leq c(\vec{i_g})\}} c(\vec{i}) \quad \leq c(i_g) \sum_{i} 1$$

$$\leq c(i_g) \cdot |\{\vec{i} | c(\vec{i}) \leq c(\vec{i_g})\}|$$

which is the complexity of evaluating the goal state, multiplied by the number of states with equal or smaller complexity. This gives slightly looser upper bounds in some cases, but illustrates that there are two competing factors involved: the growth of the complexity and the growth of the number of states. As we have seen, in some cases domain knowledge can be used to reduce the number of states bringing a policy closer to optimal.

Knowledge Can Reduce No. of States: Combining Broadening and Deepening

For rule-space searches such as those defined for the chemical domains mentioned in Section 1, we want to select both a small, but sufficient set of features (search breadth) and a small, but sufficient rule complexity (search depth). Ginsberg and Harvey write, "An attractive feature of iterative broadening is that it can easily be combined with iterative deepening . . . any of (the) fixed depth searches can obviously be performed using iterative broadening instead of the simple depth-first search" ([Ginsberg and Harvey, 1990] p. 220). This is so when the breadth bound is known *a priori*. It will be effective if the breadth bound is small. When neither exact breadth or depth is known *a priori*, and the maxima are very large (or infinite), we are left with the problem of designing a good policy for searching the (high-level) space of combinations of b, the breadth of a given search, and d the depth of a given search.

The complexity of evaluating a state in this space is $O(b^d)$. Strict iterative weakening would specify that we order the states by this complexity, and search all states such that $b^d \leq b_g^{d_g}$ (the goal state). We begin to see two things: (i) the analysis is not going to be as neat as in the previous problems, and (ii) as d grows, there will be a *lot* of different values of b to search. The second point makes us question whether the policy is going to be close to optimal; the first makes us want to transform the problem a bit anyway.

In this problem we can use the knowledge that a state $\vec{i}$ is a goal state if $\vec{i}$ is componentwise greater than or equal to $\vec{i_g}$. Since b^d can be written as $2^{d \log(b)}$, our intuition tells us that it might be a good idea to increment b exponentially (in powers of 2). We can then rescale our axes for easier analysis. Let $\hat{b} = \log(b)$, and consider integer values of $\hat{b}$. We now have the problem of searching a space where the complexity of searching state (i, j) is b^{ij}. We know that iterative weakening is a near-optimal policy for such a space. Unfortunately, the overshoot along the b dimension gets us into trouble. Given that the complexity of evaluating the (minimum-complexity) goal state is $O(2^{d_g \log(b_g)})$, the first "sufficient" state reached using our transformed dimensions would be $(\hat{b}_g, d_g)$, where $\hat{b}_g = \lceil \log(b_g) \rceil$. The difference in complexity between evaluating the minimum-complexity goal and the new goal is the difference between $O(2^{d \lceil \log(b) \rceil})$ and $O(2^{d \log(b)})$, which in the worst case approaches a factor of 2^d.

The solution to this problem is to decrease the step size of the increase of $d\hat{b}$. A satisfactory step size is found by collapsing the space onto the (single) dimension $k = d \log(b)$, and only considering integer values of k. Because we are now looking at stepping up a complexity of $O(2^{\lceil d \log(b) \rceil})$ (rather than $O(2^{d \lceil \log(b) \rceil})$), the overshoot of the minimum-complexity goal state is never more than a factor of 2, which does not affect the asymptotic complexity. Using iterative weakening along this new axis brings us to within a log factor of optimal.

Proposition: *Given a depth-first search problem where the complexity of evaluating state (b, d) is b^d (for possibly unbounded b and d), any asymptotically optimal policy for searching the space must have worst-case time complexity $O(2^m)$, where $m = d_g \log(b_g)$ (the complexity of evaluating the minimum-complexity goal state).*

Theorem: *Given a depth-first search problem where the complexity of evaluating state (b, d) is b^d, iterative weakening in integer steps along the dimension $k = d \log(b)$ gives a time complexity of $O(\hat{m} 2^{\hat{m}})$, where $\hat{m} = \lceil d_g \log(b_g) \rceil$.*

Proof: In the worst case, iterative weakening evaluates all states k such that k is an integer and $c(k) \leq c(\lceil k_g \rceil)$, where $c(k)$ is the complexity function along the k axis, and k_g is the (minimum-complexity) goal state. Thus the overall complexity of the policy is:

$$\sum_{\{k | c(k) \leq c(\lceil k_g \rceil), k \text{ is an integer}\}} c(k)$$

$$= \sum_{\{k | 2^k \leq 2^{\hat{m}}, k \text{ is an integer}\}} 2^k.$$

The states that make up the sum can be grouped into equivalence classes based on complexity. Let a state (b, d) be in class $\mathcal{C}_k$ iff $d \log(b) = k$ (for integer k). Then the overall complexity becomes: $\sum_{k=1}^{\hat{m}} |\mathcal{C}_k| 2^k$, where $|\mathcal{C}_k|$ denotes the cardinality of the set of equivalent states. The question remains as to the number of states with complexity of 2^k. The answer is the number of vectors (b, d) where $d \log(b) = k$ (for integer k). Since d is an integer, the number of such vectors is at most k, so the overall complexity is: $\leq \sum_{k=1}^{\hat{m}} k 2^k$, which is: $O(\hat{m} 2^{\hat{m}})$.♠

Corollary: *Given a depth-first search problem where the complexity of evaluating state (b, d) is b^d, iterative weakening in integer steps along the dimension $k = d \log(b)$ is within a log factor of optimal.*

Proof: The optimal complexity for this problem is $O(N) = O(2^m)$ where $m = d_g \log(b_g)$; iterative weakening has a complexity of $O(\hat{m} 2^{\hat{m}})$.

Since $\hat{m} = \lceil m \rceil$, $\hat{m} \leq m + 1$. So iterative weakening has a complexity of $O((m + 1) 2^{(m+1)}) = O(m 2^m) = O(N \log N)$. ♠

When IW is not a Good Policy

Several problem characteristics rule out iterative weakening as a near-optimal policy. The smaller the relative growth of the complexity of the states (wrt. the growth of the number of states with a given complexity), the farther from optimal the policy becomes. For example, in one dimension, if $c(i) = i$ then the optimal policy is $O(i)$ whereas iterative weakening is $O(i^2)$ even when there is only one state per equivalence class. On the other hand, the rate of growth may be large, but so too might the size of the class of states with the same complexity. In the previous sections, we saw equivalence classes of states with cardinalities whose growth was small compared to the growth of the class complexities. If, instead of counting the number of factors of k or the number of pairs that sum to k, we had an exponential or combinatorial growth in the size of the classes, iterative weakening would fail to come close to optimal. (The b^d problem was one where the number of terms grew rapidly.)

One reason for a very large growth in the size of the equivalence classes is a choice of dimensions where there is a many-to-one mapping from states into state vectors. Thus, in the chemical domains, for iterative weakening to be applicable it is essential to be able to order the terms based on prior relevance knowledge. The ordering allows a policy to choose the first b terms, instead of all possible subsets of b terms.

Conclusions

The simple policy of iterative weakening is an asymptotically optimal or near-optimal policy for searching a space where the states can be ordered by evaluation complexity, and they can be grouped into equivalence classes based on complexity, where the growth rate of the complexities is large and the growth rate of the size of the classes is small (relatively).

This has important implications with respect to the study of bias selection. If the bias selection problem that one encounters fits the criteria outlined above, it may not be profitable spending time working out a complicated scheme (*e.g.*, using more domain knowledge to guide bias selection intelligently). The time would be better spent trying to reduce the complexity of the underlying biases (*e.g.*, using more domain knowledge for lower-level search guidance). On the other hand, if the complexity of the biases is such that iterative weakening can not come close to the optimal policy, it might well be profitable to spend time building a policy for more intelligent navigation of the bias space. For example, domain knowledge learned searching with one bias can be used to restrict further the search with the next bias (see [Provost & Buchanan, 1992b]).

This paper assumed that the problem was to choose from a fixed set of biases. Another approach would be to try to find a bias, not in the initial set, that better solves the problem. By reducing the complexity of the underlying biases, as mentioned above, one is creating new (perhaps semantically based) biases with which to search. Even if iterative weakening *is* an optimal policy for selecting from among the given set of biases, a better bias might exist that is missing from the set. (As a boundary case of a semantically based bias, consider this: once you know the answer, it may be easy to prune away most or all of the search space.)

The dual search problem and combining deepening and broadening are examples of when additional knowledge of relationships between the biases can be used to come up with policies closer to optimal than strict iterative weakening. In these cases, knowledge about the subsumption of one bias by another is used to collapse the bias space onto a single dimension. In the former case, iterative weakening along the single dimension was then an optimal policy. In the breadth and depth selection problem, the knowledge about the subsumption of biases is sufficient to give a near-optimal policy. Utilizing more knowledge at the bias-selection level will not help very much unless the complexity of the underlying biases is reduced first.

Acknowledgments

I would like to thank Bruce Buchanan, Haym Hirsh, Kurt Van Lehn, Bob Daley, Rich Korf, Jim Rosenblum, and the paper's anonymous reviewers for helpful comments. This work was supported in part by an IBM graduate fellowship and funds from the W.M. Keck Foundation.

References

Buchanan, B., and T. Mitchell, 1978. Model-directed Learning of Production Rules. In Waterman and Hayes-Roth (eds.), *Pattern Directed Inference Systems*, 297-312. Academic Press.

Clark, P., and T. Niblett, 1989. The CN2 Induction Algorithm. *Machine Learning*, 3: 261-283.

Clearwater, S., and F. Provost, 1990. RL4: A Tool for Knowledge-Based Induction. In *Proceedings of the 2nd Int. IEEE Conf. on Tools for Artificial Intelligence*, 24-30. IEEE C.S. Press.

Ginsberg, M., and W. Harvey, 1990. Iterative Broadening. In *Proc of the Eighth National Conf on Artificial Intelligence*, 216-220. AAAI Press.

Korf, R., 1985. Depth-First Iterative Deepening: An Optimal Admissible Tree Search. *Artificial Intelligence* 27: 97-109.

Linial, N, Y. Mansour, R. Rivest, 1988. Results on learnability and the VC dimension. In *Proc of the 1988 Wkshp on Comp Learning Theory*, 51-60. Morgan Kaufmann.

Mitchell, T., 1980. The Need for Biases in Learning Generalizations (Tech Rept CBM-TR-117). Dept of Comp Sci, Rutgers University.

Provost, F., 1992. Policies for the Selection of Bias for Inductive Machine Learning. Ph.D. Thesis. Dept of Comp Sci, Univ of Pittsburgh.

Provost, F., 1993. Iterative Weakening: Optimal and Near-Optimal Policies for the Selection of Search Bias. Tech Rept ISL-93-2, Intelligent Systems Lab, Dept of Comp Sci, Univ of Pittsburgh.

Provost, F., and B. Buchanan, 1992a. Inductive Policy. In *Proc. of the Tenth National Conf on Artificial Intelligence*, 255-261. AAAI Press.

Provost, F., and B. Buchanan, 1992b. Inductive Strengthening: the effects of a simple heuristic for restricting hypothesis space search. In K. Jantke (Ed.), *Analogical and Inductive Inference (Lecture Notes in Artificial Intelligence* 642: 294-304. Berlin: Springer-Verlag.

Quinlan, J., 1987. Generating Production Rules from Decision Trees. In *Proceedings of the Tenth International Joint Conference on Artificial Intelligence*, 304-307. Morgan Kaufmann.

Rendell, L., 1986. A General Framework for Induction and a Study of Selective Induction. *Machine Learning* 1: 177-226. Boston, MA: Kluwer.

Simon, H., and J. Kadane, 1975. Optimal Problem-Solving Search: All-or-None Solutions. *Artificial Intelligence* 6: 235-247. North-Holland.

Slagle, J., 1964. An Efficient Algorithm for Finding Certain Minimum-Cost Procedures for Making Binary Decisions. *Journal of the ACM* 11 (3), 253-264.

Utgoff, P., 1984. Shift of Bias for Inductive Concept Learning. Ph.D. thesis, Rutgers University.

Pruning Duplicate Nodes in Depth-First Search

Larry A. Taylor and **Richard E. Korf** *
Computer Science Department
University of California, Los Angeles
Los Angeles, CA 90024
ltaylor@cs.ucla.edu

Abstract

Best-first search algorithms require exponential memory, while depth-first algorithms require only linear memory. On graphs with cycles, however, depth-first searches do not detect duplicate nodes, and hence may generate asymptotically more nodes than best-first searches. We present a technique for reducing the asymptotic complexity of depth-first search by eliminating the generation of duplicate nodes. The automatic discovery and application of a finite state machine (FSM) that enforces pruning rules in a depth-first search, has significantly extended the power of search in several domains. We have implemented and tested the technique on a grid, the Fifteen Puzzle, the Twenty-Four Puzzle, and two versions of Rubik's Cube. In each case, the effective branching factor of the depth-first search is reduced, reducing the asymptotic time complexity.

Introduction—The Problem

Search techniques are fundamental to artificial intelligence. Best-first search algorithms such as breadth-first search, Dijkstra's algorithm [Dijkstra, 1959], and A* [Hart *et al.*, 1968], all require enough memory to store all generated nodes. This results in exponential space complexity on many problems, making them impractical.

In contrast, depth-first searches run in space linear in the depth of the search. However, a major disadvantage of depth-first approaches is the generation of duplicate nodes in a graph with cycles [Nilsson, 1980]. More than one combination of operators may produce the same node, but since depth-first search does not store the nodes already generated, it cannot detect the duplicates. As a result, the total number of nodes generated by a depth-first search may be asymptotically more than the number of nodes generated by a best-first search.

---

*This research was partially supported by NSF Grant #IRI-9119825, and a grant from Rockwell International.

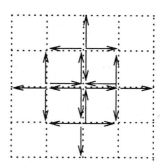

Figure 1: The grid search space, explored depth-first to depth 2, without pruning.

To illustrate, consider a search of a grid with the operators: Up, Down, Left and Right, each moving one unit. A depth-first search to depth r would visit 4^r nodes (figure 1), since 4 operators are applicable to each node. But only $O(r^2)$ distinct junctions are visited by a breadth-first search. Thus, a depth-first search has exponential complexity, while a breadth-first search has only polynomial complexity.

To reduce this effect, we would like to detect and prune duplicate nodes in a depth-first search. Unfortunately, there is no way to do this on an arbitrary graph without storing all the nodes. On a randomly connected explicit graph, for example, the only way to check for duplicate nodes is to maintain a list of all the nodes already generated. A partial solution to this problem is to compare new nodes against the current path from the root [Pearl, 1984]. This detects duplicates in the case that the path has made a complete cycle. However, as we saw in the grid example, duplicates occur when the search explores two halves of a cycle, such as up-left and left-up. Only a fraction of duplicates can be found by comparing nodes on the current path [Dillenburg and Nelson, 1993]. Other node caching schemes have been suggested [Ibaraki, 1978] [Sen and Bagchi, 1989] [Chakrabarti *et al.*, 1989] [Elkan, 1989], but their utility depends on the implementation (costs per node generation).

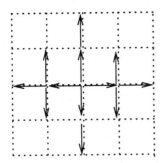

Figure 2: The grid search space, explored depth-first to depth 2, with pruning.

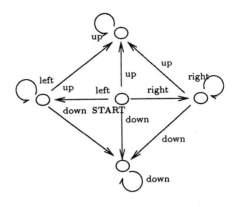

Figure 3: FSM corresponding to the search with FSM pruning, eliminating duplicate nodes.

We present a new technique for detecting duplicate nodes that does not depend on stored nodes, but on another data structure that can detect duplicate nodes that have been generated in the search's past, and nodes that will be generated in the future. This technique uses limited storage efficiently, uses only constant time per node searched, and reduces the effective branching factor, hence reducing the asymptotic time complexity of the search.

The FSM Pruning Rule Mechanism

Exploiting Structure

We take advantage of the fact that most combinatorial problems are described implicitly. If a problem space is too large to be stored as an explicit graph, then the it must be generated by a relatively small description. This means that there is structure that can be exploited. Precisely the problems that generate too many nodes to store are the ones that create duplicates that can be detected and eliminated. For this paper, a node in the search space is represented by a unique vector of values.

For example, the grid problem, the operator sequence Left-Right will always produce a duplicate node. Rejecting inverse operator pairs, including in addition Right-Left, Up-Down, and Down-Up, reduces the branching factor by one, and the complexity from $O(4^r)$ to $O(3^r)$. Inverse operators can be eliminated by a finite state machine (FSM) that remembers the last operator applied, and prohibits the application of the inverse. Most depth-first search implementations already use this optimization, but we carry the principle further.

Suppose we restrict the search to the following rules: go straight in the X-direction first, if at all, and then straight in the Y-direction, if at all, making at most one turn. As a result, each point (X,Y) in the grid is generated via a unique path: all Left moves or all Right moves to the value of X, and then all Up moves or all Down moves to the value of Y. Figure 2 shows a search to depth two carried out with these rules. Figure 3

shows an FSM that implements this search strategy. The search now has time complexity $O(r^2)$, reducing the complexity from exponential to quadratic.

Each state of this machine corresponds to a different last move made. The FSM is used in a depth-first search as follows. Start the search at the root node as usual, and start the machine at the START state. For each state, the valid transitions are given by the arrows which specify the possible next operators that may be applied. For each new node, change the state of the machine based on the new operator applied to the old state. Operators that generate duplicate nodes do not appear. This prunes all subtrees below such redundant nodes. The time cost of this optimization is negligible.

Next, we present a method for automatically learning a finite state machine that encodes such pruning rules from a description of the problem.

Learning the FSM

The learning phase consists of two steps. First, a small breadth-first search of the space is performed, and the resulting nodes are matched to determine a set of operator strings that produce duplicate nodes. The operator strings represent portions of node generation paths. Secondly, the resulting set of strings is used to create the FSM which recognizes the strings as a set of keywords. If we ever encounter a string of operators from this set of duplicates, anywhere on the path from the root to the current node, we can prune the resulting node, because we are guaranteed that another path of equal or lower cost exists to that node.

Exploratory Breadth-first Search Suppose we apply the search for duplicate strings to the grid space. In a breadth-first search to depth 2, 12 distinct nodes are generated, as well as 8 duplicate nodes, including 4 copies of the initial node (see figure 4(a)). We need to match strings that produce the same nodes, and then make a choice between members of the matched pairs of strings. We can sort the nodes by their representa-

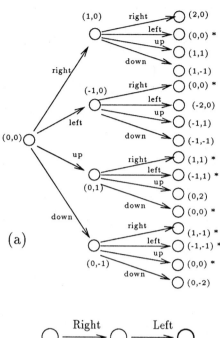

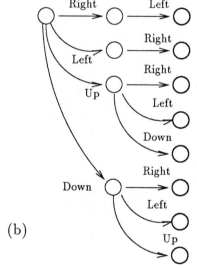

Figure 4: Tree and trie pair. (a) A tree corresponding to a breadth-first search of the grid space. Duplicates indicated by (*). (b) A trie data structure recognizing the duplicate operator strings found in the grid example. The heavy circles represent rejecting (absorbing) states.

tions to make matches, and use the cost of the operator strings to make the choices between the pairs. If we order the operators Right, Left, Up, Down, then the operator sequences that produce duplicate nodes are: Right-Left, Left-Right, Up-Right, Up-Left, Up-Down, Down-Right, Down-Left, and Down-Up (figure 4(a)).

This exploratory phase is a breadth-first search. We repeatedly generate nodes from more and more costlier paths, making matches and choices, and eliminating duplicates. The breadth-first method guarantees that duplicates are detected with the shortest possible operator string that leads to a duplicate, meaning that no duplicate string is a substring of any other. The exploratory phase is terminated by the exhaustion of available storage (in the case of the examples of this paper, disk space).

Construction of the FSM The set of duplicate operator strings can be regarded as a set of forbidden words. If the current search path contains one of these forbidden words, we stop at that point, and prune the rest of the path. Thus, we want to recognize the occurrence of these strings in the search path. The problem is that of recognizing a set of keywords (i.e., the set of strings that will produce duplicates) within a text string (i.e., the string of operators from the root to the current node).

This is the bibliographic search problem. Once the set of duplicate strings to be used is determined, we apply a well known algorithm to automatically create an FSM which recognizes the set [Aho *et al.*, 1986]. In this algorithm, a *trie* (a transition diagram in which each state corresponds to a prefix of a keyword) is constructed from the set of keywords (in this case, the duplicate operator strings). This skeleton is a recognition machine for matching keywords that start at the beginning of the 'text' string. The remaining transitions for mismatches are calculated by a 'failure transition function'. The states chosen on 'failure' are on paths with the greatest match between the suffix of the failed string and the paths of the keyword trie.

A trie constructed from the duplicate string pairs from the grid example is shown in figure 4(b). A machine for recognizing the grid space duplicate string set is shown in figure 3. Notice that the arrows for rejecting duplicate nodes are not shown. As long as the FSM stays on the paths shown, it is producing original (non-duplicate) strings. The trie for the keywords used in its construction contains these rejected paths.

Learning phase requirements All nodes previously generated must be stored, so the space requirement of the breadth-first search is $O(b^d)$, where b is the branching factor, and d is the exploration depth. The actual depth employed will depend on the space available for the exploration phase. The exploration terminates when b^d exceeds available memory or disk space. Duplicate checking can be done at a total cost of $O(N \log N) = O(b^d \log b^d) = O(db^d \log b)$ if the nodes are kept in an indexed data structure, or sorting is employed. This space is not needed during the actual problem-solving search.

The time and space required for the construction of the FSM using a trie and 'failure transition function' is at most $O(l)$, where l is the sum of the lengths of the keywords [Aho et al., 1986].

The breadth-first exploration search is small compared to the size of the depth-first problem-solving search. Asymptotic improvements can be obtained by exploring only a small portion of the problem space, as shown by the grid example. Furthermore, the exploratory phase can be regarded as creating compiled knowledge in a pre-processing step. It only has to be done once, and is amortized over the solutions of multiple problem instances. The results presented below give examples of such savings.

Using the FSM

Incorporating a FSM into a problem-solving depth-first search is efficient in time and memory. For each operator application, checking the acceptance of the operator consists of a few fixed instructions, e.g., a table lookup. The time requirement per node generated is therefore $O(1)$. The memory requirement for the state transition table for the FSM is $O(l)$, where l is the total length of all the keywords found in the exploration phase. The actual number of strings found, and the quality of the resulting pruning, are both functions of the problem description and the depth of the duplicate exploration.

Necessary Conditions for Pruning

We must be careful in pruning a path to preserve at least one optimal solution, although additional optimal solutions may be pruned. The following conditions will guarantee this. If A and B are operator strings, B can be designated a duplicate if: (1) the cost of A is less than or equal to the cost of B, (2) in every case that B can be applied, A can be applied, and (3) A and B always generate identical nodes, starting from a common node.

If these conditions are satisfied, then if B is part of an optimal solution, then A must also be part of an optimal solution. We may lose the possibility of finding multiple solutions of the same cost, however.

In all the examples we have looked at so far, all operators have unit cost, but this is not a requirement of our technique. If different operators have different non-negative costs, we have to make sure that given two different operator strings that generate the same node, the string of higher cost is considered the duplicate. This is done by performing a uniform-cost search [Dijkstra, 1959] to generate the duplicate operator strings, instead of a breadth-first search.

So far, we have assumed that all operators are applicable at all times. However, the Fifteen Puzzle contains operator preconditions. For example, when the

blank is in the upper left corner, moving the blank Left or Up is not valid.

Such preconditions may be dealt with in two steps. For purposes of the exploratory search, a generalized search space is created, which allows all possible operator strings. For the Fifteen Puzzle, this means a representation in which all possible strings in a 4x4 board are valid. This can be visualized as a "Forty-eight Puzzle" board, which is 7x7, with the initial blank position at the center.

The second step is to test the preconditions of matched A and B strings found in the exploratory search. B is a duplicate if the preconditions of A are implied by the preconditons of B. For the Fifteen puzzle, the preconditions of a string are embodied in the starting position of the blank. If the blank moves farther in any direction for string A than for string B, then there are starting positions of the blank for which B is valid, but not A. In that case, B is rejected as a duplicate. A similar logical test may be applied in other domains. A more complete description is given in [Taylor, 1992].

Experimental Results

The Fifteen Puzzle

Positive results were obtained using the FSM method combined with a Manhattan Distance heuristic in solving random Fifteen Puzzle instances.

The Fifteen Puzzle was explored breadth-first to a depth of 14 in searching for duplicate strings. A set of 16,442 strings was found, from which an FSM with 55,441 states was created. The table representation for the FSM required 222,000 words. The inverse operators were found automatically at depth two. The thousands of other duplicate strings discovered represent other non-trivial cycles.

The branching factor is defined as $\lim_{d\to\infty} N(d)/N(d-1)$, where $N(d)$ is the number of nodes are generated at depth d. The branching factor in a brute-force search with just inverse operators eliminated is 2.13. This value has also been derived analytically. Pruning with an FSM, based on a discovery phase to depth 14, improved this to 1.98. The measured branching factor decreased as the depth of the discovery search increased. Note that this is an asymptotic improvement in the complexity of the problem solving search, from $O(2.13^d)$ to $O(1.98^d)$, where d is the depth of the search. Consequently the proportional savings in time for node generations increases with the depth of the solution, and is unbounded. For example, the average optimal solution depth for the Fifteen puzzle is over 50. At this depth, using FSM pruning in brute-force search would save 97.4% of nodes generated.

Iterative-deepening A* using the Manhattan Distance heuristic was applied to the 100 random Fifteen Puzzle instances used in [Korf, 1985]. With only the inverse operators eliminated, an average of 359 million nodes were generated for each instance. The search employing the FSM pruning generated only an average of 100.7 million nodes, a savings of 72%.

This compares favorably with the savings in node generations achieved by node caching techniques applied to IDA*. The FSM uses a small number of instructions per node. If it replaces some method of inverse operator checking, then there is no net decrease in speed. The method of comparing new nodes against those on the current search path involves a significant increase in the cost per node, with only a small increase in duplicates found, compared to the elimination of inverse operators [Dillenburg and Nelson, 1993]. Although it pruned 5% more nodes, the path comparison method ran 17% longer than inverse operator checking. MREC [Sen and Bagchi, 1989], storing 100,000 nodes, reduced node generations by 41% over IDA*, but ran 64% slower per node [Korf, 1993]. An implementation of MA* [Chakrabarti et al., 1989] on the Fifteen Puzzle ran 20 times as slow as IDA*, making it impractical for solving randomly generated problem instances [Korf, 1993].

The creation of the FSM table is an efficient use of time and space. Some millions of nodes were generated in the breadth-first search. Tens of thousands of duplicate strings were found, and these were encoded in a table with some tens of thousands of states. However, as reported above, this led to the elimination of billions of node generations on the harder problems.

In addition to the experiments finding optimal solutions, weighted iterative-deepening A* (WIDA*) was also tested [Korf, 1993]. This is an iterative-deepening search, with a modified evaluation function, $f(x) = g(x) + wh(x)$, where $g(x)$ is length of the path from the root to node x, $h(x)$ is the heuristic estimate of the length of a path from node x to the goal, and w is the weight factor [Pohl, 1970]. Higher weighting allows suboptimal solutions to be found faster. This is the expected effect of relaxing the optimality criteria.

A second effect that beyond a certain value, increasing w increased the number of nodes generated, rather than decreasing it [Korf, 1993]. At $w = 3.0$, for instance, an average of only 59,000 nodes were generated. However, above $w = 7.33$, the number of nodes generated again increased. For a run at $w = 19.0$, WIDA* without pruning generates an average of 1.2 million nodes for each of 100 random puzzle instances. With FSM pruning, the average number of nodes generated is reduced to 5,590, a reduction of 99.4%. The results reported here support the hypothesis that this effect is caused by duplication of nodes through the combinatorial rise of the number of alternative paths to each node.

The Twenty-Four Puzzle

The FSM method was also employed on the Twenty-Four Puzzle. To date, no optimal solution has been found for a randomly generated Twenty-Four Puzzle instance. The exploration phase generated strings up to 13 operators long. A set of 4,201 duplicates strings was created, which produced a FSM with 15,745 states, with a table implementation of 63,000 words.

Weighted Iterative-Deepening A* (WIDA*) was applied to 10 random Twenty-Four Puzzle instances. Previously, average solution lengths of 168 moves (with 1000 problems, but at $w = 3.0$), were the shortest solutions found to that time [Korf, 1993]. With FSM duplicate pruning in WIDA*, the first ten of these problems yielded solutions at $w = 1.50$ weighting. They have an average solution length of 115, and generated an average of 1.66 billion nodes each. These solutions were found using the Manhattan Distance plus linear conflict heuristic function [Hansson et al., 1992], as well as FSM pruning. Without pruning, time limitations would have been exceeded.

The effectiveness of duplicate elimination can be measured at $w = 3.0$ with and without FSM pruning. With Manhattan Distance WIDA* heuristic search, an average of 393,000 nodes each were generated for 100 random puzzle instances. With Manhattan Distance WIDA* plus FSM pruning, an average of only 22,600 were generated, a savings of 94.23%.

Rubik's Cube

For the 2x2x2 Rubik's cube, one corner may be regarded as being fixed, with each of the other cubies participating in the rotations of three free faces. Thus, there are nine operators. The space was explored to depth seven, where 31,999 duplicate strings were discovered. An FSM was created from this set which had 24,954 states. All of the trivial optimizations were discovered automatically as strings of length two. In a brute-force search, there would be a branching factor of 9. Eliminating the inverse operators and consecutive moves of the same face, this is reduced to 6. With the FSM pruning based on a learning phase to depth seven, a branching factor of 4.73 was obtained.

For the full 3x3x3 cube, each of six faces may be rotated either Right, Left, or 180 degrees. This makes a total of 18 operators, which are always applicable. The space was explored to depth 6, where 28,210 duplicate strings were discovered. An FSM was created from this set which had 22,974 states. All of the trivial optimizations were discovered automatically as strings of length two. A number of interesting duplicates were discovered at depths 4 and 5 representing cycles of length 8. For the Rubik's cube without any pruning rules, the branching factor is 18 in a brute-force depth-first search (no heuristic). By eliminating inverse operators, moves of the same face twice in a row, and half of the consecutive moves of non-intersecting faces, the branching factor for depth first search is 13.50. With FSM pruning based on a learning phase to depth seven, a branching factor of 13.26 was obtained.

Related Work

Learning duplicate operator sequences can be compared to the learning of concepts in explanation-based learning (EBL) [Minton, 1990]. These techniques share an exploratory phase of learning, capturing information from a small search which will be used in a larger one. The purpose of these operator sequences, however, is not accomplishment of specific goals, but the avoidance of duplicate nodes. In machine learning terms, we are learning only one class of control information, i.e., control of redundancy [Minton, 1990]. We are learning nothing about success or failure of goals, or about goal interference, at which EBL techniques are directed. The introduction of macros into a search usually means the loss of optimality and an increase in the branching factor; eliminating duplicate sequences preserves optimality, and reduces the branching factor.

EBL-aided searches may be applied to general sets of operators, while the FSM technique of this paper is limited to domains which have sets of operators that may be applied at any point.

Several EBL techniques have used finite state automata for automatic proof generation [Cohen, 1987], or have used similar structures for the compaction of applicability checking for macros [Shavlik, 1990].

Conclusions

We have presented a technique for reducing the number of duplicate nodes generated by a depth-first search. The FSM method begins with a breadth-first search to identify operator strings that produce duplicate nodes. These redundant strings are then used to automatically generate a finite state machine that recognizes and rejects the duplicate strings. The FSM is then used to generate operators in the depth-first search. Producing the FSM is a preprocessing step that does not affect the complexity of the depth-first search. The additional time overhead to use the FSM in the depth-first search is negligible, although the FSM requires memory proportional to the number of states in the machine. This technique reduces the asymptotic complexity of depth-first search on a grid from $O(3^r)$ to $O(r^2)$. On the Fifteen Puzzle, it reduces the brute force branching factor from 2.13 to 1.98, and reduced the time of an IDA* search by 70%. On the Twenty-Four Puzzle, a similar FSM reduced the time of WIDA* by 94.23%. It reduces the branching factor of the 2x2x2 Rubik's Cube from 6 to 4.73, and for the 3x3x3 Cube from 13.50 to 13.26.

References

Aho, A. V.; Sethi, R.; and Ullman, J. D. 1986. *Compilers: Principles, Techniques, and Tools.* Addison-Wesley, Reading, Mass.

Chakrabarti, P. P.; Ghose, S.; Acharya, A.; and de Sarkar, S. C. 1989. Heuristic search in restricted memory. *Artificial Intelligence* 41:197–221.

Cohen, W. W. 1987. A technique for generalizing number in explanation-based learning. Technical Report ML-TR-19, Computer Science Department, Rutgers University, New Brunswick, NJ.

Dijkstra, E. W. 1959. A note on two problems in connexion with graphs. *Numerische Mathematik* 1:269–271.

Dillenburg, J. F. and Nelson, P. C. 1993. Improving the efficiency of depth-first search by cycle elimination. *Information Processing Letters* (forthcoming).

Elkan, C. 1989. Conspiracy numbers and caching for searching and/or trees and theorem-proving. In *Proceedings of IJCAI-89*. 1:341–346.

Hansson, O.; Mayer, A.; and Yung, M. 1992. Criticizing solutions to relaxed models yields powerful admissible heuristics. *Information Sciences* 63(3):207–227.

Hart, P. E.; Nilsson, N. J.; and Raphael, B. 1968. A formal basis for the heuristic determination of minimum cost paths. *IEEE Transactions on Systems Science and Cybernetics* 4(2):100–107.

Ibaraki, T. 1978. Depth_m search in branch and bound algorithms. *International Journal of Computer and Information Science* 7:315–343.

Korf, R. E. 1985. Depth-first iterative deepening: An optimal admissible tree search. *Artificial Intelligence* 27:97–109.

Korf, R. E. 1993. Linear-space best-first search. *Artificial Intelligence*. To appear.

Minton, S. 1990. Quantitative results concerning the utility of explanation-based learning. *Artificial Intelligence* 42(2–3):363–91.

Nilsson, N. J. 1980. *Principles of Artificial Intelligence.* Morgan Kaufman Publishers, Inc., Palo Alto, Calif.

Pearl, J. 1984. *Heuristics.* Addison-Wesley, Reading, Mass.

Pohl, I. 1970. Heuristic search viewed as path finding in a graph. *Artificial Intelligence* 1:193–204.

Sen, A. K. and Bagchi, A. 1989. Fast recursive formulations for best-first search that allow controlled use of memory. In *Proceedings of IJCAI-89*. 1:297–302.

Shavlik, Jude W. 1990. Acquiring recursive and iterative concepts with explanation-based learning. *Machine Learning* 5:39–70.

Taylor, Larry A. 1992. Pruning duplicate nodes in depth-first search. Technical Report CSD-920049, UCLA Computer Science Department, Los Angeles, CA 90024-1596.

Conjunctive Width Heuristics
for Maximal Constraint Satisfaction

Richard J. Wallace and Eugene C. Freuder*

Department of Computer Science

University of New Hampshire, Durham, NH 03824 USA

rjw@cs.unh.edu; ecf@cs.unh.edu

Abstract

A constraint satisfaction problem may not admit a complete solution; in this case a good partial solution may be acceptable. This paper presents new techniques for organizing search with branch and bound algorithms so that maximal partial solutions (those having the maximum possible number of satisfied constraints) can be obtained in reasonable time for moderately sized problems. The key feature is a type of variable-ordering heuristic that combines width at a node of the constraint graph (number of constraints shared with variables already chosen) with factors such as small domain size that lead to inconsistencies in values of adjacent variables. Ordering based on these heuristics leads to a rapid rise in branch and bound's cost function together with local estimates of future cost, which greatly enhances lower bound calculations. Both retrospective and prospective algorithms based on these heuristics are dramatically superior to earlier branch and bound algorithms developed for this domain.

1 Introduction

Constraint satisfaction problems (CSPs) involve finding values for problem variables subject to restrictions on which combinations of values are allowed. They are widely used in AI, in areas ranging from planning to machine vision. Many CSP applications settle for partial solutions, where some constraints remain unsatisfied, either because the problems are overconstrained or because complete solutions require too much time to compute. In fact, such applications generally settle for suboptimal partial solutions; obtaining a solution optimally close to a complete solution can be extremely difficult even for small problems (Freuder & Wallace 1992). In this paper we describe techniques that permit solving many moderately sized optimization problems within practical time bounds. (Smaller problems can be solved quickly enough for real-time applications.)

Maximal constraint satisfaction problems require solutions that optimize the number of satisfied

*This material is based on work supported by the National Science Foundation under Grant No. IRI-9207633.

constraints. Branch and bound methods (cf. Reingold et al. 1977) can be combined with constraint satisfaction techniques to find maximal solutions (Freuder & Wallace 1992) and, unlike hill climbing techniques, branch and bound can guarantee an optimal solution. This paper presents new search order heuristics for branch and bound maximal constraint satisfaction search. These heuristics permit formulation of algorithms that are in many cases markedly superior to previously studied branch and bound maximal constraint satisfaction algorithms.

The design and application of these heuristics embody three key features (using concepts discussed at greater length in subsequent sections):

Conjunctive ordering heuristics based on width: Width at a node in an ordered constraint graph has been shown to be an effective heuristic for CSPs (Dechter & Meiri 1989; there called "cardinality"). Here we show that combining this with other heuristic factors can produce conjunctive heuristics whose power is "greater than the sum of their parts". This is because, in addition to providing the successive filtering that would be expected to improve performance, certain heuristics function synergistically with width to yield a marked reduction in the search space through effective tightening of bounds.

Use of information gained in preprocessing: The effectiveness of these algorithms also depends strongly on measures of arc (in)consistency obtained for each value of each variable during preprocessing. This information is gained cheaply, in one pass through the problem before search begins. It can then used for ordering both values and variables as well as in the calculation of bounds to determine whether a given value is selected during search. While the latter procedure can only be used with retrospective algorithms, e.g., backmarking, ordering based on these measures can also be used with prospective algorithms such as forward checking.

Effective lower bound calculation: Earlier analyses of techniques for calculating lower bounds on the cost of a solution (Freuder & Wallace 1992; Shapiro & Haralick 1981) did not explore the means by which a given component of this calculation could be maximized. In particular, they did not consider the possibility of increasing the cost at the current node of the search tree as rapidly as possibly while *at the same time* maximizing the components of the lower bound that are based on future (uninstantiated) variables. Conjunctive width heuristics promote this dual effect, thus providing a kind of 'one-two punch' that raises the lower bound quickly enough to enhance pruning dramatically. From another viewpoint, this is an extension of the Fail First principle (Haralick & Elliott 1980) to the more subtle problem of lower bound calculation. Somewhat surprisingly, for some classes of problems this allows a retrospective algorithm based on backmarking and local lower bound calculations (RPO, [Freuder & Wallace 1992]) to outperform a prospective algorithm, forward checking, that uses extended lower bound calculations based on all future variables.

In the remaining sections we elucidate these properties and investigate them experimentally. In particular, we present:

(i) a set of experiments with sparse random problems that demonstrates the marked superiority of the new algorithms over the best maximal constraint satisfaction algorithms tested previously and elucidates the basis of this superior performance.

(ii) a second set of experiments that examines the range of problem parameters for which the new algorithms are superior. The parameters of greatest interest are the relative number of constraints between variables and the average *tightness* of the constraints (a tight constraint has few acceptable value-pairs).

Section 2 describes the basic features of all algorithms tested in this study. Section 3 describes results of experiments with an initial set of sparse problems. Sections 4 and 5 analyze the factors that make the new algorithms effective. Section 6 examines the range of problem parameters over which the new algorithms are superior to others. Section 7 gives our conclusions.

2 Description of the Algorithms

The algorithms discussed in this paper are all based on depth-first search with backtracking. These algorithms try to find a value for each variable in the problem drawn from its *domain*, or set of allowable values, so that the number of constraints among variables that cannot be satisfied is minimized. (In this work only binary constraints are considered.) Since these are branch and bound algorithms, they use a cost function related to constraint failure; here, this is simply the number of violated constraints in the solution, called the *distance* from a complete solution. This number is compared with the distance of the best solution found so far to determine whether the current value can be included in the present partial solution. The distance of this best solution is, therefore, an *upper bound* on the allowable cost, while the distance of the current partial solution is an elementary form of *lower bound* (i.e., the cost of a solution that includes the values chosen so far cannot be less than the current distance).

Implementing this strategy in its simplest form results

in a basic branch and bound algorithm, P-BB. More sophisticated strategies are possible that are analogous to those used to solve CSPs. Here, we consider, (i) a backmarking analogue (P-BMK) that saves the increment in distance previously derived for a value, analogous to the "mark" stored by ordinary backmark; this increment can be added to the current distance to limit unnecessary repetition of constraint checking, (ii) a forward checking analogue (P-EFC) in which constraint failures induced by values already selected are counted for each value of the future variables and can be added to the current distance to determinine whether the bound is exceeded; in addition, the sum of the smallest counts for each domain of the uninstantiated variables (other than the one being considered for instantiation) is added to the current distance to form a lower bound based on the entire problem. In this paper we are most concerned with versions of P-EFC which incorporate some form of dynamic search rearrangement. (These algorithms are described more fully in [Freuder & Wallace 1992].)

P-BMK (as well as P-BB) can incorporate tallies of constraint violations based on arc consistency checking prior to search (ACCs, for "arc consistency counts"); specifically, the ACC for a given value is the number of domains that do not support it. These are used in lower bound calculations, much as the counts used in the forward checking analogues. In addition, the values of each domain can be ordered by increasing ACCs so that values with the most support are selected first. Freuder and Wallace (1992) call the resulting algorithm RPO, in reference to its retrospective, prospective and ordering components.

The new algorithms combine the procedures just described with variable orderings based on two or three factors. The first is always the width at a node of the *constraint graph*, that represents the binary relations between variables (represented as nodes). Width at a node is defined as the number of arcs between a node and its predecessors in an ordering of the nodes of a graph (Freuder 1982). The associated heuristic, maximum (node) width, is the selection of the variable with the greatest number of constraints in common with the variables already chosen, as the next to instantiate. In a conjunctive heuristic, ties in maximum width are broken according to a second heuristic, here, either minimum domain size, maximum degree of the node associated with the variable, or largest mean ACC for a domain. Ties in both factors can be broken with a third heuristic which is also one of those just mentioned. In subsequent sections, the order in which these heuristics are applied is indicated by slashes between them: thus, in the width/domain-size/degree heuristic, ties in maximum width are broken by choosing as the next variable one with the smallest domain size, and further ties are broken by choosing the node of largest degree. It is important to note that the first variable to be instantiated is always chosen according to the second or third heuristic, since at the beginning of search all widths are zero.

3 Initial Experiments

In our initial experiments we naturally wanted problems for which the new algorithms would be likely to excel. Earlier evidence suggested that local lower bound calculation would be especially effective with problems that had sparse constraint graphs. At the same time, it was expected that P-EFC would not do as well because, due to the sparseness of the problem, the minimum counts for most future domains would be zero. In addition, we wanted problems with marked heterogeneity in the size of their domains and constraints, to insure a fair amount of inconsistency between adjacent variables.

With these ends in mind, random problems were generated as follows. Number of variables (n) was fixed at either 10, 15 or 20. To obtain sparse problems, the number of constraints was set to be $(n\text{-}1) + \text{ceiling}(n/2)$; therefore, the average degree of nodes in the constraint graph was three. Domain size and constraint satisfiability (number of acceptable value pairs) were determined for each variable and constraint by choosing a number between one and the maximum value allowed, and then choosing from the set of possible elements until the requisite number had been selected. The maximum domain size was set at 9, 12 or 15 for 10-, 15- and 20-variable problems, respectively. Note that domain sizes and constraint satisfiabilities will approximate a rectangular distribution, giving problems that are heterogeneous internally, but with have similar average characteristics. In addition, if two domains had only one element, there could be no effective constraint between them; to avoid this, domain sizes were chosen first, so that this condition could be disallowed when selecting constraints. Twenty-five problems were generated for each value of n. The mean distance for maximal solutions was always 1.2-1.6.

To measure performance we used constraint checks and nodes searched. When the two are correlated or when the former measure predominates, that measure is reported alone. Constraint checks done during preprocessing are always included in the total.

Figure 1 shows the mean performance on these problems for algorithms described in earlier work (Freuder & Wallace 1992; Shapiro & Haralick 1981) and for a conjunctive width heuristic that uses smallest domain size to break ties. First of all, note that P-EFC with dynamic search rearrangement outperforms P-EFC based on random (lexical) ordering (the best algorithm in our earlier work) by two orders of magnitude for larger problems. This is in contrast to the results of Shapiro and Haralick, who found only a slight improvement; however, their problems were more homogeneous and had complete constraint graphs. Results for P-BB and RPO are only given for 10- and 15-variable problems because of the difficulty in obtaining data for the full sample of larger problems. For P-BB, we estimate that it would take between 100 million and one billion constraint checks on average to solve the 20-variable problems.

In general, the conjunctive width algorithm outperforms all others. It requires 10^2 constraint checks on average to find an maximal solution for 10-variable problems, and for 20-variable problems its performance is still on the order of 10^4 constraint checks. In contrast, dynamic forward checking requires 10^5 constraint checks for larger problems. And this is far superior to the performance of the other algorithms. At 20 variables the range in performance covers 4-5 orders of magnitude.

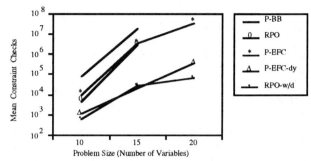

Figure 1. Performance of various algorithm on sparse random problems of varying size.

Table 1 shows results for RPO with conjunctive width heuristics based on two or three heuristic factors, for 15- and 20-variable problems. Dynamic P-EFC algorithms, some of which use value ordering based on ACCs are also shown. The most effective combinations of conjunctive heuristics used mean ACC as the first tie breaker, although at 20 variables domain size was almost as efficient. Degree, used in this capacity, produced results that were of the same order as dynamic P-EFC based on domain size, although this heuristic was sometimes effective as a second tie breaker.

Conjunctive width heuristics were also effective in combination with P-EFC, and the addition of value ordering based on ACCs led to further enhancement. The latter effect was not as large or consistent when value ordering was used with dynamic search order based on domain size; for one 20-variable problem performance was made dramatically worse, which accounted for most of the increase in the mean (cf. Table 1). As a consequence, for larger problems dynamic search rearrangement based on conjunctive width heuristics was markedly superior to the classical strategy of search rearrangement based on domain size.

Timing data was also collected for these heuristics (on a Macintosh SE/30; it was not possible to collect data for all of the weaker heuristics, but they were clearly inefficient overall). In general the pattern of results for this measure resembles that for constraint checks. However, the difference between RPO and P-EFC for a given width heuristic is generally greater than the difference in constraint checks, which indicates that the latter algorithms performed more background work per constraint check.

4 Factorial Analyses

In these new algorithms several factors work together to produce the impressive performance observed. In this section we will attempt to separate the effects of these factors experimentally.

The purpose of the first series of tests was to demonstrate that each of the separate factors did affect performance and to determine the effects of combining them. This required a factorial approach. To this end, P-BB and P-BMK were both tested in their basic form, then with either the domain value ordering based on ACCs or with ACCs used for lower bound calculations during search, and then with both factors. In addition, several ordering heuristics were tested in combination with the other factors. Finally, P-EFC with a fixed variable ordering was tested with the same variable order heuristics, as well as value ordering based on ACCs. These tests were done with the 10-variable problems since there were many conditions to run; in addition, basic features of these comparisons are shown more clearly with these smaller problems.

Table 1
Mean Constraint Checks (and Times) to Find a Maximal Solution for Conjunctive Width Heuristics

heuristics	Number of Variables (measure)		
	15 (10^3 ccks)	20 (10^3 ccks)	20 (secs)
width/dom-sz	27.1	62.8	488
width/mean-ACC	5.7	46.0	362
width/dom-sz/mean-ACC	18.1	40.3	325
width/dom-sz/degree	21.6	36.5	293
width/mean-ACC/dom-sz	4.9	35.6	240
width/mean-ACC/degree	5.6	36.3	343
width/degree/dom-sz	36.5	493.7	--
width/degree/mean-ACC	42.5	330.2	--
dynamic P-EFC - dom-sz	20.9	336.9	3098
dynam. P-EFC - dom-sz (val)	16.7	722.4	--
dynam. P-EFC - wid/dom/AC	65.1	83.0	--
dyn. P-EFC -wid/dm/AC(val)	46.0	53.7	584
dynam. P-EFC -wid/AC/dom	28.6	187.1	--
dyn. P-EFC -wid/AC/dm (val)	7.0	38.9	274

Of the many interesting features of the results (see Tables 2a and 2b) these will be noted:

(i) each of the factors, variable ordering, value ordering and use of ACCs during search, has an effect on performance (compare entries along a row); moreover, these effects can be combined to produce more impressive performance than is obtained in isolation. This is true for P-BMK as well as the basic branch and bound (P-BB).

Table 2a
Factorial Analysis of Branch and Bound Variants
(Mean Constraint Checks in 1000s)

Variable Order	P-BB	BB/val	BB/ACC	BB/ACC/v
lexical	69.8	42.9	17.1	9.5
domsz	21.0	16.0	5.9	6.7
width	6.4	3.4	1.8	1.2
mean-ACC	31.6	12.2	20.1	2.3
dom/wid	14.6	12.7	4.7	4.3
dom/ACC	14.2	13.6	4.9	5.1
wid/dom	3.7	2.5	1.5	0.8
wid/ACC	2.5	1.1	1.8	0.7

Table 2b
Factorial Analysis of Backmark and P-EFC Variants
(Mean Constraint Checks in 1000s)

Var. Order	BM	BM/v	BM/AC	BM/AC/v	EFC	EFC/v
lexical	17.1	10.6	6.8	4.5	9.6	5.5
domsz	1.4	1.8	1.0	1.2	1.0	1.1
width	2.7	1.6	1.1	0.8	2.5	1.6
mean-ACC	9.6	4.5	6.3	0.8	1.0	0.6
dom/wid	1.4	1.5	0.9	0.8	0.7	0.8
dom/ACC	1.5	1.7	1.0	1.1	0.9	0.7
wid/dom	1.2	1.1	0.8	0.6	1.1	1.1
wid/ACC	0.7	0.6	0.8	0.5	0.8	0.6

(ii) For P-BB, width at a node is superior to the other variable ordering heuristics tested. In addition, conjunctive heuristics improve performance for both width and domain size, with the former retaining its superiority.

(iii) For P-BMK the superiority of width is not as apparent when constraint checks alone are considered. However, the means for the domain size heuristic do not reflect the larger number of nodes searched. (BMK avoids many constraint checks in this case with its table lookup techniques.) At the same time, conjunctive width heuristics are consistently superior to conjunctive domain heuristics.

(iv) Width and conjunctive width heuristics are more consistently enhanced by the combination of ACCs and value ordering than other variable ordering heuristics. In this combination, they also usually outperform forward checking based on the same heuristic.

For larger problems, the trends observed with smaller problems were greatly exacerbated, and at 20-variables it was difficult to obtain data for all problems with RPO based on domain size or mean ACCs. (For both simple and conjunctive two-tiered heuristics based on domain size or mean ACC, the number of constraint checks and nodes searched reached eight or nine orders of magnitude for some problems.) For this reason, these heuristics will not be discussed further.

In addition, for larger problems the simple width heuristic is less effective overall (for 20-variable problems it was not appreciably better than dynamic forward checking), and it is here that conjunctive heuristics based on width afford significant improvement. There is also a minority of the problems of larger size that cannot be solved without an extraordinary amount of effort by either the 'pure algorithms' or by some of the partial combinations; however, at least one of the strategies that make up a combination is usually very effective. Both effects are observed for two difficult problems in the 20-variable group (Table 3; for problem #3, the width/domain-size/mean-ACC ordering gave the same results as width/domain-size). In both cases P-BMK based on width alone does poorly. For problem #3, either conjunctive ordering or use of ACCs has some effect, but not enough to make the problem easy; however, ordering domain values makes the problem trivial. In contrast, this strategy has almost no effect on problem #10 when used alone; conjunctive ordering and ACCs are both effective, and in combination with these strategies, value ordering affords further improvement, so that this problem also becomes relatively easy to solve.

Table 3
Factorial Analysis for Individual 20-Variable Problems

| | | Problem #3 | | Problem #10 | | |
		width	wid/dom	width	wid/do	w/d/ ACC
BMK	BT	84E6	36E6	18E6	4E5	9E4
	CCK	159E6	2E6	62E6	1E6	3E5
/val	BT	4E2	2E2	18E6	4E5	4E4
	CCK	1E3	8E2	60E6	1E6	1E5
/ACC	BT	53E6	31E6	2E6	1E5	4E4
	CCK	45E6	2E6	4E6	3E5	9E4
RPO	BT	1E2	1E2	2E6	1E5	1E4
	CCK	2E2	3E2	4E6	2E5	2E4

Combination algorithms are therefore effective in part because they 'cover all the bases'. However, this does not explain the peculiar effectiveness of the conjunctive width

heuristics, and there is still the question of how the different factors actually enhance branch and bound. These questions are treated in the next section.

5 Analysis of Individual Strategies

The analyses in this section assess the effects of different factors on the upper and lower bounds that are used during search, as well as interactions between factors with respect to these bounds. For ease of analysis and exposition this discussion is restricted to retrospective algorithms.

Value ordering based on ACCs should insure that good solutions are found sooner, which will reduce the upper bound more quickly. This is confirmed by the results in Figure 2, which also shows that this reduction is independent of either the variable orderings or the inclusion of ACCs in the lower bound. With this form of value ordering, a maximal solution is obtained by the fifth try in all but two of the 25 ten-variable problems. Similar results were found with larger problems.

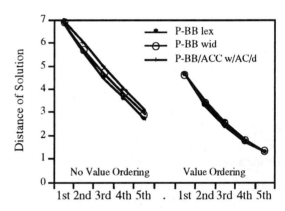

Figure 2. Mean distance (upper bound) after successive solutions found during search, with and without value ordering by increasing AC counts (10-variable problems). When a solution before the fifth was maximal, its distance was used in later group means.e 15-variable problems.

Variable ordering can influence lower bound calculations by affecting either the increase in distance (current cost) or the projected costs based on ACCs (or FC counts). To see this we will consider three orderings: lexical (a random ordering), ordering by selecting the variable with the highest mean ACC (a straightforward Fail First strategy), and the width/domain-size ordering. Figure 3 shows mean ACC as a function of position in the variable ordering for the 10-variable problems. This is the expected value to be added to the current distance in calculating the lower bound. As expected, lexical ordering shows no trend in this measure, while ordering by mean ACC shows a steep decline from the first position to the last. The width/domain-size ordering shows a sharp rise from the first to the second position, reflecting the fact that the smallest domains are almost completely supported;

thereafter, there are no obvious trends for the entire set of problems.

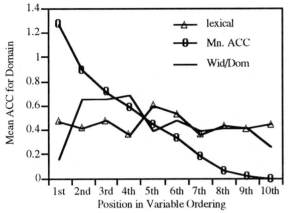

Figure 3. Mean ACCs at successive positions in variable ordering for three ordering heuristics, based on the 10-variable problems.

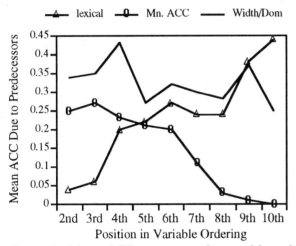

Figure 4. Mean ACCs at successive positions in variable ordering due to variables selected earlier in the search order for three ordering heuristics, based on the 10-variable problems.

Figure 4 shows a further analysis for the same problems, the mean ACC at each position due to variables that *precede* the one in question. This is the expected increase in distance that will be found during consistency checking for a value from the domain of this variable. The important points are, (i) for lexical ordering, ACCs are not translated into immediate increases in the distance until late in search, (ii) for mean ACC ordering, there is relatively little transformation of this sort (as a proportion of the mean ACC) and none late in search. To a great extent, this heuristic puts 'all its eggs in one basket' by maximizing the increase in the lower bound due to the ACC; if this strategy fails, search is likely to be very inefficient, (iii) width/domain-size ordering gives a relatively high rate of transformation of this sort

throughout the search. Since the average ACC for this ordering heuristic is also relatively high throughout search, this heuristic tends to increase the lower bound through effects on both current distance and prospective components (giving a "one-two punch" via this bound).

These analyses indicate that conjunctive width orderings are effective when they place variables likely to produce inconsistencies and ACCs (e.g., those with small domain sizes) just ahead of variables that are adjacent and are, therefore, likely to have inconsistent values. This sets up the one-two punch effect described above.

6 Varying Parameter Values

The methods described in (Freuder & Wallace 1992) were used to generate random problems varying in number of arcs in the constraint graph as well as tightness of constraints and domain size. These methods generate problems for which the expected value of these parameters can be specified, and values tend to be normally distributed around the expectations. In this discussion, number of arcs will be described in terms of the average degree of a node in the constraint graph. All problems had 20 variables; the expected degree was 3, 4, 5 or 7; the expected domain size was either 2 or 4; and for each problem density (expected degree) there were three values of tightness that differed by 0.1, beginning with the smallest value for which it was relatively easy to get problems with no solutions. In the latter case, the mean distance for maximal solutions was 2-3; for the maximum tightness the mean distance was 7-12. RPO with width/domain-size/mean-ACC was compared with four versions of dynamic forward checking, using either search rearrangement based on domain size or on the width/domain-size/mean-ACC heuristic and with or without prior value ordering based on ACCs. (Note. With this method, it was possible to generate constraints with all possible pairs; this happened with some of the smaller values for tightness. However, there were never more than a few such constraints in any problem.)

For problems of expected degree 3 (equal to that of the initial set), RPO was always better than dynamic P-EFC based on domain size, usually by an order of magnitude (e.g., 7774 ccks on average vs. 66,035 for tightness = 0.7). Hence, the effectiveness of RPO does not depend on such pecularities of the first set of problems as inclusion of variables with very small domain sizes and small maximal distances. Problem difficulty increased with constraint tightness; for the most difficult problems RPO and dynamic P-EFC using width/domain-size/mean-ACC and value ordering had about the same efficiency (71,036 vs. 68,502 mean ccks, respectively, for tightness = 0.8).

Dynamic P-EFC based on domain size did better with respect to RPO as the density of the constraint graph increased; however, the point of crossover between them varied depending on constraint tightness. For problems of low tightness (easier problems) the crossover was between 4 and 5 degrees; for problems with tighter constraints it was around 5 degrees. There was evidence that dynamic P-

EFC based on width/domain-size/mean-ACC outperforms dynamic P-EFC based on domain size up to an average degree of 7 (e.g., for the tightest constraint at degree 5, mean ccks were 220,865 and 348,074, respectively, for these algorithms).

Thus, algorithms with conjunctive heuristics outperform all others on random problems with average degree ≤ 4. Within this range, forward checking tends to be the best algorithm for problems with higher density and greater average constraint tightness, and RPO is best for problems of lower density and looser constraints. As density (average degree) increases, dynamic P-EFC based on domain size eventually predominates; this occurs sooner for problems with looser constraints (which are easier problems for these algorithms). In contrast to Experiment 1 this standard algorithm was also improved when values were ordered according to ACCs.

7 Conclusions

Conjunctive width heuristics can enhance branch and bound algorithms based on either prospective or retrospective strategies. In combination with preprocessing techniques, the resulting algorithms outperform other branch and bound algorithms by at least one order of magnitude on a large class of problems. Maximal solutions can now be obtained for some problems of moderate size (20-30 variables, depending on specific parameter values) in reasonable times. Since branch and bound can return the best solution found so far at any time during search [Freuder & Wallace 92], these new algorithms may also perform well in relation to existing algorithms that find nonoptimal solutions (e.g., [Feldman & Golumbic 90]), for an even larger class of problems.

References

Dechter, R., and Meiri, I. 1989. Experimental evaluation of preprocessing techniques in constraint satisfaction problems, In *Proceedings IJCAI-89*, Detroit, MI, p. 271-277.

Feldman, R., and Golumbic, M.C. 1990. Optimization algorithms for student scheduling via constraint satisfiability. *Comput. J.*, 33: 356-364.

Freuder, E.C. 1982. A sufficient condition for backtrack-free search. *J. Assoc. Comput. Mach.*, 29: 24-32.

Freuder, E., and Wallace, R.J. 1992. Partial constraint satisfaction. *Artif. Intell.*, 58: 21-70.

Haralick, R.M., and Elliott, G.L. 1980. Increasing tree search efficiency for constraint satisfaction problems. *Artific. Intell.*, 14: 263-313.

Reingold, E.M., Nievergelt, J., and Deo, N. 1977. *Combinatorial Algorithms. Theory and Practice.* Englewood Cliffs, NJ: Prentice-Hall.

Shapiro, L., and Haralick, R. 1981. Structural descriptions and inexact matching. *IEEE Trans. Pattern Anal. Machine Intell.*, 3: 504-519

Depth-First vs. Best-First Search: New Results *

Weixiong Zhang and *Richard E. Korf*
Computer Science Department
University of California, Los Angeles
Los Angeles, CA 90024
zhang@cs.ucla.edu, korf@cs.ucla.edu

ABSTRACT

Best-first search (BFS) expands the fewest nodes among all admissible algorithms using the same cost function, but typically requires exponential space. Depth-first search needs space only linear in the maximum search depth, but expands more nodes than BFS. Using a random tree, we analytically show that the expected number of nodes expanded by depth-first branch-and-bound (DFBnB) is no more than $O(d \cdot N)$, where d is the goal depth and N is the expected number of nodes expanded by BFS. We also show that DFBnB is asymptotically optimal when BFS runs in exponential time. We then consider how to select a linear-space search algorithm, from among DFBnB, iterative-deepening (ID) and recursive best first search (RBFS). Our experimental results indicate that DFBnB is preferable on problems that can be represented by bounded-depth trees and require exponential computation; and RBFS should be applied to problems that cannot be represented by bounded-depth trees, or problems that can be solved in polynomial time.

1 Introduction and Overview

A major factor affecting the applicability of a search algorithm is its memory requirement. If a problem is small, and the available memory is large enough, then best-first search (BFS) may be used. BFS maintains a partially expanded search graph, and expands a minimum-cost frontier node at each cycle until an optimal goal node is chosen for expansion. One important property of BFS is that it expands the minimum number of nodes among all admissible algorithms using the same cost function [2]. However, it typically requires

*This research was supported by NSF Grant No. IRI-9119825, a grant from Rockwell International, and a GTE fellowship.

exponential space, making it impractical for most applications.

Practical algorithms use space that is only linear in the maximum search depth. Linear-space algorithms include depth-first branch-and-bound (DFBnB), iterative-deepening [4], and recursive best-first search [6, 7]. DFBnB starts with an upper bound on the cost of an optimal goal, and then searches the entire state space in a depth-first fashion. Whenever a new solution is found whose cost is less than the best one found so far, the upper bound is revised to the cost of this new solution. Whenever a partial solution is encountered whose cost is greater than or equal to the current upper bound, it is pruned. DFBnB expands more nodes than BFS. In particular, when the cost function is monotonic, in the sense that the cost of a child is always greater than or equal to the cost of its parent, DFBnB may expand nodes whose costs are greater than the optimal goal cost, none of which are explored by BFS.

To avoid expanding nodes that are not visited by BFS, iterative-deepening (ID) [4] may be adopted. It runs a series of depth-first iterations, each bounded by a cost threshold. In each iteration, a branch is eliminated when the cost of a node on that path exceeds the cost threshold for that iteration. When the cost function is not monotonic, however, ID may not expand newly visited nodes in best-first order.

In this case, recursive best-first search (RBFS) [6, 7] may be applied, which always expands unexplored nodes in best-first order, using only linear space, (cf. [6, 7] for details.) Another advantage of RBFS over ID is that the former expands fewer nodes than the latter, up to tie-breaking, when the cost function is monotonic. Both ID and RBFS suffer from the overhead of expanding many nodes more than once.

Some of these algorithms have been compared before. Wah and Yu [14] argued that DFBnB is comparable to BFS if the cost function is very accurate or very inaccurate. Using an abstract model in which the number of nodes with a given cost grows geometrically, Vempaty *et al* [13] compared BFS, DFBnB and ID.

Their results are based on the solution density, the ratio of the number of goal nodes to the total number of nodes with the same cost as the goal nodes, and the heuristic branching factor, the ratio of the number of nodes with a given cost to the number of nodes of the next smaller cost. They concluded that: (a) DFBnB is preferable when the solution density grows faster than the heuristic branching factor; (b) ID is preferable when the heuristic branching factor is high and the solution density is low; (c) BFS is useful only when both the solution density and the heuristic branching factor are very low, provided that sufficient memory is available. Using a random tree, in which edges have random costs, and the cost of a node is the sum of the costs of the edges on the path from the root to the node, Karp and Pearl[3], and McDiarmid and Provan [10, 11] showed that BFS expands either an exponential or quadratic number of nodes in the search depth, depending on certain properties. On a random tree with uniform branching factor and discrete edge costs, we argued in [15] that DFBnB also runs in polynomial time when BFS runs in quadratic time. Kumar originally observed that ID performs poorly on the traveling salesman problem (TSP), compared to DFBnB [13] (cf. Section 4.2 as well).

Although DFBnB is very useful for problems such as the TSP, it is not known how many more nodes DF-BnB expands than BFS on average. Using a random tree, we analytically show that the expected number of nodes expanded by DFBnB is no more than $O(d \cdot N)$, where d is the goal depth and N is the expected number of nodes expanded by BFS (Section 2). We compare BFS, DFBnB, ID and RBFS under the tree model, and demonstrate that DFBnB runs faster than BFS in some cases, even if the former expands more nodes than the latter (Section 3). The purpose is to provide a guideline for selecting algorithms for given problems. Finally, we consider how to choose linear-space algorithms for two applications, lookahead search on sliding-tile puzzles, and the asymmetric TSP (Section 4). Our results in Sections 2 and 3 are included in [16].

2 Analytic Results: DFBnB vs. BFS

Search in a state space is a general model for problem solving. While a graph with cycles is the most general model of a state space, depth-first search explores a state space *tree*, at the cost of regenerating the same nodes arrived at via different paths. This is a fundamental difference between linear-space algorithms, which cannot detect duplicate nodes in general, and exponential-space algorithms, which can. Associated with a state space is a cost function that estimates the cost of a node. Alternatively, a cost can be associated with an edge, representing the incremental change to a node cost when the corresponding operator is applied. A node cost is then computed as the sum of the edge costs on the path from the root to the node, or the sum of the cost of its parent node and the cost of the

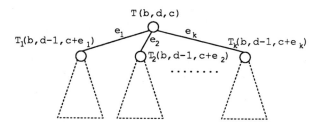

Figure 1: Recursive structure of a random tree

edge from the parent to the child. Therefore, we introduce the following tree model, which is suitable for any combinatorial problem with a monotonic cost function.

Definition 2.1 *A random tree $T(b, d, c)$ is a tree with depth d, root cost c, and independent and identically distributed random branching factors with mean b. Edge costs are independently drawn from a non-negative probability distribution. The cost of a non-root node is the sum of the edge costs from the root to that node, plus the root cost c. An* optimal goal node *is a node of minimum cost at depth d.*

Lemma 2.1 *Let $N_B(b, d)$ be the expected number of nodes expanded by BFS, and $N_D(b, d, \alpha)$ the expected number of nodes expanded by DFBnB with initial upper bound α, on $T(b, d, 0)$. As $d \to \infty$,*

$$N_D(b, d, \infty) \le (b - 1) \sum_{i=1}^{d-1} N_B(b, i) + (d - 1)$$

Proof: As shown in Figure 1, the root of $T(b, d, c)$ has k children, $n_1, n_2, ..., n_k$, where k is a random variable with mean b. Let e_i be the edge cost from the root of $T(b, d, c)$ to the root of its i-th subtree $T_i(b, d-1, c+e_i)$, for $i = 1, 2, ..., k$. The children of the root are generated all at once and sorted in nondecreasing order of their costs. Thus $e_1 \le e_2 \le ... \le e_k$, arranged from left to right in Figure 1. For convenience of discussion, let $N_D(b, d, c, \alpha)$ be the expected number of nodes expanded by DFBnB on $T(b, d, c)$ with initial upper bound α. We first make the following two observations.

First, subtracting the root cost from all nodes and the upper bound has no affect on the search. Therefore, the number of nodes expanded by DFBnB on $T(b, d, c)$ with initial upper bound α is equal to those expanded on $T(b, d, 0)$ with initial upper bound $\alpha - c$. That is

$$\left. \begin{array}{l} N_D(b, d, c, \alpha) = N_D(b, d, 0, \alpha - c) \\ N_D(b, d, c, \infty) = N_D(b, d, 0, \infty) \end{array} \right\} \quad (1)$$

Secondly, because a larger initial upper bound causes at least as many nodes to be expanded as a smaller upper bound, the number of nodes expanded by DFBnB on $T(b, d, c)$ with initial upper bound α is no less than the number expanded with initial upper bound $\alpha' \le \alpha$. That is

$$N_D(b, d, c, \alpha') \le N_D(b, d, c, \alpha), \quad \text{for } \alpha' \le \alpha \quad (2)$$

Now consider DFBnB on $T(b, d, 0)$. It first searches the subtree $T_1(b, d-1, e_1)$ (see Figure 1), expanding $N_D(b, d-1, e_1, \infty)$ expected number of nodes. Let ρ be the minimum goal cost of $T_1(b, d-1, 0)$. Then the minimum goal cost of $T_1(b, d-1, e_1)$ is $\rho + e_1$, which is the upper bound after searching $T_1(b, d-1, e_1)$. After $T_1(b, d-1, e_1)$ is searched, subtree $T_2(b, d-1, e_2)$ will be explored if its root cost e_2 is less than the current upper bound $\rho + e_1$, and the expected number of nodes expanded is $N_D(b, d-1, e_2, \rho + e_1)$, which is also an upper bound on the expected number of nodes expanded in $T_i(b, d-1, e_i)$, for $i = 3, 4, ..., k$. This is because the upper bound can only decrease after searching $T_2(b, d-1, e_2)$ and the edge cost e_i can only increase as i increases, both of which cause fewer nodes to be expanded. Since the root of $T(b, d, 0)$ has b expected number of children, we write

$$N_D(b, d, 0, \infty) \leq N_D(b, d-1, e_1, \infty) +$$
$$(b-1)N_D(b, d-1, e_2, \rho + e_1) + 1$$

where the 1 is for the expansion of the root of $T(b, d, 0)$. By (1), we have

$$N_D(b, d, 0, \infty) \leq N_D(b, d-1, 0, \infty) +$$
$$(b-1)N_D(b, d-1, 0, \rho + e_1 - e_2) + 1$$

Since $\rho + e_1 - e_2 \leq \rho$ for $e_1 \leq e_2$, by (2), we write

$$N_D(b, d, 0, \infty) \leq N_D(b, d-1, 0, \infty) +$$
$$(b-1)N_D(b, d-1, 0, \rho) + 1 \qquad (3)$$

Now consider $N_D(b, d-1, 0, \rho)$, the expected number of nodes expanded by DFBnB on $T(b, d-1, 0)$ with initial upper bound ρ. If $T(b, d-1, 0)$ is searched by BFS, it will return the optimal goal node whose expected cost is ρ, and expand $N_B(b, d-1)$ nodes on average. When $T(b, d-1, 0)$ is searched by DFBnB with upper bound ρ, only those nodes whose costs are strictly less than ρ will be expanded, which also must be expanded by BFS. We thus have

$$N_D(b, d-1, 0, \rho) \leq N_B(b, d-1) \qquad (4)$$

Substituting (4) into (3), we then write

$$N_D(b, d, 0, \infty) \leq N_D(b, d-1, 0, \infty) +$$
$$(b-1)N_B(b, d-1) + 1$$
$$\leq N_D(b, d-2, 0, \infty) +$$
$$(b-1)(N_B(b, d-1) + N_B(b, d-2)) + 2$$
$$\leq ...$$
$$\leq N_D(b, 0, 0, \infty) +$$
$$(b-1)\sum_{i=1}^{d-1} N_B(b, i) + (d-1) \qquad (5)$$

This proves the lemma since $N_D(b, 0, 0, \infty) = 0$. □

Theorem 2.1 $N_D(b, d, \infty) < O(d \cdot N_B(b, d-1))$, where N_D and N_B are defined in Lemma 2.1.

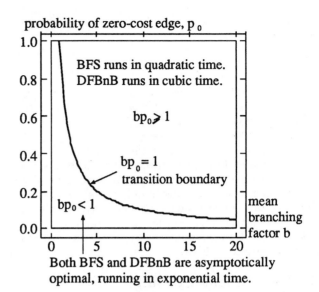

probability of zero-cost edge, p_0

BFS runs in quadratic time.
DFBnB runs in cubic time.

$bp_0 > 1$

$bp_0 = 1$
transition boundary

$bp_0 < 1$

mean branching factor b

Both BFS and DFBnB are asymptotically optimal, running in exponential time.

Figure 2: Complexity regions of tree search.

Proof: It directly follows Lemma 2.1 and the fact that $\sum_{i=1}^{d-1} N_B(b, i) < (d-1)N_B(b, d-1)$, since $N_B(b, i) < N_B(b, d-1)$ for all $i < d-1$. □

McDiarmid and Provan [10, 11] showed that if p_0 is the probability of a zero-cost edge, then the average complexity of BFS on $T(b, d, c)$ is determined by bp_0, the expected number of children of a node whose costs are the same as their parents. In particular, they proved that as $d \to \infty$, and conditional on the tree not becoming extinct, the expected number of nodes expanded by BFS is: (a) $O(\beta^d)$ when $bp_0 < 1$, where $1 < \beta < b$ is a constant; (b) $O(d^2)$ when $bp_0 = 1$, and (c) $O(d)$ when $bp_0 > 1$.

Theorem 2.2 *The expected number of nodes expanded by DFBnB on $T(b, d, 0)$, as $d \to \infty$, conditional on $T(b, d, 0)$ being infinite, is: (a) $O(\beta^d)$, when $bp_0 < 1$, where $1 < \beta < b$ is a constant; (b) $O(d^3)$ when $bp_0 = 1$, and (c) $O(d^2)$ when $bp_0 > 1$, where p_0 is the probability of a zero-cost edge.*

Proof: To use McDiarmid and Provan's result on BFS [10, 11], we have to consider the asymptotic case when $d \to \infty$. Generally, searching a deep tree is more difficult than searching a shallow one. In particular, $N_B(b, i) < N_B(b, 2i)$, for all integers i. Therefore, by Lemma 2.1 and McDiarmid and Provan's result, when $bp_0 < 1$ and $d \to \infty$,

$$N_D(b, d, 0) < 2(b-1)\sum_{i=\lfloor d/2 \rfloor}^{d-1} N_B(b, i) + (d-1)$$

$$= 2(b-1)\sum_{i=\lfloor d/2 \rfloor}^{d-1} O(\beta^i) + (d-1) = O(\beta^d)$$

The other two cases directly follow from Theorem 2.1 and McDiarmid and Provan's results on BFS. □

This theorem significantly extends and tightens our previous result in [15], which stated that the average complexity of DFBnB is $O(d^{m+1})$ on a random tree with constant branching factor, discrete edge costs $\{0, 1, 2, ..., m\}$ and $bp_0 \geq 1$. Theorem 2.2 indicates that DFBnB is asymptotically optimal as the depth of the tree grows to infinity when $bp_0 < 1$, since it expands the same order of nodes as BFS in this case, and BFS is optimal [2]. In addition, this theorem shows that, similar to BFS, the average complexity of DFBnB experiences a transition as the expected number of same-cost children bp_0 of a node changes. Specifically, it decreases from exponential ($bp_0 < 1$) to polynomial ($bp_0 \geq 1$) with a transition boundary at $bp_0 = 1$. These results are summarized in Figure 2.

3 Experimental Results

3.1 Comparison of Nodes Expanded

We now experimentally compare BFS, DFBnB, ID and RBFS on random trees. We used random trees with uniform branching factor, and two edge cost distributions. In the first case, edge costs were uniformly selected from $\{0, 1, 2, 3, 4\}$. In the second case, zero edge costs were chosen with probability $p_0 = 1/5$, and non-zero edge costs were uniformly chosen from $\{1, 2, 3, ...2^{16} - 1\}$. The comparison of these algorithms on trees with continuous edge cost distributions is similar to that with the second edge cost distribution and $bp_0 < 1$, because a continuous distribution has $p_0 = 0$, and thus $bp_0 < 1$. We chose three branching factors to present the results: $b = 2$ for an exponential complexity case, $b = 5$ for the transition case ($bp_0 = 1$), and $b = 10$ for an easy problem. The algorithms were run to different depths, each with 100 random trials. The results are shown in Fig. 3. The curves labeled by BFS, DFBnB, ID, and RBFS are the average numbers of nodes expanded by BFS, DFBnB, ID, and RBFS, respectively. The upper bound on DFBnB is based on Lemma 2.1.

The experimental results are consistent with the analytical results: BFS expands the fewest nodes among all algorithms, RBFS is superior to ID, and DFBnB is asymptotically optimal when $bp_0 < 1$ and tree depth grows to infinity. When $bp_0 > 1$ (Fig. 3(c) and 3(f)), ID and RBFS are comparable to BFS. Moreover, when $bp_0 \geq 1$ (Fig. 3(b), 3(c), 3(e) and 3(f)), DFBnB is worse than both ID and RBFS. In these cases, the overhead of DFBnB, the number of nodes expanded whose costs are greater than the optimal goal cost, is larger than the re-expansion overheads of ID and RBFS. When $bp_0 < 1$ (Fig. 3(a) and 3(d)), however, DFBnB outperforms both ID and RBFS. In addition, when $bp_0 < 1$ and the edge costs are discrete (Fig. 3(a)), the DFBnB, ID and RBFS curves are parallel to the BFS curve for

large search depth d. Thus DFBnB, ID and RBFS are asymptotically optimal, and this confirms our analysis of ID and RBFS in [16]. However, when $bp_0 < 1$ and edge costs are chosen from a large range (Fig. 3(d)), the slopes of the ID and RBFS curves are nearly twice the slope of the BFS curve, in contrast to the DFBnB curve that has the same slope as the BFS curve. This confirms our analytical result that ID expands $O(N^2)$ nodes on average when edge costs are continuous, where N is the expected number of nodes expanded by BFS [16]. This also indicates that in this case, RBFS has the same unfavorable asymptotical complexity as ID.

In summary, for problems that can be formulated as a tree with a bounded depth, and require exponential computation ($bp_0 < 1$), DFBnB should be used, and for easy problems ($bp_0 \geq 1$), RBFS should be adopted.

3.2 Comparison of Running Times

Although BFS expands fewer nodes than a linear-space algorithm, the former may run slower than the latter. Fig. 4(a) shows one example where the running time of BFS increases faster than that of DFBnB: a random binary tree in which zero edge costs were chosen with probability $p_0 = 1/5$, and non-zero edge costs were uniformly chosen from $\{1, 2, 3, ...2^{16} - 1\}$. The reason is the following. The running time of DFBnB is proportional to the total number of nodes generated, since nodes can be generated and processed in constant time. The other linear-space algorithms also have this feature. The time of BFS to process a node, however, increases as the logarithm of the total number of nodes generated. To see this, consider the time per node expansion in BFS as a function of search depth. BFS has to use a priority queue to keep all nodes generated but not expanded yet, which is exponential in the search depth, say γ^d, when $bp_0 < 1$. To expand a node, BFS first has to select the node with the minimum cost from the priority queue, and then insert all newly generated nodes into the queue. If a heap is used, to insert one node or delete the root of the heap takes time logarithmic in the total number of nodes in the heap, which is $\ln(\gamma^d) = O(d)$. This means that BFS takes time linear in the search depth to expand a node. Fig. 4(b) illustrates the average time per node expansion for both BFS and DFBnB in this case. Therefore, for some problems, BFS is not only unapplicable because of its exponential space requirement, but also suffers from increasing time per node expansion.

4 Comparison on Real Problems

4.1 Lookahead Search on Sliding-Tile Puzzles

A square sliding-tile puzzle consists of a $k \times k$ frame holding $k^2 - 1$ distinct movable tiles, and a blank space. Any tiles that are horizontally or vertically adjacent to the blank may move into the blank position. Examples of sliding-tile puzzles include the 3×3 Eight Puzzle, the

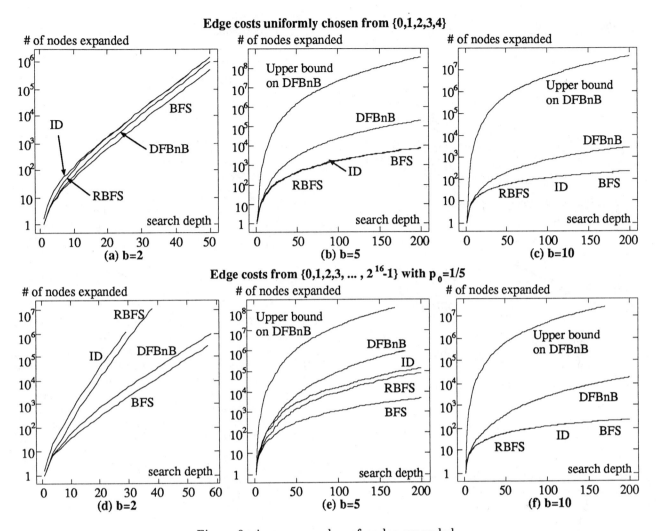

Figure 3: Average number of nodes expanded.

4 × 4 Fifteen Puzzle, the 5 × 5 Twenty-four Puzzle, and the 10 × 10 Ninety-nine Puzzle. A common cost function for sliding-tile puzzles is $f(n) = g(n) + h(n)$, where $g(n)$ is the number of moves from the initial state to node n, and $h(n)$ is the Manhattan distance from node n to the goal state, which is the sum of the number of moves along the grid of all tiles to their goal positions. Given an initial and a goal state of a sliding-tile puzzle, we are asked to find a sequence of moves that maps the initial state into the final state. To find such a sequence with minimum number of moves is NP-complete for arbitrary size puzzles [12].

In real-time settings, however, we have to make a move with limited computation. One approach to this problem, called *fixed-depth lookahead search*, is to search from the current state to a fixed depth, and then make a move toward a minimum cost frontier node at that depth. This process is then repeated for each move until a goal is reached [5].

Our experiments show that ID is slightly worse than RBFS for lookahead search, as expected. Figure 5 compares DFBnB and RBFS. The horizontal axis is the lookahead depth, and the vertical axis is the number of nodes expanded, averaged over 200 initial states. The results show that DFBnB performs better than RBFS on small puzzles, while RBFS is superior to DFBnB on large ones. The reason is briefly explained as follows. Moving a tile either increases or decreases its Manhattan distance h by one. Since every move increases the g value by one, the cost function $f = g + h$ either increases by two or stays the same. The probability that the cost of a child state is equal to the cost of its parent is approximately 0.5 initially, *i.e.* $p_0 \approx 0.5$. In addition, the average branching factors b of the Eight, Fifteen, Twenty-four, and Ninety-nine Puzzles are approximately 1.732, 2.130, 2.368, and 2.790, respectively, *i.e.* b grows with the puzzle size. Thus, bp_0 increases with the puzzle size as well, and lookahead search is

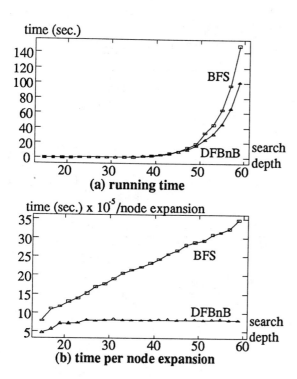

Figure 4: Running time and time per node expansion.

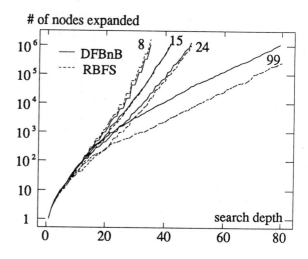

Figure 5: Lookahead search on sliding-tile puzzles.

easier on large puzzles by Theorem 2.2. As shown in Section 3, DFBnB will do better with smaller branching factors.

Unfortunately, the problem of finding a shortest solution path cannot be represented by a bounded-depth tree, since the solution length is unknown in advance. Without cutoff bounds, DFBnB cannot be applied in these cases. This limits the applicability of DFBnB, and distinguishes DFBnB from BFS, ID and RBFS. In these cases, RBFS is the algorithm of choice, since ID is worse than RBFS, as verified by our experiments.

4.2 The Asymmetric TSP

Given n cities $\{1, 2, ..., n\}$ and a cost matrix $(c_{i,j})$ that defines a cost between each pair of cities, the *traveling salesman problem* (TSP) is to find a minimum-cost tour that visits each city once and returns to the starting city. When the cost from city i to city j is not necessarily equal to that from city j to city i, the problem is the *asymmetric TSP* (ATSP). Many NP-complete combinatorial problems can be formulated as ATSPs, such as vehicle routing, no-wait workshop scheduling, computer wiring, *etc.* [8].

The most efficient approach known for optimally solving the ATSP is subtour elimination [1], with the solution to the assignment problem as a lower-bound function. Given a cost matrix $(c_{i,j})$, the *assignment problem* (AP) [9] is to assign to each city i another city j, with $c_{i,j}$ as the cost of this assignment, such that the total cost of all assignments is minimized. The AP is a generalization of the ATSP with the requirement of a single complete tour removed, allowing collections of subtours, and is solvable in $O(n^3)$ time [9]. Subtour elimination first solves the AP for the n cities. If the solution is not a tour, it then expands the problem into subproblems by breaking a subtour (cf. [1] for details), and searches the space of subproblems. It repeatedly checks the AP solutions of subproblems and expands them if they are not complete tours, until an optimal tour is found. The space of subproblems can be represented by a tree with maximum depth less than n^2.

We ran DFBnB, ID and RBFS on the ATSP with the elements of cost matrices independently and uniformly chosen from $\{0, 1, 2, 3, ..., r\}$, where r is an integer. Figures 6(a) and 6(b) show our results on 100-city and 300-city ATSPs. The horizontal axes are the range of intercity costs r, and the vertical axes are the numbers of tree nodes generated, averaged over 500 trials for each data point. When the cost range r is small or large, relative to the number of cities n, the ATSP is easy or difficult, respectively [15, 17]. Figure 6 shows that ID cannot compete with RBFS and DFBnB, especially for difficult ATSPs when r is large. RBFS does poorly on difficult ATSPs, since in this case the node costs in the search tree are unique [15, 17], which causes significant node regeneration overhead.

5 Conclusions

We first studied the relationship between the average number of nodes expanded by depth-first branch-and-bound (DFBnB), and best-first search (BFS). In particular, we showed analytically that DFBnB expands no more than $O(d \cdot N)$ nodes on average for finding a minimum cost node at depth d of a random tree, where N is the average number of nodes expanded by BFS on

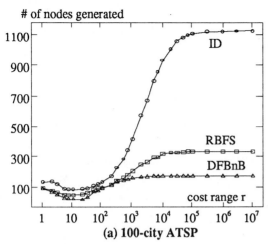

(a) 100-city ATSP

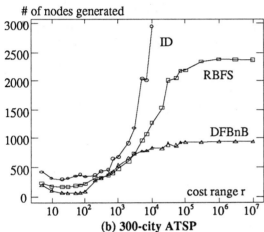

(b) 300-city ATSP

Figure 6: Performance on the ATSPs.

the same tree. We also proved that DFBnB is asymptotically optimal when BFS runs in exponential time. We then considered how to select a linear-space algorithm, from among DFBnB, iterative-deepening (ID) and recursive best-first search (RBFS). We also showed that DFBnB runs faster than BFS in some cases, even if the former expands more nodes than the latter. Our results on random trees and two real problems, lookahead search on sliding-tile puzzles and the asymmetric traveling salesman problem, show that (a) DFBnB is preferable on problems that can be formulated by bounded-depth trees and require exponential computation; (b) RBFS should be applied to problems that cannot be represented by bounded-depth trees, or problems that can be solved in polynomial time.

References

[1] Balas, E., and P. Toth, "Branch and bound methods," *The Traveling Salesman Problems*, E.L. Lawler, *et al.* (eds.) John Wiley and Sons, 1985, pp.361-401.

[2] Dechter, R., and J. Pearl, "Generalized best-first search strategies and the optimality of A*," *JACM*, **32** (1985) 505-36.

[3] Karp, R.M., and J. Pearl, "Searching for an optimal path in a tree with random cost," *Artificial Intelligence*, **21** (1983) 99-117.

[4] Korf, R.E., "Depth-first iterative-deepening: An optimal admissible tree search," *Artificial Intelligence*, **27** (1985) 97-109.

[5] Korf, R.E., "Real-time heuristic search," *Artificial Intelligence*, **42** (1990) 189-211.

[6] Korf, R.E., "Linear-space best-first search: Summary of results," *Proc. 10-th National Conf. on AI, AAAI-92*, San Jose, CA, July, 1992, pp.533-8.

[7] Korf, R.E., "Linear-space best-first search," *Artificial Intelligence*, to appear.

[8] Lawler, E.L., *et al.*, *The Traveling Salesman Problems*, John Wiley and Sons, 1985.

[9] Martello, S., and P. Toth, "Linear assignment problems," *Annals of Discrete Mathematics*, **31** (1987) 259-82.

[10] McDiarmid, C.J.H., "Probabilistic analysis of tree search," *Disorder in Physical Systems*, G.R. Gummett and D.J.A. Welsh (eds), Oxford Science Pub., 1990, pp.249-60,

[11] McDiarmid, C.J.H., and G.M.A. Provan, "An expected-cost analysis of backtracking and non-backtracking algorithms," *Proc. 12-th Intern. Joint Conf. on AI, IJCAI-91*, Sydney, Australia, Aug. 1991, pp.172-7.

[12] Ratner, D., and M. Warmuth, "Finding a shortest solution for the NxN extension of the 15-puzzle is intractable," *Proc. 5-th National Conf. on AI, AAAI-86*,, Philadelphia, PA, 1986.

[13] Vempaty, N.R., V. Kumar, and R.E. Korf, "Depth-first vs best-first search," *Proc. 9-th National Conf. on AI, AAAI-91*,, CA, July, 1991, pp.434-40.

[14] Wah, B.W., and C.F. Yu, "Stochastic modeling of branch-and-bound algorithms with best-first search," *IEEE Trans. on Software Engineering*, **11** (1985) 922-34.

[15] Zhang, W., and R.E. Korf, "An average-case analysis of branch-and-bound with applications: Summary of results," *Proc. 10-th National Conf. on AI, AAAI-92*,, San Jose, CA, July, 1992, pp.545-50.

[16] Zhang, W., and R.E. Korf, "Performance of linear-space branch-and-bound algorithms," submitted to *Artificial Intelligence*, 1992.

[17] Zhang, W., and R.E. Korf, "On the asymmetric traveling salesman problem under subtour elimination and local search," submitted, March, 1993.

Statistically-Based
Natural Language
Processing

Using an Annotated Language Corpus as a Virtual Stochastic Grammar

Rens Bod

Department of Computational Linguistics
University of Amsterdam
Spuistraat 134
NL-1012 VB Amsterdam
rens@alf.let.uva.nl

Abstract

In Data Oriented Parsing (DOP), an annotated language corpus is used as a virtual stochastic grammar. An input string is parsed by combining subtrees from the corpus. As a consequence, one parse tree can usually be generated by several derivations that involve different subtrees. This leads to a statistics where the probability of a parse is equal to the sum of the probabilities of all its derivations. In (Scha, 1990) an informal introduction to DOP is given, while (Bod, 1992) provides a formalization of the theory. In this paper we show that the maximum probability parse can be estimated in polynomial time by applying Monte Carlo techniques. The model was tested on a set of hand-parsed strings from the Air Travel Information System (ATIS) corpus. Preliminary experiments yield 96% test set parsing accuracy.

Motivation

As soon as a formal grammar characterizes a non-trivial part of a natural language, almost every input string of reasonable length gets an unmanageably large number of different analyses. Since most of these analyses are not perceived as plausible by a human language user, there is a need for distinguishing the plausible parse(s) of an input string from the implausible ones. In stochastic language processing, it is assumed that the most plausible parse of an input string is its most probable parse. Most instantiations of this idea estimate the probability of a parse by assigning application probabilities to context free rewrite rules (Jelinek, 1990), or by assigning combination probabilities to elementary structures (Resnik, 1992; Schabes, 1992).

There is some agreement now that context free rewrite rules are not adequate for estimating the probability of a parse, since they cannot capture syntactic/lexical context, and hence cannot describe how the probability of syntactic structures or lexical items depends on that context. In stochastic tree-adjoining grammar (Schabes, 1992), this lack of context-sensitivity is overcome by assigning probabilities to larger structural units. However, it is not always evident which structures should be considered as elementary structures. In (Schabes, 1992) it is proposed to infer a stochastic TAG from a large training corpus using an inside-outside-like iterative algorithm.

Data Oriented Parsing (DOP) (Scha, 1990; Bod, 1992), distinguishes itself from other statistical approaches in that it omits the step of inferring a grammar from a corpus. Instead, an annotated corpus is directly used as a stochastic grammar. An input string is parsed by combining subtrees from the corpus. In this view, every subtree can be considered as an elementary structure. As a consequence, one parse tree can usually be generated by several derivations that involve different subtrees. This leads to a statistics where the probability of a parse is equal to the sum of the probabilities of all its derivations. It is hoped that this approach can accommodate all statistical properties of a language corpus.

Let us illustrate DOP with an extremely simple example. Suppose that a corpus consists of only two trees:

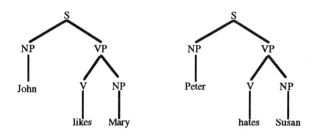

Suppose that our combination operation (indicated with ∘) consists of substituting a subtree on the leftmost identically labeled leaf node of another subtree. Then the sentence *Mary likes Susan* can be parsed as an *S* by combining the following subtrees from the corpus.

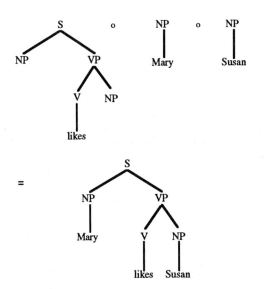

But the same parse tree can also be derived by combining other subtrees, for instance:

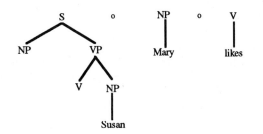

or

Thus, a parse can have several derivations involving different subtrees. These derivations have different probabilities. Using the corpus as our stochastic grammar, we estimate the probability of substituting a certain subtree on a specific node as the probability of selecting this subtree among all subtrees in the corpus

that could be substituted on that node. The probability of a derivation can be computed as the product of the probabilities of the subtrees that are combined. For the example derivations above, this yields:

$$P(\text{1st example}) = 1/20 * 1/4 * 1/4 = 1/320$$
$$P(\text{2nd example}) = 1/20 * 1/4 * 1/2 = 1/160$$
$$P(\text{3rd example}) = 2/20 * 1/4 * 1/8 * 1/4 = 1/1280$$

This example illustrates that a statistical language model which defines probabilities over parses by taking into account only one derivation, does not accommodate all statistical properties of a language corpus. Instead, we will define the probability of a parse as the sum of the probabilities of all its derivations. Finally, the probability of a string is equal to the sum of the probabilities of all its parses.

We will show that conventional parsing techniques can be applied to DOP, but that this becomes very inefficient, since the number of derivations of a parse grows exponentially with the length of the input string. However, we will show that DOP can be parsed in polynomial time by using Monte Carlo techniques.

An important advantage of using a corpus for probability calculation, is that no training of parameters is needed, as is the case for other stochastic grammars (Jelinek et al., 1990; Pereira and Schabes, 1992; Schabes, 1992). Secondly, since we take into account all derivations of a parse, no relationship that might possibly be of statistical interest is ignored.

The Model

As might be clear by now, a DOP-model is characterized by a corpus of tree structures, together with a set of operations that combine subtrees from the corpus into new trees. In this section we explain more precisely what we mean by subtree, operations etc., in order to arrive at definitions of a parse and the probability of a parse with respect to a corpus. For a treatment of DOP in more formal terms we refer to (Bod, 1992).

Subtree

A *subtree* of a tree T is a connected subgraph S of T such that for every node in S holds that if it has daughter nodes, then these are equal to the daughter nodes of the corresponding node in T. It is trivial to see that a subtree is also a tree. In the following example T_1 and T_2 are subtrees of T, whereas T_3 isn't.

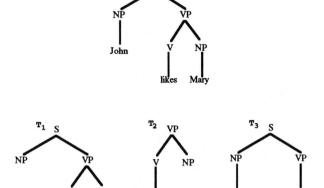

The general definition above also includes subtrees consisting of one node. Since such subtrees do not contribute to the parsing process, we exclude these pathological cases and consider as the set of subtrees the non-trivial ones consisting of more than one node. We shall use the following notation to indicate that a tree t is a non-trivial subtree of a tree in a corpus C:

$$t \varepsilon C \ =_{def} \ \exists T \in C: t \text{ is a non-trivial subtree of } T$$

Operations

In this article we will limit ourselves to the basic operation of *substitution*. Other possible operations are left to future research. If t and u are trees, such that the *leftmost non-terminal leaf* of t is equal to the *root* of u, then $t \circ u$ is the tree that results from substituting this non-terminal leaf in t by tree u. The partial function $\circ$ is called *substitution*. We will write $(t \circ u) \circ v$ as $t \circ u \circ v$, and in general $(..((t_1 \circ t_2) \circ t_3) \circ ..) \circ t_n$ as $t_1 \circ t_2 \circ t_3 \circ ... \circ t_n$.

The restriction *leftmost* in the definition is motivated by the fact that it eliminates different derivations consisting of the same subtrees.

Parse

Tree T is a *parse* of input string s with respect to a corpus C, iff the *yield* of T is equal to s and there are subtrees $t_1,...,t_n \varepsilon C$, such that $T = t_1 \circ ... \circ t_n$. The set of parses of s with respect to C, is thus given by:

$$Parses(s,C) \ = \ \{T \mid yield(T) = s \ \wedge \ \exists t_1,...,t_n \varepsilon C: T = t_1 \circ ... \circ t_n\}$$

The definition correctly includes the trivial case of a subtree from the corpus whose *yield* is equal to the complete input string.

Derivation

A *derivation* of a parse T with respect to a corpus C, is a tuple of subtrees $\langle t_1,...,t_n \rangle$ such that $t_1,...,t_n \varepsilon C$ and $t_1 \circ ... \circ t_n = T$. The set of derivations of T with respect to C, is thus given by:

$$Derivations(T,C) \ = \ \{\langle t_1,...,t_n \rangle \mid t_1,...,t_n \varepsilon C \ \wedge \ t_1 \circ ... \circ t_n = T\}$$

Probability

Subtree. Given a subtree $t_1 \varepsilon C$, a function *root* that yields the root of a tree, and a node labeled X, the conditional probability $P(t=t_1 \mid root(t)=X)$ denotes the probability that t_1 is substituted on X. If $root(t_1) \neq X$, this probability is 0. If $root(t_1) = X$, this probability can be estimated as the ratio between the number of occurrences of t_1 in C and the total number of occurrences of subtrees t' in C for which holds that $root(t') = X$. Evidently, $\Sigma_i P(t=t_i \mid root(t)=X) = 1$ holds.

Derivation. The probability of a derivation $\langle t_1,...,t_n \rangle$ is equal to the probability that the subtrees $t_1,...,t_n$ are combined. This probability can be computed as the product of the conditional probabilities of the subtrees $t_1,...,t_n$. Let $lnl(x)$ be the leftmost non-terminal leaf of tree x, then:

$$P(\langle t_1,...,t_n \rangle) \ = \ P(t=t_1 \mid root(t)=S) * \Pi_{i=2 \text{ to } n} P(t=t_i \mid root(t) = lnl(t_{i-1}))$$

Parse. The probability of a parse is equal to the probability that any of its derivations occurs. Since the derivations are mutually exclusive, the probability of a parse T is the sum of the probabilities of all its derivations. Let $Derivations(T,C) = \{d_1,...,d_n\}$, then: $P(T) = \Sigma_i P(d_i)$. The conditional probability of a parse T given input string s, can be computed as the ratio between the probability of T and the sum of the probabilities of all parses of s.

String. The probability of a string is equal to the probability that any of its parses occurs. Since the parses are mutually exclusive, the probability of a string s can be computed as the sum of the probabilities of all its parses. Let $Parses(s,C) = \{T_1,...,T_n\}$, then: $P(s) = \Sigma_i P(T_i)$. It can be shown that $\Sigma_i P(s_i) = 1$ holds.

Monte Carlo Parsing

It is easy to show that an input string can be parsed with conventional parsing techniques, by applying subtrees instead of rules to the input string (Bod, 1992). Every subtree t can be seen as a production rule $root(t) \to t$, where the non-terminals of the yield of the right hand side constitute the symbols to which new rules/subtrees are applied. Given a polynomial time parsing algorithm, a derivation of the input string, and hence a parse, can be calculated in polynomial time. But if we calculate the probability of a parse by exhaustively calculating all its derivations, the time complexity becomes exponential, since the number of derivations of a parse of an input string grows exponentially with the length of the input string.

Nevertheless, by applying *Monte Carlo techniques* (Hammersley and Handscomb, 1964), we can estimate the probability of a parse and make its error arbitrarily small in polynomial time. The essence of Monte Carlo is very simple: it estimates a probability distribution of events by taking random samples. The larger the samples we take, the higher the reliability. For DOP this means that, instead of exhaustively calculating all parses with all their derivations, we randomly calculate N parses of an input string (by taking random samples from the subtrees that can be substituted on a specific node in the parsing process). The estimated probability of a certain parse given the input string, is then equal to the number of times that parse occurred normalized with respect to N. We can estimate a probability as accurately as we want by choosing N as large as we want, since according to the Strong Law of Large Numbers the estimated probability converges to the actual probability. From a classical result of probability theory (Chebyshev's inequality) it follows that the time complexity of achieving a maximum error ε is given by $O(\varepsilon^{-2})$. Thus the error of probability estimation can be made arbitrarily small in polynomial time - provided that the parsing algorithm is not worse than polynomial.

Obviously, probable parses of an input string are more likely to be generated than improbable ones. Thus, in order to estimate the maximum probability parse, it suffices to sample until stability in the top of the parse distribution occurs. The parse which is generated most often is then the maximum probability parse.

We now show that the probability that a certain parse is generated by Monte Carlo, is exactly the probability of that parse according to the DOP-model. First, the probability that a subtree $t \varepsilon C$ is sampled at a certain point in the parsing process (where a non-terminal X is to be substituted) is equal to $P(\ t \mid root(t) = X\ )$. Secondly, the probability that a certain sequence $t_1,...,t_n$ of subtrees that constitutes a derivation of a

parse T, is sampled, is equal to the product of the conditional probabilities of these subtrees. Finally, the probability that any sequence of subtrees that constitutes a derivation of a certain parse T, is sampled, is equal to the sum of the probabilities that these derivations are sampled. This is the probability that a certain parse T is sampled, which is equivalent to the probability of T according to the DOP-model.

We shall call a parser which applies this Monte Carlo technique, a *Monte Carlo parser*. With respect to the theory of computation, a Monte Carlo parser is a probabilistic algorithm which belongs to the class of *B*ounded error *P*robabilistic *P*olynomial time (*BPP*) algorithms. BPP-problems are characterized by the following: it may take exponential time to solve them exactly, but there exists an estimation algorithm with a probability of error that becomes arbitrarily small in polynomial time.

Experiments on the ATIS corpus

For our experiments we used part-of-speech sequences of spoken-language transcriptions from the Air Travel Information System (ATIS) corpus (Hemphill et al., 1990), with the labeled-bracketings of those sequences in the Penn Treebank (Marcus, 1991). The 750 labeled-bracketings were divided at random into a DOP-corpus of 675 trees and a test set of 75 part-of-speech sequences. The following tree is an example from the DOP-corpus, where for reasons of readability the lexical items are added to the part-of-speech tags.

```
(  (S (NP *)
       (VP (VB Show)
           (NP (PP me))
           (NP (NP (PDT all))
               (DT the) (JJ nonstop) (NNS flights)
               (PP (PP (IN from)
                       (NP (NP Dallas)))
                   (PP (TO to)
                       (NP (NP Denver))))
               (ADJP (JJ early)
                     (PP (IN in)
                         (NP (DT the)
                             (NN morning)))))))  .)
```

As a measure for *parsing accuracy* we took the percentage of the test sentences for which the maximum probability parse derived by the Monte Carlo parser (for a sample size N) is identical to the Treebank parse.

It is one of the most essential features of the DOP approach, that arbitrarily large subtrees are taken into consideration. In order to test the usefulness of this feature, we performed different experiments constraining the *depth* of the subtrees. The depth of a tree is defined as the length of its longest path. The following table shows the results of seven experiments. The accuracy refers to the parsing accuracy at sample size $N = 100$, and is rounded off to the nearest integer.

depth	accuracy
≤2	87%
≤3	92%
≤4	93%
≤5	93%
≤6	95%
≤7	95%
unbounded	96%

Parsing accuracy for the ATIS corpus, sample size $N = 100$.

The table shows that there is a relatively rapid increase in parsing accuracy when enlarging the maximum depth of the subtrees to 3. The accuracy keeps increasing, at a slower rate, when the depth is enlarged further. The highest accuracy is obtained by using all subtrees from the corpus: 72 out of the 75 sentences from the test set are parsed correctly.

In the following figure, parsing accuracy is plotted against the sample size N for three of our experiments: the experiments where the depth of the subtrees is constrained to 2 and 3, and the experiment where the depth is unconstrained. (The maximum depth in the ATIS corpus is 13.)

In (Pereira and Schabes, 1992), 90.36% bracketing accuracy was reported using a stochastic CFG trained on bracketings from the ATIS corpus. Though we cannot make a direct comparison, our pilot experiment suggests that our model may have better performance than a stochastic CFG. However, there is still an error rate of 4%. Although there is no reason to expect 100% accuracy in the absence of any semantic or pragmatic analysis, it seems that the accuracy might be further improved. Three limitations of the current experiments are worth mentioning,

First, the Treebank annotations are not rich enough. Although the Treebank uses a relatively rich part-of-speech system (48 terminal symbols), there are only 15 non-terminal symbols. Especially the internal structure of noun phrases is very poor. Semantic annotations are completely absent.

Secondly, it could be that subtrees which occur only once in the corpus, give bad estimations of their actual probabilities. The question as to whether reestimation techniques would further improve the accuracy, must be considered in future research.

Thirdly, it could be that our corpus is not large enough. This brings us to the question as to how much parsing accuracy depends on the size of the corpus. For studying this question, we performed additional experiments with different corpus sizes. Starting with a corpus of only 50 parse trees (randomly chosen from the initial DOP-corpus of 675 trees), we increased its size with intervals of 50. As our test set, we took the same 75 p-o-s sequences as used in the previous experiments. In the next figure the parsing accuracy, for sample size $N = 100$, is plotted against the corpus size, using all corpus subtrees.

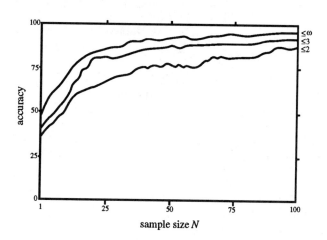

Parsing accuracy for the ATIS corpus, with depth ≤ 2, with depth ≤ 3 and with unbounded depth.

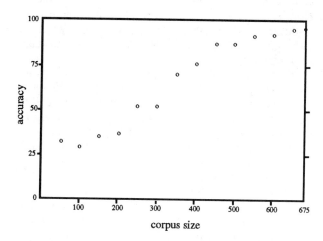

Parsing accuracy for the ATIS corpus, with unbounded depth.

The figure shows the increase in parsing accuracy. For a corpus size of 450 trees, the accuracy reaches already 88%. After this, the growth decreases, but the accuracy is still growing at corpus size 675. Thus, we would expect a higher accuracy if the corpus is further enlarged.

Conclusions and Future Research

We have presented a language model that uses an annotated corpus as a virtual stochastic grammar. We restricted ourselves to substitution as the only combination operation between corpus subtrees. A statistical parsing theory was developed, where one parse can be generated by different derivations, and where the probability of a parse is computed as the sum of the probabilities of all its derivations. It was shown that the maximum probability parse can be estimated as accurately as desired in polynomial time by using Monte Carlo techniques. The method has been succesfully tested on a set of part-of-speech sequences derived from the ATIS corpus. It turned out that parsing accuracy improved if larger subtrees were used.

We would like to extend our experiments to larger corpora, like the Wall Street Journal corpus. This might raise computational problems, since the number of subtrees becomes extremely large. Methods of constraining the number of subtrees, without loosing accuracy, should be investigated. Furthermore, in order to tackle the problem of data sparseness, the possibility of abstracting from corpus data should be included, but statistical models of abstractions of features and categories are not yet available.

Acknowledgements. The author is very much indebted to Remko Scha for many valuable comments on earlier versions of this paper. The author is also grateful to Mitch Marcus for supplying the ATIS corpus.

References

R. Bod, 1992. "A Computational Model of Language Performance: Data Oriented Parsing", *Proceedings COLING'92*, Nantes.

J.M. Hammersley and D.C. Handscomb, 1964. *Monte Carlo Methods*, Chapman and Hall, London.

C.T. Hemphill, J.J. Godfrey and G.R. Doddington, 1990. "The ATIS spoken language systems pilot corpus". *DARPA Speech and Natural Language Workshop*, Hidden Valley, Morgan Kaufmann.

F. Jelinek, J.D. Lafferty and R.L. Mercer, 1990. *Basic Methods of Probabilistic Context Free Grammars*, Technical Report IBM RC 16374 (#72684), Yorktown Heights.

M. Marcus, 1991. "Very Large Annotated Database of American English". *DARPA Speech and Natural Language Workshop*, Pacific Grove, Morgan Kaufmann.

F. Pereira and Y. Schabes, 1992. "Inside-Outside Reestimation from Partially Bracketed Corpora", *Proceedings ACL'92*, Newark.

P. Resnik, 1992. "Probabilistic Tree-Adjoining Grammar as a Framework for Statistical Natural Language Processing", *Proceedings COLING'92*, Nantes.

R. Scha, 1990. "Language Theory and Language Technology; Competence and Performance" (in Dutch), in Q.A.M. de Kort & G.L.J. Leerdam (eds.), *Computertoepassingen in de Neerlandistiek*, Almere: Landelijke Vereniging van Neerlandici (LVVN-jaarboek).

Y. Schabes, 1992. "Stochastic Lexicalized Tree-Adjoining Grammars", *Proceedings COLING'92*, Nantes.

Equations for Part-of-Speech Tagging

Eugene Charniak and **Curtis Hendrickson** and **Neil Jacobson** and **Mike Perkowitz**[*]
Department of Computer Science
Brown University
Providence RI 02912

Abstract

We derive from first principles the basic equations for a few of the basic hidden-Markov-model word taggers as well as equations for other models which may be novel (the descriptions in previous papers being too spare to be sure). We give performance results for all of the models. The results from our best model (96.45% on an unused test sample from the Brown corpus with 181 distinct tags) is on the upper edge of reported results. We also hope these results clear up some confusion in the literature about the best equations to use. However, the major purpose of this paper is to show how the equations for a variety of models may be derived and thus encourage future authors to give the equations for their model and the derivations thereof.

Introduction

The last few years have seen a fair number of papers on part-of-speech tagging — assigning the correct part of speech to each word in a text [1,2,4,5,7,8,9,10]. Most of these systems view the text as having been produced by a hidden Markov model (HMM), so that the tagging problem can be viewed as one of deciding which states the Markov process went through during its generation of the text. (For an example of a system which does not take this view, see [2].) Unfortunately, despite the obvious mathematical formulation that HMM's provide, few of the papers bother to define the mathematical model they use. In one case this has resulted in a confusion which we address subsequently. In most every case it has meant that large parts of the models are never described at all, and even when they are described the English descriptions are often vague and the occasional mathematical symbol hard to interpret as one is lacking a derivation of the equations in which it should rest.

In this paper we hope to rectify this situation by showing how a variety of Markov tagging models can be derived from first principles. Furthermore, we have implemented these models and give their performance. We do not claim that any of the models perform better than

---

[*]This research was supported in part by NSF contract IRI-8911122 and ONR contract N0014-91-J-1202.

taggers reported elsewhere, although the best of them at 96.45% is at the upper end of reported results. However, the best taggers all perform at about the same level of accuracy. Rather our goal is to systematize the "seat of the pants" knowledge which the community has already accumulated. One place where we might be breaking new ground is in techniques for handling the sparse-data problems which inevitably arise. But even here it is hard to be sure if our techniques are new since previous authors have barely mentioned their sparse-data techniques, much less formalized them. We believe that providing a clean mathematical notation for expressing the relevant techniques will take this area out of the realm of the unmentionable and into that of polite scientific discussion.

The Simplest Model

We assume that our language has some fixed vocabulary, $\{w^1, w^2, \ldots, w^\omega\}$. This is a set of words, e.g., {a, aardvark, ..., zygote }. We also assume a fixed set of parts of speech, or tags, $\{t^1, t^2, \ldots t^\tau\}$, e.g., {adjective, adverb, ..., verb}. We consider a text of n words to be a sequence of random variables $W_{1,n} = W_1 W_2 \ldots W_n$. Each of these random variables can take as its value any of the possible words in our vocabulary. More formally, let the function $V(X)$ denote the possible values (outcomes) for the random variable X. Then $V(W_i) = \{w^1, w^2, \ldots w^\omega\}$. We denote the value of W_1 by w_1, and a particular sequence of n values for $W_{1,n}$ by $w_{1,n}$. In a similar way, we consider the tags for these words to be a sequence of n random variables $T_{1,n} = T_1 T_2, \ldots, T_n$. A particular sequence of values for these is denoted as $t_{1,n}$, and the ith one of these is t_i. The tagging problem can then be formally defined as finding the sequence of tags $t_{1,n}$ which is the result of the following function:

$$T(w_{1,n}) \stackrel{\text{def}}{=} \arg \max_{t_{1,n} \in V(T_{1,n})} P(T_{1,n} = t_{1,n} \mid W_{1,n} = w_{1,n})$$

(1)

In the normal way we typically omit reference to the random variables themselves and just mention their values. In this way Equation 1 becomes:

$$T(w_{1,n}) = \arg \max_{t_{1,n}} P(t_{1,n} \mid w_{1,n})$$

(2)

We now turn Equation 2 into a more convenient form.

$$T(w_{1,n}) = \arg\max_{t_{1,n}} \frac{P(t_{1,n}, w_{1,n})}{P(w_{1,n})} \quad (3)$$

$$= \arg\max_{t_{1,n}} P(t_{1,n}, w_{1,n}). \quad (4)$$

In going from Equation 3 to 4 we dropped $P(w_{1,n})$ as it is constant for all $t_{1,n}$.

Next we want to break Equation 4 into "bite-size" pieces about which we can collect statistics. To a first approximation there are two ways this can be done. The first is like this:

$$P(t_{1,n}, w_{1,n}) = P(w_1)P(t_1 \mid w_1)P(w_2 \mid t_1, w_1)$$
$$P(t_2 \mid t_1, w_{1,2}) \ldots$$
$$P(t_n \mid t_{1,n-1}, w_{1,n-1})$$
$$P(w_n \mid t_{1,n}, w_{1,n-1}) \quad (5)$$
$$= P(w_1)P(t_1 \mid w_1)$$
$$\prod_{i=2}^{n} P(w_i \mid t_{1,i-1}, w_{1,i-1})$$
$$P(t_i \mid t_{1,i-1}, w_{1,i}) \quad (6)$$
$$= \prod_{i=1}^{n} P(w_i \mid t_{1,i-1}, w_{1,i-1})$$
$$P(t_i \mid t_{1,i-1}, w_{1,i}) \quad (7)$$

Here we simplified Equation 6 to get Equation 7 by suitably defining terms like $t_{1,0}$ and their probabilities. We derived Equation 7 by first breaking out $P(w_1)$ from $P(t_{1,n}, w_{1,n})$. In a similar way we can first break out $P(t_1)$, giving this:

$$P(t_{1,n}, w_{1,n}) = \prod_{i=1}^{n} P(t_i \mid t_{1,i-1}, w_{1,i-1})$$
$$P(w_i \mid t_{1,i}, w_{1,i-1}) \quad (8)$$

All of our models start from Equations 7 or 8, or, when we discuss equations which smooth using word morphology, modest variations of them.

Up to this point we have made no assumptions about the probabilities we are dealing with, and thus the probabilities required by Equations 7 and 8 are not empirically collectible. The models we develop in this paper differ in just the assumptions they make to allow for the collection of relevant data. We call these assumptions "Markov assumptions" because they make it possible to view the tagging as a Markov process. We start with the simplest of these models (i.e., the one based upon the strongest Markov assumptions).

We start with Equation 7 and make the following Markov assumptions:

$$P(w_i \mid t_{1,i-1}, w_{1,i-1}) = P(w_i \mid w_{1,i-1}) \quad (9)$$
$$P(t_i \mid t_{1,i-1}, w_{1,i}) = P(t_i \mid w_i) \quad (10)$$

Substituting these equations into Equation 7, and substituting that into Equation 4 we get:

$$T(w_{1,n}) = \arg\max_{t_{1,n}} \prod_{i=1}^{n} P(w_i \mid w_{1,i-1})$$
$$P(t_i \mid w_i) \quad (11)$$
$$= \arg\max_{t_{1,n}} \prod_{i=1}^{n} P(t_i \mid w_i) \quad (12)$$

Equation 12 has a very simple interpretation. For each word we pick the tag which is most common for that word. This is our simplest model.

Estimation of Parameters

Before one can use such a model however, one still needs to estimate the relevant parameters. For Equation 12 we need the probabilities of each possible tag for each possible word: $P(t^i \mid w^j)$. The most obvious way to get these is from a corpus which has been tagged by hand. Fortunately there is such a corpus, the Brown Corpus [6] and all of the statistical data we collect are from a subset of this corpus consisting of 90% of the sentences chosen at random. (The other 10% we reserve for testing our models.) So, let $C(t^i, w^j)$ be the number of times the word w^j appears in our training corpus with the tag t^i. In the obvious way $C(w^j) = \sum_i C(t^i, w^j)$. Then one approximation to the statistics needed for Equation 12 is the following estimate:

$$P(t^i \mid w^j) \overset{\text{est}}{=} \frac{C(t^i, w^j)}{C(w^j)}. \quad (13)$$

However, Equation 13 has problems when the training data is not complete. For example, suppose there is no occurrence of word w^v? First, the quotient in Equation 13 is undefined. As this is a problem throughout this paper we henceforth define zero divided by zero to be zero. But this still means that $P(t^i \mid w^v)$ is zero for all t^i.

We solve this problem by adding further terms to Equation 13. We model this after what is typically done in smoothing tri-gram models for English [7]. Thus we add a second term to the equation with weights attached to each term saying how heavily that term should be counted. That is, we are looking for an equation of the following form:

$$P(t^i \mid w^j) \overset{\text{est}}{=} \lambda_1(w^j)\frac{C(t^i, w^j)}{C(w^j)} + \lambda_2(w^j)f(t^i, w^j). \quad (14)$$

Here $f(t^i, w^j)$ is standing in for our as yet to be disclosed improvement. The two λs are the weights to be given to each term. Note that they can be different for different w and thus we have made them functions of w^j. For any w Equation 14 must sum to one over all t^i. We ensure this by requiring that the λs sum to one and that the terms they combine do so as well.

If we are primarily concerned about estimating $P(t^i \mid w^j)$ for w^j which have not been encountered before the λs can take a particularly simple form:

$$\lambda_1(w^j) = \begin{cases} 1 & \text{if } C(w^j) \geq 1 \\ 0 & \text{otherwise.} \end{cases} \quad (15)$$

With these λs the second term of Equation 14 should be the probability that a token of a word w^j which we have never seen before has the tag t^i. Obviously we cannot really collect statistics on something that has never occurred, however when we were gathering our count data in the first place we often encountered words which up to that point had not been seen. We collect statistics on these situations to stand in for those which occur in the test data. Thus, let $C_n(t^i)$ be the number of times a word which has never been seen with the tag t^i get this tag, and let $C_n()$ be the number of such occurrences in total. Then our improved probability estimation equation is this:

$$P(t^i \mid w^j) \stackrel{\text{est}}{=} \lambda_1(w^j)\frac{C(t^i, w^j)}{C(w^j)} + \lambda_2(w^j)\frac{C_n(t^i)}{C_n()} \quad (16)$$

With this improved parameter estimation function we are now able to collect statistics from our corpus and test the model thereby derived on our test corpus. The results are quite impressive for so simple a model: 90.25% of the words in the test data are labeled correctly. (The data for all of the models is summarized at the end of the paper in Figure 2.)

The "Standard" Model

The model of Equations 12 and 16 does not take any context into account. It simply chooses the most likely tag for each word out of context. Next we develop a model which does take context into account.

This time we start from Equation 8 and simplify it by making the following two Markov assumptions:

$$P(t_i \mid t_{1,i-1}, w_{1,i-1}) = P(t_i \mid t_{i-1}) \quad (17)$$
$$P(w_i \mid t_{1,i}, w_{1,i-1}) = P(w_i \mid t_{1,i}) \quad (18)$$

That is, we assume that the current tag is independent of the previous words and only dependent on the previous tag. Similarly we assume that the correct word is independent of everything except knowledge of its tag. With these assumptions we get the following equation:

$$\mathcal{T}(w_{1,n}) = \arg\max_{t_{1,n}} \prod_{i=1}^{n} P(t_i \mid t_{i-1})P(w_i \mid t_i) \quad (19)$$

This equation, or something like it, is at the basis of most of the tagging programs created over the last few years. One modification expands $P(t_i \mid t_{i-1})$ to take into consideration the last two tags [4,7]. Experimentation has shown that it offers a slight improvement, but not a great deal. We ignore it henceforth. Another modification conditions the tag probability on the tags *following* the word rather than those which preceded it [4]. However, it is easy to show that this has no effect on results.

A more important difference is that many do not use Equation 19 or the just-mentioned variants, but rather:

$$\mathcal{T}(w_{1,n}) = \arg\max_{t_{1,n}} \prod_{i=1}^{n} P(t_i \mid t_{i-1})P(t_i \mid w_i). \quad (20)$$

The difference is in the last term. This equation is found in [4,9] and is described in words in [5]. (However, while Church gives Equation 20 in [4], the results cited there were based upon Equation 19 (Church, personal communication).)

Equation 20 seems plausible except that it is virtually impossible to derive it from basic considerations (at least we have been unable to do so). Nevertheless, given the drastic Markov assumptions we made in the derivation of Equation 19 it is hard to be sure that its comparative theoretical purity translates into better performance. Indeed, the one paper we are acquainted with in which the comparison was made [1] found that the less pure Equation 20 gave the better performance. However, this was on a very small amount of training data, and thus the results may not be accurate.

To determine which, in fact, does work better we trained both on 90% of the Brown Corpus and tested on the remainder. We smoothed the probabilities using Equation 16. To use this on Equation 19 we made the following change in its form:

$$\begin{aligned} \mathcal{T}(w_{1,n}) &= \arg\max_{t_{1,n}} \prod_{i=1}^{n} P(t_i \mid t_{i-1}) \\ &\qquad \frac{P(w_i)P(t_i \mid w_i)}{P(t_i)} \quad (21) \\ &= \arg\max_{t_{1,n}} \prod_{i=1}^{n} P(t_i \mid t_{i-1})\frac{P(t_i \mid w_i)}{P(t_i)} \quad (22) \end{aligned}$$

It was also necessary to smooth $P(t_i \mid t_{i-1})$. In particular we found in our test data consecutive words with unambiguous tags, where the tags had not been seen consecutively in the training data. To overcome this problem in the simplest fashion we smoothed the probability as follows:

$$P(t_i \mid t_{i-1}) \stackrel{\text{est}}{=} (1 - \epsilon)\frac{C(t_{i-1}, t_i)}{C(t_{i-1})} + \epsilon. \quad (23)$$

Here ϵ is a very small number so that its contribution is swamped by the count data unless that contributes zero. The net effect is that when there is no data on tag context the decision is made on the basis of $P(w^j \mid t^i)$ in Equation 19 or $P(t^i \mid w^j)$ in Equation 20.

The results were unequivocal. For Equation 19 we got 95.15% correct while for the less pure Equation 20 the results were poorer, 94.09%. While this may not seem like a huge difference, a better way to think of it is that we got an 18% reduction in errors. Furthermore, given that the models have exactly the same complexity, there is no cost for this improvement.

An Improved Smoothing Model

The smoothing model of Equation 16 is very crude. This and the subsequent section improve upon it. One problem is that the model uses raw counts to estimate the probabilities for a word's tags once it has seen a word, even if only once. Obviously, if we have seen a word, say, 100 times, the counts probably give a good estimate, but for words we have seen only once they can be quite inaccurate. The improvement in this section is concerned with this problem.

In Equation 16 we collected statistics on the first occurrences of words we saw in the training data and used these statistics to predict what would happen on the first occurrences of words we saw in the test data. To improve our model we try to estimate the probability that we will next see the tag t^i as the tag for w^j despite the fact that it has never appeared as the tag for w^j before — $P(t^i\text{-new} \mid w^j)$.

$$P(t^i\text{-new} \mid w^j) \stackrel{\text{est}}{=} \begin{cases} \text{if } C(t^i, w^j) \geq 1 \quad 0 \\ \text{otherwise} \\ \quad P(\text{new tag} \mid C(w^j))P(t^i \mid \text{new tag}) \end{cases} \quad (24)$$

The first line states that that t^i cannot be new if it has already appeared as a tag of w^j. The second line says that we approximate the probability by assuming independence of the "newness" and the fact that it is the ith tag. Second it assumes that the probability of newness is only dependent on how many times we have seen w^j before. Also, rather than collect $P(\text{new tag} \mid C(w^j))$ for all possible $C(w^j)$, we have put counts into the following equivalence categories based upon how many times the word has been seen: 0, 1, 2, 3-4, 5-7, 8-10, 11-20, 21-30, 30-up. Let $\mathcal{N}(C(w^j))$ denote the frequence class for w^j. Then

$$P(\text{new tag} \mid C(w^j)) \stackrel{\text{est}}{=} P(\text{new tag} \mid \mathcal{N}(C(w^j))) \quad (25)$$

We can now use $P(t^i\text{-new} \mid w^j)$ to smooth $P(t^i \mid w^j)$ in Equation 16, giving us:

$$\begin{aligned} P(t^i \mid w^j) \stackrel{\text{est}}{=}\ & \lambda_1(w^j)\frac{C(t^i, w^j)}{C(w^j)} \\ & +\lambda_2(w^j)\frac{P(t^i\text{-new} \mid w^j)}{\sum_{i=1}^{\tau} P(t^i\text{-new} \mid w^j)} \end{aligned} \quad (26)$$

However, λ_1 and λ_2 cannot retain their definitions from Equation 15 as that assumed that any word we had seen would use the direct counts rather than the C_n's. One way to get the new λs is to use extra training data to train the HMM corresponding to Equations 22 and 26 to find a (locally) best set of λ-values as done in [7]. However, it is possible to provide an argument for what their values ought to be. If we think about an HMM for producing the part of speech given the word, for each word there would be arcs leaving the state corresponding to each possible tag. (In fact, there would be several arcs for each tag, each going to a different next state, but we ignore this.) This would appear as shown

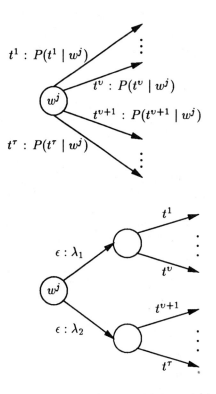

Figure 1: A Markov model for $P(t^i \mid w^j)$

on the upper portion of Figure 1. We assume that for w^j we have seen v of the tags, t^1 to t^v, and the rest, t^{v+1} to t^{τ}, have not been observed for w^j. The idea of Equation 26 is that the first term estimates the probabilities associated with the arcs t^1 to t^v, and the second term estimates the rest. To make the HMM look more like this equation we can transform it into the form on the lower portion of Figure 1 where we have introduced two ϵ (no output) transitions with probabilities $\lambda_1(w^j)$ and $\lambda_2(w^j)$, respectively. From this HMM it is easier to see the significance of these two probabilities. $\lambda_1(w^j)$ is the probability that the next occurrence of w^j has as an associated tag, a tag which has occurred with w^j before, and $\lambda_2(w^j)$ is the probability that it is a new tag for w^j. This latter term is the sum in the denominator of the second term of Equation 26.

Morphological Help for Tagging

The second improvement to our smoothing function uses the word-ending information to help determine correct tags. For example, if we have never seen the word "rakishly," then knowledge that "ly" typically ends an adverb will improve our accuracy on this word — similarly, for "randomizing."

We do not want to tackle the problem of determining the morphology of English words in this paper. Rather we assume that we have available a program which assigns roots and suffixes (we do not deal with any other kind of morphological feature) to our corpus and does so as well for those words in our test corpus which have appeared in the training corpus. For the words in the test corpus which have not appeared in the training corpus the morphological analyzer produces all possible analyses for that word and part of the problem we face is deciding between them. We should note that the morphological analyzer we had was quite crude and prone to mistakes. A better one would no doubt improve our results.

To accommodate our morphological analysis we now consider probabilities for different root-suffix combinations. Following our earlier conventions, we have a set of roots $\{r^1, \ldots, r^\rho\}$ and a set of suffixes $\{s^1, \ldots, s^\sigma\}$. $r_{1,n}$ and $s_{1,n}$ are sequences of n roots and suffixes with r_i and s_i being the ith one of each.

$$T(w_{1,n}) = \underset{t_{1,n}}{\arg\max} \sum_{r_{1,n}, s_{1,n}} P(t_{1,n}, r_{1,n}, s_{1,n} \mid w_{1,n}) \tag{27}$$

$$= \underset{t_{1,n}}{\arg\max} \sum_{r_{1,n}, s_{1,n}} \frac{P(t_{1,n}, r_{1,n}, s_{1,n}, w_{1,n})}{P(w_{1,n})} \tag{28}$$

$$= \underset{t_{1,n}}{\arg\max} \sum_{r_{1,n}, s_{1,n}} P(t_{1,n}, r_{1,n}, s_{1,n}, w_{1,n}) \tag{29}$$

$$= \underset{t_{1,n}}{\arg\max} \sum_{r_{1,n}, s_{1,n}} P(t_{1,n}, r_{1,n}, s_{1,n}) \tag{30}$$

$$= \underset{t_{1,n}}{\arg\max}$$
$$\sum_{r_{1,n}, s_{1,n}} \prod_{i=1}^{n} P(t_i \mid t_{1,i-1}, r_{1,i-1}, s_{1,i-1})$$
$$P(r_i, s_i \mid t_{1,i}, r_{1,i-1}, s_{1,i-1}) \tag{31}$$

We delete $w_{1,n}$ in going from Equation 28 to 29 because roots plus suffixes determine the words. However, this means that in all of the equations after that point there is an implicit assumption that we are only considering root as suffixes which combine to form the desired word.

Next we make some Markov assumptions.

$$P(t_i \mid t_{1,i-1}, r_{1,i-1}, s_{1,i-1}) = P(t_i \mid t_{i-1}) \tag{32}$$
$$P(r_i, s_i \mid t_{1,i}, r_{1,i-1}, s_{1,i-1}) = P(r_i, s_i \mid t_i) \tag{33}$$
$$P(r_i, s_i \mid t_i) = P(r_i \mid t_i) P(s_i \mid t_i) \tag{34}$$

The first two are just the ones we made earlier, but now with the roots and suffixes broken out. Equation 34 is new. It can be interpreted as saying that knowing the root does not help determining the suffix if we know the part-of-speech of the word. This is probably a reasonable assumption, particularly compared to the others we have made.

With these assumptions we can manipulate Equation 31 as follows:

$$T(w_{1,n}) = \underset{t_{1,n}}{\arg\max} \sum_{r_{1,n}, s_{1,n}} \prod_{i=1}^{n} P(t_i \mid t_{i-1})$$
$$P(s_i \mid t_i) P(r_i \mid t_i) \tag{35}$$

$$= \underset{t_{1,n}}{\arg\max} \sum_{r_{1,n}, s_{1,n}} \prod_{i=1}^{n} P(t_i \mid t_{i-1}) P(s_i \mid t_i)$$
$$\frac{P(r_i) P(t_i \mid r_i)}{P(t_i)} \tag{36}$$

Equation 36 is a version of Equation 19, but adapted to morphological analysis. It differs from the earlier equation in three ways. First, it includes a new term, $P(s_i \mid t_i)$, for which we now need to gather statistics. However, since the number of tags and suffixes are small, this should not provide any difficult sparse-data problems. Second, rather than needing to smooth $P(t^i \mid w^j)$ as in Equation 19, we now need to smooth $P(t^i \mid r^j)$. However, it seems reasonable to continue to use Equation 26, with r^j substituted for w^j. Finally, there is the term $P(r_i)$, and this deserves some discussion.

There was no term corresponding to $P(r_i)$ in Equation 19 as the term which would have corresponded to it was $P(w_i)$, and that was removed as it was the same for all tags. However, in Equation 36 we are summing over roots, so $P(r_i)$ is not a constant. In particular assuming that we would want our program to interpret some new word, e.g., "rakishly" as "rakish" + "ly," (or even better, "rake" + "ish" + "ly," if our morphological analyzer could handle it) it would be the $P(r_i)$ term which would encourage such a preference in Equation 36. It would do so because the probability of the shorter root would be much higher than the longer ones.

To model $P(r_i)$ we have adopted a spelling model along the lines of the one used for the spelling of unknown words in [3]. This combines a Poisson distribution over word lengths with a maximum at 5, times a distribution over letters. We adopted a unigram model for letters. Here $\mid r^j \mid$ is the length of r^j and l_i is the ith letter of r^j.

$$P(r^j) \stackrel{\text{est}}{=} \frac{5^{\mid r^j \mid}}{\mid r^j \mid!} e^{-5} \prod_{k=1}^{\mid r^j \mid} P(l_i \mid l_{i-1}) \tag{37}$$

Results

The results of our experiments are summarized in Figure 2. We trained our models on the Brown corpus with every tenth sentence removed (starting with sentence 1) and tested on these removed sentences. There were 114203 words in the test corpus. For the more basic methods we did experiments on both the full Brown corpus tag set (471 different tags) and a reduced set (186 tags). (Most of the tags in the full set are are "complex" tags in that they consist of a basic tag plus one or more

Equations	% Correct 471 Tags	% Correct 186 Tags
12 and 16	90.25	91.51
20, 16, and 23	94.09	95.04
19, 16, and 23	95.15	95.97
19, 26, and 23		96.02
36, 26, and 23		96.45

Figure 2: Results obtained from the various models

tag modifiers. For those familiar with the Brown Corpus, to get the reduced set we stripped off the modifiers "FW" (foreign word), "TL" (title), "NC" (cited word), and "HL" (headline). For the more complex techniques we only used the reduced set since the basic dynamic programming algorithm for finding the best tags runs in big-O time $= \tau^2$ where τ is the number of different tags. Using normal tests for statistical significance we find that for the interesting cases of Figure 2 a difference of .1% is significant at the 95% level of confidence.

Certain results are clear. One can get 90% of the tags correct by just picking the most likely tag for each word. Improving the model to include bigrams of tags increases the accuracy to the 95% level, with the more theoretically pure $P(w_i \mid t_i)$ performing better than $P(t_i \mid w_i)$, contrary to the results in [1]. Furthermore the improvement is much larger than the .1% required for the 95% significance level. Improvement beyond this level is possible but it gets much harder. In particular, the improvement from the more sophisticated smoothing equation, Equation 26 is minimal, only .05%. This is *not* statistically significant. However, there is reason to believe that this understates the usefulness of this equation. In particular we believe that the very crude 23 is causing extra errors when combined with the improved smoothing. Equation 23 combined with the crudeness of our morphology component also limited the improvement shown in the last line of Figure 2. Also, we should really treat endings as tag "transformers," something Equation 36 does not do. The combination of these three debilitating factors caused frequent errors in known words, and thus the figure of 96.45% was obtained when we treated known words as morphologically primitive. This improvement *is* statistically significant. We believe that fixing these problems would add another tenth of a percent or two, but better performance beyond this will require more lexical information, as that used in [10].

However, the point of this paper was to clarify the basic equations behind tagging models, rather than improving the models themselves. We hope this paper encourages tag modelers to think about the mathematics which underly their models and to present their models in terms of the equations.

References

1. BOGGESS, L., AGARWAL, R. AND DAVIS, R. *Disambiguation of prepositional phrases in automatically labelled technical text*. In *Proceedings of the Ninth National Conference on Artificial Intelligence*. 1991, 155–159.

2. BRILL, E. *A simple rule-based part of speech tagger*. In *Proceedings of the Third Conference on Applied Natural Language Processing*. 1992.

3. BROWN, P. F., DELLA PIETRA, S. A., DELLA PIETRA, V. J., LAI, J. C. AND MERCER, R. L. *An estimate of an upper bound for the entropy of english*. In *IBM Technical Report*. 1991.

4. CHURCH, K. W. *A stochastic parts program and noun phrase parser for unrestricted text*. In *Second Conference on Applied Natural Language Processing*. 1988, 136–143.

5. DeROSE, S. J. *Grammatical category disambiguation by statistical optimization*. *Computational Linguistics 14* (1988), 31–39.

6. FRANCIS, W. N. AND KUČERA, H. *Frequency Analysis of English Usage: Lexicon and Grammar*. Houghton Mifflin, Boston, 1982.

7. JELINEK, F. *Markov source modeling of text generation*. IBM T.J. Watson Research Center, Continuous Speech Recognition Group.

8. KUPIEC, J. AND MAXWELL, J. *Training stochastic grammars from unlabelled text corpora*. In *Workshop Notes, AAAI-92 Workshop on Statistically-Based NLP Techniques*. 1992, 14–19.

9. deMARCKEN, C. G. *Parsing the LOB corpus*. In *Proceedings of the 1990 Conference of the Association for Computational Linguistics*. 1990, 243–259.

10. ZERNIK, U. *Shipping departments vs. shipping pacemakers: using thematic analysis to improve tagging accuracy*. In *Proceedings of the Tenth National Conference on Artificial Intelligence*. 1992, 335–342.

Estimating Probability Distributions over Hypotheses with Variable Unification

Dekai Wu*

Department of Computer Science
The Hong Kong University of Science & Technology
Clear Water Bay, Hong Kong
dekai@cs.ust.hk

Abstract

We analyze the difficulties in applying Bayesian belief networks to language interpretation domains, which typically involve many unification hypotheses that posit variable bindings. As an alternative, we observe that the structure of the underlying hypothesis space permits an approximate encoding of the joint distribution based on marginal rather than conditional probabilities. This suggests an *implicit binding* approach that circumvents the problems with explicit unification hypotheses, while still allowing hypotheses with alternative unifications to interact probabilistically. The proposed method accepts arbitrary subsets of hypotheses and marginal probability constraints, is robust, and is readily incorporated into standard unification-based and frame-based models.

1 Introduction

The application of Bayesian belief networks (Pearl 1988) to natural language disambiguation problems has recently generated some interest (Goldman & Charniak 1990; Charniak & Goldman 1988, 1989; Burger & Connolly 1992). There is a natural appeal to using the mathematically consistent probability calculus to combine quantitative degrees of evidence for alternative interpretations, and even to help resolve parsing decisions.

However, to formulate disambiguation problems using belief networks requires an unusual form of hypothesis nodes. Natural language interpretation models (as well as many others) employ the unification operation to combine schemata; this is realized alternatively as slot-filling, role-binding, or attribute co-indexing in feature structures.

Specifically, in this paper we are concerned with the class of problems where the input context introduces a number of possible conceptual entities but the relationships between them must be inferred. This phenomenon is ubiquitous in language, for example in prepositional and adverbial attachment, adjectival modification, and nominal compounds. The process of resolving such an ambiguity corresponds to unifying two variables (or role bindings or slot fillers).

In extending the models to Bayesian belief networks, unification operations are translated to hypothesis nodes—for example *(patient g3)=r2* in figure 1—that sit alongside "regular" hypotheses concerning the features of various conceptual entities. The incorporation of binding hypotheses introduces a modelling difficulty in the context of belief networks. The strength of the unification-based paradigm rests precisely in the relatively symmetric role binding, which is subject to no constraints other than those explicitly given by the linguist or knowledge engineer. However, we argue in section 2 that this same characteristic directly resists models based on the notion of conditional independence, in particular belief networks.

In section 3 we re-analyze the structure of the underlying hypothesis space and its joint distribution. This formulation leads to an alternative approach to approximation, proposed in section 4. A natural language application dealing with nominal compound interpretation is outlined in section 5.

2 Unification Resists Conditional Independence

In conditional independence networks, the values of some hypotheses are permitted to influence others but the paths of influence are restricted by the graph, thus providing computational leverage. In the extreme, a completely connected graph offers no computational shortcuts; instead, to improve performance a distribution should be graphed with the lowest possible connectivity. In general, conditional independence networks have been applied in highly structured domains where low-connectivity approximations can be accurate. The types of domains that invite unification-oriented representations, however, resist low-connectivity approximations, because binding hypotheses have a high inherent degree of interdependence.

Typically in such a domain, there will be some number

---
*Preparation of this paper was partially supported by the Natural Sciences and Engineering Research Council of Canada while the author was a postdoctoral fellow at the University of Toronto. Much of this research was done at the Computer Science Division, University of California at Berkeley and was sponsored in part by the Defense Advanced Research Projects Agency (DoD), monitored by the Space and Naval Warfare Systems Command under N00039-88-C-0292, the Office of Naval Research under N00014-89-J-3205, the Sloan Foundation under grant 86-10-3, and the National Science Foundation under CDA-8722788.

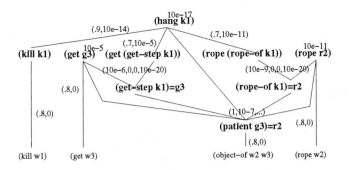

Figure 1: Example belief net from Goldman & Charniak (1991).

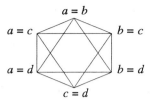

n of "free" variables $a, b, c \ldots$ that are potentially unifiable with others. A unification hypothesis is of the form $a = b$, and there are $m = \binom{n}{2}$ such hypotheses. *A priori* knowledge, like selectional restrictions, may help rule out some of these hypotheses, but many bindings will remain possible and we'll assume here that all unification hypotheses have nonzero probability. A *joint hypothesis* is an assignment of truth values to each of the m unification hypotheses.[1] The number of legal joint hypotheses is less than 2^m because of the dependence between hypotheses. For example, if $a = c$ and $b = c$ are true, then $a = b$ must also be true. In fact the number of legal joint hypotheses is equal to the number of possible partitionings of a set of n elements. Figure 2 shows the legal joint hypotheses when $n = 4$.

Hypotheses	Legal assignments
$a = b$	0 0 0 0 0 0 1 0 0 1 0 0 1 1 1
$a = c$	0 0 0 0 0 1 0 0 1 0 0 1 0 1 1
$a = d$	0 0 0 0 1 0 0 1 0 0 0 1 1 0 1
$b = c$	0 0 0 1 0 0 0 1 0 0 1 0 0 1 1
$b = d$	0 0 1 0 0 0 0 0 1 0 1 0 1 0 1
$c = d$	0 1 0 0 0 0 0 0 1 1 1 0 0 1

Figure 2: The legal joint hypotheses for $n = 4$. Each column shows a permissible truth value assignment.

Now consider the dependence relationships between unification hypotheses. The probabilities of $a = c$ and $b = c$ are not independent since they may be affected by the value of $a = b$; if $a \neq b$ then all events where $a = c$ and $b = c$ are ruled out. However, it is possible for $a = c$ and $b = c$ to be conditionally independent given $a = b$, which can be modelled by

$$a = c \text{———} a = b \text{———} b = c$$

By symmetry, all three hypotheses must be connected. This extends to larger n, so if $n = 4$, then if $a = d$ and $b = d$ are conditionally independent, it must also be conditioned on $a = b$:

---

[1] We ignore all other types of hypotheses in this section's analysis.

In general, any pair of unification hypotheses that involve a common variable must be connected. Thus for n variables, the total number of links is

$$l = n \cdot \binom{n-1}{2} = \frac{n(n-1)(n-2)}{2} = m(n-2)$$

which is $\Theta(n^3)$ or $\Theta(m^{3/2})$. This is better than a completely connected network which would be $\Theta(n^4)$ or $\Theta(m^2)$ but there are many loops nonetheless, so evaluation will be expensive. By symmetry, each of the m hypotheses is of degree

$$\frac{2l}{m} = 2(n-2)$$

and any clustering of variables will be subject to this bound.

We conclude that in domains where unification hypotheses are relatively unconstrained, the connectivity of conditional independence networks is undesirably high. This means that it is difficult to find efficient conditional probability representations that accurately approximate the desired joint probability distributions. Therefore, in the next section we reconsider the event space that underlies the joint distribution.

3 Back to Basics

Since conditional probabilities do not lend themselves well to representations involving unification hypotheses, we now examine the structure of the joint hypothesis space. Before, we considered the unification hypotheses in explicit form because we sought conditional independence relationships between them. Having abandoned that objective, here we instead consider the feature structures (or frames) that result from assigning truth values to the unification hypotheses. In other words, the unification hypotheses are left implicit, reflected by co-indexed variables (roles) in feature structures.

Figure 3 depicts the qualitative structure of the joint hypothesis space, which forms a semilattice hierarchy. We now take into consideration not only the implicit unification hypotheses, but also implicit hypotheses that specialize the features on the variables; for example, a variable of type a may be specialized to the subtype b. Each box denotes the feature structure that results from some combination of truth values over a subset of unification hypotheses and specialization hypotheses. Each small shaded box denotes a joint hypothesis specifying the truth values over *all* unification and specialization hypotheses. Thus the distinction between the shaded and non-shaded boxes is a kind of type-token distinction where the shaded boxes are tokens. Notice furthermore that role specialization and unification are intertwined: a role of type z results when a type x role and a type y role are conjoined by unifying their fillers.

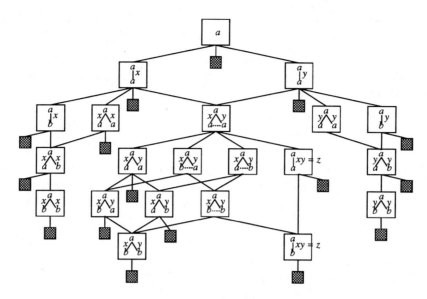

Figure 3: Simplified partial abstraction lattice for feature structures. The type b is a subtype of a; the role type z is a composite role equivalent to the conjunction xy. A dashed line indicates that the variables are "free" to be unified.

In principle, the joint distribution would be completely specified if we could enumerate the probabilities over the (shaded) tokens. We saw in the previous section that conditional probabilities are not well suited for approximately summarizing distributions over this space, because there is no way to discard large numbers of binding dependencies in the general case. However, there is another straightforward way to store distributional information, namely to record *marginal* probabilities over the abstract (non-shaded) types, i.e., the sums of probabilities over all descendant leaves. To summarize the distribution approximately, a selected subset of the marginal probabilities can be stored. Theoretically, a set of marginal probabilities induces an equivalent set of conditional probabilities over the same lattice, though it may be an unreasonably large set. If there are any independence relationships to be exploited, equivalently a subset of marginal probabilities can be omitted and the maximum-entropy principle (Jaynes 1979) can be applied to reconstruct the joint distribution.

The advantages of this formulation are: (1) fewer parameters are required since it does not encode redundant distributional information in multiple dependent conditional probabilities, (2) consistency is easier to maintain because the interdependent unification hypotheses are not explicit, (3) it facilitates an alternative *structural* approximation method for computing a conditional distribution of interest, as discussed in the next section.

4   An Approximation Based on Marginal Constraints

By itself, the marginal probability formulation can reduce probability storage requirements but does not improve computation cost. Computing maximum entropy distributions subject to large numbers of marginal constraints is infeasible in the general case. However, in many applications, includ-

ing language interpretation, the input cues are sufficient to eliminate all but a relatively small number of hypotheses. Only the distribution over these hypotheses is of interest. Moreover, the input cues may suffice to preselect a subset of relevant marginal probability constraints.

The proposed method takes advantage of these factors by dynamically creating a secondary marginal probability formulation of the same form as that above, but with far fewer constraints and hypotheses, thereby rendering the entropy maximization feasible. In the secondary formulation, only details within the desired hypothesis and constraint space are preserved. Outside this space, the minimum possible number of "dummy" events are substituted for multiple hypotheses that are not of interest. It turns out that one dummy event is required for each marginal constraint. Let $\mathcal{Q}$ be the set of token feature structures and $\mathcal{G}$ is the set of type feature structures, and $\mathcal{F} \stackrel{\text{def}}{=} \mathcal{G} \cup \mathcal{Q}$. Suppose $\mathcal{H} = \{h_1, \ldots, h_i, \ldots, h_H\} \subset \mathcal{Q}$ are the candidate hypotheses, and suppose $\mathcal{M} = \{m_1, \ldots, m_j, \ldots, m_M\} \subset \mathcal{G}$ are the abstract class types that have been preselected as being relevant, with associated marginal probabilities $P_{m_j} = P(m_j)$. Denote by $\sqsubset$ the partial ordering induced on $\mathcal{H} \cup \mathcal{M}$ by the subsumption semilattice on f-structure space.

Then we define the secondary formulation as follows. Let the set of dummy events be $\mathcal{D} = \{d_1, \ldots, d_j, \ldots, d_M\}$, one for each marginal constraint. Define $\dot{\mathcal{F}} \stackrel{\text{def}}{=} \mathcal{H} \cup \mathcal{M} \cup \mathcal{D}$ to be the *approximate event space*, and define $\dot{\mathcal{H}} \stackrel{\text{def}}{=} \mathcal{H} \cup \mathcal{D}$ to be the *approximate hypothesis space*. We construct the *approximate ordering relation* $\dot{\sqsubset}$ over $\dot{\mathcal{F}}$ according to:

$$
\begin{cases}
a \mathrel{\dot{\sqsubset}} b, & \text{if} \begin{cases} a \sqsubset b; a, b \in \mathcal{F} \\ a = m_j; b = d_j \\ a \sqsubset c; c = m_j; b = d_j \end{cases} \\
a \mathrel{\dot{\not\sqsubset}} b, & \text{otherwise}
\end{cases}
$$

Let $\dot{P}_{m_j}$ be the marginal probability constraints on $\mathcal{F}$. We use P_{m_j} as estimators for $\dot{P}_{m_j}$. (Of course, since the event space has been distorted by the structural dummy event approximation, actually $P_{m_j} \neq \dot{P}_{m_j}$.)

To estimate the distribution over the hypotheses of interest, along with the dummy events, we compute $\hat{P}_{h_i}$ and $\hat{P}_{d_i}$ such that

$$(1) \qquad \sum_{q \in \dot{\mathcal{H}}} \hat{P}_q = 1$$

while maximizing the entropy

$$(2) \qquad E = - \sum_{q \in \dot{\mathcal{H}}} \hat{P}_q \log \hat{P}_q$$

subject to the marginal constraints

$$(3) \qquad \sum_{q: q \in \dot{\mathcal{H}}, m_j \sqsubseteq q} \hat{P}_q = \dot{P}_{m_j}$$

Technical details of the solution are given in Appendix A.

Note that unlike methods for finding maximum *a posteriori* assignments (Charniak & Santos Jr. 1992) which returns the probability for the most probable joint assignment, the objective here is to evaluate the conditional distribution over a freely chosen set of joint hypothesis assignments and marginal constraints.

One of the strengths of AME is robustness when arbitrarily chosen marginals are discarded. Arithmetic inconsistencies do not arise because the dummy events absorb any discrepancies arising from the approximation. For example, if C through F are discarded from figure 4(a), then $P(A) + P(B) < P(G)$, but the remaining probability weight is absorbed by G's dummy event in (b). The ability to handle arbitrary subpartitions of the knowledge base is important in practical applications, where many different heuristics may be used to preselect the constraints dynamically. In contrast, when there are dependent unification hypotheses in a belief network, discarding conditional probability matrices can easily lead to networks that have no solution.

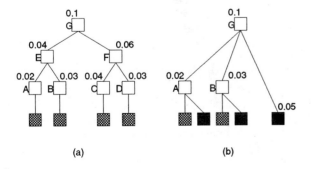

(a)   (b)

Figure 4: Robust handling of discarded marginal constraints. (a) Original KB fragment. (b) Dummy event (black) absorbing discrepancy caused by discarding marginals.

5 A Nominal Compound Interpretation Example

In this section we summarize an example from the language interpretation domain that drove the development of AME, a more detailed discussion of which is found in the companion paper (Wu 1993a). Space does not permit a description of the semantics and lexical models; see Wu (1992, 1993b). Although our modelling objectives arise solely from disambiguation problems, we believe the foregoing discussion applies nonetheless to other structured domains involving highly interdependent variable bindings with uncertainty.

The example task here is to interpret the nominal compound *coast road*,[2] which in null context most likely means a *road in coastal area* but, particularly in other contexts, can also mean other things including a *road leading to coastal area*, a *coasting road* amenable to coasting, and *Highway 1*. As is typical with novel nominal compounds, interpretation requires a wide range of knowledge. Figure 5 shows the fairly standard feature-structure notation we use to encode such knowledge; the marginal probabilities in (a) and (b) are the primary representational extension.

During interpretation, a hypothesis network as in figure 6 is dynamically constructed. Each node corresponds to a marginal constraint from the knowledge base, of the form figure 5(a)—(b). Ignoring the boldface marginals for now, the probabilities $P(coast\ and\ road)$ and $P(coast\ and\ coastal\ road)$ indicate that when thinking about roads, it is the subcategory of roads running along the coast that is frequently thought of. Similarly $P(coastal\ road)$ and $P(Highway\ 1)$ model a non-West Coast resident who does not frequently specialize coastal roads to Highway 1. Together, $P(L{:}coast)$, $P(C{:}coast{:}seacoast)$, and $P(C{:}coast{:}coasting\ accomplishment)$ indicate that the noun *coast* more frequently designates a seacoast rather than an unpowered movement. Finally, $P(C{:}NN{:}containment)$ indicates that the noun-noun construction signifies containment twice as often as $P(C{:}NN{:}linear\ order\ locative)$.

Figure 6 summarizes the results of the baseline run and four variants, from a C implementation of AME. In the base run labelled "**0:**", the AME estimate of the conditional distribution assigns highest probabilities to *road in coastal area* and *road along coastline* (features distinguishing these two hypotheses have been omitted). The next run "**1:**" demonstrates what would happen if "*coast*" more often signified *coasting accomplishment* rather than *seacoast*: the *coasting road* hypothesis dominates instead. In "**2:**" the noun-noun construction is assumed to signify linear order locatives more frequently than containment. The marginals in "**3:**" effectively reduce the conditional probability of thinking of roads along the seacoast, given one is thinking of roads in the context of seacoasts. The West Coast res-

[2] From the Brown corpus (Kučera & Francis 1967). Our approach to nominal compounds is discussed in Wu (1990), which proposes the use of probability to address long-standing problems from the linguistics literature (e.g., Lees 1963; Downing 1977; Levi 1978; Warren 1978; McDonald 1982).

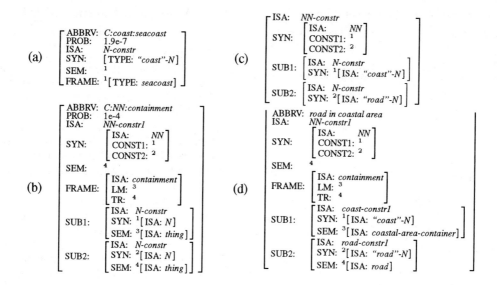

Figure 5: Feature-structures for (a) the noun *coast* signifying a seacoast, (b) a noun-noun construction signifying a containment schema, (c) an input form, and (d) a full interpretation hypothesis (the floor brackets indicate a token as opposed to type).

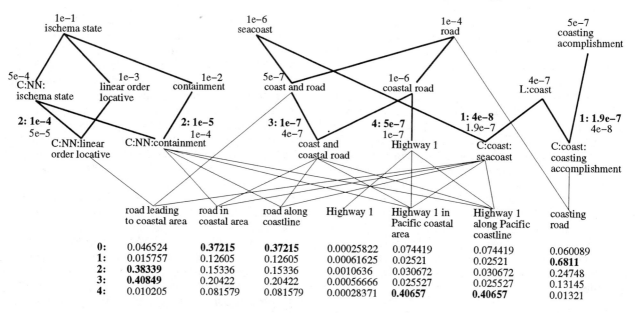

Figure 6: Estimated conditional distributions for five runs on *coast road* with varying marginal constraints. Dummy events have been omitted.

ident is modelled in "**4:**" by an increase in the marginal $P(Highway\,1)$.

6 Conclusion

We have discussed the difficulties encountered in applying Bayesian belief networks to domains like language interpretation, which involve unification hypotheses over "free" variables. We observed that the structure of the underlying joint hypothesis space permits an alternative approximate encoding based on marginal rather than conditional probabilities. This *implicit binding* formulation facilitates

a structural approximation method. For many applications, language interpretation in particular, the structural approximation is adequate and flexibility in handling unification hypotheses is quite important, whereas exact probability distribution computation is unnecessary. The method is robust and incorporates readily into unification- or frame-based models.

Acknowledgements

I am indebted to Robert Wilensky, Jerome Feldman, and the members of the BAIR and L_0 groups for many valuable discussions, as well as Graeme Hirst, Geoff Hinton, and their respective groups.

A Details of the Entropy Maximization

To solve the constrained maximization problem in equations (1)—(3), we define a new energy function with Lagrange multipliers, J, to be maximized:

$$J \stackrel{\text{def}}{=} E + \sum_{j=1}^{M} \lambda_j (\dot{P}_{m_j} - \sum_{q:q\in\mathcal{H}, m_j \sqsubseteq q} \hat{P}_q)$$

$$= -\sum_{q\in\mathcal{H}} \hat{P}_q \log \hat{P}_q + \sum_{j=1}^{M} \lambda_j (\dot{P}_{m_j} - \sum_{q:q\in\mathcal{H}, m_j \sqsubseteq q} \hat{P}_q)$$

This method is a modified version of Cheeseman's (1987) method, which applied only to feature vectors. Observe that setting the gradients to zero gives the desired conditions:

$$\nabla_\lambda J = 0 \quad \Rightarrow \quad \frac{\partial J}{\partial \lambda_j} = 0; 1 \le j \le M$$
$$\Rightarrow \quad \text{expresses all marginal constraints}$$
$$\nabla_{\hat{\mathbf{P}}} J = 0 \quad \Rightarrow \quad \frac{\partial J}{\partial \hat{P}_q} = 0; q \in \mathcal{H}$$
$$\Rightarrow \quad \text{maximizes entropy}$$

Since the partials with respect to $\hat{\mathbf{P}}$ are

$$\frac{\partial J}{\partial \hat{P}_q} = -\log \hat{P}_q - \sum_{j:m_j \sqsubseteq q} \lambda_j$$

then at $\nabla_{\hat{\mathbf{P}}} J = 0$,

$$\log \hat{P}_q = - \sum_{j:m_j \sqsubseteq q} \lambda_j$$

Defining $\omega_j \stackrel{\text{def}}{=} e^{-\lambda_j}$,

$$\hat{P}_q = \prod_{j:m_j \sqsubseteq q} \omega_j$$

the original marginal constraints become

$$\dot{P}_{m_j} = \sum_{q:m_j \sqsubseteq q} \prod_{k:m_k \sqsubseteq q} \omega_k$$

which can be rewritten

$$\dot{P}_{m_j} - \sum_{q:m_j \sqsubseteq q} \prod_{k:m_k \sqsubseteq q} \omega_k = 0$$

The last expression is solved using a numerical algorithm of the following form:

1. Start with a constraint system $X \leftarrow \{\}$ and an estimated ω vector $\langle\rangle$ of length zero.

2. For each constraint equation,

   (a) Add the equation to X and its corresponding ω_i term to $\langle \omega_1, \ldots, \omega_{i-1}, \omega_i \rangle$.

   (b) Repeat until $\langle \omega_1, \ldots, \omega_i \rangle$ settles, i.e., the change between iterations falls below some threshold:

   1. For each equation in X constraining $\dot{P}_{m_j}$, solve for the corresponding ω_j assuming all other ω values have their current estimated values.

References

BURGER, JOHN D. & DENNIS CONNOLLY. 1992. Probabilistic resolution of anaphoric reference. In *AAAI Fall Symposium on Probabilistic NLP*, Cambridge, MA. Proceedings to appear as AAAI technical report.

CHARNIAK, EUGENE & ROBERT GOLDMAN. 1988. A logic for semantic interpretation. In *Proceedings of the 26th Annual Conference of the Association for Computational Linguistics*, 87–94.

CHARNIAK, EUGENE & ROBERT GOLDMAN. 1989. A semantics for probabilistic quantifier-free first-order languages, with particular application to story understanding. In *Proceedings of IJCAI-89, Eleventh International Joint Conference on Artificial Intelligence*, 1074–1079.

CHARNIAK, EUGENE & EUGENE SANTOS JR. 1992. Dynamic MAP calculations for abduction. In *Proceedings of AAAI-92, Tenth National Conference on Artificial Intelligence*, 552–557, San Jose, CA.

CHEESEMAN, PETER. 1987. A method of computing maximum entropy probability values for expert systems. In *Maximum-entropy and Bayesian spectral analysis and estimation problems*, ed. by Ray C. Smith & Gary J. Erickson, 229–240. Dordrecht, Holland: D. Reidel. Revised proceedings of the Third Maximum Entropy Workshop, Laramie, WY, 1983.

DOWNING, PAMELA. 1977. On the creation and use of English compound nouns. *Language*, 53(4):810–842.

GOLDMAN, ROBERT P. & EUGENE CHARNIAK. 1990. A probabilistic approach to text understanding. Technical Report CS-90-13, Brown Univ., Providence, RI.

JAYNES, E. T. 1979. Where do we stand on maximum entropy. In *The maximum entropy formalism*, ed. by R. D. Levine & M. Tribus. Cambridge, MA: MIT Press.

KUČERA, HENRY & W. NELSON FRANCIS. 1967. *Computational analysis of present-day American English*. Providence, RI: Brown University Press.

LEES, ROBERT B. 1963. *The grammar of English nominalizations*. The Hague: Mouton.

LEVI, JUDITH N. 1978. *The syntax and semantics of complex nominals*. New York: Academic Press.

MCDONALD, DAVID B. 1982. Understanding noun compounds. Technical Report CMU-CS-82-102, Carnegie-Mellon Univ., Dept. of Comp. Sci., Pittsburgh, PA.

PEARL, JUDEA. 1988. *Probabilistic reasoning in intelligent systems: Networks of plausible inference*. San Mateo, CA: Morgan Kaufmann.

WARREN, BEATRICE. 1978. *Semantic patterns of noun-noun compounds*. Gothenburg, Sweden: Acta Universitatis Gothoburgensis.

WU, DEKAI. 1990. Probabilistic unification-based integration of syntactic and semantic preferences for nominal compounds. In *Proceedings of the Thirteenth International Conference on Computational Linguistics*, volume 2, 413–418, Helsinki.

WU, DEKAI, 1992. *Automatic inference: A probabilistic basis for natural language interpretation*. University of California at Berkeley dissertation. Available as UC Berkeley Computer Science Division Technical Report UCB/CSD 92/692.

WU, DEKAI. 1993a. Approximating maximum-entropy ratings for evidential parsing and semantic interpretation. In *Proceedings of IJCAI-93, Thirteenth International Joint Conference on Artificial Intelligence*, Chamberry, France. To appear.

WU, DEKAI. 1993b. An image-schematic system of thematic roles. In *Proceedings of PACLING-93, First Conference of the Pacific Association for Computational Linguistics*, Vancouver. To appear.

Trainable
Natural Language
Systems

A Case-Based Approach to Knowledge Acquisition for Domain-Specific Sentence Analysis

Claire Cardie
Department of Computer Science
University of Massachusetts
Amherst, MA 01003
E-mail: cardie@cs.umass.edu

Abstract

This paper describes a case-based approach to knowledge acquisition for natural language systems that simultaneously learns part of speech, word sense, and concept activation knowledge for all open class words in a corpus. The parser begins with a lexicon of function words and creates a case base of context-sensitive word definitions during a human-supervised training phase. Then, given an unknown word and the context in which it occurs, the parser retrieves definitions from the case base to infer the word's syntactic and semantic features. By encoding context as part of a definition, the meaning of a word can change dynamically in response to surrounding phrases without the need for explicit lexical disambiguation heuristics. Moreover, the approach acquires all three classes of knowledge using the same case representation and requires relatively little training and no hand-coded knowledge acquisition heuristics. We evaluate it in experiments that explore two of many practical applications of the technique and conclude that the case-based method provides a promising approach to automated dictionary construction and knowledge acquisition for sentence analysis in limited domains. In addition, we present a novel case retrieval algorithm that uses decision trees to improve the performance of a k-nearest neighbor similarity metric.

Introduction

In recent years, there have been an increasing number of natural language systems that successfully perform domain-specific text summarization (see [MUC-3 Proceedings 1991; MUC-4 Proceedings 1992]). However, many of the best-performing systems rely on knowledge-based parsing techniques that are extremely tedious and time-consuming to port to new domains. We estimate, for example, that the domain-dependent knowledge engineering effort for the UMass/MUC-3[1] system spanned 1500 person-hours [Lehnert et al. 1991b]. Although the exact type and form of the domain-specific knowledge required by a parser varies from system to system, all knowledge-based language processing systems rely on at least the following information: for each word encountered in a text, the system must

(1) know which *parts of speech, word senses, and concepts* are plausible in the given domain and (2) determine which part of speech, word sense, and concepts apply, *given the particular context in which the word occurs*.

Consider, for example, the following sentences from the MUC domain of Latin American terrorism:

1. The terrorists **killed** *General Bustillo*.

2. The *general* concern was that children might be **killed**.

3. In *general*, terrorist activity is confined to the cities.

It is clear that in this domain the word "general" has at least two plausible parts of speech (noun and adjective) and two word senses (a military officer and a universal entity). A sentence analyzer has to know that these options exist and then choose the noun/military officer form of "general" for sentence 1, the adjective/universal entity form in 2, and the noun/universal entity form in 3.

In addition to part of speech and word sense ambiguity, these sentences also illustrate a form of concept ambiguity with respect to the domain of terrorism. Sentence 1, for example, clearly describes a terrorist act — the word "killed" implies that a murder took place and the perpetrators of the crime were "terrorists." This is not the case for sentence 2 — the verb "killed" appears, but no murder has yet occurred and there is no implication of terrorist activity. This distinction is important in the MUC domain where the goal is to extract from texts only information concerning 8 classes of terrorist events including murders, bombings, attacks, and kidnappings. All other information should be effectively ignored. To be successful in this *selective concept extraction* task [Lehnert et al. 1991a], a sentence analyzer not only needs access to word-concept pairings (e.g., the word "killed" is linked to the "terrorist murder" concept), but must also accurately distinguish legitimate concept activation contexts from bogus ones (e.g., the phrase "terrorists killed" implies that a "terrorist murder" occurred, but "children might be killed" probably doesn't).

This paper describes a case-based method for knowledge acquisition that begins with a lexicon of only closed class words and learns the part of speech, general and specific word senses, and concept activation information for all open class words in a corpus.[2] We first create a case

---

[1]The domain for the MUC-3 and MUC-4 performance evaluations was Latin American terrorism. The general task for each system was to summarize all terrorist events mentioned in a set of 100 previously unseen texts.

[2]Closed class words are function words like prepositions, aux-

base of context-sensitive word definitions during a human-supervised training phase. After training, given an open class word and the context in which it occurs, the parser retrieves the most similar cases from the case base and then uses them to infer syntactic and semantic information for the open class word. No explicit lexical disambiguation heuristics are used, but because context is encoded as part of each definition, the same word may be assigned a different part of speech, word sense, or concept activation in different contexts.

The paper also describes the results of two experiments that explore different, but related applications of this knowledge acquisition technique. In the first application, we assume the existence of a nearly complete domain-specific dictionary and use the case base to infer the features of unknown words. In the second, more ambitious application, we assume only a small dictionary of function words and use the case base to determine the definition of *all* open class words. Although these tasks have been addressed separately in related research, our approach is the first to simultaneously accommodate both using a single mechanism.

Moreover, previous approaches to automated lexical acquisition can be classified along three dimensions: (1) the type of knowledge acquired by the approach, (2) the amount of training data required by the approach, and (3) the amount of knowledge required by the approach. [Brent 1990; Grefenstette 1992; Resnik 1992; and Zernik 1991], for example, present systems that learn either syntactic or limited semantic knowledge but not both. Statistically-based methods that acquire (usually syntactic) lexical knowledge have been successful (e.g., [Brent 1991; Church & Hanks 1990; Hindle 1990; Resnik 1992; Yarowsky 1992; and Zernik 1991]), but these require the existence of very large, often hand-tagged corpora. Finally, there exist knowledge-intensive methods that acquire syntactic and/or semantic lexical knowledge, but rely heavily on hand-coded world knowledge (e.g., [Berwick 1983; Granger 1977; Hastings et al. 1991; Lytinen & Roberts 1989; and Selfridge 1986]) or hand-coded heuristics that describe how and when to acquire new word definitions (e.g., [Jacobs & Zernik 1988 and Wilensky 1991]).

Our approach to knowledge acquisition for natural language systems differs from existing work in its:

- **unified approach to learning lexical knowledge.** The same case-based method and case representation are used to simultaneously learn both syntactic and semantic information for unknown words.

- **encoding of context as part of a word definition.** This allows the definition of a word to change dynamically in response to surrounding phrases and obviates the need for explicit, hand-coded lexical disambiguation heuristics.

- **need for relatively little training.** In the experiments described below, we obtained promising results after training on only 108 sentences. This implies that the method

iliaries, and connectives, whose meanings vary little from one domain to another. All other words (e.g., nouns, verbs, adjectives) are open class words.

may work well for small corpora where statistical approaches fail due to lack of data.

- **lack of hand-coded heuristics to drive the acquisition process.** These are implicitly encoded in the case base.

- **leveraging of two existing machine learning paradigms.** For case retrieval, we use a decision tree algorithm to improve the performance of a simple k-nearest neighbor similarity metric.

In the remainder of the paper we describe the details of the approach including the case representation, case base construction, and the hybrid approach to case retrieval. We also discuss the results of the two experiments mentioned briefly above.

Case Representation

As discussed in the last section, our goal is to learn part of speech, word sense, and concept activation knowledge for any open class word in a corpus by drawing from a case base of domain-specific, context-sensitive word definitions. However, the case representation relies on three predefined taxonomies, one for each class of knowledge that we're trying to learn. This section, therefore, first briefly describes the taxonomies and then shows how they are used in conjunction with parser-generated knowledge to construct the word definition cases.

The Taxonomies

To start, we set up a taxonomy of allowable word senses. Naturally, these reflect the goals of a particular domain. For the remainder of the paper, we will use the TIPSTER JV corpus as our sample domain. This corpus currently contains over 1300 texts that recount world-wide activity in the area of joint ventures/tie-ups between businesses. A portion of the word sense taxonomy created for the TIPSTER JV domain is shown in Figure 1. The complete taxonomy includes 14 general word senses and 42 specific word senses. They are used to describe all non-verb open class words.

General word sense Specific word sense	Description
jv-entity	party involved in a tie-up
company-name	name of a company
generic-company-name	e.g. "Co." in "Plastics Co."
government	government-affiliated entity
person	an individual
industry	type of business or industry
research	research and development
production	manufacturing, production
sales	sales, marketing, trade
facility	physical facilities
communications	broadcasting stations
factory	manufacturing sites
farm	agricultural sites
location	location expression
country	country name
city	city name
entity	generic entity

Figure 1: Word Sense Taxonomy (partial)

Concept Types	Description
tie-up	indicates a tie-up activity
tie-up-secondary	weak indicator of a tie-up
total-capitalization	total cash capitalization
ownership-%	indicates a share in the tie-up
industry	indicates the type of industry
ind-research	performed within the scope
ind-production	of the tie-up

Figure 2: Taxonomy of Concept Types (partial)

Next, we define a taxonomy of 11 domain-specific concept types which represent a subset of the relevant information to be included in the summary of each joint venture text (see Figure 2). Finally, we use a taxonomy of 18 parts of speech (not shown). The taxonomy specifies 7 parts of speech generally associated with open class words and reserves the remaining 11 parts of speech for closed class words. Although the word sense and concept taxonomies are clearly domain-specific, the part of speech taxonomy is parser-dependent rather than domain-dependent. We emphasize, however, that our approach depends not on the specifics of any of the taxonomies, only on their existence.

Representation of Cases

Each case in the case base represents the definition of a single open class word as well as the context in which it occurs in the corpus. It is a list of 39 attribute-value pairs that can be grouped into three sets of features:

- **word definition features (6)** that represent semantic and syntactic knowledge associated with the open class word in the current context
- **local context features (20)** that represent semantic and syntactic knowledge for the two words preceding and the two words following the current word
- **global context features (13)** that represent the current state of the parser

Figure 3 shows the case for the word "venture" in a sentence taken directly from the TIPSTER JV corpus. Examine first the word definition features. The open class **word** defined by this case is "venture" and its part of speech in the current context is a *noun modifier (nm)*.[3] The **gen-ws** and **spec-ws** features refer to the word's general and specific word senses. In this example, "venture" has been assigned the most general word sense, *entity*, and has no specific word senses. The **concept** feature indicates that "venture" activates the domain-specific *tie-up* concept in this context. There is also a **morphol** feature associated with the current word that indicates its class of suffix. The *nil* value used here means that no morphology information was derived for "venture."

Next, examine the local context features. For each of the two words that precede and follow the current open class

---

[3]The *noun modifier(nm)* category covers both adjectives and nouns that act as modifiers. We reserve the *noun* category for head nouns only.

word (referred to in Figure 3 as **prev1**, **prev2**, **fol1**, and **fol2**), we draw from the taxonomies to specify its part of speech, word senses, and activated concepts. The word immediately following "venture," for example, is the *noun* "firm." It has been assigned the *jv-entity* general word sense because it refers to a business, but has no specific word senses and activates no domain-specific concept in this context.

Finally, examine the global context features that encode information about the state of the parser at the word "venture." When the parser reaches the word "venture," it has recognized two major constituents — the subject and verb phrase. Neither activates any domain-specific concepts, but the subject does have general and specific word senses. These are acquired by taking the union of the senses of each word in the noun phrase. (Verbs are currently assigned no general or specific word senses.) Because the direct object has not yet been recognized, all of its corresponding features in the case are empty. In addition to specifying information about each of the main constituents, the global context features also include syntactic and semantic knowledge for the most recent low-level constituent (**last constit**). A low-level constituent can be either a noun phrase, verb, or prepositional phrase and sometimes coincides with one of the major constituents — the subject, verb phrase, or direct object. This is the case in Figure 3 where the low-level constituent preceding "venture" is just the verb.

Case Base Construction

Using the case representation described in the last section, we create a case base of context-dependent word definitions from a small subset of the sentences in the TIPSTER JV corpus. Because the goal of the approach is to learn syntactic and semantic information for only open class words, we assume the existence of a function word lexicon. This lexicon maintains the part of speech and word senses (if any apply) for 129 function words. None of the function words has any associated domain-specific concepts.

The semi-automated training phase alternately consults a human supervisor and a parser (i.e., the CIRCUS parser [Lehnert 1990]) to create a case for each open class word in the training sentences. More specifically, whenever an open class word is encountered, CIRCUS creates a case for the word, automatically filling in the global context features, the **word** and **morphol** features for the unknown word, and the local context features for the preceding two words (i.e., the **prev1** and **prev2** features). Local context features for the following two words (i.e., **fol1** and **fol2**) will be added to the case after CIRCUS reaches them in its left-to-right traversal of the sentence. The user is consulted via a menu-driven interface only to specify the current word's part of speech, word senses, and concept activation information. These values are stored in the **p-o-s**, **gen-ws**, **spec-ws**, and **concept** word definition features and are used by the parser to process the current word. When CIRCUS finishes its analysis of the training sentences, it has generated one case for every occurrence of an open class word.

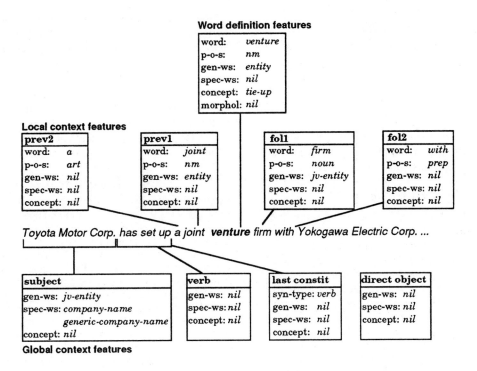

Word definition features

word:	*venture*
p-o-s:	*nm*
gen-ws:	*entity*
spec-ws:	*nil*
concept:	*tie-up*
morphol:	*nil*

Local context features

prev2	
word:	*a*
p-o-s:	*art*
gen-ws:	*nil*
spec-ws:	*nil*
concept:	*nil*

prev1	
word:	*joint*
p-o-s:	*nm*
gen-ws:	*entity*
spec-ws:	*nil*
concept:	*nil*

fol1	
word:	*firm*
p-o-s:	*noun*
gen-ws:	*jv-entity*
spec-ws:	*nil*
concept:	*nil*

fol2	
word:	*with*
p-o-s:	*prep*
gen-ws:	*nil*
spec-ws:	*nil*
concept:	*nil*

Toyota Motor Corp. has set up a joint **venture** *firm with Yokogawa Electric Corp. ...*

subject	
gen-ws:	*jv-entity*
spec-ws:	*company-name*
	generic-company-name
concept:	*nil*

verb	
gen-ws:	*nil*
spec-ws:	*nil*
concept:	*nil*

last constit	
syn-type:	*verb*
gen-ws:	*nil*
spec-ws:	*nil*
concept:	*nil*

direct object	
gen-ws:	*nil*
spec-ws:	*nil*
concept:	*nil*

Global context features

Figure 3: Case for "venture"

Case Retrieval

Once the case base has been constructed, we can use it to determine the definition of new words in the corpus. Assume, for example, that we want to know the part of speech, word senses, and activated concepts for "Toyo's" in the sentence:

Yasui said this is **Toyo's** and JAL's third hotel joint venture.

First, CIRCUS parses the sentence and creates a probe case for "Toyo's" filling in the **word** and **morphol** features of the case as well as its global and local context features using the method described in the last section.[4] The only difference between a test case and a training case is the **gen-ws**, **spec-ws**, **p-o-s**, and **concept** features for the unknown word. During training, the human supervisor specifies values for these *missing features*, but during testing they are omitted from the case entirely. It is the job of the case retrieval algorithm to find the training cases that are most similar to the probe and use them to predict values for the missing features of the unknown word. We use the following algorithm for this task:

1. Compare the probe to each case in the case base, counting the number of features that match (i.e., match = 1, mismatch = 0). Do not include the missing features in the comparison. Only give partial credit (.5) for matches on *nil*'s.

2. Keep the 10 highest-scoring cases.

3. Of these, return the case(s) whose **word** matches the unknown word, if any exist. Otherwise, return all 10 cases.[5]

4. Let the retrieved cases vote on the values for the probe's missing features.

The case retrieval algorithm is essentially a k-nearest neighbors matching algorithm (k = 10) with a bias toward cases whose **word** matches the unknown word. An interesting feature of the algorithm is that it allows a word to take on a meaning different from any it received during the training phase. However, one problem with the retrieval mechanism is that it assumes that all features are equally important for learning part of speech, word sense, and concept activation knowledge. Intuitively, it seems that accurate prediction of each class of missing information may rely on very different subsets of the feature set. Unfortunately, it is difficult to know which combinations of features will best predict each class of knowledge without trying all of them.

There are machine learning algorithms, like decision tree algorithms (see [Quinlan 1986]), however, that can be used to perform the feature specification task. Very briefly, decision tree algorithms learn to classify objects into one of *n* classes by finding the features that are most important for the classification and creating a tree that branches on each of them until a classification can be made. We use Quinlan's C4.5 decision tree system [Quinlan 1992] to select the features to be included for k-nearest neighbor case retrieval:

1. Given the cases from the training sentences as input, let C4.5 create a decision tree for each missing feature.[6]

---

[4]There is a bootstrapping problem in that the **fol1** and **fol2** features are needed to specify the probe case for "Toyo's." This problem will be addressed in the second experiment. For now, assume that the parser has access to all **fol1** and **fol2** features at the position of the unknown word.

[5]More than 10 cases will be returned if there are ties.

[6]We omit the **p-o-s**, **gen-ws**, **spec-ws**, and **concept** word definition features from training cases because those are the features

2. Note the features that occurred in each tree. This essentially produces, for each of the 4 missing attributes, a list of all features that C4.5 found useful for predicting its value.

3. Instead of invoking the case retrieval algorithm once for each test case, run it 4 times, once for each missing attribute to be predicted. In the retrieval for attribute x, however, include only the features C4.5 found to be important for predicting x in the k-nearest neighbors calculations.

By using C4.5 for feature specification, we automatically tune the case retrieval algorithm for independent prediction of part of speech, word senses, and concept activation.[7]

Experiment 1

In this section we describe an application that uses the case-based approach described above to determine the definition of unknown words given a nearly complete domain-specific dictionary. We assume the existence of the function word lexicon briefly described above (129 entries) and then create a case base of context-sensitive word definitions for all open class words in 120 sentences from the TIPSTER JV corpus. In each of 10 experiments, we remove from the case base (of 2056 instances) all cases associated with 12 randomly chosen sentences and use these as a test set.[8] For each test case, we then invoke the case retrieval algorithm to predict the part of speech, general and specific word senses, and concept activation information of its unknown word while leaving the rest of the case intact. This experimental design simulates a nearly complete dictionary in that it assumes perfect knowledge of the global and local context of the unknown word.

Figure 4 shows the average percentage correct for prediction of each feature across the 10 runs and compares them

Missing Feature	Case-Based Approach	Random Selection	Default
p-o-s	93.0%	34.3%	81.5%
gen-ws	78.0%	17.0%	25.6%
spec-ws	80.4%	37.3%	58.1%
concept	95.1%	84.2%	91.7%

Figure 4: Experiment 1 Results (% correct for prediction of each feature)

to two baselines.[9] The first baseline indicates the expected

whose values the decision trees are trying to predict. In addition, we omit the **word**, **prev1-word**, **prev2-word**, **fol1-word**, and **fol2-word** features because of their large branching factor. These "word" features are always included in the k-nearest neighbors calculations, however.

[7]Space limitations preclude the inclusion of experiments that compare the original case retrieval algorithm with the modified version. Those results are discussed in [Cardie 1993], however, which focuses on the contributions of this research to machine learning.

[8]In each experiment, a different set of 12 sentences is chosen. This amounts to a 10-fold cross validation testing scheme.

[9]Note that all results indicate performance for only the open class words. When function words are included, all percentages

accuracy of a system that randomly guesses a legal value for each missing feature based on the distribution of values across the test set. The second baseline shows the performance of a system that always chooses the most frequent value as a default. The default for the concept activation feature (*nil*) achieves quite good results, for example. (This is because relatively few words actually activate concepts in this domain.) Chi-square significance tests on the associated frequencies show that the case-based approach does significantly better than both of the baselines ($p = .01$).

Experiment 2

In the second application, we assume only a very sparse dictionary (129 function words) and use the case-based approach to acquire definitions of *all* open class words. We use the same experimental design as experiment 1 — we create a case base from 120 TIPSTER JV sentences (2056 cases) and use 10-fold cross validation. During testing, however, we now make no assumptions about the availability of definitions for words surrounding the unknown word. CIRCUS parses each test sentence and creates a test case each time an open class word is encountered, filling in the global context features, the **word** and **morphol** features for the unknown word, and the local context features for the preceding two words. If the following two words are both function words, then **fol1** and **fol2** features can also easily be specified. In most cases, however, one or both of **fol1** and **fol2** are open class words for which the system has no definition. In these cases, the parser makes an educated guess based on the training instances:

1. If the word did not appear during training, fill in the **word** features, but use *nil* as the value for the remaining **fol1** and **fol2** attributes.

2. If the word appeared during training, let each **fol1** and **fol2** feature be the union of the values that occurred in the training phase definitions.

We also relax the k-nearest neighbors matching algorithm and allow a non-empty intersection on any **fol1** or **fol2** feature to count as a full match. (Matches on *nil* still receive only half credit.) Results for experiment 2 are shown in Figure 5 along with the same baseline comparisons from ex-

Missing Feature	Case-Based Approach	Random Selection	Default
p-o-s	91.0%	34.3%	81.5%
gen-ws	65.3%	17.0%	25.6%
spec-ws	74.0%	37.3%	58.1%
concept	94.3%	84.2%	91.7%

Figure 5: Experiment 2 Results (% correct for prediction of each feature)

periment 1. Not surprisingly, all of the results have dropped somewhat; however, chi-square analysis still shows that the performance of the case-based approach is significantly better than the baselines ($p = .01$).

increase. For part of speech prediction, for example, the case-based results increase from 93.0% to 96.4%.

Conclusions

We have presented a new, case-based approach to the acquisition of lexical knowledge that simultaneously learns 3 classes of knowledge using the same case representation and requires no hand-coded acquisition heuristics and relatively little training. We create a case base of context-sensitive word definitions and use it to learn part of speech, word sense, and concept activation knowledge for unknown words. The case-based technique employs a decision tree algorithm to specify the features relevant for simple k-nearest neighbor case retrieval and allows the definition of a word to change in response to new contexts without the use of lexical disambiguation heuristics. We have tested our approach in two practical applications and found it to perform significantly better than baselines that randomly guess or choose default values for the features of the unknown word. Given results in previous work (see [Cardie 1992]), however, we believe performance can be much improved through the use of case adaptation heuristics that exploit knowledge implicit in the taxonomies that is unavailable to the learning algorithms. In addition, although this paper discusses only two applications of the approach, many more exist. Explicit domain-specific lexicons can be constructed, for example, by saving the definitions acquired during the testing phase of the experiments discussed above. Finally, we have demonstrated that the case-based technique described here is a promising approach to dictionary construction and knowledge acquisition for sentence analysis in limited domains.

Acknowledgments

I wish to thank Professor J. Ross Quinlan for supplying the C4.5 decision tree system. This research was supported by the Office of Naval Research Contract N00014-92-J-1427 and NSF Grant No. EEC-9209623, State/Industry/University Cooperative Research on Intelligent Information Retrieval.

References

Berwick, R. 1983. Learning word meanings from examples. *Proceedings, Eighth International Joint Conference on Artificial Intelligence*. Karlsruhe, Germany, pp. 459-461.

Brent, M. 1991. Automatic acquisition of subcategorization frames from untagged text. *Proceedings, 29th Annual Meeting of the Association for Computational Linguistics*. University of California, Berkeley, Association for Computational Linguistics, pp. 209-214.

Brent, M. 1990. Semantic classification of verbs from their syntactic contexts: automated lexicography with implications for child language acquisition. *Proceedings, Twelfth Annual Conference of the Cognitive Science Society*. Cambridge, MA, The Cognitive Science Society, pp. 428-437.

Cardie, C. 1993. Using Decision Trees to Improve Case-Based Learning. To appear in, P. Utgoff (Ed.), *Proceedings, Tenth International Conference on Machine Learning*. University of Massachusetts, Amherst, MA.

Cardie, C. 1992. Learning to Disambiguate Relative Pronouns. *Proceedings, Tenth National Conference on Artificial Intelligence*. San Jose, CA, AAAI Press/MIT Press, pp. 38-43.

Church, K., & Hanks, P. 1990. Word association norms, mutual information, and lexicography. *Computational Linguistics*, 16.

Granger, R. 1977. Foulup: A program that figures out meanings of words from context. *Proceedings, Fifth International Joint Conference on Artificial Intelligence*. Morgan Kaufmann, pp. 172-178.

Grefenstette, G. 1992. SEXTANT: Exploring unexplored contexts for semantic extraction from syntactic analysis. *Proceedings, 30th Annual Meeting of the Association for Computational Linguistics*. University of Delaware, Newark, DE, Association for Computational Linguistics, pp. 324-326.

Hastings, P., Lytinen, S., & Lindsay, R. 1991. Learning Words from Context. *Proceedings, Eighth International Conference on Machine Learning*. Northwestern University, Chicago, IL.

Hindle, D. 1990. Noun classification from predicate-argument structures. *Proceedings, 28th Annual Meeting of the Association for Computational Linguistics*. University of Pittsburgh, Association for Computational Linguistics, pp. 268-275.

Jacobs, P., & Zernik, U. 1988. Acquiring Lexical Knowledge from Text: A Case Study. *Proceedings, Seventh National Conference on Artificial Intelligence*. St. Paul, MN, Morgan Kaufmann, pp. 739-744.

Lehnert, W. 1990. Symbolic/Subsymbolic Sentence Analysis: Exploiting the Best of Two Worlds. In J. Barnden, & J. Pollack (Eds.), *Advances in Connectionist and Neural Computation Theory*. Norwood, NJ, Ablex Publishers, pp. 135-164.

Lehnert, W., Cardie, C., Fisher, D., Riloff, E., & Williams, R. 1991a. University of Massachusetts: Description of the CIRCUS System as Used for MUC-3. *Proceedings, Third Message Understanding Conference (MUC-3)*. San Diego, CA, Morgan Kaufmann, pp. 223-233.

Lehnert, W., Cardie, C., Fisher, D., Riloff, E., & Williams, R. 1991b. University of Massachusetts: MUC-3 Test Results and Analysis. *Proceedings, Third Message Understanding Conference (MUC-3)*. San Diego, CA, Morgan Kaufmann, pp. 116-119.

Lytinen, S., & Roberts, S. 1989. Lexical Acquisition as a By-Product of Natural Language Processing. *Proceedings, IJCAI-89 Workshop on Lexical Acquisition*.

Proceedings, Fourth Message Understanding Conference (MUC-4). 1992. McLean, VA, Morgan Kaufmann.

Proceedings, Third Message Understanding Conference (MUC-3). 1991. San Diego, CA, Morgan Kaufmann.

Quinlan, J. R. 1992. *C4.5: Programs for Machine Learning*. Morgan Kaufmann.

Quinlan, J. R. 1986. Induction of decision trees. *Machine Learning*, 1, pp. 81-106.

Resnik, P. 1992. A class-based approach to lexical discovery. *Proceedings, 30th Annual Meeting of the Association for Computational Linguistics*. University of Delaware, Newark, DE, Association for Computational Linguistics, pp. 327-329.

Selfridge, M. 1986. A computer model of child language learning. *Artificial Intelligence*, 29, pp. 171-216.

Wilensky, R. 1991. Extending the Lexicon by Exploiting Subregularities. *Tech. Report No. UCB/CSD 91/618*. Computer Science Division (EECS), University of California, Berkeley.

Yarowsky, D. 1992. Word-Sense Disambiguation Using Statistical Models of Roget's Categories Trained on Large Corpora. *Proceedings, COLING-92*.

Zernik, U. 1991. Train1 vs. Train 2: Tagging Word Senses in Corpus. In U. Zernik (Ed.), *Lexical Acquisition: Exploiting On-Line Resources to Build a Lexicon*. Hillsdale, NJ, Lawrence Erlbaum Associates, pp. 91-112.

KITSS: A Knowledge-Based Translation System for Test Scenarios

Van E. Kelly and **Mark A. Jones**

AT&T Bell Laboratories

Murray Hill, NJ 07974-0636

vek@research.att.com, jones@research.att.com

Abstract

Machine-assisted language translation systems for technical documents, guide humans through a process of selecting and composing variant partial translations. The constrained nature of technical sublanguages makes language processing aids cost-effective to build and use.

Analogously, we have developed KITSS, a *knowledge-based translation* system for converting informal English scenarios of the desired behavior of complex reactive systems into formal, executable test scripts. A trainable parser and reference resolver capture domain-specific linguistic knowledge. A logic analyzer establishes coherence in the translation process in a role comparable to a "story understander". It checks the consistency of each step of a translated test script using a theorem prover, a planner, and logic-encoded background knowledge about the system under test. This helps correct common but serious specification errors, including underspecificity, omitted steps, and even some outright mis-statements.

To evaluate how well such technology can scale, we have exercised our technology progressively on a graduated corpus of 100 behavior scenarios spanning 7 advanced calling features for a private telephone switch (PBX), successfully translating 70% into test scripts without any manual post-hoc editing. Our experience with KITSS has enabled us to identify many of the tradeoffs in accommodating informality in specification, versus demanding formality from a human agent.

Introduction

Problem Statement

Engineers who specify complex reactive systems, such as telephone switches, are often unfamiliar with expressive specification formalisms like temporal logics. Instead, they state functional requirements in thousands of stylized English prose scenarios describing linear traces of specific desired behaviors, such as Figure 1. These scenarios form an informal contract with

Action: (1.1) Place calls to stations B3 and D1 and make them busy. (1.2) Station B1 calls station B2. (1.3) B2 does not answer.

Verify: (1.4) Ringback to station B1 is replaced with Call Coverage tone.

Action: (1.5) Wait for CRI timeout at B1.

Verify: (1.6) Station B1 receives ringback again. (1.7) The call keeps ringing at station B2 (the call will not go to coverage since all the covering users are busy).

Figure 1: Sample Behavior Scenario

other engineers who will eventually validate the final product. For an initial release of new functionality, it makes economic sense to execute each required scenario manually once or twice, but for later repetitive regression testing, a manual approach is not cost-effective. Informal scenarios must be converted into formal, executable test scripts and maintained in this form. This conversion, in practice, is a laborious and costly process for test engineers, averaging several hours per scenario initially, plus revisions for subsequent product releases. When product features and versions proliferate, the cost of generating and maintaining a library of thousands of scripts only gets worse.

Solution Approach

Because the language used in informal scenarios is not really standard English but an extremely stylized technical subdialect, it seemed promising to try automated natural-language processing to speed the conversion and maintenance processes. In translation of specialized technical documents between two natural languages, say from French to Swedish, customizable interactive translator systems have recently logged clear productivity benefits over manual approaches, especially for restricted technical dialects. These tools do not replace human translators, but recast their roles as primarily one of selecting and composing partial translations suggested by the tool. We adopted this approach to structuring human-computer cooperation as one of the major paradigms for our own solution approach. As in most machine translation applications, we began with a large extant corpus which had to be substantially parsed "as we found it" in order to cost-justify our approach. It was not sufficient merely to design a suitably habitable dialect for the expression of future test scenarios.

In machine translation from one natural language to another, a direct translation of individual sentences, or even just of individual phrases and clauses, usually provides at least a marginally intelligible result, but this is not so for our task. First of all, an wide abstraction level gap must be bridged between the goal-oriented intensionality of scenarios and the procedural extensionality required in executable scripts. Oblique descriptions of actions and objects in scenarios must be identified with concrete operations and devices in a telephone switch test lab. For example, an action such as "Place a call to station B1" involves choosing a station to place the call, going off-hook, mapping "station B1" to its extension, and choosing a method for dialing (dialing digits, speed dialing, last number redial, etc.). The problems of "extensionalizing" nominal descriptions have been partially addressed by natural language database front-ends, where noun phrases are resolved using known objects and attributes in a database schema (*e.g.*, [Ballard and Stumberger 1986]), although such front-ends do not generally jump nearly as wide an abstraction gap as KITSS must. Nor have database front-ends had to deal with narrative text forms, nor have they faced head-on the history-sensitive scoping of references within narrative discourse structures.

Beyond the problems of bridging abstraction gaps on the level of individual phrases and statements, there are also "discourse level" semantic hazards in informal scenarios:

- entire steps can be left out,
- important timeouts and other "null actions" go unmentioned (*e.g.*, Figure 1, sentences 1.3, 1.7),
- actions may create "hidden" linguistic referents, such as when explicitly dialing a string of digits implicitly creates a new telephone call,
- actions and observations can be underspecified, such as in sentence 1.1 where there are several nonequivalent ways to force phones to become "busy",
- essential initialization steps and boundary conditions remain implicit, as in sentence 1.7 where the "covering users" (*i.e.*, telephone call screeners, probably secretaries) of B2 are mentioned but there were no explicit administrative steps to make B3 and D1 function in that capacity.

Sometimes, there are also just plain mistakes. A human concentrating on the purely linguistic aspects of the translation task is likely to miss at least some of these problems. An automated capability within the scenario translation process must flag such problems and guide humans in correcting them; a *story understanding* functionality is needed in addition to linguistic expertise. Although automated story understanding is very difficult in general, a telephony testing domain is, fortunately, much simpler to axiomatize than the "real" world.

An Implementation

KITSS (a.k.a. the Knowledge-based Interactive Test Scripting System) is our prototype system for formalizing and analyzing scenarios of telephone switch behavior for medium-sized private-network switches (PBX's). It was deliberately designed to integrate smoothly with an existing test process, partly automating one manual task without otherwise impacting a test engineer's job. Its translation subsystem guides the conversion of each sentence of an English scenario into an equivalent statement in WIL, a logic-based interlingua previously used in the WATSON system ([Kelly and Nonnenmann 1991]). The new natural-language technology we developed for this task includes an extremely high-performance adaptive statistical chart-parser [Jones and Eisner 1992] and a rule-based phrase converter which performs nominal reference resolution and case-frame normalization. English phrases converted into WIL can be paraphrased back into a stylized pseudo-English. Users can also directly input the pseudo-English forms as an alternative to the full English interface. No human ability to read or write WIL directly is required.

Scenario understanding and analysis is provided by a heavily instrumented "interpreter" which analyzes the translated WIL statements using a coarse black-box simulation of a telephone switch, prototyped using a theorem prover, a telephony domain theory expressed in logic, and a library of stereotypical plans for telephone usage. Whenever a scenario leads to an impossible state, such as trying to answer a telephone call which is not locally present, the interpreter summarizes the anomaly and, where possible, suggests plausible corrections, (such as answering the call from another station where it is present). Plausible elaborations of underspecified activities during the scenario, such as making a station become busy, are calculated using a planner and the plan library. Implicit initialization steps and test lab configuration conditions for test execution are also made explicit. As during translation, the analyzer keeps the human user "in the loop" for all modifications and elaborations of the WIL script, and all user interactions use pseudo-English paraphrases of WIL constructs.

A more extensive description of our system architecture, knowledge bases, user interface, and early experimental results was published in [Nonnenmann and Eddy 1992]. That paper also discusses our approach to solving the script maintenance problem for scenarios that have previously been analyzed. In the current paper we focus on the natural language translation technology, its interface with the scenario analyzer, and the lessons learned during the latter half of the project about building and maintaining a large hybrid reasoning system. In the remainder of this paper, we first describe each of the two major functions of KITSS: translating English into WIL and analyzing the translated scenario for anomalies.

Translating English into WIL

The translation of English scenarios into WIL occurs in two stages. Initially, a statistical, trainable chart parser converts English sentences into a case frame structure similar to that of a Lexical-Functional Grammar (LFG) [Kaplan and Bresnan 1982]. The case frame is then translated by a rule-driven semantic resolver into WIL. The semantic resolver performs several tasks during its translation step, including canonicalizing the case frame, handling conjunctions, and resolving definite and indefinite noun phrase references.

In many cases, there may be more than one possible WIL reading of an English sentence. This may be due to the inherent ambiguity of natural languages, or to imprecision in the parsing and reference resolution steps. The statistical chart parser computes probabilities which aid in ranking the alternatives that arise as a result of grammatical (but not referential) ambiguity. The translator, following the highly interactive design philosophy of KITSS, also includes a simple rule-driven facility which "paraphrases" WIL back into English. The choices are ranked by the probabilities from the parser. The human may select one of these translations, or else create a novel one by cut-and-pasting WIL fragments from several of the "near-misses".

Note that we are not claiming to have successfully automated the translation of English into WIL, even for the restricted English subset we use. The conditions of use that make our translation process practical are the very same ones that differentiate past research failures in *automatic* language translation from recent commercial successes in *machine assisted* translation:

- It is not necessary to produce an automatic, correct translation of every sentence.

- Human users get machine help for salvaging something useful out of incorrect "near-miss" translations (*e.g.,* cut-and-paste), and are not unduly penalized for an occasional end-run around the translator and writing directly in the target language (*i.e.,* WIL or its pseudo-English paraphrases).

- The size of each corpus to be translated is large enough to amortize customizing the translator for a particular writing style, vocabulary, and topic of discourse.

Statistical Chart-Parsing

Natural language parsers have traditionally required elaborate hand-crafted grammars which subtly depend on the chosen parsing algorithm. This has made them complex to develop and maintain, even for computational linguists. We needed a parser that could be maintained by our prospective end-users: engineers, not linguists. Instead of a large, pre-specified covering grammar, the KITSS grammar has grown incrementally from training on example sentences from our domain corpus of scenarios. The statistical chart-parsing technology used in KITSS was inspired by the recent success of statistical methods in several areas of natural language processing, including part-of-speech tagging, bilingual corpora alignment and OCR postprocessing. Statistical knowledge can be used very effectively to limit search and to order alternatives.

To "train" the parser on a sample set of sentences, a human feeds the parser a **parse tree** of the sentence (if the parser cannot already parse it correctly). Parse trees, for KITSS, are basically annotated versions of familiar elementary-school "sentence diagrams". The part-of-speech categories in KITSS were taken from the Brown Corpus [Francis and Kucera 1982]. The non-terminal categories are the standard ones in a simple linguistic theory such as S (sentence), NP (noun phrase), *etc.* The parser assists in the bracketing process by providing analyses for major sentence constituents that it can find. In addition, there is a facility for guessing parts-of-speech for new vocabulary.

Each node in the parse tree is implicitly identified with some context-free rule. Each non-terminal category also has a predefined semantic type (*slot, filler, slot-filler pair*) that is used to construct a case-frame representation. Relations such as prepositions (IN) are of type *slot*. Entities such as noun phrases (NP) or verb phrases (VP) are of type *filler*. Modifiers such as adjective phrases or prepositional phrases are of type *slot-filler pair*. To construct the case frame, the parser associates one or more semantic templates with each syntactic rule. The templates play a similar role (without unification) to the functional equations in LFG.

For example, the template (@?1 :OBJECT ?2) is associated with the rule VP -> V NP. The variable ?1 is bound to the semantic interpretation of the first right-hand side constituent (V). The template specifies that this interpretation is to spliced in and followed by the slot :OBJECT and its filler from the interpretation of the NP. A semantic template only needs to be explicitly defined for the rule if it cannot be "guessed" by the parser from the semantic types of the non-terminals and general linguistic knowledge about the heads of syntactic phrases (*e.g.,* from X-bar theory [Jackendoff 1977]). For example, for the syntactic rule VP -> VP PP, the parser will supply a default template of the form (@1 @2). In most cases, users need not explicitly specify these semantic templates.

The case frame representation includes predicate-argument information and syntactic features such as tense. It is often much "flatter' than a parse tree. Figures 2 and 3 give the parse tree and case frames for the

```
(S (VP (VP (VP (VB "Place")
             (NP (NNS "calls")))
         (PP (IN "to")
             (NP (NNS "stations")
                 (NPR (NPR "B3")
                      (CC "and")
                      (NPR "D1")))))
     (CC "and")
     (VP (VB "make")
         (SBE (NP (PPO "them"))
              (JJ "busy")))))
```

Figure 2: Parse Tree

```
(AND :CONJ1
     (PLACE :OBJECT (CALL :NUMBER PLUR)
            :TO (STATION :NUMBER PLUR
                         (AND :CONJ1
                              (:NAME "B3")
                              :CONJ2
                              (:NAME "D1"))))
     :CONJ2
     (MAKE :PRED (BE :ACTOR (THEM)
                     :ADJ-MOD BUSY)))
```

Figure 3: Case Frame

example sentence (1.1) "Place calls to stations B3 and D1 and make them busy".

Rule-Based Phrase Conversion

The second phase of the translator converts the parser's case frames into WIL logic statements describing precise facts about events in a hypothetical telephone test lab. In contrast to the large number of things that might be said in a document about testing (instructions to testers, runing commentary, explanatory headings), there is but a small number of facts specifically relevant to executing a particular test. The tasks of the phrase converter are:

- identifying references to relevant test lab actions or observations in a sentence (normalize verb concepts),

- determining which pieces of lab apparatus are to participate in the action or observed event (resolve nominal references).

- identifying simple plan-like discourse structures in the text (e.g., sequence and purpose).

- paraphrasing its fully normalized and resolved understanding of each sentence back into an English-like form.

- accepting corrections from the user in the form of edited versions of near-miss paraphrases.

With various degrees of success, the phrase converter also applies a set of rewrite rules to handle a number of natural language phenomena including syntactic transformations (e.g., active-passive), semantic

transformations (e.g., "button at station X" and "button associated with station X" are equivalent), and collective/distributive readings of conjunctions. These rewrite rules include difficult situations such as the first sentence in Figure 1 where the conjunction *and* should be interpreted as "and thus" rather than "and then". After determining a canonical representation, then the nominal descriptions are further resolved into entities in the domain model. Finally, the resulting form is converted into WIL.

For example, in our sample sentence 1.1, the phrase converter identifies the referent of "them" in the second clause, namely "B3 and D1", associates the verbs with specific WIL action predicates (`place-call` and `busy-out-station`), and links the referents of the subjects and objects of each clause with the required parameters of each action. Next, it guesses that "and", in this context, does not mean sequence ("and then") but rather purpose ("and thus"), based on the under-specificity of the first clause (calls from whom? how many?). Finally it reads "make B3 and D1 busy" distributively as "make B3 busy and make D1 busy". The final (paraphrased) translation of sentence 1.1 into WIL, is simply:

```
Busy-out station B3.
Busy-out station D1.
```

The underspecified information in the first clause of the sentence blocks its translation into WIL, and so it is dropped from the final translation as it occupies only a subsidiary discourse role. The user could, of course, re-introduce the missing information directly by typing an explicit WIL paraphrase, but in this case no harm was done.

Analyzing WIL Test Scripts

Converting each English scenario sentence correctly into a WIL formula does not guarantee that the whole sequence of formulas constitutes a valid test script. To repair the anomalies noted earlier – missing steps and null actions, underspecified and steps, implicit boundary conditions – our analysis module performs two different audit techniques on the scenario:

First, a background theory of telephony, about 250 hand-coded temporal logic axioms at present, is used to audit each scenario step in isolation; the logical conjunction of this background knowledge and the scenario step itself (*i.e.*, an action plus follow-on observations) is fed into a theorem prover, which forward-chains additional facts about the step. The background theory primarily describes user-telephone signaling conventions (ringing, tones, pickups, hangups, button-presses, lamp flashes, timeouts) and the procedural building blocks of all modern telephone call control (call origination, acceptance, rejection, bridging, transfer, redirection, drop, and hold, *etc.*). Deliberately **excluded** from this theory is any formal specification of the particular features being described in our scenarios.

Second, at each step, the scenario so far is compared with a library of hierarchically structured plans for stereotypical telephone usages, currently numbering about 70. This comparison is complex because telephone usages typically involve multiple agents, and multiple plan executions (*e.g.,* several simultaneously active telephone calls) may be interleaved within a given scenario. Furthermore, plan recognition must be updated after each scenario step in order to synchronize with the translation process, and recognition and plan instantiation (*i.e.,* fleshing out underspecified scenario actions) are freely intermixed. These requirements have forced us to engineer a complex, incremental plan recognition/instantiation algorithm based on propagating disjunctive sets of plan hypotheses regarding each scenario step.

The final desired result of this analysis is a reconstruction of the original scenario as a threaded forest of plan executions, in which every node, whether leaf or interior point, has been examined and elaborated using the background domain theory. As this is being computed, a variety of corrections and clarifications are carried out:

- calculating the detailed "state" of a telephone switch test lab before and after each scenario action using the background theory of telephony,

- finding "hidden" linguistic referents in the scenario by plan recognition, which were missed by the phrase converter. For instance, consider the fragment

  ```
  B1 goes offhook.
  B1 dials the extension of B2.
  B2 answers the call.
  ```

  There is no immediate referent here for "the call"; its identity can only be inferred by matching this fragment against plan knowledge about placing calls.

- deducing desirable but unstated intermediate observations that should be made during the course of a test (such as always making sure a phone is actually ringing before attempting to answer a call),

- determining whether each action is possible and legal in the current interpolated state, and if not, whether one single missing prior step (such as forgetting to hang up a phone – the most common error – or not waiting for a timeout to expire) could account for the discrepancy,

- elaborating details of abstract or underspecified goals (such as how to make a station "busy"). Plan selection is guided by entity types (how many calls a particular class of station can handle simultaneously), the current state (how many calls it is currently handling; which other stations are now free), and pragmatic concerns (whether it is faster to make a station busy with outgoing or incoming calls).

- Using the plan library to diagnose missing finalizations in a scenario and for selecting appropriate error recovery actions. For instance, if some action sequence implicitly activates a feature, that feature should be explicitly deactivated in case of aborting the test.

- deducing any special capabilities or privileges required by any of the participants in the scenario (*e.g.,* the ability to forward telephone calls), which need special administrative setup actions.

Finally, just as for the language translation module, the scenario analyzer had to be designed robustly so that its own failure to understand, especially on some fairly minor point, does not block KITSS from producing output. It accommodates manual on-the-fly "patching" of scenarios by cut-and-paste of WIL paraphrases, followed by incremental re-auditing. It permits the user to resolve contradictions by explicitly denying facts it has deduced and asserting others. In the face of massive apparent nonsense, it degrades gracefully, amid much complaining, to a credulous mode where most of its audits, except for plan instantiation, are disabled. This credulous mode persists until KITSS unambiguously recognizes the start of a new plan and resynchronizes itself with the scenario.

Empirical Results and Lessons Learned

We used KITSS experimentally to translate a graduated corpus of 100 scenarios covering seven advanced calling features of a private telephone switch, written by five different authors. A very experienced user of KITSS successfully converted about 70% of these scenarios into executable form, taking only a few minutes apiece, as opposed to hours without machine aid. These 70% required either zero or minimal post-hoc editing of the final output to produce a "perfect" test script, as judged by experienced test engineers. The remaining 30% were evenly divided between those requiring enough manual touch-up to nullify KITSS' productivity advantage over manual conversion, and those for which KITSS provided no useful help at all (commonly due to fatal bugs in the tricky incremental re-auditing code of the analyzer).

For about one-third of the 70% of scenarios successfully processed, KITSS degraded into "credulous" mode part of the time, requiring its human user to interpolate corrections which it otherwise would have provided. In our experiments, human performance on these troublesome cases varied over a three-fold range, even among members of our development team. This shows that although the basic technology and architecture of KITSS may be sound, more work is needed to refine it into an industrial-strength tool for general engineering use.

Emergent Natural Language Technology

The chart parser is one of the clearest research successes on the KITSS project, and the most readily transferable to other application domains. Evaluated in isolation through split-corpus experiments on a 429-sentence subset from our scenario corpus, the parser, even though still quite obviously undertrained, performed as follows:

- 77% overall chance of parsing a novel sentence correctly.
- 85% chance of success when the sentence contains no new words.
- 96% success in determining the correct parse in cases where **any** possible parses were found.
- Parsing speed averaging a few seconds per sentence and **linear** in the length of the sentence.

Thus, the parser is sufficiently accurate and predictable to be a productivity aid, and it is fast enough to be considered "real-time" for interactive use. Furthermore, most of its non-vocabulary related failures occurred with long, awkward constructions or embedded parenthetical expressions. Thus, writers can produce more parsable prose just by improving their writing style.

Our positive experience with the statistical parser convinced us that natural language parsing technology is poised for much wider exploitation as a computer interface technique. The skills required to prepare a training set for an adaptive parser are much more mundane than those formerly required to write a computational grammar from scratch; most high school students are trained in sentence diagramming, which is a form of parsing.

Although the phrase converter worked, it did not scale up nearly as gracefully as the parser. Nominal reference resolution for physical objects like calls, stations, buttons, and lamps was implemented using classification combined with a simple recency heuristic and worked reasonably well. The variability of the English language, however, worked against finding any compact set of normalization heuristics for phrases in general. Each new idiom encountered, and each significant variation in verb tense or word order, needs its own normalization rule. The number of these continues to grow linearly with the number of scenarios.

It should be noted that the 100 English scenarios which we attempted to process were originally written for humans and not machines. If a system such as KITSS were deployed earlier during the writing of the scenarios, there would be less inherent variability, and hence less of a problem with extensibility and maintainability in the phrase converter. In the end, we learned to live within the converter's limited repertoire of normalizations by performing manual touch-up on partially normalized sentences. This was still faster and easier than unassisted manual English-WIL translation.

Generic Domain Models

The scenario analyzer was the largest component of KITSS, its greatest time bottleneck, and the largest

source of lingering program bugs. Notwithstanding the obvious engineering complexity of the tightly coupled, incremental, interruptible, restartable audit routines, the greatest lessons learned from the analyzer derive from its 250-axiom, 70-plan "generic" domain model for modern telephony. While simplified models of old-fashioned telephony are common textbook exercises in formal specification, efforts to formalize modern telephony have been few and mostly unfruitful. To our knowledge, KITSS included the first formal, fully machine-interpretable model of the underpinnings of modern telephony, and it has directly catalyzed further work in this field [Zave and Jackson 1991].

The largest intellectual challenge we faced in structuring this knowledge was separating general, re-usable constraints about telephony from specific knowledge of particular features. For instance, instead of directly describing the operation of the Call Forwarding capability, we considered the general rules and constraints for redirecting calls from one location to another, of which Call Forwarding was but one example. In a pure logic notation where each axiom is textually independent, it is especially easy to write constraints that are either overly or underly general, and these have mysterious effects on the advice offered by the analyzer. Our prior work on automated specification induction using the WATSON system ([Kelly and Nonnenmann 1991]) yielded useful heuristics for tracking down and fixing such errors, but we could only apply these manually, since the size of KITSS' domain model was beyond anything WATSON's automated techniques could handle.

Engineering the plan library posed two major challenges. First of all, plans had to do double-duty for both recognition and instantiation. For instantiation, they had to be very complete and detailed, but this complicated recognizing a plan from a scenario in the presence of both interference from other interleaved plans (e.g., other telephone calls), and "observational noise" from omitted steps. We encountered a tradeoff between cluttering our plan representation with many explicit recognition cues or using a more complex set of recognition heuristics, which is the course we ultimately chose. Second, in a testing application like KITSS, deliberate plan failures are frequent, such as attempting to complete a telephone call to a busy station. We need to reason about the many ways a plan might fail, without cluttering the plan library with variants for each possible failure mode. Our compromise was to associate failures only with goals, not with individual plans, while relying on the densely hierarchical structure of the plan library (short plans, deeply nested) to help localize the point of plan failure. Again, we accepted more complex but less complete planning algorithms, in the interest of a simpler, clearer domain model.

KITSS, like many other systems that reason about actions, had to handle the "frame problem" and other non-monotonic effects, but the size, scope, and incremental growth of our domain model limited our solution approaches. Since our domain model had to be inspectable by human telephony domain experts, we wanted to keep our logic notation as "clean" as possible, uncluttered by abnormality predicates or other forms solely intended to guide non-monotonic inference. After experimentation, we solved our frame problem extra-logically by defining an arbitrary *persistence* partial order on state-predicates, enforced by controlling the order in which clauses were fed to the theorem prover. While this approach is not state-of-the-art, it worked for our domain. We would have used a more modern, general technique, had we found one appropriate for our logic that did not entail massive obfuscation of the domain knowledge base and unacceptable slowdown of the analyzer. We suggest that more empirical scaling research is needed on the practical computational demands for the currently favored methods of reasoning about actions and state.

Acknowledgements

Many individuals contributed to KITSS. Mark Jones wrote the parser, with help from his summer student, Jason Eisner. Robert Hall built the phrase converter. Van Kelly is responsible for the analyzer and its domain model of generic telephony. John Eddy, an experienced test engineer, was our in-house domain expert and designed our knowledge base ontology and taxonomic schema. Uwe Nonnenmann built the user interface and integration tested all our code. We also wish to thank Bruce Ballard, Lori Alperin Resnick, Tom Kirk, and Jim Piccarello for their technical assistance. This project would not have been possible without farsighted management support and encouragement from G. D. Bergland, Ron Brachman, and Jim Shanley.

References

Ballard B. and Stumberger D. 1986. Semantic Acquisition in TELI: A Transportable, User-Customizable Natural Language Processor. In *ACL-24 Proceedings*, pp. 20-29. Association For Computer Linguistics

Francis, W. and Kucera, H. 1982. *Frequency Analysis of English Usage.* Houghton Mifflin, Boston, 1982.

Jackendoff, R. 1977. $\bar{X}$ *Syntax: A Study of Phrase Structure.* Cambridge, MA.: MIT Press.

Jones, M.A. and Eisner, J.E. 1992. A Probabilistic Parser Applied to Software Testing Documents. In *Proc. of the 10th National Conference on Artificial Intelligence*, 322-328. San Jose, CA: AAAI Press.

Kaplan, R. and Bresnan, J. Lexical-Functional Grammar: A Formal System for Grammatical Representation. In *The Mental Representation of Grammatical Relations*, 173-281. New York: John Wiley & Sons Inc.

Kelly, V. and Nonnenmann, U. Reducing the Complexity of Specification Acquisition in *Automating Software Design*, pp. 41-64, Menlo Park, AAAI Press.

Kelly, V. and Nonnenmann, U. Inferring Formal Software Specifications from Episodic Descriptions, in *Proc. of the Sixth National Conference on Artificial Intelligence*, pp. 127-132 Menlo Park, AAAI.

Nonnenmann, U., and Eddy J.K. 1992. KITSS - A Functional Software Testing System Using a Hybrid Domain Model. In *Proc. of 8th IEEE Conference on Artificial Intelligence Applications.* Monterey, CA: IEEE.

Zave, P. and Jackson, M. Techniques for Partial Specification and Specification of Switching Systems. In *VDM '91: Formal Software Development Methods (proceedings of the Fourth International Symposium of VDM Europe).* pp. 511-525 Springer Verlag ISBN 3-540-54834-3

Automatically Constructing a Dictionary for Information Extraction Tasks

Ellen Riloff

Department of Computer Science
University of Massachusetts
Amherst, MA 01003
riloff@cs.umass.edu

Abstract

Knowledge-based natural language processing systems have achieved good success with certain tasks but they are often criticized because they depend on a domain-specific dictionary that requires a great deal of manual knowledge engineering. This knowledge engineering bottleneck makes knowledge-based NLP systems impractical for real-world applications because they cannot be easily scaled up or ported to new domains. In response to this problem, we developed a system called AutoSlog that automatically builds a domain-specific dictionary of concepts for extracting information from text. Using AutoSlog, we constructed a dictionary for the domain of terrorist event descriptions in only 5 person-hours. We then compared the AutoSlog dictionary with a hand-crafted dictionary that was built by two highly skilled graduate students and required approximately 1500 person-hours of effort. We evaluated the two dictionaries using two blind test sets of 100 texts each. Overall, the AutoSlog dictionary achieved 98% of the performance of the hand-crafted dictionary. On the first test set, the AutoSlog dictionary obtained 96.3% of the performance of the hand-crafted dictionary. On the second test set, the overall scores were virtually indistinguishable with the AutoSlog dictionary achieving 99.7% of the performance of the hand-crafted dictionary.

Introduction

Knowledge-based natural language processing (NLP) systems have demonstrated strong performance for information extraction tasks in limited domains [Lehnert and Sundheim, 1991; MUC-4 Proceedings, 1992]. But enthusiasm for their success is often tempered by real-world concerns about portability and scalability. Knowledge-based NLP systems depend on a domain-specific dictionary that must be carefully constructed for each domain. Building this dictionary is typically a time-consuming and tedious process that requires many person-hours of effort by highly-skilled people who have extensive experience with the system. Dictionary construction is therefore a major knowledge engineering bottleneck that needs to be addressed in order for information extraction systems to be portable and practical for real-world applications.

We have developed a program called AutoSlog that automatically constructs a domain-specific dictionary for information extraction. Given a training corpus, AutoSlog proposes a set of dictionary entries that are capable of extracting the desired information from the training texts. If the training corpus is representative of the targeted texts, the dictionary created by AutoSlog will achieve strong performance for information extraction from novel texts. Given a training set from the MUC-4 corpus, AutoSlog created a dictionary for the domain of terrorist events that achieved 98% of the performance of a hand-crafted dictionary on 2 blind test sets. We estimate that the hand-crafted dictionary required approximately 1500 person-hours to build. In contrast, the AutoSlog dictionary was constructed in only 5 person-hours. Furthermore, constructing a dictionary by hand requires a great deal of training and experience whereas a dictionary can be constructed using AutoSlog with only minimal training.

We will begin with an overview of the information extraction task and the MUC-4 performance evaluation that motivated this work. Next, we will describe AutoSlog, explain how it proposes dictionary entries for a domain, and show examples of dictionary definitions that were constructed by AutoSlog. Finally, we will present empirical results that demonstrate AutoSlog's success at automatically creating a dictionary for the domain of terrorist event descriptions.

Information Extraction from Text

Extracting information from text is a challenging task for natural language processing researchers as well as a key problem for many real-world applications. In the last few years, the NLP community has made substantial progress in developing systems that can achieve good performance on information extraction tasks for limited domains. As opposed to in-depth natural language processing, information extraction is a more focused and goal-oriented task. For example, the MUC-4 task was to extract information about terrorist events, such as the names of perpetrators, victims, instruments, etc.

Our approach to information extraction is based on a technique called *selective concept extraction*. Selective concept extraction is a form of text skimming that selectively processes relevant text while effectively ignoring surrounding text that is thought to be irrelevant to the domain. The work presented here is based on a conceptual sentence analyzer called CIRCUS [Lehnert, 1990].

To extract information from text, CIRCUS relies on a domain-specific dictionary of *concept nodes*. A concept node is essentially a case frame that is triggered by a lexical item and activated in a specific linguistic context. Each concept node definition contains a set of enabling conditions which are constraints that must be satisfied in order for the concept node to be activated. For example, our dictionary for the terrorism domain contains a concept node called $kidnap-passive$ that extracts information about kidnapping events. This concept node is triggered by the word "kidnapped" and has enabling conditions that allow it to be activated only in the context of a passive construction. As a result, this concept node is activated by phrases such as "was kidnapped", "were kidnapped", etc. Similarly, the dictionary contains a second concept node called $kidnap-active$ which is also triggered by the word "kidnapped" but has enabling conditions that allow it to be activated only in the context of an active construction, such as "terrorists kidnapped the mayor".

In addition, each concept node definition contains a set of slots to extract information from the surrounding context. In the terrorism domain, concept nodes have slots for perpetrators, victims, instruments, etc. Each slot has a syntactic expectation and a set of hard and soft constraints for its filler. The syntactic expectation specifies where the filler is expected to be found in the linguistic context. For example, $kidnap-passive$ contains a victim slot that expects its filler to be found as the subject of the clause, as in "the mayor was kidnapped". The slot constraints are selectional restrictions for the slot filler. The hard constraints must be satisfied in order for the slot to be filled, however the soft constraints suggest semantic preferences for the slot filler so the slot may be filled even if a soft constraint is violated.

Given a sentence as input, CIRCUS generates a set of instantiated concept nodes as its output. If multiple triggering words appear in a sentence then CIRCUS can generate multiple concept nodes for that sentence. However, if no triggering words are found in a sentence then CIRCUS will generate no output for that sentence.

The concept node dictionary is at the heart of selective concept extraction. Since concept nodes are CIRCUS' only output for a text, a good concept node dictionary is crucial for effective information extraction. The UMass/MUC-4 system [Lehnert *et al.*, 1992a] used 2 dictionaries: a part-of-speech lexicon containing 5436 lexical definitions, including semantic features for domain-specific words and a dictionary of 389 concept node definitions for the domain of terrorist event descriptions. The concept node dictionary was manually constructed by 2 graduate students who had extensive experience with CIRCUS and we estimate that it required approximately 1500 person-hours of effort to build.

The MUC-4 Task and Corpus

In 1992, the natural language processing group at the University of Massachusetts participated in the Fourth Message Understanding Conference (MUC-4). MUC-4 was a competitive performance evaluation sponsored by DARPA to evaluate the state-of-the-art in text analysis systems. Sev-

enteen sites from both industry and academia participated in MUC-4. The task was to extract information about terrorist events in Latin America from newswire articles. Given a text, each system was required to fill out a template for each terrorist event described in the text. If the text described multiple terrorist events, then one template had to be completed for each event. If the text did not mention any terrorist events, then no templates needed to be filled out.

A template is essentially a large case frame with a set of pre-defined slots for each piece of information that should be extracted from the text. For example, the MUC-4 templates contained slots for perpetrators, human targets, physical targets, etc. A training corpus of 1500 texts and instantiated templates (answer keys) for each text were made available to the participants for development purposes. The texts were selected by keyword search from a database of newswire articles. Although each text contained a keyword associated with terrorism, only about half of the texts contained a specific reference to a relevant terrorist incident.

Behind the Design of AutoSlog

Two observations were central to the design of AutoSlog. The first observation is that news reports follow certain stylistic conventions. In particular, the most important facts about a news event are typically reported during the initial event description. Details and secondary information are described later. It follows that the first reference to a major component of an event (e.g., a victim or perpetrator) usually occurs in a sentence that describes the event. For example, a story about a kidnapping of a diplomat will probably mention that the diplomat was kidnapped before it reports secondary information about the diplomat's family, etc. This observation is key to the design of AutoSlog. AutoSlog operates under the assumption that the *first* reference to a targeted piece of information is most likely where the relationship between that information and the event is made explicit.

Once we have identified the first sentence that contains a specific piece of information, we must determine which words or phrases should activate a concept node to extract the information. The second key observation behind AutoSlog is that the immediate linguistic context surrounding the targeted information usually contains the words or phrases that describe its role in the event. For example, consider the sentence "A U.S. diplomat was kidnapped by FMLN guerrillas today". This sentence contains two important pieces of information about the kidnapping: the victim ("U.S. diplomat") and the perpetrator ("FMLN guerrillas"). In both cases, the word "kidnapped" is the key word that relates them to the kidnapping event. In its passive form, we expect the subject of the verb "kidnapped" to be a victim and we expect the prepositional phrase beginning with "by" to contain a perpetrator. The word "kidnapped" specifies the roles of the people in the kidnapping and is therefore the most appropriate word to trigger a concept node.

AutoSlog relies on a small set of heuristics to determine which words and phrases are likely to activate useful concept nodes. In the next section, we will describe these heuristics and explain how AutoSlog generates complete concept node definitions.

Automated Dictionary Construction

Given a set of training texts and their associated answer keys, AutoSlog proposes a set of concept node definitions that are capable of extracting the information in the answer keys from the texts. Since the concept node definitions are general in nature, we expect that many of them will be useful for extracting information from novel texts as well. The algorithm for constructing concept node definitions is as follows. Given a targeted piece of information as a string from a template, AutoSlog finds the first sentence in the text that contains the string. This step is based on the observation noted earlier that the first reference to an object is likely to be the place where it is related to the event. The sentence is then handed over to CIRCUS which generates a conceptual analysis of the sentence. Using this analysis, AutoSlog identifies the first clause in the sentence that contains the string. A set of heuristics are applied to the clause to suggest a good *conceptual anchor point* for a concept node definition. If none of the heuristics is satisfied then AutoSlog searches for the next sentence in the text that contains the targeted information and the process is repeated.

The *conceptual anchor point heuristics* are the most important part of AutoSlog. A conceptual anchor point is a word that should activate a concept; in CIRCUS, this is a triggering word. Each heuristic looks for a specific linguistic pattern in the clause surrounding the targeted string. The linguistic pattern represents a phrase or set of phrases that are likely to be good for activating a concept node. If a heuristic successfully identifies its pattern in the clause then it generates two things: (1) a conceptual anchor point and (2) a set of enabling conditions to recognize the complete pattern. For example, suppose AutoSlog is given the clause "the diplomat was kidnapped" along with "the diplomat" as the targeted string. The string appears as the subject of the clause and is followed by a passive verb "kidnapped" so a heuristic that recognizes the pattern **<subject> passive-verb** is satisfied. The heuristic returns the word "kidnapped" as the conceptual anchor point along with enabling conditions that require a passive construction.

To build the actual concept node definition, the conceptual anchor point is used as its triggering word and the enabling conditions are included to ensure that the concept node is activated only in response to the desired linguistic pattern. For the example above, the final concept node will be activated by phrases such as "was kidnapped", "were kidnapped", "have been kidnapped", etc.

The current version of AutoSlog contains 13 heuristics, each designed to recognize a specific linguistic pattern. These patterns are shown below, along with examples that illustrate how they might be found in a text. The bracketed item shows the syntactic constituent where the string was found which is used for the slot expectation (<dobj> is the direct object and <np> is the noun phrase following a preposition). In the examples on the right, the bracketed item is a slot name that might be associated with the filler (e.g., the

subject is a victim). The underlined word is the conceptual anchor point that is used as the triggering word.

Linguistic Pattern	Example
<subject> passive-verb	<victim> was <u>murdered</u>
<subject> active-verb	<perpetrator> <u>bombed</u>
<subject> verb infinitive	<perpetrator> attempted to <u>kill</u>
<subject> auxiliary noun	<victim> was <u>victim</u>
passive-verb <dobj>[1]	<u>killed</u> <victim>
active-verb <dobj>	<u>bombed</u> <target>
infinitive <dobj>	to <u>kill</u> <victim>
verb infinitive <dobj>	threatened to <u>attack</u> <target>
gerund <dobj>	<u>killing</u> <victim>
noun auxiliary <dobj>	<u>fatality</u> was <victim>
noun prep <np>	<u>bomb</u> against <target>
active-verb prep <np>	<u>killed</u> with <instrument>
passive-verb prep <np>	was <u>aimed</u> at <target>

Several additional parts of a concept node definition must be specified: a slot to extract the information[2], hard and soft constraints for the slot, and a type. The syntactic constituent in which the string was found is used for the slot expectation. In the previous example, the string was found as the subject of the clause so the concept node is defined with a slot that expects its filler to be the subject of the clause.

The name of the slot (e.g., *victim*) comes from the template slot where the information was originally found. In order to generate domain-dependent concept nodes, AutoSlog requires three domain specifications. One of these specifications is a set of mappings from template slots to concept node slots. For example, information found in the human target slot of a template maps to a *victim* slot in a concept node. The second set of domain specifications are hard and soft constraints for each type of concept node slot, for example constraints to specify a legitimate victim.

Each concept node also has a type. Most concept nodes accept the event types that are found in the template (e.g., bombing, kidnapping, etc.) but sometimes we want to use special types. The third set of domain specifications are mappings from template types to concept node types. In general, if the targeted information was found in a kidnapping template then we use "kidnapping" as the concept node type. However, for the terrorism domain we used special types for information from the perpetrator and instrument template slots because perpetrators and instruments often appear in sentences that do not describe the nature of the event (e.g., "The FMLN claimed responsibility" could refer to a bombing, kidnapping, etc.).

Sample Concept Node Definitions

To illustrate how this whole process comes together, we will show some examples of concept node definitions gen-

---

[1]In principle, passive verbs should not have objects. However, we included this pattern because CIRCUS occasionally confused active and passive constructions.

[2]In principle, concept nodes can have multiple slots to extract multiple pieces of information. However, all of the concept nodes generated by AutoSlog have only a single slot.

erated by AutoSlog. Figure 1 shows a relatively simple concept node definition that is activated by phrases such as "was bombed", "were bombed", etc. AutoSlog created this definition in response to the input string "public buildings" which was found in the physical target slot of a bombing template from text DEV-MUC4-0657. Figure 1 shows the first sentence in the text that contains the string "public buildings". When CIRCUS analyzed the sentence, it identified "public buildings" as the subject of the first clause. The heuristic for the pattern <subject> passive-verb then generated this concept node using the word "bombed" as its triggering word along with enabling conditions that require a passive construction. The concept node contains a single variable slot[3] which expects its filler to be the subject of the clause (*S*) and labels it as a target because the string came from the physical target template slot. The constraints for physical targets are pulled in from the domain specifications. Finally, the concept node is given the type *bombing* because the input string came from a bombing template.

Id: DEV-MUC4-0657   **Slot filler:** "public buildings"
Sentence: (in la oroya, junin department, in the central peruvian mountain range, <u>public buildings</u> were bombed and a car-bomb was detonated.)

CONCEPT NODE
Name:	target-subject-passive-verb-bombed
Trigger:	bombed
Variable Slots:	(target (*S* 1))
Constraints:	(class phys-target *S*)
Constant Slots:	(type bombing)
Enabling Conditions:	((passive))

Figure 1: A good concept node definition

Figure 2 shows an example of a good concept node that has more complicated enabling conditions. In this case, CIRCUS found the targeted string "guerrillas" as the subject of the first clause but this time a different heuristic fired. The heuristic for the pattern <subject> verb infinitive matched the phrase "threatened to murder" and generated a concept node with the word "murder" as its trigger combined with enabling conditions that require the preceding words "threatened to" where "threatened" is in an active construction. The concept node has a slot that expects its filler to be the subject of the clause and expects it to be a perpetrator (because the slot filler came from a perpetrator template slot). The constraints associated with perpetrators are incorporated and the concept node is assigned the type "perpetrator" because our domain specifications map the perpetrator template slots to perpetrator types in concept nodes. Note that this concept node does not extract the direct object of "threatened to murder" as a victim. We would need a separate concept node definition to pick up the victim.

---

[3]*Variable slots* are slots that extract information. *Constant slots* have pre-defined values that are used by AutoSlog only to specify the concept node type.

Id: DEV-MUC4-0071   **Slot filler:** "guerrillas"
Sentence: (the salvadoran <u>guerrillas</u> on mar_12_89, today, threatened to murder individuals involved in the mar_19_88 presidential elections if they do not resign from their posts.)

CONCEPT NODE
Name: perpetrator-subject-verb-infinitive-threatened-to-murder
Trigger:	murder
Variable Slots:	(perpetrator (*S* 1))
Constraints:	(class perpetrator *S*)
Constant Slots:	(type perpetrator)
Enabling Conditions:	((active)
	(trigger-preceded-by? 'to 'threatened))

Figure 2: Another good concept node definition

Although the preceding definitions were clearly useful for the domain of terrorism, many of the definitions that AutoSlog generates are of dubious quality. Figure 3 shows an example of a bad definition. AutoSlog finds the input string, "gilberto molasco", as the direct object of the first clause and constructs a concept node that is triggered by the word "took" as an active verb. The concept node expects a victim as the direct object and has the type *kidnapping*. Although this concept node is appropriate for this sentence, in general we do not want to generate a kidnapping concept node every time we see the word "took".

Id: DEV-MUC4-1192   **Slot filler:** "gilberto molasco"
Sentence: (they took 2-year-old <u>gilberto molasco</u>, son of patricio rodriguez, and 17-year-old andres argueta, son of emimesto argueta.)

CONCEPT NODE
Name:	victim-active-verb-dobj-took
Trigger:	took
Variable Slots:	(victim (*DOBJ* 1))
Constraints:	(class victim *DOBJ*)
Constant Slots:	(type kidnapping)
Enabling Conditions:	((active))

Figure 3: A bad concept node definition

AutoSlog generates bad definitions for many reasons, such as (a) when a sentence contains the targeted string but does not describe the event (i.e., our first observation mentioned earlier does not hold), (b) when a heuristic proposes the wrong conceptual anchor point or (c) when CIRCUS incorrectly analyzes the sentence. These potentially dangerous definitions prompted us to include a human in the loop to weed out bad concept node definitions. In the following section, we explain our evaluation procedure and present empirical results.

Empirical Results

To evaluate AutoSlog, we created a dictionary for the domain of terrorist event descriptions using AutoSlog and compared it with the hand-crafted dictionary that we used in MUC-4. As our training data, we used 1500 texts and their associated answer keys from the MUC-4 corpus. Our targeted information was the slot fillers from six MUC-4 template slots that contained string fills which could be easily mapped back to the text. We should emphasize that AutoSlog does not require or even make use of these complete template instantiations. AutoSlog needs only an annotated corpus of texts in which the targeted information is marked and annotated with a few semantic tags denoting the type of information (e.g., victim) and type of event (e.g., kidnapping).

The 1258 answer keys for these 1500 texts contained 4780 string fillers which were given to AutoSlog as input along with their corresponding texts.[4] In response to these strings, AutoSlog generated 1237 concept node definitions. AutoSlog does not necessarily generate a definition for every string filler, for example if it has already created an identical definition, if no heuristic applies, or if the sentence analysis goes wrong.

As we mentioned earlier, not all of the concept node definitions proposed by AutoSlog are good ones. Therefore we put a human in the loop to filter out definitions that might cause trouble. An interface displayed each dictionary definition proposed by AutoSlog to the user and asked him to put each definition into one of two piles: the "keeps" or the "edits". The "keeps" were good definitions that could be added to the permanent dictionary without alteration.[5] The "edits" were definitions that required additional editing to be salvaged, were obviously bad, or were of questionable value. It took the user 5 hours to sift through all of the definitions. The "keeps" contained 450 definitions, which we used as our final concept node dictionary.

Finally, we compared the resulting concept node dictionary[6] with the hand-crafted dictionary that we used for MUC-4. To ensure a clean comparison, we tested the AutoSlog dictionary using the official version of our UMass/MUC-4 system. The resulting "AutoSlog" system was identical to the official UMass/MUC-4 system except that we replaced the hand-crafted concept node dictionary with the new AutoSlog dictionary. We evaluated both systems on the basis of two blind test sets of 100 texts each. These were the TST3 and TST4 texts that were used in the final MUC-4 evaluation. We scored the output generated by both systems using the MUC-4 scoring program. The results for systems are shown in Table 1.[7]

Recall refers to the percentage of the correct answers

that the system successfully extracted and *precision* refers to the percentage of answers extracted by the system that were actually correct. The *F-measure* is a single measure that combines recall and precision, in this case with equal weighting. These are all standard measures used in the information retrieval community that were adopted for the final evaluation in MUC-4.

System/Test Set	Recall	Precision	F-measure
MUC-4/TST3	46	56	50.51
AutoSlog/TST3	43	56	48.65
MUC-4/TST4	44	40	41.90
AutoSlog/TST4	39	45	41.79

Table 1: Comparative Results

The official UMass/MUC-4 system was among the top-performing systems in MUC-4 [Lehnert *et al.*, 1992b] and the results in Table 1 show that the AutoSlog dictionary achieved almost the same level of performance as the hand-crafted dictionary on both test sets. Comparing F-measures, we see that the AutoSlog dictionary achieved 96.3% of the performance of our hand-crafted dictionary on TST3, and 99.7% of the performance of the official MUC-4 system on TST4. For TST4, the F-measures were virtually indistinguishable and the AutoSlog dictionary actually achieved better precision than the original hand-crafted dictionary. We should also mention that we augmented the hand-crafted dictionary with 76 concept nodes created by AutoSlog before the final MUC-4 evaluation. These definitions improved the performance of our official system by filling gaps in its coverage. Without these additional concept nodes, the AutoSlog dictionary would likely have shown even better performance relative to the MUC-4 dictionary.

Conclusions

In previous experiments, AutoSlog produced a concept node dictionary for the terrorism domain that achieved 90% of the performance of our hand-crafted dictionary [Riloff and Lehnert, 1993]. There are several possible explanations for the improved performance we see here. First, the previous results were based on an earlier version of AutoSlog. Several improvements have been made to AutoSlog since then. Most notably, we added 5 new heuristics to recognize additional linguistic patterns. We also made a number of improvements to the CIRCUS interface and other parts of the system that eliminated many bad definitions[8] and generally produced better results. Another important factor was the human in the loop. We used the same person in both experiments but, as a result, he was more experienced the second time. As evidence, he finished the filtering task in only 5 hours whereas it took him 8 hours the first time.[9]

---

[4]Many of the slots contained several possible strings ("disjuncts"), any one of which is a legitimate filler. AutoSlog finds the first sentence that contains any of these strings.

[5]The only exception is that the user could change the concept node type if that was the only revision needed.

[6]We augmented the AutoSlog dictionary with 4 meta-level concept nodes from the hand-crafted dictionary before the final evaluation. These were special concept nodes that recognized textual cues for discourse analysis only.

[7]The results in Table 1 do not correspond to our official MUC-4 results because we used "batch" scoring and an improved version of the scoring program for the experiments described here.

[8]The new version of AutoSlog generated 119 fewer definitions than the previous version even though it was given 794 additional string fillers as input. Even so, this smaller dictionary produced better results than the larger one constructed by the earlier system.

[9]For the record, the user had some experience with CIRCUS but was not an expert.

AutoSlog is different from other lexical acquisition systems in that most techniques depend on a "partial lexicon" as a starting point (e.g., [Carbonell, 1979; Granger, 1977; Jacobs and Zernik, 1988]). These systems construct a definition for a new word based on the definitions of other words in the sentence or surrounding context. AutoSlog, however, constructs new dictionary definitions completely from scratch and depends only on a part-of-speech lexicon, which can be readily obtained in machine-readable form.

Since AutoSlog creates dictionary entries from scratch, our approach is related to one-shot learning. For example, explanation-based learning (EBL) systems [DeJong and Mooney, 1986; Mitchell et al., 1986] create complete concept representations in response to a single training instance. This is in contrast to learning techniques that incrementally build a concept representation in response to multiple training instances (e.g., [Cardie, 1992; Fisher, 1987; Utgoff, 1988]). However, explanation-based learning systems require an explicit domain theory which may not be available or practical to obtain. AutoSlog does not need any such domain theory, although it does require a few simple domain specifications to build domain-dependent concept nodes.

On the other hand, AutoSlog is critically dependent on a training corpus of texts and targeted information. We used the MUC-4 answer keys as training data but, as we noted earlier, AutoSlog does not need these complete template instantiations. AutoSlog would be just as happy with an "annotated" corpus in which the information is marked and tagged with event and type designations. NLP systems often rely on other types of tagged corpora, for example part-of-speech tagging or phrase structure bracketing (e.g., the Brown Corpus [Francis and Kucera, 1982] and the Penn Treebank [Marcus et al.]). However, corpus tagging for automated dictionary construction is less demanding than other forms of tagging because it is smaller in scope. For syntactic tagging, every word or phrase must be tagged whereas, for AutoSlog, only the targeted information needs to be tagged. Sentences, paragraphs, and even texts that are irrelevant to the domain can be effectively ignored.

We have demonstrated that automated dictionary construction is a viable alternative to manual knowledge engineering. In 5 person-hours, we created a dictionary that achieves 98% of the performance of a hand-crafted dictionary that required 1500 person-hours to build. Since our approach still depends on a manually encoded training corpus, we have not yet eliminated the knowledge engineering bottleneck. But we have significantly changed the nature of the bottleneck by transferring it from the hands of NLP experts to novices. Our knowledge engineering demands can be met by anyone familiar with the domain. Knowledge-based NLP systems will be practical for real-world applications only when their domain-dependent dictionaries can be constructed automatically. Our approach to automated dictionary construction is a significant step toward making information extraction systems scalable and portable to new domains.

Acknowledgments

We would like to thank David Fisher for designing and programming the AutoSlog interface and Stephen Soderland for being our human in the loop. This research was supported by the Office of Naval Research Contract N00014-92-J-1427 and NSF Grant no. EEC-9209623, State/Industry/University Cooperative Research on Intelligent Information Retrieval.

References

Carbonell, J. G. 1979. Towards a Self-Extending Parser. In *Proceedings of the 17th Meeting of the Association for Computational Linguistics*. 3–7.

Cardie, C. 1992. Learning to Disambiguate Relative Pronouns. In *Proceedings of the Tenth National Conference on Artificial Intelligence*. 38–43.

DeJong, G. and Mooney, R. 1986. Explanation-Based Learning: An Alternative View. *Machine Learning* 1:145–176.

Fisher, D. H. 1987. Knowledge Acquisition Via Incremental Conceptual Clustering. *Machine Learning* 2:139–172.

Francis, W. and Kucera, H. 1982. *Frequency Analysis of English Usage*. Houghton Mifflin, Boston, MA.

Granger, R. H. 1977. FOUL-UP: A Program that Figures Out Meanings of Words from Context. In *Proceedings of the Fifth International Joint Conference on Artificial Intelligence*. 172–178.

Jacobs, P. and Zernik, U. 1988. Acquiring Lexical Knowledge from Text: A Case Study. In *Proceedings of the Seventh National Conference on Artificial Intelligence*. 739–744.

Lehnert, W. 1990. Symbolic/Subsymbolic Sentence Analysis: Exploiting the Best of Two Worlds. In Barnden, J. and Pollack, J., editors 1990, *Advances in Connectionist and Neural Computation Theory, Vol. 1*. Ablex Publishers, Norwood, NJ. 135–164.

Lehnert, W.; Cardie, C.; Fisher, D.; McCarthy, J.; Riloff, E.; and Soderland, S. 1992a. University of Massachusetts: Description of the CIRCUS System as Used for MUC-4. In *Proceedings of the Fourth Message Understanding Conference (MUC-4)*. 282–288.

Lehnert, W.; Cardie, C.; Fisher, D.; McCarthy, J.; Riloff, E.; and Soderland, S. 1992b. University of Massachusetts: MUC-4 Test Results and Analysis. In *Proceedings of the Fourth Message Understanding Conference (MUC-4)*. 151–158.

Lehnert, W. G. and Sundheim, B. 1991. A Performance Evaluation of Text Analysis Technologies. *AI Magazine* 12(3):81–94.

Marcus, M.; Santorini, B.; and Marcinkiewicz, M. Building a Large Annotated Corpus of English: The Penn Treebank. *Computational Linguistics*. Forthcoming.

Mitchell, T. M.; Keller, R.; and Kedar-Cabelli, S. 1986. Explanation-Based Generalization: A Unifying View. *Machine Learning* 1:47–80.

Proceedings of the Fourth Message Understanding Conference (MUC-4). 1992. Morgan Kaufmann, San Mateo, CA.

Riloff, E. and Lehnert, W. 1993. Automated Dictionary Construction for Information Extraction from Text. In *Proceedings of the Ninth IEEE Conference on Artificial Intelligence for Applications*. IEEE Computer Society Press. 93–99.

Utgoff, P. 1988. ID5: An Incremental ID3. In *Proceedings of the Fifth International Conference on Machine Learning*. 107–120.

Learning Semantic Grammars with Constructive Inductive Logic Programming *

John M. Zelle and Raymond J. Mooney
Department of Computer Sciences
University of Texas
Austin, TX 78712
zelle@cs.utexas.edu, mooney@cs.utexas.edu

Abstract

Automating the construction of semantic grammars is a difficult and interesting problem for machine learning. This paper shows how the semantic-grammar acquisition problem can be viewed as the learning of search-control heuristics in a logic program. Appropriate control rules are learned using a new first-order induction algorithm that automatically invents useful syntactic and semantic categories. Empirical results show that the learned parsers generalize well to novel sentences and out-perform previous approaches based on connectionist techniques.

Introduction

Designing computer systems to "understand" natural language input is a difficult task. The laboriously hand-crafted computational grammars supporting natural language applications are often inefficient, incomplete and ambiguous. The difficulty in constructing adequate grammars is an example of the "knowledge acquisition bottleneck" which has motivated much research in machine learning. While numerous researchers have studied computer acquisition of natural languages, most of this research has concentrated on learning the syntax of a language from example sentences [Wirth, 1989; Berwick, 1985; Wolff, 1982] In practice, natural, language systems are typically more concerned with extracting the meaning of sentences, usually expressed in some sort of case-role structure.

Semantic grammars, which uniformly incorporate both syntactic and semantic constraints to parse sentences and produce semantic analyses, have proven extremely useful in constructing natural language interfaces for limited domains [Allen, 1987]. Unfortunately, new grammars must be written for each semantic domain, and the size of the grammar required for more

general applications can make manual construction infeasible. An interesting question for machine learning is whether such grammars can be automatically constructed from an analysis of examples in a given domain.

The semantic grammar acquisition problem presents a number of difficult issues. First, there is little agreement on what constitutes an "adequate" set of cases for sentence analysis; different tasks may require differing semantic representations. Therefore, the learning architecture must be general enough to allow mapping to (more or less) arbitrary meaning representations. Second, domain specific semantic constraints must be automatically recognized and incorporated into the grammar. This necessitates some form of constructive induction to identify useful semantic word and phrase classes. Finally, as in any learning system, it is crucial that the resulting grammar generalize well to unseen inputs. Given the generativity of natural languages, it is unreasonable to assume that the system will be trained on more than a small fraction of possible inputs.

In this paper we show how the problem of semantic grammar acquisition can be considered as learning control rules for a logic program. In this framework, the acquisition problem can be attacked using the techniques of inductive logic programming. We introduce a new induction algorithm that incorporates constructive induction to learn word classes and semantic relations necessary to support the parsing process. Empirical results show this to be a promising approach to the language acquisition problem.

Learning Case-Role Mapping
The Mapping Problem

Traditional case theory decomposes a sentence into a proposition represented by the main verb and various arguments such as agent, patient, and instrument, represented by noun phrases. The basic mapping problem is to decide which sentence constituents fill which roles. Though case analysis is only a part of the overall task of sentence interpretation, the problem is nontrivial even in simple sentences.

---
*This research was supported by the National Science Foundation under grant IRI-9102926 and the Texas Advanced Research Program under grant 003658114.

Consider these sentences from [McClelland and Kawamoto, 1986]:

1. The boy hit the window.
2. The hammer hit the window.
3. The hammer moved.
4. The boy ate the pasta with the cheese.
5. The boy ate the pasta with the fork.

In the first sentence, the subject, boy, is an agent. In the second, the subject, hammer, is an instrument. The role played by the subject must be determined on the grounds that boys are animate and hammers are not. In the third sentence, the subject, hammer, is interpreted as a patient, illustrating the importance of the relationship between the surface subject and the verb. In the last two sentences, the prepositional phrase could be attached to the verb (making fork an instrument of ate) or the object (cheese is an accompaniment of pasta). Domain specific semantic knowledge is required to make the correct assignment.

Previous Approaches

Recent research in learning the case-role assignment task has taken place under the connectionist paradigm [Miikkulainen and Dyer, 1991; McClelland and Kawamoto, 1986]. They argue that proper case-role assignment is a difficult task requiring many independent sources of knowledge, both syntactic and semantic, and therefore well-suited to connectionist techniques.

Connectionist models, however, face a number of difficulties in handling natural language. Since the output structures are "flat" (nonrecursive) it is unclear how the embedded propositions in more sophisticated analyses can be handled. The models are also limited to producing a single output structure for a given input. If an input sentence is truly ambiguous, the system produces a single output that appears as a weighted average of the possible analyses, rather than enumerating the consistent interpretations. We believe that symbolic techniques are more appropriate, and our approach does not suffer from these deficiencies. In addition, empirical results demonstrate that our system trains faster and generalizes to novel inputs better than its neural counterparts.

Shift-Reduce Case-Role Parsing

Variations of shift-reduce parsing have proven practical for many symbolic natural language applications [Tomita, 1986]. Our system adopts a simple shift-reduce framework for case-role mapping [Simmons and Yu, 1992]. The process is best illustrated by way of example.

Consider the sentence: "The man ate the pasta." Parsing begins with an empty stack and an input buffer containing the entire sentence. At each step of the parse, either a word is shifted from the front of the input buffer onto the stack, or the top two elements

Action	Stack Contents
(shift)	[]
(shift)	[the]
(shift)	[man, the]
(1 det)	[[man, det:the]]
(shift)	[ate, [man, det:the]]
(1 agt)	[[ate, agt:[man, det:the]]]
(shift)	[the, [ate, agt:[man, det:the]]]
(shift)	[pasta, the, [ate, agt:[man, det:the]]]
(1 det)	[[pasta, det:the], [ate, agt:[man, det:the]]]
(2 pat)	[[ate, pat:[pasta, det:the], agt:[man, det:the]]]

Figure 1: Parsing "The man ate the pasta."

on the stack are popped and combined to form a new element which is pushed back onto the stack. The sequence of actions and stack states for our simple example is shown Figure 1. The action notation *(x label)*, indicates that the stack items are combined via the role, *label*, with the item from stack position, *x*, being the head.

An advantage of assuming such a constrained parsing mechanism is that the form of structure building actions is limited. The operations required to construct a given case representation are directly inferable from the representation. In general, a structure building action is required for each unique case-role that appears in the analysis. The set of actions required to produce a set of analyses is the union of the actions required for each individual analysis.

Overview of CHILL

Our system, CHILL, (Constructive Heuristics Induction for Language Learning) is a general approach to semantic grammar acquisition. The input to the system is a set of training instances consisting of sentences paired with the desired case representations. The output is a shift-reduce parser (in Prolog) which maps sentences into case representations. The parser may produce multiple analyses (on backtracking) for a single input sentence, allowing for true ambiguity in the training set.

The CHILL algorithm consists of two distinct tasks. First, the training instances are used to formulate an overly-general parser which is capable of producing case structures from sentences. The initial parser is overly-general in that it produces many spurious analyses for any given input sentence. The parser is then specialized by introducing search control heuristics. These control heuristics limit the contexts in which certain program clauses are used, eliminating the spurious analyses. The following section details these two processes.

The CHILL Algorithm
Constructing an Overly-General Parser

A shift-reduce parser is easily represented as a logic program. The state of the parse is reflected by the contents of the stack and input buffer. Each distinct parsing action becomes an operator clause that takes the current stack and input and produces new ones. The overly-general parser is built by translating each action inferable from the training problems into a clause which implements the action. For example, the clause implementing the *(1 agt)* action is:

```
op([S1,S2|SRest], Inp, [SNew|SRest], Inp) :-
    combine(S1, agt, S2, SNew).
```

Building a program to parse a set of training examples is accomplished by adding clauses to the **op** predicate. Each clause is a direct translation of a required parsing action. As mentioned above, the identification of the necessary actions is straight-forward. A particularly simple approach is to include two actions (e.g., *(1 agt)* and *(2 agt)*) for each role used in the training examples; any unnecessary operator clauses will be removed from the program during the subsequent specialization process.

Parser Specialization

General Framework The overly-general parser produces a great many spurious analyses for the training sentences because there are no conditions specifying when it is appropriate to use the various operators. The program must be specialized by including control heuristics which guide the application of operator clauses. This section outlines the basic approach used in CHILL. More detail on incorporating clause selection information in Prolog programs can be found in [Zelle and Mooney, 1993].

Program specialization occurs in three phases. First, the training examples are analyzed to construct positive and negative control examples for each operator clause. Examples of correct operator applications are generated by finding the first correct parsing of each training pair with the overly-general parser; any subgoal to which an operator is applied in a successful parse becomes a positive control example for that operator. A positive control example for any operator is considered a negative example for all operators that do not have it as a positive example.

In the second phase, a general first-order induction algorithm is employed to learn a control rule for each operator. This control rule comprises a Horn-clause definition that covers the positive control examples for the operator but not the negative. The induction algorithm used by CHILL is discussed in the following subsection.

The final step is to "fold" the control information back into the overly-general parser. A control rule is easily incorporated into the overly-general program by unifying the head of an operator clause with the head of the control rule for the clause and adding the induced conditions to the clause body. The definitions of any invented predicates are simply appended to the program. As an example, the *(1 agt)* clause of **op** is typically modified to:

```
op([A,[B,det:the]],C,[D],C) :-
    animate(B), combine(A,agt,B,D).
animate(boy). animate(girl). ...
```

Here, a new predicate has been invented representing the concept "animate."[1] This rule may be roughly interpreted as stating: "If the stack contains two items, the second of which is a completed noun phrase whose head is animate, then attach this phrase as the agent of the top of stack."

Inducing Control Rules The induction task is to generate a Horn-clause definition which covers the positive control examples for an operator, but does not cover the negative. There is a growing body of research in inductive logic programming which addresses this problem. Our algorithm implements a novel combination of bottom-up techniques found in systems such as CIGOL [Muggleton and Buntine, 1988] and GOLEM [Muggleton and Feng, 1992] and top-down methods from systems like FOIL [Quinlan, 1990] and CHAMP [Kijsirikul *et al.*, 1992].

```
Let Pos := Positive Examples
Let Neg := Negative Examples
Let Def := Positive examples as unit clauses.
Repeat
    Let OldDef := Def
    Let S be a sampling of pairs of clauses in OldDef
    Let OldSize := TheorySize(OldDef)
    Let CurrSize := OldSize
    For each pair of clauses <C1, C2> in S
        Find_Generalization(C1,C2,Pos,Neg,NewClause,NewPreds)
        Reduce_Definition(Pos,OldDef,NewClause,NewPreds,NewDef)
        If TheorySize(NewDef) < CurrSize then
            CurrSize := TheorySize(NewDef)
            Def := NewDef
Until CurrSize = OldSize % No compaction achieved
Return Def
```

Figure 2: CHILL Induction Algorithm

Space does not permit a complete explanation of the induction mechanism, but the general idea is simple. The intuition is that we want to find a small (hence general) definition which discriminates between the positive and negative examples. We start with a most specific definition (the set of positive examples) and introduce generalizations which make the definition more compact (as measured by a CIGOL-like size metric). The search for more general definitions is carried out in a hill-climbing fashion. At each step, a number of possible generalizations are considered; the one producing the greatest compaction of the theory is implemented, and the process repeats. The basic algorithm is outlined in Figure 2.

The heart of the algorithm is the *Find_Generalization* procedure. It takes two clauses in the current definition and constructs a new clause that (empirically) subsumes them and does not cover any

---

[1]Invented predicates actually have system generated names. They are renamed here for clarity.

negative examples. *Reduce_Definition* proves the positive examples using the current definition augmented with the new generalized clause. Preferential treatment is given to the new clause (it is placed at the top of the Prolog definition) and any clauses which are no longer used in proving the positive examples are deleted to produce the reduced definition.

Find_Generalization employs three levels of effort to produce a generalization. The first is construction of the least general generalization (LGG) [Plotkin, 1970] of the input clauses. If the LGG covers no negative examples, further refinement is unnecessary. Otherwise, the clause is too general, and an attempt is made to refine it using a FOIL-like mechanism which adds literals derivable either from background or previously invented predicates. If the resulting clause is still too general, it is passed to *Invent_Predicate* which invents a new predicate to discriminate the positive examples from the negatives which are still covered.

Predicate invention is carried out in a manner analogous to CHAMP. The first step is to find a minimal-arity projection of the clause variables such that the set of ground tuples generated by the projection when using the clause to prove the positive examples is disjoint with the ground tuples generated in proving the negative examples. These ground tuples form positive and negative example sets for the new predicate, and the top-level induction algorithm is recursively invoked to create a definition of the predicate.

Experimental Results

The crucial test of any learning system is how well the learned concept generalizes to new input. CHILL has been tested on a number of case-role assignment tasks.

Comparison with Connectionism

In the first experiment, CHILL was tried on the baseline task reported in [Miikkulainen and Dyer, 1991] using 1475 sentence/case-structure examples from [McClelland and Kawamoto, 1986] (hereafter referred to as the M & K corpus). The corpus was produced from a set of 19 sentence templates generating sentences/case-structure pairs for sentences like those illustrated above. The sample actually comprises 1390 unique sentences, some of which allow multiple analyses. Since our parser is capable (through backtracking) of generating all legal parses for an input, training was done considering each unique sentence as a single example. If a particular sentence was chosen for inclusion in a training or testing set, the pairs representing all correct analyses of the sentence were included in that set.

Training and testing followed the standard paradigm of first choosing a random set of test examples (in this case 740) and then creating parsers using increasingly larger subsets of the remaining examples. All reported results reflect averages over five trials. During testing, the parser was used to enumerate all analyses for a given test sentence. Parsing of a sentence can fail

in two ways: an incorrect analysis may be generated, or a correct analysis may not be generated. In order to account for both types of inaccuracy, a metric was introduced to calculate the "average correctness" for a given test sentence as follows: $Accuracy = (\frac{C}{P} + \frac{C}{A})/2$ where P is the number of distinct analyses produced, C is the number of the produced analyses which were correct, and A is the number of correct analyses possible for the sentence.

CHILL performs very well on this learning task as demonstrated by the learning curve shown in Figure 3. The system achieves 92% accuracy on novel sentences after seeing only 150 training sentences. Training on 650 sentences produces 98% accuracy.

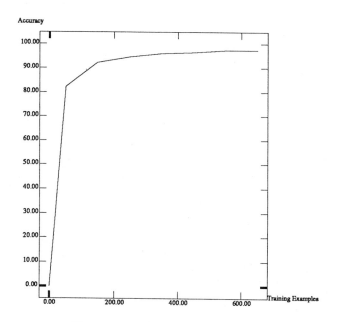

Figure 3: M & K corpus Accuracy

Direct comparison with previous results is difficult, as connectionist learning curves tend to be expressed in terms of low level measures such as "number of correct output bits." The closest comparison can be made with the results in [Miikkulainen and Dyer, 1991] where an accuracy of 95% was achieved at the "word level" training with 1439 of the 1475 pairs from the M & K corpus. Since the output contains five slots, assuming independence of errors gives an estimate of 0.95^5 or 78% completely correct parses. Interestingly, the types of inaccuracies differ substantially between systems. Neural networks always produce an output many of which contain minor errors, whereas CHILL tends to produce a correct output or none at all. From an engineering standpoint, it seems advantageous to have a system which "knows" when it fails; connectionists might be more interested in failing "reasonably."

With respect to training time, the induction algorithm employed by CHILL is a prototype implemented in Prolog. Running on a SparcStation 2, the creation of the parsers for the examples in this paper required from a few minutes to half an hour of CPU time. This compares favorably with backpropagation training times usually measured in hours or days.

It is also noteworthy that CHILL consistently invented interpretable word classes. One example, the invention of `animate`, has already been presented. This concept is implicit in the analyses presented to the system, since only animate objects are assigned to the agent role. Other invented classes clearly picked up on the distribution of words in the input sentences. The system regularly invented semantic classes such as `human`, `food`, and `possession` which were used for noun generation in the M & K corpus.

Phrase classes useful to making parsing distinctions were also invented. For example, the structure `instrumental_phrase` was invented as:

```
instr_phrase([]).
instr_phrase([with, the, X]) :- instrument(X).
instrument(fork). instrument(bat). ...
```

It was not necessary in parsing the M & K corpus to distinguish between instruments of different verbs, hence instruments of various verbs such as hitting and eating are grouped together. Where the semantic relationship between words is required to make parsing distinctions, such relationships can be learned. CHILL created one such relation: `can_possess(X,Y) :- human(X), possession(Y)`; which reflects the distributional relationship between humans and possessions present in the M & K corpus. Notice that this invented rule itself contains two invented word categories.

Although there is no *a priori* reason to suppose CHILL must invent interpretable categories, the naturalness of the invented concepts supports the empirical results indicating that CHILL is making the "right" generalizations.

A More Realistic Domain

The M & K corpus was designed specifically to illustrate the case mapping problem. As such, it does not necessarily reflect the true difficulty of semantic grammar acquisition for natural language applications. Another experiment was designed to test CHILL on a more realistic task. A portion of a semantic grammar was "lifted" from an extant prototype natural language database designed to support queries concerning tourist information [Ng, 1988]. The portion of the grammar used recognized over 150,000 distinct sentences. A simple case grammar, which produced labellings deemed useful for the database query task, was devised to generate a sample of sentence/case-structure analyses. The example pair shown in Figure 4 illustrates the type of sentences and analyses used.

An average learning curve for this domain is shown in Figure 5. The curve shows generalization results on

Show me the two star hotels in downtown LA with double rates below 65 dollars.

```
[show, theme:[hotels, det:the,
              type:[star, mod:two],
              loc:[la, casemark:in, mod:downtown],
              attr:[rates, casemark:with, mod:double,
                    less:[nbr(65), casemark:below,
                          unit:dollars]]]
 dative:me]
```

Figure 4: Example from Tourist Domain

500 sentences which differed from any used in training. The results are very encouraging. With only 50 training examples, the resulting parser achieved 93% accuracy on novel sentences. With 300 training examples, accuracy is 99%.

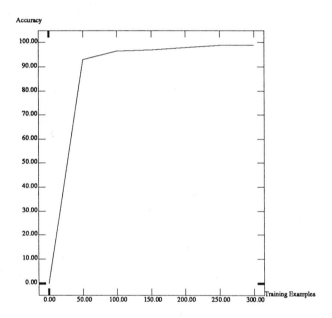

Figure 5: Tourist Domain Accuracy

Related Work

As noted in the introduction, most AI research in language acquisition has not focused on the case-role mapping problem. However, a number of language acquisition systems may be viewed as the learning of search control heuristics. Langley and Anderson [Langley, 1982; Anderson, 1983] have independently posited acquisition mechanisms based on learning search control in production systems. These systems were cognitively motivated and addressed the task of language generation rather than the case-role analysis task examined here.

Berwick's LPARSIFAL [Berwick, 1985] acquired syntactic parsing rules for a type of shift-reduce parser. His system was linguistically motivated and incorporated many constraints specific to the theory of language assumed. In contrast, CHILL uses induction techniques to avoid commitment to any specific model of grammar.

More recently an exemplar-based acquisition system for the style of case grammar used in CHILL is described in [Simmons and Yu, 1992]. Unlike CHILL, their system depends on an analyst to provide appropriate word classifications and requires detailed interaction to guide the parsing of training examples.

Recent corpus-based natural-language research has addressed some issues in automated dictionary construction [Lehnert et al., 1992; Brent and Berwick, 1991]. These systems use manually constructed parsers to "bootstrap" new patterns from analyzable text. They do not employ machine learning techniques to generalize the acquired templates or construct new features which support parsing decisions. In contrast, CHILL is a first attempt at applying modern machine learning methods to the more fundamental task of constructing efficient parsers.

Future Research

The generalization results in the experiments so far undertaken are quite encouraging; however, further testing on larger, more realistic corpora is required to determine the practicality of these techniques. Another avenue of research is "deepening" the analyses produced by the system. Applying our techniques to actually construct natural language systems will require either modifying the parser to produce final representations (e.g., database queries) or adding additional learning components which map the intermediate case structures into final representations.

Conclusion

Methods for learning semantic grammars hold the potential for substantially automating the development of natural language interfaces. We have presented a system that employs inductive logic programming techniques to learn a shift-reduce parser that integrates syntactic and semantic constraints to produce case-role representations. The system first produces an overly-general parser which it then constrains by inductively learning search-control heuristics that eliminate spurious parses. When learning heuristics, constructive induction is used to automatically generate useful semantic and syntactic classes of words and phrases. Experiments on two reasonably large corpora of sentence/case-role pairs demonstrate that the system learns accurate parsers that generalize well to novel sentences. These experiments also demonstrate that the system trains faster and produces more accurate results than previous, connectionist approaches and creates interesting and recognizable syntactic and semantic concepts.

References

Allen, James F. 1987. *Natural Language Understanding.* Benjamin/Cummings, Menlo Park, CA.

Anderson, John R. 1983. *The Architecture of Cognition.* Harvard University Press, Cambridge, MA.

Berwick, B. 1985. *The Acquisition of Syntactic Knowledge.* MIT Press, Cambridge, MA.

Brent, Micheal R. and Berwick, Robert C. 1991. Automatic acquisition of subcategorization frames from tagged text. In *Speech and Natrual Language: Proceedings of the DARPA Workshop.* Morgan Kaufmann. 342–345.

Kijsirikul, B.; Numao, M.; and Shimura, M. 1992. Discrimination-based constructive induction of logic programs. In *Proceedings of the Tenth National Conference on Artificial Intelligence,* San Jose, CA. 44–49.

Langley, P. 1982. Language acquisition through error recovery. *Cognition and Brain Theory* 5.

Lehnert, W.; Cardie, C.; Fisher, D.; McCarthy, J.; Rioloff, E.; and Soderland, S. 1992. University of massachusetts: Muc-4 test results and analysis. In *Proceedings of the Fourth DARPA Message Understanding Evaluation and Conference.* Morgan Kaufmann. 151–158.

McClelland, J. L. and Kawamoto, A. H. 1986. Mechnisms of sentence processing: Assigning roles to constituents of sentences. In Rumelhart, D. E. and McClelland, J. L., editors 1986, *Parallel Distributed Processing, Vol. II.* MIT Press, Cambridge, MA. 318–362.

Miikkulainen, R. and Dyer, M. G. 1991. Natural language processing with modular PDP networks and distributed lexicon. *Cognitive Science* 15:343–399.

Muggleton, S. and Buntine, W. 1988. Machine invention of first-order predicates by inverting resolution. In *Proceedings of the Fifth International Conference on Machine Learning,* Ann Arbor, MI. 339–352.

Muggleton, S. and Feng, C. 1992. Efficient induction of logic programs. In Muggleton, S., editor 1992, *Inductive Logic Programming.* Academic Press, New York. 281–297.

Ng, H. T. 1988. A computerized prototype natural language tour guide. Technical Report AI88-75, Artificial Intelligence Laboratory, University of Texas, Austin, TX.

Plotkin, G. D. 1970. A note on inductive generalization. In Meltzer, B. and Michie, D., editors 1970, *Machine Intelligence (Vol. 5).* Elsevier North-Holland, New York.

Quinlan, J.R. 1990. Learning logical definitions from relations. *Machine Learning* 5(3):239–266.

Simmons, R. F. and Yu, Y. 1992. The acquisition and use of context dependent grammars for English. *Computational Linguistics* 18(4):391–418.

Tomita, M. 1986. *Efficient Parsing for Natural Language.* Kluwer Academic Publishers, Boston.

Wirth, Ruediger 1989. Completing logic programs by inverse resolution. In *Proceedings of the European Working Session on Learning,* Montpelier, France. Pitman. 239–250.

Wolff, J. G. 1982. Language acquisition, data compression, and generalization. *Language and Communication* 2:57–89.

Zelle, J. M. and Mooney, R. J. 1993. Combining FOIL and EBG to speed-up logic programs. In *Proceedings of the Thirteenth International Joint conference on Artificial intelligence,* Chambery, France.

Vision
Processing

Polly: A Vision-Based Artificial Agent

Ian Horswill

MIT AI Lab

545 Technology Square

Cambridge, MA 02139

ian@ai.mit.edu

Abstract

In this paper I will describe Polly, a low cost vision-based robot that gives primitive tours. The system is very simple, robust and efficient, and runs on a hardware platform which could be duplicated for less than $10K US. The system was built to explore how knowledge about the structure the environment can be used in a principled way to simplify both visual and motor processing. I will argue that very simple and efficient visual mechanisms can often be used to solve real problems in real (unmodified) environments in a principled manner. I will give an overview of the robot, discuss the properties of its environment, show how they can be used to simplify the design of the system, and discuss what lessons can drawn for the design of other systems.[1]

Introduction

In this paper, I will describe Polly, a simple artificial agent that uses vision to give primitive tours of the 7th floor of the MIT AI lab (see figure 1). Polly is built from minimalist machinery that is matched to its task and environment. It is an example of Agre's principle of machinery parsimony [Agre, 1988], and is intended to demonstrate that very simple visual machinery can be used to solve real tasks in real, unmodified environments in a principled manner.

Polly roams the hallways of the laboratory looking for visitors. When someone approaches the robot, it stops and introduces itself and offers the vistor a tour, asking them to answer by waving their foot around (the robot can only see the person's legs and feet). When the person waves their foot, the robot leads them around the lab, recognizing and describing places as it comes to them.

Polly is very fast and simple. Its sensing and control systems run at 15Hz, so all percepts and motor commands are updated every 66ms. It also uses very little hardware (an equivalent robot could be built for approximately $10K), and consists of less than a thousand lines of Scheme code.[2] All computation is done on-board on a low-cost digital signal processor (a TI C30 with 64KW of ram). Polly is also among the best tested mobile robots to date, having seen hundreds of hours of service, and has a large behavioral repertoire.

Polly falls within the task-based or active approach to vision [Horswill, 1988][Aloimonos, 1990][Ballard, 1991][Ikeuchi and Herbert, 1990][Blake and Yuille, 1992]. While the work descrived here cannot prove the efficacy this approach, it does give an example of a large system which performs an interesting high-level task using these sorts of techniques.

Polly's efficiency is due to its specialization to its task and environment. Many authors have argued that simple machinery is often sufficient for performing intelligent behavior because of the special organizing structures of the environment (see, for example, [Rosenschein and Kaelbling, 1986][Brooks, 1986][Agre, 1988]). If we are to use such structures in a routine manner to engineer intelligent systems, then we must be able to isolate individual structures or properties of the environment and explain their computational rammifications. In this work, I have used the technique of stepwise transformation to draw out the relationships between a system specialized to its environment and a more general system. We look for a series of transformations, each of which conditionally preserves behavior given some constraint on the environment, that will transform the general system into the specialized system. The resulting derivation of the specialized system from the general system makes the additional assumptions made by the specialized system explicit. It also makes their computational rammifications explicit by putting them in correspondence with particular transformations which simplify particular computational subproblems. In effect, we imagine that the general system has been run through a "compiler" that has

---

[1]Support for this research was provided in part by the University Research Initiative under Office of Naval Research contract N00014 86 K 0685, and in part by the Advanced Research Projects Agency under Office of Naval Research contract N00014–85–K–0124.

---

[2]Not including device drivers and data structures.

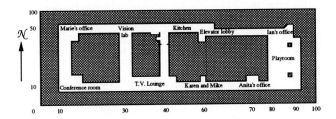

Figure 1: The approximate layout of Polly's environment (not to scale), and its coordinate system.

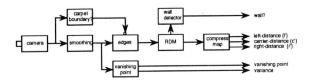

Figure 2: Portion of visual system devoted to navigation.

used declarations about the environment (constraints) to progressively optimize it until the specialized system is obtained. If we can "solve" for the declarations and associated optimizations which derive a system from a more general system, then we can reuse those optimizations in the design of future systems. Space precludes either a formal treatment of this approach or detailed analyses. See [Horswill, 1993a] or [Horswill, 1993b] for detailed discussions.

In next section, I will discuss some of the useful properties of Polly's environment and allude to the transformations which they allow. Then I will discuss the actual design of the system, including abbreviated forms of the constraint derivations for parts of the visual system. Finally, I will discusses the performance and failure modes of the system in some detail and close with conclusions.

Computational properties of office environments

Office buildings are actively structured to make navigation easier [Passini, 1984]. The fact that they are structured as open spaces connected by networks of corridors means that much of the navigation problem can be solved by corridor following. In particular, we can reduce the problem of finding paths in space to finding paths in the graph of corridors. The AI lab is even simpler because the corridor graph has a grid structure, and so we can attach coordinates to the verticies of the graph and use difference reduction to get from one pair of coordinates to another.

Determining one's position in the grid is also made easier by special properties of office environments: the lighting of offices is generally controlled; the very narrowness of their corridors constrains the possible viewpoints from which an agent can see a landmark within the corridors. I will refer to this latter property as the *constant viewpoint constraint*: that the configuration space of the robot is restricted so that a landmark can only be viewed from a small number of directions. These properties make the recognition of landmarks in a corridor an easier problem than the fully general recognition problem. Thus very simple mechanisms often suffice.

Another useful property of office buildings is that they are generally carpeted and their carpets tend to

be either regularly textured or not textured at all. The predictability of the texturing of the carpet means that any region of the image which isn't textured like the carpet is likely an object resting on the ground (or an object resting on an object resting on the ground). Thus *obstacle detection* can be reduced to *carpet detection*, which may be a simpler problem admitting simpler solutions. In the case of the MIT AI lab, the carpet has no texture and so a texture dectector suffices for finding obstacles. We will refer to this as the *background-texture constraint* (see [Horswill, 1993a] for a more detailed discussion).

Finally, office buildings have the useful property that they have flat floors and so objects which are farther away will appear higher in the image, provided that the objects rest on the floor. This provides a very simple way of determining the rough depth of such an object. We will refer to this as the *ground-plane constraint*: that all obstacles rest on a flat floor (see [Horswill, 1993a]).

Architecture

Conceptually, Polly consists of a set of parallel processes connected with fixed links (see [Brooks, 1986][Agre and Chapman, 1987][Rosenschein and Kaelbling, 1986] for examples of this type of methodology)). The actual implementation is a set of Scheme procedures, roughly one per process, with variables used to simulate wires. On each clock tick (66ms), the robot grabs a new image, runs each process in sequence to recompute all visual system outputs, and computes a new motor command which is fed to the base computer.

Physically, the robot consists of an RWI B12 robot base which houses the motors and motor control logic, a voice synthesizer, a front panel for control, a serial port for downloading, a TMS320C30-based DSP board (the main computer), a frame grabber, and a microprocessor for servicing peripherals. All computation is done on board.

Visual system

The visual system processes a 64 × 48 image every 66ms and generates a large number "percepts" from it (see figure 3) which are updated continuously. Most of these are related to navigation, although some are devoted to person detection or sanity checking of the image. Because of space limitations, we will restrict ourselves to the major parts of the navigation section.

```
open-left?     open-region?    person-direction
open-right?    blind?          wall-ahead?
blocked?       light-floor?    wall-far-ahead?
left-turn?     dark-floor?     vanishing-point
right-turn?    person-ahead?   farthest-direction
```

Figure 3: Partial list of percepts generated by the visual system.

Constraint	Computational problem
Ground plane	Depth perception
Background-texture	Figure/ground separation
Long corridor edges	Vanishing point
Strong corridor edges	Edge detection
Known camera tilt	Vanishing point
Uniform NC intersctns	Vanishing point

Figure 4: Constraints assumed by the visual system and the problems they helped to simplify. Note that "known camera tilt" is more a constraint on the agent, than on the habitat.

The central pipeline in figure 2 ("smoothing" ... "compress map") computes depth information. The major representation used here is a *radial depth map*, that is, a map from direction to distance, similar to the output of a sonar ring. Computing depth is a notoriously difficult problem. The problem is greatly simplified for Polly by the use of domain knowledge. By the ground plane constraint, we can use height in the image plane as a measure of distance. Thus the system[3]

$$\Rightarrow \boxed{F/G} \rightarrow \boxed{RDM} \rightarrow$$

can be substituted for any system which computes a radial depth map, where F/G is any system which does figure/ground separation (labeling of each pixel as figure or background), and *RDM* is a transformation from a bitmap to a vector defined by

$$RDM(x) = \min\{y | \text{the point } (x, y) \text{ isn't floor}\}$$

The effect of this is to reduce the problem of depth recovery to the figure-ground problem. The figure-ground problem is, if anything, more difficult than the depth-recovery problem in the general case so one might expect this to be a bad move. However, by the background-texture constraint, we can use any operator which responds to the presence of texture. Polly presently uses a simple edge detector (thresholded magnitude of the intensity gradient):

$$\Rightarrow \boxed{|\nabla I|} \rightarrow \boxed{RDM} \rightarrow$$

The visual system then compresses the depth map into three values, **left-distance**, **right-distance**, and **center-distance**, which give the closest distance on the left side of the image, right side, and the center third, respectively. Other values are then derived from these. For example, **open-left?** and **open-right?** are true when the corresponding distance is over threshold. **left-turn?** and **right-turn?** are true when the depth map is open on the correct side and the robot is aligned with the corridor.

The visual system also generates the vanishing point of the corridor. Bellutta *et al* [Bellutta *et al.*, 1989] describe a system which extracts vanishing points by running an edge finder, extracting straight line segments, and performing 2D clustering on the pairwise

---

[3] Here the $\Rightarrow$ symbol is used to denote input from the sensors, while $\rightarrow$ denotes signals moving within the system.

intersections of the edge segments. We can represent it schematically as:

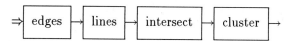

We can simplify the system by making stronger assumptions about the environment. We can remove the step of grouping edge pixels into segments by treating each edge pixel as its own tiny segment. This will weight longer lines more strongly, so the lines of the corridor must dominate the scene for this to work properly. If the edges are strong, then a simple edge detector will suffice. Polly uses a gradient threshold detector. If the tilt-angle of the camera is held constant by the camera mount, then the vanishing point will always have the same y coordinate, so we can reduce the clustering to a 1D problem. Finally, if we assume that the positions and orientations of the non-corridor edges are uniformly distributed, then we can replace the clustering operation, which looks for modes, the mean. After all these optimizations, we have the following system:

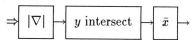

The system first computes the gradient threshold edges, then intersects the tangent line of each edge pixel with the horizontal line in which the vanishing point is known to lie, then computes the mean of the x coordinate of the intersections. The variance is also reported as a confidence measure.

The constraints assumed by these systems are summarized in figure 4. The discussion here has been necessarily brief. For a more detailed derivation, see [Horswill, 1993a].

Low-level navigation

The robot's motion is controlled by three parallel systems. The distance control system drives forward with a velocity of $\alpha(\text{center-distance} - d_{stop})$, where d_{stop} is the threshold distance for braking and α is a gain parameter. Note that it will back up if it overshoots or if it is aggressively approached. The corridor follower drives the turning motor so as to keep the vanishing point in the middle of the screen and keep **left-distance** and

Kitchen	
Position	(50, 40)
Direction	west
Veer	0
Image	...

Elevator lobby	
Position	(60, 40)
Direction	east
Veer	45
Features	right, wall

Figure 5: Example place frames.

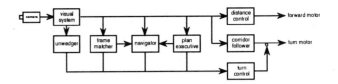

Figure 6: Architecture of the complete navigation system.

right-distance equal. The corridor follower switches into wall-following mode (keeping the wall at a constant distance) when only sees one wall. Finally, the turn unit drives the base in open-loop turns when instructed to by higher-level systems. The corridor follower is over-ridden during open-loop turns. During large turns, the distance control system inhibits forward motion so as to avoid suddenly turning into a wall. For more detailed of the low-level navigation system discussion, see [Horswill, 1993b].

Place recognition

Polly generally runs in the corridors and open spaces of the 7th floor of the AI lab at MIT. It keeps track of its position by recognizing landmarks and larger-scale "districts," which are given to it in advance. The lab, and some of its landmarks are shown in figure 1.

The corridors of the lab provide a great deal of natural constraint on the recognition of landmarks. Since corridors run in only two perpendicular directions, which we will arbitrarily designate as north-south (ns) and east-west (ew), they form natural coordinate axes for representing position. The robot's base provides rough rotational odometry which is good enough for the robot to distinguish which of four directions it is moving in, and so, in what type of corridor it must be.

Each distinctive place in the lab is identified by a pair of *qualitative coordinates*, shown in the figure. These coordinates are not metrically accurate, but they do preserve the ordering of places along each of the axes. Information about places is stored in an associative memory which is exhaustively searched on every clock tick (66ms). The memory consists of a set of frame-like structures, one per possible view of each landmark (see figure 5). Each frame gives the expected appearance of a place from a particular direction (north/south/east/west). Frames contain a place name, qualitative coordinates, and a direction and some specification of the landmark's appearance: either a 16×12 grey-scale image or a set of qualitative features (left-turn, right-turn, wall, dark-floor, light-floor). No explicit connectivity information is represented. Frames can also be tagged with a speech to give during a tour or an open-loop turn to perform.

While at first glance, this may seem to be an inefficient mechanism, it is in fact quite compact. The complete set of frames for the 7th floor requires approximately 1KByte of storage. The system can scan all the frames and find the best match at 15Hz using only a fraction of the CPU.

The system can also recognize large-scale "districts" and correct its position estimate even if it cannot determine exactly where it is. There is evidence that humans use such information (see [Lynch, 1960]). The robot presently recognizes the two long east/west corridors as districts. For example, when the robot is driving west and sees a left turn, it can only be in the southern ew corridor, so its y coordinate must be 10, regardless of its x position. This allows to robot to quickly recover from getting lost. At present, the recognition of districts is implemented as a separate computation, but I intend to fold it into the frame system.

High-level navigation

By default, the corridor follower is in control of the robot at all times. The corridor follower will always attempt to go forward and avoid obstacles unless it is overridden. Higher-level navigation is implemented by a set of independent processes which are parasitic upon the corridor follower. These processes control the robot by enabling or disabling motion, and by forcing open-loop turns. The navigator unit chooses corridors by performing difference reduction of the (qualitative) goal coordinates and the present coordinates. When there is a positive error in the y coordinate, it will attempt to drive south, or north for negative error, and so on. This technique has the advantages of being very simple to implement and very tolerant of place recognition errors. If a landmark is missed, the system need not replan its path. When the next landmark in the corridor is noticed, it will automatically return to the missed landmark. The "unwedger" unit forces the robot to turn when the corridor follower is unable to move for a long period of time (2 seconds). Finally, a set of action-sequencers (roughly plan executives for hand-written plans) are used to implement tour giving and operations such as docking. The sequencers execute a language of high level commands such as "go to place" which are implemented by sending commands to lower-level modules such as the navigator.

Performance

At present the system runs at 15Hz, but is I/O bound. The navigation system can safely run the robot at up to 1.5m/s, however, the base becomes unstable at that speed. The system is very robust, particularly the low-level locomotion system, which has seen hundreds of hours of service. The place recognition and navigation systems are newer and so less well tested. The failure modes of the component systems are summarized below.

Low-level navigation

All locomotion problems were obstacle detection problems. The corridor follower runs on all floors of the AI lab building on which it has been tested (floors 3-9) except for the 9th floor, which has very shiny floors; there the system brakes for the reflections of the overhead lights in the floor. The present system also has no memory and so cannot brake for an object unless it is actually in its field of view. The system's major failure mode is braking for shadows. If shadows are sufficiently strong they will cause the robot to brake when there is in fact no obstacle. This is less of a problem than one would expect because shadows are generally quite diffuse and so will not necessarily trigger the edge detector. Finally, several floors have multiple carpets, each with a different color. The boundaries between these carpets can thus be mistaken for obstacles. This problem was dealt with by explicitly recognizing the boundary when directly approaching it and informing the edge detector to ignore horizontal lines.

The system has also been tested recently at Brown university. There the robot had serious problems with light levels, but performed well where there was sufficient light for the camera. In some areas the robot had problems because the boundary between the floor and the walls was too weak to be picked up by the edge detector. We would expect any vision system to have problems in these cases however.

Place recognition

Place recognition is the weakest part of the system. While recognition by matching images is quite general, it is fragile. It is particularly sensitive to changes in the world. If a chair is in view when a landmark template is photographed, then it must continue to be in view, and in the same place and orientation, forever. If the chair moves, then the landmark becomes unrecognizable until a new view is taken. Another problem is that the robot's camera is pointed at the floor and there isn't very much interesting to be seen there. For these reasons, place recognition is restricted corridor intersections represented by feature frames, since they are more stable over time. The one exception is the kitchen which is recognized using images. In ten trials, the robot recognized the kitchen eight times while going west, and ten times while going east. Westward recognition of the kitchen fails completely when the water bottles in the kitchen doorway are moved however.

Both methods consistently miss landmarks when there is a person standing the the way. This often leads it to miss a landmark immediately after picking up a visitor. They also fail if the robot is in the process of readjusting its course after driving around an obstacle or if the corridor is very wide and has a large amount of junk in it. Both these conditions cause the constant-viewpoint constraint to fail. The former can sometimes cause the robot to hallucinate a turn because one of the walls is invisible, although this is rare.

Recognition of districts is very reliable, although it can sometimes become confused if the robot is driven in a cluttered open space rather than a corridor.

High-level navigation

High-level navigation performance is determined by the accuracy of place recognition. In general, the system works flawlessly unless the robot gets lost. For example, the robot has often run laps (implemented by alternately giving opposite corners as goals to the navigator) for over an hour without any navigation faults. When the robot gets lost, the navigator will generally overshoot and turn around. If the robot gets severely lost, the navigator will flail around until the place recognition system gets reoriented. The worst failure mode is when the place recognition system thinks that it is east of its goal when it is actually at the western edge of the building. In this case, the navigator unit and the unwedger fight each other, making opposite course corrections. The place recognition system should probably be modified to notice that it is lost in such situations so that the navigator will stop making course corrections until the place recognition system relocks. This has not yet been implemented however.

Getting lost is a more serious problem for the action sequencers, since they are equivalent to plans but there is no mechanism for replanning which a plan step fails. This can be mitigated by using the navigator to execute individual plan steps, which amounts to shifting responsibility from plan-time to run-time.

Conclusions

Many vision-based mobile robots have been developed in the past (see for example [Kosaka and Kak, 1992][Kriegman et al., 87] [Crisman, 1992][Turk et al., 1987]). The unusual aspects of Polly are its relatively large behavioral repertoire, simple design, and principled use of special properties of its environment.

Polly's efficiency and reliability are due to a number of factors. Specialization to a task allows the robot to compute only the information it needs. Specialization to the environment allows the robot to substitute simple computations for more expensive ones. The use of multiple strategies in parallel reduces the likelihood of catastrophic failure (see [Horswill and Brooks, 1988]). Thus if the vanishing point computation generates bad data, the depth-balancing strategy will compensate for it and the distance control system will prevent collisions until the vanishing point is corrected. Finally, the speed of its perception/control allows it to rapidly recover from errors. This relaxes the need for perfect perception and allows simpler perceptual and control strategies to be used.

Scalability is a major worry for all approaches to AI. We don't know whether an approach will scale until we try to scale it and so the field largely runs on existence proofs. Polly is an existence proof that a robust system with a large behavioral repertoire can be built using simple components which are specialized to their task and environment, but it does not show how far we can extend the approach.

One of the benefits of making constraints explicit and putting them in correspondence with transformations is that it gives us some degree of leverage in generalizing our designs. Although space precluded a detailed analysis of Polly's systems, we can see from the brief analysis of the low level navigation system that the role of the background texture constraint was to simplify the figure ground problem by allowing the substitution of a edge detector. This tells us several useful things. First, any linear filter restricted to the right band will do (see [Horswill, 1993a]). Second, if the environment does not satisfy the BTC, then any other transformation which simplifies figure ground will also do. We can even use multiple figure/ground systems and switch between them depending on the properties of the environment. Another possibility is two implement both the general system and a specialized system and switch at the behavioral level. This effectively moves the optimization from compile-time to run-time and makes the specialized system a sort of a hardware accelerator on a par with a cache memory.

Thus specialized systems need not simply be hacks. We can learn things from the design of one specialized system which are applicable to the designs of other systems, even traditional systems.

References

[Agre and Chapman, 1987] Philip E. Agre and David Chapman. Pengi: An implementation of a theory of activity. In *Proceedings of the Sixth National Conference on Artificial Intelligence*, pages 268–272, 1987.

[Agre, 1988] Philip E. Agre. The dynamic structure of everyday life. Technical Report 1085, October 1988.

[Aloimonos, 1990] John Aloimonos. Purposive and qualitative active vision. In *DARPA Image Understanding Workshop*, 1990.

[Ballard, 1991] Dana H. Ballard. Animate vision. *Artificial Intelligence*, 48(1):57–86, 1991.

[Bellutta et al., 1989] P. Bellutta, G. Collini, A. Verri, and V. Torre. Navigation by tracking vanishing points. In *AAAI Spring Symposium on Robot Navigation*, pages 6–10, Stanford University, March 1989. AAAI.

[Blake and Yuille, 1992] Andrew Blake and Alan Yuille, editors. *Active Vision*. MIT Press, Cambridge, MA, 1992.

[Brooks, 1986] Rodney A. Brooks. A robust layered control system for a mobile robot. *IEEE Journal of Robotics and Automoation*, 2(1):14–23, March 1986.

[Crisman, 1992] Jill D. Crisman. *Color Region Tracking for Vehicle Guidance*, chapter 7. In Blake and Yuille [1992], 1992.

[Horswill and Brooks, 1988] Ian Horswill and Rodney Brooks. Situated vision in a dynamic environment: Chasing objects. In *Proceedings of the Seventh National Conference on Artificial Intelligence*, August 1988.

[Horswill, 1988] Ian D. Horswill. Reactive navigation for mobile robots. Master's thesis, Massachusetts Institute of Technology, June 1988.

[Horswill, 1993a] Ian Horswill. Analysis of adaptation and environment. In submission, 1993.

[Horswill, 1993b] Ian Horswill. *Specialization of perceptual processes*. PhD thesis, Massachusetts Institute of Technology, Cambridge, 1993. forthcoming.

[Ikeuchi and Herbert, 1990] Katsushi Ikeuchi and Martial Herbert. Task oriented vision. In *DARPA Image Understanding Workshop*, 1990.

[Kosaka and Kak, 1992] A. Kosaka and A. C. Kak. Fast vision-guided mobile robot navigation using model-based reasoning and prediction of uncertainties. *Computer Vision, Graphics, and Image Processing*, 56(3), September 1992.

[Kriegman et al., 87] David J. Kriegman, Ernst Triendl, and Tomas O. Binford. A mobile robot: Sensing, planning and locomotion. In *1987 IEEE Internation Conference on Robotics and Automation*, pages 402–408. IEEE, March 87.

[Lynch, 1960] Kevin Lynch. *The Image of the City*. MIT Press, 1960.

[Passini, 1984] Romedi Passini. *Wayfinding in Architecture*, volume 4 of *Environmental Design Series*. Van Norstrand Reinhold, New York, 1984.

[Rosenschein and Kaelbling, 1986] Stanley J. Rosenschein and Leslie Pack Kaelbling. The synthesis of machines with provable epistemic properties. In Joseph Halpern, editor, *Proc. Conf. on Theoretical Aspects of Reasoning about Knowledge*, pages 83–98. Morgan Kaufmann, 1986.

[Turk et al., 1987] Matthew A. Turk, David G. Morgenthaler, Keith Gremban, and Martin Marra. Video road following for the autonomous land vehicle. In *1987 IEEE Internation Conference on Robotics and Automation*, pages 273–280. IEEE, March 1987.

Range Estimation From Focus Using a Non-frontal Imaging Camera*

Arun Krishnan and **Narendra Ahuja**
Beckman Institute
University Of Illinois
405 North Mathews Ave.,
Urbana IL 61801, U.S.A.
e-mail: arunki@vision.csl.uiuc.edu, ahuja@vision.csl.uiuc.edu

Abstract

This paper is concerned with active sensing of range information from focus. It describes a new type of camera whose image plane is not perpendicular to the optical axis as is standard. This special imaging geometry eliminates the usual focusing need of image plane movement. Camera movement, which is anyway necessary to process large visual fields, integrates panning, focusing, and range estimation. Thus the two standard mechanical actions of focusing and panning are replaced by panning alone. Range estimation is done at the speed of panning. An implementation of the proposed camera design is described and experiments with range estimation are reported.

INTRODUCTION

This paper is concerned with active sensing of range information from focus. It describes a new type of camera which integrates the processes of image acquisition and range estimation. The camera can be viewed as a computational sensor which can perform high speed range estimation over large scenes. Typically, the field of view of a camera is much smaller than the entire visual field of interest. Consequently, the camera must pan to sequentially acquire images of the visual field, a part at a time, and for each part compute range estimates by acquiring and searching images over many image plane locations. Using the proposed approach, range can be computed at the speed of panning the camera.

At the heart of the proposed design is active control of imaging geometry to eliminate the standard mechanical adjustment of image plane location, and further, integration of the only remaining mechanical action of camera panning with focusing and range estimation. Thus, imaging geometry and optics are exploited to replace explicit sequential computation. Since the camera implements a range from focus approach, the resulting estimates have the following characteristics as is true for any such approach [Das and Ahuja, 1990; Das and Ahuja, 1992b]. The scene surfaces of interest must have texture so image sharpness can be measured. The confidence of the estimates improves with the amount of surface texture present. Further, the reliability of estimates is inherently a function of the range to be estimated. However, range estimation for wide scenes using the proposed approach is faster than any traditional range from focus approach, thus eliminating one of the major drawbacks.

The next section describes in detail the pertinence of range estimation from focus, and some problems that characterize previous range from focus approaches and serve as the motivation for the work reported in this paper. The following section presents the new, proposed imaging geometry whose centerpiece is a tilting of the image plane from the standard frontoparallel orientation. It shows how the design achieves the results of search over focus with high computational efficiency. The rest of the paper presents a range from focus algorithm that uses the proposed camera, followed by the results of an experiment demonstrating the feasibility of our method. The last section presents some concluding remarks.

BACKGROUND & MOTIVATION

Range Estimation From Focus and Its Utility

Focus based methods usually obtain a depth estimate of a scene point by mechanically relocating

---

*The support of the National Science Foundation and Defence Advanced Research Projects Agency under grant IRI-89-02728 and U.S. Army Advance Construction Technology Center under grant DAAL 03-87-K-0006 is gratefully acknowledged.

the image plane, thereby varying the focus distance (v). When the scene point appears in sharp focus, the corresponding u and v values satisfy the standard lens law: $\frac{1}{u} + \frac{1}{v} = \frac{1}{f}$. The depth value u for the scene point can then be calculated by knowing the values of the focal length and the focus distance [Pentland, 1987; Darrell and Wohn, 1988; Ens and Lawrence, 1991]. To determine when a scene is imaged in sharp focus, several autofocus methods have been proposed in the past [Horn, 1968; Sperling, 1970; Tenebaum, 1971; Jarvis, 1976; Ligthart and Groen, 1982; Schlag et al., 1985; Krotkov et al., 1986; Krotkov, 1986; Darrell and Wohn, 1988; Nayar and Nakagawa, 1990].

Like any other visual cue, range estimation from focus is reliable under some conditions and not so in some other conditions. Therefore, to use the cue appropriately, its shortcomings and strengths must be recognized and the estimation process should be suitably integrated with other processes using different cues, so as to achieve superior estimates under broader conditions of interest [Abbott and Ahuja, 1990; Krotkov, 1989; Das and Ahuja, 1992a]. When accurate depth information is not needed, e.g., for obstacle avoidance during navigation, range estimates from focus or some other cue alone may suffice, even though it may be less accurate than that obtained by an integrated analysis of multiple cues.

Motivation for Proposed Approach

The usual range from focus algorithms involve two mechanical actions, those of panning and for each chosen pan angle finding the best v value. These steps make the algorithms slow. The purpose of the first step is to acquire data over the entire visual field since cameras typically have narrower field of view. This step is therefore essential to construct a range map of the entire scene. The proposed approach is motivated primarily by the desire to eliminate the second step involving mechanical control.

Consider the set of scene points that will be imaged with sharp focus for some constant value of focal length and focus distance. Let us call this set of points the SF surface[1]. For the conventional case where the image is formed on a plane perpendicular to the optical axis, and assuming that the lens has no optical aberrations, this SF surface will be a surface that is approximately planar and normal to the optical axis. The size of SF surface will be a scaled version of the size of the

image plane, while its shape will be the same as that of the image plane. Figure 1(a) shows the SF surface for a rectangular image plane.

As the image plane distance from the lens, v, is changed, the SF surface moves away, or toward the camera. As the entire range of v values is traversed, the SF surface sweeps out a cone shaped volume in three-dimensional space, henceforth called the SF cone. The vertex angle of the cone represents the magnification or scaling achieved and is proportional to the f value. Figure 1(b) shows a frustum of the cone.

Only those points of the scene within the SF cone are ever imaged sharply. To increase the size of the imaged scene, the f value used must be increased. Since in practice there is a limit on the usable range of f value, it is not possible to image the entire scene in one viewing. The camera must be panned to repeatedly image different parts of the scene. If the solid angle of the cone is ω, then to image an entire hemisphere one must clearly use at least $\frac{2\Pi}{\omega}$ viewing directions. This is a crude lower bound since it does not take into account the constraints imposed by the packing and tessellability of the hemisphere surface by the shape of the camera visual field.

If specialized hardware which can quickly identify focused regions in the image is used, then the time required to obtain the depth estimates is bounded by that required to make all pan angle changes and to process the data acquired for each pan angle.

The goal of the approach proposed in this paper is to select the appropriate v value for each scene point without conducting a dedicated mechanical search over all v values. The next section describes how this is accomplished by slightly changing the camera geometry and exploiting this in conjunction with the pan motion to accomplish the same result as traditionally provided by the two mechanical motions.

A NON-FRONTAL IMAGING CAMERA

The following observations underlie the proposed approach. In a normal camera, all points on the image plane lie at a fixed distance (v) from the lens. So all scene points are always imaged with a fixed value of v, regardless of where on the image plane they are imaged, i.e., regardless of the camera pan angle. If we instead have an image surface such that the different image surface points are at different distances from the lens, then depending upon where on the imaging surface the image of a scene point is formed (i.e., depending on the pan angle), the imaging parameter v will assume different values. This means that by controlling only the pan angle, we could achieve both goals of the

---

[1] Actually, the depth-of-field effect will cause the SF surface to be a 3-D volume. We ignore this for the moment, as the arguments being made hold irrespective of whether we have a SF surface, or a SF volume.

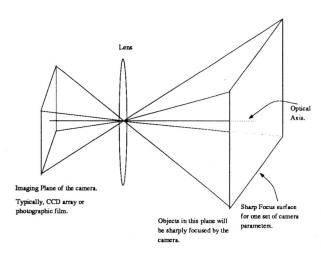

(a) SF surface

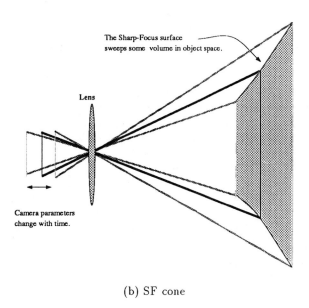

(b) SF cone

Figure 1: (a) Sharp Focus object surface for the standard planar imaging surface orthogonal to the optical axis. Object points that lie on the SF surface are imaged with the least blur. The location of the SF surface is a function of the camera parameters. (b) A frustum of the cone swept by the SF surface as the value of v is changed. Only those points that lie inside the SF cone can be imaged sharply, and therefore, range-from-focus algorithms can only calculate the range of these points.

traditional mechanical movements, namely, that of changing v values as well as that of scanning the visual field, in an integrated way.

In the rest of this paper, we will consider the simplest case of a nonstandard image surface, namely a plane which has been tilted relative to the standard frontoparallel orientation. Consider the tilted image plane geometry shown in Figure 2(a). For different angles θ, the distance from the lens center to the image plane is different. Consider a point object at an angle θ. The following relation follows from the geometry:

$$\mid \vec{OC} \mid = \frac{d \cos \alpha}{\cos(\theta - \alpha)}$$

Since for a tilted image plane, v varies with position, it follows from the lens law that the corresponding SF surface is a surface whose u value also varies with position. The volume swept by the SF surface as the camera is rotated is shown in Figure 2(b).

If the camera turns about the lens center O by an angle ϕ, then the object will now appear at an angle $\theta + \phi$. The new image distance (for the point object) will now be given by the following equation.

$$\mid \vec{OC'} \mid = \frac{d \cos \alpha}{\cos(\phi + \theta - \alpha)}$$

As the angle ϕ changes, the image distance also changes. At some particular angle, the image will appear perfectly focused and as the angle keeps changing, the image will again go out of focus. By identifying the angle ϕ at which any surface appears in sharp focus, we can calculate the image distance, and then from the lens law, the object surface distance.

As the camera rotates about the lens center, new parts of the scene enter the image at the left edge[2] and some previously imaged parts are discarded at the right edge. The entire scene can be imaged and ranged by completely rotating the camera once.

RANGE ESTIMATION ALGORITHM

Let the image plane have N x N pixels and let the range map be a large array of size **N x sN**, where **s >= 1** is a number that depends on how wide a scene is to be imaged. The kth image frame is represented by I_k and the cumulative, environment centered range map with origin at the camera center is represented by R. Every element in the range array is a structure that contains the

---

[2]Or the right edge, depending upon the direction of the rotation

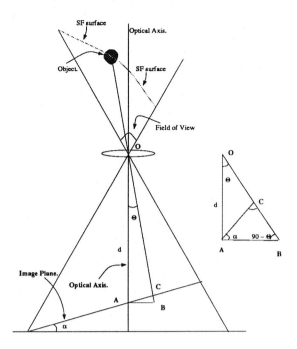

(a) Tilted Image Surface

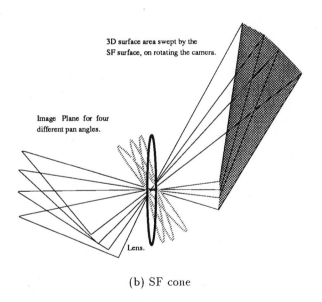

(b) SF cone

Figure 2: (a) A point object, initially at an angle of θ, is imaged at point C. The focus distance OC varies as a function of θ. When the camera undergoes a pan motion, θ changes and so does the focus distance. The SF surface is not parallel to the lens and the optical axis is not perpendicular to the SF surface. (b) The 3D volume swept by the proposed SF surface as the non-frontal imaging camera is rotated. For the same rotation, a frontal imaging camera would sweep out an SF cone having a smaller depth.

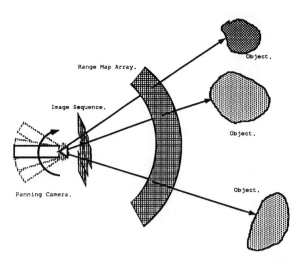

Figure 3: Panning camera, environment fixed range array, and the images obtained at successive pan angles. Each range array element is associated with multiple criterion function values which are computed from different overlapping views. The maximum of the values in any radial direction is the one finally selected for the corresponding range array element, to compute the depth value in that direction.

focus criterion values for different image indices, i.e., for different pan angles. When the stored criterion value shows a maximum, then the index corresponding to the maximum[3] can be used to determine the range for that scene point.

Let the camera start from one side of the scene and pan to the other side. Figure 3 illustrates the geometrical relationships between successive pan angles, pixels of the images obtained, and the range array elements.

Algorithm

Let $j = 0$. $\phi = 0$. Initialize all the arrays and then execute the following steps.

- Capture the jth image I_j.
- Pass the image through a focus criterion filter to yield an array C_j of criterion values.
- For the angle ϕ (which is the angle that the camera has turned from its starting position), calculate the offset into the range map required to align image I_j with the previous images. For example, Pixel $I_j[50][75]$ might correspond to the same object as pixels $I_{j+1}[50][125]$ and $I_{j+2}[50][175]$.

---

[3] Knowing the index value, we can find out the amount of camera rotation that was needed before the scene point was sharply focused. Using the row and column indices for the range point, and the image index, we can then find out the exact distance from the lens to the image plane (v). We can then use the lens law to calculate the range.

- Check to see if the criterion function for any scene point has crossed the maximum. If so, compute the range for that scene point using the pan angle (and hence v value) for the image with maximum criterion value.
- Rotate the camera by a small amount. Update ϕ and j.
- Repeat the above steps until the entire scene is imaged.

The paper [Krishnan and Ahuja, 1993] contains a pictorial representation of the above algorithm.

EXPERIMENTAL RESULTS

In the experiment we attempt to determine the range of scene points. The scene in experiment 1 consists of, from left to right, a planar surface (range = 73 in), part of the background curtain (range = 132 in), a planar surface (range = 54in) and a planar surface (range = 38 in).

The camera is turned in small steps of 50 units (of the stepper motor), that corresponds to a shift of 15 pixels (in pixel columns) between images. A scene point will thus be present in a maximum of thirty four[4] images. In each image, for the same scene point, the effective distance from the image plane to lens is different. There is a 1-to-1 relationship between the image column number and the distance from lens to image, and therefore, by the lens law, a 1-to-1 relationship between the image column number and the range of the scene point. The column number at which a scene point is imaged with greatest sharpness, is therefore also a measure of the range.

Results Among the focus criterion functions that were tried, the Tennegrad function [Tenebaum, 1971] seemed to have the best performance/speed characteristics. In addition to problems like depth of field, lack of detail, selection of window size etc., that are present in most range-from-focus algorithms, the range map has two problems as described below.

- Consider a scene point, A, that is imaged on pixels, $I_1[230][470]$, $I_2[230][455]$, $I_3[230][440]$ ... Consider also a neighboring scene point B, that is imaged on pixels $I_1[230][471]$, $I_2[230][456]$, $I_3[230][441]$ ... The focus criterion values for point A will peak at a column number that is $470 - n \times 15$ (where $0 \leq n$). If point B is also at the same range as A, then the focus criterion values for point B will peak at a column number that is $471 - n \times 15$, for the same n as that for point A. The peak column number for point A will therefore be 1 less than that of point B. If we have a patch of points that are all at the

same distance from the camera, then the peak column numbers obtained will be numbers that change by 1 for neighboring points[5]. The resulting range map therefore shows a local ramping behavior.

- As we mentioned before, a scene point is imaged about 34 times, at different levels of sharpness (or blur). It is very likely that the least blurred image would have been obtained for some camera parameter that corresponds to a value between two input frames.

To reduce these problems, we fit a gaussian to the three focus criterion values around the peak to determine the location of the real maximum. For brevity, we have not included some sample images from the experiments. Figure 4 shows two views of the range disparity values for experiment 1. Parts of the scene where we cannot determine the range disparity values due to a lack of sufficient texture are shown blank. The paper [Krishnan and Ahuja, 1993] contains more experimental results.

SUMMARY AND CONCLUSIONS

In this paper we have shown that using a camera whose image plane is not perpendicular to the optical axis, allows us to determine estimates of range values of object points. We showed that the SF surface, which appears in sharp focus when imaged by our non-frontal imaging camera, is approximately an inclined plane. When the camera's pan angle direction changes, by turning about the lens center, an SF volume is swept out by the SF surface. The points within this volume comprise those for which range can be estimated correctly. We have described an algorithm that determines the range of scene points that lie within the SF volume. We point out some of the shortcomings that are unique to our method. We have also described the results of an experiment that was conducted to prove the feasibility of our method.

References

Abbott, A. Lynn and Ahuja, Narendra 1990. Active surface reconstruction by integrating focus, vergence, stereo, and camera calibration. In *Proc. Third Intl. Conf. Computer Vision*. 489–492.

Darrell, T. and Wohn, K. 1988. Pyramid based depth from focus. In *Proc. IEEE Conf. Computer Vision and Pattern Recognition*. 504–509.

Das, Subhodev and Ahuja, Narendra 1990. Multiresolution image acquisition and surface reconstruction. In *Proc. Third Intl. Conf. Computer Vision*. 485–488.

---

[4]Roughly $\frac{512}{15}$

[5]Neighbours along vertical columns will not have this problem

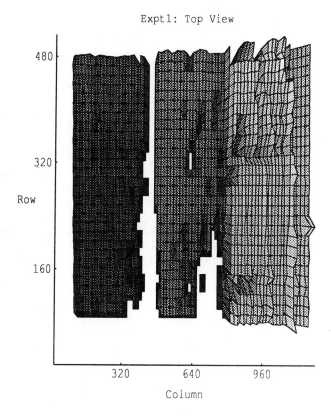

Exptl: Top View

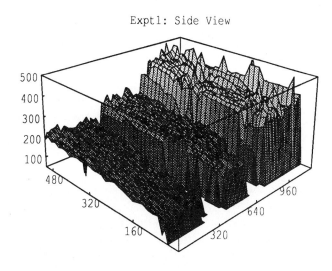

Exptl: Side View

Figure 4: Range disparities for experiment 1. Parts of the scene for which range values could not be calculated are shown blank. The further away a surface is from the camera, the smaller is its height in the range disparity map.

Das, Subhodev and Ahuja, Narendra 1992a. Active surface estimation: Integrating coarse-to-fine image acquisition and estimation from multiple cues. Technical Report CV-92-5-2, Beckman Institute, University of Illinois.

Das, Subhodev and Ahuja, Narendra 1992b. Performance analysis of stereo, vergence, and focus as depth cues for active vision. Technical Report CV-92-6-1, Beckman Institute, University of Illinois.

Ens, John and Lawrence, Peter 1991. A matrix based method for determining depth from focus. In *Proc. IEEE Conf. Computer Vision and Pattern Recognition*. 600–606.

Horn, Berthold Klaus Paul 1968. Focusing. Technical Report 160, MIT Artificial Intelligence Lab, Cambridge, Mass.

Jarvis, R. A. 1976. Focus optimisation criteria for computer image processing. *Microscope* 24:163–180.

Krishnan, Arun and Ahuja, Narendra 1993. Range estimation from focus using a non-frontal imaging camera. In *Proc. DARPA Image Understanding Workshop*.

Krotkov, E. P.; Summers, J.; and Fuma, F. 1986. Computing range with an active camera system. In *Eighth International Conference on Pattern Recognition*. 1156–1158.

Krotkov, E. P. 1986. Focusing. Technical Report MS-CIS-86-22, GRASP Laboratory, University of Pennsylvania.

Krotkov, Eric P. 1989. *Active Computer Vision by Cooperative Focus and Stereo*. New York: Springer-Verlag.

Ligthart, G. and Groen, F. C. A. 1982. A comparison of different autofocus algorithms. In *Proc. Sixth Intl. Conf. Pattern Recognition*. 597–600.

Nayar, Shree K. and Nakagawa, Yasuo 1990. Shape from focus: An effective approach for rough surfaces. In *Proc. IEEE Intl. Conf. Robotics and Automation*. 218–225.

Pentland, Alex Paul 1987. A new sense for depth of field. *IEEE Trans. Pattern Anal. and Machine Intell.* PAMI-9:523–531.

Schlag, J. F.; Sanderson, A. C.; Neuman, C. P.; and Wimberly, F. C. 1985. Implementation of automatic focusing algorithms for a computer vision system with camera control. Technical Report CMU-RI-TR-83-14, Carnegie-Mellon University.

Sperling, G. 1970. Binocular vision: A physical and a neural theory. *Amer. J. Psychology* 83:461–534.

Tenebaum, Jay Martin 1971. *Accomodation in Computer Vision*. Ph.D. Dissertation, Stanford University, Palo Alto, Calif.

Learning Object Models from Appearance *

Hiroshi Murase
NTT Basic Research Labs
3-9-11 Midori-cho, Musashino-shi
Tokyo 180, Japan
murase@siva.ntt.jp

Shree K. Nayar
Department of Computer Science
Columbia University
New York, N.Y. 10027
nayar@cs.columbia.edu

Abstract

We address the problem of automatically learning object models for recognition and pose estimation. In contrast to the traditional approach, we formulate the recognition problem as one of matching visual appearance rather than shape. The appearance of an object in a two-dimensional image depends on its shape, reflectance properties, pose in the scene, and the illumination conditions. While shape and reflectance are intrinsic properties of an object and are constant, pose and illumination vary from scene to scene. We present a new compact representation of object appearance that is parametrized by pose and illumination. For each object of interest, a large set of images is obtained by automatically varying pose and illumination. This large image set is compressed to obtain a low-dimensional subspace, called the eigenspace, in which the object is represented as a hypersurface. Given an unknown input image, the recognition system projects the image onto the eigenspace. The object is recognized based on the hypersurface it lies on. The exact position of the projection on the hypersurface determines the object's pose in the image. We have conducted experiments using several objects with complex appearance characteristics. These results suggest the proposed appearance representation to be a valuable tool for a variety of machine vision applications.

Introduction

One of the primary goals of an intelligent vision system is to recognize objects in an image and compute their pose in the three-dimensional scene. Such a recognition system has wide applications ranging from autonomous navigation to visual inspection. For a vision system to be able to recognize objects, it must have models

*This research was conducted at the Center for Research in Intelligent Systems, Department of Computer Science, Columbia University. This research was supported in part by the David and Lucile Packard Fellowship and in part by ARPA Contract No. DACA 76-92-C-0007.

of the objects stored in its memory. In the past, vision research has emphasized on the use of geometric (shape) models [1] for recognition. In the case of manufactured objects, these models are sometimes available and are referred to as computer aided design (CAD) models. Most objects of interest, however, do not come with CAD models. Typically, a vision programmer is forced to select an appropriate representation for object geometry, develop object models using this representation, and then manually input this information into the system. This procedure is cumbersome and impractical when dealing with large sets of objects, or objects with complicated geometric properties. It is clear that recognition systems of the future must be capable of acquiring object models without human assistance. In other words, recognition systems must be able to automatically *learn* the objects of interest.

Visual learning is clearly a well-developed and vital component of biological vision systems. If a human is handed an object and asked to visually memorize it, he or she would rotate the object and study its appearance from different directions. While little is known about the exact representations and techniques used by the human mind to learn objects, it is clear that the overall appearance of the object plays a critical role in its perception. In contrast to biological systems, machine vision systems today have little or no learning capabilities. Hence, visual learning is now emerging as an topic of research interest [6]. The goal of this paper is to advance this important but relatively unexplored area of machine vision.

Here, we present a technique for automatically learning object models from images. The appearance of an object is the combined effect of its shape, reflectance properties, pose in the scene, and the illumination conditions. Recognizing objects from brightness images is therefore more a problem of *appearance matching* rather than shape matching. This observation lies at the core of our work. While shape and reflectance are *intrinsic properties* of the object that do not vary, pose and illumination vary from scene to scene. We approach the visual learning problem as one of acquiring a compact model of the object's appearance under different illumination directions and object poses. The object is "shown" to the image sensor in several orientations and illumination directions. This can be accomplished using, for example, two robot manipulators; one to rotate the object while the other varies the illumination direction. The result is a very large set of object images. Since all images in the set are of the same object, any two consecutive images are correlated to large degree. The problem then is to compress this large image set into a low-dimensional representation of object appearance.

A well-known *image compression* or coding technique is based on principal component analysis. Also known as the Karhunen-Loeve transform [5] [2], this method computes the eigenvectors of an image set. The eigenvectors form an orthogonal basis for the representation of individual images in the image set. Though a large number of eigenvectors may be required for very accurate reconstruction of an object image, only a few eigenvectors are generally sufficient to capture the significant appearance characteristics of an object. These eigenvectors constitute the dimensions of what we refer to as the *eigenspace* for the image set. From the perspective of machine vision, the eigenspace has a very attractive property. When it is composed of all the eigenvectors of an image set, it is optimal in a *correlation* sense: If any two images from the set are projected onto the eigenspace, the distance between the corresponding points in eigenspace is a measure of the similarity of the images in the l^2 *norm*. In machine vision, the Karhunen-Loeve method has been applied primarily to two problems; handwritten character recognition [3] and human face recognition [8], [9]. These applications lie within the domain of pattern classification and do not use complete parametrized models of the objects of interest.

In this paper, we develop a continuous and compact representation of object appearance that is parametrized by the variables, namely, object pose and illumination. This new representation is referred to as the *parametric eigenspace*. First, an image set of the object is obtained by varying pose and illumination in small increments. The image set is then normalized in brightness and scale to achieve invariance to image magnification and the intensity of illumination. The eigenspace for the image set is obtained by computing the most prominent eigenvectors of the image set. Next, all images in the object's image set (the learning samples) are projected onto the eigenspace to obtain a set of points. These points lie on a *hypersurface* that is parametrized by object pose and illumination. The hypersurface is computed from the discrete points using the cubic spline interpolation technique. It is important to note that this parametric representation of an object is obtained *without* prior knowledge of the object's shape and reflectance properties. It is generated using just a sample of the object.

Each object is represented as a parametric hyper-surface in two different eigenspaces; the universal eigenspace and the object's own eigenspace. The *universal eigenspace* is computed by using the image sets of all objects of interest to the recognition system, and the *object eigenspace* is computed using only images of the object. We show that the universal eigenspace is best suited for discriminating between objects, whereas the object eigenspace is better for pose estimation. Object recognition and pose estimation can be summarized as follows. Given an image consisting of an object of interest, we assume that the object is not occluded by other objects and can be segmented from the remaining scene. The segmented image region is normalized in scale and brightness, such that it has the same size and brightness range as the images used in the learning stage. This normalized image is first projected onto the universal eigenspace to identify the object. After the object is recognized, the image is projected onto the object eigenspace and the location of the projection on the object's parametrized hypersurface determines its pose in the scene.

The learning of an object requires the acquisition of a large image set and the computationally intensive process of finding eigenvectors. However, the learning stage is done off-line and hence can afford to be relatively slow. In contrast, recognition and pose estimation are often subject to strong time constraints, and our approach offers a very simple and computationally efficient solution. We have conducted extensive experimentation to demonstrate the power of the parametric eigenspace representation. The fundamental contributions of this paper can be summarized as follows. (a) The parametric eigenspace is presented as a new representation of object appearance. (b) Using this representation, object models are automatically learned from appearance by varying pose and illumination. (c) Both learning and recognition are accomplished without prior knowledge of the object's shape and reflectance.

Visual Learning of Objects

In this section, we discuss the learning of object models using the parametric eigenspace representation. First, we discuss the acquisition of object image sets. The eigenspaces are computed using the image sets and each object is represented as a parametric hypersurface. Throughout this section, we will use a sample object to describe the learning process. In the next section, we discuss the recognition and pose estimation of objects using the parametric eigenspace representation.

Normalized Image Sets

While constructing image sets we need to ensure that all images of the object are of the same size. Each digitized image is first segmented (using a threshold) into an object region and a background region. The background is assigned a zero brightness value and the object region is re-sampled such that the larger of its two dimensions fits the image size we have selected for the image set representation. We now have a scale normalized image. This image is written as a vector $\hat{\mathbf{x}}$ by reading pixel brightness values from the image in a raster scan manner:

$$\hat{\mathbf{x}} = [\hat{x}_1, \hat{x}_2, \ldots, \hat{x}_N]^T \qquad (1)$$

The appearance of an object depends on its shape and reflectance properties. These are intrinsic properties of the object that do not vary. The appearance of the object also depends on the pose of the object and the illumination conditions. Unlike the intrinsic properties, object pose and illumination are expected to vary from scene to scene. If the illumination conditions of the environment are constant, the appearance of the object is affected only by its pose. Here, we assume that the object is illuminated by the ambient lighting of the environment as well as one additional distant light source whose direction may vary. Hence, all possible appearances of the object can be captured by varying object pose and the light source direction with respect to the viewing direction of the sensor. We will denote each image as $\hat{\mathbf{x}}_{r,l}^{(p)}$ where r is the rotation or pose parameter, l represents the illumination direction, and p is the object number. The complete image set obtained for an object is referred to as the **object image set** and can be expressed as:

$$\left\{ \hat{\mathbf{x}}_{1,1}^{(p)}, \ldots, \hat{\mathbf{x}}_{R,1}^{(p)}, \hat{\mathbf{x}}_{1,2}^{(p)}, \ldots, \hat{\mathbf{x}}_{R,L}^{(p)} \right\} \qquad (2)$$

Here, R and L are the total number of discrete poses and illumination directions, respectively, used to obtain the image set. If a total of P objects are to be learned by the recognition system, we can define the **universal image set** as the union of all the object image sets:

$$\left\{ \hat{\mathbf{x}}_{1,1}^{(1)}, \ldots, \hat{\mathbf{x}}_{R,1}^{(1)}, \hat{\mathbf{x}}_{1,2}^{(1)}, \ldots, \hat{\mathbf{x}}_{R,L}^{(1)}, \right. \qquad (3)$$
$$\hat{\mathbf{x}}_{1,1}^{(2)}, \ldots, \hat{\mathbf{x}}_{R,1}^{(2)}, \hat{\mathbf{x}}_{1,2}^{(2)}, \ldots, \hat{\mathbf{x}}_{R,L}^{(2)},$$
$$\cdot$$
$$\cdot$$
$$\left. \hat{\mathbf{x}}_{1,1}^{(P)}, \ldots, \hat{\mathbf{x}}_{R,1}^{(P)}, \hat{\mathbf{x}}_{1,2}^{(P)}, \ldots, \hat{\mathbf{x}}_{R,L}^{(P)} \right\}$$

We assume that the imaging sensor used for learning and recognizing objects has a linear response, i.e. image brightness is proportional to scene radiance. We would like our recognition system to be unaffected by variations in the intensity of illumination or the aperture of the imaging system. This can be achieved by normalizing each of the images in the object and universal sets, such that, the total energy contained in the image is unity, i.e. $\| \mathbf{x} \| = 1$. This brightness normalization transforms each measured image $\hat{\mathbf{x}}$ to a normalized image $\mathbf{x}$:

$$\mathbf{x} = [x_1, x_2, \ldots, x_N]^T \qquad (4)$$

where:

$$x_n = \frac{1}{\sigma} (\hat{x}_n), \quad \sigma = \sqrt{\sum_{n=1}^{N} (\hat{x}_n)^2} \qquad (5)$$

The above described normalizations with respect to scale and brightness give us normalized object image sets and a normalized universal image set. In the following discussion, we will simply refer to these as the object and universal image sets.

The images sets can be obtained in several ways. If the geometrical model and reflectance properties of an object are known, its images for different pose and illumination directions can be synthesized using well-known rendering algorithms. In this paper, we do not assume that object geometry and reflectance are given. Instead, we assume that we have a sample of each object that can be used for learning. One approach then is to use two robot manipulators; one grasps the object and shows it to the sensor in different poses while the other has a light source mounted on it and is used to vary the illumination direction. In our experiments, we have used a turntable to rotate the object in a single plane (see Fig. 1). This gives us pose variations about a single axis. A robot manipulator is used to vary the illumination direction. If the recognition system is to be used in an environment where the illumination (due to one or several sources) is not expected to change, the image set can be obtained by varying just object pose.

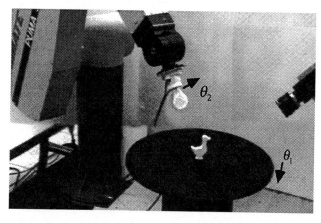

Figure 1: Setup used for automatic acquisition of object image sets. The object is placed on a motorized turntable.

Computing Eigenspaces

Consecutive images in an object image set tend to be correlated to a large degree since pose and illumination variations between consecutive images are small. Our first step is to take advantage of this correlation and compress large image sets into low-dimensional representations that capture the gross appearance characteristics of objects. A suitable compression technique is the Karhunen-Loeve expansion [2] where the eigenvectors of the image set are computed and used as orthogonal basis functions for representing individual images. Though, in general, all the eigenvectors of an image set are required for the perfect reconstruction of an object image, only a few are sufficient for the representation of objects for recognition purposes. We compute two types of eigenspaces; the universal eigenspace that is obtained from the universal image set, and object eigenspaces computed from individual object image sets.

To compute the universal eigenspace, we first subtract the average of all images in the universal set from each image. This ensures that the eigenvector with the largest eigenvalue represents the dimension in eigenspace in which the variance of images is maximum in the correlation sense. In other words, it is the most important dimension of the eigenspace. The average $\mathbf{c}$ of all images in the universal image set is determined as:

$$\mathbf{c} = \frac{1}{RLP} \sum_{p=1}^{P} \sum_{r=1}^{R} \sum_{l=1}^{L} \mathbf{x}_{r,l}{}^{(p)} \qquad (6)$$

A new image set is obtained by subtracting the average image $\mathbf{c}$ from each image in the universal set:

$$\mathbf{X} \stackrel{\triangle}{=} \left\{ \mathbf{x}_{1,1}{}^{(1)} - \mathbf{c}, \; ...., \; \mathbf{x}_{R,1}{}^{(1)} - \mathbf{c}, \; ...., \; \mathbf{x}_{R,L}{}^{(P)} - \mathbf{c} \right\} \tag{7}$$

The image matrix $\mathbf{X}$ is $N \times M$, where $M = RLP$ is the total number of images in the universal set, and N is the number of pixels in each image. To compute eigenvectors of the image set we define the *covariance matrix* as:

$$\mathbf{Q} \stackrel{\triangle}{=} \mathbf{X} \mathbf{X}^{\mathrm{T}} \qquad (8)$$

The covariance matrix is $N \times N$, clearly a very large matrix since a large number of pixels constitute an image. The eigenvectors $\mathbf{e}_i$ and the corresponding eigenvalues λ_i of $\mathbf{Q}$ are to be determined by solving the well-known eigenvector decomposition problem:

$$\lambda_i \, \mathbf{e}_i = \mathbf{Q} \, \mathbf{e}_i \qquad (9)$$

All N eigenvectors of the universal set together constitute a complete eigenspace. Any two images from the universal image set, when projected onto the eigenspace, give two discrete points. The distance between these points is a measure of the difference between the two images in the correlation sense. Since the universal eigenspace is computed using images of all objects, it is the ideal space for discriminating between images of different objects.

Determining the eigenvalues and eigenvectors of a large matrix such as $\mathbf{Q}$ is a non-trivial problem. It is computationally very intensive and traditional techniques used for computing eigenvectors of small matrices are impractical. Since we are interested only in a small number (k) of eigenvectors, and not the complete set of N eigenvectors, efficient algorithms can be used. In our implementation, we have used the *spatial temporal adaptive* (STA) algorithm proposed by Murase and Lindenbaum [4]. This algorithm was recently demonstrated to be substantially more efficient than previous algorithms. Using the STA algorithm the k most

prominent eigenvectors of the universal image set are computed. The result is a set of eigenvalues $\{ \lambda_i \mid i = 1, 2, ..., k \}$ where $\{ \lambda_1 \geq \lambda_2 \geq \; ..... \; \geq \lambda_k \}$, and a corresponding set of eigenvector $\{ \mathbf{e}_i \mid i = 1, 2, ..., k \}$. Note that each eigenvector is of size N, i.e. the size of an image. These k eigenvectors constitute the universal eigenspace; it is an approximation to the complete eigenspace with N dimensions. We have found from our experiments that less than ten dimensions of the eigenspace are generally sufficient for the purposes of visual learning and recognition (i.e. $k \leq 10$). Later, we describe how objects in an unknown input image are recognized using the universal eigenspace.

Once an object has been recognized, we are interested in finding its pose in the image. The accuracy of pose estimation depends on the ability of the recognition system to discriminate between different images of the same object. Hence, pose estimation is best done in an eigenspace that is tuned to the appearance of a single object. To this end, we compute an object eigenspace from each of the object image sets. The procedure for computing an object eigenspace is similar to that used for the universal eigenspace. In this case, the average $\mathbf{c}^{(p)}$ of all images of object p is computed and subtracted from each of the object images. The resulting images are used to compute the covariance matrix $\mathbf{Q}^{(p)}$. The eigenspace for the object p is obtained by solving the system:

$$\lambda_i{}^{(p)} \, \mathbf{e}_i{}^{(p)} = \mathbf{Q}^{(p)} \, \mathbf{e}_i{}^{(p)} \qquad (10)$$

Once again, we compute only a small number ($k \leq 10$) of the largest eigenvalues $\{ \lambda_i{}^{(p)} \mid i = 1, 2, ..., k \}$ where $\{ \lambda_1{}^{(p)} \geq \lambda_2{}^{(p)} \geq \; ..... \; \geq \lambda_k{}^{(p)} \}$, and a corresponding set of eigenvector $\{ \mathbf{e}_i{}^{(p)} \mid i = 1, 2, ..., k \}$. An object eigenspace is computed for each object of interest to the recognition system.

Parametric Eigenspace Representation

We now represent each object as a hypersurface in the universal eigenspace as well as its own eigenspace. This new representation of appearance lies at the core of our approach to visual learning and recognition. Each appearance hypersurface is parametrized by two parameters; object rotation and illumination direction.

A parametric hypersurface for the object p is constructed in the universal eigenspace as follows. Each image $\mathbf{x}_{r,l}{}^{(p)}$ (learning sample) in the object image set is projected onto the eigenspace by first subtracting the average image $\mathbf{c}$ from it and finding the dot product of the result with each of the eigenvectors (dimensions) of the universal eigenspace. The result is a point $\mathbf{g}_{r,l}{}^{(p)}$ in the eigenspace:

$$\mathbf{g}_{r,l}{}^{(p)} = [\mathbf{e}_1, \mathbf{e}_2, ..., \mathbf{e}_k]^{\mathrm{T}} (\mathbf{x}_{r,l}{}^{(p)} - \mathbf{c}) \qquad (11)$$

Once again the subscript r represents the rotation parameter and l is the illumination direction. By projecting all the learning samples in this manner, we obtain a set of discrete points in the universal eigenspace.

Since consecutive object images are strongly correlated, their projections in eigenspace are close to one another. Hence, the discrete points obtained by projecting all the learning samples can be assumed to lie on a k-dimensional hypersurface that represents all possible poses of the object under all possible illumination directions. We interpolate the discrete points to obtain this hypersurface. In our implementation, we have used a standard cubic spline interpolation algorithm [7]. Since cubic splines are well-known we will not describe them here. The resulting hypersurface can be expressed as:

$$\mathbf{g}^{(p)}(\theta_1, \theta_2) \qquad (12)$$

where θ_1 and θ_2 are the *continuous* rotation and illumination parameters. The above hypersurface is a compact representation of the object's appearance.

In a similar manner, a hypersurface is also constructed in the object's eigenspace by projecting the learning samples onto this space:

$$\mathbf{f}_{r,l}^{(p)} = \left[\mathbf{e}_1^{(p)}, \mathbf{e}_2^{(p)}, \ldots, \mathbf{e}_k^{(p)} \right]^{\mathrm{T}} \left(\mathbf{x}_{r,l}^{(p)} - \mathbf{c}^{(p)} \right) \qquad (13)$$

where, $\mathbf{c}^{(p)}$ is the average of all images in the object image set. Using cubic splines, the discrete points $\mathbf{f}_{r,l}^{(p)}$ are interpolated to obtain the hypersurface:

$$\mathbf{f}^{(p)}(\theta_1, \theta_2) \qquad (14)$$

Once again, θ_1 and θ_2 are the rotation and illumination parameters, respectively. This continuous parameterization enables us to find poses of the object that are not included in the learning samples. It also enables us to compute accurate pose estimates under illumination directions that lie in between the discrete illumination directions used in the learning stage. Fig.2 shows the parametrized eigenspace representation of the object shown in Fig.1. The figure shows only three of the most significant dimensions of the eigenspace since it is difficult to display and visualize higher dimensional spaces. The object representation in this case is a curve, rather than a surface, since the object image set was obtained using a single illumination direction while the object was rotated (in increments of 4 degrees) about a single axis. The discrete points on the curve correspond to projections of the learning samples in the object image set. The continuous curve passing through the points is parametrized by the rotation parameter θ_1 and is obtained using the cubic spline algorithm.

Recognition and Pose Estimation

Consider an image of a scene that includes one or more of the objects we have learned using the parametric eigenspace representation. We assume that the objects are not occluded by other objects in the scene when viewed from the sensor direction, and that the image regions corresponding to objects have been segmented away from the scene image. First, each segmented image region is normalized with respect to scale and brightness as described in the previous section. This

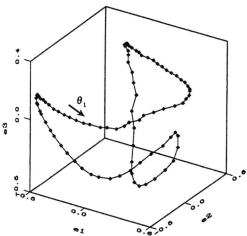

Figure 2: Parametric eigenspace representation of the object shown in Fig.1. Only the three most prominent dimensions of the eigenspace are displayed here. The points shown correspond to projections of the learning samples. Here, illumination is constant and therefore we obtain a curve with a single parameter (rotation) rather than a surface.

ensures that (a) the input image has the same dimensions as the eigenvectors (dimensions) of the parametric eigenspace, (b) the recognition system is invariant to object magnification, and (c) the recognition system is invariant to fluctuations in the intensity of illumination.

As stated earlier in the paper, the universal eigenspace is best tuned to discriminate between different objects. Hence, we first project the normalized input image $\mathbf{y}$ to the universal eigenspace. First, the average $\mathbf{c}$ of the universal image set is subtracted from $\mathbf{y}$ and the dot product of the resulting vector is computed with each of the eigenvectors that constitute the universal space. The k coefficients obtained are the coordinates of a point $\mathbf{z}$ in the eigenspace:

$$\mathbf{z} = \left[\mathbf{e}_1, \mathbf{e}_2, \ldots, \mathbf{e}_k \right]^{\mathrm{T}} (\mathbf{y} - \mathbf{c}) = \left[z_1, z_2, \ldots, z_k \right]^{\mathrm{T}} \qquad (15)$$

The recognition problem then is to find the object p whose hypersurface the point $\mathbf{z}$ lies on. Due to factors such as image noise, aberrations in the imaging system, and digitization effects, $\mathbf{z}$ may not lie exactly on an object hypersurface. Hence, we find the object p that gives the minimum distance $d_1^{(p)}$ between its hypersurface $\mathbf{g}^{(p)}(\theta_1, \theta_2)$ and the point $\mathbf{z}$:

$$d_1^{(p)} = \min_{\theta_1, \theta_2} \| \mathbf{z} - \mathbf{g}^{(p)}(\theta_1, \theta_2) \| \qquad (16)$$

If $d_1^{(p)}$ is within some pre-determined threshold value, we conclude that the input image is of the object p. If not, we conclude that input image is not of any of the objects used in the learning stage. It is important to note that the hypersurface representation of objects in eigenspace results in more reliable recognition than if the object is represented as just a cluster of the points $\mathbf{g}_{r,l}{}^{(p)}$. The hypersurfaces of different objects can intersect each other or even be intertwined, in which cases, using nearest cluster algorithms could easily lead to incorrect recognition results.

Once the object in the input image is recognized, we project the input image $\mathbf{y}$ to the eigenspace of the object. This eigenspace is tuned to variations in the appearance of a single object and hence is ideal for pose estimation. Mapping the input image to the object eigenspace gives the k-dimensional point:

$$\mathbf{z}^{(p)} = \left[\mathbf{e}_1{}^{(p)}, \mathbf{e}_2{}^{(p)}, \ldots, \mathbf{e}_k{}^{(p)}\right]^{\mathrm{T}} \left(\mathbf{y} - \mathbf{c}^{(p)}\right) \quad (17)$$

$$= \left[z_1{}^{(p)}, z_2{}^{(p)}, \ldots, z_k{}^{(p)}\right]^{\mathrm{T}} \quad (18)$$

The pose estimation problem may be stated as follows: Find the rotation parameter θ_1 and the illumination parameter θ_2 that minimize the distance $d_2{}^{(p)}$ between the point $\mathbf{z}^{(p)}$ and the hypersurface $\mathbf{f}^{(p)}$ of the object p:

$$d_2{}^{(p)} = \min_{\theta_1, \theta_2} \| \mathbf{z} - \mathbf{f}^{(p)}(\theta_1, \theta_2) \| \quad (19)$$

The θ_1 value obtained represents the pose of the object in the input image. Fig. 3(a) shows an input image of the object whose parametric eigenspace was shown in Fig. 2. This input image is not one of the images in the learning set used to compute the object eigenspace. In Fig. 3b, the input image is mapped to the object eigenspace and is seen to lie on the parametric curve of the object. The location of the point on the curve determines the object's pose in the image. Note that the recognition and pose estimation stages are computationally very efficient, each requiring only the projection of an input image onto a low-dimensional (generally less than 10) eigenspace. Customized hardware can therefore be used to achieve real-time (frame-rate) recognition and pose estimation.

Experimentation

We have conducted several experiments using complex objects to verify the effectiveness of the parametric eigenspace representation. This section summarizes some of our results. Fig. 1 in the introduction shows the set-up used to conduct the experiments reported here. The object is placed on a motorized turntable and its pose is varied about a single axis, namely, the axis of rotation of the turntable. The turntable position is controlled through software and can be varied with an accuracy of about 0.1 degrees. Most objects have a finite number of stable configurations when placed on a planar surface. For such objects, the turntable is adequate as it can be used to vary pose for each of the object's stable configurations.

We assume that the object is illuminated by the ambient lighting conditions of the environment that are not expected to change between the learning and recognition stages. This ambient illumination is of relatively low intensity. The main source of brightness is an additional light source whose direction can vary. In most of

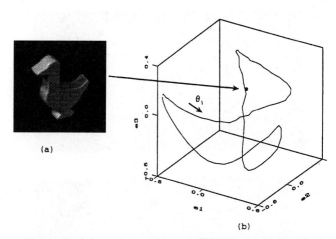

(a)

(b)

Figure 3: (a) An input image. (b) The input image is mapped to a point in the object eigenspace. The location of the point on the parametric curve determines the pose of the object in the input image.

our experiments, the source direction was varied manually. We are currently using a 6 degree-of-freedom robot manipulator (see Fig. 1) with a light source mounted on its end-effector. This enables us to vary the illumination direction via software. Images of the object are sensed using a 512×480 pixel CCD camera and are digitized using an Analogics frame-grabber board.

Table 1 summarizes the number of objects, light source directions, and poses used to acquire the image sets used in the experiments. For the learning stage, a total of 4 objects were used. These objects (cars) are shown in Fig. 4(a). For each object we have used 5 different light source directions, and 90 poses for each source direction. This gives us a total of 1800 images in the universal image set and 450 images in each object image set. Each of these images is automatically normalized in scale and brightness as described in the previous section. Each normalized image is 128×128 pixels in size. The universal and object image sets were used to compute the universal and object eigenspaces. The parametric eigenspace representations of the four objects in their own eigenspaces are shown in Fig. 4(b).

Table 1: Image sets obtained for the learning and recognition stages. The 1080 test images used for recognition are different from the 1800 images used for learning.

Learning samples	Test samples for recognition
4 objects	4 objects
5 light source directions	3 light source directions
90 poses	90 poses
1800 images	1080 images

A large number of images were also obtained to test the recognition and pose estimation algorithms. All

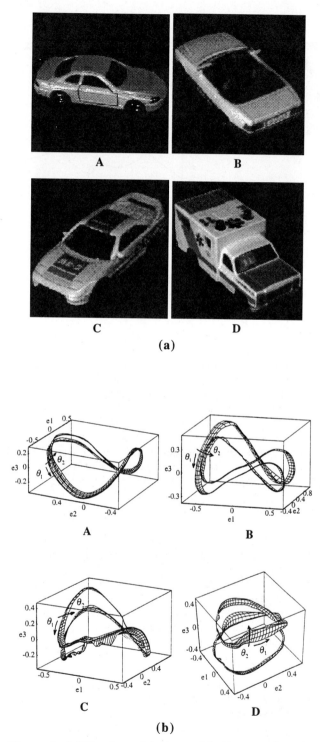

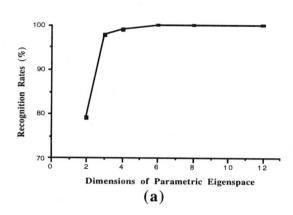

(a)

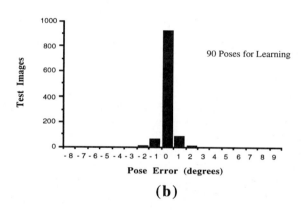

(b)

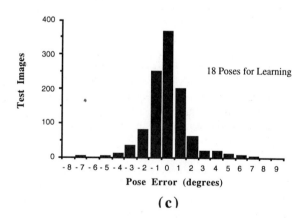

(c)

Figure 4: (a)The four objects used in the experiments. (b) The parametric hypersurfaces in object eigenspace computed for the four objects shown in (a). For display, only the three most important dimensions of each eigenspace are shown. The hypersurfaces are reduced to surfaces in three-dimensional space.

Figure 5: (a) Recognition rate plotted as a function of the number of universal eigenspace dimensions used to represent the parametric hypersurfaces. (b) Histogram of the error (in degrees) in computed object pose for the case where 90 poses are used in the learning stage. (c) Pose error histogram for the case where 18 poses are used in the learning stage. The average of the absolute error in pose for the complete set of 1080 test images is 0.5 in the first case and 1.2 in the second case.

of these images are different from the ones used in the learning stage. A total of 1080 input (test) images were obtained. The illumination directions and object poses used to obtain the test images are different from the ones used to obtain the object image sets for learning. In fact, the test images correspond to poses and illumination directions that lie in between the ones used for learning. Each input image is first normalized in scale and brightness and then projected onto the universal eigenspace. The object in the image is identified by finding the hypersurface that is closest to the input point in the universal eigenspace. Unlike the learning process, recognition is computationally simple and can be accomplished on a Sun SPARC 2 workstation in less than 0.2 second.

To evaluate the recognition results, we define the *recognition rate* as the percentage of input images for which the object in the image is correctly recognized. Fig. 5(a) illustrates the sensitivity of the recognition rate to the number of dimensions of the universal eigenspace. Clearly, the discriminating power of the universal eigenspace is expected to increase with the number of dimensions. For the objects used, the recognition rate is poor if less than 4 dimensions are used but approaches unity as the number of dimensions approaches 10. In general, however, the number of dimensions needed for robust recognition is expected to increase with the number of objects learned by the system. It also depends on the appearance characteristics of the objects used. From our experience, 10 dimensions are sufficient for representing objects with fairly complex appearance characteristics such as the ones shown in Fig. 4.

Finally, we present experimental results related to pose estimation. Once the object is recognized, the input image is projected onto the object's eigenspace and its pose is computed by finding the closest point on the parametric hypersurface. Once again we use all 1080 input images of the 4 objects. Since these images were obtained using the controlled turntable, the actual object pose in each image is known. Fig. 5(b) and (c) shows histograms of the errors (in degrees) in the poses computed for the 1080 images. The error histogram in Fig. 5(b) is for the case where 450 learning samples (90 poses and 5 source directions) were used to compute the object eigenspace. The eigenspace used has 8 dimensions. The histogram in Fig. 5(c) is for the case where 90 learning samples (18 poses and 5 source directions) were used. The pose estimation results in both cases were found to be remarkably accurate. In the first case, the average of the absolute pose error computed using all 1080 images is found to be 0.5 degrees, while in the second case the average error is 1.2 degrees.

Conclusion

In this paper, we presented a new representation for machine vision called the parametric eigenspace. While representations previously used in computer vision are based on object geometry, the proposed representation describes object appearance. We presented a method for automatically learning an object's parametric eigenspace. Such learning techniques are fundamental to the advancement of visual perception. We developed efficient object recognition and pose estimation algorithms that are based on the parametric eigenspace representation. The learning and recognition algorithms were tested on objects with complex shape and reflectance properties. A statistical analysis of the errors in recognition and pose estimation demonstrates the proposed approach to be very robust to factors, such as, image noise and quantization. We believe that the results presented in this paper are applicable to a variety of vision problems. This is the topic of our current investigation.

Acknowledgements

The authors would like to thank Daphna Weinshall for several useful comments on the paper.

References

[1] R. T. Chin and C. R. Dyer, "Model-Based Recognition in Robot Vision," *ACM Computing Surveys,* Vol. 18, No. 1, pp. March 1986.

[2] K. Fukunaga, *Introduction to Statistical Pattern Recognition,* Academic Press, London, 1990.

[3] H. Murase, F. Kimura, M. Yoshimura, and Y. Miyake, "An Improvement of the Auto-Correlation Matrix in Pattern Matching Method and Its Application to Handprinted 'HIRAGANA'," *Trans. IECE,* Vol. J64-D, No. 3, 1981.

[4] H. Murase and M. Lindenbaum, "Spatial Temporal Adaptive Method for Partial Eigenstructure Decompisition of Large Images," *NTT Technical Report No. 6527,* March 1992.

[5] E. Oja, *Subspace methods of Pattern Recognition,* Research Studies Press, Hertfordshire, 1983.

[6] T. Poggio and F. Girosi, "Networks for Approximation and Learning," *Proceedings of the IEEE,* Vol. 78, No. 9, pp. 1481-1497, September 1990.

[7] W. Press, B. P. Flannery, S. A. Teukolsky, and W. T. Vetterling, *Numerical Recipes in C,* Cambridge University Press, Cambridge, 1988.

[8] L. Sirovich and M. Kirby, "Low dimensional procedure for the characterization of human faces," *Journal of Optical Society of America,* Vol. 4, No. 3, pp. 519-524, 1987.

[9] M. A. Turk and A. P. Pentland, "Face Recognition Using Eigenfaces," *Proc. of IEEE Conference on Computer Vision and Pattern Recognition,* pp. 586-591, June 1991.

On the qualitative structure of temporally evolving visual motion fields

Richard P. Wildes

SRI David Sarnoff Research Center

Princeton, New Jersey 08543-5300

wildes@sarnoff.com

Abstract

This paper presents a qualitative analysis that relates stable structures in visual motion fields to properties of corresponding three-dimensional environments. Such an analysis is fundamental in the development of methods for recovering useful information from dynamic visual data without the need for highly accurate and precise sensing. Methodologically, the techniques of singularity theory are used to describe the mapping from image space to velocity space and to relate this mapping to the three-dimensional environment. The specific results of this paper address situations where an optical sensor is undergoing pure rotational or pure translational motion through its environment. For the case of pure rotational motion it is shown that the qualitative structure of visual motion provides information about the axes and relative magnitudes of rotation. For the case of pure translational motion it is shown that the qualitative structure of visual motion provides information about the shape and orientation of viewed surfaces as well as information about the translation itself. Further, the temporal evolution of the visual motion field is described. These results suggest that valuable information regarding three-dimensional environmental structure and motion can be recovered from qualitative consideration of visual motion fields.

Introduction

The visual motion field is the image projection of an environment that is moving relative to an optical sensor. As such, this field is a potentially rich source of information about the environment as well as the relative motion between the environment and sensor. In response to this possibility, this paper concentrates on developing an understanding of the qualitative properties of the motion field and of its relationship to an impinging visual world. In essence, this understanding is based on an analysis of stable structures in temporally evolving visual motion fields. Structural stability refers to properties that persist independently of minor perturbations to the visual motion field. In practice, this is of considerable importance as the visual motion field is not directly recoverable from optical data. Instead, only a near relative, the optical flow, the apparent motion of brightness patterns is recoverable (Horn 1986). Further, even obtaining good estimates of the optical flow has proven to be fraught with numerical difficulties. Happily, by concentrating on structurally stable properties of the visual motion field one has a rich source of information without reliance on highly accurate and precise recovery of the flow.

A great deal of research has focused on the interpretation of visual motion; general reviews are available (e.g., Hildreth & Koch 1987). Most relevant for current purposes are other qualitative analyses: The visual motion field has been decomposed into primitive fields to expose its underlying structure (Hoffman 1966; Koenderink & van Doorn 1975). The significance of stationary points has been addressed (Verri et al. 1989). Issues of uniqueness have received attention (Carlsson 1988). Interestingly, the bulk of these studies have couched their analyses in the language of dynamical systems theory (Hirsch & Smale 1974).

In contrast to prior work, this paper employs singularity theory (Arnold 1991) and its application to vector fields (Thorndike et al. 1978) to uncover and study information rich yet structurally stable properties of the flow. Presently, consideration is restricted to cases of visual motion due to either pure rotational or pure translational 3D motion. Specific contributions of this research include: First, for pure rotational 3D motion, it is shown that in principle qualitative considerations allow for the recovery of the axis of angular rotation, the direction of rotation and the ratio of the magnitudes of angular and radial rotation. Second, for pure translational 3D motion, it is shown that in principle qualitative considerations allow for the recovery of a description of viewed surface shape, information about the direction of viewed surface gradient and information about the direction of angular translation. Third, the temporal evolution of the visual motion field is described in terms of smooth changes and a set of three events marking more abrupt transitions.

Preliminary developments

For current purposes, it is useful to conceptualize of the visual motion field as a vector mapping, $\mathbf{f}$, assigning to each point $\mathbf{p} = (x, y)$ in the source space, $\mathcal{P}$, of image positions a single velocity vector $\mathbf{v} = (u, v)$ in the target space, $\mathcal{V}$, of image velocities $\mathbf{f} : \mathcal{P} \rightarrow \mathcal{V}$ or $\mathbf{v} = \mathbf{f}(\mathbf{p})$. It also is useful to introduce the Jacobian of the velocity mapping

$$\mathsf{J} = \begin{pmatrix} \frac{\partial u}{\partial x} & \frac{\partial u}{\partial y} \\ \frac{\partial v}{\partial x} & \frac{\partial v}{\partial y} \end{pmatrix}. \tag{1}$$

Singular points of the mapping $\mathbf{f} : \mathcal{P} \rightarrow \mathcal{V}$ are defined to be points $\mathbf{p}$ where $\det(\mathsf{J}) = 0$. Points that are not singular are said to be regular. In the plane, these distinctions have simple geometric interpretations: A small circle centered about a regular point in $\mathcal{P}$ will be mapped to an ellipse in $\mathcal{V}$. Correspondingly, at each of these points there is a direction, $\mathbf{a}$, that leads to the maximal change in length as the circle deforms into the ellipse. The magnitude of the determinant, $\det(\mathsf{J})$, gives the ratio of corresponding areas in $\mathcal{V}$ and $\mathcal{P}$. However, at singular points the image ellipse degenerates into a line segment; the ratio of areas is zero, i.e., $\mathsf{J}\mathbf{a} = 0$.

The structurally stable singularities of any mapping $\mathbf{f} : \Re^2 \rightarrow \Re^2$ form lines (Whitney 1955). Structurally stable properties are of interest as they are the properties that are robust to slight perturbations of the mapping, e.g., as due to varying observation conditions; for a formal definition of structural stability see (Golubitsky & Guillemin 1973). In the source space, $\mathcal{P}$, the structurally stable lines of singularity are smooth and are referred to as fold-lines. In the target space, $\mathcal{V}$, the images of the fold lines also are lines and are called folds. However, along the fold-lines are special points, called cusps, distinguished by tangency with the $\mathbf{a}$-trajectories. The image of these points in $\mathcal{V}$ appear as cusps along the folds. Since fold-lines and folds as well as cusp points and cusps form stable structures in a 2D to 2D mapping, they will serve as the focus in the following structural analysis of the visual motion field. Figure 1 illustrates the geometry of folds and cusps in the velocity mapping.

Structural analysis of visual motion

Define a Cartesian coordinate system at the center of an optical sensor with the Z-axis pointing along the optical axis. Under perspective projection a 3D point $\mathbf{P} = (X, Y, Z)$ is mapped to an image point $\mathbf{p} = (\frac{X}{Z}, \frac{Y}{Z}) = (x, y)$, where appropriate scaling is taken so that the focal length is unity. Let visual motion derive from a sensor moving through a static environment. (Alternatively, it could be assumed that a fixed sensor observes a dynamic environment.) Take the sensor's translational velocity as $\mathbf{T} = (t_x, t_y, t_z)$, while its rotational velocity is $\Omega = (\omega_x, \omega_y, \omega_z)$. Then, the equations of rigid body motion and perspective

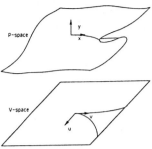

Figure 1: The velocity mapping $\mathbf{f}$ can be thought of as stretching and bending the source space of image positions, $\mathcal{P}$, in three dimensions and then projecting it into the target space of image velocities, $\mathcal{V}$. $\mathcal{P}$ is folded along fold-lines that project to folds. Cusp-points correspond to pleats along the fold-lines that project to cusps.

projection, allow the image velocity, $\mathbf{v} = (u, v)$, of an environmental point, $\mathbf{P}$, to be written as

$$u = \tfrac{1}{Z}(xt_z - t_x) + xy\omega_x - (x^2 + 1)\omega_y + y\omega_z$$
$$v = \tfrac{1}{Z}(yt_z - t_y) + (y^2 + 1)\omega_x - xy\omega_y - x\omega_z \tag{2}$$

(Horn 1986). The visual motion field is an array of velocities $\mathbf{v}$, for an imaged 3D environment. Correspondingly, the terms of the velocity Jacobian (1) can be expanded as

$$\frac{\partial u}{\partial x} = \left(\frac{\partial}{\partial x}\frac{1}{Z}\right)(xt_z - t_x) + \frac{t_z}{Z} + y\omega_x - 2\omega_y x$$
$$\frac{\partial u}{\partial y} = \left(\frac{\partial}{\partial y}\frac{1}{Z}\right)(xt_z - t_x) + x\omega_x + \omega_z$$
$$\frac{\partial v}{\partial x} = \left(\frac{\partial}{\partial x}\frac{1}{Z}\right)(yt_z - t_y) - \omega_y y - \omega_z \tag{3}$$
$$\frac{\partial v}{\partial y} = \left(\frac{\partial}{\partial y}\frac{1}{Z}\right)(yt_z - t_y) + \frac{t_z}{Z} + 2\omega_x y - \omega_y x$$

Now, consider purely rotational 3D motion. The governing conditions are $\mathbf{T} = \mathbf{0}$, while $\Omega = (\omega_x, \omega_y, \omega_z)$. In these situations the visual motion field specializes to

$$u = \omega_x xy - \omega_y(x^2 + 1) + \omega_z y$$
$$v = \omega_x(y^2 + 1) - \omega_y xy - \omega_z x \tag{4}$$

An illustration of a visual motion field due to 3D rotation is shown in the left side of Figure 2. Under pure 3D rotation, the condition for singularity, $\det(\mathsf{J}) = 0$, dictates that the expression

$$2\omega_y^2 x^2 + 2\omega_x^2 y^2 - 4\omega_x\omega_y xy + \omega_x\omega_z x + \omega_y\omega_z y + \omega_z^2 \tag{5}$$

evaluates to zero. To understand the form of the singularity in the source space, $\mathcal{P}$, consider the discriminant (Korn & Korn 1968) of the condition (5) viewed as a conic section,

$$(-4\omega_x\omega_y)^2 - 4(2\omega_y^2)(2\omega_x^2). \tag{6}$$

Since the discriminant (6) is identically equal to zero, the singular points are manifest in $\mathcal{P}$ as a parabola. This parabola describes the fold line for the case of pure rotational 3D motion.

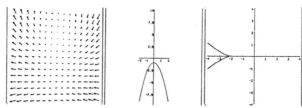

Figure 2: A visual motion field for rotation about the Z and Y axes (left). The fold-lines in the source space, $\mathcal{P}$, of image positions (middle). The corresponding folds with a cusp in the target space, $\mathcal{V}$, of image velocities (right).

In order to facilitate further analysis, a new co-ordinate system, (x', y') is now adopted so that the parabola shaped fold-line is symmetric about the y'-axis. Consideration of the related equations for the rotation of coordinate axes shows that the y'-axis is parallel to the direction $\frac{(\omega_x, \omega_y)}{\|(\omega_x, \omega_y)\|}$, i.e., the direction of the angular component of 3D rotation. Therefore, in the (x', y') coordinate system 3D rotation is given as $\Omega' = (\omega_x', \omega_y', \omega_z') = (0, (\omega_x^2 + \omega_y^2)^{\frac{1}{2}}, \omega_z)$. The form of the fold-line now can be given as

$$y' = -2\frac{\omega_y'}{\omega_z'}x'^2 - \frac{\omega_z'}{\omega_y'}. \tag{7}$$

From the equation for the fold-line in the (x', y') co-ordinate system (7) a number of observations are immediate: First, this parabola intercepts the y'-axis at $-\frac{\omega_z'}{\omega_y'}$, the ratio of radial to angular components of 3D rotation. Second, by computing the derivative with respect to x it is seen that the parabola opens at the rate $-4\frac{\omega_y'}{\omega_z'}x$, $4x'$ times the inverse of the previous ratio. Third, given the agreement in the signs of these two ratios, the parabola always opens away from the origin. An example fold-line parabola is illustrated in the middle of Figure 2.

To study the locus of singularities in the target space, $\mathcal{V}'$, the equation describing the fold-line in the source space, $\mathcal{P}'$, (7) can be substituted into the equations of the visual motion field (4) to yield

$$(u', v') = \left(-3\omega_y'x'^2 - \frac{\omega_y'^2 + \omega_z'^2}{\omega_y'}, \frac{\omega_y'^2}{\omega_z'}x'^3\right). \tag{8}$$

This set of equations can be taken as a parametric representation of the fold in $\mathcal{V}'$ with parameter x'. This curve intercepts the u'-axis at $-\frac{\omega_y'^2 + \omega_z'^2}{\omega_y'}$, the negative of the ratio of the squared magnitude of rotational motion to the angular component of rotational motion. As x' differs from zero the curve branches out symmetrically from its u'-intercept, leaving a cusp in its wake. The rate at which the fold opens can be determined by (implicitly) computing the derivative $\frac{dv'}{du'} = -\frac{\omega_y'}{\omega_z'}x'$ to see that the rate of opening (as a function of x') is determined by minus the ratio of angular to radial

rotation, $-\frac{\omega_y'}{\omega_z'}$. An illustrative example fold with cusp is shown on the right side of Figure 2.

At this point it is useful to review by noting the ways that the singularities of the velocity mapping could be used to make inferences about 3D rotational motion: First, the appearance of the fold-lines as a parabola with a single cusp-point could be taken as a signature indicative of rotational 3D motion. Second, the axis of angular rotation can be recovered as the axis of symmetry of the fold-line parabola. Third, the distance of the parabola from the origin as well as the rate of opening of the parabolic fold-line and cusped fold are all directly indicative of the relative magnitude of angular and radial rotations. Finally, notice that the singularities say nothing about 3D environmental structure. This reflects the fact that instantaneous visual motion due to purely rotational 3D motion is independent of environmental layout.

Next, consider purely translational 3D motion. The governing conditions are $\mathbf{T} = (t_x, t_y, t_z)$ while $\Omega = 0$. Correspondingly, the visual motion field specializes to

$$(u, v) = \left(\frac{1}{Z}(xt_z - t_x), \frac{1}{Z}(yt_z - t_y)\right). \tag{9}$$

Illustrations of three different visual motion fields due to 3D translation are shown in the first column of Figure 3. Under pure 3D translation, the condition for singularity, $\det(\mathbf{J}) = 0$, dictates that the expression

$$\frac{t_z}{Z}\left(\left(\frac{\partial}{\partial x}\frac{1}{Z}\right)(xt_z - t_x) + \left(\frac{\partial}{\partial y}\frac{1}{Z}\right)(yt_z - t_y) + \frac{t_z}{Z}\right) \tag{10}$$

evaluates to zero.

The translation-based singularity equation (10) involves the translation as well as the shape and pose of a surface of regard. To understand this matter consider a surface described at each point by its local tangent plane, then $n_x X + n_y Y + n_z Z = d$, where the (n_x, n_y, n_z) are normals at points on the surface (X, Y, Z). In this case, $\left(\frac{\partial}{\partial x}, \frac{\partial}{\partial y}\right) \cdot \frac{1}{Z} = \frac{(n_x, n_y)}{Z(n_x x + n_y y + n_z)}$. Substitution into (10) then yields

$$(n_x, n_y, n_z) \cdot \left(2x - \frac{t_x}{t_z}, 2y - \frac{t_y}{t_z}, 1\right) = 0.$$

This expression shows that the singularity condition holds when the local surface normal is orthogonal to

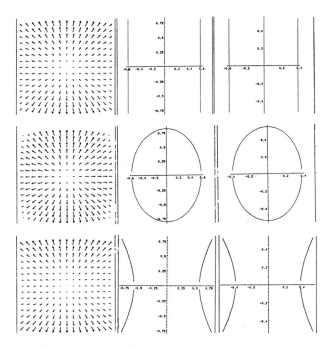

Figure 3: The left column shows visual motion fields for an observer approaching parabolic (top), elliptic (middle) and hyperbolic (bottom) surfaces. The middle column shows the fold-lines in the source space, $\mathcal{P}$, of image positions. The right column shows the folds in the target space, $\mathcal{V}$, of image velocities.

the view direction scaled by two and displaced by the focus of expansion, $t_z^{-1}(t_x, t_y)$; the locus of singularity is indicative of translation, surface shape and pose.

It is illustrative to consider in detail a particular set of examples: Let a surface be represented as a Monge patch, $(X, Y, Z(X, Y))$ with $Z(X, Y) = \frac{1}{2}\kappa_1 X^2 + \frac{1}{2}\kappa_2 Y^2 + \kappa_3 XY + pX + qY + r$ so that $\frac{1}{Z} = \frac{1 - px - qy}{r} - \kappa_3 xy - \frac{1}{2}\kappa_1 x^2 - \frac{1}{2}\kappa_2 y^2$, through second-order. When this surface model is made use of in the singularity condition (10) it is found that the locus of singularities in the source space, $\mathcal{P}$, is a quartic in x and y that can be written as the product of two conic sections. However, one of these conic sections corresponds to a degenerate situation where the underlying 3D surface recedes to infinity. Along this contour all the velocities map to a single point, $(0, 0)$. Consequently, subsequent attention will be restricted to the other conic section. To study this curve, it is convenient to immediately adopt a new coordinate system, (x', y'), by rotating the axes so as to eliminate the cross terms in xy. Following this operation, the contour can be written as

$$3\kappa_x r t_z x'^2 + 3\kappa_y r t_z y'^2 + 2(2p't_z - \kappa_x r t'_x)x \\ + 2(2q't_z - \kappa_y r t'_y)y' - 2(p't'_x + q't'_y + tz) = 0 \quad (11)$$

where it turns out that κ_x and κ_y are given by diagonalization of the coefficients of the quadratic terms in the Monge patch representation of the surface. As a point of departure on understanding the equation describing the singular points (11) suppose that there is

no angular component to translation, i.e., $t'_x = t'_y = 0$, and that the surface gradient vanishes at the origin, i.e., $p' = q' = 0$. Also, for ease of notation, primes will be dropped for the rest of this section of the paper; the fact that all calculations are being performed in the (x', y') coordinate system will be implicit. Under these conditions, equation (11) evaluates to

$$\kappa_x x^2 + \kappa_y y^2 = \frac{2}{3r}. \quad (12)$$

Consideration of this simplified singularity condition (12) shows that it describes an origin centered conic section that is: an ellipse if $sgn(\kappa_x) = sgn(\kappa_y)$, a hyperbola if $sgn(\kappa_x) = -sgn(\kappa_y)$ or parallel straight lines if $\kappa_x = 0$ or $\kappa_y = 0$, i.e., the curves are indicative of Dupin's Indicatrix for the underlying 3D surface Z. Also, the major axis of the conic section is along the x-axis if $\|\kappa_x\| < \|\kappa_y\|$ or along the y-axis if $\|\kappa_x\| > \|\kappa_y\|$. The second column of Figure 3 shows representative examples.

What conclusions can be reached about the form of the fold-lines under less restricted conditions? First, suppose that the restriction against angular translation is removed, i.e., $\mathbf{T} = (t_x, t_y, t_z)$. In this case, the form of the fold-line (12) becomes

$$\kappa_x \left(x - \frac{t_x}{3t_z}\right)^2 + \kappa_y \left(x - \frac{t_y}{3t_z}\right)^2 = \frac{18t_z^3 + t_x^2 + t_y^2}{27rt_z^3}.$$

In words, the addition of angular motion does not change the qualitative shape of the curve. However, the size is adjusted and the center moves along the axis of angular translation. Second, suppose that the surface gradient is no longer required to vanish at the origin. In this case, the fold-line equation can be written as

$$\kappa_x \left(x + \frac{2p}{3\kappa_x r}\right)^2 + \kappa_y \left(y + \frac{2q}{3\kappa_y r}\right)^2$$
$$= \frac{2}{3r}\left(1 + \frac{2}{9r^2 t_z}\left(\left(\frac{p}{\kappa_x}\right)^2 + \left(\frac{q}{\kappa_y}\right)^2\right)\right).$$

This equation shows that a surface gradient also does not change the qualitative shape of the fold-lines, although the size is altered. The center of the curve again moves in the direction specified by the surface gradient, but as weighted by the surface curvatures κ_x and κ_y. Finally, suppose that both angular translation and non-vanishing gradient are both allowed. In this case, the equation of the fold-line can be written as

$$\kappa_x\left(x + \frac{2p}{3\kappa_x r} - \frac{t_x}{3t_z}\right)^2 + \kappa_y\left(x + \frac{2q}{3\kappa_y r} - \frac{t_y}{3t_z}\right)^2 = \frac{1}{3rt_z}$$
$$\times \left(2(pt_x + qt_y + t_z) + \left(\frac{pt_z - r\kappa_x t_x}{3r\kappa_x rt_z}\right)^2 + \left(\frac{qt_z - r\kappa_y t_y}{3r\kappa_y rt_z}\right)^2\right)$$

As with the other cases, it is seen that the qualitative shape of the contour remains the same. However, now the contour's center is displaced to a point that is the vector sum of the centers for angular translation and non-vanishing gradient.

To study the locus of singularities in the target space, $\mathcal{V}$, begin by again considering the restricted situation where there is no angular translation and the surface gradient vanishes at the image origin. In this case, the corresponding equation describing the fold-line in the source space, $\mathcal{P}$, (12) can be substituted into the equations of the translational visual motion field (9). This operation yields

$$(u, v) = \left(\frac{2x}{3r}, \frac{2\left(\frac{2}{r} - 3\kappa_x x^2\right)^{\frac{1}{2}}}{r(27\kappa_y)^{\frac{1}{2}}}\right). \qquad (13)$$

This set of equations can be taken as a parametric representation of the velocity with parameter x. The shape of the corresponding fold in the target space is a parabola, ellipse of hyperbola depending on the curvature terms, κ_x and κ_y, in exactly the same way as did the fold-lines in the source space; the folds are indicative of Dupin's Indicatrix as were the fold-lines. Three examples of folds are shown in the third column of Figure 3. As in the source space, the addition of angular translation and surface gradient causes the fold conics to drift in position. However, unlike the fold-lines the folds slowly deform as they drift toward the target space periphery.

Again, it is useful to review by explicitly noting several ways that the singularities of the visual motion field can be used to interpret 3D translational motion: First, the shape of the fold-lines are indicative of the qualitative 3D surface shape. For the particular case

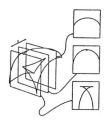

Figure 4: The swallowtail singularity describes the condition when a fold sheet and rib intersect. The swallowtail event occurs when a τ slice contains this type of intersection.

of quadratic surface patches, the fold-lines form an ellipse, hyperbola or a pair of parallel straight lines according to whether the surface is locally elliptic, hyperbolic or parabolic in shape. This same signature is apparent in the corresponding folds in the target space; however, here they can be deformed by angular translation and surface gradient. Second, the major and minor axes of the surface can be recovered from the corresponding fold-line conic section major and minor axes. Third, the directions of angular translation and surface gradient are constrained by the off-set of the fold-lines from the image origin.

Temporal evolution

In general, visual motion fields evolve in time. Correspondingly, the patterns of the singular points, the folds and cusps, vary with time. More precisely, consider a family of flows, $\{f^t : \mathcal{P} \to \mathcal{V}\}, -\infty < \sqcup < \infty$, parameterized by t, time. t can be thought of as assigning a particular time to each of the mappings in a given series. Another way of looking at matters is given by taking the family of functions f^t in tandem to define a single function $\mathbf{g} : \Re^3 \to \Re^3$ i.e., $\mathbf{g} : (x, y, t) \to (u, v, \tau)$ with the form $(u, v, \tau) = (u(x, y, t), v(x, y, t), t)$. The velocity map at any given time now corresponds to a τ slice. In the (u, v, τ)-space, the folds define surfaces called fold sheets; while, the cusps define lines in those surfaces called ribs. Additionally, a third structure of interest now presents itself, the swallowtail. A swallowtail occurs when a fold sheet and a rib intersect. The canonical form for the swallowtail singularity is

$$(u, v, \tau) = (x^4 + x^2 y + xt, y, t). \qquad (14)$$

Figure 4 illustrates the associated geometry. Of all elementary singularities, only three, the fold, cusp and swallowtail are stable with respect to general perturbations to the time dependent flow (Golubitsky & Guillemin 1973).

Typically, the stable structures of the visual motion field evolve smoothly in time. Reference to the previous section's discussion reveals much of what can be expected. For pure rotational 3D motion: As the direction of angular rotation changes, the orientation of the

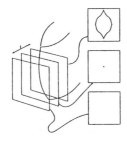 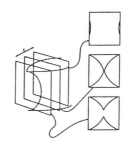

Figure 5: The lips (left) and beak to beak (right) events can occur when a τ slice is tangent to a rib.

fold-line parabola in the source space also changes as does the corresponding fold in the target space. As the ratio of angular to radial rotation changes, the fold-line parabola opens and closes and moves toward and away from the origin. Corresponding changes take place with the rate of opening of the two arms of the fold and the distance of the cusp from the origin. As time passes the fold-line and fold sweep out surfaces; the cusp creases the fold sheet with a rib. For pure translational 3D motion: As the observer moves toward or away from a surface of regard the fold-lines and folds expand and contract, without changing their characteristic shape. With angular translation the contours drift in spatial position. Again, surfaces are traced by the smooth evolution of the fold-lines and folds.

In addition to the smooth evolution of the singularities in time more abrupt change can occur. In particular, there are special points along the ribs, called events, that demark more abrupt change and that determine the overall temporal evolution. Strikingly, there are only three distinct types of events for concern in the analysis of vector fields (Thorndike *et al.* 1978). The first of these events is associated with the swallowtail singularity (14). This event occurs when a τ slice contains an intersection of a fold sheet with a rib, see Figure 4. Two additional types of events can occur when a τ slice is tangent to a curved rib: (i) In the lips event an initially structureless region becomes tangent to a rib and subsequently gives rise to a doubly cusped region. (ii) In the beak to beak event two target space regions lose their identity as the event is passed. Lips and beak to beak events are described by

$$(u, v, \tau) = (x^3 \pm xy^2 + xt, y, t),$$

respectively. Figure 5 illustrates these events.

Summary

Qualitative consideration of a visual motion field yields information about the 3D geometry and motion of an impinging environment. In this paper attention has focused on cases where an optical sensor undergoes pure rotation or pure translation. For rotation, information is available about the axes and relative magnitudes of angular and radial rotation. For translation, information is available about the shape and orientation of visible surfaces as well as about the translation itself. In either case, the structure of the flow typically evolves smoothly in time. However, on occasion discrete events occur that add greater richness to the structure.

References

Arnold, V. I. 1991. *The Theory of Singularities and Its Applications.* Cambridge University Press, NY, NY.

Carlsson, S. 1988. Information in the geometric structure of retinal flow fields. In *Proceedings of the International Conference on Computer Vision.* 629–633.

Golubitsky, M. and Guillemin, V. 1973. *Stable Mappings and their Singularities.* Springer, NY, NY.

Hildreth, E. C. and Koch, C. 1987. The analysis of visual motion: From computational theory to neuronal mechanisms. *Annual Review of Neuroscience.*

Hirsch, M. W. and Smale, S. 1974. *Differential equations, dynamical systems and linear algebra.* Academic Press, NY, NY.

Hoffman, W. C. 1966. Lie group theory of visual perception. *Journal of Mathematical Psychology* 3:65–165.

Horn, B. K. P. 1986. *Robot Vision.* MIT Press, Cambridge, MA.

Koenderink, J. J. and van Doorn, A. J. 1975. Invariant properties of the motion parallax field due to the movement of rigid bodies relative an observer. *Optica Acta* 22:717–723.

Korn, G. A. and Korn, T. M., editors 1968. *Mathematical Handbook for Scientists and Engineers, Second Edition.* McGraw-Hill, NY, NY.

Thorndike, A. S.; Cooley, C. R.; and Nye, J. F. 1978. The structure and evolution of flow fields and other vector fields. *Journal of Physics A: Mathematical and General* 11(8):1455–1490.

Verri, A.; Girosi, F.; and Torre, V. 1989. Mathematical properties of the two-dimensional motion field: From singular points to motion parameters. *Journal of the Optical Society of America A* 6(5):698–712.

Whitney, H. 1955. On singularities of mappings of euclidean spaces. i. mappings of the plane into the plane. *Annals of Mathematics* 62(3):374–410.

Invited
Talks

Tiger in a Cage
The Applications of Knowledge-based Systems (1993)

Edward A. Feigenbaum

Knowledge Systems Laboratory
Stanford University
Stanford, California 94305
feigenbaum@ksl.stanford.edu

Some pioneers of Artificial Intelligence dreamed of the super-intelligent computer, whose problem solving performance would rival or exceed human performance. Their dream has been partially realized, for narrow areas of human endeavor, in the programs called expert systems, whose behavior is often at world-class levels of competence. Their dream was partially transformed by programs that give intelligent help to humans with problems (rather than perform super-intelligently). These are called knowledge systems.

Because knowledge is of such central importance to late 20th century firms and economies, these two types of knowledge-based computer systems offer great economic and competitive leverage. The systems offer remarkable cost savings; some dramatically "hot selling" products; great return-on-investment; speedup of professional work by factors of ten to several hundred; improved quality of human decision making (often reducing errors to zero); and the preservation and "publishing" of knowledge assets of a firm. These benefits will be made vivid by descriptions of knowledge-based systems of prominence in 1993.

These stories of successful applications, repeated a thousandfold around the world, show that knowledge-based technology is a tiger. Rarely does a technology arise that offers such a wide range of important benefits of this magnitude. Yet as the technology moved through the phase of early adoption to general industry adoption, the response has been cautious, slow, and "linear" (rather than exponential). The tiger is in a cage, and we do not yet understand what the bars of the cage are made of. Are there fundamental flaws in the technology that are somehow not evident in "best practice" systems? Is there a specific set of technology transfer problems that arise with knowledge systems but not with other kinds of systems? It is important to the economy to free this competitive tiger, but to do so we must understand its cage.

Artificial Intelligence as an Experimental Science

Herbert A. Simon

School of Computer Science
Carnegie Mellon University
5000 Forbes Avenue
Pittsburgh, PA 15213

The journal *Artificial Intelligence* has experienced a rather steady drift, in recent years, from articles describing and evaluating specific computer programs that exhibit intelligence to formal articles that prove theorems about intelligence. This trend raises basic questions about the nature of theory in artificial intelligence and the appropriate form for a mature science of this discipline.

During the past 35 years of AI's history, the vast bulk of our understanding of machine intelligence has derived from experimenting: constructing innumerable programs that exhibit such intelligence, and examining and analyzing their performance. Theory has been induced by identifying components and processes that are common to many of the programs, and broad generalizations about them. Some of this theory is formal, but most takes the form of laws of qualitative structure. In this respect, artificial intelligence resembles other empirical sciences like molecular biology or geophysics much more than mathematics. Computers, however "artificial," are real objects the complexity of whose behavior cannot be captured fully in simple formalisms. There are no "Three Laws of Motion" of AI.

This talk examines the forms that theory has taken (and will take) in artificial intelligence, and shows why the progress of the discipline would be stifled by a premature or excessive preoccupation with formalizations derivable from logic and mathematics.

Video
Abstracts

A Demonstration of the "Circuit Fix-it Shoppe"

D. Richard Hipp

& Ronnie W. Smith

Department of Computer Science
Duke University
Durham, NC 27706

Abstract

The "Circuit Fix-it Shoppe" is a voice interactive dialog system which has been constructed in our laboratory. The mission of the system is to help people repair electronic circuits. The system contains a domain modeler, a reasoning system, a dialog controller, a user modeling system, an error-correcting natural language parser, and a natural language generator. A commercial speech recognizer and speech synthesizer are used for voice input and output. More detailed information about our dialog system can be found in [1] and [2].

This videotape records two live dialogs between the Circuit Fix-it Shoppe program and a user who has no special knowledge of computers, electronic repair, or our system. A brief description of the experimental setup and of the Circuit Fix-it Shoppe program precedes these dialogs.

The Circuit Fix-it Shoppe program is capable of varying its level of initiative. It can be highly directive, in which case it controls the conversation, or it may be passive, in which case the user controls the dialog, or it may take some level of initiative between these two extremes. In the first videotape demonstration, the system is running in directive mode. In this second demonstration, the system is set to operate in declarative mode. In this mode, the user is free to take the initiative and to control the conversation. Declarative mode is appropriate for users who are much more familiar with the circuit and require only minimal help from the computer.

Duration: 11 minutes 50 seconds. Tape format: VHS.

References

[1] R. W. Smith, D. R. Hipp and A. W. Biermann, "A Dialog Control Algorithm and Its Performance," Proceedings of the Third Conference on Applied Natural Language Processing, Trento, Italy, April 1-3,1992.

[2] R. W. Smith and D. R. Hipp, "Using Expectation to Enable Spoken Variable Initiative Dialog," Proceedings of the 1992 Symposium on Applied Computing, Kansas City, Missouri, March 1-3,1992.

Instructo-Soar: Learning from interactive natural language instructions (video abstract)*

Scott B. Huffman and John E. Laird
Artificial Intelligence Laboratory
The University of Michigan
Ann Arbor, Michigan 48109–2110
huffman@umich.edu

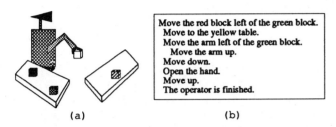

Move the red block left of the green block.
Move to the yellow table.
Move the arm left of the green block.
Move the arm up.
Move down.
Open the hand.
Move up.
The operator is finished.

(a)   (b)

Figure 1: (a). An agent in an initial situation; (b) Instructions to teach a new procedure.

Despite its ubiquity in human learning, very little work has been done in artificial intelligence on learning from natural language instructions. In this video, we present a system, Instructo-Soar, that can both behave and learn from natural language instructions. The system is described in papers elsewhere [Huffman and Laird, 1993a; Huffman and Laird, 1993b]. The type of instruction we particularly address is *situated, interactive* instruction. Situated means that the student is within the task domain, attempting to perform tasks, when instruction is given. Interactive means that the student can request instruction as needed.

Instructo-Soar can learn completely new procedures from sequences of interactive instruction, and can also learn how to extend its knowledge of previously known procedures to new situations. The video demonstrates its application in a simple robotic domain. The system starts with a small set of primitive operators. Given instructions in the form of imperative natural language sentences, it is able to learn a hierarchy of complex operators. An example instruction scenario is shown in Figure 1.

Learning procedures from instructions involves more than simply memorization of instruction sequences. Acquiring a new procedure involves learning both the procedure's goal concept, and a general implementation for the procedure.

The instructed agent can learn the goal concept of a

new procedure after performing it (an inductive learning task). Instructo-Soar uses a simple difference-of-states heuristic to induce goal concepts; everything that has changed from the initial state to the final state during execution of the new procedure is considered part of the goal of the procedure. Recent versions of the system allow the instructor to give instructional feedback to alter the induced goal as needed.

To learn a general implementation for the procedure, the applicability conditions of each instruction in the implementation sequence must be determined. Instructo-Soar uses an explanation based approach for this: the agent attempts to explain to itself (via an internal forward simulation) how each instruction leads to achievement of the goal. This explanation process indicates which features of the situation and instruction are crucial for goal achievement.

Instructo-Soar exhibits a multiple execution learning process to learn a new procedure. Initial learning is rote and episodic in nature. After executing the new procedure the first time, the system can induce the goal concept of the procedure. During future executions, the system recalls the instructions it learned by rote initially, and explains how they contribute to reaching the procedure's goal, resulting in general learning. The learning curve that results closely matches the power law of practice.

This work represents first steps towards our long-term goal of building general, instructable autonomous agents.

References

[Huffman and Laird, 1993a] Scott B. Huffman and John E. Laird. Learning from instruction: A knowledge-level capability within a unified theory of cognition. In *Proceedings of the Fifteenth Annual Conference of the Cognitive Science Society*, 1993.

[Huffman and Laird, 1993b] Scott B. Huffman and John E. Laird. Learning procedures from interactive natural language instructions. In P. E. Utgoff, editor, *Machine Learning: Proceedings of the Tenth International Conference*, June 1993.

*This research was sponsored by NASA/ONR under contract NCC 2-517.

Winning the AAAI Robot Competition

David Kortenkamp, Marcus Huber, Charles Cohen, Ulrich Raschke, Clint Bidlack, Clare Bates Congdon, Frank Koss, and Terry Weymouth

Artificial Intelligence Laboratory
The University of Michigan
Ann Arbor, MI 48109
korten@engin.umich.edu

Abstract

Last summer, AAAI sponsored a mobile robot competition in conjunction with the AAAI-92 conference in San Jose, California. Ten robots from across the country competed in the competition, with CARMEL from the University of Michigan finishing first. CARMEL is a Cybermotion K2A mobile platform with a ring of 24 sonar sensors and a single black and white CCD camera. For computing, CARMEL has three processors: one for motor control, one for sonar ring firing and one executing high-level routines such as obstacle avoidance and object recognition. All computation and power is contained entirely on-board.

The competition consisted of three stages, all taking place in a 22m by 22m arena. The first stage involved roaming the arena while avoiding obstacles (cardboard boxes) and wandering judges. The second stage involved searching for 10 distinctive objects and then visiting each of the objects. Visiting was defined as moving to within two robot diameters of the object. The robots had 20 minutes to perform this task. The third stage was a timed race to three of the objects found in stage 2 and then back home. The arena boundaries were defined by walls, and the arena floor was strewn with obstacles. Objects were ten foot tall, three-inch diameter poles. Teams could attach their own tags to the poles to allow their sensors to detect them. The objects could be seen above the obstacles, while the clearance between obstacles was a minimum of 1.5m.

Obstacle avoidance on CARMEL is done solely with its sonar sensors and has two components: (a) a unique method for detecting and rejecting noise and crosstalk with ultrasonic sensors, called error eliminating rapid ultrasonic firing (EERUF) [3]; and (b) an obstacle avoidance method called the vector field histogram (VFH) [1,2]. The VFH method uses a two-dimensional Cartesian grid, called the Histogram Grid, to represent data from ultrasonic (or other) range sensors. Each cell in the Histogram Grid holds a certainty value that represents the confidence of the algorithm in the existence of an obstacle at that location. This representation was derived from the certainty grid concept that was originally developed by Moravec and Elfes in [5]. Based on data in the Histogram Grid, the VFH method cre-

ates an intermediate data representation called the Polar Histogram. The spatial representation in the Polar Histogram can be visualized as a mountainous panorama around the robot, where the height and size of the peaks represent the proximity of obstacles, and the valleys represent possible travel directions. The VFH algorithm steers the robot in the direction of one of the valleys, based on the direction of the target location. Using VFH, CARMEL avoided obstacles while moving at speeds of up to 780 mm/sec.

Objects recognition was facilitated by tagging each pole with an omni-directional barcode. The object tag design used for CARMEL consists of a black and white stripe pattern placed upon PVC tubing with a four inch diameter, allowing the tags to be slipped over the object poles. The vision algorithm for extracting objects from an image required no preprocessing of the image. The algorithm makes a single pass over the image, going down each column of the image looking for a white-to-black transition that would mark the start of a potential object. A finite state machine keeps track of the number and spacing of the bands. After finding enough bands to comprise a tag the algorithm stores the tag id and pixel length. Once a column is complete, the eligible objects are heuristically merged with objects found in previous columns. The algorithm has an effective range of about 19 meters.

CARMEL successfully integrated high-speed obstacle avoidance with long-range vision to win the AAAI Robot competition. CARMEL placed third in stage 1 and first in stages 2 and 3. In the second stage, CARMEL found and visited all ten objects in under ten minutes; no other robot could find and visit all ten objects in under the allotted 20 minutes for stage 2. In stage 3, CARMEL finished first by visiting the three objects and returning to the start position in just under three minutes. For more details on CARMEL see [4].

References

[1] Johann Borenstein and Yoram Koren. Histogramic in-motion mapping for mobile robot obstacle avoidance. IEEE Transactions on Robotics and Automation, 7(4), 1991.

[2] Johann Borenstein and Yoram Koren. The Vector Field Histogram for fast obstacle avoidance for mobile robots. IEEE Transactions on Robotics and Automation, 7(3), 1991, pp. 278-288.

[3] Johann Borenstein and Yoram Koren. Noise rejection for ultrasonic sensors in mobile robot applications. In Proceedings of the IEEE Conference on Robotics and Automation, 1992, pp. 1727-1732.

[4] David Kortenkamp, Marcus Huber, Charles Cohen, Ulrich Raschke, Clint Bidlack, Clare Bates Congdon, Frank Koss, and Terry Weymouth. Winning the AAAI Robot Competition: A case study in integrated mobile robot design. To appear in IEEE Expert, 1993.

[5] Hans P. Moravec and Alberto Elfes. High resolution sonar maps from wide angle sonar. In Proceedings of the IEEE Conference on Robotics and Automation, 1985, pp. 19-24.

AIR-SOAR: Intelligent Multi-Level Control

Douglas J. Pearson, Randolph M. Jones, and John E. Laird
Artificial Intelligence Laboratory
The University of Michigan
1101 Beal Ave.
Ann Arbor, Michigan 48109–2122
dpearson@caen.engin.umich.edu

Autonomous systems must be able to deal with dynamic, unpredictable environments in real time. Our video describes a system for intelligent control of an airplane, within a realistic flight simulator (the Silicon Graphics flight simulator). The simulator allows asynchronous control of the plane's throttle, ailerons, elevator and other control surfaces by an external system, and it provides limited asynchronous sensing of the plane's motion. The result is a highly dynamic, real time domain in which models of the plane (and, potentially, other aircraft) are updated 20 times a second. Control of flight is complex. Unexpected events such as wind or turbulence must be responded to in a timely fashion. Further, identical control movements have different effects depending on the plane's position and environmental conditions, making precise prediction of action effects difficult. The agent must also deal with delays in feedback from its actions, waiting for the plane to respond to changes in the control surfaces. The domain requires simultaneous execution of a range of tasks at different levels of complexity and granularity, from high level maneuvers like takeoff, landing and banked turns to low level tasks such as maintaining altitude, keeping the wings level and controlling the stick.

Our autonomous agent for the flight domain is *Air-Soar* [Pearson *et al.*, 1993]. The agent is built within Soar [Laird *et al.*, 1987], a general problem solving and learning architecture. Soar solves problems by successively applying operators within problem spaces. Air-Soar reasons about flight with five problem spaces, each reasoning at a different level of granularity. In addition, the system achieves and maintains multiple goals simultaneously, both within and across levels. For example, at the highest level the system may be both climbing and turning to a new heading. Across levels, lower-level constraints may be achieved while performing higher-level goals, such as leveling the wings during a climb to a new altitude. Thus, Air-Soar supports *achievement goals*, where the goal is to reach a particular state (such as a new altitude), and *homeostatic goals*, in which constraints must be continuously maintained [Covrigaru and Lindsay, 1991; Kaelbling,

1986]. Homeostatic goals often interact with achievement goals in the flight domain. Examples include keeping the wings level while taking off, and maintaining the current altitude during a turn. Air-Soar must combine the requirements of the different types of goals to make steady progress along a flight path, without losing control by focusing only on a single aspect of the current task (such as only monitoring the altitude during a climb).

Typically, all of Air-Soar's levels are active simultaneously, trying to maintain or achieve their current goals. This hierarchical approach supports reactive behavior at multiple levels of granularity. Rather than explicitly monitoring the fact that all of the plane's flight parameters are within expected ranges, each problem space notices when the values deviate from constraints it is trying to achieve or maintain, and moves to correct them. These corrections produce changes at lower granularity levels, ultimately resulting in stick commands to control the plane.

Sensitivity at different grain sizes means that Air-Soar is able to respond to a wide range of unexpected events. For instance, after completing a turn, the plane might not be perfectly level, causing the heading to slowly change. Although the rate of change is low, after a while Air-Soar would notice the heading was no longer within range and would turn to correct it. Alternatively, if a sudden burst of turbulence caused the plane's wings to vere suddenly, then the system would react to the sudden increase in *turn rate* directly, before the heading had changed enough to be noticed.

Air-Soar is currently able to take off, level off and then follow a pre-set flight pattern including a series of turns and altitude changes, returning to land on (or near) the runway. We have simulated "turbulence" during Air-Soar runs by manually moving the mouse controlling the plane's stick while Air-Soar controls the plane. Air-Soar responds immediately to the "turbulence" and continually attempts to keep the plane on course. If the plane is flying level and is pulled out of level flight by the mouse, Air-Soar recovers by responding to the change in the plane's roll to reestablish level flight. Air-Soar's successful execution of the flight plan, together with our experiments with "turbulence", demonstrates the system's ability to perform robustly in a highly reactive, real-time domain. In addition, it highlights Air-Soar's ability to reason about multiple simultaneous goals at various levels of granularity.

References

[Covrigaru and Lindsay, 1991] Arie A. Covrigaru and Robert K. Lindsay. Deterministic autonomous systems. *AI Magazine*, 12(3):110–117, 1991.

[Kaelbling, 1986] Leslie Pack Kaelbling. An architecture for intelligent reactive systems. In Michael P. Georgeff and Amy L. Lansky, editors, *Reasoning about actions and plans: Proceedings of the 1986 Workshop*, pages 395–410. Morgan Kaufmann, 1986.

[Laird *et al.*, 1987] John E. Laird, Allen Newell, and Paul S. Rosenbloom. Soar: An architecture for general intelligence. *Artificial Intelligence*, 33(1):1–64, 1987.

[Pearson *et al.*, 1993] Douglas J. Pearson, Scott B. Huffman, Mark B. Willis, John E. Laird, and Randolph M. Jones. Intelligent multi-level control in a highly reactive domain. In Charles E. Thorpe F.C.A. Groen, S. Hirose, editor, *Proceedings of the Third International Conference on Intelligent Autonomous Systems*, pages 449–458. IOS Press, 1993.

Selective Perception for Robot Driving

Douglas A. Reece

Institute for Simulation and Training
University of Central Florida
12424 Research Parkway, Suite 300
Orlando, FL 32826

Steven A. Shafer

School of Computer Science
Carnegie Mellon University
5000 Forbes Avenue
Pittsburgh, PA 15213

Abstract

Robots performing complex tasks in rich environments need very good perception modules in order to understand their situation and choose the best action. Robot planning systems have typically assumed that perception was so good that it could refresh the entire world model whenever the planning system needed it, or whenever anything in the world changed. Unfortunately, this assumption is completely unrealistic in many real-world domains because perception is far too difficult. Robots in these domains cannot use the traditional planner paradigm, but instead need a new system design that integrates reasoning with perception. Our research is aimed at showing how a robot can reason about perception, how task knowledge can be used to select perceptual targets, and how this selection dramatically reduces the computational cost of perception.

The domain addressed in this videotape is driving in traffic. We have developed a microscopic traffic simulator called PHAROS that defines the street environment for our research. PHAROS contains detailed representations of streets, markings, signs, signals, and cars. It can simulate perception and implement commands for a vehicle controlled by a separate program. We have also developed a computational model of driving called Ulysses that defines the driving task. The model describes how various traffic objects in the world determine what actions that a robot must take. These tools have allowed us to implement robot driving programs that request sensing actions in PHAROS, reason about right-of-way and other traffic laws, and then command acceleration and lane changing actions to control a simulated vehicle.

The videotape shows three selective perception techniques that we have implemented in driving programs. Each program builds upon the concepts in the previous programs. The first, Ulysses-1, uses perceptual routines to control visual search in the scene. These task-specific routines use known objects to guide the search for others-- e.g. a routine scans "along the right side" of "the road ahead" for a sign. The second program, Ulysses-2, decides which objects are the most critical in the current situation and looks for them. It ignores objects that cannot affect the robot's actions. Ulysses-2 creates an inference tree to determine the effect of uncertain input data on action choices, and searches this tree to decide which data to sense. Finally, Ulysses-3 uses domain knowledge to reason about how dynamic objects will move or change over time. Objects that do not move enough to affect the robot can be ignored by perception. The program uses the inference tree from Ulysses-2 and a time-stamped, persistent world model to decide what to look for. When run in the PHAROS world, the techniques included in Ulysses-3 reduced the computational cost for perception by 9 to 12 orders of magnitude when compared to an uncontrolled, general perception system.

Acknowledgment

We would like to thank Jim Kocher of the Robotics Institute at Carnegie Mellon University for his work in putting together this video.

Computer Vision Research at the University of Massachusetts

Edward M. Riseman and Allen R. Hanson
with J. Inigo Thomas and Members of the Computer Vision Laboratory

Computer Science Department
University of Massachusetts
Amherst, MA 01003

Abstract

This video first summarizes current research at the University of Massachusetts on mobile vehicle navigation using landmark recognition and a partial 3D world model. We then show how landmarks and world models might be automatically acquired and updated over time.

A fundamental goal in robot navigation is to determine the "pose" of the robot - that is, the position and orientation of the robot with respect to a 3D world model, such as a hallway. In order to determine its pose, the robot identifies modeled 3D landmarks such as doors and baseboards in a 2D image of the hallway. Identifying landmarks involves determining correspondences of extracted image line segments with predicted landmark lines projected into the image. Model matching is achieved by a combinatorial optimization technique (local search) which minimizes the error in the model to data fit. From the model- data feature correspondences thus obtained, the 3D pose of the robot is computed via a non-linear optimization procedure. The best pose requires that lines in the 2D image lie on the planes formed by the corresponding 3D landmark lines and the camera center. Robust statistical methods are employed to detect outliers. Extension of the initial partial model (over time) is achieved by determining the camera pose over a sequence of images while simultaneously tracking new unmodeled features; triangulation is then used to determine the depth of these new features, allowing them to be incorporated into the 3D model.

One of our goals is to automatically construct a 3D model of the environment, without assuming the availability of an initial partial model. One technique identifies objects in the scene that are shallow in depth and which therefore can be represented by a frontal planar surface at some recovered depth. Using this model we automatically generate a path for the robot that avoids the obstacles. This shallow model has also been successfully used as the initial partial model for model extension from pose. Another 3D inference technique uses motion analysis over a sequence of images. This technique isolates and successfully corrects for a common major source of error—caused by error in the robot's motion—that has been traditionally neglected in other structure-from-motion algorithms. Model extension has also been achieved through a semi-automated method involving invariants from projective geometry. Given four points or lines on a plane, this technique is able to accurately project from the image to the model any number of such additional features on the same plane.

A test site for the UMass component of the DARPA Unmanned Ground Vehicle program, and a partial 3D model of a portion of the UMass campus has been built. Experiments are underway to use these models for landmark-based autonomous navigation, and automatic 3D model acquisition at this test site.

Acknowledgment

This work has been supported in part by the Advanced Research Projects Agency under contract numbers DAAE07-91-C-RO35 (via TACOM), and DACA76-92-C-0041, by the Defense Advanced Research Laboratories (via Harry Diamond Labs), and by the National Science Foundation under grant numbers IRI-9208920 and CDA-8922572.

A Fuzzy Controller for Flakey, the Robot

Alessandro Saffiotti, Nicholas Helft, Kurt Konolige, John Lowrance, Karen Myers, Daniela Musto, Enrique Ruspini, Leonard Wesley

Artificial Intelligence Center
SRI International
Menlo Park, CA 94025

Abstract

SRI International has a long tradition in the field of qualitative analysis and control of complex systems, starting with the development of the early mobile robot Shakey. More recently, we have developed a fuzzy controller for our new platform, Flakey. Flakey's controller can pursue strategic goals while operating under conditions of uncertainty, incompleteness, and imprecision. This controller includes capabilities for:

• Robust, uncertainty-tolerating goal-directed activity.
• Real-time reactivity to unexpected contingencies (e.g., unknown obstacles).
• Blending of multiple goals (e.g., reaching a position while avoiding static and moving obstacles).

In our approach, detailed in [2, 5], each goal is associated with a function that maps each perceived situation to a measure of desirability of possible actions from the point of view of that goal. The notion of a "control structure," is used for representing and manipulating high-level goals (and the associated desirability functions) in the fuzzy controller. Typical control structures are associated with environment features such as locations to reach, walls, or doorways. Each desirability function induces a particular "behavior"—one obtained by executing the actions with higher desirability. Many behaviors, induced by many simultaneous goals can be smoothly blended together by combining their desirability functions using the inferential procedures of fuzzy logic. The fuzzy controller prefers the actions that best satisfy each behavior. Blending of behaviors is the key to combining goal-oriented activity (e.g., trying to reach a given location) and reactivity (e.g., avoiding obstacles on the way).

Our fuzzy controller can execute a full plan, expressed as a set of control structures [3, 4]. Each control structure in a plan is associated with a fuzzy context of applicability, e.g., a corridor to follow when Flakey is near that corridor, and a door to cross when Flakey is close to that door. Sets of control structures can be generated by traditional AI planning techniques, and hence constitute a valuable link between symbolic reasoning systems and continuous control processes. We have performed experiments where Flakey planned and executed navigation tasks in an unmodified office environment during normal office activity. Thanks to the flexibility of fuzzy rules, Flakey only needs a sparse topological map of its environment, annotated with approximate metric information.

The performance of our fuzzy controller was also demonstrated at the first international robotic competition of the AAAI, held in July 1992 at San Jose, California [1]. Flakey placed second, and gained special recognition for its smooth and reliable reactivity, as exemplified by one judge's comment: "Only robot I felt I could sit or lie down in front of." (He actually did!).

References

[1] C. Congdon, M. Huber, D. Kortenkamp, K. Konolige, K. Myers, E. H. Ruspini, and A. Saffiotti. Carmel vs. Flakey: A comparison of two winners. *AI Magazine,* 14(1):49-57, Spring 1993.

[2] E. H. Ruspini. Fuzzy logic in the {Flakey} robot. Procs. of the Int. Conf. on Fuzzy Logic and Neural Networks (IIZUKA}), pages 767-770, Japan, 1990.

[3] A. Saffiotti. Some notes on the integration of planning and reactivity in autonomous mobile robots. Procs. of the AAAI Spring Symposium on Foundations of Automatic Planning, pages 122-126, Stanford, CA, 1993.

[4] A. Saffiotti, K. Konolige, and E. H. Ruspini. Now, do it! Technical report, SRI Artificial Intelligence Center, Menlo Park, California, 1993.

[5] A. Saffiotti, E. H. Ruspini, and K. Konolige. Integrating reactivity and goal-directedness in a fuzzy controller. Procs. of the 2nd Fuzzy-IEEE Conference, San Francisco, CA, 1993.